Contemporary Authors

Contemporary Authors

**A Bio-Bibliographical Guide to
Current Writers in Fiction, General Nonfiction,
Poetry, Journalism, Drama, Motion Pictures,
Television, and Other Fields**

FRANCES CAROL LOCHER

Editor

volumes **77-80**

GALE RESEARCH COMPANY • BOOK TOWER • DETROIT, MICHIGAN 48226

CONTEMPORARY AUTHORS

Published by
Gale Research Company, Book Tower, Detroit, Michigan 48226
Each Year's Volumes Are Revised About Five Years Later

Frederick G. Ruffner, *Publisher*   James M. Ethridge, *Editorial Director*

Christine Nasso, *General Editor, Contemporary Authors*

Frances Carol Locher, *Editor, Original Volumes*

Martha J. Abele, Victoria France Hutchinson, Ann Factor Ponikvar,
Nancy M. Rusin, Susan A. Stefani, Leslie D. Stone, Carolyn Thomas,
David Versical, and Barbara A. Welch, *Assistant Editors*
Norma Sawaya, Shirley Seip, Laurie M. Serwatowski,
and Johanna P. Zecker, *Editorial Assistants*

Jane A. Bowden and Otto Penzler, *Contributing Editors*
Andrea Geffner, James Carlton Obrecht,
Arlene True, and Benjamin True, *Sketchwriters*

Eunice Bergin, *Copy Editor*
Michaeline Nowinski, *Production Manager*

Special recognition is given to the staffs of
Journalists Biographical Master Index
and
Yesterday's Authors of Books for Children

Questions and Answers About
Contemporary Authors

What types of authors are included in *Contemporary Authors?* More than 54,000 living authors of nontechnical works (and such authors who have died since 1960) are represented in the series. *CA* includes writers in all genres—fiction, nonfiction, poetry, drama, etc.—whose books are issued by commercial, risk publishers or by university presses. Authors of books published only by known vanity or author-subsidized firms are not generally included. Since native language and nationality have no bearing on inclusion in *CA,* authors who write in languages other than English are also included in *CA* if their works have been published in the United States or translated into English.

Although *CA* focuses primarily on persons whose work appears in book form, the series now also encompasses prominent writers of interest to the public whose work appears in other media: newspaper and television reporters and correspondents, columnists, newspaper and periodical editors, syndicated cartoonists, screenwriters, television scriptwriters, and other media people.

Among the authors of particular interest included in this volume are Rachel Carson, Nancy Friday, Judith Guest, Alex Haley, Edith Hamilton, Dag Hammarskjoeld, Mark Hatfield, Ernest Hemingway, John Oliver Killens, Eartha Kitt, Alan Jay Lerner, Ralph Nader, David Niven, William A. Nolen, Theodore Roszak, Sylvester Stallone, and James Wight, best known for his writings under the pseudonym James Herriot.

Prominent media writers represented in this volume include Joseph Bologna, William Castle, Francis Ford Coppola, Oriana Fallaci, Martha Ellis Gellhorn, Chester Gould, Buck Henry, Kenneth Neil Herman, Fritz Lang, George Lucas, Paul Mazursky, Roman Polanski, Man Ray, Steven Spielberg, and Ritchie Yorke.

How is *Contemporary Authors* compiled? Most of the material in *CA* is furnished by the authors themselves. Questionnaires are sent regularly to authors as their new books appear and are reviewed as well as to prominent media personalities. Information provided by the authors in their questionnaires is then written in the distinctive *CA* format, and the proposed entries are sent to the authors for review and approval prior to publication.

How are entries prepared if authors do not furnish information? If authors of special interest to *CA* users fail to reply to requests for information, material is gathered from various other reliable sources. Biographical dictionaries are checked (a task made easier through the use of Gale's *Biographical Dictionaries Master Index* and *Author Biographies Master Index*), as are bibliographical sources, such as *Cumulative Book Index, The National Union Catalog,* etc. Published interviews, feature stories, and book reviews are examined, and often material is supplied by the authors' publishers.

As with entries prepared from questionnaires, sketches prepared through extensive research are also sent to the authors for approval prior to publication. If the authors do not respond, the listings are published with an asterisk (*) following them to indicate that the material has not been personally verified by the authors.

Will you please explain the unusual numbering system used for *Contemporary Authors* volumes? The unusual four-volume numbering system used today reflects *CA*'s publication history. To meet the urgent need for information about authors as quickly as possible, *CA* began as a quarterly publication, with each book carrying a single volume number. The numbering system was changed to double-volume numbers when Volumes 5-6 was published with twice as many entries as a quarterly volume. With the appearance of Volumes 25-28, the numbering system was altered once more to indicate that each physical volume of *CA* represents four of the original quarterly volumes.

Now, all *CA* volumes are available as four-volume units, including the revised volumes. As early volumes of *CA* were revised, they were combined into the four-volume units presently being issued. For example, when Volumes 1, 2, 3, and 4 were revised, the material was updated, merged into a single alphabet, and is available today as Volumes 1-4, First Revision.

An unusual number of biographical publications have been appearing recently, and the question is now often asked whether a charge is made for listings in such publications. Do authors listed in *Contemporary Authors* make any payment or incur any other obligation for their listings? Some publishers charge for listings or require purchase of a book by biographees. There is, however, absolutely no charge or obligation of any kind attached to being included in *CA*. Copies of the volumes in which their sketches appear are offered at courtesy discounts to persons listed, but less than five percent of the biographees purchase copies.

Cumulative Index Should Always Be Consulted

Since *CA* is a multi-volume series which does not repeat author entries from volume to volume, the cumulative index published in alternate new volumes of *CA* should always be consulted to locate an individual author's listing. Each new volume contains authors not previously included in the series and is revised approximately five years after its original publication. The cumulative index indicates the original or revised volume in which an author appears. Authors removed from the revision cycle and placed in the *CA Permanent Series* are listed in the index as having appeared in specific original volumes of *CA* (for the benefit of those who do not hold *Permanent Series* volumes), *and* as having their finally revised sketches in a specific *Permanent Series* volume.

For the convenience of *CA* users, the *CA* cumulative index also includes references to all entries in two related Gale series—*Contemporary Literary Criticism,* which is devoted entirely to current criticism of major authors, poets, and playwrights, and *Something About the Author,* a series of heavily illustrated sketches on juvenile authors and illustrators.

As always, suggestions from users about any aspect of *CA* will be welcomed.

CONTEMPORARY AUTHORS

Indicates that a listing has been compiled from secondary sources believed to be reliable, but has not been personally verified for this edition by the author sketched.

A

ABBOT, Charles G(reeley) 1872-1973

PERSONAL: Born May 31, 1872, in Wilton, N.H.; son of Harris and Ann Caroline (Greeley) Abbot; married Lillian E. Moore, October 13, 1897 (died, 1944); married Virginia A. Johnston, June 9, 1954. *Education:* Massachusetts Institute of Technology, B.S., 1894, M.S., 1895; University of Toronto, LL.D., 1933. *Home:* 4409 Beechwood Rd., Hyattesville, Md. 20782. *Office:* c/o Smithsonian Institution, Washington, D.C.

CAREER: Smithsonian Institution, Washington, D.C., assistant director, 1895-1906, director of Astrophysical Observatory, 1907-44, assistant secretary, 1918-27, secretary, 1928-44, research associate, 1944-73. Associated with United States Office of Science Research and Development, 1944. *Member:* National Academy of Sciences (home secretary, 1918-23), Astronomy and Astrophysics Society (vice-president, 1930), Research Corporation (director, 1928-45), American Association for Advancement of Sciences, American Philosophy Society, Washington Academy of Sciences, American Academy, Societe Astronomique de France, Sociedad astronomica de Mexico, Academy Modena, Deutsche Meterologische Gesellschaft, Royal Astronomical Society of Great Britain (associate member), Royal Meteorological Society (honorary member). *Awards, honors:* Received Draper medal from National Academy of Sciences, 1910; Rumford medal from American Academy of Arts and Sciences, 1916; Goodrich award from New York World's Fair, 1940.

WRITINGS: The Sun, D. Appleton, 1911, 2nd edition, 1929; *Everyday Mysteries,* McMillan, 1923; *The Earth and the Stars,* D. Van Nostrand, 1926, 2nd edition, 1946; *Great Inventions,* Smithsonian Institution Series, volume 12, 1932; *Adventures in a World of Science,* McMillan, 1956; *Ten Sermons, 1940-1966,* Smithsonian Institution, 1967.

AVOCATIONAL INTERESTS: Golf, tennis, bridge, classical music.

OBITUARIES: New York Times, December 18, 1973; *Washington Post,* December 18, 1973.*

(Died December 17, 1973)

* * *

ABBOTT, James H(amilton) 1924-

PERSONAL: Born November 22, 1924, in High Springs, Fla.; son of James Marion and Gussie Ann (Clark) Abbott. *Education:* University of Florida, A.A., 1947, B.A., 1948, M.A., 1950; University of California, Los Angeles, Ph.D., 1958; University of Madrid, diploma, 1968. *Home:* 443 Chautauqua, Norman, Okla. 73069. *Office:* University of Oklahoma, 780 Van Vleet Oval, Norman, Okla. 73019.

CAREER: Hope College, Holland, Mich., instructor in Spanish, 1953; University of Oklahoma, Norman, instructor, 1956-58, assistant professor, 1958-63, associate professor, 1963-68, professor of Spanish, 1968—, David Ross Boyd Professor, 1973. *Military service:* U.S. Army Air Forces, 1943-46. *Member:* Modern Language Association of America, American Association of Teachers of Spanish and Portuguese, American Council on the Teaching of Foreign Languages, South Central Modern Language Association, Sigma Delta Pi.

WRITINGS: (Editor and translator, with Lowell Dunham) Leopoldo Zea, *The Latin American Mind,* University of Oklahoma Press, 1963; (editor with Lowell Dunham) *Guide to the Improvement of the Teaching of Foreign Languages,* Oklahoma Department of Education, 1964; (editor with Dunham, Walter Frenk, and Patricia Hammond) *Oklahoma in the World,* Oklahoma Department of Education, 1972; (editor with Dunham, Frenk, and Hammond) *Azorin y Francia* (title means "Azorin and France"), Seminarios y Ediciones, 1973; *The Turpentine Still and Other Memories,* privately printed, 1975.

WORK IN PROGRESS: A collection of nostalgic sketches about life on a turpentine plantation in Florida in the 1930's; research on the dynamic concept of existence in Spanish writers of the generation of 1898.

SIDELIGHTS: Abbott has made about twenty trips to Mexico and sixteen to Spain, and has also traveled in England, France, Portugal, and Italy. He writes: "I am interested in seeing the educational level of U.S. schools improved. This is vital if the country is to survive. Abolishing practically all requirements at almost all levels has resulted in lower test scores in practically all fields. This is especially serious in the use of English, the sciences, mathematics, and foreign languages. While students in the United States are taught that how they feel about any given subject is all that matters, other countries are surpassing our country in educational goals. A democratic form of government depends on an informed electorate capable of distinguishing between propaganda and fact. A population incapable of reading critically is not in a position to vote intelligently. Students who are poorly informed are not capable of writing meaningful programs of studies for themselves. People with poor educational backgrounds can be easily manipulated by better trained persons in the mass media and in politics. The lowering of standards in public schools is already leading to the creation of private institutions with high standards; this, in turn, leads to the creation of an educated elite, a contradiction of the democratic educational system.''

* * *

ABRAMS, Joy 1941-

PERSONAL: Born March 17, 1941, in New York; daughter of Martin and Pearl Rudnick; married Kenneth L. Abrams (an attorney), April 7, 1962; children: Nancy Gayle, David Robert, Michael Joseph. *Education:* Brooklyn College of the City University of New York, B.A., 1961; Arizona State University, M.A., 1962. *Religion:* Jewish. *Residence:* Phoenix, Ariz.

CAREER: Elementary school teacher in Glendale, Ariz., 1961-62; nursery school teacher in Phoenix, Ariz., 1962-63; substitute elementary school teacher in Phoenix, 1963—. Owner of Yoga Studio, 1975—. Worked at Good Samaritan Learning Disability School, and Kivel Nursing Home. Also worked as photographic model. *Member:* Alan Foss Leukemia Society, B'nai B'rith.

WRITINGS: (With Ruth Richards) *Let's Do Yoga* (juvenile), Holt, 1975. Also author of *Look Good, Feel Good,* with Pam Gray and Richards, 1978.

WORK IN PROGRESS: Who Do I Turn To?: Learning Disabilities and Your Child, publication expected in 1981.

SIDELIGHTS: Joy Abrams writes: "At age twelve, I was ill with polio. The compassion and love shown by friends and relatives was helpful to my recovery. I always had great compassion for others, but from that time on I knew that my work someday would involve helping others. Voraciously, I read books on health and nutrition, and took courses on the subject when time allowed. I also kept writing poetry and children's books. During the summers I worked with deprived children in Manhattan.

"In 1972, I got my master's degree in elementary education and began tutoring children with learning problems, incorporating some Yoga techniques. From that my book was born. In 1975 I opened my own Yoga studio, which is a Japanese tea house where I teach Yoga, beauty, and nutrition tips to all ages.

"To have a career as well as a young family requires great discipline, as well as support and understanding from your family. Most people believe that you write a book and that's the end of it. They are not aware of the rewrites and the regular work hours writing entails.''

AVOCATIONAL INTERESTS: Travel (Macao, Hong Kong, Spain, Germany, France, Italy, Switzerland, the Caribbean).

* * *

ALLAN, Ted 1918-
(Edward Maxwell)

PERSONAL: Birth-given name Alan Herman; born January 25, 1918, in Montreal, Quebec, Canada; son of Harry and Annie (Elias) Herman; divorced; children: Julia, Norman Bethune. *Education:* Educated in Montreal, Quebec. *Politics:* Socialist. *Religion:* Humanist. *Residence:* London,

England; Toronto, Canada; and Los Angeles, Calif. *Agent:* M. Zimring, William Morris Agency, 151 El Camino, Beverly Hills, Calif. 10019.

CAREER: Author; writer for stage, screen, radio, and television. Has worked as caddy and hardware store clerk; began writing at age fifteen; later worked as actor in radio, film, and television plays. *Military service:* International Brigade in Spain; became colonel. *Member:* Screenwriters Guild, Association of Canadian Television and Radio Artists (ACTRA), Dramatists Guild, Authors League (Great Britain). *Awards, honors:* Canada Council Grant, 1956, 1970; Academy Award nomination for best original screenplay from the Academy of Television Arts and Sciences, 1975, for "Lies My Father Told Me"; Christopher Award, Virgin Islands Best Film Award, Golden Globe Best Foreign Film Award, Montreal ACTRA Award, and Canadian National ACTRA Award, all 1976, all for "Lies My Father Told Me."

WRITINGS: This Time a Better Earth (novel), Heinemann, 1939, Morrow, 1940; (with Sydney Gordon) *The Scalpel, The Sword: The Story of Doctor Norman Bethune* (non-fiction), Little, Brown, 1952, reprinted, Monthly Review Press, 1978; (under pseudonym Edward Maxwell) *Quest for Pajaro,* Heinemann, 1961; *Chu Chem: A Zen Buddhist-Hebrew Novel,* Editions Quebec, 1973; *Willie, the Squowse* (for children), J. Cape, 1977, Hastings House, 1978.

Plays: "The Money Makers," first produced in Toronto at Jupiter Theatre, 1954 (produced in London at London Arts Theatre as "The Ghost Writers," 1955); "The Legend of Pepito" (adapted from a story by B. Traven), first produced in London, 1956; (with Roger MacDougall) *Double Image* (adapted from a story by Roy Vickers; first produced in London at Savoy Theatre, 1956; produced in Paris at Michodiere Theatre as "Gog and Magog," 1960), Samuel French, 1959; "The Secret of the World," produced in London, 1964; *Oh, What a Lovely War* (first produced in London, 1964; produced on Broadway at Broadhurst Theatre, September 30, 1964), Methuen, 1965; "Chu Chem: A Zen Buddhist-Hebrew Musical" (adapted from own novel), first produced in Philadelphia, 1966; "I've Seen You Cut Lemons," produced in London at Fortune Theatre, 1970. Also author of unproduced plays, "Willie, the Squowse," "Antigone Smith," "The Service Station," and "Divorce, Divorce!"

Screenplays: "Out of Nowhere," produced by Dublin Studios, 1966; "Lies My Father Told Me," distributed by Columbia Pictures, 1975. Author of screenplays currently in production, "Love Is a Long Shot," (with John Cassavetes) "I've Seen You Cut Lemons," "Bethune," and "Them Damned Canadians Shot Louis Riel." Also author of "The Money Makers."

Author of numerous radio and television plays for Canadian Broadcasting Corp., British Broadcasting Corp., and I.T.V.

Contributor of short stories to periodicals, including *New Yorker, Harper's, London Sunday Telegraph, Canadian,* and *Colliers.*

SIDELIGHTS: "Lies My Father Told Me," based on an autobiographical story by Allan and directed by Czeck filmmaker Jan Kadar, is the story of a young Jewish boy struggling between the influences of his Orthodox grandfather and his religiously non-practicing father. Richard Schickel described the film as "a difficult movie to dislike." But he qualified that statement with: "For all its affability, 'Lies' is not a very effective work." The characters in the film, according to Schickel, are predictable stereotypes. "The minute we meet them, we can call the turns they will eventually do, just as we know, almost from the film's first minute, that Grandfather will die before it ends.'' In general, Schickel felt that the film lacked depth. ''In a film that is so predictable,'' he concluded, '' . . . a little excess is called for. We need to feel a touch of genuine desperation in this slum or of craziness in the behavior of its inhabitants, somehow the *Duddy Kravitz* ambience has been infused with the spirit of Walton's Mountain, and the result is a bland respectability—safe, pleasant, without reverberation.''

Charles Phillips Reilly, however, praised ''Lies My Father Told Me'' for being ''effulgent in its revelation of a child's discovery of love and death,'' and he found that the film ''bears an affinity to Fellini's 'Amarcord' in its affirmation of life.'' Reilly further commented that ''Ted Allan's screenplay manages to avoid bathos through an adept counterpoint of the family's relationships with their all-too-human neighbors as well as through his portrayal of Orthodox Jewish ritual. . . . And the script utilizes the honesty of children richly.''

Sharing Reilly's enthusiasm, critic Judith Crist commented that the on-location shooting at Montreal's Panet Street gave ''the seal of authenticity to place and period in 'Lies My Father Told Me.''' In addition, Crist mentioned that, ''It is more than authenticity that separates this film from the ersatz period pieces of the moment and that makes it relevant beyond time and place.'' She explained that Allan's screenplay and Kadar's direction combined to produce ''a distillation of a common past in this warm and funny and touching tale . . . capturing the child's-eye-view of adult integrity that we all have experienced.'' For Crist, the film's family conflicts being placed in a community context succeeded in ''retaining both the child's point of view and an adult appreciation thereof. As a result, beyond the humor and the lump-in-the-throat emotional involvement, the broader implications of family conflict, of the child spoiled, the father emasculated, the mother dichotomized, emerge to lend grit to the memoir and the abrasive truth that undercuts sentimentality.''

Allan told *CA:* ''The quotes from the critics confirm a strong conviction of mine; the critics who praise my work are obviously extremely intelligent; the ones who attack my work are obviously stupid and insensitive.''

BIOGRAPHICAL/CRITICAL SOURCES: Saturday Review, October 18, 1975; *Films in Review,* November, 1975; *Time,* December 1, 1975.

* * *

ALLEN, Francis R(obbins) 1908-

PERSONAL: Born November 4, 1908, in Hartford, Conn.; son of Edwin S. (an insurance executive) and Alice R. (Clark) Allen; married Gertrude Ashenfelter, February 28, 1942. *Education:* Antioch College, A.B., 1931; Columbia University, A.M., 1936; University of North Carolina, Ph.D., 1946; post-doctoral study at University of Chicago. *Politics:* ''Mostly Democrat.'' *Religion:* Episcopal. *Home:* 2236 Ellicott Dr., Tallahassee, Fla. 32312. *Office:* Department of Sociology, Florida State University, Tallahassee, Fla. 32306.

CAREER: University of Alabama, Tuscaloosa, instructor, 1946-47, assistant professor of sociology, 1947-48; Florida State University, Tallahassee, associate professor, 1948-60, professor of sociology, 1961—, professor at London Center, 1975. *Military service:* U.S. Army, 1942-46; became first lieutenant. *Member:* World Future Society (founder and

first local president, 1973-74), American Sociological Association, American Academy of Political and Social Science, American Association of University Professors (chapter president, 1963-64), Southern Sociological Society (vice-president, 1964-65).

WRITINGS: (With Laurence Foster and Morris Caldwell) *Analysis of Social Problems,* Stackpole, 1954; (with W. F. Ogburn, M. F. Nimkoff, Hornell Hart, and D. C. Miller) *Technology and Social Change,* Appleton, 1957; *Socio-cultural Dynamics: An Introduction to Social Change,* Macmillan, 1971.

WORK IN PROGRESS: Research on social change.

SIDELIGHTS: Allen writes: ''My current ideas on the subject of social change are branching out from those expressed in my volume *Socio-cultural Dynamics: An Introduction to Social Change.* In that volume I first noted various ways of looking at change (such as the economic, technological, demographic, leadership, legal, ideological, cybernetic, and other approaches); then I discussed major theories of social change (those of Marx, Durkheim, Veblen, Ogburn, Sorokin, Spengler, Toynbee, Weber, and more modern thinkers); then I endeavored to describe modern efforts to measure change (using social indicators, models, and other features); then I outlined such major processes of change as innovation, diffusion of ideas and articles, and activism; after this I outlined changes as they are occurring in developing nations (for example, in South America, Asia, and Africa); finally, I endeavored to describe the disorganization which tends to result from rapid social change, including the difficulties of making satisfactory adjustments in these circumstances (what Alvin Toffler likes to call 'Future Shock.').

''My early interests related to technology as a cause of social changes, which was largely initiated by my admiration for the ideas of the eminent sociologist, William F. Ogburn, of the University of Chicago. As a young sociologist beginning my career after military service in World War II, I took advantage of the G. I. Bill of Rights and enrolled at Chicago for post-doctoral study with Ogburn. When Ogburn retired from Chicago in 1951 he happily came to my own university (Florida State), since his collaborator and friend, Meyer Nimkoff, was chairman of the Sociology Department there; gradually I was able to develop a professional association as well as a personal friendship with this leading sociologist. Ogburn emphasized the influence of inventions (both technological and social), and it seems clear that a great amount of social change in the United States has come since 1900 from the many effects of such inventions as the automobile, airplane, telephone, radio, television, computer, and space vehicle. With Ogburn, Nimkoff, Hornell Hart, and Delbert C. Miller (all sociologists) I wrote a book a few years after this entitled *Technology and Social Change* which sought to explore further the various influences wrought by technology. I still think that technology constitutes a sizeable influence on social change although current fashion is to dwell on negative aspects of technology such as the pollution problem. Pollution has of course become a major problem in recent years, and it must be contained in industrial nations. At the same time the American and other people are still much interested in the auto, television, air conditioning, computer, etc., and systematic study of these inventions is needed. The world also needs *social inventions,* however, and systematic efforts to devise such inventions which would ameliorate conditons (or problems) involving crime, the socialization process, marital or familial problems, conditions of older people and the like, are just as much needed. This is a part of the subject that is largely neglected.

"In recent years one of the reasons that have brought a branching-out of my ideas is that the field of sociology has experienced a vast improvement in its knowledge of formulating theories and also performing research. The newer conceptions of theory construction have affected all scientific fields, of course. Thus new theories may be stated in far superior form than in earlier years; also older theories that were unsuitably stated in former times yet have present and future promise may be re-formulated. A current interest of mine (working with a former student) is to re-state the earlier theory of social change of the late British historian, Professor Arnold Toynbee. Toynbee's central idea (known as the theory of challenge and response) is that social changes in a civilization, nation, or other unit occur in relation to the way the unit (or its leaders) respond to challenges. If the nation or other unit responds successfully to the challenge (really meets it), it will rise in power-prestige, and living conditions. If it responds unsuccessfully to such challenges as war, inflation, competition, it will decline in power, prestige, and level-of-operation. If it fails dismally to meet the challenges, it will utterly fail. Civilizations will die out in the manner of the Roman experience; nations will badly decline or be conquered by others; corporations will go bankrupt. Valuable as Toynbee's essential idea seems to be, he did not state it such that it would be acceptable to the fields of history and social science. Thus his promising 'basic idea' or 'embryo-theory' has never been developed conceptually, and has not been used in research. Other basic ideas or 'general orientations' may similarly be falling into disuse because of faulty formulations.

"Advances in research procedures and methods likewise present opportunities for more adequate studies. The contemporary emphasis on *social indicators* and publication of authoritative data embodying such indicators are most helpful for research purposes (as the *Social Indicators 1976* published by the U. S. Department of Commerce in late 1977 and similar volumes published in other nations). I am also interested in developing *models* which represent the growth of some nation or other social unit and in comparing the growth models of different nations. Models may be verbal or mathematical, the latter being preferred in the world of science.

"Finally, the study of social change leads inevitably to considerations of the future. Vast interest and effort has related to studies of the future (whether of nations or of institutions like the family and the university). I have myself founded our local chapter of the World Future Society, and have helped to organize dozens of meetings devoted to forecasting the future of community or institutional subjects. I am also writing an essay on 'The Future of England' at this time, which is partly due to interest in the future of certain nations *per se* and partly due to having recently spent six months in that country. Further contributions are needed concerning the effects of scientific findings (as in biology), modern global diffusion of ideas and products, and other subjects."

AVOCATIONAL INTERESTS: European travel.

* * *

ALLEN, Kenneth S.   1913-

PERSONAL: Born September 18, 1913, in Southend, Essex, England; son of George Thomas (a builder) and Hannah Daisy (Sellar) Allen; married Avis Murton Carter, June 3, 1950; children: David Stuart, Alastair Scott, Fiona Margaret. *Education:* Attended Southend College of Art and St. Martin's School of Art. *Politics:* "Minimal." *Religion:*

"Minimal." *Home and office:* 74 Eastbury Rd., Northwood, Middlesex HA6 3 AR, England.

CAREER: Formerly employed in publicity departments of British film companies; escorted many international stars around the world; full-time writer, 1972—. *Military service:* British Merchant Navy. *Member:* Film Publicity Guild, Association of Film and Television Technicians, Poetry Club (London), Variety Club.

WRITINGS: Wings of Sail: The Story of British Ships in the Glorious Days of Sail (self-illustrated), John Crowther, 1944; *The A.B.C. of Stagecraft for Amateurs* (self-illustrated), Stacy, 1945; *Sea Captains and Their Ships*, Odhams, 1965; (editor) *Radiology in World War II*, Office of the Surgeon General, Department of the Army, 1966; *Sailors in Battle* (juvenile), Odhams, 1966; *Exploring the Cinema* (juvenile), Odhams, 1966; *Exploring the Sea*, Odhams, 1966; *The Story of London Town* (juvenile), Odhams, 1967.

Fighting Men and Their Uniforms (juvenile), Hamlyn, 1971; *Mighty Men of Valour: The Great Warriors and Battles of Biblical Times*, Smythe, 1972; (contributor) *What Do You Know?: An Illustrated History of Aircraft*, Hamlyn, 1972; *One Day in Tutankhamen's Egypt* (juvenile), Tyndall, 1973; *One Day with the Vikings* (juvenile), Purnell, 1973; *The Story of Gunpowder* (juvenile), Wayland, 1973; *One Day in Ancient Greece* (juvenile), Tyndall, 1974; *One Day in Ancient Rome* (juvenile), Tyndall, 1974; *"That Bounty Bastard": The True Story of Captain William Bligh*, R. Hale, 1976.

Also author of *The Silver Screen*, 1948; *In the Beginning*, 1948; *Crimson Harvest*, 1966; *The History of the Ship*, 1968; *Ships of Long Ago*, 1970; *Knights and Castles*, 1970; *The World's Greatest Sea Disasters*, 1970; *Fighting Ships*, 1971; *Pirates and Buccaneers*, 1971; *Battle of the Atlantic*, 1973; *Wars of the Roses*, 1973; *Transporting Goods*, 1973; *Transporting People*, 1973; *Spotlight on the Wild West*, 1973; *One Day in Roman Britain*, 1973; *Cowboys*, 1973; *One Day in Victorian Britain*, 1974; *One Day in Regency England*, 1974; *One Day in Shakespeare's England*, 1975; *Big Guns of the Twentieth Century*, 1976; *Ships and Boats*, 1976; *The London Experience*, 1977; *Lawrence of Arabia*, 1977; *Ships and Trains and Boats and Planes*, 1977.

Contributor to *Question and Answer Book, Magpie Story Book, Great Disasters, One Hundred Great Adventures,* and *Fifty Great Journeys.*

Author of radio series "Personal Appearance"; editor of cassette series "The Historymakers." Contributor to *International Encyclopedia of Aviation.*

WORK IN PROGRESS: A novel, with a film background; a book on transport; editing an anthology of spy and mystery stories.

* * *

ALLEN, Michael (Derek)   1939-

PERSONAL: Born May 4, 1939, in Peterborough, England; son of Laurence (a transport executive) and Jessie (Briggs) Allen; married Mary McLay; children: Jonathan, Rosanne. *Education:* Queens' College, Cambridge, M.A., 1961. *Home:* 81 Springfield, Bradford-on-Avon, Wiltshire BA15 1BA, England. *Agent:* Andrew Mylett, Hughes Massie Ltd., 69 Great Russell St., London WC1B 3DH, England.

CAREER: Teacher in England, 1961-72; University of Bath, Bath, England, university administrator, 1972—. *Member:* Mystery Writers of America, Crime Writers' Association (Great Britain).

WRITINGS: The Leavers, Cassell, 1963; *Spence in Petal Park*, Constable, 1977, published as *Spence and the Holiday Murders*, Walker & Co., 1978; *Spence at the Blue Bazaar*, Constable, 1979.

SIDELIGHTS: Allen told *CA:* "I am currently studying part-time for a Master of Education degree in educational management, which has led me to become interested in developing a systems approach to the novel. I think it is vital for writers of all kinds of fiction to be able to think clearly about their objectives and methods. The 'Spence' books are an attempt to combine the old-fashioned but still popular whodunit formula with an up-to-date and realistic police-procedural approach. This is a commercial mixture aimed directly at satisfying readers, but which also enables me to write about characters I find interesting."

* * *

ALLEN, Tony 1945-

PERSONAL: Born April 3, 1945, in Hayes, England. *Education:* Attended secondary school in Hayes, England. *Politics:* "Peace, love, and anarchy." *Religion:* "Peace, love, and anarchy." *Address:* c/o Rough Theatre, 32 Bravington Rd., London W.9, England.

CAREER: Writer. Also worked as arts technician and actor. *Member:* West London Free-Range Anarchists.

WRITINGS: (With John Miles) *Rough Theatre Plays*, Volume I (contains "Dwelling Unit, Sweet Dwelling Unit," first produced in London at British Oak Pub, December, 1973; "Heart of a Patriot," first produced in London at Marylands Community Centre, February, 1975; "Squat Now While Stocks Last," first produced in London, summer, 1975; "Free Milk and Orange Juice," first produced in London at Nash House, The Mall, October, 1976), Open Head Press, 1977.

Co-author of radio plays broadcast on British Broadcasting Co.: "Cloth Caps Muffler and Illfitting Suits," 1974; "Bent Triangle," 1974; "Dwelling Unit," 1975; "Two Fingers Finegan Comes Again," 1975.

WORK IN PROGRESS: "The Missionary Position," a play taking the "side of the natives in three parallel wars, the Sex War, the Class War, and the Irish War."

SIDELIGHTS: Allen writes: "I'm interested in writing theatre for the non-theatre goer, and performing it in non-theatrical settings—the street, the pubs, etc. My aim is to 'plunge the anarchic spanner of experience into the pious works of theory . . .' and to encourage people to 'gatecrash their own fantasies.'"

* * *

ALLINSON, Gary D(ean) 1942-

PERSONAL: Born August 12, 1942, in Webster City, Iowa; son of Everette J. (a businessman) and Grace Lucille (Winnie) Allinson; married Patricia Susan Bush (an editor), December 27, 1965; children: Robin John. *Education:* Attended University of Iowa, 1960-62; Stanford University, B.A. (honors), 1964, M.A., 1966, Ph.D., 1971. *Home:* 7543 Rosemary Rd., Pittsburgh, Pa. 15221. *Office:* Department of History, University of Pittsburgh, Pittsburgh, Pa. 15260.

CAREER: University of Pittsburgh, Pittsburgh, Pa., assistant professor, 1971-75, associate professor of history, 1975—. Member, Southeast Region Japan Studies Seminar. *Member:* Association for Asian Studies, Social Science History Association, International House of Japan, Phi Beta

Kappa. *Awards, honors:* Fulbright scholarship, 1975-76; Social Science Research Council fellowship, 1977; Japan Foundation fellowship, 1978-79.

WRITINGS: Japanese Urbanism: Industry and Politics in Kariya, 1872-1972, University of California Press, 1975; *Politics and Social Change in Suburban Tokyo: A Comparative Study in Urban History*, University of California Press, in press. Contributor to history and Asian studies journals.

WORK IN PROGRESS: Research on patterns of power in Japanese voluntary associations.

SIDELIGHTS: Allinson writes that his main interest is studying power and social change in modern Japan, and states that "this curiosity has been provoked by the opportunity to visit Japan on three occasions since 1964 for a total of three years. During the succeeding decade and a half, Japan has experienced sweeping social and political changes brought about by her successful economic development. These changes have caused fundamental alterations in the structure of Japanese society and the behavior of its people, particularly in the contemporary political arena, which is the focus of my interests."

AVOCATIONAL INTERESTS: Gardening, tennis, swimming, camping.

* * *

ALSOP, Gulielma Fell 1881-1978

1881—January 26, 1978; American physician, educator, medical missionary, and author. Alsop became a medical missionary in China after her graduation from Women's Medical College in Pennsylvania in 1908. In 1917 she returned to the United States and joined the faculty of Barnard College. In that same year she founded the medical department, and headed it for thirty-five years. Alsop was the author of seven books, including a history of the Women's Medical College and a book about her childhood in Pennsylvania. She died in White River Junction, Vt. Obituaries and other sources: *New York Times*, February 2, 1978.

* * *

ALSWANG, Betty 1920(?)-1978

1920(?)—April 24, 1978; American interior designer, public relations executive, and author. Alswang was a member of the board of trustees of the World Affairs Center in Westport, Conn., and the co-author of a book on the homes of famous artists and writers. She died in Westport, Conn. Obituaries and other sources: *New York Times*, April 26, 1978.

* * *

ALVIN, Juliette

PERSONAL: Born in Limoges, France; daughter of Henri and Jeanne Alvin; married William A. Robson (a professor); children: two sons, one daughter. *Education:* Attended National Conservatory of Music and Sorbonne, University of Paris; studied with Pablo Casals. *Home:* 48 Lanchester Rd., London N6 4TA, England.

CAREER: Solo cellist and music therapist; has played all over the world, including several tours of the United States, 1932-68; Guildhall School of Music and Drama, London, England, director of music therapy course, head of department of music therapy, fellow, 1975—. Lecturer at University of North Carolina, 1950-51, and at universities in England, the United States, Japan, South America, Israel,

Scandinavia, and Europe. Conducted research at Binfield Park Hospital, 1970; broadcast for British Broadcasting Corp.; appeared on television and in films.

MEMBER: International Council for Music Therapy and Social Psychiatry (vice-president), British Society for Music Therapy (founder, 1958; chairman, 1966—), American National Association for Music Therapy, Spanish Association for Music Therapy (honorary member), Brazilian Association for Music Therapy (honorary member), Argentine Association for Music Therapy (honorary member), German Association for Music Therapy (honorary member), Japanese Society for Music Therapy (honorary adviser), London Violoncello Club, Hospitality Club (University of London).

WRITINGS: 'Cello Tutor for Beginners (preface by Pablo Casals), Augener, Volume I, 1955, Volume II, 1958; *Music for the Handicapped Child,* Oxford University Press, 1965, 2nd edition, 1976; *Music Therapy,* John Baker, 1966, revised edition, Basic Books, 1976; *Report on a Research Project on Music Therapy,* British Society for Music Therapy, 1970; *Music Therapy with the Autistic Child,* Oxford University Press, 1978. Contributor to scientific, medical, and music journals. Editor of *British Journal of Music Therapy,* 1968-74.

WORK IN PROGRESS: Research on music therapy with autistic children and with the physically disabled; a book on music with mentally retarded patients.

SIDELIGHTS: Juliette Alvin writes: "Music is one of the most ancient therapeutic means used by man in magic, religion, and medicine. It works on the basic attributes of music, on the irresistible power of sound to penetrate and to create states and changes in man's behaviour. Throughout history music has been able to provoke hypnosis or catharsis, to relax or stimulate body and soul. It belongs to a concrete world of action as well as to a world of fantasy, of imagination and dreams. Music can help to make a bridge between the two worlds....

"Man has used sound to create music which in turn affects his whole being, body, mind and emotions. Music provokes in him various reactions and responses of different kinds: conscious or unconscious, emotional, mental, psychological or social. They are used towards specific therapeutic goals and create various kinds of relationship, such as perceptual, physical and motoric contact with the musical instruments; a one-to-one human rapport with the therapist or with the music group; or with the patient himself in relation to the musical experience....

"Music therapy works on unconventional approaches to music and creates a special relationship between therapist and patient. We have to discover in each of them, however ill, young, or old, some innate resonance to music. I have never found one who did not have some music in him. We may discover in him an innate gift which has never been used, or has been badly used: he may possess a hidden store of musical memories; he may have studied music at some time and abandoned it. Every child has music in him, but not always in the conventional sense. Whatever the case, the discovery has always given me a feeling of fellowship and respect for any of the patients with whom I can share something which does matter, however ill or handicapped they are."

AVOCATIONAL INTERESTS: Tennis, swimming, walking, theatre.

BIOGRAPHICAL/CRITICAL SOURCES: Therapy, November 18, 1977.

AMADO, Jorge 1912-

PERSONAL: Born August 10, 1912, in Ilheus, Bahia, Brazil; son of Joao Amado de Faria and Eulalia (Leal) Amado; married Zelia Gattai, July 14, 1945; children: Joao Jorge, Paloma. *Education:* Federal University of Rio de Janeiro, J.D., 1935. *Home:* Rua Alagoinhas 33, Rio Vermelho, Salvador, Bahia, Brazil.

CAREER: Writer. Federal deputy of Brazilian parliament, 1946-48; *Para Todos* (cultural periodical), Rio de Janeiro, Brazil, editor, 1956-59. Imprisoned for political reasons, 1935, exiled, 1937, 1941-43, 1948-52. *Member:* Brazilian Association of Writers, Brazilian Academy of Letters. *Awards, honors:* Stalin International Peace Prize, 1951.

WRITINGS—In English: Terras do sem fim, Martins (Sao Paulo), 1942, translation by Samuel Putnam published as *The Violent Land,* Knopf, 1945, revised edition, 1965, Portuguese edition reprinted, 1974; *Gabriela, cravo e canela,* Martins, 1958, translation by James L. Taylor and William L. Grossman published as *Gabriela, Clove and Cinnamon,* Knopf, 1962; *Os velhos marinheiros,* Martins, 1961, translation by Harriett de Onis published as *Home Is the Sailor,* Knopf, 1964; *A morte e a morte de Quincas Berro D'agua,* Sociedade dos Cem Bibliofilos do Brasil, 1962, translation by Barbara Shelby published as *The Two Deaths of Quincas Wateryell,* Knopf, 1965; *Os pastores da noite,* Martins, 1964, translation by de Onis published as *Shepherds of the Night,* Knopf, 1966; *Dona Flor e seus dois maridos: Historia moral e de amor,* Martins, 1966, translation by de Onis published as *Dona Flor and Her Two Husbands: A Moral and Amorous Tale,* Knopf, 1969; *Tenda dos milagres,* Martins, 1969, translation by Shelby published as *Tent of Miracles,* Knopf, 1971; *Bahia* (bilingual Portuguese-English edition), Graficos Brunner, 1971; *Tereza Batista cansada de guerra,* Martins, 1972, translation by Shelby published as *Tereza Batista: Home From the Wars,* Knopf, 1975.

Other: *O paiz do carnaval* (title means "Carnival Land"), Schmidt, 1932, reprinted, Martins, 1970; *Jubiaba,* J. Olympio, 1935, reprinted, Martins, 1971; *Mar morto* (title means" The Dead Sea"), J. Olympio, 1936, reprinted, Martins, 1974; *Suor* (title means "Sweat"), J. Olympio, 1936, reprinted, Editores Associados, 1975; *Cacau* (title means "Cocoa"), J. Olympio, 1936; *Capitaes da areia* (title means "The Beach Waifs"), J. Olympio, 1937, reprinted, Martins, 1975.

A B C de Castro Alves (title means "Life of Castro Alves"), Martins, 1941, reprinted, Publicacoes Europa-America, 1971; *Vida de Luiz Carlos Prestes, o cavaleiro da esperanca* (title means "The Life of Luiz Carlos Prestes"), Martins, 1942; *Sao Jorge dos Ilheus* (title means "St. George of Ilheus"), Martins, 1944, reprinted, 1974; *Bahia de Todos os Santos: Guia das ruas e dos misterios da cidade do Salvador* (title means "Bahia: A Guide to the Streets and Mysteries of Salvador"), Martins, 1945, reprinted, 1974; *Seara vermelha* (title means "Red Harvest"), Martins, 1946, reprinted, Publicacoes Europa-America, 1975; *Homens e coisas do Partido Comunista* (title means "Men and Facts of the Communist Party"), Edicoes Horizonte, 1946; *O amor de Castro Alves* (title means "Castro Alves's Love"), Edicoes do Povo, 1947, published as *O amor do soldado* (title means "The Soldier's Love"), Martins, 1958.

O mundo da paz: Uniao Sovietica e democracias populares (title means "The World of Peace: Soviet Union and Popular Democracies"), Editorial Vitoria, 1952; *Os subterraneos da liberdade* (title means "The Subterraneans of Freedom"; contains *Os asperos tempos* [title means "Harsh Times"], published separately, 1963; *Agonia da noite* [title means "Night's Agony"], published separately, 1961; *A luz no tunel* [title means "A Light in the Tunnel"], published separately, 1963), Martins, 1954.

Jorge Amado: Trinta anos de literatura (title means "Jorge Amado: Thirty Years of Literature"), Martins, 1961; *O poeta Ze Trindade* (title means "Ze Trindade: A Poet"), J. Ozon, 1965; *Bahia boa terra Bahia* (title means "Bahia Sweet Land"), Image (Rio de Janeiro), 1967; *O compadre de Ogun*, Sociedade dos Cem Bibliofilos do Brasil, 1969.

Jorge Amado, povo e terra: Quarenta anos de literatura (title means "Jorge Amado, His Land and People: Forty Years of Literature"), Martins, 1972; (with others) *Brandao entre o mar e o amor* (title means "Swinging Between Love and Sea"), Martins, 1973; (with others) *Gente boa* (title means "The Good People"), Editora Brasilia/Rio, 1975; (with Luis Viana Filho and Jeanine Warnod) *Porto Seguro recriado por Sergio Telles* (title means "Porto Seguro in the Painting of Sergio Telles"), Bolsa de Arte do Rio de Janeiro, 1976; *O gato malhado e a andorinha Sinha* (title means "The Cat and the Little Bird"), Editora Record, 1976; *Conheca o escritor brasileiro Jorge Amado: Textos para estudantes com exercicios de compreensao e dabate* (title means "Know the Writer Jorge Amado: Texts for Students"), edited by Lygia Marina Moraes, Editora Record, 1977; *Tieta do Agreste*, Editora Record, 1977.

Collections: *O pais do carnaval. Cacau. Suor,* Martins, 1944, reprinted, 1970; *Obras* (title means "Works"), seventeen volumes, Martins, 1944—.

SIDELIGHTS: Ranked as one of the greatest contemporary Brazilian novelists, Amado has written prolifically of his homeland and his fellow countrymen. "Bahia surely has no greater poet than Jorge Amado," wrote D. A. Yates. Critics emphasize the influence of Amado's Marxist political views on his early novels, which depict the downtrodden masses on the plantations and in the cities of Brazil. John Duncan expressed the views of many critics in his response to *Shepherds of the Night:* "Amado's world is that of the People. In this world, everyone is poor, healthy and happy. The poor are the ones who live. The rich are sick.... The difficulty, even now, seems to be that he is as much an ideologist as a novelist. He sees classes, not individuals.... His is a world where instinct, impulse and animal exuberance become the ultimate value, while the whole range of thinking man remains unexamined."

L. L. Barrow noted the evolution of Amado's work in his review of *Dona Flor and Her Two Husbands:* "In most of his earlier novels Jorge Amado showed great concern for the social problems of Brazil, offering rather rigid socialist solutions. His later works have subtler social themes, subordinated to the overall work. In his later novels, Amado's philosophy gives each person his own life, his own love and his own madness." Amado discussed the change in his writing in an interview in the *New York Times.* "As a young man I sought to put revolution into all my books and I always had a theoretical speech included. I did not realize that the reality was much more powerful than I could be," he said. When asked about the root of his success, he replied: "I write about Brazilian problems from the side of the people and I'm antielitist. I use popular language, I am no James Joyce. And in my works the people always win. I am very proud of that. My message is one of hope instead of despair."

Some of Amado's works have been translated into as many as fifty languages, and he has gained quite an international reputation.

BIOGRAPHICAL/CRITICAL SOURCES: New York Times Book Review, January 22, 1967; *Book World,* August 24, 1969; *Saturday Review,* August 28, 1971; *New York Times,* October 1, 1977.

*   *   *

AMBERG, (Martin) Hans 1913-

PERSONAL: Born May 13, 1913, in Essen, Germany; son of Oscar (a merchant) and Frieda (Gans) Amberg; married Rie Sijmons, January 12, 1938; children: Ozzie M. *Education:* Educated in Germany and Switzerland. *Home:* 26089 Ross Dr., Detroit, Mich. 48239.

CAREER/WRITINGS: Worked in Netherlands as foreign correspondent for Sweden, Hungary, and United States, 1933-42; *Dagblad van Gouda,* Gouda, Netherlands, reporter, 1937-42; worked for Dutch underground on *Cooperator Underground,* 1942-45; *Het Parool,* Amsterdam, Netherlands, special features writer, interviewer, and reporter in Europe, 1945-47; *De Spiegel,* Amsterdam, U.S. correspondent, 1947-60; U.S. correspondent and free-lance writer in Netherlands, 1960—. *Member:* Foreign Press Association, Netherlands Foreign Press Association, Netherlands Journalist Guild, Detroit Press Club.

SIDELIGHTS: Amberg told *CA:* "Working for the Dutch Underground might sound like a great heroic feat. At the time it took place, it was a natural, national duty in order to help one's country—just like every soldier on the battlefield would defend his people against the enemy."

*   *   *

AMBERG, Richard H(iller), Jr. 1942-

PERSONAL: Born October 26, 1942, in Philadelphia, Pa.; son of Richard Hiller (a journalist) and Janet Law (Volkman) Amberg; married Beverly Sharp, August 27, 1966; children: Elizabeth Law, Richard Hiller III. *Education:* Harvard University, B.A., 1964. *Home:* 409 Greenfield Drive, St. Louis, Mo. 63132. *Office:* St. Louis Globe-Democrat, 12th & Delmar, St. Louis, Mo. 63101.

CAREER/WRITINGS: Staten Island Advance, Staten Island, N.Y., assistant city editor, 1966-71; *Syracuse Post-Standard,* Syracuse, N.Y., copy editor, 1971-72; *St. Louis Globe-Democrat,* St. Louis, Mo., copy editor, feature writer, book reviewer, 1972—. Moderator of television program "Staten Island Today" for WNYC-TV in New York, N.Y., 1968-70. Alumni adviser in journalism at Harvard University, 1974—. Member of communications committee, National Perinatal Association; steering committee member, Missouri Perinatal Association; member of board of directors, St. Louis Regional Maternal and Child Health Council; member of development board, St. Louis Children's Hospital; schools and scholarships committee chairman and treasurer, Harvard Club of St. Louis; treasurer, Conway Day School, 1974—. *Member:* Naval Reserve Association (vice-president), Reserve Officers Association (vice-president). *Military service:* U.S. Naval Reserve, 1964—; active duty, 1964-66; became lieutenant commander. *Awards, honors:* Received citation from American Institute of Architects, 1970; honorable mention from Sigma Delta Chi (New York City chapter), 1971, for environmental series; honorable mention from American Academy of Pediatrics, 1976, for series on child health; Catherine O'Brien Award, 1976, for women's interest reporting.

AMBLER, Effie   1936-

EDUCATION: Bryn Mawr College, A.B., 1958; Indiana University, Ph.D., 1968. *Office:* Department of History, Wayne State University, Detroit, Mich. 48202.

CAREER: Hollins College, Hollins College, Va., assistant professor of history, 1965-66; Wayne State University, Detroit, Mich., instructor, 1966-68, assistant professor of history, 1968—. *Member:* American Historical Association, American Association for the Advancement of Slavic Studies, American Association of University Professors.

WRITINGS: Russian Journalism and Politics, 1861-1881: The Career of Aleksei S. Suvorin, Wayne State University Press, 1972.

*   *   *

ANDREOPOULOS, Spyros (George)   1929-

PERSONAL: Born February 12, 1929, in Athens, Greece; came to the United States in 1953, naturalized citizen, 1961; son of George (an engineer) and Anne (Livas) Andreopoulos; married Christine Loesch Loriaux (a teacher of French), June 6, 1958; children: Sophie. *Education:* Wichita State University, A.B., 1958. *Politics:* Democrat. *Religion:* Greek Orthodox. *Home:* 1012 Vernier Pl., Stanford, Calif. 94305. *Agent:* Raines & Raines, Inc., 475 Fifth Ave., New York, N.Y. 10017. *Office:* Medical Center, Stanford University, Stanford, Calif. 94305.

CAREER: U.S. Information Agency, Salonika, Greece, information specialist in motion picture service, 1952-53; *Wichita Beacon,* Wichita, Kan., reporter, 1954-56, assistant editor of editorial page, 1956-59; Menninger Foundation, Topeka, Kan., assistant information officer and editor of *Menninger Quarterly,* 1959-63; Stanford University, Stanford, Calif., director of News Service at Medical Center and editor of *Stanford MD,* 1963—. Consultant to National Cancer Institute. *Military service:* Royal Hellenic Air Force, 1950-52; served in Korea.

MEMBER: National Association of Science Writers (member of executive committee, 1977—), American Medical Writers Association, American Cancer Society (member of board of directors), American Association for the Advancement of Science, Association of American Medical Colleges, American Hospital Association. *Awards, honors:* Award from Council for the Advancement and Support of Education and *Newsweek,* 1975; award from American Medical Writers Association, 1975, for *Primary Care: Where Medicine Fails.*

WRITINGS: (Editor) *Medical Cure and Medical Care,* Milbank Memorial Fund, 1972; (editor) *Primary Care: Where Medicine Fails,* Wiley, 1974; (editor) *National Health Insurance: Can We Learn From Canada?,* Wiley, 1975; (with Eugene Dong) *Heart Beat* (novel), Coward, 1978. Contributor to scientific and medical journals.

WORK IN PROGRESS: A novel based on his own experiences in Greece during World War II.

SIDELIGHTS: Dong and Andreopoulos often take opposite views on events and trends at Stanford University and on other medical issues, but they share several serious concerns, which resulted in collaboration on their novel.

Andreopoulos comments: "As a science writer I became concerned that in certain areas the scientific frontiers have extended to a never-never land, and require self-imposed restraints and extraordinary caution. In our novel, we deal with the misapplication of technology. An egotistical surgeon implants a nuclear-powered artificial heart in a patient, and his gamble threatens San Francisco with a disaster with a terrible twist. All this tells me that the notion that science should gain knowledge for its own sake is not good enough. The benefits must be weighed critically against the costs of research to society."

BIOGRAPHICAL/CRITICAL SOURCES: Palo Alto Times, February 1, 1978; *San Jose Mercury,* February 9, 1978.

*   *   *

ANGELL, Judie   1937-

PERSONAL: Born July 10, 1937, in New York, N.Y.; daughter of David Gordon (an attorney) and Mildred (a teacher; maiden name, Rogoff) Angell; married Philip Gaberman (a pop and jazz music teacher and arranger), December 20, 1964; children: Mark David, Alexander. *Education:* Syracuse University, B.S., 1959. *Religion:* "Yes." *Residence:* South Salem, N.Y.

CAREER: Elementary school teacher in Brooklyn, N.Y., 1959-62; *TV Guide,* Radnor, Pa., associate editor of New York City metropolitan edition, 1962-63; WNDT-TV (now WNET-TV), New York City, continuity writer, 1963-68; writer, 1968—.

WRITINGS—For children: *In Summertime, It's Tuffy,* Bradbury, 1977; *Ronnie and Rosey,* Bradbury, 1977; *Tina Gogo,* Bradbury, 1978.

WORK IN PROGRESS: A juvenile novel about a deeply troubled adolescent girl who seeks self-importance through her anonymous phone calls; a juvenile novel dealing with the effects of advertising and consumerism.

SIDELIGHTS: Angell commented: "My background is incredibly useful to me in writing fiction for children: the childhood imaginings, the diaries, summers at camp, teaching school, some techniques and discipline, and always the music for the mood. But most important to me are the feelings I recall so well.

"I think growing up heads the list of The Hardest Things To Do In Life," she continued. "It's so hard, in fact, that some of us never get there. But even if the world changes as rapidly as it does, the feelings that we have while we're coping with those changes don't. I take a lot of those feelings, hug them, wrap them carefully in some words, and present them in a book with an invisible card that says, maybe this'll help a little—make you laugh—make you feel you're not alone."

AVOCATIONAL INTERESTS: Singing, painting, cats, listening to music.

*   *   *

ANNAS, George J.   1945-

PERSONAL: Born July 13, 1945, in St. Cloud, Minn.; son of George J., Sr. (an electrical inspector) and Margaret M. (Pallansch) Annas; married Mary Frances Roche (a respiratory therapist), August 17, 1969; children: Catherina Leona, George David. *Education:* Harvard University, B.A. (magna cum laude), 1967, J.D., 1970, M.P.H., 1972. *Home:* 57 Lake Ave., Newton Centre, Mass. 02159. *Office:* Center for Law and Health Sciences, Boston University, 209 Bay State Rd., Boston, Mass. 02215.

CAREER: Law clerk in Boston, Mass., 1970-71; Boston College, School of Law, Newton, Mass., visiting assistant professor of law and executive director of Tufts-Boston Joint Center for the Study of Law, Medicine, and the Life

Sciences, 1972-73; Boston University, Boston, Mass., director of Center for Law and Health Sciences, 1973—, assistant professor of law and medicine, 1976—. Member of Bars of Minnesota and Massachusetts. Instructor at Boston College, 1973—. Chairman of Massachusetts Health Facilities Appeals Board, 1972-75; vice-chairman of Massachusetts Board of Registration and Discipline in Medicine and chairman of its complaint committee, 1976—.

WRITINGS: The Rights of Hospital Patients, Avon, 1975; (editor with A. Milunsky, and contributor) *Genetics and the Law,* Plenum, 1976; (with L. H. Glantz and B. F. Katz) *Informed Consent to Human Experimentation: The Subject's Dilemma,* Ballinger, 1977. Also author of *Avoiding Malpractice Suits Through Informed Consent: Current Problems in Pediatrics* (monograph), 1976.

Contributor: *Psychosurgery: A Multidisciplinary Symposium,* Lexington Books, 1974; Stewart and Stewart, editors, *Safe Alternatives in Childbirth,* NAPSAC, 1976; R. Egdahl and P. Gertman, editors, *Quality Assurance in Health Care,* Aspen Systems, 1976; *Medical Malpractice,* Ballinger, 1977.

Author of columns "Legal Signs" in *Centerscope,* 1974—, "Medicolegal Clinics" in *Orthopaedic Review,* 1974—, and "Law and the Life Sciences" in *Hastings Center Report,* 1976—. Contributor to *Legal Medicine Annual.* Contributor of articles and reviews to medical and legal journals and other related magazines. Editor-in-chief of *Medicolegal News,* 1972—.

WORK IN PROGRESS: Science fiction.

* * *

ANTHONY, William P(hilip) 1943-

PERSONAL: Born January 30, 1943, in Chicago, Ill.; son of Philip (a personnel manager) and Amelia (a teacher; maiden name, Spira) Anthony; married Roselyn Griest, April 22, 1968; children: Catherine, Sarah. *Education:* Ohio University, B.B.A. (cum laude), 1965; Ohio State University, M.B.A., 1967, Ph.D., 1971. *Home:* 318 Talwood Dr., Tallahassee, Fla. 32303. *Office:* College of Business, Florida State University, Tallahassee, Fla. 32306.

CAREER: Ohio Dominican College, Columbus, instructor in business, 1968-70; Florida State University, Tallahassee, assistant professor, 1972-73, associate professor of management, 1973—, chairperson of management area, 1976—. Guest instructor at Otterbein College, winter, 1970. Member of board of directors of Tallahassee Urban League, 1973-76. Seminar leader; consultant to public and private organizations. *Member:* Academy of Management, Industrial Relations Research Association (regional president, 1975—), American Society for Training and Development, American Arbitration Association (member of national labor panel), Southern Management Association, Beta Gamma Sigma.

WRITINGS: (With Joel Haynes and Paul Wilkens) *The Social Responsibility of Business: Text and Readings in Environmental Pollution, Minority Group Employment, and Consumerism,* General Learning Corp., 1973; (with Edward Nicholson, Jr. and Robert Litschert) *Business Responsibility and Social Issues,* C. E. Merrill, 1974; (with Nicholson) *Managing Human Resources: A Systems Approach to Personnel Management,* Grid Publishing, 1977; *Participative Management,* Addison-Wesley, 1978; (with B. J. Hodge) *Organizations: An Environmental Approach,* Allyn & Bacon, 1979. Contributor of about twenty articles to business, psychology, and education journals.

WORK IN PROGRESS: An article, "Do Black and White Supervisory Styles Differ?"

SIDELIGHTS: Anthony commented: "Every manager is a human resource manager regardless of his organizational level or type of organization. Managers, from supervisors to corporate presidents, from bishops to government agency heads must deal with one key resource—people."

* * *

APPEL, Allan 1946-

PERSONAL: Born November 12, 1946, in Chicago, Ill.; son of Morris and Pearl (Dawson) Appel; married Pamela Goldberg, 1972 (divorced, 1977). *Education:* Attended University of California, Los Angeles, 1964; Columbia University, B.A., 1968; attended Jewish Theological Seminary, New York, N.Y., 1964-67; City College of the City University of New York, M.A., 1972. *Residence:* New York, N.Y. *Agent:* Lee Braff, Julian Bach Literary Agency, Inc., 3 East 48th St., New York, N.Y. 10016.

CAREER: Queensborough Community College, New York City, lecturer in English, 1972-74; Teachers & Writers Collaborative, New York City, teacher, 1974-75; Jewish Association of Services for the Aged, New York City, social worker, 1975—. Lecturer at Uppsala College, 1972-73.

WRITINGS: New Listings (poems), Inwood Press, 1974; *Not So Much Love of Flowers* (poems), Toothpaste Press, 1975; *Judah* (novel), Leisure Books, 1976. Editor of *New York Times Magazine of Poetry,* 1971-73.

WORK IN PROGRESS: A novel, tentatively titled *Survivors.*

SIDELIGHTS: Appel writes: "I've an interest in new fiction, particularly in the settings of the West Coast—Los Angeles—where I grew up. I am presently completing a book on Los Angeles in the 1850's."

* * *

APPELBAUM, Judith 1939-

PERSONAL: Born September 26, 1939, in New York, N.Y.; daughter of Robert C. (an administrator) and Harriet (a lawyer; maiden name, Fleischl) Pilpel; married Alan Appelbaum (a lawyer), April 16, 1961; children: Lynn Stephanie, Alexander Eric. *Education:* Vassar College, A.B. (with honors), 1960. *Residence:* New York, N.Y.; and Danbury, Conn. *Office: Publishers Weekly,* 1180 Avenue of the Americas, New York, N.Y. 10036.

CAREER: Harper's Magazine, New York City, editor, 1960-69; John Day Co., New York City, editor, 1970-71; *Harper's Magazine,* editor, 1971-75; *Harper's Weekly,* New York City, managing editor, 1975-76; *Atlas World Press Review,* New York City, senior consultant, 1977; *Publishers Weekly,* managing editor, 1978—. *Member:* Authors Guild of America, Committee of Small Magazine Editors and Publishers.

WRITINGS: (Editor with Tony Jones and Gwyneth Cravens) *The Big Picture: A Wraparound Book,* Harper Magazine Press, 1976; (with Nancy Evans) *How to Get Happily Published,* Harper, 1978. Contributor of articles to *Harper's, Change, Writer,* and other publications.

SIDELIGHTS: Judith Appelbaum told *CA:* "Having started out in publishing at the age of eighteen (when I got a summer job at what was then Harper & Bros. and is now Harper & Row), I developed a keen interest in the strengths and weaknesses of the modern publishing process by the mid-1970s. The book I recently wrote with Nancy Evans—*How to Get Happily Published*—is an outgrowth of that general interest and, more particularly, of a periodical called *Harper's Weekly* which a group of us founded in 1974 and which was largely written by its readers—most of whom were not professional writers but, rather, men and women from many different fields who were eager to share the valuable personal and professional insights and experiences they'd amassed during their lifetimes.

"Working on *Harper's Weekly* taught me a good deal about how—and how much—people who weren't professional writers could contribute through print to our national fund of information and ideas, and it seemed clear that ameliorating the problems such people generally face in getting published would benefit editors, publishers, and the public alike.

"In the beginning, that was the idea behind *How to Get Happily Published*, but before long it became obvious that professional writers had problems every bit as serious as those sometime writers must confront, so, in the end, we decided to try to help writers at all levels of accomplishment—as well as people who want to write for publication at some particular point in their lives for some particular reason—to break into print and to reach an appropriate and appreciative public.

"So far, our efforts have been richly rewarded, in both tangible and intangible ways, and I look forward to continued experimentation with and analysis of current opportunities in publishing."

*   *   *

ARCHER, Jeffrey (Howard) 1940-

PERSONAL: Born April 15, 1940; son of William and Lola (Cook) Archer; married Mary Weeden, 1966; children: two sons. *Education:* Attended Brasenose College, Oxford. *Politics:* Conservative. *Home:* 24 A, The Boltons, London S.W. 10, England.

CAREER: Arrow Enterprises Ltd., London, England, chairman of the board, 1968—; Conservative member of the British Parliament, 1969-74; Archer Gallery, London, director, 1969—; Arrow Films Ltd., London, chairman of the board, 1973—. Chairman, Nigeria Consultants, Inc. Member, Greater London Council for Havering, 1966-70; executive, British Theatre Museum. *Member:* Royal Society of the Arts (fellow), Oxford University Athletics Club (president, 1965), Somerset Amateur Athletics Association (president), Carlton Cricket Club, Marylebone Cricket Club.

WRITINGS: Not a Penny More, Not a Penny Less, J. Cape, 1976, Doubleday, 1977; *Shall We Tell the President?*, Viking, 1977.

*   *   *

ARCONE, Sonya 1925-1978
(Sonya Goodman)

June 27, 1925—April 18, 1978; American writer best known for incorporating her experiences as a purchaser in the garment business in her writings. Among her works are *The Golden Hammer, Cage of Light*, and *The Werewolf of Hanover*. She died in Sarasota, Fla. Obituaries and other sources: *New York Times*, April 21, 1978. (See index for *CA* sketch)

*   *   *

ARIAS-MISSON, Alain 1936-

PERSONAL: Born December 11, 1936, in Brussels, Belgium; son of Guy Misson (an architect) and May Teleki; married Nela Arias (a painter), March 25, 1963. *Education:* Harvard University, A.B. (magna cum laude), 1959. *Politics:* "Liberational but not utopian." *Religion:* Roman Catholic. *Home address:* P.O. Box 24, Clarksburg, N.J. 08510.

CAREER: Free-lance artist (visual poetry) in Europe and the United States, 1964—; currently employed as simultaneous interpreter at the United Nations. Work has been exhibited at ten one-man shows, including Tool and Santandrea in Milan, Studio Brescia in Brescia, Il Canale in Venice, Brussels Art Fair, and U.S. Information Service in Brussels, and at several hundred group exhibitions in Europe, North and South America, and Japan. *Military service:* Belgian Infantry, 1962; became lieutenant. *Member:* International Conference Interpreter Association, Poets and Writers.

WRITINGS: Confessions of a Murderer, Rapist, Fascist, Bomber, Thief; or, A Year from the Journal of an Ordinary American, Chicago Review Press and Swallow Press, 1975; *Ole the Public Poem Is Me*, Arias-Misson, Factotum Press (Brescia, Italy), 1978.

Work represented in numerous anthologies, including *The Language Experience*, edited by James F. Hoy and John Somer, Dell, 1974; *Self-Portraits*, edited by Burt Britton, Random House, 1977; *Under Fire*, edited by Somer and J. Klinkowitz, Delacorte, 1978. Contributor to art and literary reviews, including *Art Vivant, Partisan Review, Drama Review, Mizue*, and *Geijutsu Seikatsu*. Advisory editor of *Chicago Review*, 1967 and 1975, *Tafelronde*, 1968-76, *Lotta Poetica*, 1971-75, and *Factotum Art*, 1977-78.

WORK IN PROGRESS: A novel.

SIDELIGHTS: Arias-Misson told *CA:* "I have just returned to the United States after an absence of seventeen years during which I lived in North Africa, Spain, and Belgium. I am active in visual poetry, having given hundreds of exhibitions with the Lotta Poetica group (seven or eight persons) in major museums and galleries, and have been interested in an experimental approach to language, poetry, or fiction. In fiction I have developed and coined the concept of 'superfiction,' now used by various critics and writers to characterize the 'new fiction.' The core concept is a familiar one: superfiction is the fiction on (super) the language of fiction; or, the fiction of the fictions (language) of fiction. Super-super-super, the onion layers of fictive language. More precisely, *writing* mirrors or reproduces the fictive truths: superfiction at its extreme both reveals itself (like the negative of a photograph) and *disenvelops* itself (an impossible photographic procedure) from the state of (language) superalienation in which our culture is mired, by an act of ecstasis, its relationship to the superreal.

"Now I'm less concerned with experimental modes which I consider acquired than with their 'life-modes.' I'm interested in fiction-in-life and life-in-fiction. *Rebirth* is the 'biographical' or experiential justification of superfiction: this allows one to live—and to write—in the Spirit, to cut through the mesh of superalienation with His sword—the Lord's."

BIOGRAPHICAL/CRITICAL SOURCES: Flashart (Milan), 1971-72; *Annuaire des Beaux-Arts*, 1974-75; *Art Vivant*, 1975; *International Herald Tribune*, May 14, 1975; *Lotta Poetica 1971-75*, Factotum Press, 1978.

*   *   *

ARMSTRONG, Richard 1903-
(Cam Renton)

PERSONAL: Born June 18, 1903, in Northumberland, England; married wife, Edith, 1926; children: John.

CAREER: Worked in a large steel-works as an errand-boy, greaser and laborer, and crane driver, 1916-19; served in the merchant navy, 1919-36; held a variety of jobs in London, including work on a small newspaper; full-time writer, 1956—. *Awards, honors:* Carnegie Medal, 1948, for *Sea Change;* first prize in the *New York Herald Tribune* Festival of Books, 1956, for *Cold Hazard.*

WRITINGS: Mystery of Obadiah, Dent, 1943; *Sabotage at the Forge* (illustrated by L. P. Lupton), Dent, 1946, reprinted, 1962; *The Northern Maid,* Dent, 1947, reprinted, Lythway Press, 1972; *Sea Change* (illustrated by M. Leszczynski), Dent, 1948, reprinted, 1960; *The Whinstone Drift* (illustrated by M. A. Charlton), Dent, 1951; *Passage Home,* Dent, 1952; *Wanderlust: Voyage of a Little White Monkey* (illustrated by Frederick Crooke), Faber, 1952; *Danger Rock* (illustrated by Leszczynski), Dent, 1955, published as *Cold Hazard* (illustrated by C. Walter Hodges), Houghton, 1956, reprinted, 1968; *The Lost Ship* (illustrated by Edward Osmond), Dent, 1956, Day, 1958; *No Time for Tankers* (illustrated by Reg Gray), Dent, 1958, Day, 1959; *The Lame Duck* (illustrated by D. G. Valentine), Dent, 1959; *Ship Afire!* (a Literary Guild selection), Day, 1959; *Sailor's Luck,* Dent, 1959, reprinted, Lythway Press, 1974.

Horseshoe Reef (illustrated by Valentine), Dent, 1960, Duell, Sloan, 1961; *Out of the Shallows* (illustrated by Valentine), Dent, 1961; *Trial Trip* (illustrated by Valentine), Dent, 1962, Criterion Books, 1963; *Island Odyssey* (illustrated by Andrew Dodds), Dent, 1963, published as *Fight for Freedom: An Adventure of World War II* (illustrated by Don Lambo), McKay, 1966; *Storm-Path,* Dent, 1964; (under pseudonym Cam Renton) *Big Head* (illustrated by B. S. Biro), Friday Press, 1964; *The Big Sea* (Literary Guild selection), McKay, 1965; *Grace Darling, Maid and Myth,* Dent, 1965; *Greenhorn* (illustrated by Roger Payne), Nelson, 1965; *The Secret Sea* (illustrated by Yukio Tashiro), McKay, 1966; *The Early Mariners,* Benn, 1967, Praeger, 1968; *A History of Seafaring,* Benn, 1967, Praeger, 1968; *The Mutineers* (illustrated by Rus Anderson; Literary Guild selection), McKay, 1968; *The Discoverers,* Benn, 1968, Praeger, 1969; *The Merchantmen,* Praeger, 1969; (editor) *Treasure and Treasure Hunters,* Hamilton, 1969; *The Albatross* (illustrated by Anderson), McKay, 1970; *Themselves Alone,* Houghton, 1972; *Powered Ships,* Benn, 1975.

BIOGRAPHICAL/CRITICAL SOURCES: Christian Science Monitor, May 10, 1956, May 23, 1968; *New York Times,* February 16, 1958; *New York Herald Tribune,* April 13, 1958.*

*   *   *

ARUNDEL, Russell M.   1903-1978

1903—February 2, 1978; American businessman best known as the founder and president of Pepsi-Cola Bottling Co., journalist, newspaper publisher, political lobbyist, and author. Arundel gained notoriety in 1949, when a "declaration of independence" he created for his fictitious "Principality of Outer Baldonia" was criticized by the Soviet press for granting its citizens, among other rights, the right to lie. In the 1950's, he sponsored a worldwide survey of rare mammals, which was considered to be one of the first focuses on the plight of endangered species. Arundel was thought to be an effective lobbyist and among his clients were a number of sugar companies. He was the author of two books on President Franklin D. Roosevelt. He died in Washington, D.C. Obituaries and other sources: *Washington Post,* February 3, 1978.

ARVIO, Raymond Paavo   1930-

PERSONAL: Born May 22, 1930, in Jersey City, N.J.; son of Paavo Jalmar and Mae Markus (Lahti) Arvio; married Cynthia Mallory (a writer and editor), July 14, 1951; children: Jan, Rachel, Sarah, Leslie (Mrs. Michael O'Brien), Heikki, David. *Education:* Rutgers University, B.S.Ed., 1951; graduate study at Goddard College. *Politics:* "Nonpolitical." *Religion:* Society of Friends (Quakers). *Address:* c/o Sisu-Olana, Route 45, Pomona, N.Y. 10970.

CAREER: United Housing Foundation, New York, N.Y., director of publications, 1965-70; Queens College of the City University of New York, Flushing, N.Y., lecturer in home economics, 1971-76; Co-Op Education Guild, Pomona, N.Y., executive director, 1977—. *Member:* Cooperative Editorial Association, Association of Cooperative Educators, Consumer Cooperative Alliance (chairman of development committee), Authors Guild.

WRITINGS: The Cost of Dying, Harper, 1974; *Manual on Cooperative Garages,* Co-Op Education Guild, 1977. Contributor to professional journals. Editor of cooperative newsletters.

WORK IN PROGRESS: The Joy of Living, a manual on cooperative households; a textbook on radical consumerism; a series of "how-to" books for cooperatives.

SIDELIGHTS: From 1953 to 1954, Arvio was imprisoned as a conscientious objector to war.

His present concerns include basic cooperative education, new life-styles, and alternative economic systems.

*   *   *

ASCOLI, Max   1898-1978

June 25, 1898—January 1, 1978; Italian-born American political scientist, educator, newspaper editor and publisher, and author. Ascoli began his teaching career as a professor of jurisprudence in Italian universities. He was jailed briefly during the regime of Benito Mussolini for his anti-Fascist beliefs. In 1931, he left Italy for the United States where he continued with his teaching at the New School for Social Research. In 1949, he founded *Reporter,* a journal that he edited and published until its demise in 1968. Ascoli was the author of several books on fascism and democracy. He died in Manhattan, N.Y. Obituaries and other sources: *Who's Who in America,* 39th edition, Marquis, 1976; *New York Times,* January 2, 1978; *Current Biography,* Wilson, March, 1978.

*   *   *

ASHE, Mary Ann
See LEWIS, Mary (Christianna Milne)

*   *   *

ASKENASY, Hans George   1930-

PERSONAL: Born March 9, 1930, in Frankfurt am Main, Germany; came to the United States in 1949, naturalized citizen, 1954; son of Robert and Dorothea (Wernecke) Askenasy; children: Thais. *Education:* University of California, Los Angeles, M.A., 1969, Ph.D., 1973. *Residence:* Laguna Beach, Calif. *Office:* Department of Psychology, California State University, Long Beach, Calif. 90840.

CAREER: State of California, Norwalk, staff clinical psychologist, 1973—; California State University, Long Beach, assistant professor, 1974—. Licenced psychologist. *Military service:* U.S. Marine Corps, pilot, 1953-58, 1960-67; became captain. *Member:* International Society of Political Psychology, American Psychological Association, Society for the Psychological Study of Social Issues, Western Psychological Association.

WRITINGS: Are We All Nazis?, Lyle Stuart, 1978. Contributor of articles and reviews to psychology journals.

WORK IN PROGRESS: Hitler, Jews, and Genocide: The Origins of Paranoia, an examination of the causes of Hitler anti-Semitism.

SIDELIGHTS: Askenasy writes: "The issue of 'normalcy' of those engaged in mass murder, wars, pogroms, and genocide is a clinical one, though everyone seems to feel entitled to his or her opinion on it. Hannah Arendt made the case originally ('banality of evil'), but did not prove or follow through on it. In my book I argue that the Nazis who carried out the murder of six million Jews at Auschwitz and other concentration camps were neither sadists, madmen, nor monsters. Most of us would like to think they were, for then the responsibility for the atrocities they committed could be placed upon a special class of criminals or lunatics essentially different from the rest of us. Auschwitz and all it stood for could not, we like to believe, have happened here. But it is psychologically easy, I point out, to ignore responsibility when one is only an intermediate link in a chain of evil. As Stanley Milgram points out in his discussion of this subject, 'The person who assumes fully responsibility for the act has evaporated. Perhaps this is the most common characteristic of socially organized evil in modern society.' I conclude in my book that individual crime and abnormality account for only a small fraction of human destructiveness. The main cause of large-scale destructiveness is social abnormality; and it is this collective madness which we do not fully understand and with which we have not yet come to terms."

*   *   *

ASSELBROKE, Archibald Algernon 1923-

PERSONAL: Born March 27, 1923, in England; son of Albert McClain and Alice (Tidworth) Asselbroke; married Doreen Goodlough, May 20, 1945; children: Jefferson and Jonathan (twins). *Education:* Earned A.B. from Cambridge University, and M.S. from University of Bristol. *Home and office:* 103 Mew Gardens, London SW27391, England.

CAREER/WRITINGS: Department store clerk in London, England, 1946-50; bus driver, 1950; *London Express,* London, rewrite man, 1950-55, assistant editor, 1955-65; *Bucksport Point Globe,* Bucksport, Me., editor and publisher, 1965—. *Military service:* Royal Air Force, bombardier, 1942-45; became lieutenant; received Royal Flying Cross. *Member:* Amalgamated Guild of Grape Treaders and Wine Strainers.

WORK IN PROGRESS: Following Mann's Tip: Go West, completion expected, 1978.

*   *   *

AUBERJONOIS, Fernand 1910-

PERSONAL: Born September 25, 1910, in Lausanne, Switzerland; son of Rene (a painter) and Madeleine (Grenier) Auberjonois; married Laura Murat, March, 1940 (divorced, 1968); married Helga Leibke, March, 1968; children: Rene, Michel, Anne. *Education:* University of Lausanne, licence es sciences, 1933. *Politics:* Independent. *Religion:* Protestant. *Home and office:* 28 Iverna Gardens, London W.8., England.

CAREER: Havas French News Agency, New York City,

reporter, 1934-36; National Broadcasting Co. (NBC), New York City, head of French service shortwaves, 1936-42; Time-Life International, Paris, France, publishing director, 1946-47; National Broadcasting Co., head of French service, 1947-48; Voice of America, New York City, head of French service, 1948-54; *Toledo Blade,* Toledo, Ohio, and *Pittsburgh Post-Gazette,* Pittsburgh, Pa., European correspondent, 1956—. Member of editorial board of English Speaking Union, 1973—. *Military service:* U.S. Army, 1942-45; served in military intelligence in Africa, Normandy, and Germany; became major; received Legion of Merit, Croix de Guerre with three citations, and Polonia Restituta. *Member:* Association of American Correspondents in London (member of executive committee), Reform Club, Mid-Atlantic Club (secretary, 1970-76). *Awards, honors:* Overseas Press Club Citation, 1957, for foreign reporting.

WRITINGS: L'Air d'Amerique (title means "American Diaries"), Editions Fontaine, 1944; *Mon Village USA* (title means "My Village U.S.A."), Editions Mediterraneennes, 1950; *L'Ile aux feux* (novel; title means "Fire Island"), Editions Mediterranneennes, 1952. Contributor of poems to *Sewanee Review, Transition, Adam International,* and *Nouvelle Revue Francaise,* and of articles to *Horizon, New Statesman,* and other periodicals.

WORK IN PROGRESS: An autobiography entitled *Am I an American.*

SIDELIGHTS: Auberjonois told CA: "Since I am a bilingual writer, writing professionally in French and in English (American), I'm therefore interested in other cases of hybridism. I have spent half my life explaining Americans to Europeans and the other half explaining Europeans to Americans."

*   *   *

AUBIN, Henry (Trocme) 1942-

PERSONAL: Born December 16, 1942, in New Brunswick, N.J.; son of Robert Arnold (a professor) and Elisabeth Gabrielle (a teacher; maiden name, Trocme) Aubin; married Penelope Morgan (a journalist), December 22, 1968; children: Seth Morgan, Nishi Elisabeth. *Education:* Harvard University, B.A., 1964; studied at Washington Journalism Center, 1968. *Home:* 622 Victoria Ave., Westmount, Quebec, Canada H3Y 2R9. *Office: Montreal Gazette,* 1000 Rue St. Antoine, Montreal, Quebec, Canada H3C 3R7.

CAREER: Philadelphia Bulletin, Philadelphia, Pa., urban affairs reporter and Washington correspondent, 1966-70; *Washington Post,* Washington, D.C., urban affairs reporter, 1970-71; *Montreal Gazette,* Montreal, Quebec, urban affairs reporter and editorial writer, 1973—. *Military service:* U.S. Army Reserve, 1965-71. *Member:* Canadian Centre for Investigative Journalism (co-founder). *Awards, honors:* B'nai B'rith Canadian Human Rights Award, 1973; Canadian National Newspaper Award, 1973, 1976, for enterprise in reporting; Canadian National Business Writing Award, 1974, 1975, 1976.

WRITINGS: City for Sale: International Financiers Take a Major North American City by Storm, James Lorimer & Co., 1977.

SIDELIGHTS: Aubin told *CA:* "To be a journalist in Quebec is, for the moment at least, to be amidst as much cultural vigor as anywhere in North America—there's a lot of work as well as excitement being in a society which is trying to burst out on its own after centuries as a sat-upon backwater.

''As an outsider and a Franco-American, I've naturally had a somewhat different though sympathetic perspective on what's going on. The bulk of my work has been in the form of investigative newspaper articles and now *City for Sale* which examines who owns Montreal, and which became a best-seller here in French (*Les Vrais Proprietaires de Montreal*). Because the forces behind this ownership are more global than parochial, the book is also being released in Europe (*La Nouvelle Conquete de l'Amerique*) and the United States.

''Most of my stuff deals with economic power and who wields it rather than with politics, since there are so many reporters who probe the latter and since without scrutiny business is all the more easily unaccountable. I am more interested in getting the facts out on how a society is being run and letting people form their own opinions than in trying to deliberately shape those opinions.''

B

BAGIN, Don(ald Richard) 1938-

PERSONAL: Born February 3, 1938, in Philadelphia, Pa.; son of August George (a salesman) and Mildred (Bednavik) Bagin; married Carole Rennie (a teacher), September 21, 1966; children: Gary, Cathy, Brian. *Education:* Villanova University, A.B., 1959, M.A., 1961; Temple University, Ed.D., 1969. *Religion:* Roman Catholic. *Home:* 806 Westminster Blvd., Turnersville, N.J. 08012. *Office:* Department of Communications, Glassboro State College, Glassboro, N.J. 08028.

CAREER: Teacher at public schools in Souderton and Langhorne, Pa., 1959-64, publicity director, 1961-64; public relations and personnel director for public schools in Marple and Newtown, Pa., 1964-65; Glassboro State College, Glassboro, N.J., assistant professor of communications, 1965; public relations coordinator for New Jersey State Department of Education, 1965-66; Glassboro State College, associate professor, 1966-68, professor of communications, 1968—, director of public relations, 1966-68. Directed public relations for Johnson-Kosygin Summit Conference held at Glassboro State College.

MEMBER: International Association of Business Communicators, National School Public Relations Association (lecturer), Educational Press Association of America, Education Writers Association, American Association of School Administrators, National Education Association, Phi Delta Kappa.

WRITINGS: (With Frank Grazian) *Public Relations for Principals,* Pennsylvania School Boards Association, 1969; (with Dave Lefever) *How to Gain Support for Your School's Budget and Bond Issue,* Glassboro State College Press, 1970; (with Grazian and Charles Harrison) *School Communications Ideas That Work,* McGraw, 1972; *How to Start and Improve Your Public Relations Program,* National School Boards Association, 1975; (with Harrison and Grazian) *Public Relations for Board Members,* American Association of School Administrators, 1976; (with Leslie Kindred and Donald Gallagher) *The School and Community Relations,* Prentice-Hall, 1976. Author of a column in *Network* (newspaper of National Committee for Citizens in Education), and a column in *Souderton Independent,* 1962-65. Contributor to education, public relations, and communications journals. Education editor of *Souderton Independent,* 1962-65.

SIDELIGHTS: Bagin comments: "My background in education and journalism has prompted a career concern of bringing schools and the media closer. This led to developing the first graduate program in school public relations to prepare people to handle communications responsibilities for schools, colleges, and other educational entities. This program attracts journalists interested in education and educators who write well."

*   *   *

BAHAT, Dan 1938-

PERSONAL: Born October 11, 1938, in Lwow, Poland; son of Isaac and Rachel (Ungar) Bahat; married Anath Gilboa, January 19, 1971; children: Joab, Amnon, Jonathan, Nadar. *Education:* Hebrew University of Jerusalem, M.A., 1975. *Religion:* Jewish. *Home:* 3 Klausner St., Jerusalem, Israel 93388. *Office:* Israel Department of Antiquities, Jerusalem, Israel.

CAREER: Israel Department of Antiquities, Jerusalem, archaeologist, 1963—; participator in digs at Arad, Nagila, Dan, and Massada; conductor of digs at Beth-Shemesh, Zafed, Sasa, and Beth-Yerah; former district archaeologist in Galilee and Jerusalem. Adviser on the city of Jerusalem for films and television programs. *Military service:* Israeli Army, 1956—; present rank, captain.

WRITINGS: Jerusalem Atlas, Scribner, 1975. Writer of pamphlets and handbooks on the history of Jerusalem. Contributor of articles to journals.

WORK IN PROGRESS: Jerusalem Under the Crusaders.

*   *   *

BAILEY, (Corinne) Jane 1943-

PERSONAL: Born March 31, 1943, in Butte, Mont.; daughter of John Lawrence (an agricultural engineer) and Corinne Margaret (a teacher and nurse's aide; maiden name, Willey) Bailey. *Education:* University of Montana, B.A., 1965; State University of New York at Buffalo, M.A., 1967, doctoral study, 1968 and 1972-73; also attended Collegio Victoria, Guadalajara, Mexico, 1970. *Home address:* P.O. Box 26, East Glacier Park, Mont. 59434. *Office:* Blackfeet Heritage Program, Browning Public Schools, Browning, Mont. 59417.

CAREER: Erie County Department of Social Services, Buffalo, N.Y., welfare caseworker, 1967, 1968; Western Washington State College, Bellingham, instructor in English, 1969-72; State University of New York at Buffalo, instructor in poetry at Millard Fillmore College, summer, 1973; Browning Public Schools, Browning, Mont., writer, editor, and coordinator for Blackfeet Heritage Program, 1977—. Member of board of directors of Montana Media, 1977—. Has given poetry readings in Buffalo and in the Northwest. *Member:* Associated Writing Programs. *Awards, honors:* Pushcart Prize from Pushcart Press, 1976, for "Late Track."

WRITINGS: Pomegranate (poems), Black Stone Press, 1976; (editor) *Between the High Mountains and the Rainbows,* Hardin Mountain School District, 1976; *Tuning* (poems), Slow Loris Press, 1978; (editor) *The Blackfeet: Five Viewpoints,* Browning Public Schools, 1978; (editor) *Blackfeet Language Coloring Book,* Blackfeet Heritage Program, 1978.

Work anthologized in *The Pushcart Prize 1976,* edited by Bill Henderson, Avon, 1976; *Montana Poets Anthology,* edited by Lex Runciman, Cutbank Press, 1978. Contributor to literary magazines, including *Slackwater Review, Calyx, Columbia, Choice,* and *Poetry Now.* Guest editor and associate editor of *Montana Gothic,* 1975-77; contributing editor of *Kaleidoscope,* 1977.

WORK IN PROGRESS: Poems; research on Blackfoot linguistics, mythology, and history; a continuing study of book design, especially educational materials as an art form.

SIDELIGHTS: Jane Bailey writes: "When I haven't found work writing or teaching (or recently, editing and book designing), I have preferred common labor jobs such as lumber mill labor, picking fruit, or helping to scale logs. Physical work is very important to a rooted vitality. I spent five months on a Kibbutz in Israel, in 1968-69, working in the fields."

AVOCATIONAL INTERESTS: Embroidery and designing embroidery, hiking, cross-country skiing, watching birds and animals, collecting mushrooms, dancing.

*   *   *

BAIN, Robert 1932-

PERSONAL: Born September 20, 1932, in Marshall, Ill.; son of Ernest Addison (a railroader) and Gail (Clark) Bain; married Bonnie Jean Baker (a program director at a university), December 27, 1951; children: Susan Elizabeth Bain McClannahan, Robin Anne, Michael Addison. *Education:* Eastern Illinois State College (now University), B.S. (honors), 1954; University of Illinois, A.M., 1959, Ph.D., 1964. *Politics:* "Prohibitionist." *Religion:* Baptist. *Home:* 114 Milton Ave., Chapel Hill, N.C. 27514. *Office:* Department of English, University of North Carolina, Chapel Hill, N.C. 27514.

CAREER: High school English teacher in Springfield, Ill., 1954-58; University of North Carolina, Chapel Hill, assistant professor, 1964-68, associate professor, 1968-77, professor of English, 1977—. *Member:* National Council of Teachers of English, Conference on College Composition and Communication (member of executive committee, 1971-74), Society for the Study of Southern Literature, Society for the Study of Midwestern Literature, South Atlantic Modern Language Association, North Carolina-Virginia College English Association (president, 1970-71).

WRITINGS: (Editor with George F. Horner) *Colonial and Federalist American Writing,* Odyssey, 1966; (editor) John

Neal, *Seventy-Six,* York-Mail Print, Inc., 1971; (editor) George Alsop, *A Character of the Province of Mary-Land,* York-Mail Print, Inc., 1972; *H. L. Davis,* Boise State College, 1974; (with Dennis G. Donovan) *The Writer and the Worlds of Words,* Prentice-Hall, 1975; (editor with Louis D. Rubin, Jr. and Joseph M. Flora) *A Biographical Guide to Southern Literature,* Louisiana State University Press, 1979. Part-time reporter for *Illinois State Journal,* 1954-58. Editor of *Eastern State News,* 1953, and *Green Cauldron,* 1962-64; member of editorial board of *Southern Literary Journal,* 1974—.

WORK IN PROGRESS: A study of early American writing.

*   *   *

BAKER, Asa
   See DRESSER, Davis

*   *   *

BAKER, Bill 1936-

PERSONAL: Born August 9, 1936, in Coldwater, Mich.; son of Maurice (a salesman) and Martha (Mizner) Baker; married Joann Zeitz, July 11, 1959; children: Lawrence, Susan, Gordon. *Education:* University of Detroit, Ph.B. and M.A., 1960. *Home:* 14571 Park Ave., Livonia, Mich. 48154. *Office:* Detroit Free Press, 321 W. Lafayette, Detroit, Mich. 48231.

CAREER/WRITINGS: Detroit Free Press, Detroit, Mich., editor of *Detroit Magazine,* 1965-68, Sunday editor, 1968-72, assistant managing editor, 1972—. Consultant. *Member:* American Association of Sunday and Feature Editors, Comics Council (board member), Sigma Delta Chi. *Awards, honors:* Art Directors Club of Detroit gold medals.

*   *   *

BAKER, James W. 1924-
   (Jim Baker)

PERSONAL: Born June 24, 1924, in Owensboro, Ky.; son of Roy (a salesman) and Sidney (Crutcher) Baker; married Mary Louise Swickard (a writer and editor), February 21, 1948; children: Barbara E., James N., John M., Elizabeth A. *Education:* Attended DePauw University, 1942-45. *Home:* 210 Hardy Way, Worthington, Ohio 43085. *Office:* Pioneer Press Service, Inc., P.O. Box 149, Worthington, Ohio 43085.

CAREER: Columbus Dispatch, Columbus, Ohio, cartoonist, 1947-66, creator of cartoon strip "Ben Hardy," 1952-66; author of cartoon strip "Ben Hardy," and panel "As You Were" for Pioneer Press Service, Worthington, Ohio. *Member:* Ohio Historical Society. *Awards, honors:* Ohio Governor's Award, 1948; distinguished service award from Ohioana Library, 1966.

*WRITINGS—*Under name Jim Baker: *From Settlement to Statehood,* Pioneer Press Service, 1965; *Cabin in the Clearing,* Pioneer Press Service, 1965, new edition, 1974; *Frontier Medicine,* Pioneer Press Service, 1965, new edition, 1974; *Ways of the Warriors,* Pioneer Press Service, 1966, new edition, 1975; *How Our Countries Got Their Names,* Pioneer Press Service, 1973; *Naming the States,* Pioneer Press Service, 1973; *Trains of Yesteryear,* Pioneer Press Service, 1973; *Get Out and Get Under,* Pioneer Press Service, 1973; *How to Be a Kid Again,* Pioneer Press Service, 1975; *Forts in the Forest,* Heartland House, 1975; *For the Ohio Country,* Heartland House, 1976; *Benjamin Franklin, Uncommon Man,* Heartland House, 1976.

SIDELIGHTS: Baker writes: "A lucky accident of birth made me a Kentuckian on my mother's side; growing up in history-rich Ohio and artistic and literary Indiana put me where I could do what I enjoy most: draw newspaper features about American history. One is an adventure strip whose hero, Ben Hardy, participates in events in our past; the other is a two-column panel.

"I have never felt the urge to travel beyond the United States, which has provided a gold mine of fascinating and humorous anecdotes for 'As You Were,' which is all about the scalawags and buffoons as well as the giants in our social history. A lot of the material is pure nostalgia, but that's nothing to be ashamed of. The field has been overrun lately by the fast-buck boys, but it's really here to stay. A healthy interest in our collective family history and our own yesterdays is a sign of maturity in a nation. We've just begun to realize that newest isn't always best, and to appreciate selectively the good parts of what's gone before. Look at the strong steady undercurrent of interest in the Big Bands, my own first love.

"I'm a family man, enjoying four grown children, all different and all interesting to watch as they mature, and a wife who is the other half of our business; we call it the world's smallest conglomerate. For a while we were operating a newspaper syndicate, doing free-lance art and editorial work and publishing a string of books. Now it's simmered down to just the syndicate; other people take care of the books, which I hope have brought a small knowledge of American and Ohio history and a few laughs to a couple of generations so far, thanks to the cooperation of the Ohio Historical Society, among others.

"I've wanted to be a newspaper cartoonist since I was a little kid, so it doesn't bother me that I'm not rich. I just want to draw, do some wood-carving and make some furniture and muzzle-loading rifles, build a log cabin in the Ohio countryside, and take walks with our two collies through the autumn leaves."

*   *   *

BAKER, Jim
    See BAKER, James W.

*   *   *

BALCON, Michael   1896-1977

PERSONAL: Born May 19, 1896, in Birmingham, England; son of Louis and Laura Balcon; married Aileen Leatherman, 1924; children: one son, one daughter. *Residence:* Sussex, England.

CAREER: Producer of motion pictures. Worked as film salesman, c. 1920; founder and production director of Gainsborough Pictures Ltd., 1924-36; production director of Gaumont-British Picture Corporation Ltd., 1932-36; associated with Metro-Goldwyn-Mayer, 1936-38; production director of Ealing Films Ltd., 1938-59, Producer of motion pictures, including "A Yank at Oxford," 1938," "It Always Rains on Sunday," 1949, "Kind Hearts and Coronets," 1950, "The Lavender Hill Mob," 1951, "The Man in the White Suit," 1952, and "The Scapegoat," 1959. Founded film production consortium, Bryanston, 1959. Production board chairman and governor of British Film Institute, 1963-71; board chairman of British Lion Films Ltd., 1964-65. Senior fellow of Royal College of Art. *Member:* British Film Academy (fellow), British Kinematograph Society (honorary fellow), London Academy of Music and Dramatic Art (council member). *Awards, honors:* Knight First Class of

Order of Saint Olav, 1948; D. Litt. from University of Birmingham, 1967.

WRITINGS: (Co-author) *Twenty Years of British Film, 1925-1945,* Falcon Press, 1947; *Michael Balcon Presents . . . A Lifetime of Films* (autobiography), Hutchinson, 1969.

SIDELIGHTS: Balcon assembled and trained the personnel that made Ealing Studios a world-wide success during the early fifties. He also provided Alfred Hitchcock his first opportunity to direct with "The Pleasure Garden." Balcon later produced Hitchcock's popular "The Thirty-Nine Steps."

OBITUARIES: Washington Post, October 19, 1977.*

(Died October 16, 1977, in Sussex, England)

*   *   *

BALDWIN, Christina   1946-

PERSONAL: Born April 16, 1946, in Great Falls, Mont.; daughter of Leo E. Baldwin (a social service administrator) and Connie McGregor (a real estate agent; maiden name, Anderson). *Education:* Macalester College, B.A. (cum laude), 1968; graduate study at Wigerwoods Institute, 1975-76. *Politics:* "Feminist." *Religion:* Society of Friends (Quakers). *Residence:* West St. Paul, Minn. *Agent:* Meredith Bernstein, Henry Morrison, Inc., 58 West 10th St., New York, N.Y. 10011. *Office:* Dogged Determination & Doggerel Productions Ltd., 978 B. Dodd Rd., West St. Paul, Minn. 55118.

CAREER: American Friends Service Committee, peace intern in San Francisco, Calif., 1968-69, coordinator of youth affairs in Philadelphia, Pa., 1970-71; American Bicentennial Commission, St. Paul, Minn., director of community relations, 1975; Chrysalis Center for Women, Minneapolis, Minn., counselor, 1976; Community Programs in Arts and Sciences, St. Paul, writer-in-residence and teacher, 1977—. Partner in Dogged Determination & Doggerel Productions Ltd. (therapy and writing seminars), 1978—. *Member:* Author's Guild, National Organization for Women, Feminist Writers Guild, Women's Institute for Freedom of the Press, Cousteau Society.

WRITINGS: One to One: Self Understanding Through Journal Writing, M. Evans, 1977. Contributor to magazines.

WORK IN PROGRESS: Mother Box, Daughter Box, a novel on the relationship between a mother and a daughter; two nonfiction books on feelings and power, with Joy Kanehl Hoenig.

SIDELIGHTS: Christina Baldwin writes: "*One to One* grew out of over seventeen years of personal journal writing, beginning when I was fourteen years old and continuing with only one gap in the time since. I have always felt the journal to be a friendly and private place for exploring my own feelings and growth. In April, 1974, I began teaching an adult education course, exploring journal writing, and have developed various courses, workshops, and seminars on journal writing from the upper grade school to the university level. It was out of this that the book eventually grew. After working with hundreds of journal writers around the country, I believe more firmly than ever in the invaluable aid journals of many varying and individual natures grant in our lives.

"The journal also led me into my year's training in transactional analysis and gestalt therapies and provides a solid psychological basis for my journal workshops and writings in many fields. I see myself as a writer who will continue to switch from the fiction to nonfiction mode, exploring topics of interest and speaking about contemporary life. Now in my early thirties, it is exciting to feel myself taking my writing seriously and learning to struggle and grow with my own creative process.

"In my twenties I spent a total of several years working and living abroad. My countries of residence include Germany, Switzerland, Great Britain, and Israel, with travel in East Germany, Czechoslovakia, France, Spain, Norway, Sweden, Denmark, and the Netherlands. All these voyages are recorded in my journals, providing a rich and reaccessible source of writing background and ideas."

AVOCATIONAL INTERESTS: Sports (running, racquetball, cross-country skiing, and bicycling), pen and ink sketches, playing the piano.

* * *

BALDWIN, Faith 1893-1978

October 1, 1893—March 18, 1978; American author of more than sixty books of fiction, nonfiction, and poetry. Baldwin wrote constantly from 1921 until her death and often wrote a chapter a day. Her most recent works were *Thursday's Child* and *Adam's Eden*. Several of her novels have been adapted for film. She died in Norwalk, Conn. Obituaries and other sources: *The Oxford Companion to American Literature,* 4th edition, Oxford University Press, 1965; *The Reader's Encyclopedia,* 2nd edition, Crowell, 1965; *Foremost Women in Communications,* Bowker, 1970; *Longman Companion to Twentieth Century Literature,* Longman, 1970; *Todays Health,* March, 1976; *Who's Who of American Women,* 10th edition, Marquis, 1977; *New York Times,* March 20, 1978; *Washington Post,* March 21, 1978; *Newsweek,* April 3, 1978; *Time,* April 3, 1978. (See index for *CA* sketch)

* * *

BALKIN, Richard 1938-

PERSONAL: Born June 28, 1938, in New York, N.Y.; son of Leo and Mae (an actress; maiden name, Questel) Balkin; married Georgia West, April 29, 1968 (marriage ended February 1, 1977). *Education:* Attended Cornell University, 1955, Bard College, 1956, San Francisco City College, 1957, Los Angeles City College, 1958, and Hunter College (now of the City University of New York), 1959; City College of the City University of New York, B.A., 1967; graduate study at Sarah Lawrence College, 1970, and Barnard College, 1971. *Politics:* "Radicalized bourgeois liberal." *Religion:* "Skeptical pantheist." *Office:* Balkin Agency, 403 West 115th St., New York, N.Y. 10025.

CAREER: Bobbs-Merrill Co., Inc., Indianapolis, Ind., textbook salesman, 1967-70, executive editor, 1970-73; Balkin Agency, New York, N.Y., literary agent and consultant, 1973—. Instructor at Herbert H. Lehman College of the City University of New York, 1974, and University of Massachusetts, 1975. Consultant to Ford Foundation. *Member:* Independent League of Authors Agents, New York Herpetological Society.

WRITINGS: A Writer's Guide to Book Publishing, Hawthorn, 1977. Contributor to anthropology, sociology, and language journals, and to *Writer's Digest.*

WORK IN PROGRESS: My Autograph Book; A Traveler's Guide to Outer Space.

SIDELIGHTS: Balkin writes: "I was a professional student and long-term waiter until I opened my mouth to an editor while serving him a hamburger in 1967 and was offered a job.

I was happiest as a soda jerk in Los Angeles. I am fascinated by poisonous snakes and the future and am trying to figure out how to combine both and make a living thereby. My current interest is to become a father and a free man. My greatest accomplishment was becoming an ex-smoker."

* * *

BANDY, Leland A. 1935-

PERSONAL: Born June 5, 1935, in Asheville, N.C.; son of Julian A. (a minister) and Eunice (Bascom) Bandy; married Ruth Esther Beavers, November 13, 1959 (divorced, 1968); married Mary Margaret Dygert, June 25, 1972; children: Ryan Leland, Alexa Suzanne. *Education:* Bob Jones University, B.A., 1958. *Religion:* Presbyterian. *Home:* 6817 Old Stage Rd., Rockville, Md. 20852.

CAREER/WRITINGS: Sims News Bureau, Washington, D.C., reporter, 1961-64; Van der Lines Bureau, Washington, D.C., reporter, 1964-66; Columbia Newspapers, Inc., Washington, D.C., Washington bureau chief, 1966—. Notable assignments include coverage of "all presidential nominating conventions since 1964." *Military service:* U.S. Army, 1958-61. *Member:* White House Correspondents Association.

SIDELIGHTS: Bandy told *CA:* "The Carter administration is one of the most inept to arrive on the scene in some time. If he doesn't turn the economy around, Jimmy Carter may become the Democrats' Herbert Hoover. The Republican Party," he continued, "is in danger of extinction if it doesn't reverse its drift to the right. The electorate is basically middle of the road."

* * *

BARCLAY, Glen St. J(ohn) 1930-

PERSONAL: Born February 5, 1930, in Auckland, New Zealand; son of Sydney St. John and Janet (Duncan) Barclay; married Elizabeth Mead (a librarian), September 7, 1962; children: Lisa Jane, David Andrew St. J. *Education:* University of Auckland, B.A., 1955; Victoria University of Wellington, M.A., 1958; Australian National University, Ph.D., 1963. *Politics:* National Country Party. *Religion:* Anglican. *Home:* 22 Samarai St., Brisbane 4070, Queensland, Australia. *Office:* Department of History, University of Queensland, Brisbane 4067, Queensland, Australia.

CAREER: Waterside Worker's Union, Auckland, New Zealand, laborer, 1948-55; National Library of New Zealand, Wellington, library assistant at Alexander Turnbull Library, 1956-57; New Zealand Treasury, Wellington, research officer, 1958-63; University of Queensland, Brisbane, Australia, lecturer in political science, 1964-65, senior lecturer in history, 1966-69, reader in international relations, 1970—. *Member:* Society for Historians of American Foreign Relations, American Military Institute.

WRITINGS: Commonwealth or Europe?, University of Queensland Press, 1970; *Struggle for a Continent,* Sidgwick & Jackson, 1971; *The Rise and Fall of the New Roman Empire,* Sidgwick & Jackson, 1971; *Twentieth-Century Nationalism,* Weidenfeld & Nicolson, 1972; *Mind Over Matter,* Arthur Barker, 1973; (editor with Joseph M. Siracusa) *Australian-American Relations Since 1945,* Holt, 1976; (editor with Siracusa) *The Impact of the Cold War,* Kennikat, 1976; *The Empire Is Marching,* Weidenfeld & Nicolson, 1976; *Their Finest Hour,* Weidenfeld & Nicolson, 1977; *Anatomy of Horror: A Study of the Occult in Fiction,* Weidenfeld & Nicolson, 1978; *A History of the Pacific,* Sidgwick & Jackson, 1978. Contributor to political science, history, and military affairs journals, and to *Australian Outlook*.

WORK IN PROGRESS: Stars Over the Pacific: The Record of Australian-American Relations; The Cheap Detectives: A Study of the American Detective Novel.

SIDELIGHTS: When *CA* asked Barclay about his views on relations between Australia and the United States, he replied: "The most important factor influencing Australian-American relations over the next decade will certainly be the continuing decline in importance of the military alliance between the two countries, simply because of the extreme unlikelihood of any situations arising which would cause the alliance to be invoked by either party. Australia could however have an increasingly important role in Washington's strategy for a New Economic Order as a politically stable supplier of essential industrial raw materials. Cooperation between the two countries should be made easier by the very great mutual goodwill which undoubtedly exists and could be strengthened by greater personal and cultural contacts between them. The greatest immediate need is for the United States to realise more keenly that Australia must genuinely export or die, and that greater access to the American market is a matter of life and death for Australian agriculture. I have not yet visited the United States myself, but I shall be spending some months there on study leave in 1980."

Barclay added: "My interest in the occult was probably largely inspired by the martial arts, and *Mind Over Matter* was basically concerned with the occult aspects of the martial arts, and their implications for the general field of parapsychology. *Anatomy of Horror* was a literary, philosophical and psychological study of some of the more influential writers of occult fiction, such as Stoker, Le Fanu, Rider Haggard, Lovecraft, and Wheatley. I am also interested in the recent work of Raymond L. Moody (*Life After Life*) and Elizabeth Kubler-Ross."

AVOCATIONAL INTERESTS: Military history and martial arts, seventeenth and eighteenth century painting, American literature.

*   *   *

BARCLAY, William   1907-1978

PERSONAL: Born in 1907, in Wick, Caithness, Scotland; married Katherine Barbara Gillespie; children: one son, one daughter (deceased). *Education:* Earned M.A. and B.D. from University of Glasgow; also attended University of Marburg and Trinity College, Glasgow. *Home:* 8 Berridale Ave., Cathcart, Glasgow S4, Scotland.

CAREER: Ordained minister of Church of Scotland; minister of Trinity Church of Scotland, Renfrew, 1933-46; University of Glasgow, Glasgow, Scotland, lecturer in New Testament language and literature, 1946-63, professor of divinity and biblical criticism, 1963-74; writer. Visiting professor at University of Strathclyde. Bruce Lecturer, 1935; Croall Lecturer, 1955; Kerr Lecturer, 1956; Baird Lecturer, 1969-70; Sir David Own Evans and Aberystwyth Lecturer, 1969; James Reid Memorial Lecturer, 1969, 1970. Member of joint committee for New English Bible. Speaker on television and radio. *Member:* Society of New Testament Studies, Society of Old Testament Studies, National Institute of Journalists, Royal Overseas League, Royal Scottish Automobile Club. *Awards, honors:* D.D. from University of Edinburgh; named Commander of the Order of the British Empire.

WRITINGS: Ambassador for Christ: The Life and Teaching of Paul, Church of Scotland Youth Committee, 1951; reprinted, Judson Press, 1974; *And Jesus Said: A Handbook on the Parables of Jesus*, Church of Scotland Youth Committee, 1952; *The Daily Study Bible*, Saint Andrew Press, 1953-59; *And He Had Compassion on Them: A Handbook on the Miracles of the Bible*, Church of Scotland Youth Committee, 1956, Westminister Press, 1970, revised edition published as *And He Had Compassion*, Saint Andrew Press, 1975; *A New Testament Wordbook*, S.C.M. Press, 1955; *Letters to the Seven Churches*, S.C.M. Press, 1957, Abingdon, 1958; *The Letter to the Hebrews*, Saint Andrew Press, 1957; *The Letter to the Romans*, Saint Andrew Press, 1957; *More New Testament Words*, Harper, 1958; *The Mind of St. Paul*, Harper, 1958; *The Master's Men*, Abingdon, 1959; *Educational Ideals in the Ancient World*, Collins, 1959, published as *Train Up a Child: Educational Ideals in the Ancient World*, Westminster, 1959; *The Plain Man's Book of Prayers*, Fontana Books, 1959, published as *A Book of Everyday Prayers*, Harper, 1960.

The Promise of the Spirit, Westminster, 1960; *The Mind of Jesus*, S.C.M. Press, 1960; *Crucified and Crowned*, S.C.M. Press, 1961; *The Making of the Bible*, Abingdon, 1961; *Flesh and Spirit:* Abingdon, 1962; *A Guide to Daily Prayer*, Harper, 1962; *Jesus as They Saw Him: New Testament Interpretations of Jesus*, Harper, 1962; *More Prayers for the Plain Man*, Collins, 1962; *A Plain Man Looks at the Beatitudes*, Collins, 1962; *The All-Sufficient Christ*, Westminster, 1963; *Epilogues and Prayers*, S.C.M. Press, 1963, Abingdon, 1964; *Many Witnesses, One Lord*, Westminster, 1963; *Prayers for Young People*, Collins, 1963, Harper, 1967; *Turning to God: A Study of Conversion in the Book of Acts and Today*, Epworth, 1963, Westminster, 1964; *Prayers for the Christian Year*, S.C.M. Press, 1964, Harper, 1965; *Two Minutes a Day: Daily Bible Studies*, Westminster, 1964; *The Plain Man Looks at the Lord's Prayer*, Collins, 1964.

Epistle to the Hebrews, Abingdon, 1965; *A New People's Life of Jesus*, S.C.M. Press, 1965, published as *The Life of Jesus for Everyman*, Harper, 1966; (editor) *The New Testament in Historical and Contemporary Perspective: Essays in Memory of G.H.C. Macgregor*, Basil Blackwell, 1965; *The Gospel and Acts*, S.C.M. Press, Volume I: *The First Three Gospels*, 1966, revised edition published as *Introduction to the First Three Gospels*, Westminster, 1975, Volume II: *The Fourth Gospel and Acts of the Apostles*, 1976, published separately as *Introduction to John and the Acts of the Apostles*, Westminster, 1976; *Fishers of Men*, Westminster, 1966; *Seen in the Passing*, compiled by Rita F. Snowden, Collins, 1966, published as *In the Hands of God*, Harper, 1967; *The Apostles Creed for Everyman*, Harper, 1967 (published in England as *The Plain Man Looks at the Apostles' Creed*, Collins, 1967); *The Lord's Supper*, Abingdon, 1967; *Communicating the Gospel*, Drummond, 1968; *The King and the Kingdom*, Westminster, 1968; *Prayers for Help and Healing*, Harper, 1968; (editor) *The Bible and History*, Lutterworth, 1968, Abingdon, 1969; (contributor) R. E. Davies, editor, *We Believe in God*, Westminster, 1968; (author of foreword) *The Bible Speaks Again: A Guide From Holland*, translated by Annebeth Mackie, Augsburg, 1969.

God's Young Church, Westminster, 1970; *Ethics in a Permissive Society*, Harper, 1971; *Through the Year With William Barclay: Devotional Readings for Every Day*, edited by Denis Duncan, Hodder & Stoughton, 1971, published as *Daily Celebration: Devotional Readings for Every Day of the Year*, Word, Inc., 1973; *The Old Law and the New Law*, Saint Andrew Press, 1972; *By His Spirit*, Washington Review and Herald Publishing, 1972; *Introducing the Bible,* Abingdon, 1972; *Jesus Christ for Today,* Tidings, 1973; *The Plain Man's Guide to Ethics: Thoughts on the Ten Commandments,* Fontana, 1973, published as *The Ten Commandments for Today,* Harper, 1973; *Every Day With William Barclay: Devotional Readings for Every Day,* edited by Duncan, Hodder & Stoughton, 1973; *Marching On: Daily Readings for Younger People,* edited by Duncan, Westminster, 1974; *By What Authority?,* Darton, Longman & Todd, 1974, Judson Press, 1975; *William Barclay: A Spiritual Autobiography,* Eerdmans, 1975 (published in England as *Testament of Faith,* Mowbray, 1975); *Jesus of Nazareth* (based on the film by Franco Zefirelli), Collins, 1977.

Collections: *The Mind of Jesus* (contains *The Mind of Jesus* and *Crucified and Crowned),* Harper, 1961; *New Testament Words* (contains *A New Testament Wordbook* and *More New Testament Words),* S.C.M. Press, 1964; *The Beatitudes and the Lord's Prayer for Everyman* (contains *The Plain Man Looks at the Beatitudes* and *The Plain Man Looks at the Lord's Prayer),* Harper, 1975; Johnston R. McKay and James F. Miller, editors, *Biblical Studies: Essays in Honor of William Barclay,* Westminster, 1976.

Editor with F. F. Bruce of "Bible Guides" series, twenty-two volumes, Abingdon. Editor and translator of New Testament books. Author of "Barclay Introduces the Bible" (cassette set), Abingdon Audio-Graphics, 1973. Contributor to scholarly journals.

WORK IN PROGRESS: Old Testament part of *Daily Study Bible.*

SIDELIGHTS: Known as the "common man's theologian," William Barclay appealed to the masses in Great Britain through his books and radio and television broadcasts, and succeeded in communicating Christianity in terms that they could understand. "Making it interesting is a practice that ... made William Barclay one of the leading religious authors of all time, from the standpoint of both sales and reader devotion," wrote John Charles Walton in *Christianity Today.* J. D. Douglas commented on Barclay's gifts as an "extraordinary communicator." Though Douglas acknowledged theological differences between Barclay and more conservative Christians, he concluded: "William Barclay's writings and broadcasts have spoken about Christianity to many millions otherwise unreached. Those who criticize his message could well copy his method, lest he reasonably point out that he prefers his way of doing it to their way of not doing it."

BIOGRAPHICAL/CRITICAL SOURCES: Christianity Today, March 15, 1974, January 16, 1976; *William Barclay: A Spiritual Autobiography,* Eerdmans, 1975. Obituaries: *New York Times,* January 25, 1978.*

(Died January 24, 1978, in Glasgow, Scotland)

*   *   *

BARETSKI, Charles Allan 1918-

PERSONAL: Born Novmber 21, 1918, in Mt. Carmel, Pa.; son of Charles Stanley (an engineer) and Mary Ann (a linguist; maiden name, Gorzelnik) Baretski; married Gladys Edith von Nytrai Yartin (a free-lance artist and illustrator), August 19, 1950. *Education:* Rutgers University, B.A. (cum laude), 1945; Columbia University, B.S.L.S., 1946, M.S.L.S., 1951; American University, diploma in archival administration, 1951, in advanced archival administration, 1955; University of Notre Dame, M.A., 1957, Ph.D., 1958; New York University, M.A., 1965, Ph.D., 1969. *Religion:*

Roman Catholic. *Home:* 229 Montclair Ave., Newark, N.Y. 07104. *Office:* Newark Public Library, 140 Van Buren St., Newark, N.J. 07105.

CAREER: Newark Sunday Ledger, Newark, N.J., reporter, 1935; New York University, New York City, book store clerk, 1936-37; Newark Public Library, Newark, reference librarian, 1938-45, senior librarian, art and music department, 1945-54; Van Buren Branch Library, Newark, director of foreign language book collection, 1954—. Founder and director of Baretski Tutorial Service, Newark, 1935-68, Institute of Polish Culture at Seton Hall University, South Orange, N.J., 1953-54, Newark Public Library Guild, Newark, 1970, Newark Public Library Employees Union, Newark, 1971—, and Ethnic Research Archives, 1972—. Research intern, National Archives, State Department, Washington, D.C., 1951; research associate, Notre Dame University, 1956-57; faculty member, Rutgers University, 1965-66; director and lecturer, Adult Education Intercultural History Series, Newark, 1959—. President, Associated Community Councils of Newark, 1969—. Consultant to Charter Reform Movement, City Government of Newark, 1953-54, U.S. Population and Ethnohistory Research Center, Newark, 1969—, Newark Community Development Administration, Newark, 1969-70, Essex County, N.J., Office on Aging, 1971-73, and Essex County College Senior Citizen Institute, Newark, 1977—.

MEMBER: Polish-Hungarian World Federation, American Library Association, American Council of Polish Cultural Clubs (archivist-historian, 1954—; first vice-president, 1952-54, 1959-62; second vice-president, 1967-68), American Political Science Association, American Sociological Association, American Historical Association, American Society of International Law, Society of American Archivists, Polish-American History Association (assistant national editor of bulletin, 1959-60, national editor, 1961-65), American Society for Aesthetics, Society of Historians for American Foreign Relations, Immigration History Society, Galileo Galilei Educational Foundation, New Jersey Writers Society (founder and director, 1947-56), Polish University Club of New Jersey (president, 1953-54; historian, 1963-67). *Awards, honors:* Founders' Day Award from New York University, 1970, for highest excellence in doctoral studies; American Heritage award from John F. Kennedy Library for Minorities, 1972.

WRITINGS: Our Quarter Century: History of the American Council of Polish Cultural Clubs, 1948-73, American Council of Polish Cultural Clubs, 1973; (contributor) Barbara Cunningham, editor, *The New Jersey Ethnic Experience,* William H. Wise, 1977. Also editor and compiler of *The Polish Pantheon: A Roster of Men and Women of Polish Birth or Ancestry Who Have Contributed to American Culture and World Civilization,* 1958. Feature columnist, *Post Eagle* newspaper, Clifton, N.J., 1963-67. Contributor of articles to *Art in America, Opera News, Polish American Studies,* and other journals. Editor and publisher, *Ironbound Counselor* newspaper, Newark, 1965.

WORK IN PROGRESS: Our Half Century: History of the Polish University Club of New Jersey 1928-78, to be published in 1978.

SIDELIGHTS: Baretski seeks to make the public aware of "the multiple and relatively unrecognized cultural and historical contributions of all ethnic, racial, and religious groups in the U.S.A." through his writing and lecturing. His extensive experience in community service organizations has fostered his belief in "voluntarism, altruism, and self-motivation to solve the world's problems.'' He has completed fifty years of free tutoring to students of all races, creeds, and nationalities. His academic interests in U.S.-European diplomacy have led him to visit Europe intensively, and he has competence in German, French, Italian, and Slavonic languages.

*   *   *

BARNARD, J(ohn) Lawrence 1912-1977

PERSONAL: Born 1912; married Diana Kissel; children: Daphne Barnard Davis, Sylvia Barnard Brown, Pamela Barnard Ruzicka. *Education:* Graduated from Yale University, 1934. *Residence:* Stonington, Conn.

CAREER: After college graduation briefly held jobs on Wall Street and at *Time* magazine, New York, N.Y.,; U.S. State Department, former staff member at Office of Intelligence Research, American consul in Antwerp, 1954-59, consul general in Aruba, 1960, consul general in the Bahamas, 1960-66. *Wartime service:* U.S. Army, Military Intelligence, World War II; became major.

WRITINGS: Revelry by Night (novel), Doubleday, 1941; *Land of Promise* (novel), Doubleday, 1942; *Gently Down the Stream* (autobiography), Walker & Co., 1976.

SIDELIGHTS: J. Lawrence Barnard's novels were esteemed by critics but largely ignored by the public. Anatole Broyard found Barnard's autobiography a charming testimony that a sensitive individual can lead an undistinguished life and yet remain content: ''Without accomplishing anything that the world would call remarkable, he seems to have been happy all his life. If he had been a fool or a sloth, this might have been an easy matter, but on the evidence of this book he appears to be intelligent, witty, extraordinarily well balanced and filled with vitality.''

BIOGRAPHICAL/CRITICAL SOURCES: New York Times, January 1, 1977. *Obituaries: New York Times,* August 8, 1977; *AB Bookman's Weekly,* October 17, 1977.*

(Died August 5, 1977, in New York, N.Y.)

*   *   *

BARNARD, Robert 1936-

PERSONAL: Born November 23, 1936, in Burnham, England; son of Leslie (a writer) and Vera (Nethercoat) Barnard; married Mary Louise Tabor (a librarian). *Education:* Balliol College, Oxford, B.A. (with honors), 1959. *Politics:* ''Vaguely left-wing.'' *Home:* Isbjoernvei 18, 9020 Tromsdalen, Norway. *Office:* Institutt for sprak og litteratur, Universitetet, Tromsoe, 9001, Norway.

CAREER: University of New England, New South Wales, Australia, lecturer in English, 1961-66; University of Bergen, Bergen, Norway, senior lecturer in English, 1966-76; University of Tromsoe, Tromsoe, Norway, professor of English literature, 1976—. *Member:* Dickens Fellowship, Bronte Society, Crime Writers Association.

WRITINGS: Imagery and Theme in the Novels of Dickens, Norwegian University Press, 1974; *Death of an Old Goat,* Collins, 1974; *A Little Local Murder,* Collins, 1976; *Death on the High C's,* Collins, 1977.

WORK IN PROGRESS: Blood Brotherhood; Unruly Son; Death in a Cold Climate; research on a book on Evelyn Waugh.

SIDELIGHTS: Barnard told *CA:* ''I suppose I write because writing has always been around as a possibility, my father having been an author of sentimental romances. I

write detective stories because they have a ready-made framework of plot which one is more or less forced to conform to. Any 'real' novel I wrote would be horribly shapeless.''

*   *   *

BARNES, Clive (Alexander) 1927-

PERSONAL: Born May 13, 1927, in London, England; son of Arthur Lionel (an ambulance driver) and Freda Marguerite (a secretary; maiden name, Garratt) Barnes; married second wife, Patricia Amy Evelyn Winckley, June 26, 1958; children: Christopher John Clive, Joanna Rosemary Maya. *Education:* Attended King's College, London; Oxford University, B.A., 1951. *Religion:* Church of England. *Home:* 344 West 72nd St., New York, N.Y. 10023. *Office: New York Times,* 229 West 43rd St., New York, N.Y. 10036.

CAREER: Arabesque, Oxford, England, co-editor, 1950; *Dance and Dancers,* London, England, assistant editor, 1950-58, associate editor, 1958-61, executive editor, 1961-65, editor in New York City, 1965—; London County Council, London, administrative officer in town planning, 1952-61; *London Times,* London, chief dance critic, 1961-65; *New York Times,* New York City, dance critic, 1965—, daily drama critic, 1967-77; *New York Post,* New York City, drama critic, 1977—. Adjunct associate professor of journalism at New York University, 1968—. *Military service:* Royal Air Force, 1946-48. *Member:* Critics Circle London (past secretary, chairperson of ballet section), New York Drama Critics Circle.

WRITINGS: Ballet in Britain Since the War, C. A. Watts, 1953; *Frederick Ashton and His Ballets,* Dance Perspectives Foundation, 1961; (with A. V. Coton and Frank Jackson) Susan Lester, editor, *Ballet Here and Now,* Dobson, 1961; (editor with Horst Koegler) *Ballett 1965: Chronik und Bilanz des Ballettjahres,* Friedrich Verlag, 1965; (editor with Koegler) *Ballett 1966: Chronik und Bilanz des Ballettjahres,* Friedrich Verlag, 1966; (author of commentary) Jack Mitchell, photographer, *Dance Scene U.S.A.: America's Greatest Ballet and Modern Dance Companies in Photographs,* World Publishing, 1967; (editor and author of foreword) *Fifty Best Plays of the American Theatre from 1787 to the Present,* four volumes, Crown, 1969; (editor with John Gassner) *Best American Plays: Sixth Series, 1963-1967,* Crown, 1971; (author of introduction) *New York Times Directory of the Theatre,* Quadrangle, 1973; (editor) *Best American Plays: Seventh Series,* Crown, 1974; *Inside American Ballet Theatre,* Hawthorn, 1976.

Contributor of articles and reviews to periodicals, including *Dance, Nation, New Republic, Harper's,* and *Vogue.* Music, dance, drama, and film critic for *Daily Express,* London, 1956-65; dance critic for *Spectator,* London, 1959-65; executive editor of *Plays and Players, Films and Filming,* and *Music and Musicians,* 1961-65.

*   *   *

BARTON, H. Arnold 1929-

PERSONAL: Born November 30, 1929, in Los Angeles, Calif.; son of Sven Hildor Barton (a teacher); married Aina Bergman, December 29, 1960. *Education:* Pomona College, B.A., 1953; Princeton University, Ph.D., 1962. *Politics:* Democrat. *Home:* 604 South Oakland, Apt. 8, Carbondale, Ill. 62901. *Office:* Department of History, Southern Illinois University, Carbondale, Ill. 62901.

CAREER: University of Alberta, Edmonton, 1960-63, began as lecturer, became assistant professor of history; University of California, Santa Barbara, assistant professor of history, 1963-70; Southern Illinois University, Carbondale, associate professor, 1970-75, professor of history, 1975—. *Military service:* U.S. Coast Guard, 1953-57; became lieutenant junior grade. *Member:* American Historical Association, Society for the Advancement of Scandinavian Studies, Swedish Pioneer Historical Society, Immigration History Society. *Awards, honors:* National Endowment for the Humanities fellowship.

WRITINGS: (Editor) *Scandinavians and America: Essays Presented to Franklin D. Scott,* Swedish Pioneer Historical Society, 1974; *Count Hans Axel von Fersen: Aristocrat in an Age of Revolution,* Twayne, 1975; (editor) *Letters from the Promised Land: Swedes in America, 1840-1914,* University of Minnesota Press, 1975. Also author of *The Baltic Shore to the Pacific Coast: A Swedish-American Family Saga,* 1978; editor of *Clipper Ship and Covered Wagon: Essays from the Swedish Pioneer Historical Quarterly,* 1978. Contributor to history and Scandinavian studies journals. Editor of *Swedish Pioneer Historical Quarterly,* 1974—.

WORK IN PROGRESS: Scandinavia in the Revolutionary Era, 1762-1815.

SIDELIGHTS: Barton writes: "As a historian I am particularly interested in Scandinavia in the late eighteenth and early nineteenth centuries, in Scandinavian emigration, and in Scandinavians (especially Swedes) in North America. I have lived for varying lengths of time in Britain, France, Greece, and Sweden. My foreign languages include French, German, Italian, Russian, Swedish, Danish, and Norwegian."

*   *   *

BASA, Eniko Molnar   1939-

PERSONAL: Born September 7, 1939, in Huszt, Hungary; came to the United States in 1950, naturalized citizen, 1956; daughter of Julius V. (a physician) and Terezia (Fejer) Molnar; married Peter Basa (a biomedical systems analyst), November 19, 1965. *Education:* Trinity College, Washington, D.C., B.A., 1962; University of North Carolina, M.A., 1965, Ph.D., 1972. *Home:* 707 Snider Lane, Silver Spring, Md. 20904. *Office:* Library of Congress, Washington, D.C.

CAREER: Library of Congress, Washington, D.C., cataloger, 1963; University of Maryland, College Park, instructor in English, 1965-69; Dunbarton College of the Holy Cross, Washington, D.C., assistant professor of English, 1970-72; American University, Washington, D.C., part-time professorial lecturer in English, 1972-75; Hood College, Frederick, Md., part-time lecturer in English, 1975—. Participant in international conferences.

MEMBER: International Comparative Literature Association, Modern Language Association of America, American Comparative Literature Association, American Hungarian Educators Association (president, 1974-78), American Hungarian Foundation, Council on National Literatures, Southern Comparative Literature Association (member of advisory board, 1974-77; vice-president, 1977-78).

WRITINGS: (Editor) Steven C. Scheer, *Mikszath,* Twayne, 1977; *Sandor Petofi,* Twayne, 1978. General editor of Hungarian section of "Twayne World Authors Series." Contributor of articles and reviews to literature and Hungarian studies journals. Associate editor of *Comparatist;* review editor of *Hungarian Studies Newsletter;* member of

editorial board of *Canadian-American Review of Hungarian Studies.*

WORK IN PROGRESS: The "Tragedy of Man" as the Culmination of the "Poeme d'Humanite"; a book about Hungarian influences on German literature up to the middle of the nineteenth century; continuing research on Hungarian ethnic literature of the Plains states.

SIDELIGHTS: Eniko Basa told *CA:* "All aspects of Hungarian cultural activity interest me, although literary studies, translations, and the study of the Hungarian contributions to the pluralism of American literature rank high. I have participated in numerous conferences because of the opportunity these offer for contacts with others in the field."

*   *   *

BASU, Romen   1923-

PERSONAL: Born October 1, 1923, in Calcutta, India; came to the United States in 1948; married wife, Rasil (a lawyer); children: Amrita, Rekha. *Home:* 345 East 69th St., New York, N.Y. 10021.

CAREER: Writer, 1968—.

WRITINGS: A House Full of People, Navana, 1968; *Canvas and the Brush* (short stories), Firma K. L. Mikhupadhaya, 1970; *Your Life to Live,* Firma K. L. Mikhupadhaya, 1972; *A Gift of Love,* Writers Workshop (Calcutta), 1974; *The Tamarind Tree,* Writers Workshop, 1976; *Candles and Roses,* Sterling Publishers (New Delhi), 1977; *Portrait on the Roof,* Sterling Publishers, in press.

*   *   *

BATES, Betty
See BATES, Elizabeth M.

*   *   *

BATES, Elizabeth   1921-
(Betty Bates)

PERSONAL: Born October 5, 1921, in Evanston, Ill.; daughter of Alexander Willett (a civil engineer) and Elizabeth (a teacher; maiden name, Bragdon) Moseley; married Edwin R. Bates (a lawyer), September 3, 1947; children: Thomas, Daniel, Lawrence, Sarah. *Education:* Attended National Park College, 1939-40, Beloit College, 1940-41, and Katharine Gibbs Secretarial School, 1941-42. *Home:* 5 Milburn Park, Evanston, Ill. 60201.

CAREER: Worked as a secretary, 1942-48; writer, 1963—. Past member of Evanston board of directors of Rehabilitation Institute of Chicago. *Member:* Children's Reading Round Table (Chicago), Planned Parenthood Association (Chicago; member of Evanston board of directors), Off-Campus Writers Workshop (Winnetka, Ill.; member of board of directors), Garden Club of Evanston (past member of board of directors).

WRITINGS—Juvenile; under name Betty Bates: *Bugs in Your Ears* (Junior Literary Guild selection), Holiday House, 1977; *The Ups and Downs of Jorie Jenkins* (Junior Literary Guild selection), Holiday House, 1978.

WORK IN PROGRESS: Two children's books, under name Betty Bates.

SIDELIGHTS: Betty Bates writes: "Since most adult readers started to read as children, I think it's highly important to interest young people in books. For this reason, I include as much humor as possible, as well as what I hope are suspenseful plots with which my readers can identify in one way or another. I aim for tight, accurate, sensitive writing. I write in the first person, present tense, because this method suits my style and throws the reader into the story.

"I'm concerned about the plight of many young people today, who are called upon to face threatening situations, often with little adult support. One problem that worries me is the child in the disintegrating family so common in our world. In my first book, *Bugs in Your Ears,* I told the story of Carrie, whose divorced mother marries a man with three children. Carrie feels she's the outsider, that no one listens to her, that her new family has 'bugs in their ears.' In my talks with young people in schools, I've discovered many who identify with Carrie, and who are thus made to feel they're not alone in their situations.

"In *The Ups and Downs of Jorie Jenkins,* Jorie's dad, whom she adores, has a serious heart attack. Painfully she adjusts to the fact that he'll never be the same hearty, capable man he was. And she has the strength to grow from her experience.

"The world of young people fascinates me, and I feel fortunate to be a part of it."

BIOGRAPHICAL/CRITICAL SOURCES: Evanston Review, September 15, 1977; *North Shore Monthly,* April-May, 1978.

*   *   *

BATHURST, Sheila
  See SULLIVAN, Sheila

*   *   *

BATTELLE, Phyllis (Marie)   1922-

PERSONAL: Born January 4, 1922, in Dayton, Ohio; daughter of Gordon S. (a certified public accountant) and Marie (an artist; maiden name, Sides) Battelle; married Arthur Van Horn (in real estate), December 6, 1957; children: Jonathan Gordon. *Education:* Ohio Wesleyan University, B.A., 1944. *Religion:* Protestant. *Home address:* Old Church Lane, Pound Ridge, N.Y. 10576. *Agent:* Sterling Lord Agency, Inc., 660 Madison Ave., New York, N.Y. 10021. *Office:* King Features Syndicate, 235 East 45th St., New York, N.Y. 10017.

CAREER: Dayton Herald, Dayton, Ohio, police reporter, feature writer, and author of teenagers' column, 1944-47; women's editor and fashion editor for International News Service, 1947-54; King Features Syndicate, New York, N.Y., author of syndicated column "Assignment: America," 1955—. *Member:* New York Newspaperwomen's Club, Delta Gamma. *Awards, honors:* Awards from Ohio Newspaperwomen's Association, 1944-47; award from New York Newspaperwomen's Club, 1951, for domestic news coverage.

WRITINGS: (With Joseph Quinlan and Julia Quinlan) *Karen Ann: The Quinlans Tell Their Story,* Doubleday, 1977. Contributor to national magazines.

*   *   *

BATTERBERRY, Michael Carver   1932-

PERSONAL: Born April 8, 1932, in Newcastle, England; son of William J. (an executive) and June (Forsman) Batterberry; married Ariane Ruskin (a writer), May 15, 1968. *Education:* Attended Carnegie Institute of Technology (now Carnegie-Mellon University), University of Cincinnati, and Art Students League. *Home:* 1100 Madison Ave., New York, N.Y. 10028.

CAREER: Painter, designer, and writer; co-founder of design agency in Venezuela; editor-in-chief of *International Review of Food and Wine,* 1977—. Has exhibited work in Europe, South America, and the United States. Designed restaurants, hotel decor, and clubs, including the American Club in Caracas, Venezuela; appeared on television and radio programs, including "Good Morning America" and "The Joyce Brothers Program." *Awards, honors:* National award for Bonwit Teller window designs.

WRITINGS: Chinese and Oriental Art, McGraw, 1968; *Twentieth Century Art,* McGraw, 1969; (with wife, Ariane Batterberry) *Greek and Roman Art,* McGraw, 1970; *Art of the Early Renaissance,* McGraw, 1970; *Art of the Middle Ages,* McGraw, 1972; (with A. Batterberry) *Primitive Art,* McGraw, 1972; (with A. Batterberry) *Children's Homage to Picasso,* Abrams, 1973; (with A. Batterberry) *On the Town in New York,* Scribner, 1973; (with A. Batterberry) *The Pantheon Story of American Art* (Literary Guild selection), Pantheon, 1976; (with A. Batterberry) *The Bloomingdale's Book of Entertaining* (Literary Guild selection), Random House, 1976; (with A. Batterberry) *Vanity Fair,* Holt, 1977; *Mirror, Mirror: A Social History of Fashion,* Holt, 1977. Editor of "The Great Cooks Series," Random House, 1977. Contributor of articles, illustrations, and drawings to popular magazines and newspapers, including *New York, Ladies Home Journal, Playbill,* and *Travel and Leisure.* Contributing editor of *Harper's Bazaar,* 1972-73.

*   *   *

BATY, Roger M(endenhall)   1937-

PERSONAL: Born October 20, 1937, in Helena, Mont.; son of H. F. (a professor) and E. L. Baty; married Phebe Nelson; children: Iliniza, Jonathan, Marguerite. *Education:* Montana State University, B.A. (economics; honors), 1958; Merton College, Oxford, B.A. (philosophy, politics, and economics), 1961; Montana State College, teaching certificate, 1963; Stanford University, Ph.D., 1969. *Office:* Department of Intercultural/International Studies, Johnston College, Redlands, Calif. 92373.

CAREER: Johnston College, Redlands, Calif., associate professor and faculty fellow in anthropology and education, 1969—. *Military service:* U.S. Army Reserve, 1963-69. California National Guard, 1978—; present rank, sergeant. *Member:* American Anthropological Association, American Educational Research Association, Society for Intercultural Education, Training and Research.

WRITINGS: Re-Educating Teachers for Cultural Awareness, Praeger, 1971; *Regional Crafts of Mexico,* privately printed, 1978. Contributor to *America Indigena* and *International Journal of Intercultural Relations.*

WORK IN PROGRESS: Research on culture stress and adaptation and on regional crafts of Mexico.

SIDELIGHTS: Baty writes: "I consider my main accomplishment at Johnston College to be the evolution of a year-long sequence in new culture learning, involving three successive stages of preparation, experience, and reflection. The reflective phase has proved particularly important in terms of helping the student integrate and become conscious of the growth at a personal and cognitive level begun in the earlier phases. Development of this model during the past two years has been with financial help from the National Lilly Endowment, Inc.

"Philosophically, I am what might be called a 'one-worlder,' tempered by realism. While we obviously live in an interdependent world community, many psychological as well as physical and political-emotional barriers prevent true cooperation. I like to think of myself as working with those who are working toward a world community or global spaceship characterized by cooperation and mutual assistance in areas of economic and social development.

"In community terms, of crucial importance are institutions providing for stability and continuity during times of relatively rapid change. Family, school, church, are examples of such institutions which in fact are not weathering terribly well."

* * *

BAUER, Caroline Feller 1935-

PERSONAL: Born May 12, 1935, in Washington, D.C.; daughter of Abraham (a lawyer) and Alice (an adviser of foreign students; maiden name, Klein) Feller; married Peter A. Bauer (president of White Stag), December 21, 1968; children: Hilary. *Education:* Sarah Lawrence College, B.A., 1957; Columbia University, M.S., 1958; University of Oregon, Ph.D., 1971. *Home:* 15160 Southwest 133rd, Tigard, Ore. 97223. *Office:* School of Librarianship, University of Oregon, Eugene, Ore. 97034.

CAREER: New York Public Library, New York, N.Y., children's librarian, 1958, 1959, 1961; public school librarian in Carbondale, Colo., 1963-66; University of Oregon, Eugene, associate professor of library science, 1966—. Producer for KOAP-TV, 1973-74. *Member:* American Library Association, Society of American Magicians, Puppeteers of America, Bedlington Terrier Club of America.

WRITINGS: Children's Literature: A Teletext, Oregon Educational Public Broadcasting Service, 1973; *Handbook for Storytellers,* American Library Association, 1977. Contributor to *Cricket.*

Also author of *Getting It Together With Books,* 1974; *Storytelling,* 1974; *Caroline's Corner,* 1974; *Children's Literature,* 1978.

AVOCATIONAL INTERESTS: Travel (Europe, the Far and Near East, India), skiing (member of National Ski Patrol), jogging, tennis, ice skating, swimming, kayaking, horses, dogs, cooking (and eating), puppetry, magic, drawing, crafts.

* * *

BAULCH, Jerry T. 1913-

PERSONAL: Born July 14, 1913, in Alexandria, La.; son of Monte J. and Ada A. Baulch; married Sadie Renshaw (a legislative relations director), November 29, 1941; children: Velma Joan, Patricia Anne, Roberta Adeline. *Education:* Louisiana State University, B.A., 1936. *Religion:* Catholic. *Home:* 1931 Kimberly Rd., Silver Spring, Md. 20903. *Office:* Associated Press, 2021 K St. N.W., Washington, D.C. 20006.

CAREER/WRITINGS: Currently editor and reporter serving as communications and telecommunications expert for Associated Press, Washington, D.C. Notable assignments include coverage of Huey Long's career; legislatures in Arkansas, Louisiana, and Tennessee; Congressional and Washington activities; plane crashes; and riots. *Military service:* U.S. Army; served on General MacArthur's press staff and as chief news censor; received Bronze Star, Commendation Medal, and Bronze Arrowhead. *Awards, honors:* Received Certificate of Appreciation from Veterans for Salute Administration.

BAUMANN, Kurt 1935-

PERSONAL: Born August 19, 1935, in Oberhallau, Switzerland; son of Hermann (a farmer) and Verena (Bachmann) Baumann; married Iren Zweifel (a teacher), February 2, 1963; children: Mischa Clemens, Liv Tullia. *Education:* Attended Institut Minerva Zurich, 1959-62, and University of Zurich, 1962-69. *Religion:* Protestant. *Home:* Arosastrasse 6, 8008 Zurich, Switzerland.

CAREER: Goldsmith in Schaffhausen, Switzerland, 1952-56; farm worker in Ytteroey Island, Norway, 1956; goldsmith in Uppsala, Sweden, 1956-57, and Schaffhausen, 1958; writer, 1972—; college teacher of literature and history. *Military service:* Swiss Army, 1955. *Member:* Schweizerischer Schriftstellerverband.

WRITINGS—For children: Joachim der Zoellner, Nord-Sued, 1972, translation by Margaret Baker published as *Joachim the Border Guard,* A. & C. Black, 1972; *Joachim der Strassenkehrer,* Nord-Sued, translation by Baker published as *Joachim the Dustman,* A. & C. Black, 1974; *Der Schlafhund und der Wachhund,* Nord-Sued, translation by staff of Hutchinson Junior Books Ltd. published as *Dozy and Hawkeye,* Hutchinson, 1974; *Drei Koenige* (title means "The Three Kings"), Nord-Sued, 1975; *Joachim der Polizist,* Nord-Sued, translation published as *Joachim the Policeman,* A. & C. Black, 1975; *Der rote Vogel Felix* (title means "The Red Bird Felix"), Nord-Sued, 1976; *Beyond the Clouds,* translated from the original German manuscript, MacDonald & Jane's, 1976; *Micky's Kitchen Contest,* translated by Anathea Bell from the original German manuscript, Andersen Press, 1978. Also writer of two plays for children, *Der Vogel Felix,* Saverlaender Aaran, 1978, and "Nenei Joachim."

WORK IN PROGRESS—For children: The Prince and the Lute; In Televisionland; Joachim the Hotelier; a musical play, dealing with ecology.

SIDELIGHTS: Baumann writes that he was born in a small village on the Swiss side of the Rhine. Growing up in a landlocked country, he had hoped to become a sailor, but ended up as a goldsmith's apprentice. Although he has worked at many jobs over the years, he always falls back on his skill as a goldsmith to help finance continuing study.

* * *

BAXTER, James K(eir) 1926-1972

PERSONAL: Born June 29, 1926, in Brighton, Otago, New Zealand; son of Archibald Baxter (a writer); married Jacqueline Sturm, 1948; children: Hilary, John. *Education:* Attended University of Otago, 1944, and Canterbury University College; Victoria University, B.A., 1952. *Religion:* Roman Catholic. *Home:* 7 Boyle Crescent, Auckland, New Zealand. *Office:* Private Bag, Jerusalem, Wanganui River, New Zealand.

CAREER: Poet and playwright. Worked as journalist, teacher, actor, proofreader for *Christchurch Press,* 1948, brass tap grinder, 1948, freezing-worker, 1949, and postman, 1950; founded Jerusalem commune, Wanganui River, New Zealand, 1969. Member of New Zealand State Literary Fund Committee. *Awards, honors:* MacMillan Brown prize for "Convoys," 1944; UNESCO grant for travel to India and Japan, 1958; Robert Burns Fellowship, University of Otago, 1966, 1967.

WRITINGS—All poetry, except as indicated: Beyond the Palisade, Caxton Press, 1944; *Blow, Wind of Fruitfulness,* Caxton Press, 1948; (with Louis Johnson and Anton Vogt)

Poems Unpleasant, Caxton Press, 1951; *The Fallen House,* Caxton Press, 1953; *Traveller's Litany* (poem sequence), Handcraft Press, 1955; *The Iron Breadboard: Studies in New Zealand Writing* (verse parodies), Mermaid Press, 1957; (with Charles Doyle, Kendrick Smithyman, and Johnson) *The Night Shift: Poems on Aspects of Love,* Capricorn Press, 1957; *In Fires of No Return,* Oxford University Press, 1958; *Chosen Poems,* Konkan Institute of the Arts and Sciences, 1958.

Howrah Bridge and Other Poems, Oxford University Press, 1961; *Pig Island Letters,* Oxford University Press, 1966; *The Lion Skin,* University of Otago Bibliography Room, 1967; *A Death Song for M. Mouldybroke,* Caxton Press, 1967; *The Rock Woman: Selected Poems,* Oxford University Press, 1969.

Jerusalem Sonnets: Poems for Colin Durning, University of Otago Bibliography Room, 1970; *The Junkies and the Fuzz,* Wai-te-ata Press, 1970; *Jerusalem Daybook* (poems and prose), Price Milburn, 1971; *Letter to Peter Olds* (poem sequence), Caveman Press, 1972; *Four God Songs,* Futuna Press, 1972; *Ode to Auckland and Other Poems,* Caveman Press, 1972; *Autumn Testament* (poems and prose), Price Milburn, 1972; *The Tree House* (juvenile poetry), Price Milburn, 1973; *Runes,* Oxford University Press, 1973; *Two Obscene Poems,* privately printed, 1973; *The Labyrinth,* Oxford University Press, 1974. Also author of *A Small Ode on Mixed Flatting,* Caxton Press.

Other: *Recent Trends in New Zealand Poetry* (criticism), Caxton Press, 1951; *The Fire and the Anvil: Notes on Modern Poetry,* New Zealand University Press, 1955, revised edition, Cambridge University Press, 1960; *Oil* (school bulletin), School Publications, 1957; *The Coaster* (school bulletin), School Publications, 1959.

The Trawler (school bulletin), School Publications, 1961; (author of text) *New Zealand in Colour: Photographs by Kenneth and Jean Bigwood,* Reed, Volume I, 1961, Volume II, 1962 (published in Australia as *New Zealand in Colour,* Lansdowne Press, 1963); *The Old Earth Closet: A Tribute to Regional Poetry,* privately printed, 1965; *Aspects of Poetry in New Zealand* (criticism), Caxton Press, 1967; *The Man on the Horse* (lectures), University of Otago Press, 1967; *The Flowering Cross: Pastoral Articles,* New Zealand Tablet Press, 1969.

The Six Faces of Love: Lenten Lectures, Futuna Press, 1972; *A Walking Stick for an Old Man,* CMW Print, 1972; (with Ans Westra and Tim Shadbolt) *Notes on the Country I Live In,* A. Taylor, 1972; *The Bone Chanter,* edited by J. E. Weir, Oxford University Press, 1977; *The Holy Life and Death of Concrete Grady,* edited by Weir, Oxford University Press, 1977.

Plays: *The Wide Open Cage and Jack Winter's Dream: Two Plays* (contains "Jack Winter's Dream," radio play broadcast in 1958; and "The Wide Open Cage," produced in Wellington, New Zealand, 1959, produced in New York, 1962), Capricorn Press, 1959; *The Sore-Footed Man and The Temptations of Oedipus* (contains "The Sore-Footed Man," produced at Globe Theatre, Dunedin, New Zealand, 1967; and "The Temptations of Oedipus," produced in 1968), Heinemann Educational Books, 1971; *The Devil and Mr. Mulcahy and The Band Rotunda* (contains "The Devil and Mr. Mulcahy," produced in Dunedin, 1967; and "The Band Rotunda," first produced at Globe Theatre, Dunedin, July, 1967), Heinemann Educational Books, 1971.

Unpublished plays: "The Silver Plate," produced in 1961; "Three Women and the Sea," produced in 1961; "The Spots

of the Leopard," produced in New York, 1963; "Mr. Brandywine Chooses a Gravestone," produced in 1966; "The First Wife," produced in 1966; "The Bureaucrat," produced in Dunedin, 1967; "The Starlight in Your Eyes," produced in 1967; "Mr. O'Dwyer's Dancing Party," produced in 1967; "The Woman" (mime; written to precede "The Sore-Footed Man"), produced at Globe Theatre, Dunedin, 1967; "The Axe and the Mirror" (mime; written to precede "The Bureaucrat"), produced in Dunedin, 1967; "The Day Flanagan Died," produced in Dunedin, 1969; "Who Killed Sebastian," produced in 1969.

Also author of several plays, neither published nor produced, including "The Runaway Wife," "The Gentle Ones," "To Catch a Hare," "The Hero," "The Rendezvous," and "The World Is."

Work represented in anthologies, including *An Anthology of New Zealand Verse,* edited by Robert M. Chapman and J. F. Bennett, Oxford University Press, 1956; *Penguin Book of New Zealand Verse,* edited by Allen Curnow, Penguin, 1960; *Modern Poems for the Commonwealth,* edited by Maurice Wollman and John Spencer, Harrap, 1966; *Commonwealth Poems of Today,* edited by Howard Sergeant, J. Murray, 1967.

Contributor of articles to periodicals, including *Landfall, Salient Literary Issue, New Zealand Poetry Yearbook, Numbers, New Zealand Listener, Education,* and *Dominion.* Editor of school bulletins, Department of Education, Wellington, New Zealand; editor, *Numbers* magazine (Wellington, New Zealand), 1954-60.

SIDELIGHTS: Baxter was considered by many critics to be the foremost spokesman of the New Zealand wilderness and its metaphorical ramifications. His poetry and drama most often incorporated mythology, variously classical and Christian, to express his overriding concern with religion and its place in the modern world. Always present in his poems and in his life was the influence of his pacifist parents.

Vincent O'Sullivan observed that, to Baxter, myth symbolized sanity, and that logic, or the "formally educated" mind, was too superficial: "It is only the poetic mind which works deeply enough to touch the source of order." The "poetic mind" was the part of himself that Baxter liked to call the "dinosaur's egg," noted Charles Doyle, who also described the many metamorphoses of Baxter over the years from "boy prodigy of poetry" to "alcoholic rip-roarer" to "Catholic convert" and ultimately "to the final few years when he totally rejected urban materialist society and became the figure (barefoot, long-bearded, patched and baggy) whom many saw as saintlike." In his early years he often lived at variance with his poetic convictions, becoming at the end of his life "a living and vivid example of the full practice of the life of charity, the Christian life," Doyle elaborated.

Other writers have recalled Baxter's development as an artist and as a man. Peter Olds remembered, "The whole time I knew the man he was walking on a rocky road, and like any man, he took a few wrong turnings—but the words that 'belched from this rotting body' were indeed worth their weight in gold." Bill Pearson recalled Baxter reading poems in bars and discussing poetry with his bookie. Baxter himself wrote in *Landfall:* "In my late teens I developed the habit of throwing up a job, drinking for a week or so, writing for a month or so, then taking another job.... The best poems I have written (those in *Blow, Wind of Fruitfulness*) were written in this way."

Basic to an understanding of much of Baxter's poetry is a consideration of the Hero Myth, whereby fertility and springtime, personified by a Youthful Quester, are made manifest in the land by the death of the spiritually and physically dying Fisher King. Rebirth of the heretofore barren land (winter) is now possible, and the cycle of the seasons is again able to proceed. O'Sullivan pointed out that Baxter's poems abound with "the figures of regenerated return, whether as Orpheus or Antaeus or Persephone or Christ," all of whom "return not to a new world so much as the old world seen freshly." It was O'Sullivan's assessment that Baxter used the seasonal motif in conjunction with the myth of rebirth in a manner unique to modern poetry and that, when he used the Christian interpretation of the myth, he focused on the events—pain and death—preceding the subsequent resurrection. For Baxter, poetry was the true means of determining a "pattern" basic to all happenings, and his most frequent poetic device was the metaphor, which O'Sullivan labeled "the closest that natural man is going to get to truth, the golden branch which he carried as a pledge from his journey into self-knowledge/human experience/the cyclic verities." Baxter's "mythologizing is exploratory, an attempt to locate and clarify his own archetypes," wrote Doyle, who described such a dilemma as basic to the typical New Zealander who was at once part of England as well as of New Zealand.

A closely related motif is that of the city versus the wilderness. According to O'Sullivan, the "wilderness" represented to Baxter that part of him that made him different, unique, and the "City" represented "convention [and] authority." Baxter deplored the materialism of New Zealand and advocated the Maori concept of *aroha,* or love, as a means of creating a modern Civitate Dei "where men are valued for themselves, where the dead and the living and the unborn are accounted for in a cultural certainty, or in terms of orthodox Christianity, where the service of Christ is placed in one's fellow men," explained O'Sullivan. To this end, and following the examples of his brother, a conscientious objector, and his father, who had written a book, *We Will Not Cease,* about a conscientious objector in World War I, Baxter founded a Maori commune named Jerusalem on the Wanganui River in 1969, and Doyle observed the Maori influence on Baxter's writings following the establishment of Jerusalem.

Baxter's plays voiced many of the concerns of his poetry. Again and again he made use of both classical and Christian mythology to express his concepts of life in modern New Zealand. Doyle discussed the Aristotelian elements in Baxter's dramas and declared that "Baxter was well aware of the subjectivity of his plays, the likelihood that many of his characters emerged, horned or hornless, from what he once called his 'menagerie of interior selves.'" Both Doyle and Harold W. Smith found similarities between Baxter's works and Eugene O'Neill's use of ancient mythology to symbolize the contemporary world. It was Doyle's feeling, however, that more important influences were Sartre and Giraudoux and, to a lesser extent, Samuel Beckett. In a discussion of Baxter's thematic devices, Smith labeled Baxter "a Catholic Christian who is both moved and terrified at the plight of man in a world from which a transcendent God has withdrawn or been driven out." Doyle provided a list of frequent themes essential to an understanding of Baxter's plays: "Free will, death, religion, drunkenness, commitment, destitution, words, love, materialism, community, the lost garden, bureaucracy, marriage, existentialism." Smith discussed Baxter's effective use of satire and declared that, while Baxter's framework was, in many of his plays, Greek,

"the rhythms of the language [were] uniquely those of New Zealand."

AVOCATIONAL INTERESTS: Gardening, reading.

BIOGRAPHICAL/CRITICAL SOURCES: A Book of New Zealand Verse, edited by Allen Curnow, Caxton Press, 1945; *Landfall,* September, 1948, autumn, 1953, March, 1959, March, 1960, December, 1960, December, 1967, March, 1968, March, 1969, March, 1971; *Meanjin Papers,* II, number 4, 1952; E. H. McCormick, *New Zealand Literature: A Survey,* Oxford University Press, 1959; *Penguin Book of New Zealand Verse,* Penguin, 1960; Kendrick Smithyman, *A Way of Saying,* Collins, 1965; *London Magazine,* January, 1967, October, 1969; *Journal of Commonwealth Literature,* Number 4, December, 1967; J. C. Reid and G. A. Wilkes, *The Literature of Australia and New Zealand,* Pennsylvania State University Press, 1968; F. M. McKay, *New Zealand Poetry: An Introduction,* New Zealand University Press, 1970; J. E. Weir, *The Poetry of James K. Baxter,* Oxford University Press, 1970; *James K. Baxter 1926-1972: A Memorial Volume,* Alister Taylor, 1972; *Islands,* autumn, 1973, winter, 1973; *James K. Baxter Festival: 1973: Four Plays,* Victoria University Press, 1973; Charles Doyle, *James K. Baxter,* Twayne, 1976.*

(Died October 22, 1972, in Grafton,
Auckland, New Zealand)

*   *   *

BAXTER, Phyllis
See WALLMANN, Jeffrey M(iner)

*   *   *

BEACHY, Lucille   1935-

PERSONAL: Born September 24, 1935, in Sherwood, Ohio; daughter of Ezra (a teacher) and Bertha (a teacher; maiden name, Nohejl) Beachy; married Tom Mathews (a writer), June 29, 1970; children: Clea Yvette. *Education:* Goshen College, B.A., 1957. *Office: Newsweek,* 444 Madison Ave., New York, N.Y. 10022.

CAREER/WRITINGS: Newsweek, New York City, researcher, 1960-74, chief of research, 1974-76, senior editor, 1976—.

*   *   *

BEAN, Orson   1928-

PERSONAL: Name originally Dallas Frederick Burrows; born July 22, 1928, in Burlington, Vt., son of George F. (a policeman) and Marian Ainsworth (Pollard) Burrows; married Jacqueline De Sibour (an actress under name Rain Winslow), July 2, 1956 (divorced, 1962); married Carolyn Maxwell (a fashion designer) October 3, 1965; children: Michelle. *Education:* Educated in Cambridge and Boston, Mass. *Home:* 910 Chautauqua Blvd., Pacific Palisades, Calif. 90272.

CAREER: Actor and comedian. Worked as nightclub magician and comedian in Boston, Mass., area during late 1940's; became stage actor and television comedian in New York, N.Y., 1952—; has appeared in Broadway productions including "John Murray Anderson's Almanac," 1953, "Will Success Spoil Rock Hunter?," 1955, "Mr. Roberts," 1957, "Never Too Late," 1962, and "The Roar of the Greasepaint—The Smell of the Crowd," 1967; television credits include appearances on "Philco Playhouse," "The Arthur Murray Show," "Broadway TV Playhouse," "The Ed Sullivan Show," "The Jack Paar Show," and "The Tonight

Show''; has appeared as regular panelist on television quiz and game programs including ''Laugh Line,'' ''Password,'' and ''To Tell the Truth''; has appeared in films ''How to be Very, Very Popular,'' 1955, and ''Anatomy of a Murder,'' 1959. Co-producer of ''Home Movies,'' a musical farce, 1964. Founder and administrative director, Fifteenth Street School, New York City, 1964—. *Military service:* U.S. Army; served in Japan. *Member:* Screen Actors Guild, American Federation of Television and Radio Artists (AFTRA), Actors Equity Association. *Awards, honors:* Theatre World award, 1954, for role in ''John Murray Anderson's Almanac''; Obie award, 1964, for production of ''Home Movies.''

WRITINGS: Me and the Orgone, introduction by A. S. Neill, St. Martin's, 1971.

SIDELIGHTS: Bean has enjoyed a flourishing career as a television panelist, comedian, dramatic and musical comedy actor. He has given several highly acclaimed performances in roles on Broadway. But after having spent ten years in analysis, Bean felt that his personal life was less than satisfactory. He discovered the works of post-Freudian psychoanalyst Wilhelm Reich and underwent therapy with a disciple of Reich. *Me and the Orgone* is Bean's account of his experiences in Reichian therapy and how he feels it affected his emotional well-being. ''Readers drawn to this book for Bean's name as an entertainer will find their man in a serious mood, although Bean writes brightly enough,'' said *Publishers Weekly.* The reviewer went on to note that *Me and the Orgone* will appeal to those ''who are serious about discovering something about Reich's therapies, which sired, as Bean points out, the Esalen, encounter, and sensitivity groups of today.''

In addition to his participation in all phases of the entertainment business (including a period of anti-blacklist activism in the 1950's) and his involvement with Reichian psychoanalysis, Bean developed an interest in A. S. Neill's system of education. The result was the Fifteenth Street School in New York City, founded by Bean in 1964. The school was closely modeled after Neill's own school in England, Summerhill. Bean financed the school himself and holds the lofty title of administrative director, which, he points out, ''means I unclog sinks and change light bulbs.''

AVOCATIONAL INTERESTS: Collecting Laurel and Hardy films.

BIOGRAPHICAL/CRITICAL SOURCES: Newsday, April 5, 1965; *Kirkus Reviews,* March 1, 1971; *Publishers Weekly,* March 15, 1971.*

*   *   *

BEARDSLEY, Richard K(ing)   1918-1978

December 16, 1918—June 10, 1978; American anthropologist, educator, and author best known for his books about Japan. Beardsley was co-author of *Village Japan, Japanese Culture,* and *Twelve Doors to Japan.* He died in Ann Arbor, Mich. Obituaries and other sources: *American Men and Women of Science: The Social and Behavioral Sciences,* 12th edition, Bowker, 1973; *New York Times,* June 11, 1978. (See index for *CA* sketch)

*   *   *

BECK, Horace P(almer)   1920-

PERSONAL: Born September 27, 1920, in Newport, R.I.; son of H. P. (a physician) and Dorothy (Bateman) Beck; married Jane Choate (a photographer and folklorist), August 28, 1964; children: Mrs. Thomas Staatz, Thomas, Rowen. *Education:* University of Pennsylvania, M.A., 1947, Ph.D., 1952. *Politics:* ''None. After fifty years I have come to the conclusion that only the most successful criminals become politicians.'' *Religion:* None. *Residence:* Ripton, Vt. *Office:* Department of American Literature, Middlebury College, Middlebury, Vt. 05733.

CAREER: Temple University, Philadelphia, Pa., instructor, 1948-54, assistant professor of English, 1954-56; Middlebury College, Middlebury, Vt., 1956—, began as assistant professor, became associate professor, presently professor of American literature. *Military service:* U.S. Naval Reserve, active duty, 1942-46; became lieutenant junior grade. *Member:* American Folklore Society (fellow), Midwest Folklore Society, New England Folklore Society (president, 1965-66), Sigma Xi.

WRITINGS: Folklore in Maine, Lippincott, 1955; *The American Indian as a Colonial Sea-Fighter,* Mystic Seaport, 1960; *Gluscap the Liar,* Bond Wheelwright Co., 1960; (with others) *Folklore in Action,* American Folklore Society, 1964; (contributor) *Our Living Traditions,* Basic Books, 1968; *Folklore and the Sea,* Wesleyan University Press, 1973. Contributor to folklore and maritime journals.

WORK IN PROGRESS: Studies of primitive whaling and of folk art.

SIDELIGHTS: Beck writes: ''I have spent most of my life collecting folklore from the Arctic to the Caribbean, in Europe and Africa, with a chief focus on marine culture. My most illuminating experience was running aground in a rising gale off the English coast, closely followed by being caught without equipment in an Arctic blizzard.''

AVOCATIONAL INTERESTS: Seafaring, hunting, farming.

*   *   *

BECKER, Jillian (Ruth)   1932-

PERSONAL: Born June 2, 1932, in Johannesburg, South Africa; daughter of Bernard (a surgeon and member of Parliament) and Florence Louie (a translator of poetry; maiden name, Gordon) Friedman; married Gerald Becker, May, 1956 (divorced, 1972); children: Claire Eve, Lucienne Becker Pattison, Madeleine Ann. *Education:* University of the Witwatersrand, B.A., 1955. *Politics:* ''liberal—with a small 'l'.'' *Religion:* None. *Home:* 144 Hemingford Rd., London N1 1DE, England.

CAREER: Writer, 1963—. *Member:* International P.E.N., Society of Authors.

WRITINGS: The Keep (novel), Chatto & Windus, 1967, Penguin, 1971; *The Union* (novel), Chatto & Windus, 1971; *The Virgins* (novel), Gollancz, 1976; *Hitler's Children: The Story of the Baader-Meinhof Gang,* Lippincott, 1977. Contributor of stories, articles, and reviews to magazines.

WORK IN PROGRESS: A fiction work, as yet untitled; research on Karl Marx, southern Africa, the Middle East, cults of unreason, and the history of extremist politics.

SIDELIGHTS: Jillian Becker writes: ''Knowledge of what is going on in the real world in our time seems to me essential for the writing of interesting fiction. I hope to continue to write both fact and fiction. I think that the freedom we enjoy now in the Western world is under threat and we must defend it. I abhor all forms of collectivist ideology. I am a disciple of Karl Popper and F. A. Hayek. I deplore discrimination against anybody on grounds that he belongs to a special group, whether that group is designated according to race, colour, social class, etc." Her fourth book has been published in France, Germany, the Netherlands, Portugal, Great Britain, and Denmark.

BIOGRAPHICAL/CRITICAL SOURCES: Index, April, 1973; Rowland Smith, editor, *Exile and Tradition,* Longman, 1976.

* * *

BEDNARIK, Charles (Philip) 1925-
(Chuck Bednarik)

PERSONAL: Born May 1, 1925, in Bethlehem, Pa.; son of Charles Albert (a steel worker) and Mary (Pivovarnicek) Bednarik; married Emma Margetich, June 5, 1948; children: Charlene, Donna, Pamela, Carol, Jackie. *Education:* Attended University of Pennsylvania, 1945-48. *Residence:* Abingdon, Pa.

CAREER: Philadelphia Eagles (professional football team), Philadelphia, Pa., center, 1949-50, linebacker, 1950-54, center, 1954-60, linebacker, 1961-62; concrete salesman for Warner Co., 1962—. *Military service:* U.S. Army Air Forces, 1943-45; served as aerial gunner; received Air Medal with four Oak-Leaf Clusters. *Awards, honors:* Received numerous football awards as college player, including runner-up for the Heisman Memorial Trophy, 1948; named Rookie of the Year, 1949; named to the twenty-five year All American team, 1950; named to All-Pro team eight times and Pro-Bowl team seven times; selected for All-Time All-American team by *Sport* magazine, 1960, and by East Coast Athletic Conference, 1969; Hickock award as greatest professional lineman of the decade, 1962; named to National Football Hall of Fame, 1967, and National Football Foundation College Hall of Fame, 1969; named to All-time fifty-year team by National Football League, 1969.

WRITINGS: (Under name Chuck Bednarik, with Jack McCallum) *Bednarik: Last of the Sixty-Minute Men* (autobiography), Prentice-Hall, 1977.

SIDELIGHTS: Joe Namath called Chuck Bednarik "the last of the sixty-minute men." Before television made football a celebrity sport, it was not uncommon for a professional to play both offense and defense. But it was most unusual to play offensive center and defensive linebacker for an entire game. Bednarik did this four times for the Philadelphia Eagles in their last National Football League championship season in 1960. No one has done it since.

The son of Czechoslovakian immigrants, Bednarik played football with a rag-stuffed stocking until his mother saved enough coffee coupons to get him a real football. Although he admitted feeling some bitterness at coming along too early for the large salaries professional players now command, he said in his autobiography, "The players of my era were not the true pioneers of pro football but the game really became a popular sport in the fifties and I feel we made it what it is today."

AVOCATIONAL INTERESTS: Golf, music, speaking engagements.

BIOGRAPHICAL/CRITICAL SOURCES: Chuck Bednarik and Jack McCallum, *Bednarik: Last of the Sixty-Minute Men,* Prentice-Hall, 1977.*

* * *

BEDNARIK, Chuck
See BEDNARIK, Charles (Philip)

BEECHAM, Justin
See WINTLE, Justin (Beecham)

* * *

BEEMAN, Richard R(oy) 1942-

PERSONAL: Born May 16, 1942, in Seattle, Wash.; son of David E. (in business) and Dorothy (Dowds) Beeman; married Pamela Butler (a nurse), December 26, 1964; children: Kristin, Joshua. *Education:* University of California, Berkeley, B.A., 1964; College of William and Mary, M.A., 1965; University of Chicago, Ph.D., 1968. *Politics:* Democrat. *Religion:* None. *Home:* 416 Park Ave., Swarthmore, Pa. 19081. *Office:* Department of History, University of Pennsylvania, Philadelphia, Pa. 19104.

CAREER: University of Pennsylvania, Philadelphia, assistant professor, 1968-73, associate professor of history, 1973—. *Member:* Organization of American Historians, Southern Historical Association.

WRITINGS: The Old Dominion and the New Nation, 1788-1801, University Press of Kentucky, 1972; *Patrick Henry, a Biography,* McGraw, 1975. Contributor to scholarly journals.

WORK IN PROGRESS: A social history of eighteenth-century Virginia.

SIDELIGHTS: Beeman told *CA:* "I began working, quite by accident, on aspects of the history of Virginia in 1965 and I have never exhausted my interest in the subject. My one consistent concern in my Virginia research and writing has been to illuminate the larger social world of the old Dominion through a study of its political forms. I suspect that my interest in the social dimensions of political behavior will eventually impel me to undertake a larger study of the political culture of the eighteenth and nineteenth century South."

* * *

BEGLEY, Kathleen A(nne) 1948-

PERSONAL: Born March 28, 1948, in Philadelphia, Pa.; daughter of Thomas and Catherine (Harvey) Begley; married Wiley Lamar Brooks, Jr. (an assistant news director), April 19, 1977. *Education:* Temple University, B.A., 1970; Villanova University, M.A., 1974; graduate study at University of San Francisco and University of California, Berkeley, 1976. *Home:* 1660 North LaSalle St., Apt. 2002, Chicago, Ill. 60614.

CAREER: Delaware County Daily Times, Primos, Pa., general assignment reporter and author of youth column, "Coed," 1966-70; *Camden Courier Post,* Camden, N.J., urban affairs reporter and author of weekly column, "Wednesday," 1970-71; *Philadelphia Inquirer,* Philadelphia, Pa., special assignment reporter, 1971-76; *Chicago Daily News,* Chicago, Ill., feature writer for "Insight" column, 1977-78; *US* (magazine), New York, N.Y., Chicago correspondent, 1978—; Roosevelt University, Chicago, director of journalism department, 1978-79. Instructor at Temple University, 1973-75, St. Joseph's College, Philadelphia, autumn, 1975, Community College of Philadelphia, autumn, 1975, and University of California, Berkeley, autumn, 1976.

WRITINGS: Deadline (autobiography; Junior Literary Guild selection), Putnam, 1977.

WORK IN PROGRESS: Teeth, nonfiction.

SIDELIGHTS: Begley told *CA:* "When I began working on the manuscript for *Deadline,* I set up a highly organized, extremely quiet, nicely decorated office in which to write. After several days, I realized that my approach was all wrong. For ten years, I had worked in a succession of noisy, rowdy, crowded city rooms—and I had become accustomed, even dependent, on a lot of activity in my milieu. Why should I stop when it came time to write about my journalistic experiences for G. P. Putnam's young adult readers? As a result, I never worked in the office again. Instead, I did my best to simulate a newspaper office right in my dining room—brimming trash cans and all. And I never wrote a page without both the radio and the television booming into my ears.''

AVOCATIONAL INTERESTS: Travel in Europe, Great Britain, Morocco, and Brazil, needlepoint, tap dancing, gourmet cooking, embroidery.

* * *

BELAIR, Felix, Jr. 1907-1978

December 29, 1907—June 21, 1978; American journalist. Belair began his newspaper career as a telephone operator in the Washington bureau of the *New York Times* in 1929. With the exception of a five-year association with Time, Inc., Belair remained with the *New York Times* until his retirement in 1976. He had served longer on the Washington bureau than any other reporter in the history of the *Times*. Belair covered the progress of the Marshall plan, every national political convention from 1936 until 1964, and black market activities during the Vietnam War. He died in Winchester, Va. Obituaries and other sources: *New York Times,* June 23, 1978; *Washington Post,* June 24, 1978.

* * *

BELLER, Anne Scott

PERSONAL: Born in New York, N.Y.; married E. Kuno Beller, February 19, 1956 (marriage ended, 1977); children: Paul, Daniel. *Education:* Bryn Mawr College, B.A.; Temple University, M.A. *Home:* 114 Llanfair Rd., Ardmore, Pa. 19003.

CAREER: Philadelphia Board of Education, Philadelphia, Pa., research assistant, 1970-73; Franklin Institute, Philadelphia, abstractor, 1974-75; writer, 1975—. *Member:* American Association for the Advancement of Science. *Awards, honors:* French Government fellowship and Fulbright travel grant, both 1952-53.

WRITINGS: Fat and Thin: A Natural History of Obesity, Farrar, Straus, 1977; *Bed and Board: The Economics of Love, Fear, and Dependency,* Farrar, Straus, in press. Contributor to *American Journal of Clinical Nutrition.*

SIDELIGHTS: Anne Beller comments: "My training in physical anthropology stemmed from an interest in evolution, history, and the prehistory of ideas, places, and institutions. This has led me into medical history on one side and social history on the other. From there I have tended to follow my nose. I write about things that puzzle me to the point of worriment and mesmerization."

BIOGRAPHICAL/CRITICAL SOURCES: New York Times, November 2, 1977.

* * *

BENEDICT, Bertram 1892(?)-1978

1892(?)—June 18, 1978; American editor and author. Benedict joined Editorial Research Reports, a service designed to provide facts on national and international issues, in 1929,

and became part-owner in 1949. After his retirement, Benedict continued to write articles for periodicals and newspapers. He was the author of several books on history. Benedict died in Easton, Md. Obituaries and other sources: *Washington Post,* June 21, 1978.

* * *

BENFIELD, Richard E. 1940-

PERSONAL: Born October 25, 1940, in Granville, N.Y.; son of Ernest W. (an executive) and Edith H. (a teacher) Benfield; married wife, Jane N. (a dog breeder), July 3, 1967; children: Rodd Jason, Wendy Lynn. *Education:* Graduated from Bowdoin College, 1962. *Residence:* Alexandria, Va. *Office: The Record,* 1385 National Press Bldg., Washington, D.C. 20045.

CAREER/WRITINGS: Employed by *Standard Times,* New Bedford, Mass., 1962-63, and United Press International, Boston, Mass., 1963-64; *Morning Call,* Paterson, N.J., political writer and City Hall correspondent, 1964-67; *The Record,* Bergen County, N.J., political writer, 1967-69, State House correspondent and bureau chief in Trenton, N.J., 1969-73, Washington bureau chief, 1973—. Notable assignments include coverage of Kosygin and Johnson conferences, 1967, New Jersey gubernatorial campaign, 1969, and 1976 Presidential campaign. *Member:* National Press Club.

* * *

BENOIT, Emile 1910-1978

July 14, 1910—May 4, 1978; American educator, economist, and author best known for his writings on arms control. Benoit served as consultant to several organizations, including U.S. Arms Control and Disarmament Agency and U.S. Department of Defense. He wrote *Disarmament and the Economy.* Benoit died in New York, N.Y. Obituaries and other sources: *Who's Who in Consulting,* 2nd edition, Gale, 1973; *American Men and Women of Science: The Social and Behavioral Sciences,* 12th edition, Bowker, 1973; *Who's Who in the World,* 3rd edition, Marquis, 1976; *New York Times,* May 5, 1978. (See index for *CA* sketch)

* * *

BENTLEY-TAYLOR, David 1915-

PERSONAL: Born January 25, 1915, in Liverpool, England; son of Robert Martin (a bank manager) and Winifred (Hughes) Bentley-Taylor; married Jessie Mabel Moore, March 4, 1941; children: Michael Martin and Arthur John (twins), David Andrew, Rupert Paul. *Education:* Oxford University, M.A., 1936. *Religion:* Evangelical Protestant. *Home:* Swandrift, Eardisland, Leominster, Herefordshire HR6 9BU, England.

CAREER: Missionary of China Inland Mission (now Overseas Missionary Fellowship) in China, 1938-44, England, 1944-51, Indonesia, 1952-62, and England, 1962-66; International Fellowship of Evangelical Students, traveling secretary in Africa and West Asia, 1967-74; general secretary of Middle East Christian Outreach, 1974—.

WRITINGS: The Prisoner Leaps: A Diary of Missionary Life in Java, China Inland Mission Overseas Missionary Fellowship, 1961, revised edition, 1965; *The Great Volcano,* China Inland Mission Overseas Missionary Fellowship, 1965; *The Weathercock's Reward: Christian Progress in Muslim Java,* Overseas Missionary Fellowship, 1967, reprinted as *Java Saga,* 1975; *My Love Must Wait: The Story of Henry Martyn,* Inter-Varsity Press, 1976.

WORK IN PROGRESS: A biography of Augustine of Hippo.

SIDELIGHTS: Bentley-Taylor writes: "I became a Christian at eighteen and ever since my faith in Jesus Christ and desire to make the gospel known have motivated every activity. I speak German, Mandarin Chinese, and Indonesian, but use New Testament Greek most! My main interests are history and literature. I have visited universities in many parts of the world and follow all foreign affairs closely. I have visited Canada twelve times since World War II, but my main responsibilities are now concerned with Lebanon, Cypress, and the Middle East."

Commenting about his books, Bentley-Taylor added: *"The Prisoner Leaps* and *The Great Volcano* were biographical, the latter a sequel to the former. *The Weathercock's Reward,* now reprinted as *Java Saga,* is like the other two, set in Java, but it is not biographical. It aims to answer the question why there has been such a massive turning of Muslims to Christ in Java and nowhere else in the world. How did this get started? As far as I know there is no other study in English of this fascinating subject. *My Love Must Wait* was written at the request of Inter-Varsity Press who wanted to keep in print a biography of Henry Martyn. There were three previous ones. He was a remarkably gifted young man, one of the very greatest missionary linguists there has ever been, but he died at thirty-one, unmarried after completing the first Urdu and Persian New Testaments as well as an Arabic New Testament. He died in 1812, so it is a story of the Napoleonic Wars."

*   *   *

BENYO, Richard 1946-

PERSONAL: Born April 20, 1946, in Jim Thorpe, Pa.; son of Andrew Joseph, Sr. (a machinist) and Dorothy (Herman) Benyo; married Jill Wapensky, April 29, 1972. *Education:* Bloomsburg State College, B.A., 1968; also attended George Mason University, 1976-77. *Politics:* Democrat. *Religion:* Roman Catholic. *Home address:* P.O. Box 4432, Mountain View, Calif. 94040. *Agent:* Michael Larsen, 1029 James St., San Francisco, Calif. 94109. *Office:* 1400 Stierlin Rd., Mountain View, Calif. 94042.

CAREER: Times-News, Lehighton, Pa., managing editor, 1968-72; *Stock Car Racing,* Alexandria, Va., editor, 1972-77; *Runner's World,* Mountain View, Calif., managing editor, 1977—. Member of Union 76 panel of experts. *Member:* International Motor Press Association, American Automobile Racing Writers and Broadcasters Association. *Awards, honors:* Winner of American Automobile Racing Writers and Broadcasters Association writing contests, 1973-77.

WRITINGS: Superspeedway, Mason/Charter, 1977; *Return to Running,* World Publications, 1978. Editor-at-large of *Stock Car Racing.*

WORK IN PROGRESS: The Quake Creek Monster, a novel; *Going in Circles,* nonfiction on becoming a stock car racer, for Steve Smith Autosports Publishers; research for a biography of James Farrell.

SIDELIGHTS: Benyo writes: "My writing attempts to tell a story or to give some practical advice to people with like interests. A profound attempt is made to avoid profundity." *Avocational interests:* Old rock 'n' roll music, running, photography.

*   *   *

BERGAUST, Erik 1925-1978

March 23, 1925—March 1, 1978; Norwegian-born American author, poet, publisher, and lecturer. Bergaust wrote more than fifty books on rocketry, aviation, and space sciences, and edited and published numerous periodicals on air and sea exploration. He wrote *Murder on Pad 34,* an examination of an accident that resulted in the deaths of three astronauts. Bergaust also wrote two biographies of Werner von Braun. He died in McLean, Va. Obituaries and other sources: *Authors of Books for Young People,* 2nd edition, Scarecrow, 1971; *Who's Who in America,* 39th edition, Marquis, 1976; *Washington Post,* March 4, 1978. (See index for *CA* sketch)

*   *   *

BERGER, Michael (Louis) 1943-

PERSONAL: Surname is pronounced *Ber*-jer; born February 11, 1943, in Boston, Mass.; son of Clarence Quinn (an educational consultant) and Ethel J. (a social worker; maiden name, Goldberg) Berger; married Linda A. Cannizzo (a speech clinician), October 9, 1976. *Education:* Harvard University, B.A., 1965; Yale University, M.A.T., 1966; Columbia University, Ed.D., 1972. *Home:* Flat Iron Rd., Bates Acres, Great Mills, Md. 20634. *Office:* Division of Human Development, St. Mary's College of Maryland, St. Mary's City, Md. 20686.

CAREER: High school social studies teacher in Englewood, N.J., 1966-69; Marymount College, Tarrytown, N.Y., instructor in education, 1971-72; Fordham University, New York, N.Y., assistant professor of education, 1972-77, director of Institute in Urban Education, 1972-74; St. Mary's College of Maryland, St. Mary's City, associate professor of education and director of teacher education, 1977—. President of New York State Council on Social Education, 1973-74, member of executive committee, 1974-77; member of board of directors of New York State Council for the Social Studies, 1974-76; coordinator of Maryland Association of Small Teacher Education Programs, 1978—.

MEMBER: National Society for the Study of Education, National Council for the Social Studies, American Educational Studies Association, National Writers Club (professional member), Association for Supervision and Curriculum Development, Association of Teacher Educators, Phi Delta Kappa (past faculty sponsor). *Awards, honors:* Certificate of merit from Phi Delta Kappa, 1976, 1977.

WRITINGS: Violence in the Schools: Causes and Remedies, Phi Delta Kappa Educational Foundation, 1974; *The Public Education System,* F. Watts, 1977; (contributor) P. R. Baker and W. H. Hall, *The American Experience,* Volumes I and II, with teacher's guide, Oxford Book Co., 1977; *The Automobile and Social Change in Rural America, 1893-1929,* Shoe String, in press; *Firearms and Their History,* F. Watts, in press. Contributor of about forty articles and reviews to professional and popular magazines, including *Maine Life, Change, Hadassah, Antiques Journal,* and *Young World.* Book review editor for *Social Science Record,* 1974-78.

WORK IN PROGRESS: Revising picture book manuscript, *The Dream Machine;* collecting humorous articles for an anthology, *Education Is a Funny Business.*

SIDELIGHTS: Berger told *CA:* "The Public Education System* is one of the first book length attempts to explain to adolescents how American public schools operate. As such, it ought to give them a better understanding of an institution with which all of them are concerned.

"The Automobile and Social Change in Rural America will

be the first major examination of the motor car's impact on social aspects (family, community, education, religion, health, leisure, etc.) of this formerly predominant region of the United States. Another appealing aspect of this volume will be the quotation of numerous contemporary observations on the influence of the automobile. The different attitudes of the average citizen in the period 1900-1929 and today are quite startling.''

AVOCATIONAL INTERESTS: Automobile mechanics, collecting coins, stamps, ticket stubs, and pieces of Americana.

* * *

BERGERET, Ida Treat   1889(?)-1978
(Ida Treat)

1889(?)—March 25, 1978; American educator, journalist, and author. Treat was an educator at Vassar College. Earlier in her career, she was based in Paris as a correspondent for *Paris Vu.* Under the name Ida Treat, she contributed articles to the *Saturday Evening Post, Harper's,* and *Nation,* and contributed many short stories to *New Yorker.* Treat worked aboard smuggler Hendi de Montfried's ship on the Red Sea in order to obtain material for her nonfiction adventure book, *Pearls, Arms, and Hashish.* She also wrote *Primitive Hearths in the Pyrenees* and *The Anchored Heart.* She died in Poughkeepsie, N.Y. Obituaries and other sources: *New York Times,* March 26, 1978.

* * *

BERLE, Milton   1908-

PERSONAL: Surname originally Berlinger; born July 12, 1908, in New York, N.Y.; son of Moses (in painting and decorating business) and Sarah (a department store detective and theatrical manager under name Sandra Berle; maiden name Glantz) Berlinger; married Joyce Matthews, 1941 (divorced, 1947); married Ruth Cosgrove, December 9, 1953; children: Victoria Melissa, Billy. *Education:* Educated in New York City. *Address:* c/o Sagebrush Enterprises, Inc., 151 El Camino, Beverly Hills, Calif. 90212.

CAREER: Began as vaudeville performer and appeared as a child in more than fifty silent films, including a small role in "Humoresque," 1919; made debut as stage actor in New York, N.Y., 1920; returned to vaudeville circuit and later became youngest master of ceremonies on Broadway at Palace Theatre, 1931-32; appeared as star of 1936 "Ziegfeld Follies" and other shows; acted in Hollywood films, 1937-39, including "Radio City Revels," "Tall, Dark and Handsome," and "Margin for Error"; turned to night club engagements and participated in radio programs, including the "Rudy Vallee Hour," "Stop Me if You've Heard This One," and the "Milton Berle Show," 1939-48; became master of ceremonies on "Texaco Star Theatre" for both radio and television, 1948-56; guest star on television programs, radio performer, and feature actor in films, including "It's a Mad, Mad, Mad, Mad World," 1962; "The Loved One," 1968; and "Can Hieronymus Merkin Ever Forget Mercy Humpee and Find True Happiness?," 1969. *Member:* American Society of Composers and Publishers (ASCAP), American Guild of Authors and Composers, Grand Street Boys, Friar's (honorary abbot emeritus).

WRITINGS: Out of My Trunk (autobiographical), Blue Ribbon Books, 1945; (with John Roeburt) *Earthquake* (novel), Random House, 1959; (with Haskel Frankel) *Milton Berle: An Autobiography,* Delacorte, 1974.

SIDELIGHTS: "Berle's rapid gags, broad clowning, versatility, and hard work added up to video's first smash hit," wrote Jack Gould in 1948. Berle's comedy-variety series on NBC television attracted huge audiences across the country. Watching Berle's performance on "Texaco Star Theatre" each Tuesday evening became something of a national pastime and the show was considered by many to be directly responsible for popularizing the infant medium. Berle was known to his fans as "Uncle Miltie" and to the show business world as "Mr. Television."

Berle's years of experience in vaudeville and movies prepared him well for his television success. He studied the styles of popular comedians like Eddie Cantor and Al Jolson on the way to developing his own distinctive style. As part of his comedic education, Berle also collected jokes. By 1949 he claimed to have some fifty thousand jokes at his disposal.

In addition to his regular stage, screen, and television appearances, Berle has entertained for many charities and causes. As a child he entertained soldiers during World War I and later toured military hospitals for six months straight during World War II. Berle also hosted the first sixteen hour telethon in 1949 to benefit the Damon Runyon Cancer Memorial Fund.

In 1959, Berle tried his hand at writing fiction. The resulting book, *Earthquake,* is a serious novel about expatriates in Mexico and was written in collaboration with John Roeburt. "An interesting chess game has been kicked over too soon," wrote Rex Lardner in the *New York Times.* But Lardner had praise for "the Mexican interiors and exotic goings-on" in the novel. Rose Feld, in a review for the *New York Herald-Tribune,* called *Earthquake* a novel "that is individual and has dramatic color and pace." She added that the "authors bring an immediacy of portraiture [to their characters] that is both tough and perceptive."

In his 1974 autobiography, Berle tried "to come to grips with the forces that motivated his life," according to the *New York Times.* Phil Prevor wrote that it "takes on the quality of a litany: the hits and flops; the sexual conquests; the congealed sleaziness of old gossip-column tidbits.... Berle's increasing introspection reveals [that] the 'real' self he is always trying to get back to is a hungry void that can never be filled. Readers who remember Uncle Miltie will be absorbed and saddened by this book." But *Newsweek*'s Walter Clemons observed: "After the end of his reign as Mr. Television in 1956," Berle "bows off like a pro, without complaints."

AVOCATIONAL INTERESTS: Magic, pool, horse racing, golf.

BIOGRAPHICAL/CRITICAL SOURCES: Milton Berle, *Out of My Trunk,* Blue Ribbon Books, 1945; *Saturday Evening Post,* March 19, 1949; *Time,* May 16, 1949; *New York Herald-Tribune,* April 26, 1959; *New York Times,* May 3, 1959, October 6, 1974; *Newsweek,* December 2, 1974; Berle and Haskel Frankel, *Milton Berle: An Autobiography,* Delacorte, 1974.*

* * *

BERLINER, Herman A(lbert)   1944-

PERSONAL: Born April 6, 1944, in New York, N.Y.; son of Walter and Johanna (Achenbrand) Berliner. *Education:* City College of the City University of New York, B.A., 1965; City University of New York, Ph.D., 1970. *Office:* Office of the Provost, Hofstra University, Hempstead, N.Y. 11550.

CAREER: Hofstra University, Hempstead, N.Y., assistant professor, 1970-78, associate professor of economics, 1978—, associate dean, 1975-76, assistant provost, 1976-77, associate provost for budget and curriculum, 1977—. Managing editor of *American Economist*, 1975—. *Member:* American Economic Association, City University of New York Ph.D. Alumni Association (president, 1973-77).

WRITINGS: (With Dominick Salvatore) *Economics*, Monarch, 1973, 2nd edition, 1976; (with Salvatore) *Statistics*, Monarch, 1975; (editor) *Programs to Prevent or Alleviate Poverty*, Hofstra University, 1978. Contributor to economics and education journals and to *Monthly Labor Review*.

WORK IN PROGRESS: Research on the economics of higher education.

BIOGRAPHICAL/CRITICAL SOURCES: *Change*, May, 1975.

*　　*　　*

BERLONI, William 1956-

PERSONAL: Born November 19, 1956, in New Britain, Conn.; son of Fulvio (a horticulturist) and Eleanor (a factory worker; maiden name, Windish) Berloni. *Education:* Attended Central Connecticut State College, 1974-76, and New York University, 1976-77. *Religion:* Roman Catholic. *Home and office:* 14 West 68th St., Apt. 5, New York, N.Y. 10023.

CAREER: Goodspeed Opera House, East Haddam, Conn., actor, 1976—; writer, 1977—. *Awards, honors:* Award from Outer Critics Circle, 1977, for his dog's performance in the Broadway production of "Annie."

WRITINGS: *Sandy: The Autobiography of a Star*, Simon & Schuster, 1978.

WORK IN PROGRESS: Considering writing either a screenplay adapted from his book or a book on training dogs or on a dog named Arf.

SIDELIGHTS: Berloni, who is the owner-trainer of Sandy, the dog who has appeared in the Broadway production of "Annie" since 1976, writes that his main interest is pursuing a career in the performing arts.

*　　*　　*

BERNABEI, Alfio 1941-

PERSONAL: Born December 23, 1941, in Dovadola, Italy; son of Dante and Maria (Leoni) Bernabei. *Education:* Attended Wallbrook College, 1970-71; University of Reading, B.A., 1974. *Home:* 73 South Hill Park, London N.W.3, England.

CAREER: Painter and decorator, 1963; free-lance journalist, 1969; Bite Theatre Group, London, England, director, 1975—. *Military service:* Italian Army, 1962-63. *Member:* Theatre Writers Union. *Awards, honors:* Italy's National Drama Award, 1962, for "Incontri."

WRITINGS—Plays: "Incontri" (three-act; title means "Meetings"), 1962, first produced in Milan, Italy, at Centro Culturale I Rabdomanti, 1963; "The Jump" (two-act), first produced in Reading, England, at University of Reading, 1973; "Gastarbeiter" (two-act; title means "Guest Workers"), first produced in Cologne, Germany, at Katz Pott am Bonnerstrasse, 1974, English translation produced as "Gast," in Edinburgh at Edinburgh Festival, 1976; "The Bite" (one-act), first produced in London at Institute of Contemporary Art, 1975; "Grunwicks" (two-act), first produced in Edinburgh at Edinburgh Festival, 1977.

Author of "Avventura," for BBC-TV, 1971. Contributor to Italian magazines and newspapers.

WORK IN PROGRESS: A play on cultural imperialism, for Bite Theatre Group.

SIDELIGHTS: Bernabei comments: "I write plays about important social issues, placing them within a historical context. The themes of the plays so far (the insurgence of neo-fascism in parts of Europe, the Chilean coup of 1973, the plight of migrant workers, etc.) indicate the importance I attach to aspects of international politics. The aim is to provide audiences with an analysis of the dominant economic interests and their supportive cultural apparatuses."

Most of Bernabei's plays have been written for the Bite Theatre Group which he set up in 1975. The group has researched new forms of dramatic presentation, especially in the areas of language, treatment of emotion, and "decharacterization." The dramatis personae represent forces at work in history, and a constant theme is that of power and its maintenance. Bernabei has lived in France and Germany, and traveled in Latin America and Africa.

*　　*　　*

BERNSTEIN, Joanne E(ckstein) 1943-

PERSONAL: Born April 21, 1943, in New York; daughter of Murray (a lawyer) and Mildred (a teacher; maiden name, Weckstein) Eckstein; married Michael J. Bernstein (a teacher of physics), June 9, 1965; children: Robin, Andrew. *Education:* Brooklyn College of the City University of New York, B.A., 1963; Pratt Institute, M.L.S., 1966; Columbia University, Ed.D., 1971. *Home:* 3848 Maple Ave., Brooklyn, N.Y. 11224. *Office:* School of Education, Brooklyn College of the City University of New York, Brooklyn, N.Y. 11210.

CAREER: Kindergarten teacher in a public school in Brooklyn, N.Y., 1963-67; substitute teacher for elementary and secondary schools in New York City, 1967-69; Pace College, New York City, adjunct lecturer in education, 1970; New York Community College, New York City, adjunct lecturer in education, 1971; Brooklyn College of the City University of New York, Brooklyn, assistant professor of education, 1971—. *Member:* International Reading Association, Association for Childhood Education International, National Council of Teachers of English, National Association for the Education of Young Children, Foundation of Thanatology.

WRITINGS: *Loss: And How to Cope with It* (juvenile), Seabury, 1977; (with Stephen Gullo) *When People Die*, Dutton, 1977; *Books to Help Children Cope With Separation and Loss*, Bowker, 1977. Reviewer of juvenile books for *Young Children*, 1973-77.

WORK IN PROGRESS: A book about immigrant families; a book of riddles.

SIDELIGHTS: Joanne Bernstein comments: "My entire professional career—as teacher, reviewer, writer—is wrapped up in the world of publishing for children. I couldn't be more delighted with the direction life has taken!"

*　　*　　*

BERRY, Frederic Aroyce, Jr. 1906-1978

1906—February 18, 1978; American meteorologist, U.S. Navy rear admiral, and author of a book in his field. Berry, who received his master's degree in meteorology, retired from the Navy in 1957 as a specialist in weather control.

Later served as consulting meteorologist to the Naval Oceanographic Office for two years. Berry died in Arlington, Va. Obituaries and other sources: *Washington Post,* February 20, 1978.

* * *

BERTON, Peter (Alexander Menquez) 1922-

PERSONAL: Born June 11, 1922, in Bialystok, Poland; son of Claude Myron and Raissa (Menquez) Berton; married Michele Strick, August 29, 1957; children: David Adrian Strick, Jonathan Claude Kurier. *Education:* Wasada University, diploma in architecture, 1946; Columbia University, M.A., 1951, Ph.D., 1956. *Home:* 320 South Rodeo Dr., Beverly Hills, Calif. 90212. *Office:* School of International Relations, University of Southern California, 330 Von KleinSmid Center, Los Angeles, Calif. 90007.

CAREER: Supreme Command Allied Powers, Japan, deputy assistant censor, assistant chief examiner, and head of personnel and training sections, 1945-47; Eighth U.S. Army Education Center, Yokohama, Japan, instructor in Japanese and Russian, 1947-49; Library of Congress, Washington, D.C., consultant on Manchurian bibliography, 1951; Japanese interpreter, summer, 1952; University of Southern California, Los Angeles, lecturer, 1953-56, assistant professor and research associate in Soviet-Japanese relations, 1956-57; Stanford University, Stanford, Calif., assistant professor and acting curator of North Asia Collections at Hoover Institution on War, Revolution and Peace, 1957-59; University of Southern California, visiting associate professor, 1961-62, associate professor, 1964-69, professor of international relations, 1969—, coordinator of East Asian studies program, 1961—, editor of "Studies in Comparative Communism," 1970—, education director of Japanese affairs program at University of Tokyo, summer, 1960. Consultant to Ford Foundation.

MEMBER: International Studies Association, American Association for the Advancement of Slavic Studies, American Political Science Association, American Association Of University Professors, Association for Asian Studies, Western Slavic Association, Japan Society. *Awards, honors:* Grants from Ford Foundation, 1959, and Social Science Research Council, 1960-62.

WRITINGS: Manchuria: An Annotated Bibliography, Library of Congress, 1951; (co-author) *Japanese Training and Research in the Russian Field,* University of Southern California Press, 1956; *Soviet Works on China,* University of Southern California Press, 1959; (editor) *The Japanese Penetration of Korea, 1894-1910,* Stanford University Press, 1959; *The Chinese-Russian Dialogue,* two volumes, University of Southern California Press, 1964; (with Eugene Wu) *Contemporary China: A Research Guide,* Hoover Institution, 1967; (with Alvin Z. Rubenstein) *Soviet Works on Southeast Asia,* University of Southern California Press, 1967; (editor with Charles Gati) *Symposium on the Comparative Study of Communist Foreign Policy,* University of Southern California Press, 1976.

Also author of a Japanese work (title means "The Russo-Japanese Boundary, 1850-1875"), with summary in English, Kajima Institute of International Peace, 1967. Contributor to *Encyclopedia Americana* and to scholarly journals. Editor of special issue of *International Studies Quarterly,* December, 1969, and of *Studies in Comparative Communism,* 1970—.

WORK IN PROGRESS: Research on relations among Japan, China, and the Soviet Union, on Soviet-Asian relations, Japanese diplomatic history and foreign policy decision-making, the Communist press and foreign policy, Asian and Soviet bibliography, and on foreign policy and psychoanalysis.

SIDELIGHTS: Berton writes: "I was brought up in China and Japan; I have traveled in Southeast Asia, the Middle East, and Europe (with residence in England). I am fluent in Russian, German, and Japanese. At present I am very much interested in psychoanalysis and its application in my work." *Avocational interests:* Playing the violin (chamber music).

* * *

BESAS, Peter 1933-

PERSONAL: Born June 5, 1933, in Berlin, Germany; son of Alfred and Margot (Schlee) Besas; married Lucia Martinez Garcia, October 12, 1965; children: Mark. *Education:* Attended City College (now of the City University of New York), 1951-55, and Alliance Francaise (Paris), 1965. *Home and office:* 104 Calle Lagasca, Madrid 6, Spain.

CAREER: Worked in Spain as editor of *Guidepost, Castellana,* and *Fodor's Guide to Spain;* announcer for Radio Nacional in Spain; Madrid bureau chief for *Variety,* New York City; currently Madrid bureau chief for *Daily Variety,* Hollywood, Calif., and Latin American operations director for *Variety,* New York City.

WRITINGS: A Zaj Sampler (pamphlet), Stephens, 1967. Also author of *Strange Vignettes of Old Madrid,* 1969.

WORK IN PROGRESS: A historical account of travelers in Spain, *The Written Road to Spain;* a novel, *Deadline.*

* * *

BETHELL, Tom 1940-

PERSONAL: Born July 17, 1940, in London, England; came to the United States in 1962, naturalized citizen, 1974; son of Peter Paul (an editor) and Pauline (Carlile) Bethell. *Education:* Attended Royal Naval College, 1954-58; Trinity College, Oxford, M.A., 1962. *Politics:* Conservative. *Religion:* Roman Catholic. *Residence:* Washington, D.C. *Office:* Harper's, 2 Park Ave., New York, N.Y. 10016.

CAREER: Mathematics teacher at private preparatory school in Virginia, 1962-65; did jazz research in New Orleans, La., 1965-67; worked with New Orleans district attorney, Jim Garrison, on John F. Kennedy assassination investigation, 1967-68; engaged in jazz research and writing, 1969-71; managing editor of *New Orleans* magazine; associate editor of *New Orleans Courier,* 1972-74; *Washington Monthly,* Washington, D.C., editor, 1975-76; *Harper's,* New York, N.Y., Washington editor, 1976—. *Military service:* Royal Navy, 1954-58.

WRITINGS: George Lewis: A Jazzman from New Orleans, University of California Press, 1977.

WORK IN PROGRESS: Magazine writing.

SIDELIGHTS: Bethell told *CA:* "I believe in Original Sin, and I prefer the genetics of Mendel to that of Lysenko. I must have spent a fourth of my life listening to music. and I especially like Gregorian chants (which I listened to at school), Beethoven, George Lewis, Bunk Johnson, Jelly Roll Morton, and Mahalia Jackson. I detest 'modern' and experimental music of all kinds. Malcolm Muggeridge, George Orwell, and Tom Wolfe are among my favorite modern writers."

BEYER, Robert 1913(?)-1978

1913(?)—April 29, 1978; American accounting executive and author of a book in his field. Beyer became chief executive officer of the accounting firm Touche Ross & Co. in 1962. He joined the company in 1948. In 1970, the University of Wisconsin established the Robert Beyer Professorship of Managerial Accounting in his name. He died in Colorado Springs, Colo. Obituaries and other sources: *New York Times*, April 30, 1978.

* * *

BHATT, Jagdish J(eyshanker) 1939-

PERSONAL: Born February 17, 1939; came to the United States in 1961, naturalized citizen, 1976; son of Jeyshanker Mancharam and Kamala (Jeyshanker) Bhatt; married wife, Meena, January 22, 1970; children: Amar Jagdish. *Education:* University of Baroda, B.Sc. (honors), 1961; University of Wisconsin, Madison, M.S., 1963; further graduate study at University of New Mexico, 1966-67, University of California, Santa Barbara, 1968-69, and Stanford University, 1971-72; University of Wales, Ph.D., 1972. *Home:* 6 Saxony Dr., Warwick, R.I. 02886. *Office:* Department of Physics (Geology-Oceanography Unit), Rhode Island Junior College, 400 East Ave., Warwick, R.I. 02886.

CAREER: Jackson Junior College, Jackson, Mich., instructor in physics and chemistry, 1964-65; Oklahoma Panhandle State College (now University), Goodwill, instructor in geology and physical sciences, 1965-66; University of Northern Iowa, Cedar Falls, instructor in geology, summer, 1967; Stanford University, Stanford, Calif., research scholar and scientist in geology, 1971-72; State University of New York at Buffalo, assistant professor of oceanography, geology, and environmental sciences, 1972-74; Rhode Island Junior College, Warwick, assistant professor of geology and oceanography, 1974—. Geo-Resources and environmental consultant, 1972—. Member of Rhode Island Ocean Technology Task Force Committee, 1975-76. Developed courses in oceanography and programs in ocean training and off-shore technology. *Member:* International Oceanographic Foundation, Geological Society of America, Oceanic Society. *Awards, honors:* Wolfson doctoral fellowship at University of Wales, 1970-71.

WRITINGS: (Contributor) J.G.C. Anderson, A. P. Macmillan, and John Platt, editors, *Mineral Exploitation and Economic Geology*, University of Wales, 1971; *Laboratory Manual on Physical Geology*, Guymon, 1966; *Laboratory Manual on Physical Sciences*, Guymon, 1966; *Cretaceous History of Himalayan Geosyncline*, Guymon, 1966.

Environmentology: Earth's Environment and Energy Resources, Modern Press, 1975; *Geochemistry and Petrology of South Wales Main Limestone (Mississippian)*, Modern Press, 1976; *Geologic Exploration of Earth* (manual), Modern Press, 1976; *Oceanography: Exploring the Planet Ocean*, with instructor's manual, Van Nostrand, 1978. Contributor to geology journals.

WORK IN PROGRESS: Applied Oceanography: Resources, Technology, and Management, with laboratory manual; *Trace Elemental Distribution in the Marine Carbonates of the South Wales Main Limestone Series (Lower Carboniferous)*; *Exploring the Earth's History: Laboratory Manual*, publication by Modern Press expected in 1980; *Odyssey of Perception: Selected Poems*.

SIDELIGHTS: Bhatt writes that his contributions to the study of geology and oceanography include a demonstration

of the role of bacteria in the formation of nodular cherts in marine limestones, explanation of the true geochemical and geologic nature of South Wales marine limestones, and development of educational curricula on marine technology. He feels that his books provide a comprehensive treatment of contemporary issues of environmental pollution, energy resources, population, food technology, and global management of earth's resources, and a most comprehensive treatment of theoretical and practical ocean-related matters.

Sharing the ideas which motivate him as a writer, Bhatt wrote: "As a writer I have always been driven by the philosophy of local to global cooperation as the best way to fulfill the challenge of freeing ourselves from the earthly drudgeries of energy and food shortages, population and pollution dilemma, and from the rising entropy of stress per capita particularly during the present century.

"I consider that the art of organized-thoughts expression is the main business of writing. Therefore, it is a *sine qua non* that writers aim this art not for their ego-pivoting instrument of fame but use it as a powerful means of circumventing human shortcomings, including eradication of intellectual provincialism. By the same token, the art of creative communication (regardless of the writer's background as a scientist, poet, or philosopher) should consistently be affirmed as a fire of imagination ready to erode the darkness of our superfluous values, artificial barriers, wars, racism, colonialism, and various other unproductive madness permanently from the face of the planet before mankind embraces the fascinating virgin terrain of the twenty-first century. At the near end of the present century, I cannot resist the temptation of envisioning mankind's unified gift of a world society relatively free of the above mentioned scars and dilemmas. Perhaps writers, through the power of constructive expression, could significantly contribute in their own significant way. The joy of such a gift remains in the fact that we may redeem all the historic blunders we have ever made since we became to be known as *Homo sapien*, that is, man the wise, with a single mighty stroke of progress!

"Another immediate challenge writers of the world at present are facing is the issue of human rights. Although this issue transcends the planetary spatio-temporal complex of geography and history, let us not ignore equally vital issues of human responsibilities and human obligations. Writers of diversified backgrounds must keep the flame of the above-mentioned trinity in the limelight, particularly in light of the fact that it is a prerequisite for our gift to the younger generations of the next century.

"Finally, writers must make a concerted local to global effort to guard the indispensible values, including the fabric of our society—family unity—against the juggernaut technology. Although technology yields constructive fruits of communication, transportation and myriads of materialistic comforts and pleasures, its latent power of dehumanization must not be taken for granted. Otherwise we have little choice but to drown in the deluge of change.

"I have quickly flashed some of these reflections in the hope that readers of *CA* will become aware of the responsibility and challenge of writing in coming years. The art of writing demands martinet discipline of mind and dedication to one's mission in life, and unfortunately during the process of creative writing beloved ones often suffer a great deal. In the final analysis, it is worth the commitment if the quality of one's work is effective in erasing a fraction of our contemporary shadows."

BICK, Edgar Milton 1902-1978

April 3, 1902—April 8, 1978; American orthopedic surgeon, educator, and author. In addition to his private practice of orthopedics, Bick served on numerous local and national health committees. He was clinical professor emeritus at Mount Sinai Hospital and a lecturer on orthopedics at universities in New Delhi and Jerusalem. Bick died in New York, N.Y. Obituaries and other sources: *Who's Who in World Jewry*, Pitman, 1972; *Who's Who in the East*, 16th edition, Marquis, 1977; *New York Times*, April 9, 1978.

*   *   *

BIDWELL, Marjory Elizabeth Sarah (Elizabeth Ford, Mary Ann Gibbs)

PERSONAL: Born in Seaford, Sussex, England; daughter of Thomas (a surgeon) and Rozanna Marian (Kimber) Lambe; married Thomas Edward Palmer Bidwell (died, 1965); children: Timothy George. *Education:* Attended secondary school in Seaford, Sussex, England. *Politics:* "Moderate." *Religion:* Church of England. *Home:* Bedford Cottage, 36 Prince Edwards Rd., Lewes, Sussex BN7 1BE, England. *Agent:* John Cushman Associates, Inc., 25 West 43rd St., New York, N.Y. 10036.

CAREER: Writer, 1933—.

WRITINGS—Suspense novels under pseudonym Elizabeth Ford; all published by Hurst & Blackett, except as indicated: *Fog*, Chapman & Hall, 1933; *The House with the Myrtle Trees*, Lutterworth, 1942; *The Blue Cockade: A Romantic Novel of 1780*, Lutterworth, 1943; *Queen's Harbor*, 1944; *The Young Ladies' Room*, 1945; *The Irresponsibles*, 1946; *Mountford Show*, 1948; *Spring Comes to the Crescent*, 1949.

So Deep Suspicion, 1950; *Four Days in June*, 1951; *Just Around the Corner*, 1952; *English Rose*, 1953; *One Fine Day*, 1954; *Meeting in the Spring*, 1954; *Outrageous Fortune*, 1955; *The Summer at Bacclesea*, 1956; *The Empty Heart*, 1957; *The Cottage at Drimble*, 1957; *Butter Market House*, 1958.

Heron's Nest, 1960; *A Week by the Sea*, 1962; *A Holiday Engagement: A Maplechester Novel*, 1963; *No Room for Joanne: A Maplechester Novel*, 1961; *A Country Holiday*, 1966; *The Turbulent Messiters*, 1967; *The Day of the Storm*, 1971; *The Belvedere*, 1973; *Young Ann*, 1973; *A Charming Couple*, 1975; *The Amber Cat*, 1977.

Historical romances under pseudonym Mary Ann Gibbs: *A Young Man With Ideas*, P. Davies, 1950; *Enchantment: A Pastoral*, P. Davies, 1952; *A Bit of a Bounder: An Edwardian Trifle*, P. Davies, 1952; *Young Lady with Red Hair*, 1957, reprinted as *The Penniless Heiress*, Coronet, 1975; *The Guardian*, 1958; *The Years of the Nannies* (nonfiction), Hutchinson, 1960; *Horatia*, 1961; *The Apothecary's Daughter*, 1962; *Polly Kettle*, 1963, reprinted as *The Nursery Maid*, Coronet, 1975; *The Amateur Governess*, 1964, published as *The House of Ravensbourne*, Pyramid Publications, 1965; *The Sugar Mouse*, 1965; *The Romantic Frenchman*, 1967; *A Parcel of Land*, 1969.

The Year of the Pageant, 1971; *The Glass Palace*, 1973, Mason/Charter, 1975; *The Sea Urchins*, White Lion, 1973; *A Wife for the Admiral*, 1974, published as *The Admiral's Lady*, Mason/Charter, 1975; *A Most Romantic City*, Mason/Charter, 1976; *The Tempestuous Petticoat*, Mason/Charter, 1977.

Contributor of about three hundred stories and articles to magazines in England, Canada, and the United States.

WORK IN PROGRESS: Historical research.

SIDELIGHTS: Marjory Bidwell writes: "When I was born, my grandfather was a wealthy man. He owned several farms as well as large tracts of the Sussex downland, where he ran Southdown sheep. When I was about eight years old he was persuaded to invest his fortune in real estate and lost nearly all of it. My father returned to private practice of medicine, moving to the coalfields of Durham in the North, where he could earn enough to keep his family. My sister and I had a governess to teach us and when she left to get married, we went to boarding school. I think it was then I started to write: I hated the large unwelcoming school, and after my sister left I fought my home-sickness and loneliness by writing serials in my geography books.

"My husband was never strong and from early in my marriage I had to write to earn things like the rent, doctors' and dentists' bills, etc., which became increasingly difficult when he became an invalid. Since his death, however, I have found writing a great deal easier and consequently very rewarding—my enjoyment of writing has been greatly increased by the popularity my books have gained on both sides of the Atlantic."

*   *   *

BIEBER, Margarete 1879-1978

July 31, 1879—February 25, 1978; German-born American educator, archaeologist, Greek and Roman art historian, and author. Bieber wrote several books in her field, including *The History of the Greek and Roman Theatre* and *Copies of Greek Art*. She died in New Canaan, Conn. Obituaries and other sources: *The Biographical Encyclopaedia and Who's Who of the American Theatre*, James Heineman, 1966; *Directory of American Scholars*, Volume I: *History*, 6th edition, Bowker, 1974; *Archaeology*, April, 1975; *International Who's Who*, Europa, 1975; *New York Times*, February 28, 1978. (See index for *CA* sketch)

*   *   *

BIEGEL, Paul 1925-

PERSONAL: Born March 25, 1925, in Bussum, Netherlands; son of Herman (a merchant) and Madeleine (Povel) Biegel; married Marijke Straeter (a social worker), September 10, 1960; children: Leonie, Arthur. *Education:* Attended University of Amsterdam. *Home:* Keizersgracht 227, Amsterdam, Netherlands.

CAREER: "De Radiobode" (radio weekly), Amsterdam, Netherlands, editor, 1948-65; Koevesdi (press agency), Amsterdam, editor, 1965-67; Ploegsma (publishing firm), Amsterdam, editor, 1967-69; Van Holkema en Warendorf (publishing firm), Bussum, Netherlands, adviser, 1969—; free-lance writer, 1969—. Text writer for "Marten Toonder Comics." *Member:* Dutch Society of Writers (V.V.L.), Dutch Society of Literature. *Awards, honors:* Received best children's book of the year award from Collective Promotion of Dutch Books (CPNB), 1965, for *Het sleutelkruid*; award from Children's Jury of Amsterdam, 1970, for *De tuinen van Dorr*; Golden Pencil award from CPNB, 1972, for *De kleine kapitein*; Silver Pencil award from CPNB, 1972, and prize from Jan Campert Foundation, 1973, for *De twaalf rovers*; State Prize for complete works, 1973; Silver Pencil award from CPNB, 1974, for *Het olifantenfeest*.

WRITINGS—In English: *Het sleutelkruid*, Holland, 1964, translation by Guillian Hume and the author published as *The King of the Copper Mountains*, F. Watts, 1969; *Ik wou dat ik anders was,* Holland, 1967, translation by Hume and the author published as *The Seven-Times Search,* Dent, 1971; *De tuinen van Dorr,* Holland, 1969, translation by Hume and the author published as *The Gardens of Dorr,* Dent, 1975.

De twaalf rovers, Holland, 1971, translation by Patricia Crampton published as *The Twelve Robbers,* Dent, 1974, Puffin, 1977; *De kleine kapitein,* Holland, 1971, translation by Crampton published as *The Little Captain,* Dent, 1971; *Het olifantenfeest,* Holland, 1973, translation by Crampton published as *The Elephant Party,* Puffin, 1977; *De kleine kapitein in het land van waan en wijs,* Holland, 1973, translation by Crampton published as *The Little Captain and the Seven Towers,* Dent, 1973; *Het stenen beeld,* Holland, 1974, translation by Crampton published as *Far Beyond and Back Again,* Dent, 1977; *De kleine kapitein en de schat van schrik en vreze,* Holland, 1975; translation by Crampton published as *The Little Captain and the Seven Towers,* Dent, 1975; *Het spiegelkasteel,* Holland, 1976, translation by Crampton published as *The Mirror Castle,* Blackie & Son, 1979; *De dwergjes van Tuil,* Holland, 1977, translation by Crampton published as *The Dwarfs of Nosegay,* Blackie & Son, 1978; *De rover Hoepsika,* Holland, 1977, translation by Crampton published as *The Robber Hopsika,* Dent, 1978.

Other; all published by Holland, except as indicated: *De gouden gitaar* (title means "The Golden Guitar"), 1962; *Het grote boek* (title means "The Great Book"), 1962; *De kukelhaan* (title means "Crow Cockerel"), 1964; *Het lapjesbeest* (title means "Patch-Animal"), 1964; *Kinderverhalen* (title means "Children's Stories"), 1966; *De rattenvanger van Hameln* (title means "The Pied Piper of Hamlin"), 1967; *De zeven fabels uit Ubim* (title means "The Seven Fables from Ubim"), 1970; *Sebastiaan Slorp,* 1971; *Reinaart de vos* (title means "Reynard the Fox"), 1972; *De vloek van woestewolf* (title means "The Curse of Fierce Wolf"), 1974; *Twaalf sloeg de klok* (title means "Twelve Chimed the Clock"), 1974; *De brieven van de generaal* (title means "Letters From the General"), 1977; *Wie je droomt ben je zelf* (title means "You Are the Ones You Dream Of"), CPBN, 1977.

Also author of television series, "De vloek van woestewolf."

WORK IN PROGRESS: The Stories of Virgil of Nosegay.

SIDELIGHTS: Biegel told *CA:* "I was born in an estate-like home with a huge garden, two parents, two brothers, six sisters, a German maid, a gardener, and a dog. I remember a lot, but I am convinced it is the memories without words, of the years before a child has words to its disposition (Adam before he named the things of paradise) that the source of any one's creative urge lies. And the writer, for the rest of his life, tries in vain to find words for it."

* * *

BIERLEY, Paul E(dmund) 1926-

PERSONAL: Born February 3, 1926, in Portsmouth, Ohio; son of William Frederick (a shoe cobbler) and Minnie Genieve (Atkin) Bierley; married Pauline Jeanette Allison (an executive secretary), September 17, 1948; children: Lois Elaine Bierley Walker, John Emerson. *Education:* Attended Ohio University, 1947-48; Ohio State University, B. Aeronautical Engineering, 1953. *Politics:* Independent. *Religion:* Methodist. *Home:* 3888 Morse Rd., Columbus, Ohio 43219. *Office:* Ellanef Co., 4910-111 East Fifth Ave., Columbus, Ohio 43219.

CAREER: Engineer for North American Aviation, 1953-73; currently employed as engineer for Ellanef Co., Columbus, Ohio. Professional musician, 1960—, has played with Columbus Symphony Orchestra, Detroit Concert Band, and World Symphony Orchestra. Has also worked as shoe cobbler, draftsman, cartoonist, bandmaster, research and recording consultant, and in advertising sales. Member of board of advisers of Detroit Concert Band. *Military service:* U.S. Army Air Forces, 1944-46.

MEMBER: International Sousa Society (special consultant), American Bandmasters Association (research center adviser), American School Band Directors Association, Sonneck Society, Tubists Universal Brotherhood Association, National Band Association, Windjammers Unlimited. *Awards, honors:* Edwin Franko Goldman Memorial Citation from American Bandmasters Association, 1974.

WRITINGS: John Philip Sousa, American Phenomenon, Prentice-Hall, 1973; *John Philip Sousa: A Descriptive Catalog of His Works,* University of Illinois Press, 1973; *Office Fun!* (cartoons), Integrity Press, 1976. Contributor to *Dictionary of American Biography* and 6th edition of *Groves Dictionary of Music and Musicians.* Contributor to magazines and newspapers.

WORK IN PROGRESS: Books on the life and music of composer Henry Fillmore, music humor, and a local psychic; a cartoon book; continuing research on John Philip Sousa, with two books expected to result.

* * *

BIHLER, Penny 1940-

PERSONAL: Surname is pronounced *Beel*-er; born April 9, 1940, in New York, N.Y.; daughter of George H. (a businessman) and Barbara (a fashion illustrator; maiden name, Kingsley) Harter; married Charles H. Bihler (a media specialist), June 25, 1960; children: Charles, Nancy. *Education:* Douglass College, B.A., 1961. *Religion:* Protestant. *Home:* 2514 Tack Circle, Scotch Plains, N.J. 07076.

CAREER: High school English teacher in South Plainfield, N.J., 1961-62, and Scotch Plains, N.J., 1962-65; poet and writer for "Artists in the Schools" program of New Jersey Council on the Arts, 1973—; Woodbridge School District, Woodbridge, N.J., poet-in-residence for project Moppet, 1978—. Member of cultural advisory committee of Union County Cultural and Heritage Commission, 1975-76. *Member:* Haiku Society of America, Poets and Writers of New Jersey (member of board of directors, 1974-76).

WRITINGS—Books of poems: House by the Sea, From Here Press, 1975; *The Hollow Contagion* (broadside), From Here Press, 1976; (editor with Toi Derricotte, Shaun Farragher, Alice Kolb, and Lois Van Houten, and contributor) *Advance Token to Boardwalk* (anthology), Poets and Writers of New Jersey, 1977.

Work represented in anthologies, including *Fear and Fearlessness,* edited by Arlene Stone, in press. Contributor of poems and reviews to newspapers, literary journals, and popular magazines, including *New Jersey Poetry Monthly, Wind,* and *Good Housekeeping.* Member of editorial board of *Douglass Alumnae Bulletin,* 1965-77.

WORK IN PROGRESS: Bride, The Hollow Contagion, Hiking the Crevasse, and *Omens,* all books of poems; *Burying the Doll,* stories.

SIDELIGHTS: Penny Bihler writes: "Combining the skills acquired by teaching in the secondary school language arts classroom, and by conducting writing workshops in over forty schools in New Jersey, as well as for various community groups, including senior citizens, I seek to bring a greater appreciation of and participation in the arts through continuing to work in and promote the publication of quality writing, and workshops in which participants explore for themselves their capacities to create with words. As a writer I am committed both to poetry and prose that can communicate effectively and directly. These activities have repeatedly brought me into rewarding personal interaction with people of diverse age and talent. We have worked together toward common goals. I intend to keep working with people.

"I am particularly interested in the psychic—its relationship to my own writing and the use of the psychic in writing workshops. I have found my own talents in telepathy, reading others' pasts, objects, etc., to be very useful in writing workshops, particularly with children in special education classes. I believe that all of us have some degree of psychic ability that can be released into creativity.

"I am also exploring the connections between the writing of poems and short stories, having begun to write stories rather recently and finding the experience of doing so both similar and dissimilar to that of poetry.

"I am committed to all the arts. Words are my medium, and so I write. Yet I understand that place where all creativity is one, whether it be in the arts or the sciences, and I celebrate it."

AVOCATIONAL INTERESTS: Music (choral singing and playing the piano).

*   *   *

BILLINGS, Ezra
   See HALLA, R(obert) C(hristian)

*   *   *

BILLINGTON, Joy   1931-

PERSONAL: Born March 20, 1931, in Liverpool, England; came to United States in 1967; daughter of Donald Fraser (an engineer) and Jennie Ramsey (a nurse; maiden name, Sinclair) Manson; married R.B.S. Billington, 1953 (divorced); married Joseph Bonn Doty (a clergyman and headmaster), August 3, 1969; children: (first marriage) Nigel. *Education:* Educated in England. *Religion:* Episcopalian. *Home:* 1060 St. Stephen's Rd., Alexandria, Va. *Office: Washington Star,* Virginia Ave. S.E., Washington, D.C.

CAREER/WRITINGS: Singapore Standard, Singapore, reporter, 1952-55; *North Borneo News,* Sabah, columnist, 1955-57; Associated Press, New York, N.Y., editor in Bangkok, Thailand, 1957; U.S. Information Agency, Washington, D.C., editor in Bangkok, 1958-60; *London Times,* London, England, reporter, 1964-67; free-lance journalist in Washington, D.C., 1967-68; *Washington Star,* Washington, D.C., reporter, 1968—. Notable assignments include interviews with Indira Gandhi, J. Paul Getty, and King Phumiphol Aduladej of Thailand. Author of profiles for weekly column, "Embassy Row," for *Washington Star.* Contributor to *Saturday Evening Post. Member:* Washington Press Club.

SIDELIGHTS: Billington writes: "My early years in journalism coincided with the various posts of my first husband, although my first job, on the *Singapore Standard,* preceded my marriage. In 1964 I returned to England from the Far East and after a stint on a weekly (Fleet Street being disinterested in any Asian accomplishments) went to the *Times* under the dynamic editorship of Sue Puddefoot, who was revamping the previously stodgy, traditionalist women's page. In 1967 I came to Washington, since that seemed the most challenging city in which to establish a byline . . . far more so than the fairly narrow 'women's' news limitations of London newspapers. I free-lanced for a year in Washington and then came to the *Star* women's page and began to learn a whole new side of journalism—covering social events with strong political emphasis. Since then I have worked the embassy beat for several years and have continued to write profiles—probably my most satisfying work."

*   *   *

BINYON, Claude   1905-1978

October 17, 1905—February 14, 1978; American film director, screenwriter, and newspaperman. During his unsuccessful career as a news reporter, Binyon wrote one of the most-quoted headlines, "Wall Street Lays an Egg," for *Variety.* Discharged from *Variety* for "neglecting his newspaper duties," Binyon found himself working in Hollywood for Paramount Pictures. During his thirty-year career in Hollywood, Binyon wrote screenplays for such films as "Mississippi," "Arizona," "Pepe," and "Holiday Inn." He died in Glendale, Calif. Obituaries and other sources: *International Motion Picture Almanac,* Quigley, 1975; *New York Times,* March 2, 1978.

*   *   *

BISHOP, John Melville   1946-

PERSONAL: Born April 4, 1946, in North Dakota; son of John M. (a physician) and Shirley (a social worker; maiden name, Buckley) Bishop; married Naomi Hawes (an anthropologist), August 31, 1969; children: Noah. *Education:* University of California, Berkeley, B.A., 1968. *Home:* 917 East Broadway, Haverhill, Mass. 01830. *Agent:* Alan Ravage, 680 West End Ave., New York, N.Y. 10025.

CAREER: Freelance photographer, documentary cinematographer, and film editor. Also worked as survey interviewer, school bus driver, animal handler, and audio-visual technician.

WRITINGS: (With wife, Naomi Hawes Bishop) *An Ever-Changing Place,* Simon & Schuster, 1978.

Films: "Rhesus Play," 1977; "Yoyo Man," 1978.

SIDELIGHTS: Bishop writes: "I am interested in natural history and American folklife. I assisted my wife in her research on the Himalayan langur monkey in 1971-72. This first study of this particular primate niche was conducted in a remote mountain village fifty miles walk from the nearest road. The expedition forms the basis of my first book. It was my interest in primate behavior that led me into filmmaking with 'Rhesus Play.' 'Yoyo Man' is aboutt one of the early demonstrators hired to promote the yoyo during the great depression."

*   *   *

BITA, Lili

PERSONAL: Born in Zante, Greece; came to United States, 1959, naturalized citizen, 1969; daughter of George (an army general) and Eleni (a painter; maiden name, Makri) Bitas; married Michael Rethis, May 24, 1965 (divorced); married Robert Zaller (a professor and writer), January 19, 1968; children: Philip, Kimon. *Education:* Greek Conservatory of Music, fine arts degree, 1954; Athens School of Drama, fine arts degree, 1956; Trapp Conservatory of Music, Munich, certificate in piano, 1959; University of Miami,

M.A., 1978. *Politics:* "Pacifist." *Home:* 5901 Southwest 51st St., Miami, Fla. 33155.

CAREER: College of Emporia, Emporia, Kan., instructor in language, 1960-62; Siena Heights College, Adrian, Mich., instructor in music, 1962-63; University of Toledo, Toledo, Ohio, instructor in music, 1963-65; Yale University, Sterling Memorial Library, New Haven, Conn., assistant reference librarian, 1965-67; Brooklyn Conservatory of Music, Brooklyn, N.Y., instructor in music, 1967-68; guest lecturer at American universities, 1970—. Former performer in repertory companies of Theatro Technis, Laikon Theatron, and Theatron Kipos, Greece, and in premier performances of own plays. Participated in poetry therapy program of Odyssey House, and in Poetry in the Schools program in Dade County, Fla. *Member:* Alpha Psi Omega.

WRITINGS: Vimata sti Ghi (title means "Steps on the Earth"), [Athens], 1955; *Astrapes ste sarka: Lightning in the Flesh* (poems; Greek-English bilingual edition with translations by husband, Robert Zaller), Athens Printing, 1968; *Erotes: Five Love Poems,* translated by Zaller, Guevara Press, 1969; *Furies* (poems), translated by Zaller with introduction by Anais Nin, Hors Commerce Press, 1969; *Ora Mithen* (novel; title means "Zero Hour"), Guevara Press, 1971; *Skitsa apo Aima: Blood Sketches* (poems; bilingual edition with translations by Zaller), Guevara Press, 1973; (translator from Greek) Anais Nin, *A Spy in the House of Love,* Koridis, 1974; *Sacrifice, Exile, Night* (poems), Ragnarok Press, 1976; *I Crave the Bitter Sea* (poetry broadside), Ragnarok Press, 1978.

Plays: "The Judge" (one-act) first produced in Miami, Fla., at University of Miami Humanities Festival, February, 1974; "Sundays in the Cemetery" (one-act), first produced in Miami at Upstage Theatre, February, 1976; "Hyena" (one-act), first produced in Miami at Upstage Theatre, March, 1977.

Also author of "Bars," 1968, and "The First Lady of Adrian," 1976, plays as yet neither published nor produced.

Work represented in anthologies, including *Children of the Moon,* edited by Rochelle Holt, Ragnarok Press, 1973; *City Lights Anthology,* edited by Lawrence Ferlinghetti, City Lights Books, 1974; *Moving to Antarctica,* edited by Margaret Kaminski, Dustbooks, 1975.

WORK IN PROGRESS: Preparing a one-woman show, "The Greek Woman Through the Ages"; a new book of poems.

SIDELIGHTS: Lili Bita comments: "I am trying to live each minute of my life with such intensity that I will have the illusion it is a miniature universe, with all its physical and emotional presence. This way I prolong the journey and fight my fear for the one and many deaths."

* * *

BITKER, Marjorie M. 1901-

PERSONAL: Born February 9, 1901, in New York, N.Y.; daughter of Cecil Alexander (an accountant) and Rachel (Fox) Marks; married James Jacobson, December 12, 1922 (divorced, 1942); married John Mayer, October 24, 1942 (died June, 1945); married Bruno Voltaire Bitker (a lawyer), October 10, 1957; children: (first marriage) Emilie (Mrs. Frederick A. Jacobi), Margaret (Mrs. David Strange), Elizabeth (Mrs. Frank Hahn). *Education:* Barnard College, B.A. (magna cum laude), 1921; Columbia University, M.A., 1922. *Home and office:* 2330 East Back Bay, Milwaukee, Wis. 53202. *Agent:* Curtis Brown Ltd., 575 Madison Ave., New York, N.Y. 10022.

CAREER: Farrar, Straus & Giroux, New York City, editor, 1946-47; G. P. Putnam's Sons, New York City, editor, 1947-53; David McKay, New York City, editor, 1953-55; free-lance writer and editorial consultant, 1957—. Teacher of publishing procedures at Hunter College (now of the City University of New York), 1949-53. *Member:* National Book Critics Circle, National Association of Book Women, Council of Wisconsin Writers (board member, 1970-77), Friends of Wisconsin Libraries (founder and past president), Bookfellows, Friends of Milwaukee Public Library (founder and past president; currently, board member), Phi Beta Kappa. *Awards, honors:* Holder of Women's Chair of Humanistic Studies at Marquette University, 1971-72; Alumnae Recognition Award from Barnard College, 1978.

WRITINGS: Gold of the Evening, Popular Library, 1975; *A Different Flame,* Popular Library, 1976. Feature writer for *Milwaukee Journal.* Contributor to *New Yorker, American Mercury, Woman's Home Companion, Reader's Digest,* and other publications.

WORK IN PROGRESS: A semi-fictional memoir of childhood.

AVOCATIONAL INTERESTS: Music, tennis, travel (has traveled extensively in Europe, the Far East, and the Middle East).

* * *

BJORNSON, Richard 1938-

PERSONAL: Born January 16, 1938, in Oak Park, Ill.; son of Samuel (a railroad worker) and Irene (a teacher; maiden name, Lasch) Bjornson; married Aija Kuplis (a teacher), June 26, 1976. *Education:* Lawrence University, B.A., 1959; Northwestern University, M.A., 1961; Sorbonne, University of Paris, Ph.D., 1968. *Home:* 129 West Lakeview, Columbus, Ohio 43202. *Office:* Division of Comparative Studies, Ohio State University, Columbus, Ohio 43210.

CAREER: University of Maryland, College Park, instructor in English for European Division, 1963-65, 1967-68; University of Wisconsin, Madison, assistant professor of comparative literature, 1968-74; Ohio State University, Columbus, associate professor of comparative studies, 1974—. Senior Fulbright lecturer in Cameroon, 1976-77. *Member:* Modern Language Association of America, American Comparative Literature Association, American Association of Teachers of Spanish and Portuguese, Council of National Literatures, Phi Beta Kappa. *Awards, honors:* Woodrow Wilson fellowship, 1960-61; Spencer Foundation award, 1972-73.

WRITINGS: The Picaresque Hero in European Fiction, University of Wisconsin Press, 1977. Work represented in anthologies. Contributor of articles and reviews to literary journals.

WORK IN PROGRESS: The Challenge of Third-World Literature, on the relationship between social structure and literary representation in the emerging nations of Africa and South America, completion expected in 1980.

SIDELIGHTS: Bjornson writes: "As a teacher and critic, I hope to stimulate critical reflection upon commonly accepted value systems and social structures. If the assumptions behind these systems and structures can be identified, examined, and compared with those of other ages and cultures, people might become more willing to work toward a more humane, less self-destructive society. I believe that literature offers significant insights into these assumptions, and it is for that reason that I consider literary criticism to be a worthwhile endeavor. My own attitudes have been considerable influenced by Dostoevsky, the Old Testament, Marx, Orwell, the *Iliad*, Blake, Cervantes, Melville, Shakespeare, and the contemporary South American and African novelists. I have traveled extensively in Europe and Africa.''

* * *

BLADES, Ann 1947-

PERSONAL: Born November 16, 1947, in Vancouver, British Columbia, Canada; daughter of Arthur Hazelton (an administrator) and Dorothy (a teacher; maiden name, Planche) Sager; divorced. *Education:* University of British Columbia, teaching certificate, 1970; British Columbia Institute of Technology, R.N., 1974. *Home:* 14623 West Beach Dr., White Rock, British Columbia, Canada V4B 2T9.

CAREER: Elementary school teacher in Mile 18, British Columbia, 1967-68, Tache, British Columbia, 1969, and Surrey, British Columbia, 1969-71; part-time registered nurse in Vancouver, British Columbia, 1974—. *Member:* Writers' Union of Canada, Registered Nurses Association of British Columbia. *Awards, honors:* Book of the year award from Association of Children's Librarians, 1972, for *Mary of Mile 18.*

WRITINGS: Mary of Mile 18 (juvenile), Tundra Books, 1971; *A Boy of Tache* (juvenile), Tundra Books, 1973; *The Cottage at Crescent Beach*, Magook Publishers, 1977. Also illustrator of *Jacques the Woodcutter*, Oberon, 1977.

SIDELIGHTS: Ann Blades's earlier teaching positions were remote—Mile 18 is a small rural community in northern British Columbia, and Tache is an Indian Reservation on Stuart Lake—and she soon found out that the books her students read had no relation to the world they lived in. She began to write her own books soon afterwards.

BIOGRAPHICAL/CRITICAL SOURCES: Chatelaine, February, 1975; *Toronto Globe and Mail*, June 12, 1975.

* * *

BLAGOWIDOW, George 1923-

PERSONAL: Surname is pronounced Bla-*gov*-el-dov; born December 5, 1923, in Czestochowa, Poland; came to the United States in 1951, naturalized citizen, 1956; son of Pawel (a physician) and Tamara (Poszyn) Blagowidow; married Ludmilla Dobjitski (a publishing executive), November 8, 1953; children: Nicholas, Natalie, Catherine. *Education:* Institut Superieurs de Commerce, L.S.C.C.M., 1949; New York University, M.B.A., 1953, Ph.D., 1959. *Religion:* Russian Orthodox. *Home:* 86-45 Chelsea St., Jamaica, N.Y. 11432. *Agent:* Gerard McCauley Agency, Inc., 551 Fifth Ave., New York, N.Y. 10017. *Office:* Hippocrene Books, Inc., 171 Madison Ave., New York, N.Y. 10016.

CAREER: Doubleday & Co., Inc., New York City, statistician in sales, 1955-56, sales manager, 1957-62; Macmillan Publishing Co., New York City, trade sales director, 1962-66; Funk & Wagnalls Co., New York City, general manager, 1966-70; Hippocrene Books, Inc., New York City, founder and president, 1970—. Owner of Optimum Book Marketing Co., 1970—, and Compleat Strategist (games and books stores), 1976—; founder and owner of Strategy & Fantasy World (for science fiction and fantasy books and games), 1977—.

WRITINGS: Optimum Marketing of Trade Books Based on Scientific Forecasting Methodology, Bowker, 1964; (with Arnold Corbin and Claire Corbin) *Decision Exercises in Marketing*, McGraw, 1964; *The Last Train From Berlin* (novel), Doubleday, 1977.

WORK IN PROGRESS: Operation Parterre and a World War II novel.

SIDELIGHTS: Although *The Last Train From Berlin* was written to share the war experiences which have stuck in his memory, Blagowidow feels that his novel has a great deal more to offer than an entertaining experience. He feels that this book, and many novels by other writers, offer valuable information about the way other people live in other places and other times, and that fiction can be, in some cases, more informative and factual than subjective nonfiction.

About five years ago, he first heard of war simulation games; his fascination with the games, and with their marketing possibilities, led to the formation of Hippocrene Books, which specializes in books on military history, books by military figures, and distribution of war games, as well as to the establishment of his six book and games stores.

* * *

BLAIR, Clay Drewry, Jr. 1925-

PERSONAL: Born May 1, 1925, in Lexington, Va.; married wife, Joan. *Education:* Attended Tulane University and Columbia University.

CAREER: Time magazine, New York City, reporter, 1948-55; *Life* magazine, New York City, military correspondent, 1955-57; *Saturday Evening Post*, Indianapolis, Ind., associate editor, 1957-61, assistant managing editor, 1961-62, managing editor, 1962-63, editor-in-chief, 1963-64; Curtis Publishing Co., senior vice-president, executive vice-president and director, editor-in-chief, 1962-64. Writer. *Military service:* Served in U.S. Navy during World War II; became quartermaster second class; received three battle stars.

WRITINGS: The Atomic Submarine and Admiral Rickover, Henry Holt, 1954; (with James R. Shepley) *The Hydrogen Bomb: The Men, the Menace, the Mechanism*, McKay, 1954, Greenwood Press, 1971; *Beyond Courage*, McKay, 1955; (with William R. Anderson) *Nautilus 90, North*, World Publishing, 1959; *Diving for Pleasure and Treasure*, World Publishing, 1960; (with Albert Scott Crossfield) *Always Another Dawn: The Story of a Rocket Test Pilot*, World Publishing, 1960; *The Board Room*, Dutton, 1969, published as *Magazine*, Cassell, 1970; *The Strange Case of James Earl Ray, the Man Who Murdered Martin Luther King*, Bantam, 1969; *The Archbishop*, World Publishing, 1970; *Pentagon Country*, McGraw, 1971; *Survive!*, Berkeley Publishing, 1973; *Silent Victory: The U.S. Submarine War Against Japan*, Lippincott, 1975; (with wife, Joan Blair) *The Search for JFK*, Putnam, 1976; (with J. Blair) *Scuba!*, Bantam, 1977. Also author of *Valley of the Shadow*, 1955.

SIDELIGHTS: After much controversy over the use of atomic energy in submarines, it was Rear-Admiral Hyman G. Rickover who most fervently backed the development of the *Nautilus* which was finally approved. It was Clay Blair, however, who led a journalistic drive to keep Rickover in the Navy. Blair's crusade was successful and he was rewarded by being one of the first journalists allowed to go on a voyage of the *Nautilus*. His book about the submarine was described by *the New York Times Book Review* as ''exciting reading for even the non-technically inclined.... A sound treatment meriting wide acceptance.'' Blair continued the story of the *Nautilus* in his book *Nautilus 90, North*, an account of the *Nautilus's* incredible 1,830-mile journey beneath the Polar ice. The book, which was published just five months after the completion of the voyage, was a bestseller and was published in twenty-six countries.

Reviewing Blair's more recent book, *Survive!,* a *New York Times Book Review* critic wrote: "[It] cannot be called either intimate or definitive. Clearly this is an outsider's book. Blair writes as though he were himself in rarefied mountain air: short, breathless sentences, uninformed by any distinctive insight. Efficient enough, workmanlike: the excitement comes through. Blair corrects several widespread misunderstandings promulgated by early reportage. The Chilean plane crash was, in fact, an Argentinian plane crash. Much of the grisly details have been mitigated. . . ."

After noting the extensive research that was done in order to complete *The Search for JFK,* a *New York Review of Books* critic stated: "Whatever the accuracy of the authors' interpretations of the evidence, they give a rich sense of the mixture of shyness, sensitivity, and callousness that characterized Kennedy; his deliberate use of what he called his 'BP'—Big Personality; and the disabilities of having a spectacularly amoral father. A book surprisingly free of malice or prurience."

BIOGRAPHICAL/CRITICAL SOURCES: New York Times Book Review, January 17, 1954, October 3, 1954, June 26, 1955, January 4, 1959, September 4, 1960, January 8, 1961, May 4, 1969, December 19, 1971, August 19, 1973, June 6, 1976; *Newsweek,* March 31, 1969; *Atlantic Monthly,* July, 1969; *Catholic World,* July, 1971; *Choice,* July/August, 1975; *America,* November 15, 1975; *New York Review of Books,* June 10, 1976.*

*   *   *

BLICKER, Seymour 1940-

PERSONAL: Born February 12, 1940, in Montreal, Quebec, Canada. *Education:* Loyola College, Montreal, Quebec, B.A. *Home address:* c/o Val Morin Post Office, Val Morin, Quebec, Canada.

CAREER: Writer. *Member:* Writers Guild, Writers Union, Canadian Authors Association. *Awards, honors:* Received Canada Council senior arts grant.

WRITINGS: Blues Chased a Rabbit, Chateau Books, 1969; *Shmucks,* McClelland & Stewart, 1972, Morrow, 1977; *The Last Collection,* McClelland & Stewart, 1976, Morrow, 1977. Author of material for television.

*   *   *

BLOOD, Matthew
See DRESSER, Davis

*   *   *

BLYTON, Enid (Mary) 1897-1968
(Mary Pollock)

PERSONAL: Born August 11, 1897, in East Dulwich, London, England; daughter of Thomas Carey and Theresa Mary (Harrison) Blyton; married Major Hugh Alexander Pollock (an editor), 1924 (divorced December, 1942); married Kenneth F. Darrell Waters (a surgeon), 1943 (died, 1967); children: Gillian, Imogen. *Education:* Attended Guildhall School of Music, 1916, and National Froebel Union teaching school, Ipswich, 1918. *Residence:* "Green Hedges," Beaconsfield, Buckinghamshire, England.

CAREER: Teacher at a boys' preparatory school in Kent, England, 1919; private tutor to a family in Surbiton, Surrey, England, 1920; formed Darrell Waters, Ltd., with her second husband, to handle business contracts with publishers, 1950; writer and editor of poems, stories, and educational articles. Shaftesbury Society Babies Home, Beaconsfield,

committee member, 1948, later chairperson, 1954-67; also sponsored children's clubs to support other charitable organizations for children and animals. *Awards, honors:* The island of Jersey, U.K., paid tribute to Blyton's "Noddy" characters by portraying them on a 1970 commemorative stamp.

WRITINGS: Child Whispers (poems), J. Saville, 1922; *Real Fairies* (poems), J. Saville, 1923; *Responsive Singing Games,* J. Saville, 1923; *The Enid Blyton Book of Fairies,* George Newnes, 1924, reprinted, 1964; *Songs of Gladness* (music by Alec Rowley), J. Saville, 1924; *The Zoo Book,* George Newnes, 1924; *The Enid Blyton Book of Bunnies,* George Newnes, 1925; *Silver and Gold* (poems; illustrated by Lewis Baumer), Thomas Nelson, 1925; *The Bird Book* (illustrated by Ronald Green), George Newnes, 1926; *The Enid Blyton Book of Brownies,* George Newnes, 1926, reprinted, 1964; *Tales Half Told,* Thomas Nelson, 1926; *The Animal Book,* George Newnes, 1927, reprinted, 1954; *Let's Pretend* (illustrated by I. Bennington Angrave), Thomas Nelson, 1928; *Nature Lessons,* Evans Brothers, 1929; *Tarrydiddle Town,* Thomas Nelson, 1929.

Tales of Ancient Greece, George Newnes, 1930; *Tales of Robin Hood,* George Newnes, 1930; *Cheerio! A Book for Boys and Girls,* Birn Brothers, 1933; *Five Minute Tales,* Methuen, 1933; *Let's Read,* Birn Brothers, 1933; *My First Reading Book,* Birn Brothers, 1933; *Read to Us,* Birn Brothers, 1933; *The Enid Blyton Poetry Book,* Methuen, 1934; *The Old Thatch Series,* eight volumes, Johnston, 1934-35, a second series, eight volumes, Johnston, 1938-39; *The Red Pixie Book,* George Newnes, 1934; *Round the Year with Enid Blyton,* Evans Brothers, 1934; *Ten Minute Tales,* Methuen, 1934; *The Children's Garden,* George Newnes, 1935; *The Green Goblin Book,* George Newnes, 1935, abridged edition published as *Feefo, Tuppeny and Jinks,* Staples Press, 1951; *Hedgerow Tales,* Methuen, 1935; *Hop, Skip and Jump,* J. Coker, 1935; *The Tale of Mr. Wumble,* J. Coker, 1935.

The Famous Jimmy (illustrated by Benjamin Rabier), Muller, 1936, Dutton, 1937; *Fifteen Minute Tales,* Methuen, 1936; *The Yellow Fairy Book,* George Newnes, 1936; *Adventures of the Wishing Chair* (illustrated by Hilda McGavin), George Newnes, 1937; *Enid Blyton's Sunny Stories,* George Newnes, 1937-52; *The Adventures of Binkle and Flip* (illustrated by Kathleen Nixon), George Newnes, 1938; *Billy-Bob Tales* (illustrated by May Smith), Methuen, 1938; *Mr. Galliano's Circus,* George Newnes, 1938, reprinted, May Fair Books, 1962; *Boys' and Girls' Circus Book,* News Chronicle, 1939; *The Enchanted Wood,* George Newnes, 1939; *Hurrah for the Circus!* (illustrated by E. H. Davie), George Newnes, 1939; *Naughty Amelia Jane,* George Newnes, 1939.

Birds of Our Garden (illustrated by Green and Ernest Aris), George Newnes, 1940; *Boys' and Girls' Story Book,* George Newnes, 1940; *The Children of Cherry Tree Farm* (illustrated by Harry Rountree), Country Life, 1940; *Mister Meddle's Mischief* (illustrated by Joyce Mercer and Rosalind M. Turvey), George Newnes, 1940; *The Naughtiest Girl in the School,* George Newnes, 1940; *Tales of Betsy-May* (illustrated by F. Gale Thomas), Methuen, 1940; *The Treasure Hunters* (illustrated by E. Wilson and Joyce Davies), George Newnes, 1940; *Twenty Minute Tales,* Methuen, 1940; *The Adventures of Mr. Pink-Whistle,* George Newnes, 1941; *The Adventurous Four,* George Newnes, 1941; (reteller) Jean de Brunhoff, *The Babar Story Book,* Methuen, 1941 [excerpt published separately as *Tales of Babar,* Methuen, 1942]; *A Calendar for Children,* George

Newnes, 1941; *Enid Blyton's Book of the Year*, Evans Brothers, 1941, revised editon, 1950; *Five O'Clock Tales*, Methuen, 1941.

The Children of Willow Farm (illustrated by Rountree), Country Life, 1942; *Circus Days Again*, George Newnes, 1942; *Enid Blyton Happy Story Book*, Hodder & Stoughton, 1942; *Enid Blyton Readers*, Macmillan, Books 1-3, 1942, Books 4-6, 1944, Book 7, 1948, Books 10-12, 1950; *Enid Blyton's Little Books* (first of a series), Evans Brothers, 1942; *Hello, Mr. Twiddle!* (illustrated by McGavin), George Newnes, 1942; *I'll Tell You a Story* (illustrated by Eileen A. Soper), Macmillan, 1942; *I'll Tell You Another Story*, Macmillan, 1942; *John Jolly at Christmas Time*, Evans Brothers, 1942; *Land of Far-Beyond*, Methuen, 1942; *More Adventures of Willow Farm*, Country Life, 1942; *Naughtiest Girl Again*, George Newnes, 1942; *The O'Sullivan Twins*, Methuen, 1942; *Shadow, the Sheep Dog*, George Newnes, 1942; *Six O'Clock Tales* (illustrated by Dorothy M. Wheeler), Methuen, 1942.

Bimbo and Topsy (illustrated by Lucy Gee), George Newnes, 1943; *The Children's Life of Christ*, Methuen, 1943; *Dame Slap and Her School* (illustrated by Wheeler), George Newnes, 1943; *John Jolly by the Sea*, Evans Brothers, 1943; *John Jolly on the Farm*, Evans Brothers, 1943; *The Magic Faraway Tree* (illustrated by Wheeler), George Newnes, 1943; *Merry Story Book* (illustrated by Soper), Hodder & Stoughton, 1943; *Polly Piglet* (illustrated by Soper), Brockhampton Press, 1943; *Seven O'Clock Tales*, Methuen, 1943; *The Toys Come to Life* (illustrated by Soper), Brockhampton Press, 1943.

At Appletree Farm, Brockhampton Press, 1944; *Billy and Betty at the Seaside*, Valentine & Sons, 1944; *A Book of Naughty Children*, Methuen, 1944; *The Boy Next Door* (illustrated by Bestall), George Newnes, 1944; *The Christmas Book* (illustrated by Treyer Evans), Macmillan, 1944; *Come to the Circus* (illustrated by Soper), Brockhampton Press, 1944; *The Dog That Went to Fairyland*, Brockhampton Press, 1944; *Eight O'Clock Tales* (illustrated by Wheeler), Methuen, 1944; *Enid Blyton's Nature Lover's Books* (illustrated by Donia Nachshen and Noel Hopking), Evans Brothers, 1944; *Jolly Little Jumbo*, Brockhampton Press, 1944; *Jolly Story Book* (illustrated by Soper), Hodder & Stoughton, 1944; *Rainy Day Stories* (illustrated by Nora S. Unwin), Evans Brothers, 1944; *Tales from the Bible* (illustrated by Soper), Methuen, 1944; *Tales of Toyland* (illustrated by McGavin), George Newnes, 1944; *The Three Golliwogs*, George Newnes, 1944.

The Blue Story Book (illustrated by Soper), Methuen, 1945; *The Brown Family* (illustrated by E. Buhler and R. Buhler), News Chronicle, 1945; *The Conjuring Wizard and Other Stories* (illustrated by Soper), Macmillan, 1945; *Enid Blyton Nature Readers*, Macmillan, Numbers 1-20, 1945, Numbers 21-30, 1946; *The Family at Red Roofs* (illustrated by W. Spence), Lutterworth, 1945; *The First Christmas* (photographs by Paul Henning), Methuen, 1945; *Hollow Tree House* (illustrated by Elizabeth Wall), Lutterworth, 1945; *John Jolly at the Circus*, Evans Brothers, 1945; *The Naughtiest Girl Is a Monitor*, George Newnes, 1945; *Round the Clock Stories* (illustrated by Unwin), National Magazine, 1945; *The Runaway Kitten* (illustrated by Soper), Brockhampton Press, 1945; *Sunny Story Book*, Hodder & Stoughton, 1945; *The Teddy Bear's Party* (illustrated by Soper), Brockhampton Press, 1945; *The Twins Go to Nursery Rhyme Land* (illustrated by Soper), Brockhampton Press, 1945.

Amelia Jane Again, George Newnes, 1946; *The Bad Little Monkey* (illustrated by Soper), Brockhampton Press, 1946; *The Children at Happy House* (illustrated by Kathleen Gell), Basil Blackwell, 1946; *Chimney Corner Stories* (illustrated by Pat Harrison), National Magazine, 1946; *The Enid Blyton Holiday Book*, twelve volumes, Low, 1946; *The Folk of the Faraway Tree* (illustrated by Wheeler), George Newnes, 1946; *Gay Story Book* (illustrated by Soper), Hodder & Stoughton, 1946; *Little White Duck and Other Stories* (illustrated by Soper), Macmillan, 1946; *The Put-Em-Rights* (illustrated by Wall), Lutterworth, 1946; *The Red Story Book*, Methuen, 1946; *The Surprising Caravan* (illustrated by Soper), Brockhampton Press, 1946; *Tales of Green Hedges* (illustrated by Gwen White), National Magazine, 1946; *The Train That Lost Its Way* (illustrated by Soper), Brockhampton Press, 1946; *The Adventurous Four Again*, George Newnes, 1946.

At Seaside Cottage (illustrated by Soper), Brockhampton Press, 1947; *Before I Go to Sleep: A Book of Bible Stories and Prayers for Children at Night*, Latimer House, 1947; *Enid Blyton's Treasury*, Evans Brothers, 1947; *The Green Story Book* (illustrated by Soper), Methuen, 1947; *The Happy House Children Again* (illustrated by Gell), Basil Blackwell, 1947; *House-at-the-Corner* (illustrated by Elsie Walker), Lutterworth, 1947; *Jinky Nature Books*, four parts, E. J. Arnold, 1947; *Little Green Duck and Other Stories*, Brockhampton Press, 1947; *Lucky Story Book* (illustrated by Soper), Hodder & Stoughton, 1947; *Rambles with Uncle Nat* (illustrated by Unwin), National Magazine, 1947; *A Second Book of Naughty Children* (illustrated by Gell), Methuen, 1947; *The Smith Family*, three volumes, E. J. Arnold, 1947; *The Very Clever Rabbit* (illustrated by Soper), Brockhampton Press, 1947.

The Adventures of Pip, Low, 1948; *The Boy With the Loaves and Fishes* (illustrated by Walker), Lutterworth, 1948; *Enid Blyton's Bedtime Series*, two parts, Brockhampton Press, 1948; *Children of Other Lands*, J. Coker, 1948; *Come to the Circus!* (illustrated by Joyce M. Johnson; not the same as the 1944 book published under the same title), George Newnes, 1948; *Just Time for a Story* (illustrated by Grace Lodge), Macmillan, 1948; *Jolly Tales*, Johnston, 1948; *Let's Garden* (illustrated by William McLaren), Latimer House, 1948; *Let's Have a Story* (illustrated by George Bowe), Pitkin, 1948; *The Little Girl at Capernaum* (illustrated by Walker), Lutterworth, 1948; *Mister Icy-Cold*, Shakespeare Head Press, 1948; *More Adventures of Pip*, Low, 1948; *Nature Tales*, Johnston, 1948; *Now for a Story* (illustrated by Frank Varty), Harold Hill, 1948; *The Red-Spotted Handkerchief and Other Stories* (illustrated by Gell), Brockhampton Press, 1948; *The Little Button-Elves*, J. Coker, 1948; *The Secret of the Old Mill* (illustrated by Soper), Brockhampton Press, 1948; *Six Cousins at Mistletoe Farm* (illustrated by Peter Beigel), Evans Brothers, 1948; *Tales After Tea*, Laurie, 1948; *Tales of the Twins* (illustrated by Soper), Brockhampton Press, 1948; *They Ran Away Together* (illustrated by Jeanne Farrar), Brockhampton Press, 1948; *We Want a Story* (illustrated by Bowe), Pitkin, 1948.

The Bluebell Story Book, Gifford, 1949; *Bumpy and His Bus* (illustrated by Wheeler), George Newnes, 1949; *A Cat in Fairyland*, Pitkin, 1949; *Chuff the Chimney Sweep*, Pitkin, 1949; *The Circus Book*, Latimer House, 1949; *The Dear Old Snow Man*, Brockhampton Press, 1949; *Don't Be Silly, Mr. Twiddle*, George Newnes, 1949; *The Enchanted Sea*, Pitkin, 1949; *Enid Blyton Bible Pictures, Old Testament* (illustrated by John Turner), Macmillan, 1949; *The Enid Blyton*

Bible Stories, Old Testament, Macmillan, 1949; *Enid Blyton's Daffodil Story Book*, Gifford, 1949; *Enid Blyton's Good Morning Book* (illustrated by Don and Ann Goring), National Magazine, 1949; *Humpty Dumpty and Belinda*, Collins, 1949; *Jinky's Joke and Other Stories* (illustrated by Gell), Brockhampton Press, 1949; *Mr. Tumpy and His Caravan* (illustrated by Wheeler), Sidgwick & Jackson, 1949; *My Enid Blyton Bedside Book*, twelve volumes, Arthur Barker, beginning 1949; *Oh, What a Lovely Time*, Brockhampton Press, 1949; *Robin Hood Book*, Latimer House, 1949; *A Story Party at Green Hedges* (illustrated by Lodge), Hodder & Stoughton, 1949; *The Strange Umbrella*, Pitkin, 1949; *Tales After Supper*, Laurie, 1949; *Those Dreadful Children* (illustrated by Lodge), Lutterworth, 1949; *Tiny Tales*, Littlebury, 1949.

The Astonishing Ladder and Other Stories (illustrated by Soper), Macmillan, 1950; *A Book of Magic*, J. Coker, 1950; *The Enid Blyton Pennant Series*, thirty parts, Macmillan, 1950; *The Magic Knitting Needles and Other Stories*, Macmillan, 1950; *Mister Meddle's Muddles* (illustrated by Turvey and Mercer), George Newnes, 1950; *Mr. Pink-Whistle Interferes* (illustrated by Wheeler), George Newnes, 1950; *The Poppy Story Book*, Gifford, 1950; *Round the Year Stories*, J. Coker, 1950; *Rubbalong Tales* (illustrated by Norman Meredith), Macmillan, 1950; *Six Cousins Again* (illustrated by Maurice Tulloch), Evans Brothers, 1950; *Tales about Toys*, Brockhampton Press, 1950; *The Three Naughty Children and Other Stories* (illustrated by Soper), Macmillan, 1950; *Tricky the Goblin and Other Stories* (illustrated by Soper), Macmillan, 1950; *What an Adventure*, Brockhampton Press, 1950; *The Wishing Chair Again*, George Newnes, 1950; *Yellow Story Book* (illustrated by Gell), Methuen, 1950.

Benny and the Princess and Other Stories, Pitkin, 1951; *Buttercup Story Book*, Gifford, 1951; *Down at the Farm*, Low, 1951; *Father Christmas and Belinda*, Collins, 1951; *The Flying Goat and Other Stories*, Pitkin, 1951; *Gay Street Book* (illustrated by Lodge), Latimer House, 1951; *Hello Twins*, Brockhampton Press, 1951; *Let's Go to the Circus*, Odhams, 1951; *The Little Spinning Mouse and Other Stories*, Pitkin, 1951; *The Magic Snow-Bird and Other Stories*, Pitkin, 1951; *A Picnic Party with Enid Blyton* (illustrated by Lodge), Hodder & Stoughton, 1951; *Pippy and the Gnome and Other Stories*, Pitkin, 1951; *The Proud Golliwog*, Brockhampton Press, 1951; *The Runaway Teddy Bear and Other Stories*, Pitkin, 1951; *The Six Bad Boys* (illustrated by Mary Gernat), Lutterworth, 1951; *'Too-Wise' the Wonderful Wizard and Other Stories*, Pitkin, 1951; *Up the Faraway Tree* (illustrated by Wheeler), George Newnes, 1951.

Bright Story Book (illustrated by Soper), Brockhampton Press, 1952; (with W. E. Johns and others) *The Children's Jolly Book*, Odhams, 1952; *Bible Pictures, New Testament*, Macmillan, 1952; *Come Along Twins*, Brockhampton Press, 1952; *Enid Blyton Tiny Strip Books* (series), Low, 1952; *Enid Blyton's Animal Lover's Book*, Evans Brothers, 1952; *Enid Blyton's Colour Strip Books*, Low, 1952; *Enid Blyton's Omnibus* (illustrated by Jessie Land), George Newnes, 1952; *The Mad Teapot*, Brockhampton Press, 1952; *Mandy, Mops and Cubby Again*, Low, 1952; *Mandy, Mops and Cubby Find a House*, Low, 1952; *Mr. Tumpy Plays a Trick on Saucepan*, Low, 1952; *My First Enid Blyton Book* (followed by the second and third *Enid Blyton Books*), Latimer House, 1952; *My First Nature Book* (illustrated by Soper; followed by the second and third *Nature Books*), Macmillan, 1952; *The Queer Adventure* (illustrated by Meredith), Staples Press, 1952; *Snowdrop Story Book*, Gifford, 1952; *The*

Story of My Life (autobiography), Pitkin, 1952; *The Very Big Secret* (illustrated by R. Gervis), Lutterworth, 1952.

Clicky the Clockwork Clown, Brockhampton Press, 1953; *The Enid Blyton Bible Stories, New Testament*, fourteen volumes, Macmillan, 1953; *Enid Blyton's Christmas Story* (illustrated by Fritz Wegner), Hamish Hamilton, 1953; *Gobo and Mr. Fierce*, Low, 1953; *Here Come the Twins*, Brockhampton Press, 1953; (translator) *Little Gift Books* (illustrated by Pierre Probst), Hackett, 1953; *Mandy Makes Cubby a Hat*, Low, 1953; *Mr. Tumpy in the Land of Wishes*, Low, 1953; *My Enid Blyton Story Book* (illustrated by Willy Schermele), Juvenile Productions, 1953; *Snowball the Pony* (illustrated by Iris Gillespie), Lutterworth, 1953; *The Story of Our Queen* (illustrated by F. Stocks May), Muller, 1953; *Visitors in the Night*, Brockhampton Press, 1953; *Well, Really, Mr. Twiddle!* (illustrated by McGavin), George Newnes, 1953.

The Adventure of the Secret Necklace (illustrated by Isabel Veevers), Lutterworth, 1954; *The Castle Without a Door and Other Stories*, Pitkin, 1954; *The Children at Green Meadows* (illustrated by Lodge), Lutterworth, 1954; *Enid Blyton's Friendly Story Book* (illustrated by Soper), Brockhampton Press, 1954; *Enid Blyton's Marigold Story Book*, Gifford, 1954; *The Greatest Book in the World* (illustrated by Mabel Peacock), British & Foreign Bible Society, 1954; *Little Strip Picture Books* (series), Low, 1954; *The Little Toy Farm and Other Stories*, Pitkin, 1954; *Merry Mister Meddle!* (illustrated by Turvey and Mercer), George Newnes, 1954; *More About Amelia Jane* (illustrated by Sylvia I. Venus), George Newnes, 1954.

Away Goes Sooty (illustrated by Probst), Collins, 1955; *Benjy and the Others* (illustrated by Gell), Latimer House, 1955; *Bible Stories From the Old Testament* (illustrated by Lodge), Muller, 1955; *Bible Stories From the New Testament* (illustrated by Lodge), Muller, 1955; *Bimbo and Blackie Go Camping* (illustrated by Probst), Collins, 1955; *Bobs* (illustrated by Probst), Collins, 1955; *Christmas with Scamp and Bimbo*, Collins, 1955; *Enid Blyton's Little Bedtime Books*, eight volumes, Low, 1955; *Neddy the Little Donkey* (illustrated by Romain Simon), Collins, 1955; *Enid Blyton's Sooty* (illustrated by Probst), Collins, 1955; *Enid Blyton's What Shall I Be?* (illustrated by Probst), Collins, 1955; *Foxglove Story Book*, Gifford, 1955; *Gobbo in the Land of Dreams*, Low, 1955; *Golliwog Grumbled*, Brockhampton Press, 1955; *Holiday House* (illustrated by Lodge), Evans Brothers, 1955; *Laughing Kitten* (photographs by Paul Kaye), Harvill, 1955; *Mandy, Mops and Cubby and the Whitewash*, Low, 1955; *Mischief Again* (photographs by Kaye), Harvill, 1955; *Mr. Pink-Whistle's Party* (illustrated by Wheeler), George Newnes, 1955; *Mr. Tumpy in the Land of Boys and Girls*, Low, 1955; *More Chimney Corner Stories* (illustrated by P. Harrison), Latimer House, 1955; *Playing at Home* (illustrated by Sabine Schweitzer), Methuen, 1955; *Run-About's Holiday* (illustrated by Lilian Chivers), Lutterworth, 1955; *The Troublesome Three* (illustrated by Leo), Sampson Low, 1955.

The Clever Little Donkey (illustrated by Simon), Collins, 1956; *Colin the Cow-Boy* (illustrated by R. Caille), Collins, 1956; *Enid Blyton's Animal Tales* (illustrated by Simon), Collins, 1956; *Four in a Family* (illustrated by Tom Kerr), Lutterworth, 1956; *Let's Have a Party* (photographs by Kaye), Harvill, 1956; *Scamp at School* (illustrated by Probst), Collins, 1956; *Story Book of Jesus* (illustrated by Walker), Macmillan, 1956; (contributor) *Children's Own Wonder Book*, Odhams, 1956; *New Testament Picture Books 1-2*, Macmillan, 1957; *Birthday Kitten* (illustrated by

Lodge), Lutterworth, 1958; *Clicky Gets Into Trouble* (illustrated by Molly Brett), Brockhampton Press, 1958; *Mr. Pink-Whistle's Big Book*, Evans Brothers, 1958; *My Big-Ears Picture Book*, Low, 1958; *Rumble and Chuff* (illustrated by David Walsh), Juvenile Productions, 1958; (with others) *The School Companion*, New Educational Press, 1958.

Adventure of the Strange Ruby, Brockhampton Press, 1960; *Adventure Stories*, Collins, 1960; *Clicky and Tiptoe* (illustrated by Brett), Brockhampton Press, 1960; *Happy Day Stories* (illustrated by Marcia Lane Foster), Evans Brothers, 1960; *Mystery Stories*, Collins, 1960; *Old Testament Picture Books*, Macmillan, 1960; *Tales at Bedtime* (illustrated by McGavin), Collins, 1960; *Will the Fiddle* (illustrated by Lodge), Instructive Arts, 1960; *The Big Enid Blyton Book* (selections), Hamlyn, 1961; *Happy Holiday, Clicky* (illustrated by Brett), Brockhampton Press, 1961; *The Four Cousins* (illustrated by Joan Thompson), Lutterworth, 1962; *Stories for Monday*, Oliphants, 1962; *Stories for Tuesday*, Oliphants, 1962; *The Boy Who Wanted a Dog* (illustrated by Sally Michel), Lutterworth, 1963; *Enid Blyton's Sunshine Picture Story Book* (first of a series), World Distributors, 1964; *Happy Hours Story Book*, Dean, 1964; *Story Book for Fives to Sevens* (illustrated by Dorothy Hall and Grace Shelton), Parrish, 1964; *Storytime Book*, Dean, 1964; *Tell-a-Story Books*, World Distributors, 1964.

Trouble for the Twins, Brockhampton Press, 1965; *The Boy Who Came Back* (illustrated by Walker), Lutterworth, 1965; *Easy Reader* (first of a series), Collins, 1965; *Enid Blyton's Sunshine Book*, Dean, 1965; *Enid Blyton's Treasure Box*, Low, 1965; *The Man Who Stopped to Help* (illustrated by Walker), Lutterworth, 1965; *Enid Blyton's Playbook* (first of a series), Collins, 1966; *The Fairy Folk Story Book*, Collins, 1966; *Enid Blyton's Fireside Tales*, Collins, 1966; *Gift Book* (illustrated by Schermele), Purnell, 1966; *The Happy House Children*, Collins, 1966; *John and Mary* (illustrated by Fromont; series of nine books), Brockhampton Press, 1966-68; *Pixie Tales*, Collins, 1966; *Pixieland Story Books*, Collins, 1966; *Stories for Bedtime*, Dean, 1966; *Stories for You*, Dean, 1966; *Holiday Annual Stories*, Low, 1967; *Holiday Magic Stories*, Low, 1967; *Holiday Pixie Stories*, Low, 1967; *Holiday Toy Stories*, Low, 1967; *The Playtime Story Book*, Numbers 1-4, World Distributors, 1967; *Adventures on Willow Farm*, Collins, 1967; *Brownie Tales*, Collins, 1968; *The Playtime Books*, Numbers 9-12, World Distributors, 1968; *Once Upon a Time*, Collins, 1968.

Enid Blyton's A Shock for Shelia, and Other Stories, Dean, 1976; *Enid Blyton's Julia Saves Up, and Other Stories*, Dent, 1976; *Enid Blyton's The Story That Came True, and Other Stories*, Dean, 1976; *Enid Blyton's Sunnyside Stories*, Purnell, 1976; *Enid Blyton's The Train That Went to Fairyland, and Other Stories*, Dent, 1976; *Enid Blyton's Twilight Tales*, Purnell, 1976.

"Secret" series; all originally published by Basil Blackwell: *The Secret Island*, 1938, reprinted, May Fair Books, 1965; *The Secret of Spiggy Holes*, 1940, reprinted, May Fair Books, 1965; *The Secret Mountain*, 1941; *The Secret of Killimooin*, 1943; *The Secret of Moon Castle*, 1953.

"Josie, Click, and Bun" series; all illustrated by D. M. Wheeler and published by George Newnes: *The Little Tree House: Being the Adventures of Josie, Click and Bun*, 1940, reprinted as *Josie, Click and Bun and the Little Tree House*, 1951; *The Further Adventures of Josie, Click and Bun*, 1941; *Josie, Click and Bun Again*, 1946; *More About Josie, Click and Bun*, 1947; *Welcome Josie, Click and Bun*, 1952.

"St. Clare's" series; all originally published by Methuen: *The Twins at St. Clare's*, 1941; *Summer Term at St. Clare's*, 1943; *Claudine at St. Clare's*, 1944; *The Second Form at St. Clare's* (illustrated by W. Lindsay Cable), 1944; *Fifth Formers at St. Clare's* (illustrated by Cable), 1945.

"Five" series; all originally published by Hodder & Stoughton: *Five on a Treasure Island*, 1942, reprinted, Atheneum, 1972; *Five Go Adventuring Again*, 1943, published as *Five Find a Secret Way*, Atheneum, 1972; *Five Run Away Together* (illustrated by Soper), 1944, published as *Five Run Away to Danger*, Atheneum, 1972; *Five Go to Smugglers' Top*, 1945, reprinted, Atheneum, 1972; *Five Go off in a Caravan* (illustrated by Soper), 1946; *Five on Kirrin Island Again*, 1947, published as *Five Guard a Hidden Discovery*, Atheneum, 1972; *Five Go off to Camp*, 1948, published as *Five on the Track of a Spook Train*, Atheneum, 1972; *Five Get into Trouble* (illustrated by Soper), 1949, new edition published as *Five Caught in a Treacherous Plot* (illustrated by Betty Maxey), Atheneum, 1972; *Five Fall Into Adventure* (illustrated by Soper), 1950, new edition illustrated by Maxey, Atheneum, 1972; *Five on a Hike Together* (illustrated by Soper), 1951; *Five Have a Wonderful Time* (illustrated by Soper), 1952; *Five Go Down to the Sea* (illustrated by Soper), 1953; *Five Go to Mystery Moor*, 1954; *Five Have Plenty of Fun*, 1955; *Five on a Secret Trail* (illustrated by Soper), 1956; *Five Go to Billycock Hill* (illustrated by Soper), 1956; *Five Get Into a Fix* (illustrated by Soper), 1958; *Five on Finniston Farm* (illustrated by Soper), 1960; *Five Go to Demon's Rocks* (illustrated by Soper), 1961; *Five Have a Mystery to Solve* (illustrated by Soper), 1962; *Five Are Together Again* (illustrated by Soper), 1963; *Fabulous Famous Five* (illustrated by Maxey; contains *Five Get into Trouble*, *Five Fall into Adventure*, and *Five on a Hike Together*), 1974.

"Mary Mouse" series; all published by Brockhampton Press: *Mary Mouse and the Doll's House*, 1942; *More Adventures of Mary Mouse*, 1943; *Little Mary Mouse Again*, 1944; *Hallo, Little Mary Mouse* (illustrated by Olive F. Openshaw), 1945; *Mary Mouse and Her Family* (illustrated by Openshaw), 1946; *Here Comes Mary Mouse Again*, 1947; *How Do You Do, Mary Mouse*, 1948; *We Do Love Mary Mouse*, 1950; *Welcome Mary Mouse* (illustrated by Openshaw), 1950; *Hurrah for Mary Mouse*, 1951; *A Prize for Mary Mouse*, 1951; *Mary Mouse and Her Bicycle* (illustrated by Openshaw), 1952; *Mary Mouse and the Noah's Ark* (illustrated by Openshaw), 1953; *Mary Mouse to the Rescue*, 1954; *Mary Mouse in Nursery Rhyme Land*, 1955; *A Day with Mary Mouse* (illustrated by Frederick White), 1956; *Mary Mouse and the Garden Party* (illustrated by White), 1957; *Mary Mouse Goes to the Fair* (illustrated by White), 1958; *Mary Mouse Has a Wonderful Idea* (illustrated by White), 1959; *Mary Mouse Goes to Sea* (illustrated by White), 1960; *Mary Mouse Goes Out for the Day* (illustrated by White), 1961; *Fun with Mary Mouse* (illustrated by R. Paul-Hoeye), 1962; *Mary Mouse and the Little Donkey* (illustrated by Paul-Hoeye), 1964.

"Mystery" series; all originally published by Methuen: *The Mystery of the Burnt Cottage* (illustrated by J. Abbey), 1943, reprinted, British Book Center, 1973; *The Mystery of the Disappearing Cat* (illustrated by Abbey), 1944, reprinted, British Book Center, 1973; *Mystery of the Secret Room*, 1945, reprinted, British Book Center, 1975; *Mystery of the Spiteful Letters* (illustrated by Abbey), 1946, reprinted, British Book Center, 1976; *The Mystery of the Missing Necklace*, 1947, reprinted, British Book Center, 1975; *The Mystery of the Hidden House* (illustrated by Abbey), 1948, reprinted, British Book Center, 1973; *The Mystery of the Pantomime Cat*, 1949; *The Mystery of the Invisible Thief*, 1950; *The Mystery of the Vanished Prince* (illustrated by Evans), 1951; *The Mystery of the Strange Bundle* (illustrated by Evans), 1952; *The Mystery of Holly Lane* (illustrated by Evans), 1953; *The Mystery of Tally-Ho Cottage* (illustrated by Evans), 1954; *Mystery of the Missing Man* (illustrated by Lilian Buchanan), 1956; *Mystery of the Strange Messages* (illustrated by Buchanan), 1957; *The Mystery of Banshee Towers* (illustrated by Buchanan), 1961; *The Mystery That Never Was* (illustrated by Gilbert Dunlop), 1961.

"Mystery" series; all originally published by Collins: *The Rockingdown Mystery* (illustrated by Dunlop), 1949; *The Rilloby Fair Mystery* (illustrated by Dunlop), 1950; *The Rubadub Mystery* (illustrated by Dunlop), 1952; *Ring O' Bells Mystery*, 1955; *Rat-a-Tat Mystery*, 1956; *Ragamuffin Mystery*, 1959.

"Adventure" series; all originally published by Macmillan: *The Island of Adventure* (illustrated by Stuart Tresilian), 1944, published as *Mystery Island*, Macmillan, 1945; *The Castle of Adventure* (illustrated by Tresilian), 1946; *The Valley of Adventure* (illustrated by Tresilian), 1947; *The Sea Adventure* (illustrated by Tresilian), 1948; *The Mountain of Adventure*, 1949; *The Ship of Adventure* (illustrated by Tresilian), 1950; *The Circus of Adventure* (illustrated by Tresilian), 1952; *River of Adventure* (illustrated by Tresilian), 1955.

"Family" series; all published by Lutterworth; all illustrated by Ruth Gervis, except as noted: *The Caravan Family* (illustrated by William Fyffe), 1945; *The Saucy Jane Family*, 1947; *The Pole Star Family*, 1950; *The Seaside Family*, 1950; *The Buttercup Farm Family*, 1951; *The Queen Elizabeth Family*, 1951.

"Malory Towers" series; all originally published by Methuen: *First Term at Malory Towers*, 1946; *The Second Form at Malory Towers*, 1947; *Third Year at Malory Towers* (illustrated by Stanley Lloyd), 1948; *The Upper Fourth at Malory Towers*, 1949; *In the Fifth at Malory Towers* (illustrated by Lloyd), 1950; *Last Term at Malory Towers* (illustrated by Lloyd), 1951.

"Noddy" series; all originally published by Low: *Little Noddy Goes to Toyland* (illustrated by Harmsen Van Der Beek), 1949; *Hurrah for Little Noddy*, 1950; *The Big Noddy Book* (illustrated by Van Der Beek; series of eight books), 1951; *Here Comes Noddy Again*, 1951; *Noddy and Big Ears Have a Picnic*, 1951; *Noddy and His Car*, 1951; *Noddy Goes to the Seaside*, 1951; *Noddy Has More Adventures*, 1951; *Noddy Has a Shock*, 1951; *Noddy Off to Rocking Horse Land*, 1951; *A Tale of Little Noddy*, 1951; *Enid Blyton's Noddy's Ark of Books*, 1952; *Noddy and Big Ears*, 1952; *Noddy and the Witch's Wand*, 1952; *Noddy's Car Gets a Squeak*, 1952; *Noddy Colour Strip Book* (illustrated by Van Der Beek), 1952; *Noddy Goes to School*, 1952; *Noddy's Penny Wheel Car*, 1952; *Well Done, Noddy*, 1952; *New Noddy Colour Strip Book*, 1953; *The New Big Noddy Book*, 1953, reprinted as *Enid Blyton's Big Noddy Book*, Purnell, 1976; *Noddy and the Cuckoo's Nest*, 1953; *Noddy at the Seaside*, 1953; *Noddy Cut-Out Model Book*, 1953; *Noddy Gets Captured*, 1953; *Noddy Is Very Silly*, 1953; *Noddy's Garage of Books* (illustrated by Van Der Beek; five books), 1953.

Enid Blyton's Noddy Giant Painting Book, 1954; *Enid Blyton's Noddy Pop-Up Book*, 1954; *How Funny You Are, Noddy!*, 1954; *Noddy Gets into Trouble*, 1954; *Noddy and the Magic Rubber*, 1954; *Noddy's Castle of Books* (illustrated by Van Der Beek; five parts), 1954; *Noddy in Toy-*land, 1955; *Noddy Meets Father Christmas*, Low, 1955; *You Funny Little Noddy!*, 1955; *Be Brave Little Noddy!*, 1956; *A Day with Noddy*, 1956; *Enid Blyton's Noddy Playday Painting Book*, 1956; *Noddy and His Friends*, 1956; *Noddy and Tessie Bear*, 1956; *Noddy Nursery Rhymes*, 1956; *The Noddy Toy Station Books*, Numbers 1-5, 1956; *Do Look Out, Noddy!*, 1956; *Noddy and Bumpy Dog*, 1957; *Noddy's New Big Book*, 1957; *My Noddy Picture Book*, 1958; *Noddy Has an Adventure*, 1958; *The Noddy Shop Book*, Numbers 1-5, 1958; *Noddy's Own Nursery Rhymes*, 1958; *You're a Good Friend, Noddy!*, 1958; *A.B.C. with Noddy*, 1959; *Noddy and Bunkey*, 1959; *Noddy Goes to Sea*, 1959; *Noddy's Car Picture Book*, 1959.

Cheer Up, Little Noddy!, 1960; *Noddy Goes to the Fair*, 1960; *Noddy's One, Two, Three Book*, 1960; *Noddy's Tall Blue Book* (also *Green, Orange, Pink, Red,* and *Yellow Books*), 1960; *Mr. Plod and Little Noddy*, 1961; *Noddy's Toyland Train Picture Book*, 1961; *A Day at School with Noddy*, 1962; *Noddy and the Tootles*, 1962; *Noddy and the Aeroplane*, 1964; *Learn to Count with Noddy*, 1965; *Learn to Go Shopping with Noddy*, 1965; *Learn to Read About Animals with Noddy*, 1965; *Learn to Tell the Time with Noddy*, 1965; *Noddy and His Friends: A Nursery Picture Book*, 1965; *Noddy Treasure Box*, 1965; *Noddy and His Passengers*, 1967; *Noddy and the Magic Boots* [and] *Noddy's Funny Kite*, 1967; *Noddy and the Noah's Ark Adventure Picture Book*, 1967; *Noddy in Toyland Picture Book*, 1967; *Noddy Toyland ABC Picture Book*, 1967; *Noddy's Aeroplane Picture Book*, 1967.

"Secret Seven" series; all originally published by Brockhampton Press: *The Secret Seven* (illustrated by George Brook), 1949, new edition published as *The Secret Seven and the Mystery of the Empty House* (illustrated by Tom Dunnington; edited by M. Hughes Miller), Childrens Press, 1972; *The Secret Seven Adventure* (illustrated by Brook), 1950, new edition published as *The Secret Seven and the Circus Adventure* (illustrated by Dunnington; edited by Miller), Childrens Press, 1972; *Well Done, Secret Seven* (illustrated by Brook), 1951, new edition published as *The Secret Seven and the Tree House Adventure* (illustrated by Dunnington; edited by Miller), Childrens Press, 1972; *Secret Seven on the Trail* (illustrated by Brook), 1952, new edition published as *The Secret Seven and the Railroad Mystery* (illustrated by Dunnington; edited by Miller), Childrens Press, 1972; *Go Ahead Secret Seven* (illustrated by Bruno Kay), 1953, new edition published as *The Secret Seven Get Their Man* (illustrated by Dunnington; edited by Miller), Childrens Press, 1972; *Good Work, Secret Seven* (illustrated by Kay), 1954, new edition published as *The Secret Seven and the Case of the Stolen Car* (illustrated by Dunnington; edited by Miller), Childrens Press, 1972.

Secret Seven Win Through (illustrated by Kay), 1955, new edition published as *The Secret Seven and the Hidden Cave Adventure* (illustrated by Dunnington; edited by Miller), Childrens Press, 1972; *Three Cheers Secret Seven* (illustrated by Burgess Sharrocks), 1956, new edition published as *The Secret Seven and the Grim Secret* (illustrated by Dunnington; edited by Miller), Childrens Press, 1972; *Secret Seven Mystery* (illustrated by Sharrocks), 1957, new edition published as *The Secret Seven and the Missing Girl Mystery* (illustrated by Dunnington; edited by Miller), Childrens Press, 1972; *Puzzle for the Secret Seven* (illustrated by Sharrocks), 1958, new edition published as *The Secret Seven and the Case of the Music Lover* (illustrated by Dunnington; edited by Miller), Childrens Press, 1972; *Secret Seven Fireworks* (illustrated by Sharrocks), 1959, new edition published as *The Secret Seven and the Bonfire Adventure* (illustrated by Dunnington; edited by Miller), Childrens Press, 1972.

Good Old Secret Seven (illustrated by Sharrocks), 1960, new edition published as *The Secret Seven and the Old Fort Adventure* (illustrated by Dunnington; edited by Miller), Childrens Press, 1972; *Shock for the Secret Seven* (illustrated by Sharrocks), 1961, new edition published as *The Secret Seven and the Case of the Dog Lover* (illustrated by Dunnington; edited by Miller), Childrens Press, 1972; *Look Out Secret Seven* (illustrated by Sharrocks), 1962, new edition published as *The Secret Seven and the Case of Missing Medals* (illustrated by Dunnington; edited by Miller), Childrens Press, 1972; *Fun for the Secret Seven* (illustrated by Sharrocks), 1963, new edition published as *The Secret Seven and the Case of the Old Horse* (illustrated by Dunnington; edited by Miller), Childrens Press, 1972.

"Bom" series; all published by Brockhampton Press, except as noted: *Bom and His Magic Drumstick*, 1956; *Bom the Little Toy Drummer*, 1956; *Enid Blyton's Bom Painting Book*, Dean, 1956; *Bom Goes Adventuring* (illustrated by Paul-Hoeye), 1958; *Bom and the Clown*, 1959; *Bom and the Rainbow*, 1959; *Hullo Bom and Wuffy Dog* (illustrated by Paul-Hoeye), 1959; *Bom Goes to Magic Town*, 1960; *Here Comes Bom* (illustrated by Paul-Hoeye), 1960; *Bom at the Seaside* (illustrated by Paul-Hoeye), 1961; *Bom Goes to the Circus* (illustrated by Paul-Hoeye), 1961.

Plays: *A Book of Little Plays*, Thomas Nelson, 1927; *The Play's the Thing* (music by A. Rowley), Home Library Book Co., 1927, reprinted in two volumes as *Plays for the Older Children* [and] *Plays for Younger Children*, George Newnes, 1940; *Six Enid Blyton Plays*, Methuen, 1935; *The Blyton-Sharman Musical Plays for Juniors*, six parts, A. Wheaton, 1939; George H. Holroyd, editor, *Cameo Plays* (only Book 4 by Blyton), E. J. Arnold, 1939; *How the Flowers Grow, and Other Musical Plays*, A. Wheaton, 1939; *School Plays: Six Plays for School*, Basil Blackwell, 1939; *The Wishing Beam and Other Plays*, Basil Blackwell, 1939; *Finding the Tickets*, Evans Brothers, 1955; *Mr. Sly-One and Cats*, Evans Brothers, 1955; *Mother's Meeting*, Evans Brothers, 1955; *Who Will Hold the Giant?*, Evans Brothers, 1955; *Enid Blyton's Book of the Famous Play Noddy in Toyland*, Low, 1956.

Reteller: *Aesop's Fables*, Thomas Nelson, 1928; *Old English Stories*, Thomas Nelson, 1928; *Pinkity's Pranks and Other Nature Fairy Stories*, Thomas Nelson, 1928; Joel C. Harris, *Tales of Brer Rabbit*, Thomas Nelson, 1928; *The Knights of the Round Table*, George Newnes, 1930; *Tales From the Arabian Nights*, George Newnes, 1930; *The Adventures of Odysseus: Stories From World History*, Evans Brothers, 1934; *The Story of the Siege of Troy: Stories From World History*, Evans Brothers, 1934; *Tales of the Ancient Greeks and Persians: Stories From World History*, Evans Brothers, 1934; *Tales of the Romans: Stories From World History*, Evans Brothers, 1934; Harris, *Heyo, Brer Rabbit!*, George Newnes, 1938; Harris, *The Further Adventures of Brer Rabbit*, George Newnes, 1942; Harris, *Brer Rabbit and His Friends*, J. Coker, 1938; *Brer Rabbit Book* (series of eight books), Latimer House, 1948; *The Two Sillies and Other Stories*, J. Coker, 1952; Harris, *Brer Rabbit Again*, Dean, 1963; *Tales of Brave Adventure*, Dean, 1963; Harris, *Enid Blyton's Brer Rabbit's a Rascal*, Dean, 1965; *Tales of Long Ago* (selections from *Tales of Ancient Greece* and *Tales from the Arabian Nights*), Dean, 1965.

Editor: *The Teacher's Treasury*, three volumes, George Newnes, 1926; *Sunny Stories for Little Folks*, George Newnes, 1926-36; *Modern Teaching in the Infant School*, four volumes, George Newnes, 1932; *Modern Teaching: Practical Suggestions for Junior and Senior Schools*, six volumes, George Newnes, 1928; (and contributor) *Pictorial Knowledge*, ten volumes, George Newnes, 1930; *Treasure Trove Readers* (junior series), A. Wheaton, 1934; *Nature Observation Pictures*, Warne, 1935; Thomas A. Coward, *Birds of the Wayside and Woodland*, Warne, 1936; *The Children's Book of Prayers*, Muller, 1963; *Enid Blyton's Favourite Book of Fables from the Tales of La Fontaine*, Collins, 1955.

Under name Mary Pollock; all published by George Newnes, except as noted: *Children of Kidillin*, 1940; *Three Boys and a Circus*, 1940; *Adventures of Scamp*, 1943; the latter two books were reprinted together under the author's real name as *Dog Stories*, Collins, 1959; *The Secret of Cliff Castle*, 1943; *Smuggler Ben*, 1943; *Mischief at St. Rollo's*, 1947.

Also author and editor of several periodicals and annuals, including *Enid Blyton's Magazine*, [London], beginning 1953; *Playways Annual*, Lutterworth, 1953; *Enid Blyton Magazine Annual* (first of a series), Evans Brothers, 1954; *Sunny Stories Annual*, [London], 1954; *Enid Blyton's Annual*, [London], beginning 1957; *Enid Blyton's Bom Annual*, [London], 1957; *Enid Blyton's Bedtime Annual*, [Manchester], 1966; *The Big Enid Blyton Story Annual*, Purnell, 1973-76.

SIDELIGHTS: Enid Blyton originally planned to make music her career and was working towards her L.R.A.M. (Licentiate of the Royal Academy of Music) examination when she decided to become a school teacher instead. In addition to her work in the educational field, Blyton also took pleasure in writing fiction for children. As a child, Blyton was gifted with a vivid imagination and a sense for writing. At the age of fourteen, the budding author embarked on a literary career with the publication of her poem in a children's magazine edited by Arthur Mee. Since then, approximately six hundred books and countless articles have been written by Blyton. Translations of the author-educator's works can be found in ninety-three languages, including Russian, Hebrew, Indonesian, Tamil, Swahili, and Fijian.

At the peak of her writing career, Blyton usually produced six to ten thousand words a day, and still had time to play with her two daughters or read stories to them. Blyton wrote for children of all ages, with whom she was enormously popular. She deplored contemporary violence in comic books and movies, and believed that literature for young children should instill absolutely sound morals. In spite of (perhaps because of) her tremendous popularity with child readers, Blyton has been attacked by some critics and librarians who claim that her work is trivial and unreal. Some British libraries refuse to stock her books. Against this, Blyton has been solidly backed by educators and ministers of all creeds.

AVOCATIONAL INTERESTS: Gardening, reading, bridge, and golf.

BIOGRAPHICAL/CRITICAL SOURCES: Springfield Republican, March 11, 1945; *Weekly Book Review*, March 11, 1945; *New York Times*, September 15, 1946; *Saturday Review of Literature*, September 28, 1946; Enid Mary Blyton, *Story of My Life* (autobiography), Pitkin, 1952; Barbara Stoney, *Enid Blyton: A Biography*, Hodder & Stoughton, 1974.

OBITUARIES: New York Times, November 29, 1968; *Time*, December 6, 1968; *Publishers Weekly*, December 30, 1968.*

(Died November 28, 1968)

*   *   *

BOBROWSKI, Johannes 1917-1965

PERSONAL: Born April 9, 1917, in Tilsit, East Prussia, Germany (now Sovetsk, Russia); son of Gustav Bobrowski (a railroad official); married Johanna Puddrus; children: four. *Education:* Educated in Germany. *Religion:* Lutheran. *Politics:* East German Christian Democratic Union.

CAREER: Poet, novelist, short story writer. Verlag Lucie Groszer (publisher), East Berlin, East Germany, reader, 1952-59; Union Verlag (publisher), East Berlin, reader, 1959-65. *Military service:* German Army, 1939-49; prisoner of war in Russia, 1945-49, did forced labor as a miner in the Donets region. *Awards, honors:* Group 47 prize, 1962; Alma Koenig prize, 1962; Heinrich Mann prize, 1965; Charles Veillon prize, 1965; F. C. Weiskopf prize, 1967.

WRITINGS: Hans Clauert, der Maerkische Eulenspiegel (juvenile), Altberliner Verlag, 1956; *Sarmatische Zeit: Gedichte* (title means "Sarmatian Times: Poems"), Deutsche Verlags-Anstalt, 1961; *Schattenland Stroeme: Gedichte* (title means "Shadowland Streams: Poems"), Deutsche Verlags-Anstalt, 1962, 3rd edition, 1963; (editor) Johann Paul Friedrich, *Leben Fibels,* Union Verlag, 1963; (compiler) *Wer mich und Ilse sieht im Grase: Deutsche Dichter des 18. Jahrhunderts ueper die Liebe und das Frauenzimmer* (title means "Whoever Sees Me and Ilse Lying in the Grass: German Poems of the Eighteenth Century on Love and Women"), Eulenspiegel Verlag, 1964; *Levins Muehle* (novel), S. Fischer, 1964, translation by Janet Cropper published as *Levin's Mill,* Calder & Boyars, 1970; *Boehlendorff und Andere* (short stories; title means "Boehlendorff and Others"), Deutsche Verlags-Anstalt, 1965; *Mauesefest, und andere Erzaehlungen* (title means "Mouse Feast, and Other Stories"), K. Wagenbach, 1965.

Boehlendorff und Maeusefest: Erzaehlungen (title means "Boehlendorff and Mouse Feast: Stories"), Union Verlag, 1966; *Das Land Sarmatien: Gedichte* (title means "The Sarmatian Country: Poems"), Deutscher Taschenbuch Verlag, 1966; *Wetterzeichen: Gedichte* (title means "Storm Signals: Poems"), Union Verlag, 1966; *Johannes Bobrowski liest Lyrik und Prosa* (with two phonograph records; title means "Johannes Bobrowski Reads Lyric Poetry and Prose"), Union Verlag, 1966, altered edition published as *Nachbarschaft,* K. Wagenbach, 1967; *Selbstzeugnisse und Beitraege ueber sein Werk,* Union Verlag, 1967; *Der Mahner: Erzaehlungen* (title means "The Dun: Stories"), Union Verlag, 1967; *Das Tierhaeuschen* (juvenile; adaptation of *Terem-teremok* by Samuil Marshak), Kinderbuchverlag, 1967, translation by Moya Gillespie published as *The House in the Meadow,* Harvey House, 1970; *Litauische Claviere* (novel; title means "Lithuanian Pianos"), Union Verlag, 1967; *Der Mahner: Erzaehlungen und andere Prosa aus dem Nachlass* (title means "The Dun: Stories and Other Posthumous Prose"), K. Wagenbach, 1968; (translator with Guenther Deicke) Boris Pasternak, *Initialen der Leidenschaft,* Verlag Volk und Welt, 1969.

Im Windgestraeuch: Gedichte aus dem Nachlass (title means "Into the Windy Bushes: Posthumous Poems"), Deutsche Verlags-Anstalt, 1970; *Lipmanns Leib: Erzaehlungen* (title means "Lipmann's Body: Stories"), P. Reclam, 1973; *Gedichte: 1952-1965* (title means "Poems: 1952-1965"), Insel-Verlag, 1974.

English collections: *Shadow Land: Selected Poems* (contains poems from *Sarmatische Zeit* and *Schattenland Stroeme*), translated by Ruth Mead and Matthew Mead, Alan Swallow, 1966, 2nd edition, 1966; *I Taste Bitterness* (contains stories from *Boehlendorff und Maeusefest*), translated by Marc Linder, Seven Seas Publishers, 1970; (with Horst Bienek) *Selected Poems: Johannes Bobrowski and Horst Bienek* (contains poems from *Sarmatische Zeit* and *Schattenland Stroeme*), Penguin, 1971; *From the Rivers: Selected Poems,* translated by R. Mead and M. Mead, Anvil Press, 1975.

Translator of poems by Konstantin Biebl into German. Work represented in *Deutsche Lyrik auf der anderen Seite* (title means "Poetry on the Other Side"), 1960. Contributor of poetry to journals and magazines, including *Das innere Reich* and *Sinn und Form.*

SIDELIGHTS: Johannes Bobrowski spent his childhood, he said, "on both sides of the River Memel," dividing his time between Tilsit, the East Prussian town where he was born, and his grandfather's farm in Lithuania. In 1928 the family moved to the nearby city of Koenigsberg (now Kaliningrad), which is renowned for its musical and literary associations. Bobrowski went to school there, studied the classics, and learned to play the organ and the clavichord, acquiring a taste for Baroque music. Above all he experienced the sharp contrast between what he called "the patriarchal closed-inness" of village life and the sophisticated worldly preoccupations of a trading port with a rich cultural history. Bobrowski was later to become a devoted student of the history, geography, and folklore of the region in which he grew up, and a collector of books and atlases of local interest. As Brian Keith-Smith wrote in his monograph on Bobrowski, "these interests . . . gave him a peculiarly balanced combination of close attachment to the significance of local life, where the quality of the individual character and his expression meant so much, and of the detachment of an observer with a developed taste for the strict form of some of the highest achievements of classical post-Renaissance and ancient classical culture."

In 1938 the family moved again, this time to Berlin. After studying art history there for a year, Bobrowski was inducted into the German army and sent first to Poland, then to Russia. He had already tried his hand as a painter and as a composer, but had been discouraged by the greater talent of some of his friends. It was in an attempt to record his impressions of Russia that he turned to poetry, as he later explained: "I began to write near Lake Ilmen in 1941 about the Russian landscape, but as a foreigner, a German. This became [my] theme . . . the Germans and the European East—because I grew up around the River Memel, where Poles, Lithuanians, Russians and Germans lived together, and among them all the Jews—a long history of unhappiness and guilt, for which my people is to blame, ever since the days of the Teutonic Knights. Not to be undone, perhaps, or expiated, but worthy of hope and honest endeavor in German poems."

Apart from a few poems published during the war in the magazine *Das innere Reich,* Bobrowski's work did not begin to appear until he had returned from his long captivity in Russia and settled into his career as a publisher's reader in East Berlin. A group of poems was published in the important East German magazine *Sinn und Form* in 1955, and some of these were included in the West German anthology *Deutsche Lyrik auf der anderen Seite* ("Poetry on the Other Side," 1960); thereafter all of Bobrowski's poetry appeared in both East and West Germany. The most important influence on his early work was the nature poet Friedrich Klopstock, but it was Peter Huchel, the editor of *Sinn und Form,* who showed him his true direction as a poet. Bobrowski told an interviewer in 1965 that he "first read a poem of [Huchel's] in Soviet prison camp, in a newspaper, and it impressed me immensely. That's where I came to see people in a landscape—to such an extent that to this day I do not care for an unpeopled natural setting. I am no longer charmed by the elemental forces of a landscape, but by nature only when seen in connection with, and as a field of, the effective activity of man."

Most of Bobrowski's poems are concerned with what the ancient geographers called Sarmatia, the steppe country between the Vistula and the Volga. In his verse this borderland becomes archetypal and mythical, a "shadowland" alive with "the traces of peoples lost"—the old Prussians, Lithuanians, Poles, Russians, gypsies, and Jews who had lived there, their gods and heroes, languages and legends, lingering on in artifacts and cave paintings, in old songs, and superstitions, and ancient place-names. For example, "Pruzzische Elegie" ("Prussian Elegy," 1952), the longest and one of the best known of his poems, conjures up the pagan world of the Old Prussians, celebrating the simplicity and naturalness of their way of life, lamenting their extermination in the name of Christianity by the Teutonic Knights, but suggesting that something of their essence survives in the landscape itself. "Gestorbene Sprache" ("Dead Language") implies a question: Is Old Prussian dead because only traces of it remain, or is the dead language of the title actually modern German, which is unable to express the deep connections between man and nature?

A *Times Literary Supplement* critic noted that Bobrowski's poetry "is beautifully lyrical, and yet impersonal, oracular in the manner of Hoelderlin. The perceptions are enacted in language that is stark, dynamic, and almost invariably concrete, outstanding for its nervous strength and its total precision. Like his prose, it is dense in the sense of being radically condensed and richly allusive. By invoking a river or village he evokes a whole world and a whole tradition." Bobrowski favored free verse, marked by harsh German inversions, and typically began a poem with a few short and explosive substantives—what John Flores has called a "stuttering" of nouns—leading on to a final cry for communication. Bobrowski himself believed that "the language of poetry has the triadic function of *remembrance* (the mytho-historic and immediate past), *communication* (bringing the past meaningfully into the present), and the causation of *effective change* (a vision of the future)." The change he most wanted was progress towards what he called "nachbarschaft"—a sense of community and neighborly companionship between different races, and between different members of the same race.

This was also the principal theme of Bobrowski's fiction, to which he turned increasingly in his later years. Keith-Smith observed that a Bobrowski short story most often begins with "a detailed building-up of the setting with usually an emphatic concentration on the forces within it that form a link with the past.... Then comes the intrusion into that setting of the character who belongs to the past yet lingers on in the present." There is always a threat behind these stories, Keith-Smith suggested—the threat of Nazi terror, of officialdom, sometimes only of thoughtless inhumanity. Most of Bobrowski's stories were set in the pastoral "Sarmatian" world of the poems, but the eleven stories and prose sketches in his posthumous third collection, *Der Mahner*, most of them written in the highly productive last few months of his life, were more contemporary in their concerns. However, as one reviewer wrote in the *Times Liter-*

ary Supplement, here as elsewhere Bobrowski's "constant concern was Man. In these new stories his deep moral and social concerns and the sinewy classical style in which they are expressed are unchanged."

Levin's Mill, considered to be the best of Bobrowski's two novels, is set in 1874 in a Prussian village. The narrator describes how his grandfather Johann, a prosperous old German miller, ruthlessly put his young Jewish competitor out of business, but then was driven from the village himself by public disapproval. Bobrowski uses this theme to illustrate the innate hostility between the various racial and religious elements in his "Sarmatian" village, but also the mutual respect and "nachbarschaft" that enable the community to survive. H. M. Waidson wrote that the novel's style combines "the lyrical evocation of nature . . . and of human emotion, with a darting humor. Interpolated in the main narrative are a series of visionary 'hauntings' that befall the grandfather when he is unconscious and recall episodes involving his ancestors in earlier centuries, while the twentieth-century grandson who tells the story provides a present-day perspective." Bobrowski's other novel, *Litauische Claviere*, also reflects his interest in the history and folklore of his native region. It was completed only a few weeks before his premature death from peritonitis. Bobrowski was also the author of two books for children and of some outstanding translations, notably of the poetry of Boris Pasternak and the Czech poet Konstantin Biebl.

When Bobrowski died, his works were praised by an official Marxist critic as "exemplary Christian contributions to the development of the socialist literature of the nation." Peter Demetz, a western critic, complained that Bobrowski "never said a word against inhuman Soviet policies in the Baltic states," but suggested that towards the end of his life "he was feeling more and more like a speechless stranger among his people. In his last poem, 'Das Wort Mensch'/ 'The Word Man,' published posthumously on June 8, 1966, he confessed to his disgust for a society that prided itself on repeating mechanically the empty vocabulary of humanitarianism without ever being truly humane: 'Where love is lacking, do not / utter the word.'" Siegfried Mandel, however, could not agree that this poem had "the force of direct accusation against specific contemporary persecutions," and concluded that Bobrowski had chosen "in a muted voice, to pit moral vision against political expediency."

Most critics were content to regard Bobrowski as a writer in whose work humanism "again assumed a vital meaning." He is universally regarded as one of the finest and most original German poets of his generation, and his poems have been translated into all the major European languages.

BIOGRAPHICAL/CRITICAL SOURCES: Times Literary Supplement, September 21, 1962, January 14, 1965, April 20, 1967, February 22, 1968; *London Times*, September 4, 1965; *Germanic Review*, January, 1966; *Forum for Modern Language Studies*, Volume II, number 4, 1966; *Sinn und Form*, Volume XVIII, 1966; Brian Keith-Smith, editor, *Essays on Contemporary German Literature*, Volume 4: *German Men of Letters*, Oswald Wolff, 1966; Sigfrid Hoefert, *West-Ostliches in der Lyrik Johannes Bobrowskis*, Verlag Uni-Druck, 1966; Gerhard Wolf and Gerhard Rostin, *Johannes Bobrowski: Selbstzeugnisse und Beitraege ueber sein werk*, Union Verlag, 1967, revised edition, 1975; *London Magazine*, November, 1967; Siegbert Salomon Prawer, editor, *Essays in German Language, Culture and Society*, University of London Press, 1969; Keith-Smith, *Johannes Bobrowski*, Oswald Wolff, 1970; John Flores,

Poetry in East Germany, 1945-1970, Yale University Press, 1971.*

(Died September 2, 1965, in East Berlin, East Germany)

* * *

BODE, Roy E. 1948-

PERSONAL: Born July 21, 1948, in Tahoka, Tex.; son of Roy E. (a businessman) and Betty (a businesswoman; maiden name, Ingram) Bode; married Patricia Fanning, May 23, 1971 (divorced, 1973). *Education:* Attended Odessa College, 1967-69, University of Tulsa, 1969, and University of Cincinnati, 1971. *Home:* 115 East St., Washington, D.C. 20003. *Agent:* Aaron Priest, 150 East 35th St., New York, N.Y. 10016. *Office:* 995 National Press Building, Washington, D.C. 20045.

CAREER/WRITINGS: Odessa American, Odessa, Tex., reporter, 1966-69; *Tulsa Daily World,* Tulsa, Okla., reporter, 1969-70; *Dallas Times Herald,* Dallas, Tex., reporter, 1970-71; *Kentucky Post,* Cincinnati, Ohio, assistant city editor, 1971-72; *Arkansas Gazette,* Little Rock, Washington bureau chief, 1972—. Notable assignments include coverage of Nixon's resignation. *Member:* National Press Club, White House Correspondents Association. *Awards, honors:* Received Anson Johnson Award from Texas Medical Association; Texas UPI Editors award for interpretive reporting; Texas AP Managing Editors award for spot news writing.

* * *

BOGARDE, Dirk
See VAN DEN BOGARDE, Derek Jules G.U.N.

* * *

BOGGS, James 1919-

PERSONAL: Born May 28, 1919, in Marion Junction, Ala.; married Grace Lee (a writer); children: James, Wayman, Donald, Jacqueline, Thomasine, Ernestine. *Education:* Attended public schools in Bessemer, Ala. *Residence:* Detroit, Mich. *Office:* 3061 Field St., Detroit, Mich. 48214.

CAREER: Worked as field hand in Washington, ice cutter in Minnesota, and for Works Progress Administration in Detroit, Mich.; auto worker, Detroit, 1941-68; writer, 1963—.

WRITINGS: The American Revolution: Pages from a Negro Worker's Notebook, Monthly Review Press, 1963; *Racism and the Class Struggle: Further Pages from a Black Worker's Notebook,* Monthly Review Press, 1970; (with wife Grace Lee Boggs) *Revolution and Evolution in the Twentieth Century,* Monthly Review Press, 1974.

SIDELIGHTS: Referred to by John Oliver Killens as "a great ideologist for the cause of liberation," Boggs writes consistently of his political views. His *The American Revolution: Pages from a Negro Worker's Notebook* was described by A. B. Spellman as "a rambling series of brilliant and startling insights into the American past and the probable American future." Spellman called Boggs "a radical's radical. He starts from an assumption that the American power elite is innately evil, and he is not addressing people who might think otherwise."

Racism and the Class Struggle: Further Pages from a Black Worker's Notebook pursued the ideology of its earlier counterpart. "The content of these essays," reported *Kirkus Reviews,* "promotes new-leftish, black-power notions like 'internal colony' or white workers as oppressors of black people. Boggs calls, it is hard to say how seriously, for black majority power in cities and Southern counties."

Boggs has firmly established himself as a revolutionary. *Choice* noted that "what distinguishes Boggs from others who recently have written about the black movement is that he recommends complete revolution and does not accept anything less."

BIOGRAPHICAL/CRITICAL SOURCES: Nation, June 29, 1964; *Kirkus Reviews,* June 1, 1970; *Choice,* January, 1971; *Times Literary Supplement,* February 12, 1971; John A. Williams and Charles F. Harris, editors, *Amistad 2,* Random House, 1971; *Best Sellers,* November 1, 1974.*

* * *

BOGUSLAWSKI, Dorothy Beers 1911(?)-1978

1911(?)—April 3, 1978; American consultant and authority on day-care and author. Boguslawski began her career as director of the Halsey Day Nursery during the end of World War II. In 1958 she was appointed chief consultant on day-care for the overseas operations of the American Joint Distribution Committee. Her most recent publication was a guide to financing and starting a day-care center. Boguslawski died in New York, N.Y. Obituaries and other sources: *New York Times,* April 7, 1978.

* * *

BOLOGNA, Joseph

PERSONAL: Born in Brooklyn, N.Y.; married Renee Taylor (an actress and writer). *Education:* Attended Brown University.

CAREER: Actor, playwright, and author of teleplays. Has also worked for an advertising agency as a director and producer of television commercials. *Military service:* U.S. Marine Corps. *Awards, honors:* Nomination for best screenplay award from Screenwriters Guild, 1972, for "Made for Each Other"; Emmy Award from the Academy of Television Arts and Sciences, 1973, for "The Acts of Love and Other Comedies"; nominated for Emmy Award, 1975, for "Paradise."

WRITINGS: (With wife, Renee Taylor) *Lovers and Other Strangers* (four one-acts; first produced on Broadway at Brooks Atkinson Theatre, September 18, 1968), Samuel French, 1968.

Screenplays; all with Taylor: "Lovers and Other Strangers," American Broadcasting Co. (ABC), 1970; "Made for Each Other," Twentieth Century-Fox, 1971. Also author of "2," 1966.

Teleplays; all with Taylor: "Benny," Public Broadcasting System (PBS), 1971; "The Acts of Love and Other Comedies," ABC, 1973. Also author of "Honor Thy Father," 1973, and "Paradise," 1974. Contributor of scripts to television series, including "The Great American Dream Machine," and "Calucci's Department."

SIDELIGHTS: Bologna has acted in several motion pictures, including "Made for Each Other," "Lovers and Other Strangers," "Cops and Robbers," and "The Big Bus."

Christine Rose of *Writer's Digest* asked Bologna why he and his wife decided to collaborate on their writings. Bologna responded: "I guess because we each felt a lack of something writing separately. But it wasn't a question of weaknesses bringing us together. It was more a question of strengths. Renee is more instinctive and impulsive as a writer, and I am more structured. In that way, we complement each other.

"But that's technical. The important thing is that we respect each other's work and that we have the same feelings about things."

BIOGRAPHICAL/CRITICAL SOURCES: New Yorker, September 28, 1968; Commonweal, October 11, 1968; America, October 12, 1968; Writer's Digest, December, 1976.*

* * *

BOLT, Ernest C(ollier), Jr. 1936-

PERSONAL: Born July 20, 1936, in Charlotte, N.C.; son of Ernest Collier (an accountant) and Rachel (Winecoff) Bolt; married Mary Frances Pepper, May 12, 1961; children: David (deceased), Brian, Lauren. Education: Furman University, B.A., 1958; University of Georgia, M.A., 1963, Ph.D., 1966. Politics: Democrat. Religion: Baptist. Home: 55 Old Mill Rd., Richmond, Va. 23226. Office: Department of History, University of Richmond, Richmond, Va. 23173.

CAREER: University of Richmond, Richmond, Va., assistant professor, 1966-69, associate professor, 1969-76, professor of history, 1977—. Military service: U.S. Army, 1958-59. U.S. Army Reserve, 1959-64.

MEMBER: American Historical Association, Organization of American Historians, Society for Historians of American Foreign Relations, Conference on Peace Research in History, American Association of University Professors, Southern Historical Association, Virginia Historical Society, Virginia Baptist Historical Society (acting curator), Richmond Oral History Association (president, 1977-78), Phi Alpha Theta.

WRITINGS: Ballots Before Bullets: The War Referendum Approach to Peace in America, 1914-1941, University Press of Virginia, 1977.

WORK IN PROGRESS: A biography of Louis L. Ludlow, Washington correspondent and U.S. Democratic Congressman from Indiana.

SIDELIGHTS: Bolt writes: "Ballots Before Bullets examines a little known but popular and persistent twentieth century peace proposal—the idea of a direct vote of the people on declarations of war. It is the fullest account yet of the tactics of proponent Louis Ludlow and the opposition of Franklin Roosevelt, and the first published study of the war referendum movement of 1914-41. I place the history of the plan in the context of diplomatic negotiations, the peace movement, political party history, neutrality legislation, and the history of liberal reform, thus removing from obscurity the origins of the plan, the motives of its key proponents, and the reasons for its ultimate failure on the eve of World War II."

An early reviewer of the book, Professor Charles Chatfield, writes that the book "is based on scholarly use of extensive primary sources in private collections and State Department records as well as public documents, periodicals, and published works." The book, he continues, "adds important elements to the literature of the peace movements in World War I and opens new chapters in diplomatic history by describing the role of referendum plans in the League of Nations debate and in Charles Evans Hughes's negotiations for European settlement in the early 20's" Chatfield believes that Bolt relates the war referendum history "with insight to broad currents of diplomacy, politics, and peace activism."

Bolt adds: "I am continuing my study of Louis Ludlow (1873-1950) and plan a biography of the former isolationist Congressman from Indiana. Ludlow was the first Washington correspondent covering the House of Representatives to be elected to the House, and he served his Indianapolis constituency from 1929 to 1949. Ludlow represented about nineteen newspapers, was the author of five books, and served in 1927 as president of the National Press Club. In Congress he was a friend of the New Deal and foe of bureaucracy, an isolationist proponent of neutrality and limited defense, and an early advocate of the Equal Rights Amendment."

BIOGRAPHICAL/CRITICAL SOURCES: Choice, February, 1978.

* * *

BORENSTEIN, Audrey F(arrell) 1930-

PERSONAL: Born October 7, 1930, in Chicago, Ill.; daughter of Robert C. (a plumbing contractor) and Rose (Schageman) Farrell; married Walter Borenstein (a professor of Spanish language and literature), September 5, 1953; children: Jeffrey Theodore, Shari Rebecca. Education: University of Illinois, A.B., 1953, M.A., 1954; Louisiana State University, Ph.D., 1958. Home: 4 Henry Court, New Paltz, N.Y. 12561. Office: Department of Sociology, State University of New York College at New Paltz, New Paltz, N.Y. 12561.

CAREER: Louisiana State University, Baton Rouge, assistant professor of sociology, 1958-60; Cornell College, Mt. Vernon, Iowa, assistant professor of anthropology, 1965-69; State University of New York College at New Paltz, visiting assistant professor of sociology, 1970—. Member of Ulster County Council for the Arts.

MEMBER: American Association for the Advancement of Science, American Sociological Association, Associated Writing Programs, Institute of Society, Ethics, and the Life Sciences, Poets and Writers, Delta Kappa Gamma. Awards, honors: First prize in fiction from Zeitgeist, 1966, for "Rachel"; creative writing fellowship from National Endowment for the Arts, 1976-77.

WRITINGS: (Translator) Ferdinand Toennies, Custom: An Essay on Social Codes, Free Press, 1961; Redeeming the Sin: Essays on Social Science and Literature, Columbia University Press, 1978. Contributor of articles, stories, poems, and reviews to literary journals, including Antioch Review, Ascent, Kansas Quarterly and Croton Review. Editor of Hurricane Carla.

WORK IN PROGRESS: Three books of short stories; compiling a portfolio of art-poems, with Natalie Minewski; The Older Woman in Contemporary American Society, completion expected in 1979; Change of Life, a novel on aging and conversions, 1979; The Sibling Bond, 1980.

SIDELIGHTS: Audrey Borenstein comments: "Both a writer and a social scientist, I write works of fiction and nonfiction on the same theme(s), concurrently. I am interested in all aspects of anthropology, social psychology, and sociology. I write poetry, satires and novels, as well as essays and short stories. My current strong interests are in the areas of dream research and all aspects of aging."

* * *

BORLAND, Hal 1900-1978
(Harold Glen Borland; pseudonym, Ward West)

May 14, 1900—February 22, 1978; American naturalist and writer best known for his books on nature, including Hill Country Harvest, and for his editorials in the New York Times. Borland also wrote novels, children's stories, two autobiographies, and essays, the great majority of which were concerned with Borland's impressions of "the only way to live . . . waiting for the vernal equinox, seeing an apple tree blossom or coming on an old coon and her kits fishing for clams late at night." He died in Sharon, Conn. Obituaries and other sources: *The Author's and Writer's Who's Who,* 6th edition, Burke's Peerage, 1971; *World Authors, 1950-1970,* Wilson, 1975; *Publishers Weekly,* November 1, 1976; *Who's Who in America,* 40th edition, Marquis, 1977; *New York Times,* February 24, 1978. (See index for *CA* sketch)

* * *

BOSHELL, Gordon 1908-

PERSONAL: Born in 1908, in Blackburn, Lancashire, England; son of Thomas (in business) and Ada (Roberts) Boshell; married Margaret Hazel Nisbet, 1961; children: (previous marriage) David, Toby. *Education:* Attended Bradford Technical College, 1925-27. *Home:* 17 St. Osmund Close, Yetminster, Sherborne, Dorsetshire DT9 6LU, England. *Agent:* Gill Coleridge, Anthony Sheil Associates Ltd., 2/3 Morwell St., London WC1B 3AR, England.

CAREER: Yorkshire Observer, Bradford, England, reporter, 1926-30; sub-editor for provincial newspapers in England, 1930-33; insurance salesman, 1933; staff member of *Daily Express,* Manchester, England, 1933-36, *Daily Mirror,* London, England, 1936-38, *Sunday Referee,* London, 1938-39, and *Daily Mail,* London, 1939-42; British Broadcasting Corp. (BBC) Radio, London, 1940-44, began as scriptwriter, became editor of such programs as "Marching On" and "War Report"; Reuters Features Service, London, assistant editor, 1944-45; *Daily Mirror,* features editor, 1945-49; *Daily Herald,* London, features editor, 1949-51; World Health Organization, Geneva, Switzerland, information officer, 1951-57, information officer for Southeast Asia in New Delhi, India, 1957-63, for Western Pacific Region in Manila, Philippines, 1963-64, and for headquarters in Geneva, 1964-67, founder and editor of *World Health,* 1951-67; free-lance writer, 1967—.

WRITINGS: My Pen My Sword (poems), Hodder & Stoughton, 1941; *John Brown's Body* (novel), Secker & Warburg, 1942; *My Country 'Tis of Thee* (poems), W. H. Allen, 1943; *Dog's Life* (novel), Secker & Warburg, 1945; *It Happened to Me* (with own photographs), Orient Longman, 1958; *Nepal Today* (with own photographs), Orient Longman, 1960; *A Day in Ceylon* (with own photographs), Orient Longman, 1961.

Children's books: *Captain Cobwebb,* Chatto & Windus, 1967; *Captain Cobwebb's Cowboys,* Chatto & Windus, 1969; *Captain Cobwebb's Cobra,* Chatto & Windus, 1971; *The Plot against Buster the Dog,* J. Philip O'Hara, 1972; *Captain Cobwebb's Adventurers,* Macdonald & Co., 1973; *Captain Cobwebb and the Red Transistor,* Macdonald & Co., 1974; *The Secret Guardians: The Black Mercedes,* Bailey Brothers & Swinfen, 1974; *The Secret Guardians: The Million-Pound Ransom,* Bailey Brothers & Swinfen, 1975; *The Boy from Black Marsh,* Bailey Brothers & Swinfen, 1975; *Captain Cobwebb and the Crustaks,* Macdonald & Jane's, 1975; *Captain Cobwebb and the Chinese Unicorn,* Macdonald & Jane's, 1976; *The Secret Guardians: The Mendip Money-Makers,* Bailey Brothers & Swinfen, 1976; *Captain Cobwebb and the Mischief Man,* Macdonald & Jane's, 1977; *Captain Cobwebb and the Quogs,* Macdonald & Jane's, 1978; *Captain Cobwebb and the Magic Dragon,* Macdonald & Jane's, 1979.

WORK IN PROGRESS: Grey Tom, a science fiction adventure book.

SIDELIGHTS: Boshell writes: "My first children's book was written as a result of a constant loud-voiced demand, 'Tell us a story,' by two brothers, aged seven and five, when told to tuck up, shut up, and go to sleep. These stories vanished night after night into thin air, so at last I decided to write one down. I took a fortnight's holiday and wrote all day, hidden away in a remote office. Each chapter was submitted to my young editors in the evening as a continuing bed-time story. It was all very hilarious, and since that story got into print, it has been joined by many others."

Boshell's *Captain Cobwebb* books have been published in both German and Dutch. Some of his other books have been published in Norwegian.

* * *

BOSWORTH, Patricia 1933-

PERSONAL: Born April 24, 1933, in Berkeley, Calif.; daughter of Bartley C. Crum (a lawyer) and Gertrude Bosworth (a cookbook writer); married Mel Arrighi (a novelist), February 15, 1966. *Education:* Sarah Lawrence College, B.A., 1955. *Politics:* Democrat. *Religion:* Catholic. *Residence:* New York, N.Y. *Agent:* Rhoda Weyr, William Morris Agency, 1350 Avenue of the Americas, New York, N.Y. 10019.

CAREER: Woman's Day, New York City, articles editor, 1965-68; *McCall's,* New York City, senior editor, 1969-70; *Harper's Bazaar,* New York City, managing editor, 1972-73; *Viva,* New York City, executive editor, 1974-76; writer. *Member:* P.E.N., Authors Guild, Women's Media Group. *Awards, honors:* Doubleday writing fellowship.

WRITINGS: Montgomery Clift: A Biography, Harcourt, 1978. Contributor of articles to periodicals, including *Esquire, McCall's, Family Circle, New York Times,* and *Town and Country.*

WORK IN PROGRESS: Developing biographies of "contemporary women who've had a profound impact on our culture."

SIDELIGHTS: Bosworth told *CA:* "I've been most influenced by Flannery O'Connor's magnificent essays on writing, *Mystery and Manners.* I keep rereading Colette and Flaubert and am increasingly interested in Proust. The photographs of Diane Arbus inspire me as does Jacques Henri Lartique's record of one man who photographed and wrote about life for the love of it, *Diary of a Century.*

"I was inspired to write a biography of Montgomery Clift because I wanted to discover how he became (along with Marlon Brando and James Dean) one of the definitive actors of the fifties. I also wanted to explore the inner life and tragic strivings of a man who remained an enigma to even his closest friends."

AVOCATIONAL INTERESTS: Movies, biking, cooking, traveling, "getting the E.R.A. passed and raising money for public libraries."

BIOGRAPHICAL/CRITICAL SOURCES: New York Times, February 23, 1978; *New York Times Book Review,* March 5, 1978.

* * *

BOURNE, Peter
See JEFFRIES, Graham Montague

BOWER, Donald E(dward) 1920-
(Don Tower)

PERSONAL: Born July 19, 1920, in Lockport, N.Y.; son of John Jacob (a contractor) and Edith (Leonard) Bower; divorced; children: Jon C. Education: University of Nebraska, B.A., 1942. Politics: Independent. Home: 15087 East Radcliff Dr., Aurora, Colo. 80014. Office: National Writers Club, 450 South Havana, Aurora, Colo. 80012.

CAREER: D. E. Bower & Co., Inc. (publishing company), Denver, Colo., president, 1947-64; publisher of syndicated promotional material for wholesalers, 1964-66; Colorado, Denver, executive editor, 1966-70; American West Publishing Co., Palo Alto, Calif., vice-president and editor-in-chief, 1970-74; National Writers Club, Denver, director, 1974—. Publisher of Arapahoe Tribune, Littleton, Colo., 1947-64.

MEMBER: Authors Guild, American Society of Authors and Journalists, Western Writers of America, Colorado Authors League (president, 1975-76), Denver Westerners (member of board of directors, 1975—), Denver Press Club, Sigma Delta Chi (local president, 1941-42). Awards, honors: Top Hand Award from Colorado Authors League, 1969, for article "The Indian Giver," and 1976, for Fred Rosenstock: A Legend in Books and Art.

WRITINGS: Roaming the American West, Stackpole, 1970; Ghost Towns and Back Roads, Stackpole, 1972; Fred Rosenstock: A Legend in Books and Art, Northland Press, 1976. Author of detective novels under pseudonym Don Tower, published by United Graphics.

Editor; all published by American West: Edge of a Continent, 1971; Living Water, 1971; Steinbeck Country, 1972; (and author of introduction) The Magnificent Rockies, 1973; The Mighty Sierra, 1972; Living Earth, 1973; The Great Southwest, 1973; The Great Northwest, 1973.

Contributor of more than one hundred articles to magazines. Editor of American West, 1970-74.

WORK IN PROGRESS: A novel about Alexander Barclay.

SIDELIGHTS: Bower told CA: "I think the reason I kept coming back to free-lancing was that I needed the freedom and independence that a writer enjoys. Writing is, as is often said, the loneliest profession in the world, but I don't think it has the pressures that are an integral part of being an editor. It is tougher to make a living as a writer, but the sense of accomplishment is greater.

"I'm enough of an egotist to want the credit for what I do, and many times you, as an editor, practically rewrite an entire book and your name isn't even mentioned. That bothers me. I'm convinced there are some writers who are really lousy, and their style stinks, yet they receive the accolades that the editor deserves.

"What I have now is the best of all possible worlds. As the director of a writers club, I'm still involved in working with writers, something I enjoyed as an editor, and yet I don't have the spectre of the Scrooge-like publisher constantly over my shoulder."

BIOGRAPHICAL/CRITICAL SOURCES: Authorship, January, 1975.

* * *

BOWLES, Norma L(ouise)

PERSONAL: Born in Holland, Mich.; daughter of August H. (an industrialist) and Louise (a corporate director; maiden name, Kolla) Landwehr; married John Bowles (a sales consultant), October 6, 1950; children: Luisa, Kelly, John Hargrove, Norma. Education: Bryn Mawr College, A.B. (cum laude), 1942. Religion: Christian. Home: 401 Robert Lane, Beverly Hills, Calif. 90210. Office: Psi Search, 310 North San Vicente Blvd., Suite 325, Los Angeles, Calif. 90048.

CAREER: Kolla-Landwehr Foundation, Holland, Mich., founder and member of board of trustees, 1946—. Instructor for Pan American Airways, 1942-44; English teacher at a high school in Los Angeles, Calif., 1945-53. Community relations chairman of Los Angeles Women's Job Corps Center, 1965—; member of advisory committee of World Service Council, 1966—. Member of national finance committee of Young Women's Christian Association, 1966-71; member of national executive board of Achievement Rewards for College Scientists, 1970-71 (also past president; founder of local chapter, 1976). Trustee of University of California religious conference, 1960-67; trustee and vice-president of Westlake School, 1965-68.

MEMBER: American Association of Museums, Smithsonian Associates, Assistance League of Southern California, Muses of the Museum of Science and Industry, Los Angeles Chamber of Commerce (Women's Division), Interfaith Council, Friends of the Los Angeles Young Women's Christian Association (founder; president, 1968-73), Los Angeles Country Club, Salon Francais, Union Lorraine, Kildare Belvois Hunt Club (Ireland). Awards, honors: Eisenhower Gold Medal, 1960; commendation from Parapsychological Association, 1977.

WRITINGS: (With Fran Hynds and Joan Maxwell) Psi Search, Harper, 1978.

SIDELIGHTS: Norma Bowles comments: "I have always been in pioneering, educative work. This has led me to do three exhibits for the science and industry museum, on the concerns of women, research in psychic phenomena, and values awareness. Consortia, symposia, and collaborations on hard-to-convey issues particularly pique my interests. The possibility of my helping people to use more fully their unique capacities as human beings seems to be a core challenge in much that I do. I have been privileged to travel a good bit and have a wide circle of friends and acquaintances across the United States and abroad—especially in western Europe. Making contacts and ideas come together in effective and original configurations, I would suggest, is my forte."

* * *

BOWSKILL, Derek 1928-

PERSONAL: Born July 19, 1928, in Scunthorpe, England; son of Harold Fish (an engineer) and Marion (Sylvesto) Bowskill; married Jill Edwards (marriage ended); married Mary Harrison (marriage ended); children: Sara Jane Bowskill Brown. Education: Attended University of Sheffield, 1948-49, Birmingham College of St. Peter, 1950-52, and Rose Broford College of Speech and Drama, 1952-53. Politics: "Humanitarian Individualist." Religion: Atheist. Agent: Tessa Sayle, 11 Jubilee Pl., London SW3 3TE, England.

CAREER: Worked as county drama adviser in Devonshire, England, 1954-67; University of Sussex, Brighton, England, head of department of drama, film, and television, 1967-69; writer, 1969—. Media adviser to organizations and schools. Military service: British Army, 1946-48.

WRITINGS: Acting and Stagecraft Made Simple, W. H.

Allen, 1973, published as *Acting: An Introduction*, Prentice-Hall, 1977; *Person to Person: A Survey of the Intimate Personal Confrontation Business*, Allen & Unwin, 1973; *All the Lonely People*, Bobbs-Merrill, 1973; *Drama and the Teacher*, Pitman, 1974; *Swingers and Swappers*, W. H. Allen, 1975; *Photography Made Simple*, W. H. Allen, 1975; *All About Theatre*, W. H. Allen, 1975; (with Anthea Linacre) *The Male Menopause*, Muller, 1976, Brook House, 1977; *Getting On ... And Getting Off*, Harwood-Smith, 1976; *Circus, Fairground, Zoo*, J. M. Dent, 1976; *All About Cinema*, W. H. Allen, 1976; *People Need People*, Wildwood House, 1977; (with Anthea Linacre) *Men: The Sensitive Sex*, Muller, 1977. Also author of *Six Short Plays*, Longman, and *Drama in Action*, Hutchinson Educational.

Plays; all first produced in London, England: "Action" (one-act), 1969; "Re-Action" (one-act), 1969; "Gambit" (one-act), 1969; "Children of the Sun" (one-act), 1969; "Masks and Faces" (three-act), 1969; "Everybody Needs a Little Warmth" (one-act), 1969; "Legends of the Seasons" (two-act), 1969; "Gambetto" (one-act), 1970; "Gambado; or, What Shall We Do to Caroline Fairweather?" (five-act), 1970; "Woman, Angel of . . .???" (three-act), 1970.

Also author of produced plays, published by Kenyon-Deane: *Gilgamesh* (one-act), *Seaventures* (one-act), *Powers of the Earth* (one-act), and *Maker of Love* (five-act); and produced plays, published by Performance Publishing: *Lady Seeks Position* (one-act), *The Trojan War* (three-act), *Home Is* (one-act), *A Hard Sell* (one-act), *The Long Home* (one-act), *Nothing in the Telling* (one-act), and *The Third Age* (one-act).

Contributor of articles and poems to magazines.

WORK IN PROGRESS: Bowskill's Britain and *The D.I.Y. Mind Book*.

SIDELIGHTS: Bowskill writes: "In almost all my works I hope to convince someone that there is no need for him to feel inadequate, obliged, inferior, or generally BAD—as my parents instructed me to feel from my earliest memories. It has taken me half a century to understand that they were wrong."

*   *   *

BOYNTON, Searles Roland 1926-

PERSONAL: Born February 9, 1926, in Ukiah, Calif.; son of Roland Voltaire (an electrician) and Minnie (Maze) Boynton; married Marjorie Chase, August 6, 1949; children: Paige, Kevin Chase, Tambi. *Education:* Attended University of Texas, 1943-45; University of the Pacific, D.D.S., 1949. *Religion:* Presbyterian. *Home:* 711 Willow Ave., Ukiah, Calif. 95482. *Office:* 724 South Dora, Ukiah, Calif. 95482.

CAREER: Pedodontist in Ukiah, Calif., 1952—. Chairperson of Ukiah Art Commission. Elder of Presbyterian Church. *Military service:* U.S. Navy, 1943-50; became lieutenant junior grade. *Member:* Ukiah Oratorial Society (past president), Rotary (member of board of directors; vice-president). *Awards, honors:* Certificate of commendation from U.S. Congress, 1977.

WRITINGS: "The Painter Lady": A Biography of Grace Carpenter Hudson, Interface California Corp., 1978.

WORK IN PROGRESS: The Painter Lady's Sketch Book.

SIDELIGHTS: Boynton wrote to *CA:* "'One book does not an author make,' however, my family and friends are jokingly referring to me as S. Roland Boynton, the cele-brated author. My vocation is a pedodontist (children's dentist) and other than a few letters home, a term paper or two and editing the University of the Pacific dental college annual, I have written very little.

"*The Painter Lady* was accomplished after three and a half years of diligent research and an equal number of years of almost blood, sweat and tears in transcribing it into a story that would give the reader both an intellectually pleasing experience but also fulfill the demands of the public for a beautifully illustrated art book as well.

"It has added a new and interesting perspective to my life during that period between birth and death—know as middle age and perhaps will give me the joy of being remembered for something other than novacaine and amalgam.

"Most importantly, however, it has awakened Ukiah, a little community in the coastal range of California, to an awareness of its heritage as to the residence of the Vermeer of the West. Grace Hudson's estate was purchased by the city fathers of Ukiah and a museum complex is being planned that we hope will become the cultural oasis between San Francisco and Seattle."

*   *   *

BRACKETT, Leigh (Douglass) 1915-1978

December 7, 1915—March 18, 1978; American author and screenwriter. Brackett is best known for her science fiction, including *Alpha Centauri or Die!* and *The Sword of Rhiannon*. Brackett also worked with William Faulkner on the screenplay for "The Big Sleep" and wrote both "Star Wars II" and "The Long Goodbye." She died in Hollywood, Calif. Obituaries and other sources: *Foremost Women in Communications*, Bowker, 1970; *Films in Review*, August, 1976; *The Writers Directory, 1976-78*, St. Martin's, 1976; *New York Times*, March 25, 1978; *AB Bookman's Weekly*, May 8, 1978. (See index for *CA* sketch)

*   *   *

BRADFORD, M(elvin) E(ustace) 1934-

PERSONAL: Born May 8, 1934, in Fort Worth, Tex.; son of E. A. (a rancher) and Ruby (Hunter) Bradford; married Marie Jones, 1955; children: Douglas. *Education:* University of Oklahoma, B.A., 1955, M.A., 1956; Vanderbilt University, Ph.D., 1968. *Politics:* Independent. *Religion:* Baptist. *Home:* 1106 South Edwards Court, Irving, Tex. 75062. *Office:* Department of English, University of Dallas, Irving, Tex. 75062.

CAREER: U.S. Naval Academy, Annapolis, Md., instructor in English and history, 1957-59; Vanderbilt University, Nashville, Tenn., instructor in English, 1959-62; Hardin-Simmons University, Abilene, Tex., 1962-64, began as assistant professor, became associate professor of English and chairman of department; Northwestern State College, Natchitoches, La., assistant professor of English, 1964-67; University of Dallas, Irving, Tex., associate professor of English, 1967—, chairman of department, 1970-73. Member of state Democratic Committee, 1972-74. *Military service:* U.S. Naval Reserve, active duty, 1956-59; became lieutenant junior grade.

MEMBER: Modern Language Association of America, American Political Science Association, South Central Modern Language Association, Southwestern American Literature Association (president, 1975-77), Philadelphia Society, Sons of Confederate Veterans. *Awards, honors:* National Endowment for the Humanities fellow, summer,

1970, senior fellow, spring, 1977; Texas Education Association fellow, summer, 1976.

WRITINGS: (Editor and author of preface, with George Core) Richard Weaver, *The Southern Tradition at Bay,* Arlington House, 1968; *Rumors of Mortality: An Introduction to Allen Tate,* Argus Academic Press, 1969; (editor) *The Form Discovered: Essays on the Achievement of Andrew Lytle,* University & College Press of Mississippi, 1973; (editor and author of introduction) John Taylor, *Arator,* Liberty Press, 1977; *A Better Guide Than Reason: Readings in the American Revolution,* Sherwood Sugden, 1978. Contributor to literary journals, including *Southern Review, Mississippi Quarterly,* and *National Review.* Member of editorial board of *Modern Age, Occasional Review,* and *Southwestern American Literature.*

WORK IN PROGRESS: A book on Faulkner's short fiction; a book on Abraham Lincoln, with Thomas Landess.

SIDELIGHTS: Bradford writes briefly: "My main interests are American literature, history, political philosophy, and the publishing business, especially limited editions. The particular emphasis of my work is on the continuity of Anglo-American culture and on the importance of rhetoric to the study of politics and literature. My involvement with publications is through the Society for the Study of Traditional Culture which operates out of Dallas. Much of my literary criticism concerns the literature of the American South."

* * *

BRADFORD, Robert W(hitmore)   1918-

PERSONAL: Born October 14, 1918, in Melrose, Mass.; son of John W. and Mildred (Lockwood) Bradford; married Mary Jane Claflin (a college lecturer), 1944; children: three. *Education:* Dartmouth College, A.B., 1943; Columbia University, A.M., 1948; Syracuse University, Ph.D., 1957. *Residence:* Easton, Pa. *Office:* Department of English, Lafayette College, Easton, Pa. 18042.

CAREER: Syracuse University, Syracuse, N.Y., instructor in English, 1948-53; Lafayette College, Easton, Pa., instructor, 1953-57, assistant professor, 1957-63, associate professor of English, 1963—. *Member:* Modern Language Association of America, College English Association, American Association of University Professors, Danforth Associates.

WRITINGS: (With W. W. Watt) *An E. B. White Reader,* Harper, 1966.

* * *

BRAMMER, William   1930(?)-1978

1930(?)—February 11, 1978; American political press aide and author. He was press aide to Senator Lyndon B. Johnson. Brammer's study of Texas and national politics in the 1950's, *The Gay Place,* became a best-seller and won for him the Houghton-Mifflin literary fellowship award. Brammer died in Austin, Tex. Obituaries and other sources: *Washington Post,* February 14, 1978.

* * *

BRAND, Christianna
See LEWIS, Mary (Christianna Milne)

* * *

BRANDON, William   1914-

PERSONAL: Born September 21, 1914, in Kokomo, Ind.; son of William Edward (an engineer) and Mabel Olivia (Cal-

vert) Brandon; married Elizabeth Francis, August 2, 1936 (divorced, 1958); children: Mary Jane (Mrs. Martin Dodge). *Education:* Attended public schools in New Mexico and Indiana. *Residence:* St. Jeannet, France. *Agent:* Harold Ober Associates, Inc., 40 East 49th St., New York, N.Y. 10017.

CAREER: Writer. Visiting professor at University of Massachusetts, 1966-67, California State University, Los Angeles and Long Beach, 1970-71, and Long Beach only, 1974-75. *Military service:* U.S. Army Air Forces; became sergeant.

WRITINGS: The Dangerous Dead, Dodd, 1943; *The Men and the Mountain,* Morrow, 1955; *The American Heritage Book of Indians,* introduction by John F. Kennedy, American Heritage Press, 1961; *The Magic World,* Morrow, 1971; *The Last Americans,* McGraw, 1971.

Translator of works from the French, Latin, and Greek. Author of two screenplays. Work anthologized in more than a dozen collections. Contributor of several hundred stories to magazines in the United States and abroad.

WORK IN PROGRESS: The Life and White Horse of Indian Joe, a novel; a history of the Santa Fe Trail; research for "a history of liberty."

SIDELIGHTS: Brandon comments: "I like to write. I enjoy immensely the process of thinking and writing to construct what it seems to me the page must say. I'm less interested in the 'success' of the work, an objective particularly harmful, I think, to American writers."

BIOGRAPHICAL/CRITICAL SOURCES: American Historical Review, June, 1975.

* * *

BRECHT, Arnold   1884-1977

PERSONAL: Born January 26, 1884, in Luebeck, Germany; came to United States, 1933, naturalized citizen; married wife, Clara (deceased). *Education:* Educated in Germany. *Residence:* New York, N.Y.

CAREER: Served as judge and counselor in German ministry of justice before World War I; held posts in ministries of interior and finance during Weimar Republic; representative from Prussia in German Reichsrat until 1933; New School for Social Research, New York, N.Y., faculty member of University in Exile and professor of political science, international law, and public finance, 1933-54; writer. Visiting professor at Yale University, Harvard University, Princeton University, Barnard College, and Wellesley College. Served with U.S. military government in Germany, 1950. *Wartime service:* Supervised U.S. Army area-training program for Germany during World War II.

WRITINGS: Die Geshaeftsordnung der reichsministerien, ihre staatsrechtliche und geschaeftstechnische bedeutung, zugleich ein lehrbuch der bueroreform, Heymann, 1927; (with Theodor Kutzer) *Neuordnung der dezentralisation im Deutschen Reich,* Deutscher kommunal-verlag, 1928; (with Comstock Glaser) *The Art and Technique of Administration in German Ministries,* Harvard University Press, 1940, reprinted, Greenwood Press, 1971; *Prelude to Silence: The End of the German Republic,* Oxford University Press, 1944; *Federalism and Regionalism in Germany: The Division of Prussia,* Oxford University Press, 1945, reprinted, Russell, 1971.

The Political Philosophy of Arnold Brecht (essays), edited by Morris D. Forkosch, Exposition Press, 1954; *Wiedervereinigung,* Nymphenburger Verlagshandlung, 1957; *Political*

Theory: The Foundations of Twentieth-Century Political Thought, Princeton University Press, 1959; *Lebenserinnerungen,* Deutsche Verlagsanstalt, Volume I: *Aus naechster Naehe,* 1966, Volume II: *Mit der Kraft des Geistes,* 1967, abridged translation by the author of both volumes published as *The Political Education of Arnold Brecht: An Autobiography, 1884-1970,* Princeton University Press, 1970.

WORK IN PROGRESS: Another book.

SIDELIGHTS: It was Arnold Brecht, representative of Prussia in the Reichsrat, who responded to Adolph Hitler's first address as Chancellor to the German parliament in 1933. Brecht's reminder to Hitler of his oath "to abide by the Constitution and the law of the land" provoked Hitler to walk out of the legislative chambers and to dismiss Brecht from his position several days later. Brecht emigrated to the United States shortly thereafter and joined the faculty of the New School for Social Research. In a review of Brecht's autobiography, which records his experiences as an "inside" government official during the Weimar Republic and the rise of Hitler, *Virginia Quarterly Review* noted, "A sensitive writer, Brecht has transferred his political acumen to the printed page, and the result is an important, delightful memoir."

BIOGRAPHICAL/CRITICAL SOURCES: Virginia Quarterly Review, spring, 1971. Obituaries: *New York Times,* September 15, 1977; *Time,* September 26, 1977; *AB Bookman's Weekly,* January 30, 1978.*

(Died September 11, 1977, in Eutin, West Germany)

*   *   *

BREEN, (Joseph) John 1942-

PERSONAL: Born July 20, 1942, in Chicago, Ill.; son of Daniel John (a bank examiner) and Grace (a secretary; maiden name, Weiler) Breen; married Jean Keyser (a guidance counselor), June 12, 1965; children: Daniel George, Thomas John. *Education:* University of Illinois, B.A., 1964, M.A., 1965. *Home:* 20 Coburn Rd., Manchester, Conn. 06040. *Office:* Department of Journalism, U-129, University of Connecticut, Storrs, Conn. 06268.

CAREER: Champaign-Urbana Courier, Champaign-Urbana, Ill., city hall reporter, 1964-65; *Knickerbocker News,* Albany, N.Y., general assignment reporter, 1965-66, assistant editor of editorial page, 1966-68; University of Connecticut, Storrs, assistant professor, 1968-72, associate professor of journalism, 1972—. Member of Connecticut State Board of Education Joint Teacher Education Advisory Committee. *Member:* Lebanon Historical Society (member of board of directors, 1970-72), Sigma Delta Chi (member of state board of directors, 1974-76).

WRITINGS: (With Evan Hill) *A Beginner's Guide to Writing (and Thinking),* University of Connecticut Press, 1974, revised edition, 1975; (with Hill) *Reporting and Writing the News,* Little, Brown, 1977.

Work anthologized in *Our Troubled Press,* edited by Alfred Balk, Little, Brown, 1971. Contributor to professional journals and other magazines, including *Yankee* and *Reader's Digest,* and newspapers.

WORK IN PROGRESS: A nonfiction book of Chicago's neighborhoods.

SIDELIGHTS: Breen writes: "My major interest has always been politics—political extremism.

"I covered the John Birch Society as a reporter in Champaign, Ill. in the early 1960's, and wrote my master's thesis on right-wing extremism. I probably got the impetus from a classics professor at University of Illinois, Revilo P. Oliver, who was one of the founders of the Birch Society. He would give public lectures and talk about my newspaper's editor, Robert Sink, in ways that just didn't make sense. I became interested in how people could say, with such conviction, all kinds of really incredible things.

"In Albany, I did a five-part series on the local right-wingers who were threatening violence against local Parent-Teacher Association members who had planned to bring a 'Russian' speaker to the local schools to lecture on the virtues of Communism. The 'Russian' was an Albany resident who was, of course, not a Russian, or a Communist, at all. He was a salesman who played a part in the program and agreed to be 'Dr. Petrokof,' the noted Communist. He would talk about Communism and then have to defend the system under intense questioning from members of the audience, who would expose the fallacies in his system. Local zealots telephoned threats to the school; the series brought me many late-night obscene and threatening phone calls from people who still couldn't believe the whole thing was just supposed to be a lesson in civics.

"From then on, the extremism changed to the left—the campus unrest of the late sixties and early seventies. The people were younger, and the politics to the left, but the extremism was still there; people saying and doing things that made absolutely no sense.

"I have been a politician and have worked for politicians, most of whom are hard-working, hopeful people who admit, in the early hours of the morning, that they have no magic answers. It's the people who have the magic answers that have always fascinated me."

*   *   *

BRETT, Peter David 1943-

PERSONAL: Born April 23, 1943, in Jackson, Mich.; son of Benjamin T. (an eye doctor) and Fanchon (Hillsburgh) Brett. *Education:* Wayne State University, B.S., 1965; further study at University of Michigan, 1969-70. *Home:* 23 Porteous, Fairfax, Calif. 94930. *Office address:* P.O. Box 697, Ross, Calif. 94957.

CAREER: University of Michigan, Ann Arbor, laboratory technologist at Medical Center, 1968-71; writer, 1972—. Writer-in-residence at University of Colorado, 1969; consultant in technical writing. *Member:* Poets and Writers, Artists, Writers, Editors (vice-president). *Awards, honors:* Major Hopwood Award from University of Michigan, 1970, for the novel "Crossing Paradise Number Four."

WRITINGS: Ghost Rhythms (poems), Blue Cloud Quarterly, 1976; *Borrowing the Sky* (poems), Contact II, 1978. Also author of "Crossing Paradise Number Four," 1970. Feature writer for *Circus Maximus,* 1977. Contributor of more than seventy-five poems and stories to magazines, including *Dakotah Territory, Aldebaran Review, California Quarterly,* and *Sou'wester.* Editor of *Journal of Radiology,* 1970.

WORK IN PROGRESS: Sidewinder, poems and stories.

SIDELIGHTS: Brett told *CA:* "The direction my own writing has taken over the last ten-year-period is in the direction of seeing the carry-over between prose and poetry writing: very often we see today 'poetic' elements in the short story and in the novel (for example, in stream of consciousness writing), while on the other hand we see an increasingly proselike poem being written. My own recent work has been an exploration of ways to combine the traditional intensity we associate with short poems, with the continuity we find in longer prose pieces. My formal training at the university level was in the sciences. After several years experience in laboratory research, I found I wanted to figure out a way to combine my scientific training with writing—hence my work in the field of radiology—as editor, consultant, and writer. That interest is still very much intact, and I work for several organizations, for example the Sierra Club, the School of Holography in San Francisco, and Harcourt, Brace, Jovanovich Publishing Company—as a consultant.''

AVOCATIONAL INTERESTS: Mountain climbing, hiking, gardening.

*   *   *

BREWER, Jeutonne 1939-

PERSONAL: Born May 5, 1939, in Enid, Okla.; daughter of William Louis (a barber) and Ila (a hairdresser; maiden name, Sturgeon) Patten; married Chris Edward Brewer (an engineer), June 30, 1962. *Education:* Harding College, B.A., 1960; University of North Carolina, M.A., 1971, Ph.D., 1974. *Home address:* Route 2, Box 137, Jamestown, N.C. 27282. *Office:* Department of English, University of North Carolina, Greensboro, N.C. 27412.

CAREER: Junior high school English teacher in Dover, N.J., 1960-62; Warner-Chilcott Pharmaceutical Co., Morris Plains, N.J., control analysis clerk in advertising, 1962-63; junior high school English teacher in Bloomfield, N.J., 1963-64; elementary school teacher at American dependents' school in Kerpen, Germany, 1966-67; North Carolina Agricultural & Technical State University, Greensboro, workshop director of Education Professions Development Act institute, 1970-72; Greensboro College, Greensboro, N.C., instructor in English, 1972-73; University of North Carolina, Greensboro, instructor, 1973-75, assistant professor of English, 1975—. Instructor at Berlitz School in Dueren, Germany, 1966-67.

MEMBER: Linguistic Society of America, Modern Language Association of America, American Dialect Society, American Name Society, Linguistic Association of the United States, Southeastern Conference on Linguistics (member of executive committee, 1975-78). *Awards, honors:* Ford Foundation grant, 1972-73; North Carolina Humanities Committee grant, 1976.

WRITINGS: Dialect Clash in America: Issues and Answers, Scarecrow, 1977; (contributor) David L. Shores and Carole P. Hines, editors, *Papers in Language Variation,* University of Alabama Press, 1977. Contributor of articles and reviews to speech, language, and sociology journals.

WORK IN PROGRESS: A bibliography of the works of Anthony Burgess, 1956-1976; continuing research on narratives by ex-slaves, collected by Federal Writers Project.

SIDELIGHTS: Jeutonne Brewer writes that her specific interest is sociolinguistics. She has studied German, Arabic, Swahili, and Shona. Brewer comments: ''My linguistic patchwork-quilt background in Oklahoma, Texas, Arkansas, New Jersey, North Carolina, and Germany spurred my interest in regional and social dialects. I am often involved in conducting workshops for teachers; these workshops deal with the application of linguistics to such areas as language teaching, reading, and composition. My related interests include reading literature, especially writings which include dialects, and computers in the humanities.

''Traveling is a major source of enjoyment. I like to travel to other countries and learn about other cultures and languages. Being an 'outsider' in a new environment is a good way to maintain a reasonable and balanced view of cultural and linguistic differences.''

AVOCATIONAL INTERESTS: The out-of-doors, camping, fishing.

*   *   *

BRINEGAR, David F(ranklin) 1910-

PERSONAL: Born September 2, 1910, in Rulo, Neb.; son of Thomas Paine (a movingman) and Rebecca Way (a teacher; maiden name, Marsh) Brinegar; married Lorette Cooper, October 2, 1937 (deceased); children: Becky. *Education:* Attended University of Arizona, 1927-30, and Phoenix College, 1941. *Politics:* Democrat. *Religion:* Presbyterian. *Home:* 6532 East Speedway Blvd., Tucson, Ariz. 85710.

CAREER/WRITINGS: Arizona Daily Star, Tuscon, Ariz., reporter, sports editor, and assistant news editor, 1926-35; *Arizona Republic,* Phoenix, Ariz., capitol correspondent, 1935-42; *Arizona Times,* Phoenix, managing editor, capitol correspondent and editorial page columnist, 1946-48; *Arizona Soil Conservationist,* Phoenix, editor and publisher, 1949-56; *Arizona Daily Star,* associate editor, 1956-61, executive editor, 1961-74. Notable assignments include coverage of press conferences with Franklin D. Roosevelt, 1941, and Richard Nixon, 1970, and travel articles on Mexico and Japan. Contributor of articles to *Saturday Review* and other periodicals. Author of serialized novel, ''Beth Carter, WAAC.'' Consultant to Star Publishing Co. *Military service:* U.S. Army, 1942-46; became captain. *Awards, honors:* First place award in national editorial writing contest, 1969.

SIDELIGHTS: Brinegar writes: ''I entered newspaper work by accident and remained because of economic necessity. I wanted first to be a novelist, but did not have enough talent to live that way. Employers evidently felt I had a knack for newspaper work, and for two and a half years I was in charge of the *Arizona Daily Star* due to an antitrust action and the illness of the editor and publisher, W. R. Mathews, who signed the paper over to me.

''My observation is that many people fall into situations by chance and do well by them. It always has been my view that any job deserves one's best. My personal philosophies follow closely those of St. Augustine, especially in that I believe greatly in predetermination and see free will largely as the illusion that makes things work.''

*   *   *

BRISBANE, Robert Hughes 1913-

PERSONAL: Born March 21, 1913, in Jacksonville, Fla.; married wife, Kathryn; children: Phillipa. *Education:* St. John's University, B.S., 1939; Harvard University, Ph.D., 1949. *Home:* 823 Magna Carta Dr., Atlanta, Ga. 30318. *Office:* Department of Political Science, Morehouse College, 223 Chestnut St., Atlanta, Ga. 30314.

CAREER: Morehouse College, Atlanta, Ga., professor of political science, 1948—, chairman of department, 1965—. Member of editorial staff, *Encyclopaedia Britannica. Member:* American Association of University Professors, Organization of American Historians, American Political Science Association, Association for the Study of Negro Life and History, Southern Political Science Association, Alpha Phi Alpha. *Awards, honors:* Merritt travel grant, 1955; Non-Western Studies grant for study in Africa, 1963.

WRITINGS: The Black Vanguard: Origins of the Negro Social Revolution, 1900-1960, Judson Press, 1970; *Black Activism: Racial Revolution in the United States, 1954-1970,* Judson Press, 1974. Contributor of articles to journals and periodicals.

SIDELIGHTS: Saunders Redding reviewed *The Black Vanguard* for the *New York Times Book Review:* "The author brings the scholarly equipment of a political scientist and the penetrating insights of a social historian to bear upon the underlying concerns and aspirations of those American blacks who have made black nationalism an ideology and a way (or should it be 'ways'?) of life to conjure with." *New Yorker* said the book is "a sensible, readable informative account of efforts by individuals and organizations to un-do the dreadful post-Reconstruction arrangements and thus allow Negro Americans, North and South, the equal opportunities that the Constitution pledges."

BIOGRAPHICAL/CRITICAL SOURCES: New York Times Book Review, August 16, 1970; *New Yorker,* November 21, 1970; *American Historical Review,* June, 1971; *Black World,* January, 1975.*

*   *   *

BRITTAIN, William 1930-
(James Knox)

PERSONAL: Born December 16, 1930, in Rochester, N.Y., son of Knox (a medical doctor) and Dorothy (a nurse; maiden name, Sunderlin) Brittain; married Virginia Connorton (a teacher), February 6, 1954; children: James, Susan. *Education:* Attended Colgate University, 1948-50; New York State University at Brockport, B.S., 1952; Hofstra University, M.S., 1958. *Home:* 395 South Long Beach Ave., Freeport, N.Y. 11520.

CAREER: English teacher in LeRoy, N.Y., 1952-54; elementary teacher in Lawrence, N.Y., 1954-60; Lawrence Junior High School, Lawrence, remedial reading teacher, 1960—. Representative, Lawrence Teachers Association. *Member:* Mystery Writers of America.

WRITINGS: Survival Outdoors, Monarch, 1977; *All The Money in the World,* Harper, 1979. Contributor of stories to *Ellery Queen's Mystery Magazine* and *Alfred Hitchcock's Mystery Magazine,* sometimes under pseudonym James Knox.

WORK IN PROGRESS: Runyon's Onions, a mystery involving students with learning disabilities; more short stories of mystery and detection.

SIDELIGHTS: Brittain told *CA:* "It's hard to think of myself as a 'Contemporary Author'. Basically I'm a schoolteacher. Writing is a hobby. I enjoy this arrangement because it gives me the luxury of writing only when I want to and of exploring subjects that interest me. If I had to keep pounding the typewriter day after day, just to keep the bill collectors from my door, I'd be a nervous wreck in a month. The fact that the students in my classes provide the basis for many of my stories is an added bonus.

"How did I get started writing? Along with hundreds of other mystery writers, I had the guidance of Frederic Dannay, the editor of *Ellery Queen's Mystery Magazine.* I'll always be grateful for the time he spent going over those first stories with me. His help and encouragement were invaluable.

"I'm also blessed with a wife who has the patience of Job, as well as razor-sharp critical faculties. When she says a story's good, it sells. When she turns thumbs down, it comes rocketing back by return mail."

Brittain patterns his stories after the styles of many of his favorite authors, including John Dickson Carr, Ellery Queen, Agatha Christie, and Isaac Asimov. His series detective character, Mr. Strang, is a high school science teacher largely patterned after one of his former English literature teachers at Brockport, James Edmunds.

*   *   *

BRO, Margueritte (Harmon) 1894-1977

PERSONAL: Born August 5, 1894, in David City, Neb.; daughter of Andrew Davison (a preacher) and Alice (Gadd) Harmon; married Albin Carl Bro (a teaching missionary), May, 1918; children: Harmon, Kenneth, Alice, Andrew. *Education:* Cotner College, B.A., 1917; further study at Butler University, University of Chicago, and University of Nanking.

CAREER: Has worked as a teacher, pastor's assistant, editor for *Harper's,* book reviewer, and ghost writer; author.

WRITINGS—Juvenile: Why Church? (missionary stories; illustrated by Ursula H. Bostwick), Friendship Press, 1947; *Sarah* (novel), Doubleday, 1949; *Su-mei's Golden Year* (illustrated by Kurt Wiese), Doubleday, 1950; *Stub: A College Romance,* Doubleday, 1952; *Indonesia: Land of Challenge,* Harper, 1954; *Three, and Domingo* (illustrated by Leonard Weisgard), Doubleday, 1953; *The Animal Friends of Peng-U* (illustrated by Seong Moy), Doubleday, 1965; *How the Mouse Deer Became King* (illustrated by Joseph Low), Doubleday, 1966.

Other: *Al's Technique* (one-act farce), Eldridge Entertainment House, 1931; (with Frank H. O'Hara) *A Handbook of Drama,* Willett, 1938, revised and enlarged edition published as *Invitation to the Theater,* Harper, 1951; *Urban Scene,* Friendship Press, 1938; *When Children Ask,* Willett, 1940, revised edition, Harper, 1956; *Thursday at Ten,* Willett, 1942; *Every Day a Prayer* (devotional exercises), Willett, 1943; *Let's Talk about You,* Doubleday, 1945; *More Than We Are* (prayer), Harper, 1948, revised and enlarged edition, 1965; (with Harrie V. Rhodes) *In the One Spirit: The Autobiography of Harrie Vernette Rhodes,* Harper, 1951; (with Arthur A. Ford) *Nothing So Strange: Autobiography,* Harper, 1958; 1971; (with Myrtle R. Walgreen) *Never a Dull Day: An Autobiography by Myrtle R. Walgreen,* Regnery, 1963; *Today Makes a Difference! An Everyday Book of Prayer,* T. Nelson, 1970; *The Book You Always Meant to Read: The Old Testament,* Doubleday, 1974.

SIDELIGHTS: One of Bro's earliest writings is a collaborative effort with Frank H. O'Hara called *A Handbook of Drama.* A *Christian Century* reviewer wrote: "It is perhaps unfair to say at the outset that this is a highly entertaining volume. It was written to give instruction, not amusement. But diverting and delightful it certainly is, for no other reason than that Mr. O'Hara and Mrs. Bro are just naturally that way. They do not, therefore, sacrifice substance for charm. This is a practical handbook for students and teachers of drama, prepared by a very experienced teacher and director and a successful playwright."

More Than We Are, a series of inspirational essays on prayer, was reviewed by *Christian Century:* "Among books telling why and how to pray, this deserves a place of preeminence. Its excellence lies partly in its simplicity and directness, in the fact that its language is completely understandable and colloquial without being odiously intimate or flippant, and in the avoidance of conventionally pietistic phraseology."

Bro's first novel, *Sarah,* led the *New York Times* to declare: "Substantial, richly detailed, this is not only the story of an artist's development. It is also a family story which recreates an era." *Saturday Review of Literature* described it as "a thoughtful book in which a philosophy of life is analyzed by interesting, convincing people."

After living in Indonesia for a few years, Bro compiled *Indonesia: Land of Challenge.* A review appearing in *Pacific Affairs* included: "This is an attractive, personal, and warm-hearted book which contains a great deal more solid information than its apparently carefree mode of presentation indicates at first glance. What might be taken as an artless mixture of anecdote, reminiscence, and serious factual material is in fact presumably an artful device for spreading news of Indonesia to circles which might otherwise not be reached."

Mrs. Bro has lived in China, Indonesia, and Korea, as well as in Mount Carroll, Illinois, when her husband was president of Shimer College.

BIOGRAPHICAL/CRITICAL SOURCES: Christian Century, January 4, 1939, August 4, 1948; *New York Times,* October 16, 1949; *Saturday Review of Literature,* November 12, 1949; *Wilson Library Bulletin,* September, 1952; *Pacific Affairs,* June, 1955.*

(Died February 21, 1977)

*   *   *

BROME, (Herbert) Vincent 1910-

PERSONAL: Born in London, England; son of Nathaniel Gregory and Emily Brome. *Education:* Attended schools in Streatham, England; also privately educated. *Religion:* None. *Home and office:* 45 Great Ormond St., London W.C.1, England.

CAREER: Daily Chronicle, London, England, feature writer, 1930-35; editor of *Menu* (magazine), 1935-39; Ministry of Information, London, journalist, 1942-44; *Medical World,* London, assistant editor, 1944-46; writer, 1946—. Member of British Library Advisory Committee.

WRITINGS: Europe's Free Press: The Underground Newspapers of Occupied Lands Described as Far as the Censor Permits, Feature Books, 1936; *Clement Attlee* (biography), Lincolns, Prager, 1949; *H. G. Wells* (biography), Longmans, Green, 1951, Books for Libraries, 1970; *The Way Back: The Story of Lieutenant Commander Pat O'Leary,* Cassell, 1953, 2nd edition, 1957, Norton, 1958; *Aneurin Bevan* (biography), Longmans, Green, 1953; *Acquaintance With Grief* (novel), Cassell, 1954; *The Last Surrender* (novel), A. Dakers, 1954; *Six Studies in Quarrelling,* Cresset Press, 1958, Greenwood, 1973; *Sometimes at Night,* Cassell, 1959; *Frank Harris* (biography), Cassell, 1959, published as *Frank Harris: The Life and Loves of a Scoundrel,* T. Yoseloff, 1960.

We Have Come a Long Way (nonfiction), Cassell, 1962; *The Problem of Progress,* Cassell, 1963; *Love in Our Time,* Cassell, 1964; *Four Realist Novelists: Arthur Morrison, Edwin Pugh, Richard Whiting, and William Pett Ridge,* Longmans, Green, 1965; *The International Brigades: Spain, 1936-39* (nonfiction), Heinemann, 1965, Morrow, 1966; *The World of Luke Simpson,* Heinemann, 1966; *The Embassy* (novel), Cassell, 1967, reprinted, 1972; *Freud and His Early Circle: The Struggle of Psychoanalysis,* Heinemann, 1967, Morrow, 1968; *The Surgeon,* Cassell, 1967; "Man at Large" (three-act play), first produced in Edinburgh, Scotland at Princess Theatre, 1967; *The Operating*

Theatre (novel), Simon & Schuster, 1968; *The Revolution* (novel), Cassell, 1969.

Confessions of a Writer, Hutchinson, 1970; *The Brain Operators,* Cassell, 1971; *Reverse Your Verdict: A Collection of Private Prosecutions,* H. Hamilton, 1971; *The Ambassador and the Spy* (novel), Crown, 1973; *The Day of Destruction,* Cassell, 1974. Also author of *The Imaginary Crime,* 1969; *London Consequences,* 1972; *The Happy Hostage,* 1975; *Diary of a Revolution,* 1978; and *C. G. Jung: Man and Myth,* 1978. Writer of seventeen television and radio plays. Contributor to British periodicals, including *New Society, Encounter,* and *Spectator,* and to U.S. periodicals, including *Washington Post, New York Review of Books, New York Times,* and *Nation.*

WORK IN PROGRESS: A play, "Take This Thy Victim"; a novel.

SIDELIGHTS: Brome told *CA:* "I suppose I am a non-religious humanist, who regards the reformation of capitalism as just as vital as the European Reformation far back in history." *Avocational interests:* Talking.

*   *   *

BROMLEY, Dudley 1948-

PERSONAL: Born December 9, 1948, in Odessa, Tex.; son of Lee Elmo and Nellie (Brown) Bromley; married Lillian Patricia Comerford, 1969; children: Dylan Lee. *Education:* Attended University of California, Los Angeles, 1967-70. *Home:* 1752½ North Western Ave., Los Angeles, Calif. 90027. *Agent:* Lillia Levering, Box 1447, Hollywood, Calif. 90028. *Office:* 1585 Crossroads of the World #107, Los Angeles, Calif. 90028.

CAREER: Full-time writer. *Member:* Mystery Writers of America, Writers Guild of America.

WRITINGS: Crash Dive, Fearon-Pitman, 1977; *North to Oak Island,* Fearon-Pitman, 1977; *Kidnapped in Space,* Xerox, 1978; *Bad Moon,* Fearon-Pitman, 1978. Also author of story and teleplay of "Arizona Midnight," a segment of "Gunsmoke." Editor of *United States Government,* Bowmar.

WORK IN PROGRESS: Championship Tennis, with Robert Lansdorp, for Harper; "Roads to Glory," a series of six books for Fearon-Pitman.

SIDELIGHTS: Bromley told *CA:* "Because I believe it's important for writers to be entertainers first and artists second, I always try to put as much *fun* into my stories as possible. In other words, I write the kind of stories I most enjoy reading—science fiction, mystery, adventure, etc."

*   *   *

BRONSTEIN, Lynne 1950-

PERSONAL: Born December 30, 1950, in New York, N.Y.; daughter of Harry I. (a civil servant) and Sylvia (Slowes) Bronstein. *Education:* Attended Fordham University, 1968-71. *Home address:* P.O. Box 5018, Sherman Oaks, Calif. 91403.

CAREER: Writer, 1970—. *Member:* Poets and Writers, California Society of Chaparral Poets.

WRITINGS: Astray from Normalcy (poems), Animal Press, 1974; *Roughage* (poems), Animal Press, 1977. Contributor of stories and articles to California newspapers.

WORK IN PROGRESS: A novel about androgyny and love; new poems, including a long work on the Jewish heritage as seen by a child, tentatively titled "Tenement."

SIDELIGHTS: Lynne Bronstein comments: "I am trying to write works that will go at least a fraction of the way toward changing society. I write poetry that is feminist, androgynous, audacious, honest, uncompromising. I want to fight censorship, sexual hypocrisy, sexism, and anti-individualism." *Avocational interests:* Roller skating.

* * *

BROOKS, Charles V. W. 1912-

PERSONAL: Born February 6, 1912, in Palo Alto, Calif.; son of Van Wyck (a writer) and Eleanor (Stimson) Brooks; married Inez Seibert, 1936 (divorced, 1949); married Charlotte Selver (a group leader), 1961; children: Peter. *Education:* Harvard University, A.B., 1932. *Politics:* "Personally detached; theoretically socialist." *Religion:* None. *Home:* Green Gulch Farm, Sausalito, Calif. 94965. *Agent:* Sterling Lord Agency, Inc., 660 Madison Ave., New York, N.Y. 10021.

CAREER: Worked on Works Progress Administration writers' project in Washington, D.C.; employed at a shipyard and as a sheet metal worker and carpenter in San Francisco, Calif.; presently a teacher of sensory awareness.

WRITINGS: Sensory Awareness: The Rediscovery of Experiencing, Viking, 1974.

WORK IN PROGRESS: Continuing research on sensory awareness.

SIDELIGHTS: Brooks remarks: "The motivation for my book was chiefly to set down in words a study—very important to me—that has never been described. A secondary motivation, as in all creative writing, was to distill and verbalize some of my own general life experience." *Avocational interests:* Writing short stories.

* * *

BROOKS, Hunter O(tis) 1929-

PERSONAL: Born September 1, 1929, in Bluefield, W. Va.; son of Lawson (in business) and Winifred (Hunter) Brooks; married Barbara Boudreaux (a registered nurse), September 1, 1954; children: Hunter II, Christopher. *Education:* West Virginia State College, B.A., 1950, M.A., 1954; also attended Carnegie-Mellon University, University of Colorado, and University of Wyoming. *Religion:* Protestant. *Home:* 3421 Wentworth, Houston, Tex. 77004. *Office:* Department of History and Geography, Texas Southern University, Houston, Tex. 77004.

CAREER: Texas Southern University, Houston, instructor, 1954-60, assistant professor of history, 1960—. *Military service:* U.S. Army, 1951-53. *Member:* National Council for the Social Studies, Association for the Study of Afro-American Life and History, Oral History Association, Phi Alpha Theta, Sigma Rho Sigma, Phi Delta Kappa. *Awards, honors:* Carnegie Foundation fellowship, 1966.

WRITINGS: (With George W. Domke) *Man and Civilization,* W. C. Brown, 1963; (with Paula Barker and Margie E. Whatley) *Black Leadership in America,* Austin Writers Group, 1973; *Discovering Black Americans,* D. Armstrong, 1974; *History of Antioch Baptist Church,* privately printed, 1976. Contributor to *Social Education.*

WORK IN PROGRESS: Curriculum materials utilizing Texas slave narratives.

* * *

BROOKS, Nelson Herbert 1902-1978

July 18, 1902—May 8, 1978; American educator and author.

Brooks, an authority on the teaching and testing of students of foreign languages, was associate professor of French at Yale University when he retired in 1971. In 1973, he received an honorary Doctor of Letters degree from Middlebury College. His book, *Language and Language Learning,* has been translated into German, Italian, and Japanese. Brooks died in New Haven, Conn. Obituaries and other sources: *Directory of American Scholars,* Volume III: *Foreign Languages, Linguistics, and Philology,* 6th edition, Bowker, 1974; *New York Times,* May 11, 1978.

* * *

BROOKS, Terry 1944-

PERSONAL: Born January 8, 1944, in Sterling, Ill.; son of Dean O. (a printer) and Marjorie (Gleason) Brooks; married Barbara Groth, April 23, 1972; children: Amanda Leigh. *Education:* Hamilton College, B.A., 1966; Washington & Lee University, LL.B., 1969. *Home:* 1810 Ave. L, Sterling, Ill. 61081.

CAREER: Besse, Frye, Arnold & Brooks (attorneys), Sterling, Ill., partner, 1969—. *Member:* American Bar Association, Trial Lawyers of America, Illinois Bar Association, Whiteside County Bar Association.

WRITINGS: The Sword of Shannara (fantasy novel), Random House, 1977.

WORK IN PROGRESS: A sequel to *The Sword of Shannara;* a contemporary novel, dealing with men's colleges.

SIDELIGHTS: Brooks writes: "I would like to contribute something to the enhancement of fantasy as a major literary art form. Frequently confused with science fiction, often considered a non-productive time-waster, fantasy has been misunderstood for many years. It is a rich source for dreams; it is a creator of the heroes we search for in our imagination. Fantasy is beginning to surface once again in our literature, and I would like to be a part of that resurgence."

* * *

BROWDER, Sue 1946-

PERSONAL: Born January 8, 1946, in Clarinda, Iowa; daughter of Floyd Merrill and Naoma (Guthrie) Hurdle; married Walt Browder (a writer), June 17, 1967; children: Dustin, Erin. *Education:* University of Missouri, B.J., 1968. *Politics:* Liberal.

CAREER: Free-lance writer, 1974—.

WRITINGS: The New Age Baby Name Book, Workman Publishing, 1974; *The American Biking Atlas and Touring Guide,* Workman Publishing, 1974. Contributor to popular magazines, including *Saturday Review* and *Connecticut.* Editorial assistant for *Cosmopolitan,* 1971.

WORK IN PROGRESS: Research on the occult, travel in New England, bicycling, hormones, stress, and vasectomy.

* * *

BROWER, Pauline 1929-

PERSONAL: Born December 9, 1929, in Long Beach, Calif.; daughter of Mark H. and Aline (Stafford) York; married Edgar Brower (president of a division of a chemical company), August 27, 1958; children: Leslee, Cydnee, Kimberly, Kelley. *Education:* Attended Fullerton College, 1947-48; University of Southern California, Los Angeles, certificate, 1953. *Religion:* Protestant. *Home:* 2860 Woodford Circle, Rochester, Mich. 48063.

CAREER: Fullerton College, Fullerton, Calif., instructor in personality development, 1953-59; public lecturer and writer, 1953—. Organized and conducted fashion shows for women's organizations in California and Texas, 1953-65; professional model, 1953-59; consultant to Edith Rehnborg Cosmetics. *Member:* American Historical Society, Society of Children's Book Writers.

WRITINGS—All for children; all with June Behrens: *Colonial Farm,* Childrens Press, 1976; *Algonquian Indians,* Childrens Press, 1977; *Pilgrims Plantation,* Childrens Press, 1977; *Canal Boats West,* illustrated with own photographs, Childrens Press, 1978; *Lighthouse Family,* illustrated with own photographs, Childrens Press, 1979; *Harper's Ferry Blacksmith,* illustrated with own photographs, Childrens Press, 1979; *Death Valley Miners,* illustrated with own photographs, Childrens Press, 1979. Past associate editor for Northern Virginia Newspapers.

WORK IN PROGRESS: U.S. Senate Pages.

SIDELIGHTS: Pauline Brower writes: "During the last twenty years history and photography have grown to form special interests that took me into a variety of learning experiences and classrooms, to the 'Living Heritage' series I'm working on now.

"I feel privileged to have this opportunity to share the past with young children and hope that I can contribute to an awareness of their heritage.

"It is difficult but necessary that our young realize the freedoms and opportunities they came into this world with, simply by being born in the United States. My travels in various countries confirm the fact that the special opportunities I was told about as a child do exist.

"I hope that the struggles, hard work, and joys found in the different lifestyles we portray in the 'Living Heritage' series will spell out what it takes to use the opportunities that exist.

"History reveals the cycles, successful and unsuccessful, that men and women repeat at different points in time. Hopefully, with an awareness of these cycles more men and women will repeat fewer unsuccessful acts in our future."

*   *   *

BROWN, Billye Walker
 See CUTCHEN, Billye Walker

*   *   *

BROWN, Charles
 See CADET, John

*   *   *

BROWN, Clifford Waters, Jr.   1942-

PERSONAL: Born November 17, 1942, in Lawrence, Mass.; son of Clifford Waters (a textile manufacturer) and Helen (Steere) Brown. *Education:* Harvard University, A.B., 1964, A.M., 1970, Ph.D., 1970. *Home:* 180 Brown St., Providence, R.I. 02906.

CAREER: Teacher and writer, 1970—.

WRITINGS: (With George A. Kelly) *Struggles in the State,* Wiley, 1970; (with the Ripon Society) *Jaws of Victory,* Little, Brown, 1974.

WORK IN PROGRESS: The Contributing Elite, a study of individuals who donated more than one hundred dollars to Presidential candidates in 1972, with Roman B. Hedges and Lynda Watts Powell.

SIDELIGHTS: Christopher Lydon, reviewing *Jaws of Victory,* writes: "The main line of this wide-ranging, thoroughly fascinating book is an attack on something called 'strategic politics'—the 'winning is the only thing' politics of professional analysts and managers whose public purpose is defined by the power game. . . . It is the authors' argument that the Watergate raid—impelled by 'preemptive' thinking, and viewing Larry O'Brien's office at the Democratic National Committee in 'strategic' as opposed to legal or even political terms—was a perfect expression of a mentality that had come to dominate the Nixon Administration. *Jaws of Victory* is in that sense the most ambitious effort I have seen to answer the largest why's of the Watergate saga. But it is not simply an anti-Nixon polemic. Even when the book is anti-Nixon, it has a thoughtful, unpersonal sweep, a refreshing change from the 'scoop' and confessional literature of Watergate.''

BIOGRAPHICAL/CRITICAL SOURCES: New York Times Book Review, August 4, 1974.

*   *   *

BROWN, Courtney C(onrades)   1904-

PERSONAL: Born October 15, 1904, in St. Louis, Mo.; son of Alexander Hanks and Joan (McCallum) Brown; married Marjorie Warren Lawbaugh, November 6, 1930; children: Joanne Brown Finney, Roxanne Brown McDowell, Courtney Warren. *Education:* Dartmouth College, B.S., 1926; Columbia University, Ph.D., 1940. *Religion:* Congregationalist. *Home:* 4 Kent Rd., Scarsdale, N.Y. 10583. *Office:* Graduate School of Business, Columbia University, New York, N.Y. 10027.

CAREER: Investment analyst with New York Stock Exchange firms, 1927-30; investment analyst, Bankers Trust Co., 1930-35; Columbia University, New York City, 1937-41, began as instructor, became lecturer; Chase National Bank, New York City, associate director of research, 1941-42; vice-president, Commodity Credit Corp., 1942-43; deputy director of Equipment Bureau, War Production Board, 1943-44; Standard Oil Co., New Jersey, economist, 1946-54, head of Petroleum Economics Division, 1946-48, assistant head of department of coordination and economics, 1948-51, assistant to chairman of board of directors, 1951-54; Columbia University, George E. Warren Professor of Business Policy, 1963-70, Paul Garrett Professor of Public Policy and Business Responsibility, 1970-72, dean of Graduate School of Business, 1954-69, vice-president for business affairs, 1955-57; writer, 1972—. Member of board of public governors of New York Stock Exchange, 1959-62. Executive director of American Assembly, 1955-56, chairman of board of trustees, 1969—. Member of board of directors of Council for Financial Aid to Education and International Executive Service Corps. Chief of U.S. State Department's Division of War Supply and Resources, 1943-45; vice-president of the President's Famine Emergency Commission, 1946; member of President's Commission on International Trade and Investment Policy, 1970-71; chairman of New York governor's Commission on the Minimum Wage, 1965. Member of board of directors of Esso Standard Oil Co., 1952-54, Borden Co., Columbia Broadcasting System, American Electric Power Co., Union Pacific Railroad, Associated Dry Goods Corp., and Uris Buildings Corp.; member of West Side advisory board of Chemical Bank of New York Trust Co.

MEMBER: American Economic Association, Academy of Political Science (member of board of directors), Council on Foreign Relations, Scarsdale Golf Club, Century Association. *Awards, honors:* LL.D. from Miami University, Oxford, Ohio, 1959; D.B.A. from University of Sherbrooke, 1967.

WRITINGS: Liquidity and Instability, Columbia University Press, 1940; (editor with E. Everett Smith) *The Director Looks at His Job,* Columbia University Press, 1957; *Journey Toward Understanding,* [Burlington, Vt.], 1958; (with John T. Conner and Elisha Gray) *The Creative Interface,* American University, School of Business Administration, 1968; (with Conner and Gray) *The New Relationship Between Business and Government,* American University, School of Business Administration, 1968; (editor) *World Business: Promise and Problems,* Macmillan, 1970; *Putting the Corporate Board to Work,* Macmillan, 1976. Also contributor to *Contemporary Economic Problems and Trends,* 1941, and author of *Symbols and Values,* 1954, and *Political Economy of American Foreign Policy,* 1955. Editor of *Columbia Journal of World Business,* 1965-72.

WORK IN PROGRESS: The Corporate Dilemma.

* * *

BROWN, James (Wiley) 1909-

PERSONAL: Born May 12, 1909, in Laurel, Miss.; son of James Wiley (a teacher) and Emma C. (a teacher; maiden name, White) Brown; married Nancy Corbett (a teacher). *Education:* Clark College, A.B., 1931; Gammon Theological Seminary, M.Div. (religious education), 1934; Chicago Theological Seminary, M.Div. (social ethics), 1935; University of Chicago, A.M., 1957; attended Mansfield College, Oxford, summer, 1965. *Politics:* Independent. *Home:* 3905 Carmel Dr., Austin, Tex. 78721. *Office:* Huston-Tillotson College, Austin, Tex. 78702.

CAREER: Atlanta Daily World, Atlanta, Ga., reporter, 1931-34; Fisk University, Nashville, Tenn., research fellow and field investigator, studying local black housing, 1936-38; United Church of Christ, New York, N.Y., home missionary worker in Selma, Ala. and Corpus Christi, Tex., and cofounder of Mary McLeod Bethune Day Nursery, 1939-41; St. Philip's Junior College, San Antonio, Tex., registrar and director of studies, 1942-44; Huston-Tillotson College, Austin, Tex., associate professor of religion and philosophy, and chaplain, 1944-54; minister of Congregational church in Chicago, Ill., 1954-58; Jackson State College, Jackson, Miss., associate professor of humanities and social sciences, and chaplain, 1958-68; Huston-Tillotson College, professor of religion and philosophy, and director of development, 1968-71; Robert R. Moton Memorial Institute, Washington, D.C., field coordinator of Moton College Service Bureau, 1971-76; currently associated with Huston-Tillotson College. President of Hyde Park Conference of Ministers and Social Workers, 1954-58; assistant to program director of U.S. Department of Agriculture Food and Nutrition Service's Division of Child Nutrition, summers, 1970-71.

MEMBER: American Academy of Arts and Sciences, American Academy of Political and Social Science, National Association for the Advancement of Colored People (life member), Omega Psi Phi, Elks, Masons, Lions.

WRITINGS: A Reading Seminar on Great Issues, McCutchan, 1966; *Nature and Meaning: A Handbook in Philosophy,* McCutchan, 1967; (contributor) John F. Potts, editor, *Black Colleges and Federal Relations,* Moton College Service Bureau, 1973. Editor of *Amistad* (of American Missionary Association), 1936-38.

WORK IN PROGRESS: Revising *Nature and Meaning.*

AVOCATIONAL INTERESTS: Travel (Mexico, Jamaica, the Virgin Islands, western Europe).

* * *

BROWN, Roger Glenn 1941-

PERSONAL: Born April 18, 1941, in Palestine, Tex.; son of H. R. and Alva (Lee) Brown; children: Cara Leigh, Cristin Beckett. *Education:* Attended University of Texas, 1959-61, University of San Francisco, 1961, and University of California, Berkeley, 1962-68, earned A.B., M.A., and Ph.D. *Politics:* Democrat. *Religion:* Roman Catholic. *Office:* Inscape, 1629 K St., Suite 5107, Washington, D.C. 20006.

CAREER: University of San Francisco, San Francisco, Calif., lecturer in history, 1966-67; Howard University, Washington, D.C., assistant professor of African studies, 1968-71; Inscape (publishers), Washington, D.C., president, 1971—. Senior analyst for Central Intelligence Agency, 1967-77; research fellow at Hoover Institution, 1977—. Consultant on national security issues, especially international affairs in general and Europe and Asia in particular. *Member:* American Historical Association, Association of American Publishers.

WRITINGS: Fashoda Reconsidered: The Impact of Domestic Politics on French Policy in Africa, Johns Hopkins Press, 1971; (editor) Fred Ward and Charlotte Ward, *The Home Birth Book,* Doubleday, 1977; (editor) Larry Winderbaum, *The Martial Arts Encyclopedia,* Inscape, 1977; *The Politics of Technology Transfer,* Hoover Institution, in press. Contributor to *Foreign Policy.*

* * *

BROWN, Rosellen 1939-

PERSONAL: Born May 12, 1939, in Philadelphia, Pa.; daughter of David H. and Blossom (Lieberman) Brown; married Marvin Hoffman (a teacher), March 16, 1963; children: Adina, Elana. *Education:* Barnard College, B.A., 1960; Brandeis University, M.A., 1962. *Religion:* Jewish. *Home address:* Sand Hill Rd., R.F.D. 1, Peterborough, N.H. 03458. *Agent:* Virginia Barber, 44 Greenwich Ave., New York, N.Y. 10011.

CAREER: Writer. Tougaloo College, Tougaloo, Miss., member of English and American literature faculty, 1965-67; Bread Loaf Writer's Conference, Middlebury, Vt., member of fiction staff, summer, 1974; Goddard College, Plainfield, Vt., member of creative writing faculty, 1976; Boston University, Boston, Mass., visiting professor of creative writing, 1977-78. Has also participated in poets-in-the-schools programs and writing workshops. *Awards, honors:* Woodrow Wilson fellow, 1960; Howard Foundation grant, 1971-72; National Endowment for the Humanities creative writing grant, 1973-74; Radcliffe Institute fellow, 1973-75; Great Lakes Colleges new writers award, 1976, for *The Autobiography of My Mother;* Guggenheim fellow, 1976-77.

WRITINGS: Some Deaths in the Delta and Other Poems, University of Massachusetts Press, 1970; (with Marvin Hoffman, Martin Kushner, Philip Lopate, and Sheila Murphy) *Whole World Catalog #1,* Teachers and Writers Collaborative, 1972; *Street Games* (stories), Doubleday, 1974; *The Autobiography of My Mother* (novel), Doubleday, 1976; *Cora Fry* (poems), Norton, 1977.

Work anthologized in *O. Henry Prize Stories,* 1972, 1973, 1976, and *Best American Short Stories,* 1975. Contributor of poems and stories to magazines, including *Ms., Atlantic,* and *Hudson Review.*

WORK IN PROGRESS: A novel to be published by Knopf.

SIDELIGHTS: Rosellen Brown writes: "Here is a quotation from the first anthology that published a story of mine. I said then (in 1973): 'As a poet and . . . story-writer, I am compelled most by the question of how one writes richly and humanely about political problems. How one writes, that is, about anything in a setting complex enough to allow the subtle (and unsubtle) public politics of ordinary life into the frame without having to give over the whole picture to them. I spent three years in Mississippi in the mid-sixties writing (among other things) and reading movement prose and poetry the whole time, as I read Black poetry now [1977; and writing from the women's movement as well], looking for emotions more comprehensive, more delicate, than anger and contempt. Once in a great while I see them but mostly there are other purposes being served and art has become a bit of an embarrassment; decadent; the luxury of the ruling class or color (or sex). I suppose the writer I'd respect most is the kind who'd make a good gossip, a better small-time con man, a bad rabble-rouser, and a worse debater. And yet still be serious.'"

*   *   *

BROWN, Stanley C(oleman) 1928-

PERSONAL: Born May 6, 1928, in Chicago, Ill.; son of William W. (a salesman) and Marion (Coleman) Brown; married Ruth Staffelbach (a sales clerk), August 6, 1949; children: Cathryn Brown Smith, Thomas William, Elizabeth Coleman. *Education:* Attended Washington & Lee University, 1946-48; Northwestern University, B.S., 1950; Garrett Evangelical Theological Seminary, Th.M., 1954. *Politics:* Independent Republican. *Home:* 3445 Calle Alarcon, Tucson, Ariz. 85716. *Office:* Catalina United Methodist Church, 2700 East Speedway, Tucson, Ariz. 85716.

CAREER: Ordained Methodist minister, 1952; Rocky Mountain College, Billings, Mont., dean of chapel, 1955-56; pastor of United Methodist church in Mundelein, Ill., 1956-58, associate pastor in Phoenix, Ariz., 1958-63, senior pastor in Long Beach, Calif., 1963-71; Catalina United Methodist Church, Tucson, Ariz., senior pastor, 1971—.

WRITINGS: Evangelism in the Early Church, Eerdmans, 1963; (with Robert Deits) *Folly or Power?,* Hawthorn, 1975; *God's Plan for Marriage,* Westminster, 1977. Contributor to religious periodicals.

WORK IN PROGRESS: Looking to Jesus: The Answer to Our Needs, about how Christ relates to man's contemporary crises; *"The Whole World in His Hands",* short devotional essays; a third book, "a liberal's answer to fundamentalism."

SIDELIGHTS: Brown comments: "My book writing goes hand in hand with the weekly task of preparing sermons. The underlying concepts of incarnational theology, and of getting into right relationships to find life's purpose and joys, are recurrent themes in my work. My work as a pastor in this stressful time is varied, and the source of great insight into the meaning of life for this day." Brown's travels include work and study trips to the Holy Land, England, and Spain.

*   *   *

BRUEGEL, Johann Wolfgang 1905-
(John Wolfgang Bruegel)

PERSONAL: Surname is pronounced *Byoor-*gel; born July 3, 1905, in Auspitz, Austria; son of Julius (a judge) and Irene (Redlich) Bruegel; married Josephine Liebstein (a medical practitioner), March 26, 1942; children: Julian, Irene. *Education:* German University, Prague, Czechoslovakia, LL.D., 1928. *Religion:* None. *Home:* 21 Connaught Dr., London NW11 6BL, England.

CAREER: Government of Czechoslovakia, legal officer in Prague, 1929-39, in Paris and London, 1939-45, in Prague, 1945-47; translator and free-lance writer in London, 1947—. *Member:* Royal Institute of International Affairs. *Awards, honors:* Named professor by the President of Austria, 1976.

WRITINGS: (Translator) Gerald Reitlinger, *Die Endloesung* (title means "The Final Solution"), Colloquium-Verlag, 1956; (editor) *Ludwig Czech: Arbeiterfuehrer und Staatsmann* (title means "Ludwig Czech: Workers' Leader and Statesman"), Verlag der Wiener Volksbuchhandlung, 1960; (translator) Reitlinger, *Ein Haus auf Sand gebaut* (title means "The House Built on Sand"), Ruetten & Loening, 1962; (editor) Friedrich Wolfgang Adler, *Friedrich Adler vordem Ausnahmegericht* (title means "Friedrich Adler Before the Special Tribunal"), Europa Verlag, 1967; *Tschechen und Deutsche, 1918-1938,* Nymphenburger Verlagshandlung, 1967; *Czechoslovakia Before Munich: The German Minority Problem and British Appeasement,* Cambridge University Press, 1973; (editor) *Stalin und Hitler: Pakt gegen Europa* (title means "Stalin and Hitler: Pact Against Europe"), Europa Verlag, 1973; *Tschechen und Deutsche, 1939-1946* (title means "Czechs and Germans, 1939-1946"), Nymphenburger Verlagshandlung, 1974.

WORK IN PROGRESS: Research on Central Europe in general and on post-war politics in Czechoslovakia.

SIDELIHGTS: Bruegel comments that his special interests are "international law, international relations, contemporary history, and the history of the labor movement."

BIOGRAPHICAL/CRITICAL SOURCES: Aufbau, March 24, 1972.

*   *   *

BRUEGEL, John Wolfgang
See BRUEGEL, Johann Wolfgang

*   *   *

BRUNO, Harold R., Jr. 1928-

PERSONAL: Born October 25, 1928, in Chicago, Ill.; son of Harold R. (a manufacturer's representative) and Tallulah (Kandel) Bruno; married Margaret Christian (a nurse), November 12, 1959; children: Harold III, Daniel. *Education:* University of Illinois, B.S., 1950. *Politics:* Independent. *Religion:* Jewish. *Office: Newsweek,* 1750 Pennsylvania Ave. N.W., Washington, D.C. 20006.

CAREER/WRITINGS: Advertising Age, Chicago, Ill., reporter, 1950; *De Kalb Daily Chronicle,* De Kalb, Ill., sports editor, 1950-51; City News Bureau, Chicago, reporter, 1953-54; *Chicago American,* Chicago, reporter, 1954-60; *Newsweek,* New York City, reporter in Chicago bureau and overseas, 1960-63, bureau chief in Chicago, 1963-66, news editor in New York City, 1966-71, chief political correspondent and deputy bureau chief in Washington, D.C., 1971—. Notable assignments include coverage of U.S. presidential campaigns since 1960, the 1962 Chinese-Indian War, and the Watergate investigation. Lecturer. Contributor of articles to periodicals. Member of Friendship Fire Association and Port Chester Fire Patrol and Rescue Co. *Military service:* U.S. Army, 1951-53; became first lieutenant. *Member:* White House Correspondents Association, Chicago Newspaper Reporters Association, Sigma Delta Chi. *Awards, honors:* Fulbright fellowship for study in India, 1956.

* * *

BRYAN, (William) Wright 1905-

PERSONAL: Born August 6, 1905, in Atlanta, Ga.; son of Arthur Buist (an editor) and Inez (Sledge) Bryan; married Ellen Hillyer Newell, October 12, 1932; children: Ellen Newell (Mrs. Bryan Tozzer), Mary Lane (Mrs. John K. Sullivan), William Wright, Jr. *Education:* Clemson College (now University), B.S., 1926; graduate study at University of Missouri, 1926-27. *Religion:* Methodist. *Home:* 100 Wyatt Ave., P.O. Box 470, Clemson, S.C. 29631.

CAREER/WRITINGS: Greenville Piedmont, Greenville, S.C., reporter, 1924, sports editor, 1926; *Atlanta Journal,* Atlanta, Ga., reporter, city editor, managing editor, and associate editor, 1927-45, editor, 1945-53; *Cleveland Plain Dealer,* Cleveland, Ohio, editor, 1954-63; Clemson University, Clemson, S.C., vice president for development, 1964-70; free-lance writer, 1970—. Notable assignments include coverage of D-Day, June 6, 1944, the liberation of Paris, August 25, 1944, and the coronation of Queen Elizabeth II, tours of Japan and Korea to inspect the results of occupation, 1947, and a tour of NATO countries, installations, and headquarters, 1951. American Red Cross, former vice-chairman of Cleveland chapter, chairman of Atlanta Chapter, 1950; overseer and director of Sweet Briar College; first vice president of Welfare Federation of Cleveland; chairman of Georgia Press Institute, 1942. *Wartime service:* War correspondent during World War II; prisoner of war under Germans, September, 1944-January, 1945; awarded Medal of Freedom by General Eisenhower for service as war correspondent. *Member:* American Society of Newspaper Editors (president, 1952-53), Overseas Press Club, Capital City Club (Atlanta), Piedmont Driving Club (Atlanta), Nine O'Clocks Club (Atlanta), Clemson Rotary Club, Clemson Alumni Association, Poinsett Club (Greenville, S.C.), Sigma Delta Chi, Phi Kappa Psi. *Awards, honors:* Litt.D. from Clemson College (now University), 1956; LL.D. from College of Wooster, 1958; distinguished alumnus award from Clemson College, 1960.

WORK IN PROGRESS: A history of Clemson University.

SIDELIGHTS: Bryan was a guest of the Dutch government in 1974, for the thirtieth anniversary of Operation Market Garden. He was accompanied by Cornelius Ryan, author of *A Bridge Too Far,* and other former war correspondents and military officers.

* * *

BRYANT, Traphes L(emon) 1914-

PERSONAL: Given name is pronounced *Tray*-fus; born February 7, 1914, in Claremont, W. Va.; son of William Henry and Florence (Burgess) Bryant; married Doris Shawver (a systems analyst), July 3, 1946. *Education:* Attended New River State College. *Politics:* Democrat. *Home address:* Route 1, Box 63D, Pamplin, Va. 23958. *Agent:* Ruth Hagy Brod Literary Agency, 15 Park Ave., New York, N.Y. 10016.

CAREER: Chesapeake and Potomac Telephone Co., Montgomery, W. Va., linesman and telephone installer, 1938-39; Lillybrook Coal Co., Lillybrook, W. Va., electrician, 1940-41; Norfolk Naval Shipyard, Portsmouth, Va., electrician, 1941-47; General Services Administration, Washington, D.C., electrician at the White House, 1948-72; writer, 1972—. Electrician at Pearl Harbor Shipyard, 1941-42.

WRITINGS: Dog Days at the White House, Macmillan, 1975. Contributor to *Ladies Home Journal.*

SIDELIGHTS: Bryant kept a diary of special events during his years at the White House because he felt the dignitaries he met and the events he witnessed would someday be of historical interest. This diary is the basis of his book.

* * *

BUBAR, Margaret Weber 1920(?)-1978

1920(?)—May 30, 1978; American naturalist, civic leader, and writer. Bubar was the founding president of the Darien (Conn.) chapter of the National Audubon Society. She also led the Audubon tours to Trinidad and Tobago. Bubar served on many local civic committees. As a writer, she contributed articles on nature and travel to such publications as the *New York Times* and *Christian Science Monitor.* She died in Stamford, Conn. Obituaries and other sources: *New York Times,* May 31, 1978.

* * *

BUNCE, Alan 1939-

PERSONAL: Born February 2, 1939; son of Alan Coe and Ruth (Nugent) Bunce; married Joyce Elaine van Trautwig, January 31, 1965; children: Alan Elliott, John Andrew. *Education:* Earned B.A. from Yale University. *Office:* Christian Science Monitor, One Norway St., Boston, Mass. 02115.

CAREER/WRITINGS: Christian Science Monitor, Boston, Mass., New York drama critic, 1967-71, television critic, 1971-73, arts and entertainment editor, 1973—. Contributor of articles to periodicals. *Military service:* U.S. Army, 1959-61.

* * *

BURACK, Abraham Saul 1908-1978

January 31, 1908—June 29, 1978; American author, and editor and publisher of plays, books on writing, *Writer* magazine, and *Plays* magazine. Burack wrote plays and articles on writing. He co-wrote *Methods and Procedures in Federal Purchasing.* He died in Brookline, Mass. Obituaries and other sources: *Who's Who in Advertising,* 2nd edition, Redfield, 1972; *New York Times,* June 30, 1978. (See index for *CA* sketch)

* * *

BURCH, Preston M. 1884-1978

1884—April 4, 1978; American thoroughbred horse trainer and author of *The Training of Thoroughbreds,* a book that has been described as "the handbook of the trade." Burch, who once noted that experience was the key to becoming a successful trainer, was the second in three generations of his family to become a trainer. He died in Middleburg, Va. Obituaries and other sources: *New York Times,* April 5, 1978.

* * *

BURKE, John Garrett 1917-

PERSONAL: Born August 12, 1917, in Boston, Mass.; son of Edmund Joseph and Catherine (Barry) Burke; married Mary Margaret Porter (a psychologist), October 13, 1945; children: Margaret Alison Burke Ball, Kevin Garrett, Mary Eileen. *Education:* Massachusetts Institute of Technology, B.S., 1938; Stanford University, M.A., 1960, Ph.D., 1962. *Home:* 570 North Bundy Dr., Los Angeles, Calif. 90049.

Office: Department of History, University of California, Los Angeles, Calif. 90024.

CAREER: Bethlehem Steel Co., Johnstown, Pa., metallurgist, 1938-41; Cummins Diesel Engines, Inc., Pittsburgh, Pa., general manager, 1945-48; Dry Ice Converter Corp., Tulsa, Okla., president, 1948-58; University of California, Los Angeles, assistant professor, 1962-67, associate professor, 1967-71, professor of history, 1971—. *Military service:* U.S. Army Air Forces, pilot, 1941-45; became first lieutenant; received Air Medal with oak leaf cluster.

MEMBER: American Association for the Advancement of Science (fellow), American Historical Association, Society for the History of Technology, History of Science Society, British History of Science Society. *Awards, honors:* Abbott Payson Usher Award from Society for the History of Technology, 1967, for article, ''Bursting Boilers and the Federal Power.''

WRITINGS: Origins of the Science of Crystals, University of California Press, 1966; (editor) *The New Technology and Human Values,* Wadsworth, 1966, 2nd edition, 1972; (with Cyril Stanley Smith) *Atoms, Blacksmiths, and Crystals,* Clark Memorial Library (Los Angeles, Calif.), 1967; (with John C. Greene) *The Science of Minerals in the Age of Jefferson,* American Philosophical Society, 1978.

WORK IN PROGRESS: Technology in America: The Crucial Decades, 1880-1920 (tentative title).

SIDELIGHTS: Burke writes: ''From both historical and archaelogical records we know that the development of technology has been stimulated by the economic demands of society, governmental initiatives, warfare, such engineering imperatives as mechanization and efficiency, and within the past two centuries by the advance of scientific knowledge. The technological development of a society has also been conditioned by its natural environment, for example geography, climate, and natural resources; by population numbers and density; and by such cultural values as religion, ethics, and aesthetics. The effects of technological development are most clearly seen in higher standards of living, increased longevity, vastly altered working conditions, the increased complexity of technological artifacts, and the growth of such interconnected systems as transportation and communication networks. Also visible, however, are disturbing and even dangerous secondary effects, which are unintended and not visualized: environmental pollution and degradation, occupational boredom, and individual and social alienation.

''The transformation of society in the United States in the period 1880-1930 from a predominantly rural and agricultural society to one increasingly characterized by its high technology is surely a most significant and fascinating historical phenomenon. My current research interests are devoted to finding explanations of this startling change.''

*   *   *

BURKE, Ted   1934(?)-1978

1934(?)—January 1, 1978; American magazine editor and writer. Burke, editor-at-large for *Town & Country* magazine, wrote about the rich from such cities as Palm Beach and Monte Carlo. His articles were often personality profiles and travel guides to resorts and cities. Burke died in Pelham, N.Y. Obituaries and other sources: *New York Times,* January 3, 1978.

*   *   *

BURNS, Rex (Sehler)   1935-

PERSONAL: Born June 13, 1935, in San Diego, Calif. *Edu-*

cation: Stanford University, B.A., 1958; University of Minnesota, M.A., 1963, Ph.D., 1965. *Residence:* Boulder, Colo. *Agent:* Carl Brandt, Brandt & Brandt, 101 Park Ave., New York, N.Y. 10017. *Office:* University of Colorado at Denver, 1100 14th St., Denver, Colo. 80202.

CAREER: Central Missouri State University, Warrensburg, assistant professor of English, 1965-68; University of Colorado at Denver, professor of English, 1968—; writer, 1976—. Fulbright lecturer, Greece, 1969, 1970, Argentina, 1977; consultant to Denver district attorney's office, 1973-74. *Military service:* U.S. Marine Corps Reserves, active duty, 1958-61; became captain. *Member:* National American Studies Faculty, Mystery Writers of America, Authors Guild, American Studies Association, Popular Culture Association, Associaton for Retarded Citizens. *Awards, honors:* Edgar Allen Poe Award for best first novel from Mystery Writers of America, 1976, for *The Alvarez Journal;* Top Hand Award from Colorado Authors League, 1978, for *The Farnsworth Score.*

WRITINGS: The Alvarez Journal, Harper, 1975; *Success in America: The Yeoman Dream and the Industrial Revolution,* University of Massachusetts Press, 1976; *The Farnsworth Score,* Harper, 1977; *Speak for the Dead,* Harper, 1978.

WORK IN PROGRESS: Several uncompleted books including some mystery novels.

*   *   *

BUROS, Oscar Krisen   1905-1978

June 14, 1905—March 19, 1978; American educator, editor, and author. Buros, a leading authority on educational and psychological testing, was the editor and publisher of *The Mental Measurements Yearbook.* He was also head of testing for the Army's specialization training program during World War II. Buros was the author of several books and articles on testing and measurement. He died in New Brunswick, N.J. Obituaries and other sources: *American Men and Women of Science: The Social and Behavioral Sciences,* 12th edition, Bowker, 1973; *New York Times,* March 19, 1978.

*   *   *

BURROWS, E(dwin) G(ladding)   1917-

PERSONAL: Born July 23, 1917, in Dallas, Tex.; son of Millar (a scholar) and Irene (Gladding) Burrows; married Gwen Lemon (divorced, 1972); married Beth Elpern (a teacher), December 7, 1973; children: Edwin Gwynne, Daniel William, David John. *Education:* Yale University, B.A., 1938; University of Michigan, M.A., 1940. *Home:* 1952 Traver Rd., #204, Ann Arbor, Mich. 48105. *Office:* WUOM-Radio, University of Michigan, Ann Arbor, Mich. 48109.

CAREER: WUOM-Radio, Ann Arbor, Mich., manager, 1948-70; University of Wisconsin, Madison, director of National Center for Audio Experimentation, 1970-73; WUOM-Radio, executive producer, 1973—. *Military service:* U.S. Navy, 1943-46. *Member:* National Association of Educational Broadcasters (chairman of board of directors, 1967). *Awards, honors:* Major Hopwood Award from University of Michigan, 1940; Ohio State Award, 1953, for ''Radio Guild Theater,'' 1954, for ''They Fought Alone,'' 1955, for ''A Gallery of Women'' and ''Red Man in Michigan,'' 1956, for ''Tales of the Valiant,'' 1971, for ''The Tree Plumber,'' and 1974, for ''Properties''; fellow of Yaddo Foundation, 1963,

1966; Borestone Mountain Poetry Award, 1964, for "The Day Grandmother Died."

WRITINGS: The Arctic Tern (poems), Grove, 1957; Man Fishing (poems), Sumac Press, 1970; The Crossings (poems), New Moon, 1976; Kiva (poems), Ithaca House, 1976.

Broadcast plays: "All Night Store," produced by National Center for Audio Experimentation at University of Wisconsin, Madison, 1971; "Six Ecodramas," National Center for Audio Experimentation, 1971; "Circe," Canadian Broadcasting Corp., 1972; "Visiting Hours," Radio Nederland, 1972; "Properties," Earplay, Madison, Wis. 1974.

Represented in anthologies, including Accent Anthology; Best Poems of 1964; SPR: A Decade of Poems. Contributor of poems to magazines, including American Poetry Review, Epoch, Paris Review, Poetry Northwest, and Sumac.

WORK IN PROGRESS: The House of August, poems.

SIDELIGHTS: Burrows writes: "A career in public broadcasting has kept me close to the literary activity on various campuses but free of the burdens of teaching. I have been particularly interested in the recording and presentation of contemporary poetry (and other literature) as an audio experience to the listening public."

* * *

BURTON, Katherine (Kurz) 1890-1969

PERSONAL: Born in 1890 in Cleveland, Ohio; daughter of John and Louise (Bittner) Kurz; married Harry Payne Burton (an editor), 1910; children: two sons, one daughter. Education: Graduated from Western Reserve University (now Case Western Reserve University). Religion: Roman Catholic.

CAREER: Teacher in a private school; McCall's (magazine), New York City, associate editor, 1928-30, Redbook (magazine), New York City, associate editor, 1930-33; freelance writer. Awards, honors: Christopher Award, 1959; D.Litt. from St. Mary of the Springs College, 1955.

WRITINGS: Sorrow Built a Bridge: A Daughter of Hawthorne, Longmans, Green, 1937, new edition published as Sorrow Built a Bridge: The Life of Mother Alphonsa, Daughter of Nathaniel Hawthorne, Image Books, 1956; Paradise Planters: The Story of Brook Farm, Longmans, Green, 1939, reprinted, AMS Press, 1973; Andrew Carnegie: "Something of the Fairy Tale", Periwinkle Press, 1939.

His Dear Persuasion: The Life of Elizabeth Ann Seton, Longmans, Green, 1940; In No Strange Land: Some American Catholic Converts, Longmans, Green, 1942, reprinted, Books for Libraries, 1970; Brother Andre of Mount Royal, Ave Maria Press, 1943, revised edition, 1952; Celestial Homespun: The Life of Isaac Thomas Hecker, Longmans, Green, 1943; No Shadow of Turning: The Life of James Kent Stone (Father Fidelis of the Cross), Longmans, Green, 1944; Mother Butler of Marymount, Longmans, Green, 1944; His Mercy Endureth Forever, Sisters of Mercy (Tarrytown, N.Y.), 1946; According to the Pattern: The Story of Dr. Agnes McLaren and the Society of Catholic Medical Missionaries, Longmans, Green, 1946; Three Generations: Maria Boyle Ewing (1801-1864), Ellen Ewing Sherman (1824-1888), Minnie Sherman Fitch (1851-1913), Longmans, Green, 1947; Difficult Star: The Life of Pauline Jaricot, Longmans, Green, 1947; Mightily and Sweetly: The Life Story of Mother Josephine of the Sacred Heart, [Hartford, Conn.], 1948; So Surely Anchored, Kenedy, 1948; The Next Thing: Autobiography and Reminiscences,

Longmans, Green, 1949; Chaminade: Apostle of Mary, Founder of the Society of Mary, Bruce Publishing, 1949.

The Great Mantle: The Life of Giuseppe Melchiore Sarto, Pope Pius X, Longmans, Green, 1950; (with Helmut Ripperger) Feast Day Cookbook, McKay, 1951; Where There Is Love: The Life of Mother Mary Frances Siedliska of Jesus the Good Shepherd, Kenedy, 1951; Whom Love Impels: The Life of Pauline von Mallinckrodt, Foundress of the Congregation of the Sisters of Christian Charity, Kenedy, 1952; The Table of the King: The Story of Mother Gamelin, Foundress of the Sisters of Charity of Providence, Mc-Mullen Books, 1952; So Much, So Soon: Father Brisson, Founder of the Oblates of St. Francis de Sales, Benziger Brothers, 1953; The Stars Beyond the Storms: Father Etienne Pernet, Founder of the Congregation of the Little Sisters of the Assumption, Benziger Brothers, 1954; Children's Shepherd: The Story of John Christopher Drumgoole, Father of the Homeless and Founder of the Mission of the Immaculate Virgin, Kenedy, 1954.

In Heaven We Shall Rest: The Life of Vincenzo Pallotti, Founder of the Congregation of the Catholic Apostolate, Benziger Brothers, 1955; My Beloved to Me: The Life of Jeanne de Matel, Foundress of the Sisters of the Incarnate Word and Blessed Sacrament, Bruce Publishing, 1957; The Golden Door: The Life of Katharine Drexel, Kenedy, 1957; Witness of the Light: The Life of Pope Pius XII, Longmans, Green, 1958; With God and Two Ducats: The Story of the Corpus Christi Carmelites in Three Countries, 1908-1958, Carmelite Press, 1958; Lily and Sword and Crown: The History of the Congregation of the Sisters of St. Casimir, Chicago, Illinois, 1907-1957, Bruce Publishing, 1958; Make the Way Known: The History of the Dominican Congregation of St. Mary of the Springs, 1822-1957, Farrar, Straus, 1959; Faith Is the Substance: The Life of Mother Theodore Guerin, Foundress of the Sisters of Providence of Saint Mary-of-the-Woods, Indiana, Herder, 1959.

The Dream Lives Forever: The Story of St. Patrick's Cathedral, Longmans, Green, 1960; Cry Jubilee!, Sisters of St. Francis of the Third Order Regular (Allegany, N.Y.), 1960; One Thing Needful: The Biography of Mother Franziska Lechner, F.D.C., Foundress of the Daughters of Divine Charity, Kenedy, 1960; Wheat for This Planting: The Biography of Saint Mary Joseph Rossello, Foundress of the Daughters of Our Lady of Mercy, Bruce Publishing, 1960; Woman to Woman, Kenedy, 1961; Leo the Thirteenth: The First Modern Pope, McKay, 1962; The Door of Hope: The Story of Katherine Drexel (illustrated by Irene Murray), Hawthorne Books, 1963; The Bernardines, Maryview Press, 1964; Valiant Voyager: Blessed Marguerite Bourgeoys, Foundress of the Congregation de Notre Dame of Montreal, Bruce Publishing, 1964; Bells on Two Rivers: The History of the Sisters of the Visitation of Rock Island, Illinois, Bruce Publishing, 1965.

Contributor of articles to Commonweal and Sign.

SIDELIGHTS: Katherine Burton began writing after her conversion to Roman Catholicism in 1930, and most of her books are a reflection of that new-found faith. She chose to write about others who had converted to Catholicism, narrowing her scope to those Americans with New England origins. Using this method of selection, she was able to demonstrate "how these good Americans became also good Catholics and remained good Americans."

Her method of writing was criticized by many. Some reviewers felt that the fictional form of biography employed by Burton sounded too much like a novel to be called a biography.

Claiming this method was more informal, Burton contended it would attract a wider audience to read about people who were previously buried only in scholarly works.

The reviews of Burton's first biography, *Sorrow Built a Bridge,* characterize most of her other works as well. *America* noted, "*Sorrow Built a Bridge* not only tells a story of one of our foremost American women, but it tells it in such an artless, tender way that the reader cannot resist its continuous charm." Observed the *New York Times:* "The book suffers somewhat as a narrative by the emotional quality of its treatment; and the general reader must regret that the author has canalized the spiritual currents of her story with such stressing of one communion's faith. But if this is not a flawlessly written biography it is a vitally interesting one, notwithstanding. . . . It is a noble and heroic story that is told here."

BIOGRAPHICAL/CRITICAL SOURCES: New York Times, October 31, 1937; *America,* November 27, 1937; Katherine Burton, *The Next Thing: Autobiography and Reminiscences,* Longmans, Green, 1949; John A. O'Brien, editor, *Where I Found Christ,* Doubleday, 1950. Obituaries: *New York Times,* September 24, 1969.*

(Died in 1969)

*   *   *

BURTON-BRADLEY, Burton Gyrth   1914-

PERSONAL: Born November 18, 1914, in Sydney, Australia; son of Alan Godfrey (a horticulturist) and Ruby (Drayton) Burton-Bradley; married Ingeborg Roeser, October 7, 1950 (deceased). *Education:* University of Sydney, M.B. and B.S., 1946, D.T.M.&H., 1963, diploma in anthropology, 1964; University of Melbourne, D.P.M., 1956; University of New South Wales, M.D., 1969. *Office:* Mental Health Services, P.O. Box 1239, Boroko, Papua New Guinea.

CAREER: Australian Military Mission in Europe, Cologne, West Germany, medical officer, 1949-50; Psychiatric Services, Brisbane, Queensland, Australia, medical officer, 1951-57; Colombo Plan, Singapore, psychiatrist, 1957-58; Woodbridge Mental Hospital, Singapore, medical superintendent and consulting psychiatrist, 1958-59; Division of Mental Health, Port Moresby, Papua New Guinea, chief of psychiatric services, 1959-75; Mental Health Services, Boroko, Papua New Guinea, consulting psychiatrist, 1975—. Medical superintendent at Ipswich Mental Hospital, 1956-57; consulting psychiatrist at Port Moresby General Hospital, Laloki Psychiatric Center, and Bomana Corrective Institution, 1959—. Associate professor at University of Papua New Guinea, 1972-75; clinical associate professor at University of Hawaii, 1976—; lecturer at Vanderbilt University, 1973. Senior specialist at East-West Center's Institute of Advanced Projects, 1969-70. Chairman of Permanent Committee on Mental Health and Cultural Development (Papua New Guinea), 1961-75; ethnopsychiatry adviser to South Pacific Commission, 1967—; liaison officer for New Guinea, Royal Australian and New Zealand College of Psychiatrists, 1969—; member of Government of Papua New Guinea's advisory committee on the power of mercy; member of expert advisory panel on mental health of World Health Organization.

MEMBER: International College of Psychosomatic Medicine (fellow; vice-president, 1977—), International Association of Social Psychiatry (member of regional council, 1977—), World Psychiatric Association, Scientific Society of Papua New Guinea, Royal Australian and New Zealand College of Psychiatrists (fellow), Australian College of Medical Administrators (fellow), Royal College of Psychiatrists (England; fellow), Royal Anthropological Institute (fellow), Royal Society of Tropical Medicine and Hygiene (fellow), American Anthropological Association (foreign fellow), American Academy of Psychiatry and the Law, American Association for the Advancement of Science (fellow), Indian Psychiatric Society (corresponding member), Canadian Psychiatric Association (corresponding member). *Awards, honors:* Abraham Flexner Award from Vanderbilt University, 1973; Benjamin Rush Bronze Medal from American Psychiatric Association, 1974; fellowship from Foundations Fund for Research in Psychiatry, 1975.

WRITINGS: South Pacific Ethnopsychiatry, South Pacific Commission, 1967; *Mixed-Race Society in Port Moresby,* Australian National University Press, 1968; *Psychiatry and the Law in the Developing Society,* South Pacific Commission, 1970; *Longlong,* Government Printer (Port Moresby, Papua New Guinea), 1973; *Stone Age Crisis,* Vanderbilt University Press, 1975; (with Otto Billig) *The Painted Message,* Schenkman, 1978. Contributor to *Encyclopaedia of Papua New Guinea.* Contributor of more than one hundred scientific and popular articles to professional journals. Member of board of advisers of *Transcultural Psychiatric Research Review;* consulting editor of *New Guinea Psychologist.*

WORK IN PROGRESS: The Story of Laloki, "a popular account of the origin, history, and development of the only state hospital in Papua New Guinea."

SIDELIGHTS: Burton-Bradley writes: "After a career of seven years in a state hospital in Australia, I was encouraged by my wife to take an interest in the larger world. I applied for, and was appointed to, the position of Colombo Plan psychiatrist in Singapore. At that time there were no other psychiatrists in that country, and it was there, with its variety of cultural groups, that I became interested in the cultural factor in all its implications, and have been associated with the newly-developing discipline of transcultural psychiatry ever since. This deals with the overlap between anthropology and psychiatry and is a subject of popular interest that can be followed easily by any intelligent person.

"Following the *merdeka* in Singapore I came to Papua New Guinea where I have been (for the most part) the only psychiatrist in the country for the past twenty years. *Stone Age Crisis* grew out of the popular lectures I gave at Vanderbilt University in 1973.

"Not everyone shares my views, which deal with the hazards of social change in Papua New Guinea, although many do. *Longlong* is similar to *Stone Age Crisis* and can be read by anyone. *Mixed-Race Society in Port Moresby* is a popular social science account of the mixed-race people (that is, those with joint Western and indigenous ancestry) in the capital city of Papua New Guinea. The other books are perhaps a little more narrow in perspective, but are certainly not lacking in popular interest. Among the many other subjects on Papua New Guinea that I have written about are such things as cannibalism, betel-nut chewing, folk beliefs, dreams, folk healers, amok, suicide, cargo cult, drinking, gambling, and homosexuality.

"I speak Neomelanesian (pidgin English) fluently, can read German, Police Motu less fluently. I have travelled widely in the interior of Papua New Guinea over the past twenty years. I feel that this country should be publicised to the world at large. It has seven hundred distinct languages (now dialects), each one of which represents to a large extent a separate culture, with a corresponding number of varied customs. It is unique in this regard. No other country has the same diversity. Young people in particular can learn much from it."

* * *

BUSBEE, Shirlee (Elaine) 1941-

PERSONAL: Born August 9, 1941, in San Jose, Calif.; daughter of James Gatlin (a naval officer) and Helen Egan; married Howard Leon Busbee, June 22, 1963. *Education:* Burbank Business College, certificate, 1962. *Agent:* John Payne, Lenniger Literary Agency, Inc., 437 Fifth Ave., New York, N.Y. 10016. *Office:* County Parks Department, Courthouse Annex, Fairfield, Calif. 94533.

CAREER: Receptionist and typist for Marin County Title and Abstract Co., 1962-63; plant supervisor for Fairfield Title Co., 1963-66; clerk and drafting technician for Solano County Assessor's Office, 1966—; County Parks Department, Fairfield, Calif., drafting technician and secretary, 1974—.

WRITINGS: Gypsy Lady (historical romance), Avon, 1977.

WORK IN PROGRESS: Lady Vixen, a historical romance set in Louisiana and England around the battle of New Orleans.

SIDELIGHTS: Shirlee Busbee told *CA:* "I don't know why I write, I just do. I enjoy it and perhaps the reason I do write is because there are so few books on the markets these days that I enjoy reading. I have always been an avid reader; as a matter of fact, my family has often said I don't look normal without a book in one hand. I've always especially liked historical novels—Jan Wescot and Frank Yerby are two of my favorites—and so I guess when I started writing, I wanted to write the kind of book I would enjoy reading. Which I think I did in *Gypsy Lady.* I didn't set out to write the Great American Novel; I wanted to write a book that would entertain people and I consider myself an entertainer—of sorts.

"As for any personal views that I attempt to express through my writing, any such views that show up are unconscious on my part. I know I want an up-beat ending before I start writing a book and I know that right will triumph over evil. I find it very depressing to read a book in which injustice is rewarded or left unpunished, and so I try not to do that. When a person puts down one of my books I want them to be satisfied, satisfied and feeling good inside. And I want them to have enjoyed the book so much that they will go back and reread it again.

"When I am writing, I try very hard not to become sugary-sweet. I want good things for my fictional people, but not to the point of being 'goody two-shoes.' And trying to find the fine line between being touching and moving without being too sweet is very hard to do."

AVOCATIONAL INTERESTS: Reading, dogs, cats.

* * *

BUSHINSKY, Jay (Joseph Mason) 1932-

PERSONAL: Born December 8, 1932, in Buffalo, N.Y.; son of Joshua M. and Malka (Coralnik) Bushinsky; married Dvora Apte, December 30, 1952; children: Jesse, Aviv, Dahlia. *Education:* Queens College (now of the City University of New York), B.A., 1955; Yeshiva University, M.S. (education), 1959; Columbia University, M.S. (journalism), 1963. *Religion:* Jewish. *Home:* Rehov Hatsafon 5, Savyon, Israel. *Office:* 37 Pinsker St., Tel Aviv, Israel.

CAREER/WRITINGS: High school teacher of social studies in Long Island, N.Y., 1958-59, and New York City, 1959-62; *Times Herald/Record,* Middletown, N.Y., municipal reporter, 1963-64; *Miami Herald,* Miami, Fla., copy editor, 1964-66; Chicago Daily News Foreign Service, Chicago, Ill., correspondent in Tel Aviv, Israel, 1966-78; Westinghouse Broadcasting Co., New York City, correspondent and bureau chief in Tel Aviv, 1967—; *Chicago Sun-Times,* Chicago, special correspondent, 1978—. Notable assignments include coverage of the Six-Day War, the Yom Kippur War, Maalot School raid, 1974, and Anwar Sadat's visit to Jerusalem, 1977. Occasional contributor to *Christian Science Monitor,* 1967—, and contributor to other periodicals, including *Present Tense.* Contributing editor, *Atlas* and *World Press Review.* Lecturer in journalism, Tel Aviv University, 1966-70. *Military service:* U.S. Army, 1955-57. *Member:* Foreign Press Association of Israel (chairman, 1968-71), Overseas Press Club. *Awards, honors:* Overseas Press Club award for best radio spot news reporting, 1973, for coverage of Yom Kippur War.

SIDELIGHTS: Bushinsky told *CA:* "I strongly believe in the need for the American public to know about problems and developments abroad. Foreign correspondence is one of the most important aspects of journalism and I oppose efforts to curtail it in contemporary media." With regard to peace in the Middle East, Bushinsky writes that "since the Sadat visit, Israelis have been hoping for a breakthrough to peace, but disagree over the extent of concessions required on their side."

* * *

BUSSE, Thomas V(alentine) 1941-

PERSONAL: Surname is pronounced *Buss*-ee; born February 14, 1941, in Covington, Ky.; son of Louis Joseph (a postmaster) and Ruth (Neff) Busse; married Pauline Zaranka (a special education teacher), April 25, 1964; children: Kathleen Kim, Michael Douglas, Jeanne Lynn. *Education:* Thomas More College, A.B., 1961; Loyola University, Chicago, Ill., A.M., 1963; University of Chicago, Ph.D., 1967. *Residence:* Cheltenham, Pa. *Office:* Department of Educational Psychology, Temple University, Broad and Montgomery Aves., Philadelphia, Pa. 19122.

CAREER: High school mathematics teacher in Chicago, Ill., 1962-64; Institute for Juvenile Research, Chicago, medical research associate, 1964-67; Temple University, Philadelphia, Pa., assistant professor, 1967-70, associate professor, 1970-74, professor of educational psychology, 1974—, head of department, 1973-75. *Member:* American Association of University Professors (member of local executive committee, 1971-75; secretary, 1974-75), American Psychological Association, American Educational Research Association, Society for Research in Child Development, Eastern Psychological Association.

WRITINGS: (With Daniel Solomon and Robert Parelius) *Dimensions of Achievement-Related Behavior Among Lower-Class Negro Parents,* Genetic Psychology Monographs, 1969; (with Solomon, Parelius, and Kevin Houlihan) *Parent Behavior and Child Academic Achievement, Achievement Striving, and Related Personality Characteristics,* Genetic Psychology Monographs, 1971; (with Richard S. Mansfield and Lee J. Messinger) *Activities in Child and Adolescent Development,* Harper, 1974; *The Psychology of Creativity and Discovery,* Lawrence Erlbaum Associates, 1979. Contributor of more than twenty articles to psychology and education journals.

WORK IN PROGRESS: Human Development for Teachers, with Richard S. Mansfield, for Harper.

SIDELIGHTS: Busse told *CA:* "What is it that parents and teachers do to foster the development of creativity in children? How can creative persons be identified? What is the nature of the creative process? These and similar questions have concerned me for the last fifteen years. Recently my creativity research has focused on the sciences.

"The effect of first names on children continues to provide both enjoyment and scholarship. My research has shown that the desirability of first names is one of many bases for stereotyping, especially of girls. A variety of other personal characteristics (e.g., race, stature, physical attractiveness) may also, of course, produce stereotyped expectations in the eye of the beholder. In particular, it was exciting to find that the desirability of girls' first names are related to their school achievement and IQ.

"I have revived my interest in the German language, German culture, and especially German psychology. A reawakening is under way in West German psychology that should prove important for American psychologists."

*   *   *

BUTLER, Edgar W(ilbur)   1929-

PERSONAL: Born November 4, 1929, in Rapid City, S.D.; son of Edgar and Josephine (in business; maiden name, Kempter) Butler; married Patricia M. McNichols (a teacher), December 27, 1959; children: Brian E., Tracey J. *Education:* California State University, Long Beach, B.A., 1958; University of Southern California, M.A., 1962, Ph.D., 1966. *Office:* Department of Sociology, University of California, Riverside, Calif. 92521.

CAREER: University of Southern California, Los Angeles, lecturer in sociology, 1961-63; University of North Carolina, Chapel Hill, assistant professor, 1964-69; University of California, Riverside, associate professor, 1969-73; professor of sociology, 1973—, chairman of department, 1970-71, 1977—. Consultant to National Science Foundation. *Military service:* U.S. Air Force, 1952-56.

MEMBER: International Union for the Scientific Study of Population, American Association of Mental Retardation, American Association of Mental Deficiency; American Sociological Association, Society for the Study of Social Problems. *Awards, honors:* Grants from National Academy of Sciences, 1966-68, Ford Foundation, 1968, National Science Foundation, 1969-73, National Institute of Mental Health, 1972-73, 1974-76, National Institute of Education, 1974-76, and National Institute On Aging, 1976—.

WRITINGS: (Contributor) Walter Reckless, editor, *Interdisciplinary Problems in Criminology,* Ohio State University Press, 1965; (with F. Stuart Chapin, Jr., George C. Hemmens, and others) *Moving Behavior and Residential Choice: A National Survey,* National Academy of Sciences, 1969; *Urban Sociology and Ecology: A Selective Approach,* Harper, 1977; *Urban Problems and Prospects,* Goodyear Publishing, 1977; (contributor) *Research to Practice in Mental Retardation,* University Park Press, 1977; *Traditional Marriage and Emerging Alternatives,* Harper, 1978; (with Chapin and Frederick C. Patten) *Blackways in an Inner City,* University of Illinois Press, 1978. Also contributor to *Observing Behavior,* Volume I: *Theory and Applications in Mental Retardation,* edited by Gene P. Sackett, University Park Press. Contributor to *Atlas of North Carolina,* and of more than forty articles to professional journals. Associate

editor of *Social Forces;* consulting editor of *Social Science Quarterly, Demography,* and *American Journal of Mental Deficiency.*

WORK IN PROGRESS: The Other Americans, The Erotic Americans, Geothermal As a Future Alternative Energy Source; Cross-Cultural Urban Sociology; The Urban Nomads, with Edward J. Kaiser and Ronald J. McAllister; *Impaired Competence in an Urban Community,* with Tzuen-jen Lei and Wayne Usui, publication expected, 1980.

*   *   *

BYLINSKY, Gene (Michael)   1930-

PERSONAL: Born December 30, 1930, in Belgrade, Yugoslavia; came to the United States in 1949, naturalized citizen, 1955; son of Michael Ivan (a civil engineer) and Dora (Shadan) Bylinsky; married Gwen Gallegos (a singing teacher), August 15, 1955; children: Tanya, Gregory. *Education:* Louisiana State University, B.A., 1955, graduate study, 1956. *Politics:* Independent. *Religion:* Greek Orthodox. *Office: Fortune,* Time-Life Building, Rockefeller Center, New York, N.Y. 10020.

CAREER: Wall Street Journal, New York City, staff reporter in Dallas, Tex., 1957-59, San Francisco, Calif., 1959-60, and New York City, 1960-61; *National Observer,* Washington, D.C., science writer, 1961-62; Newhouse Newspapers, Washington, D.C., science writer, 1962-66; *Fortune,* New York City, associate editor, 1966—. *Military service:* U.S. Army Reserve, active duty, 1956; became captain.

MEMBER: National Association of Science Writers. *Awards, honors:* Fourteen awards for articles published in *Fortune,* including special commendations from American Medical Association, 1967, 1968, 1972, and medical journalism award, 1974; Albert Lasker Medical Journalism Award from Lasker Foundation, 1970; Deadline Award from Sigma Delta Chi, 1970, 1972; Claude Bernard Scientific Journalism Award from National Society for Medical Research, 1973, 1974; James T. Grady Gold Medal from American Chemical Society, 1976, for interpreting chemistry to the public.

WRITINGS: The Innovation Millionaires: How They Succeed, Scribner, 1976; *Mood Control,* Scribner, 1978. Contributor to magazines.

SIDELIGHTS: Bylinsky writes: "My interest in science and technology, and specifically in their applications in industry, led first to a series on innovators in high technology, in *Fortune,* and later to my book. My interests revolve around understanding and popularizing science, technology, and medicine."

AVOCATIONAL INTERESTS: Hockey, soccer, football.

*   *   *

BYRON, Christopher M.   1944-

PERSONAL: Born December 27, 1944, in Washington, D.C.; son of Edward A. (a television producer) and Catherine (an actress; maiden name, McCune) Byron; married wife, Maria (a ballet dancer); children: Janalexis. *Education:* Yale University, B.A., 1968; Columbia University, J.D., 1972. *Home:* 4 Newton Ct., Kensington Church St., London W8, England. *Agent:* William Morris Agency, 1350 Avenue of the Americas, New York, N.Y. 10019.

CAREER/WRITINGS: Time, New York, N.Y., European correspondent, 1969—. Notable assignments include the Robert Vesco securities fraud, the crisis in Northern Ireland, and the Greek junta. *Military service:* U.S. Navy, 1962-64. *Member:* International Institute for Strategic Studies.

C

CABARGA, Leslie 1954-

PERSONAL: Born October 9, 1954, in Colorado; son of Demetrio E. (an artist) and Diane Theresa (a dancer; maiden name, Seger) Cabarga; children: Casey Robbins (daughter). Education: Educated in Marlboro, N.J. Religion: "I believe in the divine self." Home and office: 1982 15th St., San Francisco, Calif. 94114.

CAREER: Free-lance illustrator, 1969—. Art director for Rock, 1970—, Outside the Net, 1971-72, and City of San Francisco, 1975—. Member: Artists in Print (Graphic Arts Union of San Francisco).

WRITINGS: "The Fleischer Story" in the Golden Age of Animation (self-illustrated), Nostalgia Press, 1976. Contributor of illustrations to national magazines, including Rolling Stone, New West, National Lampoon, and Chic, and various newspapers.

WORK IN PROGRESS: "Trying to become a publisher of art books"; Movie Ads of San Francisco and Victorian Architectural Motifs.

SIDELIGHTS: Cabarga remarks: "I am predominantly an illustrator who studies the styles of art of the twenties and thirties and tries to emulate them. Frequently I want to communicate my excitement over an art movement to others; hence my books. I foresee books in the future about architecture, hand lettering, and commercial art.

"My father has been the most influential artist in my life and now that I've reawakened his interest in art by passing work on to him, he might say the same of me.

"Other illustrators whose styles have influenced me are Andrew Loomis, Rockwell Kent, Duke Wellington (a 1930's poster designer), and of course the Fleischer Studios."

*   *   *

CADET, John 1935-
(Charles Brown, Fred Greene)

PERSONAL: Born June 8, 1935, in London, England; son of Alexis Walter (a factory worker) and Amelia (Whelan) Cadet. Education: Cheshire County Training School, teaching certificate, 1958. Home: Daroon Withaya Anuban, Soi Lang Wat Suan Dawk, Chiang Mai, Thailand.

CAREER: Civil servant in London, England, 1955-56; teacher of English in secondary school in Hampshire, England, 1958-59; teacher of English as a foreign language,

under the auspices of the British Council, in Teheran, Iran, 1960, Bangkok, Thailand, 1961-67, and Kyoto, Japan, 1968-73; writer, 1973—. Teacher at the Royal School in Bangkok's Chitrlada Palace, 1966-67. News editor of Bangkok World, 1961-66, and Thai Television and FM-Radio, 1966. Military service: British Army, 1953-55.

WRITINGS: The Ramakien, Kodansha International, 1971. Contributor of articles and stories under pseudonyms Charles Brown and Fred Greene to magazines, mainly in Southeast Asia.

WORK IN PROGRESS: Short stories; work on the Wetsundorn Chadok, a Thai version of one of the Buddhist birth-stories.

SIDELIGHTS: Cadet told CA: "I have spent most of my adult life abroad, travelling extensively and teaching in the Near and Far East and Southeast Asia. The Ramakien, a renarration of the Thai version of the Indian Ramayana, was well-received in scholarly circles, the noted American specialist in Eastern literature, Henry Willis Wells, saying of it, 'I have rarely seen a book produced with such elegance and impeccable taste and with literature and art so happily combined. The total effect comes, in my opinion, virtually to perfection.' My fiction, published so far mainly in Southeast Asia, shows my concern over the dangers to the individual of rootlessness and isolation, and expresses my conviction that social as well as individual fulfillment can be achieved only through transcendence of personal, social and cultural limitation. If you want it in a nutshell, I'm in favour of change, of radical change. And as I don't expect change to occur without a struggle, I hope to make my writing an effective weapon and to use it well."

*   *   *

CAINE, Mitchell
See SPARKIA, Roy (Bernard)

*   *   *

CALDECOTT, Moyra 1927-

PERSONAL: Born June 1, 1927, in Pretoria, South Africa; naturalized British citizen; daughter of Frederick Stanley (a receiver of revenue) and Jessy Florence (Harris) Brown; married Oliver Zerffi Stratford Caldecott (a publisher and artist), April 5, 1951; children: Stratford Stanley, Julian Oliver, Rachel Lester. Education: University of Natal,

B.A. (honors), 1949, M.A., 1950. *Politics:* "No political affiliation." *Religion:* "Religious, but no particular affiliation." *Residence:* London, England.

CAREER: University of Cape Town, Cape Town, South Africa, junior lecturer in English, 1950; teacher at high school in London, England, 1951; Central Board for Conscientious Objectors, London, art gallery assistant and clerk, 1951-52; writer, 1953—. Has given poetry readings.

WRITINGS: The Weapons of the Wolfhound (novel), Rex Collings, 1976; *The Sacred Stones* (trilogy of novels), Volume I: *The Tall Stones*, Hill & Wang, 1977, Volume II: *The Temple of the Sun*, Rex Collings, 1977, Hill & Wang, 1978, Volume III: *Shadow on the Stones*, Hill & Wang, 1978; *Adventures by Leaf Light* (juvenile), Green Tiger Press, 1978; *The Lily and the Bull* (novel), Rex Collings, 1979.

Plays: "The Runaway," British Broadcasting Corp., Overseas Service, 1960; "The Wanting Bird" (for children), first produced in London at Rosendale Junior School, 1963; "The Forty Nine Days" (three-act), first produced in California, 1978.

Work represented in anthologies, including *Gallery*, Methuen; *Rhyme and Rhythm*, Macmillan; *Reading Aloud*, Macmillan. Contributor of poems and articles to magazines, including *Outposts*, *Freeway*, *Brief*, and *British Wheel of Yoga*.

WORK IN PROGRESS: A sequel to *The Weapons of the Wolfhound*, set in the Hebrides around the twelfth century; a novel set in ancient Egypt; a science fiction novel; further adventures by Leaf Light; *The King of Shadows*, a novel set in Glastonbury, England circa 600 A.D.

SIDELIGHTS: Moyra Caldecott writes: "My chief interest is the exploration of ancient civilizations for information about a perennial wisdom that I feel is vital to our civilization, but has all but been forgotten in our exploitation of our planet for material gain.

"I have attended many adult educational courses in astronomy (I am *very* interested in space exploration) and geology. I read widely, but am mainly interested in ancient history, religious and philosophical writings, and science fiction. I do not join organizations but I attend conferences and lectures given by the Wrekin Trust (a charitable foundation for those who are committed to the exploration of their spiritual natures and the development of consciousness). I am hopeful of the *new age* when men will remember they are eternal beings in passage on the earth—each with dignity and responsibility for the whole.

"Although I am intensely interested in the working of intuition and imagination and what we loosely term the 'paranormal,' I am anxious to keep the balancing strength of reason, and a sense of discrimination."

AVOCATIONAL INTERESTS: Gardening, pottery and batik making, painting.

BIOGRAPHICAL/CRITICAL SOURCES: Times Educational Supplement, November 18, 1977.

* * *

CALDWELL, Helen F. 1904-

PERSONAL: Born July 9, 1904, in Omaha, Neb.; daughter of Lyle Sherman (an industrial engineer) and Mary (in insurance business; maiden name, Trumbull) Caldwell. *Education:* University of California, Los Angeles, A.B., 1925, M.A., 1939. *Home:* 11639 Kiowa Ave., Los Angeles, Calif. 90049. *Office:* Department of Classics, University of California, Los Angeles, Calif. 90024.

CAREER: Classical Center, Los Angeles, Calif., researcher, writer, and lecturer, 1929-35; University of California, Los Angeles, lecturer in classics, 1942-70, senior lecturer emeritus, 1970—. *Awards, honors:* Named officer of Order of the Southern Cross by the Government of Brazil, 1959; Shirley Farr fellowship from American Association of University Women, 1959-60; Rockefeller Foundation grants, 1961, 1963.

WRITINGS: (Editor of English language version) Paul Friedlander, *Plato I*, Pantheon, 1958; *The Brazilian Othello of Machado de Assis: A Study of Dom Casmurro*, University of California Press, 1960; *Ancient Poets' Guide to UCLA Gardens*, Regents of University of California, 1968; *Machado de Assis: The Brazilian Master and His Novels*, University of California Press, 1970; *Michio Ito: The Dancer and His Dances*, University of California Press, 1977.

Translator; all works of fiction by Machado de Assis: *Dom Casmurro*, Noonday Press, 1953, revised edition (with introduction), University of California Press, 1965; *What Went on at the Baroness'*, Magpie Press, 1963; (with William L. Grossman) *The Psychiatrist and Other Stories by Machado de Assis*, University of California Press, 1963; *Esau and Jacob*, University of California Press, 1965; *Counselor Ayres' Memorial*, University of California Press, 1972.

WORK IN PROGRESS: A dance motion picture.

SIDELIGHTS: Helen Caldwell writes: "Although all Machado de Assis' writing bears the stamp of genius—whether it be poetry, fiction, drama, criticism, journalism, speeches, correspondence, or the reports he made as a government administrator—it is as a fiction writer that he is of principal interest to me. In his last five novels at least, he is an artist of universal stature, so far ahead of his time in both artistic concept and narrative technique that he speaks more clearly to us today than he did to his contemporaries. In those novels he boldly created powerful, individual characters, as well as the action itself, not through realistic detail but by means of a web of allusion and symbolism: each novel is a prose poem employing the metaphor of poetry. Though the themes of all are concerned with the problem of evil, the one quality that manifests itself in every piece of Assis' fiction, in every one of his personages, is comedy, comedy in all its many forms: wit, irony, satire, parody, humor, and the rest. I consider Machado de Assis the most original spirit to have come out of Brazil's rich, four-century long literary tradition.

"Michio Ito (with whom I studied for thirteen years) pioneered artistic dance in the United States, 1916-1941. My book seeks to explain his dances in such simple terms that the reader will perceive their relation to music and resemblance to poetry, and thus come not only to a clear comprehension of dance as an art and of the distinction between art and entertainment but also to an understanding of the basis of art itself. By way of illustration Ito's career is traced from its beginning in Europe to its climax in California with the great symphonic choreographies performed in Hollywood Bowl and Pasadena Rose Bowl. Noted are sources of inspiration and the spark that passed between him and other artists: Debussy, Shaw, Yeats, Pound, Foujita, Griffes, Yamada, Stravinsky, and many more."

* * *

CAMERON, Eleanor Elford 1910-

PERSONAL: Born November 28, 1910, in St. Paul, Minn.; daughter of Albert Sydney (an insurance executive) and Ethel Mae (Canniff) Elford; married Harold William Cameron, August 29, 1933 (divorced, 1947); married William Harrison Buck (an engineer), July 30, 1977; children: Anne (Mrs. Bryan Ekren), Carol (Mrs. Joseph Fleury). *Education:* University of Washington, Seattle, B.A., 1932; University of California at Los Angeles, graduate study, 1949-50, 1960-62. *Religion:* Methodist. *Home and office:* 537 Bellevue Way S.E., #108, Bellevue, Wash. 98004. *Agent:* Elaine Markson, 44 Greenwich Ave., New York, N.Y. 10011.

CAREER: Automobile Club, San Francisco, Calif., travel counselor, 1959; University of California at Los Angeles, secretary, 1960-61; Diamond Plastics, Los Angeles, secretary, 1961-62; Northwest Artists, Bellevue, Wash., gallery administrator, 1964-66; First Methodist Church, Bellevue, secretary, 1966-67; writer, 1967—. Speaker at conferences on novel writing. *Member:* Pacific Northwest Writers Conference, Free Lance Writers of Seattle, Alpha Phi.

WRITINGS—Suspense novels: *House on the Beach,* Pocket Books, 1972; *A Place of Mischief,* Popular Library, 1972; *The Spider Stone,* Dell, 1973; *The Young Widow,* Dell, 1973; *The Curse of Casa del Monte,* Dell, 1975.

WORK IN PROGRESS: Working on a saga, as yet untitled.

SIDELIGHTS: "Though always given to 'storytelling,'" Cameron told *CA,* "my first serious interest in writing as a profession came in 1960 while I was working as a secretary at U.C.L.A." There, Cameron studied creative writing with Maren Elwood (author of several books on writing) for two years. In 1962, she continued, "determined to be a professional writer, I sold my car, most of my furniture, and went to live in the third floor apartment of my sister in Cleveland, Ohio, where for two years I continued my studies with Maren Elwood by correspondence. In 1964, I returned to the Seattle area and worked in Bellevue until 1967, when I decided to take the plunge into full-time writing. From then on, I wrote practically seven days a week, averaging six to ten hours a day.

"My first five books were suspense stories. Motivation for the first was difficulty in plotting. After that I was hooked. After my fifth book, however, I decided to try for a bigger, more comprehensive, book which I am now finishing—a tale of adventure suspense on a cross-country Canadian train. I am also gathering data on a four generation saga beginning in Cornwall, England, and ending in the Pacific Northwest.

"Writing is not a profession alone; it is a disease—one I thoroughly enjoy."

BIOGRAPHICAL/CRITICAL SOURCES: Seattle Times, January 31, 1972, March 3, 1974; *Carmel Pine Cone,* May 5, 1972; *Bellevue American,* July 20, 1972.

*   *   *

CAMPBELL, Graeme 1931-

PERSONAL: Born June 26, 1931, in Glasgow, Scotland; son of Samuel (a bank manager) and Grace (Clement) Campbell. *Education:* Royal Scottish Academy of Music and Drama, diploma, 1954. *Home:* 5 Lyndhurst Rd., London N.W.3, England.

CAREER: Performed with repertory companies in Scotland, 1954-55, and England, 1955-61; Old Vic Co., London, England, actor in London, Canada, and the United States, 1955-57; Royal Opera House, London, singer in London, Italy, Spain, and Germany, 1962-78; writer, 1962—. *Military service:* Royal Air Force, 1949-51. *Member:* British Actors Equity Association, Scottish Society of Playwrights. *Awards, honors:* Awards from Platt Arts Foundation, 1970,

for "Totem," and Scottish Education Trust, 1976, for "Small Thoughts From the Revolution."

WRITINGS—Plays: "Escape from Eden" (three-act), first produced in London, England, at Lyric Theatre, 1962; "Facets on a Golden Image" (three-act), first produced in Sheffield, England, at Crucible Theatre, 1973; "Small Thoughts from the Revolution" (two-act), first produced in Edinburgh, Scotland, at Traverse Theatre, March, 1976; "The Children," first broadcast by British Broadcasting Corp., September, 1978.

Unproduced plays: "Totem" (two-act), 1967; "Lodgings" (three-act), 1968; "Adam and Eve and Evadne" (three-act), 1970, revised, 1978; "At Base" (two-act), 1974; "Blinkers" (three-act), 1978.

SIDELIGHTS: Campbell comments: "Mainly I write politically motivated plays on the erosion of the individual. Comedy is almost always used with irony, to make the audience examine its own individual attitudes and preconceptions formed from 'received ideas.' My own beliefs are apolitical and neo-anarchist."

*   *   *

CAMPBELL, Ken 1941-
(Henry Pilk)

PERSONAL: Born December 10, 1941, in Ilford, England; son of Anthony Colin (a telegrapher) and Elsie (Handley) Campbell. *Education:* Royal Academy of Dramatic Art, diploma, 1961. *Politics:* "Anarchy and fun." *Religion:* "Forteanism." *Home and office:* Studio 96, Haverstock Hill, London N.W.3, Englandim Corrie, Fraser & Dunlop, 91 Regent St., London W1K 8RU, England.

CAREER: Actor and director, 1962—; associated with "Ken Campbell's Roadshow," 1970-73; Science Fiction Theatre of Liverpool, Liverpool, England, co-founder and artistic director, 1976—.

WRITINGS—Plays: *You See the Thing Is This* (one-act; first produced in London, March, 1970), Evans Plays, 1971; (under pseudonym Henry Pilk) *Pilk's Madhouse* (first produced in Toronto at Passe Muraille Theatre, 1973), Playwrights Co-Op, 1973; *Old King Cole* (juvenile; two-act; first produced in Stoke-on-Trent at Victoria Theatre, December, 1968), Methuen, 1976; *Jack Sheppard; or, Anything You Say Will Be Twisted* (first produced in Bolton at Octagon Theatre, April, 1969), Macmillan, 1976; (editor and translator from German) F. K. Waechter, *Schools for Clowns,* Methuen, 1977.

Unpublished plays: "One Night I Danced with Mr. Dalton," first produced by American Broadcasting Co. (ABC-TV), 1969; "Just Go Will You Harry" (one-act comedy), first produced in Stoke-on-Trent, England, at Victoria Theatre, June, 1969; "Christopher Pea" (one-act farce), first produced in Stoke-on-Trent at Victoria Theatre, June, 1970; (with Dave Hill and Andy Andrews) "Bendigo" (two-act musical), first produced in Nottingham, England at Playhouse, June, 1974; "The Great Caper" (two-act), first produced in London, England, at Royal Court Theatre, October, 1974; "Little Boy Blue; or, Skungpoomery" (two-act), first produced in Nottingham at Playhouse, April, 1975; (with Hill and Andrews) "Walking Like Geoffrey" (juvenile; two-act musical), first produced in Nottingham at Playhouse, June, 1975. Also author of "Bar Room Tales," "An Evening with Sylvester McCoy, Human Bomb," and "Stonehenge Kit the Ancient Brit."

WORK IN PROGRESS: Research for *The Men in Black,* "who warn you off serious U.F.O. research."

SIDELIGHTS: Campbell writes: "I want to get the Science Fiction Theatre of Liverpool firmly on its feet. To date, we've done five plays."

BIOGRAPHICAL/CRITICAL SOURCES: Robert Anton Wilson, *Cosmic Trigger,* And/Or Press, 1977.

* * *

CANTOR, Eli 1913-
(Agnes Wheatley)

PERSONAL: Born September 9, 1913, in Bronx, N.Y.; son of Sol M. (a typographer) and Bertha (Seidler) Cantor; married Beatrice Mink (a consultant in audio-speech disabilities), October 4, 1942; children: Ann, Fred. *Education:* New York University, B.S., 1934, M.A., 1935; Harvard University, J.D., 1938. *Politics:* "All systems need gadflies, but with age I've come to deplore rebels without proper cause." *Religion:* "All formal religions tend to be manipulative; mine is private." *Home and office:* 15 West 81st St., New York, N.Y. 10024. *Agent:* Paul Gitlin, 7 West 51st St., New York, N.Y. 10019.

CAREER: Columbia Broadcasting System, New York, N.Y., member of legal staff, 1938-39; *Esquire,* Chicago, Ill., member of editorial staff, 1940-41; Research Institute of America, New York, N.Y., editor-in-chief of *Research Institute Report,* 1941-60; Photo-Composing Room, Inc., New York City, president, 1961-65; Composing Room, Inc., New York City, chairman of board of directors, 1965-71; Royal Composing Room, New York City, chairman emeritus, 1971—; writer and consultant on management, printing, and publishing, 1971—. Director of Gallery 303, 1961-71. Lecturer at colleges and universities, including Harvard University, California State Polytechnic College, New York University, Yale University, and Pratt Institute. Chairman of board of directors of Printing Industries of Metropolitan New York, 1970-72; chairman of research-technical committee of Graphic Arts Technical Foundation, 1971—; chairman of board of directors of Printing Industries of America, 1973-74; graphics panelist for National Endowment for the Arts, 1973—; has represented his industry before the U.S. Congress. Worked for Office of War Information.

MEMBER: Advertising Typographers of America (local chairman, 1967-70), Authors Guild of Authors League of America, Harvard Club. *Awards, honors:* Awards from the graphics industry for design and leadership; O'Brien award for best short stories, 1940.

WRITINGS: *Enemy in the Mirror* (novel), Crown, 1977.

Plays: "Old Lady" (three-act), first produced in New York City at Oscar Serlin Workshop, 1943; "Our Secret Weapon" (television play), first produced in 1943; "Candy Store" (three-act), first produced in New York City at New York City Drama Festival, 1948; "The Golden Goblet" (two-act), first produced in New York City at Theatre 13, 1960; "Yes, There Are Buffalo in Italy" (one-act), first produced at Institute for Advancement of Theatre Arts, 1965. Also author of seven plays for "Armstrong Circle Theatre," 1951-52.

Work anthologized in *Anthology of Magazine Verse for 1936,* edited by Alan Pater; *O'Brien Best Short Stories,* 1940; and *100 Radio Plays,* edited by Kozlenko, 1941. Contributor of stories, poems, and articles to popular and literary magazines, including *Story, Accent,* and *Poetry.*

WORK IN PROGRESS: A gothic thriller, *Baron of Darkness,* under pseudonym Agnes Wheatley; *With Love* (tentative title), a serious novel.

SIDELIGHTS: Cantor writes: "The generational swinging of the social pendulum is my main subject. It gives some people a free, exciting ride; others it slices to pieces. Whether it 'advances' Hegelianly as it swings no one knows. My writing is concerned with the impact on individuals, for good or bad; and I am fundamentally concerned with how society is affected by the dynamics of psychological growth (or arrest) in infancy and childhood and in modern family life."

AVOCATIONAL INTERESTS: Painting, playing chamber music ("on the Cremona violin I am fortunate enough to own"), travel.

BIOGRAPHICAL/CRITICAL SOURCES: *Publishers Weekly,* January 2, 1978.

* * *

CAPECI, Dominic Joseph, Jr. 1940-

PERSONAL: Surname is pronounced Ka-*peh*-chi; born July 23, 1940, in Port Chester, N.Y.; son of Dominic Joseph (a lawyer) and Mary Rita (Cashin) Capeci; married Norma Donoghue, June 12, 1965; children: Dominic Edward, James Joseph. *Education:* University of New Mexico, B.A., 1962, M.A., 1964; University of California, Riverside, Ph.D., 1970. *Home:* 648 South McCann Ave., Springfield, Mo. 65804. *Office:* Department of History, Southwest Missouri State University, Springfield, Mo. 65802.

CAREER: Youngstown State University, Youngstown, Ohio, assistant professor of history, 1969-72; Southwest Missouri State University, Springfield, assistant professor, 1972-75, associate professor of history, 1975—. *Member:* Organization of American Historians, Association for the Study of Negro Life and History, Phi Alpha Theta.

WRITINGS: *The Harlem Riot of 1943,* Temple University Press, 1977. Contributor to history and ethnic studies journals.

WORK IN PROGRESS: A book on the 1943 Detroit race riot; studying black leaders.

SIDELIGHTS: Capeci writes: "I am interested in the multi-ethnic and multi-racial dimensions of our society, which can only be fully understood in the historical perspective. By critically analyzing and objectively depicting those dimensions, I focus on their significance in a nation whose citizenry recently has come to recognize its pluralism. Indeed, one of the most important historical (and contemporary) questions that remains to be answered is whether we can resolve past ethnic and racial conflict, and appreciate and respect—as opposed to merely recognize—our diversity. In the past and in the present, the rhetoric of democracy and humanity has been accompanied by undemocratic and, at times, repressive behavior, which does not bode well for the future of our ethnic and race relations."

* * *

CAPPO, Joseph 1936-

PERSONAL: Original name, Joseph Cacioppo; name legally changed in 1969; born February 24, 1936, in Chicago, Ill.; son of Joseph Victor (a postal clerk) and Frances (Maggio) Cacioppo; married Mary Anne Hetterick, May 6, 1967; children: Elizabeth Anne, John Joseph. *Education:* DePaul University, B.A., 1957. *Home:* 823 Monticello Place, Evanston, Ill. 60201. *Office: Chicago Sun Times,* 401 North Wabash St., Chicago, Ill. 60611.

CAREER/WRITINGS: DePaul University, Chicago, Ill.,

publicity assistant, 1957-58, director of advertising and printing, 1958-59; Hollister Publications, Wilmette, Ill., reporter and writer, 1961-62; *Chicago Daily News,* Chicago, reporter, 1962-69, business columnist, 1969-78; *Chicago Sun Times,* Chicago, business columnist, 1978—. Notable assignments include coverage of the murder of eight nurses in 1966 and the 1968 Democratic Convention, a business tour and series on Japan, and a series on self-regulation of advertising. Conducts two daily radio programs on business. Lecturer and marketing consultant to businesses. *Military service:* U.S. Army, personnel specialist, 1959-61; became specialist 4. *Member:* Delta Mu Delta (honorary member). *Awards, honors:* Award from Illinois Press Association, 1962, for best feature story; National Headliner Award, 1967, for coverage of murders of eight student nurses; distinguished alumni award from DePaul University, 1976.

SIDELIGHTS: Cappo writes: "I didn't realize that I'm not a member of any societies or organizations until I looked at the question above. I guess that stems from the fact that I never went to a journalism school or even had a course in journalism. My entree into the business was working at my college newspaper. I always stress this when I speak to groups of young people. I think there are many factors that are far more important to a journalism career than a formal education in it. That makes me wonder why so many papers require job applicants to have a journalism degree.

"As far as avocations are concerned, that's what I consider most of my free-lance work to be. I enjoy speaking and lecturing because it provides the writer with a different medium for communicating with the public . . . and a different way of listening to them."

*   *   *

CARDARELLI, Joseph 1944-

PERSONAL: Born January 21, 1944, in West Virginia; son of Joseph J. (a general contractor) and Julia (Henshaw) Cardarelli. *Education:* University of Maryland, B.S., 1965; Johns Hopkins University, M.A., 1967. *Home:* 4629 Keswick Rd., Baltimore, Md. 21210. *Office:* Maryland Institute of Art, 1300 West Mount Royal Ave., Baltimore, Md. 21217.

CAREER: Maryland Institute of Art, Baltimore, assistant professor of English, 1967—. Director of Baltimore Poetry Project, 1976-77. *Member:* American Association of University Professors.

WRITINGS: Quickly Aging Here: Some Poets of the Seventies, Doubleday, 1969; *Milano Manifesto: Concept Is Concept,* Laughing Man Press, 1975; (with Anselm Hollo and Kirby Malone) *Phantom-Pod,* Phantom House, 1978; (with Marta Beckstrom) *Practical Alien Linguistics* (poems), Phantom House, 1978.

*   *   *

CAREW, Jan (Rynveld) 1925-

PERSONAL: Born September 24, 1925, in Agricola, Guyana; son of Charles Alan (a planter) and Kathleen (Robertson) Carew; married Joy Gleason (a university lecturer), September 28, 1975; children: Lisa Gioconda, Christopher David. *Education:* Attended Howard University, 1945-46, Western Reserve University (now Case Western Reserve University), 1946-48, and Charles University, Prague, 1949-50; Sorbonne, University of Paris, M.Sc., 1952. *Home:* 1910 Orrington Ave., Evanston, Ill. 60201. *Office:* Department of African-American Studies, Northwestern University, 2003 Sheridan Rd., Evanston, Ill. 60201.

CAREER: Customs officer in British Colonial Civil Service, Georgetown, Guyana, 1940-43; price control officer for government of Trinidad, Port-of-Spain, 1943-44; artist and writer in Paris, France, and Amsterdam, Holland, 1950-51; toured as an actor with Laurence Olivier Company, 1952; University of London, London, England, lecturer in race relations, 1953-59; director of culture and adviser to the prime minister of the government of British Guyana, 1962; Latin American correspondent for *London Observer,* 1962; artist and writer under contract to Associated Television (London) on island of Ibiza, Spain, 1963-64; adviser to the publicity secretariat of the government of Ghana, 1965-66; artist and writer, commissioned by Canadian Broadcasting Co. (CBC) to do numerous programs in Toronto, Ontario, 1966-69; Princeton University, Princeton, N.J., lecturer in Afro-American studies, 1969-72; Northwestern University, Evanston, Ill., professor and chairman of department of African-American studies, 1972—. Guest lecturer at Livingston College, Douglass College, and Rutgers University, 1969-72; consultant for English language and literature programs at New York University, 1969-72; guest lecturer at University of Surinam Teacher's Training College, 1975. Held a one-man exhibition of paintings at Imperial Institute, London, 1948. Did regular weekly programs for British Broadcasting Corp. (BBC) in London, 1953-59. Toured Federal Republic of Germany as an official guest of the Ministry of Culture, 1963 and 1967; toured Soviet Union as a guest of the Soviet Writer's Union, 1963 and 1965. Director of Caribbean Foundation for Rural Development and Education in Surinam, 1975.

MEMBER: American Association of University Professors. *Awards, honors:* "The Big Pride" (television play) was selected as best play of the year by the *London Daily Mirror,* 1964; Canada Council grant, 1969, for significant contributions to the arts; Burton International Fellowship from Harvard University Graduate School of Education, 1973 and 1974; Illinois Arts Council award for fiction, 1974; American Institute of Graphic Arts Certificate of Excellence, 1974, for *The Third Gift;* Casa de las Americas award for poetry, 1977.

WRITINGS: Streets of Eternity (poetry), privately printed, 1952; *Black Midas* (novel), Secker & Warburg, 1958, published as *A Touch of Midas,* Coward, 1959; *The Wild Coast* (novel), Secker & Warburg, 1958; *The Last Barbarian,* Secker & Warburg, 1960; *Moscow Is Not My Mecca,* Secker & Warburg, 1964, published as *Green Winter,* Stein & Day, 1965; (contributor) Andrew Salkey, editor, *Breaklight* (poetry), Hamish Hamilton , 1971; (contributor) Cecil Gray, editor, *Bite In* (poetry), Thomas Nelson, 1971; *The Third Gift* (juvenile), Little, Brown, 1974; *Children of the Sun* (juvenile), Little, Brown, 1978.

Plays: "Miracle in Lime Lane" (adaptation of a play by Coventry Taylor), produced in Spanish Town, Jamaica, 1962; "The University of Hunger" (three-act), produced in Georgetown, Guyana, at Georgetown Theatre, 1966; "Gentlemen Be Seated," produced in Belgrade, Yugoslavia, 1967; *Black Horse, Pale Rider* (two-act), University of the West Indies Extra-mural Department, 1970.

Television plays; all written for Associated Television, London, 1963-64, except as indicated: "The Big Pride," "The Day of the Fox," "Exile from the Sun," "The Baron of South Boulevard," "No Gown for Peter," "The Raiders," "The Smugglers," "A Roof of Stars," "The Conversion of Tiho," "Behind God's Back," Canadian Broadcasting Co., 1969.

Radio plays; broadcast by British Broadcasting Corp., 1960-69: "Song of the Riverman," "The Riverman," "University of Hunger," "The Legend of Nameless Mountain," "Ata," "Anancy and Tiger."

Work represented in several anthologies, including *Stories from the Caribbean*, edited by Andrew Salkey, Elek, 1965, and *Carifesta Anthology*, edited by A. J. Seymour, Guyana Lithographic Co., 1972.

Contributor of articles and essays to the *New York Times*, *Saturday Review*, *New Statesman*, and other periodicals. Editor of *De Kim* (multi-lingual poetry magazine in Amsterdam), 1951, *Kensington Post* (London newspaper), 1953, and *African Review*, 1965-66; publisher of *Cotopaxi* (a third-world literary magazine), 1969.

WORK IN PROGRESS: Green Mansions of the Sun, a novel; *Sea-Drums in My Blood*, poetry; *An Anthology of Latin American Writing in Transition; The Destruction of Caribbean Civilization*, a historical account of the first forty years of the Columbia era; *A Study of Three Maroon Wars*, about the Black-Seminole wars in Florida, Palmares, and the Maroon wars in Surinam; "Pageant of the Gods," a play for the stage.

SIDELIGHTS: When asked to comment on the aspirations of Third World peoples and on how he expressed his philosophy of life through his writing, Carew shared the following passages from his novel in progress, *Green Mansions of the Sun:* ". . . His Carib hero, Kai, said that everyone has a place, a piece of terrain, a spot on earth that was his very own, like the black leopard . . . if a hunter tried to kill him, that leopard would find his spot in the forest, and once he found it—look out hunter—for on his turf, he was invincible!

"This was something that Atlassa understood, not just the trappings, but the power to make the lowliest believe in themselves. Atlassa succeeded where no one else had, he began with the most despised, he made us all see ourselves as we really were. After his return, he started out by listening to us. No one had ever listened since Christobal and his cutthroat sailors had been discovered by the Amer-indians on their beaches. . . . After that, it was a long history of colonizers shouting orders, and the colonized never talking back. After long years of listening, Atlassa showed us new images of ourselves without the distortions."

Passages from Carew's essay, "The Caribbean Writer in Exile," elaborate upon his philosophy. "The Caribbean writer today is a creature balanced between limbo and nothingness, exile abroad and homelessness at home, between the people on the one hand and the creole and the colonizer on the other. . . . The writer is, therefore, islanded in the midst of marginal tides of sorrow, despair, hope, whirlpools of anxiety, cataracts of rage. He is the most articulate member of the marginal class, articulate, that is, with the written word. There are others of his class who speak to the mind's ear with music—the calypso, raggae, the folksong—and who speak with immediacy and a sensuous ease to a much vaster audience. . . . At a time when independence, that is, an anthem, a flag and a color on the map, brings into sharper focus questions of national identity and liberation, the Caribbean writer is faced with harsh choices. The end of his marginal status is now in sight. As an honorary member of the marginal class he has both consciously and unconsciously internalized the mounting chaos that is pushing this class inexorably, not into revolution but revolutionary situations. . . . They are often unsure of what they are for, but are absolutely certain of what they're against: the corrupt, bullying, pompous, dishonest, cruel, incompetent and often mindless

regimes under which they live. . . . 'All people have a right to share the waters of the River of Life and to drink with their own cups, but our cups have been broken' laments the Carib poem-hymn. The writer, artist, musician, is directly involved in the creative process of reshaping the broken cups. . . . Therefore, while we shape exquisite new cups, we must side by side with the disinherited millions of the Third World, confront those who would deny us our fair share of the waters of the River of Life. . . .''

BIOGRAPHICAL/CRITICAL SOURCES: Journal of Black Studies, 1977.

* * *

CARLINO, Lewis John 1932-

PERSONAL: Born January 1, 1932, in New York, N.Y.; married; children: three. *Education:* Attended El Camino College; University of Southern California, B.A., M.A., 1960. *Agent:* c/o Dramatists Play Service, 440 Park Avenue South, New York, N.Y. 10016.

CAREER: Playwright, screen and television writer, motion picture director. *Military service:* U.S. Air Force. *Member:* Actors Studio (member of New York Playwrights Unit), New Dramatists Committee. *Awards, honors:* British Drama League prize in International Playwriting competition, 1960; Rockefeller Grant for Theatre; Huntington Hartford fellowship; Yaddo fellowship; Obie award; nominated for Academy award for best original screenplay, 1968, for "The Brotherhood."

WRITINGS—Plays: *The Brick and the Rose: A Collage for Voices* (first produced in Los Angeles, 1957), Dramatists Play Service, 1959; *Junk Yard* (one-act), Dramatists Play Service, 1959; *Used Car for Sale* (one-act), Dramatists Play Service, 1959; "The Beach People," first produced in Madison, Ohio, 1962; "Postlude and Snowangel," first produced in New York City, 1962; *Cages: Snowangel and Epiphany* (two one-act plays; first produced Off-Broadway, 1963), Random House, 1964; *The Dirty Old Man* (first produced in New York City, 1964), Dramatists Play Service, 1964 (also see below); *Telemachus Clay: A Collage for Voices* (first produced Off-Broadway, 1963), Random House, 1964; *The Exercise* (first produced in Stockbridge, Mass., 1967, produced on Broadway, 1968), Dramatists Play Service, 1968.

Collections of plays: *Objective Case* [and] *Mr. Flannery's Ocean* ("Objective Case" first produced in Westport, Conn., 1962; "Mr. Flannery's Ocean" [includes "Piece and Precise"], first produced in Westport, Conn., 1962), Dramatists Play Service, 1961; *Two Short Plays: Sarah and the Sax, and High Sign*, Dramatists Play Service, 1962 (also see below); *Doubletalk: Sarah and the Sax, and The Dirty Old Man* (two one-act plays; first produced Off-Broadway, 1964; "Sarah and the Sax" produced separately in London, 1971), Random House, 1964.

Screenplays: (With David Ely) "Seconds," 1966; "The Fox," 1968; *The Brotherhood*, New American Library, 1968; "The Mechanic," 1972; "The Sailor Who Fell From Grace With the Sea" (adapted from a novel by Yukio Mishima), Avco Embassy Pictures, 1976.

Television play: "In Search of America," 1971.

SIDELIGHTS: An ornithologist discovered by his wife in a homosexual act turns into a rooster who lays eggs. This theatrical metaphor is the situation of "Epiphany," which with "Snowangel" made up the bill of one-act plays called "Cages," Lewis John Carlino's first notable New York production in 1963. Although it brought many unfavorable reviews, it was impressive enough to inspire the production of his full-length play, "Telemachus Clay." Done by eleven actors sitting on barstools, this reminded one critic of "Under Milkwood" and "Spoon River." "Here and there it erupts into something wild and wonderful," Henry Hewes wrote in *Saturday Review.* And "Telemachus Clay," "for all its failings, contains solid evidence of talent and an admirable ambition to deal with human experience in larger-than-life terms."

Carlino continues to provoke mixed critical reaction with his motion picture work. Renata Adler called the screenplay of "The Fox" intelligent, and "The Brotherhood" was nominated in 1968 for the Academy award for best written original screenplay. In 1976, "The Sailor Who Fell From Grace With the Sea," written and directed by Carlino, met with critical vengeance reminiscent of that which followed his plays. Some critics, however, felt Carlino's adaptation was carefully done, and his collaboration with cameraman Douglas Slocombe was commended for its beautiful cinematography.

BIOGRAPHICAL/CRITICAL SOURCES: Theatre Arts, August, 1963; *New Yorker,* November 23, 1963, May 16, 1964, May 4, 1968; *Saturday Review,* December 7, 1963; *New Republic,* December 21, 1963; *Commonweal,* January 31, 1964; *Newsweek,* May 18, 1964.

*   *   *

CARLISLE, Regis 1955-

PERSONAL: Born November 9, 1955, in Pontiac, Colo.; son of Pedro (a fisherman) and Cloris (a plastics tester; maiden name, King) Carlisle; married Bonnie Lindahll (a poet), June 12, 1973; children: Calen, David. *Education:* Educated in Nippy Tuck, Mich. *Politics:* "I vote for the party—not the man." *Religion:* "None right now—perhaps if the tithe percentage was lowered. . . ." *Home:* 221 Lewiston Rd., Grosse Pointe Farms, Mich. 48236.

CAREER: Writer. Worked as gardener in Sands, Mich., 1974-75; pole vault instructor in Everglades Edge, Fla., 1975-77; newspaper deliverer, 1977—. *Member:* Thinkers Society (East), Grosse Pointe Ponderers Social Club, Bridge Boys. *Awards, honors:* Golden Seat Award from Thinkers Society, 1969, for *The Philosopher of Paris;* New Star on Horizon Trophy from Discoverers of Unknown Learners (DUL), 1978, for *Anarchists Unite!.*

WRITINGS: The Philosopher of Paris (novel), Dis Counte Press, 1969; *Eiffel Eyefull* (travelogue), Tourer's Guidebooks, 1969; *Europe on $1.00 a Day* (travelogue), Tourer's Guidebooks, 1970; *The Essential Relevance of Disbelief and Other Essays,* Dis Counte Press, 1971; *The Sheer Hopelessness of Life, Existence, and Social Participation* (novel), Loathers Society Press, 1973; *Pity the Thinker* (novel), Dis Counte Press, 1975; *Life Has Nothing to Do With What Happens,* Loathers Society, 1977; *Anarchists Unite!,* Organizations Ltd., 1978.

WORK IN PROGRESS: I Believe in Nihilism; two more novels about Paris, one with "Hugo, the lead character in *The Sheer Hopelessness of Life, Existence, and Social Participation*"; a chronicle of paranoia concerning one man's battle against the American Medical Association, *A Lobotomy Lurks . . . Just Ahead.*

SIDELIGHTS: Carlisle told *CA:* "Despite my unorthodox titles, all my books deal with *novel* situations. I came to writing at an early age (fourteen) but I made up in enthusiasm what I lacked in experience, knowledge, and skill. My first book, *The Philosopher of Paris,* was brought to the attention of publishers by my English teacher who thought it would be wonderful in a 'Things to Avoid' category of an English textbook. How foolish he felt when my Uncle Ned, senior editor of Dis Counte Press, accepted the manuscript for its literary worth.

"Well, that first check from the publishers convinced me that I had a future as a writer. I put the whole check (fifteen dollars!) in the bank and headed straight for the typewriter and I've been here ever since. I now devote equal time to two major themes: the foolishness of certainty and the hell of disbelief. Only man, in his unique intelligence, can realize how foolish he is. I believe my books serve as reminders of this truism."

AVOCATIONAL INTERESTS: "Searching for the metaphysical essence, exploring the existential optimism of death, expanding theosophical boundaries, peering over the horizons of mental aesthetics, and collecting stamps."

*   *   *

CARPENTER, John A(lcott) 1921-1978

August 1, 1921—May 15, 1978; American educator, post-Civil War historian, and author of works in his field. Carpenter appeared on the television series, "The American Presidency: The Men and the Office." Prominent among his writings are *Civil War Studies* and *Ulysses S. Grant.* He died in White Plains, N.Y. Obituaries and other sources: *Directory of American Scholars,* Volume I: *History,* 6th edition, Bowker, 1974; *New York Times,* May 17, 1978. (See index for *CA* sketch)

*   *   *

CARRICK, Malcolm 1945-

PERSONAL: Born June 23, 1945, in Cardiff, Wales; son of John (a publisher) and Jane (a lecturer; maiden name, Perkins) Carrick. *Education:* Attended Beckenham Art College, 1961-62, Ravens-bourne Art College, 1962-63, and Chelsea Art College, 1963-66. *Home:* 4 Palace Grove, Fox Hill, Upper Norwood SE19 2X10, England.

CAREER: Musician, composer, artist, writer.

WRITINGS—Children's books; all self illustrated, except as noted: *The Wise Men of Gotham,* Collins, 1973, Viking, 1975; *All Sorts of Everything* (not self-illustrated), Heinemann, 1973; *Mr. Pedagouge's Sneeze,* Deutsch, 1974; *The Extraordinary Hatmaker,* Transworld, 1974; *The Fairy Tale Book,* Evans Brothers, 1974; *The Farmer's Wish,* Transworld, 1975; *Make and Do,* Evans Brothers, 1975; *Splodges,* Collins, 1975, Viking, 1976; *Once There Was a Boy and Other Stories* (not self-illustrated), Penguin, 1975; *Making Magic,* Carousel, 1976; *See You Later Alligator,* Deutsch, 1976; *Tramps,* Harper, 1977; *Higgelty Pigglety,* E.M.I. Ltd., 1977; *Today Is Shrew's Day,* Harper, 1978; *Science Experiments,* Carousel, 1978; *I Can Squash Elephants,* Viking, 1978; *Horror Costumes and Makeup,* Transworld, 1978; *Making Masks,* Transworld, in press; *You'll Be Sorry, You'll Be Sorry When I'm Dead,* Harper, in press.

Author of teleplays with music, including "A Little Black Magic," 1975, and "Walkabout," 1976. Contributor of teleplays to British Broadcasting Corp., series including "Play School," "Blue-Peter," and "For My Next Trick." Composer for "Pop It Goes," 1977.

WORK IN PROGRESS: Illustrating a book by Cynthia King, *The Year of Mr. Nobody.*

SIDELIGHTS: Carrick told CA: "Interestingly, I had thought of giving up writing books for children as all the work I wanted to do was considered too graphic, too thoughtful, and introspective for English publishers and audiences. So I went to New York and found a much better reception for my particular fantasy world tinged with autobiography—as in Tramp—and my hard graphic style of illustrating—as in I Can Squash Elephants. I really consider myself an American author as only there can the full range of styles and genres I use be fullfilled."

* * *

CARSON, Rachel Louise 1907-1964

PERSONAL: Born May 27, 1907, in Springfield, Pa.; daughter of Robert Warden and Maria Frazier (McLean) Carson. Education: Pennsylvania College for Women, A.B., 1929; Johns Hopkins University, A.M., 1932; further graduate study at the Marine Biological Laboratory, Woods Hole, Mass. Religion: Presbyterian. Residence: Silver Spring, Md.

CAREER: University of Maryland, College Park, member of the zoology staff, 1931-36; U.S. Bureau of Fisheries (now the Fish and Wildlife Service), Washington, D.C., aquatic biologist, beginning, 1936, editor-in-chief, 1949-52; full-time writer, 1952-64. Instructor at Johns Hopkins University, summers, 1930-36. Member: American Ornithologists' Union, National Institute of Arts and Letters, Royal Society of Literature (fellow), Audubon Society (director in Washington, D.C.), Society of Women Geographers. Awards, honors: Eugene Saxton Memorial fellowship, 1949; George Westinghouse Science Writing award, 1950; National Book Award, 1951, for The Sea Around Us; Guggenheim fellowship, 1951-52; John Burroughs medal, 1952; Henry G. Bryant Gold Medal, 1952; Page-One award, 1952; Frances K. Hutchinson medal, 1952; silver jubilee medal from Limited Editions Club, 1954; book award from National Council of Women in the U.S., 1956; achievement award from American Association of University Women, 1956; Schweitzer medal from Animal Welfare Institute, 1962; Women's National Book Association Constance Lindsay Skinner award, 1963; New England Outdoor Writers Association award, 1963; Conservationist of the Year award from National Wildlife Federation, 1963; achievement award from Einstein College of Medicine, 1963; gold medal from New York Zoological Society; special citations from the Garden Club of America, the Pennsylvania Federation of Women's Clubs, and the Izaak Walton League of America, 1963. D.Sc. from Oberlin College, 1952; D.Litt. from Pennsylvania College for Women, 1952, Drexel Institute of Technology, 1952, and Smith College, 1953.

WRITINGS: Under the Sea-Wind: A Naturalist's Picture of Ocean Life (illustrated by Howard French), Simon & Schuster, 1941, new edition, Oxford University Press, 1952; Food from the Sea: Fish and Shellfish of New England, U.S. Government Printing Office, 1943; Food from Home Waters: Fishes of the Middle West, U.S. Department of the Interior, Fish and Wildlife Service, 1943; Fish and Shellfish of the South Atlantic and Gulf Coasts, U.S. Government Printing Office, 1944; Fish and Shellfish of the Middle Atlantic Coast, U.S. Government Printing Office, 1945.

The Sea Around Us (illustrated by Katherine L. Howe), Oxford University Press, 1951, revised edition, Watts, 1966; The Edge of the Sea (illustrated by Bob Hines), Houghton, 1955; Silent Spring (illustrated by Lois Darling and Louis Darling), Houghton, 1962; The Sense of Wonder, Harper,

1965; Life Under the Sea (selection from The Sea Around Us), Golden Press, 1968; The Rocky Coast, Macmillan, 1971.

SIDELIGHTS: Rachel Carson combined her interest in nature and her desire to write into a very successful career. She acquired her love of nature from her mother, who introduced her to the marvels of the outdoors and its creatures. As early as age ten, her writing ability was manifested in contributions to the St. Nicholas Magazine.

Under the Sea-Wind, Rachel Carson's first book, grew out of an essay entitled Undersea, which was published in Atlantic Monthly in 1937. Reviews of the book, which appeared four years later, included that written by a Books reviewer: "Miss Carson's unemotional handling of her subject matter is anything but dull. There is drama in every sentence. She rouses our interest in this ocean world and we want to watch it." A Scientific Book Club Review critic observed: "Not since the publication of Salar the Salmon has there been a volume so replete with information about sea life as this book by Rachel Carson. . . . In the three parts of the book, Miss Carson employs the device of weaving her story around certain individual creatures, although so many other animal 'personages' appear that a paradoxical sense of orderly confusion is conveyed. Here is the darting, swooping, preying struggle that has been going on for untold centuries. . . . There is poetry here, but no false sentimentality. . . ." William Beebe in Saturday Review of Literature commented: "The plethora of facts occasionally smothers the smoothness of diction, and distracts the attention from the word picture itself. . . . This is not captious criticism, but an appeal for more simple words, fewer terms of physical and faunal geography, and a greater leisureliness in description. . . ."

Miss Carson's second effort, The Sea Around Us, required a vast amount of research and two years to write. A Christian Science Monitor critic commented, "Rachel Carson has achieved that rare, all but unique phenomenon—a literary work about the sea that is comparable with the best, yet offends neither the natural scientist nor the poet." "Rare indeed," added Saturday Review of Literature, "is the individual who can present a comprehensive and well-balanced picture of such a complex entity as the sea in an easy and fluent style and in terms anyone can understand. Rachel Carson is such an individual. Many books have been written on the sea, most of them by scholars with a very detailed knowledge of some aspect of oceanography, but with a limited knowledge of popular presentation. Miss Carson's book is different." Observed Nation: "Scientifically, The Sea Around Us has its shortcomings, but it would be hard to find a style, a sensitivity, a balancing of detail more perfectly suited for the evoking of the sea." Several chapters of the book originally appeared in the New Yorker in the summer of 1951, under the title, "Profile of the Sea." A chapter entitled "Birth of an Island" was published earlier in the Yale Review, and won for its author the George Westinghouse Foundation award, given for outstanding scientific writing in a periodical. By October, 1951, sales of the book—338,000 hardcover copies—had carried it to a ninth printing, and to first place on nonfiction best-seller lists. A documentary film of the book was made by RKO, which won an Academy Award for best documentary of feature length in 1952.

"Again author Carson has shown her remarkable talent for catching the breath of science on the still glass of poetry," wrote Time concerning The Edge of the Sea. "The Edge of the Sea," commented the Christian Science Monitor, "is pitched perhaps, in a lesser key than was The Sea Around

Us, if only because the intertidal world is a more limited subject than was the whole sea itself. In her new book, Miss Carson's pen is as poetic as ever and the knowledge she imparts is profound. *The Edge of the Sea* finds a worthy place beside [her] . . . masterpiece of 1951.'' Added *Saturday Review:* ''The book has a notable feature: it appeals both to the mind's eye and to the physical eye. . . . The double impact is much stronger than if the two impressions came separately, and so *The Edge of the Sea* becomes the product of two naturalists working in close cooperation, each one scientifically trained and each an artist, the one with a pen and the other with a pencil [Bob Hines]. Together they take us on a good journey.''

Silent Spring was probably Rachel Carson's most influential, as well as most controversial book. The work, which sold over 500,000 hardcover copies, is an indictment of farmers for the use of poisonous chemical fertilizers, and points out the potentially dangerous effects of these on animals, birds, and humans. Called by *Christian Century* ''a shocking and frightening book,'' it was further critiqued by the *Christian Science Monitor* which noted: ''Miss Carson has undeniably sketched a one-sided picture. But her distortion is akin to that of the painter who exaggerates to focus attention on essentials. It is not the half-truth of the propagandist.'' Added *Saturday Review:* ''It is a devastating, heavily documented, relentless attack upon human carelessness, greed, and irresponsibility. . . . If her present book does not possess the beauty of *The Sea Around Us,* it is because she has courageously chosen, at the height of her powers, to educate us upon a sad, an unpleasant, an unbeautiful topic, and one of our own making. . . .'' Intense public concern created over the book caused President John F. Kennedy to announce a federal investigation into the problem. The report of the President's Science Advisory Committee, issued in May, 1963, agreed with the basic premise of *Silent Spring,* warning against the indiscriminate use of pesticides and urging stricter controls and more research.

Rachel Carson was in the process of finishing *The Sense of Wonder* at the time of her death from cancer in 1964. A *Publishers Weekly* reviewer observed: ''The late Mrs. Carson shares her delight in the miracles of nature, and shows one how to communicate this delight to a child, and how to share his sense of wonder. A treat for sore eyes and weary hearts.''

BIOGRAPHICAL/CRITICAL SOURCES: Scientific Book Club Review, October, 1941; *Books,* December 14, 1941; *Saturday Review of Literature,* December 27, 1941, July 7, 1951; *Christian Science Monitor,* July 5, 1951, November 10, 1955, September 27, 1962; *Nation,* August 4, 1951; *Time,* November 7, 1955; *Saturday Review,* December 5, 1955, September 29, 1962, May 16, 1964; *Life,* October 12, 1962; *Christian Century,* December 19, 1962; *Publishers Weekly,* June 19, 1967; *Instructor,* May, 1968; Henry Gilfond, *Heroines of America,* Fleet Press, 1970; Philip Sterling, *Sea and Earth: The Life of Rachel Carson,* Crowell, 1970; Frank Graham, Jr., *Since Silent Spring,* Houghton, 1970; *American Forests,* July, 1970; Donald W. Cox, *Pioneers of Ecology,* Hammond, 1971; Robert Elliott, *Banners of Courage,* Platt, 1972; Paul Brooks, *House of Life: Rachel Carson at Work,* Houghton, 1972; Jean L. Latham, *Rachel Carson Who Loved the Sea,* Garrard, 1973; C. B. Squire, *Heroes of Conservation,* Fleet Press, 1974; Ruth A. Coates, *Great American Naturalists,* Lerner, 1974; Adela Rogers St. John, *Some Are Born Great,* Doubleday, 1974; Elizabeth Anticaglia, *Twelve American Women,* Nelson-Hall, 1975.

OBITUARIES: New York Times, April 15, 1964; *Oil, Paint, and Drug Report,* April 20, 1964; *Illustrated London News,* April 25, 1964; *Publishers Weekly,* April 27, 1964; *Current Biography,* June, 1964; *Gleanings,* July, 1964.*

(Died April 14, 1964)

*   *   *

CARSWELL, Leslie
See STEPHENS, Rosemary

*   *   *

CARTER, Nick
See GRANBECK, Marilyn

*   *   *

CARTER, Nick
See WALLMANN, Jeffrey M(iner)

*   *   *

CASE, Geoffrey

PERSONAL: Born in Yorkshire, England. *Agent:* Harvey Unna & Stephen Durbridge Ltd., 14 Beaumont Mews, London W.1, England.

CAREER: Actor, writer, and theatrical director. *Member:* Writers Guild of Great Britain.

WRITINGS—Plays: ''Mr. Big,'' first produced in Manchester, England, 1970; ''Treasure Island'' (adaptation), first produced in Birmingham, England, 1972; ''Fun,'' first produced in 1973; ''The Golden Samurai'' (juvenile), first produced at Unicorn Theatre, 1975.

Also author of television plays, including ''Riding South,'' BBC-2; ''I Want to Be Like You'' (juvenile), BBC-Schools, 1976; ''Puzzles,'' BBC-2.

WORK IN PROGRESS: The English American, stories; ''Fairies and Folk Tales,'' a television film for British Broadcasting Corp.

SIDELIGHTS: Case writes: ''I write because I enjoy it more than anything else I have ever done, but the moment something comes along I enjoy more, I'll do that!''

*   *   *

CASH, Kevin   1926-

PERSONAL: Born February 22, 1926, in Manchester, N.H. *Education:* Brown University, A.B., 1948; also attended Providence College. *Home:* 782 Beech St., Manchester, N.H. 03104.

CAREER: Worked as copyboy, reporter, and feature writer for *Manchester Union Leader;* editor and writer for *Journal of Commerce, New York Herald Tribune, New York Journal-American;* writer, 1975—. *Military service:* U.S. Naval Reserves; became lieutenant. *Member:* National Press Club, Delta Kappa Epsilon.

WRITINGS: Who the Hell Is William Loeb?, Amoskeag Press, 1975.

*   *   *

CASSADY, Ralph, Jr.   1900-1978

December 30, 1900—February 22, 1978; American educator, economist, and author of works in his field. Cassady specialized in medieval marketing. Included among his works are *Price Warfare in Business Competition* and *The*

Consumer and the Economic Order. He died in Los Angeles, Calif. Obituaries and other sources: *American Men and Women of Science: The Social and Behavioral Sciences,* 12th edition, Bowker, 1973; *Who's Who in America,* 38th edition, Marquis, 1974; *New York Times,* February 25, 1978. (See index for *CA* sketch)

* * *

CASTLE, William 1914-1977

PERSONAL: Born April 24, 1914, in New York, N.Y.; married wife, Ellen; children: Georgie, Terry. *Residence:* Beverly Hills, Calif.

CAREER: Producer and director of motion pictures, screenwriter, and producer of television programs. Worked as actor and assistant director on stage in New York, 1929-39. Director of motion pictures, including "The Whistler," 1944, "The Fat Man," 1951, "House on Haunted Hill," 1959, "The Tingler," 1960, "13 Ghosts," 1960, "Mr. Sardonicus," 1961, "Strait Jacket," 1964, and "I Saw What You Did," 1965. Producer of motion pictures, including "Macabre," 1958, "Homicidal," 1961, "The Night Walker," 1965, and "Rosemary's Baby," 1968. Producer of television programs including the series "Circle of Fear," 1972. Formed production organization, 1955.

WRITINGS: Step Right Up! I'm Gonna Scare the Pants Off America (autobiography), Putnam, 1976.

Screenplays: (Author of screen story) "North to the Klondike," Universal, 1942; (with Wilfrid H. Pettitt) "Voice of the Whistler," Columbia, 1945; (with Otto Schreiber) "It's a Small World," Eagle Lion, 1950; "Bug," 1975.

SIDELIGHTS: Known for wiring theater seats to mildly shock viewers and for providing life insurance to promote "Macabre," Castle told an interviewer: "I've modeled my career on Barnum. Exploitation's the big thing in the picture business today. Stars and contents don't mean much at the box office anymore. The people who go to see pictures because of what's in them, they're a minority. Gimmicks, surprise, shock—that's what draws the crowds."

OBITUARIES: New York Times, June 2, 1977; *Washington Post,* June 3, 1977.*

(Died May 31, 1977, in Los Angeles, Calif.)

* * *

CAULFIELD, Malachy Francis 1915-
(Max Caulfield; Malachy McCoy, a pseudonym)

PERSONAL: Born May 10, 1915, in Belfast, Northern Ireland; son of Malachy (a civil servant) and Julia Mary (Campion) Caulfield; married Mary Mitchell McCoy, September 14, 1943; children: Janet Mary (Mrs. Jean Nicholas), Claire Frances (Mrs. John Maloney). *Education:* Earned B.A. from Queen's University, Belfast, Northern Ireland. *Politics:* "Idiosyncratic." *Religion:* "Latin Catholic." *Home:* Hillcroft, 61 Highview, Pinner, Middlesex HA5 3PE, England.

CAREER: Reporter and rewriter for *Irish News,* Belfast, Northern Ireland; reporter for *Daily Mirror,* London, England; news editor of *Sunday Chronicle,* London; associate foreign editor of *Daily Express,* London; chief news editor of Independent Television News, London; assistant editor of *Daily Mail* group, London; editor for *John Bull,* London. Notable assignments include coverage of nuclear development in Britain, the Suez Canal, the Irish Republican Army, and interviews with Brendan Behan, Richard Nixon,

Charles de Gaulle, Clark Gable, and Ingrid Bergman. Author of celebrity column in *TV Times,* London, 1960-70. Has appeared on British, Irish, and Canadian television and radio programs. *Member:* Press Club (London).

WRITINGS—Under name Max Caulfield, except as indicated: *The Black City* (fiction), J. Cape, 1952, New American Library, 1954; *Night of Terror* (nonfiction), Muller, 1958; *As Tomorrow Never Came* (nonfiction), Norton, 1959; (with Ellen Field) *Twighlight in Hong Kong,* Muller, 1960; *The Easter Rebellion* (nonfiction), Holt, 1963; (with Joan Paisnel) *The Beast of Jersey,* R. Hale, 1972; *The Irish Mystique* (nonfiction), Prentice-Hall, 1973; (with Winifred Young) *Obsessive Poisoner,* R. Hale, 1973; (under pseudonym Malachy McCoy) *Steve McQueen* (biography), Regnery, 1974; (with Ivor Spencer) *Pray Silence,* R. Hale, 1975; (with Linda Lee) *The Life and Tragic Death of Bruce Lee,* Star Books, 1975; *Mary Whitehouse* (biography), Mowbray, 1975; *Bruce Lee Lives?* (thriller), Star Books, 1975, Dell, 1976. Also author of *Illustrated Guide to Britain,* Reader's Digest, and *Route,* Royal Automobile Club.

Contributor of numerous articles to newspapers and magazines in the United Kingdom, United States, Europe, and Japan.

WORK IN PROGRESS: A book on exorcism with Dom Robert Petitpierre; a book on North Sea oil exploration with Denys Webster; a thriller about Alaska; a nonfiction book about British mercenaries.

SIDELIGHTS: Caulfield told *CA:* "I decided to be a writer when I was about six or seven. By the age of eight I had read *The Count of Monte Cristo, Quo Vadis, The Last Days of Pompeii,* and the entire *Three Musketeers oeuvre.* Thereafter I devoured everything in sight—boy's magazines and annuals and books of all kinds, and by sixteen had read Tolstoy, Dostoevsky, Rabelais, Boccaccio, Chaucer, Wells, Belloc, Waugh, etc., plus masses of English and Irish poetry. I had also steeped myself in history, particularly Roman history and had read Tacitus, Suetonius, and Gibbon. I had read all the great Irish epic sagas (*Deirdre of the Sorrows, Cuchulainn, Fionn MacCumhail,* etc.). Also Homer, Herodotus, etc. I was particularly attracted by humour, especially American humour and lapped up Damon Runyon, Benchley, Thurber, and Perelman.

"I played the following sports: Gaelic football and hurling, soccer, rugby, cricket, golf, tennis, bowls. I was a fair middle-distance runner and a good swimmer. I spent an inordinate amount of time from the age of twelve to twenty-eight playing poker, solo, and bridge. I have always been a film buff and until recently, attended the cinema two or three times a week. I have only two languages besides English: Latin and Gaelic. I learned to drive a car when aged five.

"I decided the best way to learn to be a writer was to become a newspaper reporter first. While acting as a staff reporter, sub-editor (rewrite man in the U.S.), theatre and film critic and parliamentary reporter in Belfast, I began writing feature articles for my own and other newspapers and magazines.

"Once in Fleet Street and working for people like Lord Beaverbrook, writing became a wholly professional activity. I nurtured the desire to become a 'creative writer,' of course, and wrote my first book, about Belfast between the wars, while I was associate foreign editor of the *Daily Express.* Thereafter writing became a way of life and remains so.

"I tend to see myself mainly as an expert on Irish affairs—particularly Irish history and topography. I am uniquely positioned to write about Northern Ireland, for instance, because I am a Belfast Catholic whose parents were both born in Southern Ireland and whose paternal family still resides there, and because I am married to a Belfast Protestant and have lived for forty years in England, thus enabling me to be reasonably objective.

"I have, however, a great love for the landscape and history of England and Wales, a fascination reinforced in a most detailed way by my work on two important (and expensive) illustrated guide books to Britain. For these two publications, I covered very considerable areas of England and all of Wales, dealing in some detail with the principal towns, villages, architectural, archaeological, historical features, plus the best routes up mountains, the best lakes and rivers and what and where to fish, plus myths and legends.

"I am, to use a hackneyed phrase, widely-travelled. I have enjoyed brief interludes as a foreign correspondent in Italy, Paris, and India. Leaving aside the Polar regions, the only continent I have not visited is Australasia.

"As a young man, I was an avid coarse fisherman. Since then I have fished for shark off Cornwall and gone on *shikari* (a tiger shoot) while a guest of my old friend, the late Maharajah of Cooch-Behar.

"Apart from literature itself, my main interests are history (with some emphasis on military history), travel, and music (classical only). I play the piano, of course. My principal form of recreation at the moment is the French *boule*. I still retain a keen interest in foreign affairs, developed to a high degree during my years as one of the principal directors of the *Daily Express* foreign staff."

* * *

CAULFIELD, Max
See CAULFIELD, Malachy Francis

* * *

CHAMBERLAIN, Anne 1917-

PERSONAL: Born September 24, 1917, in Marietta, Ohio; daughter of John Dudley (a newspaperman) and Julia (Moore) Chamberlain; married Clyde Edward Brown, October 29, 1939 (divorced, 1959); children: Dudley Chamberlain Brown, Edward Lowell Brown. *Education:* Attended Marietta College, 1935-39, and University of Cincinnati, 1936-37. *Politics:* Republican. *Religion:* Episcopalian. *Home:* 316 High School Lane, Marietta, Ohio 45750. *Agent:* Russell & Volkening, 551 Fifth Ave., New York, N.Y. 10017.

CAREER: Parkersburg News, Parkersburg, W.Va., reporter, 1944-45, book reviewer, 1944-54; *Wheeling News-Register*, Wheeling, W.Va., book reviewer, 1946-54; Marietta College, Marietta, Ohio, teacher of creative writing, 1958-70; Parkersburg Community College, Parkersburg, teacher of creative writing, 1969-74; writer. Director of Ohio Valley Writers' Conference, 1955-56. *Member:* Mystery Writers of America, MacDowell Fellows, MacDowell Colony, Marietta College Alumni Association, Washington County Historical Society. *Awards, honors:* MacDowell fellowship from MacDowell Colony, 1955; Ohioana Book award and West Virginia award, both 1959, both for *The Darkest Bough.*

WRITINGS: The Tall Dark Man, Bobbs-Merrill, 1955, reprinted, Avon, 1970; *The Soldier Room*, Bobbs-Merrill, 1956; *The Darkest Bough*, Bobbs-Merrill, 1958, published as *Possessed*, Pyramid, 1959; (contributor) A. S. Burack, editor, *Writer's Handbook, 1978*, Writer, Inc., 1978. Contributor to periodicals, including *Charm, Family Circle, New York Times Book Review, Saturday Evening Post,* and *Woman's Day.*

WORK IN PROGRESS: Citizen-Journal; collections of short stories and poetry; a new novel.

SIDELIGHTS: Anne Chamberlain told *CA:* "I've been submitting fiction, nonfiction, and poetry since the age of nine. My novels are broadly classified as 'psychological suspense.' Suspense writing appeals to me because, well-presented, it is a strong story, which holds the reader's interest, and through which can be woven the subtler arts of complex characterization, evocative atmosphere, and theme."

Chamberlain's novels have also been published in England, France, Sweden, Norway, and the Netherlands.

* * *

CHAMBLISS, William J(oseph) 1933-

PERSONAL: Born December 12, 1933, in Buffalo, N.Y.; son of Joseph H. (a realtor) and Jean (an actress and poet; maiden name, Ferguson) Chambliss; married Betty Lou Biggs, 1956 (marriage ended); children: Jeff, Kent, Lauren. *Education:* University of California, Los Angeles, B.A., 1955; Indiana University, M.A., 1960, Ph.D., 1962; postdoctoral study at University of Wisconsin, Madison, 1966-67. *Home address:* R. D. 2, Heritage Village, #B-5, Landenberg, Pa. 19350. *Office:* Department of Sociology, University of Delaware, Newark, Del. 19711.

CAREER: University of Washington, Seattle, assistant professor of sociology, 1962-66; University of Wisconsin, Madison, visiting lecturer in sociology, 1966-67; University of California, Santa Barbara, associate professor of sociology, 1967-73; University of Oslo, Oslo, Norway, professor of sociology, 1974-75; University of Stockholm, Stockholm, Sweden, professor of sociology, 1975-76; University of Delaware, Newark, professor of sociology, 1976—. Honorary professorial fellow, Faculty of Law, University College, Cardiff, Wales, 1977; visiting distinguished scholar at University of Missouri, 1978. *Military service:* U.S. Army, 1956-58.

MEMBER: American Sociological Association, Society for the Study of Social Problems, Law and Society Association. *Awards, honors:* National Institute of Mental Health grants, 1962-63, 1965-66; Russell Sage Foundation residency, 1966-67.

WRITINGS: Crime and the Legal Process, McGraw, 1969; (with Robert B. Seidman) *Law, Order and Power*, Addison-Wesley, 1971; *Boxman: A Professional Thief's Journey*, Harper, 1972; *Criminal Law in Action*, Wiley, 1975; (with Tom Ryther) *Sociology: The Discipline*, McGraw, 1975; (with Milton Mankoff) *Whose Law? What Order?*, Wiley, 1975; *On the Take*, Indiana University Press, 1978. Contributor to law and sociology journals. Editor of *Contemporary Crises;* member of editorial board of *British Journal of Law and Society;* contributing editor of *Crime and Social Justice.*

WORK IN PROGRESS: Economic Crime in Sweden.

* * *

CHAMPION, Dick
See CHAMPION, Richard Gordon

CHAMPION, Richard Gordon 1931-
(Dick Champion)

PERSONAL: Born March 25, 1931, in Elkhart, Ind.; son of Gordon (a shipping clerk) and Ruby (Jenkin) Champion; married Norma Jean Black (a college teacher and television personality), October 3, 1953; children: Jeffrey Bruce, Ashley Brooke. *Education:* Central Bible College, Springfield, Mo., B.A., 1953; also attended Drury College. *Home:* 3609 South Broadway, Springfield, Mo. 65807. *Office:* 1445 Boonville, Springfield, Mo. 65802.

CAREER: Ordained minister of Assemblies of God, 1955; assistant pastor of Assemblies of God church in Macomb, Ill., 1953-55; *Pentecostal Evangel,* Springfield, Mo., circulation manager, 1955-57; Assemblies of God Headquarters, Springfield, Mo., supervisor of youth publications and editor of *CA Herald* and *CA Guide,* 1958-64; *Pentecostal Evangel,* managing editor, 1964—. Instructor in journalism at Central Bible College, 1960—. Chairman of editors committee of Assemblies of God Headquarters, 1969-72; member of board of directors of General Council Credit Union, 1972—; participant in writers seminars and church seminars. *Member:* Evangelical Press Association (member of board of directors, 1971-73; vice-president, 1973-75; president, 1975-77), Central Bible College Alumni Association (vice-president, 1965-69).

WRITINGS: (Under name Dick Champion) *Above and Beyond,* Gospel Publishing, 1959; (under name Dick Champion) *What's Mine . . . ?,* Gospel Publishing, 1963; *Go on Singing,* Radiant Books, 1976. Author of church school material. Contributor to religious periodicals. Chairman of editorial committee of *Advance,* 1970—.

SIDELIGHTS: Champion told *CA:* "My writings have all been of a religious nature, reflecting an evangelical Christian viewpoint." *Avocational interests:* Travel, gardening.

* * *

CHANDLER, E(dwin) Russell, Jr. 1932-

PERSONAL: Born September 9, 1932, in Los Angeles, Calif.; son of Edwin Russell and Mary Elizabeth (Smith) Chandler; married Sandra Swisher, August 24, 1957 (divorced November 15, 1977); children: Heather, Holly, Timothy. *Education:* Attended Stanford University, 1950-52; University of California, Los Angeles, B.S., 1955; graduate study at University of Southern California, 1955, and New College, Edinburgh, 1955-56; Princeton Theological Seminary, M.Div., 1958. *Politics:* Republican. *Office:* Los Angeles Times, Times-Mirror Sq., Los Angeles, Calif. 90053.

CAREER: Ordained Presbyterian minister, 1958; pastor of Presbyterian church in Escalon, Calif., 1961-66; *Modesto Bee,* Modesto, Calif., reporter, 1966-67; *Washington Star,* Washington, D.C., religion editor, 1968-69; *Christianity Today,* Washington, D.C., news editor, 1969-72; *Sonora Daily Union Democrat,* Sonora, Calif., reporter, 1972-73; *Los Angeles Times,* Los Angeles, Calif., religion writer, 1974—. *Member:* Society of Professional Journalists. *Awards, honors:* James O. Supple Award from Religion Newswriters Association, 1976, for religion writing in the secular press.

WRITINGS: The Kennedy Explosion, David Cook, 1972; *Budgets, Bedrooms, and Boredom,* Regal Books (Glendale), 1976; (with wife, Sandra S. Chandler) *Your Family: Frenzy or Fun?,* Acton House, 1977; *The Overcomers,* Revell, 1978. Contributor to religious periodicals.

WORK IN PROGRESS: Behind the Wittenburg Door, for Acton House.

SIDELIGHTS: Chandler comments: "I consider myself a religion journalist. All my current writing and expertise is in this field, both from my background of seminary and pastorate, and journalistic experience. I retain my ordination in the United Presbyterian Church and speak at various writers' conferences and communications and media workshops for religious groups."

* * *

CHANDRA, Pramod 1930-

PERSONAL: Born November 2, 1930, in Banares, India; came to the United States in 1964; son of Moti (a museum director) and Shanti Devi (a writer) Chandra; children: Abhijit, Sasanka. *Education:* Georgetown University, B.S.F.S., 1951; University of Bombay, Ph.D., 1964. *Religion:* Hindu. *Office:* Department of Art, University of Chicago, 5540 South Greenwood Ave., Chicago, Ill. 60637.

CAREER: Prince of Wales Museum of Western India, Bombay, curator, 1955-64; University of Chicago, Chicago, Ill., associate professor, 1964-73, professor of art and South Asian languages and civilization, 1973—. Member of board of directors of American Academy of Banares, 1965-71, and Indian Temple Architecture Project. *Member:* Asiatic Society (Calcutta).

WRITINGS: Bundi Painting, Lalit Kala Akademi, 1959; *Catalogue of the Khajanchi Collection,* Lalit Kala Akademi, 1960; *Indian Sculptures in the Fogg Art Museum,* Harvard University, Fogg Art Museum, 1963; *Catalogue of Stone Sculpture in the Allahabad Museum,* American Institute of Indian Studies, 1971; *The Cleveland Tuti-nama and the Origins of Mughal Painting,* Akademische Druck-u Verlagsanstalt, 1976.

WORK IN PROGRESS: Mathura Sculpture; research on Mughal and Rajput Painting.

SIDELIGHTS: Chandra wrote to *CA:* "The Indian Temple Architecture Project, a joint undertaking with Indian scholars, aims to publish a history of Indian architecture combining stylistic analysis and correlation of monuments with Sanskrit canonical texts."

* * *

CHAPIN, Schuyler G(arrison) 1923-

PERSONAL: Born February 13, 1923, in New York, N.Y.; son of L. H. Paul and Leila H. (Burden) Chapin; married Elizabeth Steinway, March 15, 1947; children: Henry Burden, Theodore Steinway, Samuel Garrison, Miles Whitworth. *Education:* Attended Longy School of Music and Harvard University, both 1940-41. *Office:* School of the Arts, Columbia University, New York, N.Y. 10027.

CAREER: NBC-TV, New York City, in spot sales, 1947-51; Tex & Jinx McCrary Enterprises, New York City, general manager, 1951-53; booking director of Judson, O'Neill & Judd Division of Columbia Artists Management, 1953-59; Columbia Broadcasting System, New York City, director of Masterworks in Columbia Records Division, 1959-62, vice-president in creative services, 1962-63; Lincoln Center for the Performing Arts, New York City, vice-president for programming, 1964-69; executive producer for Amberson Enterprises, 1969-71; Metropolitan Opera Association, New York City, acting general manager, 1972-73, general manager, 1973-75; Columbia University, New York City, dean of Faculty of the Arts, 1976—. Director with Amberson Enterprises. Member of board of trustees of Naumberg Foundation, 1962—, and LeRoy Hospital (also vice-president);

vice-president of Bagby Music Lovers Foundation; chairman of Carnegie Hall Fund, 1976—. *Military service:* U.S. Army Air Forces, 1942-46; served in China-Burma-India theater; received Air Medal.

MEMBER: Century Association, Coffee House Club. *Awards, honors:* New York State Conspicuous Service Cross, 1951; Christopher Award, 1972, for television film "Beethoven's Birthday"; Emmy Award from Academy of Television Arts and Sciences, 1972, for producing "Beethoven's Birthday," and 1976, for "Danny Kaye's Look-In at the Metropolitan Opera"; honorary degrees from New York University, Hobart & William Smith College, and Emerson College.

WRITINGS: Musical Chairs: A Life in the Arts, Putnam, 1977.

WORK IN PROGRESS: A handbook for arts administrators and a possible book on funding the arts in America.

SIDELIGHTS: In a 1976 interview, Chapin said: "There is a steadily increasing interest on the part of young people in the arts. I think it's a response to a general feeling of uncertainty—an unspoken fear of tomorrow. Young people, more and more, want something they can depend on and they are looking to the arts because the arts are an outgrowth of man's sense of beauty and orderliness and purpose. Columbia's arts school should thrive and be the finest of its kind in the country. I'm going to do my best to see that that happens."

Chapin added: "*Musical Chairs* is an autobiography of my love affair with the arts, particularly the performing arts, and was written to share the joys (and the banana peels) of a life of being paid for my hobby."

*   *   *

CHAPMAN, John Roy 1927-

PERSONAL: Born May 27, 1927, in London, England; son of Albert Roy and Barbara Joyce (Fletcher) Chapman; married Betty Impey. *Education:* Attended Royal Academy of Dramatic Art, London. *Home:* 48 Wildwood Rd., London NW 11, England.

CAREER: Playwright and actor. Made stage debut at Embassy Theatre, London, 1946; stage actor in London, 1946—. Has also acted in motion pictures and television. *Member:* Dramatists Club.

WRITINGS—All plays: Dry Rot (first produced in London, 1954), English Theatre Guild, 1956; *Simple Spymen* (first produced in London, 1958), English Theatre Guild, 1960; *The Brides of March* (first produced in London, 1960), Dramatists Play Service, 1961; "This Is My Wife, Mr. Stanniforth," first produced in London, 1963; *Diplomatic Baggage* (first produced in London, 1964), English Theatre Guild, 1966; *Oh Clarence!* (first produced in London, 1968), English Theatre Guild, 1969; (with Ray Cooney) *Not Now Darling* (first produced in London, 1968, produced in New York at Brooks Atkinson Theatre, October 29, 1970), English Theatre Guild, 1970, Dramatists Play Service, 1971; (with Cooney) *My Giddy Aunt* (first produced in London, 1968), English Theatre Guild, 1970; (with Cooney) *Move Over Mrs. Markham* (first produced in London, 1971), English Theatre Guild, 1972; (with Cooney) "There Goes the Bride," first produced in London, 1974; (with Tim Fywell and Nigel Williams) "Marbles," first produced in London, 1975; "Happy Ever After," first produced in London, 1976.

Also author of film scripts, including "Dry Rot," "The Night We Dropped a Clanger," and "Nothing Barred."

Author of teleplays, including "What a Drag," "Between the Balance Sheets," and teleplay series, including "Hugh and I," "Blandings Castle," and "Happy Ever After."

AVOCATIONAL INTERESTS: Travel, reading.*

*   *   *

CHAPPLE, Steve 1949-

PERSONAL: Born January 4, 1949, in Billings, Mont.; son of Henry A. and Dorothy (Massee) Chapple. *Education:* Attended Yale University, 1967-71. *Politics:* "American and Socialist." *Religion:* "Pantheist." *Agent:* Carol Murray, 2427 10th St., Berkeley, Calif. 94710.

CAREER: Factory and antiwar organizer in Connecticut and Massachusetts, 1971-73; concert producer in Boston, Mass., 1972-73; truck driver in San Francisco, Calif., 1973-74; writer and lecturer, 1975—. Director of Entropy, Inc. Consultant to K. R. Borgenict Friendship Fund. *Member:* Students for Democratic Society, Teamsters, Hotsprings Society, Media Alliance (Northern California chapter).

WRITINGS: (With Reebee Garofalo) *Rock 'n' Roll Is Here to Pay,* Nelson-Hall, 1977; (contributor) *Media Culture,* Avon, 1978; (contributor) *Mother Jones Reader on Corporate Malpractice,* Quickfox, 1978. Contributor to numerous periodicals including *Atlantic Monthly, Christian Science Monitor, In These Times, Mother Jones, Penthouse, Playboy, Radical Therapy,* and *Rolling Stone.*

WORK IN PROGRESS: Two novels, one concerning the "Three-Fisted Reality of Contemporary America"; corporate muckraking, rock 'n' roll commentary, and Pentagon research.

SIDELIGHTS: Chapple told *CA:* "With the exceptions of Twain, Whitman, Hemingway, West, Burroughs, and Thompson, American writing of the last two hundred years has been as distinguished as breakfast cereal and controlled with the same corporate literary blandness. American writers, like the American people, must seize their culture and put an end to New York provincialism and Westchester standards."

AVOCATIONAL INTERESTS: "Fishing, dogs, political organizing, salamanders, Jewish doctors."

*   *   *

CHARD, Judy 1916-
(Doreen Gordon)

PERSONAL: Born May 8, 1916, in Gloucester, England; daughter of Thomas (an army officer) and Dorothy Isabel (Juan) Gordon; married Maurice Noel Chard (a field manager), July 26, 1941. *Education:* Educated in England. *Religion:* Church of England. *Home:* Morley Farm, Highweek, Newton Abbey, Devonshire TQ12 6NA, England.

CAREER: Writer. Has worked as a typist and personal secretary in Birmingham, London, and Wolverhampton, England. Tutor in creative writing, Workers Educational Association, Devonshire, England. *Member:* Crime Writers Association, Society of Women Writers and Journalists, Westcountry Writers Association.

WRITINGS—All published by R. Hale: Through the Green Woods, 1974; *The Weeping and the Laughter,* 1975; *Encounter in Berlin,* 1976; *The Uncertain Heart,* 1976; *The Other Side of Sorrow,* 1977; *In the Heart of Love,* 1978; *Out of the Shadows,* 1978.

Columnist, *Devon Life,* 1972—. Contributor of short stories, sometimes under pseudonym Doreen Gordon, to periodi-

cals, including *Argosy, Woman's Realm, My Weekly, Story World, London Mystery Magazine, Edgar Wallace Mystery Magazine,* and *Lady.*

WORK IN PROGRESS: Murder Casebook, for Thomson; articles.

SIDELIGHTS: Chard told *CA:* "It may be of interest to note that I started to write when I was fifty and into the last ten years I have crammed a lifetime of work and living, meeting new people, and, in fact, my whole life has changed as a result. Most important of all has been my teaching role for the Workers Educational Association, which has opened up a whole new world of helping people who are deeply interested in writing, giving them, too, a new interest."

* * *

CHASE, Ilka 1905-1978

April 8, 1905—February 15, 1978; American author and actress best known for her performances in motion pictures, including "Now, Voyager," "The Big Knife," and "Oceans 11," and plays, including "The Women" and "Present Laughter." Chase's memoirs, *Past Imperfect,* were popularly received in 1942 and she went on to write seventeen other books, including several novels and another autobiography, *Always in Vogue.* She also wrote many books about her travel experiences and appeared on the radio program, "Luncheon at the Waldorf." She died in Mexico City, Mexico. Obituaries and other sources: *Current Biography,* Wilson, 1942; *The Biographical Encyclopaedia and Who's Who of the American Theatre,* James Heineman, 1966; *Celebrity Register,* 3rd edition, Simon & Schuster, 1973; *International Motion Picture Almanac,* Quigley, 1975; *Who's Who in America,* 40th edition, Marquis, 1977; *Who's Who in the Theatre,* 16th edition, Pitman, 1977; *New York Times,* February 16, 1978; *Newsweek,* February 27, 1978; *Time,* February 27, 1978. (See index for *CA* sketch)

* * *

CHASE, Mary (Coyle) 1907-

PERSONAL: Born February 25, 1907, in Denver, Colo.; daughter of Frank Bernard (a salesman) and Mary (McDonough) Coyle; married Robert Lamont Chase (a newspaper reporter), June 7, 1928; children: Michael Lamont, Colin Robert, Barry Jerome. *Education:* Attended Denver University, 1921-23, and University of Colorado, 1923-24. *Home:* 505 Circle Dr., Denver, Colo. 80206.

CAREER: Rocky Mountain News, Denver, Colo., reporter, 1928-31; free-lance correspondent, International News Service and United Press, 1932-36; publicity director, National Youth Administration, Denver, 1941-42, Teamsters Union, 1942-44; playwright and author of books for children. *Member:* Dramatists' Guild. *Awards, honors:* William MacLeod Raine award from the Colorado Authors League, 1944; Pulitzer Prize, 1945, for *Harvey;* Litt.D., University of Denver, 1947.

WRITINGS—Plays: "Me Third," first produced in Denver, Colo., at the Federal Theatre, 1936, produced in New York as "Now You've Done It," 1937; *Sorority House* (three-act; first produced in Denver, 1939), Samuel French, 1939; *Too Much Business* (one-act), Samuel French, 1940; "A Slip of a Girl," first produced in Camp Hall, Colo., 1941; *Harvey* (three-act; first produced on Broadway at Forty-Eighth Street Theatre, November 1, 1944), Dramatists Play Service, 1950; "The Next Half Hour," first produced in New York, 1945; *Mrs. McThing* (two-act; first

produced on Broadway, February, 1952), Oxford University Press, 1952, revised edition, Dramatists Play Service, 1954; *Bernardine* (two-act; first produced on Broadway, 1952), Oxford University Press, 1953, revised edition, Dramatists Play Service, 1954; "Lolita," first produced in Abington, Va., 1954; *The Prize Play,* Dramatists Play Service, 1961; *Midgie Purvis* (two-act; first produced on Broadway, 1961), Dramatists Play Service, 1963; *The Dog Sitters* (three-act), Dramatists Play Service, 1963; *Mickey* (two-act; based on her novel, *Loretta Mason Potts*), Dramatists Play Service, 1969; *Cocktails with Mimi,* Dramatists Play Service, 1974.

For children: *Loretta Mason Potts* (novel; illustrated by Harold Berson), Lippincott, 1958; *The Wicked Pigeon Ladies in the Garden* (illustrated by Don Bolognese), Knopf, 1968.

SIDELIGHTS: Chase's work is characteristically humane and comedic. Her delicate fantasies are compounded of the most unlikely situations and people. Tales of Irish folklore told to her by an uncle introduced her to the Celtic pookas (spirits in animal forms) and banshees which appear in her writings.

The idea for *Harvey,* Chase's Pulitzer Prize winning play about an alcoholic and his imaginary six-foot white rabbit named Harvey, was conceived during World War II as a pure escapist plot. Harvey, molded after the Gaelic pooka, was originally a canary, but was changed to a human-size rabbit, which the author believed to be more advantageous to the plot. It took her two years and fifty rewrites to complete the play. It has been said that the hero of the play, Elwood P. Dowd, was created from early childhood advice received by Chase. Her mother often said: "Never be unkind or indifferent to a person others say is crazy. Often they have deep wisdom." The original production of "Harvey" starred Frank Fay and Josephine Hull and was a smash hit on Broadway, with 1775 performances. James Stewart starred in the motion picture version produced by Universal Pictures in 1950, and also in the television version presented by the Hallmark Hall of Fame, March 22, 1972, on NBC. The printed version of the play has been translated into nearly every foreign language.

Helen Hayes and Brandon de Wilde appeared in the 1952 production of "Mrs. McThing," a mixture of whimsy with fake gangsters and fairy-tale witchcraft. *Saturday Review*'s comments on the printed version included: "It is exciting to find how the charm and originality of *Mrs. McThing* come out in the printed play almost as vividly as they do on the stage with the expert playing of Helen Hayes and the other members of the fine cast. Here is a fantasy that is, too, convincing realism." Two more of Mary Chase's plays were produced as movies. RKO Radio Pictures adapted "Sorority House" in 1939, and Twentieth Century-Fox produced "Bernardine" in 1957.

Chase has also written books for children. The *Chicago Tribune*'s description of *Loretta Mason Potts* included: "How right and natural that the creator of *Harvey* and *Mrs. McThing* should now write a magical tale for boys and girls. Surely, *Loretta Mason Potts* will take her place among the memorable characters of children's literature and her story should be a favorite for a long time to come."

BIOGRAPHICAL/CRITICAL SOURCES: John E. Drewry, editor, *More Post Biographies,* University of Georgia Press, 1947; *Saturday Review,* November 15, 1952; *Cosmopolitan,* February, 1954; *Chicago Tribune,* November 2, 1958.*

CHASTENET de CASTAING, Jacques 1893-1978

April 20, 1893—February, 1978; French historian, journalist, civil servant, and author. Chastenet de Castaing began his career in the French diplomatic service and later became diplomatic correspondent for *L'Opinion*. He was former editor of *Le Temps* and the author of numerous books on French and British history. He died in Paris, France. Obituaries and other sources: *Who's Who in the World*, 3rd edition, Marquis, 1976; *The International Who's Who*, Europa, 1977; *Who's Who*, 130th edition, St. Martin's, 1978; *AB Bookman's Weekly*, May 8, 1978.

*   *   *

CHESBRO, George C(lark) 1940-

PERSONAL: Born June 4, 1940, in Washington, D.C.; son of George W. and Maxine (Sharpe) Chesbro; married Oranus Ravar (a teacher), April 4, 1969; children: Lisa, Mark. *Education:* Syracuse University, B.S., 1962. *Home:* 262 North Main St., Spring Valley, N.Y. 10977. *Agent:* William Morris Agency, Inc., 1350 Avenue of the Americas, New York, N.Y. 10019.

CAREER: High school teacher of special education classes in Rockland County, N.Y., 1962-64; Board of Cooperative Education Services, West Nyack, N.Y., special education teacher, 1964—. *Member:* Authors Guild of Authors League of America, Mystery Writers of America, American Federation of Teachers, New York State United Teachers.

WRITINGS: King's Gambit (novel), New English Library, 1976; *Shadow of a Broken Man* (novel), Simon & Schuster, 1977; *City of Whispering Stone* (novel), Simon & Schuster, 1978.

Author of "New Visions: Survival Skills for the Exceptional," an audiovisual presentation for Gamco Industries, designed to teach handicapped children and adults.

Work represented in anthologies, including *Best Detective Stories of the Year*, Dutton, 1973. Contributor of stories, poems, and articles to newspapers and to magazines, including *Fantasy and Science Fiction, If, Alfred Hitchcock's Mystery Magazine*, and *Mike Shayne Mystery Magazine*.

WORK IN PROGRESS: An untitled novel, for Simon & Schuster.

SIDELIGHTS: Chesbro comments: "I began writing in 1960, undoubtedly in response to a need to scratch some perverse psychic itch. Writing is an act by which I define myself and hold my world together. To date, my fiction has been primarily in the psychological mystery-suspense genre. I am the creator of Dr. Robert Frederickson, known to his friends as 'Mongo'—a Ph.D. criminologist, black belt karate expert, former circus headliner and private investigator who just happens to be a dwarf."

AVOCATIONAL INTERESTS: Chess, the occult, music, cinema, literature, travel (Europe, Iran).

*   *   *

CHILTON, Shirley R(ay) 1923-

PERSONAL: Born April 3, 1923, in Vancouver, Wash.; daughter of Shannon Brice and Helen Corrine (Bishop) Shafer; married F. Roy Chilton, November 21, 1952; children: Raymond, Richard, Robert. *Education:* Attended University of Washington, Seattle, 1941-43; Pepperdine University, M.B.A., 1969. *Residence:* Los Angeles, Calif. *Office:* Department of Management, Pepperdine University, 8035 South Vermont, Los Angeles, Calif. 90044.

CAREER: Daniel Reeves & Co., Los Angeles, Calif., operations manager, 1955-58; Hayden, Stone, Inc., Sherman Oaks, Calif., operations manager, branch manager, regional manager, and vice-president, 1958-69; William O'Neil & Co., Inc., Los Angeles, adviser on financial services, security analysis, and portfolios, and director of corporate planning and administration, 1969-72; Daniel Reeves & Co., managing partner, 1972-73, president, chief executive officer, and member of board of directors, 1973, chairman of board of directors, 1974—. Social worker for State of California Welfare Department; president and founder of Southern California Industry Education Council, 1968; member of board of directors of Los Angeles Institute for Urban Development, 1972; member of board of trustees of California Economic Council, 1973, and San Francisco Institute for Contemporary Studies in Economics, 1974; member of California Museum of Science and Industry's Hall of Business and Finance at University of Southern California, 1974; member of ethical conduct committee of Pacific Stock Exchange and arbitration board of New York Stock Exchange, both 1975; president of Institute for Economic Foundations, 1976—. World lecturer on gold and money markets, 1967.

MEMBER: National Association of Securities Dealers (member of arbitration board, 1975), American Finance Association, California Chamber of Commerce (member of board of directors, 1976—), Soroptimists.

WRITINGS—For children: (With husband, F. Roy Chilton, and Mary Chilton) *Economics in Action*, Rotary International, 1966; *Economics for Young People*, Children's Press, 1970; (with F. R. Chilton and Robert Chilton) *Everyone Has Important Jobs to Do*, Elk Grove Books, 1970; *Where Things We Use Come From*, Elk Grove Books, 1970; *How Things We Use Are Made*, Elk Grove Books, 1970; *How We Learned to Move About*, Elk Grove Books, 1970.

WORK IN PROGRESS: Who Killed the Goose?; a novel, with economic implications, covering the time from 1947 to the 1980's.

SIDELIGHTS: Shirley Chilton writes: "My interest in economics began with the recognition that I had been ill-prepared to exist in this socio-economic world. As I watched the people in this country move further into debt and further from each other and lose their freedom, I decided to do what little I could to bring awareness to the near calamitous position of the United States. Economics education and understanding with the social implications became the logical solution."

*   *   *

CHOMSKY, William 1896-1977

PERSONAL: Born January 15, 1896, in Russia; came to United States in 1913; naturalized citizen; son of Meyer and Esther (Korman) Chomsky; married Elsie Simonofsky, August 19, 1927 (died January 22, 1972); married Ruth Schendel, June 3, 1973; children: (first marriage) Noam A., David E. *Education:* Johns Hopkins University, B.A., 1921; University of Pennsylvania, M.A., 1925; Dropsie College, Ph.D., 1926. *Religion:* Jewish. *Home:* 6417 North Fairhill St., Philadelphia, Pa. 19126. *Office:* Department of Hebrew Languages and Literatures, Dropsie University, Philadelphia, Pa. 19132.

CAREER: Gratz College, Philadelphia, Pa., 1924-77, began as faculty member, professor of Hebrew and pedagogy, 1954-69, professor emeritus, 1969-77, chairman of faculty, 1949-69; Dropsie University, Philadelphia, professor of

Hebrew and Jewish education, 1955-77. *Member:* World Union of Jewish Studies, National Council for Jewish Education, American Academy for Jewish Research, Conference on Jewish Social Studies, Society of Biblical Literature, Histadrut Ivrith of America. *Awards, honors:* Honorary doctorate, Gratz College, 1969.

WRITINGS: (Editor and translator from the Hebrew) David Kimchi, *Hebrew Grammar (Mikhlol)*, Dropsie College for Hebrew and Cognate Learning, 1933, enlarged edition, Bloch Publishing, 1952; *How to Teach Hebrew in the Elementary Grades,* United Synagogue Commission on Jewish Education, 1946; *Teaching Hebrew,* Jewish Education Committee, 1956; *Hebrew: The Eternal Language,* Jewish Publication Society, 1957, reprinted, 1975; *Teaching and Learning: An Introduction to Jewish Education,* Jewish Education Committee, 1959; *Ha-Lashon Ha-Ivrit b'Darkhei Hitpathuthah,* Reuben Mass (Jerusalem), 1967; *Darkhei Hora'ah u'Lemidah,* Jewish Education Committee, 1968. Author of Hebrew primers and vocalized texts. Contributor to periodicals, including *Jewish Quarterly Review, Jewish Education, Modern Language Journal, Hadoar,* and *Sheviley Hahinuch.*

SIDELIGHTS: William Chomsky was one of the world's leading Hebrew grammarians. Before his death he told *CA* that the major objective of his life had been "the education of individuals who are well integrated, free and independent in their thinking, concerned about improving and enhancing the world, and eager to participate in making life more meaningful and worthwhile for all."

OBITUARIES: New York Times, July 22, 1977.*

(Died July 19, 1977, in Philadelphia, Pa.)

* * *

CHRISTENSEN, Paul 1943-

PERSONAL: Born March 18, 1943, in West Reading, Pa.; son of Kenneth Serenus and Ann Theresa Christensen; married Jane Flowers (divorced); married Catherine Ann Tensing (a teacher), August 15, 1970; children: Sean Oliver, Maxine Elizabeth. *Education:* College of William and Mary, B.A., 1967; University of Cincinnati, M.A., 1970; University of Pennsylvania, Ph.D., 1975. *Politics:* Socialist. *Home:* 206 South Sims St., Bryan, Tex. 77801. *Agent:* Frieda Wepner, Five Talents Agency, 2004½ Guadalupe, Austin, Tex. 78705. *Office:* Department of English, Texas A & M University, College Station, Tex. 77843.

CAREER: Eastern Publishing Co., Alexandria, Va., associate editor, 1967-68; Texas A & M University, College Station, instructor, 1974-76, assistant professor of English, 1976—. Creator and host of "Poetry Southwest" on KAMU-FM Radio, 1977—. *Member:* Modern Language Association of America, Poets and Writers, South Central Modern Language Association.

WRITINGS: Old and Lost Rivers (poems), Cedarshouse Press, 1977; *Missing Shoes* (poems), edited by Daniel Hoffman, BOA Editions, 1978; *Charles Olson: Call Him Ishmael* (criticism), University of Texas Press, 1978.

Work represented in anthologies, including *Seven Poets,* edited by Greg Kuzma, Best Cellar Press, 1977; *Rereadings,* edited by Kuzma, Best Cellar Press, 1978. Contributor of poems and articles to magazines, including *Shenandoah, Twentieth Century Literature, Southern Review, Boundary 2, Texas Quarterly, Epoch,* and *Prairie Schooner.* Poetry editor of *Quartet,* 1975-77. Publisher and editor of chapbooks for Cedarshouse Press.

WORK IN PROGRESS: A three-volume book of poems, *The Tituba Sequence,* "a celebration of the advent of witchcraft in Massachusetts and its heritage through the ensuing several centuries."

SIDELIGHTS: Christensen writes: "I believe a great reawakening of spirit is about to begin in the remaining years of this century that will hurl us into a renaissance of much older forms of thought and belief. Poets and writers sense this along the peripheries of their psyches and are releasing depths of imaginative energy into their work. My own poetry participates in this jubilant quest of chthonic divinity, that will sweep the exhausted empirical frame of mind I have been given clean of its walls and baffles. A new age of romance is upon us, and the best poetry of the present, my own best work as well, manifests this."

* * *

CHRISTOPHER, John
See YOUD, Samuel

* * *

CHROMAN, Nathan 1929-

PERSONAL: Born February 17, 1929, in Chicago, Ill.; son of Joel and Mary (Hertzman) Chroman; married Judie Sutton (in real estate), June 27, 1954; children: Lucie, Gina, Stacie. *Education:* Santa Anna College, A.A., 1952; also attended University of California, Los Angeles, and Loyola University. *Office:* 9171 Wilshire Blvd., Beverly Hills, Calif. 90212.

CAREER: Admitted to California Bar, 1957; attorney in Beverly Hills, Calif., 1957—. Chairman of wine judges at Los Angeles County Fair. Member of regional advisory board of B'nai B'rith Anti-Defamation League.

WRITINGS: Treasury of American Wines, Crown, 1973. Author of column on wine in *Los Angeles Times,* 1970—.

WORK IN PROGRESS: Revising *Treasury of American Wines.*

* * *

CLARK, Garel
See GARELICK, May

* * *

CLARK, Marion L. 1943-1977

CAREER: Washington Post, Washington, D.C., copy aide, then reporter for *Potomac* magazine, 1966-72, managing editor of *Potomac,* 1972-76, editor of *Potomac,* 1976—. *Awards, honors:* Co-recipient of Associated Press managing editor public service award, 1976, for coverage of the Wayne Hays scandal.

WRITINGS: (With Rudy Maxa) *Public Trust, Private Lust: Sex, Power, and Corruption on Capitol Hill,* Morrow, 1977.

BIOGRAPHICAL/CRITICAL SOURCES: Book World, June 19, 1977; *New York Times Book Review,* July 3, 1977.

OBITUARIES: New York Times, September 6, 1977; *Washington Post,* September 6, 1977.*

(Died September 4, 1977, in East Tawas, Mich.)

* * *

CLARK, Naomi 1932-

PERSONAL: Born September 6, 1932, in Eastland, Tex.; daughter of Horace Linard and Viola Gertrude (James) Gibson; married Burnice Clark (a high school teacher), April 2, 1949; children: Diane H., David B., Joel. *Education:* Attended University of Colorado, North Texas State University, Bakersfield College, and New Mexico State College; San Jose State University, B.A. (great distinction), 1965, M.A., 1968; graduate study at Oxford University, 1967; University of California, Santa Cruz, Ph.D., 1974. *Home:* 20243 Beatty Ridge Rd., Los Gatos, Calif. 95030. *Office:* Department of English, San Jose State University, San Jose, Calif. 95192.

CAREER: San Jose State University, San Jose, Calif., lecturer in English, 1974—. Coordinator of San Jose's Bicentennial Poetry Celebration, 1975-76, and Campus-Community Poetry Festival, 1976-77; has given poetry readings locally and in other parts of California. *Awards, honors:* First prize from Montalvo Poetry Competition, 1973; outstanding service award from San Jose Fine Arts Commission, 1977.

WRITINGS: (Editor with Nils Peterson and John Galm) *Discover America: Poems 1976,* San Jose State University Foundation, 1976; *Burglaries and Celebrations* (poems), Oyez Press, 1977.

Work anthologized in *California Bicentennial Poets Anthology,* edited by A. D. Winans, Second Coming Press, 1976; *Southwest: A Contemporary Anthology,* edited by Karl Kopp and Jane Kopp, Red Earth Press, 1977; *Contemporary Women Poets: An Anthology of California Poets,* edited by Jennifer McDowell, Merlin Press, 1977. Contributor of about forty poems and a story to literary journals, including *Ontario Review, Rendezvous, Big Moon, Poetry Northwest,* and *Poetry NOW.* Co-editor of a special issue of *San Jose Studies.*

WORK IN PROGRESS: A third collection of poems; *Fragment of a Gospel.*

SIDELIGHTS: Clark told *CA:* "In a recent poem, 'Letter,' the speaker ends with the statement, 'I live where/I am, weave a circle of stones,/build a fire, sing to you/and my child.' Perhaps that says what I do when I write. Making poems is for me a way of healing, of knowing, of understanding, of sharing."

BIOGRAPHICAL/CRITICAL SOURCES: Itinerary Seven, autumn, 1978.

*   *   *

CLARK, Stephen R(ichard) L(yster)   1945-

PERSONAL: Born October 30, 1945, in Luton, England; son of David Allen Richard (a teacher of engineering) and Kathleen (Finney) Clark; married Edith Gillian Metford (a researcher), July 1, 1972; children: Samuel, Dorothea. *Education:* Oxford University, B.A., 1968, M.A. and D.Phil., both 1973. *Politics:* "Left-wing Libertarian." *Religion:* Episcopalian. *Home:* 9 Clarence Dr., Glasgow G12 9QL, Scotland. *Office:* Department of Moral Philosophy, University of Glasgow, Glasgow, Scotland.

CAREER: Oxford University, Oxford, England, fellow, 1968-75; University of Glasgow, Glasgow, Scotland, lecturer in moral philosophy, 1974—. *Member:* Aristotelian Society, Vegan Society, Scottish Society for the Prevention of Vivisection.

WRITINGS: Aristotle's Man, Oxford University Press, 1975; *The Moral Status of Animals,* Oxford University Press, 1977.

WORK IN PROGRESS: Values of Knowledge and Belief; a science fiction novel; research for *The Morals of Nature.*

SIDELIGHTS: Clark writes: "I would want my philosophical studies to help clear away the prejudices and rationalizations which prevent affectionate understanding (and decent treatment) of our fellow-creatures of our own and other species; also to clear away such intellectual and emotional errors as hinder religious devotion. I am opposed to meat-farming, vivisection, obedience to any authority not ordained of God, and compulsory sex-morality. I am fond of cats, children, gadgets, and old wood."

*   *   *

CLARKE, Garry E(vans)   1943-

PERSONAL: Born March 19, 1943, in Moline, Ill.; son of Clarence H. and Gladys (Hokinson) Clarke; married Melissa Naul (an artist), May, 1975. *Education:* Cornell University, B.Mus., 1965; Yale University, M.Mus., 1968. *Religion:* Episcopal. *Home address:* Kentmere, Quaker Neck, Chestertown, Md. 21620. *Office:* Office of Dean of the College, Washington College, Chestertown, Md. 21620.

CAREER: Washington College, Chestertown, Md., assistant professor, 1968-73, associate professor of music, 1973—, acting dean, 1977, dean of the college, 1978—. Organist and choirmaster of St. Paul's Episcopal Parish in Centreville, Md.; pianist and composer; has performed in concert in the United States and Europe; served as opera coach for New Haven Opera Society. *Member:* American Association of University Professors, Council for Higher Education in Music, Music Educators National Conference, American Association for Higher Education, National Association of Schools of Music, Pi Kappa Lambda. *Awards, honors:* Received Carnegie Foundation research grant, 1964; Ford Foundation fellowship, 1965; Woodrow Wilson fellowship, 1965; Bradley-Keeler fellowship, 1966, 1967; Rena Greenwald Prize in Composition, 1967, 1968; National Endowment for the Humanities grant, 1970; Lindback Award for Distinguished Teaching, 1974.

WRITINGS: (Editor with John Kirkpatrick) Charles Ives, *Varied Air and Variations,* Merion Music, 1971; (contributor) Ives, *Five Pieces,* Merion Music, 1975; *Essays on American Music,* Greenwood Press, 1977.

Composer of works for orchestra, chamber ensembles, and solo instruments, including the opera "Westchester Limited."

AVOCATIONAL INTERESTS: Cooking, playing bridge.

*   *   *

CLARKE, Thurston   1946-

PERSONAL: Born March 11, 1946, in New York, N.Y.; son of Edwin Thurston (an investment counselor) and Nancy (a writer; maiden name, Bruff) Clarke; married Antonia Bullard (an executive), June 3, 1978. *Education:* Yale University, B.A., 1968; London School of Oriental and African Studies, M.A., 1969; Columbia University, M.B.A., 1972. *Agent:* Julian Bach Literary Agency, Inc., 3 East 48th St., New York, N.Y. 10017.

CAREER: U.S. Attorney's Office, Southern District of New York, criminal investigator 1971-72; Investor Responsibility Research Center, Washington, D.C., writer and researcher, 1973—. *Awards, honors:* Guggenheim fellow, 1978-79.

WRITINGS: (With John J. Tigue, Jr.) *Dirty Money* (nonfiction), Simon & Schuster, 1975; *The Last Caravan* (nonfiction), Putnam, 1978.

WORK IN PROGRESS: A book about the Middle East, for Putnam.

* * *

CLAY, Charles Travis 1885-1978

July 30, 1885—1978; British librarian and author. Clay, knighted in 1957, was librarian for the House of Lords from 1922 until 1956. He was the author of numerous books on archaeological subjects. Clay died in London, England. Obituaries and other sources: *Who's Who,* 130th edition, St. Martin's, 1978; *AB Bookman's Weekly,* June 19, 1978.

* * *

CLAY, Lucius D(uBignon) 1897-1978

April 23, 1897—April 17, 1978; U.S. Army general, business executive, diplomat, engineer, and author. Clay, who retired from the Army in 1949 with the rank of full general, was one of the few career soldiers to earn a four-star rank without holding a combat command. Proven to be an efficient organizer while director of material of the Army Service Forces, Clay was summoned by General Eisenhower to France in 1944 to solve problems in the shipping of supplies. His attempts were successful, and the Allied supply flow doubled in three weeks. In 1945, Clay was appointed deputy in charge of all civil affairs in post-war Germany. Two years later he became commander of the U.S. Armed Forces in Europe and military governor of Germany. Clay was largely responsible for the successful reconstruction of that country. He organized and directed the Berlin air-lift, took part in drafting the constitution of the republic, and was credited, through his currency reforms, with having given Germany one of the most stable currencies. Following his retirement from the military, Clay became chairman of the board and chief executive of Continental Can Co. and, during his eleven-year association with the firm, its sales tripled. He returned to Germany in 1961 as a member of a special mission sent by President Kennedy, and later that year he was appointed special representative with the rank of ambassador. Clay remained active in both local and national political affairs until his death. Even though he retired from business in 1973, Clay remained director or board member of some eighteen major American companies. He was the author of books on German history. Clay died in Cape Cod, Mass. Obituaries and other sources: *Current Biography,* Wilson, 1963; Lloyd C. Gardner, *Architects of Illusion,* Quadrangle, 1970; *The Papers of General Lucius D. Clay: Germany, 1945-1949,* edited by Jean Edwards Smith, Indiana University Press, 1974; *Who's Who in America,* 39th Edition, Marquis, 1976; *International Who's Who,* Europa, 1977; *Who's Who,* 130th edition, St. Martin's, 1978; *New York Times,* April 18, 1978.

* * *

CLEGG, Jerry S(tephen) 1933-

PERSONAL: Born September 29, 1933, in Heber City, Utah; son of Henry Cardwell (a farmer) and Marion (a journalist and librarian; maiden name, Davis) Clegg; married Karen M. Clarkson, June 8, 1960; children: Melissa E., Andrea M., Katherine N. *Education:* Attended Columbia University, 1953-54; University of Utah, B.A., 1955, M.A., 1959; University of Washington, Seattle, Ph.D., 1962. *Office:* Department of Philosophy, Mills College, Oakland, Calif. 94613.

CAREER: Mills College, Oakland, Calif., instructor, 1962-64, assistant professor, 1964-69, associate professor, 1970-

74, professor of philosophy, 1974—. *Military service:* U.S. Army, Russian-English voice interpreter, 1955-58. *Member:* International Platform Association, American Rock and Gem Society, Schopenhauer Society, Sierra Club.

WRITINGS: The Structure of Plato's Philosophy, Bucknell University Press, 1977. Contributor of articles on philosophy, esthetics, and history of ideas to professional journals.

WORK IN PROGRESS: A study of the parallels between cultural and linguistic theories in nineteenth- and twentieth-century intellectual history, including the positions taken by Wittgenstein, Nietzsche, Sartre, Freud, and Jung; studies on promising, faith, and self-knowledge.

SIDELIGHTS: Clegg commented: "Reviewers, to my pleasure, have accused me of writing from an oblique angle of vision with a robust common sense—a combination of qualities I would hope to have, for it is only imagination plus discipline that can gain what I think philosophy should seek; clarity and understanding."

Describing his first work in progress, Clegg continued: "The aim of the study is to demonstrate how major movements in twentieth century psychology and philosophy have sprung from similar conceptions and have been motivated by similar ambitions."

AVOCATIONAL INTERESTS: Mountaineering (in Europe, Nepal, Peru, and most of North America; "many first, but unplanned, descents down crevasses, through cornices, over ice falls, and into a varied assortment of holes, pools, and ravines"); scuba diving, lapidary, photography.

* * *

CLEW, William J(oseph) 1904-

PERSONAL: Born June 28, 1904, in Middletown, Conn.; son of Timothy J. and Anne (Taylor) Clew; married Mona Gallivan (a teacher), October 12, 1928; children: William Taylor, Harvey Taylor and Carole Clew Hoey (twins), Elizabeth Barrow (Mrs. Robert Kampmeinert). *Education:* Attended Wesleyan University, 1926-27, Columbia University, 1952, 1960, and University College, Dublin, 1977. *Politics:* Democrat. *Religion:* Roman Catholic. *Home and office address:* Middlesex Turnpike, P.O. Box 76, Haddam, Conn. 06438.

CAREER/WRITINGS: Middletown Press, Middletown, Conn., reporter, 1923-25; *Hartford Courant,* Hartford, Conn., assistant state editor, 1925-26, state editor, 1926-31, court reporter, 1931-49, assistant managing editor, 1949-66, managing editor, 1966-74, Middle East correspondent, 1974—. Contributor of travel articles and book reviews to *Hartford Courant.* Member of Operation Deep Freeze expedition to the South Pole, 1964. Member of State Freedom of Information Commission, 1977—, and Inland Wetlands Commission for Environmental Protection. *Military service:* U.S. Army, member of First Army Headquarters staff, 1942-43; became captain.

MEMBER: American Society of Newspaper Editors, Associated Press Managing Editors Association, Overseas Press Club, Explorers Club, Reserve Officers Association, Retired Officers Association, New England Associated Press News Executives Association (president, 1966), Society of the South Pole, Antarctica Press Club, Byrd Station Society, Sigma Delta Chi, Goodspeed Opera House Guild, Kiwi Club (New Zealand).

SIDELIGHTS: Clew comments: "Besides more than half a century as a journalist, I have traveled widely, going abroad at least once yearly since 1955. I have visited every continent from the Antarctic to the North Pole, except Australia. I am dedicated to accuracy in journalism and freedom of information in federal, state, and local governments.''

*   *   *

CLIFFORD, James L(owry)   1901-1978

February 24, 1901—April 7, 1978; American educator and author best known for his books on Samuel Johnson, including *Johnsonian Studies* and *Young Sam Johnson.* A colleague called Clifford "one of the most important reasons for revived popular interest in the eighteenth century." He died in New York, N.Y. Obituaries and other sources: *Directory of American Scholars,* Volume II: *English, Speech, and Drama,* 6th edition, Bowker, 1974; *The Writers Directory, 1976-78,* St. Martin's, 1976; *Who's Who in America,* 40th edition, Marquis, 1977; *Who's Who,* 130th edition, St. Martin's, 1978; *New York Times,* April 8, 1978. (See index for *CA* sketch)

*   *   *

COETZEE, J(ohn) M.   1940-

PERSONAL: Born February 9, 1940, in South Africa. *Education:* University of Cape Town, M.A., 1963; University of Texas, Ph.D., 1969. *Home address:* P.O. Box 92, Rondebosch 7700, South Africa. *Agent:* James Brown Associates, Inc., 22 East 60th St., New York, N.Y. 10022.

CAREER: International Business Machines (IBM), London, England, applications programmer, 1962-63; International Computers, Bracknell, England, systems programmer, 1964-65; State University of New York at Buffalo, assistant professor of English, 1968-71; University of Cape Town, Cape Town, South Africa, lecturer in English, 1972—. *Member:* Modern Language Association of America.

WRITINGS: Dusklands (novel), Ravan Press (Johannesburg), 1974; (translator) Marcellus Emants, *A Posthumous Confession,* Twayne, 1976; *From the Heart of the Country* (novel), Harper, 1977 (published in England as *In the Heart of the Country,* Secker & Warburg, 1977). Contributor to literature and language journals.

WORK IN PROGRESS: Another novel.

*   *   *

COLBY, Joan   1939-

PERSONAL: Born January 16, 1939, in Chicago, Ill.; daughter of Otho B. (an engineer) and Grace (an administrative assistant; maiden name, Zavek) Turbyfill; married Alan Colby (a contractor), September 5, 1959; children: Wendelin, Terry, Benjamin. *Education:* Attended College of Du Page, 1970-73. *Politics:* Independent. *Religion:* None. *Home:* 122 Timber Trail, Streamwood, Ill. 60103. *Office:* Amerad Advertising, 853 Dundee, Elgin, Ill. 60120.

CAREER: Elgin Daily Courier-News, Elgin, Ill., author of column "On the Home Front," 1966—. Author of column for Copley News Service, 1972-75. Media director for Amerad Advertising, 1975—. *Member:* National Organization for Women. *Awards, honors:* Local poetry awards.

WRITINGS: XI Poems, Interim Books, 1972; *Last Supper* (poetry), Thorp Springs Press, 1978; *Beheading the Children* (poetry), Mati, 1978.

Work anthologized in *Mothers-Daughters,* Beacon Press, 1978. Contributor of poems to literary magazines, including *Epoch, New River Review,* and *Sou'wester.*

WORK IN PROGRESS: Pioneering the Heartland.

SIDELIGHTS: Joan Colby writes: "I write out of a lifelong preoccupation with language, communication, and visionary experience. My interests are catholic but my poetry, of necessity, reflects my status as a woman. I am an avid and assiduous reader of poetry, biography, and fiction." *Avocational interests:* Playing the piano, botany.

BIOGRAPHICAL/CRITICAL SOURCES: Margins, December/January, 1973.

*   *   *

COLE, Charles Woolsey   1906-1978

February 8, 1906—February 6, 1978; American administrator, educator, diplomat, historian specializing in seventeenth-century France, and author best known for his historical works. Cole was president of Amherst College for fourteen years and then ambassador to Chile. He wrote *Colbert and a Century of French Mercantilism* and *French Mercantile Doctrines Before Colbert* as well as other history books. Cole died in Los Angeles, Calif. Obituaries and other sources: *The International Who's Who,* 39th edition, Europa, 1975; *Who's Who in America,* 40th edition, Marquis, 1977; *Who's Who,* 130th edition, St. Martin's, 1978; *New York Times,* February 8, 1978. (See index for *CA* sketch)

*   *   *

COLEMAN, Lonnie   1920-

PERSONAL: Born August 2, 1920, in Bartow, Ga.; son of John Aldine (a policeman) and Delle (a medical nurse; maiden name, Williams) Coleman. *Education:* University of Alabama, A.B., 1942. *Agent:* James Brown, James Brown Associates, Inc., 22 East 60th St., New York, N.Y. 10022.

CAREER: Free-lance writer, 1946-47; *Ladies Home Journal,* Philadelphia, Pa., associate editor, 1947-50; free-lance writer, 1950-51; *Collier's,* New York City, associate editor, 1951-52; free-lance writer, 1952-53; *Collier's,* associate editor, 1953-55; free-lance writer, 1955-61; *Good Housekeeping,* New York City, associate editor, 1961-63; *McCall's,* New York City, associate editor, 1964-72; free-lance writer, 1972—. *Military service:* U.S. Navy, 1942-46; became lieutenant senior grade. *Member:* Authors Guild of Authors League of America.

WRITINGS—Novels: Escape the Thunder, Dutton, 1944; *Time Moving West,* Dutton, 1947; *The Sound of Spanish Voices,* Dutton, 1951; *Clara,* Dutton, 1952; *Adam's Way,* Dutton, 1953; *Ship's Company,* Little, Brown, 1955; *The Southern Lady,* Little, Brown, 1958; *Sam,* McKay, 1959; *The Golden Vanity,* Macmillan, 1962; *King,* McGraw, 1967; *Beulah Land* (first novel in trilogy), Doubleday, 1973; *Orphan Jim,* Doubleday, 1975; *Look Away, Beulah Land* (second novel in trilogy), Doubleday, 1977.

Plays: —*I Cat Hattie and Kingdom Come* (three-act melodrama; first produced in Tuscaloosa at University of Alabama, 1941), L. Raines, 1942; "Jolly's Progress" (three-act), first produced in New York City at Longacre Theatre, December, 1959; "A Warm Body" (two-act comedy), first produced in New York City at Cort Theatre, April 15, 1967; "A Place for Polly" (two-act comedy; also produced under titles "A Discreet Indiscretion" and "She Didn't Say Yes"), produced on Broadway at Ethel Barrymore Theatre, April 18, 1970.

WORK IN PROGRESS: The Legacy of Beulah Land, third novel in trilogy.

COLLINS, Peter (Sheridan) 1942-

PERSONAL: Born January 23, 1942, in Colombia; son of Peter Lawton (a businessman) and Elizabeth (Sheridan) Collins; married Ly Nguyen (a student), August 1, 1973; children: Uyen Phoung Ly, Thy Hoang Nguyen. *Education:* Georgetown University, B.S.F.S., 1964; further study at Goethe Institut, 1966. *Home:* Apt. 19, Thailand Court, Soi 24, Sukhumvit, Bangkok, Thailand. *Office:* CBS News, Maneeya Building, 518/2 Ploenchit Rd., Bangkok 5, Thailand.

CAREER/WRITINGS: WTOP-News, Washington, D.C., reporter, 1966-68; Voice of America, Washington, D.C., writer, 1968-71, correspondent in Saigon, 1971-73; stringer in Saigon for American Broadcasting Co. (ABC), British Broadcasting Co. (BBC), and *Far East Review,* 1973-74; Columbia Broadcasting System (CBS) News, New York, N.Y., staff reporter in Saigon, Hong Kong, and Bangkok, 1974—. Notable assignments include coverage of wars in Laos, Cambodia, and Vietnam. *Military service:* U.S. Army, 1964-66; became first lieutenant. *Member:* Foreign Correspondents Club of Hong Kong, Foreign Correspondents Club of Thailand. *Awards, honors:* Co-winner of Overseas Press Club award for radio spot news coverage, 1975.

*   *   *

COLLOM, Jack 1931-

PERSONAL: Born November 8, 1931, in Chicago, Ill.; son of Harry Holder (a teacher) and Margaret (a teacher; maiden name, Jack) Collom; married Edeltraud Hopps, August 23, 1957 (divorced, September, 1975); married Mara Meshak (a mythologist), August 14, 1976; children: Nathaniel Johannes, Christopher Joseph, Franz Sequoya, Sierra Ava. *Education:* Colorado A & M College, B.S., 1952; University of Colorado, B.A., 1972, M.A., 1974. *Politics:* None. *Religion:* "Animism-poetry." *Home:* 957 Alpine, Boulder, Colo. 80302.

CAREER: Worked as truck driver, construction worker, and salesman; writer, 1955—; factory worker, 1956—. Instructor at University of Colorado, 1975-76. *Military service:* U.S. Air Force, 1952-56; served in Libya and Germany.

WRITINGS: Blue Heron and Ibc (poems), Grosseteste, 1972; *Ice* (poems), Lodestar Press, 1974; *Squirrel Tails* (poems), Lodestar Press, 1976. Author of privately printed books. Editor and publisher of *the* (poetry magazine), 1966-77.

WORK IN PROGRESS: Poems.

SIDELIGHTS: Collom writes: "I am just a serious poet, with an emphasis on private life and ordinary days, but I would like to get out of working so much for a living. My chief move in poetry is just to take down the mystical and magical in every day, without reference, rhythm included." *Avocational interests:* Birds, walking, drinking beer, shooting pool, reading.

*   *   *

COLTRANE, James
See WOHL, James P(aul)

*   *   *

CONANT, James Bryant 1893-1978

March 26, 1893—February 11, 1978; American educator, diplomat, chemist, and author of works in his field. Conant was president of Harvard University for twenty years. He then became the first U.S. ambassador to West Germany. Conant assisted in the development of the atom bomb, radar, synthetic rubber, and new explosives. He is also widely known for his studies on secondary education and is credited with shaping the high school as it exists today. Conant's writings include *Chemistry of Organic Compounds, Germany and Freedom: A Personal Appraisal, The American High School Today,* and *Slums and Suburbs.* In 1970, Conant wrote his autobiography, *My Several Lives: Memoirs of a Social Inventor.* He died in Hanover, N.H. Obituaries and other sources: *Current Biography,* Wilson, 1951; *The Oxford Companion to American Literature,* 4th edition, Oxford University Press, 1965; *Newsweek,* March 9, 1970, February 27, 1978; *Time,* March 16, 1970, February 27, 1978; James Conant, *My Several Lives: Memoirs of a Social Inventor,* Harper, 1970; *American Men and Women of Science: The Physical and Biological Sciences,* 12th edition, Bowker, 1971-73; *International Who's Who,* Europa, 1975; *Who's Who in America,* 40th edition, Marquis, 1977; *Who's Who,* 130th edition, St. Martin's, 1978; *New York Times,* February 13, 1978; *Washington Post,* February 13, 1978. (See index for *CA* sketch)

*   *   *

CONCONI, Charles N. 1938-

PERSONAL: Born October 25, 1938, in Ohio; son of Charles O. and Mary M. (a beautician) Conconi; children: Diana A., Collette R., Charles E. *Education:* Kent State University, B.S., 1960; Northwestern University, M.S.J., 1961. *Home and office:* 377 Massachusetts Ave., Washington, D.C. 20016. *Agent:* Philip G. Spitzer Literary Agency, 111-25 76th Ave., Forest Hills, N.Y. 11375.

CAREER: Free-lance writer. Has been press assistant to Senator Gaylor Nelson, reporter for *Washington Evening Star,* contributor to *Washingtonian* magazine, and has been associated with *Cleveland Plain Dealer, Toledo Blade, Chicago American,* and City News Bureau of Chicago. Covered the assassination of Martin Luther King, Jr. and the Poor People's Campaign; has held interviews with major political figures. Lecturer at Georgetown University; guest lecturer at colleges and universities. *Military service:* U.S. Army, 1961-63. *Member:* Washington Independent Writers (past president).

WRITINGS: (With Stewart Udall and David Osterhout) *The Energy Balloon,* McGraw, 1973; (with Toni House) *The Washington Sting,* Coward, in press. Contributor to national magazines, including *Progressive, Playgirl, Mainliner, New Republic,* and *Living Wilderness.* Washington editor of *Environmental Quality.*

*   *   *

CONROY, Frank 1936-

PERSONAL: Born January 15, 1936, in New York, N.Y.; son of Francis Philip and Helga (Lassen) Conroy; married Patty Monro Ferguson, November 21, 1958 (marriage ended); married Margaret Davidson Lee, May 5, 1975; children: Daniel, Will. *Education:* Haverford College, B.A., 1958. *Residence:* Quaise Nantucket, Mass. *Agent:* Candida Donadio & Associates, 111 West 57th St., New York, N.Y. 10019.

CAREER: Writer. *Member:* Writers Guild of America, Poets, Playwrights, Editors, Essayists, and Novelists Club, Authors Guild. *Awards, honors:* Rockefeller Foundation grant, 1960; National Foundation for the Arts and Humanities grant, 1968.

WRITINGS: Stop-time (autobiography), Viking, 1967; (contributor) Harold Hayes, editor, *Smiling Through the Apocalypse: Esquire's History of the Sixties,* McCall, 1969. Contributor to periodicals, including *New Yorker, New Times, Chicago Tribune, Boston* magazine, *Harper's,* and *New York Times* magazine.

SIDELIGHTS: "Childhood," wrote Eleanor Dienstag, "is like a dream, part nightmare, part idyll, from which the adult awakens with relief. No longer menaced by mysterious forces, the child looks up and realizes he is in command—an adult. It is a moment of utter sweetness and triumph." Conroy's book *Stop-time,* ends with that moment of realization and triumph. However, "it would be misleading to describe *Stop-time* as a memoir of childhood and leave it at that," wrote Charles Bronze in *Commonweal.* "This is not the sort of book one has read before and it resists categorization. Autobiography, yes, closet novel, yes, nonfiction chronicle, yes—but more importantly it is art, with no other purpose than the purpose of art. . . . to be accurate one would have to simply say that *Stop-time* is a book, a quite beautiful book which defines, more or less like certain poems, its own genre." *Observer Review* called *Stop-time* "an autobiography written with the imaginative freedom and variation of a novel . . . clean, witty, surprisingly mature prose, full of insights and sharp moments."

Susan Lardner described Conroy's technique in this manner: "Conroy writes with humour, in a low key, using ordinary language with such precision that he is able to bring out almost inaccessible undertones of events that have no visible roots in national history or geography or literary classics . . . the flatness of Conroy's account reflects his feeling that lessons from experience are elusive. . . ."

Hudson Review offered this opinion of Conroy: "He has no revolution to serve as a background, only modern America; he has no reputation as a writer or personage on which to capitalize; this is his first book and he is thirty-two. He has no politics or sense of history either, so if he is a child of our time, he is so by reason of his personal qualities—brooding self-absorption, passionate vague desires to be free of self and others, 'blinding' flashes of self-congratulation. . . . He does not try to make his childhood remarkable, but he does want terribly to understand it by making of its very ordinariness a sounding board for his reflections on being young . . . Conroy has written his book at the right moment, when he is still in touch with the boy he was. . . ."

New Leader called *Stop-time* "a book with so much meaningful detail, one which so nearly approximates the weight and texture of an actual life, [it] is certainly a rarity. And not only the author, but the people around him . . . are captured with a beautiful precision in the midst of the most ordinary circumstances, like fine portraits hanging on the walls of a cafeteria. If Frank Conroy at 32 cannot yet extract any final meanings from his life, he at least masterfully conveys the sense of having lived it. Boy's books can get away without deep vision—not without good eyesight."

Stop-time, reported the *New York Times Book Review* is "free of rancor, rich with the half-mad, lonely characters who people our times, is one of the finest books about growing up I have ever read; the reader cannot help recognizing a part of himself in this book. In it the author has captured that mixture of acute perception and mindlessness that is the vortex around which all memory of youth revolves."

BIOGRAPHICAL/CRITICAL SOURCES: New York Times, October 23, 1967, November 29, 1967; *Harper's Magazine,* November, 1967; *Book World,* November 12, 1967, December 3, 1967; *New York Times Book Review,* November 12, 1967; *Best Sellers,* November 15, 1967; *Time,* November 24, 1967; *New York Review of Books,* December 21, 1967; *Commonweal,* December 29, 1967; *New Yorker,* February 3, 1968; *New Leader,* February 26, 1968; *Observer,* March 10, 1968; *Listener,* March 14, 1968; *New Statesman,* March 15, 1968; *Punch,* April 10, 1968; *Books and Bookmen,* May, 1968; *Commentary,* June, 1968; *Hudson Review,* autumn, 1968; *Partisan Review,* winter, 1969; *Sewanee Review,* winter, 1969.

*   *   *

COOK, Geoffrey 1946-

PERSONAL: Born April 9, 1946, in Cleveland, Ohio; son of Arthur William (a writer) and Donna (a hospital administrator; maiden name, Christy) Cook. *Education:* Kenyon College, B.A., 1968. *Home address:* P.O. Box 18274, San Francisco, Calif. 94118.

CAREER: Writer, 1968—. *Member:* International Poetry Society, International P.E.N. (American Center), American Translators Association.

WRITINGS: Tolle Lege (poems), Moonbird Publications, 1974; *Love and Hate: Selected Translations from the Carmina of Gaius Valorius Catullus,* Outrigger Publications, 1975; *Anabasis* (poems), Fault Press, 1978; *Selections From the Miscellanea of Venantius Fortunatus,* Cherry Valley Editions, in press; *The: Texts and Explanations,* Laughing Bear Press, in press. Contributor of poems, stories, articles, and reviews to about one hundred fifty magazines. Contributing editor of *Margins* and *La Mamelle Art Contemporary.*

WORK IN PROGRESS: The Children of Marx and Coca-Cola: Small Literature in the 70's, for NFS Press; with G. P. Vimal, editing an anthology of contemporary Hindi language poets in translation, for Perivale; a translation of Menander's *Dyskolos.*

SIDELIGHTS: Cook writes: "My work has been moving more and more into non-print media. I no longer feel that a writer is necessarily one whose work is meant to end up in a book, but is one who 'plays' with language in almost any medium."

His language art pieces have been shown in museums including Joslyn Art Museum, Museum Utrecht, The Stedelijk, Gallerie Kontact, Museum of Contemporary Art of the University of Sao Paolo, and many others.

*   *   *

COOK, Mercer 1903-

PERSONAL: Born March 30, 1903, in Washington, D.C.; son of William Marion and Abbie (Mitchell) Cook; married Vashti Smith (a social worker), August 31, 1929 (died, 1969); children: Mercer, Jacques. *Education:* Amherst College, B.A., 1925; University of Paris, diploma, 1926; Brown University, M.A., 1931, Ph.D., 1936. *Religion:* Roman Catholic. *Home:* 4811 Blagden Ave. N.W., Washington, D.C. 20001. *Office:* Department of Romance Languages, Howard University, Washington, D.C.

CAREER: Howard University, Washington, D.C., assistant professor, 1927-36; Atlanta University, Atlanta, Ga., professor of French, 1936-43; University of Haiti, Port-au-Prince, professor of English, 1943-45; Howard University, professor of romance languages, 1945-60; American Society for African Culture, foreign representative, 1958-60; U.S.

ambassador to the Republic of Niger, 1961-64, and to Senegal and Gambia, 1964-66; Howard University, professor of romance languages and head of department, 1966-70, professor emeritus, 1970—. Director of African program, Congress for Cultural Freedom, 1960-61; alternate delegate to United Nations General Assembly, 1963; visiting professor, Harvard University, 1969-70.

MEMBER: Association for the Study of Negro Life and History, American Society of Composers, Authors and Publishers (ASCAP), American Association of Teachers of French, National Association for the Advancement of Colored People (NAACP), Phi Beta Kappa. *Awards, honors:* Received decorations from the Government of Haiti, 1945, the Republic of Niger, 1964, and Senegal, 1966; awarded Palmes Academiques (France); LL.D. from Amherst College, 1965, and Brown University, 1970.

WRITINGS: Five French Negro Authors (criticism), Associated, 1943; *Handbook for Haitian Teachers of English,* H. Deschamps (Port-au-Prince), c.1944; *Education in Haiti,* Federal Security Agency, Office of Education, 1948; (with Stephen Henderson) *The Militant Black Writer in Africa and the United States* (criticism), University of Wisconsin Press, 1969. Also author of *The Haitian Novel* (criticism), Gordon.

Editor: *Le Noir: Morceaux Choisis de Vingt-Neuf Francais Celebres,* American Book Co., 1934; *Portraits Americains,* Heath, 1939; *The Haitian-American Anthology: Haitian Readings from American Authors,* Imprimerie de l'Etat, 1944; *An Introduction to Haiti,* Department of Cultural Affairs, Pan American Union, 1951.

Contributor to *Journal of Negro History, Journal of Human Relations, Negro Digest, Opportunity, Phylon,* and *Crisis.*

SIDELIGHTS: Before his retirement from Howard University, Cook co-authored *The Militant Black Writer in Africa and the United States* with Stephen Henderson of Morehouse College. Hoyt Fuller noted that the book contained two excellent essays which were "expanded and edited versions of addresses delivered by the authors during the 1968 Conference on Afro-American Culture at the University of Wisconsin." Fuller further credits Cook with "drawing on his long experience as student and professor of African literature, as ambassador to two African nations, and as a personal friend to many of this century's African men of letters." *The Militant Black Writer in Africa and the United States* is, said Fuller, "all that those with a genuine interest in black literature, its past and its future need as an introduction to a rich and rewarding field of study."

BIOGRAPHICAL/CRITICAL SOURCES: Crisis, April, 1957, December, 1963; *New York Times Book Review,* October 19, 1969.*

* * *

COOPER, Harold R.   1911(?)-1978

1911(?)—April 20, 1978; American correspondent and editor. Cooper was a long-time Washington and foreign correspondent for the Associated Press. He joined the AP in Chicago in 1935 and transferred to Washington where he worked for eleven years. In 1948, Cooper moved to the foreign desk in New York and later to London where he also worked as a correspondent. He returned to New York in 1965 and was a special editor. He died in London, England. Obituaries and other sources: *New York Times,* April 21, 1978.

COOPER, Wyatt (Emory)   1927-1978

September 1, 1927—January 5, 1978; American actor, editor, and writer. Cooper was best known for his impeccable dress and flair for parties. Along with wife Gloria Vanderbilt, he was named to the International Best Dressed List in 1969. Cooper co-wrote the screenplay, "The Chapman Report," and worked with Truman Capote on the teleplay, "Glass House." He also wrote *Families: A Memoir and a Celebration.* Cooper died in New York, N.Y. Obituaries and other sources: *Authors in the News,* Volume II, Gale, 1976; *New York Times,* January 6, 1978; *Washington Post,* January 7, 1978. (See index for *CA* sketch)

* * *

COPPOLA, Francis Ford   1939-

PERSONAL: Born April 7, 1939, in Detroit, Mich.; son of Carmine (a musician and composer) and Italia (an actress; maiden name, Pennino) Coppola; married Eleanor Neil (an artist); children: Sophia, Gian-Carlo, Roman. *Education:* Hofstra University, B.A., 1959; University of California at Los Angeles, M.F.A., 1967. *Residence:* San Francisco, Calif. *Office:* American Zoetrope, 916 Kearny St., San Francisco, Calif. 94133.

CAREER: Independent screenwriter, producer and director of motion pictures. American International Pictures, Inc., Beverly Hills, Calif., began as assistant to Roger Corman, 1962, became screenwriter, dialogue director, and director of motion pictures, 1962-66, sound man, 1963; Seven Arts, Burbank, Calif., screenwriter and director, 1966-69; Paramount Pictures Corp., New York City, screenwriter, producer and director of motion pictures, 1966-74; Warner Brothers, Inc., screenwriter and director of motion pictures, 1968-69. Directed "Private Lives" for American Conservatory Theatre, 1972; staged "The Visit of the Old Lady" for San Francisco Opera Company, 1972; executive producer, "American Graffiti," Universal Pictures, 1973. Co-founder of American Zoetrope, 1969, and Directors Company, 1972. *Member:* Directors' Guild of America, Academy of Motion Picture Arts and Sciences.

AWARDS, HONORS: Received Samuel Goldwyn Award, 1962, for "Dementia 13"; award from San Sebastian International Cinema Festival, 1970, for "The Rain People"; co-winner of Academy Award for best screenplay from Academy of Motion Picture Arts and Sciences, 1970, for "Patton"; nomination for best director from Academy of Motion Picture Arts and Sciences, Academy Award for best movie, co-winner of Academy Award for best screenplay based on material from another medium, all 1972, all for "The Godfather"; named best director by Directors' Guild of America, 1972; Golden Palm award from Cannes Film Festival, nomination for best screenplay and best movie from Academy of Motion Picture Arts and Sciences, all 1974, all for "The Conversation"; Academy Award for best movie and best director, co-winner of Academy Award for best screenplay based on material from another medium, all 1974, all for "The Godfather, Part Two"; named best director by Directors' Guild of America, 1974; D.F. from Hofstra University, 1977.

WRITINGS—Screenplays: (Also director) "Dementia 13," American International, 1962; "Battle Beyond the Sun," American International, 1963; "This Property is Condemned," Paramount-Seven Arts, 1966; (with Gore Vidal) "Is Paris Burning?" Paramount, 1967; (also director) "You're a Big Boy Now," (adapted from the novel by David Benedictus) Seven Arts, 1967; (also director) " .he

Rain People," Warner Brothers-Seven Arts, 1969; (with Edmund Worth) "Patton," Twentieth Century-Fox, 1970; (with Mario Puzo; also director) "The Godfather" (adapted from the novel by Puzo), Paramount, 1972; (also director) "The Conversation," Paramount, 1974; "The Great Gatsby" (adapted from the novel by F. Scott Fitzgerald), Paramount, 1974; (with Puzo; also director) "The Godfather, Part Two," (adapted from the novel by Puzo), Paramount, 1974; (also director) "Apocalypse Now," United Artists, 1978.

WORK IN PROGRESS: "Tucker," a filmed biography of Preston Tucker, inventor of a futuristic automobile during the 1940's.

SIDELIGHTS: "You have to invent," Coppola once explained to an interviewer in reference to his latest film, "Apocalypse Now." A "mythical, highly stylized allegory of the American experience in Vietnam in 1968 and 1969," Coppola's "Apocalypse Now" was inspired by Joseph Conrad's Heart of Darkness. The film centers around the insane renegade army officer Colonel Kurtz, who establishes a stronghold in Vietnam; and an officer, Captain Willard, hired by the CIA to kill Kurtz. "The movie has two levels," said Coppola, "the level of the life on the boat and the mission and then what happens to Kurtz's mind when the film becomes surreal." In exploring the Vietnam War, Coppola is staking his career and reputation as an artist on the belief that "Apocalypse Now" will be both a commercial and artistic success. "Of course, the movie has to live in reality and practicality," Coppola said. "I'm spending $100,000 a day. Imagine the degree of control I have to have."

Control is a popular subject with Coppola. One of the few writer/director/producers in American cinema, he has maximum control of his films. Coppola recalled the difficulties involved in acquiring artistic control during the making of "The Godfather": "I wasn't given my head, by any means," he told William Murray. "A lot of the energy that went into the film went into simply trying to convince the people who held the power to let me do the film my way." Allowed to do the film his own way, after numerous battles, Coppola created what many critics have suggested is "the greatest gangster picture ever made." An increase in power was granted Coppola when he agreed to do the sequel, "The Godfather, Part Two." "I had to fight a lot of wars the first time around," Coppola said. "In 'The Godfather, Part Two' I had no interference. Paramount backed me up in every decision. The film was my baby and they left it in my hands." Coppola returned the favor by making a film Paul Zimmerman deemed "beautifully made," one of "ambition, vision, and artistic courage."

The tale "The Godfather" films tell parallels Coppola's own in that both are concerned with the acquisition of power. The Godfather, Vito Corleone, is an Italian immigrant who arrives alone in the U.S. Raised in the "Little Italy" of New York City, Corleone's rise to power is chronicled in both films, as is the transition of power to his son Michael. Explaining why he agreed to do the sequel, Coppola pointed to Michael's new power as Godfather as the reason. "I wanted to take Michael to what I felt was the logical conclusion," he said. "Michael wins every battle; his brilliance and his resources enable him to defeat all his enemies." But Coppola did not permit Michael the luxury of victory. "I didn't want him to be assassinated by his rivals. But, in a bigger sense, I also wanted to destroy Michael," said Coppola. "There's no doubt that, by the end of this picture, Michael Corleone, having beaten everyone, is sitting there alone, a living corpse." Despite the realism of the film, Coppola disdained

metaphorical interpretations or comparisons with the real Mafia. "Remember, it wasn't a documentary about Mafia chief Vito Genovese," warned Coppola. "It was Marlon Brando with Kleenex in his mouth."

Known primarily for his epic "Godfather" films and "Apocalypse Now," Coppola has also proved himself capable of making simpler, more personal, lower budgeted films. "I've made two personal movies," he said. "'The Rain People' and 'The Conversation,' and each is a small step." "The Rain People" concerns a bored housewife who, despite loving her husband, leaves him to drive around the country. The film was a critical success and remains popular at art houses. Coppola worked intermittently on the script for "The Conversation" from 1966 to 1974. Coincidentally released during the Watergate controversy, the film details the emotional breakdown and mental collapse of Harry Caul, a professional wiretapper. Caul is an aloof, cold person who remains uninvolved with his subjects until curiosity results in his own overwhelming paranoia. Surprised by Coppola's ability to create on the less-than-epic scale of the "Godfathers," critics praised "The Conversation" for being a "screenplay of the first quality" and Hollis Alpert wrote of Coppola's perception as "fascinating and rather frightening." With "The Conversation," Coppola had succeeded in combining the artistic with the purely entertaining. "Simply as a thriller," wrote Alpert, "this is inventive and unusual stuff. The clever photography aims at creating a world that is real and surreal at the same time." The success of "The Conversation" and "The Godfather, Part Two" afforded Coppola the rare honor of having two films nominated for best movie in the same year.

Coppola's cinematic ability is acknowledged by a host of critics. "Coppola stands alone as a multiple movie talent," wrote Maureen Orth, "a director who can make the blockbuster success and the brilliant 'personal film.'" And Richard Schickel considers Coppola, "A skilled popular artist—the kind of man who can blend subtly observed details with a gift for showmanship." Yet, although he is aware of his craftsmanship, Coppola sees his occupation as somewhat of a hassle. "You know what it's like to be a director?" he asked an interviewer. "It's like running in front of a locomotive. If you stop, if you trip, if you make a mistake, you get killed. How can you be creative with that thing behind you? Everyday I know it's $8000 an hour." But Coppola can't resist the power and risk involved in filmmaking. "Imagine having millions and millions of people all over the world surrendering their brain to you for two hours," he said, adding: "What would General Motors pay to have that?"

BIOGRAPHICAL/CRITICAL SOURCES: New Yorker, April 15, 1974; Saturday Review, May 4, 1974; Newsweek, November 25, 1974, December 23, 1974, June 13, 1977; Time, December 16, 1974; Playboy, July, 1975; Atlantic, August, 1976.

*   *   *

CORAM, Christopher
See WALKER, Peter N.

*   *   *

CORBETT, Thomas H(enry) 1938-

PERSONAL: Born August 19, 1938, in Chicago, Ill.; son of Thomas Cyril (a journalist) and Dorothy Marie (a copywriter; maiden name, Huttman) Corbett; married Beverly Ann Kufrovich, November 12, 1965; children: Thomas Henry Jan, Patricia Ann, Robert Cyril, James Peter. Educa-

tion: University of Michigan, M.D., 1963. *Residence:* Ann Arbor, Mich. *Office:* Department of Anesthesiology, University of Michigan Medical Center, Ann Arbor, Mich. 48109.

CAREER: University of Michigan Medical Center, Ann Arbor, intern, 1963-64, resident, 1966-70; University of Michigan Medical School, Ann Arbor, assistant professor, 1973-76, associate professor of anesthesiology, 1976—. Clinical investigator at Veteran's Hospital, Ann Arbor, 1974-77; staff anesthesiologist at Wayne County General Hospital, Wayne, Mich., 1977—. *Wartime service:* U.S. Public Health Service, 1964-66; served at Alaska Native Medical Centers in Anchorage and Barrow, Alaska, and at Laguna Indian Health Center in Laguna, N.M. *Member:* American Society of Anesthesiologists, Society for Environmental and Occupational Health, Teratology Society, New York Academy of Sciences. *Awards, honors:* U.S. Environmental Protection Agency environmental quality award, 1976, for research on toxicology of polybrominated biphenyls (PBB) following state-wide contamination of the Michigan food chain with these chemicals.

WRITINGS: Cancer and Chemicals, Nelson-Hall, 1977. Contributor of medical and scientific papers to annals of the New York Academy of Sciences, and to *Journal of the American Medical Association, Anesthesiology,* and other professional journals.

WORK IN PROGRESS: PBB: The Poisoning of Michigan; To Ease Their Pain, a novel about three young doctors in training for the specialty of anesthesiology.

SIDELIGHTS: During his residency in anesthesiology at the University of Michigan Medical Center, Corbett began to suspect that commonly used anesthetic gases might be toxic and therefore dangerous to the health of anesthesiologists who inhaled them daily in the course of their work. After reading the disturbing results of the studies carried out on the health experience of anesthesiologists, he decided to carry out tests himself, despite the lack of encouragement from his colleagues. In his study of the health experience of female nurse anesthetists in Michigan, he found that incidence of cancer in them was three times that of the general population. He also found a significantly higher rate of birth defects in the children of those anesthetists who worked during pregnancy than in the children of those who did not work. At his urging, the American Society of Anesthesiologists conducted a nationwide survey on the health experience of operating room personnel who came in contact with anesthetic gases. The results of this study supported Corbett's finding of increased incidence of birth defects in offspring of those exposed to the gases during pregnancy, and also increased incidence of liver disease and cancer. Subsequent studies led Corbett to investigate a new anesthetic, isoflurane, because its chemical structure closely resembled that of a powerful chemical carcinogen. The results of his tests on mice revealed a significant increase in the incidence of liver tumors in those exposed to isoflurane. Though at first his findings were criticized by his fellow anesthesiologists, he eventually succeeded in his campaign to convince the Federal Drug Administration to withhold approval for the marketing of the anesthetic, pending further investigation.

Corbett told *CA:* "I wrote *Cancer and Chemicals* because of the lack of knowledge on this subject on the part of the general public. I became acutely aware of this lack of knowledge while lecturing to public interest groups on the general subject of environmental contamination disasters, including

the Michigan PBB episode. My second book, *PBB: The Poisoning of Michigan,* describes the anatomy of this particular disaster, pointing out the bungling on the part of both the industries involved and the state and federal regulatory agencies. I have research interests in reproductive biology, teratology, and chemical carcinogenesis."

BIOGRAPHICAL/CRITICAL SOURCES: New Yorker, November 24, 1975.

* * *

COSLOW, Sam 1905-

PERSONAL: Born December 12, 1905, in New York, N.Y.; son of Harry (a textile designer) and Rebecca (Novitch) Coslow; married Frances King (a singer), October 30, 1953; children: Laurence, Jacqueline, Cara. *Education:* Educated in Brooklyn, N.Y. *Residence:* New York, N.Y.

CAREER: Composer and lyricist. Co-founder, Spier & Coslow, Inc., 1927, "Soundie" Industry, 1940, and RCM Productions, Inc. (now known as Famous Music Co.), 1941; producer, Paramount Pictures, 1944-45, and Mary Pickford Productions, 1945-47; went to London and wrote for film and stage musicals, 1954-55. *Member:* American Society of Composers, Authors, and Publishers (ASCAP), American Guild of Authors and Composers (AGAC). *Awards, honors:* Academy Award for producing best musical short from Academy of Motion Picture Arts and Sciences, 1943, for "Heavenly Music"; elected to Songwriters Hall of Fame, 1974.

WRITINGS: Cocktails for Two: The Many Lives of Giant Songwriter Sam Coslow (autobiography), Arlington House, 1977.

Musicals; lyricist: "Artists and Models," produced on Broadway at the Winter Garden Theatre, October 15, 1924.

Screenplays; composer and lyricist with collaborators, except as noted: "College Humor," Paramount, 1933; "Murder at the Vanities," Paramount, 1934; "Belle of the Nineties," Paramount, 1934; "One Hundred Men and a Girl," Universal, 1936; "Double or Nothing," Paramount, 1937; "Thrill of a Lifetime," Paramount, 1937; "True Confession," Paramount, 1937; "Out of This World," Paramount, 1945; (screenwriter and producer) "Copacabana," United Artists, 1947; and numerous others.

Songs; composer and lyricist with collaborators: "True Blue Lou," 1929; "Just One More Chance," 1931; "Sing You Sinners," 1931; "Moon Song," 1931; "Learn to Crow," 1932; "Down the Old Ox Road," 1933; "My Old Flame," 1934; "Cocktails for Two," 1934; "This Little Piggie," 1936; "Mister Paganini," 1936; "Blue Mirage," 1955; and numerous others.

WORK IN PROGRESS: An untitled musical comedy.

BIOGRAPHICAL/CRITICAL SOURCES: Sam Coslow, *Cocktails for Two: The Many Lives of Giant Songwriter Sam Coslow,* Arlington House, 1977.

* * *

COURAGE, James Francis 1903-1963

PERSONAL: Born February 9, 1903, in Amberley, Canterbury, New Zealand. *Education:* Attended Christ's College (Christchurch, New Zealand) and St. John's College, Oxford. *Residence:* England.

CAREER: Writer, novelist, and dramatist.

WRITINGS—All novels, except as indicated: *One House,* Gollancz, 1933; "Private History" (play), produced in London, 1938; *The Fifth Child*, Constable, 1948; *Desire Without Content*, Constable, 1950; *Fires in the Distance*, Constable, 1952; *The Young Have Secrets*, Constable, 1954; *The Call Home*, J. Cape, 1956; *A Way of Love*, Putnam, 1959; *A Visit to Penmorten*, J. Cape, 1961; *Such Separate Creatures: Stories*, edited by Charles Brasch, Caxton Press, 1973.

Work represented in *The Big Game and Other Stories*, edited by A. P. Gaskell, Caxton Press, 1947.

BIOGRAPHICAL/CRITICAL SOURCES: Times Literary Supplement, January 16, 1959.*

(Died October 5, 1963.)

*   *   *

COURSE, Edwin 1922-

PERSONAL: Born December 15, 1922, in London, England; son of Alfred (a sailor) and Alice Mansbridge (Sims) Course; married Sheila Margaret Crompton (a museum curator); children: Magnus. *Education:* London School of Economics and Political Science, London, B.Sc., 1956, Ph.D., 1957. *Office:* Department of Extra Mural Studies, University of Southampton, Southampton SO9 5NH, England.

CAREER: Clerk, 1939-41; teacher at elementary schools in London, England, 1947-56; University of Southampton, Southampton, England, lecturer, 1956-70, senior lecturer, 1970—. *Military service:* Royal Navy, 1941-46. *Member:* Chartered Institute of Transport (past section chairman), Association for Industrial Archaeology (group convener), Railway and Canal Historical Society, Society for Nautical Research (southern chairman), University of Southampton Industrial Archaeology Group (president), Hampshire Field Club (president).

WRITINGS: London Railways, Batsford, 1962; *Railways of Southern England*, Batsford, Volume I: *Main Lines*, 1972, Volume II: *Secondary and Branch Lines*, 1974, Volume III: *Independent and Light Railways*, 1976; *Rowing Holiday by Canal in 1873*, Oakwood, 1977; *The Changing Scene on British Railways*, Batsford, 1978; *Industrial Archaeology in Hampshire and Dorset*, Batsford, 1979; *The Itchen Navigation*, Oakwood, in press. Author of booklets. Contributor of more than twenty-five articles on railways to magazines. Editor of "City of Portsmouth Historical Booklets."

SIDELIGHTS: Course writes: "I do not think that I have ever written anything that has not been requested by a publisher, society, or some group. But having undertaken to write a book or article, I regard myself as responsible for reaching as many people as possible.

"I can't give any simple explanation of the quite intense satisfaction I experience in contemplating and writing about industrial archaeology. Perhaps it has something to do with the fact that my grandfather was a railwayman and my father was a sailor—or the fact that I was born in a house with the Thames and the London Arts on one side and a railway marshalling yard on the other. Certainly it is not a recent development. I still cherish my first railway picture book acquired at the age of two."

*   *   *

COUTINHO, Joaquim 1886(?)-1978

1886(?)—February 18, 1978; Portuguese-born educator, civil servant, and author. Before beginning a career in teaching, Coutinho first entered government service and became a commercial attache with the Portuguese Embassy. He was a founding faculty member of the Foreign Service School of Georgetown University and helped to establish a "junior-year abroad" program in Madrid for the university's students. Coutinho taught geopolitics, geography, and Portuguese for nearly fifty years. He received numerous awards and honors, including the Portuguese Red Cross and decorations from the Holy See and the governments of Ecuador and Portugal. He was co-author of a book on the Portuguese language. Coutinho died in Washington, D.C. Obituaries and other sources: *Washington Post*, February 22, 1978.

*   *   *

COX, Harvey (Gallagher, Jr.) 1929-

PERSONAL: Born May 19, 1929, in Phoenixville, Pa.; son of Harvey Gallagher (a painter, decorator, and transport manager) and Dorothea (Dunwoody) Cox; married Nancy Nieburger (an actress), May 10, 1957; children: Rachel Llanelly, Martin Stephen, Sarah Irene. *Education:* University of Pennsylvania, A.B. (with honors), 1951; Yale University, B.D. (cum laude), 1955; Harvard University, Ph.D., 1963. *Home:* 65 Frost St., Cambridge, Mass. 02140. *Office:* Harvard Divinity School, 45 Francis Ave., Cambridge, Mass. 02138.

CAREER: Oberlin College, Oberlin, Ohio, director of religions activities, 1955-58; ordained minister of the American Baptist Church, 1956; program associate for American Baptist Home Mission Society, 1958-63; Andover Newton Theological School, Newton Centre, Mass., assistant professor of theology and culture, 1963-65; Harvard University, Divinity School, Cambridge, Mass., associate professor of church and society, 1965-68, professor of divinity, 1968-70, Victor Thomas Professor of Divinity, 1970—, research associate in program on technology and society, 1967—. Adviser to Harvard University Divinity School department of church and society at New Delhi Conference of the World Council of Churches, 1962; fraternal worker with Gossner Mission in East Berlin, Germany, 1962-63; chairman of the board, Blue Hill Christian Center, 1963-66. *Military service:* U.S. Merchant Marine. *Member:* American Theological Association, American Association of Christian Ethics, Americans for Democratic Action, Fund for Urban Negro Development, Foundation for the Arts, Religion, and Culture (fellow).

WRITINGS: The Bible, the Church, and the Student Christian Movement (pamphlet), United Student Christian Council, 1958; *The Secular City: Secularization and Urbanization in Theological Perspective*, Macmillan, 1965, revised edition, 1966; *God's Revolution and Man's Responsibility*, Judson, 1965; *On Not Leaving It to the Snake* (essays), Macmillan, 1967; (with the members of the seminar on technology and culture at Massachusetts Institute of Technology) *Technology and Culture in Perspective*, Church Society for College Work, 1967; (editor) *The Church Amid Revolution*, Association Press, 1967; (with Mary Corita Kent and Samuel A. Eisenstein) *Sister Corita*, Pilgrim Press, 1968; (editor) *The Situation Ethics Debate*, Westminster Press, 1968; *The Feast of Fools: A Theological Essay on Festivity and Fantasy*, Harvard University Press, 1969.

The Seduction of the Spirit: The Use and Misuse of People's Religion, Simon & Schuster, 1973; (editor) *Military Chaplains: From Religious Military to a Military Religion*, American Report Press, 1973; *Turning East: The Promise and Peril of Orientalism*, Simon & Schuster, 1977.

Contributor of chapters and introductions to many books

and of articles to such magazines as *Christian Century, Commonweal,* and *Christianity Today.* Member of editorial board of *Christianity and Crisis.*

SIDELIGHTS: Harvey Cox, described by Martin Marty and others as "American Protestantism's most influential younger theologian," has attempted to bring Christianity into a more meaningful relationship to man and his problems in modern technological society by developing a secular-political theology. A "pioneer in Marxist-Christian dialogue," Cox declared, "Theology is now in a position to bring to the global struggle for human liberation a fund of images and hopes without which men might settle for less than they really deserve. It can reawaken a society that has been drugged by menial goals and vicious values. It can help us understand man better and fire his imagination more compassionately."

Not content merely to study theology on an intellectual level, Cox has sought to "do theology" by developing a lifestyle consistent with his beliefs. "Theology has to do more than think," he said. "It needs a laboratory to help us find out how to relate our thoughts to concrete action." For seven years Cox and his family lived in Roxbury, a ghetto area in Boston, in order to understand and confront the problems of the black community more compassionately. Later the Coxes tried living in a communal arrangement with another married couple so that they might mitigate the problems and abnormalities of the nuclear family. They have experimented in functioning without telephone, television, or automobile to achieve a simpler lifestyle and "more human way of living." Carrying his laboratory outside his own home, Cox has participated in innovative religious activities, including a rather unorthodox Easter/Passover celebration that he led from a discotheque through the streets of Boston in 1970. He explained it as an attempt "to 'demarginate' the Easter message by moving the celebration into a very secular setting . . . and juxtaposing the Easter symbols carefully with the images that reach people today."

Cox has sought to explore this relationship between secular culture and Christian symbols in his writing. In his first major publication, *The Secular City,* he confronted the facts of secularization and urbanization in modern society and hailed them as a means toward a renewed "Christianity." He saw secular man as fulfilling a divine rather than profane role in a technologically progressive age, in which the "Secular City" represented the coming Kingdom of God.

In *The Feast of Fools,* written in the light of the political and social upheavals of the late 1960's, Cox turned from his optimistic view of a technology-oriented secular life to seek a revitalization of religious ritual and symbol. Even though he had rejected the possibility of believing "the way our forebears did," he still found it necessary to integrate Christian symbols into his belief system after divesting them of their "negative" connotations. "Our religious crisis today comes from two sources," he explained. "The first is the use that has been made of weighty religious symbols to sanctify privilege and oppression. . . . Second, we have become so self-conscious about our symbols that we are afraid they cannot function religiously." The solution Cox offered was to "use the rich legacy of religious symbols in a self-conscious, playful way." In another interview he added, "When one approaches religious faith with a kind of playfulness, one can't become as anguished and inwardly torn up about belief and non-belief as has been popular in recent theological literature." Cox suggested that religion becomes a game in which "the symbol itself is not the ultimate reality," but merely a springboard for emotional and political liberation. Evangeli-

cals such as Dale Vree have criticized Cox for defining religious symbols by their "relative degree of cultural power" rather than their cognitive content, and for his "attempt to use their beliefs as mere tools to mobilize people for political ends."

Cox's latest book, *Turning East,* examined what he has called "America's neo-Oriental county fair" of exotic Eastern religions. After observing and participating in Eastern cults and religions, including Transcendental Meditation and Zen Buddhism, Cox discussed the dangers as well as the merits of these beliefs for Western industrialized man. In the final analysis, Cox maintained that the Judeo-Christian tradition "can still answer the human yearning for friendship, authentic experience, and even for trustworthy authority."

BIOGRAPHICAL/CRITICAL SOURCES: Daniel J. Callahan, *The Secular City Debate,* Macmillan, 1966; *New York Times Book Review,* November 19, 1967; *Commonweal,* March 15, 1968; *Time,* March 15, 1968; *Christian Century,* April 1, 1970, January 6, 1971, May 28, 1975, January 21, 1976; *Newsweek,* May 11, 1970; *New Republic,* September 29, 1973; *Christianity Today,* August 26, 1977.*

* * *

CRAIN, Sharie 1942-

PERSONAL: Born December 9, 1942, in Minocqua, Wis.; daughter of L. M. (a business executive) and Vivian (Daskam) Emmerish. *Education:* University of Wisconsin, Madison, B.S., 1964; Governors State University, M.A., 1974; currently pursuing doctoral study at Antioch College.

CAREER: Employed as director of marketing for a medical instrument company, Chicago, Ill.; partner in Buckley, Long, Crain & Associates (psychologists); employed by International Harvesting Co. in areas of college recruiting, labor-management relations, policies and procedures, and corporate personnel, served as corporate manager of women's career development, and currently as corporate manager of public affairs. Founder and director of National Migraine Foundation. Has developed audio-video training programs of career awareness for women in business. Seminar leader. Guest on national television programs. Secretary of the board and chairperson of fund-raising committee for Anti-Cruelty Society of Chicago.

WRITINGS: Taking Stock: A Woman's Guide to Corporate Success (Macmillan Book Club selection), Regnery, 1977. Author of a column in *Viva.*

WORK IN PROGRESS: Research on upward mobility for women, and on sex and business.

SIDELIGHTS: Sharie Crain writes: "The motivation to write the book was to provide other women with the benefit of my experience. The research I do provides a solid basis on which women can build appropriate success patterns in business as well as in their personal lives. Women have incredible potential—we just need to use it."

AVOCATIONAL INTERESTS: Jogging, playing the guitar, tennis, swimming, hot air ballooning.

* * *

CRANE, Richard (Arthur) 1944-

PERSONAL: Born December 4, 1944, in York, England; son of Robert Bartlet (an Anglican priest) and Nowell (Twidle) Crane; married Faynia Jeffery Williams (a theater director), September 5, 1975; children: Leo; Sabra, Teohna (stepdaughters). *Education:* Jesus College, Cambridge, B.A.

(honors), 1966, M.A., 1971. *Residence:* Brighton, Sussex, England. *Agent:* Margaret Ramsay Ltd., 14A Goodwins Court, St. Martins Lane, London WC2N 4LL, England.

CAREER: Actor, writer, and director for theater, film, and television, 1966—. Fellow in theater at University of Bradford, 1972-74; resident dramatist at National Theatre, 1974-75; fellow in creative writing at University of Leicester, 1976. *Member:* British Actors Equity, Theatre Writers Union, Edinburgh Festival Fringe Society (member of board of directors, 1973—). *Awards, honors:* Edinburgh Festival Fringe first awards from *Scotsman,* 1973, for ''Thunder,'' 1974, for ''The Quest,'' 1975, for ''Clownmaker,'' and 1977, for ''Satan's Ball.''

WRITINGS: Thunder (full-length play; first produced in Edinburgh, Scotland, at Edinburgh Festival, August, 1973), Heinemann, 1976.

Unpublished plays: ''Crippen'' (full-length music hall drama), first produced in Edinburgh at Edinburgh Festival, August, 1971; ''The Tenant'' (one-act), first produced in Edinburgh at Edinburgh Festival, August, 1971; ''Tom Brown'' (full-length musical), first produced in Bradford, England, at University of Bradford, December, 1971; ''Decent Things'' (one-act), first produced in Edinburgh at Edinburgh Festival, August, 1972; ''The Blood Stream'' (three one-act plays), first produced in Edinburgh at Traverse Theatre, November, 1972; ''Mutiny on the Bounty'' (full-length musical), first produced in Bradford at University of Bradford, December, 1972; ''Bleak Midwinter'' (full-length), first produced in Edinburgh at Pool Theatre, December, 1972.

''David, King of the Jews'' (full-length), first produced in Bradford at Bradford Cathedral, March, 1973; ''Secrets'' (full-length), first produced in Belfast at Belfast Festival, November, 1973; ''The Pied Piper'' (full-length musical), first produced in Bradford at University of Bradford, December, 1973; ''The Quest'' (full-length), first produced in Edinburgh at Edinburgh Festival, August, 1974; ''Mean Time'' (one-act), first produced in London at Royal Court Theatre Upstairs, June, 1975; ''Venus and Superkid'' (full-length musical), first produced in London at Arts Theatre and Roundhouse, June, 1975; ''Clownmaker'' (full-length), first produced in Edinburgh at Edinburgh Festival, August, 1975, produced in Westport, Conn., at White Barn Theatre, September, 1976, produced Off-Broadway at Theatre de Lys, September, 1978; ''Bloody Neighbours'' (full-length), first produced in London at National Theatre, September, 1975; ''Manchester Tales'' (full-length), first produced in Manchester, England, at Contact Theatre, November, 1975.

''Gunslinger'' (full-length), first produced in Leicester, England, at Phoenix Theatre, July, 1976; ''Nero and the Golden House'' (full-length), first produced in Edinburgh at Traverse Theatre, July, 1976; ''Satan's Ball'' (full-length), first produced in Edinburgh at Edinburgh Festival, August, 1977; ''Gogol'' (one-man, one-act), first produced in Brighton, England, at Brighton Festival, April, 1978.

Author of ''Sebastian and the Seawitch,'' a screenplay for Children's Film Foundation, 1976, and ''Rottingdean,'' BBC-TV, 1978. Co-author of ''Nice Time,'' a revue series aired on Granada Television, 1968-69, and ''The Billy West Show,'' a revue pilot, Granada Television, 1970.

WORK IN PROGRESS: ''Widespread Concern,'' a full-length play.

SIDELIGHTS: Crane comments: ''The Russian language has a word, *poshlost,* meaning 'contentment with mediocri-

ty'—the clammy hand of respectability which enshrines the second-rate. Out of this comes a dilution of spiritual values, and an easy acceptance of manipulation. I try, in plays, to uproot *poshlost* wherever it grows—in the individual, the family, entertainment, the church, the nation, et cetera. What is uncovered may be ecstasy, the 'word,' a gaping void, or Armageddon. I seek to raise questions which raise more questions, in intimate close-up or on vast canvases, and, in the process, to delight the senses with the revelation that theatre is a necessity, not a diversion.''

AVOCATIONAL INTERESTS: Swimming, tennis, walking.

* * *

CRAWFORD, Max 1938-

PERSONAL: Born August 6, 1938, in Lubbock, Tex. *Education:* Earned B.A. from University of Texas. *Residence:* San Francisco, Calif. *Agent:* Elaine Markson Literary Agency, Inc., 44 Greenwich Ave., New York, N.Y. 10011.

CAREER: Writer. *Military service:* U.S. Army, 1958-60.

WRITINGS: Waltz Across Texas (novel), Farrar, Straus, 1975; *The Backslider* (novel), Farrar, Straus, 1976.

SIDELIGHTS: Crawford comments: ''I am interested in writing and reading about certain problems of communism (Russia and China are interesting) and capitalism (American, particularly my home state of Texas) in the twentieth century.''

* * *

CRIDEN, Joseph 1916-
(Yosef Criden)

PERSONAL: Born February 8, 1916, in Buffalo, N.Y.; son of Harry (a businessman) and Ida (Wagner) Criden; married Ruth Suberman (a director of a clothing department), June 6, 1937; children: Neri, Daniel. *Education:* State University of New York at Buffalo, B.A., B.Sc.; University of California, M.Sc. *Home address:* Kibbutz Kfar Blum, Upper Galilee, Israel.

CAREER: Has worked as chief engineer for Coop Trucking Industries, chief engineering consultant for Ministry of Transportation, chief engineer for Israel Defence Forces Transportation Corp., all in Israel; presently director of Industrial Research & Development in Israel. Consulting engineer, government of Israel; chief engineer, Israel Trucking Board. *Military service:* British Army, Royal Electrical and Mechanical Engineers, 1941-46; became major.

MEMBER: Israel Institute of Architects and Engineers, Society of Automotive Engineers, Association of War Veterans, Highway Safety Officers.

WRITINGS: (Under name Yosef Criden; with Saadia Gelb) *The Kibbutz Experience: Dialogue in Kfar Blum,* Herzl Press, 1974; *Vehicle Technologies,* Israel Ministry of Labour, 1974; *Sixty Hints and One for Drivers,* Kibbutz Mevchad, 1975. Contributor to technical publications and *Automobile Club Journal.*

WORK IN PROGRESS: Revising *The Kibbutz Experience; Vehicle Technologies,* Volume II; *Handbook for Truck Drivers;* children's stories.

AVOCATIONAL INTERESTS: Classical music.

* * *

CRIDEN, Yosef
See CRIDEN, Joseph

CROSBY, Donald F(rancis) 1933-

PERSONAL: Born October 12, 1933, in Oakland, Calif.; son of Arch LeRoy and Vanda Rita Crosby. *Education:* University of San Francisco, B.A. (cum laude), 1955; Gonzaga University, M.A., 1962; Brandeis University, M.A., 1970, Ph.D., 1973. *Politics:* Democrat. *Home address:* Jesuit Community, University of Santa Clara, Santa Clara, Calif. 95053. *Office:* Department of History, University of Santa Clara, Santa Clara, Calif. 95053.

CAREER: Entered Society of Jesus (Jesuits), 1956, ordained Roman Catholic priest, 1968; Bellarmine College Preparatory, San Jose, Calif., instructor in history, 1962-65; University of Santa Clara, Santa Clara, Calif., assistant professor of history and religious studies, 1973—. *Member:* American Historical Association, Organization of American Historians, American Catholic Historical Association.

WRITINGS: (Contributor) Robert Griffith and Athan Theoharis, editors, *The Specter: Original Essays on the Cold War and the Origins of McCarthyism*, New Viewpoints Press, 1974; *God, Church and Flag: Senator Joseph R. McCarthy and the Catholic Church, 1950-1957*, University of North Carolina Press, 1978. Contributor to theology journals and *New England Quarterly*.

WORK IN PROGRESS: The American Catholic Experience in the Second World War: Rosaries, Reds, and Rivets, completion expected in 1981.

SIDELIGHTS: Crosby writes: "The most important single fact of my life is that I am a Jesuit priest. I am, however, a Jesuit priest with an obsession about the history of American Catholics, especially the manner of their participation in the larger American society. To put it obscurely, I am interested in the point of intersection between politics and Catholicism. To put it precisely, I want to find out what Catholics did, why they did it, and what kind of impact they had on the rest of these more or less United States."

AVOCATIONAL INTERESTS: "I grow house plants with a flourish and enormous success. I listen to classical music with absorption. My lust for travel is limited only by my meager budget and fleeting good sense."

BIOGRAPHICAL/CRITICAL SOURCES: London *Times*, February 11, 1978.

* * *

CROUSE, Russell M. 1893-1966

PERSONAL: Born February 20, 1893, in Findlay, Ohio; son of Hiram Powers (a newspaper editor) and Sarah (Schumacher) Crouse; married Alison Smith (a newspaperwoman), March 17, 1923 (died January, 1943); married Anna Erskine, June 28, 1945; children: (second marriage) Timothy, Lindsay Ann. *Education:* Attended public schools in Toledo, Ohio. *Residences:* New York, N.Y. and Annisquam, Mass.

CAREER: Cincinnati Commercial-Tribune, Cincinnati, Ohio, reporter, 1910; *Kansas City Star*, Kansas City, Mo., reporter and sports columnist, 1911-16; *Cincinnati Post*, Cincinnati, political reporter, 1917; reporter for *New York Globe, New York Evening Mail*, and *New York Evening Post*, 1919-31; author, dramatist, and producer. Producer, with Howard Lindsay, of several plays, including "Arsenic and Old Lace," 1940, "The Hasty Heart," 1944, "Detective Story," 1949, and "One Bright Day," 1952. Served as press agent for various people in the entertainment field, and for the Theatre Guild, beginning 1932; part-time actor. *Military service:* U.S. Navy, 1917-19. *Member:* Writers' War

Board, 1942-46, Authors' League of America (president, 1943-45), Players Club, Dutch Treat Club. *Awards, honors:* Pulitzer Prize, 1946, for *State of the Union*; D.F.A., 1951, from Ohio Wesleyan University; Antoinette Perry (Tony) Award, 1960, for *The Sound of Music*.

WRITINGS: Mr. Currier and Mr. Ives: A Note on Their Lives and Times, Doubleday, Doran, 1930; *It Seems Like Yesterday*, Doubleday, Doran, 1931; (compiler) *The American Keepsake* (illustrated by Edward A. Wilson), Doubleday, Doran, 1932; *Murder Won't Out*, Doubleday, Doran, 1932; (with wife, Anna Crouse) *Peter Stuyvesant of Old New York* (juvenile; illustrated by Jo Spier), Random House, 1954; (with A. Crouse) *Alexander Hamilton and Aaron Burr: Their Lives, Their Times, Their Duel* (juvenile; illustrated by Walter Buehr), Random House, 1958.

Plays; all with Howard Lindsay: "Anything Goes" (music and lyrics by Cole Porter), first produced in New York City at the Alvin Theater, November 21, 1934; "Red, Hot, and Blue" (music by Porter), first produced in New York City at the Alvin Theater, October 29, 1936; "Hooray for What!" (lyrics by E. Y. Harburg), first produced on Broadway at the Winter Garden Theatre, December 1, 1937; *Clarence Day's Life with Father* (three-act; first produced in New York City at the Empire Theater, November 8, 1939), Knopf, 1940, reprinted, Dramatists Play Service, 1967; *Strip for Action*, Random House, 1943; *State of the Union* (first produced in New York City at the Hudson Theater, November 24, 1945), Random House, 1946; "Clarence Day's Life with Mother," first produced in New York City at the Empire Theater, October 20, 1948.

"Call Me Madam" (music by Irving Berlin), first produced in New York City at the Imperial Theater, October 12, 1950; *Remains to be Seen* (three-act), Dramatists Play Service, 1951; *The Prescott Proposals*, Random House, 1954; *The Great Sebastians* (three-act), Random House, 1956; *Happy Hunting* (music by Harold Karr; lyrics by Matt Dubey; first produced in New York City at the Majestic Theater, December 6, 1956), Random House, 1957; *Tall Story* (three-act), Random House, 1959; *The Sound of Music* (music by Richard Rodgers; lyrics by Oscar Hammerstein II; first produced on Broadway at the Lunt-Fontanne Theatre, November 16, 1959), Random House, 1960; "Mr. President" (music by Berlin), first produced on Broadway at the St. James Theatre, October 20, 1962.

Librettist for the musical comedy, "The Gang's All Here," 1931, and librettist with Corey Ford for "Hold Your Horses," 1933.

Co-author of movie screenplays: "Mountain Music," Paramount, 1937; "The Big Broadcast of 1938," Paramount, 1938; "Artists and Models Abroad," Paramount, 1939; "The Great Victor Herbert," Paramount, 1939; "Woman's World," Twentieth Century-Fox, 1954.

SIDELIGHTS: In September, 1934, Russell Crouse met Howard Lindsay, and their collaboration on the book for the musical "Anything Goes" marked the beginning of a tremendously successful partnership. Lincoln Barnett compared Crouse and Lindsay, dramatically, to Gilbert and Sullivan. Barnett noted, however, that the former team did not experience personal conflicts as did the latter team. Crouse and Lindsay were good friends and possessed such a smooth working relationship that it was difficult to distinguish who had contributed what to the play. Lindsay liked to say that they supplemented rather than complemented one another, and added, "If any two people can be said to think alike, we do." It was commonly agreed that Lindsay possessed a greater knowledge of the theater, while Crouse had a sharper sense of humor.

The early successes of Crouse and Lindsay were all musicals. Ethel Merman starred in the production of "Anything Goes," singing the songs of Cole Porter. Paramount produced two motion pictures based on this play. Both bearing the same title as the play, the 1936 version starred Ethel Merman and Bing Crosby, the 1956 version starred Mitzi Gaynor, Donald O'Connor, and Bing Crosby. "Red, Hot, and Blue" made its debut a few years later, starring Ethel Merman and Jimmy Durante, and the following year, in 1937, Vivian Vance and Ed Wynn appeared in the production of "Hooray for What!"

Following the early achievements, Crouse and Lindsay made stage history with their adaptation of "Life with Father"—their first non-musical play. With 3,224 Broadway performances, it has been surpassed in longevity only by "The Fantasticks" and "Fiddler on the Roof." *Saturday Review of Literature* stated: "The authors of the play . . . deserve great praise for the skill with which they have turned narrative essays into drama without loss of flavor and with, if possible, a heightening of interest." "Father is a shade more graceless, Mother a shade more silly than they seemed in Clarence Day's pages," wrote a *Theatre Arts* critic, "yet the essence of that epic family is there; laughter and alarm attend its diurnal round." Following its successful adaptation as a play, "Life with Father" was also produced as a motion picture by Warner Brothers in 1947. From 1953 to 1955, it was a television series starring Leon Ames and Lurene Tuttle, with many of the episodes written by Crouse and Lindsay.

In 1946, Crouse and Lindsay won the Pulitzer Prize for "State of the Union," a political satire so timely that lines had to be changed from day to day. *New York Times* said: "If 'State of the Union' is more fun behind the footlights than under the library lamp no one has a right to complain. If some of it seems more competent than brilliant under the latter light the reader should remind himself that competence in the theatre today is prized above rubies. . . . 'State of the Union' is still an actor's paradise, even if it does not belong on the shelf with Wilde and Congreve." *Weekly Book Review* noted: "The ladies, to be sure, may be regarded as symbols of the larger forces, and no doubt Ibsen could so have manipulated them. But here they seem to suggest a too obvious triangle story, of tested audience appeal, and the triangle becomes on the authors' part a compromise which they would not permit in the political life of their hero. It is none the less a skillful and interesting play, by two men who know their theater." Spencer Tracy, Katharine Hepburn, Van Johnson and Angela Lansbury starred in the 1948 Metro-Goldwyn-Mayer motion picture based on the play, entitled "The World and His Wife."

With music by Irving Berlin, Ethel Merman starred in the theatrical production of "Call Me Madam," as well as Twentieth Century-Fox's movie adaptation in 1953. Crouse and Lindsay were also a part of the highly successful production of "The Sound of Music." With music by Richard Rodgers and words by Oscar Hammerstein, and starring Mary Martin, the show amassed 1,443 performances on Broadway, and later became a 1965 Twentieth Century-Fox motion picture starring Julie Andrews and Christopher Plummer. "Mr. President" was the last dramatic collaboration by Crouse and Lindsay. Nanette Fabray, Robert Ryan, and Anita Gillette starred in the Broadway production of the musical.

BIOGRAPHICAL/CRITICAL SOURCES: Saturday Review of Literature, November 18, 1939; *Theatre Arts*, January, 1940; *New York Times*, May 19, 1946; *Weekly Book Review*, June 9, 1946; *Life*, November 11, 1946; *Good Housekeeping*, September, 1947; L. K. Barnett, *Writing on Life*, Sloane, 1951; *Kirkus*, July 15, 1958; *Chicago Tribune*, November 2, 1958; *New York Times Magazine*, November 22, 1959; C. O. Skinner, *Life with Lindsay & Crouse*, Houghton, 1976.

OBITUARIES: New York Herald Tribune, April 4, 1966; *New York Times*, April 4, 1966; *Publishers Weekly*, April 11, 1966; *Time*, April 15, 1966; *Newsweek*, April 18, 1966; *Antiquarian Bookman*, May 2, 1966; *Britannica Book of the Year*, 1967.*

(Died April 3, 1966)

*   *   *

CROUSE, Timothy   1947-

PERSONAL: Born January 10, 1947, in New York, N.Y.; son of Russel (a playwright) and Anna (a writer; maiden name, Erskine) Crouse. *Education:* Harvard University, B.A., 1968. *Agent:* Lynn Nesbit, International Creative Management, 40 West 57th St., New York, N.Y. 10019. *Office: Village Voice*, 80 University Pl., New York, N.Y. 10003.

CAREER: U.S. Peace Corps, Washington, D.C., volunteer in Morocco, 1968-69; *Boston Herald*, Boston, Mass., rock reviewer, 1969-70; *Boston After Dark*, Boston, music editor, 1970-71; *Rolling Stone*, San Francisco, Calif., contributing editor, 1971-75; *Esquire*, New York City, author of column "Washington," 1975-76; *Village Voice*, New York, N.Y., staff writer, 1976—.

WRITINGS: The Boys on the Bus, Random House, 1973. Contributor to magazines and newspapers, including *Esquire* and *Rolling Stone*.

*   *   *

CRUMPLER, Frank H(unter)   1935-

PERSONAL: Born July 14, 1935, in Roanoke Rapids, N.C.; son of Odie B., Sr. and Margaret (Renn) Crumpler; married Glenda Dale Rosser (a teacher); children: Mark Hunter, Miriam Dawn, Michael Glenn. *Education:* Wake Forest College, B.A., 1957; Southeastern Baptist Theological Seminary, M.Div., 1961; Union Theological Seminary, Richmond, Va., D.Min., 1974. *Home:* 4782 Westhampton Dr., Tucker, Ga. 30084. *Office:* 1350 Spring St. N.W., Atlanta, Ga. 30309.

CAREER: Ordained Southern Baptist minister, 1955; pastor of Baptist churches in Charlotte, N.C., 1955-61, Durham, N.C., 1961-65, Monroe, N.C., 1965-67, Camden, S.C., 1967-70, and Richmond, Va., 1970-73; Virginia Baptist Convention, Richmond, director of evangelism, 1973-76; Southern Baptist Convention, Home Mission Board, Atlanta, Ga., director of evangelism planning and associational services, 1976—. Past president of Central Baptist Pastor's Conference of South Carolina.

WRITINGS: God Is Near, Revell, 1973; *The Invincible Cross*, Word Books, 1978. Author of church materials.

WORK IN PROGRESS: A book on personal witnessing.

SIDELIGHTS: Crumpler writes: "I am *first* devoted to evangelism and theology. I love to write because it makes possible the sharing of my ideas and convictions with so many people. Basically, I am a 'homebody.' I love being with my family and working around the house. Actually the process of writing a book would never have been possible without the patience, love, and understanding of my wife and our three precious children.

"My first book, *God Is Near,* was written while I was a pastor of a large congregation. Since I could not be with the sick and suffering every day, I put down some encouraging and comforting thoughts that I could leave by the bed or give as a gift. The book was so well received it amazed me. It is in its second printing and still much in demand.

"In *The Invincible Cross* I tried to put forth some theological views about the death of Christ which could be easily understood by laymen. The ideas are basic to New Testament teachings and I feel the book will meet a need.

"My next book is on personal witnessing. Its purpose will be to motivate and equip believers in Jesus Christ to share their faith. There are several possibilities for books which my wife and I are discussing for the future."

*　　*　　*

CRUSE, Harold

PERSONAL: Born in Petersburg, Va. *Education:* Attended Brooklyn Film Institute. *Home:* 1904 Anderson St., Ann Arbor, Mich. 48104. *Office:* Department of History, University of Michigan, Ann Arbor, Mich.

CAREER: Has worked as film editor, office clerk for Veterans Administration, film and drama critic for *New York Labor Press,* teacher of black history in free schools, researcher and writer, and political activist in New York City, 1946-67; co-founder of Jones' Black Arts Theatre and School, New York City, and served as writer, director, and stage manager, 1965-66; University of Michigan, Ann Arbor, visiting professor of history and interim director of Center for Afro-American and African Studies, 1968—. Lecturer at universities including University of London, Harvard University, University of Wales, and Yale University. *Military service:* U.S. Army, 1941-45. *Member:* Phi Kappa Phi.

WRITINGS: The Crisis of the Negro Intellectual (essays), Morrow, 1967; *Rebellion or Revolution?* (essays), Morrow, 1968.

Work represented in anthologies, including: *Black Fire: An Anthology of Black American Writing,* edited by LeRoi Jones and Larry Neal, Morrow, 1968; *Cavalcade: Negro American Writing From 1760 to the Present,* edited by Arthur P. Davis and J. Saunders Redding, Houghton, 1971; *Nommo: An Anthology of Modern African and Black American Writing,* edited by William H. Robinson, Macmillan, 1972. Contributor to *Negro Digest* and other periodicals.

SIDELIGHTS: The New Yorker called *The Crisis of the Negro Intellectual* "a book that will infuriate almost everyone." While writing for *Commonweal,* Arthur Tolbier considered the book "at times brilliant, sometimes shrill, but seldom unimportant." Tolbier noted: "The theme that weaves its way throughout the book is that attention must be paid to the plural experience in America. For the author, the key to extending the society and each of us, is to establish cultural democracy. He finds it absent outside the intellectual community."

Christopher Lasch called *The Crisis of the Negro Intellectual* a "most penetrating study" and one that will "survive as a monument of historical analysis" when "all the manifestoes and polemics of the Sixties are forgotten." Despite a few shortcomings in Cruse's analysis, Lasch agreed that "Cruse leaves no doubt of the validity of his main thesis: that intellectuals must play a central role in movements for radical change, that this role should consist of formulating 'a new political philosophy,' and that in twentieth-century American history they have failed in their work."

BIOGRAPHICAL/CRITICAL SOURCES: New Yorker, February 3, 1968; *New York Review of Books,* February 29, 1968; *Commonweal,* March 29, 1968; *Saturday Review,* May 11, 1968; *Christian Century,* November 27, 1968.*

*　　*　　*

CULBERTSON, Hugh M.

PERSONAL: Born in Michigan; son of Oscar G. (a lithographer) and Laura (a teacher; maiden name, Ferris) Culbertson; married Charlene Boyd (a teacher); children: Steven Drew, Karen Jean. *Education:* Michigan State University, B.S., 1957, Ph.D., 1966; University of Wisconsin, Madison, M.S., 1958. *Religion:* Presbyterian. *Home:* 19 Utah Pl., Athens, Ohio 45701. *Office:* School of Journalism, Lasher Hall, Ohio University, Athens, Ohio 45701.

CAREER: Cooperative Extension Service, East Lansing, Mich., assistant editor and public relations consultant, 1959-64; Ohio University, Athens, member of journalism faculty, 1964—. *Military service:* U.S. Marine Corps, 1959-60. U.S. Marine Corps Reserve, 1960-64. *Member:* Association for Education in Journalism, Mariner's Club (vice-president).

WRITINGS: (With Ralph S. Izard and Donald Lambert) *Fundamentals of News Reporting,* Kendall-Hunt, 1972, 3rd edition, 1977. Contributor of more than twenty articles to professional and literary journals. *College Press Review,* began as grassroots editor, became editor and publisher.

SIDELIGHTS: Culbertson's research on veiled attribution in the news was analyzed on national public radio and was the topic of a syndicated news column. He writes: "My primary interest has been the use of research methodology and theory in the social sciences to shed light on social problems and issues related to journalism, such as veiled attribution and the degree of subject-matter specialization among newspersons."

*　　*　　*

CULLEN, Peta
See PYLE, Hilary

*　　*　　*

CULLINANE, Leo Patrick 1907(?)-1978

1907(?)—June 21, 1978; American journalist, public relations executive, and author. Cullinane began his newspaper career when he joined the staff of the *New York Herald Tribune* in 1929. During this period he covered Roosevelt's "New Deal" administration. He wrote about some of America's important military men during World War II, while serving as a war correspondent in the South Pacific. Before his entrance into the public relations field, Cullinane worked for several congressional committees. He died in Washington, D.C. Obituaries and other sources: *Washington Post,* June 24, 1978.

*　　*　　*

CULPEPPER, Robert H(arrell) 1924-

PERSONAL: Born December 8, 1924, in Tifton, Ga.; son of James Pickren and Leona (Wansley) Culpepper; married Kathleen Sanderson (a missionary), August 21, 1948; children: Cathy Ann (Mrs. Raboteau T. Wilder, Jr.). *Education:* Mercer University, A.B., 1944; Southern Baptist Theological Seminary, B.D., 1947, Th.M., 1948, Th.D. (now Ph.D.), 1950, postdoctoral study, 1962-63; also attended Union Presbyterian Seminary, 1957, Southeastern Baptist Theological Seminary, 1968-69, and Baptist Seminary, Rueschlikon, Switzerland, 1975. *Home:* 425 A, Hoshiguma, Nishi-ku, Fukuoka 814, Japan.

CAREER: Ordained Baptist minister, 1943; bank bookkeeper in Alapaha, Ga., 1941-42; pastor of Baptist churches in Monroe County, Ga., 1943-44, and Franklin County Ky., 1948-50; Southern Baptist Convention, Foreign Mission Board, Richmond, Va., missionary to Japan, 1950—, chairman of Japan Baptist Mission, 1966-68; Seinan Gakuin University, Fukuoka, Japan, professor of theology, 1953—. *Member:* Nippon Kirisutokyo Gakkai (Christianity Learned Society of Japan).

WRITINGS: Interpreting the Atonement, Eerdmans, 1966; *Evaluating the Charismatic Movement,* Judson, 1977. Contributor to theology journals in the United States, Scotland, and Japan.

SIDELIGHTS: Culpepper writes: "After learning the rudiments of the Japanese language in Tokyo, I came to Fukuoka, Japan, to teach in the theological department of Seinan Gakuin University, a Baptist university which now has about eight thousand students. During these twenty-four years I have been helping Japanese prepare for church-related vocations. My wife and I have been actively involved in church work as well. We have started two Baptist churches, the Hirao Baptist Church and the Nagazumi Baptist Church, both in Fukora, Japan.''

*   *   *

CULVER, Kathryn
See DRESSER, Davis

*   *   *

CUNEO, Gilbert Anthony 1913-1978

June 29, 1913—April 19, 1978; American attorney and author. Cuneo was considered an expert in public contract law. He had practiced law in Washington, D.C., for thirty years and was a member of the Armed Services Board of Advisers. Cuneo was co-author of a book on government contracts and negotiations. He died in Washington, D.C. Obituaries and other sources: *Who's Who in America,* 39th edition, Marquis, 1976; *Washington Post,* April 20, 1978.

*   *   *

CURIAE, Amicus
See FULLER, Edmund (Maybank)

*   *   *

CURRY, Jennifer 1934-

PERSONAL: Born June 2, 1934, in Ryhope, England; daughter of Frederick (a businessman) and Evelyn (a teacher; maiden name, Craig) Iley; married John Curry (an air traffic controller), June 24, 1955; children: Andrew John Michael, Peter Graeme Mark. *Education:* University of London, B.A. (with honors), 1955; Moray House College of Education, Edinburgh, Scotland, diploma in education, 1965. *Home:* "Cymbeline," The Borough, Downton, Salisbury, Wiltshire, England. *Agent:* Rupert Crewe Ltd., King's Mews, Gray's Inn Rd., London WC1 N2JA, England.

CAREER: Dunfermline High School, Fife, England, assis-

tant teacher of English, 1968-70; Salisbury College of Technology, Wiltshire, England, lecturer in English and general studies, 1971-72; Open University, Salisbury Centre, England, counsellor in humanities, 1972-76; full-time writer, 1977—. *Member:* Society of Authors.

WRITINGS—All juvenile, except as indicated: *The Faces of Woman,* Harrap, 1971; *Becoming a Citizen,* Harrap, 1972; *Investigations,* Blackie & Son, 1974; *This Is the Way We Sow and Grow,* Hamlyn, 1974; *Collecting,* Hamlyn, 1975; *How Did It Start?,* Hamlyn, 1977; (editor) *Pleasure Trove* (anthology), Hamlyn, 1977; (editor) *Treasure Trove* (anthology), Hamlyn, 1977; *Woman's Own Family Garden Book* (adult nonfiction), Hamlyn, 1978.

Plays: "All for Alice" (musical adaptation of *Alice Through the Looking Glass*), produced in Salisbury, England at Cathedral School, December, 1972; "Don't Blame the Bard" (an operetta), produced in Salisbury at The Playhouse, July, 1973; "Rose Ransome" (an operetta), produced in Salisbury at The Playhouse, July, 1974; "Where There's a Will" (musical), produced in Salisbury at The Godolphin School, July, 1975; "Close Secret" (adaptation of "Theft of Magna Carta" by John Creasey), produced in Salisbury at The Playhouse, September, 1977; "Blonde on the Bonnet," first produced in London at Rock Garden Theatre, December, 1977.

WORK IN PROGRESS: A book on health foods and herbs; two plays.

SIDELIGHTS: Curry told *CA:* "Although I did a small amount of free-lance journalism even while I was at school I never intended to make a career of it. In fact, I never intended to have any career other than that of wife and mother. I married at 21, within days of graduating from university and then spent several years happily looking after my home and two sons, and cultivating my garden. However, when my children went to school I became very interested in education, so much so that at 29 I enrolled as a 'mature student' and trained to become a teacher. When I qualified I was asked by the *Times Educational Supplement,* Scotland, where I then lived, to report on educational activities for the paper, and to write several feature articles, and consequently became an educational journalist almost by accident. When I was teaching English I was very involved with studying drama and helping students to write and perform their own plays. This interest has become the most dominant in my professional life. Though I still produce one or two books each year, I now write as many plays, and find that this is by far the most exciting and immediate way in which I can make contact with those I am writing for. When I sit in a crowded theatre and see the audience responding through laughter or emotional involvement to the characters and situations I have created I feel that no vocation can possibly be more satisfying than my own."

*   *   *

CURTIS, Carol Edwards 1943-

PERSONAL: Born November 9, 1943, in Pittsburgh, Pa.; daughter of John Mantle (an engineer) and Harriet (Barnholdt) Edwards; married Lynn Alan Curtis, August 27, 1966 (divorced, 1972). *Education:* Attended the Sorbonne, University of Paris, 1963; Bard College, B.A., 1964; Boston University, M.A., 1966. *Religion:* Episcopal. *Home:* 429 East 52nd St., Apt. 4D, New York, N.Y. 10022. *Office: Business Week,* 1221 Avenue of the Americas, New York, N.Y. 10020.

CAREER/WRITINGS: Columbus Dispatch, Columbus, Ohio, Washington correspondent, 1971-72; Federal Energy

Adminstration, Washington, D.C., special assistant, 1972-75; Observer Publishing Co., Washington, D.C., senior editor for *Coal Outlook,* 1975-77; *Coal Daily* (newsletter), Washington, D.C., managing editor, 1977; *Business Week,* New York, N.Y., energy editor, 1977—. Notable assignments include coverage of the energy crisis. Participant in Presidential Classroom for Young Americans, 1975. *Member:* National Press Club (member of board of governors, 1977), Washington Press Club. *Awards, honors:* Federal Energy Administration award, 1975, for meritorious government service; National Press Club award, 1977, for serving on board of governors.

WORK IN PROGRESS: Research on the post-embargo transformation of energy policy.

SIDELIGHTS: Curtis told *CA:* "My journalistic and public service background has been focused on energy since the Arab oil embargo of 1973-74. It was then that I joined the Federal Energy Administration as a speechwriter, leaving three years later to continue to specialize in energy for newsletters and, currently, *Business Week* magazine. Within the energy field, my specialty is coal, and I have also written numerous articles on oil, gas, and nuclear energy.

"The key to achieving an effective national energy policy lies in public education," she added. "I believe that the transformation in energy economics that occurred during the 1973-74 Arab oil embargo is not yet fully understood by the person who will be most affected by it, the American consumer. Energy is an abstract concept, but its costs are real. The gradual change in our life-styles that is inevitable as energy grows more scarce and more costly will be easier if it is not forced. Government, industry, and the business and general press have an obligation to bring home to the public what a precious abstraction energy is.

"Once the public more fully understands the energy issue, it will be easier to achieve delicate environment/production tradeoffs in areas like nuclear energy, coal development, and offshore oil. A main reason these tradeoffs are so difficult to achieve now is that the arguments are left largely to vested interests, whose positions are firm. Better public understanding would, I hope, foster more enlightened policy, with a wider public participation."

* * *

CURTIS, Wade
See POURNELL, Jerry (Eugene)

* * *

CURWIN, Richard L(eonard) 1944-

PERSONAL: Born May 25, 1944. in Cambridge, Mass.; son of Louis J. (a businessman) and Ann (Fishman) Curwin; married Geri Rogoff (a teacher), February 9, 1969; children: David Louis, Andrew Stephen, Daniel Ethan. *Education:* University of Massachusetts, A.B., 1968, Ed.D., 1972; Boston State College, M.Ed., 1969. *Religion:* Jewish. *Home:* 59-2 Colony Manor Dr., Rochester, N.Y. 14623. *Office:* Office of Professional Development, National Technical Institute for the Deaf, Rochester Institute of Technology, Rochester, N.Y. 14623.

CAREER: State University of New York College at Geneseo, assistant professor of education, 1972-75; Rochester Institute of Technology, National Technical Institute for the Deaf, Rochester, N.Y., assistant professor of education and coordinator of teacher supervision, 1975—. Has conducted more than one hundred fifty workshops all over the United

States. Professional backgammon player and teacher. *Member:* Association for Supervision and Curriculum Development. *Awards, honors:* Maxi Award from *Methods and Media,* 1975, for *Developing Individual Values in the Classroom.*

WRITINGS: (With Geri Curwin, Karen Walsh, Mary Jane Simmuri, and Rose Marie Framer) *Search for Values,* Pflaum, 1972; (with Barbara Fuhrmann) *Discovering Your Teaching Self: Humanistic Approaches to Effective Teaching,* Prentice-Hall, 1975; (with wife, Geri Curwin) *Developing Individual Values in the Classroom,* Learning Handbooks, 1975; (contributor) James Bellanca and Sidney Simon, editors, *Degrading the Grading Myths: A Primer of Alternatives to Grades and Marks,* Association for Supervision and Curriculum Development, 1976; (contributor) *International and Intercultural Education for Teachers,* Foreign Area Materials Center, State University of New York Education Department, 1977; (contributor) *Migrant Heritage* (teacher's guide), with studies kit, Geneseo Migrant Center, 1977. Contributor to education journals.

WORK IN PROGRESS: (With Fuhrman and Patrick Nemarte) *Making Evaluation Meaningful: A Tour for Teachers Through the Treacherous Territory of Evaluation Learning;* (with Allen Mendler) *Three Dimensional Discipline: People to People Approaches to Classroom.*

SIDELIGHTS: Curwin writes: "My main motivation is to create better learning environments, ones that are humane, and related to me. For me, better means that they provide the opportunity for people to learn to take responsibility for themselves to make decisions and to become aware of who they are and what they wish to be."

BIOGRAPHICAL/CRITICAL SOURCES: Focus, spring/summer, 1977.

* * *

CUSHMAN, Robert F(airchild) 1918-

PERSONAL: Born November 28, 1918, in Champaign, Ill.; son of Robert Eugene (a professor) and Clarissa (a writer; maiden name, Fairchild) Cushman; married Rhea Casterline (a dietitian), July 14, 1942; children: Leslee F., Linda Cushman Ruth. *Education:* Cornell University, A.B., 1940, M.A., 1948, Ph.D., 1949. *Politics:* Democrat. *Religion:* Society of Friends (Quakers). *Home:* 27 Bennett Ave., Huntington Station, N.Y. 11746. *Office:* Department of Politics, New York University, New York, N.Y. 10003.

CAREER: Ohio State University, Columbus, instructor, 1949-52, assistant professor of political science, 1952-53; New York University, New York, N.Y., associate professor, 1953-69, professor of politics, 1969—. *Military service:* U.S. Army Air Forces, 1942-46; became sergeant. *Member:* American Political Science Association.

WRITINGS: (With father, R. E. Cushman) *Cases in Constitutional Law,* Appleton, 1958, 4th edition, Prentice-Hall, 1975, supplements, 1966-74; *Cases in Civil Liberties* (extracted from *Cases in Constitutional Law*), Appleton, 1968, 2nd edition, Prentice-Hall, 1975; (editor) R. E. Cushman, *Leading Constitutional Decisions,* 14th edition (R. F. Cushman was not associated with earlier editions), Appleton, 1969, 15th edition, Prentice-Hall, 1976. Contributor to law journals and model railroad magazines.

WORK IN PROGRESS: A book, for the lay reader as well as the professional, "to provide a new approach to the role of the Supreme Court."

AVOCATIONAL INTERESTS: Model railroad switches and trackwork, astrology.

CUTCHEN, Billye Walker   1930-
(Billye Walker Brown)

PERSONAL: Born April 23, 1930, in Oklahoma City, Okla.; daughter of William Lafayette (an accountant) and Naomi (Armstrong) Walker; married Walter Reed Brown, September 2, 1949 (divorced, August, 1971); married Paul O. Cutchen (a naval officer), April 18, 1974; children: Susan Merle (Mrs. Dennis Kresmer), Elizabeth Ann, Cynthia Lee (Mrs. Brook West). *Education:* Attended Oklahoma College for Women, 1946-47, University of Oklahoma, 1947-48, and Florida State University, 1959-60. *Residence:* Monrovia, Liberia. *Address:* 111 South Jamaica St., Warrington, Fla. 32507.

CAREER: Writer, 1966—.

WRITINGS—Under name Billye Walker Brown: (Editor with Kenneth Croft, and contributor) *Science Readings,* McGraw, 1966; *Research Ideas for Science Projects,* U.S. Agency for International Development, 1968; (with Walter R. Brown) *Science Teaching and the Law,* National Science Teachers Association, 1969.

Children's books; under name Billye Walker Brown, except as indicated: (Editor) James Haggerty, *Man's Conquest of Space,* Scholastic Book Services, 1965; (with Walter R. Brown) *Historical Catastrophes: Volcanoes,* Addison-Wesley, 1970; (with W. R. Brown) *Historical Catastrophes: Hurricanes and Tornadoes,* Addison-Wesley, 1972; (with W. R. Brown) *Historical Catastrophes: Earthquakes,* Addison-Wesley, 1974; (with W. R. Brown; under name Billye W. Cutchen) *Historical Catastrophes: Floods,* Addison-Wesley, 1975. Associate editor of "Vistas of Science," National Science Teachers Association, 1962-64. Contributor to science journals, juvenile and popular magazines, including *Jack and Jill,* and newspapers.

WORK IN PROGRESS: Villingilli, a suspense novel set in the Maldives; collecting information and photographs of Sri Lanka.

SIDELIGHTS: Billye Cutchen writes: "When I was in school, it never occurred to me that I might one day write anything for publication. Mathematics and science were my first loves, and English grammar was something to be endured, just to get through school. Fortunately, I was a conscientious student, because that subject has been a very useful tool in my work as a writer and editor of science books for students.

"When Addison-Wesley approached my former husband and me about writing a series of books for junior high school students, we started looking for a series. We were having trouble agreeing on a subject when our daughter complained to us that she was supposed to write a report on the volcanic eruption of Krakatoa in 1883. She could find information about it in the library, but nothing that was really interesting to her. When I went to the library to help her, I found that there was some really fascinating information about this volcano, but it was written long ago in the archaic fashion of the time. So we hit upon the series, 'Historical Catastrophes.' It was an interesting series to write, in that it was an adventurous learning experience. Library research and interviews were important, but travel to Iceland, to see Surtsey, and Italy, to see Vesuvius and Pompeii, gave me the feeling for the people who were really present when these events took place. Probably the most interesting experience of this sort was a flight, on a U.S. Navy aircraft, into the eye of a hurricane. In addition to being able to describe the storm itself, this flight gave me the opportunity to see how the crew of the plane treated the penetration of such a storm as a routine, fact-gathering mission. Their competence and good humor were enough to make the trip intensely interesting, but not frightening."

D

DALMAS, John
See MANDEL, Leon

*   *   *

DANIEL, Anita   1893(?)-1978

1893(?)—June 17, 1978; Romanian-born American journalist and author. Educated in France and Switzerland, Daniel worked as a free-lance writer for numerous newspapers and magazines, including the *New York Times* and *Christian Science Monitor*. During the course of her career, she interviewed leading statesmen, royalty, famous artists, and writers. She also paid several visits to Albert Schweitzer and wrote a juvenile biography about him, in addition to several travel books. Obituaries and other sources: *Authors of Books for Young People*, 2nd edition, Scarecrow, 1971; *New York Times*, June 19, 1978.

*   *   *

DANIELSON, Wayne Allen   1929-

PERSONAL: Born December 6, 1929, in Burlington, Iowa; son of Arthur Leroy (a laborer) and Bessie Ann (Bonar) Danielson; married Beverly Grace Kinsell, March 19, 1955; children: Matthew Henry, Benjamin Wayne, Grace Frances, Paul Arthur. *Education:* University of Iowa, B.A., 1952; Stanford University, M.A., 1953, Ph.D., 1957. *Home:* 2817 Glenview, Austin, Tex. 78703. *Office:* School of Communication, University of Texas, Austin, Tex. 78712.

CAREER: San Jose Mercury-News, San Jose, Calif., reporter and research manager, 1953-54; Stanford University, Stanford, Calif., acting assistant professor of journalism, 1956-57; University of Wisconsin, Madison, assistant professor of journalism, 1957-59; University of North Carolina, Chapel Hill, associate professor, 1959-63, professor of journalism, 1963-69, dean of School of Journalism, 1964; University of Texas, Austin, professor of journalism and computer science and dean of School of Communication, 1969—. James Rion McKissick Lecturer at University of South Carolina, 1977; visiting professor at University of Texas, 1967-68. Member of National Research Council advisory committee, 1968-71. Published the first computer-edited newspaper, at University of North Carolina, 1964.

MEMBER: International Communications Association, Association for Education in Journalism (chairman of publications committee, 1968-72; vice-president, 1969-70; presi-

dent, 1970-71), American Association of Schools and Departments of Journalism (vice-president, 1966-67; president, 1967-68), American Sociological Association, American Newspaper Publishers Association (member of steering committee of New Research Center, 1964-73), Associated Press Managing Editors Association, American Association for Public Opinion Research, Southern Newspaper Publishers Association (member of advisory committee of "Seminars for Newsmen," 1969-75), Southern Sociological Society, North Carolina Heart Association, Austin Natural Sciences Association (member of board of directors, 1971-76), Phi Beta Kappa, Sigma Delta Chi, Kappa Tau Alpha.

WRITINGS: (With E. L. Callihan and Harold L. Nelson) *Exercises and Tests for Journalists,* Chilton, 1961; (contributor) *Introduction to Mass Communications Research,* Louisiana State University Press, 1963; (with G. C. Wilhoit, Jr.) *A Computerized Bibliography of Mass Communication Research, 1944-1964,* Magazine Publishers Association, 1967; (with Jock Lauterer) *Only in Chapel Hill* (photographic essay; text by Danielson), Colonial Press, 1967; (with Blanche Prejean) *Programmed Newspaper Style,* American Continental Publishing, 1971. Contributor to journalism periodicals. Editor of *Journalism Abstracts,* 1963-68; member of editorial board of *Journalism Quarterly,* 1964-72.

SIDELIGHTS: Danielson writes: "Since 1959, my interest has centered on the impact of the computer on the publications industry. I took part in early experiments in the use of the computer in news writing and editing. I am now working on computerized speech synthesis from newspaper text. I believe that the computer will have a profound effect on the distribution of news and knowledge in general in the remainder of this century and in the next."

*   *   *

DANINOS, Pierre   1913-

PERSONAL: Born May 26, 1913, in Paris, France; son of Ernest (an administrator) and Andree (Ranovitz) Daninos; married Jane Marrain, September 8, 1942 (divorced, 1968); married Marie-Pierre Dourneau (a translator), October 29, 1968; children: Michele, Christian, Florence. *Education:* Educated in Paris, France. *Home:* 81 rue de Grenelle, 75007 Paris, France.

CAREER: Journalist and writer. Began as sportswriter in Wimbledon, England, 1931, became reporter; features writer for *Paris-Soir* and *Match,* beginning 1938; features editor for *France Soir,* 1946-54; chronicler for *Le Figaro,* 1951—. *Wartime service:* Liaison agent for British Army in Flanders and Dunkirk, 1940. *Awards, honors:* Prix Interallie, 1947, for *Le Carnet du bon Dieu;* Prix Courteline, 1952, for *Sonia, les autres et moi.*

WRITINGS—In English: *Comment vivre avec (ou sans) Sonia,* Plon, 1953, translation by Gerard Hopkins published as *Life With Sonia,* Penguin, 1965; *Les Carnets du Major W. Marmaduke Thompson,* Hachette, 1954, translation by Robin Farn published as *The Notebooks of Major Thompson,* Knopf, 1955 (published in England as *Major Thompson Lives in France,* J. Cape, 1955); *Le Secret du Major Thompson,* Hachette, 1956, translation by Don Cortes published as *The Secret of Major Thompson,* Knopf, 1957 (published in England as *Major Thompson and I, Pierre Daninos,* J. Cape, 1957); *Un certain Monsieur Blot,* Hachette, 1960, translation published as *A Certain Monsieur Blot,* Simon & Schuster, 1962; *Le Major tricolore,* Hachette, 1968, translation by Moura Budberg published as *Major Thompson Goes French: The New Notebooks of Major W. Marmaduke Thompson,* W. H. Allen, 1971.

Other: *Le Sang des hommes* (novel), Livraria geral franco-brasileira, 1941; *Meridiens* (novel), Julliard, 1945; *Le Roi-Sommeil* (novel), Julliard, 1946, published as *Passeport pour la nuit; ou, Le Roi-Sommeil,* Plon, 1956; *Le Carnet du bon Dieu,* La Jeune Parque, 1947, published as *Les Carnets du bon Dieu,* Plon, 1955; *L'Eternel Second* (novel), La Jeune Parque, 1949; *Sonia, les autres et moi,* Plon, 1952; *Vacances a tous prix,* Hachette, 1958.

Le Jacassin: Nouveau traite des idees recues, Hachette, 1962; *Daninoscope,* Presses de la Cite, 1963; *Snobissimo; ou, Le Desir de paraitre,* Hachette, 1964; *Le Trente-sixieme dessous,* Hachette, 1966; *Eurique et Amerope,* Plon, 1969; (with Francoise Gilles) *Le Pouvoir aux enfants,* Edition Speciale, 1969; *Ludovic Morateur; ou, Le plus que parfait* (novel), Plon, 1970; *Le Pyjama,* Grasset, 1972; *Les Nouveaux Carnets du Major W. Marmaduke Thompson,* Hachette, 1973; *Les Touristocrates,* Denoel, 1974; *La Premiere Planete a droite en sortant par la voie lactee,* Fayard, 1975; *Made in France,* Julliard, 1977.

Editor: *Savoir-vivre international: Code de la susceptibilite et des bons a travers le monde,* Ode, 1950; *Le Tour du monde du rire* (humor), Hachette, 1953; *Tout l'humour du monde* (humor), Hachette, 1958; Jean de la Fontaine, *Cent Fables,* Selection du Reader's Digest, 1963; (with Dore Ogrizek) *Etikette international,* Suedwest-Verlag, 1963.

Collections: *Sonia* (contains *Comment vivre avec (ou sans) Sonia* and *Sonia, les autres et moi*), Plon, 1957, new edition published as *Sonia; ou, Le Dictionnaire des maux courants,* 1962; *Sonia, je t'adore* (contains *Sonia, les autres et moi* and *Vacances a tous prix*), translated by Gerard Hopkins, Knopf, 1959; *Major Thompson Lives in France and Major Thompson and I,* Reprint Society, 1959; *Les Carnets du Major Thompson [and] Vacances a tous prix [and] Un certain Monsieur Blot,* Hachette, 1961, *Les Carnets et le secret du Major Thompson,* Hachette, 1964.

SIDELIGHTS: Translations or adaptions of *Les Carnets du Major Thompson* have appeared in twenty-eight countries, including England, Germany, and Sweden.

*   *   *

DARDEN, William R(aymond) 1936-

PERSONAL: Born January 1, 1936, in Lenox, Ga.; son of Levin Dawson and Avie (Lee) Darden; married Donna Kelleher (a professor), December 17, 1961; children: Kelley S., Patrick S. *Education:* Georgia Institute of Technology, B.S., 1961, M.S., 1963; University of North Carolina, Ph.D., 1966. *Office:* College of Business Administration, University of Arkansas, 225 BA, Fayetteville, Ark. 72701.

CAREER: Georgia Institute of Technology, Atlanta, instructor in business, 1962-63; Louisiana State University, Baton Rouge, assistant professor of business, 1966-69; University of Georgia, Athens, associate professor, 1969-74, professor of business, 1974-76; University of Arkansas, Fayetteville, Robert and Vivian Young Distinguished Professor of Business, 1976—. Committee member of Center for Marketing Communications; member of Athens Youth Organization; director of Macon Home for the Elderly Black; consultant to Doncaster, Inc. *Military service:* U.S. Naval Reserve, active duty, 1958-60.

MEMBER: American Marketing Association, Academy of Management, Institute of Management Science, Association for Consumer Research, American Institute of Decision Sciences (member of national council, 1974-75; member of national publications board, 1977), American Association for the Advancement of Science, American Sociological Association, American Association of University Professors (member of local executive boards, 1971-72, 1975-76), Psychometric Society, Biometric Society, Southern Marketing Association (vice-president for research, 1974), Southwestern Social Sciences Association, Southern Sociological Society, Southern Case Research Association, Sales and Marketing Executives Club, Beta Gamma Sigma, Alpha Iota Delta. *Awards, honors:* Beta Gamma Sigma scholarship, 1977-78.

WRITINGS: (Contributor) G. S. Albaum and J. C. Westing, editors, *Modern Marketing Thought,* Macmillan, 1968; (with W. H. Lucas) *The Decision Making Game,* Appleton, 1969; (editor with R. H. Lamone, and contributor) *Marketing Management and the Decision Sciences: Theory and Applications,* Allyn & Bacon, 1971; (contributor) R. L. Goble, editor, *Controversy in Marketing,* Prentice-Hall, 1972; (with wife, Donna Darden, and I. A. Robinson) *Cases in Crisis,* with teacher's manual, Austin Press, 1973; (contributor) William Wells, editor, *Life Style and Psychographics,* American Marketing Association, 1974. Contributor of more than thirty articles and reviews to marketing and business journals. Editor of *Decision Line,* 1976—; member of editorial board of *Journal of Business Research* and *Journal of Marketing.*

WORK IN PROGRESS: Research on leisure-time activities, life styles and marketing strategies, multi-variate models of consumer behavior, consumerism, and research methodology.

SIDELIGHTS: Darden writes: "My career is characterized by an interest in human behavior and a belief that these behaviors can be modelled and predicted. A corollary interest in the decision sciences has stimulated research into consumer behavior and in particular into how life styles relate to marketing strategies. These studies produced an interest in viewing other areas, such as leisure time industry, as markets. The utter fascination of modelling human behavior (not controlling it) and developing programs which predict aggregate human behavior has led to studies in product conception. In addition, these interests have led to an interest in the protection of human rights, particularly in the area of consumer rights (consumerism).

"The final spinoff from the above interests is the necessity of methodologies in the study of human behavior. I have made some contributions in the areas of attitude measurement, modelling, and computer programs for analysis."

*   *   *

DaSILVA, Leon
   See WALLMANN, Jeffrey M(iner)

*   *   *

DAVENPORT, T(homas) R(odney) H(ope)   1926-

PERSONAL: Born January 5, 1926, in Madras, India; son of Thomas and Clary May (Hope) Davenport; married Gwen Elizabeth Matthews (a teacher), July 2, 1955; children: Marian, Tony, Catherine. *Education:* Rhodes University College (now Rhodes University), B.A., 1944, M.A., 1948; Queen's College, Oxford, B.A. (honors), 1949, M.A., 1952; University of Cape Town, Ph.D., 1959. *Home:* 2 Harrismith St., Grahamstown 6140, South Africa. *Office:* Department of History, Rhodes University, Grahamstown 6140, South Africa.

CAREER: University of Cape Town, Cape Town, South Africa, lecturer, 1953-60, senior lecturer in history, 1960-65; Rhodes University, Grahamstown, South Africa, reader, 1965-75, professor of history, 1975—. Member of Grahamstown City Council, 1969-73. *Military service:* South Africa Army, gunner in Artillery, 1945. *Member:* Royal Historical Society (fellow).

WRITINGS: The Afrikaner Bond, 1880-1911, Oxford University Press, 1966; (with K. S. Hunt) *The Right to the Land,* D. Philip, 1973; *South Africa: A Modern History,* Macmillan, 1977. Contributor to *Oxford History of Africa.* Contributor to scholarly journals.

WORK IN PROGRESS: A history of South African native legislation in urban areas.

SIDELIGHTS: Davenport writes: "The writing of South African history from a liberal anti-racist viewpoint, at a moment of returning polarization and growing irrationality on both sides of the racial fence, seems to be an important task."

*   *   *

DAVIDSON, Clarissa Start
   See LIPPERT, Clarissa Start

*   *   *

DAVIES, Harriet Vaughn   1879(?)-1978

1879(?)—July 1, 1978; American social worker, university administrator, and author. Davies became a social worker in Baltimore, Md., upon graduation from Bucknell University. In 1926 she became academic adviser for women in the Columbia University adult education program. She was the author of a book about her childhood aboard her father's sailing ship. Davies died in Austin, Tex. Obituaries and other sources: *Washington Post,* July 4, 1978.

*   *   *

DAVIS, Ben Reeves   1927-

PERSONAL: Born April 1, 1927, in Huntington, Ark.; son of Lester Belton (a minister) and Jessie (Reeves) Davis; married Margaret Rogers, November 26, 1950 (divorced); children: Ben Reeves, Jr. *Education:* University of Alabama, B.A., 1949. *Religion:* Methodist. *Home:* 547 South Perry St., Montgomery, Ala. 36104. *Office:* The Advertiser Co., 200 Washington Ave., Montgomery, Ala. 36102.

CAREER/WRITINGS: Selma Times-Journal, Selma, Ala., reporter, 1949-50; *Mountain Eagle,* Jasper, Ala., managing editor, 1950-52; *Birmingham News,* Birmingham, Ala., sports writer and copy editor, 1952-56; *Tuscaloosa News,* Tuscaloosa, Ala., managing editor, 1956-64; *Montgomery Advertiser* and *Alabama Journal,* Montgomery, executive managing editor, 1964—. Member of board of directors, Montgomery United Appeal. *Military service:* U.S. Navy, 1945-46. *Member:* Associated Press Managing Editors Association, Alabama Associated Press Association (president, 1964-65), Sigma Delta Chi, Pi Kappa Phi.

*   *   *

DAVIS, Don
   See DRESSER, Davis

*   *   *

DAVIS, Maxine
   See McHUGH, Maxine Davis

*   *   *

DAVIS, Mildred

PERSONAL: Married Jerome Davis (an engineer); children: Nancy, Amy, Kathy, Pamela. *Residence:* Bedford, N.Y. *Agent:* McIntosh & Otis, Inc., 475 Fifth Ave., New York, N.Y. 10017.

CAREER: Writer. Active in community affairs. *Member:* Authors League of America. *Awards, honors:* Prize from Mystery Writers of America for first novel, *The Room Upstairs.*

WRITINGS: They Buried a Man, Simon & Schuster, 1953; *The Dark Place,* Simon & Schuster, 1955; *The Voice on the Telephone,* Random House, 1964; *The Sound of Insects,* Doubleday, 1966; *Strange Corner,* Doubleday, 1967; *Walk Into Yesterday,* Doubleday, 1967; *The Third Half,* Doubleday, 1969; *Three Minutes to Midnight,* Random House, 1971; *Tell Them What's-Her-Name Called,* Random House, 1975; *Scorpion,* Random House, 1977; (with daughter, Katherine Davis) *Lucifer Land* (historical novel), Random House, 1977.

Also author of *The Room Upstairs,* 1950, and *Suicide Hour,* 1962.

WORK IN PROGRESS: Hour of the Wolf (tentative title), a historical novel based on the Cherry Valley massacre during the American Revolution.

SIDELIGHTS: Mildred Davis told *CA:* "I got started writing at about the age of ten because my favorite activity was always reading. I chose mysteries because they were my favorite books. And of course, all writers express personal views in their writing—the way they feel about certain kinds of people, about political and social views."

AVOCATIONAL INTERESTS: Travel (Japan, Turkey, England, France, Italy, Norway, Hong Kong, Thailand, Hawaii), tennis, skiing, jogging, swimming.

*   *   *

DAWSON, Alan David   1942-

PERSONAL: Born October 13, 1942, in Toronto, Ontario, Canada; son of Alan (a news editor) and Hazel (a secretary; maiden name, Simpson) Dawson; married Eleanor Chan, April 28, 1968; children: David and Robert (twins). *Education:* McMaster University, B.A., 1962. *Home:* 83/6 Wireless Rd., Bangkok, Thailand. *Agent:* George Pipal, United

Press International-International Features Division, 220 East 42nd St., New York, N.Y. 10017. *Office:* United Press International, G.P.O. Box 608, Bangkok, Thailand.

CAREER: Metromedia Radio, Saigon, Vietnam, reporter, 1968-70; United Press International, New York, N.Y., bureau chief in Saigon, 1970-75, and Bangkok, Thailand, 1975—. *Military service:* U.S. Army, 1966-68; served in Vietnam. *Awards, honors:* National Headliner Award from Atlantic City Press Club, 1976, for foreign reporting on the end of the Vietnam war.

WRITINGS: Fifty-Five Days: The Fall of South Vietnam, Prentice-Hall, 1977.

WORK IN PROGRESS: Research on Indochina, with emphasis on the American Vietnam war.

SIDELIGHTS: Dawson remarks: "The people of the world, and specifically of the United States, will lose their self-induced amnesia of the Vietnam war and, hopefully, will wish to learn lessons from western involvement there. I hope to be able to be involved in that process."

*   *   *

DE BREFFNY, Brian   1931-

PERSONAL: Born January 14, 1931, in Ireland; married first wife Jyotsna, September 24, 1960 (divorced); married Ulli Castren, October 13, 1976; children: Sita. *Education:* Earned M.A. *Religion:* Roman Catholic. *Residence:* Ireland and Italy. *Agent:* Gillon Aitken, 17 Belgrave Place, London, S.W.1, England. *Office:* Frattina 10, Rome 00187, Italy.

CAREER: Writer, 1973—.

WRITINGS: Bibliography of Irish Family History, Mercier, 1973; (contributor) Roloff Beny, *In Italy,* Thames & Hudson, 1974; (with Rosemary Ffolliott) *The Houses of Ireland,* Viking, 1975; *The Churches and Abbeys of Ireland,* Norton, 1976; *Castles of Ireland,* Thames & Hudson, 1977; (editor) *The Irish World,* Abrams, 1977; *The Synagogue,* Macmillan, 1978. Director of *The Irish Ancestor;* administrator of *Alleluia.*

*   *   *

DEBRETT, Hal
See DRESSER, Davis

*   *   *

DEEKEN, Alfons   1932-

PERSONAL: Born August 3, 1932, in Emstek, Germany; son of Aloys and Paula (Nienaber) Deeken. *Education:* University of Munich, B.A., 1956, M.A., 1958; Fordham University, Ph.D., 1973. *Religion:* Roman Catholic. *Home and office:* Sophia University, Kioicho 7, Chiyoda-ku, Tokyo 102, Japan.

CAREER: Sophia University, Tokyo, Japan, assistant professor, 1973-75, associate professor of philosophy, 1975—. *Member:* American Catholic Philosophical Association, Japanese Society for Ethics, Philosophical Association of Japan. *Awards, honors:* Award from Catholic Press Association of America, 1974, for *Process and Permanence in Ethics.*

WRITINGS: Growing Old and How to Cope with It, Paulist/Newman, 1972; *Alt sein ist lernbar* (title means "Growing Old Can Be Learned"), Butzon & Bercker, 1973; *Oeregszuenk de Gyoezzuek* (title means "Growing Old Filled With Hope"), Prugg, 1973; *La Vejez: Periodo de Posibilidades* (title means "Old Age—A Time of Opportuni-

ties"), Paulist/Newman, 1973; *Saber Envelhecer* (title means "Knowing How to Grow Old"), Editora Vozes, 1973; *Process and Permanence in Ethics: Max Scheler's Moral Philosophy,* Paulist/Newman, 1974; *Vieilllesse heureuse: Croissance* (title means "Happy Old Age—Human Growth"), Editions Foyer Notre-Dame, 1975; *Daisen no Jinsei* (title means "The Third Phase of Life"), Nansoosha, 1975; *Tudi Starost Je Lahko Lepa* (title means "Old Age Can Be Beautiful"), Celje, 1977.

WORK IN PROGRESS: Research into the philosophy of death; a book on death and dying.

*   *   *

de la GARZA, Rodolfo O(ropea)   1942-

PERSONAL: Born August 17, 1942, in Tucson, Ariz.; son of Estevan Rios (a cook) and Sofia (Oropea) de la Garza; married Carol A. Pace, January 26, 1967 (divorced, June, 1975); married Christa Keel Meyer, June 11, 1977. *Education:* University of Arizona, B.S., 1964, M.A., 1967, Ph.D., 1972; Thunderbird Graduate School, B.F.T., 1965. *Home:* 2104 North Tejon, Colorado Springs, Colo. 80907. *Office:* Department of Political Science, Colorado College, Colorado Springs, Colo. 80903.

CAREER: U.S. Information Agency, Washington, D.C., assistant cultural affairs officer in Bolivia, 1967-69; University of Texas, El Paso, assistant professor of political science, 1972-74; Colorado College, Colorado Springs, assistant professor of political science and dean, 1974—. Member of minority affairs committee of Graduate Record Examination Board, 1975-77. Member of Colorado Springs Urban Renewal Commission; chairman of board of directors of Operation Ser; member of executive committee of local La Raza Unity Council; consultant to National Endowment for the Humanities. *Member:* American Political Science Association, Western Political Science Association. *Awards, honors:* National Endowment for the Humanities fellowship, summer, 1976.

WRITINGS: (Editor with A. Kruszewski and T. Arciniega) *Chicanos and Native Americans,* Prentice-Hall, 1973; (with F. Chris Garcia) *The Chicano Political Experience,* Duxbury, 1977. Contributor of articles on Chicano and Mexican politics to magazines.

WORK IN PROGRESS: Research on the relationship between age and personal experience with discrimination among Chicanos and on establishing the boundaries of the Mexican-American community.

SIDELIGHTS: De la Garza writes: "A major motivation in working in Chicano politics is to contribute to the creation of a body of knowledge which has been almost non-existent within the study of American politics. I would hope this will help put an end to stereotypic observations which characterize previous writings on Mexican-American politics and society."

*   *   *

de LAGUNA, Grace Mead A(ndrus)   1878-1978

September 28, 1878—February 17, 1978; American educator, philosopher, and writer. De Laguna co-founded Fullerton Philosophy Club in 1925. Her writings include *Dogmatism and Evolution* and *On Existence and the Human World.* She died in Devon, Pa. Obituaries and other sources: *New York Times,* February 25, 1978. (See index for *CA* sketch)

DELP, Michael W(illiam) 1948-

PERSONAL: Born December 21, 1948, in Michigan; son of William J. (a collector) and Frances (Kipp) Delp; married Janet Ross, September 12, 1970 (divorced, 1975). *Education:* Alma College, B.A., 1971; graduate study at Central Michigan University, 1975—. *Home address:* P.O. Box 167, Grayling, Mich. 49738.

CAREER: Crawford Ausable Schools, Grayling, Mich., teacher of English and alternative education, 1971—.

WRITINGS: A Dream of the Resurrection (poetry), Cold Mountain Press, 1976; (contributor) *The Third Coast: An Anthology of Contemporary Michigan Poetry,* Wayne State University Press, 1976. Contributor of poems to literary journals, including *East West Journal, Greenfield Review, Bitterroot,* and *Road Apple Review.* Associate editor of *Skywriting,* 1975-76.

WORK IN PROGRESS: Notebooks of Alva Stoner, a prose-poem novel; *Turning to Blood,* poems.

SIDELIGHTS: Delp writes: "Of all things, to me writing is the most vital. I believe that most of my work draws its energy from the physical environment around me. Poetry seems to be an extension of the spiritual connections found in wilderness and solitude. Much of my writing centers around my own concepts of loneliness and dreams: dream fabrics and how they influence our daily perceptions. Writing almost seems to be a curse. I write now because I feel that I have to.

"Perhaps I never really look at writing as a career. I see it as something that I have to do for my own mental health. As a young poet, I can point to the 'usual' influences: Robert Bly, Gary Snyder, and James Wright. I am also deeply grateful to Jim Harrison for his fine work. As Harrison says, a poet is only a sorcerer who is bored with his own magic.

"I think more than the actual writing, I love the distance and the feel of seeing images; actually looking at things. Much of this concentration has gone the route of photography in the last six months.

"I'd like to settle down, find forty acres, a nice cabin, a wife, and two or three dogs, learn how to play a guitar a bit better, write, build kites, grow things, and generally live quietly and intensely."

* * *

DeLYNN, Jane 1946-

PERSONAL: Born July 18, 1946, in New York, N.Y.; daughter of Wilson (a paper bag manufacturer) and Bernice (a school teacher; maiden name, Deutsch) DeLynn. *Education:* Barnard College, B.A. (cum laude), 1968; University of Iowa, M.F.A. (honors), 1970. *Agent:* Jane Rotrosen Agency, 318 East 51st St., New York, N.Y. 10022.

CAREER: Kirkus Reviews, New York, N.Y., book reviewer, 1971-76; free-lance writer, 1971—. Founding managing editor of *Fiction,* 1971-72. *Member:* Phi Beta Kappa. *Awards, honors:* Elizabeth Janeway Prize from Barnard College, 1967, for "Variations on an Obituary," and 1968, for "Collected Stories"; Book of the Month Club writing fellowship, 1968, for "Variations on an Obituary"; grant from International P.E.N., 1975.

WRITINGS: Some Do (novel), Macmillan, 1978.

Author of "Hoosick Falls" (musical play), first produced in New York City at Theater for the New City, August 8, 1974.

Work represented in anthologies, including *The Stone Wall Book of Short Fictions,* edited by Robert Coover and Kent Dixon, Stone Wall Press, 1973. Contributor to popular magazines, including *Redbook, Viva,* and *Cosmopolitan,* literary journals, including *Paris Review* and *New Dawn,* and newspapers.

WORK IN PROGRESS: A novel, *Aunts.*

SIDELIGHTS: Jane DeLynn writes: "I have always been interested in the space *between* sentences, that gap in which the 'zing' of life can be heard. I am pulled two ways in my work: toward minimalist formal experiments in which predetermined 'rules' for sentence or paragraph construction force patterns which would not occur in writing unrestricted by such (admittedly arbitrary) rules, and toward looser works of greater richness, complexity, humor.

"Politically, I am a leftist and don't understand how anyone can fail to be. I consider myself a gay feminist, but I despise the superficiality and smug insularity of most Movement-inspired writings. Temperamentally I am a skeptic, and lazy. I engage in no political actions: finding the action and discussion tedious and the possibility of success nil. I am unable to determine whether, like most people in most eras of human history, I simply believe things are getting (and have for some time been getting) worse, or whether, in fact, things *are* worse, and always will be. (I believe the latter.)"

AVOCATIONAL INTERESTS: Travel (Europe and Mexico), plays, movies, dance, music, books (novels, science, mathematics, history), sports (watching baseball, football, and tennis; swimming).

* * *

DENNIS, Carl 1939-

PERSONAL: Born September 17, 1939, in St. Louis, Mo.; son of Israel and Fay (Persuk) Dennis. *Education:* Attended Oberlin College, 1957-58, and University of Chicago, 1958-59; University of Minnesota, B.A., 1961; University of California, Berkeley, Ph.D., 1966. *Home:* 63 Ashland Ave., Buffalo, N.Y. 14222. *Office:* Department of English, State University of New York at Buffalo, Buffalo, N.Y., 14222.

CAREER: State University of New York at Buffalo, assistant professor, 1966-71, associate professor, 1971-76, professor of English, 1976—. *Awards, honors:* Robert Frost fellowship for Breadloaf Writer's Workshop, summer, 1975.

WRITINGS: A House of My Own (poems), Braziller, 1974; *Climbing Down* (poems), Braziller, 1976.

WORK IN PROGRESS: Silent Neighbors, poems.

SIDELIGHTS: Dennis writes: "I don't see myself as belonging to any particular school of poetry. Yeats was the most important early influence, but I hope that his presence is now very difficult to detect. Like him I'm interested in making my poems sound like actual speech, something that one might actually say out loud to a single listener. In Yeats's day this meant avoiding poetical ornament and mechanical rhythms. Today it also means avoiding poetry that is either too private (concerned with the play of the writer's own mind and not with an actual subject outside himself) or too public (not concerned with the particular context of speaker and listener in a dramatic situation)."

* * *

DENNIS, Peggy 1909-

PERSONAL: Born January 1, 1909, in Brooklyn, N.Y.; daughter of Meyer (a needle trades worker) and Berta (a needle trades worker; maiden name, Rubin) Karasick; married Eugene Dennis, September 4, 1928 (died, 1961); children: Tim, Eugene. *Education:* Attended University of California, Los Angeles. *Politics:* "Radical/socialist/Marxist." *Religion:* None. *Residence:* Oakland, Calif. *Office:* Creative Arts Books, 833 Bancroft Way, Berkeley, Calif. 94710.

CAREER: Communist Party activist, organizer, and journalist in the United States and abroad, 1925-76; free-lance writer, 1976—.

WRITINGS: (Editor) Eugene Dennis, *Letters from Prison*, International Publishers, 1956; *Autobiography of an American Communist: A Personal View of a Political Life, 1925-1975*, Lawrence Hill, 1977.

Contributor of articles to magazines, including *Nation, Progressive, Political Affairs, Socialist Revolution*, and *Literary Quarterly. Sunday Worker*, women's page editor, 1950-51, writer of column "Comradely Yours, Peggy Dennis," 1950-52; foreign editor of *People's World*, 1961-68.

WORK IN PROGRESS: Research for *My Mother, My Sister, and Me* (tentative title), a study of radicals and feminists, "their separate and individual experiences, compromises, and solutions"; magazine articles on current social movements.

SIDELIGHTS: Peggy Dennis writes: "All my past and future writings are related to my radical/socialist views which have all my life been consistent in commitment, however changing in the face of new experiences and the changing realities of the world around me. ... am vitally involved in the exciting responses of young radicals, academia, and seasoned political activists to the unusual personal aspects of my very candid political autobiography. There is so much to write about, to analyze and understand, as a prelude to social change."

*   *   *

de SENA, Jorge   1919-1978

November 2, 1919—1978; Portuguese educator and author of more than one hundred scholarly books, twelve volumes of poetry, and three volumes of plays. He died in Santa Barbara, Calif. Obituaries and other sources: *Directory of American Scholars*, Volume III: *Foreign Languages, Linguistics, and Philology*, 6th edition, Bowker, 1974; *Time*, June 19, 1978.

*   *   *

DeVOE, Shirley Spaulding   1899-

PERSONAL: Born July 13, 1899, in New Rochelle, N.Y.; daughter of George Lawson (a musician and composer) and Eva B. (Wood) Spaulding; married George W. DeVoe (in real estate), April 29, 1922; children: George Spaulding. *Education:* Attended Columbia University and Juilliard School; studied decorative arts at studio of Esther Stevens Brazer. *Politics:* Republican. *Religion:* Protestant. *Home address:* R.F.D. Bridgewater, Conn. 06752.

CAREER: Writer, 1950—. Lecturer and painter. Former secretary for Melville Shoe Corp. *Member:* Historical Society of Early American Decoration, American Museum (Bath, England), Smithsonian Institution, Cooper-Hewitt Museum, Antiquarian Society, New York State Historical Association, Connecticut Historical Society.

WRITINGS: The Tinsmiths of Connecticut, Wesleyan University Press, 1968; *English Papier Mache of the Geor-*

gian and Victorian Period, Wesleyan University Press, 1971. Contributor to *Oxford Dictionary of Useful Arts*. Contributor to antiques journals and *Country Life*.

WORK IN PROGRESS: The Great English Tinplate Industry; research on decorative arts, especially Japanning and Oriental lacquer work.

SIDELIGHTS: Shirley DeVoe writes: "In order to learn of the various industries, methods, and workers—all phases of the decorative arts, I made many trips to England, to libraries and museums in London, Birmingham, Wolverhampton, and Bilston, and to the Netherlands (Amsterdam and Arnem) and France. Having learned the many forms and techniques of the ornament—gold leaf, bronze, mother-of-pearl, paint, et cetera, I became interested in the history of the work."

*   *   *

DIAMOND, Martin   1919-1977

PERSONAL: Born December 19, 1919, in New York, N.Y.; son of George and Rose (Desowitz) Diamond; married Bess Sohn, August 7, 1940 (divorced, 1969); married Ann Stuart Sheldon, March 7, 1970; children: (first marriage) Katherine, Thomas; stepchildren: Samuel Sheldon, Diane Claire Sheldon. *Education:* University of Chicago, A.M., 1952, Ph.D., 1956. *Residence:* Washington, D.C.

CAREER: Illinois Institute of Technology, Chicago, instructor, 1952-53, assistant professor of political science, 1953-55; University of Chicago, Chicago, lecturer, 1952-55, assistant professor, 1955-58; Claremont Men's College and Graduate School, Claremont, Calif., associate professor of political science, 1958-64, Burnet C. Wohlford Professor of American Political Institutions, 1964-71; Northern Illinois University, De Kalb, professor of political science, 1971-77; Georgetown University, Washington, D.C., held Thomas and Dorothy Leavey chair on the Foundation of American Freedom, 1977. *Military service:* U.S. Merchant Marine, 1943-45. *Member:* American Political Science Association, Midwestern Political Science Association, Pi Sigma Alpha. *Awards, honors:* Fellow at Center for Advanced Study Behavioral Sciences, 1960-61; Rockefeller Foundation fellow, 1963-64; Relm Foundation fellow, 1966-67; fellow at Woodrow Wilson International Center for Scholars; L.H.D. from Hartford University, 1968.

WRITINGS: Essays in Federalism, Institute for Studies in Federalism, Claremont Men's College, 1961; (with Winston Mills Fisk and Herbert Garfield) *The Democratic Republic*, Rand McNally, 1966, 2nd edition, 1970; (editor with George C. S. Benson, M. Frisch, and others), *The Thirties: A Reconsideration*, Northern Illinois University Press, 1968; (with I. Kristol and G. W. Nutler) *The American Revolution: Three Views*, American Brands, 1975.

SIDELIGHTS: Senator Daniel Patrick Moynihan, Democrat of New York, referred to Mr. Diamond as "a distinguished scholar" who "almost single-handedly established the relevance of the thought and doings of the American Founders for this generation."

OBITUARIES: New York Times, July 23, 1977.*

(Died July 22, 1977, in Washington, D.C.)

*   *   *

DIBDIN, Michael   1947-

PERSONAL: Born March 21, 1947, in Wolverhampton, Staffordshire, England; son of Frederick John (a folk dance teacher and lecturer in science) and Peggy (a health visitor; maiden name, Taylor) Dibdin; married Benita Mitbrodt, January 23, 1971; children: Moselle Benita. *Education:* University of Sussex, B.A., 1968; University of Edmonton, Alberta, M.A., 1970. *Residence:* London, England. *Agent:* Elspeth Cochrane Agency, One The Pavement, London SW4 0HY, England.

CAREER: Writer. Part-time lecturer at College of Technology, Belfast, Northern Ireland, 1968. Founder of Acme Painting and Decorating, Edmonton, Alberta, 1972.

WRITINGS: The Last Sherlock Holmes Story, Pantheon, 1978; "Rough Music" (two-act play), 1978.

WORK IN PROGRESS: A volume of short prose pieces, tentatively entitled *Eros Variations.*

* * *

DICKENS, Norman
See EISENBERG, Lawrence B(enjamin)

* * *

DIEDERICH, Bernard 1926-

PERSONAL: Born July 18, 1926, in Christchurch, New Zealand; son of Bernard John (a policeman) and Stella (a nurse; maiden name, McCleavy) Diederich; married Ginette Dreyfuss, June 7, 1962; children: Jean-Bernard, Phillippe, Natalie. *Education:* Educated in Wellington, New Zealand. *Politics:* Labour. *Religion:* Roman Catholic. *Home:* Loma del Parque 150, Lomas de Vistahermosa, Mexico. *Office: Time,* 195 Reforma, Mexico City 5, Mexico.

CAREER: Currently bureau chief for *Time* magazine in Mexico City, covering Mexico, Central America, Panama, and the Caribbean. *Military service:* Served in New Zealand Merchant Marine, and U.S. Merchant Marine during World War II. *Member:* Foreign Correspondents Club of Mexico. *Awards, honors:* Maria Moors Cabot Award, 1976, for Latin American coverage.

WRITINGS: (With Al Burt) *Papa Doc: The Truth About Haiti Today,* McGraw, 1969; *Death of the Goat* (on the assassination of Dominican Republic dictator, Rafael Trujillo Molina), Little, Brown, 1978.

WORK IN PROGRESS: A book on *Finish Barque Pamir,* a four-masted sailing vessel with no engines, seized during World War II by New Zealand and sailed to San Francisco, Calif., by a young crew of forty, of which Diederich was a member.

* * *

DILLON, Bert 1937-

PERSONAL: Born June 23, 1937, in Cherokee, Okla.; son of Warren A. (a realtor) and Ruth (a realtor; maiden name, Stein) Dillon; married Susan Wienefeld (a teacher), June 4, 1966; children: Geoffrey Robery Wienfeld. *Education:* University of Colorado, B.A., 1960; Columbia University, M.A., 1963; Duke University, Ph.D., 1972. *Home:* 3800 Kilbourne Rd., Columbia, S.C. 29205. *Office:* Department of English, University of South Carolina, Columbia, S.C. 29208.

CAREER: University of South Carolina, Columbia, instructor, 1965-72, assistant professor, 1972-76, associate professor of English, 1976—, assistant dean of Arts and Letters, 1972-73, acting dean, 1973-74, director of Center for Cultural Advancement, 1973-74. *Military service:* U.S. Army, medical service, 1960-62. *Member:* Modern Language Associa-

tion of America, Mediaeval Academy of America, Southeastern Medieval Association, Classical Association, Town and Gown, Omicron Delta Kappa. *Awards, honors:* Association of Departments of English—Modern Language Association certificate, 1971.

WRITINGS: A Chaucer Dictionary, G. K. Hall, 1974; *A Malory Dictionary,* G. K. Hall, 1978. Contributor to *Annuale Mediaeval* and *Studies in Scottish Literature.*

SIDELIGHTS: Dillon told *CA:* "I have been influenced primarily by some of the romance philologists who have used the 'explication de texte' method. There are many other names for it, but that method is still a very good method for teaching and interpretation."

Dillon admits that he "probably has one of the largest libraries of useless information in the world." He firmly believes in "excursus as a pedagogical device to drive students wild," and often delivers impromptu harangues to his students of medieval literature.

AVOCATIONAL INTERESTS: Squash.

BIOGRAPHICAL/CRITICAL SOURCES: Choice, October, 1975.

* * *

DILLON, John M(yles) 1939-
(The Western Spy)

PERSONAL: Born September 15, 1939, in Madison, Wis.; son of Myles (a professor) and Elizabeth (La Touche) Dillon; married Jean Montgomery, January 2, 1965. *Education:* Oriel College, Oxford, B.A., 1962, M.A., 1964; University of California, Berkeley, Ph.D., 1969. *Home:* 1584 Leroy Ave., Berkeley, Calif. 94708. *Office:* Department of Classics, University of California, Berkeley, Calif. 94720.

CAREER: University of California, Berkeley, assistant professor, 1969-73, associate professor, 1973-76, professor of classics, 1976—. *Member:* American Philological Association.

WRITINGS: (With Brendan O'Hehir) *A Classical Lexicon to Finnegans Wake: A Glossary of the Greek and Latin in Major Works of Joyce,* University of California Press, 1977; *The Middle Platonists: A Study of Platonism, 80* B.C. *to* A.D. *220,* Duckworth, 1976, published as *The Middle Platonists: 80* B.C. *to* A.D. *220,* Cornell University Press, 1977. Columnist, under pseudonym The Western Spy, for *San Francisco Review of Books,* 1976—.

WORK IN PROGRESS: Origen, a Biography.

SIDELIGHTS: Dillon comments, "I am interested in Platonism as an intellectual force in European thought."

* * *

DiMEGLIO, John E(dward) 1934-

PERSONAL: Born July 16, 1934, in Allentown, Pa.; son of Richard A. (a barber) and Gertrude (a teacher and artist; maiden name, Ziegenfuss) DiMeglio; married Alice Britto (a teacher) November 19, 1955; children: Jean, Michael, Joseph, Stephen, Mark, Andrew. *Education:* Kutztown State College, B.S., 1955; graduate study at Lehigh University, 1956-57, 1963; University of Maine, M.A., 1967, Ph.D., 1971; postdoctoral study at Vanderbilt University, 1975. *Home:* 228 Clark St., Mankato, Minn. 56001. *Office:* Department of History, Mankato State University, Box 007, Mankato, Minn. 56001.

CAREER: High school social studies teacher in Bethlehem,

Pa., 1955-64, 1967-68; Mankato State University, Mankato, Minn., assistant professor, 1968-72, associate professor, 1972-75, professor of history, 1975—. *Member:* Organization of American Historians, Minnesota Association of History Teachers, Minnesota Association of Colleges for Teacher Education (member of executive committee, 1977-79), Minnesota Education Association, Inter-Faculty Organization. *Awards, honors:* National Endowment for the Humanities fellow, summer, 1975.

WRITINGS: Vaudeville U.S.A., Bowling Green University Popular Press, 1973. Contributor to *Dictionary of American Popular Culture,* and to *Journal of Popular Culture, Social Studies, History Teacher,* and *Variety.*

WORK IN PROGRESS: Research on violence in sport, sport history, Walt Disney, and organized crime.

SIDELIGHTS: DiMeglio comments: "Constant restlessness motivates—what new is there to learn? Where does time go? Does pop culture mirror us? Really? Is media so powerful now that the mirror is reversing, or has reversed? Why is society, despite our so-called growing sophistication, more than content to be satisfied with glitter? In-depth thinking has reached new shallows. Rip-off and 'we're number one' are leading where? Life and existence are different—but few comprehend or care. We are in a feeling and not a thinking world. What delight for tonight? What sorrow, then, tomorrow?"

* * *

DIX, William (Shepherd) 1910-1978

November 19, 1910—February 22, 1978; American librarian and author best known for his participation in organizing the international program of centralizing cataloging of the Library of Congress. Dix served as a librarian at Princeton University from 1953-75, and as president of the American Library Association. He wrote the *Amateur Spirit in Scholarship* and was also a contributor of articles to professional journals. He died in Princeton, N.J. Obituaries and other sources: *Current Biography,* Wilson, 1969; *A Biographical Directory of Librarians in the United States and Canada,* 5th edition, American Library Association, 1970; *Directory of American Scholars,* Volume II: *English, Speech, and Drama,* 6th edition, Bowker, 1974; *Who's Who in America,* 38th edition, Marquis, 1974; *New York Times,* February 23, 1978.

* * *

DOANE, Donald P(aul) 1911-

PERSONAL: Born May 14, 1911, in Lucas, Kan.; son of Ray Gue (a doctor) and Gertrude (a teacher; maiden name, Fay) Doane; married Veronica Bond, June 3, 1934; children: Linda Lou (Mrs. Alva E. King). *Education:* Attended Fort Hays Kansas State College. *Politics:* Independent. *Religion:* Protestant. *Home:* 3000 Connecticut Ave., N.W., Washington, D.C.

CAREER/WRITINGS: Journalist. *Hays Daily News,* Hays, Kan., reporter, 1931-37; Associated Press, New York, N.Y., wire editor in Kansas City, Mo., 1937-38, political reporter in Jefferson City, Mo., 1938-44, war correspondent in London, England, 1945, foreign correspondent in Germany, 1945-53; *U.S. News & World Report,* Washington, D.C., writer and assistant managing editor, 1953-77. Notable assignments include coverage of Nuremberg war crimes trials, 1945-46, Berlin blockade, 1948-49, Olympic games, 1948 and 1952, U.S. Supreme Court decisions, 1960-78, urban riots, 1964-69, Watergate, 1972-75, and Nixon impeachment proceedings, 1974. *Member:* National Press Club. *Awards, honors:* Received American Bar Association Silver Gavel award, 1976, and Certificate of Merit, 1976 and 1977.

WORK IN PROGRESS: Part-time writing for *U.S. News & World Report.*

SIDELIGHTS: Doane told *CA:* "Every newsman's dream is to be where the action is, and I was fortunate to be in Germany in the post World War II period—a reporter's paradise where there were more stories than you could write—and in Washington in a period (1953-78) of great change and important national stories. My only regret: I never got quite enough of my first love—sports writing."

* * *

DOBSON, Rosemary 1920-

PERSONAL: Born June 18, 1920, in Sydney, Australia; daughter of Arthur Austin Greaves (a civil engineer) and Marjorie (Caldwell) Dobson; married Alexander Bolton (a publisher), June 12, 1951; children: Lissant Mary, Robert Thorley Dobson, Ian Alexander. *Education:* Attended University of Sydney. *Agent:* Curtis Brown Proprietary Ltd., P.O. Box 19, Paddington 2021, New South Wales, Australia.

CAREER: Poet, 1944—. Member of editorial staff of Angus & Robertson. *Awards, honors:* Poetry prize from *Sydney Morning Herald,* 1948; four grants from Australia Council Literary Board; Myer Award, 1966.

WRITINGS—All poems, except as indicated: *In a Convex Mirror,* Angus & Robertson, 1944; *The Ship of Ice and Other Poems,* Angus & Robertson, 1948; *Child With a Cockatoo and Other Poems,* Angus & Robertson, 1955; (editor) *Australia, Land of Colour, Through the Eyes of Australian Painters,* Ure Smith, 1962; (editor and author of introduction) *Poems,* Angus & Robertson, 1963; *Cock Crow: Poems,* Angus & Robertson, 1965; (editor) *Songs for All Seasons: One Hundred Poems for Young People,* Angus & Robertson, 1967; *Rosemary Dobson Reads From Her Own Work,* with sound recording, University of Queensland Press, 1970; *Focus on Ray Crooke* (prose), University of Queensland Press, 1971; *Selected Poems,* Angus & Robertson, 1973; (translator) *Moscow Trefoil,* Australian National University Press, 1975; *Over the Frontier,* Angus & Robertson, 1978.

WORK IN PROGRESS: A new collection of poems; translations.

AVOCATIONAL INTERESTS: Art.

BIOGRAPHICAL/CRITICAL SOURCES: Quadrant, July-August, 1972; *Australian Literary Sources,* May, 1973; A. D. Hope, *Nature's Companions,* Angus & Robertson, 1974; James McAuley, *The Grammar of the Real,* Oxford University Press, 1975.

* * *

DONALDSON, (Charles) William 1935-

PERSONAL: Born January 4, 1935, in London, England; son of Charles Glen (a ship owner) and Elizabeth (Stockley) Donaldson; married Sonia Avory, June 17, 1958 (divorced, 1964); married Claire Gordon (an actress), September 1, 1967; children: Charles Sebastian Sean. *Education:* Magdalene College, Cambridge, B.A., 1958. *Politics:* Liberal. *Home:* 139 Elm Park Mansions, Park Walk, London

S.W.10, England. *Agent:* Jonathan Clowes, 19 Jeffrey's Pl., London N.1, England.

CAREER: Independent theatrical producer, 1958-71; produced about thirty shows, including "Beyond the Fringe," "The Ginger Man," "Fairy Tales of New York," and "The Promise." *Military service:* Royal Navy, 1953-55; became sub-lieutenant.

WRITINGS: (Editor) *Light Blue, Dark Blue,* Macdonald & Co., 1960; *Both the Ladies and the Gentlemen,* Talmy Franklyn, 1975, published as *Don't Call Me Madam,* Mason/Charter, 1977; *Letters to Emma Jane,* Eyre Methuen, 1977; *The Balloons in the Black Bay,* Eyre Methuen, 1978. Reviewer for *Spectator,* 1955-60.

* * *

DONIN, Hayim Halevy 1928-

PERSONAL: Birth-given name, Herman Dolnansky, legally changed, 1955; born June 3, 1928, in New York, N.Y.; son of Max and Eva (Smolensky) Dolnansky; married Tzivia Joyce Hanover, June 24, 1951; children: Haviva, David, Rena, Miriam. *Education:* Yeshiva University, B.A., 1948, rabbi, 1951; Columbia University, M.A., 1952; Wayne State University, Ph.D., 1966. *Residence:* Oak Park, Mich. *Office:* 22 Pinsker St., Jerusalem, Israel.

CAREER: Rabbi of Jewish congregation in Southfield, Mich., 1953-73; Bar-Ilan University, Ramat Gan, Israel, lecturer in religious education, 1974-76; writer, 1976—. Adjunct professor of Jewish Studies at University of Detroit, 1969-73. Vice-president of Jewish Community Council of Detroit; president of Akiva Hebrew Day School. Member of Southfield Parent-Youth Guidance Commission, 1960-68; member of Michigan Governor's Ethical and Moral Panel, 1966-68. *Member:* Association of Jewish Studies.

WRITINGS: Beyond Thyself, Bloch Publishing, 1965; *To Be a Jew,* Basic Books, 1972; *Sukkot,* Keter Publishing, 1974; *To Raise a Jewish Child,* Basic Books, 1977; *Guide to the Jewish Prayerbook,* Basic Books, in press. Contributor to *Tradition.*

SIDELIGHTS: Donin remarks: "The great success of *To Be a Jew* encouraged me to turn to writing as a full-time vocation."

AVOCATIONAL INTERESTS: Swimming, tennis.

* * *

DONNISON, Jean 1925-

PERSONAL: Born July 5, 1925, in Nottinghamshire, England; daughter of Henry Harold (a farmer) and Dorothy (a farmer; maiden name, James) Kidger; married David Vernon Donnison (a civil servant), June 30, 1950; children: Rachel, Christopher, Polly, Harry. *Education:* St. Hilda's College, Oxford, B.A. (honors), 1950; University of London, Ph.D., 1974. *Home:* 38 Douglas Rd., London N.1, England.

CAREER: Lecturer in social administration for adult evening courses, 1969-72; North-East London Polytechnic, London, England, senior lecturer in social administration, 1972—.

WRITINGS: Midwives and Medical Men: A History of Inter-Professional Rivalries and Women's Rights, Heinemann, 1976.

WORK IN PROGRESS: Research on present status of the midwife in England.

SIDELIGHTS: Jean Donnison writes: "The return of the

role of midwifery in the United States is the result of (to my mind) three factors—the growth of the consumer movement, feminism, and also the need acknowledged by the federal government to provide better obstetric care to American women and so reduce the infant and maternal mortality rates to a level equal to that of the countries leading in this field (New Zealand and several European countries).

"In England the battle is on within the medical dominated free state-financed national health service between obstetricians seeing one hundred per cent hospitalisation of delivery and the increased mechanisation of childbirth as beneficent advances, and those midwives who do not wish to be reduced to the level of the North American obstetric nurse. These women wish to retain their role as independent practitioners in their own right, legally entitled to attend, and capable of attending normal childbirth. The question of harmonization of qualifications within the European Economic Community is of topical significance when it is realised that E.E.C. midwives have longer training, higher qualifications and status, and greater professional independence than English midwives."

* * *

DORN, Phyllis Morre 1910(?)-1978

1910(?)—July 5, 1978; American artist and author. Dorn published articles in many newspapers and magazines, and wrote more than fifteen novels and numerous short stories. The *Washington Evening Star* serialized her first novel, *Lovely Little Fool.* Dorn died in Washington, D.C. Obituaries and other sources: *Washington Post,* July 7, 1978.

* * *

DOUGLASS, Amanda Hart
See WALLMANN, Jeffrey M(iner)

* * *

DOWNS, William Randall, Jr. 1914-1978

August 17, 1914—May 3, 1978; American journalist. In almost forty years as a correspondent, Downs covered such important events as the battle of Stalingrad, the D day landings at Normandy, the German surrender to Montgomery, the atomic tests at Bikini Atoll, the Berlin airlift, and the Korean War. He won a National Headliner's Club award in 1945, and an Overseas Press Club citation in 1949. At the time of his death, he was a network correspondent for the American Broadcasting Co. (ABC-TV). Obituaries and other sources: *Who's Who in America,* 39th edition, Marquis, 1976; *Washington Post,* May 4, 1978.

* * *

DRESSER, Davis 1904-1977
(Asa Baker, Matthew Blood, Kathryn Culver, Don Davis, Brett Halliday, Anthony Scott, Anderson Wayne; Hal Debrett, a joint pseudonym)

PERSONAL: Born July 31, 1904, in Chicago, Ill.; son of Justin and Mary Dresser; married Helen McCloy (a writer); married Kathleen Rollins (a writer, sometimes under joint pseudonym Hal Debrett); married Mary Savage (a writer); children: Chloe. *Education:* Educated in Texas. *Residence:* Montecito, Calif.

CAREER: Worked as engineer and surveyor, as owner of Torquil & Co. (publishing firm), as editor of *Mike Shayne's Mystery Magazine,* and as writer of mystery and Western novels. *Military service:* U.S. Army; served in cavalry.

Member: Mystery Writers of America (founding member), Western Writers of America, National Writers' Club.

WRITINGS: *Let's Laugh at Love* (novel), Hillman-Curl, 1937; *Death Rides the Pecos* (novel), Morrow, 1940; *The Hangmen of Sleepy Valley* (novel), Morrow, 1940; *Gun Smoke on the Mesa* (novel), Carlton, 1941; *Lynch-Rope Law* (novel), Morrow, 1941; (under pseudonym Anderson Wayne) *Charlie Dell* (novel), Coward, 1952; (under pseudonym Matthew Blood) *Death is a Lovely Dame* (novel), Fawcett, 1954.

All mystery novels under pseudonym Brett Halliday: *Dividend on Death,* Holt, 1939; *The Private Practice of Michael Shayne,* Holt, 1940; *The Uncomplaining Corpses,* Holt, 1940; *Tickets for Death,* Holt, 1941; *Bodies Are Where You Find Them,* Holt, 1941; *The Corpse Came Calling,* Dodd, 1942; *Michael Shayne Investigates,* Jarrolds, 1943; *Murder Wears a Mummer's Mask,* Dodd, 1943; *Blood on the Black Market,* Dodd, 1943; *In a Deadly Vein,* Dodd, 1943; *Heads You Lose,* Dodd, 1943; *Michael Shayne's Long Chance,* Dell, 1944; *Murder and the Married Virgin,* Dodd, 1944.

Dead Man's Diary [and] *Dinner at Dupre's,* Dell, 1945; *Murder Is My Business,* Dodd, 1945; *Marked for Murder,* Long, 1945; *Blood on Biscayne Bay,* Ziff-Davis, 1946; *Counterfeit Wife,* Ziff-Davis, 1947; *Michael Shayne's Triple Mystery,* Ziff-Davis, 1948; *Blood on the Stars,* Dodd, 1948; *A Taste for Violence,* Dodd, 1949; *Call for Mike Shayne,* Dodd, 1949.

This Is It, Michael Shayne, Dodd, 1950; *Framed in Blood,* Dodd, 1951; *When Dorinda Dances,* Dodd, 1951; *What Really Happened,* Dodd, 1952; *One Night With Nora,* Dodd, 1953; *She Woke to Darkness,* Dodd, 1954.

Death Has Three Lives, Dodd, 1955; *Stranger in Town,* Dodd, 1955; *The Blonde Cried Murder,* Dodd, 1956; *Weep for a Blonde,* Dodd, 1957; *Shoot the Works,* Dodd, 1957; *Murder and the Wanton Bride,* Dodd, 1958; *Fit to Kill,* Dodd, 1958; *Date With a Dead Man,* Dodd, 1959; *Target: Michael Shayne,* Dodd, 1959; *Die Like a Dog,* Dodd, 1959.

Murder Takes No Holiday, Dodd, 1960; *Dolls Are Deadly,* Dodd, 1960; *The Homicidal Virgin,* Dodd, 1960; *Michael Shayne's Torrid Twelve,* Dell, 1961; *Killer From the Keys,* Dodd, 1961; *Murder in Haste,* Dodd, 1961; *The Careless Corpse,* Dodd, 1961; *Pay-off in Blood,* Dodd, 1962; *Murder by Proxy,* Dodd, 1962; *Never Kill a Client,* Dodd, 1962; *Too Friendly, Too Dead,* Dodd, 1963; *The Corpse That Never Was,* Dodd, 1963; *The Body That Came Back,* Dodd, 1963; *A Redhead for Mike Shayne,* Dodd, 1964; *Shoot to Kill,* Dodd, 1964; *A Taste of Cognac,* Dell, 1964; *Michael Shayne's Fiftieth Case,* Dodd, 1964.

Dangerous Dames, Dell, 1965; *Nice Fillies Finish Last,* Dell, 1965; *The Violent World of Michael Shayne,* Dell, 1965; *Armed . . . Dangerous,* Dell, 1966; *Murder Spins the Wheels,* Dell, 1966; *Mermaid on the Rocks,* Dell, 1967; *Guilty as Hell,* Dell, 1967; *Violence Is Golden,* Dell, 1968; *So Lush, So Deadly,* Dell, 1968.

Under pseudonym Anthony Scott; all novels published by Godwin: *Mardi Gras Madness,* 1934; *Virgin's Holiday,* 1935; *Ladies of Chance,* 1936.

Under pseudonym Kathryn Culver; all novels: *Love Is a Masquerade,* Phoenix Press, 1935; *Too Smart for Love,* Hillman-Curl, 1937; *Green Path to the Moon,* Hillman-Curl, 1938; *Once to Every Woman,* Godwin, 1938; *Girl Alone,* Grammercy, 1939.

Under pseudonym Asa Baker; mystery novels: *Mum's the Word for Murder,* Dodd, 1938; *The Kissed Corpse,* Carlyle, 1939.

Under pseudonym Don Davis; all Westerns published by Morrow: *Return of the Rio Kid,* 1940; *Death on Teasure Trail,* 1941; *Rio Kid Justice,* 1941; *Two-Gun Rio Kid,* 1941.

Under joint pseudonym Hal Debrett; mystery novels published by Dodd: *Before I Wake,* 1949; *A Lonely Way to Die,* 1950.

SIDELIGHTS: In *Four and Twenty Bloodhounds,* edited by Anthony Boucher, Dresser wrote of his recurring character, private eye, Michael Shayne: "I think the most important characteristic in his spectacular success as a private detective is his ability to drive straight forward to the heart of the matter, without deviating one iota for obstacles or confusing side issues. He has an absolutely logical mind which refuses to be sidetracked. He acts. On impulse sometimes, or on hunches; but always the impelling force is definite logic. In every instance he calculates the risk involved carefully, weighing the results that may be attained by a certain course of action against the probable lack of results if he chooses to move more cautiously." Dresser added that once Shayne is "convinced that a risk is worth taking, he moves forward and accepts the consequences as a part of his job. It is this driving urgency and lack of personal concern more than any other thing, I think, that serves to wind up most of Mike's most difficult cases so swiftly. In time, few of his cases consume more than one or two days. This sums up Michael Shayne as I know him."

BIOGRAPHICAL/CRITICAL SOURCES: *Saturday Review of Literature,* June 26, 1948; *Chicago Sun,* July 2, 1948; Anthony Boucher, editor, *Four and Twenty Bloodhounds,* Simon & Schuster, 1950; *New York Times,* August 10, 1952, September 25, 1955; *San Francisco Chronicle,* August 31, 1952, April 29, 1956, July 23, 1961; *New York Herald Tribune Book Review,* September 25, 1955; *New York Times Book Review,* November 1, 1959, July 16, 1961.

OBITUARIES: *New York Times,* February 6, 1977; *AB Bookman's Weekly,* May 9, 1977.*

(Died February 4, 1977, in Montecito, Calif.)

*   *   *

DREW, Patricia (Mary) 1938-

PERSONAL: Born September 13, 1938, in Cornwall, England; daughter of Eric Summers (an engineer) and Elsie (a musician; maiden name, Quayle) Drew. *Education:* Portsmouth College of Art, N.D.D., 1960. *Religion:* Christian. *Home:* Howe, Watlington, Oxfordshire, England. *Agent:* Curtis Brown Ltd., 1 Craven Hill, London N.2, England.

CAREER: United Turkey Red Ltd. (textile design studio), London, England, calico printer assistant, 1960-62; freelance writer and artist, 1963—. Private art teacher, 1963—. Art work includes book illustration, commissioned portrait drawings and paintings, and design of greeting cards.

WRITINGS—Self-illustrated children's books: *Hogglespike,* Chatto & Windus, 1971; *Hogglespike and Thistle,* Chatto & Windus, 1972; *Hogglespike in Danger,* Chatto & Windus, 1973; *Spotter Puff,* Chatto & Windus, 1974; *The Dream Dragon,* Chatto & Windus, 1976; *Caramelia,* Benn, 1977.

Illustrator: David Henry Wilson, *Elephants Don't Sit on Cars,* Chatto & Windus, 1977. Also illustrator of *The Snowball,* *Sleigh,* and designer of covers for more than ten children's books.

WORK IN PROGRESS: Picture books for children.

SIDELIGHTS: Patricia Drew writes: "Animals and birds

are interesting and I have a great fondness for most of them. This has probably been the reason for the sort of books I write. The way I feel and write is possibly governed by my happy childhood, a fascinating father, and happy home background. I couldn't write a long book; I like compact sentences next to pictures which don't need words, and I find reading poetry helpful. I know I couldn't write for adults. Children's books need pictures and I'm really more artist than author.''

*   *   *

DRUMMOND, William Joe 1944-

PERSONAL: Born September 29, 1944, in Oakland, Calif.; son of Jack Martin (a carpenter) and Mary Louise (a machinist; maiden name, Tompkins) Drummond; married Faye Boykin (a teacher), June 22, 1962; children: Tammerlin, Sean. *Education:* University of California, Berkeley, B.A., 1965; Columbia University, M.S., 1966. *Politics:* Independent. *Religion:* Protestant. *Home:* 5309 Waneta Rd., Bethesda, Md. 20016. *Office: Los Angeles Times,* 1700 Pennsylvania Ave. N.W., Washington, D.C. 20006.

CAREER/WRITINGS: Los Angeles Times, Los Angeles, Calif., staff writer, 1967-71, bureau chief in New Delhi, India, 1971-74, in Jerusalem, Israel, 1974-76; U.S. Department of State, Washington, D.C., special assistant, 1976-77; Office of U.S. President, Washington, D.C., White House associate press secretary, 1977; *Los Angeles Times,* staff writer for Washington bureau, 1977—. Notable assignments include coverage of the west coast black power movement, 1967-71; Senator Robert F. Kennedy's assassination, 1968; the liberation of Bangladesh, December, 1971; India's first atomic explosion, May, 1974; Israeli rescue of hijacked airline passengers at Entebbe, July 4, 1976. *Member:* White House Fellows Association. *Awards, honors:* Received journalism award from *Vision* magazine, 1966.

WORK IN PROGRESS: A book of essays on media criticism for Random House; a year long reporting assignment for *Los Angeles Times,* examining race relations in the United States.

SIDELIGHTS: Drummond told *CA:* "Every news reporter should serve some time as a news source (which I did for ten months as associate press secretary in the White House). Jimmy Carter's Presidency is the most specialized evolution, so far, of the White House care and feeding of mass media. One of the President's closest advisers is his press secretary, Jody Powell, who has a staff of more than forty persons, including a former television network producer and half a dozen former newsmen. Press play considerations are probably more frequently brought to bear in scheduling Carter than any previous president, because of Powell's unique role in the inner sanctum. Powell is both confidential adviser and press secretary. As a result, much of what Carter does and how and when he does it is determined by the requirements of the media, which are Powell's clientele.

"In helping to implement Powell's decisions on presidential choreography I couldn't help but conclude that accommodating the press does not necessarily result in better and more informative reporting of the presidency. Instead, the press often reacted with increasing cynicism and greater criticism. I couldn't help but feel that the public was left bewildered."

DU BOIS, Shirley Graham 1906-1977
(Shirley Graham)

PERSONAL: Born November 11, 1906, in Indianapolis, Ind.; daughter of David Andrew (a Methodist minister) and Etta (Bell) Graham; married Shadrach T. McCanns; married second husband W.E.B. Du Bois (a writer, editor, and educator), February 14, 1951 (died, 1963); children: (first marriage) two sons. *Education:* Oberlin College, B.A., 1934, M.A., 1935; additional graduate study, New York University; also attended Yale University Drama School, 1939-41, and Sorbonne, University of Paris, 1946-47. *Residence:* Accra, Ghana.

CAREER: Author and dramatist. Taught music at Morgan College, Baltimore, 1930-32; supervisor of the Negro unit of the Chicago Federal Theater, 1936-39; USO director at Fort Hauchaca, Arizona, 1941-43; field secretary, NAACP, 1942-44; founding editor, *Freedomways,* 1960-63; organizing director, Ghana Television, 1964-66; English editor, Afro-Asian Writers Bureau, Peking, China, 1968. *Member:* P.E.N., Kappa Delta Pi, Sigma Delta Theta. *Awards, honors:* Julius Rosenwald fellow, 1938-40; Guggenheim fellow, 1945-47; Julian Messner Award, 1946, for *There Was Once a Slave;* Anisfield-Wolf Award, 1949, for *Your Most Humble Servant;* National Institute of Arts and Letters Award, 1950; L.H.D., University of Massachusetts, 1973.

WRITINGS: (With George D. Lipscomb) *Dr. George Washington Carver, Scientist* (illustrated by Elton C. Fax), J. Messner, 1944, reprinted, Archway, 1967; *Paul Robeson: Citizen of the World,* J. Messner, 1946, reprinted, 1971; *There Was Once a Slave: The Heroic Story of Frederick Douglass,* J. Messner, 1947, reprinted, 1968; *Your Most Humble Servant,* J. Messner, 1949, reprinted, 1965; *The Story of Phillis Wheatley* (illustrated by Robert Burns), J. Messner, 1949, reprinted, Washington Square Press, 1970; *The Story of Pocahontas* (illustrated by Mario Cooper), Grosset & Dunlap, 1953; *Jean Baptiste Pointe de Sable: Founder of Chicago,* J. Messner, 1953; *Booker T. Washington: Educator of Hand, Head, and Heart,* J. Messner, 1955; *His Day is Marching on: A Memoir of W.E.B. DuBois,* Lippincott, 1971; *Gamal Abdel Nasser, Son of the Nile: A Biography,* Third Press, 1972; *Zulu Heart,* Third Press, 1974; *Julius K. Nyerere: Teacher of Africa,* J. Messner, 1975; *A Pictorial History of W.E.B. DuBois,* Johnson, 1976.

Composer and librettist for "Tom-Tom" (an opera), produced by Cleveland Opera Co., 1932; designer, composer, and director of "Little Black Sambo" (a children's opera), 1938. Author of several plays, including "Track Thirteen," 1940; "Dust to Earth," 1941, "Elijah's Ravens," 1941, and "I Gotta Home," 1942. Contributor to periodicals, including *Black Scholar, Crisis, Etude, Freedomways,* and *Harlem Quarterly.*

SIDELIGHTS: The farm on which DuBois was born had been part of the underground railroad, and had served as a stopping point for runaway slaves en route to Canada. The farm belonged to DuBois's grandfather, a former slave who had been freed prior to the Civil War.

Though DuBois was a longtime supporter of civil rights and "leftist" causes, she was, in her later years, often "viewed in the shadow of her late husband, the black writer, co-founder of the National Association for the Advancement of Colored People and controversial civil rights crusader," *New York Times* stated. The *Times* article pointed out, however, that "Mrs. DuBois won fame on her own many years before she married Mr. DuBois, as a playwright, composer and stage director."

In 1961, the DuBoises moved to Ghana and at the invitation of then president, Kwame Nkrumah, became citizens. W.E.B. DuBois died in 1963, and in 1967, when Nkrumah's regime was ousted by a military coup, Shirley DuBois was forced to leave Ghana. She lived in Cairo for several years and attempted to come to New York in 1971. According to *New York Times*, however, the Justice Department denied DuBois a visa, maintaining that she "had been associated with more than thirty organizations on the Attorney General's list of subversive groups." But the department eventually relented and allowed DuBois to visit the United States for two months. She returned to New York City again last year to be a guest speaker at a memorial tribute to Prime Minister of China, Chou En-lai, held in the city's Chinatown.

On April 2, 1977, a memorial meeting for DuBois was held at Papaoshan Cemetery for Revolutionaries, in China. Several Chinese political figures were present at the memorial, including Deputy Prime Minister Chen Yung-kuei. The president of the Association for Friendship with Foreign Countries, Wang Ping-nan, gave the eulogy calling DuBois a "close friend" who "did a lot of work in enhancing the friendship and understanding between the Chinese people and the people of the United States and the third world."

OBITUARIES: New York Times, April 5, 1977; *Washington Post*, April 5, 1977; *AB Bookman's Weekly*, June 27, 1977; *Current Biography*, June, 1977.*

(Died March 27, 1977)

*   *   *

DUCORNET, Erica 1943-
(Rikki)

PERSONAL: Born April 19, 1943, in Canton, N.Y.; daughter of Gerard and Muriel DeGre; married Guy Ducornet (a painter and poet); children: Jean Yves. *Education:* Bard College, B.A., 1962. *Home:* La Jaleterie, Puy Notre Dame 49260, France.

CAREER: Writer, graphic artist, and illustrator. Now known professionally as Rikki. Has had exhibitions of drawings and prints all over the world, including the museums of Lille, Brussels, and Berlin, and recent one-woman shows in Paris, Toronto, and at University of Massachusetts, Amherst.

WRITINGS—Under name Rikki, except as noted: (Under name Erica Ducornet) *The Blue Bird* (juvenile; self-illustrated), Knopf, 1970; (under name E. Ducornet) *Shazira Shazam and the Devil* (Junior Literary Guild selection), Prentice-Hall, 1972; *From the Star Chamber* (poems and short fictions), Fiddlehead, 1974; *Wild Geraniums* (poems), Actual Size Press, 1975; *Weird Sisters* (poems), Intermedia, 1976; *Knife Notebook* (poems and drawings), Fiddlehead, 1977; *The Butchers Tales* (short fictions), Intermedia, 1978.

Illustrator: (Under name E. Ducornet) Mme. Leprince de Beaumont, *The Beauty and the Beast,* translated by P. H. Muir, Knopf, 1965; (under name E. Ducornet) Paris Leary and Muriel DeGre, *Jack Spratt Cook Book,* Doubleday, 1965; (under name E. Ducornet) Guy Decornet, *Silex de l'avenir* (poems; title means "Silex of the Future"), Pierre Oswald, 1966; (under name E. Ducornet) G. Ducornet, *Trophees en Selle* (poems; title means "Saddle Trophies"), Traces (Nantes, France), 1970; Susan Musgrave, *Gullband Thought Measles Was a Happy Ending,* J. J. Douglas, 1976; *The Leaves of Louise,* McClelland & Stewart, 1978.

Work represented in anthologies, including *The Stonewall Anthology,* University of Iowa Press, 1974; *Minute Fictions,* Braziller, 1977; *Women Poets of North America; Fear and Fearlessness.* Contributor of stories, poems, and drawings to literary journals, including *Prism, Phases, Radical America, Mundus Artium, Tri-Quarterly,* and *Canadian Fiction.*

WORK IN PROGRESS—Under name Rikki: Two books of poems, *The Illustrated Universe* and *Star Hotel;* a novel, *Somnolencil.*

SIDELIGHTS: Rikki told *CA:* "I write to remain lucid, and draw to remain sane! The fiction is concerned with power, madness, and obsession. Fascism. The poetry with eros and a language I like to think of as 'bone baroque.' Drawing is a pure, sensuous voyage into the joyous spaces of the self, although it demands much discipline. Writing is that difficult exploration of darkness and a coming to terms with it. Perhaps."

*   *   *

DUGAN, Michael (Gray) 1947-

PERSONAL: Born October 9, 1947, in Melbourne, Australia; son of Dennis Lloyd (a journalist) and June (Wilkinson) Dugan. *Education:* Educated in Melbourne, Australia. *Home:* 7 Sunbury Cres., Surrey Hills, 3127 Victoria, Australia.

CAREER: Writer. Vice-president of Children's Book Council of Victoria, 1977—. *Member:* International P.E.N., Fellowship of Australian Writers, Melbourne Cricket Club. *Awards, honors:* Commendation from Australian Visual Arts Foundation, 1975.

WRITINGS: Missing People (poetry), Sweeney Reed, 1970; *Returning from the Prophet* (poetry), Contempa, 1972; (editor) *The Drunken Tram* (poetry), Stockland, 1972; (editor with John Jenkins) *The Outback Reader* (prose), Outback Press, 1975; *Clouds* (poetry), Outback Press, 1975; *Publishing Your Poems,* Second Back Row Press, 1978.

Juvenile: *Travel and Transport,* Oxford University Press, 1968; *Stuff and Nonsense,* Collins, 1974; *Weekend,* Macmillan, 1976; *Nonsense Places,* Collins, 1976; *Mountain Easter,* Macmillan, 1976; *My Old Dad,* Longmans-Cheshire, 1976; *The Race,* Macmillan, 1976; *The Golden Ghost,* Macmillan, 1976; *True Ghosts,* Macmillan, 1977; *A House in a Tree,* Lion Press, 1978; *Goal,* Macmillan, 1978; *Dragon's Breath,* Gryphon, 1978; *Hostage,* Hodder & Stoughton, 1978; *Nonsense Numbers,* Thomas Nelson, 1978. Book reviewer for *Age* and *Reading Time.* Editor of *Australian Puffin Club* magazine.

WORK IN PROGRESS: A novel for teenagers.

SIDELIGHTS: Dugan writes: "My best memories of childhood are of my first eight years which were spent in the country near Melbourne. When my family moved to the suburbs of Melbourne, I took some time to adjust to the change, and it was during this period that I began to write, mainly poems and stories about the country and about my teddy bears and other toys.

"My father was a journalist and my mother wrote occasional articles and poems, so it was not surprising that I grew up wanting to be a writer. My most successful books for children have been collections of nonsense poetry.

"I live and write in a large run-down house near Melbourne which usually has lots of people staying in it or passing through. Often I escape to the country or the coast for a few days and a lot of my time is spent visiting schools to read nonsense poems and talk about what it is like being a writer.''

* * *

DUKE, Forrest R(eagan) 1918-

PERSONAL: Born November 23, 1918, in San Antonio, Tex.; son of Eward Forrest and Lucie Marie (Hipps) Duke; married Margery Norris, 1946 (marriage ended, 1954); married Phyllis Caldwell, 1960 (divorced, 1962); children: William Norris, Edward Forrest II, Forrest Reagan, Jr. *Education:* Pasadena Junior College, A.A.; also attended University of California at Los Angeles. *Home:* 4547 East Viking Rd., Las Vegas, Nev. 89121. *Office: Las Vegas Review-Journal,* 1111 West Bonanza Rd., Las Vegas, Nev. 89106.

CAREER/WRITINGS: Hearst Predate Service, New York City, assistant editor, 1944-45; King Features Syndicate, New York City, associate editor, 1945-49; Russell Birdwell and Associates, New York City, account executive, 1949-51; *People Today* magazine, managing editor, 1951-53; *Las Vegas Sun,* Las Vegas, Nev., columnist, 1954-58; *Las Vegas Review-Journal,* Las Vegas, columnist, 1958—; talk show host in Las Vegas for KORK-Radio, 1958—, and KORK-TV, 1964—. Las Vegas representative with Bill Willard of *Daily Variety* and *Variety,* 1956—. Author of column ''Vegascene'' for Vegasyndicate, 1966—. *Military service:* U.S. Army, 1941-42. *Member:* Las Vegas Press Club. *Awards, honors:* Honorary Kentucky Colonel; Honorary Kentucky Admiral.

* * *

DUKE-ELDER, Stewart 1896-1978

April 22, 1896—March 27, 1978; British ophthalmologist and author of books in his field. A distinguished eye surgeon, he treated several prominent figures, including Queen Elizabeth II, her father, King George VI, and King Edward VIII. Duke-Elder was a contributor of articles to the *British Medical Journal, Lancet,* and the *British Journal of Ophthalmology.* He died in London, England. Obituaries and other sources: *The Author's and Writer's Who's Who,* 6th edition, Burke's Peerage, 1971; *Who's Who in the World,* 2nd edition, Marquis, 1973; *The International Who's Who,* Europa, 1974; *Who's Who,* 126th edition, St. Martin's 1974; *The Writers Directory, 1976-78,* St. Martin's, 1976; *New York Times,* March 30, 1978.

* * *

DUKER, Sam 1905-1978

June 10, 1905—April 15, 1978; American educator, lawyer, editor, psychologist, and author. Duker wrote the three-volume *Time-Compressed Speech* and co-wrote *The Truth About Your Child's Reading.* He died in Fort Lee, N.J. Obituaries and other sources: *American Men and Women of Science: The Social and Behavioral Sciences,* 12th edition, Bowker, 1973; *Leaders in Education,* 5th edition, Bowker, 1974; *New York Times,* April 21, 1978. (See index for *CA* sketch)

* * *

DUNCAN, Marion Moncure 1913-1978

December 19, 1913—April 15, 1978; American insurance agent, civic leader, and author of a book on genealogy. During her tenure as president general of the Daughters of the American Revolution, Duncan strove to interest more young people in joining the DAR. She was involved in a number of genealogical societies, Bicentennial activities, and various civic groups. She died in Alexandria, Va. Obituaries and other sources: *Who's Who in America,* 38th edition, Marquis, 1974; *Washington Post,* April 22, 1978.

* * *

DUNCAN, T. Bentley 1929-

PERSONAL: Born August 9, 1929, in Caruaru, Pernambuco, Brazil; son of T. Bentley (a clergyman) and Sarah (a teacher; maiden name, Long) Duncan; married Eva Stone (an editor), September 11, 1965. *Education:* College of Wooster, B.A., 1952; University of Chicago, M.A., 1961, Ph.D., 1967. *Home:* 7851-D South Shore Dr., Chicago, Ill. 60649. *Office:* 1130 East 59th St., Chicago, Ill. 60637.

CAREER: University of Chicago, Chicago, Ill., instructor, 1965-67, assistant professor, 1967-73, associate professor of modern history, 1973—, director of Center for Latin American Studies, 1976—. *Member:* International Conference Group on Modern Portugal, American Historical Association, Conference on Latin American History, Committee on Brazilian History, Society for Spanish and Portuguese Historical Studies, Hakluyt Society, Society for the History of Discoveries, Historians of Early Modern Europe.

WRITINGS: Atlantic Islands: Madeira, the Azores, and the Cape Verdes in Seventeenth-Century Commerce and Navigation, University of Chicago Press, 1972. Contributor to *Journal of Modern History.*

WORK IN PROGRESS: Uneasy Allies: Anglo-Portuguese Diplomatic, Commercial, and Maritime Relations, 1640-1662; The Portuguese Enterprise in Asia, 1500-1750.

SIDELIGHTS: Duncan writes that he lived for a long time in Brazil; he has also traveled extensively in Spanish-speaking South America, and in Portugal, Spain, France, and England. His main interests are the Portuguese Empire, Brazilian history, and maritime and commercial history.

* * *

DUNN, Edward D. 1883(?)-1978

1883(?)—March 10, 1978; American architect, dramatist, and author. Before becoming a writer, Dunn worked as an architect in New York. Lionel Barrymore was the leading man in one of his plays, ''The Claw.'' Among Dunn's books were *Double-Crossing America: A Travel Guide* and *Caravan.* He died in Washington, D.C. Obituaries and other sources: *Washington Post,* March 16, 1978.

* * *

DUNN, Si 1944-

PERSONAL: Born March 24, 1944, in Hattiesburg, Miss.; son of Silas T., Jr. (a journalist) and Doris (Street) Dunn. *Education:* North Texas State University, B.A., 1970; also attended University of Arkansas, University of Texas, Arkansas State Teachers College (now University of Central Arkansas), and University of Houston. *Home:* 3607 Binkley, Dallas, Tex. 75205. *Office: Dallas Morning News,* Dallas, Tex. 75222.

CAREER: Arkansas Democrat, Little Rock, assistant state editor, 1966; *Denton Record-Chronicle,* Denton, Tex., reporter and photographer, 1966; *Houston Chronicle,* Houston, Tex., photographer, 1969-70; *Denton Record-Chronicle,* reporter and photographer, 1972; *Dallas Morning News,* Dallas, Tex., staff writer, 1972-75, 1976-77, 1978—.

Instructor at University of Texas at Dallas. *Military service:* U.S. Naval Reserve, active duty, 1963-65. *Member:* Society of Professional Journalists, American Radio Relay League. *Awards, honors:* Annual journalism award from National Society of Professional Engineers, 1975, for article, "Power for Here and Now."

WRITINGS: Waiting for Water (poems), Calliope Press, 1977; *The Challenge of 160* (nonfiction), 73 Magazine, 1977. Contributor to magazines and newspapers.

WORK IN PROGRESS: Two novels, one on the Vietnam war, and the other on the newspaper business; a book of poems and photographs.

SIDELIGHTS: Dunn told *CA:* "The best writing is simple writing: clear, concise, easy to read—and very difficult to achieve. The most complicated or profound concepts can be explained in terms that most people can grasp, if the writer can understand them well enough to translate them into simpler words."

AVOCATIONAL INTERESTS: Amateur radio operator, music, photography.

*   *   *

DUNNING, Bruce 1940-

PERSONAL: Born April 5, 1940, in Rahway, N.J.; son of Ranald Gardner (a chemical engineer) and Harriet (Freeman) Dunning. *Education:* Princeton University, A.B., 1962. *Politics:* None. *Religion:* None. *Office:* CBS News, 524 West 57th St., New York, N.Y. 10019.

CAREER/WRITINGS: St. Petersburg Times & Independent, St. Petersburg, Fla., reporter and arts editor, 1963-66; *International Herald Tribune,* Paris, France, features editor, 1966-69; Columbia Broadcasting System (CBS) News, New York, N.Y., reporter, 1969-70, correspondent in Saigon, 1970-73, Tokyo, 1973—. Notable assignments include coverage of the Vietnam War and an audience with Japanese emperor Hirohito. Lecturer. *Member:* Overseas Press Club, Foreign Correspondents Club of Japan. *Awards, honors:* Overseas Press Club awards, 1975.

*   *   *

DUNNING, Lawrence 1931-

PERSONAL: Born August 8, 1931, in Kansas City, Mo.; son of Lawrence M. (a wholesaler) and Elizabeth (a teacher; maiden name, Morisey) Dunning; married Barbara Adams, April 11, 1958; children: Melissa, Tracey, Jennifer. *Education:* Attended Rice Institute, 1948-49; Southern Methodist University, B.S., 1952. *Politics:* Liberal. *Religion:* Protestant. *Home:* 8008 East Jefferson Ave., Denver, Colo. 80237. *Agent:* James Brown Associates, Inc., 22 East 60th St., New York, N.Y. 10022.

CAREER: Netherlands Trade Commission, New York, N.Y., publicity writer, 1956-57; *Petroleum Information,* Denver, Colo., reporter and editor, 1957-62; Air Force Accounting and Finance Center, Denver, Colo., technical editor, 1962—. *Military service:* U.S. Air Force, 1952-56. *Member:* Colorado Authors League.

WRITINGS: Neutron Two Is Critical (novel), Avon, 1977; *Keller's Bomb* (novel), Avon, 1978.

Work anthologized in *Best American Short Stories,* 1971. Contributor to literary journals and popular magazines, including *Virginia Quarterly Review, Cavalier, Descant,* and *Seneca Review.*

WORK IN PROGRESS: A third novel; short stories.

SIDELIGHTS: Dunning comments: "The most important thing in my life is writing, and has been so for as long as I can remember. For many years my family has indulged me in what must have seemed to them a time-consuming whim, when my writing was only infrequently published and often not even paid for. It is to their credit that nothing has changed since my recent receipt of a certain amount of financial and literary attention as the result of publication of my first novel. They still expect me to work when I must and be churlish when I can't, and that is very gratifying."

BIOGRAPHICAL/CRITICAL SOURCES: Denver Post, October 23, 1977; *Lowry Airman,* October 28, 1977.

*   *   *

DURANT, David N(orton) 1925-

PERSONAL: Born July 29, 1925, in Nottingham, England; son of Edward (an agent) and Winifred (Pratt) Durant; married Christabel Wright, March 15, 1951; children: Nicholas, Jonathan, Andrew. *Education:* Thames Nautical Training College, H.M.S., 1942. *Religion:* Agnostic. *Home:* Old Hall, Bleasby, Nottingham NG14 7FU, England. *Agent:* David Higham Associates Ltd., 5-8 Lower John St., Golden Sq., London W1R 4HA, England.

CAREER: Durant & Son Ltd., Nottingham, England, founder and president, 1950-72; free-lance writer, 1970—. Lecturer at Attingham Summer School, University of Nottingham, University of Manchester, University of Sheffield, and in the United States, including Harvard University and Smithsonian Institution. Member of council of Nottingham Building Preservation Trust; architectural history consultant to Allied Breweries. *Military service:* British Merchant Marine, 1942-50. *Member:* Society of Authors, English Speaking Union.

WRITINGS: Bess of Hardwick, Atheneum, 1978; *Arbella Stuart,* Weidenfeld & Nicolson, 1978. Contributor to *Country Life* and *History Today.*

WORK IN PROGRESS: Research on Sir Walter Raleigh's settlement in Roanoke, N.C., 1584-1590.

SIDELIGHTS: Durant writes: "I always had a compulsion to write books, but the urgent necessity of earning a living intervened between reality and ambition. Now in my early fifties, I have started on a career that has matured over thirty years. I aim to produce easy to read, clear historical biographies, as a contrast to the academics, who appear mainly unable to write understandable English. I hate inefficiency and suffer from finding myself inefficient. I hate carelessness and consequently suffer again. I find writing is a very humbling trade. I am humbled twice a day on the average—it is said to be good for the soul. Nevertheless I am enjoying life for about the first time."

*   *   *

DURBRIDGE, Francis (Henry) 1912-
(Paul Temple, joint pseudonym)

PERSONAL: Born November 25, 1912, in Hull, England; son of Francis and Gertrude Durbridge; married Norah Elizabeth Lawly, 1940; children: two sons. *Education:* Attended Birmingham University. *Home:* 4 Fairacres, Roehampton Lane, London SW15 5LX, England.

CAREER: Playwright and novelist. Writer and executive producer of television series, 1952—.

WRITINGS—All novels: Send for Paul Temple, John Long, 1938; (with Charles Hatton) *Paul Temple and the*

Front Page Men, John Long, 1939; *News of Paul Temple,* John Long, 1940; *Paul Temple Intervenes,* John Long, 1944; *Paul Temple and the Front Page Men . . . 43rd Thousand,* John Long, 1948; *Send for Paul Temple Again!,* John Long, 1948; *Back Room Girl,* John Long, 1950; *Design for Murder,* John Long, 1951; *Beware of Johnny Washington,* John Long, 1951; (with James Douglas Rutherford MacConnell, under joint pseudonym Paul Temple) *The Tyler Mystery,* Hodder & Stoughton, 1957; *The Other Man,* Hodder & Stoughton, 1958; (with MacConnell, under Temple pseudonym) *East of Algiers,* Hodder & Stoughton, 1959; *A Time of Day,* Hodder & Stoughton, 1959.

The Scarf, Hodder & Stoughton, 1960; *The Case of the Twisted Scarf,* Dodd, 1961; *Portrait of Alison,* Dodd, Mead, 1962; *The World of Tim Frazier,* Dodd, Mead, 1962; *My Friend Charles,* Hodder & Stoughton, 1963; *Tim Frazier Again,* Hodder & Stoughton, 1964; *Another Woman's Shoes,* Hodder & Stoughton, 1965; *The Desperate People,* Hodder & Stoughton, 1966; *Dead to the World,* Hodder & Stoughton, 1967; *My Wife Melissa,* Hodder & Stoughton, 1967; *The Pig-Tail Murder,* Hodder & Stoughton, 1969; *The Geneva Mystery: A Paul Temple Novel,* Hodder Paperbacks, 1971; *A Man Called Harry Brent,* Hodder & Stoughton, 1971; *The Curzon Case: A Paul Temple Novel,* Coronet, 1972; *Dead to the World,* White Lion, 1972; *Bat Out of Hell,* Hodder & Stoughton, 1972; *Paul Temple and the Kelby Affair,* White Lion, 1973; *A Game of Murder,* Hodder & Stoughton, 1975; *Paul Temple and the Harkdale Robbery,* White Lion, 1976.

Plays: *Suddenly at Home,* Samuel French, 1973; *The Gentle Hook,* Samuel French, 1976; *Murder with Love,* Samuel French, 1977.

Author of screenplays for Korda and Romulus, 1954-57. Author of numerous television serials for British Broadcasting Co. (BBC), including "The Broken Horseshoe," 1952, "Portrait of Allison," 1954, "My Friend Charles," 1955, "The Other Man," 1956, "The Scarf," 1960, "The World of Tim Frazier," 1960-61, "Melissa," 1962, "Bat Out of Hell," 1964, "The Passenger," 1971, and "The Doll," 1977. Also author of radio serials for European Broadcasting Union, including "La Boutique," 1967.

Contributor of articles to periodicals, including *London Daily Mail, Birmingham Post, London Evening News,* and *Radio Times.*

SIDELIGHTS: Durbridge's teleplays and radio plays have been broadcast in over sixteen countries, including Germany, France, Italy, and the United States. *Avocational interests:* Reading and travel.

DURRANT, Theo
See OFFORD, Lenore Glen

*   *   *

DUVAL, Margaret
See ROBINSON, Patricia Colbert

*   *   *

DWORKIN, Andrea   1946-

PERSONAL: Born September 26, 1946, in Camden, N.J.; daughter of Harry and Sylvia Spiegel. *Education:* Bennington College, B.A., 1969. *Politics:* Radical feminist. *Home:* 153 Bridge St., Northampton, Mass. 01060. *Agent:* Elaine Markson, 44 Greenwich Ave., New York, N.Y. 10011.

CAREER: Writer. Has worked as a waitress, receptionist, secretary, typist, salesperson, and factory worker. *Member:* American Society of Journalists and Authors, Women's Institute for Freedom of the Press, Authors Guild.

WRITINGS: Woman Hating, Dutton, 1974; *Our Blood: Prophecies and Discourses on Sexual Politics* (essays), Harper, 1976. Contributor to periodicals, including *Village Voice, Christopher Street, America Report, Gay Community News, Ms.,* and *Social Policy.*

WORK IN PROGRESS: A feminist analysis of pornography, *Chains of Iron, Chains of Grief,* publication by Anchor expected in 1981; a novel, *Ruins.*

SIDELIGHTS: Dworkin has been called "one of the most compelling voices in the Women's Movement." Her latest book, *Our Blood,* is a collection of essays calling for abandonment of the quest for sexual equality. Dworkin finds that more radical solutions are necessary to achieve a complete social realignment of the sexes.

Dworkin's demands are revolutionary and as Carole Rosenthal pointed out, "It is difficult to remain neutral or unmoved by such passionate language and conviction." She continued: "But however strongly a reader agrees or takes issue with the essays in this book, Dworkin will never be found dull or dishonest or glib. She is a genuine visionary—bold, thoughtful, willing to take risks. *Our Blood* poses questions that enlighten us in exploring our lives; it constantly tugs and stretches at the imagination's boundaries. These are trailblazing essays. They can alter your mental map of the world."

Dworkin told *CA:* "I am a radical feminist writer concerned with illuminating and clarifying sexual and social values."

BIOGRAPHICAL/CRITICAL SOURCES: Ms., February, 1977; *New Yorker,* March 28, 1977.

E

EAMES, David 1934-

PERSONAL: Born January 12, 1934, in New York; son of Richard C. and Genevieve (Torrey) Eames; married Katherine Binger (separated, February, 1976); children: Seth, Alexander, Evan, Gillian. *Education:* Attended Bard College and Columbia University. *Home:* 444 East Eighth St., New York, N.Y. 10028. *Agent:* Paul R. Reynolds, Inc., 12 East 41st St., New York, N.Y. 10017.

CAREER: Journalist, documentary filmmaker, and writer. *Member:* Authors Guild of Authors League of America. *Awards, honors:* Citation from Hemingway Foundation, 1976, for *Family Style.*

WRITINGS: Family Style (novel), Atheneum, 1975. Contributor to *New York Times Sunday Magazine.*

WORK IN PROGRESS: A novel.

* * *

EARL, Johnrae 1919(?)-1978

1919(?)—January 10, 1978; American journalist and author. A restaurant critic and food columnist for the *Chicago Tribune,* Earl wrote ten cookbooks. For several years he was a full-time copy editor at the *Chicago Tribune* and the *American.* He died in Chicago, Ill. Obituaries and other sources: *New York Times,* January 12, 1978.

* * *

EASTHAM, Thomas 1923-
   (Thomas Harling)

PERSONAL: Born August 21, 1923, in Attleboro, Mass.; son of John Moses (a tool and die worker) and Margaret (Marsden) Eastham; married Berenice Jacqueline Hirsch, October 12, 1945; children: Scott Thomas, Todd Robert. *Education:* Attended Northwestern University, 1946-53. *Religion:* Protestant. *Home:* 2801 New Mexico Ave. N.W., Washington, D.C. 20007. *Office: San Francisco Examiner,* 110 Fifth St., San Francisco, Calif. 94119.

CAREER/WRITINGS: Chicago Herald American, Chicago, Ill., reporter, city editor, and news editor, 1945-55; *San Francisco Call Bulletin,* San Francisco, Calif., news editor, 1956-62; *San Francisco News Call Bulletin,* San Francisco, editor, 1962-65; *San Francisco Examiner,* San Francisco, executive editor, 1965—. Notable assignments include coverage of flying saucers, 1953, the Vesecky killing, 1954, and

a European travel series, 1966. Writer of comment columns, sometimes under pseudonym Thomas Harling. Instructor in media, Golden Gate University. *Military service:* U.S. Marines, 1941-45; became master technical sergeant. *Member:* International Press Institute, InterAmerican Press Institute, American Society of Newspaper Editors (member of ethics and research committees). *Awards, honors:* Nominated for Pulitzer Prize, 1955.

SIDELIGHTS: Eastham told *CA:* "Increasingly, journalism must focus on the performance of government in the people's interest—at all levels but primarily at the national level. Newspapers remain the only true 'people's lobby.'" He added: "Newsmagazines, which so adroitly address a national consensus once exposed, have trouble finding the public pulse. In democracy's eternal tug-of-war between governed and governors, newspapers must stand as the first line of defense."

* * *

EAVES, T(homas) C(ary) Duncan 1918-

PERSONAL: Born October 11, 1918, in Union, S.C.; son of Donald Matheson and Louisa Merriman (Duncan) Eaves; married Frances Juliet Caruana, June 11, 1949; children: Frances Merriman, Maria Louisa (Mrs. David Pinckney Berry, Jr.), Caroline Duncan. *Education:* Attended The Citadel, 1935-36; University of North Carolina, A.B., 1939; University of Cincinnati, M.A., 1940; Harvard University, M.A., 1943, Ph.D., 1944. *Religion:* Methodist. *Home:* 904 Lakeside Dr., Fayetteville, Ark. 72701. *Office:* Department of English, University of Arkansas, Fayetteville, Ark. 72701.

CAREER: Rutgers University, New Brunswick, N.J., instructor in English, 1944-46; College of William and Mary, Williamsburg, Va., assistant professor of English, 1946-47; University of Arkansas, Fayetteville, assistant professor, 1949-52, associate professor, 1952-57, professor of English, 1957—. Fulbright lecturer at University of Florence, 1960-61. *Member:* Modern Language Association of America, South Central Modern Language Association. *Awards, honors:* American Council of Learned Societies grants, 1943, 1967; Guggenheim fellow, 1957-58.

WRITINGS: (Editor with Mary C. Simms Oliphant) *The Letters of William Gilmore Simms,* six volumes, University of South Carolina Press, 1952-79; (with Ben D. Kimpel)

Samuel Richardson: A Biography, Clarendon Press, 1971; (editor with Kimpel) Samuel Richardson, *Pamela,* Houghton, 1971. Contributor to literature, philology, and library journals.

WORK IN PROGRESS: Research for a book on Ezra Pound's *Cantos;* research on eighteenth-century English literature.

* * *

EBEL, Suzanne
See GOODWIN, Suzanne

* * *

ECKERT, Edward K(yle) 1943-

PERSONAL: Born May 1, 1943, in Queens County, N.Y.; son of George C. (a designer) and Mildred (a store manager; maiden name, Kyle) Eckert; married Linda Marie Corroum (an antiques dealer), June 25, 1966; children: Gregory, Christopher, Daniel. *Education:* St. Bonaventure University, B.A. (magna cum laude), 1965; University of Florida, M.A., 1966, Ph.D., 1969. *Politics:* Liberal. *Religion:* Christian. *Home:* 60 South St., Cuba, N.Y. 14727. *Office address:* P.O. Box 42, St. Bonaventure, N.Y. 14778.

CAREER: St. Bonaventure University, St. Bonaventure, N.Y., assistant professor, 1971-74, associate professor of history, 1974—. Ranger-historian for Gettysburg National Military Park, summers, 1965-66, 1971. Executive couple (with his wife) for Olean Marriage Encounter, 1976-77. *Military service:* U.S. Army, Military Intelligence, 1969-72; became captain. *Member:* Organization of American Historians, American Military Institute, Southern Historical Association, Cuba Historical Society (vice-president, 1977-78), Phi Alpha Theta, Delta Epsilon Sigma. *Awards, honors:* Annual award from Florida chapter of Colonial Dames of America, 1966.

WRITINGS: The Navy Department in the War of 1812, University of Florida Press, 1973; (editor and author of introduction, with Nicholas J. Amato) *Ten Years in the Saddle: The Military Memoirs of William Woods Averill,* Presidio Press, 1978. Contributor to *Encyclopedia of Southern History.* Contributor of about thirty articles and reviews to history and military journals and popular magazines, including *American Neptune, Conservationist,* and *Yesteryears,* and to newspapers.

WORK IN PROGRESS: A college-level textbook on U.S. military history; a modern interpretative biography of Jefferson Davis.

SIDELIGHTS: Eckert commented: "I try to spend time with my family, for it is from my relationship with my wife and children that I find the self-fulfillment and acceptance which enables me to function effectively as a teacher and historian. Life to me is a continuing experience which we try to sample together."

Eckert told *CA* that his interest in the Civil War Era "stems from viewing it as the grand climax of American issues since discovery. The role of minorities, the constitutional balance of parts and center, and majority rule vs. individual liberties are all climaxed in this epic struggle. The South is in each American; the tragic struggle of a people to preserve an identity based upon an evil system.

"Southern history demonstrates to me that a social system based upon an immoral choice is eventually doomed. It provides me with a hope for mankind's ability to survive. The war brings together two systems of life that seem inimical,

yet at the end of the era (1877), a South that never existed had overwhelmed a real North." Eckert concluded, "The mystery of humanity's struggle with itself is capsulized and emphasized in the American Civil War."

AVOCATIONAL INTERESTS: Hiking, camping.

* * *

ECO, Umberto 1932-

PERSONAL: Born January 5, 1932, in Alessandria, Italy; son of Guilio and Giovanna (Bisio) Eco; married Renate Ramge (a teacher), September 24, 1962; children: Stefano, Carlotta. *Education:* University of Turin, Ph.D., 1954. *Home:* Via Melzi d'Eril 23, Milano, Italy. *Office:* Universita di Bologna, Via Guerrazzi 20, Bologna, Italy.

CAREER: Employed by Italian Television, 1954-59; University of Turin, Turin, Italy, assistant lecturer, 1956-63, lecturer in aesthetics, 1963-64; University of Milan, Milan, Italy, lecturer on faculty of architecture, 1964-65; University of Florence, Florence, Italy, professor of visual communications, 1966-69; Milan Polytechnic, Milan, professor of semiotics, 1970-71; University of Bologna, Bologna, Italy, professor of semiotics, 1971—. Adviser for scholarly series, Casa Editrice Bompiani, Milan. *Military service:* Italian Army, 1958-59. *Member:* International Association for Semiotic Studies (secretary-general), James Joyce Foundation (honorary trustee).

WRITINGS: Il problema estetico in san Tommaso (title means "The Aesthetic Problem in Saint Thomas"), Edizioni di "Filosofia," 1956, 2nd edition, 1970; *Filosofia in liberta,* Taylor (Turin), 1958, 2nd edition, 1959.

(Editor with G. Zorzoli) *Storia figurata delle invenzioni dalla selce scheggiata al volo spaziali,* Bompiani, 1961, translation by Anthony Lawrence published as *The Picture History of Inventions from Plough to Polaris,* Macmillan, 1963, 2nd Italian edition, Bompiani, 1968; *Opera aperta: forma e indeterminazione nelle poetiche contemporanee,* Bompiani, 1962, 2nd edition, 1967; *Diario minimo,* Mondadori, 1963, 3rd edition, 1966; *Apocalittici e integrati: Comunicazioni di massa e teoria della cultura di massa,* Bompiani, 1964, 3rd edition, 1968.

(Editor with Oreste del Buono) *Il caso Bond,* Bompiani, 1965, translation by R. Downie published as *The Bond Affair,* Macdonald, 1966; *Le poetiche di Joyce dalla 'Summa'' al "Finnegan's Wake",* 2nd edition, Bompiani, 1966; *Appunti per una semiologia delle comunicazioni visive,* Bompiani, 1967; (author of introduction) Mimmo Castellano, *Noi vivi,* Dedalo libri, 1967; *La struttura assente,* Bompiani, 1968; *La definizione dell'arte* (title means "The Definition of Art"), U. Mursia, 1968; (editor) *L'arte come mestiere,* Bompiani, 1969; (editor with Remo Faccani) *I Sistemi di segni e lo strutturalismo sovietico,* Bompiani, 1969.

Le Forme del contenuto, Bompiani, 1971; (editor with Cesare Sughi) *Cent'anni dopo,* Bompiani, 1971; (editor with Jean Chesneaux and Gino Nebiolo) *I fumetti di Mao,* Laterza, 1971, translation by Frances Frenaye published as *The People's Comic Book: Red Women's Detachment, Hot on the Trail, and Other Chinese Comics,* Anchor Press, 1973; (editor) *Estetica e teoria dell'informazione,* Bompiani, 1972; (contributor) *Documenti su il nuovo medioevo,* Bompiani, 1973; *Il segno,* ISEDI (Milan), 1973; *Il costume di casa: Evidenze e misteri dell'ideologia italiano,* Bompiani, 1973; *Trattato di semiotica generale,* Bompiani, 1975, translation published as *A Theory of Semiotics,* Indiana University Press, 1976.

Contributor to *Espresso, Corriere della Sera, Times Literary Supplement,* and other journals and periodicals.

WORK IN PROGRESS: Research on the general theory of communications and on the semiotics of texts (semantics and pragmatics of literary languages).

SIDELIGHTS: Eco writes: "I think that the duty of a scholar is not only to do scientific research but also to communicate with people through various media about the most important issues of social life from the point of view of his own discipline."

BIOGRAPHICAL/CRITICAL SOURCES: Christian Science Monitor, November 29, 1963; *New York Times Book Review,* December 1, 1963; *Science,* November 8, 1963.

* * *

EDEN, (Robert) Anthony 1897-1977

PERSONAL: Born June 12, 1897, in Durham, England; son of William (a baronet) and Sybil Frances (Grey) Eden; married Beatrice Helen Beckett, 1923 (divorced, 1950); married Clarissa Anne Spencer Churchill, 1952; children: Simon (died, 1945), Nicholas. *Education:* Graduated from Christ Church, Oxford (first class honors), 1922. *Politics:* Conservative.

CAREER: Member of British Parliament, 1923-57; appointed parliamentary private secretary to under secretary of Home Office, 1925, and foreign secretary, 1926; served as under secretary for foreign affairs, 1931-34, Lord Privy Seal (minister without portfolio) in charge of League of Nations affairs, 1934-35, cabinet member in charge of ministry for League of Nations affairs, 1935, foreign secretary, 1935-38, secretary of state for dominion affairs, 1939, secretary of state for war, 1940, foreign secretary, 1940-45, leader of House of Parliament, 1942-45, deputy leader of opposition party, 1945-51, foreign secretary and deputy prime minister, 1951-55, prime minister, 1955-57; writer, 1957-77. Foreign correspondent for *Yorkshire Post.* Appointed privy councilor, 1934. Trustee of National Gallery, 1935-49; chancellor of University of Birmingham, beginning 1945; director of Westminster Bank, beginning 1946; justice of the peace for Warwickshire. *Military service:* British Army, 1915-18, King's Royal Rifle Corps; became brigade major; earned Military Cross. *Awards, honors:* D.C.L. from Oxford University, 1936, University of Durham, 1937, and Cambridge University, 1938; LL.D. from McGill University, 1950; dubbed Knight of the Garter, 1954; named Earl of Avon, 1961.

WRITINGS: Places in the Sun (collected articles), J. Murray, 1926; *Foreign Affairs,* Harcourt, 1939, reprinted, Kraus Reprint, 1971; *Freedom and Order: Selected Speeches, 1939-46,* Faber & Faber, 1947, Houghton, 1948; *Days for Decision,* Faber & Faber, 1949, Houghton, 1950; *Full Circle: The Memoirs of Anthony Eden,* Houghton, 1960; *Facing the Dictators: The Memoirs of Anthony Eden, Earl of Avon,* Houghton, 1962; *The Reckoning: The Memoirs of Anthony Eden, Earl of Avon,* Houghton, 1965; *Toward Peace in Indochina,* Houghton, 1966; *The Suez Crisis of 1956,* Beacon Press, 1968; *Another World: 1897-1917,* A. Lane, Doubleday, 1977.

SIDELIGHTS: During a political career that spanned more than three decades, Anthony Eden was recognized as "a distinguished parliamentarian and a statesman of exceptional experience and determination," to borrow the words of British Prime Minister James Callaghan at Eden's death. When Eden was appointed foreign secretary in 1935, he became the youngest man to hold that post in more than eighty years. His skillful negotiations with Mussolini and Hitler, and subsequent resignation in 1938 in protest of Neville Chamberlain's appeasement policy, led Callaghan to eulogize Eden as "a staunch opponent of fascism and fascist dictators." Reinstated as foreign secretary for the duration of World War II, Eden helped to solder and forge relations among the Allies as well as to construct policies that would guide Britain's foreign relations in the postwar years. After an interlude of Labour Party government, Eden returned with the Conservatives in 1951 to reassume his position as foreign secretary and deputy prime minister under Winston Churchill, whom he succeeded as prime minister in 1955.

Eden's actions during the Suez Crisis of 1956 provoked a public outcry that, coupled with ill health, forced him to resign from public office in 1957. In response to Nasser's move to nationalize the Suez Canal, Eden directed a joint Anglo-French invasion of the Suez, but later succumbed to American pressure for a cessation of hostilities. In his memoirs he defended his actions against accusations that he sought to maintain British imperialism. Comparing Nasser to Hitler and Mussolini, Eden denounced the military dictatorship in Egypt and likened a failure to respond to Nasser's action to Chamberlain's appeasement of Hitler. In the final analysis, he acknowledged that history would be his judge.

OBITUARIES: Washington Post, January 15, 1977; *Newsweek,* January 24, 1977; *Time,* January 24, 1977; *Current Biography,* March, 1977.*

(Died January 14, 1977, in Wiltshire, England)

* * *

EGAN, Robert 1945-

PERSONAL: Born February 10, 1945, in Cambridge, Mass.; son of Christopher Edward (a physician) and Mary (Collins) Egan; married Marlene Joan Walker, August 11, 1970; children: Kevin P. Knarr and Duncan D. Knarr (stepsons). *Education:* Harvard University, B.A. (magna cum laude), 1966; Stanford University, Ph.D., 1972. *Office:* Department of Dramatic Art, University of California, Santa Barbara, Calif. 93106.

CAREER: Columbia University, New York, N.Y., assistant professor of English, 1970-77; University of California, Santa Barbara, assistant professor of dramatic art, 1977—. Actor and director with Shakespeare festivals, summer stock productions, and regional theaters. *Member:* Modern Language Association of America, Shakespeare Society of America, Renaissance Society of America.

WRITINGS: Drama Within Drama: Shakespeare's Sense of His Art in "King Lear," "The Winter's Tale," and "The Tempest," Columbia University Press, 1975. Contributor of articles and reviews to scholarly journals.

WORK IN PROGRESS: A study of artistic self-consciousness in twentieth-century drama; research on *Macbeth* and *Measure for Measure.*

SIDELIGHTS: Egan writes: "I have followed parallel careers, in theatre and as a teacher-critic of dramatic literature. My hope is that my practical experience has informed my ideas and critical approaches, and my ambition is to write and teach in ways that are as useful to actors and directors as they are to scholars and students."

* * *

EISEMAN, Alberta 1925-

PERSONAL: Born November 2, 1925, in Venice, Italy;

came to the United States in 1941, naturalized citizen, 1947; daughter of Alberto and Xenia (Oreffice) Friedenberg; married Alfred S. Eiseman, Jr. (a printing representative), September 22, 1946; children: Margot, Nicole. *Education:* Cornell University, B.A., 1945; also attended New School for Social Research. *Politics:* "Usually Democrat." *Religion:* Jewish. *Home and office:* 5 Hidden Hill, Westport, Conn. 06880. *Agent:* McIntosh & Otis, Inc., 475 Fifth Ave., New York, N.Y. 10017.

CAREER: Member of editorial staffs of *Seventeen* magazine and Doubleday & Co.; employed by WOV-Radio, New York City; *New York Times Book Review,* New York City, reviewer of children's books, 1952-65; free-lance writer for children, 1956—. Member of board of trustees of Westport Public Library. *Member:* Authors League of America, American Civil Liberties Union, American Jewish Committee, Save Venice, Inc., Connecticut Trust for Historic Preservation. *Awards, honors:* Award from Seventeenth Summer Literary Competition, 1957, for *Monica.*

WRITINGS—For children: (With Ingrid Sladkus) *Monica,* Dodd, 1957; *Candido,* Macmillan, 1965; (with Sladkus) *Skate to a Mountain Song,* Macmillan, 1966; *The Guest Dog,* Random House, 1968; *From Many Lands* (Junior Literary Guild selection), Atheneum, 1970; *Manana Is Now: The Spanish-Speaking in the United States,* Atheneum, 1973; *Rebels and Reformers,* Doubleday, 1976; *The Sunday Whirligig,* Atheneum, 1977. Author of "The Immigrants" (cassette series), Mass Communications, Inc., 1975. Contributor of articles and reviews to magazines and newspapers, including *Connecticut, Publishers Weekly,* and *New York Times.*

WORK IN PROGRESS: A book with daughter, Nicole Eiseman, for Atheneum; historical research for another book.

SIDELIGHTS: Alberta Eiseman writes: "My interests are varied—scattered, I often think. I consider it my great good fortune that I have been able to take a subject that appeals to me, deepen my own knowledge with research, then share it with a young audience. My work is all based on research, even the books I have written for the very young. *The Sunday Whirligig,* for example, was the result of the first folk art exhibit I ever saw. I was intrigued by a group of whirligigs, but it was only after I read up on them—who made them, how they were used, in what part of the country and what period—that a story began to take shape. My books for older readers on the history of immigration and ethnic groups grew out of the realization that my daughters and their friends, elementary and junior high school students at that time, were not sufficiently aware of the wondrously varied backgrounds of their contemporaries. This led to a rethinking of my own years as a refugee, and of American history as it is usually taught. The research that I did produced three books, but more than that, it has given me a far better understanding of the American experience, and of many of today's trends."

AVOCATIONAL INTERESTS: The outdoors (swimming, sailing, and gardening in the summer; walking and cross-country skiing in the winter), theater, movies, fine architecture, "good talk with friends and family," travel.

* * *

EISENBERG, Lawrence B(enjamin)
(Norman Dickens)

PERSONAL: Born in New York, N.Y.; son of Oscar (a furrier) and Mildred (Rubinfeld) Eisenberg; married Barbara Smith (a travel agent), December 12, 1954; children: Mindy,

Paul. *Education:* Brooklyn College (now of the City University of New York), B.A., 1949; Columbia University, M.A., 1952. *Religion:* Jewish. *Residence:* New York, N.Y.

CAREER: Affiliated with *New York Herald Tribune,* 1950-55, WNEW-TV, 1955-57, WABC-TV, 1957-59, CBS-TV, 1959-61, and M.S.E.I.G. Public Relations, 1961-64, all New York City; Mahoney/Wasserman Public Relations, New York City, staff member, 1964—. *Military service:* U.S. Navy, 1944-45.

WRITINGS: *The Villa of the Ferromonte* (novel), Simon & Schuster, 1974; (under pseudonym Norman Dickens) *Jack Nicholson: The Search for a Superstar,* New American Library, 1975. Contributor to *Cosmopolitan.*

WORK IN PROGRESS: Cissie Love, Superstar, a novel; *Sex in Israel.*

SIDELIGHTS: Eisenberg writes: "When I die impoverished, I want my ashes thrown in Swifty Lazar's face."

* * *

EKSTEINS, Modris 1943-

PERSONAL: Born December 13, 1943, in Riga, Latvia; son of Rudolfs Erhards (a clergyman) and Biruta (a library technician; maiden name, Vajeiks) Eksteins. *Education:* University of Toronto, B.A., 1965; Oxford University, B.Phil., 1967, D.Phil., 1970. *Home:* 8 Glencairn Ave., Toronto, Ontario, Canada M4R 1M5. *Office:* Department of History, Scarborough College, University of Toronto, West Hill, Ontario, Canada M1C 1A4.

CAREER: University of Toronto, Scarborough College, West Hill, Ontario, assistant professor, 1970-75, associate professor of history, 1975—. *Member:* American Historical Association. *Awards, honors:* Woodrow Wilson fellowship, 1965-66; Rhodes scholarship, 1965-68; Canada Council research grants, 1971-72, 1976-77.

WRITINGS: Theodor Heuss und die Weimarer Republik (title means "Theodor Heuss and the Weimar Republic"), Klett, 1969; *The Limits of Reason,* Oxford University Press, 1975. Contributor to history journals.

WORK IN PROGRESS: The First World War and the European Imagination.

* * *

ELDER, Karl 1948-

PERSONAL: Born July 7, 1948, in Beloit, Wis.; son of Amos L. and Anna Mae (Greife) Elder; married Brenda Kay Olson, August 23, 1969; children: Seth Wade. *Education:* Northern Illinois University, B.S. in Ed., 1971, M.S. in Ed., 1974; Wichita State University, M.F.A., 1977. *Politics:* Libertarian-Anarchist. *Religion:* Atheist. *Home:* 803 East Powell, Springfield, Mo. 65807. *Office:* Department of English, Southwest Missouri State University, Springfield, Mo. 65802.

CAREER: Southwest Missouri State University, Springfield, instructor in English, 1977—. *Military service:* U.S. Army, 1971-73. *Awards, honors:* Lucien Stryk Award for poetry, 1974; Illinois Arts Council award for poetry, 1975, and project completion grant, 1977.

WRITINGS: Can't Dance an' It's Too Wet to Plow (poetry), Prickly Pear Press, 1975. Work represented in *Interface: Literature and Its Dispositions (1972-1975),* Margin Books, 1976. Contributor of poetry and prose to more than fifty journals, including *Folio, Chicago Review, Small Pond, Margins,* and *Wisconsin Review.* Poetry editor, *Seems,* 1973—.

WORK IN PROGRESS: Run, a novel; *The Celibate,* a volume of poems; a sequence of phobia poems.

SIDELIGHTS: Karl Elder wrote: "To paraphrase Dali, rapture and delirium are the only true realms of art. I've begun to believe it. And like Dali, like Stevens and Pater, I've come to a similar conclusion that the most difficult task facing any artist is that of becoming himself—the goal of existing in an intense state of awareness while adhering to the reality that is one's mind. Considering the protean quality of human consciousness, that each individual is bound by perpetual change, it's a wonder one retains a style for any given period, let alone an aesthetic. Consequently, I have made the conscious effort to allow myself to 'become' Karl Elder, to never remain attached to a wholly consistent methodology. If I am able to project for an audience a macabre, seemingly incongruent and inappropriate attitude of joy in the face of pain—through hyperbole, sarcasm, and even cynicism—then I am very close to what I currently want to accomplish."

BIOGRAPHICAL/CRITICAL SOURCES: Sunflower, January 30, 1976, May 9, 1977.

*   *   *

ELIASON, Joyce 1934-

PERSONAL: Born May 14, 1934, in Manti, Utah; daughter of Perry Carlton (a rancher) and Ada (Jensen) Eliason; married Allan Dotson, April, 1955 (divorced, 1962); married Stuart Margolin, August 5, 1966 (divorced April 9, 1975); children: (first marriage) Polly, Jill. *Education:* Attended University of Utah. *Home:* 950 North Ogden Dr., Los Angeles, Calif. 90046. *Agent:* Elaine Markson Literary Agency, Inc., 44 Greenwich Ave., New York, N.Y. 10011.

CAREER: TV Guide, Radnor, Pa., 1959-76, field editor in Salt Lake City, Utah, and Los Angeles, Calif.; free-lance writer, 1976—. Professional actress at University of Utah, 1954-64, and for Pasadena Playhouse Repertory Co., 1965-66. *Member:* Writers Guild of America, Authors Guild of Authors League of America.

WRITINGS: Fresh Meat/Warm Weather, Harper, 1974; *Laid Out,* Harper, 1976.

Also author of television scripts, including "James at Fifteen" and "Love American Style." Contributor to *New Dawn.*

WORK IN PROGRESS: A novel about the contemporary West; a three-act play for two actors; a screenplay.

*   *   *

ELLER, William 1921-

PERSONAL: Born April 11, 1921, in Janesville, Wis.; son of Benjamin L. (a railroad station-master) and Winifred (a teacher; maiden name, Macmillan) Eller; married Betty Jean Sanders (an artist), October 20, 1944; children: Charles B. *Education:* Wisconsin State University (now University of Wisconsin), Platteville, B.S., 1942; University of Iowa, M.A., 1949, Ph.D., 1950. *Home:* 42 Briar Hill Rd., Orchard Park, N.Y. 14127. *Office:* Department of Elementary and Remedial Education, Baldy Hall, State University of New York at Buffalo, Amherst, N.Y. 14260.

CAREER: High school teacher of mathematics in New Lisbon, Wis., 1942-43; University of Oklahoma, Norman, associate professor of education and director of Reading Laboratory, 1951-54; University of Iowa, Iowa City, associate professor of education and director of Educational Clinic,

1954-62; State University of New York at Buffalo, Amherst, professor of elementary and remedial education, 1962—, chairman of department, 1964-75. *Military service:* U.S. Army Air Forces, navigator, 1943-47; became captain.

MEMBER: International Reading Association (member of board of directors, 1971-74; president, 1977-78), National Reading Conference (president, 1961), National Council of Teachers of English, American Educational Research Association.

WRITINGS: (With B. Y. Welch) *Introduction to Literature,* Ginn, 1964, 3rd edition, 1970; (with Ruth Reeves) *The Study of Literature,* Ginn, 1964, 3rd edition, 1970; (senior author) *The Laidlaw Reading Program,* one hundred eight volumes (for teachers and students), with workbooks, tests, and kits, Laidlaw Brothers, 1976-77. Co-author of "A Corner on Reading," a monthly column in *Early Years.*

WORK IN PROGRESS: Laidlaw Reading Program books for seventh and eighth grades, publication expected in 1980.

*   *   *

ELLIOTT, Lesley 1905-
(Lesley Gordon)

PERSONAL: Born August 5, 1905, in England; daughter of Harry Braine (a small tool salesman) and Mabel Jane (a fashion designer; maiden name, Statham) Gordon; married Frederick Allan Bannister, August 26, 1927 (died, 1970); married Stuart Randall Elliott, 1970 (deceased); children: (first marriage) Rosemary Ann (Mrs. Raymond Few), Hilary Clare (Mrs. Keith Atkinson). *Education:* Educated in East Orange, N.J. and in England. *Home:* 1 Honeysuckle Cottage, Horley Row, Horley, Surrey, England. *Agent:* Webb & Bower, 21 Southernhay W., Exeter, Devonshire, England.

CAREER: Free-lance writer, 1930—. *Member:* Garden History Society.

WRITINGS—Under name Lesley Gordon: *Sorrowful and Not-So-Sorrowful Tales,* Samuel French, 1937; *The Jenny Lou Books* (juvenile), three volumes, Lutterworth, 1940; *Snips and Snails* (juvenile poems), Lutterworth, 1941; *A Pageant of Dolls* (history), Edmund Ward, 1954; (with Esmee Mascall) *Moppit and Co* (juvenile), Kinheim, Vitgeverij, Heilloo, 1955; *Peepshow Into Paradise: A History of Toys,* Harrap, 1958; *Poorman's Nosegay: Flowers From a Cottage Garden,* Collins, 1973; *Green Magic: Flowers, Plants, and Herbs in Lore and Legend,* Viking, 1977. Contributor of articles, stories, and poems to magazines since 1930, including American antiques journals.

WORK IN PROGRESS: Research for a book on marriage customs and folklore.

SIDELIGHTS: Gordon told *CA:* "My writing career has always played second to my family life. I did, however, try out my story/how-to-make ideas on my own children, so that Easter, summer holiday, and Christmas plays were previewed in our home and appeared in the women's magazines the following year, providing that they had been voted successful by the home critics. Now that the home critics have homes of their own I prefer to concentrate on more demanding writing."

AVOCATIONAL INTERESTS: Travel (France, the Netherlands, Germany, Italy), sculpture, painting (especially flowers), botanical illustration, bookbinding and marbelling, garden history, gardening, collecting old books (especially flower and gardening books).

ELLIS, Ron(ald Walter) 1941-

PERSONAL: Born September 12, 1941, in Southport, England; son of Walter (an engineer) and Isobel (Sherlock) Ellis. *Education:* Attended Liverpool Polytechnic. *Politics:* "Right wing conservative." *Religion:* Christian. *Home:* The Grange, Rawlinson Road, Southport, Merseyside, England.

CAREER: Worked as a branch librarian in Southport, England; full-time disc jockey, 1970—; sports commentator and disc jockey for British Broadcasting Corp. (BBC-Radio), 1976—; professional singer and songwriter. Worker's Education Association lecturer in creative writing in Liverpool, England, 1975—; northern promotions manager for WEA Records, 1976-77.

WRITINGS: Diary of a Discotheque (poetry), Nirvana Books, 1978. Also author of a column appearing monthly in *Disco International*. Contributor of articles to *Knave, Cockade, Club/International,* and other British periodicals.

WORK IN PROGRESS: First Glass and *Second Glass,* detective novels.

SIDELIGHTS: Ellis told *CA:* "When *Diary of a Discotheque* was published in 1977, W.E.A. Records released an album of its greatest hits entitled 'Ron Ellis Discotheque Show Collection,' and I tour the country promoting them as a disc jockey." Ellis's record credits include "Northern Soul," 1975, "Boys on the Dole," 1978, and "Hot California Nights," 1978.

* * *

ELLITHORPE, Harold (Earle) 1925-

PERSONAL: Born June 25, 1925, in Denver, Colo.; son of Earle Day (a mechanic) and Gertrude Mary (Donahue) Ellithorpe; married Janie Yen Ho Yen Tran, May 12, 1966; children: Don, John. *Education:* University of Denver, A.B., 1948, M.A., 1949. *Politics:* "No affiliations." *Religion:* "None." *Home and office:* 1B Gardena Ct., 2 Kennedy Ter., Hong Kong.

CAREER/WRITINGS: U.S. Air Force, Denver, Colo., instructor, 1950-55; free-lance correspondent in United States, Southeast Asia, Asia, and Hong Kong, 1966—. Notable assignments include coverage of Vietnam War. Contributor to *Time, Newsweek, Life, Fortune, Asia* magazine, *National Review, London Sun, China Letter,* and over three hundred other periodicals. Former partner and manager of Empire News/Photography. *Military service:* U.S. Army Air Corps, 1943-46. U.S. Air Force Reserves, 1951-56; became first lieutenant. *Member:* Foreign Correspondents Club of Hong Kong (chairman of professional committee and member of board of governors, 1975-76).

WORK IN PROGRESS: A dramatic work on Mao Tse-Tung; research on role of press in Vietnam War.

SIDELIGHTS: Ellithorpe told *CA:* "I have been involved both as a university student and as a journalist with the problem of communist ideology and its manifestations, and much of my work concerns the study and analysis of this phenomenon of our times. The current focus of my attention is on China and the Maoist variant."

* * *

ELSON, Robert T(ruscott) 1906-

PERSONAL: Born June 21, 1906, in Cleveland, Ohio; son of John Truscott (in hardware) and Katharine (Logue) Elson; married Georgina E. MacKinnon, December 28, 1928; children: John Truscott, Katharine Ellen Elson Zadravec, Elizabeth Elson Mahlfeld, Brigid Mary, Robert Anthony. *Education:* Attended University of British Columbia. *Religion:* Roman Catholic. *Home address:* P.O. Box 1523, East Hampton, N.Y. 11937.

CAREER: Daily Province, Vancouver, British Columbia, reporter, 1924-28; *Tribune,* Winnipeg, Manitoba, promotion manager, 1930-32; *Daily Province,* sports editor, 1932-34, news editor, 1934-39; *News-Herald,* Vancouver, editor and publisher, 1939; Southam Newspapers of Canada, Washington correspondent, 1941-43; Time Inc., New York, N.Y., contributing editor of *Time,* 1943-44, Washington chief for Time Inc., 1944-48, assistant executive editor of *Fortune,* 1948-49, chief of correspondents for U.S. & Canadian News Service, 1949, national affairs editor, 1949-58, assistant managing editor, 1954, deputy managing editor, 1955-58, general manager of *Life,* 1958-60, London correspondent for Time-Life, 1960-64, corporate historian, 1964-71; free-lance writer, 1971—. *Member:* Nature Conservancy, Council on Foreign Relations.

WRITINGS: Time Inc.: The Intimate History of a Publishing Enterprise, 1923-1941, edited by Duncan Norton-Taylor, two volumes, Atheneum, 1968; *The World of Time Inc.,* Atheneum, 1971; *Prelude to War,* Time-Life, 1976.

BIOGRAPHICAL/CRITICAL SOURCES: New York Times Book Review, November 24, 1968; *New Leader,* December 2, 1968; *Commonweal,* December 30, 1968.

* * *

EMBER, Carol R(uchlis) 1943-

PERSONAL: Born July 7, 1943, in Brooklyn, N.Y.; daughter of Hyman (a writer and educator) and Elsie (an actuary; maiden name, Kardonsky) Ruchlis; married Melvin Ember (a professor of anthropology), March 21, 1970. *Education:* Antioch College, B.A., 1965; attended Cornell University, 1965-66; Harvard University, Ph.D., 1971. *Office:* Department of Anthropology, Hunter College of the City University of New York, 695 Park Ave., New York, N.Y. 10021.

CAREER: Hunter College of the City University of New York, New York, N.Y., lecturer, 1970-71, assistant professor, 1971-74, associate professor of anthropology, 1975—. *Member:* American Anthropological Association, Society for Cross-Cultural Research.

WRITINGS: (With husband, Melvin Ember) *Anthropology,* Appleton, 1973, 2nd edition, Prentice-Hall, 1977; (with M. Ember) *Cultural Anthropology,* Appleton, 1973, 2nd edition, Prentice-Hall, 1977.

WORK IN PROGRESS: Research on sex and mating in birds, humans, and other mammals.

SIDELIGHTS: Ember told *CA* that her main research interests include cross-cultural variation in marriage, family, and kinship, as well as sex differences and sex roles.

* * *

EMY, Hugh (Vincent) 1944-

PERSONAL: Born November 5, 1944, in Guildford, Surrey, England; son of Ernest H. (a banker) and Moira (Borland) Emy; married Elizabeth A. Gloster, May 14, 1971; children: Antony C., Mathew B. *Education:* London School of Economics and Political Science, B.Sc., 1966, Ph.D., 1969. *Home:* 8 The Woodland, Glen Waverley, Melbourne, Victoria 3150, Australia. *Office:* Department of Politics, Monash University, Clayton, Victoria 3168, Australia.

CAREER: Monash University, Clayton, Australia, lecturer, 1969-73, senior lecturer, 1973-75, professor of politics, 1975—.

WRITINGS: Liberals, Radicals, Social Politics, 1892-95, Cambridge University Press, 1973; *The Politics of Australian Democracy: An Introduction to Political Science,* Macmillan (Australia), 1974, revised edition published as *The Politics of Australian Democracy: Fundamentals in Dispute,* 1978; *Public Policy: Problems and Paradoxes,* Macmillan (Australia), 1977.

WORK IN PROGRESS: Research on Australian politics, political theory, and public policy.

SIDELIGHTS: Emy told *CA:* "Recent writings on Australian politics analyse the deficiencies in the framework of accountability in the modern state, with special reference to the Westminster model. They argue that problems in political investigation reflect problems in democratic theory as a whole. Public policy writings treat this field as a type of social theory, finding the intellectual significance of public policy in the renewed search for methods of social control in the modern state."

*   *   *

ERDOES, Richard   1912-

PERSONAL: Born July 7, 1912, in Vienna, Austria; son of Richard (an opera singer) and Maria (Schrom) Erdoes; married Elsie Schulhof (an artist), 1940 (deceased); married Jean Sternbergh (an artist), June 24, 1951; children: (second marriage) David Richard, Eric Peter, Jacqueline. *Education:* Attended Berlin Academy of Art, Academy for Applied Arts, Vienna, Austria, and Academie de la Grande Chaumiere. *Politics:* "Non-phony liberal." *Religion:* "Father Jewish, mother Roman Catholic, one aunt Mohammedan; take part in Indian ceremonies." *Home and office:* 251 West 89th St., New York, N.Y. 10024; and 110 Vigil Lane, Santa Fe, N.M. 87501. *Agent:* Peter Basch, 322 West 72nd St., New York, N.Y. 10023.

CAREER: Free-lance artist, illustrator, muralist, photographer, writer, and maker of educational films. Owner of Studio 46 (graphic arts studio). Lecturer at Yale University, Long Island University, Princeton University, Dartmouth College, City College of the City University of New York, Pratt Institute, and New School for Social Research. Has had one-man and group shows of his work. Active in American Indian civil rights movements.

MEMBER: Authors Guild of Authors League of America, Society of Illustrators, Artists Equity. *Awards, honors:* Awards from American Institute of Graphic Arts, Viennese Museum of Applied Arts, Art Directors Club of New York, and Society of Illustrators.

WRITINGS—All self-illustrated: *The Pueblo Indians,* Funk, 1967; *Lame Deer, Seeker of Visions* (biography), Simon & Schuster, 1971; *The Sun Dance People,* Knopf, 1972; *The Rain Dance People,* Knopf, 1976; *The Sound of Flutes,* Knopf, 1976; *Yuwipi* (novel), Avon, 1977; *A Social History of the Western Saloon,* Knopf, in press.

For children: *A Picture History of Ancient Rome,* Macmillan, 1962; *The Green Tree House,* Dodd, 1965; *Peddlers and Vendors Around the World,* McGraw, 1965; *Policemen Around the World,* McGraw, 1966; *Musicians Around the World,* McGraw, 1967; *Ireland: Bewitching Wonderland,* Dodd, 1968.

Also illustrator of Alexander King, *Memoirs of a Certain Mouse,* McGraw; James Joyce, *The Cat and the Devil,* Dodd; and Theodore Geisel, *Come Over to My House,* Random House.

Author of scripts for educational filmstrips on Native American life. Contributor of stories, articles, illustrations, and photographs to major national magazines, first in Austria, then in the United States, including *Smithsonian, Signature, Life, Saturday Evening Post,* and *Camera 35.*

WORK IN PROGRESS: A historical novel, tentatively titled *La Hermana,* edited by Clover Swann, for Fawcett; *The Eye of the Heart,* a biography of a militant Sioux medicine man, for Harper; *Woman From He-Dog,* a biography of a young Sioux woman-activist, for Simon & Schuster; *Seven-Up,* a juvenile novelette about contemporary Sioux life, for Knopf; three chapters for *Our Fascinating Indian Heritage* (tentative title), for Reader's Digest Press.

SIDELIGHTS: Erdoes writes: "I am an old artist, but a young writer. For thirty years I lived in New York making my living as a magazine illustrator and photographer. I got into serious writing accidentally in 1970.

"My early outlook and first writings were influenced by a cosmopolitan European upbringing in a family of actors and opera singers. Later, I was strongly influenced by a short and modest spell in the European Underground resisting the Nazis. In this country, after twelve happy years in a profitable ivory tower, I was struck by the shock and outrage of first-hand experience of conditions on American Indian reservations.

"I was doing a painting and photography portfolio for *Life* on a Sioux Indian reservation when I was befriended by an old and almost totally illiterate Sioux medicine man, Lame Deer, who unfortunately died recently. He picked me to write his life story [which has been published in French, Dutch, Norwegian, and German].

"I found writing so rewarding that ninety per cent of my time is now devoted to it. I do artwork and photography now only on prestige projects which tickle my fancy.

"Travel is one of my hobbies, and I have been lucky to have made this into a paid hobby. I have had assignments as an artist and photographer to go exploring in three continents, and lately I have also had writing travel assignments."

AVOCATIONAL INTERESTS: Skiing, climbing, wandering on Indian reservations.

*   *   *

ERIKSSON, Edward   1941-

PERSONAL: Born July 7, 1941, in Brooklyn, N.Y.; son of Edward Erik (a machinist) and Anna (Movchan) Eriksson; married Charlotte Bertrand, April 9, 1966; children: Edward, Jennifer, Eve. *Education:* Brooklyn College of the City University of New York, B.A., 1962; University of Iowa, M.A., 1965. *Home:* 342 East Broadway, Port Jefferson, N.Y. 11777. *Office:* Department of English, Suffolk Community College, Selden, N.Y. 11784.

CAREER: Burlington Community College, Burlington, Iowa, instructor in English and speech, 1965-66; Suffolk Community College, Selden, N.Y., instructor, 1966-69, assistant professor, 1969-72, associate professor, 1972-78, professor of English, 1978—. Active as performer with Long Island Dinner Theatre. *Member:* Poetry Society of America.

WRITINGS: Focus on the Written Word, Edutex, 1973.

Plays: "Good Citizenship" (two-act), first produced in St. James, N.Y. at Community Free Theatre, November 25, 1977; "The Misogynist," a two-act.

Author of television script "Whitman on Long Island," 1974. Contributor of poems to magazines.

WORK IN PROGRESS: A book on historical cycles, 3600 B.C. to 2100 A.D.

SIDELIGHTS: Eriksson describes himself as "romantically an internationalist. I am familiar with French, Italian, Swedish, and classical Greek." He has also conducted trips to England for the purpose of studying Shakespeare.

* * *

ESKEY, Kenneth 1930-

PERSONAL: Born June 6, 1930, in Pittsburgh, Pa.; son of Kenneth D. (a doctor) and Anne (Volz) Eskey; married Jane P. Yahres, October 20, 1956; children: Clifford, Matthew. *Education:* Northwestern University, B.S.J., 1952, M.S.J., 1955. *Religion:* Presbyterian. *Home:* 5102 Baltimore Ave., Washington, D.C. 20016. *Office:* Scripps-Howard Newspapers, 777 14th St. N.W., Washington, D.C. 20005.

CAREER/WRITINGS: Pittsburgh Press, Pittsburgh, Pa., education writer, 1955-69; Scripps-Howard Newspapers, Washington, D.C., editorial writer, 1970—. Notable assignments include coverage of business and economic affairs, with a special series on a California referendum to cut property taxes 57%. *Military service:* U.S. Navy, 1952-54. *Member:* Pittsburgh Press Club (president, 1967-68), Sigma Delta Chi.

SIDELIGHTS: Eskey suggests that programs for journalism students should include more training in business and economics reporting.

* * *

EVANS, Bergen (Baldwin) 1904-1978

September 19, 1904—February 4, 1978; American educator, author, and television personality best known as master of ceremonies for "The Last Word" and "Down You Go." Evans received a Peabody Award in 1957 for his work in broadcasting. A renowned authority on the English language, he wrote *A Dictionary of Contemporary American Usage, Word-a-day,* and *Comfortable Words.* Evans died in Highland Park, Ill. Obituaries and other sources: *The Author's and Writer's Who's Who,* 6th edition, Burke's Peerage, 1971; *Who's Who in America,* 39th edition, Marquis, 1976; *New York Times,* February 5, 1978; *Washington Post,* February 6, 1978; *Newsweek,* February 13, 1978; *Time,* February 20, 1978. (See index for *CA* sketch)

* * *

EVANS, Nancy 1950-

PERSONAL: Born April 12, 1950, in Philadelphia, Pa.; daughter of Charles Restrick (a driver) and Charlotte (a teacher; maiden name, Burr) Evans. *Education:* Skidmore College, B.A. (highest honors), 1972; Columbia University, M.A., 1974. *Politics:* Democrat. *Religion:* Protestant. *Home:* 155 East 88th St., New York, N.Y. 10028. *Agent:* Meredith Bernstein, Henry Morrison, Inc., 58 West 10th St., New York, N.Y. 10011.

CAREER: College English, Middletown, Conn., copy editor, 1972-73; Wesleyan University, Middletown, Conn.,

teacher of literature course, 1973; Harper's Magazine Co., New York, N.Y., associate editor of *Harper's Weekly,* 1974-76; writer, 1976—. Lecturer at Womanschool and other gatherings. *Member:* Authors Guild of Authors League of America, Women's Ink, Phi Beta Kappa.

WRITINGS: (Contributor) Susan Cornillon, editor, *Images of Women in Fiction,* Popular Press, 1972; (with Judith Appelbaum) *How to Get Happily Published,* Harper, 1978. Contributor to popular magazines, including *Ms.* (under pseudonym Mary Ann Eliot), *Family Circle, Glamour, Esquire, Writer,* and *Seventeen.* Editor of *Encyclopedia of the American Woman,* 1972-73.

SIDELIGHTS: Nancy Evans writes: "Judith Appelbaum and I are hopeful of expanding the range of participants in the publishing process by making known the rules of the game as well as encouraging alternatives such as the thousands of small presses and little magazines, and the self-publishing option. We are also concerned with the already-published author who too often feels disappointed and bitter by the lack of attention and consideration he receives from his publisher. The atrocity stories often exchanged among authors can be minimized if and when authors know that only a handful of books get the publisher's money and manpower behind them; the rest are left to sink or swim on their own merit or luck; and given this state of affairs, that it is the author who needs to roll up his sleeves and get in there to make sure his book reaches as many of its natural readers as is humanly possible. The point is that in the 1970's, with forty thousand books published each year and bestsellerdom uppermost in most publishers' minds, an author can no longer afford—literally—to end his job when the manuscript is turned in."

* * *

EZELL, Macel D. 1934-

PERSONAL: Born April 23, 1934, in Rutherfordton, N.C.; son of L. D. (a carpenter) and Alma (Scoggin) Ezell; married Carol Jean Ridgway (a teacher), November 3, 1956; children: Macel Lynn (daughter), Rachel Beth. *Education:* Furman University, B.A., 1960; Texas Christian University, M.A., 1963, Ph.D., 1969. *Home:* 1860 Melrose, East Lansing, Mich. 48823. *Office:* Department of American Thought and Language, Michigan State University, East Lansing, Mich. 48824.

CAREER: Temple Junior College, Temple, Tex., instructor in history, 1963-65; Michigan State University, East Lansing, instructor in American thought and language, 1967—. *Military service:* U.S. Navy, 1954-58. *Member:* American Historical Association, Society for the Study of Midwest Literature, Canadian Association for American Studies.

WRITINGS: McCarthyism: Twentieth-Century Witch Hunt (booklet), Steck, 1970; (contributor) E. D. Malpass, editor, *Personalities and Policies,* Texas Christian University Press, 1977; *Unequivocal Americanism: Right-Wing Novels in the Cold War Era,* Scarecrow, 1977. Contributor of articles and reviews to history and American studies journals, and to *Intellect.*

WORK IN PROGRESS: Studying Canadian right-wing movements and ideologies.

F

FABE, Maxene 1943-

PERSONAL: Born May 22, 1943, in Atlanta, Ga.; daughter of Robert (an artist) and Miriam (Timmer) Fabe. *Education:* Attended Earlham College, 1961-62; University of Cincinnati, B.A. (high honors), 1965; University of Pennsylvania, M.A., 1966. *Home:* 420 East 80th St., New York, N.Y. 10021. *Agent:* Elaine Markson Literary Agency, Inc., 44 Greenwich Ave., New York, N.Y. 10011. *Office:* 1 Bank St., New York, N.Y. 10014.

CAREER: Thomas Y. Crowell Co., New York City, publicist for children's books, 1968-70; taxicab driver in New York City, 1970-71; writer for horror comic books, 1971-72; Thomas Y. Crowell Co., publicist for children's books, 1972-76; free-lance writer, 1976—. Staff member of Miami University writers workshop, 1974.

WRITINGS: Death Rock (novel), Popular Library, 1972; *Beauty Millionaire: The Life of Helena Rubenstein*, Crowell, 1972; (contributor) Judy Fireman, editor, *The Television Book*, Workman Publishing, 1977; *Game Shows*, Doubleday, 1978. Contributor to magazines and newspapers, including *New Times, Mademoiselle, Village Voice, Creem, Penthouse*, and *Apartment Life.*

WORK IN PROGRESS: A second novel; a feminist psychology book.

SIDELIGHTS: Maxene Fabe writes: "Because I think we grow up too truncated from our childhoods, all my work tries to bridge that gap, whether by explaining how our 'lost' childhoods affect us adults, or by describing the fun things from childhood (games, for example) adults still cling to. In general, I think the best books and the best ideas can't be labeled adult or children's. The core of the best reaches the child in all of us."

* * *

FABER, Adele 1928-

PERSONAL: Born January 12, 1928, in New York, N.Y.; daughter of Morris (a furrier) and Betty (Kamay) Meyrowitz; married Leslie Faber (a guidance counselor), August 27, 1950; children: Carl, Joanna, Abram. *Education:* Queens College (now of the City University of New York), B.A., 1949; New York University, M.A., 1950. *Home:* 351 I.U. Willets Rd., Roslyn Heights, N.Y. 11577.

CAREER: New York School of Printing, New York, N.Y.,

teacher of speech, 1950-51; high school English teacher in Brooklyn, N.Y., 1952-58; Long Island University, C. W. Post College, Greenvale, N.Y., leader of parent workshops, 1975—. Workshop teacher at New School for Social Research, 1976. Lecturer and consultant; guest on national television and radio programs. *Awards, honors:* Christopher Award, 1975, for *Liberated Parents/Liberated Children.*

WRITINGS: (With Elaine Mazlish) *Liberated Parents/Liberated Children* (Book-of-the-Month Club selection), Grosset, 1974; (with Mazlish) *Breaking Barriers: A Workshop Series in Human Relations Skills for Teenagers*, Salvation Army, 1976.

Television scripts: "The Princess," ABC-TV, 1975; "Mr. Sad-Sack," ABC-TV, 1975; "You Can Live With Your Family" (three-part series), CBS-TV, 1976.

WORK IN PROGRESS: "Liberated Parents' Workshop," a tape presentation supplemented by workbooks, with Elaine Mazlish.

SIDELIGHTS: Adele Faber comments: "As a child I remember wincing at the ways adults spoke to children. It was generally accepted that if you loved your child it was alright to order him about, call him names, subject him to sarcasm, deny his feelings, and tell him what was wrong with him—loud and often. I knew exactly what Dr. Haim Ginott [she studied with him for ten years] meant when he said, 'The children . . . no more scratches on their souls.' Yet as a parent I soon discovered that being 'nice' was not enough. It was the search for another way to live with children that launched me into writing *Liberated Parents/Liberated Children* and my present work with parents and teachers. I'm never bored. The question of how people can communicate more honestly and helpfully remains eternally fascinating to me."

* * *

FABIAN, Robert (Honey) 1901-1978

January 31, 1901—June 14, 1978; British detective, journalist, and author. A former head of Scotland Yard's Flying Squad, Fabian was one of Britain's most famous sleuths. His cases served as the basis for a television series and numerous films. After retiring from the Yard, Fabian wrote a book about his exploits, *Fabian of the Yard*, and two best-selling detective novels. He also wrote crime feature stories for a chain of British newspapers. In 1939, Fabian received the King's Police Medal for dismantling a bomb placed by the Irish Republican Army in Piccadilly Circus. He died in Epsom, England. Obituaries and other sources: Robert Fabian, *Fabian of the Yard: An Intimate Record,* Naldrett Press, 1950; *Current Biography,* Wilson, 1954; Leonard Gribble, *Great Manhunters of the Yard,* Roy, 1968; *New York Times,* June 15, 1978; *Washington Post,* June 17, 1978; *Time,* June 26, 1978.

* * *

FADER, Shirley Sloan 1931-

PERSONAL: Born February 24, 1931, in Paterson, N.J.; daughter of Samuel Louis (a surgeon) and Miriam (a teacher; maiden name, Marcus) Sloan; married Seymour J. Fader (a professor), June 26, 1951; children: Susan Deborah, Steven Micah Kimhi. *Education:* University of Pennsylvania, B.S., 1952, M.S., 1953. *Home and office:* 377 McKinley Blvd., Paramus, N.J. 07652.

CAREER: Writer. *Member:* American Society of Journalists and Authors (national vice-president, 1976-77; member of national executive council, 1976-79), Authors Guild, Authors League of America, Women's Ink.

WRITINGS: The Princess Who Grew Down (juvenile), Lion Press, 1968; *From Kitchen to Career,* Stein & Day, 1978. Author of columns "People and You" and "Jobsmanship," in *Family Weekly,* 1971—.

WORK IN PROGRESS: Jobsmanship, essays collected from her columns.

* * *

FAHS, Sophia Blanche Lyon 1876-1978

1876—April 17, 1978; American Unitarian minister, educator, and author of children's books and religious texts. In her teaching and writings, Fahs tried to break away from didacticism and to emphasize the human side of Jesus. At the age of eighty-two, she was ordained a Unitarian minister. Fahs died in Hamilton, Ohio. Obituaries and other sources: *Religious Education,* November, 1976; *New York Times,* April 19, 1978.

* * *

FAIRBAIRN, Garry L. 1947-

PERSONAL: Born June 5, 1947, in Arcola, Saskatchewan, Canada; son of Clarence B. and Evangeline E. (Hurlbert) Fairbairn; married Lorna E. Bratvold, December 9, 1977. *Education:* Carleton University, B.A. (with honors), 1968, M.A., 1969; additional study at University of Manitoba. *Politics:* None. *Home:* 1039-2001 North Adams St., Arlington, Va. 22201. *Office:* Canadian Press, Room 600, 2021 K St. N.W., Washington, D.C. 20006.

CAREER/WRITINGS: Canadian Press, Ottawa, Ontario, reporter and editor in Ottawa, 1969, and 1971-73, photo editor in Montreal, Quebec, 1969-70, reporter and editor in Toronto, Ontario, 1970-71, correspondent in Regina, Saskatchewan, 1973-76, correspondent in Washington, D.C., 1976—. Notable assignments include coverage of the FLQ crisis in Quebec, 1970; the U.S. presidential campaign of 1976; and numerous federal and provincial elections. Editor, Saskatchewan Press Club magazine, 1975. *Member:* National Press Club (U.S.), National Historical Society (U.S.), U.S. Naval Institute, Foreign Correspondents Association, Saskatchewan Journalists Association (membership secretary, 1975, president, 1976).

SIDELIGHTS: Fairbairn told *CA:* "Being a Canadian correspondent in Washington often produces the best of both worlds. Sources treat you as a fellow American but also realize your stories are unlikely to stir up political trouble for them in the United States. The advantages, however, end at the level of elected politicians who realize that giving you an interview gains them no votes. The foreign correspondent's job in Washington is made incomparably easier by the openness of the bureaucracy. U.S. reporters may have their complaints about bureaucratic pronouncements, but even an aide to Nixon would hesitate to adopt the extreme zippered-lip style of Canadian civil servants."

AVOCATIONAL INTERESTS: Military/diplomatic history, science fiction, dining, motorcycling, conflict simulations.

BIOGRAPHICAL/CRITICAL SOURCES: Saskatchewan Journalist, October, 1976.

* * *

FALLACI, Oriana 1930-

PERSONAL: Born June 29, 1930, in Florence, Italy; daughter of Edoardo (a cabinet maker and politician) and Tosca (Cantini) Fallaci; lived with Alexandros Panagulis (a political activist; died May 1, 1976). *Education:* Attended University of Florence. *Politics:* Liberal socialist. *Religion:* None. *Office:* c/o Rizzoli Editore Corp., 712 Fifth Ave., New York, N.Y. 10019.

CAREER: Writer. Special correspondent for *Europeo* (Italian magazine) since 1950's; formerly reporter for *Epoca* (Italian magazine). Has interviewed internationally known figures, including Nguyen Cao Ky, Yasir Arafat, the Shah of Iran, Henry Kissinger, Walter Cronkite, Indira Gandhi, Golda Meir, Nguyen Van Thieu, Ali Bhutto, and Willy Brandt. *Awards, honors:* Has twice received St. Vincent prize for journalism; Bancarella Prize, 1971, for *Nothing and So Be It;* Doctorate in Letters honoris causa from Columbia College (Chicago).

WRITINGS: I sette peccati di Hollywood (title means "The Seven Sins of Hollywood"), preface by Orson Welles, Onganesi (Milan), 1958; *Il sesso inutile: Viaggio intorno all donna,* Rizzoli (Milan), 1961, translation by Pamela Swinglehurst published as *The Useless Sex,* Horizon Press, 1964; *Penelope alla guerra* (novel), Rizzoli, 1962, translation by Swinglehurst published as *Penelope at War,* Joseph, 1966; *Gli antipatici,* Rizzoli, 1963, translation by Swinglehurst published in England as *Limelighters,* Joseph, 1967, published as *The Egotists: Sixteen Surprising Interviews,* Regnery, 1968; *Se il sole muore,* Rizzoli, 1965, translation by Swinglehurst published as *If the Sun Dies,* Atheneum, 1966; *Niente a cosi sia* (on Vietnam), Rizzoli, 1969, translation by Isabel Quigly published as *Nothing, and So Be It,* Doubleday, 1972; *Quel giorno sulla Luna,* Rizzoli, 1970; *Intervista con la Storia,* Rizzoli, 1974, translation by John Shepley published as *Interview With History,* Liveright, 1976; *Lettera a un bambino mai nato,* Rizzoli, 1975, translation by Shepley published as *Letter to a Child Never Born,* Simon & Schuster, 1976.

Contributor of numerous articles to periodicals throughout the world, including *New Republic, New York Times Magazine, Life, McCall's, La Nouvelle Observateur,* and *La Gaceta Illustrada.*

WORK IN PROGRESS: A long novel.

SIDELIGHTS: "I do not feel myself to be, nor will I ever succeed in feeling like, a cold recorder of what I see and hear. On every professional experience I leave shreds of my heart and soul; and I participate in what I see or hear as though the matter concerned me personally and were one on which I ought to take a stand (in fact I always take one, based on a specific moral choice)," Fallaci stated in the preface to *Interview With History.*

But while Fallaci's morality has seldom been questioned (Josiah Bunting III, in fact, has called her "a woman of transcendant moral courage"), her interviewing techniques are highly controversial. According to Francine du Plessix Gray, Fallaci combines "the psychological insight of a great novelist and the irreverence of a bratty quiz kid." Known for her abrasive interviewing tactics, Fallaci has been described as a practitioner of "surgical journalism." She herself admitted that she "make(s) psychological violence" on her interview subjects. When a subject refuses to cooperate with Fallaci, he becomes, commented David Sanford, "a bastard, a fascist, an idiot."

Fallaci denies her reputation as a brutal interrogator. She told Sally Moore that Americans invented that abrasive character. "What I am—forgive an act of pride—is courageous," Fallaci explained. "Most of our colleagues don't have the guts to ask the right questions. I asked Thieu, 'How corrupt are you?'"

The objectivity that other journalists strive for is meaningless to Fallaci. She has said that she hates the term objectivity: she prefers to use the words "honest" and "correct" when describing her reportage. Each of her interviews, she told Jordan Bonfante, "is a portrait of myself. They are a strange mixture of my ideas, my temperament, my patience, all of these driving the questions."

Although Ted Morgan, for one, has complained that Fallaci "wants to be more than a brilliant interviewer, she wants to be an avenging angel," Fallaci defends her unique approach to journalism on the grounds that she is not simply a journalist but a historian as well. She told Bonfante: "A journalist lives history in the best of ways, that is in the moment that history takes place. He lives history, he touches history with his hands, he looks at it with his eyes, he listens to it with his ears." To Jonathan Cott, she explained: "I am the judge. I am the one who decides. Listen: if I am a painter and I do your portrait, have I or haven't I the right to paint you as I want?"

Fallaci's subjects are chosen because of their importance to her. She told *CA:* "The travel to the moon was so important for me that I wrote a book on it (*If the Sun Dies*); the Vietnam war marked me so deeply that I wrote a book about it (*Nothing and So Be It*); politics is so important to me, I am so involved in it (I always was, since a teenager) that I wrote a book of 'politics' in my opinion (*Interview With History*); feminism and the abortion issue marked me so much that from them I got inspired to write my book, *Letter to a Child Never Born.*"

Power is what most fascinates Fallaci. She told Moore that those in powerful positions intrigue her because they "rule our lives, command us, decide if we live or die, in freedom or in tyranny." No holds are barred in a Fallaci interview with a powerful person. Her interview with Henry Kissinger in 1972 may be a case in point. "Why I agreed to it, I'll never know," Kissinger said afterwards. In the now famous interview, Kissinger described himself as the lone cowboy of American foreign policy, for which he was ridiculed by the press and the public. According to Fallaci, "There is only one person who is guilty of that interview, and it is him (Kissinger). Because he said what he said and he knows it. He knows that a tape exists and he said those words. So he should blame himself and nobody else."

Fallaci is not always antipathetic to her subjects. Although Kissinger, Robert Kennedy, and the Shah of Iran (among others), did not win her favor, Fallaci's favorite interview subjects include Golda Meir, Indira Gandhi, and Willy Brandt. Tapes of many of Fallaci's interviews are housed at the Boston University Library.

Fallaci discussed major influences on her work with *CA*. She wrote: "Born in an antifascist family, I was always involved in politics on the opposition side. (One grandfather was an anarchist, one grandfather was with Mazzini.) I was a child of the resistence against the Nazis and Fascists (took part in it as a little Vietcong). I went to work in a newspaper as a reporter at the age of sixteen when women were extremely rare in journalism and were contributors rather than reporters. I always wanted to be a writer, was always politically engaged. The final fact that marked my life (and even work) was my union with the poet and Greek Resistance leader Alexandros Panagulis, who was condemned to death in 1968 and was killed by political assassination on May 1st, 1976. We lived together for three years, that is from the moment he left prison until he died. It was a great love."

BIOGRAPHICAL/CRITICAL SOURCES: New York Times Book Review, February 5, 1967, February 13, 1977; *Esquire,* November, 1968, June, 1975; *Life,* February 21, 1969; *Washington Post,* February 23, 1972, March 13, 1972, May 18, 1976; *New York Times,* January 25, 1973; *Time,* October 20, 1975; *Rolling Stone,* June 17, 1976; *New Yorker,* February 21, 1977; *People,* March 14, 1977; *New York,* May 22, 1978.

*   *   *

FALLON, Jack
    See FALLON, John W(illiam)

*   *   *

FALLON, John W(illiam) 1924-
    (Jack Fallon)

PERSONAL: Born December 4, 1924, in Lawrence, Mass.; son of John W. and Harriet W. (Welch) Fallon; married Margaret H. Ford (a chemist), June 9, 1951; children: John, Dan, Mary (Mrs. William Choquette), Matthew, Julie, Margaret. *Education:* U.S. Naval Academy, B.S., 1947; Boston University, M.A., 1951. *Politics:* Democrat. *Religion:* Roman Catholic. *Home:* 96 North Rd., Chelmsford, Mass. 01824. *Office:* Blue Cross of Massachusetts, 100 Summer St., Boston, Mass.

CAREER: Sanders Associates, Inc., Nashua, N.H., publications manager, 1953-59; Sylvania Electronic Systems, Waltham, Mass., publications manager, 1959-68; EG & G Inc., Bedford, Mass., publications manager, 1968-69; Sanders Associates, Inc., publications manager, 1969-71; TME/JMR Corps, Salem, N.H., director of corporate information, 1971-74; Blue Cross of Massachusetts, Boston, writer for technical publications, 1974—. Member of summer faculty at Massachusetts Institute of Technology; instructor for Civil Service Commission, colleges, and government agencies. *Military service:* U.S. Army Air Forces, aviation cadet, 1943-44. U.S. Navy, 1944-50, 1951-53; became lieutenant senior grade. *Member:* Outdoor Writers Association, Outdoor Writers Association of America (New England).

WRITINGS—Under name Jack Fallon: *Teaching Your*

Children to Fish, Winchester Press, 1974; *All About Surf Fishing,* Winchester Press, 1975. Author of monthly features in *Soundings, Fisherman's Voice,* and *New Hampshire Outdoorsman.*

WORK IN PROGRESS: Outdoor writing, especially on marine recreation in the Northeast; outdoor photography and writing for product promotion and public relations.

SIDELIGHTS: Fallon writes: "My books are vehicles for sharing the preeminent privilege of incendiary sunrises, incandescent sunsets, stormy days, and starry nights. I wouldn't swap places with any person on this planet, past, present, or future."

* * *

FALLS, Joe 1928-

PERSONAL: Born May 2, 1928, in New York, N.Y.; son of Edward (a policeman) and Anna (Zincak) Falls; married Rose Gentile (divorced December 19, 1973); married Mary Jane Erdei (a secretary), October 10, 1975; children: Robert, Kathleen, Susan, Janet, Michael. *Religion:* Roman Catholic. *Home:* 8115 Deerwood Rd., Clarkston, Mich. 48016. *Office: Detroit Free Press,* 321 West Lafayette, Detroit, Mich. 48231.

CAREER: Associated Press, New York, N.Y., copy boy, 1946-51, sports writer, 1951-53; Associated Press, Detroit, Mich., sports editor, 1953-56; *Detroit Times,* Detroit, baseball writer, 1956-60; *Detroit Free Press,* Detroit, baseball writer, 1960-65, sports editor and author of column, 1966—. Member of committee of Oakland County Community for Retarded Citizens. *Awards, honors:* Named Michigan sports writer of the year by National Sportscasters and Sports Writers Association seven times; named runnerup for national sports writer of the year five times.

WRITINGS: Man in Motion (biography of Bo Schembechler), School-Tech Press, 1973; *The Detroit Tigers,* Macmillan, 1975; *The Boston Marathon,* Macmillan, 1977. Author of a column in *Sporting News.*

* * *

FANNING, Robbie 1947-

PERSONAL: Born January 30, 1947, in West Lafayette, Ind.; daughter of J. Edwin (a sociologist) and Roberta (a home economist; maiden name, Edwards) Losey; married Anthony David John Fanning (a writer), 1969; children: Kali Koala. *Education:* Attended Knox College, 1964-66; University of the State of New York in Albany, B.S., 1978. *Residence:* Menlo Park, Calif. *Agent:* Elyse Sommer, Inc., Box E, 962 Allen Lane, Woodmere, N.Y. 11598. *Office:* P.O. Box 2634, Menlo Park, Calif. 94025.

CAREER: Lecturer and teacher at short-term workshops on needlework and self-publishing all over the United States, 1974—. Teacher of machine and ethnic embroidery, running for families, photography for textiles, comic book art, cartooning, and self-publishing. Volunteer worker in children's department of local public library, and previously at Peninsula Conservation Center. *Member:* International Guild of Craft Journalists, Authors, and Photographers, National Standards Council, Embroiderers Guild of America, American Crafts Council, Committee of Small Magazine Editors and Publishers, Center for the History of American Needlework (member of advisory council), California Writers, California Crafts Museum (member of board of directors), Peninsula Stitchery Guild (chairwoman, 1974).

WRITINGS: Decorative Machine Stitchery, Butterick,

1976; (with husband, Tony Fanning) *Here and Now Stitchery* (on ethnic embroidery), Butterick, 1978; (with T. Fanning) *Keep Running,* Simon & Schuster, 1978. Author of weekly column "Stitches," in *Country Almanac.* Contributor to national magazines and newspapers, including *Better Homes and Gardens, Good Housekeeping Needlecraft, California Living, Women's Almanac,* and *Consumer's Gazette.* Editor and publisher of *Open Chain.*

WORK IN PROGRESS: A book on bicycling; a juvenile novel; a book on time management; a detective novel; a book on machine quilting; a self-published textile almanac; a biography of Morris DeCamp Crawford, completion expected in 1980.

SIDELIGHTS: Robbie Fanning writes: "As a writer, I love to communicate clearly and simply my personal enthusiasms, to act as a catalyst between people and ideas, and then to listen and watch the rest of the world. Our family is interested in living a full, meaningful, joyful life. The three of us are getting ready for a cross-country bike trip which is taking all our time. As for other interests, I can only say that a librarian once asked us to check off our reading interests— after checking every category she had, we added one more: life."

* * *

FANTINI, Mario D.

PERSONAL: Born in Philadelphia, Pa. *Education:* Temple University, B.S., 1957, M.A., 1958; Harvard University, C.A.G.S., 1960, Ed.D., 1961. *Office:* School of Education, University of Massachusetts, Amherst, Mass. 01003.

CAREER: Worked as an elementary school teacher, high school teacher, and teacher of mentally retarded and emotionally disturbed children; Syracuse University, Syracuse, N.Y., senior research associate, and director of urban teacher preparation program, school social work program, and scholastic rehabilitation program for emotionally disturbed children, 1962-64; Ford Foundation, New York, N.Y., program officer, beginning 1965; State University of New York at New Paltz, project director of grant to establish regional cooperation, beginning 1972, faculty exchange scholar, beginning 1974; currently professor and dean of education at University of Massachusetts, Amherst. Adjunct professor at Antioch College, Opne University, Walden University, and Inter-American University of Puerto Rico; lecturer at Harvard University and Yale University; member of advisory board at University of San Francisco and Kent State University. Member of National Advisory Council of Supplementary Centers and Services, 1968; adjunct member of National Commission on Resources for Youth. Demonstration teacher in public schools in Philadelphia, Pa.; staff director of special projects for Syracuse public schools. Has testified before Koerner Commission on Civil Disorders; guest on television and radio programs; consultant to Institute for the Advancement of Urban Education and National Committee for Citizens in Education. *Member:* American Association of School Administrators, Association for Supervision and Curriculum Development, Phi Delta Kappa.

WRITINGS: (With Gerald Weinstein) *Toward a Contact Curriculum,* Anti-Defamation League, B'nai B'rith, 1967; *Taking Advantage of the Disadvantaged* (monograph), Ford Foundation, 1967; *Alternatives for Urban School Reform* (monograph), Ford Foundation, 1968; (with Weinstein) *The Disadvantaged: Challenge to Education,* Harper, 1968; (with Weinstein) *Making Urban Schools Work,* Holt, 1968;

(with Milton A. Young) *Designing Education for Tomorrow's Cities,* Holt, 1968.

(With Marilyn Gittell and Richard Magat) *Community Control and the Urban School,* Praeger, 1970; (with Weinstein) *Toward Humanistic Education: A Curriculum of Affect,* Praeger, 1970; (with Gittell) *Decentralization: Achieving Reform,* Praeger, 1973; *Public Schools of Choice: A Plan for the Reform of American Education,* Simon & Schuster, 1974; *What's Best for the Children?: Resolving the Power Struggle Between Parents and Teachers,* Doubleday, 1974; *Alternative Education: A Source Book for Parents, Teachers, Students, and Administrators,* Doubleday, 1976. Also co-editor of *Alternative Education: Resources for Improving Education.*

Contributor: Arthur B. Shostak, editor, *Sociology in Action,* Dorsey, 1960; Lester and Olui Crow, editors, *Mental Hygiene for Teachers,* Macmillan, 1963; *Readings in the Methods of Education,* Odyssey, 1964; A. Harry Passow, editor, *Teaching and Learning in Depressed Areas,* Teachers College Press, 1966; (author of foreword) Marilyn Gittell, *Participants and Participation,* Praeger, 1967; Alvin Taffler, editor, *The Schoolhouse in the City,* Praeger, 1968; (author of foreword) Naomi Levine, *The School Crisis,* Popular Library, 1969; Troy V. McKelvey and Austin D. Swanson, editors, *Urban School Administration,* Sage Publications, 1969; Gittell and Alan G. Hevesi, editors, *The Politics of Urban Education,* Praeger, 1969; Ronald and Beatrice Gross, editors, *Radical School Reform,* Simon & Schuster, 1969.

Schools for the Seventies, Center for the Study of Instruction, National Education Association, 1970; (author of foreword) Francesco Cordasco, Maurie Hillson, and Henry A. Bullock, editors, *The School in the Social Order: A Sociological Introduction to Educational Understanding,* International Textbook Co., 1970; Richard L. Hart and J. Galen Saylor, editors, *Student Unrest: Threat or Promise?,* Association for Supervision and Curriculum Development, 1970; Arthur W. Foshay, editor, *The Professional as an Educator,* Teachers College Press, 1970; J. A. Lauwerys and D. G. Scanlon, editors, *The World Yearbook of Education, 1970: Education in Cities,* Harcourt, 1970; Louis J. Rubin, editor, *Improving In-Service Education,* Allyn & Bacon, 1971; Richard B. Heidenreich, editor, *Urban Education,* College Readings, Inc., 1971; Roy P. Fairfield, editor, *Humanistic Frontiers in American Education,* Prentice-Hall, 1971; (author of preface) Dennis L. Roberts II, editor, *Planning Urban Education,* Educational Technology Publications, 1972; (author of foreword) James Haskins, *Black Manifesto for Education,* Morrow, 1973.

Francis A. J. Ianni, editor, *Conflict and Change in Education,* Scott, Foresman, 1974; Harvey F. Clarizio, editor, *Contemporary Issues in Educational Psychology,* Allyn & Bacon, 2nd edition (Fantini was not included in 1st edition), 1974; C. Glenn Hass and other editors, *Readings in Curriculum,* Allyn & Bacon, 3rd edition (Fantini was not included in earlier editions), in press; Malcolm Provus, editor, *Trainers of Teacher Trainers,* University Press of Virginia, in press; William Cave and Mark Chesler, editors, *Sociology of Education,* Macmillan, in press; *Cities, Communities, and the Young,* Routledge & Kegan Paul, in press; John Johansen and other editors, *American Education,* W. C. Brown, 2nd edition (Fantini was not included in 1st edition), in press; Ianni, editor, *Education and Social Problems,* Scott Foresman, in press; Edmund C. Short, editor, *Contemporary Thought on Public School Curriculum Leadership,* W. C. Brown, in press. Also contributor to *The Formative Process: Early Childhood Education, Challenge and Choice in American Education, Children of the Cities, The Social Cultural Foundations of Education, Development in Adolescence,* and *Contemporary Adolescence: Readings.*

Contributor to *World Book Encyclopedia,* and of articles and reviews to newspapers, education journals, and popular magazines, including *Saturday Review.* Member of editorial board of *Principal.*

*   *   *

FARADAY, Ann 1935-

PERSONAL: Born in 1935 of British parents; married John Wren-Lewis (an author and theologian); children: Fiona Claire. *Education:* University College, London, B.Sc., 1964, Ph.D., 1969. *Office:* Ragged Mountain Center for Dream Research, Virginia.

CAREER: Full-time author and lecturer. Founder and director of Ragged Mountain Center for Dream Research. *Member:* Association for Humanistic Psychology.

WRITINGS: Dream Power, Coward McCann, 1972; *The Dream Game,* Harper, 1974.

WORK IN PROGRESS: A third book.

BIOGRAPHICAL/CRITICAL SOURCES: Washington Post, March 28, 1972; *New York Post,* April 8, 1972; *Chicago Tribune,* May 23, 1972; *Los Angeles Times,* June 25, 1972; *San Francisco Sunday Examiner and Chronicle,* September 10, 1972, November 24, 1974; *Los Angeles Free Press,* September 15, 1972; *Reader's Digest,* September, 1972, March, 1975; *Tropic* (Sunday magazine of *Miami Herald*), April 29, 1973; *McCall's,* October, 1974; *Boston Globe,* December 1, 1974; *Los Angeles Herald-Examiner,* December 8, 1974; *Psychology Today,* February, 1975; *Detroit Free Press,* May 3, 1976.

*   *   *

FARHI, Moris 1935-

PERSONAL: Born July 5, 1935, in Ankara, Turkey; son of Hayim Daniel (a businessman) and Palomba (Koenka) Farhi; married Monique Hassid, April 14, 1957 (divorced, 1975). *Education:* American College, Istanbul, B.A., 1954; Royal Academy of Dramatic Arts, diploma, 1956. *Politics:* Socialist. *Religion:* Jewish. *Home:* 24 Heathgate, London NW11 7AN, England. *Agent:* A. D. Peters Ltd., 10 Buckingham St.,London WC2N 6BV, England.

CAREER: Actor in plays, films, and television. *Member:* British Actors Equity, Crime Writers Association, Writers Guild, Society of Authors.

WRITINGS: "From the Ashes of Thebes" (play), first produced in New York at the Mercury Theatre, 1969; *The Pleasure of Your Death,* Constable, 1972.

Also author of a filmscript, "The Primitives," Borjer/Rank, 1960; and numerous teleplays, including "From the Ashes," 1969.

WORK IN PROGRESS: The Last of Days, an epic novel; *Journey Through the Wilderness,* a novel; *Jesus and Judas,* a "reconstruction and reinterpretation"; teleplays.

SIDELIGHTS: Farhi told *CA:* "My work centers on the theme of 'man's search for sanctity.' My major influence has been William Saroyan. My viewpoint is that man, much as he aspires to social morality, can never achieve it." Farhi speaks Turkish, French, Spanish, Italian, and English. *Avocational interests:* Theology, travel, sports, politics, and Israel.

FARR, Dorothy M(ary) 1905-

PERSONAL: Born May 18, 1905, in Stourbridge, England; daughter of Arthur William (an accountant) and Elizabeth (Peters) Farr. Education: University of Birmingham, B.A. (honors), 1926; University of London, diploma, 1927; University of Leeds, Ph.D., 1948. Politics: Conservative. Religion: Church of England. Home: Greenways, 100 Norton Rd., Stourbridge, West Midlands D48 2A9, England.

CAREER: Teacher of English and history at girls' high school in Stourbridge, England, 1929-30, and English at girls' high school in Manchester, England, 1930-34; City of Leeds College of Education, Leeds, England, 1934-51, began as lecturer, became senior lecturer in English; City of Liverpool College of Education, Liverpool, England, principal, 1951-65; free-lance writer, 1965—. Member of Dudley Family Practitioner Committee, 1974. Member: English Association, Soroptimist International (Stourbridge).

WRITINGS: Thomas Middleton and the Drama of Realism, Oliver & Boyd, 1973. Contributor to Modern Language Review.

WORK IN PROGRESS: John Ford and the Caroline Theatre; a study of dominant imagery and its dramatic function in Shakespeare's Jacobean tragedies.

SIDELIGHTS: Dorothy Farr writes: "My aim in literary research has been to take a new look at some of the major Jacobean and Caroline dramatists in whom, in particular Middleton and Ford, the English theatre has latterly shown a revival of interest. I am convinced that the contemporary stage can learn a great deal from their work and stage management.

"Drama, verse speaking, and the theatre have always been among my main interests and I have had a good deal of experience as an amateur producer. As a trained speaker I believe that the spoken word has a major place in education at all levels, and particularly in higher education."

AVOCATIONAL INTERESTS: Music (playing violin), going to concerts.

*   *   *

FAST, Jonathan David 1948-

PERSONAL: Born April 13, 1948, in New York, N.Y.; son of Howard (a writer) and Bette (Cohen) Fast. Education: Attended Princeton University, 1966-68; Sarah Lawrence College, B.A., 1970; also attended University of California, Berkeley, 1970. Religion: "Zen Judist." Residence: Weston, Conn. Agent: Sterling Lord Agency, Inc., 660 Madison Ave., New York, N.Y. 10021.

CAREER: Composer, 1961—; writer, 1972—. Member: Writer's Guild (West).

WRITINGS: The Secrets of Synchronicity (novel), New American Library, 1977; Mortal Gods (novel), Harper, 1978.

Film scripts: "Two Missionaries"; "The Thrill Show Hero"; "Love Al Dente"; "Prisoner of Space" (adaptation of Secrets of Synchronicity), CBS Television.

WORK IN PROGRESS: A novel, The Sacrifice; "I have a large telescope and am trying to locate all the 'Messier' objects, but it is difficult because it rains so much in Connecticut."

SIDELIGHTS: Fast writes: "In my books I try primarily to entertain, secondarily to put across my world view—namely that life is an illusion, that we are sleepwalkers, that the matters we suffer and weep over are inconsequential in the cosmic scheme. I believe that man has the potential of sanity, although frankly at times I doubt it."

*   *   *

FATEMI, Nasrollah S(aifpour) 1910-

PERSONAL: Born June 15, 1910, in Iran; came to the United States in 1946, naturalized citizen, 1960; son of Saifulama (a land owner) and Touba Fatemi; married Shayesteh Ostowar, May 10, 1932; children: Faramarz S., Fariborz S., Farivar S. Education: Stuart Memorial College, B.A. (honors), 1932; Columbia University, M.A., 1949; New School for Social Research, Ph.D., 1954. Religion: Moslem. Home: 47 Chestnut Ridge Rd., Saddle River, N.J. 07458. Office: Graduate Institute for International Studies, Fairleigh Dickinson University, Teaneck, N.J. 07666.

CAREER: Isfahan (daily newspaper), Tehran, Iran, editor and publisher, 1932-46; Province of Isfaham, Iran, member of legislative council, 1933-39, vice-president of council, 1936-39; mayor of Shirez, Iran, 1939-41; governor-general of Fars Province, Iran, 1941-43; member of Iranian Parliament (and of its foreign relations committee), 1943-47; supervisor of Iranian students in United States, 1948-49; lecturer at Asia Institute, 1949; economic and political adviser to the permanent delegation from Iran to the United Nations, 1949-53; Princeton University, Princeton, N.J., professor of political science, 1950-55; Iranian delegate to the United Nations, 1952-53; Fairleigh Dickinson University, Teaneck, N.J., professor of social science, 1955—, distinguished professor of international affairs, 1971—, chairman of department of political science, 1960-65, dean of Graduate School, 1965-70, director of Graduate Institute for International Studies, 1971—. Chairman of executive committee of Inter-University Centre (Dubrovnik, Yugoslavia). Represented Iran at UNESCO national conference, 1948, and International Congress of Americanists, 1949.

MEMBER: International Association of University Presidents (member of executive committee; member of steering committee of North America Council), Royal Academy of Arts and Sciences (fellow). Awards, honors: Special award from UNESCO Sufi Book Week, 1972, for the monograph Sufism: Message of Brotherhood, Harmony, and Hope; LL.D. from Kyung Hee University, 1973; leadership citation from International Association of University Presidents, 1975.

WRITINGS: A Diplomatic History of Persia, Whittiers Books, 1951; Oil Diplomacy, Russell, 1954; (with Thibaut de Saint Phalle) The Dollar Crisis, Fairleigh Dickinson University Press, 1964; Problems of Balance of Payments and Trade, Fairleigh Dickinson University Associated University Press, 1974; Multinational Corporations, A. S. Barnes, 1975, 2nd edition, 1976; Sufism: Message of Brotherhood, Harmony, and Hope (monograph), A. S. Barnes, 1976. Contributor to professional journals and newspapers in English and Persian.

WORK IN PROGRESS: Research on multinational corporations and international banking.

*   *   *

FATIGATI, (Frances) Evelyn 1948-

PERSONAL: Born February 4, 1948, in Washington, Mo.; daughter of Alfred Herbert (a factory owner) and Frances Philips (Munroe) de Buhr; married Richard Francis Fatigati (a journalist), November 15, 1974. Education: Attended

Mills College, 1966-67; University of Iowa, B.A., 1971. *Home:* 853 East State St., Mason City, Iowa 50401.

CAREER: Free-lance writer, 1975—.

WRITINGS: Bzzz: A Beekeeper's Primer, Rodale Press, 1976; *Garden on Greenway Street* (fiction), Rodale Press, 1977.

WORK IN PROGRESS: A Stitch in Time, "a simple approach to sewing practical, comfortable clothes using geometric shapes—squares, rectangles, circles—demonstrating that sewing can be logical and fun, a puzzle rather than a puzzlement."

SIDELIGHTS: Evelyn Fatigati comments: "I allow myself to believe that my writing is inspired by environmentally conscionable ideals and by the desire to present loving characters as positive role models for readers. But the truth is that writing is very hard work, and I will tackle one hundred unappealing tasks before I make myself sit down at the typewriter. Motivation for me, comes in envisioning the end result, in the reward of getting the job done."

* * *

FAUROT, Albert 1914-

PERSONAL: Born March 7, 1914, in Lamar, Mo.; son of Ira N. (a clergyman) and Grace (Hiatt) Faurot. *Education:* Park College, A.B., 1936; Oberlin College, M.A., 1940; studied piano in London, England, 1939; private studies with Frank Mannheimer. *Religion:* Presbyterian. *Office:* Silliman University, Dumaguete City, Philippines 6501.

CAREER: Foochow College, Foochow, China, member of faculty, 1936-39; Hwa Nan College, Foochow, China, member of faculty, 1940-49; Kobe College, Kobe, Japan, member of faculty, 1950-52; Silliman University, Dumaguete City, Philippines, member of faculty, 1952—. *Awards, honors:* Ford Foundation writing grants, 1967, 1970, 1974; bronze plaque from U.S. Embassy, 1976, for service to American music.

WRITINGS: Culture Currents of the World, Silliman University Press, 1967; *Culture Currents of World Art,* New Day Publishers, 1974; *Concert Piano Repertoire,* Scarecrow, 1974; (with Frederic Chang) *Team Piano Repertoire,* Scarecrow, 1976; *Prayers of Great Men,* New Day Publishers, 1976; (with Isabel Vista) *Culture Currents of World Music,* New Day Publishers, 1977. Contributor of poems and articles to music journals.

WORK IN PROGRESS: Some Things I Finally Figured Out (tentative title), memoirs of his life in Asia.

SIDELIGHTS: Faurot writes: "My deepest interests are in music, art, culture, religion, and my books are an attempt to share my enthusiasm with students and others. *Concert Piano Repertoire* captures in print the comments on piano music which accompany my lecture recitals. The series called 'Culture Currents' traces the Orient-Occident exchanges and influences that I have observed in forty years of life in Asia."

* * *

FEATHERSTONE, D.
See WARREN, David

* * *

FEENEY, Leonard 1897-1978

February 15, 1897—January 30, 1978; American Roman Catholic priest and author. Feeney, a Jesuit, was dismissed

from that society and also was excommunicated in 1953 because he preached that salvation could not be obtained outside the Catholic Church. However, in 1972, Pope Paul VI removed the issue of excommunication. Feeney was the spiritual director of a lay organization for students near Harvard University, and later formed a religious order called "The Slaves of the Immaculate Heart of Mary." He was the author of numerous books on theological subjects. Feeney died in Massachusetts. Obituaries and other sources: *The Authors and Writer's Who's Who,* 6th edition, Burke's Peerage, 1971; *The Writers Directory, 1976-78,* St. Martin's, 1976; *New York Times,* February 1, 1978; *Washington Post,* February 3, 1978.

* * *

FELBER, Stanley B. 1932-

PERSONAL: Born March 17, 1932, in New York, N.Y.; son of Jack (a pattern maker) and Lillian Felber; married Estelle Sherman (a teacher), April 9, 1960; children: Michael, Rachel. *Education:* Brooklyn College (now of the City University of New York), B.A., 1953; University of Wisconsin, Milwaukee, M.S., 1964; also attended New York University, University of Wisconsin, Madison, and Hunter College of the City University of New York. *Home:* 9026 North Iroquois Rd., Milwaukee, Wis. 53217. *Office:* Department of English, Milwaukee Area Technical College, 1015 North Sixth St., Milwaukee, Wis. 53203.

CAREER: High school English teacher in Brooklyn, N.Y., 1957-59; Milwaukee Area Technical College, Milwaukee, Wis., instructor in English, 1962—, chairman of department, 1966-74, associate dean, 1976—. *Military service:* U.S. Army, 1953-55. *Member:* National Council of Teachers of English, Council for Occupational Education, American Vocational Association, Wisconsin Association for Vocational and Adult Education.

WRITINGS: (With Arthur Koch) *What Did You Say? A Guide to Oral and Written Communication,* Prentice-Hall, 1973, revised edition published as *What Did You Say? (Again): A Guide to Effective Communication,* 1978. Contributor to English and education journals.

SIDELIGHTS: Felber comments: "My primary professional concern—improving communication skills—is reflected in my careers in teaching, writing, and educational administration." *Avocational interests:* Travel (Spain, England), photography.

* * *

FENADY, Andrew 1928-

PERSONAL: Born October 4, 1928, in Toledo, Ohio. *Education:* Attended University of Toledo, 1946-50. *Office:* Fenady Associates, 249 North Larchmont Blvd., Los Angeles, Calif. 90004.

CAREER: Fenady Associates, Los Angeles, Calif., founder and independent producer of motion pictures, including "Stakeout on Dope Street," 1958, "The Young Captives," 1959, "Ride Beyond Vengeance," 1966, and "Chisum," 1970. Has also worked as a screenwriter, actor, television producer.

WRITINGS: The Man With Bogart's Face, Regnery, 1977.

Also author of screenplays, including "Stakeout on Dope Street," Warner Bros., 1958, "The Young Captives," Paramount, 1959, "Ride Beyond Vengeance," Columbia, 1966, "Hondo and the Apaches," Metro-Goldwyn-Mayer, 1967, and "Chisum," Warner Bros., 1970. Contributor of scripts to television series, including "The Rebel," "Branded," "Hondo," and "Mission: Impossible."

BIOGRAPHICAL/CRITICAL SOURCES: New York Times Herald Tribune, April 24, 1958; *New York Times,* April 24, 1958, September 29, 1966, July 30, 1970; *Variety,* April 27, 1966.*

* * *

FENELON, Fania 1918-

PERSONAL: Given name, Fania Goldstein; born September 2, 1918, in Paris, France; daughter of Jules (an engineer) and Marie (Bernier) Goldstein; divorced. *Education:* Attended Paris Conservatory of Music, 1934. *Home:* "Les Irlandais," Batiment B, Esc. 4, 94110 Arcueil, France. *Agent:* Opera Mundi, 100 Ave. Raymond Poincare, 75016 Paris, France.

CAREER: Professional singer; teacher of piano and voice. *Wartime service:* Member of the French Resistance, 1940-43; prisoner at Auschwitz, 1943-45. *Awards, honors:* First prize in piano from Paris Conservatory of Music, 1934; Legion of Honor.

WRITINGS: (With Marcelle Routier) *Sursis pour l'orchestre,* Stock, 1976, translation published as *Playing for Time,* Atheneum, 1977 (published in England as *Musicians of Auschwitz,* M. Joseph, 1977).

WORK IN PROGRESS: A second book.

SIDELIGHTS: Fania Fenelon told *CA:* "My book bears witness of my experience as an inmate of a German concentration camp, but from the viewpoint of a musician who lived in special conditions (we had individual beds, a shower every day, comparatively clean clothes, and heat). But we shared the same hunger as all the inmates in the camp. As the Women's Orchestra, we had to play music seventeen hours a day—gay, light music and marching music—while our eyes witnessed the marching of thousands of people to the gas chambers and ovens."

In an interview published in the *Washington Post,* Fenelon continued: "I have never felt guilty, never. Guilt is something one feels when you have a choice. But I had no choice. I can't feel guilty because I survived. And if anything, the orchestra survived because of me, because, for instance, I could orchestrate, without that they might have been disbanded. And even then, we could have been killed any minute."

Asked why she waited so long before sharing her story, she replied: "Because, I first wanted to have a life and I have had a very interesting life. And because I never have felt so acutely that Nazism is coming back, and I wanted to tell my story, to put a drop in that big ocean which is fascism."

BIOGRAPHICAL/CRITICAL SOURCES: Paris Match, April 24, 1976; *New York Times,* January 7, 1978; *Washington Post,* March 3, 1978.

* * *

FENTON, Mildred Adams 1899-

PERSONAL: Born in 1899, near West Branch, Iowa; married Carroll Lane Fenton (an author and illustrator), 1921 (died November 16, 1969). *Education:* Attended University of Iowa and University of Chicago. *Residence:* New Brunswick, N.J.

CAREER: University of Cincinnati, Cincinnati, Ohio, acting curator, 1926-29; Rutgers University, New Brunswick, N.J., curator of Geological Museum, 1944-46; writer.

WRITINGS—For adults; all with husband, Carroll Lane Fenton: *Records of Evolution,* Haldeman-Julius, 1924; *The Rock Book,* Doubleday, 1940; *The Story of the Great Geologists,* Doubleday, Doran, 1945, reprinted, Books for Libraries, 1969, revised and enlarged edition published as *Giants of Geology,* Doubleday, 1952; *Rocks and Their Stories,* Doubleday, 1951; *The Fossil Book: A Record of Prehistoric Life,* Doubleday, 1958.

For young people; all with C. L. Fenton: *Mountains* (illustrated by the authors), Doubleday, Doran, 1942, reprinted, Books for Libraries, 1969; *The Land We Live On,* Doubleday, Doran, 1944; *Worlds in the Sky* (illustrated by the authors), J. Day, 1950, revised edition, 1963; *Riches From the Earth* (illustrated by the authors), J. Day, 1953, reprinted, 1970; *Our Changing Weather,* Doubleday, 1954; *Prehistoric Zoo* (illustrated by C. L. Fenton), Doubleday, 1959; *In Prehistoric Seas* (illustrated by C. L. Fenton), Doubleday, 1963.*

* * *

FERGUSON, Mary Anne 1918-

PERSONAL: Born July 25, 1918, in Charleston, S.C.; daughter of William (a lawyer) and Anne (Walker) Heyward; married Alfred Riggs Ferguson (a professor and editor), May 23, 1948 (died, 1974); children: Margaret W., Jean Ferguson Carr, Lucy Ferguson Allen. *Education:* Duke University, A.B., 1938, M.A., 1940; Ohio State University, Ph.D., 1965. *Politics:* Democrat. *Religion:* Episcopal. *Home:* 37 Ridge Hill Rd., Scituate, Mass. 02066. *Office:* Department of English, College I, University of Massachusetts, Harbor Campus, Boston, Mass. 02125.

CAREER: University of North Carolina, Chapel Hill, instructor in English, 1945-46; University of Connecticut, New London, instructor in English, 1946; Queens College (now of the City University of New York), Flushing, N.Y., instructor in English, 1947; Ohio Wesleyan University, Delaware, part-time instructor in English, 1948-62; Ohio State University, Columbus, instructor in English, 1963-64; Ohio University, Athens, visiting professor of English, 1965-66; University of Massachusetts, Boston, assistant professor, 1966-69, associate professor, 1969-74, professor of English and women's studies, 1974—.

MEMBER: Modern Language Association of America (member of Commission on the Status of Women, 1970-73), Mediaeval Academy of America, Phi Beta Kappa. *Awards, honors:* E. Howald fellowship from Ohio State University, 1968-69; National Endowment for the Humanities grant, 1972-74; Carnegie Foundation fellowship, 1974-75.

WRITINGS: (Editor) *Images of Women in Literature,* Houghton, 1973, 2nd edition, 1977; *Bibliography of English Translations from Medieval Sources,* Columbia University Press, 1974. Contributor to language and literature journals.

WORK IN PROGRESS: A book on Willa Cather's creation of the myth of the pioneer woman; research on Sherwood Anderson and his image of women and on Eudora Welty's *Losing Battles* as a comic epic.

SIDELIGHTS: Mary Anne Ferguson writes: "My interest in women's studies was a direct result of my realization that a discriminatory nepotism law was keeping me from professional advancement. My work on the Commission on the Status of Women for three years led me first to teach a course and then to edit an anthology, one of the first in the field. As a result of this change, I am now writing in the field of twentieth-century American literature."

AVOCATIONAL INTERESTS: Swimming, snorkeling, New England.

* * *

FERNANDO, Lloyd 1926-

PERSONAL: Born May 31, 1926, in Sri Lanka; married Marie Therese Consigliere (a college lecturer in English), March 31, 1962; children: Eva Marie, Jacqueline Sunetra. *Education:* University of Singapore, B.A. (honors; philosophy) and B.A. (honors; English), 1958; University of Leeds, Ph.D., 1964. *Home:* 126 Jalan Bukit Pantai, Kuala Lumpur, Malaysia. *Office:* Department of English, University of Malaya, Kuala Lumpur, Malaysia.

CAREER: University of Malaya, Kuala Lumpur, professor of English, 1967—. *Member:* International Association for the Study of Commonwealth Literature and Language Studies, International Association of University Professors of English, International Association for the Study of Anglo-Irish Literature, Modern Language Association of America. *Awards, honors:* Fellowship from Pennsylvania State University, 1973.

WRITINGS: (Editor) *Twenty-Two Malaysian Stories,* Heinemann, 1968; (editor) *New Drama One, New Drama Two,* Oxford University Press, 1972; *Scorpion Orchid* (novel), Heinemann, 1976; *"New Women" in the Late Victorian Novel,* Pennsylvania State University Press, 1977. Contributor to language and literature journals, and to *Ariel* and *Southern Review.*

WORK IN PROGRESS: Editing a book of Asian verse in English.

SIDELIGHTS: Fernando comments briefly: "I am interested in defining and, where possible, illustrating (through editions of works) the place of literature in the cultural context of the modern world." *Avocational interests:* Watching movies.

* * *

FERRANTE, Don
See GERBI, Antonello

* * *

FERRIS, Helen Josephine 1890-1969

PERSONAL: Born November 19, 1890, in Hastings, Neb.; daughter of Elmer E. (a minister) and Minnie (Lum) Ferris; married Albert B. Tibbets, February 12, 1924. *Education:* Vassar College, B.A., 1912.

CAREER: Correspondent for a Poughkeepsie, N.Y., and a New Jersey newspaper, 1909-12; member of educational department staff, John Wanamaker Stores, 1912-18; editor of *Guardian,* 1921-23, and *American Girl,* 1923-28; associate editor of *Youth's Companion,* 1928-29; editor-in-chief of Junior Literary Guild, 1929-59; writer. *Wartime service:* Served on the Commission on Training Camp Activities of the War Work Council, 1918-19. *Member:* Phi Beta Kappa. *Awards, honors:* Child Study Association Children's Book Committee award, 1950, for *Partners: The United Nations and Youth.*

WRITINGS: Girls' Clubs, Their Organization and Management: A Manual for Workers, Dutton, 1918, new edition, 1926; *Producing Amateur Entertainments: Varied Stunts and Other Numbers With Program Plans and Directions,* Dutton, 1921; (with Virginia Moore) *Girls Who Did: Stories of Real Girls and Their Careers* (illustrated by Harriet

Moncure), Dutton, 1927; *This Happened to Me: Stories of Real Girls as Told to Helen Ferris,* Dutton, 1929; *Dody and Cap-tin Jinks* (illustrated by Grace Paull), Doubleday, Doran, 1939; *Tommy and His Dog, Hurry* (illustrated by Ruth Wood), Doubleday, 1944; *Watch Me, Said the Jeep* (illustrated by Tibor Gergely), Garden City Publishing, 1944; (with Eleanor Roosevelt) *Partners: The United Nations and Youth,* Doubleday, 1950; (with Roosevelt) *Your Teens and Mine,* Doubleday, 1961.

Editor: (With Alice M. Kimball) *Girl Scout Short Stories,* Doubleday, Page, 1925; *Adventure Waits: A Book of Adventure Stories for Girls* (illustrated by Beth K. Morris), Harcourt, 1928; *Loves Comes Riding: Stories of Romance and Adventure for Girls* (illustrated by Morris), Harcourt, 1929; *When I Was a Girl: Stories of Five Famous Women as Told by Themselves* (illustrated by Curtiss Sprague), Macmillan, 1930; (with Anne H. Choate) *Juliette Low and the Girl Scouts,* Girl Scouts, 1931; *Five Girls Who Dared: The Girlhood Stories of Five Courageous Girls as Told by Themselves* (illustrated by Allan McNab), Macmillan, 1931, reprinted, Books for Libraries, 1971; *P. T. Barnum, Here Comes Barnum* (illustrated by Frank Dobias), Harcourt, 1932; (with Grace T. Huffard and L. M. Carlisle) *My Poetry Book,* Winston, 1934; *Challenge: Stories of Courage and Love for Girls* (illustrated by Marguerite de Angeli), Doubleday, Doran, 1936; *Love's Enchantment: Story Poems and Ballads* (illustrated by Vera Bock), Doubleday, 1944, reprinted, Books for Libraries, 1969; *Writing Books for Boys and Girls: A Young Wings Anthology of Essays,* Junior Literary Guild, 1952; *Favorite Poems, Old and New* (illustrated by Kay L. Smith and Leonard Weisgard), Doubleday, 1957; *Girls, Girls, Girls: Stories of Love, Courage, and the Quest for Happiness,* F. Watts, 1957; *Brave and the Fair: Stories of Courage and Romance,* Winston, 1960; *Time of Discovering: Stories of Girls Who Found Clues to Careers,* F. Watts, 1961; *Time of Starting Out: Stories of Girls on Their First Jobs,* F. Watts, 1962; *Time of Understanding: Stories of Girls Learning to Get Along with Their Parents,* F. Watts, 1963.

SIDELIGHTS: Helen Ferris's long and diverse career included both writing and editing. One of her earlier writing efforts was *Dody and Cap-tin Jinks,* of which a *New York Times* critic commented: "Dody, the publishers say, is the author's own mother, which may account for the perfect understanding of a little girl's desires and the intimate tone of family fun which runs through the story, but the skill with which it is told is the author's own. Grace Paull's illustrations, pleasantly reminiscent of the early nineteen hundreds, are as droll and sprightly as ever, although the ubiquitous smiles on all the faces are a trifle wearisome."

Reviewing *Favorite Poems, Old and New,* a *Saturday Review* critic wrote: "Drawing on the happy memories of her childhood joy in poetry, Helen Ferris has selected some 700 poems, from those which are the classics of all literature to those of today's creative poets for children. She has prefaced this collection with an introduction that paints a perfect picture of family reading and the effect on small children of mothers and fathers who take time to enjoy books together."

BIOGRAPHICAL/CRITICAL SOURCES: New York Times, January 7, 1940; *Saturday Review,* November 16, 1957. Obituaries: *New York Times,* September 29, 1969; *Publishers Weekly,* October 13, 1969.*

(Died September 28, 1969)

FERRIS, Tom
  See WALKER, Peter N.

* * *

FERRO, Marc 1924-

PERSONAL: Born December 24, 1924, in Paris, France; son of Jacques Ferro; children: Eric, Isabelle. *Education:* Educated in France. *Home:* 38 Rue de Tourville, 78100 St. Germain en Laye, France. *Office:* Ecole des Hautes Etudes, Blvd. Raspail, 75006 Paris, France.

CAREER: Professor of history at Ecole Pratique des Hautes Etudes, Paris, France. *Military service:* Volontaire Magris Vercors, 1944. *Awards, honors:* Officer palmes academiques.

WRITINGS: La Revolution de 1917, Aubier, 1967, abridged version published as *La Revolution russe de 1917,* Flammarion, 1967, translation by J. L. Richards published as *The Russian Revolution of February 1917,* Prentice-Hall, 1972; (with others) *La Revolution d'octobre et le mouvement ouvrier europeen* (title means "The October Revolution and the European Workers' Movement"), Etudes et documentation internationales, 1967; *La Grande Guerre, 1914-1918,* Gallimard, 1969, translation published as *Great War, 1914-1918,* Routledge & Kegan Paul, 1973.

Les Dictionnaires du savoir moderne (title means "Dictionaries of Modern Knowledge"), Denoel, 1971; (editor) *L'-Histoire de 1871 a 1971,* Centre d'etude et de promotion de la lecture, 1971; (with Rene Girault) *De la Russie a l'U.R.S.S.* (title means "From Russia to the U.S.S.R."), Nathan, 1974; *Cinema et Histoire* (title means "Cinema and History"), Denoel, 1977.

Also writer of films on Lenin, China, Cuba, and Marxism.

WORK IN PROGRESS: Comment on raconte l'histoire aux enfants (title means "How to Teach Children About History"); *Des Soviets a la bureaucratie;* "Une histoire de la medecine" (title means "A History of Medicine"), a film.

* * *

FETHERLING, Dale 1941-

PERSONAL: Born September 5, 1941, in Baltimore, Md.; son of George S. (a machinist) and Mary Emma (Jones) Fetherling; married Rae Patterson, December 26, 1966; children: Dane, Jill. *Education:* West Virginia University, A.B., 1963; Northwestern University, M.S.J., 1964. *Residence:* La Jolla, Calif. *Office: Los Angeles Times,* Times-Mirror Sq., Los Angeles, Calif. 90053.

CAREER: Oregonian, Portland, Ore., reporter, 1968; *Minneapolis Tribune,* Minneapolis, Minn., reporter, 1968-72; *Los Angeles Times,* Los Angeles, Calif., reporter for Orange County edition in Costa Mesa, 1973-76, and in Los Angeles, 1977—, editor, San Diego County edition, 1978—. Instructor at Orange Coast College, 1976-77. *Military service:* U.S. Naval Reserve, active duty, 1964-68; served in Asia; became lieutenant, junior grade. *Member:* Phi Beta Kappa. *Awards, honors:* Award of merit from Illinois State Historical Society, 1974, for *Mother Jones, the Miners' Angel.*

WRITINGS: Mother Jones, the Miners' Angel, Southern Illinois University Press, 1974.

WORK IN PROGRESS: A novel; research on Carl Sandburg's newspaper writing.

SIDELIGHTS: Fetherling told *CA:* "The *Mother Jones* book is a portrait of a spectacular female labor organizer and agitator, the first detailed study of Mary Harris Jones (1830-1930)."

AVOCATIONAL INTERESTS: Sports, gardening, backpacking.

* * *

FIALKOWSKI, Barbara 1946-

PERSONAL: Born July 18, 1946, in Philadelphia, Pa.; daughter of Marion M. and Leona (Lankford) Fialkowski; married William McMillen (a university lecturer), January 17, 1970; children: Christopher Fialkowski McMillen. *Education:* Temple University, B.S., 1969; Ohio University, M.A., 1971, Ph.D., 1976. *Home:* 236 Crim St., Bowling Green, Ohio 43402. *Office:* Department of English, Bowling Green State University, Bowling Green, Ohio 43402.

CAREER: Bowling Green State University, Bowling Green, Ohio, assistant professor of English and creative writing, 1976—. *Member:* Modern Language Association of America, Bowling Green Faculty Association.

WRITINGS: Framing (collection of poems), Croissant Press, 1977.

Work anthologized in *The Sound of a Few Leaves,* Rook Press, 1977; *What Is That Country Standing Inside You?,* Explorations Press. Contributor to magazines, including *New Letters, Shenandoah, Greenfield Review,* and film magazines.

WORK IN PROGRESS: The Villain's Hit, poems; *The Knife on the Cutting Board;* a book on film and poetry.

* * *

FINGARETTE, Herbert 1921-

PERSONAL: Born January 20, 1921, in New York, N.Y.; son of David and Jeannette Fingarette; married Leslie S. Swabacker, January 23, 1945; children: Ann Fingarette Hasse. *Education:* University of California, Los Angeles, A.B., 1947, Ph.D., 1949. *Home:* 1507 Alameda Padre Serra, Santa Barbara, Calif. 93103. *Office:* Department of Philosophy, University of California, Santa Barbara, Calif. 93106.

CAREER: University of California, Santa Barbara, instructor, 1948-51, assistant professor, 1951-57, associate professor, 1957-62, professor of philosophy, 1962—. *Military service:* U.S. Army, 1943-46; became second lieutenant.

WRITINGS: The Self in Transformation, Basic Books, 1963; *On Responsibility,* Basic Books, 1967; *Self-Deception,* Routledge & Kegan Paul, 1969; *Confucius: The Secular as Sacred,* Harper, 1972; *The Meaning of Criminal Insanity,* University of California Press, 1972; (with daughter, Ann Fingarette Hasse) *Mental Disability and Criminal Responsibility,* University of California Press, 1978. Contributor to philosophy journals.

* * *

FINLER, Joel W(aldo) 1938-

PERSONAL: Born July 1, 1938, in New York, N.Y.; son of Bennett (an economist) and Matilda (Hay) Finler. *Education:* Oberlin College, B.A. (cum laude), 1959; additional study at University College, London, and Slade School of Fine Art. *Home:* 7A Belsize Sq., London N.W.3, England.

CAREER: U.S. Department of Agriculture, Washington, D.C., economist, 1957-63; Bath Academy of Art, Corsham, England, and Maidstone College of Art, Maidstone, England, lecturer in cinema history, 1964-68; writer, 1967—. *Member:* British Film Institute. *Awards, honors:* Henry J. Haskell graduate fellowship, 1968-69.

WRITINGS: Stroheim, Studio Vista, 1967, University of California Press, 1968; (co-editor and author of introduction) Jean Renoir, *The Rules of the Game,* Simon & Schuster, 1970; (editor and author introduction) Eric von Stroheim, *Greed,* Simon & Schuster, 1972; (contributor) *Masterworks of the French Cinema,* Harper, 1974; *All-Time Movie Favorites,* Longmeadow Press, 1976. Contributor to *Time Out in London, International Times, Ink,* and *Friends.*

WORK IN PROGRESS: The Rules of the Game Book; The Story of the Movies in Color; The Early Career of Jean Renoir, 1924-1935.

SIDELIGHTS: Finler told *CA:* "Putting my career into perspective I recognize the extent to which my own career as a writer was related to the general cultural climate of the early sixties when the cinema (along with rock music) acquired a new 'respectability.' A large number of American universities began or expanded their departments of film. Around 1963 I recognized that it would be possible to make a viable career out of writing and lecturing on film, drawing on my own wide interests in the visual arts along with music, literature, and the social sciences. Probably typical of the period was my initial attraction to the serious ('art house') films of foreign directors like Godard, Antonioni, and Renoir, and to classic silent directors like D. W. Griffith and Stroheim (although, as a film critic, I also reviewed some of the more 'commercial' releases and was particularly interested in the work of the underground filmmakers).

"However, during more recent years I've come to value more highly the contribution of the American cinema, both the Hollywood of the thirties and forties and the work of that new generation of young directors brought up on the cinema, like myself, who emerged during the sixties, including Francis Ford Coppola, Brian de Palma, Martin Scorsese, Steven Spielberg, and others, testifying to the continuing vigor of the American cinema. It appears unfortunate to me that even with the fading of the French and Italian 'new wave,' many serious film-goers, particularly in the United States, still tend to be more interested in foreign films than in the new American cinema.

"In spite of the boom in film book publishing during the past ten years, the vast riches of the American cinema have only just begun to be explored in depth. They offer a challenge to the film historian unmatched by the films of any other country. The studio system, for example, provides a fascinating continuity of production for a period of forty-odd years and reflects a real and continuing commitment to filmmaking which produced a fair number of bad films, but a surprisingly large number of good ones while preserving a remarkably high standard overall. Thus, my current book in progress, *The Story of the Movies in Color,* in spite of its popular sounding title, represents a serious attempt to reassess the development of the American cinema during the years 1935-55 when color was first introduced and developed side-by-side with black-and-white for a period of twenty years. The phenomenon of the color film provides a new perspective for examining Hollywood at its peak and then in decline. This work has developed from my previous book on Hollywood, *All Time Movie Favorites,* which represented a first step in this new direction, and I similarly plan to illustrate the book from my own extensive collection of thirty-five millimeter color film frames, stills, and posters."

*   *   *

FIRTH, Robert E.   1921-

PERSONAL: Born December 19, 1921, in Minnesota; son of William E. (a telegrapher) and Loa (Budd) Firth; married Morna Y. Lequier (a secretary), August 28, 1943; children: Holly Howell, Francis E. *Education:* Union College, Lincoln, Neb., B.A., 1948; University of Nebraska, M.A., 1952, Ph.D., 1960. *Politics:* Republican. *Religion:* Seventh-Day Adventist. *Home:* 133 North George, Berrien Springs, Mich. 49103. *Office:* Department of Business Administration, Andrews University, Berrien Springs, Mich. 49103.

CAREER: Maplewood Academy, Hutchinson, Minn., accountant, 1948-52; Union College, Lincoln, Neb., 1952-64, began as assistant professor, became associate professor of business administration; Andrews University, Berrien Springs, Mich., professor of business administration, 1964—, chairman of department. Private consultant. *Military service:* U.S. Army, combat medic, 1942-46; became sergeant; received Bronze Star. *Member:* Academy of Management, American Business Law Association.

WRITINGS: Public Power in Nebraska, University of Nebraska Press, 1962; *Guidelines for Committees and Board Members,* Review & Herald, 1973.

WORK IN PROGRESS: A casebook on church institutions.

*   *   *

FISCH, Edith L.   1923-

PERSONAL: Born March 3, 1923, in New York, N.Y.; daughter of Hyman (a lawyer) and Clara (Lond) Fisch; married Steven L. Werner (a lawyer), December 14, 1963 (deceased). *Education:* Brooklyn College (now of the City University of New York), B.A., 1945; Columbia University, LL.B., 1948, LL.M., 1949, J.Sc.D., 1950. *Home:* 250 West 94th St., New York, N.Y. 10025. *Office:* Lond Publications, Pomona, N.Y. 10970.

CAREER: Admitted to New York State bar, 1948, U.S. Supreme Court bar, 1957; Conrad & Smith, New York City, associate, 1951-57; Brodsky, Linett & Altman, New York City, counsel, 1973—. Assistant professor at New York Law School, 1962-65. Educational director and member of board of trustees of Foundation for Continuing Legal Education, 1964—. President of Lond Publications, 1958—. *Member:* National Association of Women Lawyers, Academy of Political Science, National Women's Committee (director), American Association of University Women, American Arbitration Association (member of national panel), New York Women Lawyers Association (president, 1970-71), New York State Trial Lawyers Association, Association of the Bar of the City of New York, Brooklyn College Lawyers Group (member of board of governors, 1963-65), Brooklyn College Alumni Association, Columbia University Alumni Association, Friends of Columbia Libraries, Princeton Club.

WRITINGS: The Cy Pres Doctrine in the United States, Matthew Bender, 1950; (editor with Mortimer D. Schwartz) *State Laws on the Employment of Women,* Scarecrow, 1953; (with Matthew Foner and Albert P. Blaustein) *Lawyers in Industry,* Oceana, 1956; *Fisch on New York Evidence,* privately printed, 1959, 2nd edition, 1976; *The Feasibility of Formulating a Code of Evidence for the State of New York,* privately printed, 1966; (editor) *New York Charter and Code,* Williams Press, 1973; (with Doris Jonas Freed and Esther R. Schachter) *Charities and Charitable Foundations,* privately printed, 1974. Contributor to law journals.

SIDELIGHTS: Fisch told *CA* that she was the first woman

professor of law in the state of New York, the first woman on the faculty of New York Law School, the first woman to receive the J.Sc. D. degree from Columbia University's Law School, and the first graduate of the Law School to receive every degree offered there.

AVOCATIONAL INTERESTS: Playing the piano, reading, travel, eating in gourmet restaurants, the company of fellow lawyers.

* * *

FISCHER, Bruno 1908-
(Russell Gray)

PERSONAL: Born June 29, 1908, in Germany; came to the United States in 1913, naturalized citizen, 1919; son of Herman (a grocer) and Sarah (Metzger) Fischer; married Ruth Miller (a school secretary), March 20, 1934; children: Adam, Nora Fischer Ernst. *Education:* Graduated from Rand School of Social Science. *Politics:* Social Democrat. *Religion:* Jewish. *Home and office address:* Three Arrows, R. D. 3, Putnam Valley, N.Y. 10579. *Agent:* Lenniger Literary Agency, Inc., 437 Fifth Ave., New York, N.Y. 10016.

CAREER: Long Island Daily Press, Long Island City, N.Y., reporter, 1929-31; editor of *Labor Voice,* 1931-32, and *Socialist Call,* 1934-36; Macmillan Publishing Co., Inc., New York City, executive editor, 1961-65; Arco Publishing Co., Inc., New York City, education editor, 1965-70; writer, 1970—. *Member:* Authors Guild of Authors League of America, Mystery Writers of America, Social Democrats, Workmen's Circle.

WRITINGS—Mystery novels: So Much Blood, Greystone Press, 1939; *The Hornet's Nest,* Morrow, 1943; *Quoth the Raven,* Doubleday, 1944; *The Dead Men Grin,* McKay, 1945; *The Spider Lily,* McKay, 1946; *The Pigskin Bag,* Ziff-Davis, 1946; *Kill to Fit,* Five Star Mysteries, 1946; *More Deaths Than One,* Ziff-Davis, 1947; *The Bleeding Scissors,* Ziff-Davis, 1948; *The Restless Hands,* Dodd, 1948.

The Angels Fell, Dodd, 1950; *The Silent Dust,* Dodd, 1950; *The House of Flesh,* Fawcett, 1950; *The Lady Kills,* Fawcett, 1951; *The Paper Circle,* Dodd, 1951; *Fools Walk In,* Fawcett, 1951; *The Fast Buck,* Fawcett, 1952; (editor) *Crook's Tour,* Dodd, 1953; *Run for Your Life,* Fawcett, 1953; *So Wicked My Love,* Fawcett, 1954; *Knee-Deep in Death,* Fawcett, 1955; *Murder in the Raw,* Fawcett, 1957; *Second-Hand Nude,* Fawcett, 1958; *The Lustful Ape,* Fawcett, 1959; *The Girl Between,* Fawcett, 1960; *The Evil Days,* Random House, 1973. Contributor of about five hundred stories, some under pseudonym Russell Gray, and several hundred articles to magazines.

WORK IN PROGRESS: A mystery novel.

SIDELIGHTS: Fischer, whose books have been translated into eleven foreign languages, writes: "Though I've had my flings at editing and newspaper writing, I am essentially a free-lance writer—setting my own pace, working at home, being pretty much independent. I'm a story-teller, in particular, a recounter of mysteries, dedicated wholly to the printed word."

* * *

FISHER, M(ary) F(rances) K(ennedy) 1908-
(Mary Frances Parrish)

PERSONAL: Born July 3, 1908, in Albion, Mich.; daughter of Rex Brenton (an editor) and Edith Oliver (Holbrook) Kennedy; married Alfred Young Fisher, 1929 (divorced, 1938); married Dillough Parrish, 1940 (died, 1942); married

Donald Friede, 1945 (divorced, 1951); children: (third marriage) Anna Kennedy Friede Maginnis, Kennedy Wright. *Education:* Attended University of California, Los Angeles, and University of Dijon, 1929-32. *Residence:* Glen Ellen, Calif. *Agent:* Russell & Volkening, Inc., 551 Fifth Ave., New York, N.Y. 10017.

CAREER: Writer, 1937—.

WRITINGS: (Under name Mary Frances Parrish) *Serve It Forth,* Harper, 1937; (under Parrish name) *Consider the Oyster,* Duell, Sloan & Pearce, 1941; (under Parrish name) *How to Cook a Wolf,* Duell, Sloan & Pearce, 1942, revised edition, 1951; (under Parrish name) *The Gastronomical Me,* Duell, Sloan & Pearce, 1943; *Here Let Us Feast: A Book of Banquets,* Viking, 1946; *Not Now But Now,* Viking, 1947; *An Alphabet for Gourmets,* Viking, 1949; (editor and translator) Jean Anthelme Brillat-Savarin, *The Physiology of Taste,* Limited Editions Club, 1949, reprinted, Knopf, 1971.

The Art of Eating: The Collected Gastronomical Works of M. F. K. Fisher, World Publishing, 1954, reprinted as *The Art of Eating: Five Gastronomical Works,* Vintage, 1976; *A Cordiall Water: A Garland of Odd and Old Receipts to Assauge the Ills of Man or Beast,* Little, Brown, 1961; *The Story of Wine in California,* University of California Press, 1962; *Maps of Another Town: A Memoir of Provence,* Little, Brown, 1964; (author of introduction) Robert Louis Stevenson, *Napa Wine,* J. E. Beard, 1965; *The Cooking of Provincial France,* Time-Life, 1968; *With Bold Knife and Fork,* Putnam, 1969; *Among Friends,* Knopf, 1971.

SIDELIGHTS: Fisher wrote: "I continue to be interested in the problems of aging. I enjoy the practice and contemplation of adapting the need to eat to the need to be properly nourished."

* * *

FISHER, Richard B(ernard) 1919-

PERSONAL: Born May 7, 1919, in Cleveland, Ohio; son of Sidney L. (a manufacturer) and Marjorie (Kohn) Fisher; divorced; children: Anne (Mrs. Richard Buchanan), Meg, Sara. *Education:* Yale University, B.A., 1941, M.A., 1947, Ph.D., 1953; Brunel University, M.Sc., 1978. *Politics:* Labour. *Religion:* "Non-practicing Jew." *Residence:* London, England. *Agent:* Pat Feeley, 52 Vanderbilt Ave., New York, N.Y. 10017.

CAREER: San Francisco State College, San Francisco, Calif., instructor in social sciences, 1950-53; Academic Reprints, Palo Alto, Calif., founder and manager, 1952-56; Paper Editions Book Club, Palo Alto, founder and manager, 1953-56; Western Publishing Co., New York City, editor, 1956-62; McGraw-Hill Book Co., New York City, manager of paperback books, 1962-66; Sphere Books Ltd., London, England, managing director, 1966-68; writer, 1968—. *Military service:* U.S. Army Air Forces, 1942-45; received Silver Cross and three Distinguished Flying Crosses. *Member:* Brain Research Association, Phi Beta Kappa.

WRITINGS: (With G. A. Christie) *A Dictionary of Drugs,* Schocken, 1971, 3rd edition, 1975; (with Christie) *How Drugs Work,* Allen Lane, 1973; *The Chemistry of Consciousness,* Barrie & Jenkins, 1975; *Joseph Lister, 1827-1912,* Stein & Day, 1977; *Syrie Maugham* (illustrated biography), Duckworth, 1978; *The Brain Manual,* Paddington Press, 1979.

Author of "Joseph Lister's Nervous Breakdown," first aired on BBC-Radio, June 22, 1977. Contributor to British newspapers, including *Observer Colour* magazine.

WORK IN PROGRESS: Dictionary of Mental Health, for the layman.

SIDELIGHTS: Fisher told *CA:* "I became interested in drugs and how they work in the body because of the vast proliferation of new medicines we have experienced since World War II. To understand drug action, I had to learn some biochemistry to say nothing of anatomy, histology, and pathology. It was through my interest in drugs, especially psychomimetic drugs, that I began to look more closely at how that most unique organ, the human brain, works. But I am an historian, which explains my interest in biography, first (in order of writing) Syrie Maugham, who was an interior decorator, and then the great surgeon, Joseph Lister. I expect to continue to write about the ever-expanding biological sciences, as an historian and reporter."

AVOCATIONAL INTERESTS: Book binding, tending his small city-garden.

*   *   *

FITSCHEN, Dale 1937-

PERSONAL: Born October 13, 1937, in St. Louis, Mo.; son of Jacob J. and Flora (Freihaut) Fitschen; married Marilyn Olsen (an artist and illustrator), February 10, 1962; children: Romy, Jean-Claire, Samantha. *Education:* Washington University, St. Louis, Mo., B.A., 1960; also attended Roosevelt University, 1960-62, and University of Chicago, 1962-65. *Home:* 1029 South Clinton, Oak Park, Ill. 60304. *Office:* Regional Transportation Authority, Marina City, Chicago, Ill. 60601.

CAREER: Victor Rouse Associates, Chicago, Ill., urban planner, 1972-73; Chicago Transportation Authority, Chicago, transportation planner, 1973-75; Regional Transportation Authority, Chicago, transportation planner, 1975—. Founder of local Co-Op Kindergarten, 1970; member of South Shore Food Co-Op and Co-Op Gardens, both 1974—.

WRITINGS: (Illustrated by wife, Marilyn Fitschen) *Rotten Hair! Rotten Snags!* (juvenile), Follett, 1975.

WORK IN PROGRESS: Two children's books.

SIDELIGHTS: Fitschen commented that he has been reading and telling stories to his children for ten years and they were the ones who persuaded him and their mother to make books. *Avocational interests:* Literature, the outdoors, gardening, game playing.

*   *   *

FITZGERALD, Hiram E(arl) 1940-

PERSONAL: Born November 12, 1940, in Columbia, Pa.; son of Harry E. and Esther C. (McCachren) Fitzgerald; married Dolores Catherine Koncar (a teacher), December 15, 1962; children: Steven Scott, Stephanie Kay, Katherine Koncar. *Education:* Lebanon Valley College, B.A., 1962; University of Denver, M.A., 1964, Ph.D., 1967. *Politics:* Democrat. *Religion:* Eastern Orthodox. *Home:* 1922 Mendota Dr., East Lansing, Mich. 48823. *Office:* Department of Psychology, Michigan State University, East Lansing, Mich. 48824.

CAREER: Michigan State University, East Lansing, assistant professor, 1967-71, associate professor, 1971-76, professor of psychology, 1976—. *Member:* International Society for Developmental Psychobiology, American Association for the Advancement of Science, Society for Research in Child Development, Society for Psychophysiological Research, American Psychological Association (fellow), Pav-

lovian Society of America, Midwestern Psychological Association, Michigan Association for Infant Mental Health. *Awards, honors:* Fulbright senior scholar, 1973-74; Lebanon Valley College alumni citation, 1978.

WRITINGS: (With Yvonne Brackbill and L. M. Lintz) *A Developmental Study of Classical Conditioning* (monograph), Society for Research in Child Development, 1967; (editor with J. P. McKinney) *Developmental Psychology: Studies in Human Development,* Dorsey, 1970, revised edition, 1977; (with E. A. Strommen) *Programmed Learning Aide for Developmental Psychology,* Learning Systems Co., 1972; (editor with Charles Cofer) *Psychology: A Programmed Modular Approach,* Learning Systems Co., 1975; (with McKinney and Strommen) *Developmental Psychology: The Infant and Young Child,* Dorsey, 1977; (with McKinney and Strommen) *Developmental Psychology: The School Age Child,* Dorsey, 1977; (with McKinney and Strommen) *Developmental Psychology: The Adolescent and Young Adult,* Dorsey, 1977. Contributor to psychology journals.

WORK IN PROGRESS: Research on attentional processes in speech disfluencies, infant learning and attention, infant auditory perception, adults' reactions to infants' physical appearance, effects of group day care on infants and toddlers, developmental intervention for children with behavioral dysfunctions.

SIDELIGHTS: Fitzgerald writes: "I am committed to the scientific study of human development so that we can better understand how to rear human beings so that they can attain their utmost potential. My work with colleagues in Yugoslavia and Mexico has been deeply satisfying for it has demonstrated time and again that when the needs of children are given primary emphasis, scientists from diverse cultures can work cooperatively toward the elimination of conditions which produce a profound human suffering and unhappiness."

AVOCATIONAL INTERESTS: Athletics (golf, swimming), gardening, travel.

*   *   *

FITZGERALD, Michael G(arrett) 1950-

PERSONAL: Born December 14, 1950, in El Dorado, Ark.; son of John F. (an electrician) and Tommye (Murphy) Fitzgerald. *Education:* Southern State College (now South Arkansas University), B.B.A., 1972. *Politics:* "Like most Southerners, Democrat, though I vote for the man, not the party." *Religion:* Southern Baptist. *Home:* 1310 Harold Ellen, El Dorado, Ark. 71730. *Office:* Southwestern Electric Power Co., 428 Travis, Shreveport, La. 71156.

CAREER: Southwestern Electric Power Co., Shreveport, La., accountant, 1972—.

WRITINGS: Universal Pictures: A Panoramic History in Words, Pictures, and Filmographies, Arlington House, 1977.

WORK IN PROGRESS: A book on the early 1940's, including casts, credits, and plots for all feature films and serials released in those six years.

SIDELIGHTS: Fitzgerald told *CA:* "My favorite movie studio has always been Universal, or, as it was called in the 1950's, Universal-International. A fellow Arkansan, Julie Adams, was the top female star in those years and, like many other Arkansans, I went to each new Julie Adams film. (I still do, in fact.) In 1964 came cablevision, and a great deal more to watch on television, since there were many more stations to see. I saw the Universal serial, 'Flash Gordon Conquers the Universe' with Anne Gwynne, an actress who caught my eye. I began watching old films to see her, and the interest grew. She was a bridesmaid at Deanna Durbin's wedding, and her co-star in two movies. Durbin, and similar personalities, like Gloria Jean and Susanna Foster, became more of my favorites. Now these are 'Star' actors. A real actor is one who can play many different types of roles and be believable. My most favorite character star is Rosemary De Camp, an actress I have admired since I can remember. It is Miss De Camp, a beautiful woman inside and out, to whom I dedicated my book."

*   *   *

FLAMM, Gerald R(obert)   1916-
(Jerry Flamm)

PERSONAL: Born July 13, 1916, in San Francisco, Calif.; son of David Aaron (a police officer) and Sophie (Frucht) Flamm; married Esther Zwerling, October 25, 1942; children: Daniel L., Kenneth L., David S. *Education:* University of California, Berkeley, A.B., 1941, graduate study, 1967-69. *Politics:* Democrat. *Religion:* Jewish. *Home:* 1619 Funston Ave., San Francisco, Calif. 94122.

CAREER: United Press International and *New York Herald Tribune,* New York City, correspondent and reporter for Mexico City bureaus, 1940-41; *San Francisco Call Bulletin,* San Francisco, Calif., reporter and staff writer, 1946-50; Pan American World Airways, Latin American Division, Miami, Fla., public relations representative in Rio de Janeiro, Brazil, 1950-53; *San Francisco Chronicle,* San Francisco, Calif., rewriteman, 1953; *San Francisco Call Bulletin,* reporter and staff writer, 1953-56; Office of Messrs. Rockefeller, International Basic Economy Corp., and Jackson Hole Preserve, Inc., New York City, public relations director for the Caribbean in San Juan, Puerto Rico, 1956-65; California State Legislature, Sacramento, publications coordinator to the Assembly, 1965-67; San Francisco Redevelopment Agency, San Francisco, Calif., business development specialist, 1967—. Interim confidential secretary to the mayor of San Francisco, 1970-71, assistant director and acting director of mayor's Office of Economic Development, 1973-76. *Military service:* U.S. Marine Corps, communications officer, 1942-46; served in the Pacific and China; became major.

WRITINGS—Under name Jerry Flamm: *Good Life in Hard Times: San Francisco's Twenties and Thirties,* Chronicle Books, 1977. Contributor of articles and photographs to magazines and newspapers, including *San Francisco* and *California Living.*

SIDELIGHTS: Flamm told *CA:* "*Good Life in Hard Times: San Francisco's Twenties and Thirties* is a personal memoir of my home town, San Francisco, and the surrounding Bay area. It deals with events, places, and people with which, and with whom, I was personally involved or familiar with through family members or friends. It is not a detailed history, or a dull chronological record. The book is illustrated with more than 125 photographs gathered over two years, and touches on a gamut of scenes ranging from the old baseball park to the 50-cent-with-wine Italian restaurants to the highly competitive, cutthroat newspaper days.

"My own feelings about my city? There have been changes in population and the skyline, and a switch in many life styles, just as in other big cities. However, San Francisco still retains much of its beauty and charm, and still—I believe—is one of the most fascinating and enjoyable cities in the world in which to live and work."

FLAMM, Jerry
See FLAMM, Gerald R(obert)

*   *   *

FLECK, Henrietta   1903-

PERSONAL: Born September 22, 1903, near Papillion, Neb.; daughter of John Peter and Wilhelmina (Prinz) Fleck; married Dale Houghton (a professor of marketing and a business executive), June 6, 1956. *Education:* Attended Peru Teachers College, 1921-23; University of Nebraska, B.Sc., 1928; Columbia University, M.Sc., 1932; Ohio State University, Ph.D., 1944. *Home:* 6100 Vine St., H-45, Lincoln, Neb. 68505.

CAREER: Rural school teacher in Elkhorn, Neb., 1921-22; high school teacher of home economics and English in Shelby, Neb., 1923-25, and Bloomington, Neb., 1926-27; Riverside Community Hospital, Riverside, Calif., dietitian, 1929; Santa Barbara Cottage Hospital, Santa Barbara, Calif., dietitian, 1929-30; University of Delaware, Newark, instructor in home economics, 1932-42; Illinois State Normal University, Normal, professor of home economics and chairman of department, 1944-46; New York University, New York, N.Y., chairman of home economics department, 1946-71, professor of home economics, 1971-72, professor emerita, 1972—, part-time professor, 1972-76, 1978—.

MEMBER: National Education Association (president of home economics department, 1953-55), American Home Economic Association, American Dietetic Association, American Educational Research Association, National Council for Family Relations, American Association of University Professors, National Society for the Study of Education, Omicron Nu, Pi Lambda Theta. *Awards, honors:* Sc.D. from University of Nebraska, 1970.

WRITINGS: A Recipe Primer, Heath, 1949; (author of revision with Helen Hovey and Gladys Peckham) *Woman's Home Companion Cookbook,* Collier, 1950; (author of introduction) *The Complete Book of Home Sewing,* Pocket Books, 1952; *A First Cookbook for Boys and Girls,* Alumni Publications, 1953; *How to Evaluate Students,* McKnight & McKnight, 1953; (with Elizabeth Munves) *Everybody's Book of Modern Diet and Nutrition,* Dell, 1955; (with Munves and Louise Fernandez) *Exploring Home and Family Living,* Prentice-Hall, 1959, 4th edition, 1977; *Introduction to Nutrition,* Macmillan, 1962, 3rd edition, 1976; (with Munves and Fernandez) *Living With Your Family,* Prentice-Hall, 1965; *Toward Better Teaching of Home Economics,* Macmillan, 1968, 2nd edition, 1974. Also author of *The Co-Ed Cookbook,* 1967.

General editor of "College Home Economics Texts," Macmillan, 1957-63. Contributor of about two-hundred-fifty articles to home economics, medical, and nutrition journals, and to other magazines, including *Modern Miss,* and newspapers. Contributing editor of *Forecast,* 1949-62.

WORK IN PROGRESS: A third edition of *Toward Better Teaching of Home Economics;* a fourth edition of *Introduction to Nutrition.*

SIDELIGHTS: Henrietta Fleck writes: "One of my most important goals in life is to be a good teacher, not only in the classroom but in my writing. My philosophy in teaching and writing is to focus on the development of the student or the reader—add something worthwhile to their lives. The content taught or written is a means to that end.

"In my nutrition classes and in my nutrition text, I try to help students and readers to make wise selections of food for an adequate diet if they are meat-eaters, vegetarians, eat in fast food restaurants, have strong cultural eating patterns, are trying to lose weight, or have a limited food budget. In addition, I attempt to weave in the influences of society, including government, international influences, the hungry world, farming and business, marketing, and countless other factors. Personal development is stressed in my high school text through building self concept, becoming expert in the skills for living, and appreciating the importance of wholesome home and family life. In my methods text, my major objective is to develop humane teachers, ones who are supportive, understanding, loving, interested, and who provide a creative learning environment.''

*   *   *

FLEMING, Guy
See MASUR, Harold Q.

*   *   *

FLEMING, Jennifer Baker 1943-

PERSONAL: Born July 28, 1943, in New York, N.Y.; daughter of Theodore G. and Doris I. (Balch) Baker; divorced; children: Robert Michael, Jr., Kathleen. *Education:* Antioch College, B.A., 1975. *Residence:* Philadelphia, Pa. *Agent:* Virginia Barber, 44 Greenwich Ave., New York, N.Y. 10011. *Office:* Women's Resource Network, 4025 Chestnut St., Philadelphia, Pa. 19104.

CAREER: Burlington County Community Action Program, Burlington, N.J., co-founder, 1964-67; New Jersey Community Action Training Institute, Trenton, N.J., trainer, 1965-67; Economic Opportunity Corp., New Brunswick, N.J., program development specialist and community organizer, 1967-68; Camden County Council on Economic Opportunity, Camden County, N.J., program evaluator, 1968-69; Women's Center, Philadelphia, Pa., co-director, 1970-71; Women in Transition, Inc., Philadelphia, founder and co-director, 1971-77; Women's Resource Network, Inc., Philadelphia, founder and director, 1977—. Board member of Burlington County branch of National Association for the Advancement of Colored People, Burlington County Human Relations Council, Burlington County Welfare Rights Organization, Woman Against Abuse, and Women's Way. Consultant to law enforcement agencies, criminal justice systems, universities, and women's groups on wife abuse and issues involving minority women.

WRITINGS: (With others) *Women in Transition: A Feminist Handbook on Separation and Divorce*, Scribner, 1975; *For Better, For Worse: A Feminist Handbook on Marriage and Other Options*, Scribner, 1977. Contributor to *Harper's Bazaar*.

WORK IN PROGRESS: A manual for people interested in and working on the battered woman issue.

SIDELIGHTS: Jennifer Fleming writes: ''I am a woman whose career is based upon a commitment to combat the forces of sexism, racism, and class bias. I believe that it is possible to help create a peaceful revolution through touching base with one's own power and utilizing it constructively on both a personal and political level.''

*   *   *

FLEMING, Macklin 1911-

PERSONAL: Original surname, Stainback; name legally changed; born September 6, 1911, in Chicago, Ill.; son of Ingram Macklin (governor and Supreme Court justice of Hawaii) and Hazel (Caldwell) Stainback; married Polly Naething; children: Penelope Fleming Young, Frances, Ingram. *Education:* Yale University, B.A., 1934, LL.B., 1937. *Politics:* Democrat. *Home:* 331 North Carmelina Ave., Los Angeles, Calif. 90049. *Office:* Court of Appeal, 3580 Wilshire Blvd., Los Angeles, Calif. 90010.

CAREER: Admitted to State Bars of New York, 1938, and California, 1946; Sullivan & Cromwell, New York, N.Y., attorney, 1937-39; U.S. Government, Bituminous Coal Division, Washington, D.C., counsel, 1939-41; private practice of law in San Francisco, Calif., 1949; assistant U.S. attorney in San Francisco, 1949-53, special assistant U.S. attorney for northern district of California, in San Francisco, 1953-54; Mitchell, Silberberg & Knupp, Los Angeles, Calif., trial lawyer, 1954-59; Superior Court, Los Angeles, judge, 1959-64; Court of Appeal, Los Angeles, justice, 1964—. Extension lecturer at University of California, Los Angeles, 1955-66. Special counsel to California's director of finance, 1959; counsel for American Civil Liberties Union, 1954. President of Southern California Yale Scholarship Foundation; director of Los Angeles Center Theatre Group; past chairman of Los Angeles County Art Museum's Far Eastern Art Council; member of board of trustees of Friends of Santa Monica Mountain Parks; member of World Peace Through Law Center, Institute of Judicial Administration, International Commission of Jurists, and Los Angeles Committee on Foreign Relations. *Military service:* U.S. Army, 1941-46; served in Europe; became captain.

MEMBER: American Bar Association, Foreign Policy Association, Selden Society, Los Angeles County Bar Association, Bar Association of the City of New York. *Awards, honors:* LL. D. from Pepperdine University, 1968.

WRITINGS: The Price of Perfect Justice, Basic Books, 1974; *Of Crimes and Rights*, Norton, 1978.

*   *   *

FLORES, John 1943-

PERSONAL: Born September 27, 1943, in Alexandria, Va.; son of Angel (a professor and writer) and Kate (a writer; maiden name, Berger) Flores; married Susan McKevitt, December 21, 1963 (divorced, 1974); married Ana Perez (an education director), August 23, 1975; children: Diana, Andrea. *Education:* Queens College of the City University of New York, B.A., 1964; Yale University, M.A., 1965, Ph.M., 1966, Ph.D., 1968. *Home:* 84 Sterling Pl., Brooklyn, N.Y. 11217. *Office:* Center for Puerto Rican Studies, City University of New York, 445 West 59th St., New York, N.Y. 10019.

CAREER: Stanford University, Stanford, Calif., assistant professor of German, 1968-74; City University of New York, New York, N.Y., research director at Center for Puerto Rican Studies, 1976—. *Awards, honors:* Award from *Choice*, for *Poetry in East Germany*.

WRITINGS: Poetry in East Germany: Adjustments, Revisions, and Provocations, 1945-1970, Yale University Press, 1970; (co-author) *Cuaderno de Cultura*, Center for Puerto Rican Studies, City University of New York, 1976; *The Insular Vision: Pedreira's Interpretation of Puerto Rican Culture*, Center for Puerto Rican Studies, University of New York, 1977.

WORK IN PROGRESS: By Virtue of Omission: Notes on Applying Walter Benjamin; essays on aspects of Puerto Rican literature and cultural theory; editing *Landmarks in Puerto Rican Literature: A Reader*; translating *Memoirs of Bernardo Vega*.

SIDELIGHTS: Flores told *CA:* "I am attempting to apply knowledge and methods gained while studying and teaching German and European traditions to the field of Puerto Rican and so-called 'Third World' culture. I am also transferring from a more conventional academic setting into one where the emphasis is on collective learning, research, and writing."

*   *   *

FLUCHERE, Henri 1914-

PERSONAL: Born July 31, 1914, in France; came to the United States in 1925, naturalized citizen, 1935; son of Armand H. (a draftsman) and Emma (Aubanel) Fluchere; married Ruth Allen, 1944 (divorced, January, 1946); married Maud Elliot Hall (a musician), September 4, 1946; children: Peter, Michael, Marion. *Education:* Attended Brooklyn College (now of the City University of New York), 1933-35, City College (now of the City University of New York), 1935-36, and Columbia University, 1946-48. *Politics:* Democrat. *Religion:* Episcopalian. *Home and office:* 21 Oak St., Irvington, N.Y. 10533.

CAREER: Free-lance writer, 1950—. Art director for McGraw's Technical Writing Service, 1950-53. Irvington village trustee, 1958-60, police commissioner, 1958-60, and acting mayor, 1959-60. Consultant on wines and gastronomy. *Military service:* U.S. Army, Intelligence, 1942-46; became master sergeant; received Purple Heart. *Member:* American Wine Society.

WRITINGS: (With John Musacchia and M. J. Grainger) *Airbrush Techniques*, Reinhold, 1953; (with Musacchia and Grainger) *Watercolor*, Reinhold, 1954; *Wines*, Western Publishing, 1973, enlarged edition, 1974. Author of "The Westchester Winetaster," a weekly column in Westchester newspapers, 1965-74. Editor of *Consumer Wineletter*, 1973—.

*   *   *

FOERSTER, Lotte B(rand) 1910-
(Lotte Brand Philip)

PERSONAL: Born May 27, 1910, in Hamburg, Germany; came to the United States in 1941; daughter of Friedrich Wilhelm (a merchant) and Anna (a merchant; maiden name, Majuol) Brand; married Herbert Leopold Philip (divorced); married Otto H. Foerster (a professor; deceased). *Education:* University of Freiburg, Ph.D., 1937. *Religion:* Lutheran. *Home:* 58 West 68th St., New York, N.Y. 10023. *Office:* Queens College of the City University of New York, Flushing, N.Y. 11367.

CAREER: Jewelry and button designer in New York, N.Y., and Providence, R.I.; Bryn Mawr College, Bryn Mawr, Pa., lecturer in art history, 1960; New York University, New York, N.Y., became professor of art history, 1961; Queens College of the City University of New York, Flushing, N.Y., professor of art history, 1961—.

MEMBER: College Art Association of America, Verband Deutscher Kunsthistoriker. *Awards, honors:* Fellowships from American Association of University Women, Belgian American Educational Association, and National Endowment for the Humanities; also awarded Bollinger fellowship and Fulbright fellowship.

WRITINGS—Under name Lotte Brand Philip: *Hieronymous Bosch*, Abrams, 1955; *The Ghent Altarpiece and the Art of Jan Van Eyck*, Princeton University Press, 1971. Contributor to German and American scholarly periodicals.

WORK IN PROGRESS: A comprehensive book on the art of Hieronymous Bosch.

SIDELIGHTS: Foerster told *CA:* "My career as a teacher, art historian, art expert, and writer was greatly delayed by an unfortunate tangle of circumstances connected with my foreign university degree, my lack of teaching experience, and the college structure in the United States at the time of my immigration to this country. I had escaped the persecutions of the Hitler regime in Germany at the last minute, arriving in the United States as late as in 1941.

"Though working successfully as a jewelry designer, I started to put up a desperate fight for a chance to return to my original profession, the history of fine arts. Finally in 1960 a teaching position was offered to me. Today I am working as a professor of art history in my field of specialization which is the art of the Gothic and Renaissance periods in northern Europe. I greatly enjoy the contact with our American students and the rewarding response to my scholarly publications. Since my entire work is based on a new view of the history of art—according to which I am placing the work of art back into its original context—I have been called a pioneer and a revolutionary in my field."

*   *   *

FOGEL, Robert W(illiam) 1926-

PERSONAL: Born July 1, 1926, in New York, N.Y.; son of Harry G. and Elizabeth Fogel; married Enid Morgan, April 2, 1950; children: Steven Dennis, Michael Paul. *Education:* Cornell University, A.B., 1948; Columbia University, A.M., 1960; Johns Hopkins University, Ph.D., 1963. *Home:* 50 Garden St., Cambridge, Mass. 02138. *Office:* Department of Economics and History, Harvard University, 1737 Cambridge St., Cambridge, Mass. 02138.

CAREER: Johns Hopkins University, Baltimore, Md., instructor in economics, 1958-59; University of Rochester, Rochester, N.Y., assistant professor of economics, 1960-64; University of Chicago, Chicago, Ill., associate professor, 1964-65, professor of economics and history, 1965-75; Harvard University, Cambridge, Mass., professor of economics and history, 1975—, Taussig Research Professor, 1973-74. Ford Foundation visiting research professor at University of Chicago, 1963-64; professor of economics and history at University of Rochester, autumns, 1968-75; Pitt Professor of American History and Institutions at Cambridge University, 1975-76; centennial professor at Texas A & M University, 1976; lecturer at dozens of schools in the United States, Australia, Belgium, Canada, France, Germany, England, Japan, Norway, Sweden, Scotland, the Soviet Union, Israel, Ireland, Denmark, and the Netherlands. Member of Mathematical Social Science Board, 1965-72.

MEMBER: American Academy of Arts and Sciences (fellow), National Academy of Sciences, American Association for the Advancement of Science (fellow), Econometric Society (fellow), Economic History Association (member of board of trustees, 1972—; president, 1977-78), Royal Historical Society (fellow), Economic History Society (Glasgow; honorary vice-president, 1967), Columbia University Seminar in Economics and History (associate), Phi Beta Kappa. *Awards, honors:* Social Science Research Council grant, 1966; grant from Mathematical Social Science Board, 1966; National Science Foundation grants, 1967, 1970, 1972, 1974, 1976, 1978; Fulbright grant, 1968; Arthur H. Cole Prize from Economic History Association, 1968; Ford Foundation fellowship, 1970; Schumpeter Prize from Harvard University, 1971; Bancroft Prize in American History from Columbia University, 1975.

WRITINGS: The Union Pacific Railroad: A Case in Premature Enterprise, Johns Hopkins Press, 1960; *Railroads and American Economic Growth: Essays in Econometric History*, Johns Hopkins Press, 1964; (editor with S. L. Engerman, and contributor) *The Reinterpretation of American Economic History*, Harper, 1971; (editor with W. O. Aydelotte and A. G. Bogue, and contributor) *The Dimensions of Quantitative Research in History*, Princeton University Press, 1972; (with Engerman) *Time on the Cross: The Economics of American Negro Slavery*, Little, Brown, 1974. Also author of a Japanese book (title means "Ten Lectures on the New Economic History"), Nan-un-do, 1977.

Contributor: Bruce Mazlish, editor, *The Railroad and the Space Program*, M.I.T. Press, 1965; Ralph Andreano, editor, *New Views on American Economic Development*, Schenkman, 1965; Ross M. Robertson and James L. Pate, editors, *Readings in United States Economic and Business History*, Houghton, 1966; Robertson and A. W. Coats, editors, *Essays in American Economic History*, Arnold, 1969; Allan G. Bogue and other editors, *The West of the American People*, Peacock Press, 1970; Robert Swierenga, editor, *Quantification in American History*, Atheneum, 1970; Andreano, editor, *The New Economic History*, Wiley, 1970; Gerald D. Nash, editor, *Issues in American Economic History*, 2nd edition, Heath, 1972; Peter Temin, editor, *The New Economic History*, Penguin, 1973. Contributor of about twenty-five articles to economic, history, and law journals. General editor of "Quantitative Studies in History" series, Princeton University and Mathematical Social Science Board, 1971-76. Member of editorial board of *Explorations in Economic History*, 1970—, and *Journal of the Social Science History Association*, 1976—.

WORK IN PROGRESS: Mortality in North America, 1650-1910.

SIDELIGHTS: Fogel's books have been published in Spain, Italy, the United Kingdom, and Japan.

*   *   *

FOLEY, Allen Richard   1898-1978

November 11, 1898—February 16, 1978; American educator, historian, and author. Foley wrote *What the Old-Timer Said* and co-wrote *Since the Civil War*. He taught at Dartmouth College from 1924 to 1964. He died in Norwich, Vt. Obituaries and other sources: *New York Times*, February 18, 1978. (See index for *CA* sketch)

*   *   *

FOLSOM, Robert S(lade)   1915-

PERSONAL: Born April 29, 1915, in Cincinnati, Ohio; son of William Cumner (a civil engineer) and Mary H. (Slade) Folsom; married Florence M. Towle (an art gallery manager), March 14, 1942; children: William Bartram, John Edward. *Education:* Tufts University, A.B., 1938; Fletcher School of Law and Diplomacy, A.M., 1939, M.A.L.D., 1940, Ph.D., 1945; attended National War College, 1954-55. *Politics:* Independent. *Home:* 1200 North Nash St., Apt. 509, Arlington, Va. 22209.

CAREER: U.S. Department of State, Diplomatic Service, Washington, D.C., third secretary and vice-consul of American embassy in Port-au-Prince, Haiti, 1941-45, second secretary and consul of American legation in Budapest, Hungary, 1945-48, consul at American consulate general in Canton, China, 1948-49, Hong Kong, 1949, and Saigon, Indochina, 1949-50, first secretary and consul of American

embassy in Mexico City, Mexico, 1950-52, charge d'affaires at American embassy in Port-au-Prince, 1952-54, deputy director of Office of Inter-American Affairs, 1955-58, consul general in Thassaloniki, Greece, 1958-64, on special duty, 1964-65, member of foreign service board of examiners, 1965-67, country director for Cyprus affairs, 1967-69; writer, 1970—.

WRITINGS: Handbook of Greek Pottery, Faber, 1967; *Attic Black-Figured Pottery*, Noyes Press, 1975; *Attic Red-Figured Pottery*, Noyes Press, 1976.

WORK IN PROGRESS: Myths of the Greek Gods; Legends of the Greek Heroes; I, Diomedes.

SIDELIGHTS: Folsom writes: "During my tour in Greece, I became fascinated by the country, its history and people, with the small coins and bits of ancient pottery that I found (I had been greatly intrigued during summers, while in college, by Indian pottery and other artifacts that I found in New Mexico). Accordingly, I talked with Greek archaeologists, showed them my potsherds, and studied. My *Handbook* grew out of my own notes on Greek pottery. Further research produced the two following books. The current books are preliminary to a book I hope to do for my grandson to read when he is nine or ten years old."

*   *   *

FONER, Jack D(onald)   1910-

PERSONAL: Born December 14, 1910, in New York, N.Y.; son of Abraham (a garage owner) and Mary (Smith) Foner; married Lila Kraitz (a painter), June 14, 1942; children: Eric, Tom. *Education:* City College (now of the City University of New York), A.B., 1932; Columbia University, A.M., 1933, Ph.D., 1960. *Politics:* Democrat. *Home:* 205 West End Ave., New York, N.Y. 10023.

CAREER: City College (now of the City University of New York), New York, N.Y., instructor in American history, 1933-42; public lecturer, 1950-68; Colby College, Waterville, Maine, associate professor, 1969-73, professor of American and Afro-American history, 1973-76, professor emeritus, 1976—. Assistant director of Hampshire Lodge, 1956-68. *Military service:* U.S. Army, Quartermaster Corps, 1942-45; became staff sergeant. *Member:* American Historical Association, American Association of University Professors, Phi Beta Kappa. *Awards, honors:* Fellow of Leopold Schepp Foundation, 1972-73.

WRITINGS: (Co-author) *History of Modern Europe*, College Entrance Examination Board, 1937; *The United States Soldier Between Two Wars: Army Life and Reforms, 1865-1898*, Humanities Press, 1970; *The Blacks and the Military in American History: A New Perspective*, Praeger, 1974. Also author of *The Socializing Role of the Military*, U.S. Government Printing Office.

WORK IN PROGRESS: Ethnic and Racial Minorities and the U.S. Military Academies; Jews and the Military in American History; Labor and Radical Groups and the U.S. Military.

BIOGRAPHICAL/CRITICAL SOURCES: Colby College Alumnus, winter, 1975; *Waterville Sentinel*, May 28, 1976, July 30, 1976.

*   *   *

FORBES, Clarence A(llen)   1901-

PERSONAL: Born September 6, 1901, in Colebrook, N.H.; son of Allen Allison (a farmer) and Mamie (Corcoran)

Forbes; married Florence Lemaire, September 1, 1924; children: Jacqueline Forbes Kehoe, Charmian Forbes Clanin, Rodney, Roland, Joyce Forbes Nolan. *Education:* Bates College, A.B., 1922; University of Illinois, A.M., 1924, Ph.D., 1928. *Politics:* Democrat. *Religion:* Roman Catholic. *Home:* 21 East Jeffrey Pl., Columbus, Ohio 43214.

CAREER: University of Cincinnati, Cincinnati, Ohio, instructor in classics, 1925-27; University of Nebraska, Lincoln, assistant professor, 1927-36, associate professor, 1936-42, professor of classics, 1942-48; Ohio State University, Columbus, professor of classics, 1948-71; St. Louis University, St. Louis, Mo., professor of classics, 1972-73; writer, 1973—. *Member:* North American Society for Sport History, American Classical League, Archaeological Institute of America, American Philological Association, Classical Association of the Middle West and South (president, 1950-51). *Awards, honors:* Litt.D. from University of Nebraska, 1971.

WRITINGS: Greek Physical Education, Century Co., 1929; *Neoi,* American Philological Association, 1933; (with Harold S. Wilson) *Gabriel Harvey's Ciceronianus,* University of Nebraska Press, 1945; *Firmicus Maternus: The Error of the Pagan Religions,* Newman Press, 1970; (with Gertrude Drake) *The "Christiad" of Marco Girolamo Vida: Text and Translation,* Southern Illinois University Press, 1978.

SIDELIGHTS: Forbes told *CA:* "For more than half a century I've had a strong interest in the sport, athletics, gymnasia, and physical education of ancient Greece. Hence came membership in the North American Society for Sport History, which was founded in 1973."

AVOCATIONAL INTERESTS: Travel (Greece, Italy, and Roman areas of France and Great Britain).

* * *

FORD, Elizabeth
   See BIDWELL, Marjory Elizabeth Sarah

* * *

FORD, Hilary
   See YOUD, Samuel

* * *

FORD, Stephen 1949-

PERSONAL: Born August 23, 1949, in Toronto, Ontario, Canada; naturalized U.S. citizen, 1963; son of Henry E. (in advertising) and Irene (a boutique owner; maiden name, Packer) Ford. *Education:* Charles Morris Price School of Journalism, diploma, 1969; Camden County Community College, A.A., 1971; also attended New School for Social Research, 1975. *Politics:* "Liberal democrat." *Religion:* Episcopal. *Home:* 2008 County Lane, West Trenton, N.J. 08628.

CAREER/WRITINGS: Courier Post, Cherry Hills, N.J., reporter, 1967-68; Suburban News Group, Cherry Hills, assistant editor, 1969-70; Lorraine Publishing Co., Bordentown, N.J., managing editor, 1970-74; Newspaper Enterprise Assoc., New York, N.Y., associate editor, 1974-76; *Detroit News,* Detroit, Mich., staff writer, 1976-78; freelance writer, 1978—. Notable assignments include coverage of Betty Ford and the 1976 Democratic convention. Creater and writer of column, "Sounds," syndicated by Newspaper Enterprise Assoc. Contributor to *Rolling Stone, Gig, Cue,* and *Circus. Member:* American Civil Liberties Union

(ACLU), Detroit Press Club, Willingboro Amateur Astronomy Society, Sigma Delta Chi. *Awards, honors:* New Jersey Press Association Award, 1971, for best story by individual in investigative reporting, and 1972, for general excellence.

WORK IN PROGRESS: A series of articles on Jamaica's political atmosphere; writing and delivering commentary on the music industry for WWWW-FM in Detroit.

SIDELIGHTS: "I started as a general assignment reporter drifting into political reporting," Ford told *CA,* "but became intrigued with rock music coverage though most reporting is on a superficial level and written for a ten year old mentality. I concentrate on quality rock and entertainment reporting."

When asked what he thought of rock and roll's influence on our culture, Ford responded: "The effect of rock music on contemporary society is incalculable. From its initial impact in the fifties to its current role in daily life, rock's detractors have predicted its imminent demise. It is a death long coming. But rather than rock's supporters losing interest in the state of the art, rock continues to gain broader public acceptance. Adults reviled once by rock's side effects, such as long hair or less-inhibited clothing styles, now sport hair creeping over shirt collars. They wear more casual clothing obviously inspired by rock musicians.

"Rock music will continue as a significant influence in American culture but on a different plane due to its gradual integration with other forms of entertainment (rock variety shows on television, televised award presentations, Hollywood's growing interest in films with a rock theme), and as such, will have an impact but less distinct.

"To summarize, don't envision rock as a dinosaur lacking the good sense to roll over and die. It shall be around for a long time but in a vein wholly different from its origin: viz. there are 'golden oldie' stations, 'big band' stations, mellow, mainstream and all news stations. Rock 'n roll kept its promise to radio as a refreshing breath but it can't help getting stale. The generations of the late fifties, sixties and early seventies will remain faithful to rock's staleness like older generations stay with the Dorseys, Glen Miller and Duke Ellington."

AVOCATIONAL INTERESTS: History, astronomy.

* * *

FOREMAN, Gene 1934-

PERSONAL: Born November 20, 1934, in Fremont, Ohio; son of Clemons W. (a farmer) and Louise (Vogel) Foreman; married Jo Ann Baldwin, December 14, 1957; children: Harry, Valerie, Susan, Jo Claire, Nell Rose. *Education:* Arkansas State College, B.A., 1956. *Home:* 1010 Darby-Paoli Rd., Berwyn, Pa. 19312. *Office: Philadelphia Inquirer,* 400 North Broad St., Philadelphia, Pa. 19101.

CAREER/WRITINGS: Arkansas Gazette, Little Rock, Ark., reporter, 1957, assistant city editor, 1958-60, state editor, 1960-62; *New York Times,* New York, N.Y., copy editor, 1962; *Pine Bluff Commercial,* Pine Bluff, Ark., managing editor, 1963-68; *Arkansas Democrat,* Little Rock, managing editor, 1968-71; *Newsday,* Garden City, N.Y., executive news editor, 1971-73; *Philadelphia Inquirer,* Philadelphia, Pa., managing editor, 1973—. *Military service:* U.S. Army Reserve, 1956-67, active duty, 1956-57; became major. *Member:* Sigma Delta Chi.

* * *

FOREMAN, Russell 1921-

PERSONAL: Born December 15, 1921, in Melbourne, Australia; son of Ralph John (a farmer) and Monica (Mulcare) Foreman; married Mary Shipton (a consular official). *Education:* Educated in Melbourne, Australia. *Home:* Il Corneto, Panzano-in-Chianti, 50020 Florence, Italy.

CAREER: Department of Aircraft Production, 1935-45, began as draftsman in Sydney, Australia, became project engineer in Melbourne, Australia; Murray Valley Newspapers, Victoria, Australia, editor, 1946-49; currently director of English worship at Villa Mercede, Florence, Italy. Founder of Russell Foreman School of Painting. Committee member of Lega del Chianti. *Member:* Society of Authors, Authors Club, Carlton Club, Royal Melbourne Yacht Squadron.

WRITINGS: (With Max Meldrum) *The Science of Appearances,* Shepherd Press, 1950; *Long Pig* (novel), McGraw, 1958; *Sandalwood Island* (novel), Heinemann, 1960; *O Arquipelago da Morte,* Editoria Civilizacao Brasileireira, 1960; *Prede Bianche,* Rizzoli Milano, 1961; *La Carne Humana,* Editorial Planeta, 1966; *The Ringway Virus* (novel), Millington, 1976, Little, Brown, 1977; *Virus,* Bancho Shobo, 1977. Also author of *Oneata,* 1959.

SIDELIGHTS: Foreman writes: "My novels show a desire to educate through entertainment. *Long Pig* and *Sandalwood Island* are historical fiction written to explain the effect of European entry into the Southwest Pacific with special reference to the Sandalwood wars beginning with the discovery of sandalwood in the Fiji Islands in 1800. A later novel, *The Ringway Virus,* tries to explain how human interference with the environment could cause mutations in viruses (such as influenza) which could have catastrophic effects for mankind."

* * *

FORMAN, Harrison 1904-1978

June 15, 1904—January 31, 1978; American explorer, aviator, photographer, journalist, and author. Forman was best known for his coverage of the Sino-Japanese conflict in the 1930's, the Chinese government under Chiang Kai-shek, and the Japanese bombardment of Shanghai in 1937. Forman received criticism during the close of the conflict between Chinese nationalists and Communists because he favored Mao Tse-tung's communist leadership though he didn't believe Mao was an advocate of communism. He was also among the first Americans to explore Tibet. Forman's books include *Through Forbidden Tibet, Changing China,* and *Report From Red China.* He died in New York, N.Y. Obituaries and other sources: *The Author's and Writer's Who's Who,* 6th edition, Burke's Peerage, 1971; *Authors of Books for Young People,* 2nd edition, Scarecrow, 1971; *The Writers Directory, 1976-78,* St. Martin's, 1976; *Who's Who in America,* 40th edition, Marquis, 1977; *New York Times,* February 2, 1978. (See index for *CA* sketch)

* * *

FORREST, Derek W(illiam) 1926-

PERSONAL: Born February 15, 1926, in Liverpool, England; son of Walter and Edith (Leech) Forrest; married Pamela Jones (a teacher), August 21, 1953; children: Tansy. *Education:* Keble College, Oxford, B.A., 1951, M.A., 1954; University of London, Ph.D., 1956. *Politics:* None. *Religion:* None. *Residence:* Wirral, England. *Office:* Department of Psychology, Trinity College, University of Dublin, Dublin, Ireland.

CAREER: Research psychologist in Farnborough, England,

1951-52; University of London, London, England, lecturer in psychology, 1952-62; University of Dublin, Trinity College, Dublin, Ireland, reader, 1962-66, professor of psychology, 1966—, head of department, 1966—, and fellow. Consultant in clinical psychology. *Military service:* Royal Navy, 1944-47. *Member:* British Psychological Society, Psychological Society of Ireland, Royal Geographical Society, Eugenics Society.

WRITINGS: Francis Galton: The Life and Work of a Victorian Genius, Elek Books, 1974. Contributor to psychology, medical, and history of science journals.

WORK IN PROGRESS: Research for biographies of W. T. Stead and William and Henry James; a book on the history of hypnotism; research on the nature of love.

SIDELIGHTS: Forrest commented, "I am fascinated by the vitality, optimism, and hypocrisy of Victorian England and the impact of scientific discoveries on that culture." *Avocational interests:* European travel, the sea, most sports.

* * *

FORRESTAL, Dan J(oseph), Jr. 1912-

PERSONAL: Born September 2, 1912, in St. Louis, Mo.; son of Dan Joseph (a merchant) and Kathryn (Otto) Forrestal; married Esther L. Witte, October 5, 1940; children: Dan Joseph III, Patrick G., Elizabeth Katherine (Mrs. William R. Reinus). *Education:* Attended St. Louis University, 1930-32, and Harvard University, 1948. *Religion:* Roman Catholic. *Home:* 431 Conway Lake Dr., St. Louis, Mo. 63141. *Office:* 7701 Forsyth Blvd., St. Louis, Mo. 63105.

CAREER: St. Louis Globe-Democrat, St. Louis, Mo., 1926-47, variously sports writer, feature editor, war correspondent, and assistant managing editor; Monsanto Co., St. Louis, assistant director of industrial and public relations, 1947-58, director of public relations, 1958-74; Forrestal & Associates, Inc. (public relations counseling agency), St. Louis, president, 1974—. Foreign correspondent, representing North American Newspaper Alliance and Columbia Broadcasting System, 1945-46. St. Louis University, member of president's council, chairman of public relations committee, 1956-68; member of board, St. John's Mercy Hospital. *Member:* Public Relations Society of America (national president, 1957; member of seminar committee, 1958-76, chairman, 1967), Overseas Press Club, Manufacturing Chemists' Association (chairman of public relations committee, 1967-67), Sigma Delta Chi, Harvard Club (New York City); Noonday Club and St. Louis Club (both St. Louis). *Awards, honors:* St. Louis University Alumni Merit Award, 1961; Gold Plate Award, American Academy of Achievement, 1974; Gold Anvil Award, Public Relations Society of America, 1974.

WRITINGS: (With Richard W. Darrow and others) *The Dartnell Public Relations Handbook,* Dartnell Corp., 1967, revised edition, 1978; *Faith, Hope and Five Thousand Dollars: The Story of Monsanto,* Simon & Schuster, 1977. Contributor of articles on communications and related subjects to journals.

WORK IN PROGRESS: Two histories of American corporations, one on the Williams Companies in Tulsa, Okla., the other on the Seven-Up Bottling Company in St. Louis, Mo.

SIDELIGHTS: Reviewing *Faith, Hope and Five Thousand Dollars,* a critic from the *St. Louis Globe-Democrat* wrote: "Forrestal details the careers of the presidents . . . and of the many talented managers and scientists the company has attracted through the years. He describes some of the brilliant methods by which Monsanto products have achieved market and technical leadership. In all, he does a remarkable job of sorting out what must have been a complex, tangled skein of corporate history and personalities, putting them in order and serving them up to his readers with clarity, balance, and a touch of class.''

In an article about company histories, Forrestal wrote: ''Why launch a company history in the first place? The most frequent reason is the anniversary. Milestones, after all, deserve notice. Indeed, many companies have had Horatio Alger-type startups meriting both current review and permanent record.

''A bit more pragmatically, some corporate executives feel there are lessons for tomorrow to be found in case histories of yesterday. George Santayana, Spanish poet and philosopher put it this way: 'Those who cannot remember the past are condemned to repeat it.' ''

BIOGRAPHICAL/CRITICAL SOURCES: Women's Wear Daily, November 15, 1977; *St. Louis Globe-Democrat*, December 24-25, 1977; *Public Relations Journal*, February, 1978.

* * *

FORT, John 1942-

PERSONAL: Born September 4, 1942; son of Tomlinson (a university professor) and Madeline (Scott) Fort; married Joan Murphey, September 15, 1962; children: Lulah Ellis, John Porter, Cynthia Joan. *Education:* Attended University of the South, 1961-62; University of Southern California, B.A., 1965. *Home address:* Seaside Plantation, Edisto Island, S.C. 29438.

CAREER: Headmaster of private day school in Charleston, S.C., 1970-72; Sea Pines Co., Hilton Head Island, S.C., resort development manager, 1973-74; Tallulah's, Inc. (retail clothing chain), Hilton Head Island, president, 1974—.

WRITINGS: June the Tiger, Little, Brown, 1975.

WORK IN PROGRESS: A companion book to *June the Tiger*.

SIDELIGHTS: Fort comments: ''My major interests center around my farm, where I raise race horses and play polo. Polo essentially occupies all my leisure time.''

* * *

FOSBURGH, Pieter Whitney 1914(?)-1978

1914(?)—March 5, 1978; American conservationist, naturalist, magazine editor, and author. Fosburgh, founder and editor of the *Conservationist,* resigned after a ten-year association with the journal published by the New York State Conservation Department in protest of an experimental pheasant-rearing project in which fifteen-thousand birds had died of botulism. Fosburgh later served as president of North Woods Club, a private association for wildlife conservation. He was conservation adviser to the New York state legislature, and the author of numerous books and magazine articles on conservation. Obituaries and other sources: *New York Times*, March 7, 1978.

* * *

FOX, Levi 1914-

PERSONAL: Born August 28, 1914, in Leicestershire, England; son of John William and Julia (Stinson) Fox; married Jane Richards (marriage ended); children: Roger James, Elizabeth Jane, Patricia Mary. *Education:* Oriel College,

Oxford, B.A. (first class honors), 1936, M.A., 1938; University of Manchester, M.A., 1938. *Home:* 27 Welcombe Rd., Stratford-upon-Avon, England. *Office:* Shakespeare Centre, Stratford-upon-Avon, England.

CAREER: Shakespeare Centre, Stratford-upon-Avon, England, director of Shakespeare Birthplace Trust, 1945—. *Military service:* British Army, 1940-43. *Member:* International Shakespeare Association (deputy chairman), Royal Society of Literature (fellow), Royal Historical Society (fellow), Society of Antiquarians (fellow). *Awards, honors:* Received doctorate from George Washington University, 1964; New York University medal, 1964; named officer of the Order of the British Empire, 1964; named deputy lieutenant of County of Warwick, 1967.

WRITINGS: The Administration of the Honor of Leicester in the Fourteenth Century, E. Backus, 1940; *The History of Coventry's Textile Industry*, privately printed, 1944; *Leicester Castle* (pamphlet), Leicester Publicity and Development Department, 1944; *Coventry's Heritage: An Introduction to the History of the City*, Coventry Evening Telegraph, 1947, 2nd edition, 1957; (with Percy Russell) *Leicester Forest*, E. Backus, 1948; *Shakespeare's Town, Stratford-upon-Avon: A Pictorial Record with Historical Introduction and Descriptions*, H. & J. Busst, 1949; *Stratford-upon-Avon*, Garland Publishing, 1949.

(Author of introduction and notes) Gerald Gardiner, *Oxford: A Book of Drawings*, Garland Publishing, 1951; *Stratford-upon-Avon: An Appreciation*, Jarrolds, 1952; *The Borough Town of Stratford-upon-Avon*, privately printed, 1953; (editor) *English Historical Scholarship in the Sixteenth and Seventeenth Centuries*, Oxford University Press, 1956; *Stratford-upon-Avon: Official Guide*, privately printed, 1958; *William Shakespeare: A Concise Life* (pamphlet), Jarrolds, 1959; *Shakespeare's Town and Country*, Cotman House, 1959.

Shakespeare's Stratford-upon Avon: A Souvenir in Colour With Historical Descriptions, J. Salmon, 1962; *Shakespeare's Birthplace: A History and Description*, Jarrolds, 1963; (editor) William Shakespeare, *Sonnets*, Cotman House, 1963; *Stratford-upon-Avon in Colour: A New Pictorial Guide*, Jarrolds, 1963; *The Shakespearian Properties*, Jarrolds, 1964, new edition, 1975; *The Shakespeare Anniversary Book*, Jarrolds, 1964; (editor) *Correspondence of the Reverend Joseph Greene: Parson, Schoolmaster, and Antiquary, 1712-1790*, H.M.S.O., 1965; *Celebrating Shakespeare: A Pictorial Record of the Celebrations Held at Stratford-upon-Avon During 1964 to Mark the Four-Hundredth Anniversary of the Birth of William Shakespeare*, privately printed, 1965; *New Place: Shakespeare's Home* (pamphlet), Jarrolds, 1966; *A Country Grammar School: A History of Ashby-de-la-Zouch Grammar School Through Four Centuries, 1567 to 1967*, Oxford University Press, 1967; *The Shakespeare Book*, Jarrolds, 1969, new edition, 1972.

Shakespeare's England, Putnam, 1972; *In Honour of Shakespeare: The History and Collections of the Shakespeare Birthplace Trust*, Jarrolds, 1972; *A Splendid Occasion: The Stratford Jubilee of 1769* (pamphlet), V. Ridler, 1973; *Stratford Past and Present: A Pictorial Record of the Ancient Town of Stratford*, Oxford Illustrated Press, 1975; *Stratford-upon-Avon and the Shakespeare Country*, Jarrolds, 1975.

Contributor to Shakespeare studies journals.

WORK IN PROGRESS: Research on historical records of Stratford-upon-Avon and Warwickshire.

FOX, Robert 1943-

PERSONAL: Born February 2, 1943, in Brooklyn, N.Y.; son of Charles and Mary (Wilkes) Fox; married Susan Goldstein (a teacher), 1967; children: Joshua. *Education:* Brooklyn College of the City University of New York, B.A., 1967; Ohio University, M.A., 1970. *Home address:* Route 4, Pomeroy, Ohio 45769. *Office:* Ohio Arts Council, 50 West Broad St., Columbus, Ohio 45769.

CAREER: Ohio University, Athens, instructor in English, 1969-71; Rider College, Trenton, N.J., writer-in-residence, 1971-72; Ohio University, assistant editor of publications, 1973-77; Ohio Arts Council, Columbus, poet-in-residence, 1977—. *Awards, honors:* Finalist for Iowa Letters Award, 1974, 1975.

WRITINGS: Destiny News (stories), December Press, 1977. Work represented in anthologies, including *Concerns, Currents, and Composition,* 1971; *Three Stances of Modern Fiction,* 1972; *Literature: An Introduction,* 1973; *Literature: Fiction,* 1974; and *Challenge of Conflict,* 1977. Contributor of poems and stories to magazines, including *Trace, Prism International, Salmagundi,* and *North American Review.*

WORK IN PROGRESS: Second Chance, a novel; *Tuscarora Tunnel's Last Touchdown,* a novel; *Confessions of a Dead Politician,* a novel; *Whom Is the Real Pronto Bananas,* a novel; *Wind Poems,* poetry; *Other World,* poetry; *Love Stories and Other Tales,* short stories; *Deadent Planet,* a novel, with Matthew Paris.

SIDELIGHTS: Fox told *CA:* "I write about what is real and accessible, and also about what is not 'real' in everyday terms. Some of my writing is described as surreal. I do not exercise in techniques of surrealism; rather, my interest is to push to and beyond the limits of consciousness, to discover what the imagination is capable of creating and knowing."

* * *

FOXLEY, William M(cLachlan) 1926-1978

PERSONAL: Born August 8, 1926, in Salt Lake City, Utah; son of William L. (a fingerprint expert) and Grace (a teacher; maiden name, McLachlan) Foxley; married Norma Noall (a teacher), December 16, 1948; children: William N., Louise Foxley Spencer, Janice Foxley Billings, Laura. *Education:* McCune School of Music and Art, B.Mus., 1954; Brigham Young University, B.A., 1954, Ph.D., 1969; University of Utah, M.F.A., 1955. *Home:* 2691 North 700 E., Provo, Utah 84601. *Office:* Department of Music, Brigham Young University, Provo, Utah 84602.

CAREER: Church of Jesus Christ of Latter-day Saints, General Music Committee, Salt Lake City, Utah, field representative, 1949-69; Brigham Young University, Provo, Utah, associate professor of music, 1969-78. *Military service:* U.S. Army, 1944-46. *Member:* Music Teachers National Association (regional first vice-president), Music Teachers National Conference, American Guild of Organists, Utah Music Teachers Association (past president).

WRITINGS: Organ Study Guide, Brigham Young University Press, 1974; *Piano Study Guide and Workbook Course Outline,* Brigham Young University Press, 1975, revised edition, 1975. Editor of *Utah Music Educator.*

WORK IN PROGRESS: Revising *Organ Study Guide;* research on music history.

AVOCATIONAL INTERESTS: Swimming, photography.

(Died in 1978)

FRANCIS, C.D.E.
 See HOWARTH, Patrick (John Fielding)

* * *

FRANCIS, Clare 1946-

PERSONAL: Born April 17, 1946, in Thames Ditton, Surrey, England; daughter of Owen and Joan (Norman) Francis; married Jacques Redon (a teacher), July 8, 1977. *Education:* University of London, B.Sc., 1967. *Home:* Fleet House, 9A Captains Row, Lymington, Hampshire, England.

CAREER: Beecham Products Ltd., London, England, in marketing, 1968-70; Robertsons Foods Ltd., London, product manager, 1970-73; writer, 1973—. *Member:* Royal Cruising Club, Seaview Yacht Club. *Awards, honors:* Chichester Award from Royal Yacht Squadron of England, 1976; member of Order of the British Empire, 1978.

WRITINGS: Come Hell or High Water, Pelham Books, 1976; *Woman Alone,* McKay, 1977; *Victoire Atlantique* (title means "Atlantic Victory"), Librairie Arthaud, 1977; *Come Wind or Weather,* Pelham Books, 1978. Contributor to yachting magazines in the United States, Europe, and England.

SIDELIGHTS: Clare Francis writes: "My books tell the story of my participation in the 1976 Singlehanded Transatlantic Race in which I was the first British woman entry. Out of 125 starters, only 70 finished in what was the hardest race ever. There were three gales and a storm during which five boats sank and two men lost their lives. I finished thirteenth to take the women's trophy and the record for the fastest ever time by a woman singlehanded.

"*Come Wind or Weather* tells the story of my entry, as the first woman skipper of a large ocean racer, in the 1977-78 Whitbread Round the World Race. This unique race takes yachts between forty-five and eighty feet long down into the notorious Southern Ocean, round the 'three capes' which include the famous Cape Horn. The book chronicles the exciting events of the 27,000 mile, seven month race, from the hurricane force winds and icebergs my boat encountered at sixty degrees south, to the calms and burning heat of the Equatorial regions."

* * *

FRANCK, Sebastian
 See JACOBY, Henry

* * *

FRANK, Joseph (Nathaniel) 1918-

PERSONAL: Born October 6, 1918, in New York, N.Y.; married Marguerite J. Straus, May 11, 1953; children: Claudine, Isabelle. *Education:* Attended New York University, 1937-38, University of Wisconsin, Madison, 1941-42, and University of Paris, 1950-51; University of Chicago, Ph.D., 1960. *Home:* 24 Haslet Ave., Princeton, N.J. 08540. *Office:* Department of Comparative Literature, Princeton University, 326 East Pyne, Princeton, N.J. 08540.

CAREER: Bureau of National Affairs, Washington, D.C., editor, 1942-50; American Embassy, Paris, France, special researcher, 1951-52; Princeton University, Princeton, N.J., Christian Gauss Lecturer, 1954-55, lecturer in English, 1955-56; University of Minnesota, Minneapolis, assistant professor of English, 1958-61; Rutgers University, New Brunswick, N.J., 1961-66, began as associate professor, became professor of comparative literature; Princeton University, professor of comparative literature, 1966—, professor of Slavic studies, 1966-68, director of Christian Gauss Seminars in Criticism, 1966—. Visiting professor at Harvard University, spring, 1965. *Member:* Modern Language Association of America, American Association for the Advancement of Slavic Studies, American Academy of Arts and Sciences (fellow). *Awards, honors:* Fulbright scholar in Paris, 1950-51; Guggenheim fellow, 1956-57; award from National Institute of Arts and Letters, 1958; American Council of Learned Societies grants, 1961-62, 1964-65, 1967-68, 1970-71; Bollingen Foundation grant, 1962; award from National Endowment for the Arts for article, "N. G. Chernyshevsky: A Russian Utopia"; James Russell Lowell Prize from Modern Language Association of America, 1977; Christian Gauss Award from Phi Beta Kappa, 1977.

WRITINGS: The Widening Gyre: Crisis and Mastery in Modern Literature, Rutgers University Press, 1963; (contributor) R.W.B. Lewis, editor, *Malraux: A Collection of Critical Essays,* Prentice-Hall, 1964; (editor) R. P. Blackmur, *A Primer of Ignorance,* Harcourt, 1967; (author of introduction) Paul Valery, *Masters and Friends* (essays), Princeton University Press, 1968; *F. M. Dostoevsky: The Seeds of Revolt (1821-1849),* Princeton University Press, 1976.

Work represented in *American Literary Anthology II,* Random House, 1968. Contributor of about fifty articles and reviews to literary journals, including *Critical Inquiry, Times Literary Supplement, Dissent,* and *Encounter.*

WORK IN PROGRESS: Another book on Dostoevsky, for Princeton University Press.

* * *

FRANK, Sheldon 1943-

PERSONAL: Born June 7, 1943, in Philadelphia, Pa.; son of Maxwell (a shipping clerk) and Reba (Kazze) Frank; married Winifred Carter Millikin (a dancer), August 24, 1968. *Education:* Harvard University, A.B. (magna cum laude), 1965; University of Chicago, graduate study, 1968-72. *Home and office:* 34 Greene St., New York, N.Y. 10013.

CAREER: Writer, 1972—. *Member:* Phi Beta Kappa. *Awards, honors:* Woodrow Wilson honorary fellowship, 1968; National Endowment for the Arts creative writing fellowship for fiction, 1974-75.

WRITINGS: (With Sally Banes and Tem Horwitz) *Sweet Home Chicago* (guidebook), Chicago Review Press, 1974; (with Banes and Horwitz) *Our National Passion: Two Hundred Years of Sex in America,* Follett, 1976. Contributor to *Encyclopaedia Britannica* and *The People's Almanac II.* Contributor of stories, articles, and reviews to magazines and newspapers, including *Fiction Midwest, Chicago Review, National Observer, Chicago Reader, New Republic,* and *New York Times Book Review.*

WORK IN PROGRESS: Now's the Time, a novel.

* * *

FRANKE, Christopher 1941-

PERSONAL: Born December 25, 1941, in Cleveland, Ohio; son of Norman (an accountant) and Jeannette (a dog breeder; maiden name, Hanford) Franke. *Education:* Attended Ohio State University, 1961-62, and Cuyahoga Community College, 1967-74. *Home:* 4208½ Whitman Ave., Cleveland, Ohio 44113.

CAREER: Everyman (magazine), Cleveland, Ohio, editor, 1972-74, 1977—. *Member:* Poets' League of Greater Cleveland (vice-president, 1977—). *Awards, honors:* Grant from Coordinating Council of Literary Magazines, 1975.

WRITINGS: Title (poetry), Poetry Center, Cleveland State University, 1975; *S.* (poetry), Deciduous, 1977.

WORK IN PROGRESS: Untitled, a collection of poems; *ARTicles,* a collection of poem-collages and concrete poems; *The Collected Critical Works of Christopher Franke.*

SIDELIGHTS: Franke writes: "In my poetry, I have a propensity for plurisignation and pun. I like the presumptuousness of sesquipedalians, whether I use them or not. Yet where meaning may lack clarity (because, to borrow from the vernacular, 'Who knows what it all means'), I like a clarity of intention. In writing, I feel a certain playfulness, and I want to engage. Whether I do a one-word concrete poem, a collage, or a 'sonnet,' where, I have done what I would have done and a reader is able to 'appreciate' this occurrence, intention will have its realization. The heaviness of this paragraph incites me to say, 'Just read my poems. Either you will react to them, or you will not.'"

* * *

FRANKEL, Eliot 1922-

PERSONAL: Born August 2, 1922, in New Jersey; married Charlotte Hartman (a public relations worker); children: Charles, Mark. *Education:* Rutgers University, Litt.B., 1943; graduate study at Vanderbilt University, 1946-47. *Office:* NBC News, 30 Rockefeller Plaza, New York, N.Y.

CAREER/WRITINGS: Nashville Tennessean, Nashville, Tenn., reporter, 1946; *Newark Evening News,* Newark, N.J., reporter, 1947-50; currently works for National Broadcasting Co., New York, N.Y. Notable assignments include pioneering the early satellite coverage of European news, including the Winston Churchill funeral. Associate adjunct professor at Long Island University, 1972-73, and New York University, 1974-75. Member of Municipal Cable TV Committee, Tenafly, N.J. *Military service:* U.S. Army Air Corps, 1943-46; served as correspondent for India-China Hump Express, 1944-46. *Member:* Academy of Television Arts and Sciences, Investigative Reporters and Editors Association, Sigma Delta Chi. *Awards, honors:* American Medical Association award in journalism, 1971; Emmy award, 1972, for best television magazine program; American Bar Association awards, 1971, 1972, 1973, and 1974; also winner of Peabody, Columbia Dupont, and Ohio State Awards.

* * *

FRANKLIN, Colin 1923-

PERSONAL: Born October 8, 1923, in London, England; son of Ellis Arthur (a banker) and Muriel (Waley) Franklin; married Charlotte Hajnal-Konyi, January 4, 1950; children: Simon, Jacob, Daniel, Noah, Gideon. *Education:* St. John's College, Oxford, M.A., 1949. *Home address:* Home Farm, Culham, Oxford, England.

CAREER: Routledge & Kegan Paul (publishers), London, England, vice-chairman, 1959-70; antiquarian bookseller in Oxford, England, 1970—. *Military service:* Royal Naval (Volunteer) Reserve, 1942-45; became lieutenant. *Member:* Royal Society of Antiquaries (fellow), Designer Bookbinders (honorary fellow), Athenaeum Club, Garrick Club, Savile Club. *Awards, honors:* Casberd Exhibitioner at St. John's College, Oxford.

WRITINGS: *The Private Presses,* Studio Vista, 1969; *Emery Walker,* Cambridge University Press, 1973; *Themes in Aquatint,* Book Club of California, 1978. Contributor to periodicals.

WORK IN PROGRESS: *Gordon Craig; Early Colour Printing;* memoirs.

AVOCATIONAL INTERESTS: "Pleasure and distraction."

* * *

FRANKS, C(harles) E(dward) S(elwyn) 1936-

PERSONAL: Born October 23, 1936, in Toronto, Ontario, Canada; married wife, Daphne; children: Caroline, Peter, Timothy. *Education:* Queen's University, Kingston, Ontario, B.A. (honors), 1959; Oxford University, D.Phil., 1973. *Office:* Department of Political Studies, Queen's University, Kingston, Ontario, Canada.

CAREER: Member of department of political studies at Queen's University, Kingston, Ontario.

WRITINGS: The Canoe and White Water (nonfiction), University of Toronto Press, 1977.

WORK IN PROGRESS: A book on the politics of peaceful nuclear power.

* * *

FRANTZ, Ralph Jules 1902-

PERSONAL: Born November 1, 1902, in Springfield, Ohio; son of George Franklin (an industrialist) and Lillian R. (Schaefer) Frantz; married Loulette Isabelle Desrumeaux, March, 1926 (died January 28, 1967); married Lillian Maxine Moore (a librarian), June 15, 1968. *Education:* Attended Wittenberg College (now University) and Sorbonne, University of Paris. *Politics:* Democrat. *Religion:* None. *Home:* 362 Plaza Rd. N., Fair Lawn, N.J. 07410.

CAREER: Springfield Sun, Springfield, Ohio, reporter and sports editor, 1919-22; *Cleveland Times,* Cleveland, Ohio, 1922-25, began as reporter, became state editor, assistant city editor, then Sunday editor; *Chicago Tribune-New York Daily News* European edition, Paris, France, 1925-34, began as copy editor, became night editor, then managing editor; *New York Herald Tribune,* New York, N.Y., 1935-66, began as copy editor, became assistant night editor, telegraph editor, then Long Island editor; *Record,* Hackensack, N.J., 1966-71, began as copy editor, became market final editor; free-lance writer, 1971—. Lifetime member of board of trustees of Correspondents Fund. *Member:* Overseas Press Club (founding life member; vice-president, 1950-55).

WRITINGS: (Contributor) Hugh Ford, editor, *The Left Bank Revisited,* Pennsylvania State University Press, 1972. Contributor to magazines and newspapers. Member of advisory board of *Lost Generation Journal.*

WORK IN PROGRESS: Research on Elliot Paul.

SIDELIGHTS: Frantz writes: "Having been a working newspaperman for more than fifty years, and having edited millions of words of bad writing, I have no desire to contribute to the flood. I enjoy reading and rejoice over good writing. My own writing is straightforward without literary pretensions.

"Now retired, when I do write something occasionally, it is for pleasure, rather than profit. I have cooperated with a number of writers, giving them freely of my recollections of the Paris years, 1925-34, and anecdotes about my colleagues and acquaintances of those days, among whom were Elliot

Paul, William L. Shirer, Waverley Root, Sterling Noel, Eugene Jolas, O. W. (Tom) Riegel, David Darrah, Vincent Sheean, Jay Allen, George Seldes, and many others."

* * *

FRARY, Michael 1918-

PERSONAL: Born May 28, 1918, in Santa Monica, Calif.; son of Earl (an architect) and Henrietta (Chittenden) Frary; married Gloria Marvin, 1942 (divorced, 1951); married Peggy Finch, July 19, 1951; children: Michael, Mark, David. *Education:* University of Southern California, B.Arch., 1940, M.F.A., 1941; also attended Chicago Art Institute, 1941, Escuela de Bellas Artes, San Miguel de Allende, Mexico, 1949, and Academie de la Grande Chaumiere, 1949-50. *Home:* 3409 Spanish Oak Dr., Austin, Tex. 78731. *Office:* Department of Art, University of Texas, Austin, Tex. 78712.

CAREER: Assistant art director for major motion picture companies (Goldwyn, Paramount, and Universal Studios), 1945-48; University of California, Los Angeles, instructor in art, 1945-48; instructor in art at Chouinard Art Institute, Los Angeles City College, and San Antonio Art Institute, 1949-52; University of Texas, Austin, professor of art, 1952—. Has had more than one hundred-seventy solo exhibitions since 1954, including one at National Gallery; work is represented in about fifty museums and other public collections, including the National Collection, Washington, D.C. *Military service:* U.S. Navy, 1941-45; became lieutenant.

MEMBER: National Watercolor Society (past member of board of directors), Southwestern Watercolor Society (honorary life member), Texas Watercolor Society (regional director). *Awards, honors:* More than one hundred-twenty awards from art institutions and organizations, including Butler Institute of American Art, National Watercolor Society, Texas Watercolor Society, and Oklahoma Art Center.

WRITINGS: Impressions of the Big Thicket (paintings and drawings; text by Bill Owens), University of Texas Press, 1973; *Impressions of the Texas Panhandle* (text and paintings), Texas A & M University Press, 1977; *Impressions of the Texas Gulf Coast* (text and paintings), Texas A & M University Press, 1979.

Illustrator: Bill Brett, *Stolen Steers,* Texas A & M University Press, 1977.

WORK IN PROGRESS: Impressions of the Rio Grande, text and paintings, publication by Texas A & M University Press expected in 1980.

BIOGRAPHICAL/CRITICAL SOURCES: Southwestern Art, Volume II, number 4, December, 1970.

* * *

FRATTI, Mario 1927-

PERSONAL: Born July 5, 1927, in L'Aquila, Italy; came to United States, 1963, naturalized citizen, 1974; son of Leone and Palmira (Silvi) Fratti; married Lina Fedrigo, 1953 (marriage ended); married Laura Dubman, 1964; children: three. *Education:* Ca' Foscari University, Venice, Italy, Ph.D., 1951. *Home:* 145 West 55th St., New York, N.Y. 10019. *Agent:* Bruce Savan, 120 West 57th St., New York, N.Y. 10019.

CAREER: Rubelli Publishers, Venice, Italy, translator, 1953-63; *Sipario,* Milan, Italy, drama critic, 1963-66; Columbia University, New York City, professor, 1967; Adelphi College, New York City, professor, 1967-68; Hunter College of the City University of New York, New York City, professor, 1967-78; playwright. Drama critic for *Ridotto, Paese Sera,* and *L'Ora,* all 1963-73. *Military service:* Italian Army, 1951-52; became lieutenant. *Member:* Drama Desk (New York City), Outer Circle (New York City). *Awards, honors:* RAI-Television Prize, 1959; Ruggeri Prize, 1960, 1967, 1969; Golden Mask Award, 1960; Bologna Award, 1961; Vallecorsi Award, 1964; Lentini-Rosso di San Secondo Award, 1964; Unasp-Enars Prize, 1967, 1969; Arta-Terme Award for radio drama, 1973.

WRITINGS—Plays; except as indicated: "Il Campanello" (produced in Milan, 1958), published in *Ridotto,* 1958, translation as "Doorbell" (produced in New York City, 1970) published in *Ohio University Review,* 1971; "La Menzogna" (title means "The Lie"; produced in Milan, 1959), published in *Cynthia,* 1963; "A" (produced in Rome, 1965), published in *Ora Zero,* 1959; *Volti: Cento Poesie* (poetry; title means "Faces: One Hundred Poems"), Editione Mariano, 1960; "La Partita" (title means "The Game"; produced in Pesaro, 1960), published in *Ridotto,* 1960; "Il Rifuto" (produced in Mantua, 1960), published in *Dramma,* 1965, translation as "The Refusal" (produced in New York City, 1972) published in *Races* (see below); *In Attesa* (produced in La Spezia, 1960), E.I.S.T. (Rome), 1964, translation as "Waiting" (produced in New York City, 1970) published in *Poet Lore,* 1968.

"Il Ritorno" (produced in Bologna, 1961), published in *Ridotto,* 1961, translation as "The Return" (produced in New York City, 1963) published in *Masterpieces of the Italian Theatre,* Collier, 1967; "La Domanda" (title means "The Questionnaire"; produced in La Spezia, 1961), published in *La Prora,* 1962; "Flowers From Lidice," published in *L'Impegno,* 1961, and in *Dramatics,* 1972; *L'Assegno,* Pellegrini, 1961, translation as "The Third Daughter" published in *First Stage,* 1966; *Confidenze* (produced in Rome, 1962), E.I.S.T., 1964, translation as "The Coffin" (produced in New York City, 1967) published in *Four Plays* (see below); "Gatta Bianca" (produced in Rome, 1962), published in *Dramma,* 1962, translation as "White Cat" published in *Races* (see below); "Il Suicidio" (produced in Spoleto, 1962), published in *Cynthia,* 1962, translation as "The Suicide" (produced in New York City, 1965) published in *New Theatre of Europe II,* edited by Robert W. Corrigan, Dell, 1964.

"La Gabbia" (produced in Milan, 1963), published in *Cynthia,* 1962, translation as "The Cage" (produced in New York City, 1966) published in *New Theatre of Europe II* (see above); "The Academy" (produced in New York City, 1963), published as *L'Accademia,* E.I.S.T., 1964, and as "The Academy" in *Masterpieces of Italian Theatre* (see above); "La Vedova Bianca" (produced in Milan, 1963), published in *Ridotto,* 1972, translation published as *Mafia* (produced in Tallahassee, Fla., 1966), Proscenium Press, 1971; *La Telefonata* (produced in Rome, 1965), E.I.S.T., 1964, translation as "The Gift" (produced in New York City, 1966) published in *Four Plays* (see below); "I Seduttori" (title means "The Seducers"; produced in Venice, 1972), published in *Dramma,* 1964; "I Frigoriferi" (produced in Pistoia, 1965), published in *Ora Zero,* 1964, translation as "The Refrigerators" (produced in New York City, 1971) published in *Modern International Drama,* 1970.

"Le Spie" (title means "The Spies"), produced in Pescara, 1967; *Eleonora Duse* (produced in Sarasota, Fla., 1967), Breakthrough Press, 1972; "Il Ponte" (produced in Pesaro, 1967), published in *Ridotto,* 1967, translation published as *The Bridge* (produced in New York City, 1972), McGraw,

1970; "The Victim" (produced in Sacramento, Calif., 1968), published as *La Vittima,* Lo Faro, 1972; "Che Guevara" (produced in Toronto, 1968; produced in New York City, 1971), published in *Enact* (New Delhi), 1970, and in *Costume* (Bergamo), 1972; "Unique" (produced in Baltimore, 1968), published in *Ann Arbor Review,* 1971; "L'Amico Cinese" (produced in Fano, 1969), published in *Ridotto,* 1969, translation as "The Chinese Friend" (produced in New York City, 1972), published in *Enact,* 1972; *L'Ospite Romano* (title means "The Roman Guest"; produced in Pesaro, 1971), E.N.A.R.S., 1969.

"La Panchina del Venerdi" (produced in Milan, 1970), translation as "The Friday Bench" (produced in New York City, 1971) published in *Four Plays* (see below); *Betrayals,* Pellegrini, 1970, published in *Drama and Theatre,* 1970; "The Wish" (produced in Denton, Tex., 1971), published in *Four Plays* (see below); "The Other One" (produced in New York City, 1971), published in *Races* (see below); "The Girl With a Ring on Her Nose" (produced in New York City, 1971), published in *Janus,* 1972; "Too Much" (produced in New York City, 1971), published in *Janus,* 1972; "Cybele," produced in New York City, 1971; "The Brothel" (produced in New York City, 1972), published in *Mediterranean Review,* 1971; "The Family" (produced in New York City, 1972), published in *Enact,* 1971. Also author of "The Piggy Bank," produced in New York City, 1978, and "The Biggest Thief in Town," produced in New York City, 1978. Also author of "Chile 1973," "Madam Senator," "Rapes," "Fire," "Dialogue With a Negro," "Originality," and "Patty Hearst."

English collections: *Four Plays* (includes "The Coffin," "The Gift," "The Friday Bench," and "The Wish"), Edgemoor, 1972; *Races: Six New Plays* (includes "Rapes," "Fire," "Dialogue With a Negro," "White Cat," "The Refusal," and "The Other One"), Proscenium Press, 1972. Also author of *The Family [and] The Chinese Friend,* Breakthrough Press, *The Seducers [and] The Roman Guest,* Drama Bookshop, *The Cage [and] the Suicide,* Drama Bookshop, and *The Academy [and] the Return,* Drama Bookshop.

WORK IN PROGRESS: A play, "Sundays"; a musical, "Nights With Nino."

*　　　*　　　*

FREE, James S(tillman) 1908-

PERSONAL: Born November 5, 1908, in Gordo, Ala.; son of James S. (a lumberman) and Nettie (Bell) Free; married Ann Cottrell (a free-lance writer), February 24, 1950; children: Elissa Blake. *Education:* University of Alabama, B.A., 1929; Columbia University, B.Litt., 1930. *Politics:* Democrat. *Home:* 4700 Jamestown Rd., Washington, D.C. 20016. *Office:* 1750 Pennsylvania Ave. N.W., Suite 1320, Washington, D.C. 20006.

CAREER/WRITINGS: Reporter for *Birmingham News,* Birmingham, Ala., *Richmond Times-Dispatch,* Richmond, Va., and *Washington Star,* Washington, D.C., 1935-41; *Chicago Sun,* Chicago, Ill., staff writer for Washington bureau, 1941-42, 1945-46; *Raleigh News & Observer,* Raleigh, N.C., Washington correspondent, 1947-53; *Birmingham News,* Washington correspondent, 1947—. Notable assignments include coverage of national political conventions, 1948-76, the Berlin Crisis, 1961, and follow-up reaction from NATO countries, 1962. Contributor to *New Yorker, Collier's,* and *New Republic. Military service:* U.S. Naval Reserve, 1942-68; served in the Pacific during World War II;

retired as captain. *Member:* White House Correspondents Association, National Press Club, Sigma Delta Xi (president, Washington chapter, 1977-78), Gridiron Club, International Club of Washington.

SIDELIGHTS: James Free writes that he has "concentrated on integrating national development—primarily out of Washington—in terms of impact on area of readerships. Also, to a lesser degree, I have written about the impact—or image—of Alabama personalities and events on the nation, as reflected in Washington. While emphasis has been on congressional and administration activity and reaction, national defense has been a high priority interest."

* * *

FREEDMAN, Richard 1932-

PERSONAL: Born February 14, 1932, in New York, N.Y.; son of Hyman (a dentist) and Bertha (Zimmerman) Freedman; married Helen Baird (a computer programmer), September 5, 1969; children: David, Pamela. *Education:* New York University, A.B., 1952, M.A., 1953; Columbia University, M.S., 1954, Ph.D., 1967. *Politics:* Democrat. *Religion:* "Mozart." *Home:* 144 Clark St., Newton, Mass. 02159. *Office:* Department of English, Simmons College, 300 Fenway, Boston, Mass. 02115.

CAREER: Columbia University, New York, N.Y., instructor in English, 1959-64; Simmons College, Boston, Mass., instructor, 1964-66, assistant professor, 1966-70, associate professor. 1970-74, professor of English, 1974—. Member of National Endowment for the Humanities panel, 1970-75. *Member:* National Book Critics Circle, Jane Austen Society, Mencken Society.

WRITINGS: The Novel, Newsweek, 1975.

WORK IN PROGRESS: A book on opera in literature.

SIDELIGHTS: Freedman told *CA:* "In my tenth year as a professional book-reviewer, I still feel wild excitement whenever a book-mailer arrives on my desk, not merely at the prospect of some money (hardly munificent), but because my attitude to new books is that of an obstetrician, however hardened, to new babies. Too often recently that excitement turns to ashes within the first few pages of a designedly illiterate, totally unedited spy or disaster 'thriller.' I am appalled at the amount of space lavished by the few remaining American book reviews on such trash, especially in comparison to the supposedly poverty-stricken British reviews, and am equally appalled at the speed with which the few good books find themselves relegated to the remainder shelves.

"I am a lifetime Anglophile, but the penury of my profession has only allowed me one year (1972-73) so far in Britain. As it happened, it was the year of Watergate, which made me homesick for my native country, Looneyland West. My second and third favorite islands are Manhattan and Martha's Vineyard, which should unite and form a new country called Civilization."

* * *

FREEMAN, Don 1908-1978

PERSONAL: Born August 11, 1908, in San Diego, Calif.; son of Mortimer Roy (a salesman) and Hazel (Currier) Freeman; married Lydia Cooley (an artist), June 30, 1931; children: Roy Warren. *Education:* Attended San Diego School of Fine Arts and Art Students League of New York. *Address:* 1932 Cleveland Ave., Santa Barbara, Calif. 93103.

CAREER: Author and illustrator. Worked as jazz trumpeter, free lance artist, painter, and print-maker; graphic artist with the *New York Times* and *New York Herald Tribune* for more than twenty years. *Awards, honors:* Received Book World Children's Spring Book Festival Award, 1953, for *Pet of the Met;* runner-up for Caldecott Medal, 1958, for *Fly High, Fly Low;* award from Southern California Council on Literature for Children and Young People, 1962, for *Come Again, Pelican,* and 1976, for *Will's Quill;* Commonwealth Club of California Silver Medal, 1975, for *The Paper Party.*

WRITINGS—All for children; all self-illustrated; all published by Viking, except as noted: *It Shouldn't Happen* (American wit and humor), Harcourt, 1945; *Come One, Come All!* (autobiography), Rinehart, 1949; (with wife, Lydia Freeman) *Chuggy and the Blue Caboose,* 1951; (with L. Freeman) *Pet of the Met,* 1953; *Beady Bear,* 1954; *Mop Top,* 1955, reprinted, 1970; *Fly High, Fly Low,* 1957; *The Night the Lights Went Out,* 1958; *Norman the Doorman,* 1959; *Space Witch,* 1959.

Cyrano the Crow, 1960; *Come Again, Pelican,* 1961; *Ski Pup,* 1963; *Botts, the Naughty Otter,* Golden Gate Junior Books, 1963; *The Turtle and the Dove,* 1964; *Dandelion,* 1964; *A Rainbow of My Own,* 1966; *The Guard Mouse,* 1967; *Add-a-Line Alphabet,* Golden Gate Junior Books, 1968; *Corduroy,* 1968; *Tilly Witch,* 1969; *Quiet! There's a Canary in the Library,* Golden Gate Junior Books, 1969.

Forever Laughter, Golden Gate Junior Books, 1970; *Hattie the Backstage Bat,* 1970; *Penguins of All People!,* 1971; *Inspector Peckit,* 1972; *Flash the Dash,* Childrens Press, 1973; *The Paper Party,* 1974; *The Seal and the Slick,* 1974; *Will's Quill,* 1975; *The Chalk Box Story,* Lippincott, 1976; *Bearymore,* 1976; *A Pocket for Corduroy,* 1978.

Illustrator: William Saroyan, *The Human Comedy,* Harcourt, 1943, revised edition, 1971; James Thurber, *White Deer,* Harcourt, 1945; Justin B. Atkinson, *Once Around the Sun,* Harcourt, 1951; Julia L. Sauer, *Mike's House,* Viking, 1954; Jane Randolph, *Circus in Peter's Closet,* Crowell, 1955; Ann N. Clark, *Third Monkey,* Viking, 1956; Anne H. White, *The Uninvited Donkey,* Viking, 1957; Clyde R. Bulla, *Ghost Town Treasure,* Crowell, 1958; Dorothy Koch, *Monkeys Are Funny That Way,* Holiday, 1962; Saroyan, *My Name Is Aram,* Harcourt, 1963; Clark, *This for That,* Golden Gate Junior Books, 1965; Myra B. Brown, *Best Friends,* Golden Gate Junior Books, 1967; Elizabeth Hall, *Voltaire's Micromegas,* Golden Gate Junior Books, 1967; Ruth A. Sonneborn, *Seven in a Bed,* Viking, 1968; Helen Bauer, *California Indian Days,* Doubleday, 1968; Brown, *Best of Luck,* Golden Gate Junior Books, 1969; Robert Burch, *Joey's Cat,* Viking, 1969; Julia Cunningham, *Burnish Me Bright,* Pantheon, 1970; Jacklyn M. Matthews, *Edward and the Night Horses,* Golden Gate Junior Books, 1971; Elizabeth K. Cooper, *The Wild Cats of Rome,* Golden Gate Junior Books, 1972; Cunningham, *Far in the Day,* Pantheon, 1972; Marjorie Thayer, *The Christmas Strangers,* Childrens Press, 1976.

SIDELIGHTS: Don Freeman played trumpet in a jazz band while attending art school in New York City. He supplemented his income by doing drawings of the theater, which appeared in the *New York Times* and the *New York Herald Tribune.* Drawing soon became his only means of livelihood when he forgot his trumpet on the subway. *Come One, Come All!,* an autobiography, relates these events in detail. The *New York Herald Tribune Book Review* called it "a warm and mellow book, one to cheer up any one who has lived to see the hopes of his youth realized." The *Christian*

Science Monitor commented: "His book does more than affectionately chronicle life and amusing adventures in Manhattan. It traces the maturing of an artist. A riffle through its profusion of illustrations 'drawn from memory' establishes Mr. Freeman's claim to the name."

Freeman believed his books for children to be a form of theatrical expression. All of his stories stem from personal experiences or direct observation of the experiences of others. With his wife, Lydia, Don Freeman wrote *Pet of the Met*, described by the *Chicago Sunday Tribune* as "a riot of bold color, spirited action, and amusing text." The *New York Herald Tribune Book Review* commented: "The text is brief and dramatic; the big, bold, full-color pictures are dashing, humorous and full of the spirit of the beloved old Met. What a laugh it would have given Mozart!" A *New York Times* reviewer wrote: "The economical prose (scarcely more than captions) is perfectly integrated with the pictures. In the latter the intensity of color, the vigor of line heighten the theatrical effect of both setting and plot."

The Turtle and the Dove was reviewed by a *Christian Science Monitor* critic who wrote: "Adult readers may find the story pleasantly allegorical. Be that as it may, it is still a delightful tale for very young children, done with the gentle Don Freeman touch. His quiet, reassuring, blue-gray drawings are delicately excellent, and readers will close the book with a wistful sigh."

Freeman told *CA*: "Creating picture books for children fulfills all my enthusiasms and interests and love of life." A one-man show of his paintings and graphics was presented at the Margo Feiden Galleries in New York City in 1976. Several of his books for children have been adapted into filmstrips.

BIOGRAPHICAL/CRITICAL SOURCES: Kirkus, September 15, 1949; *Christian Science Monitor*, November 10, 1949, May 7, 1964; *New York Times*, November 13, 1949, April 12, 1953, October 6, 1957; *New York Herald Tribune Book Review*, December 11, 1949, May 17, 1953, November 17, 1957; *Chicago Sunday Tribune*, June 7, 1953.

OBITUARIES: New York Times, February 3, 1978.

(Died February 1, 1978, in New York, N.Y.)

* * *

FREEMAN, Harry 1906-1978

PERSONAL: Born March 8, 1906, in Brooklyn, N.Y.; son of Isaac (a businessman) and Stella (Lvovitch) Freeman; married Vera Shapiro (an economist), October 7, 1927. *Education:* Cornell University, B.A., 1926; further study at Columbia University, 1928-29. *Home:* 22 East 89th St., New York, N.Y. 10028. *Office:* 50 Rockefeller Plaza, New York, N.Y. 10020.

CAREER/WRITINGS: Brooklyn Daily Eagle, Brooklyn, N.Y., reporter, 1926-27; *New Masses*, New York City, editorial assistant, 1926; *Daily Worker*, New York City, reporter, then foreign editor, 1927; Tass (Soviet news agency), correspondent, 1929-30, assistant managing editor, then managing editor of New York bureau, 1930-78. Notable assignments include coverage of U.S. election campaigns beginning 1932, both Democratic and Republican national conventions beginning 1936, and the founding conference of the United Nations, 1945. *Member:* Foreign Press Association (vice-president, 1946-48), United Nations Correspondents Association (founder; member of standing committee, 1946-48), National Press Club, Academy of Political Science, Phi Beta Kappa, Phi Kappa Phi. *Awards, honors:*

Order of People's Friendship, 1976, for contributions to Soviet-American understanding.

SIDELIGHTS: Freeman founded and became secretary of the short-lived Proletarian Artists and Writers whose membership included such notable writers as Upton Sinclair, John Dos Passos, and Van Wyck Brooks.

OBITUARIES: New York Times, January 15, 1978; *Time*, January 30, 1978.*

(Died January 13, 1978, in Manhattan, N.Y.)

* * *

FREESE, Arthur S. 1917-

PERSONAL: Born November 16, 1917, in New York, N.Y.; son of David and Hattie (Seidel) Freese; married Ruth N. Wilson (an executive), May 28, 1958. *Education:* New York University, B.S., 1935. *Religion:* Unitarian-Universalist. *Home and office:* 137 East 36th St., New York, N.Y. 10016.

CAREER: Writer. *Member:* American Society of Journalists and Authors, National Association of Science Writers, Authors Guild, Authors League of America, Mystery Writers of America, Mensa.

WRITINGS: Management of Temporomandibular Joint Problems, Mosby, 1962; *Careers in the Medical Sciences*, Dutton, 1972; *Headaches: The Kinds and the Cures*, Doubleday, 1973; *Pain*, Putnam, 1974; *Aspirin and Your Health*, Pyramid Publications, 1974; *Occult Medicine*, Dial, 1975; *Dr. Finneson on Low Back Pain*, Putnam, 1975; *Managing Your Doctor*, Stein & Day, 1976; *Your Kidneys, Their Care, and Their Cure*, Dutton, 1976; *Hypnosis for You*, Popular Library, 1976; *Help for Your Grief*, Schocken, 1977; *The Miracle of Vision*, Harper, 1977; *Arthritis*, New American Library, 1978; *The End of Senility*, Arbor House, 1978. Contributor to encyclopedias, including *Reader's Digest Medical Encyclopedia*. Contributor to most national popular magazines.

WORK IN PROGRESS: A book on drugs for Basic Books; a book on medical care for Simon & Schuster.

SIDELIGHTS: Freese writes: "My major interest is in the medical, psychiatric, and social science area—but I feel strongly that such books should be scientifically responsible and medically accurate. Pushing gimmicky ideas in order to make a bestseller is, to me, utterly irresponsible and a moral and ethical betrayal of whatever talents an author has, an insult, in essence, to the profession he or she claims to follow."

* * *

FREW, David R(ichard) 1943-

PERSONAL: Born January 20, 1943, in Erie, Pa.; son of John R. (a salesman) and Margaret M. (a personnel manager; maiden name, Huffman) Frew; married Mary Ann Borgia (a professor), November 6, 1966; children: Kristin, Cheryl, David. *Education:* Gannon College, B.S., 1964, M.A., 1967; Kent State University, D.B.A., 1970. *Religion:* Roman Catholic. *Home:* 529 Shenley Dr., Erie, Pa. 16505. *Office:* Center for Management Development, Gannon College, Perry Sq., Erie, Pa. 16505.

CAREER: Basic Industries, Cleveland, Ohio, industrial engineer, 1964-67; Singer Corp., Philadelphia, Pa., manager of industrial engineering, 1967-68; Kent State University, Kent, Ohio, instructor in operations research, 1968-70; Gannon College, Erie, Pa., assistant professor, 1970-72, associate professor of organization theory and behavior, 1973—, director of business administration program, 1971—, co-director of Center for Management Development. Faculty member for American Sterilizer Corp. Educational Division, 1971— (has directed more than fifty seminars on motivation and communication). *Member:* Academy of Management, American Institute of Decision Sciences, American Sociological Association, American Institute of Industrial Engineers.

WRITINGS: The Management of Stress, Nelson-Hall, 1976. Contributor of more than twenty articles to administration and management journals and to local magazines. Contributing editor of *Erie Today.*

* * *

FRIDAY, Nancy 1937-

PERSONAL: Born August 27, 1937, in Pittsburgh, Pa.; daughter of Walter (a financier) and Jane (Colbert) Friday; married W. H. Manville (a writer), October 20, 1967. *Education:* Attended Wellesley College. *Home:* 1108 Southard St., Key West, Fla. 33040. *Agent:* Betty Anne Clarke, International Creative Management, 20 West 51st St., New York, N.Y. 10019.

CAREER: San Juan Island Times, San Juan, Puerto Rico, reporter, 1960-61; editor, *Islands in the Sun* (magazine), 1961-63; free-lance writer, 1963—.

WRITINGS—Nonfiction: *My Secret Garden,* Trident, 1973; *Forbidden Flowers,* Pocket Books, 1975; *My Mother/My Self,* Delacorte, 1977; *His Secret Garden,* Delacorte, in press.

SIDELIGHTS: My Mother/My Self concerns the relationship between mothers and daughters—what Friday has termed "the great untalked about subject" and "the last taboo." Friday's interest in the mother/daughter bond grew out of her research on women's sex fantasies, when she realized the powerful effects of the bond on daughters' sexual development. But, as she told Judy Klemesrud, when she approached her male literary agent with an outline for the book, he said "What about their fathers?" Friday then acquired a woman agent who sold the book quickly.

Before writing *My Mother/My Self,* Friday interviewed more than 300 women, as well as psychologists and sociologists. What she discovered was that, contrary to popular belief, mother love is seldom perfect.

Guilt is a major theme in a mother/daughter relationship. Friday told Sally Moore that both mothers and daughters "feel inappropriately guilty—guilty for what they could have done, or think they should have done or been, and guilty for wanting emotional independence. We call it guilt, but it's really a suffocating dependency and fear of loss. This not only grips us all our lives but often increases after a mother's death." Anger is another unresolved emotion. Friday continued: "It mostly comes from daughters who were taught to be dependent and passive, to control their emotions, to keep their hands off their bodies, never air their emotions, their rage, their competitive feelings. We are angry at the person who taught us not to express what we feel."

Friday has suggested that in order to lessen the conflict with their daughters, mothers should raise them as they raise their sons. Because mothers "don't train their daughters in courage the way they train their sons," Friday explained to Klemesrud, "women are frightened people. They just haven't had the repetitious practice of the difficulties of life. They grow up packed in cotton wool." Friday also feels that "mothers should free their daughters to sometimes turn to surrogate mothers—such as aunts or teachers—without resenting it," according to Klemesrud. "The fact is," Friday commented to Klemensrud, "we need more than one mother for every child."

BIOGRAPHICAL/CRITICAL SOURCES: People, December 19, 1977; *New York Times,* December 30, 1977; *New York Times Book Review,* February 12, 1978.

* * *

FRIED, Frederick 1908-

PERSONAL: Born December 11, 1908, in Brooklyn, N.Y.; son of Samuel Isaac (a watchmaker) and Rachel (Wachtel) Fried; married Sadie Brown (marriage ended, 1948); married Mary McKenzie Hill (an artist and writer), September 17, 1949; children: Robert Frederick, Rachel Banks. *Education:* Mechanics Institute, certificate, 1932. *Politics:* "Progressive Democrat." *Religion:* "Born Jewish." *Home and office:* 875 West End Ave., New York, N.Y. 10025.

CAREER: Artist in New York, N.Y., 1934-37; Department Store Union, New York City, business manager, 1937-42; worked as art director for advertising agency in New York, 1948-53; Bonwit Teller, New York City, art director, 1955-62; Smithsonian Institution, Washington, D.C., fellow and consultant, 1966—. Union organizer in New York City, 1937-42. *Military service:* U.S. Army Air Forces, Intelligence, 1942-45; received four battle stars. *Member:* Musical Box Society International (historian), National Carousel Association (founder; honorary life member), South Street Seaport (founding member).

WRITINGS: A Pictorial History of the Carousel, A. S. Barnes, 1964; *Fragmentary Landmarks,* Brooklyn Museum, 1966; *Artists in Wood,* C. N. Potter, 1970; (with Edmond Gillon, Jr.) *New York Civic Sculpture,* Dover, 1976; (with wife, Mary Fried) *The Uncelebrated American Arts,* Pantheon, 1978; *The Encyclopedia of American Coin-Operated Machines,* J.W.S. Publishing, 1978. Contributor to art magazines and art preservation journals.

WORK IN PROGRESS: Architectural Ornamentation from the Mid-Nineteenth to the Early Twentieth Century.

SIDELIGHTS: Fried told *CA:* "I am a collector. The history of each item or group is important to me. In nearly all instances the names or makers were unknown. I consider my great contribution the erasure of 'Artist Unknown' from wall cards in museums and collections with the replacement of a name, date, and provenance. This adventure into research is a continuing thing. My lectures show the procedure of discovery, as an aid to students in the techniques of research. I warn my students not to rely on newspaper or magazine articles—my research shows they quote each other with all errors from the first to the last."

* * *

FRIED, Marc (Allen) 1922-

PERSONAL: Born May 29, 1922, in Newport, R.I.; son of Max (a painter) and Anna (Masserman) Fried; married Joan Zilbach (a psychiatrist), May 1, 1953; children: Lise, Diana, Susanna, Alan. *Education:* City College (now of the City University of New York), B.S.S., 1943, graduate study, 1946-47; Harvard University, Ph.D., 1955. *Home:* 36 Amory St., Brookline, Mass. 02146. *Office:* Laboratory of Psychosocial Studies, Boston College, Chestnut Hill, Mass. 02167.

CAREER: Cleveland State Hospital, Cleveland, Ohio, psychologist, summer, 1949; Harvard University, Cambridge, Mass., research analyst at Russian Research Center, 1950-53; psychologist, Massachusetts Mental Health Center, 1953-56; Harvard University, Center for Community Studies, 1957-66, began as coordinator of research, became research director; Boston College, Chestnut Hill, Mass., research professor of human sciences, 1964—, director of Institute of Human Sciences, 1965-67, 1970-72, director of Laboratory of Psychosocial Studies, 1973—. Research assistant at Boston Psychopathic Hospital, summer, 1948; research associate and lecturer at Harvard University Medical School, 1957-67; lecturer at Brandeis University, 1953-54; associate psychologist, and later psychologist at Massachusetts General Hospital, 1957-67. Member of board of directors of Center for Child and Family Studies, 1962-65, Boston Social Service Exchange, 1962-68, and Council on Social Data Systems, 1965-70; member of executive board of Brookline Council on Planning and Development, 1969-77; member of executive committee and board of directors of Coolidge Corner Community Corp., 1977—; president of Arts Group of Brookline, 1964-68. Member of advisory panel for National Cooperative Highway Research Program, 1972—; member of review committee for National Institute of Mental Health, 1964-68, and Center for the Study of Metropolitan Problems, 1975—; consultant to Social Security Administration. *Military service:* U.S. Army, Infantry, 1943-46.

MEMBER: American Psychological Association, American Association for the Advancement of Science, American Orthopsychiatric Association, Society for the Psychological Study of Social Issues, Massachusetts Psychological Association (member of board of directors, 1966-68), Brookline Mental Health Association. *Awards, honors:* Grants from National Institute of Mental Health, 1958-64, 1966-67, 1971-75, 1975-76, 1975-78, U.S. Civil Rights Commission, 1966, U.S. Office of Economic Opportunity, 1968-70, and Charles F. Kettering Foundation, 1974-75, 1975-76.

WRITINGS: The World of the Urban Working Class, Harvard University Press, 1973.

Contributor: Leonard J. Duhl, editor, *The Urban Condition,* Basic Books, 1963; Duhl, editor, *Urban America and the Planning of Mental Health Services,* Group for the Advancement of Psychiatry, 1964; Mildred Kantor, editor, *Mobility and Mental Health,* C. C Thomas, 1965; Sam B. Warner, Jr., editor, *Planning for a Nation of Cities,* M.I.T. Press, 1966; Bernard Friedan and Robert Morris, editors, *Urban Planning and Social Policy,* Basic Books, 1968; Leigh M. Roberts, Norman S. Greenfield, and Milton H. Miller, editors, *Comprehensive Mental Health: The Challenge of Evaluation,* University of Wisconsin Press, 1968; Daniel P. Moynihan, editor, *On Understanding Poverty: Perspectives from the Social Sciences,* Basic Books, 1969; John Kosa, Aaron Antonovsky, and Irving Kenneth Zola, editors, *Poverty and Health: A Sociological Analysis,* Harvard University Press, 1969; Helen McGill Hughes, editor, *Cities and City Life,* Allyn & Bacon, 1970; Joseph Eaton, editor, *Migration and Social Welfare,* National Association of Social Workers, 1971; Joe R. Feagin, editor, *The Urban Scene: Myths and Realities,* Random House, 1973.

Contributor of about twenty articles to professional journals and to newspapers. Member of editorial board and editor of "Research Notes," *Journal of the American Institute of Planners,* 1963-65; advisory editor of *International Journal of Psychiatry,* 1963—.

WORK IN PROGRESS: Race- and Income-Integrated

Housing; research on the meaning of community in modern urban life and on the impact of unemployment on adaptation.

* * *

FRIED, Marc B(ernard) 1944-

PERSONAL: Born April 25, 1944, in New York, N.Y.; son of Bernard J. (a dentist) and Celia (a teacher; maiden name, Paisner) Fried. *Education:* Attended Queens College of the City University of New York, 1960-61, and Ulster County Community College, 1965-66; State University of New York College at New Paltz, B.S., 1968. *Religion:* None. *Home address:* Sand Hill Rd., R.F.D., Gardiner, N.Y. 12525.

CAREER: Professional musician, 1961-75; farmer in Gardiner, N.Y., 1974—. Chairman of Shawangunk Democratic Committee, 1973-77.

WRITINGS: The Early History of Kingston and Ulster County, N.Y., Ulster County Historical Society, 1975.

SIDELIGHTS: Fried writes: "Since early childhood, I have been inspired by the great physical beauty of my immediate environment: from a simple wood- and coal-heated frame house on ten acres, a broad view that looks out over the woods, meadows, and farms of the Wallkill Valley, to the white cliffs of the Shawangunk Mountains. The setting, to which my family moved when I was a year old, has been crucial in establishing my curiosity about, and eventual scholarship in, local history, my love of nature and the outdoors, my later political activism as an environmentalist, and my determination never to become caught up in the desperate irrelevancies of urban or suburban life, acquisitiveness, or the forty-hour week.

"I have always considered my fourteen-year musical career (I played the drums) a bit of an anomaly. It took me to such diverse locations as Grossinger's Hotel, the Officers' Club at Thule Air Force Base in Greeland, and Carnegie Hall. It made few demands on my time, and provided me adequately with a subsistence income, which is all that I've ever required."

On politics, Fried commented: "Now that we are no longer dropping bombs on people in Indochina, our greatest political horror is the ecological collision course on which this nation and much of the western and westernized world is charted. The problems of industrial and nuclear pollution, resource depletion, and overpopulation will almost certainly bring an eventual collapse of industrialized society as we know it, and may well threaten the existence of our species. Given the moral, social, and political history of the human race, I am not optimistic that any change in political styles or systems can prevent the unfolding debacle. But my pessimism does not seriously diminish for me the demonstrated value of pragmatic political action toward specific near- and medium-term goals. I have worked for such goals both as a private citizen and through the Democratic Party."

And on religion: "Most religions have directly or indirectly led people to lower their expectations and limit their options in this life, while holding out the hope of unlimited reward in an afterlife. My own lack of belief in an afterlife has led me to a total commitment to this life here on Earth—to its variety, its beauty, its enormous possibilities in terms of human relationships, self-discovery and self-realization, and experiencing the natural world in all its diversity. If I have a 'religion,' it is to proceed with this life—and to proceed within a framework of social and moral consciousness and historical and cultural perspective."

AVOCATIONAL INTERESTS: Gardening, camping, hiking, winter mountaineering, hitchhiking around the country, rock music at local bars, "spending long afternoons with my cat on my lap, a pipe in my mouth, and a fire in the fireplace."

BIOGRAPHICAL/CRITICAL SOURCES: Kingston Daily Freeman, September 28, 1975, March 7, 1976.

* * *

FRIEDMAN, Josephine Troth 1928-
(Joy Troth Friedman)

PERSONAL: Born October 23, 1928, in Bryn Mawr, Pa.; daughter of Edward Pemberton and Eleanor (Adams) Troth; married Jere Howard Friedman (a graphic designer), August 4, 1954; children: Edward P., Stephen T. *Education:* Attended Philadelphia College of Art, 1947-51. *Home and office:* 508 Midland Ave., Berwyn, Pa. 19312.

CAREER: Free-lance illustrator, 1951—. *Member:* Authors Guild, Authors League of America, Philadelphia Children's Reading Round Table.

WRITINGS—Self-illustrated children's books; all under name Joy Troth Friedman: *What's So Important About . . . ,* Grosset, 1972; *Look Around and Listen,* Grosset, 1974. Illustrator of books and periodicals for children.

SIDELIGHTS: Joy Friedman comments: "I started to write as a result of illustrating. The idea for my first book grew from something that one of my children did in school." Friedman's books have been published in England, Argentina, Sweden, Denmark, Finland, Germany, the Netherlands, Belgium, and France.

* * *

FRIEDMAN, Joy Troth
See FRIEDMAN, Josephine Troth

* * *

FRIEDMAN, Sara Ann 1935-

PERSONAL: Born October 4, 1935, in New York, N.Y.; daughter of Daniel J. (an attorney) and Ruth (a camp director; maiden name, Gordon) Riesner; married Victor Friedman (an attorney), June 21, 1958; children: Eric, Diana, Michael. *Education:* Attended Smith College, 1954-56; Barnard College, B.A., 1957. *Politics:* Democrat. *Religion:* Jewish. *Home:* 7 West 95th St., New York, N.Y. 10025. *Agent:* McIntosh & Otis, Inc., 475 Fifth Ave., New York, N.Y. 10017.

CAREER: Batten, Barton, Durstine and Osborn (advertising agency), New York City, secretary, 1957-58; Bobbs-Merrill Co., New York City, editorial assistant, 1958-59; *Signal* (magazine servicing military industrial complex), Washington, D.C., editorial assistant, 1959-61; Grolier, Inc., New York City, assistant editor, 1963-65; free-lance writer, 1965—. Volunteer for civil rights movement, Congress of Racial Equality, and WMCA Call for Action. Chairperson of West Side Fair Housing Committee, and Materials and Education Committee of the Friends of the Bronx Zoo.

WRITINGS: (With Lois Schwartz) *No Experience Necessary* (employment guide), Dell, 1971; (with David Jacobs) *Police: A Precinct at Work,* Harcourt, 1975; *How Was School Today, Dear?: Fine, What's for Dinner?,* Reader's Digest Press, 1977; (with Alice Shick) *Zoo Year,* Lippincott, 1978. Writer for the series "Family" on ABC-TV.

WORK IN PROGRESS: Mushrooms: A Celebration; Hummingbirds Fly Backwards, a novel dealing with the plight of the Maya in Yucatan.

SIDELIGHTS: Sara Friedman writes: "My interests are broad, border on the esoteric, and reflect the fact that I view writing as probably three parts life commitment to one part profession. Fortunately, I am financially able to indulge these interests, because until recently they have not worked to my professional advantage.

"Essentially, I write more to learn, to explore, to grow, than to sell. I use writing as an expression of love and source of truth, my typewriter acting as final challenger forcing me to confront the blank page and refusing to let my fingers move until they answer all questions honestly. I am also interested in developing the skills of language, narrative, imagery, and the communication of ideas so that others will respond as I do in my happiest reading experiences. As a result, whether the form is fiction or nonfiction, the market juvenile or adult, the subject mushrooms or police, and the method solitary or collaborative, I have learned something important from every book I have written—and each one has been better than the last. At the same time I surely do not denigrate million dollar movie or paperback sales and would love to share my thoughts with millions of readers. But I can only do what I can do, when I can do it."

* * *

FROHLICH, Norman 1941-

PERSONAL: Born September 30, 1941, in Winnipeg, Manitoba, Canada; son of Israel and Sarah (Alberstat) Frohlich; married Roberta Stein (a writer), September 4, 1966; children: Katherine, Daniel, Jonah. *Education:* University of Manitoba, B.Sc. (honors), 1963; Rutgers University, M.S., 1965; Princeton University, M.A., 1968, Ph.D., 1970. *Home:* 373 Oxford St., Winnipeg, Manitoba, Canada R3M 3H9. *Office:* Management Committee, Cabinet, 330 Legislative Blvd., Winnipeg, Manitoba, Canada.

CAREER: University of Texas, Austin, assistant professor, 1971-74, associate professor of government, 1974-75; Cabinet Management Committee, Winnipeg, Manitoba, program audit officer, 1976—. *Member:* American Political Science Association, Public Choice Society. *Awards, honors:* Outstanding academic book award, 1971, for *Political Leadership and Collective Goods.*

WRITINGS: (With Joe Oppenheimer and Oran Young) *Political Leadership and Collective Goods,* Princeton University Press, 1972; (with Oppenheimer) *Modern Political Economy,* Prentice-Hall, 1978.

WORK IN PROGRESS: Continuing research on mathematical-economic models of politics with a growing emphasis on bureaucratic-administrative behavior and Canadian politics.

* * *

FUJIWARA, Michiko 1946-
(Michiko Saito)

PERSONAL: Born December 6, 1946, in Yokohama, Japan; daughter of Tatsuo (a painter) and Kiyoko Saito; married Masami Fujiwara, October 6, 1974; children: Ken, Jun. *Education:* Attended Kuwasawa Design Institute, 1965-68. *Home:* 4-19-15 Kitazawa, Setagaya-ku, Tokyo, Japan.

CAREER: Associated with Shufu to Seikatsu (publishers), 1967-68; Matsukiya Department, Yokohama, Japan, graphic designer, 1968-69; Japan Advertising Center, Tokyo, illustrator, 1969-70; free-lance illustrator and writer, 1970—.

WRITINGS: (Under name Michiko Saito) *Jenny's Journey* (self-illustrated juvenile), McGraw, 1974.

Illustrator: Elizabeth Ando, *Japanese Cooking*, Knopf, 1978. Also illustrator of *The World Is Narrower*, by Masako Osodo.

SIDELIGHTS: Michiko Fujiwara writes that she came to New York in 1972, planning to stay for three months. Instead, she remained two years, wrote a book, and designed Christmas cards. Since returning to Japan in 1974, she has illustrated book covers, made animal masks for a children's television program, and continued writing. After a longer writing career, she intends to visit New York again.

* * *

FULLER, Edmund (Maybank) 1914-
(Amicus Curiae)

PERSONAL: Born March 3, 1914, in Wilmington, Del.; married Ann Graham, 1936; children: four. *Residence:* Kent, Conn.

CAREER: Writer. Teacher at New School for Social Research, 1940-43, South Kent School, 1952-63, Columbia University, 1952-54, and St. Stephens School, 1965-66. Trustee and chairman of academic committee, Wykeham Rise School.

WRITINGS—Fiction: *A Star Pointed North*, Harper, 1946; *Brothers Divided*, Bobbs-Merrill, 1951; *The Corridor*, Random House, 1963; *Flight*, Random House, 1970.

Nonfiction: *A Pageant of the Theatre*, Crowell, 1941, revised edition, 1965; *John Milton* (juvenile; illustrated by Robert Ball), Harper, 1944; *George Bernard Shaw: Critic of Western Morale*, Scribner, 1950; *Vermont: A History of the Green Mountain State*, State Board of Education, 1952; *Tinkers and Genius*, Hastings House, 1955; *Man in Modern Fiction: Some Minority Opinions on Contemporary American Writing*, Random House, 1958; *Peter the Apostle* (juvenile), Doubleday, 1961; *Books With Men Behind Them*, Random House, 1962; *Successful Calamity: A Writer's Follies on a Vermont Farm*, Random House, 1966; *Charles Williams' All Hallows' Eve*, Seabury, 1967; (with David E. Green) *God in the White House: The Faiths of American Presidents*, Crown, 1968; *Prudence Crandall: An Incident of Racism in Nineteenth-Century Connecticut*, Wesleyan University Press, 1971; (co-author) *Myth, Allegory, and Gospel: An Interpretation of J. R. R. Tolkien, C. S. Lewis, G. K. Chesterton, and Charles Williams*, Bethany Fellowship, 1974.

Editor: *Thesaurus of Quotations*, Crown, 1941; *Thesaurus of Anecdotes*, Crown, 1942, published as *2500 Anecdotes for All Occasions*, Doubleday, 1961; *Thesaurus of Epigrams*, Crown, 1943; (under pseudonym Amicus Curiae) *Law in Action: An Anthology of the Law in Literature*, Crown, 1947; (with Hiram C. Haydn) *Thesaurus of Book Digests*, Crown, 1949; Leo Stein, *Journey Into the Self: Being the Letters, Papers, and Journals of Leo Stein*, Crown, 1950; *Mutiny!*, Crown, 1953; Feodor Dostoyevsky, *The Brothers Karamazov*, Dell, 1956; *The Christian Idea of Education*, Yale University Press, 1957-62; Samuel Langhorne Clemens, *Mark Twain*, Dell, 1958; (with Olga Achtenhagen) *Four American Novels*, Harcourt, 1959; Plutarch, *Lives of the Noble Romans*, Dell, 1959; Plutarch, *Lives of the Noble Greeks*, Dell, 1959; Francois Voltaire, *Voltaire*, Dell, 1959; Thomas Bullfinch, *Mythology: A Modern Abridgement*, Dell, 1959.

(With Blanche J. Thompson) *Four Novels for Appreciation*, Harcourt, 1960; Honore de Balzac, *Balzac: Five Stories*, Dell, 1960; (with Achtenhagen) *Four Novels for Adventure*,

Harcourt, 1960; (with O. B. Davis) *Four American Biographies*, Harcourt, 1961; *Schools and Scholarship: The Christian Idea of Education*, Yale University Press, 1962; (with B. J. Kinnick) *Adventures in American Literature*, Harcourt, 1963; (with Davis) *Three World Classics*, Harcourt, 1963; John Donne, *The Showing Forth of Christ: Sermons*, Harper, 1964; *The Great English and American Essays*, Avon Books, 1964; Samuel Johnson, *Selections From The Lives of the English Poets [and] Preface to Shakespeare*, Avon Books, 1965; Henry Wadsworth Longfellow, *Poems* (illustrated by John Ross and Clare Romano Ross), Crowell, 1967; *Affirmations of God and Man: Writings for Modern Dialogue*, Association Press, 1967; (with Davis) *The Idea of Man: An Anthology of Literature*, Harcourt, 1967; James Boswell, *The Life of Samuel Johnson, LL.D.*, Heron Books, 1969; (with Davis) *Introduction to the Essay*, Hayden, 1971; *Time of Turbulence: Research Cases for Freshman English*, Crowell, 1972.

Editor; all by William Shakespeare, all published by Dell: *Hamlet*, 1966; *Julius Caesar*, 1966; *The Merchant of Venice*, 1966; *Henry IV, Part One*, 1968; *As You Like It*, 1968; *Romeo and Juliet*, 1968; *A Midsummer Night's Dream*, 1968.

SIDELIGHTS: Edmund Fuller's first novel, *Star Pointed North*, was reviewed by a *New York Times* critic who wrote: "With his fast-moving, well-written, at times beautiful historical novel based on the life of Frederick Douglass, Edmund Fuller has performed a double service. He has bridged an aching gap in American history; and he has done this in a thoroughly enjoyable book in which a great man is handled with dignity and warmth, in which a Negro hero is treated as the American hero that he was." *Kirkus Reviews* noted: "A biographical novel about the famous Negro abolitionist, Frederick Douglass, which reads more like history than fiction, but a pretty thrilling piece of history at that. The most vivid and engrossing part of the book deals with Douglass' life as a slave." A later effort, *The Corridor*, was critiqued in the *New York Times Book Review*: "As a novel, *The Corridor* is tidy and skillful. What lifts it above mere adequacy is the author's underlying, passionate belief in married happiness as the greatest boon on earth. It is his conviction—and he proves it—that this boon is not just occasionally or accidentally attainable."

Fuller has also written several books of literary criticism, among them *Man in Modern Fiction*. A *Chicago Sunday Tribune* reviewer called the book "probably the most thoroughgoing and intelligent attack so far made on the filth and insanity now being dished up in fiction. . . . Fuller names names and cites examples. Some writers he condemns in toto, others only in part. He does not blow out the gas to see how dark it is; instead, he gives due meed of praise to those who have retained their sanity and decency. . . ." *Kirkus Reviews* saw the book as "a welcome change from the coterie judgments of the academic critics . . . penetrating, to the point, and worthy of study by readers, writers, and editors," adding, "Others may enjoy Mr. Fuller's wit and devastating gift for demolishing popular idols." In contrast, the *New York Times* critic wrote: "Though Mr. Fuller's book is entertaining and a praiseworthy act of debunking, it is not altogether satisfactory. He has concentrated his attention on a very narrow segment of contemporary fiction and, within that, on a number of novels which are not, in fact, very distinguished as literature, however significant their success may be sociologically. . . ." *Saturday Review* added, "The troubling part of his book is that he doesn't want to institute censorship, he sees no way of converting William March,

John Steinbeck, James Jones, Gerald Tesch, and the rest to Christianity, the Judaeo-Christian tradition, or even 'humanism,' so that, beyond a general call to repentance addressed to readers and writers, he can only lament the short-sighted vision of novelists. . . .''

BIOGRAPHICAL/CRITICAL SOURCES: Kirkus Reviews, September 1, 1946, March 1, 1958; *New York Times,* November 3, 1946, June 1, 1958; *Saturday Review,* May 17, 1958; *Chicago Sunday Tribune,* May 18, 1958; *New Yorker,* May 25, 1963; *New York Times Book Review,* May 26, 1963.*

* * *

FULLER, Lon (Luvois) 1902-1978

June 15, 1902—April 8, 1978; American educator and author best known for his books on law. Fuller taught law for forty-eight years. His writings include *Human Purpose and Natural Law* and *The Morality of Law.* He died in Cambridge, Mass. Obituaries and other sources: *New York Times,* April 10, 1978. (See index for *CA* sketch)

* * *

FULWEILER, Howard Wells 1932-

PERSONAL: Born August 26, 1932, in Media, Pa.; son of Howard W. (a clergyman) and Mary Louise (Boyles) Fulweiler; married Sally Nichols, December 28, 1953; children: Peter, John, Mary, Ann. *Education:* University of South Dakota, B.A., 1954, M.A., 1957; University of North Carolina, Ph.D., 1960. *Politics:* Democrat. *Religion:* Episcopal. *Home:* 601 South Greenwood, Columbia, Mo. 65201. *Office:* Department of English, University of Missouri, Columbia, Mo. 65201.

CAREER: University of Missouri, Columbia, assistant professor, 1960-64, associate professor, 1964-70, professor of English, 1970—, chairman of department, 1967-71. *Military service:* U.S. Army, 1954-56; became first lieutenant. *Member:* Modern Language Association of America, American Association of University Professors, Tennyson Society, Midwest Modern Language Association.

WRITINGS: Letters From the Darkling Plain: Language and the Grounds of Knowledge in the Poetry of Arnold and Hopkins, University of Missouri Press, 1972. Contributor to literature journals and church magazines.

WORK IN PROGRESS: Critical research on Tennyson.

SIDELIGHTS: Fulweiler told *CA:* "*Letters From the Darkling Plain* considers the role of poetry as a source of knowledge in the secular and technological society which had its beginnings in the nineteenth century. The study of Tennyson in progress will consider Tennyson as a representative figure in the evolution of consciousness which took place in Western civilization between the eighteenth and the twentieth centuries.''

* * *

FURNAS, J(oseph) C(hamberlain) 1905-

PERSONAL: Born November 24, 1905, in Indianapolis, Ind.; son of Isaiah George (in business) and Sally Elizabeth (Chamberlain) Furnas; married Helen Winthrop Levinson. *Education:* Harvard University, A.B. (cum laude), 1927. *Residence:* Southern New Jersey. *Agent:* Brandt & Brandt, 101 Park Ave., New York, N.Y. 10017.

CAREER: Writer, 1927—. *Member:* Phi Beta Kappa, Harvard Club, Century Association, Nassau Club. *Awards, honors:* Anisfield-Wolff nonfiction award 1948, for *Anatomy of Paradise.*

WRITINGS: (With Ernest M. Smith) *Sudden Death, and How to Avoid It,* Simon & Schuster, 1935; *The Prophet's Chamber* (novel), Morrow, 1935; *Many People Prize It* (novel), Morrow, 1937; *So You're Going to Stop Smoking!,* Simon and Schuster, 1939; *How America Lives,* Holt, 1941; *Anatomy of Paradise: Hawaii and the Islands of the South Seas,* Sloane, 1948.

Voyage to Windward: The Life of Robert Louis Stevenson, Sloane, 1951; *Goodbye to Uncle Tom* (nonfiction), Sloane, 1956; *The Road to Harper's Ferry: Facts and Follies of the War on Slavery* (nonfiction), Sloane, 1959; *The Devil's Rainbow* (novel), Harper, 1962; *The Life and Times of the Late Demon Rum* (nonfiction), Putnam, 1965; *Lightfoot Island* (novel), Atheneum, 1968; *The Americans: A Social History of the United States, 1587-1914* (first book of trilogy), Putnam, 1969; *Great Times: An Informal Social History of the United States, 1914-1929* (second book of trilogy), Putnam, 1974; *Stormy Weather: Crosslight on the Nineteen Thirties, An Informal Social History of the United States, 1929-41* (third book of trilogy), Putnam, 1978.

G

GABRIEL, H(enry) 1922-

PERSONAL: Born October 2, 1922, in Glasgow, Scotland; son of Samuel and Esther (Tarant) Gabriel; married Tessa Winton, 1946; children: two sons, one daughter. *Education:* Educated in Glasgow, Scotland. *Home:* 42 Terregles Dr., Glasgow G41 4RN, Scotland.

CAREER: Playwright, 1967—. Has worked as gardener, upholsterer, garment cutter, mill worker, leathercraft designer, and sales representative. *Member:* Scottish Society of Playwrights.

WRITINGS—Plays: "Clear Vision" (one-act), first produced in Edinburgh, Scotland, at Royal Mile Centre, August, 1976; "We're All Implicated" (one-act), first produced in Edinburgh at Royal Mile Centre, August, 1976; "Tamburlaine Was Right Great" (one-act), first produced in Glasgow, Scotland, at Glasgow Citizen's Theatre, December 12, 1976; "In the Light of Day" (one-act), first produced in Glasgow, Scotland, at Glasgow Citizen's Theatre, December 12, 1976.

Unproduced plays: "Promises" (one-act), 1971; "What Would People Think" (one-act), 1973; "On Stage—Off Stage," 1974; "Points of View"; "The Competitors" (three-act).

WORK IN PROGRESS: "A Question of Third Degree," a three-act play.

SIDELIGHTS: Gabriel writes: "The irrational and 'absurd' in life, the incidental and co-incidental, more or less, dictate the genre of play which emerges from my pen. And invariably, a brand of humour, which I do not consciously strive for, though not so clear-cut in the text, highlights itself in performance. The problem of Identity, and the conflict between Art and Life, intrigue me to the extent that I am anti-naturalist as far as the Modern Theatre is concerned."

*   *   *

GACH, Gary 1947-

PERSONAL: Born November 30, 1947, in Los Angeles, Calif.; son of Eugene Hugh and Shirley Carla (Pfeiffer) Gach. *Education:* Attended University of California, Riverside, 1964, and University of California, Los Angeles, 1965-67; San Francisco State University, B.A., 1970. *Residence:* San Francisco, Calif. *Office:* c/o William E. Taggart, Jr., 220 Montgomery, Suite 440, San Francisco, Calif. 94104.

CAREER: Worked as longshoreman, 1967; *Sun-Reporter,* San Francisco, Calif., typesetter, 1968; worked as clerk in a second-hand bookstore, 1969-76, screen actor, 1977, and legal secretary, 1978—. Founder of Esira, Inc., 1970. Guest lecturer at University of California, Los Angeles, San Francisco Community College, and Pacific Institute of East-West Studies. Has given readings. *Member:* American Academy of Poets.

WRITINGS: Preparing the Ground (poems), Heirs Press, 1975. Contributor of poems, translations, and reviews to magazines, including *City, Maitreya, American Poetry Review,* and *Rolling Stone.* Editor of *Cable Television Guide,* 1977.

WORK IN PROGRESS: Map and Grain; Call Theatre for Title.

SIDELIGHTS: Gach writes: "*Preparing the Ground* is an edition of fifteen years' writing, perhaps judged best by what I do next." His work has been translated into Arabic and Italian.

*   *   *

GAINZA PAZ, Alberto 1899-1977

PERSONAL: Born March 16, 1899, in Buenos Aires, Argentina; son of Alberto and Zelmira (Paz) Gainza; married Elvira Castro Soto, June 17, 1922; children: Alberto, Maximo, Elvira, Ezequeil, Jose, Angelica, Zelmira, Jorge. *Education:* University of Buenos Aires, law degree, 1921. *Home:* 1324 Villanueva, Buenos Aires, Argentina. *Office: La Prensa,* Avenida de Mayo 567, Buenos Aires, Argentina.

CAREER/WRITINGS: La Prensa, Buenos Aires, Argentina, staff member, 1922-43, editor and publisher, 1943-51, 1956-77. Exiled in Uruguay and the United States, 1951-55. *Member:* Inter-American Press Association (honorary chairman of the board), Overseas Press Club (honorary member). *Awards, honors:* Americas Foundation award, 1950, for "promoting hemispheric solidarity"; Freedom House prize, 1951; honorary Dr. Journalism from Northwestern University, 1951; LL.D. from Columbia University, 1951; Sigma Delta Chi fellowship, 1952; Theodore Brent award, 1956; Maria Moors Cabot award, 1968, for journalistic excellence; awarded Golden Pen of Freedom, 1970.

SIDELIGHTS: As editor and publisher of the internationally respected *La Prensa,* Gainza Paz received world-wide attention in 1951 when Argentine dictator Juan Peron confiscated the newspaper in a labor dispute. Gainza Paz became a symbol of the struggle of journalists to maintain a free press amidst opposition from authoritarian government forces. After Peron was overthrown in 1955, Gainza Paz regained control over *La Prensa* and continued the "long tradition of independent, objective journalism" which his grandfather had established when he founded the paper in 1869.

OBITUARIES: New York Times, December 27, 1977; *Washington Post*, December 27, 1977.*

(Died December 26, 1977, in Buenos Aires, Argentina)

* * *

GALLAHUE, David L(ee) 1943-

PERSONAL: Born February 15, 1943, in Niagara Falls, N.Y.; son of Douglas (a printer) and Loretta (a file clerk) Gallahue; married Elnora Bredenberg; children: David Lee, Jr., Jennifer. *Education:* Indiana University, B.S., 1964; Purdue University, M.S., 1967; Temple University, Ed.D., 1970. *Religion:* Evangelical Christian. *Office:* Indiana University, Bloomington, Ind. 47401.

CAREER: Indiana University, Bloomington, assistant professor, 1970-74, associate professor of physical education, 1974—, assistant dean for research and development, 1977—. Owner and director of Challengers Day Camp, 1973—. Public lecturer and director of workshops on a national and international level. Consultant to Creative Playgrounds Equipment Corp. *Member:* American Alliance of Health, Physical Education and Recreation, Educational Press Association, Parents Without Partners (member of board of directors), Phi Delta Kappa, Phi Epsilon Kappa.

WRITINGS: (Contributor) Maryhelen Vannier, editor, *Teaching Physical Education in Elementary Schools*, Saunders, 5th edition, 1973, 6th edition, 1978; *Let's Move*, Kendall/Hunt, 1974; *A Conceptual Approach to Moving and Learning*, Wiley, 1975; *Developmental Play Equipment for Home and School*, Wiley, 1975; *Motor Development and Movement Experiences for Young Children*, Wiley, 1976; *Fundamental Movement: A Developmental and Remedial Approach*, Saunders, 1978. Writer of filmstrip "Yes I Can!: Movement and the Developing Self." Editor-in-chief of *Physical Educator*, 1973—.

WORK IN PROGRESS: Research on the effects of developmental play equipment on the physical fitness and motor development of elementary school children.

SIDELIGHTS: Gallahue comments: "Writing must be a labor of love. The financial rewards are too uncertain and often too meager in the textbook market for it to be anything else. For the most part, writing is hard work. It is time-consuming, demanding of one's complete attention and long-range commitment. It is, however, a tremendous thrill to see a completed manuscript in print and to be able to express your views to thousands of people all over the world."

* * *

GALLOWAY, Jonathan F(uller) 1939-

PERSONAL: Born December 2, 1939, in Washington, D.C.; son of George Barnes (a political scientist) and Eilene Marie (a political scientist; maiden name, Slack) Galloway; married Judith Collier Wells (a nursery school teacher), September 5, 1964; children: Matthew, Jennifer, Anne. *Education:* Swarthmore College, B.A., 1961; Columbia University, Ph.D., 1967. *Home:* 771 Green Briar Lane, Lake Forest, Ill. 60045. *Office:* Department of Politics, Lake Forest College, Lake Forest, Ill. 60045.

CAREER: Lake Forest College, Lake Forest, Ill., instructor, 1966-67, assistant professor, 1967-72, associate professor of political science, 1972—. President of Northern Illinois Citizens Against the Anti-Ballistic Missile, 1968-69. *Member:* International Institute of Space Law, International Studies Association, American Political Science Association.

WRITINGS: The Politics and Technology of Satellite Communications, Heath, 1972. Contributor to international studies journals.

WORK IN PROGRESS: A book on multinational corporations; research on the problem of corporate bribery abroad; technology transfer policy and the question of geostationary orbit.

SIDELIGHTS: Galloway writes: "I believe the moral problem of our time is the creation of a more just world order. I also believe that the teaching of the next generation of citizens of the country and of the world is a sacred trust of this generation. The innovation of communications satellites is an example of one technology which has served the general interest of mankind, this in spite of the serious economic and political controversies surrounding the diffusion of the capability. However, many technologies transferred by governments and multinational corporations do not have the same advantages for world order, e.g. armaments and nuclear power facilities. One of the prime responsibilities of contemporary scholarship should be to weigh the pros and cons of various technologies in light of their impact on world order and human rights."

* * *

GAMERMAN, Martha 1941-

PERSONAL: Born June 13, 1941, in New York, N.Y.; daughter of Oscar (a realtor and certified public accountant) and Sarah (Berlinsky) Sapir; married Kenneth Gamerman (a producer of educational materials), December 25, 1958; children: Amy, Nancy, Ellen. *Education:* Queens College (now of the City University of New York), B.A., 1962. *Home:* 257 Barnard Rd., Larchmont, N.Y. 10538.

CAREER: Roslyn High School, Roslyn, N.Y., teacher of English, 1962-64; writer, 1975—. Teacher of writing and poetry workshops for children.

WRITINGS: Trudy's Straw Hat (juvenile), Crown, 1977.

WORK IN PROGRESS: Another picture book; an adventure story for older readers.

SIDELIGHTS: Martha Gamerman writes: "One winter, when my children were very young, we moved from New York to Chicago. It was cold, and we were lonely, so we spent many hours in the children's room of the local library. We read hundreds of books together that winter. I loved them as much as my children did. And I remained fascinated and delighted long after my children outgrew them. My interest in children's literature had taken firm hold.

"I remember my own childhood as a sequence of unadulterated pleasures and uncomfortable dilemmas. And those childhood predicaments are the material for my stories. Wanting things we can't have, trying to find good friends, and being afraid of strangers, are some of the problems I remember and want to explore. I think of my stories as illustrated conversations about those old dilemmas."

* * *

GANNON, Robert I(gnatius) 1893-1978

April 20, 1893—March 12, 1978; American Jesuit priest,

educator, administrator, and author. Gannon was president of Fordham University from 1936 to 1949. He delivered eulogies for both Francis Cardinal Spellman and Pope Pius XII. Among Gannon's writings are two collections of speeches, *After Black Coffee* and *After More Black Coffee*, and an autobiography, *The Poor Old Liberal Arts*. He died in New York, N.Y. Obituaries and other sources: *Current Biography*, Wilson, 1945, May, 1978; *International Who's Who*, Europa, 1975; *The Writers Directory, 1976-78*, St. Martin's, 1976; *New York Times*, March 13, 1978; *Washington Post*, March 15, 1978. (See index for *CA* sketch)

* * *

GANS, Roma 1894-

PERSONAL: Born February 22, 1894, in St. Cloud, Minn.; daughter of Hubert W. (a musician and businessman) and Mary Anne (Ley) Gans. *Education:* Columbia University, B.S., 1926, Ph.D., 1940. *Politics:* Democrat. *Religion:* Roman Catholic. *Home and office address:* Wayside Lane, West Redding, Conn. 06896.

CAREER: Junior high school mathematics teacher in Clearwater, Minn., 1917; high school mathematics teacher in St. Cloud, Minn., 1918-23; director of primary grades at community school in St. Louis, Mo., 1924-25; assistant superintendent of schools and research director in Superior, Wis., 1925-29; Columbia University, Teachers College, New York, N.Y., 1929-59, began as assistant professor, then associate professor, professor of education, 1940-59; writer, 1959—. Co-founder and chairman of New York City's Citizens Committee for Children. Vice-president of New York State Liberal Party. Member of editorial boards, Thomas Y. Crowell Co. and Harper & Row. Lecturer at colleges and universities in Canada, Italy, England, and the United States, including University of Pennsylvania and University of Illinois. *Awards, honors:* Awards from Child Study Association International and Delta Kappa Gamma, 1963, for *Common Sense in Reading.*

WRITINGS: A Study of Critical Reading Comprehension in the Intermediate Grades, Teachers College, Columbia University, 1940, reprinted, AMS Press, 1972; *Guiding Children's Reading Through Experiences: Practical Suggestions for Teaching*, Teachers College, Columbia University, 1941; (with Celia Burns Stendler and Millie Almy) *Teaching Young Children in Nursery School, Kindergarten, and the Primary Grades*, World Book Co., 1952; *Common Sense in Teaching Reading: A Practical Guide*, Bobbs-Merrill, 1963; *Common Sense in Teaching Reading*, Bobbs-Merrill, 1963; *Fact and Fiction About Phonics*, Bobbs-Merrill, 1964. Also author of *Reading Is Fun*, published by Teachers College, Columbia University.

Children's books; all published by Crowell: *Birds Eat and Eat and Eat*, 1963; *The Wonder of Stones*, 1963; *It's Nesting Time*, 1964; *Icebergs*, 1964; *Birds at Night*, 1968; *Hummingbirds in the Garden*, 1969; *Bird Talk*, 1971; *Water for Dinosaurs and You*, 1972; *Millions and Millions of Crystals*, 1973; *Oil: The Buried Treasure*, 1975; *Caves*, 1976. Contributor of several hundred articles to education journals.

* * *

GARBARINO, Merwyn S(tephens)

PERSONAL: Born in New York, N.Y.; daughter of Henry Clay (a certified public accountant) and Marie (Jenkins) Stephens; married Harold L. Garbarino (deceased). *Education:* University of Colorado, B.A., 1950; Northwestern University, M.A., 1964, Ph.D., 1966. *Politics:* Independent. *Reli-*

gion: Agnostic. *Office:* Department of Anthropology, University of Illinois at Chicago Circle, Chicago, Ill. 60680.

CAREER: University of Illinois at Chicago Circle, Chicago, assistant professor, 1966-71, associate professor, 1972-76, professor of anthropology, 1977—. *Member:* American Anthropological Association, American Ethnological Association, Authors Guild, Authors League of America.

WRITINGS: Big Cypress: A Changing Seminole Community, Holt, 1972; (with Rachel R. Sady) *People and Cultures*, Rand McNally, 1975; *Native American Heritage*, Little, Brown, 1976; *Sociocultural Theory in Anthropology*, Holt, 1977. Contributor to *World Book Encyclopedia* and to professional journals.

WORK IN PROGRESS: Research on Algonkian tribes of the northeast and central Atlantic states.

* * *

GARCIA, Mario R(amon) 1947-

PERSONAL: Born February 15, 1947, in Cuba; came to the United States in 1962, naturalized citizen, 1970; son of Mario D. (a watchmaker) and Maria O. (Suarez) Garcia; married Maria Nobo, October 11, 1969. *Education:* University of South Florida, B.A., 1969; University of Miami, Coral Gables, Fla., M.A., 1972, D.A., 1976. *Religion:* Roman Catholic. *Home:* 204 Sheatree Lane, North Syracuse, N.Y. 13212. *Office:* Newhouse School of Public Communications, Syracuse University, Syracuse, N.Y. 13210.

CAREER: Miami-Dade Community College, Miami, Fla., instructor, 1970-73, assistant professor of journalism, 1973-76, director of student publications, 1974-77; Syracuse University, Newhouse School of Public Communications, Syracuse, N.Y., associate professor of graphic arts, 1977—. Guest lecturer at universities; graphic design consultant. *Member:* Association for Education in Journalism, Community College Journalism Association, National Council of College Publications Advisers, Sigma Delta Chi.

WRITINGS: The (New) Adviser: Learning the Craft, Columbia Scholastic Press, 1974. Contributor to journalism education journals. Founder and editor, *Community College Journalist* magazine, 1972-74.

WORK IN PROGRESS: Contemporary Newspaper Design: A Structural Approach.

SIDELIGHTS: Garcia writes about his forthcoming book: "My book will describe new trends in newspaper typography and design, with emphasis on the structural approach to page design, the new front page and case studies of American newspapers which have successfully redesigned themselves for a new look. The book is an outgrowth of lectures and consulting engagements with colleges, universities and newspapers around the country. It will be aimed at college students, but can also be utilized by professional newspaper editors."

* * *

GARDINER, Muriel 1901-

PERSONAL: Born November 23, 1901, in Chicago, Ill.; daughter of Edward (a businessman) and Helen (Swift) Morris; married Julian Gardiner, May 20, 1930 (divorced, 1932); married Joseph Buttinger (a writer), August 1, 1939; children: Constance (Mrs. Harold Harvey). *Education:* Wellesley College, B.A., 1922; attended Oxford University, 1923-25; University of Vienna, M.D., 1938. *Politics:* "At heart a socialist! Usually vote Democratic.'' *Religion:* ''No affilia-tion.'' *Home and office address:* R.R. 1, Box 264, Penning-ton, N.J. 08534.

CAREER: Psychiatrist and psychoanalyst in Pennington, N.J., beginning, 1948, until retirement. Adjunct professor at Rutgers University, 1955-59. Volunteer psychiatric worker in prisons, 1966—. *Member:* American Psychoanalytic As-sociation, Philadelphia Association for Psychoanalysis.

WRITINGS: (Co-author and editor) *The Wolf-Man,* Basic Books, 1971; *The Deadly Innocents,* Basic Books, 1976. Contributor to psychoanalytic journals.

WORK IN PROGRESS: An autobiography, dealing with her work in the Socialist underground movement in Vienna, 1934-38.

SIDELIGHTS: Muriel Gardiner comments that her inter-ests have included literature and history, education, psy-chology, psychoanalysis, and medicine. She has traveled extensively, including periods of work with archaeologists.

AVOCATIONAL INTERESTS: Travel, skiing, the arts.

*   *   *

GAROFALO, Reebee
   See GAROFALO, Robert L.

*   *   *

GAROFALO, Robert L.   1944-
   (Reebee Garofalo)

PERSONAL: Born November 18, 1944, in Topeka, Kan.; son of Mario Louis (a doctor) and Evelyn (Pellegrino) Garo-falo. *Education:* Yale University, B.A., 1967; Harvard Uni-versity, Ed.D., 1974. *Home:* Main Street, Franconia, N.H. 03580. *Office:* Franconia College, Franconia, N.H. 03580.

CAREER: Training and Research Institute for Residential Youth Centers (TRI-RYC, Inc.), New Haven, Conn., co-founder, 1968, field specialist, 1968-69, director of in-service training, 1969-70; Entropy, Inc., Cambridge, Mass., concert producer, accountant, funding-board liaison, 1972-74; Fran-conia College, Franconia, N.H., member of social sciences faculty, 1975—, director of community services, 1975-76, dean of students, 1976-77, director of development, 1977—. Field reader, Office of Student and Youth Affairs, Office of Education, 1972.

WRITINGS: (Contributor) Elizabeth Southerland, editor, *Letters From Mississippi,* McGraw, 1965; (under pseud-onym Reebee Garofalo; with Steve Chapple) *Rock 'n' Roll Is Here to Pay: The History and Politics of the Music Indus-try,* Nelson-Hall, 1977. Contributor to *Mother Jones.*

*   *   *

GARRITY, Richard (George)   1903-

PERSONAL: Born August 11, 1903, in Tonawanda, N.Y.; son of Richard J. (a canal boatman) and Wilhelmina (Kohler) Garrity; married Mildred E. Daubney, December 20, 1928; children: Marjorie, Carolyn, James, Sandra, Lynette, Timo-thy. *Education:* Attended elementary school in Tonawanda, N.Y. *Politics:* Republican. *Religion:* Presbyterian. *Home:* 22 Catherine St., Tonawanda, N.Y. 14150.

CAREER: Canal boathand, 1915-17; tugboat fireman, 1918-23; licensed steam tugboat engineer, 1924-70; coal passer on a lumber hooker, 1924; papermill worker, 1925; millwright, 1937-39; foreman in a water-treatment plant, 1940; shipyard diesel mechanic, 1941-43; Great Lakes Towing Co., Buffalo, N.Y., steam tugboat engineer, 1943-70; writer, 1970—.

Member: Canal Society of New York State, Niagara County Historical Society, Historical Society of the Tona-wandas (charter member).

WRITINGS: Recollections of the Erie Canal, Historical Society of the Tonawandas, 1966, revised edition, 1971; (contributor) George E. Condon, editor, *Stars in the Water: The Story of the Erie Canal,* Doubleday, 1974; *Canal Boat-man: My Life on the Upstate Waterways,* Syracuse Univer-sity Press, 1977.

WORK IN PROGRESS: Research on transportation in New York State before the building of the Erie Canal.

SIDELIGHTS: In the foreword to *Canal Boatman* Lionel D. Wyld wrote: ''Here is that rarity in publishing: a manu-script chock full of Americana that is not only significant but interestingly written—a book by an author whose life and work have been intimately bound up with the famed Big Ditch which has been referred to in more romantic literature as 'the shining ribbon of water.' there are few other books like this one about any of the canals, and none so completely by a person who has lived and worked on the waterways of upstate New York.''

In an interview with a local New York state newspaper Garrity commented: ''It's the unusual things that happened that you remember the most, but the book is basically about the day-to-day life of the Canal Boatmen and their families. I lived through the changes on these waterways and I saw the change from animal power to steam, to diesel, and finally, to diesel-electric. I was on the boats that carried lumber, pig-iron and gravel. The Erie was always animal powered and open barges. They were usually privately owned and every-one took their families aboard with them. That was the time when those songs were made up and the canal was friendly place to live.''

According to Garrity, the end of the Erie came in about 1917 when the friendly existence of family and privately owned barges was halted with the introduction of company-owned tugging crews. Now the canals are used mostly for pleasure boating rather than for transportation.

BIOGRAPHICAL/CRITICAL SOURCES: Richard Garr-ity, *Canal Boatman: My Life on the Upstate Waterways,* Syracuse University press, 1977; *Tonawanda News,* De-cember 1, 1977.

*   *   *

GARTNER, Michael G(ay)   1938-

PERSONAL: Born October 25, 1938, in Des Moines, Iowa; son of Carl D. (an editor) and Mary M. (Gay) Gartner; mar-ried Barbara Jeanne McCoy, May 25, 1968; children: Mel-issa. *Education:* Carleton College, B.A., 1968; New York University, J.D., 1969. *Home:* 5315 Waterbury Rd., Des Moines, Iowa 50312. *Office:* 715 Locust St., Des Moines, Iowa 50304.

CAREER/WRITINGS: Admitted to the Bar of New York State; *Wall Street Journal,* New York, N.Y., 1960-74, be-came page one editor; *Des Moines Register* and *Des Moines Tribune,* Des Moines, Iowa, executive editor and vice-pres-ident, 1974—. *Member:* American Bar Associations, New York City Bar Association, New York County Bar Associa-tion.

*   *   *

GASH, Jonathan
   See GRANT, John

GATES, Norman T(immins) 1914-

PERSONAL: Born October 4, 1914, in New York, N.Y.; son of Benjamin D. (a confectioner) and Amy (Timmins) Gates; married Gertrude Morre, April 29, 1933; children: Marilyn L. Gates Hart, Norman E., Patricia A. Gates Winder. *Education:* Attended Dickinson College, 1931-32; University of Pennsylvania, B.A. (honors), 1965, M.A., 1967, Ph.D., 1969. *Home:* 520 Woodland Ave., Haddonfield, N.J. 08033. *Office address:* Rider College, P.O. Box 6400, Lawrenceville, N.J. 08648.

CAREER: E. W. Twitchell, Inc., Philadelphia, Pa., began as clerk, became manager, 1935-50; N. T. Gates Co. (packaging materials firm), Pennsauken, N.J., president, 1950-67; Rider College, Lawrenceville, N.J., assistant professor, 1969-74, associate professor, 1974-77, professor of English, 1977—. *Member:* Modern Language Association of America, American Association of University Professors, College English Association, Browning Society, Melville Society, British Museum Society, Northeast Modern Language Association, Friends of Dickinson Library, Friends of University of Pennsylvania Library.

WRITINGS: The Poetry of Richard Aldington: A Critical Evaluation and an Anthology of Uncollected Poems, Pennsylvania State University Press, 1974; *A Checklist of the Letters of Richard Aldington,* Southern Illinois University Press, 1977. Contributor to *The Reader's Encyclopedia of English Literature.* Contributor of articles and reviews to literature journals and literary magazines, including *Ohio Review* and *Texas Quarterly.*

WORK IN PROGRESS: Richard Aldington: The Russian View, with Robert J. Winter; *Richard Aldington: Selected Letters,* with Miriam J. Benkovitz.

SIDELIGHTS: Gates comments: "I suppose the most interesting biographical detail of my life is the fact that I am now embarked on my second career. Beginning in industry, I went back to college in middle age and entered my present academic career at a time when most of us are thinking about retirement. If there is time, I would like to spend the last part of my life writing poetry and fiction."

* * *

GAULDIE, Enid 1928-

PERSONAL: Born January 29, 1928, in Liverpool, England; daughter of William E. and Annie (Green) Macneilage; married William Sinclair Gauldie (an architect), December 5, 1949; children: Robin, Alison, Becca. *Education:* University of St. Andrews, M.A., 1947, B.Phil., 1967. *Politics:* "Leftish." *Religion:* None. *Home and office:* Waterside, Invergowrie by Dundee, Scotland.

CAREER: University of St. Andrews, St. Andrews, Scotland, librarian, 1948; research historian in Dundee, Scotland, 1967-69; writer, 1969—. Visiting lecturer at University of Dundee. Member of board of governors of Duncan of Jordanstone College of Art.

WRITINGS: (With Lenman and Lythe) *Dundee Textile Industry,* Abertay Historical Society, 1969; *Cruel Habitations: A History of Working Class Society,* Allen & Unwin, 1974. Author of school broadcasts. Contributor to women's magazines.

WORK IN PROGRESS: The Scottish Miller, a history of corn milling, publication by John Donald; an article on rural housing, to be included in *The Victorian Countryside,* edited by Mingay, publication by Routledge & Kegan Paul.

SIDELIGHTS: Enid Gauldie writes: "I have a very usual feminine career, shredded between the demands of a husband, children, and writing, and ambitions to have a perfect home, perfect parties, perfect friends, all falling short in reality!"

AVOCATIONAL INTERESTS: Art, country life, politics, friends.

* * *

GECKLE, George L. 1939-

PERSONAL: Surname is pronounced *Jeck*-el; born December 2, 1939, in Danbury, Conn.; son of George L. (a businessman) and Dorothy (Hill) Geckle; married Justine V. Carroll (a librarian), August 19, 1961; children: George, Richard. *Education:* Middlebury College, Middlebury, Vt., A.B. (cum laude), 1961; University of Virginia, M.A., 1962, Ph.D., 1965. *Home:* 303 Southwood Dr., Columbia, S.C. 29205. *Office:* Department of English, University of South Carolina, Columbia, S.C. 29208.

CAREER: University of Wisconsin—Madison, assistant professor of English, 1965-68; University of South Carolina, Columbia, assistant professor, 1968-70, associate professor, 1970-74, professor of English, 1974—, director of university honors program, 1970-73, director of graduate program in English, 1974-76, 1977-78, chairman of English department, 1978—. *Member:* Modern Language Association of America, Shakespeare Association of America, South Atlantic Modern Language Association, Southeastern Renaissance Conference.

WRITINGS: (Editor) *Twentieth Century Interpretations of "Measure for Measure"* (essays), Prentice-Hall, 1970; *John Marston's Plays* (nonfiction), Fairleigh Dickinson University Press, in press. Contributor of articles to journals including *Shakespeare Quarterly, Texas Studies in Literature and Language, James Joyce Quarterly, Modern Fiction Studies, Comparative Drama, PMLA, Papers* of the Bibliographical Society of America, and others.

WORK IN PROGRESS: A book on Christopher Marlowe's plays in performance, completion expected in 1980.

AVOCATIONAL INTERESTS: Golf, basketball, handball, poker.

* * *

GEDDA, George 1941-

PERSONAL: Born January 7, 1941, in Valley Stream, N.Y.; son of Hilding E. (an accountant) and Mildred Gedda; married Irene Lewin, February 16, 1973; children: Deborah, Sara. *Education:* Attended Southern Methodist University, 1958-62. *Office:* Associated Press, 2021 K St. N.W., Washington, D.C. 20006.

CAREER/WRITINGS: Associated Press, New York, N.Y., Latin American correspondent, 1968-75, State Department correspondent, 1975—. Notable assignments include reporting trips to Cuba and most other Latin American countries, coverage of the Panama Canal treaty negotiations, and coverage of virtually all state visits by foreign leaders during the Ford and Carter administrations. *Military service:* U.S. Army, active duty, 1965. *Member:* State Department Correspondents Association (vice-president).

SIDELIGHTS: Gedda told *CA:* "The opportunity to watch the foreign policy process at work and to report on it daily is both absorbing and challenging."

GEERTZ, Hildred 1927-

PERSONAL: Surname pronounced Gertz; born February 12, 1927 in New York, N.Y.; daughter of Walter Rendell (a writer) and Helen (a writer; Anderson) Storey; married Clifford Geertz (an anthropologist), October 30, 1948; children: Erika, Benjamin. *Education:* Antioch College, B.A., 1948; Radcliffe College, Ph.D., 1956. *Office:* Department of Anthropology, Princeton University, Princeton, N.J. 08540.

CAREER: Field research in Java, Indonesia, 1952-54; Smith College, Northampton, Mass., instructor in sociology, 1956-57; engaged in field research in Bali, Indonesia, 1957-58, and Menlo Park, Calif., 1959; University of California, Berkeley, instructor, 1960; University of Chicago, Chicago, Ill., lecturer in social science, 1963-64; engaged in field research in Rabat, Morocco, 1964, and in Sefrou, Morocco, 1965-66; University of Chicago, lecturer, 1967; returned to field work in Sefrou, 1968-69; University of Chicago, assistant professor of social science, 1969-70; Princeton University, Princeton, N.J., visiting lecturer, 1970-71, associate professor, 1971-75, professor of anthropology, 1975—, chairperson of department, 1973—. *Awards, honors:* Rockefeller Foundation grant for research in Bali, Indonesia, 1957-58; National Institute of Mental Health grant for field research in Sefrou, Morocco, 1965-66, 1968-69; Social Science Research Council grant for research in Europe on Balinese paintings, 1978-79.

WRITINGS: The Javanese Family: A Study in Kinship and Socialization, Free Press of Glencoe, 1961; (editor and author of introduction) Raden Adjeng Kartini, *Letters of a Javanese Princess,* preface by Eleanor Roosevelt, Norton, 1964; (contributor) Paul Bohannon and John Middleton, editors, *Marriage, Family, and Residence,* Natural History Press, 1968; (contributor) Robert A. LeVine, editor, *Culture and Personality: Contemporary Readings,* Aldine, 1974; (with husband, Clifford Geertz) *Kinship in Bali,* University of Chicago Press, 1975; (with Lawrence Rosen and C. Geertz) *Meaning and Order in Moroccan Society,* Cambridge University Press, in press. Contributor to *Psychiatry, Journal of the Royal Anthropological Institute, Journal of Asian Studies,* and other periodicals.

WORK IN PROGRESS: The Idea of a Painting: The Emergence of a New Graphic Genre in Bali in the 1930's.

SIDELIGHTS: Hildred Geertz actively speaks Indonesian, Javanese, French, and Moroccan Arabic. Geertz also has some competence in Dutch, German, Spanish, and Balinese.

*   *   *

GELLER, Bruce 1930-1978

October 13, 1930—May 21, 1978; American television producer, director, and writer. Geller, winner of six Emmy awards, was the creator and executive producer of the successful television series, "Mission Impossible," and "Mannix." He also wrote scripts for such series as "Dr. Kildare" and "The Rebel." Geller produced and directed the popular "Rawhide" series in the 1960's. He died in Montecito, Calif. Obituaries and other sources: *The ASCAP Biographical Dictionary of Composers, Authors, and Publishers,* American Society of Composers, Authors and Publishers, 1966; *Who's Who in World Jewry,* Pitman, 1972; *International Motion Picture Almanac,* Quigley, 1975; *Who's Who in America,* 39th edition, Marquis, 1976; *Washington Post,* May 23, 1978; *Newsweek,* June 5, 1978.

GELLHORN, Martha Ellis 1908-

PERSONAL: Born 1908, in St. Louis, Mo.; daughter of George and Edna (Fischel) Gellhorn; married Ernest Hemingway (a writer), November 21, 1940 (divorced December 21, 1945); married T. S. Matthews, 1954 (divorced, 1963); children: George Alexander. *Education:* Attended Bryn Mawr College. *Office:* Morgan Guaranty Trust Co., 31 Berkeley Square, London W.I., England.

CAREER: Collier's Weekly, war correspondent in Spain, 1937-38, in Finland, 1939, in China, 1940-41, in England, Italy, France, and Germany, 1943-45, in Java, 1946; *Guardian,* London, England, war correspondent in Vietnam, 1966, in Israel, 1967; freelance journalist in Europe and Asia, 1967—.

WRITINGS: What Mad Pursuit (novel), Stokes, 1934; *The Trouble I've Seen* (short stories), Morrow, 1936; *A Stricken Field* (novel), Duell, Sloan & Pierce, 1940; *The Heart of Another* (short stories and sketches), Scribner, 1941; *Liana* (novel), Scribner, 1944; *The Wine of Astonishment* (novel), Scribner, 1948; *The Honeyed Peace* (short stories), Doubleday, 1953; *Two by Two* (short stories), Simon & Schuster, 1958; *The Face of War* (collected news articles), Simon & Schuster, 1959; *His Own Man* (novel), Simon & Schuster, 1961; *Pretty Tales for Tired People* (short stories), Simon & Schuster, 1965; *The Lowest Trees Have Tops* (novel), M. Joseph, 1967, Dodd, Mead, 1969; *The Weather in Africa* (fiction), Penguin, 1978; *Travels With Myself and Another* (nonfiction), Penguin, 1978.

SIDELIGHTS: Many reviewers of Gellhorn's books have commented on what they feel is the obvious influence of her first husband, Ernest Hemingway. Describing Gellhorn's "method of expression," Rose Field called it "Pure Hemingway . . . romantic under a surface of hardness . . . bitter with disenchantment . . . frank with physical and functional details." Some criticisms concerning the "Hemingway influence" have been considerably more derogatory. *New Yorker* stated, "Perhaps . . . she has read too carefully the works of Mr. Hemingway—an admirable trait in a wife but dangerous for a writer of fiction."

However, other reviewers, while acknowledging certain similarities between the styles of Gellhorn and Hemingway, have stressed the importance of viewing Gellhorn as a definite talent in her own right. One such observation came from the *Springfield Republican:* "It is almost inevitable that readers who know that Martha Gellhorn is the wife of Ernest Hemingway should look for 'influences' of his writings on hers. . . . But those who recall gratefully the strength and clarity of Miss Gellhorn's *A Stricken Field* have no desire or need to justify her art by or through her marriage to one of the great contemporary stylists . . . Miss Gellhorn needs no other recommendation beyond her own talents."

A war correspondent for many years, Gellhorn has drawn on personal experiences for several of her novels. Though she has received much praise for her sound psychological handling of war and war related subjects, she is sometimes criticized for being "overly journalistic." *Springfield Republican,* however, countered this accusation by offering that, "If this is in any sense true, it may well be that the chaotic world with which she deals demands of writers just the unelaborated and disciplined technic which is peculiarly hers." And, J. H. Thompson found Gellhorn's journalistic writing to be "sensitive as litmus paper."

Discussing *The Wine of Astonishment,* Gellhorn's 1948 novel of war, Benell Braunstein declared that the novelist "has come closer to that subject than any other American woman writer. Her war is a *Farewell to Arms* kind of intimate drama in which nothing is sacred but an individual's integrity and where courage and honor really have no meaning except in a very personal and social way." Walter Havinghurst echoed that opinion, claiming that "Miss Gellhorn's novel brings the public war to bear on a private consciousness, on a man's hopes and wishes, on his humanity."

A collection of four stories recalling Gellhorn's experiences with the Federal Emergency Relief, *The Trouble I Have Seen* received generally favorable reviews. Though D. B. Collins attacked Gellhorn's numerous "lapses into sentimentality" he subsequently praised the "honest amount of courage, tenderness, selflessness, and love in the characters," and stated that Gellhorn "has been not only scrupulous but skillful in showing these truly human qualities flowering in the very depths of misery." *Boston Transcript* commented that "Miss Gellhorn has limitless sympathy and a sensitivity which makes this book compelling in its simplicity, fearlessness, and honesty." C. H. Grattan focused on Gellhorn's effective treatment of the "abominable cruelty, short-sightedness, and general all-around social imbecility of those who defame the relief recipients *en masse*." E. H. Walton said that "Miss Gellhorn has been able to identify herself with these victims of depression. She writes well; she is not patronizing; her insight, for an outsider, is compassionate and shrewd." And Graham Greene noted that "her masculine characters are presented as convincingly as her female, and her writing is hard and clear."

A Stricken Field deals with war time experiences in Prague. While reviewers have generally agreed on its literary shortcomings, they have praised its journalistic merits. E. H. Walton, for example, had this to say: "Because it wavers so on the borderline of fiction, *A Stricken Field* is a hard book to appraise. Considered as a novel it is something of a failure—lacking as it does most of the elements that give a novel pith and point—yet it's material is so poignant and so well handled that one cannot dismiss it lightly. Miss Gellhorn, as she has previously proved, is an admirable reporter." Reiterating that judgement, Marianne Hauser claimed that Gellhorn, "a journalist by profession, is at her best when describing general events or sketching the political background. If her individual characterizations lack vitality, she knows how to describe a crowd."

In 1959 Gellhorn published *The Face of War*, a collection of news articles covering World War II, as well as wars in Finland, China, and Spain. Edward Weeks termed it a "vivid, militant book," and *Booklist* called it a "haunting panorama of tragedy and suffering." Isabel Quigly felt that "these articles arouse, to a remarkable degree, feelings that are retrospectively violent."

Aside from being a capable journalist, Gellhorn has proven herself to be comfortable with comedy and whimsy. Reviewing *His Own Man*, which chronicles the adventures of an expatriate living in Paris, Charles Rolo hailed it as "a mortality tale . . . felicitously conceived and executed with wit, gaiety and toughness of mind, and perfect control." Similarly, David Dempsey acclaimed Gellhorn's "rare sense of comic style" in the novel he felt was "written with such verve, such effervescence of wit, that it is like taking a bubble bath, with a well-iced absinthe on the side."

BIOGRAPHICAL/CRITICAL SOURCES: Spectator, May 22, 1936; *Boston Transcript*, October 10, 1936; *New Republic*, October 21, 1936, February 28, 1944; *American Review*, December, 1936; *New York Times*, March 10, 1940, March 23, 1958; *Saturday Review of Literature*, Octo-

ber 9, 1940; *New Yorker*, November 1, 1941; *Books*, November 2, 1941; *Yale Review*, winter, 1942; *Springfield Republican*, January 16, 1944; *Weekly Book Review*, January 16, 1944; *Nation*, January 22, 1944; *Times Literary Supplement*, December 30, 1944, March 7, 1958, June 29, 1967; *New York Herald Tribune Book Review*, October 3, 1948, March 16, 1958; *Time*, March 17, 1958; *Atlantic*, March, 1959; *Chicago Tribune*, March 1, 1959; *Booklist*, March 15, 1959; *Guardian*, September 11, 1959; *Best Sellers*, March 1, 1969.

* * *

GEORGE, Collins Crusor 1909-

PERSONAL: Born June 30, 1909, in Washington, D.C.; son of John S. (a letter carrier) and Margaret (Crusor) George. *Education:* Howard University, A.B., 1929; Harvard University, A.M., 1932; University of Southern California, A.M., 1938. *Politics:* Democrat. *Home:* 1525 Cherboneau St., Detroit, Mich. 48027.

CAREER/WRITINGS: A. and T. College, Greensboro, N.C., teacher of English, 1932-33; Langston University, Langston, Okla., teacher of French and German, 1933-35; Lemoyne College, Memphis, Tenn., teacher of French and German, 1935-42; *Pittsburgh Courier*, Pittsburgh, Pa., reporter, war correspondent, managing editor of Washington, D.C., and Detroit, Mich., branches, 1944-52; *Detroit Free Press*, Detroit, staff member, 1953-61, music critic, 1961-75. Music columnist for *Birmingham Eccentric*, Birmingham, Mich., 1968—. Conductor of classical music program for WQRS-FM, Detroit. *Member:* American Newspaper Guild, Music Critics Association, Sigma Delta Chi, Omega Psi Phi, Detroit Historical Society.

* * *

GEORGE, Susan Akers 1934-

PERSONAL: Born June 29, 1934, in Akron, Ohio; daughter of Walter Thomas, Jr. (an insurer) and Edith (Vance) Akers; married Charles-Henry George (a financial and administrative director of a building firm), May 12, 1956; children: Valerie, Michel, Stephanie. *Education:* Smith College, B.A., 1956; Sorbonne, University of Paris, lic. es phil., 1967; Ecole des Hautes Etudes en Sciences sociales, doctoral study, 1974—. *Residence:* Paris, France.

CAREER: Transnational Institute, Amsterdam, Netherlands, fellow, 1973—. *Member:* Phi Beta Kappa.

WRITINGS: How the Other Half Dies: The Real Reasons for World Hunger, Penguin, 1976, revised edition, Allan Held, Osmun & Co., 1977.

WORK IN PROGRESS: Continuing research on agribusiness and "food-power"; research on development and economics.

SIDELIGHTS: Susan George writes: "My life is in France but my feelings and interests are still very much American. My political education came about through the Vietnam war against which I was an active militant. Moving from militancy (with no time to write anything longer than a tract) toward a general concern with poverty and oppression in the underdeveloped countries was natural—and hunger is the most basic of oppressions. It is also a question of politics and I have tried to write in a simple and lively way in order to make this clear to the general, non-specialized reader."

AVOCATIONAL INTERESTS: Gardening, opera.

GERACI, Philip C. 1929-

PERSONAL: Born September 22, 1929, in Frederick, Md.; son of Phil (a printer) and Grace (Royston) Geraci; married Dorothy Schaffer, June 17, 1950; children: Philip James, Ronald Blair, Jeffrey Alan. *Education:* University of Maryland, B.S., 1953, M.A., 1961. *Home:* 7 Winifred Ct., Burtonsville, Md. 20730. *Office: Burtonsville Shopper,* 3537 Spencerville Rd., Burtonsville, Md. 20730.

CAREER: Washington Star, Washington, D.C., writer and photographer, 1953-57; *High Fidelity,* Great Barrington, Mass., associate editor, 1957-59; *Airlift,* Washington, D.C., managing editor, 1959-61; *Popular Mechanics,* Washington, D.C., Washington correspondent, 1961-70; *Burtonsville Shopper,* Burtonsville, Md., editor and publisher, 1975—. Director of photojournalism program at University of Maryland, 1964—. *Military service:* U.S. Air Force, military correspondent, 1947-50; became sergeant. *Member:* Photographic Society of America, Professional Photographers of America, National Press Photographers Association, Association for Education in Journalism, Aviation-Space Writers Association, Sigma Delta Chi. *Awards, honors:* Photographic awards, including citations from Photographic Society of America.

WRITINGS: Photojournalism: Making Pictures for Publication, Kendall/Hunt, 1973; *Radio,* Doubleday, in press. Contributor to technical and popular journals, including *Popular Science, Popular Photography,* and *Coronet.*

SIDELIGHTS: Geraci writes: "Journalism has been a lifelong interest, from high school and military days, through a succession of publications, to university teaching and community journalism publishing. I am chiefly interested in bringing life to journalism through visuals, design, sharp editing, and sprightly writing. I deplore 'in-depth' treatments as traditional cop-outs by journalists too lazy to learn new techniques or too stubborn to admit the reading public is not interested."

*   *   *

GERARD, David 1923-

PERSONAL: Born October 19, 1923, in Glasgow, Scotland; son of Hugh and Julia Caroline (Price) Gerard. *Education:* University of London, B.A., 1955. *Home:* The Hollies, Southgate, Aberystwyth, Wales. *Office:* College of Librarianship, Llanbadarn Fawr, Aberystwyth, Wales.

CAREER: Liverpool Public Libraries, Liverpool, England, member of staff, 1946-54, librarian in charge of special collections, 1951-54; Exeter City Libraries, Exeter, England, deputy city librarian, 1955-57; Nottingham City Libraries, Nottingham, England, deputy chief librarian, 1957-64, city librarian, 1964-68; currently senior lecturer in library science at College of Librarianship, Aberystwyth, Wales. *Military service:* Royal Air force, photographer, 1942-46. *Member:* Classical Association (life member), Library Association (life member; president of East Midlands branch, 1967-68). *Awards, honors:* Churchill traveling fellowship for the United States, 1967.

WRITINGS: (Editor) *Libraries and the Arts,* Bingley, 1970; (editor) *Libraries and Leisure,* Diploma Press, 1975; (translator) Lucien Febvre and Henri-Jean Martin, *The Coming of the Book,* New Left Books, 1976. Contributor to *Encyclopedia of Library and Information Science* and to library journals.

WORK IN PROGRESS: Translating *Print, Power, and Public Opinion in Seventeenth-Century France,* two volumes, by Henri-Jean Martin.

SIDELIGHTS: Gerard comments: "I suppose my interests are largely centered on libraries as a focus for a reading public: the purpose of the public library in society. From this comes an interest in the history of the printed book, the reading public as it has evolved, and indeed in the history of libraries as a phenomenon of both popular and elite cultures.

"Apart from this I have spent much time tape recording. Primarily this is related to the D. H. Lawrence collection held at Nottingham, and the recordings of friends and relatives of his. Later I began tape recording the views and reminiscences of contemporary British writers, for example Angus Wilson, John Wain, Malcolm Bradbury, John Braine, Brigid Brophy, Iris Murdoch, and Raymond Williams. Later still I began to record conversations with distinguished British librarians.

"The living voice says so much more (in terms of tone and nuance) than the printed word: this is why it seems to me there is value in having a record of someone worthwhile in sound. The route from librarian to writer is not long, and fairly self-evident. At present I'm engaged in making a film about D. H. Lawrence, and audio-recording a version of Ben Jonson's *Staple of News,* a play that has much to say about news and newsmongers, and therefore is relevant to a course I teach, 'The History and Evolution of British Journalism.'"

*   *   *

GERBER, David A(llison) 1944-

PERSONAL: Born September 28, 1944, in Chicago, Ill.; son of Joseph S. (a lawyer) and Janet (Hellman) Gerber; married Carolyn W. Korsmeyer (a college professor), January 17, 1975. *Education:* Northwestern University, B.A., 1966; Princeton University, Ph.D., 1970. *Home:* 133 Woodward Ave., Buffalo, N.Y. 14214. *Office:* Department of History, State University of New York at Buffalo, North Campus, Amherst, N.Y. 14261.

CAREER: Princeton University, Princeton, N.J., instructor in history, 1970-71; State University of New York at Buffalo, North Campus, Amherst, assistant professor, 1971-77, associate professor of history, 1977—. Participant (and adviser) in public radio programs. *Member:* American Historical Association, Organization of American Historians, Association for the Study of Negro Life and History, Immigration History Society, History of Education Society, Phi Beta Kappa. *Awards, honors:* Ford Foundation fellowship in ethnic studies, 1971; Shelby Cullom Davis Center for Historical Research fellow, 1973.

WRITINGS: Black Ohio and the Color Line, 1860-1915, University of Illinois Press, 1976. Contributor of articles and reviews to history journals.

WORK IN PROGRESS: Buffalo, New York: The Making of a Pluralistic Community, 1825-1880.

SIDELIGHTS: Gerber comments: "I am interested in what is unique about Americans, their communities, their patterns of social interaction, and their culture."

*   *   *

GERBER, Israel J(oshua) 1918-
(Ben Mordechai)

PERSONAL: Born July 30, 1918, in New York, N.Y.; son of Max (a businessman) and Sadie Leah (Schuster) Gerber; married Sydelle Reba Katzman, January 9, 1943; children: Barbara Jane Gerber Parker, Sharon May, Wayne Scott. *Education:* Yeshiva University, B.A., 1939; City College (now of the City University of New York), M.S., 1940; Boston University, Ph.D., 1950. *Politics:* "I generally vote Democratic." *Home:* 5727 Riviera Dr., Charlotte, N.C. 28211. *Office:* Department of Psychology, Johnson C. Smith University, Charlotte, N.C. 28216.

CAREER: Ordained rabbi, 1941; public school teacher in New York, N.Y., 1941-42; rabbi of Jewish congregations in Plymouth, Mass., 1943-44, Fitchburg, Mass., 1944-53, Dothan, Ala., 1953-59, and Charlotte, N.C., 1959-72; Johnson C. Smith University, Charlotte, N.C., professor of psychology, 1972—. Professor at Livingstone College, 1961—; University of North Carolina at Charlotte, lecturer, 1968-71, director of Institute for Jewish Studies, 1972—; lecturer at Queens College, 1971—. Chaplain at Boston Psychopathic Hospital, 1948-50; director of Southeast Council of Union of American Hebrew Congregations; member of executive board of Central Conference of American Rabbis and National Council on Crime and Delinquency. President of Houston County Mental Health Association, 1956-59; member of Charlotte-Mecklenburg Council on Human Relations and local Citizens Safety Association; vice-president of Mental Health Association of Charlotte and Mecklenburg County, 1963-65; president of Mecklenburg County Society for Crippled Children and Adults, 1966-69. Chairman of Hearthstone Halfway House, 1970; member of board of trustees of Florence Crittenden Home; member of board of directors of Big Brothers, 1971—; member of board of governors of Institute for Pastoral Care. *Military service:* U.S. Army Reserve, chaplain, 1949-54, active duty, 1951-52; became captain.

MEMBER: American Psychological Association, American Academy of Religion, Jewish Chaplains Association, Society for the Scientific Study of Religion, American Association of University Professors, National Association of Biblical Instructors, Academy of Religion and Mental Health, Southeast Psychological Association, North Carolina Psychological Association, Alabama Psychological Association, Mecklenburg County Psychological Association, B'nai B'rith (Dothan chapter president, 1956-59), Masons, Rotary International, Elks, Kiwanis. *Awards, honors:* Interfaith award from Junior Women's League, 1962; special award from North Carolina Society of Crippled Children and Adults, 1963; brotherhood award from National Conference of Christians and Jews, 1964.

WRITINGS: Psychology of the Suffering Mind, Jonathan David, 1950; *Man on a Pendulum,* American Press, 1956; *Immortal Rebels,* Jonathan David, 1963; (contributor) *Rabbinical Counseling,* Bloch Publishing, 1966; *The Heritage Seekers,* Jonathan David, 1977. Contributor of articles to magazines, under pseudonym Ben Mordechai.

WORK IN PROGRESS: Research on attitude change and the wisdom of Job; studying Jewish communities in South Africa, Rhodesia, Japan, Taiwan, Hong Kong, Bangkok, the Philippines, Buenos Aires, Egypt, Iran, and Romania, with regard to both the historical and present-day situations.

*   *   *

GERBI, Antonello   1904-1976
(Don Ferrante)

PERSONAL: Born May 15, 1904, in Florence, Italy; son of Edmo (a stockbroker) and Iginia (Levi) Gerbi; married Herma Schimmerling, January 11, 1940; children: Daniele, Alessandro. *Education:* University of Rome, D.Law, 1925; postdoctoral study at University of Berlin, London School of Economics and Political Science, and University of Vienna, all 1929-31.

CAREER: Employed by a stockbroker in Milan, Italy, 1925-27; barrister at Court of Appeals in Milan, 1927-29; Banca Commerciale Italiana, Milan, chief of economic department and editor of bank publications, including *Rassegna Trimestrale,* 1932-39; University of Rome, Rome, Italy, lecturer in the history of ideas, 1933; Royal University, Milan, lecturer in philosophy and political thought, 1936-38; writer in Lima, Peru, 1938; Banco de Credito del Peru, Lima, chief of economic department, 1940-48; Banca Commerciale Italiana, senior economist and member of board of directors, 1948-70. Attended international congresses in England, the Netherlands, Australia, and the United States. *Awards, honors:* Rockefeller Foundation fellow, 1929-31; Ordine del Sol, Lima, 1948.

WRITINGS: La Politica del Settecento (title means "The Politics of the Eighteenth Century"), Laterza, 1928; *La Politica del Romanticismo: Le Origini* (title means "The Politics of Romanticism: Its Origins"), Laterza, 1932; *Il Peccato di Adamo ed Eva: Storia della Ipotesi di Beverland* (title means "The Original Sin of Adam and Eve: A History of Beverland's Hypothesis"), La Cultura, 1933.

El Peru en Marcha: Ensayo de Geografia Economica (title means "The Progress of Peru: An Essay on Economic Geography"), Banco de Credito del Peru, 1941, 2nd edition, 1943; (with Joao Normano) *The Japanese in South America: An Introductory Survey With Special Reference to Peru,* Institute of Pacific Relations, 1943; *Diego de Leon Pinelo Contra Justo Lipsio: Una de las primeras polemicas sobre el Nuevo Mundo* (title means "Pinelo Versus Lipsius: One of the First Polemics About the New World"), [Lima], 1945; *Viejas Polemicas sobre el Nuevo Mundo: En el umbral de una conciencia americana* (title means "Old Polemics About the New World: On the Threshold of an American Ideology"), Banco del Credito del Peru, 1946, published as *La Disputo del Nuovo Mondo: Storia di una polemica, 1750-1900,* Ricciardi, 1955, revised and enlarged translation by Jeremy Moyle published as *The Dispute of the New World: The History of a Polemic, 1750-1900,* University of Pittsburgh Press, 1973.

(Editor) Benedetto Croce, *Filosofia—Poesia—Storia,* Ricciardi, 1952; *La natura delle Indie Nove* (title means "The Nature of the New Indies"), Ricciardi, 1975.

Contributor of articles and reviews to magazines and newspapers, often under pseudonym Don Ferrante.

SIDELIGHTS: Gerbi spent his childhood in Tuscany, and the World War I years in Rome. His stay in Rome was important for him, because it helped him to develop his sense of history and love of scholarship. While there he also developed an interest in politics. Though not a party member, he became a steady contributor to a Social-Democratic daily newspaper, *La Giustizia,* and, under the pseudonym Don Ferrante, acquired a wide reputation.

That newspaper was suppressed by the Fascist government in 1925, and the next few years were filled with uncertainty for Gerbi. He became interested in film and acquainted the Italian public with contemporary European film and film stars through his writings. During his postdoctoral study in Europe, 1929-31, he reported to Italian readers on cultural matters, films, music, and on trends which would soon engulf Germany in Nazism.

He also chose a new career in economic research. The racial legislation enacted by the Fascist government in 1938 seemed to end his career in Italy. To avoid dismissal, he was transferred to Peru, where he remained until 1948, when he returned to Italy permanently.

Gerbi's health began to fail almost simultaneously with his mandatory retirement from the bank; he recovered in the spring of 1976, but died soon after at his country house in Civenna.*

(Died July 26, 1976)

* * *

GERRIETTS, John 1912-

PERSONAL: Born May 11, 1912, in Chicago, Ill.; son of John D. (an accountant) and Mary C. (Graber) Gerrietts. *Education:* Loyola University, Chicago, Ill., A.B., 1934, M.A., 1937, Ph.D., 1954. *Office:* Department of English, Loyola University, Chicago, Ill. 60611.

CAREER: Loyola University, Chicago, Ill., associate professor, 1955-60, professor of English, 1960—, chairman of department, 1958-73. Member of executive committee of Illinois Study Center for the Preparation of English Teachers, 1964-67, chairman, 1965-66; member of faculty advisory committee of Illinois Board of Higher Education, 1966-68. *Member:* Association of Departments of English (member of executive committee, 1963-65), National Council of Teachers of English.

WRITINGS: A Manual for Teacher (to accompany *Reading for Writing* by Maurice B. McNamee), Rinehart & Co., 1958; (with Stanley A. Clayes) *Ways to Poetry,* Harcourt, 1975. Contributor to English and education journals.

* * *

GERULAITIS, Leonardas Vytautas 1928-

PERSONAL: Born November 6, 1928, in Kaunas, Lithuania; came to the United States in 1950, naturalized citizen, 1954; son of Zenonas (a military general) and Elena (Pileika) Gerulaitis; married Renate Keppler (a professor), August 20, 1960. *Education:* University of Michigan, A.B., 1956, M.A.,1957, M.A.L.S., 1963, Ph.D., 1969. *Home:* 388 West Maryknoll, Rochester, Mich. 48063. *Office:* Department of History, Oakland University, Rochester, Mich. 48063.

CAREER: Oakland University, Rochester, Mich., assistant professor, 1963-70, associate professor of history, 1970—. *Military service:* U.S. Air Force, 1951-55. *Member:* American Historical Association, Mediaeval Academy of America, Renaissance Society of America, Society for Italian Historical Studies, American Catholic Historical Association, American Association of University Professors.

WRITINGS: Printing and Publishing in Fifteenth-Century Venice, American Library Association, 1976.

WORK IN PROGRESS: Research on the cultural history of the Renaissance, especially on the hermetic tradition.

SIDELIGHTS: Gerulaitis writes: "The major problem confronting me is to understand how knowledge is transmitted. It is relatively easy to communicate information. What I find so fascinating about the Renaissance period is a shift from one mode of perceiving reality to another, a change in human consciousness. In a way it was a step backwards in order to leap forward. Probably the most original contribution was the magical/hermetical tradition, which has to be studied anew taking into account the recent findings of humanistic psychology."

* * *

GHIGNA, Charles 1946-

PERSONAL: Surname is pronounced *Geen*-ya; born August 25, 1946, in New York; son of Charles Vincent and Pa-

tricia (Pelletier) Ghigna; married Nancy Minnicks, June 24, 1967 (divorced June 5, 1973); married Debra Holmes (a model), August 2, 1975; children: (first marriage) Julie Ann. *Education:* Florida Atlantic University, B.A., 1968, M.A., 1969; also attended Edison Community College, 1964-66, University of South Florida, 1968-69, and Florida State University, 1974. *Home:* 204 West Linwood Dr., Birmingham, Ala. 35209. *Office:* Department of Creative Writing, Alabama School of Fine Arts, 820 18th St. N., Birmingham, Ala. 35203.

CAREER: High school English teacher in Fort Myers, Fla., 1968-73; Edison Community College, Fort Myers, Fla., instructor in creative writing, 1973; National Council of Teachers of English, Urbana, Ill., poetry editor of *English Journal,* 1974; Alabama School of Fine Arts, Birmingham, poet-in-residence, 1974—; Creekwood Colony for the Arts, Hurtsboro, Ala., director, 1975—. Creator, director, and performer on "Cabbages and Kings" (children's television series), Alabama Educational Television, 1976. Has given more than one hundred readings at colleges and secondary schools. *Awards, honors:* Mary Roberts Rinehart fellowship, 1977; first prize in poetry from *Writer's Digest,* 1977, for "Divers."

WRITINGS: Plastic Tears (poems), Dorrance, 1973; *Stables* (poetry chapbook), Creekwood Press, 1976; *Cockroach* (one-act play), Contemporary Drama Service, 1977. Work represented in *Southern Poetry: The Seventies,* edited by Guy Owen, North Carolina State University, 1977. Contributor of more than two hundred poems to magazines and newspapers, including *Harper's, Kansas Quarterly, Texas Quarterly, Christian Science Monitor, Highlights for Children, Southern Poetry Review,* and *Folio.*

WORK IN PROGRESS: Southern Bred, poems; children's books.

AVOCATIONAL INTERESTS: Sky-diving, jogging, restoring his fifty-two-year-old home.

BIOGRAPHICAL/CRITICAL SOURCES: Birmingham, January, 1975; *Alabama Arts,* summer, 1975; *Writer's Digest,* July, 1977.

* * *

GIBBS, Mary Ann
See BIDWELL, Marjory Elizabeth Sarah

* * *

GIBSON, Alexander Dunnett 1901-1978

October 6, 1901—May 1, 1978; American educator and author of books in his field. Gibson, who studied in France, taught French for more than forty years. He was also active in local civic affairs and served on many state committees. Gibson died in McIndoe, Vt. Obituaries and other sources: *Who's Who in American Politics,* 4th edition, Bowker, 1974; *New York Times,* May 4, 1978.

* * *

GIBSON, Gifford Guy 1943-

PERSONAL: Born January 21, 1943, in Tullahoma, Tenn.; married Iloika Vegh. *Agent:* Evelyn Oppenheimer, 7929 Meadow Park, Dallas, Tex.

CAREER: Writer, 1975—.

WRITINGS: Missing Nuclear Weapons, Pacific News Service, 1975; *Scent of Cruelty,* Pacific News Service, 1975; *By Her Own Admission* (biography), Doubleday, 1977.

WORK IN PROGRESS: A novel "on the theme that survival is becoming our highest obligation"; a screenplay; an opera libretto; and an essay.

SIDELIGHTS: Gibson remarks briefly: "My writing alone is my *public* life. What I want known about me or what I have to say I do in print. Like Borges, I write for myself and a few friends, and to help ease the passage of time."

*   *   *

GIBSON, Margaret 1944-

PERSONAL: Born February 17, 1944, in Philadelphia, Pa.; daughter of John Spears (an engineer) and Mattie (a teacher; maiden name, Doyle) Ferguson; married Ross Gibson, August 27, 1966 (divorced, May, 1974); married David McKain (a poet and teacher), December 27, 1975. *Education:* Hollins College, B.A., 1966; University of Virginia, M.A., 1967. *Politics:* Socialist. *Religion:* Society of Friends (Quakers). *Home and office address:* R.F.D. 1, Matson Rd., Norwich, Conn. 06360.

CAREER: Madison College, Harrisonburg, Va., instructor in English, 1967-68; Virginia Commonwealth University, Richmond, instructor in English, 1968-70; George Mason University, Fairfax, Va., assistant professor of English, 1970-75; writer, 1975—. *Member:* Phi Beta Kappa. *Awards, honors:* Woodrow Wilson fellowship, 1967.

WRITINGS: Lunes, Some of Us Press, 1972; *On the Cutting Edge,* Curbstone Press, 1975; (editor with others) *Landscape and Distance: Contemporary Poets from Virginia,* University Press of Virginia, 1975; *Signs,* Louisiana State University Press, in press.

WORK IN PROGRESS: Three Women, a novel; a book of poems.

SIDELIGHTS: Margaret Gibson writes: "A serious commitment to writing came early, thanks to encouragement from Louis Rubin and other teachers. Slow development in writing parallels slow, steady personal growth. A stay at Yaddo in summer, 1975, was invaluable personally and professionally.

AVOCATIONAL INTERESTS: Feminism, gardening, radical politics.

*   *   *

GIDDINS, Gary 1948-

PERSONAL: Born March 21, 1948, in Brooklyn, N.Y.; son of Leo a (businessman) and Alice (a decorator; maiden name, Gelber) Giddins; married Susan Rogers (a writer and publicist), April 23, 1972. *Education:* Grinnell College, B.A., 1970. *Religion:* Jewish. *Home:* 145 East 15th St., New York, N.Y. 10003. *Agent:* Curtis Brown, Ltd., 575 Madison Ave., New York, N.Y. 10022. *Office: Village Voice,* 80 University Pl., New York, N.Y. 10003.

CAREER/WRITINGS: Hollywood Reporter, Hollywood, Calif., film critic, 1972; *Down Beat,* Chicago, Ill., contributing editor, 1972-73; *Village Voice,* New York City, writer and author of column, "Weather Bird," 1973—. Author of jazz columns in *Hifi/Stereo,* 1975-78, and in *New York,* 1975—. Radio producer and disc jockey, WBAI-FM, New York City, 1975—. Teacher of jazz history at New York University School of Continuing Education, 1977—. Contributor of articles to periodicals, including *Esquire, New York Times, New Times,* and *Melody Maker.* Fellow at Smithsonian Colloquium on jazz criticism, 1974. *Member:* Music Critics Association. *Awards, honors:* ASCAP-Deems Taylor Award, 1976 and 1977, for music criticism.

WORK IN PROGRESS: Riding on a Blue Note, "a book on matters relating to the blues idiom in the past decade," for Dial; a book on recent jazz (1958-1980) for Oxford University Press; a book on recorded jazz for Vintage.

SIDELIGHTS: Giddins comments: "A trend back to acoustic jazz implies a previous trend away from acoustic jazz. In the wake of the rock, it was inevitable that jazz musicians would investigate the expanded coloration made possible by electric instruments both for musical and commercial reasons. But the mainstream of jazz creativity has always been acoustic, and probably always will be if for no other reasons than economics and portability. The reasons several pop/jazz musicians have returned to the acoustic fold include a prevalent middle-of-the-road backlash against loud pop, a desire to realign themselves with the jazz tradition, and chiefly, the respect any good pianist has for a good acoustic instrument, no matter how complex and sophisticated the electric imitations. Of course, electric jazz will continue to be part of the canvas."

"My background is in literature and I hope to bring a broader scope to jazz criticism than is usually encountered. It's a great, multifarious world of music, and one which sheds particular light on both the country that created and rejected it, and the speed with which an art can evolve and decay and be reborn in a technocracy. My immediate influences among music critics were Martin Williams and Dan Morgenstern."

*   *   *

GIDLOW, Elsa 1898-

PERSONAL: Born December 29, 1898, in England; came to the United States in 1920, naturalized citizen, 1938; daughter of Samuel Ault (a lecturer) and Alice May (Rommel) Gidlow. *Education:* Attended McGill College (now University). *Politics:* "Radical (go back to roots of social wrongs)." *Religion:* "Taoist—if anything." *Home address:* Camino del Canyon, Muir Woods, Mill Valley, Calif. 94941.

CAREER: Worked as editor and journalist for industrial house organs, 1918-21; *Pearson's* Magazine, New York, N.Y., began as poetry editor, became associate editor until 1926; *Pacific Coast Journal of Nursing,* San Francisco, Calif., editor, 1926-28; traveled in Europe, 1928-29; editor of a Western Trade Journals magazine; free-lance writer, 1940-68. Founder and owner of Druid Heights Books (publishing company). *Member:* Society for Comparative Philosophy (treasurer; board member).

WRITINGS: On a Grey Thread (poems), Will Ransom, 1923; *California Valley With Girls* (poems), privately printed, 1932; *From Alba Hill* (poems), privately printed, 1933; *Wild Swan Swinging* (poems), privately printed, 1954; *Letters From Limbo* (poems), privately printed, 1956; *Moods of Eros* (poems), Druid Heights Books, 1970; *Makings for Meditation* (poems), Druid Heights Books, 1973; *Ask No Man Pardon* (essay), Druid Heights Books, 1975; *Sapphic Songs* (poems), Diana Press, 1976. Contributor to several hundred magazines in England, Canada, and the United States, including *Canadian Bookman, San Francisco Review, Forum,* and *Pacific Weekly.*

WORK IN PROGRESS: An autobiography; a novel.

SIDELIGHTS: Elsa Gidlow told *CA* that the themes of her poetry include lyrical love, politics, protest, mysticism, and nature. *Avocational interests:* Organic gardening (vegetables, fruits, and flowers).

BIOGRAPHICAL/CRITICAL SOURCES: Alan Watts,

In My Own Way, Random House, 1973; *American Poetry Review,* January-February, 1978.

*   *   *

GIFFORD, Thomas (Eugene) 1937-

PERSONAL: Born May 16, 1937, in Dubuque, Iowa; son of Eugene A. and Mabel (Maxwell) Gifford; married Kari Sandven (divorced); married Camille d'Ambrose (an actress); children: Thomas, Rachel. *Education:* Harvard University, A.B., 1959. *Agent:* Julian Bach Literary Agency, Inc., 3 East 48th St., New York, N.Y. 10017.

CAREER: Houghton Mifflin Co., Boston, Mass., college textbook salesman in Minneapolis, Minn., 1960-68; *Twin Citian,* Minneapolis, editor-in-chief, 1968-69; Tyrone Guthrie Theatre, Minneapolis, director of public relations, 1970; Sun Newspapers, Minneapolis, editor and author of column, 1971-75; free-lance writer, 1975—. President of Deja-Vu, Inc. (advertising agency). *Awards, honors:* Special Scroll Award from Mystery Writers of America, 1977, for *The Cavanaugh Quest.*

WRITINGS: The Wind Chill Factor, Putnam, 1975; *The Cavanaugh Quest* (mystery novel), Putnam, 1976; *The Man From Lisbon,* McGraw, 1977.

*   *   *

GILBERT, Edwin 1907-1976

PERSONAL: Born in 1907, in Mannheim, Germany; married Virginia Smith, 1941 (divorced, 1973); children: Holly. *Education:* Graduated from University of Michigan.

CAREER: Writer. Worked for Broadway theatrical agency. *Military service:* Served in U.S. Army Air Forces during World War II.

WRITINGS—Novels: The Squirrel Cage, Doubleday, 1947; *Damion's Daughter,* Doubleday, 1949; *The Hot and the Cool,* Doubleday, 1953; *Native Stone,* Doubleday, 1956; *Silver Spoon,* Lippincott, 1957; *The Hourglass,* Lippincott, 1959; *The New Ambassadors,* Lippincott, 1961; *American Chrome,* Putnam, 1966; *The Beautiful Life,* Putnam, 1966; *Jamey: A Novel of a Period, 1967-1968,* Trident, 1969; *Newport,* Little, Brown, 1971; *Connecticut Circle,* Putnam, 1972; *A Season in Monte Carlo,* Arbor House, 1976.

Other: (With Leonard Spigelgass) "All Through the Night" (screenplay), Warner Bros., 1942; (with Everett Freeman) "Larceny, Incorporated" (screenplay; adapted from the play, "The Night Before Christmas," by Laura Perelman and S. J. Perelman), Warner Bros., 1942. Also author of plays, including "The Golden Journey," 1936, and "To Soothe the Savage Beast," (with Virginia Smith) "Virginia Reel," and "Hot Nocturne." Contributor of articles to *Vanity Fair* and *Mademoiselle.* Contributor of lyrics to "New Faces of 1936."

SIDELIGHTS: Gilbert's novels have consistently received praise for their realistic depictions of the worlds they portray. A critic for *New Yorker* called *The Squirrel Cage* "a compendium of information on Hollywood jargon and mores. . . ." Critics also applauded *The Hot and the Cool* because it "effectively recreates the childish, brilliant, and frenetic world" of modern jazz.

George Goodman, Jr. noted that Gilbert was "a writer whose versatility brought him commercial success as a dramatist, scriptwriter, and novelist."

BIOGRAPHICAL/CRITICAL SOURCES: New Yorker, October 4, 1947; *Saturday Review,* September 26, 1953.

OBITUARIES: New York Times, August 29, 1976; *AB Bookman's Weekly,* October 4, 1976.*

(Died August 24, 1976, in Cannes, France)

*   *   *

GILBERT, Julie Goldsmith 1949-

PERSONAL: Born July 21, 1949, in New York, N.Y.; daughter of Henry (a publisher) and Janet (an actress; maiden name, Fox) Goldsmith; married John L. Weisman (employed by a magazine), July 7, 1973. *Education:* Attended Boston University, 1965-67. *Politics:* Democrat. *Religion:* Jewish. *Home:* 5500 Friendship Blvd., Chevy Chase, Md. 20015. *Agent:* Robert Lantz, Lantz Office, Inc., 114 East 55th St., New York, N.Y. 10022.

CAREER: Professional actress (on stage, in film, commercials, also soap opera and dinner theater), 1967-72; writer, 1972—. *Member:* Writers Guild of America, Actors Equity, Screen Actors Guild, American Federation of Television and Radio Artists. *Awards, honors:* Fellow of Bread Loaf Writers Conference, 1972.

WRITINGS: Umbrella Steps, Random House, 1972. Author of "Abracadabra" (three-act play), first produced as a staged reading, 1973. Author of the screenplay version of *Umbrella Steps.*

WORK IN PROGRESS: Those Kids (tentative title), a novel, completion expected in 1980; "Honey, I'm Home," a three-act play.

SIDELIGHTS: Julie Gilbert comments: "I consider people-watching vital to my existence. It can be an art form if practised with regularity and dedication. Just plant me on a park bench in New York in the spring, and I'll never ask for more pleasure."

*   *   *

GILBERT, Neil 1940-

PERSONAL: Born September 18, 1940, in New York, N.Y.; son of Allan (a salesman) and Ida (Bedzin) Gilbert; married Barbara Feinstein (a scientist), June 3, 1963; children: Evan, Jesse. *Education:* Brooklyn College of the City University of New York, B.A., 1962; University of Pittsburgh, M.S.W., 1965, Ph.D., 1968. *Office:* Department of Social Welfare, University of California, Berkeley, Calif. 94720.

CAREER: University of California, Berkeley, assistant professor, 1969-73, associate professor, 1973-77, professor of social welfare, 1977—. Fellow at United Nations Research Institute for Social Development, 1975-76. Research director for Pittsburgh mayor's committee on human resources, 1966-68.

WRITINGS: Clients or Constituents, Jossey-Bass, 1970; (with Harry Specht) *The Model Cities Program: A Comparative Analysis of Participating Cities—Process, Product, Performance, and Predictions,* U.S. Government Printing Office, 1973; (with Specht) *Dimensions of Social Welfare Policy,* Prentice-Hall, 1974; (editor with Specht) *The Emergence of Social Work and Social Welfare,* F. T. Peacock, 1976; (with Specht) *Coordination of Social Services: An Analysis of Community, Organizational, and Staff Characteristics,* Praeger, 1977; (editor with Specht) *Planning for Social Welfare: Issues, Models, and Tasks,* Prentice-Hall, 1977; (with Specht) *The Dynamics of Community Planning,* Ballinger, 1978; (with Specht and Henry Miller) *Introduction to Social Work Methods,* Prentice-Hall, in press.

Contributor: Roger Miller, editor, *Race, Research, and Reason,* National Association of Social Workers, 1969; Jack Rothman, editor, *Issues in Race and Ethnic Relations,* F. T. Peacock, 1976; Warren Bennis and other editors, *The Planning of Change,* Holt, 3rd edition (Gilbert was not included in earlier editions), 1976; Harry Specht and Ann Vickery, editors, *Integrating Methods of Social Work Practice,* Allen & Unwin, 1977.

Editor of Prentice-Hall series on social work, and Praeger series on social services. Contributor to *Encyclopedia of Social Work.* Contributor of more than twenty articles to journals in the social sciences.

* * *

GILL, Alan
See GILLEPSIE, Alfred

* * *

GILLESPIE, Alfred 1924-
(Alan Gill)

PERSONAL: Born May 19, 1924, in Brooklyn, N.Y.; son of John F. (a veterinarian) and Lillian (Blankley) Gillespie; married Jean Hollis, April 18, 1953; children: Kevin. *Education:* Attended Brooklyn College (now of the City University of New York) and University of Rochester. *Politics:* Democrat. *Religion:* Roman Catholic. *Home:* 14 Dailey Dr., Croton-on-Hudson, N.Y. 10520. *Agent:* Emilie Jacobson, Curtis Brown Ltd., 575 Madison Ave., New York, N.Y. 10022.

CAREER: New York Herald Tribune Syndicate, New York City, manager of syndicate, 1949-54; Time, Inc., New York City, manager of renewal promotions for *Time,* 1954-55; manager of direct mail promotions for *This Week* (magazine), 1955-59; creative director of Burnaford & Co. (promotions), 1959-60; account executive for Donahue & Coe, 1960-62; New York Herald Tribune Syndicate, syndicated columnist, 1961-64; Curtis Publishing, New York City, promotion director, 1964-69; Time, Inc., member of promotion staff, 1969-71; *Travel and Leisure,* New York City, promotion director, 1971-73; free-lance writer, 1973—. *Military service:* U.S. Naval Reserve, active duty; served in Pacific theater. *Awards, honors:* National magazine award for fiction from *Redbook,* 1970, for story "Tonight at Nine-Thirty-Six."

WRITINGS: Gilliam Unbuttoned (novel), Little, Brown, 1977.

Stories anthologized in *The Best American Short Stories, 1970,* edited by Martha Foley and David Burnett, Houghton, and *Redbook's Famous Fiction,* 1977. Author of daily television column under pseudonym Alan Gill, syndicated by New York Herald Tribune Syndicate to about thirty newspapers, 1961-64. Contributor of stories and articles, sometimes under pseudonym Alan Gill, to popular magazines, including *Good Housekeeping, Show, Saturday Evening Post,* and *TV Guide.*

WORK IN PROGRESS: Eye of the Hermit (tentative title), a novel.

* * *

GILLINGS, Richard John 1902-

PERSONAL: Born October 30, 1902, in London, England; son of John George (a British Army officer) and Winifred Susan (a shorthand typist; maiden name, Sibley) Gillings; married Esme Victoria Salisbury, June 27, 1925; children:

Kevin John Raoul, Barrie Roderick D'Arcy. *Education:* Sydney University, B.Sc. (honors), 1922, M.Ed. (honors), 1951. *Politics:* "General." *Religion:* Church of England. *Home:* 14 The Mall, Turramurra, Sydney, New South Wales, 2074, Australia. *Office:* School of History and Philosophy of Science, University of New South Wales, P.O. Box 1, Kensington, 2033, Sydney, Australia.

CAREER: Mathematics master in various high schools in New South Wales, Australia, 1924-46; Balmain Teachers' College, Balmain, New South Wales, lecturer in mathematics, 1947-50; Sydney University, Sydney Teachers' College, Sydney, New South Wales, lecturer in mathematics, 1951-62; University of New South Wales, School of History and Philosophy of Science, Kensington, senior lecturer in mathematics of ancient Egypt and Babylon, 1963-69; writer, 1969—. Sole director of Problems Bureau of Mathematics Association of New South Wales, 1939—; business manager and member of editorial committee of *Australian Mathematics Teacher,* 1945-56; member of standing committee of convocation at Sydney University, 1950-55; co-founder with wife of Calligraphic Art & Pen Co., Sydney, 1957. *Military service:* New South Wales Voluntary Defense Corps, 1941-45; became intelligence officer. *Member:* Royal Life Saving Society, Australian National Ski Federation. *Awards, honors:* Silver medal from Royal Life Saving Society, 1920.

WRITINGS: Crazy Cards or Bizarre Bridge, Newcastle, 1934; *Graphs: Columnar, Locus, Complex* (holograph), Australian Publishing Co., 1941; (with Victor R. Outten) *Mathematical Tables,* Australian Publishing Co., 1944, 5th edition, 1961; *A Brief History of British Weights, Measures, Decimal Currency, Signs, and Symbols,* New South Wales University Press, 1964, 2nd edition, 1968; *Mathematics in the Time of the Pharaohs,* M.I.T. Press, 1972. Contributor to *Dictionary of Scientific Biography,* 1978. Contributor of about one hundred articles to journals in his field.

WORK IN PROGRESS: Enlarged and illustrated edition of *Crazy Cards or Bizarre Bridge; Grim Fairy Tails* (for adults reading to children); *Mathematics Can Be Fun.*

SIDELIGHTS: Gillings told *CA:* "Of all books and articles written by me in scientific journals, *Mathematics in the Time of the Pharaohs* is clearly my outstanding performance. To date, it is the only book of its kind in the world. It has been favorably reviewed in over thirty journals and newspapers, in English, French, German, Russian, and Swedish languages." Gillings admitted, however, that "its sale price of twenty-five dollars may militate against high sales."

Gillings has also been an active athlete throughout his life, excelling in swimming, life-saving, sculling, skiing, tennis, and lawn bowling. In 1936 he became the first man to ski on Barrington Tops in New South Wales. During the Olympic Games in Melbourne in 1956, Gillings acted as the French announcer for boxing. He participated as a lawn bowling competitor in the British Empire Commonwealth Games of 1958 and 1962.

BIOGRAPHICAL/CRITICAL SOURCES: Smith's Weekly (New South Wales), November 26, 1949; *Science,* May 11, 1973.

* * *

GINNINGS, Harriett W.
See HARRIETT

GIPE, George 1933-

PERSONAL: Surname rhymes with "ripe"; born February 3, 1933, in Baltimore, Md.; son of George Albert and Marjorie (Showell) Gipe; married Nancy Ellen Boylan, April 23, 1960; children: Lawrence Charles, George David. *Education:* Western Maryland College, B.A., 1956; graduate study at University of Glasgow, 1956-57. *Politics:* "Anti-Republican." *Home:* 17400 Bruehl Rd., Upperco, Md. 21155. *Agent:* Elaine Markson, 44 Greenwich Ave., New York, N.Y. 10011. *Office:* WMAR-TV, 6400 York Rd., Baltimore, Md. 21212.

CAREER: WJZ-TV, Baltimore, Md., cameraman, 1958-61; WMAR-TV, Baltimore, Md., writer-producer, 1962—. *Military service:* U.S. Army Reserve, 1956-65, active duty, 1956; became captain. *Member:* American Society for Baseball Research, Johann Strauss Society of Great Britain.

WRITINGS: Coney Island Quickstep (novel), Crowell, 1977; *Sportslog* (off-beat history of American sports), Doubleday, 1978. Contributor to a variety of popular magazines, including *Sports Illustrated, Mad, American Heritage, Ms.,* and *Alfred Hitchcock Mystery Magazine.*

SIDELIGHTS: Gipe told *CA:* "I write because I enjoy the experience, and unlike many writers, thoroughly enjoy re-writing as well. Yet I'm not sure I would do it if I were denied an audience. Writing just for myself doesn't seem like much fun. I suppose that makes me very 'commercial,' but I need the anticipation of putting my work before readers or viewers to make things happen. When I'm at the typewriter, I feel I'm the best writer in the world. Later, of course, the world informs me I'm mistaken, but by that time the work is finished, so I'm ahead!"

* * *

GIRARD, Joe 1928-

PERSONAL: Born November 1, 1928, in Detroit, Mich.; son of Antony (an automobile assembly worker) and Grace (Stabile) Girard; married June Krantz, June 2, 1951; children: Joe, Grace. *Education:* Attended high school in Detroit, Mich. *Politics:* Independent. *Religion:* Roman Catholic. *Residence:* Grosse Pointe Shores, Mich. *Office:* Joe Girard Productions, Inc., 16546 East Nine-Mile Rd., East Detroit, Mich. 48021.

CAREER: Building contractor in Detroit, Mich., 1960-65; Merollis Chevrolet, Detroit, Mich., new car and truck salesman, 1966—. President of Joe Girard Productions, Inc., 1976—. *Military service:* U.S. Army, 1947. *Awards, honors:* Golden Plate Award from American Academy of Achievement, 1975.

WRITINGS: How to Sell Anything to Anybody, Simon & Schuster, 1978. Also creator of videotapes.

WORK IN PROGRESS: Research for a book on personal achievement; training materials for a salesman's school.

SIDELIGHTS: Girard told *CA:* "My viewpoints on achievement and success are goal-oriented, with the conviction that any person can set out to what he wishes to do if he makes up his mind to it. I lecture to young people on this subject."

BIOGRAPHICAL/CRITICAL SOURCES: Adcrafter, November 4, 1977.

* * *

GIRAUD, Marcel 1900-

PERSONAL: Born April 7, 1900, in Nice, France; married wife, Fernande, August 16, 1926; children: Paulette, Annie, Jean-Marc. *Education:* Attended University of Aix and University of Paris. *Home:* 3 rue Paradis, 06000 Nice, France.

CAREER: Professor of North American history at College de France, Paris. *Awards, honors:* Rockefeller Foundation scholarship, 1934-35, and 1947.

WRITINGS: Le Metis Canadien (title means "The Half-Breed Canadian"), Paris Institute of Ethnology, 1947; *Histoire de la Louisiane francaise* (title means "History of French Louisiana"), Presses Universitaires de France, Volume I: *Le Regne de Louis XIV* (title means "The Reign of Louis XIV"), 1953, translation by Joseph C. Lambert published as *A History of French Louisiana,* Louisiana State University Press, 1974, Volume II: *Annees de transition* (title means "Years of Transition"), 1958, Volume III: *L'Epoque de John Law* (title means "The Era of John Law"), 1966, Volume IV: *La Louisiane apres le systeme de Law* (title means "Louisiana After the System of Law"), 1974; *Histoire du Canada* (title means "History of Canada"), Presses Universitaires de France, 1966. Contributor to journals in his field.

WORK IN PROGRESS: Volume V of *Histoire de la Louisiane francaise.*

SIDELIGHTS: Giraud told *CA:* "I specialized in the field of North American history after meeting the first American soldiers who landed in France in 1918. From that time on, I developed a major interest in the western provinces of Canada and the United States."

* * *

GIVENS, John 1943-

PERSONAL: Born September 24, 1943, in California; son of Boyd (a salesman) and Eleanor (Shuman) Givens; married Yasuko Tokumaru (a weaver), May, 1974. *Education:* California State University, Fresno, B.A., 1966; University of Iowa, M.F.A., 1976. *Residence:* San Francisco, Calif. *Agent:* Russell & Volkening, Inc., 551 Fifth Ave., New York, N.Y. 10017.

CAREER: Teacher of English as a second language in Pusan, South Korea, 1966-69, and Kyoto, Japan, 1970-74; San Francisco Community College, San Francisco, Calif., teacher of English as a second language, 1976—.

WRITINGS: Sons of the Pioneers (novel), Harcourt, 1977. Contributor of stories to *Fiction International* and *Hawaii Review.*

WORK IN PROGRESS: A novel.

SIDELIGHTS: Givens writes: "My main interest is Japan, as well as the rest of northeast Asia. My second language is Japanese; I spent four years studying and practicing traditional Japanese calligraphy. Now I intend to divide my time between Japan and California. At present, I am interested in the weight of the past, and a corresponding loss of satisfaction in the present."

* * *

GLASER, Dianne E(lizabeth) 1937-

PERSONAL: Born August 29, 1937, in Bronx, N.Y.; daughter of James and Elizabeth Jackson; married Marvin E. Glaser (a creative director), November 9, 1957; children: Tamara, Sean, Carey, Dane, Amber, Quinn, Tristan. *Education:* Attended University of Alabama, Huntsville, 1956-57. *Home and office:* 1135 McNichol Lane, Chattanooga, Tenn. 37421.

CAREER: Writer, 1971—. *Awards, honors: The Diary of Trilby Frost* was named book of the year by American Library Association, 1977.

WRITINGS—For children: *Amber Wellington, Daredevil,* Walker & Co., 1975; *Amber Wellington, Witchwatcher,* Walker & Co., 1976; *The Diary of Trilby Frost,* Holiday House, 1976; *Summer Secrets,* Holiday House, 1977; *The Case of the Missing Six,* Holiday House, 1978.

* * *

GLASER, Isabel Joshlin 1929-

PERSONAL: Born June 7, 1929, in Birmingham, Ala.; daughter of Notreab and Kathleen (Sigler) Joshlin; married Melvin William Glaser, November 7, 1953 (died, 1966); children: Susan Elaine, Stephen Philip. *Education:* Attended Randolph-Macon Woman's College, 1947-49; George Peabody College for Teachers, B.A., 1951; also attended Baldwin-Wallace College, Ohio University, Kent State University, and Memphis State University. *Religion:* Methodist. *Home:* 5383 Mason Rd., Memphis, Tenn. 38117.

CAREER: High school teacher of English and Spanish in Tennessee, 1951-53; elementary school teacher in Ohio, 1953-66; free-lance writer, 1968—. Research assistant for John Kennedy Foundation at George Peabody College for Teachers, 1976; director of creative writing workshops; has given readings at universities and on radio.

MEMBER: National League of American Pen Women (local president, 1974-76), National Federation of Press Women, Ozark Writers and Artists Guild, Tennessee Woman's Press and Authors Club (vice-president, 1974-75), Poetry Society of Tennessee, Tennessee Literary Arts Association. *Awards, honors:* Local, state, and national awards for poetry, fiction, and nonfiction include first prizes from Biennial Convention of Pen Women, 1974, for adult fiction, lyric poetry, and general poetry, Ozark Writers and Artists Guild, 1975, for modern poetry and for poetry on a country theme, Poetry Society of Tennessee, 1975, 1976, Tennessee Woman's Press and Authors Club, 1976, for poetry, and Mid-South Poetry Festival, 1976.

WRITINGS: *Old Visions, New Dreams* (poems), Old Hickory Review Press, 1977. Work represented in *Prize Poems, 1973,* National Federation of State Poetry Societies. Contributor of stories, poems, articles, and reviews to adult and juvenile magazines, including *Prairie Schooner, Child Life, Wind, My Weekly Reader, Mississippi Review, Southern Poetry Review,* and *Twigs.*

WORK IN PROGRESS: *On the Line,* a book of stories; poetry, *The Girl Who Did Not Shake the Pears.*

SIDELIGHTS: Isabel Glaser writes: "Since 1968, I have free-lanced fiction, poetry, and now and then articles and book reviews. As a writer, I have also been actively involved in the promotion of writing and other art forms, both my own and that of others throughout the area. In 1974 and 1975, I served as the judge of fiction and poetry contests on state, regional, and national levels."

* * *

GLASS, Ian Cameron 1926-

PERSONAL: Born May 27, 1926, in Scotland; son of John and Christine (McGregor) Glass; married Terry Johnson King (an author). *Office: Miami News,* One Herald Plaza, Miami, Fla. 33101.

CAREER/WRITINGS: Employed by *London Daily Express,* London, England, 1950-65; *Miami News,* Miami, Fla., features editor, 1965—. Author of self-syndicated travel column with wife Terry Johnson King, appearing in eighteen newspapers. Notable assignments include coverage of the British invasion of Anguilla, Jamaica's ties with Cuba, and a series on life in Cuba under Castro.

SIDELIGHTS: Glass told *CA:* "As a vocation I write features, and as an avocation I write travel, much of which I coauthor with my wife, Terry Johnson King. We spend every weekend traveling throughout Latin America, the Bahamas and Caribbean, logging about a quarter of a million air miles a year."

* * *

GLOVER, Dennis 1912-
(Peter Kettle)

PERSONAL: Born December 10, 1912, in Dunedin, New Zealand; son of Henry Lawrence (a dental surgeon) and Lyla (a writer; maiden name, Matthews) Glover; married third wife, Gladys Evelyn; children: Rupert. *Education:* University of Canterbury, B.A., 1934. *Politics:* Socialist. *Religion:* Church of England. *Home:* 4/537 Broadway, Strathmore, Wellington 3, New Zealand.

CAREER: Reporter, 1932-34; Caxton Press, Christchurch, New Zealand, founder and managing director, 1934-51; tutor in typography, 1960-68; free-lance writer, 1968—. Lecturer, 1933-36. Typography consultant. *Military service:* Royal Navy, 1940-44. Royal New Zealand Naval (Volunteer) Reserve, 1943-51; became lieutenant commander; received Distinguished Service Cross.

MEMBER: International P.E.N. (past president of New Zealand Center), Friends of Turnbull Library (past president), University Club. *Awards, honors:* D.Litt. from Victoria University of Wellington; Jesse McKay Award from International P.E.N., 1957, for poetry; Queen Elizabeth II grant, 1975.

WRITINGS: *Hot Water Sailor* (prose), A. H. & A. W. Reed, 1956; *Bedside Book* (prose and poetry), A. H. & A. W. Reed, 1959; *Enter Without Knocking* (poems), Pegasus Press, 1971; *Dancing to My Tune* (prose and poetry), Catspaw, 1975; *Wellington Harbour* (poems), Catspaw, 1976. Contributor to magazines, sometimes under pseudonym Peter Kettle.

WORK IN PROGRESS: *Come High Water,* poems; *Or Hawk or Basilisk,* poems; *Hawks and Handsaws,* "satires and frivolities."

SIDELIGHTS: Glover remarks: "What is done is done, and forgotten. I scribble because it's in my nature. Muchly praised, I am, honestly, quite indifferent. I never send things overseas—the world can wag on without me."

* * *

GLOVER, Harry 1912-

PERSONAL: Born April 1, 1912, in Coventry, England; son of William (an engineer) and Ada Glover; married Grace Thirza (an artist), July 23, 1937; children: Gay Glover Swift, Joy Glover Gammon. *Education:* Attended Coventry School of Art, 1928-30; Royal College of Art, A.R.C.A., 1933, A.T.D., 1934. *Religion:* Church of England. *Home:* Keresforth House, Barnsley S70 6RE, England.

CAREER: School of Art, Barnsley, England, principal, 1938-72; writer and artist, 1972—. *Military service:* British Army, 1940-46; became major; mentioned in dispatches. *Member:* Kennel Club.

WRITINGS—All self illustrated: *The Batsford Book of Dogs*, Batsford, 1970; *The Batsford Book of the Poodle*, Batsford, 1974; *Toy Dogs*, David & Charles, 1977; *A Standard Guide to Pure Bred Dogs*, Macmillan, 1977.

Author of ''Comment,'' a column in *Our Dogs*, 1972—.

SIDELIGHTS: Glover writes: ''I am recognised as an authority on dogs, and have judged dogs in seventeen countries. I have also lectured and broadcast on dogs, and served as commentator at the Crufts Show. I am a painter of dogs and illustrator of dog books, and in retirement, I am busier than ever before.'' *Avocational interests:* Angling, photography, growing roses, jewelry, vintage cars.

*   *   *

GODDEN, Jon   1906-

PERSONAL: Born August 3, 1906, in India; daughter of Arthur (an agent) and Norah (Hingley) Godden; married Nigel Baughan, September 14, 1930 (died, 1931); married Roland Oakley, October 26, 1936 (divorced). *Education:* Attended art school in England, 1922-25. *Residence:* Kent, England. *Agent:* Curtis Brown Ltd., 1 Craven Hill, London W2 3GP, England.

CAREER: Writer, 1947—. *Member:* International P.E.N.

WRITINGS—Novels: *The Bird Escaped*, Rinehart, 1947; *The House by the Sea*, Rinehart, 1948; *The Peacock*, Rinehart, 1950; *The City and the Wave*, Rinehart, 1950; *The Seven Islands*, Knopf, 1956; *Mrs. Panopoulis*, Knopf, 1959; *A Winter's Tale*, Knopf, 1961; *In the Sun*, Knopf, 1965; (with sister, Rumer Godden) *Two Under the Indian Sun*, Knopf, 1966; (with R. Godden) *Shiva's Pigeons*, Knopf, 1972; *Mrs. Starr Lives Alone*, Knopf, 1972; *Ahmed and the Old Lady*, Knopf, 1976.

WORK IN PROGRESS: A novel.

AVOCATIONAL INTERESTS: Travel in India, Africa, and Japan.

*   *   *

GODFREY, William
See YOUD, Samuel

*   *   *

GODSON, John   1937-

PERSONAL: Born October 23, 1937, in Sydney, Australia; son of John B. and Hilda M. (Kettley) Godson. *Education:* Educated in Australia. *Politics:* ''Apolitical—most politicians are crooks.'' *Religion:* ''I don't believe in being brainwashed.'' *Agent:* Anne Harrel, 32 Winsham Grove, London SW11 6NE, England. *Office:* Case Postale, 4, 1217-Meyrin-2, Switzerland.

CAREER: Radio announcer with Riverina Broadcasting Co., Ltd., 1953-55; radio announcer with Canberra Broadcasters, Ltd., 1955-57; Television Corporation, Ltd., Sydney, Australia, television news reader/presenter, 1957-61; news and current affairs editor with Amalgamated Wireless Australia, Ltd. (radio network), 1961-63; British Broadcasting Corp., London, England, news and current affairs producer/director, 1964-70; writer, 1970—. Consultant to British Broadcasting Corp., numerous European television and radio networks, European newspapers, and law firms. *Military service:* Australian National Service, 1953.

WRITINGS: Unsafe at Any Height, Blond, 1970, Simon & Schuster, 1971; *Runway*, Stacey, 1973, Scribner, 1974; *Papa India: The Trident Tragedy*, Compton Press, 1974; *The*

Rise and Fall of the DC-10, McKay, 1975; *The Airline Pilot*, Macmillan, 1976; *Clipper 806*, Contemporary Books, 1978. Also author of *An Eye for an Eye* (in Arabic), 1974. Author of television documentaries, including ''The Disaster of the DC-10,'' 1975, and ''The Ghost of Bravo November,'' 1978. Contributor of articles to periodicals in England, Germany, and the Netherlands.

WORK IN PROGRESS: The Ghost of Bravo November.

SIDELIGHTS: Godson told *CA:* ''My interest in researching why civil air crashes occur dates from 1963—the initial intriguing question being WHY. It was soon discovered that crashes were confined to relatively few airlines—usually the bigger, more sloppily managed ones. With regards to the motivation to continue. I think the reason one goes on is because the public is kept in complete ignorance about air disasters.

''At the time of the crash the public hears a lot of mainly press speculation. The press's difficulties are, to a certain extent, understood. Crashes very rarely happen in the right places, therefore they have to use amateurs and stringers who, for the most part, try and drag statements out of people who just happen to be nearby. These people usually know nothing about aircraft, but can certainly say some headline-creating words: words which rarely have any basis in fact. So, soon after the crash, the public is fed, in the main, with rubbish. Then, everyone forgets about it because these things take so long to investigate. By the time the investigation is complete, the press assumes that no one is interested anyway.

''There is also the angle that the press is scared of losing precious revenue from the airlines by printing anything bad about them. This is especially true in America. So, the public very rarely hears the truth.

''It is in this aura of keeping people in the dark that the air carriers have been literally able to get away with murder. I don't think any aircraft manufacturer received such a shock as when, within twenty-four hours of the DC-10 crashing at Paris, I was on European radio and television accusing them of manslaughtering those 346 persons who were on board. It was evident, well within that time, that the DC-10 had been negligently designed and manufactured.''

Discussing his reputation, Godson reported to *CA:* ''I have never been invited to join air safety organizations because they must feel my work is too 'reactionary.' However, it is known that my books and writings have been quoted or cited at many of the meetings of such groups without formal acknowledgment.

''Practically every European newspaper, along with the *New York Times* and the *Washington Post*, has attacked me for my work—however their logic of argument has largely been misfounded and can be proven wrong. The point is that if they don't attack me, they lose airline advertising (or so they think).''

Godson speaks French and German.

AVOCATIONAL INTERESTS: Flying, photography, skiing, driving, travel.

*   *   *

GOERING, Helga
See WALLMANN, Jeffrey M(iner)

*   *   *

GOLDBERG, Sidney   1931-

PERSONAL: Born March 1, 1931, in New York, N.Y.; son

of Emanuel (a manufacturer) and Florence (Fishbein) Goldberg; married Lucianne Steinberger (a literary agent); children: Joshua, Jonah. *Education:* University of Michigan, B.A., 1950, M.A., 1952; further study at New York University, 1952-53. *Politics:* Republican. *Religion:* Jewish. *Home:* 255 West 84th St., New York, N.Y. 10024. *Office:* United Feature Syndicate, 220 East 42nd St., New York, N.Y. 10017.

CAREER/WRITINGS: Washington Post, Washington, D.C., copy boy, 1955; *World Week,* New York City, foreign editor, 1955-57; North American Newspaper Alliance, New York City, associate editor, 1957-60, executive editor, 1960—; United Feature Syndicate, New York City, managing editor, 1972—. President of Bell-McClure Syndicate, 1971. Notable assignments include securing and editing top-name byliners from all fields. *Military service:* U.S. Army, 1953-55. *Member:* Overseas Press Club, Dutch Treat Club.

* * *

GOLDENSOHN, Barry 1937-

PERSONAL: Born April 26, 1937, in New York, N.Y.; son of Joseph (a teacher) and Shirley (a ballerina; maiden name, Friedburg) Goldensohn; married Lorrie Sanchez-Myer (a professor, poet, and critic), August 5, 1956; children: Matthew, Rachel. *Education:* Oberlin College, B.A., 1957; University of Wisconsin, Madison, M.A., 1959. *Office:* School of Humanities and Arts, Hampshire College; Amherst, Mass. 01002.

CAREER: Illinois Institute of Technology, Chicago, instructor in English and philosophy, 1959-61; Kent State University, Kent, Ohio, instructor in English, 1961-62; Pacific High School, Palo Alto, Calif., co-founder and teacher, 1962-65; Goddard College, Plainfield, Vt., faculty member in literature and writing, 1965—; Hampshire College, Amherst, Mass., dean of School of Humanities and Arts, 1977. Visiting professor of creative writing, University of Iowa Writers Workshop, 1972-77. *Awards, honors:* Borestone Mountain poetry award, 1968, for "Nomos, Logos"; grant from Vermont Arts Council, 1976; National Endowment for the Humanities fellowship, 1977.

WRITINGS: (Author of introduction) Jonathan Swift, *Gulliver's Travels,* Collier, 1962; *St. Venus Eve* (poems), Cummington Press, 1972; *Uncarving the Block* (poems), Vermont Crossroads Press, 1977.

Work anthologized in *Best Poems of 1968,* Borestone Foundation. Contributor of poems to magazines, including *Poetry, Yale Review,* and *Massachusetts Review.* Poetry editor of *Iowa Review,* 1971-72.

WORK IN PROGRESS: More poetry; editing a volume of Swift's poems.

* * *

GOLDIN, Stephen 1947-
(Charles Stephens)

PERSONAL: Born February 28, 1947, in Philadelphia, Pa.; son of David H. (a salesman) and Frances (a bookkeeper; maiden name, Cohen) Goldin; married Kathleen McKinney (a novelist, under pseudonym Kathleen Sky), September 2, 1972. *Education:* University of California, Los Angeles, B.A., 1968. *Politics:* Liberal. *Religion:* "A fundamental belief in the human race." *Residence:* California. *Agent:* Joseph Elder, 150 West 87th St., #6D, New York, N.Y. 10024.

CAREER: Navy Space Systems Activity, El Segundo,

Calif., physicist and space scientist, 1968-71; manager of a grocery store in Rosemead, Calif., 1972; *Jaundice Press* (underground newspaper), Van Nuys, Calif., editor, 1973-74; free-lance writer, 1974—. Director of Merriment House (creative consultants). *Member:* World Future Society, Authors Guild, Science Fiction Writers of America, Society for Creative Anachronism, Los Angeles Science Fantasy Society. *Awards, honors:* Citation from Science Fiction Writers of America, 1973, for editing *The Alien Condition.*

WRITINGS: (Editor) *The Alien Condition* (stories), Ballantine, 1973; *Herds,* Laser Books, 1975; *Caravan,* Laser Books, 1975; *Scavenger Hunt,* Laser Books, 1976; *Finish Line,* Laser Books, 1976; *Assault on the Gods,* Doubleday, 1977; *Mindflight,* Fawcett, 1978.

"Family d'Alembert" series; all published by Pyramid Publications, except as indicated: (With E. E. Smith) *Imperial Stars,* 1976; *Stranglers' Moon,* 1976; *The Clockwork Traitor,* 1977; *Getaway World,* 1977; *Appointment at Bloodstar,* Jove Books, 1978.

Editor of *San Francisco Ball,* 1973-74, and Science Fiction Writers of America *Bulletin,* 1975-77.

WORK IN PROGRESS: Five novels in the "Family d'-Alembert" series, including *The Purity Plot,* all for Jove Books; *Trek to Madworld,* a "Star Trek" novel, Bantam; under pseudonym Charles Stephens, *Cowalker* (tentative title), an occult/spy novel, Geis; *A World Called Solitude,* a science fiction novel, Doubleday; *Nightshade,* with wife, Kathleen Sky; research for *A Lion in the State,* a novel about Greek General Alcibiades.

SIDELIGHTS: Goldin writes: "I have written science fiction almost exclusively so far, because that's what I prefer to read. I like the freedom, the chance to exercise my imagination, to break away from the humdrum of everyday existence and explore new dimensions that give me fresh insights into contemporary reality. My wife is also a science fiction writer, and virtually everything either of us does is a collaboration to some extent. She designs the costumes my characters wear and does the interior decorating for the rooms I describe, while I provide her with scientific explanations for phenomena in her books. We have no children because our lifestyle is basically a selfish one; our books are our children. They make no demands on us, don't eat, wear clothes, or have problems with members of the opposite sex. They also leave home very early and begin supporting us, which children seldom do.

"My own personal philosophy of life, if such it can be called, is that each person should accept the responsibility for his actions. We live in a society with other people, and we must learn that everything we do has a consequence that may affect others. If we started to think about how our actions might affect those around us, instead of just ourselves, society would be able to work with a lot fewer problems. I've elaborated on this philosophy in more depth in my novel *Assault on the Gods,* and it's a theme that underlies all my work.

"In addition, my novels tend to have positive endings, because I believe that there is no problem so great that it can't be solved by the application of human ingenuity. My characters usually learn to solve their own problems to some degree of satisfaction."

AVOCATIONAL INTERESTS: Travel (England, France, Italy, Germany, Switzerland, and the Netherlands; attended World Science Fiction Convention in Heidelberg), reading, collecting original cast Broadway show albums, collecting board games, doing crossword and other word puzzles.

GOLDMAN, Alvin I(ra) 1938-

PERSONAL: Born October 1, 1938, in Brooklyn, N.Y.; son of Nathan A. and Frances K. (Krugman) Goldman; married Holly Smith (a professor), June 15, 1969; children: Raphael. *Education:* Columbia University, B.A., 1960; Princeton University, M.A., 1962, Ph.D., 1965. *Home:* 1205 Linwood, Ann Arbor, Mich. 48103. *Office:* Department of Philosophy, University of Michigan, Ann Arbor, Mich. 48109.

CAREER: University of Michigan, Ann Arbor, assistant professor, 1963-69, associate professor, 1969-73, professor of philosophy, 1973—, chairman of department, 1977—. Fellow of Center for Advanced Study in the Behavioral Sciences, 1975-76. *Member:* American Philosophical Association, American Association of University Professors. *Awards, honors:* Woodrow Wilson fellow, 1960-61; Danforth fellow, 1960-63; Guggenheim fellow, 1975-76.

WRITINGS: A Theory of Human Action, Prentice-Hall, 1970. Contributor to philosophy journals.

WORK IN PROGRESS: Research on theory of knowledge.

* * *

GOLDMARK, Peter C(arl) 1906-1977

PERSONAL: Born December 2, 1906, in Budapest, Hungary; came to United States in 1933, naturalized citizen, 1937; son of Alexander and Emmy Goldmark; married Muriel Gainsborough Evans, 1936; married second wife, Frances Charlotte Trainer, January 12, 1940 (divorced); married third wife, Diane Davis; children: (second marriage) Frances Massey, Peter Carl Jr., Christopher, Andrew; (third marriage) Jonathan, Susan. *Education:* Attended the University of Berlin; University of Vienna, B.S., 1930, Ph.D., 1931. *Residence:* Stamford, Conn.

CAREER: Pye Radio, Ltd., Cambridge, England, television engineer in charge department, 1931-33; consulting engineer for several television and radio companies, New York City, 1933-36; Columbia Broadcasting System (CBS), New York City, chief engineer in television department, 1936-44, director of engineering research, and development, 1944-50, vice president of engineering research and development department, 1950-72, president of CBS laboratories, 1972; Goldmark Communications Corporation, Stamford, Conn., founder, scientist, and president, 1972-77. Visiting professor at University of Pennsylvania and Fairfield University; fellow, Franklin Institute, and Harvard University. Former head of Antipoverty Office, Stamford. Member of Smithsonian Council. *Wartime service:* Harvard University, group leader of Radio Research Laboratory, 1942-45; U.S. Navy, member of Office of Scientific Research and Development, 1944. *Member:* British Television Society (fellow), American Institute of Electrical Engineers (fellow), Institute for Radio Engineers (fellow), American Physical Society (fellow), Society of Motion Picture Engineers (fellow).

AWARDS, HONORS: Morris N. Liebmann Memorial Award from the Institute of Electrical and Electronics Engineers, Inc., 1946, for electronic research; medal from the Television Broadcasters Association, 1954; Vladimir K. Zworykin Prize Award from the Institute of Electrical and Electronics Engineers, Inc., 1961, for development and utilization of electronic television; George Washington Award, 1967, for contributions to science; National Urban Service Award, 1967, for efforts in War on Poverty; David Sarnoff Gold Medal Award from the Society of Motion Picture and Television Engineers, 1969, for pioneering contributions to communications; Elliott Cresson Medal from the Franklin Institute, 1969, for development of long-playing record, color television broadcast system, and electronic recording; Progress Medal Award from the Society of Motion Picture and Television Engineers, 1970; Industrial Research Medal from the Society of Motion Picture and Television Engineers, 1972; Carnegie Mellon Award, 1972; Golden Omega Award, 1973; National Governors Council Award, 1973; Harold Pender Award from the University of Pennsylvania, 1974; Trustee Award from the National Academy of Television Arts and Sciences, 1975; National Medal of Science from President Jimmy Carter, 1977, for development of communications sciences for education, entertainment and culture. D.Sc. from Fairfield University, 1967, and Polytechnic Institute of Brooklyn, 1968; D.H.L., Dartmouth College, 1974.

WRITINGS: (With Lee Edson) *Maverick Inventor: My Turbulent Years at CBS,* Saturday Review Press, 1973; *The New Rural Society,* Cornell University, 1973.

SIDELIGHTS: While working at Columbia Broadcasting System, Goldmark invented the long-playing phonograph record and was instrumental in the development of color television and electronic video recording. After his retirement from CBS, Goldmark founded the Goldmark Communications Corporation, a subsidiary of Warner Communications Inc., in order to pursue his interest in the "New Rural Society." By devising a communications system to link rural inhabitants with such urban conveniences as entertainment, business, government, and medical centers, Goldmark hoped to halt the flow of people into cities and make the countryside a more appealing place to live. The project was funded by two $326,000 grants from the Department of Housing and Urban Development through Fairfield University.

In his memoirs, Goldmark reflected on the effect his inventions had on business: "As I look back, I think my contributions were, somewhat ironically, not so much the invention itself or in innovation (a word I prefer because it means putting an invention to work), but in its gadfly impact on industry.

"The development of the long-playing record impelled the recording industry including RCA, the giant of the communications business, to change for the better its historical pattern of record production. My work in color television resulted, I think, in bringing color to the public a decade faster than it might otherwise have come, though not exactly in the form I intended.

"Finally electronic video recording, though it ended up without the auspices of CBS, fired up the video cassette business into the potential multimillion-dollar industry whose fruits we are beginning to enjoy today."

AVOCATIONAL INTERESTS: Playing the piano and the cello, tennis, skiing.

BIOGRAPHICAL/CRITICAL SOURCES: New York Times, May 7, 1972; Peter C. Goldmark and Lee Edson, *Maverick Inventor: My Turbulent Years at CBS,* Saturday Review Press, 1973. Obituaries: *New York Times,* December 8, 1977; *Washington Post,* December 9, 1977.*

(Died December 7, 1977, in Port Chester, N.Y.)

* * *

GOLDSMITH, Donald 1943-

PERSONAL: Born February 24, 1943, in Washington, D.C.; son of Raymond William (an economist) and Selma

(Fine) Goldsmith; married Rose Marien, April 10, 1975; children: Rachel Evelyn. *Education:* Harvard University, B.A., 1963; graduate study at University of California, Los Angeles, 1963-64; University of California, Berkeley, Ph.D., 1969. *Office:* Interstellar Media, 1655 12th Ave., San Francisco, Calif. 94122.

CAREER: State University of New York at Stony Brook, assistant professor, 1972-74; Interstellar Media, San Francisco, Calif., president, 1974—. *Member:* International Astronomical Union, American Astronomical Society, Astronomical Society of the Pacific (member of board of directors).

WRITINGS: (With Donald Levy) *From the Black Hole to the Infinite Universe,* Holden-Day, 1974; *The Universe,* W. A. Benjamin, 1976; (editor) *Scientists Confront Velikovsky,* Cornell University Press, 1977; (with Tobias Owen) *The Search for Life,* W. A. Benjamin, 1979.

SIDELIGHTS: Goldsmith writes: "My goal is to increase the popular awareness of astronomy. Members of the public, often taught that their ignorance of astronomy, and of science in general, is so great as to be insuperable, deserve a chance to learn for themselves some of the flood of new information that has come to us in the era of space exploration. The established channels of education seem relatively uninterested in this job, and large parts of the public are eager to obtain new knowledge through new means. No doubt exists in my mind that the public's interest in the universe at large continue to grow, or that they see 'established' scientists as deliberately cutting themselves off from the chance to link up with the universe. Hence pseudo-scientific works, such as those of Velikovsky, Von Daeniken, and Castaneda, have a tremendous popularity, for they offer their readers a chance to see the world as far stranger than the 'straight,' scientific view, without having to think about how we know such things. My overall desire in writing about science is to encourage people to ask what we think we know, why we think we know it, and to what extent the average reader must accept the voice of authority rather than thinking for herself or himself."

* * *

GOLDSTONE, Harmon H(endricks) 1911-

PERSONAL: Born May 4, 1911, in New York, N.Y.; son of Lafayette A. (an architect) and Aline May (Lewis) Goldstone. *Education:* Attended Columbia University, 1924-28, M.Arch., 1936; Harvard University, S.B. (cum laude), 1932, graduate study, 1933-35. *Residence:* New York, N.Y. *Office:* Goldstone & Hinz, 104 East 40th St., New York, N.Y. 10016.

CAREER: Harrison & Fouilhoux, New York City, architectural designer, 1936-41; Office of the Coordinator of Inter-American Affairs, Washington, D.C., director of control room, 1941-42; Harrison, Fouilhoux & Abramovitz, New York City, designer and project architect, 1946-52; International Basic Economy Corp., Housing Corp., New York City, worked on technical missions in Israel, 1949, and Paris, 1952-53; Harmon H. Goldstone, New York City, architect and principal, 1953-55; Goldstone & Dearborn, New York City, partner, 1955-70; Goldstone, Dearborn & Hinz, New York City, partner, 1970-73; Goldstone & Hinz, New York City, partner, 1973—. Vice-chairman of junior council of Museum of Modern Art, 1953-59; member of New York City Planning Commission, 1962-68; chairman of New York City Landmarks Preservation Commission, 1968-73; member of New York Society Library board of trustees,

1978. *Military service:* U.S. Army Air Forces, 1942-46; became technical sergeant.

MEMBER: American Institute of Architects (fellow), National Academy of Design (associate), National Institute of Architectural Education (member of board of trustees, 1947-50), Municipal Art Society (president, 1960-61), New York Historical Society (member of board of trustees, 1969—), Harvard Club of New York City, Century Association. *Awards, honors:* Honor award from New York Society of Architects, 1972, and certificate of merit from New York State Association of Architects, 1973, both for design of Greenacre Park; president's medal from Municipal Art Society, 1974.

WRITINGS: (With mother, Aline L. Goldstone) *Lafayette A. Goldstone: A Career in Architecture,* privately printed, 1964; (with Martha Dalrymple) *History Preserved: A Guide to New York City Landmarks and Historic Districts,* Simon & Schuster, 1974; (author of introduction) Andrew Alpern, *Apartments for the Affluent,* McGraw, 1975; (contributor) David Kotlar, *David Kotlar Jubilee Volume,* Am Hassefer, Ltd., 1975; (contributor) *Preservation and Conservation: Principles and Practices,* Preservation Press, 1976. Contributor to architecture journals.

WORK IN PROGRESS: Architectural design.

SIDELIGHTS: Goldstone's designs include hotels, the Aquatic Bird House of Bronx Zoo, Rockefeller Archive Center, and Osborne Laboratories of Marine Sciences.

* * *

GOLDSTONE, Herbert 1921-

PERSONAL: Born June 5, 1921, in Mount Pleasant, Pa.; son of Sol (a salesman) and Rose (a bookkeeper; maiden name, Lurie) Goldstone; married Carol Davis, July 7, 1957 (divorced, June, 1972); children: Beth, Ann. *Education:* University of Chicago, A.B., 1942; Harvard University, M.A., 1947, Ph.D., 1951. *Politics:* "Leftist." *Religion:* Jewish. *Home:* 54 Windham St., Willimantic, Conn. 06226. *Office:* Department of English, University of Connecticut, Storrs, Conn. 06268.

CAREER: Cornell University, Ithaca, N.Y., instructor in English, 1951-55; State University of New York College at Cortland, assistant professor, 1955-62, associate professor of English, 1962; University of Connecticut, Storrs, assistant professor, 1962-66, associate professor, 1966-74, professor of English, 1974—. Chairman of board of directors of Windham Area Community Action Program, 1974-76. *Military service:* U.S. Army, 1942-46. *Awards, honors:* Fulbright scholarship.

WRITINGS: A Casebook on "The Cherry Orchard", Allyn & Bacon, 1965; (editor with Irving Cummings) *Poets and Poems,* Wadsworth, 1967; (editor with Cummings and Thomas Churchill) *Points of Departure,* Prentice-Hall, 1969; *In Search of Community: The Achievement of Sean O'Casey,* Mercier Press, 1973.

WORK IN PROGRESS: A critical study of the plays of John Osborne.

* * *

GONZALES, Sylvia Alicia 1943-

PERSONAL: Born December 16, 1943, in Arizona; daughter of Nazario Antonio (an accountant) and Aida (Lopez) Gonzales. *Education:* University of Arizona, B.A., 1966; graduate study at Antioch College, 1971-72; University of

Massachusetts, Ed.D., 1974. *Politics:* Democrat. *Home:* 1544 Glenpine Dr., San Jose, Calif. 95125. *Office:* Department of Mexican American Graduate Studies, San Jose State University, San Jose, Calif. 95192.

CAREER: U.S. Congress, Washington, D.C., receptionist, 1967; U.S. Civil Rights Commission, Washington, D.C., social science analyst, 1968, personnel management specialist, 1969-70; Model Cities, Tucson, Ariz., assistant coordinator, 1970-71; San Jose State University, San Jose, Calif., assistant professor of Mexican American studies and bilingual education, 1974—. Co-founder and member of board of directors of Interstate Research Associates, 1968—, and National Congress of Hispanic American Citizens (El Congreso), 1971-74; associate of Women's Institute for Freedom of the Press, 1977. Member of University of Massachusetts Center for Curriculum Studies, 1976—. Member of National Institute of Education Hispanic women's advisory committee and national advisory committee on desegregation and education concerns of the Hispanic community; delegate-at-large to U.S. State Department International Women's Year Conference, 1977. Adviser to board of directors of Biblioteca Latino Americano at San Jose City Library, 1974-75.

MEMBER: National Association for Bilingual Education, National Women's Studies Association (executive director, 1977; member of coordinating council), National Women's Political Caucus, Mexican American Women's National Association, Conference of Inter American Women Writers, Consortium on Peace Research, Education, and Development, United Professors of California (member of executive board, 1976). *Awards, honors:* Scholarship from Argentina's "Experiment in International Living," 1965; certificate of excellence from Chicano literature contest at Chicano Cultural Center (Bakersfield, Calif.), 1975-76, for *Chicana Evolution.*

WRITINGS: Consortium of Colleges and Universities for Chicanos and American Indians in Higher Education, U.S. Atomic Energy Commission, 1971; (editor) *Women in Action,* Office of Federal Programs, U.S. Civil Service Commission, 1971; *La Chicana Piensa* (title means "The Chicana Thinks"), Spartan Bookstore (San Jose State University), 1974; (editor) *Que Tal Anthology,* Spartan Bookstore (San Jose State University), 1975; (contributor) Phillip Ortega and Carlos Conde, editors, *The Chicano Literary World, 1974,* New Mexico Highlands University, 1975; *The Chicana Perspective: A Design for Self-Awareness,* Spartan Bookstore (San Jose State University), 1976; (contributor) Lipman-Blumen, editor, *Women's Research Compendium,* National Institute of Education, 1976; (contributor) Kathleen Blumhagen and Walter Johnson, editors, *Women's Studies Symposium,* Greenwood Press, 1977; (contributor) Beverly Lindsay, editor, *Comparative Perspectives of Third World Women: Social Educational and Career Patterns,* Pennsylvania State University, 1977; (contributor) Dexter Fisher, editor, *The Third Woman,* Houghton, 1977; (contributor) Arnulfo Trejo, editor, *The Mexican Americans as We See Ourselves,* University of Arizona Press, in press.

Work anthologized in *An Anthology of Bay Area Poets,* edited by C. Peeden, Stanford University, 1977. Contributor of about fifteen articles and stories to magazines, including *Ms., Caracol,* and *Peace Corps Training Journal,* and newspapers.

WORK IN PROGRESS: A Pictorial Essay of the Hispanic Women in the United States; an autobiographical novel.

SIDELIGHTS: Sylvia Gonzales comments: "As a minority in this country, caught between two worlds of language, culture, and history, it was important to have a voice, particularly in the early years. My own predicament inspired me to seek, understand, and interpret the broader experience of humankind in order to find my place in the world. I grew to love people, cultures, differences, in a way that I had not been loved or accepted. I wrote of my experiences, my perceptions. I traveled throughout Latin America seeking my roots, Europe in my search for universality, and the barrios of the United States to share with my people. I love music and the arts of all peoples for the stories they have to tell."

BIOGRAPHICAL/CRITICAL SOURCES: La Luz, December, 1974; *La Cosecha: Journal of the Chicano,* Volume I, number 1, 1976; *The Third Woman,* Houghton, 1977.

*   *   *

GONZALEZ, Arturo 1928-

PERSONAL: Born June 5, 1928, in New York, N.Y.; son of Arturo (an exporter) and Katherine (Phippen) Gonzalez. *Education:* Brown University, A.B., 1952. *Politics:* Independent. *Home:* Carroll House, 12 St. Alphonsus Ave., Dublin, Ireland. *Agent:* Betty Marks, 51 East 42nd St., New York, N.Y. 10017. *Office:* Merrywood House, Honingham, Norfolk, England.

CAREER: Time-Life, New York, N.Y., member of marketing staff, 1952-57; marketing director for *Time, Life,* and *Fortune,* 1957-61, and *Reader's Digest* international editions, 1961-63; creative director of *Asia* magazine, 1963-71; marketing director of *Life International,* 1971—; currently London bureau chief of *Maclean's Magazine* and free-lance journalist. Lecturer at University of Indiana, New York University, and New School for Social Research. *Military service:* U.S. Navy, 1946-48.

MEMBER: International P.E.N., American Society of Authors and Journalists, Society of American Travel Writers, Institute for Strategic Studies, Overseas Press Club. *Awards, honors:* Best Magazine Article of the Year award from Pacific Area Travel Association, 1967; George Hedman travel award, 1970.

WRITINGS: Eugene H. Nickerson: Statesman of a New Society, James H. Heineman, 1964. Contributor of more than a thousand articles to magazines, including *Saturday Review, McCall's, People, Realities,* and *Ladies Home Journal,* and of syndicated feature articles to newspapers.

WORK IN PROGRESS: Feature articles.

SIDELIGHTS: Gonzalez comments: "I write on whatever interests me. I have been on assignments to all seven continents (including Vietnam, the South Pole, Beirut, Belfast, Quemoy-Matsu, Rhodesia, South Africa, and the Golan Heights), and photograph as well as write."

*   *   *

GOOCH, Bob
See GOOCH, Robert M.

*   *   *

GOOCH, Robert M(iletus) 1919-
(Bob Gooch)

PERSONAL: Born November 20, 1919, in Troy, Va.; son of Octavious Price (a farmer) and Lola (Williams) Gooch; married Virginia Winn (a teacher), October 24, 1943; children: Pamela Gooch Huff, Patricia Gooch McClaugherty. *Education:* University of Virginia, B.A., 1943. *Politics:*

Independent. *Religion:* Southern Baptist. *Home and office address:* P.O. Box 194, Troy, Va. 22974.

CAREER: Gooch & Winn, Inc. (insurance company), Charlottesville, Va., president and insurance agent, 1947-73; writer, 1973—. Vice-president of Fluvanna County Development Corp. *Military service:* U.S. Marine Corps, 1943-47. U.S. Marine Corps Reserve, 1947-65; became lieutenant colonel.

MEMBER: Outdoor Writers Association of America (member of board of directors), Mason-Dixon Outdoor Writers Association (past president), Virginia Outdoor Writers Association (past president), Ruritan Club (president). *Awards, honors:* Awards from Mason-Dixon Outdoor Writers Association, 1974, for "Stripers the Santee-Cooper Way" in *Outdoors,* July, 1974, and 1976, for "Wildlife Refuge Crisis" in *Virginia Wildlife,* May, 1976; award from Safari Club, 1975, for "Turkey Dogs and Fall Hunting: A Family Tradition" in *Field and Stream,* September, 1975.

WRITINGS—All under name Bob Gooch: *The Weedy World of the Pickerels,* A. S. Barnes, 1970; *Squirrels and Squirrel Hunting,* Tidewater, 1972; *Bass Fishing,* Tidewater, 1975; *In Search of the Wild Turkey,* Greatlakes Living Press, 1978. Author of "Virginia Afield," syndicated column appearing in about thirty newspapers, 1962—, and "Virginia Report and West Virginia Report in *Outdoor Life,* 1970—. Contributor of more than three hundred articles to major outdoor magazines.

WORK IN PROGRESS: Coveys and Singles; Land You Can Hunt; Spinning for Trout.

SIDELIGHTS: Gooch writes: "My current production schedule is a weekly newspaper column, a weekly magazine article, a monthly column, an article for *Turkey Call* twice a year, and a book each two years. I shoot all my own photographs for illustrations and travel regularly all over the North American continent. I am primarily a rod and gun writer, but touch on outdoors generally."

*   *   *

GOOCH, Stan(ley Alfred) 1932-

PERSONAL: Born June 13, 1932, in London, England; son of Albert Alfred (a clerk) and Annie Emily (Gatty) Zuch; married Ruth Senior, April 1, 1961 (divorced, 1965). *Education:* King's College, London, B.A. (honors), 1955; Birkbeck College, London, B.Sc. (honors), 1963. *Politics:* None. *Religion:* None. *Home and office:* 11 Crossfield Rd., London N.W.3, England. *Agent:* A. D. Peters & Co., 10 Buckingham St., London W.C.2, England.

CAREER: Teacher and head of modern language department at boys' school in London, England, 1958-61; teacher of maladjusted children at special schools in London, 1961-64; senior research psychologist for National Children's Bureau, 1964-68; free-lance writer, 1968—. Lecturer in psychology at Hatfield College of Technology, 1965, and at Brunel University, 1968.

WRITINGS: (With M. L. Kellmer Pringle) *Four Years On,* Humanities, 1966; *Total Man,* Allen Lane, 1972, Holt, 1973; *Personality and Evolution,* Wildwood House, 1973; *The Neanderthal Question,* Wildwood House, 1977; *The Paranormal,* Wildwood House, 1978. Contributor to education and psychology journals.

WORK IN PROGRESS: The Religious Impulse and *Bearers of the Message* (a study of ancient knowledge), publication by Wildwood House expected in 1980.

SIDELIGHTS: Gooch writes: "I became a writer out of a deep dissatisfaction with current (psychological, cultural, religious), accounts of the nature, evolution, and potential of man. Also, although successful in my earlier career, I had never found a job which could satisfy me. I have now been a full-time writer (and writing consultant, ghost writer, and journalist) for ten years, and the thought of ever being anything else has never entered my head. My greatest satisfaction has been in seeing my allegedly wild ideas and my name increasingly appearing in books by significant authors (Colin Wilson, Lyall Watson, Arthur Janov, etc.)."

*   *   *

GOODE, Ruth 1905-
(Ruth Seinfel; Julia Rainer, a pseudonym)

PERSONAL: Born May 1, 1905, in Brooklyn, N.Y.; daughter of Henry (in life insurance) and Helen (Greenberg) Seinfel; married Gerald Goode (a writer and former publicist), June 27, 1927; children: Daniel, Judith. *Education:* Smith College, B.A., 1925. *Agent:* Curtis Brown Ltd., 575 Madison Ave., New York, N.Y. 10022. *Office: MD Medical Newsmagazine,* 30 East 60th St., New York, N.Y. 10022.

CAREER: New York Evening World, New York City, reporter, 1926-26; *Nation,* New York City, junior editor, 1926-27; *New York Evening Post,* New York City, reporter and women's page editor, 1927-33; free-lance writer, 1933-57; *MD Medical Newsmagazine,* New York City, senior staff writer, 1957—.

WRITINGS: (Under name Ruth Seinfel) *Lady Buyer* (fiction), Covici Friede, 1933; (with S. Hurok) *Impresario,* Random House, 1946; (with Alyce Pollock) *Don Gaucho* (fiction), Whittlesey House, 1950; (with Gertrude Mackenzie) *My Love Affair With the State of Maine,* Simon & Schuster, 1955; (under pseudonym Julia Rainer; with husband under pseudonym Jerome Rainer) *Sexual Pleasure in Marriage,* Messner, 1959, 2nd edition, Simon & Schuster, 1969; (with Benjamin F. Miller) *Man and His Body,* Simon & Schuster, 1960; (under pseudonym Julia Rainer; with Jerome Rainer) *Sexual Adventure in Marriage,* Messner, 1965; (with Aaron Sussman) *The Magic of Walking,* Simon & Schuster, 1967; *People of the Ice Age* (juvenile), Macmillan, 1973; *A Book for Grandmothers,* Macmillan, 1976; *People of the First Cities* (juvenile), Macmillan, 1977. Ghostwriter of about nineteen books on medical, health, and educational subjects.

SIDELIGHTS: Goode told *CA:* "Ghostwriting, often denigrated, is the ideal profession for anyone who wants a continuing education without having to go to school. One studies under the best teachers, people who care deeply about their work and want to tell the world what they know. Anatomy and physiology, medicine, child learning, the arts of parenthood, and whole schools of psychotherapy were opened up to me in this way, long before I became a staff writer for a medical magazine. Professional writers are indispensable in a world in which all too few people who have something to say know how to say it in a book for the general reader. In time one turns to writing one's own books about one's own deepest interests. Mine are paleontology and archaeology; travel, especially to ancient sites; walking, which includes people-watching as well as bird-watching; and grandmothering."

*   *   *

GOODELL, Rae 1944-

PERSONAL: Born May 16, 1944, in Cambridge, Mass.;

daughter of Harrison B. and Dorothy Parsons (Whitten) Simpson; married Ross Goodell (a software engineer), August 28, 1965; children: Maia. *Education:* Pomona College, B.A. (magna cum laude), 1967; Stanford University, M.A., 1971, Ph.D., 1975; postdoctoral study at Massachusetts Institute of Technology, 1975-76. *Residence:* Watertown, Mass. *Agent:* Word Guild, 119 Mount Auburn St., Cambridge, Mass. 02138. *Office:* Department of Humanities, Massachusetts Institute of Technology, Cambridge, Mass. 02139.

CAREER: Claremont Courier, Claremont, Calif., reporter, 1967-68; U.S. Peace Corps, Washington, D.C., teacher of English and computer applications in Kandahar, Afghanistan, 1968-69; *Edubusiness,* New York, N.Y., West Coast correspondent, 1970; Massachusetts Institute of Technology, Cambridge, research associate in oral history program, 1976-77, assistant professor of science writing, 1977—. *Member:* National Association of Science Writers, American Association for the Advancement of Science, Association for Education in Journalism, Phi Beta Kappa. *Awards, honors:* Mellon postdoctoral fellow, 1975-76; National Science Foundation grant, 1975—.

WRITINGS: (Contributor) Peter Spain and others, editors, *A Direct Broadcast Satellite for Education and Development in Africa?,* Institute for Communications Research, Stanford University, 1972; (contributor) David Rubin and David Sachs, editors, *Mass Media and the Environment,* Praeger, 1972; *The Visible Scientists,* Little, Brown, 1977. Contributor to *Funk and Wagnalls New Encyclopedia Yearbook* and to periodicals, including *America Illustrated, Sciences,* and *Washington Post.*

WORK IN PROGRESS: Research on public involvement in the DNA debate, science critics in the DNA debate, and public understanding of science.

SIDELIGHTS: Goodell told *CA:* "*The Visible Scientists* describes the handful of science celebrities, such as Margaret Mead, Linus Pauling, Barry Commoner, and Carl Sagan, who regularly make news talking about today's pressing technological problems. It suggests that, given rapid changes taking place in science, in the media, and in society, scientists must become more responsive to public interest and public involvement. The controversy that has erupted recently over the safety of recombinant DNA research illustrates the same changes, and a dilemma: neither scientists nor the public know how to handle the complex scientific issues now affecting present and future life."

* * *

GOODMAN, Rebecca Gruver   1931-
(Rebecca Gruver)

PERSONAL: Born November 3, 1931, in St. Joseph, Mo.; daughter of Arthur L. (an engineer) and Dana (Brooks) Gruver; married Phil P. Goodman (a businessman), June 17, 1972. *Education:* Stanford University, B.A., 1954; University of California, Berkeley, M.A., 1956, Ph.D., 1964. *Home:* 70 East 10th St., New York, N.Y. 10003.

CAREER: Hunter College of the City University of New York, New York, N.Y., lecturer, 1961-64, instructor, 1964-69, assistant professor of history, 1969-73, adjunct assistant professor, 1973—. *Member:* American Historical Association, Organization of American Historians, Society for Historians of American Foreign Relations, Institute for Research in History.

WRITINGS—Under name Rebecca Gruver: (Editor)

American Nationalism, 1783-1830, Putnam, 1970; (contributor) Armin Rappaport and Richard Traina, editors, *Present in the Past,* Macmillan, 1972; *An American History,* Appleton, 1972, 2nd edition, Addison-Wesley, 1976, abridged edition, 1978.

WORK IN PROGRESS: A book on the diplomatic career of John Jay.

* * *

GOODMAN, Sonya
See ARCONE, Sonya

* * *

GOODWIN, John R(obert)   1929-

PERSONAL: Born November 3, 1929, in West Virginia; son of John Emory (a glassworker) and Ruby Iona (Everly) Goodwin; married Betty Lou Wilson, June 2, 1952; children: Elizabeth Ann Goodwin Paugh, John R., Jr., Mark Edward Wilson, Matthew Emory, Luke Jackson. *Education:* Earned B.S. and J.D. from West Virginia University. *Politics:* Democrat. *Religion:* Protestant. *Home:* 427 Mildred Ave., Morgantown, W. Va. 26505. *Office:* Department of Business and Economics, Armstrong Hall, West Virginia University, Morgantown, W. Va. 26505.

CAREER: Manager of West Virginia Supply & Equipment Co., 1958-63; attorney in Morgantown, W. Va., 1964—; West Virginia University, Morgantown, professor of business law, 1964—. Mayor of Morgantown, 1964-65. Special prosecuting attorney for Monongalia County, W. Va., 1965; city attorney for Morgantown, 1965-66. Chairman of local Sanitary Board, 1964-66. *Military service:* U.S. Army, Infantry, 1952-55; became first lieutenant.

MEMBER: American Bar Association, American Business Law Association, National Association of Business Law Teachers (founder). *Awards, honors:* Award from National Claimant's Counsel, 1964, for "Tort Liability for Mental Injury"; award from Beta Gamma Sigma, 1970.

WRITINGS: Twenty Feet from Glory (nonfiction), McClain Printing Co., 1970; *Business Law: Principles, Documents, and Cases,* Irwin, 1972, revised edition, 1976; (coauthor) *Travel and Lodging Law,* Grid Publishing, 1978. Contributor to *Advocate* and *Infantry School Journal.* Editor of *Business Law Review* and *Business Law Letter.*

WORK IN PROGRESS: A book on the Custer battle in 1876; a book on court-appointed lawyers; a book on travel in the United States, based on his family's experiences; a third edition of *Business Law: Principles, Documents, and Cases.*

SIDELIGHTS: Goodwin writes: "My life has gone from living in poverty to finding that the world is full of nice things. As I acquired the means, I began to move out of the small circles that had enclosed me to discover what was out there. In this transition, I believe, lies an important story which I intend to tell in the near future."

* * *

GOODWIN, Suzanne
(Suzanne Ebel; Cecily Shelbourne, a pseudonym)

PERSONAL: Born in London, England; daughter of Clement (a director) and Charlotte (a musician; maiden name, Collins) Ebel; married John Goodwin (publicity director for National Theatre), October, 1948; children: Marigold Goodwin Sebastian, James, Timothy. *Education:* Educated at Roman Catholic convent schools in England and Belgium.

Home: 52-A Digby Mansions, Hammersmith Bridge Rd., London W6 9DF, England. *Agent:* Curtis Brown Ltd., 1 Craven Hill, London W.2, England.

CAREER: Former journalist for *London Times;* Young & Rubicam, New York, N.Y., public relations director in London office, 1950-72; full-time writer, 1972—. *Awards, honors:* Best Romantic Novel of the Year award for *Journey from Yesterday,* 1964.

WRITINGS—Under name Suzanne Ebel; all romantic novels, except as indicated: *Journey From Yesterday,* Collins, 1964; *The Half Enchanted,* Collins, 1965; *The Love Campaign,* Collins, 1966; *A Perfect Stranger,* Collins, 1967; *Name in Lights,* Collins, 1967; *A Most Auspicious Star,* Collins, 1968; *Somersault,* Collins, 1969; *Portrait of Jill,* Collins, 1970; *Dear Kate,* Collins, 1970; *To Seek a Star,* Collins, 1971; *The Family Feeling,* Collins, 1972; *Girl by the Sea,* Collins, 1973; *Guide to the Cotswolds* (nonfiction), Ward, Lock, 1973; *Music in Winter,* Collins, 1974; *A Grove of Olives,* Collins, 1975; *River Voices,* Collins, 1976; *London's Rivergate* (nonfiction), Luscombe, 1976; *The Double Rainbow,* Collins, 1977; *A Rose in the Heather,* Collins, 1978.

Under pseudonym Cecily Shelbourne: *Stage of Love,* Putnam, 1977.

Author of "Chords and Dischords" (radio play), aired by British Broadcasting Corp. in 1975. Contributor of stories to magazines.

WORK IN PROGRESS: A historical novel, set in Victorian times.

SIDELIGHTS: Suzanne Goodwin writes: "I have written since I was a teenager. I write regularly every day, sometimes for as long as nine hours. I feel that writing has something strongly in common with painting: it catches the mood, the character, the flavour of life. We own a flat in the south of France, I speak fluent French, and the French influence of art and nature has an effect on my writing, as the English atmosphere does."

*   *   *

GORDON, Doreen
   See CHARD, Judy

*   *   *

GORDON, Janet
   See WOODHAM-SMITH, Cecil (Blanche Fitzgerald)

*   *   *

GORDON, Lesley
   See ELLIOTT, Lesley

*   *   *

GORDON, Robert A(aron)   1908-1978

July 26, 1908—April 7, 1978; American educator, economist, and author of works in his field. Gordon was best known for his expertise in business cycles and mass labor manipulation. He was an advisor to three presidents and devised the current means of unemployment computation. Gordon wrote *Business Fluctuations* and *Business Leadership in the Large Corporation,* among others. He died in Berkeley, Calif. Obituaries and other sources: *Business Week,* March 3, 1973; *American Men and Women of Science: The Social and Behavioral Sciences,* 12th edition,

Bowker, 1973; *Who's Who in America,* 40th edition, Marquis, 1977; *New York Times,* April 9, 1978. (See index for *CA* sketch)

*   *   *

GOSLING, J(ustin) C(yril) B(ertrand)   1930-
PERSONAL: Born April 26, 1930, in Wolverhampton, England; son of Vincent Samuel (a lawyer) and Dorothy (Smith) Gosling; married Angela Margaret Clayton, September 2, 1958; children: Samuel, Rachel, Elizabeth, Thomas. *Education:* Oxford University, B.A., 1953, B.Phil. and M.A., both 1955. *Office:* St. Edmund Hall, Oxford University, Oxford OX14 1QA, England.

CAREER: Oxford University, Oxford, England, Fereday research fellow at St. John's College, 1955-58, lecturer in philosophy at Wadham and Pembroke Colleges, 1958-60, fellow at St. Edmund Hall, 1960—, tutor, 1960-67, senior tutor in philosophy, 1967-72, senior proctor of the university, 1977-78. *Member:* Aristotelian Society, Mind Association.

WRITINGS: Pleasure and Desire, Oxford University Press, 1969; (contributor) J. J. Macintosh and S. C. Coval, editors, *The Business of Reason,* Routledge & Kegan Paul, 1969; *Plato,* Routledge & Kegan Paul, 1973; *Plato: Philebus,* Oxford University Press, 1975; (contributor) R. S. Peters, editor, *Nature and Conduct,* Macmillan, 1975. Contributor to scholarly periodicals.

WORK IN PROGRESS: Ancient Greek Theories of Pleasure.

*   *   *

GOTTLIEB, Darcy   1922-
PERSONAL: Born March 13, 1922, in Los Angeles, Calif.; daughter of Allan Kerr (an electrical engineer) and Lenorah (Darrow) Thompson; married Arnold Friedman, June, 1947 (divorced July 4, 1964); married Sidney Gottlieb (a professional photographer and musician), June 7, 1965; children: (first marriage) Laura Janine. *Education:* University of California, Berkeley, B.A., 1945; Hunter College of the City University of New York, M.A., 1961; also attended University of Hong Kong, University of Grenoble, and University of Wisconsin, Madison. *Residence:* Woodstock, N.Y. *Agent:* Betty Marks, 51 East 42nd St., New York, N.Y. 10017.

CAREER: English teacher and department head at private school in New York City, 1957-73; The Woman School, New York City, instructor in creative writing, 1976—. Instructor at State University of New York College at New Paltz, autumn, 1977. Chairman of literary arts committee of Ulster County Council of the Arts, 1977. *Member:* Poetry Society of America (member of executive board, 1977-78). *Awards, honors:* Poetry Society of America awards, including Dylan Thomas Award, 1966, for "When the Music Players Came to Our House," and Christopher Morley Award, 1977, for "Two Specks of Matter Communicate as They Drift Through the Universe."

WRITINGS: No Witness but Ourselves (poems), University of Missouri Press, 1973.

Work anthologized in *For Neruda, for Chile* and *New York Times Book of Verse.* Contributor of poems to literary journals and popular magazines, including *American Scholar, Seventeen, Mademoiselle,* and *Voices International.*

WORK IN PROGRESS: Another collection of poems; a book of short stories; literary criticism.

SIDELIGHTS: Darcy Gottlieb writes: "'Someday I know that I will be a writer' are the first words written in my journals, which have been kept for nearly thirty years. All that I am at this point in my life stems from that basic statement. The way has been filled with detours and I started late in achieving some degree of recognition, but there has never been any turning back from the dedication that becomes only more ingrained with each creative endeavor. Poems insist on being born, coming always from inside, often after many years between the event or feeling that lies behind them. My journals are a sourcebook for my creative thought process, as well as my poems, and provide a record of my journey as a woman as well as a poet."

*   *   *

GOTTSCHALK, Stephen 1940-

PERSONAL: Born April 2, 1940, in Los Angeles, Calif.; son of William (in business) and Lenore (Gunbiner) Gottschalk; married Mary Van Urk, April 12, 1975; children: Laird (stepson). *Education:* Occidental College, B.A., 1962; University of California, Berkeley, M.A., 1963, Ph.D., 1969. *Home:* 350 Arden Rd., Menlo Park, Calif. 94025.

CAREER: U.S. Naval Postgraduate School, Monterey, Calif., assistant professor, 1969-72, associate professor of history, 1972-75; writer, 1975—. Member of board of directors of Twelve Acres (institution for the mentally retarded).

WRITINGS: The Emergence of Christian Science in American Religious Life, University of California Press, 1973; *Beyond the Painted Paradise: A Synoptic Study of American Culture,* University of California Press, 1979.

WORK IN PROGRESS: Co-editing *Sources and Documents in American Culture* with Christopher Wagstaff.

SIDELIGHTS: Gottschalk writes: "I am primarily interested in the relation of religion to other phases of culture (art, music, literature, philosophy, etc.), particularly in the nineteenth and twentieth centuries. I am particularly concerned with seeing how the arts, together with other aspects of culture, interrelate as expressions of more basic attitudes that have their origin in religion. My main field of study at present is American culture, though I look at it against the background of European culture. Understanding the relation between the two is, I feel, a most fruitful field for inquiry in intellectual and cultural history."

*   *   *

GOTTSEGEN, Gloria Behar 1930-

PERSONAL: Born November 15, 1930, in New York, N.Y.; daughter of Marco (an antiquarian) and Flora (Salti) Behar; married Monroe G. Gottsegen (a psychologist), April 14, 1951; children: Abby Jean, Paul Richard. *Education:* New York University, B.A., 1950, Ph.D., 1967; City College (now of the City University of New York), M.A., 1951. *Residence:* Harriman, N.Y. *Office:* Department of Specialized Services in Education, Herbert H. Lehman College of the City University of New York, Bronx, N.Y. 10468.

CAREER: Jewish Child Care Association, New York, N.Y., remedial psychologist, 1956-59; Bronx Consultation Center, Bronx, N.Y., supervising psychologist, 1961-68; Herbert H. Lehman College of the City University of New York, Bronx, assistant professor, 1968-75, associate professor of psychology and education, 1975—, chairperson, department of specialized services in education, 1976—. *Member:* American Psychological Association (member of council, 1976; president of Division of Humanistic Psychology, 1976-77), American Orthopsychiatric Association, Association for Humanistic Psychology, Eastern Psychological Association, New York State Psychological Association (president of Division of School Psychology, 1975-76; member of board of directors, 1976-77), Psi Chi, Phi Delta Kappa.

WRITINGS: (Editor with husband, M. G. Gottsegen) *Professional School Psychology,* Grune, Volume I, 1960, Volume II, 1963, Volume III, 1969; (editor with M. G. Gottsegen and Leonard Blank) *Confrontation: Encounters in Self and Interpersonal Awareness,* Macmillan, 1971; *Group Behavior: A Guide to Information Sources,* Gale, in press; *Humanistic Psychology: A Guide to Information Sources,* Gale, in press. Co-editor of school psychology section of *International Encyclopedia of Psychiatry, Psychology, Psychoanalysis, and Neurology,* 1974-77. Associate editor of *Psychotherapy: Theory, Research, and Practice,* 1976—.

*   *   *

GOULD, Chester 1900-

PERSONAL: Born November 20, 1900, in Pawnee, Okla.; son of Gilbert R. (a newspaperman) and Alice (Miller) Gould; married Edna Gauger, November 6, 1926; children: Jean (Mrs. Richard O'Connell). *Education:* Attended Oklahoma A. & M. College (now Oklahoma State University), 1919-21; Northwestern University, diploma, 1923. *Residence:* Woodstock, Ill. *Office: Chicago Tribune,* Tribune Tower, 435 N. Michigan Ave., Chicago, Ill. 60611.

CAREER: Chicago American, Chicago, Ill., cartoonist for syndicated comic strip "Fillum Fables," 1924-29; *Chicago Daily News,* Chicago, ad illustrator, 1929-31; Chicago Tribune-New York News Syndicate, Chicago, creator of "Dick Tracy" comic strip syndicated to over five hundred newspapers, 1931—. *Member:* National Cartoonists Society, Woodstock Country Club, Lambda Chi Alpha. *Awards, honors:* National Cartoonists Society Reuben Award for outstanding cartoonist, 1959; has also received numerous awards from law enforcement agencies and police departments, including the Police Athletic League Award, 1949, and the Associated Police Communications Officers Award, 1953.

WRITINGS: Dick Tracy and Dick Tracy, Jr., and How They Captured "Stooge" Viller, Cupples & Leon, 1933; *How Dick Tracy and Dick Tracy, Jr., Caught the Racketeers,* Cupples & Leon, 1934; *Dick Tracy, Ace Detective,* Whitman Publishing, 1943; *Dick Tracy Meets the Night Crawler,* Whitman Publishing, 1945; *The Celebrated Cases of Dick Tracy, 1931-1951,* edited by Herb Galewitz, Chelsea House, 1970.

SIDELIGHTS: In 1921 Chester Gould came to Chicago to try to work as a cartoonist for the *Chicago Tribune.* During the next decade, he bombarded publisher Joseph Patterson with over sixty ideas for comic strips, "trying everything," Gould said, "the beautiful girl strip, the office boy, the smart aleck, the oddball, the believe-it-or-not cartoon, even a comic feature on sports; but none of them quite clicked." During those years, Gould remembered, he worked "on every paper in Chicago except the *Evening Post,* which went bankrupt or I probably would have ended up working on that too." Early in 1931 Gould began working on a comic strip about a policeman named Plainclothes Tracy, using as inspiration his personal sense of outrage at the Chicago mobs. On August 13, 1931, Gould received a telegram from Patterson stating: "Your Plainclothes Tracy has possibilities. Would like to see you when I go to Chicago next. Please call *Tribune* office Monday about noon for an appointment." At the interview, Patterson studied the drawings Gould submitted. "This name's too long," Patterson said. "Tracy's not bad, but Plainclothes—let's see. George ... Sam ... Dick? Yeah. They call cops 'dicks.' Call him Dick Tracy. Now why don't you start with Tracy visiting his girl? Her father runs a grocery store and they live over the store. Crooks rob the place while Tracy's there, and they murder the old man. Tracy swears vengeance and that's how he becomes a detective." Thus on October 4, 1931, Dick Tracy made his first appearance in the *Detroit Mirror*. Eight days later the *New York News* began running the strip. "It took a couple of months to catch on," Gould recalled, "then it grew like wildfire."

In the beginning weeks of his career, Tracy was a "hard hitting amateur who dealt with criminals with fists, black-jack or gun; his prowess won him an appointment as a city detective." Tracy, called by Ellery Queen "the world's first procedural detective of fiction, in the modern sense," became for Gould and many others the "All-American boy grown up, dressed in a snap-brim hat, natty striped tie, and black sack suit, whose private life is perpetually Spartan," characterized as a "tall, four-square man with his jutting (meatchopper bulldozer) chin, his grim mouth and tight-lipped smile, his eagle's-beak of a nose." Millions of people across the country were thrilled by Tracy's exploits chasing felons across the page, an "absolutely honest and incorruptible defender of the faith with his Rock of Gibraltar sense of duty." Gould said, "I decided that if the police couldn't catch the gangsters, I'd create a fellow who would." And the list of criminals Tracy chased in the early days is indeed impressive; by 1951 he had brought the likes of Stooge Viller, The Blank, Little Face Finney, The Mole, B-B Eyes, 88 Keyes, Pruneface and Mrs. Pruneface, The Brow, Vitamin Flintheart, Flattop Sr., Shakey, Breathless Mahoney, Mumbles, Shoulders and Sketch Paree to justice. And in the process he was shot no less than twenty-seven times; he was slugged, pistol-whipped, gassed, chloroformed, dragged from a speeding car, tortured, burned, near-drowned, frozen, buried alive, mangled, and subjected to dozens of other "gruesome, sinister, fiendish" experiences. Accused of being too realistic in his depiction of violence, Gould told *Newsweek:* "Blood in itself is not repulsive. Any mother with small children who get hurt knows what blood is. Police work is the most bloody and miserable on earth. Any policeman on night duty sees far more blood than I ever put in my strip. Of course, brutality for its own sake is taboo."

Dick Tracy's appearance in the early 1930's influenced other media, particularly the police procedural story in novels, radio, and movies. Gould told Ellery Queen: "I feel that Dick Tracy has set a pattern for much of the very excellent entertainment in crime detection and police work. And I think the strip has definitely been a tremendous influence in the lives of the writers who have worked in these media." Gould's own inspiration for strips, however, did not come from the hard-boiled writing of the time. "I got most of my inspiration," he said, "from a boyhood love of Sherlock Holmes. I was also a great follower of Edgar Allan Poe. I didn't follow many of the so-called 'popular' things that came in after 'Dick Tracy.' I followed the newspapers almost exclusively—the police news and all the information about the operation of gangsters and the war against them. And it really is a war that the police are constantly engaged in."

In his pursuit of criminals, Gould's Tracy has not only been a persistent legman and investigator, he has also been vigilant enough to utilize the possibilities created by modern technology, frequently before anyone else. On January 21, 1946, for example, Tracy introduced the two-way wrist radio; in 1947 he was the first to use closed-circuit television ("teleguard") to monitor criminal activities, and he was the first to adapt the television for a burglar alarm. Gould recently has had Tracy using a two-way wrist television set. Tracy's techniques also incorporate the most modern of police detection, as in the use of tracer bullets as early as 1937, and the use of the iodine blowgun and wet-film process to find fingerprints. Tracy is as at home in the most modern police laboratory as he is at the scene of a crime.

And in the finest police tradition, the current mystery aside, Tracy has left no case unsolved.

AVOCATIONAL INTERESTS: Golf, swimming, jogging, poker, driving.

BIOGRAPHICAL/CRITICAL SOURCES: Saturday Evening Post, December 17, 1949; *Holiday,* June, 1958; *Newsweek,* October 16, 1961; *The Celebrated Cases of Dick Tracy,* 1931-1951, edited by Herb Galewitz, Chelsea House, 1970; *Washington Post,* January 15, 1971.*

*   *   *

GOULD, Lois 1938(?)-

PERSONAL: Daughter of a cigar manufacturer and Jo Copeland (a fashion designer); married Philip Benjamin (a reporter, 1959 (deceased); married Robert E. Gould (a psychiatrist), September 14, 1967; children: (first marriage) Tony, Roger. *Education:* Attended Wellesley College.

CAREER: Journalist and writer. Former police reporter and editor of *Long Island Star Journal;* former executive editor of *Ladies Home Journal.*

WRITINGS—All novels except as indicated: *Such Good Friends,* Random House, 1970; *Necessary Objects,* Random House, 1972; *Final Analysis,* Random House, 1974; *A Sea Change,* Simon & Schuster, 1977; *Not Responsible for Personal Articles* (essays), Random House, 1978. Contributor of articles to *New York Times* magazine and *McCall's.* Columnist for *New York Times,* 1977.

SIDELIGHTS: Lois Gould has been peripherally associated with the feminist movement in literature for several years. Indeed, after the publication of her first novel, *Such Good Friends,* Diana Gerrity called her one of the "ranking dramatic muses" of the movement. But her writing represents more a popularization of feminism than a politicization of literature.

The titles of a few of Gould's essays ("Good Manners for Liberated Persons," "How to Liberate Your Entire Family in Your Own Home," and "Pornography for Women") illustrate this point. Critics are divided, in fact, over whether to place her in a feminist or a pornographic tradition. W. G. Rogers wrote of *Such Good Friends:* "I do not believe in banning anything in print, but this book (like one of those X-rated films) might well bear the sign, 'Persons under eighteen not admitted.'" On the other hand, Joel Lieber called the same novel "an important, awful, believable book," adding, "Many men will resent it, but the novel will change the lives of many women."

In subsequent novels, Gould has been accused of riding the wave of feminism without contributing to its depths. Sara Blackburn pointed out that the flap copy of *Necessary Objects* "is written with a women's liberationist consciousness that is entirely absent from the novel itself." Similarly the

New Yorker called *Final Analysis* "a slick romance . . . which is occasionally quite funny but pushes feminism and enlightenment-through-psychiatry in the same way that old-fashioned romances used to push love and moral rectitude."

A Sea Change generally baffled the critics, but succeeded at least in diverting their attention from comparing Gould's work to that of Jacqueline Susann. Instead, they tried to define and extract the meaning of the maze of symbols—mostly of "maleness" and "femaleness"—that permeate the novel. Anne Tyler called the book "a generalization on the very nature of male and female," but urged the reader to "ignore the polemics [and] read it as a bizarre fantasy."

In a collection of essays entitled *Not Responsible for Personal Articles,* Gould examined such issues as female pornography, liberation of the family, and the cost of traditional courtesies to the liberated woman. Judith Viorst concluded: "If I am moved to argument, surely that's part of what makes this book worthwhile. For by challenging readers to think through old positions and consider new ones, it encourages us to distinguish reason from rote. And by offering us an essentially quite sane and humane point of view, it offers the hope that even after the lines of division are drawn, we still can find ourselves on the same side."

BIOGRAPHICAL/CRITICAL SOURCES: New York Times Book Review, June 2, 1970, October 15, 1972, September 19, 1976, February 26, 1978; *Saturday Review,* June 13, 1970; *Christian Science Monitor,* September 24, 1970; *New Yorker,* April 22, 1974; *Contemporary Literary Criticism,* Volume 4, Gale, 1975; *Ms.,* February, 1978; *Washington Post,* February 23, 1978; *People,* April 10, 1978; *New York Times,* April 21, 1978.*

*   *   *

GOULD, Stephen Jay   1941-

PERSONAL: Born September 10, 1941, in New York, N.Y.; son of Leonard (a court reporter) and Eleanor (an artist; maiden name, Rosenberg) Gould; married Deborah Lee (an artist), October 3, 1965; children: Jesse, Ethan. *Education:* Antioch College, A.B., 1963; Columbia University, Ph.D., 1967. *Office:* Museum of Comparative Zoology, Harvard University, Cambridge, Mass. 02138.

CAREER: Harvard University, Cambridge, Mass., assistant professor, 1967-71, associate professor, 1971-73, professor of geology, 1973—.

WRITINGS: Ever Since Darwin, Norton, 1977; *Ontogeny and Phylogeny,* Harvard University Press, 1977. Author of "This View of Life," a monthly column in *Natural History.* Contributor of more than a hundred articles to scientific journals.

WORK IN PROGRESS: An elementary geology textbook, with Salvador Luria; a popular book on biological determinism (racism and sexism), with Gar Allen.

*   *   *

GRAAF, Peter
See YOUD, Samuel

*   *   *

GRAEDON, Joe (David)   1945-

PERSONAL: Born August 8, 1945, in New York, N.Y.; son of Sid (a literary agent) and Helen (Ars) Graedon; married wife, Theresa Lynn (a medical anthropologist and professor), August 27, 1970; children: David Emil. *Education:*

Pennsylvania State University, B.S., 1967; University of Michigan, M.S., 1971. *Home:* 215 Pineview Rd., Durham, N.C. 27707. *Agent:* Sid Graedon, R.D. #1, Box 60-B, New Hope, Pa. 18938. *Office:* Department of Pharmacology, Duke University, Durham, N.C. 27706.

CAREER: New Jersey Neuro-Psychiatric Institute, Princeton, research assistant in pharmacology, 1967-69; Benito Juarez Autonomous University, Oaxaca, Mexico, professor of pharmacology, 1972-74; teacher of adult education course on medicine in Doylestown, Pa., 1975; Duke University, Durham, N.C., guest lecturer in pharmacology, 1976—. Contributor and consultant to KABC-TV, Los Angeles. *Member:* American Association for the Advancement of Science, Society of Neuroscience. *Awards, honors:* National Institute of Health fellowship, 1969-71.

WRITINGS: The People's Pharmacy: A Guide to Prescription Drugs, Home Remedies, and Over-the-Counter Medications, St. Martin's, 1976. Contributor to *Esquire* and to professional journals.

WORK IN PROGRESS: Another trade book on popular pharmacological issues; a textbook of pharmacology for allied health students.

SIDELIGHTS: Graedon believes that the drug-buying public is ignorant of the effects of various items, from aspirin to antacids, and may actually be doing more harm than good to themselves by using many drugs. Graedon also warns that price differences don't necessarily mean quality differences and that brand name drugs don't always offer a higher quality cure than generic ones. "If doctors, the Federal Food and Drug Administration and pharmacists did their jobs properly, there would be no need for my book," he said.

BIOGRAPHICAL/CRITICAL SOURCES: New York, August 23, 1976; *Detroit News,* October 4, 1976; *Chicago Sun-Times,* October 13, 1976; *Chicago Tribune,* November 24, 1976.

*   *   *

GRAEME, Bruce
See JEFFRIES, Graham Montague

*   *   *

GRAEME, David
See JEFFRIES, Graham Montague

*   *   *

GRAHAM, Carlotta
See WALLMANN, Jeffrey M(iner)

*   *   *

GRAHAM, (George) Kenneth   1936-

PERSONAL: Born March 24, 1936, in Scotland; son of George Herdman and Cordelia Graham; married Sheila Welham, 1961; children: Angus, Evan. *Education:* University of Glasgow, M.A,, 1957; further study at Yale University, 1959-60; Jesus College, Oxford, D.Phil., 1962. *Office:* Department of English Literature, University of Sheffield, Sheffield, England.

CAREER: University of Aberdeen, Aberdeen, Scotland, assistant lecturer in English, 1960-63; University of Southampton, Southampton, England, 1963-76, began as lecturer, became senior lecturer in English; University of Sheffield, Sheffield, England, professor of English, 1976—.

WRITINGS: English Criticism of the Novel, 1860-1900,

Oxford University Press, 1965; (editor) *Tales of Edgar Allan Poe,* Oxford University Press, 1966; *Henry James: The Drama of Fulfillment, an Approach to the Novels,* Oxford University Press, 1975.

WORK IN PROGRESS: Research on nineteenth- and twentieth-century fiction.

* * *

GRAHAM, Margaret Bloy 1920-

PERSONAL: Born November 2, 1920, in Toronto, Ontario, Canada; daughter of Malcolm Robert (a physician) and Florence (a nurse; maiden name, Bloy) Graham; married Gene Zion, July, 1948 (divorced, 1968); married Oliver W. Holmes (a merchant ship officer), August, 1972. *Education:* University of Toronto, B.A., 1943; further study at New York University and New School for Social Research. *Address:* c/o Harper & Row, 10 East 53rd St., New York, N.Y. 10022.

CAREER: Artist. Gibbs & Cox, New York City, draftsman, 1944-45; Conde Nast Publications, New York City, artist, 1946-56. *Awards, honors: All Falling Down* was named a Caldecott honor book, 1952, *The Storm Book,* 1953.

WRITINGS: Be Nice to Spiders, Harper, 1968; *Benjy and the Barking Bird,* Harper, 1970; *Benjy's Dog House,* Harper, 1972; *Benjy's Boat Trip,* Harper, 1977.

Illustrator: Gene Zion, *All Falling Down,* Harper, 1951; Charlotte Zolotow, *The Storm Book,* Harper, 1952; Zion, *Hide and Seek Day,* Harper, 1954; Zion, *The Summer Snowman,* Harper, 1955; Zion, *Really Spring,* Harper, 1956; Zion, *Harry the Dirty Dog,* Harper, 1956; Zion, *Dear Garbage Man,* Harper, 1957; Zion, *No Roses for Harry!,* Harper, 1958; Zion, *Harry and the Lady Next Door,* Harper, 1960; Zion, *The Meanest Squirrel I Ever Met,* Scribner, 1962; Zion, *The Sugar Mouse Cake,* Scribner, 1964; Zion, *Harry by the Sea,* Harper, 1965; Shirley Gordon, *The Green Hornet Lunchbox,* Houghton, 1970; Jack Prelutsky, *The Pack Rat's Day,* Macmillan, 1974.

BIOGRAPHICAL/CRITICAL SOURCES: Saturday Review/World, December 4, 1973.

* * *

GRAHAM, Shirley
See DU BOIS, Shirley Graham

* * *

GRAINGER, J(ohn) H(erbert) 1917-

PERSONAL: Born October 10, 1917, in Kirklinton, Cumberland, England; son of William Herbert (a civil servant) and Margaret (Coates) Grainger; married Eileen Butterfield; children: Elizabeth. *Education:* St. Catharine's College, Cambridge, B.A. (honors), 1939. *Home:* 6 Knibbs St., Turner, Canberra, Australian Capital Territory, Australia. *Office:* Australian National University, Canberra, Australian Capital Territory, Australia.

CAREER: Employed by British Colonial Service in British Somaliland, 1946-47; schoolmaster in Surrey, England, 1947-50; Cornwall County Council, Cornwall, England, extramural tutor, 1950-59; Welsh College of Advanced Technology, Cardiff, lecturer, 1959-61; Australian National University, Canberra, 1962—, began as lecturer, currently reader. *Military service:* British Army, 1940-46; served in Kenya and the Middle East; became major.

WRITINGS: Character and Style in English Politics, Cambridge University Press, 1969; (contributor) D. Southgate, editor, *The Conservative Leadership,* Macmillan, 1974. Contributor to magazines and newspapers, including *Nation, Cambridge Quarterly,* and *Quadrant.*

WORK IN PROGRESS: Research on the ideology of British politics.

* * *

GRANBECK, Marilyn 1927-
(Nick Carter, Ben Grant, Adam Hamilton, Clayton Moore, Van Saxon)

PERSONAL: Born September 7, 1927, in Brooklyn, N.Y.; daughter of Rudolph (a machinist) and Irene (Jacobsen) Podest; married Robert Granbeck, December 31, 1949 (divorced, 1972); children: Christine Ellen, Leslie Carolyn, Robert Alan, Laurie Ann. *Education:* Brooklyn College (now of the City University of New York), B.A., 1947. *Residence:* Westlake Village, Calif. *Agent:* Richard Curtis, 156 East 52nd St., New York, N.Y. 10022.

CAREER: Institute of Paper Chemistry, Appleton, Wis., research chemist, 1947-48; Krimko Corp., Chicago, Ill., research chemist, 1948-50; University of Minnesota, Minneapolis, research chemist, 1952-58; writer, 1962—. *Member:* Mystery Writers of America (regional vice-president of Southern California chapter, 1976-79), Authors Guild, Minneapolis Writers Workshop (president, 1967-68).

WRITINGS: A Career in Metals and Plastics, Dillon, 1974; (under pseudonym Clayton Moore) *End of Reckoning,* Berkley Publishing, 1974; (under Moore pseudonym) *The Corrupters,* Berkley Publishing, 1974; (under pseudonym Adam Hamilton, with Arthur Moore) *Zaharan Pursuit,* Berkley Publishing, 1974; (under Hamilton pseudonym, with A. Moore), *Xander Pursuit,* Berkley Publishing, 1974; (under Hamilton pseudonym, with A. Moore) *Yashar Pursuit,* Berkley Publishing, 1975; (under Hamilton pseudonym, with A. Moore) *Wyss Pursuit,* Berkley Publishing, 1975; (under pseudonym Van Saxon, with A. Moore) *Hollywood Hit Man,* Zebra Publications, 1975; (under pseudonym Ben Grant) *Alice Dies Twice,* Major, 1975; *The Hidden Box Mystery,* Scholastic Book Services, 1975; (under pseudonym Nick Carter), *Assignment Intercept,* Award, 1976; *Social Work Careers,* F. Watts, 1977; *Summer at Ravenswood,* Scholastic Book Services, 1977; *The Magician's Daughter,* Manor, 1977; *Celia,* Jove, 1977; *Elena,* Jove, 1977; *Winds of Desire,* Jove, 1978; *The Mystery of the Jade Princess,* Scholastic Book Services, 1979.

WORK IN PROGRESS: A historical romance set in New York, Pittsburgh, and Cairo, Ill. in 1849.

SIDELIGHTS: Marilyn Granbeck writes to *CA:* "A recurrent back injury that made it impossible for me to stand in a laboratory was the incentive to turn to writing. I believe in keeping fit by jogging, swimming, regular exercise. I love to travel and find that the most interesting (and easy) part of getting into a book. I have no competency in foreign languages, though I have been struggling with Spanish since my high school days. I was not a good history student and am now learning all the history I didn't in school."

* * *

GRANBY, Milton
See WALLMANN, Jeffrey M(iner)

GRANDY, Richard (Edward) 1942-

PERSONAL: Born December 6, 1942, in Pittsburgh, Pa.; son of Richard S. (a businessman) and Elizabeth (a teacher; maiden name, Greiner) Grandy. *Education:* University of Pittsburgh, B.A., 1963; Princeton University, M.A., 1965, Ph.D., 1967. *Agent:* David Rosenthal, 425 Riverside Dr., New York, N.Y. 10025. *Office:* Department of Philosophy, Caldwell Hall, University of North Carolina, Chapel Hill, N.C. 27514.

CAREER: Princeton University, Princeton, N.J., assistant professor of philosophy, 1967-74; University of North Carolina, Chapel Hill, associate professor of philosophy, 1974—. *Member:* American Philosophical Association, Association for Symbolic Logic, Philosophy of Science Association, American Association for the Advancement of Science. *Awards, honors:* Woodrow Wilson fellowship, 1966-67; National Science Foundation postdoctoral fellowship, 1970-71; American Council of Learned Societies fellowship, 1976.

WRITINGS: Theories and Observation in Science, Prentice-Hall, 1973; *Advanced Logic for Applications,* D. Reidel, 1977. Contributor to philosophy journals.

WORK IN PROGRESS: Research on the nature of rationality and cognition.

*   *   *

GRANSDEN, Antonia 1928-

PERSONAL: Born October 7, 1928, in Somersetshire, England; daughter of Stephen Coleby (a sheepskin manufacturer) and Hilda Lucy (Street) Morland; married Karl Watts Gransden, 1958; married second husband, Jonathan Harrison (a university professor), 1978; children: (first marriage) Katherine, Deborah. *Education:* Somerville College, Oxford, B.A. (first class honors), 1951; University of London, Ph.D., 1957. *Office:* Department of History, University of Nottingham, University Park, Nottingham NG7 2RD, England.

CAREER: British Museum, London, England, assistant keeper of manuscripts, 1952-60, superintendent of students' room, 1960-62; Buckland Hall, Berkshire, England, tutor in mediaeval history, 1963-65; University of Nottingham, Nottingham, England, assistant lecturer, 1965-66, lecturer, 1966-73, reader in mediaeval history, 1973—, editor of "Nottingham Mediaeval Studies," 1977—. *Member:* Royal Historical Society (fellow), Society of Antiquarians (fellow).

WRITINGS: The Letter-Book of William of Hoo, Sacrist of Bury St. Edmunds, 1280-1294, Suffolk Records Society, 1963; *The Customary of the Benedictine Abbey of Eynsham in Oxfordshire,* Corpus Consuetudinum Monasticarum, 1963; *The Chronicle of Bury St. Edmunds, 1212-1301,* Thomas Nelson, 1964; *The Customary of Bury St. Edmunds,* Henry Bradshaw Society, 1973; *Historical Writing in England, circa 550 to circa 1307,* Routledge & Kegan Paul, 1974. Contributor of articles and reviews to history journals.

WORK IN PROGRESS: Historical Writing in England, circa 1307 to circa 1485, publication by Routledge & Kegan Paul.

*   *   *

GRANT, Ben
See GRANBECK, Marilyn

GRANT, John 1933-
(Jonathan Gash)

PERSONAL: Born September 30, 1933, in Bolton, Lancashire, England; son of Peter Watson (a mill worker) and Anne (a mill worker; maiden name, Turner) Gash; married Pamela Richard (a nurse), February 19, 1955; children: Alison Mary, Jacqueline Clare, Yvonne. *Education:* University of London, M.B. and B.S., 1958; Royal College of Surgeons and Physicians, M.R.C.S. and L.R.C.P., 1958; also earned D.Path., D.Bact., D.H.M., M.D., and D.T.M.H. *Home:* Silver Willows, Chapel Lane, West Bergholt, Colchester, Essex CO6 3EF, England. *Agent:* David Bolt, Bolt & Watson, 8 Storey's Gate, London S.W.1, England.

CAREER: General practitioner in London, England, 1958-59; pathologist in London and Essex, England, 1959-62; clinical pathologist in Hannover and Berlin, Germany, 1962-65; University of Hong Kong, Hong Kong, lecturer in clinical pathology and head of division, 1965-68, microbiologist in Hong Kong and London, 1968-71; University of London, School of Hygiene and Tropical Medicine, London, head of bacteriology unit, 1971—. *Military service:* British Army, Medical Corps; became major. *Member:* International College of Surgeons (fellow), Royal Society of Tropical Medicine (fellow).

*WRITINGS—*Under pseudonym Jonathan Gash: *The Judas Pair* (novel), Harper, 1977.

Author of "Terminus" (play), first produced in England at Chester Festival, November, 1976. Contributor of poems to *Record.*

*WORK IN PROGRESS—*Under pseudonym Jonathan Gash: *Gold in Gemini,* a sequel to *The Judas Pair; Jade Woman,* a novel about a high-class Hong Kong prostitute; *Pontiff,* a novel; a book of Lancastershire-dialect poems.

SIDELIGHTS: The basis for Grant's first novel was formed during his undergraduate days, when he worked in London junk shops, on the canals, in movie theaters, and as an antique-stall attendant in the street markets.

One of his current interests is the Lancastershire dialect. He writes: "I feel strongly that the vigour and dynamism of dialect should not be relegated by class feelings to a merely quaint pictorial function. It is time dialect poetry grew into the modern age."

AVOCATIONAL INTERESTS: Music ("I play a few instruments; choral music"), history, antiques, Chinese language, Oriental cultures, religion.

*   *   *

GRAVA, Sigurd 1934-

PERSONAL: Born September 25, 1934, in Latvia; came to the United States in 1950, naturalized citizen, 1955; son of Nikolajs (a lawyer) and Matilde Grava; married Ruth Kucko (a librarian), July 27, 1957; children: Lars. *Education:* City College (now of the City University of New York), B.C.E., 1955; Columbia University, M.S., 1957, Ph.D., 1965. *Home:* 401 West 118th St., New York, N.Y. 10027. *Office:* Division of Urban Planning, Columbia University, Avery Hall, New York, N.Y. 10027.

CAREER: Columbia University, New York, N.Y., instructor, 1960-64, assistant professor, 1965-67, associate professor, 1968-71, professor of urban planning, 1972—. Technical director for planning at Parsons Brinckerhoff, 1976—. Active in civic affairs; consultant to United Nations. *Military service:* U.S. Coast Guard, 1958. *Member:* American Institute of Planners, American Society of Civil Engineers, American Society of Planning Officials, Tau Beta Pi, Chi Epsilon, City Club of New York (member of board of trustees).

WRITINGS: Urban Planning Aspects of Water Pollution Control, Columbia University Press, 1969. Contributor to technical journals.

WORK IN PROGRESS: Research on transportation planning with low-investment systems.

AVOCATIONAL INTERESTS: International travel.

*   *   *

GRAY, Martin 1926-

PERSONAL: Born April 27, 1926, in Warsaw, Poland; came to United States in 1947, naturalized citizen, 1952; son of Henry (an industrialist) and Ida (Feld) Gray; married Dina Cult, December 12, 1959 (died October 3, 1970); married Virginia Eraerts, March 6, 1976; children: (first marriage) Nicole, Suzanne, Charles, Richard (all died October 3, 1970), (second marriage) Barbara. *Education:* Educated in Poland. *Home:* Les Barons, 83141 Tanneron, France. *Office:* Dina Gray Foundation, 8 rue de Babylone, 75007 Paris, France.

CAREER: Wholesale antique dealer, in New York, N.Y., 1950-60; agriculturalist in Tanneron, France, 1960-70; founder and president of Dina Gray Foundation, Paris, France, 1971—; writer and lecturer, 1971—. *Military service:* Warsaw ghetto fighter, 1939-43; arrested and sentenced to concentration camps, including Treblinka, from which he escaped. Soviet Army, 1944-46; became captain; participated in the battle of Berlin; received numerous decorations, including Order of Alexandre Nevsky, Order of the Fatherland's War, Order of the Red Star, Medal of Berlin, and Medal of Victory. *Awards, honors:* Dag Hammarskjold prize, 1973, for *Au nom de tous les miens.*

WRITINGS: (With Max Gallo) *Au nom de tous les miens,* Laffont, 1971, translation by Anthony White published as *For Those I Loved,* Little, Brown, 1972; *Le Livre de la vie: Pour trouver le bonheur, le courage, et l'espoir,* Laffont, 1973, translation published as *A Book of Life: To Find Happiness, Courage, and Hope,* Seabury, 1975; *Les Forces de la vie,* Laffont, 1975, translation published as *The Force of Life,* New American Library, 1978; *Les Pensees de notre vie* (title means "Thoughts of Our Life"), Laffont, 1977; *La Vie renaitra de la nuit* (title means "Life Arises Out of Night"), Laffont, 1977. Writer of a weekly column in *Bonne Soiree* (women's magazine).

SIDELIGHTS: Gray's books express his response to the tragedies which have marred his life. After losing his family in the Warsaw ghetto and the concentration camps of Poland during World War II, he established a new life for himself in the United States and later on his estate in France, seeking happiness through his relationship with his wife and children. When all of them perished in a forest fire in 1970, he refused to submit to despair, deciding instead to establish the Dina Gray Foundation as a memorial to his wife. The foundation's goal is to fight against natural disasters, fires, and pollution which menace the life of man just as war has in the past.

When asked about coping with personal tragedy, Gray told *CA:* "I am not a philosopher, a scientist, nor a saint. I am simply a man who has had lots of experiences, and I've learned not from books but from life. I know no recipes. I know no infallible methods. When it comes to such serious questions to such grave problems as courage, hope, and happiness, no miracles. In fact the only, the only true miracle, is Life, and it is in life that one must find the resources that give the means to achieve courage, hope, and happiness. What is important in our life is to know oneself. To learn to utilize the unsuspected forces that are in us and to share them. Herein is the true meaning of man's life. A life reduced to itself is no life. It is an amputation of life.

"Unselfishly we must turn toward others. Not to be an adversary but a friend. It is not always easy but it is the only way finally to be at peace with oneself.

"Life is always to go beyond."

*   *   *

GRAY, Russell
See FISCHER, Bruno

*   *   *

GRAYEFF, Felix 1906-

PERSONAL: Born February 6, 1906, in Koenigsberg, East Prussia, Germany; son of Nahum (a corn merchant) and Sarah (Feltenstein) Grayeff; married Marianne Zander (a teacher), January 17, 1943; children: Leonie Sara (Mrs. Allen Breeds), Michael Norbert. *Education:* University of Freiburg, Ph.D., 1930; University of Koenigsberg, state degree, 1931; also attended University of Heidelberg, University of Vienna, and University of Berlin. *Politics:* None. *Home:* 42 Friern Park, London N.12, England.

CAREER: College teacher in Greek and Latin classics in Koenigsberg and Berlin, Germany, in Adelaide, Australia, 1931-38; university lecturer in Dunedin, New Zealand, 1939-52; college teacher in Greek and Latin in York and London, England, 1952-56; full-time writer, 1956—. University of Tuebingen, guest lecturer, 1952, 1964, visiting professor, 1965-66. *Member:* P.E.N., Royal Institute of Philosophy, Hellenic Society (London).

WRITINGS: Der Freiheitskampf der Makkabaeer (title means "The Freedom Struggle of the Maccabeans"), Schocken Verlag, 1934; *The Political Organization of Peace,* Whitcombe & Tombs, 1941; *Deutung und Darstellung der theoretischen Philosophie Kants: Ein Kommentar zu den grundlegenden Teilen der Kritik der reinen Vernunft,* Felix Meiner, 1951, translation by David Walford published as *Kant's Theoretical Philosophy: A Commentary to the Central Parts of the Critique of Pure Reason,* Manchester University Press, 1970, reprint of German edition, 1977; *Heinrich der Achte* (title means "Henry VIII"), Claassen Verlag, 1961; *Lucien Bonaparte,* Claassen Verlag, 1966; *Versuch ueber das Denken* (title means "An Essay on Thinking"), Felix Meiner, 1966; *Aristotle and His School,* Duckworth, 1974; *Descartes,* Goodall, 1977; *Joan of Arc, Legends and Truth,* Goodall, 1978.

Contributor of articles to scholarly journals. Co-editor of *Kant-Studien,* 1953—.

WORK IN PROGRESS: Papers on *Aristotle and His School; Jeremiah: Das Leben des Propheten im Licht der Geschichte* (title means "Jeremiah: A Historical Account of the Prophet's Life"); *Historical Re-appraisals,* a book of essays relating to French history; a treatise on ethics.

SIDELIGHTS: Grayeff writes: "My migration from Germany to English-speaking countries in my early thirties has made a profound impact on my thinking and writing. I had received my full education in Germany but was still flexible enough to absorb English approaches to philosophical problems and I believe that my work has greatly profited in many respects by my ability to synthesise English and German cultural influences.''

* * *

GREALIS, Walt(er) 1929-

PERSONAL: Born February 18, 1929, in Toronto, Ontario, Canada. *Home:* 426 Merton St., Toronto, Ontario, Canada M4G 1B3. *Office:* RPM Music Publications, 6 Brentcliffe Rd., Toronto, Ontario, Canada M4F 342.

CAREER/WRITINGS: Royal Canadian Mounted Police, western Canada, constable, 1947-52; Toronto City Police, Toronto, Ontario, officer, 1952-58; employed by St. George Hotel, Bermuda, 1958-59, O'Keefe Breweries, Toronto, 1959-62, and *London Records,* Toronto, 1962-64; *RPM* Music Publications, Toronto, publisher and editor, 1964—. Notable assignments include long range coverage of the music industry in Canada. Lecturer.

SIDELIGHTS: Grealis told *CA:* "In 1964 when *RPM* began there was no trade paper in Canada on the record and music industries. Over the thirteen years that *RPM* has published, a domestic industry was born in Canada. *RPM*'s encouragement of Canadians to enter the creative areas of record production was a contributing factor to the birth of this new industry in Canada. *RPM* also encouraged a star system for Canadian artists with such events as the Juno Awards, Big Country Awards, and brought the industry together through our Communication Series of meetings, seminars and conventions.''

BIOGRAPHICAL/CRITICAL SOURCES: Toronto Star, May 11, 1974.

* * *

GREEN, David 1942-

PERSONAL: Born February 9, 1942, in New York, N.Y.; son of Herman J. (a professor) and Selma (a professor; maiden name, Berenson) Green; married Norma J. Stewart, August 6, 1976; children: Shoshana Leslie. *Education:* Cornell University, B.A. (honors), 1962, Ph.D., 1967; Stanford University, M.A., 1963. *Politics:* "Jewish Anarchism." *Religion:* "Anarchistic Judaism." *Home:* 920 Temperance St., Saskatoon, Saskatchewan, Canada. *Office:* Department of History, University of Saskatchewan, Saskatoon, Saskatchewan, Canada.

CAREER: Ohio State University, Columbus, assistant professor of history, 1967-68; University of Saskatchewan, Saskatoon, special lecturer, 1969-70, assistant professor, 1970-72, associate professor, 1972-77, professor of history, 1977—. Visiting assistant professor at Cornell University, summers, 1969-70. Fellow of Center for Advanced Study in the Behavioral Sciences, 1971-72. *Member:* Canadian Association for Latin American Studies, Canadian Association of University Teachers, Canadian Professors for Peace in the Middle East. *Awards, honors:* Woodrow Wilson fellow, 1962-63; American Council of Learned Societies fellow, 1971-72.

WRITINGS: (Contributor) Barton J. Bernstein, editor, *Politics and Policies of the Truman Administration,* Quadrangle, 1970; *The Containment of Latin America: A History of the Myths and Realities of the Good Neighbor Policy,* Quadrangle, 1971. Contributor to history and Latin American studies journals.

WORK IN PROGRESS: The Agony of American Conservatism (tentative title).

SIDELIGHTS: In 1968, Green was fired from Ohio State University for burning his draft card. He was convicted in 1969, and his probation was terminated in 1970.

He writes: ''I am becoming more and more interested in the links between political language and the growth of government power. As I become more skeptical about the ability of any government to do anybody any good, I also become more interested in the techniques politicians use to convince their constituents that government is acting in the constituents' interests, and is doing things for the constituents which they could not possibly do for themselves. Thus my indicated political and religious preferences are no joke; they represent many years of self-searching.''

* * *

GREEN, Edith Pinero 1929-

PERSONAL: Born November 7, 1929, in Jersey City, N.J.; daughter of Jose Luis (an industrial realtor) and Maxine (Auerbach) Pinero; married Julius Green (a businessman), March 15, 1959; children: Jason, Jeremy. *Education:* Centenary Junior College, A.A., 1950; New School for Social Research, B.A., 1965. *Residence:* New York, N.Y. *Agent:* Elaine Markson Literary Agency, Inc., 44 Greenwich Ave., New York, N.Y. 10011.

CAREER: Gotham Vladimir Advertising Agency, New York, N.Y., assistant to chairman of board of directors, 1955-62; writer, 1971—. *Member:* Mystery Writers of America.

WRITINGS—Mystery novels: *Mark of Lucifer,* Dell, 1974; *The Death Trap,* Dell, 1975; *A Woman's Honor,* Dell, 1976; *Rotten Apples,* Dutton, 1977.

WORK IN PROGRESS: Deadfall (tentative title), a mystery novel; *Quesheba's Daughter,* a historical romance, the first volume of a series.

* * *

GREEN, Fitzhugh 1917-

PERSONAL: Born September 12, 1917, in Jenkintown, Pa.; son of Fitzhugh (an Arctic explorer, naval officer, and author) and Natalie Wheeler (Elliot) Green; married Patricia Peerson, June 25, 1953 (divorced, 1970); children: Penelope. *Education:* Attended Princeton University, 1936-40; Boston University, M.A., 1963. *Religion:* Fundamentalist. *Home:* 3630 Prospect St. N.W., Washington, D.C. 20007.

CAREER: Vick Chemical Co., New York City, sales and advertising executive, 1946-49; *Life,* New York City, advertising sales promotion executive, 1950-52; Federal Trade Commission, Washington, D.C., assistant to the chairman, 1953-54; U.S. Information Agency, Washington, D.C., director of operations in Laos, 1955-56, and Israel, 1956-58, chief of private enterprise division, 1958-60, director in Belgian Congo, 1960, and in the Republic of Congo, Leopoldville, 1960-62, representative at U.S. Mission to the United Nations, 1964-65, deputy director of personnel and training, 1965-66, deputy director of operations in the Far East, 1968-70; U.S. Senate, Washington, D.C., staff expert on foreign affairs, oceanography, 1966-68; U.S. Environmental Protection Agency, Washington, D.C., associate administrator, 1971-77. Lecturer. Psychological warfare consultant, American University, 1959; representative, United Nations Conference on Human Environment, 1972. Deputy vice-chairman, National Citizens for Eisenhower, 1954; Republican candidate for Congress, Rhode Island, 1970. Director, Boys Harbor. *Military service:* U.S. Navy,

1942-46; became lieutenant. *Member:* Metropolitan Club, Federal City Club, New York Explorers Club, Newport Country Club, Burning Tree Country Club, Racquet and Tennis Club.

WRITINGS: Fitz Jr. with the Fleet, Brewer, Warren & Putnam, 1931; *A Change in the Weather,* Norton, 1977.

Contributor of articles to periodicals, including *Washington Post, Washingtonian, Providence Journal/Bulletin, Foreign Service Journal,* and *Sea Technology.*

WORK IN PROGRESS: A novel and a nonfiction work on propaganda.

SIDELIGHTS: Green told *CA:* "I believe strongly that citizens with good educations should participate in public service, as a career or at least as additional duty to their other chosen occupations. I believe in citizen solutions to problems, or government at local level before the mammoth federal establishment gets involved. I believe in strong local and federal attention to needed environmental protection constraints, plus conservation of wild life, wetlands, etc. People should particularly support Nature Conservancy attempts to put underdeveloped acreage in trust for the future. From a personal standpoint, I intend to write for the balance of my life on the many areas of activity in which I have had experience."

CA asked Green if he favored the creation of a Department of the Environment. He responded: "I would favor such a department. Like the new Energy Department, a Department of the Environment would bring together all the aspects of the field of the environment. Weather modification, pollution control, review of environmental impact statements, and protection of fish and wildlife are now all located in different corners of the government. Like severed parts of a snake, each is still twitching independently with little or no coordination. Since the environment is a complex but integrated mechanism of nature, so should the government's administrative dealings with it be orchestrated singly, under one command. The new department should include two brand-new functions: national land use management, and planning for control of urban transportation (vital because most city air pollution comes from cars, buses, and trucks). Environment, energy and the related economic matters could then all be handled within the cabinet, with presidential attention to the major decisions. At the highest level, fair and reasonable trade-offs could be made to maintain both the health of our people and that of our economy.

"The disadvantage of such a department would be mainly the inefficiencies which change always brings to the bureaucracy. We had it when the EPA was formed; but it can be overcome, as we managed to do in the EPA."

* * *

GREEN, Maurice B(erkeley) 1920-

PERSONAL: Born September 25, 1920, in London, England; son of Walter Michael (a civil servant) and Margaret (a teacher; maiden name, Nimmy) Green; married Doreen Evelyn Catherine Nayler (a catering manager), August 15, 1942; children: Sally Green Whitehead, Patrick, Richard, Andrew. *Education:* Imperial College of Science, London, A.R.C.S., 1940, B.Sc., 1940, Ph.D., 1955. *Religion:* Society of Friends (Quakers). *Home:* 12 Ashley Dr., Hartford, Northwich, Cheshire CW8 3AQ, England. *Office:* Imperial Chemical Industries Ltd., Heath, Runcorn, Cheshire WA7 4QD, England.

CAREER: Wellcome Foundation Ltd., London, England,

research chemist, 1944-47; May & Baker Ltd., Dagenham, England, research chemist, 1947-58; Imperial Chemical Industries Ltd., Runcorn, England, research manager, 1958—. Visiting lecturer at University of Stirling; visiting fellow at University of Salford. *Member:* European Weed Research Society, Association of Professional Scientists and Technologists (president), Royal Institute of Chemistry, Society of Chemical Industry (member of council, 1964-74; chairman of pesticides group, 1972-74), Biodeterioration Society, American Chemical Society (fellow).

WRITINGS: (Contributor) Hans Suschitzky, editor, *Polychlorinated Aromatic Compounds,* Plenum, 1974; *Pesticides: Boon or Bane?,* Westview Press, 1976; *Chemicals for Crop Protection and Pest Control,* Pergamon, 1977; *Eating Oil: A Study of Energy Usage in Food Production,* Westview Press, 1978. Contributor of articles and reviews to scientific journals.

WORK IN PROGRESS: Research on pesticides, agricultural chemistry, and energy usage in agriculture.

SIDELIGHTS: Green writes that there is a "need to give the public a balanced view of pesticides so that they can be used for maximum good with minimum risk. There is also a need for the public to realize the extent to which its standard of living depends on the use of limited, irreplaceable fossil fuel resources, and the need to conserve these. The driving force for all I do (including writing) is my concept of Quaker service and my commitment to Christ."

AVOCATIONAL INTERESTS: Bridge, travel, including the United States.

* * *

GREEN, Robert D(avid) 1942-

PERSONAL: Born April 20, 1942, in St. Petersburg, Fla.; son of Samuel J. and Margaret (Lang) Green. *Education:* University of Florida, B.S.J., 1964. *Home:* 1600 South Eads St., Arlington, Va. 22202. *Office:* Reuters News Agency, 615 National Press Bldg., Washington, D.C. 20045.

CAREER/WRITINGS: Fort Lauderdale News, Fort Lauderdale, Fla., sports writer, 1965-67; employed by Reuters News Agency in Washington, D.C., 1967—. Notable assignments include coverage of the White House, Congress, and Watergate. *Military service:* U.S. Air Force Reserve, 1966-71. *Member:* National Press Club, Sigma Delta Chi.

* * *

GREEN, Roland (James) 1944-

PERSONAL: Born September 2, 1944, in Bradford, Pa.; son of James Ernest (a teacher) and Bertha (a librarian; maiden name, Cohen) Green; married Frieda A. Murray (in management), November 8, 1975. *Education:* Oberlin College, B.A., 1966; University of Chicago, M.A., 1968, doctoral study, 1968—. *Home:* 629 West Oakdale, Chicago, Ill. 60657. *Agent:* Lurton Blassingame, 60 East 42nd St., New York, N.Y. 10017.

CAREER: Writer, 1973—. *Member:* Science Fiction Writers of America, American Military Institute, U.S. Naval Institute.

WRITINGS: Wandor's Ride (heroic fantasy), Avon, 1973; *Wandor's Journey* (historic fantasy), Avon, 1975; *Wandor's Voyage* (heroic fantasy), Avon, 1978; *Wandor's Flight* (heroic fantasy), Avon, 1979. Contributor to *Illinois Schools Journal.*

WORK IN PROGRESS: Little War of Aphrodite and *And*

All the Trumpets Sounded, both with Michael Bradley; *Kara the Exile,* with Laurence Nichols.

SIDELIGHTS: Green writes: "My work has been heavily influenced by my long-standing interest in history (especially military and naval) and political science. This interest has greatly affected my choice of material, and I think it has helped me build and depict realistic imaginary worlds. The four "Wandor" books are part of a series which will eventually run to at least seven and possibly ten books laid in the same fantasy world and focused on the same characters."

* * *

GREEN, Samuel 1948-

PERSONAL: Born December 2, 1948, in Sedro Wolley, Wash.; son of Andrew W. and Vera Jean (Todd) Green; married Sally K. Purdy (an architectural assistant), December 18, 1971; children: Lonnie Robert. *Education:* Highline Community College, A.A. (honors), 1972; Western Washington State College, B.A. (honors), 1973, M.A., 1975; further graduate study at University of Washington, Seattle, 1975-76. *Home:* 17023 Fifth Ave. N.E., Seattle, Wash. 98155. *Office:* King County Arts Commission, Seattle, Wash.

CAREER: Schwary & Associates, Inc., Seattle, Wash., director of communications, 1975-77; artist-in-residence at public schools in the Tacoma, Wash., area and for Tacoma's gifted children's program, 1977; Mission Creek Youth Camp (for juvenile offenders), Belfair, Wash., artist-in-residence and teacher, 1977—. Editor and publisher of Jawbone Press, 1974—. Guest speaker at University of Washington, Seattle, Tacoma Community College, Highline Community College; and teacher at correctional and penal institutions; conducts poetry workshops; artist-in-residence for King County Arts Commission. Has given local readings at public gatherings and on radio programs. *Military service:* U.S. Coast Guard, 1966-70; served in Vietnam and Antarctica. *Awards, honors:* National Endowment for the Arts fellow, 1976; Centrum Foundation scholarship, 1977.

WRITINGS: Gillnets (poems), Cold Mountain Press, 1978.

Work anthologized in *Intro 6,* edited by George Garrett, Doubleday, 1974. Contributor of poems to literary journals, including *Poetry Northwest, Poet & Critic, Poetry Now,* and *Southern Poetry Review.* Editor of *Jawbone,* 1974—; co-editor of *Poetry Exchange.*

WORK IN PROGRESS: A collection of letter poems; a collection of poems "in a variety of voices."

SIDELIGHTS: Green comments: "Beside my own writing, I am involved in the study of making fine books. Since I plan eventually to publish full-size books, in addition to the chapbook series I now edit, I'm learning hand papermaking and hand bookbinding. Not enough attention is paid to fine books, like those produced by such presses as Copper Canyon Press and Graywolf Press."

* * *

GREENBERG, Simon 1901-

PERSONAL: Born January 8, 1901, in Russia; came to the United States in 1905, naturalized citizen, 1924; son of Morris (a wine expert) and Bessie (Chaidenko) Greenberg; married Betty Davis, December 13, 1925; children: Moshe, Daniel Asher. *Education:* City College (now of the City University of New York), B.A., 1922; attended American School of Oriental Studies and Hebrew University of Jerusalem, 1924-25; Jewish Theological Seminary, rabbi and M.H.L., 1925; Dropsie College, Ph.D., 1932. *Home:* 420 Riverside Dr., New York, N.Y. 10025. *Office:* Jewish Theological Seminary, 3080 Broadway, New York, N.Y. 10027.

CAREER: Jewish Theological Seminary, New York, N.Y., lecturer, 1932-40, associate professor, 1940-46, professor of education, 1946-72, professor of homiletics, 1948-72, provost, 1946-52, vice-chancellor and faculty vice-president, 1952; initiator and administrator of Israel Project in Jerusalem, 1972—. Rabbi of Jewish congregation in Philadelphia, Pa., 1925-46. Director of University of Judaism, 1948-58, president, 1958-66, chancellor, 1966-72. Executive director of United Synagogue of America, 1950-53.

MEMBER: American Association for Jewish Education, Religious Education Association, Rabbinical Assembly of America (president, 1938-40), Educators Assembly of United Synagogue of America, Conference on Science, Philosophy, and Religion (fellow). *Awards, honors:* D.D. from Jewish Theological Seminary, 1958; Sam Rothberg Award from Hebrew University of Jerusalem, 1977, for contributions to Jewish education in the diaspora; Mordecai M. Kaplan Medal from University of Judaism, 1977.

WRITINGS: Living as a Jew Today, Behrman, 1939; *The Ideals and Values of the Prayer Book,* Jewish Theological Seminary, 1940; *The Harishon Textbook Series,* five volumes, United Synagogue of America, 1941; *The First Year in the Hebrew School: A Teacher's Guide,* United Synagogue of America, 1945; *Foundation of a Faith,* Burning Bush Press, 1968; *Words of Poetry,* privately printed, 1970; *The Ethical in the American and Jewish Heritage,* Ktav, 1977.

WORK IN PROGRESS: A Jewish Philosophy of Life.

SIDELIGHTS: Greenberg writes: "Since 1972 I have been spending some six months of the year in Jerusalem. I initiated and have been guiding and nurturing the seminary's special Israel Project devoted to building joint educational projects with Israeli institutions for developing more effective methods for transmitting Jewish religio-cultural values while maintaining a policy of freedom of thought and intellectual integrity. We have met with considerable response particularly from a goodly number of intellectuals identified with the non-religious kibbutzim (communal settlements)."

* * *

GREENE, Ellin 1927-

PERSONAL: Born September 18, 1927, in Elizabeth, N.J.; daughter of Charles M. and Dorothea (Hooten) Peterson; married K. Richard Greene, June 24, 1962 (marriage ended, 1976). *Education:* Douglass College, A.B., 1953; Rutgers University, M.L.S., 1957, currently pursuing doctoral study. *Home and office:* 113 Chatham Lane, Point Pleasant, N.J. 08742.

CAREER: Free Public Library, Elizabeth, N.J., children's librarian, 1953-57, specialist working with groups of children, 1957-59; New York Public Library, New York, N.Y., assistant in storytelling and group work specialist, 1959-64, children's specialist in Bronx, 1964-65, storytelling specialist and assistant coordinator of children's services, 1965-67; Rutgers University, New Brunswick, N.J., adjunct faculty member in children's literature, storytelling, and library service to children, 1968—. Children's literature specialist at National College of Education, 1976-77; juror of children's films for Educational Film Library Association; lecturer and consultant.

MEMBER: American Library Association, National Council of Teachers of English, Association for Library Service to Children, Authors Guild, Authors League of America, American Crafts Council, Psi Chi. *Awards, honors:* Tangley Oaks fellowship, 1977-78.

WRITINGS: Recordings for Children: A Selected List, New York Public Library, 1964; *Stories: A List of Stories to Tell and to Read Aloud,* 6th edition, New York Public Library, 1965; *Films for Children: A Selected List,* New York Library Association, 1966; (editor) Mary E. Wilkins, *The Pumpkin Giant* (juvenile), Lothrop, 1970; (editor) Wilkins, *Princess Rosetta and the Popcorn Man* (juvenile), Lothrop, 1971; (with Madalynne Schoenfeld) *A Multimedia Approach to Children's Literature: A Selective List of Films, Filmstrips, and Recordings Based on Children's Books,* American Library Association, 1972, 2nd edition, 1977; *Clever Cooks: A Concoction of Stories, Charms, Recipes, and Riddles,* Lothrop, 1973, published as *Clever Cooks: A Ready-Mix of Stories, Recipes, and Riddles,* Scholastic Book Services, 1977; (editor) Laurence Houseman, *The Rat-Catcher's Daughter* (stories), Atheneum, 1974; (with Augusta Baker) *Storytelling: Art and Technique,* Bowker, 1977; *Midsummer Magic: A Garland of Stories, Charms, and Recipes,* Lothrop, 1977. Contributor to *World Book Encyclopedia* and *Top of the News.*

WORK IN PROGRESS: An anthology of articles on storytelling, for Bowker.

SIDELIGHTS: Ellin Greene comments briefly: "I have a deep interest in literature, especially imaginative literature, including folk and fairy tales, fantasy, and poetry for both adults and children."

AVOCATIONAL INTERESTS: Dance, theater, gardening, the seashore, yoga, meditation.

*   *   *

GREENE, Fred
See CADET, John

*   *   *

GREENHOUSE, Linda 1947-

PERSONAL: Born January 9, 1947, in New York, N.Y.; daughter of H. Robert (a physician) and Dorothy (Greenlick) Greenhouse. *Education:* Radcliffe College, B.A., 1968; Yale University, M.S.L., 1978. *Office: New York Times,* 1920 L St. N.W., Washington, D.C. 20036.

CAREER/WRITINGS: New York Times, New York, N.Y., assistant to James Reston, 1968-69, local staff member, 1969-73, local political staff member, 1974—, state legislative bureau chief, 1976-77, U.S. Supreme Court correspondent, 1978—. Notable assignments include coverage of "the silence" at West Point, 1973, and the New York City fiscal crisis, 1975-76. *Awards, honors:* Ford Foundation fellowship for journalists at Yale Law School, 1977-78.

*   *   *

GREGORY, James 1912-

PERSONAL: Born May 11, 1912, in Manchester, England; son of William Stothert (an accountant) and Nora (Keogh) Gregory; divorced; children: Donald Michael, Leonora. *Education:* University of London, B.A. (honors), 1935, diploma in education, 1937. *Politics:* Socialist. *Religion:* Society of Friends (Quakers). *Home and office:* 167 High St., Queenborough, Isle of Sheppey, Kent, England.

CAREER: Teacher in Manchester and London, England, 1937-43; National Farm Survey, Rothamstead, England, research analyst, 1943-44; International Sugar Council, London, economist, 1944-45; United Nations Relief & Rehabilitation Administration, Belgrade, Yugoslavia, distribution officer, 1945-47; University of Nottingham, Nottingham, England, organizer of extramural studies for Derbyshire, 1947-48; United Nations International Children's Fund, Belgrade, administrative officer, 1948-49; engaged in free-lance teaching, journalism, and educational broadcasting in London, 1949-52; Secondary Teachers College, Bangkok, Thailand, lecturer in geography, 1952-55; high school geography teacher in Kitimat, British Columbia, 1955-57; headmaster of London Missionary Society schools in Western Samoa, 1957-60; University of Singapore, Singapore, senior lecturer in geography, 1960-63; University of Ghana, Extra-mural Studies Department, Accra, senior lecturer in geography and research fellow, 1963-65; Furzedown College of Education, London, senior lecturer in the geography of Southeast Asia and the Soviet Union, 1965-77; Furzedown Students' Hostels, London, warden, 1977—. Member of board of directors of Andongreg Ltd. (tourism and publishing company). *Military service:* Royal Air Force, 1941. *Member:* Royal Geographical Society (fellow), Society for Cultural Relations with the U.S.S.R. (member of executive council), Great Britain-U.S.S.R. Association.

WRITINGS: (With D. W. Shave) *The U.S.S.R.: A Geographical Survey,* Harrap, 1944; *Land of the Soviets,* Penguin, 1945; (with W.J.F. Horrabin) *An Atlas of the U.S.S.R.,* Penguin, 1945; *Russian Land, Soviet People: A Geographical Approach to the U.S.S.R.,* Harrap, 1968; *My First World of Geography* (juvenile), Hamlyn, 1975, published as *My World of Geography,* Hamlyn-American, 1977; (editor) *An Outline Geography of the U.S.S.R.,* Collets, 1976; *Moscow,* Book Society of Canada, in press; *Siberia,* Book Society of Canada, in press. Writer for British Broadcasting Corp. educational broadcasts. Contributor to magazines and newspapers, including *Times Educational Supplement* and *Reporter.* Editor of *Teaching and Learning,* 1961-63.

WORK IN PROGRESS: A novel, completion expected in 1982; "lavishly illustrated" children's books, one on Siberia.

SIDELIGHTS: Gregory writes: "As a student of geography during the Great Depression of the 1930's, I became interested in what was often called the 'Russian experiment,' and first visited the U.S.S.R. in 1935. I then made my special area of study the geography of the U.S.S.R., about which almost nothing was known, became proficient in the Russian language, and visited the U.S.S.R. almost every year thereafter, visiting almost every part of the country. My work also took me to Yugoslavia, Thailand, Canada, Samoa, Malaya, Singapore, and Ghana, and I became intensely interested in the relationship between people and their environment.

"I became convinced that human relationships, irrespective of nationality, creed, or colour, were the most important factors in life, and my own search for an ideal partner led to four marriages, not one to a British woman. Now, at the age of sixty-five, I believe that at last I have found the ideal woman, and she happens to be English.

"I want to convey something of the wonder and unity of the world and its inhabitants to young people, and I am looking forward to writing books for young children. I have also started work on a novel, based on the experiences of my own life, hoping to show the younger generation that mature love, a deep caring relationship, which I myself have only recently attained, is the most valuable asset in life. I hope also to show that, to avoid prejudice and understand one's fellow men and women, it is essential to judge any society or culture in relation to its stage in historical evolution, and the natural environment.''

* * *

GREGORY, Ruth W(ilhelmine) 1910-

PERSONAL: Born February 20, 1910, in West Point, Neb.; daughter of Edward George (a hotel owner) and Wilhelmine (Plieth) Gregory. *Education:* University of Nebraska, A.B., 1933; University of Wisconsin, Madison, L.S. (magna cum laude), 1938. *Religion:* Episcopalian. *Home and office:* 2035 Walnut St., Waukegan, Ill. 60085.

CAREER: Lincoln City Library, Lincoln, Neb., general assistant, 1934-36; *Rotarian,* Chicago, Ill., librarian in editorial department, 1937; Stevens Point Public Library, Stevens Point, Wis., acting librarian, 1938-39; Waukegan Public Library, Waukegan, Ill., associate librarian, 1939, head librarian, 1939-76, librarian emeritus, 1976—. Instructor at Drexel University, summer, 1962, and University of Wisconsin, Madison, summer, 1966. Member of Illinois State Library Advisory Committee, 1967-76; member of executive committee of North Suburban Regional Library Advisory Council, 1972-73; member of advisory council of University of Wisconsin Library School, 1974-75, and University of Illinois Library School, 1974-77; library consultant. Executive secretary of Waukegan City Planning Commission, 1950-57; member of board of directors of Lake County Crippled Children's Clinic, 1952—, Family Service Agency, 1954-60, North Lake County Mental Health Society, 1954-62, and Lake County Museum of History, 1962-64 (vice-president of board of directors, 1962-63); member of Lake County Fine Arts Council, 1965-69.

MEMBER: American Association of University Women (member of local board of directors, 1944-50; local president, 1949-51), American Library Association (member of council, 1951-54; president of Public Libraries Division, 1954-55; member of executive board, 1956-60), Illinois City Managers Association (chairman of publication committee, 1960-64), Public Library Association, Illinois League of Women Voters, P.E.O. Sisterhood, Illinois Library Association (vice-president, 1946-47; president, 1947-48), Lake County Woman's Management Association (honorary member), Waukegan Women's Club, Chicago Library Club, Altrusa (honorary member), Kappa Delta. *Awards, honors:* Civic service award from Fraternal Order of Eagles, 1963; award from Lake County Mental Health Society, 1965; Avis Community Award, 1966; citation from Illinois Library Association, 1976.

WRITINGS: Library Service to Adults, American Library Association, 1962; (editor) *Waukegan, Illinois: Its Past, Its Present,* Waukegan League of Women Voters, 1959, 3rd edition, 1967; (with Lester L. Stoffel) *Public Libraries in Cooperative Systems,* American Library Association, 1971; *Anniversaries and Holidays,* American Library Association, 3rd edition (Gregory was not associated with earlier editions), 1975. Contributor to library journals. *Public Libraries,* editor, 1947-48, member of editorial committee, 1948-52; editor of *ASD Newsletter,* 1967.

WORK IN PROGRESS: Anniversaries and Holidays, 4th edition, for American Library Association; books on library systems and library administration.

SIDELIGHTS: Ruth Gregory comments: "Mary Emogene Hazeltine's 2nd edition of *Anniversaries and Holidays* was published in 1944. I had been a member of her last class at the University of Wisconsin. To be responsible, many years later, for a complete revision of her book was comparable to picking up a torch. My interest in the writing of other professional material has been a natural follow-up to a long-time participation in workshops and other library association activities.''

BIOGRAPHICAL/CRITICAL SOURCES: Illinois Libraries, February, 1977.

* * *

GRICE, Julia (Haughey) 1940-

PERSONAL: Born May 28, 1940, in Battle Creek, Mich. *Education:* Albion College, B.A., 1962. *Residence:* Detroit, Mich. *Agent:* Lenniger Literary Agency, Inc., 437 Fifth Ave., New York, N.Y. 10016.

CAREER: Public assistance caseworker for State of Michigan, 1963-66; writer. Speaker at various conferences. *Member:* Detroit Women Writers (president, 1976-77).

WRITINGS: Lovefire (novel), Avon, 1977. Contributor of more than one hundred fifty articles to popular magazines.

WORK IN PROGRESS: Two novels, tentatively titled *Emeraldfire* and *Aurora Wind,* for Avon; *Daughters of the Flame,* a family saga; another romantic historical novel.

SIDELIGHTS: Julia Grice writes: "My writing 'apprenticeship' lasted about ten years, during which period I taught myself how to write and wrote six books which were never published. One, a nonfiction book for expectant mothers, did sell but was reneged upon by the publisher. Each time I was rejected I started another book, and eventually, with my seventh book, I had a sale. I feel that none of my early work was wasted as I learned from my mistakes and actually taught myself how to write. It was my agent who suggested that I try romantic historical novels—he felt I would do well with them. I was reluctant to try, but finally gathered my courage together and did so.''

Grice told Diane Pawlowski: "When I begin to work a really strange thing happens. I'll be working away at the typewriter and I can almost see the characters, as if they were on a fuzzy TV. Only they're in my mind. And I not only see and hear them, but smell them as well.

"It's like when we were kids and played 'Let's Pretend,' only this is much more intense. It's as if I'm in another world, as if I'm in a trance. Two hours are gone and it's like no time has passed at all.''

BIOGRAPHICAL/CRITICAL SOURCES: Detroit News, November 20, 1977.

* * *

GRIFFIN, David Ray 1939-

PERSONAL: Born August 8, 1939, in Wilbur, Wash.; son of Troy A. (a driller of water wells) and Ella (Ratcliffe) Griffin; married Carolyn Bartell, June 16, 1963 (divorced, 1978); children: Lydia Beth. *Education:* Northwest Christian College, B.A., 1962; University of Oregon, M.A., 1963; Claremont Graduate School, Ph.D., 1968. *Politics:* Democrat. *Religion:* Protestant. *Home:* 1466 Wells Ave., Claremont, Calif. 91711. *Office:* Department of Philosophy of Religion, School of Theology at Claremont, Claremont, Calif. 91711.

CAREER: University of Dayton, Dayton, Ohio, assistant professor of philosophy of religion, 1968-73; School of Theology at Claremont, Claremont, Calif., associate professor of philosophy of religion and executive director of Center for Process Studies, both 1973—. *Member:* American Academy of Religion, Society for the Study of Process Philosophies.

WRITINGS: A Process Christology, Westminster, 1973; *God, Power, and Evil: A Process Theodicy,* Westminster, 1976; (with John B. Cobb, Jr.) *Process Theology: An Introductory Exposition,* Westminster, 1976; (editor with Cobb) *Mind in Nature: Essays on the Interface of Science and Philosophy,* University Press of America, 1976; (editor with Thomas J. J. Altizer) *John Cobb's Theology in Process,* Westminster, 1977; (editor with Donald Sherburne) A. N. Whitehead, *Process and Reality,* Free Press, 1978. Contributor of about twenty-five articles to philosophy and theology journals.

WORK IN PROGRESS: Dialogues on God and Evil; "a treatment of the relations between religion and ethics, with a special focus on the idea of enjoyment," tentatively titled *God and Enjoyment.*

SIDELIGHTS: Griffin comments: "Most of my work is on issues that I think are of central importance in a world-view capable of sustaining a sense of the meaning and importance of life, and an ethical stance adequate to the needs of the present and future situation of the world, with its hunger, diminishing resources, and potential ecological disaster. I have found the 'process' view of reality suggested by Alfred North Whitehead to be the most adequate, so my work revolves around his vision."

* * *

GRIFFIN, John Q(uealy) 1948-

PERSONAL: Born November 15, 1948, in White Plains, N.Y.; son of John H. (a retailer) and Patricia (Schwan) Griffin; married Claire Janosik (a writer and editor), April 3, 1976. *Education:* Wesleyan University, Middletown, Conn., B.A., 1970. *Home:* 3 Rose St., Somerville, Mass. 02143. *Office: Exceptional Parent,* 708 Statler Office Building, Boston, Mass. 02116.

CAREER: Educreative Systems, Inc., New York, N.Y., project manager, 1973-75; *Exceptional Parent,* Boston, Mass., managing editor, 1975—. Worked as psychiatric aide, leather worker, and housepainter.

WRITINGS: (Editor) James Olsen and Maryanne Johnson, *Exiles From the American Dream,* Walker & Co., 1974; *Motorcycles on the Move,* Lerner, 1976; (contributor) Ellen Janosik and Jean Miller, editors, *Theory and Practice of Family Health,* McGraw, 1979. Contributor to magazines.

* * *

GRIFFITH, Patricia Browning 1935-

PERSONAL: Born November 9, 1935, in Fort Worth, Tex.; daughter of Robert (a civil servant) and Alonza Lee (Johnston) Browning; married William Byron Griffith (a professor of philosophy), June 16, 1960; children: Flannery. *Education:* Baylor University, B.A., 1958. *Home:* 1215 Geranium St. N.W., Washington, D.C. 20012. *Agent:* Betty Anne Clarke, International Creative Management, 40 West 57th St., New York, N.Y. 10019.

CAREER: Fort Worth Star-Telegraph, Fort Worth, Tex., news reporter, 1957; Rogers & Cowan (public relations), New York City, secretarial assistant, 1958-59; employed by American Civil Liberties Union, New York City, 1960; Yale University, New Haven, Conn., secretary, 1960-62; free-lance writer, 1962—. George Washington University, instructor in fiction writing, 1974-77; teaches a private prose

seminar; has taught writing workshops. Conducts interviews on "Washington Review on the Air," for WAMU-FM. Consultant to Washington, D.C. Arts Commission. *Member:* Washington Writers Center (member of board of directors), Washington Women's Art Center. *Awards, honors:* National Endowment for the Arts literary fellow, 1978.

WRITINGS: The Future Is Not What It Used to Be (novel), Simon & Schuster, 1970.

Work anthologized in *O. Henry Prize Stories,* 1970, 1976. Contributor of stories, articles, and reviews to *Harper's* and *Paris Review* and to newspapers. Member of founding editorial staff of *Washington Review of the Arts,* presently fiction editor.

WORK IN PROGRESS: Big Moments, a novel about a returning Vietnam veteran; *Tennessee Blue,* a novel set mainly in Washington about a journalist, "not a typical 'Washington novel' but rather like my first novel also set in Washington, about the ordinary people living in the surreal setting of Washington, D.C."; short stories, experimenting in new styles.

SIDELIGHTS: Griffith writes that she is "involved in the more experimental cultural life of Washington, D.C.—small press publishing, literary readings, multi-media arts." She is interested in writing about "the unusual atmosphere of this city, a 'lost' community without full voting rights, an interesting city that happens to be the company town of the federal government."

* * *

GRIGGS, Tamar 1941-

PERSONAL: Born December 4, 1941, in Tacoma, Wash.; daughter of Chauncey Leavenworth and Johanna (Clement) Griggs. *Education:* Attended Barnard College, 1960-62, and Simon Fraser University, 1976—. *Office:* Whale Workshops, 3316 West 3rd Ave., Vancouver, British Columbia, Canada V6R 1L4.

CAREER: Whale Workshops, Vancouver, British Columbia, instructor, 1971—. Poet, dancer, and artist. *Member:* Friends of Whales (founder).

WRITINGS: There's a Sound in the Sea: A Child's Eye-View of the Whale, Scrimshaw Press, 1975.

WORK IN PROGRESS: "Developing a curriculum for teachers on whales."

SIDELIGHTS: Griggs told *CA,* "I have a passion for the sea, having spent my childhood in it, on it, and near it."

BIOGRAPHICAL/CRITICAL SOURCES: Whalewatcher, May, 1972; *National Geographic,* December, 1976.

* * *

GRIMES, Nikki 1950-

PERSONAL: Born October 20, 1950, in New York, N.Y.; daughter of James (a violinist and composer) and Bernice L. (a keypunch operator; maiden name, McMillan) Grimes; children: Tawfiqa (daughter; deceased). *Education:* Rutgers University, B.A., 1974. *Religion:* "Born Again Christian." *Residence:* New York, N.Y. *Agent:* Joan Daves, 515 Madison Ave., New York, N.Y. 10022.

CAREER: Blackafrica Promotions, Inc., New York, N.Y., talent coordinator, 1970-71; Rutgers University, Livingston College, New Brunswick, N.J., instructor in English, 1971-74; researcher, 1974-75; free-lance writer and photographer, 1975—. Producer of "The Kid Show" on WBAI-Radio. Has lectured at colleges, universities, and workshops, including

Pratt Institute, City University of New York, Studio Museum of Harlem, University of Massachusetts, and New York University. *Member:* Rutgers Institute of Jazz Studies (associate member), Livingston College Community of Arts and Letters. *Awards, honors:* Ford Foundation grant for Africa, 1974-75.

WRITINGS: Poems By, CB Broadside Publications, 1970; *Growin'* (juvenile novel), Dial, 1977; *Something on My Mind* (poems for children), Dial, 1978.

Work anthologized in *Night Comes Softly,* edited by Nikki Giovanni. Contributor to *Collier's Encyclopedia.* Contributor to magazines and newspapers, including *Blackstage, Black World, Time Capsule,* and *Critique.*

WORK IN PROGRESS: A Willingness to Fly, "a novel based on the loss of my daughter [by drowning] and the changes it brought to my life"; editing *Reaching for a Smile,* an anthology of poems by and about black women; "Dumas Lives!," a musical play based on the life and work of black poet, Henry Dumas.

SIDELIGHTS: Nikki Grimes writes: "I began writing when I was six years old. I found it easiest to communicate my feelings on paper. Later on, as a teenager, I decided, unequivocally, that I was to be a writer.

"I was most influenced by James Baldwin who, when I was just seventeen, offered me his advice and counsel. He taught me the value of mastering the mother tongue. But more importantly, he drummed into me the value of a writer maintaining his integrity as an artist and as a human being. I am an avid student of languages, among which are Spanish, Swahili, and Arabic.

"That the quality and quantity of literature for the black child is limited is common knowledge. However, lodging a complaint is not a solution to the problem. The responsibility for creating quality literature and learning materials for black children rests with the black writer. I, for one, have accepted that responsibility and, while I do not write for children alone, I write for children first.

"In general, my fiction is autobiographical. My life and travels have been difficult, but, in surmounting those difficulties, I have learned much that I wish to share. There's no better way to do that than through my work."

AVOCATIONAL INTERESTS: Apartment gardening, interior decorating, handcrafts (crocheting-sewing).

* * *

GRIMES, Paul 1924-

PERSONAL: Born May 8, 1924, in New York, N.Y. *Residence:* New York, N.Y. *Office: New York Times,* 229 West 43rd St., New York, N.Y. 10036.

CAREER/WRITINGS: New York Times, New York City, copy editor and foreign correspondent, 1957-66; *Philadelphia Bulletin,* Philadelphia, Pa., foreign correspondent and editor of special projects, 1966-74; *New York Times,* foreign affairs writer and travel columnist, 1974—. Teacher of journalism and world affairs at Columbia University, Katherine Gibbs School, New York University, and Temple University.

* * *

GRIMSTED, Patricia Kennedy 1935-

PERSONAL: Born October 31, 1935, in Elkins, W.Va.; daughter of John A. (a newspaper and television executive) and Bruce (Lee) Kennedy; married David A. Grimsted, 1960 (divorced, 1974); children: Jennifer Sea, Rolf Davidson, Almon John. *Education:* Attended University of Lausanne, 1952-53, and Swarthmore College, 1953-55; University of California, Berkeley, B.A. (honors), 1957, M.A., 1959, Ph.D., 1964; also attended Middlebury College, summer, 1958. *Residence:* Cambridge, Mass. *Office:* Ukrainian Research Institute, Harvard University, 1581-83 Massachusetts Ave., Cambridge, Mass. 02138.

CAREER: Bucknell University, Lewisburg, Pa., lecturer in history, 1965-67; University of Maryland, College Park, lecturer, 1968-70; American University, Washington, D.C., visiting associate professor, 1970-71, adjunct professor of history, 1971-72; Harvard University, Cambridge, Mass., currently research associate at Russian Research Center, senior fellow at Ukrainian Research Institute, 1974—. Research associate at Harvard University's Russian Research Center, summer, 1964, 1967-68, fellow of Radcliffe Institute, 1967-69; Columbia University, Russian Institute, research associate, 1969-74, senior fellow, 1969-70; visiting research professor at University of Warsaw, 1977.

MEMBER: International Council on Archives, American Historical Association, Society of American Archivists, American Association for the Advancement of Slavic Studies. *Awards, honors:* Woodrow Wilson grant, summer, 1962; American Philosophical Society grant, summer, 1967; American Council of Learned Societies grants for the Soviet Union, 1969, 1972; International Research and Exchanges Board grant for the Soviet Union, 1970, senior exchange scholarships for the Soviet Union, 1973, 1976, research grant for Poland, 1973, travel grants for Scandinavia and Western Europe, 1976, and the Ukraine, 1978; National Endowment for the Humanities research grants, 1973-75, 1975-78; Waldo Gifford Leland Prize from Society of American Archivists, 1973, for *Archives and Manuscripts in the U.S.S.R.,* Volume I: *Moscow and Leningrad.*

WRITINGS: The Foreign Ministers of Alexander I: Political Attitudes and the Conduct of Russian Diplomacy, 1801-1825, University of California Press, 1969; *Archives and Manuscript Repositories in the U.S.S.R.,* Volume I: *Moscow and Leningrad,* Princeton University Press, 1972, supplement, Inter Documentation Co., 1976, Volume II: *Estonia, Latvia, Lithuania, and Belorussia,* Princeton University Press, 1978; (contributor) Bill Katz, editor, *Library Literature,* Volume VI: *The Best of 1975,* Scarecrow, 1976; (editor) *Archives and Manuscript Collections in the U.S.S.R.: Finding Aids on Microfiche,* Inter Documentation Co., Volume I: *Moscow and Leningrad,* 1976, Volume II: *Estonia, Latvia,* 1978. Contributor of articles and reviews to history, Slavic studies, and archivists' journals and newspapers.

WORK IN PROGRESS: Archives and Manuscript Repositories in the U.S.S.R., Volume III: *The Ukraine and Moldavia,* for Princeton University Press.

* * *

GROSS, Beatrice 1935-

PERSONAL: Born January 23, 1935, in New York, N.Y.; daughter of Leonard I. and May (Osterman) Schaap; married Ronald Gross (a writer), June 4, 1956; children: Elizabeth Emily, Peter Jordan. *Education:* Syracuse University, B.A., 1956; attended Columbia University, 1956-57; Bank Street College of Education, M.S., 1958. *Home and office:* 17 Myrtle Dr., Great Neck, N.Y. 11021.

CAREER: New York University, New York, N.Y., lecturer in School for Continuing Education, 1968—. Associate professor at State University of New York College at Old Westbury, 1972-76. Consultant. *Member:* National Education Association, American Association of University Professors, Authors Guild of Authors League of America. *Awards, honors:* Distinguished achievement award from Educational Press Association of America, 1974, for "A Nation of Learners"; S.U.N.Y. Faculty Exchange Scholars award for distinguished scholarship.

WRITINGS: (Editor with husband, Ronald Gross) *Radical School Reform,* Simon & Schuster, 1970; (contributor) *Open Education,* Bantam, 1972; (editor with R. Gross) *Will It Grow in a Classroom?,* Dell, 1974; (editor with R. Gross) *The Children's Rights Movement,* Doubleday, 1977; (editor) *Teaching under Pressure,* Goodyear Publishing, 1978. Contributor to newspapers, education and film journals, and popular magazines, including *Saturday Review, Christian Science Monitor, Parent's Magazine,* and *New York Times Magazine.*

SIDELIGHTS: Beatrice Gross writes: "My main interest lies in documenting successes and failures with children and enabling adults and children to take greater control over their lives. Speaking of the Gross & Gross team, writers have called us 'the Bonnie and Clyde of education' and 'popularizers in the best sense of the word.' I like both descriptions."

* * *

GROSSMAN, Martin (Allen) 1943-

PERSONAL: Born June 15, 1943, in Chicago, Ill.; son of Leon (a photographer) and Esther (Immerman) Grossman; married Julia Becker (an administrator), June 15, 1971; children: Sarah Esther. *Education:* Michigan State University, B.A., 1969; University of Oregon, M.F.A., 1972. *Politics:* Independent. *Religion:* Jewish. *Home:* 511 Campbell, Kalamazoo, Mich. 49007. *Office:* Department of English, Western Michigan University, Kalamazoo, Mich. 49001.

CAREER: Doubleday Book Shop, San Francisco, Calif., assistant manager, 1969-70; Koobdooga Books, Eugene, Ore., buyer and assistant manager, 1970-73; Kellogg Community College, Battle Creek, Mich., instructor in English, 1973-74; Western Michigan University, Kalamazoo, instructor in English, 1974—. *Member:* Associated Writing Programs, Coordinating Council of Literary Magazines. *Awards, honors:* Grants from Coordinating Council of Literary Magazines, 1972-78, National Endowment for the Arts, 1976, P.E.N. Writer's Fund, 1977, and Michigan Council for the Arts, 1977-78.

WRITINGS: The Arable Mind (poetry chapbook), Blue Mountain Press, 1977. Contributor of poems to literary magazines, including *Antioch Review, American Poetry Review, Dragonfly, Midatlantic Review,* and *Raccoon.* Editor of *Skywriting.*

WORK IN PROGRESS: Standing Without Feet (tentative title), poems.

* * *

GROSSMAN, Mary Louise 1930-

PERSONAL: Born July 18, 1930, in Minneapolis, Minn.; daughter of Arthur D. (a professor) and Minnie M. (Watson) Whedon; married Shelly Grossman (a writer and photographer; died, 1975); children: Keith, Julie. *Education:* Carleton College, B.A., 1952. *Home and office:* 955 Camino Santander, Santa Fe, N.M. 87501.

CAREER: Free-lance writer and filmmaker, 1962—. Member of board of directors of Southwest Foundation for Audio-Visual Resources. *Member:* Santa Fe Canyon Association (member of board of directors). *Awards, honors:* Award from *Time,* 1970, for "Vanishing Wilderness," a television series.

WRITINGS: (With John Hamlet) *Birds of Prey of the World,* (illustrated by husband, Shelly Grossman), C. N. Potter, 1964; (with S. Grossman and Hamlet) *The Struggle for Life in the Animal World* (juvenile), Grosset, 1967; (with S. Grossman and Hamlet) *Our Vanishing Wilderness,* Grosset, 1969; (with S. Grossman) *Understanding Ecology* (juvenile), Grosset, 1970; (with S. Grossman) *How and Why Wonder Book of Ecology* (juvenile), Grosset, 1971. Contributor to "Life Nature Library" series, 1963-65.

Films: (Writer and co-producer with S. Grossman) "Life in Parched Lands," Time-Life, 1968; "The Golden Eagle," Films, Inc., 1968; "Vanishing Wilderness" (series), Public Broadcasting System, 1970; "Black Coal, Red Power," Public Broadcasting System, 1972; "The Hopi Way," Films, Inc., 1973; "Man in His Environment" (series), Field Museum of Natural History, 1975-80.

Contributor to popular magazines, including *Sports Illustrated* and *American Heritage.*

WORK IN PROGRESS: A book on the ecology of wildflowers; "When the Rivers Run Dry," a film about water in the Southwest.

SIDELIGHTS: Mary Louise Grossman writes: "The 'Vanishing Wilderness' television series dealt with the effects of man-made changes on the environment and wildlife of the North American continent. 'Man in His Environment,' composed of seven short films, was created for a new hall in the Field Museum. In the first theater, natural laws are shown; in the second theater, nature is meddled with by Man, natural laws are broken by over-consumption, overpopulation and pollution; finally the producers go back to the origins of civilization in western Europe to question whether our institutions are able to cope with present massive environmental problems. The show provides some alternatives to disaster."

* * *

GROVER, John W(agner) 1927-

PERSONAL: Born June 21, 1927, in Moorefield, W. Va.; son of Leon Rex (a bacteriologist) and Evalyn DeChant (a musician; maiden name, Wagner) Grover; married Philippa R. Eby (an occupational therapist), April 5, 1952; children: Jessica, Amy, Ava. *Education:* Harvard University, A.B., 1952, M.D., 1956; postgraduate study at Cambridge University, 1959-61. *Politics:* "Democrat/Independent." *Religion:* Episcopal. *Home:* 10 Rolling Lane, Weston, Mass. 02193. *Office:* Massachusetts General Hospital, 1 Hawthorne Pl., Boston, Mass. 02114.

CAREER: Massachusetts General Hospital, Boston, intern and resident in surgery, 1956-59, gynecologist, 1964—; Boston Hospital for Women, resident in obstetrics and gynecology, 1961-64, obstetrician, 1964—. Member of Massachusetts governor's Commission on the Status of Women, 1972-74. *Military service:* U.S. Navy, 1945-49; became communications technician first class.

MEMBER: American Medical Association, American College of Obstetricians and Gynecologists, American Fertility Society, American Association of Sex Educators and Counselors, Massachusetts Medical Society, Boston Obstetrical Society, Appalachian Mountain Club. *Awards, honors:*

Award from Association of American Film Librarians, 1977, for ''Gentle Birth.''

WRITINGS: (With Dick Grace) *V.D.: The ABC's,* Prentice-Hall, 1972.

Films: ''Not Me Alone'' (childbirth film), Polymorph Films, 1970; ''Gentle Birth,'' Polymorph Films, 1976.

WORK IN PROGRESS: A book about childbirth.

SIDELIGHTS: Grover writes: ''As a practicing obstetrician-gynecologist, I have long been convinced of the value of helping men and women understand themselves better through the experience of childbirth and parenting. I have also been positive about healthy education on sexuality for teenagers. I am convinced of the 'personhood' of the newborn. I believe in a positive approach to the process of bonding and attachment experienced by parents and their newborn. We must facilitate those actions that lead to healthy on-going relationships between newborns and their parents.''

AVOCATIONAL INTERESTS: Hiking, climbing, music (singing, playing, listening), winemaking, weaving, jogging.

*   *   *

GRUENSTEIN, Peter 1947-

PERSONAL: Born April 20, 1947, in New York, N.Y.; son of Harry H. (a businessman) and Jacqueline (a teacher; maiden name, Zoberman) Gruenstein. *Education:* Beloit College, B.A., 1969; attended University of Wisconsin, Madison, 1969-70; George Washington University, J.D. (honors), 1973. *Religion:* Jewish. *Home:* 1500 Arlington Blvd., #1020, Arlington, Va. 22209. *Agent:* Philip G. Spitzer Literary Agency, 111-25 76th Ave., Forest HIlls, N.Y. 11375. *Office:* FANS, 1028 Connecticut Ave., Washington, D.C. 20036.

CAREER: Legislative aide to U.S. Representative Les Aspin in Washington, D.C., 1971-73; free-lance writer, 1972-73; Capitol Hill News Service, Washington, D.C., bureau chief, 1973-76; free-lance writer, 1976-77; currently affiliated with FANS, Washington, D.C.

WRITINGS: (With John Hanrahan) *Last Frontier: The Marketing of Alaska,* Norton, 1977. Contributor to newspapers and to popular magazines, including *Playboy, Nation,* and *Progressive.*

*   *   *

GRUVER, Rebecca
See GOODMAN, Rebecca Gruver

*   *   *

GUARD, Dave
See GUARD, David

*   *   *

GUARD, David 1934-
(Dave Guard)

PERSONAL: Born October 19, 1934, in Honolulu, Hawaii; son of Carl Jackson (a civil engineer) and Marjorie Elizabeth (a secretary; maiden name, Kent) Guard; married Gretchen Ballard (an art director), 1957; children: Catherine Kent, Thomas Jonathan, Sally. *Education:* Stanford University, B.A., 1956. *Home and office:* 107 Degas Rd., Portola Valley, Calif. 94025.

CAREER: Musical performer, 1957—; leader of the original

''Kingston Trio,'' 1957-61, and ''Whiskeyhill Singers,'' 1962; adviser to ''Jazz Meets Folk'' on Australian Broadcasting Corp. Television, 1964; host of ''Dave's Place'' on Australian Broadcasting Corp. Television, 1965; guitar teacher in Portola Valley, Calif., 1968-75; concert performer, 1976—. President of Britannia Enterprises Ltd., 1960—; director of Granada Music Broadcast Music, Inc., 1961-66. Member of singing group ''Hassilev, Settle, & Guard,'' 1974; songwriter and musical arranger; recording artist for Capitol Records and in Australia. Lecturer at colleges.

AWARDS, HONORS: Seven Gold Records from Recording Industry Association of America, 1957-61, as part of ''Kingston Trio''; performed with ''Whiskeyhill Singers'' on Academy Award-winning soundtrack of ''How the West Was Won''; Grammy Award from National Academy of Recording Arts and Sciences, 1958, for ''Tom Dooley,'' as best country and western single recording, and 1959, for ''At Large,'' as best folk music album.

WRITINGS—Under name Dave Guard: *Colour Guitar,* Britannia Enterprises, 1967; *Colour Guitar Primer,* Britannia Enterprises, 1971; *Colour Guitar Reader,* Britannia Enterprises, 1973; (with wife, Gretchen Guard) *Deirdre: A Celtic Legend,* Celestial Arts, 1977; *Halemano: A Legend of Hawaii,* Celestial Arts, 1978; *Grace O'Malley: Irish Pirate Queen,* Celestial Arts, in press. Contributor to *Peninsula.*

WORK IN PROGRESS: ''Pure Gabby,'' an album of music by Gabby Pahinui, for Hula Records.

BIOGRAPHICAL/CRITICAL SOURCES: Baggelaar and Milton, *Folk Music: More Than Just a Song,* Crowell, 1976; *Peninsula,* January, 1977.

*   *   *

GUEST, Judith 1936-

PERSONAL: Born March 29, 1936, in Detroit, Mich.; daughter of Harry Reginald (a business person) and Marion Aline (Nesbit) Guest; married husband, Larry (a data processing executive), August 22, 1958; children: Larry, John, Richard. *Education:* University of Michigan, B.A., 1958. *Residence:* Edina, Minn.

CAREER: Writer. Employed as teacher in public grade schools in Royal Oak, Mich., 1964, Birmingham, Mich., 1969, and Troy, Mich., 1975. *Member:* Detroit Women Writers, Authors Guild, P.E.N. American Center. *Awards, honors:* Janet Heidinger Kafka Prize from University of Rochester, 1977, for *Ordinary People.*

WRITINGS: *Ordinary People* (Book-of-the-Month Club selection), Viking, 1976. Contributor to periodicals, including *The Writer.*

WORK IN PROGRESS: Another novel; research for possible novel on Emanuel Swedenberg.

SIDELIGHTS: Guest's *Ordinary People* is unusual for two reasons. One is that it was the first unsolicited manuscript to be accepted by Viking Press since 1949. Contrary to custom, Guest sent the manuscript without a preceding letter of inquiry and without the usual plot synopsis and outline that many publishing houses require. The second unusual fact about *Ordinary People* is that it was written by a forty-year-old housewife and mother who had begun writing seriously just six years prior to her first published manuscript.

Ordinary People concerns the recovery of a seventeen year old boy returning from an eight-month stay at a mental hospital after attempting suicide. Reviews of the book, which have been generally favorable, are typified in this comment by Walter Clemons: "*Ordinary People* is an unpretentious, expert piece of popular fiction. Perhaps it solves a little too patly some of the problems it raises—particularly in the very entertaining sessions between Conrad and his likable psychiatrist. But the feelings in the book are true and unforced. Guest has the valuable gift of making us like her characters; she has the rarer ability to move a toughened reviewer to tears."

A *New Yorker* critic stated that "Guest steers a brave and fearless course through the potentially hazardous waters of nervous breakdowns, suburban neuroses, and the angst of high-school life with hardly a ripple in her sails," and added that while many of the characters and events described are stock, "all are described so sharply and economically that one forgets that one has been in these waters many times before." However, the critic agreed with Clemons that the psychiatric sessions fall a bit short: "The boy's encounters with a charismatic psychiatrist, despite gallant efforts at an original note (the psychiatrist says 'kiddo' a lot, serves his patients coffee, and is very nimble and hairy), are something of a trial."

Melvin Maddocks made similar observations, commenting that *Ordinary People* though "quite good" is "thoroughly conventional." He further explained that Guest deals with "themes appropriate to Greek tragedy. But she must deal with them in the terms of the well-made suburban novel. Panic equals the rattle of father's ice cube in one-too-many martinis. Despair equals the hundred small ways a Christmas Day falls apart, even when the keys to a new Le Mans for Conrad lie under the tree. Loneliness gets spelled out in the instructions on a frozen TV dinner." If a bit irritated with the flawlessness of the plot and dialogue, Maddox conceded: "Give the author credit though. She has written a truly haunted story in which agony gives gloss a run for the money. The Furies in her suburbs are real, even if she seems to banish them with a spray of Airwick."

Comparing the adolescent struggle in *Ordinary People* with those of *The Catcher in the Rye* and *A Separate Peace*, John Breslin predicted that Guest's book would join the others as "a favorite, even cultic, text both for the journeyers themselves and for their mentors." He noted that though the novel's only flaw may "lie in its very neatness," a "harsh note of realism, carefully prepared for from the very beginning of the novel, saves Judith Guest from the sentimentality that hovers around the edges of her plot." And he was most impressed with Guest's dialogue: "She captures the verbal games men play, whether in a high school locker room or a psychiatrist's office, to keep their emotions well padded and safe from attack. But she knows, too, the sound of the language we all speak in the privacy of our own heads—the eliptical, ironic, sometimes punishing, sometimes defensive commentary that accompanies our public performance."

Lore Dickstein echoed the praise of Guest's dialogue: "The dialogue Conrad has with himself, his psychiatrist, his friends, his family, all rings true with adolescent anxiety, but offered the opinion that the dialogue "is the small hard kernel of brilliance in the novel; the rest is deeply flawed." Dickstein concluded that the author, while stylistically awkward at times, exhibits potential: "Guest has a raw, unpolished talent, but she also has a passionate honesty and sensitivity that cannot be bought from a mail-order Writer's School."

Guest herself feels that she has not developed the character of Conrad's mother to the fullest, but is otherwise satisfied with her book: "It's a first novel, and as a first novel it

pleases me." She is presently experiencing mixed feelings about giving interviews: "Let's face it. It's great fun for a while to have people ask you questions and talk about yourself. But after a while with every interview you give away a big chunk of yourself. You could look up one day and find there's nothing left for you. When that happens, I'll quit."

BIOGRAPHICAL/CRITICAL SOURCES: Washington Post, July 4, 1976; *Newsweek*, July 12, 1976; *New York Times Book Review*, July 16, 1976; *Time*, July 19, 1976; *New Yorker*, July 19, 1976; *Writer*, January, 1977; *Bookviews*, January, 1978; *Contemporary Literary Criticism*, Volume 8, Gale, 1978.

* * *

GUILDS, John C(aldwell, Jr.) 1924-

PERSONAL: Surname rhymes with "child's"; born February 27, 1924, in Columbia, S.C.; son of John Caldwell (a college president) and Lucille (Folk) Guilds; married Carolee Green Heriot, July 3, 1947; children: Carolee Heriot Guilds Calabrese, Reba Lucille, John Caldwell III. *Education:* Wofford College, A.B., 1947; Duke University, A.M., 1949, Ph.D., 1954. *Politics:* Democrat. *Religion:* Episcopal. *Home:* 4396 Fiesta Lane, Houston, Tex. 77004. *Office:* College of Humanities and Fine Arts, University of Houston, Houston, Tex. 77004.

CAREER: Duke University, Durham, N.C., instructor in English, 1949-52; Clemson University, Clemson, S.C., assistant professor of English, 1952-54; East Central State College, Ada, Okla., associate professor of English, 1954-56; Texas Tech University, Lubbock, associate professor, 1956-59, professor of English, 1959-64, chairman of department, 1962-64; University of South Carolina, Columbia, professor of English and chairman of department, 1964-70, vice-provost, 1970-75; University of Houston, Houston, Tex., dean of College of Humanities and Fine Arts, 1975—. Smith-Mundt Professor at University of Damascus, 1959-60. Member of fellowship selection committee for American Council of Learned Societies, 1974—; member of South Carolina Committee on the Humanities, 1971-75. *Military service:* U.S. Army, Infantry, 1943-46; served in European theater; received Bronze Star and Purple Heart.

MEMBER: International Association of University Professors of English, Modern Language Association of America, American Studies Association, Modern Humanities Research Association, South Atlantic Modern Language Association (honorary life member), South Atlantic Association of Departments of English (president, 1971), Phi Beta Kappa, Phi Kappa Phi, Kiwanis. *Awards, honors:* American Philosophical Society grant, 1970.

WRITINGS: (Editor) *Nineteenth-Century Southern Fiction*, C. E. Merrill, 1970; (editor with Richard J. Calhoun) *Tricentennial Anthology of South Carolina Literature, 1670-1970*, University of South Carolina Press, 1971; (editor) William Gilmore Simms, *Stories and Tales*, University of South Carolina Press, 1974.

Also contributor to *The Poetry of Community: Essays on the Southern Sensibility of History and Literature*, 1972. General editor of "The Centennial Edition of the Writings of William Gilmore Simms," 1969-75. Contributor to professional journals.

WORK IN PROGRESS: A biography of William Gilmore Simms.

GURNEY, A(lbert) R(amsdell), Jr.   1930-
(Pete Gurney)

PERSONAL: Born November 1, 1930, in Buffalo, N.Y.; son of Albert Ramsdell (in real estate) and Marion (Spaulding) Gurney; married Mary Goodyear, 1957; children: George, Amy, Evelyn, Benjamin. *Education:* Williams College, B.A., 1952; Yale University, M.F.A., 1958. *Home:* 20 Sylvan Ave., West Newton, Mass. 02165. *Office:* Department of the Humanities, Massachusetts Institute of Technology, Cambridge, Mass. 02139.

CAREER: Teacher of English and Latin at high school in Belmont, Mass., 1959-60; Massachusetts Institute of Technology, Cambridge, professor of humanities, 1960—. *Military service:* U.S. Navy, 1952-55. *Member:* Phi Beta Kappa. *Awards, honors:* Everett Baker Teaching Award, Massachusetts Institute of Technology, 1969; Drama Desk Award, 1971; Rockefeller playwright-in-residence award, 1977.

WRITINGS—Novels: The Gospel According to Joe, Harper, 1974; *Entertaining Strangers,* Doubleday, 1977.

Plays: "Love in Buffalo," produced in New Haven, Conn., 1958; "Tom Sawyer" (musical), first produced in Kansas City, Mo. at Starlight Theatre, July, 1959; "The Bridal Dinner," produced in Cambridge, Mass., 1962; (under pseudonym Pete Gurney) *Around the World in Eighty Days* (two-act musical; based on the book by Jules Verne), Dramatic Publishing, 1962; *The Rape of Bunny Stuntz* (one-act; first produced in New York City at Playwrights Unit, Cherry Lane Theatre, 1964), Samuel French, 1964; *The Comeback* (one-act; first produced in Cambridge, Mass. at Image Theatre, May, 1964), Dramatists Play Service, 1966; *The Golden Fleece* (one-act; first produced in Los Angeles at Mark Taper Forum, June, 1968, produced in New York City, 1968), Samuel French, 1967; *The Problem* (one-act; first produced in London at King's Head Theatre, March, 1973; produced in New York City, January, 1978), Samuel French, 1968; *The Open Meeting* (one-act comedy; first produced in Boston at The Atora Coffee House Theatre, January, 1965), Samuel French, 1968; *The David Show* (one-act; first produced in Tanglewood, Mass., 1966; produced in New York City at Players Theatre, October, 1968), Samuel French, 1968; "Tonight in Living Color" (contains "The David Show" and "The Golden Fleece"), first produced together in New York City at Actors Playhouse, June 10, 1969; *The Love Course* (one-act; first produced in Boston, 1970; produced in London at King's Head Theatre, July, 1974; produced in New York City, 1976), Samuel French, 1969.

Scenes From American Life (two-act; first produced in Tanglewood, Mass., 1970; produced in New York City at Forum Theatre, March, 1971), Samuel French, 1970; *The Old One-Two* (one-act; first produced in Waltham, Mass., 1973; produced in London at King's Head Theatre, August, 1975), Samuel French, 1971; *Children* (two-act; suggested by short story, "Goodbye, My Brother," by John Cheever; first produced in London at Mermaid Theatre, April, 1974; produced in New York City at Manhattan Theatre Club, November, 1976), Samuel French, 1975; *Who Killed Richard Cory?* (one-act; first produced in New York City at Circle Repertory Theatre, March, 1976). Samuel French, 1976; "The Middle Ages," first produced in Los Angeles at Mark Taper Forum Laboratory, 1977; "The Wayside Motor Inn," first produced in New York City at Manhattan Theatre Club, 1977.

Author of Screenplay, "The House of Mirth," 1972. Work

represented in anthologies, including *The Best Short Plays, 1955-56,* edited by Margaret Mayorga, Beacon Press, 1956; *The Best Short Plays, 1957-58,* edited by Mayorga, Beacon Press, 1958; *The Best Short Plays, 1969,* edited by Stanley Richards, Chilton, 1970; *The Best Short Plays, 1970,* edited by Richards, Chilton, 1971.

SIDELIGHTS: "The Golden Fleece" was broadcast by National Educational Television (N.E.T.) on "N.E.T. Playhouse," November 8, 1969.

*   *   *

GURNEY, Peter
See GURNEY, A(lbert) R(amsdell) Jr.

*   *   *

GWALTNEY, John Langston   1928-

PERSONAL: Born September 25, 1928, in Orange, N.J.; son of Stanley and Mabel (Harper) Gwaltney; married wife, Judith; children: Karen, Peter. *Education:* Upsala College, B.A., 1952; New School for Social Research, M.A., 1957; Columbia University, Ph.D., 1967. *Home:* 153 Strong Ave., Syracuse, N.Y. 13210. *Office:* Department of Anthropology, Syracuse University, Syracuse, N.Y. 13210.

CAREER: Henry George School of Social Science, New York, N.Y., lecturer, 1958; State University of New York College at Cortland, Cortland, assistant professor, 1967-69, associate professor of anthropology, 1969-71; Syracuse University, Maxwell Graduate School of Citizenship and Public Affairs, Syracuse, N.Y., associate professor of anthropology, 1971—. Consultant to projects of national science organizations. *Member:* American Anthropological Association (fellow), American Ethnological Society, American Association for the Advancement of Science (member of Committee on Opportunities in Science), National Science Foundation, Latin American Anthropology Group. Society for Applied Anthropology. *Awards, honors:* Ruth Benedict Memorial Award; John Hay Whitney Foundation fellow; National Endowment for the Humanities senior fellow; American Council of Learned Societies fellow; grant-in-aid from State University of New York, American Philosophical Society, and Social Science Research Council; faculty research fellowship from State University of New York; summer faculty grant from New York State Education Department.

WRITINGS: The Thrice Shy: Cultural Accommodations to Blindness and Other Disasters in a Mexican Village, Columbia University Press, 1970; *Role of Expectation of Blindness in an Oaxaca Village,* Columbia University Press, 1970; (contributor) H. Fried, editor, *Explorations in Anthropology,* Crowell, 1973; (contributor) *Renaissance 2,* Yale University Press, 1973. Contributor of articles to journals, including *Natural History, American Scholar, American Anthropologist,* and *Phylon.*

WORK IN PROGRESS: Research on the concept of native anthropology; a book of Afro-American life histories "which is a non-exotic, indigenously derived description of the core Black American nation."

SIDELIGHTS: Gwaltney, a blind anthropologist, has done fieldwork among the Ethiopian Hebrew Congregation and Commandment Keepers in Harlem, urban Afro-Americans in the Northeastern states, Highland Chinantec Indians of Oaxaca, Mexico, Shinnecock and Poospatuck Indians of Long Island, and the Maroons of St. Elizabeth Parish, Jamaica. He told *CA* that his "major teaching and research interests are Black ecumeny, minority-majority relations, ethnicity, social race hierarchies, the status of the handicapped, sexism, and speciesism. Area interests include the Caribbean, Meso-america and West Africa.''

* * *

GYORGYEY, Clara 1936-

PERSONAL: Born May 23, 1936, in Budapest, Hungary; came to the United States in 1957, naturalized citizen, 1963; daughter of Leslie (an engineer) and Charlotte (Mendel) Takacs; married Ferenc A. Gyorgyey (a medical historian), February 20, 1960; children: Katalin, Maria. *Education:* University of Budapest, B.A., 1954; Institute of Foreign Languages, Budapest, Hungary, M.A., 1955; Yale University, M.A.T., 1959. *Politics:* "Consistently anti-Communist." *Religion:* "In time of calamity." *Home:* 42 Derby Ave., Orange, Conn. 06477. *Agent:* Marton Agency, 96 Fifth Ave., New York, N.Y. 10011.

CAREER: Yale University, New Haven, Conn., research assistant, 1957-60, instructor in English, 1960—. Director of student plays at Gyorgyey Theatre, 1967-76; chairwoman of Yale University Woman's Organization Drama Club and Connecticut Arts Council nominating committee for the literary Nobel Prize, 1977. *Member:* International P.E.N.

(president of Writers-in-Exile Center), Modern Language Association of America, American Hungarian Educators Association, Authors' League, Arpad Academy, Yale University Woman's Organization.

WRITINGS: Edgar Allan Poe and Walt Whitman in Hungary, Hungarian Academy of Science, 1976; (translator) Ferenc Karinthy, *Ephepheh* (novel), Corvina, 1977; (translator and contributor) *The Anthology of Hungarian Poetry, 1400-1700,* Jupiter Press, 1977; (translator) Peter Mueller, *The Celebrity* (novel), Potocsnyi, 1978; (translator) Istvan Orkeny, *Catgame and Tot Family* (two novels), Doubleday, 1979; *Ferenc Molnar, the Perpetual Emigre,* Twayne, 1979.

Translator of scripts: Imre Sarkady, "Man on the Pillar" (two-act play), first produced in North Haven, Conn., at Pumpkin Hall, 1976; Orkeny, "Catsplay" (two-act play), first produced in Washington, D.C. at Arena Theater, 1977; Orkeny, "Keysearchers" (two-act play), first produced in Washington, D.C. at Arena Theater, 1977; Mueller, "The Captain" (motion picture script), 1978.

SIDELIGHTS: Clara Gyorgyey writes: "As one of the much-celebrated Hungarian freedom fighters of 1956, I am still in awe; it's a miracle that we've survived. And we are everywhere! It can happen only in America that a Hungarian is teaching English with an accent. This year I'll be going to Australia—the only continent I haven't visited yet."

H

HACKER, Marilyn 1942-

PERSONAL: Born November 27, 1942, in New York, N.Y.; daughter of Albert Abraham (a management consultant) and Hilda (a teacher; maiden name, Rosengarten) Hacker; married Samuel R. Delang (a writer), August 22, 1961 (separated, December, 1974); children: Iva Alyxander Hacker-Delang. *Education:* New York University, B.A., 1964. *Politics:* Feminist. *Residence:* New York, N.Y. *Agent:* Frances Collin, 141 East 55th St., New York, N.Y. 10022.

CAREER: Poet. Antiquarian bookseller in London, England, 1971-76. *Member:* P.E.N., Poetry Society of America. *Awards, honors:* Lamont Poetry Selection of Academy of American Poets and New York YWHA Poetry Center discovery award, both 1973, both for *Presentation Piece;* National Book Award in Poetry, 1975, for *Presentation Piece;* Jenny McKeen Moore fellowship for writers at George Washington University, 1976-77.

*WRITINGS—*Poems: *Presentation Piece,* Viking, 1974; *Separations,* Knopf, 1976. Editor, *City,* 1967-70, and *Quark* (a speculative fiction quarterly), 1970-71.

WORK IN PROGRESS: Editing and writing an introduction to a volume of H.D.'s poems about women, to be published by Out & Out Books; compiling and editing an H.D. newsletter, with Mario Pousot.

SIDELIGHTS: Verse forms included in Hacker's award-winning first book, *Presentation Piece,* are sonnets, sestinas, villanelles, blank verse, and heroic couplets. Some reviewers have commented that Hacker's adherence to formal structure has resulted in poems that are nothing more than technical exercises. Norma Procopiow wrote, "The poems seem created, not with urgency or commitment, but to display craftmanship." Similarly, Ben Howard found the more formal poems of the group to "fall victim to artifice," while finding the poems in freer forms to be "more convincing."

Peter Meinke, however, lauded Hacker's poems for showing "the rich possibilities inherent in structure." He continued: "I suppose it is still fashionable to think that intellect and wit are somehow incompatible with deeply felt poetry—one can't be romantic and ironic at the same time—but *Presentation Piece* encourages me to think that the fashion may be changing."

Hacker's wit is often mentioned favorably in reviews of her poetry. Christopher Ricks commented: "Marilyn Hacker stands squarely, and very elegantly, in the indirect T. S. Eliot line. She is sharp-eyed and -edged, cool, very acute about sophistication and its falsities, and very witty. Her wit is at its best when it is at one with her humor and her good humor."

The use of language in Hacker's poems has impressed several critics. Honor Moore said that the poems seem "as much about language as life. There is something very disturbing about her images, the kind of disturbance you feel jostling through an unfamiliar street: everything is too vivid." Howard noted: "Over and again one encounters images of the body, especially the tongue; of salt upon the tongue; of the sea, cliffs, a beach; of lovers awakening. And it becomes apparent that the poet is attempting to formulate, in these and related images, a language of instinct and feeling—of a woman's bodily awareness—and to express the body's longings, including its 'inadmissible longings' as they are shaped and repressed in personal relationships."

BIOGRAPHICAL/CRITICAL SOURCES: Book World, May 26, 1974; *New Republic,* September 7, 1974; *New York Times Book Review,* January 12, 1975, August 8, 1976; *Poetry,* April, 1975; *Ms.,* April, 1975; *Contemporary Literary Criticism,* Gale, Volume 5, 1976, Volume 9, 1978; *Nation,* September 18, 1976; *Times Literary Supplement,* October 29, 1976.

*　　*　　*

HACKETT, Philip 1941-

PERSONAL: Born April 10, 1941, in Boston, Mass.; son of Paul (an artist) and Mary (Addario) Hackett. *Education:* Attended University of New Mexico, City College of San Francisco, San Francisco State College, Saddleback College, and Bridgewater State College. *Politics:* Independent. *Religion:* None. *Home address:* P.O. Box 424, Astor Station, Boston, Mass. 02123.

CAREER: Writer and poet. Worked in public relations. Founder, organizer, and director of poetry readings at Boston Center for the Arts, Poets' Lib, Poetry on the Plaza, and Poetry in the Gallery (all in Boston), Laguna Beach Free Poets, and other Laguna Beach locations; founder and director of Laguna Beach International Poetry Festival, 1972, 1974, 1975; has given readings throughout California and New England. *Military service:* U.S. Army, 1960-63. *Awards, honors:* National Poetry Press award, 1970, for "Homage to Picasso."

WRITINGS: (Editor) *Poetry on the Plaza,* City Printers, 1977. Work represented in *Five Poets,* April Publications, 1978. Contributor of poems to magazines and newspapers, including *Stone Country, Bardic Echoes, Human Voice Quarterly, Poetry East-West,* and *Orion.*

WORK IN PROGRESS: Selected Poems of Philip Hackett.

AVOCATIONAL INTERESTS: International travel (Germany, Austria, England, France, Belgium, the Netherlands, Luxembourg, Switzerland, Italy).

* * *

HACKETT, Roger F(leming) 1922-

PERSONAL: Born October 23, 1922, in Kobe, Japan; American citizen born abroad; son of Harold Wallace (a college administrator) and Anna (Powell) Hackett; married Caroline Gray, August 24, 1946; children: Anne (Mrs. Daniel J. Buckley), David Gray, Brian Vance. *Education:* Carleton College, B.A., 1947; Harvard University, M.A., 1949, Ph.D., 1955. *Home:* 2122 Dorset Rd., Ann Arbor, Mich. 48104. *Office:* Department of History, University of Michigan, Ann Arbor, Mich. 48109.

CAREER: Northwestern University, Evanston, Ill., instructor, 1953-55, assistant professor, 1955-59, associate professor of history, 1959-61; University of Michigan, Ann Arbor, associate professor, 1961-66, professor of history, 1966—, chairman of department, 1975-77, director of Center for Japanese Studies, 1968-71. *Military service:* U.S. Marine Corps, 1942-46; became captain. *Member:* American Historical Society, Association for Asian Studies (member of executive committee and board of directors, 1966-69), Japan Society.

WRITINGS: (Contributor) Marius Jansen, editor, *Changing Japanese Attitudes Toward Modernization,* Princeton University Press, 1965; (contributor) Robert Ward, editor, *Political Development in Modern Japan,* Princeton University Press, 1968; *Yamagata Aritomo in the Rise of Modern Japan, 1838-1922,* Harvard University Press, 1971; (contributor) John Harrison, editor, *Enduring Scholarship Selected from the Far Eastern Quarterly-The Journal of Asian Studies, 1941-1971,* University of Arizona Press, 1972; (contributor) Arthur Tiedeman, editor, *An Introduction to Japanese Civilization,* Columbia University Press, 1974. Editor of *Journal of Asian Studies,* 1959-62.

WORK IN PROGRESS: Research on the role of the military in the modern development of Japan, attempting to "assess the economic, social, and political impact on nineteenth-and early twentieth-century Japan of the organization of a modern military system based on universal conscription."

* * *

HAGEN, Uta 1919-

PERSONAL: Born June 12, 1919, in Goettingen, Germany; daughter of Oskar Frank (a professor) and Thyra (Leisner) Hagen; married Jose Ferrer (an actor), December 8, 1938 (divorced, June 1948); married Herbert Berghof (a director, actor, and teacher), January 25, 1957; children: Leticia Ferrer Teuscher. *Education:* Attended Royal Academy of Dramatic Art, 1936, and University of Wisconsin, 1937. *Residence:* New York, N.Y. *Agent:* Lucy Kroll, 390 West End Ave., New York, N.Y. 10024. *Office:* Herbert Berghof Studio, 120 Bank St., New York, N.Y. 10014.

CAREER: Actress for stage, television, and motion pic-

tures, 1937—. Notable roles include stage performances in "The Sea Gull," 1938, "Othello," 1943, "Angel Street," 1948, "A Streetcar Named Desire," 1948, "The Country Girl," 1950, "Saint Joan," 1951, "Tovarich," 1952, "Who's Afraid of Virginia Woolf," 1962, and "The Cherry Orchard," 1968; television performances on "Playhouse 90," "KRAFT Theatre," "CBS Playhouse," and numerous other network shows; motion picture performance in "The Other," Warner Bros., 1972, "The Boys From Brazil," 1978. Co-founder and acting teacher at HB Studio, New York City, 1947—. *Awards, honors:* Antoinette Perry Award (Tony), New York Drama Critics' Award, and the Donaldson Award, all 1951, all for her portrayal of Georgie in "The Country Girl"; Tony Award and Drama Critics' Circle Award, both 1963, both for her portrayal of Martha in "Who's Afraid of Virginia Woolf?"; Doctor of Fine Arts from Smith College, 1978.

WRITINGS: Respect for Acting, 1972; *Love for Cooking,* Macmillan, 1976.

WORK IN PROGRESS: Need for Nature.

SIDELIGHTS: Hagen commented: "Imitation in acting as well as in all other art forms is the death of art."

BIOGRAPHICAL/CRITICAL SOURCES: Edward R. Murrow, *This I Believe,* Simon & Schuster, 1954.

* * *

HAIGHT, Amanda 1939-

PERSONAL: Born December 18, 1939, in Los Angeles, Calif.; daughter of George (a producer) and Justine (an actress; maiden name, Chase) Haight; married Leigh Caines (a farmer); children: Justine Gwendolen, Rebecca Anne. *Education:* Earned Dr.Phil. from University of London. *Home:* Bells Line Rd., Nilpin, New South Wales, Australia 2758.

CAREER: Writer. Has also worked as a teacher, interpreter, guide, and for the Russian Service of the British Broadcasting Co. (BBC).

WRITINGS: Anna Akhmatova: A Poetic Pilgrimage, Oxford University Press, 1976.

SIDELIGHTS: Haight's literary biography of Anna Akhmatova, a Russian poet, authority on Alexander Pushkin, and "ultimately victorious heroine of the struggle for women's liberation," was reviewed by Clarence Brown in the *New York Times Book Review:* "Of all Akhmatova's many foreign visitors during the last years of her life, none, I daresay, was more intimately and frequently received than Amanda Haight, a brilliant young American-born English student of Russian literature, who met her great friend in 1964, and has now written the first full-scale biography. She was able to draw upon her close acquaintance not only with Akhmatova but also with most of Akhmatova's lifelong friends, such as the gifted Lydia Chukovskaya, and, no less important, upon her own impressive knowledge of 'Soviet reality.'"

BIOGRAPHICAL/CRITICAL SOURCES: New York Times Book Review, December 26, 1976.

* * *

HALEY, Alex (Palmer) 1921-

PERSONAL: Born August 11, 1921, in Ithaca, N.Y.; son of Simon Alexander (a professor) and Bertha George (a teacher; maiden name, Palmer) Haley; married Nannie Branch, 1941 (divorced, 1964); married Juliette Collins, 1964 (divorced); children: Lydia Ann, William Alexander, Cynthia Gertrude. *Education:* Attended Elizabeth City Teachers College, 1937-39. *Office:* Kinte Corporation, 1801 Avenue of the Stars, Los Angeles, Calif. 90067.

CAREER: U.S. Coast Guard, 1939-59, retiring as chief journalist; free-lance writer, 1959—. Founder and president of Kinte Corporation, Los Angeles, Calif., 1972—. Adviser to African American Heritage Association, Detroit, Mich. *Member:* Authors Guild, Society of Magazine Writers. *Awards, honors:* Litt. D. from Simpson College, 1970; special citation from National Book Award committee, 1977, for *Roots;* special citation from Pulitzer Prize committee, 1977, for *Roots.*

WRITINGS: (With Malcolm X) *The Autobiography of Malcolm X,* Grove, 1965; *Roots: The Saga of an American Family,* Doubleday, 1976. Initiated "Playboy Interviews" feature for *Playboy,* 1962. Contributor to periodicals, including *Reader's Digest, New York Times Magazine, Harper's,* and *Atlantic.*

WORK IN PROGRESS: My Search for Roots, an account of how *Roots* was researched and written; a study of Henning, Tenn., where Haley was raised.

SIDELIGHTS: Haley's book *Roots* is seldom mentioned without the word phenomenon tacked on. Combined with the impact of the televised "mini-series," *Roots* has become a "literary-television phenomenon" and a "sociological event," according to *Time.* By April, 1977, almost two million hardcover copies of the book had been sold and 130 million people had seen all or part of the eight episode television series.

Although critics generally lauded Haley for his accomplishment, they seemed unsure whether to treat *Roots* as a novel or as a historical account. While it is based on factual events, dialogue, thoughts, and emotions of characters are fictionalized. Haley himself described the book as "faction," a mixture of fact and fiction. Lance Morrow contended that *Roots* "cannot be evaluated merely as history or merely as an entertainment. As either one of those, it fails. Yet as both, in resonance with the long, complex American experience on the subject, *Roots* is extremely powerful." While finding the mixture of fact and fiction somewhat inconvenient to the reader who finds himself "having to keep the peace" between them in his mind, Jervis Anderson said that it would be "ungenerous to press this charge against Haley too strongly, considering the stern necessity that drove him—his desire to see and understand himself more wholly.... In composing his work of 'faction,' Haley may have felt the need to do what many of the rest of us must: complete ourselves, as best we can, by an act of imagination." And despite the fictional characterizations, Willie Lee Rose suggested that Kunte Kinte's parents Omoro and Binte "could possibly become the African proto-parents of millions of Americans who are going to admire their dignity and grace." *Newsweek* found that Haley's decision to fictionalize was the right approach: "Instead of writing a scholarly monograph of little social impact, Haley has written a blockbuster in the best sense—a book that is bold in concept and ardent in execution, one that will reach millions of people and alter the way we see ourselves."

Some concern was voiced, especially at the time of the television series, that racial tension in America would be aggravated by *Roots.* But while *Time* reported several incidents of racial violence following the telecast, it commented that "most observers thought that in the long term, *Roots* would improve race relations, particularly because of the televised version's profound impact on whites.... A broad consensus

seemed to be emerging that *Roots* would spur black identity, and hence black pride, and eventually pay important dividends." Some black leaders viewed *Roots* "as the most important civil rights event since the 1965 march on Selma," according to *Time.* Vernon Jordan, executive director of the National Urban League called it "the single most spectacular educational experience in race relations in America."

Haley has heard only positive comments from both blacks and whites. He told William Marmon: "The blacks who are buying books are not buying them to go out and fight someone, but because they want to know who they are. *Roots* is all of our stories. It's the same for me or any black. It's just a matter of filling in the blanks—which person, living in which village, going on what ship, across the same ocean, slavery, emancipation, the struggle for freedom.... The white response is more complicated. But when you start talking about family, about lineage and ancestry, you are talking about every person on earth. We all have it; it's a great equalizer.... I think the book has touched a strong, subliminal cord." Lucille Clifton commented that Haley's accomplishment of "finding and assigning true names is one beyond words, like grace; it is grace. It is what the poet spends her/his life trying for. The naming of things."

But there was also concern, according to *Time,* that "breast-beating about the past may turn into a kind of escapism, distracting attention from the present. Only if *Roots* turns the anger at yesterday's slavery into anger at today's ghetto will it really matter." And James Baldwin wrote: "*Roots* is a study of continuities, of consequences, of how a people perpetuate themselves, how each generation helps to doom, or helps to liberate, the coming one—the action of love, or the effect of the absence of love, in time. It suggests, with great power, how each of us, however unconsciously, can't but be the vehicle of the history which has produced us. Well, we can perish in this vehicle, children, or we can move on up the road."

Since the publication of *Roots* in October, 1976, Haley has signed at least 500 books daily, spoken to an average of 6,000 people a day, and has traveled round trip coast-to-coast at least once a week, according to *People.* Stardom has taken its toll on Haley. *New Times* reported that on a recent trip to his ancestral village in Africa, Haley complained: "You'll find that people who celebrate you will kill you. They forget you are blood and flesh and bone. I have had days and weeks and months of schedules where everything from my breakfast to my last waking moment was planned for me.... Someone has you by the arm and is moving you from room to room. Then people *grab* at you. You're actually pummeled—hit with books—and you ask yourself, 'My God, what *is* this?'"

Although Haley now wishes that he were famous "one day a month," stardom was not always a problem. Upon retiring from the Coast Guard in 1959, he decided to become a free-lance writer and headed for Greenwich Village, rented a basement apartment, and "prepared to starve," as he told John Baker. Unwilling to take a job because he wanted to devote his full energies to writing, he came close to starving. "One day," he related to Baker, "I was down to 18 cents and a couple of cans of sardines, and that was *it.*" The next day a check came for an article he had written and he struggled on. Today the 18 cents and cans of sardines are framed and hang in the library of his home as symbols of his "determination to be independent."

BIOGRAPHICAL/CRITICAL SOURCES: Publishers Weekly, September 6, 1976; *Saturday Review,* September

18, 1976; *New York Times Book Review*, September 26, 1976, January 2, 1977, February 27, 1977; *Newsweek*, September 27, 1976, February 14, 1977; *New York Times*, October 14, 1976; *Time*, October 18, 1976, February 14, 1977; *New York Review of Books*, November 11, 1976; *Ms.*, February, 1977; *New Yorker*, February 14, 1977; *Forbes*, February 15, 1977; *National Review*, March 4, 1977; *New Republic*, March 12, 1977; *People*, March 28, 1977; *Ebony*, April, 1977; *New Times*, July 8, 1977; *Contemporary Literary Criticism*, Volume 8, Gale, 1978.

* * *

HALEY, James L(ewis) 1951-

PERSONAL: Born December 14, 1951, in Tulsa, Okla.; son of Kenneth Houston (in business) and Georgia (Lewis) Haley. *Education:* University of Texas, Arlington, B.A., 1975; graduate study at University of Texas, Austin, 1976—. *Politics:* "Avenging liberal." *Religion:* Christian. *Home:* 3507 Banton Rd., Austin, Tex. 78722. *Office:* Urban Law Review, School of Law, University of Texas, 2500 Red River, Austin, Tex. 78705.

CAREER: Big Thicket Association, Saratoga, Tex., executive assistant to the president, 1973; executive director of Wildlands Preservation Society, 1973—. Tennis instructor at University of Texas, Arlington, and at country clubs. Member of Biblical Studies Center at University of Texas. *Member:* Alpha Chi, Phi Alpha Delta.

WRITINGS: The Buffalo War: The History of the Red River Indian Uprising of 1874, Doubleday, 1976; *T'Inde: A History and Culture-Portrait of the Apache Indians*, Doubleday, in press. Contributor to *American Heritage*. Editor-in-chief of *Urban Law Review*, 1977—.

WORK IN PROGRESS: A biography of P. T. Barnum; novels; a play; research on nature education, conservation, parks and reserves, and urban and environmental law.

SIDELIGHTS: Haley comments: "I am still sufficiently awed by the prospect of people paying money to read *my* thoughts as to have little to communicate; and my bibliography is too short to give me much right to if I wanted.

"For now, let me venture that I am much concerned with the artistic responsibility of a writer to reach his readers on a heart-to-heart level. In the future I would like to see my creative writing deal with the classical literary masonry of good, solid craft. My professional writing in the conservation field will likely question the place of conservation in politics. Taking care of our planet has become a matter of pro-or-con labels that are gross oversimplifications. Conservation should be a matter of daily personal hygiene, but advocates on both sides of the fence insist on keeping boxed categories of heroes, villains, bugaboos, and crusades."

AVOCATIONAL INTERESTS: Camping, nature and wildlife photography, tennis.

* * *

HALL, F. H. 1926-

PERSONAL: Born June 12, 1926, in Ohio; son of F. H. (a soldier) and Norma E. (Kern) Hall. *Education:* Ohio University, B.A., 1950, M.A., 1955. *Politics:* "Not as liberal as I used to be." *Home:* 13661 Iyopawa Island, Coldwater Lake, Coldwater, Mich. 49036. *Agent:* Philip G. Spitzer Literary Agency, 111-25 76th Ave., Forest Hills, N.Y. 11375. *Office:* Millersburg Military Institute, Millersburg, Ky. 40348.

CAREER: Worked as instructor in English and tennis and as wrestling coach; currently employed by Millersburg Military Institute, Millersburg, Ky. *Military service:* U.S. Army; paratrooper, served in Europe and Korea; received Silver Star. *Member:* Authors Guild of Authors League of America.

WRITINGS: In the Lamb White Days, Bobbs-Merrill, 1975.

SIDELIGHTS: Hall comments: "I like to write and read history—principally the early history of North American exploration, and read about, work on, and sail cruising sailboats on the Great Lakes. The sailing and history of sailing on the lakes has become an obsession." *Avocational interests:* Tennis, hiking.

* * *

HALL, Haywood 1898-
(Harry Haywood)

PERSONAL: Born February 13, 1898, in South Omaha, Neb.; son of Haywood (a meatpacker) and Harriet (Thorpe) Hall; married Gwendolyn Midlo (a college professor), 1955; children: Haywood, Becky. *Education:* Attended Communist University of the Toilers of the East (KUTVA), 1926-28, and Lenin School, 1928-30. *Politics:* Communist. *Religion:* None. *Office:* 201 Eastern Parkway, #5F, Brooklyn, N.Y. 11238.

CAREER: Communist Party organizer, 1925-59, and 1977—. *Military service:* U.S. Army, 1917-18. U.S. Merchant Marine, 1942-50.

WRITINGS—Under name Harry Haywood: *Negro Liberation*, International Publishers, 1948, reprinted, Liberator Press, 1975; *For a Revolutionary Position on the Negro Question*, Liberator Press, 1975; *Black Bolshevik: Autobiography of an Afro-American Communist*, Liberator Press, 1978. Author of Communist pamphlets.

WORK IN PROGRESS: Collecting previous writings.

SIDELIGHTS: Haywood has spent his life working toward socialist revolution in the United States. He was the first American communist to contend that blacks constitute an oppressed nation in the deep South, with full rights to self-determination, and he has continued to fight for this position ever since. He led the fight against the right-wing takeover of the Communist Party in the United States, especially what he considered to be its betrayal of the black liberation movement. Today, he is still active in the Party.

His autobiography sums up his experiences in the revolutionary movement. The son of former slaves, Haywood's experiences took him from the Midwest to the Soviet Union, during the early years of socialist construction, and then back to the United States during the years that saw people march in defense of the "Scottsboro Boys," the building of the militant and revolutionary Alabama Sharecroppers Union, and campaigns against fascism and war. Then, Haywood feels, the Party lost its great initiative, not, as so many others have written, because of the repression of McCarthyism, but because of its own internal weaknesses. The book concludes with his analysis of the black revolt of the 1960's, and his own optimistic outlook for the future of the revolutionary and people's movement in the United States.

Hall was an American volunteer in the Spanish Civil War.

* * *

HALL, Richard H(ammond) 1934-

PERSONAL: Born October 6, 1934, in Philadelphia, Pa.;

son of Edwin L. (an engineer) and Carol (Van Bolt) Hall; married Sharon Miller, June 21, 1958; children: Thomas S. M., Julie H. *Education:* Denison University, A.B., 1956; Ohio State University, M.A., 1958, Ph.D., 1961. *Home:* 16 Turner Lane, Loundonville, N.Y. 12211. *Office:* Department of Sociology, State University of New York at Albany, 1400 Washington Ave., Albany, N.Y. 12222.

CAREER: Indiana University, Bloomington, instructor, 1961-64, assistant professor, 1964-66, associate professor of sociology, 1966-67; University of Minnesota, Minneapolis, associate professor, 1967-70, professor of sociology, 1970-77, chairman of department, 1976-77; State University of New York at Albany, professor of sociology, 1977—. Visiting professor at University of Vermont, 1974-75. Program manager for National Science Foundation, 1971-72. Member of National Ski Patrol. *Member:* American Sociological Association (member of board of directors, 1968-72), Midwest Sociological Society (president, 1976-77). *Awards, honors:* Grants from National Science Foundation, 1965-77, and National Institute of Mental Health, 1970.

WRITINGS: Occupations and the Social Structure, Prentice-Hall, 1969, revised edition, 1975; *Organizations: Structure and Process,* Prentice-Hall, 1972, revised edition, 1977; (editor) *The Formal Organization,* Basic Books, 1972; (with L. W. Goodman, S. Green, P. Hammond, and M. C. Taylor) *The Structure of Society,* Heath, 1975. Contributor to journals in the social sciences. Member of editorial board of *American Journal of Sociology, Administrative Science Quarterly, Sociology of Work and Occupations, Sociological Quarterly,* and *Organization and Administrative Sciences.*

WORK IN PROGRESS: Interorganizational Relationships.

SIDELIGHTS: Hall comments briefly: "I'm currently interested in examining organizations in their political context, as actors seeking to improve their competitive positions."

* * *

HALLA, R(obert) C(hristian) 1949-
(Ezra Billings)

PERSONAL: Born February 16, 1949, in Oshkosh, Wis.; son of Floyd E. (a factory foreman) and Laura B. (a seamstress; maiden name, Roberts) Halla; married Janet L. Gramoll, August 23, 1969; children: Joshua Aaron. *Education:* University of Wisconsin—Oshkosh, B.S., 1973. *Home address:* P.O. Box 252, 395 Blaine St., Iola, Wis. 54945. *Office:* Krause Publications, Iola, Wis. 54945.

CAREER: Wisconsin Review, Oshkosh, fiction editor, 1972-73; Oshkosh Truck Corp., Oshkosh, editor and writer, 1973-75; Harley-Davidson, Milwaukee, Wis., writer, 1977; Wolfsong Publications, Iola, Wis., editor and publisher, 1977—; Krause Publications, Iola, associate editor, 1977—. Judge of poetry contests. *Member:* Committee of Small Magazine Editors and Publishers, Coordinating Council of Literary Magazines, Society of Automotive Historians, Associated Writing Programs.

WRITINGS: (With Dale David) *River Bottom* (poetry), Broken Arrow Press, 1973; *Adventures of a Freelance Farmer* (poetry), River Bottom Press, 1976. Author of "The Woods in the Seasons," a column in *View.* Contributor of stories, poems, features, and reviews to magazines, sometimes under pseudonym Ezra Billings. Editor of *River Bottom,* 1973-77.

WORK IN PROGRESS: River Boy, River Town, River,

poems; long poem cycles on King Arthur and on the wives of Henry VIII; research on the history of Wisconsin counties.

SIDELIGHTS: Halla comments: "My main interest, which is obvious in my own writing, is a need to define the human condition in terms of my own past and present, and perhaps by that road come to a larger understanding of universals. I am also interested in Wisconsin history and lore and in the phenomenon of one-room schoolhouses. As for the writing of others, I am dedicated to the small press and continue to do what little is in my power to further the small press and the writings therein."

* * *

HALLIDAY, Brett
See DRESSER, Davis

* * *

HAMILTON, Adam
See GRANBECK, Marilyn

* * *

HAMILTON, Charles Vernon 1929-

PERSONAL: Born October 19, 1929, in Muskogee, Okla.; son of Owen and Viola (Haynes) Hamilton; married Dona Louise Cooper, October 5, 1956; children: Carol, Valli. *Education:* Roosevelt University, B.A., 1951; Loyola University, Chicago, Ill., J.D., 1954; University of Chicago, M.A., 1957, Ph.D., 1963. *Office:* Department of Political Science, Columbia University, New York, N.Y. 10027.

CAREER: Albany State College, Albany, Ga., instructor in political science, 1957-58; Tuskegee Institute, Tuskegee, Ala., assistant professor of political science, 1958-60; Rutgers University, New Brunswick, N.J., instructor in political science, 1963-64; Lincoln University, Lincoln University, Pa., instructor in political science, 1964-67; Roosevelt University, Chicago, Ill., professor of political science, 1967-69; Columbia University, New York, N.Y., professor of political science, 1969—. *Military service:* U.S. Army, 1948-49.

MEMBER: National Association for the Advancement of Colored People (NAACP), American Political Science Association (vice-president, 1972-73). *Awards, honors:* John Hay Whitney fellowship, 1962; Lindback Distinguished Teaching award, Lincoln University, 1965; University of Chicago Alumni award and Roosevelt University Alumni award, both 1970.

WRITINGS: Minority Politics in Black Belt Alabama, McGraw, 1962; (with Stokley Carmichael) *Black Power: The Politics of Liberation in America,* Vintage, 1967; *The Black Preacher in America,* Morrow, 1972; (co-author) *The Social Scene,* Winthrop, 1972; *The Black Experience in American Politics,* Putnam, 1973; *The Bench and the Ballot: Southern Federal Judges and Black Voters,* Oxford University Press, 1973. Contributor to scholarly journals.

SIDELIGHTS: Political Science Quarterly calls *The Bench and the Ballot* "a general chronicle of one aspect of the civil rights struggle." *Choice* says that Hamilton "has done us a service with his detailed treatment of the handling of a sampling of voting rights cases by U.S. district judges in the South. Three judicial types are analyzed: the judge who aggressively enforces the law and seeks justice; the racist judge who obstructs justice; the racist judge who is willing to be educated to dispense justice." The reviewer goes on to call *The Bench and the Ballot* "a very readable lesson on the effectiveness of using the courts to administer the law." Daniel Morrisey states that the book "serves as a provocative monograph on the relationship between the law and social change. . . ." He adds that "Hamilton strongly hints that economic independence is almost a precondition to political freedom."

Saturday Review reports that in *Black Power: The Politics of Liberation in America* the authors "have set down the philosophy and concept of Black Power as it has painfully emerged out of the urban and rural black ghettos these last thirteen years. Their accomplishment is extraordinary." The reviewer contends that the book is "surely the most important document to have come forth from the whole black-white arena of public affairs, perhaps the most significant single piece of writing in this area since the 1954 Supreme Court decision declaring public school segregation unconstitutional. . . ."

BIOGRAPHICAL/CRITICAL SOURCES: Saturday Review, November 11, 1967; *Christian Science Monitor,* November 18, 1967; *Political Science Quarterly,* March, 1974; *Choice,* March, 1974, April, 1974; *Commonweal,* April 26, 1974.*

*   *   *

HAMILTON, Edith   1867-1963

PERSONAL: Born August 12, 1867, in Dresden, Germany; daughter of Montgomery and Gertrude (Pond) Hamilton. *Education:* Bryn Mawr College, B.A. and M.A., both 1895; further study at University of Leipzig and University of Munich, 1895-96. *Religion:* Presbyterian. *Residence:* Washington, D.C.; and Bar Harbor, Me.

CAREER: Bryn Mawr School, Baltimore, Md., headmistress, 1896-1922; full-time writer, beginning 1922. *Member:* National Institute of Arts and Letters, American Academy of Arts and Letters, P.E.N. *Awards, honors:* Mary E. Garrett European fellow at the Universities of Leipzig and Munich, 1895-96; D.Litt. from the University of Rochester, 1949, University of Pennsylvania, 1953, and Yale University, 1959; National Achievement Award, 1950; was named an honorary citizen of Athens, Greece, and received the Greek Golden Cross of the Order of Benefaction, 1957; Constance Lindsay Skinner Award from Women's National Book Association, 1958.

WRITINGS: The Greek Way, Norton, 1930, reprinted, Avon, 1973, enlarged editions published as *The Great Age of Greek Literature,* Norton, 1942, and *The Greek Way to Western Civilization,* New American Library, 1948; *The Roman Way,* Norton, 1932, reprinted, Avon, 1973; *The Prophets of Israel,* Norton, 1936, new edition published as *Spokesmen for God: The Great Teachers of the Old Testament,* 1949; *Mythology* (illustrated by Steele Savage), Little, Brown, 1942, reprinted, New American Library, 1971; *Witness to the Truth: Christ and His Interpreters,* Norton, 1948; *The Echo of Greece,* Norton, 1957; *The Ever-Present Past,* Norton, 1964; Doris Fielding, editor, *A Treasury of Edith Hamilton* (selections), Norton, 1969.

Other: (Translator) *Three Greek Plays: Prometheus Bound, Agamemnon, The Trojan Women,* Norton, 1937, reprinted, 1965; (editor) Plato, *The Collected Dialogues of Plato, including Letters,* Pantheon Books, 1961; (translator) Euripides, *The Trojan Women,* Bantam Books, 1971.

Contributor of articles to periodicals, including *Atlantic Monthly, Saturday Review,* and *Theatre Arts Monthly.*

SIDELIGHTS: The classics were a part of Edith Hamilton's life as early as age seven when she read *Six Weeks' Preparation for Caesar* in Latin. Upon her graduation from college, where she majored in Latin and Greek, Hamilton became headmistress of Bryn Mawr School. There, for over a quarter of a century, she instilled in her students an understanding of classical values. Her theories of education were modeled on the beliefs of the greatest civilization before ours—the Greeks. Whereas we believe in the mass education of all young—a view that Miss Hamilton described as "magnificent," but also criticized for its tendency to produce similar minds—the Greeks emphasized differences, and thus a kind of educational freedom which enabled each individual to develop his own specific talents independently. Hamilton pointed to television as one factor contributing to the "deadly commonplace" nature of our education—millions of children see the same thing at the same time.

Many of these same ideas can be expanded to include the whole of society. In her acceptance speech for the Constance Lindsay Skinner Award, reprinted in *Publishers Weekly,* Miss Hamilton explained: "The picture which Thucydides gives of the age of Pericles is of a nation of independent individuals, wanting to be let alone to do their own work but closely bound together by a love of country. . . . A great . . . , good and enduring republic it must be along such lines. The Athenians kept their eyes fixed on the individual boy growing up . . . to meet life's changes with grace. Only an ideal, [but] . . . not the way I look at it. Ideals have tremendous power. When ideals are low they fade out and are forgotten; great ideals have had power of persistent life."

Edith Hamilton's first book was published after her retirement from her position as headmistress at age 63. *The Greek Way* was an interpretation of the Greek mind and spirit, and applied the Greek ideal to civilization today. The comments of reviewers were mixed. *Outlook* wrote: "The book is delightful reading throughout—and good sound sense, too. Of the greater writers who have discussed the Greek way of life and thought, none has expressed himself in a manner more likely to appeal to the common reader. The atmosphere of ponderous erudition which hangs over the usual work of scholarship on the Greek period is absent from Edith Hamilton's work." Added *Saturday Review:* "Miss Hamilton makes little demands on any sort of special knowledge of antiquity in her readers, but she succeeds in conveying an atmosphere and getting us to share in her admiration of the Greek spirit." Negative comments included a review in *New Statesman,* which read: "This book is an American interpretation of Greek civilisation. It is written in a sustained, but deadly vein of enthusiasm. . . . The style is that of the direct statement with seventy-five per cent of the statements unsupported by documentation." Five new chapters were added when the book was published as *The Great Age of Greek Literature* in 1942. *Churchman* described it as "a treasury of inspiration for those who would appreciate the contribution of ancient Greece to the civilization of the world." *The Greek Way* enjoyed a long popularity, proven when it was chosen by the Book-of-the-Month Club in 1957—twenty-seven years after its first publication. The sequel to *The Greek Way, The Echo of Greece,* was published in 1957.

The Roman Way described a way of life as it was presented in the works of ancient poets such as Plautus and Virgil, and attempted to apply these thoughts to the modern world. A *Theatre Arts Monthly* critic commented: "*The Greek Way* established Miss Hamilton's reputation as a scholar and as an interpreter to the modern mind of Greek civilization. . . . Her pen here is more pliant, her choice of phrase and epithet more sure, and her ability to point her argument just as persuasive. The fact that her preference is always for the Greek way has put her on her mettle among these brilliant Romans, and she does them all full justice."

Hamilton retold the stories of classical mythology in her book *Mythology*. A review of the book in *Nation* noted: "In a prose at once edged and colorful, she has thrown the whole of even familiar Greek and Norse mythology into a fresh and luminous context. She has never overpressed suggestions and intimations. She has distilled into incidental observations the whole meaning of mythology itself to the modern scholar." The *New York Times* added: "Its merit is largely derived from the author's interest in Greek and Roman myths, which she sees not merely as outworn fancies of dead antiquity, but as living fables not wholly deprived of meaning for our time. Created when the world was young, there is in them, as in most things engendered in humanity's youth, a quality of timelessness, inherent, and unforgettable."

John Mason Brown, in his book, *Seeing More Things*, described Edith Hamilton as a citizen of both the ancient and the modern worlds, "equally at home with the best of both." He called her a woman "who would be unusual in any period; in ours she is unique." In a speech reprinted in *Publishers Weekly*, Virginia Matthews added, "As she distilled and interpreted to us what was the finest and best of the world two thousand years ago, so have her own books represented what is best in American literature today."

BIOGRAPHICAL/CRITICAL SOURCES: Outlook, May 28, 1930; *New Statesman,* September 20, 1930; *Saturday Review,* November 15, 1930; *Theatre Arts Monthly,* March, 1933; *New York Times,* May 24, 1942; *Nation,* September 19, 1942; *Churchman,* March 15, 1943; John Mason Brown, *Seeing More Things,* Whittlesey House, 1948; *Publishers Weekly,* March 17, 1958; *Life,* September 15, 1958; *Saturday Review,* June 22, 1963; Doris F. Reid, *Edith Hamilton: An Intimate Portrait,* Norton, 1967; Hope Stoddard, *Famous American Women,* Crowell, 1970. Obituaries: *New York Times,* June 1, 1963; *Time,* June 7, 1963; *Newsweek,* June 10, 1963; *Publishers Weekly,* June 10, 1963; *Current Biography,* July, 1963.*

(Died May 31, 1963)

*   *   *

HAMMARSKJOELD, Dag (Hjalmar Agne Carl) 1905-1961

PERSONAL: Born July 29, 1905, in Joenkoeping, Sweden; son of Hjalmar L. (a judge and former prime minister) and Agnes (Almquist) Hammarskjoeld. *Education:* Uppsala University, B.A., 1925, M.A., 1928, LL.B., 1930; Stockholm University, Ph.D., 1934.

CAREER: Secretary of Swedish Government commission on unemployment, 1930-34; University of Stockholm, Stockholm, Sweden, associate professor of political economics, 1933; Bank of Sweden, Stockholm, secretary, 1935-36; Swedish Ministry of Finance, Stockholm, under-secretary, 1936-45; Swedish Ministry of Foreign Affairs, economic advisor, 1946-49, under-secretary of state, 1949-51; minister of state, 1951-53; United Nations, New York, N.Y., secretary-general, 1953-61. Member of Swedish Board of Foreign Exchange, 1940-48; chairman of board of governors of Bank of Sweden, 1941-48; Swedish delegate to Paris Conference, 1947; chief delegate to and vice-chairman of executive committee of Organization for European Eco-

nomic Cooperation, 1948-49; vice-chairman of Swedish delegation to United Nations General Assembly, 1952-53. *Member:* Swedish Academy, Swedish Tourist Association (vice-president, 1950), Swedish Mountaineers (chairman, 1945-52). *Awards, honors:* LL.D. from University of Pennsylvania, Amherst College, Columbia University, Carleton College, McGill University, Princeton University, Johns Hopkins University, University of California, Uppsala University, Harvard University, Cambridge University, Yale University, and Ohio University.

WRITINGS—In English: *Speeches,* edited by Wilder Foote, Norstedt, 1962, published as *Servant of Peace: A Selection of Speeches and Statements of Dag Hammarskjoeld, Secretary-General of the United Nations, 1953-61,* Harper, 1962; *Markings,* translated by Leif Sjoeberg and W. H. Auden from the original Swedish manuscript, Knopf, 1964; *The Light and the Rock: The Vision of Dag Hammarskjoeld,* edited by T. S. Settel, Dutton, 1966; *Hammarskjoeld: The Political Man,* edited by Emery Kelen, Funk & Wagnalls, 1968; *Public Papers of the Secretaries-General of the United Nations,* Volume II: *Dag Hammarskjoeld: 1953-56,* Volume III: *Dag Hammarskjoeld: 1956-57,* Volume IV: *Dag Hammarskjoeld: 1958-61* (Hammarskjoeld not associated with Volume I), edited by Andrew W. Cordier and Foote, Columbia University Press, 1969.

Other writings: *Konjunkturspridningen: En teoretisk och historisk undersoekning* (title means "A Theoretical and Historical Survey of Market Trends"), Norstedt, 1933; (editor) *Svensk natur: En antologi,* [Stockholm], 1949; (translator into Swedish) Saint-John Perse, *Chronique: Kroenika* (bilingual edition containing Perse's original work and Hammarskjoeld's translation), Bonnier (Stockholm), 1960; *Fraan Sarek till Havaeng* (travel), Svenska turistfoereningen, 1961; (contributor) Karl N. Dahl, compiler, *Afrika,* Universitetsforlaget (Oslo), 1961.

SIDELIGHTS: Though Dag Hammarskjoeld left his mark upon the pages of history through his distinguished career as a statesman and spokesman for international cooperation, it was his posthumously published journal, *Markings,* that shed light upon the personal thoughts of the United Nations secretary-general who had been called "a private face in a public place." His reflections and meditations complement the historical accounts of his achievements during his terms as chief executive of the United Nations, revealing the ideals and convictions which shaped his decisions and policies. To neglect his personal document is to write only a fragment of history, for Hammarskjoeld himself declared: "The greatest contribution to international life that anyone can render—is to represent frankly and consistently what survives or emerges as one's own. Far from demanding that we abandon or desert ideals and interests basic to our personality, international service thus puts us under the obligation to let those ideals and interests reach maturity and fruition in a universal climate."

In the introduction to *Markings* W. H. Auden discussed the philosophy of life which formed Hammarskjoeld's vision of his mission. "Two themes came to preoccupy his thoughts," wrote Auden. "First, the conviction that no man can do properly what he is called upon to do in this life unless he can learn to forget his ego and act as an instrument of God. Second, that for him personally, the way to which he was called would lead to the Cross, i.e., to suffering, worldly humiliation, and the physical sacrifice of his life." In 1957, Hammarskjoeld wrote: "If you fail, it is God, thanks to your having betrayed him, who will fail mankind. You fancy you can be responsible *to* God: can you carry the responsibility *for*

God?'' Pointing out the danger of misinterpretation inherent in such a statement, Auden emphasized that Hammarskjoeld radiated a humility in his actions as secretary-general of the United Nations that confounded his critics' charges of megalomania.

Because Hammarskjoeld believed that the chief executive of an international organization such as the United Nations must play a large role in order to protect the interests of small nations, he suffered much abuse from the leaders of nations who perceived any expression of favoritism towards their opponents. A *London Times* writer summarized the opposition he endured: ''Belgians could rage at him over the Congo; Israelis accuse him of kowtowing to Nasser; to a large section of the British population he was deeply suspect at the time of Suez; two months before his death President de Gaulle was prepared to snub him over Bizerta; to the Russians, above all, he had in his last year become anathema, and after the death of Lumumba, Hammarskjoeld was for them 'a man who has sullied himself with foul murder.' '' Perhaps the climax of furious criticism directed against Hammarskjoeld involved accusations by the Soviet Union during the Congo controversy that the secretary-general was not neutral. Calling for Hammarskjoeld's replacement, the Soviets demanded a ''troika'' leadership within the United Nations, comprised of representatives from the West, the Communist nations, and the non-aligned nations. But most of the member states supported Hammarskjoeld in contesting this concept as ''liable to deprive the organization of effective executive direction.'' In the final analysis, the *London Times* spoke for most of the world in its assessment of Hammarskjoeld's contribution to the international forum: ''If the nations of the world ever achieve a unified government no man would have a higher claim to count as one of its founding fathers. The possibilities as well as the perils of world organization were exemplified in the career of this resolute and indefatigable Swede.''

BIOGRAPHICAL/CRITICAL SOURCES: Dag Hammarskjoeld, *Markings,* Knopf, 1964; *New York Times Book Review,* October 18, 1964; *New Statesman,* October 30, 1964; *New Yorker,* October 31, 1964; *Saturday Review,* October 31, 1964; *New Republic,* November 14, 1964; T. S. Settel, editor, *The Light and the Rock: The Vision of Dag Hammarskjoeld,* Dutton, 1966. Obituaries: *London Times,* September 19, 1961.*

(Died September 17, 1961, near Ndola, Northern Rhodesia)

* * *

HAMMARSKJOLD, Dag
See HAMMARSKJOELD, Dag (Hjalmar Ange Carl)

* * *

HANCOCK, Lyn 1938-

PERSONAL: Born January 5, 1938, in Fremantle, West Australia; daughter of Edward (a businessman) and Doris (Williams) Taylor; married David Hancock (a publisher and wildlife biologist), 1963 (divorced, 1974). *Education:* Earned associate and licentiate diplomas from University of West Australia, and teaching certificate from Graylands Teachers College; Simon Fraser University, B.Ed., 1977, graduate study, 1977– ; attended London Royal Academy of Music, and Trinity College, London.

CAREER: Private teacher of speech, drama, and mime, Perth, West Australia, 1954-59; elementary and secondary school teacher in Perth; London, England; Montreal, Quebec; and Vancouver, British Columbia, 1957-75; Wildlife Conservation Centre, Victoria, British Columbia, secretary, lecturer, and animal caretaker, 1964-73; author, journalist, and researcher. *Member:* Friends of the Sea Otter. *Awards, honors:* Pacific Northwest Booksellers award, 1973, for *There's a Seal in My Sleeping Bag;* British Columbia Television scholarship, 1976; Francis H. Kortright Outdoor Writing Award, 1978, for *There's a Raccoon in My Parka.*

WRITINGS: (With David Hancock) *Wild Islands,* Hancock House, 1970; *There's a Seal in My Sleeping Bag,* Collins & Knopf, 1972; *The Mighty Mackenzie,* Hancock House, 1974; *There's a Raccoon in My Parka,* Doubleday, 1977; *There's a Cougar in My Classroom,* Doubleday, 1978. Regular columnist, *Victorian,* 1969-75. Contributor of articles and reviews to *Canadian Geographic Journal, Westworld, Victoria Daily Times, Arctic in Colour, Daily Colonist,* and other periodicals.

WORK IN PROGRESS: The Controversial Cougar; An Ape Came out of My Hatbox (tentatively titled book about raising a gibbon in a classroom); a book on Arctic travel experiences.

SIDELIGHTS: Hancock told *CA:* ''I have a pet raccoon asleep on my typewriter as I try to print this. I find life to be a grand adventure every day—you never know what's around the corner. Ever since I can remember in Australia, perhaps at the age of eight, I sought adventures. I had the desire to be where other feet had not trod. I would have liked to be Columbus and to discover America. I planned to leave Australia and see the world as soon as I completed my teaching degree. I travelled to Malaysia, Africa, Europe and Britain, living with the people as much as possible. Then I came to America to earn the money home to Australia and thought that living was all over. 'Now I will become an old maid, live in an apartment, teach speech and drama and have a cockatoo for a companion,' I said to myself. Instead, on the eve of my departure I married a Canadian biologist, played nursemaid to a seal, macaw, a gibbon, four cougars, a myriad of sea birds and the rest of a continuous menagerie, and began to write books and articles. Now nature and travelling have a purpose, and life has extra significance.

''I entered university to study wildlife and communication of wildlife values seriously. I want to motivate others to enjoy what has become important to me. No longer do I want to list countries, their museums, galleries, and old historic sites as places to see just to say that I have seen them.

''I am still interested in travel—but to places like the north which are empty and remote. I have rubber boated down the Inside Passage between Alaska and Washington; hitchhiked by bush plane across the Arctic Islands and throughout the Northwest Territories; bushwhacked in 100 mile circles from the Alaska Highway; bussed and driven around interior New Guinea; and hiked wherever the wilderness called.

''I think my greatest joy is to wander in the wilderness beside a raccoon, or a bear, or a cougar. I like to watch the way they explore their world and to share it with them.

''I look forward to the day when all the animals I have encountered live in print—a gibbon called Gypsy, a bear called Bubu, a seal like Sam, a cougar like Tom, a raccoon like Rocky. . . . Now on my desk and interfering with the ribbon on my typewriter is a raccoon called Tobasco. He makes a mess but one day he will make a story.''

HANDELMAN, John R(obert) 1948-

PERSONAL: Born July 6, 1948, in New York, N.Y.; son of Samuel Robert (a dentist) and Thelma (Leal) Handelman; married Barbara Borgersen, June 30, 1973; children: Christina Brooke. *Education:* Hamilton College, A.B., 1970; Syracuse University, M.A., 1972, Ph.D., 1974. *Home:* 412 Confederate Circle, Lexington, Va. 24450. *Office:* Department of Politics, Washington & Lee University, Lexington, Va. 24450.

CAREER: Washington & Lee University, Lexington, Va., assistant professor of politics, 1973—. *Member:* International Studies Association, American Political Science Association, Southern Political Science Association.

WRITINGS: Introductory Case Studies for International Relations, Rand McNally, 1974. Contributor to political science journals.

WORK IN PROGRESS: Research on the relationship between non-national actors and the foreign relations bureaucracy of the People's Republic of China.

* * *

HANDKE, Peter 1942-

PERSONAL: Born December 6, 1942, in Griffen, Carinthia, Austria; married; children: one daughter. *Education:* Attended a Jesuit seminary, and University of Graz, 1961-65. *Home:* 53 rue Cecille-Dinant, F-92140 Clamart, France. *Office:* c/o Suhrkamp Verlag, Postfach 4229, 6000 Frankfurt am Main, Federal Republic of Germany.

CAREER: Dramatist, novelist, poet, essayist, and screenwriter, 1966—. *Awards, honors:* Gerhart Hauptmann Prize, 1967; Schiller Prize, 1972; Buechner Prize, 1973.

WRITINGS—Fiction: *Die Hornissen* (novel; title means "The Hornets"), Suhrkamp, 1966; *Der Hausierer* (novel; title means "The Peddler"), Suhrkamp, 1967; *Begruessung des Aufsichtsrats* (experimental prose pieces; title means "Welcoming the Board of Directors"), Residenz Verlag, 1967, also published in *Peter Handke* (see below); *Die Angst des Tormanns beim Elfmeter* (novel), Suhrkamp, 1970, translation by Michael Roloff published as *The Goalie's Anxiety at the Penalty Kick,* Farrar, Straus, 1972; *Der kurze Brief zum langen Abschied* (novel), Suhrkamp, 1972, translation by Ralph Manheim published as *Short Letter, Long Farewell,* Farrar, Straus, 1974; *Die Stunde der wahren Empfindung* (novel), Suhrkamp, 1975, translation by Manheim published as *A Moment of True Feeling,* Farrar, Straus, 1977; *Die linkshaendige Frau: Erzaehlung* (novel), Suhrkamp, 1976, translation published as *The Left-Handed Woman,* Farrar, Straus, 1978.

Plays: "Publikumsbeschimpfung" (first produced in Frankfurt at Theater am Turm, June 8, 1966), published in *Publikumsbeschimpfung und Andere Sprechstuecke* (see below), translation by Roloff published as "Offending the Audience" in *Kaspar and Other Plays* (see below); "Selbstbezichtigung" (first produced in Oberhausen at Staedtische Buehnen, October 22, 1966), published in *Publikumsbeschimpfung und Andere Sprechstuecke* (see below), translation by Roloff published as "Self-Accusation" in *Kaspar and Other Plays* (see below); "Weissagung" (first produced in Oberhausen at Staedtische Buehnen, October 22, 1966), published in *Publikumsbeschimpfung und Andere Sprechstuecke* (see below), translation by Roloff published as "Prophecy" in *The Ride Across Lake Constance and Other Plays* (see below).

"Hilferufe" (first produced in Stockholm, September 12, 1967), published in *Deutsches Theater der Gegenwart 2,* 1967, translation by Roloff published as "Calling for Help" in *Drama Review,* fall, 1970, and in *The Ride Across Lake Constance and Other Plays* (see below); *Kaspar* (produced simultaneously in Frankfurt at Theater am Turm and in Oberhausen at Staedtische Buehnen, May 11, 1968), Suhrkamp, 1968, translation by Roloff under same title (produced in New York at the Brooklyn Academy of Music, February, 1973) published in *Kaspar and Other Plays* (see below), also published separately, Methuen, 1972; "Das Mundel will Vormund sein" (first produced in Frankfurt at Theater am Turm, January 31, 1969), published in *Theatre Heute,* February, 1969, and in *Peter Handke* (see below), translation by Roloff published as "My Foot My Tutor" in *Drama Review,* fall, 1970, and in *The Ride Across Lake Constance and Other Plays* (see below).

Quodlibet (first produced in Basle at Basler Theater, January 24, 1970), published in *Theater Heute,* March, 1970, also privately printed, 1970, translation by Roloff published under same title in *The Ride Across Lake Constance and Other Plays* (see below); *Wind und Meer: 4 Hoerspiele* (title means "Wind and Sea: Four Radio Plays"), Suhrkamp, 1970; *Der Ritt ueber den Bodensee* (first produced in Berlin at Schaubuehne am Halleschen Ufer, January 23, 1971), Suhrkamp, 1971, translation by Roloff as *The Ride Across Lake Constance* (produced in New York at the Forum, Lincoln Center, January, 1972) published in *The Contemporary German Drama,* edited by Roloff, Equinox Books, 1972, published separately, Methuen, 1973 (also see below); *Die Unvernuenftigen sterben aus* (first produced in Zurich, April, 1974), Suhrkamp, 1973, translation by Roloff and Karl Weber published as *They Are Dying Out,* Methuen, 1975 (also see below); "A Sorrow Beyond Dreams," produced in New York City at Marymount Manhattan Playhouse, June, 1977.

German collections: *Publikumsbeschimpfung und Andere Sprechstuecke* (includes "Publikumsbeschimpfung," "Selbstbezichtigung," and "Weissagung"), Suhrkamp, 1966; *Peter Handke: Prosa, Gedichte, Theaterstuecke, Hoerspiel, Aufsaetze* (includes "Begruessung des Aufsichtsrats," "Publikumsbeschimpfung," and "Das Mundel will Vormund sein"), Suhrkamp, 1969; *Stuecke* (title means "Plays"), Suhrkamp, 1972; *Stuecke 2,* Suhrkamp, 1973.

English collections: *Kaspar and Other Plays* (includes "Kaspar," "Offending the Audience," and "Self-Accusation"), translated by Roloff, Farrar, Straus, 1969; *Offending the Audience* (includes "Offending the Audience" and "Self-Accusation"), translated by Roloff, Methuen, 1971; *The Ride Across Lake Constance and Other Plays* (includes "Prophecy," "Calling for Help," "My Foot My Tutor," "Quodlibet," and "They Are Dying Out"), translated by Roloff and Karl Weber, Farrar, Straus, 1976.

Other: *Die Innenwelt der Aussenwelt der Innenwelt* (poems), Suhrkamp, 1969, abridged translation by Roloff published as *The Innerworld of the Outerworld of the Innerworld,* Seabury, 1974; (compiler) *Der gewoehnliche Schrecken* (title means "The Ordinary Terror"), Residenz Verlag, 1969; *Deutsche Gedichte* (title means "German Poems"), Euphorion-Verlag, 1969.

Chronik der laufenden Ereignisse (film scenario; title means "Chronicle of Current Events"), Suhrkamp, 1971; *Ich bin ein Bewohner des Elfenbeinturms* (essays; title means "I Live in an Ivory Tower"), Suhrkamp, 1972; *Wunschloses Unglueck* (biography), Residenz Verlag, 1972, translation by Manheim published as *A Sorrow Beyond Dreams,* Farrar, Straus, 1975; *Als das Wuenschen noch geholfen hat* (poems), Suhrkamp, 1974, translation by Roloff published as *Nonsense and Happiness,* Urizen Books, 1976; *Falsche Bewegung* (film scenario; title means "False Move"), Suhrkamp, 1975; *Three by Peter Handke* (contains *A Sorrow Beyond Dreams, Short Letter Long Farewell, The Goalie's Anxiety at the Penalty Kick*), Avon, 1977; (and director) "The Left-Handed Woman" (screenplay), 1978.

WORK IN PROGRESS: A journal; also a novel—"a personal odyssey"—set in the Rocky Mountains and in Austria.

SIDELIGHTS: Nicholas Hern is one of a number of critics who have suggested that Handke's legal training may have been an important influence on his prose style, pointing out that "most of his plays and novels consist of a series of affirmative propositions each contained within one sentence. . . . The effect . . . is not unlike the series of clauses in a contract or will or statute-book, shorn of linking conjunctions. It is as if a state of affairs or a particular situation were being defined and constantly redefined until the final total definition permits of no mite of ambiguity." Handke's prose has reminded other readers of the propositions making up Ludwig Wittgenstein's *Tractatus Logico-Philosophicus,* and the inquiries into language of Wittgenstein and the French structuralists touch on themes that are central to Handke's work. Discussing his more strictly literary masters, Handke said in 1977 that Faulkner remains the most important of all writers to him.

Handke's remarkable style was first displayed in the experimental prose pieces he wrote and published in magazines while still at the university, and in *Die Hornissen,* which reminded reviewers of the French "new novel." This first novel appeared in the spring of 1966 and was generally well received, but it was not this alone that made him overnight a figure to be reckoned with on the German literary scene. In April, 1966, Handke went to the United States to participate in the twenty-eighth convention of Group 47, the famous association of German writers, which that year met in Princeton, N.J. On the last day of the conference Handke, then aged twenty-four, made the first move in a deliberate campaign of what came to be called "Handke-Publicity." In his book on Group 47 Siegfried Mandel wrote: "Shaking his Beatle-mane, Handke . . . railed against what he had been listening to: impotent narrative; empty stretches of descriptive (instead of analytical) writing pleasing to the ears of the older critics; monotonous verbal litanies, regional and nature idyllicism, which lacked spirit and creativeness. The audience warmed up to the invective with cheers, and later even those whose work had been called idiotic, tasteless, and childish came over to congratulate the Group 47 debutant and to patch things up in brotherly fashion. . . . As he stood among a circle of interviewers—a thin, energetic figure with thick, dark sunglasses—it became clear that he had arrived as a spokesman for the young and hitherto silent clique and reestablished confidence in the rejuvenating capacity of the group."

This assessment was fully confirmed a few months later, when Handke's first play was the major hit in a week of experimental new drama in Frankfurt. *Offending the Audience,* in which all the comfortable assumptions of bourgeois theatre are called in question and the audience is systematically mocked and insulted, was and has remained highly popular in German theatres. To a lesser extent, the same is true of Handke's other early "sprechstuecke"—plays which all in various ways investigate the role of language in defining the individual's social identity.

The power of language is the theme also of *Kaspar,* Handke's first full-length play. It is a matter of record that in 1828 in Nuremberg a sixteen-year-old boy was discovered who had apparently been confined all his life in a closet, and who was physically full-grown but mentally a baby. This was Kaspar Hauser, whose story has intrigued a number of writers, and who in Handke's play is indoctrinated with conventional moral precepts in the process of being taught to speak. As Nicholas Hern put it, "the play is an abstract demonstration of the way an individual's individuality is stripped from him by society, specifically by limiting the expressive power of the language it teaches him." Robert Brustein rejected the play's thesis, but found it all the same "sometimes penetrating, sometimes brilliant, always permeated by a fierce, if rather cold, intensity." In Germany *Kaspar* was voted play of the year, and it is regarded as one of the most important postwar German plays.

A number of other plays have followed, for radio, television, and the stage. The most discussed of these was Handke's second full-length play, *The Ride Across Lake Constance,* which, most critics thought, also dealt with the problems of communication, though in a baroque and bewildering fashion that fascinated even some reviewers, like Clive Barnes, who could make no sense of it at all. Hern wrote that in this play "Handke has moved from a Wittgensteinian distrust of language to a Foucaultian distrust of what our society calls reason. His play is by no means surrealist in externals only: it parallels the surrealists' cardinal desire—the liberation of men's minds from the constraints of reason. Thus Handke continues to demonstrate that the consistently *anti*-theatrical stance which he has maintained throughout his dramatic writing can none the less lend concrete theatrical expression to abstract, philosophical ideas, thereby generating a new and valid form of theatre."

Meanwhile, Handke had been establishing a second reputation as one of the most important of the young German novelists. His first success in this form was *The Goalie's Anxiety at the Penalty Kick,* which reflects the same preoccupations as his plays. As Russell Davies wrote, when Handke's alienated hero Bloch commits an apparently pointless murder, "it is the problem of language itself which upsets his mind and stomach. . . . One comes to realise that Handke is demonstrating how similar to the toils of madness are the inner wranglings of the writer as he fights to order his world." Frank Conroy called the book "an ambitious tour de force in which Handke deals with the interrelationships of man, external reality and time."

The partly autobiographical novel *Short Letter, Long Farewell,* about a young Austrian writer's haphazard journey across the United States to a dangerous meeting with his estranged wife, had a mixed but generally favorable reception. And there was little but praise for *A Sorrow Beyond Dreams,* Handke's profoundly sensitive account of his mother's life, which ended in suicide. Michael Wood wrote of it that "Handke's objective tone is a defense against the potential flood of his feelings, of course, but it is also a act of piety, an expression of respect: this woman's bleak life is not to be made into 'literature'. . . . Handke's mother is important not because she is an especially vivid case but because she is *not,* because she is one of many." Dramatized as a monologue by Daniel Freudenberger, it was staged by the Phoenix Theatre at the Marymount Manhattan Theatre early in 1977, and greatly praised.

Some reviewers were disappointed by *A Moment of True Feeling,* another fictional study in alienation, but Stanley Kauffmann was deeply impressed. He suggested that

Handke was moving toward "the novel as poem" and concluded that "this new book proves further that, in power and vision and range, he is the most important new writer on the international scene since Beckett."

Handke has written: "I myself would support Marxism every time as the only possibility of solution . . . but not its pronouncement in play, in the theatre." His refusal to use his plays and novels as vehicles for political propaganda has been much criticized by the New Left in Germany, but Handke maintains that literature and political commitment are incompatible. "It would be repugnant to me to twist my criticism of a social order into a story or to aestheticize it into a poem," he says in one of his essays. "I find that the most atrocious mendacity: to manipulate one's commitment into a poem or to make literature out of it, instead of just saying it loud."

BIOGRAPHICAL/CRITICAL SOURCES—Books: Guenter Heintz, *Peter Handke*, Klett, 1971; Nicholas Hern, *Peter Handke: Theatre and Anti-Theatre*, Wolff, 1971; Elizabeth Boa and J. H. Reid, *Critical Strategies: German Fiction in the Twentieth Century*, McGill-Queens University Press, 1972; Henning Rischbieter, *Peter Handke*, Friedrich, 1972; Siegfried Mandel, *Group 47*, Southern Illinois University Press, 1973; Michael Scharang, editor, *Uber Peter Handke*, Suhrkamp, 1973; Uwe Schultz, *Peter Handke*, Friedrich, 1973; Frederick Ungar, editor, *Handbook of Austrian Literature*, F. Ungar, 1973; Henning Falkenstein, *Peter Handke*, Colloquium Verlag, 1974; Richard Gilman, *The Making of Modern Drama*, Farrar, Straus, 1974; *Contemporary Literary Criticism*, Gale, Volume 5, 1976, Volume 8, 1978.

Articles: *Text und Kritik*, Number 24, 1969 (Handke issue); *Universitas*, February 25, 1970; *New Republic*, February 28, 1970, September 28, 1974; *Drama Review*, fall, 1970; *New York Times*, January 30, 1977, March 22, 1971, June 17, 1978; *Times Literary Supplement*, April 21, 1972, December 1, 1972; *London Times*, May 15, 1972, November 13, 1973, December 9, 1973; *New York Times Book Review*, May 21, 1972, September 15, 1974, April 27, 1975, July 31, 1977, June 18, 1978; *Performance*, September-October 1972; *New York Review of Books*, May 1, 1975, June 23, 1977; *Publishers Weekly*, September 12, 1977; *Newsweek*, July 3, 1978.

*   *   *

HANDLER, Meyer Srednick   1905-1978

June 3, 1905—February 9, 1978; American journalist. For nearly thirty years, Handler was a foreign correspondent in Europe for the *New York Times* and United Press International. During World War II, he covered many major events, including the fall of France, the London blitz, and Germany's invasion of the U.S.S.R. In addition, he wrote on the Nuremberg trials, Yugoslavian Tito's rise to head-of-state, and the civil rights movement in the United States during the 1960's. He came to know several black leaders, among them Martin Luther King, Jr. and Malcolm X. Besides reporting, he taught at the University of Indiana and Tuft University's Fletcher School of Law and Diplomacy. Handler spoke fluent French, Russian, Italian, German, Serbo-Croatian, and Bulgarian. He was author of the introduction to *The Autobiography of Malcolm X*. He died in Santa Barbara, Calif. Obituaries and other sources: *New York Times*, February 11, 1978.

HANES, Bailey C(ass)   1915-

PERSONAL: Born January 6, 1915, in Shawnee, Okla.; son of Bailey R. (a peace officer) and Roxanna (a nurse; maiden name, Cass) Hanes; married Effie L. Merritt, July 18, 1935; children: Bailey Frank. *Education:* Attended Oklahoma State University, 1933-42. *Religion:* Episcopalian. *Home and office:* 965 Osage Ave., Santa Fe, N.M. 87501.

CAREER: J. H. Hereford Farm, Macomb, Okla., manager and co-owner, 1936-42; Boeing Aircraft Co., Wichita, Kan., draftsman, 1942-43; Vocational Education for National Defense, instructor in aircraft sheet metal in Langston, Okla., 1942-43; Tinker Airforce Base, Oklahoma City, Okla., aircraft mechanic and instructor, 1943; Guthrie Furniture Sales, Guthrie, Okla., manager and co-owner, 1944-48; Sooner State Loan Co., Guthrie, owner and manager, 1948-76. *Member:* Lions (member of board of directors). *Awards, honors:* Award from Oklahoma Writers Association, 1969, for *Bill Doolin, Outlaw O.T..*

WRITINGS: The Complete Bulldog, Delinger's, 1956; *The New Complete Bulldog*, Howell Book, 1966, 3rd edition, 1973; *Bill Doolin, Outlaw O.T.* (biography), University of Oklahoma Press, 1968; *Bill Pickett, Bulldogger*, University of Oklahoma Press, 1977.

WORK IN PROGRESS: Tom Mix, Cowboy Deluxe; Moses Bradley Carson, Brother of Kit; 101 Ranch at Kenton, California.

SIDELIGHTS: Hanes writes: "Writing is my golf game, I do it for the hell of it." Hanes is also a licensed dog show judge and judges bulldogs and Boston terriers.

*   *   *

HANLON, Emily   1945-

PERSONAL: Born April 26, 1945, in New York, N.Y.; daughter of Stuart (a teacher) and Evelyn (Green) Hanlon; married Edward Tarasov, June 25, 1966; children: Natasha, Nicholas. *Education:* Barnard College, B.A., 1967. *Home address:* Chapman Rd., R.F.D. 1, Yorktown Heights, N.Y. 10598. *Agent:* Florence Crowthers, 17 Murchison Place, White Plains, N.Y. 10605.

CAREER: Occupation Day Center, New York, N.Y., teacher of mentally retarded adults, 1972-74; creative writing teacher at elementary school in Yorktown Heights, N.Y.; writer. *Member:* Authors Guild of Authors League of America.

WRITINGS—For children: *What If a Lion Eats Me and I Fall into a Hippopotamus' Mud Hole?*, Delacorte, 1975; *How a Horse Grew Hoarse on the Site Where He Sighted a Bare Bear*, Delacorte, 1976; *It's Too Late for Sorry* (young adult novel), Bradbury, 1978.

WORK IN PROGRESS: The Swing, a juvenile novel.

SIDELIGHTS: Emily Hanlon told *CA:* "As *The Swing* is now under consideration for publication, I am currently working on a young adult novel concerning the friendship between two seventeen year old girls in their senior year of high school. I am trying to capture in this book the essence of a friendship that goes beyond good times and happy days to become a meaningful experience and an influencing force in an individual's life.

"I have been writing ever since I can remember, although I began writing with thoughts of publication about six years ago. My first books were picture books but I find writing novels for older children and teenagers more satisfying. I also write poetry."

AVOCATIONAL INTERESTS: Gardening.

HANNIFIN, Jerry (Bernard) 1917-

PERSONAL: Born April 5, 1917, in Boise, Idaho; son of John Bernard and Isbella (Munn) Hannifin; married Betty Johnson, May 10, 1949 (marriage ended, 1956); married Rieck Kerber, June 14, 1963; children: (first marriage) Consuelo (Mrs. Donald Scardino). *Education:* Boise Junior College, A.A., 1938; University of California, Berkeley, B.A., 1943; also attended Fresno State College. *Politics:* Independent. *Religion:* Roman Catholic. *Home:* 1500 Massachusetts Ave. N.W., Washington, D.C. 20005. *Office:* 888 16th St. N.W., Washington, D.C. 20006.

CAREER: Boise Capitol News, Boise, Idaho, reporter, 1938-39; United Press International, New York City, staff correspondent from the West Coast, Mexico, and Central America, 1939-46; Time, Inc., New York City, correspondent, 1947—, chief of Time-Life bureaus in Mexico City, 1949, Seattle, Wash., 1950, Atlanta, Ga., 1954-55, Buenos Aires, 1967, and Rio de Janiero, 1968-69, Washington correspondent for *Time,* 1969—, editor of *Life en Espanol,* 1951-53. Member of Florence and Daniel Guggenheim Commission for Aeronautical Safety and Laura Taber Barbour Award Board; member of board of directors of Foundation for Community Creativity; consultant to Human Factors in Aviation Safety Foundation.

MEMBER: International Aviation Club, Aerospace Writers Association (national vice-president, 1956—), National Press Club, National Space Club, National Aviation Club (vice-president, 1967-69), International Society of Air Safety Investigators, Association des Amis de Musee de l'Air, International Club, Washington Press Club, Aero Club. *Awards, honors:* Strebie-Dobbin Writing Award, 1968; aerospace writing award from National Space Club, 1977.

WRITINGS: Who Brought the Word, Summer Institute of Linguistics Press, 1965.

SIDELIGHTS: Hannifin writes: "My main concern is aviation safety, all factors concerned, mechanical and human. I was senior delegation member during two visits to the Soviet Union in 1968 and again in 1973, leading a delegation of U.S. aerospace writers, reporting the Soviet aviation and space effort. We were the first American writers and reporters to visit the Yakolev Plant near Moscow, and the Tupolev production line at Voronezh, where the Soviets are building their 'SST.'"

* * *

HANRAHAN, John D(avid) 1938-

PERSONAL: Born September 8, 1938, in Fort Dodge, Iowa; son of James L. and Frances (a secretary; maiden name, Chock) Hanrahan; married Deborah Barger (a political activist), February 6, 1971; children: Timothy J. and John F. *Education:* University of Iowa, B.A., 1960. *Politics:* District of Columbia Statehood Party. *Home:* 1505 Q St. N.W., Washington, D.C. 20009.

CAREER: Davenport Daily Times (now *Quad-City Times-Democrat*), Davenport, Iowa, assistant sports editor, 1960-61, local political reporter, 1963-64; *Montgomery County Sentinel,* Rockville, Md., reporter, 1964-66; *Washington Star,* Washington, D.C., local reporter, 1966-68; *Washington Post,* Washington, D.C., local reporter, 1968-74, assistant local editor, 1974-75; writer, 1975—. *Military service:* U.S. Army, 1961-63. *Member:* Newspaper Guild, Washington Independent Writers. *Awards, honors:* Award from Maryland-Delaware Press Association, 1966, for local government reporting; award from American Political Science Association, 1971, for local government reporting.

WRITINGS: (With Peter Gruenstein) *Lost Frontier: The Marketing of Alaska,* Norton, 1977; *Government for Sale,* American Federation of State, County, and Municipal Employees, 1977. Contributor to magazines and newspapers, including *Progressive, More,* and *Inquiry.*

* * *

HARCOURT, Palma

PERSONAL: Born in Jersey, Channel Islands; married Jack H. Trotman. *Education:* Attended Jersey Ladies College; earned M.A. from St. Anne's College, Oxford. *Home:* Champ de Rousset, Mont Felard, St. Lawrence, Jersey, Channel Islands. *Agent:* Murray Pollinger, 4 Garrick St., London W.C.2, England.

CAREER: Writer. *Member:* Crime Writers' Association (Britain), Army and Navy Club (London).

WRITINGS: Climate for Conspiracy, Collins, 1974; *A Fair Exchange,* Collins, 1975, McKay, 1976; *Dance for Diplomats,* Collins, 1976; *At High Risk,* Collins, 1977; *Agents of Influence,* Collins, 1978; *A Sleep of Spies,* Collins, 1979.

* * *

HARDIN, Robert 1934-

PERSONAL: Born October 5, 1934, in Hot Springs, Ark.; son of Ernest (a salesman) and Ruby (Davis) Hardin; married Nancy Abolin, October, 1960 (divorced, 1966); married Cynthia Krane (a ballet teacher), December 23, 1967. *Education:* Attended Columbia University, 1960; Lincoln University, LL.B., 1976. *Politics:* None. *Religion:* None. *Home:* 100 South St., Sausalito, Calif. 94965. *Agent:* James Oliver Brown, James Brown Associates, Inc., 22 East 60th St., New York, N.Y. 10022.

CAREER: Encore Litho, New York, N.Y., vice-president, 1965-71; Art Sales Unlimited, Inc., Raleigh, N.C., president, 1971-74; C.B.R., Inc., San Francisco, Calif., president, 1974—. *Military service:* U.S. Army, 1957-60; became sergeant. *Member:* Mystery Writers of America.

WRITINGS: Amateur Hour (mystery), Bobbs-Merrill, 1977.

WORK IN PROGRESS: God-Damned Murders, a mystery novel; research for *Warpath,* a novel about terrorism.

SIDELIGHTS: Hardin writes: "The personal view I expressed in *Amateur Hour* is one of the solitary task of a defense attorney standing against all of the resources of the State and Society (in the form of newspapers, radio and television) and of his success working within the confines of the system, using the system's own rules to win. I personally think that the defense attorney in our own society is one of the bulwarks against a police state. On a smaller note, my novel has no sex and no violence in it whatsoever, as all of the murders have taken place before the book begins. Everything in the plot is after the fact. I also attempted to depict the hero and his family as happy (not to say contented) members of society who were simply caused to confront it by circumstance."

AVOCATIONAL INTERESTS: Flying small airplanes (has private pilot's license), sailing, all spectator sports.

* * *

HARDING, A(nthony) F(ilmer) 1946-

PERSONAL: Born November 20, 1946, in Bromley, England; married Lesley Eleanor Forbes (a librarian), 1976. *Education:* Corpus Christi College, Cambridge, B.A., 1968,

M. A. and Ph. D., both 1973. *Office:* Department of Archaeology, University of Durham, 46 Saddler St., Durham DH1 3NU, England.

CAREER: British Museum, London, England, research assistant for department of prehistoric and Romano-British antiquities, 1972-73; University of Durham, Durham, England, lecturer in archaeology, 1973—.

WRITINGS: (With J. M. Coles) *The Bronze Age of Europe,* Methuen, 1978.

WORK IN PROGRESS: Studying thematic approaches to European prehistory, especially Bronze Age, paleoserology, and archaeological excavations in northern England, especially "henge-monuments."

*   *   *

HARE, Ronald 1899-

PERSONAL: Born August 30, 1899, in Durham, England; son of Frederick (a physician) and Elizabeth (Roxby) Hare; married Barbara Thurgarland Wintle (a musician), June 6, 1932 (died, 1966); children: Timothy Richard Frederick Thurgarland. *Education:* Birkbeck College, London, M.B.B.S., 1924, M.D., 1935. *Home:* 15 Warwick Sq., Flat 3, London, England. *Agent:* Curtis Brown Ltd., 1 Craven Hill, London W.2, England.

CAREER: St. Mary's Hospital, London, England, bacteriological researcher, 1925-30; Queen Charlotte's Maternity Hospital, London, England, bacteriological researcher, 1931-36; University of Toronto, Toronto, Ontario, lecturer in hygiene and preventive medicine and research associate at Connaught Laboratories, 1936-46; University of London, St. Thomas Hospital Medical School, London, England, professor of bacteriology, 1946-64, professor emeritus, 1964—, consulting bacteriologist, 1951—. Member of council of Wright-Fleming Institute, 1952-60, and Nuffield Institute of Comparative Medicine, 1960-68; member of Fountains & Carshalton Group hospital management committee, 1966-71. Examiner for Universities of London, Malaya, Birmingham, the West Indies, East Africa, and Ibadan. *Military service:* British Army, 1917-18; served in France.

MEMBER: Royal Society of Medicine (member of council, 1965-68), Pathological Society of Great Britain, British Society of Immunology, British Medical Association. *Awards, honors:* Catherine Bishop Harman Prize from British Medical Association, 1928, and Nicholls Prize from Royal Society of Medicine, 1935, both for research on streptococci.

WRITINGS: Pomp and Pestilence, Gollancz, 1954; *An Outline of Bacteriology and Immunity,* Longmans, Green, 1956, 3rd edition, 1967; *Bacteriology and Immunity for Nurses,* Longmans, Green, 1961, 4th edition, Churchill, 1975; *The Birth of Penicillin and the Disarming of Microbes,* Allen & Unwin, 1970. Contributor to scientific and medical journals.

WORK IN PROGRESS: The Discovery of Penicillin.

AVOCATIONAL INTERESTS: Painting (water colors).

*   *   *

HARKER, Ronald 1909-

PERSONAL: Born August 13, 1909, in Grassington, Yorkshire, England; son of Edward Henry (an automobile engineer) and Mabel (Boothman) Harker; married Joan Mary Ellis, February 3, 1933; children: Gillian (Mrs. Philip Levy), Carolyn (Mrs. John Burge), Quentin, Jeremy. *Education:* Attended secondary school in Skipton, Yorkshire, England.

Home: Court Ing, Main St., Grassington, Skipton, Yorkshire, England.

CAREER: Bradford Telegraph & Argus, Bradford, England, 1929-38, began as reporter, became sub-editor; *News Chronicle,* London, England, sub-editor, 1938-42, chief foreign sub-editor, 1946-53, night editor, 1953-56; *Observer,* London, 1956-74, began as night editor, became editor for Foreign News Service; free-lance writer, 1974—. *Military service:* British Army, Intelligence Corps, 1943-44. Indian Army, public relations unit, 1944-46; served in India and Ceylon; became captain.

WRITINGS: Digging Up the Bible Lands, Bodley Head, 1972, Walck, 1973.

WORK IN PROGRESS: Collating conference and seminar proceedings of a London-based organization of scientists, economists, and philosophers on the future of world energy resources and food production, with a book expected to result.

*   *   *

HARKNESS, Edward 1947-

PERSONAL: Born April 19, 1947, in Bremerton, Wash.; son of Harry Lincoln (a cost analyst) and Doris May (a college instructor; maiden name, Houston) Harkness; married Linda Ann Lovan (a teacher), July 13, 1974; children: Devin Charles. *Education:* University of Washington, Seattle, B.A., 1970; University of Montana, M.F.A., 1973. *Politics:* "In full understanding of the absurdity of the situation, I voted for McCarthy in 1976." *Religion:* "Born-again atheist." *Home:* 12119 Nile Rd., Naches, Wash. 98937.

CAREER: Poet, 1973—. Member of poet-in-the-schools and poet-in-the-community programs in Montana, Idaho, and Washington. *Awards, honors:* Branford Millar Poetry Prize from *Portland Review,* 1976, for "Checking the Well at Night."

WRITINGS: Long Eye Lost Wind Forgive Me (poetry), Copper Canyon Press, 1975; *Caretaker* (poetry), Confluence Press, 1978. Contributor of poems to periodicals, including *American Poetry Review, Poetry Northwest, New Letters, Northwest Review,* and *Ploughshares.*

WORK IN PROGRESS: Autobiography of a Pathological Liar (tentative title), a book-length poem.

SIDELIGHTS: Harkness writes: "I can't explain my need to write. I'm not prolific, not very inventive. My poems tend to be private and therefore of little importance to anyone but me. Now and then a friend will say something nice about one of my poems. I have no literary theories or ideologies—if I did I doubt I could convey them, even to myself.

"This is something I've never said to anyone: most things in life seem to me confusing or ridiculous. I admire but secretly despise people who have everything worked out, who find nothing odd about tying one's shoe or needle-nose pliers."

*   *   *

HARLING, Thomas
See EASTHAM, Thomas

*   *   *

HARPER, Bill
See HARPER, William A(rthur)

*   *   *

HARPER, Floyd H(enry) 1899-1978

1899—February 21, 1978; American economist, statistician,

and author of a book in his field. A former economist with the Army Corps of Engineers, Harper concentrated on writing studies and reports on goods that can be transported via waterways. Obituaries and other sources: *American Men and Women of Science: The Social and Behavioral Sciences,* 12th edition, Bowker, 1973; *Washington Post,* February 23, 1978.

* * *

HARPER, William A(rthur) 1944-
(Bill Harper)

PERSONAL: Born November 11, 1944, in Glendale, Calif.; son of William Adams (a musician) and Mary (a writer; maiden name, Storms) Harper; married Carol Ann Johnson (a teacher), August 5, 1967; children: Christopher Sean, Michael Lee, Eric Storm. *Education:* California State University, Northridge, B.A., 1965; University of Southern California, Ph.D., 1971. *Politics:* Democrat. *Religion:* Roman Catholic. *Home:* 1430 College Dr., Emporia, Kan. 66801. *Office:* Division of Health, Physical Education, Recreation & Athletics, Emporia State University, 1200 Commercial St., Emporia, Kan. 66801.

CAREER: Emporia State University, Emporia, Kan., assistant professor, 1969-73, associate professor of health, physical education, recreation, and athletics, 1973—. Part-time assistant professor of philosophy, Emporia State University, 1970—. Member of summer faculty at University of Washington, Seattle, 1976.

MEMBER: American Alliance of Health, Physical Education and Recreation (member of national research council), National College of Physical Education Association for Men, Society for Phenomenological and Existential Philosophy, Kansas Association for Health, Physical Education and Recreation (research chairman, 1971; vice-president, 1972), Phi Epsilon Kappa (past chapter president). *Awards, honors:* Grants from United Ministries in Higher Education, 1974-75, 1975-76.

WRITINGS: (With E. C. Davis, Donna Mae Miller, and Roberta Park) *The Philosophic Process in Physical Education,* Lea & Febiger, 1961, 3rd edition, 1977; (contributor) Jack Wilmore, editor, *Exercise and Sport Science Reviews,* Volume II, Academic Press, 1974; (contributor under name Bill Harper) Brian Fahey and Dorothy Allen, editors, *Being Human in Sport,* Lea & Febiger, 1977; (contributor) Richard Rivenes, editor, *Foundations of Physical Education,* Houghton, 1978. Contributor to physical education journals, and to *Dynamic Years* and *Quest.* Editor of *Play Factory Advocate,* 1973-77.

WORK IN PROGRESS: A series of short studies on play; a children's story.

SIDELIGHTS: Harper writes: "Our age is not particularly playful. We are well-ordered, regular, and tidy. I am not particularly playful. I am well-ordered, regular, and oh so tidy. So, I guess I am stumped about why such potentially 'playfull' humans seem to rather enjoy being mechanical. With Lewis Carroll, such a preference reduces most people to the mental condition of 'a coffee-mill or a mangle.'

"I am now doing a series of short studies on play. My effort is directed toward finding a proper format for writing on a subject that laughs in your face. I am playing hide 'n seek with play. It is winning at the moment. If it ever comes out of hiding long enough for me to capture it, a playful monograph may result. If it refuses to come out of hiding, you will never hear from me again."

AVOCATIONAL INTERESTS: "I may not play much, but I do toy around with vegetable gardening, breadmaking, the classical guitar, and just about any sport there is. While looking out for my game (the kind you hunt, i.e., play) I have occasion to jog a lot, too."

BIOGRAPHICAL/CRITICAL SOURCES: Sports Illustrated, October 13, 1975.

* * *

HARRAGAN, Betty Lehan 1921-

PERSONAL: Born June 2, 1921, in Milwaukee, Wis.; daughter of Charles Joseph and Marie Ann (Caswell) Lehan; married David Joseph Harragan, January 2, 1962 (deceased); children: Kathleen Ann. *Education:* Attended Milwaukee State Teachers College, 1939-41; Marquette University, A.B., 1944; Columbia University, A.M., 1947. *Politics:* "Women's Equality." *Home and office:* 541 East 20th St., New York, N.Y. 10010.

CAREER: Worked for Allis Chambers, Columbia Broadcasting System, and Newell-Emmett Advertising Agency; New York Telephone Co., New York City, women's editor of employee publications, 1950-56; Ruth Lundgren Co., New York City, 1957-63, executive vice-president, 1960-63; J. Walter Thompson Co., New York, N.Y., senior public relations writer, 1963-72; Betty Harragan & Affiliates (consultants on women's employment), New York City, principal, 1972—. Faculty member of Womanschool, 1975—.

MEMBER: National Organization for Women, National Women's Political Caucus, Authors Guild of Authors League of America.

WRITINGS: Games Mother Never Taught You: Corporate Gamesmanship for Women, Rawson Associates, 1977. Contributor to magazines.

WORK IN PROGRESS: Corporate Gameswomen, "on the emerging new power brokers," for Rawson Associates.

SIDELIGHTS: Betty Harragan writes: "My interests and expertise are solely directed toward moving women into economic power positions. Today's young women have all the qualifications for success except that nobody tells them the truth about real-life conditions in the world of business. I am a businesswoman, a writer, and an activist in the woman's rights movement and I expect all my writing to be a conjunction of those facets. In line with that, I teach a course for professional/executive women at the Womanschool in New York on playing corporate politics and find it immensely gratifying to observe genuine progress on their jobs by my students."

* * *

HARRIETT 1905-

PERSONAL: Legal name, Harriett Wilcoxen Ginnings; professionally known as Harriett; born May 12, 1905, in Lewistown, Ill.; daughter of George Ray (a farmer) and Sylvia (Black) Wilcoxen; married Harold Ginnings, June 22, 1928 (divorced); children: Brett (Mrs. Richard Johnson Bell). *Education:* Attended Western Illinois Teachers College (now Western Illinois University), 1924-27; further part-time study at various schools of art, drama, speech, and fashion. *Politics:* Republican. *Religion:* Episcopalian. *Home and office:* 135 East 54th St., New York, N.Y. 10022. *Agent:* Evelyn Singer Agency, Inc., P.O. Box 163, Briarcliff Manor, N.Y. 10510.

CAREER: Teacher of commerce in Illinois schools, 1927-

30; Berlitz School of Languages, Minneapolis, Minn., English teacher, 1943; Colwell Press, New York City, apprentice, 1944; free-lance writer, designer, and illustrator, 1944-59; Grosset & Dunlap, Inc., New York City, assistant to art director, 1959-62; Grollier, Inc., New York City, assistant editor of *Book of Knowledge,* 1962-63; Macfadden-Bartel Corp., New York City, medical editor-writer, 1963-73; free-lance writer, designer, and illustrator, 1973—. Book designer and illustrator for Harvey House, Inc., 1964-67; writing instructor at Famous Writers School, Westport, Conn., 1966-67. Appears on television as guest artist and actress, 1953—, producer of children's television show "The Magic Slate," 1956; member of little theatre troupe, "Fable Valley Puppets," 1961-62; member of puppet troupe, "We Three!", 1975—. Has exhibited art work at major advertising agencies in New York City; permanent collections of her work housed at Western Illinois University Memorial Library, Macomb, and Lila Acheson Wallace Memorial Library, Lewistown, Ill. *Member:* National Academy of Television Arts and Sciences, American Federation of Television and Radio Arts, Screen Actors Guild, Society of Illustrators, Puppeteers of America, Art Students League, Puppetry Guild of Greater New York (liaison officer, 1964-65).

WRITINGS: (Adapter and illustrator) Hans Christian Andersen, *The Emperor's New Clothes,* Maxton, 1948; *Animal ABC* (self-illustrated), Whitman Publishing, 1949; *Froggie Went A-Courtin'* (self-illustrated), Harvey House, 1967; *First Lady of India: The Story of Indira Gandhi,* Doubleday, 1969; (with Mario Martino) *Emergence,* Crown, 1977.

Illustrator: *My First Adventure in Pianoland,* G. Shirmer, 1953; *Learning to Use Arithmetic, 2,* Heath, 1953; *The Travel Play and Coloring Book,* Grosset, 1961; *Crosswords for the Connoisseur #4,* Grosset, 1962; Richard George Van Gelder, *The Professor and the Mysterious Box,* Harvey House, 1964; *The Professor and the Vanishing Flags,* Harvey House, 1965; Florence Dorothy Wood, *The Bear Family,* Harvey House, 1966; *Baby's Own Horoscope,* Time Pattern Research Institute, 1971.

Author and illustrator of the "It Is Easy to Draw" series. Contributor of articles to periodicals. Associate editor, *The Gold Leaf Question and Answer Library, Interior Design,* 1964; editor of employees newsletter, St. Clare's Hospital and Health Center, 1969-72.

WORK IN PROGRESS: A book on puppetry; creating toys for manufacturing.

SIDELIGHTS: Harriett told *CA:* "I'd like to feel I have a special understanding of children. If you're honest with them, you'll always hold them, and if you love them, they'll love you. I cannot stress too greatly the importance of reading and creative playing. What one learns, one becomes. And knowledge is the one possession that can never be taken away."

*   *   *

HARRIS, Fred (Roy) 1930-

PERSONAL: Born November 13, 1930, in Walters, Okla.; son of Fred B. (a farmer) and Alene (Person) Harris; married LaDonna Crawford (an administrator), April 8, 1949; children: Kathryn Tijerina, Byron, Laura. *Education:* University of Oklahoma, B.A., 1952, LL.B., 1954. *Politics:* Democrat. *Home address:* P.O. Box 1203, Corrales, N.M. 87048. *Office:* Department of Political Science, University of New Mexico, Albuquerque, N.M. 87131.

CAREER: Admitted to Oklahoma Bar, 1954; Harris, New-

combre, Redman & Doolin, Lawton, Okla., founder and senior partner, 1954-64; member of Oklahoma Senate, 1956-64; member of U.S. Senate from Oklahoma, 1964-73; Peoples Policy Center (public interest and research organization), Washington, D.C., president, 1973-75; campaigned for Democratic U.S. presidential nomination, 1975-76; University of New Mexico, Albuquerque, professor of political science, 1976—. Member of National Advisory Commission on Civil Disorders, 1967-68. Chairperson of Democratic National Committee, 1969-70. Adjunct professor of government, American University, 1973-75. *Member:* Phi Beta Kappa.

WRITINGS—Nonfiction: *Alarms and Hopes,* Harper, 1967; *Now Is the Time,* McGraw, 1971; *The New Populism,* Saturday Review Press, 1973; *Potomac Fever,* Norton, 1977; *Participation: The Ideal and the Reality of Democracy in America,* Scott, Foresman, in press.

SIDELIGHTS: Harris, the "neo-populist" candidate for president in 1976, was the emotional, if not the practical, favorite of Democratic liberals, as several political commentators have noted. Harris's neopopulism was described by Philip Terzian as "a spellbinding combination of affirmative action, Naderism, youthophilia, elitist-baiting, and good old fashioned legislative know-how." Although Harris began his career as a moderate Democratic senator from Oklahoma, during the late 1960's he drifted leftward politically and became known as a critic of the country's maldistribution of wealth.

Harris's presidential campaign was predicated, wrote Jules Witcover, "on a perception of an electorate that is tired of old trappings, that yearns for a new kind of open, straightforward candidate and politics, but that is justifiably suspicious of anyone who projects himself as different from the pack of old jacks." In a 1974 memo outlining his campaign plans, Harris wrote about himself as candidate: "The candidate must be plain-spoken, candid, open. He must demonstrate, from the very first and even in little things, that he will tell the people the truth. None of this 'people are asking me to run' business. No coy 'non-candidate' status. . . . The candidate must articulate in blunt language the real frustrations that people rightly feel because of elitism, privilege, bigness, and concentrated power. No twelve-point programs and new bureaucracies, but common sense steps to diffuse economic and political power more widely."

The style of Harris's campaign was in accordance with his political stance. He ran what Whitcover termed a "guerilla-type campaign," crossing the country with his family in their camper, sponsoring $4.76 a plate fund-raising dinners, and generally conducting the campaign in a manner that made "Jimmy Carter look like John Connally" (according to Jeff Greenfield).

Many Democrats likened Harris to George McGovern and avoided supporting him for that reason. They feared that if Harris became the Democratic nominee, he would be defeated in the national election, like McGovern, because he was perceived by the electorate as a "radical." Harris explained the difference between him and McGovern to Stanley Cloud: "I never tell people that they ought to do something because it's morally right. I show how it's in their own self-interest. My dad used to listen to McGovern and then say, 'Well, it sounds fine, but when's he gonna start talking to me?' Dad was right, and that's what I try to do—talk a language that ordinary people can understand."

After bowing out of the race for the presidential nomination, Harris wrote his political memoirs. In the book *Potomac*

Fever, he discussed his own case of "Potomac Fever": Harris felt that he concerned himself more with Washington and neglected his home state of Oklahoma. Colman McCarthy thought that Harris misdiagnosed his affliction—that instead Harris was suffering from "Potomac Blahs." Harris's problem, according to McCarthy, "was in believing that he, the mighty liberal and champion of the little guy, could bring on reforms quickly. He couldn't, and he got the Potomac Blahs.... The value of Harris's book is what it says about one person's failure to deal with the frustrations of reform."

In another review of the book, Les Whitten described Harris: "With his penultimate shirt button open, flesh showing through the gap, a suit too small, a 1930's hairstyle, he was a portrait in noble disorganization—caused by doing too much for others, his wife, LaDonna, and himself, in that order. Sometimes, he was a sudden dry handful of Dust Bowl wit in our surprised faces." But Whitten complained: "*That* vivid Harris isn't enough in evidence in this book, and it is badly flawed thereby.... We hear too much about Harris's 'deeply seated concern with the issues,' and far too little about how, imaginatively, often bumblingly, always humanly, he tried to deal with the issues." Although Harris's book contains disappointments, they are not, according to Whitten, "fatal ones." He continued, "Lumpy as the book is, it still flashes with the precursors of the better, more anecdotal book Harris has inside him."

Philip Terzian was also drawn to the anecdotal humor of the book. He commented: "If Hollywood had any imagination, it would buy the rights for this book of Fred Harris's memoirs and film it as a political *Pilgrim's Progress* of the past two decades. Except, of course, it would require a script writer with more humor than Bunyan to bring the tale off, because Fred Harris's career has not only been instructive, but funny."

Harris told *CA:* "In Moscow once, the Soviet Union's Americanologist chief, Georgi Arbatov, and I were talking, and I mentioned that I was at a disadvantage in commenting on the Soviet economic and political system, as compared to his ability to comment on ours, because the Soviet system was not open to outside researchers. 'That's no disadvantage for you,' he replied. 'We study your system, but we still cannot understand it.'

"The American system looks simple, but it is a labyrinth of complexity. I enjoy writing about it, to make it more understandable—not just *how* a bill goes through Congress, but also *why,* for example—to point the way for citizen participation and suggest ways to make participation opportunities better."

BIOGRAPHICAL/CRITICAL SOURCES: Myra MacPherson, *Power Lovers,* Putnam, 1975; *Newsweek,* November 3, 1975, December 22, 1975; *Time,* December 22, 1975; *Progressive,* January, 1976, July, 1977; *Book World,* May 15, 1977; *New Republic,* May 21, 1977; *New York Times Book Review,* June 5, 1977.

* * *

HARRIS, Richard N(elson) 1942-

PERSONAL: Born January 17, 1942, in New York, N.Y.; son of Nelson (a salesman) and Elizabeth (Hurst) Harris; married Linda Mancke; children: Pamela, Debra, Richard, Jennifer Leigh. *Education:* West Virginia Wesleyan College, B.A., 1964; Boston University, M.A., 1965; Tufts University, Ph.D., 1970; Hunter College of the City University of New York, M.S.W., 1974. *Residence:* Valley Stream, N.Y.

Office: Department of Sociology and Anthropology, St. John's University, Jamaica, N.Y. 11439.

CAREER: St. John's University, Jamaica, N.Y., assistant professor, 1975-78, associate professor of sociology and social work, 1978—. Staff therapist at Institute for Advanced Study in Rational Psychotherapy, 1974—. Counselor for New York City Community Sex Information, 1974-78. *Member:* National Association of Social Workers, American Association of Marriage and Family Counseling (clinical member).

WRITINGS: The Police Academy: An Inside View, Wiley, 1973; *Rational Emotive Therapy: Simple But Not Easy,* Rational Living, 1978.

WORK IN PROGRESS: Directive Casework: A Rational-Emotive Approach.

SIDELIGHTS: Harris comments: "One of the greatest pleasures that motivates my vocational work is helping others and myself with our emotional problems. I especially enjoy training clinicians to become more aware of their own emotional problems and to intervene more effectively with the problems of others."

* * *

HARRIS, Warren G(ene) 1936-

PERSONAL: Born January 29, 1936, in Newark, N.J.; son of Frank G. (an aviation executive) and Maude (Friedman) Harris. *Education:* Queens College (now Queens College of the City University of New York), B.A., 1957. *Home:* 205 West 57th St., New York, N.Y. 10019. *Agent:* William Morris Agency, 1350 Avenue of the Americas, New York, N.Y. 10019.

CAREER: Quigley Publications, New York City, reporter and film reviewer for *Motion Picture Daily* and *Motion Picture Herald,* 1957-59; Paramount Pictures, New York City, publicity executive, 1959-69; unit publicist for motion pictures in New York City and Europe, 1970-72; writer, 1972—.

WRITINGS: Gable and Lombard, Simon & Schuster, 1974. Contributor to film journals.

WORK IN PROGRESS: Collaborating with Eddie Fisher on his own autobiography, for publication by Harper.

* * *

HARRISON, Barbara Grizzuti 1934-

PERSONAL: Born September 14, 1934, in Brooklyn, N.Y.; daughter of Dominick (a printer) and Carmela (Di Nardo) Grizzuti; married W. Dale Harrison, July, 1960 (marriage ended, 1968); children: Joshua Paul, Anna Edyth. *Religion:* Roman Catholic. *Residence:* Brooklyn, N.Y. *Agent:* Georges Borchardt, Inc., 145 East 52nd St., New York, N.Y. 10022.

CAREER: Writer. Worked as secretary, 1958-60.

WRITINGS: Unlearning the Lie: Sexism in School, Liveright, 1969; *Visions of Glory: A History and a Memory of the Witnesses of Jehovah,* Simon & Schuster, 1978. Contributor to magazines.

SIDELIGHTS: Barbara Harrison has lived in Tripoli, Bombay, Hyderabad, and Guatemala City.

* * *

HARRISON, J(ames) P.

EDUCATION: Yale University, B.A., 1954; Columbia

University, M.A., 1960, Ph.D., 1965. *Home:* 404 Riverside Dr., New York, N.Y. 10025. *Office:* Department of History, Hunter College of the City University of New York, New York, N.Y. 10021.

CAREER: Richmond News Leader, Richmond, Va., reporter, 1957-58; Barnard College, New York, N.Y., part-time visiting lecturer in history, 1966; Columbia University, New York City, visiting professor of political science, 1969-71; Hunter College of the City University of New York, New York City, professor of history, 1975—. *Military service:* U.S. Air Force, pilot, 1955-57.

MEMBER: American Historical Association, Association of Asian Studies, Amnesty International (chairman of board of directors, 1971-73). *Awards, honors:* Ford Foundation fellowship for Hong Kong, 1962-63.

WRITINGS: Modern Chinese Nationalism, Hunter College of the City University of New York, 1969; *The Communists and Chinese Peasant Rebellions,* Atheneum, 1969; *The Long March to Power: A History of the Chinese Communist Party, 1921-1972,* Praeger, 1972.

SIDELIGHTS: Harrison writes: "In my research and writings on Chinese Communism, I have attempted to understand the forces which created the greatest revolution in history, and how the Communists were able to take leadership of that revolution against overwhelming odds. Similarly my present work on the victory of the Vietnamese communists against even greater odds aims to examine similar interactions of economic and social conditions with ideology and leadership. I have sought interviews with participants in these extraordinary events in China and Vietnam, and have made trips to both countries. But the students of these complex and highly controversial revolutions must rely primarily on research in such documents as exist, and on the scholarly studies of these documents. I am able to pursue these in English, French, Russian, and Chinese."

*　　*　　*

HASHMI, Alamgir 1951-

PERSONAL: Born November 15, 1951, in Lahore, Pakistan; came to the United States in 1974; son of Sharif Ahmed (a professor) and Naseem (Akhter) Hashmi. *Education:* University of the Panjab, M.A., 1972. *Home address:* c/o Beatrice Stoerk, Hulfteggstrasse 27, CH-8400, Winterthur, Switzerland. *Office:* Department of English, University of Louisville, Louisville, Ky. 40208.

CAREER: Government College, Lahore, Pakistan, tutor in English, 1972-73; Forman Christian College, Lahore, lecturer in English, 1973-74, faculty adviser, *Folio,* 1973-74; University of Louisville, Louisville, Ky., part-time lecturer in English, 1975—. Broadcaster and editor for Writers' Workshop on Radio Pakistan, 1972-74. *Member:* International Poetry Society, Association for Asian Studies, Modern Poetry Association, Sondhi Translation Society, George Eliot Fellowship. *Awards, honors:* Poetry prize from All-Pakistan Creative Writing Contest at University of Lyallpur, 1972, for "The Telegram."

WRITINGS: The Oath and Amen: Love Poems, Dover, 1976. Contributor to literature and Asian studies journals. Assistant editor of *Ravi,* 1971-72; editor of *English* (Lahore), 1972-74; guest editor of *New Quarterly,* 1978.

WORK IN PROGRESS: Poems; research on formalist criticism; critical work on modern Urdu poetry; a book length collection of poems, *Assonances.*

SIDELIGHTS: Hashmi writes: "Many of my poems deal

with multicultural experience, and since my arrival in the United States, I think, there has been some 'displacement' of imagery, and occasionally, perhaps a colloquialism may have been too apposite or forceful to avoid merely because o its status (or caste?) in the society of language.

"My 1976 book is a collection of 'love poems' mostly, though it also contains a section called "Distractions," as a countermovement, set against the unity of theme in the main body of the work. Because of the thematic nature of this volume several other poems that I may have liked to publish at the time, as they were contemporaneous with several of those which are in the book, were kept out. Of course, love is an important and enduring theme in my work so far, but I have written and published dozens of poems on other subjects as well."

BIOGRAPHICAL/CRITICAL SOURCES: New Quarterly, January, 1978.

*　　*　　*

HATFIELD, Mark O(dom) 1922-

PERSONAL: Born July 12, 1922, in Dallas, Ore.; son of Charles Dolin (a railroad construction blacksmith) and Dovie (a teacher; maiden name, Odom) Hatfield; married Antoinette Kuzmanich (a teacher and counselor), July 8, 1958; children: Elizabeth, Mark Odom, Jr., Theresa, Charles Vincent. *Education:* Willamette University, B.A., 1943; Stanford University, A.M., 1948. *Politics:* Republican. *Religion:* Baptist. *Home address:* P.O. Box 2416, Newport, Ore. 97365. *Office:* Room 463, Senate Office Bldg., Washington, D.C. 20510.

CAREER: Willamette University, Salem, Ore., instructor, 1949, associate professor of political science and dean of students, 1950-56; Oregon state representative, 1951-55; Oregon state senator, 1955-57; Oregon secretary of state, 1957-59; governor of Oregon, 1959-67; U.S. senator from Oregon, 1967—. Republican National Convention, delegate, 1952, 1956, 1960, 1964, 1968, member of convention resolutions committee, 1952, 1956, chairman of Oregon delegation, 1960, 1964, 1968, keynoter and temporary chairman, 1964, nominator for Richard M. Nixon, 1960, seconded Nixon's nomination, 1968. Member of Senate committees for Appropriations, Energy and Natural Resources, Indian Affairs, and Rules and Administration, and of subcommittees for Foreign Operations, Public Works, Interior, Agriculture, State-Justice-Commerce-Judiciary, Energy Research and Development, Parks and Recreation, and Public Lands and Resources. Trustee of Willamette University, George Fox College, Western Conservative Baptist Seminary, and Dag Hammarskjold College. *Military service:* U.S. Navy, 1943-45; served in Pacific; became lieutenant junior grade. *Member:* American Legion, Japanese Diet (honorary member), Croation Fraternal Union, Mason, Grange, Shriners. *Awards, honors:* Annual War Memorial Award from New York Republican Club, 1967; Award for Conservatism from Izaak Walton League of America; Eleanor Roosevelt Humanitarian Award; Freedom Award for Distinguished Leadership in Combating Communism from Order of Lafayette, 1967; Robert A. Taft Memorial Award, 1967.

WRITINGS: Not Quite So Simple, Harper, 1968; *Conflict and Conscience,* Word, Inc., 1971; (author of introduction) *The Economics of Defense: A Bipartisan Review of Military Spending,* Praeger, 1971; (with others) *Amnesty?: The Unsettled Question of Vietnam,* Sun River Press, 1973; *Between a Rock and a Hard Place,* Word, Inc., 1976.

SIDELIGHTS: Mark Hatfield's struggle to live out his

Christian faith in the context of his role as a U.S. senator has often placed him "between a rock and a hard place," as he so aptly entitled his latest book. Grappling with the conflicts between obeying God and working within an imperfect political process, Hatfield has become convinced that his commitment to Jesus Christ requires him to follow Christ's example of servanthood in his own role as a political leader. Because his entire philosophy of life has been shaped by his relationship to Jesus Christ, his political stands have expressed these deep convictions. In seeking to take action in accordance with his understanding of God's standards of justice, the Senator has incurred the displeasure of both the political establishment and Christians who disagree with his views.

After serving two terms as governor of Oregon, Hatfield was elected to the U.S. Senate in 1966, during the height of the Vietnam war. Because his faith had led him to question whether our foreign policy goals justified the suffering that American troops were inflicting upon the Vietnamese people, the new Republican senator openly expressed his opposition to the war. Dismayed that the war had continued without the Constitutional sanction of a declaration of war by Congress, Hatfield joined with George McGovern in 1970 to introduce the Hatfield-McGovern amendment to cut off funds to finance the war. In taking this position, he alienated himself from his constituents, the Republican Party in his state, and even fellow Christians who criticized his refusal to support the President's policies. Though agonizing deeply over this situation, Hatfield continued to follow his conscience and called for national repentance at the National Prayer Breakfast held soon after the signing of the Paris Peace Accords in 1973. Condemning the idolatry of civil religion which used the name of God to justify policies because they were "American," Hatfield challenged his listeners to obey God's commands for righteousness and justice, and to become "Christ's messengers of reconciliation and peace." Even though Hatfield criticized only the national spirit of self-righteousness, the media and the White House regarded his speech as a personal attack on President Nixon and his war policies. Once again Hatfield came under attack for his views.

Undaunted in his struggle to "bring the political realm into an authentic relationship with biblical faith," Hatfield introduced a Senate resolution in December, 1973, to proclaim April 30, 1974, as a National Day of Humiliation, Fasting, and Prayer. He was influenced by similar proclamations by Lincoln during the Civil War, and sought healing for national divisions through this expression of national repentance. The measure passed the Senate quickly, and even though it remained buried in a House committee, thousands of Americans did take part in the observance. During the Bicentennial year Hatfield refused to follow the majority in lauding the virtues of American society, but instead continued to plea for a revolution in the minds and hearts of the American people. In an address given at the National Prayer Breakfast in January, 1976, Hatfield drew comparisons between the biblical "year of jubilee" and the Bicentennial celebration. The inscription on the Liberty Bell, "Proclaim liberty throughout all the land unto all the inhabitants thereof," originally heralded the year of jubilee in Israel during which the Israelites were commanded to free their slaves, forgive their debtors, and seek justice for the oppressed. Hatfield urged Americans likewise to celebrate the Bicentennial "not through pageantry but through concrete acts that flowed from a deeper commitment to God's justice."

Hatfield's convictions have led him to speak out on other

issues facing the national government, especially the problems of poverty and world hunger. He has challenged Americans to reexamine their materialistic lifestyles and to recognize that "the world's food and resources belong to all humanity and must be shared for the benefit of all." Convinced that federal government programs are not always the best instruments for meeting the needs of people, Hatfield has urged Christians to respond collectively in their communities to provide for the needy, and to look beyond their own national borders to the hungry of the fourth world nations. But Hatfield has also defended governmental intervention on behalf of the poor, declaring: "Let us not hide from our duty by utilizing metaphoric excuses decrying socialism—creeping or otherwise—protesting the welfare state or painting pictures of big government as a type of antichrist. The evangelical conscience takes its authority not from John Locke's concept of property or William Buckley's concepts of strictly limited government, but from the New Testament."

A leader in environmental legislation in both his home state of Oregon and in the Senate, Hatfield has consistently opposed the destruction and misuse of natural resources. His commitment to the environment has been partly influenced by the Biblical injunction to "replenish the earth" and care for God's creation. Equally concerned about the welfare of people in a deteriorating environment, Hatfield has maintained: "We must each live and act in ways that demonstrate loving stewardship of the whole of creation for all of humanity. In so doing, we must fashion those environments, in our cities and in the country, which truly nurture the whole person, and his or her relationship to creation."

Hatfield has also vocalized his opposition to the neutron bomb, warning that "deployment of these nuclear warheads will lower the threshold for nuclear war—making a nuclear confrontation more likely." Rejecting the argument that such weapons would serve as a more credible deterrent to the Soviet Union in Europe, he has maintained that we cannot predict the reaction of the adversary, or be guaranteed that limited nuclear warfare would remain limited. Despite our goal of restricted use, the danger of escalation would always exist. Hatfield has also expressed concern that production of the neutron bomb would encourage other nations to exert pressure on the United States in attempts to obtain such a weapons system for themselves. In Hatfield's opinion, developing these weapons would both "impede progress toward the arms-limitation goal of our foreign policy" and risk further nuclear proliferation throughout the world.

An acute sensitivity to the problems of depersonalization and alienation in modern bureaucratic-industrial society has shaped Hatfield's commitment to establishing participatory democracy through decentralization. Warning against the tendency towards tyranny bred by centralization of economic and political power, the Senator has encouraged the growth of neighborhood governments engaged in solving local problems, and has called for worker involvement in the management of their companies. Such decentralization would restore individual dignity and recognize individual needs and aspirations, without undermining the role of federal legislation to protect the environment, the poor, and other vulnerable interests from exploitation.

Though actively involved in seeking political change, Hatfield has rejected the idea that true justice will be established by "reforming the existing structures." Viewing his task as one of calling the nation to conform to God's standards, he has defined success not by visible results but by his faithfulness to God's commands. Mark Hatfield has set his ultimate hope on the Kingdom that God will establish, and committed himself to the Christian community whose sacrificial life-style "demonstrates the shape of God's new order in the midst of a fallen world."

BIOGRAPHICAL/CRITICAL SOURCES: Mark Hatfield, *Conflict and Conscience,* Word, Inc., 1971; *Time,* September 27, 1971; *Christian Century,* February 21, 1973, March 27, 1974; *Christianity Today,* March 26, 1976, June 18, 1976; Hatfield, *Between a Rock and a Hard Place,* Word, Inc., 1976; *U.S. News and World Report,* July 27, 1977.

* * *

HAUGHEY, John C. 1930-

PERSONAL: Surname rhymes with "joy"; born September 27, 1930, in White Plains, N.Y.; son of Patrick and Eleanor (Boyle) Haughey. *Education:* Earned A.B. from Bellarmine College, Ph.L. from Fordham University, S.T.B. and S.T.L. from Woodstock College, and S.T.D. from Catholic University of America. *Home:* 1419 35th St. N.W., Washington, D.C. 20007. *Office:* 1322 36th St. N.W., Washington, D.C. 20007.

CAREER: Entered Society of Jesus (Jesuits); ordained Roman Catholic priest; Georgetown University, Washington, D.C., faculty member in department of theology, 1963-68; associate editor of *America,* 1968-74; Woodstock Theological Center, Washington, D.C., associate member, 1974—. Member of theology faculty at Fordham University, 1973-75.

WRITINGS: The Conspiracy of God, Doubleday, 1976; *Should Anyone Say Forever?,* Doubleday, 1977; (editor and contributor) *Theological Reflections on Charismatic Renewal,* Charismatic Renewal Services, 1977; (editor and contributor) *The Faith That Does Justice,* Paulist Press, 1977. Contributor to theology journals.

WORK IN PROGRESS: A "justice Christology," for Doubleday; directing a seminar series on government decision-making at Georgetown University, with publication expected to result.

* * *

HAWES, William (Kenneth) 1931-

PERSONAL: Born March 6, 1931, in Grand Rapids, Mich.; son of William Kenneth, Sr. (a motor equipment supervisor) and C. Elizabeth (Tibble) Hawes; married Ella Margaret Plant (an educator), August 13, 1961; children: William Kenneth III, Robert Ernest. *Education:* Eastern Michigan University, A.B., 1955; University of Michigan, M.A., 1956, Ph.D., 1960; also attended University of St. Thomas, 1969, and Museum Fine Arts School, Houston, Tex., 1970. *Home:* 2240 Glen Haven, Houston, Tex. 77030. *Office:* School of Communication, University of Houston, Houston, Tex. 77004.

CAREER: Eastern Michigan University, Ypsilanti, instructor in English and speech, 1956-60; Texas Christian University, Fort Worth, assistant professor of radio, television and film, and director of program, 1960-64; University of North Carolina, Chapel Hill, visiting assistant professor and director of radio program, 1964-65; University of Houston, Houston, Tex., associate professor, 1965-76, professor of radio, television, and film, 1976—, executive officer for radio-television-film faculty, 1978. Adjunct professor of biomedical communications, School of Allied Health Sciences, University of Texas, 1975—. Manager of KTCU-FM Radio,

1960-64, WUNC-FM Radio, 1964-65, and KUHF-FM Radio, 1965-69; executive producer of KTVT-TV series, "The Future We Face," 1960-64; member of production staff at WTOP-TV, summer, 1965; producer and host of KHTV-TV series "College News Conference" and "News on Campus," 1967-73, executive producer of "Campus Workshop," 1973—; executive producer of films, including "Farewell to All the Ghosts and Goblins of Circumstance," 1974, "The Second Door," 1977, and "H.M.S. Pinafore"; producer-director of "Holden's Heroes" for Variable Annuity Life Insurance Co., 1971. Owner and associate director of Children's Playhouse (preschool), 1972—. Instructor on WJRT-TV, 1959; instructor at National Music Camp (Interlochen), 1959. *Military service:* Michigan Air National Guard, 1950-54. U.S. Air Force, 1951-53.

MEMBER: International Radio and Television Society, Institute for International Education, Broadcast Education Association, American Film Institute, Speech Communication Association of America, Texas Association of Broadcasters. *Awards, honors:* Hopwood Award in Drama from University of Michigan, 1957, for "Reach for a Dream"; fellowships from International Radio and Television Society, 1973, 1974, 1975.

WRITINGS: (Contributor) Robert L. Hilliard, editor, *Radio Broadcasting: Introduction to the Sound Medium,* Hastings House, 1967, revised edition, 1975; (contributor) Hilliard, editor, *Television Broadcasting,* Hastings House, 1964, revised edition, 1978; (editor) *Pornography Cinema: Community Standards,* University of Houston, 1975; *The Performer in Mass Media,* Hastings House, 1978. Contributor of articles and reviews to professional journals and newspapers.

WORK IN PROGRESS: Divine Decision: The Rehabilitation of a Criminal.

SIDELIGHTS: Hawes writes: "*The Performer in Mass Media* is a comprehensive guide for those who aspire to be on camera and or microphone, including media professional and community experts (doctors, advocates, ministers, etc.). It is a realistic view of what it takes to become a performer and what the performer's environment consists of with chapters on appearance, voice, movement, talent, studios and preparation of materials."

* * *

HAYAMI, Yujiro 1932-

PERSONAL: Born November 26, 1932, in Tokyo, Japan; son of Kannosuke and Chiyoko Hayami; married Takako Suzuki. *Education:* University of Tokyo, B.A., 1956; Iowa State University, Ph.D., 1960. *Home:* 6-8-14 Okusawa, Setagaya, Tokyo, Japan. *Office:* Faculty of Economics, Tokyo Metropolitan University, Yakumo, Meguro-ku, Tokyo, Japan.

CAREER: Tokyo Metropolitan University, Tokyo, Japan, professor of economics, 1966—. *Awards, honors:* American Agricultural Economic Association, distinguished publication award, 1971, for "Factor Prices and Technical Change in Agricultural Development," and outstanding article award, 1976, for "Efficiency and Equity of Public Research: Rice Breeding in Japan's Economic Development."

WRITINGS: Agricultural Development: An International Perspective, Johns Hopkins Press, 1971; *A Century of Agricultural Growth in Japan,* University of Tokyo Press, 1975; *Anatomy of Peasant Economy,* International Rice Research Institute, 1978.

WORK IN PROGRESS: Changes in Agrarian Institutions in Asia.

* * *

HAYES, Bartlett (Harding, Jr.)   1904-

PERSONAL: Born August 5, 1904, in Andover, Mass.; son of Bartlett Harding (a stock broker and farmer) and Marjorie (Scull) Hayes; married Clare Wadleigh, September 15, 1932; children: Bridget, Deborah, Hilary, Delia-Maria Hayes Thompson. *Education:* Harvard University, A.B., 1926. *Politics:* Independent Republican. *Religion:* Independent Episcopal. *Home:* 24 Phillips St., Andover, Mass. 01810.

CAREER: Art teacher at private school in Andover, Mass., 1933-69; director of Addison Gallery of American Art, 1940-69; Seminar for Asiatic Museum Curators, Honolulu, Hawaii, lecturer, 1969-70; American Academy, Rome, Italy, director, 1970-73; consultant and writer, 1973—. Member of board of directors of Learning Disabilities Foundation, 1976—; member of Council for the Arts, Massachusetts Institute of Technology, 1973—, board of overseers of Strawberry Banke, 1973—, art advisory committee of Mt. Holyoke College, 1975—, and museum collections committee, Essex Institute, 1976—. Director, Centennial Exhibition of School of Museum of Fine Arts, Boston, 1977. Member of board of trustees of St. Gaudens Memorial, and Institute of Contemporary Art. *Military service:* U.S. Army, Field Artillery, 1926; became second lieutenant. *Member:* American Academy of Arts and Sciences (fellow), American Association of Museums, College Art Association of America, Society for Preservation of New England Antiquities, Trustees of Public Reservations, Bostonian Society, Newburyport Maritime Society.

WRITINGS: (With Mary Rathbun) *A Layman's Guide to Modern Art,* Oxford University Press, 1948; (editor with Sara Weeks) *Search for the Real,* Hans Hofman Addison Gallery, Phillips Academy, 1948; *The Naked Truth and Personal Vision,* Addison Gallery, Phillips Academy, 1954; (editor) *Art Education for Scientist and Engineer,* M.I.T. Press, 1957; *American Drawings,* Shorewood, 1965; (with Nina Kaiden) *Artist and Advocate,* Renaissance Editions, 1967; *Art and Nature* (monograph), Holt, 1973; *Up From the Ground,* Holt, 1973. Contributor to magazines, including *Antiques* and *Glamour,* and newspapers.

WORK IN PROGRESS: A Vestryman's Guide to Contemporary Church Architecture.

SIDELIGHTS: Hayes comments: "Charles Eames recently wrote: 'As a society, we now put much more of our total energy into teaching than into learning.' I might counter by noting that one learns more by teaching than by being taught and that there is an army of teachers working in behalf of our present society."

* * *

HAYES, Dorsha

PERSONAL: Born in Galesburg, Ill.; daughter of Frederick Jay and Caroline (Rice) Bentley; married Paul Hayes, June 19, 1936 (died, 1969). *Education:* Attended Columbia University and University of Chicago. *Home:* 1647 First Ave., New York, N.Y. 10028.

CAREER: Professional dancer; member of Fokine Ballets, soloist in Broadway musical productions, and concert artist; co-founder of off-Broadway Theater of the Dance. Writer. Lecturer for Harold Peat Bureau, 1942. Director of workshops; has given readings and lectures.

MEMBER: International P.E.N., Poetry Society of America (past vice-president), Academy of American Poets, National League of American Pen Women, Composers, Authors, and Artists of America, C. J. Jung Foundation (past member of board of directors), Analytical Psychology Club (past vice-president), Pen and Brush, New York Women Poets, Daughters of the Cinncinati. *Awards, honors:* Awards from *Poet Lore,* National Federation of State Poetry Societies, and New York Women Poets.

WRITINGS: The American Primer, Alliance Book Corp., 1941; *Mrs. Heaton's Daughter,* Ziff-Davis, 1943; *Chicago: Crossroads of American Enterprise,* Messner, 1944; *Who Walk with the Earth* (stories and essays on the labor movement), Harper, 1945, reprinted, AMS Press, 1977; *The Bell-Branch Rings: Selected Poems,* William Bauhan, 1972; *Bell-Branch, Ring Again* (poems), Branden Press, 1975.

Work represented in anthologies. Contributor of articles and poems to magazines and newspapers, including psychology journals and *Lyric.*

WORK IN PROGRESS: A book on technique in poetry.

* * *

HAYES, Paul Martin   1942-

PERSONAL: Born February 12, 1942, in London, England; son of Richard Oswald (an engineer) and Margaret Jessie (Ward) Hayes; married Linda Constable, June 26, 1966 (divorced November 25, 1975). *Education:* University of Dijon, diploma, 1960; St. John's College, Oxford, B.A., 1963; University of Marburg, diploma, 1961; Oxford University, M.A., 1967, D.Phil., 1969; also attended University of Lausanne, University of Oslo, and Institute for Higher International Studies (Geneva, Switzerland). *Politics:* Conservative. *Religion:* Church of England. *Home:* 3 Pound Close, Yarnton, Oxford, England. *Office:* Keble College, Oxford University, Oxford OX1 3PG, England.

CAREER: Oxford University, Oxford, England, lecturer at Keble College, 1964-65, faculty lecturer, 1965-73, fellow and tutor at Keble College, 1965—, lecturer in modern history, 1973—, dean of Keble College, 1966-74, 1977—. *Member:* Oxford University Hockey Club, Oxford University Cricket Club.

WRITINGS: Quisling, David & Charles, 1971; *Fascism,* Allen & Unwin, 1973; *The Nineteenth Century, 1814-1880,* A. & C. Black, 1975; *The Twentieth Century, 1880-1939,* A. & C. Black, 1978. Contributor of articles and reviews to history, education, and popular journals.

WORK IN PROGRESS: Writing about the part played by British ambassadors to Berlin, 1866-1939, in influencing British policy.

SIDELIGHTS: Hayes told *CA:* "*Quisling* is a study of the personality of the man in relation to his historical achievements. For what it is worth, his *first* wife, now a resident of California, described it as the only work written on Quisling which showed any real understanding of the man.

"*Fascism* is a study of the interaction of beliefs and organisations/leaders in the interwar years. It tries to examine and analyse the basic beliefs of the fascists and to evaluate the contemporary and long-term importance of these men and their ideas.

"*The Nineteenth Century, 1814-1880* and *The Twentieth Century, 1880-1939* are two studies that cover the period 1814-1939, looking at the historical developments very much through the eyes of contemporary observers. This is accompanied by an attempt to analyze these views from an historical vantage point—and to put *British* decisions in the context of *world* developments.''

AVOCATIONAL INTERESTS: Attending concerts, plays, and artistic exhibitions.

* * *

HAYWOOD, Harry
   See HALL, Haywood

* * *

HAZZARD, Lowell B(restel)   1898-1978

February 6, 1898—January 28, 1978; American clergyman, educator, and author. Hazzard taught at Wesley Theological Seminary in Washington, D.C., Ohio Wesleyan University, and Illinois Wesleyan University. He served as a pastor at churches in Peoria, Pittsfield, and Quincy, Illinois. He was author of books on the subject of religion. Hazzard died in Pontiac, Ill. Obituaries and other sources: *Directory of American Scholars,* Volume IV: *Philosophy, Religion, and Law,* 6th edition, Bowker, 1974; *Who's Who in America,* 38th edition, Marquis, 1974; *Washington Post,* February 2, 1978.

* * *

HEADSTROM, Richard   1902-

PERSONAL: Born February 21, 1902, in Cambridge, Mass.; son of John Birger and Anna (Wiebe) Headstrom; married Ruth H. Hemmerdinger, 1934; children: John Richard. *Education:* Massachusetts Institute of Technology, S.B., 1924; additional study at Harvard University. *Home:* 1144 Cornish St., Aiken, S.C. 29801.

CAREER: Science teacher in private and public schools in Massachusetts, 1939-64. Associate curator and workshop lecturer, New England Museum of Natural History, 1938-43; curator, David Mason Little Museum of Natural History, 1939-42; curator of entomology and workshop teacher, Worcester Museums of Science and Industry, 1942-64; lecturer in natural science, Boston Center for Adult Education, 1946-49; entomologist of Dover, Mass., 1953-56; educational director, Daniels School of Forestry, Wildlife Management, and Aquatic Biology, 1955-59. Writer. Member of Dover Municipal Tree Committee, Medway Municipal Conservation Committee, and Massachusetts Committee on Conservation of the National Association of Biology Teachers. Assistant director of children's summer camps and director of nature study programs; director and judge of science fairs. Established Dover's wildlife sanctuary. Has been interviewed on radio programs. *Member:* Harvard Club of South Carolina. *Awards, honors:* Named honorary member of Sioux Indian Tribe, 1945; outstanding children's science book award from National Science Teachers Association and Children's Book Council, 1972, for *Frogs, Toads, and Salamanders as Pets;* Chickadee Award from Massachusetts Audubon Society, 1975.

WRITINGS: The Origin of Man, Princeton University Press, 1921; *The Story of Russia: A History of Russia from the Earliest Times to 1933,* Stokes Publishing, 1933; *Adventures with a Microscope* (juvenile), Stokes Publishing, 1941; *Birds' Nests,* Washburn, 1949; *The Living Year,* Washburn, 1950; *Birds' Nests of the West,* Washburn, 1951; *Garden Friends and Foes,* Washburn, 1954; *Adventures With a Hand Lens* (juvenile), Lippincott, 1962; *Adventures With Insects* (juvenile), Lippincott, 1963; *Adventures With Fresh-*

water Animals (juvenile), Lippincott, 1964; *Nature in Miniature,* Knopf, 1968; *A Complete Field Guide to Nests in the United States,* Washburn, 1970; *Lizards as Pets* (juvenile), Lippincott, 1971; *Whose Track Is It?,* Washburn, 1971; *Frogs, Toads, and Salamanders as Pets* (juvenile), Washburn, 1972; *Spiders of the United States,* A.S. Barnes, 1973; *Your Insect Pet,* McKay, 1973; *The Beetles of North America,* A.S. Barnes, 1977; *The Families of Flowering Plants,* A.S. Barnes, 1978; *Lobsters, Crabs, Shrimps, and Their Relatives,* A.S. Barnes, 1978; *Your Reptile Pet,* McKay, in press.

Booklets: *Whose Nest Is That?* Massachusetts Audubon Society, 1944, revised edition, 1965; *Animals and the Garden,* Organic Gardening Publishing Co., 1945; *Whose Track Is That?,* Massachusetts Audubon Society, 1950; *Animal Homes,* Massachusetts Audubon Society, 1951; *Butterfly Chrysalides,* Worcester Museums of Science and Industry, 1951; *Moth Cocoons,* Worcester Museums of Science and Industry, 1952; *Insect Webs,* Worcester Museums of Science and Industry, 1953.

Newspaper columns: ''Naturalist's Corner,'' in *Medford Record,* 1938—; ''Nature's Corner,'' in *Boston Transcript,* 1939-40; ''Hunting with a Microscope,'' in *Boston Transcript,* 1940-41; nature writer and care of pets column in *Boston Globe,* 1941-45; ''Animals in Your Scrapbook,'' in *Boston Herald,* 1945-46; ''Animals in Your Backyard,'' in *Worcester Telegram,* 1964-67; ''Palmetto Wildlife,'' in *Columbia State,* 1965-67.

Contributor to *Encyclopaedia Britannica, Encyclopedia of the Biological Sciences,* and *Massachusetts Educational Guide.* Contributor of about three thousand articles to science, literature, and philosophy journals, including *Science, Naturalist, Personalist,* and *Organic Gardening.*

* * *

HEALEY, B. J.
   See HEALEY, Ben J.

* * *

HEALEY, Ben J.   1908-
   (B. J. Healey; J. G. Jeffreys, a pseudonym)

PERSONAL: Born June 26, 1908, in Birmingham, England; son of William Henry (an engraver) and Alice (Owen) Healey; married Muriel Rose Herd, January 15, 1951. *Education:* Attended Birmingham School of Art and University of Birmingham, 1926-30. *Politics:* Conservative. *Religion:* Church of England. *Home:* 19 Granard Ave., Putney, London SW15 6HH, England. *Agent:* Barthold Fles, Barthold Fles Literary Agency, 507 Fifth Ave., New York, N.Y. 10017.

CAREER: Worked as stage designer for theatres, 1939-45; artist and designer in film industry; currently full-time writer. *Member:* Royal Horticultural Society.

WRITINGS—Under name Ben Healey: *Waiting for a Tiger,* Harper, 1965; *The Terrible Pictures,* Harper, 1967; *The Vespucci Papers,* G. K. Hall, 1972; *The Stone Baby,* Lippincott, 1973; *The Horstmann Inheritance,* R. Hale, 1975.

Under name B. J. Healey: *The Plant Hunters* (nonfiction), Scribner, 1975; *A Gardner's Guide to Plant Names,* Scribner, 1975.

Under pseudonym J. G. Jeffreys: *The Thief Taker,* Manor Books, 1975; *Conspiracy of Poisons,* Walker & Co., 1977.

WORK IN PROGRESS: Research for *A World History of Gardening;* research for a historical novel.

SIDELIGHTS: Healey writes that before World War II he worked as a stage designer for theaters, but spent a lot of time traveling in Europe, mostly on foot. After the war, he worked in the film industry. His first book, which was successful, was written for his own amusement.

AVOCATIONAL INTERESTS: Antique books; bibliography.

*   *   *

HEARN, Charles R(alph)   1937-

PERSONAL: Born October 19, 1937, in Thompsonville, Ill.; son of Hubert R. (a carpenter) and Lillian (Pulley) Hearn; married Pamela Hindman (a college professor), August 12, 1962; children: Stephen, Melissa. *Education:* Southern Illinois University, B.S., 1959, M.A., 1960; University of Minnesota, Ph.D., 1971. *Politics:* Democrat. *Religion:* Episcopalian. *Home:* 2031 Kevin Dr., Cape Girardeau, Mo. 63701. *Office:* Department of English, Southeast Missouri State University, Cape Girardeau, Mo. 63701.

CAREER: Southern Illinois University, Carbondale, lecturer in English, 1960-62; University of Minnesota, Minneapolis, part-time instructor in English, 1965-67; Southeast Missouri State University, Cape Girardeau, assistant professor, 1967-76, associate professor of English and director of American studies program, 1976—. *Member:* American Studies Assocation, National Council of Teachers of English, Midwest Modern Language Association.

WRITINGS: The American Dream in the Great Depression, Greenwood Press, 1977.

WORK IN PROGRESS: Research on popular formula literature and the twentieth-century American novel.

SIDELIGHTS: Hearn writes: "My main interest is in the kind of research and writing that brings together and integrates diverse sources, including the popular and the 'serious' in the realm of literature. I believe that a major accomplishment of my 1977 book, *The American Dream in the Great Depression*—and this has been emphasized in the reviews that have appeared thus far—is that the inclusion of materials like popular magazine stories, best-selling novels, and widely read how-to-succeed guidebooks along with the works of major writers leads to a more balanced view of the decade than one finds in intellectual histories and literary studies that ignore the popular dimension. My major research interest at present is in writers who have been popular with the general public but have not gained critical acceptance as major writers."

*   *   *

HECHINGER, Fred M(ichael)   1920-

PERSONAL: Born July 7, 1920, in Nuremberg, Germany; came to the United States in 1937, naturalized citizen, 1943; son of Julius (a physician) and Lilly (Niedermaier) Hechinger; married Grace Bernstein (a writer and teacher), 1958; children: Paul David, John Edward. *Education:* Attended New York University, 1937-38; City College (now of the City University of New York), A.B., 1943; graduate study at University of London, 1945. *Home:* 40 East 88th St., New York, N.Y. 10028. *Office:* New York Times Co. Foundation, 229 West 43rd St., New York, N.Y. 10036.

CAREER: Times Educational Supplement, London, England, correspondent, 1946-47; *Bridgeport Sunday Herald,* Bridgeport, Conn., education editor and foreign correspondent, 1947-50; *New York Herald Tribune,* New York City, education editor, 1950-56; *Bridgeport Sunday Herald,* associate publisher and executive editor, 1956-59; *New York Times,* New York City, education editor, 1959-69, member of editorial board, 1969-77, assistant editor of editorial page, 1976; New York Times Co. Foundation, New York City, president, 1977—. Adjunct professor at Hunter College and Queens College, both of the City University of New York, 1973—; special lecturer at New School for Social Research. Member of board of directors of American-Scandinavian Foundation. *Military service:* U.S. Army, Military Intelligence, 1943-46; served in England.

MEMBER: Education Writers Association (president, 1956), Academy of Educational Development (member of board of directors), American Public Relations Association, Phi Beta Kappa (past president), Century Association, Coffee House. *Awards, honors:* Member of Order of the British Empire; awards from Education Writers Association, 1948, 1949, 1952, 1964, 1973, 1975; George Polk Memorial Award, 1950, 1951; Fairbanks Award, 1952; Townsend Harris Medal, 1968; editorial writing award from Society of Silurians, 1971, 1977; honorary doctorates include LL.D. from Kenyon College, 1955, Bates College, 1963, University of Notre Dame, 1963, and Knox College, 1966; L.H.D. from Bard College, 1956, Washington College, 1965, Wilkes College, 1968, Rider College, 1972, Paine College, 1972, and Trinity College, 1973; D.Journalism from St. Joseph's College, 1970; also received a degree from City College of the City University of New York.

WRITINGS: New Approaches, Fund for Advancement of Education, 1955; *An Adventure in Education: Connecticut Points the Way,* Macmillan, 1956; *Worrying About College* (pamphlet), Public Affairs Press, 1958; *The Big Red Schoolhouse,* Doubleday, 1959, revised edition, 1962; (with wife, Grace Hechinger) *Teen-Age Tyranny,* Morrow, 1963; (editor) *Pre-School Education Today,* Doubleday, 1966; (with G. Hechinger) *The New York Times Guide to New York City Private Schools,* Simon & Schuster, 1968; (with G. Hechinger) *Growing Up in America,* McGraw, 1975.

Author of a column in *Washington Post,* 1947-50. Foreign correspondent for Overseas News Agency, 1948-50; special writer for *This Week,* 1946-59. Contributor to professional journals and popular magazines, including *Harper's* and *McCall's.* Education editor of *Parents' Magazine,* 1957-59; contributing editor of *Saturday Review.*

*   *   *

HEFFERNAN, Michael   1942-

PERSONAL: Born December 20, 1942, in Detroit, Mich.; son of Joseph W. (a refrigeration contractor) and Susan (a teacher; maiden name, Schneider) Heffernan; married Anne M. Miller, August 14, 1968 (divorced June 9, 1975); married Kathleen Spigarelli (a teacher), August 9, 1975; children: (second marriage) Joseph William Rinaldo. *Education:* University of Detroit, A.B., 1964; University of Massachusetts, M.A., 1967, Ph.D., 1970. *Politics:* "Democrat (habitual)." *Religion:* "Roman Catholic (disgruntled)." *Home:* 715 West Eighth St., Pittsburg, Kan. 66762. *Office:* Department of English, Pittsburg State University, Pittsburg, Kan. 66762.

CAREER: Oakland University, Rochester, Mich., instructor in English, 1967-69; Kansas State College, Pittsburg, assistant professor of English, 1969-77; Pittsburg State University, Pittsburg, Kan., associate professor of English, 1977—. Member of board of advisers of creative writing panel, Kansas Arts Commission, 1971—, and board of directors of Associated Kansas Writing Programs. *Member:* Poetry Society of America. *Awards, honors:* Woodrow Wilson fellowship, 1964; Bread Loaf Writers' Conference scholarship, 1977; National Endowment for the Arts creative writing fellowship, 1978.

WRITINGS: Booking Passage (poetry), Bookmark, 1973; *In Front of All These People* (poetry), Blue Period Books, 1977; *A Figure of Plain Force* (poetry), Chowder Chapbooks, 1978.

Work anthologized in *Heartland II: Poets of the Midwest*, edited by Lucien Stryk, Northern Illinois University Press, 1975. Contributor of poems and reviews to literary journals, including *Poetry, American Poetry Review, Poetry Northwest,* and *Shenandoah.*

WORK IN PROGRESS: The Cry of Oliver Hardy, a book of poems; a study of the work of William Carlos Williams, with special emphasis on *Paterson Five.*

SIDELIGHTS: Heffernan writes: "My poems are efforts at speech in the Anglo-American dialect. I read very little contemporary poetry in translation, and I no longer write like William Carlos Williams. My heroes are Robert Frost, William Butler Yeats, Dante Alighieri, and Mahon O'Heffernan, a sixteenth-century ancestor who deplored the demise of the Gaelic poetry of his time at the hands of the Sassenach. For my part, I begrudge the dying of the language of the heart and head under the current electric din. I want to make one poem that can make someone weep or laugh or want to make love in the twenty-fifth century."

* * *

HEFLIN, Donald
See WALLMANN, Jeffrey M(iner)

* * *

HEINEMANN, Katherine 1918-
(Kaki)

PERSONAL: Born August 13, 1918, in St. Louis, Mo.; daughter of Herbert N. and Elsa (Straus) Arnstein; married Morton D. May, December 30, 1937 (divorced, 1949); married Sol Heinemann (a physician), July 8, 1950; children: (first marriage) David A., Philip F.,; (second marriage) Kate Heinemann Taucher. *Education:* Attended Connecticut College, 1936-37; Washington University, St. Louis, Mo., B.S. (honors), 1950, M.A., 1956. *Politics:* "Generally conservative." *Home and office:* 4252 Ridge Crest Dr., El Paso, Tex. 79902.

CAREER: University of Texas, El Paso, instructor in English, 1968-74; writer, 1974—. Has given readings in Texas, New Mexico, and Missouri. *Member:* International P.E.N., American Association of University Women, Modern Language Association of America, Kappa Delta Pi.

WRITINGS: Brandings (poems), Cummington Press, 1968. Author of "Young Sprouts," a review column for juvenile books in *El Paso Times*, 1965-66. Contributor of poems, articles, and reviews to literary journals and popular magazines, occasionally under pseudonym Kaki, including *Forum, Western Review,* and *Prairie Schooner.*

WORK IN PROGRESS: The Barbed Wire (tentative title), poems; a monograph on Robert McAlmon.

SIDELIGHTS: Katherine Heinemann has said that many of her poems spring, not from quiet meditation, but from her active, and sometimes adventurous, non-professional life. She has traveled extensively in Europe, the Middle East, Mexico, and Central and South America, with a special interest in the archaeology of Mexico and Peru. She partici-

pated in an excavation at the sacred well of Chichen Itza and an excursion by dugout canoe to remote Mayan ruins at Yaxchilan. She has also visited other ruins in Yucatan, Quintana Roo, Bolivia, and Macchu Picchu.

* * *

HELLER, Reinhold (August Friedrich) 1940-

PERSONAL: Born July 22, 1940, in Fulda, Germany; came to the United States in 1949, naturalized citizen, 1955; son of Friedrich (a baker) and Brigitte (a seamstress; maiden name, Schueler) Heller; married Vivian Hall (an instructor in French), June 11, 1966; children: Frederik Andreas, Erik Reinhold. *Education:* St. Joseph's College, Philadelphia, Pa., B.S., 1963; Indiana University, M.A., 1966, Ph.D., 1968; also attended University of Oslo, 1966. *Office:* Department of Art, Cochrane-Woods Art Center, University of Chicago, 5540 S. Greenwood Ave., Chicago, Ill. 60637.

CAREER: University of Pittsburgh, Pittsburgh, Pa., assistant professor, 1968-73, associate professor, 1973-76, professor of fine arts, 1976-78; University of Chicago, Chicago, Ill., professor of art, 1978—. *Member:* College Art Association of America, Modern Language Association of America.

WRITINGS: The Art of Wilhelm Lehmbruck, Macmillan, 1972; *Munch: The Scream*, Viking, 1973. Contributor to art magazines, including *Art Quarterly, Art Bulletin, Artforum, Kunst og Kultur,* and *Gazette des Beaux-Arts.*

WORK IN PROGRESS: Expressionism: Style, Iconography and Ideology of an Art Movement; Vincent Van Gogh: His Public Reception; research on the history of art criticism.

SIDELIGHTS: Heller told *CA:* "Realizing that art is but a part of an historical social structure, I have sought to study the interactions between the arts, between the personality of the artist and the demands of a public, between art and the society in which it is produced. The process of this study not only is intended to make the art of the past more meaningful and comprehensible today, but also to present the history of art as model or warning for the artistic process of today and its political situation."

* * *

HELLIE, Ann 1925-

PERSONAL: Born June 16, 1925, in Williamsport, Pa.; daughter of LaVerne H. and Ruth (Stewart) Shea; married Charles W. Hellie (president of a graphic communications company), July 2, 1946; children: Charles Michael, Stephen Shea, Mary Elizabeth, John Stewart. *Education:* Bucknell University, B.A., 1946; also attended West Chester State College, 1958-59, and University of Michigan, 1975-76. *Home and office:* 2909 Brockman Blvd., Ann Arbor, Mich. 48104. *Agent:* John K. Payne, Lenniger Literary Agency, Inc., 437 Fifth Ave., New York, N.Y. 10016.

CAREER: Xerox University Microfilms Division, Ann Arbor, Mich., editorial room assistant, 1963-64; Jacobson's (department store chain), Ann Arbor, Mich., department manager, 1973-76; Graphic Communications, Inc., Plymouth, Mich., executive vice-president, 1976—. *Member:* Detroit Women Writers. *Awards, honors:* Award from Chicago Book Clinic, 1974, for *Brian and the Long, Long Scarf;* award from Printing Industries of America, 1975, for *Brian and the Long, Long Scarf.*

WRITINGS—For children: The Box of Important Things, Western Publishing, 1968; *Once I Had a Monster,* Western Publishing, 1969; *Brian and the Long, Long Scarf,* Carol-rhoda, 1973. Contributor of stories (including children's stories), poems, articles, and reviews to magazines.

WORK IN PROGRESS: Research on Hellenistic society for *Dark Festival,* a historical romance; *Balderdash,* a children's novel about baseball; *The Terrible Something New,* a children's picture book.

SIDELIGHTS: Hellie told *CA:* "I write because I cannot help it. It is the work I am here to do and I am not happy unless I am doing it. Though I have been writing since I learned to put words on a page, I did not try to market my work until I was forty. It took a lot of nerve and much prodding from my excellent creative writing teacher to let that first big envelope slip into the mailbox. It took one year for me to get back a check instead of rejection slips. I am still working on the realization that the piles of agonies in my chosen field are topped with whipped cream and cherries.

"My philosophy? It is a good time to be alive. When I see or hear dark stories of the world we live on, I recall the sight of this earth from outer space suspended in black velvet, a beautiful jewel of a planet. And I write because I want to make it shine for others, especially children, as it does for me. This does not mean that I believe in writing only happy things. Tears and laughter both breed rainbows. I wonder though how good the current trend called 'realism' is, the trend that follows that which is, at the moment, newsworthy. What is real? I think 'real' can best be found at The Back of the North Wind, through The Door in the Wall, in Narnia, on the Mushroom Planet, with The Midnight Fox, with Charlotte at the fair, and in the many books that wash away the rougher ores of life to show the gems within. And so I like to bring my readers to the edge of fantasy where they can draw upon their own inner brightness and use it to help polish this great jewel, earth."

AVOCATIONAL INTERESTS: "Travel, reading, the study of history, biological and space science, needlework, speaking to and teaching people about creative writing."

* * *

HELM-PIRGO, Marian 1897-

PERSONAL: Born March 25, 1897, in Lwow, Poland; came to United States in 1952, naturalized citizen, 1958; son of Adam (a colonel in the military) and Klementyna (de Novak) Helm-Pirgo. *Education:* Attended Technical University of Lwow, 1918-20; Technical University of Warsaw, degree in architecture, 1925; attended Warsaw School of Fine Arts, 1926-28. *Religion:* Roman Catholic. *Residence:* New York, N.Y. *Address:* c/o Polish Institute of Arts and Sciences in America, 59 East 66th St., New York, N.Y. 10021.

CAREER: Self-employed architect in Zakopane, Poland, 1928-34; director of construction in Upper Silesia, 1930-32; Silesian Technical Scientific Institution, Katowice, Poland, lecturer in building construction, 1930-32; Bureau of Building Supervision, Lwow, Poland, director, 1932-39; imprisoned by Soviets, 1939-41; Ministry of Works, London, England, architectural assistant, 1949-52; architect in New York, N.Y., 1952—. Paintings exhibited in Warsaw, Lwow, Lodz, and Katowice, Poland, and at Cromwell Gallery and Guildhall Art Gallery, London. *Military service:* Austria-Hungarian Army, Artillery, 1915-18; served on Russian and Italian fronts; received five decorations. Polish Army, 1918-28, 1941-49, participated in defense of Lwow, 1918-19, and war for independence of Poland against Bolsheviks, 1919-21; instructor at Military-Geographic Institute, 1920-28, and at military training centers; served in Russia, the Middle East, and Italy during World War II; became major; received ten decorations.

MEMBER: Polish Army Veterans Association of America, Polish Institute of Arts and Sciences in America, Polish Ex-Combatant Association (Great Britain), Polonia Technica (New York). *Awards, honors:* First prize from Association of Polish Town Planners, 1929, for regulation and development plan for the city of Bedzin; Golden Cross of Merit from the government of the Republic of Poland, 1939, for work in Lwow; Polonia Restituta from the government of the Republic of Poland (in Exile), 1973, for work in science and art.

WRITINGS—In English: *Virgin Mary, Queen of Poland* (historical essay), Polish Institute of Arts and Sciences in America, 1957, 2nd edition, 1966; *Royal Dragoons: Immortal Love* (historical novel), Bicentennial Publishing Corp., 1976.

In Polish: *Kartoznawstwo i wojskowe wyzykanie terenu* (title means "Cartography and Military Use of the Terrain"), Zaklad Narodowy im Ossolinskich, 1928; *Podanie o Helmie* (title means "The Legend of Helm"), Gebethner i Wolf, 1931; *Grota Stradecka* (title means "The Grotto of Stradcz"), Dom Ksiazki Polskiej, 1932; *O wlasciwe traktowanie zagadnien architektonicznych i podniesienie poziomu budownictwa* (title means "For Raising the Standard of Architecture and Building Crafts"), Stowarzyszenie Architektow Rzeczypospolitej Polskiej, 1936; *W okowach i w walce* (title means "In Fetters and Fight"), Ksiegarnia Polska, 1946; *Poczatki kartografi wojskowej w Polsce odrodzonej, 1918-20* (title means "The Beginnings of Military Cartography in Restored Poland, 1918-20"), Polski Instytut Naukowy w Ameryce, 1971. Contributor to journals in Poland, the United States, and Canada.

WORK IN PROGRESS: Studying Polish-Soviet affairs.

SIDELIGHTS: Before he left Poland, Helm-Pirgo was widely recognized for his work in uncovering and restoring the "old city" of Lwow. His interest in this project included membership in the Society of Lovers of the Past of Lwow. He had written a manuscript on the subject of restoring old Lwow, which was to be published by that society, but after his arrest and stay in Russian prisons and Siberian concentration camps during World War II, and the incorporation of the eastern provinces of the Polish Republic into the Soviet Union, the manuscript was lost along with all his other possessions.

He remained in England and, while exhibiting his art work and working in the Ministry of Works, served as president of the London-based Society of Polish Architects Abroad until his immigration to the United States.

He writes: "The previous subjugations, as well as the present oppression of the Polish nation caused by the Yalta agreement and the Soviet-Russian domination of Poland had a substantial influence on my activity and my writings. I reflect my attachment to Poland's past and traditions in almost all my accomplishments in Poland and abroad. *Virgin Mary, Queen of Poland* is not only a historic presentation of the loftiest ideals professed by the Polish nation, but is also an appeal to mankind to contribute to the moral obligation to achieve justice and freedom for all. *Royal Dragoons* also has a remarkable ideological aim.

"I state in its introduction: 'If this story is of interest to the reader and reflects, moreover, to a certain extent not only the events and life in Poland in the middle of the seventeenth century, but also the historical rights of the Polish nation, I shall consider my intention fulfilled.'"

HELPER, Rose

PERSONAL: Born in Port Arthur, Ontario, Canada; came to the United States in 1947; daughter of Aaron (a furrier) and Fanny Leah (Strejevsky) Helper. *Education:* University of Toronto, M.A., 1945; University of Chicago, Ph.D., 1958. *Religion:* Jewish. *Home:* 2565 West Bancroft St., Toledo, Ohio 43607. *Office:* Department of Sociology, Anthropology, and Social Work, University of Toledo, 2801 Bancroft St., Toledo, Ohio 43606.

CAREER: New York University, New York, N.Y., research associate at Research Center for Human Relations, 1951-52; Indiana State Teachers College (now State University), Terre Haute, assistant professor of sociology, 1959; University of Toledo, Toledo, Ohio, assistant professor, 1959-66, associate professor, 1966-71, professor of sociology, 1971—. Research fellow at Fisk University, 1945-47. Member of Toledo Community Housing Resources Board.

MEMBER: International Sociological Association, American Sociological Association, Society for the Study of Social Problems, Society for the Psychological Study of Social Issues, Society for the Study of Symbolic Interaction, Midwest Sociological Society, North Central Sociological Association, Pi Gamma Mu, Phi Kappa Phi, Alpha Kappa Delta. *Awards, honors:* Grant from Commission on Race and Housing, Fund for the Republic, Ford Foundation, 1955-56.

WRITINGS: Racial Policies and Practices of Real Estate Brokers, University of Minnesota Press, 1969. Contributor to professional journals. Guest editor of *Sociological Focus,* 1970-71.

WORK IN PROGRESS: Research on social interaction in racially mixed residential neighborhoods.

SIDELIGHTS: Rose Helper writes: "My undergraduate major was modern languages and my minor was philosophy. While I love these fields of study, the great thought and beauty of expression of the French and German writers, I felt a concern from my childhood about certain social problems and wanted to get closer to the field of human relations.

"In my work as researcher and presenter of research findings in written form, there is a deep satisfaction in finally arriving at the result of one's study. If not deemed presumptuous, there may also be a sense of having had a hand in the great task of moving the frontiers of knowledge, in as careful a way as one could, slightly, ever so slightly, forward, but still forward.

"I have found the work as teacher of sociology deeply moving. It is a privilege to work with young minds and to introduce them to new ideas. It is good when you find that there is thinking, reflection, assessment going on in those young minds, as when they take issue with you and think carefully enough to base their objections on factual grounds. There is no doubt about it, I love to teach, and if I live to be a hundred, I'll still be teaching.

"One main task for teachers and writers is, I think, to get people, including ourselves, to overcome their prejudices, their stereotyping, so that they will judge individual persons on the basis of their qualifications, achievements, and character, and *not* on the basis of sex, age, race, color, height, physical handicap, ethnic background, religion, or any criterion other than the intrinsic worth of the person as a human being and a member of social groups."

AVOCATIONAL INTERESTS: Bowling, physical fitness classes, travel (France, England, Mexico, Italy, Guatemala, Israel).

HEMINGWAY, Ernest   1899-1961

PERSONAL: Born July 21, 1899, in Oak Park, Ill.; son of Clarence Edmunds (a physician) and Grace (a music teacher; maiden name, Hall) Hemingway: married Hadley Richardson, September 3, 1921 (divorced March 10, 1927); married Pauline Pfeiffer (a writer), May 10, 1927 (divorced November 4, 1940); married Martha Gellhorn (a writer), November 21, 1940 (divorced December 21, 1945); married Mary Welsh (a writer), March 14, 1946; children: (first marriage) John Hadley Nicanor; (second marriage) Patrick, Gregory. *Education:* Educated in Oak Park, Ill. *Residence:* Ketchum, Idaho; and Finca Vigia, Cuba.

CAREER: Writer, 1917-61. *Kansas City Star,* Kansas City, Mo., cub reporter, 1917-18; ambulance driver for Red Cross Ambulance Corps in Italy, 1918-19; *Co-operative Commonwealth,* Chicago, Ill., writer, 1920-21; *Toronto Star,* Toronto, Ontario, covered Greco-Turkish War, 1920, European correspondent, 1921-24; covered Spanish Civil War for North American Newspaper Alliance, 1937-38; war correspondent in China, 1941; war correspondent in Europe, 1944-45. *Awards, honors:* Pulitzer Prize, 1953, for *The Old Man and the Sea;* Nobel Prize for Literature, 1954; Award of Merit from American Academy of Arts & Letters, 1954.

WRITINGS—Novels: *The Torrents of Spring: A Romantic Novel in Honor of the Passing of a Great Race* (parody), Scribner, 1926, published with a new introduction by David Garnett, J. Cape, 1964, reprinted, Scribner, 1972; *The Sun Also Rises,* Scribner, 1926, published with a new introduction by Henry Seidel Canby, Modern Library, 1930, reprinted, Scribner, 1969 (published in England as *Fiesta,* J. Cape, 1959); *A Farewell to Arms,* Scribner, 1929, published with new introductions by Ford Madox Ford, Modern Library, 1932, Robert Penn Warren, Scribner, 1949, John C. Schweitzer, Scribner, 1967; *To Have and Have Not,* Scribner, 1937, J. Cape, 1970; *For Whom the Bell Tolls,* Scribner, 1940, published with a new introduction by Sinclair Lewis, Princeton University Press, 1942, reprinted, Scribner, 1960; *Across the River and Into the Trees,* Scribner, 1950, reprinted, Penguin with J. Cape, 1966; *The Old Man and the Sea,* Scribner, 1952; *Islands in the Stream,* Scribner, 1970.

Short stories, except as indicated: *Three Stories & Ten Poems,* Contact (Paris), 1923; *In Our Time,* Boni & Liveright, 1925, published with additional material a new introduction by Edmund Wilson, Scribner, 1930, reprinted, Bruccoli, 1977 (also see below); *Men Without Women,* Scribner, 1927; *Winner Take Nothing,* Scribner, 1933; *Fifth Column and the First Forty-nine Stories* (stories and a play), Scribner, 1938, stories published separately as *First Forty-nine Stories,* J. Cape, 1962, play published separately as *The Fifth Column: A Play in Three Acts,* Scribner, 1940, J. Cape, 1968 (also see below); *The Snows of Kilimanjaro and Other Stories,* Scribner, 1961; *The Short Happy Life of Francis Macomber and Other Stories,* Penguin, 1963; John M. Howell, compiler, *Hemingway's African Stories: The Stories, Their Sources, Their Critics,* Scribner, 1969; *The Nick Adams Stories,* preface by Philip Young, Scribner, 1972.

Other works: *in our time* (miniature sketches), Three Mountain Press (Paris), 1924 (also see above); *Today Is Friday* (pamphlet), As Stable Publications (Englewood, N.J.), 1926; *Death in the Afternoon* (nonfiction), Scribner, 1932; *God Rest You Merry Gentlemen,* House of Books, 1933; *Green Hills of Africa* (nonfiction), Scribner, 1935, reprinted, Penguin with J. Cape, 1966; *The Spanish Earth* (commentary and film narration), introduction by Jasper Wood, J. B. Savage (Cleveland, Ohio), 1938; *The Spanish War* (monograph), Fact, 1938; (editor and author of introduction) *Men at War: The Best War Stories of All Time* (based on a plan by William Kozlenko), Crown, 1942; *Voyage to Victory,* Crowell-Collier, 1944; *The Secret Agent's Badge of Courage,* Belmont Books, 1954; *Two Christmas Tales,* Hart Press, 1959; *A Moveable Feast* (reminiscences), Scribner, 1964.

Omnibus volumes: Malcolm Cowley, editor, *The Portable Hemingway* (contains *The Sun Also Rises, A Farewell to Arms, To Have and Have Not, For Whom the Bell Tolls,* and short stories), Viking, 1944; *The Essential Hemingway* (contains one novel, novel extracts, and twenty-three short stories), J. Cape, 1947, reprinted, 1964; Charles Poore, editor and author of foreword, *The Hemingway Reader,* Scribner, 1953; *Three Novels: The Sun Also Rises, A Farewell to Arms, and The Old Man and the Sea,* each with separate introductions by Malcolm Cowley, Robert Penn Warren, and Carlos Baker, respectively, Scribner, 1962; Gene Z. Hanrahan, editor, *The Wild Years* (collection of journalism), Dell, 1962; William White, editor, *By-line, Ernest Hemingway: Selected Articles and Dispatches of Four Decades,* Scribner, 1967; *Fifth Column and Four Stories of the Spanish Civil War,* Scribner, 1969 (also see above); Matthew J. Bruccoli, editor, *Ernest Hemingway, Cub Reporter: Kansas City Star Stories,* University of Pittsburgh Press, 1970; Bruccoli, editor, *Ernest Hemingway's Apprenticeship: Oak Park, 1916-1917,* Bruccoli Clark / NCR Microcard Editions, 1971; Charles Scribner, Jr., editor, *The Enduring Hemingway: An Anthology of a Lifetime in Literature,* Scribner, 1974.

Unpublished manuscripts: "The Garden of Eden" (novel); "The Dangerous Summer" (nonfiction about travels in Spain).

SIDELIGHTS: "The writer's job is to tell the truth," Ernest Hemingway once said. When he was having difficulty writing he reminded himself of this, as he explained in his memoirs, *A Moveable Feast.* "I would stand and look out over the roofs of Paris and think, 'Do not worry. You have always written before and you will write now. All you have to do is write one true sentence. Write the truest sentence that you know.' So finally I would write one true sentence, and then go on from there. It was easy then because there was always one true sentence that I knew or had seen or had heard someone say."

Hemingway's personal and artistic quests for truth were directly related. As Earl Rovit noted: "More often than not, Hemingway's fictions seem rooted in his journeys into himself much more clearly and obsessively than is usually the case with major fiction writers.... His writing was his way of approaching his identity—of discovering himself in the projected metaphors of his experience. He believed that if he could see himself clear and whole, his vision might be useful to others who also lived in this world."

The public's acquaintance with the personal life of Hemingway was perhaps greater than with any other modern novelist. He was well-known as a sportsman and *bon vivant* and his escapades were covered in such popular magazines as *Life* and *Esquire.* Hemingway became a legendary figure, wrote John W. Aldridge, "a kind of twentieth-century Lord Byron; and like Byron, he had learned to play himself, his own best hero, with superb conviction. He was Hemingway of the rugged outdoor grin and the hairy chest posing beside a marlin he had just landed or a lion he had just shot; he was Tarzan Hemingway, crouching in the African bush with ele-

phant gun at ready, Bwana Hemingway commanding his native bearers in terse Swahili; he was War Correspondent Hemingway writing a play in the Hotel Florida in Madrid while thirty Fascist shells crashed through the roof; later on he was Task Force Hemingway swathed in ammunition belts and defending his post singlehanded against fierce German attacks." Anthony Burgess declared: "Reconciling literature and action, he fulfilled for all writers, the sickroom dream of leaving the desk for the arena, and then returning to the desk. He wrote good and lived good, and both activities were the same. The pen handled with the accuracy of the rifle; sweat and dignity; bags of *cojones.*"

Hemingway's search for truth and accuracy of expression is reflected in his terse, economical prose style, which is widely acknowledged to be his greatest contribution to literature. What Frederick J. Hoffman called Hemingway's "esthetic of simplicity" involves a "a basic struggle for absolute accuracy in making words correspond to experience." For Hemingway, William Barrett commented, "style was a moral act, a desperate struggle for moral probity amid the confusions of the world and the slippery complexities of one's own nature. To set things down simple and right is to hold a standard of rightness against a deceiving world."

In a discussion of Hemingway's style, Sheldon Norman Grebstein listed these characteristics: "first, short and simple sentence constructions, with heavy use of parallelism, which convey the effect of control, terseness, and blunt honesty; second, purged diction which above all eschews the use of bookish, latinate, or abstract words and thus achieves the effect of being heard or spoken or transcribed from reality rather than appearing as a construct of the imagination (in brief, verisimilitude); and third, skillful use of repetition and a kind of verbal counterpoint, which operate either by pairing or juxtaposing opposites, or else by running the same word or phrase through a series of shifting meanings and inflections."

One of Hemingway's greatest virtues as a writer was his self-discipline. He described how he accomplished this in *A Moveable Feast.* "If I started to write elaborately, or like someone introducing or presenting something, I found that I could cut that scrollwork or ornament out and throw it away and start with the first true simple declarative sentence I had written.... I decided that I would write one story about each thing that I knew about. I was trying to do this all the time I was writing, and it was good and severe discipline." His early training in journalism as a reporter for the *Kansas City Star* and the *Toronto Star* is often mentioned as a factor in the development of his lean style. Later, as a foreign correspondent he learned the even more rigorously economic language of "cablese," in which each word must convey the meaning of several others. While Hemingway acknowledged his debt to journalism in *Death in the Afternoon* by commenting that "in writing for a newspaper you told what happened and with one trick and another, you communicated the emotion to any account of something that has happened on that day," he admitted that the hardest part of fiction writing, "the real thing," was contriving "the sequence of motion and fact which made the emotion and which would be valid in a year or ten years or, with luck and if you stated it purely enough, always ..."

Although Hemingway has named numerous writers as his literary influences, his contemporaries mentioned most often in this regard are Ring Lardner, Sherwood Anderson, Ezra Pound, and Gertrude Stein. Malcolm Cowley assessed the importance of Stein and Pound (who were both friends of Hemingway) to his literary development, while stressing that the educational relationship was mutual. "One thing he took partly from her [Stein] was a colloquial—in appearance—American style, full of repeated words, prepositional phrases, and present participles, the style in which he wrote his early published stories. One thing he took from Pound—in return for trying vainly to teach him to box—was the doctrine of the accurate image, which he applied in the 'chapters' printed between the stories that went into *In Our Time;* but Hemingway also learned from him to bluepencil most of his adjectives." Hemingway has commented that he learned how to write as much from painters as from other writers. Cezanne was one of his favorite painters and Wright Morris has compared Hemingway's stylistic method to that of Cezanne. "A Cezanne-like simplicity of scene is built up with the touches of a master, and the great effects are achieved with a sublime economy. At these moments style and substance are of one piece, each growing from the other, and one cannot imagine that life could exist except as described. We think only of what is there, and not, as in the less successful moments, of all of the elements of experience that are not."

While most critics have found Hemingway's prose exemplary (Jackson J. Benson claimed that he had "perhaps the best ear that has ever been brought to the creation of English prose"), Leslie A. Fiedler complained that Hemingway learned to write "through the eye rather than the ear. If his language is colloquial, it is *written* colloquial, for he was constitutionally incapable of hearing English as it was spoken around him. To a critic who once asked him why his characters all spoke alike, Hemingway answered, 'Because I never listen to anybody.'"

Hemingway's earlier novels and short stories were largely praised for their unique style. Paul Goodman, for example, was pleased with the "sweetness" of the writing in *A Farewell to Arms.* "When it [sweetness] appears, the short sentences coalesce and flow, and sing—sometimes melancholy, sometimes pastoral, sometimes personally embarrassed in an adult, not adolescent, way. In the dialogues, he pays loving attention to the spoken word. And the writing is meticulous; he is sweetly devoted to writing well. Most everything else is resigned, but here he makes an effort, and the effort produces lovely moments."

But in his later works, particularly *Across the River and Into the Trees* and the posthumously published *Islands in the Stream,* the Hemingway style degenerated into near self-parody. "In the best of early Hemingway it always seemed that if exactly the right words in exactly the right order were not chosen, something monstrous would occur, an unimaginably delicate internal warning system would be thrown out of adjustment, and some principle of personal and artistic integrity would be fatally compromised," John Aldridge wrote. "But by the time he came to write *The Old Man [and the Sea]* there seems to have been nothing at stake except the professional obligation to sound as much like Hemingway as possible. The man had disappeared behind the mannerism, the artist behind the artifice, and all that was left was a coldly flawless facade of words." Foster Hirsch found that Hemingway's "mawkish self-consciousness is especially evident in *Islands in the Stream.*" *Across the River and Into the Trees,* according to Philip Rahv, "reads like a parody by the author of his own manner—a parody so biting that it virtually destroys the mixed social and literary legend of Hemingway." And Carlos Baker wrote: "In the lesser works of his final years . . . nostalgia drove him to the point of exploiting his personal idiosyncrasies, as if he hoped to persuade readers to accept these in lieu of that powerful union of objective

discernment and subjective response which he had once been able to achieve."

But Hemingway was never his own worst imitator. He was perhaps the most influential writer of his generation and scores of writers, particularly the hard-boiled writers of the thirties, attempted to adapt his tough, understated prose to their own works, usually without success. As Clinton S. Burhans, Jr., noted: "The famous and extraordinarily eloquent concreteness of Hemingway's style is inimitable precisely because it is not primarily stylistic: the *how* of Hemingway's style is the *what* of his characteristic vision."

It is this organicism, the skillful blend of style and substance, that made Hemingway's works so successful, despite the fact that many critics have complained that he lacked vision. Hemingway avoided intellectualism because he thought it shallow and pretentious. His unique vision demanded the expression of emotion through the description of action rather than of passive thought. In *Death in the Afternoon,* Hemingway explained, "I was trying to write then and I found the greatest difficulty, aside from knowing truly what you really felt, rather than what you were supposed to feel, was to put down what really happened in action; what the actual things were which produced the emotion you experienced."

Even morality, for Hemingway, was a consequence of action and emotion. He stated his moral code in *Death in the Afternoon:* "What is moral is what you feel good after and what is immoral is what you feel bad after." Lady Brett Ashley, in *The Sun Also Rises,* voices this pragmatic morality after she has decided to leave a young bullfighter, believing the break to be in his best interests. She says: "You know it makes one feel rather good deciding not to be a bitch. . . . It's sort of what we have instead of God."

Hemingway's perception of the world as devoid of traditional values and truths and instead marked by disillusionment and moribund idealism, is a characteristically twentieth-century vision. World War I was a watershed for Hemingway and his generation. As an ambulance driver in the Italian infantry, Hemingway had been severely wounded. The war experience affected him profoundly, as he told Malcolm Cowley. "In the first war I was hurt very badly; in the body, mind, and spirit, and also morally." The heroes of his novels were similarly wounded. According to Max Westbrook they "awake to a world gone to hell. World War I has destroyed belief in the goodness of national governments. The depression has isolated man from his natural brotherhood. Institutions, concepts, and insidious groups of friends and ways of life are, when accurately seen, a tyranny, a sentimental or propagandistic rationalization."

Both of Hemingway's first two major novels, *The Sun Also Rises* and *A Farewell to Arms,* were "primarily descriptions of a society that had lost the possibility of belief. They were dominated by an atmosphere of Gothic ruin, boredom, sterility and decay," John Aldridge wrote. "Yet if they had been nothing more than descriptions, they would inevitably have been as empty of meaning as the thing they were describing." While Alan Lebowitz contended that because the theme of despair "is always an end in itself, the fiction merely its transcription, . . . it is a dead end," Aldridge believed that Hemingway managed to save the novels by salvaging the characters' values and transcribing them "into a kind of moral network that linked them together in a unified pattern of meaning."

In the search for meaning Hemingway's characters necessarily confront violence. Omnipresent violence is a fact of existence, according to Hemingway. Even in works such as *The Sun Also Rises* in which violence plays a minimal role, it is always present subliminally—"woven into the structure of life itself," William Barrett remarked. In other works violence is more obtrusive: the wars in *A Farewell to Arms* and *For Whom the Bell Tolls,* the hostility of nature which is particularly evident in the short stories, and the violent sports such as bullfighting and big game hunting that are portrayed in numerous works.

"Hemingway is the dramatist of the extreme situation. His overriding theme is honour, personal honour: by what shall a man live, by what shall a man die, in a world the essential condition of whose being is violence?" Walter Allen wrote. "These problems are posed rather than answered in his first book *In Our Time,* a collection of short stories in which almost all of Hemingway's later work is contained by implication."

The code by which Hemingway's heroes must live (Philip Young has termed them "code heroes") is contingent on the qualities of courage, self-control, and "grace under pressure." Irving Howe has described the typical Hemingway hero as a man "who is wounded but bears his wounds in silence, who is defeated but finds a remnant of dignity in an honest confrontation of defeat." Furthermore, the hero's great desire must be to "salvage from the collapse of social life a version of stoicism that can make suffering bearable; the hope that in direct physical sensation, the cold water of the creek in which one fishes or the purity of the wine made by Spanish peasants, there can be found an experience that can resist corruption."

Hemingway has been accused of exploiting and sensationalizing violence. However, Leo Gurko remarked that "the motive behind Hemingway's heroic figures is not glory, or fortune, or the righting of injustice, or the thirst for experience. They are inspired neither by vanity nor ambition nor a desire to better the world. They have no thoughts of reaching a state of higher grace or virtue. Instead, their behavior is a reaction to the moral emptiness of the universe, an emptiness that they feel compelled to fill by their own special efforts."

If life is an endurance contest and the hero's response to it is prescribed and codified, the violence itself is stylized. As William Barrett asserted: "It is always played, even in nature, perhaps above all in nature, according to some form. The violence erupts within the patterns of war or the patterns of the bullring." Clinton S. Burhans, Jr., is convinced that Hemingway's "fascination with bullfighting stems from his view of it as an art form, a ritual tragedy in which man confronts the creatural realities of violence, pain, suffering, and death by imposing on them an esthetic form which gives them order, significance, and beauty."

It is not necessary (or even possible) to understand the complex universe—it is enough for Hemingway's heroes to find solace in beauty and order. Santiago in *The Old Man and the Sea* cannot understand why he must kill the great fish he has come to love, Burhans noted. Hemingway described Santiago's confusion: "I do not understand these things, he thought. But it is good we do not try to kill the sun or the moon or the stars. It is enough to live on the sea and kill our brothers."

Despite Hemingway's pessimism, Ihab Hassan declared that it is "perverse to see only the emptiness of Hemingway's world. In its lucid spaces, a vision of archetypal unity reigns. Opposite forces obey a common destiny; enemies discover their deeper identity; the hunter and the hunted

merge. The matador plunges his sword, and for an instant in eternity, man and beast are the same. This is the moment of truth, and it serves Hemingway as symbol of the unity which underlies both love and death. His fatalism, his tolerance of bloodshed, his stoical reserve before the malice of creation, betray a sacramental attitude that transcends any personal fate...."

Death is not the ultimate fear: the Hemingway hero knows how to confront death. What he truly fears is *nada* (the Spanish word for nothing)—existence in a state of nonbeing. Hemingway's characters are alone. He is not concerned with human relationships as much as with portraying man's individual struggle against an alien, chaotic universe. His characters exist in the "island condition," Stephen L. Tanner has noted. He compared them to the islands of an archipelago "consistently isolated [and] alone in the stream of society."

Several critics have noted that Hemingway's novels suffer because of his overriding concern with the individual. *For Whom the Bell Tolls,* a novel about the Spanish Civil War, has engendered controversy on this matter. While it is ostensibly a political novel about a cause that Hemingway believed in fervently, critics such as Alvah C. Bessie were disappointed that Hemingway was still concerned exclusively with the personal. "The cause of Spain does not, in any *essential* way, figure as a motivating power, a driving, emotional, passional force in this story," Bessie wrote. "In the widest sense, that cause is actually *irrelevant* to the narrative. For the author is less concerned with the fate of the Spanish people, whom I am certain he loves, than he is with the fate of his hero and heroine, who are *himself.* . . . For all his groping the author of the *Bell* has yet to integrate his individual sensitivity to life with the sensitivity of every living human being (read the Spanish people); he has yet to expand his personality as a novelist to embrace the truths of other people, everywhere; he has yet to dive deep into the lives of others, and there to find his own." But Mark Schorer contended that in *For Whom the Bell Tolls* Hemingway's motive is to portray "a tremendous sense of man's dignity and worth, an urgent awareness of the necessity of man's freedom, a nearly poetic realization of man's *collective* virtues. Indeed, the individual vanishes in the political whole, but vanishes precisely to defend his dignity, his freedom, his virtue. In spite of the ominous premium which the title seems to place on individuality, the real theme of the book is the relative unimportance of individuality and the superb importance of the political whole."

Hemingway's depiction of relationships between men and women is generally considered to be his weakest area as a writer. Leslie Fiedler has noted that he is only really comfortable dealing with men without women. His women characters often seem to be abstractions rather than portraits of real women. Often reviewers have divided them into two types: the bitches such as Brett and Margot Macomber who emasculate the men in their lives, and the wish-projections, the sweet, submissive women such as Catherine and Maria (in *For Whom the Bell Tolls*). All of the characterizations lack subtely and shading. The love affair between Catherine and Frederic in *A Farewell to Arms* is only an "abstraction of lyric emotion," Edmund Wilson commented. Fiedler complained that "in his earlier fiction, Hemingway's descriptions of the sexual encounter are intentionally brutal, in his later ones, unintentionally comic; for in no case, can he quite succeed in making his females human. . . . If in *For Whom the Bell Tolls* Hemingway has written the most absurd love scene in the history of the American novel, this is not because he lost momentarily his skill and authority; it is a give-away—a moment which illuminates the whole erotic content of his fiction.''

In 1921, when Hemingway and his family moved to the Left Bank of Paris (then the literature, art, and music capital of the world), he became associated with other American expatriates, including F. Scott Fitzgerald, Archibald MacLeish, E. E. Cummings, and John Dos Passos. These expatriates and the whole generation which came of age in the period between the two world wars came to be known as the "lost generation." For Hemingway the term had more universal meaning. In *A Moveable Feast* he wrote that being lost is part of the human condition—that all generations are lost generations.

Hemingway also believed in the cyclicality of the world. As inscriptions to his novel *The Sun Also Rises,* he used two quotations: first, Gertrude Stein's comment, "You are all a lost generation"; then a verse from Ecclesiastes which begins, "One generation passeth away, and another generation cometh; but the earth abideth forever. . . ." The paradox of regeneration evolving from death is central to Hemingway's vision. The belief in immortality is comforting, of course, and Hemingway evidently found comfort in permanence and endurance. According to Steven R. Phillips, Hemingway discovered permanence in "the sense of immortality that he gains from the otherwise impermanent art of the bullfight, in the fact that the 'earth abideth forever,' in the eternal flow of the gulf stream and in the permanence of his own works of art." Hemingway's greatest depiction of endurance is in *The Old Man and the Sea* in which "he succeeds in a manner which almost defeats critical description," Phillips claimed. "The old man becomes the sea and like the sea he endures. He is dying as the year is dying. He is fishing in September, the fall of the year, the time that corresponds in the natural cycle to the phase of sunset and sudden death. . . . Yet the death of the old man will not bring an end to the cycle; as part of the sea he will continue to exist."

Hemingway was inordinately proud of his own powers of rejuvenation, and in a letter to his friend Archibald Mac-Leish, he explained that his maxim was: "*Dans la vie, il faut (d'abord) durer.*" ("In life, one must [first of all] endure.") He had survived physical disasters (including two near-fatal plane crashes in Africa in 1954) and disasters of critical reception to his work (*Across the River and Into the Trees* was almost universally panned). But due to his great recuperative powers he was able to rebound from these hardships. He made a literary comeback with the publication of *The Old Man and the Sea,* which is considered to be among his finest works. In 1954 he was awarded the Nobel Prize for Literature. But the last few years of his life were marked by great physical and emotional suffering. He was no longer able to write—to do the thing he loved the most. Finally Hemingway could endure no longer and, in 1961, he took his own life.

Several of Hemingway's works have been adapted for motion pictures, including *A Farewell to Arms, For Whom the Bell Tolls,* and *To Have and Have Not.*

BIOGRAPHICAL/CRITICAL SOURCES—Selected periodicals: *New Masses,* November 5, 1940; *Kenyon Review,* winter, 1941; *New Yorker,* May 13, 1950; *Yale Review,* spring, 1969; *Mediterranean Review,* spring, 1971; *New York Review of Books,* December 30, 1971; *Arizona Quarterly,* spring, 1973; *American Scholar,* summer, 1974; *Modern Fiction Studies,* summer, 1975; *Midwest Quarterly,* spring, 1976; *Southwest Review,* winter, 1976; *Georgia Review,* summer, 1977.

Selected books: Ernest Hemingway, *Death in the Afternoon,* Scribner, 1932; Carlos Baker, *Hemingway: The Writer as Artist,* Princeton University Press, 1956; W. M. Frohock, *The Novel of Violence in America,* Southern Methodist University Press, 1957; Wright Morris, *The Territory Ahead: Critical Interpretations in American Literature,* Harcourt, 1958; Maxwell Geisman, *American Moderns: From Rebellion to Conformity,* Hill & Wang, 1958; J. B. Priestley, *Literature and Western Man,* Harper, 1960; Leslie A. Fiedler, *Love and Death in the American Novel,* Criterion, 1960; Carlos Baker, editor, *Ernest Hemingway: Critiques of Four Major Novels,* Scribner, 1962; Earl H. Rovit, *Ernest Hemingway,* Twayne, 1963; Frederick J. Hoffman, *The Modern Novel in America,* Regnery, revised edition, 1963; Irving Howe, *A World More Attractive: A View of Modern Literature and Politics,* Horizon Press, 1963; Hemingway, *A Moveable Feast,* Scribner, 1964; Walter Allen, *The Modern Novel,* Dutton, 1964; Fiedler, *Waiting for the End,* Stein & Day, 1964; Philip Rahv, *The Myth and the Powerhouse,* Farrar, Straus, 1965; Philip Young, *Ernest Hemingway,* University of Minnesota Press, revised edition, 1965; Max Westbrook, editor, *The Modern American Novel: Essays in Criticism,* Random House, 1966; John W. Aldridge, *Time to Murder and Create: The Contemporary Novel in Crisis,* McKay, 1966; Young, *Ernest Hemingway: A Reconsideration,* Pennsylvania State University Press, 2nd edition, 1966; A. E. Hotchner, *Papa Hemingway: A Personal Memoir,* Bantam, 1966; Anthony Burgess, *The Novel Now: A Guide to Contemporary Fiction,* Norton, 1967; Burgess, *Urgent Copy: Literary Studies,* Norton, 1968; David Madden, editor, *Tough Guy Writers of the Thirties,* Southern Illinois University Press, 1968; Leo Gurko, *Ernest Hemingway and the Pursuit of Heroism,* Crowell, 1968; Robert O. Stephens, *Hemingway's Nonfiction: The Public Voice,* University of North Carolina Press, 1968; William Seward, *My Friend Ernest Hemingway,* A. S. Barnes, 1969; Carlos Baker, *Ernest Hemingway: A Life Story,* Scribner, 1969; Delbert E. Wylder, *Hemingway's Heroes,* University of New Mexico Press, 1969; Matthew J. Bruccoli and C. E. Frazer Clark, Jr., editors, *Fitzgerald-Hemingway Annual,* Bruccoli Clark Books, 1969-76, Gale, 1977.

Chaman Nahal, *The Narrative Pattern in Ernest Hemingway's Fiction,* Fairleigh Dickinson, 1971; Ihab Hassan, *The Dismemberment of Orpheus: Toward a Postmodern Literature,* Oxford University Press, 1971; William Barrett, *Time of Need: Forms of Imagination in the Twentieth Century,* Harper, 1972; Leicester Hemingway, *My Brother, Ernest Hemingway,* Fawcett, 1972; Sheldon N. Grebstein, *Hemingway's Craft,* Southern Illinois University Press, 1973; Alfred Kazin, *Bright Book of Life: American Novelists and Storytellers from Hemingway to Mailer,* Little, Brown, 1973; Arthur Waldhorn, *Ernest Hemingway,* McGraw, 1973; Malcolm Cowley, *A Second Flowering: Works and Days of the Lost Generation,* Viking, 1973; *Contemporary Literary Criticism,* Gale, Volume 1, 1973, Volume 3, 1975, Volume 6, 1976, Volume 8, 1978; Jose L. Castillo-Puche, *Hemingway in Spain,* Doubleday, 1974; Richard Astro and Jackson J. Benson, editors, *Hemingway in Our Time,* Oregon State University Press, 1974; Linda W. Wagner, editor, *Ernest Hemingway: Five Decades of Criticism,* Michigan State University Press, 1974; Benson, editor, *The Short Stories of Ernest Hemingway: Critical Essays,* Duke University Press, 1975; Kenneth H. Baldwin and David K. Kirby, editors, *Individual and Community: Variations on a Theme in American Fiction,* Duke University Press, 1975; John

Updike, *Picked-Up Pieces,* Knopf, 1975; Sarah P. Unfried, *Man's Place in the Natural Order: A Study of Ernest Hemingway's Major Works,* Gordon Press, 1976; Mary Welsh Hemingway, *How It Was,* Knopf, 1976; Michael S. Reynolds, *Hemingway's First War: The Making of a Farewell to Arms,* Princeton University Press, 1976; Gregory H. Hemingway, *Papa: A Personal Memoir,* Houghton, 1976; Scott Donaldson, *By Force of Will: The Life in Art and Art in the Life of Ernest Hemingway,* Viking, 1977; Richard E. Hardy and John G. Cull, *Hemingway: A Psychological Portrait,* Banner Books, 1977; Anthony Burgess, *Ernest Hemingway and His World,* Scribner, 1978.*

(Died July 2, 1961, in Ketchum, Idaho)

*   *   *

HENDERSON, Mary C. 1928-

PERSONAL: Born July 16, 1928, in Newark, N.J.; daughter of Thomas and Divina (Gionatasio) Malanga; married Robert Morton Henderson (a library administrator), February 14, 1953; children: James M., Douglas A., Stuart A. *Education:* Douglass College of Rutgers University, B.A. (honors), 1949; University of Pittsburgh, M.A., 1951; New York University, Ph.D., 1973; also attended Columbia University and Hunter College of the City University of New York. *Home:* 859 Meadow Lane, Franklin Lakes, N.J. 07417. *Office:* Theatre and Music Collection, Museum of the City of New York, Fifth Ave. at 103rd St., New York, N.Y. 10029.

CAREER: Rowitt & Lewitt Advertising, Newark, N.J., copywriter, 1951-52; WOR-Mutual, New York City, in public relations, 1952; Biow Advertising, New York City, in television production, 1952; A. H. Bull Steamship Co., New York City, administrative assistant, 1953-56; Adelphi University, Garden City, N.Y., adjunct instructor in speech and costume, 1955-60; American University, Washington, D.C., costumer, 1960-64; William Patterson College of New Jersey, Wayne, instructor in speech and theatre, 1966-72; Montclair State College, Upper Montclair, N.J., assistant professor of speech and theatre, 1973-74; Museum of the City of New York, New York, N.Y., assistant curator, 1975-77, associate curator of theater and music collection, 1977-78, curator of theatre and music collection, 1978—. Adjunct lecturer, New York University, 1977—, special lecturer in theatre, Columbia University, 1977—. Guest on television and radio programs.

MEMBER: International Society of Performing Arts Museums and Libraries, American Society for Theatre Research, Theatre Library Association, American Theatre Wing, Theatre Historical Society, American Theatre Association, National Society of Literature and the Arts, Modern Language Association of America, American Association of University Professors, New York Historical Society, Phi Beta Kappa.

WRITINGS: The City and the Theatre, James T. White, 1973. Contributor to history and performing arts journals. Editor of *Performing Arts Resources.*

WORK IN PROGRESS: A two-volume history of theatrical photography, the first volume covering the nineteenth century.

SIDELIGHTS: Mary Henderson writes: "I consider myself a theatre historian and teacher, and my writing and career will continue to reflect my personal considerations. My interest is mostly in the area of social history—I see theatre as social history and social history as theatre and my job as

curator of a theatre collection affords me the opportunity to develop my ideas. My dream is to buy part of a mountain in Vermont, for escape, to recoup my energies, with an occasional foray into New York City for stimulation."

AVOCATIONAL INTERESTS: Travel, sculpture.

*   *   *

HENDERSON, Richard B(eveir) 1921-

PERSONAL: Born November 27, 1921, in Washington, D.C.; son of Reagan Latimer (a printer) and Catherine (Snyder) Henderson; married Dorothy Tschoepe, May 30, 1944; children: Richard B., Jr., Thomas, DeWitt. *Education:* Southwest Texas State College (now University), B.A., 1949; University of Maryland, M.A., 1950, Ph.D., 1960. *Politics:* Democrat. *Home address:* P.O. Box 505, San Marcos, Tex. 78666. *Office:* Department of Political Science, Southwest Texas State University, San Marcos, Tex. 78666.

CAREER: Southwest Texas State University, San Marcos, instructor in government, summer, 1949; University of Maryland, College Park, instructor in government, 1950-51; Southwest Texas State University, assistant professor of government, 1951-53; University of Maryland, instructor in government, 1954-55; Southwest Texas State University, assistant professor, 1955-57, associate professor, 1957-63, professor of political science, 1963—, chairman of Division of Social Sciences, 1962-65, and department of government, 1965-69. *Military service:* U.S. Army Air Forces, 1942-46; served in Pacific theater; became first lieutenant; received three Bronze Stars.

MEMBER: National Audubon Society, Smithsonian Society, Southwestern Social Science Association, Texas Association of College Teachers, Alpha Chi, Pi Sigma Alpha, Pi Gamma Mu. *Awards, honors:* Prize from Texas Institute of Letters, 1970, and award of excellence from Theta Sigma Phi, 1971, both for *Maury Maverick.*

WRITINGS: Maury Maverick: A Political Biography, University of Texas Press, 1970. Contributor to *Dictionary of American Biography;* also contributor to *Congressional Quarterly Almanac* and *National Observer.*

WORK IN PROGRESS: Studying contributions of U.S. Senator James Hillhouse to early American political thought.

SIDELIGHTS: Henderson writes: "My current academic and personal interest runs to the neo-Malthusian brand of futurology, with emphasis on ecological concerns."

AVOCATIONAL INTERESTS: Bird watching, motorcycles and motorcycle mechanics, carpentry, camping.

*   *   *

HENDREN, Ron 1945-

PERSONAL: Born August 3, 1945, in Pinehurst, N.C.; son of Isaac E. and Emily (Williams) Hendren; married Jeanne Elizabeth Plough, July 10, 1976. *Education:* University of North Carolina at Chapel Hill, B.A., 1967. *Home:* 29 Marin Ave., Sausalito, Calif. 94965.

CAREER/WRITINGS: Staff assistant to Sargent Shriver, 1969; legislative assistant to U.S. Senator Stephen M. Young, 1970, and B. Everett Jordan, 1971; *Los Angeles Times,* Los Angeles, Calif., author of syndicated column, "In Washington," 1972—. Visiting lecturer at University of Maryland, College Park, 1976-77. Commentator "About Washington" on WRC-Television, Washington, D.C., 1976-

77; commentator for KQED-Television, San Francisco, Calif., 1978—.

SIDELIGHTS: Hendren told *CA:* "The purpose of commentary, as I see it, is not so much to persuade people to adopt your point of view, but rather to make them think about political issues of the day that affect their lives, by writing and talking about those issues imaginatively, thoughtfully, and with the primary goal of informing."

*   *   *

HENLE, Jane   1913-

PERSONAL: Born July 14, 1913, in Cleveland, Ohio; daughter of Leo (a merchant) and Pearl (a physician; maiden name, Hahn) Henle. *Education:* Smith College, A.B., 1934; Columbia University, M.A., 1935, Ph.D., 1954. *Home address:* P.O. Box 404, Ridgefield, Conn. 06877.

CAREER: Columbia University, New York, N.Y., lecturer in art history, 1955-71; Marymount College, Tarrytown, N.Y., instructor, 1971-74, assistant professor of art history, 1974—. *Member:* American Institute of Archaeology.

WRITINGS: Greek Myths: A Vase Painter's Notebook, Indiana University Press, 1973.

WORK IN PROGRESS: Mycenaean Linear B.

*   *   *

HENRICKS, Kaw
See WOLFE, Charles Keith

*   *   *

HENRY, Buck   1930-

PERSONAL: Birth given name Buck Henry Zuckerman; born December 9, 1930, in New York, N.Y.; son of Paul (a general in U.S. Army Air Forces) and Ruth (an actress; maiden name, Taylor) Zuckerman; divorced. *Education:* Dartmouth College, B.A., 1952. *Office:* 760 North La Cienega Blvd., Los Angeles, Calif. 90069.

CAREER: Writer for television and motion pictures; actor. Toured with stage production of "Life With Father," 1948; actor in play, "No Time for Sergeants," and in Broadway productions of "Fortress of Glass," and "Bernardine," both 1952; performed with improvisational theatre group, The Premise, 1960. Motion picture performances include, "The Graduate," 1967, "Catch-22," 1970, "Taking Off," 1971, and "The Man Who Fell From Earth," 1976. Performed on television series, including "The Steve Allen Show." Co-director of the motion picture, "Heaven Can Wait," Paramount, 1978. Producer of pilot for "Captain Nice" series, National Broadcasting Company (NBC); occasional guest host for NBC's "Saturday Night Live." *Military service:* U.S. Army, 1952-54, served as helicopter mechanic, and with Seventh Army Repertory Company touring Germany. *Awards, honors:* Co-winner of Emmy Award from National Academy of Television Arts and Sciences, 1966, for "Get Smart"; Writers Guild of America award for best written American comedy, 1967, Academy Award Nomination, 1967, and British Film Academy award for best script, 1969, all for "The Graduate."

WRITINGS—All screenplays: (With Theodore Flicker) "The Troublemaker," Janus, 1964; (with Calder Willingham) "The Graduate" (adapted from Charles Webb's novel), Avco-Embassy, 1967; "Candy" (adapted from novel by Terry Southern and Mason Hoffenberg), Cinerama, 1969; "The Owl and the Pussycat" (adapted from Bill Man-

hoff's play), Columbia, 1970; "Catch-22" (adapted from Joseph Heller's novel), Paramount, 1970; (with Robert Benton and David Newman) "What's Up, Doc?" (based on story by Peter Bogdanovich), Warner Brothers, 1972; "The Day of the Dolphin" (based on Robert Merle's novel), Avco-Embassy, 1973.

Creator, with Mel Brooks, and story editor of "Get Smart"; creator, author, and producer of "Quark." Contributor to television series, "The Steve Allen Show," and "That Was the Week That Was," NBC. Comedy writer for more than one hundred comedians, including Steve Allen, Bill Dana, Jonathan Winters, and the Smothers Brothers.

SIDELIGHTS: "Buck Henry is one of the greatest unknown celebrities of our time," said Paul D. Zimmerman. Similarly Marcia Seligson described Henry as "the hottest screenwriter in America. Still anonymous to the public, mind you. But *very* hot." If Henry is anonymous it is due in part to his role as screenwriter. Though movie fans can usually identify the stars and directors of current films few can name the screenwriters. The other part seems to be Henry's own choice. "He does his best to confuse the issue," Zimmerman explained, "by telling reporters that he is only impersonating himself, that he took the name Buck because his parents named him Linda and that he divides his time between loitering at Bloomingdale's and contemplating a death leap from his New York apartment." When asked why he consistently evades questions about his personal life, Henry answered, "I don't think it's any of my business and I certainly don't want to hear about it."

Following his military service in Korea, Henry spent six years looking for work as an actor. Zimmerman described this period as "vigorous, total unemployment, characterized by a great deal of sleep." It was during this time that Henry, along with fellow hoaxster Alan Abel, founded the Society for Indecency to Naked Animals (SINA). Posing as SINA's president, G. Clifford Prout, Henry made television appearances and speaking engagements calling for the dressing of all animals—in private homes as well as in zoos and pounds. On one occasion Prout (Henry) demonstrated his convictions by attempting to dress San Francisco Zoo's baby elephant in boxer shorts, and was subsequently interviewed by Walter Cronkite. Reportedly, Cronkite was quite upset to find that SINA was a joke.

Mike Nichols, director of "The Graduate," met Henry through a mutual friend, George Segal. He chose Henry to work with him on the film after rejecting the attempts of two other screenwriters. Nichols recalled, "I thought Buck was the funniest and most serious guy I'd ever met—simultaneously." Leonard Stern, executive producer of "Get Smart" remembered one of Henry's creations for the show, a large dog that would feign heart attacks to avoid spying missions. "Buck is the most imaginative writer I know, with the most bizarre sense of mischief," Stern said. While Henry often works in collaboration with good friends and admits that such working conditions make for more fun, he maintains, "I don't think rosy camaraderie is necessary to make great films."

One of Henry's particular talents in screenwriting is tailoring lines to the personalities of the actors. Recalling the role Henry developed for him in "The Owl and the Pussycat," George Segal stated: "What Buck wrote for my part was an aspect of myself, specific to the character and also specific to me personally." Henry's early writing for many different comedians helped him to develop this ability along with the skill of adapting a writer's tone to the screenplay. He told

Newsweek: "The good screenwriter should be able to see a movie in his head or, at the very least, hear it. But it's not enough to have a good ear for dialogue. You have to know where the beats and pauses are."

BIOGRAPHICAL/CRITICAL SOURCES: New Republic, December 23, 1967; *Variety,* December 18, 1968, November 4, 1970, March 8, 1972; *Cue,* July 5, 1969; *Christian Science Monitor,* July 10, 1970; *New York Times Magazine,* July 19, 1970; *Nation,* July 20, 1970; *Newsweek,* October 19, 1970; *New York Times,* November 22, 1970, March 29, 1971, May 16, 1971; *Life,* April 7, 1972.

* * *

HENRY, Frances 1931-

PERSONAL: Born December 24, 1931, in Germany; married W. Mischel, April 6, 1952 (divorced, 1959); married J. Henry (a professor), November 10, 1960; children: Terrence, Miriam. *Education:* Brooklyn College (now of the City University of New York), B.A., 1953; Ohio State University, M.A., 1955, Ph.D., 1958. *Home:* 47 Wembley Rd., Toronto, Ontario, Canada. *Office:* York University, Toronto, Ontario, Canada.

CAREER: McGill University, Montreal, Quebec, assistant professor, 1963-72; York University, Toronto, Ontario, professor, 1972—.

WRITINGS: McGill Studies in Caribbean Anthropology, McGill University Press, 1967; *Stress and Response in Fieldwork,* Holt, 1969; *Forgotten Canadians: The Blacks of Nova Scotia,* Longmans Canada, 1973; (editor) *Ethnicity in the Americas,* Mouton & Co., 1976.

WORK IN PROGRESS: Research on racism in Canada.

* * *

HERBERT, Anthony B(ernard) 1930-

PERSONAL: Born April 17, 1930, in Herminie, Pa.; son of Charles E. (a coal miner) and Mary (Theibert) Herbert; married Marygrace Natale, September 12, 1952; children: Toni-Junell. *Education:* University of Pittsburgh, B.A., 1956; University of Georgia, M.S., 1968, Ph.D., 1975. *Agent:* Gerard McCauley, Gerard McCauley Agency, Inc., 551 Fifth Ave., New York, N.Y. 10017.

CAREER: U.S. Army, Infantry, 1947-72, retiring as lieutenant colonel; Medical University of South Carolina, Charleston, internship and lecturer in psychology, beginning 1975; currently licensed psychologist in private practice, Denver, Colo. Served in Korea, Africa, the Middle East, Europe, South America, the Dominican Republic, and Vietnam; instructor at U.S. Army Combat and Service School Training Centers; associate therapist and instructor in hypnotherapy and natural childbirth at Martin Army Hospital, Ft. Benning, Ga., 1958-59; associate professor of military sciences and lecturer in psychology at University of Georgia, 1966-68; inspector general in Vietnam, 1968-69; associate professor of humanitites and psychology, Fitzsimmons Army Hospital, 1976-77. *Member:* American Psychological Association, Charleston Psychological Association, Psi Chi. *Awards, honors*—Military: More than fifty international and national decorations, including Silver Star, Bronze Star, and Purple Heart. Other: Awarded New York State Medal of Honor; American Civil Liberties Union National Award, 1972.

WRITINGS: (With Robert L. Niemann) *Conquest to Nowhere,* Keystone, 1955; (with James T. Wooten) *Soldier,* Holt, 1973. Also author of *13 Best Short Stories of World War Two and Korea,* 1968.

SIDELIGHTS: Herbert gained national attention in 1971 when he charged his Army superiors with ignoring reports of atrocities in Vietnam. After the Army ruled in favor of the superior officers and Herbert took an early retirement, he wrote *Soldier,* his account of the alleged field brutalities and the failure to investigate them. Herbert told *CA* that the three court suits filed by officers he criticized in *Soldier* were subsequently dropped, but that he had gone to court against CBS ("Sixty Minutes") and *Atlantic* for libel.

In an article about Herbert and his charges against CBS, *Time* reported: "In a half-hour '60 Minutes' segment in 1973, Lando and correspondent Mike Wallace challenged a number of Herbert's allegations, and interviewed fellow officers unable to substantiate them. Herbert sued Lando, Wallace, and CBS for libel demanding that Lando answer questions about his state of mind when he prepared the program. Lando balked, and in January a judge ordered him to comply." In November, 1977, a final decision was made by federal appeals court Chief Judge Irving R. Kaufman in Manhattan who declared such judicial delving into editorial thought unconstitutional. He stated: "Such an inquiry unquestionably puts a freeze on the free interchange of ideas within the newsroom." Herbert and his attorneys have now taken their appeal to the U.S. Supreme Court.

BIOGRAPHICAL/CRITICAL SOURCES: New York Times, March 13, 1971; *Playboy,* July, 1972, November, 1972; *Newsweek,* January 29, 1973; *Time,* February 12, 1973, November 21, 1977; *Saturday Review,* February, 1973.

* * *

HERLIN, Hans 1925-

PERSONAL: Born December 24, 1925, in Germany. *Home:* D8911 Unterfinning, Ammersee, West Germany.

CAREER: Worked as editor, 1950-56, newspaper editor, 1956-63, managing editor and editor-in-chief, 1969-72; free-lance writer, 1972—.

WRITINGS: (With Renate Herlin) *Die moderne Hausfrau* (title means "Modern Housewife"), Lanzenreiter-Verlag, 1954; *Udet: Eines Mannes Leben und die Geschichte seiner Zeit,* Nannen-Verlag, 1958, translation by Mervyn Savill published as *Udet: A Man's Life,* Macdonald & Co., 1960, German edition reprinted as *Der Teufelsflieger: Ernst Udet und die Geschichte seiner Zeit,* Heyne, 1974; *Verdammter Atlantik* (title means "Damned Atlantic"), Nannen-Verlag, 1959.

Kain, wo ist dein Bruder Abel?: Die Flieger von Hiroshima und Nagasaki (title means "Cain, Where Is Your Brother Abel?: The Flyers of Hiroshima and Nagasaki"), Nannen-Verlag, 1960; *Kein gelobtes Land: Die Irrafhrt der "St. Louis"* (title means "The Voyage of the St. Louis"), Nannen-Verlag, 1961, reprinted as *Die Riese der Verdammten,* Heyne, 1977; *Die Welt des Uebersinnlichen* (title means "The World of Psi"), Moderne Verlags GmbII, 1965; *Freunde* (novel), Droemer Knaur, 1974, translation by Eric Mosbacher published as *Commemorations,* St. Martin's, 1975; *Feuer im Gras* (novel), Droemersche, 1976, translation by C. C. Winston published as *Which Way the Wind,* St. Martin's, 1978; *Tag-und Nachgeschicten* (short stories; title means "Day and Night Stories"), Droemersche, 1978.

WORK IN PROGRESS: A novel set in Germany.

HERMAN, Kenneth Neil 1954-

PERSONAL: Born May 20, 1954, in Brooklyn, N.Y.; son of David (an accountant) and Doris (an office manager; maiden name, Arnold) Herman; married Sharon Jayson (a reporter), January 7, 1978. *Education:* Miami-Dade Community College, A.A., 1973; Florida Atlantic University, B.A., 1975. *Religion:* Jewish. *Home:* 1325 South 77 Sunshine Strip, Apt. H-10, Harlingen, Tex. 78550. *Office:* Associated Press, P.O. Box 711, Harlingen, Tex. 78550.

CAREER/WRITINGS: Lufkin News, Lufkin, Tex., reporter, 1975-77; Associated Press, New York, N.Y., newsman in Dallas, Tex., 1977-78, correspondent in Harlingen, Tex., 1978—. *Awards, honors:* Pulitzer Prize for meritorious public service and National Headliner Award for outstanding reporting, both 1977, both for series on U.S. Marine Corps.

SIDELIGHTS: Herman was praised by *Lufkin News* editor Joe Murray as "the best thing that happened to me when he walked in here." Murray was referring to Herman's Pulitzer Prize winning coverage of the boot camp beating of Pvt. Lynn E. McClure, U.S.M.C. Herman's story led to a presidential inquiry and a congressional investigation of Marine recruiting and boot camp procedures.

BIOGRAPHICAL/CRITICAL SOURCES: Editor & Publisher, April 23, 1977, May 21, 1977.

*   *   *

HERRIOT, James
See WIGHT, James Alfred

*   *   *

HERRMANN, Nina 1943-

PERSONAL: Born December 1, 1943, in Gettysburg, Pa.; daughter of Philip August and Sarah (Neely) Herrmann. *Education:* Northwestern University, B.S., 1961; University of Chicago, M.A., 1975. *Home:* Chicago, Ill. *Office:* Rehabilitation Institute of Chicago, 345 East Superior, Chicago, Ill. 60611.

CAREER: United Press International (UPI), Chicago, Ill., writer-editor, 1965-67; National Broadcasting Company (NBC)-Television News, New York, N.Y., reporter, 1967-68; WGN-Television News, Chicago, reporter, 1968-73; Children's Memorial Hospital, Chicago, chaplain, 1973-74; State of Illinois, Office of the Attorney General, Chicago, administrative assistant, 1974-76; ordained Presbyterian minister, 1976; Rehabilitation Institute of Chicago, Chicago, chaplain, 1976—. *Member:* American Congress of Rehabilitation Medicine.

WRITINGS: Go Out in Joy, John Knox, 1977. Contributor to *War Cry* (Salvation Army magazine).

WORK IN PROGRESS: Writing a second book.

SIDELIGHTS: Herrmann's studies at the divinity school of the University of Chicago led her into her first encounter with terminal patients at a children's hospital. Watching the sickness and pain that the children had to tolerate each day brought about a change in her life and the resignation of her television job. *Go Out in Joy!* was based on her experiences in the hospital.

Herrmann told *CA* that her goal is to "listen and to help each person reaffirm his own value in the eyes of God and his fellow man and to help society realize that a person who is physically handicapped is a *person* first."

BIOGRAPHICAL/CRITICAL SOURCES: People, May 5, 1978.

HESS, Thomas B. 1920-1978

July 14, 1920—July 13, 1978; American art critic, editor, and author. Hess was editor of *Arts News* magazine for twenty-five years before becoming chairman of twentieth-century art at the Metropolitan Museum of Art in New York. A strong supporter of modern art, he organized important art exhibits that toured the United States and Europe. Hess was also an art critic for *Le Monde* and *New York* magazine. He was author of books on abstract expressionist artists Willem De Kooning and Barnett Newman. He died in Manhattan, N.Y. Obituaries and other sources: *Who's Who in American Art,* Bowker, 1973; *Who's Who in America,* 38th edition, Marquis, 1974; *New York Times,* July 14, 1978.

*   *   *

HEWES, Jeremy Joan 1944-

PERSONAL: Born March 4, 1944, in Toledo, Ohio; daughter of George Robert (a lawyer) and Laura (Robins) Hewes. *Education:* Duke University, A.B., 1966; attended Radcliffe College, 1966; University of Michigan, M.A., 1968, further graduate study, 1968-69. *Home:* 111-B Seventh Ave., San Francisco, Calif. 94118. *Office:* Graduate School of Business Administration, University of California, Berkeley, Calif. 94720.

CAREER: Lahey Clinic Foundation, Boston, Mass., editor, 1966-67; University of Michigan, Ann Arbor, publications editor for Medical Center's hospital systems improvement program, 1967-68; University of California, San Francisco, editor for department of ophthalmology, 1969-72, and department of otolaryngology, 1972-73; free-lance editor and writer, 1973-75; University of California, Berkeley, senior editor of *California Management Review,* 1975—. Educational materials editor for Northeast Community Mental Health Services, Inc., 1972-73. Member of state committee of America the Beautiful Fund, Inc., Volunteers to Beautify Our Schools, Inc., and Network.

WRITINGS: (With Christopher Swan and Eileen Douse) *Cable Car,* Ten Speed Press, 1973; *Build Your Own Playground!,* Houghton, 1975; (with E. E. Shev) *Good Cops/Bad Cops,* San Francisco Book Co., 1977. Contributor to magazines and newspapers. Editor of *Archives of Physical Medicine and Rehabilitation,* 1967-71, and *West Words,* 1969-70; co-editor of *Wordsworth,* 1977—.

WORK IN PROGRESS: Two film scripts, "Hoops" and "The Soda Pop War," both with Ron Jones; research for a book on community-based social change, *Little-Known Saints.*

SIDELIGHTS: Jeremy Hewes told *CA* that vital issues for herself include "nature and human beings: enhancing people's understanding of their own worth and power. The sharing of others' lives and community experiences is essential to the human future." *Avocational interests:* Writing music (contemporary and folk music; also the title songs for her films).

*   *   *

HEWITT, Jean D(aphne) 1925-

PERSONAL: Born August 15, 1925, in Ipswich, England; came to the United States in 1948, naturalized citizen, 1957; daughter of Basil J. (an engineer) and Jessie (Wright) White; married Eric J. Hewitt, May 21, 1949 (died February 26, 1976); children: Gordon J., Geoffrey L. *Education:* Queen Elizabeth College, London, B.Sc., 1945; Columbia University, M.S., 1949. *Agent:* Curtis Brown Ltd., 575 Madison

Ave., New York, N.Y. 10022. *Office: Family Circle,* 488 Madison Ave., New York, N.Y. 10022.

CAREER: Evans Research & Development Corp., New York City, head of home economics department, 1953-61; *New York Times,* New York City, food reporter and food critic, 1961-75; *Family Circle,* New York City, food and equipment editor, 1975—. *Member:* American Home Economics Association, Home Economists in Business, Electrical Women's Round Table, Institute of Food Technologists, Women in Communications. *Awards, honors:* R. T. French Tastemaker Awards, for *The New York Times Large Type Cookbook, The New York Times Main Dish Cookbook, The New York Times Natural Foods Cookbook,* and *The New York Times Weekend Cookbook.*

WRITINGS: The New York Times Large Type Cookbook, Quadrangle, 1969; *The New York Times Main Dish Cookbook,* Western Publishing, 1969; *The New York Times Natural Foods Cookbook,* Quadrangle, 1971; *The New York Times Heritage Cookbook,* Putnam, 1972; *The New York Times Weekend Cookbook,* Quadrangle, 1974; *The New York Times Southern Heritage Cookbook,* Putnam, 1976; *The New York Times New England Heritage Cookbook,* Putnam, 1977; *Family Circle's Quick and Easy Menu Cookbook,* Times Books, 1978. Contributor to popular magazines, including *House and Garden* and *Town and Country.*

SIDELIGHTS: Hewitt told *CA:* "In grade school I won an academic prize and stunned the principal by asking for a cookbook. I still have it. I knew then I wanted to work with food. Since, I have made it my vocation through teaching, research and development and journalism, and my avocation through cooking for family and friends in my home. Home is a weekend place near the ocean in Rhode Island where I satisfy my craving for fresh fish. This is also where I work on cookbooks in a room with a floor-to-ceiling library of cookbooks and a view of Block Island Sound."

* * *

HEYNEN, Jim 1940-

PERSONAL: Born July 14, 1940, in Sioux County, Iowa; son of Hilbert (a farmer) and Alice (Klein) Heynen; married DeLaine Bliek, August 16, 1960 (divorced June 7, 1967); married Carol Jane Bangs (a poet and scholar), August 1, 1973; children: Emily Jane. *Education:* Calvin College, B.A., 1960; University of Iowa, M.A., 1965; University of Oregon, M.F.A., 1972. *Religion:* Protestant. *Home address:* c/o Howard Berry, 1059 Bayberry Rd., Lake Oswego, Ore. 97034. *Office:* Centrum Fort Worden State Park, Port Townsend, Ore. 98368.

CAREER: University of Michigan, Ann Arbor, lecturer in English, 1967-68; Calvin College, Grand Rapids, Mich., instructor in English, 1969-70; poet, 1970-74; University of Oregon, Eugene, visiting instructor in English, summer, 1975; program director in arts administration for Idaho Commission on the Arts, 1975-76; Centrum Fort Worden State Park, Port Townsend, Ore., program director, 1976—. *Awards, honors:* National Endowment for the Arts fellowship, 1974; United States-United Kingdom exchange fellowship from U.S. State Department, 1977.

WRITINGS: Sioux Songs (translations), Blue Cloud Press, 1976; *Notes From Custer* (poems), Bear Claw Press, 1976; *The Boys* (prose fables), Gray Wolf Press, 1978. Contributor to literary journals and popular magazines, including *Redbook, Prairie Schooner, Carleton Miscellany,* and *Midwest Quarterly.*

WORK IN PROGRESS: Morning Chores, poems; a novel.

SIDELIGHTS: Heynen writes: "Most of my work is rural in subject and/or sentiment; even when I am not writing on rural subjects, my esthetic is clearly non-urbane. I am interested in developing a distinctively rural American esthetic, one which I would not call a sentimental ruralism, but rather a clear and even harsh acceptance of the earth and animal presence in our historical and contemporary lives."

* * *

HIDDEN, (Frederick) Norman 1913-

PERSONAL: Born October 24, 1913, in Portsmouth, England. *Education:* Brasenose College, Oxford, M.A., diploma in education; also attended University of Michigan. *Home:* 2 Culham Court, Granville Rd., London N4 4JB, England.

CAREER: Former elementary school teacher in Macclesfield, England, Goole, England, and Hornchurch, England; Adrian College, Adrian, Mich., former lecturer in English; College of All Saints, London, England, senior lecturer in English, 1964-75; writer and lecturer, 1975—. Creator of Poets' Picnic; member of council of National Book League and advisory council of English Speaking Board. Has given readings of his poems at theaters, schools, and other public places, and broadcast on British radio and television. Past borough councillor and candidate for Parliament. *Military service:* British Army, liaison to U.S. Army headquarters in Europe.

MEMBER: Poetry Society of Great Britain (member of executive committee, 1967-73; chairman of general council, 1968-71; vice-president, 1974—), English Association (member of executive committee, 1967—).

WRITINGS: These Images Claw (poems), Outposts Publications, 1966; (co-editor) *National Anthology of Student Poetry,* Institute of Education Students Association, University of London, 1968; (editor) *Say It Aloud* (poetry anthology), Hutchinson, 1972; *Dr. Kink and His Old Style Boarding School: Fragments of Autobiography,* Workshop Press, 1973; (editor) *Over to You* (poetry anthology), English Speaking Board, 1975.

Work represented in *Pick of the Year's Short Stories.* Contributor of articles and poems to magazines and newspapers. Founding editor of *New Poetry,* 1967—.

BIOGRAPHICAL/CRITICAL SOURCES: Teacher, September 22, 1972; *Guardian,* January 9, 1973.

* * *

HIGDON, David Leon 1939-

PERSONAL: Born March 22, 1939, in Oklahoma City, Okla.; son of Elmer Ray (a farmer) and Gertrude Vernoyce (Petricek) Higdon; married Mary Ann Johnston (a librarian), August 29, 1958; children: David, Liana, Andrew. *Education:* Attended Oklahoma State University, 1957-58; Oklahoma City University, B.A. (magna cum laude), 1962; University of Kansas, M.A., 1964, Ph.D., 1968. *Religion:* Episcopal. *Home:* 3309 61st, Lubbock, Tex. 79413. *Office:* Department of English, Texas Tech University, Box 4530, Lubbock, Tex. 79409.

CAREER: Southern Methodist University, Dallas, Tex., assistant professor of English, 1968-71; Texas Tech University, Lubbock, assistant professor, 1971-74, associate professor, 1974-78, professor of English, 1978—. *Member:* Modern Language Association of America, American Association of University Professors, Rocky Mountain Modern Language Association, South-Central Modern Language

Association. *Awards, honors:* American Philosophical Society grants, 1972, 1977.

WRITINGS: Time and English Fiction, Macmillan, 1977; (editor) Joseph Conrad, *Almayer's Folly* (critical edition), Cambridge University Press, in press. Editor of *Conradiana.*

WORK IN PROGRESS: The Visible Past: The Contemporary British Novel.

* * *

HIGGINS, George V(incent) 1939-

PERSONAL: Born November 13, 1939, in Brockton, Mass. *Education:* Boston College, B.A., 1961, J.D., 1967; Stanford University, M.A., 1965. *Address:* c/o Little Brown, 34 Beacon St., Boston, Mass. 02106. *Office:* George V. Higgins, Inc., 100 Federal St., Boston, Mass.

CAREER: Newspaper reporter for *Journal* and *Evening Bulletin,* Providence, R.I., 1962-63; reporter for Associated Press, 1963-64; Massachusetts Office of the Attorney General, Boston, member of staff, 1969-70; Office of U.S. Attorney for Massachusetts, Boston, assistant U.S. Attorney, 1970-73, special assistant U.S. Attorney, 1973-74; George V. Higgins, Inc., Boston, attorney and president, 1974—. Novelist.

WRITINGS: The Friends of Eddie Coyle (novel), Knopf, 1972; *The Digger's Game* (novel), Knopf, 1973; *Cogan's Trade* (novel), Knopf, 1974; *A City on a Hill* (novel), Knopf, 1975; *The Friends of Richard Nixon* (nonfiction), Little, Brown, 1975; *The Judgement of Deke Hunter* (novel), Little, Brown, 1976; *Dreamland* (novel), Little, Brown, 1977.

Work represented in anthologies, including *The Best American Short Stories 1973,* edited by Martha Foley, Houghton, 1973; *They Don't Dance Much,* edited by James Ross, Southern Illinois University Press, 1975. Contributor of short fiction to journals and periodicals, including *Arizona Quarterly, Massachusetts Review, Cimarron Review, North American Review, Esquire,* and *Atlantic.*

SIDELIGHTS: The fiction of George V. Higgins has met with uniformly appreciative reception, with most critics focusing on his extensive use of dialogue to study his characters' psychology as the typifying element of his writing.

Time reviewer Martha Duffy wrote of *The Friends of Eddie Coyle:* "Almost the whole book is dialogue, and it is truly a bravura performance. Higgins is a master of the colorful street language heard around Boston. Throughout the novel, without quaintness or self-parody, he is able to sustain long arias of criminal shoptalk." Duffy noted that "Higgins cheerfully admits to logorrhea," an admission additionally borne out by the fact that *Eddie Coyle,* Higgins's first published novel, is actually the eleventh he has written, Higgins having "junked the other ten."

Christopher Lehmann-Haupt echoed Duffy's critique of Higgins's use of dialogue: "Its dialogue eats at one's nerve endings. Its ironies—of a world in which hoods and cops depend on one another to eke out their mean livings; of betrayals and double-crosses and loyalties to self-preservation; of the women's liberation movement rearing its head just when it is least expected—these are corrosive enough. The craft with which Higgins controls his reader's comprehension of who is who and doing what to whom makes the book worth reading not only once but twice. And the ending is as hard as a set of metal knuckles in the face." Walter Clemons stated: "Higgins' pungent, ironic dialogue precisely registers the feints and formalities of a world in which unguarded

speech can be fatal. He risks confusing us in order to make us sink or swim as his characters must learn to do."

In a review of *The Digger's Game,* a writer for *New Republic* noted: "The book is flawless of its kind—never a false word, phrase, rhythm, gesture; its 'kind' being the fictional equivalent of a 'gangster' film that has never been made, for the book is free of the least sentimentality that inevitably mars by prettifying or magnifying the best of those films. . . . Talk [is] Higgins' and the book's chief pleasure. Higgins lets his talkers run on at reckless length; he encourages them, eggs them on to floods of filth, a kind of brutal patois of the gutter . . . all of it used with metric precision." *New York Times Book Review* critic James Mills disliked Higgins's "boring" and "annoying" use of "descriptive prose" but conceded that "the dialogue here is perfect."

Cogan's Trade received both positive and negative commentary. J. D. O'Hara panned the "drab obscenities and . . . endless drivel" prevalent throughout the novel, and O. L. Bailey suggested the need of a "dictionary of slang" to understand fully the criminal argot. On a more positive note, a *Newsweek* critic declared: "The narrative, the criminal design, winds twistingly around a series of set pieces in which the action is suspended, often for chapters at a time, while the gangsters talk about sex and marriage, their weight and root-canal work. To these people the banal frustrations of life are more important than the taking of it. This is a fine comic device. . . ."

A City on a Hill represented a departure for Higgins from his usual crime-oriented plot and deals with politics and politicians. Phoebe Adams labeled the dialogue "shrewd and tough and funny" and suggested that it "should be followed with the ear as much as the eye." Christopher Lydon found the dialogues "elliptical, digressive, confusing . . . and implausible" but admitted that "part of Higgins's success is that the conversations . . . have the undeniable sound of primary-source material on life in Washington in the seventies."

The Friends of Richard Nixon is Higgins's account of the Watergate scandal. Some reviewers found Higgins's treatment sketchy in view of his experience with law and courtroom procedure. M. H. Freedman expressed disappointment in Higgins's failure to provide penetrating commentary on the question of "lawyers' ethics," noting that "his treatment of those questions is infrequent and superficial." *Newsweek*'s P. D. Zimmerman declared that Higgins "views the seismic events of the last Nixon years through the narrow prism of his own prejudices as a former U.S. attorney," adding: "His casting of heroes and villains often inverts common sense. . . . The value of Higgins's abrasive, showy account lies in his forensic savvy. He offers a tipster's tour of the stratagems that guided the cover-up, right down to a play-by-play analysis of the . . . courtroom and committee-room performance of Richard Nixon's felonious friends."

In a review of *Dreamland,* a *Kirkus* critic observed: "As a brocaded reupholstery of the familiar son-learns-truth-about-father motif, *Dreamland* furnishes rather leaden arm chair detection. But as a sort of cerebral morality play—livened by the details of Back Bay milieux and those bristling tongue wars—it may be the ideal George V. Higgins for homes in which *The Friends of Eddie Coyle* would be highly unwelcome guests."

BIOGRAPHICAL/CRITICAL SOURCES: New York Times, January 25, 1972; *Newsweek,* February 7, 1972, March 25, 1974, October 13, 1975; *Time,* February 21, 1972;

New Republic, March 17, 1973, March 30, 1974; *New York Times Book Review,* March 25, 1973, March 31, 1974, March 30, 1975, October 26, 1975, September 12, 1976; *Atlantic,* May, 1975; *Contemporary Literary Criticism,* Gale, Volume 4, 1975, Volume 7, 1977; *Times Literary Supplement,* September 24, 1976; *Kirkus,* June 15, 1977.*

* * *

HIGGINS, John A(loysius) 1931-

PERSONAL: Born March 20, 1931, in Brooklyn, N.Y.; son of John A. (a bank manager) and Margaret (McGrath) Higgins; married Elizabeth S. Browne (an executive assistant director), December 26, 1955; children: John, Neil, Patrick, Brendan, Robert. *Education:* St. John's University, Jamaica, N.Y., B.A. (magna cum laude), 1953, Ph.D., 1968; New York University, M.A., 1959. *Home:* 714 Thomas Ave., Baldwin, N.Y. 11510. *Office:* Department of Teacher Preparation, York College of the City University of New York, Jamaica, N.Y. 11451.

CAREER: High school English teacher in Hewlett, N.Y., 1956-61, and Oceanside, N.Y., 1961-69; York College of the City University of New York, Jamaica, N.Y., assistant professor of English, 1969—. Editor for Barnell Loft, Inc. Adjunct professor at Nassau Community College and Queensborough Community College. *Military service:* U.S. Army, 1953-55. *Member:* National Council of Teachers of English, College English Association.

WRITINGS: F. Scott Fitzgerald: A Study of the Stories, St. John's University Press, 1971; *Comp/Mods: Discovering Writing Skills,* Crowell, 1976. Contributor to English teaching journals.

WORK IN PROGRESS: A novel for young adults; stories for children.

SIDELIGHTS: Higgins told *CA:* "*F. Scott Fitzgerald: A Study of the Stories* is a scholarly work that examines the one hundred sixty-odd stories of Fitzgerald on their own merits and in relation to his novels. His work in the short stories sharpened his literary skills and gave him a reservoir from which to draw material for his novels. He emerges as a major contributor to the short story, though not an innovator in the genre.

"*Comp/Mods* is a writing text-workbook for college students whose basic skills need sharpening. It is flexible in organization and attempts to simplify most concepts. It is designed for either individual self-teaching or for full-class use.

"From my teaching of children's literature I have become interested in writing stories for young people. I have completed two stories at the picture-storybook level and am working on a young adult novel that contrasts life in the suburbs with that in the inner-city's changing neighborhoods."

* * *

HILL, Adrian Keith Graham 1895-1977

PERSONAL: Born March 24, 1895, in Charlton, Kent, England; son of Graham Hill; married Dorothy Margaret Whitley; children: one son. *Education:* Attended Royal College of Art. *Home:* Old Laundry Cottage, Midhurst, Sussex, England.

CAREER: Artist and writer. Life master and lecturer in anatomy, Westminster School of Art, 1935-38; external examiner for teachers certificate, University of Durham, 1938-39; appointed under the Pilgrim Trust grant to depict the changing face of Britain, 1940; art lecturer to Her Majesty's Forces, 1943-44; governor of Chichester School of Art, 1951-62, and Midhurst Grammar School, 1957-67. Presenter of the television program, "Sketch Club," British Broadcasting Corporation (BBC), London. Works represented in Victoria and Albert Museum, Bradford Corporation Art Gallery, and various municipal galleries; held one-man exhibitions in 1938, 1940, 1961, 1964, 1966, and 1968. *Member:* British Association of Art Therapists (president, 1966), British Society of Aesthetics (founder member), Federation of British Artists (governor, 1968), Royal Institute of Oil Painters (former president), Chichester Art Society (president, 1969), Midhurst Art Society (president, 1972), St. James Art School (vice-president, 1947), National League of Hospital Friends (vice-president, 1950); Ancient Monuments Society (vice-president, 1960). *Military service:* Honourable Artillery Company (HAC), 1914-1919; became lieutenant. *Awards, honors:* Awarded De Lasizo Silver and Bronze Medals by Royal Society of British Artists; Prix Catherine-Hadot from Academie Nationale de Medicine, 1947.

WRITINGS: On Drawing Trees, Pitman, 1936, revised edition, 1957; *On the Mastery of Water Colour Painting,* Pitman, 1939, new edition, 1961; *Art Versus Illness,* Allen & Unwin, 1945; *Trees Have Names,* Faber, 1949; *A Book of Trees,* Faber, 1951; *The Pleasures of Painting, with Practical Demonstrations,* Pitman, 1953; *Adventures in Line and Tone,* Allen & Unwin, 1955; *The Beginners Book of Oil Painting,* Blandford, 1958, Emerson, 1959; *What Shall We Draw?,* Emerson, 1959; *The Beginners's Book of Water Painting,* Emerson, 1959; *Painting as a Hobby,* Stanley Paul, 1959.

Knowing and Drawing Trees, Faber, 1960; *Sketching and Painting Indoors,* Pitman, 1961; *Sketching and Painting Out of Doors,* Pitman, 1961; *Countryside,* Longacre, 1961; *The Studio Book of Basic Anatomy,* Studio Books, 1962; *Faces and Figures,* Blandford, 1962; *How to Draw,* Pan Books, 1963, published as *You Can Draw,* Hart, 1966; *The Handbook of Learning to Draw,* Barker, 1964; *How to Paint Landscapes and Seascapes,* Blandford, 1964; *On Drawing and Painting Trees,* Pitman, 1964; *The Beginner's Book of Drawing and Painting Flowers,* Blandford, 1965; *Drawing and Painting Architecture in Landscape,* Blandford, 1966; *How to Paint in Water Colour,* Pitman, 1967; *Further Steps in Oil Painting,* Blandford, 1970.

SIDELIGHTS: Mr. Hill's paintings were represented in the Victoria and Albert Museum. He was popularly known for his art instruction television program, and for a variety of his self-help art books. One in particular was his *Art Versus Illness,* which was geared toward the art therapy movement. As an official War Artist, Mr. Hill retained a collection of 190 war pictures at the Imperial War Museum in London, and at the headquarters of the Honourable Artillery Company.

OBITUARIES: AB Bookman's Weekly, September 5, 1977.*

(Died June 22, 1977, in England)

* * *

HILL, Carol (Dechellis) 1942-

PERSONAL: Born January 20, 1942, in New Jersey; divorced. *Education:* Chatham College, B.A., 1961. *Home:* 52 West Ninth St., New York, N.Y. 10011. *Agent:* Lynn Nesbit, International Creative Management, 40 West 57th St., New York, N.Y. 10019. *Office:* William Morrow & Co., Inc., 105 Madison Ave., New York, N.Y. 10016.

CAREER: Crown Publishers, New York City, publicist, 1965-67; Bernard Geis Associates, Inc., New York City, publicist, 1967-69; Pantheon Books, New York City, publicist, 1971-73, editor, 1971-73; Random House, New York City, publicity manager, 1973-74; William Morrow & Co., Inc., New York City, senior editor, 1974—. Has also worked as an actress.

WRITINGS: "Mother Loves" (play), produced in New York, 1967; *Jeremiah 8:20* (novel), Random House, 1970; (with Bruce Davidson) *Subsistence U.S.A.* (pictorial work), edited by Jamie Shalleck, Holt, 1973; *Let's Fall in Love* (novel), Random House, 1975. Contributor of short stories to *Playboy* and *Viva.*

SIDELIGHTS: "One gets an overwhelming sense of *deja vu* from this contemporary fable," said Martin Levin of *Jeremiah 8:20,* Carol Hill's first novel. Robert A. Gross was more specific in his observation: "Hill has gotten down the madness of our times—racism, obsessions with money, sex and power, loss of contact with the past—and given us a vision of the future that is at once a desperate comedy and a harrowing rehearsal of the apocalypse."

John Leonard compared *Jeremiah 8:20* to Sartre's *Nausea,* "written from a lower middle-class rather than an academic point of view. Francis is the perfect American victim," continued Leonard, "—trying to buy a personality, connect 'it is' with 'I feel', break the code, learn the happiness trick, merge with the advertisements—and the reader is victimized right alongside of him." *Time* praised Hill's ability to handle "crowd situations that many more experienced writers avoid—or simply flub," saying "riots, nightclub scenes, eight-way conversations around a boardinghouse dinner table bring out her gift for orchestrating many elements without losing the tone or clarity of individual voices." Leonard best summarized the effect of Hill's title character Jeremiah: "If you can't identify with him, you probably can't identify with yourself."

Sponsored by the Ford Foundation, Hill's *Subsistence U.S.A.* was a joint effort with photographer Bruce Davidson. Roy Bongartz complimented Hill for "keeping at bay the sentimentality that threatens any project involving a portrayal of country folk or self-sustaining citizens or old-timers or individuals in the United States." Yet, Bongartz found the book's strength lessened by "the subjects themselves [who] see life through fogs of old hopes or worn-out romanticism," for the reader often "feels the actual life is still hidden from him, as maybe it also is hidden from those who are living it."

Commenting on the grand scale of *Let's Fall in Love,* Annie Gottlieb said: "At its best, this comic novel is to the sexual and international politics of the seventies what Busby Berkeley musicals were to the Depression. Totally unrealistic, wildly exaggerated, and for just that reason refreshing—extravagant fantasy salted with self-irony." "Forget the plot," suggested Jonathan Yardley, "and read *Let's Fall in Love* for the laughs and the sex, both of which are first class."

BIOGRAPHICAL/CRITICAL SOURCES: Newsweek, May 11, 1970; *New York Times,* May 21, 1970; *Best Sellers,* June 1, 1970; *New York Times Book Review,* June 14, 1970, October 21, 1973, April 14, 1974, June 2, 1974; *Time,* June 29, 1970; *Village Voice,* August 27, 1970; *Nation,* October 25, 1975.*

HILL, Ellen Wise 1942-
(Nellie Hill)

PERSONAL: Born August 16, 1942, in Rockford, Ill.; daughter of F. Leroy (a machine-tool designer) and Ellen (a bookseller; maiden name, Mayo) Hill; married William P. Sildar, April 10, 1966 (divorced, June, 1969). *Education:* Attended Washington University, St. Louis, Mo., 1960-61; New York University, B.A., 1965. *Home and office:* 79 Ulloa St., San Francisco, Calif. 94127.

CAREER: Member of editorial staffs of publishers, magazines, stockbrokers, architects, a wine company, and a wig company, 1966—; free-lance writer, 1974—. *Awards, honors:* Fellowships for Yaddo Colony, 1974, Macdowell Colony, 1975, and Ossabaw Island, 1976.

WRITINGS—Under name Nellie Hill: (With Elizabeth Keeler and David Hoag) *Astrolabes* (poems), Peace & Pieces Press, 1975; (with Keeler) *Having Come This Far* (poems), privately printed, 1977.

WORK IN PROGRESS—Under name Nellie Hill: *In the Country of No Language,* poems; *Along for the Ride or The Autobiography of Sunday Jenks,* a novel; another novel; stories; poems.

SIDELIGHTS: Nellie Hill writes: "When I began taking karate, I saw that I'd found the perfect antidote for the blocks I'd been experiencing in the novel I was writing. I began to dream that the people I was writing about, both the imaginary ones and the quasi-real, were attacking me. I fended them off and was able to bring the novel to a finish. I also discovered that the physical communication of karate had leaked from the classes into my poetry. Thanks to my unconscious processes, none of my classmates, relatives, and friends will recognize themselves as the creatures I've turned them into—parrots, hibiscus flowers, palm trees, rain, oceans, and men carrying coconuts.

"The feeling of those early karate classes has stayed with me, especially when I'm taking a long walk by an Illinois river or hiking in the coastal woods of northern California. It's a feeling for direct movement, and this feeling correlates with the action of language I care about. Whatever I write, poems or novels, I write in order to move into a new awareness by means of shock of imagery and phrase hung on a narrative or a thread of feeling.

"In the karate class, you practice variations of the same drills over and over. You're always pushed to a new limit, pushed to learn a new way of seeing the basic idea. This changes your awareness of your body. You discover new capabilities and new connections.

"Fiction and poetry can do the same thing for one's view of self and of life, for both writer and reader. This is why I write: to remain aware of my feelings for life and of my connection with myself and others."

BIOGRAPHICAL/CRITICAL SOURCES: Mill Valley Record, June 29, 1977.

*   *   *

HILL, Nellie
See HILL, Ellen Wise

*   *   *

HILLERS, Delbert R(oy) 1932-

PERSONAL: Born November 7, 1932, in Chester, S.D.; son of William Albert and Emma (Gienapp) Hillers; married Patricia Mays Turnbaugh, June 28, 1958; children: Eve Elizabeth, Samuel Thomas. *Education:* Concordia College, Milwaukee, Wis., diploma, 1952; Concordia Seminary, St. Louis, Mo., B.A., 1954, B.D., 1957; Johns Hopkins University, M.A., 1958, Ph.D., 1963. *Home:* 604 Hollen Rd., Baltimore, Md. 21212. *Office:* Department of Near Eastern Studies, Johns Hopkins University, Baltimore, Md. 21218.

CAREER: Concordia Senior College, Fort Wayne, Ind., instructor in Hebrew and the ancient Near East, 1958-60; Johns Hopkins University, Baltimore, Md., assistant professor, 1963-66, associate professor, 1966-70, professor, 1970—, W. W. Spence Professor of Semitic Languages, 1971—, chairman of department of Near Eastern studies, 1976—. Annual professor at American School of Oriental Research (Jerusalem), 1968-69; Schaff Lecturer at Pittsburgh Theological Seminary, 1970. *Member:* Biblical Colloquium, Society of Biblical Literature, American Oriental Society, Phi Beta Kappa. *Awards, honors:* American Philosophical Society grant, 1968-69.

WRITINGS: Treaty-Curses and the Old Testament Prophets, Pontifical Biblical Institute, 1964; *Covenant: The History of a Biblical Idea,* Johns Hopkins Press, 1969; *Lamentations: The Anchor Bible,* Doubleday, 1972; (contributor) H. A. Hoffner, Jr., editor, *Orient and Occident,* Neukirchener Verlag, 1973; (editor) *Discoveries in the Wadi ed-Daliyeh,* American Schools of Oriental Research, 1974. Contributor to *Encyclopaedia Britannica* and *Encyclopedia Judaica.* Contributor of about twenty articles to scholarly journals in the United States and other countries. Co-editor of *Bulletin of the American Schools of Oriental Research,* 1965-68, editor, 1969-73.

SIDELIGHTS: Hillers participated in archaeological expeditions in Jordan, 1962, 1963, 1966, 1968, and in Syria, 1975.

* * *

HINCHLIFFE, Arnold P. 1930-

PERSONAL: Born December 3, 1930, in Dewsbury, Yorkshire, England. *Education:* University of Manchester, M.A., Ph.D.; Yale University, M.A. *Home:* 19 Craigweil Ave., Didsbury, Manchester, England. *Office:* Department of English, University of Manchester, Manchester, England.

CAREER: Currently senior lecturer in English literature at University of Manchester, Manchester, England. *Military service:* British Army, Royal Engineers, 1948-50; became sergeant.

WRITINGS: Private File (poems), Manchester Institute of Contemporary Arts, 1967; *Harold Pinter,* Twayne, 1967; (editor with C. B. Cox) *Casebook on "The Wasteland,"* Macmillan, 1968; *The Absurd: Critical Idiom Number 5,* Methuen, 1969; *British Theatre, 1950-1970,* Basil Blackwell, 1974; *Modern Verse Drama: Critical Idiom Number 32,* Methuen, 1977.

WORK IN PROGRESS: Casebook on Dramatic Criticism Since Ibsen, for publication by Macmillan.

* * *

HIRO, Dilip

PERSONAL: Born in Sind, Pakistan. *Education:* Virginia Polytechnic Institute and State University, M.S. in industrial engineering. *Home:* 31 Waldegrave Rd., Ealing, London W5 3HT, England.

CAREER: Writer. *Awards, honors:* Award from Chicago Film Festival, 1975, for "A Private Enterprise."

WRITINGS: A Triangular View (novel), Dobson, 1969; *Black British, White British,* Eyre & Spottiswoode, 1971, revised edition, Monthly Review Press, 1973; *To Anchor a Cloud: A Play in Three Acts* (first produced in London, England at Collegiate Theatre, September 25, 1970), Writers Workshop (Calcutta, India), 1972; *The Untouchables of India,* Minority Rights Group (London), 1975; *Inside India Today,* Routledge & Kegan Paul, 1976, revised edition, Monthly Review Press, 1977; "A Clean Break: A Play in One Act," first produced in London, England at Ravi Shankar Hall, November 24, 1977.

"A Private Enterprise" (feature film), January, 1975; "Apply, Apply, No Reply" (television play), BBC-TV, June 12, 1976; "A Matter of Honor" (television play), Granada Television, 1976. Author of scripts for television serial "Parosi," 1977-78. Contributor to magazines, including *New Society,* and newspapers.

WORK IN PROGRESS: Research in the Middle East, for a book, publication by Oxford University Press.

* * *

HIRSCH, Fred 1931-1978

July 6, 1931—January 11, 1978; Austrian-born British educator, editor, economist, and author of works in his field. Hirsch was an advisor to the International Monetary Fund for several years. His writings include *Money International* and *Social Limits to Growth.* He died in Leamington Spa, England. Obituaries and other sources: *New York Times,* January 12, 1978; *Washington Post,* January 14, 1978. (See index for *CA* sketch)

* * *

HIRSCHI, Travis 1935-

PERSONAL: Born April 15, 1935, in Rockville, Utah; son of Warren G. and Orra (Terry) Hirschi; married Anna Yergensen, September 3, 1955; children: Kendal, Nathan, Justine. *Education:* University of Utah, B.S., 1957, M.S., 1958; University of California, Berkeley, Ph.D., 1968. *Home address:* Hillcrest Dr., West Sand Lake, N.Y. 12196. *Office:* School of Criminal Justice, State University of New York at Albany, Albany, N.Y. 12222.

CAREER: University of Washington, Seattle, 1967-71, began as assistant professor, became associate professor of sociology; University of California, Davis, professor of sociology, 1971-77; State University of New York at Albany, professor of sociology, 1977—. Chairman of National Institute of Mental Health's crime and delinquency review committee, 1976-78. *Military service:* U.S. Army, 1958-60. *Awards, honors:* C. Wright Mills Award from Society for the Study of Social Problems, 1968, for *Delinquency Research.*

WRITINGS: (With Hanan Selvin) *Delinquency Research,* Free Press, 1967; *Causes of Delinquency,* University of California Press, 1969.

* * *

HISS, Tony 1941-

PERSONAL: Born August 5, 1941, in Washington, D.C.; son of Alger (a lawyer) and Priscilla (Fansler) Hiss. *Education:* Harvard University, B.A., 1963. *Home:* 29 West Tenth St., New York, N.Y. 10011. *Agent:* Helen Brann, 14 Sutton Pl. S., New York, N.Y. 10022. *Office: New Yorker,* 25 West 43rd St., New York, N.Y. 10036.

CAREER: *New Yorker*, New York City, reporter and writer, 1963—. Bartender at All State Cafe, New York City, 1976-77. Has taught writing workshops in New York City and Berkeley, Calif. *Member:* Coffee House Club (New York City).

WRITINGS: The Giant Panda Book, Golden Press, 1973; (with Rogers E. M. Whitaker) *All Aboard with E. M. Frimbo, World's Greatest Railroad Buff*, Grossman, 1975; (with G. Allard) *Know-How: A Fix-It Book for the Clumsy But Pure of Heart*, Little, Brown, 1976; *Laughing Last: Alger Hiss*, Houghton, 1977.

Contributor of articles and reviews to periodicals, including *New York Times Book Review, Harper's, Rolling Stone,* and *Saturday Review.* Publisher of *Real World,* 1974—; editor of *Plaza Newsletter,* 1976—.

WORK IN PROGRESS: Editing *Henry Chung's Hunan Cookbook* for Crown; writing *The Old Curmudgeon* with Whitaker for Knopf ("based on the *New Yorker*'s beloved 'Talk-of-the-Town' character").

AVOCATIONAL INTERESTS: Growing roses and tomatoes on the deck behind his apartment.

BIOGRAPHICAL/CRITICAL SOURCES: New York Times Book Review, February 20, 1977; *Book World,* February 20, 1977; *Newsweek,* February 28, 1977; *New York Times,* March 15, 1977; *New Republic,* April 2, 1977; *Saturday Review,* April 2, 1977.

* * *

HO, Minfong 1951-

PERSONAL: Born January 7, 1951, in Rangoon, Burma; daughter of Rih-Hwa (an economist) and Lienfung (a chemist and writer; maiden name, Li) Ho; married John Value Dennis, Jr. (a soil scientist), December 20, 1976. *Education:* Attended Tunghai University, 1967-69; Cornell University, B.A. (honors), 1973. *Religion:* Agnostic. *Home:* 7 Leedon Park, Singapore 10, Singapore. *Office:* Multiple Cropping Project, Faculty of Agriculture, Chiengmai University, Chiengmai, Thailand.

CAREER: Starlight Plywood Factory, Singapore, manual worker, 1973; *Straits Times*, Singapore, journalist, 1973-75; Chiengmai University, Chiengmai, Thailand, lecturer in department of mass communications, 1976—. Trade union representative, 1973-75. *Awards, honors:* First prize from Council of Interracial Books for Children, 1973, for *Sing to the Dawn.*

WRITINGS: Sing to the Dawn (juvenile), Lothrop, 1975. Author of "Hsin Nu-Ren," a column in Singapore *Sunday Times.* Contributor to economic journals.

WORK IN PROGRESS: Sky on Fire (tentative title), a novel based on the ideals and experiences of Thailand's student movement during the brief "democratic period," 1973-76.

SIDELIGHTS: Minfong Ho writes: "Writing, in itself, is like the sound of one hand clapping—incomplete, silent, and without impact. Only when the writer as the one hand, and the reader as the other, confront each other is there that clap, that spark of communication which makes literature alive.

"When I wrote *Sing to the Dawn,* it was in moments of homesickness during the thick of winter in upstate New York, when Thailand seemed incredibly far away. Writing about the dappled sunlight and school children of home brought them closer to me; it aired on paper that part of me which couldn't find any place in America. The story was not meant to be read—it was only one hand clapping.

"The manuscript was later published (through no effort of mine). Suddenly a whole new dimension of writing opened up to me: it became a communicative rather than cathartic activity. I had always written, but now I would have readers!

"Since then I've returned home to Singapore and Thailand, and I've continued to write. I've also worked in prisons and plywood factories; I have transplanted rice seedlings and helped a peasant woman give birth; I have attended trade union meetings in stuffy attics and international conferences in plush hotels. There is so much, so much beauty and so much pain in the world around me which I want to write about—because I want to share it.

"Hopefully, young readers in America will understand better, through some of my stories, the youth around me in Asia. And hopefully too, some lone foreign student stuck in a snowbound university in America somewhere will pick up a copy of my book one day, and in reading it, feel just a shade less homesick. The sound of such claps will be deeply exhilarating."

AVOCATIONAL INTERESTS: Swimming, hiking, growing things.

BIOGRAPHICAL/CRITICAL SOURCES: Human Values in Children's Books, Racism and Sexism Resource Center for Educators, 1976.

* * *

HOFFMAN, Alice 1952-

PERSONAL: Born March 16, 1952, in New York, N.Y. *Education:* Adelphi University, B.A., 1973; Stanford University, M.A., 1975. *Residence:* New York, N.Y. *Agent:* Elaine Markson Literary Agency, Inc., 44 Greenwich Ave., New York, N.Y. 10011.

CAREER: Writer, 1975—. *Awards, honors:* Mirelles fellow, Stanford University, 1975; Bread Loaf fellowship, summer, 1976.

WRITINGS: Property of (novel), Farrar, Straus, 1977. Contributor of stories to *Ms., Fiction, American Review,* and *Playgirl.*

WORK IN PROGRESS: Esther the White.

SIDELIGHTS: Hoffman told *CA:* "I think I most often write about women's ability or inability to come to terms with their own identity and independence. For me *Property of* is about victims who in turn victimize the women around them. The novel I am now working on, *Esther the White,* is about the relationship of a young woman to her family and their past in her effort to begin a separate life. So I suppose my main concern is the search for identity and continuity, and the struggle inherent in that search."

* * *

HOFFMAN, Elizabeth P(arkinson) 1921-

PERSONAL: Born March 23, 1921, in Pittsburgh, Pa.; daughter of William Sterrett (an electrical engineer) and Elizabeth (a teacher; maiden name, Hill) Parkinson; married James William Hoffman (a free-lance writer and editor), April 2, 1944; children: William Sterrett, Charles Harran, Lloyd Abbott, Elizabeth Whedon Hoffman Crawford. *Education:* Dickinson College, A.B., 1942; attended New York University, 1943; Drexel University, M.S. in L.S., 1961. *Politics:* Republican. *Religion:* Presbyterian. *Home:* 805

Beechwood Rd., Havertown, Pa. 19083. *Office:* Department of Library Science, Villanova University, Villanova, Pa. 19085.

CAREER: Elementary school teacher in Havertown, Pa., 1958-66; Pennsylvania Department of Education, Harrisburg, coordinator in Division of School Libraries, 1966, director of division, 1966-75; Villanova University, Villanova, Pa., associate professor of library science and chairman of department, 1975—. Part-time teacher at Villanova University, 1968-75.

MEMBER: American Library Association (member of council, 1972-77; chairman of legislation committee, 1973-76), American Association of School Librarians (chairman of supervisors section, 1971-72; chairman of legislation section, 1976-78), Pennsylvania Library Association, Beechwood Civic Association (president, 1976-77). *Awards, honors:* Special award from Pennsylvania School Library Association, 1971; distinguished service award from Pennsylvania Library Association, 1973; citation from Pennsylvania senate, 1975.

WRITINGS: Palm Reading Made Easy, Simon & Schuster, 1971; *This House Is Haunted,* Contemporary Perspectives, Inc., 1977; *Palm Reading,* Contemporary Perspectives, Inc., 1977; *Here a Ghost, There a Ghost,* Messner, 1978; *A History of State School Library Agencies,* Library Trends, 1978. Editor of *Report Card* (bulletin of Pennsylvania Library Association), 1968-75.

WORK IN PROGRESS: A book on haunted houses around the country.

SIDELIGHTS: Elizabeth Hoffman writes: "My writing deals with my profession—library science—or my hobby—a component of parapsychology. I've investigated haunted houses, and taught and lectured on palm reading as well as hauntings. Living in a haunted house helps." *Avocational interests:* European travel.

* * *

HOFFMAN, Stanley 1944-

PERSONAL: Born August 2, 1944, in Brooklyn, N.Y. *Education:* Brooklyn College of the City University of New York, B.A., 1966; University of Rochester, M.A., 1972. *Politics:* "None whatever." *Religion:* "Eclectic." *Home:* 2312 Avenue I, Brooklyn, N.Y. 11210.

CAREER: Haile Selassie University, Addis Ababa, Ethiopia, instructor in English, 1966-67; Brooklyn College of the City University of New York, Brooklyn, N.Y., adjunct assistant professor of English and creative writing, 1973-75, 1977-78.

WRITINGS: Solomon's Temple (novel), Viking, 1974.

WORK IN PROGRESS: A new novel.

SIDELIGHTS: Hoffman told *CA:* "I write because I have no choice and couldn't imagine myself doing anything else unless it's playing major league baseball (honest!). My favorite poets are Edmund Spenser and William Yeats, and my favorite ntvelists are Dickens, Dostoyevsky, and George Eliot, all of whom have greatly influenced my work—as well as Henry Miller who gives me solace when I think I'm probably going to starve. So for what I write about, my books alone can answer that better than I ever can, and I can only refer you to whatever has—or will be—published."

In a *Newsweek* review of *Solomon's Temple,* Walter Clemmons wrote: "Offhand, a day-to-day log of a weight-loss regimen strikes me as far down on the list of promising subjects

for a novel." Clemmons wondered why he found "this Jewish ugly duckling's progress from schlemiel to swan" entertaining. He explained: "Stanley Hoffman has the obsessive energy of a born comic novelist who could make bookkeeping dramatic if he put his mind to it. When a superb girl . . . invades Solomon's life with the natural force of a tornado, the story becomes psychologically complex and oddly touching."

BIOGRAPHICAL/CRITICAL SOURCES: New York Times Book Review, March 24, 1974; *Newsweek,* May 20, 1974; *Contemporary Literary Criticism,* Volume 5, Gale, 1976.

* * *

HOGAN, Judy 1937-

PERSONAL: Born May 27, 1937, in Hutchinson, Kan.; daughter of William Robert (a clergyman) and Margaret (Roys) Stevenson; married Tom Fordham, 1960 (divorced, 1965); married Terry M. Hogan (a professor of economics), May 12, 1967 (divorced February, 1976); children: (first marriage) Amy; (second marriage) Timothy Michael, Virginia Lynn. *Education:* University of Oklahoma, B.A. (cum laude), 1959; graduate study at Indiana University, 1959-60, and University of California, Berkeley, 1964-68. *Politics:* Democrat. *Religion:* Protestant. *Home address:* P.O. Box 209, Carrboro, N.C. 27510. *Office:* Committee of Small Magazine Editors and Publishers, South Distribution Cooperative, Carrboro, N.C. 27510.

CAREER: University of North Carolina, Chapel Hill, extension, instructor in writing, autumn, 1974; Committee of Small Magazine Editors and Publishers, South Distribution Cooperative, Carrboro, N.C., coordinator, 1974—. Organized poetry reading series in Chapel Hill and Durham, N.C.,1974—, and radio program series, 1976—. *Member:* Committee of Small Magazine Editors and Publishers (national chairwoman, 1975-78). *Awards, honors:* Woodrow Wilson fellowship, 1959-60.

WRITINGS: Cassandra Speaking (poems), Thorp Springs Press, 1977; (editor) *Eat Your Natchos: Texas COSMEP Anthology,* Carolina Wren Press, 1977. Contributor of poems and articles to magazines and newspapers, including *North Carolina Sun.* Guest co-editor of *Hyperion Poetry Journal,* 1969—.

WORK IN PROGRESS: Poems; a diary.

SIDELIGHTS: Judy Hogan writes: "I have, since beginning a small poetry journal with Foster and Paul Foreman in 1969 (*Hyperion Poetry Journal*), become deeply involved in the contemporary small press movement, and my major energy apart from my writing and bringing up three children, has gone there since 1974. I believe this is a great literary age, and a wonderful time for a writer to be alive. Many writers are too caught up in technical competence, though; we need more writers concerned with their own whole development as well as with the health of their society; my radio program series emphasizes these points and also the vitality of the oral tradition newly alive in our time; the effect of reading aloud on one's development."

* * *

HOGAN, Michael 1943-

PERSONAL: Born July 14, 1943, in Newport, R.I.; son of Francis Xavier (a businessman) and Anna (Mack) Hogan; married Cynthia Hooper, April 1, 1964 (divorced, 1967); children: Francis Garrison. *Education:* Attended Stonehill

College, 1961-64; University of Arizona, B.A., 1977, LL.B. *Home:* 2839 East Mabel, Tucson, Ariz. 85716. *Agent:* Ryan Getty, 4705 Sinclair Ave., Austin, Tex. 78756.

CAREER: Cold Mountain Press, Austin, Tex., associate editor, 1972-76; Cochise College, Douglas, Ariz., writer-in-residence, 1977—. *Member:* Committee of Small Magazine Editors and Publishers. *Awards, honors:* Received award from International P.E.N., 1975; Joseph Fels Award, 1976; Pushcart Prize from Pushcart Press, 1976; National Endowment for the Arts fellowship, 1976-77.

WRITINGS: Letters for My Son, Unicorn Press, 1975; *If You Ever Get There,* Emerald City Press, 1975; *Soon It Will Be Morning,* Cold Mountain Press, 1976; *Risky Business,* Great Raven Press, 1977; *Dust,* Harry Reese, 1977; (editor) *Do Not Go Gentle,* University of Arizona Press, 1977. Guest editor of *Greenfield Review.* Editor for Pushcart Press, 1977-78.

WORK IN PROGRESS: Revising *Living Is No Laughing Matter: A Primer on Existential Optimism;* translating contemporary Mexican poets, with Richard Shelton.

SIDELIGHTS: Hogan writes: "My first book was published while I was in prison. It was well-received by critics because it was written in prison and the work *defined the place,* instead of the opposite. Convinced of the efficacy of writing as a tool to define one's life, I've recently begun setting up writing workshops for ex-offenders, under the auspices of the U.S. Department of Labor."

* * *

HOGNER, Nils 1893-1970

PERSONAL: Born July 22, 1893, in Whitinsville, Mass.; son of a doctor; married Dorothy Childs (an author), July 23, 1932. *Education:* Attended Rhodes Academy, Copenhagen, Denmark, Royal Academy of Arts, Stockholm, Sweden, Boston School of Painting, and the School of the Museum of Fine Arts, Boston. *Home:* Hemlock Hill Herb Farm, Litchfield, Conn. 06759.

CAREER: University of New Mexico, Albuquerque, art instructor, 1930-32; artist, illustrator, and mural painter. Member of board of directors, American Artists Professional League. *Military service:* Served in France with the American Expeditionary Force during World War I. *Member:* National Society of Mural Painters (treasurer), Architectural League of New York (vice-president), Salmagundi Club.

WRITINGS—All self-illustrated, except as noted: (With Guy Scott) *Cartoon Guide Of New York City,* J. J. Augustin, 1938; *The Lost Tugboat,* Abelard, 1952; *Boldy,* Abelard, 1953; *Dynamite, the Wild Stallion,* Aladdin Books, 1953; *Jean's Whale,* Abelard, 1955; *Sad Eye, the Clown,* Abelard, 1956; *Farm for Rent,* Abelard, 1958; *Jimmy's First Roundup,* Abelard, 1959; *Tanny,* Walck, 1960; *Molly the Black Mare,* Walck, 1962; *The Devil Stallion,* Walck, 1967; *The Nosy Colt* (illustrated by Richard Lebenson), Walck, 1973.

Illustrator: Idella Purnell, *Pedro the Potter,* Thomas Nelson, 1935; Alice Gall and Fleming C. Crew, *Top of the World,* Oxford University Press, 1939; Glenn Balch, *Indian Paint: The Story of an Indian Pony,* Crowell, 1942, reprinted, 1970; Marion Gill MacNeil, *Between Earth and Sky,* Oxford University Press, 1944; Lucile McDonald, *Bering's Potlatch,* Oxford University Press, 1944; Ralph Godwin De Voe, *Calling All Ducks,* Crowell, 1945; Edwin Burtis, editor, *All the Best Dog Poems,* Crowell, 1946; De Voe, *Ad-*

ventures of Midgie, Crowell, 1946; Frances Fullerton Neilson, *Ten Commandments in Today's World,* Thomas Nelson, 1946; Gall and Crew, *Winter Flight,* Oxford University Press, 1949; Gall and Crew, *Here and There and Everywhere,* Oxford University Press, 1950; Olga Townsend, *White-Tailed Deer,* Whittlesey, 1951; Crew, *More the Merrier,* Oxford University Press, 1952; Ruth Hepburn Protheroe, *Little Chief of the Gaspe,* Abelard, 1955; Ruth Hubbell Dudley, *Our American Trees,* Crowell, 1956; Helene Jamieson Jordan, *Seeds by Wind and Water,* Crowell, 1962.

Illustrator; all written by wife, Dorothy Hogner: Navajo Winter Nights, Thomas Nelson, 1935; *Education of a Burro,* Thomas Nelson, 1936; *Little Esther,* Thomas Nelson, 1937; *Santa Fe Caravans,* Thomas Nelson, 1937; *Lady Bird,* Oxford University Press, 1938; *Westward, High, Low, and Dry,* Dutton, 1938; *Old Hank Weatherbee,* Oxford University Press, 1939; *Pancho,* Thomas Nelson, 1939; *Summer Roads to Gaspe,* Dutton, 1939; *Don't Blame the Puffins,* Oxford University Press, 1940; *Stormy, the First Mustang,* Oxford University Press, 1941 (published in England as *Stormy, the First American Mustang,* Hutchinson, 1944); *The Animal Book: American Mammals North of Mexico,* Oxford University Press, 1942; *Children of Mexico,* Heath, 1942; *The Bible Story,* Oxford University Press, 1943; *Our American Horse,* Thomas Nelson, 1944; *Reward for Brownie,* Oxford University Press, 1944; *Farm Animals and Working and Sporting Breeds of the United States and Canada,* Oxford University Press, 1945; *Unexpected Journey: The Story of a Dog,* Creative Age Press, 1945; *Winky, King of the Garden,* Oxford University Press, 1946; *Blue Swamp,* Oxford University Press, 1947; *Barnyard Family,* Oxford University Press, 1948; *Daisy: A Farm Fable,* Oxford University Press, 1949.

Dusty's Return, Oxford University Press, 1950; *The Wild Little Honker,* Oxford University Press, 1951; *Snowflake,* Oxford University Press, 1952; *Earthworms,* Crowell, 1953; *Herbs From the Garden to the Table,* Oxford University Press, 1953; *The Horse Family,* Oxford University Press, 1953; *The Dog Family,* Oxford University Press, 1954; *Wide River,* Lippincott, 1954; *Rufus,* Lippincott, 1955; *Spiders,* Crowell, 1955; *The Cat Family,* Oxford University Press, 1956; *Frogs and Polliwogs,* Crowell, 1956; *Conservation in America,* Lippincott, 1958; *Snails,* Crowell, 1958; *Grasshoppers and Crickets,* Crowell, 1960; *Water Over the Dam,* Lippincott, 1960; *A Fresh Herb Platter,* Doubleday, 1961; *Butterflies,* Crowell, 1962; *Water Beetles,* Crowell, 1963; *Gardening and Cooking on Terrace and Patio,* Doubleday, 1964; *Moths,* Crowell, 1964; *A Book of Snakes,* Crowell, 1966; *Weeds,* Crowell, 1968; *Birds of Prey,* Crowell, 1969.

SIDELIGHTS: Nils Hogner and his wife, Dorothy, enjoyed the outdoors and frequently made camping trips throughout the United States, Canada, and Mexico. Their shared interest in wildlife and their combined skills in art and literature resulted in numerous books. One of their earlier books together was *Westward, High, Low, and Dry.* "Though the places Mr. and Mrs. Hogner visit are barren, the book is not. . . . To obtain the full essence of these places the Hogners not only give the reader their own experiences but the results of their reading in government bulletins, scholarly modern works, and narratives of the early explorers and travelers. . . . The result is a charming, simple account with no theatricals, no great descriptions, or philosophical analyses arising from the sights, but just what it is meant to be—a good, interesting travel book," commented a critic for *Saturday Review.*

AVOCATIONAL INTERESTS: Gardening, fishing, camping.

BIOGRAPHICAL/CRITICAL SOURCES: Saturday Review of Literature, January 22, 1938; *Commonweal,* February 11, 1938; *Chicago Sunday Tribune,* July 13, 1952; *New York Times,* August 3, 1952.*

(Died July 30, 1970)

* * *

HOLLAND, Cecil Fletcher 1907-1978

December 10, 1907—June 22, 1978; American journalist and author. While a reporter for the *Washington Star,* Holland covered the Army-McCarthy hearings and, from 1940 to 1968, all presidential and congressional campaigns. For eight years, he was administrative assistant to Republican Senator Robert P. Griffin of Michigan. He wrote *Morgan and His Raiders,* a highly praised Civil War book. Holland died in Washington, D.C. Obituaries and other sources: *Who's Who in American Politics,* 4th edition, Bowker, 1974; *New York Times,* June 24, 1978.

* * *

HOLLES, Everett R. 1904(?)-1978

1904(?)—June 8, 1978; American foreign correspondent, radio commentator, public relations director, lecturer, and, author. Holles served as a correspondent for the *New York Times* and United Press. He was a commentator for CBS news and lectured on foreign affairs. As an assistant to the chairman of the Atomic Energy Commission, Holles helped plan the first conference on the peaceful uses of atomic energy. He wrote a book entitled *Unconditional Surrender.* Holles died in La Jolla, Calif. Obituaries and other sources: *New York Times,* June 10, 1978.

* * *

HOLMES, Michael Stephan 1942-

PERSONAL: Born August 24, 1942, in Houston, Tex.; son of Sidney (in sales) and Malvina (Demain) Holmes; married Reva Aronson (an administrative assistant), December 26, 1966. *Education:* Rice University, B.A., 1964; University of Wisconsin, Madison, M.S., 1965, Ph.D., 1969. *Home:* 313 10th St., Racine, Wis. 53403.

CAREER: University of Wisconsin, Parkside, assistant professor of history, 1969-76; University of Wisconsin, Milwaukee, lecturer in history, 1976—. *Member:* Organization of American Historians, Southern Historical Association.

WRITINGS: The New Deal in Georgia: An Administrative History, Greenwood Press, 1975; (contributor) Judith Merrick, editor, *A Grassroots History of Racine County,* Racine County Historical Society, 1978. Also contributor to *Racine: Growth and Change in a Wisconsin County,* edited by N. C. Burckel, 1977. Contributor to history journals.

WORK IN PROGRESS: A biography of Georgia Senator Richard B. Russell; research on the depression in Racine and on Georgia's first aid for the depression.

* * *

HONAN, Park 1928-

PERSONAL: Born September 17, 1928, in Utica, N.Y.; married, 1952; children: three. *Education:* University of Chicago, M.A., 1951; University of London, Ph.D., 1959. *Office:* Department of English, University of Birmingham, Birmingham B15 2TT, England.

CAREER: Connecticut College, New London, instructor, 1959-61, assistant professor of English, 1961-62; Brown University, Providence, R.I., assistant professor, 1962-65, associate professor of English, 1965-68; University of Birmingham, Birmingham, England, lecturer, 1968, currently senior lecturer in English. Managing editor of *Novel: A Forum on Fiction,* 1967—. *Member:* Modern Language Association of America. *Awards, honors:* Guggenheim fellowship, 1962-63.

WRITINGS: Browning's Characters: A Study in Poetic Techniques, Yale University Press, 1961; (co-editor) *Shelley,* Dell, 1962; (author of introduction) *Falkland,* Cassell, 1967; (with William Irvine) *The Book, the Ring, and the Poet: A Biography of Robert Browning,* McGraw, 1974. Contributor to literature journals.

* * *

HONEYCOMBE, Gordon 1936-

PERSONAL: Born September 27, 1936, in Karachi, India; son of Gordon Samuel (a sales manager) and Dorothy Louise (Fraser) Honeycombe. *Education:* Oxford University, M.A. (honors), 1961. *Agent:* A. D. Peters & Co., 10 Buckingham St., London WC2N 6BU, England.

CAREER: Radio Hong Kong, Hong Kong, announcer, 1956-57; Scottish Home Service, Glasgow, radio announcer, 1958; actor, 1960-61; Royal Shakespeare Co., Stratford-on-Avon, England, actor, 1962-63; television actor, 1964; Independent Television News, London, England, newscaster, 1965-77; author, playwright, and lecturer, 1978—. Performed in television series including "That Was the Week That Was" and "The Foundation," in plays including "Late Night Joys" and "Playback 625," and in motion pictures including "The Commuter" and "The Medusa Touch." Recorded "Stuff and Nonsense" (poems for children), for Thames Television, 1975 and 1976. Has continued to work as actor and performer, and producer. *Military service:* British Army, Royal Artillery, 1955-57; served in Hong Kong. *Awards, honors:* Silver Medal from New York Film and Television Festival, 1975, for "Time and Again."

WRITINGS: "The Miracles" (two-act play) first produced in Oxford, England at Pusey House Chapel, February, 1960; *The Redemption* (two-act play; first produced in Cosett, England at Cosett Civic Theatre, 1970), Methuen, 1964; *Neither the Sea nor the Sand* (novel), Hutchinson, 1969, Weybright, 1970; *Dragon Under the Hill* (novel), Hutchinson, 1972, Simon & Schuster, 1973; *Adam's Tale* (nonfiction), Hutchinson, 1974; *Red Watch* (nonfiction), Hutchinson, 1976; "The Princess and the Goblins" (two-act musical play), first produced in Graet Ayton, England at Rosehill Theatre, November, 1976.

Teleplays: "The Golden Vision," first broadcast by British Broadcasting Corp. (BBC), April 17, 1968; "Time and Again," first broadcast by Westward Television (England), November 11, 1975.

Adaptor of dramatizations, including "Paradise Lost," first broadcast by BBC-Radio 4, November 4, 1974; "God Save the Queen" (two-act dramatized anthology), first produced in Chichester, England at Chicester Festival Theatre, June 12, 1977; "A King Shall Have a Kingdom" (two-act dramatized anthology), first produced in York, England at Theatre Royal, October 16, 1977; "Lancelot and Guinevere," first broadcast by BBC-Radio 4, December 18, 1977.

WORK IN PROGRESS: The Edge of Heaven, a fictional love story set in Cyprus.

SIDELIGHTS: Honeycombe's book *Red Watch* is the true story of a fatal fire and the men who fought it. Its publication coincided with the first national fireman's strike in Britain, and according to Honeycombe, indirectly led to his resignation as a television newscaster. (He had also written an article in support of the fireman for a national newspaper, *The Daily Mail,* which was another contributing factor to his resignation.)

Honeycombe told *CA:* "I happened to get to know this particular Watch at this particular fire station in London through a charity event. Six months later they had to deal with the worst fire in central London that year (1974). I was not at the fire, but afterwards I heard the firsthand accounts of the men who had fought the blaze. Seven people, including one Red Watch fireman, died. I thought it was a story well worth telling, for no one then knew or cared about what a fireman's job entailed and it was a story never told before. Strangely, it was while I was writing the book that I learned that my great-grandfather, Samuel Honeycombe, had been the first captain and founder of the Northfleet Fire Brigade in Kent, in 1885."

AVOCATIONAL INTERESTS: Brass-rubbing, genealogy, darts, tavli, curry, crosswords, pigs, mountains, and the sea.

* * *

HONIG, Louis 1911-1977

PERSONAL: Born in 1911; married wife, Miriam; children: Louis, Jr., Ann Honig Nadel, Sue Honig Weinstein. *Residence:* San Francisco, Calif.

CAREER: Former director of Honig-Cooper & Harrington; board chairman of Foote, Cone & Belding (advertising agency). Investor and backer of *Ramparts.*

WRITINGS: For Your Eyes Only: Read and Destroy! (novel), Charles Publishing, 1972.

OBITUARIES: New York Times, July 19, 1977.*

(Died July 15, 1977, in San Francisco, Calif.)

* * *

HOOD, Graham 1936-

PERSONAL: Born November 6, 1936, in Birmingham, England; came to the United States in 1961; son of Stanley G. and Lillian (Franklin) Hood; married Gale Frackelton, August 5, 1961; children: Sarah, Jorin. *Education:* Earned M.A. from Keble College, Oxford; further graduate study at Courtauld Institute of Art, London. *Home:* Benjamin Waller House, Williamsburg, Va. 23185. *Office:* Colonial Williamsburg Foundation, Williamsburg, Va. 23185.

CAREER: Wadsworth Atheneum, Hartford, Conn., curator of European decorative arts, 1961-64; Yale University, Art Gallery, New Haven, Conn., associate curator of Garvan Collection, 1964-68; Detroit Institute of Arts, Detroit, Mich., curator of American art, 1968-71; Colonial Williamsburg Foundation, Williamsburg, Va., vice-president and director of Division of Collections, 1971—. Adjunct professor at Wayne State University, 1968-71; lecturer at University of Michigan, 1970-71, and College of William and Mary, 1974—. Member of board of visitors of Boston University, 1976-79; member of advisory council of Institute of Early American History and Culture, 1977-80. *Member:* Dunlap Society (member of advisory council, 1975—), Hampton Roads Educational Telecommunications Association (director, 1977).

WRITINGS: American Pewter at Yale: Catalogue of the Garvan and Other Collections of Pewter, Art Gallery, Yale University, 1965; (with Kathryn C. Buhler) *American Silver: Garvan and Other Collections in the Yale University Art Gallery,* two volumes, Yale University Press, 1970; *American Silver: A History of Style, 1650-1900,* Praeger, 1971; *Bonnin and Morris of Philadelphia: The First American Porcelain Factory, 1770-1772,* University of North Carolina Press, 1972; (co-author) *The Williamsburg Collection of Antique Furnishings,* Holt, 1973; (author of foreword) Mildred B. Lanier, *English and Oriental Carpets at Williamsburg,* Colonial Williamsburg Foundation, 1975; (author of foreword) Rupert Gentle and Rachael Field, *English Domestic Brass, 1680-1810, and the History of Its Origins,* Elek, 1975.

(Author of foreword) John D. Davis, *English Silver at Williamsburg,* University Press of Virginia, 1976; (author of foreword) John D. Dolmetsch, *Rebellion and Reconciliation: Satirical Prints on the Revolution at Williamsburg,* University Press of Virginia, 1976; (author of foreword) Wallace B. Gusler and James D. Lavin, *Decorated Firearms, 1540-1870, From the Collection of Clay P. Bedford,* University Press of Virginia, 1977; (author of foreword) John C. Austin, *Chelsea Porcelain at Williamsburg,* University Press of Virginia, 1977; *Charles Bridges and William Deering: Two Virginia Painters, 1735-1750,* University Press of Virginia, 1978.

Editor of "Williamsburg Decorative Art Series," Colonial Williamsburg Foundation; consulting editor of "American Decorative Arts Series," Praeger, 1969-75. Contributor of more than twenty-five articles and reviews to arts journals. Member of editorial board of *Art Quarterly,* 1968-71; editorial consultant for *American Art Journal,* 1969—.

* * *

HOOKER, (Peter) Jeremy 1941-

PERSONAL: Born March 23, 1941, in Warsash, England; son of Aubrey Wastie (a horticultural advisory officer) and Ivy (an elementary school teacher; maiden name, Mould) Hooker; married Susan Mary Hope Gill (a physiotherapist), February 24, 1968; children: Joseph Llewelyn, Emily Teleri. *Education:* University of Southampton, B.A., 1963, M.A., 1965. *Home:* Brynbeidog, Llangwyryfon, Aberystwyth, Dyfed, Wales. *Office:* Department of English, University of Wales, University College, Aberystwyth, Wales.

CAREER: University College of Wales, Aberystwyth, lecturer in twentieth-century English literature, 1965—. *Member:* Yr Academi Gymreig, Powys Society, David Jones Society. *Awards, honors:* Eric Gregory Award for Poetry, 1969; literature prize from Welsh Arts Council, 1975, for *Soliloquies of a Chalk Giant,* bursary, 1976-77.

WRITINGS: (Editor) *Poems '71,* Gwasg Gomer, 1971; *The Elements* (poems), Christopher Davies, 1972; *John Cowper Powys,* University of Wales Press, 1973; *Soliloquies of a Chalk Giant* (poems), Enitharmon Press, 1974; *David Jones: An Exploratory Study,* Enitharmon Press, 1975; *Landscape of the Daylight Moon* (poems), Enitharmon Press, 1977; *David Jones and John Cowper Powys: A Comparative Study,* Enitharmon, 1978; *Solent Shore* (poems), Carcanet New Press, 1978. Contributor to literary journals, including *Anglo-Welsh Review, Planet, Poetry Wales,* and *Poetry National Review.*

WORK IN PROGRESS: A selection of critical essays, 1969-75.

SIDELIGHTS: Hooker writes: "My principal concern, as

poet and critic, is with place—specific places in their totality of non-human, historical and personal meanings—and displacement. This derives from experience of attachment and mobility, continuity and change, and leads to belief in cultural and local differences, and opposition to centralizing forces and images, romanticizing of the past, and falsification of the present."

* * *

HOPKINS, J. L. 1938-

PERSONAL: Born August 5, 1938, in Orange, N.J.; son of John L. (an investment banker) and Anita (Bradshaw) Hopkins; married Ellen Ann Ragsdale (a writer), June 24, 1977. *Education:* Princeton University, B.A., 1960. *Home:* 8 Rue Brooks, Tangier, Morocco.

CAREER: American School of Tangier, Tangier, Morocco, vice-chairman of board of trustees, 1968—.

WRITINGS: The Attempt (novel), Viking, 1967; *Tangier Buzzless Flies* (novel), Atheneum, 1972. Contributor of stories to magazines, including *New Yorker, Penthouse,* and *Transatlantic Review.*

WORK IN PROGRESS: Two novels, *All I Wanted Was Company* and *Xenophobic Dogs.*

SIDELIGHTS: Hopkins writes: "Tangier is strategically located on the northwest tip of Africa. The Atlantic lies to the west, the more placid Mediterranean to the east. One can look north across the Straits of Gibraltar to Spain, or south in the direction of the Grand Atlas and the Sahara. One cannot live in Tangier without feeling the influences from all these quarters.

"I've lived in Morocco sixteen years and have done all my creative work here. I arrived in Tangier after two years of travel in Peru, Europe and Africa. During those travels I kept an extensive journal (and still do), and by the time I came here, to teach at The American School of Tangier, I was resolved to try my hand at fiction. I've been at it ever since. Not surprisingly, my work largely reflects my travel experiences, and I have continued to travel, almost exclusively in Africa and South America, always returning to Tangier. I have tended to see my characters against broad natural backdrops which usually dominate them. My Saharan adventures have been decisive in this respect. Man is small, his days are numbered, his objectives minuscule; this does not, however, prevent his spirit from soaring.

"In my present work the characters are brought into much larger focus. The American School of Tangier, which I continue to serve as a member of the Board of Trustees, has a tradition of presenting Greek tragedy. These student productions are staged with much force and integrity. The harsh moral lessons contained in these classics and the awful logic that sustains them has for many years held a deep and almost mysterious fascination for me. In the novel I am about to conclude, the characters are deliberately punished far in excess of their guilt. It is in this very excess of suffering, I hope, that their dignity will be revealed.

"Here in Tangier we enjoy the comforts of the past, the conveniences of the present, and vistas that have not yet been much tampered with. The limitations and advantages of life outside America seem to balance each other out. Not a day passes that I don't question my existence here or think about returning to America. But so far, I haven't budged."

* * *

HOPKINS, Nicholas S(nowden) 1939-

PERSONAL: Born February 20, 1939, in Boston, Mass.; son of Frank Snowden (a foreign service officer) and Ruth (Hazen) Hopkins; married Ferial Ghazoul; children: Omar, Ziyad. *Education:* Harvard University, B.A., 1960; attended Ecole Pratique des Hautes Etudes, 1960-61; University of Chicago, M.A., 1964, Ph.D., 1967. *Office:* Department of Sociology, Anthropology, and Psychology, American University in Cairo, 113 Sharia Kasr el Aini, Cairo, Egypt.

CAREER: New York University, New York, N.Y., assistant professor, 1967-73, associate professor of anthropology, 1973-75; American University in Cairo, Cairo, Egypt, associate professor of anthropology, 1975—. *Member:* International African Institute, American Anthropological Association, African Studies Association, Middle East Studies Association (acting executive secretary, 1973-74), Royal Anthropological Institute, Societe des Africanistes.

WRITINGS: Popular Government in an African Town: Kita, Mali, University of Chicago Press, 1972; (editor with June Nash and Jorge Dandler) *Popular Participation in Social Change: Cooperatives, Collectives, and Nationalized Industry,* Mouton, 1976; (editor with Saad Eddin Ibrahim) *Arab Society in Transition,* American University in Cairo, 1978. Contributor to anthropology, African studies, and Middle East studies journals.

WORK IN PROGRESS: Continuing research on the anthropology of the Middle East and Africa.

SIDELIGHTS: Hopkins told *CA:* "*Popular Government in an African Town,* based on my doctoral research, deals with the patterns and processes of local politics and relates these politics to development efforts. *Popular Participation in Social Change* is a collection of original studies that came out of a conference held in conjunction with the ninth International Congress of Anthropological and Ethnological Sciences held in Chicago in 1973. The studies deal with problems and prospects of cooperatives in fomenting social change in various parts of the world; many of the authors are from the countries they are analyzing and have been involved as activists in cooperative movements there.

"*Arab Society in Transition,*" Hopkins continued, "is a collection of readings on the society, culture, and politics of the Arab world. It was designed to fill a need at American University in Cairo where students must take a course on Arab society. The theme of the collection is the current phase of the process of change in the Arab world: change in national-local relationships, change in agriculture and industry, urbanization, demographic change, change in ideology and religion, change in family structure and sex roles, and change in national politics and economics."

Hopkins has traveled in West and North Africa, the Middle East, Europe, and the Caribbean. He speaks French, German, Arabic, and Bamanakan.

* * *

HORNBAKER, Alice 1927-

PERSONAL: Born February 3, 1927, in Cincinnati, Ohio; daughter of Albert (a restaurant proprietor) and Ida (a restaurant proprietor; maiden name, Frisch) Golder; married Joseph B. Hornbaker, Jr. (in dairy management), June 25, 1949; children: Christopher A., Holly Jo, Joseph B. III. *Education:* San Jose State College (now University), B.A., 1949. *Residence:* Cincinnati, Ohio. *Office: Cincinnati Enquirer,* Cincinnati, Ohio 45201.

CAREER: San Jose Mercury-News, San Jose, Calif., reporter, feature writer, and assistant women's editor, 1949-

55; free-lance writer and photographer, 1955-68; Children's Home Society, San Jose, director of public information, 1968-71; public information director for California United Fund, 1971; Writer's Digest School, Cincinnati, Ohio, editorial director, 1971-75; free-lance writer and photographer, 1975—. Teacher of adult writing courses. *Member:* Women in Communications, Ohio Newspaper Women's Association, Sigma Delta Chi. *Awards, honors:* Award from Cincinnati Editors Association, 1973, for feature story "Broken Heart Mended"; Health Journalism Award from American Chiropractic Association, 1977, for series of health stories; first place in feature writing from Ohio Newspaper Women's Association, 1977, for several stories.

WRITINGS: Preventive Care: Easy Exercise Against Aging, Drake, 1974. Feature writer for "People Today," in *Cincinnati Enquirer,* 1976—. Contributor to national magazines, including *Modern Maturity.*

WORK IN PROGRESS: Working in collaboration with a medical doctor on a book about successful dieting for a lifetime of slimness.

SIDELIGHTS: Hornbaker told *CA:* "My book on aging reinforces my personal belief that we need to practice preventive maintenance of health in the same manner management does it for its factory machinery. That not only includes checkups, but planned, regular exercise and moderation in diet. I have seen elderly people completely turned around and put back into the mainstream of life by simply adding moderate exercise to their every day lifestyle."

* * *

HOROWITZ, Elinor Lander

PERSONAL: Born in New Haven, Conn.; daughter of Harry P. (a lawyer) and Gertrude (Pearson) Lander; married Norman H. Horwitz (a neurosurgeon); children: Erica, Joshua, Anthony. *Education:* Smith College, A.B. *Home:* 3807 Bradley Lane, Chevy Chase, Md. 20015. *Agent:* Henriette Neatrour, Curtis Brown Ltd., 575 Madison Ave., New York, N.Y. 10022.

CAREER: Writer.

WRITINGS: The Strange Story of the Frog Who Became a Prince (juvenile), Delacorte, 1971; *The Soothsayer's Handbook,* Lippincott, 1972; *Communes in America: A Place Just Right,* Lippincott, 1972; *Capital Punishment U.S.A.,* Lippincott, 1973; *Mountain People, Mountain Crafts,* Lippincott, 1974; *When the Sky Is Like Lace* (juvenile), Lippincott, 1974; *Contemporary American Folk Artists,* Lippincott, 1975; *The Bird, the Banner and Uncle Sam: Images of America in Folk and Popular Art,* Lippincott, 1976; *A Child's Garden of Sculpture,* Washingtonian Books, 1976; *Madness, Magic and Medicine: The Treatment and Mistreatment of the Mentally Ill,* Lippincott, 1977. Contributor to *Washington Star, Washington Post,* and national magazines.

AVOCATIONAL INTERESTS: Art, environment, science, travel, natural science.

* * *

HOROWITZ, Gene 1930-

PERSONAL: Born March 12, 1930, in Bayonne, N.J.; son of Morris (in the milk business) and Elsie (Popper) Horowitz. *Education:* City College (now of the City University of New York), B.A., 1957; New York University, M.A., 1959. *Politics:* "Unconvinced." *Religion:* "Born Jewish, now

atheist." *Home and office:* 20 East 35th St., New York, N.Y. 10016. *Agent:* Julie Coopersmith, 8 West 14th St., New York, N.Y.

CAREER: English teacher in junior and senior high schools in Chappaqua, N.Y., 1957-64; writer, 1965—. *Military service:* U.S. Army, 1951-53. *Member:* International P.E.N., National Gay Task Force, Friends of Mozart. *Awards, honors:* Award from Edward Lewis Wallant Association and New Jersey novelist of the year award from Secondary School Teachers of New Jersey, both 1966, for *Home Is Where You Start From.*

WRITINGS—All novels: *Home Is Where You Start From,* Norton, 1966; *A Catch in the Breath,* Norton, 1968; *Mr. Jack and the Greenstalks,* Norton, 1970.

WORK IN PROGRESS: Four novels.

SIDELIGHTS: Horowitz remarked: "Writing helps me live my life as an always-renewing work-in-progress. Each work completed, published or not, brings me to the end of a problem faced and prepares me for what may be upcoming. Music—Mozart particularly—rubs out the roughest edges of my life.

"Although recently my work has not met with easy acceptability, I nevertheless proceed with it," Horowitz continued. "Publishing has become a 'figures' business, and the so-called 'middling writer,' who may or may not make a million for his publisher, tends to be excluded. The standard by which that writer's work is evaluated becomes anything but aesthetic. The realistic writer fights this paradox: the impressionable television viewer tends to think that the *illusion* of Farrah Fawcett-Majors is reality and not the life lived outside the television room. One, of course, impinges on the other, but who finally will read in America? Television has become the 'book' I used to pick up when there was time, as a young boy. But compare Dickens to Kojak. I shudder when I try to imagine the maturity of the generation now 'into TV.'"

* * *

HOTALING, Edward 1937-

PERSONAL: Born October 16, 1937, in Saratoga Springs, N.Y.; son of Charles A. and Elizabeth (Husek) Hotaling; married Marthe Vincent (a travel executive), January 24, 1970; children: Gregory, Luc. *Education:* Syracuse University, B.A., 1959; University of Minnesota, M.A., 1961. *Home:* 5342 32nd St. N.W., Washington, D.C. 20015. *Office:* National Broadcasting Co., 4001 Nebraska Ave. N.W., Washington, D.C. 20016.

CAREER: International Herald-Tribune, Paris, France, reporter, 1962-67; free-lance journalist, 1967—. Chief of Columbia Broadcasting System-News bureau in Beirut, 1974-75; covered celebrations for Iran's twenty-five-hundredth anniversary, 1971, the wars in Cyprus, 1974, and Lebanon, 1975, and Nixon's and Kissinger's Middle East trips, 1974-75. Staff writer for WRC-TV (National Broadcasting Co.), 1977—. *Military service:* U.S. Army Reserve, active duty, 1961. *Member:* Saratoga Springs Historical Society.

WRITINGS: The Arab Blacklist Unveiled, Landia, 1977. Author of column "Los Angeles" in *Art News,* 1969-70. Contributor to popular magazines, including *Business Week.* Contributing editor of *Art News,* 1969-70.

SIDELIGHTS: Hotaling told *CA:* "*The Arab Blacklist Unveiled* is a study of the Arab Boycott, its history, operation, and impact on U.S. and world trade." *Avocational interests:* History, travel, tennis.

HOTTOIS, James W.   1943-

PERSONAL: Born June 16, 1943, in Batavia, N.Y.; son of George I. and Ethel (Holly) Hottois; married Suanne Burdette, August 14, 1965; children: Jo-Elle, Robert Paul. *Education:* State University of New York at Albany, B.A., 1965; State University of New York at Buffalo, Ph.D., 1971. *Home:* 4882 Mount Ashman Dr., San Diego, Calif. 92111. *Office:* Department of Political Science, University of San Diego, San Diego, Calif. 92110.

CAREER: Grinnell College, Grinnell, Iowa, assistant professor of political science, 1969-73; presently affiliated with University of San Diego, San Diego, Calif. *Member:* American Political Science Association, Southern Political Science Association, Western Political Science Association.

WRITINGS: The Sex Education Controversy, Heath, 1975.

*   *   *

HOUCHIN, Thomas D(ouglas)   1925-

PERSONAL: Born July 15, 1925, in Mattoon, Ill.; son of George Walter and Zella Mathilda (Miller) Houchin. *Education:* University of Iowa, B.A., 1946, M.A. (speech pathology), 1950; Harvard University, A.M. (linguistics), 1955; Columbia University, Ed.D., 1963. *Religion:* Episcopal. *Home address:* P.O. Box 621, Ansonia Station, New York, N.Y. 10023. *Office:* Division of Humanities, St. John's University, Staten Island, N.Y. 10301.

CAREER: Speech clinician for public schools in Fairmont, Minn., 1946-48; Minnesota State Crippled Children's Services, St. Paul, speech consultant, 1948-50; Nebraska State Department of Education, Lincoln, supervisor of speech and hearing therapy, 1950-52; Emerson College, Boston, Mass., assistant professor, 1956-58, associate professor of speech, 1958-60; St. John's University, Staten Island, N.Y., professor of speech, 1960—. *Member:* International Phonetic Association (life member), International Association of Logopedics and Phoniatrics, American Speech and Hearing Association (chairman of committee on international affairs), American Dialect Society.

WRITINGS: Children with Speech and Hearing Problems (monograph), Nebraska State Department of Education, 1950; *How to Help Adults with Aphasia,* Public Affairs Press, 1964; *Directory for Spanish-Speaking New York,* Quadrangle, 1971; *The Sounds of American English,* AMSCO College Publications, 1976. Contributor to professional journals.

SIDELIGHTS: Houchin comments: "My interests in Latin America have led me to international involvement in speech pathology and audiology and in contemplated writing for and consulting in the Spanish-speaking Americas as a bilingual."

*   *   *

HOUCK, Carter   1924-

PERSONAL: Born May 2, 1924, in Washington, D.C.; daughter of David Thomas (a farmer) and Eliza (Mason) Greene; married Louis Talmadge Houck, February 3, 1945 (divorced, December, 1965); children: Linda Page, Carl Thomas. *Education:* Attended College of William and Mary, 1941-43, University of Connecticut, 1962-65, and Hunter College of the City University of New York, 1965-68. *Politics:* Independent. *Religion:* Episcopalian. *Home:* 16 West 16th St., Apt. 12DS, New York, N.Y. 10011.

CAREER: Sewing teacher for Singer Sewing Co., 1943-44; pattern maker for Butterick, 1944-45; *Fort Worth Star-Telegram,* Fort Worth, Tex., author of column "Sewing," 1950-51; *Parents' Magazine,* New York, New York, author of column "Sewing," 1962-72; *Lady's Circle,* New York City, editor of *Needlework,* 1971-78, and *Patchwork,* 1971—. Part-owner of Rag Doll (fabric shop), 1968-74. *Member:* New York Embroiderers Guild, Appalachian Mountain Club (vice-chairperson of executive committee).

WRITINGS: (With Joanne Schreiber) *Betty Crocker's Good and Easy Sewing Book for You and Your Family,* Universal Publishing, 1972; *Warm as Wool, Cool as Cotton: Natural Fibers and Fabrics and How to Work with Them,* illustrated by Nancy Parker, Seabury, 1975; *American Quilts and How to Make Them,* photography by Myron Miller, Scribner, 1975; *The Big Bag Book,* photography by Miller, Scribner, 1977. Contributor to magazines, including *Appalachia, Trail Walker,* and *Action Vacations.*

WORK IN PROGRESS: A book on white-work embroidery, for Dover; a book on boat designs for three types of simple embroidery, with Myron Miller, for Scribner.

SIDELIGHTS: Carter Houck writes: "As a small child growing up on a farm a mile from the highway in the Virginia Piedmont, I had to do a great deal of making my own fun. The Depression struck farming in that area an almost deadly blow when I was five years old, which meant that new cars, movies, coats that weren't hand-me-downs from wealthy city cousins, and a lot of other things I never missed, were unknown to me. What I did have was a horse, a whole menagerie of pets, including occasional wild ones that boarded for a while, and a great deal of delightful neglect. That sort of neglect enabled me to climb trees and swing from the branches, use the tools in my father's workshop, sew on my mother's treadle machine, and sometimes play wild imaginative games with my brother. I still hold conversations with cats, dogs, horses, or any other animals that will hold still for long enough to listen.

"I lived with an assortment of very different relatives, mostly in cities. One uncle had an exquisite townhouse in Washington, D.C., which is now a parking lot. One aunt lived on the Main Line of Philadelphia, complete with swimming pool and tennis court, cottage at the shore, and two bratty children. One aunt was the penurious widow of a minister. She counted the grains of sugar on the cereal, the drops of water in the shower, and all of my sins.

"As life has a habit of doing, all things come full circle, and the little girl who'd used the treadle machine as a rainy-day toy headed straight for design school and the Big City.

"I have never lost the habit of writing down descriptions of things I see, places I go, emotions that I cannot share easily. I carry a camera now when I travel, but I find that words paint a clearer picture for me. I see many things around me in terms of needlework designs, and I want to share these things that are a pleasure to me with anyone who will listen. Teaching small groups isn't enough—I can reach a much larger audience by writing. I do, however, like the contact and feedback of teaching workshops.

"When anyone comes to me and asks about being a writer or designer and about working free-lance, I suggest that being used to being alone and keeping oneself amused are helpful character traits. Being creative alone is only possible if being alone is comfortable and even fun."

HOUGAN, James Richard   1942-
   (Jim Hougan)

PERSONAL: Name originally James Richard Edwards; name legally changed, 1960; born October 14, 1942, in Brooklyn, N.Y.; son of Stephen Buhl Edwards (a stockbroker and night watchman) and Doris (Daly) Edwards Hougan; married Carolyn Johnson, December 16, 1966; children: Daisy Case, Matthew Edwards. *Education:* University of Wisconsin—Madison, B.S., 1966; attended Centro Interculturales de Documentacion, Cuernavaca, Mexico, 1971. *Politics:* "Pessimistic." *Home:* 3431-A South Stafford, Arlington, Va. 22206. *Agent:* Elaine Markson Literary Agency, Inc., 44 Greenwich Ave., New York, N.Y. 10011. *Office:* 1723 Lamont St. N.W., Washington, D.C. 20010.

CAREER: Social worker in Chicago, Ill., 1966; *Capital Times,* Madison, Wis., investigative reporter, 1968-71; *Harper's,* New York, N.Y., Washington editor, 1976—. Member of board of directors of Carolyn Bridge & Land Co., 1968—. *Member:* Sigma Delta Chi. *Awards, honors:* Fellowships from Alicia Patterson Foundation and Rockefeller Foundation, 1971-72.

WRITINGS—Under name Jim Hougan: *Anticipating Machine* (poems), Quixote Press (Madison, Wis.), 1969; *Decadence* (nonfiction), Morrow, 1975; *Spooks* (nonfiction), Morrow, 1978. Contributor to popular and literary magazines, including *Nation, Playboy, Oui, Quixote,* and *Crawdaddy,* and newspapers.

WORK IN PROGRESS: Dragonette (tentative title), a novel set in Haiti, for Morrow.

SIDELIGHTS: Hougan writes: "My vocational and avocational interests are impossible to separate in that each influences the other in ways that are often quite direct. Family, friends, mystery, money, and travel are the things most important to me. It would be nice to have clarity about political and religious matters, but I don't. From time to time, I have certainties about these things but, in retrospect, never clarity.

"I am presently involved in various efforts to obtain information on a number of subjects from the Central Intelligence Agency—utilizing the Freedom of Information Act."

*   *   *

HOUGAN, Jim
   See HOUGAN, James Richard

*   *   *

HOUGHTON, Bernard   1935-

PERSONAL: Born August 23, 1935, in Liverpool, England; son of Edward and Agnes Houghton; married Margaret McNamara, May 7, 1964; children: Russell, Romilly. *Education:* University of London, M.A., 1970. *Politics:* Socialist. *Home:* 9 Hathaway Rd., Liverpool, England. *Office:* Department of Library and Information Studies, Liverpool Polytechnic, Liverpool, England.

CAREER: Liverpool Polytechnic, Liverpool, England, senior lecturer in library science, 1965—. *Member:* Library Association (fellow).

WRITINGS—All published by Bingley: *Technical Information Sources,* 1967, 2nd edition, 1972; *Information Work Today,* 1967; *Computer-Based Information Retrieval Systems,* 1968; *Standardization for Documentation,* 1969; *Mechanical Engineering: The Sources of Information,* 1970;

Out of the Dinosaurs, 1972; *Scientific Periodicals,* 1975; *On-Line Information Retrieval Systems,* 1977; *Patent Systems and Their Documentation,* in press. Contributor to *Jazz Journal.*

WORK IN PROGRESS: An evaluation of Medline for the provision of drug information; research on the optimization of journal holdings in special libraries.

AVOCATIONAL INTERESTS: Foreign travel, the English countryside; literature, especially English poetry; music, especially jazz; cricket, "real ale."

*   *   *

HOULDEN, J(ames) L(eslie)   1929-

PERSONAL: Born March 1, 1929, in Knutsford, England; son of James and Lily (Snow) Houlden. *Education:* Queen's College, Oxford, B.A., 1952, M.A., 1956; further graduate study at Cuddesdon College, Oxford, 1953-55. *Home:* 33 Raleigh Court, Lymer Ave., London SE19 1LS, England. *Office:* King's College, University of London, Strand, London WC2R 2LS, England.

CAREER: Ordained Anglican priest, 1955; assistant priest at Anglican church in Hunslet, England, 1955-58; Theological College, Chichester, England, chaplain, 1958-60; Oxford University, Oxford, England, fellow and chaplain of Trinity College, 1960-70, principal of Cuddesdon College, 1970-77; University of London, London, England, lecturer in New Testament studies, 1977—. Member of Church of England Liturgical Commission and Doctrine Commission. *Military service:* British Army, 1947-49; became sergeant. *Member:* Society for New Testament Studies.

WRITINGS: Paul's Letters From Prison, Penguin, 1970, revised edition, S.C.M. Press, 1977; *Ethics and the New Testament,* Penguin, 1973; *The Johannine Epistles,* A. & C. Black, 1973; *The Pastoral Epistles,* Penguin, 1976; *Patterns of Faith,* S.C.M. Press, 1977; *Explorations in Theology III,* S.C.M. Press, 1978. Contributor of articles and reviews to magazines.

WORK IN PROGRESS: Research on the interaction between the New Testament and Christian doctrine.

SIDELIGHTS: Houlden told *CA:* "Three of my books are commentaries on books of the New Testament. *Ethics and the New Testament* is an attempt to move out from exegesis into questions of interpretation and application: how does the diversity of the New Testament teaching, showing the early Christian congregations grappling with ethical problems, affect our sense of the New Testament's usefulness and our own handling of moral questions? *Patterns of Faith* tackles doctrinal issues by a similar method. The New Testament displays great diversity in patterns of doctrine and in doctrinal emphasis. It reflects a variety of response to the impact of Jesus, according to the variety of culture and circumstance of those receiving it. This leads to reflection on the proper nature and task of doctrinal statement today, which so often fails to take sufficiently into account the findings of New Testament scholarship. This is, in other words, a methodological exercise, with wide-range implications.

"The most recent book," Houlden continued, "consists of essays on doctrinal subjects published in periodical and collections over the past twelve years. Most of them illustrate the principles expounded in *Patterns of Faith,* applying them to topics as varied as the Doctrine of the Trinity and the Ordination of Women. There is an underlying conviction that much confusion of faith could be avoided if historical criticism, so widely accepted with regard to the Bible, were applied also to the history of doctrine: this leads to a clarification of what is properly involved in doctrinal statement and of the dynamics of Christian faith.''

*   *   *

HOUSEHOLD, Geoffrey (Edward West) 1900-

PERSONAL: Born November 30, 1900, in Bristol, England; son of Horace W. (a lawyer) and Beatrice (Noton) Household; married Ilona Zsoldos-Gutman, 1942; children: Geoffrey Andrew, Nicolette Ilona, Anna Celia. *Education:* Magdalen College, Oxford, first class honors in English literature, 1922. *Home:* Church Headland, Whitchurch, Aylesbury, Buckinghamshire, England.

CAREER: Engaged in commerce in Europe, the United States, South America, and the Near East, 1922-35; writer, 1935—. *Military service:* Served in the Intelligence Corps, 1939-45; became lieutenant colonel; awarded Territorial Decoration and mentioned in dispatches.

*WRITINGS—*Novels: *The Third Hour,* Chatto & Windus, 1937, Little, Brown, 1938; *Rogue Male,* Little, Brown, 1939, reprinted, 1971; *Arabesque,* Little, Brown, 1948, reprinted, International Publications Service, 1969; *The High Place,* Little, Brown, 1950, reprinted, White Lion, 1972; *A Rough Shoot,* Little, Brown, 1951; *A Time to Kill,* Little, Brown, 1951; *Fellow Passenger,* Little, Brown, 1955; *Watcher in the Shadows,* Little, Brown, 1960, reprinted, M. Joseph, 1972; *Thing to Love,* Little, Brown, 1963; *Olura,* Little, Brown, 1965; *The Courtesy of Death,* Little, Brown, 1967; *Dance of the Dwarfs,* Little, Brown, 1968; *Doom's Caravan,* Little, Brown, 1971; *The Three Sentinels,* Little, Brown, 1972; *The Lives and Times of Bernardo Brown,* M. Joseph, 1973, Little, Brown, 1974; *Red Anger,* Little, Brown, 1975; *Hostage London: The Diary of Julian Despard,* Little, Brown, 1977.

Short stories: *The Salvation of Pisco Gabar, and Other Stories,* Chatto & Windus, 1938, Little, Brown, 1940; *Tales of Adventurers,* Little, Brown, 1952; *The Brides of Solomon, and Other Stories,* Little, Brown, 1958; *Sabres on the Sand, and Other Stories,* Little, Brown, 1966.

For children: *The Spanish Cave* (illustrated by Henry C. Pitz), Little, Brown, 1936, reprinted, Longmans, Green, 1965 (published in England as *The Terror of Villadonga,* Hutchinson, 1936); *The Exploits of Xenophon* (illustrated by Leonard E. Fisher), Random House, 1955 (published in England as *Xenophon's Adventure,* Bodley Head, 1961); *Prisoner of the Indies* (illustrated by Warren Chappell), Little, Brown, 1967; *Escape Into Daylight,* Little, Brown, 1976.

Autobiography: *Against the Wind,* M. Joseph, 1958, Little, Brown, 1959.

SIDELIGHTS: Rogue Male is perhaps Household's best known work. It is a psychological novel of an English sportsman from a family of excellent financial standing who suddenly desires to assassinate a European dictator. "*Rogue Male,*" commented a *Books* critic, "is one of the most original adventure tales of recent times, a book with a delightfully dry, bitter tang of intelligent dramaturgy.... Mr. Household's dish is a pungent combination of dramatic and lyric ingredients. It is exciting to consume." The *New York Times* commented: "The author is thoroughly adroit, but what the reader feels is not deftness or 'swift pace,' but a breath-taking, uninterrupted concentration. As a work of imagination *Rogue Male* is an almost overpowering tour de force. And in its spare, tense, desperately alive narrative it will keep, long after the last page is finished, its hold from

the first page upon the reader's mind. Its deepest and broadest suggestion the reader must find for himself, if he will.''

Another novel, *Fellow Passenger,* won this praise from a *Times Literary Supplement* reviewer, who wrote: "The pleasure that arises from reading the work of a real craftsman is the keener as it grows rarer.... A comedy thriller in which the comedy is comic and the thrills thrill would alone be worth the reader's money. But Mr. Household has a great deal more to offer than this. His book is admirably constructed, highly entertaining, and elegantly written." And *The Three Sentinels,* one of Household's most recent novels, was called a "sophisticated thriller, an intricate moral confrontation," by the *New York Times.*

Household's books of short stories have also generally won favor with critics. A *New Republic* critic, writing about *The Salvation of Pisco Gabar, and Other Stories,* commented: "Household is a natural story-teller; vivid prose, good selection, interest, and fun, too. But there is more in it. He has ranged just about everywhere, going with a quick eye for the human and absurd, but no malice, in fellowship and with gusto." However, a reviewer for *Christian Science Monitor* noted that while "the flair for the strange and bizarre can, of course, be a fascinating quality in a writer, ... Mr. Household does not always succeed in rendering his effective. His settings are convincing, but his characters, like his plots, are apt to seem thin, and the result to appear but a flitting of shadows over the landscape."

Of *Tales of Adventurers,* another book of short stories, the *Chicago Tribune* commented that the stories are "crisply told, admirably constructed, and designed to hold the reader by means of a skillful combination of violence and subtlety." The *New York Times* wrote: "Ironic humor and a hard-driving pace that never falters are the hallmarks of these tales. Mr. Household's comic touch is sure, even when the laughter hovers on the brink of tragedy—as it does in nearly all of the entries." *Saturday Review* noted that the book "reveals his suberb craftsmanship for the short story. Some of them have a bizarre climax, others are the essence of danger and fear combined with a kind of gruesome humor."

Household has also written a few books for young people. *Prisoner of the Indies* was described by the *New York Times* as "one of the best juvenile historical novels of the year. It's tough stuff. Its author makes no compromises for young readers. His material is complex and sometimes demanding. His language, though simple, is mature and sometimes challenging. But for devotees of historical adventure, his book is pure delight...."

Household's autobiography, *Against the Wind,* was thus described by a *Booklist* critic: "Quietly reported in a somewhat formal style, the events of [Household's] life are not given a false air of adventure but are presented with appreciation of the variety in the situations and aspects of society met as a representative of commercial interests from banking to selling printer's ink, and as a special agent in the Near East during World War II.... The interest is for the literary—rather than the adventure-minded." *New Yorker* wrote: "Mr. Household, though a painfully self-taught writer, is a born raconteur with a nicely balanced sense of irony and an amused attitude toward the world and himself. This adventure story, with its honesty and its little fillips of absurdity, is one of his most delightful books." The *New York Times* called it a "revealing book, warm with memories and glowing with humor and humility."

In 1941, Twentieth Century-Fox adapted Household's *Rogue Male* into a motion picture, "Man Hunt," and in

1953, United Artists produced "Shoot First," based on *A Rough Shoot.*

BIOGRAPHICAL/CRITICAL SOURCES: Books, August 27, 1939; *Christian Science Monitor,* February 1, 1939; *New York Times,* August 27, 1939, June 1, 1952, January 25, 1959, May 12, 1972; *New Republic,* April 29, 1940; *Chicago Tribune,* June 8, 1952, February 20, 1955; *Saturday Review,* July 5, 1952; Geoffrey Household, *Against the Wind,* Little, Brown, 1959; *New Yorker,* February 14, 1959; *Booklist,* February 15, 1959; *New York Times Book Review,* July 28, 1968.

* * *

HOWARD, Dick 1943-

PERSONAL: Born August 30, 1943, in Cleveland, Ohio; son of Sherwin H. (a salesman) and Patricia (Roth) Howard; married Brigitte Delaquaize (a librarian), 1967; children: Marc Alan. *Education:* Rice University, B.A., 1965; graduate study at University of Paris, 1966-67, and University of Bonn, 1969-70; University of Texas, M.A., 1967, Ph.D., 1970. *Office:* Department of Philosophy, State University of New York at Stony Brook, Stony Brook, N.Y. 11794.

CAREER: Southern Illinois University, Carbondale, assistant professor of philosophy, 1970-71; State University of New York at Stony Brook, visiting assistant professor, 1971-72, assistant professor, 1972-75, associate professor of philosophy, 1975—. *Member:* American Philosophical Association, Society for Phenomenology and Existential Philosophy, Hegel Society of America. *Awards, honors:* Fulbright fellowship for France, 1966-67; Alliance Francaise Fribourg fellow, 1967-68; National Defense Education Act fellowship for Germany, 1969-70; National Endowment for the Humanities younger humanist fellowship for University of Tuebingen, 1973-74; Research Institute on International Change fellow, Columbia University, 1978.

WRITINGS: On Marx's Critical Theory, Telos Press, 1970; (editor) *Selected Political Writings of Rosa Luxemburg,* Monthly Review Press, 1971; (editor with Karl E. Klare) *The Unknown Dimension: European Marxism Since Lenin,* Basic Books, 1972; *The Development of the Marxian Dialectic,* Southern Illinois University Press, 1972; (contributor) Garth Gillan, editor, *The Horizons of the Flesh,* Southern Illinois University Press, 1973; (editor with Dean Savage) *The New Working Class: The Writings of Serge Mattel,* Telos Press, 1975; *The Marxian Legacy,* Urizen, 1978; *The Return of the Political,* Duquesne University Press, 1978. Member of editorial board of *Telos.*

WORK IN PROGRESS: A book on the political sphere, publication by Macmillan expected in 1979; a book on Marxism, with Andrew Arato and Jean Cohen, publication by Telos expected in 1979.

SIDELIGHTS: Howard writes: "My books, articles, and teaching are all the product of the political experience of the New Left in the 1960's, here and in Europe. In one manner or another, my goal is to formulate the self-understanding of that movement, and to contribute to its revivification. That takes both the personal form of teaching and political and editorial activity, and a philosophical and journalistic cast as well. It means keeping up on current events and theoretical developments in Europe as well as here, and writing in the European languages for their publications as well. The difficulties in the 1970's center around practical political questions (what to do in this *apparently* quiescent period, whether to join this or that group) and the theoretical work of Marx and its influence (whether to try to create the 'Marxist

culture' the United States never really had, or whether the problems in Marx, such as my *Marxian Legacy* criticizes, demand jettisoning Marx)."

* * *

HOWARTH, Patrick (John Fielding) 1916-
(C.D.E. Francis)

PERSONAL: Born April 25, 1916, in Calcutta, India; son of Frank Fielding (an insurance manager) and Edith Margaret Morrison (Brodie) Howarth. *Education:* St. John's College, Oxford, M.A. (honors), 1937. *Politics:* Liberal. *Religion:* Church of England. *Home:* 219A King's Rd., London SW3 5EJ, England. *Agent:* A. D. Peters & Co., 10 Buckingham St., London WC2N 6BU, England. *Office:* 21 Ebury St., London S.W.1, England.

CAREER: Baltic Institute, Gdynia, Poland, editor, 1938-39; British Embassy, Warsaw, Poland, first information secretary, 1945-47; British Home Civil Service, London, staff member of Ministry of Town and Country Planning and Ministry of Housing and Local Government, 1948-53; Royal National Lifeboat Institution, London, public relations officer and editor of *Lifeboat,* 1953—. *Military service:* British Army, 1940-45, Special Operations Executive, 1941-45; became major. *Member:* Society of Authors, Special Forces Club, Marylebone Cricket Club.

WRITINGS: The Year Is 1851 (history), Collins, 1951; *The Dying Ukrainian* (fiction), Bodley Head, 1953; *A Matter of Minutes* (fiction), Wingate, 1953; (editor) *Special Operations,* Routledge & Kegan Paul, 1955; *Questions in the House* (history), Bodley Head, 1956; (under pseudonym C.D.E. Francis) *Portrait of a Killer* (detective novel), Hammond & Hammond, 1956; *The Lifeboat Story* (history), Routledge & Kegan Paul, 1957; *How Men Are Rescued From the Sea* (history), Routledge & Kegan Paul, 1961; *Squire: Most Generous of Men* (biography), Hutchinson, 1963; *Play Up and Play the Game* (literary criticism), Eyre Methuen, 1973; *Lifeboats and Lifeboat People* (history), White Lion, 1974; *When the Riviera Was Ours* (history), Routledge & Kegan Paul, 1977.

Author of long poems "Play Back a Lifetime" and "The Four Seasons," both broadcast by British Broadcasting Corp. Contributor to magazines, including *History Today, Punch,* and *Time and Tide.*

WORK IN PROGRESS: "The Boy from Over the Hill," a long poem for four voices; research for a book on Special Operations Executive in World War II, for Routledge & Kegan Paul.

SIDELIGHTS: Howarth writes: "As a boy I wrote rather good immature poetry; I won the poetry prize at Rugby School, and narrowly missed winning the Newdigate Prize at Oxford; I had my verses commended by such distinguished figures as Siegfried Sassoon and C. S. Lewis. Suddenly the ability to write poetry left me, and in the preoccupation of war and post-war diplomacy I wrote virtually nothing. In 1948 I began the initial research for the first of my various books of social history and criticism, which for a time I interspersed with novels. Then, at the age of fifty, the capacity to write poetry returned, and the work to which I attach most importance is the series of three long poems [broadcast by British Broadcasting Corp.]. Before, during, and after World War II I travelled extensively and I have broadcast for the BBC in five languages."

HOWE, Richard J. 1937-

PERSONAL: Born May 24, 1937, in Boston, Mass.; son of William T. (a minister) and Hazel (Jameson) Howe; married Marie-Claude Herve, July 1, 1967; children: Corentine, Cedric. *Education:* Tufts University, B.A., 1959; Columbia University, M.S., 1960; further study at Alliance Francaise, University of Paris, 1964-67. *Home:* 245 Henry St., Brooklyn Heights, N.Y. 11201. *Office: Vision,* 641 Lexington Ave., New York, N.Y. 10022.

CAREER/WRITINGS: Minneapolis Tribune, Minneapolis, Minn., reporter, 1960-62; *Chicago Daily News,* Chicago, Ill., general-assignment reporter, 1962-64; *International Herald Tribune,* Paris, France, news editor, 1964-67; freelance writer for *Reader's Digest* in Paris, 1967-69; *Wall Street Journal,* New York City, Philadelphia correspondent, 1969-70; *Vision* (European financial magazine), Paris, U.S. bureau chief in New York City, 1970—. Notable assignments include coverage of the Black Muslims' annual convention, and international economic and financial news. Contributor of articles to *Reader's Digest, Selection du Reader's Digest, Opera, Boston Globe, Atlantic Community Quarterly,* and *Atlas World Press Review.*

* * *

HSIA, Adrian (Rue Chun) 1938-

PERSONAL: Surname is pronounced Shya; born November 25, 1938, in Chungking, China; son of Yun Foo (a film producer) and Hak Shun (Yang) Hsia; married Ruth Weimar, November 22, 1960; children: Ariane. *Education:* Attended University of Cologne, 1957-62; Free University of Berlin, Dr.Phil., 1965. *Office:* Department of German, McGill University, P.O. Box 6070, Montreal, Quebec, Canada H3C 3G1.

CAREER: University of Cologne, Cologne, Germany, lecturer in German, 1965-68; McGill University, Montreal, Quebec, lecturer, 1968-69, assistant professor, 1969-72, associate professor of German literature, 1972—. *Member:* Canadian Association of University Teachers of German, Canadian Comparative Literature Association, Modern Language Association of America, Deutsche Gesellschaft Ostasienkunde. *Awards, honors:* Canada Council grants and fellowships.

WRITINGS: Die Kurzgeschichten von D. H. Lawrence (title means "The Short Stories of D. H. Lawrence"), Free University of Berlin, 1965; *D. H. Lawrence: Die Charaktere seiner Kurzgeschichten in Handlung und Spannung* (title means "D. H. Lawrence: Characters, Plot and Suspense of His Short Stories"), Bouvier, 1968; *Die chinesische Kulturrevolution: Zur Entwicklung der Widersprueche in der chinesischen Gesellschaft,* Hermann Luchterland, 1971, translation published as *The Chinese Cultural Revolution,* Orbach & Chambers, 1972, McGraw, 1973; *Hermann Hesse und China: Darstellung, Materialien und Interpretation* (title means "Hermann Hesse and China: Description, Material and Interpretation"), Suhrkamp, 1974; (editor) *Hermann Hesse im Spiegel der zeitgenoessischen Kritik* (title means "Hermann Hesse in the Mirror of Contemporary Criticism"), Francke, 1975. Also author of numerous articles.

WORK IN PROGRESS: Research on the Sino-German literary relationship; *Hermann Hesse and his Readers; The German Novel of Enlightenment.*

SIDELIGHTS: Hsia writes: "My publications reflect a cosmopolitan background: Chinese by birth, German by choice, living in French Canada, teaching in an English university."

BIOGRAPHICAL/CRITICAL SOURCES: Martin Pfeifer, editor, *Hermann Hesses Weltweite Wirkung* (title means "World-wide Reception of Hermann Hesse"), Suhrkamp, 1977.

* * *

HSIAO, Katharine H(uei-Ying Huang) 1923-

PERSONAL: Born May 13, 1923, in Peking, China; came to the United States in 1948, naturalized citizen, 1961; daughter of Hsien-Cheng Huang (a civil servant) and Shu-chen Liu; married Liang-lin Hsiao (a professor of economics), September 12, 1948; children: Georgia Angella, Gilbert Lynn, Katharine Jean. *Education:* Southwestern University (China), B.A., 1943; graduate study at University of Toronto, 1947-48; Columbia University, M.A., 1959, Ph.D., 1966. *Home:* 4386 Hulman St., Terre Haute, Ind. 47803. *Office:* Department of Economics, Indiana State University, Terre Haute, Ind. 47809.

CAREER: Canadian Embassy, Chungking, China, instructor in Chinese, 1943-46; National Bureau of Economic Research, New York, N.Y., research assistant, 1953-54; Moravian College, Bethlehem, Pa., instructor in economics, 1956-59; Indiana State University, Terre Haute, assistant professor, 1964-69, associate professor, 1969-73, professor of economics, 1973—. Member of Young Women's Christian Association Hyte Community Center, Terre Haute Symphony, and Terre Haute Mental Health Association. *Member:* American Economic Association, American Statistical Association, American Association for Asian Studies, American Association of University Professors (local president, 1976-77), Indiana Academy of Social Sciences.

WRITINGS: Money and Monetary Policy of Communist China, Columbia University Press, 1971.

WORK IN PROGRESS: Research on monetary policy and economic development in Taiwan.

SIDELIGHTS: Hsiao told *CA* of *Money and Monetary Policy of Communist China:* "This book is the first comprehensive study made of monetary economics in the People's Republic of China. It examines the role and structure of money and banking, the nature of monetary policy, and how well the monetary mechanism has helped to control the inflation generated by a rapid rate of economic development."

* * *

HUANG, Stanley S(hang) C(hien) 1923-

PERSONAL: Born January 21, 1923, in Shanghai, China; came to the United States in 1947, naturalized citizen, 1962; son of Dien-Ching and Ching-Chong (Nee) Huang; married Aileen Yueh, February 14, 1954. *Education:* St. John's University, Shanghai, China, B.A., 1944; University of Illinois, M.A., 1948; New York University, M.B.A., 1956, Ph.D., 1966. *Home:* 48 Stonicker Dr., Lawrenceville, N.J. 08648. *Office:* Department of Finance, Rider College, Lawrenceville, N.J. 08648.

CAREER: St. John's University, Jamaica, N.Y., instructor, 1957-60, assistant professor, 1960-66, associate professor of finance, 1966-69; Rider College, Lawrenceville, N.J., associate professor, 1969-73, professor of finance, 1973—. *Member:* American Finance Association, American Economic Association, American Financial Management Association.

WRITINGS: Corporate Earning Power and Valuation of Common Stock, Investors Intelligence, Inc., 1968; *Techniques of Investment Analysis*, International Textbook Co., 1972; *A New Technical Approach to Stock Market Timing*, Investors Intelligence, Inc., 1973. Contributor to finance journals.

WORK IN PROGRESS: A book on investments.

*   *   *

HUBBARD, L(afayette) Ron(ald)   1911-

PERSONAL: Born March 13, 1911, in Tilden, Neb.; son of Harry Ross (a naval officer) and Dora May (Waterbury de Wolfe) Hubbard; married Mary Sue Whipp, October 30, 1952; children: Diana Meredith de Wolfe (Mrs. Jonathan Horwich), Mary Suzette Rochelle, Arthur Ronald Conway. *Education:* Attended George Washington University, 1930-34, and Princeton University, 1945. *Home:* Saint Hill Manor, East Grinstead, Sussex, England. *Agent:* Forrest Ackerman, Ackerman Sci-Fi Agency, 2495 Glendower Ave., Hollywood, Calif. 90027.

CAREER: Writer of aviation and travel articles, mystery, and science fiction, 1930-50; explorer, 1934—; organizer and director of Hubbard Foundation for public interests, 1950; founder of Church of Scientology, 1952; director of international humanitarian organizations, 1952-66; resigned all directorships to devote full time to research, 1966; engaged in research and international programs to resolve drug abuse, 1966—; engaged in experimental work in music and photography, 1974—. Leader of expeditions, including Caribbean Motion Picture Expedition, 1931, West Indies Minerals Survey Expedition, 1932, and Alaskan Radio Experimental Expedition for U.S. government, 1940. Carried out research and developed technology for better education, 1964-71. *Military service:* Served in World War II. *Awards, honors:* New York Explorers Club Flag for geological expeditions, 1940, 1961, 1968; Highest Certificate of Merit from Governor of Louisiana, 1974; Ingrams West Award, 1977, for *Dianetics: The Modern Science of Mental Health*, the twenty-seven year best seller; Tully Marketing Business Administration Award, 1977, for contributions of technology in the field of marketing.

WRITINGS—Nonfiction; all published by Publications Organization except as noted: Dianetics: The Modern Science of Mental Health, Hermitage House, 1950; *Dianetics: The Evolution of a Science*, 1950, 11th edition, American St. Hill Organization, 1974; *Scientology 0-8*, 1950, 3rd edition, American St. Hill Organization, 1970; *Advanced Procedure and Axioms*, 1951, 3rd edition, American St. Hill Organization, 1971; *Dianetics: The Original Thesis*, 1951; *Handbook for Preclears*, 1951, 2nd edition, Hubbard Scientology Organization, 1962; *Introduction to Scientology Ethics*, 1951, 4th edition, American St. Hill Organization, 1973; *Notes on the Lectures*, 1951; *Science of Survival*, 1951; *Self Analysis*, 1951, 6th edition, American St. Hill Organization, 1968; *Child Dianetics*, 1951, 6th edition, 1975.

Electropsychometric Auditing, Scientific Press, 1952; *A Key to the Unconscious*, Scientific Press, 1952; *Scientology: 88*, Hubbard Association of Scientologists, 1952; *Scientology: What to Audit*, Scientific Press, 1952; *Scientology: A History of Man*, 1952; *Scientology 8-80*, 1952; *How to Live Though an Executive*, 1953, 5th edition, Department of Publications World Wide, 1968; *Scientology 8-8008*, 1953, 8th edition, American St. Hill Organization, 1967; *The Creation of Human Ability*, 1954; *Dianetics '55*, 1955, 9th edition, American St. Hill Organization, 1973; *The Problems of*

Work, 1956; *Scientology: The Fundamentals of Thought*, 1956; *Scientology: Clear Procedure Issue One*, 1957; *Have You Lived Before This Life?*, 1958, 3rd edition, 1978; *Axioms and Logics*, 1958; *Background and Ceremonies of the Church of Scientology*, 1959.

The Book of E-Meter Drills, 1961; *E-Meter Essentials*, 1961; *Control and the Mechanics of Start, Change, Stop*, 1962; *The Book of Case Remedies*, 1964; *Scientology: A New Slant on Life*, 1965; *Introduction to the E-Meter*, 1966; *Scientology and the Bible*, compiled by Catherine Briggs and others, Department of Publications World Wide, 1967; (contributor) Richard Farley, editor, *All About Radiation*, 1967; *Level 0 Professional Auditors Bulletins*, 1968; *Level One Professional Auditors Bulletins*, 1968; *Collected Magazine Articles*, 1968; *Collected Magazine Articles II*, 1968; *Mission into Time*, 1968; *The Phoenix Lectures*, 1968, 3rd edition, American St. Hill Organization, 1974; *When in Doubt, Communicate*, compiled by Ruth Minshull and Edward M. Lefson, Scientology Ann Arbor, 1969.

The Basic Dianetics Picture Book, 1972; *The Basic Scientology Picture Book*, 1972; *Organizational Executive Course*, ten volumes, 1974; *The Management Series*, American St. Hill Organization, 1974; *Dianetics and Scientology Technical Dictionary*, 1975; *Dianetics Today*, 1975; *The Technical Bulletins of Dianetics and Scientology*, ten volumes, 1976; *Volunteer Minister's Handbook*, 1976; *Modern Management Technology Defined*, 1976; *Hubbard Communications Office Policy Letter Subject Index Under Likely Titles*, edited by Pat Brice, 1976.

Science fiction, except as noted: *Buckskin Brigades*, Macaulay, 1937, reprinted, Theta, 1977; *Death's Deputy*, illustrated by Lou Goldstone, Fantasy Publishing, 1948; *Slaves of Sleep*, Shasta, 1948; *Final Blackout*, Hadley, 1948, reprinted, Garland Publishing, 1975; *The Kingslayer*, Fantasy Publishing, 1949; *Triton, and Battle of Wizards*, Fantasy Publishing, 1949; *Typewriter in the Sky* [and] *Fear: Two Novels*, Gnome Press, 1951, reprinted as *Fear* [and] *Typewriter in Sky*, Popular Library, 1977, *Fear* reprinted separately, Galaxy Publishing, 1957; *Return to Tomorrow*, Ace Books, 1954, reprinted, Garland Publishing, 1975; *Ole Doc Methuselah* (short stories), Daw Books, 1970; *Fear and the Ultimate Adventure*, Berkley Publishing, 1970; *Hymn of Asia: An Eastern Poem* (poetry), Publications Organization, 1974; *Seven Steps to the Arbiter*, Major Books, 1975.

Also author of "Treasure Island" and "Dive Bomber," screenplays produced by Columbia.

Contributor of short stories to *Astounding Science Fiction, Thrilling Wonder Stories, Adventure, Argosy, Detective Fiction Weekly, Western Story Magazine*, and other magazines.

WORK IN PROGRESS: "Research into current justices/injustices of individuals toward development of sane and equal justice for all; further research into advanced technologies of Dianetics and Scientology."

SIDELIGHTS: Hubbard writes: "The first principle of my own philosophy is that wisdom is meant for anyone who wishes to reach for it. It is the servant of the commoner and king alike and should never be regarded with awe.... The second principle of my own philosophy is that it must be capable of being applied. Learning locked in mildewed books is of little use to anyone and therefore of no value unless it can be used. The third principle is that any philosophical knowledge is only valuable if it is true or if it works. These three principles are so strange to the field of philosophy, that I have given my philosophy a name: SCIENTOL-

OGY. This means only 'knowing how to know.' A philosophy can only be a *route* to knowledge. It cannot be crammed down one's throat. If one has a route, he can then find what is true for him. And that is Scientology. Know Thyself . . . and the truth shall set you free. Therefore, in Scientology, we are not concerned with individual actions and differences. We are only concerned with how to show Man how he can set himself or herself free. . . .

"I have seen much human misery. As a very young man I wandered through Asia and saw the agony and misery of overpopulated and underdeveloped lands. I have seen people uncaring and stepping over dying men in the streets. I have seen children less than rags and bones. And amongst this poverty and degradation I found holy places where wisdom was great, but where it was carefully hidden and given out only as superstition. Later, in Western universities, I saw Man obsessed with materiality and with all his cunning, I saw him hide what little wisdom he really had in forbidding halls and make it inaccessible to the common and less favored man. I have been through a terrible war and saw its terror and pain uneased by a single word of decency or humanity. . . .

"Blinded with injured optic nerves, and lame with physical injuries to hip and back, at the end of World War II, I faced an almost non-existent future. . . . I yet worked my way back to fitness and strength in less than two years, using only what I knew and could determine about Man and his relationship to the universe. I had no one to help me; what I had to know I had to find out. And it's quite a trick studying when you cannot see.

"I became used to being told it was all impossible, that there was no way, no hope. Yet I came to see again and walk again, and I built an entirely new life. It is a happy life, a busy one and I hope a useful one. My only moments of sadness are those which come when bigoted men tell others all is bad and there is no route anywhere, no hope anywhere, nothing but sadness and sameness and desolation, and that every effort to help others is false. I know it is not true.

"So my own philosophy is that one share what wisdom he has, one should help others to help themselves, and one should keep going despite heavy weather for there is always a calm ahead. . . . If things were a little better known and understood, we would all lead happier lives. And there is a way to know them and there is a way to freedom. The old must give way to the new, falsehood must become exposed by truth, and truth, though fought, always in the end prevails."

BIOGRAPHICAL/CRITICAL SOURCES: Newsweek, September 23, 1974; *Time*, April 5, 1976.

*   *   *

HUBER, Joan 1925-

PERSONAL: Born October 17, 1925, in Bluffton, Ohio; daughter of Lawrence Lester and Hallie (Althaus) Huber; married Anton Rytina, July 13, 1946 (divorced, 1969); married William Form (a professor), February 5, 1971; children: (first marriage) Nancy, Steven. *Education:* Pennsylvania State University, B.A., 1945; Western Michigan University, M.A., 1963; Michigan State University, Ph.D., 1967. *Politics:* Democrat. *Religion:* Episcopalian. *Home:* 612 LaSell, Champaign, Ill. 61820. *Office:* Department of Sociology, University of Illinois at Urbana-Champaign, Urbana, Ill. 61801.

CAREER: University of Notre Dame, South Bend, Ind.,

assistant professor of sociology, 1967-71; University of Illinois at Urbana-Champaign, Urbana, assistant professor of sociology, 1971-73, associate professor of sociology, 1973—. *Member:* American Sociological Association (member of council, 1975-78), Sociologists for Women in Society (president, 1971-73), Society for the Study of Social Problems (member of board of directors, 1974-77), American Association of University Women (past local president; past member of state board of directors), Phi Beta Kappa. *Awards, honors:* National Science Foundation grant, 1978-80.

WRITINGS: (Editor) *Changing Women in a Changing Society*, University of Chicago Press, 1973; (with husband, William Form) *Income and Ideology*, Free Press, 1973; (editor with Paul Chalfant) *The Sociology of American Poverty*, Schenkman, 1974. Member of editorial board of *American Journal of Sociology, Social Forces, Pacific Sociological Review, Sociological Quarterly*, and *Social Science Quarterly*, beginning 1971.

WORK IN PROGRESS: Research on the social bases of sex-role ideologies.

SIDELIGHTS: Joan Huber told *CA:* "During fifteen years as a housewife, I achieved dizzying heights of power in Coshocton, Ohio. My name typically appeared several times a week on the Women's Page of the local paper, amidst the new cookie recipes. But I had always wanted to write, hence I finally entered graduate school in sociology so that I would have something to write about. Actually I preferred philosophy, but I correctly perceived that my age, sex, maritally-induced geographic immobility, and the poor job market for philosophers made that choice impossible. In 1967 I attained a Ph.D. after driving a hundred thousand miles in Michigan winters. By 1969 a divorce—always a consciousness-raising experience for women—and the emergence of the new women's movement drew my interest to an almost completely unresearched area, sex stratification. Because many of my male academic colleagues believe that the women's movement will soon fade away, I am especially interested in the sociodemographic changes which spawned the current movement. Unless we humans obliterate ourselves with atom bombs—should this event occur, the women's movement will disappear along with the energy crisis and flush toilets—women's shift to human status is probably irreversible."

*   *   *

HUEBEL, Harry Russell 1943-

PERSONAL: Born March 13, 1943, in Cape Girardeau, Mo.; son of Harry (a janitor) and M. A. Huebel; married Kathy Myrick, October 5, 1968; children: Anne, David. *Education:* Southeast Missouri State University, B.S., 1964; Washington State University, Ph.D., 1970. *Home:* 734 Santa Elena, Kingsville, Tex. 78363. *Office:* Department of History, Texas A & I University, Kingsville, Tex. 78363.

CAREER: Texas A & I University, Kingsville, assistant professor, 1969-72, associate professor of history, 1972—. *Member:* American Studies Association, Popular Culture Association.

WRITINGS: (Editor) *Things in the Driver's Seat: Readings in Popular Culture*, Rand McNally, 1972; *Jack Kerouac and the Contemporary West*, Boise State University Press, in press. Contributor to popular culture and other scholarly journals. Member of advisory board for *Readings in American History*, Dushkin, 1975-78, and *Rendezvous: Journal of Arts and Letters*.

WORK IN PROGRESS: American autobiography.

HUFANA, A(lejandrino) G.   1926-

PERSONAL: Born October 22, 1926, in San Fernando, La Union, Philippines; son of Alejandro H. and Abdona (Gurtiza) Hufana; married Julita Quiming (a nursing instructor), November 28, 1957; children: Aleta, Leni, Zayda, Sharon. *Education:* University of the Philippines, A.B., 1952, M.A., 1961; further study at University of California, Berkeley, 1957-58; Columbia University, M.S., 1969. *Home:* 54 Mabini St., Area I, University of the Philippines, Diliman, Quezon City, Philippines. *Office:* Library, Cultural Center of the Philippines, Roxas Blvd., Manila, Philippines.

CAREER: University of the Philippines, Quezon City, instructor, 1956-64, assistant professor, 1964-71, associate professor, 1971-75, professor of English and comparative literature, 1975—, principal researcher in Iloko literature, 1972—; Cultural Center of the Philippines, Manila, director of the library, 1970—. Poet, Playwright, and artist. Managing editor, University of the Philippines Press, 1965-66. Technical assistant for Office of the President, 1966-68, research fellow, 1974—. Chairman of Palanca Memorial Awards in Literature, 1966-68, 1970-74; co-ordinator and chairman of Cultural Center of the Philippines Writing Contest, 1971—; chairman of independence celebration subcommittee on literature, Republic Cultural Heritage Awards, 1972-73. *Military service:* Served with North Luzon guerrillas, 1944; Reserve Officers Training Corps (R.O.T.C.), 1948-50.

MEMBER: American Library Association, Philippine Library Association, Philippine Writers Union, P.E.N. International, Fulbright Students Association of the Philippines, GUMIL (Association of Iloko Writers; president, 1972-76). *Awards, honors:* Fulbright fellowship, 1957-58; Rockefeller fellow in creative writing, University of California, Berkeley, 1961-62; Republic Cultural Heritage Award from the Philippine government, 1965, for literature; John D. Rockefeller III fellow in library science, Columbia University, 1968-70.

WRITINGS—Poetry: *13 Kalisud,* Collegian New Review, 1955; *Sickle Season: Poems of a First Decade, 1948-1958,* Kuwan, 1959; *Poro Point: An Anthology of Lives,* University of the Philippines, 1961; *The Wife of Lot and Other New Poems,* Diliman Review, 1971; *Obligations,* University of the Philippines, 1974; *Sieg Heil: An Epic of the Third Reich,* Tala, 1975; *Imelda Romualdez Marcos: A Tonal Epic,* Konsensus, 1975.

Plays: "Man in the Moon," first produced in La Union, 1956, revised version first produced in Manila, 1972; *Curtain Raisers: First Five Plays,* University of the Philippines Social Science Research Council, 1964. Also author of "The Unicorn," and "Salidom-ay."

Other: *Mena Pecson Crisologo and Iloko Drama,* Diliman Review, 1963; (editor) *Aspects of Philippine Literature,* University of the Philippines, 1967; (editor) *A Philippine Cultural Miscellany,* University of the Philippines, Part I, 1968, Part II, 1970; *Notes on Poetry,* Diliman Review, 1973; (editor) *Introduction to Literature,* Alemar Phoenix, 1974; (editor) *Philippine Writings,* Regal, 1977.

Contributor of articles, poems, and plays to periodicals, including *Panorama, Pamana, Beloit Poetry Journal,* and *Literature East and West.* Co-founding editor, *Signatures,* 1955, *Comment,* 1956-67, *University College Journal,* 1961-72, and *Heritage,* 1967-68; editor, *Panorama,* 1959-61, and *Pamana,* 1971—.

WORK IN PROGRESS: Kalisuds I-XXXIX; Oratorios: A Poet's Journey; Filipinas: A National Epic.

SIDELIGHTS: Hufana told *CA:* "Joyce's 'smithy of the soul' does not only apply to his area of writing—his native Ireland—but is increasingly my own realization as I try to comprehend this culturally complex creature called 'Filipino.' This is enough forge—crucible, if you will—for me presently; the alternative is to remain inchoate among all viable peoples, or those who are asserting themselves rightly or wrongly, in the contemporary world."

BIOGRAPHICAL/CRITICAL SOURCES: Collegian New Review, January, 1954; *Manila Times,* November 26, 1961; *The Wayward Horizon,* Community Publishers, 1961; *Philippine Writing 2,* 1963; *Graphic,* September 8, 1966; Leonard Casper, *New Writing From the Philippines,* Syracuse University Press, 1966; *Chronicle,* July 1, 1967.

*   *   *

HUGHES, James W(ilfred)   1934-

PERSONAL: Born June 24, 1934, in Michigan; son of Enoch and Isabelle (a bookkeeper; maiden name, Blommer) Hughes. *Education:* State University of New York College at Buffalo, B.S., 1960; University of New Mexico, M.A., 1962, Ed.D., 1966. *Home:* 2173 Bonnie Brae, Rochester, Mich. 48063.

CAREER: Elementary school teacher in North Colonie, N.Y., 1960-61; U.S. Agency for International Development, Washington, D.C., curriculum consultant for government of Kenya, 1966-68; State University of New York College at Buffalo, associate professor of elementary education, 1968; Oakland University, Rochester, Mich., assistant professor, 1969-71, associate professor, 1971-74, professor of education, 1974—. Member of National Education Association projects in Nepal and Kenya.

WRITINGS—Juvenile "Enchantment of Africa" series; all with John Allan Carpenter; all published by Children's Press: *Enchantment of Uganda,* 1973; ... *Tanzania,* 1973; ... *Rhodesia,* 1974; ... *Chad,* 1976; ... *Ghana,* 1977; ... *the Ivory Coast,* 1977; ... *Libya,* 1977; ... *Cameroon,* 1978; ... *the Congo,* 1978; ... *the Islamic Republic of Mauritania,* 1978; ... *Gabon,* 1978.

"Our World Today" series; all with Harold D. Drummond: *The Eastern Hemisphere,* Allyn & Bacon, in press; *Journey Through the Americas,* Allyn & Bacon, in press; *Journey Through Many Lands,* Allyn & Bacon, in press.

Also author of "Our National Heritage Series," East African Publishing House. Contributor of articles to education journals.

SIDELIGHTS: Hughes told *CA:* "In approaching the books on Africa, I personally was very concerned about trying to (a) present a representative picture and/or feel for a nation, without (b) stereotyping and producing misconceptions. Too often books about Africa treated the content mainly from a Eurocentric base, and I was trying to avoid that. I have been critical of other peoples books, so it was my turn to put my typewriter where my mouth had been. I felt that "omission of content" had been a problem of many books. So I purposely hunted down data on history of a nation that illustrated history of a nation prior to Europeanization of Africa. I hunted down both historical and contemporary figures of note, and tried to maintain or add balance so both male and female figures were presented in books. I tried to highlight "differences" rather than try to shade them into 'similarities,' which to me destroys the unique aspects of anything. I hope to have readers enjoy the differences, appreciate the differences, and become comfortable with differences. However I doubt that all that comes through, but for me as a writer in selecting content, I guess you'd say that I screen my content through these objectives, and thus my selection of content hopefully lends itself more to these goals, than to a haphazard bla bla.

"As co-author of these books I had to adhere to senior author's guidelines, and he had final editorial rights, not me. So I tried to know him better, and tried to 'educate him' about an approach to certain topics when and if I felt it might be 'delicate' or mistreated, if one was not careful. Mr. Carpenter is a very delightful human being and so that task was not a troublesome one. As far as dealing with 'rapid change,' that was not really an aspect one was sure could come through within books as structured as these. However I did try to illustrate the best I could the terrible 'legacy of colonialism' that most nations had to overcome, the enormous problems that a nation must face in shifting from a 'tribal alligence' to one of 'nationalism,' and in shifting economically from a single (or narrow based) crop or mineral raw material exporter economy to one of diversification and more balanced between import-export. So many factors of latter day twentieth century have been forced upon the people of this continent (Africa) and rapid change is an ever present way of life for contemporary Africans. In my simple way I often tried to get at this through the contrasts in generation gap of lives of kids in the third chapter of each book. Of course the chapter dealing with the 'Nation Today' was another one, but often less 'human interest,' one might say."

Commenting on his time in Africa, Hughes continued: "I have travelled in more than half the nations of Africa. I recently spent two years living in Nepal, based in the capital city, Kathmandu. It was a fascinating experience. I never 'planned' on doing international work in education, but my life has taken me through many unusual events and places. I have no regrets, and yet I feel at times like those experiences are but dreams in my 'memory bank.' I feel that at times because so many friends and colleagues have never experienced some of those remote and crazy things I have done, and no one really seems comfortable hearing too many tales (I don't blame them at times). But they have no common basis on which to share, to sympathize, to even empathize. It's all too foreign, too unfamiliar, and can make others uncomfortable.

"I love sharing my thoughts and experiences through writing. The writing is a great outlet. I hope that something of the wonder of it all—the people, places, and events—comes through and helps spark some interest, enthusiasm, comfortableness of strange places for the readers of things I write. I hope kids never become so 'Americanized' that they deny themselves the opportunity to know and appreciate the differences of other cultures, their people and their places."

* * *

HUGHES, John L(ewis) 1938-

PERSONAL: Born July 14, 1938, in Pontypridd, Wales; son of Glyn Lewis (a baker) and Blodwen (Jones) Hughes; married Enid Pamela Anstes, February 1, 1960; children: Mark, Glyn, Karl. *Education:* University of Cardiff, B.Ed., 1974. *Politics:* Socialist. *Religion:* Baptist. *Home and office:* 4 Assessment Centre, Counterpool Rd., Kingswood, Bristol, England. *Agent:* Curtis Brown Ltd., 1 Craven Hill, London W2 3EP, England.

CAREER: Assessment Centre, Bristol, England, deputy headmaster (assessing the needs of highly disturbed, delinquent adolescent boys), 1976—. Has also worked as head of special education, Rumney Comprehensive School, Cardiff, Wales. *Military service:* British Army, Infantry, machinegunner and marksman, 1957-59; served in Cyprus. *Member:* National Association of Schoolmasters.

WRITINGS: Tom Jones Slept Here (novel), Gwasg Gomer, 1971; *Before the Crying Ends* (novel), Braziller, 1977.

Plays: "The Alphabet" (three-act), first produced in Cardiff, Wales, 1974; "Shifts" (three-act), first produced in Cardiff, 1978. Author of "Tom Jones Slept Here" (radio play), British Broadcasting Corp., 1974.

WORK IN PROGRESS: Another Kind of Jericho, a novel about dogs, from the dog's point of view.

SIDELIGHTS: Hughes comments: "I write because something peculiar in my ego id compels me to do so. Writing is a form of acting out—same as an escape valve. Obviously, I loathe and detest writing. I despise it. Having to write a story is the thing I hate most. Writing is my punishment for having committed some despicable crime in some past life—I suspect that I was probably a mass murderer of blind babies thousands of years ago. Nothing is more punitive to me than the process of inventing and describing a story. I claim, however, to be a proper writer, for only proper writers feel this way."

* * *

HUGHES, Monica 1925-

PERSONAL: Born November 3, 1925, in Liverpool, England; daughter of Edward Lindsay (a mathematician) and Phyllis (Fry) Ince; married Glen Hughes (in city government), April 22, 1957; children: Elizabeth, Adrienne, Russell, Thomas. *Education:* Educated privately in England and Scotland. *Home:* 13816 110-A Ave., Edmonton, Alberta, Canada T5M 2M9.

CAREER: Dress designer in London, England, 1948-49, and Bulawayo, Rhodesia, 1950; bank clerk in Umtali, Rhodesia, 1951; National Research Council, Ottawa, Ontario, laboratory technician, 1952-57; full-time writer, 1975—. *Military service:* Women's Royal Naval Service, 1943-46. *Member:* Alberta Writers Federation, Hand Weavers, Spinners and Dyers of Alberta, Edmonton Weavers Guild.

WRITINGS—For children: Gold-Fever Trail, John LeBel, 1974; *Crisis on Conshelf Ten,* Copp, 1975, Atheneum, 1977; *Earthdark,* Hamish Hamilton, 1977; *The Tomorrow City,* Hamish Hamilton, 1978; *The Ghost Dance Caper,* Hamish Hamilton, 1978.

Work represented in *Magook,* McClelland & Stewart, 1977. Formerly author of craft column, "The Craft Corner," in *Edmonton Sunday Sun.*

WORK IN PROGRESS: Science fiction for teenagers.

SIDELIGHTS: Monica Hughes writes: "Though born in England, I spent my next six years in Egypt. Then back to London, where I was exposed to all the great museums and art galleries. Then to Edinburgh, where I attended private school and read voraciously, especially science fiction and books of high adventure. Then to boarding school, first in the west of Scotland, and then overlooking the Yorkshire moors—cold and lonely.

"I studied dress designing after the war, but wandering seemed to be in my blood, and I went to Rhodesia, and later to Canada. I worked mostly at testing materials and aircraft, and during (and after) coffeebreaks indulged in much speculation about life on Mars and the pros and cons of flying saucers and ESP. It was great fun, and instead of crossing Canada as I had planned, and then going on to Australia, I stayed on and on.

"I still wandered, working in Cornwall, Ontario, on the St. Lawrence Seaway and Power Project, then living in London, Ontario, and Toronto. During these years of moving and small babies I wrote sporadically.

"Finally, my husband was transferred to the Prairies, and here in Edmonton all my creative instincts have suddenly jelled. I embroidered, designing wall-hangings that were actually published, and with the proceeds I bought a tapestry loom, on which I have been working for seven years. At about the same time, I read a book on writing for children, discarded all my uncompleted adult novels, and turned to juvenile writing.

"Science fiction is my first love. I cannot write 'ethnic' writing, not about my pioneer roots. I feel like a wanderer, an observer, and I love to speculate—'what if.' I like to explore the feelings, the needs and ideals of young people in the world of tomorrow, hopefully bringing a universality to the specific.

"I care very much about our planet and what we are doing to it, and about the people of the Third World and the underprivileged at home, and what we are doing to them."

*   *   *

HULL, David L(ee) 1935-

PERSONAL: Born June 15, 1935, in Hancock County, Ill.; son of James Robert (a salesman) and Alberta (Bouseman) Hull. *Education:* Illinois Wesleyan University, A.B., 1960; Indiana University, Ph.D., 1964. *Residence:* Chicago, Ill. *Office:* Department of Philosophy, University of Wisconsin, Milwaukee, Wis. 53201.

CAREER: University of Wisconsin, Milwaukee, assistant professor, 1964-66, associate professor, 1966-71, professor of philosophy, 1971—. Visiting assistant professor of philosophy at Indiana University, 1966; visiting associate professor at University of Chicago, 1972. *Member:* Society of Systematic Zoology (member of council), Philosophy of Science Association, American Philosophical Association.

WRITINGS: Darwin and His Critics, Harvard University Press, 1973; *Philosophy of Biological Science,* Prentice-Hall, 1974. Member of editorial board of *Systematic Zoology* and *Philosophy of Science.*

WORK IN PROGRESS: Research on the social structure of research communities.

*   *   *

HULME, Hilda Mary 1914-

PERSONAL: Born June 13, 1914, in Stoke on Trent, England; daughter of Samuel and Mary Hulme; married Aslam Mohamed. *Education:* University of London, B.A. (honors), 1935, M.A., 1937, Ph.D., 1947. *Home:* 97 Swains Lane, Highgate, London N6 6PJ, England.

CAREER: University of London, London, England, lecturer, 1944-59, senior lecturer, 1959-72, reader in English, 1972-76. Writer, 1951—.

WRITINGS: (Editor) William Shakespeare, *Julius Caesar,* Longmans, Green, 1959; (editor) Shakespeare, *Richard II,* Longmans, Green, 1961; *Explorations in Shakespeare's Language: Some Problems of Lexical Meaning in the Dramatic Text,* Longmans, Green, 1962, Barnes & Noble, 1963; (editor) Shakespeare, *Henry V,* Longmans, Green, 1963; *Yours That Read Him: An Introduction to Shakespeare's Language,* Ginn, 1972.

WORK IN PROGRESS: Continuing research on Shakespeare's language.

*   *   *

HUMPHREY, Henry (III) 1930-

PERSONAL: Born April 26, 1930, in Mineola, N.Y.; son of Henry, Jr. (an editor) and Cathleen (Murphy) Humphrey; married Deirdre O'Meara (a writer), July 20, 1977; children: Nora Alexandra, Maud Gonne, Daphne O'Meara, Eloise Arnold, Deirdre Mary. *Education:* Attended New York University, 1949-51. *Home:* 166 Newtown Turnpike, Weston, Conn. 06883. *Agent:* Anita Diamant, Writer's Workshop, Inc., 51 East 42nd St., New York, N.Y. 10017; and Betty Marks, 51 East 42nd St., New York, N.Y. 10017.

CAREER: Channel 5-Television, New York City, film director, 1952-57; Cunningham & Walsh (advertising agency), New York City, account executive, 1957-62; Doherty, Clifford, Shenfield & Steers (advertising agency), New York City, account executive, 1962-63; Sullivan, Stauffer, Colwall & Bayles (advertising agency), New York City, account executive, 1963-65; free-lance photographer and writer for children, 1965—.

WRITINGS—For children; all with own photographs: *What Is It For?,* Simon & Schuster, 1969; *What's Inside,* Simon & Schuster, 1972; *Sights and Sounds of Flying,* Little, Brown, 1972; *Farm,* Doubleday, 1978.

WORK IN PROGRESS: A children's book, *When Is Now?,* with wife Diedre Humphrey, publication by Doubleday expected in 1980.

SIDELIGHTS: Humphrey writes: "I don't know if it's ever inevitable that someone becomes an author, but I suppose my hide would have to have been even thicker than it is for me to have avoided it. My father is an editor; my sister is a poet and professor of creative writing; my wife is an author, and so is her father. My friends include Nils Bodecker and Richard and Patsy Scarry who, as everybody knows, are enormously successful in writing and illustrating books for children.

"But, strangely enough, I didn't consciously try to become an author. I'm a photographer specializing in a photojournalistic approach to pictures for corporate brochures and annual reports. I got an idea for a photographic children's book *What Is It For?* which would show children the end use of some very familiar objects found in cities and towns everywhere (manhole cover, not-for-deposit mailbox, standpipe connector, etc.). I thought it would be fine if a couple of thousand were published, then I could put one under my arm and show corporate prospects what a clever photographer I am. It was picked by the *New York Times* as one of the ten best illustrated children's books of the year, and Simon & Schuster went back on press with the book almost immediately. 'Well, this is fun!' I thought to myself, and I've been hopelessly hooked on children's books ever since.

"I can't imagine a more important audience to reach than young people. They can be so enthusiastic, but so easily turned off by boredom. One of the best parts of doing books is receiving an occasional letter from a reader to whom the book meant something.

"Where do ideas come from? I'm trained to see things. Some of them I don't understand and my curiosity is piqued. What I want more than anything is that my books will excite curiosity in my readers."

HUMPHREY, William 1924-

PERSONAL: Born June 18, 1924, in Clarksville, Tex. *Education:* Attended Southern Methodist University and University of Texas. *Residence:* Lexington, Va. *Address:* c/o Alfred A. Knopf, Inc., 201 East 50th St., New York, N.Y. 10022.

CAREER: Writer. *Awards, honors:* National Institute of Arts and Letters grant, 1962.

WRITINGS: The Last Husband and Other Stories, Morrow, 1953; *Home From the Hill* (novel), Knopf, 1958; *The Ordways* (novel), Knopf, 1965; *A Time and a Place: Stories,* Knopf, 1968; *The Spawning Run: A Fable,* Knopf, 1970; *Proud Flesh* (novel), Knopf, 1973; *Ah, Wilderness: The Frontier in American Literature,* Texas Western Press, 1977; *Farther Off From Heaven* (memoir), Knopf, 1977. Contributor of short stories to *Esquire* and *Saturday Evening Post.*

SIDELIGHTS: Humphrey's first book, *The Last Husband and Other Stories,* was an impressive first book. "Mr. Humphrey successfully brings off the usually awkward match of satire with sympathy," wrote D. M. Culhane about a few of the stories. And Pearl Kazin of *New York Times* noted that Humphrey "has the kind of skilled and persuasive originality which only the most respected practitioners of the short-story art can claim."

Home From the Hill, his first novel, brought Humphrey widespread critical attention. Jean Holzhauer wrote that "Humphrey's virtues are a sense of the masculine character, of family estrangements and family love, and the ability to dramatically develop these in a recognizable social framework." Reviewing the novel in *Chicago Tribune,* Fanny Butcher deemed Humphrey "a major American novelist in the making." Butcher also noted that "he has in his writing qualities which every novelist strives for."

The Ordways also received critical praise. A *Time* review summed it up lavishly: "Good writings is rare enough. Storytelling is an even rarer skill. A genuinely comic vision is beyond price. *The Ordways* has all three."

Humphrey's favorite locale is the Southwest, especially East Texas. As in his first two novels, *A Time and a Place* takes place in this area where Humphrey spent his childhood. Commenting on the characters that populate Humphrey's second collection of stories, Janice Elliott wrote that Humphrey "writes beautifully . . . of oil prospectors, farmers, Indians, children, in a deceptive, lolloping style that is in fact precise, and, for all its good humour, carries a sombre message." And Granville Hicks referred to Humphrey's characters as "rough people in a rough age, but there was drama in their lives, and Humphrey knows how to reveal it to us."

Many of Humphrey's writings are compared to those of William Faulkner. In reviewing *Home From the Hill,* William Hogan wrote: "*Home From the Hill* is a kind of lucid Faulkner in this serious novel which observes the mental and physical crack-up of an East Texas small-town. It is a kind of healthy *As I Lay Dying* . . . in which a young author's cosmos is less awry than Faulkner's, and his syntax is far more agreeable." Walter Allen commented on the similarity to Faulkner in *New Statesman.* "What Mr. Humphrey gives us," Allen wrote, "is a piece of Faulkner in which the obscurities have been clarified and the crooked made straight." And in a review of *A Time and A Place,* Granville Hicks commented, "Humphrey is a storyteller in the tradition of Mark Twain and William Faulkner." But Hicks also distinguished between Faulkner and Humphrey. "He [Humphrey] forgives more, grieves less torturedly, converts more to folklore. . . ." Perhaps Elizabeth Janeway established the relation between Faulkner and Humphrey when she wrote of Humphrey: "He's too good a writer to copy Faulkner, any more than he's copying Chekhov or Mark Twain, both of whom are recalled by various pages in *The Ordways.* What Humphrey does is accept the vision that Faulkner and others have bequeathed to their heirs, and build on it."

Humphrey abandoned the "Faulknerian" style in *The Spawning Run.* The story of the salmon's journey to its spawning place was also a critical success for Humphrey. Christopher Lehmann-Haupt wrote, "What Humphrey has done in his chronicle of a fishing trip to Wales is to artfully compare the life cycle of the salmon with that of elderly British fishermen."

In his most recent book, *Farther Off From Heaven,* Humphrey returned to Texas for the locale. An autobiographical story of his years in Texas before the death of his father, *Farther Off From Heaven* garnered more praise for Humphrey. Thomas Lask called attention to Humphrey's "prose that is precise and exact in detail, yet one that imparts to the events a feeling of distance, of happenings far away. . . ." And *Saturday Review*'s Peter Shaw praised Humphrey's "incomparable portrait of small-farm and small-town America, both as they looked on the outside and felt on the inside."

BIOGRAPHICAL/CRITICAL SOURCES: New York Times, April 12, 1953, November 5, 1970, June 15, 1977; *Commonweal,* May 8, 1953, February 28, 1958; *Chicago Tribune,* January 12, 1958; *San Francisco Chronicle,* January 30, 1958; *New Statesman,* April 12, 1958, February 28, 1969; *New York Times Book Review,* January 31, 1965, November 3, 1968, May 22, 1977; *Time,* February 5, 1965; *Book World,* November 3, 1968; *Saturday Review,* November 9, 1968, May 28, 1977; *New Leader,* December 30, 1968; *Observer Review,* November 20, 1970.*

* * *

HUMPHREYS, (Travers) Christmas 1901-

PERSONAL: Born February 15, 1901, in London, England; married Aileen Faulkner, December 17, 1927 (died, 1975). *Education:* Trinity Hall, Cambridge, M.A. and LL.B., 1923. *Politics:* None. *Religion:* Buddhist. *Home:* 58 Marlborough Place, London N.W.8, England.

CAREER: Author and lawyer. Called to the Bar in England, 1924. Worked in British judicial system as junior council to treasury for certain appeals, 1932, junior prosecution council in Central Criminal Court, 1934, recorder of Deal, 1942-56, senior prosecution council to the Crown in Central Criminal Court, 1950-59, bencher, 1955, recorder of Guildford, 1956-68, and judge in Central Criminal Court, 1968-76. *Member:* Buddhist Society (formerly Buddhist Lodge; founder and president), Shakespearean Society (vice-president).

WRITINGS: The Great Pearl Robbery of 1913, Heinemann, 1929; *Seven Murderers,* Heinemann, 1931; *The Menace in Our Midst,* Chapman & Hall, 1933; *The Development of Buddhism in England,* Buddhist Lodge, 1937; *Studies in the Middle Way,* C. W. Daniel, 1940, Macmillan, 1959; *Poems of Peace and War,* Favil Press, 1941; *Seagulls, and Other Poems,* Favil Press, 1942; *Karma and Rebirth,* J. Murray, 1943; *Shadows and Other Poems,* Favil Press, 1945; *Via Tokyo,* Hutchinson, 1948; *Zen Buddhism,* Heinemann, 1949, Macmillan, 1957; *Buddhism,* Penguin, 1951, revised edition, Barnes & Noble, 1962; (editor) *A Buddhist Student's Manual*, Buddhist Society, 1956; *Walk On*, Buddhist Society, 1956; *Concentration and Meditation: A Manual of Mind Development*, J. M. Watkins, 1959.

The Way of Action, Macmillan, 1960; (editor) *The Wisdom of Buddhism*, Random House, 1960; *Zen Comes West*, Macmillan, 1960; *A Popular Dictionary of Buddhism*, Arco, 1962, Citadel, 1963; (editor) *The Mahatma Letters to A. P. Sinnett From the Mahatmas M. & K.H.*, 3rd edition and revised, Theosophical Publishing House, 1962; *Zen: A Way of Life*, English Universities Press, 1962, Emerson, 1965; *Basic Buddhism*, Buddhist Society, 1965; (editor) Helene Petrovna Blavatsky, *An Abridgement of The Secret Doctrine*, Theosophical Publishing House, 1966; *The Field of Theosophy*, Theosophical Publishing House, 1966; (editor) *The Sutra of Hui-neng*, 4th edition and revised, Theosophical Publishing House, 1966, new edition, Hyperion Press, 1973; *Sixty Years of Buddhism in England (1907-1967): A History and a Survey*, Buddhist Society, 1968; *An Invitation to the Buddhist Way of Life for Western Readers*, Schoken, 1969, published in England as *The Buddhist Way of Life*, Allen & Unwin, 1969; (editor) Suzuki, *The Field of Zen: Contributions to The Middle Way*, Buddhist Society, 1969.

(Editor) *The Wisdom of Buddhism*, Harper, 1970; *Buddhist Poems: A Selection, 1920-70*, Allen & Unwin, 1971; *A Western Approach to Zen*, Allen & Unwin, 1972; (editor) *Some Sayings of the Buddha, According to the Pali Canon*, Oxford University Press, 1973; *Exploring Buddhism*, Theosophical Publishing House, 1974; *The Search Within*, Sheldon Press, 1977; *Both Sides of the Circle* (memoirs), Allen & Unwin, 1978.

*   *   *

HUNGERFORD, Mary Jane 1913-

PERSONAL: Born August 30, 1913, in Chicago, Ill.; daughter of Ethelbert Arthur (in public relations) and Mary Jane (Walker) Hungerford; married Charles H. Lawrance (an environmental engineer), November 22, 1947; children: Kenneth Arthur, Lois Ruth, Robert Jefferson. *Education:* Attended Boston University, 1930-32; Columbia University, M.A., 1937, Ph.D., 1947. *Politics:* Liberal. *Religion:* Unitarian-Universalist. *Home:* 1340 Kenwood Rd., Santa Barbara, Calif. 93109. *Office:* 1840 South Elena, Suite 205, Redondo Beach, Calif. 90277; and 800 Garden St., Suite 1, Santa Barbara, Calif. 93101.

CAREER: Professional dancer with Virginia Hall Johnson group, 1936-38, and Lester Horton Dance group, 1938-40; University of Washington, Seattle, instructor in hygiene, 1945-46; Montclair State Teachers College, Upper Montclair, N.J., member of faculty, 1946-47; New Haven State Teachers College, New Haven, Conn., lecturer in family relations and marriage and family counselor, 1948-53; American Institute of Family Relations, South Bay branch, Redondo Beach, Calif., director of education department, 1954—; East Los Angeles Junior College, Los Angeles, Calif., instructor in marriage and the family, 1968—. Physical education teacher, specializing in dance, at University of Oregon at Columbia, University of Southern California, Louisiana State University, Mary Washington College, and University of Virginia, 1933-53. Public lecturer; guest on television and radio programs.

MEMBER: International College of Applied Nutrition (first vice-president), International Childbirth Education Association (founder; life member; past president), International Platform Association, American Association of Marriage

and Family Counselors, National Council on Family Relations (regional branch chairman), Society for the Scientific Study of Sex, American Association of Sex Educators and Counselors, American League of Women Voters, California Association of Marriage and Family Counselors, Southern California Association of Marriage and Family Counselors, Childbirth Education Association of Los Angeles (founder; first president).

WRITINGS: Creative Tap Dancing, Prentice-Hall, 1938; *Childbirth Education*, C. C Thomas, 1972. Also author of *Some Fundamentals of Breast-Feeding, Summary of Labor and Birth, Some Basic Principles Concerning Sex Education for Your Children*, and *Dating Do's and Don'ts: For Men and Women*, all published by American Institute of Family Relations, and of *Happiness Is Good Human Relations*, 1977. Contributor to professional journals. Editor of *Preparing for Parenthood* (newsletter), 1958-74.

WORK IN PROGRESS: Research on hypoglycemia and the glucose tolerance test.

SIDELIGHTS: Mary Hungerford comments: "I am very active in the field of nutrition, especially as it relates to mental health. I lecture and write on the subject for periodicals."

AVOCATIONAL INTERESTS: Sailing, tennis, gardening, bicycling, reading, classical music.

*   *   *

HUNT, E. K. 1937-

PERSONAL: Born November 13, 1937, in Blanding, Utah; son of Emery R. and Minerva (Kartchner) Hunt; divorced; children: Jeffrey, Andrew. *Education:* University of Utah, B.S., 1961, Ph.D., 1966. *Politics:* Socialist. *Religion:* Unitarian-Universalist. *Residence:* Riverside, Calif. *Office:* Department of Economics, University of California, Riverside, Calif. 92506.

CAREER: University of California, Riverside, associate professor of economics, 1969—.

WRITINGS: (With Jesse G. Schwartz) *A Critique of Economic Theory*, Penguin, 1972; (with Howard J. Sherman) *Economics: An Introduction to Traditional and Radical Approaches*, Harper, 1972, 3rd edition, 1978; *Property and Prophets*, Harper, 1972; *Social Harmony and Class Conflict: A History of Economic Doctrines*, Wadsworth, in press.

*   *   *

HUNTER, Edward 1902-1978

July 2, 1902—June 24, 1978; American journalist and author best known for his books on brainwashing, a term he reportedly originated. Hunter edited and published *TACTICS*, a journal on psychological warfare, and served as a specialist in psychological warfare during World War II. Among his writings are *Brain-Washing in Red China* and *Brainwashing: From Pavlov to Powers*. He died in Arlington, Va. Obituaries and other sources: *The Author's and Writer's Who's Who*, 6th edition, Burke's Peerage, 1971; *The Writers Directory, 1976-78*, St. Martin's, 1976; *Who's Who in America*, 40th edition, Marquis, 1977; *Washington Post*, June 26, 1978. (See index for *CA* sketch)

*   *   *

HUNTER, William B(ridges), Jr. 1915-

PERSONAL: Born June 7, 1915, in Louisville, Ky.; son of William B. (a banker) and Florence (Porter) Hunter; married

Margaret Jackson, August 31, 1940; children: William, James, Sarah (Mrs. R. Thompson Wright), Penelope. *Education:* Princeton University, A.B., 1937; Vanderbilt University, M.A., 1939, Ph.D., 1946. *Politics:* Democrat. *Religion:* Presbyterian. *Home:* 9031 Kapri Lane, Houston, Tex. 77025. *Office:* Department of English, University of Houston, Houston, Tex. 77004.

CAREER: Wofford College, Spartanburg, S.C., professor of English and chairman of department, 1946-57; Baylor University, Waco, Tex., professor of English, 1957-59; University of Idaho, Moscow, professor of English and head of humanities, 1959-65; Macalester College, St. Paul, Minn., chairman of English, 1965-68; University of New Hampshire, Durham, professor of English, 1968-74; University of Houston, Houston, Tex., professor of English, 1974—. *Member:* Modern Language Association of America, Milton Society of America (president), South Central Modern Language Association.

WRITINGS: The Complete Poetry of Ben Jonson, Doubleday, 1963; *Bright Essence* (studies in Milton), University of Utah Press, 1971; *The English Spenserians,* University of Utah Press, 1977. General editor of *A Milton Encyclopedia,* Bucknell University Press, 1977—. Contributor to academic journals.

WORK IN PROGRESS: A Milton Encyclopedia, eight volumes; an edition of Milton's *Treatise on Civil Power* and *Considerations Touching Means to Remove Hirelings Out of the Church,* for Yale University Press.

SIDELIGHTS: Hunter told *CA:* "The *Milton Encyclopedia* has been a tremendous time consumer for years, involving editing thousands of pages from about one hundred fifty world-wide contributors and reading proofs interminably. One does not learn much new from editing an encyclopedia, but he comes to some sense of perspective on what is already known."

AVOCATIONAL INTERESTS: Music, travel.

* * *

HUTTON, Ginger
    See HUTTON, Virginia Carol

* * *

HUTTON, James 1902-

PERSONAL: Born November 30, 1902, in Scotland; son of John and Elizabeth (Arthur) Hutton. *Education:* Cornell University, B.A., 1924, M.A., 1925, Ph.D., 1927. *Home:* 123 Roberts Pl., Ithaca, N.Y. 14850. *Office:* Department of Classics, Cornell University, Goldwin Smith Hall, Ithaca, N.Y. 14853.

CAREER: Columbia University, New York City, instructor in Greek and Latin, 1926-27; Cornell University, New York City, instructor, 1927-29, assistant professor, 1929-38, professor, 1938-61, Kappa Alpha Professor of Classics, 1961-68, professor emeritus, 1968—, chairman of department, 1946-52, member of department of comparative literature, 1927-43. *Member:* Modern Language Association of America, American Philological Association, Phi Beta Kappa, Phi Kappa Phi. *Awards, honors:* Guggenheim fellow, 1958-59.

WRITINGS: The Greek Anthology in Italy, Cornell University Press, 1935; *The Greek Anthology in France and in Latin Writers of the Netherlands,* Cornell University Press, 1946, revised edition, Johnson Reprint, 1967. Co-editor of "Cornell Studies in Classical Philology." Contributor of articles and reviews to scholarly periodicals.

WORK IN PROGRESS: Peace Themes in Renaissance Poetry; translating and writing introduction and notes for *Aristotle's Poetics.*

* * *

HUTTON, Virginia Carol 1940-
    (Ginger Hutton)

PERSONAL: Born August 30, 1940, in Phoenix, Ariz.; daughter of Don M. (a salesman) and Ellen (Martins) Wiley; divorced; children: Kimberly Rose, Richard Dean. *Education:* Attended Phoenix College and Arizona State University. *Residence:* Phoenix, Ariz. *Office: Arizona Republic,* 120 East Van Buren, Phoenix, Ariz. 85004.

CAREER/WRITINGS: United Press International, New York, N.Y., radio wire writer in Phoenix, Ariz., 1959; *Glendale News,* Glendale, Ariz., reporter and feature writer, 1961; *Phoenix Gazette,* Phoenix, reporter and feature writer, 1962-63, 1964-65; *Arizona Republic,* Phoenix, writer, 1969—, writer of "At the Capitol Column," 1970—, assistant women's editor, 1973-77, writer of "Reflections" column, 1976—, women's editor, 1977—. Contributor to local and national publications, sometimes under name Ginger Hutton. *Member:* Society of Professional Journalists (secretary, 1973-74; vice-president, 1974-75; president, 1975-76), Arizona Press Club. *Awards, honors:* National Catherine L. O'Brien honorable mention, 1970, for story on divorcees' problems, and 1977, for column comparing minor everyday problems to those of people fighting loneliness or handicaps.

SIDELIGHTS: Hutton comments: "In 1970 I innovated a women's page column 'At the Capitol Column' dealing with 'human interest' legislation. In 1976 I began a personal column 'Reflections' which reflects both seriously and humorously on everything from politics to childrearing."

* * *

HUXLEY, Elspeth Josceline 1907-

PERSONAL: Born July 23, 1907, in London, England; daughter of Major Josceline and Eleanor Lillian (Grosvenor) Grant; married Gervas Huxley (a tea commissioner), 1931 (died, 1971); children: Charles. *Education:* Reading University, diploma, 1927; attended Cornell University, 1927-28. *Home:* Green End Oaksey near Malmesbury, Wiltshire, England.

CAREER: Author and broadcaster. Assistant press officer, Empire Marketing Board, London, England, 1929-32; member of general advisory council, British Broadcasting Corp. (BBC), 1952-59. Member, Monckton Advisory Commission on Central Africa, 1959. Justice of the peace for Wiltshire, 1946-77.

WRITINGS—Novels: Murder at Government House, Harper, 1937; *Murder on Safari,* Harper, 1938; *Red Strangers,* Harper, 1939; *Death of an Aryan,* Methuen, 1939, published as *The African Poison Murders,* Harper, 1940; *The Walled City,* Lippincott, 1948; *I Don't Mind if I Do,* Chatto & Windus, 1950; *A Thing to Love,* Chatto & Windus, 1954; *The Red Rock Wilderness,* Morrow, 1957; *The Merry Hippo,* Chatto & Windus, 1963, published as *The Incident at the Merry Hippo,* Morrow, 1964; *A Man from Nowhere,* Chatto & Windus, 1964, Morrow, 1965.

Nonfiction: *White Man's Country: Lord Delamere and the Making of Kenya,* Macmillan, 1935, Praeger, 1967; *Atlantic Ordeal: The Story of Mary Cornish,* Chatto & Windus, 1941, Harper, 1942; (with Margery Perham) *Race and Politics in Kenya,* Faber, 1944, Greenwood, 1975; *Settlers of*

Kenya, Longmans, Green, 1948, Greenwood, 1975; *The Sorcerer's Apprentice: A Journey Through East Africa,* Chatto & Windus, 1948, Greenwood, 1975; *Four Guineas,* Chatto & Windus, 1954, reprinted, Greenwood, 1974; *No Easy Way,* [Nairobi], 1957; *A New Earth,* Morrow, 1960, Greenwood, 1973; *Suki,* Morrow, 1964; *Forks and Hope,* Chatto & Windus, 1964, published as *With Forks and Hope,* Morrow, 1964; *Back Street New Worlds: A Look at Immigrants in Britain,* Chatto & Windus, 1964, Morrow, 1965; *Brave New Victuals: An Inquiry into Modern Food Production,* Chatto & Windus, 1965; *Their Shining El Dorado: A Journey Through Australia,* Morrow, 1967; *The Challenge of Africa,* Aldus, 1971; (compiler) *The Kingsleys: A Biographical Anthology,* Allen & Unwin, 1973; *Livingstone and His African Journeys,* Saturday Review Press, 1974; *Florence Nightingale,* Putnam, 1975; *Gallipot Eyes,* Weidenfeld & Nicolson, 1976; *Scott of the Antarctic,* Weidenfeld & Nicolson, 1977, Atheneum, 1978.

Autobiography: *The Flame Trees of Thika,* Morrow, 1959; *The Mottled Lizard,* Chatto & Windus, 1962, published as *On the Edge of the Rift,* Morrow, 1962; *Love Among the Daughters: Memories of the Twenties in England and America,* Morrow, 1968.

SIDELIGHTS: Travel has always been a major part of Elspeth Huxley's life. At the age of five she moved with her family to Kenya, where her father had started a coffee plantation about forty miles from Nairobi. She spent most of her childhood and adolescence in Africa, although she returned to England during World War I to attend school. After receiving her degree from Reading University in 1927, she went to the United States for a year. After her marriage, she continued traveling with her husband, whose work in tea sales promotion took them all over the globe. In 1967 they bought a farm in Wiltshire, England, and settled down to produce milk, pigs, and roses.

Much of Huxley's writing is based on her experiences in the various places she has been. Her first book, *White Man's Country,* is a biography of Lord Delamere and a history of the British colonization of Kenya. But while the objectivity of her historical account has been questioned, the book has been praised as "the most comprehensive account of the pioneer activities in farming and politics of European colonization" in East Africa.

For a time Huxley wrote novels and detective stories, and even these are generally set in Africa. But her most widely appreciated work is her autobiography. The first two volumes, *The Flame Trees of Thika* and *On the Edge of the Rift,* which concerned her childhood in Kenya, were best sellers. With the third volume, *Love Among the Daughters,* she abandoned Africa as a subject and focused her skills on recapturing the spirit of her student days both at Reading in England and Cornell in the United States. Anne Freemantle reviewed *Love Among the Daughters* in the *New York Times Book Review:* "With the clarity of thought of a brilliant and witty mind scientifically trained, Elspeth Huxley expresses herself in scalpel-precise language." And Peggy Shonbrun, in *Book World,* likened the volume to "the accounts of the several Mitfords" about their youth in England, and concluded that Mrs. Huxley's "eye for the patterns of English country manners and morals is so sharp and her writing so pleasant that a more deserved comparison might be with Jane Austen."

BIOGRAPHICAL/CRITICAL SOURCES: Nature, August 3, 1935; *Times Literary Supplement,* December 2, 1965, May 25, 1967; *Observer,* May 21, 1967, September 29, 1969; *Punch,* July 19, 1967, October 9, 1968; *Atlantic,* July, 1967; *New York Times Book Review,* September 22, 1968; *Book World,* November 3, 1968.*

* * *

HYER, James Edgar   1923-

PERSONAL: Born May 5, 1923, in Honolulu, Hawaii; son of James Edgar III and Audrey N. (Bryant) Hyer; married Mildred Danielson (a teacher and writer), August 7, 1953; children: James Edgar V, Melanie Jean. *Education:* Oregon College of Education, B.S., 1955; University of Oregon, M.Ed., 1958; Oregon State University, M.S., 1966. *Religion:* Lutheran. *Home:* 3791 Hawthorne, Eugene, Ore. 97402. *Office:* Bethel Public Schools, 4640 Barger, Eugene, Ore. 97402.

CAREER: Employed by police departments, 1948-52; elementary school teacher in Culp Creek, Ore., 1953-56, and Eugene, Ore., 1956-59; junior high school teacher in Eugene, Ore., 1959-62; Science Research Associates, Chicago, Ill., associate science editor, assistant department head of science editorial staff, and director of development for elementary science project, 1962-63; Bethel Public Schools, Eugene, Ore., science teacher at Cascade Junior High School, 1963—. Instructor at University of Puget Sound, summers, 1967-75, and University of Oregon, summer, 1976. Field editor for Science Research Associates, 1963-64; science education consultant. *Military service:* U.S. Navy, Flying Boat Squadrons, 1941-47.

MEMBER: Oregon Education Association, Oregon Classroom Teachers Association (vice-president, 1960-61; president, 1961-62), Bethel Education Association (past vice-president and president). *Awards, honors:* Science writing award from National Education Association and Oregon Education Association, 1966; National Science Foundation scholarships, 1960, 1961, 1963, 1964.

WRITINGS: (With wife, Mildred Hyer) *Science Fun* (juvenile), McKay, 1973. Contributor of more than one hundred-fifty articles to education journals, children's magazines, and newspapers.

WORK IN PROGRESS: Spiders Galore, nonfiction for children; a teaching system for junior high school science programs.

SIDELIGHTS: Hyer told *CA:* "I feel strongly about 'hands-on' activity for children. In my opinion, children develop a wholesome, lasting interest in what they study, and a better understanding of most concepts when involved with their hands as well as their minds. Since the subject of science lends itself well to the kind of teaching that involves 'hands-on' activity, I like to teach science. My early teaching was in the elementary school, but I moved into secondary science because this was an area where I could employ many 'hands-on' activities in my teaching and devote full time to the development of a special program of this type.

"At this time, the teaching I do with children, involves material I have written to go with a text which provides for individualization; more capable students are permitted to move faster than others. In addition, provisions are made for constant feedback. Since it involves the completion of sequential tasks, I refer to this type of program as 'performance task teaching.' Fortunately, nearly any good text can be employed in this type of teaching, when the teacher prepares the accompanying materials. I do not lecture because I feel that most children do not learn well from lectures, and this type of teaching can cause bright students to develop confidence in learning that has limited use. Encouraging the ability of capable children to develop skills which permit them to experiment and/or innovate, as is provided for with lab work (hands-on activity) in an individualized program helps these people learn how to proceed on their own and (hopefully) prepare them for discovering things in the future that are not yet known.

''Most of all, I try to be enthusiastic and encourage my students to be the same.''

*   *   *

HYNDS, Frances Jane   1929-

PERSONAL: Born October 27, 1929, in Martin, Tenn.; daughter of Loyd Orion (a clergyman) and Hunter Elizabeth (Goad) Hynds. *Education:* McMurry College, B.S., 1951; University of Southern California, M.A., 1960; further study at University of California, Los Angeles, 1961. *Home:* 1033 North Carol Dr., #107, Los Angeles, Calif. 90069. *Office:* Fran Hynds, 310 North San Vicente Blvd., Suite 325, Los Angeles, Calif. 90048.

CAREER: McMurry College, Abilene, Tex., director of publicity, 1951-53; Oklahoma City University, Oklahoma City, Okla., director of public relations, 1953-55; Knickerbocker Hotel, Hollywood, Calif., director of promotion, 1955-56; Joe Leighton & Associates, Inc., Hollywood, account executive, 1956-65; Fran Hynds Public Relations, Los Angeles, Calif., owner, 1965-75; Fran Hynds, Los Angeles, Calif., communications consultant, 1975—. Senior lecturer at University of Southern California, 1977. Member of National Public Relations Council for Human Services, 1968-73; organizer and coordinator of California Equal Rights Amendment Coalition, 1972; member of Los Angeles Human Relations Commission and Public Relations Commission, 1968, and Status of Women Committee, 1975.

MEMBER: Public Relations Society of America (member of board of directors, 1975-77), Women in Communications (past local president, 1969-70; member of board of directors, 1969-72), Los Angeles Publicity Club (member of board of directors, 1960-63), Los Angeles Advertising Women, Theta Sigma Phi (local president, 1969-70). *Awards, honors:* Silver Radio Award from Southern California Broadcasters, 1968; creative partnership award from Los Angeles Young Women's Christian Association, 1970; first place award from Los Angeles Advertising Women, 1971; commendation from California Museum of Science and Industry, 1971.

WRITINGS: (With Norma Bowles and Joan Maxwell) *Psi Search: Psychic Phenomena,* Harper, 1978.

SIDELIGHTS: Fran Hynds writes: ''I have come to realize from personal experience the tremendous strength that is the uniqueness of each individual being. With that realization, I have developed an interest and a commitment in assisting human beings to explore and develop their particular uniqueness. Because of an innate ability to synthesize information and to envision potential, I usually find my thinking process is different from other creative people. The longer I live, the more comfortable this inherently uncomfortable position becomes to me. I have become aware that it is now a matter of personal integrity to express this part of myself, and while I am not always popular, I usually make a contribution that no one else makes. I believe the world would function more effectively if, as a society, we would truly cultivate and nurture individual uniqueness. This is my life goal.''

I

IGLAUER, Edith

PERSONAL: Born in Cleveland, Ohio; daughter of Jay and Bertha (Good) Iglauer; married Philip Paul Hamburger, December 24, 1942 (divorced, 1966); married John Heywood Daly (a commercial salmon troller), March 1, 1976; children: (first marriage) Jay Philip, Richard Shaw. Education: Wellesley College, B.A., 1938; attended Zimmern School, Geneva, Switzerland, 1937; Columbia University, M.S., 1939. Politics: Democrat. Religion: None. Home address: P.O. Box 116, Garden Bay, British Columbia, Canada V0N 1S0. Agent: Joan Daves, 515 Madison Ave., New York, N.Y. 10022. Office: New Yorker, 25 West 43rd St., New York, N.Y. 10036.

CAREER: Princeton University, Princeton, N.J., writer and editor for local government survey, 1939-40; McCall's, New York, N.Y., writer for national defense section, 1940-41; Office of War Information, Washington, D.C., writer and editor in radio newsroom, and White House press conference representative for Eleanor Roosevelt, 1941-44; Cleveland News, Cleveland, Ohio, war correspondent in Mediterranean theater, 1945; free-lance writer, 1945—. Member: Authors Guild of Authors League of America, American Civil Liberties Union, Writers Union of Canada, Cosmopolitan Club.

WRITINGS: The New People: The Eskimo's Journey into Our Time, Doubleday, 1966; Denison's Ice Road, Dutton, 1975. Contributor of numerous articles to major national magazines, including New Yorker, Harper's, Atlantic, and MacLean's, and newspapers.

WORK IN PROGRESS: Revising The New People: The Eskimo's Journey Into Our Time, with an epilogue, for Douglas & McIntyre; magazine articles.

SIDELIGHTS: Iglauer told CA: "Both of my books are about the Canadian North, where I went in 1961 to report on the development of the first Eskimo cooperatives for New Yorker magazine. I was lucky enough to be present at the second meeting of the first cooperative, which was in a community hall which the Eskimos had built in a lonely spot near the mouth of Ungava Bay. The Eskimos then lived in tents in the surrounding area which is now a thriving community called Port Nouveau-Quebec.

"I was led by my curiosity about the western Arctic to Yellowknife, in the Northwest Territories," Iglauer continued. "There I met John Denison who was building ice roads to mines in uninhabited areas. After I had been in Yellowknife for some weeks, I did a New Yorker story on the opening of the ice road between Yellowknife, on Great Slave Lake, and Port Radium, on Great Bear Lake. I drove the 325 miles in trucks with the crew that annually builds this ice highway. My story was later greatly expanded to become my second book.

"Since then I have written a number of pieces about Canada, including a profile of Prime Minister Trudeau. I have also written two pieces on air pollution, one of which resulted in a law requiring the New York power companies to change to a relatively sulfur-free oil in the fuel they use."

Iglauer concluded: "My husband was a commercial salmon fisherman. I plan to write something on my experiences fishing with him, as well as on salmon enhancement."

*   *   *

IGNOTUS, Paul 1901-1978

July 1, 1901—April 1, 1978; Hungarian-born British journalist and writer best known for his book on his experiences in a Communist labor camp, Political Prisoner. Ignotus left Hungary three years before it entered World War II as a German ally. Three months after he returned to Hungary in 1949, he was arrested and convicted as a British spy. He was released after serving seven years. Ignotus also wrote The Paradox of Maupassant, a study of the French writer. He died in London, England. Obituaries and other sources: The Author's and Writer's Who's Who, 6th edition, Burke's Peerage, 1971; The Writers Directory, 1976-78, St. Martin's, 1976; New York Times, April 2, 1978. (See index for CA sketch)

*   *   *

IHIMAERA, Witi 1944-

PERSONAL: Born February 7, 1944, in Gisborne, New Zealand; son of Tame Czar, Jr. (a farmer) and Julia (Keelan) Ihimaera; married Jane Cleghorn, May 9, 1970; children: Jessica Kiri, Olivia Ata. Education: Attended University of Auckland, 1962-66; Victoria University of Wellington, B.A., 1970. Home: 11 Hungerford Rd., Wellington 3, New Zealand. Office: Ministry of Foreign Affairs, Wellington, New Zealand.

CAREER: Post Office, Headquarters, Wellington, New Zealand, journalist, 1969-72; Ministry of Foreign Affairs,

Wellington, New Zealand, diplomatic officer, 1973—. Member of Queen Elizabeth II Arts Council of New Zealand. *Member:* International P.E.N., Maori Writers and Artists Society of New Zealand. *Awards, honors:* Burns fellow at University of Otago, 1975.

WRITINGS: Pounamu, Pounamu (short stories; title means "Greenstone, Greenstone"), Heinemann, 1972; *Tangi* (novel; title means" Mourning"), Heinemann, 1973; *Whanau* (novel; title means "Family"), Heinemann, 1974; *Maori* (nonfiction), New Zealand Government Printer, 1975; *The New Net Goes Fishing* (short stories), Heinemann, 1976; (editor with D.S. Long) *Into the World of Light* (collection of contemporary Maori writing), Queensland University Press, 1978. Contributor to New Zealand magazines, including *Islands* and *Landfall*.

WORK IN PROGRESS: A sequel to *Tangi*.

SIDELIGHTS: Ihimaera writes: "There are two landscapes to New Zealand, the Maori and the Pakeha (European). I began writing and continue writing to ensure that the Maori landscape of New Zealand is taken into account. I am Maori. I write about Maori people. They are my commitment—and I am committed not only in my writing, but also in my career and my whole life."

BIOGRAPHICAL/CRITICAL SOURCES: World Literature Written in English, April, 1977.

* * *

IKO, Momoko 1940-

PERSONAL: Born March 30, 1940, in Wapato, Wash.; daughter of Kyokuo (a farmer and laborer) and Natsuko (Kagawa) Iko. *Education:* University of Illinois, B.A. (honors), 1961; also attended Instituto Allende and University of Iowa. *Home:* 1719 West Carmen St., Chicago, Ill. 60640.

CAREER: High school English teacher in Chicago, Ill., 1961-64; Ridgeway Hospital, Chicago, Ill., teacher of emotionally disturbed elementary school children, 1964-65; writer, 1965—. Head of gerontology project for Japanese American Service Committee, 1975; staff writer for KABC-TV and KNBC-TV, 1976. *Member:* Writers Guild (East). *Awards, honors:* Playwriting awards from East-West Players, 1970, for "Gold Watch," and 1971, for "Old Man"; playwriting grant from Rockefeller Foundation, 1976, for "Flowers and Household Gods"; National Endowment for the Arts grant, 1977.

WRITINGS—Plays: "Gold Watch" (two-act), first produced in Los Angeles, Calif., at Inner City Cultural Center, spring, 1972; "When We Were Young" (two-act), first produced in Los Angeles, Calif., by East-West Players, autumn, 1974.

Unproduced plays: "Old Man" (one-act); "Flowers and Household Gods" (two-act).

Films; for Japanese-American Service Committee: "Social Services: Seeking a Human Dimension," 1975; "Issei: A Quality for Survival," 1975; "Values and Attitudes I, II, III," 1975.

Work anthologized in *Aiiieeee: Anthology of Asian-American Writers,* Howard University Press, 1975; *Counterpoint: Perspectives on Asian America,* University of California Press.

WORK IN PROGRESS: A novel; "Second City Flat," a two-act play.

IMAMURA, Shigeo 1922-

PERSONAL: Born August 14, 1922, in San Jose, Calif.; son of Keijiro and Hisako (Tachibana) Imamura; married Isako Maegami, April 23, 1963; children: Yoko Imamura Iwashita, Akiko Imamura Abe, Mitsuko (deceased). *Education:* Matsuyama University, diploma, 1943; University of Michigan, B.A., 1953, M.A., 1964. *Home:* 1410 Chester Rd., Lansing, Mich. 48912. *Office:* English Language Center, Michigan State University, East Lansing, Mich. 48824.

CAREER: Teacher and supervisor of English as a second language at schools in Japan, 1949-55; Ehime University, Matsuyama, Japan, assistant professor of English as a second language, 1955-61, associate director of English Teaching Institute, 1956-61; Michigan State University, East Lansing, assistant professor of English as a second language, 1961-62; Ehime University, assistant professor of English, 1962-63; Michigan State University, assistant professor, 1963-64, associate professor of English as a second language, 1966—, director of English Language Center, 1964-73. Visiting professor at University of San Francisco, 1974-76. *Military service:* Imperial Japanese Naval Air Force; became lieutenant senior grade.

MEMBER: National Association for Foreign Student Affairs (chairman, 1973-74), Association of Teachers of English as a Second Language (chairman, 1973-74), Consortium of Intensive English Programs (chairman, 1966-68), Teachers of English to Speakers of Other Languages, Linguistic Society of America.

WRITINGS: Current Problems in Secondary School English Teaching, Ehime University, 1964; (editor with James Ney) *Readings from Samuel Clemens,* with instructor's manual, Blaisdell, 1969; (editor with Ney) *Readings on American Society,* Blaisdell, 1969; (editor with Ney) *Readings in the Philosophy of Science,* with instructor's manual, Blaisdell, 1969; *Basic Knowledge for Studies in the United States,* Kenkyusha, 1972; (editor) *Japan and America: Readings in Education,* Bunri, 1974; *Shin Amerika ryugaku e no michi* (title means "The Way to Study in the United States"), Taishukan, 1975. Contributor to language journals.

SIDELIGHTS: Imamura told *CA:* "English as a second/foreign language continues to be of vital importance for international inter-change and understanding. I am devoted to its research and teaching."

* * *

INGRAM, Gregory Keith 1944-

PERSONAL: Born March 20, 1944, in Pittsburgh, Pa.; son of Harry (a civil engineer) and Dorothy (Burket) Ingram; married Elizabeth Smith (a teacher), September 17, 1966; children: Eliot Courtney, Carleton Douglas, Dabney Chatwin. *Education:* Swarthmore College, B.S., 1965; Oxford University, B.A., 1967, M.A., 1972; Harvard University, M.A., 1969, Ph.D., 1972. *Home:* 5708 33rd St. N.W., Washington, D.C. 20015. *Office:* World Bank, 1818 H St. N.W., Washington, D.C. 20433.

CAREER: National Bureau of Economic Research, New York, N.Y., research analyst, 1969-71; Harvard University, Cambridge, Mass., assistant professor, 1971-75, associate professor of economics, 1975—. Economist for World Bank, 1977—. Director of staff research for National Academy of Science's committee on costs and benefits of automotive emission control, 1974; member of National Research Council committee on urban activity systems; participant in U.S.-Soviet Union Cooperative on Computer Applications in

Transportation (Moscow), 1975. *Member:* American Economic Association, Econometric Society.

WRITINGS: (With J. F. Kain and J. R. Ginn) *The Detroit Prototype of the NBER Urban Simulation Model,* Columbia University Press, 1972; (with Frank Grad and others) *The Automobile and the Regulation of Its Impact on the Environment,* University of Oklahoma Press, 1975; (editor) *Residential Location and Urban Housing Markets,* Ballinger, 1977.

WORK IN PROGRESS: Examining patterns of urban development in developing countries, especially in Bogota, Colombia.

SIDELIGHTS: Ingram told *CA:* "My writings and current research deal with economic phenomena that occur within cities, the analysis of which requires the incorporation of a spatial dimension. I believe that we can enhance our understanding of such phenomena (transport, housing, pollution, etc.) by combining empirical studies with computer based models. This approach is present in nearly all of my work."

* * *

IRVINE, Betty Jo 1943-

PERSONAL: Surname rhymes with "turban"; born July 13, 1943, in Indianapolis, Ind.; daughter of Edward and Marie (Sassower) Kish; and married John Mark Irvine (an attorney), January 28, 1967; children: Sara Rebecca. *Education:* Indiana University, A.B. (with distinction), 1966, M.L.S., 1969, doctoral study, 1969-75. *Agent:* Jan B. Herron, 121 Pinewood, Bloomington, Ind. 47401. *Office:* Fine Arts Library, Indiana University, Bloomington, Ind. 47401.

CAREER: Indiana University, Bloomington, slide librarian, 1966-68, assistant fine arts librarian, 1968-69, fine arts librarian and part-time instructor in fine arts, both 1969—, assistant director of university libraries, 1974-75, chairperson of librarians' advisory committee, 1972-73, member of president's council on the humanities, 1972—. Guest member of faculty at State University of New York at Buffalo, 1969. Leader of workshops and public speaker. Reviewer for National Endowment for the Humanities, 1977.

MEMBER: Art Libraries Society of North America (cofounder of Illinois-Indiana chapter, 1974), American Library Association (chairperson of art section, 1978-79), Special Libraries Association, College Art Association (member of national steering committee, 1971-75), Indiana Council of Teachers of English, Indiana University Librarians Association (president, 1974-75), Pi Lambda Theta. *Awards, honors:* Officer's grant from Council on Library Resources, 1971.

WRITINGS: Slide Libraries: A Guide for Academic Institutions and Museums, Libraries Unlimited, 1974; (contributor) Pearce S. Grove, editor, *Nonprint Media in Academic Libraries,* American Library Association, 1975. Contributor of articles and reviews to library journals. Member of advisory board of "Art Bibliographies," Clio Press, 1972—.

WORK IN PROGRESS: Research on power expression as a measurement of effective library management, planning of art library facilities, and preservation of art library materials, including books, slides, and photographs.

SIDELIGHTS: Irvine writes: "Since 1970 I have been involved in the planning and design of a new fine arts library to be in the projected Indiana University Academic and Art Museum Building, scheduled to begin construction in 1978. During this project I have had the opportunity to work with I. M. Pei and his architectural associates who were awarded the contract for the building. Having the opportunity to work on this projected library has allowed me to work with an internationally acclaimed group of architects. Such an experience can be both exhilarating and frustrating and I would be delighted to share my thoughts with any interested colleagues."

AVOCATIONAL INTERESTS: Chess, yoga, tennis, hypnosis.

* * *

ISAACS, Edith Somborn 1884-1978

June 18, 1884—May 8, 1978; American author. Isaacs wrote a variety of skits, sketches, and plays that were performed by professional theatre groups, civic groups, and university theatres. Her book, entitled *Love Affair With a City,* is about her husband's work as a New York City politician and businessman. Isaacs died in New York, N.Y. Obituaries and other sources: *New York Times,* May 9, 1978.

* * *

ITZIN, Catherine 1944-

PERSONAL: Born May 29, 1944, in Iowa City, Iowa; daughter of Frank H. (in social work) and Neva (a social worker; maiden name, Smith) Itzin; married R. J. Hawkes, September 3, 1966 (divorced, July, 1976); children: Caitlin Sarah, Nicholas Charles. *Education:* University of Iowa, B.A., 1967; University of London, M.Phil., 1970. *Home and office:* 8 Brief St., London SE5 9RD, England. *Agent:* Michael Imison, Jan van Loewen Ltd., 81 Shaftesbury Ave., London W.1, England.

CAREER: City Literary Institute, London, England, lecturer in English drama and playwriting, 1971—. Script editor and producer of radio drama for British Broadcasting Corp., 1973-74. Member of House of Commons Current Arts and Policy Advisory Committee, 1975-76. Manager of Loughborough Infants School, 1976-77; governor of Loughborough Juniors School, 1977-78. *Member:* British Theatre Institute (founder; member of council, 1972—), Theatre Writers Union, Phi Beta Kappa. *Awards, honors:* Second prizes from BBC-TV competition for new writers, 1969, for "I'll Huff and I'll Puff," and Platt Arts Foundation playwriting competition, 1970, for "The Gifts of the Magi."

WRITINGS: Alternative Theatre Handbook, TQ Publications, 1976; *New Playwrights Directory,* TQ Publications, 1977; *Political Theatre and the Politics of the Theatre from 1968-1978,* Eyre Methuen, 1979; *Splitting Up,* Virago, 1979; *British Alternative Theatre Directory,* John Offord Publications, 1979.

Plays: "Cuckolds" (one-act), first produced in London, England, at Little Theatre, May 1, 1970; "Infants, Lunatics, and Married Women" (one-act radio play), performed on stage in New York, N.Y., at Westbeth Feminist Collective, October 13, 1974. Also author of two unproduced plays, "I'll Huff and I'll Puff," and "The Immaculate Misconception."

Author of "Everything of Any Value Is Theatrical" (documentary on futurism), BBC-Radio 3, 1978. Co-founder of TQ Publications, and co-editor of its *Theatre Quarterly, Theatrefacts,* and *New Plays,* 1971-77; drama critic for *Tribune,* 1972—, *Time Out,* and *Plays and Players.*

WORK IN PROGRESS: "Splitting Up," a play based on interviews with single parent women; "Ssshhh . . . I.T.T.: A Living Newspaper on American Labour in Chile," a two-act play about International Telephone & Telegraph and U.S. government involvement in the Chilean coup of 1973.

SIDELIGHTS: Catherine Itzin writes: "I am an expatriate American who has settled in England. As the drama critic for *Tribune,* the independent socialist weekly newspaper of the Labour movement, I have been committed to promoting new writing, particularly socialist and feminist theatre, and chronicling the development of political theatre in Britain in the seventies. As a playwright I am concerned with socialist and feminist issues. As a theatre editor I have been concerned with documenting the best of historical and contemporary theatre and with the international dissemination of theatre information."

* * *

IVERS, Larry E(dward) 1936-

PERSONAL: Born September 9, 1936, in Vincennes, Ind.; son of Isaac N. (a farmer) and Doris (Smith) Ivers; married Kristin Feaster (a paralegal assistant), July 12, 1958; children: Robin, Brian. *Education:* Attended Augustana College, Rock Island, Ill., 1954-55; University of Omaha, B.G.E., 1965. *Home and office address:* Box C, Eagle Grove, Iowa 50533.

CAREER: U.S. Army, parachutist, ranger, and combat infantryman, 1955-69, served in Vietnam, leaving service as major; attorney at law, 1972—. Attorney for Wright County, Iowa, 1975-76. *Member:* American Bar Association, Council for Abandoned Military Posts, Company of Military Historians, Iowa Bar Association, Iowa Historical Society, Georgia Historical Society, South Carolina Historical Society.

WRITINGS: *Colonial Forts of South Carolina,* University of South Carolina Press, 1970; *British Drums on the Southern Frontier,* University of North Carolina Press, 1974. Contributor to history and military journals.

WORK IN PROGRESS: A book on the Yamassee War in southeastern North America, 1715-1720.

SIDELIGHTS: Ivers writes that his goal is "to present colonial politics, society, economics, and warfare from the viewpoint of the common settler."

J

JACKSON, Derrick 1939-

PERSONAL: Born February 3, 1939, in Cleethorpes, England; son of Herbert James (a bookbinder) and Doris (Schofield) Jackson; married Kathleen Joan Meadowcroft (an educator), August 22, 1964; children: Wendy Fiona, Mark Andrew. Education: Leicester College of Art, N.D.D., 1961, A.T.D., 1962. Religion: Methodist. Home: 46 Berkeley Rd., Loughborough, Leicestershire LE11 3SJ, England. Office: Department of Design and Visual Communications, Loughborough College of Art and Design, Radmoor Rd., Loughborough, England.

CAREER: Southport College of Art, Southport, England, assistant lecturer in graphic design, 1962-70; Loughborough College of Art and Design, Loughborough, England, lecturer, 1970-77, senior lecturer in graphic design, 1977—, also lecturer in calligraphy. Free-lance designer, illustrator, and calligrapher, working on house styles, catalogs, sign systems, brochures, typography, and exhibitions, with personal, civic, and commissioned calligraphy. Member: Society of Industrial Artists and Designers. Awards, honors: Second prize from Caxton Watermark competition, 1975.

WRITINGS: Lighthouses of England and Wales, David & Charles, 1975.

WORK IN PROGRESS: Research into maintenance and development of lighthouses; an introductory book on the teaching and practice of calligraphy.

SIDELIGHTS: Jackson writes: "My interest in lighthouses began as a world-wide study, developed through philatelic studies (I own a five-volume collection on lighthouses) into an in-depth study of the working of the lights around our coastline, most of which I have visited."

*   *   *

JACKSON, Edgar (Newman) 1910-

PERSONAL: Born July 10, 1910, in Cold Spring Harbor, N.Y.; son of Edgar Starkey (a clergyman) and Abbie (Newman) Jackson; married Estelle Miller, 1934; children: Edgar D. (deceased), James W. (deceased), Lois Estelle. Education: Ohio Wesleyan University, A.B., 1932; graduate study at Drew Theological Seminary, 1932-34, and Union Theological Seminary, New York, N.Y., 1934-35; earned B.D. and M.Div. from Yale University; further graduate study at Postgraduate Center for Psychotherapy, 1949-52, and Columbia University, 1954. Home address: Washington Rd.,

Corinth, Vt. 05039. Agent: Ann Elmo Agency, Inc., 52 Vanderbilt Ave., New York, N.Y. 10017.

CAREER: Ordained Methodist minister, 1933; pastor of Methodist churches in Centerport, N.Y., Thomaston, Conn., New Haven, Conn., Winsted, Conn., Bridgeport, Conn., and Mamaroneck, N.Y. Visiting professor at University of Minnesota, 1964-66; professor at Royalton College, 1968-72; adjunct professor at Union Graduate School, 1972—; Danforth lecturer at Brooklyn College of the City University of New York; Ritter lecturer at Congregational School of Theology; lecturer at dozens of universities, seminaries, religious and medical conferences, and military schools in the United States, Japan, the Philippines, England, Germany, Italy, Greece, and Iceland, including Columbia University and St. John's University, Jamaica, N.Y.; member of board of trustees of New England Institute. Clinical psychologist at Veterans Administration Hospital; chaplain at U.S. Air Force General Hospital; director and chairman of advisory board of New Rochelle Guidance Center. Guest on several hundred local and national television and radio programs; consultant to medical, religious, and military groups.

MEMBER: Association for Humanistic Psychology, National Council on Family Relations, Hastings Institute. Awards, honors: Essay award from National Cancer Society; Freedoms Foundations award; named honorary chaplain of U.S. House of Representatives; D.D. from Ohio Wesleyan University, 1959.

WRITINGS: This Is My Faith, Abingdon, 1951; How to Preach to People's Needs, Abingdon, 1956; Understanding Grief: Its Roots, Dynamics, and Treatment, Abingdon, 1957; (with Russell Dicks) Facing Ourselves, Abingdon, 1961; Green Mountain Hero (juvenile historical novel), Lantern Press, 1961; You and Your Grief, Channel Press, 1961; The Pastor and His People, Channel Press, 1963; For the Living, Channel Press, 1963; (with M. K. Bowers, Knight, and Lawrence LeShan) Counseling the Dying, Thomas Nelson, 1963; Telling a Child About Death, Channel Press, 1965; The Christian Funeral, Channel Press, 1967; Understanding Prayer: Its Roots, Disciplines, and Growth, World Publishing, 1968; Group Counseling: A Dynamic Resource for the Church, Pilgrim Publications, 1969; Though We Suffer, Graded Press, 1971; When Someone Dies, Fortress, 1971; Coping With the Crises in Your Life, Hawthorn, 1974;

Parish Counseling, Jason Aronson, 1975. Also author of *A Psychology for Preaching,* Channel Press.

Contributor: Herman Feifel, editor, *The Meaning of Death,* McGraw, 1959; *Catastrophic Illness,* National Cancer Institute, 1966; Earl Grollman, editor, *Explaining Death to Children,* Beacon Press, 1967; *Growth Through Grief* (monograph), Forest Hospital, 1968; *Sociologia de la Muerte* (title means "The Sociology of Death"), Tribuna Medica, 1974. Also contributor to *But Not to Lose,* 1968, *Death and Bereavement,* 1969, *Religion and Bereavement,* 1972, and *Children and Dying,* 1974, all edited by Austin Kutscher, and to *Concerning Death,* 1974.

Contributor of more than three hundred articles to religious and professional journals, and a wide variety of popular magazines, including *Modern Bride, Successful Farmer, Adult Student,* and *Yankee.* Member of editorial advisory boards.

WORK IN PROGRESS: The Many Faces of Grief; Health Is Up to You; Mobilizing the Life Force, with Lawrence LeShan; *With Further Ado: A Guide for Program Chairpersons; Mysticism, Man, and Meaning; The Varieties of Pastoral Language; Pastoral Care of Children and Their Families.*

SIDELIGHTS: Jackson comments briefly that he has "spent a life-time trying to interpret the findings of the personality sciences to the care-giving professions."

*   *   *

JACKSON, James P(ierre)   1925-

PERSONAL: Born December 10, 1925, in Paris, France; son of Kenneth M. and Germaine (Lepaute) Jackson; married Charlene Duncan, August 10, 1957; children: Keith Allen, Glenn Stuart. *Education:* University of Missouri, A.B., 1950, M.A., 1957. *Home:* 105 Terry Lane, Washington, Mo. 63090.

CAREER: Missouri Department of Conservation, Jefferson City, conservation education consultant, 1951-61; junior high school science teacher in Ladue, Mo., 1961-63; Washington Public High School, Washington, Mo., biology teacher, 1963—, chairman of science department, 1965—. Member of advisory council for University of Missouri's School of Forestry, Fisheries, and Wildlife. *Military service:* U.S. Navy, 1944-46; became lieutenant junior grade. *Member:* Conservation Federation of Missouri (member of board of directors), Audubon Society of Missouri (past president).

WRITINGS: The Biography of a Tree (self-illustrated with photographs), Jonathan David, 1978. Contributor to national wildlife and other outdoor magazines.

WORK IN PROGRESS: A book of articles and photographs prepared originally for *American Forests* magazine.

SIDELIGHTS: Jackson writes: "As one whose educational training and lifelong interests have been in natural science, I consider myself a specialist. Part of my motivation consistently has been the protection and preservation of our natural heritage. I am a devoted environmentalist. The outlet for such devotion is my writing combined with my photographic efforts. I strive for accuracy and quality in both media.

"*The Biography of a Tree* is a fictionalized story about a long-lived white oak tree, about the effects it had on other life forms of the forest, and about how it was affected by them. Too many nature stories tend to glorify their heroes by making them unrealistically human. My effort was to depict the struggles and successes of the growing, and finally aging

tree, in terms of the limitations imposed upon it by nature. The tree is presented as a unique form of life with unique ways of coping with its own problems."

*   *   *

JACOB, Herbert   1933-

PERSONAL: Born February 10, 1933, in Augsburg, Germany; came to the United States in 1940, naturalized citizen, 1946; son of Ernest I. and Annette (Loewenberg) Jacob; married Joan Forbstein, August, 1957 (marriage ended, 1967); married Lynn Carp, August 19, 1968; children: Joel B., David S., Jenny E., M. Max. *Education:* Harvard University, A.B., 1954; Yale University, M.A., 1955, Ph.D., 1960. *Religion:* Jewish. *Home:* 2234 Asbury Ave., Evanston, Ill. 60201. *Office:* Department of Political Science, Northwestern University, 1890 Sherdan Rd., Evanston, Ill. 60201.

CAREER: Tulane University, New Orleans, La., assistant professor of political science, 1960-62; University of Wisconsin—Madison, associate professor, 1964-67, professor of political science, 1967-69; Northwestern University, Evanston, Ill., professor of political science, 1969—, department chairperson, 1974-77. *Military service:* U.S. Army, 1955-57. *Member:* American Political Science Association (member of executive council, 1975-77), Law and Society Association (member of board of directors), Midwest Political Science Association.

WRITINGS: German Administration Since Bismarck, Yale University Press, 1963; *Justice in America,* Little, Brown, 1965, 3rd edition, 1977; (editor with Kenneth N. Vines) *Politics in the American States,* Little, Brown, 1965, 3rd edition, 1976; *Debtors in Court,* Rand McNally, 1969; (with Robert Weissberg) *Elementary Political Analysis,* McGraw Hill, 1970, 2nd edition, 1975; *Urban Justice,* Prentice-Hall, 1973; (with James Eisenstein) *Felony Justice,* Little, Brown, 1977. Also editor of *Potential for Reform of Criminal Justice,* Sage Publications.

WORK IN PROGRESS: A book on justice in American cities; editing a book on American lawyers.

SIDELIGHTS: Jacob writes: "When I was growing up, my father took us on vacation trips and we would stop at every major university library and look at the catalogue to see whether our family was represented. My maternal grandfather was a German poet and novelist; my paternal grandfather was a Biblical exegesist. I am sure that is part of my own motivation for becoming a writer.

"So far I have written two kinds of books. The first are attempts to illumine parts of the political process with new data and new insights into those data—for instance, my new book with Jim Eisenstein, *Felony Justice,* in which I believe we develop new ways to understand the workings of American criminal courts. The second type of writing seeks to make new fields accessible to students—*Justice in America* was the first text to bring together the many research findings of socio-legal researchers, and *Politics in the American States* popularized a whole new way of examining American state politics. I avoid the polemical although some day I hope to have time to write my own interpretation of political life.

"Writing is a lonely art, as is photography—the other form through which I attempt to express and communicate my view of the world. Whether in front of the typewriter or in the darkroom, I enjoy solitude while communicating with the world at large."

JACOBS, Lewis 1906-

PERSONAL: Born April 22, 1906, in Philadelphia, Pa.; son of Walter and Lillian Jackson; married Lillian Wilentz (an artist); children: Ellen Freyer, Carol Mendez. *Education:* Attended Pennsylvania Academy of Fine Art. *Home:* 9 Grace Court W., Great Neck, N.Y. 11021. *Office:* 41 West 47th St., New York, N.Y. 10036.

CAREER: Has worked as screenwriter and test director of motion pictures in Hollywood, Calif.; writer, 1939—; screenwriter, photographer, director and producer of motion pictures in New York City, 1950—. Instructor in cinema at City College of New York (now City College of the City University of New York) and New York University; visiting professor of cinema at Pratt Institute, and Philadelphia College of Art. Filmmaker for many companies and corporations including Ford Motor Co., Monsanto Chemical Co., U.S. Steel, and Burlington Industries. *Member:* International Cinematographers, Directors Guild of America, Barnes Foundation, Society of Cinema Studies. *Awards, honors:* Winner of six international awards and twenty-two American awards for films; received Silver Star Award from Philadelphia College of Art, 1976.

WRITINGS: The Rise of the American Film, Harcourt, 1939, new edition, Teachers College Press, 1968; (editor) *Introduction to the Art of the Movies,* Noonday Press, 1960; (compiler) *The Emergence of Film Art,* Hopkinson & Blake, 1969; (compiler) *The Movies as Medium,* Farrar, Straus, 1970, reprinted, Octagon Books, 1973; (compiler) *The Documentary Tradition, From Nanook to Woodstock,* Hopkinson & Blake, 1971; (selector, arranger, and author of introduction) *The Compound Cinema: The Film Writings of Harry Alan Potamkin,* Teachers College Press, 1977. Contributor of articles to film journals and encyclopedias. Founder of *Experimental Cinema.*

SIDELIGHTS: Jacobs told *CA:* "Vernon Louis Parrington's book, *Main Currents in American Thought,* turned me to writing about motion pictures—Albert Barnes's teaching provided me with a 'plastic' conception of structure."

Jacobs served as a juror at numerous film festivals in Venice and West Berlin.

*   *   *

JACOBS, Norman (Gabriel) 1924-

PERSONAL: Born February 28, 1924, in New York, N.Y.; son of Joseph (a salesman) and Beatrice (Esserman) Jacobs; married Margaret Ayres, August 20, 1956; children: Laurie, Charles. *Education:* City College (now of the City University of New York), B.S., 1943; Harvard University, A.M., 1950, Ph.D., 1951. *Politics:* None. *Religion:* Buddhist. *Home:* 312 South Willis, Champaign, Ill. 61820. *Office:* Department of Sociology, University of Illinois, Urbana, Ill. 61801.

CAREER: Taiwan Normal University, Taipei, lecturer in sociology and English, 1955-57; American University, Washington, D.C., research scientist on China, 1957-59; Agency for International Development, Community Affairs Division, Fars, Iran, community development adviser, 1959-61; University of Kansas, Lawrence, assistant professor, 1962-63, associate professor, 1963-65, professor of sociology and Asian studies, 1965; University of Illinois, Urbana, professor of sociology and Asian studies, 1965—. Fulbright professor at Prasarnmitr College and Thammasat University, 1965-66, and Keio University, 1968-69; Fulbright researcher at Korean Institute for Buddhist Studies,

1975. *Military service:* U.S. Army, Military Intelligence, 1943-46; served in Japan; became first lieutenant. *Member:* Association for Asian Studies, Indian Sociological Society.

WRITINGS: Characteristics of the Japanese Agricultural Cooperative Association (mongraph), Supreme Commander Allied Forces in Japan, 1946; (with C. C. Vermeule) *Japanese Coinage,* Numismatic Review Press, 1953, revised edition, 1972; *The Origin of Modern Capitalism and Eastern Asia,* University of Hong Kong Press, 1958; (contributor) Werner J. Cahnman and Alvin Boskoff, editors, *Sociology and History: Theory and Research,* Free Press of Glencoe, 1964; *The Sociology of Development,* Praeger, 1966; (contributor) Irving Louis Horowitz, editor, *Studies in Comparative International Development,* Volume II, Washington University Press, 1966; *Modernization Without Development,* Praeger, 1972; (contributor) *Technology and Social Change in East Asia,* Iowa State University Press, 1973; (contributor) John Barratt and other editors, *Accelerated Development in Southern Africa,* Macmillan, 1974; *The Korean Road to Development,* Praeger, in press. Contributor to *Handbook of Iran* and *Modern World Coins.* Contributor of about twenty articles to academic and numismatic journals.

WORK IN PROGRESS: Feudalism, Patrimonialism, and Japanese Development, completion expected in 1981.

SIDELIGHTS: Jacobs comments: "I have devoted some forty years to the study of and working in Asia, focused upon the problems of change and modernization and its institutional roots. I have used this experience to develop a comparative sociological framework for the analysis of social phenomena. This framework assumes that the various societies of plains Asia, regardless of their diversity, share in common certain social characteristics and that these characteristics are qualitatively different from those associated with pre-industrial feudal societies in the west *and* in Japan. My study and work in Asia has convinced me that these differences are significant for understanding the differing reaction to the challenge of modernization and development between the west and Asia. In my writings I have attempted to apply these ideas and framework to various Asian societies in the hope of clarifying the process and pinpointing the needs of directed social change in contemporary Asia."

*   *   *

JACOBSON, Michael F. 1943-

PERSONAL: Born July 29, 1943, in Chicago, Ill.; son of Larry and Janet (Siegel) Jacobson. *Education:* University of Chicago, B.A., 1965; graduate study at University of California, San Diego, 1965-67; Massachusetts Institute of Technology, Ph.D., 1969. *Office:* Center for Science in the Public Interest, 1755 S St. N.W., Washington, D.C. 20009.

CAREER: Research associate, Salk Institute for Biological Studies, 1970-71; Center for the Study of Responsive Law, Washington, D.C., technical consultant, 1970-71; Center for Science in the Public Interest, Washington, D.C., co-director, 1971-77, executive director, 1977—.

WRITINGS: Eater's Digest: The Consumer's Factbook of Food Additives, Doubleday, 1972; *How Sodium Nitrite Can Affect Your Health,* Center for Science in the Public Interest, 1973; (with Sandy Kageyama) *Scorecard for Better Eating,* Center for Science in the Public Interest, 1973; *Nutrition Scoreboard,* Avon, 1975; (editor with Catherine Lerza) *Food for People, Not for Profit,* Ballantine, 1975. Contributor to *Time-Life Science Annual.* Contributor of about one dozen articles to magazines, including *Progressive, Smithsonian, Instructor,* and *Newsday,* and to newspapers.

JACOBY, Henry 1905-
(Sebastian Franck, Andre Martin)

PERSONAL: Born in 1905, in Berlin, Germany; came to the United States in 1941. *Education:* Graduated from Deutsche Hochschule fuer Politik (German College for Politics). *Home:* 28 Rue de Vermont, CH-1202 Geneva, Switzerland.

CAREER: Editor of an underground newspaper during Nazi period, and served several years in prison; economist for U.S. federal government; served with Food and Agriculture Organization of United Nations in Washington, Rome, and Geneva; presently representing Amnesty International at United Nations, Geneva.

WRITINGS—In English: *Die Buerokratisierung der Welt: Ein Beitrag zur Problemgeschichte,* Luchterhand, 1969, translation by Eveline L. Kanes published as *The Bureaucratization of the World,* University of California Press, 1973.

Other: *Zur Kritik der politischen Moral: Kritik des politischen Verhaltens—Ein Beitrag zur Konzeption einer neuen sozialistischen Bewegung,* Bollwerk-Verlag, 1947, reprinted, Prolit-Buchvertrieb, 1972; *Soziologie der Freiheit: Otto Ruehles Auffassung vom Sozialismus—Eine Gedenkschrift,* A. J. Schotola, 1951; (editor) Otto Ruehle, *Bauplaene fuer eine neue Gesellschaft,* Taschenbuch-Verlag, 1971; *Beitraege zur Soziologie der sozialistischen Idee,* Focus Verlag, 1973; *Alfred Adler's Individualpsychologie und dialektische Charakterkunde,* Fischer-Taschenbuch-Verlag, 1974. Contributor to *Socialist Call, Politics,* and other periodicals, sometimes under pseudonyms Sebastian Franck and Andre Martin.

* * *

JACOBY, Russell 1945-

PERSONAL: Born April 23, 1945, in New York, N.Y. *Education:* Attended University of Chicago, 1963-64; University of Wisconsin, Madison, B.A., 1967; University of Rochester, M.A., 1968, Ph.D., 1974; graduate study at Ecole Pratique des Hautes Etudes, 1969-70. *Home:* 22A Paloma Ave., Venice, Calif. 90291. *Office:* Department of History, University of California, Los Angeles, Calif. 90024.

CAREER: Boston University, Boston, Mass., lecturer in social science, 1972-73; Brandeis University, Waltham, Mass., scholar-in-residence, spring, 1975; University of California, Los Angeles, acting assistant professor of history, 1976—. *Member:* International Pessimists Society (vice-president, 1975—).

WRITINGS: (Contributor) Paul Breines, editor, *Critical Interruptions: New Left Perspectives on Herbert Marcuse,* Herder, 1970; *Social Amnesia: A Critique of Conformist Psychology from Adler to Laing,* introduction by Christopher Lasch, Beacon Press, 1975. Contributor of articles and reviews to scholarly journals. Member of editorial staff of *Telos.*

AVOCATIONAL INTERESTS: "Saving the Big Apple, defending the Knicks, and finding—or founding—a bookstore in Los Angeles."

* * *

JACOT, B. L.
See JACOT de BOINOD, Bernard Louis

JACOT de BOINOD, Bernard Louis 1898-1977
(B.L. Jacot)

February 25, 1898—September, 1977; British novelist and short story writer best known for his biography of Guglielmo Marconi who invented the wireless radio. Jacot de Boinod also wrote such novels as *The Tulip Tree* and *Crying for the Moon.* He died in England. Obituaries and other sources: *AB Bookman's Weekly,* February 6, 1978. (See index for *CA* sketch)

* * *

JAKOBSON, Roman 1896-

PERSONAL: Born October 11, 1896, in Moscow, Russia; came to the United States in 1941, naturalized citizen, 1952; son of Osip and Anna (Volpert) Jakobson; married Krystyna Pomorska, September 28, 1962. *Education:* Lazarev Institute of Oriental Languages, A.B. (with silver medal), 1914; University of Moscow, A.M., 1918; University of Prague, Ph.D., 1930. *Office:* 301 Boylston Hall, Harvard University, Cambridge, Mass. 02138.

CAREER: University of Moscow, Moscow, Russia, research associate, 1918-20; Moscow Dramatic School, Moscow, Russia, professor of orthoepy, 1920; Masaryk University, Brno, Czechoslovakia, assistant professor, 1933-34, visiting professor, 1934-37, associate professor of Russian philosophy and old Czech literature, 1937-39; University of Copenhagen, Copenhagen, Denmark, visiting lecturer in phonology, 1939; University of Oslo, Oslo, Norway, visiting lecturer in linguistics, 1939-40; University of Uppsala, Uppsala, Sweden, visiting lecturer in Russian, 1940-41; Ecole Libre des Hautes Etudes, New York City, professor of linguistics, 1942-46; Columbia University, New York City, visiting professor, 1943-46, T. G. Masaryk Professor of Czechoslovak Studies, 1946-49; Harvard University, Cambridge, Mass., Samuel Hazzard Cross Professor of Slavic Languages, Literatures, and General Linguistics, 1949-67, professor emeritus, 1967—, fellow of Center for Cognitive Studies, 1967-69. T. G. Masaryk Professor at Institut de Philologie et d'Histoire Orientales et Slaves, 1943-46; professor at Massachusetts Institute of Technology, 1957-67, professor emeritus, 1967—; visiting professor at Yale University, 1967, 1971, Princeton University, 1968, Brown University, 1969-70, Brandeis University, 1970, College de France, 1972, Catholic University of Louvain, 1972, New York University, 1973, and Bergen University, 1976. Fellow of Center for Advanced Study in the Behavioral Sciences, 1959, 1961; visiting fellow at Salk Institute for Biological Studies, 1966-69. President of International Council of Phonetic Sciences, 1948-61; honorary president of Tokyo Institute for the Advanced Study of Language, 1967—; vice-president of International Committee of Slavists, 1958-76; consultant to UNESCO.

MEMBER: International Society of Phonetic Sciences (vice-president, 1970—), Association Phonetique Internationale (honorary member), International Association for Semiotic Studies (vice-president, 1969—), Linguistic Society of America (president, 1956), American Anthropological Association, Acoustic Society of America, American Academy of Arts and Sciences (fellow), American Association for Armenian Studies and Research (honorary member), Academy of Aphasia (honorary member), Center for Byzantine Studies (honorary member), Norwegian Academy of Sciences (foreign member), Royal Danish Academy of Science and Letters (foreign member), Serbian Academy of Sciences (foreign member), Polish Academy of Science (foreign member), Royal Netherlands Academy of Sciences (foreign member), Irish Academy of Sciences (foreign member), Italian Academy of Sciences in Bologna (foreign member), British Academy (foreign member), Finnish Academy of Sciences (foreign member), Finno-Ugric Society (honorary member), Royal Society of Letters of Lund (honorary member), Associazione Italiana di Studi Semiotica (honorary member), Circolo Semiologico Siciliano (honorary member), Phonetic Society of Japan (honorary member), Philological Society (England; honorary member), Royal Anthropological Institute of Great Britain and Ireland (honorary member), Mediaeval Academy.

AWARDS, HONORS: Chevalier de la Legion d'Honneur, 1947; A.M. from Harvard University, 1949; D.Litt. from Cambridge University, 1960, University of Chicago and University of Oslo, 1961, University of Uppsala and University of Michigan, 1963, University of Grenoble and University of Nice, 1966, University of Rome and Yale University, 1967, Charles University and Purkyne University, 1968, University of Zagreb, 1969, Ohio State University, 1970, University of Louvain, 1972, University of Tel Aviv and Harvard University, 1975, and Columbia University, 1976; D.Sc. from University of New Mexico, 1966, and Clark University, 1969; awards from American Council of Learned Societies, 1960, National Slavic Honor Society, 1967, and American Association for the Advancement of Slavic Studies, 1970; gold medal from Slovak Academy of Science, 1968; Johns Hopkins University centennial scholar, 1975; Boston College presidential bicentennial award, 1976.

WRITINGS—In English: (with Gunnar M. Fant and Morris Halle) *Preliminaries to Speech Analysis,* M.I.T. Press, 1952; (with Halle) *Fundamentals of Language,* Mouton (Netherlands), 1956, revised edition, 1971; (with L. L. Hammerich) *Low German Manual of Spoken Russian, 1607,* Danish Academy of Sciences, Volume I, 1961, Volume II, 1970; *Selected Writings,* five volumes, Mouton, 1962-79; *Child Language, Aphasia and Phonological Universals,* Mouton, 1968; (with L. G. Jones) *Shakespeare's Verbal Art,* Mouton, 1970; *Studies on Child Language and Aphasia,* Mouton, 1971; *Bibliography of Publications,* Mouton, 1971; *Main Trends in the Science of Language,* [New York], 1973; (editor and author of foreword) *N. S. Trubetzkoy's Letters and Notes,* Mouton, 1975; *Pushkin and His Sculptural Myth,* Mouton, 1975; (with Stephen Rudy) *Yeats' "Sorrow of Love" Through the Years,* Peter de Ridder Press, 1977; (with Linda R. Waugh) *The Sound Shape of Language,* Indiana University Press, 1978.

Other: *Kindersprache, Aphasie und allgem eine Lautgesetze* (title means "Children's Language, Aphasia, and General Sound Laws"), [Uppsala], 1941, 2nd edition, [Frankfurt], 1970; *Essais de linguistique generale* (title means "Essays in General Linguistics"), Editions de Minuit (Paris), Volume I, 1963, Volume II, 1973; *Language enfantin et aphasie* (title means "Children's Language and Aphasia"), Editions de Minuit, 1969; *Linguistica, Poetica, Cinema* (title means "Linguistics, Poetics, Cinema"), Editora Perspectiva, 1970; *Form und Sinn* (title means "Form and Meaning"), W. Mink Verlag, 1973; *Questions de Poetique* (title means "Questions of Poetics"), Editions de Seuil (Paris), 1973; *Coup d'oeil sur le developpement de la semiotique* (title means "Glance on the Development of Semiotics"), Indiana University Press, 1975; *Gremesse di storia letteraria Slava* (title means "Foundations of Slavic Literary History"), Il Saggiatore (Milan), 1975; *Aufsaetze zur Linguistik und Poetik* (title means "Contributions to Linguistics and

Poetics"), Nymphenburger Verlag (Munich), 1976; *Six lecons sur le son et le sens* (title means "Six Lectures on Sound and Meaning"), Editions de Minuit, 1976; *Hoelderlin-Klee-Brecht: Zur Wortkunst dreier Gedichte* (title means "Hoelderlin-Klee-Brecht: The Verbal Art of Two Poems"), Suhrkamp Verlag, 1976; *Der Grammatische aufbau der Kindersprache* (title means "The Grammatical Structure of Children's Language"), Rheinisch-Westfaelische Akademie, 1977; *Lo suiluppo della semiotica* (title means "Development of Semiotics"), Studi Rampiane (Milan), 1978. Also author of *Saggi di linguistica generale* (title means "Studies in General Linguistics"), 1966, and *Fonema e Fonologia* (title means "Phoneme and Phonology"), 1967.

SIDELIGHTS: Jakobson's works have been translated into more than fifteen languages, including Portuguese, Swedish, Serbo-Croatian, Hungarian, Korean, and Hebrew.

BIOGRAPHICAL/CRITICAL SOURCES: Roman Jakobson: A Bibliography of His Writings, Mouton, 1971; Elmar Holenstein, *Roman Jakobson's Approach to Language,* Indiana University Press, 1976; Linda R. Waugh, *Roman Jakobson's Science of Language,* Lisse, 1976; Ladislav Matejka, editor, *Sound, Sign, and Meaning,* University of Michigan, 1976; Daniel Armstrong and C. M. van Schooneveld, editors, *Roman Jakobson: Echoes of His Scholarship,* Lisse, 1977.

*　　*　　*

JAMES, Edward
See MASUR, Harold Q.

*　　*　　*

JAMESON, Kenneth (Ambrose) 1913-

PERSONAL: Born May 21, 1913, in Blackwell, England; son of Robert Barnecott (a timber merchant) and Elsie May (Birchley) Jameson; married Marion Lucy Muckley, June 19, 1937 (divorced, 1956); married Norma Marion Salt (a college lecturer), January 4, 1957; children:(first marriage) Andrew Leigh, Susan Isobel Marion. *Education:* Attended Birmingham School of Music, 1921-36, Laird School of Art, 1947-52, and Bath Academy of Art, 1953-54; University of Bristol, certificate in education, 1954. *Politics:* Liberal. *Religion:* Church of England. *Home:* 111 Hayes Way, Beckenham, Kent BR3 2RR, England.

CAREER: Ripon Cathedral, Ripon, England, lay clerk and tenor in choir, 1936-46; art master of school in Birkenhead, England, 1947-56; art teacher and head of department at school in London, England, 1956-60; Inner London Education Authority Inspectorate, London, England, art inspector, 1960-73; writer, 1973—. Painter (with exhibitions), 1939—. Lecturer on art, especially children's art; children's art advisor to British Broadcasting Corp., preschool groups, and commercial firms; past chairman of Schools Council art committee. *Military service:* Royal Air Force, 1940-45; became sergeant. *Member:* Royal Society of Arts (fellow; life member), Royal Cambrian Academy of Art.

WRITINGS—All self-illustrated: *You Can Draw,* Watson-Guptill, 1967; *Pre-School and Infant Art,* Studio Vista, 1968, published in the United States as *Art and the Young Child,* Viking, 1969; *Flower Painting for Beginners,* Watson-Guptill, 1968; *Starting with Abstract Painting,* Watson-Guptill, 1970; *Junior School Art,* Reinhold, 1971; *Seeing Colour,* Educational Supply Association, 1972; (with Pat Kidd) *Preschool Play,* Reinhold, 1974; *Painting: A Complete Guide,* Viking, 1975; (with Brenda Crowe) *What's a House?* (study of preschool paintings), Galt Toys

Ltd., 1978; (co-author) Aubrey Thomas, editor, *Reader's Digest Mother Care Book,* Reader's Digest Press, 1978. Contributor to education and art journals in England and the United States.

WORK IN PROGRESS: "A self-motivating" practical art textbook for high school students.

SIDELIGHTS: Jameson writes: "In all my writing I have been motivated by two considerations. The first is a sympathetic understanding of the art problems of the amateur; and this motivation springs, I believe, from the fact that I consider myself to be an amateur painter. In spite of the help I have received from tutors and academic institutions, for which I am grateful, I believe myself to be a self-taught artist. The second consideration is the abiding belief that practical participation in, and experience of, any of the arts, particularly the graphic and plastic arts, is a means to education in a total sense. Hence my two most important studies, *Art and the Young Child* and *Junior School Art,* are aimed at helping to educate those special kinds of amateur, the school child and the preschool child."

*   *   *

JANTZEN, Steven L(loyd)   1941-

PERSONAL: Born October 31, 1941, in White Plains, N.Y.; son of William Lloyd (in sales) and Elizabeth (Lauckhardt) Jantzen; married Geraldine Sermattei, July 22, 1967; children: David Scott, Douglas Steven. *Education:* Dartmouth College, B.A. (summa cum laude), 1963; Harvard University, M.A.T., 1964; Princeton University, M.A., 1970. *Home:* 62 Meadowbrook Rd., Short Hills, N.J. 07078.

CAREER: High school history teacher in Newton, Mass., 1964, and teacher of government and economics in Tenafly, N.J., 1964-65; Chilton Book Co., Philadelphia, Pa., editorial assistant, 1965-66; American Education Publications, Middletown, Conn., assistant editor and author of study guides, 1966-67; Education Development Center, Newton, Mass., editor, 1970-71; Scholastic Magazines, Inc., New York, N.Y., curriculum specialist and writer, 1971-76; free-lance writer, 1976—. *Member:* Phi Beta Kappa.

WRITINGS: Hooray for Peace, Hurrah for War (juvenile), Knopf, 1971; *Winning Ideas in the Social Studies,* Teachers College Press, 1977; *The Scholastic American Citizenship Program* (juvenile), Scholastic Magazines, Inc., 1977; (contributor) Franklin G. Myers, editor, *The World's a Stage* (juvenile), Prentice-Hall, 1977; (with Ira Peck) *A Nation Conceived and Dedicated* (juvenile), 2nd edition (Jantzen was not associated with 1st edition), Scholastic Magazines, Inc., 1978; (with Peck) *Old Hate, New Hope* (juvenile), 2nd edition (Jantzen was not associated with 1st edition), Scholastic Magazines, Inc., 1978.

WORK IN PROGRESS: Macmillan Grammar and Composition: Grade 6, for Macmillan; *Scholastic Writing Program: Grade 8,* for Scholastic Magazines, Inc.

SIDELIGHTS: Jantzen writes: "The word 'textbook,' I think, must be one of the ugliest, most unpleasant words in our language. Whenever I tell people that I am writing such a dreadful thing, they nearly gag with bad memories. I like to think that I can write texts for school kids which are better than a bad memory. I want to inject as much humanity, humor, and imagination into them as my editors and publishers will allow. For example, of all the pale and innocuous characters we meet regularly in history texts, James Madison must be about the palest and most bloodless. I think it helps to mention—as I have done in one American history

text—that Madison suffered from a frostbitten nose during Washington's inauguration. The detail is of course insignificant historically—but it is also human and real, qualities which have been, until now, absent from most textbooks.

"I should say too that I am the founder of an imaginary corporation called Inspirations, Inc. Membership in this corporation is freely offered to anyone who, as my business card states, is willing 'to share talents and ideas for the public good.'"

*   *   *

JARRELL, Mary Von Schrader   1914-

PERSONAL: Surname accented on second syllable; born May 2, 1914, in St. Louis, Mo.; daughter of Alleyne (a physician and surgeon) and Irene (Bond) Von Schrader; married Melville Garton (an architect), June 18, 1936 (divorced July, 1951); married Randall Jarrell (a poet, critic, and teacher), November 8, 1952 (died in 1965); children: Alleyne Von Schrader Garton Boyette, Beatrice Farquhar Garton Hofer. *Education:* Stanford University, B.A., 1936. *Politics:* Democrat. *Religion:* Episcopalian. *Agent:* McIntosh & Otis, Inc., 475 Fifth Ave., New York, N.Y. 10017. *Office address:* P.O. Box 8584, Greensboro, N.C. 27410.

CAREER: California State Relief Administration, San Bernadino and Los Angeles, medical case worker, 1937-39; Huntington Memorial Hospital, Pasadena, Calif., receptionist in cancer clinic, 1940-46. Gives poetry readings for city school enrichment programs.

WRITINGS: Jerome: The Biography of a Poem, Grossman, 1970; *The Knee-Baby* (for children), Farrar, Straus, 1973; (editor with David Bromwich) *Kipling, Auden, and Company,* Farrar, Straus, 1978. Author with Cheryl Seaver of teleplay, "Randall Jarrell, 1914-1965," Public Broadcasting System. Contributor to periodicals, including *American Poetry Review, Parnassus, Harper's,* and *Shenandoah.*

WORK IN PROGRESS: Editing the *Selected Letters of Randall Jarrell;* a story, "The Letter in the Library."

SIDELIGHTS: Jarrell told *CA:* "When I married Randall Jarrell, I had a handful of notes from agent Harold Ober and editor Edward Weeks, and two half-finished cathedrals. One of these was to have been a big Steinbeckian novel about the American-born Japanese in California after World War II. The other was to have been a grand Proustian novel about an aristocratic circle of Bostonians, mostly spinsters, residing in Pasadena. However, as I have written in a memoir, 'The Group of Two': 'To be married to Randall was to be encapsulated with him. He wanted, and we had, an around-the-clock inseparability. We took three meals a day together, every day. I went along to his classes and he went along on my errands. I watched him play tennis, he picked out my clothes.' She continued, "He re-made me into an opera-ballet buff, a tennis-football-sportscar fan, and a nineteenth century nut. After fourteen years of participating so intimately in his habits, hobbies, tastes and activities I could scarcely tell where he left off and I began. When he was accidentally struck by a car and killed I was re-made again—into a lone person with a vast cultural legacy to sort through, re-evaluate and, possibly, benefit from.

"I discarded specator sports," Jarrell recalled, "as they were no fun without Randall. But I kept what I could of the rest and I went back to writing—not to my old cathedrals which I no longer regretted were half-finished but marvelled at their getting half-built—but to the subject I knew best: Randall Jarrell and his work. In the editing of, or active involvement with his six posthumous books and two Caedmon recordings I have written everything from book-and-record-jacket copy to Forewords and Afterwords." She is also writing essays and memoirs.

Jarrell described her writing schedule, "Beginning in the fall I write half a day for half a year." The time not spent writing is activity filled: "In my free time I read Homer, Shakespeare, The Bible, and works by European, Russian, and English nineteenth-century writers which inspires me to visit their lands. I will also, at the drop of a hat, visit the Kennedy Center or Lincoln Center to see Messrs Richardson, Scofield, Gielgud, and Nureyev, and to hear Monserrat-Caballe, Vickers, Fisher-Dieskau, and Carreras, as well as Brendel, Abbado, and Boehme. I am a frequenter of galleries here and abroad, accompanied by Sir Kenneth Clark's words and a special interest of my own in the French impressionists and Vermeer. I hope to see all the Vermeers there are.

"Summers I stay home. I live in a shady oak and pine grove with an almost hidden swimming pool where my faculty friends join me to cool off. In August my family comes to visit for several weeks and we play and read and talk around the pool. After Labor Day when my daughters go back to their husbands and my grandchildren go back to their schools, a familiar restlessness and mounting anxiety signal that I am about to forsake all others and write. Each year I routinely procrastinate and become irritable but nothing satisfies this extraordinary craving except to give in to it and to the unnatural (to me) isolation and inwardness my writing requires. I fight it, but I do it. I don't know why. But I do it."

*   *   *

JEFFREYS, J. G.
See HEALEY, Ben J.

*   *   *

JEFFREYS-JONES, Rhodri   1942-

PERSONAL: Born July 28, 1942, in Carmarthen, Wales; son of Thomas Ieuan (a college president) and Nancy (Watkins) Jeffreys-Jones; married Janetta Carolina Minkiewicz (a teacher), August 15, 1970; children: Gwenda Ludwika, Marie Rowena. *Education:* University College of Wales at Aberystwyth, B.A., 1963; further study at University of Michigan, 1964-65, and Harvard University, 1965-66; Cambridge University, Ph.D., 1967. *Home:* 9 Ethel Ter., Edinburgh EN10 5NB, Scotland. *Office:* Department of History, University of Edinburgh, 50 George Sq., Edinburgh, Scotland.

CAREER: Cambridge University, Cambridge, England, tutor in history, 1966-67; University of Edinburgh, Edinburgh, Scotland, lecturer in history, 1967—, convenor of North American Studies Program, 1974-77. Council candidate for Labour Party, 1971. Director of Scottish Universities Summer School, 1976. *Member:* British Association for American Studies, Society for Historians of American Foreign Relations. *Awards, honors:* Award from Institute for Historical Research's Twenty-Seven Foundation, 1969; fellow of Charles Warren Center at Harvard University, 1971-72; British Academy overseas fellowship, 1975.

WRITINGS: American Espionage: From Secret Service to CIA, Free Press, 1977; *Violence and Reform in American History,* New Viewpoints, 1978. Contributor to Irish studies, American studies, and education journals.

WORK IN PROGRESS: The Social Bases of American Diplomacy, completion expected in 1981.

SIDELIGHTS: Jeffreys-Jones writes: "I am interested in furthering British expertise in the fields of American history and politics. Such expertise is essential to a continuing good relationship between Great Britain and the United States. Too often in the past, British media have broadcast without question American opinions and self-criticisms. Yet there is scope for an independent, British critique of American affairs, particularly concerning the relationship between domestic social problems and external policy, and particularly at the present juncture, when, in relation to such commodities as oil, U.S. conservationists, wage-earners, consumers, and statesmen find themselves confronted with scarcities that have traditionally affected Britain and European countries."

AVOCATIONAL INTERESTS: Vegetable gardening, Welsh language and culture.

*   *   *

JEFFRIES, Graham Montague   1900-
(Peter Bourne, Bruce Graeme, David Graeme)

PERSONAL: Born May 23, 1900, in London, England; son of William Henry and Elizabeth Charlotte (Montague) Jeffries; married Lorna Helene Louch, April 7, 1925; children: Roderic, Guillaine Lois Jeffries Hughes. *Education:* Privately educated. *Residence:* Kent, England.

CAREER: Writer, 1920—. Has also worked as free-lance journalist, literary agent, and film writer/producer.

WRITINGS—All under pseudonym Bruce Graeme, except as noted: *Blackshirt,* Dodd, 1925; *The Trail of the White Knight,* Harrap, 1926, Doran, 1927; *La Belle Laurine,* Unwin, 1926, revised edition published as *Laurine,* Phillip Allan, 1935; *The Return of Blackshirt,* Dodd, 1927; *Passion, Murder, and Mystery* (nonfiction), Hutchinson, 1928; *Hate Ship,* Dodd, 1928; *The Story of Buckingham Palace* (nonfiction), Hutchinson, 1928, revised edition, Howard Baker, 1970; *Trouble!,* Lippincott, 1929; *Adventures of Blackshirt,* Dodd, 1929 (published in England as *Blackshirt Again,* Hutchinson, 1929); *The Story of St. James's Palace* (nonfiction), Hutchinson, 1929.

Through the Eyes of the Judge, Lippincott, 1930; *The Penance of Brother Alaric,* Hutchinson, 1930; *A Murder of Some Importance,* Lippincott, 1931; *Unsolved,* Hutchinson, 1931, Lippincott, 1932; *Gigins Court,* Hutchinson, 1932; *Alias Blackshirt,* Dodd, 1932; *The Imperfect Crime,* Hutchinson, 1932, Lippincott, 1933; *Impeached!,* Hutchinson, 1933; (under pseudonym David Graeme) *Monsieur Blackshirt,* Lippincott, 1933; *Epilogue,* Hutchinson, 1933, Lippincott, 1934; *An International Affair,* Hutchinson, 1934; *Public Enemy—No. 1,* Hutchinson, 1934, published as *John Jenkin, Public Enemy,* Lippincott, 1935; (under pseudonym David Graeme) *The Vengeance of Monsieur Blackshirt,* Harrap, 1934, Lippincott, 1935; *Satan's Mistress,* Hutchinson, 1935; *Madame Spy,* Phillip Allan, 1935; *Blackshirt the Audacious,* Hutchinson, 1935, Lippincott, 1936; *Not Proven,* Hutchinson, 1935; *Cardyce for the Defense,* Hutchinson, 1936; (under pseudonym David Graeme) *The Sword of Monsieur Blackshirt,* Lippincott, 1936; *Blackshirt the Adventurer,* Hutchinson, 1936; *Mystery on the Queen Mary,* Hutchinson, 1937, Lippincott, 1938; *Blackshirt Takes a Hand,* Hutchinson, 1937; *Disappearance of Roger Tremayne,* Hutchinson, 1937; *A Century of Buckingham Palace* (nonfiction), Hutchinson, 1937; *The Story of Windsor Castle* (nonfiction), Hutchinson, 1937; *Racing Yacht Mystery,*

Hutchinson, 1938; *Blackshirt: Counter Spy*, Hutchinson, 1938; (under pseudonym David Graeme) *The Inn of Thirteen Swords*, Harrap, 1938; *The Man from Michigan*, Hutchinson, 1938, published as *The Mystery of the Stolen Hats*, Lippincott, 1939; *Body Unknown*, Hutchinson, 1939; *Blackshirt Interferes*, Hutchinson, 1939; *Poisoned Sleep*, Hutchinson, 1939.

All published by Hutchinson, except as noted: *Thirteen in a Fog*, 1940; *Blackshirt Strikes Back*, 1940; *The Corporal Died in Bed*, 1940; *Seven Clues in Search of a Crime*, 1941; *Son of Blackshirt*, 1941; *Encore Allain!*, 1941; *House with Crooked Walls*, 1942; *Lord Blackshirt*, 1942; *News Travels By Night*, 1943; *A Case for Solomon*, 1943; *Calling Lord Blackshirt*, 1943; *Work for the Hangman*, 1944; *Ten Trails to Tyburn*, 1944; *The Coming of Carew: A Fantasy in Crime*, 1945; *A Case of Books*, 1946; *Without Malice*, 1946; *A Brief for O'Leary, and Two Other Episodes in His Career*, 1947; (under pseudonym Peter Bourne) *Drums of Destiny*, Putnam, 1947 (published in England as *Black Saga*, Hutchinson, 1947); *No Clues for Dexter*, 1948; *And a Bottle of Rum*, 1949; *Tigers Have Claws*, 1949; (under pseudonym Peter Bourne) *Flames of Empire*, Putnam, 1949.

(Under pseudonym Peter Bourne) *Dupe of Destiny*, 1950; *Cherchez la Femme*, 1951; (under pseudonym Peter Bourne) *Ten Thousand Shall Die*, 1951; *Dead Pigs at Hungry Farm*, 1951; (under pseudonym Peter Bourne) *The Golden Rod*, Putnam, 1951; *Lady in Black*, 1952; (under pseudonym Peter Bourne) *Gateway to Fortune*, Putnam, 1952; *Mr. Whimset Buys a Gun*, 1953; *Suspense*, 1953; *The Way Out*, 1954; (under pseudonym Peter Bourne) *Twilight of the Dragon*, Putnam, 1954; *So Sharp the Razor*, 1955; *Just an Ordinary Case*, 1956; (under pseudonym Peter Bourne) *When God Slept*, Putnam, 1956; *The Accidental Clue*, 1957; *The Long Night*, 1958; (under pseudonym Peter Bourne) *The Court of Love*, 1958; *Boomerang*, 1959.

(Under pseudonym Peter Bourne) *Soldiers of Fortune*, 1962, Putnam, 1963; *The Undetective*, 1962, London House & Maxwell, 1963; (under pseudonym David Graeme) *The Drums Beat Red*, Harrap, 1963; *Almost Without Murder*, 1963; *Holiday for a Spy*, 1963; (under pseudonym Peter Bourne) *Black Gold*, 1964; *Always Expect the Unexpected*, 1965; *The Devil Was a Woman*, 1966; (under pseudonym Peter Bourne) *Fall of the Eagle*, 1967; *Much Ado About Something*, 1967; *Never Mix Business with Pleasure*, 1968; *Some Geese Lay Golden Eggs*, 1968; *Blind Date for a Private Eye*, 1969; *The Quiet Ones*, 1970; *The Lady Doth Protest*, 1971; *Tomorrow's Yesterday*, 1972; *Danger in the Channel*, Kaye & Ward, 1973; *Two and Two Make Five*, 1973; *The Snatch*, 1976; *Two Faced*, 1977.

WORK IN PROGRESS: Another novel.

SIDELIGHTS: While working as a literary agent in 1922, Jeffries submitted his first novel (which was rejected) and short story (which was accepted) about Blackshirt, one of the enduring rogues of fiction. After numerous stories and novels featuring the cracksman and adventurer, all written under the Bruce Graeme pseudonym, the author tired of the character and the series was continued by his son, Roderic Jeffries (under the name Roderic Graeme).

Graham Montague Jeffries told *CA:* "My motivation is simply a love of writing. My major avocational interest is travel—there have been ten visits to the United States and countless trips to France and Spain. I have also traveled to Holland, Italy, Austria, Morocco, Algiers. I speak indifferent French, even less Spanish."

BIOGRAPHICAL/CRITICAL SOURCES: Chris Stein-

brunner and Otto Penzler, *Encyclopedia of Mystery and Detection*, McGraw, 1975.

* * *

JENNER, Chrystie 1950-

PERSONAL: Born October 6, 1950, in Washington; daughter of Carlos H. (a foreman) and Chrystal D. (a counselor) Crownover; married William Bruce Jenner (an athlete), December 16, 1972. *Education:* Attended Graceland College. *Office:* Sports Media Sales, 1901 Avenue of the Stars, #630, Century City, Los Angeles, Calif. 90067.

CAREER: United Air Lines, San Francisco, Calif., flight attendant, 1972-76; 8618, Inc., Malibu, Calif., vice-president, 1976—. Co-founder of C. J. and Dr. Varnish (house remodeling business). Counselor and public speaker for Los Angeles Rape Crisis Center. *Member:* National Organization of Women.

WRITINGS: I Am Chrystie, Les Femmes, 1977.

WORK IN PROGRESS: Bruce and Chrystie Jenner's Guide to Fitness for Tempo Books; two stories of Olympic goals and personal independence and how they support and contradict each other.

* * *

JENSEN, Merrill 1905-

PERSONAL: Born July 16, 1905, in Elkhorn, Iowa; son of John M. (a farmer) and Julia (Seymour) Jensen; married Genevieve M. Privet, December 24, 1929; children: Julanne (Mrs. David G. Pease). *Education:* University of Washington, Seattle, B.A., 1929, M.A., 1931; University of Wisconsin, Madison, Ph.D., 1934. *Home:* 2823 Century Harbor Rd., Middleton, Wis. 53562. *Office:* 5227 Humanities Building, University of Wisconsin, 435 North Park St., Madison, Wis. 53706.

CAREER: University of Washington, Seattle, 1935-44, began as instructor, became associate professor of history; University of Wisconsin—Madison, associate professor, 1944-47, professor of history, 1947—, Vilas Research Professor of History, 1964—, chairman of department, 1961-64. Harmsworth Professor of American History at Oxford University, 1949-50; lecturer at University of Tokyo, 1955, University of Ghent, 1960, and Doshisha University, 1961, 1971. Member of advisory committee of Conference Board on International Exchange of Persons, 1962-72. *Member:* Organization of American Historians (president, 1969-70).

WRITINGS: The Articles of Confederation: An Interpretation of the Social-Constitutional History of the American Revolution, 1774-1781, University of Wisconsin Press, 1940, 3rd edition, 1959; *The New Nation: A History of the United States During the Confederation, 1781-1789* (History Book Club selection), Knopf, 1950; (editor) *Regionalism in America*, University of Wisconsin Press, 1951; (editor) *English Historical Documents*, Volume VI: *American Colonial Documents to 1776*, Oxford University Press, 1955.

The Making of the American Constitution, Van Nostrand, 1964; (editor) *Tracts of the American Revolution, 1763-1776*, Bobbs-Merrill, 1967; *The Founding of a Nation: A History of the American Revolution, 1763-1776* (History Book Club selection), Oxford University Press, 1968; *The American Revolution Within America*, New York University Press, 1974; (editor) *The Documentary History of the First Federal Elections, 1788-1790*, University of Wisconsin Press, Volume I, 1976, Volume II, 1979; (editor) *The Documentary History of the Ratification of the Constitution*, State Historical Society of Wisconsin Press, Volume I, 1976, Volume II, 1976, Volume III, 1978.

Contributor: (Author of introduction) R. G. Adams, *Political Ideas of the American Revolution*, Barnes & Noble, 1959; Ray Billington, editor, *The Reinterpretation of Early American History: Essays in Honor of John Edwin Pomfret*, Huntington Library, 1966; C. Vann Woodward, editor, *The Comparative Approach to American History*, Basic Books, 1968; (author of introduction) Joseph Galloway, *Historical and Political Reflections on the Rise and Progress of the American Rebellion*, Johnson Reprint, 1972; *Fundamental Testaments of the American Revolution*, Library of Congress, 1973.

Contributor to history and political science journals. Member of editorial board of *Mississippi Valley Historical Review* and *American Quarterly*.

WORK IN PROGRESS: Editing third volume of *The Documentary History of the First Federal Elections, 1788-1790*, for University of Wisconsin Press; editing further volumes of *The Documentary History of the Ratification of the Constitution*, for State Historical Society of Wisconsin Press.

*   *   *

JENSEN, Peter
See WALLMANN, Jeffrey M(iner)

*   *   *

JEPSEN, Stanley M(arius)   1912-

PERSONAL: Born June 8, 1912, in Wheeling, W.Va.; son of Marius C. (a baker) and Paulina (Schultz) Jepsen; married Mildred E. Cuthbert, January 24, 1941 (died March 6, 1944); married Ruth Barrett, December 26, 1946 (died April 6, 1977); children: Jeffrey S., Holly J. (Mrs. Curtis B. Maloy), Jenny K., Erica J. *Education:* University of Idaho, B.S., 1954, M.F., 1955. *Religion:* Protestant. *Home:* 7205 Oakridge Ave., Chevy Chase, Md. 20015. *Office:* Forest Service, U.S. Department of Agriculture, Washington, D.C. 20250.

CAREER: Glacier National Park, Glacier Park, Mont., seasonal ranger, summers, 1953-54; Philmont Scout Ranch, Cimarron, N.M., forester, 1955; high school teacher of forestry and life science in Weaverville, Calif., 1955-56; Miller Freeman Publications, Portland, Ore., associate editor of *Timberman* and *Lumberman*, 1956-61; American Forest Institute, Washington, D.C., director of education, 1961-64; U.S. Department of Agriculture, Forest Service, Washington, D.C., chief of Conservation Education Branch, 1964-74, group contacts coordinator in Office of Information, 1974—. *Member:* National Audubon Society, Wheaton Club of Ohio, Xi Sigma Pi. *Awards, honors:* Essay award from Western Forestry & Conservation Association, 1953, for "The Production and Conservation of Water."

WRITINGS: Trees and Forests, A. S. Barnes, 1969; *The Gentle Giants*, A. S. Barnes, 1971; *The Coach Horse: Servant with Style*, A. S. Barnes, 1977; (with Philip Weber) *Heroes in Harness*, A. S. Barnes, in press. Contributor to foresters' journals.

WORK IN PROGRESS: Over the Years, poems; *Grandpa's Woodpile*, children's stories.

SIDELIGHTS: Jepsen writes: "My interest in nature and the out-of-doors goes back to my boyhood on a farm in Delaware County, Ohio. This led me to choose forestry as a career, and to study forestry at the University of Idaho."

AVOCATIONAL INTERESTS: Hunting, fishing, horseback riding, working with horses, gardening, bird watching.

*   *   *

JEROME, Lawrence E(dmund)   1944-

PERSONAL: Born January 15, 1944, in Glen Cove, N.Y.; son of George L. (a civil engineer) and Gladys (Roberts) Jerome. *Education:* Florida State University, B.S., 1965, M.S., 1966; further graduate study at Stanford University, 1966-70. *Politics:* None. *Religion:* None. *Residence:* Cupertino, Calif. 95014.

CAREER: Writer and environmental activist, 1971—. *Member:* American Humanist Association, Oceanic Society, Sylvan-Dale Committee for Legal EIRs, Zetetic Committee for the Scientific Investigation of Claims of the Paranormal, Phi Eta Sigma, Pi Mu Sigma, Sigma Pi Sigma, Phi Kappa Phi, Omicron Delta Kappa. *Awards, honors:* National Aeronautics & Space Administration fellowship, 1966-70.

WRITINGS: (With Bart Bok) *Objections to Astrology*, Prometheus Books, 1975; *Astrology Disproved*, Prometheus Books, 1977. Author of column "Scienvironment," in *Groundswell*. Contributor of articles and a story to *Oceans, Humanist, Leonardo*, and *Foreground*.

WORK IN PROGRESS: The Compleat Atheist; The PCB Story; Innovative Statistics, with educational statistical game set.

SIDELIGHTS: Jerome writes: "Impact writing is my immediate goal. Our inherited world must be viewed with considerable skepticism. Societal myths abound which require serious questioning if we are to progress into the twenty-first century in any orderly fashion. Particularly destructive are misconceptions regarding man's use of the environment, aided and abetted by political and religious naivete."

*   *   *

JESCHKE, Susan   1942-

PERSONAL: Born October 18, 1942, in Cleveland, Ohio; daughter of Aaron (a dentist) and Victoria (a teacher; maiden name, Virnick) Kochman. *Education:* Attended School of Visual Arts, and Brooklyn Museum School. *Residence:* Brooklyn, N.Y.

CAREER: Illustrator and writer.

WRITINGS—Self-illustrated children's books: *Firerose*, Holt, 1974; *Sidney*, Holt, 1975; *The Devil Did It*, Holt, 1975; *Rina and Zeppo*, Windmill Books, 1976; *Victoria's Adventure*, Holt, 1976; *Mia, Grandma, and the Genie*, Holt, 1977.

Illustrator: Joan Tate, *Wild Boy*, Harper, 1973; Lucile Clifton, *The Times They Used to Be*, Holt, 1974; Johanna Hurwitz, *Busybody Nora*, Morrow, 1976; Hurwitz, *Nora and Mrs. Mind-Your-Own-Business*, Morrow, 1977.

SIDELIGHTS: Susan Jeschke remarks: "Love, death, supernatural events, and grotesqueries—are all uppermost in my mind." *Avocational interests:* Movies, books, animals, travel in Italy.

*   *   *

JESSEN, Carl A.   1887(?)-1978

1887(?)—June 19, 1978; American educator, journalist, and author. Jessen was the former chief of the secondary school section of the U.S. Office of Education. After his retirement, he was elected executive secretary for the Cooperative Study of Secondary Education. Jessen published articles in educational magazines and was the author of *Mignonette and Other Poems.* He died in Washington, D.C. Obituaries and other sources: *Washington Post,* June 22, 1978.

* * *

JESSUP, Philip C(aryl) 1897-

PERSONAL: Born January 5, 1897, in New York, N.Y.; son of Henry Wynans and Mary Hay (Stotesbury) Jessup; married Lois Walcott Kellogg, July 23, 1921; children: Philip C., Jr. *Education:* Hamilton College, A.B., 1919; Yale University, LL.B., 1924; Columbia University, A.M., 1924, Ph.D., 1927. *Home:* Windrow Rd., Norfolk, Conn. 06058.

CAREER: Admitted to the Bar of Washington, D.C., 1925, and the Bar of New York State, 1927; Columbia University, New York City, lecturer, 1925-27, assistant professor, 1927-29, associate professor, 1929-35, professor, 1935-46, Hamilton Fish Professor of International Law and Diplomacy, 1946-61, Jacob Blaustein Lecturer, 1970; International Court of Justice, United Nations, The Hague, Netherlands, judge, 1961-70; Council on Foreign Relations, New York City, Whitney H. Shepardson senior research fellow, 1970-71; Wellesley College, Wellesley, Mass., Barnett Miller Lecturer, 1971; jurist, 1971—; chairman of Permanent Austro-Swedish Commission for Arbitration and Reconciliation, 1976—. Member of Parker & Duryea (a law firm), 1927-43. Assistant solicitor for U.S. Department of State, 1924-25; assistant to Elihu Root at Permanent Court of International Justice in Geneva, 1929; legal adviser to American ambassador to Cuba, 1930; associate director of Naval School of Military Government and Administration, 1942-44; chief of personnel and training division for Office of Foreign Relief and Rehabilitation Operations, 1943; assistant secretary general of United Nations Relief and Rehabilitation Administration, 1943; assistant secretary general of U.N. Monetary and Financial Conference at Bretton Woods, 1944; U.S. delegate to San Francisco Conference, 1945; U.S. representative to U.N. Committee on Progressive Development and Codification of International Law, 1947; U.S. representative at various sessions of U.N. Security Council and General Assembly, 1948-53; U.S. ambassador-at-large, 1949-53; chairman of Chile-Norway Permanent Conciliation Commission, 1958—; honorary member of governing council of International Institute for Unification of Private Law, 1967—. *Military service:* U.S. Army, 1917-18; received Hungarian Cross of Merit, Class II, and Nacional do Cruzeiro do Sul (Brazil); named National Order of Cedars grand officer (Lebanon).

MEMBER: International Law Association (honorary president, 1970-73), Institut de Droit International (first vice-president, 1973-75), American Society for International Law (honorary president, 1969-73, 1976—), American Philosophical Society, American Academy of Arts and Sciences, Century Club, Cosmos Club. *Awards, honors:* LL.D. from Hamilton College, 1937, Western Reserve University (now Case Western Reserve University), 1941, Brown University, 1949, Rutgers University, 1950, Seoul National University, 1950, Middlebury College, 1950, Yale University, 1964, St. Lawrence University, 1966, University of Michigan, 1966, Columbia University, 1970, Johns Hopkins University, 1970, Brandeis University, 1971, Colby College, 1973, University of Pennsylvania, 1976; J.D. from Oslo University, 1946; Dr. hon. c. from University of Paris, 1948; Litt. D. from University of Hanoi, 1950; L.C.D. from Colgate University, 1950, Union College, 1951. Awarded Hudson Gold Medal from American Society of International Law, 1964; Fowler Harper fellow at Yale Law School, 1966; distin-

guished public service award from Connecticut Bar, 1970; Wolfgang Friedman Award from Columbia University Law School, 1973; Columbia University School of Law Alumni Association medal for excellence, 1976; Graduate Faculties Alumni of Columbia University award for excellence, 1976.

WRITINGS: The Law of Territorial Waters and Maritime Jurisdiction, G. A. Jennings, 1927, reprinted, Kraus Reprint, 1970; *American Neutrality and International Police,* World Peace Foundation, 1928; *The United States and Treaties for the Avoidance of War,* Carnegie Endowment for International Peace, 1928; *The Permanent Court of International Justice,* Carnegie Endowment for International Peace, 1929; *The United States and the World Court,* World Peace Foundation, 1929, reprinted, Johnson Reprint, 1970; *The United States and the Permanent Court of International Justice,* Carnegie Endowment for International Peace, 1931; *International Security: The American Role in Collective Action for Peace,* Council on Foreign Relations, 1935, reprinted, Greenwood Press, 1975; (editor) *Neutrality: Its History, Economics, and Law,* four volumes, Columbia University Press, 1935-36, reprinted, Octagon, 1973; (editor with Francis Deak) *A Collection of Neutrality Laws, Regulations, and Treaties of Various Countries,* two volumes, Carnegie Endowment for International Peace, 1939, reprinted, Kraus Reprint, 1976.

The International Problem of Governing Mankind, Claremont Men's College, 1947; *A Modern Law of Nations,* Macmillan, 1948, reprinted with a new preface by the author, Archon Books, 1968; (with Adolf Lande and Oliver J. Lissitzyn) *International Regulation of Economic and Social Questions,* Carnegie Endowment for International Peace, 1955; (with Lissitzyn) *Opinion of Philip C. Jessup and Oliver J. Lissitzyn With Respect to the United States Senate's Attempt to Repeal the Federal Power Act in Its Relation to the Niagara Through the Use of the Treaty-Making Power,* Power Authority of the State of New York, 1955; *Transnational Law,* Yale University Press, 1956; (editor) *Atoms for Power,* American Assembly, 1957; *The Use of International Law,* University of Michigan Law School, 1959; (with Howard J. Taubenfeld) *Controls for Outer Space and the Antarctic Analogy,* Columbia University Press, 1959; *The Price of International Justice,* Columbia University Press, 1971; *The Birth of Nations,* Columbia University Press, 1974.

Contributor to journals in his field. Supervising editor of *Columbia University Studies in History, Economics, and Public Law,* 1929-33; member of editorial boards of *American Journal of International Law, World Politics,* and *International Organization.*

WORK IN PROGRESS: Research and writing of memos on international law problems in U.S. federal courts.

SIDELIGHTS: Jessup told *CA:* "Experience as a doughboy on the Belgian and French fronts in World War I led me to devote my life to measures calculated to promote peace and avoid war. I consulted Elihu Root and chose a career in international law." Looking back on Jessup's distinguished career, former Secretary of State Dean Acheson called him a "diplomatist," distinguishing him from the rabble of "diplomats" who had denigrated the latter term, and comparing him instead to the sixteenth century "fathers" of modern diplomacy, Cardinals Wolsey of England and Richelieu of France. Jessup's service as U.S. representative to the United Nations and ambassador-at-large between 1948 and 1953 prompted Acheson to praise his diplomatic skills, especially as they manifested themselves in the secret negotiations concerning the Soviet blockade of Berlin and the resolution of the potentially divisive question of German participation in the defense of Europe. Recalling the leadership role against Soviet intransigence that the United States played in NATO and the United Nations during 1950, Acheson also credited Jessup with helping to inspire and create confidence and trust in American integrity on the part of the nations within those organizations. According to Acheson, this creation of trust fulfilled the primary purpose of diplomacy as Cardinal Richelieu had conceived it.

In *The Birth of Nations,* Jessup drew upon his diplomatic experience to describe the "nationhood explosion" which has occurred during the last several decades. F. H. Soward noted: "This sprightly volume is concerned . . . with events preceding the birth of such nations as Korea, Indonesia, Morocco, Tunisia, Libya, Somalia, and Israel, with the abortive empire of Bao Dai where the United States played too 'paternalistic' a role, the stillbirth of Eritrea, and the illegitimate child, Manchukuo, 'the prime example of puppetry. . . .' Students of diplomacy and international relations will profit from the painstaking description Jessup presents of how policies are formed and negotiations conducted."

Besides recounting many of the historical details of these events, Jessup expressed his views about the conduct of American foreign policy in general. Rupert Emerson observed: "Jessup pleads for a restoration of the old-established system under which American foreign policy was directed by the State Department, under a Secretary of State actually in charge of the formulation and execution of foreign policy. 'It is a tragic error,' he writes, 'to relegate the State Department and the Foreign Service to a status in which they would be no more important in foreign policy than the dinosaur is of current ecological significance.'"

BIOGRAPHICAL/CRITICAL SOURCES: Wolfgang Friedmann, Louis Hendin, and Oliver Lissitzyn, editors, *Transnational Law in a Changing Society: Essays in Honor of Philip C. Jessup,* Columbia University Press, 1972; Philip C. Jessup, *The Birth of Nations,* Columbia University Press, 1974; *New York Times Book Review,* May 19, 1974; *Pacific Affairs,* fall, 1974; *Nation,* November 9, 1974.

*   *   *

JIMENEZ, Janey (Renee) 1953-

PERSONAL: Born January 1, 1953, in Van Nuys, Calif.; daughter of Raymond Lopez and Frances (Estrada) Jimenez. *Education:* Los Angeles Valley Junior College, A.A., 1972; San Diego State University, B.A., 1974, graduate study, 1976—; further study at Federal Law Enforcement Training Center (Glynco, Ga.), 1975. *Religion:* Roman Catholic. *Residence:* San Diego, Calif. *Agent:* Tony Mendez, 140 East 56th St., New York, N.Y. 10022.

CAREER: U.S. Bureau of Prisons, Metropolitan Correctional Center, San Diego, Calif., correctional officer, 1974-75; U.S. Marshals Service, San Francisco, Calif., U.S. Deputy Marshal, 1975-76; currently working as an investigative intern with Federal Defenders, San Diego. *Member:* International Association of Chiefs of Police, Western Society of Criminology.

WRITINGS: (With Ted Berkman) *My Prisoner,* Sheed Andrews & McMeel, 1977.

SIDELIGHTS: Janey Jimenez will never forget the day she began her job as U.S. Deputy Marshall in San Francisco. Her first assignment that day, September 29, 1975, was to take Patty Hearst to the hospital. That and the months of

guarding her throughout the long, widely publicized trial profoundly influenced the life of the young Chicana who became close friends with Patty. In *My Prisoner,* she tells the story of their friendship and shares her intimate knowledge of the enigmatic Patty Hearst. Nancy Faber called the book "a sympathetic, highly personal portrait of a troubled and confusing young woman."

Jimenez told *CA:* "I am currently enrolled in the criminal justice administration program at San Diego State University, working on a master's degree. I am also working as an investigative intern for Federal Defenders in San Diego, the legal agency that represents defendants who cannot afford to hire private attorneys. I find the work of an investigator to be very challenging. After I complete my internship I figure I will have gained the experience of working on both sides of the system (locking the prisoner up, and now viewing the defendant as an individual and trying to prevent him/her from being put behind bars). I also believe that from this experience I will be able to decide whether or not I want to pursue my career in the field of law, which at this point I most certainly do."

When asked how her experience as Deputy U.S. Marshal for Patricia Hearst influenced her ideas about the criminal justice system, Jimenez replied: "I always wanted to help people no matter who they were or what they had, and especially those who were victims of society. My experience with the trial of Patty Hearst has only reinforced these feelings. It will be impossible for me to change the system, but at least I can only hope that with me being a part of it and seeing the victim as a 'human being' and not labeling him/her, this in turn will be my contribution. There should definitely be justice, but new attitudes and approaches must be developed so that we do not send people to prison or death knowing they are innocent."

BIOGRAPHICAL/CRITICAL SOURCES: New York Daily News, January 28, 1976, October 20, 1977; *New York Post,* February 2, 1976; *San Francisco Chronicle,* February 24, 1976, July 28, 1976; *People* Magazine, March 1, 1976, October 18, 1976, October 3, 1977; *Los Angeles Times,* March 7, 1976; *San Francisco Examiner,* October 5, 1976; *Kirkus Reviews,* September 1, 1977; *Publishers Weekly,* September 12, 1977; *Courier Post,* November 4, 1977; *San Diego Evening Tribune,* November 14, 1977; *San Diego Union,* November 14, 1977, March 27, 1978; *Chicago Tribune,* November 20, 1977.

*   *   *

JOFFE, Joyce 1940-

PERSONAL: Born June 5, 1940, in South Africa; daughter of Max and Saura (Leiserowitz) Joffe; married Francis Treuherz (a lecturer), July 7, 1968; children: Stefan, Sasha. *Education:* University of Wales, B.Sc., 1963. *Religion:* Atheist. *Home:* 27 Milman Rd., London N.W.6, England.

CAREER: Engaged in paleontology research, 1963-67; worked as editor, 1966-70, and teacher, 1971—. *Member:* Alternative Society.

WRITINGS: Conservation, Doubleday, 1968. Contributor to *All About Science.*

SIDELIGHTS: Joyce Joffe writes: "I have 'eco-guilt'—concern about rising population, dwindling resources. It prompted *Conservation,* and now, after ten years, it prompts me to return to the university to qualify as a nutritionist. Perhaps I can make some contribution to alleviating an ill or two." *Avocational interests:* Chamber music, playing viola.

JOHNS, Claude J., Jr. 1930-

PERSONAL: Born August 28, 1930, in Jacksonville, Fla.; son of Claude J. and Agnes (Dugger) Johns; married Rachel Sutton (a counselor), September 1, 1956; children: Michael R., Kenneth Patrick. *Education:* Florida State University, B.S., 1952, M.S., 1953; University of North Carolina, Ph.D., 1964; University of Denver, M.A., 1975. *Politics:* Democrat. *Religion:* Episcopal. *Home:* 29 Alles Dr., Greeley, Colo. 80631. *Office:* Michener Library, University of Northern Colorado, Greeley, Colo. 80639.

CAREER: U.S. Air Force, career officer, retiring as lieutenant colonel, 1976; professor of political science and director of libraries at U.S. Air Force Academy, 1961-76; University of Northern Colorado, Greeley, dean of library services, 1976—. Member of board of directors of Colorado Springs Symphony Association, 1972-76, and board of trustees of Colorado Springs Fine Arts Center, 1975-76.

MEMBER: American Library Association, Special Libraries Association, American Association of University Professors, American Society for Information Science, Mountain Plains Library Association, Colorado Library Association. *Awards, honors*—Military: Legion of Merit. Other: John Cotton Dana Lecturer for Special Libraries Association, 1974-75.

WRITINGS: American Defense Policy, Johns Hopkins Press, 1968; *Handbook of Library Regulations,* Dekker, 1977. Contributor to *Encyclopedia of Library and Information Science.* Contributor of articles and reviews to professional journals.

WORK IN PROGRESS: Collective Bargaining in College and University Libraries.

SIDELIGHTS: Johns comments: "My primary interest is in library administration, especially personnel and fiscal areas; also in collective bargaining and unionization in college and university libraries."

* * *

JOHNSON, James E(dgar) 1927-

PERSONAL: Born March 26, 1927, in Johnson City, N.Y.; son of Willis B. and Margeurite Johnson; married wife, Louella (a teacher), 1948; children: Kathleen L., Richard W. *Education:* Triple Cities College of Syracuse University (now State University of New York Harpur College), B.A., 1950; State University of New York at Buffalo, M.A., 1953; Syracuse University, Ph.D., 1959. *Home:* 1065 Carlton Dr., St. Paul, Minn. 55112. *Office:* Department of History, Bethel College, 3900 Bethel Dr., St. Paul, Minn. 55112.

CAREER: Youngstown State University, Youngstown, Ohio, assistant professor of history, 1959-61; Bethel College, St. Paul, Minn., associate professor, 1961-67, professor of history, 1967—. Member of summer faculty at Syracuse University, 1959-69. *Military service:* U.S. Naval Reserve, active duty, 1945-46. *Member:* American Historical Association, Organization of American Historians, Immigration History Society, Conference on Administrative History, Conference on Faith and History, Minnesota Historical Society, Social Welfare History Group, Pi Gamma Mu. *Awards, honors:* Grants from National Endowment for the Humanities and Minnesota American Revolution Bicentennial Commission, both 1976.

WRITINGS: The Irish in America, Lerner, 1966; *The Scots and Scotch-Irish in America,* Lerner, 1966; (contributor) Richard Pierard, Robert Clouse, and Robert Linder, editors, *Protest and Politics,* Attic Press, 1969; (contributor)

Pierard, Clouse, and Linder, editors, *The Cross and the Flag,* Creation House, 1972; (contributor) Carol George, editor, *"Remember the Ladies": New Perspectives on Women in American History,* Syracuse University Press, 1975. Contributor of articles and reviews to social studies and religious periodicals.

WORK IN PROGRESS: A manuscript dealing with the history of child welfare in America.

* * *

JOHNSON, Ralph W(hitney) 1923-

PERSONAL: Born October 11, 1923, in Barberton, Ohio; son of H. V. (an attorney) and Hazel Irene (Whitney) Johnson, married Anne Goodman (an art gallery owner), Sept. 27, 1950; children: Brady, Jill, Grant. *Education:* Attended Lehigh University, 1943-44; University of Oregon, B.S., 1947, J.D., 1949; Hague Academy of International Law, diploma, 1961. *Office:* School of Law, University of Washington, JB-20 Condon Hall, Seattle, Wash. 98105.

CAREER: Admitted to Oregon Bar; attorney, practising in Eugene, Ore., 1949-50, and Seattle, Wash., 1952-55; University of Washington, Seattle, assistant professor, 1955-58, associate professor, 1958-61, professor of law, 1961—, adjunct professor at Institute for Marine Studies, 1973—, and Institute for Environmental Studies, 1974—. Visiting scholar at London Institute for Advanced Legal Studies, 1961-62. Member of National Science Foundation task forces on weather modification, and National Academy of Sciences committee on outer continental shelf environmental studies. Consultant to U.S. Senate, Stanford Research Institute, and Hudson Institute. *Military service:* U.S. Army, Infantry, 1944-46, Judge Advocate General's Corps, 1950-52.

MEMBER: International Council of Environmental Law, International Association for Water Law, Washington State Bar Association, Order of Coif. *Awards, honors:* Ford Foundation grant for England, 1961-62; National Science Foundation grant for Europe, 1973-75.

WRITINGS: (With D. R. Van Cleve) *Management of the High Seas Fisheries of the Northeastern Pacific* (monograph), University of Washington, Seattle, 1963; *The Law of Interbasin Transfers,* National Technical Information Service, 1972; (with Robert G. Fleagle, James A. Crutchfield, and M. F. Abdo) *Weather Modification in the Public Interest,* University of Washington Press, 1973; *The Impact of Public Law 280 Upon the Administration of Criminal Justice on Indian Reservations,* National American Indian Court Judges Association, 1974; (with Jay V. White) *Cases and Materials for Indian Court Judges,* National American Indian Court Judges Association, 1976; (with Gardner M. Brown) *Cleaning Up Europe's Waters: Economics, Management, Policies,* Praeger, 1976.

Contributor: *Developments in the Law of the Sea, 1958-1964,* British Institute of International and Comparative Law, 1964; *The Fisheries: Problems in Resource Management,* University of Washington Press, 1965; *The Law of the Sea,* Ohio State University Press, 1967; *Human Dimensions in the Atmosphere,* National Center for Atmospheric Research, 1968; *Weather Modification and the Law,* Southern Methodist University Press, 1968; Albert D. Garretson, Robert D. Hayton, and Cecil J. Olmstead, editors, *The Law of International Drainage Basins,* Ocean Press, 1968; C. Johnson and S. Lewis, editors, *Contemporary Developments in Water Law,* University of Texas Press, 1970; Taubenfeld, editor, *Controlling the Weather: A Study of Law and Regulatory Processes,* Dunellen, 1970.

Contributor to *Yearbook of World Affairs,* and of more than twenty articles to law and environmental studies journals.

* * *

JOHNSON, Sherman Ellsworth 1896-1978

July 31, 1896—April 28, 1978; American educator, researcher, agriculture consultant, agricultural economist, and author. Johnson began his career in Washington, D.C., as a researcher and later worked for the government in the Bureau of Agricultural Economics. During World War II, he served as the director of food productions for the War Food Administration and, in 1959, was the agricultural consultant to the government of India. Johnson received the Distinguished Federal Civilian Service Medal from the president in 1963. He is the author of numerous articles and several books, including an autobiography, *From St. Croix to the Potomac: Reflections of a Bureaucrat.* Johnson died in Strasburg, Va. Obituaries and other sources: *American Men and Women of Science: The Social and Behavioral Sciences,* 12th edition, Bowker, 1971-73; *Who's Who in America,* 39th edition, Marquis, 1975; *Washington Post,* May 4, 1978.

* * *

JOHNSON, Stanley J. F. 1920(?)-1978

1920(?)—March 22, 1978; American news correspondent on foreign affairs. As a correspondent for the Associated Press in Moscow, Johnson covered the succession battle between Nikita S. Khrushchev and other Soviet leaders. He also covered early Soviet space achievements and Berlin Wall diplomacy. Johnson died in New York, N.Y. Obituaries and other sources: *New York Times,* March 3, 1978.

* * *

JOHNSTON, (William) Arnold 1942-

PERSONAL: Born May 31, 1942, in Cambuslang, Scotland; came to the United States in 1951, naturalized citizen, 1962; son of James Reid (a laborer) and Eliza (Arnold) Johnston; married June La Valley, July 27, 1963 (divorced September 8, 1968); married Kristin Lucille Tyrrell (a librarian), September 16, 1972. *Education:* Wayne State University, Ph.B., 1963; University of Delaware, M.A., 1965, Ph.D., 1970. *Home:* 1012 North Fletcher, Kalamazoo, Mich. 49007. *Office:* Department of English, Western Michigan University, Kalamazoo, Mich. 49001.

CAREER: Western Michigan University, Kalamazoo, assistant professor, 1966-72, associate professor of English, 1972—. Member of board of directors of New Vic Theatre, 1973-75, vice-president of board, 1975-76, president, 1976—; has given poetry readings throughout Michigan. Professional singer (from folk to popular music, including his own compositions) at bars and colleges, on radio and television, 1968—; actor with college, civic, and repertory groups, 1966—, and for radio and television commercials. *Member:* American Association of University Professors (member of local bargaining council, 1975-76, and collective bargaining negotiation team, 1976-77; chief negotiator, 1977—).

WRITINGS: The Witching Voice (three-act play about Robert Burns; first produced in Kalamazoo, Mich., at New Vic Theatre, February, 1973), Western Michigan University Press, 1973; (editor) *There Aren't Any Snakes in Ireland,* Department of English, Western Michigan University, 1973; (editor) *The Trial Balloon,* Department of English, Western Michigan University, 1975.

Author of "Scrimshaw" (two-act play), first produced in Kalamazoo, Mich., at New Vic Theatre, February, 1975.

Author of radio series "Songbag," for WMUK-Radio, 1969, and "The Lavender Hill Mob Sings," WMUK-Radio, 1969, a television documentary, "Casting the Spell: The Making of a Play," Western Michigan University, 1973, and individual scripts for WMUK-Radio, "'Fourth of July' Moore and the Battle of Tebb's Bend," 1975, and "The Great Steamboat Race," 1975.

Work represetned in anthology edited by Jack I. Biles and Robert Evans, University of Kentucky Press, 1978. Songwriter and composer for local play productions. Head writer and script supervisor for "Voices from Michigan's Past," WMUK-Radio, 1975. Contributor to literary journals, including *Human Voice, Colorado Quarterly, Midwest Quarterly,* and *Stuffing Box.*

WORK IN PROGRESS: Another play; continuing research on contemporary drama and fiction.

SIDELIGHTS: Johnston writes: "My Scottish background is important to 'The Witching Voice' and to two record albums ('Poems and Songs of Robert Burns,' Aural Press, 1970, and 'Burns in Poetry, Song, and Prose,' CMS Records, Inc., 1971), as well as my one-man program of Burns' works."

* * *

JOHNSTONE, William D(avid) G(ordon) 1935-

PERSONAL: Born in 1935, in Grosse Pointe Farms, Mich.; married wife, Gloria, 1970; children: two. *Education:* Attended Michigan State University, 1953-56. *Agent:* Julian Bach Literary Agency, Inc., 3 East 48th St., New York, N.Y. 10017. *Office:* Johnstone & Johnstone, Inc., 19790 Mack Ave., Grosse Pointe Woods, Mich. 48236.

CAREER: Real estate broker in Grosse Pointe Woods, Mich., 1956—.

WRITINGS: For Good Measure (nonfiction), Holt, 1975.

WORK IN PROGRESS: Lister's Guide to Marketing Residential Real Estate.

* * *

JOINER, Charles A(drian) 1932-

PERSONAL: Born August 26, 1932, in West Frankfort, Ill.; son of LeRoy and Audrey (Ballard) Joiner; married Doris Kendig, December 28, 1961. *Education:* Southern Illinois University, B.A., 1954, M.A., 1955; University of Illinois, Ph.D., 1958. *Home:* 237 West Highland, Philadelphia, Pa. 19118. *Office:* Department of Political Science, Temple University, Philadelphia, Pa. 19122.

CAREER: Congressional fellow of the American Political Science Association, 1958-59; Michigan State University, East Lansing, assistant professor of political science and public administration specialist of the Institute for Community Development, 1959-61; National Institute of Administration, Saigon, Vietnam, public administration consultant, 1961-62; Temple University, Philadelphia, Pa., professor of political science, 1962—, director of public administration program, 1963-68, 1974—, chairman of department of political science, 1963-68, 1976—, chairman of executive council of the Center for the Study of Federalism, 1976—, chairman of administrative council of Academy for Public Service Executive Development, 1977—. Consultant and adviser to Lebanese University and national Civil Service Commission of Lebanon under auspices of Ford Foundation, 1968-70.

Visiting professor at University of Illinois, 1963. Consultant to various governmental organizations.

MEMBER: International Political Science Association, International Institute of Administrative Science, American Academy of Political and Social Science, American Association of University Professors, American Political Science Association, American Society for Asian Studies, American Society for Public Administration, National Association of Schools of Public Affairs and Administration, International Studies Association, Asia Society, Southeast Asia Development Advisory Group, Lebanese Political Science and Public Administration Association, Comparative Administration Group, Section on International and Comparative Administration, Society for International Development, Peace Research Conference, Inter-University Consortium for Political Behavior Research, Midwest Asian Studies Association, Midwest Political Science Association, Northeastern Political Science Association, Eastern Regional Organization for Public Administration, Southern Political Science Society, Southwest Political and Social Science Association, Western Political Science Association, Pennsylvania Political Science and Public Administration Association, Phi Beta Kappa, Pi Sigma Alpha.

WRITINGS: Activities and Financial Arrangements of Local Government Within Calhoun County, Michigan, Institute for Community Development, Michigan State University, 1960; *Local Government Finances and Functions, Branch County, Michigan,* Institute for Community Development, Michigan State University, 1961; *Dynamics of Administrative Situations,* National Institute of Administration (Saigon), 1962; *Public Administration in the Saigon Metropolitan Area,* Vietnam Advisory Group, Michigan State University, 1962, published as *Saigon: Public Administration in a Southeast Asian Metropolitan Area,* Agency for International Development, 1963; *Organizational Analysis,* Michigan State University Press, 1964; (contributor) Wesley R. Fishel, editor, *Vietnam: Anatomy of a Conflict,* Peacock Press, 1968; *Lebanese Civil Service Education and Training,* Republic of Lebanon, 1969; (contributor) Jerry M. Tinker, editor, *Strategies of Revolutionary Warfare,* Chand (New Delhi), 1969.

Higher Education in Lebanon and the United States, Ford Foundation, 1971; (editor with John C. Donnell) *Electoral Politics in South Vietnam,* Lexington Books, 1974; *The Politics of Massacre: Political Processes in South Vietnam,* Temple University Press, 1974; *Fedayeen and Arab World Politics, General Learning Corp.,* 1975.

Contributor to *Colliers Encyclopedia,* 1969, 1973, *Encyclopedia of World Political Parties,* 1976, and of articles to *Asian Survey, Current History,* and other journals in his field. Manuscript reader for political science journals.

WORK IN PROGRESS: Research on the future of public service and public policy education in the United States; *Development Administration, Technical Assistance, and the Politics of Oil Revenues; Public Administration Systems Analysis; Political Biography of Ngo Dinh Diem; The Decline and Fall of South Vietnam; Efficacy of Public Service Quota Systems; Lebanon's Political and Administrative Tragedy.*

* * *

JONES, Annabel
See LEWIS, Mary (Christianna Milne)

JONES, Elizabeth Orton 1910-

PERSONAL: Born June 25, 1910, in Highland Park, Ill.; daughter of George Roberts (a musician) and Jessie Mae (Orton) Jones. *Education:* University of Chicago, Ph.B., 1932; Ecole des Beaux Arts, Fontainebleau, France, diploma, 1932; attended School of the Art Institute of Chicago, 1932. *Residence:* Mason, N.H.

CAREER: Author, artist, and illustrator. Received commissions to do murals for the Crotched Mountain Center, Greenfield, N.H., and University of New Hampshire Library. Her works have been exhibited in numerous galleries, including O'Brien Galleries, Chicago, and the Smithsonian Institution. *Member:* New Hampshire Art Association, Cambridge (Mass.) Art Association, Delta Kappa Gamma. *Awards, honors:* Charles Muller Prize, Chicago Society of Etchers, 1939; Caldecott Medal, runner-up, 1944, for *Small Rain: Verses From the Bible,* and winner, 1945, for *Prayer for a Child;* M.A., Wheaton College, 1955.

WRITINGS—All self-illustrated: *Ragman of Paris and His Ragamuffins,* Oxford University Press, 1937; (with Thomas Orton Jones) *Minnie the Mermaid,* Oxford University Press, 1939; *Maminka's Children,* Macmillan, 1940, reprinted, 1968; *Twig,* Macmillan, 1942, reprinted, 1966; *Big Susan,* Macmillan, 1947, reprinted, 1967; (reteller) *Little Red Riding Hood,* Simon & Schuster, 1948; *How Far Is It to Bethlehem?,* Horn Book, 1955. Also author and editor of the *Mason Bicentennial Book, 1768-1968.*

Illustrator: Bible, *David,* Macmillan, 1937; Gladys L. Adshead, *Brownies—Hush!,* Oxford University Press, 1938, reprinted, Walck, 1966; Cornelia Lynde Meigs, *Scarlet Oak,* Macmillan, 1938; Association for Childhood Education (International), *Told Under the Magic Umbrella: Modern Fanciful Stories for Young Children,* Macmillan, 1939, reprinted, 1967; Mabel Leigh Hunt, *Peddler's Clock,* Grosset, 1943; Jessie Mae Jones, editor, *Small Rain: Verses from the Bible,* Viking, 1943, reprinted, 1974; Rachel Field, *Prayer for a Child,* Macmillan, 1944, reprinted, 1973; Eleanor Farjeon, *Prayer for Little Things,* Houghton, 1945; J. M. Jones, *Secrets,* Viking, 1945; J. M. Jones, editor, *Little Child: The Christmas Miracle Told in Bible Verses,* Viking, 1946; J. M. Jones, editor, *This Is the Way: Prayers and Precepts from World Religions,* Viking, 1951; St. Francis of Assisi, *Song of the Sun,* Macmillan, 1952; Elizabeth Bridgman, *Lullaby for Eggs,* Macmillan, 1955; Robbie Trent, *To Church We Go,* Follett, 1956.

SIDELIGHTS: In her Caldecott Medal acceptance speech, Jones commented: "Drawing is very like a prayer. Drawing is a reaching for something away beyond you. As you sit down to work in the morning, you feel as if you were on top of a hill. And it is as if you were seeing for the first time."

BIOGRAPHICAL/CRITICAL SOURCES: Caldecott Medal Books: 1938-1957, Horn Book, 1957.*

* * *

JONES, Faustine Childress 1927-

PERSONAL: Born December 3, 1927, in Little Rock, Ark.; daughter of Perrine M. C. (Patterson) Thomas; married James Theoplius Jones, June 20, 1948 (divorced, June, 1977); children: Yvonne Dianne, Brian Vincent. *Education:* Dunbar Junior College, diploma, 1946; University of Arkansas at Pine Bluff, A.B. (summa cum laude), 1948; University of Illinois, A.M., 1951, Ed.D., 1967; also attended University of Chicago and Indiana University, Gary. *Politics:* Democrat. *Religion:* Methodist. *Residence:* Silver Spring,

Md. *Office:* School of Education, Howard University, 2400 Sixth St. N.W., Washington, D.C. 20059.

CAREER: Junior high school librarian in public schools in Gary, Ind., 1955-60, high school teacher, 1960-62, 1964-67; University of Illinois at Chicago Circle, Chicago, assistant professor of education, 1967-69; Howard University, Washington, D.C., assistant professor of education, 1969-70; Federal City College, Washington, D.C., associate professor of adult education, 1970-71; Howard University, associate professor, 1971-73, professor of education, 1973—, chairman of School of Education foundations department, 1972-73, 1976—, area coordinator of social foundations, 1973-77, senior fellow at Institute for the Study of Educational Policy, 1974-77. Workshop leader and participant. Regular speaker at Washington International Center. Member of advisory board of University of the District of Columbia.

MEMBER: American Educational Studies Association (member of national executive board and executive council), American Association for Higher Education, Philosophy of Education Society, John Dewey Society (member of national executive committee), Society of Professors of Education, Commission of Professors of Adult Education, National Council of Negro Women (member of Commission on Higher Education), Adult Education Association of Metropolitan Washington, Phi Delta Kappa, Alpha Kappa Mu, Kappa Delta Pi, Delta Tau Kappa.

WRITINGS: (Contributor) Lawrence E. Gary and Aaron Favors, editors, *Restructuring the Educational Process: A Black Perspective,* Institute for Urban Affairs and Research, Howard University, 1975; *The Changing Mood in America: Eroding Commitment?,* Howard University Press, 1977. Contributor of more than forty articles and reviews to education and black studies journals.

WORK IN PROGRESS: A study of the alumni of Dunbar High School in Little Rock, Ark.; research on desegregation.

SIDELIGHTS: Faustine Jones comments: "Growing up in Arkansas with a concerned, strong family and with dedicated teachers, I was shaped to enjoy learning, and to appreciate its value. It was deemed an obligation to know, and to use knowledge in behalf of one's people. That love of knowledge, and sense of obligation has carried over to my adult life and shaped my rearing of my own children and my relationships with students over time."

CA asked Jones about the results of her Dunbar study and her views on desegregation. She responded: "Initial examination of the responses from the alumni of Dunbar High School, Little Rock, Arkansas reveals that this public school successfully educated large numbers of unselected black youth from 1930 to 1955, when it was converted into a junior high school under the desegregation process. To put it another way, Dunbar made a positive difference in the adult lives of its alumni, irrespective of their family background and social class status. Contributory factors are yet to be identified through analysis of the data.

"As public policy, desegregation was designed to abolish the previously established policy of forced segregation, end discriminatory practices against blacks and other nonwhites related to education, occupation, income, housing, and life chances, and to remedy the grossly unequal conditions which had resulted from mandatory segregation of the races over time. Thus desegregation is a very positive, desirable public policy, quite in line with the highest tenets of American democracy. However, some of the practices which have

occurred in the name of desegregation are very negative; latent and manifest consequences of some of these practices are in many ways destructive to the black group. For example, NEA figures reveal that between 1954 and 1970 discrimination via desegregation employment practices resulted in the loss of 31,584 black teachers, and might be costing black educators a quarter of a billion dollars annually. Black principals had been discharged or demoted to the point where in the fall of 1970 the *New Republic* carried an article describing the situation in its title as 'The Black Principal: Another Vanishing American.' Black students have suffered, as well. They have been pushed out of school, suspended in disproportionate numbers, excluded from extracurricular activities, tracked into segregated classes, and confronted with condescension or hostility.

"Positive consequences have come in increased access to public accommodations, in voting rights which when exercised resulted in real increases in the number of black and other concerned elected officials, and in increased access to educational opportunity in higher education. Thus desegregation, including school desegregation, has in practice become a 'mixed blessing' since it has both positive and negative overtones.

"For blacks and other minorities, desegregation is necessary, though not sufficient, to full and open access to all parts of the society, with the means to participate fully in that society. The policy is positive in intent; it is up to people to see that the implementation of the policy is positive in practice. Segregation in all societal institutions should be eradicated. The difficulty is that where segregation was explicit and overt, it is now often implicit and covert, and much harder to combat because it is difficult to prove. Two examples will illustrate my point. There are today white employers who tell white applicants that they cannot be employed because a black or a woman must be employed under affirmative action programs. The white male applicant becomes hostile and disgusted, angry at blacks and women, when in fact statistics show that most desirable, rewarding jobs still are given to white males. In the specific example, the white male applicant probably never seeks to find evidence of who was employed when he was not. The chances are that some other white male was employed, not a black or a female. Such statements from employers hurt affirmative action efforts. While affirmative action policies and programs usually are thought of as directly related to equality of opportunity, their practical effect also is to desegregate. The second example is with the Supreme Court's decisions. The 1977 Dayton, Ohio case with respect to school segregation was decided on the principle of *segregative intent,* and in the future blacks and other minorities claiming that school boards have failed to desegregate will have to prove segregative intent on the boards' part. Decisions of school boards which had the effect of maintaining segregated schools are necessary, but not sufficient, to prove segregative intent. The key question is, 'How does one prove *intent*?' Thus from 1954-1977 Court decisions have moved from the very clear *Brown* mandate to desegregate with all deliberate speed to the Dayton mandate which calls for proving segregative intent.

"I would like to see humane, positive-ly oriented leaders emerge who will guide America more quickly toward the realization of equality and justice for those groups which still have less than parity. I would like to see Americans work together as people—as policy-makers and recipients of policies made—to meet the human needs and solve the man-made problems so evident in America in the direction of the greater good. Segregation/desegregation problems are man-made, and capable of solution.''

* * *

JONES, Gayl 1949-

PERSONAL: Born November 23, 1949, in Lexington, Ky.; daughter of Franklin (a cook) and Lucille (Wilson) Jones. *Education:* Connecticut College, B.A., 1971; Brown University, M.A., 1973, D.A., 1975. *Home:* 400 Maynard, Ann Arbor, Mich. 48108. *Office:* Department of English, University of Michigan, Ann Arbor, Mich. 48109.

CAREER: University of Michigan, Ann Arbor, assistant professor of English, 1975—. *Member:* Authors Guild of Authors League of America. *Awards, honors:* Howard Foundation award, 1975; National Endowment for the Arts fellowship, 1976; fellowship from Michigan Society of Fellows, 1977-79.

WRITINGS: Corregidora (novel), Random House, 1975; *Eva's Man* (novel), Random House, 1976; *White Rat* (stories), Random House, 1977.

WORK IN PROGRESS: Research on sixteenth- and seventeenth-century Brazil and on settlements of escaped slaves, such as Palmares.

SIDELIGHTS: Critics have found Jones's works to be bleak, even brutal at times, but most agree that she is a powerful writer. Charles Larson, for example, called her novels ''imaginative . . . characterized by their sharp, dramatic intensity,'' and he said that Jones's short stories ''though fragmented, have an ethereal beauty reminiscent of the stories in Jean Toomer's *Cane.*'' Accordingly, Mel Watkins made these observations about *Corregidora* and *Eva's Man:* '' Despite the grisly, often lurid, nature of her theme and the acerbic narrative tone, the author's tightly controlled prose and perceptive characterization gave those novels a lyrical, bittersweet quality.''

Newsweek described *Eva's Man* as a ''taut, compelling excursion into the lower depths of sexuality,'' and observed that ''Jones's writing powerfully blends narrative and lyricism. Her people speak a spare, lean, Southern black language . . . but she can move into a fluid, almost feverish style that rushes thoughts and images together with surreal speed.''

Eva's Man makes ''being a woman sound very depressing,'' according to John Updike. The exploration of ''femaleness as experienced by American blacks,'' Updike said, began with *Corregidora* and is continued in *Eva's Man*—this time ''with a sharpened starkness, a power of ellipsis that leaves darker gaps between its flashes of rhythmic, sensuously exact dialogue and visual symbol.'' However, Updike noted that Jones fell short with her characterization of Eva and lost effect with her fragmented, dreamlike style: ''Miss Jones apparently wishes to show us a female heart frozen into rage by deprivation, but the worry arises, as it did not in *Corregidora,* that the characters are dehumanized as much by her artistic vision as by their circumstances. *Eva's Man* is a room with a lot of pictures on the wall but not much furniture to lean on.''

Watkins found similar problems with *White Rat:* ''It is the lack of character development that finally makes this assemblage of misfits and neurotics unbelievable or, worse, uninteresting. Without the sensitive probing of personality and history that readily defined Ursa in *Corregidora* and Eva in *Eva's Man* most of these tales seem arbitrarily depressed and bleak despite our awareness that such situations and people exist.''

Darryl Pinckney observed an imbalance of characterization in Jones's novels which he called ''indictments against black men.'' He explained: ''Only the women seem capable of reflection, affection without completely impure motives. While they address each other in scorn and pity, they also show a tremendous intimacy and sympathy. . . . Gayl Jones places her heroines between victory and defeat where deprivation is a narcotic. Though they are women of intense and complicated feelings, their severity suggests an impasse.'' Though he found ''hints of fragmentation and strain in the conception of *Eva's Man,*'' Pinckney acknowledged the novel's merit: ''Opaque, flat, peculiar, in her fiction Gayl Jones has presented problems that are living, historical and important additions to the current American—not just black—scene. These novels are genuinely imaginative creations.''

With *White Rat,* Jones proved herself capable of presenting the male viewpoint with sensitivity. Charles R. Larson stated: ''The basic theme is that of the long-suffering black male, striving to make the best of a bad situation he himself created. Though White Rat agonizes over his relationship with his wife and child, in the end he accepts the responsibility for their well-being. In this story and in several others, Jones has created a refreshing image of the black male—so frequently maligned in recent fiction and sociology.''

''I see men and women conditioned to look at sexuality in different ways,'' Jones told Margo Jefferson. ''What a woman sees as hurt or sexual abuse a man may see as something else entirely.'' Said Jefferson: ''[Jones] explores this conflict like a photographer, studying a single object from different angles. Jones sees the sexual and the psychological as inextricably bound together—she calls the sexual explicitness of her books as much metaphor as fact. And she is fascinated by the way people carry their histories into every encounter and relationship.''

Jones has said that she used to picture herself as a ''maker of generations.'' She explained: ''That can be 'translated' into something in my own life. Ever since I was a kid I never really wanted or thought of myself as having children. At first, I thought, of course, that that was the natural thing that happened, that women naturally grew up and got married and had children. So I thought since that was what 'naturally' happened, it would happen to me, too. I decided that I wouldn't get married till I was in my late twenties, though—which was unusual for the kind of community I grew up in. But then, when I was twelve, for some reason, I learned that you didn't just naturally grow up and get married and have children. So since I was twelve I decided that I wasn't going to ever get married or have children. And then something happened. I was going along—feeling that way—not feeling guilty about it or anything—not even thinking that other people might care about that kind of decision—that whatever I chose to do was okay. I didn't think about how parents might feel. In fact, I thought as long as it was something that I'd decided, it was okay. But then I realized that when you make that kind of a decision, you're not just making it for yourself, you're making it for your mother and your grandmother—I speak of the women here for another personal reason—and your great-grandmother; that it's not just you making that decision for yourself but you're making it for all the generations that came before you.

''What made me realize this,'' Jones continued, ''was talking to my mother. I really didn't think it mattered, you know. I'd never even thought about it—how she might feel. Because I didn't see it that way. And we were talking and I said I wasn't going to have any children or didn't want to have any children and then she asked me, 'What about the generations?' And then I realized it wasn't just me. And ever since then I've had this tremendous feeling of guilt, you know. I don't know if I should call it guilt, but . . . ambivalence. Right now, I'm not doing anything about generations.''

Jones told *CA:* "I have no specific philosophy or theory of writing, except 'to write'; I enjoy the process of storytelling. I am interested in Kentucky and Brazillian history, psychology of language, oral storytelling traditions, and how these can be applied to creative writing.''

AVOCATIONAL INTERESTS: Reading fifteenth- and sixteenth-century English and Spanish ballads.

BIOGRAPHICAL/CRITICAL SOURCES: Contemporary Literary Criticism, Gale, Volume 6, 1976; *Newsweek,* April 12, 1976; *New York Times Book Review,* May 17, 1976; *New Republic,* June 19, 1976; *New Yorker,* August 9, 1976; *Yale Review,* autumn, 1976; *Washington Post,* October 21, 1977; *New York Times,* December 28, 1977; *Massachusetts Review,* winter, 1977.

* * *

JONES, Hardin Blair 1914-1978

June 11, 1914—February 16, 1978; American physicist, physiologist, educator, and author. An authority on carcinogens, in the 1950's Jones was one of the first scientists to alert the public to the hazards of cigarette smoking. He was a professor at the University of California, Berkeley, where he co-founded the Donner Laboratory. In his controversial book, *Sensual Drugs,* Jones linked marijuana smoking with brain damage and genetic disorders. He died in Berkeley, Calif. Obituaries and other sources: *American Men and Women of Science: The Physical and Biological Sciences,* 12th edition, Bowker, 1971-73; *New York Times,* February 18, 1978.

* * *

JORDAN, Hope Dahle 1905-

PERSONAL: Born December 9, 1905, in Mt. Horeb, Wis.; daughter of Otto Bjorn (a merchant) and Bertha (Locke) Dahle; married Claude D. Jordan (a recreational therapist); children: David, Hope (Mrs. Richard Kellman). *Education:* University of Wisconsin, Madison, B.A., 1928; also attended Columbia University, 1930, and University of Michigan, 1938. *Home:* 625 Kurtis Dr., Elm Grove, Wis. 53122.

CAREER: General Outdoor Advertising Co., New York, N.Y., in public relations, 1928-31; writer, 1933—. *Member:* Society of Children's Book Writers, Council for Wisconsin Writers, Fictioneers. *Awards, honors:* Awards from Council for Wisconsin Writers, 1968, for *Haunted Summer,* and 1970, for *Supermarket Sleuth.*

WRITINGS—For young people: Take Me to My Friend, Lothrop, 1962, reprinted as *Three Dangerous Days,* Scholastic Book Services, 1964; *Haunted Summer,* Lothrop, 1967; *Talk About the Tarchers,* Lothrop, 1968; *Supermarket Sleuth,* Lothrop, 1969; *The Fortune Cake,* Lothrop, 1972, reprinted as *Danger at Loud Lake,* Archway, 1974; *Stranger in Their Midst,* Lothrop, 1974.

Contributor to popular adult and juvenile magazines, including *Ladies Home Journal, Seventeen, Reader's Digest, Ingenue,* and *Collier's.*

SIDELIGHTS: Hope Jordan writes: "Like most authors, it's easy for me to write about my characters, but so, so difficult to write about myself.

"I was raised in a small Wisconsin town, Mt. Horeb, under ideal conditions, I realize now. Wonderful parents, and grandparents in the home next door—both houses having large libraries crammed with books. My father provided a tennis court, swings, skis, skates, golf clubs, saxophones, drums, piano, typewriter, and every year there was a new 'hired girl' from Norway to help my mother while learning English and finding a husband.

"For me, this meant time to read and read. However, I never meant to write novels. I majored in advertising, went to New York to have a great career, and absolutely loathed the city and was bored by the career.

"It was in my office on Park Avenue that I began writing short stories. Because of my husband's business, we transferred to a number of cities, and this kept me at writing despite discouragements, because I was forever a stranger where we lived, and it was simpler to make friends at the typewriter than in real life.

"My first novel was begun as a short story for *Seventeen* during a heavy Wisconsin snowstorm. It kept snowing, and I kept writing—and six weeks later I had my novel ready to market. Not even my husband knew I'd written a book until after I'd sold it.

"I thoroughly enjoy writing for young people. It pleases me that they think I'm about sixteen and am writing a true experience (even my first editor thought that).''

AVOCATIONAL INTERESTS: Golf, swimming, hiking, knitting, crocheting, embroidery, travel (especially London).

* * *

JORDAN, Leonard [a pseudonym] 1935-
(Nicholas Brady, Lee Chang, Glen Chase, Nelson De Mille, Richard Gallagher, March Hastings, Robert Novak, Philip Rawls, Bruno Rossi, Cynthia Wilkerson)

PERSONAL: Born in 1935, in New Bedford, Mass.; married twice (first marriage ended by divorce, second by death); children: (first marriage) Deborah. *Education:* Michigan State University, B.A., 1961. *Residence:* New York, N.Y. *Agent:* Elaine Markson Literary Agency, Inc., 44 Greenwich Ave., New York, N.Y. 10011.

CAREER: Writer, 1971—. Has also worked as a public relations representative, social worker, bartender, cab driver, and waiter. *Military service:* U.S. Army, 1954-57. *Member:* Writers Guild of America (East).

WRITINGS: Operation Perfidia (spy thriller), Warner, 1975; *The Bar Studs,* Fawcett, 1976; *Hype* (novel), Fawcett, 1977.

All crime novels, except as indicated: (Under pseudonym March Hastings) *Private Sessions* (romantic comedy), Midwood Books, 1974; (under pseudonym Bruno Rossi) *The Worst Way to Die,* Leisure Books, 1974; (under Rossi pseudonym) *Night of the Assassins,* Leisure Books, 1974; (under Rossi pseudonym) *Headcrusher,* Leisure Books, 1974; (under pseudonym Robert Novak) *The Thrill Killers,* Belmont-Tower, 1974; (under pseudonym Nelson De Mille) *The Terrorists,* Leisure Books, 1974.

(Under pseudonym Philip Rawls) *Streets of Blood,* Manor, 1975; (under pseudonym Lee Chang) *The Year of the Boar,* Manor, 1975; (under pseudonym Nicholas Brady) *Shark Fighter* (adventure novel), Belmont-Tower, 1976; (under pseudonym Glen Chase) *Where the Action Is,* Leisure

Books, 1977; (under Brady pseudonym) *Inside Job*, Belmont-Tower, 1978; (under pseudonym Cynthia Wilkerson) *Sweeter Than Candy* (romantic comedy), Belmont-Tower, 1978; (under pseudonym Richard Gallagher) *The Doom Platoon* (war novel), Belmont-Tower, 1978.

WORK IN PROGRESS: Two novels, a thriller set in Europe during the final months of World War II, and a contemporary love story.

SIDELIGHTS: Jordan comments: "After writing sixteen published novels and numerous unpublished ones, I still don't understand how and why I write, and apologize for not being able to enlighten the reader further."

* * *

JOSEPH, Marjory L(ockwood) 1917-

PERSONAL: Born October 10, 1917, in Milan, Ohio; daughter of Ernest J. (a grain dealer) and Bertha E. (a secretary; maiden name, Allyn) Lockwood; married William D. Joseph (a teacher), August 11, 1941; children: Nancy Joyce Joseph David. *Education:* Ohio State University, B.Sc., 1939, M.Sc., 1952; Pennsylvania State University, Ph.D., 1962. *Home:* 10612 Collett Ave., Granada Hills, Calif. 91324. *Office:* Department of Home Economics, California State University, 18111 Nordhoff St., Northridge, Calif. 91330.

CAREER: Costume designer, 1941-44; Ruth Harris, Inc., New York, N.Y., supervisor of custom design shop workrooms, 1944-46; MarJay Dress Shop, Milan, Ohio, co-owner and manager, 1946-48; high school home economics teacher in Birmingham, Ohio, and Berlin Heights, Ohio, 1948-51; Juniata College, Huntingdon, Pa., instructor, 1952-55, assistant professor, 1955-58, associate professor of home economics, 1958-62, chairman of Textiles & Clothing Division, 1954-58, chairman of department, 1958-62; California State University, Northridge, associate professor, 1962-66, professor of home economics, 1966—, chairman of department, 1969—. Instructor at Pennsylvania State University, 1956-62. Home economics consultant.

MEMBER: American Association of Textile Chemists and Colorists, American Home Economics Association, American Society for Testing and Materials, Association of Dyers and Colourists, Association of College Professors of Textiles and Clothing (member of executive board, 1971-73), American Institute of Chemists (fellow), California Home Economics Association (district president, 1968-70), Sigma Delta Epsilon, Delta Theta Tau, Omicron Nu.

WRITINGS: (Contributor) *Fabrics, Fashions, and Facilities,* American Home Laundry Manufacturers Association, 1965; *Introductory Textile Science,* Holt, 1966, 2nd edition, 1972; (with Audrey G. Gieseking) *Illustrated Guide to Textiles,* Plycon, 1971, 2nd edition, 1973; *Essentials of Textiles: Textiles for the Consumer,* Holt, 1976; (with husband, William D. Joseph) *Research Tools for Home Economists,* Plycon, 1976, 2nd edition, in press. Contributor of articles and reviews to home economics journals and to *Science for the Farmer.*

WORK IN PROGRESS: With Nancy Owens and Dorothy Blackman, *Advanced Textile Science,* for Plycon.

* * *

JOSEPHSON, Matthew 1899-1978

February 15, 1899—March 13, 1978; American editor and author. Josephson started his writing career as a poet but soon discovered his forte was history and biography. In the 1920's he lived in Paris, where he hobnobbed with American and French writers, including Paul Eluard, Andre Breton, Louis Aragon, E. E. Cummings, William Carlos Williams, and Malcolm Cowley. While in France Josephson served as an associate editor of *Broom* and contributing editor to *transition.* When he returned to the United States, he took a position on the editorial staff of the *New Republic.* Among his biographies are *Zola and His Time, Jean-Jacques Rousseau, Victor Hugo, Stendhal, Edison,* and *Al Smith: Hero of the Cities.* His best-known book, *The Robber Barons,* traces the lives of such captains of industry as John D. Rockefeller, Andrew Carnegie, and J. P. Morgan. He died in Santa Cruz, Calif. Obituaries and other sources: *The Oxford Companion to American Literature,* 4th edition, Oxford University Press, 1965; *The Reader's Encyclopedia,* 2nd edition, Crowell, 1965; Matthew Josephson, *Infidel in the Temple: A Memoir of the Nineteen-Thirties,* Knopf, 1967; *The Penguin Companion to American Literature,* MacGraw, 1971; *Who's Who in America,* 39th edition, Marquis, 1976; *New York Times,* March 14, 1978; *Time,* March 27, 1978.

* * *

JOSHI, Shivkumar 1916-

PERSONAL: Born November 16, 1916, in Ahmedabad, India; son of Girijashanker and Taralakshmi (Mehta) Joshi; married Satyavati Mehta (a teacher), November 1, 1952; children: Ruchir. *Education:* Gujrat College, B.A. (honors), 1937. *Politics:* "Secular-moderate!" *Religion:* Hindu. *Home:* 162/19 Lake Gardens, Calcutta, West Bengal, India 700-045. *Office:* 154 J. Bajaj St., Calcutta, West Bengal, India 700-007.

CAREER: Partner in wholesale cloth business, Calcutta, India, 1937—. Writer, 1950—. *Member:* P.E.N. Executive (West Bengal), Gujrati Sahitya Parishad (member of central committee). *Awards, honors:* Kumar Medal, 1952; Narmad gold medal, 1959; Sangeet Nrutyanatak Akademi award, 1964; Ranjeetram gold medal, 1970, for contributions to Gujrati playwrighting.

WRITINGS—He Never Slept So Long (three-act play), Writers Workshop (Calcutta), 1972.

Also author of numerous novels, plays, and short stories in Indian languages. Translator of plays and novels from Bengali into Gujarati. Editor of *Kesudan* (literary and art magazine), 1954-61.

WORK IN PROGRESS: Two plays and a novel.

SIDELIGHTS: Joshi writes: "I was active as a freedom fighter, in a nonviolent way, during 1930 and 1932, and more actively during the 1942-43 'Quit India' movement by Gandhi. More recently, I protested vehemently against Indira Gandhi's emergency days during 1975-77, through writings, lectures and open discussions in seminars."

Joshi was a delegate to the International Theatre Institute conference in Budapest in 1969, and was invited to the World Theatre Festival in Nancy (France) in 1975. He has also traveled to Greece, Austria, Czechoslovakia, Germany, Holland, Denmark, Great Britain, the United States, and Japan. Among his vocational interests he includes directing plays, photography, and art criticism.

* * *

JUREK, Martin 1942-

PERSONAL: Born February 22, 1942, in Worcester, England; separated; children: Caroline. *Education:* Oxford

University, M.A., 1963. *Home:* 4605 Warren St. N.W., Washington, D.C. 20016. *Office: Financial Times,* 1325 E St. N.W., Washington, D.C. 20004.

CAREER/WRITINGS: Financial Times, London, England, staff member of foreign desk in London, 1966-69, correspondent in Washington, D.C., 1969-70, New York bureau chief, 1970-72, foreign news editor in London, 1972-75, U.S. editor in Washington, D.C., 1975—. Notable assignments include coverage of Calaveras (Calif.) Frog Jump, 1965, and Saudi Arabian Soccer Cup Final, 1973.

SIDELIGHTS: Jurek told *CA:* "I could write that I have this passion for communication, the representation of complex views and ideas in comprehensible form and all the usual claptrap. But I won't. All I would say is that I do this job because I happen to like it, than which there is no higher endorsement."

*   *   *

JUVILER, Peter H(enry) 1926-

PERSONAL: Born March 26, 1926, in London, England; came to the United States in 1939, naturalized citizen, 1945; son of Adolphe A. (an industrial organizer) and Katie (a pianist; maiden name, Henry) Juviler; married Nina Lawford (a graphic artist), December 20, 1956; children: Gregory, Geoffry. *Education:* Yale University, B.E., 1948, M.E., 1949; Columbia University, M.A., 1954, Ph.D., 1960. *Home:* 305 Riverside Dr., New York, N.Y. 10025. *Office:* Department of Political Science, Barnard College, Columbia University, New York, N.Y. 10027.

CAREER: Sperry Gyroscope Co., Lake Success, N.Y., project engineer, 1949-52; Princeton University, Princeton, N.J., instructor in politics, 1957-58; Columbia University, New York City, instructor in government, 1959-60; Hunter College of the City University of New York, New York City, instructor, 1960-63, assistant professor of political science, 1963-64, chairman of Russian studies program, 1961-64; Columbia University, Barnard College, associate professor, 1964-74, professor of political science, 1974—, member of academic advisory board of Center for the Study of Human Rights, 1978—. Citizen Exchange Corps, member of board of trustees, 1971-77, member of advisory board, 1977—; member of American Council of Learned Societies committee on Soviet studies, 1971-75. *Military service:* U.S. Navy, electronic technician, 1944-46.

MEMBER: American Political Science Association, American Association for the Advancement of Slavic Studies, American Association of University Professors. *Awards, honors:* Ford Foundation grant, 1976-78.

WRITINGS: (Editor with Henry W. Morton, and contributor) *Soviet Policy-Making: Studies of Communism in Transition,* Praeger, 1967; (contributor) C. D. Kerner, editor, *The Soviet Union and Democratic Society,* Verlag Herder, 1968; (contributor) Kerner, editor, *Marxism, Communism, and Western Society,* Verlag Herder, 1972; (contributor) Morton and Rudolf L. Tokes, editors, *Soviet Politics and Society in the 1970's,* Free Press, 1974; (contributor) Donald D. Barry and George Ginsburgs, editors, *Contemporary Soviet Law: Essays in Honor of John N. Hazard,* Nijhoff, 1974; *Revolutionary Law and Order: Politics and Social Change in the U.S.S.R.,* Free Press, 1976; (contributor) Alexander Dallin, Dorothy Atkinson, and Gail W. Lapidus, editors, *Women in Russia,* Stanford University Press, 1977; (contributor) Barry, Ginsburgs, and Peter B. Maggs, editors, *The Individual and the State in Soviet Law,* Sijthoff, 1977. Also contributor to *Foreign Affairs: A Fifty-Year Bibliography,* Council on Foreign Relations. Contributor to *Encyclopedia on Russia and the Soviet Union,* and of more than a dozen articles to scholarly journals and newspapers.

WORK IN PROGRESS: Delinquents and Authority: The Soviet Experience; research on family and criminal law in the Soviet Union since Stalin, on analysis of political movements in political science, and on resistors and authority.

SIDELIGHTS: Juviler writes: "My interest in comparative and communist studies, especially in the U.S.S.R., grew out of a personal crisis during the Korean War when I was doing secret work on radar control systems with Sperry. After our unnecessary embroilment with the Chinese, I decided to go back to study political science and the Russian area so as to be a better informed technician. Once at Columbia University, I stayed on in political science, began to teach, and have been a teacher and researcher ever since.

"My writing has grown out of a desire to convey my experiences and impressions during the nine field visits I have had to the U.S.S.R. between 1955 and 1977—Soviet-U.S. exchanges I have considered vital to our understanding of the U.S.S.R. and Soviet people and to the building of bridges that will survive the moments of crisis that crop up periodically in U.S.-Soviet relations. Another student and I organized the first visit of graduate students to the U.S.S.R. after Stalin (in two groups, 1954-55). The country was still so cut off that I acted not only as a visitor in early 1955, but also as a correspondent and movie photographer, there being few journalists in Russia then. In 1958-59, my interest in the exchanges was deepend as a member of the first U.S.-Soviet exchange under the new cultural agreement (the Zarubin-Lacey agreement). I spent the school year researching at Moscow University and traveling in the U.S.S.R. Later visits included a semester at Moscow University and, most recently, academic coordination of a seminar on administration of justice in the summer of 1977. The visit to the U.S.S.R. with a group of criminal justice specialists, especially at this time of tension over human rights, provided a unique opportunity for observation and interchange with Soviet jurists.

"I have traveled recently in the Andean countries after teaching a short seminar on Colombia to an American school aboard a sailing ship where my wife was teaching. I took away with me impressions of great Indian civilizations of the past and Indian poverty and struggles of the present—poverty, fantastic beauty, and the sinister fear that was gripping Chile at the time I visited it.

"My vocational interests now center increasingly on teaching and research in the area of authority and resistance to it. This touches for me on the behavior of inmates and staffs of various types of institutions, especially prisons, and on the relationships between resistors and authority from ancient times to the present. My interest in this came out of the study of law and compulsion in social change, with detailed study of Soviet law, and out of the teaching of a course on modern political movements, as well as out of an ongoing concern with human rights and my writing and research about Soviet and American efforts to deal with problems of conformity and deviance in the family and in crime prevention. In this sense, my recent book on Soviet responses to crime, *Revolutionary Law and Order,* my articles and chapters on family and criminal law, and the manuscript I am now completing on delinquency and authority in the U.S.S.R., are all leading toward this new phase in my research and writing. That will still leave time for such involvements as go with my trusteeship in the Citizen Exchange Corps, a nonprofit non-political organization that sends a counterpart group of citizens to the U.S.S.R. on intercultural travel visits.''

AVOCATIONAL INTERESTS: ''My avocation is to promote exchanges, non-violent solution of problems (hence the activities and frustrations of several years in the peace movement during the Vietnam war).''

K

KAHN, Hannah 1911-

PERSONAL: Born June 30, 1911, in New York, N.Y.; daughter of David and Sarah (Seigelbaum) Abrahams; married Frank M. Kahn (deceased); children: Melvin A., Daniel Lyon, Vivian Dale. *Education:* Florida Atlantic University, B.A., 1972; also attended Miami Dade Community College. *Politics:* Liberal Democrat. *Religion:* Jewish. *Home:* '40 Northeast 69th St., Miami, Fla. 33138.

CAREER: Whitecraft Industries, Miami, Fla., interior decorator, 1937—. Guest lecturer at Barry College; faculty member at Miami Dade Community College. Past member of board of directors of Florida Council for Retarded Children; has conducted poetry seminars.

MEMBER: Academy of American Poets (member of advisory board), Poetry Society of America (southern vice-president), Poetry Society of Virginia, Poetry Society of Georgia, Dade County Association for Retarded Citizens (charter member; past president), Phi Lambda Phi. *Awards, honors:* Winner of more than twenty-five awards for poetry from societies in Virginia, Florida, and Georgia, and from *Lyric* magazine.

WRITINGS: Eve's Daughter (poems), Hurricane House, 1963; (editor with Orma Jean Surbey) *Wind Song* (poems), Olivant, 1969.

Represented in anthologies, including *I Hear My Sisters Saying,* Crowell; *Poetry: The Essence of Being Human,* McGraw. Contributor of more than four hundred poems to popular magazines and newspapers, including *Harper's, Saturday Review, Commonweal,* and *Saturday Evening Post.* Poetry review editor for *Miami Herald.*

WORK IN PROGRESS: Ride a Wild Horse (tentative title), poems.

SIDELIGHTS: Hannah Kahn writes: "Ever since I was a child I loved poetry, but it never occurred to me that I might myself someday be a poet. I had little formal education; went to work when I was fifteen. Though born in New York, I lived in a small town from ages twelve to fifteen. I was ill during those years and did not attend high school (which was five miles away). I had acceptances from literary magazines such as *American Scholar* before I continued my education. At the age of fifty I started—one night a week—taking classes at Miami Dade Community College. Twelve years later at age sixty-two I got my degree."

BIOGRAPHICAL/CRITICAL SOURCES: William C. Doster, editor, *The Differing Eye,* Glencoe Press, 1970; Richard P. Janero and D. E. Gearhart, editors, *Human Worth,* Holt, 1972.

* * *

KAHN, James M. 1903(?)-1978

1903(?)—March 7, 1978; American journalist and author. Over a period of fifty years, Kahn worked for a number of New York City newspapers, most notably at the *New York Sun,* Where he was the sports editor, and at the *Brooklyn Eagle,* where he was the managing editor. The author of two books about baseball, Kahn covered the Yankees in the heydays of Babe Ruth, Lou Gehring, and Tony Lazzeri. One of the highlights of his career was being given the bat with which Ruth had hit his sixtieth home run in 1927. Kahn died in New York City. Obituaries and other sources: *New York Times,* March 8, 1978.

* * *

KAHN, Joan 1914-

PERSONAL: Born April 13, 1914, in New York, N.Y.; daughter of Ely Jacques and Elsie Plant (Mayer) Kahn. *Education:* Attended Barnard College. *Residence:* New York, N.Y. *Office:* Harper & Row Publishers, Inc., 10 East 53rd St., New York, N.Y. 10022.

CAREER: Free-lance writer, 1935-45; Harper & Row Publishers, Inc., New York, N.Y., reader, 1945-46, editor, 1946—. *Member:* International P.E.N., Authors Guild, Mystery Writers of America, National Arts Club, Art Students League of New York.

WRITINGS: Ladies and Gentlemen, Said the Ringmaster (self-illustrated; juvenile,), Knopf, 1938; *To Meet Miss Long* (novel), Lippincott, 1943; *Open House* (novel), Lippincott, 1946; *Seesaw* (juvenile), Harper, 1964; *You Can't Catch Me* (juvenile), Harper, 1976; *Hi, Jock, Run Around the Block* (juvenile), Harper, 1978.

Editor; all collections of mystery and suspense stories: *The Edge of the Chair,* Harper, 1967; *Hanging by a Thread,* foreword by Ogden Nash, Houghton, 1969; *Some Things Dark and Dangerous* (juvenile), Harper, 1970; *Some Things Fierce and Fatal,* Harper, 1971; (and author of introduction) *Trial and Terror,* Houghton, 1973; *Some Things Strange and Sinister,* Harper, 1973; (and author of introduction)

Open at Your Own Risk, Houghton, 1975; *Some Things Weird and Wicked: Twelve Stories to Chill Your Bones,* Pantheon, 1976; *Chilling and Killing,* Houghton, 1978.

Contributor to magazines, including *Writer.*

SIDELIGHTS: Joan Kahn wrote in *Writer* magazine: "Edgar Allan Poe started the mystery story proper about a hundred twenty years ago. . . . From Poe until about twenty years ago, the mystery novel enveloped its core of life-into-death with clues and with puzzles. . . . When the mystery novel shifted to the suspense novel, the game side became less important, and the people involved in the book's story became more important. . . . I do prefer people to puzzles. I get tired of games pretty quickly and doubt that I could have spent as many years in the business as I have," she analyzed, "if the whodunit had not turned into the suspense novel when it did. . . . I'm certainly not keen about verbosity or padding for padding's sake . . . but I think a suspense novel has to be able to move freely in any manner that suits it best. All I ask of a book is that it's good reading, believable, and the best the author can do at the moment."

Kahn reflected: "Even after all the years I've been reading novels of suspense, I'm still excited by the new books coming along. . . . And though there are days when I wish no one was ever let near a typewriter again, I expect to go on reading suspense novels eagerly (and not just the ones I've published), because I think suspense novels are getting better all the time."

BIOGRAPHICAL/CRITICAL SOURCES: Writer, February, 1969.

* * *

KAKI

See HEINEMANN, Katherine

* * *

KAKUGAWA, Frances H(ideko) 1936-

PERSONAL: Born February 22, 1936, in Kapoho, Hawaii; daughter of Sadame and Matsue Kakugawa. *Education:* University of Hawaii, B.Ed., 1959. *Home:* 2649 Varsity Pl., #208, Honolulu, Hawaii 96826. *Office:* State Department of Education, Honolulu, Hawaii.

CAREER: Teacher in elementary schools in Hilo, Hawaii, 1959-62, and Jackson, Mich., 1962-63; State Department of Education, Honolulu, Hawaii, supervisory teacher in Hilo, 1963-72, curriculum writer in Honolulu, 1972—. Gives poetry readings and lectures.

WRITINGS: Sand Grains (poems), Naylor, 1970; *White Ginger Blossom* (poems), Naylor, 1971; *Golden Spike* (poems), Naylor, 1973; *The Path of Butterflies* (poems), Naylor, 1976. Contributor of articles and poems to journals.

WORK IN PROGRESS: Poems.

SIDELIGHTS: Kakugawa told *CA:* "My poetry and I have often become elements of surprise because of our marked-changing-switching contrast between idealism and reality. Nothing would please me more than to be able to write poetry and short stories and to be read by a larger audience—or to be able to afford being a full-time writer."

* * *

KALLENBACH, Joseph E(rnest) 1903-

PERSONAL: Born October 27, 1903, in Tuscumbia, Mo.; son of J. Edward (in garage and auto supply business) and Hattie (Maylee) Kallenbach; married Jessamine Shively (a

librarian), August 30, 1939; children: Julie Anne Kallenbach Lambdin, Jobina Louise Kallenbach Del Monico, Jennifer Lynn Kallenbach Bannon. *Education:* Central Missouri State College (now University), B.S., 1926; University of Missouri, M.A., 1928; University of Michigan, Ph.D., 1939. *Politics:* Independent. *Religion:* Congregationalist. *Home:* 1745 Glenwood Rd., Ann Arbor, Mich. 48104. *Office:* Department of Political Science, University of Michigan, 5625 Haven Hall, Ann Arbor, Mich. 48104.

CAREER: Marshalltown Junior College, Marshalltown, Iowa, instructor in social science, 1928-30; Iowa State College (now University), Ames, instructor in government, 1930-33; University of Michigan, Ann Arbor, instructor, 1939-42, assistant professor, 1942-48, associate professor, 1948-53, professor of political science, 1953-73, professor emeritus, 1973—. Hearing officer for War Labor Board, 1944-45; labor arbitrator, 1945—. *Member:* American Political Science Association, American Studies Association, American Academy of Arbitrators, National Municipal League, Midwest Political Science Association, Southern Political Science Association, Phi Beta Kappa.

WRITINGS: Federal Cooperation With the States Under the Commerce Clause, University of Michigan Press, 1942, reprinted, Greenwood Press, 1968; *The American Chief Executive: The Presidency and the Governorship,* Harper, 1966; (with wife, Jessamine Kallenbach) *American State Governors, 1776-1976,* Volume I, Oceana, 1977. Contributor to law and political science journals.

WORK IN PROGRESS: American State Governors, 1776-1976, Volumes II and III with wife, Jessamine Kallenbach, for Oceana.

* * *

KANE, Frank R. 1925-

PERSONAL: Born April 24, 1925, in Chicago, Ill.; son of Frank George (a writer) and Mabel (Bell) Kane; married Mary Ellen Turnbull (a secretary), September 2, 1950; children: Sheila Kane Fraser, Julie, Nancy, Ann. *Education:* University of Michigan, B.A., 1948; Cornell University, M.S., 1952. *Religion:* Congregational. *Home:* 1011 Potomac Lane, Alexandria, Va. 22308. *Office:* 1280 National Press Bldg., Washington, D.C. 20045.

CAREER/WRITINGS: Ann Arbor News, Ann Arbor, Mich., reporter, 1948-51; *Toledo Blade,* Toledo, Ohio, reporter, 1952-63, assistant city editor, 1963-66, city editor, 1966-69, member of Washington bureau staff, 1969—. Notable assignments include coverage of AFL-CIO merger, 1955, President Nixon's trip to Soviet Union, 1972, President Ford's trip to Japan, 1974, and to People's Republic of China, 1975, and numerous political conventions. *Military service:* U.S. Navy, 1943-46; became ensign. *Member:* National Press Club, Federal City Club (Washington). *Awards, honors:* Received award from Northwestern Ohio chapter of Sigma Delta Chi for distinguished contributions to journalism; Headliner Award from Ohio Press Club.

SIDELIGHTS: Kane told *CA:* "I became interested in journalism because my father had been a top-notch reporter for *Detroit News* who later went into advertising. While working at *Ann Arbor News,* I also became interested in labor reporting and eventually did a year's graduate study at Cornell in labor relations."

* * *

KANTER, Rosabeth Moss 1943-

PERSONAL: Born March 15, 1943, in Cleveland, Ohio;

daughter of Nelson Nathan (an attorney) and Helen (a teacher; maiden name, Smolen) Moss; married Stuart A. Kanter, June 15, 1963 (died March 24, 1969); married Barry A. Stein (a management consultant), July 2, 1972. *Education:* Attended University of Chicago, 1962-63; Bryn Mawr College, B.A. (magna cum laude), 1964; University of Michigan, M.A., 1965, Ph.D., 1967; post-doctoral study at Harvard University, 1975-76. *Residence:* Cambridge, Mass. *Office:* Department of Sociology, Yale University, New Haven, Conn. 06520.

CAREER: University of Michigan, Ann Arbor, instructor in sociology, 1967; Brandeis University, Waltham, Mass., assistant professor of sociology, 1967-73; Harvard University, Cambridge, Mass., associate professor of administration, 1973-74; Brandeis University, associate professor of sociology, 1974-77; Yale University, New Haven, Conn., associate professor, 1977—, professor of sociology, 1978—. Partner in Good Measure, Cambridge, Mass. Visiting scholar at Newberry Library, 1973, and Harvard University, 1975—; fellow of Center for Advanced Study in the Behavioral Sciences, 1978-79. Blazer Lecturer at University of Kentucky, 1974; Davidson Lecturer at University of New Hampshire, 1975; faculty member at Young Presidents' Organization of International University (Hong Kong), 1976; lecturer at universities and colleges. Member of planning task force of Cambridge Institute's New City Project, 1969-71; expert witness before Equal Employment Opportunities Commission, 1976-77; consultant to Russell Sage Foundation, Ford Foundation, and U.S. Department of State.

MEMBER: American Sociological Association, American Orthopsychiatric Association, American Legal Studies Association, National Training Laboratories Institute for Applied Behavioral Science (dean, 1973—), Society for the Study of Social Problems, Society for the Psychological Study of Social Issues, Sociologists for Women in Society, Law and Society Association, Eastern Sociological Society (member of executive committee, 1975-78), Yale Club (New York City and New Haven). *Awards, honors:* U.S. Office of Education grant, 1971-72; National Institute of Mental Health grant, 1972-74; Guggenheim fellowship, 1975-76.

WRITINGS: Commitment and Community: Communes and Utopias in Sociological Perspective, Harvard University Press, 1972; (editor and contributor) *Communes: Creating and Managing the Collective Life,* Harper, 1973; (editor with Marcus Millman, and contributor) *Another Voice: Feminist Perspectives on Social Life and Social Science,* Doubleday, 1975; *Work and Family in the United States: A Critical Review and Research and Policy Agenda,* Russell Sage Foundation, 1976; *Men and Women of the Corporation,* Basic Books, 1977; (editor) *Life in Organizations,* Basic Books, 1979.

Contributor: J. Rabow, J. A. Winter, and M. Chesler, editors, *Vital Problems for American Society,* Random House, 1968; C. G. Bennello and D. Roussopoulos, editors, *The Case for Participatory Democracy,* Richard Grossman, 1971; M. Gordon, editor, *The Nuclear Family in Crisis,* Harper, 1972; Rabow, editor, *Sociology: Students and Society,* Goodyear Publishing, 1972; L. K. Howe, editor, *The Future of the Family,* Simon & Schuster, 1972; A. Effrat, editor, *Perspectives on Political Sociology,* Bobbs-Merrill, 1972; M. P. Effrat, editor, *The Community: Approaches and Applications,* Free Press, 1974; J. Heiss, editor, *Marriage and Family Interaction,* Rand McNally, 2nd edition (Kanter was not included in 1st edition), 1976; *Schooling and Capitalism,* Routledge & Kegan Paul, 1976; W. R. Burke, editor, *Current Issues and Strategies in Organization Develop-*

ment, Behavioral Publications, 1976; W. Feigelman, editor, *Sociology Full Circle,* Praeger, 2nd edition (Kanter was not included in 1st edition), 1976; M. Rosenbaum and A. Snadowsky, editors, *The Intensive Group Experience,* Free Press, 1976; A. Sargent, editor, *Beyond Sex Roles,* West Publishing, 1976; M. Blaxall and B. Reagan, editors, *Women and the Workplace: The Implications of Occupational Segregation,* University of Chicago Press, 1976.

Contributor of about thirty-five articles and reviews to sociology, education, psychology, and psychiatry journals. Member of editorial board of *Journal of Applied Behavioral Science,* 1970-73, "Rose Monograph Series," American Sociological Association, 1973-76, and *American Sociologist,* 1977—; associate editor of *Sociological Symposium,* 1972-76, and *Sociological Inquiry,* 1973-76; consulting editor of *Journal of Voluntary Action Research,* 1972-76, and *American Journal of Sociology,* 1975-77; associate editor of *American Sociological Review,* 1977—.

WORK IN PROGRESS: Management As If People Mattered, for Harper.

*   *   *

KANTOR, Hal 1924-

PERSONAL: Born June 27, 1924, in New York, N.Y.; son of Seymour Charles (a businessman) and Mary Helen (Maizel) Kantor; married Lora Gail Weld, June 3, 1966. *Education:* New York University, B.S., 1948. *Politics:* Democrat. *Home and office:* 1290 Bolton, Morro Bay, Calif. 93442.

CAREER: Long Island Daily Press, New York City, sportswriter, 1945-48; *Confidential,* New York City, investigative reporter, 1958; Nevada Nuclear Test Site, Las Vegas, in publicity and public information, 1963-64; *Coast-Valley Weekly,* Greenleaf, Ore., owner and publisher, 1972-74; basketball referee, 1972-75. Free-lance writer. Member of Silverton, Ore. City Planning Commission. *Military service:* U.S. Army Air Forces, 1942-45, prisoner of war, 1943-45; served in European theater; received Purple Heart, Air Medal, three battle stars.

WRITINGS: The Vegas Trap, Pinnacle Books, 1970; *The Town That Saw No Evil,* Major Books, 1977.

Also author of filmscripts for U.S. Department of Defense. Author of column "Cabbages and Kings" in *Silverton Appeal-Tribune.*

WORK IN PROGRESS: The Life and Times of John Warren, a historical novel set in Oregon.

SIDELIGHTS: Kantor writes that his own writing was inspired by his grandfather, A. A. Kantor, a co-founder of one of the first Jewish newspapers in this country, the *Daily Forward. Avocational interests:* Gardening, fishing, golf, Las Vegas.

*   *   *

KANTROWITZ, Arnie 1940-

PERSONAL: Born November 26, 1940, in Newark, N.J.; son of Morris (a salesman) and Jean (Zabarsky) Kantrowitz. *Education:* Rutgers University, Newark, N.J., B.A., 1961; New York University, M.A., 1963. *Office:* Department of English, College of Staten Island, Staten Island, N.Y. 10301.

CAREER: WNEW-TV, New York, N.Y., promotion writer, 1961-62; State University of New York College at Cortland, instructor in English, 1962-63; College of Staten Island, Staten Island, N.Y., assistant professor of English,

1965—. Vice-president of Gay Activists Alliance, 1971; member of Christopher Street Liberation Day Committee, 1976, National Gay Task Force, and Gay Academic Union.

WRITINGS: Under the Rainbow: Growing Up Gay (autobiography), Morrow, 1977. Contributor of articles and poems to magazines, including *Advocate, College English,* and *Washington Square Review,* and newspapers.

WORK IN PROGRESS: Native Moments (tentative title), a novel based on the life of Walt Whitman.

SIDELIGHTS: Kantrowitz writes: "My primary subjects are gay liberation and mysticism. I am fond of fresh blueberries."

*   *   *

KAPLAN, Johanna 1942-

PERSONAL: Born December 29, 1942, in New York, N.Y.; daughter of Max (a teacher) and Ruth (a social worker; maiden name Duker) Kaplan. *Education:* New York University, B.A., 1964; Columbia University, M.A., 1966. *Politics:* Democrat. *Religion:* Jewish. *Home:* 411 West End Ave., New York, N.Y. 10024. *Agent:* Russell & Volkening, 551 Fifth Ave., New York, N.Y. 10017. *Office:* P.S. 106, 1450 Madison Ave., New York, N.Y. 10029.

CAREER: Teacher of emotionally disturbed children in New York City Public Schools and at Mount Sinai Hospital, New York, N.Y., 1966—. *Member:* Authors Guild, P.E.N. *Awards, honors:* New York State Council on the Arts grant, 1973; National Endowment for the Arts grant, 1973; National Book Award nomination and Jewish Book Award from Jewish Book Council, both 1976, for *Other People's Lives.*

WRITINGS: Other People's Lives, Knopf, 1975. Contributor of short stories and reviews to *Commentary* and to *Harper's.*

WORK IN PROGRESS: An untitled novel.

SIDELIGHTS: "It doesn't seem possible that any literary vitality can still be squeezed out of Jewish life in the Bronx," said Pearl K. Bell for *New Leader.* Yet Bell conceded that Johanna Kaplan's stories in *Other People's Lives* "abundantly prove that the chicken soup has not yet turned into water." She continued, "[Kaplan] has a sharp but affectionate eye for ultraliberal hypocrites and upwardly mobile families that finally make it from Intervale Avenue to Mount Vernon, so their snotty children can brag: 'I don't live in the disgusting Bronx anymore.'"

A reviewer for *Book List* referred to *Other People's Lives* as "sardonically fitful perceptions in brief and at length of alien cultures." In praise of Kaplan's first book, a *Kirkus Reviews* critic predicted further success for the author who "has an attuned eye, ear, and heart all going for her."

BIOGRAPHICAL/CRITICAL SOURCES: Kirkus Reviews, February 1, 1975; *Book List,* March 1, 1975; *New Leader,* June 9, 1975.

*   *   *

KARMEN, Roman Lazarevich 1906-1978

November 29, 1906—April, 1978; Russian film maker, screenwriter, journalist, and author. One of the Soviet Union's most prominent film makers, Karmen's documentary motion pictures covered such topics as the Spanish Civil War, the invasion of Russia by the Germans, the Nuremburg trials, life in the Soviet Union, and Vietnam. His books include *In India* and *No Pasaran.* In 1960, Karmen received the Lenin Prize. Obituaries and other sources: *Who's Who in the World,* 2nd edition, Marquis, 1973; *The International Who's Who,* Europa, 1977; *New York Times,* April 30, 1978.

*   *   *

KARP, Laurence E(dward) 1939-

PERSONAL: Born April 26, 1939, in Paterson, N.J.; son of Mark (a teacher) and Cecilia (a teacher; maiden name, Sandelson) Karp; married Myra Osterweil (a home economist), July 29, 1962; children: Steven, Erin. *Education:* Attended Rutgers University, 1956-59; New York University, M.D., 1963; University of Washington, Seattle, postdoctoral study, 1970-72. *Religion:* "No formal affiliation." *Home:* 2557 Perkins Lane W., Seattle, Wash. 98199. *Agent:* Ann Elmo Agency, Inc., 52 Vanderbilt Ave., New York, N.Y. 10017. *Office:* Department of Obstetrics and Gynecology, School of Medicine, University of Washington, Seattle, Wash. 98195.

CAREER: Bellevue Hospital, New York, N.Y., intern, 1963-64, first-year resident, obstetrician and gynecologist, 1964-65; Sinai Hospital, Baltimore, Md., second-year resident, obstetrician and gynecologist, 1967-68; University of Texas Medical Center, San Antonio, Tex., third-year resident, obstetrician and gynecologist, 1968-69, instructor, 1969-70; University of Washington, Seattle, fellow in reproductive genetics, 1970-72, assistant professor, 1972-76, associate professor of obstetrics and gynecology, 1977—. Associate professor at University of California, Los Angeles, and Harbor General Hospital, 1976-77; director of obstetrics and gynecology education at Swedish Hospital (Seattle), 1977—. *Military service:* U.S. Navy, 1965-67; became lieutenant. *Member:* American Society of Human Genetics, American Academy for the Advancement of Science, American College of Obstetricians and Gynecologists, Writers Guild.

WRITINGS: Genetic Engineering: Threat or Promise?, Nelson-Hall, 1976; *The View from the Vue,* Jonathan David, 1977. Member of editorial advisory board of *American Journal of Medical Genetics.*

WORK IN PROGRESS: A novel dealing with late adolescent self-discovery and religious fanaticism; a novel, *The Glory, Jest, and Riddle.*

SIDELIGHTS: Karp writes: "My book-length writing originated as an offshoot of my teaching work, but with deeper involvement in counseling situations, I became more interested in the dynamics of individual motivations than in group responses, and am now trying to explore and express these through fiction.

"As I explained in my first book, I see genetic engineering as a far more complex issue than one might suppose from the treatment it has received in the lay press. Basically, I think the field is one which offers enormous promise for being able to deal more effectively with our genetic problems, including presently unsatisfactory reproductive options. Proceeding, as science customarily does, one step at a time, I believe that there will be ample opportunity for humans to adjust psychologically to new developments.

"Genetic engineering has been misrepresented as a field whose pursuit would lead us to a *Brave New World* existence. This is a specious argument: to my mind, there is no genetic engineering technique that would make it easier for us to fall under a dictator's power. And misuse of genetic engineering by an established tyrant would be no more horrific than the torture and brainwashing techniques already available."

KARPMAN, Harold L(ew) 1927-

PERSONAL: Born August 23, 1927, in Belvedere, Calif.; son of Samuel (a pharmacist) and Dora (Kastleman) Karpman; married wife Rodelle (an artist and designer), June 24, 1955; children: David, Laura. *Education:* University of California, B.A., 1950, M.D., 1954. *Office:* 414 North Camden Dr., Beverly Hills, Calif. 90210.

CAREER: Los Angeles County General Hospital, Los Angeles, Calif., intern, 1954-55; Beth Israel Hospital, Boston, Mass., assistant resident, 1955-57; Los Angeles County General Hospital, cardiovascular trainee, 1957-58; Cardiovascular Medical Group of Southern California, Inc., Beverly Hills, physician, 1958—. Clinical instructor at University of Southern California, 1958-64, assistant clinical professor, 1964-71, associate clinical professor, 1971—; associate clinical professor at University of California, Los Angeles, 1972—. Affiliated with Cedars-Sinai Medical Center, University of California Medical Center, and Memorial Hospital of Southern California. Member of medical advisory board of Cardio-Dynamics Laboratories, Inc.; chief of coronary care unit and Electrocardiographic Laboratory, both at Westside Hospital. Examiner for California Industrial Accident Commission and California Department of Vocational Rehabilitation. Participant in more than sixty local, national, and international professional conferences and seminars; presented about ten exhibits at professional meetings. Consultant to RAND Corp. *Military service:* U.S. Navy, 1945-46.

MEMBER: International College of Angiology (fellow), American Thermographic Society (charter member; fellow; vice-president, 1970-71; president, 1971-72), American College of Physicians (fellow), American College of Cardiology (fellow), American College of Chest Physicians (fellow), American College of Angiology (fellow), American Medical Association, American Heart Association, American Society of Internal Medicine, California Medical Association, California Heart Association, California Society of Internal Medicine, Los Angeles County Medical Association, Los Angeles County Heart Association, Alpha Omega Alpha. *Awards, honors:* San Bruno Community House Award, 1953; Oliver P. Douglas Award from Los Angeles County Heart Association, 1958; fellow of Heart Research Foundation, 1958-59.

WRITINGS: (With Myron Prinzmetal and others) *The Auricular Arrhythmias,* C. C Thomas, 1962; (with S. B. Bleifer and D. J. Bleifer) *Dynamic Electrocardiography in Medical Engineering,* Year Book Medical Publishers, 1974; *Your Second Life,* J. P. Tarcher, 1975. Contributor of about forty articles to medical and scientific journals.

WORK IN PROGRESS: A medically oriented adventure novel.

SIDELIGHTS: Karpman commented: "*Your Second Life* is a book about heart attacks which was written from the patient's view point using dialogue and action to simplify the mystery of heart abnormalities. Most books dealing with the heart provide more information than patients can absorb, often require more concentration than they can maintain (especially if they are convalescing), and the books are frequently terribly boring. The patients find these books difficult to read even though they are intended for laymen because they are, for all of these reasons, doctor oriented. They are written to educate but usually present the necessary material in a formal, pedantic, 'doctor-like' fashion. *Your Second Life* was written in order to provide a book which is patient oriented, to give the patients the information

they deserve in a way which they will find entertaining as well as instructive."

* * *

KARSAVINA, Tamara 1885-1978

March 10, 1885—May 26, 1978; Russian-born ballerina and author of an autobiography and textbooks on ballet. Heralded as one of the finest ballerinas of her age, Karsavina was a key figure in the transition from the old style of ballet to a newer, more dramatic style. Among her most notable performances were the title roles in "Thamar" and "Firebird," and roles as the Ballerina Doll in "Petrouchka," the Girl in "Specter of the Rose," and Pimpinella in "Pulcinella." Vaslev Nijinsky, the famous male dancer, was her partner in several ballets. The Russian Revolution compelled Karsavina to flee to England, where she resided for the rest of her life. After her retirement from the stage in 1933, Karsavina continued to teach and write on ballet; one of her pupils was Dame Margot Fonteyn. She died in London, England. Obituaries and other sources: Tamara Karsavina, *Theatre Street: The Reminiscences of Tamara Karsavina,* Dutton, 1931; Lillian Moore, *Artists of the Dance,* Dance Horizons, 1969; *Who's Who,* 130th edition, St. Martin's, 1978; *New York Times,* May 28, 1978; *Washington Post,* May 30, 1978; *Time,* June 12, 1978.

* * *

KARSCH, Robert F(rederick) 1909-

PERSONAL: Born November 12, 1909, in Farmington, Mo.; son of Fred M. (a merchant) and Emma (Sackmann) Karsch; married Ruth Wilson, August 24, 1940; children: Michael P. *Education:* Westminster College, Fulton, Mo., A.B., 1932; Vanderbilt University, M.A., 1934; University of Missouri, Ph.D., 1948. *Politics:* Republican. *Religion:* Protestant. *Home:* 717 Westport Dr., Columbia, Mo. 65201. *Office:* Institute of Public Administration, University of Missouri, 315 Middlebush Hall, Columbia, Mo. 65201.

CAREER: Westminster College, Fulton, Mo., instructor, 1935-37, assistant professor, 1937-40, associate professor, 1940-42, professor of political science and chairman of department, 1942-46; University of Missouri—Columbia, instructor, 1947-48, assistant professor, 1948-49, associate professor, 1949-54, professor of political science, 1954—, chairman of department, 1958-64, director of Institute of Public Administration, 1975—. Visiting professor at University of New Mexico, 1950, and Jadavpur University, 1964-65; lecturer in Japan and Korea. Member of Columbia city council, 1955-61, and Missouri Elections Commission, 1975-80; consultant to state and local government.

MEMBER: American Society for Public Administration, American Guild of Organists, Missouri Political Science Association (president, 1966-67), Missouri Institute of Public Administration. *Awards, honors:* Award from Missouri Institute of Public Administration, 1977.

WRITINGS: The Government of Missouri, Lucas Brothers, 1951, 14th edition, 1978; (with Peggy Elzea) *Missouri: The Living Constitution,* Lucas Brothers, 1974. Also author of *I'm From Missouri: The State Constitution at Work,* Lucas Brothers. Contributor to law, public administration, and education journals. Member of editorial board of *Midwest Review of Public Administration,* 1970—.

SIDELIGHTS: Robert Karsch told *CA:* "In 1946 I wrote the music for the University of Missouri's 'Fight, Tiger!,' now the official 'fight song' of the University. About a year ago there was some national listing which included it in the ten most distinctive university fight songs. My hobby is classical pipe organ. I have been a regular church organist from 1925." Karsch also listed international travel as another interest.

* * *

KATZ, Alfred 1938-

PERSONAL: Born April 15, 1938, in Yaroslaw, Poland; came to the United States in 1949, naturalized citizen, 1955; son of Israel and Rosa Katz; married Merrily Waxman (a teacher), December 25, 1966; children: Sharon, Ari. *Education:* Yeshiva University, B.A., 1960; Columbia University, M.A., 1962; New York University, Ph.D., 1966. *Home:* 317 West Oakridge Ave., Peoria, Ill. 61604. *Office:* Department of Political Science, 439 Bradley Hall, Bradley University, Peoria, Ill. 61625.

CAREER: Bradley University, Peoria, Ill., assistant professor, 1967-71, associate professor, 1971-77, professor of political science, 1977—. *Member:* American Political Science Association, American Association of University Professors, Midwest Political Science Association, Polish Institute of Arts and Sciences.

WRITINGS: Poland's Ghettos at War, Twayne, 1970; *Government and Politics in Contemporary Israel,* University Press of America, 1978. Contributor of articles and reviews to academic journals.

SIDELIGHTS: Katz told *CA:* "In *Poland's Ghettos at War,* a study of Jewish resistance during World War II, I purpose to disprove the mistakenly common belief that the Jews went to their deaths like sheep, without any form of resistance. The book also analyzes the internal organization of ghetto life.

"*Government and Politics in Contemporary Israel* is an updated study of Israel's political prowess," Katz continued, "a study of its economic, social, and foreign policies. The Yom Kippur War of 1973 changed Israel's society from a smug, self-confident nation into a more reserved nation, distrustful of its governmental structure and of society at large. Also, Israel's economic and foreign policies have undergone greater questioning by a larger segment of the population."

* * *

KATZ, Fred E(mil) 1927-

PERSONAL: Born November 10, 1927, in Germany; came to the United States, naturalized citizen; son of Max and Jenny (Gruenebaum) Katz; married Pearl Gottlieb (an anthropologist); children: Michael, Deborah, Jennifer. *Education:* Guilford College, A.B., 1952; University of North Carolina, M.A., 1956, Ph.D., 1961. *Home:* 2105 Avenue Rd., Toronto, Ontario, Canada.

CAREER: University of Missouri, Columbia, assistant professor of sociology, 1962-65; State University of New York at Buffalo, associate professor, 1965-69, professor of sociology, 1970-72; Tel Aviv University, Tel Aviv, Israel, professor of sociology, 1972—. Professor at State University of New York at Buffalo, 1977-78. Researcher at University of Toronto's Urban Center, 1977-78. *Military service:* U.S. Army, 1953-55. *Member:* American Sociological Association.

WRITINGS: (With Garland Lewis and Greta Holmes) *An Approach to the Education of Psychiatric Nurses,* National League for Nursing, 1962; *Autonomy and Organization,*

Random House, 1968; (editor) *Contemporary Sociological Theory,* Random House, 1971; *Structuralism in Sociology,* State University of New York Press, 1976.

WORK IN PROGRESS: Environmental Responses to Social Movements.

* * *

KATZENBACH, Maria 1953-

PERSONAL: Born October 29, 1953, in New Haven, Conn.; daughter of Nicholas de B. (a lawyer) and Lydia P. S. (a psychotherapist) Katzenbach. *Education:* Attended Barnard College, 1973-74; Princeton University, B.A. (summa cum laude), 1976; graduate study at Yale University. *Residence:* New Haven, Conn. *Agent:* Charles Neighbors, Inc., 240 Waverly Pl., New York, N.Y. 10014.

CAREER: Writer, 1975—. *Member:* Phi Beta Kappa. *Awards, honors:* First prize in Amy Loveman Poetry Contest at Barnard College, 1974, for "Galliard" and "Summer Weather"; Princeton University Ward Mathis Prize for Short Fiction co-winner, 1975, for "The Passenger," and Francis Lemoyne Page Prize co-winner, 1976, for *The Grab.*

WRITINGS: The Grab (novel), Morrow, 1978. Work anthologized in *Intro Seven* and *Intro Eight.* Contributor to *Denver Quarterly.*

WORK IN PROGRESS: Poetry; research on her great-uncle, Adrian Luskin, and New York City at the turn of the last century, for a biographical novel "concerning especially the women he loved and failed"; a contemporary novel that is her response, in part, to D. H. Lawrence's *Women in Love.*

SIDELIGHTS: Maria Katzenbach writes: "I am committed to the family and the myths attending it, to the way character is created within families by memory. My 'Luskins' are based on my mother's family, who are so prone to 'fictionalizing' themselves in the stories passed down to the next generation that I feel I am adding my personal familial vision to a collected story. Women have dominated the family's myth of itself—I am listening to them."

AVOCATIONAL INTERESTS: Dance, women's history, theatre.

* * *

KAUFMAN, I(sadore) 1892-1978
(William Weer)

March 14, 1892—February 28, 1978; Austrian-born journalist and author. One of the founders of the American Newspaper Guild, Kaufman was the chairman of the *Brooklyn Eagle*'s Newspaper Guild chapter in 1955, when a long strike resulted in the folding of the newspaper. Writing under the byline of William Weir, his assignments for the *Brooklyn Eagle* included coverage of Charles Lindbergh's flight across the Atlantic, the Lindbergh kidnapping case, and the gangland wars of the Prohibition. Kaufman, who had been a correspondent during World War II, wrote *American Jews in World War II,* an account of the heroic feats performed by Jews in the armed forces. He died in New York, N.Y. Obituaries and other sources: *New York Times,* March 8, 1978.

* * *

KAUR, Sardarni Premka 1943-

PERSONAL: Born July 1, 1943, in Seattle, Wash.; daughter of Marc Lyngae and Josephine (Skarpness) Venable. *Educa-*

tion: Attended University of Washington, Seattle. *Politics:* Democrat. *Home address:* Route 1, Box 132-D, Espanola, N.M. 87532. *Office:* Route 1, Box 129, Espanola, N.M. 87532.

CAREER: Sikh minister in Los Angeles, Calif., 1972—. Administrative director and vice-president of 3HO Foundation, 1976—; vice-president of Sikh Dharma Brotherhood. Secretary-general of Khalsa Council. Member of Interreligious Council of Southern California and Women's Interfaith Council.

WRITINGS: (Translator) Yogi Bhajan, *Peace Lagoon,* Brotherhood of Life Books, 1971; *Guru for the Aquarian Age,* Spiritual Community, 1973. Contributing editor of *Beads of Truth,* 1972—.

WORK IN PROGRESS: Handbook for Living, the teachings of Yogi Bhajan, categorized in chapters which relate to everyday living; *Yoga Is Life,* quotations and photographs of Yogi Bhajan.

SIDELIGHTS: Sardarni Kaur writes: "In 1968, I began the conscious search for a spiritual teacher. I was living in Los Angeles, and the manager of 'Help' restaurant told me about Yogi Bhajan, who had just begun teaching in the United States. I set up a private lesson with him, and began attending his meditation classes and other lectures. He very quickly utilized my secretarial skills by having me type an English translation of the major prayer of the Sikhs. He told me that one day I would write his biography, and he soon put me to work studying the various translations of Sikh scripture. Then he requested me to remain in one room for forty-five days, revising and editing certain portions of the 'Siri Guru Granth Sahib' which was later titled *Peace Lagoon.*

"My motivation has been a love for Truth in its highest form, which is what God is to a Sikh, and the gratitude for the precious opportunity to serve humanity in the highest and most meaningful way. I could have found satisfaction in nothing less in my life, and indeed frustration and futility was all I could see until my deepest longings were fulfilled in finding a man on this earth who knew what to change, how to change it and what to change it into.

"I had also been the main photographer for recording the growth and history of Yogi Bhajan and the 3HO Foundation."

*   *   *

KAY, Reed 1925-

PERSONAL: Born March 29, 1925, in Boston, Mass.; son of Israel (an engraver) and Leah (Shalman) Kay; married Frieda Hymowitz (a bacteriologist), February 19, 1946; children: Jonathan, Susannah. *Education:* Attended School of the Museum of Fine Arts, Boston, Mass., 1941-43, 1946-49. *Home:* 109 Rawson Rd., Brookline, Mass. 02146. *Office:* School of Visual Arts, Boston University, 855 Commonwealth Ave., Boston, Mass. 02215.

CAREER: School of the Museum of Fine Arts, Boston, Mass., instructor in painting, 1951-55; Boston University, Boston, instructor, 1956-57, assistant professor, 1957-62, associate professor, 1962-68, professor of art, 1968—. Instructor at Skowhegan School of Painting and Sculpture, 1952, 1954-60. Has exhibited drawings and paintings in the United States, with a concentration in the New England area. *Military service:* U.S. Army, 1943-45; received Purple Heart.

WRITINGS: The Painter's Companion: A Basic Guide to Studio Methods and Materials, Webb Books, 1961, revised edition published as *The Painter's Guide to Studio Methods and Materials,* Doubleday, 1972. Contributor to *World Book Encyclopedia.*

SIDELIGHTS: "I paint from nature, in response to the landscape, people and objects around me. I try to understand those visual aspects of the subject that cause me to be interested in it in the first place, and to find ways to recreate those qualities on the canvas.

"When teaching in the studio, I try to encourage the student to understand what he sees in terms of the way forms originate and function and the ways that their volumes are distributed through the space that they occupy. I feel that the student can best develop his own personal style when he understands the technical and stylistic achievements of the tradition.

"My writing stresses the responsibility of the painter to select materials and techniques that will be as durable as possible, so that his pictures may age with a minimum of change. At the same time, the artist must select those materials and methods that will enable him to reach his own aesthetic objectives."

AVOCATIONAL INTERESTS: Travel (France and Italy).

*   *   *

KEATS, Ezra Jack 1916-

PERSONAL: Born March 11, 1916, in Brooklyn, N.Y.; son of Benjamin (a waiter) and Augusta (Podgainy) Keats. *Education:* Attended public schools in New York, N.Y. *Home:* 444 East 82nd St., New York, N.Y. 10028.

CAREER: Author and illustrator of books for children. Worked as muralist for Works Progress Administration (WPA) during Depression; instructor, School of Visual Arts, New York City, 1947-48, and Workshop School, New York City, 1955-57; *Military service:* U.S. Army Air Forces, camouflage expert during World War II. *Member:* P.E.N., Author's Guild, Society of Illustrators. *Awards, honors:* Caldecott Medal, 1963, for *The Snowy Day; Boston Globe-Horn Book* award for illustration, 1970, for *Hi, Cat!;* Brooklyn Art Books for Children citation, 1973, for *The Snowy Day.*

WRITINGS—All self-illustrated: (With Pat Cherr) *My Dog Is Lost!,* Crowell, 1960; *The Snowy Day,* Viking, 1962; *Whistle for Willie,* Viking, 1964; *John Henry: An American Legend,* Pantheon, 1965; *Jennie's Hat,* Harper, 1966; (compiler) *God Is in the Mountain,* Holt, 1966; *Peter's Chair,* Harper, 1967; *A Letter to Amy,* Harper, 1968; (compiler) *Night,* Atheneum, 1969; *Goggles,* Macmillan, 1969; *Hi, Cat!,* Macmillan, 1970; *Apt. 3,* Macmillan, 1971; *Pet Show!,* Macmillan, 1972; *Skates!,* F. Watts, 1973; *Psst! Doggie—,* F. Watts, 1973; *Dreams,* Macmillan, 1974; *Kitten for a Day,* F. Watts, 1974; *Louie,* Greenwillow Books, 1975.

Illustrator: Elisabeth C. Lansing, *Jubilant for Sure,* Crowell, 1954; Frances Carpenter, *Wonder Tales of Dogs and Cats,* Doubleday, 1955; Lansing, *Sure Thing for Shep,* Crowell, 1956; George S. Albee, *Three Young Kings,* F. Watts, 1956; William McKellar, *Wee Joseph,* McGraw-Hill, 1957; Tillie S. Pines, *Indians Knew,* McGraw-Hill, 1957; Pines and Joseph Levine, *Pilgrims Knew,* McGraw-Hill, 1957; Pines and Levine, *Chinese Knew,* McGraw-Hill, 1958; Dorothea F. Fisher, *And Long Remember,* McGraw-Hill, 1959; Eleanor A. Murphey, *Nihal of Ceylon,* Crowell, 1960; Paul Showers, *In the Night,* Ambassador, 1961; Patricia M. Martin, *The Rice Bowl Pet,* Crowell, 1962; Solveig P. Russell, *What Good Is a Tail?,* Bobbs-Merrill, 1962; Ruth

P. Collins, *The Flying Cow,* Walck, 1963; Lucretia P. Hale, *The Peterkin Papers,* Doubleday, 1963; Ann N. Clark, *Tia Maria's Garden,* Viking, 1963; Millicent E. Selsam, *How to Be a Nature Detective,* Harper, 1963; Maxine W. Kumin, *Speedy Digs Downside Up,* Putnam, 1964; Ann McGovern, *Zoo, Where Are You?,* Harper, 1964; John Keats, *The Naughty Boy,* Viking, 1965; Richard Lewis, editor, *In a Spring Garden,* Dial Press, 1965; Esther R. Hautzig, *In the Park,* Macmillan, 1968; *The Little Drummer Boy* (words and music by Katherine Davis), Macmillan, 1968; *Over in the Meadow,* Four Winds Press, 1971; Lloyd Alexander, *The King's Fountain,* Dutton, 1971; Myron Levoy, *Penny Tunes and Princesses,* Harper, 1972.

SIDELIGHTS: Ezra Keats's first solo effort at writing took the form of a children's book, *The Snowy Day,* which won the Caldecott Medal in 1963. His previous experience had been illustrating the works of f other authors. Florence B. Freeman, writing in *Elementary English,* noted that for Keats, "this was a new experience in illustration." She added: "Text and drawings reinforce each other to provide an integrated experience for eye and ear. The illustrations, in paint and collage, with simple forms, delicate patterns, and a variety of textures, are not merely visual representations of the text, [but] another way of telling about Peter's day. From the pictures we see that Peter is a Negro child. It's direct and lyrical quality leads the adult reader to recognize that Keats was not trying to do an 'ethnic' book. Children come in different colors, and Peter is brown. To children, this is a book about a child."

The Snowy Day was reviewed by a *Horn Book* critic, who wrote: "In this mood book, never static but sparkling with atmosphere in lovely water-color pictures, a small boy experiences the joys of a snowy day. The brief, vividly expressed text points out his new awareness of the sight and texture of snow (the crunch, crunch of his feet making tracks), the sound (the plop of snow smacked off a tree with a stick), and the fun of playing with snow—then his thinking and thinking about the outdoor adventures later in warm bathtub and bed, while more snowflakes fall."

One of Keats's most recent efforts is *Dreams,* which was reviewed by *Horn Book:* "The artist's skillful combination of acrylic painting and collage has never been more effectively employed. The rich hues of sunset, the muted sky of night, and the brilliant blue of early morning form an impressive but not overwhelming background; and the evanescent nature of dreams is delightfully conveyed."

In 1967, the Weston Woods Studio's film version of *Whistle for Willie* was shown at the Second Teheran International Festival of Film for Children in Iran, which Keats attended as an U.S. delegate and as guest of honor of the Empress. Earlier, at the Venice Film Festival, the Weston Woods Studio adaptation of *The Snowy Day* won the prize for the best children's film.

BIOGRAPHICAL/CRITICAL SOURCES: Commonweal, November 16, 1962; *Saturday Review,* December 15, 1962; *Horn Book,* February, 1963, June, 1964, December, 1974; *Publishers Weekly,* March 11, 1963, January 16, 1973; *Elementary English,* January, 1969; *American Artist,* September, 1971; *Milwaukee Journal,* March 28, 1974; *Children's Literature Review,* Volume 1, Gale, 1976.*

* * *

KEATS, Mark 1905-

PERSONAL: Born August 11, 1905, in New York, N.Y.; son of David (a storekeeper) and Gizelle Katie (Marcus) Keats; married Nina Julia Hall, September 26, 1932 (separated); children: Mary Ann Keats Luna, Steven G. *Education:* Syracuse University, B.S., 1927, graduate study, 1929; further graduate study at Cornell University, 1930, and University of Wisconsin, Madison, 1932. *Religion:* "Jewish secularist." *Home:* 4948 Rosewood Ave., #4, Los Angeles, Calif. 90004. *Office:* Westside Jewish Community Center, 5870 West Olympic Blvd., Los Angeles, Calif. 90036.

CAREER: Los Angeles County Social Service, Los Angeles, Calif., case worker, 1940-45; Los Angeles County Probation Department, Los Angeles, deputy probation officer, 1945-48; Los Angeles Jewish Centers, Los Angeles, currently serving as group worker specialist in intercultural programming, adult programming, and senior adult programming. Officer of Los Angeles County community coordinating council, 1955-58. *Member:* Society of Children's Book Writers, American Civil Liberties Union, Common Cause, Coalition for Economic Survival, Los Angeles Jewish Secular Cultural Club. *Awards, honors:* National bicentennial award from Play, Inc., 1976, for "Peter Salem, Black Minuteman."

WRITINGS: Sancho and His Stubborn Mule (juvenile), William R. Scott, 1944; *Sancho, Pronto, and the Engineer* (juvenile), Blaine-Ethridge, 1976; *Peter Salem, Black Minuteman* (one-act play), Plays, 1976. Also author of *Gertrudis Bocánegro: Joan of Arc of Mexico,* 1969, *Jose Maria Morelos,* 1970, and *Miguel Hidalgo y Costilla,* 1970, all monographs.

Unpublished plays: "Gertrude Bocanegra" (one-act), first produced in Los Angeles at Eastside Jewish Community Theatre, September, 1954; "Oh Modin" (oratorio), first produced in Los Angeles at Yublon Center, December, 1976.

Author of "Evolution of Sports in History," a column in *Labor Paper,* 1939-40. Contributor of short story to *Jewish Currents.*

WORK IN PROGRESS: Two novellas for children, *Pepito, Boy Folk Singer* and *Abraham and Auntie's Magic Garden;* original folktales; folktale plays for children; research on international folklore.

AVOCATIONAL INTERESTS: Photography, raising houseplants, foreign films, plays, activity in civil rights programs.

* * *

KEELER, Mary Frear 1904-

PERSONAL: Born January 1, 1904, in State College, Pa.; daughter of William (a chemistry professor and research scientist) and Julia (Reno) Frear; married John B. Keeler, June 30, 1938 (deceased); children: Shirley Keeler Bebout. *Education:* Pennsylvania State University, B.A., 1924; Yale University, M.A., 1929, Ph.D., 1933. *Politics:* Democrat. *Religion:* Presbyterian. *Home:* 302 West 12th St., Frederick, Md. 21701. *Office:* Yale Center for Parliamentary History, Yale University, New Haven, Conn. 06520.

CAREER: University of Wyoming, Laramie, instructor in history, 1929-31; New Jersey College for Women, New Brunswick, instructor, 1931-32; Pennsylvania State University, University Park, instructor, 1933-37, assistant professor of history, 1937-38; Vassar College, Poughkeepsie, N.Y., lecturer in history, 1952-53; Wellesley College, Wellesley, Mass., lecturer in history, 1953-54; Hood College, Frederick, Md., lecturer, 1954-58, professor of history, 1958-71, dean of faculty, 1954-69; Yale University, New

Haven, Conn., research associate in history, 1974-76, executive editor at Yale Center for Parliamentary History, 1974—.

MEMBER: American Historical Association, Conference on British History (member of executive committee, 1972-77), American Association of University Women (member of state board of directors, 1938-40, 1973-74; chairman of national fellowships awards committee, 1955-61), Royal Historical Society (fellow), Berkshire Conference of Women Historians, Phi Kappa Phi. *Awards, honors:* American Association of University Women fellowship, 1935-36; Folger Shakespeare Library senior fellowship, 1971-72.

WRITINGS: The Long Parliament, 1640-1641, American Philosophical Society, 1954; (editor) *Bibliography of British History: Stuart Period,* revised edition, Clarendon Press, 1970 (Keeler was not associated with earlier edition); (editor) *Accounts of Sir Francis Drake's West Indian Voyage, 1585-86,* Cambridge University Press, 1976; (editor with R. C. Johnson, M. J. Cole, and W. B. Bidwell) *Commons Debates, 1628,* Yale University Press, Volume I, 1977, Volume II, 1977, Volume III (edited by Keeler), 1977, Volume IV, 1978.

WORK IN PROGRESS: Editing *Commons Debates, 1628,* with R. C. Johnson, M. J. Cole, and W. B. Bidwell, publication of Volumes V and VI expected by Yale University Press, 1979-80; research on seventeenth-century Parliamentary committees.

SIDELIGHTS: Keeler told *CA:* "I have done a great deal of work on biographies of members of Parliament and on their activities while serving. Another object of my studies has been the procedure by which business was done, with special emphasis on the formation of committees and their development as means of shaping policies."

* * *

KEENAN, Martha 1927-

PERSONAL: Born May 29, 1927, in San Jose, Calif.; daughter of Leo (a life insurance salesman) and Jeannette (Bookmyer) Wagner; married Robert Keenan (an elementary school principal), September 12, 1953; children: Susan, Kathryn. *Education:* San Jose State College (San Jose State University), B.A., 1949. *Residence:* Santa Clara, Calif.

CAREER: Secretary, 1950-56; writer, 1965—.

WRITINGS: The Mannerly Adventures of Little Mouse (juvenile), Crown, 1977. Contributor of stories to children's magazines, including *Jack and Jill, Humpty Dumpty,* and *Highlights for Children.*

SIDELIGHTS: "I began to write when my children were young," Keenan told *CA,* "and chose children's stories because of them. I continue to write because I enjoy it and because I feel it is needed."

* * *

KEENLEYSIDE, T(erence) A(shley) 1940-

PERSONAL: Born January 2, 1940, in Hartford, Conn.; son of Edward A. (a physician) and Margaret E. (an actress; maiden name, Wilson) Keenleyside; married Dorothy Anne Pointing (a teacher), September 8, 1962; children: Karen Anne, Deborah Ashley, Timothy Aldworth. *Education:* University of Toronto, B.A., 1962; University of London, Ph.D., 1966. *Religion:* None. *Home:* 833 Homedale Blvd., Windsor, Ontario, Canada N8S 2S8. *Office:* Department of Political Science, University of Windsor, Windsor, Ontario, Canada N9B 3P4.

CAREER: Toronto Daily Star, Toronto, Ontario, part-time reporter, 1960-62; Canadian Department of External Affairs, Ottawa, Ontario, diplomat in Ottawa, New York, N.Y., Thailand, and Indonesia, 1966-71; University of Windsor, Windsor, Ontario, assistant professor, 1971-75, associate professor of political science, 1975—. *Member:* Canadian Political Science Association, Canadian Society for Asian Studies, Canadian Institute of International Affairs (member of local executive committee, 1972—; branch president, 1975-77).

WRITINGS: The Common Touch (political novel), Doubleday, 1977. Contributor to Canadian and Pacific studies journals.

WORK IN PROGRESS: A novel; research on Canadian foreign service officers, Canadian foreign policy independence, and Indian foreign policy.

SIDELIGHTS: Keenleyside comments: "My writing thus far has been largely based on my experiences in the Canadian foreign service. The purpose of my political novel was to draw the attention of as large an audience as possible to the shortcomings in the relations of western states with developing countries, particularly in Southeast Asia."

BIOGRAPHICAL/CRITICAL SOURCES: Windsor This Month, November, 1977; *Windsor Star,* December 24, 1977.

* * *

KEEP, David (John) 1936-

PERSONAL: Born December 4, 1936, in Bedford, England; son of Ralph Henry (a toolmaker) and Mildred (a secretary; maiden name, Ford) Keep; married Carolyn Jean Herbert (a teacher), August 1, 1962; children: Nicholas Herbert, Philippa Ruth. *Education:* New College, Oxford, B.A., 1960, M.A., 1963; Wesley House, Cambridge, B.A., 1962; attended University of Zurich, 1962-63; University of Sheffield, Ph.D., 1971. *Home:* Heatherdene, Woodbury, Exeter EX5 1NR, England.

CAREER: Ordained Methodist minister, 1964; pastor of Methodist churches in Coalville, England, 1963-64, and Belper, England, 1964-66; high school teacher of religion and history in Bedford, England, 1966-71; Rolle College, Exmouth, England, senior lecturer in religious studies, 1971—. *Military service:* Royal Air Force, 1955-57. *Member:* Ecclesiastical History Society, National Association of Teachers in Further and Higher Education, Southwest Writers Association, Devonshire Association, Oxford Union Club, Zwingliverein.

WRITINGS: History Through Stamps, David & Charles, 1975. Contributor to regional and ecclesiastical history journals.

WORK IN PROGRESS: "Continuing interest in the influence of the Zurich reformer, Heinrich Bullinger, on the English Protestant Church."

SIDELIGHTS: Keep told *CA:* "The idea of writing *History Through Stamps* came when I was teaching world affairs and found I often turned to the stamp catalogue for dates and names. My own knowledge of history and geography was extended by stamp collecting when I was a boy, and though I specialise in Great Britain and Switzerland now, I retain a general collection, especially of issues before 1939. I hoped the book would encourage people to collect stamps as clues to the world around them, rather than simply for investment."

AVOCATIONAL INTERESTS: Russia (has visited the Soviet Union).

KELDYSH, Mstislav V(sevolodovich) 1911-1978

February 10, 1911—June 24, 1978; Russian scientist, mathematician, administrator, and author of books in his field. An expert on space mathematics and aerodynamics, Keldysh supported cooperation between the United States and the Soviet Union on space research. While he was president of the Soviet Academy of Sciences from 1961 to 1975, Keldysh refuted the politically popular "school of biology" theory promulgated by Trofim Lysenko. His refutation brought about a new interest in the science of genetics in the Soviet Union. He received the Stalin Prize twice, in 1942 and 1946. Obituaries and other sources: *Current Biography,* Wilson, 1962; *Who's Who in the World,* 2nd edition, Marquis, 1973; *The International Who's Who,* Europa, 1977; *Time,* July 10, 1978; *Washington Post,* June 27, 1978.

* * *

KELLEY, William Melvin 1937-

PERSONAL: Born in 1937, in New York, N.Y.; son of William (an editor) and Narcissa Agatha (Garcia) Kelley; married Karen Gibson (a designer), December, 1962; children: Jessica, Ciratikaiji. *Education:* Educated at Harvard University. *Address:* c/o Doubleday & Co., Inc., 277 Park Ave., New York, N.Y. 10017.

CAREER: Free-lance writer. Taught at the New School for Social Research, 1965-67; State University of New York at Geneseo, writer-in-residence, spring, 1965. *Awards, honors:* Dana Reed Prize from Harvard University, 1960; Bread Loaf Scholar, 1962; John Hay Whitney Foundation award and Rosenthal Foundation award, 1963, both for *A Different Drummer; Transatlantic Review* award, 1964, for *Dancers on the Shore.*

WRITINGS—All published by Doubleday: *A Different Drummer* (novel), 1962; *Dancers on the Shore* (short stories), 1964; *A Drop of Patience* (novel), 1965; *dem* (novel), 1967; *Dunfords Travels Everywhere* (novel), 1970.

Contributor to periodicals, including *Accent, Urbanite, Negro Digest, Partisan Review, New York Times Magazine, Mademoiselle, Jazz and Pop.*

Work represented in anthologies, including *The Best Short Stories by Negro Writers: An Anthology from 1899 to the Present,* edited by Langston Hughes, Little, Brown, 1967; *The Young American Writers,* edited by Richard Kostelanetz, Funk, 1967; *Dark Symphony: Negro Literature in America,* edited by James A. Emanuel and Theodore Gross, Free Press, 1968; *Native Sons: A Critical Study of Twentieth-Century Negro American Authors,* edited by Edward Margolies, Lippincott, 1968; *Brothers and Sisters: Modern Stories by Black Americans,* edited by Arnold Adoff, Macmillan, 1970; *The Black Man and the Promise of America,* edited by Lettie J. Austin, Lewis W. Fenderson, and Sophia P. Nelson, Scott, Foresman, 1970; *Right On! Anthology of Black Literature,* edited by Bradford Chambers and Rebecca Moon, New American Library, 1970; *Harlem: Voices from the Soul of Black America,* edited by John Henrik Clarke, New American Library, 1970; *From the Roots: Short Stories by Black Americans,* edited by Charles L. James, Dodd, 1970; *Black Experience: An Anthology of American Literature for the 1970's,* edited by Francis E. Kearns, Viking, 1970; *Black American Literature: Essays, Poetry, Fiction, Drama,* edited by Darwin T. Turner, Merrill, 1970; *Black Literature in America,* edited by Houston A. Baker, Jr., McGraw-Hill, 1971; *Cavalcade: Negro American Writing From 1760 to the Present,* edited by Arthur P. Davis and J. Saunders Redding, Houghton, 1971; *Black Insights: Significant Literature by Black Americans, 1760 to the Present,* edited by Nick Aaron Ford, Ginn, 1971; *Black Writers of America: A Comprehensive Anthology,* edited by Richard K. Barksdale and Keneth Kinnamon, Macmillan, 1972; *New Black Voices,* edited by Abraham Chapman, New American Library, 1972; *Afro-American Writing: An Anthology of Prose and Poetry,* edited by Richard A. Long and Eugenia W. Collier, New York University Press, 1972.

WORK IN PROGRESS: Days of Our Years.

SIDELIGHTS: The title of William Melvin Kelley's first novel, *A Different Drummer,* is far more than just a favorite phrase remembered from Thoreau's "If a man does not keep pace with his companions, perhaps it is because he hears a different drummer. Let him step to the music which he hears, however measured or far away." That belief in the worth of the individual and his basic rights is the basis for all of Kelley's writing. With the success of his first novel, Kelley explained that he was interested, among other things, in exploring "the plight of Negroes, *as individual human beings,* in America."

Hugh J. Ingrasci has noted Kelley's concern with the individual. "The world Kelley portrays," wrote Ingrasci, ". . . projects a life of possibilities, one wherein the struggle to eliminate racial inequities is viable, but only for the individual who hammers away at exploitation with one irresistible conviction: that each human person has too great a value to allow others to regard him as a mere social commodity." It matters little if one "wins his battle with the society he finds," said Ingrasci, ". . . it is his belief that he is humanly equal to anyone else that has set him free, and not the prospect of attaining social justice."

Kelley criticizes reviewers who lump all black authors into one category for creating what he calls the "Negro literary ghetto." In the preface to *Dancers on the Shore,* he wrote: "An American writer who happens to have brown skin faces this unique problem: Solutions and answers to the Negro Problem are very often read into his work. At the instant they open his book, the readers begin to search fervently, and often with honest concern, for some key or answer to what is happening today between black and white people in America.

"At this time, let me say for the record that I am not a sociologist or a politician or a spokesman. Such people try to give answers. A writer, I think, should ask questions. He should depict people, not symbols or ideas disguised as people."

In another interview, Kelley stated: "It isn't that I'm naive, that I'm trying to divorce myself from the racial struggle, but I don't think it should enter into my art in such a way that my writing becomes propagandistic. If my novels are so strongly tied to the times the book would have no reason to live once the present struggles are over—if indeed, they ever will be over. I want my books to have reason to exist."

While critics have unanimously found merit in Kelley's novels, they have sometimes found that he writes almost too facilely. Writing about *dem,* Dan Jaffe said: "The texture of the language, the settings, and the dialogue, give the reader a sense of life, of the alienation of a confused white man who suspects he is on the periphery of a life-rhythm more natural and substantial than his own. Unfortunately, the rest of the novel is slick and stagey by comparison." Frank C. Shapiro commented that the main character of *dem* was not quite believable and wrote, "There are good scenes in this unsatisfying book, and good writing, too, but on the whole, reading *dem* is like watching a basketball player, in perfect form, fake out a guard, arch for a pivot shot, and miss.'' But in a discussion of the same novel, Robert Bone said: ''Kelley turns to an overt satire of the ways of white people. His present mood is bitter, disillusioned, alienated to the point of secession from American society. The expatriate impulse, however, has found in satire a controlling form. Kelley's images are able to encompass his negative emotions. The result is a sharp increase in perception for the victims of his satire.''

H. T. Anderson commented that Kelley's latest novel, *Dunfords Travels Everywhere*, ''exasperates and exhausts,'' and contended that Kelley ''seems to be making an aesthetic of obscurity.'' However, Christopher Lehmann-Haupt praised Kelley's use of a ''black form of the dreamlanguage of James Joyce's *Finnegans Wake* . . . to escape the strictures of the conventional (white) novel. . . . The idea has released in Kelley a creative exuberance that was being choked with bitterness in his last book *dem*.'' Although Lehmann-Haupt found that some parts of the novel don't work, he commended Kelley for ''the way the 'real' surface is undermined, so that finally it threatens to splinter into hallucination at every moment.''

BIOGRAPHICAL/CRITICAL SOURCES—Books: William Melvin Kelley, preface to *Dancers on the Shore*, Doubleday, 1964; David Littlejohn, *Black on White*, Grossman, 1966; Roy Newquist, *Conversations*, Rand McNally, 1967; Sherley Anne Williams, *Give Birth to Brightness*, Dial, 1972; Roger Whitlow, *Black American Literature: A Critical History*, Nelson Hall, 1973.

Articles: *New York Times Magazine*, May 20, 1962; *New York Times Book Review*, June 17, 1962, May 2, 1965, September 24, 1967, November 8, 1970; *Negro Digest*, October, 1962, January, 1967, March, 1967, May, 1968, November, 1969; *Esquire*, August, 1963; *Reporter*, May 21, 1964; *Commonweal*, July 3, 1964; *Saturday Review*, April 17, 1965, October 28, 1967; *Prairie Schooner*, spring, 1968; *Book World*, October 22, 1967; *New York Times*, September 7, 1970; *Best Sellers*, October 1, 1970; *New York Review of Books*, March 11, 1971; *Studies in Black Literature*, summer, 1971, fall, 1972, winter, 1974, fall, 1975.

* * *

KELSON, Allen H(oward) 1940-

PERSONAL: Born May 4, 1940, in Chicago, Ill.; son of Ben (a retailing executive) and Esther (Ashkinaze) Kelson; married Carla S. Lipson (a dining critic and keyliner), August 18, 1976; children: David, Melina. *Education:* Attended University of Illinois, Chicago, 1957, and Urbana, 1958; Roosevelt University, B.A., 1965. *Residence:* Highland Park, Ill. *Office: Chicago* Magazine, 500 North Michigan, Chicago, Ill. 60611.

CAREER: Sears, Roebuck & Co., Chicago, Ill., catalog copywriter, 1962-64, sales promotion writer, 1964-67, director of special projects and catalog sales, 1967-68; *Chicago* magazine, Chicago, editor-in-chief, 1968—. Principal of Kelson Kapuler Advertising, 1962-68; public relations director and advertising manager of WFMT-Radio, Chicago, 1968-70. Lecturer for National Association of FM Broadcasters, 1970, National Retail Merchants Association, 1973, and National Restaurant Association, 1975. Board member of Les Gourmets of Illinois, 1972-74, International Visitors Center of Chicago, 1975—, and Friends of Highland Park Library, 1975—; member of advisory board of Walt Disney Magnet School, 1974-75. *Member:* American Society of

Magazine Editors, Chicago Press Club. *Awards, honors:* Merit award from Chicago Advertising Club, 1965; certificate of excellence from ''Cover '75''.

WRITINGS: (Editor) *Chicago GuideBook*, Regnery, 1972, 2nd edition, 1973; (editor) *Chicago GuideYear*, Photopress, 1972, 3rd edition, 1975. Author with wife, Carla Kelson, of monthly column of gourmet dining in *Chicago;* contributor to other magazines.

SIDELIGHTS: Kelson writes: ''In the course of my work—and the growth of the publication I've helped to create—I've come to realize that personal and business success are dependent on the same standards of performance that distinguish good restaurants: neither businesses nor people should attempt more than they are capable of doing well, nor must they attempt to appear to be other than what they are. If one manages to do well all one purports to be able to do well, reasonable people will neither expect more nor properly demand more than they will receive; they will, in other words, be satisfied with the performance.''

* * *

KEMP, Jerrold E(dwin) 1921-

PERSONAL: Born April 23, 1921, in New York, N.Y.; son of Irving (a manufacturer of women's wear) and Clementine Kemp; married Dorothy P. Gallon, December 31, 1949. *Education:* University of Florida, B.S., 1942; University of Miami, Coral Gables, Fla., M.S., 1952; Indiana University, D.Ed., 1956. *Home address:* Box 106, Mount Hamilton Rd., San Jose, Calif. 95140. *Office:* Instructional Resources Center, San Jose State University, San Jose, Calif. 95192.

CAREER: Science teacher in public schools in Miami, Fla., 1949-52; Indiana University, Bloomington, assistant professor of education, 1952-58; San Jose State University, San Jose, Calif., associate professor, 1958-64, professor of education, 1964—. *Military service:* U.S. Army Air Forces, 1942-47; became lieutenant colonel. *Member:* Association for Educational Communications and Technology (president, 1972-73), National Society for Performance and Instruction, Phi Delta Kappa.

WRITINGS: Planning and Producing Audiovisual Materials, Prentice-Hall, 1975; *Instructional Design: A Plan for Unit and Course Development*, Fearon, 1977.

WORK IN PROGRESS: Measuring Cost Effectiveness and Efficiency in Instructional Programs.

SIDELIGHTS: Kemp writes: ''Presently, my major interests and contributions are in the area of instructional development for educational and training organizations.

''Instructional development is the application of systematic planning. It gives consideration to setting objectives for learning, selecting techniques and resources to accomplish objectives, and then measuring the degree to which the objectives are accomplished.''

* * *

KEMPSTER, Norman 1936-

PERSONAL: Born January 4, 1936, in Sacramento, Calif.; son of Roy D. (a teacher) and Viola A. (Cox) Kempster; married Jane Leon (an editor), June 30, 1957; children: Jill, David. *Education:* California State University at Sacramento, B.A., 1957; further study at Stanford University, 1967-68. *Home:* 111 Devon Court, Silver Spring, Md. 20910. *Office: Washington Star*, 225 Virginia Ave. S.E., Washington, D.C. 20026.

CAREER/WRITINGS: United Press International, New York, N.Y., bureau chief in Olympia, Wash., 1961-66, assistant bureau chief in Sacramento, Calif., 1966-69, White House correspondent, 1969-73; *Washington Star,* Washington, D.C., White House correspondent, 1973—. Notable assignments include coverage of President Nixon's trip to China, Nixon's resignation, and an interview with President Ford. Contributor of articles to periodicals, including *Finance. Military service:* U.S. Army, 1959-61. *Member:* White House Correspondents Association (member of board of directors), Washington Press Club, Olympia Press Club (president).

* * *

KENNEDY, James Y(oung) 1916-

PERSONAL: Born May 21, 1916, in Pecos, Tex.; son of James Wayland (a laborer) and Martha Jane (Tompson) Kennedy; married Annette Pera, July 1, 1975 (divorced January 1, 1976). *Education:* Attended New Mexico Military Institute, 1937; University of Oklahoma, B.S., 1941; Southern Methodist University, M.S., 1959. *Home address:* P.O. Box 2, Chatsworth, Calif. 91311.

CAREER: Lockheed Aircraft, Burbank, Calif., aircraft designer, 1941, 1945; Convair, Fort Worth, Tex., nuclear aircraft designer, 1950-59; Rockwell International, Los Angeles, Calif., nuclear rocket designer, 1960-69, laser designer, 1972. *Military service:* U.S. Aviation Service, flying cadet, 1938; U.S. Navy, radio technician, 1945.

WRITINGS: South Seas Odyssey: An Escape (nonfiction), Great Lakes Living Press, 1977.

SIDELIGHTS: Kennedy writes: "Always active with a variety of interests, I engaged in wrestling and football in high school and college. Later it was archery, skiing, scuba diving, prospecting for gold, and flying. After sailing the South Seas alone on my own boat for four years, my interests lie mainly in my two-hundred-acre mountain retreat overlooking the San Fernando Valley and in amateur ham radio."

* * *

KENNEL, LeRoy E(ldon) 1930-

PERSONAL: Born March 29, 1930, in Nebraska; son of Peter R. (a clergyman) and Anna (Reeb) Kennel; married R. Pauline Graybill (a teacher), July 26, 1954; children: Jon, Rita, Janice, Jay. *Education:* Hesston Junior College, A.A., 1949; Goshen College, B.A., 1952; University of Iowa, M.A., 1953; Goshen Biblical Seminary, B.D., 1954; Michigan State University, Ph.D., 1966. *Politics:* Democrat. *Home:* 757 22nd St., Lombard, Ill. 60148. *Office:* Department of Communication, Bethany Theological Seminary, Oak Brook, Ill. 60521.

CAREER: Ordained Mennonite pastor, 1955; pastor of Mennonite church in Lombard, Ill., 1954-66, and of Presbyterian church in Chicago, Ill., 1966-67; Bethany Theological Seminary, Oak Brook, Ill., associate professor, 1969-76, professor of communication, 1976—. *Member:* North American Academy of Liturgy, Academy of Homiletics, Speech Communication Association of America, Religious Speech Communication Association, Association for Professional Education for the Ministry, Screen Educators Society.

WRITINGS: Mennonites: Who and Why, Herald Press, 1966; *Ecology of the Airwaves,* Herald Press, 1971. Contributor of articles and reviews to magazines. Editor of *Faith and Art,* 1972-74.

WORK IN PROGRESS: Communication and Celebration; Perspectives for Preaching.

SIDELIGHTS: Kennel writes: "Forthcoming publications presume that Christian communication has roots in biblical and history-heritage matters, but also appreciates and appraises our mass-mediated culture. To tell the whole story as it is requires that knowledge and experience be combined and integrated in contextual situations. Communication publications can do that with the story, interrelating storybook (bible), storytellers (history and heritage), and storyland (the times of our lives). Communication arts awaken all of the senses. Both classical and contemporary principles and methods of preparing and presenting messages that speak to pastoral and prophetic needs, concern for appropriate theories and theology, and search for forms and styles for the church as it celebrates the presence and power of God as experienced in the life of the community, need emphasis."

* * *

KENT, Leonard J. 1927-

PERSONAL: Born December 21, 1927, in Brooklyn, N.Y.; married; children: four. *Education:* Long Island University, B.A., 1953; New York University, M.A., 1955; Yale University, Ph.D., 1965. *Office:* Department of English, Quinnipiac College, Hamden, Conn. 06518.

CAREER: Elementary and high school teacher until 1960; Quinnipiac College, Hamden, Conn., instructor, 1960-64, assistant professor, 1964-65, associate professor, 1965-67, professor of English, 1967-69, chairman of department, 1965-69; Chico State College, Chico, Calif., professor of English and dean of Graduate School, 1969-71; Quinnipiac College, professor of English and president of the college, 1971—. Member of executive committee of Connecticut Conference of Independent Colleges; president of Connecticut Council on Higher Education. *Awards, honors:* Grant from National Translation Center, 1967.

WRITINGS: (Editor with N. Berberova) Leo Tolstoy, *Anna Karenina,* Modern Library, 1950, revised edition, Random House, 1965; (editor) *Collected Tales and Plays of Nikolai Gogol,* Pantheon, 1964; *The Subconscious in Gogol and Dostoevsky, and Its Antecedents,* Mouton & Co., 1969; (translator and editor) *Selected Writings of E. T. A. Hoffmann,* University of Chicago Press, 1969; (editor) *Graduate Education Today and Tomorrow,* University of New Mexico Press, 1972; (translator and editor) Ernst Theodor Amadeus Hoffmann, *Tales,* University of Chicago Press, 1972. Contributor to journals.

* * *

KERMAN, Judith (Berna) 1945-

PERSONAL: Born October 5, 1945, in Bayside, N.Y.; daughter of Harry (a comptroller) and Betty (a secretary; maiden name, Zeltsman) Kerman. *Education:* University of Rochester, B.A. (honors), 1967; State University of New York at Buffalo, M.A., 1972, Ph.D., 1977. *Politics:* "Left feminist." *Religion:* "Working on it." *Home:* 704 Crescent Ave., Crescent, N.Y. 14216. *Office:* Office for Credit-Free Programs, Hayes A, Room 3, State University of New York at Buffalo, Buffalo, N.Y. 14214.

CAREER: Macmillan & Co., New York, N.Y., copy editor trainee in textbook department, 1967; Jewish Guild for the Blind, New York, N.Y., social group worker, 1967-68; Aetna Life & Casualty Co., Hartford, Conn., computer programmer, 1968-69; CALSPAN Corp., Cheektowaga,

N.Y., computer programmer, 1969-70; substitute teacher at public schools in Buffalo, N.Y., 1971, and at children's psychiatric hospital in West Seneca, N.Y., 1971-73; State University of New York at Buffalo, coordinator of Office for Credit-Free Programs, 1973—, counseling intern, 1974-75, adjunct instructor in human dimensions of family and community relations, autumn, 1974. Artist and teacher at Allentown Arts Laboratory, 1971; music director and teacher at Buffalo Theatre Workshop, 1970-72; part-time lecturer at Empire State College, Niagara Frontier Learning Center, 1975—; poet-in-residence at Center for Employment and Perceptual Arts (CEPA) Gallery, 1976-77; has given poetry readings. Soprano concert soloist and choral singer, 1964-72.

MEMBER: International P.E.N. (American Center), National University Extension Association (professional member), Modern Language Association of America, Committee of Small Magazine Editors and Publishers, Coordinating Council of Literary Magazines, Women's Caucus on Modern Languages. *Awards, honors:* Grants from Coordinating Council of Literary Magazines, 1973, 1977.

WRITINGS: Obsessions (poetry chapbook), Intrepid Press, 1974; *The Jakoba Poems* (chapbook), White Pine Press, 1976; *Mothering* (prose poem), Uroboros Books, 1978.

Plays: "Skyscraper," first produced in Hartford, Conn., at Image Theatre, 1969; "Dream of Rain" (verse play), first produced in Buffalo, N.Y., at American Contemporary Theatre, January, 1976. Also author of "Equinox," "Ariadne," and "Wine Bottle Piece."

Contributor of articles to *Jewish Currents, Cats, Scene,* and *RT: A Journal of Radical Therapy,* and poems to literary periodicals, including *Hanging Loose, Rapport, Nebula,* and *Niagara.* Founder and editor of *Earth's Daughters: A Feminist Arts Periodical,* 1971—, and *Beefsteak Begonia,* 1976.

WORK IN PROGRESS: A college-level creative writing textbook; "Daughters," a long poem; folklore research on language of citizens' band radio and its changes under the impact of mass access.

SIDELIGHTS: Judith Kerman writes: "I am fascinated by the junction of thought/feeling images, which include mythic, psychological, biological dimensions and are too narrowly labelled 'Jungian' and/or 'Gestaltist'—I find that willy-nilly this is what my poems do, and where they seem most informative as well as compelling and rich, both to me and to my readers. My critical work about Merwin also follows this direction. I try to allow the poem to create its own world, and to tell me about its proper form and content, never to impose extraneous ideas but to use all my craft and skill to allow the poem to become what it needs to be. I earn my living as an administrator, and struggle against the canard that poets must be disorganized and impractical by nature."

AVOCATIONAL INTERESTS: Photography, handcrafts, hiking, nature study, raising and showing cats, folk singer, guitarist, pianist.

* * *

KERNS, Robert Louis 1929-

PERSONAL: Born May 1, 1929, in Cedar Rapids, Iowa; son of William Edward and Nellie (Sawyer) Kerns; married Jean Adair Slater, May 20, 1961; children: William Patrick, Heather Adair. *Education:* University of Iowa, B.A., 1956; Syracuse University, M.A., 1970. *Politics:* Democrat. *Reli-*

gion: Presbyterian. *Home:* 10503 Orange Grove Dr., Tampa, Fla. 33618. *Office:* Department of Mass Communications, University of South Florida, Tampa, Fla. 33620.

CAREER: Davenport Morning Democrat, Davenport, Iowa, staff photographer, 1955-56; *Cedar Rapids Gazette,* Cedar Rapids, Iowa, picture editor, 1958-60; Goodyear Tire & Rubber, Akron, Ohio, photojournalist and director of photography for public relations, 1960-64; Syracuse University, Syracuse, N.Y., 1964-72, began as assistant professor, became associate professor of mass communications; University of South Florida, Tampa, associate professor of mass communications and coordinator of visual communications, 1972—. Director of photographic workshops and tours; consultant to industrial publications.

MEMBER: International Association of Business Communicators (member of local board of directors; president, 1977), Society of Professional Journalists, Professional Photographers of America, National Press Photographers Association, Association for Education in Journalism, Florida Industrial Editors Association, Carrollwood Civic Association (member of board of directors). *Awards, honors:* About two hundred photography awards.

WRITINGS: (Co-author) *Creative News Photography,* University of Iowa Press, 1961; *History of Photography: A Chronology,* Syracuse University Press, 1971; *Photojournalism With a Purpose,* Prentice-Hall, in press. Also author of *Introduction to Photography,* 1969.

* * *

KESSLER, Leonard P. 1921-

PERSONAL: Born October 28, 1921, in Ohio; married wife, Ethel; children: Kim, Paul. *Education:* Earned B.F.A. from Carnegie Institute of Technology. *Residence:* Rockland County, N.Y.

CAREER: Author and illustrator. *Military service:* U.S. Army; became staff sergeant. *Awards, honors:* New York Times best illustrated children's books award, 1954, 1955, and 1957.

WRITINGS: What's in a Line? (self-illustrated), W. R. Scott, 1951; *World without Color,* S. Gabriel Sons, 1953; (with John G. McCullough) *Farther and Faster* (self-illustrated), Crowell, 1954; (with wife, Ethel Kessler) *Plink, Plink! Goes the Water in My Sink,* Doubleday, 1954; (with E. Kessler) *Crunch, Crunch,* Doubleday, 1955; (with E. Kessler) *Peek-a-Boo: A Child's First Book,* Doubleday, 1956; (with E. Kessler) *Big Red Bus* (self-illustrated), Doubleday, 1957; *Art Is Everywhere,* Dodd, 1958; (with E. Kessler) *The Day Daddy Stayed Home* (self-illustrated), Doubleday, 1959, reprinted, 1971; (with E. Kessler) *I Have Twenty Teeth—Do You?,* Dodd, 1959.

(With E. Kessler) *Kim and Me,* Doubleday, 1960; (with E. Kessler) *Do Baby Bears Sit in Chairs?* (self-illustrated), Doubleday, 1961; *The Duck on the Truck,* Grosset, 1961; *I Made a Line,* Wonder Books, 1962; *The Worm, the Bird, and You: A Long and Short Look at the World About You,* Dodd, 1962; (with E. Kessler) *All Aboard the Train* (self-illustrated), Doubleday, 1964; *Here Comes the Strikeout* (self-illustrated), Harper, 1965; *Mr. Pine's Purple House* (self-illustrated), Wonder Books, 1965; *The Sad Tale of the Careless Klunks* (self-illustrated), Dodd, 1965; (with E. Kessler) *Are You Square?* (self-illustrated), Doubleday, 1966; *Kick, Pass, and Run* (self-illustrated), Harper, 1966; *Mrs. Pine Takes a Trip* (self-illustrated), Grosset, 1966; *Are We Lost, Daddy?,* Grosset, 1967; *Did You Ever Hear a*

Klink Say Please? (self-illustrated), Dodd, 1967; *Last One in Is a Rotten Egg* (self-illustrated), Harper, 1969; *Soup for the King* (self-illustrated), Grosset, 1969.

A Tale of Two Bicycles: Safety on Your Bike (self-illustrated), Lothrop, 1971; *On Your Mark, Get Set, Go! The First All Animal Olympics* (self-illustrated), Harper, 1972; (with E. Kessler) *Our Tooth Story: A Tale of Twenty Teeth* (self-illustrated), Dodd, 1972; *Paint Me a Picture, Mr. Pine* (illustrated by John Kuzich), Ginn, 1972; (with E. Kessler) *Slush Slush!* (self-illustrated), Parents' Magazine Press, 1973; (with E. Kessler) *Splish Splash* (self-illustrated), Parents' Magazine Press, 1973; *Who Tossed That Bat? Safety on the Ballfield and Playground* (self-illustrated), Lothrop, 1973; (with E. Kessler) *All for Fall* (self-illustrated), Parents' Magazine Press, 1974; *The Forgetful Pirate* (self-illustrated), Garrard, 1974; (with E. Kessler) *What's Inside the Box?*, Dodd, 1976; *Ghosts and Crows and Things with O's*, Scholastic Book Services, 1976; (with E. Kessler) *What Do You Play on a Summer Day?*, Parents' Magazine Press, 1977.

Illustrator: Miriam Schlein, *Fast Is Not a Ladybug*, W. R. Scott, 1953; Schlein, *Heavy Is a Hippopotamus*, W. R. Scott, 1954; Schlein, *It's about Time*, W. R. Scott, 1955; Hyman and Alice Chanover, *Pesah Is Coming*, United Synagogue Book Service, 1956; H. and A. Chanover, *Pesah Is Here*, United Synagogue Book Service, 1956; Lily Edelman, *Sukkah and the Big Wind*, United Synagogue Book Service, 1956; Lenore Klein, *What Would You Do, If?*, W. R. Scott, 1956; John Bryan Lewellen, *Tommy Learns to Fly*, Crowell, 1956; Schlein, *Deer in the Snow*, Abelard-Schuman, 1956; Maryalicia Crowell, *Horse in the House*, W. R. Scott, 1957; Jean Fiedler, *Teddy and the Ice Cream Man*, Abelard-Schuman, 1957; Lewellen, *Tommy Learns to Drive a Tractor*, Crowell, 1958; Franklyn Mansfield Branley, *A Book of Moon Rockets for You*, Crowell, 1959, revised edition, 1970; Branley, *A Book of Satellites for You*, Crowell, 1959, revised edition, 1971.

Branley, *Big Trucks, Little Trucks*, Crowell, 1960; Lucia and James L. Hymes, *Hooray for Chocolate and Other Easy-to-Read Jingles*, W. R. Scott, 1960; Branley, *A Book of Planets for You*, Crowell, 1961, revised edition, 1966; Mike McClintock, *What Have I Got*, Harper, 1961; Muriel Rukeyser, *I Go Out*, Harper, 1961; James Playsted Wood, *The Elephant in the Barn*, Harper, 1961; Carla Greene, *What Do They Do? Policemen and Firemen*, Harper, 1962; Jacqueline Harris Straus, *Let's Experiment! Chemistry for Boys and Girls*, Harper, 1962; Branley, *A Book of Astronauts for You*, Crowell, 1963; Greene, *Doctors and Nurses, What Do They Do?*, Harper, 1963; Greene, *Soldiers and Sailors, What Do They Do?*, C. Paul Jackson, *How to Play Better Baseball*, Crowell, 1963, reissued, Scholastic Book Service, 1971; Greene, *Railroad Engineers and Airplane Pilots, What Do They Do?*, Harper, 1964; L. and J. L. Hymes, *Oodles of Noodles, and Other Hymes' Rhymes*, Young Scott Books, 1964; Solveig Paulson Russell, *Indian Big, Indian Little*, Bobbs-Merrill, 1964.

Rochelle Scott, *Colors, Colors, All Around*, Grosset, 1965; Branley, *A Book of the Milky Way Galaxy for You*, Crowell, 1965; Augusta R. Goldin, *Ducks Don't Get Wet*, Crowell, 1965, reissued, 1976; Greene, *Where Does a Letter Go?*, Harvey House, 1966; Klein, *What Is an Inch?*, Harvey House, 1966; Branley, *A Book of Stars for You*, Crowell, 1967; Greene, *Animal Doctors, What Do They Do*, Harper, 1967; Greene, *Truck Drivers, What Do They Do?*, Harper, 1967; Klein, *How Old is Old?*, Harvey House, 1967; Harry Milgrom, *Adventures With a Straw*, Dutton, 1967; Branley,

A Book of Mars for You, Crowell, 1968; Jackson, *How to Play Better Basketball*, Crowell, 1968; James Duncan Lawrence, *Binky Brothers, Detectives*, Harper, 1968; Milgrom, *Adventures With a Paper Cup*, Dutton, 1968; Branley, *A Book of Venus for You*, Crowell, 1969; Klein, *Just a Minute: A Book About Time*, Harvey House, 1969; Molly Whisman, *My Hideout*, Harper, 1969.

Branley, *A Book of Outer Space for You*, Crowell, 1970; Lawrence, *Binky Brothers and the Fearless Four*, Harper, 1970; Edna Mitchell Preston, *The Boy Who Could Make Things*, Viking, 1970; Henry Walker, *Illustrated Baseball Dictionary for Young People*, Harvey House, 1970; Mannis Charosh, *The Ellipse*, Crowell, 1971; Greene, *Cowboys, What Do They Do?*, Harper, 1972; Jackson, *How to Play Better Football*, Crowell, 1972; Harley Knosher, *Basic Basketball Strategy*, Doubleday, 1972; Richard J. Margolis, *Homer the Hunter*, Macmillan, 1972, reissued as *Homer and the Ghosts*, 1976; Melvin Berger, *The New Water Book*, Crowell, 1973; Branley, *A Book of Flying Saucers for You*, Crowell, 1973; Peggy Parish, *Two Many Rabbits*, Macmillan, 1974; Anne Catharina Vestly, *Hello, Aurora*, Crowell, 1974; Branley, *A Book of Planet Earth for You*, Crowell, 1975; Nina and Herman Schneider, *Science Fun for You in a Minute or Two*, McGraw, 1975; Nancy Jewell, *The Family Under the Moon*, Harper, 1976; N. and H. Schneider, *Got a Minute? Quick Experiments You Can Do*, Scholastic Book Service, 1976.*

* * *

KETTLE, Peter
See GLOVER, Dennis

* * *

KEYSER, (George) Gustave 1910-

PERSONAL: Surname is pronounced *Kai*-zer; born February 19, 1910, in Cumberland, Md.; son of Charles Frank and Lydia Ann (Pyle) Keyser; married Sarah Bolton Newland, December 20, 1946 (divorced, October, 1956); children: Dale (Mrs. Christopher Farrin), Gregory. *Education:* Attended high school in Alleghany County, Md. *Politics:* Independent. *Religion:* "Golden Rule." *Home:* 4912 Gaston Ave., Apt. J, Dallas, Tex. 75214.

CAREER: Office of the Secretary of War, Washington, D.C., position classification analyst, 1940-44, position classification analyst in Atlanta Field Office, 1944-52; U.S. Department of the Army, Washington, D.C., civilian personnel management specialist in Atlanta, Ga., 1952-59, and Dallas, Tex., 1959-71; writer, 1971—.

MEMBER: International Poetry Society, World Poetry Society Intercontinental, International Platform Association, Centro Studi e Scambi Internazionali, Western World Haiku Society (co-founder), Poetry Society of America, Poetry Society of Texas, Dallas Museum of Fine Arts. *Awards, honors:* Outstanding civilian performance award and official commendation from U.S. Army deputy chief of staff; "voice of the year award" from *Human Voice Quarterly*, 1971, for *Listen Softly*.

WRITINGS: Listen Softly (poems and drawings), Olivant, 1971.

Work represented in several anthologies, including *Responding Four*, Ginn, 1973; *Action English Two*, Gage Educational Publishing, 1973; *Art: Choosing and Expressing*, Benefic, 1977. Contributor of about nine hundred articles and poems, and some drawings, to about ninety magazines, including *Wormwood Review, Voices International, Bitterroot, American Haiku,* and *Westways.* Contributing editor of *Dragonfly.* Associate editor of *Modern Haiku.*

WORK IN PROGRESS: The Morning Moon, a haiku collection; *This Small Daughter,* a senryu collection; *Once Upon a Turbulent Time,* poems; *Chats on the Haiku,* a collection of articles; *Tabernacle Tales,* poems.

SIDELIGHTS: Keyser writes: "It seems to me that too much is made of motivation and influence. Writers, and particularly poets, should be merely their individual selves, their own persons and personalities. They should not be influenced (or perhaps even exploited) by anyone else.

"Virtually all of my own poetry speaks for the 'traditional' human and social values: man-woman relationships, home, children, self-responsibility, and self-respectability. Thoughtfulness, consideration, and fairness in our treatment of others. This may sound religious, but it is not meant to. It is purely human in the largest and best sense of that word. I am not a political or social activist beating a self-styled drum for some crusade or another; not a street marcher. I believe in common-sense behavior."

AVOCATIONAL INTERESTS: Numismatics, conchology, gemology, classic cars, pioneer aircraft, model railroading, fine graphic arts, books, travel.

BIOGRAPHICAL/CRITICAL SOURCES: Poetry Society of America Bulletin, January, 1972; *Dallas Times Herald,* July 14, 1974; *Modern Haiku,* Volume V, number 4, 1974.

*   *   *

KEZDI, Paul   1914-

PERSONAL: Born November 13, 1914, in Monor, Hungary; came to the United States in 1951, naturalized citizen, 1957; son of Walter and Anna (Buday) Kezdi; married second wife, Anita Bournakis, April 29, 1965; children: Melinda Kezdi Griesman, Ann Kezdi Radcliffe, Laura J., Paula C., Chris Kezdi Argites (stepson). *Education:* Budapest Junior College, B.A., 1934; attended Budapest Business College, 1935; Pazmany Peter University, M.D., 1942. *Office:* Cox Heart Institute, Wright State University, 3525 Southern Blvd., Dayton, Ohio 45429.

CAREER: University Hospitals, Budapest, Hungary, intern, 1941-42, resident in internal medicine, 1942-44; worked for United Nations Relief & Rehabilitation Administration Camp Hospital, Allendorf, Germany, 1945-47; University Hospitals, Frankfurt-am-Main, Germany, resident in internal medicine, 1947-51; Methodist Hospital, Madison, Wis., intern, 1952; Northwestern University, Medical School, Chicago, Ill., fellow in cardiology, 1953-54, clinical assistant, 1954-56, clinical associate, 1956-58, assistant professor, 1958-62, associate professor of medicine, 1962-65, program director of Cardiovascular Research Center, 1962-65; Ohio State University, Columbus, clinical professor of medicine, 1965-76; Wright State University, Dayton, Ohio, research director at Cox Heart Institute, 1965-67, director of institute, 1967—, clinical professor, 1975-76, professor of medicine, 1976—, associate dean for research affairs at School of Medicine, 1976—. Licensed in Illinois, 1954, and Ohio, 1965; diplomate of American Board of Internal Medicine, 1961; certified educational counsel for foreign medical students. Instructor at Pazmany Peter University, 1940-42; professor at Indiana University, 1965-73. Assistant attending physician at Wesley Memorial Hospital, 1954-61, director of heart station, 1954-65, associate attending physician, 1961-65; adjunct physician at Passavant Memorial Hospital,

1958-65; active staff physician at Charles F. Kettering Memorial Hospital, 1965—, director of research, 1968-76. Member of board of trustees of Kettering Community Improvement Corp.; member of program project committee of National Heart and Lung Institute, 1966-69; consultant to National Center for Health Services Research and Development, 1968-69.

MEMBER: International Society of Cardiology (member of Scientific Council on Hypertension), International Society of Hypertension, American Medical Association, American College of Cardiology (fellow), American College of Chest Physicians (fellow), American Heart Association (fellow; member of executive committee of Council on Circulation; local president and member of board of trustees, 1974—), American Physiological Society, American Federation for Clinical Research, American Association for the Advancement of Science, Central Society for Clinical Research, Dayton Society of Internal Medicine. *Awards, honors:* National Institutes of Health grants, 1962-65, 1966-72, 1972-75, 1973-79, 1975-77.

WRITINGS: (Editor) *Baroreceptors and Hypertension,* Pergamon, 1967; *You and Your Heart,* Atheneum, 1977.

Contributor: I. H. Page and J. W. McCubbin, editors, *Renal Hypertension,* Year Book Medical Publishers, 1968; J. H. Moyer and A. N. Brest, editors, *Cardiovascular Disorders,* F. A. Davis, 1968; J. N. Moyer, G. Onesti, and K. E. Kim, editors, *Hypertension: Mechanism and Management,* Grune, 1973; L. T. Harmison, editor, *Research Animals in Medicine,* National Heart and Lung Institute, 1973; S. Julius and M. D. Esler, editors, *The Nervous System in Arterial Hypertension,* C. C Thomas, 1974. Contributor of more than one hundred articles to scientific and medical journals. Member of editorial board of *Journal of Electrocardiology,* 1968-73, *American Journal of Physiology,* 1970—, and *Journal of Applied Physiology.*

*   *   *

KGOSITSILE, Keorapetse (William)   1938-

PERSONAL: Born September 19, 1938, in Johannesburg, South Africa; came to United States in 1961; married wife, Melba. *Education:* Educated in Africa; further study at Lincoln University, University of New Hampshire, New School for Social Research, and Columbia University. *Office:* North Carolina Agricultural and Technical State University, Greensboro, N.C. 27411.

CAREER: North Carolina Agricultural and Technical State University, Greensboro, poet-in-residence, 1971—. Member of staff, *Black Dialogue* and *Spearhead. Awards, honors:* Conrad Kent Rivers award, 1969; National Endowment for the Arts grant, 1970.

WRITINGS: Spirits Unchained (poems), Broadside Press, 1969; *For Melba* (poems), Third World Press, 1970; *My Name Is Afrika* (poems), Doubleday, 1971; (editor) *The Word Is Here: Poetry From Modern Africa,* Doubleday, 1973. Contributor of poetry to anthologies and to periodicals, including *Transition* and *Guerrilla.*

SIDELIGHTS: Although Kgositile has lived in the United States for several years, his poetry is considered "African" in its consideration of the themes of black unification and liberation. In *My Name Is Africa,* according to *Booklist,* "passionate poems of the horror of black slavery in Africa and America symbolize universal suffering of the oppressed. Rhythmic and rhetorical calls to action, contemplations on black leaders, and acute observations couched in authentic dialogue are preceded by a characteristically penetrating and artistic introduction by Gwendolyn Brooks.''

In *For Melba,* Christopher Scott wrote in *Books Abroad,* "Kgositsile employs the medium of his love for his wife Melba to make a rather political statement. Revolutionary nationalism, as the poet sees it, has its foundation in the (concrete of) the family unit, both nuclear and extended. It would seem that for revolutionary nationalism the health of the personal and familial building blocks of society is causally related to the health of the nation. Kgositsile's message to his black brothers and sisters is, finally, 'Let us stop playing games.''' The poems of *For Melba,* Scott added, trace the "physical and spiritual movement of the poet (and, by extension, all black people) in his personal and consequently political struggle for dignity.''

Choice claimed Kgositsile's *The Word Is Here: Poetry from Modern Africa* is an "attractive, original, and highly recommended collection of recent poetry from Africa.''

BIOGRAPHICAL/CRITICAL SOURCES: Books Abroad, spring, 1971; *Booklist,* September 1, 1971; *Christian Century,* March 14, 1973; *Choice,* October, 1973.*

*   *   *

KIDDER, Rushworth M(oulton) 1944-

PERSONAL: Born May 8, 1944, in Providence, R.I.; son of George W. (a professor) and Ruth (Rushworth) Kidder; married Anne Elizabeth Davidson, June 11, 1966; children: Heather, Abby. *Education:* Amherst College, B.A., 1965; Columbia University, M.A., 1966, Ph.D., 1969. *Religion:* Christian Scientist. *Home:* 289 Patton, Wichita, Kan. 67208. *Office:* Department of English, Wichita State University, Wichita, Kan. 67208.

CAREER: Wichita State University, Wichita, Kan., assistant professor, 1969-74, associate professor of English, 1974—.

WRITINGS: Dylan Thomas: The Country of the Spirit, Princeton University Press, 1973; *E. E. Cummings: An Introduction to the Poetry,* Columbia University Press, 1979. Contributor to literature journals and newspapers.

WORK IN PROGRESS: E. E. Cummings, the Painter, a book of plates of Cummings' paintings, with brief text; *E. E. Cummings: A Concordance to the Complete Poems.*

SIDELIGHTS: Kidder told *CA:* "What originally interested me in Thomas and Cummings was the capacity they shared for writing poems of praise that are neither cynical nor sentimental—a talent few of their contemporaries could or wanted to match. My work with Cummings led me into his paintings and into an investigation of some of the relationships between his poetry and painting. It's been a little-known side of his career—those I talk to generally respond, 'I didn't know he painted!'—and, I think, a significant one: he wanted for years to become 'primarily a painter,' but his poetry was simply more successful than his painting. He pursued both arts equally throughout his career, however, and left behind literally thousands of paintings and drawings.

"What I'm finally trying to come to terms with are the aesthetic interrelations between poetry and the visual arts. Such interrelations have usually been studied by comparing the works of different individuals; I'm excited by the prospect of seeing how a single mind encounters, with significant skill, both these two areas.

"As a writer and researcher who is also a teacher, I feel a certain responsibility to translate some of these ideas out of the scholarly idiom and make them available to a literate but nonspecialized audience—which is what I've tried to do as a contributor on poetry and painting for *The Christian Science Monitor* and in writing *E. E. Cummings the Painter.*''

*   *   *

KIEFER, Warren 1929-

PERSONAL: Born December 18, 1929, in Paterson, N.J.; son of Harold Birck (an insurance executive) and Margaret (McFadden) Kiefer; married Ann Kaser, 1953 (divorced, 1960); married Mariana Doebbeling (a painter), September 19, 1962; children: Alden, Kathleen Alexandra. *Education:* University of New Mexico, B.A., 1951; University of Maryland, M.A., 1954. *Home:* Villa Angela, Chaco, Argentina; and Punta del Este, Uruguay. *Agent:* Harold Ober Associates, Inc., 40 East 49th St., New York, N.Y. 10017.

CAREER: Manager of public relations for Latin America, Pfizer International, 1954-57; free-lance television producer and president of Trans-Africa Films, Inc., 1958-65; feature film producer, 1965-75; rancher (raising and training horses) in Chaco, Argentina, 1974—. *Military service:* U.S. Marine Corps, pilot, 1951-53; served in Korea; became captain; received Bronze Star. *Member:* Authors League of America, Squash Club (Buenos Aires), Club Ippico Aleman, Sociedad Rural Argentina. *Awards, honors:* Edgar Allen Poe Award from Mystery Writers of America, 1973, for *The Lingala Code.*

WRITINGS: Pax (novel), Random House, 1958; *The Lingala Code* (mystery novel), Random House, 1972; *The Pontius Pilate Papers* (novel), Harper, 1975; *The Kidnappers* (novel), Harper, 1977; *The Snow Queen* (novel), Harper, 1979.

Feature films: "Castle of the Living Dead," 1965, "Michael Strogoff," 1967, "The Outrider," 1968, "Juliette de Sade," 1969, "Dominoes," 1970, "Farewell to the King," 1973.

Author of about twenty-five documentary films produced in Africa, the Middle East, and Europe. Television writer and director, 1958-72.

*   *   *

KIESER, Rolf 1936-

PERSONAL: Born May 14, 1936, in Switzerland; came to the United States in 1964, naturalized citizen, 1971; son of R. Paul (a merchant) and Molly (Frueh) Kieser. *Education:* Attended London School of Economics and Political Science, 1962-63; University of Zurich, 1957-64, Ph.D., 1964. *Home:* 82 Irving Pl., New York, N.Y. 10003. *Office:* Department of German and Scandinavian, Queens College of the City University of New York, Flushing, N.Y. 11367.

CAREER: Queen's College of the City University of New York, Flushing, N.Y., instructor, 1965-66, assistant professor, 1967-71, associate professor, 1972-75, professor of German, 1976—, chairman of department of German and Scandinavian, 1973-76. *Member:* Modern Language Association of America, American Association of Teachers of German, Swiss-American Historical Society (vice-president, 1971—), Northeast Modern Language Association.

WRITINGS: England's Appeasement Politics, Keller Winterthur, 1964; (with Max Kirch) *Functional German,* American Book Co., 1967; *Max Frisch: Das literarische Tagebuch* (title means "Max Frisch: The Literary Diary"), Huber, 1975. Contributor of articles on contemporary German literature to American, German, and Swiss magazines.

WORK IN PROGRESS: German Exile Literature in Switzerland; research on Kaiser, Musil, Brecht, and Thomas Mann in Switzerland, and on Jakob Schaffner.

SIDELIGHTS: Kieser told *CA: "Max Frisch: The Literary Diary* is an attempt to prove the eminent Swiss writer's role as an innovator of the concept of prose fiction by creating an artistic narrative genre (the diary) which reflects the linguistic and philosophical principles of a literature increasingly irreverent of distinctions between literary genres.''

*   *   *

KILLENBERG, George A(ndrew)   1917-

PERSONAL: Born March 30, 1917, in St. Clair County, Ill.; son of George W. (a building contractor) and Lavina Helen (Ruhl) Killenberg; married Therese M. Murphy, June 3, 1943; children: George M., Mary C. (Mrs. F. Quinn Riley), John A., Terry M., Susan M. *Education:* St. Louis University, B.A., 1954, M.A., 1958. *Religion:* Roman Catholic. *Home:* 3042 Hatherly Dr., Bel-Nor, Mo. 63121. *Office:* 710 North 12th St., St. Louis, Mo. 63101.

CAREER/WRITINGS: Worked in public relations, 1935-41; *St. Louis Globe-Democrat,* St. Louis, Mo., member of staff, 1941—, city editor, 1956-66, managing editor, 1966—. Director, Mid-American Press Institute; member of board of directors, Boys Town Missouri, 1960—, Missouri Society for Crippled Children, St. Louis Council on Alcoholism; member of advisory board, Marillac College. *Military service:* U.S. Army, 1942-46. *Member:* Sigma Delta Chi, Press Club (president, 1964), Media Club (St. Louis).

*   *   *

KILLENS, John Oliver   1916-

PERSONAL: Born January 14, 1916, in Macon, Ga.; married wife Grace; children: Jon C., Barbara E. Wynn. *Education:* Attended Edward Waters College, Morris Brown College, Atlanta University, Howard University, Terrel Law School, Columbia University, and New York University. *Home:* 1392 Union St., Brooklyn, N.Y. 11212.

CAREER: Member of staff, National Labor Relations Board, 1936-42, and 1946; free-lance writer, 1954—. Lecturer and writer-in-residence, Howard University, 1971-72; lecturer and teacher of creative writing, New School for Social Research; writer-in-residence, Fisk University; lecturer and adjunct professor, Columbia University; also lecturer at Southern University, Cornell University, Rutgers University, Brandeis College (now Brandeis University), Springfield College, Western Michigan University, and Savannah State College. *Military service:* U.S. Army, Pacific Amphibian Forces, 1942-45. *Member:* American Poets, Playwrights, Editors, Essayists, and Novelists (member of executive board), Black Academy of Arts and Letters (vice-president), Harlem Writers Guild (founder and past chairperson). *Awards, honors:* Recipient of numerous awards from local organizations, including Afro Art Theatre, Brooklyn National Association for the Advancement of Colored People, and Brooklyn Association for the Study of Negro Life and History.

WRITINGS: Youngblood (novel), Dial, 1954; *And Then We Heard the Thunder* (novel), Knopf, 1962; *The Cotillion; or, One Good Bull is Half the Herd* (novel), Simon & Schuster, 1966; *'Sippi* (novel), Simon & Schuster, 1967; *Slaves* (novel), Pyramid, 1969; *Black Man's Burden* (essays), Simon & Schuster, 1971; *Great Gittin' Up Morning: A Biography of Denmark Vesey,* Doubleday, 1972; *A Man Ain't Nothin But a Man* (young adult), Little, Brown, 1975.

Plays: (With Loften Mitchell) "Ballad of the Winter Soldier,'' first produced in Washington, D.C., at Lincoln Center Philharmonic Hall, 1964; "Lower Than Angels,'' first produced in New York City, 1965.

Screenplays: "Odds Against Tomorrow,'' Belafonte Productions/United Artists, 1960; (with Herbert J. Biberman) "Slaves,'' Theatre Guild, 1969.

Nonfiction and short stories represented in anthologies, including *The State of the Nation,* edited by David Boroff, Prentice-Hall, 1966; *Voices From the Soul of Black America,* edited by Raman K. Singh and Peter Fellowes, Crowell, 1970; *Black Insights: Significant Literature by Black Americans, 1760 to the Present,* edited by Nick Aaron, Ginn, 1971; and *Nommo: An Anthology Of Modern African and Black American Literature,* edited by William H. Robinson, Macmillan, 1972.

Contributor to periodicals, including *Ebony, Black World, The Black Aesthetic, African Forum, Library Journal,* and *Arts in Society.*

SIDELIGHTS: Among the motivating influences behind Killens's writings are the words of his great grandmother, "The half ain't never been told.'' Killens believes that "Western man has nothing more or new to say to humankind'' and that the time is long overdue "for Black men to speak, to create a new vision for mankind, a vision oriented to man, not to things.''

Killens started writing during World War II in the South Pacific and has been "scribbling madly ever since.'' He abandoned his ideas of becoming a doctor or lawyer despite three years of law studies at night and the protests of his in-laws, for he said: "By then I knew that writing was the thing for me. It would be my raison d'etre, and nothing else would matter. . . . I found out of course that writing was the damnedest, hardest, loneliest buck a man could make, especially if that man was Black.

"Black kids today have the motivation, the image . . . a tradition for aspiring to become writers,'' noted Killens. "There was no such image or tradition when I grew up in Macon, Georgia.'' He credited Langston Hughes, Richard Wright, and Margaret Walker with having the "greatest impact'' on his career. "Langston,'' he said, ". . . was the first Black writer who reached me way down yonder by myself in the wilderness of Georgia. . . . He was the only person in New York among the 'established' writers who welcomed me into the club upon the publication of *Youngblood.*'' Killens admired the "awesome, unadulterated power'' of Richard Wright's writing. "He made me believe that a Black writer could make the literate world sit up and take notice. He taught me,'' said Killens, ". . . that you don't have to be a timid writer. You can be bold, you can say what you have to say without holding anything back.'' Margaret Walker's *For My People* also received great praise from Killens: "In terms of Black and beautiful rhythms it taught me more than any other piece of Literature. . . . I am always under the influence of the flowing, rhythmic beauty of that poem.'' *Youngblood,* Killens's first novel, was written in black dialect called by some "Afro-Americanese'' after attempts using "proper language to tell their story'' failed. Killens said: "I write out of a Black thing, out of Black necessity. I write in a Black idiom to be dug by Black folks in the first instance, and for all people in the second.''

And Then We Heard Thunder came out of Killens's army experiences. John Howard Griffen called this a "big, polyphonic, violent novel about Negro soldiers in World War II'' and commented on its message—the "hideous irony of asking the Negro to fight (in segregated units) and die in order to preserve the very freedoms he could not enjoy at home." Griffen also mentioned the "Negro soldier's common motto, the Double V for Victory: victory against Fascism overseas and victory against Fascism at home" and said the "reader, living all the indignities of the Negro soldier, sees clearly how it looked from the other side of the color line. Discrimination in the armed forces has been eliminated. But the deep wounds of Negro soldiers have not. This novel magnificently illumines the reason why. Their second victory—against Fascism at home—is slow in coming."

The essays of *Black Man's Burden* produced, in the words of Frank Cordasco, "a sardonic inversion of Kipling's magnanimous mandate, and a wry commentary on the image white legend has imposed on Negroes and which is accepted by many of them." He called the book a "pastiche of perceptive, sharply delineated vignettes animated by the twin engines of hate and despair."

A fictional "Johnny Carson Show" introduction typifies the tone of *The Cotillion,* the book Killens called his "black, black comedy": "Tonight, ladies and gentlemen, we have a most distinguished guest by the name of Jomo Mamadou Zero the Third. He is the most terrifying Black militant the world has ever known. He's so bad he's scared of his own self. He makes Malcolm X look like Little Lord Fauntleroy. Give him a big hand, ladies and gentlemen. He's making plans right now to overthrow our wonderful government and kill every white person in the good old U.S.A. Come right in and sit down, Brother Zero, and tell us all about it." Phoebe Adams said a white cast and author in this "social comedy about the debutante racket would be as trite as a Doris Day movie," but with black characters and a "black author [who] is a wily blend of clown and porcupine, the moribund plot bounces merrily back to life." Acknowledging this as a non-traditional novel, J. R. Frakes said everything is "triple life-size, every character, . . . gesture, . . . speech, . . . emotion, . . . action. . . . The whole laughing, howling, bursting career of the book zooms like a caricature-missile toward the biggest Everlasting Yea . . . to 'the real world,' the black nation, Afro-natural hairdos, dashikis, Negritude."

Killens wrote: "I think I'm a man who has made a helluva lot of mistakes in my life, but I have always been in there pitching. I have always worked for Black liberation, but I've changed my mind a million times about how . . . to achieve it." Echoing Santayana, Killens believes that blacks must study their past to improve their lives or "Black history will repeat itself instead of moving up."

BIOGRAPHICAL/CRITICAL SOURCES: Midwest Journal, summer, 1954; *Crisis,* October, 1954, April, 1965; *Time,* October 26, 1959; *Saturday Review,* January 26, 1963, March 12, 1966, March 6, 1971; *Best Sellers,* February 1, 1963, October 1, 1965, March 15, 1972; *New York Herald Tribune Books,* April 14, 1963; *Negro Digest,* November, 1967; *New York Times,* March 2, 1969, March 28, 1969, March 27, 1970, May 29, 1972; *Newsweek,* May 26, 1969; *New York Times Book Review,* January 17, 1971; *Atlantic,* February, 1971; *Black World,* June, 1971; *Freedomways,* 1971; John A. Williams and Charles F. Harris, editors, *Amistad Two,* Random House, 1971; *New York Review of Books,* April 2, 1972; *Christian Science Monitor,* May 4, 1972.*

*   *   *

KING, Richard H. 1942-

PERSONAL: Born March 2, 1942, in Knoxville, Tenn.; son

of Dewey Dawson and Dorothy (Howell) King; married Nancy Landreth (a teacher), August 14, 1967. *Education:* University of North Carolina, A.B. (honors), 1963; Yale University, M.A., 1966; University of Virginia, Ph.D., 1971. *Home:* 406 E St. S.E., Washington, D.C. 20003. *Office:* Department of History, Federal City College, 425 Second St. N.W., Washington, D.C.

CAREER: Stillman College, Tuscaloosa, Ala., instructor in history, 1965-66; Federal City College, Washington, D.C., 1968—, began as instructor, became assistant professor, and associate professor of history. Fulbright lecturer at University of Nottingham, 1977-78. *Member:* Phi Beta Kappa. *Awards, honors:* Fulbright fellow, 1963-64.

WRITINGS: The Party of Eros, University of North Carolina Press, 1972. Contributor of articles and reviews to scholarly and popular journals, including *New Leader, Salmagundi,* and *New South.*

WORK IN PROGRESS: Narcissus Grown Analytical: Race and Politics in Southern Thought, 1930-55, for publication by Oxford University Press.

SIDELIGHTS: King commented that his main interests are Freud and psychological thought, and Southern politics and culture.

AVOCATIONAL INTERESTS: Sports, music (country and western, bluegrass).

*   *   *

KING, Robert L. 1950-

PERSONAL: Born June 20, 1950, in Tennessee; son of Herbert (a teacher) and Ruth (a nurse; maiden name, Dulaney) King; married Laura Sessions (a newspaper editor), August 6, 1974. *Education:* Earlham College, A.B., 1973; Columbia University, M.S., 1974. *Religion:* Baptist. *Home:* 1302 Sunset Dr., Johnson City, Tenn. 37601 (permanent); and 110 North Ohio Trail, Medford, N.J. 08055. *Office: Courier-Post,* Cherry Hill, N.J. 08002.

CAREER/WRITINGS: Press-Chronicle, Johnson City, Tenn., reporter, 1968-73; Associated Press, New York, N.Y., correspondent in Paris, 1971-72; *Miami Herald,* Miami, Fla., reporter, 1974-75; *Courier-Post,* Cherry Hill, N.J., political editor, 1975—. Contributing writer to Gannett News Service. *Member:* New Jersey Society of Professional Journalists. *Awards, honors:* U.S. Human Rights Commission fellowship, 1974; special award from New Jersey Society of Professional Journalists, 1976, for investigative reporting; media award from New York State Bar Association, 1976; citation from Scripps-Howard Newspaper Foundation, 1976, for public service reporting; silver gavel from American Bar Association, 1977, for reporting; Paul Tobenkin Award from Columbia University School of Journalism, 1977, for reporting on discrimination; citation from New Jersey Press Association, 1977, for reporting on election campaign financing; media award from New Jersey Bar Association, 1977; feature writing award from Gannett Newspapers, 1977; citation from Philadelphia Press Association, 1977, for outstanding reporting by an individual.

SIDELIGHTS: King wrote: "I've traveled extensively in Europe where I worked as a correspondent. At one point I studied international human rights law at the University of Strasbourg and the Council of Europe. My primary writing interests have always been in government, national and international affairs." His notable assignments have included coverage of the Paris Peace Talks, the presidential campaign of 1976, and New Jersey state politics from 1975-78.

KING, Terry Johnson 1929-1978

May 29, 1929—March 10, 1978; American journalist and author who in 1977 began a series of articles on her fight against cancer after being told she had about a year to live. King served as columnist, music editor, and lifestyle editor of the *Miami Daily News*. Her writings include *The Neutron Beam Murder* and *The Noose of Red Beads*. Obituaries and other sources: *New York Times*, March 12, 1978. (See index for *CA* sketch)

*   *   *

KINNARD, Douglas (Leo) 1921-

PERSONAL: Born September 13, 1921, in Morristown, N.J.; son of Frederick Henry (a businessman) and Mary (Toomey) Kinnard; married Wade Tyree (an English professor), July 6, 1951; children: Frederick Douglas. *Education:* U.S. Military Academy, B.S., 1944; Princeton University, M.S., 1948, M.A., 1972, Ph.D., 1973. *Home:* 343 South Prospect St., Burlington, Vt. 05401. *Office:* Department of Political Science, University of Vermont, Burlington, Vt. 05401.

CAREER: U.S. Army, officer, 1944-70, retiring as brigadier general; University of Vermont, Burlington, associate professor of political science, 1973—, director of area and international studies, 1976—. Served as special assistant to supreme commander Allied headquarters, Paris, 1961-64; commander of 24th infantry division artillery, Germany, 1964-65; chief of operations analysis of U.S. military assistance command, Vietnam, 1966-67; chief of staff, II Field Force, Vietnam, 1969-70. Consultant on national security affairs. *Member:* International Institute for Strategic Studies, International Studies Association, American Political Science Association, Northeast Political Science Association, Association of Graduates of U.S. Military Academy, Princeton Graduate Alumni Association, Nassau Club, Army and Navy Club, Princeton Club. *Awards, honors—Military:* Distinguished Service Medal, Distinguished Flying Cross, and numerous others.

WRITINGS: President Eisenhower and Strategy Management, University Press of Kentucky, 1977; *The War Managers*, University Press of New England, 1977. Contributor of articles to *Journal of Politics, Polity, Journal of Political and Military Sociology, Public Opinion Quarterly*, and *Midwest Review of Public Administration*.

WORK IN PROGRESS: The Secretary of Defense; articles on foreign and defense policy matters.

*   *   *

KINNICUTT, Susan Sibley 1926-
(Susan Sibley; Susan Shelby)

PERSONAL: Born August 5, 1926, in Spencer, Mass.; daughter of John Russell (a businessman) and Charlotte (Chace) Sibley; married Lincoln N. Kinnicutt, February 26, 1944 (divorced, 1972); children: Lincoln, Michael, Katherine Susan, Mark. *Education:* Attended University of Hartford, Hartford College for Women, University of North Carolina, and Appalachian State University. *Religion:* Congregationalist. *Home and office address:* Hartland Hill Rd., Woodstock, Vt. 05091; and 1405 Mesquite, Carefree, Ariz. 85331. *Agent:* Marcia Higgins, William Morris Agency, 1350 Avenue of the Americas, New York, N.Y. 10019.

CAREER: Writer, 1948—. Worked as waitress, counselor, teacher, probation officer's assistant, singer, and model. Paintings are exhibited throughout New England; writer-in-

residence at St. Andrew's College, Laurinburg, N.C. Member of West Hartford Conservation Commission.

MEMBER: Sierra Club, National Trust for Historic Preservation, Southern Vermont Artists, Society of Southwest Authors, Vermont Academy of Arts and Sciences, Conservation Council of North Carolina, North Carolina Writers Conference, Association for the Preservation of Tennessee Antiquities, Rutland Area Artists Association, and numerous other organizations. *Awards, honors:* First prize from Tar Heel Writers Round Table short story contest, 1976, for "Head of the Family"; first prize from Charlotte Writers short story contest, 1976, for "Sandy's Castle."

WRITINGS—Under name Susan Sibley: Woodsmoke (novel), Blair, 1977; *What's Left Is Right: A Cookbook for the Desperate Houseperson*, Kinford Press, 1977. Contributor of stories to magazines, under pseudonym Susan Shelby, including *Cimarron Review, Mississippi Review, St. Andrews Review, Old Hickory Review*, and *Sanskrit*.

WORK IN PROGRESS: Lucky in the Morning and *A Joy and a Comfort*, novels; *Sandy's Castle*, stories; short stories.

SIDELIGHTS: Susan Kinnicutt writes: "Although I had led a full life with volunteer work and social activities, in 1972, at the time of my divorce, I wanted to really sink my teeth into something. I had written all my life, but had never done much with my stories. So I took courses, attended conferences, buckled down, and changed my life entirely. Writing is my career now. I'm dedicated, and find it very rewarding in terms of new friends, experiences, and most of all a sense of self-respect."

AVOCATIONAL INTERESTS: Golf, painting, music, bridge, gardening, conservation, politics, children, reading.

*   *   *

KIRBY, (George) Blaik 1928-

PERSONAL: Born April 14, 1928, in London, Ontario, Canada; son of Frederick Blaiklock and Winnifred T. (Pyle) Kirby; married Margaret Ruth Brubacher (a teacher), September 29, 1956; children: David Blaiklock. *Education:* University of Toronto, B.A., 1948, further study, 1969-75. *Politics:* "Cynic and iconoclast." *Religion:* Anglican. *Residence:* Toronto, Ontario, Canada. *Office: Toronto Globe and Mail*, 444 Front St. W., Toronto, Ontario, Canada M5V 2S9.

CAREER/WRITINGS: Reporter, critic, and copy editor for daily newspapers in Sudbury, Calgary, Winnipeg, and Ottawa, all Canada, 1948-55; *Toronto Daily Star*, Toronto, Ontario, copy editor, 1955-58, photo editor, 1959-60, music critic, 1960, film critic, 1961, classical record critic and entertainment feature writer, 1961-64; Reuters News Agency, London, England, copy editor, 1964-66; *Toronto Globe and Mail*, Toronto, nightlife critic, 1967—, television critic, 1970—. Notable assignments include coverage of the Northern Ontario Natural Gas Co. scandal, 1958, and interviews with most major television and night life personalities. *Awards, honors:* Southam fellowship in journalism, University of Toronto, 1978-79.

SIDELIGHTS: Kirby writes: "My job as a television and nightlife writer is to act as a consumer reporter in those areas, to inform the public of what is going on and what it signifies under the surface. NOT to engage in an ego trip or power trip by exerting anything other than an informative and advisory function. Accordingly, I write in a comparatively impersonal way, to communicate facts rather than make a name for myself."

KIRKENDALL, Richard Stewart 1928-

PERSONAL: Born April 11, 1928, in Spokane, Wash.; son of Roland P. (a salesman) and Marjorie (Monfort) Kirkendall; married Joan Carol Nelson, August 19, 1950; children: Thomas Reed, Andrew John, Theodore Nelson. *Education:* Gonzaga University, B.A., 1950; University of Wisconsin—Madison, M.S., 1953, Ph.D., 1958. *Politics:* Democrat. *Home:* 2715 Bluff Court, Bloomington, Ind. 47401. *Office:* Organization of American Historians, 112 North Bryan St., Bloomington, Ind. 47401.

CAREER: Wesleyan University, Middletown, Conn., instructor in history, 1955-58; University of Missouri—Columbia, assistant professor, 1958-61, associate professor, 1961-67, professor of history, 1967-73; Indiana University at Bloomington, professor of history, 1973—, director of oral history project, 1973—. *Military service:* U.S. Naval Reserve, active duty, 1950-52. *Member:* American Historical Association, Organization of American Historians (executive secretary, 1973—), Agricultural History Society, Southern Historical Association, Alpha Sigma Nu.

WRITINGS: Social Scientists and Farm Politics in the Age of Roosevelt, University of Missouri Press, 1966; (editor) *The Truman Period as a Research Field,* University of Missouri Press, 1967, revised edition published as *The Truman Period as a Research Field: A Reappraisal,* 1972; (editor) *The New Deal: The Historical Debate,* Wiley, 1973; *The Global Power: The United States Since 1941,* Allyn & Bacon, 1973; *The United States, 1929-1945: Years of Crisis and Change,* McGraw, 1974; (with John Schutz) *The American Republic,* Forum Press, 1977.

WORK IN PROGRESS: The Early Life of a Global Power: The United States in the Truman Period, for Indiana University Press; *Missouri Since 1920,* for University of Missouri Press.

* * *

KIRKHAM, George L. 1941-

PERSONAL: Born November 15, 1941; married; children: three. *Education:* San Jose City College, A.A., 1962; California State University, San Jose, B.A. (with distinction), 1964, M.S., 1966; University of California, Berkeley, D.Crim., 1972. *Home address:* Route 2, Box 197C, Tallahassee, Fla. 32301. *Office:* School of Criminology, Florida State University, Tallahassee, Fla. 32306.

CAREER: California Department of Corrections, assistant, 1964, correctional counselor at Correctional Training Facility in Soledad, 1965-66; Langley-Porter Neuropsychiatric Facility, San Francisco, Calif., intern, 1966-67; San Jose City College, San Jose, Calif., instructor in social science, 1968-70; Stanford Research Institute, Stanford, Calif., research criminologist in Systems Analysis Division, 1970-71; Florida State University, Tallahassee, assistant professor, 1971-76, associate professor of criminology, 1976—. Assistant professor at California State University, San Jose, and research associate at its Center for Interdisciplinary Studies, 1968-70; faculty member at University of Houston, 1975. Intern at Mount Zion Hospital Outpatient Psychiatric Clinic, 1966-67; juvenile group counselor for Santa Clara County Juvenile Probation Department, 1967. Police patrolman in Jacksonville, Fla., summer, 1973; part-time police officer in Tallahassee, Fla., 1974—; agent for Broward County Sheriff's Department Organized Crime Division, summer, 1975; deputy sheriff in detective division of Leon County, Fla., 1977. Consultant to Law Enforcement Assistance Administration and U.S. Treasury Department.

MEMBER: Alpha Kappa Delta, Psi-Chi, Tau Delta Phi, Alpha Gamma Sigma. *Awards, honors:* Grants from Law Enforcement Assistance Administration, 1972, 1973, 1974; distinguished service award from Reserve Officers Association of America, 1974; outstanding service awards from Florida Peace Officers Association, 1974, Ohio Association of Chiefs of Police, Optimist International, 1975, and California Association of Administration of Justice Educators, 1976; Golden Eagle Award from Council on International Nontheatrical Events, 1974, for film "Minorities and the Police"; Freedoms Foundation Award, 1975, for article "What a Professor Learned When He Became a Cop"; Chris Plaque from Columbus Film Festival, 1975, for "Police Ethics"; J. Edgar Hoover Award, 1976; recognition award from Southern Police Institute, 1976.

WRITINGS: Signal Zero (autobiography), Lippincott, 1976. Also author of *Introduction to Law Enforcement,* Harper.

Contributor: Edward Sagarin, editor, *Sex on the American Scene,* Dell, 1962; Sagarin, editor, *Odd Man In: Societies of Deviants in America,* Quadrangle, 1968; Simon Dinitz and Walter C. Reckless, editors, *Critical Issues in the Study of Crime,* Little, Brown, 1968; James M. Henslin, editor, *Studies in the Sociology of Sex,* Appleton, 1971; Donal E. J. MacNamara and Frank Reidel, editors, *The Police: Problems and Prospects,* Praeger, 1975.

Educational films; for Harper: "Police: The Human Dimension," 1974; "Police Authority and Discretion," 1974; "Minorities and the Police," 1974; "Police and the Community," 1974; "Police Ethics," 1974; "Internal Adaptation to Stress in Policing," 1976; "External Adaptation in Policing," 1976; "The Police Marriage: Personal Issues," 1976; "The Police Marriage: Social Issues," 1976; "Police Children: Problems and Issues," 1976. Contributor to criminology, law, and sociology journals, and *Reader's Digest.*

* * *

KIRSNER, Douglas 1947-

PERSONAL: Born April 22, 1947, in Melbourne, Australia; son of Gordon (a manufacturer's agent) and Sadie (a manufacturer's agent) Kirsner. *Education:* University of Melbourne, B.A., 1968, diploma in criminology, 1972; Monash University, M.A., 1974. *Politics:* Socialist. *Home:* 632 Canning St., North Carlton, Victoria, Australia. *Office:* School of Humanities, Deakin University, Geelong, Victoria, Australia.

CAREER: University of Melbourne, Parkville, Australia, tutor in philosophy, 1971-75; Deakin University, Geelong, Victoria, Australia, lecturer in philosophy and history of ideas, 1976—.

WRITINGS: (Editor with John Playford) *Australian Capitalism: Toward a Socialist Critique,* Penguin, 1972; *The Schizoid World of Jean-Paul Sartre and R. D. Laing,* Humanities, 1976.

WORK IN PROGRESS: A psychoanalytic interpretation of the work of Samuel Beckett, with particular reference to the metaphor of the birth experience.

SIDELIGHTS: Kirsner writes: "I am generally interested in modern developments in psychoanalysis, particularly in the 'spin-offs' in other areas, and in enhancing our understanding of authors as persons reflecting the general mood of our time. I consider that the mood of advanced western capitalist societies can be characterized as schizoid in the sense that there seems to be a pervasive crisis of a failure of basic trust in ourselves and others. This crisis is largely sociologically determined by the growth of rapid capitalist technologization which has transformed technical reason into truth itself. I believe that the effect on culture and the way we relate to ourselves and the world can be understood through extensions of the work of the British 'object relations' school of psychoanalysis (Winnicott, Fairbairn, Klein, Guntrip), but I am most concerned not to be psychologically reductionist. I want to understand what it is about particular authors such as Kafka, Sartre, and Beckett that makes them representative of our period and can help us understand it, and what it is about the period that makes these authors possible."

*   *   *

KISTLER, Mark O(liver)   1918-

PERSONAL: Born April 21, 1918, in New Tripoli, Pa.; son of Howard C. (a farmer) and Emma T. (Herber) Kistler; married Jo Ann Rohde (a teacher), August 25, 1948; children: Stephen, Matthew. *Education:* Dickinson College, A.B., 1938; Columbia University, A.M., 1941; University of Illinois, Ph.D., 1948. *Politics:* Republican. *Religion:* Protestant. *Home:* 1604 River Ter., East Lansing, Mich. 48823. *Office:* Department of German, Michigan State University, East Lansing, Mich. 48824.

CAREER: Dickinson College, Carlisle, Pa., instructor in German, 1942-44; Temple University, Philadelphia, Pa., assistant professor of German, 1948-49; Michigan State University, East Lansing, assistant professor, 1949-61, associate professor,1961-68, professor of German, 1968—. *Member:* Modern Language Association of America, American Association of Teachers of German.

WRITINGS: Drama of the Storm and Stress, Twayne, 1969.

WORK IN PROGRESS: Research on Lessing and Fontane.

*   *   *

KITT, Eartha (Mae)   1928-

PERSONAL: Born January 26, 1928, in North, S.C.; daughter of William (a sharecropper) and Anna Mae (Riley) Kitt; married William McDonald, June, 1960 (divorced, 1965); children: Kitt (daughter). *Education:* Educated in New York, N.Y. *Residence:* Beverly Hills, Calif. *Agent:* Jordan Karlin, 449 South Beverly Drive, Beverly Hills, Calif. 90212.

CAREER: Singer, dancer, actress, and nightclub performer. Toured United States, Mexico, and South America as a dancer and singer with Katherine Dunham dance troupe, 1944-49; made European nightclub debut at Carroll's, Paris, France, 1949; played Helen of Troy in Orson Welles's production of "Faust," Paris, 1951; made American nightclub debut at La Vie En Rose, New York City. Play performances include "New Faces," 1952, "Mrs. Patterson," 1954, "Shinbone Alley," 1957, and "Jolly's Progress," 1959, all in New York City; toured with production companies of "The Skin of Our Teeth," and "The Owl and the Pussycat"; opened in "Timbuktu" as Princess-Sahleem-La-Lume, Kennedy Center, Washington, D.C., January 14, 1978. Motion picture performances include "New Faces," 1954; "Accused," 1957; "The Mark of the Hawk," Universal, 1958; "Anna Lucasta," Paramount, 1959; "Synanon," 1965; also acted in two French films. Television appearances include "The Ed Sullivan Show," "Colgate Comedy Hour," "I Spy," "Batman," and "Police Woman." Recorded albums with RCA Victor include "That Bad Eartha," "Down to Eartha," "St. Louis Blues," and "Thursday's Child"; has also recorded albums with European companies. Recorded dramatic readings include "Black Pioneers in American History: Nineteenth Century," with Moses Gunn, Caedmon, 1968; "Folk Tales of the Tribes of Africa," Caedmon, 1968. *Awards, honors:* Golden Rose First Place Award for best special of the year from Montreux Film Festival, 1962, for "This is Eartha"; Woman of the Year award from National Association of Black Musicians, 1968.

WRITINGS: Thursday's Child (autobiography), Duell, Sloan & Pearce, 1956; *Alone with Me* (autobiography), Regnery, 1976.

SIDELIGHTS: "In essence, I'm a sophisticated cotton picker," wrote Kitt in *Alone With Me.* Despite her childhood of poverty and instability, she has achieved international recognition and success.

While living with an aunt in a Puerto Rican-Italian section of New York City, Kitt learned several languages and polished her talents for singing and dancing. Her first break came at age sixteen, in the form of a scholarship with the Katherine Dunham Dance Group. This break led Kitt to Europe and sparked a nightclub career that has taken her, by her own accounting, to ninety-two countries.

In a long list of acknowledgements at the beginning of *Alone With Me,* Kitt included: "*My country,* which hasn't allowed me to work here but which takes a more than healthy chunk of my income because I refuse to be intimidated to leave it." The series of events which precipitated that sentiment began in January, 1968, with her participation, by the invitation of First Lady Mrs. Lyndon Johnson, in the first "Woman Doers' Luncheon" at the White House. The topic for discussion at the meeting was to be "Why is there so much juvenile delinquency in the streets of America?"

It was a subject in which Kitt took a very personal interest. Over the years, she had helped organize numerous anti-poverty and anti-crime groups; she had visited ghettos and talked with their residents wherever she worked; she had formed dance workshops in Harlem and Watts. She accepted the White House invitation with "a grave sense of personal commitment," paying her own transportation expenses to attend.

Before she went, she talked with a group called the Mothers of Watts about the discussion topic. Their feeling was that the war in Vietnam was a direct cause of street crime among the young in several ways: the drain on the economy, the disproportionate number of minorities being sent to war, and—worst of all—the fact that those with criminal records were deferred while the law-abiding young men were drafted. Kitt wanted to raise the issue of Vietnam, among many others, at the luncheon.

"But," as she said, "things got a little out of hand—to say the least." She described her growing chagrin at the lack of seriousness among many guests and the careful staging for a "surprise" visit by President Johnson. "I was most definitely getting upset," Kitt recalled. "I hadn't flown from Los Angeles to Washington, D.C., to watch a show."

Miss Kitt said in *Alone With Me,* "With God as my witness, I had no intention of launching a diatribe against the war in Vietnam. But the reaction to my statements precluded my saying much more." *Newsweek,* January 29, 1968, quoted her remarks to Mrs. Johnson as follows: "I think we have missed the main point at this luncheon. We have forgotten the main reason we have juvenile delinquency . . . there's a war going on and America doesn't know why. Boys I know across the nation feel it doesn't pay to be a good guy. They figure that with a [crime] record they don't have to go off to Vietnam. . . . No wonder the kids rebel and take pot, and Mrs. Johnson, in case you don't understand the lingo, that's marijuana. . . .''

Kitt went on in her book to describe the effect of this incident on her career. ''After the White House luncheon and the press it received, I became persona non grata in my own country . . . club contracts were cancelled or 'lost' with the contractors refusing to draw up new ones. The television quiz show on which I was a semi-regular never invited me back and the phones stopped ringing.'' Finally, in 1974, she began once more to get nightclub bookings in the United States.

In a recent article for *Washington Post*, Lon Tuck stated: ''It was not until 1975, however, that Kitt learned through newspaper reports that an upshot of that incident was the assembling of a Secret Service dossier filled with gossip about her personal life, but concluding she was no immediate threat to the Republic. A CIA document quoted a 1956 source in Paris as saying Kitt had 'a lurid sex life' . . . Kitt replied, 'I have always lived a very clean life. I have nothing to be ashamed of. I have nothing to be afraid of, and I have nothing to hide.''' Later, when Jack Anderson's Washington, D.C. office disclosed the extent to which the various government intelligence agencies had investigated Kitt's activities, both before and after the 1968 luncheon, the recovery of her career was accelerated.

Kitt returned to the White House in February, 1978. She and her sixteen year old daughter, Kitt McDonald, were among several hundred guests invited to a reception in honor of the tenth anniversary of the restoration of Ford's Theatre. According to *Time*, Kitt commented: ''First I thought I shouldn't go. Now I'm very glad I went. Mr. Carter looked at me and he smiled as though he understood.''

Tuck observed that throughout Kitt's conversations and writings there remains a strong consistency: ''She describes her life as a success story, in which disaster, for a citizen of the world, has been only a temporary setback.'' In Kitt's own words: ''Overall, I've had a very good life, a life of cotton and caviar. And the cotton years have made the caviar years far more savory than they would have been had my early life been an easy one.''

BIOGRAPHICAL/CRITICAL SOURCES: Eartha Kitt, *Thursday's Child,* Duell, Sloan & Pearce, 1956; *Newsweek,* January 29, 1968; Kitt, *Alone with Me,* Regnery, 1976; *Washington Post,* January 19, 1978; *Time,* February 13, 1978.*

*   *   *

KLADSTRUP, Don(ald) 1943-

PERSONAL: Born September 4, 1943; son of Don (a businessman) and Ruth (Coon) Kladstrup; married Petie Sarlette (a teacher), August 27, 1966; children: Regan, Kwan-li. *Education:* University of Iowa, B.A., 1965; Iowa State University, M.S., 1967; attended University of Minnesota, 1967-70. *Home:* 200 East 74th St., Apt. 3B, New York, N.Y. 10021. *Office:* Columbia Broadcasting System (CBS) News, 524 West 57th St., New York, N.Y. 10019.

CAREER/WRITINGS: WCCO-TV, Minneapolis, Minn., reporter, 1967-75; Columbia Broadcasting System (CBS), New York, N.Y., reporter and special correspondent, 1975—.

KLANN, Margaret L. 1911-

PERSONAL: Born December 30, 1911, in Chicago, Ill.; daughter of Ernest H. (a managerial businessman) and Frieda (Lafrentz) Klann. *Education:* Attended Chicago Teachers College, 1929-32; University of Illinois, B.S., 1933; Colorado State College of Education, M.A., 1942. *Residence:* Tempe, Ariz.

CAREER: High school teacher in Glendale, Ariz., 1935-44, and South Pasadena, Calif., 1944-45; Arizona State University, Tempe, instructor, 1945-48, assistant professor, 1948-54, associate professor, 1954-76, archery coach, 1945-76; writer, 1976—. Assistant coach of U.S. Archery Team at World Championships in Canberra, 1977. *Member:* American Alliance for Health, Physical Education and Recreation, National Archery Association (member of Olympic archery sports committee, 1969—), Arizona Association for Health, Physical Education and Recreation. *Awards, honors:* Named coach of the year by College Division of National Archery Association, 1975.

WRITINGS: Target Archery, Addison-Wesley, 1968. Also author of *Advanced Target Archery for Shooters and Coaches.*

WORK IN PROGRESS: The College Division of the National Archery Association, a pamphlet.

*   *   *

KLEIN, Jeffrey B. 1948-

PERSONAL: Born January 15, 1948, in Scranton, Pa.; son of Harold H. (a doctor) and Helen (Blum) Klein; married Judith Weinstein (a psychologist), August 9, 1971. *Education:* Columbia University, B.A., 1969; San Francisco State University, M.A., 1973. *Religion:* Jewish. *Office: Mother Jones,* 607 Market St., San Francisco, Calif. 94105.

CAREER/WRITINGS: University of California, Berkeley, instructor in English and creative writing, 1973—; *Mother Jones,* San Francisco, Calif., editor, 1976—. Notable assignments include coverage of repression and terror in Soviet Union and a profile of Larry Flynt. Contributor to *American Scholar, New York Times Book Review,* and *North American Review.*

WORK IN PROGRESS: ''A novel set in 1992 about a radical senator running for the presidency on the platform that he will end the nation's cancer epidemic; a collection of articles on contemporary dissidents.''

SIDELIGHTS: Klein told *CA:* ''I am by conviction a democratic socialist and by inclination a psychological observer. I like to combine these two in my writing in order to deflate radical pretenders and help develop an intelligent honest American left.''

*   *   *

KLEIN, Stanley D. 1936-

PERSONAL: Born July 7, 1936, in New York, N.Y.; son of Benjamin (a certified public accountant) and Dora (Wides) Klein; married Rona Bornstein (a psychiatrist), July 29, 1972; children: Steve Martin. *Education:* Lehigh University, B.A., 1957; Clark University, M.A., 1960, Ph.D., 1963. *Politics:* Democrat. *Home:* 280 Beacon St., Boston, Mass. 02116. *Office: Exceptional Parent,* 20 Providence St., Boston, Mass. 02116.

CAREER: Clark University Psychological Clinic, Worcester, Mass., staff member, 1957-62; Worcester Youth Guidance Center, Worcester, clinical psychology intern, 1960-61, consulting psychologist, 1965-66; Douglas A. Thom Clinic for Children, staff psychologist, 1962-64, director of research, 1964-66; intern, 1960-61, clinical psychologist in private practice, 1963—. Boston University, Boston, Mass., School of Fine and Applied Arts, lecturer in psychology, 1963-65, School of Medicine, instructor, 1965-66, assistant professor of psychiatry, 1966-68, assistant project director of Mental Health Center Studies Unit, 1966-68; Simmons College, School of Social Work, Boston, special lecturer in clinical psychology, 1966-69; University of Massachusetts—Boston, assistant professor, 1967-71, associate professor of psychology, 1971-73; faculty member, Massachusetts Psychological Center, 1974; Emmanuel College, Division of Continuing Education, Boston, lecturer, 1975; Lesley College, Graduate School of Education, Cambridge, visiting associate professor, 1975-76, associate professor of special education, 1976-77; associate professor of psychiatry, New England College of Optometry, 1977—. *Exceptional Parent*, Boston, founding editor, 1971-73, editor-in-chief, 1973-76, editor, 1976—. Child psychologist for program, "At Your Service," WEEI-Radio, Boston, 1965; member of advisory panel, Handicapped Awareness Project, WGBH-TV, 1976—. Member of task force on special education, Massachusetts Mental Retardation Planning Project, 1963-65; member of board of directors, Citizens for the Boston Public Schools, 1966-67; special assistant to mayor, 1968, and consultant to mayor's office, Boston, 1969; member of coordinating council on drug abuse, City of Boston, 1969-72. Field reader in Learning Disabilities Program, Division of Innovation and Development, Bureau of Education for the Handicapped, 1976—; reviewer of manuscripts, Seymour Lawrence, Inc., 1976—; member of editorial advisory board, Action for Children's Television, 1976—. *Member:* National Association for Retarded Citizens, Massachusetts Association for Retarded Citizens (member of board of trustees of Retardate Trust), Phi Beta Kappa. *Awards, honors:* Commendation from National Media Awards Committee, American Psychological Foundation, 1975, for *Psychological Testing of Children: A Consumer's Guide.*

WRITINGS: The Psychological Testing of Children: A Consumer's Guide, Psy-Ed Corp., 1975, 2nd edition, Exceptional Parent Press, 1977. Writer of papers for professional symposia, panels, and workshops. Contributor of articles to journals in his field.

*   *   *

KLEINFELD, Judith S. 1944-

PERSONAL: Born May 29, 1944, in Dayton, Ohio; married Andrew Kleinfeld (a lawyer), June 18, 1967; children: Daniel, Rachel. *Education:* Wellesley College, B.A., 1966; Harvard University, Ed.M., Ed.D. *Religion:* Jewish. *Home:* 216 Newland Building, Fairbanks, Alaska 99701. *Office:* Institute of Social and Economic Research, University of Alaska, Fairbanks, Alaska 99701.

CAREER: University of Alaska, Fairbanks, associate professor of psychology, 1969—. *Member:* American Educational Research Association, American Psychological Association, National Indian Education Association, Phi Beta Kappa.

WRITINGS: Cognitive Strengths of Eskimos and Implications for Education, Institute of Social, Economic, & Government Research, University of Alaska, 1970; (with Thomas A. Morehouse) *Manpower Needs in Alaska State and Local Government,* Institute of Social, Economic, & Government Research, University of Alaska, 1970; *Alas-*

ka's *Urban Boarding Home Program: Interpersonal Relationships Between Indian and Eskimo Secondary Students and Their Boarding Home Parents,* Institute of Social, Economic, & Government Research, University of Alaska, 1972; *Effective Teachers of Indian and Eskimo High School Students,* Institute of Social, Economic, & Government Research, University of Alaska, 1972; *A Long Way From Home: The Effects of Public High Schools on Village Children Away from Home,* Center for Northern Educational Research, University of Alaska, 1973; (with Peter Jones and Ron Evans) *Land Claims and Native Manpower: Staffing Regional Villages and Corporations Under Alaska Native Claims Settlement of 1971,* Alaska Native Foundation and Institute of Social, Economic, & Government Research, University of Alaska, 1973; (with Karen Kohout) *Alaska Natives in Higher Education,* University of Alaska, 1974. Contributor to academic journals.

WORK IN PROGRESS: I Am Very Happy I Went There (tentative title), a study of a Catholic boarding school; research on the effects of oil and gas development on North Slope Eskimos.

SIDELIGHTS: Judith Kleinfeld writes: "I have been fundamentally concerned with ways to increase the educational development of Alaskan Indian and Eskimo children. The developmental period of adolescence is my particular interest."

*   *   *

KLINEBERG, Stephen L(ouis) 1940-

PERSONAL: Born March 12, 1940, in New York, N.Y.; son of Otto (a professor) and Selma Ruth (Gintzler) Klineberg; married Margaret Kersey, June 16, 1962; children: Geoffrey Morris, Katharine Douglas. *Education:* Haverford College, B.A., 1961; University of Paris, diploma, 1963; Harvard University, Ph.D., 1966. *Home:* 2109 Goldsmith, Houston, Tex. 77030. *Office:* Department of Sociology, Rice University, Houston, Tex. 77001.

CAREER: Harvard University, Cambridge, Mass., instructor in social relations, 1965-66; Princeton University, Princeton, N.J., assistant professor of sociology, 1966-72; Rice University, Houston, Tex., associate professor of sociology, 1972—. Member of board of managers of Haverford College, 1970—. *Member:* American Sociological Association, American Psychological Association, Society for the Psychological Study of Social Issues.

WRITINGS: (With T. J. Cottle) *The Present of Things Future: Explorations of Time in Human Experience,* Free Press, 1974. Contributor to journals.

WORK IN PROGRESS: A book on the psychological dimensions of social change and the future.

*   *   *

KLOTTER, James C(hristopher) 1947-

PERSONAL: Born January 17, 1947, in Lexington, Ky.; son of John C. (a university dean) and Marjorie (Gibson) Klotter; married Freda Jean Campbell (a teacher), December 28, 1966; children: Karen, Christopher, Katherine. *Education:* University of Kentucky, B.A., 1968, M.A.Ed., 1969, Ph.D., 1976. *Politics:* Independent. *Home:* 1048 Pinebloom Dr., Lexington, Ky. 40504. *Office:* Kentucky Historical Society, P.O. Box H, Frankfort, Ky. 40601.

CAREER: Kentucky Historical Society, Frankfort, research analyst, 1973-75, assistant editor of *Register*, 1975—, assistant director of publications, 1976—, editor of *Bulletin*,

1976—. Instructor at University of Kentucky, 1976-77. Public lecturer on local history. *Military service:* U.S. Army, 1970-71; became first lieutenant. *Member:* Organization of American Historians, Southern Historical Association, Kentucky Historical Society, Kentucky Civil War Round Table, Filson Club, Phi Alpha Theta.

WRITINGS: William Goebel: The Politics of Wrath, University Press of Kentucky, 1977; (with Hambleton Tapp) *Kentucky: Decades of Discord, 1865-1900,* Kentucky Historical Society, 1977.

WORK IN PROGRESS: A book on twentieth-century Kentucky history, for Kentucky Historical Society; research on the Breckinridges of Kentucky; a study of Kentucky boss Ben Johnson; research on Appalachia and on feuds and Kentucky's image of violence.

SIDELIGHTS: James Klotter writes: "Historians are increasingly turning to detailed examinations of the state and regional settings in their efforts to understand our national experience. In this we can learn much. At the same time, historians should always remember that they are not writing solely for their fellow scholars, but for a larger public as well. While this is a difficult task, if it can be achieved the results are more meaningful for the historian, for the public, and for the future."

* * *

KNIKER, Charles Robert 1936-

PERSONAL: Surname is pronounced Ka-*nick*-ker; born August 20, 1936, in Austin, Tex.; son of Theodore S. (a banker) and Alice (a teacher; maiden name, Steger) Kniker; married Carrol Ann Sumner, June 6, 1959 (died January 21, 1960); married Eleanor LeAnn Orth (a nursing instructor), December 29, 1962; children: (second marriage) Theodore, Timothy Scott. *Education:* Elmhurst College, B.A., 1958; Eden Seminary, B.D., 1962; San Francisco Theological Seminary, M.A., 1966; Columbia University, Ed.D., 1969. *Home:* 2111 Ashmore Circle, Ames, Iowa 50010. *Office:* Department of Secondary Education, Iowa State University, 218 Curtiss Hall, Ames, Iowa 50010.

CAREER: Ordained minister of United Church of Christ, 1962; pastor of United Church of Christ in Wellston, Mo., 1962-64, and Congregational church in Park Ridge, N.J., 1967-68; Hofstra University, Hempstead, N.Y., instructor in education, 1968-69; Iowa State University, Ames, assistant professor, 1969-72, associate professor, 1972-76, professor of education, 1976—. Member of Iowa Educators Task Force on Teaching About Religion in Public Schools, 1975—. *Member:* Religious Education Association, History of Education Society, American Educational Studies Association, Phi Delta Kappa (local president).

WRITINGS: (Editor with Glenn Smith) *Myth and Reality,* Allyn & Bacon, 1972, 2nd edition, 1975; *You and Values Education,* C. E. Merrill, 1977; *The Values of Physical Activities,* J. Weston Walch, 1977.

Author of "Mirror of America," a filmstrip, Perfection Form, 1976. Contributor to educational journals.

WORK IN PROGRESS: Research on the Chautauqua Literary and Scientific Circle, the first successful book club in the United States, and on human relations training.

SIDELIGHTS: Kniker comments: "In my career I have moved from a direct concern for religious education to a more general concern regarding the development of personal and social value systems. In my professional work I am moving from writing about how teachers can be value educa-

tors to how we can better assess whether our values efforts have 'paid off.' One of the related areas of interest is the values of physical activities."

* * *

KNOPF, Kenyon A(lfred) 1921-

PERSONAL: Born November 24, 1921, in Cleveland Heights, Ohio; son of Harold C. and Emma (Underwood) Knopf; married Madelyn Trebilcock, March 28, 1953; children: Kristin Lee, Mary George. *Education:* Kenyon College, A.B., 1942; Harvard University, M.A., 1949, Ph.D., 1949. *Office:* Whitman College, Walla Walla, Wash. 99362.

CAREER: Grinnell College, Grinnell, Iowa, instructor, 1949-51, assistant professor of economics and business, 1951-55, associate professor, 1955-60, Jentzen Professor of Economics, 1961-67; Whitman College, Walla Walla, Wash., professor of economics and dean of college, 1967-70, dean of faculty and provost, 1970—, acting president, 1974-75. Visiting professor at Butler University, summer, 1954. Public interest director of Federal Home Loan Bank of Seattle; president of Walla Walla County Human Services Administration Board, 1975-76; member of Walla Walla Mental Health Board, 1968-76. City councilman in Grinnell, 1964-67. *Military service:* U.S. Army Air Forces, 1943-46.

MEMBER: American Economic Association, American Conference of Academic Deans (chairman of executive committee, 1975), American Association for Higher Education, Phi Beta Kappa. *Awards, honors:* Social Science Research Council grant, 1951-52.

WRITINGS: (Editor with J. H. Stauss) *The Teaching of Elementary Economics,* Holt, 1960; (with Robert H. Haveman) *The Market System,* Wiley, 1966, 3rd edition, 1978; (editor) *Introduction to Economics,* ten volumes, Wiley, 1966, 2nd edition, seven volumes, 1970.

* * *

KNOX, Collie T. 1897-1977

PERSONAL: Born in 1897; son of Edmund Francis Vesey Knox (a lawyer and member of parliament); married Gwendoline Frances Mary Mitchell, 1944 (divorced, 1948). *Education:* Attended Royal Military College, Sandhurst (now Royal Military Academy). *Home:* 10E Sussex Heights, St. Margarets Place, Brighton, East Sussex BN1 2FQ, England.

CAREER: British Army, began as regular commissioned officer in Queen's Royal Regiment; alternately served as member of Royal Flying Corps and captain on staff at War Office during World War I; served with Queen's Royal Regiment during Irish rebellion at Londonderry and County Cork; captain on staff in India, Uganda, and Sudan; lieutenant-colonel in Sudan Defence Force, 1925; *Daily Express,* London, England, staff member, 1928-33; *Daily Mail,* London, special columnist, beginning 1933, columnist, 1945-55; *Morning Telegraph,* New York, N.Y., London columnist and drama critic, 1955-77; free-lance writer and journalist, 1955-77. Contributor to Ministry of Information and to service publications during World War II; director of public relations, Entertainments National Service Association, London, 1943-45; former feature writer, Newnes and Pearson Publications and Daily Mirror Group.

WRITINGS: Collie Knox Calling, Chapman & Hall, 1937; *It Might Have Been You* (autobiography) Chapman & Hall, 1938; *Draw Up Your Chair,* Chapman & Hall, 1938; *Collie Knox Again,* Chapman & Hall, 1938; *Collie Knox Re-Calls,*

Chapman & Hall, 1940; *Atlantic Battle,* Methuen, 1941; *Heroes All,* Hodder & Stoughton, 1941; (compiler) *For Ever England* (anthology), Cassell, 1943; *The Un-Beaten Track,* Cassell, 1944; *It Had To Be Me* (autobiography), Methuen, 1947; *People of Quality,* Macdonald & Co., 1947; *Voices of British Radio: Original Portraits and Personal Stories,* David Waddington Publications, 1948; *We Live and We Learn,* W. H. Allen, 1951; *Steel at Brierley Hill: The Story of Round Oak Steel Works, 1857-1957,* Newman Neame, 1957. Writer of lyrics for over thirty songs.

AVOCATIONAL INTERESTS: Golf and lawn tennis.

BIOGRAPHICAL/CRITICAL SOURCES: Collie Knox, *It Might Have Been You* (autobiography) Chapman & Hall, 1938; Collie Knox, *It Had To Be Me* (autobiography), Methuen, 1947. Obituaries: *AB Bookman's Weekly,* October 17, 1977.

(Died May, 1977, in England)

*   *   *

KNOX, James
    See BRITTAIN, William

*   *   *

KNUEMANN, Carl H(einz)   1922-

PERSONAL: Surname is pronounced *New*-man; born November 15, 1922, in Bydgoszcz, Poland; came to the United States in 1954, naturalized citizen, 1960; son of Carl H. (an industrialist) and Marta (Huebner) Fenski Knuemann; married Carolyn Goldberg (a journalist), September 4, 1954 (divorced May 20, 1960); married Anneliese Ruetsch (an accountant), May 18, 1961; children: Patricia E. *Education:* University of Berlin, B.A., 1943; also attended Berlin University, 1947-51, and Duke University, 1951. *Politics:* Democrat. *Religion:* Lutheran. *Home and office:* 3755 Jocelyn St. N.W., Washington, D.C. 20015.

CAREER: British Military Government, Berlin, Germany, civilian analyst, 1947-51; British Broadcasting Corp., German Service, Berlin, reporter, 1951-52; U.S. Embassy, Bonn, Germany, political analyst, 1953-54; *Daily Telegraph,* London, England, reporter and office manager in Berlin, 1954; government contractor in sociological research in Washington, D.C., 1955-63; U.S. Department of Health, Education and Welfare, Washington, D.C., public health service analyst, 1963-71; president of Atlantic Standard Publishing Co., 1971—. *Wartime service:* Danish Anti-Nazi Resistance Movement, 1943-44.

MEMBER: White House and State Department Correspondents Association, U.S. Senate Press Gallery Correspondents Association, District of Columbia Sociological Society, District of Columbia Polo Association. *Awards, honors:* Fulbright scholarship for Duke University, 1951.

WRITINGS: (With Jerome D. Schein) *Directory of Health and Social Services for the Deaf,* Gallaudet College, 1962; (with Carolyn G. Knuemann) *Berlin Symphony of a Metropolis,* Staneck-Verlag, 1964. Contributor to magazines and newspapers in German and English, including *Jewish Week, Washington Kaleidoscope,* and *Journal of Commerce.* Editor, Washington Briefs News Service, 1956—.

WORK IN PROGRESS: Modern Weapons Markings, a book on manufacturers' names and code marks; *Documents of German History, 1862 to 1972; International Social Security Systems,* publication expected in 1980: an autobiography, *You Are Telling Me?*

SIDELIGHTS: Knuemann writes: "My news service is geared to report and interpret events in their political, social, and special group context. General human rights aspects are prominently examined, the interests of German-Americans and the Jewish-European groups are specifically observed. The questions of personal liberties are always discussed. Defense, education, health, foreign affairs, and economics are topics especially observed."

BIOGRAPHICAL/CRITICAL SOURCES: Washington New Approach, March, 1972.

*   *   *

KOCH, Stephen   1941-

PERSONAL: Surname is pronounced Coke; born May 8, 1941, in St. Paul, Minn.; son of Robert Fulton (a lawyer) and Edith (Bayard) Koch. *Education:* Attended University of Minnesota, 1959-60; City College of the City University of New York, A.B., 1962; Columbia University, M.A., 1965. *Religion:* Episcopalian. *Home:* 432 Lafayette St., New York, N.Y. 10003. *Agent:* Maxine Groffsky, 2 Fifth Ave., New York, N.Y. 10011.

CAREER: Writer; Columbia University, New York, N.Y., instructor in fiction writing, 1977—. *Member:* Phi Beta Kappa.

WRITINGS: Night Watch (novel), Harper, 1969; *Stargazer: Andy Warhol's World and His Films,* Praeger, 1972. Author (and host) of "Eye-to-Eye," a television series for Public Broadcasting System. Contributor of articles and reviews to literary journals.

AVOCATIONAL INTERESTS: Films and filmmaking.

*   *   *

KOHLER, Julilly H(ouse)   1908-1976

PERSONAL: Born October 18, 1908, in Cincinnati, Ohio; married John M. Kohler (an executive), 1933; children: John M., Jr., William C., Julilly Housman, Marie Cabot. *Education:* Wellesley College, diploma, 1930. *Residence:* Riverbend, Wis.

CAREER: Author of books for children. Trustee, Wellesley College and Ripon College. *Awards, honors:* Sears Roebuck Civic Development Medal for leadership in saving Wisconsin Indian mounds.

WRITINGS: Farmer Collins, Childrens Press, 1947; *Football Trees,* Childrens Press, 1947; (with Paul Andrew Witty) *You and the Constitution of the United States,* Childrens Press, 1948; *Daniel in the Cub Scout Den,* Aladdin Books, 1951; *The Boy Who Stole the Elephant,* Knopf, 1952; *Harmony Ahead,* Aladdin Books, 1952; *Friend to All,* Aladdin Books, 1954; *"Crazy as You Look!",* Knopf, 1954; *"The Sun Shines Bright",* Crowell, 1956; *Razzberry Jamboree,* Crowell, 1957; *Plants and Flowers to Decorate Your Home,* Western Publishing, 1977.

SIDELIGHTS: Kohler's *The Boy Who Stole the Elephant* was dramatized for the "Disney Hour" television series in 1971.

OBITUARIES: New York Times, December 28, 1976; *AB Bookman's Weekly,* February 14, 1977.*

(Died December 24, 1976, in Sheboygan, Wis.)

*   *   *

KOO, Samuel   1941-

PERSONAL: Born December 23, 1941, in Seoul, Korea;

came to United States, 1966; son of H. N. (a politician) and Namkil (an educator; maiden name, Park) Koo; married Myung-Wha Chung (a concert cellist), May 15, 1971; children: Jennifer, Leslie. *Education:* Korean University, B.A., 1965; Columbia University, M.S., 1968. *Religion:* Presbyterian. *Home:* 78 Clinton Ave., Dobbs Ferry, N.Y. 10522. *Office:* Associated Press, Room 452 United Nations Bldg., New York, N.Y. 10020.

CAREER/WRITINGS: Korea Herald, Seoul, diplomatic correspondent, 1964-66; Associated Press, New York, N.Y., world news editor, 1970—, United Nations correspondent, 1974—. Notable assignments include coverage of United Nations general assemblies, 1973—. *Awards, honors:* Henry Taylor Award from Columbia University, 1968.

WORK IN PROGRESS: A book on the "planetary management" aspect of the United Nations.

* * *

KORB, Lawrence J(oseph) 1939-

PERSONAL: Born July 9, 1939, in New York, N.Y.; son of Joseph Anthony (an office manager) and Katherine (a secretary; maiden name, McKenna) Korb; married Ann Guttmann (a registered nurse), August 20, 1966; children: Mary, Karen, Julia, Lawrence J. *Education:* Athenaeum of Ohio, B.A., 1961; St. John's University, Jamaica, N.Y., M.A., 1962; State University of New York at Albany, Ph.D., 1969. *Religion:* Roman Catholic. *Home:* 79 Fischer Circle, Portsmouth, R.I. 02871. *Office:* Department of Management, U.S. Naval War College, Newport, R.I. 02840.

CAREER: University of Dayton, Dayton, Ohio, assistant professor of political science, 1968-71; U.S. Coast Guard Academy, New London, Conn., associate professor of history and government, 1971-75; U.S. Naval War College, Newport, R.I., professor of management, 1975—. Adjunct scholar at American Enterprise Institute; consultant to National Security Council and Office of the Secretary of Defense. *Military service:* U.S. Navy, 1962-66; served in Vietnam; became lieutenant senior grade. *Member:* International Studies Association (member of governing council).

WRITINGS: The Joint Chiefs of Staff: The First Twenty-Five Years, Indiana University Press, 1976; *The System for Educating Military Officers,* University of Pittsburgh Press, 1976; *The Price of Preparedness,* American Enterprise Institute, 1977; *Changing Priorities in Defense,* American Enterprise Institute, 1978; *Organizing for National Security,* University of Kentucky Press, 1979; *The Fall and Rise of the Pentagon,* Greenwood Press, 1979; (with Sam Sarkesinn) *Carter's Defense Policy,* Westview Press, 1979. Contributor to military, public administration, and education journals.

SIDELIGHTS: Korb writes: "I research and write about national security organization, process, and policy. The thrust of my work has been to analyze the manner in which post World War II administrations have formulated national security policy and the implications of those policies."

* * *

KORS, Alan Charles 1943-

PERSONAL: Born July 18, 1943, in Jersey City, N.J.; son of Samuel and Belle (a teacher; maiden name, Silber) Kors; married Erika Wallace (an illustrator), May 30, 1975. *Education:* Princeton University, B.A. (summa cum laude), 1964; Harvard University, M.A., 1965, Ph.D., 1968. *Home:* 3909 Spruce St., Philadelphia, Pa. 19104. *Office:* Department of History, University of Pennsylvania, Philadelphia, Pa. 19104.

CAREER: University of Pennsylvania, Philadelphia, assistant professor, 1968-73, associate professor of history, 1973—. *Member:* American Society for Eighteenth-Century Studies, American Historical Association, American Civil Liberties Union, Phi Beta Kappa. *Awards, honors:* American Council of Learned Societies fellowship, 1975-76.

WRITINGS: (Editor with Edward Peters) *Witchcraft in Europe,* University of Pennsylvania Press, 1972; *D'Holbach's Coterie: An Enlightenment in Paris,* Princeton University Press, 1976; (contributor) Marc Pachter, editor, *Abroad in America,* Addison-Wesley, 1976. Contributor to journals. Book review editor of *Eighteenth-Century Studies,* 1976-78.

WORK IN PROGRESS: The Origins and Development of French Atheism, 1660-1789.

SIDELIGHTS: Kors commented: "My work, essentially, is an effort to study the formation and development of world views in the context of the intellectual and social fabric of seventeenth- and eighteenth-century France. I am particularly interested in the process by which European minds of this period generated changes in and alternatives to traditional Judeo-Christian conceptions of reality and its components."

* * *

KORTY, Carol 1937-

PERSONAL: Born January 4, 1937, in Albany, N.Y.; daughter of Frederick H. (a business executive) and H. Louise (a teacher; maiden name, Herrlich) Tweedie; married John Korty (a filmmaker), March 29, 1958 (divorced, 1964). *Education:* Antioch College, B.A., 1959; Sarah Lawrence College, M.A., 1966; studied dance with top professionals, including Merce Cunningham, Jose Limon, and Martha Graham's school. *Politics:* Socialist. *Religion:* Society of Friends (Quakers). *Home:* 15 Perkins Sq., Jamaica Plain, Boston, Mass. 02130. *Agent:* Alice Bach, 175 East 79th St., New York, N.Y. 10021. *Office:* Department of Theater, Boston University, 855 Commonwealth Ave., Boston, Mass. 02215.

CAREER: Antioch College, Yellow Springs, Ohio, teaching associate in theater and dance, 1966-67; State University of New York College at Brockport, instructor, 1967-68, assistant professor, 1968-71, associate professor of theater, 1971-72; University of Massachusetts, Amherst, associate professor of theater, 1972-75; Children's Museum, Boston, Mass., drama developer, 1975-76; Boston University, Boston, visiting associate professor of theater, 1977—. Children's theater evaluator for New York State Council on the Arts, 1969-72. Danced with Charles Weidman Dance Co. (solo member), 1961-62, National Company of "My Fair Lady," 1962-63, New York City Opera, 1963, Music Fair Enterprises, 1963, Merle Marsicano Dance Co. (solo member), 1964-65, and Richard Bull Dance Co., 1970-71.

MEMBER: International Association of Theatre for Children and Young People (member of executive board), Children's Theatre Association of America, University and College Theatre Association.

WRITINGS—For children: Plays from African Folktales: With Ideas for Acting, Dance, Costumes, and Music, Scribner, 1975; *Silly Soup: Ten Zany Plays with Songs and Ideas for Making Them on Your Own,* Scribner, 1977.

Unpublished plays: "The Shape We're In" (one-act), first produced in Brockport, N.Y., at State University College, fall, 1968; "Beginnings" (one-act), first produced in Brockport at State University College, fall, 1970; "Score for May Fest" (festival score), first produced in Brockport at State University College, spring, 1971; "Sometimes I'm a Ladybug and Sometimes I'm Angry" (one-act), first produced in Amherst, Mass., at University of Massachusetts, winter, 1974; "If I Were a Kid Back Then . . . " (one-act), first produced in Boston at Children's Museum, spring, 1976.

WORK IN PROGRESS: Turning Stories into Plays.

SIDELIGHTS: Carol Korty writes: "I certainly never intended becoming a writer. Although I read a great deal when I was growing up, when it came to choosing a career, I was too busy changing ideas to focus on any one goal. I took a long time to realize you could be interested in a subject without having to consider it your life work: florist, farmer, nurse, politician, teacher, reformer, explorer, artist, historian, anthropologist. By the time I was twenty, however, I knew I wanted to perform professionally in theater as an actress or dancer. I earned a degree in theater and moved to New York City to begin professional study. After a few exciting years of that and a couple more performing, I returned to school to study choreography. I became excited about theater again, and before I knew it, I had picked children's theater as a focus.

Children's theater was an exciting discovery because it demanded that I use all of myself and incorporated most of the things I'd wanted to do. I got into writing simply because I couldn't find plays that dealt with issues I was interested in. I want a play to make you see yourself and the world in a new way. I also want it to address some of the really important questions of life for which there are no clear answers: questions about birth, death, love, loss, fear, wishes, dreams. I like to try making plays about these things because it helps me understand my own life more clearly. I also love the whole process of getting a play ready, or working collaboratively with other artists, and then of watching an audience enjoy what we have made."

*   *   *

KOSTIUK, Hryhory 1902-
(Boris Podoliak)

PERSONAL: Born October 12, 1902, in Boryshkivtsi, Ukraine; came to United States in 1952, naturalized citizen, 1958; son of Alexander (a farmer) and Hanna (Sudak) Kostiuk; married Raisa Butko (a bank accountant), September 28, 1941; children: Theodor. *Education:* University of Kiev, M.A., 1925-29; Research Institute of the History and Theory of Literature, Kharkiv, Ukraine, Ph.D., 1929-32. *Home:* 69 Monona Ave., Rutherford, N.J. 07070. *Office:* Ukrainian Academy of Arts and Sciences in the United States, 206 West 100th St., New York, N.Y. 10025.

CAREER: Kharkiv Institute of Education, Kharkiv, Ukraine, assistant professor of literature history, 1931-33; Luhansk Institute of Education, Luhansk, Ukraine, professor of history, 1933-35; teacher, writer, and editor at displaced persons' camps in Ulm, Stuttgart, and Munich, Germany, 1945-51; Research Program on the Union of Soviet Socialist Republics, New York City, historian, political scientist, and researcher, 1952-54; Columbia University, New York City, lecturer in Russian, 1954-56; Institute for the Study of the Union of Soviet Socialist Republics, New York City, historian, political scientist, and researcher in New York and Munich, 1956-63; Columbia University, archivist

for Archives of Russian and East European History and Culture, and chairman of V. Vynnychenko archives, 1963—.

MEMBER: International P.E.N. Club for Exiles (member of board of directors, 1967-74), Ukrainian Writers Association in Exile (chairman, 1954-75; honorary chairman, 1975—), Ukrainian Academy of Arts and Sciences in the United States, Institute for the Study of the Union of Soviet Socialist Republics.

WRITINGS: Panas Mirny (critical biography), State Publishing House, 1930; (editor) *M.U.R. Almanac,* Volume I, [Stuttgart], 1946; *The Fall of Postyshev,* translated by Lois Weinert, Research Program on the Union of Soviet Socialist Republics, 1954; (editor) Valerian Pidmohylhyj, *Misto* (title means "The City"), Ukranian Academy of Arts and Sciences in United States, 1954; (editor) Mykola Kulish, *Works,* Ukranian Academy of Arts and Sciences in United States, 1955.

Stalinist Rule in the Ukraine: A Study of the Decade of Mass Terror, 1929-1939, Stevens, 1960; (editor) M. A. Plevako, *Articles, Studies, and Bio-Bibliographic Materials,* Ukranian Academy of Arts and Sciences in United States, 1961; *Teoria i diisnist do problemy vy vchennia teorii, taktyky i stratehii bil' shovyzmu v natsional'nomu pytanni* (title means "Theory and Reality on the Problem of Study on the Theory, Tactics, and Strategy of Bolshevism in the Nationality Question"), Sucasnist, 1971; *Volodymyr Vynnychenko and His Last Novel,* [New York], 1971; *Chronicle of Literary Life in Diaspora,* Sucasnist, 1971; (editor) Paulo Fylypovych, *Literature,* Ukranian Academy of Arts and Sciences in United States, 1971; *The Damned Years, 1935-1940,* Diyaloh, in press.

Contributor of articles and reviews, some under pseudonym Boris Podoliak, to English-langauge and Ukrainian scholarly journals. Editor of *Slovo,* 1962-68.

WORK IN PROGRESS: Diary of Volodymyr Vynnychenko, Volume I: *1911-1920;* editing works of Mykola Khvylovy, five volumes; editing his own articles and reviews on Vynnychenko, and his other literary critiques and reviews.

BIOGRAPHICAL/CRITICAL SOURCES: Times Literary Supplement, February 17, 1961; *American Political Review,* September, 1961; *Slavonic Review,* October, 1961; *Svoboda,* October, 1962; *Nowi Dni,* October, 1972.

*   *   *

KRAINES, Samuel H(enry) 1906-

PERSONAL: Born April 30, 1906, in Chicago, Ill.; son of Louis and Rose (Mutterperl) Kraines; married Ruth Jaffe, May 29, 1934; children: Richard, David, Gerald. *Education:* University of Illinois, M.D., 1930. *Address:* 1321 East 56th St., Chicago, Ill. 60637.

CAREER: Cook County Hospital, Chicago, Ill., general internship, 1930-31; Johns Hopkins Hospital, Baltimore, Md., resident in psychiatry, 1930-31; Boston Psychopathic Hospital, Boston, Mass., resident in psychiatry, 1931-32; private practice of psychiatry in Chicago, 1933—. Assistant professor at University of Illinois, 1933-50, and Rush Medical College, 1976—. Clinical clerk at Queen's Square Neurologic Hospital (London), 1937-38. *Military service:* U.S. Army, Medical Corps, 1942-46; became lieutenant colonel. *Member:* American Psychiatric Association, Central Neuropsychiatric Society, Illinois Psychiatric Society, Chicago Neurological Society, Sigma Xi.

WRITINGS: Therapy of the Neuroses and Psychoses,

Macmillan, 1941; (with E. S. Thetford) *Managing Your Mind,* Macmillan, 1943; *Managing Men,* Herschfeld Press, 1946; (with Thetford) *Live and Help Live,* Macmillan, 1951; *Mental Depressions and Their Treatment,* Macmillan, 1957; (with Thetford) *Help for the Depressed,* C. C Thomas, 1972. Contributor of about fifty articles to scientific journals.

WORK IN PROGRESS: Research on the physical origins of emotion and consciousness.

SIDELIGHTS: When asked if depression was increasing in American society, Kraines replied: "I doubt it. Like cancer, we see more because we recognize more. But there is another factor. In the past, man was concerned with the evils that befell him, whether they were the devil or the struggle for a livelihood. His attention was directed away from himself. Today man cries 'Mea Culpa'—what is wrong with me.

"If there were a thermometer that could measure the degree of the depressive illness then and now, the temperature would register the same. Only the awareness of possible causes differs."

Kraines's books have been translated into Swedish, Italian and Japanese.

* * *

KRAMER, Bernard M(ordecai) 1923-

PERSONAL: Born December 23, 1923, in Brooklyn, N.Y.; son of Hyman S. (a manufacturer) and Fannie (Seiden) Kramer; married Barbara Maysles (an artist), March 16, 1947; children: Rosalyn, Miriam, Philip. *Education:* Brooklyn College (now at the City University of New York), B.A., 1944; Harvard University, M.A., 1946, Ph.D., 1950. *Home:* 18 Bemuth Rd., Newton, Mass. 02161. *Office:* Department of Psychology, University of Massachusetts, Boston Harbor Campus, Boston, Mass. 02125.

CAREER: University of Chicago, Chicago, Ill., research assistant in race relations, 1948-50; New York State Mental Health Commission, Syracuse, N.Y., research psychologist, 1950-53; R. E. Diety Co., Syracuse, N.Y., industrial works, 1953-57; Massachusetts Mental Health Center, Boston, research psychologist, 1957-60; Tufts University, Boston, Mass., assistant professor, 1960-63, associate professor of preventive medicine, 1963-72; University of Massachusetts, Boston, professor of psychology, 1972—. Member of board of directors of Boston Medical Foundation; technical adviser to Falk Medical Fund.

MEMBER: American Psychological Association, Society for the Psychological Study of Social Issues.

WRITINGS: Day Hospital, Grune, 1962; (editor with Henry Wechsler and Leonard Solomon) *Social Psychology and Mental Health,* Holt, 1970; (editor with Charles V. Willie and Bertram S. Brown) *Racism and Mental Health,* University of Pittsburgh Press, 1973; (editor with Robert M. Hollister and Seymour S. Bellin) *Neighborhood Health Centers,* Lexington Books, 1974. Contributor to psychology journals.

WORK IN PROGRESS: Research on the nature of prejudice and on individuality and collectivity; revising Gordon W. Allport's *The Nature of Prejudice;* a book about "public and private interests in the lives of individuals and groups."

* * *

KRAUSKOPF, Konrad B(ates) 1910-

PERSONAL: Born November 30, 1910, in Madison, Wis.; son of Francis Craig (a chemist) and Maude (Bates) Krauskopf; married Kathryn Isabel McCune, January 1, 1936; children: Karen Krauskopf Hyde, Frances Krauskopf Conley, Karl Bowen, Marion Krauskopf Foerster. *Education:* University of Wisconsin, Madision, A.B., 1931; University of California, Berkeley, Ph.D (chemistry), 1934; Stanford University, Ph.D. (geology), 1939. *Politics:* Democrat. *Religion:* Protestant. *Home:* 806 La Mesa, Menlo Park, Calif. 94025. *Office:* Department of Geology, Stanford University, Stanford, Calif. 94305.

CAREER: University of California, Berkeley, instructor in chemistry, 1934-35; Stanford University, Stanford, Calif., acting instructor, 1935-39, assistant professor, 1939-42, associate professor, 1942-50, professor of geochemistry, 1950-76, professor emeritus, 1976—. Geologist for U.S. Geological Survey, 1942—. Civilian chief of geographic section for U.S. Army in Tokyo, 1947-49.

MEMBER: American Association for the Advancement of Science, Geological Society of America (president, 1967), American Geological Institute (president, 1964), Geochemical Society (president, 1970), Society of Economic Geologists, American Geophysical Union, National Academy of Science. *Awards, honors:* Fulbright and Guggenheim fellowships for Norway, both 1952-53; National Science Foundation fellowship for Germany, 1960-61; Day Medal from Geological Society of America, 1961; D.Sc. from University of Wisconsin, Milwaukee, 1971.

WRITINGS: Fundamentals of Physical Science, McGraw, 1941, 6th edition (with Arthur Beiser), 1971; *The Physical Universe,* McGraw, 1960, 4th edition, 1978; *Introduction to Geochemistry,* McGraw, 1967, 2nd edition, 1979; *The Third Planet,* Freeman, Cooper, 1974; (with Beiser) *Introduction to Earth Science,* McGraw, 1975. Contributor to scientific journals.

AVOCATIONAL INTERESTS: Travel (Mexico, Japan, Norway, Germany, France, Greece, Jordan, Brazil, Soviet Union).

* * *

KRING, Hilda Adam 1921-

PERSONAL: Born January 3, 1921, in Munich, Germany; American citizen born abroad; daughter of Alfons F. and Anna H. Adam; married Frederick S. Kring (a professor), May 4, 1946. *Education:* Millersville State College, B.S.Ed., 1942; University of Pittsburgh, M.Litt., 1952; University of Pennsylvania, Ph.D., 1969. *Politics:* Independent. *Religion:* Christian. *Home and office address:* Grove City College, Grove City, Pa. 16127.

CAREER: High school teacher of English, social studies, and German in Gap, Pa., 1942-46; high school English teacher in Johnstown, Pa., 1946-47, Sidman, Pa., 1947-48, and Davidsville, Pa., 1948-56; Slippery Rock State College, Slippery Rock, Pa., supervisor, 1956-58; high school English teacher in Slippery Rock, Pa., 1958-67; Grove City College, Grove City, Pa., professor of literature and communication arts, 1967—. *Member:* National Council of Teachers of English, American Folklore Society, National Historic Communal Societies Association, Pennsylvania Folklore Society, Pennsylvania Council of Teachers of English, Pennsylvania Association of Teacher Educators, Delta Kappa Gamma (Lambda chapter). *Awards, honors:* Named Pennsylvania teacher of the year by State Department of Education, 1967.

WRITINGS: The Harmonists: A Folk Cultural Approach, Scarecrow, 1973; (contributor) Buxton, editor, *The Many*

Faces of Teaching, University of South Carolina Press, 1978. Also author of plays, including "The Bird That Couldn't Sing," and "Pumpity, Pump, Pump." Contributor to literature and folklore journals. Member of editorial board of *Pennsylvania Folklore.*

WORK IN PROGRESS: Research on the variety of foods found in "The Last Supper."

SIDELIGHTS: Hilda Kring writes: "My main interest is folk religion. I travel every summer; often, it is to pilgrimage sites to gather material and empathy for my folk religion classes." Among the pilgrimage sites she has visited are Iona, Glastonbury, Santiago de Compestalo, Lourdes, Fatima, Eichstaett, Rome, Jerusalem.

* * *

KRIPPENDORFF, Klaus 1932-

PERSONAL: Born March 21, 1932, in Frankfurt, Germany; came to the United States in 1961; son of Herbert R. A. (an engineer) and Charlotte (Barthel) Krippendorff; married Sultana Alam (a community worker), December 31, 1965; children: Kaihan Pascal, Heike Prya. *Education:* Ulm School of Design, diploma, 1961, and Princeton University, 1961-62; University of Illinois, Ph.D., 1967. *Home:* 4533 Osage Ave., Philadelphia, Pa. 19143. *Office:* Annenberg School of Communications, University of Pennsylvania, Philadelphia, Pa. 19104.

CAREER: University of Pennsylvania, Philadelphia, associate professor of communications, 1965—. *Member:* International Communication Association (member of board of directors), American Cybernetics Association (member of board of directors), American Society for Cybernetics, Society for General Systems Research. *Awards, honors:* M.A. from University of Pennsylvania, 1971; award from *Journal of Communication,* 1971, for "On Generating Data in Communication Research."

WRITINGS: (Editor with G. Gerbner, O. R. Holsti, W. J. Paisley, P. J. Stone) *The Analysis of Communication Content,* Wiley, 1969; (editor) *Communication and Control in Society,* Gordon & Breach, in press. Contributor to journalism, sociology, cybernetics, and communications journals.

WORK IN PROGRESS: Research on spectral analysis of relations; a book, *Content Analysis.*

* * *

KRISHER, Bernard 1931-

PERSONAL: Born August 9, 1931, in Frankfurt, Germany; son of Joseph (a furrier) and Fella (Solnica) Krisher; married Akiko Yaginuma, May 1, 1960; children: Deborah, Joseph. *Education:* Queens College (now of the City University of New York), B.A., 1953; Columbia University, certificate in international reporting, 1962. *Politics:* Independent. *Religion:* Jewish. *Home:* 34-20 6-chome, Jingumae, Shibuya-ku, Tokyo, Japan. *Office: Newsweek,* Asahi Building, 6-6-7 Ginza 6-chome, Chuoku, Tokyo, Japan.

CAREER: New York World-Telegram & Sun, New York City, staff writer, 1955-59, assistant editor of magazine, 1959-61; *Newsweek,* New York City, correspondent, 1963—, Tokyo bureau chief, 1968—. *Military service:* U.S. Army, 1954-55; served in Germany. *Member:* Council on Foreign Relations, Foreign Correspondents Club (Tokyo), Tokyo Lawn Tennis Club.

WRITINGS: (With Alan Levy and James Cox) *Draftee's Confidential Guide,* Indiana University Press, 1957; *Interview,* translated by Osamu Senna, Simul Press, 1977.

SIDELIGHTS: Krisher told *CA:* "A journalist's worst enemy is cynicism, a disease which hits too many reporters once they have 'seen it all,' and one must be on constant guard against it, trying to approach each assignment as though it were the very first one. The journalist's best friend is his consuming interest and enthusiasm in people and events; as long as he retains that fervor and nervousness for each day's assignment or interview—then his freshness is contagious and reaches the reader who—living out his humdrum existence at some monotonous, routine job—relies on the reporter to be his eyes and ears to the world.

"Journalists generally know only a little about everything and not very much about anything particular. They must, however, have the ability to draw information and opinions out from those who know. A good knowledge of people and psychology is essential in drawing out information from an often reluctant, shy or unwilling source. This may, depending on the occasion, require tact, flattery or confrontation. You must always try to know your subject and his reaction, lest you fail to draw him out. The process is very much like luring a mouse into its trap.

"In the past, interviews usually formed the information the reporter drew on to write his story, interspersed with some quotes or paraphrases from his subject. The reporter divided what was important and what was irrelevant and then fashioned his story on his own subjective perception based on the information he had collected. In recent years the question-answer interview—where the reporter draws the subject out but lets him speak in his own words, printing the text of his answers to the questions—has become increasingly popular, both among readers and those interviewed, for it gives the personalities themselves the unfettered opportunity to communicate directly with the public. This technique, however, has its pluses and minuses. While it bars the reporter or publication from inserting its own subjective interpretation, it also gives a potentially dangerous demagogue the opportunity to disseminate self-serving, false and potentially harmful views to the public. The fact, however, that many such interviews appear everywhere, probably tends to cancel out such a danger.

"The most difficult and rewarding interviews in *Interview* were with President Sukarno of Indonesia (1964) and of course, *the* most important interview of my life, with Emperor Hirohito of Japan. Both involved considerable planning and strategy, since both Sukarno and the Emperor had never before given exclusive interviews. Sukarno's reason for not meeting with journalists before, was a basic shyness (hard to believe), of being publicly embarassed or humiliated. With the Emperor it was precedent: no Emperor of Japan had ever given an exclusive interview in 2,000 years."

* * *

KROMMINGA, John H(enry) 1918-

PERSONAL: Born August 25, 1918, in Grundy Center, Iowa; son of Diedrich (a professor) and Kathryn (Van Laaten) Kromminga; married Claire Ottenhoff, June 30, 1943; children: Kathryn Kromminga Greenfield, Connie Kromminga Hoelsema, John Richard. *Education:* Calvin College, A.B., 1939; Calvin Seminary, B.D., 1942; Princeton Theological Seminary, Th.D., 1948. *Politics:* Republican. *Home:* 3335 Burton St. S.E., Grand Rapids, Mich. 49506. *Office:* Calvin Seminary, 3233 Burton St., Grand Rapids, Mich. 49506.

CAREER: Ordained Christian Reformed minister, 1943; pastor of Christian Reformed churches in Newton, N.J.,

1943-46, Des Plaines, Ill., 1946-49, and Grand Haven, Mich., 1949-52; Calvin Seminary, Grand Rapids, Mich., assistant professor, 1952-56, professor of church history, 1956—, president of seminary, 1956—. Participant in lecture tour of the Pacific, including New Zealand, Australia, Sri Lanka, the Philippines, and Taiwan; also lectured in Korea. Member of Grand Rapids Historical Commission. *Member:* American Society of Church History, American Society of Reformation Research.

WRITINGS: Who Is John Calvin? (pamphlet), Christian Reformed Publishing House, 1949; *The Christian Reformed Church: A Study in Orthodoxy,* Baker Book, 1949; *You Shall Be My Witness,* Eerdmans, 1954; *In the Mirror,* Guardian Publications, 1957; *Thine Is My Heart,* Zondervan, 1959; (contributor) Jacob T. Hoogstra, editor, *John Calvin, Contemporary Prophet,* Baker Book, 1959.

Teaching Theology in an Era of Change (pamphlet), Calvin Seminary, 1963; *All One Body We,* Eerdmans, 1970; (contributor) Elmer Towns, editor, *A History of Religious Educators,* Baker Book, 1975. Contributor to *Encyclopedia Americana, Twentieth Century Encyclopedia of Religious Knowledge, Baker's Dictionary of Christian Ethics,* and *Christelijke Encyclopaedie.* Contributor to theology journals.

SIDELIGHTS: Kromminga writes: "Contemporary society is in danger of losing its heritage from the past by reason of its intense concentration on the present. This observation applies to American society no less than to those of other countries, and to Christians no less than other members of society.

"Christians need to be renewed in their consciousness of belonging to the Body of Christ. This means not only an awareness of other groups of Christians alongside of their own—an awareness which is growing—but also to an awareness of belonging to an ongoing tradition. This latter awareness is fading and needs to be revived.

"The benefits of such an awareness are readily evident. The great minds of the past, such as John Calvin and Abraham Kuyper in the Reformed tradition, have provided Christians with a vision which they can ill afford to lose. The Christian Church is like a nation, which the Bible calls the people of God. Although its circumstances change, it has a basic continuity, founded on Scripture and shaped by its history. It cannot understand its role in the present or its prospects for the future without knowing that rich tradition.

"How to encourage that revival is a more difficult subject. Adult education classes, the study of Christian hymnology, historical references in sermons, and Christian biographies can serve to that end. Ministers and teachers have a special responsibility in this regard, and seminaries must be well aware of their duty to equip their students to discharge that responsibility."

AVOCATIONAL INTERESTS: Travel (including Europe, Kenya, Nigeria, South Africa, and Japan).

* * *

KRUEGER, Hardy 1928-

PERSONAL: Born April 12, 1928, in Berlin, Germany; son of Max (an engineer) and Gustl (Meier) Kruger; married Renate Densow (an artist), December, 1951 (divorced, 1965); married Francesca Marazzi (an artist), December, 1965 (divorced); children: Christiane Kruger Bockelmann, Malaika, Hardy, Jr. *Education:* Educated in Berlin, Germany. *Home:* Neuhauserstrasse 3, 8 Munich 2, Germany.

Agent: Michael Meller, Mohn-Bertelsmann Corp., 620 Fifth Ave., New York, N.Y.

CAREER: Screen actor, 1945—. Has worked on films in Germany, England, France, Yugoslavia, Israel, Italy, and the United States, including "Hatari," "Flight of the Phoenix," "The Defector," "The Battle on the Neretva," "The Red Tent," and "The Secret of the Santa Vittoria." Founder and part-owner of Momella Game Lodge and Momella Farm Ltd. (Tanzania), 1961—. *Military service:* German Army, 1945; taken prisoner by American forces in May, 1945, and escaped several weeks later. *Awards, honors:* Grand Prix du Cinema Francais, 1960; Prix Femina, 1961; named best actor in Yugoslavia, 1970.

WRITINGS: Eine Farm in Afrika (title means "A Farm in Africa"), Rowohlt, 1970; *Sawimbulu,* Scholz-Mainz Verlag, 1972; *Wer Stehend Stirbt, Lebt Laenger,* R. S. Schulz-Verlag, 1974, translation by Daniel Main Waring published as *The Upside Down Tree,* Citadel, 1977.

WORK IN PROGRESS: Two novels, *Horizons* and *Miriam.*

AVOCATIONAL INTERESTS: Maintaining game reserve near Kilimanjaro in Tanzania, flying gliders and small planes.

* * *

KRUGER, Hardy
See KREGER, Hardy

* * *

KRUPAT, Edward 1945-

PERSONAL: Born August 31, 1945, in Bronx, N.Y.; son of Milton (a civil servant) and Ruth (Oberfeld) Krupat; married Barbara Riemer (a speech therapist), June 16, 1968; children: Jason, Michael. *Education:* New York University, B.A., 1965; University of Michigan, Ph.D., 1971. *Home:* 151 Elgin St., Newton Centre, Mass. 02159. *Office:* Department of Behavioral Sciences, Massachusetts College of Pharmacy, 179 Longwood Ave., Boston, Mass. 02159.

CAREER: Rutgers University, New Brunswick, N.J., assistant professor of psychology, 1970-72; Boston College, Chestnut Hill, Mass., assistant professor of psychology, 1972-77; Massachusetts College of Pharmacy, Boston, associate professor of behavioral sciences and chairman of department, 1977—. *Member:* American Psychological Association, American Association of University Professors, Environmental Design Research Association, Eastern Psychological Association.

WRITINGS: Psychology Is Social, Scott, Foresman, 1975; *People in Cities: The Urban Environment and Its Effects,* Brooks/Cole, in press. Contributor to psychology and sociology journals.

* * *

KUCZYNSKI, Pedro-Pablo 1938-

PERSONAL: Born October 3, 1938, in Lima, Peru; came to the United States in 1959; son of Maxime H. (a physician) and Madeleine (a professor of linguistics; maiden name, Godard) Kuczynski; married Jane Casey (a free-lance radio broadcaster), June 29, 1962; children: Carolina M., Alexandra L., John-Michael M. *Education:* Oxford University, B.A., 1959, M.A., 1961; Princeton University, M.P.A., 1961. *Politics:* None. *Residence:* Pittsburgh, Pa. *Office:* Halco Mining, 900 TWO Allegheny Center, Pittsburgh, Pa. 15212.

CAREER: World Bank & International Finance Corp., Washington, D.C., economist, 1961-67; Central Reserve Bank of Peru, Lima, deputy director general, 1967-69; International Monetary Fund, Washington, D.C., senior economist, 1969-71; World Bank & International Finance Corp., chief economist on Latin America, 1971-73; Kuhn Loeb & Co. International, New York, N.Y., vice-president and partner, 1973-75; World Bank & International Finance Corp., chief economist of International Finance Corp., 1975-77; Halco Mining, Pittsburgh, Pa., president and chief executive officer, 1977—. Professor at Catholic University of Peru, 1967-69; lecturer at other universities. Director of Peruvian Merchant Navy, 1967-69; adviser to Central Bank of Venezuela, 1974-75. *Member:* American Economic Association.

WRITINGS: (Contributor) Hellman and Rosenbaum, editors, *Latin America: The Search for a New International Role,* Sage Publications, 1975; *Peruvian Democracy Under Economic Stress: An Account of the Belaunde Administration, 1963-1968,* Princeton University Press, 1977; (contributor) R. Bond, editor, *Contemporary Venezuela,* Council on Foreign Relations, 1977; *The Economic Evaluation of Latin America Since the 1930's: A Synopsis,* Princeton University Press, in press. Contributor to periodicals, including *Euromoney.*

WORK IN PROGRESS: The Economic Development of Latin America Since 1945.

AVOCATIONAL INTERESTS: Piano, flute, squash rackets, running.

*   *   *

KUHNE, Marie (Ahnighito Peary)   1893-1978
(Marie Ahnighito Peary)

1893—April 16, 1978; Greenland-born lecturer, authority on the Arctic, and author. The daughter of Rear Admiral Robert Peary, the famous North Pole explorer, Kuhne wrote a biography of her father and in 1932 headed an expedition to Cape York, Greenland, to erect a monument in his honor. Concerned about the plight of the Eskimos, Kuhne was decorated by the King of Denmark for her work on their behalf. She also wrote children's books about the Arctic. She died in Brunswick, Me. Obituaries and other sources: *New York Times,* April 19, 1978.

*   *   *

KULESHOV, Arkady A.   1914-1978

Byelorussian poet, editor, and journalist. The head of the Union of Soviet Writers, Kuleshov published several volumes of poetry, including *Blossoming of the Earth, Communist,* and *The Dread Thicket.* He was a reporter for a number of newspapers between 1933 and 1941 and served as a correspondent during World War II. Kuleshov translated poetry into the Byelorussian language, edited the magazine *Literature and Art,* and directed the script department of the Byelorussian Film Studios. He was awarded two Stalin Prizes, an Order of Lenin, and an Order of the Red Banner. Obituaries and other sources: *New York Times,* February 10, 1978.

*   *   *

KUO Mo-Jo   1892-1978

November, 1892—June 12, 1978; Chinese poet, novelist, playwright, essayist, and historian. Kuo was a literary and political figure of long standing in China. His immense output of books included *Goddess, Fallen Leaves, The Bronze Age,* and *Starry Canopy,* as well as Chinese translations of the works of Goethe, Nietzsche, Marx, Turgenev, and Galsworthy. During World War II he wrote anti-Japanese propaganda. Although Kuo announced his conversion to Marxism in 1924, he did not join the Communist party until 1958. He was a vice-chairman for both the National People's Congress and the Chinese People's Political Consultative Conference, and also president of the Academy of Sciences. In 1951 Kuo received the Stalin Peace Prize. While he did briefly fall into disfavor with authorities at the beginning of the Cultural Revolution in 1966, Kuo managed to emerge with his reputation intact. Obituaries and other sources: David Tod Roy, *Kuo Mo-Jo: The Early Years,* Harvard University Press, 1971; *Who's Who in the World,* 2nd edition, Marquis, 1973; *Cassell's Encyclopaedia of World Literature,* revised edition, Morrow, 1973; *Dictionary of Oriental Literatures,* Basic Books, 1974; *The International Who's Who,* Europa, 1977; *New York Times,* June 14, 1978; *Washington Post,* June 14, 1978; *Time,* June 26, 1978.

*   *   *

KUTSCHER, Charles L(awrence)   1936-

PERSONAL: Born September 8, 1936, in Harvey, Ill.; son of Vernon C. (a salesman) and Nell (a secretary and administrator; maiden name, Owings) Kutscher; married Irene Coffin (a teacher), June 11, 1960; children: Cheryl Sue, Nancy Lynne. *Education:* Georgetown College, Georgetown, Ky., B.A., 1958; University of Illinois, M.A., 1961, Ph.D., 1962. *Home address:* Route 80, Fabius, N.Y. 13063. *Office:* Department of Psychology, Collondale Laboratory, Syracuse University, Syracuse, N.Y. 13210.

CAREER: Syracuse University, Syracuse, N.Y., assistant professor, 1962-67, associate professor, 1967-73, professor of psychology, 1973—. *Member:* American Association for the Advancement of Science, American Psychological Association, Animal Behavior Society, Eastern Psychological Association.

WRITINGS: (Editor) *Readings in Comparative Studies of Animal Behavior,* Xerox Education Group, 1971; (with P. A. Renquist, W. J. Meyer, and others) *Discovering Psychology,* Science Research Associates, 1977. Contributor to scientific journals.

WORK IN PROGRESS: Hormonal Determinants of Blood Pressure; research on the physiology of taste aversion in rodents.

SIDELIGHTS: Kutscher writes: "I am concerned about the relevance of animal models in bio-medical research for problems of importance to man. For example, what can studies of rodent blood pressure tell us about human blood pressure? I am particularly interested in the biological mechanisms which mediate behavior."

*   *   *

KUTTNER, Paul   1931-

PERSONAL: Born September 20, 1931, in Berlin, Germany; son of Paul (a physician) and Margarete (a piano teacher; maiden name, Fraenkel) Kuttner; married Myrtil Romegialli, September, 1956 (divorced, 1960); married Ursula Timmermann, 1963 (divorced, 1970). *Education:* Educated in Berlin, Germany and Dorset, England. *Religion:* "Firm believer in the Universal Creator, but not in organized religion." *Home:* 37-26 87th St., Jackson Heights, N.Y. 11372. *Office:* Guinness Book of World Records, 26th floor, Two Park Ave., New York, N.Y. 10016.

CAREER: Der Weg (weekly newspaper), Bern, Switzerland, political, economic and cultural reporter, and correspondent in London, England, 1946-47; *London News Chronicle*, London, England, U.S. correspondent, 1948; *What's On in London—The London Week*, London, England, columnist in Hollywood, Calif. and New York City, 1948-56; Watson-Guptill Publications, Inc., New York City, salesperson, 1954-62; *Guinness Book of World Records*, New York City, publicity director, 1966—. Social worker with Bureau of Displaced Persons, Church World Service, 1948-53.

WRITINGS—Novel: *The Man Who Lost Everything*, Sterling, 1977.

Juvenile; translator from the German; all published by Sterling: Katharina Zechlin, *Creative Enamelling and Jewelry Making*, 1965; T. M. Schegger, *Make Your Own Mobiles*, 1965; A. Pflunger, *Karate: Basic Principles*, 1967; Susanne Strose, *Coloring Papers*, 1968; Strose, *Potato Printing*, 1968; Strose, *Candle Making*, 1968; Elmar Gruber, *Nail Sculpture*, 1968; Peter and Susanne Bauzen, *Flower Pressing*, 1972; Charles H. Paraquin, *Eye-Teasers: Optical Illusions and Puzzles*, 1976.

WORK IN PROGRESS: Absolute Proof, for Sterling; a play, "Odyssey Without End."

SIDELIGHTS: Kuttner told *CA:* "Having been raised on the Spahn Ranch of *Mittel Europa* (Nazi Germany) in the 1930's, the melodrama and the tragedy of that era have left an indelible stamp on my mind, my writing, and the skepticism of my lifestyle. Melodrama: visiting my father at Berlin's Universum Film Aktiengesellschaft (UFA) movie studio where he was doctor-in-residence, watching Emil Jannings perform before the cameras, my filmed conversation with Hitler, and observing the political, racial, and cultural madness of the Nazi era in Berlin until 1939. Then the tragedy: my parents murdered in a concentration camp, my sister, Annemarie, forced to live underground, and later dying of cancer, and I on my own at the age of eight, in England, where I spent my summer vacations with the chairman of Lloyd's of London and was wounded by a V-1 flying bomb. These early events influenced my life more than any single work or writer.

"In the end," Kuttner recalled, "it was literature—Shakespeare, Tolstoy, Shaw, Forster, Greene, Salinger, Hemingway, Wolfe, Goethe—which generously and mercifully opened my eyes to look at the world with a clearer vision. Literature let me see life from a less hunted and more tranquil, contemplative perspective. It, more than any person, became my balm—the motivating factor that finally triggered my determination to settle down after a restless life and two marriages and write, write, write."

AVOCATIONAL INTERESTS: Photography, amateur film-directing, oil painting.

L

LACEY, Jeannette F.

PERSONAL: Born in Colorado; daughter of George (a carpenter) and Jeannette Adams; married Richard E. Fields (died, 1942); married Gerald F. Lacey (a contractor), February 29, 1952. *Education:* University of Northern Colorado, B.A.; University of Denver, M.A. *Politics:* Democrat. *Religion:* Protestant. *Home:* 7300 West 33rd Ave., Wheat Ridge, Colo. 80033.

CAREER: Former teacher at University of Manitoba, Winnipeg, University of Colorado, Denver, University of Northern Colorado, Greeley, and University of Denver, Denver, Colo.; currently assistant superintendant of public schools in Denver.

WRITINGS: Young Art: Nature and Seeing, Van Nostrand, 1973.

*   *   *

LACY, Gerald M(orris) 1940-

PERSONAL: Born September 18, 1940, in Greenville, Tex.; son of James M. (a professor of English) and Jennie (a teacher; maiden name, Titus) Lacy. *Education:* East Texas State University, B.A., 1963; University of Texas, Ph.D., 1969. *Home and office address:* P.O. Box 10954, Angelo State University, San Angelo, Tex. 76901.

CAREER: Angelo State University, San Angelo, Tex., assistant professor, 1969-75, associate professor of English, 1975—. Tutor at University of Manchester, 1971-72. *Military service:* U.S. Marine Corps, 1959-61. *Member:* South Central Modern Language Association. *Awards, honors:* Leverhulme fellow at University of Manchester, 1971-72; National Endowment for the Humanities research grant, 1977-78.

WRITINGS: (Editor) D. H. Lawrence, *The Escaped Cock,* Black Sparrow Press, 1973; (editor) *The Letters of D. H. Lawrence to Thomas and Adele Seltzer,* Black Sparrow Press, 1976; *A Calendar of the Letters of D. H. Lawrence,* University of Texas Press, 1976. Member of editorial board of "The Letters of D. H. Lawrence," Cambridge University Press.

WORK IN PROGRESS: A critical study of Anne Sexton; editing the German letters of D. H. Lawrence; editing *The Letters of D. H. Lawrence,* Volume VI, publication by Cambridge University Press expected in 1985.

La GUMINA, Salvatore John 1928-

PERSONAL: Born November 21, 1928, in Brooklyn, N.Y.; son of Giacomo (a plasterer) and Maria (a seamstress; maiden name, Madonia) La Gumina; married Juliana Heath, August 18, 1956; children: Frank, Mary, John, Cristine. *Education:* Attended St. Mary's College, St. Mary, Ky., 1951-52; Duquesne University, B.Ed., 1955; St. John's University, Jamaica, N.Y., M.S.Ed., 1957, Ph.D., 1966. *Religion:* Roman Catholic. *Home:* 32 Fairview Rd., West Massapequa, N.Y. 11758. *Office:* Department of History and Political Science, Nassau Community College, Garden City, N.Y. 11530.

CAREER: Factory worker in New York, N.Y. and Pittsburgh, Pa., 1946-55; public school teacher in Massapequa, N.Y., 1956-61; Nassau Community College, Garden City, N.Y., assistant professor, 1961-65, associate professor, 1965-68, professor of history and political science, 1968—. *Member:* American Historical Association, American Italian Historical Association (president). *Awards, honors:* Freedoms Foundation award, 1961, for radio series "Your Heritage, America: Its Principles and Challenges"; State University of New York fellowships, 1967-68.

WRITINGS: (Editor) *Ethnicity in American Life: The Italian-American Experience* (pamphlet), American Italian Historical Association, 1969; *Vito Marcantonio: The People's Politician,* Kendall/Hunt, 1969; (contributor) S. M. Tomasi and Madeline Engel, editors, *The Italian Experience in the United States,* Center for Migration Studies, 1970; (editor with Francesco Cordasco) *Italians in the United States: A Bibliography of Reports, Texts, Critical Studies, and Related Material,* Oriole, 1972; *An Album of Italian-Americans,* F. Watts, 1972; *WOP!: A Documentary History of Anti-Italian Discrimination in the United States,* Straight Arrow Press, 1973; (editor with Frank J. Cavaioli) *The Ethnic Dimension in American Society,* Holbrook, 1974. Contributor to history and Italian studies journals in the United States and Italy, to *Newsday,* and to newspapers. Editor of radio series "Your Heritage, America: Its Principles and Challenges" for WHLZ-Radio, 1961-62.

WORK IN PROGRESS: Studying the Italian-American immigration experience.

*   *   *

LALLY, Michael 1942-

PERSONAL: Born May 25, 1942, in Orange, N.J.; son of

James A. and Irene (Dempsey) Lally; married Carol Lee, August 8, 1964 (divorced); children: Caitlin Maeve, Miles Aaron. *Education:* University of Iowa, B.A., 1968, M.F.A., 1969. *Home:* 190 A Duane St., New York, N.Y. 10013. *Office:* 801 Second Ave., New York, N.Y. 10017.

CAREER: Trinity College, Washington, D.C., instructor, 1969-74; Franklin Library, New York, N.Y., editor, 1976—. Poet and musician. Member of board of directors of Print Center, 1972-77, and Washington Film Classroom, 1972; founder and president of Some of Us Press, 1972-75; founder and director of Mass Transit Poetry Project, 1972-76. *Military service:* U.S. Air Force, 1962-66.

MEMBER: National Book Critics Circle, Poetry Society of America, P.E.N. *Awards, honors:* Discovery award from New York Poetry Center, 1972, for "92nd Street 'Y' "; National Endowment for the Humanities fellow, 1974; award from New York Poets Foundation, 1974.

WRITINGS—Poetry: What Withers, Doones Press, 1970; *The Lines Are Drawn,* Asphalt Press, 1970; *Stupid Rabbits,* Morgan Press, 1971; *MCMLXVI Poem,* Nomad Press, 1971; *The South Orange Sonnets,* Some of Us Press, 1972; *Late Sleepers,* Pellet Press, 1973; *My Life,* Wyrd Press, 1975; *Rocky Dies Yellow,* Blue Wind Press, 1975; *Dues,* Stonewall Press, 1975; (editor) *None of the Above,* Crossing Press, 1976; *Catch My Breath* (prose and poems), Lucky Heart Books, 1977; *In the Mood,* Titanic Books, 1978; *Just Let Me Do It,* Vehicle Editions, 1978. Contributor to more than two hundred magazines. Editor of periodicals, including *Iowa Defender, Daily Iowan, Campus Underground,* and *Washington Review of the Arts;* reviewer for *Washington Post* 1975—, author of column, "Alternate Currents," for *Village Voice,* 1978—.

WORK IN PROGRESS: A novel; several collections of poems, including *In the Recent Future.*

SIDELIGHTS: Lally comments: "I started out as a musician (piano and bass), mostly jazz, so music, especially American music, has been a great source of inspiration for my work and the generating force behind my ideas on structure and movement, both in poetry and prose."

BIOGRAPHICAL/CRITICAL SOURCES: Sun and Moon Quarterly, spring, 1976.

* * *

LAMPSON, Robin 1900-1978

February 2, 1900—1978; American poet and novelist. Lampson's best-known books were two novels written in free verse, *Laughter Out of the Ground* and *Death Loses a Pair of Wings.* He was also a contributor to periodicals and a writer of historical works on California. He died in Orangevale, Calif. Obituaries and other sources: *AB Bookman's Weekly,* June 19, 1978.

* * *

LANDO, Barry Mitchell 1939-

PERSONAL: Born June 8, 1939, in Vancouver, British Columbia, Canada; son of Edmond (a lawyer) and Edith (Mitchell) Lando; married Moreno Fernande (a travel agent); children: Jeffrey Alain, Dominique Sylvie. *Education:* Harvard University, B.A. (magna cum laude), 1961, graduate study, 1961-62; also attended Columbia University, 1962-63. *Religion:* Jewish. *Office:* CBS News, 2020 M St. N.W., Washington, D.C. 20036.

CAREER/WRITINGS: Time, New York City, correspon-

dent in Latin America, 1963-67; Columbia Broadcasting System (CBS), New York City, 1967-78, associate producer of "CBS News," then producer of "CBS News" and "Sixty Minutes"; American Broadcasting Co. (ABC), European producer of "0-20," 1978—. Contributor to periodicals including *Atlantic, Christian Science Monitor, New Republic, Toronto Globe and Mail,* and *Washington Monthly. Awards, honors:* Received Emmy Award from Academy of Television Arts and Sciences, 1973, for "The Selling of Colonel Herbert"; George Polk Award, 1978, for "Sixty Minutes."

* * *

LANDON, H(oward) C(handler) Robbins 1926-

PERSONAL: Born March 6, 1926, in Boston, Mass.; son of William Grinell (a writer) and Dorothea Le B. (a musician; maiden name, Robbins) Landon; married Christa Fuhrmann, March 13, 1951 (divorced); married Else Radant, November 6, 1957. *Education:* Attended Swarthmore College, 1943-44; Boston University, B.Mus., 1947. *Religion:* Episcopalian. *Home:* Anton Frankgasse 3, Vienna 1180, Austria. *Agent:* Georges Borchardt, Inc., 145 East 52nd St., New York, N.Y. 10022.

CAREER: Haydn Society, Vienna, Austria, secretary general, 1949-52; writer, 1952—. Visiting professor at Queens College of the City University of New York, 1969; Regis Professor at University of California, Davis, 1970, 1975; honorary professorial fellow of University of Wales University College in Cardiff, 1971—. *Military service:* U.S. Army, 1947-48; served in Austria. *Member:* Zentralinstitut fuer Mozartforschung, Internationale Stifftung Mozarteum. *Awards, honors:* D.Mus. from Boston University, 1969, and Queen's University, Belfast, 1974; service cross for art and science from Austrian Government, 1973.

WRITINGS: The Symphonies of Joseph Haydn, Barrie & Rockliff, 1955; (editor with Donald Mitchell) *The Mozart Companion,* Barrie & Rockliff, 1956; *The Collected Correspondence and London Notebooks of Joseph Haydn,* Barrie & Rockliff, 1959; *Beethoven: A Documentary Biography,* Thames & Hudson, 1970; *Haydn: Chronicle and Works,* Indiana University Press, Volume III, 1976, Volume IV, 1977, Volume V, 1977, Volume II, 1978, Volume I, in press. Also editor of critical editions of works by Haydn, Mozart, Johann Christian Bach, Johann Michael Haydn, and other eighteenth-century composers.

Television programs: "Haydn," British Broadcasting Corp. (BBC)-TV, 1964; "Vivaldi," BBC-TV, 1965; "Mozart," BBC-TV, 1966; "Monteverdi," BBC-TV, 1967; "Beethoven" (three programs), BBC-TV, 1970; "Haydn's 'Linfefelta delusa' in Tuscany," French Television, 1974.

Author of a lecture series for BBC.

SIDELIGHTS: Landon comments briefly: "I speak and write in English, German, French, and Italian. For fifteen years I lived in a Tuscan hill town (Buggiano Castello, Pistoia, 1959-74). I now have a country cottage in Austria near the Czech border where I write. I am a practicing musician (organ, piano), but specialize on eighteenth-century Austrian music."

AVOCATIONAL INTERESTS: Swimming, travel, walking, cooking.

* * *

LANDRETH, Catherine 1899-

PERSONAL: Born July 20, 1899, in Dunedin, New Zealand; daughter of Robert and Elizabeth (Faulkes) Landreth. *Education:* University of Otago, B.Sc., 1920; Iowa State University, M.S., 1926; University of California, Berkeley, Ph.D., 1936. *Politics:* Democrat. *Religion:* Protestant. *Home:* 2465 Hilgard Ave., Berkeley, Calif. 94709.

CAREER: University of Chicago, Chicago, Ill., assistant professor of home economics, 1936-38; University of California, Berkeley, professor of home economics and psychology, 1938-64. Summer lecturer at University of Hawaii, Oregon State University, and University of Arizona. *Member:* Sigma Xi, Omicron Nu, Delta Phi Upsilon. *Awards, honors:* Fulbright grant for Victoria University, 1959.

WRITINGS: The Education of the Young Child, Wiley, 1942; *The Psychology of Early Childhood,* Knopf, 1958; *Early Childhood: Behavior and Learning,* Knopf, 1967; *Preschool Learning and Teaching,* Harper, 1972. Contributor to professional journals.

WORK IN PROGRESS: Research for books on human behavior, for the general reader.

SIDELIGHTS: Catherine Landreth told *CA* that "keeping one foot in each of two countries, the United States and New Zealand, I think, stimulates my awareness of the influences of the social climate on human development."

* * *

LANDY, David 1917-

PERSONAL: Born June 4, 1917, in Savannah, Ga.; son of Charles Edwin (a merchant) and Tillie (Rabinowitz) Landy; married Louise Fleming (a macrame artist and teacher), March 18, 1949; children: Laura Louise, Lisa Ann, Jonathan Fleming. *Education:* Armstrong Junior College, A.A., 1948; University of North Carolina, B.A., 1949, M.A., 1950; Harvard University, Ph.D., 1956. *Home:* 60 Endicott St., Newton Highlands, Mass. 02161. *Office:* Department of Anthropology, University of Massachusetts, Boston, Mass. 02125.

CAREER: Boston University, Boston, Mass., lecturer in anthropology, 1953-58; Harvard University, Cambridge, Mass., research associate in anthropology, 1956-60; University of Pittsburgh, Pittsburgh, Pa., associate professor, 1960-63, professor of anthropology, 1963-70, chairman of department, 1963-70; University of Massachusetts, Boston, professor of anthropology, 1970—, chairman of department, 1970-75. *Military service:* U.S. Army, Signal Corps, 1944-46; became staff sergeant.

MEMBER: American Anthropological Association (fellow), Society for Applied Anthropology (fellow), American Association for the Advancement of Science (fellow), American Society for Ethnohistory (member of executive board, 1963), American Ethnological Society, Society for Medical Anthropology (member of executive committee, 1977—), American Association of University Professors, Faculty-Staff Union (University of Massachusetts; member of steering committee, 1977—).

WRITINGS: Tropical Childhood: Cultural Learning and Transmission in a Rural Puerto Rican Community, University of North Carolina Press, 1959; (with Milton Greenblatt) *Halfway House,* U.S. Department of Health, Education & Welfare, 1965; (editor and contributor) *Culture, Disease, and Healing: Studies in Medical Anthropology,* Macmillan, 1977. Contributor of articles and reviews to anthropological and behavioral science journals. Associate editor of *Ethnology,* 1961-70; member of manuscript review committee of *Behavioral Science,* 1970—.

WORK IN PROGRESS: Investigating social-cultural correlates of magical death and studying the anthropology of death, with a book expected to result.

SIDELIGHTS: Tropical Childhood is based on two years of research in Puerto Rico and nearly one year in a rural community studying the socialization process in the context of local cultural and social structure. Landy's approach combines participant observation, interviews, projective doll play, and descriptive and statistical analyses of data. Landy's next book, *Halfway House,* is a participant observation study of a transitional residence for discharged female psychiatric patients in Boston based on interviews with residents and staff. It is the first full-length study of a half-way house in the United States.

Culture, Disease, and Healing represents the first attempt to put together a series of representative studies in medical anthropology and to present an integrated approach to the field.

Landy writes that while "emphases in studies of magical (voodoo) death have been mainly on physiological and psychological factors," his own current research attempt is "to discover and analyse social-cultural correlates. Related studies in the anthropology of death are an attempt to survey the literature in this field and see whether an integrated approach can be defined to the study of this most important but relatively neglected aspect of anthropology."

* * *

LANG, Fritz 1890-1976

PERSONAL: Born December 5, 1890, in Vienna, Austria; came to United States, 1934; naturalized U.S. citizen, 1939; son of Anton (an architect) and Paula (Schlesinger) Lang; married Thea von Harbou (a writer), 1920 (divorced, 1933). *Education:* Attended College of Technical Science in Vienna, 1908, and Academy of Graphic Art in Munich, 1911; also studied painting in Paris. *Home:* 1501 Summitridge Dr., Beverly Hills, Calif. 90210.

CAREER: Screenwriter, director, and producer of motion pictures. Associated with Decla Bioscop Company in Berlin, Germany, 1919-34, and Metro-Goldwyn-Mayer, 1934-37. Director of motion pictures, including "Liliom," 1935, "You Only Live Once," 1937, "Return of Frank James," 1940, "Western Union," 1941, "Man Hunt," 1941, "Ministry of Fear," 1945, "Cloak and Dagger," 1946, "Rancho Notorious," 1952, "The Big Heat," 1953, and "Beyond a Reasonable Doubt," 1956. Actor in "Contempt," 1963. *Military service:* Served in Austrian Army during World War I. *Awards, honors:* Received commander's cross Order of Merit from Federal Republic of Germany; Golden Ribbon Motion Picture Art award from German Federal Government; Order of Arts and Letters (officer) from France; Order of the Yugoslavian Flag with golden wreath, 1971; honorary professorship from University of Vienna, 1973.

WRITINGS—Published screenplays: *M,* Simon & Schuster, 1968; *Metropolis,* Simon & Schuster, 1970.

Screenplays; screenwriter and director; all with wife, Thea von Harbou Lang: "Halbblut" (released in U.S. as "The Weakling"), Decla Bioscop, 1919; "Der Muede Tod" (released in U.S. as "Destiny"), Decla Bioscop, 1921; "Dr. Mabuse, Der Spieler" (released in U.S. as "Dr. Mabuse, the Gambler"), Decla Bioscop, 1922; "Siegfried," Decla Bioscop, 1924; "Metropolis," Decla Bioscop, 1927; "Spione" (released in U.S. as "The Spy"), Decla Bioscop, 1927; "Spione" (adapted from the motion picture), 1928;

"Kriemhild's Revenge," 1928; "Frau im Mond" (released in U.S. as "The Girl in the Moon"), 1928; "M," 1933; "Das Testament des Dr. Mabuse" (released in U.S. as "The Last Will of Dr. Mabuse"), 1933.

Other screenplays; all as screenwriter and director: "The Last Will of Dr. Mabuse" (adapted from the motion picture), produced in France, 1935; (with Bartlett Cormick) "Fury," Metro-Goldwyn-Mayer, 1936; (with Bertolt Brecht) "Hangmen Also Die," United Artists, 1943; "The 1,000 Eyes of Dr. Mabuse," produced in Germany, 1960.

SIDELIGHTS: Lang began his career as an artist but turned to films as a means of income after being hospitalized with a war injury. Prior to World War I, he had traveled in Europe, Asia, Africa, and the South Seas supporting himself by peddling his art on postcards and to newspapers. During an exhibition of his paintings in Paris, Lang was informed that war had broken out and he hurried back to his native Vienna. Inducted into the Austrian Army, Lang was wounded several times and eventually spent a year recuperating in the hospital. With little to entertain himself, he began writing short stories, screenplays, and ideas for films. Surprisingly good, many of the crime oriented scripts were purchased by filmmakers in Berlin and soon after leaving the hospital, Lang accepted a position as script reader with Decla Bioscop. Rising quickly to scenario writer and then to director, Lang made his first film in 1919. "The Weakling" explored the theme of self-destructive love, one which Lang would turn to many times in later films such as "Liliom," "The Woman in the Window," and "Rancho Notorious."

Lang followed "The Weakling" with a pair of lengthier projects. In 1922, he filmed the first of three Dr. Mabuse films, "Dr. Mabuse, the Gambler." Mabuse was a sinister criminal of such magnitude that in the second film, "The Last Will of Dr. Mabuse," the evil doctor mouthed Nazi slogans with little change of character from the pre-Nazi original. It was this second Mabuse film that resulted in Lang's departure from Germany. The Nazi censors had banned the film but, in recognizing Lang's talents, had offered him the opportunity to make pro-Nazi films. Hating the Nazi's intensely and fearing they would eventually discover his Jewish ancestry, Lang returned home after meeting with propaganda minister Joseph Goebbels and stuffed his pockets with his possessions. He fled to France whereupon he remade "The Last Will of Dr. Mabuse."

Lang's other lengthy project was a two-part motion picture based on the Nordic legends of Siegfried. Collectively referred to as "Die Nibelungen," the work is comprised of "Siegfried" and "Kriemhild's Revenge." An immensely ambitious project, "Die Nibelungen" creatively employed the same myths which had been used decades earlier by composer Richard Wagner in his opera, "The Ring of the Nibelung."

Between the Mabuse and Nibelungen projects is one of Lang's two great films, "Metropolis." The futuristic tale of capitalist excess in a world faced with tyranny and overpopulation, "Metropolis" was the forerunner of such diverse films as "The Day the Earth Stood Still" and Chaplin's "Modern Times." Lang conceived his expressionist vision when he gazed upon the skyline during a brief visit to New York City. He returned to Germany and recreated one of the most strikingly innovative and original sets in film history. Shot in stark contrasts with lighting that lent a nightmarish quality to the film, "Metropolis" is recognized today as a milestone in cinema.

Oddly enough, Lang himself had little regard for the film. "I didn't like the picture," he once said, "thought it was silly and stupid. . . ." It is not certain why Lang hated "Metropolis." Possibly, its popularity among the Nazis he so despised and the realization of some of the concepts suggested in the film swayed his assessment. In an interview with Peter Bogdanovich, Lang commented, "Should I say now that I like 'Metropolis' because something I have seen in my imagination comes true—when I detested it after it was finished?"

Lang's one film that rivals "Metropolis" on innovative and thematic grounds is "M." Filmed in 1933, the year before he left Germany, "M" is the often horrifying, often sympathetic study of a psychopathic child murderer. It follows the child murderer's progress as he is seen alone in his room, aware of his madness, to his stalking the children, to becoming stalked himself by both the police and the underworld in what is one of the most chilling climaxes in cinema.

Among the first German sound films, "M" is recognized as much for its innovative soundtrack as for its bizarre story. Lang used sound sparingly in the film but with great effect. One of the more noted scenes in the film occurs when the killer's shadow drifts across the screen towards that of a little girl. The camera cuts to an empty dinner table and then back to where the killer and girl were. All the while, voiced over the soundtrack is the mother's cry for the daughter. The cries become more urgent as the camera cuts between the two places. But where the killer and child once stood, now drifts only a balloon, the device the murderer used to initially acquaint himself with the girl. Further, Lang identified sound with the killer by having him whistle the opening bars of Grieg's "In the Hall of the Mountain King." As Albin Krebs commented, the killer's whistle "threads through the film, ominously foreboding his appearances."

With "Metropolis" and "M," Lang had spent the maximum of his talents. Later films such as "You Only Live Once," "Return of Frank James," "Ministry of Fear," and "The Big Heat," all made in the United States, showed his obsession with the darker side of human nature. "I am profoundly fascinated by cruelty, fear, horror and death," Lang once said. "My films show my preoccupation with violence, the pathology of violence."

Lang never enjoyed the notoriety in the United States that he had in Germany. Although his films were still technically competent and interesting, he abandoned his innovative and stylized approach to cinema in favor of exploring his themes through specific genres such as the western and the gangster film. He returned to Germany in 1958 to make two films, "While the City Sleeps" and the third Mabuse, "The 1,000 Eyes of Dr. Mabuse," but the films were poorly received by both the public and the critics. After appearing as himself in Jean Luc-Godard's "Contempt," Lang removed himself from the film world but he never forgot his contributions to the art form which he helped shape. When interviewed by Mary Blume, who confronted Lang with his Hollywood-evolved reputation as a "difficult" director, he replied, somewhat bitterly: "Difficult! Do you know what that means? It means you're a perfectionist. Hollywood hates perfectionists."

BIOGRAPHICAL/CRITICAL SOURCES: Sight and Sound, summer, 1955, autumn, 1955, winter, 1961-62, summer, 1967; *Films and Filming,* June, 1962; Paul M. Jensen, *The Cinema of Fritz Lang,* A. S. Barnes, 1968; Lotte Eisner, *Fritz Lang,* Oxford University Press, 1977. Obituaries: *New York Times,* August 3, 1976; *Washington Post,* August 4, 1976.*

(Died August 2, 1976, in Beverly Hills, Calif.)

LANGDON, Charles 1934-

PERSONAL: Born August 13, 1934, in Newton, Mass.; son of Lloyd J. and Mary (DeDoming) Langdon; married Laura Macchiarini (a clerk and calligrapher), July 2, 1965; children: Matthew D. Education: University of Colorado, B.A., 1958. Home: 298 East Park Ave., Durango, Colo. 81301. Office: Southwest Library System, Miller Student Center, Durango, Colo. 81301.

CAREER: Stanford University Press, Palo Alto, Calif., proofreader, 1965-66; Durango Herald, Durango, Colo., sports editor, 1967-68, feature editor, 1968-71; Southwest Library System, Durango, reference librarian, 1973—. Directed local ice hockey program for young people, 1968-70. Worked in public relations for Purgatory Ski Area, 1970-73. Military service: U.S. Army, Public Information Office, 1958-60. Awards, honors: Ann Hafen Woodbury Poetry Award from Colorado Poetry Society, 1974, for "My Lost Brother."

WRITINGS—One-act plays: "Socrates Is," first produced in Durango, Colo., at Diamond Circle Theatre, April 5, 1969; "Footlocker," first produced in Denver, Colo., at Changing Scene, July 2, 1970; "Unidentified Flying Angel," first produced in Denver at Changing Scene, February 3, 1971; "The Supreme Equal," first produced in Denver at Changing Scene, May 9, 1972; "The Imperial Hero Explains," first produced in Denver at Changing Scene, September 7, 1973. Contributor to magazines and newspapers, including Colorado Outdoors, Rocky Mountain Review, and Skier's Gazette.

WORK IN PROGRESS: The Mountains and the Sea, a novel for young adults; The Backyard Astronomer, notes and meditations on the night sky as seen through a small telescope.

SIDELIGHTS: Langdon writes: "In a literary sense, I'm a sprinter who is learning to be a long-distance runner. I am learning to enjoy every line that I write and rewrite. It will take me some time, but I will reach my goal. And my goal is to create books and full-length plays which people will enjoy reading and seeing as much as they have enjoyed my shorter works."

*   *   *

LANKEVICH, George J(ohn) 1939-

PERSONAL: Born April 23, 1939, in New York, N.Y.; son of George C. and Madeline Lankevich; married Josette Napolitano, July 24, 1965; children: George M., Christine. Education: Fordham College (now University), B.S., 1959; Columbia University, M.A., 1960, Ph.D., 1967. Office: Department of History, Bronx Community College of the City University of New York, Bronx, N.Y. 10453.

CAREER: Bronx Community College of the City University of New York, Bronx, N.Y., professor of history, 1975—.

WRITINGS: Boston: A Chronological/Documentary History, Oceana, 1974; (with Wallace Sokolsky) Ideas that Made Modern History, Kendall/Hunt, 1976; Milwaukee: A Chronological/Documentary History, Oceana, 1977; The Presidency of Gerald Ford, Oceana, 1977.

WORK IN PROGRESS: Histories of Atlanta and the Texas republic.

*   *   *

LANZILLOTTI, Robert F(ranklin) 1921-

PERSONAL: Born June 19, 1921, in Washington, D.C.; son of Vincent and Gilda Lanzillotti; married Patricia J. Jackson; children: Robert, Donna. Education: American University, B.A., 1947, M.A., 1948; University of California, Berkeley, Ph.D., 1952. Politics: Republican. Religion: Roman Catholic. Home: 2135 Northwest 28th St., Gainesville, Fla. 32607. Office: College of Business Administration, University of Florida, Gainesville, Fla. 32611.

CAREER: Employed by Carnegie Corp. New York, 1957-59; member of Washington State Governor's Advisory Expenditure Council, 1959-60, Michigan State University, East Lansing, professor of economics, 1961-68, chairman of department, 1969; University of Florida, Gainesville, professor of economics, 1969—, director of Public Policy Research Center. Member of permanent subcommittee on investigations, U.S. Senate Committee on Government Operations, 1962, and U.S. Price Commission, 1971-73; member of board of trustees of Michigan Council on Economic Education, 1964-68, and Florida governor's economic advisory board, 1973—. Member of board of directors of First City National Bank, Gainesville, 1973—, and Jim Walter Corp., 1977—. Consultant to federal and state agencies. Military service: U.S. Navy, 1943-46; became lieutenant commander; received two Bronze Stars.

MEMBER: American Economic Association, American Association of University Professors (local president, 1954-55), Southern Economic Association (first vice-president, 1972-73), Western Economic Association (member of executive committee, 1952-54), Phi Beta Kappa (local president, 1966-67).

WRITINGS: (With R. D. Tousley) The Spokane Wholesale Market: An Economic Analysis, Washington State University Press, 1952; The Hard-Surface Floor Covering Industry: A Case Study of Market Structure and Competitive Behavior in Oligopoly, Washington State University Press, 1955; (with J. B. Dirlam and A. D. H. Kaplan) Pricing in Big Business, Brookings Institution, 1958; (contributor) Walter Adams, editor, The Structure of American Industry, Macmillan, 1961; Pricing, Production, and Marketing Policies of Small Manufacturers, Washington State University Press, 1964; (contributor) Adams, editor, The Structure of American Industry, Macmillan, 1971; Phase II in Review: The Price Commission Experience, Brookings Institution, 1975; (contributor) A. P. Jacquemin and H. W. deJong, editors, Markets, Corporate Behavior, and the State, Nijhoff, 1976; Micro and Macro Economic Effects of Regulation Through Mandated Standards, University of Florida Press, 1978. Also author of Banking Structure in Michigan, 1945-1963, 1966. Contributor to Encyclopaedia Britannica. Contributor of about thirty articles to professional journals and to Challenge and other magazines.

*   *   *

LAPHAM, Lewis H(enry) 1935-

PERSONAL: Born January 8, 1935, in San Francisco, Calif.; son of Lewis Abbot (a banker) and Jane (Foster) Lapham; married Joan Brooke Reeves, August 10, 1972; children: Lewis Anthony Polk, Elizabeth Sophia. Education: Yale University, B.A., 1956; further study at Cambridge University, 1956-57. Home: 988 Fifth Ave., New York, N.Y. 10021. Office: Harper's, 2 Park Ave., New York, N.Y. 10016.

CAREER/WRITINGS: San Francisco Examiner, San Francisco, Calif., reporter, 1957-60; New York Herald Tribune, New York City, reporter, 1960-62; Saturday Evening Post, New York City, writer, 1963-67; Life, New York City, writer, 1968-70; *Harper's,* New York City, managing editor, 1971-75, editor, 1975—. *Member:* Yale Club, Coffee House Club, National Golf Links.

* * *

LAPIDUS, Morris 1902-

PERSONAL: Born November 25, 1902, in Odessa, Russia; son of Leon (a manufacturer) and Eva (Sherman) Lapidus; married wife, Beatrice, February 22, 1929; children: Richard Louis, Alan Harvey. *Education:* Attended New York University, 1921-23; Columbia University, B. Arch., 1927. *Politics:* Democrat. *Religion:* Jewish. *Home:* 3 Island Ave., Miami Beach, Fla. 33139. *Agent:* Julian Bach Literary Agency, Inc., 3 East 48th St., New York, N.Y. 10017. *Office:* 1301 Dade Blvd., Miami Beach, Fla. 33139.

CAREER: Morris Lapidus, Kornblath, Harle, & Liebman (architectural firm), Miami Beach, Fla., partner, 1957-60; Morris Lapidus, Harle & Liebman, Miami Beach, partner, 1960-62; Morris Lapidus-Liebman Associates, Miami Beach, partner, 1962-63; Morris Lapidus Associates, Miami Beach, president and principal, 1964—. Vice-president of Miami Beach Chamber of Commerce, 1967-69. *Member:* American Institute of Architects.

WRITINGS: Architecture: A Profession and a Business, Van Nostrand, 1967; *An Architecture of Joy,* E. A. Seemann, 1977. Contributor to architecture journals.

* * *

LARSEN, Carl 1934-
(Edna Poots-Booby)

PERSONAL: Born August 28, 1934, in Orange County, Calif.; son of Carl T. (a clerk) and Lucille (Porter) Larsen; married Celeste Rhodes (a college instructor), May 30, 1970; children: Catherine, Shoshana, David, Adam, Jason. *Education:* Attended El Camino College, 1954-56, and Actor's Studio, 1960-61. *Politics:* Liberal. *Religion:* None. *Home and office:* 84 Susquehanna Ave., Lock Haven, Pa. 17745. *Agent:* Foley Agency, 34 East 38th St., New York, N.Y. 10016.

CAREER: Western Freight Association, New York, N.Y., dispatcher, 1960-75; free-lance writer, 1975—. *Member:* Dramatists Guild. *Awards, honors:* National Endowment for the Arts grant, 1978-79.

WRITINGS: Notes From a Machine Shop (poems), Hennypenny Press, 1956; *The Journal of an Existentialist Villain* (poems), Hennypenny Press, 1957; *Arrows of Longing* (poems), Hearse Chapbooks, 1958; *Onan's Seed* (novel), Seven Poets Press, 1960; (with Jim Singer) *The Beat Generation Cook Book,* Seven Poets Press, 1961; *The Plot to Assassinate the Chase Manhattan Bank* (poems), Seven Poets Press, 1962; *The Naked and the Dead and the Catcher in the Rye and the Sick and the Sad and the Sorry Meet Frankenstein* (poems), Hors Commerce Press, 1963; *The Book of Eric Hammerscoffer* (novel), Tarot Press, 1964; *The Toad King* (poems), Goosetree Press, 1964; *The Popular Mechanics Book of Poetry,* Mimeo Press, 1966; *Ol' Peckerhead* (fiction), Samasdat, 1975; *The Midvale Chronicle* (fiction), New Earth Books, 1977; *The Amalgamated Lugwart Company Spare Parts Catalogue* (fiction), Cornerstone Press, 1977.

Plays: "The Census Bureau" (one-act), first produced in New York City at Riverdale Church, 1962; "The Plot to Assassinate the Chase Manhattan Bank" (one-act), first produced in New York City at Theatre East, 1963; "Who's Afraid of Edward Albee?" (one-act), first produced in New York City at Theatre East, 1963; "The Clocks" (one-act), first produced in New York City at Fulton Theatre, 1965; "Funny Side Up" (one-act), first produced in San Francisco, Calif., at Revue Theater, 1965; "You Guys Kill Me" (one-act), first produced in New York City at Fulton Theater, 1969; "Sue Loves Frankenstein" (two-act), first produced in New York City at Fulton Theater, 1970; "Several Objects Passing Charlies Greeley" (one-act), first produced in Milwaukee, Wis., at Milwaukee Repertory Theatre, 1972.

Writer and co-producer for radio series, "The Sowbelly Show," for WBPZ-AM-FM Radio, 1975-76. Author of syndicated weekly column, "Frying Pan Follies," 1977—.

Contributor to literary magazines, sometimes under pseudonym Edna Poots-Booby.

WORK IN PROGRESS: The Sands of Sorrow, a collection of radio sketches; *Frying Pan Follies,* a collection of newspaper columns; *Only a Gringo Would Die for an Anteater,* a biography, to be published by W. W. Norton.

SIDELIGHTS: Larsen writes: "An avowed humorist is either funny, or not. And I've found that social protest goes down a lot easier with a teaspoon of sugar. I've always felt like a sort of tourist on this funny planet; here to take pictures, to gather a few anecdotes (for the folks back on Betelgese), and—The Writer's Sacred Responsibility—to spread as much Chaos and Confusion as is possible, amongst the natives."

* * *

LARSON, Kris 1953-

PERSONAL: Born February 7, 1953, in Bangor, Maine; son of Vincent Karl (a general practitioner of medicine) and Elizabeth (a registered nurse; maiden name, Nief) Larson. *Education:* Attended University of Maine, 1971-73. *Politics:* Independent. *Religion:* "Agnostic; freethinker—Christian?" *Home address:* High St., East Machias, Me. 04630.

CAREER: Writer, 1972—. Has worked as blueberry raker, stableboy, housepainter, groundskeeper, and gardener. Former librarian of East Machias. *Member:* Maine Archaeological Society, Cutler Association, East Machias Historical Society (past vice-president).

WRITINGS: Groundwork (poetry), Salt-Works Press, 1974; *Second Thoughts* (poetry), Salt-Works Press, 1976. Sports writer for *Quoddy Times.*

WORK IN PROGRESS: Poems.

SIDELIGHTS: Larson writes: "Writing is uncertain territory, especially writing poems. I've been doing it for nearly six years, but it seems like only six weeks because of the uncertainty. There are times when not even my closest, and most supporting, friends are able to budge me from the doldrums. It takes that one good poem to start the process again and lead me to believe, if only temporarily, that I'm a poet, after abandoning other vocations."

* * *

LARSON, Orvin Prentiss 1910-

PERSONAL: Born April 18, 1910, in Minneapolis, Minn.; son of Magnus (a clergyman) and Laura (Oleson) Larson; married Ruth Holten, November 28, 1934 (died July, 1941); married Ruth Hetland, August 19, 1951; children: Karen, Erik, Kristi. *Education:* Augustana College, B.A., 1932; University of Iowa, M.A., 1937, Ph.D., 1939. *Home:* 230 Park Ave., Freeport, N.Y. 11520. *Office:* Department of

Speech, Brooklyn College of the City University of New York, Bedford & Ave. H., Brooklyn, N.Y. 11210.

CAREER: University of Denver, Denver, Colo., assistant professor of speech, 1939-40; University of Hawaii, Honolulu, instructor in English, 1940-41; Indiana University, Bloomington, professor of speech and theatre, 1941-43, acting chairperson of department of speech, 1943-45; Brooklyn College of the City University of New York, Brooklyn, N.Y., professor of speech, 1946—, chairperson of department of speech and theatre, 1952-72.

WRITINGS: (With Lee Norvelle and Raymond G. Smith) *Speaking Effectively,* Dryden, 1957; *American Infidel* (biography of Robert G. Ingersoll), Citadel, 1962; *When It's Your Turn to Speak,* Harper, 1962, revised edition, 1971.

WORK IN PROGRESS: The Wizard of the Great White Way, a biography of David Belasco.

* * *

LASKOWSKI, Jerzy 1919-

PERSONAL: Born April 12, 1919, in Cracow, Poland; came to the United States in 1952; married Janina Domanska (an artist), 1953. *Education:* Attended Lwow University.

CAREER: Staff correspondent for several Polish newspapers, 1936-39; later became editor for a newspaper published in Iraq and Palestine; writer. *Military service:* Enlisted in the Polish army, 1939; later joined the French Foreign Legion; served with the Second Polish Corps in the Middle East and Italy, 1942-45; became lieutenant.

WRITINGS: Master of the Royal Cats (illustrated by wife, Janina Domanska), Seabury, 1965; *The Dragon Liked Smoked Fish* (illustrated by Domanska), Seabury, 1967; (editor and translator) *Casanova's Book of Numbers and the Daily Horoscope,* Vulcan Books, 1975. Also author of *Tobruk* (poetry), published in Tel Aviv.

Plays: "The End of Adventure," produced in England in 1948; "Beautiful Helen" (a musical comedy), produced in England in 1949. Also writer of "Scandal in 'The Black Cat," 1934, "Case No. 113," produced in Palestine, and "The Dream of the Severed Head," 1976. Contributor of articles to newspapers during World War II.

SIDELIGHTS: Laskowski began creating stories and plays at an early age, and by the time he was eighteen, the young writer had already had his first book published and his first play performed on stage. Some of Laskowski's poems and plays have been translated into Hebrew and French.

* * *

LAU, Joseph S(hui) M(ing) 1934-

PERSONAL: Born July 9, 1934, in Hong Kong; came to United States in 1961, naturalized citizen, 1976; son of Wingfun and Sin-wen Lau; married Yu-shan Liu; children: Peter, Samuel. *Education:* National Taiwan University, B.A., 1960; Indiana University, Ph.D., 1966. *Office:* Department of East Asian Languages and Literature, University of Wisconsin, Madison, Wis. 53706.

CAREER: Chinese University of Hong Kong, Hong Kong, lecturer in English, 1968-71; University of Singapore, Singapore, senior lecturer in English, 1971-72; University of Hawaii, Honolulu, associate professor of Chinese literature, 1972-73; University of Wisconsin, Madison, professor of Chinese, 1977—. *Member:* American Comparative Literature Association, Association for Asian Studies. *Awards, honors:* American Council of Learned Societies fellow, 1975.

WRITINGS: Ts'ao Yu: A Study in Literary Influence, Hong Kong University Press, 1970; (editor) *Chinese Stories from Taiwan,* Columbia University Press, 1977; (editor with Y. W. Ma) *Traditional Chinese Stories: Themes and Variations,* Columbia University Press, 1978; (editor with C. T. Hsia and Leo Ou-fan Lee) *Modern Chinese Stories and Novellas,* Columbia University Press, in press.

Co-editor, "Chinese Translation" series, Indiana University Press, 1978—. Translator of works by Bernard Malamud and Saul Bellow into Chinese.

WORK IN PROGRESS: A translation from the Chinese, with Christopher Rand, of Ts'ao Yu's four-act play, *The Wilderness,* to be published by Hong Kong University Press.

* * *

LAUDIN, Harvey 1922-

PERSONAL: Born September 24, 1922, in Brooklyn, N.Y.; son of Abraham (an insurance agent) and Luella (a club woman; maiden name, Laudin) Levin; married Gloria Singer (a guidance counselor), May 31, 1948; children: Alan, David, Joyce. *Education:* Queens College (now of the University of New York), B.A., 1947; Hofstra University, M.S., 1963; New York University, M.A., 1970, Ed.D., 1974. *Home:* 10 Oakfield Ave., Freeport, N.Y. 11520. *Office:* C. W. Post College, Long Island University, Greenvale, N.Y. 11548.

CAREER: Long Island University, C. W. Post College, Greenvale, N.Y., lecturer, summer, 1969, instructor, 1969-74, assistant professor of sociology, 1974—, college representative to American Indian Conference, coordinator of archaeological excavation at Shinnecock Indian Reservation, 1977. Had a one-man American Indian exhibition, 1978; guest speaker for television documentary program, "Long Island Indians," produced at Hofstra University; adviser to Suffolk County Indian and Archaeological Museum and Black History Museum. *Member:* American Indian Historical Society, Eastern Sociological Society, Kappa Delta Pi (Beta Pi chapter).

WRITINGS: Victims of Culture, C. E. Merrill, 1973; *The Shinnecock Powwow: A Study of Culture Change,* University Microfilm, 1973; (contributor) Hernan LaFontaine, editor, *Bilingual Education,* Avery, 1978. Contributor to sociology and education journals.

WORK IN PROGRESS: Education of American Indians into Indian Americans.

SIDELIGHTS: Laudin writes: "Since 1973, I have traveled thirty thousand miles, visiting American Indian reservations and Canadian Indian reserves, photographing and taping ceremonies, interviews, and places, including museums and other locations related to native Americans and Canadians."

* * *

LAURENCE, William Leonard 1888-1977

PERSONAL: Surname legally changed in 1906; born March 7, 1888, in Salantai, Lithuania; came to United States in 1905, naturalized citizen, 1913; son of Lipman and Sarah (Preuss) Siew; married Florence Davidow, December 19, 1931. *Education:* Attended Harvard University, 1908-11, 1914-15, 1921, and University of Besancon, Besancon, France, 1919; Boston University, LL.B., 1925. *Residence:* Majorca, Spain.

CAREER: New York World, New York City, reporter,

1926-30; *New York Times*, New York City, science reporter, 1930-56, science editor, 1956-64, science editor emeritus, 1964-77. Notable assignments include coverage of the first nuclear test blast in Alamogordo, N.M., 1945, the atomic bombing of Nagasaki, Japan, 1945, and the hydrogen bomb tests in the Pacific, 1956. Science consultant to New York World's Fair, 1964-65; consultant on scientific affairs, National Foundation-March of Dimes, 1964-66; former secretary of board of trustees, Hall of Science, New York City. Visiting professor, Graduate School of Education, Yeshiva University, 1959-60. *Military service:* U.S. Army, Signal Corps, 1917-19.

MEMBER: National Association of Science Writers (founding member; president, 1939-40), Overseas Press Club, National Press Club, American Association for the Advancement of Science (fellow), P.E.N., Dramatists Club, Authors League of America, Sigma Delta Chi, Harvard Club (New York City), Society of Silurians, Players Club, Dutch Treat Club. *Awards, honors:* Pulitzer Prize, 1937, for reporting of the Harvard Tercentenary Conference of Arts and Sciences, and 1946, for the eye-witness account of the atomic bombing of Nagasaki, Japan; citation from Army Surgeon General, 1945; Westinghouse Distinguished Science Writers Award, American Association for the Advancement of Science, 1946; award from Society of Silurians, 1946; medal for distinguished service in journalism, University of Missouri, 1947; Lasker Award, 1950; George Polk Memorial Award, 1950; Page One Award, 1950; Gold Medal, American Chemical Society, 1958. D.Sc. from Boston University, 1946, and Stevens Institute of Technology, 1951; L.H.D. from Grinnell College, 1951, and Yeshiva University, 1957.

WRITINGS: Dawn Over Zero: The Story of the Atomic Bomb, Knopf, 1946, reprinted, Greenwood Press, 1972; *The Hell Bomb*, Knopf, 1951; *Men and Atoms: The Discovery, the Uses, and the Future of Atomic Energy*, Simon & Schuster, 1959. Also author of *The New Frontiers of Science*, 1964. Contributor of articles to journals in his field.

SIDELIGHTS: A *New York Times* reporter wrote: "Laurence was one of the country's first full-time science reporters, and his biggest exclusive was the dawn of the nuclear age. With a style that often relied on vivid, but simple, imagery, he put technical subjects into terms that a layman could understand. He was a science reporter who conceived of his beat as the universe."

Laurence was the only journalist to witness the first test blast of the atomic bomb at Alamagordo, N.M., in 1945, and also the only newspaperman allowed to fly on the atomic-bomb mission over Nagasaki, Japan. He was warmly nicknamed "Atomic Bill" by his colleagues at the *New York Times*.

OBITUARIES: New York Times, March 20, 1977; *Newsweek*, March 28, 1977.*

(Died March 19, 1977, in Majorca, Spain)

* * *

LAURY, Jean Ray 1928-

PERSONAL: Born March 22, 1928, in Doon, Iowa; daughter of Ralph (an electrician) and Alice (a teacher; maiden name, Kloek) Ray; married Frank B. Laury, September 18, 1952 (divorced); married Stan Bitters (a sculptor and writer), October 3, 1971; children: (first marriage) Tom, Lizabeth. *Education:* Northern Iowa University, B.A., 1950; Stanford University, M.A., 1956. *Politics:* Liberal. *Religion:* Protestant. *Home and office:* 25090 Auberry Rd., Clovis, Calif. 93612.

CAREER: Free-lance designer, 1958—; writer, 1966—. Former teacher at California State University, Fresno.

WRITINGS: Applique Stitchery, Reinhold, 1966; *Quilts and Coverlets: A Contemporary Approach*, Van Nostrand, 1970; *Doll Making: A Creative Approach*, Van Nostrand, 1970; (with Joyce Aiken) *Handmade Rugs From Practically Anything*, Countryside Press, 1971; *Wood Applique*, Van Nostrand, 1973; (with Aiken) *Creating Body Coverings*, Van Nostrand, 1973; *New Uses for Old Laces*, Doubleday, 1974; (with Ruth Milliken Law) *Handmade Toys and Games: A Guide to Creating Your Own*, Doubleday, 1975; *A Treasury of Needlecraft Gifts for the New Baby*, Taplinger, 1976; (with Aiken) *The Total Tote Bag Book: Designer Totes to Craft and Carry*, Taplinger, 1977; *The Creative Woman's Getting-It-All-Together-at-Home Handbook*, Van Nostrand, 1977.

WORK IN PROGRESS: Writing fiction; art work for exhibitions; commissioned art work.

SIDELIGHTS: Jean Laury writes: "My primary interest has always been in the folk arts, and the contemporary survival of these arts. I am concerned with the art in people's everyday lives, the arts they live with. More recently I have been concerned with the problems of women who try to fill multiple roles of homemaking, motherhood, and serious commitment to art."

AVOCATIONAL INTERESTS: Travel in Mexico, Guatemala, Kenya, Germany, Italy; wildlife, skiing, reading.

* * *

LAVERTY, Carroll D(ee) 1906-

PERSONAL: Born November 3, 1906, in Omaha, Neb.; son of Jesse Dee (in business) and Mabel (Horr) Laverty; married H. Marion Smith, July 28, 1935; children: Penelope (Mrs. Wayne O. Wilson), Alan Tim. *Education:* University of Colorado, A.B., 1933, A.M., 1934; Duke University, Ph.D., 1951. *Politics:* Democrat. *Religion:* Episcopal. *Home:* 503 Angus, College Station, Tex. 77840.

CAREER: Reporter for *Muskogee Daily Phoenix* and *Okmulgee Daily Times*, 1928-31; University of Colorado, Boulder, instructor in English, 1934-37; Texas A & M University, College Station, 1939-73, began as instructor, became professor of English, emeritus professor, 1973—; writer, 1973—. *Military service:* U.S. Navy, 1944-45. *Member:* Modern Language Association of America, National Council of Teachers of English, Sigma Delta Chi.

WRITINGS: (Editor with Harrison Hierth and Harry Kroitor) *The Unity of English*, Harper, 1971. Contributor of articles, poems, and reviews to journals, including *American Literature, Transcendental Quarterly*, and *Isis*.

WORK IN PROGRESS: Poetry; research on Edgar Allan Poe and William Butler Yeats, on literary theory, and on relations between science and literature.

SIDELIGHTS: Laverty writes: "Vital is keeping the humanities alive in a technological world. The old concept of a broadly educated man is disappearing under the high specialization demanded by technology. Respect for *the man,* the human being, is being replaced by respect for the technologist, the narrow specialist. Literature, as always, along with history and philosophy, for example, is being ignored more than ever; it is fighting a continuing battle for survival; but the present emphasis on material things and material success is gaining against it. Note the fact that the humanities get comparatively little money for research as compared with science.

"The only way of reversing the trend that I can see is to insist that both science and literature have an absolutely vital part to play in our civilization and to insist on their working together and helping each other rather than engaging in a tacit competition. Each has much to contribute to the other, and together they can do more for civilization than either working separately can do."

* * *

LAWRENCE, Josephine   1890(?)-1978

PERSONAL: Born in Newark, N.J.; daughter of Elijah Wiley and Mary Elizabeth (Barker) Lawrence; married Artur Platz, 1940 (died, 1965). *Education:* Attended New York University. *Politics:* Democrat. *Religion:* Presbyterian. *Residence:* Newark, N.J.

CAREER: Newark Sunday Call, Newark, N.J., beginning 1915, began as staff member, became editor of the household service department and children's page; *Newark Sunday News,* Newark, women's page editor and author of weekly column. *Member:* Authors League, New Jersey Women's Press Club.

WRITINGS—For children: *Man in the Moon Stories* (from radio broadcasts), Cupples & Leon, 1922; *Rosemary,* Cupples & Leon, 1922; *The Adventures of Elizabeth Ann,* Barse & Hopkins, 1923; *Elizabeth Ann at Maple Spring,* Barse & Hopkins, 1923; *Rainbow Hill,* Cupples & Leon, 1924; *Linda Lane,* Barse & Hopkins, 1925; *Elizabeth Ann and Doris,* Barse & Hopkins, 1925; *Linda Lane Helps Out,* Barse & Hopkins, 1925; *The Berry Patch,* Cupples & Leon, 1925; *Next Door Neighbors,* Cupples & Leon, 1926; *The Unhappy Paper Doll,* Barse, 1928; *The Two Little Fellows' Secret,* Barse, 1928; *Flying Cloud and His Rocking Horse,* Barse, 1928; *Linda Lane's Problems,* Barse, 1928; *The Jolly Holly Berrys,* Barse, 1928; *The Toys' Christmas Party,* Barse, 1928; *Red Arrow: A Warrior,* Barse, 1928; *The Policeman Cat,* Barse, 1928; *Perry and Polly's Pictures,* Barse, 1928; *Mr. White Helps Santa Claus,* Barse, 1928; *Elizabeth Ann and Uncle Doctor,* Barse, 1928; *The Dollville Railroad,* Barse, 1928; *Eagle Feather: The Laughing Indian,* Barse, 1928; *Linda Lane's Big Sister,* Barse, 1929; *The Two Little Fellows in April,* Barse, 1929; *Elizabeth Ann's Houseboat,* Barse, 1929; *Glenna,* Cupples & Leon, 1929; *Christine,* Cupples & Leon, 1930; *Wind's in the West,* Cupples & Leon, 1931.

Adult novels: *Head of the Family,* Aventine Press, 1932; *Years Are So Long* (Book-of-the-Month Club selection), Stokes, 1934; *If I Have Four Apples* (Book-of-the-Month Club selection), Stokes, 1935; *The Sound of Running Feet,* Stokes, 1937; *Bow Down to Wood and Stone,* Little, Brown, 1938; *A Good Home With Nice People,* Little, Brown, 1939; *But You Are So Young,* Little, Brown, 1940; *No Stone Unturned,* Little, Brown, 1941; *There Is Today,* Little, Brown, 1942; *Tower of Steel,* Little, Brown, 1943; *Let Us Consider One Another,* Appleton-Century, 1945; *Double Wedding Ring,* Appleton-Century, 1946; *The Pleasant Morning Light,* McGraw, 1948; *My Heart Shall Not Fear,* McGraw, 1949.

The Way Things Are, McGraw, 1950; *The Picture Window,* Morrow, 1951; *Song in the Night,* Morrow, 1952; *The Web of Time,* Harcourt, 1953; *The Gates of Living,* Harcourt, 1955; *The Empty Nest,* Harcourt, 1956; *The Prodigal,* Harcourt, 1957; *The Ring of Truth,* Harcourt, 1958; *All Our Tomorrows,* Harcourt, 1959; *Hearts Do Not Break,* Harcourt, 1960; *I Am in Urgent Need of Advice,* Harcourt, 1962; *In the Name of Love,* Harcourt, 1963; *Not a Cloud in the Sky,* Harcourt, 1964; *In All Walks of Life,* Harcourt, 1968; *Retreat With Honor,* G. K. Hall, 1973; *Under One Roof,* Harcourt, 1975. Also author of *The Amiable Meddlers,* 1961; writer of radio series for children, "Man in the Moon."

SIDELIGHTS: Josephine Lawrence's first novel for adults, *Head of the Family,* appeared in 1932, a time of economic depression, but also a time of artistic and social consciousness. And Lawrence, like many of her fellow writers of that day, focused her work on a variety of social issues, both economic and domestic. The milieu she used was middle-class Newark, New Jersey, where she has lived and worked all her life.

The unusual quality of Lawrence's fiction is that her social consciousness persisted past the Depression, World War II, and the affluent fifties. Consequently, critics tended to be less kind to her as her work became less fashionable; she has been seen, more and more, as didactic, and at least one critic has called her propagandistic. However, she has maintained a steady following of readers, and among her reviewers there has been a continual thread of appreciation of her work. In 1936, for example, Lewis Gannett wrote that "Miss Lawrence is not a subtle novelist, but she achieves a simple, hard hitting reality; her problems are real, and if the characters are stock types, they are genuine types." And in 1960, Caroline Turnstall similarly remarked: "Miss Lawrence is no great stylist, her characters are not memorable, her plots are episodic. But the slice of life that she sets out to detail is as real as the people next door."

Sinclair Lewis once said that "as important as her striking into motives in middle class America is Miss Lawrence's unusual power of seeing and remembering the details of daily living, each petty, yet all of them together making up the picture of an immortal human being."

Lawrence's novel *Years Are So Long* was made into a film, "Make Way for Tomorrow," in 1937.

BIOGRAPHICAL/CRITICAL SOURCES: New York Herald Tribune, January 1, 1936, August 28, 1960; *Obituaries: New York Times,* February 24, 1978.*

(Died February 22, 1978, in New York, N.Y.)

* * *

LAWSON, Philip J.   1908(?)-1978

1908(?)—May 15, 1978; American engineer, educator, and author of books in his field. Lawson was a former director of special projects for the Cushing & Nevell Technical Design Corp. and at one time taught at Pratt Institute. He died in New York, N.Y. Obituaries and other sources: *New York Times,* May 16, 1978.

* * *

LAZARUS, Arthur   1892(?)-1978

1892(?)—February 12, 1978; American management and financial consultant, lecturer, and author. The first director of the Cost Accounting Bureau for the U.S. Chamber of Commerce, Lazarus wrote articles and a book on business subjects. At one time he was a management consultant for corporate clients of the Metropolitan Life Insurance Co.; later he directed his own management consulting business. He died in Washington, D.C. Obituaries and other sources: *New York Times,* February 13, 1978.

LEASKA, Mitchell A(lexander) 1934-

PERSONAL: Surname is pronounced Lee-as-ka; born September 8, 1934, in Putnam, Conn.; son of Nicholas Naum (in real estate) and Flora (Ginalis) Leaska. Education: Brown University, A.B., 1956; Emerson College, M.A., 1958; New York University, Ph.D., 1968. Home: 310 East 55th St., New York, N.Y. 10022. Office: New York University, 829 Shimkin Hall, New York, N.Y. 10003.

CAREER: Teacher at private school in New York City, 1958-64; Brooklyn College of the City University of New York, Brooklyn, N.Y., lecturer in English, 1964-66; New York University, New York City, instructor, 1966-68, assistant professor, 1968-70, associate professor, 1970-72, professor of English education, 1972—, director of humanities program in Paris, summer, 1974. Member: Modern Language Association of America, National Council of Teachers of English.

WRITINGS: The Voice of Tragedy, Robert Speller, 1964; Virginia Woolf's Lighthouse: A Study in Critical Method, Columbia University Press, 1970; (editor) The Pargiters by Virginia Woolf: Novel-Essay Portions of the Years, New York Public Library, 1977; The Novels of Virginia Woolf: From Beginning to End, John Jay Press, 1977. Contributor to library journals and Virginia Woolf Quarterly.

WORK IN PROGRESS: Editing Pointz Hall, a novel by Virginia Woolf, original title, Between the Acts, publication expected in 1982.

BIOGRAPHICAL/CRITICAL SOURCES: Ariel: A Review of International English Literature, January, 1971.

*   *   *

LEAVIS, F(rank) R(aymond) 1895-1978

July 14, 1895—April 14, 1978; British author, editor, and literary critic who was best known for his boldness of opinion and his conservative view of English literature. He advocated "The Great Tradition," wherein he traced the moral tradition of English letters from its seventeenth century origins to the twentieth century, ultimately claiming that in the fiction of Jane Austen, George Eliot, Henry James, Joseph Conrad, and D. H. Lawrence, "we have the successors of Shakespeare; for in the nineteenth century and later the poetic and creative strength of the English language goes into prose fiction." Leavis was equally staunch in his criticism of the modern in literature and life, which he found lacking in moral earnestness. A teacher at four different British universities and the founding editor of the literary journal Scrutiny, he also published over two dozen books in his career. He died in Cambridge, England. Obituaries and other sources: The Oxford Companion to English Literature, 4th edition, Oxford University Press, 1967; The Author's and Writer's Who's Who, 6th edition, Burke's Peerage, 1971; The Penguin Companion to English Literature, McGraw, 1971; Cassell's Encyclopaedia of World Literature, revised edition, Morrow, 1973; Webster's New World Companion to English and American Literature, World Publishing, 1973; Universities Quarterly, winter, 1975; Who's Who in Twentieth Century Literature, Holt, 1976; The Writer's Directory, 1976-78, St. Martin's, 1976; Who's Who in the World, 3rd edition, Marquis, 1976; Ronald Hayman, Leavis, Rowman & Littlefield, 1977; The International Who's Who, Europa, 1977; Who's Who, 130th edition, St. Martin's, 1978; Washington Post, April 19, 1978. (See index for CA sketch)

LEBOVITZ, Harold Paul 1916-

PERSONAL: Born September 11, 1916, in Cleveland, Ohio; son of Isaiah and Celia (Levy) Lebovitz; married Margie Glassman (a secretary), February 20, 1938; children: Neil Ross, Lynn Gail. Education: Western Reserve University (now Case Western Reserve University), B.A., 1938, M.A., 1942. Residence: University Heights, Ohio. Office: Cleveland Plain Dealer, 1801 Superior Ave., Cleveland, Ohio 44114.

CAREER: High school teacher of chemistry and mathematics (and athletic coach) in Euclid, Ohio, 1938-48; Cleveland News, Cleveland, Ohio, sports reporter and columnist, 1948-60; Cleveland Plain Dealer, Cleveland, columnist, 1960-64, sports editor, 1964—. Director of Cleveland Jewish News, 1971—; member of board of directors of Cleveland Jewish Community Center, 1962-63. Baseball umpire, 1937-40; football official, 1940-71; basketball official, 1940-60; inventor of "Four Square Tennis," an outdoor playground game.

MEMBER: American Sports Editors Association (president, 1965-66; member of board of directors, 1966-67), Baseball Writers Association (president, 1964), Ohio Sports Editors Association (president, 1965-66), Ohio Football Officials Association, Cleveland Football Officials Association, Cleveland Umpires Association, Sigma Delta Chi. Awards, honors: Ten awards from Cleveland Newspaper Guild, 1948-60; more than twenty-five writing awards, including top sports writer from Cortron Twelve of the Atlantic Fleet, 1961, and top feature writer from Sporting News, 1963-64.

WRITINGS: (With Leroy Paige) Pitchin' Man, American News, 1949; (with Phil R. Gillman) Springboards to Science, Wiley, 1968. Author of column in Sporting News, 1976—. Contributor to sports magazines.

*   *   *

LEBRA, Takie Sugiyama 1930-

PERSONAL: Born February 6, 1930, in Japan; came to the United States in 1958, naturalized citizen, 1971; daughter of Tarosaku (a mason) and Kimi (Saigusa) Sugiyama; married William Lebra (a professor of anthropology), April 25, 1963. Education: Tsuda College, teaching certificate, 1951; Gakushuin University, B.A., 1954; University of Pittsburgh, M.A., 1960, Ph.D., 1967. Home: 3625 Woodlawn Terrace Pl., Honolulu, Hawaii 96822. Office: Department of Anthropology, University of Hawaii, Honolulu, Hawaii 96822.

CAREER: University of Hawaii, Honolulu, lecturer, 1968-71, associate professor of anthropology, 1971—. Member: American Anthropological Association (fellow), American Sociological Association, Japanese Ethnological Society, Japanese Sociological Society. Awards, honors: National Science Foundation grant, 1976-78.

WRITINGS: (Editor with husband, W. P. Lebra) Japanese Culture and Behavior: Selected Readings, University Press of Hawaii, 1974; (contributor) W. P. Lebra, editor, Youth, Socialization, and Mental Health, University Press of Hawaii, 1974; (contributor) Koichi Ogino, Hitoshi Aiba, and Hiroshi Minami, editors, Rinsho shakai shinrigaku no kiso (title means "Theories in Clinical Social Psychology"), Seishinshobo, 1975; (contributor) R. H. Lauer, editor, Social Movements and Social Change, Southern Illinois University Press, 1976; Japanese Patterns of Behavior, University Press of Hawaii, 1976; (contributor) William Newell, editor, The Ancestors, Mouton, 1976; (contributor) W. P.

Lebra, editor, *Culture-Bound Syndromes, Ethnopsychiatry and Alternate Therapies,* University Press of Hawaii, 1976; (contributor) David Landy, editor, *Culture, Disease, and Healing: Studies in Medical Anthropology,* Macmillan, 1977. Contributor to academic journals.

WORK IN PROGRESS: Japanese Women, an ethnographic study with a focus on adult socialization.

SIDELIGHTS: Takie Lebra comments: "My areas of interest from the standpoint of social and psychological anthropology are religious conversion, moral values, acculturation, and social exchange. I have conducted field research several times in Japan."

* * *

LEDERER, Chloe 1915-

PERSONAL: Born April 4, in Sparta, Ontario, Canada; daughter of LeRoy A. (a farmer) and B. Jean (Smale) Harvey; married Howard E. Lederer (a physician); children: Robert, Joel (stepsons). *Education:* Attended University of Western Ontario and College of Art, Toronto, Ontario; New York University, B.S., 1954. *Religion:* Quaker. *Home:* 149 Summit Ave., Hackensack, N.J. 07601. *Office:* WBGO-FM, 345 High St., Newark, N.J. 07102.

CAREER: Elementary school teacher in London, Ontario, 1937-41, in New York, N.Y., 1948-54, and in Philadelphia, Pa., 1954-56; WBGO-FM, Newark, N.J., writer and broadcaster, 1957—. *Wartime service:* British Intelligence, 1941-45, served as member of staff in New York, N.Y. *Member:* Authors Guild, Society of Children's Book Writers, Bergen County Humane Society/Lost Pet (secretary; member of board of directors, 1971-72). *Awards, honors:* National Council for Social Studies Notable Children's Book Award, 1971, for *Down the Hill of the Sea;* Japan Prize, for radio script "Harriet Tubman"; National Association of Educational Broadcasters award; Ohio awards for radio scripts, "Tales That Live" and "Neighbors."

WRITINGS: Down the Hill of the Sea, Lothrop, 1971. Also author of radio programs and stories for children.

WORK IN PROGRESS: Zan the Ciander; a biography of Pearl Buck; several stories for children; travel articles based on trips to Africa, Lapland, the Caribbean, and the Mackenzie River delta area.

SIDELIGHTS: Lederer told *CA* that though she'd had an early interest in writing, it became directed when she joined the Writer's Laboratory at the Bank Street College of Education in New York City. "From a newspaper clipping," she said, "a radio script evolved and then my first book."

Most of her writing has been for children, but she is strongly interested in the relationship between man and nature, an interest reflected in all areas of her work. She maintains a broad affiliation with groups concerned with "earth saving," like the Audubon Society, the National Wildlife Federation, Wolf Sanctuary, Whale Protection, and the Smithsonian Institution. She is active in their causes and has attended international conferences such as the Endangered Species Symposium, Earthcare, and the Fragile Earth.

* * *

LEDERER, Muriel 1929-

PERSONAL: Born May 31, 1929, in Chicago, Ill.; daughter of Arnold Philip (in manufacturing) and Stella (in real estate; maiden name, Franklin) Natenberg; married Frederick E. Lederer (a manufacturer's sales representative), February 16, 1952; children: Jill, William, Margaret. *Education:* Attended Vassar College, 1947-50; Lake Forest College, B.A., 1951. *Home:* 756 Lincoln Ave., Winnetka, Ill. 60093. *Agent:* Anita Diamant, 51 East 42nd St., New York, N.Y. 10017.

CAREER: Free-lance writer, 1953—. Lecturer and public relations consultant. *Member:* American Society of Journalists and Authors (director-at-large, 1976-78).

WRITINGS: Guide to Career Education, Quadrangle, 1974; *New Job Opportunities for Women,* Publications International, 1975; *Blue-Collar Jobs for Women,* Dutton, 1979. Author of nationally syndicated weekly newspaper column, "Memo to a Working Woman." Contributor to magazines and newspapers, including *Seventeen, McCall's, Viva, Woman's Day,* and *Science and Mechanics.*

* * *

LEE, Lance 1942-

PERSONAL: Born August 25, 1942, in New York, N.Y.; son of David (a television producer) and Lucile (Wilds) Levy; married Jeanne Barbara Hutchings (a medical technologist), August 30, 1963; children: Heather, Alyssa. *Education:* Attended Boston University, 1960-62; Brandeis University, B.A., 1964; Yale University, M.F.A., 1967. *Residence:* Pacific Palisades, Calif. 90272.

CAREER: University of Bridgeport, Bridgeport, Conn., lecturer in speech and drama, 1967, 1968; Southern Connecticut State College, New Haven, instructor in creative writing, 1968; University of Southern California, Los Angeles, senior lecturer, 1968-69, assistant professor of drama, 1969-71; University of California, Los Angeles, lecturer in drama, 1971-73; free-lance writer, 1973—. Delegate to assembly of Community Relations Conference of Southern California, 1973-75; member of Citizens Advisory Committee for Topanga Canyon State Park; founding chairman of coordinating council for Santa Monica Mountains and Seashore State Park Advisory Committees, 1972-74.

MEMBER: Dramatists Guild, Authors League of America, Sierra Club, Save San Francisco Bay Association. *Awards, honors:* Arts of the Theatre Foundation Fellowship, 1966-67; Rockefeller Foundation grant, 1971; National Endowment for the Arts creative writing fellowship, 1976-77; travel grant from Theatre Communication Group, 1976.

WRITINGS—Plays: "Rasputin" (three-act), first produced in New Haven, Conn., at Yale University School of Drama, April, 1967; "Fox, Hound, and Huntress" (one-act), first produced in Los Angeles, Calif., at Odyssey Theatre, August, 1971; "Gambits" (one-act), first produced under title "Hollinrake's Gambit" at Eugene O'Neill Memorial Theatre Center, July, 1975; "Time's Up" (two-act), first produced at Goodman Theatre Center, November, 1976.

Work represented in *Playwrights for Tomorrow,* Volume X, University of Minnesota Press, 1973. Contributor of poems, stories, and articles to journals, including *Coast, Riverside Quarterly, Literary Review,* and *Midwest Poetry Review.*

WORK IN PROGRESS: "On the Line," and "Two of a Kind," both screenplays; a play, "Life Scenes"; a volume of poems, *Surroundings.*

* * *

LEE, Laurie 1914-

PERSONAL: Born June 26, 1914, in Stroud, Gloucestershire, England; married Catherine Francesca Polge, 1950; children: Jesse Frances. *Education:* Educated in Stroud, England. *Home:* Slad, Gloucestershire, England.

CAREER: Poet, writer. Worked as clerk in Stroud, England, and as builder's laborer in London, England; documentary filmmaker for Post Office film unit in Cyprus, India, and Assam, during World War II; publications editor for Ministry of Information, 1944-46; worked with Green Park film unit, 1946-47; caption writer-in-chief for Festival of Britain, 1950-51. *Member:* Royal Society of Literature. *Awards, honors:* Atlantic Award, 1944; Society of Authors Travelling Award, 1951; Member of the Order of the British Empire, 1952; Foyle's Poetry Award, 1955; W. H. Smith Award for Literature, 1959-60.

WRITINGS: *The Sun My Monument* (poems), Hogarth, 1944; *Land at War,* H.M.S.O., 1945; (with Ralph Keene) *A Film in Cyprus,* Longmans, Green, 1947; *The Bloom of Candles* (poems), Lehmann, 1947; *The Voyage of Magellan* (verse play), Lehmann, 1948; *A Rose for Winter,* Hogarth, 1955; *My Many-Coated Man* (poems), Deutsch, 1955; *Cider With Rosie* (autobiography), Hogarth, 1959, published as *Edge of Day: A Boyhood in the West of England,* Morrow, 1960; *Poems,* Vista, 1960; *The First Born,* Hogarth, 1964; *As I Walked Out One Midsummer Morning* (autobiography), Deutsch, 1969; *I Can't Stay Long* (collected prose pieces), Deutsch, 1975, Atheneum, 1976.

SIDELIGHTS: At the age of nineteen, Lee left his home and walked to London, taking little else with him than his violin and the determination to never again have an employer. Both have remained with him throughout the years. If writing should fail him, Lee said, he will survive on his violin: "A little time ago I went busking with it just to see what the going rate was. . . . I keep in practice."

Cider With Rosie, one of Lee's best known works, is a memoir of his boyhood in England which was very warmly received by critics and the reading public. When it was published in the United States under the title *The Edge of Day,* T. S. Matthews stated: "Good books don't always sell; the best seller lists are usually swamped by the second- and third-rate. But now and then, once in a blue moon, a book appears that deserves its success. This time the moon is blue, and *The Edge of Day* is the book."

After publishing *Cider With Rosie,* Lee returned to his home town and bought a cottage there. "It took me a long time to go back," he said. "I had to have some success behind me." According to the *London Times:* "There was some vexation when the villagers recognized themselves in the book, then he was accepted. They even sell his books at the local pub." Lee recalled, "At first they wouldn't touch them with tongs."

A collection of prose pieces written over a thirty-year period, *I Can't Stay Long,* is Lee's most recent publication. Criticisms of the book have been polarized. Robert Nye, for example, found that "Little in [the book] is deeply thought or felt through." He further commented: "Nice is perhaps an appalling word, but it suits Mr. Lee. There is a niceness in him both in the old sense of being minutely and delicately precise, and in the modern colloquial sense of being agreeable."

Other reviews of *I Can't Stay Long* were more favorable. Sylvia Secker noted: "When Lee drops his purple mantle he can write with a vivid, spare imagery that makes one realize how closely allied are the eyes of the poet and the painter: 'the bright-backed cows standing along the dykes like old china arranged on shelves,' 'motionless canals, full of silver light, lap the houses likes baths of mercury.' One is no longer reading but looking at the work of an old Dutch Master." *New Yorker* praised the book's imagery, citing as example Lee's recollection of adolescence: "I don't think I ever discovered sex, it seemed to be always there—a vague pink streak running back through the landscape as far as I can remember." This type of writing, *New Yorker* said, shows Lee "at his most characteristically expressive." The review further stated: "Mr. Lee's writing—almost precious, almost naive—has a tone and intensity that are truly entirely his own, and are inimitably pleasing."

BIOGRAPHICAL/CRITICAL SOURCES: *New York Times Book Review,* March 27, 1960; *London Times,* December 21, 1975; *Times Literary Supplement,* January 30, 1976; *New Yorker,* February 23, 1976; *Christian Science Monitor,* April 5, 1976.

* * *

LEE, Linda 1947-

PERSONAL: Born June 23, 1947, in Rush City, Minn.; daughter of Robert Edward (a welder and blacksmith) and Edna (a storekeeper; maiden name, Halverson) Lee. *Education:* Attended University of Minnesota; Columbia University, B.A., 1969, graduate study, 1969. *Home and office:* 315 West 71st St., New York, N.Y. 10023. *Agent:* Elaine Markson Literary Agency, Inc., 44 Greenwich Ave., New York, N.Y. 10011.

CAREER: Farrar, Straus & Giroux, New York, N.Y., assistant editor, 1970-74; writer, 1974—.

WRITINGS: *One by One* (fiction), Simon & Schuster, 1977.

WORK IN PROGRESS: *The Hand Book,* on the hands and use of gestures, with Jim Charlton, for Prentice-Hall; *Minnesota Medical* (tentative title), for Fawcett.

SIDELIGHTS: Linda Lee comments: "My primary motivation was and is earning a living. To be able to do so by writing interesting, compelling stories is one of the wonders of living."

* * *

LEE, Warren M. 1908-

PERSONAL: Born October 24, 1908, in Mount Etna, Iowa; son of Charles Warren (a farmer) and Carrie (De Voss) Lee; married Margaret Robertson, November 30, 1933 (died March 17, 1966); married Evelyn Geneva Dawson (a teacher), August 28, 1966; children: Byron George, Milton Charles. *Education:* University of Iowa, B.A., 1931, M.A., 1932, Ph.D., 1941. *Home:* 500 South University, Vermillion, S.D. 57069.

CAREER: University of Minnesota, Minneapolis, instructor, 1933-36; University of South Dakota, Vermillion, professor, 1938-75, professor emeritus, 1975—, director of theater, 1938—, dean of fine arts, 1951—. Founder and director of Black Hills Playhouse, 1946-75; chairman of South Dakota Arts Council, 1966-71. *Awards, honors:* Warren M. Lee Center for the Fine Arts was named for him in 1975.

WRITINGS—Plays: *Shave and a Haircut, Six Bits,* Dramatic Publishing, 1940. Also author of "Trouble Shooter," "Saint Louie," "Penny Anarchy," and "Legend of Devil's Gulch."

WORK IN PROGRESS: *Handbook for Adventure in the Arts.*

* * *

LEGGETT, Stephen 1949-

PERSONAL: Born July 9, 1949, in Michigan; son of Charles

William and Helen (Schroeder) Leggett; married Cindi McMillan, July 5, 1974. *Education:* Central Michigan University, B.I.S., 1978. *Home address:* Route 3, Steinberg Rd., Manistee, Mich. 49660.

CAREER: Manistee County Historical Museum, Manistee, Mich., assistant curator, 1974-75; writer, 1975—. Part-time musician in bars and coffee houses.

WRITINGS: Wild Apples (poems), Great Outdoors Press, 1973; *Monk Poems,* Cat's Pajamas Press, 1975; *The Gift of Water, the Gift of Fire* (poems), Cold Mountain Press, 1978. Contributor to literary journals and popular magazines, including *Nation, Epoch, Greenfield Review,* and *Dacotah Territory.*

WORK IN PROGRESS: The Forest of Symbols, poems, completion expected about 1980; research on changes and constants in soil-tilling rites, land tenure, and descent systems of Trobriand Islands, New Guinea.

SIDELIGHTS: Leggett writes: "My work as a poet has led me increasingly in the direction of anthropology, and I expect my work in the future to be grounded in that discipline. Few areas of inquiry have proven as vital to my understanding of what it is a poet does, or ought to do. Malinowski and other field workers have shown the utilitarian value of songs, charms, and recitative pieces in certain cultures, where an oral literature might carry an incredible amount of essential taxonomic data. On another level, in his work among such cultures as the Caduveo and the Tupi of South America, Levi-Strauss has called attention to the transformational aspect of mythic material, which must mediate Nature and Culture, Life and Death. I would expect nothing less of poetry: to be taxonomic and useful, to mediate between Nature and Culture, between Life and Death, to confront directly Humankind's most ancient and desperate concerns."

*   *   *

LEHMANN, Rosamond (Nina) 1901-

PERSONAL: Born February 3, 1901, in London, England; daughter of Rudolph Chambers (a magazine staff member) and Alice Marie (Davis) Lehmann; married Leslie Ruciman (divorced); married Wogan Philipps (divorced); children: one son, one daughter, Sally (died, 1962). *Education:* Attended Cambridge University. *Home:* 70 Eaton Square, London S.W. 1, England.

CAREER: Author. Co-director of John Lehmann, Ltd. (a publishing company), beginning 1946. *Member:* International P.E.N. (former president of English Centre; former international vice-president), Society of Authors. *Awards, honors:* Commandeur dans l'Ordre des Arts et Lettres, 1968.

WRITINGS—Novels: *Dusty Answer,* Holt, 1927, reprinted, Harcourt, 1975; *A Note in Music,* Holt, 1930; *Invitation to the Waltz,* Holt, 1932, reprinted, Harcourt, 1975; *The Weather in the Streets,* Reynal, 1936; *The Ballad and the Source,* Reynal, 1945, reprinted, Harcourt, 1975; *The Echoing Grove,* Harcourt, 1953; *A Sea-Grape Tree,* Harcourt, 1977.

Other writings: *A Letter to a Sister,* Harcourt, 1932; *No More Music* (play), Collins, 1939; (editor with others) *Orion: A Miscellany 1-3,* three volumes, Nicholson & Watson, 1945-46; *The Gipsy's Baby and Other Stories,* Collins, 1946, Reynal, 1947; (translator from the French) Jacques Lemarchand, *Genevieve,* Lehmann, 1947; (translator from the French) Jean Cocteau, *Children of the Game,* Harvill, 1955, published as *The Holy Terrors,* New Directions, 1957; (with

W. Tudor Pole) *A Man Seen Afar,* Spearman, 1965; *The Swan in the Evening: Fragments of an Inner Life,* Harcourt, 1967.

Also author, with Cynthia Sandys, of *Letters from Our Daughters,* College of Psychic Studies.

SIDELIGHTS: Lehmann was categorized early in her career, in the days before Women's Liberation and feminist criticism, as a "woman's writer." Primarily a romantic novelist, she seeks to explore the inner lives, the "sensibilities," of her heroines, who are often young girls. Indeed, her first novel, *Dusty Answer,* dealt with adolescent lesbianism, though its mode was romantic, if not sentimental.

Critical response to *Invitation to the Waltz,* her third book, characterizes Lehmann's work. Doris Cunningham simply called the novel "delicate, subtle, and appealing," while the *New York Times* described it as "utterly charming." Similarly, Amy Loveman wrote, "Her smiling tenderness depicts with deft and humorous strokes the little sum of nothings that make up a girl's world at seventeen."

In the 1940's, when *The Ballad and the Source* appeared, reviewers pinned down the nature of Lehmann's fiction. Isabelle Mallet remarked that this fifth novel "retains her original feminine flavor." Labelling it "a distinctly feminine novel," Richard Watts noted, "The men who appear in it are comparatively dim as contrasted with the vivid yet mysterious women who play its central roles." But with the appearance of *The Echoing Grove* in 1953, another note was struck. Brendan Gill wrote: "Miss Lehmann's skill is such that male readers, though resentful of being harrowed in the name of entertainment . . . will gamely follow her to her dark journey's end."

In *The Swan in the Evening,* Lehmann recounted her mystical experiences following the death of her only daughter. Jean Stafford observed: "She presents her case so gracefully, so unaggressively, with so fine a care to maintain her humor and her level head, that one feels rude in refusing her refreshments of nectar and ambrosia . . . but nevertheless one feels oneself withdrawing, flushed, stammering an apology as if, in a house one had thought well-known, one had by accident opened the door to an altogether strange room and had confronted a scene that was none of one's business." Echoing Stafford's sentiments, V. S. Pritchett declared: "*The Swan in the Evening* embarrasses because it puts the reader in the position of being an intruder on a terrible private grief." But D. C. Goddard maintained that "no one of any sensitivity is likely to remain unmoved, for there are few authors living who write more beautifully than Miss Lehmann."

Lehmann's latest novel, *The Sea-Grape Tree,* seems to reflect her new-found mystical beliefs. Pamela Hansford Johnson wrote, "This is a very strange novel with enchantment in its very strangeness." The characters, she felt, "seem part of a fairy story in a fairy place. Nevertheless, Miss Lehmann's book is haunting beyond a first reading. . . . This novel is in the best sense romantic."

BIOGRAPHICAL/CRITICAL SOURCES: New York Times Book Review, October 30, 1932, April 1, 1945, July 14, 1968, October 9, 1977; *Saturday Review of Literature,* November 5, 1932; *Commonweal,* January 4, 1933; *New Republic,* April 9, 1945; E. Bowen, *Collected Impressions,* Knopf, 1950; *New Yorker,* May 23, 1953; *New Statesman,* December 22, 1967; *Book World,* April 21, 1968; *Contemporary Literary Criticism,* Volume 5, Gale, 1976.*

LEONARD, Thomas C(harles) 1944-

PERSONAL: Born October 17, 1944, in Detroit, Mich.; son of Vincent C. (a certified public accountant) and Virginia (a librarian; maiden name, Damm) Leonard; married Carol Hurlbut (a psychologist), August 25, 1969; children: Peter S. Education: University of Michigan, B.A. (high honors), 1966; graduate study at Queens University, Belfast, 1966-67; University of California, Berkeley, Ph.D., 1973. Home: 1315 McGee, Berkeley, Calif. 94703. Office: School of Journalism, University of California, 607 Evans, Berkeley, Calif. 94720.

CAREER: Columbia University, New York, N.Y., assistant professor of history, 1973-76; University of California, Berkeley, assistant professor of journalism, 1976—. Member: American Historical Association. Awards, honors: Woodrow Wilson fellow, 1967-68; Ford Foundation fellow, 1967-72.

WRITINGS: Above the Battle: War-Making in America from Appomattox to Versailles, Oxford University Press, 1978. Contributor to American Quarterly and American Heritage.

WORK IN PROGRESS: A book on the expose in American journalism.

SIDELIGHTS: Leonard comments: "I consider myself a cultural historian and I offer this perspective to the professional journalists I help train at Berkeley."

* * *

LEONARD, Tom 1944-

PERSONAL: Born August 22, 1944, in Glasgow, Lanarkshire, Scotland; married, 1971. Education: Graduate study at University of Glasgow. Home: 56 Eldon St., Glasgow G3 6NJ, Scotland.

CAREER: Poet. Awards, honors: Scottish Arts Council bursary, 1971.

WRITINGS: Six Glasgow Poems, Midnight Publications, 1969; A Priest Came on at Merkland Street (poems), Midnight Publications, 1970; Poems, E. & T. O'Brien, 1973; Bunnit Husslin, [Glasgow], 1975; (with Alex Hamilton and James Kelman) Three Glasgow Writers: A Collection of Writings, Molendinar Press, 1976. Author of "If Only Bunty Was Here" (radio play), broadcast by Radio Scotland, 1977.

WORK IN PROGRESS: Research on James Thomson.

* * *

LERNER, Alan Jay 1918-

PERSONAL: Born August 31, 1918, in New York, N.Y.; son of Joseph J. (founder of Lerner Stores, Inc.) and Edith Lerner; married Ruth O'Day Boyd, 1940 (divorced, 1947); married Marion Bell (a singer), 1947 (divorced, 1949); married Nancy Olson (an actress), 1950 (divorced, 1957); married Micheline Muselli (a lawyer), December, 1957 (marriage ended); married Karen Gunderson; children: Susan, Liza, Jennifer, Michael. Education: Attended Juilliard School of Music, 1936, 1937; Harvard University, B.S., 1940.

CAREER: Lyricist, librettist, screenwriter, and producer of motion pictures and Broadway musicals. Worked as advertising copywriter for Lord & Thomas Agency, 1940-42. Member of President's Committee for the Cultural Center in Washington, D.C., 1962. Member: Players, Lambs, Shaw Society. Awards, honors: Received New York Drama Crit-

ics Circle Award, 1947, for "Brigadoon"; Academy Awards for best story and best screenplay from Academy of Motion Picture Arts and Sciences, 1951, for "An American in Paris"; Christopher Award, 1954; New York Drama Critics Circle Award, Donaldson award, and Antoinette Perry ("Tony") Award, all 1956, all for "My Fair Lady"; Academy Awards for best screenplay and for best song from Academy of Motion Picture Arts and Sciences, 1958, for "Gigi"; Grammy Award, 1965, for "On a Clear Day You Can See Forever"; Choate Alumni Seal; elected to Songwriters Hall of Fame, 1971; co-winner, with Frederick Loewe, of Tony Award, 1974.

WRITINGS—Lyricist: (And librettist) Brigadoon (musical play; first produced in 1947), music by Frederick Loewe, Coward, 1947; (and librettist) Paint Your Wagon (musical play; first produced on Broadway, November, 1951), music by Loewe, Coward, 1952; (and librettist) My Fair Lady (musical play; adapted from the play, "Pygmalion," by George Bernard Shaw; first produced on Broadway at Mark Hellinger Theatre, March 15, 1956), music by Loewe, Coward, 1956; (and librettist) Camelot (musical play; adapted from the book, The Once and Future King, by T. H. White; first produced in 1960), music by Loewe, Random House, 1961; Lerner & Loewe Song Book, music by Loewe, Simon & Schuster, 1962; (author of introduction) Great Songs of Broadway, Quadrangle, 1973; (with Shaw) Pygmalion (contains "Pygmalion" and "My Fair Lady"; the former by Shaw, the latter by Lerner), New American Library, 1975.

Librettist and lyricist; music by Loewe, except as noted: "Life of the Party" (adapted from the play, "The Patsy," by Barry Connor), first produced in Detroit, 1942; "What's Up?," first produced on Broadway at National Theatre, November 11, 1943; "The Day Before Spring," first produced in 1945; "Love Life" (music by Kurt Weill), first produced in 1948; "On a Clear Day You Can See Forever" (music by Burton Lang), first produced in 1965; "Coco" (music by Andre Previn), first produced on Broadway at Mark Hellinger Theatre, December 18, 1969; "Lolita, My Love" (adapted from the novel, Lolita, by Vladimir Nabokov; music by John Barry), first produced in Philadelphia, 1971; "Gigi" (adapted from own screenplay), first produced in 1973; "Music, Music," first produced in 1974; "1600 Pennsylvania," first produced in 1975.

Screenwriter and lyricist: "Royal Wedding," Metro-Goldwyn-Mayer (MGM), 1951; "An American in Paris," MGM, 1951; "Brigadoon" (adapted from own musical play), MGM, 1954; "Gigi" (adapted from the novel by Colette), MGM, 1958; "My Fair Lady" (adapted from own musical play), Warner Brothers, 1967; "Paint Your Wagon" (adapted from own musical play), Paramount, 1969; "On a Clear Day You Can See Forever" (adapted from own musical play), 1970.

Also author of radio scripts for programs including "Philco Hall of Fame" and "Music Society of Lower Basin Street."

SIDELIGHTS: With Frederick Loewe, Lerner became one of the most prominent figures of the musical stage. After an initial success with Life of the Party, the team of Lerner and Loewe went on to create huge broadway hits, including "Paint Your Wagon," "Camelot," and "On a Clear Day You Can See Forever." But their greatest triumph was their musical, "My Fair Lady."

The musical adaptation of George Bernard Shaw's "Pygmalion," "My Fair Lady" opened on Broadway to praise which never let up. New York Times critic Brooks Atkinson proclaimed it "a wonderful show" and praised Lerner's "crisp adaptation and his sardonic lyrics." Celebrating its second year on Broadway, Atkinson deemed "My Fair Lady" "the most civilized play of its time and one of the finest of the century."

After Loewe became ill, Lerner collaborated with composers such as Andre Previn and Leonard Bernstein but the plays were not greeted with the same critical applause as those done with Loewe.

BIOGRAPHICAL/CRITICAL SOURCES: New York Times, March 16, 1956, March 9, 1958; David Ewen, *Great Men of American Popular Song,* Prentice-Hall, 1970; Lehman Engel, *Their Words Are Music,* Crown, 1975.*

*   *   *

LERNOUX, Penny (Mary)   1940-

PERSONAL: Born January 6, 1940, in Los Angeles, Calif.; daughter of Maurice (a chemist) and Beatrice Lernoux; married Denis Nahum (a businessman), May 1, 1972. *Education:* University of Southern California, B.A., 1961. *Home and office:* Apartado Aereo 22413, Bogota, Colombia. *Agent:* International Creative Management, 40 West 57th St., New York, N.Y. 10019.

CAREER: Hollywood Citizen News, Hollywood, Calif., reporter, 1961; U.S. Information Agency, Washington, D.C., foreign service officer in Bogota, Colombia, and Rio de Janeiro, Brazil, 1961-63; Copley News Service, chief of bureaus in Caracas, Venezuela, 1964-67, and Buenos Aires, Argentina, 1967-70, South American correspondent from Bogota, 1970-74; free-lance writer, 1974—.

MEMBER: Overseas Press Club, Women in Communications, Center for Inter-American Relations, Phi Beta Kappa, Phi Kappa Phi. *Awards, honors:* Citations from Overseas Press Club, 1969, 1970; Tom Wallace Award from Inter-American Press Association, 1973; press award from Latin American Studies Association, 1975; grant from Alicia Patterson Foundation, 1976.

WRITINGS: (With Mari Wesche and Rolf Wesche) *South America,* Ginn, 1974. Contributor to magazines, including *Newsweek, Washington Post,* and *Inquiry.* Latin American editor of *Nation.*

WORK IN PROGRESS: A book on human rights and the Latin American Catholic Church, for Doubleday.

SIDELIGHTS: Penny Lernoux writes: "My principal motivation has always been to try to explain to and interest U.S. readers in the peoples of Latin America. My principal areas of interest are human rights, political, economic, and social matters in the form of investigative reporting."

*   *   *

LESIEUR, Henry R(ichard)   1946-

PERSONAL: Surname is pronounced Les-yer; born April 9, 1946, in Pawtucket, R.I.; son of Richard A. (a letter carrier) and Claire (Collette) Lesieur; married Helen M. Menard, June 15, 1968; children: Matthew H., Bethany J. *Education:* Providence College, A.B., 1968; University of Massachusetts, M.A., 1973, Ph.D., 1976. *Home:* 27 Northgate Apts., Burlington, Vt. 05401. *Office:* Department of Sociology, University of Vermont, Burlington, Vt. 05401.

CAREER: McGill University, Montreal, Quebec, assistant professor of sociology, 1975-77; University of Vermont, Burlington, assistant professor of sociology, 1977—. *Military service:* U.S. Army, 1968-70; served in Vietnam. *Member:* American Sociological Association, American Society of Criminology, Society for the Study of Social Problems, American Civil Liberties Union.

WRITINGS: The Chase: The Career of the Compulsive Gambler, Doubleday, 1977. Contributor to *British Journal of Criminology.*

WORK IN PROGRESS: Research on shoplifting and white-collar crime.

*   *   *

LEVIS, Larry   1946-

PERSONAL: Born September 30, 1946, in Fresno, Calif.; son of William Kent (a farmer) and Carol (Mayo) Levis; married Barbara Campbell, January 29, 1969 (divorced); married Marcia Southwick (a poet), March 8, 1975. *Education:* California State University, Fresno, B.A., 1968; Syracuse University, M.A., 1970; University of Iowa, Ph.D., 1974. *Home:* 1024 Crestland Ave., Columbia, Mo. 65201. *Office:* 218 Arts & Science, University of Missouri, Columbia, Mo. 65201.

CAREER: California State University, Los Angeles, lecturer in English, 1970-72; University of Missouri, Columbia, assistant professor of English, 1974—. *Member:* Modern Language Association of America, P.E.N., Academy of American Poets. *Awards, honors:* International Poetry Forum U.S. award, 1971, for *Wrecking Crew; The Afterlife* was the 1976 Lamont poetry selection.

WRITINGS: Wrecking Crew (poetry), University of Pittsburgh Press, 1972; *The Rain's Witness* (pamphlet), Southwick Press, 1975; *The Afterlife* (poetry), University of Iowa Press, 1977. Co-editor of *Missouri Review,* 1977—.

WORK IN PROGRESS: A volume of poems.

SIDELIGHTS: Levis told *CA:* "The landscapes in which I live always have a powerful and direct, although often delayed, effect on my poetry. The most important landscape, for me, is that of my childhood: the central valley of California."

He added: "My themes have changed since *Wrecking Crew.* The poems are far less overtly political, and, in *The Afterlife,* much more personal. By personal I do not mean 'confessional' at all. I mean the creation of a private, familial mythology which intends to be representative rather than idiosyncratic. However, I don't know what this third volume is going to do; I'm too busy simply writing it to know yet."

*   *   *

LEVITAS, Maurice   1917-

PERSONAL: Born February 1, 1917, in Dublin, Ireland; son of Harry (a presser) and Leah (Rick) Levitas; married Elizabeth Scott, February, 1941 (divorced); married Jacqueline Litterland (a journalist), April, 1966 (separated); children: William Stuart, Diana, Ruth, Daniel, Rachel, John Benjamin. *Education:* University of London, B.Sc., 1958. *Politics:* Communist. *Religion:* None. *Home:* 4 Fleming Field, Shatham Colliery, Durham DH6 2JF, England. *Office:* Faculty of Education, New College, University of Durham, Durham DH1 3HP, England.

CAREER: Upholsterer, 1932-35; plumber, 1935-37, 1939-42; teacher in secondary schools in London and Lincolnshire, both England, 1949-66; University of Durham, New College, Durham, England, member of education faculty, 1966—. *Military service:* International Brigades, soldier in British battalion, 1937-39. British Army, 1942-47.

WRITINGS: Marxist Perspectives in the Sociology of Education, Routledge & Kegan Paul, 1974. Contributor to *Marxism Today.*

WORK IN PROGRESS: Research on division of labor and on teaching as a profession.

SIDELIGHTS: When questioned about the educational opportunities for working class children, Levitas told *CA:* "Denial to working class children of conditions for full human development stems from their class identity. The working class in general are normally denied full human development. This is because their position in the 'ensemble of social relations' makes each devote his life to a confined task in the division of labour which thus reduces him to only part of a man. His identity is defined by his occupation. And even this limited opportunity for self-expression is further limited by its function—not as a contribution to the well-being of society—but as a means to a living. He is compelled to place this emphasis upon his work because his and his dependent's economic security is always marginal.

"The analogous components in the terms of existence of the dominant capitalist class are offset by its members' economic and social powers. These open up access to a world of human achievement and to scope for development and expression. There are limits here too, but the limits are only the historically given conditions of reproducing their power in the web of human interaction.

"The reproduction of that power and of its complementary powerlessness of the working class depends upon family socialization and formal education. For the dominant social classes formal education tends to be human-developmental, for the working class it tends to be instrumental—centered upon an ultimate occupational role. Both modes of formal education are provided, governed, and overlooked by the dominant social class.

"The pre-requisites exist in modern capitalist society for its transformation. This involves a first step of making the working class politically dominant. Working class political parties and trade unions represent this potentiality. But so also do the growing pressure from the working class for 'the common school', for 'the common curriculum'. Whether before or after 'the first step' educational change in this direction facilitates larger changes to be accomplished. Finally, the more teachers define their professional commitments in terms of their responsibility to the all-round human development of their pupils—refuting the notion that selection for ultimate occupational statuses is their 'function'—the greater will be their contribution to the social revolution already in progress and gathering force."

* * *

LEVY, Elizabeth 1942-

PERSONAL: Born April 4, 1942, in Buffalo, N.Y.; daughter of Elmer Irving and Mildred (Kirschenbaum) Levy. *Education:* Brown University, B.A. (cum laude), 1964; Columbia University, M.A.T., 1968. *Home:* 201 West 16th St., New York, N.Y. 10011. *Agent:* Elaine Markson Literary Agency, Inc., 44 Greenwich Ave., New York, N.Y. 10011.

CAREER: American Broadcasting Co., New York City, editor and researcher in news department, 1964-66; Macmillan Co., New York City, assistant editor, 1967-69; New York Public Library, New York City, writer in public relations, 1969; JPM Associates (urban affairs consultants), New York City, staff writer, 1970-71; free-lance writer, 1971—. *Member:* Authors Guild of Authors League of

America, Mystery Writers of America. *Awards, honors: Struggle and Lose, Struggle and Win* was named outstanding book of the year by the *New York Times,* 1977.

WRITINGS: The People Lobby: The SST Story, Delacorte, 1973; *Something Queer Is Going On* (juvenile; My Weekly Reader Book Club selection), Delacorte, 1973; *Nice Little Girls* (juvenile), Delacorte, 1974; *Lawyers for the People,* Knopf, 1974; *By-Lines: Profiles in Investigative Journalism,* Four Winds Press, 1975; *Something Queer at the Ballpark* (juvenile; selection of Junior Literary Guild), Delacorte, 1975; *Lizzie Lies a Lot* (juvenile), Dell, 1976; *Something Queer at the Library* (juvenile), Delacorte, 1977; (with cousin, Robie H. Harris) *Before You Were Three: How You Began to Walk, Talk, Explore, and Have Feelings* (alternate selection of Book-of-the-Month Club), Delacorte, 1977; (with Mara Miller) *Doctors for Today: Profiles of Six Who Serve,* Knopf, 1977; (with Tad Richards) *Struggle and Lose, Struggle and Win: The United Mineworkers Story,* Four Winds Press, 1977; (with Earl Hammond and Liz Hammond) *Our Animal Kingdom,* Delacorte, 1977.

Plays: (Co-author) "Croon" (one-act), first produced in New York, N.Y., at Performing Garage, March 28, 1976; (co-author) "Never Waste a Virgin" (two-act), first produced in New York City at Wonderhorse Theatre, December 3, 1977.

WORK IN PROGRESS: Come Out Smiling, a novel for teenagers; books on nuclear energy and birth control, both for teenagers.

SIDELIGHTS: Elizabeth Levy told *CA:* "I'm usually asked why I write on such a wide variety of subjects. Since I try to make my living just from writing and primarily from children's books, I need to have a number of projects going at one time. This may not be the best road to sanity, but it seems to be the only way I can pay the rent.

"Even if it weren't a necessity, I'd probably continue to write both fiction and nonfiction. I often work with another person on nonfiction, and I write on political subjects of issues that interest me. I try to write about 'radicals' wherever I can find them, and I have a very liberal definition of radical.

"Collaborating is a partial solution to the anxiety and loneliness of writing. I'd much rather talk about my work than write, and I like to excitement of two people sharing our reactions to the same facts or the same interview."

* * *

LEVY, Michael R(ichard) 1946-

PERSONAL: Born May 17, 1946, in Dallas, Tex.; son of Harry A. and Florence (Friedman) Levy; married Rebecca Schulman (an artist), January 19, 1969; children: Anne Rachel, Mara Elizabeth, Tobin Janel. *Education:* University of Pennsylvania, B.S., 1968; University of Texas, J.D., 1972. *Home address:* P.O. Box 146, Austin, Tex. 78767. *Office address: Texas Monthly,* P.O. Box 1569, Austin, Tex. 78767.

CAREER/WRITINGS: Texas Monthly, Austin, Tex., founder and publisher, 1972—. Chairman of the board and president, Mediatex Communications Corp., Austin, 1972—. Admitted to Texas Bar, 1972. *Member:* Headliners Club.

* * *

LEVY, Morton 1930-

PERSONAL: Born August 1, 1930, in Worcester, Mass.;

son of Maurice (a salesman) and Bessie (Rosenblatt) Levy; married Barbara Fischer, December 29, 1956; children: Myra, Emily, Michael. *Education:* Worcester Junior College, A.A., 1950; Northwestern University, B.B.A., 1954. *Politics:* Democrat. *Religion:* Jewish. *Residence:* San Francisco, Calif. *Office:* Accountants for the Public Interest, 233 Sansome St., San Francisco, Calif. 94104.

CAREER: Lido Lanes (bowling center), Newark, Calif., general manager, 1960-61; Harb, Levy & Weiland (certified public accountants), San Francisco, Calif., partner, 1962-72; San Francisco Accountants for the Public Interest, San Francisco, Calif., executive director, 1972-74; National Association of Accountants for the Public Interest, San Francisco, Calif., executive director, 1975—. Former instructor at Golden Gate University. Member of advisory committee of National Housing Law Project Multifamily Demonstration Program.

MEMBER: American Institute of Certified Public Accountants, American Accounting Association, National Association of Accountants, National Council for the Public Assessment of Technology (member of advisory board), California Society of Certified Public Accountants, San Francisco Mental Health Association (member of board of directors). *Awards, honors:* Community service award from American Jewish Congress of Northern California, 1969.

WRITINGS: Accounting Goes Public, University of Pennsylvania Press, 1977. Contributor to accounting journals.

*   *   *

LEVY, Robert 1926-

PERSONAL: Born October 1, 1926, in New York, N.Y.; son of Mack and Reggy (Steinbrecher) Levy; married Corinne Schlissel, April 26, 1953; children: Randall Mark, Meredith Robin. *Education:* City College (now of the City University of New York), B.S.S., 1949. *Home:* 42 Wedgewood Dr., Westbury, N.Y. 11590. *Office: Dun's Review,* 666 Fifth Ave., New York, N.Y. 10019.

CAREER/WRITINGS: Tide, New York City, senior editor, 1950-53; *Time,* New York City, contributing editor, 1953-55; *Forbes,* New York City, senior editor, 1955-59; Manning Public Relations Firm, New York City, vice-president, 1960-63; Elgin Watch Co., New York City, director of public relations, 1963-64; Ruder & Finn, New York City, senior associate, 1965; *Dun's Review,* New York City, senior editor, 1966—. *Military service:* U.S. Army Air Force, 1945-46; became staff sergeant. *Member:* New York Financial Writers Association. *Awards, honors:* Lincoln University Humanitarian Award, 1952-53, for a series of articles entitled "The Negro Market."

SIDELIGHTS: When questioned about the most engaging aspect of his work, Levy responded, "That which comes with the territory of a business writer: responsibility for reporting what is happening in U.S. industry and taking the measure of the movers and shakers of American business—the liveliest beat in journalism."

*   *   *

LEWANDOWSKI, Dan 1947-

PERSONAL: Born March 5, 1947, in Detroit, Mich.; son of Jerome (a postal clerk) and Lottie (Kruszewski) Lewandowski. *Education:* University of Michigan, B.A., 1970. *Home address:* P.O. Box 1466, Vail, Colo. 81657.

CAREER: Ross Enterprises, Flint, Mich., copywriter, 1970-71; Omnimedia, Inc., Tampa, Fla., copywriter, 1971-

74; waiter, 1974-77; *New Vail* (magazine), Vail, Colo., staff writer, 1977—. *Military service:* U.S. Marine Corps Reserve, 1967-70.

WRITINGS: Perhaps It Was in Vail, Bobbs-Merrill, 1977.

SIDELIGHTS: Lewandowski remarks: "I like to think the field of literature is wider than that which is encompassed by gothic romances, murder mysteries, and toppling government stories."

*   *   *

LEWIS, Albert 1885(?)-1978

1885(?)—April 6, 1978; Polish-born producer and screenwriter. "Cabin in the Sky," "The Jazz Singer," and "Rain" were all Broadway hits which Lewis produced. The stories behind these shows and others are recounted in his book, *First Nights in the New York Theatre: 1900 to 1960.* Lewis also wrote screenplays, including "Oh, You Beautiful Doll" and "Meet Me in St. Louis." In his later years he was a television producer. He died in Beverly Hills, Calif. Obituaries and other sources: *New York Times,* April 10, 1978.

*   *   *

LEWIS, George 1943-

PERSONAL: Born April 16, 1943, in Bakersfield, Calif.; son of George Ira (a civil servant) and Lynn (Harris) Lewis; married Jane Cook (a wholesale importer), August 22, 1964. *Education:* Attended University of the Pacific, 1960-61; San Diego State University, A.B., 1964. *Politics:* Independent. *Religion:* "No church affiliation." *Home:* 149 Litchfield Lane, Houston, Tex. 77125. *Office:* NBC News, 4615 Southwest Freeway, Houston, Tex. 77027.

CAREER: KFMB-TV, San Diego, Calif., reporter, 1962-69; KNBC, Los Angeles, Calif., reporter, 1969-70; National Broadcasting Co. (NBC) News, New York, N.Y., correspondent, 1970—. Notable assignments include coverage of the Vietnam war, 1970-72, the fall of Saigon, 1975, the Houston mass murders, 1973, and the 1976 U.S. presidential campaign. *Member:* Radio-TV News Directors Association, Houston Press Club, Sigma Delta Chi. *Awards, honors:* Silver Medal from New York Film and Television Festival, 1967, for documentary on operation room nurses; Emmy nomination, 1968, for documentary "Operation Thanks."

SIDELIGHTS: Lewis told *CA:* "After almost two years residence in the Far East, my wife and I maintain an active interest in Asian affairs. Her business has taken her back to Asia since then and she and I contemplate future trips there. We are hoping to visit the People's Republic of China before the end of the year. I speak a smattering of Spanish which isn't exactly useful in Asia. Both of us ski (badly) and enjoy tennis and bicycling when time permits. Time doesn't usually permit."

*   *   *

LEWIS, Mary (Christianna Milne) 1907-
(Mary Ann Ashe, Christianna Brand, Annabel Jones, Mary Roland, China Thompson)

PERSONAL: Born December 17, 1907, in Malaya; daughter of Alexander Brand (a rubber planter) and Nancy (Irving) Milne; married Roland Swaine Lewis (a surgeon); children: Victoria. *Education:* Educated in India and England. *Politics:* Conservative. *Home:* 88 Maida Vale, London W.9, England. *Agent:* Am Heath, Brandt & Brandt, 101 Park Ave., New York, N.Y. 10017.

CAREER: Novelist and free-lance writer. Has also worked as a salesperson, governess, dancer, model, and secretary. *Member:* Crime Writers Association (chairperson, 1973), Mystery Writers of America, Detection Club. *Awards, honors:* Received two awards for best short story from Mystery Writers of America.

WRITINGS—Under pseudonym Mary Ann Ashe: *Alas for Her That Met Me,* Star Books, 1976; *A Ring of Roses,* Star Books, 1976, published under pseudonym Christianna Brand, W. H. Allen, 1977.

All under pseudonym Christianna Brand; all mystery novels, except as indicated: *Death in High Heels,* Bodley Head, 1941, Scribner, 1954; *Heads You Lose,* Bodley Head, 1942, Dodd, 1943; *Green for Danger,* Dodd, 1945, reprinted, M. Joseph, 1973; *The Crooked Wreath,* Dodd, 1947 (published in England as *Suddenly at His Residence,* Bodley Head, 1947, reprinted, M. Joseph, 1973); *Welcome to Danger* (children's novel), Dodd, 1948 (published in England as *Danger Unlimited,* Foley House, 1949); *Death of Jezebel,* Dodd, 1948, reprinted, Ian Henry, 1977; *Cat and Mouse,* Knopf, 1950, reprinted, Avon, 1976; *London Particular,* M. Joseph, 1952, published as *Fog of Doubt,* Scribner, 1953; *Tour de Force,* Scribner, 1955; *The Three-Cornered Halo,* Scribner, 1957; *Heaven Knows Who* (nonfiction), Scribner, 1960; *Naughty Children: An Anthology* (for children), Gollancz, 1962, Dutton, 1963; *Nurse Matilda* (for children), Brockhampton Press, 1963, Dutton, 1964; *What Dread Hand?* (short stories), M. Joseph, 1964; *Nurse Matilda Goes to Town* (for children), Brockhampton Press, 1966, Dutton, 1967; *Nurse Matilda Goes to Hospital* (for children), Brockhampton Press, 1969; *Brand X* (short stories), M. Joseph, 1974; *The Honey Harlot,* W. H. Allen, 1978.

Under pseudonym Annabel Jones: *The Radiant Dove* (romantic fiction), St. Martin's, 1974.

Under pseudonym Mary Roland: *The Single Pilgrim,* Crowell, 1946.

Under pseudonym China Thompson: *Starrbelow* (romantic mystery), Scribner, 1958, reprinted under Brand pseudonym, Brook House, 1977.

Contributor to periodicals, including *Chicago Tribune, Saturday Evening Post,* and *Ellery Queen's Mystery Magazine.* Work represented in anthology, *Best Police Stories,* edited by Roy Vickers, Faber, 1966.

WORK IN PROGRESS: A mystery, under pseudonym Christianna Brand, *The Rose in Darkness.*

SIDELIGHTS: Mary Lewis writes: "What is my aim? To write good, readable (saleable) entertainment books and above all to write them well. I detest illiterate writing, I detest bad style, bad grammar, bad punctuation. At four years of age, I read fluently; and I was brought up on the classics and I hope I may say that I really can't write other than in good style.

"I write in a sort of rat's nest of papers all over two desks; and a book is for some time a sort of rat's nest of ideas in my mind, until it slowly and painfully clears to what is a strong plot, highly involved, but, one hopes, easy to read and understand. I write largely crime stories and these I believe may be brought to a very highly skilled craft; but I don't claim as some do that they are an art form.

"My pet loves are good literature, paintings, and Siamese cats. My hates are sloppy work, dirt in any form (mental or physical), and noise.

"As a girl I was very poor, cold, and hungry and I have known a great deal of suffering—for many years, for personal family reasons I was able to write hardly at all so that there has been a long gap in my work. It was a bitter sacrifice—of money, of recognition, above all of talent wasted; but people are more important than anything else and that's the end of it. Compassion is all—and everything adds up to being a writer. We are what we remember, and as a writer, we become a sort of sponge that soaks up our experience and emerges in what we have to say.

"Nowadays, everything is fine and I am working again. Knock on wood!"

BIOGRAPHICAL/CRITICAL SOURCES: Julian Symons, editor, *The Hundred Best Crime Stories,* London Sunday Times, 1959.

* * *

LEZAMA LIMA, Jose 1910-1976

PERSONAL: Born December 19, 1910, in Campamento Militar de Columbia, Cuba. *Education:* Earned law degree from University of Havana. *Residence:* Havana, Cuba.

CAREER: In private law practice in Cuba, 1938-40; worked for various government agencies in Cuba, 1940-59; National Council of Culture, Havana, director of the department of literature and publications, beginning 1959. Poet, essayist, and novelist.

WRITINGS: La fijeza, Origenes, 1949; *Analecta del reloj* (essays), Origenes, 1953; *El padre Gaztelu en la poesia,* Origenes, 1955; *La expresion Americana* (lectures), Ministerio de Educacion, 1957; *Tratados en la Habana,* Universidad Central de Las Villas, 1958; *Dador* (poems), [Havana], 1960; *Anotologia de la poesia cubana,* Consejo Nacional de Cultura, 1965; *Orbita de Lezama Lima,* Union Nacional de Escritores y Artistas, 1966; *Paradiso* (novel), Union Nacional de Escritores y Artistas, 1966, translation by Gregory Rabassa published under same title, Farrar, Straus, 1974; *Los grandes todos,* ARCA, 1968; *Lezama Lima* (anthology), J. Alvarez, 1968; *Posible imagen de Jose Lezama Lima* (poems), Llibres de Sinera, 1969; *La expresion Americanos* (essays), ARCA, 1969; *Esferaimagen,* Tusquets Editor, 1970; *La cantidad hechizada* (essays), UNEAC, 1970; *Poesia completa* (poems), Instituto del Libro, 1970; *Las eras imaginarias,* Editorial Fundamentos, 1971; *Algunos tratados en La Habana,* Editorial Anagrama, 1971; *Introduccion a los vasos orficos,* Barral Editores, 1971; *La cantidad hechizada,* Jucar, 1974.

Also author of *Muerte de Narciso,* 1937; *Enemigo rumor,* 1941; *Aventuras siglosas,* 1945; *Aristides Fernandez,* 1950.

Co-founding editor, *Verbum,* 1937, *Nadie parecia,* 1943, and *Origenes,* 1945-56.

SIDELIGHTS: Lezama Lima's *Paradiso,* according to *Publishers Weekly,* "prompted critics to refer to him as 'the Proust of the Caribbean.'" The novel was released in the United States, France, Italy, and several Latin American countries.

BIOGRAPHICAL/CRITICAL SOURCES: Washington Post, April 14, 1974; *New York Review of Books,* April 18, 1974; *New York Times Book Review,* April 21, 1974; *Village Voice,* April 25, 1974; *New Republic,* June 15, 1974; *Contemporary Literary Criticism,* Volume 4, Gale, 1975. *Obituaries: New York Times,* August 10, 1976; *Publishers Weekly,* August 23, 1976.*

(Died August 9, 1976, in Havana, Cuba)

LIBO, Lester M(artin) 1923-

PERSONAL: Born September 18, 1923, in Chicago, Ill.; son of Leopold (a salesman) and Anita (a saleswoman; maiden name, Pearl) Libo; married Elizabeth Laws, June 9, 1949 (divorced, January, 1960); married Shirley Sims (a psychologist), September 14, 1963 (divorced, March, 1978); children: Gina Libo Manchester, Victor, Felicia. *Education:* Attended Central Young Men's Christian Association College, Chicago, Ill., 1941-43, and University of California, Berkeley, 1946; Stanford University, A.M., 1948, Ph.D., 1951. *Home:* 1520 University Blvd., Apt. 305, Albuquerque, N.M. 87102. *Agent:* John Brockman Associates, Inc., P.O. Box 376, Planetarium Station, New York, N.Y. 10024. *Office:* Department of Psychiatry, School of Medicine, University of New Mexico, Albuquerque, N.M. 87131.

CAREER: University of Michigan, Ann Arbor, research associate, 1950-53; University of Maryland, School of Medicine, Baltimore, assistant professor of medical psychology, 1953-57; New Mexico Department of Public Health, Santa Fe, director of mental health, 1957-62; University of New Mexico, Albuquerque, associate professor, 1963-70, professor of psychiatry and psychology, 1970—. Visiting professor at University of Bergen, 1969-70. Executive director of New Mexico General Addictions Treatment Effort, Albuquerque, 1972-73; vice-chairman of New Mexico Board of Psychologist Examiners, 1972-77. *Military service:* U.S. Army, combat infantryman, 1943-46; served in European theater; became staff sergeant; received three battle stars.

MEMBER: American Psychological Association (fellow), Association for Humanistic Psychology, American Orthopsychiatric Association (fellow), Biofeedback Society of America, American Association of Biofeedback Clinicians, New Mexico Psychological Association (president, 1965). *Awards, honors:* National Institute of Mental Health fellow, 1969-70.

WRITINGS: Attitude Prediction in Labor Relations (monograph), Graduate School of Business, Stanford University, 1948; *Measuring Group Cohesiveness* (monograph), Institute of Social Research, University of Michigan, 1951; (with C. R. Griffith) *Mental Health Consultants,* Jossey-Bass, 1968; *Is There Life After Group?,* Anchor Books, 1977. Contributor to psychology journals, and of nonfiction articles to science fiction and detective magazines.

WORK IN PROGRESS: Research on biofeedback, relaxation, and stress management.

SIDELIGHTS: Libo told *CA:* "*Is There Life After Group?* offers suggestions to people considering entering an intensive encounter or sensitivity group, and to people who have participated in such a group and desire to maintain their personal growth gains. There is solid evidence, reviewed in this book, that intensive short-term groups can be effective, safe, and long-lasting."

AVOCATIONAL INTERESTS: Travel in Europe and Mexico, tennis, sailing, skiing, jazz and chamber music, reading contemporary fiction.

*   *   *

LIDDLE, William 1925-

PERSONAL: Born April 9, 1925, in Palisade, Colo.; son of William (an engineer) and Rena (a teacher; maiden name, Beattie) Liddle; married Ruth L. Reeds, June 5, 1949 (died April 14, 1971); married Mary Ann Loos (a teacher), January 18, 1975; children: Kevin, Jeffrey, Eric, Susan, Brian. *Education:* University of California, Los Angeles, B.A., 1949; Colorado College, M.A., 1953; University of Delaware, Ph.D., 1964; postdoctoral study at University of Reading, 1973-74. *Religion:* Methodist. *Home:* 2641 North Chelton Rd., Colorado Springs, Colo. 80909. *Office:* Department of Education, Colorado College, Colorado Springs, Colo. 80907.

CAREER: Junior high school teacher of English, social studies, vocal music, and dramatics in Colorado Springs, Colo., 1949-54, guidance counselor, 1955-57, chairman of department of English, 1954-57, teacher in adult school, 1953-59; Colorado College, Colorado Springs, instructor, 1955-62, assistant professor of education, 1962-63, visiting professor, 1963—; Colorado Springs Public Schools, Colorado Springs, supervisor of secondary education, 1957-60, assistant director, autumn, 1963, director of elementary education, 1964-74, administrative assistant in instructional services, 1974-75, director, 1975—, principal of Pike School, 1976-77. Instructor at Colorado University, 1957-59, University of Delaware, 1960-62, and Western State College, 1965-72; visiting lecturer at University of Reading, 1973-74. Member of State Department Accreditation Committee and Colorado Advisory Board on Reading. *Military service:* U.S. Army Air Forces, 1944-46.

MEMBER: International Reading Association (president of Colorado council; state president; member of state board of directors), National Education Association (life member), National Society for the Study of Education, American Association of University Professors, National Conference for Research in English, Association for Supervision and Curriculum Development (member of national board of directors; local and state president), Classroom Teachers Association (past vice-president; president), Community Education Association, Parent Teachers Association (member of state board of directors), Directors and Supervisors Association (president), College Reading Association, Tri-State Association for Supervision and Curriculum Development, Colorado Education Association (regional zone chairman), Colorado Association of Specialists in Education, State Department of Classroom Teachers (vice-president), Colorado Schoolmasters Association, Pi Gamma Mu. *Awards, honors:* National Science Foundation grant, 1957; Reading Dynamics Corp. fellowship, 1960-62; Holt, Rinehart & Winston, Inc. grant, 1961-62; certificate of merit from Colorado International Reading Association, 1968.

WRITINGS: Reading for Concepts, Volumes A-H, with tape cassettes, McGraw, 1970; *Oral Comprehension Program for Pre-School and Kindergarten: Early Approaches to Reading Skills,* Economy Publishing, 1971; (with Ethel Clifford) *Color Me Safe* (juvenile), Unified College Press, 1976; (with Clifford) *Color Me Healthy* (juvenile), Unified College Press, 1976; (with Clifford) *Color Me Friendly* (juvenile), Unified College Press, 1976; (with Clifford) *Color Me Growing* (juvenile), Unified College Press, 1976. Contributor to education and reading journals. Member of advisory board of *Harcourt, Brace School Dictionary.*

WORK IN PROGRESS: Diagnosis of Comprehension Problems; Reading in Content Area; Evolution of Concept Development.

*   *   *

LIEW, Kit Siong 1932-

PERSONAL: Born October 16, 1932, in North Borneo; son of Sang and Yueh-yung (Hung) Liew; married Elizabeth Anne Piggott (an English teacher), January 30, 1961; children: Frances, Alice, Marcus, Imogen. *Education:* University of Tasmania, B.A., 1958, diploma in education, 1959; Australian National University, Ph.D., 1968. *Home:* 27 Princes St., Sandy Bay, Hobart, Tasmania 7005, Australia. *Office:* Department of History, University of Tasmania, Box 252C, Hobart, Tasmania 7001, Australia.

CAREER: Elementary school teacher in Jesselton, North Borneo, 1952-54; Sabah College, Jesselton, North Borneo, senior master of history, 1959-61; University of Tasmania, Hobart, Australia, lecturer, 1966-71, senior lecturer in history, 1972—.

MEMBER: Australian Institute of International Relations, Asian Studies Association of Australia, Australian University Staff Association, Asian Studies Teachers Association of Tasmania. *Awards, honors:* Myer Foundation grant, 1969; Social Science Research Council of Australia travel grant, 1969-70; British Council grant for England, 1972.

WRITINGS: Struggle for Democracy, University of California Press, 1971.

WORK IN PROGRESS: Studying British-Chinese relations in the Republican period.

SIDELIGHTS: Liew writes: "*Struggle for Democracy* is a study of China's pre-Republican revolutionary movements centered around the political career of Sung Chiao-jen, 1882-1913. Brought up in China's classical tradition and having successfully passed the traditional imperial examination for the first degree, he went to a modern school in Wuchang in 1902 and subsequently turned against the Manchu regime. After participating in an abortive uprising in Changsha, the capital of his native province Hunan, he fled to Japan at the end of 1904. Here he continued his tertiary education, and at the same time engaged in revolutionary activities among the Chinese students in Tokyo. He, together with Sun Yat-sen and others, founded the T'ung-meng-hui which played a leading role in overthrowing the Manchu dynasty in the 1911 revolution. After the establishment of the Republic of China, Sung became a leading political figure in his attempt to secure parliamentary democracy by curbing the dictatorial tendencies of the president Yuan Shih-k'ai. But he failed in the attempt. While his colleagues were rejoicing over their successes in the Republic's first national election, his political foes struck and Sugn Chiao-jen lost his life at the hands of an assassin at the Shanghai railway station.

"In discussing the aspirations of Sung Chiao-jen and his fellow-revolutionaries, and in analyzing the factors which helped or hampered their efforts to shape China's future, this book aims to shed light on the nature of the 1911 revolution and its consequences. It is the author's contention that although the 1911 revolution failed to achieve its goals of democracy and independence for China, it marks an important and even inevitable stage in modern China's development. No students could adequately comprehend subsequent revolutionary movements in China without a good understanding of this event."

* * *

LI Ling-Ai

PERSONAL: Born in Honolulu, Hawaii; daughter of Li Khai-Fai (a surgeon) and Kong Tai-Heon'g (a surgeon). *Education:* University of Hawaii, B.A., 1930; further study in Chinese, music, and Chinese theatre, 1932-36. *Politics:* Republican. *Religion:* "Christian-Confucian." *Home:* 360 West 55th St., New York, N.Y. 10019.

CAREER: Peking Institute of Fine Arts, Peking, China, director of theatre, 1933-36; co-producer and technical ad-

viser of Academy award-winning documentary film "Kukan," 1938-43; "Ripley's Believe It or Not" Far Eastern department, New York, N.Y., director, 1940-53; lecturer to associated clubs throughout the United States, 1943-68; lecturer, 1943—; full-time writer, 1968—. Director of theatre programs for American Bureau of Medical Aid to China fund raising program, 1940-46; member of board of directors, *Sun Chung Kwock Bo* (Chinese language paper); consultant to National Nationalities Program of National Federation of Republican Women, 1958-62; organizer and lecturer for Chinese cooking course given by Chinese Cultural Center in New York, 1975—. *Member:* Overseas Press Club of America, Hawaii-Chinese History Center, Women's American-Oriental Club of New York (member of advisory board), Woman Pays Club of Women in the Arts (New York; member of advisory board). *Awards, honors:* Bicentennial Woman of the Year from National Association of Women Artists of America, 1975.

WRITINGS: (Contributor) Harry Carr, *Riding the Tiger,* Houghton, 1934; *Children of the Sun in Hawaii,* Heath, 1946; *Life Is for a Long Time,* Hastings House, 1972.

WORK IN PROGRESS: Teardrops in the Wind, an account of her personal experiences in China during the 1930's; *Recipes from a Chinese Courtyard.*

SIDELIGHTS: Li Ling-Ai attributes her success as a writer and lecturer to the influence of her family during her childhood. She grew up sixth in a family of nine children, and was constantly exposed to many different kinds of people, largely because of her parents' medical profession. She remembers "conversations with parents, visiting dignitaries, scholars, writers, artists, missionaries, laborers, the sick, the old, and the young around the big dining table at home." Because her parents were often called away in emergencies, she learned at an early age to cook meals and entertain guests by singing, dancing, and playing the violin. She gives much credit to her parents, whose goal was "to train the children the best way within their means, physically, mentally, and spiritually, to take their places in a continually changing modern world, and to add rather than to subtract from life wherever they might go."

When asked about motivation for her work, Li Ling-Ai told *CA:* "I seek to show 'a way of life.' The theme of all my work, whether in writing, lecturing, movie-making, or just plain everyday living, is 'Kukan—Heroic Courage Under Bitter Suffering.' The twenty years spent in writing *Life Is for a Long Time* was to justify the faith in me of both my American friends and my Chinese relatives. The writing was my attempt to bring about a transliteration of the rhythm and mood on a lifestyle based largely on instinctive and creative reactions against a predominantly scientific and mathematical screen of another lifestyle, in order to finally distill a clear picture of a bigger pattern of human existence for others to see, perhaps to understand, and maybe to remember."

* * *

LILLEY, Peter 1943-

PERSONAL: Born August 23, 1943, in Kent, England; son of Arnold Francis (a personnel officer) and Lilian Violet (Elliott) Lilley. *Education:* Clare College, Cambridge, B.A., 1965. *Religion:* Anglican. *Home:* 17 Montford Pl., London S.E.11, England. *Agent:* Curtis Brown Ltd., 1 Craven Hill, London, England. *Office:* W. Greenwell & Co., Bow Bells House, Bread St., London EC4M 9EL, England.

CAREER: Marketing and Economic Research Ltd., London, England, project leader, 1965-68; Maxwell Stamp Associates Ltd., London, senior economic consultant, 1968-72; W. Greenwell & Co., London, investment analyst, 1972—. National chairman of Bow Group, 1973, 1974. Conservative candidate for Parliament from Tottenham, 1974. Member of board of governors of Bethnal Green Adult Education Institute, Henry Fawcett Schools, and Beaufoy School. *Member:* Society of Investment Analysts, London Oil Analysts Group.

WRITINGS: A Europe of States, C.P.C., 1965; *Do You Sincerely Want to Win?: The Security Problem in Northern Ireland,* Bow Publications, 1972, revised edition, 1972; *The Alternative Manifesto,* Bow Publications, 1973; *Lessons for Power,* Bow Publications, 1974; (contributor) Christopher West, editor, *Inflation: A Management Guide to Company Survival,* Associated Business Publishers, 1976; (with Samuel Brittan) *The Delusion of Incomes Policy,* Maurice Temple Smith Ltd., 1977; (contributor) Robert Skidelsky, editor, *The End of the Keynesian Era,* Macmillan, 1977.

WORK IN PROGRESS: A book on the economics of racial discrimination; a "political thriller" novel.

SIDELIGHTS: Lilley writes: "The underlying theme of my work so far has always been the supreme importance of man's freedom of moral choice. In my economic writings I have tended to concentrate on defending and urging enlargement of the sphere of market choice. I emphasise the moral superiority of the market (versus political choice), since in the market men bear both the costs and rewards of their own choices. Thus *The Delusion of Incomes Policy* sought to provide, in addition to a comprehensive analysis of the empirical effectiveness of incomes controls, a philosophical exegesis of the vanity of imposing an artificial system of 'fair' rewards. As a result the book initiated a rethink of the case for incomes policies which had been thought desirable by almost all informed opinion in Britain since the war. The *Times,* itself long sympathetic to pay controls, unprecedentedly devoted its entire leader columns to a remarkably favourable discussion of the book.

"In my political writings I have emphasised that, where collective choices must be made, those who will the end must will the means. Thus in *Do You Sincerely Want to Win?* I spelt out the means necessary to extirpate terrorism in Ulster and exposed the policy of appeasement of the I.R.A. then being pursued. Coming from the chairman-elect of the Bow Group (a reputedly leftish group of conservative intellectuals) this attack on official policy angered the Conservative Government almost as much as the I.R.A. (whose leaders had cooperated during my researches). Nonetheless it was hailed both by the liberal Manchester *Guardian* and Northern Ireland premier, Brian Faulkner, who described it as the 'best thing ever written about Ulster's security problem.'"

*   *   *

LIMPERT, John A.   1934-

PERSONAL: Born March 15, 1934, in Appleton, Wis.; son of John and Olga (Lindstrom) Limpert; married Jean A. Vincent (a pharmacist), July 3, 1975. *Education:* University of Wisconsin, B.S., 1959; further study at Stanford University, 1959-60. *Office: Washingtonian,* 1828 L St. N.W., Washington, D.C. 20036.

CAREER/WRITINGS: United Press International, New York, N.Y., reporter and regional editor in Minneapolis, Minn., St. Louis, Mo., and Detroit, Mich., 1960-64; San Jose Sunpapers, San Jose, Calif., managing editor, 1965-67; *Washingtonian,* Washington, D.C., editor, 1969—. *Awards,*

honors: Congressional fellow, 1968; American Political Science Association reporting award, 1970, for an article on air pollution.

SIDELIGHTS: Limpert told *CA:* "The economics of freelancing are awful. We now are willing to pay $1,000 to $1,500 for major articles—which is a lot of money by city magazine standards—but for two to four weeks work that's not very good pay. Most of all, we look for writers who really know and care about their subjects. Too many writers think they can take average material and with flashy writing make a magazine piece out of it. We look more and more for good research and clear writing. Also, not many writers know what the material means—that's the difference between a newspaper story and a magazine article: What does it all mean?"

*   *   *

LINDAMAN, Edward B.   1920-

PERSONAL: Born May 6, 1920, in Davenport, Iowa; son of a clergyman and Lillian (Hammer) Lindaman; married Geraldine Metcalf. *Education:* Eveleth Junior College (now Mesabi Community College), A.S., 1939. *Religion:* Presbyterian. *Home:* 215 West Hawthorne Rd., Spokane, Wash. 99207. *Office:* Whitworth College, Spokane, Wash. 99251.

CAREER: North American Aviation, Inc., Los Angeles, Calif., in production control, 1940-50; American Helicopter Co., Inc., Manhattan Beach, Calif., assistant to the president, 1951-53; North American Aviation, Inc., Autonetics Division, Anaheim, Calif., general supervisor in project administration, 1954-63; North American Rockwell, Space Division, Downey, Calif., director of program control on Apollo Spacecraft project, 1963-69; Whitworth College, Spokane, Wash., president, 1970—. Member of board of directors of Key Tronic, Inc. President of Northwest Regional Foundation, 1975—; national chairman of EXPO'74 environmental symposium series; chairman of governor's Task Force on Alternatives for Washington, 1985, 1974-76; member of board of directors of San Francisco Theological Seminary, 1967—.

MEMBER: Association of American Colleges, Young Men's Christian Association (member of national council, 1976—; local president, 1974-75), Independent Colleges of Washington, Presbyterian College Union, United Presbyterian Men (national president, 1967). *Awards, honors:* D.H.L. from Tarkio College, 1966; D.Sc. from Chapman College, 1970.

WRITINGS: Space: A New Direction for Mankind, Harper, 1969; *Thinking in the Future Tense,* Broadman, 1978.

WORK IN PROGRESS: Choosing Your Futures: A Resource for Planning, with Ronald Lippitt, for Broadman.

SIDELIGHTS: Lindaman writes: "*Thinking in the Future Tense* will attempt to help the reader become at least an amateur 'futurist.' It will aid him in learning how to talk about the future for himself (or herself), rather than merely parroting well-known futurists."

*   *   *

LINDENAU, Judith Wood   1941-

PERSONAL: Born May 22, 1941, in Zanesville, Ohio; daughter of Vernon Earl (a construction worker) and Jean (Hogan) Wood; married John R. Lindenau (a musician), June 29, 1963; children: Jonathan, Sarah. *Education:* Baldwin-Wallace College, B.A., 1963; University of South Dakota, M.A., 1964. *Religion:* Unitarian-Universalist.

Home: 4501 Lakeview Dr., Interlochen, Mich. 49643. *Office:* Green Lake Township, P.O. Box 22, Interlochen, Mich. 49643.

CAREER: University of South Dakota, Vermillion, instructor in English and creative writing, 1964-69; Interlochen Arts Academy, Interlochen, Mich., instructor in flute, English, and creative writing, and chairman of creative writing, 1969-71; Ferris State College, Big Rapids, Mich., instructor in English, 1973—. Trustee of Green Lake Township, 1974-77, township supervisor, 1977-78. *Member:* Academy of American Poets.

WRITINGS: (With Elaine Edelman and Jill Haldeman) *Noeva: Three Women Poets,* University of South Dakota Press, 1975. Contributor of poems to literary journals, including *South Dakota Review, Washout Review, Firelands Arts Review,* and *Wheatfield.*

WORK IN PROGRESS: The Chilling Season (tentative title), poems and prose poems based on surrealism in art and music.

SIDELIGHTS: Judith Lindenau comments: "I am a woman with a wide variety of interests and skills, from politics and land use planning to music and art, but I believe that all activity must be a result of the search for the center of Self—it is that search which is the motivation and, I hope, the end result of what I write."

*   *   *

LINDENMEYER, Otto J. 1936-

PERSONAL: Born October 2, 1936, in New York; son of Otto and Helen (Malovany) Lindenmeyer; married Esther Vega (a nurse), November 28, 1963; children: Elizabeth, Deborah, Jennifer, Veronica. *Education:* Fordham University, B.A., 1957; University of Heidelberg, diploma, 1959; New York University, M.A., 1963. *Religion:* Roman Catholic. *Home:* 652 Union Ave., Holtsville, N.Y. 11742. *Office:* Heffley and Browne School, 188 Montague St., Brooklyn, N.Y. 11201.

CAREER: Educational Heritage, Inc., Yonkers, N.Y., associate editor of "Negro Heritage Library," 1963-66; Bellwether Publishing Co., New York, N.Y., project editor for *Negro Almanac,* 1966-68; Columbia Broadcasting System, New York City, series consultant for "Of Black America," 1968; teacher at Heffley and Browne School, Brooklyn, N.Y. Editorial director for Scanfax Systems. *Military service:* U.S. Army, Cavalry, editor of *Cavalier,* 1959-62. *Awards, honors:* George Foster Peabody Award from University of Georgia School of Journalism, 1968, for "Of Black America."

WRITINGS: Black and Brave (juvenile), McGraw, 1970; *Black History: Lost, Stolen, or Strayed,* Avon, 1970.

WORK IN PROGRESS: A Pictorial History of America's Black Fighting Men; Branches; The Court Reporter's Almanac.

SIDELIGHTS: Lindenmeyer comments: "I am branching out from black subjects into other ethnic materials. *Branches* is a 1968 manuscript originally titled 'Nicodemus, Unincorporated,' about an all-black town in Kansas. I teach court reporting in New York and have worked up a reference volume on this subject."

*   *   *

LINDHEIM, Irma Levy 1886-1978

December 9, 1886—April 10, 1978; American Zionist leader and author. Lindheim was president of Hadassah in 1926-28, and later a pioneer in Palestine, where she settled on a kibbutz in 1933. Dividing her time between Israel and the United States, Lindheim, an honorary life member of the World Zionist executive board and congress, also helped organize the League for Labor in Palestine and worked to create fellowships for American youths to study in Israel. She wrote *The Immortal Adventure* in 1928, and her autobiography, *Parallel Quest: A Search of a Person and a People,* in 1962. She died in Berkeley, Calif. Obituaries and other sources: *Who's Who in World Jewry,* Pitman, 1972; *New York Times,* April 11, 1978. (See index for *CA* sketch)

*   *   *

LINDQUIST, E(veret) F(ranklin) 1901-1978

June 4, 1901—May 13, 1978; American educator and author. The director of the University of Iowa's testing program, Lindquist wrote the National Merit Scholarship tests and a number of books on intelligence testing and measurement. Lindquist supervised the writing of educational development tests for the Armed Forces Institute during World War II. After the war he was an educational consultant to the military government of Germany. Obituaries and other sources: *American Men and Women of Science: The Social and Behavioral Sciences,* 12th edition, Bowker, 1973; *Who's Who in America,* 39th edition, Marquis, 1976; *New York Times,* May 16, 1978.

*   *   *

LINDSAY, Robert 1924-

PERSONAL: Born November 27, 1924, in Durham, N.C.; son of Albert and Emily (Sheridan) Lindsay; married Mary Anne Phillips, January 3, 1950; children: Phillips S., Nancy Beth Lindsay Seldomridge. *Education:* University of Wisconsin, Madison, B.A., 1953, M.A., 1954; University of Minnesota, Ph.D., 1965. *Home:* 11 Hillside Court, St. Paul, Minn. 55108. *Office:* School of Journalism and Mass Communication, University of Minnesota, Minneapolis, Minn. 55455.

CAREER: WKOW-News, Madison, Wis., news director, 1948-50; United Press International, New York, N.Y., editor in Wisconsin, 1952-53; WHA-TV, Madison, commentator, 1954-57; University of Minnesota, Minneapolis, instructor, 1957-65, assistant professor, 1965-70, professor of mass communication and international relations, 1970—. Lecturer at University of Wisconsin, Madison, 1952-57, and at universities and journalism training centers in Africa, Asia, Latin America, and Europe, 1957—. U.S. State Department specialist in Latin America, Asia, and Africa, 1965—; senior program specialist for space communication, UNESCO, Paris, 1968-69. *Military service:* U.S. Marine Corps, 1941-45, 1950-52; became captain. U.S. Marine Corps Reserve, 1952-66.

MEMBER: International Press Institute, International Institute of Communications, International Communication Association, International Association for Mass Communication Research, International Communication Development Council (chairman, 1970-72), International Studies Association, Institut International de Droit Spatial, Inter American Press Association, American Society for Eighteenth Century Studies, American Association for the Advancement of Science, American Society of International Law, British Institute of International and Comparative Law, Canadian Institute of International Affairs, Centre d'Etude des Consequences Generales des Grandes Techniques Nouvelles, Colegio National de Comunicacion, Communication Association of the Pacific, Asian Mass Communication Information and Research Center, Foreign Policy Association, Radio Television News Directors Association, Minnesota Press Club, Geneva Press Club (Switzerland). *Awards, honors:* Fellowship from Foundation for Public Relations Research and Education, 1959 and 1967; Ariel Award from Citizens Committee on Public Education, 1960; grants from University of Minnesota for Bolivia, 1967, and Ecuador, 1976; grant from U.S. Department of State for worldwide study of mass communication development, 1977.

WRITINGS: This High Name, University of Wisconsin Press, 1956.

Contributor: Robert L. Chatten and Oscar Pena, editors, *La Prensa en Funcion del Desarrollo,* [La Paz, Bolivia], 1966; H. J. Skornia and J. W. Kitson, editors, *Problems and Controversies in Television and Radio,* Pacific Books, 1968; Chatten and Pena, editors, *La Television de Hoy,* [Quito, Ecador], 1972; H. D. Fischer and J. C. Merrill, editors, *International and Intercultural Communication,* Hastings House, 1976; P. Dumont-Frenette, editor, *Le Destin des relations publiques,* [Montreal], 1977.

Contributor of hundreds of articles to professional, scholarly, and mass circulation journals in the United States and abroad.

WORK IN PROGRESS: A book on communication development.

SIDELIGHTS: Lindsay lists his research concerns as: communication and international affairs; mass communication policy and training in developing countries; freedom of information, in its international aspects; satellite communications.

*   *   *

LIPMAN, Samuel 1934-

PERSONAL: Born June 7, 1934, in Los Gatos, Calif.; son of Max (in real estate) and Jane (Pinsky) Lipman; married Jeaneane Dowis (a concert pianist), April 18, 1963; children: Edward. *Education:* San Francisco State College, B.A., 1956; University of California, Berkeley, M.A., 1958; Julliard School, special student, 1959-62; has studied music privately with Pierre Monteux, Darius Milhaud, and Rosina Lhevinne. *Religion:* Jewish. *Home:* 340 Riverside Dr., New York, N.Y. 10025. *Office: Commentary,* 165 East 56th St., New York, N.Y. 10022.

CAREER: Concert pianist, 1943—; Aspen Music Festival and School, Aspen, Colo., member of piano faculty, 1971—; Waterloo Music Festival and School, Stanhope, N.J., member of piano faculty, 1976—; *Commentary,* New York City, music critic, 1976—. *Member:* American Historical Association, Harmonie Club (New York City). *Awards, honors:* Woodrow Wilson fellow, 1956; Deems Taylor Award, 1977, from American Society of Composers, Authors & Publishers, for "outstanding articles about music and its creators."

WRITINGS: The Revaluation of Music, Basic Books, 1979. Contributor of articles to *Times Literary Supplement* and *Music Journal.*

SIDELIGHTS: Lipman wrote to *CA:* "My current interests are two: the inability of modernism to find a wide musical audience, and the failure of serious music to expand or even retain its social base. At this point it seems clear that these twin disabilities suggest that the entire musical enterprise, as traditionally conceived, is presently in a wounded and par-

lous state. Though I remain committed to that enterprise, despite its problems, I can see no point in the artificial and professional optimism so endemic today among the publicists and administrators of music.

"I have concertized widely in the United States and Canada, appearing in recital and under such major conductors as Abravanel, Comissiona, Fiedler, Fricsay, Horenstein, and Monteux. In 1975, I gave the New York premiere of the Elliott Carter piano concerto in Carnegie Hall with the American Symphony. I made my New York recital debut in Town Hall in 1955, and my orchestral debut at Lewisohn Stadium in New York in 1956. I have appeared in nationally televised programs on both NBC and PBS, and have recorded for RCA and CRI."

*   *   *

LIPPERT, Clarissa Start 1917-
(Clarissa Start Davidson, Clarissa Start)

PERSONAL: Born March 28, 1917, in St. Louis, Mo.; daughter of George M. (a civil engineer) and Ada (Huebel) Start; married E. Gary Davidson (a lawyer), May 14, 1938 (died, March, 1967); married Raymond J. Lippert, December 21, 1972; children: (first marriage) Bruce Benton. *Education:* University of Missouri, B.J., 1936. *Politics:* Republican. *Religion:* Lutheran. *Home address:* Route 4, Box 196, High Ridge, Mo. 63049.

CAREER: St. Louis Post-Dispatch, St. Louis, Mo., author of column "The Little Woman," 1938-72; Blue Barn (antique shop), High Ridge, Mo., operator, 1972—. Past member of Missouri Commission on the Status of Women. *Member:* Missouri Press Women (past president), Advertising Women of St. Louis (past president), Theta Sigma Phi (past president), Fenton Garden Club. *Awards, honors:* National headliner award from Theta Sigma Phi, 1958, for column in *St. Louis Post-Dispatch;* award from Missouri Writers Guild, 1970, for *Never Underestimate the Little Woman;* top ten award from National Federation of Press Women, 1971.

WRITINGS—All under name Clarissa Start, except as indicated: (Under name Clarissa Start Davidson) *God's Man: The Story of Pastor Niemoeller,* Ives Washburn, 1959; (under name Clarissa Start Davidson) *When You're a Widow,* Concordia, 1968, published as *On Becoming a Widow,* Pyramid Publications, 1973; *Never Underestimate the Little Woman,* Concordia, 1969; *Look Here, Lord* (Catholic Digest Book Club selection), Augsburg, 1972; *Flowers Forever,* Donley Press, 1974; *Webster Groves,* privately printed, 1975.

WORK IN PROGRESS: A book on antiques; a book on second marriages.

SIDELIGHTS: Clarissa Lippert writes: "I have always written, for the most part in newspaper columns and books, about my personal life, as I find writing about the things close at hand and familiar has the widest reader appeal."

AVOCATIONAL INTERESTS: Gardening.

*   *   *

LLERENA AGUIRRE, Carlos (Antonio) 1952-

PERSONAL: Born March 31, 1952, in Arequipa, Peru; came to the United States in 1971, naturalized in 1975; son of Eduardo (a lawyer) and Susana (a teacher; maiden name, Aguirre Dongo) Llerena Salinas; married Debbie Hall (an artist), May 18, 1974. *Education:* Attended Universidad Federico Villarreal, 1970; Ringling School of Art, certificate, 1974; New York School of Visual Arts, B.A., 1978. *Home:* 105-28 65th Ave., 6B, Forest Hills, N.Y. 11375.

CAREER: School of Visual Arts, New York, N.Y., teacher of illustration and media communications, 1975—. Freelance artist (woodcuts, etchings, drawings). *Awards, honors:* Art awards include certificate of merit from New York City Society of Illustrators, 1976, for drawing "Hunger"; award of distinction from *Communication Arts,* 1977, for drawings from *Sticks and Stones;* gold medal from New York City Art Directors' Club, 1977, for drawing "The Brontes' Halloween."

WRITINGS: The Fair at Kanta (self-illustrated; juvenile), Holt, 1975; *Sticks and Stones* (self-illustrated; juvenile), Holt, 1977; (illustrator) William O. Steele, *Talking Bones: Secrets of Indian Burial Mounds,* Harper, 1978. Contributor of illustrations to popular magazines, including *Harper's, Saturday Review, Ms., Psychology Today,* and *Esquire,* and to newspapers.

WORK IN PROGRESS: The Witch of Queros, a self-illustrated children's book, publication by Harper expected in 1980.

SIDELIGHTS: Llerena Aguirre writes: "I have traveled extensively through the Peruvian Andes where I have recorded, in several sketchbooks, its people, their traditions and landscapes. During these trips I was inspired to create *The Fair at Kanta* and *Sticks and Stones.*

"Much of my time is spent creating etchings, woodcuts, and paintings of Peruvian motifs. I want to portray my people as I see them through their individual expressions of humanity.

"As well as art, I've studied several Peruvian instruments. Among them are the Quena, an ancient notched pre-Columbian flute, the Antara, a pentatonic pan-pipe, and the Charango, a mandolin-like instrument made with the shell of an armadillo. During my trips to the mountains I originally learned the flute under Moises La Torre, Roberto Roman, and Alejandro Vivanco."

*   *   *

LOCKMILLER, David A(lexander) 1906-

PERSONAL: Born August 30, 1906, in Athens, Tenn.; son of G. F. (a banker) and Lotta May (Ulrey) Lockmiller; married Alma Russell, September 23, 1930; children: F. Russell, Carlotta Elizabeth (Tillman). *Education:* Emory University, B.Ph., 1927, M.A., 1928; Cumberland University, LL.B., 1929; University of North Carolina, Ph.D., 1935; also attended University of Chicago, University of Paris, and Oxford University. *Politics:* Republican. *Religion:* Methodist. *Home and office address:* P.O. Box 1372, Sedona, Ariz. 86336.

CAREER: Attorney in Monett, Mo., 1929-34; North Carolina State University, Raleigh, professor of history, 1935-42; University of Chattanooga, Chattanooga, Tenn., president, 1942-59; Ohio Wesleyan University, Delaware, president, 1959-61; National Home Study Council, Washington, D.C., executive director, 1961-72; editorial consultant and writer, 1972—. Member of Bars of Missouri, Arkansas, Tennessee, Oklahoma, North Carolina, Ohio, and U.S. Supreme Court. U.S. delegate to Argentina's Sesquicentennial.

MEMBER: American Historical Association, Association of American Colleges, Southern Historical Association, Phi Beta Kappa, Phi Kappa Phi, Omicron Delta Kappa, Phi Delta Phi, Blue Key, Cosmos Club, Rotary International (local president; district governor), Kiwanis (honorary member). *Awards, honors:* LL.D. from Cumberland Uni-

versity, 1942, and Emory University, 1954; Litt.D. from University of Chattanooga, 1960; L.H.D. from American University, 1961, and Tennessee Wesleyan College, 1962.

WRITINGS: Magoon in Cuba, University of North Carolina Press, 1938, 2nd edition, 1969; *Sir William Blackstone,* University of North Carolina Press, 1938, 2nd edition, 1969; *History of North Carolina State College,* privately printed, 1939; *The Consolidation of the University of North Carolina,* University of North Carolina Press, 1942; *General Enoch H. Crowder,* University of Missouri Press, 1955; *Scholars on Parade,* Macmillan, 1964. Contributor to encyclopedias; contributor of articles and reviews to history and law journals.

WORK IN PROGRESS: Panorama of World Universities.

AVOCATIONAL INTERESTS: International travel.

*   *   *

LOCKWOOD, Mary
See SPELMAN, Mary

*   *   *

LOGAN, John 1923-

PERSONAL: Born January 23, 1923, in Red Oak, Iowa; son of James Borland (an accountant) and Agnes (Kemmers) Logan; married Mary Guenevere Minor (a librarian), September 9, 1945 (divorced); children: John, Theresa, Christina, Peter, Alice, David, Mark, Stephen, Paul. *Education:* Coe College, B.A., 1943; State University of Iowa, M.A., 1949. *Home:* 1396 Amherst, Buffalo, N.Y. 14216. *Office:* Department of English, State University of New York, Buffalo, N.Y. 14214.

CAREER: St. John's College, Annapolis, Md., tutor in great books, 1947-51; Notre Dame University, South Bend, Ind., assistant professor, 1951-55, associate professor of English, 1955-63; San Francisco State University, San Francisco, Calif., visiting professor of English, 1965-66; State University of New York at Buffalo, professor of English, 1966—. *Member:* International P.E.N. *Awards, honors:* Miles modern poetry prize from Wayne State University, 1968; Rockefeller Foundation grant, 1969; Morton Dauwen Zabel Award from National Institute of Arts & Letters, 1974, for poetry.

WRITINGS—All poems, except as indicated: *A Cycle for Mother Cabrini,* Grove, 1955; *Ghosts of the Heart,* University of Chicago Press, 1960; *Spring of the Thief,* Knopf, 1963; *Zig Zag Walk,* Dutton, 1969; *Anonymous Lover,* Liveright, 1973; *Poem in Progress,* Dryad, 1974; *The House That Jack Built* (autobiographical fiction), University of Nebraska Press, 1974.

Contributor of fiction and criticism to periodicals, including *New Yorker, Sewanee Review, Kenyon Review,* and *Chicago Review.* Founder and editor of *Choice;* poetry editor of *Critic* and *Nation.*

WORK IN PROGRESS: Only the Dreamer Can Change the Dream, poems; *The Panic Round,* short stories.

*   *   *

LOGGINS, William Kirk 1946-

PERSONAL: Born October 20, 1946, in Dickson, Tenn.; son of Hick Farris (a farmer) and Mary Lee (Robertson) Loggins. *Education:* Vanderbilt University, B.A., 1968. *Office: Nashville Tennessean,* 1750 Pennsylvania Ave. N.W., Washington, D.C. 20006.

CAREER/WRITINGS: Dickson County Herald, Dickson, Tenn., editor, 1968-72; *Nashville Tennessean,* Nashville, Tenn., reporter, 1972-75, Washington correspondent, 1975—. Stringer for *Rolling Stone,* 1975.

SIDELIGHTS: Loggins told *CA:* "I fell into journalism for lack of anything better to do, but have now become fairly committed to it. It greatest pleasures, to me, are exact observation and calling public figures to task. I have become more and more concerned with the apparently casual and haphazard operation of government at all levels and the perhaps concomitant disappearance of traditional social structure."

* * *

LOHR, Thomas F. 1926-

PERSONAL: Born June 17, 1926, in Governeur, N.Y.; son of Frederick T. (an engineer) and Elfred (an actress; maiden name, Chilton) Lohr; married June Curtis (a decorator), February 14, 1950; children: Jennifer, Phoebe, Fred, Philip. *Education:* Brown University, A.B., 1941; Columbia University, M.A., 1952; Harvard University, Ph.D., 1955. *Politics:* Conservative. *Religion:* Christian. *Home address:* R.D. 2, Box 387, Coopersburg, Pa. 18036. *Office:* Department of Psychology, Muhlenberg College, Allentown, Pa. 18104.

CAREER: Muhlenberg College, Allentown, Pa., 1954—, began as assistant professor, became professor of psychology. *Military service:* U.S. Army Air Forces, 1941-45, prisoner of war, 1943-45; became first lieutenant; received Air Medal and Purple Heart.

WRITINGS: The Mechanics of the Mind, Venture Books, 1971.

* * *

LOUGHMILLER, Campbell 1906-

PERSONAL: Born October 19, 1906, near Canton, Tex.; son of George J. (a farmer and businessman) and Tommie (Richards) Loughmiller; married Lynn O. Nicolaides (a naturalist-historian, educator, and writer), September 1, 1935; children: Camelia Sue Loughmiller Lambert, Grover C. *Education:* Attended Weatherford Junior College, 1925-26, and Texas Technological College (now Texas Tech University), 1927-29; University of California, Berkeley, B.A., 1934, graduate study, 1934-35; Southern Methodist University, M.Ed., 1954. *Religion:* Methodist. *Home and office address:* Route 1, Box 498, Whitehouse, Tex. 75791. *Agent:* Evelyn Oppenheimer, 4505 Fairway, Dallas, Tex. 75219.

CAREER: Seaman, 1926-31; Department of Public Welfare, Crescent City, Calif., director, 1935-36; State Relief Administration, Del Norte County, Calif., director, 1935-36; Farm Security Administration, Dallas, Tex., chief of community and family services, 1936-39; City-County Welfare Department, Dallas, director, 1939-43; U.S. Office of Labor, War Food Administration, Chicago, Ill., assistant regional director, 1943-46; Camp Woodland Springs, Dallas, founder and camp director, 1946-66; mental health and education consultant, 1966—. Member of Texas United Community Services; member of board of directors of Texas Conservation Council; past member of board of directors of Dallas Community Planning Council, and Dallas Children's Bureau.

MEMBER: National Association of Social Workers, Outdoor Education Association, American Camping Association (past member of national board of directors; past state president), Audubon Society, Wilderness Society, Sierra Club, Texas Mental Health Society (past member of board

of directors), Texas Social Welfare Association (past member of board of directors), Nature Conservancy of Texas (past president). *Awards, honors:* Special award from Texas chapter of American Camping Association, 1952; LL.B. from George Marshall Law School, 1975; certificate from American Association for State and Local History, 1977, for *Big Thicket Legacy.*

WRITINGS: (With wife, Lynn Loughmiller) *Camping and Christian Growth,* Abingdon, 1953; (with L. Loughmiller) *Let's Go Camping,* Abingdon, 1953; *Wilderness Road,* Hogg Foundation for Mental Health, 1966; (with L. Loughmiller) *Big Thicket Legacy,* University of Texas Press, 1977. Contributor to professional journals.

WORK IN PROGRESS: Camping With Kids in Trouble: An Adventure in Education.

SIDELIGHTS: Camp Woodland Springs is an outdoor program for delinquent and emotionally handicapped children. Loughmiller and his wife lived on the grounds, raising their own children in a wilderness area just outside the city of Dallas. His interest in camping and canoeing, especially on wild rivers, has taken him all over the United States, Central and South America, and around the rest of the world, including a three-week camping trip in the Arctic.

AVOCATIONAL INTERESTS: Nature photography, "visiting with people."

* * *

LOVE, Kennett 1924-

PERSONAL: Born August 17, 1924, in St. Louis, Mo.; son of John Allan (a businessman) and Mary (a painter; maiden name, Potter) Love; married Felicite Pratt, June 27, 1946 (divorced, 1969); married Melinda Reed, December 21, 1973; children: Mary Christy Love Sadron, Suzanna, John, Nicholas. *Education:* Columbia University, A.B., 1948; also attended Princeton University. *Politics:* "Pacifist." *Religion:* Episcopalian. *Home:* Hotel des Artistes, 1 West 67th St., New York, N.Y. 10023. *Agent:* Curtis Brown Ltd., 60 East 56th St., New York, N.Y. 10022.

CAREER: Hudson Dispatch, Union City, N.J., reporter, 1948; *New York Times,* New York, N.Y., foreign correspondent, 1948-62; *U.S.A. 1* (magazine), New York City, associate editor, 1962; U.S. Peace Corps, Washington, D.C., planner and evaluator, 1963-64; Princeton University, Princeton, N.J., research associate, 1964-67; American University in Cairo, Cairo, Egypt, professor, 1971-73; American Broadcasting Corp., New York, N.Y., correspondent from Cairo, 1973-74; writer. *Military service:* U.S. Navy, Air Force, 1943-45. *Member:* Middle East Institute, Overseas Press Club of America.

WRITINGS: Suez: The Twice-Fought War, McGraw, 1969, revised edition, Longman, 1970. Contributor to national and professional journals, including *New Leader, Show,* and *Washington Monthly,* and newspapers.

WORK IN PROGRESS: An autobiography; a play, short stories.

SIDELIGHTS: Love comments: "My experiences as a co-founder of the 'war tax resistance movement' in the 1960's influenced my political thinking. Other strong influences are professional theater training and the sea. I am now sailing a forty-one foot yawl around the world with my wife. We began sailing in the Mediterranean and have sailed from New York to Hawaii. My present writing is coming out of a pervasive transition from journalism and historical work into fiction."

LOVE, Philip H(ampton)   1905-1977

PERSONAL: Born December 19, 1905, in Baltimore, Md.; son of Philip H. (a real estate broker) and Madeline S. (a musician; maiden name, McDonald) Love; married Ann Purcell (an artist), December 29, 1928; children: Ann (Mrs. Edward A. Greene). *Education:* Attended Landon School of Cartooning, 1918-19, and Calvert Hall College, 1919-22. *Home and office:* 3015 Beech St. N.W., Washington, D.C. 20015. *Agent:* Toni Mendez, 140 East 56th St., New York, N.Y. 10022.

CAREER: Baltimore Times, Baltimore, Md., cartoonist, 1922; free-lance cartoonist and writer, 1923-29; *Baltimore Post,* Baltimore, feature writer, 1929-31; *Washington Star,* Washington, D.C., reporter, 1931-35, assistant city editor, 1935-38, associate Sunday editor, 1938-45, Sunday magazine editor, 1945-63, feature editor and columnist, 1963-70; *Greater Buffalo Press,* Buffalo, N.Y., editor, 1971-77; columnist for McNaught syndicate, 1971-77; *Profiles* magazine, Westport, Conn., columnist and cartoonist, 1973-77. Lecturer in journalism at George Washington University, 1942-52; guest lecturer at American University, 1947-77. Columnist and special writer for North American Newspaper Alliance, Bell-McClure Syndicate, 1963-71. Writer of syndicated column, "Love on Life." Consultant to newspapers. *Member:* National Press Club, American Association of Sunday and Feature Editors, White House Correspondents Association.

WRITINGS: Andrew W. Mellon: The Man and His Works, Coggins, 1929; *Phil Love Talks of the Comics,* Metropolitan Sunday Newspaper, 1964. Contributor of short stories and verse to magazines and newspapers.

OBITUARIES: Washington Post, August 18, 1977; *Washington Star,* August 18, 1977.

(Died August 17, 1977, in Washington, D.C.)

*   *   *

LOVELACE, Earl   1935-

PERSONAL: Born in 1935, in Trinidad; married. *Residence:* Trinidad. *Office:* c/o Henry Regnery Co., 180 N. Michigan Ave., Chicago, Ill. 60601.

CAREER: Novelist. Has also worked as an agricultural assistant for the Jamaican Civil Service. *Awards, honors:* British Petroleum Independence Award, 1965, for *While Gods Are Falling.*

WRITINGS: While Gods Are Falling (novel), Collins, 1965, Regnery, 1966; *The Schoolmaster* (novel), Regnery, 1968.

SIDELIGHTS: Lovelace's *The Schoolmaster,* a novel about the building of a school in the remote Trinidad village of Kumaca, was reviewed by Martin Levin in the *New York Times Book Review:* "*The Schoolmaster* is a folk fable with the clean, elemental structure of Steinbeck's *The Pearl.* But unlike *The Pearl,* Mr. Lovelace tells his story from the inside looking out, using the unsophisticated accents of everyday speech to lead to a Homeric conclusion." Levin added that Lovelace is a "writer of elegant skills, with an infectious sensitivity to the heady Carribean [sic] atmosphere."

BIOGRAPHICAL/CRITICAL SOURCES: New York Times Book Review, October 30, 1966, November 24, 1968; *New Statesman,* January 5, 1968.*

*   *   *

LUBIN, Isador   1896-1978

June 9, 1896—July 6, 1978; American economist, statistician, educator, and author of books in his field. A special adviser to President Franklin D. Roosevelt, Lubin was considered one of the most prominent members of the New Deal "Brain Trust." Lubin began his career in government service in 1918, when he served as a statistician in the Food Administration. After World War I he held various teaching positions until he was named commissioner of the Bureau of Labor Statistics in 1933. During President Harry Truman's administration, Lubin served as U.S. representative to the Economic and Social Council of the United Nations. From 1953 to 1959 he worked as the industrial commissioner of the state of New York. He died in Annapolis, Md. Obituaries and other sources: *Current Biography,* Wilson, 1953; *Who's Who in World Jewry,* Pitman, 1972; *American Men and Women of Science: The Social and Behavioral Sciences,* 12th edition, Bowker, 1973; *Who's Who in America,* 39th edition, Marquis, 1976; *The International Who's Who,* Europa, 1977; *Washington Post,* July 8, 1978.

*   *   *

LUBOW, Robert E.   1932-

PERSONAL: Born March 25, 1932, in New York, N.Y.; son of Harry and Sima (Szmerkovitz) Lubow; married Karol Solomon, August 14, 1953 (died, 1970); married Malka Lerner, December 15, 1970; children: David, Susan, Michael, Oren. *Education:* New York University, B.A., 1953; Washington State University, M.S., 1955; Cornell University, Ph.D., 1958. *Home:* 13 Shalom Aleichem St., Herzlia-Pituah, Israel. *Office:* Department of Psychology, Tel-Aviv University, Ramat-Aviv, Israel.

CAREER: General Electric Advanced Electronic Center, Ithaca, N.Y., research psychologist, 1958-63; North Carolina State University, Raleigh, assistant professor, 1963-65, associate professor, 1965-70, professor of psychology, 1970-71; Tel-Aviv University, Ramat-Aviv, Israel, professor of psychology, 1971—. Visiting fellow, Yale University, 1977-78. *Member:* American Psychological Association, Psychonomic Society, American Association for the Advancement of Science. *Awards, honors:* Career development award from National Institutes for Health, 1963-68.

WRITINGS: The War Animals, Doubleday, 1977. Contributor to psychology journals.

WORK IN PROGRESS: A book, as yet untitled, on the relationship between basic research with animals and human problem solving and knowledge, to be published by Lippincott.

*   *   *

LUCAS, George   1944-

PERSONAL: Born May 14, 1944, in Modesto, Calif.; son of George (a retail merchant) and Dorothy; married Marcia Griffin (a film editor). *Education:* Modesto Junior College, A.A.; University of Southern California, B.A. *Residence:* San Anselmo, Calif. *Office address:* c/o Jane Bay, P.O. Box 186, San Anselmo, Calif. 94960.

CAREER: Worked as film editor for U.S. Information Agency; assistant to Francis Ford Coppola for "The Rain People," 1969; director of motion pictures and writer, 1971—. *Member:* Writers Guild of America, Academy of Motion Picture Arts and Sciences, Screen Directors Guild. *Awards, honors:* Received Third National Student Film Festival Award, 1967-68, for "THX 1138:4EB"; best screenplay award from New York Film Critics and from National Society of Film Critics, and nominations from

Academy of Motion Picture Arts and Sciences for best screenplay, best director, and best film, all 1973, all for "American Graffiti"; best film award from Los Angeles Film Critics, nominations from Academy of Motion Picture Arts and Sciences for best director and best film, all 1977, all for "Star Wars"; and numerous other film awards.

WRITINGS: American Graffiti, Grove, 1974; *Star Wars,* Ballantine, 1976.

Screenplays: (With Walter Murch; and director) "THX 1138," released by Warner Brothers, 1971; (with Gloria Katz and Willard Huyck; and director) "American Graffiti," Universal, 1973; (and director) "Star Wars," Twentieth Century-Fox, 1977. Also author of three alternate "Star Wars" scripts; developer of unproduced script, "Apocalypse Now."

WORK IN PROGRESS—Screenplays: "Radioland Murders"; "More American Graffiti"; a sequel to "Star Wars"; "Raiders of the Lost Ark."

SIDELIGHTS: "I was at a film conference with George Cukor," recalled Lucas, "and he detested the fact that everyone called us filmmakers. He said, 'I'm not a filmmaker. A filmmaker is like a toymaker, and I'm a director.' Well, I'm a filmmaker. I'm very much akin to a toymaker. I like to make things move, and I like to make them move myself." As both writer and director of three films, Lucas belongs to the exclusive circle of American filmmakers (along with Francis Ford Coppola, Woody Allen, Robert Altman, and a few others) referred to as auteurs. "He is a pure filmmaker," said Coppola of Lucas. "He really only wants to put on film the things he loves. He has few pretentions about making 'great films' or 'great art,' and consequently he comes closer than most." Lucas himself stated: "Just give me the tools and I'll make the toys. I can sit forever doodling on my movie. I don't think that much whether it's going to be a great movie or a terrible movie, or whether it's going to be a piece of art or a piece of shit."

Unlike most of his peers, Lucas was not a film buff as an adolescent. After an auto accident ruined his hopes of becoming a racer, he enrolled at a community college, worked as a mechanic's assistant, and began photographing automobiles. Through a mechanic he met noted cinematographer, Haskell Wexler. Encouraged by Wexler, Lucas entered the University of Southern California's film school where he gained notoriety for his determination. "When I got to film school," Lucas told *Film Quarterly,* "the other students said, 'You really can't make movies here. They don't give you enough film, they don't let you keep the camera for very long.' Well, I made eight films at USC, ranging from one minute to twenty-five minutes. It was difficult, and there were lots of barriers, but it wasn't impossible."

Lucas's early ability to overcome obstacles carried over into his professional career. His "American Graffiti" was turned down by numerous studios before Universal agreed to make it provided Coppola would produce. Ultimately doing the film on a minimal budget ($750,000), a twenty-eight night shooting schedule, and a $20,000 salary, Lucas saw the film become the eleventh largest grossing one to date. After the success of "American Graffiti," Lucas took his idea for "Star Wars" around to various studios (including Universal) where he was refused repeatedly until Twentieth Century-Fox accepted the script and provided him with an $8.5 million budget.

Lucas's first film, "THX 1138," suffered at the box office and received mixed reviews. Stephen Farber referred to it as "a dazzling technical achievement; it revealed Lucas's con-

trol of all the resources of film—sound as well as image. Unfortunately, it also exhibited the most common failings of the science-fiction genre: the ideas (drawn from Orwell and Huxley) were rather stale, and the whole movie was rather cold and arid; the zombie characters could not really stir our sympathy." Lucas's own regret was not that it had been poorly received but that, unlike "Star Wars," it was an end in itself. "When I did 'THX 1138,' I realized that I put in an enormous amount of effort that I will never be able to use again. I know the world of 'THX 1138.' I could make movies about 'THX 1138' forever but it took so much time and so much energy to develop all that stuff, and then it got touched upon in one movie."

Disturbed with his reputation as a result of "THX 1138," Lucas resolved to contradict his image. "After I finished 'THX 1138,' I was considered a cold, weird director, a science-fiction sort of guy who carried a calculator. And I'm not like that at all. So, I thought, maybe I'll do something exactly the opposite." But in "American Graffiti," Lucas was careful not to alter his style, just his degree of personalization. "'American Graffiti' has the same technical flair," wrote Faber, "but Lucas's work with the actors reveals a new talent; the film has a depth of feeling missing from 'THX 1138.'" Lucas explains the differences simply: "'THX 1138' is very much the way that I am as a filmmaker. 'American Graffiti' is very much the way I am as a person—two different worlds really."

Hailed upon release as an appropriate addition to the nostalgia craze, "American Graffiti" proved to be much more than just an extension of a fad. "The film is about change," said Lucas. "It's about the change in rock and roll, it's about the change in a young person's life at eighteen when he leaves home and goes off to college; and it's also about the cultural change that took place when the fifties turned into the sixties—when we went from a country of apathy and non-involvement to a country of radical involvement." The film was also a step forward for Lucas as a filmmaker. He showed the studios that a film could be done unconventionally—almost exclusively at night and without traditional plot—and still be commercially successful. "What's interesting about 'American Graffiti,'" said actor Dustin Hoffman, "is that millions of people are willing to go to a movie that breaks away from conventional plot."

After the more conventional "Star Wars" was released, Lucas told Paul Scanlon that he wished to pursue the experimental direction of "American Graffiti" further: "What I want to do now is take my craft in the other direction, which is telling stories without plots and creating emotions without understanding what is going on in terms of purely visual and sound relationships."

Upon release, "Star Wars" was immediately praised by critics. *New Yorker* reviewer Penelope Gilliatt called it "amazing" and "exuberantly entertaining," while *Time* referred to it as "a grand and glorious film that may well be the smash hit of 1977, and certainly is the best movie of the year so far." Lucas was less enthusiastic. "'Star Wars' is about twenty-five percent of what I wanted it to be," he said. "It's still a good movie but it fell so short of what I wanted it to be." Asked what inspired him, Lucas replied: "I wanted to make a space fantasy that was more in the genre of Edgar Rice Burroughs; that whole other end of space fantasy that was there before science took it over in the fifties. I saw that kids today don't have westerns, they don't have pirate movies, they don't have that stupid serial fantasy life that we used to believe in."

Thematically, all three films are similar. "Both 'THX 1138' and 'American Graffiti' are saying the same thing," said Lucas, "that you don't have to do anything; it is still a free country." Speaking of "Star Wars," he added: "I was also working with themes that I worked with in 'THX 1138' and 'American Graffiti,' of accepting responsibility for your actions and that kind of stuff." Lucas is a zealous believer in his themes. "Everybody says, 'the country's rotten, we've fought for change but doesn't work. It's hopeless.' Well, life isn't that way," said Lucas. "It wasn't that way for THX 1138, it wasn't that way for Curt Henderson [character in "American Graffiti"], and it isn't that way for me. When they said I could never get into the film business, I said, 'Well, okay, but I'll try anyway.' Anybody who wants to do anything can do it. It's an old hokey American point of view, but I've sort of discovered that it's true." Lucas justifies the mood change of "American Graffiti" and "Star Wars" away from the sterility and oppressive sense of "THX 1138": "I realized after 'THX 1138' that people don't care about how the country's being ruined. All that movie did was to make people more pessimistic, more depressed, and less willing to get involved in trying to make the world better. So I decided that this time I would make a more optimistic film that makes people feel positive about their fellow human beings."

Lucas is frequently considered with Martin Scorsese, Brian De Palma, and Steven Spielberg, as the new wave in American film, but he eschews comparisons. "Some of my friends," Lucas said, "are more concerned about art and being considered a Fellini or an Orson Welles, but I've never had that problem. I just like making movies."

AVOCATIONAL INTERESTS: Anthropology, sociology, auto racing, comic and illustrator art, antique toys.

BIOGRAPHICAL/CRITICAL SOURCES: Film Quarterly, spring, 1974; *New Yorker,* May 30, 1977; *Time,* May 30, 1977; *Rolling Stone,* August 25, 1977.

* * *

LUCAS, T(homas) E(dward) 1919-

PERSONAL: Born June 24, 1919, in Chicago, Ill.; son of Frank Cook (in business) and Ann (Quinliven) Lucas; married Lise Michiko Endo (an artist), January 21, 1955; children: Thomas E., Jr. *Education:* Attended Northwestern University, 1937-38; University of Chicago, M.A., 1948; attended University of Illinois, 1948-49; University of Denver, Ph.D., 1963. *Home:* 108 Connett Pl., South Orange, N.J. 07079. *Office:* Department of English, Seton Hall University, South Orange, N.J. 07079.

CAREER: U.S. Air Force, career officer, 1942-45 and 1951-69, psychological warfare officer in Korea and Tokyo, 1952-55, and headquarters squadron commander for Western Air Defense Forces, 1956-58, associate professor of English at U.S. Air Force Academy, 1959-69, retiring as major; Seton Hall University, South Orange, N.J., professor of English, 1969—, chairperson of department, 1976—. Has also taught in Japan. *Member:* Modern Language Association of America, Modern Humanities Research Association, American Association of University Professors.

WRITINGS: Elder Olson, Twayne, 1972. Contributing editor of annual bibliography for Modern Humanities Research Association, 1964-70.

WORK IN PROGRESS: A book on Melville's literary theories; a collection of poems.

SIDELIGHTS: Lucas writes: "My book on Elder Olson is

the first book-length study both of its subject and of 'Chicago Criticism' in general. It has had good critical reception. I have recently read my poems at a number of poetry readings to enthusiastic response. I have received a letter of thanks from the brother of the Emperor of Japan, Prince Takamatsu, for my work with Japanese students and was rather well-known in that country."

* * *

LUCAS, W(ilmer) F(rancis, Jr.) 1927-

PERSONAL: Born September 1, 1927, in Brooklyn, N.Y.; son of Wilmer Francis (a certified public accountant) and Inez (a teacher; maiden name, Williams) Lucas; married Cleo Melissa Martin (a professor of history), February 18, 1969; children: Alain Francis. *Education:* Attended New York University, 1945-48. *Religion:* Episcopalian. *Home and office:* 1936 Prospect Pl., Knoxville, Tenn. 37915.

CAREER: New York Amsterdam News, New York City, United Nations correspondent, 1959-60; Howard News Syndicate, New York City, associate editor in United Nations Bureau, 1960-61; New School for Social Research, New York City, lecturer in comparative Afro-American literature, 1962-68; Knoxville College, Knoxville, Tenn., writer-in-residence, 1968-70; University of Tennessee, Knoxville, director of Black Experience Institute, 1970-71, lecturer at Educational Opportunities Planning Center, 1971-72, co-director of humanities summer program, 1972, instructor in humanities, 1972-73; full-time writer, 1973—. Special guest lecturer for colleges, universities, and civic organizations. Visiting lecturer in English at Lincoln University, 1966-67; research consultant for Opportunities Industrial Center, 1967-68. Founder and executive director of Carpetbag Theatre, 1971—; past member of theater arts advisory council for Tennessee Arts Commission and Knoxville City Commission for the Arts. Chairman of Duke Ellington Cancer Center Fund.

MEMBER: Authors Guild of Authors League of America, American Comparative Literature Association, Popular Culture Association (state coordinator), American Film Institute, American Federation of Musicians, Black Merit Academy, Duke Ellington Society.

WRITINGS: Bottom Fishing: A Novella and Other Stories, Carpetbag Press, 1974.

Plays: "Patent Leather Sunday" (one-act), first produced in Lincoln University, Pa., spring, 1967; "Fandangos for Miss X" (one-act), first produced in Philadelphia, 1969; "Aunt Lottie's Wake" (one-act), first produced in Knoxville at Carpetbag Theatre, 1972; "Africa Too Young" (one-act), first produced in Knoxville at Carpetbag Theatre, 1972; "Elevator Stomp" (one-act), first produced in Knoxville at Carpetbag Theatre, 1973; "The Planet of President Pandora" (three-act), first produced in Knoxville at Carpetbag Theatre, May, 1977. Also author of several one-act plays done in workshops.

Contributor to magazines and local newspapers in Haiti and the United States. Associate editor of *African Heritage,* 1963-64; book review editor of Negro Book Club, 1964-65, and *East Village Other,* 1968-69; contributing editor of *News Illustrated,* 1965-66, and *Our Voice,* 1970-72; editor-at-large and author of column "At Last" in *Kenyana-Spectrum,* 1974-75.

WORK IN PROGRESS: Tropical Philadelphia, an experimental novel; *An Okra Venue,* a novel of regional aperture; *Bottom Fishing Revisited* (or *BF II*), a further collection of short stories.

SIDELIGHTS: Lucas writes: "Having lived in Appalachia for nearly ten years without direct recourse to the mainstream of the publishing industry (except via perfunctory correspondence), I am in pursuit of a more constant and responsible liaison with the industry which I hope will see fit to afford me greater publishing opportunities. Without the aid of both agent and publisher who are equally cogently empathetic and imaginative, the source of much material I am capable of is becoming a still-born legacy that will one day arise like Lazarus in my lifetime.

"The sense of being a New Yorker and Yankee to boot still is primary in my consciousness, and will be there till the end. As an avid reader of all media, I am not only a bibliophile, but also an activist in issues that relate to the projection of the Carpetbag Theatre that I founded in 1971 to bring responsible theatre to the community in which I live. Trying to bring the past and the future to the present is virtually literary social work that I now feel can stand on its own. In the beginning it was social concern (and equally economic), and now it reverts to its true original premise of aesthetics in the quality of its own genre and milieu.

"My work bears the indelibility of cultural pluralism in a world in which I have traveled in both fact and imagination. The two are indistinguishable but hopefully the sense of art survives. The sophisticated truth and the real truth is the bridge that is being built on which we can all stand. I live both in the attic as well as the cellar. In between I survive.'

"My relationship to the south by exposure is no less than an exposure to my environment, I am by nature eternally curious, and a voyeur of sorts whose previous apprenticeship to people, places and problems of the arts is already history. I now concentrate on my family, my work, and my theatre."

AVOCATIONAL INTERESTS: "Gigging" with other musicians with his vibraharp, fiction, literary criticism, creative living.

* * *

LUCKETT, Hubert Pearson 1916-

PERSONAL: Born November 18, 1916, in Cameron, Tex.; son of Henry Lee (a machinist) and Adelia (Pearson) Luckett; married Joleigh Cohn (divorced, 1961); married Dorothy Whipple (an artist), July 20, 1962; children: Daniel, Arleigh, Terence, James. *Education:* Attended University of Texas, 1935-42. *Politics:* Democrat. *Home:* 72 Colonial Ave., Dobbs Ferry, N.Y. 10522. *Office: Popular Science,* 380 Madison Ave., New York, N.Y. 10017.

CAREER/WRITINGS: Christianson-Leibermann Studios, Austin, Tex., photographer, 1942-45; *Popular Science,* New York, N.Y., photographer, 1945-54, technical editor, 1954-65, executive editor, 1965-70, editor-in-chief, 1971—. Writer, performer, and director for National Educational Television. Union Free School District Three Board of Education in Dobbs Ferry, N.Y., member, 1961-66, president, 1965-66; trustee of Village of Dobbs Ferry, 1967-70. *Member:* American Society of Magazine Editors (executive board member), Overseas Press Club, Dutch Treat Club.

* * *

LUCKETT, Karen Beth 1944-

PERSONAL: Born November 1, 1944, in Canton, Miss.; daughter of Gustus (a civil servant) and Georgia (a nurse; maiden name, Craig) Luckett. *Education:* Attended high school in Columbus, Ga. *Politics:* Democrat. *Religion:* Roman Catholic. *Home:* 864 Peachtree Dr., Columbus, Ga. 31906.

CAREER: Writer, 1971—. *Member:* Freedom for Handicaps.

WRITINGS: Short Stories for Boys and Girls, Exposition Press, 1972.

WORK IN PROGRESS: A picture book for children; writing for juvenile magazines.

* * *

LUTHER, Edward T(urner) 1928-

PERSONAL: Born February 11, 1928, in Nashville, Tenn.; son of Eligah T. (a foundryman) and Matilda (McCall) Luther; married Patricia Worthy (a program secretary), September 17, 1955; children: Margaret Kennedy, Daniel Edward. *Education:* Vanderbilt University, B.A., 1950, M.S., 1951. *Politics:* "Liberal-leaning Independent." *Religion:* Methodist. *Home:* 838 Summerly Dr., Nashville, Tenn. 37209. *Office:* Tennessee Division of Geology, G-5 State Office Building, Nashville, Tenn. 37219.

CAREER: Tennessee Geological Survey, Nashville, geologist, 1951-57; Tennessee Valley Authority, Chattanooga, fuels engineer on planning staff, 1957; Tennessee Geological Survey, assistant director, 1958—. Part-time instructor at University of Tennessee, 1956-57, 1976-78. Consultant on coal geology and reserves. Cartographer. *Military service:* U.S. Navy, 1946-48; served in Pacific theater. *Member:* Geological Society of America (fellow; vice-chairman of Coal Geology Division, 1970, chairman, 1971), Association of Professional Geological Scientists (member of state management board, 1977-78), Tennessee Academy of Science (chairman of Geology-Geography Section, 1959).

WRITINGS: Our Restless Earth: The Geologic Regions of Tennessee, University of Tennessee Press, 1977. Contributor to technical and popular journals, including *Tennessee Conservationist.*

WORK IN PROGRESS: Research on the early history of the gold-producing areas of the southeastern United States in the first half of the nineteenth-century, for a historical novel linking frontier Tennessee with the California gold rush.

SIDELIGHTS: Luther writes: "I have always wanted to be a writer, but was never interested in a conventional English-major type of approach. I am happy with my career as a geologist, and have been reasonably successful, but the urge to write persists. I have gone through the usual beginning writer's syndrome (creative writing course, unpublished short stories, etc.), but have had success only in the field of popularized science articles.

"My own taste in reading is strongly bent toward the novel form, and on the theory that one writes best the kind of material he most enjoys reading, I look forward someday to attempting a novel. I have always felt that my training in geology would be an advantage in such an endeavor, in particular for setting a scene and avoiding some of the unlikely material so common in fiction that deals in any way with mining, oil drilling, or even so overworked a topic as the perils encountered by wagon trains during the gold rush."

* * *

LYNNE, James Broom 1920-
(James Quartermain)

PERSONAL: Born October 31, 1920, in London, England; married Catherine Joan Redmore, 1948; children: three. *Education:* Attended St. Martin's School of Art, London.

Home: Gissings, East Bergholt, Colchester, Essex, England. *Agent:* A. D. Peters, 10 Buckingham St., Adelphi, London, England.

CAREER: Free-lance graphic artist specializing in book design, playwright, and novelist. William Larkins Studio, London, England, art director, 1960-61; Service Advertising, London, storyboard director, 1962-66; Macdonald and Co. (publishers), London, art editor, 1966-69; art school lecturer in London, 1970-72. *Wartime service:* Served with the Civil Defense, 1940-45.

WRITINGS: The Trigon (play; first produced in London, 1962; produced Off-Broadway at Stage 73, October 9, 1965), J. Cape, 1963; "Ketch," first produced in London, 1963; *Tobey's Wednesday,* Macdonald & Co., 1967, published as *The Wednesday Visitors,* Doubleday, 1968; *The Marchioness,* Macdonald & Co., 1968, Doubleday, 1969; *Drag Hunt,* M. Joseph, 1969; (under pseudonym James Quartermain) *The Diamond Hook,* Doubleday, 1970; (under pseudonym) *The Man Who Walked on Diamonds,* Doubleday, 1972; (under pseudonym) *Rock of Diamonds,* Doubleday, 1972; *The Commuters,* Doubleday, 1973; *The Colonel's War,* W. H. Allen, 1975; (under pseudonym) *The Diamond Hostage,* Constable, 1975; *Verdict,* W. H. Allen, 1976; *Jet Race,* Putnam, 1978.

Teleplays: "The Jokers," 1961; "The Living Image," 1963; "Wanted: Single Gentleman," 1967.

Radio plays: "Charlie and Duke," 1963; "Return Visit," 1965; "The Duke and Duckett," 1965; "Top People Have Rows, Too," 1965; "To the Home Office, with Love," 1965; "Trilogy: The Applicant, The Golden Marathon, The High Place," 1967.

WORK IN PROGRESS: Research visits to South Africa, Sierra Leone, and Liberia for a novel set in the world of diamonds.

SIDELIGHTS: Lynne's novels are popular and have excited praise from the critics. Most acclaimed are those written under his pseudonym James Quartermain. These suspense novels feature Corbo, a security officer for Diamonds, Ltd., who was ranked by a *New York Times Book Review* critic as "a cut above most of his kind."

Lynne told *CA:* "With *The Commuters, The Colonel's War,* and *Verdict,* I have entered the world of 'faction'—novels combining fact with fiction. All three books contain much autobiographical material. In *The Commuters,* I draw on childhood memories and on my adult experiences as a commuter to London. In *The Colonel's War,* I relate my own wartime experiences in Civil Defense and security liason with the American forces in Mayfair, London. *Verdict* was written after observation of trial procedure at the Old Bailey, London's central criminal court. In *Jet Race* I express my love of flying and aircraft and of world travel. But this book also contains an expression of my sympathy with, and support for, the Israeli cause, but with an understanding of the Arab States and their problems and a not entirely unsympathetic view of the PLO and the PLA.

"My ambition as a writer is simply to become a first-class entertainer. 'Art' is accidental. Artists and writers, composers too, work to an audience—very few work in an ivory tower and shield their work from vulgar, public gaze. I want to entertain and, maybe, instruct a little and knock down a few Aunt Sallies."

BIOGRAPHICAL/CRITICAL SOURCES: New York Times, October 11, 1965; *New York Times Book Review,* April 11, 1967, March 17, 1968; *Times Literary Supplement,* April 20, 1967; *New Yorker,* July 12, 1969; *Best Sellers,* September 1, 1970.

M

MABOGUNJE, Akin(lawon) L(adipo) 1931-

PERSONAL: Born October 18, 1931, in Kano, Nigeria; son of Joseph Omotunde (a bookkeeper) and Janet Adeola (a trader; maiden name, Atewologun) Mabogunje; married Titilola Ogunmekan (a chief magistrate), December 28, 1957; children: Folasade (daughter), Oluseun (son), Adegboyega (son), Adebimpe (daughter), Olusola (son). *Education:* University of Ibadan, B.A., 1953; University of London, B.A. (honors), 1956, M.A., 1958, Ph.D., 1961. *Religion:* Christian. *Home:* 13 Oba Olagbegi St., Bodija Estate, Ibadan, Nigeria. *Office:* Department of Geography, University of Ibadan, Ibadan, Nigeria.

CAREER: University of Ibadan, Ibadan, Nigeria, assistant lecturer, 1958-60, lecturer, 1960-63, senior lecturer, 1963-65, professor of geography, 1965—. Member of Western Nigeria Economic Advisory Council, 1967-71, and Federal Public Service Review Commission, 1972-74; chairman of Western State Forestry Commission, 1968-76; consultant to Nigerian National Census Board, 1973-75, and Nigerian Federal Capital Development Authority, 1976—; chairman of Nigerian Council for Management Development, 1976—; member of board of trustees of Population Council, 1977—. Visiting professor at Northwestern University, 1963, 1967, University of Goteborg, 1970, University of Rio de Janeiro, 1975, and Stockholm School of Economics, 1976; Commonwealth visiting professor at universities in England. Member of board of directors and vice-president of Pan-African Institute for Development, 1972—; consultant to the United Nations.

MEMBER: International Geographical Union (first vice-president), Nigerian Geographical Association (former president), Association of American Geographers, Institute of British Geographers, Regional Science Association, Regional Studies Association. *Awards, honors:* David Livingstone Memorial Gold Medal from American Geographical Society, 1972; D.Econ. from Stockholm School of Economics, 1973; Murchison Award from Royal Geographical Society, 1975; D.Letters from Michigan State University, 1976.

WRITINGS: Yoruba Towns, Ibadan University Press, 1962; (editor) *The City of Ibadan,* Cambridge University Press, 1967; (editor) *Pathfinder Atlas for Nigeria,* Collins, 1967; *Urbanization in Nigeria,* Africana Publishing, 1969; (editor) *Kainji: A Nigerian Man-Made Lake,* Nigerian Insti-

tute of Social and Economic Research, Volume I, 1970, Volume II, 1973; (with J. D. Omer-Cooper) *Owu in Yoruba History,* Ibadan University Press, 1971; *Growth Poles and Growth Centres in the Regional Development of Nigeria,* United Nations Research Institute for Social Development, 1971; *Regional Mobility and Resource Development in West Africa,* McGill-Queens University Press, 1972; (co-author) *Regional Planning and National Development in Tropical Africa,* Ibadan University Press, 1977; (with J. E. Hardoy and R. P. Miora) *Shelter Provision in Developing Countries,* Wiley, 1978; *On Developing and Development* (compilation of lectures), Ibadan University Press, in press.

WORK IN PROGRESS: Development Geography, to be published by Hutchinson Publishing.

SIDELIGHTS: Akin Mabogunje told *CA:* "Most of my early books were concerned with an examination and description of urbanization in Nigeria and some of its consequences for the pattern of development in the country. More recently, the emphasis of my work has shifted to development itself and to the crucial role of spatial and regional planning in achieving the goals of structural transformation implied in the very concept of development. Such planning is people-based and begins with consideration of how their present distribution in rural settlements and urban centres over the national space inhibit or facilitate effective utilization and exploitation of the natural resources of the country. Spatial planning is seen as a way of providing a systematic and concrete dimension to social and economic programmes of development. It is my contention in many of these publications that a critical study of the development effort of virtually all present-day advanced industrial countries will reveal a strong and all-pervasive preoccupation with the spatial reorganization of their society during the vital period of its transformation from preindustrial to industrial."

*   *   *

MACAULAY, Stewart 1931-

PERSONAL: Born April 7, 1931, in Atlanta, Ga.; son of Ralph S. and Mildred L. (Morgan) Macaulay; married wife, March 20, 1953; children: four. *Education:* Stanford University, A.B., 1952, LL.B., 1954. *Office:* School of Law, University of Wisconsin, Madision, Wis. 53706.

CAREER: Law clerk to chief judge of U.S. Court of Appeals, 1955-56; University of Chicago, Chicago, Ill., instructor in law, 1956-57; University of Wisconsin—Madison, professor of law, 1957—. Visiting professor at State University of New York at Buffalo, 1972-73. Fellow of Center for Advanced Study in the Behavioral Sciences, 1966-67. Director of Chile Law Program at International Legal Center in Santiago, 1970-72.

WRITINGS: Law and the Balance of Power: The Automobile Manufacturers and Their Dealers, Russell Sage Foundation, 1966; (with Lawrence M. Friedman) *Law and the Behavioral Sciences,* Bobbs-Merrill, 1969, 2nd edition, 1977; (with Jacqueline Macaulay) *Adoptive Placement of Black Children: A Case Study of Discretion and Legal Norms,* JAI Press, 1978. Contributor to *International Encyclopedia of Comparative Law,* and to law and social studies journals.

* * *

MacCAFFREY, Isabel Gamble 1924-1978

August 2, 1924—May 19, 1978; American educator and author of critical works on Spenser and Milton. An authority on English Renaissance literature, MacCaffrey was the first woman to chair the history and literature department at Harvard University. Obituaries and other sources: *Directory of American Scholars,* Volume II: *English, Speech, and Drama,* 6th edition, Bowker, 1974; *Who's Who in America,* 39th edition, Marquis, 1976; *New York Times,* May 21, 1978.

* * *

MacDOUGALL, Fiona
See MacLEOD, Robert F.

* * *

MACE, Elisabeth 1933-

PERSONAL: Born April 16, 1933, in London, England; daughter of Arthur (an engineer) and Ivy (Harvey) Cox; married David Mace (a teacher of creative studies), July 28, 1956; children: Anna Victoria, Simon Harvey. *Education:* University of Reading, B.A. (honors), 1956. *Politics:* "Not interested." *Home:* 1 Inglenook, Main St., East Keswick, Leeds, Yorkshire, England. *Agent:* David Higham Associates Ltd., 5-8 Lower John St., Golden Sq., London W1R 4HA, England.

CAREER: Teacher of elementary and preschool children in Cheltham, and Boston Spa, England, 1970-76; Boston Spa Junior School, Boston Spa, part-time teacher of French, English, and art to elementary school children, 1976—.

WRITINGS: Ransome Revisited (science fiction; juvenile), Deutsch, 1975, published as *Out There,* Greenwillow, 1978; *Travelling Man* (sequel to preceding book), Deutsch, 1976; *The Ghost Diviners* (fantasy novel; juvenile), Thomas Nelson, 1977; *The Rushton Inheritance* (fantasy novel; juvenile), Deutsch, 1978; *Brother Enemy* (history; young adult), Deutsch, in press.

WORK IN PROGRESS: Research on the "paranormal" for a series of stories (not necessarily ghost stories).

SIDELIGHTS: Elisabeth Mace wrote: "I have always been interested in children's literature, and what children themselves choose to read, or reject or dislike. Science fiction for this age range is a subject which excites but often disappoints its readers. Science fiction, to me, is far more than space opera. Similarly, there's more to ghosts than visitations from the dead!"

AVOCATIONAL INTERESTS: Music (especially choral singing), patchwork, dress designing, and dressmaking.

* * *

MacGREGOR, Bruce (Alan) 1945-

PERSONAL: Born June 21, 1945, in Tucson, Ariz.; son of John Irving (a school superintendent) and Frances (a teacher; maiden name, Gleason) MacGregor; married Kathleen M. Ogan (a publishers assistant), March 26, 1970; children: Haig, Ann. *Education:* Stanford University, B.S., 1968, doctoral study, 1973—; University of Oregon, M.S., 1971; Antioch-Putney College, M.A.T., 1971. *Home:* 100-C Escondido Village, Stanford, Calif. 94305.

CAREER: Free-lance writer. Associate member of Stanford Linear Accelerator, Stanford, Calif., 1975—. Lecturer at Stanford University, 1976—.

WRITINGS: The South Pacific Coast, Howell North, 1968; *A Narrow Gauge Portrait: South Pacific Coast,* Glenwood, 1975; *A Centennial History of Newark,* privately printed, 1976; (with Ted Benson) *Portrait of a Silver Lady,* Pruett, 1977. Contributor to *San Francisco Chronicle.*

WORK IN PROGRESS: An environmental and photographic essay on the south San Francisco Bay as a wilderness area; short sketches of high energy physicists.

SIDELIGHTS: MacGregor comments: "I am increasingly concerned with man's concepts of his own survival in nature, and am courting a concept called a 'survival paradigm,' or story, as a genre for man's self-expression of his own survival strategies. A collected anthology of survival paradigms is a first step. The creation of new ones, based on a heavily technologized society, may be a second."

* * *

MacISAAC, David 1935-

PERSONAL: Born June 22, 1935, in Boston, Mass.; son of John L. (a marketing clerk) and Mary (a credit manager; maiden name, Mullen) MacIsaac; married Charlotte Wade, July 19, 1959; children: Donna Marie, Paul, Pamela, Patrick. *Education:* Trinity College, Hartford, Conn., A.B., 1957; Yale University, A.M., 1958; Duke University, Ph.D., 1970. *Politics:* "Eccentric." *Office:* Woodrow Wilson International Center for Scholars, Smithsonian Institution, Washington, D.C. 20560.

CAREER: U.S. Air Force, career officer, 1958—, personnel officer with Strategic Air Command in Texas, 1959-61, and at Torrejon Air Base in Spain, 1961-64, instructor at Air Force Academy, 1964-66, assistant professor, 1968-70, associate professor, 1971-76, professor of history, 1976—, member of Air Force Advisory Group in Vietnam, 1971, visiting professor at U.S. Naval War College, 1975-76; present rank, lieutenant colonel. Fellow of Woodrow Wilson International Center for Scholars, at Smithsonian Institution, 1978-79. *Member:* Air Force Association, United States Naval Institute, American Committee on the History of the Second World War, Inter-University Seminar on the Armed Forces and Society, Phi Beta Kappa. *Awards, honors*—Military: Bronze Star. Other: Woodrow Wilson fellowship, 1958.

WRITINGS: (Contributor) M. D. Wright and Lawrence Paszek, editors, *Soldiers and Statesmen: Proceedings of the Fourth Military History Symposium,* U.S. Government Printing Office, 1973; (editor) *The Military and Society: Proceedings of the Fifth Military History Symposium,* U.S. Government Printing Office, 1975; *Strategic Bombing in World War II: The Story of the U.S. Strategic Bombing*

Survey, Garland Publishing, 1976; (editor and author of introductions) *The U.S. Strategic Bombing Survey,* ten volumes, Garland Publishing, 1976; (contributor) David H. White, editor, *Proceedings of The Citadel Conference on War and Diplomacy,* Citadel, 1976. Contributor to *Dictionary of American History.* Contributor of about thirty articles and reviews to history and military journals.

WORK IN PROGRESS: The Air Force and Strategic Air Power: From Hiroshima to the New Look.

SIDELIGHTS: MacIsaac writes: "I have lived and traveled in Spain and Vietnam, preferring the former, especially Pamplona. My writing thus far has been pretty straightforward stuff, history and all that, but I have a good (*not* autobiographical) novel or two up my sleeve."

*   *   *

MACKAY, Barbara E.   1944-

PERSONAL: Born October 22, 1944, in New York, N.Y.; daughter of Charles E. and Agnes (Talbot) Mackay. *Education:* Wellesley College, B.A., 1966; Johns Hopkins University, M.A., 1968, M.A., 1974, D.F.A., 1974. *Home:* 1302 East 11th Ave., Denver, Colo. 80218. *Office: Denver Post,* Fifteenth St., Denver, Colo. 80202.

CAREER/WRITINGS: Saturday Review, New York City, drama critic, 1973-75; *Film International,* New York City, film critic, 1974-75; *L'Espresso,* Rome, Italy, drama critic, 1975-76; *Denver Post,* Denver, Colo., drama critic, 1976—.'

*   *   *

MacKEITH, Ronald Charles   1908-1977

February 22, 1908—October, 1977; British physician, editor, and author of books on pediatrics. A world-renowned pediatrician, MacKeith was editor of the highly regarded journal, *Developmental Medicine and Child Neurology.* He died in England. Obituaries and other sources: *Who's Who,* 128th edition, St. Martin's, 1976; *AB Bookman's Weekly,* February 6, 1978.

*   *   *

MACKEY, Mary   1945-

PERSONAL: Born January 21, 1945, in Indianapolis, Ind.; daughter of John Edward (a physician) and Jean (an art museum director; maiden name, McGinness) Mackey. *Education:* Harvard University, B.A., 1966; University of Michigan, M.A., 1967, Ph.D., 1970. *Home address:* P.O. Box 9183, Berkeley, Calif. 94709. *Agent:* Carol Murray, 2427 10th St., Berkeley, Calif. 94710. *Office:* Department of English, California State University, 6000 J St., Sacramento, Calif. 95819.

CAREER: Indianapolis Star, Indianapolis, Ind., feature writer, 1965; California State University, Sacramento, assistant professor, 1972-76, associate professor of English, 1976—. *Member:* Feminist Writers Guild (founder and member of national steering committee). *Awards, honors:* Woodrow Wilson fellowship, 1966-67.

WRITINGS: Immersion (novel), Shameless Hussy Press, 1972; *Split Ends* (poems), Ariel Press, 1974; *One Night Stand* (poems), Effie's Press, 1977; (editor with Mary MacArthur) *Chance Music* (anthology), Gallimaufry, 1977; *Skin Deep* (poems), Gallimaufry, 1978; *McCarthy's List* (novel), Doubleday, 1979.

Author of "Silence" (screenplay), 1974; "As Old As You Feel" (television documentary), Columbia Broadcasting System, 1978.

WORK IN PROGRESS: Arabesque (tentative title), poems; *Women and Violence in the Cinema;* a sequel to *McCarthy's List.*

SIDELIGHTS: Mary Mackey writes: "I get tired of reading about women who suffer, and suffer, and suffer. Right now I want my women characters to be strong, self-sufficient, mildly pig-headed, and happy as hell. I used to see life as high tragedy. Lear and Cordelia. Lady Macbeth with blood on her hands. Now I see it as an on-going Goon Show. With myself as one of the prime goons, of course."

AVOCATIONAL INTERESTS: Cats, cooking, weightlifting.

*   *   *

MacLEOD, Robert F.   1917-
(Fiona MacDougall)

PERSONAL: Born October 15, 1917, in Chicago, Ill.; son of Ernest F. (a photographer) and Martha (Womer) MacLeod; divorced; children: Robert F., Jr., Merrill Scott, Edward Jay, Ian Dana. *Education:* Dartmouth College, B.A., 1939. *Religion:* Protestant. *Home:* 110 Colony Dr., Malibu, Calif. 90265. *Office:* 8831 Sunset Blvd., Los Angeles, Calif. 90069.

CAREER/WRITINGS: Town and Country, New York City, advertising manager, 1946-49; *Harper's Bazaar,* New York City, publisher, 1950-60; *Seventeen,* New York City, publisher, 1961-62; *Teen,* Los Angeles, Calif., publisher and editor, 1965-76. Illustrator of books under pseudonym Fiona MacDougall.

*   *   *

Mac LIAIMMHOIR, Micheal
See Mac LIAMMOIR, Micheal

*   *   *

Mac LIAMMHOIR, Micheal
See Mac LIAMMOIR, Micheal

*   *   *

Mac LIAMMOIR, Micheal   1899-1978
(Micheal Mac Liaimmhoir, Micheal Mac Liammhoir)

October 25, 1899—March 6, 1978; Irish actor, designer, director, and playwright. Mac Liammoir established, with Hilton Edwards, the innovative Dublin Gate Theatre in 1928 where he acted in and designed over three hundred productions. Among his best known career performances were "The Importance of Being Oscar," a solo recitation of Oscar Wilde passages that played in four continents, and "I Must Be Talking to My Friends," a one-man celebration of Ireland through the words of its literary figures. Mac Liammoir's many writings include plays, articles, short stories, and translations. He died in Dublin, Ireland. Obituaries and other sources: *The Biographical Encyclopaedia and Who's Who of the American Theatre,* James Heineman, 1966; Micheal Mac Liammoir, *An Oscar of No Importance . . . Being an Account of the Author's Adventures With His One-man Show About Oscar Wilde, The Importance of Being Oscar,* Heinemann, 1968; *McGraw-Hill Encyclopedia of World Drama,* McGraw, 1972; *Modern World Drama: An Encyclopedia,* Dutton, 1972; *The Writer's Directory, 1976-78,* St. Martin's, 1976; *The International Who's Who,* Europa, 1977; *Who's Who in the Theatre,* 16th edition, Pitman, 1977; *Who's Who,* 130th edition, St. Martin's, 1978; *New*

York Times, March 7, 1978; *Time,* March 20, 1978. (See index for *CA* sketch)

* * *

MACOMBER, Daria
   See ROBINSON, Patricia Colbert

* * *

MALIK, Hafeez 1930-

PERSONAL: Born March 17, 1930, in Lahore, Pakistan; son of Abdul Khaliq (a revenue officer) and Sardar (a teacher; maiden name, Begum) Malik; married Lynda Pollock (a professor of sociology); children: Cyrus, Dean. *Education:* Government College, Lahore, Pakistan, B.A., 1949; University of the Punjab, diploma, 1952; Syracuse University, M.S., 1955, M.A., 1957, Ph.D., 1961. *Politics:* Independent. *Religion:* Islam. *Home:* 315 Arden Rd., Gulph Mills, Conshohocken, Pa. 19428. *Agent:* Susan Hausman, Villanova University, Villanova, Pa. 19085. *Office:* Villanova University, 138 Tolentine Hall, Villanova, Pa. 19085.

CAREER: Villanova University, Villanova, Pa., assistant professor, 1961-63, associate professor, 1963-67, professor of political science and history, 1967—. Director of American Institute of Pakistan Studies; president of Pakistan American Foundation; member of Pakistan Council and National Seminar on Pakistan/Bangladesh, 1970-75. *Member:* Association for Asian Studies, American Association of University Professors, American Political Science Association, American Historical Association, Asia Society (chairman, 1971), Pi Sigma Alpha.

WRITINGS: Muslim Nationalism in India and Pakistan, foreword by Hans Kohn, Public Affairs Press, 1963; *Iqbal: Poet-Philosopher of Pakistan,* Columbia University Press, 1971; *Sir Sayyid Ahmad Khan's History of the Bijnor Rebellion,* Michigan State University Press, 1972; *Shah Waliullah and the Muslim Renaissance in India,* Islamabad National Commission on Historical and Cultural Research, 1977; *Sir Sayyid Ahmad Khan's Educational Philosophy,* Islamabad National Commission on Historical and Cultural Research, 1977.

White House correspondent. Associate editor of *Islam and the Modern Age,* 1969, and *Islam Awr Aser-i Jadid,* 1969; editor of *Journal of South Asian and Middle Eastern Studies,* 1977—.

WORK IN PROGRESS: Sir Sayyid Ahmad Khan and Muslim Modernization in India.

BIOGRAPHICAL/CRITICAL SOURCES: The East Indians and the Pakistanis in America, Lerner, 1972.

* * *

MALIKIN, David 1913-

PERSONAL: Born July 17, 1913, in New York, N.Y.; son of Morris and Anna (Becker) Malikin; married; children: Patricia Clow. *Education:* City College (now of the City University of New York), B.S., 1953, M.S., 1956; New York University, Ph.D., 1961. *Home:* 40 Walker Ave., Rye, N.Y. 10580. *Office:* Department of Rehabilitation Counseling, New York University, 34 Stuyvesant St., New York, N.Y. 10003.

CAREER: Long Island University, Brooklyn, N.Y., assistant professor of guidance counseling, 1960-62; New York University, New York, N.Y., assistant professor, 1962-64, associate professor, 1965-67, professor of rehabilitation

counseling, 1967—. Consultant to schools, foundations, hospitals, and government agencies. *Member:* American Psychological Association, National Rehabilitation Association, American Association of University Professors, New York State Psychological Association. *Awards, honors:* "Best Book on a Medical Subject by Non-Physician Authors" award from American Association of Medical Writers, 1976, for *Contemporary Vocational Rehabilitation.*

WRITINGS: Vocational Rehabilitation of the Disabled: An Overview, New York University Press, 1968; *Social Disability,* New York University Press, 1973; *Contemporary Vocational Rehabilitation,* New York University Press, 1976; (with Helen Green) *The Role of the Family in Rehabilitation,* New York University Press, 1979. Contributor to professional journals.

SIDELIGHTS: Malikin writes that his particular interest is services to the disabled around the world. He has traveled widely in Europe, Asia, Latin America, and the Middle East. He comments: "In my opinion the United States offers the most comprehensive rehabilitation services in the world but fails in one major area, employment. There is no guarantee that a rehabilitated individual will find a job. Some governments, for example in Scandinavia, guarantee a disabled person a job when he is considered ready. If we could do the same it would make rehabilitation a much more meaningful experience."

* * *

MALONE, Michael (Christopher) 1942-

PERSONAL: Born November, 1942, in North Carolina; son of Thomas Patrick (a psychiatrist) and Faylene (Jones) Malone; married Maureen Quilligan (a professor of English), May 17, 1975; children: Margaret Elizabeth. *Education:* Attended Syracuse University; earned B.A. and M.A. from University of North Carolina; further graduate study at Harvard University. *Politics:* Democrat. *Religion:* Episcopalian. *Home:* 16 Edgewood, New Haven, Conn. 06511. *Agent:* Elaine Markson Literary Agency, Inc., 44 Greenwich Ave., New York, N.Y. 10011.

CAREER: Writer. Instructor at various colleges. *Member:* Authors Guild of Authors League of America.

WRITINGS: Painting the Roses Red (novel), Random House, 1975; *The Delectable Mountains* (novel), Random House, 1977; *Pschetypes* (nonfiction), Dutton, 1977; *Star Sex: Men in the Movies,* Dutton, 1978; *American Vamp,* Quadrangle, 1978. Contributor of articles and reviews to popular magazines, including *Viva, Nation, Human Behavior,* and *Harper's.*

WORK IN PROGRESS: Dingley on the Rampage, a novel.

* * *

MANDEL, Leon 1928-
   (John Dalmas)

PERSONAL: Born July 31, 1928, in Chicago, Ill.; son of Leon and Edna Horn (Seligmann) Mandel; married Olivia Lee Eskridge, June 12, 1953; children: Leon, Olivia. *Education:* Attended Cornell University, 1946, 1950-53, Columbia University, 1949, and Hastings College of Law, 1962. *Home and office:* 3450 San Mateo Ave., Reno, Nev. 89509. *Agent:* Jacques de Spoelberch, Jacques de Spoelberch, Inc., South Norwalk, Conn.

CAREER: Salesman, manager, and partner in auto retail business in California, 1954-61; *Autoweek,* San Francisco,

Calif., 1963-67, began as associate editor, became managing editor and editor; *Car and Driver,* New York, N.Y., 1967-71, began as managing editor, became editor; *Autoweek,* 1971-74, began as editorial director, became publisher; currently consultant for SRI International, and television commentator in Reno, Nev. *Member:* Auto Racing Writers and Broadcasters, Sierra Nevada Sports Writers, Airedale Terrier Club of America, Benedict Arnold Society, Admiral Jellicoe Historical Society.

WRITINGS: (With Peter Revson) *Speed With Style,* Doubleday, 1974; *Driven: The American Four-Wheeled Love Affair,* Stein & Day, 1977; (with Phillip Finch; under pseudonym John Dalmas) *No Place to Hide* (suspense novel), Coward, 1977. Also author of *The American Diet,* in press. Contributor to television and sports magazines and to popular journals and newspapers, including *True* and *Newsday.*

WORK IN PROGRESS: Two suspense novels.

SIDELIGHTS: Mandel remarks: "A decent career can be made by taking the automobile seriously—all the while waiting to be run over. As for motivation, there are mortgage payments, college tuitions, and food bills."

*   *   *

MANLEY, John F(rederick) 1939-

PERSONAL: Born February 20, 1939, in Utica, N.Y.; son of John A. and Gertrude (Donahue) Manley; married; children: John, Laura. *Education:* LeMoyne College, B.S., 1961; Syracuse University, Ph.D., 1966. *Office:* Department of Political Science, Stanford University, Stanford, Calif. 94306.

CAREER: University of Wisconsin—Madison, assistant professor, 1966-69, associate professor of political science, 1969-71; Stanford University, Stanford, Calif., associate professor of political science, 1971—. Fellow of Center for Advanced Study in the Behavioral Sciences, 1976-77. *Member:* American Political Science Association. *Awards, honors:* Guggenheim fellowship, 1974-75.

WRITINGS: The Politics of Finance, Little, Brown, 1970; *American Government and Public Policy,* Macmillan, 1976. Contributor to political science journals.

*   *   *

MARAIS, Josef 1905-1978

November 17, 1905—April 27, 1978; South African-born American singer, guitarist, composer, and author. Marais and his wife, Miranda, were popular folk singers who toured the United States, Europe, and Israel. Marais wrote a children's book, co-authored four plays with his wife, and composed scores for musicals. He died in Los Angeles, Calif. Obituaries and other sources: *The ASCAP Biographical Dictionary of Composers, Authors, and Publishers,* American Society of Composers, Authors, and Publishers, 1966; *Encyclopedia of Folk, Country, and Western Music,* St. Martin's, 1969; *Authors of Books for Young People,* 2nd edition, Scarecrow, 1971; *Who's Who in the World,* 3rd edition, Marquis, 1976; *New York Times,* May 3, 1978.

*   *   *

MARCUS, Mordecai 1925-

PERSONAL: Born January 18, 1925, in Elizabeth, N.J.; son of Sidney (a bookdealer) and Mary (Swerdlow) Marcus; married Erin Jenean Gasper, June 3, 1955; children: Paul, Emily. *Education:* Brooklyn College (now of the City University of New York), B.A., 1949; New York University, M.A., 1950; University of Kansas, Ph.D., 1958. *Politics:* "Desperate." *Religion:* "Uncertain." *Home:* 822 Mulder Dr., Lincoln, Neb. 68510. *Office:* Department of English, University of Nebraska, Lincoln, Neb. 68588.

CAREER: University of Kansas, Lawrence, instructor in English, 1952-58; Purdue University, West Lafayette, Ind., instructor, 1958-60, assistant professor of English, 1960-65; University of Nebraska, Lincoln, assistant professor, 1965-66, associate professor, 1966-72, professor of English, 1972—. *Member:* Modern Language Association of America, National Association for Psychoanalytic Criticism.

WRITINGS: Five Minutes to Noon (poems), Best Cellar Press, 1971; *Return From the Desert* (poems), Newedi Press, 1977. Contributor of articles and poems to more than sixty magazines, including literature and aesthetics journals.

WORK IN PROGRESS: Poems; stories.

BIOGRAPHICAL/CRITICAL SOURCES: Nantucket Review, May, 1975.

*   *   *

MARGULIES, Herbert F(elix) 1928-

PERSONAL: Born September 11, 1928, in New York; son of Joseph (an artist) and Mary (Polisuk) Margulies; married Francine Kornzweig (an instructor in English), September 12, 1954; children: Karen, Eric Ned, Daniel, Laura. *Education:* Reed College, B.A., 1950; University of Wisconsin—Madison, M.A., 1951, Ph.D., 1955. *Home:* 118 Hawaii Loa St., Honolulu, Hawaii 96821.

CAREER: Iowa State Teachers College (now University of Northern Iowa), Cedar Falls, instructor, 1955-59; University of Hawaii, Honolulu, assistant professor, 1959-63, associate professor, 1963-68, professor of history, 1968—. *Member:* American Historical Association, Organization of American Historians.

WRITINGS: The Decline of the Progressive Movement in Wisconsin, 1890-1920, State Historical Society of Wisconsin, 1968; *Senator Lenroot of Wisconsin: A Political Biography, 1900-1929,* University of Missouri Press, 1977. Contributor to history and regional studies journals.

WORK IN PROGRESS: Research on the court martial system, 1920, and the presidency in the twentieth century.

*   *   *

MARKANDAYA, Kamala
See TAYLOR, Kamala (Purnaiya)

*   *   *

MARMON, William F., Jr. 1942-

PERSONAL: Born June 10, 1942, in Richmond, Va.; son of William Fain Marmon; married Lucretia McCalmont, October, 1972. *Education:* Princeton University, B.A., 1964. *Home:* 16413 Akron St., Pacific Palisades, Calif. 90272. *Office: Time,* 450 N. Roxbury Dr., Beverly Hills, Calif. 90210.

CAREER/WRITINGS: Time, New York City, staff member, 1966—, bureau chief in Jerusalem, 1973-75, and Beirut, 1975-76, correspondent in Los Angeles, 1977—. *Member:* University Club.

*   *   *

MARRONE, Robert 1941-

PERSONAL: Surname is pronounced Ma-*rown;* born June

25, 1941, in New York, N.Y.; son of Ernest V. (a stock-broker) and Joan (Leonardi) Marrone; children: Jason. *Education:* Adelphi University, B.A., 1963; Texas Christian University, M.A., 1966; State University of New York Downstate Medical Center, Ph.D., 1967, postdoctoral study, 1967-68. *Religion:* Buddhist. *Home:* 1157 48th St., Sacramento, Calif. 95819. *Office:* Department of Psychology, California State University, 6000 J St., Sacramento, Calif. 95825.

CAREER: Licensed clinical psychologist, state of California, 1978—. California State University, Sacramento, assistant professor, 1968-72, associate professor, 1973-78, professor of psychology, 1978—, chairman of department of experimental studies, 1973-74. Director of Kriya Workshop, 1974-76. Member of field faculty at Humanistic Psychology Institute, 1975—. *Member:* Lomi Associates International, Association for Humanistic Psychologists, Sigma Xi. *Awards, honors:* National Aeronautics and Space Administration (NASA) fellowship, 1967, 1968.

WRITINGS: (With Richard Rasor) *Behavior Observation: Analysis,* Holt, 1973. Contributor to professional journals. Editor of *Journal of Humanistic and Interdisciplinary Studies,* 1977.

WORK IN PROGRESS: Research on mind/body confluence and new approaches to therapy, such as imagery, lomi, rolfing, and psychodrama, as well as body therapies.

SIDELIGHTS: Marrone commented: "I am trained as an experimental psychologist. I have spent the past seven years in transition toward a humanist/existential/psychotherapeutic perspective. This dramatic change, manifested in my courses and workshops, will hopefully come to another fruition in my writings in progress, especially writing on the role of the body in psychotherapy."

*   *   *

MARROW, Alfred J.   1905-1978

March 8, 1905—March 3, 1978; American psychologist, businessman, and author. An authority on group dynamics and industrial psychology, Marrow was president of the National Academy of Professional Psychologists. He served as president and chairman of the board of the Harwood Manufacturing Co. from 1940 to 1976. *Management by Participation* is Marrow's best-known book. He died in New York, N.Y. Obituaries and other sources: *Who's Who in World Jewry,* Pitman, 1972; *American Men and Women of Science: The Social and Behavioral Sciences,* 12th edition, Bowker, 1973; *New York Times,* March 4, 1978.

*   *   *

MARSDEN, Peter Richard Valentine   1940-

PERSONAL: Born April 29, 1940, in London, England; son of Sidney L. V. and Emily Sylvia (Lynde) Marsden; children: Paul Stephen Valentine, Mark Richard Valentine. *Education:* Attended Kilbnan Polytechnic, 1957. *Politics:* None. *Religion:* Church of England. *Home:* 21 Meadow Lane, Lindfield, Sussex RH16 2RJ, England. *Office:* Museum of London, London Wall, London E.C.3, England.

CAREER: Museum of London, London, England, archaeologist, 1959—. *Member:* Society of Antiquaries (fellow), Society for Nautical Research (member of council), Council for Nautical Archaeology (member of council), Press Club of London.

WRITINGS: The Wreck of the Amsterdam, Hutchinson, 1974, Stein & Day, 1975. Contributor to magazines and newspapers.

WORK IN PROGRESS: The Archaeology of Ships for Elek; research for a book on Sir Francis Drake and his voyage around the world, 1577-80.

SIDELIGHTS: Marsden writes that his interest in old ships and archaeology, exploration, and discovery, is motivated by "extreme curiosity." *Avocational interests:* Planetary geology (including Earth).

*   *   *

MARSH, Clifton E.   1946-

PERSONAL: Born August 10, 1946, in Los Angeles, Calif.; son of Clifton H. and Margaret Marsh; married Tobie Burton, October 6, 1970 (divorced, May, 1972); married Johnnie Hill, October 22, 1976; children: (second marriage) Mecca Shanara. *Education:* California State University, Long Beach, B.A., 1969, M.A., 1971; Syracuse University, Ph.D., 1977. *Home:* 710 Ridge St., Charlottesville, Va. 22903. *Office:* Office of Afro-American Affairs, University of Virginia, 4 Dawson's Row, Charlottesville, Va. 22903.

CAREER: California State University, Long Beach, instructor in Afro-American studies, 1969-70; Direction Sports, Inc., Los Angeles, Calif., regional director, 1970-71; Central City Community Mental Health Center, Los Angeles, program coordinator, 1971-72; Syracuse University, Syracuse, N.Y., instructor in sociology, 1973-74; State University of New York College at Cortland, instructor in sociology, 1974-75; Tompkins Cortland Community College, Dryden, N.Y., adjunct professor of sociology, summer, 1975; Virginia Union University, Richmond, instructor in sociology, 1975-77; University of Virginia, Charlottesville, assistant professor of sociology, 1977—, associate dean of academic affairs for Office of Afro-American Affairs, 1977—. Member of Poettential Theatre. Consultant with Morse Associates. *Member:* American Sociological Association.

WRITINGS—Books of poems: Journey to Shanara, Shanara Publications, 1973; (editor and contributor) *Harambee,* State University of New York College at Cortland, 1974; *Summer '72,* Shanara Publications, 1975.

Contributor of poems and stories to magazines, including *Black Folk, Afro-American Quarterly,* and *Journal of Black Poetry,* and to newspapers. Editor of *Black Voice* (newspaper).

WORK IN PROGRESS: Research on Latin American history, Black nationalist movements, and charisma and leadership.

SIDELIGHTS: Marsh comments: "My father was the greatest single motivating force in my life. Now he is dead and I gain motivation from within, trying to find inner peace; to find proper diet and exercise, and trying to grow as a person. Travel has been my most inspirational resource. Travels include Mexico, Denmark, Sweden, Holland, Germany, Belgium, Luxembourg, Puerto Rico, and the Virgin Islands."

*   *   *

MARSH, Meredith   1946-

PERSONAL: Born January 26, 1946, in Philadelphia, Pa.; daughter of Murray Forbes (an executive) and Marilyn (Seiders) Marsh; married Barton Jannen Bernstein (a historian), August 9, 1967. *Education:* Attended Bennington College, 1963-65, and Pennsylvania Academy of Fine Arts, 1965-66. *Religion:* None. *Residence:* Palo Alto, Calif.

CAREER: Free-lance artist (painter), 1967-71; writer, 1971—.

WRITINGS: I Had Wild Jack for a Lover (novel), Coward, 1977.

WORK IN PROGRESS: Another novel.

SIDELIGHTS: Meredith Marsh writes: "A ready access to one's own daydreams is both a handicap and a source of considerable, ambiguous power.

"In the fourth grade, the teacher inaugurated a 'creativity hour,' and when I stopped boggling at such a forbidding title and realized that we were only required to do more formally what we all presumably did at home—play—I wrote, each day, a chapter of a novel, "Wolfe: The Story of a Wolf." In those days, what I wanted to be when I grew up was a wild animal. To my immense surprise, this literary extension of the plastic animals I made up stories about all day at home brought me great social success.

"Bennington College, which I expected to be a Mecca, was a culture shock. My first English teacher, Bernard Malamud, whom I had never heard of, had us write short stories so he might single out any nascent talent. Not singled out, I tucked my hurt pride into the proverbial drawer and concentrated instead on acting and painting, where I met a more welcoming reception from teachers.

"In Cambridge and later in Palo Alto, I drew from the model wherever I could find one and painted in a studio at home. I had just begun to branch out from that homemade studio—selling some work, getting one painting into a juried show—when we decamped to Illinois. With the confidence gained from having painted tenaciously, yet with no one to inspect my studio, I worked up the courage to try to write a short story. Gradually I had realized that writing was what I most wanted to do. I was not at all sure, however, whether or not I could write. I spent the next six years finding out.

"I write novels in order to discover and grasp what I make of the world. Since for me the world is a mysterious web of stories, my redesign of it must also be a story, full of the suspense of discovery. And since this web is transparent, yet has infinite layers, so must the language of the story be both clear and many-layered.

"Like modern art, recent serious fiction has often sought to become more abstract, and less representational, less concerned with the kinds of illusion and meaning that eventually send the reader back to examine her own life in a new light. But I would argue that human experience and meaning—and the dialogue that a book inspires with the reader—are the irreducible elements of literature. A book is certainly made of words, but words are not material in the sense that paint is, or even color. Pure sound is not poetry, it's music. A word resonates in our minds in a different way. In fact, our language is so rich with accretion that nearly every word shimmers with associations. Words mean."

*　　*　　*

MARSHALL, George (Nichols) 1920-

PERSONAL: Born July 4, 1920, in Bozeman, Mont.; son of J. Wallace (a professor and editor) and Grace (Nichols) Marshall; married Barbara Ambrose, June 17, 1947 (divorced, 1967); children: Charles Hopkinson. Education: Tufts University, A.B., 1939, S.T.B., 1941, A.M., 1943; Columbia University, M.A.,1945; Harvard University, S.T.M., 1947; Walden University, Ph.D., 1975. Politics: Independent. Residence: Boston, Mass. Office: Church of the Larger Fellowship, 25 Beacon St., Boston, Mass. 02108.

CAREER: Ordained Unitarian-Universalist minister, 1943; pastor of Unitarian-Universalist churches in Natiek, Mass., 1941-43, Plymouth, Mass., 1946-52, and Niagara Falls, N.Y., 1952-60; Church of the Larger Fellowship, Boston, Mass., pastor and religious editor, 1960—. Associate director of extension for Boston's Unitarian-Universalist Association, 1960-70. Military service: U.S. Army Air Forces, chaplain, 1943-46; became captain. Member: Albert Schweitzer World Confederation, Albert Schweitzer Fellowship (member of board of directors), Planned Parenthood Federation, Smithsonian Associates, Unitarian Historical Society, Pilgrim Society, New England Memorial Society. Awards, honors: Wendell Willkie Award from Freedom House, 1949; D.D. from Meadville/Lombard Theological School, 1976.

WRITINGS: (Contributor) Voices of Liberalism, Volume II, Beacon Press, 1951; Church of the Pilgrim Fathers, Beacon Press, 1955; On an Understanding of Albert Schweitzer, Philosophical Library, 1966; The Challenge of a Liberal Faith, Pyramid Publications, 1970, revised edition, Family Library, 1975; (with David Poling) Schweitzer, a Biography, Doubleday, 1971; Buddha, The Quest for Serenity, Beacon Press, 1978. Editor of Bulletin for Religious Liberals, 1960—.

WORK IN PROGRESS: Dying in American Society, a general book on coping with death and grief; an anthology; a biography.

SIDELIGHTS: Marshall writes: "I am dividing material from extensive research on traditional and modern attitudes and practices regarding death and funeral practices into two books. The more general book is Dying in American Society. My earlier pamphlet, 'When a Family Faces Death,' has been distributed to memorial societies and churches. I was an 'expert' witness at Federal Trade Commission hearings in 1976."

*　　*　　*

MARSHALL, Paule 1929-

PERSONAL: Born April 9, 1929, in Brooklyn, N.Y.; married Kenneth E. Marshall, 1950 (divorced, 1963); children: Evan. Education: Brooklyn College (now of the City University of New York), B.A. (cum laude), 1953; attended Hunter College (now of the City University of New York), 1955. Home: 407 Central Park West, New York, N.Y. 10025.

CAREER: Worked as librarian in New York Public Libraries; Our World magazine, New York, N.Y., staff writer, 1953-56; free-lance writer and lecturer on Black literature at colleges and universities including Oxford University, Columbia University, Michigan State University, Lake Forrest College, and Cornell University. Member: Phi Beta Kappa. Awards, honors: Guggenheim fellowship, 1960; Rosenthal Award from the National Institute of Arts and Letters, 1962; Ford Foundation grant, 1964-65; National Endowment for the Arts grant, 1967-68.

WRITINGS: Brown Girl, Brownstones (novel), Random House, 1959; Soul Clap Hands and Sing (short stories), Atheneum, 1961; The Chosen Place, The Timeless People, Harcourt, 1969. Contributor of articles and short stories to periodicals.

SIDELIGHTS: Marshall began writing before her tenth birthday and has become "one of the best novelists writing in the United States" and "almost too gifted" according to Henrietta Buckmaster in a Christian Science Monitor review of The Chosen Place, The Timeless People.

In her review of the same book, Nikki Giovanni wrote: "The sheer emotion of *The Chosen Place* can be 'whelming.' To say overwhelming would be to put an onus on the book, and there is no such word as 'underwhelming' (though some things do 'underwhelm' us). There are times when control is lost, and in the effort to show, we feel Mrs. Marshall pushing our heads. But that would be in line with her collective historical need; call it an irresistable impulse. And it adds rather than detracts from our involvement. Technically the book is expert, so, every now and then it was a good feeling to see Mrs. Marshall's firm hand pushing us along."

Soul Clap Hands and Sing, a collection of four stories, took its title from lines in William Butler Yeats's "Sailing to Byzantium." *Kirkus Review* praised Marshall for having "suddenly expanded a private sense of race and color into an enormously wide, almost mystic, sense of the shimmering chiaroscuro of life itself in its mixed moods and human destinies.... The complexity and range of meaning is dazzling, and it is a remarkable achievement. *Saturday Review* commended her for having "escaped the cliches that must doubly tempt every Negro writing today; and she has given us a vision, precise and compassionate, of solitary lives that yet participate in the rich, shifting backgrounds of cultures near and remote."

The *New York Times Book Review* called *The Chosen Place, The Timeless People* "one of the four or five most impressive novels ever written by a black American." Richard Rhodes for *Book World* said, "if the characters are faulty and the story sometimes ponderous, it is also sometimes unforgettable."

Lloyd W. Brown discussed Marshall's fiction: "Paule Marshall's major themes are both significant and timely. Her West Indian background (Barbadian parentage) enables Paule Marshall to invest her North American materials with a Caribbean perspective, and in the process she invokes that Pan-African sensibility which has become so important in contemporary definitions of Black identity. Secondly, her treatment of the Black woman links her ethnic themes with the current feminist revolt. Finally, the ethnic and sexual themes are integrated with the novelist's interest in the subject of power."

BIOGRAPHICAL/CRITICAL SOURCES: Kirkus Review, July 1, 1959, July 15, 1961; *Booklist,* October 15, 1959, September 15, 1961; *Guardian,* August 19, 1960; *London Times,* August 19, 1960; *Saturday Review,* September 16, 1961; *New York Times Book Review,* November 30, 1969; *Book World,* December 28, 1969; *Christian Science Monitor,* January 22, 1970; *Negro Digest,* January 1970; *Novel,* winter, 1974.*

* * *

MARTIN, Albro 1921-

PERSONAL: Born November 21, 1921, in Clarksville, Ark.; son of Albro and Fannie (Taylor) Martin. *Education:* George Washington University, B.A., 1948; Harvard University, M.A., 1949; Columbia University, Ph.D., 1970. *Politics:* Independent. *Religion:* "No affiliation." *Home:* 6 Soldiers Field Park, #421, Boston, Mass. 02163. *Office:* 215 Baker Library, Harvard University, Soldiers Field, Boston, Mass. 02163.

CAREER: U.S. Department of Agriculture, Washington, D.C., economist, 1949-52; American Machine & Foundry Co., New York, N.Y., assistant manager of commercial research, 1954-57; J. Walter Thompson Co., New York City, account research executive, 1957-66; State University of New York College at New Paltz, visiting professor of history, 1968-69; American University, Washington, D.C., associate professor of history, 1970-76. Writer. Economic and marketing consultant. Lecturer in business administration and teacher of business history, 1952-66. *Military service:* U.S. Army Air Forces, 1943-46.

MEMBER: American Historical Association, Organization of American Historians, Economic History Association, Business History Conference (member of board of trustees), Phi Beta Kappa, Phi Kappa Phi, Harvard Club. *Awards, honors:* American economic history prize from Columbia University, 1970, for *Enterprise Denied;* Binkley-Stephenson Prize from Organization of American Historians, 1975, for "Trouble Subject of Railroad Regulation in the Gilded Age: A Reappraisal."

WRITINGS: Enterprise Denied: Origins of the Decline of American Railroads, 1897-1917, Columbia University Press, 1971; *James J. Hill and the Opening of the Northwest,* Oxford University Press, 1976. Contributor to professional journals. Editor of *Business History Review.*

WORK IN PROGRESS: A People in Motion: The Mobility Revolution in American Life, publication by Oxford University Press expected in 1981.

SIDELIGHTS: Martin commented: "I am interested in the impact of business enterprise on American life, especially its cultural, political, and social aspects. As a corollary, I am interested in studying those aspects of the American experience that demanded those developments of an entrepreneurial nature that did, in fact, change American society."

* * *

MARTIN, Andre
See JACOBY, Henry

* * *

MARTIN, Dwight 1921-1978

May 27, 1921—April 9, 1978; American journalist. Martin was a senior editor of *Newsweek* magazine and a former correspondent for *Time* magazine. His notable assignments included coverage of the final months of the Communist revolution in China, the Korean War, and the Berlin Wall crisis. He died in Millbrook, N.Y. Obituaries and other sources: *Who's Who in the World,* 3rd edition, Marquis, 1976; *New York Times,* April 10, 1978; *Washington Post,* April 11, 1978.

* * *

MARTIN, William C. 1937-

PERSONAL: Born December 31, 1937, in San Antonio, Tex.; son of Lowell Curtis (in agribusiness) and Joe Bailey (Brite) Martin; married Patricia Summerlin, December 31, 1957; children: Rex William, Jeffrey Summerlin, Elisabeth Dale. *Education:* Abilene Christian College, B.A., 1958, M.A., 1960; Harvard University, Ph.D., 1969, B.D., 1973. *Politics:* Democrat. *Religion:* Protestant. *Home address:* P.O. Box 941, Houston, Tex. 77001. *Agent:* Gerard F. McCauley, P.O. Box 456, Cranbury, N.J. 08512. *Office:* Department of Sociology, Rice University, Houston, Tex. 77001.

CAREER: Traveling salesman for Southwestern Co., summers, 1956-61; high school instructor and chaplain in Wellesley, Mass., 1964-68; Rice University, Houston, Tex., associate professor of sociology, 1968—, master of Richardson

College, 1976—. President of House of the Carpenter and Fellowship for Racial and Economic Equality. Member of executive board of Houston Council on Human Relations. *Member:* American Sociological Association, Society for the Scientific Study of Religion, Religious Research Association, Popular Culture Association.

WRITINGS: The Layman's Bible Encyclopedia, Southwestern Co., 1964; *These Were God's People: A Layman's Bible History,* Southwestern Co., 1966; *Christians in Conflict,* Center for the Scientific Study of Religion, 1972. Contributor to popular magazines, including *Atlantic, Harper's, Esquire,* and *Texas Monthly.*

WORK IN PROGRESS: The Electric Preacher: Mass Evangelism in America.

* * *

MARTINSON, Harry (Edmund) 1904-1978

PERSONAL: Born May 6, 1904, in Jaemshoeg, Blekinge, Sweden; son of Martin Olofsson (a sea captain); married Moa Swartz, 1929 (marriage ended, 1940).

CAREER: Worked as a seaman and a stoker throughout the world from the end of World War I until 1927; writer, 1927—. *Awards, honors:* Nobel Prize for Literature, 1974.

WRITINGS—In English: Kap Faerval!, A, Bonnier, 1933, translation by Naomi Walford published as *Cape Farewell,* Putnam, 1934; *Naesslorna blomma* (novel), A. Bonnier, 1935, reprinted, 1966, translation by Walford published as *Flowering Nettle,* Cresset, 1935; *Vaegen till Klockrike* (novel), A. Bonnier, 1948, translation by M. A. Michael published as *The Road,* J. Cape, 1955, Reynal, 1956; *Aniara: En revy om maenniskan i tid och rum* (epic poem), A. Bonnier, 1956, adaptation by Hugh McDiarmid and Elspeth Harley Shubert published as *Aniara: A Review of Man in Time and Space,* Knopf, 1963, reprinted, Avon, 1976; (contributor) Robert Bly, compiler and translator, *Friends You Drank Some Darkness,* Beacon Press, 1975.

Other works; all published by A. Bonnier, except as noted: *Vaegen ut* (novel; title means "The Way Out"), 1936, reprinted, 1974; *Svaermare och harkrank,* 1937; *Midsommardalen,* 1938; *Det enkla och det svaara,* 1939; *Verklighet till doeds* (title means "Realism Unto Death"), P. A. Norstedt, 1941; *Passad* (poems; title means "Trade Wind"), 1945, reprinted, 1966; *Cikada* (poems; title means "Cicada"), 1953; *Lotsen fraan Moluckas: En radiospel om den portugisiske sjoe fararen Magellans vaerldsomsegling, 1519-1522,* FIB's Lyrikklubb, 1954; *Gaesen i Thule* (poems; title means "The Grasses in Thule"), 1958; *Dikter* (poems), 1959; *Vagnen* (poems; title means "The Wagon"), 1960; *Den forlorade jaguaren,* 1961; (editor) *Vishetens ord i oester,* Bokfoerlaget Piccolo, 1962; *Utskit fraan en graestuva,* 1963; (with Bjoern von Rosen) *Bestiarium: Omfattande djur och faaglar fraan allo jordens laender och historiens aaldrar infaangade med tankens snaror vid stranden av sjoen Sillen sommaren 1963,* 1964; *Tre knivar fraan Wei* (play; title means "Three Knives from Wei"), 1964; *Vinden paa marken, och andra naturstycken,* 1964; *Vildbukettan: Naturdikter i urval av Ake Runnquist,* 1965.

Dikter om ljus och moerker, 1971; *Tuvor* (poems), 1973; *Dikter, 1929-1953* (poems), 1974; *Dikter, 1958-1973,* 1974.

Collections: *Dikter, Ur Kap Farvael, Naturstycken, Kalender,* [and] *Vaegen till Klockrike,* 1974; *Midsommardalen, Det enkla och det svaara, Utsikt fraan en graestuva,* 1974; *Resor utan maal* [and] *Kap farvael!,* 1974.

Also author of *Spoekskepp* (poems; title means "Ghost Ship"), 1926, *Nomad* (poems; title means "Nomad"), 1931; *Modern lyrik* (poems; title means "Modern Poems"), 1931; *Resor utan maal* (title means "Journeys Without a Goal"), 1932.

OBITUARIES: New York Times, February 12, 1978.*

(Died February 11, 1978, in Stockholm, Sweden)

* * *

MARTINSON, Tom L. 1941-

PERSONAL: Born November 7, 1941, in Portland, Ore.; son of Alfred T. and Mildred A. Martinson; married Paula N. Kaminska, June 3, 1965; children: Laura D. *Education:* University of Oregon, B.A., 1963; University of Kansas, Ph.D., 1969. *Home:* 3516 North Royal Oak Dr., Muncie, Ind. 47304. *Office:* Department of Geography and Geology, Ball State University, Muncie, Ind. 47306.

CAREER: University of Colorado, Boulder, visiting assistant professor of geography, 1966-67; Ball State University, Muncie, Ind., assistant professor, 1967-73, associate professor, 1973-75, professor of geography, 1975—, director of Institute for International Studies, 1967-74. *Member:* Conference of Latin Americanist Geographers (member of board of directors, 1973—; vice-chairman of board, 1974-76; chairman of board, 1976-78; executive secretary, 1978—), Association of Amerian Geographers, American Geographical Society, Latin American Studies Association, National Council for Geographic Education.

WRITINGS: (Editor with Barry Lentnek and Robert Carmin) *Geographic Research on Latin America: Benchmark 1970,* Ball State University, 1971; *Introduction to Library Research in Geography,* Scarecrow, 1972; (with Gerald Showalter) *Research Guide to Colombia,* Pan American Institute of Geography and History, 1975. Contributor to *Handbook of Latin American Studies.* Contributor of more than thirty articles to professional journals. Editor of *Geographical Survey,* 1975—.

WORK IN PROGRESS: Writing about the geography of Latin America, space perception, and instructional methodology.

SIDELIGHTS: Martinson comments: "I have always been fascinated with the spatial characteristics of personal and cultural interaction. Viewed in this light, geography has been and doubtless will continue to be the glass through which I view the world and thus discover myself."

* * *

MASINTON, Charles G(erald) 1938-

PERSONAL: Born May 28, 1938, in LeVeta, Colo.; son of Charles Julius (a grocer and local politician) and Lola Louise (Ladurini) Masinton; married Martha Claire Tait (a freelance editor), September 21, 1963; children: Carolyn Neal, Martha Claire. *Education:* University of Colorado, B.A., 1961; University of Oklahoma, Ph.D., 1966. *Home:* 709 Mississippi St., Lawrence, Kan. 66044. *Office:* Department of English, University of Kansas, Lawrence, Kan. 66045.

CAREER: Punahou Academy, Honolulu, Hawaii, instructor in English, 1961-62; University of Oklahoma, Norman, instructor in English, 1965-66; University of New Mexico, Albuquerque, assistant professor of English, 1966-67; University of Kansas, Lawrence, assistant professor, 1967-71, associate professor, 1971-77, professor of English, 1977—. *Member:* Phi Beta Kappa. *Awards, honors:* Danforth Associate, 1970.

WRITINGS: Christopher Marlowe's Tragic Vision: A Study in Damnation, Ohio University Press, 1972; *J. P. Donleavy: The Style of His Sadness and Humor,* Bowling Green University Popular Press, 1975. Contributor to *Ohio University Review.*

WORK IN PROGRESS: The Myth of the New Beginning in Contemporary American Fiction, "dealing with the recurrent image of the protagonist who 'heads for the territory' or otherwise withdraws from American society, usually at the end of the novel; works dealing with the opposing image—the integration of the hero into society at the end of a novel—are also a part of the fabric of the study."

SIDELIGHTS: Masinton wrote: "My major teaching area is American literature, with a concentration in twentieth-century fiction (both pre- and post-World War II), but I also teach modern American drama rather frequently and thus tend to think of myself as a modernist rather than a scholar of the entire range of American literature. My teaching of pre-1900 American literature is mostly survey in nature."

* * *

MASSEY, Irving (Joseph) 1924-

PERSONAL: Born June 15, 1924, in Montreal, Quebec, Canada; came to the United States in 1944; son of Alexander (a commercial traveler) and Ida (a poet; maiden name, Zukofsky) Massey; married Arlene H. Reichenbach (divorced, 1971); married Susan Thompson (divorced, 1975); children: Melez, Ephraim, Rachel. *Education:* McGill University, B.A., 1944; Columbia University, M.A., 1945; Harvard University, M.A., 1946, Ph.D., 1954. *Religion:* Jewish. *Home:* 332 Ashland Ave., Buffalo, N.Y. 14222. *Office:* Department of English and Comparative Literature, State University of New York at Buffalo, Clemens Hall, Buffalo, N.Y. 14260.

CAREER: Wayne State University, Detroit, Mich., instructor in English, 1946-50; Brandeis University, Waltham, Mass., instructor, 1954-56, assistant professor of English, 1956-60; McGill University, Montreal, Quebec, assistant professor of comparative literature, 1960-64; State University of New York at Buffalo, associate professor of English, 1964-69; McGill University, professor of English, 1969-70; State University of New York at Buffalo, professor of English, 1970—. Visiting professor at University of Wisconsin—Madison and Concordia University, Montreal, Quebec. *Member:* Modern Language Association of America, International Association for Literature and Philosophy, American Comparative Literature Association, Keats-Shelley Society.

WRITINGS: (Editor and translator from the French) Alfred de Vigny, *Stello: A Session with Doctor Noir,* McGill-Queen's University Press, 1962; (editor) *Posthumous Poems of Shelley,* McGill-Queen's University Press, 1969; *The Uncreating Word: Romanticism and the Object,* Indiana University Press, 1970; *The Gaping Pig: Literature and Metamorphoses,* University of California Press, 1976. Contributor of about thirty-five articles and reviews to professional journals.

WORK IN PROGRESS: A book on literature and ethics.

SIDELIGHTS: Massey told *CA:* "In the midst of my work on ethics, I find myself reverting to my old preoccupation with the disjunction between images and language. I am writing a paper on that subject now."

AVOCATIONAL INTERESTS: Spending time on his farm in Nova Scotia.

MASSIE, Robert K(inloch) 1929-

PERSONAL: Born January 9, 1929, in Lexington, Ky.; son of Robert K. and Mary (Kimball) Massie; married Suzanne Rohrbach (a writer), December 18, 1954; children: Robert, Susanna, Elizabeth. *Education:* Yale University, B.A., 1950; Oxford University, B.A., 1952. *Home address:* Irvington, N.Y. 10533.

CAREER: Collier's, New York City, reporter, 1955-56; *Newsweek,* New York City, writer and correspondent, 1956-62; *USA-1,* New York City, writer, 1962; *Saturday Evening Post,* New York City, writer, 1962-65; freelance writer, 1965—. *Military service:* U.S. Naval Reserves, 1952-55; became lieutenant, junior grade. *Member:* Authors League.

WRITINGS: Nicholas and Alexandra (biography), Atheneum, 1967; (with wife, Suzanne Massie) *Journey,* Knopf, 1975.

WORK IN PROGRESS: Peter the Great.

SIDELIGHTS: Robert Payne reviewed *Nicholas and Alexandra* for the *New York Times Book Reivew:* "Massie's canvas is the whole of Russia, the Czar and Czarina merely the focal points. His aim has been to paint in some 500 pages the decline and fall of Czarist Russia and to show the actors in the drama as they were. He has read most of the books, and he knows how to select the revealing passages. What emerges is a study in depth of the reign of Nicholas, and for perhaps the first time we meet the actors in the drama face to face in their proper setting." The *Observer* reported that Massie "embarked on the task because, finding himself the father of a hemophilic son, reading everything he could lay hands on to help him to cope, he became fascinated by the sad case of the Tsarevich Alexis, the effects of this tragedy on the conduct of his parents, and the impact of Rasputin on the course of history."

Massie's *Journey,* co-written with his wife Suzanne, is the story of their struggle to come to terms with their son's hemophilia. Elizabeth Hegeman reviewed *Journey* for the *New York Times Book Review:* "*Journey* is remarkable not just because the Massies met the challenge, but because their book makes it possible to believe that their experiences opened to them a self-awareness they otherwise never would have known." "The substance of the book," Hegeman added, "shifts from the mastery of pain to the mastery of life, and it is done in part by a turning outward in contrast to the Romanovs' secretiveness and withdrawal. The authors skillfully weave into their story important information about hemophilia in order to dispel harmful misinformation. They are determined to try to change those American institutions that fail to support the chronically ill." Peter Stoler reviewed *Journey* for *Time:* "Its portrait of Bobby Massie's enduring courage and the decency and devotion of those who helped him makes *Journey* a remarkable human document. Beyond that, the Massies' analysis of how the disease is handled and mishandled by American medicine is a model of reportorial precision and reformist zeal."

"Nicholas and Alexandria," filmed by Columbia Pictures in 1971, is based on Massie's book.

BIOGRAPHICAL/CRITICAL SOURCES: New York Times Book Review, August 20, 1967, May 11, 1975; *Observer,* January 14, 1968; *Time,* May 19, 1975.

* * *

MASUR, Harold Q. 1909-
(Guy Fleming, Edward James)

PERSONAL: Born January 29, 1909, in New York, N.Y.;

son of Jacob (a manufacturer) and Rose (Barondess) Masur. *Education:* New York University, B.S., 1932, J.D., 1934. *Home:* 520 East 20th St., New York, N.Y. 10009.

CAREER: Admitted to the Bar of New York State, 1935; attorney at law, 1935—. Legal Counsel to Mystery Writers of America. Instructor in writing at New York University, Iona College Writers' Conference, and Cape Cod Writers' Conference. Consultant on war games for Joint Chiefs of Staff, Department of Defense. *Member:* Mystery Writers of America (chairman of grievance committee, 1969—; chairman of Edgar Allan Poe awards dinner, 1971—; president, 1974). *Awards, honors:* Story Teller's Award from Mutual Broadcasting Co.

WRITINGS: Bury Me Deep, Simon & Schuster, 1947; *Suddenly a Corpse,* Simon & Schuster, 1949; *You Can't Live Forever,* Simon & Schuster, 1951; *So Rich, So Lovely, and So Dead,* Simon & Schuster, 1952; *The Big Money,* Simon & Schuster, 1954; *Tall, Dark, and Deadly,* Simon & Schuster, 1956; (editor) *Dolls Are Murder,* Lion Books, 1957; *The Last Gamble,* Simon & Schuster, 1958 (published in England as *The Last Breath,* Boardman, 1958); *Send Another Hearse,* Simon & Schuster, 1960; *The Name Is Jordan,* Pyramid, 1962; *Make a Killing,* Random House, 1964; *The Legacy Lenders,* Random House, 1967; *The Attorney,* Random House, 1973.

Also editor of *Murder Most Foul,* Walker; associate editor of Alfred Hitchcock anthologies; author of television plays and motion pictures; writer of short stories, sometimes under pseudonyms Guy Fleming and Edward James.

WORK IN PROGRESS: Research on investment banking for a book about Wall Street to be published by Random House.

SIDELIGHTS: Masur told *CA:* "The writing of mystery fiction affords me deep satisfaction because it is perhaps the only area in life in which man's problems are solved through logic and malefactors brought to justice. Oh, that it would be truly so on God's green footstool!"

*   *   *

MATA, Daya 1914-

PERSONAL: Birth-given name, Faye Wright; born January 31, 1914; daughter of Clarence Aaron and Rachel (Terry) Wright. *Education:* Attended Self-Realization teacher's training course. *Home and office:* Self-Realization Fellowship, 3880 San Rafael, Los Angeles, Calif. 90065.

CAREER: Entered Self-Realization Fellowship (monastic order), 1921, minister of headquarters chapel, 1935, church treasurer, 1939-71, lecturer on the teachings of the fellowship, 1952—, president of the U.S. fellowship and its branches in Canada, Mexico, South America, Europe, Africa, Australia, New Zealand, and Asia, and of its Yogoda Satsanga Society of India and church branches in India. President of Yogoda Mahayidyala, Yogoda Homeopathic Mahavidyalaya, Yogoda Vidalaya, Yogoda Kanya Vidyalaya, Yogoda Sangeet Kala Bharati, Yogoda Shilpa Kala Bharati, Yogoda Bal-Krishnalaya, and Yogoda Sevashran Hospital, Ranchi, as well as elementary and secondary schools and colleges in Surakhet, Anandapur, and medical clinics and hospitals, all sponsored by Self-Realization Fellowship Church.

WRITINGS: Only Love: A Book of Spiritual Counsel, Self-Realization Fellowship, 1976. Contributor to church magazines.

WORK IN PROGRESS: A companion volume for *Only Love;* record albums on spiritual counsel.

SIDELIGHTS: Daya Mata's record albums include "A Heart Aflame," "God First," and "Is Meditation on God Compatible with Modern Life?"

She writes: "As president of an international yoga society, I have made five world lecture-tours, but my primary responsibility is overseeing the administrative work of the organization's centers in various countries and spiritual guidance involved in the monastic and lay programs of the society.

"The essence of all my talks or writings centers on these two themes: 1) We can never know God through blind faith or outer forms of worship alone. We must take up deep meditation in order to reach Him, and that is man's purpose on Earth. 2) The only lasting answer to all individual or world problems lies in developing our latent spiritual potentials through scientific methods of Yoga meditation."

*   *   *

MATTHEWS, Jacklyn Meek
See MEEK, Jacklyn O'Hanlon

*   *   *

MAXWELL, Edward
See ALLAN, Ted

*   *   *

MAZMANIAN, Arthur B(arkev) 1931-

PERSONAL: Born April 21, 1931, in Detroit, Mich.; son of Egishe H. (a farmer) and Lucy (a teacher; maiden name, Hovagimian) Mazmanian; married Irene Boyle (a teacher), December 11, 1960; children: Ian, Tarah. *Education:* School of the Museum of Fine Arts, Boston, Mass., diploma, 1962; Goddard College, B.A., 1967; Tufts University, M.F.A., 1974. *Politics:* Democrat. *Home:* 481 Main St., Hudson, Mass. 01749. *Office:* Department of Art, Framingham State College, Framingham, Mass. 01701.

CAREER: Farmer in Hudson, Mass., 1950-62; De Cordova Museum, Lincoln, Mass., instructor in art, 1963-66; Craft Center School, Worcester, Mass., instructor in art, 1965-73; Framingham State College, Framingham, Mass., assistant professor of art, 1973—. *Awards, honors:* Clarissa Bartlett traveling scholarships from Boston Museum of Fine Arts, 1962, for museum study in England, Holland, France, and Italy, and 1971, for study of architecture in Switzerland and southern Italy.

WRITINGS: The Structure of Praise: A Design Study/Architecture for Religion in New England From the Seventeenth Century to the Present, Beacon Press, 1970.

WORK IN PROGRESS: Research on book illustration and Shaker design.

SIDELIGHTS: Mazmanian commented: "*The Structure of Praise* was an attempt at visually communicating good design concepts. The format was used to reach a larger audience than I can reach in the classroom, and the book is unusual because its author, illustrator (there are more than two hundred photographs and drawings), and designer are one. I tried to make the book, in all of its parts, as well designed and as beautiful as the structures that are the subject of the study."

*   *   *

MAZUR, Gail 1937-

PERSONAL: Born November 10, 1937, in Cambridge, Mass.; daughter of Manuel (in antiques business) and

Mildred (a teacher; maiden name, Rosenberg) Beckwith; married Michael Mazur (an artist), December 28, 1958; children: Daniel Isaac, Kathe Elizabeth. *Education:* Smith College, B.A., 1959; studied with Robert Lowell, 1975-77. *Home:* 5 Walnut Ave., Cambridge, Mass. 02140.

CAREER: Cambridge Center for Adult Education, Cambridge, Mass., instructor in poetry, 1973—. Founder and director of Blacksmith House poetry program, 1973—, editor for Blacksmith Press, 1974—. Member of board of directors of "Book Affair"; has given readings from her works throughout New England and the Tennessee poetry circuit, and served as juror for poetry competitions. *Member:* Poetry Society of America. *Awards, honors:* Fellowship for Ossabaw Island, 1975; National Endowment for the Arts fellow, 1978.

WRITINGS: Nightfire (poems), David R. Godine, 1978.

Work anthologized in *Blacksmith Anthologies; Io Anthology; Baseball, I Gave You the Best Years of My Life.* Contributor to literary periodicals, including *Antioch Review, Nantucket Review, Ploughshares,* and *Sun.*

WORK IN PROGRESS: Letting Go (working title), a second volume of poems.

SIDELIGHTS: Mazur writes: "I began the poetry readings in the Blacksmith House Coffeeshop (the original building, by the way, of Longfellow's Village Smithy), hoping to create a place for the poetry community to meet and listen to poetry. The whole project succeeded far beyond my first tentative dream: the readings are crowded every week; we all look forward to those evenings and the sense of a real world of poetry which the program supports; in concert with the Grolier Bookshop, the Blacksmith sponsors an annual poetry prize reading, two or three poets each spring. The anthologies (Blacksmith Press) grew naturally from these reading: what writer doesn't want to see a literary event documented? For me, what began without much forethought or ambition has blossomed into a mission: to keep the thing going, to support and validate the work of poets, to make a dent in the isolation writers feel in their working life. I'm hooked on readings now, can't imagine I'll stop. And of course, the stimulation for me, as a poet, has been tremendous."

*   *   *

MAZURSKY, Paul 1930-

PERSONAL: Birth-given name, Irwin; born April 25, 1930, in Brooklyn, N.Y.; married wife, Betsy, March 14, 1953. *Education:* Attended Brooklyn College (now of the City University of New York). *Residence:* New York, N.Y.; and Beverly Hills, Calif.

CAREER: Screenwriter, actor, director, and producer of motion pictures. Writer and performer with Herb Hartig in comedy act, "Igor and H," and with Larry Tucker in semi-improvisational revue, "Second City"; writer with Tucker for television series, "The Danny Kaye Show"; actor in plays, including "The Seagull" and "Major Barbara," and motion pictures, including "Fear and Desire," 1953, "Blackboard Jungle," 1955, "Alex in Wonderland," 1971, "Blume in Love," 1973, "A Star Is Born," 1976, and "An Unmarried Woman," 1978. *Awards, honors:* Received nomination for best screenplay with Larry Tucker from Writers Guild, 1968, for "I Love You, Alice B. Toklas!"; Writers Guild Award, and nomination for best screenplay from Academy of Motion Picture Arts and Sciences, both with Tucker, both 1969, both for "Bob & Carol & Ted & Alice";

nomination for best film and with Josh Greenfield for best screenplay from Academy of Motion Picture Arts and Sciences, both 1974, both for "Harry and Tonto"; has also received other film awards.

WRITINGS—Screenplays: (With Larry Tucker) "I Love You, Alice B. Toklas," Warner Brothers, 1968; (with Tucker, and director) "Bob & Carol & Ted & Alice," Columbia, 1969; (with Tucker, and director) "Alex in Wonderland," Metro-Goldwyn-Mayer, 1970; (and director) "Blume in Love," Warner Brothers, 1973; (with Josh Greenfield, and director) *Harry and Tonto* (released by Twentieth Century-Fox, 1974), Dutton, 1974; (and director) "Next Stop, Greenwich Village," Twentieth Century-Fox, 1976; (and director) "An Unmarried Woman," Twentieth Century-Fox, 1978.

SIDELIGHTS: "I know I'm always looking to find out a little bit more about who I am," Mazursky told an interviewer. For Mazursky, this often means using his past experiences as subject matter for his films. His personal, intimate looks into neurotic life in America have earned him a reputation as one of the more compassionate filmmakers working today. "There are two kinds of movies," Mazursky said, "movies made out of passion and movies made to make money. They're both authentic, but the pictures I've loved were made out of passion."

Mazursky mined his early experiences as an aspiring actor in "Next Stop, Greenwich Village." The film is a recreation of the early fifties in New York City and adeptly captures the spirit of the young actor in the days when improvisation, method acting, and Marlon Brando were considered radical elements in the theatre. The film follows Larry Lapinsky's experiences of moving into his own apartment, struggling in an actor's school, and winning a part in a movie. Mazursky himself endured many of the same experiences with the culmination of his efforts being the acquisition of the starring role in Stanley Kubrick's first feature film, "Fear and Desire." Like the character of Larry Lapinsky, Mazursky also entertained the notion of winning an Academy Award: "I mean, I was on the screen for about an hour," Mazursky recalled; "I went crazy; I raped Virginia Leith . . . I figured I couldn't miss."

Another closely autobiographical film by Mazursky is "Alex in Wonderland." The story of a successful filmmaker who is faced with artistic uncertainty and ennui, "Alex in Wonderland" is often viewed today as an Americanized version of Fellini's classic, "8½." In the film, Mazursky attempts to show the obstacles which stand in the way of the independent filmmaker. Mazursky himself appears in the film as a Hollywood producer who tries to lure Alex, the filmmaker, into directing any of several abominable projects. The film portrays the plight of the independent artist negotiating with his own creativity while trying to avoid the trendy and pretentious California lifestyle. "Listen," said Mazursky, "I think if Solzhenitsyn moved to L.A., within a few months he's have a hot tub, be doing TM, be writing a movie and probably have two wives."

Mazursky has covered the swinger's lifestyle in two other films, "Bob & Carol & Ted & Alice," and "Blume in Love." The former, his first directorial effort, is a sarcastic expose of the hypocrisy involved in open marriage offering a puckish view of consciousness raising and sexual communication. "Blume in Love" is a more serious examination of the trends and hypocrisy in contemporary male/female relationships. It concerns a woman who leaves her husband, Blume, when she discovers his infidelity. She moves in with a musician. Blume, who is still in love with his wife, feigns a liberated attitude towards the arrangement in order to maintain their friendship. The interactions of the three people, combined with Blume's attempts to revive the relationship with his ex-wife, provide a thought provoking glimpse of modern life seen from a humorous viewpoint. Regarded by critics as a funny, but real, film, "Blume in Love" proved Mazursky's assertion that "the best humor usually comes from the truth."

A film that stands out as unique in the Mazursky canon is "Harry and Tonto." Described by Penelope Gilliatt as a film of travel that is "both fine and very matter-of-fact," "Harry and Tonto" tells the story of an old man forced to leave his apartment in New York City. Together with his cat, Tonto, Harry travels across the country. In the process he meets his four-times-married daughter, his son who lives in California and boozes the days away, an old girlfriend gone senile, and an ambitious prostitute. The film is a cavalcade of characters, with Mazursky giving even the least important characters a depth not seen in most films. Mazursky doesn't like cliches and feels that an audience can recognize a realistic character: "The moviegoer's attitude moves from 'I know *him*' to 'I *know* him!'" he said. "Harry and Tonto" proved to be one of Mazursky's more popular films both financially and critically. Much of the success was due to his ability to impose a unique, personal, quality to the characters. "In their quest," wrote Gilliatt, "they summon up far more about children, time, friendship than more orthodox film characters do."

Mazursky's most recent film, "An Unmarried Woman," received the most critical praise. Comments ranged from Richard Corliss's simple "splendid," to Andrew Sarris's weighty assessment that "'An Unmarried Woman' is the best American film I have seen in several years." It is the story of Erica, a woman married for sixteen years, whose husband leaves her for a younger woman. Following Erica as she deals with her new situation, Mazursky's film offers an insight into the personal and emotional struggle for independence which men and women can relate to. "You don't have to live in New York or L.A., his creative turfs, to love Mazursky," wrote David Anson, "his world of affluent, neurotic Americans plunging headlong into the social and sexual upheavals of the seventies is everywhere about us." As a critic for *Time* noted, Mazursky "has the terrain down pat." And in his highly personal films, Mazursky is equally at ease with male or female protagonists. "As a joke," said Mazursky, "I told one interviewer: 'I am the unmarried woman.' I don't know, is that a joke? I guess there are similarities."

In a medium dominated by oversaturation and a desire to repeat the successful, it is surprising that Mazursky has been able to make his highly personal studies. "I don't even know what commercial means," he told one interviewer. "I suppose I could look at the weekly grosses in *Variety* and say, 'Ah, I should make 'Jaws.' But, you know my stuff. If I did 'Jaws,' the shark would be just a little bit neurotic, and he'd be worrying about some other bigger shark, and wondering why these men are out to kill him. He'd be a shark with an identity crisis." Like filmmakers Robert Altman, Francis Ford Coppola, and Woody Allen, Mazursky has made the films he chooses without worrying about the desires of the studios. "Altman and I have only one thing in common," Mazursky said. "We're both unafraid. The studios don't scare us. I believe if you've got the passion and the talent you can get a lot of things made."

BIOGRAPHICAL/CRITICAL SOURCES: New York

Times, January 17, 1971; *New Yorker*, August 26, 1974; *Village Voice*, February 16, 1976, March 6, 1978; *Time*, March 6, 1978; *Newsweek*, March 13, 1978.*

*   *   *

McANDREW, John   1904-1978

May 4, 1904—February 18, 1978; American art historian, museum curator, educator, and author of books in his field. A former curator at the Museum of Modern Art in New York City, McAndrew was the founder and chairman of Save Venice Inc., an organization dedicated to restoring water-damaged art and buildings. Earlier in his career, McAndrew taught at Vassar College and served as director of the Wellesley College art museum. He died in Venice, Italy. Obituaries and other sources: *Directory of American Scholars,* Volume I: *History,* 6th edition, Bowker, 1974; *Who's Who in American Art,* 12th edition, Bowker, 1976; *New York Times,* February 20, 1978.

*   *   *

McAULEY, James J(ohn)   1936-

PERSONAL: Born January 8, 1936, in Dublin, Ireland; came to the United States in 1966; son of J. Noel (a pilot) and Maureen (McCarthy) McAuley; married Joan McNally, October 28, 1958 (divorced September 4, 1968); married Almut R. Nierentz (a translator and teacher), September 6, 1968; children: J. Michael, Anthony J., Kevin B., Owen, Rory G. *Education:* National University of Ireland, University College, Dublin, B.A., 1962; University of Arkansas, M.F.A., 1971. *Politics:* "Moderate Socialist?" *Home:* 624 Lincoln St., Cheney, Wash. 99004. *Office:* Department of English, Eastern Washington University, Cheney, Wash. 99004.

CAREER: Electricity Supply Board, Dublin, Ireland, journalist, 1954-66; *North West Arkansas Times,* Fayetteville, reporter, 1967; Lycoming College, Williamsport, Pa., assistant professor of English, 1968-70; Eastern Washington University, Cheney, assistant professor, 1970-73, associate professor, 1973-78, professor of English, 1978—. Lecturer at Dublin's Municipal Gallery of Modern Art, 1965-66; visiting lecturer at University of Victoria, 1975. Member of board of trustees of Spokane Allied Arts Council, 1971-76. *Member:* Associated Writing Programs. *Awards, honors:* National Endowment for the Arts fellowship, 1972; Washington governor's award for poetry, 1976, for *After the Blizzard.*

WRITINGS: Observations (poems), Mount Salus Press, 1960; *A New Address* (poems), Humanities, 1965; *Draft Balance Sheet: Poems, 1963-1969,* Humanities, 1970; *After the Blizzard* (poems), University of Missouri Press, 1976.

Author of "The Revolution" (five-part verse satire), first produced in Dublin, Ireland, by Lantern Theatre Co., 1966. Contributor of articles, poems, and reviews to magazines in Ireland, England, Canada, and the United States. Art critic for *Kilkenny,* 1960-66; associate editor of *Poetry Ireland,* 1962-66; member of editorial board for Associated Writing Programs.

WORK IN PROGRESS: A fifth book of poems; a novel.

SIDELIGHTS: McAuley comments: "I hope that my writings reflect those subjects and attitudes which I consider vital." *Avocational interests:* Travel.

*   *   *

McBRIDE, Donald O(pie)   1903-1978

June 1, 1903—June 25, 1978; American engineer, government official, and author. Director of the Tennessee Valley Authority from 1966 to 1975, McBride wrote *TVA and the National Defense.* He began his career as an enginner in Oklahoma, where he was named chairman of the Oklahoma Resources and Planning Board, and later became secretary-manager of the National Reclamation Association. At the time of his appointment to the TVA directorship, McBride was serving on the staff of U.S. Senator A. S. Mike Monroney. He died in Fort Wayne, Ind. Obituaries and other sources: *Who's Who in American Politics,* 4th edition, Bowker, 1974; *Who's Who in America,* 39th edition, Marquis, 1976; *New York Times,* June 28, 1978.

*　*　*

McCAFFREY, Phillip 1945-

PERSONAL: Born December 14, 1945, in Mobile, Ala.; son of Hugh C. (a lawyer) and Leatrice (Surratt) McCaffrey; married Lee DeAngelis (a medical researcher), August 10, 1968. *Education:* Fordham University, B.A., 1968; University of Pennsylvania, Ph.D., 1972. *Home:* 110 Homeland Ave., Baltimore, Md. 21212. *Office:* Department of English, Loyola College, 4501 North Charles St., Baltimore, Md. 21210.

CAREER: Loyola College, Baltimore, Md., assistant professor, 1972-77, associate professor of English, 1977—, director of creative writing workshop. *Member:* Modern Language Association of America, Mediaeval Academy of America, Associated Writing Programs, South Atlantic Modern Language Association. *Awards, honors:* Woodrow Wilson fellowship, 1968-69.

WRITINGS: Cold Frames (poems), Samsidat, 1976. Contributor of articles and poems to literary journals, including *New York Quarterly, Poetry Now,* and *Beloit Poetry Journal.*

*WORK IN PROGRESS—*Poems: *Body Time; Naming the Carnival;* and *Weights and Measures.*

SIDELIGHTS: McCaffrey told *CA:* "My work carries the past into the future. *Naming the Carnival* is a world in which old myths appear in twentieth-century disguises, our new myths. The continuum—between past and future, between writer and reader—is always in the language, which is our most enduring myth."

*　*　*

McCAUGHEY, Robert A(nthony) 1939-

PERSONAL: Born April 13, 1939, in Pawtucket, R.I.; son of John F. (an accountant) and Helen (Galleshaw) McCaughey; married Ann Ballantyne (a personnel counselor), August 30, 1965; children: Hannah, John. *Education:* University of Rochester, A.B. (summa cum laude), 1961; University of North Carolina, M.A., 1965; Harvard University, Ph.D., 1969. *Religion:* Roman Catholic. *Home:* 40 East 88th St., New York, N.Y. 10027. *Office:* Department of History, Barnard College, Columbia University, New York, N.Y. 10027.

CAREER: Columbia University, Barnard College, New York, N.Y., assistant professor, 1969-73, associate professor of history, 1974—. *Military service:* U.S. Navy, Supply Corps, 1961-65; became lieutenant. *Member:* American Historical Association, American Association of University Professors.

WRITINGS: Josiah Quincy: The Last Federalist, Harvard University Press, 1974. Contributor to law and political science journals. Member of board of editors of *Political Science Quarterly.*

WORK IN PROGRESS: A history of the development of foreign studies in American universities.

SIDELIGHTS: McCaughey told *CA* that his research interests are increasingly directed to the historical and contemporary workings of American academe.

*　*　*

McCLELLAN, A(rchibald) W(illiam) 1908-

PERSONAL: Born May 29, 1908, in London, England. *Education:* Attended secondary school in London, England. *Home:* Rosemount, Llanon, Dyfed, Wales.

CAREER: Tottenham Public Libraries and Museum, London, England, director, 1945-65; assistant town clerk of Haringey, London, 1965-68; research fellow at College of Librarianship in Wales, 1969-75; writer, 1975—. Has broadcast talks on British Broadcasting Corp. (BBC). *Member:* Library Association. *Awards, honors:* Fellow of Library Association, 1973.

WRITINGS: The Reader, the Library, and the Book, Bingley, 1973; *The Logistics of a Public Library Bookstock,* Association of Assistant Librarians, 1977. Contributor of about thirty articles to library journals.

WORK IN PROGRESS: Language, Literacy, Reading, and Readers; Readers and Reading.

*　*　*

McCLORY, Robert J(oseph) 1932-

PERSONAL: Born June 8, 1932, in Chicago, Ill.; son of Guy T. (a postal clerk) and Alice (a teacher; maiden name, Branick) McClory; married Margaret A. McComish (a curriculum consultant), November 20, 1971; children: Jennifer. *Education:* St. Mary of the Lake Seminary, Mundelein, Ill., B.A., 1954, M.A., 1957; Northwestern University, M.S.J., 1971. *Religion:* Roman Catholic. *Home:* 7510 North Bell, Chicago, Ill. 60645. *Agent:* Dominick Abel Literary Services, 498 West End Ave., #12C, New York, N.Y. 10024. *Office: Chicago Daily Defender,* 2400 South Michigan, Chicago, Ill. 60616.

CAREER: Roman Catholic priest in Chicago archdiocese, and associate pastor of Roman Catholic churches in Winnetka and Chicago, Ill., 1958-70, left the priesthood in 1971; Loyola University, Chicago, lecturer in theology, 1960-64; associate pastor of parish in Chicago, 1964-71; *Chicago Daily Defender,* Chicago, reporter and city editor and staff writer, 1971—. *Awards, honors:* Best feature story award from National Newspaper Publishers Association, 1976, for "Why Johnny's Teacher Can't Read" (about Chicago State University); best news story award, 1977, for "Black School Board Members Rebel."

WRITINGS: Fighting Your Way Through the Welfare Jungle, Rockford Library Press, 1973; *The Man Who Beat Clout City* (biography), Swallow Press, 1978. Correspondent for *Race Relations Reporter,* 1972-75, and *National Catholic Reporter,* 1976—. Contributor to magazines, including *Sepia, U.S. Catholic,* and *Midwest,* and to newspapers.

WORK IN PROGRESS: Research on discrimination in the United States, reverse discrimination, and problems and trends in the Roman Catholic Church.

SIDELIGHTS: McClory writes: "I was a Roman Catholic priest from 1958 to 1970, working largely in racially changing areas. I have worked for the black-owned *Chicago Daily Defender* since 1971. My second book is the story of the eight-year struggle of black policeman Renault Robinson against bias on the Chicago police force. My main professional interest is interracial relations and authority problems in the Catholic Church."

BIOGRAPHICAL/CRITICAL SOURCES: New York Times, August 20, 1977; *Chicago Reader,* August 26, 1977; *Chicago Sun-Times,* January 4, 1978.

*   *   *

McCONAGHA, Alan   1932-

PERSONAL: Born July 26, 1932, in Appleton, Wis.; son of William A. (a professor) and Jessie Mae (a professor; maiden name, Pate) McConagha; married Barbara Melamed, June 22, 1966; children: William Arthur, Megan Mara, Adam Cameron. *Education:* Attended Lawrence University, 1950-51; Earlham College, A.B., 1954; University of Wisconsin, M.A., 1955, special student, 1955-56. *Home:* 4802 Newport Ave., Bethesda, Md. 20016. *Office: Minneapolis Tribune,* 940 National Press Bldg., Washington, D.C. 20045.

CAREER/WRITINGS: Montgomery Advertiser, Montgomery, Ala., reporter, 1956-57; *Minneapolis Tribune,* Minneapolis, Minn., currently correspondent in Washington, D.C. Notable assignments include coverage of the African drought, 1974, Richard Nixon's visits to the Soviet Union and Egypt, 1974, Palestinian activities, 1975, and the Israeli election, 1977.

*   *   *

McCONE, R(obert) Clyde   1915-

PERSONAL: Born September 30, 1915, in Redfield, S.D.; son of Robert A. (a farmer) and Ruth (Smart) McCone; married Angeline Schmidt (a teacher), July 14, 1943; children: Robert Clyde, Jr., Evangeline McCone Pearson. *Education:* Wessington Springs College, B.A., 1946; South Dakota State University, M.S., 1956; Michigan State University, Ph.D., 1961. *Religion:* Wesleyan. *Home:* 1901 Snowden Ave., Long Beach, Calif. 90815. *Office:* Department of Anthropology, California State University, 1250 Bellflower Blvd., Long Beach, Calif. 90840.

CAREER: Pastor of churches in South Dakota and Montana, 1943-54; South Dakota State University, Brookings, instructor in anthropology, 1956-57; California State University, Long Beach, 1961—, began as assistant professor, professor of anthropology, 1970—. *Member:* American Anthropological Association (fellow), Society of Applied Anthropology (fellow), American Association for the Advancement of Science, American Scientific Affiliation, Royal Anthropological Institute of Great Britain and Ireland (fellow), Creation Research Society, California Teachers Association.

WRITINGS: (Contributor) *Symposium on Creation,* Baker Book, Volume I, edited by Henry M. Morris, 1968, Volume II, edited by Donald W. Patton, 1970, Volume IV, edited by Patton, 1972; *Man and His World,* Creation Science Research Center, 1971; (contributor) Mark Tuttle, editor, *About School: Essays by Scholars Investigating Christian Higher Education,* Lanthorn, 1972; (editor) *Science, Culture, and Glossolalia,* 49er Shops Bookstore, 1978; *Culture and Controversy: An Investigation of the Tongues of Pentacost,* Dorrance, 1978. Contributor to anthropology and scientific journals.

WORK IN PROGRESS: The Phenomena of Man.

SIDELIGHTS: McCone writes: "I am interested in the mystery of the distinctiveness of the cultures of western civilization. These cultures are exclusively the cultural medium of the advancement of natural sciences and they are also the exclusive cultural medium for the advancement of supernatural and supercultural claims of Christianity. In some recent writings I have extended the realm of applied anthropology to the area of Biblical interpretation and Christian controversy. In *The Phenomena of Man* I develop the dimensions of the moral order in which man moves and has his being and which also must provide the framework for the study of man."

*   *   *

McCONNELL, Allen   1923-

PERSONAL: Born March 22, 1923, in Long Branch, N.J.; son of Burt Morton (a writer) and Gertrude (an executive secretary; maiden name, Allen) McConnell; married Brigitte Brandis (a psychologist), 1964; children: Roderick, Fiona, Dugald. *Education:* Brown University, B.A., 1946; graduate study at University of Chicago, 1946-48; Columbia University, M.A., 1950, Ph.D., 1954. *Religion:* Episcopalian. *Home:* 28 Orchard St., Glen Head, N.Y. 11545. *Office:* Department of History, Queens College of the City University of New York, Flushing, N.Y. 11367.

CAREER: Brown University, Providence, R.I., instructor, 1951-54, assistant professor of political science, 1954-59; Queens College of the City University of New York, Flushing, N.Y., instructor, 1960-61, assistant professor, 1962-64, associate professor, 1965-69, professor of history, 1970—. *Military service:* U.S. Army Air Forces, 1943-46. *Member:* American Historical Association, American Association for the Advancement of Slavic Studies. *Awards, honors:* Social Science Research Council grant, 1956-57; American Philosophical Society grant, 1966-67.

WRITINGS: A Russian Philosophe: Alexander Radishchev, Nijhoff, 1964; *Tsar Alexander I,* Crowell, 1970. Contributor to history and Slavic studies journals.

WORK IN PROGRESS: Articles.

*   *   *

McCORMICK, Mona

PERSONAL: Born in Cleveland, Ohio; daughter of Benjamin (a newspaperman) and Mildred (a social worker; maiden name, Hogan) McCormick. *Education:* University of Iowa, B.A., 1952; Pratt Institute, M.L.S., 1965; further graduate study at University of South Dakota, summer, 1971. *Home:* 8561 Villa La Jolla Dr., Apt. J, La Jolla, Calif. 92037. *Office:* Central University Library, University of California, San Diego, Calif.

CAREER: National Broadcasting Co. (NBC) TV News, New York City, researcher for news specials, 1954-64; New York Public Library, New York City, 1965-67, began as reference librarian, at Hamilton Fish branch, became senior librarian at Donnell Reference Center; *New York Times,* New York City, assistant to head librarian, 1967-70; Rosebud Sioux Reservation, Rosebud, S.D., volunteer high school librarian and teacher, 1970-72; Western Behavioral Sciences Institute, La Jolla, Calif., research associate, 1972-76; editorial assistant to Jonas Salk, 1976-78; University of California, San Diego, member of staff in central university library, 1978—.

WRITINGS: Who-What-Where-How-Why Made Easy: A Guide to the Practical Use of Reference Books, Quadrangle, 1971; (contributor) John Lubans, Jr., editor, *Educating the Library User*, H. W. Wilson, 1974; *Stepfathers; What the Literature Reveals* (monograph), Western Behavioral Sciences Institute, 1974; *Probation: What the Literature Reveals* (monograph), Western Behavioral Sciences Institute, 1974; *Robbery Prevention: What the Literature Reveals* (monograph), Western Behavioral Sciences Institute, 1975; (with Ray Johnson) *Too Dangerous to Be at Large*, Quadrangle, 1975; *Primary Education for the Disadvantaged: What the Literature Reveals* (monograph), Western Behavioral Sciences Institute, 1976. Contributor to *New York Times Encyclopedic Almanac*, 1970.

* * *

McCOY, Malachy
See CAULFIELD, Malachy Francis

* * *

McCOY, Tim(othy John Fitzgerald) 1891-1978

April 10, 1891—January 29, 1978; American actor and author of his autobiography. Prior to his career as a cowboy movie star in more than eighty films, McCoy had been a cowhand and an authority on Indians in Wyoming. In his later years, McCoy toured with circuses and Wild West Shows. His television program, "The Tim McCoy Show," won an Emmy award. He died in Nogales, Ariz. Obituaries and other sources: Ernest Corneau, *Hall of Fame of Western Film Stars*, Christopher, 1969; *Who's Who in America*, 38th edition, Marquis, 1974; Tim McCoy and Ronald McCoy, *Tim McCoy Remembers the West: An Autobiography*, Doubleday, 1977; *American Heritage*, June, 1977; *International Motion Picture Almanac*, Quigley, 1977; *New York Times*, January 31, 1978.

* * *

McCROSKEY, James C(layborne) 1936-

PERSONAL: Born October 6, 1936, in Platte, S. D.; son of James C. (a dentist) and Sally Sue (a teacher; maiden name, Chastain) McCroskey; married, 1957 (marriage terminated); children: Kellie C., James C., Patrick S., Linda L., Lisa L. *Education:* Southern State College (now University of South Dakota at Springfield), B.S., 1957; University of South Dakota, Vermillion, M.A., 1959; Pennsylvania State University, Ed.D., 1966. *Office:* Department of Speech Communication, West Virginia University, Morgantown, W. Va. 26506.

CAREER: High school speech teacher in Scotland, S.D., 1957-58, and Watertown, S.D., 1958-60; University of Hawaii, Honolulu, instructor in speech, 1960-61; Old Dominion College (now University), Norfolk, Va., instructor in speech, 1961-63; Pennsylvania State University, State College, instructor in speech, 1963-66; Michigan State University, East Lansing, assistant professor of communication, 1966-69; Illinois State University, Normal, associate professor of communication, 1969-72; West Virginia University, Morgantown, professor of communication and chairman of department of speech communication, 1972—. *Member:* International Communication Association (vice-president, 1972-74), Speech Communication Association of America, American Forensic Association, Eastern Communication Association (vice-president, 1977; president, 1978-79), Western Speech Communication Association.

WRITINGS: Introduction to Rhetorical Communication, Prentice-Hall, 1968, 3rd edition, 1978; (with Mark L. Knapp and Carl E. Larson) *Introduction to Interpersonal Communication*, Prentice-Hall, 1971; (contributor) *Speech Commu-nication Behavior*, Prentice-Hall, 1971; (with Michael Burgoon and Judee Heston) *Small Group Communication*, Holt, 1974; (with Lawrence Wheeless) *Introduction to Human Communication*, Allyn & Bacon, 1976; (with Thomas Hurt and Michael Scott) *Communication in the Classroom*, Addison-Wesley, 1977; (with John A. Daly) *Relational Communication*, Prentice-Hall, in press. Contributor of about sixty articles to professional journals.

WORK IN PROGRESS: With Virginia P. Richmond, *Communication Problems of Children* and *Communication in Educational Organizations*.

SIDELIGHTS: McCroskey wrote: "My primary purpose in writing is to diffuse information about human communication processes generated from empirical research."

* * *

McCUNE, Shannon 1913-

PERSONAL: Born April 6, 1913, in Sonch'on, Korea; son of George Shannon (a missionary) and Helen (a missionary; maiden name, McAfee) McCune; married Edith Blair, June 30, 1936; children: Antoinette McCune Kennedy, Shannon McCune Wagner, George Blair. *Education:* College of Wooster, B.A. (honors), 1935; Syracuse University, M.A., 1937; Clark University, Ph.D., 1939. *Home:* 1617 Northwest Seventh Pl., Gainesville, Fla. 32603. *Office:* Department of Geography, University of Florida, Gainesville, Fla. 32611.

CAREER: Ohio State University, Columbus, member of faculty of geography, 1939-47; Colgate University, Hamilton, N.Y., member of faculty of geography and chairman of department, 1947-55; University of Massachusetts, Amherst, provost, 1955-61; United Nations Educational, Scientific & Cultural Organization (UNESCO), Paris, France, director of department of education, 1961-62; U.S. Civil Administration of the Ryukyu Islands, Naha, Okinawa, civil administrator, 1962-64; University of Illinois, Champaign-Urbana, adjunct professor of geography and staff associate, 1964-65; University of Vermont, Burlington, president, 1965-66, research professor of geography, 1966-67; Columbia University, New York, N.Y., adjunct professor of geography, 1967-69; University of Florida, Gainesville, professor of geography, 1969—, chairman of department, 1969-75. Fulbright professor at Tokyo University, 1953-54, and Soong-Jun University, 1975-76; visiting professor at University of Hawaii, 1976; member of summer or visiting faculty at Miami University, Oxford, Ohio, Harvard University, University of Chicago, Washington University, St. Louis, Mo., University of Minnesota, McGill University, and Johns Hopkins University. Served with U.S. Board of Economic Warfare and U.S. Economic Administration in Washington, D.C., 1942-43, India, 1943-44, Ceylon, 1944, and China, 1944-45; deputy director of Far East Program Division for U.S. Economic Cooperation Administration, 1950-51.

MEMBER: American Geographical Society (director, 1967-69), American Oriental Society, American Association for the Advancement of Science, American Association of University Professors, National Council for Geographic Education, Association of American Geographers (member of council; vice-president), Association for Asian Studies (member of board of directors), Association of Japanese Geographers, Korean Geographical Society, Phi Beta Kappa, Sigma Xi, Phi Kappa Phi, Phi Beta Kappa Associates. *Awards, honors:* Medal of Freedom, 1946; Pandit Madan Mohan Malaviya Medal from National Geographic Society of India, 1950; LL.D. from Clark University, 1960, University of Massachusetts, 1962, and Eastern Nazarene College, 1966; founders award from Hampshire College, 1970; National Science Foundation grant, 1970.

WRITINGS: Korea's Heritage: A Regional and Social Geography, Tuttle, 1956; *Korea: Land of Broken Calm,* Van Nostrand, 1966; *Geographical Aspects of Agricultural Changes in the Ryukyu Islands,* University of Florida Press, 1975; *The Ryukyu Islands,* David & Charles, 1975. Contributor of more than a hundred-twenty articles to academic journals.

WORK IN PROGRESS: The Zone of Conflict in the Far East: A Descriptive Political Geography.

SIDELIGHTS: McCune writes: "Having been born in Korea of American parents and having been trained as a geographer, I have specialized in research and writing on the Far East and expect to continue to do so."

McCune has traveled in Asia, Europe, the Arab states, Africa, and Latin America, has carried on field work in central India, and conducted research in the Far East, especially in the zone of conflict between Japan and China, gathering material on the political geography of the area.

*   *   *

McDANIEL, Walton Brooks   1871-

PERSONAL: Born March 4, 1871, in Cambridge, Mass.; son of Samuel Walton (a clergyman and lawyer) and Georgiana Frances (Brooks) McDaniel; married Alice Corinne Garlichs, 1899 (deceased); married Helen C. Stock Brown (a teacher), April 1, 1950. *Education:* Harvard University, A.B., 1893, M.A., 1894, Ph.D., 1899; also attended University of Berlin, 1897-98, University of Rome, and Sorbonne, University of Paris. *Politics:* Independent. *Religion:* Unitarian-Universalist. *Home:* 1620 Maple Ave., Haddon Heights, N.J. 08035.

CAREER: Harvard University, Cambridge, Mass., instructor in Greek and Latin, 1899-1901, instructor at Radcliffe College, 1900-01; University of Pennsylvania, Philadelphia, instructor, 1901-03, assistant professor, 1903-09, professor of Latin language and literature, 1909-37, professor emeritus, 1937—, chairman of department. Annual professor at American Academy in Rome, 1920-21; has lectured around the United States. *Member:* American Philosophical Association (president, 1921), American Philosophical Society, Archaeological Institute of America (fellow), American Association for the Advancement of Science (fellow), Classical Association of the Atlantic States, Phi Beta Kappa. *Awards, honors:* LL.D. from University of Pennsylvania, 1975.

WRITINGS: Roman Private Life and Its Survivals, Marshall Jones Co., 1924, reprinted, Cooper Square, 1963; *Conception, Birth, and Infancy in Ancient Rome and Modern Italy,* privately printed, 1948; *Riding a Hobby in the Classical Lands,* Department of Classics, Harvard University, 1971. Also author of *Guide for the Study of English Books on Roman Private Life,* Service Bureau for Classical Teachers. Contributor to learned journals.

SIDELIGHTS: McDaniel has traveled often, and has spent long periods of time in Italy and Greece. During his career as an academician and specialist on Roman private life, he collected Roman antiquities that illustrate Roman private life. His extensive collection is now on display at Harvard University. *Avocational interests:* Collecting shells (especially fossil shells).

McDERMOTT, A(gnes) Charlene Senape   1937-

PERSONAL: Born March 11, 1937, in Hazleton, Pa.; daughter of Charles (a restauranteur) and Conjetta (Ranieri) McDermott; divorced; children: Bob, Lise, Jamie. *Education:* University of Pennsylvania, B.A. (honors), 1956, Ph.D., 1964; graduate study at University of California, Berkeley, 1960-61; postdoctoral study at University of Amsterdam, 1965-66, and University of Wisconsin—Madison, 1971-72. *Home:* 602 Camino Espanol N.W., Albuquerque, N.M. 87107. *Office:* Department of Philosophy, University of New Mexico, Albuquerque, N.M. 87131.

CAREER: Applied mathematician, programmer and logical designer for industrial firms, including Burroughs Corp., Sperry Rand, and Lawrence Radiation Laboratories, 1957-59; Drexel Institute of Technology, Philadelphia, Pa., instructor in mathematics, 1962-63; State University of New York College at Buffalo, assistant professor of philosophy, 1964-65; Hampton Institute, Hampton, Va., assistant professor of philosophy, 1966-67; University of Wisconsin—Milwaukee, assistant professor of philosophy, 1967-70; University of New Mexico, Albuquerque, associate professor of philosophy, 1970—, chairperson of Asian Studies Program. Visiting associate professor at University of California, Berkeley, summer, 1973, and winter, 1974, University of Washington, Seattle, summer, 1974, and University of Hawaii, autumn, 1975.

MEMBER: American Philosophical Association (member of executive board), Phi Beta Kappa, Pi Mu Epsilon. *Awards, honors:* American Association of University Women fellowship, 1965-66; National Endowment for the Humanities fellowship, 1971-72.

WRITINGS: Ratnakirti's Ksanabhangasiddhi Vyatirekatmika: An Eleventh-Century Buddhist Logic of "Exists", Reidel of Dordrecht, 1969, Humanities, 1970; (contributor) Min Kiyota and Elvin Jones, editors, *Buddhist Meditation in Theory and Practice,* University Press of Hawaii, 1976. Contributor of articles and reviews to journals. Review editor, *Journal of Buddhist Philosophy.*

WORK IN PROGRESS: Translating and analyzing a medieval Western "speculative" grammatical text and the Tibetan Buddhist (Sa-skya pandita) treatise on logic.

*   *   *

McDILL, Edward L.   1930-

PERSONAL: Born October 14, 1930, in Gadsden, Ala.; son of Ed N. (a cotton buyer) and Grace (Little) McDill; married Mary J. Sexton (divorced, June, 1976); children: Mark E., Ellen K. *Education:* Jacksonville State University, B.A., 1952; University of Alabama, M.A., 1956; Vanderbilt University, Ph.D., 1959. *Office:* Department of Social Relations, Johns Hopkins University, Baltimore, Md. 21218.

CAREER: Vanderbilt University, Nashville, Tenn., assistant professor, 1959-63, associate professor of sociology, 1964-65; Johns Hopkins University, Baltimore, Md., associate professor, 1965-69, professor of social relations and chairman of department, 1970—, co-director of Center for Social Organization of Schools, 1975—. *Military service:* U.S. Army, Artillery, 1952-54; became first lieutenant. *Member:* American Sociological Association, American Association for the Advancement of Science, American Educational Research Association, Southern Sociological Society. *Awards, honors:* Social Science Research Council fellowship, 1961-62; Ford Foundation fellowship, 1969-70.

WRITINGS: Strategies for Success in Compensatory Edu-

cation, Johns Hopkins Press, 1969; *Structure and Process in Secondary Schools,* Johns Hopkins Press, 1973; (editor with James McPartland) *Violence in the Schools,* Heath, 1976. Contributor of about thirty articles to social science journals.

WORK IN PROGRESS: Sociological research on the educational and occupational attainment of twenty thousand students who completed high school in 1972.

* * *

McDONOUGH, Sheila 1928-

PERSONAL: Born December 13, 1928, in Calgary, Alberta, Canada; daughter of B. T. (a purchasing officer) and M. J. (a journalist; maiden name, Simmons) McDonough; married Michel Despland (a professor), August 13, 1969; children: Emma, Alexis. *Education:* McGill University, B.A., 1952, M.A., 1955, Ph.D., 1963. *Politics:* "Feminist." *Religion:* "Feminist." *Home:* 464 Claremont, Montreal, Quebec, Canada. *Office:* Department of Religion, Concordia University, Montreal, Quebec, Canada.

CAREER: Teacher of comparative religion at universities in Lahore, Pakistan, 1957-60, and Birmingham, England, 1963-64; Concordia University, Montreal, Quebec, assistant professor, 1964-68, associate professor, 1968-75, professor of religion, 1975—. *Member:* Canadian Society for the Study of Religion, Society for Values in Higher Education.

WRITINGS: Islam and the West, Sh. Chulam Ali, 1960; *The Authority of the Past,* AAR Monograph Series, 1970; *Jinnah: Maker of Modern Pakistan,* Heath, 1970; (contributor) Aziz Ahmed, editor, *Readings in Muslim Self-Statement in the Indo-Pakistan Sub-Continent,* Columbia University Press, 1970; (contributor) D. Little, editor, *Essays on Islamic Civilization,* Brill, 1976. Contributor to *Encyclopaedia Britannica,* and to scholarly journals, including *Journal of World History* and *Studies in Religion.*

SIDELIGHTS: Sheila McDonough writes: "Some of my former students at Kinnaird College for Women in Lahore, Pakistan are now running a women's institute. Here at Concordia University I teach 'women and religion' as well as 'comparative religion' courses. We are beginning a new women's institute for inter-disciplinary women's studies here. For my views, I encourage you to see my article in *Studies in Religion* (Volume 6, number 5, 1977)."

* * *

McELRATH, William N. 1932-

PERSONAL: Surname is accented on first syllable; born March 1, 1932, in Murray, Ky.; son of Hugh M. (a dentist) and Gladys (Thomas) McElrath; married Elizabeth F. Hendricks (a missionary), August 28, 1958; children: Timothy Paul, James Conrad. *Education:* Murray State University, B.A., 1953; Southern Baptist Theological Seminary, B.D., 1956, Th.M., 1959. *Home:* 1016 Pineview Dr., Raleigh, N.C. 27606. *Office:* Southern Baptist Foreign Mission Board, 3806 Monument Ave., Richmond, Va. 23230.

CAREER: Music and youth director of Baptist church in Louisville, Ky., 1955-57; pastor of Baptist church in Carroll County, Ky., 1957-59; Baptist Sunday School Board, Nashville, Tenn., editor, 1959-64; Southern Baptist Foreign Mission Board, Richmond, Va., missionary, 1964—. Camp counselor in Louisville, 1954-55; school teacher in Louisville, 1958-59. *Member:* Indonesian Baptist Mission (member of executive committee, 1970-73, 1975-77), Indonesian Baptist Literature Society (editorial coordinator, 1966—). *Awards, honors:* Prizes from Broadman for hymns.

WRITINGS: Butch Discovers America (juvenile), with teacher's manual, Home Mission Board, Southern Baptist Convention, 1961; *Great Passages of the Bible* (with teacher's manual), Broadman, 1962; *Jamie Ireland, Freedom's Champion,* Broadman, 1964; *A Bible Dictionary for Young Readers,* Broadman, 1965; *Music in Bible Times* (with teacher's edition), Convention Press, 1966; *Me, Myself, and Others* (with teacher's edition), Convention Press, 1968; *Bible Guidebook,* Broadman, 1972; *Winding Road,* Convention Press, 1973, 2nd edition, Broadman, 1976; *To Be the First: The Adventures of Adoniram Judson, America's First Foreign Missionary,* Broadman, 1976; *Four Fishers for Men: An Anytime Play (or Easter Play) for Teens,* Broadman, 1978.

Librettos: *Samuel!,* Broadman, 1970; *God's Word in Their Hearts,* Broadman, 1975.

Author of hymns. Work anthologized in *Junior Hymnal,* Broadman, 1964.

WORK IN PROGRESS: A children's book on music in missions; an Indonesian-language programmed instruction text on the Book of Acts; an Indonesian-language book (title means "Practical Bible Handbook"), three volumes.

SIDELIGHTS: McElrath comments: "While continuing to write in my mother tongue, I have also been writing and editing in Indonesian for more than a decade now. Knowledge of one language and culture enriches understanding of the other—and that works in both directions.

"A major part of my ministry is developing Asian authors. Besides giving individual guidance to editorial colleagues and writers whose works we publish, I also lead workshops for Christian writers of Indonesia, Malaysia, Singapore, and the Philippines."

* * *

McFADDEN, Charles Joseph 1909-

PERSONAL: Born April 30, 1909, in Philadelphia, Pa.; son of Charles and Hannah (Callahan) McFadden. *Education:* Villanova University, A.B., 1932; Augustinian College, Washington, D.C., S.T.L., 1935; Catholic University of America, M.A., 1936, Ph.D., 1938. *Office:* Department of Philosophy, Villanova University, Villanova, Pa. 19085.

CAREER: Entered Order of St. Augustine, 1927, ordained Roman Catholic priest, 1935; Villanova University, Villanova, Pa., professor of philosophy, 1938—. Professor at Rosemont College, 1940-56; professor of medical ethics at Mercy Catholic Medical Center, 1940-66.

WRITINGS: The Metaphysical Foundations of Dialectical Materialism, Catholic University of America Press, 1938; *The Philosophy of Communism,* Benziger, 1939, revised edition, 1963; *Medical Ethics for Nurses,* F. A. Davis, 1946; *Medical Ethics,* F. A. Davis, 1949, 6th edition, 1967; *Reference Manual for Medical Ethics,* F. A. Davis, 1949; *The Dignity of Life,* Our Sunday Visitor, 1976; *Challenge to Morality,* Our Sunday Visitor, 1978.

SIDELIGHTS: McFadden's works have been translated into Spanish, Portuguese, and Chinese.

* * *

McFADDEN, Cyra 1937-

PERSONAL: Born December 2, 1937, in Great Falls, Mont.; daughter of Cyrill James and Patricia Ann (Montgomery) Taillon; married Leroy Hinze, 1956 (divorced, 1964); married John A. McFadden (an export trader), May

30, 1964; children: Caroline Taillon, Lee. *Education:* San Francisco State University, B.A. (magna cum laude), 1972, M.A. (honors), 1974. *Residence:* Mill Valley, Calif. *Agent:* Elaine Markson Literary Agency, Inc., 44 Greenwich Ave., New York, N.Y. 10011.

CAREER: San Francisco State University, San Francisco, Calif., part-time instructor in English, 1972-76; writer, 1976—. *Awards, honors:* Fellowship from Dutch Ministry of Education, 1973.

WRITINGS: (Contributor) Caroline Shrodes, editor, *A Rhetoric Reader,* Harper, 1974; *The Serial* (novel), Knopf, 1977. Contributor of articles and reviews to literary journals and popular magazines, including *Nation, McCall's, New York Times Magazine,* and *Smithsonian.*

WORK IN PROGRESS: A novel; film script for *The Serial,* for Paramount.

SIDELIGHTS: Cyra McFadden told *CA:* "My book is social satire. So is much of my other published writing. I think seeing things at a slant is an involuntary reflex for me, like a tic in the eyelid. *Avocational interests:* Reading.

*   *   *

McGINLEY, Phyllis 1905-1978

March 21, 1905—February 22, 1978; American poet, essayist, and writer of children's stories who, in 1961, won a Pulitzer Prize for *Times Three: Selected Verse From Three Decades.* Proud of her role as a housewife, McGinley often celebrated suburban living with her "light verse," but many of her poems bore a serious overtone. Her goal, she once said, was to try "to narrow the gulf between light and serious verse," and she hoped that her work would perhaps lead her readers "into greater poetry." In addition to the Pulitzer Prize, McGinley's numerous other honors include membership in the National Institute of Arts and Letters, honorary degrees from colleges and universities, and awards from several Catholic literary groups. Her writing career spanned four decades, in which time she wrote eighteen books and contributed to *New Yorker, America, Atlantic,* and many other publications. McGinley died in New York, N.Y. Obituaries and other sources: *Current Biography,* Wilson, 1961, April, 1978; *The Oxford Companion to American Literature,* 4th edition, Oxford University Press, 1965; Everett S. Allen, *Famous American Humorous Poets,* Dodd, 1968; *Books Are by People: Interviews With 104 Authors and Illustrators of Books for Young Children,* Citation Press, 1969; *Catholic World,* August, 1970; *Longman Companion to Twentieth Century Literature,* Longman, 1970; *The Author's and Writer's Who's Who,* 6th edition, Burke's Peerage, 1971; *Authors of Books for Young People,* 2nd edition, Scarecrow, 1971; *The Penguin Companion to American Literature,* McGraw, 1971; *Celebrity Register,* 3rd edition, Simon & Schuster, 1973; *Contemporary Poets,* 2nd edition, St. Martin's, 1975; *Time,* March 31, 1975, March 6, 1978; *Who's Who in Twentieth Century Literature,* Holt, 1976; *The Writer's Directory, 1976-78,* St. Martin's, 1976; *The International Who's Who,* Europa, 1977; *Who's Who of American Women,* 10th edition, Marquis, 1977; *New York Times,* February 23, 1978; *Washington Post,* February 24, 1978; *Newsweek,* March 6, 1978; *AB Bookman's Weekly,* May 8, 1978. (See index for *CA* sketch)

*   *   *

McGINNIES, Elliott M(orse) 1921-

PERSONAL: Born September 19, 1921, in Buffalo, N.Y.; son of Elliott M. (an accountant) and Mabel (Hussong) McGinnies; married Bessie Yeh (an economist), January 25, 1967; children: Michelle, Lisa, Amy. *Education:* State University of New York at Buffalo, B.A., 1943; Brown University, M.A., 1944; Harvard University, Ph.D., 1948. *Home:* 8321 Sligo Creek Parkway, Takoma Park, Md. 20012. *Office:* Department of Psychology, American University, Washington, D.C. 20016.

CAREER: University of Alabama, Tuscaloosa, assistant professor of psychology, 1947-52; University of Maryland, College Park, associate professor, 1952-56, professor of psychology, 1957-70; American University, Washington, D.C., professor of psychology, 1970—, chairman of department, 1973—. Fulbright professor in Taiwan, 1976-77. Consultant to Department of the Navy. *Military service:* U.S. Army, 1943. *Member:* American Psychological Association, Eastern Psychological Association, Sigma Xi.

WRITINGS: Social Behavior: A Functional Analysis, Houghton, 1970; (with C. B. Ferster) *The Reinforcement of Social Behavior,* Houghton, 1971; (with B. T. King) *Attitudes, Conflict, and Social Change,* Academic Press, 1972. Contributor of about fifty articles to professional journals.

WORK IN PROGRESS: Revising *Social Behavior: A Functional Analysis.*

AVOCATIONAL INTERESTS: Sailing, tennis, swimming, piano, travel (Europe, the Far East, Micronesia; speaks French, German, and Japanese).

*   *   *

McGREAL, Ian Philip 1919-

PERSONAL: Born August 27, 1919, in Brockville, Ontario, Canada; son of Michael (an educator) and Elsie (MacLaurin) McGreal; married Patricia Aeschliman (a photographer), February 23, 1946; children: Patrick, Colin, Derek. *Education:* Oberlin College, B.A., 1940, M.A. (English), 1941; Brown University, M.A. (philosophy), 1946, Ph.D., 1947. *Home:* 3724 Laguna Way, Sacramento, Calif. 95825. *Office:* Department of Philosophy, California State University, Sacramento, Calif. 95819.

CAREER: Brown University, Providence, R.I., instructor in philosophy, 1947-48; Southern Methodist University, Dallas, Tex., assistant professor of philosophy, 1948-54; University of Maryland, College Park, lecturer in the humanities, 1954-55; California State University, Sacramento, professor of philosophy, 1955—. *Military service:* U.S. Army, Field Artillery, 1942-45; became first lieutenant; received Air Medal with three oak leaf clusters. *Member:* American Philosophical Association. *Awards, honors:* Ford Foundation fellow, 1951; Carnegie Foundation fellow, 1952.

WRITINGS: The Art of Making Choices, Southern Methodist University Press, 1953; (editor and contributor) *Masterpieces of World Philosophy,* Harper, 1961; (editor and contributor) *Masterpieces of Christian Literature,* Harper, 1963; *Analyzing Philosophical Arguments,* Chandler Publishing, 1967; *Problems of Ethics,* Chandler Publishing, 1970. Contributor to philosophy journals.

WORK IN PROGRESS: Revising *Analyzing Philosophical Arguments* and *Problems of Ethics; Emotive Logic,* for the general public.

SIDELIGHTS: McGreal comments: "I have been interested in making ideas clear, especially ideas of considerable importance to human beings. My present concern is to make the work and meaning of two Maidu painters (Frank Day and Dalbert Castro) known to the general public."

McHALE, Tom 1942(?)-

EDUCATION: Temple University, B.S., 1963; also attended University of Pennsylvania and University of Iowa. Office: Monmouth College, West Long Branch, N.J. 07764.

CAREER: Worked as waiter and on a kibbutz; Monmouth College, West Long Branch, N.J., writer-in-residence, 1971—. Awards, honors: Guggenheim fellowship, 1974.

WRITINGS—All novels: Principato, Viking, 1970; Farragan's Retreat, Viking, 1971; Dooley's Delusion, Droke-Hallux, 1971; Alinsky's Diamond: A Love Story, Lippincott, 1974; School Spirit, Doubleday, 1976; The Lady From Boston, Doubleday, 1978.

SIDELIGHTS: The publication of Principato brought numerous favorable reviews and a certain hope among critics for even better things to come. A Time reviewer wrote, "He already has a formidable mastery of technique, as well as a deeper insight into the clash between time and eternity."

Principato was followed by Farragan's Retreat, of which a critic for Saturday Review wrote: "Even whackier than McHale's first novel, Principato, this furiously nutty book tells of the methodical extermination of a rich Irish Catholic family living, for as long as its members last, in Philadelphia. Tasteful it isn't; blackly hilarious it is."

Both novels were of the grotesque. Both, according to John Breslin, bore "the marks of their Philadelphia origins where the strong ethnic ties and bitter conflicts of Irish and Italians share a common root in the soil of cultural Catholicism."

Speaking about his childhood, McHale told the Philadelphia Inquirer: "I went to parochial schools and a Jesuit high school. Everybody in town seemed Catholic, pro-Joe McCarthy, and very patriotic." The sameness among the townspeople gave him a biased view. McHale said: "I never knew an un-Catholic until as a teenager I worked summers as a waiter in the Poconos at a Jewish resort called Tamamint. I learned who Lenny Bruce was."

In Alinsky's Diamond, McHale abandoned the Philadelphia setting, but maintained the heavy anti-Catholic tone and black comedy of his earlier books. America's Gerard Reedy wrote: "McHale is still as funny as any novelist writing today. Alinsky's Diamond ... moves far beyond fragmental comic effects to a comic vision of life." Reedy saw maturation in McHale's work in that Alinsky's Diamond expressed a deeper "sympathy for the human predicaments of illusion, death, unbelief and infidelity which are his subjects."

Published in 1976, School Spirit was deemed "powerful," "ironic," and "hilarious" by Commonweal. Richard R. Lingeman described it as "laced with a flaying satire and a sharp eye for the stubborn irrefragability of the sin of pride in all its guises." Of McHale, Lingeman wrote: "In the church, Mr. McHale might be classed as one of those impish, irreverent carved figures, often with their tongues sticking out, that medieval craftsmen hid about under seats and other visually inaccessible places in cathedrals. That is, he employs a good deal of black humor, and his characters are twisted with pride, greed, piety." McHale himself noted: "I write about men seeking balance, stability, amid the madness that often surrounds them."

BIOGRAPHICAL/CRITICAL SOURCES: Time, June 29, 1970, September 30, 1974; New Yorker, April 17, 1971; Saturday Review, January 22, 1972; New Republic, October 19, 1974; America, October 26, 1974; Harper's, November, 1974, May, 1975; Philadelphia Inquirer, December 15, 1974; Contemporary Literary Criticism, Gale, Volume 3, 1975, Volume 5, 1976; Commonweal, March 14, 1975, December 3, 1976; New York Times, May 21, 1976, January 30, 1978.*

McHUGH, Maxine Davis 1899(?)-1978
(Maxine Davis)

American journalist, former Washington reporter and magazine writer, and author. She worked in Europe, and covered such events as the World Economics Conference, the British-Indian Round Table Conferences, and the assembly of the League of Nations. McHugh also studied political, social, and economic conditions in various countries and interviewed such world leaders as Mahatma Gandhi. McHugh, who chose to write under her maiden name, is the author of eight books on medical and social problems, including two best sellers, The Lost Generation and Sexual Responsibility of Woman. She was a contributor of articles to Ladies Home Journal, Good Housekeeping, McCall's, Saturday Evening Post, Cosmopolitan, and other periodicals. McHugh died in Washington, D.C. Obituaries and other sources: Washington Post, May 23, 1978.

* * *

McINNES, Neil 1924-

PERSONAL: Born September 6, 1924, in Sydney, Australia; son of William Neil and Mary (Burke) McInnes; married June B. Turner; children: Rose, Genevieve, Berenice. Education: Attended University of Sydney, 1942-47. Home: 39 Ave. Mozart, Paris 75016, France.

CAREER: Statesman, Calcutta, India, reporter, 1948-51; Capital, Calcutta, editor, 1951-55; Barron's, New York, N.Y., associate editor, 1965—.

WRITINGS: (With Arnold Toynbee and others) The Impact of the Bolshevik Revolution, Oxford University Press, 1967; The Western Marxists, Library Press, 1972; The Communist Parties of Western Europe, Oxford University Press, 1975. Author of weekly column, "The World at Work," in Barron's, 1974—. Contributor to Washington Papers.

* * *

McINTOSH, Carey 1934-

PERSONAL: Born February 4, 1934, in New York, N.Y. Education: Harvard University, B.A., 1955, Ph.D., 1964; Cambridge University, M.A., 1959. Residence: Providence, R.I. Office: Brown University, Providence, R.I. 09212.

CAREER: Teacher of English at schools in Palm Springs, Calif., and West Hartford, Conn., 1955-57; Harvard University, Cambridge, Mass., senior tutor and assistant dean, 1959-64, assistant professor of English, beginning 1964; University of Rochester, Rochester, N.Y., assistant professor, until 1974, associate professor of English, beginning 1974; University of California, Santa Barbara, associate professor of English, 1974-76; Brown University, Providence, R.I., dean of freshmen, 1976—. Member: Modern Language Association of America, American Association for Eighteenth-Century Studies. Awards, honors: Danforth associate.

WRITINGS: The Choice of Life: Samuel Johnson and the World of Fiction, Yale University Press, 1973. Contributor to language journals.

WORK IN PROGRESS: English Evolving: Studies in Nominal Prose, Style, and Social Class, 1611-1759.

* * *

McKEE, Christopher (Fulton) 1935-

PERSONAL: Born June 14, 1935, in Brooklyn, N.Y.; son of William R. (a college professor) and Frances (Manning)

McKee; married Linda (Mitchell) Maloney, October 12, 1957 (divorced October 15, 1971); married Olivia Frederick (an educator), April 26, 1974; children: Sharon Frances, David Bruce. *Education:* University of St. Thomas, Houston, Tex., A.B., 1957; University of Michigan, A.M.L.S., 1960. *Home address:* P.O. Box 272, Grinnell, Iowa 50112. *Office:* Burling Library, Grinnell College, Grinnell, Iowa 50112.

CAREER: Washington & Lee University, Lexington, Ky., catalog librarian, 1958-62; Southern Illinois University, Edwardsville, social science librarian, 1962-66, book selection officer at Lovejoy Library, 1967-69, assistant director of Lovejoy Library, 1969-72, assistant professor, 1962-71, associate professor, 1971-72; Grinnell College, Grinnell, Iowa, college librarian, 1972—, associate professor, 1972-77, Samuel R. and Marie-Louise Rosenthal Professor, 1977—. Member of Iowa State Library advisory council, 1976-77; member of executive committee of Iowa OCLC Council, 1976-77; chairman of Iowa Private Academic Librarians, 1977-78. *Member:* Organization of American Historians, Society for Nautical Research (fellow), American Military Institute, U.S. Naval Institute, Iowa Library Association, Inter-University Seminar on Armed Forces and Society (fellow). *Awards, honors:* Newberry Library fellow, summers, 1974 and 1976; National Endowment for the Humanities fellow, 1978.

WRITINGS: Edward Preble: A Naval Biography, 1761-1807, Naval Institute Press, 1972. Contributor of articles and reviews to history and military journals.

WORK IN PROGRESS: A Gentlemanly, an Elegant, and Very Honorable Station: The Naval Establishment and Its Officers, 1794-1815.

SIDELIGHTS: McKee comments: "In my writing on American naval history I am particularly concerned with the interaction between the individual human person and the institutions and larger movements of his or her times. To me that individual's story is endlessly fascinating and a valid way of looking at history. Moreover, my concern is always with the less-noticed persons whose role in the development of an institution may have been as significant as that of more famous historical figures."

*   *   *

McKILLOP, Menzies   1929-

PERSONAL: Given name is pronounced *Min*-gis; born August 20, 1929, in Oban, Scotland; son of Dugald (a baker) and Christina (Menzies) McKillop; divorced. *Education:* University of Glasgow, M.A., 1951. *Politics:* "Apolitical." *Religion:* Buddhist. *Home:* 8 Fergus Ct., Glasgow G20 6AR, Scotland. *Agent:* Rosica Colin, 4 Hereford Sq., London SW7 4TU, England.

CAREER: Glasgow Education Authority, Glasgow, Scotland, teacher, 1956-75; writer, 1975—. *Military service:* British Army, 1951-53; served in Hong Kong.

WRITINGS: "The Future Pit" (three-act play), first produced in Minneapolis, Minn., at Guthrie Two Theatre, February, 1976. Writer of about thirty radio plays for British Broadcasting Corp., Canadian Broadcasting Corp., and South African Broadcasting Corp., including: "Bats," 1973; "Meeting," 1974; "Essence of Woman," 1976; "The Love Drink," 1977; "Tristan's Gift," 1977; "A Scottish Artist's Reply to Just Criticism," 1977; and "Violets Rooted by a Sepulchre," 1978.

Work represented in anthologies, including *Scottish Poetry,*

Volumes II-V, Edinburgh University Press, 1967-70, *Scottish Love Poems,* Canongate Publishing, 1975, and *Guthrie New Theatre,* Volume I, Grove, 1976.

WORK IN PROGRESS: "The Love Drink," a story.

SIDELIGHTS: McKillop comments: "I am interested in writing science fiction and love stories. I think good writing should be as unselfconscious as possible. I write in English not in Scots, although Scots is my fireside language. A Scottish writing in Scots is often in danger of becoming over sugary and sentimental because the connotations of Scots are highly emotional."

*   *   *

McKINZIE, Richard D.   1936-

PERSONAL: Born July 31, 1936, in Lebanon, Ind.; son of Kenneth R. (a farmer) and Mary (a bookkeeper; maiden name, Newby) McKinzie; married Kathleen O'Connor, June 6, 1964 (divorced, November, 1971); married Norma Stratemeier, December 12, 1973. *Education:* Indiana State Teachers College (now State University), B.A., 1959; Indiana University, M.A., 1963, Ph.D., 1969. *Home:* 5911 Wornall Rd., Kansas City, Mo. 64113. *Office:* Department of History, University of Missouri, 5100 Rockhill Rd., Kansas City, Mo. 64110.

CAREER: North Texas State University, Denton, assistant professor of history, 1966-69; University of Missouri, Kansas City, associate professor of history, 1969—, chairman of department, 1977—. Fulbright professor at Trinity College, Dublin, 1975-76. Oral historian for foreign affairs at Harry S Truman Library (Independence, Mo.), 1972-74. *Military service:* U.S. Army, 1956-58; became sergeant. *Member:* American Historical Association, Organization of American Historians, Society for Historians of American Foreign Relations.

WRITINGS: The New Deal for Artists, Princeton University Press, 1973; (with John G. Clark, David M. Katzman, and Theodore A. Wilson) *Three Generations in Twentieth-Century America: Family, Community, and Nation,* Dorsey, 1977.

WORK IN PROGRESS: America's Accidental Empire (tentative title), a history of the U.S. foreign aid program as an instrument of foreign policy, 1941-53, with Theodore A. Wilson.

SIDELIGHTS: McKinzie writes: "Over the years, it seems to me, historians have made the past overly intellectual and irrelevant to most people by focusing sharply upon an elite corps of decision makers and their most articulate critics (who left convenient records). I have become more concerned with analyzing and explaining how it was to be alive for people at different points on the social spectrum."

*   *   *

McLAUGHLIN, Joseph F., Jr.   1919-1978

1919(?)—February 25, 1978; American columnist and author best known for the "Tell It to Joe" column of the *Boston Herald American.* McLaughlin's column, which started in 1961, covered the problems of individuals in business and government. He died in Boston, Mass. Obituaries and other sources: *New York Times,* February 27, 1978.

*   *   *

McRAE, Robert (Forbes)   1914-

PERSONAL: Born June 27, 1914, in Winnipeg, Manitoba,

Canada; son of Duncan (a clergyman) and Susan (Rodgers) McRae; married Nora Frances Beacock (a teacher), September 1, 1950; children: Kiloran, Alison, Ellen. *Education:* University of Toronto, B.A., 1936, M.A., 1938; Johns Hopkins University, Ph.D., 1946. *Home:* 29 Dunbar Rd., Toronto, Ontario, Canada M4W 2X5.

CAREER: University of Toronto, Toronto, Ontario, instructor, 1945-46, lecturer, 1946-48, assistant professor, 1948-56, associate professor, 1956-60, professor of philosophy, 1960—. *Military service:* Royal Canadian Navy, 1940-45; became lieutenant commander. *Member:* Canadian Philosophical Association, American Society for Eighteenth Century Studies. *Awards, honors:* Nuffield Foundation fellowship, 1951-52; Canada Council fellowship, 1972-73.

WRITINGS: The Problems of the Unity of the Sciences: Bacon to Kant, University of Toronto Press, 1961; (contributor) R. J. Butler, editor, *Cartesian Studies,* Basil Blackwell, 1972; *Leibniz: Perception, Apperception, and Thought,* University of Toronto Press, 1976. Contributor to philosophy journals. Member of editorial committee for "Collected Works of J. S. Mill," 1963—.

WORK IN PROGRESS: Research on philosophy of science in the seventeenth and eighteenth centuries.

* * *

McWHIRTER, George 1939-

PERSONAL: Born September 26, 1939, in Belfast, Northern Ireland; son of James (a fitter) and Margaret (a fruit merchant; maiden name, McConnell) McWhirter; married Angela Coid (a teacher), December 26, 1963; children: Grania, Liam. *Education:* Queen's University of Belfast, B.A., 1961, diploma, 1962; University of British Columbia, M.A., 1970. *Home:* 4637 West 13th Ave., Vancouver, British Columbia, Canada V6R 2V6. *Office:* Department of Creative Writing, University of British Columbia, Vancouver, British Columbia, Canada.

CAREER: Teacher in public schools in Kilkeel, Northern Ireland, 1962-64, Bangor, Northern Ireland, 1964-65, Barcelona, Spain, 1965-66, and Port Alberni, British Columbia, 1966-68; University of British Columbia, Vancouver, assistant professor, 1970-76, associate professor of creative writing, 1976—. *Member:* League of Canadian Poets, Canadian Association for Irish Studies. *Awards, honors:* Commonwealth Poetry Prize from The Commonwealth Institute and National Book Society (Great Britain), 1972, for *Catalan Poems.*

WRITINGS: Catalan Poems, Oberon Press, 1971; *Body Works* (stories), Oberon Press, 1974; *Bloodlight for Malachi McNair* (poems), Kanchenjunga Press, 1974; *Queen of the Sea* (poems), Oberon Press, 1976; *Twenty-Five* (poems), Fiddlehead Press, 1978.

Prism International, associate editor, 1970-77, advisory editor, 1978—; editor of *Words from Inside,* 1974-75.

WORK IN PROGRESS: A creative writing textbook.

SIDELIGHTS: McWhirter told *CA:* "My purpose in poetry is simply to make sense through the senses and in bringing my self to my senses, do so for others, if I have the skill. People, places, and things predominate—as with Neruda—more and more the beauty of what is common and what is used. The purpose of the creative writing textbook is to teach the use of these skills—the power of the particular, the ability to ratiocinate and to superimpose one effect or insight on another."

BIOGRAPHICAL/CRITICAL SOURCES: Canadian Journal of Irish Studies, July, 1977.

* * *

MEDDIS, Ray 1944-

PERSONAL: Born July 23, 1944, in Sunderland, England; son of William Wilson and Mary (Howarth) Meddis; married Valerie Clark, July 7, 1965; children: Christopher, William. *Education:* University of London, B.A. (honors), 1965, Ph.D., 1969. *Home:* 14 Chester Close, Loughborough LE11 3BD, England. *Office:* Department of Human Sciences, University of Technology, Loughborough LE11 3TU, England.

CAREER: University of London, Bedford College, London, England, lecturer in psychology, 1965-74; University of Technology, Loughborough, England, lecturer in psychology, 1974—. *Member:* British Psychological Society (associate member).

WRITINGS: Elementary Analysis of Variance, McGraw, 1973; *Statistical Handbook for Non-Statisticians,* McGraw, 1975; *The Sleep Instinct,* Routledge & Kegan Paul, 1977.

WORK IN PROGRESS: Research on cognition and statistical analysis of ranked data.

SIDELIGHTS: "*The Sleep Instinct,*" Meddis explained, "outlines a theory that may serve no important function in modern man, but helps animals to survive by causing them to rest in a safe place for prolonged periods in each day."

* * *

MEEHAN, Daniel Joseph 1930-1978
(Danny Meehan)

1930(?)—March 29, 1978; American dancer, singer, actor, composer, and author. In 1964, Meehan was nominated for a Tony Award for his performance with Barbra Streisand in the Broadway musical "Funny Girl." Meehan appeared in summer theatres, night clubs, and on television series, including "Quincy, and "Eight Is Enough." He has written many songs that were made popular by well known performers, such as Nat (King) Cole, Lena Horne, Helen Reddy, Sammy Davis, Jr., and popular group, Blood, Sweat and Tears. Meehan also wrote the lyrics to the soundtrack for the motion picture "Joe." He died in New York, N.Y. Obituaries and other sources: *The ASCAP Biographical Dictionary of Composers, Authors, and Publishers,* American Society of Composers, Authors and Publishers, 1966; *New York Times,* March 30, 1978.

* * *

MEEHAN, Danny
See MEEHAN, Daniel Joseph

* * *

MEEK, Jacklyn O'Hanlon 1933-
(Jacklyn Meek Matthews, Jacklyn O'Hanlon)

PERSONAL: Born December 5, 1933, in California; children: Margaret, Stephen, Clifford, Anne, Catherine, John. *Education:* Attended private high school in San Francisco, Calif. *Politics:* Democrat. *Religion:* Christian Scientist. *Residence:* Santa Barbara, Calif.

CAREER: Writer. Operator of a boarding house in Santa Barbara, Calif.

WRITINGS—For children: (Under name Jacklyn Meek Matthews) *Edward and the Night Horses,* Golden Gate,

1970; (under name Jacklyn O'Hanlon) *Fair Game*, Dial, 1977; (under name O'Hanlon) *The Other Michael*, Dial, 1977; (under name O'Hanlon) *The Door*, Dial, 1978.

WORK IN PROGRESS: Always Be Green, a fantasy, under name Jacklyn O'Hanlon.

SIDELIGHTS: Jacklyn Meek remarks: "It's simple—I write for children. They have always been my focus and concern. They are very discriminating, so I must be careful and as *truthful* as I can be—for young people will not be deceived or fooled. I *love* writing. It is a privilege to work at it."

* * *

MELLOWS, Joan

PERSONAL: Born in England; daughter of William (an accountant) and Constance Richardson (a teacher; maiden name, Taylor) Melloy; married Ian Arthur Mellows (an oil company executive), February, 1952; children: Caroline Susan Hodson Mellows Bradley, William Anthony Neligan. *Education:* St. Hugh's College, Oxford, M.A., 1951. *Politics:* Conservative. *Religion:* Church of England. *Home:* White Tower, Westacres, Esher, Surrey, England.

CAREER: Writer. Worked as advertising copywriter, 1947-52, lecturer in English, 1953-55, information officer, 1956-58, assistant organizer of Nigerian World Exhibition, 1959-60, and contact officer for National Health Service, 1970-72.

*WRITINGS—*Novels: *Friends at Knoll House*, Fawcett, 1972; *A Family Affair*, Fawcett, 1974; *Harriet*, Fawcett, 1976. Contributor to periodicals.

WORK IN PROGRESS: A modern novel; an early nineteenth-century novel.

SIDELIGHTS: Joan Mellows lived for nine years in Nigeria, two years in the United States, eight years in France, and two years in Zaire. She writes that her main interests are sixteenth- to early nineteenth-century history, literature, and theater.

* * *

MELOSI, Martin Victor 1947-

PERSONAL: Born April 27, 1947, in San Jose, Calif.; son of Elmo Victor (an accountant) and Nancy (Rossi) Melosi; married Carolyn Ronchetto (an accountant), June 19, 1971; children: Gina Michelle. *Education:* University of Montana, B.A., 1969, M.S., 1971; University of Texas, Ph.D., 1975. *Politics:* Democrat. *Home:* 1107 Westover, College Station, Tex. 77840. *Office:* Department of History, Texas A & M University, College Station, Tex. 77843.

CAREER: University of Texas at Austin, instructor in history, 1973-75; Texas A & M University, College Station, instructor, 1975-76, assistant professor of history, 1976—. Visiting instructor at Oklahoma Baptist University, 1975; guest lecturer at University of Rhode Island, 1977. Participant and chairman in professional conferences.

MEMBER: American Historical Association, Organization of American Historians, Public Works Historical Society, American Society for Environmental History, Society for Historians of American Foreign Relations, Society of the History of Technology, Phi Kappa Phi, Phi Alpha Theta. *Awards, honors:* Rockefeller Foundation fellow, 1976-77.

WRITINGS: The Shadow of Pearl Harbor: Political Controversy Over the Surprise Attack, 1941-1946, Texas A & M University Press, 1977; *Practical Environmentalist: Sanitary Engineer George E. Waring, Jr.* (monograph), Public Works Historical Society, 1977; (editor and contributor) *Urban Pollution in Historical Perspective: Environmental Degradation and Reform in American Cities, 1850-1930*, University of Texas Press, 1979. Contributor of more than a dozen articles and reviews to history and environmental studies journals.

WORK IN PROGRESS: Environmental Challenge in the City: The Refuse Problem and Municipal Reform, 1850-1920, publication by Texas A & M University Press; a book studying the role of children in urban sanitation reform, 1896-1920.

SIDELIGHTS: Martin Melosi told *CA:* "My primary research interests at the present time are concentrated in the area of urban environmental studies. Until very recently, historians have neglected the important relationship between humans and their physical surroundings. What has become known as Environmental History still has not expanded sufficiently to include careful examination of the impact of the urban environment on city dwellers. How did industrialism influence the quality of life in the cities? What were the social and political effects of environmental pollution? When did urbanites develop an environmental consciousness? These questions and many more provide rich avenues of exploration for the historian. Currently, I am examining the extent and impact of municipal and industrial waste in American cities. What appears to be a rather mundane subject for historical inquiry is really very significant. For a study of urban waste not only can tell us about the degree to which refuse pollution posed a health problem in our past, but also how contemporaries reacted to a growing environmental crisis in the cities. What did nineteenth-century Americans believe constituted a reasonable quality of life? Were they willing to condone an unhealthy and aesthetically debilitating environment for the sake of economic gain? How did urbanites feel about the squandering of natural resources that aggravated the growing problem of waste?

"I don't believe it is enough for historians of the environment to simply conduct scholarly research which will reach only a limited audience. Armed with evidence about the state of the environment, the historian can provide valuable data and insightful analyses to policy makers with an eye to improving current environmental problems. Without historical perspective on the environment and the reactions of humans to it, current efforts to minimize pollution and establish livable physical surroundings may prove difficult. It is the responsibility of the environmental scholar to lend his expertise to the fight to preserve environmental quality."

AVOCATIONAL INTERESTS: Tennis, photography, gardening, piano, science fiction.

* * *

MENZIES, Robert Gordon 1894-1978

December 20, 1894—1978; Australian politician, former prime minister, and author of several books on law and government. Menzies began his political career in 1928, and served as prime minister of Australia from 1949-66. He established the Liberal party and was firmly against the "downward threat" of Communism. Menzies also served in the Legislative Assembly and Council of Victoria, and represented the district of Kooyong in the Australian Federal Parliament. Menzies contributed articles to magazines, including *Scribner's, New Yorker, Reader's Digest*, and *American Mercury*, and wrote a biographical novel in 1936. He died in Melbourne, Australia. Obituaries and other sources: *Current Biography*, Wilson, 1950; *The Authors and*

Writers Who's Who, 6th edition, Burke's Peerage, 1971; *The Writers Directory, 1976-78,* St. Martin's, 1976; *The International Who's Who,* Europa, 1977; *Time,* May 29, 1978.

* * *

MEREDITH, James Howard 1933-

PERSONAL: Born June 25, 1933, in Kosciusko, Miss.; son of Moses Cap and Roxie (Patterson) Meredith; married Mary June Wiggins, December 16, 1956; children: John Howard, Joseph Howard, James Henry. *Education:* Attended Jackson State College, 1960-62; University of Mississippi, B.A., 1963; attended University of Ibadan, Nigeria, 1964-65; Columbia University, J.D., 1968. *Home:* 427 Eastview St., Jackson, Miss. 39209.

CAREER: Civil rights worker; has also worked as stockbroker, in real estate, and as an investor, 1967—. Lecturer on racial problems. Republican candidate for U.S. Congress, 1972. *Military service:* U.S. Air Force, 1951-60. *Member:* Phi Alpha Delta.

WRITINGS: Three Years in Mississippi (autobiography), Indiana University Press, 1966.

SIDELIGHTS: In autumn, 1962, James Meredith became the first black person to enroll in the University of Mississippi. Called by the *New York Times* a "man of extraordinary courage, self-confidence and stubborness," Meredith weathered campus riots and the resistence of state officials and succeeded in graduating in 1963. At one point thousands of Federal troops were called on campus to assist him. Meredith explained his role at the university: "Because of my 'Divine Responsibility' to advance human civilization, I could not die. If one places society above self, and I do, life never ends. Everything I do, I do because I must; and everything that I must do, I do."

Meredith's autobiographical *Three Years in Mississippi* was published in spring, 1966. Meredith explained that he published his book with Indiana University Press rather than a commercial publisher because the academic publisher was "willing to let me write the book I wanted to write.... There are some things involved in this society that can only be told by a Negro. Some things are best said by the personal construction you give them." *Newsweek* reviewed the book, saying: "Seldom is a piece of violent history so dispassionately dissected by one of its participants as it has been by James Meredith in this three-years-later study of his breakthrough at the University of Mississippi. Part report and part legal brief, part manifesto, part tract, it is a valuable and fascinating account."

Shortly after the publication of his book, Meredith was shot while marching for civil rights in Mississippi. Before the shooting, radio reporter Sherwood Ross asked Meredith if he felt the non-violent approach would work. "The time has come," Meredith answered, "when Negroes have got to work for their rights. Nonviolence is not in the American tradition. The American tradition is to get out and work for what you want, to fight for what you want. I'm tired of all this begging and all this pleading. We've got to assert our rights."

Since 1966, *Newsweek* reported, Meredith "has shifted attention from the educational and political battles of his past and has become a model of the new black entrepreneur." Meredith said, "There will come a time when I'll be needed to help out. I want to prepare myself to be ready."

BIOGRAPHICAL/CRITICAL SOURCES: Newsweek, April 18, 1966, March 27, 1967, December 23, 1968; *Book Week,* April 24, 1966; *New Yorker,* May 21, 1966; *Saturday Review,* May 28, 1966; *Life,* June 17, 1966; *Nation,* June 27, 1966; *National Review,* June 28, 1966; *New York Times Book Review,* July 3, 1966.*

* * *

MERIWETHER, Louise

EDUCATION: New York University, B.A.; University of California at Los Angeles, M.S., 1965. *Home:* 1691 East 174th St., Apt. 7D, Bronx, N.Y. 10472.

CAREER: Worked as a legal secretary in New York and California, 1950-61; *Los Angeles Sentinal,* Los Angeles, Calif., reporter, 1961-64; Universal Studios, Universal City, Calif., story analyst, 1965-67; free-lance writer, 1967—. *Member:* Authors Guild, Watts Writers Workshop, Harlem Writers Guild.

*WRITINGS—*All published by Prentice-Hall, except as noted: *Daddy Was a Number Runner* (novel), 1970; *The Freedom Ship of Robert Small* (juvenile), 1971; *The Heart Man: The Story of Daniel Hale Williams* (juvenile), 1972; *Don't Ride the Bus on Monday: The Rosa Parks Story* (juvenile), 1973; (contributor) Mary Helen Washington, editor, *Black-Eyed Susans,* Anchor Press, 1975. Contributor to periodicals.

SIDELIGHTS: Paule Marshall reviewed *Daddy Was a Number Runner* in the *New York Times Book Review:* "In her perceptive and moving first novel about the social death of one Harlem family, Meriwether reaches deeply into the lives of her characters to say something about the way black people relate to each other—the customs, traditions and manners that bind up together and sustain our underground life. It is her expression of this tribal or communal quality of black life, its group solidarity and sharing, that lends such strength and humanity to the novel."

In *Black-Eyed Susans,* Meriwether wrote: "After the publication of my first novel, *Daddy Was a Number Runner,* I turned my attention to black history for the kindergarten set, recognizing that the deliberate omission of Blacks from American history has been damaging to the children of both races. It reinforces in one a feeling of inferiority and in the other a myth of superiority."

Meriwether's next three books were biographies of Robert Small, a slave who piloted a Confederate ship into Yankee waters and earned a promotion in the Union Army, Daniel Hale Williams, a black heart surgeon who performed the first successful open-heart surgery, and Rosa Parks.

BIOGRAPHICAL/CRITICAL SOURCES: Saturday Review of Literature, May 23, 1970, December 11, 1971; *New York Times Book Review,* June 28, 1970; *New Yorker,* July 11, 1970; *Kirkus Reviews,* June 15, 1972, December 15, 1973; Mary Helen Washington, editor, *Black-Eyed Susans,* Anchor Press, 1975.

* * *

MERRIMAN, Ann Lloyd 1934-

PERSONAL: Born October 5, 1934, in Lynchburg, Va.; daughter of Corrie Flemming and Mary (Whitten) Lloyd; married Kenneth Lee Merriman (a custom builder), September 5, 1958; children: Diane Paige. *Politics:* "Conservative." *Home:* 2707 Skipwith Rd., Richmond, Va. 23229. *Office: Richmond News Leader,* 333 East Grace St., Richmond, Va. 23213.

CAREER/WRITINGS: Richmond News Leader, Richmond, Va., editorial assistant, 1956-63, associate editor, 1963—, book editor, 1966—. Fields of specialty include economics, labor, Congress, Social Security, taxes, crime, welfare, education, abortion, capital punishment, the Supreme Court, and national health insurance. *Masthead*, editor, 1976-77, contributor of articles. *Member:* American Society of Newspaper Editors, National Conference of Editorial Writers (secretary, 1978), Virginia Press Association (co-chairman of news committee, 1974), Virginia Press Women (president, 1972-74), Sigma Delta Chi (Richmond chapter). *Awards, honors:* Virginia Press Association second place award, 1969, and first place award, 1970, for editorial series, third-place award, 1977, for editorials; Press Woman of the Year award from Virginia Press Women, 1975.

SIDELIGHTS: Merriman told *CA:* "It is my belief that it is a conflict of interest for a journalist to belong to any organization other than a professional one."

Merriman has participated in numerous journalism panels and seminars and was among twelve American journalists involved in a cultural exchange with the Soviet Union in 1975. She was also one of a dozen journalists who toured Taiwan in 1977.

*   *   *

MESTHENE, Emmanuel George   1920-

PERSONAL: Born August 19, 1920, in New York, N.Y.; son of Emmanual and Georgette (Anzolinou) Mesthene; married Ruth Allgeier, January 29, 1944; children: Laura, Donald, James. *Education:* Columbia University, B.S., 1948, M.A., 1949, Ph.D., 1964. *Home:* 12 Lafayette St., New Brunswick, N.J. 08901.

CAREER: American Viscose Corp., New York City, sales engineer, 1939-42; Columbia University, New York City, lecturer in philosophy, 1948-51; Adelphi College, Garden City, N.Y., lecturer in philosophy, 1948-51; Bantam Books, New York City, editor, 1951-53; Rand Corp., Santa Monica, Calif., research staff member, 1953-64; Harvard University, Cambridge, Mass., director of program on technology and society and member of business school faculty, 1964-73; Rutgers University, New Brunswick, N.J., dean of Livingston College, 1974-77, professor of philosophy, 1974—. Consultant to Office of Special Assistant to the President on Science and Technology, 1960, and U.S. Senate Subcommittee on National Policy Machinery, 1961. Staff director of advisory group on science policy for Organization for Economic Cooperation and Development (OECD), 1962-64. Part-time professional musician, 1941—. Founder and manager of American Bach Society, 1950-53, Collegium Musicum of Washington, 1954-56, Collegium Musicum of Los Angeles, 1958-60, and Rand Chamber Orchestra, 1958-61. Has given numerous recitals. *Military service:* U.S. Army, 1942-46. *Member:* American Philosophical Association, American Political Science Association, American Association for the Advancement of Science.

WRITINGS: How Language Makes Us Know, M. Nijoff, 1964; (editor) *Ministers Talk About Science,* Organization for Economic Cooperation and Development, 1965; (contributor) John P. Anton, editor, *Naturalism and Historical Understanding,* State University of New York Press, 1967; (editor) *Technology and Social Change,* Bobbs-Merrill, 1967; *Technological Change: Its Impact on Man and Society,* Harvard University Press, 1970; (contributor) Robin Marris, editor, *The Corporate Society,* Macmillan, 1974.

Also author of technical reports. Contributor to *Philosophy and Phenomenological Research, Science, Saturday Review, Theology Today,* and other periodicals.

METZ, William   1918-

PERSONAL: Born May 31, 1918, in Los Angeles, Calif.; son of William C. (a machinist) and Eva (Hudson) Metz; married Polly Tuttle, May 15, 1951; children: Susan Meredith, Jeffrey William. *Education:* University of Redlands, B.A., 1942; University of California, Los Angeles, M.S., 1960. *Politics:* Independent. *Religion:* Protestant. *Home:* 4321 Bridle Way, Reno, Nev. 89509. *Office:* Department of Journalism, University of Nevada, Reno, Nev. 89507.

CAREER: Honolulu Star-Bulletin, Honolulu, Hawaii, reporter and copy editor, 1947-56; *Pismo Times,* Pismo Beach, Calif., editor and publisher, 1956-59; Bradley University, Peoria, Ill., assistant professor of journalism, 1960-69; University of Nevada, Reno, associate professor of journalism, 1969—. Editor and publisher of *Grove City Press,* 1956-59. Has interviewed Presidents Eisenhower and Truman; covered Communist conspiracy trials of the 1950's. *Military service:* U.S. Navy, 1943-46; served in Pacific theater; became lieutenant junior grade. *Member:* Association for Education in Journalism, National Press Photographers Association, American Civil Liberties Union, Common Cause, Kappa Tau Alpha, Sigma Delta Chi.

WRITINGS: Newswriting: From Lead to "30", Prentice-Hall, 1977.

SIDELIGHTS: Metz told *CA:* "My turn from sixteen years of newspaper work to college teaching resulted partly from the deterioration of editing standards that began with the introduction of TTS tape. In my opinion, news writing has improved over the years, while the quality of editing has declined steadily during the same time. It seemed to me that I could make a greater contribution to the news profession by teaching than by meeting the lessening demands of newspaper management. There is no greater thrill than to do a good job of reporting and writing, and then to see your work in print, and the greatest satisfaction and deepest pleasures have come to me while working on newspapers. But there is satisfaction, too, in helping to prepare young people to enter journalism."

AVOCATIONAL INTERESTS: Playing tennis, travel, "tending my acre of sagebrush."

*   *   *

MEYER, William R(obert)   1949-

PERSONAL: Born August 19, 1949, in New York, N.Y.; son of Robert A. and Frances (Duncan) Meyer; married Antoinette Cavuoto (a public relations manager). *Education:* New School for Social Research, B.A., 1974; New York University, M.A., 1976. *Residence:* New York, N.Y. *Agent:* Dominick Abel Literary Agency, 498 West End Ave., New York, N.Y. 10024.

CAREER: Ivy Film, New York, N.Y., researcher and writer, 1975; free-lance writer, 1975—. *Member:* American Film Institute, Society for Cinema Studies.

WRITINGS: Warner Brothers Directors: The Hard Boiled, the Comic, and the Weepers, Arlington House, 1978; *The Film Buff's Catalog,* Arlington House, 1978.

WORK IN PROGRESS: The Making of the Great Westerns; a novel; research for a book about television.

SIDELIGHTS: Meyer writes: "As a film historian/critic, my job is to illuminate the best and worst in the cinema, and those who make movies. To do this is an intelligent, yet simple, engaging fashion is my duty as a writer. There is much that still needs to be done in the field of cinema studies.

There are films to be uncovered, preserved, and screened, thousands of live and works that wait for research and analysis. In a way, anyone performing any of these duties is like a detective, searching for, and hopefully finding, a shred of truth. We are hard-boiled dicks on the prowl for the good and the great, the classic and the corny, in musty repertory theatres, wide-screen palaces, or late-night television.

"My impossible dream is to help chart the production of every movie, determine the contributions of directors, writers, actors, technicians, producers, and studios. After this, we can take a long coffee break and wait for next year's films."

AVOCATIONAL INTERESTS: Music, baseball.

* * *

MICHAEL, Manfred
See WINTERFELD, Henry

* * *

MICHAELSON, L(ouis) W. 1920-

PERSONAL: Born March 27, 1920, in Denver, Colo.; son of Max and Helen (Weiner) Michaelson; married wife, Anne; children: Marcy, David. *Education:* University of Denver, B.A., 1954, Ph.D., 1969; University of Iowa, M.A., 1956. *Home:* 1400 West Lake St., Fort Collins, Colo. 80521. *Agent:* Ruth Cantor, 211 42nd St., New York, N.Y. 10010. *Office:* Department of English, Colorado State University, Fort Collins, Colo. 80521.

CAREER: Colorado State University, Fort Collins, assistant professor of creative writing, 1958—, tennis coach, 1969-72. *Member:* Phi Beta Kappa.

*WRITINGS—*All poems: *New Shoes on an Old Man,* Pierian Press, 1968; *Songs of My Divided Self,* Southwest Press, 1969; *Everyone Revisited,* Prairie Gate Press, 1974. Contributor of stories and poems to popular magazines, including *Esquire, Saturday Evening Post, Saturday Review,* to journals, and to newspapers. Contributor of reviews to *New York Times.*

WORK IN PROGRESS: A novella, *Summer Work.*

AVOCATIONAL INTERESTS: Travel in Mexico.

* * *

MICHEL, Sandra (Seaton) 1935-
(Sandy Michel)

PERSONAL: Surname is pronounced like "Michael"; born January 30, 1935, in Hancock, Mich.; daughter of Donald Wylie (a banker) and Mary Luciel (Finlayson) Seaton; married Philip Raymond Michel (a chemical engineer), July 28, 1956; children: John Donald, David Duncan, Timothy Douglas, Kristin. *Education:* Attended Stanford University, 1953-56. *Home:* 608 Whitby Dr., Wilmington, Del. 19203. *Office:* Lenape Publishing Ltd., 608 Whitby Dr., Wilmington, Del. 19203.

CAREER: Concordia News, Wilmington, Del., editor, 1971—. President of Lenape Publishing Ltd. Director of Technology Associates, Inc. Member of local school district desegregation task force; works with deaf children, the elderly, and prisoners.

MEMBER: International Society of Poets, National League of American Pen Women (literary chairman of Diamond State branch, 1977-78), National Federation of American Press Women, First State Writers (president, 1972-75). *Awards, honors:* First place in First State Writers national poetry contest, 1976, for "The Underground Railroad."

*WRITINGS—*Under name Sandy Michel: *My Name Is Jaybird* (fiction; juvenile), Houghton, 1972; *No More Someday* (poetry), Lenape Publishing, 1973; (editor) *In a Walled Garden,* Lenape Publishing, 1974; (editor) *Touch of Spring,* Lenape Publishing, 1975; (editor) *Anita Mia,* Lenape Publishing, 1976; *The D & N Story* (on Detroit & Northern Savings & Loan Association), Detroit & Northern Savings Loan Association, in press.

Plays: (Co-author) "Red, Bleached and Blue" (two-act), first produced in Hohokus, N.J., at Hohokus Players Theatre, April 8, 1969; (co-author) "Now-How" (two-act), first produced in Hohokus, at Hohokus Players Theatre, March 15, 1971. Contributor to *Delaware Today* and *New Directions for Women in Delaware.*

WORK IN PROGRESS: Topta, juvenile fiction.

SIDELIGHTS: Sandy Michel comments: "I like to write—to read—to fantasize. I have wanted to be a writer since first learning to read. Vital subjects are a lack of censorship by right, left, government, men, or women. Guidelines become restrictions very easily."

BIOGRAPHICAL/CRITICAL SOURCES: Town Talk, June 25, 1975.

* * *

MICHEL, Sandy
See MICHEL, Sandra (Seaton)

* * *

MICHELSON, Edward J(ulias) 1915-

PERSONAL: Born April 3, 1915, in Northampton, Mass.; son of Isadore Henry and Fanny (Avrich) Michelson; married Dorothea Adair Pohlman (a college professor), February 3, 1938; children: Kathleen (Mrs. Frederick Davis Meloan), Paul, Emily. *Education:* Williams College, B.A., 1937. *Home:* 2153 Florida Ave. N.W., Washington, D.C. 20008. *Office:* 1032 National Press Bldg., Washington, D.C. 20045.

CAREER: St. Louis Post-Dispatch, St. Louis, Mo., reporter, 1937-38; Westinghouse Electric Co., New York City, writer in public relations division, 1939-40; Columbia Broadcasting System (CBS), New York City, day editor in international shortwave news division, 1941-44; War Department, Washington, D.C., special assistant in the Office of the Secretary of War and member of strategic services unit, 1946; associate of Robert S. Allen (syndicated columnist), 1946-50; Washington correspondent for North American Newspaper Alliance and New England dailies, 1946—; *Forbes,* New York City, Washington editor, 1956-63; *Printer's Ink,* New York City, Washington editor, 1958-63; *Ocean Science News,* Washington, D.C., associate editor, 1958-63; *Science and Technology,* New York City, Washington editor, 1969—. Research director for U.S. House water resources subcommittee, 1951. Notable assignments include coverage of European Common Market, 1958-59, European Common Agricultural Policy, 1960, and aerospace market survey, 1964, United States trade with Mexico, 1966, Bogota, 1968, and Japan, 1971, and East-West trade, 1967. *Wartime service:* Served with Office of Support Services, 1944-46. *Member:* National Press Club, White House Correspondents Association.

WRITINGS: (Editor) Wright Patman, *Our American Government,* Ziff-Davis, 1948. Contributor to *Saturday Evening Post, Esquire, American Legion Magazine, Montreal Star,* and *World.* Book editor for Reynal & Hitchcock; consulting editor in book division of U.S. News and World Report Inc.

WORK IN PROGRESS: Reports on preparations for the 1980 census, U.S. bilateral and multilateral foreign trade/economic policies, and foreign markets for U.S. technology.

SIDELIGHTS: When asked about tensions in trade relations between the United States and other countries, Michelson told *CA:* "Much of the tension in trade relations with Japan and the European Community, especially the Federal Republic of Germany, stems from our having a representative government, as against parliamentary or cabinet governments in our trading partners' countries. Our leadership has to respond to midterm 1978 election moods of voters, and to the 1980 Presidential campaign, with protectionism as a major problem. Secondly, we are no longer as great a superpower as in the post World War II period. We can't stymie such developments as West Germany's nine billion dollar nuclear plants deal with Brazil, or Japan's turning to China as a market for steel and steel products, and to Brazil, for say, jeans and other commodities. Other major industrial nations balk at unemployment rates that we tolerate and at pressures which would fire up inflation in their economies."

*   *   *

MILLDYKE, (John) William   1937-

PERSONAL: Born April 10, 1937, in Kearney, Neb.; son of John W. and Irene (Dow) Milldyke; married Doris Evans, August 28, 1960; children: Sonja Lynne, Michelle Marie. *Education:* Nebraska State College, B.A., 1958; further study at University of Nebraska, 1959-60. *Home:* 66 High St., Amersham, Buckinghamshire HP7 0DS, England. *Office:* ABC News, 8 Carburton St., London W1P 7DT, England.

CAREER/WRITINGS: KHGI-TV, Kearney, Neb., news director, 1960-62; WOI-Radio and Television, Ames, Iowa, news director, 1962-68; American Broadcasting Co. (ABC) News, New York, N.Y., producer in Washington, D.C., 1968-71, senior European producer and London bureau manager, 1971—. Notable assignments include coverage of the Indo-Pakistan War, war in the Middle East, 1973, the end of the Viet Nam War, Nixon's 1975 Middle East trip, the Kissinger shuttles. Assistant professor of journalism, Iowa State University, Ames, 1963-67; lecturer in journalism, University of Nebraska, 1974. *Member:* International Press Institute, Radio-Television News Directors Association (assistant chairman of committee on ethics and standards, 1963), British Academy of Film and Television Arts, Association of American Correspondents in London.

SIDELIGHTS: Milldyke told *CA* he is interested in creative broadcast journalism, "making broadcast journalism more useful to the American public and increasing its contribution to their understanding of world events." He added, "I hope to use the continuing development of new tools of our trade to the end of speeding up this information process and continuing an effort to provide this information in a meaningful and understandable way."

*   *   *

MILLER, Byron Strongman   1912(?)-1978

1912(?)—April 16, 1978; American realty investor and author. Miller was interested in the ocean liners that traveled between the United States and Europe, and made more than forty Atlantic crossings. He wrote the book *Sail, Stream and Splendour.* Miller died in Manhattan, N.Y. Obituaries and other sources: *New York Times,* April 20, 1978.

MILLER, Charles   1918-

PERSONAL: Born October 27, 1918, in New York, N.Y.; son of Philip Lee (a lawyer) and Rose (Shimberg) Miller. *Education:* Harvard University, A.B., 1941. *Residence:* New York, N.Y. *Agent:* Lucianne Goldberg, 255 West 84th St., New York, N.Y. 10024.

CAREER: Employed in public affairs positions, 1948-68, including work with Pfizer International, 1963-68; free-lance writer, 1968—. *Military service:* U.S. Army, 1942-46; became sergeant.

WRITINGS—Nonfiction: *The Lunatic Express,* Macmillan, 1971; *Battle for Bundu,* Macmillan, 1974; *Khyber,* Macmillan, 1977. Contributor of articles and reviews to popular magazines, including *Reader's Digest, Saturday Review, Saturday Evening Post, New Republic,* and *Travel,* and newspapers.

WORK IN PROGRESS: Research for books on the American Revolution, and the U.S. Marine Corps.

SIDELIGHTS: Miller writes: "Between 1948 and 1968, I was a sort of journeyman editor and publicist, doing book reviews and magazine pieces on the side. Also during this period, I somehow got interested in Africa and went there a number of times. In 1968 I severed my ties with the corporate world (actually it was the other way around), and became a full-time writer. Knowing there was a lot of money to be made in this line of work, I began researching *The Lunatic Express,* an informal history of the opening up of East Africa and the building of the Uganda Railway. This was followed by *Battle for Bundu,* an account of the East African campaign of World War I. Both books received mouth-watering reviews and sold dozens of copies in the United States alone. Flushed with success and dwindling funds, I turned to an even more remote quarter of the globe, to try my hand at a narrative history of Afghanistan, the Khyber Pass, and the northwest frontier of British India, and at the risk of seeming immodest, I recommend it warmly. Right now, I'm employed as a mail room clerk.

"My work comes under the heading of popular history, a term I don't like much because it suggests comic books. I'd rather think of myself as a storyteller who writes in a historical framework. While I feel an almost compulsive obligation to keep faith with the facts, my main objective is to tell a story—as dramatically and suspensefully and entertainingly as I can."

AVOCATIONAL INTERESTS: Singing (Miller is a member of Village Singers); sleeping.

*   *   *

MILLER, Jane (Judith)   1925-

PERSONAL: Born October 6, 1925, in Sydney, Australia; daughter of Peter and Thelma (Thomson) Lawrence; divorced. *Education:* Educated in Australia. *Residence:* London, England. *Agent:* Jonathan Clowes Ltd., 19 Jeffreys Pl., London N.W.1, England.

CAREER: Free-lance photographer and writer for children. *Awards, honors: Birth of a Foal* was named "Outstanding Science Book for Children, 1977" by National Science Teachers Association Children's Book Council Joint Committee.

WRITINGS—For children: *Foxglove Farm,* Dent, 1975; *Birth of a Foal,* Lippincott, 1977; *Lambing Time,* Dent, 1978.

WORK IN PROGRESS: Other children's books.

SIDELIGHTS: Jane Miller told *CA:* "I lived for five years in India (Calcutta and Ahmedabad respectively), and for a year and a half in the northern part of Thailand (Nan province) where my husband was doing an anthropological field study in the early 1950's.

"My other work in photography is with a variety of books, magazines, and papers on a free-lance basis," she added. "I also supply natural history pictures for greeting cards, etc. My favourite subjects are animals, where possible in their natural surroundings. I spend hours waiting for the right moment to capture the desired photography, or often the unexpected one that just happens. You have to be relaxed with your subject and use a form of telepathy. In photographing for my books on animals for children, I first have to get the confidence of the animals just by being with them and talking to them, so that after a time they get used to me and I am able to concentrate on the photography."

* * *

MINER, Matthew
    See WALLMANN, Jeffrey M(iner)

* * *

MINES, Stephanie   1944-

PERSONAL: Born May 21, 1944, in Bronx, N.Y.; daughter of Sidney B. and Muriel (a secretary; maiden name, Newman) Mines; children: Sierra Carol Mines-Buryn. *Education:* Attended Los Angeles State College, 1963-65, and University of Pittsburgh, 1965-67; San Francisco State College, B.A., 1971. *Home:* 143 Moffitt St., San Francisco, Calif. 94131.

CAREER: Writer, 1968—. Telephone operator, 1963-65; secretary for San Francisco Art Commission, 1970-72. Teacher of creative writing workshops. *Awards, honors:* Joseph Henry Jackson Award from San Francisco Foundation, 1977, for *Solitary Woman.*

WRITINGS: Two Births (poems), Random House, 1972; (editor) *Noe Valley,* Cassandra, 1973; (editor) *Quasar,* Cassandra, 1974; *Belly Poems,* Cassandra, 1977.

WORK IN PROGRESS: The Woman Who Loves Jazz, a novel; *The Names,* stories; *Solitary Woman,* poems and prose poems; *Nadia,* a long prose poem in novella form.

SIDELIGHTS: Mines told *CA:* "I work to continue the tradition of Anais Nin—by which I mean the development of the literature of the inner life, the literature of beauty, the literature that unites personal (internal) with external reality.

"For four years I have been working with children to evoke from them their own language. In all my work I want to release true and natural creativity into fluid productivity. This is what I aim for in my own writing as well as in my teaching. I am constantly seeking, developing, and experimenting with exercises in spontaneous writing—writing which helps bring the unconscious into consciousness.

"The work I do with music and dance," Mines continued, "is necessarily secondary to my writing. However, I have been developing the integration of music and poetry and I have presented more than sixteen readings using both music and words, and often including movement as well. I use music to support language and to indicate the similarities between the two forms of expression, I want to emphasize the possibility of language being used to communicate feeling as well as thought.

"All this work—writing, teaching, music, and dance—I consider to be healing work. It is work which releases stored imaginings, wishes, and fantasies. It also heals the damage done by the separation of mind from imagination, of creativity from intuition, of dream from daily life. I consider my work to be going in the direction of integration, both personal and cultural. I believe in a gentle and intimate approach to education, a sharing, responding, communicating experience rather than forced feeding."

* * *

MINTZER, Yvette   1947-

PERSONAL: Born August 3, 1947, in New York, N.Y.; daughter of Abe and Esther (a secretary; maiden name, Mentlik) Mintzer. *Education:* City College of the City University of New York, B.A., 1969. *Home:* 128 Post Ave., New York, N.Y. 10034.

CAREER: Inwood Press, New York, N.Y., business manager, 1974—. Poetry teacher for schools, libraries, and community centers, 1973—.

WRITINGS: Dreamline Express (poetry), Inwood Press, 1975; "Komachi" (one-act play), first produced in New York, N.Y., at Open Space, November, 1977.

WORK IN PROGRESS: The Planting Moon, poems.

* * *

MIRON, Dan   1934-

PERSONAL: Born November 13, 1934, in Tel Aviv, Israel; son of Arieh (an agriculturist) and Malka (Singer) Miron; married Yael Schocken, August 1, 1961 (died August 20, 1975); children: David Eliezer, Menachem Uriel. *Education:* Hebrew University of Jerusalem, B.A., 1957, M.A., 1959; Columbia University, Ph.D., 1967. *Religion:* Jewish. *Home:* 10 Efrata St., Jerusalem, Israel. *Office:* Department of Hebrew Literature, Hebrew University of Jerusalem, Jerusalem, Israel.

CAREER: Jerusalem Academy of Music, Jerusalem, Israel, music teacher, 1953-59; currently professor of Hebrew literature at Hebrew University of Jerusalem. Assistant professor at University of Tel Aviv, 1956-58; professor at Max Weinreich Center (New York City). *Military service:* Israel Army, 1956-58. *Member:* Musad Bialik Curatorium.

WRITINGS: A Traveler Disguised, Schocken, 1973.

Also author of *Chayim Hazaz,* 1959, and *Arba Panim Basifrut Haivrit Bat Yameynu,* 1962.

* * *

MISSILDINE, (Whitney) Hugh   1915-

PERSONAL: Born July 23, 1915, in Des Moines, Iowa; son of Carl Seymore (an attorney) and Myrtle (Mathis) Missildine; married Alice Hughes, December 24, 1940; children: Nancy (Mrs. Michael Donaldson), Daniel Whitney. *Education:* Iowa State University, A.B., 1936, M.D., 1939. *Politics:* Republican. *Religion:* Protestant. *Home:* 2483 Coventry Rd., Columbus, Ohio 43221. *Office:* 695 Bryden Rd., Columbus, Ohio 43205.

CAREER: Psychiatrist in private practice, 1949—; Ohio State University, College of Medicine, Columbus, professor of psychiatry, 1949—. Director of Children's Mental Health Center, Columbus, 1949-58. *Military service:* U.S. Army, Medical Corps, 1941-45; became major; received Bronze Star. *Member:* American Medical Association, American Psychiatric Association.

WRITINGS: Your Inner Child of the Past, Simon & Schuster, 1963; *Your Inner Conflicts: How to Solve Them,* Simon & Schuster, 1975. Editor of *Feelings and Their Medical Significance,* 1959-77.

SIDELIGHTS: Missildine writes: "I am particularly interested in home attitudes which affect children and the influence of past home attitudes on the self-attitudes and feelings of adults."

* * *

MITCHELL, Adam
See PYLE, Hilary

* * *

MITCHELL, Frank
See MITCHELL, George Francis

* * *

MITCHELL, George Francis   1912-
(Frank Mitchell)

PERSONAL: Born October 15, 1912; son of David William (a merchant) and Frances (Kirby) Mitchell; married Lucy Margaret Gwynn (an educator), January 20, 1940; children: Lucy Elizabeth (Mrs. Christophe Compos), Rosamond Frances. *Education:* Trinity College, Dublin, B.A., 1934, M.A., 1937. *Home address:* Townley Hall, Drogheda, County Louth, Ireland. *Office:* Department of Botany, Trinity College, University of Dublin, Dublin 2, Ireland.

CAREER: University of Dublin, Trinity College, Dublin, Ireland, lecturer in geology, 1934-50, reader in Irish archaeology, 1950-65, professor of quaternary studies, 1965—, fellow, 1944, junior dean, 1945-51, registrar, 1952-67, senior lecturer, 1968-70, senior fellow, 1974—. Visiting faculty member at Cambridge University, University of Colorado, and Cornell University. *Member:* International Union for Quaternary Research (president, 1969-73), Royal Irish Academy (president, 1976-79), Royal Society (fellow), Prehistoric Society (honorary corresponding member). *Awards, honors:* Rockefeller Foundation grant, 1952; D.Sc. from Queen's University of Belfast, 1976, and National University of Ireland, 1977; Fil. Dr. from University of Uppsala, 1977.

WRITINGS—Under name Frank Mitchell: (Contributor) T. W. Moody and F. X. Martin, editors, *The Course of Irish History,* Mercier Press, 1967; (contributor) Donald Walker and R. G. West, editors, *Studies in the Vegetational History of the British Isles,* Cambridge University Press, 1970; *The Irish Landscape,* Collins, 1976; (editor and contributor) *Treasures of Early Irish Art,* Metropolitan Museum of Art, 1977; (contributor) D. V. Ager and M. Brooks, editors, *Europe from Crust to Core,* Wiley, 1977; (contributor) F. W. Shotton, editor, *Recent Studies in the British Quaternary,* Clarendon Press, 1977.

WORK IN PROGRESS: Research on history, archaeology, and geology.

SIDELIGHTS: Mitchell writes: "When I edited the college undergraduate magazine many years ago, my prose style was reported on as 'homely if ugly'; it is a source of constant amazement to me that my writing is now generally clear, and sometimes interesting. My geological wanderings have brought me to almost all the corners of the earth. My book *The Irish Landscape* endeavours to portray the countryside from earliest geological time to the present day, with a few conjectures for the future. Though it is *not* a coffee-table book, it has been well reviewed, and I am satisfied with it."

BIOGRAPHICAL/CRITICAL SOURCES: Irish Times, June 13, 1959; *New Yorker,* October 31, 1977; *New York Review of Books,* May 4, 1978.

* * *

MITCHELL, Joseph (Quincy)   1908-

PERSONAL: Born July 27, 1908, in Fairmont, N.C.; son of Averette Nance (a farmer) and Elizabeth Amanda (Parker) Mitchell; married Therese Dagny Engelsted Jacobsen (a photographer), February 27, 1931; children: Nora Therese (Mrs. John L. R. Sanborn), Elizabeth Kristin (Mrs. Henry Curtis). *Education:* Attended University of North Carolina, 1925-29. *Home:* 44 West 10th St., New York, N.Y. 10011. *Agent:* Harold Ober Associates, 40 East 49th St., New York, N.Y. 10017. *Office:* New Yorker Magazine, Inc., 25 West 43rd St., New York, N.Y. 10036.

CAREER: New York World, New York City, reporter, 1929-30; *New York Herald Tribune,* New York City, reporter, 1930-31; *New York World-Telegram,* New York City, reporter, 1931-38; *New Yorker,* New York City, staff writer, 1938—. *Member:* National Institute of Arts and Letters (vice-president, 1971; secretary, 1972-74), Society of Architectural Historians, Society for Industrial Archeology, James Joyce Society, Friends of Cast-Iron Architecture, Gypsy Lore Society (England), Century Association. *Awards, honors:* Award from National Institute of Arts and Letters, 1965.

WRITINGS: My Ears Are Bent (collection of newspaper articles), Sheridan, 1938; *McSorley's Wonderful Saloon,* Duell, 1943; *Old Mr. Flood,* Duell, 1948; *The Bottom of the Harbor,* Little, Brown, 1960; (with Edmund Wilson) *Apologies to the Iroquois [With] A Study of the Mohawks* (the former by Wilson, the latter by Mitchell), Farrar, Straus, 1960; *Joe Gould's Secret,* Viking, 1965.

SIDELIGHTS: There is unity between the subject of Joseph Mitchell's writing and the object of his own enthusiasms. His membership in such strikingly diverse organizations as Friends of Cast-Iron Architecture and the James Joyce Society should not surprise his readers. Mitchell is concerned with lower Manhattan, with its inhabitants and landmarks, in much the way Joyce was preoccupied with Dublin. Though Mitchell grew up in rural North Carolina and has written a series of stories about people he knew in his youth, most of his journalism and fiction celebrate the lives of New York characters from the waterfront, the Bowery and Greenwich Village.

In 1952 Mitchell explained his work in *North Carolina Authors: A Selective Handbook.* He said, "I specialized for years in writing about outcasts and cranks and about unusual groups—the fishmongers and fishwives in Fulton Market, the people on the Bowery, a band of gypsies, a band of Mohawk Indians who have no fear of heights and work as riveters on skyscrapers and bridges." Malcolm Cowley, the literary critic, said of this, "In his somewhat narrow field, which is that of depicting curious characters, Joseph Mitchell is the best reporter in the country."

Stanley Edgar Hyman, another prominent critic, took exception to the term "reporter," suggesting that Mitchell "is a reporter only in the sense that Defoe is a reporter." He maintained that Mitchell belongs to a literary and not merely journalistic tradition that includes William Faulkner and Saul Bellow, as well as James Joyce and Daniel Defoe. He has traced in Mitchell's work literary archetypes such as Ishmael, the Wandering Jew, and the Flying Dutchman. The implication is that beyond the surface of accurate detail and engaging humor, Mitchell confronts the same serious issues as does the best of our literature and should be judged accordingly.

BIOGRAPHICAL/CRITICAL SOURCES: New York Times Book Review, July 25, 1943; *New Republic,* July 26, 1943; *North Carolina Authors: A Selective Handbook,* University of North Carolina Extension Library, 1952; *New Leader,* December 6, 1965; Brendan Gill, *Here at the New Yorker,* Random House, 1975.

* * *

MITCHELL, W(illiam) O(rmond)   1914-

PERSONAL: Born March 13, 1914, in Weyburn, Saskatchewan, Canada; son of Ormond S. and Margaret Letitia (MacMurray) Mitchell; married Merna Lynne Hirtle, August 15, 1942; children: Ormond Skinner, Hugh Hirtle, Willa Lynne. *Education:* Attended University of Manitoba, 1932-34; University of Alberta, B.A., 1942. *Politics:* Liberal. *Religion:* Presbyterian. *Home:* 3031 Roxboro Glen Rd., Calgary, Alberta, Canada.

CAREER: Worked variously as a salesman, teacher, seaman, and high school principal; University of Calgary, Alberta, writer-in-residence, 1968-71; full-time writer, 1971—. *Member:* Delta Kappa Epsilon. *Awards, honors:* President's medal from University of Western Ontario, 1953; *Maclean's Magazine* Novel Award, 1953; Stephen Leacock Memorial Medal for best humorous book by a Canadian author, 1962, for *Jake and the Kid.*

WRITINGS—All novels, except as indicated: *Who Has Seen the Wind,* Little, Brown, 1947; *The Alien,* serialized in *Maclean's Magazine,* 1953-54, revised edition published as *The Vanishing Point,* Macmillan, 1973; *Jake and the Kid,* Macmillan, 1961; *The Kite,* Macmillan, 1962; *The Black Bonspiel of Wullie MacCrimmon* (short story), Frontiers Unlimited, 1965; *The Devil's Instrument* (play; produced in Ottawa at the National Arts Center, 1972), Simon & Pierre, 1973. Also author of radio scripts for Canadian Broadcasting Co.

Work represented in *Best American Short Stories,* 1946, and *Three Worlds of Drama,* edited by J. P. Livesley, Macmillan, 1966. Contributor to various periodicals, including *Liberty, Maclean's Magazine, Atlantic Monthly, Canadian Forum, Queen's Quarterly,* and *Ladies' Home Journal.*

SIDELIGHTS: "Beautifully written, with unusual insight and sensitivity, [*Who Has Seen the Wind*] is a first novel of high merit," wrote Dorothy Sparks in the *Chicago Sun Book Week.* The preface of the book contains explanations of Mitchell's expectations of the novel which Samuel Roddan summed up in *Canadian Forum* as "an attempt to present through the mind and feeling of a young boy on the Saskatchewan prairie . . . 'the ultimate meaning of the cycle of life.'" By virtue of the many favorable critiques it received, *Who Has Seen the Wind* met the standards its author set. Richard Sullivan wrote: "Here is a first novel which measures up fully to its author's own specifications; it turns out to be exactly what Mr. Mitchell declares in advance it is to be. Furthermore, it is a piece of brilliantly sustained prose, a very beautiful, keen, perceptive rendering of human beings engaged in the ordinary yet profoundly—almost mysteriously—meaningful drama of every day."

Fourteen years elapsed between *Who Has Seen the Wind* and the publication of Mitchell's next novel. During that time Mitchell published a story in serial form called *The Alien.* Some twenty-one years later, Mitchell remodeled the serial into a novel that he published under the name of *The Vanishing Point.* The story, however, remained basically the same—a white man on an Indian reservation who functions as school teacher and Indian agent, and his experiences with the Indians, government officials, his students, and a particular student with whom he later becomes romantically involved. The title comes from an early experience of the main character, Carlyle Sinclair. W. H. New recounted the incident in *Canadian Forum:* "Carlyle learns in elementary school of the 'vanishing point'—the arbitrary horizon point where 'parallel' lines must meet if a drawing is to have a three-dimensional perspective. He is punished then because, dimly trying to make his work more than an exercise, he disobeys instructions; he adds trees and telephone poles to his picture to make it more realistic." Throughout the novel, according to New, Sinclair is "constantly discovering the extent to which illusion confuses the real world in which he must live." "The overall effect," wrote New, "is one of moral disarray, against which Mitchell's quiet humanitarianism seems both idealistic and remarkably kind."

Mitchell's *Who Has Seen the Wind* has recently been published in French, and his plays have been produced on CBC since 1947.

AVOCATIONAL INTERESTS: Dramatics, angling, riding.

BIOGRAPHICAL/CRITICAL SOURCES: Kirkus Reviews, February 1, 1947; *New York Times,* February 23, 1947; *New York Herald Tribune Weekly Book Review,* March 2, 1947; *San Francisco Chronicle,* March 13, 1947; *Booklist,* March 15, 1947; *Canadian Forum,* April, 1947, May-June, 1974; *Chicago Sun Book Week,* August 17, 1947.*

* * *

MITCHISON, Naomi Margaret (Haldane)   1897-

PERSONAL: Born November 1, 1897, in Edinburgh, Scotland; daughter of John Scott (a physiologist and philosopher) and Kathleen (Trotter) Haldane; married Gilbert Richard Mitchison (a lawyer and member of Parliament), February, 1916 (died, 1970); children: Denis Antony, Murdoch, Lois Godfrey, Avrion, Valentine Arnold-Forster. *Education:* Attended St. Anne's College, Oxford. *Politics:* British Labour Party. *Residence:* Carradale, Campbeltown, Argyll, Scotland.

CAREER: Writer and playwright, 1923—. Labour candidate for Parliament for the Scottish Universities Constituency, 1935; member of the Argyll County Council, 1945-1966; member of the Highland Panel, Scotland, 1947-65; member of the Highland and Island Advisory Council, Scotland, 1966—. *Wartime service:* Served as a volunteer nurse during World War I. *Member:* P.E.N. *Awards, honors:* Received the Palmes de l'Academie Francaise, 1921.

WRITINGS—Novels: *The Conquered,* Harcourt, 1923, reprinted, Dufour, 1959; *Cloud Cuckoo Land,* J. Cape, 1925, Harcourt, 1926, reprinted, Hodder & Stoughton, 1967; *The Corn King and the Spring Queen,* Harcourt, 1931, reprinted, Scholarly Press, 1972; *The Powers of Light* (illustrated by Eric Kennington), Pharos, 1932; (with Wyndham Lewis) *Beyond This Limit,* J. Cape, 1935; *We Have Been Warned,* Constable, 1935, Vanguard, 1936; *The Blood of the Martyrs,* Constable, 1939, Whittlesey House, 1948; *The Bull Calves* (illustrated by Louise Richard Annand), J. Cape, 1947; *The Big House,* Faber, 1950; *Lobsters on the Agenda,* Gollancz, 1952; *Travel Light,* Faber, 1952; *To the Chapel Perilous,* Allen & Unwin, 1955; *Behold Your King,* Muller,

1957; *Memoirs of a Space Woman*, Gollancz, 1962, Berkeley Publishing, 1973; *When We Become Men*, Collins, 1965; *Cleopatra's People*, Heinemann, 1972; *Solution Three*, Warner, 1975.

Short stories: *When the Bough Breaks, and Other Stories*, Harcourt, 1924, reprinted, Arno, 1977; *Black Sparta: Greek Stories*, Harcourt, 1928; *Barbarian Stories*, Harcourt, 1929, reprinted, Arno, 1977; *The Delicate Fire: Short Stories and Poems*, Harcourt, 1933, reprinted, Arno, 1977; *The Fourth Pig*, Constable, 1936; *Five Men and a Swan*, Allen & Unwin, 1958.

Plays: (With Lewis E. Gielgud) *The Price of Freedom* (three-act), J. Cape, 1931; *An End and a Beginning, and Other Plays*, J. Cape, 1937; (with Gielgud) *As It Was in the Beginning* (three-act), J. Cape, 1939; "The Corn King," first produced in London, England, 1950; (with Denis Macintosh) *Spindrift* (three-act), Samuel French, 1951.

For children: *Nix-Nought-Nothing: Four Plays for Children*, J. Cape, 1928; *The Hostages, and Other Stories for Boys and Girls* (illustrated by Logi Southby), J. Cape, 1930, Harcourt, 1931, reprinted, Parrish, 1964; *Graeme and the Dragon* (illustrated by Pauline Baynes), Faber, 1954; *The Land the Ravens Found* (illustrated by Brian Allderidge), Collins, 1955; *Little Boxes* (illustrated by Louis Annand), Faber, 1956; *The Far Harbour* (illustrated by Martin Thomas), Collins, 1957; *Judy and Lakshmi* (illustrated by Avinash Chandra), Collins, 1959.

The Rib of the Green Umbrella (illustrated by Edward Ardizzone), Collins, 1960; *The Young Alexander the Great* (illustrated by Betty Middleton-Sandford), Roy, 1961; *Karensgaard: The Story of a Danish Farm*, Collins, 1961; *The Young Alfred the Great* (illustrated by Shirley Farrow), Parrish, 1962, Roy, 1963; *The Fairy Who Couldn't Tell a Lie* (illustrated by Jane Paton), Collins, 1963; *Alexander the Great* (illustrated by Rosemary Grimble), Longmans, Green, 1964; *Henny and Crispies*, New Zealand School Publications, 1964; *Ketse and the Chief* (illustrated by Christine Bloomer), Thomas Nelson, 1965; *Friends and Enemies* (illustrated by Caroline Sassoon), Collins, 1966, Day, 1968; *Highland Holiday*, New Zealand School Publications, 1967; *The Big Surprise*, Kaye & Ward, 1967; *African Heroes* (illustrated by William Stobbs), Bodley Head, 1968, Farrar, Straus, 1969; *Don't Look Back*, Kaye & Ward, 1969; *The Family at Ditlabeng* (illustrated by Joanna Stubbs), Collins, 1969, Farrar, Straus, 1970; *Sun and Moon* (illustrated by Barry Wilkinson), Bodley Head, 1970, Thomas Nelson, 1973; *The Danish Teapot* (illustrated by Patricia Frost), Kaye & Ward, 1973; *Snake!* (illustrated by Polly Loxton), Collins, 1976.

Other: *The Laburnum Branch* (poems), J. Cape, 1926; *Anna Comnena*, Howe, 1928; *Comments on Birth Control*, Faber, 1930; *Boys and Girls and Gods*, Watts, 1931; *The Home and a Changing Civilisation*, John Lane, 1934; *Naomi Mitchison's Vienna Diary*, H. Smith & R. Haas, 1934; (with Richard H. S. Crossman) *Socrates*, Hogarth, 1937, Stackpole, 1938; *The Moral Basis of Politics*, Constable, 1938, reprinted, Kennikat, 1971; *The Kingdom of Heaven*, Heinemann, 1939; (with Macintosh) *Men and Herring*, Serif Books, 1949; *The Swan's Road* (illustrated by Leonard Huskinson), Naldrett Press, 1954; *Other People's Worlds*, Secker & Warburg, 1958; *Presenting Other People's Children*, P. Hamlyn, 1961; (with George W. L. Paterson) *A Fishing Village on the Clyde*, Oxford University Press, 1961; *Return to the Fairy Hill*, J. Day, 1966; *The Africans*, Blond, 1970; *Sunrise Tomorrow: A Story of Botswana*, Farrar, Straus, 1973; *Small Talk: Memories of an Edwardian Childhood*, Bodley Head,

1973; *A Life for Africa: The Story of Bram Fischer*, Merlin Press, 1973; *Oil for the Highlands?*, Fabian Society, 1974; *All Change Here: Girlhood and Marriage*, Bodley Head, 1975.

Editor: *An Outline for Boys and Girls and Their Parents*, Gollancz, 1932; *Re-Educating Scotland*, Scoop Books, 1944; Frederic Bartlett and others, *What the Human Race Is Up To*, Gollancz, 1962.

Work represented in anthologies, including *The Year 2000*, Collier Macmillan, 1970; *Scottish Short Stories*, Oxford University Press, 1970; and *Nova 1*, Dell, 1971.

SIDELIGHTS: An author whose works span five decades, Naomi Mitchison originally wanted to be a scientist. An incomplete education made her turn to writing.

Naomi Mitchison's early writings were primarily historical novels and short stories, all of which included the basic theme of conflict of loyalties. *The Conquered* tells the story of the Gallic War between 58 B.C. and 46 B.C. A *Saturday Review* critic wrote, "She has, as it were by miracle, got back into the air and mood of the time she writes about: she creates and re-creates. The splendour and the mystery come easy to her. She is at home. Mrs. Mitchison's touch never falters. She never condescends to the pedantry of archaic speech on the one hand or of distracting colloquialism on the other. And she rises without effort to eloquence and, beyond eloquence, to poetry."The *New York Times* observed: "The author has made an interesting story against a colorful background, a background that in its essentials seems as accurately as it is graphically pictured. True, she frequently forgets in the conversation of her people, especially in their expletives, that they are not modern Britons. The result is an often jarring note that seems the more regrettable because of the care and the excellence with which otherwise she has recreated the time and the scene."

More recently, Naomi Mitchison has been writing for children. Of *Young Alexander the Great*, *Horn Book* commented, "In an English series of brief fictionalized biographies, this has much to offer the student of ancient history. Presenting a conversation-filled picture of fourth-century B.C. life at the court of Philip of Macedon, it discusses activities and thinking of the time, from the point of view of the young heir Alexander who with his famous companions studied with Aristotle, the 'best brain of his generation.' Short chapters separately concern literature, sports, hunting, Alexander's acquiring a Bucephalos, scientific knowledge, and Greek ideas of self-discipline, the middle way, and the brotherhood of man. In 'What Happened Afterward' the author adds, 'What is so exciting is that his [Alexander's] ideas went far beyond those of his tutor.' Authentic and interesting." The *New York Times* added, "Alexander is wholly believable—eager, curious, hotheaded, spoiling for battle but surprisingly merciful. Poetic in feeling, lucid in style, this study is not for those who read as they run but for serious readers."

Naomi Mitchison became interested in politics and in social problems when her husband ran for Parliament. She helped establish the first birth control clinics in London, and became involved in political action with the counter-revolution in Austria in 1934 and with sharecroppers in Arkansas in 1935. She traveled to Russia in 1932 and 1952.

BIOGRAPHICAL/CRITICAL SOURCES: Saturday Review, May 26, 1923; *New York Times*, October 28, 1923 *New York Times Book Review*, May 28, 1961; *Horn Book*, June, 1961.

MITGANG, Lee D. 1949-

PERSONAL: Born November 12, 1949, in New York, N.Y.; son of Herbert (a writer and journalist) and Shirley (an attorney; maiden name, Kravchick) Mitgang. *Education:* University of Michigan, B.A., 1971; London School of Economics and Political Science, M.A., 1972; further study at Northwestern University, 1976. *Religion:* Jewish. *Residence:* Brooklyn, N.Y. *Office:* Associated Press, 50 Rockefeller Plaza, New York, N.Y. 10020.

CAREER/WRITINGS: United Press International, New York City, business writer, 1972-74; Associated Press, New York City, urban affairs writer, 1974—. Member of Media Advisory Board of Scientists' Institute for Public Information. *Awards, honors:* Frank E. Gannett fellow of journalism at Northwestern University, 1976; John Hancock Award, Gerald Loeb Award from University of California, Los Angeles, and University of Missouri Business Journalism Award, all 1977, all for a four-part series on pensions.

SIDELIGHTS: Mitgang writes: "I hope I have been, and continue to be, a part of the ground-breaking in journalism that will lead to a public understanding of the problems affecting the nation's cities and the poor who live in them. That has been my sole writing aim for the past three years, and I expect the subject to keep me busy for years to come."

* * *

MOLESWORTH, Charles 1941-

PERSONAL: Born September 1, 1941, in Houston, Tex.; son of Charles H. (a plumber) and Anne (a clerk; maiden name, Fetsch) Molesworth; married Carol Choinski (a knitter), July 17, 1965; children: Helen, James. *Education:* University of St. Thomas, Houston, Tex., B.A., 1962; Hollins College, M.A., 1964; State University of New York at Buffalo, Ph.D., 1967. *Politics:* "Utopian Socialist." *Home:* 68-54 136th St., Flushing, N.Y. 11367. *Office:* Department of English, Queens College of the City University of New York, Flushing, N.Y. 11367.

CAREER: Queens College of the City University of New York, Flushing, assistant professor, 1967-71, associate professor, 1972-77, professor of English, 1978—. Member of editorial board of *Salmagundi.* Fulbright-Hays senior lecturer at Abo Akademi and Turun Yliopisto, Turku, Finland, 1975-76. *Member:* Thoreau Society.

WRITINGS: (Contributor) Robert Boyers, editor, *Contemporary Poetry in America: Essays and Interviews,* Schocken, 1974; *Common Elegies,* New Rivers Press, 1977. Contributor to *Contemporary Poets,* 1975; also contributor of more than fifty articles, poems, and reviews to literary journals, including *Poetry, Nation, New American Review,* and *Salmagundi.*

WORK IN PROGRESS: A book of poems; a book on Thoreau and Henry Adams.

SIDELIGHTS: Molesworth comments: "I have lived in New York City, fascinated and repelled by such an environment, for ten years, having begun as a foot-shuffling country boy. I teach because I want to, and I write reviews and essays for the same reason; I write poetry because I cannot *not* do so. I think almost all publishers in America are corrupt or illiterate or both. I lament the low state of reviewing and poetry publishing in our time and have tried to do something about it. To read is an art."

* * *

MONTAGU, Ewen (Edward Samuel) 1901-

PERSONAL: Born March 29, 1901, in London, England; son of Lord Swaythling and Gladys (Goldsmid) Montagu; married Iris Rachel Solomon, June 14, 1923; children: Jeremy Peter Samuel, Jennifer Iris Rachel. *Education:* Attended Harvard University, 1919-20; Trinity College, Cambridge, B.A. and LL.B., both 1923, M.A., 1946. *Religion:* Jewish. *Home:* 24 Montrose Court, Exhibition Rd., London SW7 2QQ, England.

CAREER: Called to the Bar at Middle Temple, 1924; practised law in London, England, 1924-60; lawyer on Western Circuit, 1924-60; King's/Queen's counsel, 1939—; bencher at Middle Temple, 1948—, treasurer, 1968; judge advocate of the Fleet, 1945-73. Recorder of Devizes, 1944-51, and Southampton, 1951-60; chairman of Hampshire quarter sessions, 1951-60, and Middlesex sessions, 1956-69, judge, 1969. Past president of United Synagogue and of Jewish Memorial Council; past chairman of Central Council of Magistrates' Courts Committees and of Pioneer Health Centre. *Military service:* Royal Navy, Inteligence, 1939-45; became lieutenant commander; received Order of the British Empire and Order of the Crown of Yugoslavia; became Commander of Order of the British Empire; named honorary captain of Royal Naval Reserve, 1973.

MEMBER: Anglo-Jewish Association, Bar Yacht Club (founder; past commodore), Royal Ocean Racing Club, Royal Yachting Association. *Awards, honors:* Award from Royal Yachting Association.

WRITINGS: The Man Who Never Was (nonfiction), Evans Brothers, 1953, Lippincott, 1954; *The Archer-Shee Case* (nonfiction), David & Charles, 1974; *Beyond Top Secret U* (nonfiction), P. Davies, 1977, published as *Beyond Top Secret Ultra,* Coward, 1978.

SIDELIGHTS: Montagu writes: "I have taken a considerable part in the administration of the Jewish Community in England as well as a part in the administration of the Bar. I have been very interested in penology and criminology, and in the fostering of health and the prevention and cure of drug addiction.

"I have travelled all over the United States (except for the Deep South), and visited Australia, Singapore, and Hong Kong as Judge Advocate of the Fleet, our nearest equivalent to the American Judge Advocate General of the Navy."

During World War II, Montagu dealt with deciphered German and neutral messages, among other things with Hitler's communications with commanders on all fronts and with the Japanese and Vichy-French, Spanish, and German Secret Service messages. He was the Naval representative dealing with double agents, and from 1940 was the sole regular supplier of naval "information" from the United Kingdom to the Germans. He also took part in all British strategic deceptions of the Germans, and it was one of the more spectacular of these that he described in *The Man Who Never Was.*

AVOCATIONAL INTERESTS: Most sports and games, including fly-fishing, hunting ("in the American sense of that word"), golf, tennis, swimming, skiing, and photography, off-shore cruising and racing sailboats.

* * *

MONTGOMERY, Charles F(ranklin) 1910-1978

April 14, 1910—February 21, 1978; American educator, art administrator, and author of books in the field of American decorative art and antiques. Montgomery was a professor of art history at Yale University and curator of the Mabel Brady Garvan and Related Collections of American Art who organized the "American Art, 1750-1800" exhibition in

1976 that sent Yale to the Victoria and Albert Museum in London. He died in New Haven, Conn. Obituaries and other sources: *Who's Who in American Art,* Bowker, 1973; *New York Times,* February 22, 1978; *AB Bookman's Weekly,* May 8, 1978.

*   *   *

MONTINI, Giovanni Battista (Enrico Antonio Maria)
  See PAUL VI, Pope

*   *   *

MOODIE, T(homas) Dunbar   1940-

PERSONAL: Born August 16, 1940, in Cape Town, South Africa; came to the United States in 1976; son of Graham D. (a soldier) and Sheila D. (a teacher; maiden name, Gow) Moodie; married Meredith Aldrich (a teacher), December 18, 1966; children: Mary Jane, James, Benjamin. *Education:* Rhodes University, B.S.S., 1960, B.S.S. (honors), 1961; Oxford University, B.A. (honors), 1964, M.A., 1970; Harvard University, Ph.D., 1971. *Religion:* Anglican. *Home:* 57 High St., Geneva, N.Y. 14456. *Office:* Department of Anthropology and Sociology, Hobart & William Smith Colleges, Geneva, N.Y. 14456.

CAREER: Wellesley College, Wellesley, Mass., instructor in sociology, 1966-68; University of Massachusetts, Boston, instructor in sociology, 1970-71; University of Natal, Durban, South Africa, senior lecturer in sociology, 1971-74; University of the Witwatersrand, Johannesburg, South Africa, professor of sociology, 1975-76; Hobart & William Smith Colleges, Geneva, N.Y., professor of sociology, 1976—. Member of Princeton's Institute for Advanced Study, 1972-73.

WRITINGS: The Rise of Afrikanerdom, University of California Press, 1975; (contributor) George Zollschan, editor, *On Doing Sociology: An Inaugural Lecture,* University of the Witwatersrand Press, 1976. Author of articles.

WORK IN PROGRESS: Research on black gold miners in South Africa and on the concept of secularization.

SIDELIGHTS: Moodie told *CA:* "*The Rise of Afrikanerdom* attempts to uncover the ideological sources of the Afrikaner's moral commitment to separate development and to assess the importance of the Afrikaner civil religion in the crucial 1948 Nationalist election victory. A close and careful account is given of the role played by Afrikaner political ideology in political events in South Africa before 1948. The final chapter is a brief description of current controversies within Afrikanerdom. The book thus helps us to understand the present-day leaders of the dominant Afrikaner elite in South Africa by recreating with historical detail the social and cultural context in which they were reared. During the last twenty years, I believe that the ideological force of the exclusivist Afrikaner civil religion has been muted by a much more pragmatic commitment to continued white political and economic domination in South Africa. White English-speaking South Africans have thereby been drawn into the Afrikaner camp. There is no evidence that the will of this white group to rule in South Africa has slackened despite recent events."

*   *   *

MOONBLOOD, Q.
  See STALLONE, (Michael) Sylvester

MOORE, Clayton
  See GRANBECK, Marilyn

*   *   *

MOORE, Janet Gaylord   1905-

PERSONAL: Born June 2, 1905, in Hanover, N.H.; daughter of Frank Gardner (a professor) and Anna B. (a children's librarian; maiden name, White) Moore. *Education:* Vassar College, B.A., 1927; also studied at Art Students League, New York, N.Y. *Politics:* Democrat. *Religion:* Protestant. *Home address:* Sand Beach Rd., Stonington, Maine 04681.

CAREER: Art teacher at private elementary school in New York, N.Y., 1939-43; Chance Vought Aircraft, Stratford, Conn., in production illustration, 1943-45; art teacher and head of department at secondary school in Shaker Heights, Ohio, 1947-60; Cleveland Museum of Art, Cleveland, Ohio, supervisor for clubs and adult groups, 1961-67, associate curator, 1967-72, curator in department of art history and education, 1972; writer and artist, 1973—. Adjunct assistant professor, Case Western Reserve University, 1967-72. Paintings have been shown in group and solo exhibitions. *Awards, honors:* Newberry Honor Award from American Library Association, 1970, for *The Many Ways of Seeing.*

WRITINGS: The Many Ways of Seeing: An Introduction to the Pleasures of Art (juvenile), World Publishing, 1969; *The Eastern Gate: An Invitation to the Arts of China and Japan* (for young adults), Collins & World, 1978.

SIDELIGHTS: Janet Moore has lived in Paris, Rome, and Peking. She writes: "*The Many Ways of Seeing* came out of my experience in secondary school. *The Eastern Gate* comes out of my experience with young people and adult groups in the oriental galleries at the Cleveland Museum of Art, and out of travel in China, Japan, and Taiwan. Both books owe something to my own experience as a painter."

*   *   *

MORDECHAI, Ben
  See GERBER, Israel J(oshua)

*   *   *

MORLEY, Hugh   1908(?)-1978

1908(?)—March 8, 1978; American priest, journalist, and author. Morley became a member of the Capuchin Franciscans in 1928 and served for fifteen years as the representative of the International Catholic Union of the Press at the United Nations. He was appointed executive director for the Conference of International Catholic Organization headquarters in Paris. Morley wrote the book *The Pope and the Press,* and was editor for religious publications, including *Seraphic Chronicle, Mission Almanac,* and *Cowl and View.* He died in New York, N.Y. Obituaries and other sources: *New York Times,* March 10, 1978.

*   *   *

MORRIS, John N(elson)   1931-

PERSONAL: Born June 18, 1931, in Oxford, England; came to the United States in 1931; son of Charles (a teacher) and Charlotte (Maurice) Morris; married Anne de La Chapelle, May 27, 1966; children: Julia, John, Richard. *Education:* Hamilton College, A.B., 1953; Columbia University, Ph.D., 1964. *Office:* Department of English, Washington University, St. Louis, Mo. 63130.

CAREER: University of Delaware, Newark, instructor in

English, 1956-58; Columbia University, New York, N.Y., lecturer, 1958-60, instructor, 1960-64, assistant professor of English, 1964-67; Washington University, St. Louis, Mo., associate professor, 1967-71, professor of English, 1971—. *Military service:* U.S. Marine Corps Reserve, active duty, 1953-55; became first lieutenant. *Member:* Modern Language Association of America, American Association of University Professors.

WRITINGS: Versions of the Self: Studies in Autobiography, Basic Books, 1966; *Green Business* (poems), Atheneum, 1970; *The Life Beside This One* (poems), Atheneum, 1974. Contributor of poems, articles, and reviews to literary journals and popular magazines, including *New Yorker, Hudson Review, Yale Review,* and *Poetry.*

WORK IN PROGRESS: Poems.

* * *

MORRIS, W. R. 1936-

PERSONAL: Born July 8, 1936, in Reagan, Tenn.; son of Robert W. (a plant manager) and Estelle (Jowers) Morris; married Carolyn Archer; children: Angel, Crystal, Renee, Lance Jay. *Education:* Attended high school in Cahokia, Ill. *Politics:* Independent. *Religion:* Baptist. *Home address:* P.O. Box 737, Lexington, Tenn. 38351.

CAREER: Free-lance writer, 1969—. *Military service:* U.S. Air Force, 1954-56. *Member:* National Writers Club, American Society of Composers, Authors and Publishers, American Legion, Veterans of Foreign Wars. *Awards, honors:* "Walking Tall" Award from T & B Associates, 1976, for *The Twelfth of August.*

WRITINGS: The Twelfth of August, Aurora, 1971. Author of television script, "Sugar Man," Memphis Productions, 1972.

WORK IN PROGRESS: The King of the Moonshiners; Monument to Justice: Buford Pusser.

SIDELIGHTS: Morris comments: "It was John Howard Griffin, author of *Black Like Me,* who encouraged me to pursue a professional writing career. He was my chief critic for several months. Later, I became interested in the colorful law enforcement officer of McNairy County, Tenn., Sheriff Buford Pusser, and wrote *The Twelfth of August.* From that book and the movie 'Walking Tall,' Pusser became a national hero."

* * *

MORRISON, Hobe 1904-

PERSONAL: Born March 24, 1904, in Philadelphia, Pa.; son of J. I. (an accountant) and Agnes (Miller) Morrison; married Elizabeth Ann Smith, March 15, 1946 (divorced, December, 1962); married Toni Darnay (an actress), November 20, 1964; children: Christopher, Randolph, Douglas. *Education:* Educated in Pennsylvania. *Home:* 7 West 16th St., New York, N.Y. 10011. *Office: Variety,* 154 West 46th St., New York, N.Y. 10036.

CAREER/WRITINGS: Philadelphia Record, Philadelphia, Pa., drama editor and critic, 1933-37; *Variety,* New York, N.Y., drama editor and critic, 1937—. Columnist and reviewer for *Bergen Record,* 1958-69, and for *Passaic Herald-News,* 1969—. *Member:* New York Drama Critics Circle, Players, Coffee House Club.

SIDELIGHTS: Morrison told *CA:* "There is a shortage of good writing—there always has been. The shortage of good writing may be more serious now than in the past. But few

critics seem to recognize that in Neil Simon we have the most talented and prolific playwright since Shakespeare—at least in the field of serious comedy.

"Few filmed plays," Morrison continued, "are as good as the staged versions because the film hasn't the reality or immediacy of the stage." *Avocational interests:* Crossword puzzles, walking, and bird-watching.

* * *

MORTON, Marian J(ohnson) 1937-

PERSONAL: Born May 19, 1937, in Boston, Mass.; daughter of David L. Johnson (a lawyer) and Jean (Inglish) Lincoln; married Geoffrey A. Morton (a teacher), September 5, 1959; children: Margaret, Elizabeth, John, Sarah. *Education:* Smith College, B.A., 1959, Case Western Reserve University, M.A., 1963, Ph.D., 1970. *Politics:* Democrat. *Religion:* None. *Home:* 3061 Fairfax Rd., Cleveland Heights, Ohio 44118. *Office:* Department of History, John Carroll University, University Heights, Ohio 44118.

CAREER: Heights Sun Press, Cleveland, Ohio, reporter, 1959-60; *Cleveland Press,* Cleveland, reporter, 1960-61; John Carroll University, Cleveland, visiting lecturer, 1970-72, assistant professor, 1972-77, associate professor of history, 1977—. *Member:* Organization of American Historians, American Studies Association, Ohio Academy of History.

WRITINGS: The Terrors of Ideological Politics: Liberal Historians in a Conservative Mood, Case Western Reserve, University Press, 1972. Contributor to *Antioch Review.*

WORK IN PROGRESS: Research on women's history, family history, and popular culture.

SIDELIGHTS: Morton told *CA:* "In an undergraduate institution where teaching is stressed, authorship is a luxury. For a full-time teacher with a full-time family, writing is almost an impossibility."

* * *

MOSCATI, Sabatino 1922-

PERSONAL: Born November 24, 1922, in Rome, Italy; married Anna Enrico; children: two daughters. *Education:* Attended Pontifical Biblical Institute, and University of Rome. *Residence:* Rome, Italy. *Office:* Istituto di Studi del Vicino Oriente, Universita di Roma, 00100 Rome, Italy.

CAREER: University of Florence, Florence, Italy, professor of history of religion, 1950-51, professor of Hebrew and Semitic languages, 1951-52; Oriental Institute, Naples, Italy, professor of Hamito-Semitic philology, 1953-54; University of Rome, Rome, Italy, professor of Semitic philology, 1954—. Visiting professor at Pacific School of Religion, 1956, and at University of Wales; director of Institute of Near Eastern Studies; president of Center of Studies for Phoenician and Punic Civilization; vice-president of Institute for the Orient. *Member:* Pontifical Academy of Archaeology, Accademia dei Lincei, Italian Academic Union (president). *Awards, honors:* Awarded President of Italy's National Prize for the moral, historical, and philological sciences, 1964.

WRITINGS—In English: Storia e civita dei Semiti, Laterza, 1949, translation published as *Ancient Semitic Civilizations,* Putnam, 1957, 3rd edition, 1960; *Il profilo dell'Oriente mediterraneo: Panorami di civilta preclassiche,* Edizioni Radio Italiana, 1956, translation published as *The Face of the Ancient Orient: A Panorama of Near Eastern Civilizations in Pre-Classical Times,* Anchor Books, 1960, 2nd edition, 1962; *Le antiche civilta semitiche*, Editori Laterza, 1958, translation published as *Ancient Semitic Deities*, University of Rome, 1958; *The Semites in Ancient History*, University of Wales Press, 1959.

Le origini della narrativa storica nell'arte del Vincino Oriente antico, Accademia nazionale dei Lincei, 1961, translation published as *Historical Art in the Ancient Near East*, Centro di Studi Semitici, 1963; (editor with others) *An Introduction to the Comparative Grammar of the Semitic Languages: Phonology and Morphology*, Harrassowitz, 1964; *Il mondo dei Fenici*, Saggiatore, 1966, translation by Alastair Hamilton published as *The World of the Phoenicians*, Praeger, 1968; *L'archeologia*, 1975, translation published as *Archaeology*, Watts, 1975.

Other writings: *L'Oriente antico*, Vallardi, 1952; *Oriente in nuova luce: Saggi sulle civilta dell'Asia anteriore*, Sansoni, 1954; *I predecessori d'Israele: Studi sulle piu antiche genti semitiche in Siria e Palestina*, Bardi, 1956; *Chi furono i Semiti?*, Accademia nazionale dei Lincei, 1957.

Lezioni di linguistica semitica, Centro di studi semitici, 1960; *Scoprendo l'antico Oriente*, Laterza, 1962; *Antichi imperi d'Oriente*, Saggiatore, 1963; *Archeologia mediterranea: Missioni e scoperte recenti in Asia, Africa, Europa*, Feltrinelli, 1966; *La penetrazione fenicia e punica in Sardegna*, Accademia nazionale dei Lincei, 1966; *Avventure archeologiche*, Casini, 1968; *Fenici e Cartaginesi in Sardegna*, Saggiatore, 1968.

Le stele puniche di Nora nel Museo nazionale di Cagliari, Consiglio nazionale delle ricerche, 1970; *Civilta sul Mediterraneo*, Istituto geografico De Agostini, 1971; *Italia sconosciuta*, Mondadori, 1971; *Tra Caragine e Roma*, Rizzoli, 1971; *I fenici e Cartagine*, Unione tipografico-editrice torinese, 1972; (with Anna Maria Bisi and Enrico Acquaro) *Italia archeologica*, Istituto geografico De Agostini, 1973; *Problematica della civilta fenicia*, Consiglio nazionale delle ricerche, 1974; (with Andre Parrot and Maurice Chebab) *Les Pheniciens*, Gallimard, 1975; *Le pietre parlano*, Mondadori, 1976.

Also author of *L'epigrafia ebraica antica*, 1951, *L'alba della civilta*, 1976, *Vita privata e vita sociale nell'antichita*, 1976, and *I Cartaginesi in Italia*.

Contributor to *Journal of Near Eastern Studies*, *Journal of Biblical Literature*, *Catholic Biblical Quarterly*, and other scholarly journals.

*   *   *

MOULTON, Edward C. 1936-

PERSONAL: Born July 7, 1936, in Epworth, Burin, Newfoundland, Canada; married; children: two. *Education:* Memorial University of Newfoundland, B.A., 1957, M.A., 1960; University of London, Ph.D., 1964. *Office:* Department of History, University of Manitoba, 500 Dysart Rd., Winnipeg, Manitoba, Canada R3T 2M8.

CAREER: Vice-principal of public school in Grand Bank, Newfoundland, 1957-58; University of Manitoba, Winnipeg, assistant professor, 1964-69, associate professor of history, 1969—, chairman of Asian studies committee, 1971—, and World University Service Committee, 1973-75. President of Shastri Indo-Canadian Institute, 1971-74, director of summer program in India, 1973. *Member:* Association for Asian Studies, Canadian Society for Asian Studies. *Awards, honors:* Book award from Grolier Society, 1957; Canada Council fellow, summer, 1966.

WRITINGS: Lord Northbrook's Indian Administration,

1872-1876, Asia Publishing House, 1969; (contributor) A. J. A. Morris, editor, *Edwardian Radicalism, 1900-1914*, Routledge & Kegan Paul, 1974. Contributor of articles and reviews to history journals.

*   *   *

MOUNTBATTEN, Richard
See WALLMANN, Jeffrey M(iner)

*   *   *

MOWAT, David 1943-

PERSONAL: Born March 16, 1943, in Cairo, Egypt; son of Robert Case (a historian) and Renee (Sutton) Mowat. *Education:* New College, Oxford, B.A. (honors), 1964; University of Sussex, further study, 1964-66. *Agent:* Michael Imison, Dr. Jan Van Loewen Ltd., 81-83 Shaftesbury Ave., London W1V 8BX, England.

CAREER: Playwright. Cilcennin fellow at University of Bristol, 1973-75. *Awards, honors:* Arts Council bursary awards, 1969, 1970, and 1976.

WRITINGS—Plays: Anne-Luse and Other Plays (contains "Anne-Luse," first produced in Edinburgh, Scotland, 1968, produced in London, 1971, and in New York City, 1972; "Jens," first produced in Falmer, England, 1965, produced in London, 1969; "Purity," first produced in Manchester, England, 1969, produced in London, 1970, and in New York City, 1972), Calder & Boyars, 1970; *The Others* (first produced in London, 1970), Calder & Boyars, 1973.

Unpublished, produced plays: "Pearl," first produced in Brighton, England, 1966; "1850," first produced in London, 1967; "Dracula," first produced in Edinburgh, 1969, produced in London, 1973; "The Normal Woman, and Tyyppi," first produced in London, 1970; "Adrift," first produced in Manchester, 1970; "Most Recent Least Recent," first produced in Manchester, 1970; "Innuit," first produced in London, 1970; "Liquid," first produced in London, 1971; "The Diabolist," first produced in London, 1971; "John" (three-act), first produced in London, 1971; "Amalfi" (based on Webster's "The Duchess of Malfi"), first produced in Edinburgh, 1972; "Phoenix-and-Turtle," first produced in London, 1972; "Morituri," first produced in London, 1972; "My Relationship with Jane," first produced in London, 1973; "Come" (one-act), first produced in London, 1973; "Main Sequence," first produced in Bristol, 1974; "The Collected Works" (three-act), first produced in London, 1974; (and composer of musical score) "The Memory Man," first produced in Bristol, 1974; (and composer of musical score) "The Love Maker," first produced in Bristol, 1974; (and composer of musical score) "X to C," first produced in Bristol, 1975.

Unpublished, unproduced plays: "Fat-Man: The Exercise of Power."

Stories and a play represented in anthologies, including *New Writers Eleven*, Calder & Boyars, 1975; *The London Fringe Theatre*, edited by Victor Mitchell, Burnham House, 1976.

*   *   *

MOXHAM, Robert Morgan 1919-1978

September 15, 1919—March 23, 1978; American geophysicist and author. He served with the U.S. Geological Survey, and was president of the D.C. Civil War Roundtable and a member of the Alexandria Civil War Roundtable and the American Revolutionary War Roundtable. Moxham wrote several books on the history of northern Virginia. He died in

Fairfax, Va. Obituaries and other sources: *American Men and Women of Science,* 13th edition, Bowker, 1976; *Washington Post,* March 25, 1978.

* * *

MULLINS, Helene 1899-

PERSONAL: Born July 12, 1899, in New Rochelle, N.Y.; daughter of Timothy J. (a train dispatcher) and Marie (an actress; maiden name, McCall) Gallagher; married Ivan Mullins, October 1, 1919 (divorced, 1957); married Linne Johnson (a transportation Salesman), November 28, 1958. *Education:* Attended convent boarding schools. *Religion:* "Seeker." *Home:* 16 West 16th St., New York, N.Y. 10011.

CAREER: Writer, 1923—. Has given poetry readings at universities and women's clubs, and on radio programs.

WRITINGS: (With sister, Marie McCall) *Paulus Fy* (novel), Robert McBride, 1924; *Earthbound* (poems), Harper, 1929; *Convent Girl* (novel based on her own experiences), Harper, 1930; *Balm in Gilead* (poems), Harper, 1930; *Streams from the Source* (poems), Caxton Press, 1938; *The Mirrored Walls* (poems), Twayne, 1970. Work represented in *The Diamond Anthology,* edited by Charles Angoff, Gustav Davidson, Hyacinth Hill, and A. M. Sullivan, Poetry Society of America, 1971. Contributor of poems and stories to magazines and newspapers, including *Commonweal, New Yorker, American Scholar,* and *Saturday Review.*

WORK IN PROGRESS: A semi-autobiographical novel set in New York City; poems.

SIDELIGHTS: Helene Mullins writes: "I started writing stories out of homesickness in the convent boarding school. I was brought up as a Roman Catholic, in fear of hell and damnation, and when my sister and I were taken home I joined a public library and read Fraser's *Golden Bough,* which helped to free me. After an almost fatal automobile accident in 1935, and unconsciousness for three weeks, I returned to consciousness with a feeling of living a posthumous existence. My poetry has matured greatly since then, but it is not in the current mode." Her poems have been recorded at Fairleigh Dickinson University.

BIOGRAPHICAL/CRITICAL SOURCES: Saturday Review, August 8, 1970.

* * *

MUNGER, Robert Boyd 1910-

PERSONAL: Born July 28, 1910, in Santa Cruz, Calif.; son of Albert Luke (in business) and Pearl (Weakley) Munger; married Edith Borkgren (a clinical psychologist), February 1, 1938; children: Marilyn Star Munger Brown, Monica Rae. *Education:* University of California, Berkeley, B.A., 1932; Princeton Theological Seminary, B.D., 1936. *Politics:* Democrat. *Home:* 1844 East Midwick Dr., Altadena, Calif. 91001. *Office:* Fuller Theological Seminary, 135 North Oakland, Pasadena, Calif. 91101.

CAREER: Ordained United Presbyterian minister; pastor of Presbyterian churches in South Hollywood, Calif., 1936-45, Berkeley, Calif., 1945-62, and Seattle, Wash., 1962-69; currently affiliated with Fuller Theological Seminary, Pasadena, Calif. *Awards, honors:* D.D. from Whitworth College, 1948.

WRITINGS: What Jesus Says, Revell, 1955; *New Life to Live,* Regal Books, 1973; *Jesus, Man of His Word,* Regal Books, 1974.

WORK IN PROGRESS: A book on renewal of the local congregation.

SIDELIGHTS: Munger writes that he has spent considerable time abroad studying the missionary work of the church.

BIOGRAPHICAL/CRITICAL SOURCES: Theology: News and Notes, June, 1976.

* * *

MUNSON-BENSON, Tunie 1946-

PERSONAL: Born August 15, 1946, in Chicago, Ill.; daughter of George Randall (a painter and decorator) and Violet May (an executive secretary; maiden name, Seaberg) Munson; married Peter Lorimer Benson (a psychologist), June 7, 1969; children: Liv Christina. *Education:* Augustana College, Rock Island, Ill., B.A. (magna cum laude), 1968. *Religion:* Lutheran. *Residence:* Minneapolis, Minn.

CAREER: Conde Nast Publications, New York, N.Y., junior copywriter for *Vogue,* 1968-69; elementary school teacher in Wallingford, Conn., 1969-70, and Aurora, Colo., 1971-73; free-lance writer, 1973-75; Earlham College, Richmond, Ind., part-time lecturer in children's literature, 1975-77. Public lecturer on children's literature. *Member:* Ann Arbor Writers, Detroit Women Writers, Earlham Writers.

WRITINGS: (Under name Tunie Munson) *A Fistful of Sun* (juvenile), Lothrop, 1974. Contributor to magazines, including *American Baby.* Guest editor-in-chief of *Mademoiselle,* 1968.

WORK IN PROGRESS: 7-8-9! (tentative title), a juvenile picture book.

SIDELIGHTS: Tunie Munson-Benson writes: "I continue to resist the dubious status of grownup. My happiest hours have been spent with children—my own, students, neighborhood friends—and writing has become a natural extension of my love for them, a way to weave my life into the lives of these special persons, and a rewarding means to that end. A fledgling's attempt at a first book (which has as its setting a loft open to sun and sky, inviting flight) has led me to a loft of my own, where I try my wings and, through writing, believe that someday, I too may 'fly.' I'm a pusher of children's books, and addicted to all kinds. I'm partial to the child within me . . . and others."

AVOCATIONAL INTERESTS: Weaving on a floor loom.

BIOGRAPHICAL/CRITICAL SOURCES: Mademoiselle, August, 1968.

* * *

MURPHY, Arthur Lister 1906-

PERSONAL: Born February 8, 1906, in Dominion, Nova Scotia, Canada; son of George Henry and Helena Josephine (MacNeil) Murphy; married Mary Sylvia Shore, September 14, 1932; children: Arthur Lister, Jr., Paul Edward, Sylvia Joanne Carr. *Education:* Dalhousie University, B.A., 1926, M.D. and C.M., 1930; postdoctoral study at Montreal General Hospital. *Home:* 6009 Inglis St., Halifax, Nova Scotia, Canada. *Agent:* Ray Johnson, 408 West 57th St., New York, N.Y. 10019.

CAREER: Halifax Infirmary, Halifax, Nova Scotia, assistant and attending surgeon, 1933-60; Victoria General Hospital, Halifax, assistant and attending surgeon, 1934-70; Dalhousie University, Halifax, assistant professor, 1934-44, associate professor of surgery, 1944-70; writer. University Grants Committee, Province of Nova Scotia, part-time member, 1963-68, chairman, 1968—. Member of Halifax Board of Trade; director of Nova Scotia Trust Co. Founding president of Neptune Theatre Foundation, 1963-66; director of National Theatre School. *Member:* Canadian Medical Association, Canadian Authors Association, Writers Guild of America, American College of Surgeons (fellow and governor), Nova Scotia Medical Society (past president), Halifax Medical Society (past president), Phi Rho Sigma, Royal Nova Scotia Yacht Squadron, St. Margaret's Sailing Club. *Awards, honors:* Malcolm Honor Award, 1930; *Canadian Drama* award, 1962; Dominion Drama Festival Shield, 1963; LL.D. from St. Francis Xavier University, 1966.

WRITINGS: The Story of Medicine, Ryerson, 1954.

Plays: "The Sleeping Bag," first produced in Halifax at Neptune Theatre, July 19, 1966; "The Breadwinner," first produced in St. John, New Brunswick at Rothesay Playhouse, 1967; *The First Falls on Monday* (first produced in Lindsay, Ontario, at the Karwartha Festival, 1967), University of Toronto Press, 1972; "Charlie," first produced in Halifax at Neptune Theatre, August 4, 1967; "Tiger! Tiger!," first produced in Halifax at Neptune Theatre, March 17, 1970.

Script-writer for "Dr. Kildare" and "Ben Casey" television series. Also author of non-commercial radio and television dramas for Canadian Broadcasting Co. (CBC), and of various scientific papers and essays.

SIDELIGHTS: Murphy is one of the few Canadian playwrights to have as many as five plays professionally produced. Nevertheless, his work for the theatre is generally little known, and only one of his plays, "The First Falls on Monday," has been published. This play is a historical work, based on the two days preceding the Canadian confederation. His other historical drama, "Tiger! Tiger!," follows the story of the eighteenth century anatomist, John Hunter, and was a box office success when it was produced in 1970. "Charlie" presents a serious treatment of the plight of Cape Breton miners. Murphy's two other full-length works, "The Sleeping Bag" and "The Breadwinner," are both comedies. Murphy's most popular work, however, combined his dual talents of playwright and physician. As a script-writer for both the "Ben Casey" and "Dr. Kildare" television shows, he reached an audience of millions during the 1960's.*

* * *

MURPHY, George E(dward) 1948-

PERSONAL: Born December 30, 1948, in Winthrop, Mass.; son of George E. (owner of a delivery service) and Mary Agnes (Forristall) Murphy; married Rosemary Harrington, July 1, 1972; children: Madigan Rose. *Education:* Boston College, B.A. (summa cum laude), 1972; Bridgewater State College, M.A.T., 1977; attending Goddard College. *Home:* 108 Canal St., Green Harbor, Mass. 02041. *Office:* Hingham Public Schools, 41 Pleasant St., Hingham, Mass. 02043.

CAREER: Hingham Public Schools, Hingham, Mass., writing teacher, 1972—. Owner of Bear Essential Books, 1977—, and Wampeter Press, 1978—, both Green Harbor, Mass. *Member:* National Council of Teachers of English, Committee of Small Press Magazine Editors & Publishers, Massachusetts Council of Teachers of English.

WRITINGS: Bicycle & Other Gifts (poems), privately printed, 1976; *Teddy: A Christmas Story* (for children), Bear Essential Books, 1977; *Encounters* (poems), Wampeter Press, 1977; "The Meaning of It All" (six-act musical; first produced in Winthrop, Mass. at Memorial Auditorium, 1971; (adapter from Kurt Vonnegut's novel of the same name) "Mother Night" (three-act play; first produced in

Hingham, Mass. at Town Auditorium, 1976. Editor of *Tendril,* 1977—. Contributor of poems to periodicals, including *Aspect, Applecart, Dark Horse,* and *Stone.*

WORK IN PROGRESS: Calligraphy, a book of poems.

SIDELIGHTS: Murphy writes: "I am becoming increasingly interested in establishing small press production companies. At Wampeter Press, I have just published a volume of poems by Elizabeth McKim, entitled *Burning Through.*

"My other great love is the teaching of writing. I work full time in the public school system of Hingham, Massachusetts, and find my work there challenging, stimulating, and rewarding. Some of my former students are now beginning to get published."

* * *

MURPHY, Romaine 1941-

PERSONAL: Born April 8, 1941, in New York; daughter of Louis (a scholar) and Josephine (Costa) Romaine; children: Dionys. *Education:* College of New Rochelle, A.B., 1960; Fordham University, M.A., 1963; currently pursuing doctoral study at New York University. *Residence:* Tarrytown, N.Y.

CAREER: Daemon College, Buffalo, N.Y., instructor in English, 1963-65; high school English teacher in New York; *Gravida Poetry Quarterly,* Hartsdale, N.Y., editor, 1973—. Adjunct professor at College of New Rochelle, 1978. Member of National Coordinating Council of Literary Magazines, 1977.

WRITINGS: The Molly Bloom Poems, Pulp Press, 1977.

* * *

MURPHY, Sharon M. 1940-

PERSONAL: Born August 2, 1940, in Milwaukee, Wis.; daughter of Adolph L. (an engineer) and Margaret Ann (Hirtz) Feyen; married James E. Murphy (a journalist and professor); children: Shannon Lynn, Erin Ann. *Education:* Marquette University, B.A. (cum laude), 1965; University of Iowa, M.A., 1970, Ph.D., 1973. *Residence:* Milwaukee, Wis. *Office:* Department of Mass Communication, University of Wisconsin, P.O. Box 413, Milwaukee, Wis. 53201.

CAREER: Roman Catholic nun of the Society of the Divine Savior, 1957-68; teacher in elementary schools in Wisconsin, 1959-63, and secondary schools in Milwaukee, Wis., 1963-69; Kirkwood Community College, Cedar Rapids, Iowa, instructor, 1970-72, coordinator of publications in community relations, 1970-71; University of Iowa, Iowa City, instructor in journalism, 1972-73; University of Wisconsin, Milwaukee, assistant professor of mass communication, 1973—. Fulbright professor at University of Nigeria, 1977-78. Reporter for *Milwaukee Sentinel,* 1967; *WorldWide,* stringer, editor, 1967-68. Member of research team for National Center for Educational Communication, 1972; member of Wisconsin Journalism Teacher-Advisor Council (member of executive committee, 1965-68); coordinator of workshops and seminars.

MEMBER: Association for Education in Journalism (chairman of National Curriculum Commission), Women in Communications (head of national continuing education committee, 1974-76; regional vice-president), Journalism Education Association, Sigma Delta Chi, Kappa Tau Alpha. *Awards, honors:* Special recognition award from Catholic School Press Association, 1966.

WRITINGS: (With Donald Wigal) *Screen Experience: An*

Approach to Film, Pflaum, 1969, 2nd edition, in press; (with Virginia Woodring and others) *Laboratory Manual for Journalism in the Mass Media,* Ginn, 1970; (with husband, James Murphy) *Supervision of High School Publications,* Bureau of Correspondence Study, University of Iowa, 1973; *Other Voices: Black Chicano and American Indian Press,* Pflaum, 1974; (contributor) Malcolm S. MacLean, Jr. and Albert D. Talbott, editors, *Use of Simulation and Games for Mass Communication Education: A Symposium,* University of Iowa Press, 1974; *Freedom to Be . . . in Communications* (monographs), four volumes, Journalism Education Association, 1976; (contributor) Marilyn Sealine, editor, *Communication Altogether: A Guide to Media for Use in Schools,* Women in Communications, in press. Contributor to education, journalism, and religious journals.

WORK IN PROGRESS: Research on human communication, approaches to simulation in teaching news writing and evaluation, case studies on roles of women in the press, and case studies of selected Chicano and native American newspapers.

*   *   *

MURRAY, Joan 1945-

PERSONAL: Born August 6, 1945, in New York, N.Y.; daughter of Charles George (a building inspector) and Vera (a typist and translator; maiden name, Bjork) Schwetje; married James Murray (a counselor), August 29, 1964; children: James Charles. *Education:* Hunter College of the City University of New York, B.A., 1969; New York University, M.A., 1970, doctoral study, 1970-72. *Home:* 39 Granger Pl., Buffalo, N.Y. 14222.

CAREER: Herbert H. Lehman College of the City University of New York, New York, N.Y., instructor in English, 1970-74; free-lance writer, 1974—. Coordinator of Bronx Poets Alliance, 1974-77. *Member:* International Women's Writing Guild, Poets and Writers, Poets and Writers of New Jersey, Sigma Tau Delta. *Awards, honors:* Named artist of the month by Bronx Council on the Arts, 1976.

WRITINGS: Egg Tooth (poetry; self-illustrated), Sunbury Press, 1975. Work represented in anthologies, including *In the Looking Glass: 21 Modern Short Stoires by Women,* edited by Nancy Dean and Myra Stark, Putnam, 1977, and *Mothers, Daughters,* edited by Lyn Lifshin, Beacon Press, 1978. Contributor of poems and articles to literary journals and popular magazines, including *Atlantic Monthly, Ms.,* and *College English,* and to newspapers.

WORK IN PROGRESS: A novel; a book of poems; a book of stories; editing an anthology of poems.

SIDELIGHTS: Joan Murray comments: "My writing takes shape from my own experience: a working-class background, feminism, social protest, family life, urban and rural visions and encounters. Though I write in free form, my poems have been praised for their lyrical qualities (I have a musical ear that tunes me to their rhythms and tones) and their strong imagery (I worked as an artist and seek strong visual texture in writing). Critics have noted too the accessibility or immediacy of my poems for the reader. Subjects may vary from a raw murder on a city street to an ironic musing in an old country graveyard. Though my fiction is less autobiographical and sometimes experimental in form, it most often takes root from my own life or the things I've witnessed."

MURRAY, K(atherine) M(aud) Elisabeth 1909-

PERSONAL: Born December 3, 1909, in Cambridge, England; daughter of Harold James R. (an inspector of schools) and Kate Maitland (Crosthwaite) Murray. *Education:* Somerville College, Oxford, B.A. (honors), 1931, B.Litt., 1933. *Religion:* Church of England. *Home address:* Upper Cranmore, Heyshott, Midhurst, Sussex GU29 ODL, England.

CAREER: Ashburne Hall, Manchester, England, tutor and librarian, 1935-37; Oxford University, Somerville College, Oxford, England, Mary Somerville research fellow, 1937-38; Cambridge University, Girton College, Cambridge, England, assistant tutor and registrar, 1938-44, domestic bursar, 1942-44, junior bursar, 1944-48; Bishop Otter College of Education, Chichester, England, principal, 1948-70; writer, 1970—. Chichester District Council, member, 1973—, vice-chairman of planning committee, 1976—. *Member:* Society of Antiquaries (fellow), Sussex Archaeological Society (chairman of council, 1964-77; president, 1977—). *Awards, honors:* Mond student at British School of Archaeology in Jerusalem, 1933.

WRITINGS: The Constitutional History of the Cinque Ports, Manchester University Press, 1935; *The Register of Daniel Rough, Common Clerk of Romney,* Records Branch, Kent Archaeological Society, 1945; *Caught in the Web of Words: James Murray and the Oxford English Dictionary,* Yale University Press, 1977. Contributor to history and archaeology journals.

WORK IN PROGRESS: A history of the parish of Heyshott, Sussex.

SIDELIGHTS: Murray writes that she is interested in conservation, walking, and archaeology. "I am only an amateur archaeologist. I became interested at school in Colchester and during my time at Oxford, when I became president of the Oxford University Archaeological Society. I excavated on weekends at a Saxon site near Oxford and on vacations at Colchester (a Roman site). As a student of the British School of Archaeology in Jerusalem I joined the Samaria expedition for one season."

Murray also commented that her last book was a biography of her grandfather, Sir James A. H. Murray, first editor of *The Oxford English Dictionary.*

*   *   *

MURRAY, Thomas J(oseph) 1943-

PERSONAL: Born May 5, 1943, in Sioux City, Iowa; son of Joseph Allan (a farmer) and Alice (Kenaley) Murray; married Molly Fifield (a landscape architect), March 8, 1975. *Education:* Iowa State University, B.S., 1966; University of Wisconsin—Madison, M.S., 1975. *Religion:* Roman Catholic. *Office:* College of Engineering, University of Wisconsin, 1500 Johnson Dr., Room 729, Madison, Wis. 53706.

CAREER: University of Wisconsin—Madison, writer and editor for College of Engineering, 1967—. Consultant to National Academy of Sciences.

WRITINGS: (With Reid A. Bryson) *Climates of Hunger,* University of Wisconsin Press, 1977. Contributor to *Wisconsin State Journal.*

WORK IN PROGRESS: Writing on energy, especially efficient use of energy for residential purposes.

*   *   *

MURRAY-BROWN, Jeremy 1932-

PERSONAL: Born June 20, 1932, in India. *Education:* Attended New College, Oxford, 1952-55. *Home:* 35 Brook Green, London W.6, England. *Agent:* Harold Matson Co., Inc., 22 East 40th St., New York, N.Y. 10016.

CAREER: Writer.

WRITINGS: Kenyatta, Dutton, 1973; *Faith and the Flag,* Allen & Unwin, 1977.

* * *

MYERS, R(obert) E(ugene)   1924-

PERSONAL: Born January 15, 1924, in Los Angeles, Calif.; son of Harold Eugene and Margaret (Anawalt) Myers; married Patricia A. Tazer, August 17, 1956; children: Edward E., Margaret A., Hal R., Karen. *Education:* University of California, Berkeley, A.B., 1955; Reed College, M.A., 1960; further graduate study at University of Minnesota, 1960-63; University of Georgia, Ed.D., 1968. *Politics:* Democrat. *Religion:* Protestant. *Home:* 2846 Northwest Angelica Dr., Corvallis, Ore. 97330. *Office:* 942 Lancaster Dr. N.E., Salem, Ore. 97310.

CAREER: Elementary school teacher in Oregon, California, and Minnesota, 1954-61; Augsburg College, Minneapolis, Minn., assistant professor of education, 1962-63; University of Oregon, Eugene, assistant professor of education, 1963-66; elementary school teacher in Eugene, 1966-67; University of Victoria, Victoria, British Columbia, associate professor of education and associate director of teacher education, 1968-70; Oregon State System of Higher Education, Teaching Research Division, associate research professor of education, 1970-73; Northwestern, Inc., Portland, Ore., filmmaker, 1973-74; University of Portland, Portland, associate professor of education, 1974-75; free-lance film producer, 1975-77; Oregon State Department of Education, Salem, learning resources specialist, 1977—. Visiting professor at San Diego State University, Northeastern Louisiana University, Winona State University, Oregon College of Education, University of Victoria, Paine College, and Texas Tech University. Has appeared on television programs. *Military service:* U.S. Merchant Marine, 1943-45.

MEMBER: National Association for Gifted Children (member of board of directors, 1974-77), Oregon Teachers of the Able and Gifted. *Awards, honors:* Outstanding book award from Pi Lambda Theta, 1972, for *Creative Learning and Teaching;* Golden Eagle from Council on International Nontheatrical Events, 1973, for "Feather."

WRITINGS: (Contributor) E. Paul Torrance, editor, *Rewarding Creative Behavior,* Prentice-Hall, 1965; (with Torrance) *Creative Learning and Teaching,* Dodd, 1970.

For children: *Invitations to Thinking and Doing,* with teacher's guide (with Torrance), Ginn, 1965; *Invitations to Speaking and Writing Creatively,* with teacher's guide (with Torrance), Ginn, 1965; *Can You Imagine?,* with teacher's guide (with Torrance), Ginn, 1965; *Plots, Puzzles, and Ploys,* with teacher's guide (with Torrance), Ginn, 1966; *For Those Who Wonder,* with teacher's guide (with Torrance), Ginn, 1966; *Stretch,* with teacher's guide (with Torrance), Perceptive, 1968; *It's a Butterfly!,* with audio cassette, United Learning, 1977; *It's a Dolphin!,* with audio cassette, United Learning, 1977; *It's a Squirrel!,* with audio cassette, United Learning, 1977; *It's a Toad!,* with audio cassette, United Learning, 1977; *It's an Alligator!,* with audio cassette, United Learning, 1977.

Films: "Feather" (juvenile), ACI Media, 1973; "Flexibility," Teaching Research, 1973; "Learning Sets," Teaching Research, 1973; "Perseveration," Teaching Research, 1973; "Inducing a Creative Set: The Magic Net," Teaching Research, 1973; "Elephants" (juvenile), ACI Media, 1974.

Filmstrip series for young people: "Animal Friends," A.I.M.S. Instructional Media, 1974; "Exploring the Unexplained," United Learning, 1974; "Investigating the Unknown," United Learning, 1974; "Sing Along with Animals," United Learning, 1975; "Hand Tools: An Introduction to Working with Wood and Plastic," A.I.M.S. Instructional Media, 1975.

WORK IN PROGRESS: Revising *Creative Learning and Teaching;* studying gifted and talented children.

SIDELIGHTS: Myers writes: "My motivation for writing has always had two sides: self-expression and professional reasons. The latter generally deal with helping young people become more creative. I am interested in intelligence, learning, instructional materials and techniques, motivation, and personality. I've done research in all these areas.

"I'm still not convinced I was meant to be a college teacher. During the past few years, I have been producing films and audio cassettes to be used to improve courses which prepare college students for teaching. I'm also engaged in preparing films for educational television. My main goal, however, is to produce recordings and filmstrips which will become superior instructional tools."

N

NABOKOV, Nicolas 1903-1978

April 4, 1903—1978; Russian-born American composer, educator, and author. Cousin to novelist Vladimir Nabokov, he was best known for his organization of international music festivals in Rome, Tokyo, and Paris during the 1950's and early 1960's. Nabokov composed two operas, five ballets, three symphonies, and several works for voice and orchestra. He was an educator of music history, composition, and theory. He wrote *Old Friends and New Music* and *Bagazh: Memoirs of a Russian Cosmopolitan.* Nabokov died in Manhattan, N.Y. Obituaries and other sources: *Who's Who in America,* 38th edition, Marquis, 1974; *Time,* April 17, 1978.

* * *

NADER, Ralph 1934-

PERSONAL: Born February 27, 1934, in Winsted, Conn.; son of Nadra (a restaurant owner) and Rose (Bouziene) Nader. *Education:* Princeton University, B.A., 1955; Harvard University, LL.B., 1958. *Office address:* P.O. Box 19367, Washington, D.C. 20026.

CAREER: Admitted to the Bar of Connecticut, 1958, the Bar of Massachusetts, 1959, and the Bar of U.S. Supreme Court; research assistant to Harold J. Berman (a Harvard University law professor), 1958; private practice of law in Hartford, Conn., 1959—; University of Hartford, Hartford, lecturer in history and government, 1961-63; U.S. Labor Department, Washington, D.C., consultant dealing with automobile safety, 1964-65; Princeton University, Princeton, N.J., lecturer, 1967-68; founder of Center for Study of Responsive Law, 1969, and of Public Interest Research Group, Center for Auto Safety, Profiles for Auto Safety, and Project for Corporate Responsibility. Consumer advocate. *Military service:* U.S. Army, 1959. *Member:* American Bar Association, American Academy of Arts and Sciences, Phi Beta Kappa. *Awards, honors:* Nieman Fellows award, 1965-66; named one of ten Outstanding Men of the Year by U.S. Junior Chamber of Commerce, 1967; first annual Public Defender Award from *New Republic,* 1969.

WRITINGS: *Unsafe At Any Speed: The Designed-in Dangers of the American Automobile,* Grossman, 1965; (with Lowell Dodge and Ralf Hotchkiss) *What To Do With Your Bad Car,* Grossman, 1970; *Beware,* Law-Arts, 1971; (editor with others) *Whistle Blowing: The Report of the Conference on Professional Responsibility,* Grossman, 1972; (editor) *The Consumer and Corporate Accountability,* Harcourt, 1973; (with Kate Blackwell) *You and Your Pension,* Viking, 1973; (editor with Mark Green) *Corporate Power in America,* Viking, 1973; (with Donald Ross) *Action for a Change: A Student's Manual for Public Interest Organizing,* Viking, 1973; *Working on the System: A Comprehensive Manual for Citizen Access to Federal Agencies,* Basic Books, 1974.

(With others) *The Commerce Committees: A Study of the House and Senate Commerce Committees* (also see below), Viking, 1975; (with others) *The Environment Committees: A Study of the House and Senate Interior, Agriculture and Science Committees* (also see below), Viking, 1975; (with others) *The Judiciary Committees: A Study of the House and Senate Judiciary Committees* (also see below), Viking, 1975; (with others) *The Revenue Committees: A Study of the House Ways and Means and the Senate Finance Committees and the House and Senate Appropriations Committees* (also see below), Viking, 1975; (with others) *The Money Committees: A Study of the House and Senate Banking and Currency Committees* (also see below), Viking, 1975; (with others) *Ruling Congress: A Study of How the Senate and House Rules Govern the Legislative Process* (also see below), Viking, 1975; *The Ralph Nader Congress Project* (collection of previous six titles), six volumes, Viking, 1975.

(With others) *Government Regulation: What Kind of Reform?,* American Enterprise, 1976; (with Green and Joel Seligman) *Taming the Giant Corporation,* Norton, 1976; (editor with Green) *Verdicts on Lawyers,* Crowell, 1976; *The White House,* Viking, 1977; (with John Abbotts) *The Menace of Atomic Energy,* Norton, 1977.

Author of introduction: Edward F. Cox, Robert C. Fellmeth and John E. Schultz, *The Nader Report on the Federal Trade Commission,* Baron, 1969; John C. Esposito and Larry J. Silverman, *Vanishing Air: The Ralph Nader Study Group Report on Air Pollution,* Grossman, 1970; Robert C. Fellmeth, *The Interstate Commerce Omission: The Ralph Nader Study Group Report on the ICC and Transportation,* Grossman, 1970; James S. Turner, *The Chemical Feast: The Ralph Nader Study Group Report of Food Protection and the Food and Drug Administration,* Grossman, 1970; Morton Mintz and Jerry S. Cohen, *America Inc.: Who Owns and Runs the U.S.,* Dial, 1971; David Leinsdorf and Donald Etra, *Citibank: Ralph Nader's Study Group Report on First National City Bank,* Grossman, 1973.

Contributor of articles to *Saturday Review, New Republic,* and other periodicals. Contributing editor of *Ladies Home Journal,* 1973—.

SIDELIGHTS: Nader's father once told a reporter: "We made Ralph understand that working for justice is a safe-guard of our democracy," and that remark may reveal the roots of the younger Nader's immense energy and dedication as the foremost consumer advocate in the United States. Actually, he prefers to be called a "people's law-yer," and views his legal profession in moral and ethical terms. "The most important thing a lawyer can do is become an advocate of powerless citizens," he said. "I am in favor of lawyers without clients. Lawyers should represent systems of justice."

Nader's work for powerless citizens began after he had handled several automobile accident damage suits. The fact that effort was rarely made to discover whether the car, rather than the driver, could be at fault sparked Nader's own investigations. He wrote *Unsafe At Any Speed,* which carefully documented safety defects in American cars, and then he proceeded to Washington, D.C., where he played a key role in governmental studies of auto-safety and the ultimate passage of law-enforced safety standards.

In 1969, following an investigation of the Federal Trade Commission, Nader helped establish the Center for Study of Responsive Law, a non-profit, foundation-funded organization. Staffed, to a large extent, by college, graduate, and law students, the Center came to be known as "Nader's Raid-ers" and initiated studies of several federal commissions as well as a variety of consumer problems.

In addition to his battle against the power of large corporations, Nader and his associates have made significant contributions in such areas as meat inspection, mental health and old age care, water and air pollution, nuclear power, and technological data gathering. He is generally acknowledged as the "founder" of the current nationwide consumer movement; his work in the late 1960's is seen as directly linked to the establishment of consumer affairs commissions in most major cities and to the public's newly stimulated concern with product safety and value.

Nader himself, however, remains dedicated to more than consumer matters; he is principally concerned with the use and misuse of corporate and institutional power. He sees citizenship and community action as the fundamental modes for insuring democracy in a corporate/industrial state. As a first step toward such insurance he seeks, as he has said, "to create a new dimension to the legal profession. What we have now is a democracy without citizens. No one is on the public's side. And the bureaucrats in the administration don't think the government belongs to the people. . . . I hope a new generation of lawyers will begin to change that."

BIOGRAPHICAL/CRITICAL SOURCES: Newsweek, January 22, 1968; *Life,* October 3, 1969; R. F. Buckhorn, *Nader: The People's Lawyer,* Prentice-Hall, 1972; Jay Acton, *Ralph Nader: A Man and a Movement,* Warner, 1972; Charles McCarry, *Citizen Nader,* Saturday Review Press, 1972; David Sanford, *Me & Ralph: Is Nader Unsafe for America?,* New Republic Book Company, 1976.*

* * *

NAKATANI, Chiyoko 1930-

PERSONAL: Born January 16, 1930, in Tokyo, Japan; daughter of Teisuke (an industrial engineer) and Toshiko (Sato) Nagano; married Sadahiko Nakatani (a university professor), March 5, 1953. *Education:* Attended Tokyo National University of Fine Arts and Music, 1948-52. *Home:* 3-784 Sekimachi, Nerimaku, Tokyo, Japan 177.

CAREER: Writer and illustrator of books for children. Has also given painting lessons to children. *Member:* Japanese Board on Books for Young People. *Awards, honors:* Prize from Kodansha Publishing Co., 1970, for *Machi no nezumi to inaka no nezumi* (title means "A Town Mouse and a Country Mouse").

WRITINGS—All self-illustrated: *The Day Chiro Was Lost* (translated from original Japanese), World Publishing, 1969; *Taro to iruka,* Fukuinkan, 1969, translation published as *Fumio and the Dolphins,* World Publishing, 1970; *Machi no nezumi to inaka no nezumi* (adapted from Ruri Nagano's translation of an English adaptation of Aesop's fable, "A Town Mouse and a Country Mouse"), Fukuinkan, 1971; *Boku no uchi no dobutsuen,* Fukuinkan, 1971, translation published as *The Zoo in My Garden,* Crowell, 1973; *My Teddy Bear* (translated from original Japanese), Crowell, 1975; *My Day on the Farm* (translated from original Japanese), Crowell, 1976.

Also illustrator of more than twenty books for children, including Soya Kiyoshi, *Ruru no tanjobi* (title means "The Kitten Ruru's Birthday"), [Japan], 1971; Eriko Kishida, *The Lion and the Bird's Nest,* Crowell, 1973.

SIDELIGHTS: Nakatani told *CA:* "Since my childhood I liked to draw pictures imagining scenes of my favorite fairy tales. After graduating from the university I held after-school painting classes for children in my home. It was in those days that I began to illustrate children's books with enthusiasm. I wished to give good picture books to children in order to add a good element to their environment.

"I take interest in traveling," Nakatani continued. "I especially like to go to places, such as mountains and stock farms, which are not contaminated by modern civilization. I have a country house at the seaside, one hundred fifty kilometers from Tokyo. The house is situated in a beautiful place between the Pacific Ocean and the mountains. I draw pictures and try lithographs there. During spring and summer holidays, my beloved nephews often come from Tokyo to stay for several days. I enjoy taking a walk, fishing, and swimming with them. When I am observing children's emotions, new ideas for books spring inside me.

"When I illustrate children's books, I like to draw realistic pictures in order to express the scenes of the stories. I consider the rhythms of lines and the harmony of colors to be most important."

BIOGRAPHICAL/CRITICAL SOURCES: Bettina Hurli-mann, *Seven Houses,* Bodley Head, 1976.

* * *

NAKHLEH, Emile A. 1938-

PERSONAL: Born May 25, 1938, in Palestine; came to the United States in 1960, naturalized citizen, 1970; son of Abdalla and Labibeh (Shiban) Nakhleh; married Mary Bird (a science teacher), December 25, 1965; children: Charles Walid, Richard Riyad. *Education:* St. John's University, Collegeville, Minn., B.A., 1963; Georgetown University, M.A., 1966; American University, Ph.D., 1968. *Politics:* "Respect for Human Rights." *Religion:* Melkite. *Home:* 35 Park Dr., Emmitsburg, Md. 21727. *Office:* Department of History and Political Science, Mount St. Mary's College, Emmitsburg, Md. 21727.

CAREER: Mount St. Mary's College, Emmitsburg, Md.,

assistant professor, 1967-71, associate professor, 1971-76, professor of history and political science, 1976—, chairman of department, 1975—. Lecturer for Foreign Service Institute. Member of local planning and zoning commission, 1971-75, and member of city council. Consultant to Abbot Associates. *Member:* International Studies Association, American Political Science Association, American Society of International Law, Middle East Institute, Middle East Studies Association, Pi Sigma Alpha. *Awards, honors:* Fulbright senior fellowship, 1972-73.

WRITINGS: Arab-American Relations in the Persian Gulf, American Enterprise Institute for Public Policy Research, 1975; *The United States and Saudi Arabia: A Policy Analysis,* American Enterprise Institute for Public Policy Research, 1975; (editor with wife, Mary B. Nakhleh) *Emmitsburg: History and Society,* Emmitsburg Chronicle Press, 1976; *Bahrain: Political Development in a Modernizing Society,* Lexington Books, 1976. Contributor to Middle East studies journals.

WORK IN PROGRESS: Research on U.S. foreign policy in the Persian Gulf and Arabian Peninsula and on the Palestine conflict.

SIDELIGHTS: Nakhleh writes: "I am an American professor of Palestinian origin. My family and I reside in Maryland, to which we have become attached. I enjoy being involved in local politics. I have traveled extensively and have done field research in Bahrain, Saudi Arabia, Qatar, Israel, and the West Bank. I support a peaceful solution to the Palestine conflict. Furthermore, I am professionally interested in the making and execution of American foreign policy, particularly in the eastern Mediterranean, the Middle East, the Persian Gulf, and the Indian Ocean."

* * *

NALLIN, Walter E.   1917(?)-1978

1917(?)—April 26, 1978; American educator and author. In addition to his teaching positions at universities in New York, N.Y., Nallin also performed in professional orchestras on NBC, CBS, and independent radio stations as a clarinet recitalist and conductor. He wrote *The Musical Idea: A Consideration of Music and Its Ways.* Nallin died in Ridgewood, N.J. Obituaries and other sources: *New York Times,* April 28, 1978.

* * *

NAPIER, William
See SEYMOUR, William

* * *

NASKE, Claus-M(ichael)   1935-

PERSONAL: Born December 18, 1935, in Stettin, Germany; son of Alfred (an army officer) and Kaethe (Salomon) Naske; married Dinah Ariss (a teacher), May 20, 1960; children: Natalia-Michelle Nau-geak, Nathaniel-Michael Noah. *Education:* University of Alaska, B.A., 1961; University of Michigan, M.A., 1964; Washington State University, Ph.D., 1970. *Politics:* Independent. *Office:* Department of History, University of Alaska, Fairbanks, Alaska 99701.

CAREER: Farm laborer in Palmer, Alaska, 1954-56; surveyor in Palmer and Fairbanks, Alaska, 1957-61, and Monterey, Calif., 1962; Bureau of Indian Affairs, Barrow, Alaska, teacher, 1964-65; Juneau-Douglas Community College, Juneau, Alaska, instructor in history and political science, 1965-67; University of Alaska, Fairbanks, 1969—, began as

assistant professor, became professor of history. Member of board of directors of Pacific Northwest History Conference, 1970—; chairman of board of directors of Alaska Humanities Forum; consultant to Bureau of Land Management. *Military service:* U.S. Army Reserve, 1961.

MEMBER: American Historical Association, Organization of American Historians, Association for Canadian Studies in the United States, Canadian Historical Association, Alaska Historical Society, Tanana-Yukon Historical Society (past president).

WRITINGS: An Interpretive History of Alaskan Statehood, Alaska Northwest Publishing, 1973. Contributor to *Alaska Journal.*

WORK IN PROGRESS: E. L. "Bob" Bartlett of Alaska; A Modern History of Alaska; research on Ernest Gruening, territorial governor of Alaska, 1939-53, and on coal mining in Alaska.

SIDELIGHTS: Naske comments: "I am damn glad I made it to America and was able to leave Europe behind. American society is fascinating—I wake up each morning, realizing with great joy that I am doing what I want to do, and getting paid for it on top of it all. What a life!"

* * *

NASON, Alvin   1919-1978

June 10, 1919—January 28, 1978; American educator, research biochemist, and author best known for his contribution to research on enzyme processes in various forms of life. An educator of biology at Johns Hopkins, Nason wrote more than one hundred papers on the use of nitrogen as a life source by plants. From 1957 to 1978, Nason was the editor-in-chief of *Analytical Biochemistry* magazine. He was the author of two textbooks. Nason died in Baltimore, Md. Obituaries and other sources: *American Men and Women of Science,* 13th edition, Bowker, 1976; *Who's Who in America,* 39th edition, Marquis, 1976; *The Writers Directory, 1976-78,* St. Martin's, 1976; *New York Times,* January 31, 1978; *Washington Post,* January 31, 1978.

* * *

NATHANSON, Yale S(amuel)   1895-

PERSONAL: Born March 25, 1895, in Philadelphia, Pa.; son of Joseph Oscar (a linguist) and Esther (Goldberg) Nathanson; married wife Nola, May 6, 1925 (deceased); married Juliet Eshner (a physician), September 27, 1930; children: Josephine Wright, Erika. *Education:* Attended Lock Haven State Normal School; University of Pennsylvania, B.Sc., 1923, M.A., 1924, Ph.D., 1930. *Religion:* Jewish. *Home and office:* 2048 Pine St., Philadelphia, Pa. 19103.

CAREER: University of Pennsylvania, Philadelphia, instructor in psychology, 1927-37; Temple University, Philadelphia, assistant professor of speech correction, 1937-45; director, Psychological Resource Center, 1945-69; psychologist in private practice, Philadelphia, 1969—. Lecturer at colleges and universities, including Philadelphia College of Art, American University, and University of Massachusetts. Consultant to U.S. Department of Health, Education, and Welfare and Bureau of Vocational Rehabilitation. Regular commentator on national radio programs for NBC and CBS. *Military service:* U.S. Army, served in World War I and 1942-45; became lieutenant colonel. *Member:* American Psychological Association (fellow), American Speech and Hearing Association (fellow), Professional Rehabilitation Workers with the Adult Deaf.

WRITINGS: *So Winds the River* (novel), Impress House, 1972. Author of numerous textbooks. Author of nationally syndicated columns, including "Odd Facts about Yourself."

WORK IN PROGRESS: *Glorious Transition,* completion expected in 1978.

SIDELIGHTS: Nathanson told *CA:* "My greatest attention currently is in the field of deafness. Some years ago I adopted an eight and a half year old refugee who had no speech. I devoted myself to learning total communication, teaching her. She has now graduated from college (specialized in art), speaks well (of course, cannot hear), and is a delightful, most unusual, and beautiful character."

*   *   *

NAUMANN, Oscar E(dward)   1912-

PERSONAL: Born June 15, 1912, in New York, N.Y.; son of Oscar C. and Josephine (Ridder) Naumann; married Maria Martinez, May 30, 1942; children: Nancy (Mrs. Thomas Jones, Jr.), Melinda Maria (Mrs. Darryl Bates), Victoria Ridder. *Education:* Attended Columbia University, 1930-33. *Home:* 2722 Cortland Pl. N.W., Washington, D.C. 20008. *Office:* 1325 E St. N.W., Washington, D.C. 20004.

CAREER/WRITINGS: *Journal of Commerce,* New York, N.Y., reporter in New York City, 1940-42, and Washington, D.C., 1942-50, Washington bureau chief, 1950—. Notable assignments include coverage of war effort and price controls, 1942-45. *Member:* National Press Club, Capitol Hill Club, Overseas Writers Club, International Club, Chesapeake Yacht Club, Zeta Psi.

*   *   *

NEFF, Donald   1930-

PERSONAL: Born October 15, 1930, in York, Pa.; son of Harry and Gertrude (Kessler) Neff. *Education:* Attended York College, 1950-52, and New York University, 1952-53. *Home:* 2 Diskin, Kiryat Wolfson, Rahavia, Jerusalem, Israel. *Office: Time,* Beit Agron, Jerusalem, Israel.

CAREER/WRITINGS: *Los Angeles Mirror-News,* Los Angeles, Calif., reporter, 1955-58; United Press International, New York City, reporter in Los Angeles, 1958-60; *Los Angeles Times,* Los Angeles, reporter, 1960-63, correspondent in Tokyo, 1963-64; *Time,* New York City, correspondent in Viet Nam, 1965-66, contributing editor, 1967-68, Houston bureau chief, 1968-70, Los Angeles bureau chief, 1970-73, senior editor, 1973-75, Jerusalem bureau chief, 1975—. Notable assignments include coverage of the Apollo moonlanding program, the Mariner Mars program, the U.S. presidential campaign, 1972, the Sinai interim agreement, 1976, and Anwar Sadat's visit to Jerusalem, 1977.

*   *   *

NELSON, James C(ecil)   1908-

PERSONAL: Born October 5, 1908, in Bickleton, Wash.; son of James Christian (a farmer) and Anna (Boysen) Nelson; married Helen Catherine Sands (a history teacher), October 24, 1935; children: James Christian, Richard William. *Education:* University of Washington, Seattle, B.A., 1930; Ohio State University, M.A., 1931; University of Virginia, Ph.D., 1934. *Politics:* Republican. *Religion:* Unitarian-Universalist. *Home and office:* Northeast 1036 D St., Pullman, Wash. 99163.

CAREER: U.S. Department of Commerce, Washington, D.C., chief of Transportation Division, 1945-47; Washington State University, Pullman, professor of economics, 1947-74, professor emeritus, 1974—. Research fellow at Brookings Institution, 1933-34. Guest professor of Monash University and University of British Columbia. Consultant to state legislatures and federal agencies. *Member:* American Economic Association, American Society of Traffic and Transportation (founder member), Transportation Research Forum (founder member), American Association of University Professors (past local president), Western Economic Association, Phi Beta Kappa, Beta Gamma Sigma. *Awards, honors:* Social Science Research Council grant, 1938-39; award from American Economic Association, 1971, in recognition of outstanding contributions to scholarship in the field of transportation and public utilities.

WRITINGS: *Railway Transportation and Public Policy,* Brookings Institution, 1959; (with T. D. Heaver) *Railway Pricing under Commercial Freedom: The Canadian Experience,* Center for Transportation Studies, University of British Columbia, 1977; *Regulatory Performance of Surface Freight Transport in Australia, Britain, Canada, and the United States,* National Bureau of Economic Research, 1979. Contributor to economic and transportation studies journals.

SIDELIGHTS: Nelson writes: "I write to apply economic theory to transport problems, and to explain what appear to be economic solutions for public policy. I was the original American economist to analyze the economic effects of Interstate Commerce Commission regulation of motor carriers and later comers, restrictive of competition and protective regulation lessening competition, encouraging rate cartels, fragmenting markets, and contributing to the decline of the U.S. railways. I am the 'father' of transport deregulation in the United States, an issue to which much attention is being given by the Congress, the White House, the Interstate Commerce Commission, and the public in the 1970's."

Nelson has conducted research in Australia, Canada, and western Europe.

*   *   *

NELSON, Kent   1943-

PERSONAL: Born April 21, 1943, in Cincinnati, Ohio. *Home address:* P.O. Box 413, Ouray, Colo. 81427.

CAREER: Writer.

WRITINGS: *The Tennis Player and Other Stories,* University of Illinois Press, 1977.

*   *   *

NELSON, W(esley) Dale   1927-

PERSONAL: Born March 16, 1927, in Bremerton, Wash.; son of Andrew Lee (a logger) and Alice Levelle (Newby) Nelson; married Beverly Strobeck, May 8, 1950 (divorced, 1966); married Joyce Ellen Miller, December 31, 1966; children: Eric Christopher, Kirsten Lee, Barbara West, Mark Andrew. *Education:* University of Puget Sound, A.B., 1949; University of Washington, M.L.S., 1951. *Religion:* Episcopalian. *Home:* 8048 Fairfax Rd., Alexandria, Va. 22308. *Office:* Associated Press, 2021 K St., Washington, D.C. 20006.

CAREER/WRITINGS: *Tacoma News Tribune,* Tacoma, Wash., reporter, 1951-52; Associated Press, New York, N.Y., newsman in Boise, Idaho, 1952-59, Seattle, Wash., 1959-67, correspondent in Olympia, Wash., 1967-73, newsman in Washington, D.C., 1973—. Notable assignments include coverage of the Alaska earthquake, 1964, the U.S. Supreme Court, 1974-76, and the Watergate tapes. Contributor to periodicals, including articles in the *Washington Post* and poetry in *New Yorker* and *New York Times*. *Military service:* U.S. Navy, 1945. *Member:* Washington Press Club. *Awards, honors:* Washington State Sigma Delta Chi award for reporting, 1965.

* * *

NESBITT, Paul H(omer) 1904-

PERSONAL: Born August 15, 1904, in Savanna, Ill.; son of Thomas Elmer (a merchant) and Estelle (Grayless) Nesbitt; married Antoinette Rogers, March 18, 1927 (divorced, 1945); married Helen Stone Devine, October 22, 1954; children: Thomas R., James R. *Education:* Beloit College, B.A., 1926; University of Chicago, M.A., 1930, Ph.D., 1938. *Politics:* Republican. *Religion:* Congregationalist. *Home:* 9-I Northwood Lake, Northport, Ala. 35476. *Office:* P.O. Box 1456, University, Ala. 35486.

CAREER: Beloit College, Beloit, Wis., assistant professor, 1930-35, associate professor, 1935-37, professor of anthropology, 1937-45, curator of Logan Museum, 1935-45; National Museum of Guatemala, Guatemala City, technical director, 1946-48; Arctic-Desert-Tropic Information Center, Maxwell Air Force Base, Ala., director and film consultant, 1948-67; University of Alabama at Tuscaloosa, University, professor of anthropology and chairman of department, 1967-74, professor emeritus, 1974—. Leader of archaeology and life science expeditions to Algeria, France, Mexico, Yucatan, Puerto Rico, Venezuela, Greenland, Panama, and Southeast Asia. *Military service:* U.S. Army Air Corps, Office of Strategic Services, 1943-45; became captain.

MEMBER: Arctic Institute of North America, American Anthropological Association (fellow), Society for American Archaeology (fellow), American Association for the Advancement of Science (fellow), American Association of Physical Anthropologists, Alabama Academy of Science (vice-president, 1965), Sigma Xi, Beta Theta Pi, Explorers Club, Rotary International, University Club, North River Yacht Club. *Awards, honors:* Lapham Medal from Wisconsin Historical Society, 1946, for contributions to Wisconsin archaeology.

WRITINGS: The Ancient Mimbrenos, Beloit College, 1931; *Starkweather Ruin,* Beloit College, 1938; (editor) *U.S. Air Force Survival Manual,* U.S. Government Printing Office, 1950, revised edition, 1954; *Ethnic Minorities,* Air University, 1951, 4th edition, 1956; (with Alonzo W. Pond and William H. Allen) *The Survival Book,* Van Nostrand, 1962; (contributor) H. Herman Friis, editor, *U.S. Polar Expeditions,* Ohio University Press, 1970; (contributor) Edward Moseley and Edward Terry, editors, *Yucatan: A World Apart,* University of Alabama Press, 1978; *A Pilot's Survival Manual,* Van Nostrand, in press. Contributor to professional magazines, including *American Antiquity, Explorers Club,* and *Southeastern Latin Americanist.*

* * *

NETTELS, Elsa 1931-

PERSONAL: Born May 25, 1931, in Madison, Wis.; daughter of Curtis Putnam (a historian) and Elsie (Patterson) Nettels. *Education:* Cornell University, B.A., 1953; University of Wisconsin, Madison, M.A., 1955, Ph.D., 1960. *Home:* 201 Indian Springs Rd., Williamsburg, Va. 23185. *Office:* Department of English, College of William and Mary, Williamsburg, Va. 23185.

CAREER: Mt. Holyoke College, South Hadley, Mass., instructor, 1959-62, assistant professor of English, 1963-67; College of William and Mary, Williamsburg, Va., assistant professor, 1967-69, associate professor, 1969-75, professor of English, 1975—. *Member:* Modern Language Association of America, Joseph Conrad Society, South Atlantic Modern Language Association. *Awards, honors:* Award from South Atlantic Modern Language Association, 1975, for *James and Conrad.*

WRITINGS: James and Conrad, University of Georgia Press, 1977. Contributor to literature and library journals.

WORK IN PROGRESS: Research on nineteenth-century American literature, especially fiction.

* * *

NEWMAN, Coleman J. 1935-

PERSONAL: Born February 17, 1935, in Montreal, Quebec, Canada; son of Leon Yehuda (a manufacturer) and Annie (Dubin) Newman; married wife, Frances Margaret, May 7, 1962 (separated, 1977); children: Rafael, Adam, Zoe. *Education:* Sir George Williams University, B.A., 1959; graduate study at University of Toronto, 1959-60, and Marianapolis College, 1967-68. *Politics:* Socialist. *Residence:* Vancouver, British Columbia, Canada. *Agent:* Timothy Seldes, Russell & Volkening, Inc., 551 Fifth Ave., New York, N.Y. 10017. *Office:* Department of Creative Writing, University of British Columbia, Vancouver, British Columbia, Canada.

CAREER: Sir George Williams University, Montreal, Quebec, lecturer in English, 1960-66; McGill University, Montreal, assistant professor of English, 1966-71; Sir George Williams University, assistant professor of English, 1971-72; University of British Columbia, Vancouver, assistant professor of creative writing, 1972—. Assistant professor at MacDonald College, 1966-71, and Sir George Williams University, 1967-69. Has given readings from his work.

MEMBER: Writers Union of Canada, University of British Columbia Faculty Association. *Awards, honors:* Woodrow Wilson fellowship, 1959; Lieutenant-Governor General's Medal for Creative Expression, 1959; first prize in short story category from Canadian Broadcasting Corp. Canadian Writing Competition, 1963.

WRITINGS: We Always Take Care of Our Own, McClelland & Stewart, 1965; (co-author) *New Canadian Writing, 1969* (stories), Clarke, Irwin, 1969; *A Russian Novel,* New Press, 1973.

Also author of plays broadcast by Canadian Broadcasting Corp., including "All the State Children Got Shoes" (radio play), "The Jam on Garry's Books" (radio play), "A Work of Art" (radio and television play), "The Last Potato" (radio play), and "The Birth of a Salesman" (television play).

Contributor of about sixty stories, poems, articles, and reviews to literary journals, including *Canadian Forum, Fiddlehead, Tamarack Review,* and *Quarry. Prism International,* associate editor, 1972-74, 1975, acting editor-in-chief, 1974-75.

WORK IN PROGRESS: A collection of short stories and a collection of poems; novels, including *Conversations of a Father and Son, The Zen Thief, The Longest Undefended Border in the World,* and *Red Zinger* (working title).

NEWMYER, R. Kent 1930-

PERSONAL: Born May 18, 1930, in Nebraska; married, December 22, 1956; children: two sons, one daughter. Education: Doane College, B.A., 1952; University of Nebraska, Ph.D., 1959. Home: 19 Center St., Mansfield Center, Conn. 06250. Office: Department of History, University of Connecticut, Storrs, Conn. 06268.

CAREER: University of Connecticut, Storrs, professor of history, 1960—. Military service: U.S. Army, 1952-54; became sergeant.

WRITINGS: The Supreme Court Under Marshall and Taney, Crowell, 1968.

WORK IN PROGRESS: A biography of Supreme Court justice Joseph Story.

*   *   *

NEWTON, Ray C(lyde) 1935-

PERSONAL: Born September 26, 1935, in Denver, Colo.; son of Louis W. and Thelma (Sipe) Newton; married Patricia Boekhaus (a teacher), December 27, 1956; children: Sheri, Lynn, William. Education: Fort Hays Kansas State University, A.B., 1957; South Dakota State University, M.S., 1961; further graduate study at New Mexico Highlands University, 1968, and University of Texas, 1971-72. Religion: Methodist. Home: 1520 Appalachian, Flagstaff, Ariz. 86001. Office: Department of Journalism, Northern Arizona University, Box 6001, Flagstaff, Ariz. 86011.

CAREER: Rush County News, LaCrosse, Kan., reporter, 1957-59; Santa Fe New Mexican, Santa Fe, reporter, 1961-63; New Mexico Highlands University, Las Vegas, director of public information and public relations, 1963-73; Northern Arizona University, Flagstaff, associate professor of journalism and chairman of department, 1973—. Special correspondent for Associated Press New Mexico Bureau, 1963-71; reporter and photographer for KGGM-TV, 1964-71; public speaker and communications consultant.

MEMBER: Associated Press Managing Editors Association, Association for Education in Journalism, Football Writers of America, American Heart Association (chairman of board of directors), Arizona Press Association, Sigma Delta Chi, Kiwanis International (district chairman). Awards, honors: Citation from Public Relations Society of America, 1967; citation from American Heart Association, 1972, for public relations; citation from Boy Scouts of America, 1977, for outstanding media contributions to Boy Scout program.

WRITINGS: Propaganda and Persuasion, with filmstrip, Prentice-Hall, 1975. Contributor of articles and photographs to professional journals and recreation magazines.

WORK IN PROGRESS: Research for APME Redbook; research for Mountainwest magazine on best fishing spots; research for National Geographic on Arizona.

SIDELIGHTS: Newton writes: "Circumstances largely beyond my control have directed the vocational-professional direction of my life. In most instances, I happened to be at the right place at the right time to get the right assignment.

"Over the years, I have turned from the generalist to the specialist in terms of journalistic interests. Presently, my efforts are by and large aimed at developing professional skills and attitudes among younger writers—college students, in this case. My central focus has been upon developing students who combine ecological-environmental interests with writing, my thought being that knowledgeable environmental writers will be drawing the prime assignments and writing the major stories of the coming decades.

"I have traveled overseas on assignments—the South Pacific notably, where I wrote of the economy, customs, and cultures of persons living there for Associated Press. I also worked as a consultant in Mexico, training journalists in Nuevo Leon—a challenging experience. In all, journalism has been rewarding and stimulating."

*   *   *

NICHOLS, Jeannette 1931-

PERSONAL: Born May 24, 1931, in New Haven, Conn.; daughter of Sylvester E. and Cona (Alderson) Nichols; married Shepard Murdock (a contractor), December 14, 1974. Home: 5 Glen Haven Rd., East Haven, Conn. 06513. Office: Jonathan Edwards College, Yale University, New Haven, Conn. 06513.

CAREER: Poet.

WRITINGS: Mostly People (poems), Rutgers University Press, 1966; Emblems of Passage (poems), Rutgers University Press, 1968.

WORK IN PROGRESS: Another book of poems.

*   *   *

NICHOLS, Peter
See YOUD, Samuel

*   *   *

NICKERSON, Betty 1922-

PERSONAL: Born June 26, 1922, in Fort Scott, Kan.; came to Canada, 1954; daughter of Clarence T. (a stonemason) and Helen (a caterer; maiden name, Smiley) Smith; married, July 25, 1942 (divorced); children: Stephen, Michael, Marki (daughter). Education: Attended Oregon State University, 1939-42, and Goucher College, 1943-44; University of Utah, B.A., 1946; University of Manitoba, M.A., 1965; graduate study at McGill University, 1972. Home: Rideau Rd., Kars, Ontario, Canada K0A 2E0. Office: All About Us/Nous Autres, Inc., Box 1985, Ottawa, Ontario, Canada K1P 5R5.

CAREER: Canadian Broadcasting Corp. (CBC), Winnipeg, Manitoba, performer in television arts and crafts series, 1957-65; EXPO-67, Montreal, Quebec, consultant for "Man the Creator" exhibit, 1967; Man and His World (permanent exhibition), Montreal, director and exhibitor of "From Youth With Love," 1968; All About Us/Nous Autres, Inc. (foundation for young Canadian writers and artists), Ottawa, founder and national coordinator, and project director for literary quarterly, Nous Journal, 1972—. Consultant for UNESCO "Education Through Art" project, 1967-68; Canadian national committee of United Nations Children's Fund, member, 1967-68, conductor of study tour in India and Thailand; member of Advisory Committee on Human Rights. Member: Association of Cultural Executives, Society for Education Through Art, Phi Beta Kappa. Awards, honors: India Council fellowship, 1967; British Council fellowship, 1968; Canada Council travel grant, 1972.

WRITINGS: How the World Grows Its Food, McGraw, 1966; Celebrate the Sun, Lippincott, 1969; Chi: Letters from Biafra, New Press (Toronto), 1970; (editor) Girls Will Be Women, All About Us, 1976. Also author of Of You and Me: A Contemporary View of Human Rights, 1977.

WORK IN PROGRESS: Ring of Changes, a book on cultural interaction in Canadian society; Ceremony in Aneverly, a utopian novel of a society based on positive human interaction; research on creativity in children.

SIDELIGHTS: Nickerson wrote: "My interests and concern for many years has centered around what people can do when they do their very best. This particularly applies to young people and their creative efforts. When people try to do their very best, they create marvelous paintings, poems, structures, families, communities, and this, to me, is a vitally important survival skill. When human beings try to make things better, to make them beautiful, or to make them work well, they are never destructive or hurtful to themselves, to others, or to their environment.

"Despite the ugliness, meanness, greed, and hurt that surrounds us, I remain convinced that human beings have the power to make a paradise of beauty, caring, and growth. It could happen if we all did our best to make things better, so I try in whatever ways come to hand—only a little of it is writing. For the past four years I have directed a project to discover the creativity of young Canadians, kids of six to eighteen. And it has been a magnificent experience. My respect for young writers and artists, for the ability of young people to state the conditions, needs, hopes, joys, and concerns of the world they are growing into increases daily.

"Kids respond to the idea of making responsible statements, and they appear willing to make the effort to act responsibly and with imagination. The real difficulty is in finding a way in which their ideas can enter the mainstream of society, and I'm certain that is true not only in Canada, but in all the world. If I can do anything to help bring that about, I do it. The world will be a reasonable place if we who live in it act reasonably—as individuals, citizens, workers, artists, parents—human beings. I believe that we could combine all our skills, customs, and knowledge taking the best of them, and make a masterpiece of human achievement from our best pieces. These are the things I write about, especially for young people."

*   *   *

NICKERSON, Jane Soames

PERSONAL: Education: Earned B.A. from Oxford University. *Home address:* P.O. Box 458, Oyster Bay, N.Y. 11771.

CAREER: Secretary to journalist Hilaire Belloc; writer.

WRITINGS: A Short History of North Africa, from Pre-Roman Times to the Present: Libya, Tunisia, Algeria, Morocco, Devin-Adair, 1961; (editor) Hilaire Belloc, *Belloc,* Allen & Unwin, 1970; *Homage to Malthus,* Kennikat, 1975. Also author of *The English Press* and *The Coast of Barbary.* Translator of *The Origins of the First World War* (from the French) and of *The Political and Social Doctrine of Fascism* (from the Italian).

*   *   *

NIEBUHR, Richard R. 1926-

PERSONAL: Born March 9, 1926, in Chicago, Ill.; son of H. Richard (a teacher) and Florence Marie (Mittendorf) Niebuhr; married Nancy Mullican, October 14, 1950; children: R. Gustav, Sarah Louise. *Education:* Harvard University, A.B., 1947; attended Westminster Theological College, Cambridge, England, 1948-49; Union Theological Seminary, New York, N.Y., B.D., 1950; Yale University, Ph.D., 1955. *Politics:* Democrat. *Office:* Study of Religion, Harvard University, Harvard Union, Cambridge, Mass. 02138.

CAREER: Ordained Congregational minister; pastor of Congregational church in Cornwall, Conn., 1950-52; Vassar College, Poughkeepsie, N.Y., lecturer in religion, 1954-56; Harvard University, Cambridge, Mass., assistant professor, 1956-59, associate professor, 1959-63, Lamont Professor of Divinity, 1963—. *Member:* American Academy of Arts and Sciences, American Theological Society, Phi Beta Kappa.

WRITINGS: Resurrection and Historical Reason, Scribner, 1957; *Schleiermacher on Christ and Religion,* Scribner, 1964; (contributor) Funk, editor, *Schleiermacher as Contemporary,* Herder, 1970; *Experiential Religion,* Harper, 1972. Associate editor of *Harvard Theological Review,* 1964-74; member of editorial committee of "The Works of Jonathan Edwards."

WORK IN PROGRESS: Visual and Spatial Elements in Religious Imagination; research on Samuel Taylor Coleridge.

SIDELIGHTS: Niebuhr comments: "Teaching, my occupation, is my strongest motivation for writing."

AVOCATIONAL INTERESTS: The arts, photography (especially American landscape and documentary photography), wilderness travel.

*   *   *

NIEMI, John A. 1932-

PERSONAL: Born December 6, 1932, in Ironwood, Mich.; son of Arvo J. and Eva (Remes) Niemi; married Muriel Tomkins, December 11, 1968. *Education:* Gogebic Community College, A.A., 1952; Michigan State University, B.A., 1954; University of Alaska, M.Ed., 1963; University of California, Los Angeles, Ed.D., 1967. *Politics:* Independent. *Religion:* Lutheran. *Home:* 807 Ridge Rd., #901, DeKalb, Ill. 60115. *Office:* Northern Illinois University, 204 Gabel Hall, DeKalb, Ill. 60115.

CAREER: University of Alaska, Fairbanks, assistant to the president, 1961-62, head of evening, off-campus, and correspondence department, 1962-64; University of California, Los Angeles, extension specialist, 1964-66; University of British Columbia, Vancouver, associate professor of adult education, 1966-75; Northern Illinois University, DeKalb, professor of adult education, 1975—. *Member:* Adult Education Association of the United States (chairman of Commission on Research in Adult Education, 1972-74), National Association for Public Continuing and Adult Education, Northwest Adult Education Association (president, 1974-75).

WRITINGS: (Editor with Darrell V. Anderson, and contributor) *Adult Education and the Disadvantaged Adult,* Syracuse University Publications in Continuing Education, 1970; (editor) *Mass Media and Adult Education,* Educational Technology Publications, 1971; (editor with Daniel C. Jessen, and contributor) *Directory of Resources in Adult Education,* ERIC Clearinghouse in Career Education, 1976; (with Stanley M. Grabowski and Elizabeth Kuusisto) *Research and Investigation in Adult Education Register,* ERIC Clearinghouse in Career Education, 1976. Contributing editor of *Educational Broadcasting,* 1971—; international book review editor of *Adult Leadership,* 1971-74; associate editor of *Lifelong Learning: The Adult Years,* 1977—.

WORK IN PROGRESS: Revising *Adult Education and the Disadvantaged Adult.*

SIDELIGHTS: Niemi writes: "As an adult educator, I have focused my writing on the learning needs of culturally different groups and on means whereby to deliver educational programs, which include both traditional and nontraditional (mass media) approaches.''

* * *

NIES, Judith 1941-

PERSONAL: Born September 23, 1941, in Boston, Mass.; daughter of Charles Raymond (a factory worker) and Lillian (Farrell) Nies; married J. Hugh McFadden, October 28, 1967 (divorced, 1974); children: Cristina Alexandra. *Education:* Tufts University, B.A., 1962; Bologna Center for International Studies, certificate, 1964; also attended University of Paris, 1964; Johns Hopkins School of Advanced International Studies, M.A., 1965. *Home and office:* 84 Pleasant St., Marblehead, Mass. 01945. *Agent:* Elaine Markson Literary Agency, Inc., 44 Greenwich Ave., New York, N.Y. 10011.

CAREER: Women's International League for Peace and Freedom, Washington, D.C., director of Washington office, 1968-69; U.S. Congress, Washington, D.C., special assistant and speechwriter for Congressman Donald M. Fraser, 1969-72; State of Massachusetts, Boston, assistant secretary of environmental affairs, 1975; Judith Nies Associates, Marblehead, Mass., writer and communications consultant, 1976—. Member of board of directors of North Shore Woman's School. *Member:* Women's Equity Action League.

WRITINGS: (Editor with Erwin Knoll) *American Militarism 1970*, Viking, 1969; (editor with Knoll) *War Crimes and the American Conscience*, Holt, 1970; *Seven Women: Portraits from the American Radical Tradition*, Viking, 1976. Contributor to national magazines, including *Progressive* and *Ms.*

WORK IN PROGRESS: Roads Not Yet Taken, a guidebook to Massachusetts through the eyes of women writers; *Who Shall Preach?: Essays on Women Priests in America.*

SIDELIGHTS: Judith Nies writes: ''My professional work experience has mostly been in politics. My writing has generally dealt with questions of women and power. The two activities—the direct practical experience in politics and the synthesizing through writing—are intertwined.

''Although in my writing I use the vocabulary of history and politics, I am also concerned with dreams, folklore, awareness, memory, and collective consciousness. Underlying the topics I choose is a sense that in women's consciousness of the past there is power for the future. I do not think that the personal is separate from the political or that emotions are irrelevant to history. It is a distorted vision of the historian's craft that has kept history a story of the wars of kings and the hero's quest for power.''

AVOCATIONAL INTERESTS: Travel, architecture, archaeology, art (''with a small 'a' ''), juggling (''which a friend has called a personal metaphor, because it is an ancient art, it involves balance, concentration, symbolism of women's role in modern culture, and it is fun'').

* * *

NIIZAKA, Kazuo 1943-

PERSONAL: Born April 14, 1943, in Saitam, Japan; son of Seisaku (a restaurant manager) and Kikue (a restaurant manager) Niisaka. *Education:* Attended industrial high school in Kitatoshima, Japan. *Home:* 22-1 Shirako 2-chome, Wako-shi, Saitam-ken, Japan.

CAREER: Nanboku-Sha Co. (advertising agency), Tokyo,

Japan, clerk, 1963-65; Niisaka's Studio, Tokyo, manager and kite designer, 1975—. *Member:* Dobiren (Association of Japanese Illustrators of Children's Books).

WRITINGS—Children's books; all self-illustrated: *Nohara de Dotten To*, Shiko-Sha, 1971, adaptation by Henry Stanton published as *Clouds*, Addison-Wesley, 1975; *Todai no Himawari* (title means ''Sunflower at Lighthouse''), Fukuinkan, 1973; *Yoake no Umi* (title means ''Sea at Dawn''), Shiko-Sha, 1974; *Musubi* (title means ''Knots for Fun''), Fukuinkan, 1975; *Hatsumei Dako* (title means ''Let's Have Fun With Kites''), Fukuinkan, 1975.

Illustrator: Yoshihiko Funasaki, *Ashita Tonde Ike* (title means ''Fly Away Tomorrow''), Kaisei-Sha, 1975. Illustrator for ''Ikuji-Ran,'' a column on child care in *Tokyo Shinbun.*

WORK IN PROGRESS: The White Owl's Adventure, the story of a last owl searching for his mother; a love story for adults, *Shiro-Fukuro-No-Boken.*

SIDELIGHTS: As a child, Niizaka enjoyed drawing and reading. Then he spent a whole year in blindness. When his eyesight returned, he appreciated his vision much more and began painting, which led to a career of writing and illustration. *Avocational interests:* Making ceramics, reading.

* * *

NISSENBAUM, Stephen 1941-

PERSONAL: Born January 13, 1941, in Jersey City, N.J.; son of Alexander W. (a businessman) and Claire (Willner) Nissenbaum; married Judith Schwartz (a musician), February 3, 1962; children: Paul, Jon, Jeffrey, Daniel. *Education:* Harvard University, A.B., 1961; Columbia University, M.A., 1963; University of Wisconsin, Ph.D., 1968. *Home:* 180 Lincoln Ave., Amherst, Mass. 01002. *Office:* Department of History, University of Massachusetts, Amherst, Mass. 01002.

CAREER: University of Massachusetts, Amherst, assistant professor, 1968-72, associate professor of history, 1972—. *Member:* American Historical Association, Organization of American Historians, American Studies Association. *Awards, honors:* John H. Dunning Prize from American Historical Association, 1974, and nomination for National Book Award, 1975, both for *Salem Possessed;* National Endowment for the Humanities Fellowship, 1976-77; Charles Warren Fellowship, 1976-77.

WRITINGS: (Editor) *The Great Awakening at Yale College,* Wadsworth, 1972; (editor with Paul Boyer) *Salem-Village Witchcraft,* Wadsworth, 1972; (with Boyer) *Salem Possessed: The Social Origins of Witchcraft,* Harvard University Press, 1974; (editor with Boyer) *The Salem Witchcraft Papers,* Da Capo Press, 1977.

WORK IN PROGRESS: Research on Nathaniel Hawthorne and on nineteenth century sexuality.

* * *

NIVEN, (James) David (Graham) 1910-

PERSONAL: Born March 1, 1910, in Kirriemuir, Scotland; son of William Edward Graham Niven (a lieutenant) and Henriette (Degacher) Niven Comyn-Platt; married Primula Rollo, 1940 (died May 21, 1946); married Hjordis Tersmeden, January 14, 1948; children: David, James Graham, Kristina, Fiona. *Education:* Attended Royal Military College, Sandhurst. *Home:* Chateau D'Oex, Vaud, Switzerland. *Office:* c/o Coutts & Co., 440 Strand, London W.C. 2, England.

CAREER: Worked as journalist, whiskey salesman, laundry deliveryman, lumberjack in Canada, indoor pony racing promoter, and was a founder of Four Star Television, 1952. As a motion picture actor, has appeared in more than seventy films, including: "A Feather in Her Hat," 1935; "The Charge of the Light Brigade," 1936; "The Prisoner of Zenda," 1937; "Dawn Patrol," 1938; "Wuthering Heights," 1939; "Raffles," 1940; "Spitfire," 1943; "A Matter of Life and Death," 1945; "Stairway to Heaven," 1946; "The Bishop's Wife," 1947; "Kiss in a Dark," 1949; "The Moon Is Blue," 1953; "The King's Thief," 1955; "Around the World in 80 Days," 1956; "Separate Tables," 1958; "Please Don't Eat the Daisies," 1960; "The Guns of Navarone," 1961; "55 Days at Peking," 1963; "The Pink Panther," 1964; "Lady L," 1966; "Casino Royale," 1967; "The Impossible Years," 1968; "The Extraordinary Seaman," 1969; "Vampira," 1974. Also acted in television series "The David Niven Show," 1959-64, and "The Rogues," 1964-65. *Military service:* Highland Light Infantry, served in Malta. British Army, 1939-45, served in Belgium, Holland, Germany, and Normandy; became lieutenant colonel. *Awards, honors:* American Legion of Merit, 1945; Golden Globe Award for Best Comedy Performance of the Year, 1953, for "The Moon Is Blue"; National Academy of Motion Picture Arts and Sciences "Oscar" for Best Performance by an Actor, 1958, and New York Film Critics' Award, 1960, both for "Separate Tables."

WRITINGS: Once Over Lightly (novel), Prentice-Hall, 1951 (published in England as *Round the Rugged Rocks,* Cresset Press, 1951); *The Moon's a Balloon* (autobiography), Putnam, 1971; *Bring on the Empty Horses* (nonfiction), Putnam, 1975.

SIDELIGHTS: In his autobiography *The Moon's a Balloon,* David Niven described life at Elstree, the first of several schools he was to attend: ". . . sadistic masters and the school bullies tying small boys to hot radiators . . . mad matrons . . . ex-naval cooks with fingernails like toenails doling out their nauseous confections. . . . Thus began a long and multi-phased career of occasional study and frequent expulsions." At another school, Heatherdown, Niven was to discover his comedic talents after he was removed from the school choir as a "bad risk," and he became the "bellows man" on the church organ. Niven recalled, "It took careful preparation, but I could generally arrange matters so that a rude noise could be subtly injected into the proceedings usually just after an Amen."

At a school for "difficult boys" Niven came into his own as a dramatic actor during shoplifting sprees at the local candy store. Niven assumed the task of providing a distraction by bursting a paper bag full of marbles. At the critical moment the "crash of falling glass turned all heads; many willing souls stooped to aid the poor little boy, who even on occasions could summon up a few tears of embarrassment." Nevertheless, Niven managed to finish school (although not without incident) respectably at Stowe.

His subsequent success as a cadet at the Royal Military Academy, Sandhurst, resulted in his commission into the Highland Light Infantry. Niven's years with the Infantry were spent in Malta and were chiefly marked by his introduction to Trubshawe, a fellow officer who was to remain his lifelong friend, and with whom Niven created an appalling spectacle when they arrived at a Fancy-Dress Ball outfitted as goats.

After resigning his commission Niven found his way to Hollywood where he signed on as an extra and was immediately typecast as "Anglo-Saxon type No. 2008." His first part was to portray a Mexican in a "Hopalong Cassidy" feature. He eventually signed with Samuel Goldwyn, and his first speaking part, in "Rose Marie," was apparently cut and another actor hired to take his place. He met with more success as a poet in "A Feather in Her Hat." Niven's portrayal of Captain Lockert in "Dodsworth" resulted in the only review he has saved: "In this picture we were privileged to see the great Samuel Goldwyn's latest discovery—all we can say about this actor ? is that he is tall, dark and not the slightest bit handsome." The review appeared in the *Detroit Free Press,* and Niven keeps it in his bathroom.

Following a distinguished career with the Second Battalion during World War II, Niven with his wife and two sons returned to Hollywood and moviemaking. His English wife Primmie died tragically in a fall shortly after their return. Two years later during the filming of "Bonnie Prince Charlie" in England, Niven met Hjordis Tersmeden and ten days later they were married.

In 1953 Niven appeared in the film "The Moon Is Blue." His performance won him the Golden Globe award for comedic portrayal. In 1956, Niven acted the part of Phileas Fogg in "Around the World in 80 Days," perhaps his best known role. A reviewer for the *New Yorker* termed his performance admirable, and the film won the Academy Award for the Best Picture of the Year in 1956.

The role of the British major in "Separate Tables" won Niven the Academy Award for Best Performance by an Actor in 1958. Based on Sir Terence Rattigan's play, the film and its actors netted overwhelmingly positive reviews. The *New York Herald Tribune* declared that it "is no denial of the superb quality of this film to point out that its dominant quality is the brilliance of its acting. David Niven's is a delicate and touching performance in a difficult role." Bosley Crowther of the *New York Times* wrote: "David Niven starts weakly and gains strength so that his final scene of gathering valor is one of the best in the film." Of his Oscar Niven said, "Whatever the background and however sentimental the vote, it's a lovely feeling to accept first prize."

Niven's first novel *Once Over Lightly* deals with the adventures of an Englishman in Hollywood. A. F. Otis, in a review for the *Chicago Sunday Tribune,* said the "farcical parts are very funny." A reviewer for the *New York Herald Tribune Book Review* noted that the "target is diversion, and it is well hit," although A. H. Weiler declared that Niven's "first venture seems unlikely to earn a literary Oscar."

The Moon's a Balloon, an autobiographical look at Niven's growing-up years and his acting career, takes its title from an E. E. Cummings's poem. *Time*'s Brad Darrach noted that "Niven offers himself as a tough, ambitious international playboy—a well-preserved specimen of that almost extinct species, the gilded barfly." And G. M. Fraser, in a review for *Book World,* stated that Niven "has given evidence . . . of more character and sensitivity than his fans probably ever gave him credit for."

Bring on the Empty Horses is a collection of vignettes and reminiscences of past and present Hollywood and its most famous personalities. N. J. McNeil of *Best Sellers* called it "newsy, charmingly written, and in part scandalous, perceptive, personal, and honest." In a review for *New York Times Book Review,* W. F. Buckley noted that the book possessed "a narrative tension from the beginning, and an ear for piquancy, an eye for the amusing and absurd and the poignant. The compulsion of the entertainer, in Niven's case a blend of exuberance, skill, and good manners . . . keeps the book moving.... Some of the portraits ... approach art, and easily surpass entertainment.'' In *National Review* Priscilla L. Buckley stated that the ''slightest incident ... becomes Laurel and Hardy-esque in his retelling of it.'' Buckley additionally pointed to Niven's ''capacity for friendship, an unbridled delight in the idiotic, and the native and irrepressible irreverence'' he brings to bear on his selection of anecdotes.

In a *Holiday* interview with Janet Graham, Niven said: ''Writing scares the pants off me—it's so difficult. I used to wake and remember things in the middle of the night and jot them on a pad by my bed. I found it fascinating to lift up a stone in my memory and find that all sorts of little things would wriggle out that I had entirely forgotten about.''

AVOCATIONAL INTERESTS: Shooting, fishing, golf, tennis, oil painting, water skiing, swimming.

BIOGRAPHICAL/CRITICAL SOURCES: Chicago Sunday Tribune, November 18, 1951; *New York Times,* November 18, 1951; *New York Herald Tribune Book Review,* December 16, 1951; *New Yorker,* October 27, 1956; *Newsweek,* October 29, 1956; *Time,* October 29, 1956, February 7, 1972; *Filmfacts,* 1958/59; David Niven, *The Moon's a Balloon,* Putnam, 1971; *Book World,* January 16, 1972; *New York Times Book Review,* January 30, 1972, September 21, 1975; *Holiday,* January, 1973; *Best Sellers,* December, 1975; *National Review,* January 23, 1976.*

*   *   *

NOLAN, Tom   1948-

PERSONAL: Born January 15, 1948, in Montreal, Quebec, Canada; came to the United States in 1952, naturalized citizen, 1957. *Education:* Attended University of California, Los Angeles, 1962-66. *Home and office address:* P.O. Box 48465, Los Angeles, Calif. 90048. *Agent:* Elaine Markson Literary Agency, Inc., 44 Greenwich Ave., New York, N.Y. 10011.

CAREER: Motion picture and television actor, 1953-69, including appearances in ''The Seven Year Itch,'' ''An Affair to Remember,'' ''A Star Is Born,'' and ''Buckskin''; writer, 1966—.

WRITINGS: (Contributor) Jonathan Eisen, editor, *The Age of Rock,* Random House, 1969; *The Allman Brothers Band,* Chappell, 1976; *Jimi Hendrix,* Chappell, 1977. Contributor to magazines, including *Oui, West, Rolling Stone,* and *New Times,* and newspapers. Contributing editor of *New West.*

*   *   *

NOLEN, William A(nthony)   1928-

PERSONAL: Born March 20, 1928, in Holyoke, Mass.; son of James R. (a judge) and Katherine Margaret (Dillon) Nolen; married Joan Scheibel, November 28, 1953; children: James, Joan, William, Anna, Julius, Mary. *Education:* College of the Holy Cross, A.B., 1949; Tufts University, M.D., 1953. *Residence:* Litchfield, Minn. *Office:* Litchfield Clinic, 35 East Fourth St., Litchfield, Minn. 55355.

CAREER: Bellevue Hospital, New York, N.Y., surgical intern, 1953-54, resident, 1954-55, 1957-60; Litchfield Clinic, Litchfield, Minn., general surgeon, 1960—. Diplomate, American Board of Surgery. *Military service:* U.S. Army Reserve, 1955-57; became captain. *Member:* American College of Surgeons (fellow), American Medical Association, Society of Journalists and Authors, Authors League of America, Minnesota Surgical Society. *Awards, honors:*

Howard Blakeslee Award from American Heart Association, 1977, for *Surgeon Under the Knife.*

WRITINGS: The Making of a Surgeon, Random House, 1970; *Spare Parts for the Human Body,* Random House, 1971; *A Surgeon's World,* Random House, 1972; *Healing: A Doctor in Search of a Miracle,* Random House, 1975; *Surgeon Under the Knife,* Coward, 1976; *The Baby in the Bottle: A Review of the Edelin Case,* Coward, 1978. Author of column ''A Doctor's World,'' in *McCall's* magazine, 1971—. Contributor of articles to medical journals and popular periodicals, including *Esquire* and *Today's Health.* Member of editorial board, *Minnesota Medicine;* contributing editor, *Medical Economics.*

WORK IN PROGRESS: Work on book reviews.

SIDELIGHTS: ''I am forty-seven years old and have high blood pressure. My father died at fifty-eight of 'heart trouble'. I exercise vigorously at least five times a week, try to keep my weight at respectable levels, take pills to regulate my blood pressure, don't smoke cigarettes. Yet, despite all that I do to prevent it, the possibility of heart attack threatens my horizon. Whenever I notice a twinge in my chest as I run around the tennis court, it occurs that this may be it—my first, and possibly my last, heart attack,'' wrote Dr. Nolen in the beginning of his article on coronary surgery for *Esquire* magazine. He revised the rest of the article because he did suffer angina (heart pains), underwent a coronary bypass operation, and wrote about it later, without, perhaps the usual and expected surgeon's detachment. ''As my editor at *Esquire* said, with apologies, 'Going through the operation ought to make for a better piece.' I reluctantly agreed and revised the original manuscript.''

Nolen's book *Surgeon Under the Knife* is an account of his own struggle with heart problems and with his final decision to undergo surgery for the first time. A reviewer for *Time* called it ''an exciting life-and-death story—his own—and also [one that] provides useful insights that should help less informed surgery patients.'' As a surgeon Nolen is familiar with the coronary bypass procedures and during his own hospital stay acknowledged, according to *Time,* ''that his fellow doctors gave him unusually cordial treatment—possibly, one young resident slyly suggested, because he might write another book. But his special status and posh private room did not protect him from 'screwups'. Several times wrong pills were delivered; a blood test meant for him was taken from the patient next door. Once a nurse even forgot to hook up the crucial heart monitor. Nolen's advice to patients: keep aware of the number and variety of prescribed pills, ask why X-rays are being ordered and demand explanations of everything.''

Nolen's first book, *The Making of a Surgeon,* also provided a candid and revealing look into the medical world, specifically the training of surgical interns and residents at Bellevue Hospital in New York City. Michael Crichton, reviewing for *Book World,* wrote: ''This is an astonishing, superb book, and it works on many levels. As an anecdotal, rambling account of a young surgeon's training, it is remarkable for its wit and honesty. As a chronicle of life in a big municipal hospital ... it is a horror story told in straight-forward, ghastly detail. As a description of how men work against impossible odds, it is both human and heroic in a fascinating way. Nothing quite like it has ever been written about American medicine before.... Many people, including many physicians, may be upset by the book. They will call it too blunt, too crude, too dirty, too gross. It is none of those things; it is accurate.''

In an interview with *Publishers Weekly,* Dr. Nolen stated: "A lot of doctors thought I was a traitor to the profession when *The Making of a Surgeon* was published.... There was a lot of heat and a lot of static, but, as you can see they didn't drum me out of the profession. I just don't see why there has to be so much mystery to medicine." Describing his views on doctor-patient relationships Nolen told the interviewer: "I've learned to be very careful what I say in front of a patient coming out of anaesthesia.... What upsets patients can bore the hell out of us doctors, but we've got to be conscious always of how patients feel. Through their eyes I've come to see myself better, and writing itself has made me a better doctor." *Publishers Weekly* described *A Surgeon's World* as a book that "will hardly enhance Nolen's popularity among doctors, but since patients are his true concern, it is a good bet that the audience that made his initial literary effort a major success will be considerably widened and even more informed about surgery, medical practice, and the doctor-patient relationship."

BIOGRAPHICAL/CRITICAL SOURCES: William A. Nolen, *The Making of a Surgeon,* Random House, 1970; *Newsweek,* December 14, 1970; *Book World,* December 27, 1970; *Time,* January 4, 1971, May 31, 1976; Nolen, *A Surgeon's World,* Random House, 1972; *Publishers Weekly,* November 13, 1972; *Esquire,* August, 1973, February, 1976; *New York Times Book Review,* February 2, 1975; Nolen, *Surgeon Under the Knife,* Coward, 1976; *New York Times,* June 13, 1978.

* * *

NOLTE, Carl William 1933-

PERSONAL: Born August 22, 1933, in San Francisco, Calif.; son of William Charles and Mary (Roche) Nolte; married Mary Cunningham, July 19, 1958 (divorced, 1968); children: Laura, Lynn. *Education:* City College of San Francisco, A.A., 1953; University of San Francisco, B.S., 1955. *Home:* 2123 Leavenworth St., San Francisco, Calif. 94133. *Office: San Francisco Chronicle,* 901 Mission St., San Francisco, Calif. 94119.

CAREER/WRITINGS: University of San Francisco, San Francisco, Calif., athletic news director, 1957-59, director of public information, 1959-61; *San Francisco Chronicle,* San Francisco, 1961—, began as copy editor, assistant city editor for special projects, 1970—. Lecturer in journalism at San Francisco State University, 1969—. President of *Feed/back* magazine (journalism review), 1974—. *Military service:* U.S. Army, 1955-57. U.S. Army Reserve, 1957-61; became staff sergeant. *Member:* Newspaper Guild (president of Western regional council, 1971), San Francisco Oakland Newspaper Guild (president, 1969-70).

* * *

NOORBERGEN, Rene 1928-

PERSONAL: Born September 26, 1928, in the Netherlands; son of R. B. (in the furniture business) and E. T. J. (Reuter) Noorbergen; married Judie D. Hammond; children: Dawn Elisabet, Wendy Judith, Randall Berend. *Education:* Earned B. A. from Loma Linda University; also attended University of Groningen, Atlantic Union College, and University of Tennessee, Chattanooga. *Religion:* Seventh-day Adventist. *Home address:* P.O. Box N, Collegedale, Tenn. 37315. *Office:* Department of Behavioral Science, Southern Missionary College, Collegedale, Tenn. 37315.

CAREER: Chief European correspondent for *Soldier Illustrated,* 1956-57; Camera Press Ltd., London, England, rov-

ing correspondent, 1957-62; roving correspondent for *Epoque,* 1962-66; Ford Motor Co., Dearborn, Mich., managing editor in public relations publications department, 1966-69; free-lance writer, 1969—; Southern Missionary College, Collegedale, Tenn., writer-in-residence, 1974—. *Member:* Psi Chi.

WRITINGS: (With Jeane Dixon) *Jeane Dixon: My Life and Prophecies,* Morrow, 1969; *You Are Psychic,* Morrow, 1971; *Ellen G. White: Prophet of Destiny,* Keats Publishing, 1972; *Charisma of the Spirit,* Pacific Press Publishing Association, 1973; *Glossolalia: Sweet Sounds of Ecstasy,* two volumes, Pacific Press Publishing Association, 1973; *The Ark File,* Pacific Press Publishing Association, 1974; *Programmed to Live,* Pacific Press Publishing Association, 1975; *The Soul Hustlers,* Zondervan, 1976; *Secrets of the Lost Races,* Bobbs-Merrill, 1977; *Deathcry of an Eagle,* Zondervan, 1979. Contributor to magazines and newspapers in the United States and abroad. Roving member of editorial staff of *National Wildlife* and *International Wildlife.*

SIDELIGHTS: Noorbergen's assignments as a journalist have included U.S. armed forces' intervention in Lebanon, the Cuban revolution, the Dalai Lama's escape from Tibet, fighting in Laos and Vietnam, Trujillo's assassination, guerilla actions in Haiti, the Hungarian revolt, Noah's ark expeditions, Irish terrorist activities, and black revolts in the United States.

* * *

NORDLINGER, Eric A. 1939-

PERSONAL: Born September 18, 1939, in Frankfurt, Germany; son of Leo and Kate (Levi) Nordlinger; children: Alexandra. *Education:* Cornell University, A.B., 1961; Princeton University, M.A., 1963, Ph.D., 1966. *Home:* 11 Kennedy Rd., Cambridge, Mass. 02138. *Office:* Department of Political Science, Brown University, Providence, R.I. 02192.

CAREER: Brandeis University, Waltham, Mass., 1965-71, began as assistant professor, became associate professor of political science; Brown University, Providence, R.I., 1971—, began as associate professor, became professor of political science. Research fellow at Harvard University, 1975—. *Awards, honors:* National Science Foundation grants, 1968, 1973; Ford Foundation grant, 1970, fellowship, 1971.

WRITINGS: The Working Class Tories: Authority, Deference, and Stable Democracy, University of California Press, 1967; (editor) *Politics and Society: Studies in Comparative Political Sociology,* Prentice-Hall, 1970; *Decentralizing the City,* M.I.T. Press, 1972; *Conflict Regulation in Divided Societies,* Center for International Affairs, Harvard University, 1972; *Soldiers in Politics: Military Coups and Governments,* Prentice-Hall, 1977. Contributor to political science journals. Member of editorial board of *Public Policy.*

* * *

NORDQUIST, Barbara K(ay) 1940-

PERSONAL: Born August 29, 1940, in California; daughter of Peter (a teacher) and Alice (a teacher) Altpeter; married Myron Harry Nordquist (an attorney), December 28, 1963; children: Nels, Silvy, Ingrid. *Education:* Oregon State University, B.S., 1962; Cornell University, M.S., 1963; U.S. International University, Ph.D., 1969. *Politics:* Republican. *Religion:* Lutheran. *Home:* 5110 Duvall Dr., Bethesda, Md. 20016. *Office:* Department of Microenvironmental Studies and Design, Howard University, Washington, D.C. 20059.

CAREER: San Diego State College, San Diego, Calif., assistant professor of home economics, 1963-70; Howard University, Washington, D.C., associate professor of home economics, 1970—. *Member:* American Home Economics Association, Costume Society of America, Association of College Professors of Textiles and Clothing (member of regional board of directors, 1975-77), Textile Museum, Museum of African Art, Smithsonian Associates, District of Columbia Home Economics Association.

WRITINGS: (With Jean Mettam and Peggy Hoyle) *Creative West African Fashion,* Textile Book Service, 1973; *The Complete Guide to Pattern Making,* Drake, 1974. Author of costume and textile catalogs and slide show programs. Contributor of articles and reviews to home economics and art journals.

WORK IN PROGRESS: Folk Textiles; African Costume.

SIDELIGHTS: Barbara Nordquist comments: "My African research began when I came to Howard University. I have developed a large collection of traditional West African dress and textiles for the school, in addition to a collection of traditional American dress. The African research is to appeal to the students of African heritage, to increase their awareness and interest."

*   *   *

NOREEN, Robert Gerald   1938-

PERSONAL: Born January 2, 1938, in Gresham, Ore.; son of Oscar E. and Floella M. (Jacobs) Noreen; married Carole Stone (a psychotherapist), June 24, 1961; children: Kirstin Joanne, Eric Davin. *Education:* University of Chicago, B.A., 1960, M.A., 1963, Ph.D., 1969. *Religion:* Anglican. *Office:* Department of English, California State University, Northridge, Calif. 91330.

CAREER: Northwestern University, Evanston, Ill., instructor in English, 1965-68; California State University, Northridge, assistant professor, 1968-71, associate professor, 1972-76, professor of English, 1977—, coordinator of liberal studies program, 1973—.

WRITINGS: (Editor with Walter Graffin) *Perspectives for the Seventies,* Dodd, 1971; *Saul Bellow: A Reference Guide,* G. K. Hall, 1977.

WORK IN PROGRESS: The Composing Process.

*   *   *

NORRIS, Kenneth S(tafford)   1924-

PERSONAL: Born August 11, 1924, in Los Angeles, Calif.; son of Robert DeWitt (an engineer) and Jessie (an artist; maiden name, Matheson) Norris; married Phyllis Stout; children: Susan, Nancy, Barbara, Richard. *Education:* University of California, Los Angeles, B.A., 1945, M.A., 1950; Scripps Institute of Oceanology, Ph.D., 1959. *Politics:* "Democrat mostly." *Office:* Environmental Studies Board, University of California, Santa Cruz, Calif. 95064.

CAREER: Curator of Marineland of the Pacific, 1954-60; University of California, Los Angeles, lecturer, 1960-65, associate professor, 1965-69, professor of zoology, 1969-72, director of Oceanic Institute, 1968-71; University of California, Santa Cruz, professor of natural history, 1972—. *Military service:* U.S. Naval Reserve, active duty, 1942-46; became lieutenant junior grade. *Member:* American Association for the Advancement of Science, American Society of Ichthyologists and Herpetologists, Ecological Society of America, American Society of Mammalogists, Society for the Study of Evolution. *Awards, honors:* Mercer Award from Ecological Society of America, 1965; fellows award from California Academy of Sciences, 1977.

WRITINGS: Whales, Dolphins, and Porpoises, University of California Press, 1966; *The Porpoise Watcher,* Norton, 1974.

O

OCHILTREE, Thomas H. 1912-

PERSONAL: Surname pronounced *Oak*-hill-tree; born June 2, 1912, in Indianapolis, Ind.; son of Samuel Paxton (a journalist) and Mabel (a telegrapher; maiden name, Shannon) Ochiltree; married Jewel Doty (a real estate agent), May 17, 1941; children: Scott Huston, Thomas H. II. *Education:* Earned B.A. from De Pauw University. *Politics:* Independent. *Religion:* Presbyterian. *Home and office:* 308 C St. S.E., Washington, D.C. 20003.

CAREER/WRITINGS: Indianapolis Times, Indianapolis, Ind., state-house reporter, 1934-40; *Louisville Courier-Journal,* Louisville, Ky., Indiana correspondent, 1940-42; Associated Press, New York, N.Y., United Nations correspondent and European diplomatic correspondent in London, 1942-66; Panax Newspapers, East Lansing, Mich., Washington correspondent. Notable assignments include coverage of gangsters John Dillinger and Baby Face Nelson, the coronation of Queen Elizabeth II, several Middle East wars and revolts, the death of Pope John XXIII, the coronation of Pope Paul VI, and interviews with Soviet Premier Khrushchev. *Member:* National Press Club, Sigma Delta Chi.

SIDELIGHTS: Ochiltree wrote: ''I have spent a lifetime in journalism, as my late father did before me. Having grown up in a newspaper-wire service environment, I began writing obits, and covering club luncheons and high school sports as soon as I was old enough to write a declarative sentence.

I have lived for a time in many of the world's great cities, met many saints and sinners, and enjoyed it all.''

*   *   *

O'CLAIR, Robert M. 1923-

PERSONAL: Born February 28, 1923, in Nashua, N.H.; son of Edward J. (an engineer) and Mary (in real estate; maiden name, Matheson) O'Clair; married Margaret Gysh, June 2, 1969; children: (from previous marriage) Michael, Hanna. *Education:* Harvard University, B.A. (summa cum laude), 1949, M.A., 1950, Ph.D., 1956. *Politics:* Democrat. *Religion:* Unitarian-Universalist. *Office:* Department of English, Manhattanville College, Purchase, N.Y. 10577.

CAREER: Harvard University, Cambridge, Mass., lecturer in English and Allston Burr Senior Tutor at Kirkland House, both 1956-61; Manhattanville College, Purchase, N.Y., assistant professor, 1961-62, associate professor, 1962-68, pro-

fessor of English, 1968—. *Military service:* U.S. Army, 1942-46; became staff sergeant. *Member:* Phi Beta Kappa.

WRITINGS: (Editor with Richard Ellmann) *The Norton Anthology of Modern Poetry,* Norton, 1973; (with Ellmann) *Modern Poems: An Introduction to Poetry,* Norton, 1976.

WORK IN PROGRESS: A critical edition of Jane Austen's *Mansfield Park,* for Norton.

*   *   *

O'CONNOR, Jack
See O'CONNOR, John Woolf

*   *   *

O'CONNOR, John Joseph 1904-1978

November 9, 1904—June 5, 1978; American educator, editor, and author. O'Connor was a professor of history at Georgetown University. He was also founder and former president of the Catholic Interracial Council. O'Connor was a member of various race relation groups, and he served as a spokesman during the late 1940's and 1950's promoting programs that would possibly bring these groups together. O'Connor was the recipient of the James J. Hoey Award and received a citation from the National Association for the Advancement of Colored People (NAACP) for his contributions on behalf of human rights. He was contributing editor of *Commonweal,* managing editor of *Logistics Magazine,* and columnist for the *Interracial Review.* O'Connor was the author of six books. He died in Washington, D.C. Obituaries and other sources: *Washington Post,* June 8, 1978.

*   *   *

O'CONNOR, John Woolf 1902-1978
(Jack O'Connor)

January 22, 1902—January 20, 1978; American author and editor. O'Connor taught as an associate professor of journalism at University of Arizona before becoming the arms and ammunition editor of *Outdoor Life* magazine in 1939, a position he held for over thirty years. In addition to two novels written in the 1930's, he published more than a dozen books on hunting and contributed articles and stories to national magazines. O'Connor is best known for *The Rifle Book,* considered by many hunters to be the classic, complete book on rifles. He died aboard the S. S. *Mariposa* while returning to San Francisco from Hawaii. Obituaries and other sources: *Who's Who Among Pacific Northwest Authors,* 2nd edition, Pacific Northwest Library Association, 1969; *Who's Who in America,* 39th edition, Marquis, 1976; *New York Times,* January 24, 1978. (See index for *CA* sketch)

* * *

O'CONNOR, Patrick

PERSONAL: Born in Ardrossan, Scotland; son of Daniel and Margaret (Dooley) O'Connor; married Vicki Snellgrove (a cartographer), February 11, 1950; children: Fiona. *Education:* "Self-educated." *Residence:* London, England. *Agent:* Sterling Lord Agency, Inc., 660 Madison Ave., New York, N.Y. 10021.

CAREER: Employed by an oil refinery, 1936-38; British Admiralty, London, assistant in chart depot, 1944-47; actor and producer, 1947-60; full-time writer, 1960—. Conducts research for an international journal subscription agent and antiquarian publisher. *Military service:* British Merchant Navy, 1939-44. *Member:* International P.E.N.

WRITINGS: Down the Bath Rocks (novel), Gill & Macmillan, 1971; *In a Marmalade Saloon* (novel), Hutchinson, 1974; *Across the Western* (novel), Houghton, 1976.

Plays: "The Wooden Box" (one-act), first produced in Santa Maria, Calif., at Ernest Righetti High School, October 26, 1971; "A Bit Like Ginger Rogers" (three-act), first broadcast by British Broadcasting Corp., May 12, 1971.

Also author of "A Marmalade Saloon" (documentary for television), British Broadcasting Corp, 1975.

Work represented in *Best Short Plays—1968,* Chilton, 1968. Contributor to magazines and newspapers, including *Sight and Sound, First Stage,* and *Now International.*

WORK IN PROGRESS: The fourth novel in a series, *Into the Strong City,* about a fictional Patrick O'Connor; two plays; a satire.

SIDELIGHTS: O'Connor writes: "One of my critics, Auberon Waugh, wrote, 'O'Connor avoids all the obvious traps of being an Irish novelist in the post-Joycean era.' One can only continue to try to avoid the traps while resisting being deflected from the path laid down by the master. I believe my method of presenting dialogue to be original. I aim at a more *graphic* form of writing."

O'Connor continued: "Taken in sequence my novels, although complete works in themselves (and cannot be described as 'autobiographical novels'), portray (1) childhood; (2) a youth in the back streets; (3) a young man goes to war—all written strictly from the point of view of the 'I' at that particular stage of development, scrupulously eschewing adult hindsight. The fourth, *Into the Strong City,* describes 'maturing, learning, loving' and touches on the problems of consciousness, identity and dream, and the mystery of 'self.' Whenever feasible I use real locations and sometimes characters in the series. But what is reality? Could the 'I' of the series, living on in the novels (it is to be hoped), have as much claim to 'existence' as the writer who is (arguably) merely a passing dream in the cosmic consciousness?"

AVOCATIONAL INTERESTS: All the arts (contemporary and classical), extra-sensory perception and the paranormal.

BIOGRAPHICAL/CRITICAL SOURCES: Hibernia, December 3, 1971.

ODELL, Rice 1928-

PERSONAL: Born August 19, 1928, in Lake Forest, Ill.; son of William Rice (a businessman) and Frances (a sculptress; maiden name, Robbins) Odell; married Sheila Bateman (a secretary), June, 1962; children: Colin, Denise. *Education:* Stanford University, B.A., 1950. *Religion:* None. *Home:* 4323 Murdock Mill Rd. N.W., Washington, D.C. 20016.

CAREER: Washington Daily News, Washington, D.C., reporter and author of column "Washington Business," 1953-67; *Conservation Foundation Letter,* Washington, D.C., editor, 1967—. *Military service:* U.S. Army, Counterintelligence Corps, 1951-53. *Member:* Washington Independent Writers. *Awards, honors:* Front Page Award from Washington Newspaper Guild, 1965, for public service reporting.

WRITINGS: The Saving of San Francisco Bay, Conservation Foundation, 1972. Contributor to magazines, including *Audubon, Nation's Business, Smithsonian, Washingtonian,* and *World,* and to newspapers.

WORK IN PROGRESS: A series of articles on telephone rate regulation.

* * *

O'DONOGHUE, Bryan 1921-

PERSONAL: Born June 21, 1921, in Ireland; son of W. J. and Agnes Mary O'Donoghue; married wife, Ethne (a handweaver), August 9, 1947; children: Rosemary, Miriam, Robert, David, Finnian, Ann, Hilary. *Education:* Attended secondary school in Dublin, Ireland. *Politics:* Conservative. *Religion:* Roman Catholic. *Home address:* Box 696, Fort Victoria, Rhodesia. *Agent:* Lurton Blassingame, 60 East 42nd St., New York, N.Y. 10017. *Office:* P.O. Box 641, Fort Victoria, Rhodesia.

CAREER: Writer.

WRITINGS: Little Game Hunter, Collins, 1968; *The Pattern of Things: Animal Stories of Africa,* Collins, 1969; *Wild Animal Rescue* (juvenile), Dodd, 1971; *Black Rhino Rescue,* Perskor, 1976; *Green Place,* Perskor, 1977. Contributor of about one hundred-twenty stories to magazines.

WORK IN PROGRESS: Two books.

* * *

OFFERLE, Mildred 1912-

PERSONAL: Born January 3, 1912, in Barnum, Minn.; daughter of John Sprague (a house painter) and Lilian (a teacher; maiden name, Ortman) Goodell; married Martin A. Offerle, August 31, 1938; children: Caroline. *Education:* Duluth Teachers College, diploma, 1932; Mankato State University, B.S., 1966. *Politics:* Democrat. *Religion:* Christian. *Home:* 105 Third St. S.W., Madelia, Minn. 56062.

CAREER: Rural school teacher in Mapleton, Minn., 1932-33; elementary school teacher in Barnum, Minn., 1933-38; Madelia Schools, Madelia, Minn., elementary teacher, 1964-66. Writer, 1945—. Active in civic and church affairs.

MEMBER: World Poetry Society, Centro Studi e Scambi Internazionali, National Education Association, American Poetry League, Minnesota Education Association, Madelia Teacher's Association, League of Minnesota Poets, Southwest Minnesota Reading Teachers Association, Southwest Minnesota Arts and Humanities Society, Southwest Minnesota Poets Association, Sorosis of Madelia.

WRITINGS: Crystal Wells (poems), Candor Press, 1950; *The Long Cry* (novel), Concordia, 1960; *Moods and Thoughts* (poems), Prairie Press, 1970. Contributor of poems and children's stories to magazines.

WORK IN PROGRESS: Revising a historical novel; poems.

SIDELIGHTS: Mildred Offerle writes: "I have always been interested in writing my thoughts down on paper. Early in 1945 my mother sent me a clipping describing the work of the League of Minnesota Poets and inviting the poets of the state to join. I joined the group and it opened a whole new world of people and interest to me. Since then my poems have been published on three continents.

"History and historical places have always intrigued me. I have been an avid reader of biographies and historical novels. One day when I ran out of reading material, I suddenly felt that I would like to write one of my own. I began with a story idea and added writing and researching to my reading.

"I believe that each writer must individually face the truth that each work published may have a wide influence on the thoughts and actions of others. None of us knows how many persons a single one of our ideas may touch. It is my sincere hope that as my writings are read, the readers may gain not only the enjoyment of reading but perhaps some added help and strength."

*   *   *

OFFIT, Avodah K. 1931-

PERSONAL: Born November 18, 1931, in New York, N.Y.; daughter of Abraham David (an engineer) and Carrie (a teacher; maiden name, Fortgang) Komito; married Sidney Offit (a teacher and writer), August, 1952; children: Kenneth, Michael. *Education:* Hunter College (now of the City University of New York), A.B., 1952; New York University, M.D., 1967. *Religion:* Jewish. *Home and office:* 23 East 69th St., New York, N.Y. 10021. *Agent:* Candida Donadio Associates, Inc., 111 West 57th St., New York, N.Y. 10019.

CAREER: Lenox Hill Hospital, New York City, intern, 1967-68; Payne Whitney Psychiatric Clinic, New York City, resident, 1968-71; psychiatrist with private practice in New York City, 1971—. Head of sexual therapy at Lenox Hill Hospital, 1972—. Member of local Democratic County Committee, 1967—.

MEMBER: American Medical Association, American Psychiatric Association, American Medical Writers' Association. *Awards, honors:* Blanche Colton Williams playwriting award, 1952; Bread Loaf writing scholarship, 1961; *The Sexual Self* was chosen by *Psychology Today,* in 1977, as the best human sexuality book.

WRITINGS: (Contributor) Grunebaum and Christ, editors, *Contemporary Marriage: Structure, Dynamics, Therapy,* Little, Brown, 1976; *The Sexual Self,* Lippincott, 1977. Also author of plays. Contributor of articles and a story to psychology journals and popular magazines, including *Intellectual Digest, Harper's Bazaar, Saturday Evening Post,* and *Glamour.*

WORK IN PROGRESS: Another book on human sexuality.

SIDELIGHTS: Avodah Offit comments: "As a person trained to write English long before learning medical jargon, my ambition has been to unite the literary and medical viewpoint in a prose that professionals in both fields can appreciate. The subject of human sexuality lends itself ideally to

this union." *Avocational interests:* Reading, writing poetry, painting, swimming.

*   *   *

OFFORD, Lenore Glen 1905-
(Theo Durrant, a joint pseudonym)

PERSONAL: Born October 24, 1905, in Spokane, Wash.; daughter of Robert Alexander (a newspaper editor) and Catherine (a piano teacher; maiden name, Grippen) Glen; married Harold R. Offord (a division chief in U.S. Forest Service), September 17, 1929; children: Judith Marie Offord Kennedy. *Education:* Mills College, Oakland, Calif., B.A., 1925; graduate study at University of California, 1925-26. *Home:* 641 Euclid Avenue, Berkeley, Calif. 94708. *Agent:* Frances Collin, 141 East 55th St., New York, N.Y. 10022.

CAREER: San Francisco Chronicle, San Francisco, Calif., reviewer of science-fiction literature, 1950—. Writer.

MEMBER: Crime Writers Association (England), Mystery Writers of America, Baker Street Irregulars, The Scowrers and Molly Maguires of San Francisco. *Awards, honors:* Edgar Allan Poe Award from Mystery Writers of America, 1951, for criticism; received titular investiture of "The Old Russian Woman" from the Baker Street Irregulars, 1963.

WRITINGS: Murder on Russian Hill, Macrae-Smith, 1938; *Cloth of Silver,* Macrae-Smith, 1939; *Angels Unaware,* Macrae-Smith, 1940; *The Nine Dark Hours,* Duell, Sloan & Pearce, 1941; *Clues to Burn,* Duell, Sloan & Pearce, 1942; *Skeleton Key,* Duell, Sloan & Pearce, 1943; *The Glass Mask,* Duell, Sloan & Pearce, 1944; *My True Love Lies,* Duell, Sloan & Pearce, 1947; *The Smiling Tiger,* Duell, Sloan & Pearce, 1949; (with others; under joint pseudonym Theo Durrant) *The Marble Forest,* Knopf, 1951; *Enchanted August* (juvenile), Bobbs-Merrill, 1956; (with Joseph Henry Jackson) *The Girl in the Belfry,* Gold Medal, 1957; *Walking Shadow,* Simon & Schuster, 1959.

SIDELIGHTS: Jacques Barzun and Wendell Hertig Taylor, in *A Catalogue of Crime,* described Offord as "a respectable member of the retreaded 'Had-I-But-Known' school, with several substantial works to her credit. Mrs. Offord reviews detective fiction . . . writes good light verse, and shows a nice wit in all she does."

*   *   *

O'HANLON, Jacklyn
See MEEK, Jacklyn O'Hanlon

*   *   *

O'HIGGINS, Donal Peter 1922-

PERSONAL: Born September 9, 1922, in Republic of Ireland; son of Thomas (a former Irish Defense Minister) and Agnes (McCarthy) O'Higgins; married Theresa Mary Sharpe. *Education:* Attended Clongowes Wood College (Ireland) and University College (Dublin). *Religion:* Roman Catholic. *Home:* 18 Zion Rd., Rathgar, Dublin, Irish Republic.

CAREER/WRITINGS: Former correspondent in Far East, Burma, India, and Egypt, for Reuters News Agency; United Press International, New York City, correspondent, 1946-49, bureau manager in Dublin, Ireland, 1949-53, foreign desk worker at headquarters in New York City, 1953-59, correspondent in Ireland, 1959—. Notable assignments include coverage of the Hindu-Moslem confrontations in India and the conflict in Northern Ireland.

OJANY, Francis Frederick 1935-

PERSONAL: Born July 17, 1935, in Olasi, Kenya; son of Owuor (a tribal elder) and Olesi Ojany; married Agnes Ochido (an administrative assistant); children: Rachel, Richard, Lucy, Deborah, Peter, Jonathan, Hazel. *Education:* Makerere University, B.A. (honors), 1960; University of Birmingham, M.A., 1963. *Religion:* Protestant. *Home address:* P.O. Box 36, Koru, Kenya. *Office:* Department of Geography, University of Nairobi, P.O. Box 30197, Nairobi, Kenya.

CAREER: University of Nairobi, Nairobi, Kenya, Rockefeller assistant lecturer, 1963-64, lecturer, 1964-72, senior lecturer in geography, 1972—, chairman of department, 1977—. *Member:* Kenya Geographical Society. *Awards, honors:* Commonwealth scholarship for University of Birmingham, 1960-63.

WRITINGS: (With R.B. Ogendo) *Kenya: A Study in Physical and Human Geography,* Longmans, 1973. Contributor to geography journals. Editor of *Kenyan Geographer;* member of editorial board of *Habitat,* 1976—.

WORK IN PROGRESS: A geomorphology book, with special emphasis on East Africa.

SIDELIGHTS: Ojany lists his main interests as geomorphology, especially of tropical areas, and the geography of Africa.

Avocational interests: Geology, history.

*   *   *

O'KEEFE, M(aurice) Timothy 1943-

PERSONAL: Born March 7, 1943, in New York, N.Y.; son of Maurice Edward (a bakery manager) and Jeanne (a nurse; maiden name, Murphy) O'Keefe; married; children: Timothy Patrick. *Education:* Washington and Lee University, B.A. (cum laude), 1965; University of North Carolina, M.A., 1967, Ph.D., 1968. *Home:* 597 Brookwood Lane, Maitland, Fla. 32751. *Agent:* (photography) Bruce Coleman, Inc., 15 East 36th St., New York, N.Y.; and 16a/17a Windsor St., Uxbridge, Middlesex, England. *Office:* Department of Communications, Florida Technological University, Orlando, Fla. 32816.

CAREER: Richmond News Leader, Richmond, Va., staff reporter, 1961-65; Florida Technological University, Orlando, assistant professor, 1968-72, associate professor of communications, 1972—. *Member:* Conservation, Education, Diving, and Archeology Museums International (member of advisory board), Outdoor Writers Association of America, Association for Education in Journalism, Florida Outdoor Writers Association, Delta Tau Kappa. *Awards, honors:* First place award from Florida Magazine Association, 1974, for "March of the Aliens," and 1977, for "The Mighty St. Johns"; awards from Florida Outdoor Writers Association, 1974, for "World Wide Skindivers Guide," and 1975, for photography and radio broadcasting; first place in Evinrude-OWAA Writing Competition, 1977; other awards for in-depth reporting, editorials, and historical features.

WRITINGS: (Contributor) Michael Goodstadt, editor, *Research Methods in Drug Abuse Education,* Addiction Research Foundation (Toronto), 1974; (with K. G. Sheinkopf) *Advertising Principles and Practices,* College & University Press, 1975; (contributor) Joseph Roucek, editor, *Social Control in the 70's,* Greenwood Press, 1978.

Short story represented in *Witch's Brew,* edited by Alfred Hitchcock, Random House, 1977. Contributor of articles and photographs to professional journals and popular magazines, including *Florida Naturalist, Boatmaster, Southern Sea,* and *Sport Diver.* Editor of *International Divers Guide,* 1973—; field editor of *Florida Sportsman,* 1973—; senior writer, *Southern Outdoors,* 1978—.

Contributor of photographs to *Time-Life Nature Science Annual,* 1975; Fred Fedler, *An Introduction to the Mass Media,* Harcourt, 1978; *The Ocean Realm,* National Geographic Society, 1978.

WORK IN PROGRESS: First Underwater Christmas, a children's book; an untitled children's book on undersea creatures.

SIDELIGHTS: O'Keefe writes: "Outside of scholarly publications, my writing has been concerned with environment-ecology as well as the recreational aspects of scuba diving and other water-oriented sports. I am concerned with increasing pollution and destruction of the natural habitat and the effect of this on both nature and man; I attempt in my writing to show the importance, benefits, and pleasures of the outdoors, which hopefully will bring about a greater appreciation and concern for it."

AVOCATIONAL INTERESTS: Travel (the Caribbean, Soviet Union, Australia, Ireland).

*   *   *

OKIGBO, Christopher (Ifenayichukwu) 1932-1967

PERSONAL: Born in 1932, in Ojoto, Nigeria; son of James (a school teacher) Okigbo; married wife, Sefi, in 1963; children: Ibrahimat (daughter). *Education:* University of Ibadan, B.A., 1956.

CAREER: Nigerian Department of Research and Information, Lagos, Nigeria, private secretary to the Minister, 1955-56; affiliated with Nigerian Tobacco Company and United Africa Company; Fiditi Grammar School, Fiditi, Nigeria, Latin teacher, 1959-60; University of Nigeria, Nsukka, assistant librarian, 1960-62; Cambridge University Press, Ibadan, Nigeria, Nigerian representative, 1962-66; founder of small publishing company with Chinua Achebe in Enugu, 1967. Member of editorial staff of Mbari Press. *Military service:* Biafran Defense Forces, 1967; became major; killed in action. *Awards, honors:* Dakar Festival of Arts first prize for *Limits,* 1966 (refused); posthumously awarded Biafran National Order of Merit.

WRITINGS—Poetry: *Heavensgate,* Mbari Press, 1962; *Limits,* Mbari Press, 1964; *Labyrinths, With Path of Thunder,* Africana, 1971. Works represented in anthology "African Writers Series," Number 62, Heinemann, 1971. Contributor of poetry to periodicals, including *Transition* and *Black Orpheus.* Co-editor of *Transition.*

SIDELIGHTS: "There wasn't a stage when I decided that I definitely wished to be a poet," Okigbo once commented, "there was a stage when I found that I couldn't be anything else."

Paul Theroux calls Okigbo "an obscure poet, possibly the most difficult poet in Africa." He suggests two approaches to Okigbo's work. One is to examine the words he used, many springing from his wide knowledge of other writers, and all having a special meaning in the context of his own work. The other is to "listen to his music." According to Theroux, one can hear three separate melodies in it: "the music of youth, the clamour of passage (that is, growing up) and lastly, the sounds of thunder."

Part of the difficulty, according to S. D. Anozie, lies in the fact that "Okigbo's poetry is constantly exploring two irregular dimensions of myth . . . myth as a privileged religious mode of cognition" and myth, with totem, as "affective and even evaluative in a given cultural context." Anozie also notes the derivative nature of the poet's work, the "wide range of references to and echoes of other poets," which further obscure his poetry.

In Theroux's opinion, *Heavensgate* and *Limits* express the "music of growth," a music which also suggests the danger inherent in growing up. The bird imagery running through both poems is related to the speaker, the poet who appears in all of Okigbo's work and would seem to represent Okigbo himself. *Silences* and *Distances* speak of the disillusionments which can follow maturation and the loss of innocence. "It is safe to say that very few poems achieve the music and harmony that *Silences* does," Theroux commented. *Distances*, however, is characterized by pain, shocking images such as that of the "horizontal stone" which represents a morgue slab holding a corpse, and the repetition of the line, "I was the sole witness to my homecoming," indicating solitude at the attainment of maturity.

Okigbo felt none of the conflict between old and new that often seems to pose a problem for educated Africans. He often went back to his village for festivals and major religious ceremonies, and his own religion combined Christian and pagan elements. In an interview with Marjory Whitelaw, he described the family shrine which housed their ancestral gods, the male Ikenga and the female Udo, whom he considered different aspects of the same force represented by the Christian god. Unlike others in his family, he never made sacrifices to these deities, but he declared: "My creative activity is in fact one way of performing these functions in a different manner. Every time I write a poem, I am in fact offering a sacrifice." Okigbo's maternal grandfather, of whom he was believed to be a reincarnation, was the priest of a shrine to Idoto, the river goddess, and the poet's idea of his own priesthood is apparent in much of his writing.

In spite of this oneness with his background and the local themes and images which abound in his work, Okigbo did not adhere to the literary concept of negritude, which, he felt, emphasized racial differences. He told Marjory Whitelaw: "I think I am just a poet. A poet writes poetry and once a work is published it becomes public property. It's left to whoever reads it to decide whether it's African poetry or English. There isn't any such thing as a poet trying to express African-ness. Such a thing doesn't exist. A poet expresses himself."

His interest in social and political change in his own country, however, formed an inseparable part of his work. Okigbo told Whitelaw of his conviction that the poet in any society could not examine his own identity in isolation, but that "any writer who attempts a type of inward exploration will in fact be exploring his own society indirectly." Okigbo's concern for humanity was perhaps best expressed in his commitment to the Biafran secession. He lost his life in August, 1967, fighting as a volunteer for the Biafran forces.

Anozie wrote: "Nothing can be more tragic to the world of African poetry in English than the death of Christopher Okigbo, especially at a time when he was beginning to show maturity and coherence in his vision of art, life and society, and greater sophistication in poetic form and phraseology. Nevertheless his output, so rich and severe within so short a life, is sure to place him among the best and the greatest of our time."

BIOGRAPHICAL/CRITICAL SOURCES: Journal of

Commonwealth Literature, July, 1970; *Books Abroad,* spring, 1971; Sunday Anozie, *Christopher Okigbo,* Africana, 1972; Bruce King, editor, *Introduction to Nigerian Literature,* Africana, 1972.*

(Died August, 1967)

* * *

OLDROYD, Harold 1913-

PERSONAL: Born December 24, 1913, in Batley, Yorkshire, England; son of Oliver (a mill worker) and Drusilla (Walker) Oldroyd; married Joan Mary Preston (a secretary), May 15, 1944; children: David Preston. *Education:* Christ's College, Cambridge, B.A., 1935, M.A., 1939. *Home:* 88 Park Ave. E., Ewell, Epsom, Surrey KT17 2PA, England.

CAREER: British Museum (Natural History), London, England, assistant keeper, 1936-51; principal scientific officer, 1951-64, senior principal scientific officer, 1964-73; writer, 1958—. *Military service:* Royal Air Force, pilot, 1941-46; became flight lieutenant. *Member:* Institute of Biology (fellow), Royal Entomological Society (fellow; vice-president, 1952), Royal Society of Arts (fellow), Societe Royal Belge d'Entomologie (honorary member).

WRITINGS: Collecting, Preserving, and Studying Insects (all ages), Macmillan, 1958, 2nd edition, 1970; *Insects and Their World* (all ages), British Museum, 1960, University of Chicago Press, 1962, 3rd edition, 1973; *The Natural History of Flies,* Weidenfeld & Nicolson, 1964, Norton, 1966; *Elements of Entomology* (all ages), Weidenfeld & Nicolson, 1968, Universe Books, 1969; *The Insects in Your Garden* (children), Penguin, 1976.

Translator: R. Jeannel, *Introduction to Entomology,* Hutchinson, 1960; Remy Chauvin, *The World of an Insect,* Weidenfeld & Nicolson, 1967; Heinz J. Bogen, *Modern Biology,* Weidenfeld & Nicolson, 1968; Roger Buvat, *Plant Cells,* Weidenfeld & Nicolson, 1969; Etienne Grandjean, *Ergonomics of the Home,* Taylor & Francis, 1973; (with Roger Abbot, Marguerite Biederman-Thorson) Werner Nachtigall, *Insects in Flight,* Allen & Unwin, 1974; Grandjean and Alfred Gilgen, *Environmental Factors in Urban Planning,* Taylor & Francis, 1976. Co-editor of *Journal of Natural History,* 1964—.

WORK IN PROGRESS: Children's books on flowers and ladybirds, for Angus & Robertson; "Lives of Insects," to be included in *Insects: An Illustrated Survey,* for Hamlyn; an English-German German-English biological dictionary for Verlag Eugen Ulmer.

SIDELIGHTS: Oldroyd writes: "During my working life, professional scientists have despised 'popular' writing as being unworthy of their intellectual powers. I do not agree. I think that the presentation and dissemination of scientific knowledge is as important as the original research. I have therefore tried to balance the detailed scientific work which was my professional occupation, with original books and translations addressed to a more general public, including some children's books."

AVOCATIONAL INTERESTS: Photography (especially close-up photography of insects and flowers in natural settings).

* * *

OLNEY, James 1933-

PERSONAL: Born July 12, 1933, in Marathon, Iowa; son of Norris G. (a lawyer and banker) and Doris (Hawk) Olney;

married Judith Wall (a cooking teacher), June 26, 1967; children: Nathan. *Education:* Iowa State University, B.A., 1955; Columbia University, M.A., 1958, Ph.D., 1964. *Home:* 1500 Forest Hills Plaza, Durham, N.C. 27707. *Office:* Department of English, North Carolina Central University, Durham, N.C. 27707.

CAREER: Drake University, Des Moines, Iowa, assistant professor of English, 1963-67; Cuttington College and Divinity School, Monrovia, Liberia, Fulbright lecturer in English, 1967-69; North Carolina Central University, Durham, professor of English, 1970—. Visiting professor at Northwestern University, 1964, and Amherst College, 1978-79. *Military service:* U.S. Army, 1955-57. *Member:* Modern Language Association of America, African Studies Association. *Awards, honors:* Frances G. Wickes fellowship, 1972-73; National Endowment for the Humanities senior fellowship, 1975-76.

WRITINGS: Metaphors of Self: The Meaning of Autobiography, Princeton University Press, 1972; *Tell Me Africa: An Approach to African Literature,* Princeton University Press, 1973; *The Rhizome and the Flower: The Perennial Philosophy, Yeats and Jung,* University of California Press, 1979; (editor and translator) *Autobiography: Essays Theoretical and Critical,* Princeton University Press, 1979.

* * *

ONDAATJE, Michael   1943-

PERSONAL: Born December 9, 1943, in Ceylon. *Agent:* Jill Dargeon, 160 East 84th St., New York, N.Y. 10028. *Office:* Department of English, Glendon College, 2275 Bayview Ave., Toronto, Ontario, Canada.

CAREER: Member of English faculty at Glendon College, Toronto, Ontario; hound breeder and hog breeder. Inventor of Dragland hog feeder, 1975. *Awards, honors:* Canadian Governor General's Award for Literature, 1970.

WRITINGS: The Dainty Monsters (poems), Coach House Press, 1967; *The Man With Seven Toes* (poems), Coach House Press, 1969; *The Collected Works of Billy the Kid* (poetry and prose), Norton, 1970; *Rat Jelly* (poems), Coach House Press, 1973; *Coming Through Slaughter* (prose), Anansi, 1976, Norton, 1977.

Films: "Sons of Captain Poetry," Canadian Filmmakers Distribution Center, 1970; "Carry on Crime and Punishment," Canadian Filmmakers Distribution Center, 1972; "The Clinton Special," Canadian Filmmakers Distribution Center, 1974.

BIOGRAPHICAL/CRITICAL SOURCES: Fiddlehead, spring, 1968; *Saturday Night,* July, 1968; *New York Times Book Review,* April 24, 1977.

* * *

O'NEILL, Eugene   1922-

PERSONAL: Born August 23, 1922, in New York, N.Y.; son of Robert J. (in business) and Catherine (McMahon) O'Neill; married Marie C. Lodato, June 2, 1951; children: Robert, John. *Education:* City College (now of the City University of New York), B.A., 1943; Columbia University, M.A., 1947, Ed.D., 1963. *Politics:* Democrat. *Religion:* Roman Catholic. *Home:* 19 Wellington Rd., Garden City, N.Y. 11530. *Office:* Department of History, State University of New York Agricultural and Technical Institute in Farmingdale, Farmingdale, N.Y. 11738.

CAREER: Seton Hall University, South Orange, N.J., as-

sistant professor of history, 1947-52; St. John's University, Jamaica, N.Y., associate professor of history, 1956-65; State University of New York Agricultural and Technical Institute in Farmingdale, Farmingdale, New York, professor of general education, 1965—, dean of instruction, 1967-73. *Military service:* U.S. Army Air Forces, 1942-45; became sergeant; received five battle stars. *Member:* American Historical Association.

WRITINGS: Origin of New York National Parks, 1800-1920, University of Michigan Press, 1963.

WORK IN PROGRESS: "An analysis of the western world's response to the four major crises from 1800 to present."

* * *

OPPENHEIM, Irene   1928-

PERSONAL: Born July 26, 1928, in New York, N.Y.; daughter of Samuel (a physician) and Bessie (a teacher; maiden name, Gersten) Gartner; married Don B. Oppenheim (a psychologist and college administrator), June 22, 1947; children: Ellen, Wendy, Barbara. *Education:* Pratt Institute, B.S., 1949; New York University, M.A., 1959, Ph.D., 1961. *Home:* 40 Van Dyke Rd., Princeton, N.J. 08540.

CAREER: Teacher in public schools in New York City, 1949-50, in Newark, N.J., 1954-55, and in Irvington, N.J., 1957-59; Montclair State College, Montclair, N.J., assistant professor of home economics, 1959-63; New York University, New York City, assistant professor, 1963-65, associate professor of home economics, 1965-68; New Jersey Department of Education, Trenton, consultant on consumer education and home economics, 1969-72; writer, 1972—. Member of public service advisory committee of U.S. Food & Drug Administration, 1964-65; consultant to U.S. Department of Health, Education & Welfare.

MEMBER: American Home Economics Association, American Council on Consumer Interests (vice-president, 1964-65; president, 1965-66), New Jersey Home Economics Association (vice-president), Pi Lambda Theta, Omicron Nu.

WRITINGS: The Family as Consumers, Macmillan, 1965; *Management of the Modern Home,* Macmillan, 1972, 2nd edition, 1976; *Consumer Skills,* with workbook and teacher's guide, Charles A. Bennett, 1977. Contributor to periodicals.

WORK IN PROGRESS: Living Today.

SIDELIGHTS: Oppenheim told *CA:* "My books and articles are concerned with helping people get the most from their resources. This is the role of the consumer in our society."

* * *

ORLOVITZ, Gil   1918-1973

PERSONAL: Born June 7, 1918, in Philadelphia, Pa.; married wife Maralyn (separated); children: one daughter, two sons. *Education:* Attended Temple University and Columbia University. *Residence:* New York, N.Y.

CAREER: Writer. Has worked as editor and free-lance television script writer; paperback editor for Universal Publishing and Distributing Corp., 1960-69.

WRITING: The Statement of Erica Keith and Other Stories, Poems, and a Play, Miscellaneous Man, 1957; *Something to Tell Mother: A Story,* American Letters Press,

1959; (editor) *Award Avant-Garde Reader,* Award Books, 1965; *Milkbottle H* (novel), Calder & Boyars, 1967, Dell, 1968; *Ice Never F* (novel), Calder and Boyars, 1970.

Poems: *Concerning Man,* Banyan Press, 1947; *Keep to Your Belly,* L. Brigants/Intro, 1952; *The Diary of Dr. Eric Zeno,* Inferno Press, 1953; *The Diary of Alexander Patience,* Inferno Press, 1958; *The Papers of Professor Bold,* Hearse Press, 1958; *Selected Poems,* Inferno Press, 1960; *The Art of the Sonnet,* Hillsboro Publications, 1961; *Five Sonnets,* Goosetree Press, 1964; *Couldn't Say. Might Be Love,* Barrie & Rockliff, 1969; *More Poems,* Fiddlehead, 1972.

Plays: "Stevie Guy," published in *Quarterly Review of Literature,* 1952; "Noone," produced Off-Broadway at Provincetown Playhouse, 1953; "Stefanie," first produced in New York City at Amato Theatre, 1954; "Todt and Thor," read in New York City at Gallery East, 1955; "Case of a Neglected Calling Card" (Produced in New York City at Dramatic Workshop, 1952), published in *The Statement of Erica Keith and Other Stories, Poems, and a Play,* Miscellaneous Man, 1957; "Gray," published in *Literary Review,* 1959.

Author of screenplay, "Overexposed," Columbia, 1956. Contributor of stories and plays to journals, including *Quarterly Review of Literature, Intro, Whetstone, Colorado Quarterly,* and *Literary Review.*

SIDELIGHTS: "It will ultimately be found that the extent and depth of my esthetic is so fabulous and of such variety and texture and sheer wonder that my work will be adjudged second to none at any time in the history of art," said Orlovitz. According to poet Hale Chatfield, Orlovitz also "alleges unhesitatingly that America has so far produced two poets worthy of the name: Emily Dickinson and himself, and he rates himself as America's best novelist since James and Melville." Chatfield explained, however, that "much of Orlivitz's startling self-assertiveness is undoubtedly bravado caused by the great quantity of disappointment and frustration he has had to endure."

The disapointment Chatfield referred to is that Orlovitz had not received the recognition that many critics felt he deserved. Robin Nye, for example, found *Milkbottle H* to be a "major work of fiction by any standards" and he was apalled at the neglect of it on the part of American publishers. Nye admitted that this could be attributed, at least in part, to the "nightmarishness" of the book's content, and to the complexity of its "moblie structure of interlocking metaphors." He maintained, though, that this neglect is "the embarrassment of fashionable American writers who have recognised its greatness while being unable to persuade publishers to risk money; it is the badge of the publishing world's failure to issue work which, because of its very goodness of art, is not commercially viable."

Kevin Sullivan commented that *Milkbottle H* "is a no-novel, and Gil Orlovitz is a no-novelist, which is to say a writer, and essentially a poet, whose explosive, sprawling, non-stop prose insists constantly on its own self-sufficiency. To the traditional eye it will appear as formless as lava and as uncontainable, for there is in fact no container for the verbal energies at work here, no plot, no beginning and no end to the rush and crush of language."

Perhaps, as Chatfield suggested, the "present day, with its emphasis on the poem as both an object and an experience, might be a good day for Gil Orlovitz. That the poem is its own primary objective is certainly one of the major critical assumptions of our time."

BIOGRAPHICAL/CRITICAL SOURCES: *Poetry,* September, 1959; *Americas,* January, 1964; *Scotsman,* April 10, 1965; *New Statesman,* May 26, 1967; *Times Literary Supplement,* June 8, 1967, July 24, 1969; *London,* August, 1967; *Listener,* November 2, 1967; *Time,* January 12, 1968; *New York Times,* January 16, 1968; *Book World,* February 1, 1968; *New York Times Book Review,* February 4, 1968; *Best Sellers,* February 15, 1968; *Carleton Miscellany,* spring, 1968; *Hudson Review,* spring, 1968; *Kenyon Review,* Number 4, 1969.

OBITUARIES: *New York Times,* September 8, 1973.*

(Died July 10, 1973)

* * *

ORMEROD, Roger 1920-

PERSONAL: Born April 17, 1920, in Wolverhampton, Staffordshire, England; son of William Robert (an engineer) and Dora Adelaide (Brommage) Ormerod; married Barbara Joyce Wright, March 31, 1952. *Education:* Educated in Wolverhampton, England. *Home:* 3 The Crescent, Tettenhall Wood, Wolverhampton WV6 8LA, England. *Agent:* Harvey Unna & Stephen Durbridge Ltd., 14 Beaumont Mews, Marylebone High Street, London W1N 4HE, England.

CAREER: Writer. Has worked in various positions, including postman and clerk; clerk in county court, Wolverhampton, England, 1937-48; inspector for Department of Social Security, 1948-72.

WRITINGS—All mystery novels; published by R. Hale: *Time to Kill,* 1974; *The Silence of the Night,* 1974; *Full Fury,* 1975; *A Spoonful of Luger,* 1975; *Sealed with a Loving Kill,* 1976; *The Colour of Fear,* 1976; *A Glimpse of Death,* 1976; *Too Late for the Funeral,* 1977; *This Murder Come to Mind,* 1977; *A Dip Into Murder,* 1978.

Writer of teleplays, including *I'll Go Along With That,* December, 1971 and *All Too Tidy,* August, 1973.

WORK IN PROGRESS: Research on civil engineering, soil mechanics, cranes, wagons and medicine for a novel tentatively entitled *The Far Side of the Bridge.*

SIDELIGHTS: Ormerod told *CA:* "I am principally interested in human motivation in respect of crimes, rather than the mechanics of them. My main intention is to entertain rather than to instruct." *Avocational interests:* Amateur tailoring, wine making, stereo photography and high fidelity.

* * *

ORNSTEIN, Dolph 1947-

PERSONAL: Born July 4, 1947, in New York, N.Y.; son of David (a businessman) and Miriam (Hoffman) Ornstein; married Ehlah Pascal (an artist), December 21, 1975. *Education:* Miami University, Oxford, Ohio, B.A., 1968; earned M.B.Ch.B. from University of Dundee. *Home:* 545 Frederick St., San Francisco, Calif. 94117. *Office:* San Francisco Medical Research Foundation, Inc., P.O. Box 7583, Rincon Annex, San Francisco, Calif. 94120.

CAREER: San Francisco Medical Research Foundation, San Francisco, Calif., president, 1976—. *Member:* Orthomolecular Medical Society, Association for the Advancement of Medical Hypnosis.

WRITINGS: (Author of preface) Steven Chang, *The Complete Handbook of Acupuncture,* Celestial Arts, 1976; *Medicine Today, Healing Tomorrow,* Celestial Arts, 1977; *Hypertension: The Relationship of Stress to Its Pathogenesis,* San Francisco Medical Research Foundation, Inc., 1977.

WORK IN PROGRESS: Research on the use of sound, light, and color in healing, and on the relationship between the seven notes in the musical scale, seven colors, and seven glandular systems of the human organism.

SIDELIGHTS: Ornstein writes: *"Medicine Today, Healing Tomorrow* is essentially a personal statement as to who I am and my feelings about what the world and universe really are. It is difficult to say what particularly influenced me to reach such conclusions; however, I am convinced that we are continuously being guided along a path of ever-increasing freedom and self-understanding if we will only become aware of it.

"The movement of my life has been one of great mystery, excitement, and awe. As a medical doctor trained in a materialistic, mechanistic framework I have been led out of these limiting ideas, to recognize that man is not material at all but spirit, a form of conditioned light, if you like, with unlimited freedom and creative possibilities. The concept of time and death as ideas have been shown to be illusory and as such, much of what I thought the world to be has been revealed as illusory as well. The teachers and friends who have led and are still leading me to greater understanding are deep philosophers of the Cabalah and the Tarot. The creative world of the artist has revealed to me the joy, spontaneity, and beauty of the spirit of man. I realized that beauty, creativity, and silence in the writings of Carl Jung are the essential components of life itself.

"To me, healing is a process of recognition, self-understanding, and awareness. Disease is illusion in that, as we are part of a perfectly-balanced universal thought-world-system, we ourselves must partake of the universal order as well. As it is known in the East, the only sin is the sin of separation, and the sin of separation is based on ignorance. Once we know and recognize our true natures we are free and we become creative, moment to moment experiencing life as movement, rhythm, and beauty—ever-new, ever-mysterious, ever-changing. I realize that the quality of life is totally determined by one's attention and one's desire, and it appears that we are all led in our own unique ways to realize that it is *all right* and it has always been all right.

"As a researcher, philosopher, and doctor, I am extremely interested in the use of sound, music, light, and color in healing. To me healing is a process of raising consciousness. There is no such thing as a cure; there is only understanding. Beauty is the great healer because it is a true reflection of ourselves. It is the artist who feels and knows the inherent magnificence of creation, who brings it forth in his own work. There is only one life, one will, and we are all aspects of this one.

"It is my desire and firm conviction that art and science will recognize each other and create environments which are uplifting, knowing that to uplift, support, and care for each other is in reality to care for oneself. Duality is illusion and duality is the hallmark of the world. As a teacher and doctor, I am bringing out this simple truth in order that we can progress, evolve, and recognize the miracle which we are and which life is. Fear is the cause of disease and fear does not exist."

* * *

O'ROURKE, P. J. 1947-

PERSONAL: Born November 14, 1947, in Toledo, Ohio; son of Clifford Bronson (an auto salesman) and Delphine (a school administrator; maiden name, Loy) O'Rourke. *Education:* Miami University, B.A., 1969; Johns Hopkins Univer-

sity, M.A., 1970. *Politics:* Libertarian. *Religion:* None. *Residence:* New York, N.Y. *Office: National Lampoon,* 635 Madison Ave., New York, N.Y. 10022.

CAREER: Worked as writer and editor of underground newspapers in Baltimore, Md., and New York City, 1968-71; *New York Herald,* New York City, feature editor, 1971-72; free-lance writer, 1972-73; *National Lampoon,* New York City, executive editor and managing editor, 1973-77, editor-in-chief, 1978—. *Awards, honors:* Woodrow Wilson fellow, 1969-70; received Merit Award from Art Directors Club, 1973; Gold Award, 1975; Merit Award from Society of Publication Designers, 1976; other awards for visual excellence for *National Lampoon.*

WRITINGS: (Editor with Douglas C. Kenney, and contributor) *The 1964 High School Yearbook,* National Lampoon, 1974. Also author of *Nancy Adler Poems,* 1970, and *Our Friend the Vowel,* 1976, both poetry books.

SIDELIGHTS: O'Rourke told *CA:* "I write because I don't know how to do anything else." *Avocational interests:* Automobiles, graphic arts, industrial design.

* * *

OSMAN, John 1907(?)-1978

1907(?)—June 12, 1978; American economic historian and author of books in his field. A specialist in the study of cities, Osman served as vice-president of the Ford Foundation and was a senior fellow at Brookings Institute. He was an organizer of urban and regional economic studies and directed the urban policy conference program. During his retirement he remained active and served as a consultant for urban policy and management at Brookings. He died in Garden City, S.C. Obituaries and other sources: *Washington Post,* June 29, 1978.

* * *

OSTER, Jerry 1943-

PERSONAL: Born January 22, 1943, in Carlsbad, N.M.; son of Ted (a book dealer) and Mildred (a book dealer; maiden name, Pobar) Oster. *Education:* Columbia University, B.A., 1964. *Residence:* New York, N.Y. *Office: New York Daily News,* 220 East 42nd St., New York, N.Y. 10014.

CAREER/WRITINGS: United Press International, New York City, reporter, 1965-66; Reuters, Ltd., New York City, reporter, 1966-69; *New York Daily News,* New York City, deskman, feature writer, and movie critic, 1970—.

* * *

OSTERLUND, Steven 1943-

PERSONAL: Born September 11, 1943, in Akron, Ohio; son of Frank August (a businessman) and Betty Louise (Butler) Osterlund. *Education:* Attended Ashland College, 1961-62, 1963-66, University of Akron, 1962-63, Kent State University, 1966-67, and Akron Art Institute. *Politics:* "If any, quite liberal." *Residence:* Akron, Ohio.

CAREER: Akron Public Library, Akron, Ohio, assistant reference librarian, 1962-66; University of Western Ontario, London, assistant reference librarian, 1967-68; Lambton College, Sarnia, Ontario, faculty member in creative writing, 1969; *Sarnia Observer,* Sarnia, Ontario, reporter, 1969-70; writer, 1970—. Radio writer in Canada. Faculty member at Fanshawe College, 1976-77. Artist, with more than a hundred paintings in private collections, and five exhibitions. *Awards, honors:* Writing grant from Abraham Woursell Foundation, 1971-76, for University of Vienna; Ontario Arts Council grants, 1976, 1977.

WRITINGS: Sign on a Door (poems), Commonwealth Press, 1971; *Fumigator: An Outsider's View of Irving Layton,* Kilally Press, 1975; *Twenty Love Poems,* Windflower Press, 1976; *Pendulum* (poems), Open Chord Press, 1977; *Awakening* (poems), Open Chord Press, 1977.

Work anthologized in *New Directions #20, Aspen Anthology,* and *The New Salt Creek Reader.* International correspondent for *Poesie Vivante,* 1966. Contributor of more than a hundred poems to literary journals in the United States and Canada and abroad, including *Massachusetts Review, Tamarack Review, Nation, Open Places,* and *Canadian Forum.* Editor of *Orange Bear Reader,* 1970—; past editor of *Stuffed Crocodile.*

WORK IN PROGRESS: In a Town of Steel, memoirs; *Mysteries of the World* (tentative title), poems; *The Private Life: Poems, 1965-1977; Holes,* poems; *A Bowl of Burning Stones,* poems; *The Eye Doctor* (tentative title), stories; a collection of love poems and ink-wash drawings; a trilogy of short novels, *The Listener, Liars,* and *The Traveler.*

SIDELIGHTS: Osterlund writes: "I started writing at an early age according to my mother, who encouraged me endlessly. Works important to me personally, to my growth, were those of many Ohio writers, especially James Purdy, who I consider one of America's best contemporary writers of prose fiction. I wrote poetry during my student years, but everything before 1965 was garbage.

"Then came Vietnam and the most important change in my life: I protested the whole disaster, and finally 'dodged' the draft by moving to Canada on the advice of my father (who served honorably in the U.S. Navy). The move threw me out of myself, out of my native land, into a cultural experience I could never have imagined.

"It was the age-old story of the starving (literally) artist. I met the Canadian poet Irving Layton, the single most important personal influence to my work and my life. During the decade in Canada my work came to life. I was removed enough from America to be able to view events in its turbulent history with some objectivity. I also traveled to France and Sweden. Some American writers and poets stood by me steadfastly during these years, encouraging me through their letters: Henry Miller, James Purdy, James Laughlin, and Irving Layton.

"My background is a mixed bag. My father was born in Philadelphia, but lived in Lisbon until he was seventeen. He spoke several languages, played a beautiful guitar and mandolin, and was a marvelous graphic artist. My mother was from a family line that included the founders of Salem, Mass.; she was the great reader of literature.

"I consider *life* vital, and it is so sadly lacking from recent American writing. I leaned toward many writers because it was my nature to embrace the whole. I don't give a damn for 'regional' writing; I want the universal or nothing at all. The poet should speak for all men and women on this planet or he fails those who went before him, and he fails the gods. My work ranges from the introspective, rather dark vision of an outsider (which I am) to the passionate outbursts of a somewhat angry (but mostly loving) man. I like poems—the language—to go straight to the heart. I like passion. I want to taste a poem, or a line of prose, feel it on my skin. I loathe surrealism, or 'new' surrealism as it is practiced at present. I find most new poetry unreadable. The poets are playing tricks; they seem to have forgotten (or forsaken) the language.

"While my work may at times be dark and painful, I am a lover of life, of great music, books, wine, women (Woman), and all of the life-giving sources. I will reflect this in my writings or die trying, a happy failure!"

*   *   *

OSTROFF, Anthony J(ames) 1923-1978

November 9, 1923—April 9, 1978; American poet and teacher who was one of the first American intellectuals to protest U.S. involvement in Vietnam. As a professor of rhetoric at University of California at Berkely from 1949 to 1969, and as a professor of humanities at Portland's Lewis and Clark College since 1969, Ostroff earned numerous fellowships and poetry awards. Despite these awards, and the 1962 publication of *Imperatives,* he admitted several years ago that he had only recently begun the work that he most wished to do—writing poetry. Ostroff published his last book of verse, *A Fall in Mexico,* in 1977, and at the time of his death was preparing *Five Cold Days,* a collection of short stories, for publication. He died in Pacific City, Ore. Obituaries and other sources: *World Authors, 1950-1970,* Wilson, 1975; *The Writers Directory, 1976-78,* St. Martin's, 1976; *Who's Who in the West,* 16th edition, Marquis, 1978; *New York Times,* April 13, 1978. (See index for *CA* sketch)

*   *   *

O'SULLIVAN, Joan (D'Arcy)

PERSONAL: Born in New York, N.Y.; daughter of Timothy J. and Edna (D'Arcy) O'Sullivan; married Archie Vassiliades, June 1, 1956; children: Darcy, Demitra. *Education:* Attended Fordham University, 1943-47. *Office:* King Features, 235 East 45th St., New York, N.Y. 10017.

CAREER: New York Sun, New York City, educational reporter, 1945-47, feature writer, 1947-50; King Features, New York City, feature writer, 1950-67, women's editor and author of column, "Women's Ways," 1967-76, senior editor and author of column, "Living Today," 1976—. *Member:* Newswomen's Club of New York (president, 1958-60; member of board of directors, 1961—; vice-president, 1974-78). *Awards, honors:* Prize story award from Newswomen's Club of New York, and citation from New York Department of Commerce, both 1951, both for series on women who originate their own business.

WRITINGS: One Hundred Ways to Popularity, Macmillan, 1961. Home editor of *New York Mirror,* 1964-67.

*   *   *

OTT, Maggie Glen
See OTT, Virginia

*   *   *

OTT, Virginia 1917-
(Maggie Glenn Ott)

PERSONAL: Born October 14, 1917, in Milo, Iowa; daughter of James Byron (a farmer) and Margaret (a milliner; maiden name, Glenn) Hall; married Clifford Raymond Ott (an Episcopal priest), September 29, 1940; children: Frances M. (Mrs. James Bly), Paula L. (Mrs. Edward Payne), Virginia Rae (Mrs. J. George Bly), Theodore Jeffrey and Terence James (adopted twins). *Education:* Simpson College, B.A., 1939; University of Minnesota, M.A.L.S., 1966; other graduate study at University of North Dakota and University of Nebraska. *Politics:* Republican. *Religion:* Episcopalian. *Home:* 116 South Ninth St., Nebraska City, Neb. 68410. *Office:* Hayward School, Nebraska City, Neb. 68410.

CAREER: High school English teacher and librarian in Fonda, Iowa, 1954-62; elementary school teacher in Hallock, Minn., 1962-65, 1967-70; media director at junior high school in Jamestown, N.D., 1971-76; Hayward School, Nebraska City, Neb., media director and librarian, 1976—. Member of North Dakota governor's advisory council on libraries, 1974-76. Teacher of creative writing.

MEMBER: P.E.O. Sisterhood, American Library Association, American Association of School Librarians, National Education Association, Parent Teacher Association (life member), Nebraska Educational Media Association, Nebraska Education Association, Federated Womans Club, Nebraska City Education Association, Delta Kappa Gamma, Pi Delta Kappa, Eastern Star (worthy matron).

WRITINGS: (With Gloria Swanson) *Man with a Million Ideas* (juvenile), Lerner, 1977. Contributor to state library news publications.

WORK IN PROGRESS: A biography of Dr. Anne Carlsen, administrator of Crippled Children's Hospital/School in Jamestown, N.D., with Gloria Swanson; research for a series on the "late pioneer Midwest," for middle grades, based on the experiences of her mother, under pseudonym Maggie Glenn Ott.

SIDELIGHTS: Virginia Ott writes: "My roots go deep into mid-America. One grandmother came from County Down, Ireland, in the 1850's. Otherwise, my ancestors have been here since the early 1700's and followed the frontier to the Middle West. I was raised on family lore. We were all readers—from a Carnegie Library. Every Saturday afternoon I traveled around the world via stereoptican viewers.

"Writing became my avocation. Five children, a full-time job, and life in a rectory leave little time for any activity requiring long concentration. My writing is often done in spurts, in pencil, on yellow legal pads. Having a co-author was good for me.

"I am tremendously interested in a children's approach to religion and I am concerned about the necessity for exercise, nutrition, and mental activity in the field of geriatrics.

"I like being a librarian/media director. I believe the 'book' is generic—appearing today in more and more forms, adaptable for print and non-print. It is an exciting time to be working with children, teachers, and media."

AVOCATIONAL INTERESTS: Reading (especially Louis L'Amour westerns and twentieth-century poetry).

*   *   *

OWEN, George Earle 1908-

PERSONAL: Born March 26, 1908, in Christiansburg, Va.; son of George Elvy (a clergyman) and Ethel (Berry) Owen; married Margaret Frances Richards (a clergywoman), May 23, 1936; children: Mary Devon (Mrs. Gordon Covert O'Brien), Anne Franklin (Mrs. Alvin Marcus Fountain II), Margaret Earle (Mrs. Gerald Daniel Clark, Jr.), Deborah Elizabeth. *Education:* Bethany College, Bethany, W.Va., A.B., 1931; University of Chicago, M.A., 1938; Union Theological Seminary, New York, N.Y., B.D., 1940; Columbia University, Ed.D., 1943. *Home:* 5354 Julian Ave., Indianapolis, Ind. 46219.

CAREER: Ordained minister of Christian Church (Disci-

ples of Christ), 1928; pastor of churches in Bolivar, Pa., 1928-31, Tazewell, Va., 1931-35, and Winchester, Va., 1935-37, associate pastor in New York, N.Y., 1939-40; Christian Church (Disciples of Christ), Richmond, Va., area director of religious education for Virginia, Maryland, Delaware, and the District of Columbia, 1940-42; Union Theological Seminary, Buenos Aires, Argentina, professor of church history, and vice-president and head of department, 1943-48; United Christian Missionary Society, Indianapolis, Ind., field representative, 1949-50; Union Theological Seminary, Manila, the Philippines, professor of philosophy, and head of department, 1951-55; United Christian Missionary Society, executive secretary for missionary selection and training, and dean of College of Missions, 1955-57, chairman of Division of General Departments, 1957-67; General Office of the Christian Church, Indianapolis, Ind., assistant to the general minister and the president, and editor of yearbook and directory, 1967-73; writer, 1973—. Member of board of directors and executive committee of Tougaloo College, 1965—; member of board of directors of Irvington Historic Landmarks Foundation, 1970-72, and Colegio Ward.

MEMBER: American Bible Society (member of board of directors, 1968-71), Indiana Historical Society, Disciples of Christ Historical Society (life member), Irvington Historical Society (president, 1970-72), Contemporary Club of Indianapolis, Indianapolis Literary Club, Brevard Poetry Club, Indianapolis Athletic Club. *Awards, honors:* Distinguished service award from Disciples of Christ churches in the Tagalog area of the Philippines, 1954; D.D. from Bethany College, Bethany, W.Va.

WRITINGS: Faith and Freedom: The Problem of Religious Freedom and the Christian Answer, Philippine Federation of Christian Churches, 1953; *Education for Mission and Change,* Christian Board of Publication (St. Louis, Mo.), 1964; *A Century of Witness,* Christian Church Services, Inc., 1975; *The Nature of Prayer,* Christian Church Services, Inc., 1977. Contributor of articles and reviews to religious magazines. Editor of *River Plate Reflections,* 1943-48; member of board of directors of *Religion in American Life,* 1968-72.

WORK IN PROGRESS: Lessons Learned from Experience, an autobiography.

SIDELIGHTS: Owen told *CA:* "A rewarding experience while at the seminary in Buenos Aires was preparing Christian leaders for working in all of Latin America. Five of my former students are now bishops, one is president of the seminary, and one is in a top-level position in the World Council of Churches."

*   *   *

OWEN, Roger C(orey) 1928-

PERSONAL: Born September 14, 1928, in Port Arthur, Tex.; son of Richard B. and Evelyn (Corey) Owen; married Suzanne Martinez, 1951; children: five. *Education:* Michigan State University, B.A., 1953; University of Arizona, M.A., 1957; University of California, Los Angeles, Ph.D., 1962. *Home:* 25 Duck Pond Rd., Glen Cove, N.Y. 11542. *Office:* Department of Anthropology, Queens College of the City University of New York, Flushing, N.Y. 11367.

CAREER: University of California, Los Angeles, field director of Paipai Interdisciplinary Research Project, 1958-59; University of California, Santa Barbara, instructor, 1959-61, assistant professor, 1961-64, associate professor of anthropology, 1964-67; Queens College of the City University of New York, Flushing, N.Y., professor of anthropology, 1967—. Visiting professor at Fundacao Escola de Sociologia e Politica, 1964-65; visiting lecturer at University of Arizona, summers, 1968, 1974, Sweetbriar College, 1972, University of California, Irvine, 1972, and Widener College, 1975. Consultant to National Science Foundation, General Motors, Educational Associates, Inc., Department of Health, Education and Welfare, and Wenner-Gren Foundation.

MEMBER: American Anthropological Association (fellow), American Association for the Advancement of Science, Current Anthropology (associate), American Ethnological Society (member of council, 1966-69), Southwestern Anthropological Association (president, 1963-64), Sigma Xi. *Awards, honors:* Grants from Licensed Beverages Industries, Inc., 1964-66, National Science Foundation, 1966-67, and Holt, Rinehart & Winston, 1969-71.

WRITINGS: (Editor with others) *The North American Indians: A Sourcebook,* Macmillan, 1967; (contributor) Walter Buckley, editor, *Readings in Modern Systems Research for the Behavioral Scientist,* Aldine, 1968; *Inquiring About Cultures,* with databook and teacher's guide, Holt, 1972, revised edition published as *Inquiring About Cultures: Anthropology and Sociology,* 1976. Contributor to *Handbook of Middle American Indians* and *Encyclopedia of Indians of the Americas.* Contributor of more than thirty articles and reviews to anthropology journals.

WORK IN PROGRESS: The Anthropology of Native North America, for Macmillan.

* * *

OWENS, John R(obert) 1926-

PERSONAL: Born May 29, 1926, in Ilion, N.Y.; son of Albert E. (a farmer) and Anna Mae (Rowlands) Owens; married Elizabeth Bauman (a teacher), August 4, 1962; children: John R., Jr., David. *Education:* Syracuse University, B.A., 1949, M.A., 1952, Ph.D., 1956. *Politics:* Independent. *Religion:* Protestant. *Home:* 527 Rutgers Dr., Davis, Calif. 95616. *Office:* Department of Political Science, University of California, Davis, Calif. 95616.

CAREER: Wesleyan University, Middletown, Conn., instructor in political science, 1953-56; University of Michigan, Ann Arbor, instructor in political science, 1956-59; University of California, Davis, assistant professor, 1959-66, associate professor, 1966-71, professor of political science, 1971—. *Military service:* U.S. Navy, 1944-46. *Member:* American Political Science Association, Western Political Science Association, University of California Faculty Club, Pi Sigma Alpha, Pi Gamma Mu. *Awards, honors:* Fulbright scholar in Japan, 1976.

WRITINGS: (Editor with Phillip J. Stuadenraus) *The American Party System,* Macmillan, 1965; *A Wildlife Agency and Its Possessive Public,* Bobbs-Merrill, 1965; (with Edmond Constantine and Lewis Weschler) *Party Politics in California,* Macmillan, 1970; *Trends in Campaign Spending in California,* Citizens Research Foundation, 1973.

WORK IN PROGRESS: Research on campaign spending and political reform.

* * *

OWER, John 1942-

PERSONAL: Born January 17, 1942, in Palmerston North, New Zealand; son of John Rattray (a geologist) and Jessie (Barnasconi) Ower; married Patricia Baxter, July 14, 1965; children: Katherine. *Education:* University of Alberta, B.A. (with honors), 1963, M.A., 1965, Ph.D., 1972. *Politics:* Conservative. *Religion:* Roman Catholic. *Home:* #221 Chateau de Ville Apts., Columbia, S.C. 29208. *Office:* Department of English, University of South Carolina, Columbia, S.C. 29208.

CAREER: College St. Jean, Edmonton, Alberta, lecturer, 1966-68; St. Francis Xavier University, Antigonish, Nova Scotia, lecturer, 1968-69; University of Alberta, Edmonton, sessional lecturer, 1969-70; University of Tennessee at Chattanooga, assistant professor of English, 1970-72; University of Waikato, Hamilton, New Zealand, lecturer in English, 1972-73; University of South Carolina, Columbia, assistant professor of English, 1973—. *Military service:* Served briefly in Canadian Air Force Reserve. *Member:* South Atlantic Modern Language Association. *Awards, honors:* Woodrow Wilson fellowship, 1963-64; Fellow of Massey College, University of Toronto, 1963-64; Canada Council Post-Doctoral Research fellowship, 1975-76; South Carolina Arts Commission fellowship, 1976-77; Winthrop College poetry award, 1977, for *Legendary Acts.*

WRITINGS: Legendary Acts (poems), University of Georgia Press, 1977.

Contributor: George Woodcock, editor, *Poets and Critics: Essays from Canadian Literature 1966-1974,* Oxford University Press, 1974; Woodcock, editor, *Colony and Confederation: Early Canadian Poets and Their Background,* University of British Columbia Press, 1974; Lorraine McMullen, editor, *Twentieth Century Essays on Confederation Literature,* Tecumseh Press, 1976; Jac Tharpe, editor, *Tennessee Williams: A Tribute,* University Press of Mississippi, 1977; Frank Tierney, editor, *The Crawford Symposium,* University of Ottawa Press, 1978.

Contributor of articles, reviews, and poems to more than fifty scholarly journals and reviews, including *Canadian Literature, Fitzgerald/Hemingway Annual, Modern Fiction Studies, Southern Poetry Review, Southern Humanities Review,* and *Paris Review.*

WORK IN PROGRESS: A book on Edith Sitwell; a volume of verse.

SIDELIGHTS: John Ower told *CA:* "I started writing poetry as a teenager, most of it appallingly bad. My juvenilia have mercifully been destroyed. As an undergraduate at the University, I was motivated by a Canadian poet, Eli Mandel. I started submitting poetry to Canadian magazines. I had a few acceptances, but by 1968 I was so discouraged I gave up circulating. At that time in Canada six editors could make or break your career. In 1972 I went to New Zealand—change of scene and a 2½ hour per week teaching load—I don't know why I ever came back—started me writing again. And I published a couple of poems in New Zealand magazines.

"I've always regarded poetry as something an educated gentleman should do in his spare time, and I frankly never took my own work terribly seriously until the acceptance of my volume and the awarding of the South Carolina Arts Commission Individual Artist Fellowship in Literature in 1976. I am now becoming somewhat more ambitious, although not to the point of consistently collecting rejection slips from the New York 'slicks' as do most of my poet friends. I am presently working on a second volume of poetry which I will have in circulation in a short while.

"I regard myself as strongly supported and encouraged by other people.

''Poetry in general: Most modern American poetry can be fitted into one or more variations of bad Romanticism. I regard myself as following in the modern metaphysical tradition of T. S. Eliot, although I do feel a lot of inspiration from Blake and Shelley. I'm more and more emphasizing discipline, control, and craft. I am experimenting a good deal with rhymed forms. Despite this, I must confess that I work by inspiration and that most of the first drafts of my poems are produced in less than a day. However, I do a good deal of revision. I was also very much influenced in writing by the 'Toronto School' of myth and symbol critics founded by Northrop Frye.

''I am very much disturbed by the contemporary myth of the 'victim poet.' I have no desire to be a suicide, an alcoholic, or to indulge in any of the varieties of sexual misbehavior. I am very straight and square. I don't drink much any-more—diabetes in the family. Despite my personal predilec-tions my first volume of poetry obviously reflects and was partly written in reaciton to a deeply disturbed sensibility (*mine*). I've sometimes defined my poetry as intellect tortured by emotion, emotion tortured by intellect, and both torturing sound.

''I have for some time been a fancier of snakes, but recently understandable objections of my wife and fear of the land-lord have combined to make me give up my last pet python, Nathan.

''Other than the usual financial tensions, etc., affecting most married couples in the late '70's, I lead a relatively quiet family life. I find my daughter a great delight, and she's in-spired me to write a number of poems from the perspective of childhood. I am a convert to Roman Catholicism and have now been in the Church twelve years. I consider religion a very, very important part of my outlook.''

P

PACOSZ, Christina V(ivian) 1946-

PERSONAL: Born October 12, 1946, in Detroit, Mich.; daughter of Walter Frank (an automobile company employee) and Sophia (a cleaning woman; maiden name, Kostrzewski) Pacosz. *Education:* Wayne State University, B.S.Ed., 1970. *Politics:* "Anarchist." *Religion:* "Pagan." *Home:* 4511 North Kirby, Portland, Ore. 97217.

CAREER: Teacher of special education at public schools in Detroit, Highland Park, and Croswell, all Mich., 1970-73, and Estacada, Ore., 1973-76; writer, 1976—. Poet-in-residence of Portland Metropolitan Arts Commission.

WRITINGS: Shimmy Up to This Fine Mud, Poets Warehouse, 1976.

SIDELIGHTS: Christina Pacosz comments: "I view my poetry as magic, as ritual, as healing in a shamanistic sense. Feminism and the loving support of many women have been vital to my work. Poetry has the power to change people and cultural viewpoints. That is my aim in writing, but first I change myself."

* * *

PALMER, Kenneth T. 1937-

PERSONAL: Born March 22, 1937, in Glen Ridge, N.J.; son of Leland Kenneth and Thelma (Townsend) Palmer; married Janice Ruof, March 15, 1969. *Education:* Amherst College, B.A., 1959; Pennsylvania State University, M.A., 1961, Ph.S., 1964. *Politics:* Republican. *Religion:* Congregationalist. *Home:* 4 Pinewood St., Orono, Maine 04473. *Office:* Department of Political Science, University of Maine, Orono, Maine 04473.

CAREER: Pennsylvania State University, State College, instructor in political science, 1963-64; Hamilton College, Clinton, N.Y., assistant professor of political science, 1964-67; Franklin & Marshall College, Lancaster, Pa., assistant professor of political science, 1967-69; University of Maine, Orono, associate professor of political science, 1969—. Research assistant at Brookings Institution, 1973—. Member of Orono Board of Zoning Appeals. *Member:* American Political Science Association, National Municipal League, Delta Sigma Rho.

WRITINGS: (With Nelson P. Guild) *Introduction to Politics,* Wiley, 1968; *State Politics in the United States,* St. Martin's, 1972, new edition, 1977; (with others) *The Legisla-*

tive Process in Maine, American Political Science Association, 1973; (with James Horan) *Studies in American Politics,* MSS Information Corp., 1974. Contributor to *Collier's Encyclopedia* and to political science journals.

WORK IN PROGRESS: Co-author of *America's Changing Federalism* for Brookings Institution.

* * *

PALMER, Raymond Edward 1927-

PERSONAL: Born April 1, 1927, in Bristol, England; son of Walter Edward (a businessman) and Emily Alice (Randall) Palmer; married Joan Parker (a sculptor), December 18, 1954. *Education:* Attended U.S. Air Force College, Tokyo, Japan, 1948. *Home:* 1 Lyme Farm Rd., Lee, London SE12 8JE, England.

CAREER: Bristol Evening World, Bristol, England, junior reporter, 1944; *British Commonwealth Forces Newspaper,* Tokyo, Japan, bureau chief, 1947-48; *Bristol Evening Post,* Bristol, reporter and author of column "Radio Notes," 1949-50; Central Office of Information, Manchester, England, press officer, 1950-52; Reuters Ltd., London, England, journalist, 1952-54; Associated Press, London, staff writer and editor, 1954-67; free-lance writer, 1967—. *Military service:* British Army, Royal Army Service Corps, 1945-49; became sergeant. *Member:* International Federation of Journalists, National Union of Journalists.

WRITINGS: The Making of a Spy, Crown, 1977; *Tools and Techniques of Espionage,* Crown, 1978. Contributor to popular magazines in the United States and England, including *Reader's Digest, Cosmopolitan, Penthouse,* and *Catholic Digest,* and to newspapers.

WORK IN PROGRESS: A book of "faction," on intelligence and deception in summer of 1940; research on contemporary history since 1930, with particular reference to the role played by intelligence and espionage agents in the shaping of world affairs.

SIDELIGHTS: Palmer writes: "My writing is mainly nonfiction, about intelligence and espionage matters; I have many friends and contacts among former intelligence officers from a number of countries. My interests are now turning toward a blend of fiction and fact to produce 'factional' novels in this field, based on expert background knowledge. I have travelled extensively in Spain, and visited France, Belgium, Holland, Germany, Italy, Switzerland, Egypt, Ceylon, Hong Kong, China, Singapore, and Japan."

BIOGRAPHICAL/CRITICAL SOURCES: Spectator, February 26, 1954; *World's Press News,* February 26, 1954; *Bookseller,* February 27, 1954; *United Kingdom Press Gazette,* October 4, 1971.

*   *   *

PANTER, Gideon G. 1935-

PERSONAL: Born April 24, 1935, in Montreal, Quebec, Canada; son of Philip E. (a professor) and Nehamah (a teacher; maiden name, Serlin) Panter; widower; children: Danielle, Ethan, Abigail. *Education:* Cornell University, B.A., 1956, M.D., 1960. *Office:* 653 Park Ave., New York, N.Y. 10021.

CAREER: Columbia-Presbyterian Medical Center, New York, N.Y., resident, 1960-65; private practice in obstetrics and gynecology, 1965—. Assistant professor at Cornell University. Assistant attending obstetrician and gynecologist at New York Hospital—Cornell Medical Center. *Member:* New York County Medical Society.

WRITINGS: Now That You've Had Your Baby, McKay, 1976.

SIDELIGHTS: Panter comments that his two special interests are teaching and informing the lay public on health and medical matters.

*   *   *

PAPASHVILY, George 1898-1978

August 23, 1898—March 29, 1978; Russian-born American sculptor and humorist best known for his best-seller, *Anything Can Happen.* Papashvily's writings, all of which he co-authored with his wife, Helen Waite Papashvily, were based on real-life encounters he experienced in the process of becoming a U.S. citizen and on his life in America. He was highly praised for his work by various critics. He wrote five books, including a collection of Georgian folklore and a primer about how to co-exist with dogs. *Anything Can Happen* sold 600,000 copies, was a Book-of-the-Month selection, was translated into fifteen foreign languages, including Urdu, and was finally made into a motion picture. Papashvily's last written work was *Home and Home Again.* He was also an apprenticed swordmaker and a successful sculptor of animals. Papashvily died in Cambria, Calif. Obituaries and other sources: *Current Biography,* Wilson, 1945; *Who's Who in American Art,* Bowker, 1973; *New York Times,* March 31, 1978; *Time,* April 10, 1978.

*   *   *

PARK, George 1925-

PERSONAL: Born January 8, 1925, in Boston, Mass.; son of Edward C. (a lawyer) and Fentress (Kerlin) Park; married Alice Roach, August 12, 1948; children: Nicholas, Thomas, Geoffrey, Laura. *Education:* Attended Yale University, 1942-47; University of Chicago, M.A., 1951, Ph.D., 1958; Cambridge University, postdoctoral study, 1958-59. *Home address:* Mount Scio Rd., St. John's, Newfoundland, Canada A1C 5H3. *Office:* Department of Anthropology, Memorial University of Newfoundland, St. John's, Newfoundland, Canada A1C 5S7.

CAREER: Freeport Journal-Standard, Freeport, Ill., journalist, 1947-48; Ohio University, Athens, assistant professor of sociology, 1952-61; senior research fellow, East African Institute of Social and Economic Research, 1961-63; University of Pittsburgh, Pittsburgh, Pa., Mellon research fellow, 1963-64; Pitzer College, Claremont, Calif., associate

professor, 1964-67, professor of social anthropology, 1967-69; Memorial University of Newfoundland, St. John's, professor of anthropology, 1969—. *Military service:* U.S. Marine Corps Reserve, active duty, 1943-46; became captain.

WRITINGS: The Idea of Social Structure, Doubleday, 1974.

WORK IN PROGRESS: A book on the Kinga people of Tanzania; a book on local politics in northern Norway.

SIDELIGHTS: Park told *CA:* "*The Idea of Social Structure* examines a small number of exotic societies at close range, and argues that the idea of social structure (which is *not* simple and is generally ignored or misunderstood) is needed by anyone wanting more than a haphazard insight into behaviour in typical human situations. I take it this behaviour is what most of us ultimately want to comprehend, not the myths and models people have in their heads. Mine is a different path than the one Claude Lévi-Strauss takes in pursuit of structure, though we criss-cross here and there. When I come to predicting the kind of society toward which we may be headed I see good reason for expecting continued turbulence but little for anticipating a return to the egalitarian structures in which our kind evolved."

*   *   *

PARK, Richard L(eonard) 1920-

PERSONAL: Born March 29, 1920, in Savannah, Ga.; son of Leonard (a certified public accountant) and Alice (Farrell) Park; married Donna Divine (a consultant), May 1, 1960. *Education:* Northwestern University, S.B., 1942; Harvard University, M.A., 1948, Ph.D., 1951. *Politics:* Democrat. *Home:* 2220 Washtenaw Ave., Ann Arbor, Mich. 48104. *Office:* Department of Political Science, University of Michigan, Ann Arbor, Mich. 48109.

CAREER: University of California, Berkeley, assistant professor of political science, 1953-59, chairman of Center for South Asia Studies, 1953-59; University of Michigan, Ann Arbor, associate professor of political science, 1959-62; Asia Foundation, San Francisco, Calif., representative to India, 1962-64; University of Pittsburgh, Pittsburgh, Pa., professor of political science and dean of social sciences, 1964-66; University of Michigan, professor of political science, 1966—. Vice-president and chairman of board of trustees of American Institute of Indian Studies. Consultant to Ford Foundation, U.S. State Department, and Council on International Exchange of Scholars. *Military service:* U.S. Army Air Forces, 1942-46; became captain.

MEMBER: Association for Asian Studies (secretary-treasurer, 1971-76; vice-president, 1977-78; president, 1978-79), American Political Science Association, Institute of Historical Studies (fellow), Council on Foreign Relations, Asiatic Society (Calcutta).

WRITINGS: (Editor with S. V. Kogekar, and contributor) *State Reports on the Indian General Elections, 1951-52,* Popular Book Co. (Bombay, India), 1956; (with Albert Mayer and McKim Marriott) *Pilot Project, India,* University of California Press, 1958; (editor with Irene Tinker, and contributor) *Leadership and Political Institutions in India,* Princeton University Press, 1959; (with R. A. Scalapino and Guy Pauker) *U.S. Foreign Policy: Asia,* U.S. Senate Committee on Foreign Relations, 1959.

India's Political System, Prentice-Hall, 1967, revised edition (with Bruce Bueno de Mesquita), 1979; (contributor) Roy Macridis, editor, *Foreign Policy in World Politics,* Prentice-Hall, 5th edition, 1976; (contributor) George T.

Yu, editor, *Intra-Asian International Relations*, Westview Press, 1977; (with Stephen P. Cohen) *India: Emergent Power?*, Crane, Russak, 1978; (editor) *Social Change in Modern India*, Michigan State University Asian Studies Center, 1978. Also editor of *Patterns of Change in Modern Bengal*, 1978.

Contributor to annals of American Academy of Political and Social Science. Member of editorial board of *Asian Survey* and *Asian Forum*.

WORK IN PROGRESS: Samuel Walliker, Victorian Postmaster; a book on the revolutionary movement in Bengal, 1905-1934; a personal memoir on M. N. Roy, founder of the Communist Party of India and of Mexico.

SIDELIGHTS: Park comments: "About fifteen years of residence in India since 1943 have shaped my career and my writing interests. Hindi, some Bengali, and French have been used in my work. One of my major writing tasks will be a personal study of my experiences in India since 1943, concentrating on direct observations of the changes that took place from the old British regime to the present."

AVOCATIONAL INTERESTS: Music (classical European and Asian).

* * *

PARKER, David Marshall 1929-

PERSONAL: Born January 3, 1929, in Hawaii; son of George Henry (a lieutenant commander in U.S. Navy) and Dorothy (a Navy nurse; maiden name, Wright) Parker; married Joanne Ostroga (a psychologist), February 23, 1973. *Education:* San Diego State College, A.B., 1960; University of California, Los Angeles, M.A., 1963, Ph.D., 1964. *Politics:* Republican. *Home:* 13745 Chandler, Van Nuys, Calif. *Office:* Department of Psychology, California State University, 18111 Nordhoff, Northridge, Calif. 91330.

CAREER: California State University, Northridge, assistant professor, 1963-68, associate professor, 1968-76; professor of psychology, 1976—. Has also worked as welder, mechanic, and flight engineer. *Military service:* U.S. Air Force, 1946-50. *Member:* American Association for the Advancement of Science, Sigma Xi.

WRITINGS: Ocean Voyaging, de Graff, 1975; *Offshore*, Time-Life, 1976. Also author of forewords of books for Time-Life, including *Motor Boating and Sailing*, 1975, *Yachting*, 1975, *The Hardy Boatman*, 1977, and *Sea*, 1978. Contributor to psychology and boating magazines.

WORK IN PROGRESS: Research on the physiology of motion sickness and the psychology of stress.

SIDELIGHTS: Parker writes: "I am a believer in individualism, and in the right of man to challenge established thinking. I wrote my book to stand in contradiction to the vast erroneous literature on sailing. I am, and probably will be a rebel. I am *not* a liberal, but might rightfully be called a libertarian."

* * *

PARKER, Robert 1920-

PERSONAL: Born November 13, 1920, in Garland, Ark.; son of Robert E. (a teacher) and Theresa (a teacher; maiden name, Ebonham) Parker; married Elizabeth Sass, May 27, 1944; children: Doris Ruth, Carol Elizabeth. *Education:* Attended Arkansas Polytechnic College, 1937-39; University of Missouri, B.J., 1941. *Home:* 6 Summit Rd., Port Washington, N.Y. 11050. *Office:* Time, Inc., Rockefeller Center, New York, N.Y. 10020.

CAREER/WRITINGS: Arkansas Gazette, Little Rock, Ark., reporter, 1941-42, 1945-48; Time, Inc., New York, N.Y., correspondent, 1948—, deputy chief of correspondents, 1965-72, news editor in Europe, 1973-75. *Military service:* U.S. Naval Reserve, 1942-45; became lieutenant.

* * *

PARKER, Willie J. 1924-

PERSONAL: Born July 1, 1924, in Smith County, Tenn.; son of J. D. (a farmer) and Bess (Warren) Parker; married Margaret Faye Gibbs, February 2, 1947; children: Rita Elaine, William Ronald. *Education:* Attended George Peabody College for Teachers. *Religion:* Baptist. *Home:* 2312 Revere Pl., Nashville, Tenn. 37214. *Agent:* Bill Reiss, Paul R. Reynolds, Inc., 12 East 41st St., New York, N.Y. 10017. *Office:* U.S. Fish & Wildlife Service, Federal Building, P.O. Box 290, Nashville, Tenn. 37214.

CAREER: Tennessee wildlife officer supervisor in Greenbrier, 1948-57; U.S. Fish & Wildlife Service, Washington, D.C., special wildlife agent in Kentucky, 1957-66, special agent in charge of office in Annapolis, Md., 1966-74, and Nashville, Tenn., 1974—. *Military service:* U.S. Navy, air bomber; received Air Medal and Distinguished Flying Cross.

WRITINGS: Halt: I'm a Federal Game Warden, McKay, 1977.

WORK IN PROGRESS: See How They Die, the story of the mourning dove; a college textbook on wildlife law enforcement.

SIDELIGHTS: Parker writes: "I have been committed to wildlife conservation and wise use for some forty years. Writing is an attempt to share my knowledge and experience with less fortunate people who have not been able to spend their entire lives in the realm of wildlife."

* * *

PARKERSON, John 1885(?)-1978

1885(?)—March 18, 1978; American writer, newspaperman, and author. He began his career at the age of ten by publishing a newspaper in his hometown of Franklin, La. Parkerson was a cub reporter for the *Los Angeles Times* before he was sent to Europe by the Associated Press to cover World War I. After organizing Fox Newsreel and Trans Radio Wireless Press, he returned to Europe to cover World War II. Parkerson wrote *Looking Back to Glory*, a collection of war stories. He died in Ormond Beach, Fla. Obituaries and other sources: *New York Times*, March 21, 1978.

* * *

PARMET, Robert D(avid) 1938-

PERSONAL: Born December 11, 1938, in New York, N.Y.; son of Isaac and Fanny (Scharf) Parmet; married Joan Bernice Levy, June 8, 1963; children: Andrew Charles. *Education:* City College (now of the City University of New York), B.A., 1960; Columbia University, M.A., 1961, Ph.D., 1966. *Home:* 1 Highland Pl., Great Neck, N.Y. 11020. *Office:* Department of History and Philosophy, York College of the City University of New York, 150-14 Jamaica Ave., Jamaica, N.Y. 11451.

CAREER: City College of the City University of New York, New York, N.Y., lecturer in history, 1962-65; Newark State College, Union, N.J., assistant professor of history, 1965-67; York College of the City University of New

York, Jamaica, N.Y., assistant professor, 1967-70, associate professor, 1971-77, professor of history, 1978—. *Member:* American Historical Association, Organization of American Historians, Academy of Political Science, Southern Historical Association, Connecticut Historical Society, New York State Labor History Association.

WRITINGS: (With Ira M. Leonard) *American Nativism, 1830-1860,* Van Nostrand, 1971; *Labor and Immigration in Industrial America,* Twayne, in press. Contributor to history journals.

SIDELIGHTS: Parmet commented to *CA:* "Both antebellum and late nineteenth-early twentieth century nativism served opportunistic purposes. The Know-Nothing movement of the 1850's exploited anti-immigrant and anti-Catholic sentiment to gain political power during a period of sectional division over the slavery issue and rapid social change.

"Between the Civil War and the Great Depression, American workers of northern and western European descent combined economic and racial fears to form labor organizations and secure immigration exclusion and restriction. A successful anti-Chinese campaign led to attacks on southern and eastern Europeans as well as other Asians. Despite considerable evidence that the unwelcome Europeans could be organized and serve the cause of labor with distinction, the American Federation of Labor, guided by Samuel Gompers, fought bitterly until their entry was curtailed."

*   *   *

PARRISH, Mary Frances
    See FISHER, M(ary) F(rances) K(ennedy)

*   *   *

PATTERSON, Lindsay 1942-

PERSONAL: Born July 22, 1942, in Bastrop, La.; son of James Harrison (a physician and dentist) and Frances Adele (a teacher; maiden name, Lindsay) Patterson. *Education:* Virginia State College, B.A.

CAREER: Writer. Worked as an account executive for Harrison Advertising Agency; was an editorial assistant for writer, Langston Hughes; visiting lecturer at Hunter College of the City University of New York, 1974-75; co-host of "Celebrity Hour" on WRVR-FM Radio and "Patterson and Coombs: Black Conversations" on WPIX-TV. *Military service:* U.S. Army, correspondent for *Stars and Stripes* in Europe, feature writer and managing editor for *Patton Post,* served in Germany.

AWARDS, HONORS: Award from National Foundation on the Arts and Humanities; three MacDowell Colony fellowships; two Edward Albee Foundation fellowships.

WRITINGS: (Editor and author of introduction) *The Negro in Music and Art,* Publishers Co., 1967, 2nd edition, 1968; (editor and author of introduction) *Anthology of the American Negro in the Theatre: A Critical Approach,* Publishers Co., 1967, 2nd edition, 1968; (editor) *An Introduction to Black Literature in America: From 1946 to the Present,* Publishers Co., 1968; (editor and author of introduction) *Black Theater: A Twentieth-Century Collection of the Work of Its Best Playwrights,* Dodd, 1971; (editor and author of introduction) *A Rock Against the Wind: Black Love Poems, an Anthology,* Dodd, 1973; (editor and author of introduction) *Black Films and Film-Makers: A Comprehensive Anthology from Stereotype to Superhero,* Dodd, 1975; (editor) *A Critical Study of the Best Black Playwrights,* Dodd, 1978; *Diary*

of an Aging Young Writer: An Autobiography, Morrow, 1978. Also editor of *Black Theater,* New American Library.

Anthologized in *The Best Short Stories by Negro Writers; Young Black Storytellers; The World of Language.* Contributor of more than thirty stories, articles, and reviews to popular magazines, including *New Leader, Saturday Review, Essence,* and *Freedomways,* and to newspapers. Feature writer and columnist, *Associated Negro Press.*

WORK IN PROGRESS: The Plot, a novel; "Roper," a screenplay; "Rock Against the Wind," a play on black love; "Black Magazine" for television.

SIDELIGHTS: Patterson writes: "My primary interest is fiction and I feel that my career as a fiction writer is just beginning. My aim is to write high quality fiction about blacks, with popular appeal."

*   *   *

PAUL, (John) Anthony 1941-

PERSONAL: Born May 30, 1941, in Caernarvon, Wales; son of Leslie Douglas (a musician) and Elizabeth (Lloyd-Jones) Paul; married Rita Moretti, August, 1966; children: Alexandra. *Education:* New College, Oxford, B.A. (honors), 1962. *Politics:* Social Democrat. *Religion:* "None at present." *Home:* Zocherstraat 15, Amsterdam, Netherlands. *Agent:* Tessa Sayle, 11 Jubilee Pl., London SW3 3TE, England.

CAREER: Teacher in Italy, 1962-63; International Language Centre, London, England, teacher, 1963-71; University of Amsterdam, Institute of Translation Studies, Amsterdam, the Netherlands, lecturer in English, 1972—.

WRITINGS: A Present From Hugo (novel), Collins, 1966; (translator) Giuliano Procacci, *A History of the Italian People,* Weidenfeld & Nicolson, 1970, Penguin, 1973; *Down the Rabbit Hole* (novel), Secker & Warburg, 1972; *The Tiger Who Lost His Stripes* (for children), Andersen Press, 1978. Also translator of scripts for BBC-TV.

WORK IN PROGRESS: Two novels; children's stories; poems.

SIDELIGHTS: Paul commented briefly: "My two published novels were more or less comic, with touches of parody and satire. While I have not lost interest in social comedy, I find myself now trying to work towards a greater economy and poetic concentration of effect."

*   *   *

PAUL, Anthony (Marcus) 1937-

PERSONAL: Born June 17, 1937, in Brisbane, Australia; son of Arthur Aubrey (a manufacturer) and Grace (Brodie) Paul; married Anne Carse (a gemmologist), May 2, 1964; children: Anthony Brodie, Bruce Bradley. *Education:* Attended University of Queensland, 1955-59, and Macalester College, 1961-62. *Home:* 9 Jade House, 47-C Stubbs Rd., Hong Kong.

CAREER: United Press International, New York, N.Y., correspondent and copy editor on international desk, 1963-65; *Reader's Digest,* Pleasantville, N.Y., associate editor of international editions, 1965-67, editor-in-chief for Australia and New Zealand, 1967-71, roving editor in Asia and the Pacific, 1971—. *Military service:* Royal Australian Air Force, 1950-59; became flying officer. *Member:* Foreign Correspondents Club of Hong Kong (president, 1977-78), American Club of Hong Kong, American National Club of Sydney (Australia), Royal Hong Kong Yacht Club.

WRITINGS: (With John Barron) *Murder of a Gentle Land,* Crowell, 1977, published in England as *Peace With Horror,* Hodder & Stoughton, 1977.

WORK IN PROGRESS: Shanghai, 1937-1949.

* * *

PAUL VI, Pope   1897-1978

September 26, 1897—August 6, 1978; Italian Roman Catholic pontiff, archbishop of Milan, diplomat, priest, and author. Born Giovanni Battista Enrico Antonio Maria Montini, Pope Paul was the 262nd successor to the seat of St. Peter and the spiritual leader of the world's 600 million Catholics. Often referred to as the "Pilgrim Pope," Paul was the most traveled pope. He visited sixteen countries on six continents, including his unprecedented arrivals in Third World nations. He was also the most accessible pope, granting audiences frequently and to such notable Americans as Martin Luther King, Jr. and Betty Friedan. Paul was a close friend of his predecessor John XXIII and John's personal choice as his successor to the papacy. The first cardinal to be named by John, Paul was elected pope on June 21, 1963, and continued the work of the Second Vatican Council that John had called in October, 1962. During his fifteen-year reign, Paul initiated numerous changes within the church, including the vernacularization of the liturgy, the allowance of contemporary music and dance in religious services, and the granting to the bishops of some collegial authority with the pope. He also internationalized the Curia in the Vatican and appointed 110 new cardinals, among them the first black and Chicano bishops in the United States in this century, nineteen black and Asian cardinals, and the first black archbishop in South Africa. Ecumenism was another of Paul's concerns, and in 1966 he made the first papal visit to the Archbishop of Canterbury since England's break with Rome in the sixteenth century. Likewise he met with the Orthodox Patriarch Athenagoras I in 1964, the first of three meetings to be held between these two religious leaders. Author of two controversial encyclicals, *Populorum Progressio* ("On the Progress of Peoples") and *Humanae Vitae* ("Of Human Life"), Paul was often under fire from both conservatives and liberals within the church. His first encyclical was a strong statement of support for the poor and oppressed peoples of the Third World and was said to have given support to social activists in those areas. *Humanae Vitae,* published in 1968, denounced all forms of artificial contraception and saw opposition from theologians and bishops, as well as laity. Paul was the author of numerous papers on such subjects as world peace, the church in Africa, and the family. In addition, he was the author of a book of dialogues with French philosopher Jean Guitton, in which he stated what he had often practiced, the allowance of dissent within his church. Pope Paul VI died in Castel Gandolfo, Italy. Obituaries and other sources: *Current Biography,* Wilson, 1963; *Who's Who in the World,* 3rd edition, Marquis, 1976; *Washington Post,* August 7, 1978; *Newsweek,* August 21, 1978; *Time,* August 21, 1978.

* * *

PEARY, Marie Ahnighito
See KUHNE, Marie (Ahnighito Peary)

* * *

PECK, Anne Merriman   1884-

PERSONAL: Born July 21, 1884, in Piermont-on-Hudson, N.Y.; daughter of a clergyman; children: one son. *Educa-*

tion: Attended Hartford Art School and New York School of Fine and Applied Art. *Residence:* Tucson, Ariz.

CAREER: Author and illustrator of books for children; painter. Instructor in writing and illustrating for children, University of Arizona Extension Division.

WRITINGS—Juvenile: (Self-illustrated) *A Vagabond's Provence,* Dodd, Mead, 1929; (self-illustrated) *Storybook Europe,* Harper, 1929; *Young Germany,* R. McBride, 1931; (self-illustrated) *Roundabout Europe,* Harper, 1931; (with Enid Johnson; self-illustrated) *Wings over Holland,* Macmillan, 1932; (with Johnson; self-illustrated) *Roundabout America,* Harper, 1933; (self-illustrated) *Young Mexico,* R. McBride, 1934, enlarged edition, 1948; (with Johnson; self-illustrated) *Young Americans from Many Lands,* Whitman, 1935; (with Edmond A. Meras) *France: Crossroads of Europe,* Harper, 1936; (with Meras) *Spain in Europe and America,* Harper, 1937; (self-illustrated) *Rene and Paton,* Whitman, 1938; (with Johnson; self-illustrated) *Ho for Californy!,* Harper, 1939.

Belgium (illustrated by Alexandre Serebriakoff), Harper, 1940; (self-illustrated) *Roundabout South America,* Harper, 1940; *The Pageant of South American History,* Longmans, Green, 1941, 3rd edition, McKay, 1962; (self-illustrated) *Manoel and the Morning Star,* Harper, 1943; (self-illustrated) *Young Canada,* R. McBride, 1943; *The Pageant of Canadian History,* Longmans, Green, 1943, 2nd edition, McKay, 1963; (self-illustrated) *The Pageant of Middle American History,* Longmans, Green, 1947; (with Johnson) *Big, Bright Land,* Grosset, 1947; (self-illustrated) *Southwest Roundup,* Dodd, Mead, 1950; *Jo Ann of the Border Country,* Dodd, Mead, 1952; (self-illustrated) *The March of Arizona History,* Arizona Silhouettes, 1962; (with Dorothy and Frank Getlein) *Wings of an Eagle: The Story of Michelangelo* (illustrated by Lili Rethi), Hawthorn Books, 1963.

Illustrator: Charlotte M. Yonge, *Little Lucy's Wonderful Globe,* Harper, 1927; Alice Dussauze, *Little Jack Rabbit,* Macmillan, 1927; Rene Bazin, *Juniper Farm,* Macmillan, 1928; Enid Johnson, *Runaway Balboa,* Harper, 1938; Hope H. Newell, *Steppin and Family,* Oxford University Press, 1942; Newell, *Cinder Ike,* Nelson, 1942; Newell, *Little Old Woman Carries On,* Nelson, 1947; Newell, *Story of Christina,* Harper, 1947; Christine N. Govan, *Mr. Hermit Miser and the Neighborly Pumpkin,* Aladdin, 1949; Gertrude Crampton, *Pottlebys,* Aladdin, 1949; Crampton, *More Pottleby Adventures,* Aladdin, 1950; Catherine Blanton, *Trouble on Old Smoky,* Whittlesey House, 1951; Crampton, *Further Pottleby Adventures,* Aladdin, 1951; (with Margaret Ruse) Newell, *The Little Old Woman Who Used Her Head, and Other Stories,* Nelson, 1973.

SIDELIGHTS: The *New York Times* reviewed *Vagabond's Provence:* "Her book will be wholly delightful to people who enjoy this kind of informal traveling.... There is much history in the book, but all historical references are narrated in a style so fresh and lively that the whole work, whether engaged with the immediate surroundings or the ancient past, is keyed upon a human note that makes its narrative as entertaining as it is informing about a little-known place and people."

BIOGRAPHICAL/CRITICAL SOURCES: New York Times, July 28, 1929, October 13, 1929, July 9, 1950.*

* * *

PECK, Ira   1922-

PERSONAL: Born August 13, 1922, in New York; son of

Louis (a silk worker) and Henrietta (Mazurar) Peck; married Virginia DePaolo, August 16, 1969. *Education:* Attended Harvard University, 1940-42. *Home:* 313 East Devonia Ave., Mount Vernon, N.Y. 10552. *Office:* Scholastic Books & Magazines, 50 West 44th St., New York, N.Y. 10036.

CAREER: PM (newspaper), New York City, feature writer, 1943-48; free-lance writer, 1948-50; Dell Publishing Co., Inc., New York City, editor, 1950-52; Popular Library, Inc., New York City, editor, 1953-64; employed by Scholastic Books & Magazines, New York City, 1964—.

WRITINGS—Young adult, all published by Scholastic Book Services: *The Russian Revolution*, 1967; *Life and Words of Martin Luther King, Jr.*, 1968; *Battle of Britain*, 1970; *Patton*, 1970; *The Last Czar*, 1972; *The Life and Words of Jesus Christ*, 1973; *The Life and Words of St. Francis of Assisi*, 1973; *Battle of Midway*, 1976; *Raid at Entebbe*, 1977; *Scholastic Sociology*, in press.

SIDELIGHTS: Peck writes: "I have been told that my chief asset as a writer is a prose style that is easy to read (simple, clear) and interesting. Narrative writing seems to be my forte. I have always believed that the best way to say anything in writing is the simplest way. If a reader can't understand your book or is confused by it, you have failed him."

*   *   *

PEEBLES, Dick 1918-

PERSONAL: Born July 4, 1918, in Oil City, Pa.; son of Herbert (a salesman) and Sarah (Hagen) Peebles; married Mary T. Holman (a secretary), November 7, 1949; children: Michael, Timothy. *Education:* Educated in Erie, Pa. *Religion:* Roman Catholic. *Home:* 9103 McAvoy Dr., Houston, Tex. 77074. *Office: Houston Chronicle*, 801 Texas Ave., Houston, Tex. 77002.

CAREER/WRITINGS: Erie Dispatch-Herald, Erie, Pa., sports writer, 1936-41; *Sharon Herald*, Sharon, Pa., sports editor, 1941-42; *San Antonio Express*, San Antonio, Tex., sports editor, 1946-58; *Houston Chronicle*, Houston, Tex., sports editor, 1958—. Notable assignments include coverage of World Series, Super Bowls, National Opens, the Olympics, All-Star games, and heavyweight championship fights. Contributor of stories to *Golf Magazine, Golf World*, and *Top Sports Stories. Military service:* U.S. Army, 1942-46; became sergeant. *Member:* Baseball Writers Association of America, American Football Writers Association, National Football Writers Association, National Golf Writers Association, Texas Sports Writers Association (president). *Awards, honors:* Headliners Club Award.

*   *   *

PEEL, Robert 1909-

PERSONAL: Born May 6, 1909, in London, England; came to the United States in 1921, naturalized citizen, 1940; son of Arthur J. (a writer) and Anne (Monk) Peel. *Education:* Harvard University, B.A. (highest honors), 1931, M.A., 1940. *Politics:* Independent. *Religion:* Christian Scientist. *Home:* 790 Boylston St., Boston, Mass. 02199. *Office:* First Church of Christ, Scientist, Christian Science Center, Boston, Mass. 02115.

CAREER: Harvard University, Cambridge, Mass., instructor in English, 1931-36; Principia College, Elsah, Ill., associate professor of English and philosophy, 1936-42; *Christian Science Monitor*, Boston, Mass., editorial writer, 1946-53; First Church of Christ, Scientist, Boston, editorial con-

sultant, 1953—. Member of board of trustees of Zion Research Foundation. *Military service:* U.S. Army, counterintelligence, 1942-46; received Bronze Star. *Member:* Authors Guild of Authors League of America, Phi Beta Kappa, Harvard Club. *Awards, honors:* Sohier Award from Harvard University, 1932, for *The Creed of a Victorian Pagan*.

WRITINGS: The Creed of a Victorian Pagan, Harvard University Press, 1932; *Christian Science: Its Encounter with American Culture*, Holt, 1958; *Mary Baker Eddy: The Years of Discovery*, Holt, 1966; *Mary Baker Eddy: The Years of Trial*, Holt, 1971; *Mary Baker Eddy: The Years of Authority*, Holt, 1977.

Contributor: Erwin D. Canham, editor, *Awakening: The World at Mid-Century*, Longmans, Green, 1951; Helen Wood Bauman, editor, *Mary Baker Eddy: A Centennial Appreciation*, Christian Science Publishing Society, 1966; A. H. and L. G. Kuscher, editors, *Religion and Bereavement*, Health Sciences, 1972. Contributor of poems, articles, and reviews to magazines and newspapers in England, Australia, and the United States, including *American Literature, Voices*, and *Journal of Pastoral Counseling*.

WORK IN PROGRESS: Research on trends in contemporary religion and science.

SIDELIGHTS: Peel writes: "With an education that included schooling in several different countries, I seemed firmly embarked on a career of academic teaching and literary criticism. But a plunge into the socio-political scene as a journalist following World War II and a constantly deepening interest in the practical and conceptual relations of Christian Science to a decreasingly religious society led me finally into an area combining all these interests.

"Until very recently there have been two streams of historiography of Christian Science and its founder, one hagiographic, the other muckraking. My aim has been to give a clear, frank, thoroughly documented account that would avoid both these extremes and at the same time relate this little-understood subject intelligibly to the vital currents of thought in the past century and a half. With the help of a vast amount of hitherto unused material from the archives of the Church of Christ, Scientist, I have found (and, I hope, presented) a Mary Baker Eddy whose contribution to the religious culture of our age needs radical reassessment.

"I look at my rather tentative first book on Christian Science and the solid trilogy that followed as a first step toward such a reassessment. At the same time I've found unexpected delight in the sheer detective work involved in historical study in a remarkably controversial area—work in which my earlier counterintelligence training has had its value. If writing itself is both a joy and an agony, I find unmixed satisfaction in the pursuit of truth through what Mrs. Eddy herself described as 'the interlaced ambiguities of being.'"

*   *   *

PEI, Mario A(ndrew) 1901-1978

February 16, 1901—March 2, 1978; Italian-born educator, philologist, linguist, and author. Pei wrote numerous books on the use and teaching of language, including *One Language for the World, Language for Everybody*, and *Language of the Specialists*. He believed language to be "mankind's most important invention" and devoted his teaching to making linguistics a pleasure to study. In addition to his works on linguistics, Pei wrote novels and some books on world politics. Fluent in several languages, Pei taught Romance philology at Columbia University for more than thirty years. He died in Montclair, N.J. Obituaries and other sources: *Current Biography*, Wilson, 1968, May, 1978; *Directory of American Scholars*, Volume III: *Foreign Languages, Linguistics, and Philology*, 6th edition, Bowker, 1974; *The Writers Directory, 1976-78*, St. Martin's, 1976; *Who's Who in America*, 40th edition, Marquis, 1977; *New York Times*, March 5, 1978; *Washington Post*, March 10, 1978. (See index for *CA* sketch)

*   *   *

PELL, Derek 1947-

PERSONAL: Born December 9, 1947, in New York, N.Y.; son of William D. (a photographer) and Betty Jane (an advertising food stylist; maiden name, Johnson) Pell. *Education:* Attended Art Institute of Chicago. *Politics:* "There's no government like no government." *Religion:* "Book Worship." *Residence:* New York, N.Y. *Agent:* Ron Bernstein Agency, 200 West 58th St., New York, N.Y. 10019.

CAREER: Writer. Worked as dishwasher, file clerk, landscaper, proofreader, and book reviewer. Founded Not Guilty Bookshop and Press, 1968. *Member:* Powys Society.

WRITINGS: Frozen Sunlight, Black Journal Books, 1968; *Uncle Sam*, Black Journal Books, 1968; *Scar Mirror*, Cat's Pajama Press, 1977; *Had Lunch Here On the Patio, 1947*, Not Guilty Press, 1978; *The Invention of Style* (poem), Not Guilty Press, 1978.

"Doktor Bey" series: *Doktor Bey's Suicide Guidebook*, Dodd, 1977; *Doktor Bey's Bedside Bug Book*, Harcourt, 1978; *Doktor Bey's Handbook of Strange Sex*, Avon, 1978.

Contributor of articles, photographs, and fiction to periodicals, including *New York Times, Village Voice, Rolling Stone, Crawdaddy*, and *New York*. Editor of literary magazine, *Not Guilty*.

WORK IN PROGRESS: Doktor Bey's Book of Brats; a satire with John Jacob, *The Book of Instructions;* a novel, *Flats and Wings;* a biography of John Cowper Powys.

SIDELIGHTS: Pell told *CA:* "I began writing as a strict surrealist poet, evolved into protest/prose and, eventually, satire. I am a collage artist as well, now blending text and artwork in a series of strange (humorous) volumes resurrecting the nineteenth century in the form of the mysterious Doktor Bey. I have no desire to be a guest on 'Tonight.'"

*   *   *

PENROD, James 1934-

PERSONAL: Born July 22, 1934, in Provo, Utah; son of Kellar Joseph (a mechanic) and Rose (a nurse; maiden name, Zobell) Penrod. *Education:* Attended University of Utah, 1954, Brigham Young University, 1954-55, and American School of Dance, 1955-58; University of Southern California, B.A., 1963; University of California, Irvine, M.F.A., 1974. *Home:* 4645 Greentree, Irvine, Calif. 92715. *Office:* School of Fine Arts, University of California, Irvine, Calif. 92664.

CAREER: American School of Dance, Hollywood, Calif., teacher, 1959-65; University of California, Irvine, assistant professor, 1966-72, associate professor of fine arts, 1973—. Co-director of Penrod-Plastino Movement Theatre and Dancer's Dance Co. Professional dancer on television, in films, at international festivals, and for dance companies; choreographer of about fifty ballets, musical comedies, and theater pieces. *Member:* Dance Notation Bureau, Screen Actors Guild, Screen Extra's Guild, American Federation of Television and Radio Artists, American Guild of Musical Artists, American Guild of Variety Artists. *Awards, honors:* Grant from Creative Arts Institute, 1971.

WRITINGS: (With Janice Gudde Plastino) *The Dancer Prepares*, Mayfield, 1970; *Movement for the Performing Artist*, Mayfield, 1974.

WORK IN PROGRESS: A book on ballet technique; research on movement notations, effort-shape, kinesics, dance, and theater.

SIDELIGHTS: Penrod writes: "My primary professional activities are teaching dance notation, ballet and modern dance techniques, choreographing, and dancing myself. I am currently engaged in related research activities that systematically analyze movement qualitatively as well as quantitatively; for example, effort-shape, kinesics, choreometrics, and linguistics (its nonverbal aspects). I am actively engaged in presenting dance concerts and demonstrations locally in the primary and secondary schools and nationally in colleges and universities, as choreographer and as co-director with Janice Gudde Plastino of the Penrod Plastino Movement Theatre."

*   *   *

PEREZ, Louis C(elestino) 1923-

PERSONAL: Surname is accented on first syllable; born February 7, 1923, in DePue, Ill.; son of Celestino (a laborer) and Luisa Isabel (a seamstress; maiden name, Alvarez) Perez; married Grace Esther Rogge (a librarian), August 12, 1950; children: Alison Louise, David William, Roberta Elaine. *Education:* Brooklyn College (now of the City University of New York), B.A. (cum laude), 1950; University of Michigan, M.A. (honors), 1951, Ph.D., 1957. *Office:* Department of Spanish, Italian, and Portuguese, Pennsylvania State University, 357 North Burrowes Bldg., University Park, Pa. 16802.

CAREER: Williams College, Williamstown, Mass., instructor, 1955-58, assistant professor, 1958-62, associate professor of Romanic languages, 1962-67; Pennsylvania State University, University Park, professor of Spanish, 1967—. *Military service:* U.S. Merchant Marine, 1942-46. *Member:* Modern Language Association of America, American Association of Teachers of Spanish and Portuguese, Sigma Delta Pi.

WRITINGS: (With Federico Sanchez Escribano) *Afirmaciones de Lope de Vega sobre preceptiva dramatica a base de cien comedias* (title means "Assertions of Lope de Vega About Dramatic Precepts, Based on a Study of One Hundred Plays"), Consejo Superior de Investigaciones Científicas, 1961; (editor) Ernesto Sabato, *El Tunel* (title means "The Tunnel"), Macmillan, 1965; (editor with Leon F. Lyday) Eduardo Caballero Calderon, *Ancha es Castilla* (title means "Broad Is Castile"), Van Nostrand, 1971; *La Apologia en defensa de las comedias que se representan en Espana de Francisco Ortiz* (title means "Apology in Defense of the Dramas Which Are Presented in Spain, By Francisco Ortiz"), Estudios de Hispanofila, (Chapel Hill, North Carolina), 1977.

WORK IN PROGRESS: Research on the literature of Spain's Golden Age.

*   *   *

PERKIN, Harold (James) 1926-

PERSONAL: Born November 11, 1926, in Stoke-on-Trent, England; son of Robert James (a builder) and Hilda (Dillon)

Perkin; married Joan Griffiths, 1948; children: Deborah, Julian. *Education:* Jesus College, Cambridge, B.A. (first class honors), 1948, M.A., 1952. *Home:* Borwicks, Caton, Lancaster LA2 9NB, England; and 1(0) Grove End House, Grove End Road, London NW8, England. *Office:* Centre for Social History, University of Lancaster, Lancaster LA1 4YG, England.

CAREER: University of Manchester, Manchester, England, assistant lecturer in extramural education, 1950-51, lecturer in Social history, 1951-65; University of Lancaster, Lancaster, England, senior lecturer, 1965-67, professor of social history, 1967—, founding director of Centre for Social History, 1976—. *Military service:* Royal Air Force, education officer, 1948-50. *Member:* Royal Historical Society (fellow), Social History Society (founding chairman), Association of University Teachers (past president), Economic History Society, Labour History Society, History of Education Society, Cumberland and Westmorland Antiquarian and Archaeological Society.

WRITINGS: The Origins of Modern English Society, 1780-1880, Routledge & Kegan Paul, 1969; *New Universities in the United Kingdom,* Organization for Economic Co-operation and Development, 1969; *Key Profession: The History of the Association of University Teachers,* Routledge & Kegan Paul, 1969; *The Age of the Railway,* Panther Books, 1970; *History: An Introduction for the Intending Student,* Routledge & Kegan Paul, 1970; *The Age of the Automobile,* Quartet Books, 1976. Contributor of more than thirty articles to periodicals. Editor of "Studies in Social History," Routledge & Kegan Paul, 1957—. Editor of *Newsletter* of Social History Society.

WORK IN PROGRESS: Elites in British Society Since 1880, for Social Science Research Council; long-term research on English society, mainly since 1880, with special reference to professionalization and the role of higher education.

SIDELIGHTS: Perkin comments briefly: "As the first professor of social history in Britain, my aim is to encourage research in and teaching of social history (of all periods and places) as widely as possible."

* * *

PERKIN, Robert L(yman)   1914-1978

March 18, 1914—January 28, 1978; American reporter, writer, director, and author. He served as a reporter on the editorial staff for the *Rocky Mountain News* and became director of information services for the University of Colorado. Perkin was also a science writer for the Colorado Medical Society, and a book editor from 1951-63. He wrote a historical book, *The First 100 Years.* Perkin died in Denver, Colo. Obituaries and other sources: *Who's Who in Public Relations (International),* 4th edition, PR Publishing, 1972; *Who's Who in the West,* 14th edition, Marquis, 1974; *New York Times,* January 31, 1978.

* * *

PERKINS, David   1928-

PERSONAL: Born October 25, 1928, in Philadelphia, Pa.; son of Dwight and Esther (Williams) Perkins. *Education:* Harvard University, A.B. (summa cum laude), 1951, A.M., 1952, Ph.D., 1955. *Home:* 23 Sparks St., Cambridge, Mass. 02138. *Office:* Department of English, Harvard University, Warren House, Cambridge, Mass. 02138.

CAREER: Harvard University, Cambridge, Mass., assis-

tant professor, 1959-60, associate professor, 1960-65, professor of English, 1965—, chairman of department, 1976—. *Military service:* U.S. Army, 1955-57. *Member:* Modern Language Association of America, American Academy of Arts and Sciences, Keats-Shelley Association, Phi Beta Kappa. *Awards, honors:* Guggenheim fellowship, 1961-62; Fulbright fellowship for University of Goettingen, 1968-69.

WRITINGS: The Quest for Permanence: The Symbolism of Wordsworth, Shelley, and Keats, Harvard University Press, 1955; *Wordsworth and the Poetry of Sincerity,* Harvard University Press, 1964; *English Romantic Writers,* Harcourt, 1967; (contributor) *The English Romantic Poets: A Review of Research and Criticism,* Modern Language Association of America, 1972; *History of Modern Poetry,* Volume I, Harvard University Press, 1976.

WORK IN PROGRESS: Volume II of *History of Modern Poetry.*

* * *

PERKINS, R(ichard) Marlin   1905-

PERSONAL: Born March 28, 1905, in Carthage, Mo.; son of Joseph Dudley (a judge) and Mynta Mae (Miller) Perkins; married Elise More, September 12, 1933 (divorced October, 1953); married Carol M. Cotsworth, August 13, 1960; children: (first marriage) Suzanne. *Education:* Attended University of Missouri, 1924-26. *Politics:* Republican. *Religion:* Episcopalian. *Address:* 52 Aberdeen Pl., St. Louis, Mo. 63105.

CAREER: St. Louis Zoo, St. Louis, Mo., curator of reptiles, 1926-38; Buffalo Zoo, Buffalo, N.Y., curator, 1938-44; Lincoln Park Zoo, Chicago, Ill., director, 1944-62; St. Louis Zoo, director, 1962-70, director emeritus, 1970—. Originator of the television programs "Zoo Parade", 1949-57, and with Don Meier, "Wild Kingdom", 1962—; member of Hillary's Expedition on Yeti Investigation, Himalayas, 1960. *Member:* International Union of Directors of Zoological Gardens, World Wildlife Fund, East African Wildlife Society, American Society of Ichthyologists and Herpetologists, American Society of Mammalogists, American Association of Zoological Parks and Aquariums, Missouri Athletic Club, Adventurers Club (Chicago), Explorers Club (New York City). *Awards, honors:* Has received numerous awards for "Zoo Parade," including the Peabody Award, 1950, Look Award, and Sylvania Award; has received several awards for "Wild Kingdom", including four Emmy Awards; has received doctorates from universities and colleges, including University of Missouri, 1971, Rockhurst College, and Northland College.

WRITINGS: Animal Faces (illustrated with own photographs), Foster & Stewart, 1944; (with Peggy Tibma) *One Magic Night: A Story from the Zoo* (illustrated by Katherine Evans), Regnery, 1952; *Zooparade* (illustrated by Paul Bransom and Seymour Fleishman), Rand McNally, 1954; (with wife, Carol M. Perkins) *"I Saw You from Afar": A Visit to the Bushmen of the Kalahari Desert,* Atheneum, 1965; (author of introduction) Richard Cromer, *The Miracle of Flight* (illustrated by Joseph Cellini), Doubleday, 1968; (author of introduction) Allan W. Eckert, *Bayou Backwaters* (illustrated by Cellini), Doubleday, 1968; (author of introduction) A. W. Eckert, *In Search of a Whale* (illustrated by Cellini), Doubleday, 1970; (author of introduction) Robert Martin, *Yesterday's People* (illustrated by Richard Cuffari), Doubleday, 1970; (author of introduction) Lewis Wayne Walker, *Survival under the Sun* (illustrated by Jean Zallinger), Doubleday, 1971.

SIDELIGHTS: Perkins's interest in animals began when he was a young boy growing up in the Midwest. At the age of twenty-one, Perkins was hired as a workman at the St. Louis Zoo, and within two weeks was put in charge of the reptiles. During his stay as curator of the reptiles, the young zoologist expanded the snake collection by going on numerous hunting expeditions to Illinois and the southern States. At each of the wildlife parks where he was employed, Perkins used his unique flair for combining the entertainment and educational aspects of zoos.

While working at the Buffalo Zoo, Perkins organized the material for his first book, *Animal Faces.* In this publication Perkins studied and compared various facial expressions of animals. A *New York Times* critic observed, "The photographs are beautifully done, and they go far toward proving the author's contention that the faces of animals are just as revealing as are those of human beings." In an article for *Weekly Book Review,* May Lamberton Becker commented, "I have seen many good books about wild animals, but none has interested me more than this."

Perkins later utilized the theatrics of animal behavior to create the television program "Zoo Parade." A zoologist always runs the risk of being injured while handling wild animals, and Marlin Perkins was no exception. It was during a rehearsal for the television show in April of 1951 that Perkins encountered one of several close calls with death after being bitten by a three-and-a-half-foot rattlesnake.

In 1962 Perkins developed the television series "Wild Kingdom" along with Don Meier. Acclaimed for its emphasis on animal conservation, "Wild Kingdom" has been honored by almost every wildlife organization in the United States. In an article for *Variety,* a critic noted, "Superb photography and editing and the actual physical participation of the narrators keep the show at high tempo."

The author-zoologist departed from the world of animals and wrote about a primitive African civilization in *"I Saw You from Afar": A Visit to the Bushmen of Kalahari Desert.* A *New York Times* critic wrote, "This delightful little book, 50-odd pages of well-chosen words and photographs, opens a window on the world of the Bushmen. . . . The Perkinses admired these resourceful nomads, and their enthusiasm is contagious."

AVOCATIONAL INTERESTS: Photography, scuba diving, archaeology.

BIOGRAPHICAL/CRITICAL SOURCES: Weekly Book Review, March 19, 1944; *New York Times,* April 16, 1944; Lynn and Gray Poole, *Scientists Who Work Outdoors,* Dodd, 1963; *New York Times Book Review,* May 9, 1965; *Variety,* January 15, 1969.

*　　*　　*

PERMAN, Dagmar Horna 1926(?)-1978

1926(?)—May 26, 1978; Czechoslovakian-born American educator, social activist, and author. An associate professor of history at Georgetown University, Perman was also interested in the social issues of the present. She was known nationally for her help in organizing a group of southeastern Pennsylvania citizens in a legal fight against the land development company, Charnita Inc., which disregarded local and national laws involving fair trade practices. Perman fled her native Czechoslovakia in 1948 at the onset of the Communist takeover. She was the author of several books, including *The Shaping of the Czechoslovakian State.* Perman died in Jerusalem, Israel. Obituaries and other sources:

Directory of American Scholars, Volume I: *History,* 6th edition, Bowker, 1974; *Washington Post,* May 31, 1978.

*　　*　　*

PEROUTKA, Ferdinand 1895(?)-1978

1895(?)—April 20, 1978; Czechoslovakian journalist and author. Imprisoned by the Nazis in the Dachau and Buchenwald concentration camps, Peroutka later fought the Communists in his native country. He founded the political weekly *Pritomost* in 1924, which became a leading voice of Czechoslovakian liberalism between the two world wars. He was also editor-in-chief of the weekly newspaper *Dnesek* and the daily *Svobodne Noviny.* Peroutka was head of the Czechoslovak service of Radio Free Europe in New York from 1950 until his retirement in 1964, but continued writing a weekly column for that service. He wrote several plays and novels. Peroutka died in Queens, N.Y. Obituaries and other sources: *New York Times,* April 21, 1978.

*　　*　　*

PERRY, Roger 1933-

PERSONAL: Born August 4, 1933, in Enfield, England; son of Gerald Alfred Amos and Frances Mary (Everett) Perry; married Shirley Pettifer, December 18, 1974. *Education:* Christ's College, Cambridge, B.A., 1957, M.A., 1961. *Home address:* Trapalanda, Bradfield St. George, Suffolk, England. *Office:* British Ministry of Overseas Development, Christmas Island, Gilbert Islands.

CAREER: British Broadcasting Corp., Bristol, England, field research assistant in natural history unit, 1958-62; UNESCO, Department for the Advancement of Science, Charles Darwin Research Station, Galapagos Islands, Ecuador, director, 1964-70; British Ministry of Overseas Development, Christmas Island, Gilbert Islands, wildlife adviser, 1977—. Conducted field studies in the northern Andes, 1957-58, 1971, 1972, the Amazon, 1962-63, and Patagonia, 1973, 1974, 1975. *Military service:* British Army, Airborne Division, 1952-54. *Member:* Royal Geographical Society (fellow), Ecuadorian Institute of Natural Sciences (honorary member).

WRITINGS: The Galapagos Islands, Dodd, 1972; *Patagonia: Windswept Land of the South,* Dodd, 1974; *Wonders of Llamas,* Dodd, 1977. Contributor to magazines, including *Country Life, Illustrated London News, Wildlife,* and *Pacific Discovery.*

AVOCATIONAL INTERESTS: Mountain travel.

*　　*　　*

PETERSEN, Clarence G. 1933-

PERSONAL: Born February 14, 1933, in Chicago, Ill.; son of Ludvig (an engineer) and Sigrid (Hegerlund) Petersen; married Isabell A. Vaughn, May 19, 1956 (divorced, 1976); children: Judith Anne, Karen Sue. *Education:* Attended University of Illinois, 1952-54; Michigan State University, B.A., 1955. *Politics:* Independent. *Religion:* Agnostic. *Home:* 4633 Kirchoff Rd., Apt. 28, Rolling Meadows, Ill. 60008. *Office:* Chicago Tribune, 435 North Michigan Ave., Chicago, Ill. 60611.

CAREER: City News Bureau of Chicago, Chicago, Ill., reporter, 1953-55; Life Newspapers, Chicago, reporter, 1958; *Chicago Tribune,* Chicago, reporter, editor, and columnist, 1958—, writer of "Paperbacks" column in *Chicago Tribune Book World,* 1964—. Has given speeches on broadcasting and on books.

WRITINGS: The Bantam Story, Bantam, 1970, revised edition, 1975.

* * *

PETREMENT, Simone   1907-

PERSONAL: Born June 6, 1907, in Nemours, France; daughter of Francois (a military officer) and Gabrielle (Bonnaud) Petrement. *Education:* Ecole Normale Superieure and Universite de Paris, Agregation de philosophie, 1931, Doctorat es lettres, 1947. *Residence:* Paris suburbs, France.

CAREER: Taught literature and philosophy in secondary schools in Caen and Grenoble, France, 1931-36; Bibliotheque Nationale, Paris, France, 1937-64, began as librarian, became head librarian; writer, 1964—. *Member:* Association des Amis d' Alain, Association pour l'etude de la pensee de Simone Weil. *Awards, honors:* Chevalier de la Legion d'-Honneur; Officier de l'Order National du Merite; Fondation Broquette-Gonin prize from l'Academie Francaise, 1974, for *La Vie de Simone Weil.*

WRITINGS: Le Dualisme dans l'histoire de la philosophie et des religions (title means "Dualism in the History of Philosophy and Religions"), Gallimard, 1946; *Le Dualisme chez Platon, les Gnostiques et les Manicheens* (title means "The Dualism of Plato, the Gnostics, and the Manicheans"), Presses Universitaires de France, 1947; *La Vie de Simone Weil,* Fayard, 1973, translation by Raymond Rosenthal published as *Simone Weil: A Life,* Pantheon, 1977. Contributor to various journals, including *Critique, La Revue de Metaphysique et de Morale,* and *Le Contrat Social.*

WORK IN PROGRESS: Research on primitive Christianity, and especially on the history of Gnosticism.

SIDELIGHTS: Simone Petrement told *CA:* "I owe to the philosopher Alain (Emile Chartier, known under the name of Alain, 1861-1951, who was my teacher at Lycee Henri-IV as well as that of Simone Weil) my love of philosophy and my conviction that, contrary to the most widespread opinion, philosophy can reach Truth in certain domains. We know a great deal more about the world than the ancient philosophers, but in certain fundamental matters (such as ethics, methods of reasoning, and the study of the nature and task of the mind), certain very ancient philosophies are always beautiful and true. The philosophy of platonic inspiration has reappeared periodically during the course of history under new forms, and perhaps it shall always reappear.

"There is also true philosophy in the theologies of platonic inspiration. I have especially concerned myself with the study of certain platonic forms of Christianity."

Simone Petrement has contributed in an editorial capacity to the posthumous publication of many of Simone Weil's works.

* * *

PHILIP, Lotte Brand
See FOERSTER, Lotte B(rand)

* * *

PHILLIPPI, Wendell Crane   1918-

PERSONAL: Born July 4, 1918, in Zionsville, Ind.; son of Jesse F. and Bernice (Brock) Phillippi; married Georgiana Pittman, January 10, 1942; children: Frank B., Ann D. *Education:* Indiana University, A.B., 1940. *Religion:* Episcopalian. *Home:* 4151 North Pennsylvania, Indianapolis, Ind. 46205. *Office: Indianapolis News,* 307 North Pennsylvania, Indianapolis, Ind. 46206.

CAREER/WRITINGS: Indianapolis News, Indianapolis, Ind., copy editor, 1940-46, state editor, 1946-47, city editor, 1947-52, assistant managing editor, 1952-62, managing editor, 1962—. *Military service:* U.S. Army, 1941-45; became major; received Silver Star, Bronze Star with cluster, and Purple Heart. U.S. Army Reserve, 1962-63; became major general.

MEMBER: American Society of Newspaper Editors, Associated Press Managing Editors Association (member of board of directors, 1963-66, 1969-72; president, 1971-72), Army Association (past president), Mid America Press Institute (member of board), Indianapolis Press Club, Indianapolis Chamber of Commerce, Indianapolis Urban League (member of board), Indianapolis Chamber of Commerce, American Legion, Sigma Delta Chi, Sigma Nu, Contemporary Club, Indianapolis Athletic Club.

* * *

PHILLIPS, Alan
See STAUDERMAN, Albert P(hilip)

* * *

PHILLIPS, Julien L(ind)   1945-

PERSONAL: Born June 16, 1945, in Minneapolis, Minn.; daughter of Iver C. and Florence (Brill) Lind; married Jeffrey H. Phillips (a teacher), August 10, 1968. *Education:* University of Minnesota, B.A., 1967, Ph.D., 1977; University of Illinois, M.A., 1968. *Home:* 3931 Upton Ave N., Minneapolis, Minn. 55412.

CAREER: Free-lance theater designer, actress, and director in Minneapolis, Minn., 1968-71; University of Minnesota, Minneapolis, instructor in theater arts and costumer, 1971-76; free-lance writer, 1976—. Active in Twin Cities area community theater.

WRITINGS: Stars of the Ziegfeld Follies, Lerner, 1972. Theater reviewer for *Minnesota Daily,* 1976-77.

WORK IN PROGRESS: Research on theory and practical use of masks in the plays of Eugene O'Neill.

SIDELIGHTS: Julien Phillips writes: "I have always felt that artistic expression is vital to mankind's existence; I feel that understanding of others' artistic efforts not only promotes tolerance but increases the likelihood of continued growth."

* * *

PHILLIPS, Margaret McDonald   1910(?)-1978

1910(?)—May 18, 1978; American painter, educator, and author of books in her field. Phillips, a renowned painter, received acclaim for her portraitures of such figures as Indira Gandhi, Richard M. Nixon, and John Sutherland Bonnell. She was head of the portrait-painting department at the New York Phoenix School of Design. Phillips was the recipient of the Nancy Ashton Prize and a woman of the year citation. She was founder and president of the honorary society, Fifty American Artists. Phillips died in Queens, N.Y. Obituaries and other sources: *Who's Who in American Art,* Bowker, 1973; *New York Times,* May 23, 1978.

* * *

PHILLIPS, Robert L(eRoy), Jr.   1940-

PERSONAL: Born May 4, 1940, in Wadesboro, N.C.; son of Robert LeRoy (a banker) and Mary (a teacher; maiden name, Holland) Phillips; married Lucy McIntyre (a teacher), December 27, 1967; children: Robert McIntyre, Shandy Llewellyn. *Education:* Davidson College, B.A., 1962; University of North Carolina, M.A., 1963, Ph.D., 1970. *Home:* 206 Woodlawn, Starkville, Miss. 39759. *Office address:* P.O. Box 2625, Mississippi State, Miss. 39762.

CAREER: North Carolina Central University, Durham, instructor, 1969-70; Mississippi State University, Mississippi State, associate professor, 1970—. *Military service:* U.S. Army, 1963-65; served in Germany; became lieutenant. U.S. Army Reserve; became captain. *Member:* Modern Language Association of America, Society for the Study of Southern Literature, South Atlantic Modern Language Association, South Central Modern Language Association. *Awards, honors:* National Endowment for the Humanities grant.

WRITINGS: Antebellum Mississippi Stories, Mississippi Library Commission, 1976; *Richard Harding Davis,* Twayne, in press.

Author of "A Climate for Genius," a series for Mississippi Authority Educational Television network. Editor of *Newsletter of the Society for the Study of Southern Literature;* book review editor of *Mississippi Quarterly.*

* * *

PICK, Robert   1898-1978

March 1, 1898—April 7, 1978; Austrian-born novelist, editor, and translator. Pick was editor and member of the executive board for Alfred A. Knopf, Inc., and reviewer for the Book-of-the-Month Club and *Saturday Review of Literature.* In addition to translating a number of volumes from German and writing the biography of Empress Marie Theresa, Pick wrote the novels *The Terhoven File, The Guests of Don Lorenzo,* and *The Escape of Socrates.* He died in New York, N.Y. Obituaries and other sources: *New York Times,* April 8, 1978. (See index for *CA* sketch)

* * *

PICKERILL, Don   1928-

PERSONAL: Born November 23, 1928, in Parsons, Kan.; son of Earl Ray and Inez (Milks) Pickerill; married Maurine Bilger, May 29, 1949; children: Mark, Tim, Todd. *Education:* L.I.F.E. Bible College, graduated, 1952; Pasadena Nazarene College, M.A., 1956; also attended Fuller Theological Seminary, University of Southern California, and University of Judaism. *Home:* 2900 Manhattan, La Crescenta, Calif. 91214. *Office:* 2424 Colorado Blvd., Los Angeles, Calif. 90041.

CAREER: Ordained minister, 1952; pastor of church in La Crescenta, Calif., 1952-64; Christian Assembly, Los Angeles, Calif., pastor, 1969—. Associate counselor, American Institute of Family Relations, Los Angeles, Calif., 1956-58. Faculty member at L.I.F.E. Bible College, 1956-76. *Military service:* U.S. Navy, 1946-47.

WRITINGS: Learning to Live in the Love of God, Whitaker Books, 1973.

WORK IN PROGRESS: The Model Church.

SIDELIGHTS: Pickerill told *CA:* "My most current interest is in ecclesiology and the renewal of the church. Much attention is given to the ecumenical and charismatic movement.

"I'm senior minister of a congregation of nearly one thousand people, which is experiencing renewal especially in intergenerational education and life-related ministries."

Pickerill leads annual tours of the Bible lands.

PICKLES, (Maud) Dorothy   1903-

PERSONAL: Born August 8, 1903, in Bridlington, Yorkshire, England; married William Pickles (a university teacher, writer, and broadcaster), December 15, 1928; children: Judith Louis. *Education:* University of Leeds, B.A. (first class honors), 1925, M.A., 1927; attended University of Paris, 1925-27; London School of Economics and Political Science, B.Sc. (first class honors), 1936. *Home:* White Hatch, 29 Detillens Lane, Limpsfield, Oxted, Surrey, England.

CAREER: University of London, London School of Economics and Political Science, London, England, assistant lecturer in French, 1935-40; Ministry of Information, London, administrative official, 1939-44; free-lance writer, broadcaster, and lecturer, 1945—. Visiting professor at Columbia University, 1960; part-time lecturer at London School of Economics and Political Science, 1958—.

WRITINGS: The French Political Scene, Thomas Nelson, 1937; (with husband, William Pickles) *Is France Still a Democracy?* (pamphlet), Gollancz, 1940; (with W. Pickles) *France Faces Fascism* (pamphlet), Gollancz, 1940; *France* (pamphlet), Oxford University Press, 1944; *France Between the Republics,* Contact Press, 1946, reprinted, Russell & Russell, 1971.

Introduction to Politics, Sylvan Press, 1951, 3rd edition, Methuen, 1976; *French Politics: The First Ten Years of the Fourth Republic,* Royal Institute of International Affairs, 1953; *France: The Fourth Republic,* Methuen, 1954, revised edition, 1958, reprinted, Greenwood Press, 1976; *France: Our Unknown Neighbour* (pamphlet), British Broadcasting Corp., 1956; *The Fifth French Republic,* Praeger, 1960, revised edition, 1965; *Algeria and France,* Praeger, 1963; *France,* Oxford University Press, 1964; *The Uneasy Entente,* Oxford University Press, 1966.

Democracy, Batsford, 1970, Basic Books, 1972; *The Government and Politics of France,* Methuen, Volume I, 1972, Volume II, 1973. Contributor to *Annual Register of World Affairs* and *Encyclopaedia Britannica.* Contributor to academic journals, including *International Affairs* and *Contemporary Review,* and to *World Today.*

SIDELIGHTS: Dorothy Pickles's books have been translated into Dutch, Spanish, Arabic, Greek, and Hindi. *The Fifth French Republic* has also been published in braille.

* * *

PIERATT, Asa B.   1938-

PERSONAL: Born August 30, 1938, in Kalamazoo, Mich.; son of Asa B. and Ella May Pieratt. *Education:* Kalamazoo College, B.A., 1961; University of Michigan, A.M.L.S., 1965; also studied at Universidad de los Andes, 1959, Jane Greenfield Bindery, 1968-69, and Columbia University, 1969-70. *Home:* 72 Welsh Tract Rd., Apt. 102, Newark, Del. 19711. *Office:* Library, University of Delaware, Newark, Del. 19711.

CAREER: University of Michigan, Ann Arbor, member of library staff, 1962-64; Miami-Dade Junior College, Miami, Fla., assistant periodicals librarian, 1965-66, periodicals librarian, 1966; Bowling Green State University, Bowling Green, Ohio, serials librarian, 1966-67; University of New Haven, West Haven, Conn., head of acquisitions department and chief bibliographer, 1967-70, technical services librarian, 1970-73; University of Delaware, Newark, acquisitions librarian, 1973—. *Member:* American Library Association, Association of College and Research Libraries, Delaware Library Association, Philadelphia Acquisitions

Information Network, Philobiblon Club. *Awards, honors:* Light fellowship, 1959, for Universidad de los Andes.

WRITINGS: (Contributor) Seymour Lawrence, editor, *The Vonnegut Statement:* Delacorte, 1973; *Kurt Vonnegut, Jr.: A Descriptive Bibliography and Annotated Secondary Checklist,* Shoe String, 1974; *Donald Barthelme: A Descriptive Bibliography,* Shoe String, 1978; *Postcard Pageantry: Celebrations of Major and Minor Expositions, Fairs, and Events in Early Twentieth-Century America,* Darien House, 1978. Contributor to library journals and *Hobbies.* Editor of *Courier* of South Jersey Postcard Club.

* * *

PIERCE, Edward T. 1917(?)-1978

1917(?)—February 22, 1978; American physicist and author. He was an expert on electricity in atmosphere. Pierce was the author of seventy books and articles on meteorological physics. He died in San Francisco, Calif. Obituaries and other sources: *New York Times,* February 23, 1978.

* * *

PIERMAN, Carol J. 1947-

PERSONAL: Born October 16, 1947, in Lima, Ohio; daughter of James H. (a farmer) and Ellin J. Pierman. *Education:* l'Institut de Touraine, certificate, 1967; Bowling Green State University, B.A., 1969, M.F.A., 1972. *Home address:* P.O. Box 324, Ottawa, Ohio 45875.

CAREER: Writer, 1968—. Member of editorial staff of Thirteenth Moon, Inc., 1975-76, member of board of directors, 1976-77. Has read poems on radio programs. *Member:* Modern Language Association of America, American Association of University Professors.

WRITINGS: Passage (poems), Madeira Press, 1977. Contributor of poems and reviews to literary magazines.

WORK IN PROGRESS: A book of poems.

SIDELIGHTS: Pierman writes: "My work ranges from the nearly autobiographical (long narrative line) to the more densely imaginative (dream sequence). The poets I have read most lately are Denise Levertov, Randall Jarrell and Lorine Niedecker. I don't necessarily try to imitate them, except in that I consider them standards by which to work."

* * *

PILK, Henry
See CAMPBELL, Ken

* * *

PLEASANTS, Samuel A(ugustus III) 1918-

PERSONAL: Born September 26, 1918, in Oakland, Calif.; son of Samuel Augustus, Jr. (a lawyer) and Fay (Crawford) Pleasants; married Elsie Marie Walter (a professor of chemistry), September 21, 1947; children: Ellen, Elizabeth, Samuel Augustus IV. *Education:* Columbia University, B.A., 1940, M.A., 1941, Ph.D., 1947. *Home:* 47 Linden Ter., Leonia, N.J. 07605. *Office:* Department of History and Political Science, Fairleigh Dickinson University, Teaneck, N.J. 07666.

CAREER: Walter Hervey Junior College, New York City, instructor in history, 1946-53; Fairleigh Dickinson University, Teaneck, N.J., assistant professor, 1953-60, associate professor, 1960-63, professor of history, government, and law, 1963—. *Military service:* U.S. Naval Reserve, active duty as gunner's mate, 1942-46; served in Europe and Asia.

Member: Society of American Historians, American Society for Legal History, Organization of American Historians, Early American Seminars at Columbia, Delta Chi. *Awards, honors:* Travel grant from Fairleigh Dickinson University, 1959, for West Africa, the Middle East, and the Soviet Union; award from Government of Korea, 1963.

WRITINGS: Fernando Word of New York, Columbia University Press, 1948; *The Bill of Rights,* C. E. Merrill, 1969; *The Declaration of Independence,* C. E. Merrill, 1970; *The Articles of Confederation,* C. E. Merrill, 1971. Contributor to philosophy, history, and education journals.

WORK IN PROGRESS: Studying Stephen Langton and his work with the Magna Carta; research on James Otis, 1770-1775.

SIDELIGHTS: Pleasants commented on his work in progress: "My interest in Langton came about as a result of my research on the Magna Carta. History takes a different perspective of events as time passes. In the 17th century it was regarded by Coke as a bill of rights reflecting his difficulties with the Stuart monarchs. In the 20th century it has come in the minds of some to have an economic connotation. It was in revolt against this sort of causation that I came across references to the Archbishop Stephen Langton and his work in the late 12th century and the early years of the 13th century in France and England.

"My interest in James Otis goes back to my interest in 18th century America and the rising opposition to the monarchy in the colonies. One of the most interesting personalities is James Otis whose brilliant mind may have been permanently damaged by a blow received from a British customs agent in Boston. There seems to be some evidence of an emotional instability as far back as his days at Harvard. He came from a very distinguished family in Massachusetts politics and mercantilism and has provided me with many problems in historical research."

* * *

PODOLIAK, Boris
See KOSTIUK, Hryhory

* * *

POLANSKI, Roman 1933-

PERSONAL: Born August 18, 1933, in Paris, France; married Barbara Kwiatkowski (an actress; divorced, 1961); married Sharon Tate (an actress), January, 1968 (died, 1969). *Education:* Polish National Film Academy, diploma, 1959. *Residence:* Paris, France.

CAREER: Actor in Poland in radio, 1945-47, in stage productions, 1947-53, and in films, 1953-61; assistant film director with Kamera (a cinema production company), in Poland, 1959-61; director, screenwriter, actor, 1963—. Director of motion pictures, including "Le Gros et le Maigre," 1960, and "Chinatown," 1974. Actor in motion pictures, including "The Fearless Vampire Killers; or, Pardon Me But Your Teeth Are in My Neck," 1967, "Chinatown," 1974, and "The Tenant," 1976. Signed contract with Compton Group, London, England, 1966, and with Paramount Pictures, Los Angeles, Calif., 1967. Founder, with Gene Gutowski, of Cadre Films Ltd., 1964. *Awards, honors:* Winner of more than ten international awards including one for experimental pictures from Brussels World Fair, 1958, for "Two Men and a Wardrobe"; Grand Prize from Tours Film Festival, 1961, for "Mammals"; received Critics Award from Venice Film Festival, 1962, International Film Critics Award, 1962, nomination for Academy Award for best foreign language film from Academy of Motion Picture Arts and Sciences, 1964, all for "Knife in the Water"; received Critics Prize from Venice Film Festival, 1965, and Silver Bear Award from Berlin Film Festival, 1965, both for "Repulsion"; received award from Venice Film Festival and Golden Bear Award from Berlin Film Festival, both 1966, both for "Cul-de-Sac"; nomination for Academy Award for best screenplay from Academy of Motion Picture Arts and Sciences, 1968, for "Rosemary's Baby"; best English language film award from National Board of Review of Motion Pictures, 1971, for "Macbeth"; best director award from Society of Film and Television Arts, Golden Globe award for best director from Hollywood Foreign Press, nomination for Academy Award for best director from Academy of Motion Picture Arts and Sciences, all 1975, all for "Chinatown"; and numerous other film awards.

WRITINGS: Polanski: Three Film Scripts (contains "Knife in the Water," "Repulsion," "Cul-de-Sac"), Harper, 1975.

Screenplays: (And director) "Rozbijemy Zabawe" (released in U.S. as "Break Up the Dance"), 1957; (and director) "Dwaj Ludzie Z Szafa" (released in U.S. as "Two Men and a Wardrobe"), 1957; (and director) "Gdy Spadaja Anioly" (released in U.S. as "When Angels Fall"), 1959; (and director) "Lampa" (released in U.S. as "The Lamp"), 1959; (co-author and director) "Ssaki" (released in U.S. as "Mammals"), 1961; (co-author and director) "Noz W Wodzie" (released in U.S. as "Knife in the Water"), 1961; (with Gerard Brach, and director) "A River of Diamonds," 1963; "Aimez-Vous Les Femmes?" (released in U.S. as "Do You Like Women?"), 1963; (with Brach, and director) "Repulsion," Compton-Cameo, 1965; (with Brach, and director) "Cul-de-Sac," Compton-Cameo, 1966; (with Brach, and director) "The Fearless Vampire Killers; or, Pardon Me But Your Teeth Are in My Neck," Metro-Goldwyn-Mayer, 1967; (and director) "Rosemary's Baby" (adapted from the novel by Ira Levin), Paramount, 1968; (with Kenneth Tynan, and director) "Macbeth" (adapted from the play by William Shakespeare), Playboy Productions/Caliban Films, 1971; (with Brach, and director), "What?," Carlo Ponti, 1973; (with Brach, and director) "The Tenant" (adapted from the novel by Roland Topor), 1976.

WORK IN PROGRESS: Directing the motion picture "Tess," adapted from the novel, *Tess of the d'Urbervilles,* by Thomas Hardy.

SIDELIGHTS: "What I like is a realistic situation where things don't quite fit in," Polanski once told an interviewer. "I like to begin with a mood, an atmosphere. My ideas are not exact. I begin to people the atmosphere with characters—I like to be frightened." One of the few surrealists in modern cinema and admittedly influenced by Franz Kafka and Samuel Beckett, Polanski establishes a mood of terror by focusing on bizarre incidents occurring within normal surroundings. "We had nothing really for it but verbal concepts," said Polanski of his first feature film, "Knife in the Water." "I knew I wanted to do film in Poland's lake country; I knew I wish to do picture with only four people in it and nobody in background, no extras. When we start, I have nothing more in mind than a scene in which there are two men in sailboat and one falls into water. Why? Don't know, except I am fascinated early by mood, atmosphere, people reacting to some heightened situation such as terror."

Like surrealists Salvador Dali and Luis Bunuel, Polanski concentrates on the unusual within the usual which, in his case, provides a mood of terror evident in many of his films. In reference to "Repulsion," his study of a knife murderess, Polanski commented: "I decided to make a picture about a psychopathic girl. My aim was simply to show what she could see and feel." "Cul-de-Sac," Polanski's favorite of his own films, is about two criminals seeking refuge on an island inhabited by a transvestite and his flirtatious wife; "Rosemary's Baby" concerns a woman raped by Satan; and "The Tenant" is described by Penelope Gilliatt as "a poetic nightmare about punishment imposed on an unguilty man who merely entertained great fear of guilt."

By consistently developing a mood of terror and concentrating on the unusual, Polanski has been pegged by critics as a "master of the macabre" and as one preoccupied with the supernatural. Polanski adamantly refuses to accept this critical summation. "When you start talking about someone's career," he said, "your mind puts him in a certain category, and I was put in the category of 'master of the macabre,' which is as close to me as being a Buddhist monk." Polanski sees himself as a scrutinizer of the human reaction to unfamiliar situations within normal environments, as in "Knife in the Water" and "Cul-de-Sac." "I'm not preoccupied with the macabre," he said. "I'm rather more interested in the behavior of people under stress, when they are no longer in comfortable, everyday situations where they can afford to respect the conventional rules and morals of society. You can really learn something about a person when he's put into circumstances in which civilized values place his own identity, even his very being, in jeopardy." "The Tenant" typifies this loss of identity. "It is a serious, exact film about the ache of exile," wrote Gilliatt. "Exile from the country. Exile from gender. Exile from the person whom others recognize as the self but whom the self, at times of extreme self-questioning or torment, can find quite foreign."

Because of the prevalent mood of terror in his films, and the often strange subject matter, many of Polanski's films contain intimated and often explicitly detailed violence. This has led to accusations by critics that his films display excessive and irrelevant gore. Polanski has refuted these accusations repeatedly. "I suspect what bothers people in my films is not the amount of violence that's shown, but the realism, the authenticity of it." His "Macbeth," described by Tom Burke as "relentlessly bloody," was defended in its depiction of violence by Vincent Canby. "The violence," wrote Canby, "together with the blood it makes flow, is surely part of what 'Macbeth' is all about, I think it represents excellent Shakespearean moviemaking, a real interpretation of the text."

"You have to show violence the way it is," Polanski told an interviewer. "If you don't show it realistically then that's immoral and harmful. If you don't upset people, then that's obscenity." In another interview, Polanski elaborated on the philosophy that underlies his filming of violence. "If there's violence in the movies it's merely a reflection of life. You know, censorship endorses murder on the screen as long as it's committed in a 'clean way.' But if you show them killing in a real, an agonizing, way, with spitting blood like it usually happens—because very few people die immediately on the spot—if you show that, it's no good. But that's the way it is." Polanski has accused the film industry of approving efficient violence: "If there is violence on the screen that can make people act violently in their lives, it's the Hollywood conception of violence. It's the western where the bad guy aggravates you so much for ninety minutes that, when the good guy gets rid of him in a tidy way, you feel relieved and happy. So what develops in young minds is that when somebody is bad enough, you can get rid of him—and without a mess. This is murder committed the 'clean' way, murder that can be endorsed by movie-rating authorities who miss its real meaning. To me, this is immorality.''

A filmmaker of artistic integrity, Polanski is considered a unique talent by his peers. Jack Nicholson, an actor and director himself, once said of Polanski: ''There is no director alive with Roman's genius.'' And film producer Robert Evans told Tom Burke: ''He is not an easy person, very difficult to crack, but once you do, there is no man and no filmmaker like him.'' However, Polanski himself is ambiguous in his summation of his abilities. ''In movies, stamina is sometimes more important than talent,'' he said. ''You have to be stubborn in this business.'' Assessing the task of directing, Polanski added: ''Art is involving an audience through aesthetic technique. This is what I want. I know what I want and I fight like hell to get what I want. I'm a maniac when I do films. I know it.''

BIOGRAPHICAL/CRITICAL SOURCES: New York Times, November 14, 1965, December 22, 1971, February 22, 1976, June 25, 1976; Ivan Butler, *The Cinema of Roman Polanski,* A. S. Barnes, 1970; *Esquire,* September, 1971; *Playboy,* September, 1971; *New York Times Magazine,* December 12, 1971; *New Yorker,* July 1, 1974, July 3, 1976; *Newsweek,* July 1, 1974; *Rolling Stone,* July 18, 1974; *Variety,* August 28, 1974; *Village Voice,* July 26, 1976; *New York Post,* May 2, 1977.

*   *   *

POLK, Ralph Weiss 1890-1978

January 26, 1890—January 26, 1978; American teacher and author. His *The Practice of Printing* was recognized as the standard text in letterpress printing. An honorary life member of the Graphic Arts Education Guild, Polk also wrote *Elementary Platen Presswork* and *Composition Manual.* He died in North Manchester, Ind. Obituaries and other sources: *AB Bookman's Weekly,* May 8, 1978. (See index for *CA* sketch)

*   *   *

POLLACK, Peter 1911-1978

March 21, 1911—May 13, 1978; American director, writer, and author. He served as director of the South Side Community Art Center in Chicago from 1939-42, and briefly served as field director of the American Red Cross in Iran and Egypt. Pollack was curator, writer, and lecturer in photography at the Art Institute of Chicago and was appointed director of the American Federation of Arts in 1962. He wrote two books, *The Picture History of Photography* and *Understanding Primitive Art.* He died in Sarasota, Fla. Obituaries and other sources: *Who's Who in American Art,* Bowker, 1973; *New York Times,* May 16, 1978.

*   *   *

POLLOCK, Mary
See BLYTON, Enid (Mary)

*   *   *

POLLOWITZ, Melinda Kilborn 1944-

PERSONAL: Born September 22, 1944, in Petoskey, Mich.; daughter of Glenn Ludlow (a salesman) and Jeanne (Arthur) Kilborn; married S. Morton Pollowitz (a salesman), May 24, 1969; children: Greg, Rebecca. *Education:* University of Michigan, B.A., 1966. *Home:* 2937 Via Alvarado, Palos Verdes, Calif. 90274.

CAREER: Jacobson's (department store chain), Jackson, Mich., accessories buyer, 1966-69; writer, 1969—. *Member:* Society of Children's Book Writers, Surfwriters.

WRITINGS: Cinnamon Cane (juvenile), Harper, 1977.

WORK IN PROGRESS: Mandy's Angels, on alcoholism.

SIDELIGHTS: Melinda Pollowitz writes: ''Does an adult ever again feel the zing—the inexpressible joys or the wrenching despairs—he did as a young teenager? I think not, which is why I write for kids—they are wide open and always responsive, if I remember my own emotional ups and downs as a teenager well enough to convey in my books a feeling, a happening, a code of honor that can speak to them. It's a terrific audience and it keeps me always on my toes, always reading to keep up with them, always hammering away at stories I hope are interesting enough to compete with the busy life of today's active teenager.''

*   *   *

POMPER, Philip 1936-

PERSONAL: Born April 18, 1936, in Chicago, Ill.; married in 1961; children: three. *Education:* University of Chicago, B.A., 1959, M.A., 1961, Ph.D., 1965. *Office:* Department of History, Wesleyan University, Middletown, Conn. 06457.

CAREER: Wesleyan University, Middletown, Conn., instructor, 1964-65, assistant professor, 1965-71, associate professor, 1971-76, professor of history, 1976—. *Member:* American Historical Association, American Association for the Advancement of Slavic Studies, Connecticut Academy of Arts and Sciences. *Awards, honors:* Travel grants for the Soviet Union from Interuniversity Committee on Travel Grants, 1962-63, and International Research & Exchanges Board, 1972-73; Ford Foundation fellow in Amsterdam, 1963-64; Social Science Research Council fellow, 1968-69.

WRITINGS: The Russian Revolutionary Intelligentsia, Crowell, 1970; *Peter Lavrov and the Russian Revolutionary Movement,* University of Chicago Press, 1972. Contributor to academic journals.

WORK IN PROGRESS: Nechaev: A Study of Youth, Violence, and Revolution.

*   *   *

POOTS-BOOBY, Edna
See LARSEN, Carl

*   *   *

POPKIN, Richard H(enry) 1923-

PERSONAL: Born December 27, 1923, in New York, N.Y.; son of Louis (a public relations specialist) and Zelda (a writer; maiden name, Feinberg) Popkin; married Juliet Greenstone (a teacher), June 9, 1944; children: Jeremy, Margaret, Susan. *Education:* Columbia University, A.B., 1943, A.M., 1945, Ph.D., 1950; graduate study at Yale University, 1945-46. *Religion:* Jewish. *Home:* 418 South Meramec, Clayton, Mo. 63105. *Office:* Department of Philosophy, Washington University, St. Louis, Mo. 63130.

CAREER: University of Connecticut, Storrs, instructor in philosophy, 1946-47; State University of Iowa, Iowa City, assistant professor, 1947-58, associate professor of philosophy, 1958-60; Harvey Mudd College, Claremont, Calif., professor of philosophy, 1960-63; University of California, San Diego, professor of philosophy, 1963-73; Washington University, St. Louis, Mo., professor of philosophy, 1973—. *Military service:* U.S. Army, 1943. *Member:* American Society for Eighteenth-Century Studies (member of executive board, 1973-76), American Philosophical Association (vice-president of Western Division, 1962), Renaissance Society of America, Phi Beta Kappa. *Awards, honors:* Nicholas Murray Butler Medal from Columbia University, 1977.

WRITINGS: (With Avrum Stroll) *Philosophy Made Simple,* Doubleday, 1957; *The History of Scepticism from Erasmus to Descartes,* Van Gorcum & Co., 1960, revised edition, 1964, Harper, 1968, 4th edition, University of California Press, 1979; (with Stroll) *Introduction to Philosophy,* Holt, 1961, revised edition, 1979; (editor and translator) Pierre Bayle, *Historical and Critical Dictionary: Selections,* Bobbs-Merrill, 1965; (editor with David Norton) *David Hume's Historical Writings: Selections,* Bobbs-Merrill, 1965; (editor and author of introduction) *Readings in the History of Philosophy: The Sixteenth and Seventeenth Centuries,* Free Press, 1966; *The Second Oswald,* Avon, 1966, revised edition, Deutsch, 1967; (editor with Stroll) *Readings in Philosophy,* Holt, 1972, revised edition, 1979; (with Stroll) *Philosophy and the Human Spirit: A Brief Introduction,* Holt, 1973.

Contributor: Frank N. Magill, editor, *Masterpieces of World Philosophy in Summary Form,* Salem Press, 1961; C. M. Turbayne, editor, *Studies on Bishop Berkeley,* Bobbs-Merrill, 1970; R. B. Palmer, editor, *Philomathes: Studies and Essays in the Humanities in Memory of Philip Merlan,* Nijhoff, 1971; Josiah Thompson, editor, *Kierkegaard: A Collection of Critical Essays,* Doubleday, 1972; Craig Walton and John P. Anton, editors, *Philosophy and the Civilizing Arts: Essays Presented to Herbert W. Schneider,* Ohio University Press, 1974; Edward P. Mahoney, editor, *Philosophy and Humanism: Renaissance Essays in Honor of Paul Oskar Kristeller,* E. J. Brill, 1976; Kenneth R. Merrill and Robert W. Shahan, editors, *David Hume, Many-Sided Genius,* University of Oklahoma Press, 1976.

Also contributor to Paul Dibon, editor, *Pierre Bayle: Le Philosophe de Rotterdam,* 1959; V. C. Chapell, editor, *Hume,* 1966; *Expanding Horizons of Knowledge About Man,* Yeshiva University, 1967; *Naturalism and Historical Understanding: Essays on the Philosophy of John H. Randall, Jr.,* 1967; *The Critical Spirit: Essays in Honor of Herbert Marcuse,* 1967; Imre Lakatos and Alan Musgrave, editors, *Problems in the Philosophy of Science,* 1968; N. S. Carl and R. H. Grimm, editors, *Perception and Personal Identity: Proceedings of the 1967 Oberlin Colloquium in Philosophy,* 1969; *Physics, Logic, and History,* Plenum, 1970; *Essays in Honor of Ernest C. Mossner,* Edinburgh University Press, 1974; *Big Brother and the Holding Company,* Ramparts, 1974; *Woman in the Eighteenth Century, and Other Essays,* McMaster University, 1976.

Author of introduction: Henry Van Leeuwen, *The Problem of Certainty in English Thought, 1630-1690,* Nijhoff, 1963; Joseph Glanvill, *Essays on Several Important Subjects in Philosophy and Religion,* Johnson Reprint, 1970; Donald Freed and Mark Lane, editors, *Executive Action,* Dell, 1973; Isaac La Peyrere, *Men Before Adam,* Olms Reprint, 1979; La Peyrere, *Du Rappel des Juifs* (title means "The Recall of the Jews"), Olms Reprint, 1979; Stillingfleet, *Three Attacks on Locke,* Olms Reprint, 1980.

Contributor to *Encyclopaedia Britannica, Catholic Encyclopedia, Encyclopedia of Philosophy, Encyclopedia Judaica,* and *Dictionary of the History of Ideas.* Contributor of nearly two hundred articles and reviews to scholarly journals and popular magazines, including *Ramparts.*

WORK IN PROGRESS: Isaac La Peyrere and His Influence and *Selected Essays,* both for Austin Hill Press.

PORTER, Jonathan 1938-

PERSONAL: Born March 25, 1938, in Boston, Mass.; son of Eliot F. (a photographer) and Aline (a painter; maiden name, Kilham) Porter; married Zoe Barter (a cooking teacher), June 20, 1959. *Education:* Harvard University, A.B., 1960; University of Colorado, M.A., 1963; University of California, Berkeley, Ph.D., 1971. *Home:* 6603 Elwood Dr. N.W., Albuquerque, N.M. 87107. *Office:* Department of History, University of New Mexico, Albuquerque, N.M. 87131.

CAREER: University of New Mexico, Albuquerque, instructor, 1969-71, assistant professor, 1971-74, associate professor of history, 1974—. *Member:* Association for Asian Studies (Western Conference; chairman, 1973-74; executive secretary, 1974—), Social Science History Association, Society for Ch'ing Studies. *Awards, honors:* Social Science Research Council fellowship, 1968-69; American Council of Learned Societies grant, 1976-77.

WRITINGS: Tseng Kuo-fan's Private Bureaucracy, Center for Chinese Studies, University of California, Berkeley, 1972. Contributor to Ch'ing studies journals.

WORK IN PROGRESS: Research on bureaucracy, specialization, and the sociology of science in China.

SIDELIGHTS: Porter has traveled and conducted research in Taiwan, Japan, Hong Kong, Thailand, Cambodia, Malaysia, and Singapore; he speaks Chinese. He comments: "My travels in Taiwan and other countries of Asia have led to an interest in popular religion and culture in the Chinese communities of that area; I hope to eventually write a photographic essay on that subject."

*   *   *

PORTUGES, Paul 1945-

PERSONAL: Born September 16, 1945, in Los Angeles, Calif.; son of Joe (a jet mechanic) and Rose (Glickstein) Portuges; married Maureen Riley (a florist), May 1, 1971; children: Amin. *Education:* University of California, Los Angeles, B.A., 1968; University of California, Berkeley, M.A., 1971, Ph.D., 1975. *Home:* 3888 Fairfax Rd., Santa Barbara, Calif. 93110. *Agent:* Buzz Erikson, 233 Via Sevilla, Santa Barbara, Calif. 93109. *Office:* Department of English, University of Southern California, University Park, Los Angeles, Calif. 90007.

CAREER: University of California, Berkeley, lecturer in composition and literature, 1971-73; Universite de Provence, Aix-en-Provence, France, professor of American studies, 1973-74; University of Southern California, Los Angeles, assistant professor of English and creative writing, 1974—. *Awards, honors:* Fulbright fellow, 1973-74.

WRITINGS: Saving Grace (poetry), Gondwana Publications, 1973; *Hands Across the Earth* (poetry), Gondwana Publications, 1975; (translator) *Aztec Birth: Songs and Flowers,* Mudborn Press, 1978; *The Visionary Poetics of Allen Ginsberg,* Ross-Erickson Publications, 1978.

WORK IN PROGRESS: A biography of Allen Ginsberg; *Survival,* poems; "Fall of America," a screenplay.

AVOCATIONAL INTERESTS: Buddhist meditation, travel in Mexico, Central America, and Europe.

*   *   *

POTTER, James H(arry) 1912-1978

November 10, 1912—March 15, 1978; American educator and author. He specialized in mechanical engineering and was professor of the subject at Stevens Institute of Technology. Potter was a fellow of the Royal Academy of Arts in London, elected as a fellow of the American Society of Mechanical Engineers in 1964, and in 1972, he became a Benjamin Franklin fellow of the Royal Society. In 1971, he was decorated officer de L'Orde des Palmes Academiques in Paris. He wrote numerous books, some of which were on engineering. Potter died in Hoboken, N.J. Obituaries and other sources: *American Men and Women of Science: The Physical and Biological Sciences,* 12th edition, Bowker, 1971-73; *New York Times,* March 22, 1978.

* * *

POTTER, Robert D(ucharme) 1905-1978

February 5, 1905—March 18, 1978; American physicist, editor, and author of scientific books and articles. Potter was a founder and past president of the National Association of Science Writers. The former executive director of the Medical Society of the County of New York, he served as editor of its official publication, *New York Medicine.* As a research assistant at the Carnegie Institute from 1939 to 1940, Potter operated the atom smasher, thereby participating in the first American experiments on fission of the uranium atom. He died in Miami, Fla. Obituaries and other sources: *American Men and Women of Science: The Physical and Biological Sciences,* 12th edition, Bowker, 1971-73; *New York Times,* March 22, 1978.

* * *

POURNELLE, Jerry (Eugene) 1933-
(Wade Curtis)

PERSONAL: Born August 7, 1933, in Shreveport, La.; son of P. Eugene (a radio station owner) and R. Ruth (Lewis) Pournelle; married Roberta Jane Isdell (a reading specialist), July 18, 1960; children: Alexander, Francis Russell, Phillip, Richard Stefan. *Education:* University of Washington, B.S., 1954, M.S., 1957, Ph.D., 1964. *Politics:* Republican. *Religion:* "Anglo-Catholic." *Home:* 12051 Laurel Terrace, Studio City, Calif. 91604. *Agent:* Lurton Blassingame, Blassingame, McCauley & Wood, 60 East 42nd St., New York, N.Y. 10017.

CAREER: Boeing Co., Seattle, Wash., aviation psychologist and research engineer, 1957-63; Aerospace Corp., San Bernardino, Calif., manager of special studies, 1964; systems scientist for North American Aviation, 1964-65; Pepperdine University, Los Angeles, Calif., professor of history and political science, 1964-68; executive assistant to mayor of Los Angeles and director of research, Los Angeles, 1969; writer and consultant, 1969—. Member of Republican Party Board of Governors, San Bernardino Co., 1960-64; chairman of board, Seattle Civic Playhouse, 1962-63; member of board of directors, Ocean Living Institute. Adviser to numerous futurist and space-oriented organizations. *Member:* Science Fiction Writers of America (president, 1973-74), American Institute of Aeronautics and Astronautics, Operations Research Society of America, American Academy of Arts and Sciences (fellow), Institute for Strategic Studies, University Professors for Academic Order (director, 1971). *Awards, honors:* Bronze Medal from American Security Council, 1967; John W. Campbell Award, 1974.

WRITINGS: (With Stefan Possony) *The Strategy of Technology,* Dunellen, 1970; *A Spaceship for the King,* Daw, 1972; (editor) *2020 Vision,* Avon, 1972; (with Larry Niven) *The Mote in God's Eye,* Simon & Schuster, 1975; *Birth of Fire,* Laser, 1976; (with Niven) *Inferno,* Pocket Books,

1976; *West of Honor,* Laser, 1976; *The Mercenary,* Pocket Books, 1977; *High Justice,* Pocket Books, 1977; (with Niven) *Lucifer's Hammer,* Playboy Press, 1977.

Also author of *Human Temperature Tolerance in Astronautic Environments,* 1959, *Stability and National Security,* 1968, *Congress Debates Viet Nam,* 1971, *The Right to Read,* 1971, and *Escape From the Planet of the Apes,* 1973.

Under pseudonym Wade Curtis: *Red Heroin,* Berkeley Publishing, 1967; *Red Dragon,* Berkeley Publishing, 1970.

Science columnist, *Galaxy Science Fiction Magazine.* Contributor of articles to *Analog* and *American Legion* magazine.

WORK IN PROGRESS: Science fiction novels with Larry Niven, *Oath of Fealty* and *Krishna's Fist; The War of the Gods,* a Bronze Age historical for Simon & Schuster.

SIDELIGHTS: Pournelle told *CA:* "I write because you work inside and sitting down and there is no heavy lifting. I tell stories, rather than 'contribute to literature.' I hike, fish, swim, sail small boats, swing a sword as Knight Marchal of the West in the Society for Creative Anachronism, keep dogs but not cats, raise boys, drink beer, and sing lewd songs. I've traveled over most of the world and want to do so again when I get this book done. What's vital is that I make money at this business because nobody would work that hard if they weren't paid."

* * *

POWELL, (John) Craig 1940-

PERSONAL: Born November 16, 1940, in Australia; son of Frederick and Ilma (an office worker; maiden name, Makin) Powell; married Janet Dawson, October 16, 1965; children: Edwin (deceased), Katie, Matthew. *Education:* University of Sydney, B.Med. and B.Surg., 1965; further study at New South Wales Institute of Psychiatry, 1969-70. *Home:* 799 Dulaney Dr., London, Ontario, Canada N6C 3W3. *Office:* London Psychiatric Hospital, London, Ontario, Canada N6A 4L1.

CAREER: Royal Prince Alfred Hospital, Sydney, Australia, junior resident medical officer, 1965; Western Suburbs Hospital, Sydney, senior resident medical officer, 1966; salaried assistant in family practice to Dr. John Rigney, Fairfield, Sydney, 1967; Parramatta Psychiatric Hospital, Sydney, staff psychiatrist, 1968-72; Brandon Mental Health Centre, Brandon, Manitoba, team III clinical director, 1972-75; St. Joseph's Hospital, London, Ontario, chief resident in psychiatry, 1976; London Psychiatric Hospital, London, Ontario, staff psychiatrist, 1976—. *Member:* Australian and New Zealand College of Psychiatrists, League of Canadian Poets. *Awards, honors:* Award from *Poetry* (Australia), 1964, for "Four Portraits"; award from Henry Lawson Festival, 1969, for poem "Tree and River Bank."

WRITINGS—Books of poems: *A Different Kind of Breathing,* South Head Press, 1966; *I Learn by Going,* South Head Press, 1968; *A Country Without Exiles,* South Head Press, 1972; *Rehearsal for Dancers,* Turnstone Press, 1977. Author of "Craig Powell on Poetry," a weekly column in *Brandon Sun,* 1974-75. Contributor to poetry magazines.

WORK IN PROGRESS: Induced Psychosis, on casualties of encounter-style groups in Ontario.

SIDELIGHTS: Powell told *CA:* "I've had almost a life-long fascination with psychoanalysis, and began reading Freud at the age of fourteen. That was what induced me to take medicine as a career, rather then entering some field more in keeping with my literary enthusiasm. I am currently training with the Canadian Institute of Psychoanalysis, and am more attracted to object relations theory and Kohut's work on narcissism than to the original writings of Freud which, these days, are mainly of historical interest.

"The introspection and the detailed attention to interpersonal relationships that are essential to my psychiatric work can also be seen in my poems. However, the poems have a music and an impulse of their own. All the same, psychotherapy, when it is done well, has some of the qualities of poetry—it proceeds by feeling and intuition rather than strict logic, and tries to form linkages between elements that previously did not seem to belong together."

BIOGRAPHICAL/CRITICAL SOURCES: Poetry Australia, Number 49.

*   *   *

POWER, (Patrick) Victor 1930-

PERSONAL: Born October 16, 1930, in Dublin, Ireland; came to the United States in 1966, naturalized citizen, 1973; son of Patrick Joseph (a banker) and Kathleen (a writer; maiden name, Murphy) Power; married Marybel Killian (a writer), November 4, 1968; children: Ann Allen, Lynn Goldsberry, Kim Goldsberry. *Education:* St. John's College, Waterford, Ireland, B.A., 1951, B.D.,1954; University of Iowa, M.A., 1968, M.F.A., 1970, Ph.D., 1971. *Politics:* Democrat. *Religion:* Roman Catholic. *Home:* 5801 North Sheridan, #3D, Chicago, Ill. 60660. *Agent:* Joel Ostrow, #1425, 1 North LaSalle, Chicago, Ill. *Office:* Department of Human Services, City of Chicago, 640 North LaSalle, Chicago, Ill. 60610.

CAREER: Ordained Roman Catholic priest, 1954, for diocese of Waterford and Lismore, Ireland; pastor of Roman Catholic churches in England, Ireland, and the United States, 1954-68, legally released from obligations of the priesthood in 1968; King Abdulaziz University, Jeddah, Saudi Arabia, head of English literature department, 1971-72; City of Chicago, Ill., Department of Human Services, director of public services, 1972-77, coordinator of program services, 1978—. Lecturer at Loyola University, Chicago, Ill., 1973, and Columbia College, Chicago, Ill., 1978. Producer for WSUI-Radio and WMT-TV (Iowa).

MEMBER: Dramatists Guild, Poets and Writers, Chicago Press Club, Chicago Headliners Club, Chicago Council on Fine Arts, Sigma Delta Chi, Kappa Tau Alpha. *Awards, honors:* First prize from *Oireachtas* national Gaelic literary contest, 1959, for "Aisling 'sna Comaraigh," and 1962, for "Umar na hAimleise"; first prize of Cork Drama Festival and All-Ireland contest, 1964, for "Young Men in a Hurry"; first prize from All-Ireland Drama Contest, 1966, for "Blood Brothers"; second prize from Illinois Arts Council, 1974, for "The Escape."

WRITINGS—Plays: "Umar na hAimleise" (three-act), first produced in Dublin at Damar Hall, 1962; "Who Needs Enemies" (three-act), first produced in Iowa City at University of Iowa, April, 1971; "The Escape" (two-act), first produced in Chicago at Happy Medium Theatre, 1974; "Johnnie Will" (two-act), first produced in Chicago at Body Politic Theatre, March 17, 1977; "Mother Jones" (two-act), first produced in Chicago at Body Politic Theater, November 2, 1978.

Radio plays: "Aisling 'sna Comaraigh," broadcast on Radio Eireann, 1960; "Young Men in a Hurry," first broadcast in 1964, broadcast on Radio Telefis Eireann, 1978; "The Mudnest" (three-act), broadcast on WSUI Radio, Iowa.

Work represented in anthologies, including *Story: The Yearbook of Discovery,* edited by Whit Burnett, Four Winds Press, 1969; *Drama and Theater,* State University of New York College at Fredonia, 1972. Contributor to professional and popular journals, including *North American Review, New Statesman,* and *Eire-Ireland.*

WORK IN PROGRESS: Circle of Knives, a novel; another novel (working title, *The O'Hare Triangle*); translating *Apple on the Tree Top,* a novel by his brother, Richard Power.

SIDELIGHTS: Power told *CA:* "I learned much from being a priest—the calling leaves a stamp which is difficult, indeed impossible, to obliterate. My plays are mainly about change—rural, urban, religious, political, and shifting values between the younger and older generation. My new novel is set in Chicago and is a thriller—hope it will be exciting enough to be a movie."

*   *   *

POWERS, Bill 1931-

PERSONAL: Born February 3, 1931, in Brooklyn, N.Y.; son of Robert J. (a steelworker) and Delia (Thompson) Powers; married Suzy Martin, October 26, 1965 (divorced, 1970); children: Michael, James. *Education:* Attended Pratt Institute, 1956-58, and Mexico City College, 1959. *Home:* 72 Barrow St., New York, N.Y. 10014. *Agent:* Elaine Markson, 44 Greenwich Ave., New York, N.Y. 10011.

CAREER: Free-lance commercial artist in New York City, 1956-65; Second Story Players, New York City, theatrical director, 1965-68; free-lance writer and photographer, 1969—. *Military service:* U.S. Air Force, 1951-55; became sergeant. *Member:* American Society of Magazine Photographers. *Awards, honors:* Obie award, 1967, for general excellence of productions.

WRITINGS—Juvenile: Break Him Down!, F. Watts, 1977; *The Weekend,* F. Watts, 1978; *Flying High,* F. Watts, 1978; *Love Lost, and Found,* F. Watts, 1979.

WORK IN PROGRESS: "Sweet Arsenic," a film script.

*   *   *

POWERS, Edward A(lvin) 1941-

PERSONAL: Born March 10, 1941, in West Virginia; son of Edward (a construction engineer) and Noyedell (Smith) Powers; married Joyce K. Small (a speech clinician), September 15, 1961; children: Paige Marie, Courtney Britt. *Education:* Alma College, B.A., 1962; Indiana University, M.A., 1964; Ohio State University, Ph.D., 1967. *Politics:* Democrat. *Religion:* Presbyterian. *Home:* 1214 Truman, Ames, Iowa 50010. *Office:* Department of Sociology and Anthropology, Iowa State University, Ames, Iowa 50011.

CAREER: Iowa State University, Ames, instructor, 1967-68, assistant professor, 1968-72, associate professor, 1972-76, professor of sociology, 1976—. *Member:* American Sociological Association, Gerontological Society, Midwest Sociological Society (member of board of directors, 1976-78), Midwest Council for Social Research in Aging (president, 1976—). *Awards, honors:* Fellowship from Midwest Council for Social Research in Aging, 1970-72.

WRITINGS: (With J. P. Golinvaux) *The Aged in an Affluent Society,* Iowa State University, 1971; *Process in Relationships,* West Publishing, 1974, 2nd edition, 1976; *Encounter with Family Realities,* West Publishing, 1977.

WORK IN PROGRESS: At My Grandmother's Knee, with J. K. Powers.

POWERS, Robert M(aynard) 1942-

PERSONAL: Born November 9, 1942, in Lexington, Ky.; son of Ralph D. and Eddie M. (Vaughn) Powers; married Patricia L. Burgdorf, September 1, 1961 (divorced, 1970); married Lee Welcyng (a writer), July 12, 1977; children: Michelle M. *Education:* University of Edinburgh, certificate, 1968; University of Arizona, B.A., 1969. *Agent:* Alexandria Hatcher Agency, 150 West 55th St., New York, N.Y. 10019. *Office address:* P.O. Box 11628, Denver, Colo. 80211.

CAREER: Writer, 1970—. *Member:* American Society of Journalists and Authors, Authors Guild of Authors League of America, National Space Institute, Aviation/Space Writers Association, Royal Astronomical Society of Canada, Webb Society (London). *Awards, honors:* Richard Grand Foundation grant for legal and educational research, 1968.

WRITINGS: Viking Mission to Mars, Martin-Marietta, 1975; *Planetary Encounters,* Stackpole, 1978; *Turquoise,* Stackpole, 1978; *Space Shuttle,* Stackpole, in press. Science editor of *Denver.*

WORK IN PROGRESS: First Landing, publication by Stackpole expected in 1980; *Unicorns Seldom Die,* a science fiction novel for Doubleday; *Future Body,* for Stackpole.

SIDELIGHTS: Powers writes: "I had the misfortune, at the age of five, to be given a college astronomy textbook to find an answer to what should have been an innocent childish question. From that time on, I was burned by space. Having gone through science fiction books at a regular rate since very young, I turned to making telescopes. Somewhere in the mid-sixties, while working at a job I detested, I saw via television a Ranger vehicle impact on the Moon. I quit my job and began writing about space."

* * *

POYNTER, Nelson 1903-1978

December 15, 1903—June 15, 1978; American publisher and newspaper manager. As chairman of the board of the *St. Petersburg Times* and the *Evening Independent,* Poynter took liberal stands on many controversial issues. His paper was one of the first to call on President Nixon to resign or face impeachment proceedings during the Watergate investigation of 1972. The *St. Petersburg Times* won the Pultizer Prize for public service because of Poynter's firm editorial positions. He died in St. Petersburg, Fla. Obituaries and other sources: *Who's Who in America,* 38th edition, Marquis, 1974; *New York Times,* June 17, 1978; *Newsweek,* June 26, 1978.

* * *

PRESSAU, Jack Renard 1933-

PERSONAL: Born November 16, 1933, in Curtisville, Pa.; son of Wilson Leo (a mining engineer) and Mary Virginia (Jenkins) Pressau; married Gail Girdwood, December 23, 1955 (divorced March 22, 1973); married Jane Todd (a professor and college librarian), April 8, 1973; children: Susan Ellen, Jeffrey Glenn, Cara Lynn; Nancy Suzanne Jones (stepdaughter). *Education:* Indiana University of Pennsylvania, B.S., 1955; Pittsburgh Theological Seminary, M. Div., 1958; Presbyterian School of Christian Education, M.C.E., 1959; University of Pittsburgh, Ph.D., 1965. *Home address:* Route 2, Box 327, Clinton, S.C. 29325. *Office:* Presbyterian College, Box 975, Clinton, S.C. 29325.

CAREER: Ordained Presbyterian minister, 1959; associate pastor of Presbyterian church in Elmira, N.Y., 1959-62;

Presbyterian College, Clinton, S.C., counselor, 1972-75. Member of board of directors of Beckman Center for Mental Health Services, 1974-77 (chairman of board, 1976-77); member of board of directors of Parents Without Partners. *Member:* Religious Education Association, Religious Research Association, Professors and Researchers in Religious Education, Association of Church Teachers, Association of Presbyterian Church Educators, American Association of University Professors, Alston Wilkes Society (member of board of directors), Phi Mu Alpha (life member of Sinfonia).

WRITINGS: I'm Saved, You're Saved—Maybe, John Knox, 1977, leader's guide, privately printed. Contributor to religious journals.

WORK IN PROGRESS: A methods book in Christian education.

SIDELIGHTS: Pressau comments: "I consider myself a career church educator with special skills in religious developmental and learning psychology. I taught psychology courses from 1966-75 in addition to my Christian education courses and try to bring to the church contributions from that social science. I have a side-vocation of helping small congregations, with preaching and pastoral care."

AVOCATIONAL INTERESTS: Music (playing the bass violin).

* * *

PREUSSLER, Otfried 1923-

PERSONAL: Born in 1923, in Reichenberg (Liberec), Bohemia; children: three daughters. *Residence:* Germany.

CAREER: Author. *Awards, honors:* German Children's Book Prize, 1972, and European prize for books for young people, 1973, both for *Krabat.*

WRITINGS: The Little Water-Sprite (translation by Anthea Bell of *Der Kleine Wassermann;* illustrated by Winnie Gayler), Abelard, 1960; *The Little Witch* (translation by Bell of *Die Kleine Hexe;* illustrated by W. Gayler), Abelard, 1961; *The Wise Men of Schilda* (translation by Bell of *Bei Uns in Schilda;* illustrated by F. J. Tripp), Abelard, 1962; *Der Raeuber Hotzenplotz,* K. Thienemann (Stuttgart), 1962, translation by Bell published as *The Robber Hotzenplotz* (illustrated by Tripp), Abelard, 1964; *Thomas Scarecrow* (translation by Bell of *Thomas Vogelschreck;* illustrated by W. Gayler), Abelard, 1963; (editor) Josef Lada, *Kater Mikesch, Geschichten vom Kater, der Sprechen Konnte,* 3rd edition, Sauerlaender (Aarau, Switzerland), 1964; *The Little Ghost* (translation by Bell of *Das Kleine Gespenst;* illustrated by Tripp), Abelard, 1967; *Die Abenteuer des Starken Wanja,* Arena (Wuerzburg, Germany), 1968, translation by Bell published as *The Adventures of Strong Vanya* (illustrated by Herbert Holzing), Abelard, 1970; (editor) Z. K. Slaby and others, *Das Geheimnis der Orangenfarbenen Katze* (illustrated by Tripp), K. Thienemanns, 1968; *Neues vom Raeuber Hotzenplotz: Noch eine Kasperlgeschichte* (illustrated by Tripp), Thienemann, 1969, translation by Bell published as *The Further Adventures of the Robber Hotzenplotz: A Story about Kasperl* (illustrated by Tripp), Abelard, 1971; (editor) Josef Kolar, *Kater Schnurr mit den Blauen Augen* (translation of *Z Deniku Kocoura Modroocka;* illustrated by Siegfried Wagner), Oesterreichischer Bundesverlag (Vienna), 1969.

Krabat, Arena, 1971, translation by Bell published as *The Satanic Mill,* Abelard, 1972; *Die Dumme Augustine* (illustrated by Herbert Lentz), K. Thienemann, 1972; *Jahrmarkt in Rummelsbach* (illustrated by Lentz), K. Thienemann,

1973; *The Final Adventures of the Robber Hotzenplotz* (translated from the German by Bell), Abelard, 1975; *The Green Bronze Bell* (illustrated by Holzing), Hamish Hamilton, 1977; *Die Flucht nach Aegypten* (novel), R. Piper, 1978.

BIOGRAPHICAL/CRITICAL SOURCES: Chicago Sunday Tribune, October 22, 1961; *New York Times Book Review,* March 25, 1973; *Times Literary Supplement,* March 25, 1977.*

* * *

PREVERT, Jacques (Henri Marie) 1900-1977

PERSONAL: Born February 4, 1900, in Neuilly-sur-Seine, France; son of Andre (a clerk) and Suzanne (Catusse) Prevert; married Simone Dienne, April 30, 1925 (marriage ended); married Janine Tricotet, March 4, 1947. *Education:* Educated in Paris, France. *Home:* Cite Veron, 82 Blvd. de Clichy, 75018 Paris, France.

CAREER: Poet, screenwriter, and dramatist. Held exhibitions of collages in Paris, 1957, and Antibes, 1963. *Awards, honors:* Grand prix from Societe des auteurs et compositeurs dramatiques, 1973; grand prix national from *Cinema,* 1975.

WRITINGS—In English: *Paroles* (poems), Editions du Point du Jour, 1945, revised and augmented edition, Gallimard, 1966, translation by Lawrence Ferlinghetti published as *Selections from 'Paroles,'* City Lights, 1958; (with Albert Lamorisse) *Bim, le petit ane,* Guilde du livre, 1951, translation by Bette Swados and Harvey Swados published as *Bim, the Little Donkey,* Doubleday, 1973; (author of introduction) *Couleur de Paris* (photography by Peter Cornelius), La Bibliotheque des Arts, 1961, translation by Jonathan Griffin and Margaret Shenfield published as *Paris in Colour,* Thames & Hudson, 1962, Bramhall House, 1963; (author of preface) *Les Halles: L'Album du coeur de Paris* (illustrated by Romain Urhausen), Editions des Deux-Mondes, 1963, translation published as *Les Halles: The Stomach of Paris,* Atlantis Books, 1964; *To Paint the Portrait of a Bird—Pour faire le portrait d'un oiseau* (English-French edition with translations by Ferlinghetti), Doubleday, 1971.

Poetry: (With Andre Verdet) *Histoires* (title means "Stories"), Editions du Pre aux clercs, 1946; *Grand bal du printemps* (title means "Grand Ball of Spring"; photography by Izis Bidermanas), Guilde du livre, 1951 (also see below); *Charmes de Londres* (title means "The Charms of London"; photography by Bidermanas), Guilde du livre, 1952 (also see below); *Lumieres d'homme* (title means "Lights of Man"), Guy Levis Mano (G.L.M.), 1955; (with Joseph L. Artigas) *Miro,* Maeght, 1956; (contributor) Henry Decanaud, *La Pierre dans le souffle* (title means "The Stone in the Wind"), Seghers, 1959; *Histoires et d'autres histoires* (title means "Stories and Other Stories"), Gallimard, 1963; *Varengeville* (illustrated by Georges Braque), Maeght, 1968; *Choses et autres* (title means "Things and Others"), Gallimard, 1972.

Other works: (With Paul Grimault) *La Bergere et le ramoneur* (title means "The Shepherdess and the Chimney-Sweep"), Les Gemeaux, 1947; *Contes pour les enfants pas sages* (title means "Stories for Naughty Children"), Editions du Pre aux clercs, 1947; (with Camilla Koffler) *Le Petit Lion* (title means "The Little Lion"; photography by Ylla), Arts et metiers graphiques, 1947; (contributor) Joseph Kosma, *Le Rendezvous: Ballet en trois tableaux* (piano scores), Enoch, 1948; (with Verdet) *C'est a Saint Paul de Vence,* Nouvelle Edition, 1949; *Spectacle* (poems, plays, and prose), Gallimard, 1949, reprinted, 1972.

Des Betes (title means "The Animals"; photography by Ylla), Gallimard, 1950; *Guignol* (title means "Puppet Show"; illustrated by Elsa Henriquez), Guilde du livre, 1952; *Lettre des Iles Baladar* (title means "Letter From the Baladar Islands"), Gallimard, 1952; *L'Opera de la lune* (title means "Moon Opera"; music by Christiane Verger), Guilde du livre, 1953; *La Pluie et le beau temps* (title means "Rain and Fine Weather"), Gallimard, 1955; (with Georges Ribemont-Dessaignes) *Joan Miro,* Maeght, 1956; (with Ribemont-Dessaignes) *Arbres* (title means "Trees"), Gallimard, 1956, 2nd edition, 1976; *Images* (title means "Pictures"), Maeght, 1957; *Dix-sept chansons de Jacques Prevert* (title means "Seventeen Songs by Jacques Prevert"; music by Joseph Kosma), Folkuniversitetets Foerlag, 1958; *Portraits de Picasso* (title means "Portraits of Picasso"; photography by Andre Villers), Muggiani, 1959.

(Contributor) Ylipe, *Magloire de Paris,* Losfeld, 1961; (with Max Ernst) *Les Chiens ont soif* (title means "The Dogs Are Thirsty"), Pont des Arts, 1964; *Jacques Prevert presente "Le Circle d'Izis"* (title means "Jacques Prevert Presents 'The Circle of Izis'"; photography by Bidermanas), A. Sauret, 1965; (with Helmut Grieshaber) *Carl Orff: Carmina burana,* Manus Presse, 1965; *Georges* (illustrated by Ribemont-Dessaignes), Cagnes, 1965; (contributor) Alexander Calder, *Calder,* Maeght, 1966; *Fatras* (self-illustrated), Livre de poche, 1966; (contributor) Cesare Vivaldi, *Mayo,* Instituto editoriale italiano, 1968; *Imaginaires* (title means "Make-Believe"), A. Skira, 1970; *Fromanger,* Fall, 1971; (with Andre Pozner) *Hebdomadaires* (interview; title means "Weeklies"), G. Authier, 1972; (with Rene Bertele) *Images de Jacques Prevert* (title means "Pictures by Jacques Prevert"), Filipacchi, 1974.

Also author of *Le Cheval de Troie,* 1946, *L'Ange garde-chiourme,* 1946, and *Vignette pour les vignerons,* 1951.

Collections: Guy Jacob, Andre Heinrich, and Bernard Chardere, *Jacques Prevert* (screenplays), Imprimerie du Bugey, 1960; J. H. Douglas and D. J. Girard, editors, *Poemes,* Harrap, 1961; Teo Savory, adapter, *Prevert II,* Unicorn Press, 1967; Andree Bergens and David Noakes, editors, *Prevert vous parle* (title means "Prevert Speaks to You"), Prentice-Hall, 1968; *Poesies* (includes "Spectacles" and "La Pluie et le beau temps"), Newton Compton, 1971; Joel Sadler, *A travers Prevert* (title means "Through Prevert"), Gallimard, 1975; *Grand bal du printemps, suivi de Charmes de Londres* (collection of two works of poetry first published separately; see above), Gallimard, 1976.

Screenplays: *Les Amants de Verone,* La Nouvelle Edition, 1949; "Les Visiteurs du soir," published in *Deux films francais: Les Visiteurs du soir* [and] *Le Feu follet,* edited by Robert M. Hammond and Marguerite Hammond, Harcourt, 1965; *Les Enfants du paradis,* Lorrimer Publishing, 1968, translation by Dinah Brooke published as *Children of Paradise,* Simon & Schuster, 1968; *Le Jour se leve,* translated by Brooke and Nicola Hayden, Simon & Schuster, 1970; *Drole le drame,* Balland, 1974. Also author of screenplays for "L'Affaire est dans le sac," "Quai des brumes," "Lumiere d'ete," "Les Portes de la nuit," "La Bergere et le ramoneur," and "Notre Dame de Paris," and of dialogue for "Les Amours celebres."

Also author of farces, pantomimes, ballets, and skits, including "Baptiste" and "La Famille tuyau de poele" (title means "Top-hat Family"), 1935, and of lyrics for numerous popular songs set to music by Joseph Kosma.

Work represented in numerous anthologies, including *Let's Get a Divorce,* edited by E. R. Bentley, Hill & Wang, 1958;

and *Selections from French Poetry,* edited by K. F. Canfield, Harvey House, 1965. Contributor to *Coronet, Kenyon Review, Poetry,* and other periodicals.

SIDELIGHTS: Marcel Carnet, the producer with whom Prevert collaborated on several major films, commented on Prevert's death: "Jacques Prevert is the one and only poet of the French cinema. He created a style, original and personal, reflecting the soul of the people. His humor and poetry succeeded in raising the banal to the summit of art."

OBITUARIES: New York Times, April 12, 1977; *AB Bookman's Weekly,* June 20, 1977.*

(Died April 11, 1977, at Omonville-La-Petite, France)

*   *   *

PRICE, Anthony   1928-

PERSONAL: Born August 16, 1928, in Hertfordshire, England; son of Walter Longsdon (an engineer) and Kathleen (an artist; maiden name, Lawrence) Price; married Ann Stone (a registered nurse), June 20, 1953; children: James, Simon, Katherine. *Education:* Earned M.A. (with honors) from Merton College, Oxford. *Home:* Wayside Cottage, Horton-cum-Studley, Oxfordshire. *Agent:* A. P. Watt & Son, 26/28 Bedford Row, London WC1R 4HL. *Office:* Oxford Times, Osney Mead, Oxford.

CAREER: Writer. *Oxford Times,* Oxford, England, editor, 1972—. *Military service:* British Army; became captain. *Member:* Guild of British Newspaper Editors, Crime Writers Association (England), The Detection Club. *Awards, honors:* Silver Dagger from Crime Writers' Association, 1971, for *The Labyrinth Makers;* Golden Dagger of the Crime Writers' Association (England), 1974, for *Other Paths to Glory.*

WRITINGS: The Labyrinth Makers, Gollancz, 1970, Doubleday, 1971; *The Alamut Ambush,* Gollancz, 1971, Doubleday, 1972; *Colonel Butler's Wolf,* Gollancz, 1972, Doubleday, 1973; *October Men,* Gollancz, 1973, Doubleday, 1974; *Other Paths to Glory,* Gollancz, 1974, Doubleday, 1975; *Our Man in Camelot,* Gollancz, 1975, Doubleday, 1976; *War Game,* Gollancz, 1976.

WORK IN PROGRESS: The '44 Vintage.

*   *   *

PRICE, Leo   1941-

PERSONAL: Born August 13, 1941, in Findlay, Ohio; son of Dale (a farmer) and Angelene (Ricard) Price; married Sandy Anderson, September 4, 1962; children: Michael Lee, Tamela Sue. *Religion:* United Methodist. *Home:* 11355 Neapolis-Waterville Rd., Whitehouse, Ohio 43571. *Office:* Campbell Soup Co., Napoleon, Ohio 43545.

CAREER: Employed by Fisher Cheese Co., Wapakoneta, Ohio, 1962-63; employed by Campbell Soup Co., Napoleon, Ohio, 1963-66; farmer, 1966-68; Campbell Soup Co., in shipping, 1968—. Writer, cartoonist, and illustrator. Union steward, 1975—.

WRITINGS—Self-illustrated children's books: *The Tree That Always Said No,* Daughters of St. Paul, 1973. Contributor to local church publications.

WORK IN PROGRESS: Hoover Wants to Help, The Hopeless Tree, The Fearful Forest, The Raging River; all self-illustrated children's books, the first two to be published by Daughters of St. Paul.

SIDELIGHTS: Untrained as a writer or artist, Price's children's stories have been well-received by local children for

several years. Purposely published by a non-profit organization, his only goal so far has been to help children develop moral values. Some day he hopes to be able to write full-time.

AVOCATIONAL INTERESTS: Painting and restoring cars and trucks; painting portraits and landscapes in oil.

BIOGRAPHICAL/CRITICAL SOURCES: Ohio West News, October, 1974.

*   *   *

PRITCHARD, Norman Henry II   1939-

PERSONAL: Born October 22, 1939, in New York, N.Y. *Education:* Washington Square College, B.A., 1961; further study at New York University, 1961-63, and Columbia University, 1962. *Office:* 131 East 70 St., New York, N.Y. 10021.

CAREER: Writer. Poet-in-residence at Friends Seminary, 1968—; New School for Social Research, New York, N.Y., instructor in poetry, 1969—. Co-chairman of National Standing Committee on Poetry for American Festival of Negro Arts, 1963-64. *Member:* Audubon Society, Asia Society, St. George's Society of New York.

WRITINGS: The Matrix: Poems 1960-1970, Doubleday, 1970; *Eecchhooeess,* New York University Press, 1971.

Contributor: Ishmael Reed, editor, *Yardbird Reader I,* Yardbird Publishing Cooperative, 1969; Walter Lowenfels, editor, *In a Time of Revolution,* Random House, 1969; Clarence Major, editor, *The New Black Poetry,* International Publishing Co., 1969; Adam David Miller, editor, *Dices and Black Bones,* Houghton, 1970; Richard Kostelanetz, editor, *In Youth,* Ballantine, 1972; Abraham Chapman, editor, *New Black Voices,* New American Library, 1972; Arnold Adoff, editor, *The Poetry of Black America,* Harper, 1972. Also contributed to recording *Destinations: Four Contemporary American Poets,* Mono, 1965.

WORK IN PROGRESS: Poems 1970-1975, Origins: An Anthology of Transreal Writing, and a novel, *The Mundus.*

SIDELIGHTS: Pritchard, who specializes in poetic word games and concrete poetry, accents his poems with specific designs. "Pritchard's *Eecchhooeess* is full of visual oddities, sight gags, and thisss sssort of thinggg," *Choice* reported. And a reviewer for *Hudson Review* commented: "Anyone interested in N. H. Pritchard will want to experience his absolutely unique brand of word-magic."

BIOGRAPHICAL/CRITICAL SOURCES: Hudson Review, Spring, 1972; *Choice,* September, 1972.*

*   *   *

PROBERT, Walter   1925-

PERSONAL: Born January 13, 1925, in Portland, Ore.; son of Raymond and Mildred Marie (Pyburn) Probert; married Barbara Louise Stevenson, March 22, 1952; children: Richard Walter, James Stevenson. *Education:* Attended Alfred University, 1944; University of Oregon, B.S., 1948, J.D., 1951; Yale University, J.S.D., 1957. *Home:* 1929 Northwest 14th Ave., Gainesville, Fla. 32605. *Office:* College of Law, University of Florida, Gainesville, Fla. 32611.

CAREER: Admitted to Oregon bar, 1951; attorney in Portland, Ore., 1951-52; Western Reserve University (now Case Western Reserve University), Cleveland, Ohio, assistant professor, 1953-57, associate professor of law, 1957-59; University of Florida, Gainesville, professor of law, 1959—. Visiting professor at Northwestern University, 1960-61,

University of Texas, summer, 1970, and University of Washington, Seattle, 1972-73; visiting research professor at University of Denver, 1966-67; lecturer at Balliol College, Oxford, 1968. Director of National Science Foundation law and social science program, 1973-74. *Military service:* U.S. Army, 1943-46; became first lieutenant.

MEMBER: International Association for Philosophy of Law and Social Philosophy, Association of American Law Schools (member of panel of advocates), American Trial Lawyers Association, American Psychology-Law Society, American Society for Political and Legal Philosophy, American Arbitration Association (member of national panel of arbitrators), Law and Society Association, Society for Health and Human Values, Oregon Bar Association, Coif, Delta Theta Phi, Order of St. Ives. *Awards, honors:* National Foundation for the Humanities research grant, 1968; Educational Testing Service grant, 1968.

WRITINGS: (Contributor) R. D. Henson, editor, *Landmarks of the Law,* Harper, 1960; *Law, Language, and Communication,* C. C Thomas, 1972. Contributor to law journals. Faculty editor of *Western Reserve University Law Review,* 1953-59.

WORK IN PROGRESS: The Ethics of Lawyers.

SIDELIGHTS: Commenting briefly on the ethics of lawyers, Probert told *CA:* "Most lawyers are pragmatically amoral, mainly because clients want them to be."

* * *

PROSSER, H(arold) L(ee) 1944-

PERSONAL: Born December 31, 1944, in Springfield, Mo.; son of Harold and Marjorie (maiden name, Firestone) Prosser; married Grace Eileen Wright, November 4, 1971; children: Rachael Maranda. *Education:* Santa Monica College, A.A., 1968; attended California State University, Northridge, 1968-69; Southwest Missouri State University, B.S., 1974; has studied under writers Paul Bowles, Alan Casty, and Christopher Isherwood. *Home:* 1313 South Jefferson Ave., Springfield, Mo. 65807.

CAREER: Writer, 1963—.

WRITINGS: Dandelion Seeds: Eighteen Stories, Angst, 1974; *The Capricorn and Other Fantasy Stories,* Angst, 1974; *The Cymric and Other Occult Poems,* Mafdet Press, 1976; *The Day of the Grunion and Other Stories,* Mafdet Press, 1977; *Spanish Tales,* Mafdet Press, 1977. Contributor to magazines, including *Nitty-Gritty, Fate, Antaeus,* and *Dialogue.*

WORK IN PROGRESS: The Hyperboreans, a novel; *Summer Wine,* stories; *A Gathering of Secret Places,* autobiographical sketches.

SIDELIGHTS: Prosser writes: "I feel it is the duty of any good writer to create in clear, concise, correct English if he truly wants to communicate and share with the reader. To do otherwise is to be dishonest. Don't write for a select elite, for when they are gone your work dies with them; but do write for the common man and woman—like Hemingway, Dickens, Twain, and Poe did—for they are the ones who will keep your work alive long after you're gone. It is all right to experiment creatively, but remember you're writing for the reader as well as yourself, and if the reader fails to understand, then you've accomplished nothing of lasting value.

"The two greatest influences on my writing have been writers Paul Bowles and Christopher Isherwood. I learned my skills through hard work and study, and experimentation, but these two individuals taught me the ropes. Without their early influence and encouragement, I wouldn't be writing today."

Novelist Thomas Carlisle has commented: "H. L. Prosser's prose does for the imagination what Nathaniel West did for Hollywood—rips it wide open and exposes the guts of raw mind. Prosser is a highly sensitive and perceptive writer, and he gives credence to the concept that humanity's only infinite resource is the imagination."

BIOGRAPHICAL/CRITICAL SOURCES: Angst Review, January, 1977.

* * *

PRUDDEN, Bonnie 1914-

PERSONAL: Born January 29, 1914, in New York, N.Y.; daughter of Harry J. (a newspaper representative) and Nell (Russell) Prudden; children: Joan Hirschland Meijer, Susan Hirschland Sussman. *Education:* Attended Columbia University Extension. *Home address:* Prospect Hill, Stockbridge, Mass. 01262. *Agent:* Willis Wing, Falls Village, Conn. 06031. *Office:* Institute for Physical Fitness, Stockbridge, Mass. 01262.

CAREER: Director of New York City and Westchester ski patrols and Red Cross disaster units, 1939-49; Institute for Physical Fitness, Stockbridge, Mass., director, 1950—. Appeared on television programs, including "Home Show" and "Today"; presented "Fit for Life," national workshops for older people. *Awards, honors:* Safety award from Eastern Amateur Ski Association; M.H. from Springfield College; grant from *Reader's Digest,* 1974.

WRITINGS: Improve Your Body (manual), Equitable Life, 1959; *Bonnie Prudden's Fitness Book: A Picture Guide With Exercises and Reducing Plans,* Ronald, 1959; *Executive Fitness* (manual), Equitable Life, 1960; *How to Keep Slender and Fit After Thirty,* Geis, 1961, revised and enlarged edition, 1969; *Fitness for You* (talking book for the blind), Library of Congress, 1964; *How to Keep Your Child Fit From Birth to Six,* Harper, 1964; *Teenage Fitness,* Harper, 1965; *Quick Rx for Fitness,* Grosset, 1965; *Bowling and Fitness* (manual), American Machine & Foundry, 1967; *Fit for Life* (manual), Girls Clubs of America, 1967; *Fitness From Six to Twelve,* Harper, 1972; *Your Baby Can Swim,* Reader's Digest Press, 1974; *How to Keep Your Family Fit and Healthy,* Reader's Digest Press, 1975; *Exer-Sex,* Bantam, in press.

Films: "Peter and the Koos," Institute for Physical Fitness, 1967; "Keep Fit: Be Happy" (filmstrips with manuals), Pathescope Educational Films, 1971; "Alive and Feeling Great," Girls Clubs of America, 1974; "Your Baby Can Swim," Institute for Physical Fitness, 1974.

Columnist for *Sports Illustrated.* Contributor to professional journals and popular magazines.

WORK IN PROGRESS: After Fifty (tentative title); research for a book on erasing pain with a trigger point release.

SIDELIGHTS: Bonnie Prudden writes: "The Institute for Physical Fitness is a teaching organization. It provides workshops, clinics, seminars, and lecture-demos, all having to do with physical fitness. We produce books, records, films, equipment, etc. We design programs for schools, recreation groups, businesses. And we have a very large medical referral department dealing with soft tissue damage.

"I got into the physical fitness business by accident. I noticed my children went downhill physically when they entered school. Investigation showed physical education to be useless inactivity, causing all sorts of ills to children. I had been a concert dancer and had been interested in exercise. I was influenced by Dr. Hans Kraus' therapeutic exercises so I changed dance to exercise and vice versa. This was very successful. Using a medical posture test on my students I found they were, by medical standards, unfit. I started to test everywhere, produced the report that 'shocked the President' (Eisenhower) and I was on my way. This led to the President's Council for Physical Fitness. My present research in progress shows that twenty years hasn't helped!''

Her record albums include: ''Keep Fit: Be Happy,'' Volume I, 1960, Volume II, 1961; ''Fit to Ski,'' 1962; ''Fitness for Baby and You,'' 1962; ''Executive Fitness,'' 1963; ''Teenage Fitness,'' 1963.

*   *   *

PUDNEY, John (Sleigh)   1909-1977

January 19, 1909—November, 1977; British poet, fiction writer, and journalist. Pudney became popular in the 1930's with his short stories and first novel, *Jacobson's Ladder*. Further acclaim came during World War II when some of his lyrics were used in the popular film, ''The Way to the Stars.'' His novels are characterized by ''a penchant for fantasy and social comedy, a graceful and witty style,'' while his poems have been labeled ''masculine, honest, agreeable, unpretentious.'' In addition to fiction and poetry, Pudney's many writings include nonfiction and children's books ''which are rewarding,'' he once wrote, ''not only because they are fun but because they stay in print and prosper.'' He died in England. Obituaries and other sources: *The New Century Handbook of English Literature*, revised edition, Appleton, 1967; *The Who's Who of Children's Literature*, Schocken, 1968; *Longman Companion to Twentieth Century Literature*, Longman, 1970; *The Author's and Writer's Who's Who*, 6th edition, Burke's Peerage, 1971; *The Penguin Companion to English Literature*, McGraw, 1971; *Contemporary Poets*, 2nd Edition, St. Martin's, 1975; *International Motion Picture Almanac*, Quigley, 1975; *World Authors, 1950-1970*, Wilson, 1975; *Contemporary Novelists*, 2nd edition, St. Martin's, 1976; *The Writer's Directory, 1976-78*, St. Martin's, 1976; *AB Bookman's Weekly*, February 6, 1978. (See index for *CA* sketch)

*   *   *

PUETTE, William J(oseph)   1946-

PERSONAL: Born December 15, 1946, in Cleveland, Ohio; son of John David (an electrical engineer) and Helen (Ayers) Puette; married Carol Naganuma, June 24, 1972; children: Seamus Toranosuke. *Education:* St. Vincent College, B.A., 1969; Edinboro State College, M.A., 1972. *Home:* 3928 Maunaloa Ave., Honolulu, Hawaii 96816.

CAREER: High school English teacher in Maui, Hawaii, 1969-73; Notre Dame Women's College, Kyoto, Japan, lecturer in English, 1973-75; Honolulu Community College, Honolulu, Hawaii, lecturer in language arts, 1975—. Lecturer at Leeward Community College, 1976—. Has done volunteer work in a state mental institution.

WRITINGS: The Rain That Swells the Water (poems), Shore Press, 1973; *Bridge of Glass* (poems), Kiu Press, 1976.

WORK IN PROGRESS: Lode River, a book-length poem.

SIDELIGHTS: Puette writes: ''In each of my books, in-

cluding *Lode River*, I have addressed the image of water. Each work comes from a different point of view and from a different stage in my life. I trust it to nourish me and bring my poetry to its ultimate conclusion. In *Lode River*, I'm trying to synthesize and extend traditional and mythic symbolism of rivers as an inspirational force.''

*   *   *

PURSELL, Carroll W(irth), Jr.   1932-

PERSONAL: Born September 4, 1932, in Visalia, Calif.; son of Carroll Wirth (in sales) and Ruth Irene (a teacher; maiden name, Crowell) Pursell; married Joan Young (a librarian), January 28, 1956; children: Rebecca Elizabeth, Matthew Carroll. *Education:* University of California, Berkeley, B.A., 1956, Ph.D., 1961; University of Delaware, M.A., 1958. *Politics:* Democrat. *Religion:* None. *Home:* 624 Chelham Way, Santa Barbara, Calif. 93108. *Office:* Department of History, University of California, Santa Barbara, Calif. 93106.

CAREER: Case Institute of Technology (now Case Western Reserve University), Cleveland, Ohio, assistant professor of history, 1963-65; University of California, Santa Barbara, assistant professor, 1965-69, associate professor, 1969-76, professor of history, 1976—. Andrew W. Mellon Distinguished Professor of the Humanities at Lehigh University, 1974-76; research professor at University of Wisconsin, Milwaukee, 1977. *Member:* American Historical Association, American Studies Association, Organization of American Historians, History of Science Society, Society for the History of Technology, Phi Beta Kappa.

WRITINGS: (Editor with Melvin Kranzberg) *Technology in Western Civilization*, Oxford University Press, 1968; *Early Stationary Steam Engines in America*, Smithsonian Institution, 1969; (editor) *Readings in Technology and American Life*, Oxford University Press, 1969; (editor) *Military-Industrial Complex*, Harper, 1972; (editor) *From Conservation to Ecology*, Crowell, 1973. Contributor to scholarly journals.

WORK IN PROGRESS: Editing essays on the bicentennial history of American technology; studying the ideology of industrial research.

*   *   *

PYE, Lloyd (Anthony, Jr.)   1946-

PERSONAL: Born September 7, 1946, in Houma, La.; son of Lloyd A. (an optometrist) and Nina Jo (Boyles) Pye. *Education:* Tulane University, B.S., 1968. *Politics:* ''I'm for whatever strikes me as positive and against whatever strikes me as negative.'' *Religion:* ''Overall, it probably does more harm than good.'' *Agent:* Sterling Lord Agency, Inc., 660 Madison Ave., New York, N.Y. 10021.

CAREER: Writer, 1977—. *Military service:* U.S. Army, Military Intelligence, 1968-69. *Member:* Authors Guild of Authors League of America.

WRITINGS: That Prosser Kid (novel), Arbor House, 1977.

SIDELIGHTS: Pye writes: ''My basic motivation is to tell entertaining stories that many people can and will read and enjoy. In short, I want to be commercial. To say any more at such an early point in my career would probably be presumptuous.'' *Avocational interests:* Racquetball, international travel.

PYK, Ann Phillips 1937-

PERSONAL: Surname sounds like "peek"; born July 27, 1937, in New Rochelle, N.Y.; daughter of Walter Thomson (a contractor) and Dorothy (Fleischman) Phillips; married Jan Christian Pyk (an illustrator), September 25, 1965; children: Wha Mi. *Education:* Hollins College, B.A., 1959; attended Sorbonne, University of Paris, 1957-58. *Residence:* Southampton, N.Y. *Agent:* Henry Morrison, Inc., 58 West 10th St., New York, N.Y. 10011.

CAREER: Housemother at a home for neglected children, 1959; American Society of Civil Engineers, New York City, editor of technical publications, 1959-67; Macmillan Publishing Co., Inc., New York City, associate editor, 1970-73; free-lance writer and editor, 1973—. *Member:* Authors Guild of Authors League of America.

WRITINGS—Juveniles: (Translator) Ulf Loefgren, *What*Ever*You*Want*, Putnam, 1972; (translator) Max Lundgren, *Matt's Grandfather*, Putnam, 1972; (reteller) *The Hammer of Thunder*, Putnam, 1973; (translator) Kerstin Sundh, *August Can Do Everything*, Putnam, 1973.

WORK IN PROGRESS: A collection of children's writings; a craft book.

SIDELIGHTS: Pyk told *CA:* "I feel that the children's book market is flooded with thin story lines and overly decorative or 'cute' books. Illustrations are, of course, very important for young children and if the story line is strong enough, words may even be eliminated entirely, occasionally; however, overly decorative illustrations (or what I call 'noisy' illustrations) proliferate. I believe that too much is assumed about children by those who are making the books for them. We should consider them as human beings—full of curiosity, discrimination, and most of the feelings that adult human beings share.

"It seems to me that children are bombarded by both television and literature with violence and hyperactivity. More simple, but strong, quiet themes are needed, e.g., about times alone, private times, and private thoughts—shared or not shared. Fantasies are marvelous and nonfiction is too, but whatever the nature of the story, the children should not be talked down to and should not be overstimulated needlessly. Life is stimulating enough if it is presented with clarity and simplicity and honesty."

* * *

PYLE, Hilary 1936-
(Peta Cullen, Adam Mitchell)

PERSONAL: Born July 14, 1936, in Dublin, Ireland; daughter of William Fitzroy (a university professor) and Patricia (Conerney) Pyle; married Maurice Carey (dean of Cork); children: Colm, Sorcha, Duinseach, Manus. *Education:* Trinity College, Dublin, B.A., 1958; Cambridge University, M.Litt., 1960. *Religion:* Church of Ireland. *Residence:* Cork, Ireland.

CAREER: Employed by Ulster Museum, Belfast, Northern Ireland, 1961-62; art critic for *Irish Times,* 1963-69, and *Irish Independent,* 1969—. Lecturer at National Gallery of Ireland, 1970—, and Cork School of Art, 1976—. Art critic for Radio Eireann, 1969—.

WRITINGS: James Stephens: His Work and an Account of His Life, Routledge & Kegan Paul, 1965; *Portraits of Patriots,* Allen Figgis, 1966; *Jack B. Yeats: A Biography,* Routledge & Kegan Paul, 1970; (with J. White) *Jack B. Yeats: Drawings and Paintings,* Secker & Warburg, 1971; *You Can Say That Again,* Association for Promoting Christian Knowledge, 1977. Author of exhibition catalogs. Contributor to *Thieme-Becker Dictionary of Art History.* Contributor to magazines, including *Studies* and *Hibernia.* Art critic, under pseudonyms Adam Mitchell and Peta Cullen, for *Sunday Independent,* 1969—.

WORK IN PROGRESS: Catalogue Raisonne of Jack B. Yeats; Words and Paint, essays on Jack B. Yeats; a study of Mary Delaney's eighteenth-century drawings.

* * *

PYROS, John 1931-

PERSONAL: Born January 9, 1931, in New York, N.Y.; son of Andreas and Anastasia (Kalograkos) Pyrovolikos; married Sheila B. Weinstein (a professor of language studies); children: Andrea. *Education:* Brooklyn College (now of the City University of New York), B.A., 1953; New York University, M.A., 1963, Ph.D., 1973. *Home and office:* Dramatika Productions, 390 Riverside Dr., #10B, New York, N.Y. 10025. *Agent:* Helen Walls, 2202 St. James St., Philadelphia, Pa. 19103.

CAREER: Junior high school English teacher at public school in Patchogue, N.Y., 1957, private school in Oakland, N.J., 1958, and public school in Levittown, N.Y., 1959; teacher in public schools in New York, N.Y., 1960-67; Lincoln University, Lincoln University, Pa., assistant professor of theatre arts and film, and head of theater, 1968-70; University of Alabama, University, assistant professor of English and drama, and associate director of theater, 1970-71; Cumberland County College, Vineland, N.J., associate professor of humanities, 1971-73; Philadelphia Filmmakers Cooperative, Philadelphia, Pa., curator, 1973-76; instructor at Pasco-Hernando Community College, autumn, 1977; WMNF, Tampa, Fla., cultural director, 1978—. Assistant professor at Southern University, 1966-67; coordinator of Rutgers University experimental theater (Camden), summer, 1976. Curator of 3:19 Art Galleries, 1967-68. Director of children's theater for Boys Club of New York, 1964-66; stage manager and actor with Philadelphia 76 Co., 1976; actor with Popi Productions, 1977. Social worker for New York City Youth Board, 1960, Neighborhood Youth Corps, 1964, and Philadelphia Department of Public Welfare, 1975. Film judge; theatrical director and producer; president of Dramatika Productions.

MEMBER: American Theatre Association, Speech Communication Association of America, Dramatists Guild, University Film Association. *Awards, honors:* Playwright award from Bertholt Brecht-Marilyn Monroe Foundation, 1963.

WRITINGS: Moving Out (film study), Sneak Preview, 1974.

Plays: "Death of Mozart" (one-act), first produced in Philadelphia at Young Men's Hebrew Association Center Stage, February, 1976; "Three Plays," first produced in Philadelphia at T. C. Playhouse, January, 1977.

Reporter for *White Plains Reporter-Dispatch,* 1965. Contributor of articles, short plays, fiction, and reviews to magazines and newspapers, including *Encore, Small Press Review, Margins, Cineste,* and *Nitty Gritty.* Editor and publisher of *Dramatika,* 1968—.

WORK IN PROGRESS: Greek Films; Occult Films; "Our Town Too," a full-length play.

SIDELIGHTS: Pyros comments: "A concern for aesthetics alone is insufficient to explain the chaos of our times. There's something else. I seek that something else."

Q

QUALEY, Carlton C(hester) 1904-

PERSONAL: Born December 17, 1904, in Spring Grove, Minn.; son of Ole O. (an implement dealer) and Clara (Knatterud) Qualey; married Elizabeth Cummings, April 29, 1933; children: John, Mary. *Education:* St. Olaf College, B.A., 1929; University of Minnesota, M.A., 1930; Columbia University, Ph.D., 1938. *Religion:* Unitarian-Universalist. *Home:* 2110 Carter Ave., St. Paul, Minn. 55108. *Office:* Minnesota Historical Society, St. Paul, Minn. 55101.

CAREER: Columbia University, New York, N.Y., associate professor of history, 1936-44; Swarthmore College, Swarthmore, Pa., associate professor of history, 1944-45; Columbia University, associate professor of history, 1945-46; Carleton College, Northfield, Minn., professor of history, 1946-70; Minnesota Historical Society, St. Paul, director of ethnic history project, 1973—. Visiting professor at Northwestern University, Stanford University, Cleveland State University, Carleton College, and Augsburg College.

MEMBER: American Historical Association, Organization of American Historians, Immigration History Society, Norwegian-American Historical Association, American Association of University Professors. *Awards, honors:* Shevlin fellow, University of Minnesota, 1932-33; received grants from Hill Foundation, 1954-55, Bush Foundation, 1973-78, and National Endowment for the Humanities, 1976-78; fellow of Huntington Library, 1968.

WRITINGS: Norwegian Settlement in the United States, Norwegian-American Historical Association, 1938, reprinted, Arno, 1970; *Thorstein Veblen,* Columbia University Press, 1968; *People of Minnesota,* Minnesota Historical Society, 1978. Contributor of articles and reviews to academic journals. Editor of *Immigration History Newsletter,* 1973—; member of editorial board of Norwegian-American Historical Association.

WORK IN PROGRESS: A survey of the population of Minnesota, 1850-1970, "dealing especially with native and foreign stocks."

AVOCATIONAL INTERESTS: Skiing, sailing.

* * *

QUARTERMAIN, James
See LYNNE, James Broom

QUENEAU, Raymond 1903-1976

PERSONAL: Born February 21, 1903, in Le Havre, France; son of Auguste (a businessman) and Josephine (Mignot) Queneau; married Janine Kahn; children: Jean-Marie. *Education:* Earned licence from University of Paris. *Office:* Gallimard, 5 rue Sebastien-Bottin, 75007 Paris, France.

CAREER: Comptoir national d'escompte (bank), Paris, France, employee, beginning 1927; reporter for *L'Intransigeant,* 1936-38; Gallimard (publishing house), Paris, reader, beginning 1938, secretary general, beginning 1941, director of *Encyclopedie de la Pleiade,* 1955-75; member of l'-Academie Goncourt (France's top literary jury), 1951-76.

WRITINGS—In English: *Le Chiendent* (novel), Gallimard, 1933, reprinted, 1974, enlarged edition with an article by Jean Queval and notes by Nicole Onfroy, Bordas, 1975, translation by Barbara Wright of first French edition published as *The Bark Tree,* Calder & Boyars, 1968, New Directions, 1971; *Loin de Rueil* (novel), Gallimard, 1944, reprinted, 1967, translation by H. J. Kaplan published as *The Skin of Dreams,* New Directions, 1948; *Exercices de style,* Gallimard, 1947, revised edition, 1973, translation by Wright published as *Exercises in Style,* New Directions, 1958; (compiler) Alexandre Kojeve, editor, *Introduction a la lecture de Hegel,* Gallimard, 1947, abridged translation by James H. Nichols, Jr. published as *Introduction to the Reading of Hegel,* Basic Books, 1969.

Le Dimanche de la vie (novel), Gallimard, 1951, reprinted, 1973, translation by Wright published as *The Sunday of Life,* New Directions, 1977; *Zazie dans le metro* (novel), Gallimard, 1959, translation by Wright published as *Zazie,* Harper, 1960; *Les Fleurs bleues* (novel), Gallimard, 1965, enlarged edition with introduction and notes in English edited by Wright, Methuen, 1971, translation by Wright published as *The Blue Flowers,* Atheneum, 1967 (published in England as *Between Blue and Blue,* Bodley Head, 1967); *Le Vol d'Icare,* Gallimard, 1968, translation by Wright published as *The Flight of Icarus,* New Directions, 1973.

Other works; novels: *Gueule de Pierre,* Gallimard, 1934; *Chene et chien,* Denoel, 1937; *Odile,* Gallimard, 1937, reprinted, 1969; *Un Rude Hiver* (title means "A Hard Winter"), Gallimard, 1939, reprinted, 1968; *Les Temps meles* (title means "Mixed-Up Times"), Gallimard, 1941; *Pierrot mon ami* (title means "Pierrot, My Friend"), Gallimard,

1943, reprinted, 1965; *On est toujours trop bon avec les femmes* (title means "One Is Always Too Nice With Women"), Gallimard, 1971.

Poetry: *Les Ziaux,* Gallimard, 1943; *Une Trouille verte,* Editions de minuit, 1947; *L'Instant fatal,* Gallimard, 1948; *Petite cosmogonie portative* (title means "A Portable Little Cosmogony"), Gallimard, 1950; *Si tu t'imagines, 1920-1951* (title means "If You Imagine"), Gallimard, 1952, revised edition published as *Si tu t'imagines, 1920-1948,* 1968; *Le Chien a la mandoline* (title means "The Dog on the Mandolin"), Verviers, 1958, enlarged edition, 1965; *Sonnets,* Editions Hautefeuille, 1958; *Cent mille milliards de poemes* (title means "One Hundred Thousand Billion Poems"), Gallimard, 1961; *Courir les rues* (title means "Running the Streets"), Gallimard, 1967; *Battre le campagne,* Gallimard, 1968; *Fendre les flots,* Gallimard, 1969; *Bonjour Monsieur Prassinos,* F. A. Parisod, 1972.

Other writings: *Les Derniers Jours* (title means "The Last Days"), Gallimard, 1936, reprinted with a preface by Olivier de Magny, Societe Cooperative (Lausanne), 1965; *Bucoliques,* Gallimard, 1947; *Joan Miro; ou, Le Poete prehistorique* (title means "Joan Miro; or, The Prehistoric Poet"), A. Skira, 1949; (with Queval) *Rendez-vous de juillet* (title means "Rendezvous in July"), Chavane, 1949; *Batons, chiffres, et lettres* (title means "Sticks, Figures, and Letters"), Gallimard, 1950, new edition, 1965; (editor with A. J. Arberry and others) *Les Ecrivains celebres* (title means "Famous Writers"), three volumes, L. Mazenod, 1951-53, 3rd edition, 1966; (editor) *Anthologie des jeunes auteurs* (title means "Anthology of Young Authors"), Editions J.A.R., 1955; (editor) *Histoire des litteratures* (title means "History of Literatures") three volumes, Gallimard, 1955-58; (compiler) *Pour une bibliotheque ideale* (title means "For an Ideal Library"), Gallimard, 1956; *Lorsque l'esprit* (title means "When the Spirit"), Collection Q, 1956; (contributor) *Le Declin du romantisme: Edgar Poe* (title means "The Decline of Romanticism: Edgar Poe"), L. Mazenod, 1957.

Les Oeuvres completes de Sally Mara (title means "The Complete Works of Sally Mara"), Gallimard, 1962; *Entretiens avec Georges Charbonnier* (title means "Conversations with Georges Charbonnier"), Gallimard, 1962; *Bords: Mathematiciens, precurseurs, encyclopedistes* (illustrated by Georges Mathieu), Hermann, 1963; *Une Histoire modele* (title means "A Model History"), Gallimard, 1966; *Texticules* (lithographies by Sebastien Hadengue), Galerie Louise Leiris, 1968; *De quelques langages animaux imaginaires et notamment du langage chien dans "Sylvie et Bruno"* (title means "Of Several Imaginary Animal Languages, Notably the Dog Language in 'Sylvie and Bruno'"), L'Herne, 1971; *Le Voyage en Grece* (title means "The Voyage to Greece"), Gallimard, 1973; *Morale elementaire* (title means "Elementary Ethics"), Gallimard, 1975. Also author of *La Litterature potentielle,* 1973.

Collections: *Saint Glinglin* (with a new version of "Gueule de Pierre" and "Les Temps meles"), Gallimard, 1948; *Variations typographiques sur deux poemes de Raymond Queneau* (title means "Typographic Variations of Two Poems by Raymond Queneau"; typography by Jean Vodaine), [Paris], 1964; *L'Instant fatal, precede de Les Ziaux* (collection of two works of poetry first published separately), Gallimard, 1966; *Chene et chien* (includes "Chene et chien," revised version of "Petite cosmogonie portative," and "Le Chant de Styrene"), preface by Yvon Belaval, Gallimard, 1969; *Raymond Queneau en verve* (title means "Raymond Queneau Alive!"), edited by Jacques Bens, P. Horay, 1970;

Raymond Queneau: Poems, translated by Teo Savory, Unicorn Press, 1971.

Documentary films: "Le Lendemain," "Arithmetique," "Champs-Elysees," "Le Chant du Styrene."

Film dialogues: "Monsieur Ripois," 1953; "La Mort en ce jardin," 1956; "Un couple," 1960; "Le Dimanche de la vie," 1967.

SIDELIGHTS: Most critics trace the roots of Queneau's literary style to his involvement with Andre Breton and the Surrealist movement in the 1920's. Queneau's poetry and novels reflect the Surrealist rebellion against established bourgeois literary values and the rule of reason which restrains literature from the irrational forces of the subconscious mind. Influenced by the linguistic games in the novels of Joyce and by Celine's use of colloquial language, Queneau seemed to delight in "upsetting the rules and regulations of the written language." Tom Bishop noted: "In Queneau's hands, language—vocabulary, spelling, syntax—is manipulated, squeezed, and pulled until it fairly explodes and becomes a 'neo-language' of slang and colloquialisms."

Because Queneau played such games with language, translation of his works from the French is not an easy task. A *Times Literary Supplement* reviewer commented: "Translation is, in a sense, the whole of Raymond Queneau's art. The task of translating him in turn into an alien language and cultural context is virtually impossible." Reviewers generally praised Barbara Wright for her attempts to capture in English the spirit of the slang and puns which dominate his work.

In the introduction to *The Bark Tree,* her translation of Queneau's first novel, Wright briefly answered the question "What is *Le Chiendent* about?" by declaring, "It is not *about* anything, it *is* something." Philip Carrow added: "In other words, it is how life is. Told by Queneau in his own way. If you like it is about nothingness, that uniquely twentieth century malaise diagnosed again and again by Lawrence, and here made into a poem, a song, and behind this erudite man's comic virtuosity, a cry of anguish." Noting the philosophical character of the novel, Bishop observed: "Queneau set out to do a modern slang translation of Descartes' *Discourse on Method;* fortunately, he was carried further than he expected and produced this strange, hilarious novel, which is a masterpiece of black humor and at the same time a meaningful, philosophic meditation.... [He] clearly views life as absurd (already!) and dwells insistently (though playfully) on the shadowy line that divides the actual from the imagined.... [He] is cynical but not pessimistic. No one who writes as funny a book as this could really be a pessimist." In retrospect, many critics called *Le Chiendent* the forerunner of existential novels such as Sartre's *La Nausee.*

A *Times Literary Supplement* reviewer noted the mathematical and rhyme-filled structure of *Les Fleures bleues* and Queneau's preoccupation with form over content. By imposing a rigorous structure upon the novel, Queneau turned it into poetry and thereby met "the implicit challenge of Valery and Andre Breton, who both dismissed the novel-form because it was banal and gratuitous." And yet Queneau purposely undermined the structures he created in many of his novels, as if to mock literature as a mode of expression. Roland Barthes observed: "As soon as each element of the traditional universe solidifies, Queneau dissolves it, undermines the novel's security: literature's solidity curdles; everything is given a double aspect, made unreal, whitened by that lunar light which is an essential theme of deceit and a theme characteristic of Queneau."

Echoing this theme of "creator as destroyer," Vivian Mercier cited Queneau's epitaph to *Zazie dans le metro, Ho plasas ephanisen* ("He who created it razed it to the ground"), and applied this phrase to several of his novels. "They remind us of those notoriously elaborate pieces of contemporary 'sculpture' in the Dadaist tradition that, when set in motion, more or less destroy themselves," he wrote. Other critics were quick to point out that this "destructive" tendency did not constitute "murder," but rather an attempt to create a new synthesis of the traditional written language and the evolving spoken language. Although critics disagreed over this point, Maurice Nadeau emphasized the existence of a consensus on one issue: "Queneau's work lies at the heart of the problems which have arisen in our time regarding the relation between literature and life and between expression and communication."

BIOGRAPHICAL/CRITICAL SOURCES: Life, March 24, 1967; *Times Literary Supplement,* May 25, 1967, September 19, 1968; *Books and Bookmen,* October, 1968; *Saturday Review,* August 7, 1971; *Contemporary Literary Criticism,* Gale, Volume 2, 1974, Volume 5, 1976. Obituaries: *New York Times,* October 26, 1976; *AB Bookman's Weekly,* January 3, 1977.*

(Died October 25, 1976, in Paris, France)

* * *

QUEST, Linda (Gerber) 1935-

PERSONAL: Born November 8, 1935, in York, Pa.; married, May 29, 1964. *Education:* Pennsylvania State University, B.A., 1957, M.A., 1959; University of Pennsylvania, Ph.D., 1964. *Residence:* Brooklyn, N.Y. *Office:* Department of Social Sciences, Pace University, New York, N.Y. 10038.

CAREER: American Academy of Political and Social Science, Philadelphia, Pa., editorial assistant, 1960-64; Adelphi University, Garden City, N.Y., assistant professor of political science, 1964-69; Pace University, New York, N.Y., professor of political science, 1969—. *Member:* World Future Society, American Political Science Association, American Academy of Political and Social Science, Association for Research and Enlightenment (member of board of trustees, 1976-78), Institute for Sub/Urban Governance (member of advisory board, 1974—), Phi Beta Kappa.

WRITINGS: Politics of Hope, Association for Research and Enlightenment, 1971; *Peace by Choice,* Association for Research and Enlightenment, 1974. Contributor to *A.R.E. Journal* and *Beacon.*

WORK IN PROGRESS: Systematic comparative analysis of future-oriented movements/organizations, chiefly those with utopian leanings and emphasis on the development of human potentials, with a view to their possible impacts on or contributions to public affairs.

SIDELIGHTS: Linda Quest writes: "Writing for publication is a service to nonspecialists and to general readers who are interested in my specialty but either not equipped or not interested in doing the research themselves."

* * *

QUINN, David B(eers) 1909-

PERSONAL: Born April 24, 1909, in Dublin, Ireland; son of David and Albertina (Devine) Quinn; married Alison Moffat Robertson (an indexer), October 30, 1937; children: Nicholas R. K., Roderick E. N., Brigid L. S. A. Quinn Wainwright. *Education:* Queen's University, Belfast, B.A.

(first class honors), 1931, M.A., 1957, D.Litt., 1958; King's College, London, Ph.D., 1934. *Home:* 9 Knowsley Rd., Liverpool L19 0PF, England.

CAREER: University of Southampton, Southampton, England, assistant lecturer, 1934-37, lecturer in history, 1937-39; Queen's University of Belfast, Belfast, Northern Ireland, lecturer in history, 1939-44; British Broadcasting Corp., European Service, London, England, sub-editor in Czechoslovakian section, 1943; University of Wales, University College of Swansea, professor of history and chairman of department, 1944-57; University of Liverpool, Liverpool, England, Andrew Geddes and John Rankin Professor of Modern History, 1957-76, professor emeritus, 1976—. British Council visiting scholar in New Zealand, 1967, and Hungary, 1972; James Pinckney Harrison visiting professor at College of William & Mary, 1969-70; visiting professor at St. Mary's College of Maryland, 1976-78. Member of council of Institute of Early American History and Culture, 1968-70.

MEMBER: Royal Historical Society (fellow; member of council, 1951-55, 1956-60; vice-president, 1964-68; Prothero lecturer, 1975), Royal Irish Academy, Societe des Americanistes, Hakluyt Society (member of council, 1950-54, 1957-60; vice-president, 1960—), Society for the History of Discoveries (member of editorial board, 1974—; council member, 1975-77), Colonial Society of Massachusetts (corresponding member). *Awards, honors:* Fellow of Folger Shakespeare Library, 1957, 1959-63, John Carter Brown Library, 1963-64, 1970, and Henry E. Huntington Library, 1964; Leverhulme research fellow, 1963; D.Litt. from Memorial University of Newfoundland, 1964, and New University of Ulster, 1975; D.H.L. from St. Mary's College of Maryland, 1978.

WRITINGS: (Editor and author of introduction) *The Voyages and Colonising Enterprises of Sir Humphrey Gilbert,* two volumes, Hakluyt Society, 1940, reprinted, Kraus Reprint, 1967; *Raleigh and the British Empire,* Hodder & Stoughton, 1947, Macmillan, 1949, revised edition, English Universities Press, 1962; (editor) *The Roanoke Voyages, 1584-1590: Documents to Illustrate the English Voyages to North America Under the Patent Granted to Walter Raleigh in 1584,* two volumes, Hakluyt Society, 1955.

(With Paul Hope Hulton) *The American Drawings of John White, 1577-1590,* Universty of North Carolina Press, 1964; (author, with R. A. Skelton, of introduction) Richard Hakluyt, *The Principall Navigations, Voiages, and Discoveries of the English Nation,* Cambridge University Press, 1965; *The New Found Land: The English Contribution to the Discovery of North America,* Associates of John Carter Brown Library, 1965; *The Elizabethans and the Irish,* Cornell University Press, 1966; (editor) George Percy, *Observations Gathered Out of "A Discourse on the Plantation of the Southern Colony in Virginia by the English,"* University Press of Virginia, 1967; *A Study Introductory of the Facsimile Edition of Richard Hakluyt's "Divers Voyages" (1582) to Which Is Added a Facsimile of "A Short and Briefe Narration of the Two Navigations to Newe Fraunce"* translated by John Florio, two volumes, Theatrum Orbis, 1968; *Sebastian Cabot and Bristol Exploration,* Bristol Branch, Historical Association, 1968.

(Editor) *North American Discovery, circa 1000-1612,* Harper, 1971; (with William Patterson Cumming and Skelton) *The Discovery of North America,* Elek, 1971, American Heritage Press, 1972; (editor with N. M. Cheshire) Stephen Budaeus Parmenius, *The New Found Land of Stephen*

Parmenius, University of Toronto Press, 1972; (editor with wife, A. M. Quinn) Hakluyt, *Virginia Voyages From Hakluyt,* Oxford University Press, 1973; *England and the Discovery of America, 1481-1620, From the Bristol Voyages of the Fifteenth Century to the Pilgrim Settlement at Plymouth: The Exploration, Exploitation, and Trial-and-Error Colonization of North America by the English,* Knopf, 1974; (with Cumming, S. E. Hillier, and Glyndwr Williams) *The Exploration of North America, 1634-1776,* Elek, 1974; (editor) *The Hakluyt Handbook,* two volumes, Hakluyt Society, 1974; *The Last Voyage of Thomas Cavendish,* [Chicago], 1975; *North America From Earliest Discovery to First Settlements: The Norse Voyages to 1612,* Harper, 1977; *New American World: A Documentary History of North America from Earliest Times to 1612,* five volumes, Arno, 1978.

Also author of *The Port Books or Petty Customs Accounts of Southampton for the Reign of Edward IV,* two volumes, 1937-38. Contributor to *Historia Mundi,* Volume 8, and to history journals.

WORK IN PROGRESS: Editing *The New England Voyages, 1602-1608* with A. M. Quinn, publication by Hakluyt Society expected in 1980; a facsimile edition of Richard Hakluyt's *A Particuler Discourse* (known as *Discourse of Western Planting*), for Hakluyt Society.

SIDELIGHTS: Quinn writes: "In the earliest stages of my academic studies I involved myself mainly in the expansion (or re-expansion) of England into Ireland in the sixteenth century. This led me to search for evidence of the earliest English explorations of the Atlantic beyond Ireland, and ultimately to North America, and to the working out of the gradually increasing involvement of England in the lands across the ocean. But America proved to have attractions of its own. The interplay with the native Amerindian society of successive groups of English, Portuguese, French, and Spanish explorers and settlers provided a challenging and endless exercise in the interrelationship of historic forces. I have therefore increasingly attempted to see the early European interventions in North America as one small part of the European out-thrust into the overseas world, which has laid the foundations for our modern history. In this my studies and teaching have taken me far afield, but I still remain specially attached to Ireland and eastern North America where

I began. The historian in my time has leaped ahead from local and regional preoccupations to a world view. He is realizing only now how intimately this has involved him in and with the other sciences of humanity and of the earth, and how long it will take him to reach an understanding of the evolving phases of human intercourse. Generations of effort lie ahead of him, if he is given this time. My own part in all this has been a tiny one, the illuminating of a few small facets of human experience in Ireland and North America, until they are overshadowed by fresh discoveries and fresh insights in a constantly changing context of historical experience."

* * *

QUINN, Edward 1932-

PERSONAL: Born January 5, 1932, in Brooklyn, N.Y.; son of Edward and Margaret (Conway) Quinn; married Gail Murphy (a teacher), September 1, 1956; children: Deirdre, Colin, David, Jenny. *Education:* Brooklyn College (now of the City University of New York), B.A., 1958; New York University, M.A., 1959, Ph.D., 1963. *Home:* 54 East Eighth St., New York, N.Y. 10003.

CAREER: City College of the City University of New York, New York, N.Y., assistant professor, 1965-70, associate professor, 1970-75, professor of English, 1975—. *Military service:* U.S. Army, 1952-53; became sergeant; received Bronze Star.

WRITINGS: (Editor with Oscar James Campbell) *Reader's Encyclopedia of Shakespeare,* Crowell, 1966; (editor with Paul Dolan) *The Sense of the Sixties,* Free Press, 1968; (editor) *King Lear,* Crowell, 1968; (editor with John Gassner) *Reader's Encyclopedia of World Drama,* Crowell, 1969; (editor with Dolan) *Relevants,* Free Press, 1970; (editor with Robert Lilienfeld and Rodman Hill) *Interdiscipline,* Free Press, 1972; (with James Rooff) *Major Shakespearean Tragedies,* Free Press, 1973; (with Doland) *Sense of the Seventies,* Oxford University Press, 1978; (editor) *How to Read Shakespearean Tragedy,* Harper, 1978.

SIDELIGHTS: Quinn comments: "My books reflect two major interests: Shakespeare, on the one hand, and the quality and style of American life in the past two decades."

R

RABINOWITCH, Eugene   1901-1973

PERSONAL: Born August 26, 1901, in St. Petersburg, Russia (now Leningrad, U.S.S.R.); son of Isaac and Zinaida (Weinlud) Rabinowitch; married Anna Mejerson, March 12, 1932; children: Alexander and Victor (twins). *Education:* Educated in Russia and Germany; University of Berlin, Ph.D., 1926. *Residence:* Albany, N.Y.

CAREER: University of Goettingen, Goettingen, Germany, research associate, 1929-33; worked with Niels Bohr in Copenhagen, Denmark, 1933-34; University of London, University College, London, England, staff member, 1934-38; Massachusetts Institute of Technology, Cambridge, Mass., instructor, 1939-44; University of Chicago, Chicago, Ill., senior chemist on "Manhattan Project," 1944-46; University of Illinois, Urbana, professor of botany and biophysics, 1947-68; State University of New York, Albany, professor of chemistry and biology and director of Center for Science and the Future of Human Affairs, 1968-73; Woodrow Wilson International Center for Scholars, Washington, D.C., fellow, 1973. Organizer of Pugwash Conferences, 1957-73; member of Center for Advanced Studies, Princeton, N.J., 1966-68.

MEMBER: Federation of Atomic Scientists (founder), American Chemistry Society, American Physics Society, American Biophysics Society. *Awards, honors:* D.H.L., Brandeis University, 1960; D.Sc., Dartmouth College, 1964; Kalinga Prize from UNESCO, 1965; Kettering Award from American Society of Plant Physiology, 1967; D.Sc., Columbia College, Chicago, 1967; D.Sc., Alma College, 1970; medal from American Academy of Arts and Sciences, 1972.

WRITINGS: Periodisches system, F. Enke, 1930; (translator with others) Richard von Mises, *Probability, Statistics, and Truth,* Macmillan, 1939; *Photosynthesis and Related Processes,* two volumes, Interscience Publishers, 1945-56; *Minutes to Midnight: The International Control of Atomic Energy,* Bulletin of the Atomic Scientists, 1950; (editor with Joseph Jacob Katz) *The Chemistry of Uranium,* McGraw, 1951; (author of revision and contributor) Selig Hecht, *Explaining the Atoms,* Viking, 1954; *The Photochemistry of Uranyl Compounds,* Technical Information Service, 1955; *The Dawn of a New Age: Reflections on Science and Human Affairs,* University of Chicago Press, 1963; (with R. Linn Belford) *Spectroscopy and Photochemistry of Uranyl Compounds,* Macmillan, 1964; (with Govindjee) *The Role of Chlorophyll in Photosynthesis,* W. H. Freeman, 1965; (editor with Morton Grodzins) *The Atomic Age: Forty-Five Scientists and Scholars Speak,* Simon & Schuster, 1968; (editor with Richard S. Lewis) *Man on the Moon: The Impact on Science, Technology and International Cooperation,* Basic Books, 1970; (editor with son, Victor Rabinowitch) *Views on Science, Technology and Development,* Pergamon, 1975. Also author of *Grundbegriffe der Chemie,* A. Unger.

Founding editor, with Hyman Goldsmith, of *Science and Public Affairs,* the bulletin of the Federation of Atomic Scientists, 1945-73.

SIDELIGHTS: A leading authority in the field of photosynthesis, Rabinowitch worked in a wide range of disciplines. In addition to his achievements in chemistry and biophysics, he was also a poet, translator, and skilled journalist. But his most lasting contribution to mankind may prove to be his inexhaustible campaign for nuclear arms control.

During World War II, Rabinowitch served as a senior chemist on the "Manhattan Project," which produced America's first nuclear weapons. However, along with several of his colleagues, Rabinowitch was an early opponent of the use of these weapons, recognizing, even in 1945, that the atomic bomb was more than a matter of military tactics. In 1945, he contributed to the Franck report issued by seven scientists (the "Committee on Social and Political Implications") who opposed surprise use of the bomb on a Japanese city.

From then until his death, Rabinowitch worked relentlessly to educate the public on the significance and dangers of atomic energy. As he put it at a Pugwash Conference in 1970: "The future of our nation, the fate of our children and grandchildren, and the survival of the whole human race, depend on successful adjustment of mankind to the new facts of its existence on earth, created by science and technology. Science and technology have made possible weapons so destructive that a future war could totally destroy both sides, and even endanger the survival of mankind." Yet he also saw science and technology as the source of humanity's salvation. "We must find ways," he continued, "to change the direction of our technology, from preparing for war and raising production for production's sake, to rational efforts for the common weal of all, seeking to satisfy legitimate needs of all men without further unnecessary deterioration of our environment."

Thus Rabinowitch became, as many have called him, "the conscience of science" and a leading figure in the organization of world scientists. Along with Hyman Goldsmith, he founded in 1945 *Science and Public Affairs,* the bulletin of the Federation of Atomic Scientists. As editor-in-chief, he made the bulletin the mouthpiece of efforts to establish international controls for atomic energy. While the bulletin also addresses itself to such issues as the relation between science and other disciplines like religion, ethics, law, and art, its principal concern is epitomized by the bulletin clock which symbolizes nuclear doomsday as midnight and its advent only minutes away.

The Pugwash Conferences were another of Rabinowitch's major accomplishments. These conferences were meetings of the international science community, with representatives from capitalist and communist nations alike, devoted to finding scientific solutions to the problems created by modern science. Rabinowitch helped organize the first conference in 1957, and until his death in 1973 he remained an active and articulate participant.

In 1972, the American Academy of Arts and Sciences awarded Eugene Rabinowitch a special medal recognizing his unique contribution "in fostering international cooperation among scientists. His unceasing efforts to ensure the rational application of science and technology to the pressing problems of mankind have earned him the respect and appreciation of members of the scientific community throughout the world." And as Ralph E. Lapp noted in a eulogy, "the fact that no nuclear weapons have been used in anger, though they are stockpiled by the tens of thousands, is a singular achievement," attestable at least in part to Rabinowitch's spread of nuclear awareness.

BIOGRAPHICAL/CRITICAL SOURCES: Science and Public Affairs, June, 1973.*

(Died May 15, 1973, in Washington, D.C.)

* * *

RAE, Douglas W(hiting) 1939-

PERSONAL: Born May 2, 1939, in Indianapolis, Ind.; son of W. Douglas (a clergyman) and Katherine (Whiting) Rae; married Natalie Bradley, 1965 (divorced, 1972); married Ulla Kasten (an editor), 1973; children: (first marriage) Hugh, Katherine, Kimberley. *Education:* Indiana University, B.A., 1962; University of Wisconsin, Madison, M.A., 1965, Ph.D., 1967. *Politics:* "Libertarian socialist." *Home:* 319 Crown St., New Haven, Conn. 06520. *Office:* Department of Political Science, Yale University, New Haven, Conn. 06511.

CAREER: University of Vermont, Burlington, instructor in political science, 1964-65; Syracuse University, Syracuse, N.Y., assistant professor of political science, 1966-67; Yale University, New Haven, Conn., assistant professor, 1967-71, became associate professor, 1971, presently professor of political science. Fellow of Center for Advanced Studies in the Behavioral Sciences, 1972-73. Member of publications committee of Yale University Press. *Member:* American Political Science Association. *Awards, honors:* Hurfurth Prize, 1967; Guggenheim fellowship for England, 1969-70.

WRITINGS: The Political Consequences of Electoral Laws, Yale University Press, 1967, 2nd edition, 1971; (with Michael Taylor) *The Analysis of Political Cleavages,* Yale University Press, 1977. Contributor to *Handbook of Political Science* and to political science journals in the United States and abroad. Member of editorial board of *American*

Political Science Review, Comparative Political Studies, and *British Journal of Political Science.* Consulting editor for Random House.

WORK IN PROGRESS: Democracy and the Fair Economy of Public Liberty.

* * *

RAHL, James A(ndrew) 1917-

PERSONAL: Born October 8, 1917, in Wooster, Ohio; son of James Blaine (a pharmacist) and Harriet (Munson) Rahl; married Jean Mayberry, September 5, 1942; children: James Andrew, Jr. *Education:* Northwestern University, B.S., 1939, J.D., 1942. *Politics:* Democrat. *Religion:* Methodist. *Home:* 2426 Marcy Ave., Evanston, Ill. 60201. *Office:* School of Law, Northwestern University, 357 East Chicago Ave., Chicago, Ill. 60611.

CAREER: Admitted to the Bar of Ohio, 1942, the Bar of Illinois, 1950, and the Bar of U.S. Supreme Court; Northwestern University, Chicago, Ill., lecturer in speech, 1939-41; Office of Price Administration, Washington, D.C., attorney, 1942-43; Northwestern University, assistant professor, 1946-50, associate professor, 1950-53, professor of law, 1953—, Owen L. Coon Professor, 1974—, dean of School of Law, 1972-77. Counsel with Chadwell, Kayser, Ruggles, McGee & Hastings, 1952—. Resident partner of a firm in Brussels, Belgium, 1963-64. Faculty member at Salzburg Seminar on American Studies, 1967, 1972. Member of U.S. Attorney General's committee to study antitrust laws, 1953-55, White House task force on antitrust policy, 1967-68, United Nations Committee on Trade and Development's group of experts, 1973, and Illinois governor's committee on ethics, 1976-77. *Military service:* U.S. Army, 1943-46; became second lieutenant.

MEMBER: American Bar Association, American Law Institute, American Society of International Law, American Association of University Professors, Illinois Bar Association, Chicago Bar Association, Chicago Council of Lawyers, Law Club of Chicago (president, 1976-77). *Awards, honors:* Ford Foundation travel grant, 1968.

WRITINGS: (With Green, Pedrick, and others) *Cases on Torts,* West Publishing, 1959, 3rd edition, 1977; (with Green, Pedrick, and others) *Cases on Injuries to Relations,* West Publishing, 1959, 3rd edition, 1977; (editor and contributor) *The Common Market and American Antitrust: Overlap and Conflict,* McGraw, 1970. Also co-author of *Northwestern University of Law: A Short History.* Contributor to law journals. Editor-in-chief of *Illinois Law Review,* 1941-42.

WORK IN PROGRESS: Cases and Materials for a Study of Antitrust Law; A Comparative Study of the Impact of Antitrust Laws on International Business.

SIDELIGHTS: Rahl writes: "My principal field is antitrust law, and my area of concentration is American and foreign laws pertaining to international business activity. I have devoted about seventeen years to this area, engaging in research, writing, speaking, and consulting, with a number of extended trips to Europe."

* * *

RAINER, Julia
  See GOODE, Ruth

* * *

RAMSAY, Raymond (Henry) 1927-

PERSONAL: Born July 4, 1927, in Morden, Manitoba,

Canada; came to the United States in 1927; son of Henry Hastings and Anne Vinetta (Oke) Ramsay. *Education:* Concordia College, Moorhead, Minn., B.A., 1951. *Politics:* Democrat. *Religion:* "Undecided." *Home address:* P.O. Box 2284, Station A, Berkeley, Calif.

CAREER: Free-lance writer, 1977—. Has worked as clerk, salesman, crop picker, construction worker, and night security guard; worked as singer and actor, with North Star Singers, 1951-52, Magic Theater of Berkeley, 1968-72, in feature film "Roseland," and stage production "Macbeth"; model for Bay Area Model's Guild, 1959-64. Assistant director of Studio C Galleries of Berkeley, 1959-64, and Berkeley Art Festival, 1962-65. Member of Berkeley Citizens Action, Agape Foundation, and Center for the Study of Democratic Institutions. *Member:* Authors Guild of Authors League of America, Cousteau Society, American Civil Liberties Union, Berkeley H. P. Lovecraft Society (founder; vice-president).

WRITINGS: No Longer on the Map (nonfiction), Viking, 1972; *Instead of a Blade* (satire and verse), Yardbird Press, in press. Author of "The Roving Ratfink," a column in *Berkeley Barb*, 1965-69, and "Xavier Hammerberg," a science fiction column, *Berkeley Barb*, 1973-76. Editor of *Progressive Times*, 1948-49.

WORK IN PROGRESS: An eyewitness history of Berkeley, Calif. in the 1960's; a book on Bouvet Island.

SIDELIGHTS: Ramsay writes: "I have had a lifelong interest in history and geography. I picked the subject for my first book because no one else had used it. The same is true in my shorter writing. I consider it vital to find out as much as possible about whatever subject I write about.

"I've felt a need to write ever since I was a little kid. I don't really hope to change the world much by my writing, but I hope it might make some difference. My advice to an aspiring writer is this: Keep working at it. It may take awhile. It took me a long while, so keep up hope. If you want to write, you will write, regardless."

AVOCATIONAL INTERESTS: Science fiction and fantasy, "every kind of off-beat history."

* * *

RAMSEY, Arthur Michael 1904-

PERSONAL: Born November 14, 1904, in England; son of Arthur Stanley (a mathematics don at Cambridge Universtiy) and Agnes (Wilson) Ramsey; married Joan Alice Hamilton, April 8, 1942. *Education:* Cambridge University, B.A., 1927, M.A., 1930, B.D., 1950; also attended Cuddesdon Theological College. *Home:* The Old Vicarage, Cuddesson, Oxford, England.

CAREER: Ordained deacon in Church of England, 1928, and priest, 1929; Church of St. Nicholas, Liverpool, England, curate, 1928-30; Lincoln Theological College, Oxford, England, subwarden, 1930-36; Boston Parish Church, Lincolnshire, England, lecturer, 1936-38; St. Benedict's Church, Cambridge, England, 1938-40; University of Durham, Durham, England, Van Mildert Professor of Divinity, 1940-50; Cambridge University, Cambridge, Regius Professor of Divinity, 1950-52; bishop of Durham, 1952-56; archbishop of York, 1956-61; archbishop of Canterbury, 1961-74. Examining chaplain to bishop of Chester, 1932-39. Select preacher to Cambridge University, 1934, 1940, 1948; canon, Durham Cathedral, 1940-50; select preacher to Oxford University, 1945-46; fellow of Magdalene College, Cambridge, 1950-52; canon of Caistor and prebendary, Lincoln Cathe-

dral, 1951-52; Hulsean Preacher, Cambridge University, 1969-70. Trustee of British Museum, 1963-69.

MEMBER: World Council of Churches (president, 1961-68), Cambridge Union (president, 1926). *Awards, honors:* Honorary Master of the Bench, Inner Temple, 1962; doctorate in divinity from University of Durham, 1951, University of Edinburgh, University of Leeds, University of Hull, and Cambridge University, all 1957, Victoria University of Manchester, 1961, and University of London, 1962; D.Cl. from Oxford University, 1960, and University of Kent, 1966; D.Litt. from University of Keele, 1967; honorary fellow of Magdalene College, Cambridge, 1952—, Merton College, Oxford, 1974—, and Keble College, Oxford, 1975—.

WRITINGS: The Gospel and the Catholic Church, Longmans, Green, 1936; *The Resurrection of Christ,* Presbyterian Board of Christian Education, 1946; *The Glory of God and the Transfiguration of Christ,* Longmans, Green, 1949; *F. D. Maurice and the Conflicts of Modern Theology,* Cambridge University Press, 1951; *Durham Essays and Addresses,* S.P.C.K., 1956; *Oratory and Literature,* English Association, 1960; *Introducing the Christian Faith,* S.C.M.P., 1961; *Unity, Truth, and Holiness,* Fellowship of St. Alban and St. Serbius, 1961; *The Narratives of the Passion,* Mowbray, 1962; *Christianity and the Supernatural,* Althone, 1963; *Image Old and New: On the Problem of Finding New Ways to State Old Truths,* Forward Movement, 1963; *Canterbury Essays and Addresses,* Seabury, 1964; *Beyond Religion?,* S.P.C.K., 1964; *Christ Crucified, for the World,* Mowbray, 1964; *Sacred and Secular: A Study in the Other Worldly and This Worldly Aspects of Christianity,* Longmans, Green, 1965; *The Meaning of Prayer,* Morehouse, 1965; *Problems of Christian Belief,* BBC Publications, 1966; *God, Christ, and the World: A Study in Contemporary Theology,* Morehouse, 1969; (with Leon-Joseph Cardinal Suenens) *The Future of the Christian Church,* Morehouse, 1970; *The Christian Priest Today,* S.P.C.K., 1972; (with Robert E. Terwillizer and A. M. Allchin) *The Charismatic Christ,* Morehouse, 1973; *Canterbury Pilgrim,* S.P.C.K., 1974; (with others) *Come Holy Spirit,* Morehouse, 1976.

SIDELIGHTS: When Ramsey succeeded to the episcopacy of York in 1956, many feared that his Anglo-Catholicism would prove a threat to Christian reunion. But he retired as Archbishop of Canterbury, eighteen years later, "to a chorus of nearly unqualified praise—including comparisons with such giants of English ecclesiastical history as Saint Anselm and Thomas a Becket," according to *Newsweek*. The *Newsweek* article also stated that: "In a fitting farewell to Ramsey's episcopacy, the House of Commons last week approved a reform that he has been advocating since becoming Primate—the granting of ecclesiastical affairs to the Church of England. The church's historic ties with the state will remain. The Queen is still its Supreme Governor and the Prime Minister will continue to appoint its bishops. But Church officials may now reform doctrine and liturgy without approval from . . . Parliament."

Ramsey has been affectionately regarded for his engaging lack of pretension and his "folksy episcopal style." Describing his own perception of God, he said, "I enjoy Him. I think about Him, tell Him of my worries."

One of Ramsey's dreams was to see Anglican reconciliation with Roman Catholicism. He helped further that cause in 1966 when he became the first Archbishop of Canterbury since 1937 to officially visit Rome, exchanging a "kiss of peace" with Pope Paul VI.

In his writings, Ramsey has been less conciliatory. For example, in "The Menace of Fundamentalism," an article published in 1956, Ramsey attacked fundamentalism as heretical, singling out American evangelist Billy Graham as a preacher of the "grossest doctrines." Most of Ramsey's full-length works, however, have been either studies of the New Testament or broad expositions of Christian doctrine.

BIOGRAPHICAL/CRITICAL SOURCES: J. B. Simpson, *The Hundredth Archbishop of Canterbury,* 1960; *Newsweek,* December 16, 1974.*

* * *

RAND, Christopher 1912-1968

PERSONAL: Born February 14, 1912, in New York, N.Y.; married Margaret Aldrich, 1934 (divorced, 1952); married Miriam Ervin, 1961 (divorced, 1962); children: Christopher, Jr., Richard, Mary, Payson, Diana. *Education:* Yale University, B.A., 1934. *Religion:* Buddhist. *Residence:* Salisbury, Conn.

CAREER: Worked as a journalist for Time, Inc., and the *San Francisco Chronicle* during the 1930's and early 1940's; Office of War Information, Washington, D.C., member of staff in China, 1943-45; *New York Herald Tribune,* New York City, correspondent in China, 1945-48, correspondent in Japan and Korea, 1949-51; *New Yorker,* New York City, staff member, 1951—. *Awards, honors:* Neiman fellow, 1948-49; co-winner of George Polk Award for best foreign reporting, 1949, for "Asia's Red Riddle" series in the *New York Herald Tribune.*

WRITINGS: Hongkong: The Island Between, Knopf, 1952; *A Nostalgia for Camels,* Little, Brown, 1957; *The Twain Shall Meet,* Gollancz, 1957; *The Puerto Ricans,* Oxford University Press, 1958; *Grecian Calendar,* Oxford University Press, 1962; *Christmas in Bethlehem, and Holy Week at Mount Athos,* Oxford University Press, 1963; *The Holy Land at Christmastime,* Oxford University Press, 1963; *Cambridge, U.S.A.: Hub of a New World,* Oxford University Press, 1964; *Mountains and Water,* Oxford University Press, 1965; *Los Angeles: The Ultimate City,* Oxford University Press, 1967; *Changing Landscape: Salisbury, Connecticut,* Oxford University Press, 1968; *Making Democracy Safe for Oil: Oilmen and the Islamic East,* Atlantic Monthly Press, 1975.

Co-founder, *Coast.*

SIDELIGHTS: Rand's life as a journalist led him to travel to many exotic lands, including Hong Kong, Singapore, Macao, and India. He smoked opium in Hong Kong, encountered guerillas in Afghanistan, and lived with lepers in the Belgian Congo. Rand once walked over one hundred miles through the Sinkiang Province in China while being pursued by Communist troops; on another occasion he was held hostage by five Chinese youths who had mistaken him for a Russian. The *New York Times* claimed that Rand was "equally adept at reporting on places and on people—familiar or strange."

OBITUARIES: New York Times, September 27, 1968; *New Yorker,* October 12, 1968.*

(Died September 26, 1968)

* * *

RAND, Peter 1942-

PERSONAL: Born February 23, 1942, in San Francisco, Calif.; son of C. T. and M. A. (Demott) Rand; married M.

Bliss Inui (a researcher and reporter), December 19, 1976. *Education:* Johns Hopkins University, M.A., 1976. *Agent:* Phoenix Literary Agency, 150 East 74th St., New York, N.Y. 10021.

CAREER: Antaeus, New York City, advisory fiction editor, 1970-72; *Washington Monthly,* Washington, D.C., editor, 1973; New York University, New York City, lecturer, 1976-77; Columbia University, New York City, lecturer, 1977—. *Member:* P.E.N., Poets and Writers. *Awards, honors:* Creative Artists Public Service Award, 1977.

WRITINGS—All novels: *Firestorm,* Doubleday, 1969; *The Time of the Emergency,* Doubleday, 1977.

SIDELIGHTS: Rand is interested in working in old age homes and prisons.

* * *

RANKIN, Robert P(arks) 1912-

PERSONAL: Born July 28, 1912, in Pueblo, Colo.; son of John R. and Irene (Parks) Rankin; married Madge Slayden, June 8, 1938; children: Jim C., Jo Suzzane Rankin Ballard. *Education:* California State University, San Jose, A.B., 1935; Union Theological Seminary, New York, N.Y., M.A. (religion), 1938; University of California, Berkeley, M.A. (sociology), 1953, Ph.D., 1958. *Politics:* Democrat. *Home address:* Route 2, Box 318, Chico, Calif. 95926. *Office:* Department of Sociology, California State University, Chico, Calif. 95926.

CAREER: Sequoia National Park Service, Ash Mountain, Calif., ranger and surveyor, summers, 1930-35; ordained Methodist minister, 1939; pastor of Methodist churches in El Cerrito, Santa Rosa, Orland, and Red Bluff, all Calif., 1938-53; California State University, Chico, assistant professor, 1953-58, associate professor, 1958-63, professor of sociology, 1963-75, professor emeritus, 1975—, chairperson of department, 1964-66 and 1975-77. Chairman of board of directors of Family Service Association of Butte and Glenn Counties. *Military service:* U.S. Naval Reserve, chaplain, active duty, 1945-46. *Member:* American Sociological Association, National Council on Family Relations, Pacific Sociological Association.

WRITINGS: (With Ritchie P. Lowry) *Sociology, Social Science, and Social Concern,* Scribner, 1969, 3rd edition, 1977. Contributor to sociology journals.

WORK IN PROGRESS: Research on divorce, especially in relation to welfare and children, based on California data.

SIDELIGHTS: Rankin writes: "My writing has been in connection with my classroom teaching in the field of sociology and reflects my long range involvement in research focusing upon religion and family.

"Within the sociology of the family, there is great need for more data and analysis relative to divorce and its implication for children involved, for family readjustment, and for related social problems such as child support and social welfare. Currently I am working with Kingsley Davis, Distinguished Professor of Sociology at University of Southern California, Los Angeles, California, in seeking research grants for the detailed analysis of California data on marital dissolution from 1966-1977. California has collected a remarkable body of information about the divorcing population but very little rigorous analysis has taken place. Our goal is to study these data with special emphasis upon the impact of divorce upon children and upon their support, economic and emotional. Beyond this we will include divorce findings on a national and international basis."

RANNEY, (Joseph) Austin 1920-

PERSONAL: Born September 23, 1920, in Courtland, N.Y.; son of Frank Addison and Florence Edith Ranney; married Elizabeth Ann Mackay, September 21, 1946; children: Joseph Austin III, Douglas Mackay, Gordon Charles, David Frank. Education: Northwestern University, B.S., 1941; University of Oregon, M.A., 1943; Yale University, Ph.D., 1948. Politics: Democrat. Home: 3930 Plymouth Cir., Madison, Wis. 53705. Office: Department of Political Science, University of Wisconsin, Madison, Wis.

CAREER: Yale University, New Haven, Conn., instructor in political science, 1945-47; University of Illinois, Urbana, member of faculty, 1946-59, professor of political science, 1959-63, associate dean of graduate college, 1958-61; University of Wisconsin—Madison, professor of political science, 1963—. Council chairman, Inter-University Consortium for Political Research, 1963-64; chairman of committee for governmental and legal processes, Social Sciences Research Council, 1964-72; member, Congressional Committee on Political Activity of Government Employees, 1966-67.

MEMBER: International Political Science Association, American Academy of Arts and Letters (fellow). Awards, honors: Social Science Research Council, research award, 1961; National Science Foundation, fellowship, 1970-71; Center for Advanced Study in the Behavioral Sciences, fellow, 1974-75.

WRITINGS: The Doctrine of Responsible Party Government, University of Illinois Press, 1954; (with Willmoore Kendall) Democracy and the American Party System, Harcourt, 1956; The Governing of Men, Holt, 1958; Illinois Politics, New York University Press, 1960; (editor) Essays on the Behavioral Study of Politics, University of Illinois Press, 1962; Pathways to Parliament: Candidate Selection in Britain, University of Wisconsin Press, 1965; Curing the Mischiefs of Faction: Party Reform in America, University of California, 1975. Contributor of articles and essays to scholarly journals. Managing editor, American Political Science Review, 1965-71.

SIDELIGHTS: Ranney is considered by many to be a penetrating commentator on party politics in America. He believes that historically reform has provided a convenient alternative to either abolishing political parties or making them pragmatically cohesive governing and electoral organizations. His most recent book, Curing the Mischiefs of Faction: Party Reform in America, is concerned with three main periods of political reform in America. Ranney argues that party rules and procedures have never been politically neutral and he describes how candidates and factions have won or lost as a result of each of the major reforms.

BIOGRAPHICAL/CRITICAL SOURCES: Reporter, March 14, 1963; American Political Science Review, September, 1965; Times Literary Supplement, November 4, 1965, August 27, 1976; Christian Science Monitor, August 26, 1975; Choice, October, 1975; Annals of the American Academy, January, 1976; Political Science Quarterly, Spring, 1976.

*   *   *

RAOUL, Anthony
See WILMOT, Anthony

*   *   *

RATHER, L(elland) J(oseph) 1913-

PERSONAL: Born December 22, 1913, in College Station, Tex.; son of James Burness (a chemist) and Corinne (Carson) Rather; married Eleanor Knight, 1940 (divorced, 1958); married Ingeborg Arnold, 1959 (died, 1965); children: Patricia, Leland, Noel. Education: Johns Hopkins University, A.B., 1934, M.D., 1939; University of Chicago, M.S., 1936. Home: 28 Pearce Mitchell Pl., Stanford, Calif. 94305.

CAREER: Stanford University, Stanford, Calif., assistant professor, 1946-51, associate professor, 1951-57, professor of pathology, 1957-76, professor emeritus, 1976—. Consultant to National Institutes of Health, U.S. Department of Agriculture, and U.S. Surgeon General. Member, American Board of Pathology. Military service: U.S. Army, 1942-46; became captain. Awards, honors: Welch Medal from American Association for the History of Medicine, 1976, for medical history writing.

WRITINGS: (Editor and translator) Disease, Life, and Man: Selected Essays of Rudolf Virchow, Stanford University Press, 1958; Mind and Body in Eighteenth-Century Medicine, University of California Press, 1965; (editor and translator, with John Sharp) Pedro Lain-Entralgo, The Therapy of the Word in Classical Antiquity, Yale University Press, 1970; Addison and the White Corpuscles, University of California Press, 1972; The Genesis of Cancer: A Study in the History of Ideas, Johns Hopkins Press, 1978; The Dream of Self-Destruction: Reflections on Wagner's "The Ring of the Nibelung," Louisiana State University Press, in press.

WORK IN PROGRESS: "A study of metaphor, simile and analogy in the language of medicine and the medical sciences; a study of Johannes Mueller's work on the structure and chemistry of tumors."

*   *   *

RAY, Man 1890-1976

PERSONAL: Born August 27, 1890, in Philadelphia, Pa.; married Donna Loupov (a poet), 1914 (divorced); married Juliet Browner (a dancer), 1946. Education: Attended National Academy of Design, 1908. Residence: Paris, France.

CAREER: Painter, filmmaker, photographer, art constructor. Held first one-man exhibition in New York, N.Y., 1915.

WRITINGS: Self Portrait (autobiography), Little, Brown, 1963. Also author of screenplays, including "Retour a la raison" (title means "The Return to Reason"), 1923, "Emak Bakia," 1927, (with Robert Desnos) "L'Etoile de Mer" (title means "Star of the Sea"), 1927, and "Les Mysteres du Chateau de De" (title means "The Mysteries of the Chateau of the Dice"), 1929. Art work represented in collections, including Photographs by Man Ray, J. T. Soby, 1934, published as Man Ray: Photographs, 1920-1934, East River Press, 1975; and in numerous U.S. and foreign catalogs. Co-designer and co-editor with Marcel Duchamp of New York Dada, April, 1921.

SIDELIGHTS: Ray's early art implied Dadaism but showed Cubist tendencies and was not well received. At the same time, Marcel Duchamp, a Dadaist, was popular in artist's circles for his "Nude Descending a Staircase." After meeting Duchamp, Ray also became a Dadaist.

Dadaism began in Switzerland in 1916 when a group of artists decided to show their contempt for rationality through their art. The word "dada" is French for hobbyhorse and by adopting this title, the Dadaists were also attempting to mock prevalent art modes.

Ray arrived in France in 1921 and was quickly received into the inner circle of Dadaists. But by this time, Dadaism was evolving under the influence of Andre Breton into Surrealism. Ray was a key member of the Surrealist movement and his work was featured at the first Surrealist art show in 1925.

Like fellow Surrealists Luis Bunuel and Salvador Dali, Ray too became involved in filmmaking. Ray's flair for film lead to an interest in photography and by the late 1920's, Ray had developed a new means of photographic art. His technique, which he called "painting with light," involved placing objects on photographic paper to create silhouettes when developed. He later referred to these photos as "Rayograph prints."

Ray also applied Surrealist concepts to the creation of abstract objects. Among his most famous objects are "The Gift," a flatiron with nails glued to the surface, and "Object to be Destroyed," which was a metronome with a photograph of an eye clipped to the stem.

In later years, Ray disavowed any Dadaist or Surrealist classification. "Painting to me is a secret activity that expresses my private life," he said. Ray was devoted primarily to making adjustable wooden mannequins and working on several manuscripts. He believed no two works of his were alike.

OBITUARIES: New York Times, November 19, 1976.*

(Died November 18, 1976, in Paris, France)

* * *

RAYNER, William 1929-

PERSONAL: Born January 1, 1929, in Barnsley, England; son of Thomas (a civil servant) and Lily (Fisher) Rayner; married Pamela Ross (a secretary), November 1, 1954; children: Simon Thomas, Christopher Philip, William Ian. *Education:* Oxford University, B.A., 1952. *Politics:* Social Democrat. *Religion:* "Uncertain." *Home:* Spurriers Close, West Porlock, nr. Minehead, Somerset, England.

CAREER: Has worked as a teacher of English in England and Africa; full-time writer.

WRITINGS: The Reapers, Faber, 1961; *The Tribe and Its Successors* (nonfiction), Faber, 1962; *The Barebones,* Faber, 1963; *The Last Days,* Morrow, 1968; *The Knifeman,* Morrow, 1969; *The World Turned Upside Down,* Morrow, 1970; *Stag Boy* (juvenile), Collins, 1972, Harcourt, 1973; *Seth & Belle & Mr. Charles and Me: The Bloody Affray at Lakeside Drive,* Simon & Schuster, 1972; *Big Mister* (juvenile), Collins, 1974; *The Trial to Bear Paw Mountain,* Collins, 1974, Ballantine, 1976; *A Weekend With Captain Jack,* Collins, 1975, Ballantine, 1977; *The Day of Chominuka,* Collins, 1976, Atheneum, 1977; *Eating the Big Fish,* Collins, 1977, published as *The Interface Assignment,* Atheneum, 1977.

WORK IN PROGRESS: "I am at present involved in widescale research concerning the period of the Industrial Revolution in its social and political as well as its economic aspects, including developments in America as well as in England. I hope a series of novels will result eventually."

SIDELIGHTS: Rayner's interests extend to history, comparative religion, and politics. *Avocational interests:* Vegetable gardening.

* * *

READ, Jan
See READ, John Hinton

READ, John Hinton 1917-
(Jan Read)

PERSONAL: Born in 1917, in Sydney, Australia; married Maria Teresa Manjon-Alonso; children: one son. *Education:* Attended St. Andrews University. *Home:* 18 Lowndes Sq., London SW1X, 9HB, England.

CAREER: Worked as a research scientist and university lecturer, 1939-46; scriptwriter for motion pictures and television, 1947—; Gainsborough Pictures, London, England, scenario editor, 1947-49; Rank Organisation, London, assistant to the executive producer, 1950-52; Triangle Film Productions, London, director, 1952-73; free-lance writer. *Member:* Writers Guild. *Awards, honors:* Commonwealth Fund fellow in cinematography, 1946-47; chevalier of Spanish wine order of San Miguel, 1977.

WRITINGS—Under name Jan Read: (With Antonio Mingote) *History for Beginners,* Thomas Nelson, 1960; *The Wines of Spain and Portugal,* Faber, 1973, Hippocrene, 1974; *The Moors in Spain and Portugal,* Faber, 1974, Rowman & Littlefield, 1975; *War in the Peninsula,* Faber, 1977; (with wife, Maite Manjon) *The Paradores of Spain,* Mason Charter, 1977; *Guide to Wines in Spain and Portugal,* Pitman, 1977, Monarch, in press; (with Manjon) *The Flavours of Spain,* Cassell, 1978.

Screenplays: "The Blue Lamp," Eagle Lion, 1951; "White Corridors," Rank Organisation, 1953; (with Beverly Cross) "Jason and the Argonauts," Paramount, 1959; (with Nigel Kneale) "First Men in the Moon," Columbia, 1964. Also author of screenplays "The Haunted Strangler," 1958, and "Street Corner."

Also author of teleplays for television series, including "Dr. Finlay's Casebook," "Robin Hood," "Sherlock Holmes," and "Danger Man."

Contributor of articles to periodicals, including *Journal of the Chemical Society, Hollywood Quarterly, History Today,* and *Burlington.*

SIDELIGHTS: Read told *CA:* "My first interests were in photography and cinema, but, unable to obtain a union ticket in Hollywood, I turned to writing when working as an assistant, first to Louis de Rochemont at Twentieth Century-Fox and then to Fritz Lang at Universal Pictures Corp. I have travelled widely in Spain and Portugal since 1951, my particular interests being their history and wines. My wife (Maite Manjon) is an accomplished cook and in recent years we have collaborated on a series of books on gastronomy, and in the near future these will embrace books on Scotland and Portugal. I take most of the photographs to illustrate my books. Having as a child in St. Andrews had a nannie who was the daughter of an Open Champion, I naturally play golf!"

* * *

RECKORD, Barry

PERSONAL: Born in Jamaica. *Education:* Attended Oxford University, 1952. *Residence:* Jamaica.

CAREER: Playwright and author of teleplays. Has also worked as a theatrical director.

WRITINGS: "Adella," first produced in London, 1954, revised version produced as "Flesh to a Tiger," London, 1958; "You in Your Small Corner," first produced in Cheltenham, England, 1960; *Skyvers* (first produced in London, 1963), J. Calder, 1977; "Don't Gas the Blacks," first produced in London, 1969; "A Liberated Woman," first produced in New York City, 1970; *Does Fidel Eat More Than Your Father: Conversations in Cuba,* Praeger, 1971; "Give the Gaffers Time to Love You," first produced in London, 1973; "X," first produced in London, 1977.

Also author of teleplays, including "In the Beautiful Caribbean," 1972, and "Club Havana," 1975. Author of radio play "Malcolm X," 1973.

Work represented in anthologies, including *New English Dramatists 9,* Penguin, 1966.

SIDELIGHTS: The *Times Literary Supplement* reviewed *Does Fidel Eat More Than Your Father: Conversations in Cuba:* "Mr. Reckord's book, despite the silly title, is a serious and thorough study of liberty and equality in Cuba today. It makes a lot of sense to compare Cuba, as he does, not with Western or Eastern Europe but with the poverty-stricken depressed areas of other West Indian islands." The *Times Literary Supplement* also added that Reckord's book reveals most clearly "the growing disparity between what the third world wants and expects and what the developed world believes it ought to want."

BIOGRAPHICAL/CRITICAL SOURCES: New York Times Book Review, July 18, 1971; *Times Literary Supplement,* September 3, 1971.*

*   *   *

REDFIELD, Alden   1941-

PERSONAL: Born May 10, 1941, in Englewood, N.J.; son of John Alden (a banker) and Lucy (Bancroft) Redfield; married Judith Omond Chute (an antiques dealer), August 22, 1966; children: Laura Margaret, Edmund Bancroft. *Education:* University of Arizona, B.A. (with distinction), 1964; Harvard University, M.A., 1966, Ph.D., 1973. *Politics:* Independent Republican. *Religion:* Plymouth Brethren. *Home:* 216 East Parkway Dr., Columbia, Mo. 65201. *Office: Museum Scope,* 5 Strollway Centre, 11 East Ninth St., Columbia, Mo. 65201.

CAREER: American Museum of Natural History, New York, N.Y., research assistant, 1960-63; University of Missouri, Columbia, instructor in anthropology and director of Museum of Anthropology, 1968-73; museum consultant and writer, 1973—. Owner of Hotel Tipton, California Commercial Hotel, Ritz Theater, Clarksburg Lodge Hall, Boone's Lick Vending, and Hotel Tipton Antiques, 1973-77, and Museumscope's Antiques, 1976—; co-owner of Paperback Exchange Book Store, Columbia, Mo. President of board of directors of Columbia Montessori School, 1972-74. Adjunct professor at Stephens College, 1976—. Conducted archaeological field studies in Xalapa, Mexico, summer, 1964, Yugoslavia, summer, 1967, and Luxembourg, summer, 1972. Guest on television and radio programs.

MEMBER: Amnesty International, American Association of Museums, Society for American Archaeology, Museum Stores Association, British Museum Association, Midwest Museum Conference, Southern Anthropological Society, Missouri Museums Associates, Columbia Montessori Society (president, 1973-75), Tenafly Nature Center, Park Hill Improvement Association (president, 1977-78).

WRITINGS: Lace Place: A Dalton Project Site, Arkansas Archaeological Society, 1970; *Dalton Project Notes,* Volume I, Museum of Anthropology, University of Missouri, 1971; (with Sheila Lewis) *The Care of Osteological Collections,* Museum of Anthropology, University of Missouri, 1972; (editor) *Anthropology Beyond the University,* University of Georgia Press, 1972; *Indians of the Midwest* (juvenile

coloring book), Museum of Anthropology, University of Missouri, 1972. Editor of "Museum Briefs" for Museum of Anthropology, University of Missouri, 1969-73. Contributor of more than twenty articles and reviews to anthropology and archaeology journals. Co-editor of Missouri Museums Associates *Newsletter,* 1972-74; editor of *Museum Scope,* 1976—.

WORK IN PROGRESS: Editing *Entrada,* a historical novel by Nina Eldred Bancroft.

SIDELIGHTS: Redfield writes: "My primary interest in museology is the educational potential of displays and the museum. As an archaeologist I gathered data; as a museologist I used it to educate the public. A display, however, is extremely limited, so books, magazines, stories, and other printed materials are needed to continue any education begun in a museum. I have worked in Mexico and Yugoslavia, and found that learning the languages, even badly, made a major difference in the excitement and fun of being abroad. This sort of extra diversion is what I want to work into my writings."

*   *   *

REDMONT, Dennis Foster   1942-

PERSONAL: Born December 8, 1942, in Washington, D.C.; son of Bernard S. (a foreign correspondent) and Joan (Rothenberg) Redmont; married Maria Manuela Paixao de Magalhaes, April 16, 1968; children: Michael Andrew, Rodrigo Brian. *Education:* Oberlin College, B.A., 1962; Columbia University, M.S. (with honors), 1963. *Home:* Via Alessandro Poerio 59, Apt. 7, Rome, Italy. *Office:* Associated Press, Piazza Grazioli 5, Rome, Italy 00186.

CAREER/WRITINGS: Associated Press, New York, N.Y., world services editor, 1963-65, correspondent in Lisbon, Portugal, 1965-67, newsman in Rome, 1967-70, bureau chief in Rio de Janeiro, 1970-75, and Rome, 1975—. Notable assignments include coverage of Pope Paul VI's trips to Latin America and Turkey, the first diplomatic kidnappings by Brazilian Guerrillas, General Antonio Spinola's coup attempt in Portugal, and the May, 1968, revolution in Paris. Member of board of trustees, Overseas School of Rome. *Member:* Overseas Press Club, Stampa Estera, Circolo Romano Giornalisti Sportivi, Brazil Foreign Press Association (president, 1974-75). *Awards, honors:* Carl Dipman Award in journalism, 1963; International fellow, Columbia University, 1963.

SIDELIGHTS: Redmont writes: "The most engaging aspect of my work in Rome is certainly the ferment which currently affects all the Mediterranean countries which AP Rome serves as hub: Communist efforts to enter the Italian government; the sun setting on the lives of Pope Paul VI and Marshall Tito and Constantine Karamanlis; Turkey torn apart between East and West and violent Left and Right wing groups; Greece struggling to enter modern Europe; Malta going its own strange course aided by Libya and China. The work in Italy is significantly different from my work in South America, because the countries AP Rome supervises (Greece, Turkey, Yugoslavia, Libya, Malta, etc.) are so radically different in their problems. Furthermore, I was in Brazil at a time when economic growth and very little politics were foremost in the minds of Brazilians." Redmont is fluent in French, Portuguese, Spanish, Latin, and German.

AVOCATIONAL INTERESTS: Tennis, skiing, the Eastern Mediterranean and Latin America.

REED, Bobbie (Butler) 1944-

PERSONAL: Born July 10, 1944, in Neosho, Mo.; daughter of Robert Moore (a clergyman) and Wilma Dean (Eidson) Butler; married Jerold Lynn Reed, July 5, 1963 (marriage ended, 1973); children: Jonathan Robert, Peter Michael Jay. *Education:* Orange Coast College, A.A., 1976; California State University, Los Angeles, M.P.A., 1978. *Home:* 8147 Kaula Dr., Fair Oaks, Calif. 95628. *Office:* Department of Health, 774 p St., Sacramento, Calif. 95814.

CAREER: State Department of Transportation, Los Angeles, Calif., coordinator of PERMIS (computerized personnel information file), 1972-73; California Department of Health, Sacramento, assistant to chief of consultation unit, 1973-74, supervisor of facilities information unit, 1974-75; Fairview State Hospital, Costa Mesa, Calif., director of staff development services, 1975-78; Health Manpower Services, Sacramento, staff services manager, 1978—. Public relations coordinator for Sacramento Concerned Citizens Coalition.

WRITINGS—All published by Regal Books: (With Rex E. Johnson) *Bible Learning Activities: Youth,* 1974; (with Lowell E. Brown) *Your Sunday School Can Grow,* 1974; (with Monroe Marlow) *Teacher Planbook: Adult,* 1975; (with Johnson and C. Edward Reed) *Teacher Planbook: Youth,* 1975; (with C. E. Reed) *Creative Bible Learning: Youth,* 1977; (with Marlow) *Creative Bible Learning: Adult,* 1977; *Developing a Single Adult Ministry,* 1977. Also author of *Single on Sunday,* 1978. Writer of church school material for Gospel Light Publications. Contributor to magazines, including *Teach.* Contributing editor, *Valley Visitor,* 1966, and *World Opportunities,* 1970; managing editor, *Solo.*

WORK IN PROGRESS: A book for parents of adolescents, to provide assistance in letting go, in developing desirable characteristics in youth, and in learning to accept young people as individuals with inherent worth.

SIDELIGHTS: Reed told *CA:* "I was raised in Brazil from the ages of nine to fifteen, living in the jungle with a tribe of Indians." Finding herself camp cook and official interpreter for the Indian workers by the time she was ten years old, Reed noted, "The older men would come to me and ask me to write down their customs and rituals."

When she returned to the United States, Reed found she didn't fit in. She told Allison Deerr: "My values were not [American children's] values. And, while they had been playing, I had been working. I'm still not very good at playing." She is convinced that her Brazilian experience developed in her a great sense of independence, however: "We had a lot of discussions about beliefs and values. Values I held were my own. I owned them because I had worked them through myself."

BIOGRAPHICAL/CRITICAL SOURCES: Time, January, 1957; *Costa Mesa Daily Pilot,* September 16, 1975.

* * *

REED, Daniel 1892(?)-1978

1892(?)—February 9, 1978; American actor, director, and author. In 1912, Reed made his first Broadway appearance in "Oliver Twist". He was founder of the Town Theatre of Columbia, S.C. In 1926, Reed joined the Eastman Theatre in Rochester, N.Y., as director. He wrote "Scarlet Sister Mary," which had a Broadway run, and "Black April" for Paul Robeson. He died in Montrose, N.Y. Obituaries and other sources: *New York Times,* February 12, 1978.

REED, Elizabeth Liggett 1895-

PERSONAL: Born May 30, 1895, in New Castle, Pa.; daughter of Joseph C. (a businessman) and Ida (an artist; maiden name, Boyd) Reed. *Education:* Presbyterian Training School, Baltimore, Md., diploma, 1916; Columbia University, B.S., 1941; graduate study at Union Theological Seminary, New York, N.Y. *Politics:* Democrat. *Home:* 742 Plymouth Rd., Claremont, Calif. 91711.

CAREER: Director of religious education at various churches in New York City, South Orange, N.J., and Springfield, Mass., 1924-29, 1937-53; parish religion education teacher in New York City, and curriculum writer for Pilgrim Press, 1929-33; Syracuse Area Council of Churches, Syracuse, N.Y., director of department of Christian education, 1953-67; writer, 1967—. *Member:* National League of American Pen Women, Theta Chi Beta.

WRITINGS: Bible Homes and Homes Today, Pilgrim, 1937; *When Jesus Was a Boy and When Jesus Grew Up* (juvenile), Pilgrim, 1948; *Let's Go to Nazareth* (juvenile), Westminster, 1948; *Helping Children With the Mystery of Death,* Abingdon, 1970. Also author of church school curricula for Congregational Publishing, 1930-34. Contributor to education and religious periodicals.

WORK IN PROGRESS: Seven Blue Jays and Me; a book about Francis of Assisi, for young people; a book about great people, for children.

SIDELIGHTS: Elizabeth Reed writes: "My special interest has been children in neglected areas of the United States. I worked in a Presbyterian mission in South Philadelphia, organized and taught Sunday and day school in the mountains of Virginia; served on the National Council of Churches' Committee for Summer Projects for children in neglected areas, and helped with work in mining towns of Pennsylvania and a migrant camp in New York State. I have lectured on death and dying at churches and colleges since 1970."

* * *

REEVE, F(ranklin) D(olier) 1928-

PERSONAL: Born September 18, 1928, in Philadelphia, Pa.; son of Richard and Anne Reeve; married Helen Schmidinger (a professor); children: Alison, Brock, Mark. *Education:* Princeton University, A.B., 1950; Columbia University, Ph.D., 1958. *Residence:* Higganum, Conn. *Agent:* Phyllis Seidel, 164 East 93rd St., New York, N.Y. 10028.

CAREER: Worked as longshoreman and truck driver; Columbia University, New York, N.Y., 1952-61, began as instructor, became assistant professor of Slavic languages; Wesleyan University, Middletown, Conn., professor of Russian, 1962-66, adjunct professor of letters, 1968—. Exchange professor in Soviet Union, 1961; visiting professor at Oxford University, 1964, Connecticut College, 1970, and Yale University, 1972. Justice of the peace and member of Democratic Town Committee in Haddam. *Member:* International P.E.N., Poetry Society of America. *Awards, honors:* Literature award from American Academy-National Institute, 1970.

WRITINGS: (Editor and translator) *An Anthology of Russian Plays,* Vintage, Volume I, 1961, reprinted as *Nineteenth-Century Russian Plays,* Norton, 1973, Volume II, 1963, reprinted as *Twentieth-Century Russian Plays,* Norton, 1973; *Aleksandr Blok: Between Image and Idea,* Columbia University Press, 1962; (editor) *Great Soviet Short Stories,* Dell, 1962; (editor) Lev Nikolaevich Tolstoi,

Resurrection: A Novel in Three Parts, Limited Editions Club, 1963; *Robert Frost in Russia,* Little, Brown, 1964; *On Some Scientific Concepts in Russian Poetry at the Turn of the Century,* Center for Advanced Studies, Wesleyan University (Middletown, Conn.), 1966; *The Russian Novel,* McGraw, 1966; *In the Silent Stones* (poems), Morrow, 1968; (editor and translator) *Contemporary Russian Drama,* Pegasus, 1968; *The Red Machines* (novel), Morrow, 1968; *Just over the Border* (novel), Morrow, 1969.

The Brother (novel), Farrar, Straus, 1971; *The Blue Cat* (poems), Farrar, Straus, 1972; *White Colors* (novel), Farrar, Straus, 1973; *The Wild Swans* (novel), Ellis, 1978. Contributor of articles and reviews to magazines.

WORK IN PROGRESS: A novel with an international setting.

SIDELIGHTS: Reeve writes: "I have traveled to Eastern Europe (lived in Russia), to Western Europe (lived in Paris and London), and around the United States. There is much more I want to see: Alaska, Peru, and the South Seas."

AVOCATIONAL INTERESTS: Sailing, skiing, fly fishing, backpacking.

*   *   *

REEVES, Gregory Shaw   1950-

PERSONAL: Born May 15, 1950, in Chicago, Ill.; son of Roy H. (a chef) Reeves. *Education:* Attended University of Frankfurt, 1970-71, and University of Marburg, 1972; University of Chicago, B.A., 1973. *Religion:* None. *Home:* 3623 Gillham Rd., Kansas City, Mo. 64111. *Office: Kansas City Star,* 1729 Grand Ave., Kansas City, Mo. 64108.

CAREER/WRITINGS: Ottawa Daily Times, Ottawa, Ill., reporter, 1973-74; *Kankakee Daily Journal,* Kankakee, Ill., reporter, 1974-75; *Belleville News-Democrat,* Belleville, Ill., reporter, 1976; *Kansas City Star,* Kansas City, Mo., reporter and contributor to weekly magazine, 1976—. Notable assignments include coverage of the ongoing East-West German espionage conflict, and series on corruption in county government, victims of crime, and court reform. Contributor of articles to *Atlas World Press Review* and to various newspapers. *Member:* Kansas City International Relations Council. *Awards, honors:* First-place award for investigative reporting from United Press International, 1974, for a series on corruption in county government in Ottawa, Ill.; first-place award for in-depth reporting for public service from Associated Press, 1975, for a series on victims of crime; John J. McCloy fellowship for reporting and travel in West Germany from Columbia University Graduate School of Journalism and American Council on Germany, 1977.

WORK IN PROGRESS: A series of twenty-four articles on East and West Germany.

SIDELIGHTS: When asked about the political situation in Germany, Reeves wrote: "I feel terrorism in West Germany arose in large part out of frustration with the ruling political parties. A large minority of young persons in the country are committed socialists and are seeking real change. The fact that none of the major parties in the Federal Republic is providing it has helped spawn extremist groups, mostly on the left. My hope for West Germany is that it is able to solve its problems. My hope for the United States is that we recognize and support the progressive socialist tradition in Europe rather than backing conservative or reactionary forces."

REHAK, Peter (Stephen)   1936-

PERSONAL: Born June 9, 1936, in Bratislava, Czechoslovakia; came to Canada, 1949; naturalized citizen, 1955; son of Richard and Helen (Gross) Rehak; married Louise Jean Rouse, June 30, 1962; children: Anna Elizabeth, Ellen, Emilia. *Education:* McGill University, B.A., 1959. *Residence:* Toronto, Canada. *Office address:* Canadian Broadcasting Corp., P.O. Box 500, Station A, Toronto, Canada M5W 1E6.

CAREER/WRITINGS: Windsor Star, Windsor, Ontario, reporter, 1959-60; *Vancouver Sun,* Vancouver, British Columbia, reporter, 1960; *Canadian Press,* Toronto, Ontario, editor, 1960-62; Associated Press, New York, N.Y., newsman in Frankfurt, Germany, 1961-64, editor of foreign desk, 1964-66, newsman in Bonn, Germany, 1967, correspondent in Prague, Czechoslovakia, 1968, Vienna, Austria, 1969, and Bonn, Germany, 1969-73; Time-Life News Service, correspondent in Ottawa, Ontario, 1973-75, bureau chief in Toronto, 1975-76; Canadian Broadcasting Corp., Toronto, producer of "The National" (evening newscast), 1976—. Notable assignments include coverage of Soviet invasion of Czechoslovakia, President Nixon's visit to Romania, 1969, Willy Brandt's rise to power in West Germany, and President Carter's inaugural. *Member:* Graduate Society of McGill University. *Awards, honors:* Managing Editors Award from Associated Press, 1968; Overseas Press Club award, 1969, for best reporting from abroad; George Polk Award from Overseas Press Club, 1969.

SIDELIGHTS: Rehak told *CA:* "The Soviet-led invasion of Czechoslovakia was the most moving story I ever covered. The invading armies destroyed the hope of a small nation in the center of Europe. Everyone in the country—foreigner or native—was affected by the drive to reform the Soviet-style government and everyone was infected by the optimism of the natives. The final and powerful blow to the hope of liberalization was a great emotional disappointment to all. The tension was heightened by the clandestine resistance against the invaders—most of it passive. The show of support for reformist leader Alexander Dubcek eventually forced the Soviet Union to restore him to power—even though only temporarily. The world's attention turned to other matters after a few weeks. But those who were on the scene will never forget the experience."

*   *   *

REID, William J(ames)   1928-

PERSONAL: Born November 14, 1928, in Detroit, Mich.; son of James MacKnight and Sophie Amelia Reid; married wife, Jean, April 2, 1954 (divorced); married Audrey Dowling (a professor), 1972; children: Valerie, Steven. *Education:* University of Michigan, B.A., 1951, M.S.W., 1953; Columbia University, D.S.W., 1963. *Home:* 6019 Ingleside, Chicago, Ill. 60637. *Office:* 969 East 60th St., Chicago, Ill. 60637.

CAREER: University of Chicago, Chicago, Ill., professor, 1962—, George Herbert Jones Professor, 1975. Visiting professor at Smith College. Director of Center for Casework Research, of Community Service Society (New York City), 1965-68. *Member:* National Association of Social Workers, Council on Social Work Education, Phi Beta Kappa.

WRITINGS: (With Anne Shyne) *Brief and Extended Casework,* Columbia University Press, 1969; (with Laura Epstein) *Task Centered Casework,* Columbia University Press, 1972; (with Epstein) *Task-Centered Practice,* Columbia University Press, 1977; *The Task-Centered System,*

Columbia University Press, 1978; (with Charles Garvin and Audrey Smith) *The Work Incentive Experience,* Allanheld & Osmun, 1978. Editor-in-chief of "Social Work Research and Abstracts," Council on Social Work Education. Associate editor of *Social Science Review.*

WORK IN PROGRESS: Research on Social Work, publication by Columbia University Press expected in 1980.

SIDELIGHTS: Reid comments: "Most of my books concern methods of short-term individual and family counseling, particularly one such approach—the task-centered model—developed by my colleagues and me."

* * *

REILLY, John H(urford) 1934-

PERSONAL: Born October 31, 1934, in Penn Yan, N.Y.; son of Thomas Angelo and Mildred (Hurford) Reilly. *Education:* Syracuse University, B.A., 1956; graduate study at University of Montpellier, 1956-57; University of Wisconsin, Madison, M.A., 1958, Ph.D., 1964. *Home:* 10 Park Ave., Apt. 19A, New York, N.Y. 10016. *Office:* Department of Romance Languages, Queens College of the City University of New York, Kissena Blvd., Flushing, N.Y. 11367.

CAREER: Bowling Green State University, Bowling Green, Ohio, instructor in French, 1961-63; Queens College of the City University of New York, Flushing, N.Y., lecturer, 1963-64, instructor, 1964-66, assistant professor, 1967-71, associate professor, 1971-78, professor of French, 1978—, chairman of department, 1970—. *Member:* Modern Language Association of America, American Association of Teachers of French, American Council on the Teaching of Foreign Languages, Northeast Conference on the Teaching of Foreign Languages.

WRITINGS: (Editor) Jean Giraudoux, *Intermezzo,* Appleton, 1967; *Arthur Adamov,* Twayne, 1974; *Jean Giraudoux,* Twayne, 1979. Contributor to theater history and Romance language journals.

* * *

REIS, Claire Raphael 1889-1978

1889—April 11, 1978; American founder of music organizations and author of books on composers. Known as a supporter of contemporary composers, Reis was appointed to the New York Committee on the Use of Leisure Time by President Franklin D. Roosevelt. A founding member of the League of Composers, she served as chairman of the board for twenty-five years. The group brought recognition to foreign and American composers, most notably to Aaron Copland. For ten years, Reis chaired the People's Music League, which she also helped found. She is author of an autobiography, *Composers, Conductors and Critics,* and of *Composers in America,* a reference book. Reis died in New York, N.Y. Obituaries and other sources: *New York Times,* April 13, 1978.

* * *

RELYEA, Suzanne 1945-

PERSONAL: Born August 6, 1945, in Goshen, N.Y.; daughter of Richard J. (an attorney) and Marjorie (Greene) Relyea. *Education:* New York University, B.A., 1968; Yale University, M.Phil., 1971, Ph.D., 1972. *Residence:* Cambridge, Mass. *Office:* Department of French, University of Massachusetts, Harbor Campus, Boston, Mass. 02125.

CAREER: University of Massachusetts, Harbor Campus, Boston, instructor, 1972, assistant professor of French, 1973—. *Member:* Modern Language Association of America, American Society of Seventeenth Centuryists, North East Modern Language Association.

WRITINGS: Signs, Systems, and Meanings: A Contemporary Semiotic Reading of Four Moliere Plays, Wesleyan University Press, 1976.

WORK IN PROGRESS: An article, "The Sign's Desire: Colette's Creation of the Real"; signifying systems in Madame de Sevigne's letters.

SIDELIGHTS: Suzanne Relyea comments: "My interest is in analyzing literary works through an examination of their internal dynamics—that which enables them to produce meaning and how they produce meaning, and the reader's complicity in the production of meaning. My assumption is that a work is a semiotic system in interaction with the larger linguistic system in which it participates. I'm in seventeenth-century French literature and also teach writing (English) to students who need special skills work."

* * *

REMARQUE, Erich Maria 1898-1970

PERSONAL: Born June 22, 1898, in Osnabrueck, Germany; came to United States in 1939, naturalized citizen, 1947; son of Peter Maria (a bookbinder) and Anna Maria Remarque; married first wife, 1923 (divorced, 1932); married Ilsa Intta Zambota, 1938 (divorced); married Paulette Goddard, February 25, 1958. *Education:* Attended University of Munster. *Residence:* New York, N.Y.

CAREER: Novelist and playwright. Worked variously as a teacher, stonecutter, drama critic, salesman for a tombstone company, test driver for a Berlin tire company, advertising copywriter for an automobile company, and organist at an insane asylum. *Military service:* Germany Army, served on Western front during World War I. *Member:* German Academy of Speech and Poetry. *Awards, honors:* German Grand Cross Merit.

WRITINGS—Novels: Im Westen nichts Neues, Kiepenheuer & Witsch, 1928, reprinted, 1968, translation by A. W. Wheen published as *All Quiet on the Western Front,* Little, Brown, 1929, reprinted, 1969; *Der Weg zurueck,* Im Propylaen-verlag, 1931, translation by Wheen published as *The Road Back,* Little, Brown, 1931; *Drei Kameraden,* Querido Verlag, 1937, abridged edition, American Book Co., 1941, complete original edition reprinted, Desch, 1969, original edition translated by Wheen published as *Three Comrades,* Little, Brown, 1937; *Liebe deinen Naechsten,* Querido Verlag, 1941, translation by Denver Lindley published as *Flotsam,* Little, Brown, 1941; *Arc de Triomphe,* F. G. Micha, 1946, translation by Walter Sorell and Lindley published as *Arch of Triumph,* Appleton-Century, 1945.

Der Funke Leben, Kiepenheuer & Witsch, 1952, 6th edition, 1972, original edition translated by James Stern published as *Spark of Life,* Appleton-Century, 1952; *Zeit zu Leben und Zeit zu Sterben,* Kiepenheuer & Witsch, 1954, translation by Lindley published as *A Time to Live and a Time to Die,* Harcourt, 1954, published as *Bobby Deerfield,* Fawcett, 1977; *Der Schwarze Obelisk,* Kiepenheuer & Witsch, 1956, translation by Lindley published as *The Black Obelisk,* Harcourt, 1957; *Der Himmel kennt keine Guenstlinge,* Kiepenheuer & Witsch, 1961, translation by Richard Winston and Clara Winston published as *Heaven Has No Favorites,* Harcourt, 1961; *Die Nacht von Lissabon,* Robin Productions, 1961, translation by Ralph Manheim published as *The Night in Lisbon,* Harcourt, 1964; *Schatten im Paradies,* Droemer Knaur, 1971, translation by Manheim published as *Shadows in Paradise,* Harcourt, 1972.

Other: "The Last Act" (film script), 1955; "Die lezte Station" (play; title means "The Last Station"; produced in 1956), adaptation by Peter Stone published as *Full Circle,* Harcourt, 1974.

Assistant editor of *Sportbild* (illustrated sports magazine).

SIDELIGHTS: All Quiet on the Western Front is unquestionably Remarque's best known and most enduring work. Originally written in German, it has been translated into more than two dozen languages and made into three separate film versions. Its antimilitary tone led to its censorship by the Nazis, who also exiled its author.

When this semi-autobiographical novel was published in English, it met nearly unequivocal praise. T. R. Ybarra wrote, "To the best of my knowledge, nothing written about the War while it was still being fought or since the armistice, in any one of the countries engaged in it or in any neutral land, has done to readers what this book has done." Herbert Read called it "the Bible of the common soldier, the Tommy in the front-line who month after month endured the mess and stink of death, and all the loud riot of killing, the testament of the only man who is competent and worthy to speak of the war."

An example of neorealism, *All Quiet on the Western Front* has been appreciated for its directness and simplicity. "The book is starkly simple, thoroughly lacking in all bugle calls, all flag waving, all false patriotism," observed K. Schriftgiesser. "It is just War." F. E. Hill found Remarque's narrative to have "the lean savagery of an Ibsen tragedy," and *Catholic World* added: "The author's style is unfurbished, unapologetic, unemotional. In its masterful directness, it transmits with almost equal force the whole range of the war's reverberating hell-tones of agony and horror; the dreadful intimacy of the men with fiendish reality, their gleeless, death-dodging humor; their ominous, half-courageous, half-indifferent comradeship." Joseph W. Krutch concluded: "Remarque tells his plain tale with a sort of naivete which is the result, not of too little experience, but of too much. He has given up rhetoric because it is inadequate and given up analysis because he has gone through more than can ever be analyzed."

BIOGRAPHICAL/CRITICAL SOURCES: Nation and Atheneum, April 27, 1929; *Boston Transcript,* June 1, 1929; *New York Herald Tribune,* June 2, 1929; *Nation,* July 10, 1929; *Outlook,* July 31, 1929; *Catholic World,* November, 1929; *Saturday Review,* May 22, 1954; *Newsweek,* April 1, 1957.*

(Died September 25, 1970, in Locarno, Switzerland)

*   *   *

RENOIR, Alain 1921-

PERSONAL: Born October 31, 1921, in Cagnes-sur-Mer, France; came to the United States in 1941, naturalized citizen, 1944; son of Jean (a motion picture writer) and Catherine (an actress; maiden name, Hessling) Renoir; married Jane E. Wagner, February 10, 1948; children: John, Peter, Anne. *Education:* University of California, Santa Barbara, B.A., 1949; Harvard University, A.M., 1951, Ph.D., 1955. *Office:* Department of English, University of California, Berkeley, Calif. 94720.

CAREER: Motion picture cameraman in France, 1937-39,

and North Africa, 1940-41; Ohio University, Athens, acting instructor in English, 1952-53; Williams College, Williamstown, Mass., instructor in English, 1953-55; University of California, Berkeley, assistant professor, 1955-61, associate professor, 1961-67, professor of English, 1967—, chairman of Division of Interdisciplinary and General Studies, 1969-74. *Military service:* French Army, Cavalry, 1939-40. U.S. Army, Artillery, 1942-45; served in Pacific theater; became second lieutenant; received Bronze Star.

MEMBER: Modern Language Association of America, Mediaeval Academy of America, American Philological Association, Philological Association of the Pacific Coast (past member of governing board; second vice president, 1977-78; first vice president, 1978-79; president, 1979-80), California Classical Association (past president). *Awards, honors:* Fellow of Center for Advanced Study in the Humanities, at University of Wisconsin, Madison, 1963-64.

WRITINGS: The Poetry of John Lydgate, Harvard University Press, 1967. Contributor to *Manual of the Writings in Middle English.* Contributor of about sixty articles and reviews to academic journals in the United States, England, Germany, Finland, Sweden, Denmark, the Netherlands, and Belgium.

WORK IN PROGRESS: Research on the old high German *Hildebrandslied,* on medieval courtly love, on oral-formulaic composition, on *Beowulf,* and on problems of translation.

*   *   *

RENSHAW, Samuel 1892-

PERSONAL: Born March 10, 1892, in Lancaster, Ohio; son of Samuel and Susan (Daubenmeier) Renshaw; married Vivian Hart, June 24, 1931; children: Carolyn Renshaw McKelvey, Thomas. *Education:* Ohio University, A.B., 1914; Ohio State University, M.A., 1923, Ph.D., 1928. *Home:* 2675 Coventry Rd., Columbus, Ohio 43221.

CAREER: Ohio State University, Columbus, assistant professor, 1925-27, associate professor, 1928-29, professor of psychology, 1929-72, professor emeritus, 1972—. Civilian director of recognition training for U.S. Navy, 1943-44. *Member:* American Psychological Association, American Association for the Advancement of Science. *Awards, honors:* Gold medal from U.S. Navy.

WRITINGS: A Bibliography on Learning, H. L. Hedrick, 3rd edition, 1936; (with Vernon L. Miller and Dorothy P. Marquis) *Children's Sleep: A Series of Studies on the Influence of Motion Pictures; Normal Age, Sex, and Seasonal Variations in Motility; Experimental Insomnia, the Effects of Coffee; and the Visual Flicker Limens of Children,* Macmillan, 1933, reprinted as *Children's Sleep,* Arno, 1970. Also author of *PsychOptics.*

*   *   *

RENTON, Cam
See ARMSTRONG, Richard

*   *   *

RESKIND, John
See WALLMANN, Jeffrey M(iner)

*   *   *

REUTHER, Victor G(eorge) 1912-

PERSONAL: Born January 1, 1912, in Wheeling, W. Va.;

son of Valentine (a labor leader) and Anna (Stocker) Reuther; married Sophie Goodlavich, July 18, 1936; children: Carole Luise Reuther Hill, Eric Val, John Stocker. *Education:* Attended University of West Virginia, 1929-30, and College of the City of Detroit (now Wayne State University), 1930-33. *Politics:* Democrat. *Religion:* Methodist. *Agent:* Nancy F. Wechsler, 437 Madison Ave., New York, N.Y. 10022. *Office:* 3701 Porter St. N.W., Washington, D.C. 20016.

CAREER: Kelsey-Hayes Wheel Co., Detroit, Mich., assembly line worker, 1935-37; United Automobile Workers Union (UAW), Detroit, Indiana director, 1937-38, defense employment coordinator, 1944-47, director of education, 1948-52; Congress of Industrial Organizations (CIO), Washington, D.C., European director based in Paris, 1953-54, director of International affairs, 1955; UAW, director of international affairs and administrative assistant to the president, 1956-72; writer, 1972—. Member of executive committee of International Metalworkers Federation; National Council of Churches of Christ, vice-chairperson of the commission on the church and economic life and member of the commission on religion and race. Served on President Eisenhower's Committee on Government Contracts and on President Johnson's National Advisory Council on Education of Disadvantaged Children. Active in establishment of joint international labor programs. Lecturer. *Member:* Americans for Democratic Action (member of national executive committee). *Awards, honors:* Doctor of Laws Degree from Wayne State University.

WRITINGS: The Brothers Reuther and the Story of the UAW: A Memoir, Houghton, 1976. Contributor of articles to periodicals in the United States and abroad.

WORK IN PROGRESS: Research on trade unions, multinational corporations, and foreign policy.

SIDELIGHTS: The Reuther brothers, Walter, Roy, and Victor, have been closely identified with the growth of industrial unionism in the second third of this century. Victor has written a book about the brothers which, according to Paul D. Zimmerman, "is as much an official history of the United Auto Workers as it is a personal memoir." A. H. Raskin wrote: "It would be an exaggeration, of course, to suggest that this somewhat Homeric memoir of Victor G. Reuther, the last surviving brother, puts the Reuther story in full perspective. It is much too partisan for that." Nonetheless, he found that, "The Reuther story, so full of sadness, is still a testament to all that is best in the American dream."

Before settling in Detroit and beginning labor union organization, Victor and Walter (later to become president of the UAW and of the Industrial Union Department of the AFL-CIO), spent three years traveling in Europe and Asia. They traveled by bicycle and lodged with farm families and at inexpensive inns. They spent two years in a Ford sponsored worker-exchange program in the Soviet Union. The brothers witnessed the beginnings of the Nazi government in Europe and the growth of Stalin's despotism in Soviet Russia. As a result of their first-hand experiences and observations, the Reuthers have been strongly pro-democratic, anti-fascist, and anti-communist leaders ever since, according to Victor Reuther. This repeated assertion is "one of the striking aspects of the book," Zimmerman noted.

AVOCATIONAL INTERESTS: Woodworking, photography, and gardening.

BIOGRAPHICAL/CRITICAL SOURCES: Newsweek, May 17, 1976; *New York Times Book Review,* June 13, 1976; *New York Times,* June 21, 1976; *Book World,* July 25, 1976; *National Review,* September 3, 1976.

REX, Barbara (Clayton)   1904-

PERSONAL: Born May 30, 1904, in Philadelphia, Pa.; daughter of Paul (a broker) and Helen (Brown) Clayton; married Walter Rex (a broker; died, 1956); children: Walter, Barbara Rex Darsey. *Residence:* Chestnut Hill, Pa.; Nantucket, Mass. *Agent:* Harold Ober Associates, Inc., 40 East 49th St., New York, N.Y. 10017. *Office:* c/o W. W. Norton & Company, Inc., 500 Fifth Ave., New York, N.Y. 10056.

CAREER: Worked as free-lance consultant editor; writer, 1967—.

WRITINGS—All novels: *Vacancy on India Street,* Norton, 1967; *Saints and Innocents,* Norton, 1972; *I Want to Be in Love Again,* Norton, 1977.

WORK IN PROGRESS: A novel, as yet untitled.

SIDELIGHTS: Barbara Rex told *CA:* "When I was doing a newspaper column, I was much influenced by Thoreau. Now I read almost nothing but fiction, and am re-reading all of Iris Murdoch and E. Bowen. The stylists passionately interest and concern me. How else does one improve? Right now I am on a Joyce Cary binge. Having had almost no education, I am self-taught, and my sights are high. I write about women, about their relationships, endlessly fascinating. Only strivers really interest me. For what writer is not one?"

*   *   *

RHEA, Nicholas
See WALKER, Peter N.

*   *   *

RHIE, Schi-Zhin   1936-

PERSONAL: Born October 17, 1936, in Korea; came to the United States in 1969; son of Sung-Choon (a businessman) and Tansil (Choi) Rhie; married Sowon Kahng (a teacher), August 9, 1965; children: Ann, Julie, Grace. *Education:* Seoul National University, B.A., 1958, M.A., 1964; further study at Goethe Institute, 1967-69; Rosary College, River Forest, Ill., M.A.L.S., 1971. *Home:* 18 Donald Pl., Elizabeth, N.J. 07208. *Office:* Library, Kean College, Union, N.J. 07083.

CAREER: Minjung Publishing Co., Seoul, Korea, proofreader (German), 1958-62; high school teacher and librarian in Sungchung, Korea, 1962-64; Seoul National University, Seoul, instructor in German, 1964-67; Metro Catalog Cards Co., Chicago, Ill., cataloger, 1970-71; Elmhurst College, Elmhurst, Ill., catalog librarian, 1971-73; Center for Research Libraries, Chicago, cataloger, 1973; Kean College, Union, N.J., catalog librarian, 1973—.

WRITINGS: Ich lerne Deutsch (title means "I Learn German"), two volumes, Silhak-Sa, 1968; *Soon-Hee in America* (bilingual children's book; with own photographs), Hollym International Corp., 1977. Contributor to *Korean Culture.*

WORK IN PROGRESS: The Koreans in America, with his own photographs.

SIDELIGHTS: Rhie has traveled all around the world, especially to visit European museums and architects. His second book, for children, was intended less as a textbook, than as a bridge between two cultures. Simultaneously published in Korea, to show Korean children a glimpse of an American child's daily life, Rhie hopes that it will show American children that Korean-American children are not different simply because they look different. The book and its photographs show everyday events from the life of his youngest daughter.

BIOGRAPHICAL/CRITICAL SOURCES: Union Independent, April 21, 1977, November 3, 1977; *Elizabeth Daily Journal,* November 17, 1977.

*   *   *

RIBAR, Joe 1943-

PERSONAL: Born May 5, 1943, in Hudson, N.Y.; son of Joseph Peter, Sr. (a cook) and Irene (Stokes) Ribar; married Margaret Lawsing Fox, August 30, 1966 (divorced, 1973). *Education:* Attended New School for Social Research, 1968, and University of Iowa, 1969; Bard College, A.B., 1969. *Home:* 24 Allen St., Hudson, N.Y. 12534.

CAREER: Random House, Inc., New York City, order processing supervisor for School and Library Service, 1966-68; Praeger Publishers, New York City, Phaidon liaison, 1970; WNET, New York City, poet-in-residence, 1974; Project Whale, Hudson, N.Y., director, 1975; writer. Has worked as police dispatcher and food stamp "outreach" worker. *Awards, honors:* J. D. Rockefeller honorarium, 1971; National Endowment writing grant, 1973; grant from America the Beautiful Fund of New York, 1974, for a whaling history of Hudson, N.Y.

WRITINGS: Book of the Buffalo (poems), Figtree Press, 1971.

Co-author of "Sweet Verticality," a feature-length videotape, 1974, and "Biohsea," a shorter videotape.

WORK IN PROGRESS: The Madonnas; research on local history and nineteenth-century American poets.

SIDELIGHTS: Ribar writes: "I am interested in the natural world. I look for my material where I grew up, which is where I live."

*   *   *

RICE, Stan 1942-

PERSONAL: Born November 7, 1942, in Dallas, Tex.; son of Stanley Travis (a salesman) and Margaret (Cruse) Rice; married Anne O'Brien (a novelist), October 14, 1961. *Education:* Attended North Texas State University, 1960-61; San Francisco State University, B.A., 1963, M.A., 1965; also attended University of California, Berkeley, 1964. *Home:* 2800 Claremont Blvd., Berkeley, Calif. 94705. *Office:* Departments of Creative Writing and English, San Francisco State University, 1600 Holloway, San Francisco, Calif. 94132.

CAREER: San Francisco State University, San Francisco, Calif., assistant professor, 1965-71, associate professor, 1971-76, professor of English and creative writing, 1977—, assistant director of Poetry Center, 1966-74. *Awards, honors:* Regional first prizes from Academy of American Poets, 1964 and 1965; National Endowment for the Arts grants, 1965 and 1972; San Francisco Foundation Joseph Henry Jackson Award, 1968, for manuscript, *Eye;* Edgar Allan Poe Award, 1977, for *Whiteboy.*

WRITINGS: Some Lamb (poems), Figures, 1975; *Whiteboy* (poems), Mudra, 1976. Author of radio poem, "Elegy," KPFA Pacifica Foundation.

WORK IN PROGRESS: Holy Whole (tentative title), poems.

SIDELIGHTS: Rice comments: "I am committed to a vigorous and exciting poetry that can be read aloud, that is not contemptuous of its audience, and yet makes no compromise to mediocre taste or subject matter. I would bring every means to my disposal to achieve this public poetry: televi-

sion, radio, you name it. Poetry is now either an excellent private art *or* a lousy public art—I'd very much like to make an excellent public art and claim again the ancient social role of poetry as public language at its best."

*   *   *

RICHARDS, Caroline 1939-

PERSONAL: Born August 8, 1939, in Atkinson, Neb.; daughter of John M. and Hildred Higgins; married Howard C. Richards (a philosopher), July 26, 1965; children: Shelley Demaris, Laura Mary. *Education:* University of Colorado, B.A., 1960; Stanford University, Ph.D., 1970. *Agent:* Elaine Markson Literary Agency, Inc., 44 Greenwich Ave., New York, N.Y. 10011. *Office:* Box 105, Earlham College, Richmond, Ind. 47374.

CAREER: Brooklyn College of the City University of New York, Brooklyn, N.Y., instructor in history, 1964-65; Santiago College, Santiago, Chile, teacher of English and history, 1966-69; Earlham College, Richmond, Ind., assistant professor of history, 1974—.

WRITINGS: Coup d'Etat (novel), Harcourt, 1978.

WORK IN PROGRESS: A historical novel about Chile in the nineteenth century.

SIDELIGHTS: Caroline Richards writes: "I have spent many years in Latin America. I am profoundly interested in the economic and social problems of the developing areas and in the relationship between politics and culture. I have taught in several humanities programs which attempt to integrate history, literature, and philosophy."

*   *   *

RICHARDSON, James 1950-

PERSONAL: Born January 1, 1950, in Bradenton, Fla.; son of James E. (an engineer) and Betty (Behrer) Richardson. *Education:* Princeton University, A.B., 1971; University of Virginia, M.A., 1973, Ph.D., 1975. *Home address:* P.O. Box 439, Cambridge, Mass. 02138. *Office:* Department of English, Harvard University, 38 Kirkland St., Cambridge, Mass. 02138.

CAREER: Harvard University, Cambridge, Mass., assistant professor of English, 1975—. *Member:* Modern Language Association of America, P.E.N., Associated Writing Programs. *Awards, honors:* National Endowment for the Humanities fellowship, 1978-79.

WRITINGS: Reservations (poems), Princeton University Press, 1977; *Thomas Hardy: The Poetry of Necessity,* University of Chicago Press, 1977.

WORK IN PROGRESS: Second Guesses, poems; *The Elegiac Consciousness: A Study of Nineteenth-Century Poetry.*

*   *   *

RICHARDSON, Richard C(olby), Jr. 1933-

PERSONAL: Born September 10, 1933, in Burlington, Vt.; son of Richard C. and Florence (Barlow) Richardson; married Patricia Barnhart, December 21, 1954; children: Richard C. III, Michael Donald, Christopher Robin. *Education:* Castleton State College, B.S., 1954; Michigan State University, M.A., 1958; University of Texas, Ph.D., 1963. *Home:* 126 Loma Vista, Tempe, Ariz. 85282. *Office:* Center for Higher and Adult Education, Arizona State University, Tempe, Ariz. 85281.

CAREER: Vermont College, Montpelier, instructor in social studies and counselor, 1958-61; St. Louis Community College, St. Louis, Mo., dean of student personnel services and of instruction, 1963-67; Northampton County Area Community College, Bethlehem, Pa., president, 1967-77; Arizona State University, Tempe, professor of education and director of Center for Higher and Adult Education, 1977—. Adjunct professor at Pennsylvania State University, 1973-77; visiting lecturer at Lehigh University, 1967-77. Vice-chairman of board of directors of Easton Hospital, 1975-77. Member of Minsi Trails Council (Boy Scouts of America). *Military service:* U.S. Marine Corps, 1954-57; became captain. U.S. Marine Corps Reserve, 1959-67.

MEMBER: American Association of University Professors, American Educational Research Association, Association for the Study of Higher Education, American Association of Higher Education (member of board of directors, 1970-73), American Council on Education (member of board of directors, 1971-72), American association of Community and Junior Colleges, Phi Delta Kappa. *Awards, honors:* Litt. D. from Lafayette College, 1973.

WRITINGS: (With Clyde Blocker and Robert Plummer) *The Two Year College: A Social Synthesis,* Prentice-Hall, 1965; (with Blocker) *Student's Guide to the Two Year College,* Prentice-Hall, 1968; *Interim Campus: Starting a New Community Junior College,* American Association of Community and Junior Colleges, 1968; (with Blocker and Louis Bender) *Governance for the Two Year College,* Prentice-Hall, 1972; (with Kenneth Mortimer) *Collective Bargaining: Six Case Studies,* Center for the Study of Higher Education, Pennsylvania State University, 1977. Contributor to education journals and *Change.*

WORK IN PROGRESS: A book on finance and planning.

SIDELIGHTS: Richardson writes: "Many of my colleagues in community colleges stress the unique characteristics of their institutions. Service with such groups as the National Board on Graduate Education and the board of directors of the American Council on Education has convinced me that the commonalities among two and four year institutions of higher education are more important than their differences. From a university position, I will be able to share the experiences I've had with the community college movement. Equally important, I'll be able to pursue, through research and writing, the challenges which all post-secondary institutions must confront."

AVOCATIONAL INTERESTS: Golf, fishing, hunting, hiking.

* * *

RICKS, Nadine 1925-

PERSONAL: Born February 20, 1925, in Texas; daughter of Sidney Leeman (a rancher) and Mabel (Bollinger) Wilson; married Albert Conwell Ricks (a stockbroker), May 5, 1944; children: Cynthia Ann (Mrs. E. H. Littlejohn), Connie Jean (Mrs. R. Engel), Richard Allan. *Education:* University of Texas, B.A., 1954; University of Nebraska, M.A., 1964. *Religion:* Presbyterian. *Home:* 471 Oak Hill Ter., Lompoc, Calif. 93436. *Office:* Allan Hancock College, 800 South College Ave., Santa Maria, Calif. 93454.

CAREER: Aroostook State Teachers College, Presque Isle, Me., instructor in English, 1960; University of Nebraska, Lincoln, instructor in English, 1964-67; Allan Hancock College, Santa Maria, Calif., instructor in English, 1967—.

WRITINGS: (With Marilyn Marsh) *Patterns in English,* Scribner, 1969; (with Marsh) *How to Write Your First Research Paper,* Wadsworth, 1971.

WORK IN PROGRESS: Writing for religious periodicals.

* * *

RIDPATH, Ian (William) 1947-

PERSONAL: Born May 1, 1947, in Ilford, Essex, England; son of Alfred William J. (an engineer) and Irene F. (Walton) Ridpath. *Education:* Educated in England. *Politics:* Liberal. *Religion:* "I believe in the future of the human race." *Home and office:* 35 Oakwood Gardens, Ilford, Essex 1G3 9TY, England. *Agent:* James Brown Associates, Inc., 25 West 43rd St., New York, N.Y. 10036.

CAREER: University of London Observatory, London, England, member of lunar group, 1966-68; *Science in Action,* IPC Magazines, London, staff writer, 1968-69; BPC Publishing, London, member of editorial staff, 1969-71; freelance writer, 1971—. Lecturer. *Member:* National Union of Journalists, Association of British Science Writers, Federation of Astronomical Societies (vice-president).

WRITINGS: Discovering the Universe (juvenile), Macdonald & Co., 1974; *Worlds Beyond,* Harper, 1975; *Man and Materials* (juvenile), Volume I: *Coal,* Volume II: *Gas,* Volume III: *Minerals,* Volume IV: *Oil,* Volume V: *Plastics,* Volume VI: *Stone,* Addison-Wesley, 1975; (editor) *Encyclopedia of Astronomy and Space,* Crowell, 1976; (editor) *Stars and Space Seventy-Seven,* Independent Newspapers, 1976; *Signs of Life* (juvenile), Kestrel, 1977; *Stars and Planets,* Hamlyn, 1978; *Messages from the Stars,* Harper, 1978. Contributor to "Library of Modern Knowledge" series, Reader's Digest Press, to magazines, including *New Scientist,* and to newspapers all over the world. Former editor of *Hermes.*

WORK IN PROGRESS: Continuing research on astronomy and space.

SIDELIGHTS: Ridpath writes: "I have a strong and continuing interest in amateur astronomy. Much of my time when not writing about astronomy and space is devoted to voluntary work on behalf of astronomical societies in the United Kingdom. My recent writings have concentrated on the subject of extraterrestrial life and the search for its existence, which I consider the major science story of our day. I am also a supporter of the space colony concept of Professor Gerard O'Neill, and my writings have discussed its implications for the future of mankind, with particular reference to the role of colonies in interstellar travel and communications. Equally, I have criticized the pseudo-scientific movement, notably the works of Erich von Daniken and the UFOlogists. I believe that science fact is more exciting and rewarding than science fiction."

* * *

RIKKI
See DUCORNET, Erica

* * *

RITNER, Peter Vaughn 1927(?)-1976

PERSONAL: Married Susan Rennie (a professor). *Education:* Attended Massachusetts Institute of Technology, Harvard University, and Columbia University. *Home:* 340 Riverside Dr., New York, N.Y.

CAREER: Became feature editor of *Saturday Review of Literature* in 1950; later joined Macmillan Publishing Co., where he worked for ten years before becoming vice-president and director for the general publishing division of World Publishing Co.

WRITINGS: The Death of Africa (nonfiction), Macmillan, 1960; *The Society of Space* (essays), Macmillan, 1961; *Red Carpet for the Shah* (novel), Morrow, 1975; *The Passion of Richard Thynne* (novel), Morrow, 1976.

SIDELIGHTS: Ritner worked with Walt W. Rostow, Theodore C. Sorensen, Jim Bouton, and Jacques Cousteau during his years with Macmillan. Ritner was also responsible for negotiating the purchase of Albert Speer's memoirs for Macmillan. *Avocational interests:* Pianist, authority on Beethoven and other composers.

OBITUARIES: New York Times, October 28, 1976.*

(Died, October 27, 1976)

*   *   *

RITSOS, Giannes
   See RITSOS, Yannis

*   *   *

RITSOS, Yannis   1909-
   (Giannes Ritsos)

PERSONAL: Born May 1, 1909, in Monemvasia, Greece; son of Eleftherios (a land-owner) and Eleftheria (Vouzounara) Ritsos; married Fallitasa Georgiades (a medical doctor), 1954, children: Erie. *Education:* Educated in Greece. *Religion:* Greek Orthodox. *Home:* 39 M. Koraka St., Athens 219, Greece.

CAREER: Poet. Angelopoulos (law firm), Athens, Greece, law clerk, 1925; Mitzopoulos-Oeconomopoulos (notaries for National Bank of Greece), Athens, clerk, 1925-26; Lawyer's Association, Athens, assistant librarian, 1926; confined to a sanatorium because of tuberculosis, 1927-31; employed by a music theatre during the 1930's; National Theatre of Greece, Athens, member of Chorus of Ancient Tragedies, 1938-45; Govostis (publisher), Athens, editor and proofreader, 1945-48, 1952-56; full-time writer, 1956—. Former actor and dancer for Lyriki Skini (Athens Opera House). *Member:* European Community of Writers, Society of Greek Writers, Society of Greek Dramatists, Comite des Gens des Lettres, Societe des Ecrivains et Compositeurs Dramatiques Francais, Academy of Meinz, Academy Mallarme. *Awards, honors:* State Prize Award for Poetry (Greece), 1956; Grand Prix International de la Biennale de Poesie de Knokke (Belgium), 1972; International Prize "Georgi Dimitroff" (Bulgaria), 1974; honorary doctorate from Salonica University (Greece), 1975; Grand Prix Francais de la Poesie "Alfred de Vigny," 1975; International Prize for Poetry "Etna-Taormina" (Italy), 1976; International Prize for Poetry "Seregno-Brianza" (Italy), 1976; Lenin Prize for Peace, 1977.

WRITINGS—Poetry in English: Romiosyne, Kedros, 1966, translation by O. Laos published as *Romiossyni,* Dustbooks, 1969; *Dekaochto lianotragouda tes pikres patridas,* Kedros, 1973, translation by Amy Mims published as *Eighteen Short Songs of the Bitter Motherland,* North Central Publishing, 1974; *Diadromos kai skala,* Kedros, 1973, translation by Nicos Germanacos published as *Corridor and Stairs,* Goldsmith Press (Ireland), 1976.

Poetry collections in English: *Poems of Yannis Ritsos,* translated by Alan Page, Oxonian Press, 1969; *Romiossini and Other Poems,* translated by Dan Georgakas and Eleni Paidoussi, Quixote Press, 1969; *Gestures and Other Poems, 1968-1970,* translated by Nikos Stangos, Cape Golliard, 1971; *Contradictions,* translated by John Stathatos, Sceptre Press, 1973; *Vannis Ritsos: Selected Poems,* translated by

Stangos, Penguin, 1974; *The Fourth Dimensions: Selected Poems of Yannis Ritsos,* translated and introduced by Rae Dalven, David R. Godine, 1977; *Chronicle of Exile,* translated and introduced by Minas Savvas, Wire Press, 1977.

Other poetry: *Trakter* (title means "Tractors"), Govostis, 1934; *Pyramides* (title means "Pyramids"), Govostis, 1935; *Epitaphios,* Rizospastis, 1936; *To tragoudi tes adelphes mou* (title means "The Song of My Sister"), Govostis, 1937; *Earini Symphonia* (title means "Spring Symphony"), Govostis, 1938; *To emvatirio tou okeanou* (title means "The March of the Ocean"), Govostis, 1940; *Palia Mazurka se rythmo vrohis* (title means "An Old Mazurka in the Rhythm of the Rain"), Govostis, 1942; *Dokimasia* (title means "Trial"), Govostis, 1943; *O syntrofos mas* (title means "Our Comrade"), Govostis, 1945.

O anthropos me to gary fallo (title means "The Man with the Carnation"), Politikes Ke Logotechnikes Ekdoseis (p.L.E.; Bucharest?), 1952; *Agrypnia* (title means "Vigil"), Pyxida, 1954; *Proino astro* (title means "Morning Star"), [Athens], 1955; *He sonata tou selenophotos* (title means "Moonlight Sonata"), Kedros, 1956; *Croniko* (title means "Chronicle"), Kedros 1957; *Apochairetismos* (title means "Farewell"), Kedros, 1957; *Hydria* (title means "The Urn"), Kedros, 1957; *Cheimerine diaugeia* (title means "Winter Limpidity"), Kedros, 1957; *Petrinos Chronos* (title means "Stony Time"), P.L.E., 1957; *He Geitonies tou Kosmou* (title means "The Neighborhoods of the World"), P.L.E., 1957; *Otan erchetai ho xenos* (title means "When the Stranger Comes"), Kedros, 1958; *Any potachti Politeia* (title means Unsubjugated City"), P.L.E., 1958; *He architectoniki ton dentron* (title means "The Architecture of the Trees"), P.L.E., 1958; *Hoi gerontisses k'he thalassa* (title means "The Old Women and the Sea"), Kedros, 1959.

All published by Kedros: *To parathyro* (title means "The Window"), 1960; *He gephyra* (title means "The Bridge"), 1960; *Ho mavros Hagios* (title means "The Black Saint"), 1961; *Pieimata Tomos I* (title means "Poems Volume I"), 1961; *Pieimata Tomos II* (title means "Poems Volume II"), 1961; *To nekro spiti* (title means "The Dead House"), 1962; *Kato ap' ton iskio tou vounou* (title means "Beneath the Shadow of the Mountain"), 1962; *To dentro tis phylakis Kai he gynaikes* (title means "The Prison Tree and the Women"), 1963; *Martyries* (title means "Testimonies I"), 1963; *Dodeka pieimata gia ton Kavaphe* (title means "12 Poems for Cavafy"), 1963; *Pieimata Tomos III* (title means "Poems Volume III"), 1964; *Paichnidia t'ouranou kai tou nerou* (title means "Playful Games of the Sky and the Water"), 1964; *Philoktetes,* 1964; *Orestes,* 1966; *Martyries* (title means "Testimonies II"), 1966; *Ostrava,* 1967.

Petres, Epanalepseis, Kinklidoma (title means "Stones, Repetitions, Railings"), 1972; *He epistrophe tes Iphigeneias* (title means "The Return of Iphigenia"), 1972; *He Helene* (title means "Helen"), 1972; *Cheironomies* (title means "Gestures"), 1972; *Tetarte distase* (title means "Fourth Dimension"), 1972; *Chrysothemis,* 1972; *Ismene,* 1972; *Graganda,* 1973; *Ho aphanismos tis Milos* (title means "The Annihilation of Milos"), 1974; *Hymnos kai threnos gia tin Kypro* (title means "Hymn and Lament for Cyprus"), 1974; *To Kapnismeno tsoukali* (title means "The Soot-black Pot"), 1974; *To kodonostasio* (title means "Belfry"), 1974; *Ho tichos mesa ston Kathrephti* (title means "The Wall in the Mirror"), 1974; *Chartina* (title means "Papermade"), 1974.

He Kyra ton Ambelion (title means "The Lady of the Vineyards"), 1975; *He teleftaia pro Anthropou ekatontaeteia* (title means "The Last Century Before Humanity"), 1975; *Epikairika* (title means "Circumstantial Verse"), 1975; *Ho hysterographo tis doxas* (title means "The Postscript of Glory"), 1975; *Hemerologia exorias* (title means "Diaries in Exile"), 1975; *Mantatofores*, 1975; *Pieimata Tomos IV* (title means "Poems Volume IV"), 1975; *To thyroreio* (title means "Conciergerie"), 1976; *To makrino* (title means "Remote"), 1977; *Gignesthai* (title means "Becoming"), 1977.

Other writings: *Pera ap'ton iskio ton Kyparission* (title means "Beyond the Shadow of the Cypress Trees"; three-act play; first produced in Bucharest at National Theatre, January, 1959), P.L.E., 1958; "Mia gynaika plai sti thalassa" (title means "A Woman by the Sea"; three-act play), first produced in Bucharest, 1959; *Meletimata* (title means "Essays"), Kedros, 1974.

Translations of work represented in anthologies, including *The Penguin Book of Socialist Verse,* edited by A. N. Bold, Penguin, 1970; and *Modern Greek Poetry: From Cavafy to Elytis,* & Schuster, 1973 edited by K. Friar, Simon & Schuster, 1973.

Translator of French, Rumanian, and Czechoslovakian poetry into Greek.

SIDELIGHTS: The hardship and misfortune that Yannis Ritsos experienced in his early years undoubtedly spurred his creative genius. His wealthy family suffered financial ruin during his early childhood, and soon afterward his father and sister became insane. Tuberculosis claimed his mother and an older brother, and later confined Ritsos himself to a sanatorium in Athens for several years. Poetry and the revolutionary movement in Greece became the sustaining forces in his tragedy-ridden life, but because his writing was so controversial, Ritsos also endured much political persecution. One of his most celebrated works, the "Epitaphios," a lament inspired by the assassination of a worker in a large general strike in Salonica, was actually burned by the Metaxas dictatorship, along with many other books, in a "Ceremony" enacted in front of the Temple of Zeus in 1936. After the end of the second World War and the annihilation of the National Resistance Movement, Ritsos was exiled for four years to the islands of Lemnos, Makronisos, and Ayios Efstratios. His books were also banned and he was not allowed to publish again until 1954. On April 21, 1967, the day of the Colonels' coup d'etat, Ritsos was again deported and subsequently kept under house arrest until the winter of 1970. His works were banned again until 1972.

Ritsos's poetry has been translated into forty-three different languages and is widely read in Greece. His theatrical plays and many of his long poems have been presented on the stage, radio, and television in France, Belgium, Holland, Czechoslovakia, Poland, and Rumania. Various composers have also set his poetry to music. Mikis Theodorakis's inspired songs from "Epitaphios," "Romiosyni," and the "Eighteen Short Songs of the Bitter Motherland" have been sung constantly throughout all the critical moments of recent Greek history, having become a kind of second national anthem for the progressive forces in Greece.

BIOGRAPHICAL/CRITICAL SOURCES: Times Literary Supplement, March 10, 1972, July 18, 1975; *American Poetry Review,* September-October, 1973; *Books Abroad,* winter, 1974; *Yannis Ritsos: Selected Poems,* introduced by Peter Bien, Penguin, 1974; *Contemporary Literary Criticism,* Gale, Volume 6, 1976; Rae Dalven, *The Fourth Dimension: Selected Poems of Yannis Ritsos,* David R. Godine, 1977.

RIVERS, Clarence Joseph 1931-

PERSONAL: Born September 9, 1931, in Selma, Ala.; son of Clarence Rufus and Lorraine (Echols) Rivers. *Education:* St. Mary's Seminary, Cincinnati, Ohio, B.A., 1952, M.A., 1956; Union Graduate School, Yellow Springs, Ohio, Ph.D., 1978; additional graduate work at Xavier University, Cincinnati, Ohio, Yale University, Institut Catholique, Paris, and Catholic University of America. *Office:* Stimuli, Inc., 17 Erkenbrecher Ave., Cincinnati, Ohio 45220.

CAREER: Ordained Roman Catholic priest, 1956; Archdiocese of Cincinnati, Cincinnati, Ohio, priest, 1956—. Taught high school English in Cincinnati and was part-time assistant pastor of St. Joseph's and Assumption parishes, both in Cincinnati, 1956-66; Stimuli, Inc. (religious education consultants), Cincinnati, president, 1969—. National Office for Black Catholics, Washington, D.C., founder and first director of department of culture and worship, 1971-74, consultant. Narrator for television documentaries. *Member:* North American Academy of Liturgy, Martin Luther King Fellows, Liturgical Commission of the Archdiocese of Cincinnati. *Awards, honors:* Gold Medal of Catholic Art Association for "An American Mass Program," 1966; several public service awards.

WRITINGS: Celebration (devotions), Seabury, 1969; *Reflections* (meditations), Herder & Herder, 1970; *Soulfull Worship* (liturgies), National Office for Black Catholics, 1974.

Musical compositions: "An American Mass Program"; "Brotherhood of Man"; "Resurrection."

WORK IN PROGRESS: The Spirit in Worship, a book; "Turn Me Loose," a musical play based on the life of Frederick Douglass; "The Continuity of African Culture in the Western Hemisphere," a television series; a television script of worship for CBS.

SIDELIGHTS: "You're going to have a good time," Rivers promises congregations when he conducts services. His greatest challenge has been to provide spiritual enrichment to members of the Roman Catholic Church. He told one congregation that the Church must be "more responsive to the Black worship tradition.... The Church must not allow the brilliant glory of her traditional and familiar worship forms to blind her to other possibilities, to prevent her from appropriating with appreciation a new vitality within her midst, a vitality, a life, new to her, but conceived long ago in the ancient and fertile womb of Mother Africa.

"The worship of God ought to be responsibly planned," Rivers continued, "but ought not be so rigidly predictable that the unforseen is unallowed in every case. For, while there need be structure and form, the Spirit is nonetheless free. God is not by fixed formula captured; He comes! And His presence is energizing, His actions oft appear spontaneous. His worship is spirited, alive, moving."

After attending a service conducted by Rivers, Chuck Stone said the priest "wove together the divine threads of Catholic prayers, African drumming and black American Gospel music," and commented, "Only the Heavenly Father could have pulled it off."

BIOGRAPHICAL/CRITICAL SOURCES: Philadelphia Daily News, August 5, 1976; *Catholic Telegraph,* May 27, 1977.

*   *   *

ROACH, James P. 1907-1978

December 20, 1907—March 16, 1978; American journalist

best known for his unique literary style. While sports editor for the *New York Times* from 1958 to 1973, Roach covered sports in the United States and overseas, including the Olympic games in Tokyo in 1964. Earlier, as a writer on horse races, he received nine publisher's awards for his work. After retiring from the *New York Times,* he became the information director of the New York State Racing and Wagering Board. Roach died in New York, N.Y. Obituaries and other sources: *Who's Who in America,* 38th edition, Marquis, 1974; *New York Times,* March 17, 1978.

* * *

ROBARD, Jackson
See WALLMANN, Jeffrey M(iner)

* * *

ROBERSON, (Charles) Ed(win)   1939-

PERSONAL: Born December 26, 1939, in Pittsburgh, Pa.; son of Charles Ned (a trucker) and Elizabeth (a teacher of handicapped children; maiden name, Burley) Roberson; married Rhonda Wiles (an attorney), May 6, 1973; children: Lena Illiniza. *Education:* University of Pittsburgh, B.A., 1967. *Home:* 5 Petunia Dr., #1-F, North Brunswick, N.J. 08902. *Office:* Department of English, Rutgers University, Scott Hall, New Brunswick, N.J. 08903.

CAREER: Has worked in various positions in Pittsburgh, Pa., including advertising assistant at Film Graphics, tankman at Pittsburgh Zoological Society, and lecturer in English at Community College of Allegheny County; University of Pittsburgh, Pittsburgh, instructor in English, until 1973; Rutgers University, New Brunswick, N.J., assistant professor of English, 1973—. Research assistant on expedition to Alaska, 1961, and off the Bermuda Reef, 1962; member of U.S. El Sangay expeditions to Peru and Ecuador (mountaineering expeditions), 1963, and Ecuador, 1975. *Awards, honors:* Poetry prize from *Atlantic Monthly,* 1963.

WRITINGS: When Thy King Is a Boy, University of Pittsburgh Press, 1970; *Etai-Eken,* University of Pittsburgh Press, 1975.

Work anthologized in *New Directions, Number Twenty-Two,* New Directions, 1970; *The Poetry of the Negro,* edited by Bontemps and Hughes, 1970; *Out of This World,* edited by Gildner and Gildner.

WORK IN PROGRESS: Ultimal Solo: This Week's Concerts, a series of lyrics "developed from experiments with change and outburst/interruption."

BIOGRAPHICAL/CRITICAL SOURCES: Don L. Lee, *Dynamite Voices,* Broadside Press, 1971; Eugene Redmond, *Drum Voices,* Doubleday, 1976.

* * *

ROBERTS, Donald Alfred   1897-1978

November 11, 1897—April 27, 1978; American educator and expert on the works of seventeenth-century writer John Milton. An educator in English at the City College of the City University of New York, Roberts was also editor of the *Complete Prose Works of John Milton,* and founder of the Milton Society of America. He contributed articles on Milton and his writings to *National Encyclopedia, Dictionary of American Biography,* and to various periodicals, including *Nation, New York Times Book Review,* and *Commonweal.* He died in Martha's Vineyard, Mass. Obituaries and other sources: *New York Times,* April 28, 1978.

ROBERTS, Grant
See WALLMANN, Jeffrey M(iner)

* * *

ROBINSON, Charles E(dward)   1941-

PERSONAL: Born January 14, 1941, in Farmington, W.Va.; son of Charles Edward (an insurance salesman) and Amy (Flynn) Robinson; married Peggy Jean Kemno, August 24, 1963; children: Clare, John. *Education:* Mount St. Mary's College, Emmitsburg, Md., A.B. (summa cum laude), 1962; Temple University, Ph.D., 1967. *Religion:* Roman Catholic. *Residence:* Newark, Del. *Office:* Department of English, University of Delaware, Newark, Del. 19711.

CAREER: University of Delaware, Newark, instructor, 1965-67, assistant professor, 1967-73, associate professor of English, 1973—. Guest professor at University of Essen, 1972. Trustee of Thomas More Oratory. *Member:* Modern Language Association of America (member of executive committee, 1970-74), Anglo-American Associates, Keats-Shelley Association, Byron Society (member of American board of directors, 1976-81; treasurer of International Byron Council, 1976-79), Phi Kappa Phi. *Awards, honors:* American Council of Learned Societies grant, 1972.

WRITINGS: Shelley and Byron: The Snake and Eagle Wreathed in Fight, Johns Hopkins Press, 1976; (editor and author of introduction) *Mary Shelley: Collected Tales and Stories, with Original Engravings,* Johns Hopkins Press, 1976. Contributor to literature and language journals.

WORK IN PROGRESS: Research for a literary biography of Charles Ollier, nineteenth-century publisher, writer, and editor; research on English Romantic writers, especially Percy Shelley, Mary Shelley, and Leigh Hunt.

* * *

ROBINSON, Derek   1932-
(Dirk Robson)

PERSONAL: Born April 12, 1932, in Bristol, England; son of Alexander (a policeman) and Margaret (MacAskill) Robinson; married Sheila Collins, April 29, 1968. *Education:* Downing College, Cambridge, B.A., 1956, M.A., 1958. *Politics:* "Left of centre, drifting slowly right." *Religion:* None. *Residence:* Bristol, England. *Agent:* John Farquharson Ltd., Bell House, Bell Yard, London WC2A 2JU, England.

CAREER: McCann-Erickson Advertising, London, England, copywriter, 1956-60; BBDO Advertising, New York, N.Y., copywriter, 1960-66; writer, 1966—. *Military service:* Royal Air Force, 1951-53. *Member:* Society of Authors, Writers' Guild of Great Britain, Authors Guild, Oxford and Cambridge Club.

WRITINGS: Rugby: Success Starts Here, Pelham Books, 1969; *Goshawk Squadron* (novel), Viking, 1971; *Rotten With Honor* (novel), Viking, 1973; *A Shocking History of Bristol,* Abson Books, 1973; *Kramer's War* (novel), Viking, 1977.

Under pseudonym Dirk Robson; all published by Abson: *Krek Waiter's Peak Bristle,* 1970; *Son of Bristle,* 1971; *Bristle Rides Again,* 1972; *Sick Sundered Yers of Bristle,* 1974.

Author of radio and television scripts for British Broadcasting Corp. Honorary editorial adviser to Rugby Football Union, 1966-76.

WORK IN PROGRESS: Get Squash Straight, nonfiction; a novel about World War II intelligence operations, mainly in Spain and Portugal.

SIDELIGHTS: Robinson writes: "I did not set out to be a 'war' novelist, but somehow the problem of violence, of man's appetite for war, seems to arise again and again. All three novels have been about attitudes to war—the phony glamour of the World War I air war, the confused logic of the Cold War, the ambivalence of an English island occupied by the Nazis. They are all political in the sense that I deliberately set out to make the reader re-assess his opinions. Other than that they are just meant to be good stories, with action, conflict, and humour. Especially humour, which I consider to be the acid test of any novel.

"The 'Bristle' books are a series of small, cheap, funny books written in the dialect of Bristol, inspired by the 'Strine' books from Australia. They sell steadily."

*   *   *

ROBINSON, Patricia Colbert 1923-
(Margaret Duval, Daria Macomber)

PERSONAL: Born November 4, 1923, in Pittsburgh, Pa.; daughter of Charles Francis II (an industrialist) and Marie (a painter; maiden name, Benton) Colbert; married Emmett Robinson (a professor of fine arts and theater director), June 30, 1950; children: Jennet Colbert Robinson-Greene, Alix Patricia. *Education:* Attended Trinity College, 1941-42; Cornell University, B.A., 1945. *Religion:* Episcopalian. *Home:* 76 Ashley Ave., Charleston, S.C. 29401. *Agent:* Curtis Brown Ltd., 60 East 56th St., New York, N.Y. 10022.

CAREER: Writer.

WRITINGS: (With Nancy Stevenson; under pseudonym Daria Macomber) *Return to Octavia,* New American Library, 1964; (with Stevenson; under pseudonym Macomber) *A Clearing in the Fog,* World Publishing, 1970; (with Stevenson; under pseudonym Margaret Duval) *Savage Summer,* Dell, 1976.

Three-act plays; all produced in Charleston, S.C., at Dock Street Theatre: "Syllabub," "Hiddydoddy," "Jubalee," "Rare Fine Towne," "The Burning Tide," and "The Rackleigh Rebels."

*   *   *

ROBINSON, Ray(mond Kenneth) 1920-

PERSONAL: Born December 4, 1920, in New York, N.Y.; son of Louis H. (a lawyer) and Lillian (Hoffman) Robinson; married Phyllis Cumins (a writer), September 18, 1949; children: Nancy, Stephen, Tad. *Education:* Columbia University, B.A., 1941, further study, 1941-42. *Home:* 530 East 90th St., New York, N.Y. 10028. *Agent:* Sterling Lord Agency, Inc., 660 Madison Ave., New York, N.Y. 10028. *Office:* *Seventeen* magazine, 850 Third Ave., New York, N.Y. 10022.

CAREER: Real, New York City, editor, 1955-57; *Pageant,* New York City, managing editor, 1957-59; *Coronet,* New York City, senior editor, 1959-61; *Good Housekeeping,* New York City, articles editor, 1961-69; *Seventeen* magazine, New York City, managing editor, 1969—. Instructor at New York University, 1977. *Military service:* U.S. Army, 1942-46. *Member:* American Society of Magazine Editors (executive committee).

WRITINGS: (With Constantine Callinicos) *The Mario Lanza Story,* Coward, 1960; (editor) *Baseball Stars, 1961,* Pyramid Books, 1961; *Ted Williams,* Putnam, 1962; *Stan Musial: Baseball's Durable Man,* Putnam, 1963; *Speed Kings of the Basepaths,* Putnam, 1964; *Greatest World Se-*

ries Thrillers, Random House, 1965; *Baseball's Most Colorful Managers,* Putnam, 1969; *The Greatest Yankees of Them All,* Putnam, 1969. Work represented in anthologies, including *Fireside Book of Baseball,* Simon & Schuster, 1956, *Second Fireside Book of Baseball,* Simon & Schuster, 1958; *Best Sports Stories of 1958,* Dutton, 1958, and *Best Short Stories of 1959,* Dutton, 1959.

*   *   *

ROBINSON, Rose

PERSONAL: Born in Chicago, Ill. *Education:* Earned B.A. from School of the Art Institute (Chicago, Ill.); also attended University of Chicago, DePaul University, Western Reserve University (now Case Western Reserve University), and University of Washington. *Office:* c/o Crown Publishers, Inc., 419 Park Ave. S., New York, New York 10016.

CAREER: Author.

WRITINGS: Eagle in the Air (novel), Crown, 1969. Contributor of articles to various periodicals.

*   *   *

ROBSON, Dirk
See ROBINSON, Derek

*   *   *

ROBY, Kinley E. 1929-

PERSONAL: Born August 2, 1929, in Westbrook, Me.; son of George and Margaret Roby; married Mary Linn (a writer and teacher); children: Linn Roby-Mueller, Kinley Christopher. *Education:* University of Maine, B.A., 1951, M.Ed., 1956; Pennsylvania State University, Ph.D., 1970. *Office:* Department of English, Northeastern University, Boston, Mass. 02115.

CAREER: Currently professor of English at Northeastern University, Boston, Mass.

WRITINGS: A Writer at War: Arnold Bennett, 1914-1918, Louisiana State University Press, 1972; *The King, the Press, and the People: A Study of Edward VII,* Barrie & Jenkins, 1975.

*   *   *

ROCKEFELLER, John Davison III 1906-1978

March 21, 1906—July 10, 1978; American philanthropist, patron of the arts, executive, and author. Rockefeller, named after his oil baron grandfather, was chairman, director, or trustee of numerous organizations, many of which are family interests. These included the Lincoln Center for the Performing Arts, the Rockefeller Foundation, and the Performing Arts Panel of Rockefeller Brothers Fund. Committed to the belief that the quality of life would improve with population control, he was appointed chairman of the U.S. Commission on Population Growth in the American Future by President Richard M. Nixon. In 1951, he served as a consultant to John Foster Dulles's peace mission to Japan, and was part of the American delegation that signed the peace treaty with that country. Rockefeller's collection of American and Asian art will be given to the Asia Society which he founded. He received many honors for his philanthropic work, including a Special Tony Award of the American Theatre Wing. He was author of *The Second American Revolution: Some Personal Observations,* a study of the division between today's youth and blacks, and the establishment. Rockefeller also wrote the foreword to *Protecting Our Children From Criminal Careers,* and articles for *Life* and *Rotarian.* He died in Westchester County, N.Y. Obituaries and other sources: *Current Biography,* Wilson, 1953; *The Biographical Encyclopaedia and Who's Who of American Theatre,* James Heineman, 1966; *Celebrity Register,* 3rd edition, Simon & Schuster, 1973; *New York Times,* July 11, 1978.

* * *

RODDICK, Alan (Melven) 1937-

PERSONAL: Born July 22, 1937, in Belfast, Northern Ireland; son of George (an accountant) and Margaret (a nurse; maiden name, Trotter) Roddick; married Patricia Woods (a librarian), February 21, 1959; children: Janet, Susannah, Helen, Matthew. *Education:* Attended Auckland University College, 1956; University of Otago, B.D.S., 1960. *Home:* 42 Albert St., Invercargill, New Zealand. *Office:* 79 Don St., Invercargill, New Zealand.

CAREER: Dentist in Invercargill, New Zealand, 1961—. *Member:* New Zealand Dental Association, P.E.N.

WRITINGS: The Eye Corrects (poetry), Blackwood & Janet Paul, 1967; (editor) Charles Brasch, *Home Gound* (poems), Caxton Press, 1975. Contributor of articles and reviews to New Zealand magazines. Editor of "Poetry," a monthly radio program for New Zealand Broadcasting Corp. Radio, 1968-69, 1973-74.

WORK IN PROGRESS: The Poetry of Allen Curnow; Collected Poems of Charles Brasch.

* * *

RODGERS, Joann Ellison 1941-
(Eve Scott)

PERSONAL: Born January 10, 1941, in Baltimore, Md.; daughter of Max Milton and Dorothy (Hirschhorn) Ellison; married George Greeley Rodgers (a journalist), September 15, 1963 (separated); children: Adam, Jared. *Education:* Boston University, B.S. (magna cum laude), 1962; Columbia University, M.S. (cum laude), 1964. *Religion:* Jewish. *Home:* 12104 Ridge Valley Dr., Owings Mills, Md. 21117. *Agent:* Elaine Markson Literary Agency, 44 Greenwich Ave., New York, N.Y. 10011. *Office: Baltimore News American,* Lombard and South St., Baltimore, Md. 21203.

CAREER/WRITINGS: Patriot Ledger, Quincy, Mass., reporter, 1960-63; *New York Herald Tribune,* New York City, stringer, 1963-64; *Baltimore News American,* Baltimore, Md., general assignment reporter, 1964-66, life science writer, 1966—; Hearst Newspapers, New York City, national medical writer, 1966—, author of syndicated column "Medical Beat," 1973—; *Mademoiselle,* New York City, health columnist, 1977—. Notable assignments include coverage of annual meetings of national medical organizations, and the Twelfth International Cancer Congress in Florence, Italy. Contributor to *Ladies Home Journal, Women's Day, Family Health, Saturday Review, New York Times Magazine, National Observer,* and *Cosmopolitan,* and to *Seventeen* under pseudonym Eve Scott. Stringer for *Medical World News.* Medical script consultant to Group W Station, Baltimore (WJZ-TV); panelist for "FACE to Fact," WMAR-TV, Baltimore

MEMBER: National Association of Science Writers (board member, 1972—), American Association for the Advancement of Science (sponsor of science writing fellow, 1977), Council for the Advancement of Science Writing (member of

board of directors, 1977—). *Awards, honors:* American Medical Association Journalism Award, 1965; Lasker Medical Journalism Award, 1965; Medical Journalism Award for Excellence from Maryland Optometric Association, 1974; American Heart Association National Science Writing Award, 1975; Claude Bernard Science Journalism Award, 1977; Cystic Fibrosis Foundation Science Writing Award, 1977; Multiple Sclerosis Society Award, 1977.

SIDELIGHTS: Joann Rodgers told *CA:* "The role of the science writer has evolved in the past 15 years from that of a hit-and-run interpreter of science and health to that of a trend-finder and surveyor of important science and public policy issues. Nevertheless, the demands of daily journalism and of magazine journalism require still attention to news. The task today is to flesh out the news with perspective to give readers enough information to sort out for themselves the science pertinent to their own lives and to society in general. Preventive medicine, with very few exceptions (immunizations, for example, or Pap smears), is still a twinkle in the eyes of public health specialists. There is still very little of a concrete nature that one can do to actually prevent the largest killers—heart disease, cancer, stroke—or the familial ailments that are epidemic—diabetes, some forms of arthritis—or mental disorders. Many of my articles report progress on the preventive front, but most often, they attempt to get across the message that science is a process, not a finite story."

* * *

RODNEY, Robert M(orris) 1911-

PERSONAL: Born August 21, 1911, in Gary, Ind.; married Isobel Kathleen Wilson, June 11, 1938; children: Robert Morris, Jr., Judith Louise. *Education:* Trinity College, Hartford, Conn., B.S., 1935; University of Michigan, M.A., 1936; University of Wisconsin, Madison, Ph.D., 1946. *Home:* 417 Silver Lane, Billings, Mont. 59102.

CAREER: Pennsylvania State College (now University), State College, instructor in English composition, 1936-38, 1940-42; Union College, Schenectady, N.Y., assistant professor of English, 1946-48; Northeast Missouri State College (now University), Kirksville, professor of English and head of language and literature division, 1948-56; Northern Illinois University, DeKalb, associate professor, 1956-60, professor of English, 1960-67; Eastern Montana College, Billings, professor of English and dean of liberal arts, 1967-76; writer, 1976—. *Military service:* U.S. Air Force Reserve, 1950-71; became major.

WRITINGS: (Editor with Minnie M. Brashear) *The Art, Humor, and Humanity of Mark Twain,* University of Oklahoma Press, 1959; (editor with Brashear) *The Birds and Beasts of Mark Twain,* University of Oklahoma Press, 1966; (with William R. Seat, Jr.) *Focus on Spelling,* Sernoll, 1967; (editor with Martin Kallich and Jack Gray) *A Book of the Sonnet: Poems and Criticism,* Twayne, 1973. Contributor to history and education journals.

WORK IN PROGRESS: Mark Twain Abroad: 1870-1970; American Writers Abroad.

SIDELIGHTS: Rodney writes: "Other than training, teaching, and scholarship attendant on a forty-year college teaching career, my interests have focused on the vital part that a long succession of American 'literary ambassadors' have played in Anglo-American and European-American political and cultural relations, with emphasis on Mark Twain. Research into the matter has taken me twice to England and twice to the Continent and through a dozen major

American libraries. The results are offered as a reminder that Americans have an important literary as well as political and economic legacy of past achievements in world affairs."

* * *

ROGERS, Linda (Hall) 1944-

PERSONAL: Born October 10, 1944, in Port Alice, British Columbia; daughter of Ormande James (a lawyer) and Patricia (a theatrical producer; maiden name, Wilgress) Hall; married Ian Rogers (a farmer), June 11, 1966; children: Sasha, Keefer, Tristan. *Education:* University of British Columbia, B.A., 1966, M.A., 1970. *Politics:* "Liberal/socialist or vice versa." *Religion:* Anglican. *Home address:* R.R. 1, Chemainus, British Columbia, Canada V0R 1K0.

CAREER: Writer, 1972—. Public relations chairwoman for Vancouver Status of Women Coordinating Council, 1971-73. *Awards, honors:* Canada Council scholarship, 1961.

WRITINGS—Poetry: *Music for a Human Silence*, Anak, 1972; *Funeral of Hours*, Fiddlehead, 1972; *Music for Moondance*, Fiddlehead, 1974; *Some Breath*, Fiddlehead, 1976; *This Is a List*, Fiddlehead, 1977. Contributor of articles and reviews to *Canadian Literature* and *Books in Canada*.

WORK IN PROGRESS: Queens of the Next Hot Star (tentative title), a self-illustrated book about Maggie Jack, an old Indian woman.

SIDELIGHTS: Linda Rogers writes: "I am a farmer and a mother, occupations which obviously affect my view of the world and explain my preoccupation with regeneration, the harmony of landscape and people who live and die in it. My poetry is lyrical and quite spare. I think the image is sufficient as objective correlative and do not care much for overt didacticism. I live in a beautiful house on a beautiful farm and grow beautiful food and children and have great enthusiasm for the well-made and lovely. I study music and art and have a great love for and interest in the life and culture of the native people who live near us. I am very lucky but not, I hope, insensitive to the inequities of this world. My favorite writer is Lady Murasaki."

AVOCATIONAL INTERESTS: Gardening, spinning wool, playing the piano, baking bread.

* * *

ROGERS, W(illiam) G(arland) 1896-1978

February 29, 1896—March 1, 1978; American literary, music, and art editor of the Associated Press, which he joined as a reporter in 1943. Rogers also reviewed books for the *New York Times, Saturday Review, New York Herald Tribune,* and *New York Post.* He was the author of a dozen books, including *When This You See, Remember Me: Gertrude Stein in Person* and *Wise Men Fish Here: The Story of Frances Steloff.* He died in Altoona, Pa. Obituaries and other sources: *Authors of Books for Young People,* 2nd edition, Scarecrow, 1971; *The Writer's Directory, 1976-78,* St. Martin's, 1976; *New York Times,* March 2, 1978; *AB Bookman's Weekly,* May 8, 1978. (See index for *CA* sketch)

* * *

ROGERS, Warren (Joseph, Jr.) 1922-

PERSONAL: Born May 6, 1922, in New Orleans, La.; son of Warren Joseph and Rose Agatha (Tennyson) Rogers; married Hilda Kenny, December 23, 1943 (deceased); married Alla Bilajiw, December 26, 1973; children: (first mar-

riage) Patricia Ann, Sean. *Education:* Attended Tulane University, 1940-41, and Louisiana State University, 1951. *Home:* 1622 30th St. N.W., Washington, D.C. 20007. *Office:* 1619 Massachusetts Ave. N.W., Washington, D.C. 20036.

CAREER: New Orleans Tribune, New Orleans, La., began as copy boy, became cub reporter, 1939-41; *New Orleans Item,* New Orleans, La., copyreader and author of column "A. Labas," 1945-47; Associated Press, New York City, reporter in Baton Rouge, La., 1947-51, and Washington, D.C., 1951-53, diplomatic correspondent in Washington, 1953-59; *New York Herald Tribune,* New York City, military affairs correspondent with assignments abroad, 1959-63; Hearst Newspapers, Washington, D.C., chief Washington correspondent with foreign assignments, 1963-66; *Look,* New York City, Washington editor, 1966-69, chief of Washington Bureau, 1969-70; *Los Angeles Times,* Los Angeles, Calif., military foreign affairs correspondent attached to Washington Bureau, 1970-71; Chicago Tribune-New York News Syndicate, Washington, D.C., author of Washington column "Countdown," 1971-73; National Forest Products Association, Washington, D.C., vice-president in public affairs, 1973—. *Military service:* U.S. Marine Corps Reserve, active duty, 1941-45.

MEMBER: National Press Club (president, 1972), Federal City Club, Gridiron Club. *Awards, honors:* Best reporting from abroad citation from Overseas Press Club, 1963.

WRITINGS: The Floating Revolution, McGraw, 1962; *Outpost of Freedom,* McGraw, 1965.

* * *

ROJAN
See ROJANKOVSKY, Feodor Stephanovich

* * *

ROJANKOVSKY, Feodor Stepanovich 1891-1970 (Rojan)

PERSONAL: Born December 24, 1891, in Mitava, Russia; came to the United States in 1941; son of a school administrator; children: Tanya. *Education:* Attended Moscow Fine Arts Academy, 1912-14. *Residence:* Bronxville, N.Y.

CAREER: Began illustrating children's books during the Russian Revolution; art director of both a fashion magazine and a book publishing company, also stage decorator in Poland, beginning 1920; worked for an advertising agency, motion pictures studios, and several publishing firms in Paris, France, 1927-41; associated with the Artists and Writers Guild, New York City, 1941-51. *Military service:* Russian Imperial Army, infantry reserve officer, 1914-17. *Awards, honors:* Limited Edition Club's Silver Medal of the Silver Jubilee, 1953; Caldecott medal, 1956, for *Frog Went A-Courtin'* edited by John Langstaff; Art Directors Club Gold Medal.

WRITINGS—All self-illustrated: *The Great Big Animal Book,* Simon & Schuster, 1950; *The Great Big Wild Animal Book,* Simon & Schuster, 1951; *Animals in the Zoo,* Knopf, 1962; *Animals on the Farm,* Knopf, 1967; *F. Rojankovsky's ABC: An Alphabet of Many Things,* Golden Press, 1970.

Illustrator: Esther Holden Averill and Lila Stanley, editors, *Daniel Boone: Historic Adventures of an American Hunter among the Indians,* Domino Press (Paris), 1931; Averill, *Powder: The Story of a Colt, a Duchess and the Circus,* H. Smith & R. Haas, 1933; Rose Celli, *Les Petits et les Grands,* Flammarion (Paris), 1933, translation published as *Wild*

Animals and Their Little Ones, Artists & Writers Guild, 1935; Averill, *Flash: The Story of a Horse, a Coach-Dog and the Gypsies*, Faber, 1934; Averill, *The Voyages of Jacques Cartier*, Domino Press, 1937, published as *Cartier Sails the St. Lawrence*, Harper, 1956; Jean Mariotti, *Tales of Poindi* (translated from the French by Averill), Domino Press, 1938.

Hans Christian Andersen, *Old Man Is Always Right*, Harper, 1940; Algernon Blackwood, *Adventures of Dudley and Gilderoy*, edited by Marion B. Cothren, Dutton, 1941; *The Tall Book of Mother Goose*, Harper, 1942; Rudyard Kipling, *How the Camel Got His Hump*, Garden City Publishing, 1942; Kipling, *How the Leopard Got His Spots*, Garden City Publishing, 1942; Kipling, *How the Rhinoceros Got His Skin*, Garden City Publishing, 1942; Kipling, *The Elephant's Child*, Garden City Publishing, 1942; Hazel Lockwood, *Golden Book of Birds*, Simon & Schuster, 1943; *Tall Book of Nursery Tales*, Harper, 1944; Georges Duplaix, *Animal Stories*, Simon & Schuster, 1944, published as *Animal Tales*, Golden Press, 1971; *Pictures from Mother Goose*, Simon & Schuster, 1945; Andersen, *Ugly Duckling*, Grosset, 1945.

Bible, *Golden Bible: From the King James Version of the Old Testament*, edited by Jane Werner Watson, Simon & Schuster, 1946, published as *The Golden Bible: Stories From the Old Testament*, Golden Press, 1966; Kipling, *Butterfly That Stamped*, Garden City Publishing, 1947; Kipling, *The Cat That Walked by Himself*, Garden City Publishing, 1947; Covelle Newcomb, *Cortez: The Conqueror*, Random House, 1947; *The Three Bears*, Simon & Schuster, 1948, new edition edited by Kathleen N. Daly, Golden Press, 1967; G. Duplaix, *Gaston and Josephine*, Simon & Schuster, 1948; Kathryn and Byron Jackson, *Big Farmer Big*, Simon & Schuster, 1948; Phyllis McGinley, *A Name for Kitty*, Simon & Schuster, 1948; Elsa Ruth Nast, *Our Puppy*, Simon & Schuster, 1948; *Favorite Fairy Tales*, Simon & Schuster, 1949; K. Jackson and B. Jackson, *The Big Elephant*, Simon & Schuster, 1949, reprinted, Western Publishing, 1974.

Mikhail Mikhailovich Prishvin, *Treasure Trove of the Sun* (translated from the Russian by Tatiana Balkoff-Drowne), Viking, 1952; Claire Huchet Bishop, *All Alone*, Viking, 1953; Elizabeth Jane Coatsworth, *Giant Golden Book of Cat Stories*, Simon & Schuster, 1953; Coatsworth, *Giant Golden Book of Dog Stories*, Simon & Schuster, 1953; Nicholas Kalashnikoff, *My Friend Yakub*, Scribner, 1953; Florence Esther Tchaika, *Trouble at Beaver Dam*, Messner, 1953; Coatsworth and Kate Barnes, *Horse Stories*, Simon & Schuster, 1954; Dorothy Clarke Koch, *I Play at the Beach*, Holiday House, 1955; John Langstaff, editor, *Frog Went A-Courtin'*, Harcourt, 1955.

Felix Riesenberg, *Balboa: Swordsman and Conquistador*, Random House, 1956; Langstaff, *Over in the Meadow*, Harcourt, 1957; Jane Thayer, *The Outside Cat*, Morrow, 1957; *More Mother Goose Rhymes*, Simon & Schuster, 1958; Kathleen Daly, *Wild Animal Babies*, Western Publishing, 1958; Jean Fritz, *The Cabin Faced West*, Coward, 1958; Bible, *Catholic Child's Bible*, edited by J. W. Watson and Charles Hartman, Simon & Schuster, 1958; Ann Rand, *Little River*, Harcourt, 1959.

Daniel Defoe, *Robinson Crusoe*, edited by Anne-Terry White, Golden Press, 1960; Bible, *Holy Bible*, edited by Watson and Hartman, Guild Press, 1960; Carl Memling, *Ten Little Animals*, Golden Press, 1961; Dimitry Varley, *The Whirly Bird*, Knopf, 1961; Rand, *So Small*, Harcourt,

1962; *The Dog and Cat Book*, Golden Pleasure, 1963; Aileen Lucia Fisher, *A Cricket in a Thicket*, Scribner, 1963; Jeanette Krinsley, *The Cow Went over the Mountain*, Western Publishing, 1963; C. Memling, *I Can Count*, Golden Press, 1963; (illustrator with others) *The Tall Book of Let's Pretend*, E. Ward, 1964.

Marie Colmont, *Christmas Bear* (translated by Constance Hirsch), Golden Press, 1966; John Graham, *A Crowd of Cows*, Harcourt, 1968; Guy Daniels, editor and translator, *The Falcon Under the Hat: Russian Merry Tales and Fairy Tales*, Funk, 1969; Carol E. Lester, *To Make a Duck Happy*, Harper, 1969; Nina Rojankovsky, editor, *Rojankovsky's Wonderful Picture Book: An Anthology*, Golden Press, 1972; Bill Hall, *A Year in the Forest*, McGraw, 1975.

Under pseudonym Rojan: Lida, *Panache l'ecureuil*, Flammarion (Paris), 1934, translation by G. Duplaix published as *Pompom, the Little Red Squirrel*, Harper, 1936; Lida, *Froux, le lievre*, Flammarion, 1935, translation by G. Duplaix published as *Fluff, the Little Wild Rabbit*, Harper, 1937; Lida, *Plouf, Canard Sauvage*, Flammarion, 1935, translation by G. Duplaix published as *Plouf, the Little Wild Duck*, Harper, 1936, reprinted, Golden Press, 1966; Lida, *Bruin, the Brown Bear* (translated from the French by Lily Duplaix), Harper, 1937, reprinted, Golden Press, 1966; Lida, *Scuff, the Seal* (translated from the French by L. Duplaix), Harper, 1937, reprinted, Golden Press, 1966; Y. Lacote, *Children's Year* (adapted from the French by Margaret Wise Brown), Harper, 1937; Lida, *Spiky, the Hedgehog* (translated from the French by L. Duplaix), Harper, 1938, reissued, Golden Press, 1966; Lida, *The Kingfisher* (translated from the French by L. Duplaix), Harper, 1940; Lida, *Cuckoo* (translated from the French by L. Duplaix), Harper, 1942.

SIDELIGHTS: "I became an illustrator of children's books. I did it because I was an artist and loved nature and loved children," Rojankovsky explained in his Caldecott medal acceptance paper. The author-illustrator's decision to become an artist however, was influenced by several factors and events. As a child, Rojankovsky visited a small zoo with his father. This excursion introduced the budding illustrator to the world of bears, tigers, monkeys, and other wild animals. Rojankovsky's fascination for the animals inspired him to recreate his vision of the zoo creatures with color crayons and paper, and would later play a central role in several of his picture books.

The author-illustrator was also influenced by the numerous books in his father's library. The drawings in the *Bible* and John Milton's *Paradise Lost* (both illustrated by the French artist, Gustave Doré) occupied a good deal of young Rojankovsky's time and helped in guiding him toward an art career. The outbreak of World War I disrupted Rojankovsky's studies at the Moscow Fine Arts Academy, but it did not deter the young artist from painting and drawing. Although Rojankovsky was wounded while serving with the Russian Army, he continued to paint war subjects while recuperating from his injuries. These sketches became the artist's first published work, and eventually led to his profession of book illustrator.

BIOGRAPHICAL/CRITICAL SOURCES: New York Times, November 15, 1942; *San Francisco Chronicle*, May 13, 1962; Lee Bennett Hopkins, *Books Are by People*, Citation Press, 1969; *Publishers Weekly*, June 29, 1970; *Bulletin of the Center for Children's Books*, September, 1970.

OBITUARIES: New York Times, October 13, 1970; *Publishers Weekly*, November 9, 1970.*

(Died October 12, 1970)

ROJKO, Anthony J.   1918(?)-1978

1918(?)—June 27, 1978; American economist and author. Rojko headed the commodities program area of the U.S. Department of Agriculture, where he was an authority in projecting future worldwide food resources and needs. He is author of several books on the subject of agriculture economics. Rojko died in Washington, D.C. Obituaries and other sources: *Washington Post,* June 30, 1978.

*   *   *

ROKEBY-THOMAS, Anna E(lma)   1911-

PERSONAL: Born May 10, 1911, in Crieff, Ontario, Canada; daughter of Frederick Edwin (a farmer) and Jane Ann (McAninch) Roszell; married Howard R. Rokeby-Thomas (an Anglican minister), August 10, 1936; children: Emily Ann Nairne (Mrs. J. William McLean), David Earnest Roszell, Derwyn Evan Howard. *Education:* Guelph General Hospital School of Nursing, diploma, 1934; also attended Anglican Womens' College, 1935-36. *Religion:* Anglican Church of Canada. *Home:* 74 Jackson Ave., Kitchener, Ontario, Canada N2H 3P1.

CAREER: Victorian Order of Nurses, Guelph, Ontario, nurse, 1934-35; nurse in Canadian Arctic, 1936-39; writer, 1939—; St. Thomas-Elgin General Hospital, St. Thomas, Ontario, nurse, 1952-60; Toronto General Hospital, Toronto, Ontario, nurse, 1960-65.

WRITINGS—For children: *Ningiyuk's Igloo World,* Moody, 1972; *Ning's Igloo Romance: A Sequel to Ningiyuk's Igloo World,* Moody, 1975. Contributor of articles and photographs of the Canadian Arctic to adult periodicals and stories to children's magazines, including *Jack & Jill, Young World,* and *Discovery.*

WORK IN PROGRESS: Short stories and books.

SIDELIGHTS: Anna Rokeby-Thomas writes: "I was born on a farm in the lovely Ontario countryside. Our family was a large one and there was always a lot of fun and laughter—as well as hard work.

"As far back as I can remember I had a tendency to daydream and before I was eight years old I was making up stories in my imagination.

"My troubles started as I grew older and began writing the stories down on paper. I had the best parents in the world, but they thought my writings were utter foolishness and would get me nowhere. In spite of the fact that I excelled in school compositions they discouraged every writing attempt. Consequently, I did a lot of writing in hidden corners.

"A nursing career was approved for me and I went in training with my younger sister. My writing dreams lay dormant during those years. After my marriage, the ambition and desire to write flared up. I took night classes in writing and soon had the thrill of seeing both stories and articles in print.

"I was very fortunate to have a unique background to write about. We lived for some years among the primitive Eskimos and I made a vow then that I would write a book about an Eskimo girl and tell my readers what it is really like to live in an igloo. I have been able to do this. The story reads like one of my persistent dreams in a world of fantasy, but the background *is* authentic."

AVOCATIONAL INTERESTS: Travel (Great Britain, Europe, and North America) and gardening.

*   *   *

ROLAND, Mary
See LEWIS, Mary (Christianna Milne)

ROLLAND, Barbara J(une)   1929-

PERSONAL: Born June 4, 1929, in Chippewa Falls, Wis.; daughter of Joel J. (a mechanic) and Mildred (a teacher; maiden name, Kelly) Nystrom; married Guy W. Long, 1951 (divorced, 1964); married Alvin E. Rolland (a teacher), October 31, 1965; children: (first marriage) John J., Cynthia Long Jackson. *Education:* University of Wisconsin, Eau Claire, B.A., 1960; University of Wisconsin, Madison, M.A., 1963; further graduate study at Institut de Phonetique, 1964. *Home address:* Route 5, Box 296, Chippewa Falls, Wis. 54729. *Office:* Department of Foreign Languages, University of Wisconsin, HHH352, Eau Claire, Wis. 54701.

CAREER: University of Wisconsin, Eau Claire, instructor, 1963-78, assistant professor of French, 1960—. Consultant of English as a second language for State of Wisconsin, 1976—; director of English for non-English-speaking students in public schools of Eau Claire, 1975—. *Member:* American Association of Teachers of French, National Association for Foreign Student Affairs, Teachers of English to Speakers of Other Languages, Wisconsin Association of Foreign Language Teachers, Pi Delta Phi (sponsor), Phi Kappa Phi.

WRITINGS: (With Edith O'Connor and Martine Meyer) *Le Francais: Langue et Culture* (title means "French: Language and Culture"), Van Nostrand, 1974, revised edition, in press; (contributor) Frank Grittner, editor, *Careers, Communication, and Culture,* National Textbook Co., 1974.

Author of "International Employment and You," an audio-visual presentation.

WORK IN PROGRESS: Le Francais dan les affaires (title means "French in Business"); *English Composition for Foreign Students.*

SIDELIGHTS: Barbara Rolland writes: "All my books were written to fill what I thought was a gap—either because I could not find a book which I considered adequate for a particular course or because students had many unanswered questions which I considered important. I'm concerned about careers for foreign language students and the contribution which a liberal arts person can make to the professional fields. I'm concerned, too, that teaching materials be presented as fully but as simply and clearly and logically as possible."

*   *   *

ROSEN, R(ichard) D(ean)   1949-

PERSONAL: Born February 18, 1949, in Chicago, Ill.; son of Sol A. and Carolyn (Baskin) Rosen. *Education:* Attended Brown University, 1967-68; Harvard University, B.A., 1972. *Residence:* Cambridge, Mass. *Agent:* Erica Spellman, International Creative Management, 40 West 57th St., New York, N.Y. 10016.

CAREER: Playboy, Chicago, Ill., assistant editor, 1968-69; Peasant Stock Restaurant, Somerville, Mass., chef, 1971; *Boston Phoenix,* Boston, Mass., arts editor, 1972-77, author of columns "The Fat and the Lean," 1972-73, 1975-77, and "Printed Matters," 1974-75; Harvard University, Cambridge, Mass., teacher of expository writing, 1975-76; *Boston,* Boston, Mass., staff writer and author of column "Dining Out," 1977—.

WRITINGS: Me and My Friends, We No Longer Profess Any Graces: A Premature Memoir, Macmillan, 1971; *Psychobabble: Fast Talk and Quick Cure in the Era of Feeling,*

Atheneum, 1977. Contributor to magazines, including *New Times* and *New Republic.*

SIDELIGHTS: Rosen told *CA:* "*Me and My Friends, We No Longer Profess Any Graces: A Premature Memoir,* is a collection of personal essays embracing such subjects as adolescence ("The Metaphors of a Suburban Dilettante"), poetry ("Go Away Richard Brautigan, You're Not Helping College Poetry Anyway"), food ("Hot Sausage Links: An Allegory of American Politics"), and baseball ("The Story of Baseball").

"*Psychobabble,* also non-fiction, is a critique of what I call the Cult of Candor, and of the debasement of language and psychological thinking by various popular therapies and quick cures prominent in the 1970's.

"What both of my books have in common is the attempt to be as articulate as possible about the intersections of my own character and currents of popular culture."

* * *

ROSEN, S. McKee 1902(?)-1978

1902(?)—June 2, 1978; American educator, foreign aid specialist, and author whose most notable achievement was aiding in the development of the Marshall Plan following World War II. Rosen was chairman of the department of political science at Chicago's Central YMCA College for ten years before taking a position with the Bureau of the Budget in 1942. After retiring from the Agency for International Development, he taught at George Washington University's graduate school of business and public administration for eight years. He wrote or edited several books on topics in his field, and contributed many articles to professional journals. Rosen died in Washington, D.C. Obituaries and other sources: *Washington Post,* June 8, 1978.

* * *

ROSENBERG, Harold 1906-1978

February 2, 1906—July 11, 1978; American author, educator, and art critic who helped legitimize the school of abstract Impressionism by recognizing its place in art history as "action painting." Rosenberg held a variety of posts in his career, including national art editor of the "American Guide" series, lecturer at various universities, and professor at University of Chicago, before becoming art critic of the *New Yorker* in 1967. Previously limited to writing for smaller magazines, Rosenberg's *New Yorker* position gave his "supple essays, rich in the texture of paradox," a larger readership than ever before. In addition to books on art criticism, he also published poems, translations, and studies of artists Arshile Gorky, Barnett Newman, and Willem de Kooning. Rosenberg died in East Hampton, N.Y. Obituaries and other sources: *Who's Who in World Jewry,* Pitman, 1972; *Who's Who in American Art,* Bowker, 1973; *World Authors, 1950-1970,* Wilson, 1975; *Who's Who in America,* 39th edition, Marquis, 1976; *New York Times,* July 13, 1978; *Newsweek,* July 24, 1978; *Time,* July 24, 1978. (See index for *CA* sketch)

* * *

ROSENBLATT, Gary 1947-

PERSONAL: Born February 25, 1947, in Baltimore, Md.; son of Morris (a rabbi) and Esther (Friedlander) Rosenblatt; married Judith Turk (a teacher), June 15, 1969; children: Avi, Talia. *Education:* Yeshiva University, B.A., 1968; graduate study at City College of the City University of New York, 1968-70. *Religion:* Jewish. *Residence:* Baltimore, Md. *Office:* Baltimore Jewish Times, 2104 North Charles St., Baltimore, Md. 21218.

CAREER/WRITINGS: London Jewish Chronicle, London, England, assistant New York correspondent, 1969-70; *TV Guide* magazine, New York City, national programming sports editor, 1970-72; *New York Times,* New York City, free-lance writer, 1972; *Jewish Week-American Examiner,* New York City, assistant editor, 1972-74; *Baltimore Jewish Times,* Baltimore, Md., editor, 1974—. Contributor of articles to *National Observer, Moment, Jewish Digest,* and *National Jewish Monthly. Member:* Sigma Delta Chi. *Awards, honors:* Smolar Award for excellence in North American Jewish journalism, 1974 and 1977, for best news coverage.

SIDELIGHTS: Rosenblatt writes: "I write from the special vantage point of my job as editor of a Jewish weekly, as a person who, five years ago, was writing copy for *TV Guide* and who preferred, and chose—eyes open—the professional and personal satisfaction of being able to concentrate on analyzing the Middle East or exploring various aspects of Jewish community life. Jewish journalism is hardly an easy field to break into. There are few editorial positions, the salary does not compare to the secular press, there is no glamour and little recognition. But I chose it, and I do not ask for sympathy. It does have its rewards, not measurable in terms of wealth or prestige. Among those rewards is the daily exposure to the problems and promise of the American Jewish community—to its power structure, its paranoia, its potential and its priorities. And if, significantly, those priorities do not include a vital Fourth Estate, on a good day that can be seen as an exciting challenge. . . .

"How does one reconcile the ethic of journalistic honesty with the ethic of Jewish responsibility?" Rosenblatt wonders. He concludes that "it comes down to a sense of balance, a balance between truth and morale, between public discourse and communal responsibility, between serving the needs of the community as it perceives those needs and serving needs that may not be widely perceived, that may even be devalued." In the final analysis, it is the "sense of involvement with the destiny of a community" that leads Rosenblatt to view Jewish journalism as "more than a job," as, indeed, "a calling."

BIOGRAPHICAL/CRITICAL SOURCES: Moment, November, 1977.

* * *

ROSENTHAL, Edwin Stanley 1914-

PERSONAL: Born June 18, 1914, in Far Rockaway, N.Y.; son of Siegfried and Alpha Korn (Kastner) Rosenthal; married Hilda Thorpe (divorced); married Valerie Jean Day, July 26, 1965; children: Jack William. *Education:* Attended Yale University, 1932-33, and University of Arizona, 1933-35; University of Wisconsin, B.A., 1936. *Politics:* Democrat. *Religion:* Protestant. *Home address:* Springfield, Witnesham, Ipswich, England. *Office:* 114 Clifford's Inn, London E.C.4, England.

CAREER/WRITINGS: Buffalo Times, Buffalo, N.Y., reporter, 1936-37; *Houston Press,* Houston, Tex., assistant sports editor, 1938; *San Francisco Examiner,* San Francisco, Calif., world fair writer, 1939; *Mission Daily Times,* San Francisco, sports editor, 1940; *San Francisco Call-Bulletin,* San Francisco, sports make-up, 1940-42; United Press International, New York City, desk editor in London, 1946-49, foreign desk editor in New York City, 1950-51; Reuters

Ltd., London, England, feature editor, 1952-73. Notable assignments include coverage of Franklin Roosevelt's visit to Buffalo, N.Y., 1936, 1948 Olympics, Geneva Summit Conference, and Richard Nixon's visit to London, England, 1958. Reporter and editor for *Yank* magazine and *Stars and Stripes* during World War II. Member of East Anglian area Community Council and editor of their monthly newsletter and Christmas magazine. Chairman of Queen's Silver Jubilee Committee in East Anglian area. *Military service:* U.S. Army, 1942-46; became staff sergeant. *Member:* Overseas Press Club of America, Society of California Pioneers.

WORK IN PROGRESS: A history of James W. Marshall, the discoverer of gold; history of Hangtown (Placerville).

SIDELIGHTS: Rosenthal told *CA:* "I have always tried to be honest in my reporting and editing of the news. For forty years, I was employed by such huge media organizations as Scripps-Howard, Hearst, the U.S. Army, the United Press, and Reuters. Early in my news career, I learned that the news that is not printed may often be as important as the news that is 'fit' to print. The most vital issue today, in my opinion, is freedom to enjoy youth, marriage, children, and old age. Two forces compete on these major issues: Soviet Communism and Capitalism. I sincerely do not know which one will win. But Patrick Henry said all this long before I was born."

BIOGRAPHICAL/CRITICAL SOURCES: Margaret Parton, *Laughter on the Hill,* McGraw, 1945.

* * *

ROSS, H(ugh) Laurence   1934-

PERSONAL: Born May 12, 1934, in New York, N.Y.; son of Laurence (in business) and Ruth (a professor; maiden name, Buxbaum) Ross; married Judith Atkins (in business), May 31, 1965; children: Mark. *Education:* Swarthmore College, A.B. (honors), 1955; Harvard University, M.A., 1957, Ph.D., 1959. *Office:* Department of Sociology, State University of New York, Buffalo, N.Y. 14261.

CAREER: Northwestern University, Evanston, Ill., instructor in sociology and staff behavioral scientist at Traffic Institute, 1959-60; New York University, New York, N.Y., assistant professor, 1960-64, associate professor of sociology and anthropology and chairman of department, 1964-67; University of Denver, Denver, Colo., professor of sociology and law, 1967-78; State University of New York at Buffalo, professor of sociology, 1978—. Director of National Science Foundation program in law and social sciences, 1976-78. Fulbright lecturer at University of Louvain, 1969-70; visiting scholar of American Bar Foundation, 1972; distinguished visiting scholar at Oxford University's Centre for Socio-Legal Studies, 1976. Committee member and task force member of National Research Council's Highway Research Board; member of National Safety Council's committee on alcohol and drugs, 1972—. City councilman of Georgetown, Colo., 1975-76; police commissioner, 1975-76.

MEMBER: American Sociological Association, Society for the Study of Social Problems (member of board of directors, 1973-75), Law and Society Association (member of board of trustees, 1972-75, 1977-80), Society for the Preservation and Encouragement of Barber Shop Quartet Singing in America, Georgetown Historical Society (member of board of directors, 1971-76; vice-president, 1973-75). *Awards, honors:* Russell Sage Foundation resident at Center for the Study of Law and Society, University of California, 1963-64; research grants from Council on Law-Related Studies, 1971, and National Science Foundation, 1974-75; Metropolitan Life Award from National Safety Council, 1973.

WRITINGS: (Editor and contributor) *Perspectives on the Social Order,* McGraw, 1963, 3rd edition, 1973; (contributor) Stanton Wheeler, editor, *On Record: Files and Dossiers in American Life,* Russell Sage Foundation, 1969; (with Erwin O. Smigel) *Crimes Against Bureaucracy,* Van Nostrand, 1970; *Settled Out of Court: A Sociological Study of Insurance Claims Adjustment,* Aldine, 1970; (contributor) Freda Adler and G. O. W. Mueller, editors, *Politics, Crimes, and the International Scene,* North-South Center Press, 1972; (with Steven de Batselier) *Les Minorites Homosexuelles* (title means "Homosexual Minorities"), Editions Duculot, 1973; (contributor) Stephen Israelstam and Sylvia Lambert, editors, *Alcohol, Drugs, and Traffic Safety* (proceedings), Addiction Research Foundation of Ontario, 1975. Contributor of about thirty-five articles to professional journals. Associate editor of *Social Problems,* 1960-61; member of editorial board of *Journal of Law and Human Behavior,* 1975—.

WORK IN PROGRESS: "Continued studies of law in action: the outcomes of law as applied by bureaucracies and experienced by the general public."

SIDELIGHTS: Ross told *CA:* "The bulk of my work runs to the study of law in action as defined here, where existing literature is fairly well limited to consideration of the police. My interest extends to insurance adjusters, accountants, auditors, inspectors, and other bureaucrats. A further interest is in the deterrence question generalized, the abilities and limitations of law in affecting human behavior."

* * *

ROSS, Tony   1938-

PERSONAL: Born August 10, 1938, in London, England; son of Eric Turle Lee (a magician) and Effie Ross; married Carole Jean D'Arcy (divorced); children: Philippa, George, Alexandra. *Education:* Liverpool College of Art, diplomas, 1960, 1961. *Politics:* None. *Religion:* Methodist. *Home:* 5 Timber St., Macclesfield, Cheshire, England.

CAREER: Smith Kline & French Laboratories, graphic designer, 1962-64; Brunnings Advertising, art director, 1964-65; Manchester Polytechnic, Manchester, England, lecturer, 1965-72, senior lecturer in illustration, 1972—. Consultant in graphic design. *Member:* Society of Industrial Artists and Designers.

*WRITINGS—*All self-illustrated juveniles: *Tales from Mr. Toffy's Circus,* six volumes, W. J. Thurman, 1973; (editor) *Goldilocks and the Three Bears,* Andersen, 1976; *Hugo and the Man Who Stole Colors,* Follett, 1977; (editor) *The Pied Piper of Hamelin,* Andersen, 1977; *Hugo and the Wicked Winter,* Sidgwick & Jackson, 1977; *Norman and Flop Meet the Toy Bandit,* W. J. Thurman, 1977; (editor) *Little Red Riding Hood,* Andersen, 1978; *Hugo and Oddsock,* Andersen, 1978; (editor) *Mother Goose,* Andersen, 1979; *The Greedy Little Cobbler,* Andersen, 1979.

Illustrator: Iris Grender, *Did I Ever Tell You . . . ,* Hutchinson, 1977; Grender, *The Second Did I Ever Tell You,* Hutchinson, 1977. Contributor of cartoons to magazines, including *Punch* and *Town.*

WORK IN PROGRESS: Writing and illustrating *Jack and the Beanstalk* and *Dear Mole;* illustrating Jon Talbot's *The Most Unusual Computer,* to be published by Kaye & Ward; illustrating *Two Monkey Tales,* to be published by Longmans.

SIDELIGHTS: Ross writes: "As a small child in England during the war, I learned respect for children's things. Toys and books were scarce, therefore treasured. Christmas was the time for new books, and unwittingly, on the living room rug, I met Beatrix Potter, E. H. Shepard, Arthur Rackham, Edward Ardizzone, and surprisingly enough, Gustave Dore. Once I was given my grandfather's copy of *Don Quixote* illustrated by Dore. I do not remember liking the stern engravings, although I was impressed by them, and for the first time, I became aware of the illustrator's craft. I was eight years old.

"My training as an etcher, and my liking of graphic, rather than fine, artists, gave me a love of black line on white paper. My colours tend to be transparent inks and watercolours, laid lightly, not obscuring the line. To me, a children's illustrator is a creator of worlds for kids, and so I prefer to write my own texts. I like telling stories, I like to see children laugh, I like to draw."

AVOCATIONAL INTERESTS: Sailing small boats, cats, the monarchy, collecting toy soldiers, lamb cutlets.

BIOGRAPHICAL/CRITICAL SOURCES: Graphis 177.

*   *   *

ROSSITER, Margaret W(alsh)   1944-

PERSONAL: Born July 8, 1944, in Malden, Mass.; daughter of Charles Aston (a teacher) and Mary (a government employee; maiden name, Madden) Rossiter. *Education:* Radcliffe College, A.B. (cum laude), 1966; University of Wisconsin, Madison, M.S., 1967; Yale University, M.Phil., 1969, Ph.D., 1971. *Politics:* Democrat. *Home:* 2410 Oak St., Berkeley, Calif. 94708.

CAREER: University of California, Berkeley, acting assistant professor, 1973-74, lecturer in history, 1975-76, research associate in the history of science and technology, 1976—. Distinguished visiting lecturer at California State University, Sacramento, 1977. *Member:* History of Science Society (member of council, 1974-76), American Association for the Advancement of Science, American Historical Association, Society for History of Technology (member of board of editors, 1978-82), Agricultural History Society. *Awards, honors:* National Science Foundation fellow at Brown University, 1972-72; fellow of Harvard University's Charles Warren Center for Studies in American History, 1972-73.

WRITINGS: The Emergence of Agricultural Science: Justus Liebig and the Americans, Yale University Press, 1975; (contributor) Alexander Oleson and Sanborn C. Brown, editors, *The Pursuit of Knowledge in the Early American Republic,* Johns Hopkins Press, 1976; (contributor) Oleson, editor, *Knowledge in American Society,* Johns Hopkins Press, in press. Contributor to education and scientific journals, and to *New England Quarterly.*

WORK IN PROGRESS: A history of women scientists in the United States, 1830-1970.

SIDELIGHTS: Margaret Rossiter writes: "I have been interested in the history of science since high school, especially nineteenth- and twentieth-century history of biology, agriculture, chemistry, and women (I can't think of anything else I would rather read about). A summer job at the Smithsonian Institution in 1966 confirmed my interest, and I've been at it ever since."

AVOCATIONAL INTERESTS: Travel (Europe, the Soviet Union, the Far East).

*   *   *

ROSSMAN, Evelyn
See ROTHCHILD, Sylvia

ROSTEN, Norman   1914-

PERSONAL: Born January 1, 1914, in New York, N.Y.; married Hedda Rowinski (a psychologist and free-lance writer), 1940; children: Patricia. *Education:* Brooklyn College (now of the City University of New York), B.A., 1935; New York University, M.A., 1936; further graduate study at University of Michigan, 1937-38. *Home:* 84 Remsen St., Brooklyn, N.Y. 11201. *Agent:* Harold Ober, Inc., 40 East 49th St., New York, N.Y. 10017.

CAREER: Poet, playwright, and novelist. Employed by New York Federal Theatre, 1939-40; contributed special scripts to United Service Organizations, Council for Democracy, Writers War Board, Office of War Information, and Armed Forces Radio during World War II. *Member:* Writers Guild of America. *Awards, honors:* Avery Hopwood Award in poetry and drama from University of Michigan, 1938; Yale Series of Younger Poets Award, 1940, for *Return Again, Traveler;* Guggenheim fellowship, 1941-42; National Theatre Conference Award, 1942, for "This Proud Pilgrimage"; American Academy of Arts and Letters Award, 1945; Ford Foundation grant, 1965.

WRITINGS—All poetry, except as noted: *Return Again, Traveler,* Yale University Press, 1940; *The Fourth Decade and Other Poems,* Farrar & Rinehart, 1943; *The Big Road,* Rinehart, 1946; *Songs for Patricia,* Simon & Schuster, 1951; *The Plane and the Shadow,* Bookman, 1953; *Thrive Upon the Rock,* Trident, 1965; *Under the Boardwalk* (fiction), Prentice-Hall, 1968; *Over and Out* (fiction), Braziller, 1972; *Marilyn: An Untold Story* (nonfiction), New American Library, 1973.

Plays: "This Proud Pilgrimage," first produced in Ann Arbor, Mich., at University Theatre, January, 1938, produced Off-Broadway, 1942; "First Stop to Heaven," first produced on Broadway at Windsor Theatre, January 5, 1941; "Mardi Gras," first produced in Philadelphia at Walnut Street Theatre, January 11, 1954; *Mister Johnson* (based on novel by Joyce Cary; first produced on Broadway at Martin Beck Theatre, March 29, 1956), published in *Theatre '56,* Random House, 1956, published separately by Dramatists Play Service, 1969; *A View From the Bridge* (screenplay based on play by Arthur Miller), Continental Publishing, 1962; "The Golden Door," first produced Off-Broadway, 1966; *Come Slowly Eden: A Portrait of Emily Dickinson* (first produced Off-Broadway at Theatre de Lys, December 5, 1966), Dramatists Play Service, 1967.

Also author of radio verse plays for such series as "Cavalcade of America," "Treasury Star Parade," "Hello, Americans," and of documentary films for International Business Machines (IBM Corp.) and Western Electric. Work represented in anthologies, including *Treasury Star Parade,* 1942, *Radio's Best Plays,* 1947, *The Heart of Spain,* 1952, and *The New Yorker Book of Poems,* 1969. Contributor to periodicals, including *Antioch Review, Holiday, New York Times, Newsday,* and *Travel and Leisure.*

WORK IN PROGRESS: New and Selected Poems; a fiction work, *Dying in Miami.*

SIDELIGHTS: "I do not belong to that school which holds to the curious belief that poetry is written for poets and should be as difficult and obscure as possible. Poetry . . . should neither exhaust nor confuse, but invigorate and clarify." Although Rosten thus defined his aesthetic several decades ago—when critics were still describing him as a "young poet"—it is still possible to view his more complete opus in the light of these words. For Rosten has been nothing if not a poet of communication. He has written for a popular audience in the honorable tradition of such poets as Edwin Arlington Robinson, Robert Frost, and Carl Sandburg. Like his predecessors, Rosten avoided artificiality and egocentricity in his verse while stressing a colloquial expression of American reality. These qualities surfaced in such works as *The Big Road,* a book-length narrative poem about the Alcan Highway and the drama of road-building.

In keeping with his concern with the popularity of poetry, Rosten turned early in his career to radio as a medium for his words. During the 1940's he wrote poetic dramas for a variety of radio shows, including Orson Welles's "Hello, Americans," thus reaching a much larger audience than could ever be attained by poets who stick to the more conventional printed page. So impressive was Rosten's radio work during the early forties that in 1945 he was honored with an American Academy of Arts and Letters Award for his "exploration of the Radio as a new medium for poetry."

After a number of plays produced both on and off-Broadway, as well as after six volumes of poetry, Rosten abandoned drama for the novel. He explained the turn in his career in the *New York Times:* "The playwright is in eclipse because of the distrust of the Play. The distrust of the Play is, to my mind, related to the distrust of language—a distrust particularly evidenced by the young, and for good reason. They see the language of officialdom, of public discourse, government pronouncements and military communiques, so debased as to bring the entire purpose of communication into doubt.... A play represents a world governed by speech and action. If you don't trust the mechanism of language, you literally resist words."

To reach the popular audience, a writer must avoid such resistance, and in his two novels to date Rosten appears to have done so. When Ronald Sukenick reviewed *Under the Boardwalk,* he likened its author to both Mark Twain and Sherwood Anderson, thus placing Rosten in the American tradition of writing about ordinary people. Indeed, Sukenick explained that the book is "about the pain of petty existence engulfing people who are aware, however dimly, that their lives should be something better." Then he went on to call it "a gentle, human, funny, and beautifully written successor" to Anderson's stories.

Other critics had additional praise for *Under the Boardwalk.* Thomas Lask lauded its "honesty and solidity of detail" and Paul Kresh called it "a poet's novel ... simple, declarative and clean-carpentered." *Over and Out,* which appeared in 1972, was not as consistently appreciated, but it too earned positive reviews. Josephine Herdin wrote: "Wry and ridiculous, outlandish and obvious, *Over and Out* is an entertainment, a very sophisticated slapstick."

BIOGRAPHICAL/CRITICAL SOURCES: Thomas Yoseloff, editor, *Seven Poets in Search of an Answer,* B. Ackerman, 1944; *New York Times Book Review,* September 1, 1968, November 5, 1972; *Saturday Review,* November 2, 1968; *New York Times,* January 16, 1969, May 16, 1971.

*   *   *

ROSZAK, Theodore 1933-

PERSONAL: Born in 1933; son of Anton and Blanche Roszak; married wife, Betty; children: Kathryn. *Education:* University of California, Los Angeles, B.A., 1955; Princeton University, Ph.D., 1958. *Office:* Department of History, California State University, Hayward, Calif. 94542.

CAREER: Stanford University, Stanford, Calif., instructor in history, 1959-63; *Peace News,* London, England, editor,

1964-65; currently professor of history at California State University, Hayward. *Awards, honors:* Guggenheim fellowship, 1971-72.

WRITINGS: (Editor) *The Dissenting Academy,* Pantheon, 1968; *The Making of a Counter Culture: Reflections on the Technocratic Society and Its Youthful Opposition,* Doubleday, 1969; (editor with wife, Betty Roszak) *Masculine/Feminine: Readings in Sexual Mythology and the Liberation of Women,* Harper, 1969; (editor) *Sources: An Anthology of Contemporary Materials Useful for Preserving Personal Sanity While Braving the Great Technological Wilderness,* Harper, 1972; *Where the Wasteland Ends: Politics and Transcendence in Post-Industrial Society,* Doubleday, 1972; *Pontifex: A Revolutionary Entertainment for the Mind's Eye Theater,* Anchor Books, 1974; *Unfinished Animal: The Aquarian Frontier and the Evolution of Consciousness,* Harper, 1975; *Person/Planet,* Doubleday, 1978.

SIDELIGHTS: The upheaval of American culture by youthful dissidents during the 1960's spawned numerous critiques and interpretations by academics and lay observers alike. When Roszak's book, *The Making of a Counter Culture,* appeared in 1969, Robert Gross hailed it as "the best guide yet published to the meaning ... of youthful dissent not only in the U.S. but throughout the world's advanced industrial societies." Roszak analyzed the influence of such "intellectual gurus" as Herbert Marcuse, Paul Goodman, and Allan Ginsberg on the radical movement, adding a sympathetic but detached critique of its aims and accomplishments.

While critics commended Roszak's lucid portrayal and "imaginative understanding" of the formation of a counter culture, many found fault with his indictment of "objective consciousness" as the root of the evils of modern society. According to Kenneth Keniston, Roszak attacked the "'scientific' way of experiencing the world that involves a sharp separation between objective and subjective knowledge, an alienated detachment from other people, and the mechanization of knowledge and experience." But Keniston and other critics pointed out Roszak's imprecision in dealing with the nuances between technology, technocracy, and techniques. Robert Wolff contended that Roszak failed to distinguish between the methodology of science and the men, particularly the social scientists, who "confuse functional rationality with reason itself," and perpetuate the evils of depersonalization, economic exploitation, and political domination. Identifying the hatred of reason as "the greatest temptation of the fledgling intellect," Wolff concluded: "Despite the very great sophistication of his analysis, Roszak succumbs in the end to exactly the same sin of misology."

Graham Chedd interpreted Roszak's ideas differently, concluding that Roszak took issue not with science itself, but with the twentieth century view that "seeing the world through the eyes of science is the only way of looking at it." Refuting the view that Roszak was the "dark angel leading the evil forces of mindless irrationality," Chedd emphasized that Roszak called for a "synthesis between science and other modes of consciousness, which includes mystical traditions, aesthetic experiences, and many others."

While Henrietta Buckmaster was willing to accept Roszak's tendency "to join the young in throwing out technocratic achievement with the bathwater," acknowledging his determination to establish the dichotomy and demand a choice between "a better man or a better machine," other critics parted company with Roszak precisely at this point. Keniston observed: "[Roszak] fails to notice that the same counter culture that rejects careerism, materialism, and science is built upon, implicitly accepts and often caricatures much of the rest of American society. Specifically, the counter culture takes for granted the technology, the institutions and the economy necessary to provide its own material base." A *Times Literary Supplement* reviewer echoed these sentiments, protesting, "It is all very well to despise techniques, so long as one can remain confident that the necessary technical experts are manning their various stations and continuously devoting their energies, not to the attainment of cosmic consciousness but to the maintenance and improvement of their skills."

Most critics refused to become mesmerized by Roszak's "dithyrambic" prose in celebration of the shaman, subjectivity, and the symbiotic system of nature, finding his alternative to technocratic civilization inadequate if not thoroughly detrimental to the soundness of his work. Pointing out the anti-political character of a solution based upon "expanding consciousness," Keniston called for a synthesis which would incorporate both "visionary imagination" and "objective consciousness" into a world view that would deal concretely with social and political problems. Kingsley Widmer concurred with those who doubted the possibility of achieving political ends without political means, declaring, "The counter culture must really counter, offering something rather more specific and radical than a magical change in sensibility, or else, as we can sympathetically fear with Roszak, we shall sure go under to domination, despoilation, and destruction of any humane culture at all."

Where the Wasteland Ends led Owen Barfield to enter the arena in defense of Roszak's critique of technological society. Heralding the book's "merits as a literary and intellectual product," Barfield wrote: "In the second book [Roszak's] own 'countering' passes from strident protest into quiet, if emphatic, argument. It goes much deeper, inasmuch as its blows are aimed, not primarily at our 'power structures' etc. and our ruthlessly technological civilization themselves, but through them at the historical and metaphysical roots from which they spring. His quarry now is not modern life, whether plutocratic, bourgeois or proletarian, but the 'mindscape' it expresses." Barfield echoed Roszak's plea for a transformation of this 'mindscape' and the restoration of an "intercommunion between man and nature."

While earlier reviewers had criticized Roszak's emphasis on spiritual transformation as "apolitical," Richard Falk defended Roszak's views in his review of *Unfinished Animal,* declaring: "At bottom lies Roszak's belief that 'the medicine of the body politic must deal with us as whole persons, or its best intentions will go awry....' But at the same time Roszak is unsympathetic with those who deploy all their energies in the search for an inner transformation. He argues elaborately that the kind of cultural renewal he proposes implies that ethical concern for the well-being of others is given priority over the pursuit of personal salvation."

Roszak suggested that readers of *CA* refer to the introduction of his latest book, *Person/Planet,* for his response to many of the "hasty and prejudicial criticisms" he has received.

BIOGRAPHICAL/CRITICAL SOURCES: New York Times Book Review, September 7, 1969, November 30, 1975; *Newsweek,* September 15, 1969; *Village Voice,* October 30, 1969; *Life,* November 7, 1969; *Christian Science Monitor,* February 19, 1970; *Times Literary Supplement,* April 16, 1970; *New Scientist,* March 4, 1971; *Time,* September 11, 1972; *Saturday Review,* September 23, 1972; *Denver Quarterly,* Volume 9, spring/winter, 1974-75; *America,* November 29, 1975; *Nation,* September 4, 1976.

*   *   *

ROTH, Herrick S. 1916-

PERSONAL: Born March 19, 1916, in Omaha, Neb.; son of Joseph and Rhea (Smith) Roth; married Marjorie Land, April 25, 1941; children: Wayne, Alan, Martin. *Education:* University of Denver, A.B., M.A.; also attended University of California, Berkeley, 1939-40. *Politics:* Democrat. *Religion:* Presbyterian. *Home:* 2887 South Monroe, Denver, Colo. 80210. *Office:* H.S.R. Associates, Inc., 1665 Grant, Denver, Colo. 80223.

CAREER: Junior high school teacher in public schools in Denver, Colo., 1938-51; Colorado Federation of Teachers, Denver, executive secretary, 1951-61; Colorado Labor Council, Denver, president, 1962-73; University of Denver, Denver, adjunct professor of business administration, 1973-74; Colorado State Department of Labor, Denver, executive director, 1975; Lewis & Co., Englewood, Colo., director of program development, 1976-77; H.S.R. Associates, Inc., Denver, president and chief associate consultant, 1977—. Moderator of television series, "Herrick Roth's Roundup," for KBTV-TV, 1962—. Member of Colorado General Assembly, 1949-51, chairman of Senate and House of Representatives education committees, 1957-61. *Military service:* U.S. Army, Signal Corps, 1941-46; served in Pacific theater; became captain.

MEMBER: American Economic Association, Industrial Relations Research Association, American Federation of Teachers (national vice-president, 1952-57, 1962-72), Phi Delta Kappa, Lambda Chi Alpha, Omicron Delta Kappa.

WRITINGS: Labor: The Two-Faced Movement, Mason/Charter, 1975. Author of column in *Rocky Mountain Journal.* Contributor to education and labor journals.

SIDELIGHTS: Roth comments: "My one book was motivated by the Colorado American Federation of Labor-Congress of Industrial Organization's endorsement of George McGovern and our refusal to bow down to George Meany, who sent a trustee to take over our organization. We held a federal court order against Meany for fourteen months.

"I was also among the first members of the U.S. Army in Hiroshima in 1945. As a result I am convinced war is no alternative and the Vietnamese War was a disaster."

*   *   *

ROTH, Mark J(oseph) 1941-

PERSONAL: Born June 27, 1941, in New York, N.Y.; son of Sam (a salesman) and Rose (a bookkeeper; maiden name, Fried) Roth. *Education:* Harpur College, B.A., 1963; University of Wisconsin, Madison, M.A., 1964. *Home:* 782 Dearborn St., Teaneck, N.J. 07666.

CAREER: Kent State University, Kent, Ohio, instructor in English, 1964-70; writer.

WRITINGS: (With Sally Walters) *Bicycling Through England,* McKay, 1976. Contributor to *Christian Science Monitor, Bike World,* and *Beaver.*

WORK IN PROGRESS: A book on bicycling in Denmark.

SIDELIGHTS: Roth told *CA:* "I had visited Britian a couple of times before bicycling there. When I did bicycle I realized how little I had been aware of trees and birds and topography. The idea of the book is to encourage more people to use bicycling (and walking) as a means of coming in contact with another land and people.''

* * *

ROTH, Richard H(enry) 1949-

PERSONAL: Born April 27, 1949, in New York, N.Y.; son of Morton W. (a manufacturer) and Floren Levinson (Shivitz) Roth. *Education:* Union College, B.A., 1970; Columbia University, M.S., 1972. *Residence:* Washington, D.C. *Office:* CBS News, 2020 M St. N.W., Washington, D.C. 20036.

CAREER/WRITINGS: WROW-Radio, Albany, N.Y., reporter and anchorman, 1968-69; WTEN-TV, Albany, legislative correspondent, 1969-71; Columbia Broadcasting System (CBS) News, New York, N.Y., reporter and assignment editor, 1972-73, reporter in the Chicago bureau, 1973-74, bureau chief and correspondent in Moscow, 1974-76, Washington correspondent, 1976—. Notable assignments include coverage of Hurricane Agnes, the indictment and arraignment of John Mitchell and Maurice Stans, President Ford's Eastern European trip, 1975, the Soyuz and Apollo joint space mission, and an interview with Andrei Sakharov after he received his 1975 Nobel Peace Prize. *Awards, honors:* Associated Press Broadcasters award for best spot news coverage, 1970, for coverage of an Albany, N.Y., antiwar demonstration.

* * *

ROTHCHILD, Sylvia 1923-
(Evelyn Rossman)

PERSONAL: Born January 4, 1923, in New York, N.Y.; daughter of Samuel and Bertha (Neuberger) Rosner; married Seymour Rothchild (an executive), July 7, 1944; children: Alice, Judith, Joseph. *Education:* Attended Brooklyn College of the City University of New York. *Religion:* Jewish. *Home and office:* 19 Hilltop Rd., Brookline, Mass. 02167.

CAREER: Writer. Premier Crystal Laboratories, New York, N.Y., supervisor, 1942-45; Jewish Young Men's and Women's Association, Rochester, N.Y., director of adult activities, 1945-47; study group leader, 1947-72. Lecturer at colleges and universities, including Bryn Mawr College, Massachusetts Institute of Technology, Wheaton College, Boston University, and Radcliffe Institute. Director of Golden Age Club at Hecht House. Cellist with Newton and Boston civic orchestras. *Member:* Brookline Art Association, Copley Society. *Awards, honors:* Jewish Book Award, 1961, for *Keys to a Magic Door.*

WRITINGS: Keys to a Magic Door (biography of Peretz), Farrar, Straus, 1960; *Sunshine and Salt,* Simon & Schuster, 1964. Author of weekly column, ''Reviews and Reflections,'' in *Jewish Advocate,* 1962—. Contributor of articles and reviews, sometimes under pseudonym Evelyn Rossman, to magazines and newspapers, including *Boston Phoenix* and *Herald Traveler.*

WORK IN PROGRESS: A collection of short pieces about Vienna; short stories and a film script on Jerusalem.

SIDELIGHTS: Sylvia Rothchild writes: ''The Jewish experience in America has been an ongoing concern. Fiction and nonfictional pieces have focused on history, sociology or literature that provides perspective and information about the varieties of adjustments and transformations in individuals and communities.''

ROTHSTEIN, Samuel 1902(?)-1978

1902(?)—April 17, 1978; Polish-born rabbi, journalist, and Hebrew scholar who escaped to Palestine during the Nazi occupation in World War II. While still in Poland, Rothstein edited *Dos Yiddische Togblatt,* a daily newspaper. In 1947, he immigrated to New York City where he became a regular contributor to the *Jewish Morning Journal,* and wrote a daily column for the *Daily Forward.* He died in Brooklyn, N.Y. Obituaries and other sources: *New York Times,* April 19, 1978.

* * *

ROUTH, Porter W(roe) 1911-

PERSONAL: Surname is pronounced like ''Ruth''; born July 14, 1911, in Lockhart, Tex.; son of Eugene Coke (an editor) and Mary (Wroe) Routh; married Ruth Elizabeth Purtle, June 7, 1936; children: Charles, Elizabeth Ann, Dorothy, Susan, Lelia. *Education:* Oklahoma Baptist University, A.B. (honors), 1934; graduate study at Southern Baptist Theological Seminary, 1937-38, University of Missouri, 1938-39, and George Peabody College for Teachers, 1946. *Politics:* Independent. *Home:* 3426 Hampton Ave., Nashville, Tenn. 37215. *Office:* 460 James Robertson Parkway, Nashville, Tenn. 37219.

CAREER: Oklahoma Baptist Convention, Oklahoma City, secretary of brotherhood and promotion, 1942-43; *Baptist Messenger,* Oklahoma City, editor, 1943-45; Southern Baptist Convention, Nashville, Tenn., senior secretary, 1945-51, treasurer, 1951—, executive secretary-treasurer of executive committee, 1951—. Member of executive committee and general council of Baptist World Alliance; member of national council of Boy Scouts of America. Chairman of Tennessee governor's advisory committee on developmental disabilities. Has appeared on television and radio programs. *Member:* American Bible Society (member of board of managers). *Awards, honors:* LL.D. from Oklahoma Baptist University, 1952, and Georgetown University, 1978; D.D. from Wake Forest University, 1978.

WRITINGS: My World Too, Broadman, 1945; *Meet the Presidents,* Broadman, 1963; *Seventy-Seven Thousand Churches,* Broadman, 1963; *Chosen for Leadership,* Broadman, 1976; *Waiting in the Wings,* Broadman, 1978. Contributor to denominational periodicals. Editor of *Quarterly Review,* 1945-51.

AVOCATIONAL INTERESTS: International travel (including Iron Curtain countries); television talk shows.

* * *

ROUTTENBERG, Max Jonah 1909-

PERSONAL: Born March 22, 1909, in Montreal, Quebec, Canada; came to the United States in 1927, naturalized citizen, 1940; son of Harry David (a teacher) and Dora (Garmaise) Routtenberg; married Lilly Soloway (a writer), September 24, 1931; children: Ruth Routtenberg Seldin, Naomi Routtenberg Rotenberg (deceased), Aryeh. *Education:* Attended McGill University, 1925-27; New York University, B.Sc., 1930; Jewish Theological Seminary, M.H.L., 1932, D.H.L., 1949. *Politics:* Democrat. *Home:* 61 Maine Ave., Rockville Centre, N.Y. 11570.

CAREER: Rabbi of Jewish congregation in Reading, Pa., 1932-48; Rabbinical Assembly, New York City, executive vice-president, 1948-51; Jewish Theological Seminary, New York City, executive vice-president, 1951-54, visiting professor, 1954—; Temple B'Nai Sholom, Rockville Centre,

N.Y., rabbi, 1954-72; writer, 1972—. Lecturer at Institute of Social and Religious Studies. Director of Seminary College of Jewish Music and Cantors Institute; president of Rabbinical Assembly, 1964-66; member of American Jewish Committee and New York Board of Rabbis. *Military service:* U.S. Army, senior chaplain, 1942-45; served in England; became major. *Awards, honors:* D.D. from Jewish Theological Seminary, 1966; Sabato Morais Fellowship from Herbert Lehman Institute of Ethics, 1967.

WRITINGS: (Contributor) F. Ernest Johnson, editor, *Patterns of Ethics,* Harper, 1960; *Seedtime and Harvest* (essays and commentaries), Bloch Publishing, 1969; *Decades of Decision* (lectures and studies), Bloch Publishing, 1973; *One in a Minyan and Other Stories,* Ktav, 1977. Contributor of stories, articles, and reviews to religious magazines, including *Reconstructionist, National Jewish Monthly,* and *Commentary.*

WORK IN PROGRESS: Ethics of the Fathers, a critical commentary.

SIDELIGHTS: Routtenberg writes: "My credo is formulated in *Seedtime and Harvest* as follows: I believe that the single, most important quality of the human spirit is the quality of spiritual receptivity, the hospitality of heart and mind, which permits me to entertain new ideas, meet new people, expose myself to new experiences. It is a quality that enables me to feel at home in the whole wide world and to share with my fellow man the joy and privilege of helping establish God's kingdom here on earth.

"My major interest is the teaching of Judaism, using all the media available to me—the pulpit, the classroom, the lecture platform, the press, television, and the written word in books, magazines, etc. I have traveled extensively in Europe and Israel; I speak and write in English, Hebrew, and Yiddish."

*   *   *

ROVIN, Jeff 1951-

PERSONAL: Born November 5, 1951, in Brooklyn, N.Y.; son of Herman (an engineer) and Ada (a secretary; maiden name, Michaelson) Rovin; married Leslie Stevens, July 27, 1975; children: Michael Alexander. *Agent:* Jet Associates, 124 East 84th, Suite 4A, New York, N.Y. 10028.

CAREER: National Periodicals, New York, N.Y., magazine editor, 1972; Country Studios, Danbury, Conn., advertising copywriter, 1972-73; Warren Publishing Co., New York, N.Y., magazine editor, 1973-74; Seaboard Periodicals, New York City, magazine editor, 1974-75; free-lance writer, 1975—.

WRITINGS: A Pictorial History of Science Fiction Films, Lyle Stuart, 1975; *Hollywood Detective: Garrison* (detective novel), Manor Books, 1975; *The Hindenburg Disaster* (historical novel), Manor Books, 1975; *Hollywood Detective: The Wolf* (detective novel), Manor Books, 1975; *Of Mice and Mickey* (history of the Mickey Mouse Club), Manor Books, 1975; *The Fabulous Fantasy Films,* A. S. Barnes, 1977; *From Jules Verne to Star Trek* (on science fiction films), Drake, 1977; *The Films of Charlton Heston,* Lyle Stuart, 1977; *The Supernatural Movie Quizbook,* Drake, 1977; *The Great Television Series* (on "the doctors, lawyers, cowboys, policemen, and other heroes"), A. S. Barnes, 1977; *From the Land Beyond Beyond* (the films and lives of special effects men Ray Harryhausen and Willis O'Brien), Berkley, 1977; *Movie Special Effects,* A. S. Barnes, 1977; *Mars!* (on the fact and fantasy of Mars, includ-

ing astronomy, science fiction films, literature, rocket shots, and the future), Corwin, 1978; *The Book of Dinosaurs,* Berkley, 1978; *The UFO Movie Quizbook,* New American Library, 1978. Author of a science and media column in *Analog,* and of "Graveyard Examiner" in *Famous Monsters.*

WORK IN PROGRESS: Starship, a novel of political intrigue, 1985-2040; a science fiction novel, for Harcourt; a historical trilogy.

SIDELIGHTS: Rovin remarks: "Briefly, I love all forms of writing, which is why I have selected it as a career! I would add, however, that I try to be commercial first—and artistic only as far as commercial parameters allow. I find the two surprisingly compatible!"

BIOGRAPHICAL/CRITICAL SOURCES: People, October 17, 1977.

*   *   *

ROWE, David Knox

EDUCATION: Earned B.A. from Haverford College; earned M.Sc. from New York University; earned M.A. and Ph.D. from Columbia University; also attended New School for Social Research, Cornell University, and Southern Methodist University. *Office:* c/o American Management Association, Inc., 135 West 50th St., New York, N.Y. 10020.

CAREER: Has worked as a manager of Industrial Relations Division for Pfaudler-Permutit Co., Paramus, N.J., as a corporate director in personnel and labor relations for S. Klein Department Stores, New York City, as vice-president in personnel and labor relations for Southland Corp., Dallas, Tex., as assistant to the vice-president of industrial relations for General Dynamics Corp., New York City, as vice-president in industrial relations for Macke Co., Cheverly, Md., and as president of MPI & Associates, New York City. Lecturer at New York School of Industrial and Labor Relations, Cornell University and Southern Methodist University; professor at Maryland State College. Director of Towson State University's Institute of Management. Member of retail advisory council of C. W. Post College, Long Island University. Consultant to the mayors of New York City and Philadelphia.

MEMBER: American Society of Personnel Administration, American Society of Public Administration, American Society of Training Directors, Industrial Relations Research Institute, Society of Personnel Administration, Employee Relations Resources Institute (member of board of directors). *Awards, honors:* Award of merit from Institute of Applied Psychology.

WRITINGS: The Policies and Procedures of Executive Search, Executive Advertising Services, Inc., 1966; *The Sales Training Manual for Executive Search Consultants,* Executive Advertising Services, Inc., 1966; *Industrial Relations Management for Profit and Growth,* American Management Association, 1971; (contributor) *Personnel Management: Policies and Practices,* Prentice-Hall, 1971; *Employee Relations Programming for Company Managers,* E. H. Friend & Co., 1973. Also author of *The Management Productivity Index,* 1976; *The Management Efficiency Index,* 1976; *The Management Productivity Index,* in press. Contributor to *American Management Handbook.* Editor of many company newsletters.

*   *   *

ROY, G(eorge) Ross 1924-

PERSONAL: Born August 20, 1924, in Montreal, Quebec,

Canada; came to the United States in 1958; son of A. Carlyle (a horticulturist) and Georgina (Ross) Roy; married Lucie Jehl, December 21, 1954; children: Madeleine. *Education:* Sir George Williams University, B.A., 1950; University of Montreal, M.A., 1951, Ph.D., 1959; University of Strasbourg, diploma, 1954; Sorbonne, University of Paris, Doctorat d'Universite, 1958. *Home:* 4160 Eastwood Dr., Columbia, S.C. 29206. *Office:* Department of English, University of South Carolina, Columbia, S.C. 29208.

CAREER: Royal Military College, St. Jean, Quebec, lecturer in English, 1954-56; University of Alabama, University, assistant professor of English, 1958-61; University of Montreal, Montreal, Quebec, assistant professor, 1961-62, associate professor of English, 1962-63; Texas Tech University, Lubbock, professor of English and comparative literature, 1963-65; University of South Carolina, Columbia, professor of English and comparative literature, 1965—, chairman of comparative literature program, 1974—. Member of board of governors of Scottish-American Foundation, 1971—. *Military service:* Royal Canadian Air Force, flying officer, 1942-46.

MEMBER: International Comparative Literature Association, Modern Language Association of America, American Comparative Literature Association, Association for Scottish Literary Studies (vice-president, 1973—), Society of Antiquaries (fellow), South Atlantic Modern Language Association, Universities Committee on Scottish Literature (Scotland), Edinburgh Bibliographical Society.

WRITINGS: Twelve Modern French Canadian Poets, Ryerson, 1958; *Le sentiment de la nature dans la poesie canadienne anglaise* (title means "The Sentiment of Nature in English Canadian Poetry"), Nizet, 1961; *Robert Burns: An Exhibition,* University of Nevada Press, 1962; *Robert Burns,* Department of English, University of South Carolina, 1966; *Robert Burns: An Exhibition,* Northern Illinois University, 1972; (contributor) Donald A. Low, editor, *Critical Essays on Robert Burns,* Routledge & Kegan Paul, 1975; (editor of revision) *The Letters of Robert Burns,* two volumes, Clarendon Press, 1978. Editor of "Bibliographical Series," Department of English, University of South Carolina, 1966-75, and Scottish Poetry Reprints, 1970—. Contributor to *New Cambridge Bibliography of English Literature,* 1971, and to literature and Scottish studies journals. Founding editor of *Studies in Scottish Literature,* 1963—.

WORK IN PROGRESS: A computerized bibliography of Scottish poetry to 1900, publication expected in 1983.

SIDELIGHTS: Roy writes: "A major interest is Robert Burns, both editing and collecting editions of his works. I possess what is no doubt the largest privately-owned collection of Burns material in the world. This collection was started by my grandfather, W. Ormiston Roy of Montreal, to whom I owe my interest in Scottish literature. The collection contains one of only two known copies of the first edition of Burns's *Merry Muses of Caledonia* (1799)."

AVOCATIONAL INTERESTS: Philately, travel (Europe, Africa), gastronomy.

*   *   *

ROY, Joaquin 1943-

PERSONAL: Born July 9, 1943, in Barcelona, Spain; son of Joaquin and Asuncion (Cabrerizo) Roy; married Barbara Ann Lucas; children: Nuria Elizabeth, Alexander Miguel. *Education:* Colegio H. Maristas, B.Letras, 1960; University of Barcelona, lic. en derecho, 1966; Georgetown University,

M.S., 1970, Ph.D., 1973. *Home:* 443 Alcazar Ave., Coral Gables, Fla. 33134. *Office:* Department of Foreign Languages, University of Miami, Coral Gables, Fla. 33124.

CAREER: Instructor in Spanish at American high school in Barcelona, Spain, 1965-67, lecturer in Spanish history, 1966-67; high school Spanish teacher in Baltimore, Md., 1967-68; Georgetown University, Washington, D.C., visiting instructor in Spanish, summers, 1968-71; Johns Hopkins University, School of Advanced International Studies, Washington, D.C., instructor in Spanish, 1969, 1970-71; Emory University, Atlanta, Ga., instructor, 1971-73, assistant professor of Romance languages, 1973-76, director of Latin American studies, 1973-76; University of Miami, Coral Gables, Fla., assistant professor, 1976-77, associate professor of foreign languages and Latin American studies, 1977—.

MEMBER: Instituto Internacional de Literature Iberoamericana, American Council on the Teaching of Foreign Languages, American Association of Teachers of Spanish and Portuguese, Latin American Studies Association, Linguistic Society of America, Modern Language Association of America, South Atlantic Modern Language Association, South Eastern Conference on Latin American Studies, Southern Conference on Language Teaching (member of advisory council, 1972). *Awards, honors:* American Council of Learned Societies travel grant for Spain, 1975; Organization of American States fellowship for research in Argentina.

WRITINGS: Julio Cortazar ante su sociedad (title means "Julio Cortazar and Argentine Culture"), Peninsula, 1974; (editor and contributor) *Narrativa y critica de Nuestra America* (title means "Latin American Fiction and Criticism"), Castalia, 1976. Contributor of articles, translations, and reviews to Spanish studies journals and newspapers. Editorial assistant for Pan American Health Organization *Gaceta/Gazette,* 1970; contributing editor of *Urogallo,* 1974—.

WORK IN PROGRESS: Editing *Los Estados Unidos vistos en espanol* (title means "The United States as Seen by Spanish and Latin American Writers"), an anthology; *Iberoamerica: Entre la novela y el ensayo* (title means "Latin America: Between Novel and Essay"); research on Argentine poetry, Ortega and Argentina, the sociolinguistics of Catalan, teaching of literature, Galdos and Bunuel, March and Garcilaso, Espriu and Bartra, and Martinez Estrada and Argentine fiction.

SIDELIGHTS: Roy told *CA:* "All my writings have an interdisciplinary nature and try to explain different aspects of different culture. The United States has become a central topic of my recent research, as has the evolution of Latin American intellectual history."

*   *   *

RUBIN, David M. 1945-

PERSONAL: Born May 19, 1945, in Cleveland, Ohio; son of Arthur L. (a businessman) and Gertrude (Berkowitz) Rubin; married Christina Press (a journalist), August 22, 1971. *Education:* Columbia University, B.A. (cum laude), 1967; Stanford University, M.A., 1968, Ph.D., 1972. *Residence:* New York, N.Y. *Office:* Department of Journalism, New York University, 1021 Main Building, New York, N.Y. 10003.

CAREER: New York University, New York, N.Y., associate professor of journalism, 1971—, chairman of department. Faculty member of Manhattanville College, 1974—;

Stanford University, summer, 1975. Sports director and business manager of WKCR-FM Radio, 1965-67; football commentator for WFAS-AM Radio, 1973. *Member:* Association for Education in Journalism, American Civil Liberties Union, Kappa Tau Alpha.

WRITINGS: (With William L. Rivers) *A Region's Press: Anatomy of Newspapers in the San Francisco Bay Area,* Institute of Governmental Studies, 1971; *Independent Teenager* (edited by Peter M. Sandman), Macmillan, 1971; (with Sandman and David B. Sachsman) *Media: An Introductory Analysis of American Mass Communications,* Prentice-Hall, 1972, 2nd edition, 1976; (editor with Sandman and Sachsman) *Media Casebook: An Introductory Reader in American Mass Communications,* Prentice-Hall, 1972; *The Media: Press, Radio, and Television in a Free Society,* American Education Publications, 1972; (with David Peter Sachs) *Mass Media and the Environment: Water Resources, Land Use, and Atomic Energy in California,* Praeger, 1973; (contributor) John Cairns, Jr. and Kenneth L. Dickson, editors, *The Environment: Costs, Action, Conflicts,* Dekker, 1974. Contributor to academic and literary magazines and newspapers. Associate editor of *More,* 1975—; reviewer for *Quill,* 1973—.

* * *

RUBIN, William 1927-

PERSONAL: Born August 11, 1927, in New York, N.Y. *Education:* Columbia University, A.B., 1949, M.A., 1952, Ph.D., 1959; also attended University of Paris. *Home:* 425 East 58th St., New York, N.Y. 10021; and Plan de la Tour, Paris, France. *Office:* Department of Painting and Sculpture, Museum of Modern Art, 11 West 53rd St., New York, N.Y. 10019.

CAREER: Sarah Lawrence College, Bronxville, N.Y., professor of art history, 1952-67; Museum of Modern Art, New York, N.Y., chief curator of painting and sculpture, 1968—, director of department, 1973—. Professor at City University of New York, 1960-67; adjunct professor at Hunter College of the City University of New York, 1954-64, and New York University, 1969—; lecturer at Columbia University, 1954—. Has had exhibitions in the United States and France. *Member:* College Art Association of America, American Society of Aesthetics.

WRITINGS: Matta, Museum of Modern Art, 1957; *Modern Sacred Art and the Church of Assy,* Columbia University Press, 1961; *Dada, Surrealism, and Their Heritage,* Museum of Modern Art, 1968; *Dada and Surrealist Art,* Abrams, 1969; *Frank Stella,* Museum of Modern Art, 1970; *Picasso in the Collection of the Museum of Modern Art,* Museum of Modern Art, 1972; *Miro in the Collection of the Museum of Modern Art,* Museum of Modern Art, 1973; *The Paintings of Gerald Murphy,* Museum of Modern Art, 1974; *Anthony Caro,* New York Graphic Society, 1975; (with Carolyn Lanchner) *Andre Masson,* Museum of Modern Art, 1976; (editor) *Cezanne: The Late Work,* New York Graphic Society, 1977. Contributor to professional magazines. American editor of *Art International,* 1959-64.

WORK IN PROGRESS: Matisse in the Collection of the Museum of Modern Art, for Museum of Modern Art.

* * *

RUDDICK, Sara 1935-

PERSONAL: Born February 17, 1935, in Toledo, Ohio; daughter of Alan Bevington (a lawyer) and Eleanor (Wilcox) Loup; married William Ruddick (a professor); children: Harold Tyrrell, Elizabeth Ellen. *Education:* Vassar College, B.A., 1957; Harvard University, Ph.D., 1964. *Politics:* Feminist. *Home:* 110 Bleecker St., New York, N.Y. 10012. *Office:* New School for Social Research, 66 West 12th St., New York, N.Y. 10011.

CAREER: Writer. New School for Social Research, New York, N.Y., faculty member in philosophy, biology, and literature, 1967—.

WRITINGS: (With Pamela Daniels) *Working It Out,* Pantheon, 1977. Contributor to anthologies and journals.

WORK IN PROGRESS: A book, tentatively titled *Male Thought, Women's Culture, Human Work;* various articles.

* * *

RUDIS, Al 1943-

PERSONAL: Born December 9, 1943, in St. Gallen, Switzerland; son of Joseph (a car mechanic) and Rose (a bookkeeper; maiden name, Schkolnick) Rudis; married wife, Ruth, March 22, 1970; children: Rachel Rebecca. *Education:* Attended Northwestern University; University of Arizona, B.A., 1966; further study at University of Chicago. *Politics:* Liberal. *Religion:* Jewish. *Home:* 736 Leamington, Wilmette, Ill. 60091. *Office: Chicago Sun-Times,* 401 North Wabash, Chicago, Ill. 60611.

CAREER/WRITINGS: Arizona Daily Star, Tucson, Ariz., writer and editor, 1960-65; *Stars and Stripes,* Darmstadt, Germany, editor, 1965; *Chicago Sun-Times,* Chicago, Ill., editor and popular music critic, 1966—. Chicago correspondent for *Melody Maker* and *Performance.* Contributor of articles to periodicals, including *Hit Parader, Creem, FM Guide, Circus* and *Zoo World. Member:* American Newspaper Guild.

AVOCATIONAL INTERESTS: Music, theater, films, literature, and travel.

* * *

RUEFF, Jacques (Leon) 1896-1978

August 23, 1896—April 23, 1978; French author and government economic official who was a leading figure behind France's financial reform in the 1950's. A professor, jurist, and advisor to the French and foreign governments, Rueff was also a distinguished author and poet and the first economist elected to the elite French Academy. As an economist, he advocated a return to the gold standard as a cure for economic instability and often criticized John Maynard Keynes and the monetary practices of the United States, especially its payment deficits. Rueff wrote five major books in his career, including *The Age of Inflation,* as well as economic pamphlets, articles, reports, an opera-ballet, his memoirs, and a detailed dissertation on his concept of the social order and a new liberalism. He died in Paris, France. Obituaries and other sources: *Current Biography,* Wilson, 1969, June, 1978; *Who's Who in the World,* 3rd edition, Marquis, 1976; *The International Who's Who,* Europa, 1977; *Who's Who,* 130th edition, St. Martin's, 1978; *New York Times,* April 25, 1978; *Washington Post,* April 25, 1978; *Time,* May 8, 1978. (See index for *CA* sketch)

* * *

RUTHERFORD, Ward 1927-

PERSONAL: Born October 27, 1927, in Richmond, England; son of Edward Thomas (a marine engineer) and Lydia (a journalist; maiden name, Jones) Rutherford; married Marilyn Aikens Cowes (a teacher), August 5, 1955; children: Sarah Julia, Luke Edward, Martin Richard. *Education:* Educated in the United Kingdom. *Politics:* Radical. *Religion:* Anglican. *Home:* 76 Stanford Ave., Brighton, Sussex BN1 6FE, England. *Agent:* Douglas Rae, 28 Charing Cross Rd., London W1, England.

CAREER: Channel Television, Jersey, United Kingdom, head of news, 1962-65; British Broadcasting Corp. (BBC), London, reporter, 1965-67; writer. Member, Teilhard Centre for the Future of Man. *Member:* Writers Guild, Crime Writers Association, Society of Sussex Authors.

WRITINGS: The Gallows Set, Bles, 1969; *Great Big Laughing Hannah,* Bles, 1970; *Kasserine: Baptism of Fire,* Ballantine, 1970; *The Fall of the Philippines,* Ballantine, 1971; *The Untimely Silence,* Hamish Hamilton, 1972; *Genocide: The Persecution of the Jews,* Ballantine, 1973; *The Russian Army in World War I,* Cremonesi, 1975; *Jersey,* David & Charles, 1976.

Plays: "Fingers," first performed in Worthing, England, at the Connaught Theatre, November 24, 1976.

SIDELIGHTS: Rutherford told *CA:* "As a writer my motivation has always been the belief that modern, western man feels himself to be lost. I believe that this arises from the lack of those central certainties he once obtained from religious belief. His criteria for behavior have thus become negative ones, i.e. why shouldn't I do this or that—rather than positive ones. I realize that it is impossible to expect humanity to return to the old religious ideas with their very rigid structures and that many ethical and moral ideas have been irreversibly changed (sexual morality, for instance, by the advent of the contraceptive pill). On the other hand, I am utterly convinced that humanity needs to find for itself some central, extrinsic point of reference and that, indeed, the need is realized, if only on a sort of subconscious level. My own hints on achieving this arise from the writings of Pierre Teilhard de Chardin. What is basic to this, it seems to me, is his notion that man is deeply enmeshed in his evolutionary process, which with the development of the reflective mind is now become conscious. It is from this that modern man must derive his ideas about himself and about his attitudes to his fellow man, whether or not this includes the notion of a personal or any other kind of God. As I am not a propagandist writer I have never sought to canvas these views through my work, but rather to use them as a matrix out of which my books and their ideas arise."

*   *   *

RYDING, William W.   1924-

PERSONAL: Born May 11, 1924, in Detroit, Mich.; son of Reuben (in public relations) and Esther (Benson) Ryding; married Mary Dedes, September 4, 1949; children: Erik Sven. *Education:* University of Michigan, B.A., 1948, M.A., 1949; graduate study at University of Lyons, 1949-50; Columbia University, Ph.D., 1961. *Home:* 13 Sylvan St., Rutherford, N.J. 07070. *Office:* Department of Languages, Fairleigh Dickinson University, Rutherford, N.J. 07070.

CAREER: Western Illinois State University, Macomb, instructor in English, 1954-55; Augustana College, Rock Island, Ill., assistant professor of French, 1955-56; Wayne State University, Detroit, Mich., assistant professor of French, 1956-58; Columbia University, New York, N.Y., assistant professor of French, 1958-67; Fairleigh Dickinson University, Rutherford, N.J., associate professor, 1967-71, professor of French, 1971—. *Military service:* U.S. Army Air Forces, 1943-46. *Member:* Modern Language Association of America, Mediaeval Academy of America, American Association of University Professors. *Awards, honors:* Fulbright fellowship for France, 1949-50; grant for France from Council for Research in the Humanities, summer, 1963.

WRITINGS: (With Jean Sareil) *Au Jour le Jour: A French Review,* Prentice-Hall, 1967; *Structure in Medieval Narrative,* Mouton, 1971; *Petite Revision de Grammaire Francaise* (title means "Short Review of French Grammar"), Harper, 1975. Contributor of articles and reviews to *Romanic Review, Speculum,* and *Symposium.* Member of editorial board of Fairleigh Dickinson University Press.

WORK IN PROGRESS: Research on medieval narrative forms, Old Provencal poetry, and applied linguistics.

*   *   *

RYE, Anthony
  See YOUD, Samuel

S

SACKREY, Charles 1936-

PERSONAL: Born July 19, 1936, in Sacramento, Calif.; son of C. Melvin and Anece (a painter; maiden name, Swearingen) Sackrey; children: John, Ponteir. *Education:* University of Texas, B.A., 1961, M.A., 1963, Ph.D., 1965. *Home:* 2504 East Fourth St., Tulsa, Okla. 74104. *Office:* Department of Economics, University of Tulsa, Tulsa, Okla. 74104.

CAREER: Smith College, Amherst, Mass., assistant professor, 1968-71, associate professor of economics, 1972-73; Hampshire College, Amherst, visiting lecturer, 1974; coordinator of low income housing program in Springfield, Mass., 1975-76; University of Massachusetts, Amherst, associate professor of economics, 1976-77; University of Tulsa, Tulsa, Okla., associate professor of economics, 1977—.

WRITINGS: The Political Economy of Urban Poverty, Norton, 1973. Contributor of stories and poems to magazines. Co-editor of *Westbere Review,* 1978—.

WORK IN PROGRESS: An economics book, with Cadwell Ray.

SIDELIGHTS: Sackrey writes: "As co-editor of *Westbere Review* I am interested in printing stories not selected for publication by profit-making corporations. I combine the editing of *Westbere Review* with my work in economics for several reasons. First, both social science and literature (that is, nonfiction) are themselves incomplete. Social scientists are typically ignorant of all but their narrow fields; and literary people are often unaware, in varying degrees, of the more analytical writing among academic social theorists. Frankly, I would not enjoy concentrating all my efforts on either of these broad areas.

"Second, reading the stories and poems that come my way as editor of *WR* remind me, each time I receive one, that the people that lie just the other side of all the statistical data have very individual tales to tell. It is an affliction of our times, I think, that so much statistical data is being gathered; for one consequence is that 'poverty,' 'alienation,' and other obvious results of American capitalism, are known to people ordinarily as this number or that one. Having 'fiction' passing through my life in manuscripts keeps me reminded of all this.

"Finally, economics research and writing is really an attendant feature of my great love: classroom teaching. I like economics because it's more political than most disciplines; however, I like it most because having advanced degrees in the subject allows me a ticket into the classroom. Writing comes to me with much anxiety and trepidation; editing is easier yet; teaching is what I guess I finally do the best, and all the rest works to the extent that it makes me better in the class."

* * *

SAGAN, Miriam 1954-

PERSONAL: Born April 27, 1954, in New York, N.Y.; daughter of Eli Jacob (a writer) and Frimi (a teacher; maiden name, Gillen) Sagan. *Education:* Harvard University, B.A., 1975; Boston University, M.A., 1977, doctoral study, 1977—. *Politics:* "Socialist/feminist." *Home:* 15 Leland St., #1, Jamaica Plain, Mass. 02130.

CAREER: New England Conservatory of Music, Boston, Mass., teacher of poetry, 1975-76; writer, 1976—. *Member:* Poets and Writers. *Awards, honors:* Poetry award from *Mademoiselle,* 1974, for "Order of Things."

WRITINGS: Dangerous Body (poems), Samisdat, 1976; *Vision's Edge* (poems), Samisdat, 1978.

Work anthologized in *One Hundred Flowers Anthology* and *Fighter's Peace Anthology.* Contributor of poems and reviews to literary magazines, including *Ploughshares, Northwest, Boston Phoenix,* and *Bardic Echoes.* Co-editor of *Aspect.*

WORK IN PROGRESS: Another book of poems, *The Escape Artist.*

* * *

ST. CLAIR, William

PERSONAL: Born in Great Britain. *Education:* Oxford University, B.A., 1960. *Home:* 52 Eaton Pl., London S.W.1, England.

CAREER: Employed by British Ministry of Defence, 1961-66, Foreign Office, 1966-69, and Her Majesty's Treasury, 1969—. *Member:* Byron Society (joint-chairman, 1978—). *Awards, honors:* Heineman Award from Royal Society of Literature, 1973, for *That Greece Might Still Be Free.*

WRITINGS: Lord Elgin and the Marbles, Oxford University Press, 1967; *That Greece Might Still Be Free,* Oxford University Press, 1972; (editor) *Trelawny's Adventures of a*

Younger Son, Oxford University Press, 1974; *Trelawny, the Incurable Romancer,* Vanguard, 1978. Contributing editor of *Shelley and His Circle.*

*   *   *

SAITO, Michiko
    See FUJIWARA, Michiko

*   *   *

SALSINI, Paul E(dward) 1935-

PERSONAL: Born June 9, 1935, in Hubbell, Mich.; son of Louis (a copper miner) and Josephine (Consani) Salsini; married Barbara Kienlen (a reporter), September 12, 1959; children: James, Laura, John. *Education:* Marquette University, B.S., 1958. *Religion:* Roman Catholic. *Home:* 2405 East Stratford Court, Shorewood, Wis. 53211. *Office: Milwaukee Journal,* 333 West State St., Milwaukee, Wis. 53201.

CAREER: Milwaukee Journal, Milwaukee, Wis., reporter, 1959-70, state editor, 1970—. Lecturer at Marquette University.

WRITINGS: Frank Lloyd Wright, SamHar Press, 1971; *Cole Porter,* SamHar Press, 1972. Author of "Wisconsin," in *Americana Annual,* 1967—.

SIDELIGHTS: Salsini writes: "As state editor, I am concerned about our coverage of the news of Wisconsin—that it be fair and thorough, but especially that it tell the real significance of the news. There should be a greater effort, I believe, in telling readers what the news events mean to them personally. I am also concerned about the future of reporting in this age of changing technology. But the quality of students in my Marquette classes indicates that the future of journalism is in good hands."

*   *   *

SANDBERG, Larry 1944-

PERSONAL: Born May 10, 1944, in New York, N.Y.; son of Max (a dentist) and Anne (an office manager; maiden name, Beizer) Sandberg. *Education:* City College of the City University of New York, B.A., 1964; graduate study at Yale University, 1964-68. *Residence:* Denver, Colo. *Office:* 155 East 4th St., New York, N.Y. 10009.

CAREER: Boston University, Boston, Mass., instructor in classical languages, 1968-70; guitarist and singer, 1970—. Music teacher at Denver Folklore Center, 1973—; lecturer at colleges. *Member:* American Federation of Musicians, American Federation of Labor-Congress of Industrial Organizations, Broadcast Music, Inc. *Awards, honors:* Deems Taylor Award from American Society of Composers, Authors and Publishers, 1977, for *The Folk Music Source Book.*

WRITINGS: (With Dick Weissman) *The Folk Music Source Book,* Knopf, 1976; *Chords and Tunings for Fretted Instruments,* Oak, 1977; *The Banjo Case Chord Book,* Oak, 1978; (editor) *Banjo Styles,* Oak, 1978.

WORK IN PROGRESS: A banjo maintenance and repair manual; technical projects on guitar playing; traditional music pedagogy.

*   *   *

SAUNDERS, Doris E(vans) 1921-

PERSONAL: Born August 8, 1921, in Chicago, Ill.; daughter of Alvesta Stewart (in insurance business) and Thelma (in real estate; maiden name, Rice) Evans; married Vincent Ellsworth Saunders, Jr., October 28, 1950 (divorced, August, 1963); children: Ann Camille (Mrs. Charles J. Vivian), Vincent Ellsworth III. *Education:* Roosevelt University, B.A., 1951; Boston University, M.S. and M.A., both 1977. *Politics:* Democrat. *Religion:* Episcopalian. *Residence:* Chicago, Ill. *Office:* Johnson Publishing Co., 820 South Michigan Ave., Chicago, Ill. 60605.

CAREER: Chicago Public Library, Chicago, library assistant, 1942-46, principal reference librarian, 1946-49; Johnson Publishing Co., Chicago, librarian, 1949-66, director of book division, 1961-66; Information, Inc., Chicago, president, 1966-68; Chicago State College, Chicago, director of community relations, 1968-70; University of Illinois at Chicago Circle, Chicago, staff associate in chancellor's office, 1970-73; Johnson Publishing Co., director of book division, 1973—. Host of radio program, "The Think Tank," 1971-72; writer and producer of television program "Our People," 1968-70. Member of board of directors of South Side Community Art Center.

MEMBER: Black Academy of Arts and Letters (member of board of directors), Special Libraries Association (state president, 1960-61), Association of American Publishers, American Booksellers Association, National Association of Media Women, Inc., National Association for the Advancement of Colored People (member of local board of directors), Publicity Club of Chicago, Friends of the Chicago Public Library (member of board of directors), Alpha Gamma Pi.

WRITINGS: (Editor) *The Day They Marched,* Johnson Publishing Co. (Chicago, Ill.), 1963; (editor) *The Kennedy Years and the Negro,* Johnson Publishing Co. (Chicago, Ill.), 1964; (editor) *The Ebony Handbook,* Johnson Publishing Co. (Chicago, Ill.), 1974; (with Gerri Major) *Black Society,* Johnson Publishing Co. (Chicago, Ill.), 1976. Also author of *The Life and Times of William L. Dawson,* 1978. Columnist for *Chicago Daily Defender,* 1966-70, and *Chicago Courier,* 1970-73. Contributor to professional journals. Associate editor of *Negro Digest,* 1962-66.

*   *   *

SAUVANT, Karl P(eter) 1944-

PERSONAL: Born September 20, 1944, in Georgenswalde, Germany; came to the United States in 1968; son of Hans-Dieter (a civil servant) and Ilse (Groeger) Sauvant. *Education:* Free University of Berlin, B.A., 1968; University of Pennsylvania, M.A., 1969, Ph.D., 1975; attended University of Michigan, summer, 1972. *Home:* 347 East 51st St., Apt. 4A, New York, N.Y. 10022. *Office:* Centre on Transnational Corporations, United Nations, Room BR-1081, New York, N.Y. 10017.

CAREER: Lower Saxon Provincial Assembly, Hanover, Germany, legislative assistant, spring, 1967; Foreign Policy Research Institute, Philadelphia, Pa., research assistant, 1970-71, research associate, 1971-72, part-time employee, 1972-73; United Nations, Secretariat, New York, N.Y., associate economic affairs officer at Centre for Development Planning, 1973-75, officer of Centre on Transnational Corporations, 1975—. Guest lecturer at Rosemont College, 1970. Research associate at Institut fuer Fuehrungslehre, 1973-74.

MEMBER: International Studies Association, Academy of International Business, American Economic Association, American Political Science Association, Deutsche Vereinigung fuer Politische Wissenschaft. *Awards, honors:* Humboldt Award from Humboldt Gymnasium, 1965, for outstanding achievements in community affairs; Free University, Berlin, exchange scholar at University of Pennsylvania, 1968-69; Fulbright travel grant, 1968.

WRITINGS: (Editor with David Burtis, Farid G. Lavipour, and Steven Ricciardi) *Multinational Corporation-Nation State Interaction: An Annotated Bibliography,* Foreign Policy Research Institute, 1971; (contributor) Friedrich Fuerstenberg, editor, *Industriesoziologie III: Analysen der Beziehungen zwischen Industrie und Gesellschaft seit 1945* (title means "Industrial Sociology III: Analyses of the Relations Between Industry and Society since 1945"), Luchterhand Verlag, 1975; (with Bernard Mennis) *Emerging Forms of Transnational Community: Transnational Business Enterprise and Regional Integration,* Lexington Books, 1976; (contributor) Klaus Jurgen Gantzel, editor, *Zur Multinationalisierung des Kapitals* (title means "The Multinationalization of Capital"), Deutsche Vereinigung fuer Politische Wissenschaft, 1976; (editor with Lavipour, and contributor) *Controlling Multinational Enterprises: Problems, Strategies, Counterstrategies,* Westview Press, 1976; (editor with Hajo Hasenpflug, and contributor) *The New International Economic Order: Confrontation or Cooperation between North and South?,* Westview Press, 1977; (editor with Odette Jankowitsch) *The Third World: Basic Documents of the Non-Aligned Countries,* Oceana, 1978. Contributor to academic journals.

WORK IN PROGRESS: Research on international economic questions, especially the North-South dimension, and on transnational enterprises, especially their socio-cultural impact.

*   *   *

SAXON, Bill
   See WALLMANN, Jeffrey M(iner)

*   *   *

SAXON, Van
   See GRANBECK, Marilyn

*   *   *

SCARBROUGH, George (Addison)   1915-

PERSONAL: Born October 20, 1915, in Benton, Tenn.; son of William Oscar (a farmer) and Louise Anabel (McDowell) Scarbrough. *Education:* University of Tennessee, student, 1935-36, M.A., 1954; attended University of the South, 1941-43; Lincoln Memorial University, B.A., 1947; graduate study at State University of Iowa, 1957. *Politics:* Independent. *Religion:* Unitarian. *Home:* 100 Darwin Lane, Oak Ridge, Tenn. 37830.

CAREER: Newspaperman and farmer in eastern Tennese, 1937-43; teacher of English at various secondary schools in Tennessee, 1943-64; Hiwassee College, Madisonville, Tenn., English instructor, 1965-67; Chattanooga City College, Chattanooga, Tenn., professor of English, 1968; freelance writer and journalist, 1968—. Has given poetry readings at schools and workshops, including Appalachian State University, State University of New York, Carson-Newman College, and Cumberland Valley Writers Conference. *Member:* Poetry Society of America, Southern Appalachian Writers' Co-op, Book Discussion Club (Oak Ridge, Tenn.), Friends of Oak Ridge Library. *Awards, honors:* Actor's Award from Lincoln Memorial University, 1947; Borestone Mountain Award, 1961, for "Noon Baptism"; Mary Rugeley Ferguson Poetry Award from *Sewanee Review,* 1964, for

"Return: August Afternoon"; nomination for W. D. Weatherfor Award from Berea College, 1978, for *George Scarbrough: New and Selected Poems;* grants from Carnegie Foundation, 1956 and 1975, P.E.N. (American branch), 1975, and Authors League, 1976.

WRITINGS—All poems: *Tellico Blue,* Dutton, 1949; *The Course Is Upward,* Dutton, 1951; *Summer So-Called,* Dutton, 1956; *George Scarbrough: New and Selected Poems,* Iris Press, 1977. Poems represented in numerous anthologies, including *Forever the Land,* edited by Russell Lord, Harper, 1950, *The Current Voice: Readings in Contemporary Prose,* edited by Don L. Cook and others, Prentice-Hall, 1971, *Traveling America With Today's Poets,* edited by David Kheridian, Macmillan, 1977, and *Southern Poetry: The Post Fugitive Era,* Louisiana State University Press, 1978. Contributor of poems to such magazines as *Atlantic, Harper's, Poetry,* and *Saturday Review,* and of articles on travel and conservation to *Land, Mountain Life and Work, Progressive Farmer,* and *Appalachian Journal.*

WORK IN PROGRESS: Two more books of verse; a novel entitled *A Summer Ago.*

SIDELIGHTS: Scarbrough told *CA:* "As a teacher of creative writing both on the high school and the college level, I have been careful to stress that a poetic renaissance does not happen simply because thousands of people happen to be writing publishable verse. My great ambition is to find a college campus on which I can stress to all interested students the values of language to the would-be writer, a need that is crying in these days of slack attention to the graces of formalized speech, days in which even syntax and correct grammatical forms, not to mention shades of meanings of words, are regarded as old hat and unnecessary to the young scribe. Learning, as such, is adjudged superfluous. All these are reasons I preached, John in the wilderness, that all of us know something, a little, but nobody knows enough. The poetic classroom is disorganized. Poets in America wait for the great one, the teacher, to enter the door.

"As a born dirt farmer, I have dirt, soil, under my nails. I keep it there figuratively, as a reminder. Interstate highways can never quite by-pass the land. It is always there, as is the art of spreading manure on lonely ground between the river and the mountain. And wood doves still call in the remote county places. All this, despite the high smokestacks of Oak Ridge and the atomic honey the bees make from the old flowering pear trees of disappeared farms.

"I am a kind of writing spider that catches only what his net is capable of catching—which means, only, that I am limited to my own time, place, and my sense of values of these. I am not a regional writer. I am a southern writer, with a difference: that difference being that I was born north of the majority of slavery, in the shadow of the southern Appalachians, not of the mountains but nurtured by them. I wish to write out for America what it meant to be such an individual in such a time and in such a place."

BIOGRAPHICAL/CRITICAL SOURCES: John W. Warren and others, editors, *Tennessee Belles-Lettres: A Guide to Tennessee Literature,* Morrison, 1977; *Mossy Creek Journal,* Spring, 1977; *Chattanooga Times,* May 22, 1977; *Select Press Review,* Summer, 1977; *Appalachian Journal,* winter, 1977-78.

*   *   *

SCHAEFER, Ted   1939-

PERSONAL: Born July 10, 1939, in Philadelphia, Pa.; son

of Albert Leslie (a technical writer) and Martha (a planetarium lecturer; maiden name, Crawford) Schaefer; married Tricia Snyder (an actress and singer); children: Jennifer, Beth. *Education:* University of Missouri, B.A., 1962, M.A., 1969. *Politics:* Liberal. *Home:* 712 Hillside, Antioch, Ill. 60002. *Office:* Department of English, College of Lake County, Grayslake, Ill. 60030.

CAREER: University of Missouri, Columbia, instructor in English, 1968-69; *Co-Op City Times,* New York, N.Y., reporter, 1970; College of Lake County, Grayslake, Ill., instructor in English, 1971-73; University of Missouri, instructor in English, 1974; College of Lake County, instructor in English, 1976—. *Military service:* U.S. Army, editor of newspaper in Frankfurt, Germany, 1963-66. *Awards, honors:* Award from Illinois Arts Council, 1978, for poem "Natural Protection."

WRITINGS: After Drought (poems), Raindust Press, 1976; *The Summer People* (poems), Singing Wind Publications, 1978. Contributor of articles and poems to literary journals, popular magazines, and newspapers, including *Saturday Review, New Letters, Northwest Review,* and *Midatlantic Review.*

WORK IN PROGRESS: Poems and stories.

SIDELIGHTS: Schaefer writes: "Coming to poetry from years of journalism and fiction-writing, I find I prefer to read and write clear, direct verse that has a dramatic movement. Ideally, my favorite poetry would combine the richness of language of Wallace Stevens with the muscular directness of William Carlos Williams. Stevens says, 'Accuracy of observation is the equivalent of accuracy of thinking.'"

* * *

SCHAEFFER, Edith (Seville) 1914-

PERSONAL: Born December 3, 1914, in Wenchow, Chekiang, China; daughter of George H. (a missionary) and Jessie (Merritt) Seville; married Francis A. Schaeffer (a minister and writer), July 6, 1935; children: Priscilla, Susan, Deborah, Franky. *Education:* Attended Beaver College. *Home:* Chalet le Chardonnet, Chesieres, Switzerland. *Office:* L'Abri Fellowship, Huemoz, Switzerland.

CAREER: Writer and lecturer. Missionary in Switzerland, 1948—; co-founder of L'Abri Fellowship, 1955—.

WRITINGS: L'Abri, Tyndale, 1969; *Hidden Art,* Tyndale, 1971; (with husband, Francis Schaeffer) *Everybody Can Know,* Tyndale, 1973; *What Is a Family?,* Revell, 1975; *Christianity Is Jewish,* Tyndale, 1975; *A Way of Seeing,* Revell, 1977; *Affliction,* Revell, 1978.

Author of column "Witness Stand" in *Christianity Today,* 1974—. Contributor to Christian periodicals.

WORK IN PROGRESS: "The Two Trees."

SIDELIGHTS: Edith Schaeffer writes: "In this day of broken continuity, it may be interesting to know that I met my husband when I was seventeen and he was twenty, that we wrote every day to each other through the next years of college, and married a few days after he graduated (while I was still a senior), and have now been married for forty-three years. My earning money during the depression days when my husband was going through seminary took the form of dressmaking, and designing and making leather belts and buttons. Creativity born of necessity brought forth furniture and other forms of interior decoration where 'something' came forth from 'nothing' except an odd collection of materials—leather, fabrics from factory sales, barrels and nail

kegs, old automobile seats, paint—plus imagination and hard work. We have lived through a variety of situations from those seminary days, on through three different 'pastorates,' and then in Switzerland for now thirty years. Added to indoor ingenuity to create an atmosphere and a home, has always been a 'togetherness' in landscaping and gardening, planting and watching grow while weeding and cultivating, then harvesting—whether in a butter-tub on our first tin-roof garden, or in a large field in the Swiss Alps. The feel of soil, the wonder of seed buried and bursting forth into amazing fruitfulness is something that has been a part of our years of relationship as a couple and as a family—not to be dismissed as simply a 'hobby.' Concrete, shutting off growth of plants, is dangerous to the growth of human beings and to relationships, as the miles of cemented atmosphere surrounding so many human beings seal off a whole dimension of understanding that is essential. Human relationships are not theoretical to us, nor do we write from an 'ivory tower' with 'theories.'

Our family has consisted of three daughters and one son, all married, and now thirteen grandchildren. All three daughters and their husbands are central in the work of L'Abri in Switzerland and England, and our artist son Franky is a film maker making now a second series of films with his father. My 'work' includes traveling and speaking, writing, counseling a large variety of people, and being my husband's 'assistant' in the periods of shooting film and in the strenuous time of seminars. My 'method of writing' (a too frequent question) happens to be 'in my head' after first having *lived* much of what I think I should put on paper, as well as having given in personal counsel, or in lectures, in a variety of places, the content of what I later put on paper. When I sit down at a typewriter, it flows directly into chapters rather rapidly—although with years of preparation as to what is so rapidly coming forth! I send the manuscript or put it personally in the hands of the editor, as is. Every author is different!"

AVOCATIONAL INTERESTS: Cross country skiing, swimming, walking in the mountains, gardening, preparing a diversity of surprises for her children and grandchildren, letter writing, bread-making, cooking for large groups.

* * *

SCHAEFFER, Francis A(ugust) 1912-

PERSONAL: Born January 30, 1912, in Philadelphia, Pa.; son of Francis A. and Bessie (Williamson) Schaeffer; married Edith Seville (a writer), July 6, 1935; children: Priscilla, Susan, Deborah, Franky. *Education:* Hampden-Sydney College, A.B. (magna cum laude), 1935; Faith Theological Seminary, B.D., 1938. *Home:* Chalet le Chardonnet, Chesieres, Switzerland. *Office:* L'Abri Fellowship, Huemoz, Switzerland.

CAREER: Ordained Presbyterian minister, 1938; pastor in United States, 1938-48; missionary in Switzerland, 1948—; president of L'Abri Fellowship, Huemoz, Switzerland, 1955—. Lecturer. *Awards, honors:* LL.D. from Gordon College, 1971.

WRITINGS: The God Who Is There, Inter-Varsity Press, 1968; *Escape From Reason,* Inter-Varsity Press, 1968; *Death in the City,* Inter-Varsity Press, 1969; *The Church at the End of the Twentieth Century,* Inter-Varsity Press, 1970; *Pollution and the Death of Man: The Christian View of Ecology,* Tyndale, 1970; *The Mark of the Christian* (booklet), Inter-Varsity Press, 1970; *True Spirituality,* Tyndale, 1971; *The Church Before the Watching World,* Inter-Varsity Press, 1971; *Genesis in Space and Time,* Inter-Varsity Press, 1972; *He Is There and He Is Not Silent,* Tyndale, 1972; *Basis Bible Studies,* Tyndale, 1972; *The New Super-Spirituality* (booklet), Inter-Varsity Press, 1972; *Back to Freedom and Dignity,* Inter-Varsity Press, 1972; (with wife, Edith Schaeffer) *Everybody Can Know,* illustrated by son, Franky Schaeffer, Tyndale, 1973; *Art and the Bible* (booklet), Inter-Varsity Press, 1973; *No Little People: Sixteen Sermons for the Twentieth Century,* Inter-Varsity Press, 1974; *Two Contents, Two Realities* (booklet), Inter-Varsity Press, 1974; *Joshua and the Flow of Biblical History,* Inter-Varsity Press, 1975; *No Final Conflict* (booklet), Inter-Varsity Press, 1975; *How Should We Then Live?: The Rise and Decline of Western Thought and Culture,* Revell, 1976; *What Ever Happened to the Human Race?,* Revell, 1979.

WORK IN PROGRESS: A film version of *What Ever Happened to the Human Race?*

SIDELIGHTS: Summarizing the influence of Schaeffer on contemporary society, *Eternity* magazine declared: "Francis A. Schaeffer is something of an evangelical phenomenon. Judging by the popularity of his books, he has more influence with today's youth—from members of the dropout world to the disillusioned heirs of evangelicalism—than any other one man." Stephen Board elaborated on Schaeffer's reputation: "His presentation of Christianity, linked as it has been to the larger culture and to formal philosophy, has attracted the attention of academics in philosophy and apologetics.... Schaeffer, an orthodox Protestant, has earned a respectful hearing among skeptics and discriminating believers, not only for his gracious sensibilities but for the rational plausibility of his world view." Though Schaeffer has been described as a theologian, a philosopher, and a cultural historian, he views himself primarily as an evangelist and defines his task as "first of all, giving honest answers to honest questions to get the blocks out of the way so that people will listen to the Gospel as a viable alternative, and then secondly, showing them what Christianity means across the whole spectrum of life." For Schaeffer, this means confronting twentieth-century man with the results of humanism (or "man's starting with himself alone") and proposing the Christian alternative to answer the questions humanism leaves unanswered.

Most of Schaeffer's books have grown out of lectures and discussions at L'Abri Fellowship, the Christian community he and his wife founded in the Swiss Alps in 1955. L'Abri gradually became known throughout Europe and beyond as "a place where one could discuss the great twentieth century questions quite openly" and literally thousands of people have sought and found answers to their questions about life's meaning there since 1955. In his books as well as his lectures, Schaeffer has sought to relate biblical Christianity to philosophical questions and contemporary culture.

Schaeffer's latest and most ambitious project, the book and film series *How Should We Then Live?,* has received widespread attention in the United States and Europe. The book draws together many themes from Schaeffer's previous works to propose an interpretation of the development of modern culture. Schaeffer analyzes the process by which Western culture deviated from biblical Christianity and eventually threw off the constraints of a biblical world-view in order to celebrate the autonomy that man craves. As he traces the results and implications of man's search for total autonomy, Schaeffer sets forth his case for Christianity as the only system that fits the philosophical and practical facts of man's existence.

How Should We Then Live? suffered under the pens of some reviewers because of its brevity. James Daane criticized its "sweeping generalities" and lack of highly reasoned and intellectual analysis. D. Keith Mano quipped: "Western thought from Augustus' Rome to Fellini's 'Roma' doesn't readily compress inside 288 pages: one might better pack for the Arctic with an attache case." But Mano hastened to add that "[Schaeffer's] theology is applied theology," and that he is "a powerful and accurate summarizer." Hailing Schaeffer as a "sentinel phenomenon," Mano urged his audience to read *How Should We Then Live?* as "part of a good education."

Schaeffer himself explained his limited aim in his author's note: "In no way does this book make a pretense of being a complete chronological history of Western culture. It is questionable if such a book could even be written. This book is, however, an analysis of the key moments in history which have formed our present culture, and the thinking of the people who brought those moments to pass. This study is made in the hope that light may be shed upon the major characteristics of our age and that solutions may be found to the myriad of problems which face us as we look toward the end of the twentieth century."

The approach that offended Daane and Mano was a purposeful attempt on Schaeffer's part to communicate on a level that the average man could understand. Thomas Morris noted, "His style and treatment are popular rather than philosophically rigorous so that he may reach a larger audience and have a more widespread effect on the church and on the world." Schaeffer himself elucidated his aims in an interview with the editors of *Christianity Today:* "I worked for a year and a half to try to remove all technical language from the book and from the film script. It was hard going to remove philosophical terminology and still have philosophical concepts! ... If I'm right that the shipyard worker has the same questions as the intellectual, and if I've been able to get rid of the technical language, then perhaps this message will get to a wider audience than anything we've done so far."

Edith Schaeffer explained the way in which the title *How Should We Then Live?* was chosen for the book and film series. The phrase came from a verse in the book of Ezekiel which caught her husband's attention one day as he deliberated whether to continue through the "long dark tunnel of work [which] stretched out with no end in view." Translating the situation in Ezekiel's day into modern terms, Edith Schaeffer wrote: "The question today is: 'If humanism has been a failure, if there is no satisfying answer to life that starts with man, and leaves God out of it all, if the concept of an impersonal universe has brought forth the chaotic situation that surrounds us, *how should we then live?* What is the answer to life?' The question needs to be placed in men's and women's minds to shake them, to make them think. We have a responsibility to do something that people will hear, as they would hear a trumpet blast."

BIOGRAPHICAL/CRITICAL SOURCES: Edith Schaeffer, *L'Abri,* Tyndale, 1969; *Eternity,* March, 1973; Thomas V. Morris, *Francis Schaeffer's Apologetics: A Critique,* Moody, 1976; Francis A. Schaeffer, *How Should We Then Live?,* Revell, 1976; *Christianity Today,* October 8, 1976; *National Review,* March 18, 1977; *Christian Century,* October 12, 1977.

*   *   *

SCHAFER, R(aymond) Murray 1933-

PERSONAL: Born July 18, 1933, in Sarnia, Ontario, Canada; son of Harold J. (an accountant) and Belle (Rose) Schafer; married Phyllis Mailing, July, 1960 (divorced, 1970); married Jean Elliott, October, 1970; children Christopher and Nicholas (stepchildren). *Education:* Attended University of Toronto, 1954-56. *Home address:* R.R.5, Bancroft, Ontario, Canada K0L 1C0. *Agent:* Harold Ober Associates, Inc., 40 East 49th St., New York, N.Y. 10017.

CAREER: Memorial University of Newfoundland, St. John's, artist in residence, 1962-64; Simon Fraser University, Burnaby, British Columbia, lecturer in music, 1965-70, professor of communication studies, 1970-75. Composer and writer, 1970—. Director of World Soundscape Project, 1972—. Member, Broadcast Music Inc., Canada. *Member:* Canadian League of Composers, Phi Mu Alpha.

WRITINGS: British Composers in Interview, Faber, 1961; *The Composer in the Classroom,* Berandol Music (Canada), 1965; *Ear Cleaning,* Berandol Music, 1967; *The New Soundscape,* Berandol Music, 1968; *When Words Sing,* Berandol Music, 1969; *The Rhinoceros in the Classroom,* Universal Edition, 1970; *The Book of Noise,* Price Milburn, 1971; *E.T.A. Hoffmann and Music,* University of Toronto Press, 1975; *Creative Music Education,* Schirmer Books, 1976; *Smoke* (novel), privately printed, 1976; *The Tuning of the World,* Knopf, 1977; (editor) *Ezra Pound and Music,* New Directions, 1977.

Musical compositions include: "Canzoni for Prisoners," 1961-62; "Loving," 1966; "From the Tibetan Book of the Dead," 1968; "No Longer Than Ten Minutes," 1970; "In Search of Zoroaster," 1971; "Miniwanka," 1972. Has made several recordings of his compositions.

BIOGRAPHICAL/CRITICAL SOURCES: Peter Such, *Soundprints,* Clark, Irwin, 1975; *Contemporary Canadian Composers,* Oxford University Press, 1976.

*　　*　　*

SCHIER, Ernest L. 1918-

PERSONAL: Born March 25, 1918, in New York, N.Y.; son of David T. (a pharmacist) and Celia (a businesswoman; maiden name, Reiss) Schier; married Marjorie Poore (a writer); children: Johanna, Jennifer, Harry D., William A. *Education:* Educated in New York, N.Y. *Office: Philadelphia Bulletin,* 30th and Market Sts., Philadelphia, Pa. 19101.

CAREER/WRITINGS: Washington Times Herald, Washington, D.C., drama critic, 1946-54; Arena Stage, Washington, D.C., publicist, 1954-55; *Philadelphia Daily News,* Philadelphia, Pa., editor and columnist, 1956-58; *Philadelphia Bulletin,* Philadelphia, drama and film critic, and columnist, 1958—. Contributor of articles to periodicals, including *Pennsylvania Gazette* and *Toronto Star.* Instructor in drama and playwriting, Villanova University. Director, National Critics Institute, O'Neill Theater Center. *Military service:* U.S. Air Force, 1943-46. *Member:* American Theatre Critics Association (co-founder).

*　　*　　*

SCHLACHTER, Gail Ann 1943-

PERSONAL: Born April 7, 1943, in Detroit, Mich.; daughter of Lewis E. (an attorney) and Helen (Blitz) Goldstein; married Alfred S. Schlachter, June 18, 1964 (divorced, 1973); children: Sandra Elyse, Eric Brian. *Education:* Attended Santa Monica City College, 1960-62; University of California, Berkeley, B.A., 1964; University of Wisconsin, Madison, M.A. (history and education), 1966; M.A. (library science), 1967; University of Minnesota, Ph.D., 1971; at-

tending University of Southern California. *Home:* 1204 Marina Circle, Davis, Calif. 95616. *Office:* Library, University of California, Davis, Calif. 95616.

CAREER: University of Wisconsin, Madison, director of Industrial Relations Reference Center and Social Science Graduate Reference Center, 1967-68; University of Minnesota, Minneapolis, lecturer in library science, 1969-70; University of Southern California, Los Angeles, assistant professor of library science, 1971-74; California State University Library, Long Beach, head of department of social sciences, 1974-76; University of California, Davis, assistant university librarian, 1976—.

MEMBER: American Library Association, American Association of Library Schools, Special Libraries Association, Committee of Small Magazine Editors and Publishers, American Association of University Professors, California Library Association (chapter president, 1977-78), Beta Phi Mu, Alpha Gamma Sigma, Alpha Mu Gamma. *Awards, honors:* Ford Foundation Area fellowship, 1965; Higher Education Act fellowship, 1968-70.

WRITINGS: Library Science Dissertations, 1925-1972: An Annotated Bibliography, Libraries Unlimited, 1974; *Directory of Internships, Work Experience Programs, and On-the-Job Training Opportunities,* Ready Reference Press, 1976; *Minorities and Women: A Guide to Reference Literature in the Social Sciences,* Reference Service Press, 1977; *Directory of Financial Aids for Women,* Reference Service Press, 1978; *Student Guide to Financial Aid in Public Administration,* University of Southern California, 1978; *Alcoholism: A Guide to the Literature,* Gale, in press. Editor of "Facsimile Reprint Series," California State University, Long Beach; and of *Critique: Journal of Southern California Public Policy,* 1976. Contributor to library journals.

*　　*　　*

SCHMIDGALL, Gary 1945-

PERSONAL: Born June 14, 1945, in Los Angeles, Calif. *Education:* Stanford University, A.B., 1967, Ph.D., 1974; City University of New York, postdoctoral study, 1976-77. *Office:* Department of English, University of Pennsylvania, Philadelphia, Pa. 19104.

CAREER: Stanford University, Stanford, Calif., lecturer in English, 1974-76; University of Pennsylvania, Philadelphia, assistant professor of English, 1977—.

WRITINGS: Literature As Opera, Oxford University Press, 1977.

WORK IN PROGRESS: Shakespeare and the Courtly Aesthetic; a general study of the musical settings of important poetry.

BIOGRAPHICAL/CRITICAL SOURCES: New York Times, January 5, 1978.

*　　*　　*

SCHNEIR, Miriam 1933-

PERSONAL: Born March 28, 1933, in New York; daughter of Abraham and Ida (Weinstein) Blumberg; married Walter Schneir (a writer), July 14, 1957; children: Jason, Frances, Nicholas. *Education:* Attended Antioch College, 1950-52, and Queens College (now of the City University of New York), 1952-55. *Politics:* Independent socialist. *Residence:* Pleasantville, N.Y. 10570.

CAREER: Elementary school teacher in New York, N.Y., 1955-58; Child Development Center, New York City, teacher, 1958-60; writer, 1960—. *Member:* International P.E.N., American Historical Association. *Awards, honors:* Macdowell Colony fellowship.

WRITINGS: (With husband, Walter Schneir) *Invitation to an Inquest: A New Look at the Rosenberg-Sobell Case,* Doubleday, 1965; (editor) *Feminism: The Essential Historical Writings,* Random House, 1972; (with DePauw and Hunt) *Remember the Ladies: Women in America, 1750-1815,* Viking, 1976.

Writer for "The Unquiet Death of J. and E. Rosenberg," a television documentary, 1972-73. Contributor to magazines, including *Ms., Nation,* and *Liberation,* and newspapers.

WORK IN PROGRESS: A feminist history of seventeenth-century America, for Random House.

* * *

SCHOFER, Lawrence 1940-

PERSONAL: Born December 30, 1940, in Baltimore, Md.; son of George and Rebecca (Levine) Schofer; married Jane E. Winter (a librarian), August 9, 1966; children: Ethan, Alexander. *Education:* Johns Hopkins University, B.A., 1962; University of California, Berkeley, M.A., 1963, Ph.D., 1970. *Politics:* "Kathedersozialist." *Religion:* Jewish. *Home:* 419 West Mount Pleasant Ave., Philadelphia, Pa. 19119.

CAREER: University of Pennsylvania, Philadelphia, assistant professor of history, 1969-77; free-lance writer and researcher, 1977—. *Member:* American Historical Association, Association for Jewish Studies, Economic History Association, Social Science History Association, Phi Beta Kappa. *Awards, honors:* National Endowment for the Humanities fellow, 1977-78.

WRITINGS: The Formation of a Modern Labor Force: Upper Silesia, 1865-1914, University of California Press, 1975. Contributor to *Journal of Social History.*

WORK IN PROGRESS: The Jewish Communities of Berlin and Warsaw, 1850-1939: Migration, Urbanization, and Occupational Choice.

SIDELIGHTS: Schofer comments: "I have had one year of research in Poland, 1967-68, and one year in West Berlin, 1974-75. I am planning to leave the academic world and pursue a career in health care administration, building on a longtime interest in the institutions of the welfare state. Successful historical research involves defining important topics and developing strategies for understanding those problems. Health care planning should provide the opportunity to use those same skills in a socially useful occupation."

AVOCATIONAL INTERESTS: Woodworking, canoeing, bicycling.

* * *

SCHOLBERG, Henry 1921-

PERSONAL: Born May 29, 1921, in Darjeeling, India; son of Henry Caesar (a missionary) and Ella (a missionary; maiden name, Conrad) Scholberg; married Phyllis Nelson (a teacher), June 16, 1951; children: Andrew David, Daniel Lester, Naomi. *Education:* University of Illinois, B.A., 1943; University of Minnesota, B.S., 1954, M.A., 1962. *Politics:* Democrat. *Religion:* United Methodist. *Home:* 195 Windsor Lane, St. Paul, Minn. 55112. *Office:* Ames Library of South Asia, University of Minnesota, Minneapolis, Minn. 55455.

CAREER: Onamia Journal, Onamia, Minn., editor, 1946-

48; *Brainerd Daily Dispatch,* Brainerd, Minn., sports editor, 1948-49; *State Democrat-Farmer-Labor News,* Minneapolis, Minn., editor, 1949-50; high school librarian in Columbia Heights, Minn., 1954-61; University of Minnesota, Minneapolis, librarian at Ames Library of South Asia, 1961—, instructor, 1961-66; assistant professor, 1966-74; associate professor, 1974—, chairman of South Asia microform project executive committee, 1976-77. Member of Footlighters Community Theater, 1961-68, president, 1966-67; has acted in and directed plays at the university and in community theater productions. Chairman of Anoka County Democrat-Farmer-Labor Party, 1956-62; chairman of District 49-A Democrat-Farmer-Labor Party, 1970-71.

MEMBER: International Association of Orientalist Librarians, American Library Association, Association for Asian Studies, Historical Society of Pondicherry (India), Minnesota Library Association (president, 1966-67).

WRITINGS: The Boy King: A Play About India for Children of All Nations (three-act; first produced in St. Paul, Minn., April 24, 1964), Callimachus, 1964; *The District Gazetteers of British India: A Bibliography,* Inter Documentation Co., 1970; *Une Bibliographie des Francais dans l'Inde* (title means "A Bibliography of the French in India"), Historical Society of Pondicherry, 1973; *Saroja: A Play in Three Countries* (three-act), Writers Workshop (Calcutta), 1977.

Unpublished plays: "Good Night, Ruth" (one-act), first produced in Minneapolis at University of Minnesota Theatre, December 4, 1963; "Ranjit Is Home" (one-act), first produced in Columbia Heights, Minn. at Community Methodist Church, January, 1964; "Mafia Jones" (one-act), first produced in Minneapolis, 1965; "The People Race" (one-act), first produced in Minneapolis, April 7, 1967; "But the Greatest of These" (three-act), first produced in Mussoorie, India, September 27, 1970; "Benjamin: A Christmas Play" (one-act), first produced at Community Methodist Church, December 18, 1971; "Rahab and the Spies" (one-act), first produced at Community Methodist Church, February 9, 1975; "Saul of Tarsus" (one-act), first produced at Community Methodist Church, February 29, 1976; "The Story of Ruth" (one-act play), first produced in Mapleton, Minn., May 12, 1977; "The Golden Candlesticks" (one-act play), first produced in St. Francis, Minn., December 4, 1977.

Unproduced plays: "The Day Jesus Came Back" (one-act), 1963; "And They Shall Die" (one-act), 1964; "The Final Hour," 1965; "Another Time, Another Country" (three-act), 1965; "Thaddeus" (three-act), 1966; "The Brother Keeper" (one-act), 1966; "The Assassin" (three-act), 1967; "How Would You Like Your Daughter to Marry One?" (one-act), 1971; "The Day Martin Luther King Got Shot: A Nightmare in One Act," 1973; "The Man Who Turned the World Upside Down: A Dramatic Reading," 1975; "Calcutta 1851: A Play in Two Acts."

Television plays: "I Was Hungry," WTCN-TV, March 19, 1972; "The Waiting Room," WCTN-TV, February 18, 1973; "The Knowledge Tree," WCTN-TV, February 3, 1974; "Pontius Pilate and the Dream of Claudia," WCTN-TV, March 26, 1978. Contributor of articles and reviews to library journals.

WORK IN PROGRESS: A Golden Jubilee Author-Subject Index to the Journal of Indian History; a bibliography of the Portuguese to India, publication expected, 1980.

SIDELIGHTS: Scholberg writes: "Because of my upbringing in India, much of my writing and research is concerned with that country. However, I have written numerous plays that have nothing to do with India: many of Biblical and non-Biblical themes. I have tried to maintain versatility in my writing, doing comedy and tragedy, the sacred and the profane, and sometimes combining all of these elements in a single play. Recently, however, I have been sticking to religious drama but look forward to getting back to secular subjects.''

AVOCATIONAL INTERESTS: Theater, chess, tennis.

* * *

SCHONBORG, Virginia 1913-

PERSONAL: Born October 20, 1913, in Newport, R.I.; daughter of Charles and Sadie (Weaver) Schonborg. *Education:* Smith College, A.B., 1935; Bank Street College of Education, M.S., 1950. *Home address:* P.O. Box 97, Cape Porpoise, Maine 04014. *Agent:* Dorothy Markinko, McIntosh & Otis, Inc., 475 Fifth Ave., New York, N.Y. 10017.

CAREER: Bank Street College of Education, New York, N.Y., director of interns and adviser, 1970—.

WRITINGS—Juveniles: *The Salt Marsh,* Morrow, 1969; *Subway Singer,* Morrow, 1970. Contributor to *Childhood Education.*

WORK IN PROGRESS: City Time (tentative title), a book of poems for children; a self-illustrated story for young children.

SIDELIGHTS: Virginia Schonborg told *CA:* ''I am interested in the role that poverty plays in a child's life. I have had a special thing for city children, but since living here in Maine I have a special thing for all children. With conflict between painting and writing, my solution is illustrating my own books. Time spent working with so-called 'vicinity' young adults has made me more intelligent about life!''

* * *

SCHOONOVER, Shirley 1936-

PERSONAL: Born February 25, 1936, in Biwabik, Minnesota; daughter of John Arvo (a farmer) and Clara (Knuutinen) Waisanen; married LeRoie C. Schoonover (divorced); children: Noel. *Education:* Attended University of Minnesota and University of Nebraska. *Politics:* Independent. *Home and office:* 456 Julian Pl., Kirkwood, Mo. 63122. *Agent:* Sterling Lord Agency, Inc., 660 Madison Ave., New York, N.Y. 10021.

CAREER: Hovland-Swanson, Lincoln, Neb., fashion coordinator during 1960's; University of Nebraska, Lincoln, instructor in education during 1960's; University of Rochester, Rochester, N.Y., assistant professor of English, 1970-74; writer. *Member:* Lincoln Community Playhouse. *Awards, honors:* O. Henry Award, 1962, for ''The Star Blanket,'' and 1964, for ''Old and Country Tale.''

WRITINGS: Mountain of Winter (fiction), Coward, 1965; *Sam's Song* (fiction), Coward, 1969. Work has been represented in anthologies, including *Best Short Stories of 1970,* edited by Martha Foley. Contributor of criticism, articles, and short stories to *New York Times Book Review, Atlantic,* and *Holiday.* Assistant editor, *Prarie Schooner,* during 1960's.

WORK IN PROGRESS: Flowers for Leah, a novel; *Finns,* a novel based on characters and material in *The Kalevala,* the Finnish folk epic.

SIDELIGHTS: Shirley Schoonover told *CA:* ''Motivation for writing my books does not change: to write something approaching the truth about a situation, the people in it. I find that most of my writing goes into the waste basket, that I write a lot and cut more. Recently wrote a few haiku for Warren Benson, the composer; seventeen syllables was exactly how many I had in my head for the material I chose: vegetables, toadstools, ferns. But I had just, a week before, completed four hundred plus pages of *Finns I,* the first part of a large thing I'm tackling about the Finns in *The Kalevala.* That is a work of love. The language and the poetry, the imagery of that long folk poem is somehow soul satisfying, nurturing, invigorating. I hope the books I'm writing will be a dot as enchanting.

''The book I'm working on now, *Flowers for Leah,* is about a woman who discovers that her marriage, her life, have been based on myth and fantasy, and that it is peopled by strangers who are isolated from each other and from themselves. While all good marriages are different, bad marriages have a similarity: an intangible monster that takes on carnality, blood and bone, and that monster (in Leah's marriage) is the child, the lover, the inevitable destroyer of the marriage. Well, that's not all the book is about, it's also about the undersea life that women have. Leah, I hope, illuminates that aspect of womanhood.''

In the midst of a flurry of reviews characterizing Schoonover's book *Sam's Song* as just another erotic novel born of the feminist wave of writing, Martin Levin asked: ''When is a dirty book not a dirty book?'' He answered: ''When it is a *cri de coeur,* in which whatever detritus there is exists as part of the structure of personality.'' He went on to say that ''Schoonover is a literary artist who is not interested in practicing elementary Freud any more than she is using her protagonist as a medium for tittering scatology. Her narrator is a thoroughly homogenized mixture of ambiguous urges, detoured maternal feelings, sharply bitter humor, ethnic (Finnish) traces. In short, she has soul—one that is lost in a 'black forrest' of obsession, whose outcry shrills with compelling urgency.''

BIOGRAPHICAL/CRITICAL SOURCES: New York Times Book Review, March 9, 1969; *Best Sellers,* March 15, 1969; *Times Literary Supplement,* April 23, 1970.

* * *

SCHOTT, Penelope Scambly 1942-

PERSONAL: Born April 20, 1942, in Washington, D.C.; daughter of Elihu (a lawyer) and Marian (in market research; maiden name, Goldstein) Schott; children: Daniel, Rebecca. *Education:* University of Michigan, B.A., 1963; Queens College of the City University of New York, M.A., 1968; City University of New York, Ph.D., 1971. *Religion:* None. *Home address:* 118 Washington St., Box 215, Rocky Hill, N.J. 08553.

CAREER: Rutgers University, Douglass College, New Brunswick, N.J., assistant professor of English, 1971—. Member of board of directors of Middlesex County Council on the Arts. *Member:* Poetry Society of America. *Awards, honors:* Award from Poetry Society of America, 1974, for ''The Orangetrees.''

WRITINGS: My Grandparents Were Married for Sixty-Five Years (chapbook), Fairleigh Dickinson University, 1977. Contributor of poems and articles to literary journals and national magazines, including *Ms.* and *Literary Review.*

WORK IN PROGRESS: A narrative poem, ''Morbidezza.''

SCHOYER, B. Preston 1912(?)-1978

1912(?)—March 13, 1978; American author of four novels based on his experiences in China. During World War II, Schoyer headed an effort directed by the Army Air Forces intelligence service that led American pilots stranded in East China to safety. A former correspondent in Hong Kong for Worldwide Press Service and executive director of the National Committee on United States-China Relations, he was executive director of the Yale China Association. Schoyer wrote *The Foreigners, The Indefinite River, The Ringing of the Glass,* and *The Typhoon's Eye.* He contributed articles on China, the Far East, and Hong Kong to *Saturday Review, Reporter, New York Times Magazine,* and *New Yorker.* He died in Stamford, Conn. Obituaries and other sources: *New York Times,* March 14, 1978; *AB Bookman's Weekly,* May 8, 1978.

* * *

SCHULMAN, Bob
See SCHULMAN, Robert

* * *

SCHULMAN, Robert 1916-
(Bob Schulman)

PERSONAL: Born July 7, 1916, in New York, N.Y.; son of Samuel (an electrical engineer) and Becky (Yuster) Schulman; married Eleanor Langham, March 17, 1943 (divorced, 1976); married Louise Tachau (a civic volunteer worker), November 4, 1976; children: Rebecca (Mrs. Stephen P. McIntyre). *Education:* New York University, B.S., 1936; Columbia University, M.S., 1937. *Politics:* Independent. *Religion:* Jewish. *Residence:* Louisville, Ky. *Agent:* Curtis Brown Ltd., 575 Madison Ave., New York, N.Y. 10022. *Office: Courier-Journal & Louisville Times,* 525 West Broadway, Louisville, Ky. 40202.

CAREER: St. Louis Post-Dispatch, St. Louis, Mo., reporter, 1937-39; St. Louis Community Chest, St. Louis, producer and scriptwriter, 1939-40; *St. Louis Star-Times,* St. Louis, reporter, 1940-41, feature writer, 1946-51; Time, Inc., New York, N.Y., staff correspondent, 1951-53, bureau chief, 1953-60; King Broadcasting Co., Seattle, Wash., director of documentaries and editorials, 1960-66; Design for Washington, Inc., Seattle, executive director, 1966-67; *Courier-Journal and Louisville Times,* Louisville, Ky., commentator in "One Man's Opinion" and writer for magazine section, 1968-73, media critic, 1973—. Media commentator on National Public Radio, 1977-78. Chairman of Seattle Municipal Arts Commission, 1960-61. *Military service:* U.S. Army, Air Transport Command, 1942-46; served in the North Atlantic and the Caribbean; became captain.

MEMBER: Society of Professional Journalists. *Awards, honors:* Award from Ohio State University, 1961, for "Lost Cargo," a television documentary; award from National Association of Education Writers, 1969, for an article on community colleges; award from American Political Science Association, 1970, for an article on state legislatures; award from Sigma Delta Chi, 1971, for a television editorial on strip mining.

WRITINGS: John Sherman Cooper: The Global Kentuckian, University Press of Kentucky, 1976.

Author (under name Bob Schulman) of "Lost Cargo" (documentary film), King Broadcasting, 1960. Author of "In All Fairness," a column featured in *An Open Press,* published by National News Council. Contributor to popular magazines, including *Saturday Evening Post, Sports Illustrated,* and *Quill.*

WORK IN PROGRESS: A biography of Greenwich Village cafe operator Romany Marie.

* * *

SCHWARTZ, Barry 1938-

PERSONAL: Born January 19, 1938, in Philadelphia, Pa.; son of Albert (a merchant) and Ann (Pogach) Schwartz; married Janet Cline (a teacher), August 25, 1962; children: Harald, Sarah. *Education:* Temple University, B.S., 1962; University of Maryland, M.A., 1964; University of Pennsylvania, Ph.D., 1970. *Home:* 225 Atkinson Dr., Athens, Ga. 30606. *Office:* Department of Sociology, University of Georgia, Athens, Ga. 30602.

CAREER: Fairfax County Juvenile & Domestic Relations Court, Fairfax, Va., senior probation officer, 1963-65; University of Chicago, Chicago, Ill., assistant professor of sociology, 1970-77; University of Georgia, Athens, associate professor of sociology, 1977—. *Military service:* U.S. Army, 1956-58. *Member:* American Sociological Association.

WRITINGS: Queuing and Waiting: Studies in the Social Organization of Access and Delay, University of Chicago Press, 1975; (editor) *The Changing Face of the Suburbs,* University of Chicago Press, 1976. Contributor to sociology, criminology, and education journals.

WORK IN PROGRESS: Vertical Classification, on metaphors usually employed in the description of authority; research on time costs of medical care and on the social psychology of authority.

* * *

SCHWARZ, Robert 1921-

PERSONAL: Born May 6, 1921, in Vienna, Austria; came to the United States in 1940, naturalized citizen, 1946; son of Samuel and Dora (Schwebel) Schwarz; married; children: Claire. *Education:* Emory University, A.B., 1944; Syracuse University, M.A., 1946; University of Wisconsin, Madison, Ph.D., 1952. *Office:* Department of Philosophy, Florida Atlantic University, Boca Raton, Fla. 33431.

CAREER: Carnegie-Mellon University, Pittsburgh, Pa., instructor, 1948-51, assistant professor, 1951-57, associate professor of history, 1957-64; Florida Atlantic University, Boca Raton, professor of history, 1964-65, professor of philosophy, 1965—, chairman of department, 1965-76, administrative director of humanities program, 1972—. Member of summer faculty at Georgetown University, 1966-67; guest lecturer at University of Aachen, University of Bonn, and University of Duisburg, 1976; professor at Florida State University's Overseas Study Center in Florence, Italy, 1977-78. Liaison officer for Danforth Foundation, 1969-75. Former chairman of board of managers of Florida Atlantic University Press. Guest on television and radio programs.

MEMBER: American Committee for the History of the Church Struggle, American Academy of Political and Social Science, American Catholic Philosophical Association, Conference Group of Central European History, Habsburg Committee, Institut fuer Oesterreichkunde, Southern Historical Association (European section), Florida Teachers of History, Florida Philosophical Association, Phi Beta Kappa, Phi Kappa Phi, Phi Alpha Theta, Phi Sigma Tau. *Awards, honors:* Grants from Jewish Claims Commission, 1961, American Philosophical Society, 1966, Memorial Foundation for Jewish Culture, 1966, and Ludwig Boltzman Institut fuer Geschichte der Arbeiterbewegung, 1970.

WRITINGS: (Contributor) Ludwig Schaefer, David Fowler, and Jacob Cooke, editors, *Problems in Western Civilization,* Scribner, 1965, revised edition, 1968; (contributor) Josef Fraenkel, editor, *The Jews of Austria,* Vallentine & Mitchell, 1967, 2nd edition, 1970; *Sozialismus der Propaganda* (title means "Socialism of Propaganda"), Europa-Verlag, 1976. Contributor of nearly one hundred articles and reviews to history, philosophy, and social studies journals.

WORK IN PROGRESS: Hitler's Forgotten Nazis, with Bruce Pauley.

SIDELIGHTS: Schwarz's main interests are Central European history, existentialism, Zen Buddhism, and political philosophy. He has conducted research in Italy, Germany, and England. Commenting briefly on his writings, he told *CA:* "*Hitler's Forgotten Nazis* explores the history of the Nazi movement in Austria since 1918. I am particularly interested in Christian existentialism as well, and have published essays on Nicholas Berdyaev. I am also beginning a study of the great transmitters of Buddhism in the English-speaking world."

* * *

SCHWEBEL, Stephen M(yron) 1929-

PERSONAL: Born March 10, 1929, in New York, N.Y.; son of Victor (a businessman) and Pauline (Pfeffer) Schwebel; married Louise Ingrid Nancy Killander, August 2, 1972; children: Jennifer Pauline Anna, Anna Nina Cecilia. *Education:* Harvard University, B.A. (magna cum laude), 1950; graduate study at Cambridge University, 1950-51; Yale University, LL.B., 1954. *Home:* 1917 23rd St. N.W., Washington, D.C. 20008. *Office:* U.S. Department of State, Washington, D.C. 20510.

CAREER: Admitted to Bars of New York, 1955, U.S. Supreme Court, 1965, and District of Columbia, 1976; World Federation of United Nations Associations, New York City, director of United Nations headquarters office, 1950-53; White & Case (attorneys), New York City, associate, 1954-59; Harvard University, Cambridge, Mass., assistant professor of law, 1959-61; U.S. State Department, Washington, D.C., assistant legal adviser on United Nations affairs, 1961-66, special assistant to assistant secretary of state for international organization affairs, 1966-67; Johns Hopkins University, School of Advanced International Studies, Washington, D.C., professor of international law, 1967—, Edward B. Burling Professor of International Law and Organization, 1973—. U.S. State Department lecturer in India, 1952; visiting lecturer at Cambridge University, 1957, and Dag Hammarskjold Institute, 1967; visiting professor at Australian National University, 1969; Carnegie lecturer at Hague Academy of International Law, 1972; lecturer at U.S. Navy War College, 1966-68, and National War College, 1970-77. U.S. State Department, special representative on Micronesian claims, 1966-72, counselor on international law, 1973-74, deputy legal adviser, 1974—; legal adviser for U.S. delegations to the United Nations General Assembly, 1961-64; member of United Nations International Law Commission, 1977—. Member of executive committee of Commission to Study the Organizations of Peace, 1948-61; national chairman of Collegiate Council for the United Nations, 1948-50; president of International Student Movement for the United Nations, 1950-51; member of board of trustees for Trust for Education on the United Nations, 1958-61; member of advisory board, Center for Oceans Law and Policy, 1975—. News analyst for "The World This Week" on WHDH-Radio, 1947-49, and other programs for Worldwide Broadcasting Foundation and major American networks.

MEMBER: International Law Association (member of executive committee of American branch, 1968—), Inter-American Institute for International Legal Studies (associate member), American Society of International Law (executive vice-president, 1967-73; member of executive council, 1967—), American Law Institute, American Bar Association, American Association for the United Nations (member of board of directors, 1948-50), American Foreign Service Association, Council on Foreign Relations, British Institute of International and Comparative Law, Washington Institute of Foreign Affairs, Association of the Bar of the City of New York, Phi Beta Kappa, Cosmos Club, Harvard Club, Athenaeum Club. *Awards, honors:* Knox Memorial fellowship from Harvard University, 1950-51; Gherini Prize from Yale University Law School, 1954.

WRITINGS: The Secretary-General of the United Nations, Harvard University Press, 1952; (editor) *The Effectiveness of International Decisions,* Oceana, 1971. Contributor to law journals and newspapers, including *Washington Post.* Editor of *American Journal of International Law,* 1967—; chairman of editorial advisory committee of *International Legal Materials,* 1967-73; member of advisory board of *Law and Policy in International Business,* 1968—.

WORK IN PROGRESS: Studying international rivers as special rapporteur for the United Nations international law commission on non-navigational uses of international water courses.

* * *

SCHWOERER, Lois G.

PERSONAL: Born in Roanoke, Va.; daughter of Edward Shelley (a businessman) and Emma Hester Green; married Frank Schwoerer (a nuclear engineer), June 25, 1949; children: John Arnold. *Education:* Smith College, B.A. (summa cum laude), 1949; Bryn Mawr College, M.A., 1952, Ph.D., 1956. *Residence:* Chevy Chase, Md. *Office:* Department of History, George Washington University, Washington, D.C. 20052.

CAREER: Teacher of social studies at private school in Bryn Mawr, Pa., 1949-51; Bryn Mawr College, Bryn Mawr, Pa., instructor in history, 1954-55; University of Pittsburgh, Pittsburgh, Pa., lecturer in history, 1962-63; George Washington University, Washington, D.C., associate professorial lecturer, 1964-65, assistant professor, 1965-68, associate professor, 1968-75, professor of history, 1976—, chairwoman of Commission on Equal Opportunity, 1973-75.

MEMBER: American Historical Association, Conference on British Studies, Renaissance Society of America, Phi Beta Kappa. *Awards, honors:* American Philosophical Society grant, 1971-72; annual prize from Berkshire Conference of Women Historians, 1974-75, for *No Standing Armies!;* National Endowment for the Humanities senior fellowship, 1975.

WRITINGS: No Standing Armies!: The Antiarmy Ideology in Seventeenth-Century England, Johns Hopkins Press, 1974. Also contributor to *Three British Revolutions.* Contributor of articles and reviews to history and library journals.

WORK IN PROGRESS: A book on the Declaration of Rights and the Bill of Rights.

* * *

SCORER, Richard 1919-

PERSONAL: Born August 30, 1919, in Lincoln, England;

son of Eric West (a solicitor) and Maud (a teacher; maiden name, Segar) Scorer; married Dorothy Joan Toft, December 20, 1944 (died November 30, 1964); married Margaret Valmai Ross (a magistrate), July 10, 1965; children: Beatrice Scorer Shire, Margaret, Valerie Scorer Martin, Jason (deceased), Richard, Josephine. *Education:* Cambridge University, M.A., 1947, Ph.D., 1950; attended New York University, 1968. *Politics:* Labour. *Religion:* Humanist. *Office:* Department of Mathematics, Imperial College, University of London, London S.W.7, England.

CAREER: University of London, Imperial College, London, England, lecturer in meteorology, 1949-57, reader in applied mathematics, 1957-62, reader in theoretical mechanics, 1962—. Alderman of London's Borough of Merton, 1971-78. *Military service:* Royal Air Force, 1941-45; became flight lieutenant.

MEMBER: Royal Meteorological Society (fellow), Royal Aeronautical Society (fellow), Institute of Mathematics and Its Applications (fellow), Royal Society of Health (fellow), Conservation Society. *Awards, honors:* Buchan Prize from Royal Meteorological Society, 1954; National Science Foundation grant, 1968, for New York University; named honorary associate of Imperial College, London, 1972.

WRITINGS: (With F. H. Ludlam) *Further Outlook,* Wingate, 1953; *Natural Aerodynamics,* Pergamon, 1958; *Weather,* Phoenix House, 1959; (with Ludlam) *Cloud Study,* J. Murray, 1959; (with Henry Wexler) *A Colour Guide to Clouds,* Pergamon, 1963; *Air Pollution,* Pergamon, 1968; (with Wexler) *Cloud Studies in Colour,* Pergamon, 1968; *Pollution in the Air,* David & Charles, 1973; *Clouds of the World: A Complete Colour Encyclopaedia,* Stackpole, 1973; *The Clever Moron,* Routledge & Kegan Paul, 1977; *Environmental Aerodynamics,* Wiley, 1977. Contributor to scientific journals. Editor of *Weather,* 1956-58, and *International Journal of Air Pollution,* 1959-65.

WORK IN PROGRESS: A book on "Joan of Arc and our time."

AVOCATIONAL INTERESTS: Politics, pollution, conservation, international travel (United States, Australia, Canada, New Zealand, Japan, France, Italy, Spain, Scandinavia, Germany, Czechoslovakia, East Africa, the Middle East, India, Pakistan).

*   *   *

SCOTT, Anthony
See DRESSER, Davis

*   *   *

SCOTT, Eve
See RODGERS, Joann Ellison

*   *   *

SCOTT, Gavin   1936-

PERSONAL: Born May 16, 1936, in Montreal, Canada; son of R. B. Y. (a professor) and Kathleen (a teacher; maiden name, Cordingly) Scott; married Margaret Sue, March 11, 1961 (divorced, 1974); children: Rachel Lisle (deceased), Jennifer Alison, Catherine Abigail. *Education:* Attended Harvard University, 1954-59. *Home address:* P.O. Box 18, Georgeville, Quebec, Canada. *Office address:* P.O. Box 30421, Nairobi, Kenya, Africa.

CAREER/WRITINGS: Time-Life News Service, New York, N.Y., bureau chief in Montreal, Quebec, 1959-61, correspondent in Ottawa, Ontario, 1961-62, bureau chief in

Buenos Aires, Argentina, 1962-66, correspondent in Madrid, Spain, 1966, deputy bureau chief in London, England, 1966-68, bureau chief in Boston, Mass., 1968-69, Beirut, Lebanon, 1969-72, Saigon, South Vietnam, 1972-74, Madrid, 1974-76, roving correspondent in Africa, 1976—. Notable assignments include coverage of the Six Day War, 1967, Jordan Civil War, 1970, war in Indochina, 1972-74.

*   *   *

SCOTT, J(ohn) D(ick)   1917-

PERSONAL: Born February 26, 1917, in Lanarkshire, Scotland; son of Alexander and Margaret Gourlay (Allardice) Scott; married Helen Elizabeth Whittaker, 1941; children: two sons. *Education:* Earned M.A. (with honors) from University of Edinburgh. *Home:* Apt. 101, 1517 30th St. N.W., Washington, D.C. 20007.

CAREER: Novelist. Ministry of Aircraft Production, London, England, assistant principal, 1940-44; Cabinet Office, London, historian, 1944; *Spectator,* London, literary editor, 1953-56; *Finance and Development,* Washington, D.C., editor, 1963—.

WRITINGS—Novels: *The Cellar,* Pilot Press, 1947, published as *Buy It for a Song,* Pelligrini & Cudahy, 1948; *The Margin,* Pilot Press, 1949, Knopf, 1950; *The Way to Glory; or, The Last Night of the Holidays,* Knopf, 1952; *The End of an Old Song,* Eyre & Spottiswoode, 1953, Knopf, 1954; *The Pretty Penny,* Eyre & Spottiswoode, 1963, Harcourt, 1964.

Other: *Life in Britain,* Morrow, 1956; (contributor) Hessel Hall and Christopher Wrigley, editors, *Studies of Overseas Supply,* H.M.S.O., 1956; (with Richard Hughes), *The Administration of War Production,* H.M.S.O., 1956; *The Siemens Brothers, 1858-1958,* Weidenfeld & Nicolson, 1958; *Look at Post Offices,* Hamish Hamilton, 1962; *Vickers: A History,* Weidenfeld & Nicolson, 1963, Mystic, 1964; (with Michael Postan) *Design and Development of Weapons,* H.M.S.O., 1964.

Work represented in anthologies, including *Pick of Today's Short Stories 4,* edited by John Pudney, Putnam, 1953.

SIDELIGHTS: Scott's first novel, *The Cellar,* written just after World War II, concerned an English fighter pilot shot down over France. The novel revolves around pilot Aubrey Grey's attempts to escape the Nazis and return to England. Hubert Kupferberg wrote in *New York Herald Tribune Weekly Book Review:* "Telling two stories at once is a difficult trick, and that J. D. Scott so nearly brings it off in *Buy It for a Song* is a considerable tribute to his resourcefulness as a novelist.... Mr. Scott tells the stories alternately, by contrasting the flyer's London diary with a manuscript of his life in France. The diary, like most diaries, is of only moderate interest to an outsider, and most of the attractiveness of Mr. Scott's book has to do with his swift story of Aubrey Grey's escape through France." A review which appeared in *Times Literary Supplement* reported that "the novel is carefully constructed, and written in a style that is simple and pleasant to read. All the characters are convincing and well observed, but they are subsidiary to Aubrey, and the gradual undermining of his self-confidence holds the reader's interest throughout the book."

Scott's second novel, *The Margin,* is about corruption within government and filmmaking. John Cournos described the book in *Saturday Review:* "The reputation of bureaucrats for stuffiness is confirmed by the shrewd author of this book, which describes the British species in particular...."

As a contrast the author offers us also a glimpse of the more anarchic movie world, which is anything but stuffy if just as bad in other respects.''

The Way to Glory is a love story. A review in *Atlantic Monthly* described Scott's characterization: "Mr. Scott has a talent for making his people interesting; his touch is light and sure; and he consistently registers an intelligent comment on human behavior in the contemporary world." John Raymond wrote in *New Statesman* that "Mr. Scott is a novelist's novelist. . . . His book contains no waste matter, there are no ends left lying about." J. H. Jackson echoed that concept in the *San Francisco Chronicle:* "It may be that Mr. Scott is a novelist's novelist: men who write with his firm, disciplined brilliance often are most enjoyed by other writers, who know how and where to admire the technical niceties. But he will also entertain many a reader who simply likes a piece of well-written fiction. . . .''

The End of an Old Song depicts Scott's contemporary Scotland. Roger Pippett wrote in *New York Times* that the book "is one of those rare novels in which life blows across the pages. . . ." In *New Statesman* Walter Allen observed: "Of the English novelists who have emerged since the war Mr. Scott strikes me as being in the best sense the most sheerly professional, and in nothing is this more clearly seen than in his treatment of the contemporary scene. He is essentially of the present, and he knows what is going on in the present. . . .

"In Mr. Scott we have an authentic instance of the novelist as historian of his times."

Concentrating on contemporary Britain, Scott wrote *Life in Britain.* Edwin Tetlow wrote about the book in *Saturday Review:* "There is always satisfaction in meeting thoroughly professional work. . . . One receives that satisfaction in J. D. Scott's new guide to British institutions, traditions, and contemporary life. *Life in Britain* is an admirable production." Also written on British life, *The Pretty Penny* depicts the life of one British citizen forced into conformity in order to succeed. Martin Levin wrote in the *New York Times Book Review:* "Mr. Scott works up his hero's escapade into a solidly entertaining adventure novel that is also a minor commentary on the Americanization of British life."

BIOGRAPHICAL/CRITICAL SOURCES: Times Literary Supplement, January 17, 1948, August 12, 1949; *New York Herald Tribune Weekly Book Review,* March 14, 1948; *New York Times,* August 20, 1950, February 14, 1954; *Commonweal,* September 15, 1950; *Saturday Review,* October 14, 1950, September 29, 1956; *New Statesman,* May 17, 1952; *San Francisco Chronicle,* July 29, 1952; *Atlantic Monthly,* August, 1952; *New York Times Book Review,* September 13, 1964.*

* * *

SCOTT, Jack B(rown) 1928-

PERSONAL: Born January 2, 1928, in Greensboro, N.C.; son of Lacy Allen (a business manager) and Mamie B. Scott; married Eleanor Caslick (a registered nurse), June 8, 1954; children: Ann Wiley, Edward Allen, Caroline Brown, John Thomas. *Education:* Davidson College, B.A., 1949; Columbia Theological Seminary, M.Div., 1952; Dropsie University, Ph.D., 1976. *Home:* 552 Moye Dr., Montgomery, Ala. 36109. *Office:* 1020 Monticello Court, Montgomery, Ala. 36111.

CAREER: Ordained Presbyterian minister, 1952; Board of World Missions, Nashville, Tenn., missionary in Korea,

1952-57; pastor of Presbyterian churches in Springfield, Ky., 1958-60, and Clinton, Miss., 1961-66; Reformed Theological Seminary, Jackson, Miss., chairperson of Old Testament department, 1966-76, professor of Old Testament, 1976-77; Committee on Christian Education, Montgomery, Ala., writer, consultant, 1977—. *Member:* Society of Biblical Literature, American Association of Professors of Hebrew.

WRITINGS: The Book of Hosea, Baker Book, 1968; *God's Plan Unfolded,* Tyndale House, 1978.

WORK IN PROGRESS: A sequel to *God's Plan Unfolded,* from the New Testament.

SIDELIGHTS: Scott told *CA:* "Semitic linguistics, Biblical studies, archaeology, ancient history are my special areas of interest. I do extensive writing for laymen in the areas noted above, and I write quarterlies for guided Bible study."

* * *

SCOTT, James Frazier 1934-

PERSONAL: Born July 9, 1934, in Atchison, Kan.; son of James B., Jr. and Helen (Frazier) Scott; married Carolyn Davis (an arts council administrator), June 17, 1961; children: Adrienne T., James Davis. *Education:* Rockhurst College, B.S., 1955; University of Kansas, M.A., 1957, Ph.D., 1960. *Home:* 7567 Cornell, St. Louis, Mo. 63130. *Office:* Department of English, St. Louis University, St. Louis, Mo. 63103.

CAREER: University of Kentucky, Lexington, instructor in English, 1960-62; St. Louis University, St. Louis, Mo., assistant professor, 1962-65, associate professor, 1965-69, professor of English, 1969-72; Ruhr University, Bochum, West Germany, guest professor, 1972-76; St. Louis University, professor of English, 1976—. *Member:* Modern Language Association of America, American Association of University Professors, Phi Beta Kappa. *Awards, honors:* Alexander von Humboldt Foundation fellowship, 1974-76.

WRITINGS: Film: The Medium and the Maker, Holt, 1975. Contributor to journals, including *Mosaic, Victorian Studies,* and *American Quarterly.*

WORK IN PROGRESS: Speed as an Aesthetic Reference Point in the Modern American Arts: Film, Photography, and Literature; The Ecological Imagination: Literature and Photography of the American Southwest.

SIDELIGHTS: Scott writes: "I am interested chiefly in the social dimension of the arts, with considerable emphasis upon the newer mass media (film, television, etc.). I consider a familiarity with European communications systems vital to an understanding of American culture, because such systems show us the experience of other advanced industrial societies in dealing with such questions as advertising, government subsidy of the arts, tax-supported television, press syndicates and conglomerates, etc. I also consider teaching an important means of maintaining the critical perspectives necessary for good writing."

* * *

SCOTT, Jeffrey
See USHER, Shaun

* * *

SCOTT, Paul (Mark) 1920-1978

March 25, 1920—March 1, 1978; British literary critic, playwright, poet, and author. Scott was praised for his four-volume work, *The Raj Quartet,* a fictionalized account of events leading to the demise of English control in India. He also wrote a critical work entitled *Essays by Divers Hands,* in addition to poetry and plays. His other novels, some of which have been adapted for television, include *A Male Child, Chinese Love Pavilion, Johnnie Sahib,* and *The Mark of a Warrior.* Scott died in London, England. Obituaries and other sources: *World Authors, 1950-1970,* Wilson, 1975; *The Writers Directory, 1976-78,* St. Martin's, 1976; *New York Times,* March 3, 1978.

* * *

SCOTT, William R(eese) 1907-

PERSONAL: Born April 5, 1907, in Media, Pa.; son of William Reese and Mary Bringhurst Scott; married Matilda Fassitt (a painter), October 2, 1937; children: Joan F., Claire Scott Friedman, W. Reese, Jr., Louisa Scott Knowles. *Education:* University of Pennsylvania, B.A. (honors), 1928, J.D. (honors), 1938; attended Harvard University, 1947. *Politics:* Independent. *Religion:* Independent. *Home:* 9 Salt Spray Lane, Cape Elizabeth, Maine 04107.

CAREER: Attorney in Doylestown, Pa., 1931-34; Scott Paper Co., Philadelphia, Pa., vice-president and general counsel, member of board of directors, and member of executive committee, 1934-72; writer. Member of Pennsylvania Supreme Court Bar. Past member of board of directors of Brunswick Pulp and Paper Co.; past member of board of governors of Pennsylvania Economy League and of its executive committee of Eastern Division; former associate trustee of University of Pennsylvania; former trustee of University of Pennsylvania Press. *Member:* Phi Beta Kappa, Phi Beta Kappa Associates.

WRITINGS: Cry Into the Night (poetry), Olivant, 1969; *A Breaking Thread* (poetry), Olivant, 1971. Contributor of poems to magazines.

WORK IN PROGRESS: Random Thoughts, poems; *Something of Nature,* poems.

SIDELIGHTS: Scott writes: "My motivation in writing poetry is the need to express thoughts and feelings in a way which may interest and stimulate the thoughts and emotions of others. I believe that each individual is, in the last analysis, alone in the universe, but that is not synonomous with 'lonely.' There may be friends and relatives; but, in the end, he is alone within himself. One of the most complete and inspiring experiences is to be alone and realize, if only for a brief moment, that being truly alone is to be a unique and individual identity within the infinity and eternity of total existence."

AVOCATIONAL INTERESTS: Reading, singing, painting, swimming, tennis.

* * *

SEAGLE, William 1898-1977

January 14, 1898—December 31, 1977; American trial examiner and author. Seagle served as senior attorney for the Petroleum Board, as specialist in Indian affairs for the U.S. Department of Interior, and as trial examiner for the National Labor Relations Board. His writings include *The Quest for Law, Men of Law: From Hammurabi to Holmes, Law: The Science of Inefficiency* and articles contributed to such magazines as *Harper's, Atlantic Monthly,* and *New Republic.* A member of Mystery Writers of America, Seagle also wrote *Acquitted of Murder.* He died in Washington, D.C. Obituaries and other sources: *The Author's and Writer's Who's Who,* 6th edition, Burke's Peerage, 1971; *Who's*

Who in America, 39th edition, Marquis, 1976; *Washington Post,* January 3, 1978. (See index for *CA* sketch)

* * *

SEAMAN, Don F(erris) 1935-

PERSONAL: Born June 12, 1935, in Peebles, Ohio; son of Roy (a farmer) and Junia (Garmen) Estel; married Anna Hawkins (a professor), June 6, 1965; children: Roy, Linda. *Education:* Ohio State University, B.S., 1958, M.S., 1965; Florida State University, Ph.D., 1968. *Religion:* Methodist. *Home:* 1912 Carter Creek, Bryan, Tex. 77801. *Office:* College of Education, Texas A & M University, College Station, Tex. 77843.

CAREER: County extension agent for Ohio Cooperative Extension Service, 1961-65; assistant state coordinator of higher education for Florida Board of Regents, Office of Academic Affairs, 1967-68; Mississippi State University, Mississippi State, assistant professor of adult education, 1968-71; Texas A & M University, College Station, associate professor of adult education, 1971—. Visiting professor at Mississippi State University, 1972. Member of board of directors of Appalachian Adult Basic Education Center, 1969-70; member of Commission of Professors of Adult Education, 1969-70; consultant to Delta Opportunities Corp. *Military service:* U.S. Army, 1969-71.

MEMBER: Adult Education Association, National Association for Public Continuing Adult Education, Texas Association for Continuing Adult Education, Texas Association for Community Service and Continuing Education, Phi Delta Kappa, Kappa Delta Pi.

WRITINGS: (With M. Donnie Dutton) *The High School: Establishing a Successful G.E.D. Program,* Prentice-Hall, 1972; (with Dutton) *Understanding Group Dynamics in Adult Education,* Prentice-Hall, 1972; (with wife, Anne Seaman) *The General Educational Performance Index,* Steck, 1975; *Techniques of Adult Education: A Research Review and Synthesis,* Education Research Information Center for Career Education, Ohio State University, 1977. Contributor to education journals.

* * *

SEDYCH, Andrei
See ZWIBAK, Jacques

* * *

SEIDMAN, Laurence Ivan 1925-

PERSONAL: Surname is pronounced *Side*-man; born March 8, 1925, in New York, N.Y.; son of Leo (in business) and Ida (Witkin) Seidman; married Marion Nesler (a teacher of physically handicapped infants), June 12, 1947; children: Douglass, Susan, Leslie. *Education:* City College (now of the City University of New York), B.B.A., 1947; New York University, M.Ed., 1949, Ed.D., 1969. *Home:* 140 Hill Park Ave., Great Neck, N.Y. 11548. *Office:* School of Education, C. W. Post College, Long Island University, Greenvale, N.Y. 11548.

CAREER: Elementary school teacher in New York, N.Y., 1949-51, and Long Island, N.Y., 1956-70; Long Island University, C. W. Post College, Greenvale, N.Y., associate professor of education, 1971—. Member of National Humanities Faculty of Concord, Mass.; consultant to school systems. *Military service:* U.S. Army, first aid man in Infantry, 1943-45; served in Italy; received Bronze Star.

WRITINGS: Once in the Saddle: The Cowboys' Frontier,

1866-1896, Knopf, 1973; *Fools of '49: The California Gold Rush, 1848-1856*, Knopf, 1976. Also author of scripts for filmstrips, Hawkhill Enterprises.

SIDELIGHTS: Seidman writes: "My special field of interest is the utilization of folk songs and ballads to teach the humanities and the full range of our country's history. I have folk songs as a vehicle to 'turn students on' and to get them excited about their heritage and traditions. Folk songs are catalysts which open up students to emotional and intellectual exploration of their cultural and historic backgrounds. But they are more than just history. Put into their proper settings and time slots, folk songs lead to insights into the economic, social, political, and moral issues of their day.

"I sing 'with' students, not 'for' students. I am not an entertainer, nor do I use an instrument. Anybody can sing, and when you sing for your own pleasure and interest, rather than for someone else or for a mark, it is a whole new ballgame. I am not a music teacher, merely one of the folk. I give courses in the 'ballad of America' which train teachers to utilize folk songs and ballads in working with their classes. It is an area which transcends grade levels, age levels, and subject areas. It is an interdisiplinary, multimedia approach, so that in my classes I will often have teachers from kindergarten through high school, as well as librarians and media people.

"It is through my interest in folk songs that I became a writer. The more I listened to and sang folk songs about cowboys, whalers, loggers, and miners, the more I became curious about them and their life style. So I started reading and the more I read, the more I understood and enjoyed the songs. I learned so much, that I decided to try it out with my students in my fifth grade class. And I've been singing ever since. I have sung with thousands of students of all ages and I have never met one who did not like to sing, once the pressure was off and they were singing for themselves and because they found the song beautiful and attractive."

Seidman added: "In 1963-64 I took a year's sabbatical and, with the entire family, camped for a year in Europe and Africa, living in a tent and moving southward with the seasons—an exhilarating and rewarding experience. Our camping trip abroad has left us with many rich dividends. We really got to know people, made loads of friends with other campers and always dropped the invitation to 'stop in and see us if you're in New York.' As a result, just about everyone we met has come over to visit us. We've had campers stay at our house from Tasmania, New Zealand, Japan, and most of Europe. In return we have visited many of them in their homes and being good correspondents, have kept up friendships for these many years. Our children feel that the world is their oyster and have many homes open to them when and if they travel abroad. Our experiences led us to sharing our home with an exchange student from Colombia, Fernando Cadena. In return, my son, Douglass, spent two summers down in South America in Colombia and speaks Spanish fluently. Above all, we have memories of wonderful places and marvelous people and a conviction that people throughout the world share the same hopes, needs, and emotions. They may all satisfy their needs, desires, and emotions differently, but we are much more alike than we are different."

AVOCATIONAL INTERESTS: Hiking, camping.

* * *

SEINFEL, Ruth
  See GOODE, Ruth

SELDIS, Henry 1925-1978

February 21, 1925—February 20, 1978; German-born art critic, educator, and author. A critic for the *Los Angeles Times* for twenty years and winner of the Frank Mather award for art criticism, Seldis helped Los Angeles become a popular center of contemporary art. He supported the works of such artists as Henry Moore, Jacques Lipchitz, and Georgia O'Keefe, and is credited with organizing various exhibitions of modern art. Seldis was also an educator at California State College and other institutions. He was author of *Henry Moore in America*. He died in Los Angeles, Calif. Obituaries and other sources: *Who's Who in America*, 38th edition, Marquis, 1974; *New York Times*, February 28, 1978.

* * *

SELIGMAN, Germain 1893-1978

February 25, 1893—March 27, 1978; French-born American art dealer, collector of French art, and author who, through exhibitions, brought to light the talents of many artists, including Picasso and Toulouse-Lautrec. He was a key figure in obtaining the works of prominent artists for the Boston Museum of Fine Arts and other institutions. Among other awards, Seligman received the Croix de Guerre and was made commander of the Legion of Honor. He was author of *Merchants of Art: Eighty Years of Professional Collecting*, the story of the art dealership begun by his father, and *Oh Fickle Taste* and an award-winning monograph on Roger de la Fresnaye. He died in New York, N.Y. Obituaries and other sources: *New York Times*, March 29, 1978.

* * *

SELLERS, Bettie M(ixon) 1926-

PERSONAL: Born March 30, 1926, in Tampa, Fla.; daughter of William S. (a farmer) and Rebecca P. Mixon; married Ezra L. Sellers, March 1, 1946 (divorced, April, 1977); children: Carol (Mrs. James R. Story), David, Molly. *Education:* La Grange College, B.A., 1958; University of Georgia, M.A., 1966; further graduate study at Middlebury College, 1973, and Worcester College, Oxford, 1977. *Religion:* Methodist. *Home address:* P.O. Box 274, Young Harris, Ga. 30582. *Office:* Division of Humanities, Young Harris College, Young Harris, Ga. 30582.

CAREER: Young Harris College, Young Harris, Ga., instructor in English, 1965—, chairman of Division of Humanities, 1975—. *Member:* Poetry Society of America, South Atlantic Modern Language Association, Southeastern Conference of Teachers of English, Southeastern Writers, New York Poetry Forum, Delta Kappa Gamma. *Awards, honors:* Award from *Sunstone Review*, 1975, for "I Hear the Owl Calling"; three awards from Hollywood/South Florida Poetry Institute, 1977, for "Evensong for Amanda," "Indian Corn," and "Complaint to Betelgeuse"; Shel McDonald Dramatic Poetry Award from National Federation of State Poetry Societies, 1977, for "For Rebecca, with Tempered Sadness."

WRITINGS: Westward from Bald Mountain (chapbook of poems and drawings), privately printed, 1974; *Spring Onions and Cornbread* (poems), Pelican, 1977.

WORK IN PROGRESS: Complaint to Betelgeuse, poems.

SIDELIGHTS: Bettie Sellers writes: "One of the poems in *Complaint to Betelgeuse* is called 'I Know This Road.' That sums up my feelings about writing—a time and place that each writer knows and about which he/she does the best writing. My place is North Georgia, my home the Blue Ridge Mountains."

SEMMEL, Bernard 1928-

PERSONAL: Born July 23, 1928, in New York, N.Y.; son of Samuel (a restaurateur) and Tillie (Beer) Semmel; married Maxine Loraine Guse, March 19, 1955; children: Stuart Mill. *Education:* City College (now of the City University of New York), B.A., 1947; Columbia University, M.A., 1951, Ph.D., 1955; postdoctoral study at London School of Economics and Political Science, 1959-60. *Home:* 6 Woodbine Ave., Stony Brook, N.Y. 11790. *Office:* Department of History, State University of New York at Stony Brook, Stony Brook, N.Y. 11790.

CAREER: National Citizens Commission for the Public Schools, New York, N.Y., in research and public relations, 1951-54; Council for Financial Aid to Education, New York City, in public relations, 1954-55; Park College, Parkville, Mo., assistant professor of history, 1956-60; State University of New York at Stony Brook, Stony Brook, worked as assistant professor, and as associate professor, currently professor of history. Visiting professor at Columbia University, 1966-67, seminar associate, 1968—.

MEMBER: American Historical Association, Economic History Society, Conference for British Studies, U.S. Strategic Institute, Royal Historical Society (fellow). *Awards, honors:* Rockefeller Foundation fellowship, 1959-60; American Council of Learned Societies fellowship, 1964-65; Guggenheim fellowships, 1967-68, 1974-75; Lehrman Institute fellowship, 1974-76.

WRITINGS: Imperialism and Social Reform, Harvard University Press, 1960; *The Governor Eyre Controversy,* MacGibbon & Kee, 1962, published in the United States as *Jamaican Blood and Victorian Conscience,* Houghton, 1963, and *Democracy versus Empire,* Doubleday, 1969; (editor) *Occasional Papers of T. R. Malthus,* Burt Franklin, 1963; *The Rise of Free Trade Imperialism,* Cambridge University Press, 1970; (editor and translator) E. Halevy, *The Birth of Methodism in England,* University of Chicago Press, 1971; *The Methodist Revolution,* Basic Books, 1973. Editor of *Journal of British Studies,* 1969-74.

WORK IN PROGRESS: Continuing research on liberalism, imperialism, the Pax Britannica, and socialism.

*   *   *

SENDAK, Jack

PERSONAL: Born in Brooklyn, N.Y.; son of Philip and Sarah (Schindler) Sendak. *Residence:* Brooklyn, N.Y.

CAREER: Author of books for children. *Military service:* Served in U.S. Army during World War II. *Awards, honors:* In 1972, *The Magic Tears* received the Children's Book Showcase award, and was selected as the *New York Times* Choice of Best Illustrated Children's Books of the Year.

WRITINGS: The Happy Rain (illustrated by brother, Maurice Sendak), Harper, 1956; *Circus Girl* (illustrated by M. Sendak), Harper, 1957; *The Second Witch* (illustrated by Uri Shulevitz), Harper, 1965; *The King of the Hermits and Other Stories* (illustrated by Margot Zemach), Farrar, Straus, 1966; *Martze* (illustrated by Mitchell Miller), Farrar, Straus, 1968; *The Magic Tears* (illustrated by Miller), Harper, 1971.

SIDELIGHTS: In a review of *Circus Girl,* a *San Francisco Chronicle* critic wrote, "The story has a Hans Christian Andersen quality, an approach to ordinary living that makes it a dream world, a world that young children love." Added *Saturday Review:* "The full-page illustrations done in soft blues and pinks have a quaint unforgettable quality which

makes this a book that will intrigue both adults and children." On the other hand, the *New York Times* commented "Unfortunately most readers will be like Flora on her tightrope—very much up in the air as to the point of this almost surrealistic dilemma.... After Jack Sendak's *The Happy Rain* one expected a more distinguished book than this. Maurice Sendak's illustrations, depicting a range of moods and expressions, are, however, worth the price of admission." Noted *Kirkus:* "Despite Maurice Sendak's delightful illustrations in black and white, little Flora's unfortunate misapprehensions are just not very entertaining."

"*The King of the Hermits and Other Stories* should be—must be—folk tales from some mid-European countries," remarked a *Book Week* reviewer, "but instead they are original tales made up by Jack Sendak, with an unbelievable folk-tale quality about them. Three stories are included, each filled with humor, magic, and mystery, and illustrated in black and white with Margot Zemach's gorgeously awful monsters.... Strange, offbeat, and welcome are these unusual tales!" A *Young Reader's Review* critic added: "These are simple tales, simply told. Most children will enjoy them because of their originality, but few will penetrate beneath the surface to the themes. It doesn't matter—they are fun to read or hear...."

Noted the *New York Times Book Review* concerning *Martze:* "A parable about illusion and reality? A morality tale of good and evil? We do not know, nor are we meant to know. Mr. Sendak's talent is for the mysterious; and, though new, his stories seem to have passed through generations, told around flickering fires and embellished with each new rendering...."

BIOGRAPHICAL/CRITICAL SOURCES: Kirkus, October 1, 1957; *San Francisco Chronicle,* November 10, 1957; *New York Times,* January 26, 1958; *Young Reader's Review,* April, 1967; *Book Week,* May 21, 1967; *New York Times Book Review,* July 21, 1968.*

*   *   *

SENIOR, Donald 1940-

PERSONAL: Born January 1, 1940, in Philadelphia, Pa.; son of Vincent E. (a business executive) and Margaret (Tiernan) Senior. *Education:* Passionist Seminary College, Chicago, Ill., B.A., 1963; University of Louvain, lic. theology, 1970, S.T.D., 1972. *Home:* 5401 South Cornell Ave., Chicago, Ill. 60615. *Office:* Catholic Theological Union, 5401 South Cornell Ave., Chicago, Ill. 60615.

CAREER: Entered Passionist Religious Congregation, 1960, ordained Roman Catholic priest, 1967; Catholic Theological Union, Chicago, Ill., assistant professor, 1972-77, associate professor of New Testament studies, 1977—. Member of Roman Catholic/Southern Baptist Scholars Dialogue, 1977—. Has appeared on Chicago's Catholic television network, CTN/C. *Member:* Society of Biblical Literature, Catholic Biblical Association of America, Catholic Theological Society, Chicago Society of Biblical Research.

WRITINGS: Matthew: A Gospel for the Church, Franciscan Herald, 1973; *Matthew: Read and Pray,* Franciscan Herald, 1974; *Jesus: A Gospel Portrait,* Pflaum, 1975; *The Passion Narrative According to Matthew,* University of Louvain Press, 1975; *Invitation to Matthew,* Doubleday, 1977. Creator of a tape cassette series, "The Gospel of Mark." Contributor of articles and reviews to professional and popular magazines. Associate editor of *Bible Today* and *Catholic Biblical Quarterly.*

WORK IN PROGRESS: Research on the Gospels, particularly on their presentation of the death of Jesus.

SIDELIGHTS: Senior writes: "My career has been shaped by two main influences: my professional training in critical biblical scholarship, and my vocation as a Catholic priest. I have tried to keep faith with both by serious scholarship and by a heavy schedule of lectures and writings to disseminate the results of biblical scholarship for the sake of Christians interested in contemporary interpretation of the Bible. I have had the opportunity to travel and lecture throughout the United States and Canada, have spent five years in Europe, and in 1977, spent five months in Korea, Japan, and the Philippines lecturing to and learning from people there. All of this helps me understand more about the art of interpreting a treasured tradition in a new world."

* * *

SEYMOUR, Miranda
See SINCLAIR, Miranda

* * *

SEYMOUR, William Napier 1914-
(William Napier)

PERSONAL: Born September 8, 1914, in London, England; son of Charles Hugh Napier (a soldier) and Mary (Philips) Seymour; married Mary Hambro, April 28, 1945; children: Carolyn Seymour Hanbury, Sarah Seymour Page, Arabella Seymour Elwes. *Education:* Educated at private school in Windsor, England. *Home:* Falconer's House, Crichel, Wimborne, Dorsetshire BH21 5DR, England.

CAREER: British Army, career officer in Scots Guards, 1934-49, served in Palestine, 1936, in the Middle East, 1939-41, in the Far East, 1942-44, and in Malaya, 1948-49, affiliated with staff college, Quetta, Pakistan, 1943, mentioned in dispatches; retired as major, 1949. Crichel Estate, Wimborne, England, land agent, 1949-70, manager of Crichel Woodlands, 1970—. *Member:* Royal Institution of Chartered Surveyors (fellow).

WRITINGS: (Under name William Napier) *Lands of Spice and Treasure*, Aldus Books, 1971; *Ordeal by Ambition*, Sidgwick & Jackson, 1972; *Battles in Britain and Other Political Background*, Sidgwick & Jackson, 1976; Contributor to magazines and newspapers, including *Country Life* and *History Today*.

WORK IN PROGRESS: Sovereigns' Legacies, for Sidgwick & Jackson.

* * *

SHANNON, Ellen 1927-

PERSONAL: Born August 14, 1927, in Decatur, Ill.; daughter of Harley Foss (an educator) and Blon Nova (an educator; maiden name, Smith) Carmichael; married Richard Shannon (an actor), May 16, 1959; children: Kathleen, Michael, Amy. *Education:* University of Illinois, A.B., 1950; University of Delaware, M.A., 1954. *Politics:* "liberal (small 'l')." *Religion:* Episcopalian. *Home:* 964 17th St., Astoria, Ore. 97103. *Agent:* Collier Associates, 280 Madison Ave., New York, N.Y. 10016. *Office:* Department of English, Clatsop Community College, 16th & Jerome, Astoria, Ore. 97103.

CAREER: Clatsop Community College, Astoria, Ore., instructor in English, 1966—.

WRITINGS: American Dictionary of Culinary Terms, A.

S. Barnes, 1962, reprinted as *The Cook in the Kitchen*, 1974; *The Expectation Cookbook*, A. S. Barnes, 1965, reprinted as *The Expectant Mother's Guide to Happy Eating*, 1975; *A Layman's Guide to Christian Terms*, A. S. Barnes, 1969.

WORK IN PROGRESS: An abridged edition of Marcel Proust's *Remembrance of Things Past; Traveling Together*, an account of family travels through Europe, emphasizing useful information on such subjects as budgeting; *So Wondrous a Magic: A Biography of the Irish Poet James Clarence Mangan*.

SIDELIGHTS: Ellen Shannon writes: "My family and my curiosity have motivated most of my published writings. However, my admiration for Proust's work, and a desire to see it more readily accessible, have inspired me to spend the most time on editing his masterpiece. In between times, teaching absorbs the lion's share of my attention—and I would travel half of every year if I could!"

* * *

SHARMA, Partap 1939-

PERSONAL: Born December 12, 1939, in Lahore, India (now Pakistan); son of Baij Nath (a civil engineer and farmer) and Dayawati (Pandit) Sharma; married Susan Amanda Pick, October 21, 1971; children: Kiran Namrita, Tara Natasha. *Education:* St. Xavier's College, Bombay, India, B.A. (honors), 1959. *Politics:* "Democratic, anti-censorship, but no political party." *Religion:* Hindu. *Home:* 105 Olympus, Altamount Rd., Bombay 400 026, India. *Office:* Flat 5B, Block 6, Shyam Nivas, Bhulabhai Desai Rd., Bombay 400 026, India. *Agent:* Oliver Swan, Collier Associates, 280 Madison Ave., New York, N.Y. 10016.

CAREER: Indian National Theatre, Bombay, playwright and director of English drama, 1961—. Chief free-lance commentator for newsreels and documentaries produced by Films Division (Bombay), 1960— (also producer-director); host of "What's the Good Word?," a program for Television Centre (Bombay), 1975-76; actor in Hindi feature films.

MEMBER: Cine Artistes Association, Radio Advertisers and Producers Association of India, Commentators Guild, National Centre for the Performing Arts, Films Division Film Study Group, Club Mahabaleshwar, Amateur Riders Club. *Awards, honors:* Silver Gazelle from the President of India, 1971, for lead role in feature film "Phir Bhi" (title means "Even Then"); national award for best Hindi film of the year for "Phir Bhi"; first prize from RAPA, 1976, for best voice in radio-spots.

WRITINGS: A Touch of Brightness (three-act play; first produced on the West End at Royal Court Theatre, March 5, 1967), Grove, 1967; *The Surangini Tales* (juvenile), Harcourt, 1973; *Dog Detective Ranjha* (juvenile), Macmillan, 1977.

Plays: "Bars Invisible" (three-act), first produced in Bombay at Indian National Theatre, June 10, 1961; "The Word" (three-act), first produced in Bombay at Bombay Arts Festival, March 26, 1966; "The Professor Has a Warcry" (five-act), first produced in Bombay at Impermanent Theatre, January 15, 1970.

Documentary film scripts: "The Framework of Famine," 1967; "The Flickering Flame," 1974; "Kamli," 1976.

Work represented in anthologies, including *Twenty-Five Years of Indian Independence*, edited by Jag Mohan, Vikas, 1973; *Young Winter's Tales 5*, edited by M. R. Hodgkin, Macmillan (London), 1974; *Aspects of Indian Literature*, edited by Suresh Kohli, Vikas, 1975; *Young Winter's Tales*

8, edited by Hodgkin, Macmillan, 1978. Contributor of stories and articles to magazines.

WORK IN PROGRESS: The Passport Racket and two other novels, a trilogy touching on contemporary events in India.

SIDELIGHTS: Sharma comments: "Stories are perhaps a way of making more coherent and comprehensible the bewildering complexity of the world. I learn and discover as I write and I try to share what I have understood. This began with me when I was a child, before I could read, and when I needed to deduce a story to explain the pictures in a book. But that is just the technique; the aim is to uncover an aspect of the truth. The truth isn't always palatable. Two of my documentaries and a play have been banned. The High Court reversed the ban on the play; it is now a text in three Indian universities."

* * *

SHARP, Ansel M(iree) 1924-

PERSONAL: Born June 25, 1924, in Rome, Ga.; son of Joseph Albert (a state fire marshall) and Mattie Belle (Miree) Sharp; married Martha Martin (a drama professor); children: Courtney, Alison. *Education:* Howard College, B.A., 1949; University of Virginia, M.A., 1950; Louisiana State University, Ph.D., 1956. *Office:* Department of Economics, Oklahoma State University, Stillwater, Okla. 74075.

CAREER: Auburn University, Auburn, Ala., instructor in economics, 1950-52; William Jewell College, Liberty, Mo., professor of economics and head of department, 1955-56; University of Cincinnati, Cincinnati, Ohio, assistant professor of economics, 1956-57; Oklahoma State University, Stillwater, assistant professor, 1957-64, professor of economics, 1964—. Economic adviser to Government of Kenya, 1966-68. *Member:* American Economic Association, Southern Economic Association. *Awards, honors:* Grants from Ford Foundation, 1966-68, and Joint Council on Economic Education, 1970-73.

WRITINGS: (With Robert L. Sandmeyer) *Oklahoma Tax Effort and Service Effort: A Study in Interstate Comparisons,* Research Foundation, Oklahoma State University, 1961; *State and Local Government General Expenditures and Revenues: Past and Future Trends,* Research Foundation, Oklahoma State University, 1965; *The Cost of Hospital Illness in Oklahoma,* Research Foundation, Oklahoma State University, 1966; (with R. W. Leftwich) *Economics of Social Issues,* with instructor's manual and student guide, Business Publications, 1974, 3rd edition, 1978; (with Sandmeyer, Jack Robinson, and Larkin Warner) *Oklahoma State Expenditures: A Functional Analysis of State Government Expenditures in Fiscal 1973,* Kerr Foundation, 1974; (contributor) *Management Policies in Local Government Finance,* Municipal Finance Officers Association, 1975; (with Kent Olsen) *The Economics of Public Finance and Expenditures,* West Publishing, 1978. Contributor to professional journals.

* * *

SHEARER, Ronald A(lexander) 1932-

PERSONAL: Born June 15, 1932, in Trail, British Columbia, Canada; son of James (a mechanic) and Mary Ann (Smith) Shearer; married Renate E. Selig (a social planner), December 22, 1956; children: Carl, Bruce. *Education:* University of British Columbia, B.A., 1954; Ohio State University, M.A., 1955, Ph.D., 1959. *Residence:* Vancouver, Brit-

ish Columbia, Canada. *Office:* Department of Economics, University of British Columbia, 2075 Westbrook Pl., Vancouver, British Columbia, Canada V6T 1W5.

CAREER: University of Michigan, Ann Arbor, assistant professor of economics, 1958-62; Royal Commission on Banking & Finance, Toronto, Ontario, economist, 1962-63; University of British Columbia, Vancouver, assistant professor, 1963-65, associate professor, 1965-70, professor of economics, 1970—.

WRITINGS: (Editor) *Exploiting Our Economic Potential,* Holt, 1968; (editor) *Trade Liberalization and a Regional Economy,* University of Toronto Press, 1971; (with David Bond) *The Economics of the Canadian Financial System,* Prentice-Hall, 1972, revised edition, 1979; (with Bond and Helen B. O'Bannon) *Money and Banking,* Harper, 1972.

WORK IN PROGRESS: Research on Canadian monetary history, 1920-1934.

* * *

SHELBOURNE, Cecily
See GOODWIN, Suzanne

* * *

SHELBY, Susan
See KINNICUTT, Susan Sibley

* * *

SHELDON, Scott
See WALLMANN, Jeffrey M(iner)

* * *

SHENOY, B(ellikoth) R(aghunath) 1905-

PERSONAL: Born June 3, 1905, in Bellikoth, South Canara, India; son of B. Janardhan and Siree Shenoy; married Anasuya Kamath, 1938; children: Sudha (daughter), Subodh (son), Siddharth (son). *Education:* Banaras Hindu University, M.A., 1930; London School of Economics and Political Science, London, M.Sc., 1933. *Religion:* "Theosophy." *Home and office:* Economics Research Centre, D-390 Defence Colony, New Delhi 110024, India.

CAREER: University of Ceylon (now University of Sri Lanka), Colombo, lecturer in economics, 1936-42; University of Bombay, Bombay, India, professor of economics and principal of Lalbhai Dalpthbai Arts College in Ahmedabad, 1942-45; Reserve Bank of India, Bombay, director of rural economics and monetary research, 1945-49; International Monetary Fund, Bombay, India, head technical representative in the Far East, 1948-51, alternate executive director, representing India, 1951-53; Gujarat University, Ahmedabad, professor of economics and director of School of Social Sciences, 1954-68; Economics Research Centre, New Delhi, India, director, 1968—. Sir William Meyer Lecturer at University of Madras, 1955-56; lecturer at other Indian universities. Member of Ceylon board of commissioners of currency, 1940-42; member (and member of board of directors) of Bombay Bullion Exchange, 1948-49. *Member:* Indian Economic Association (president, 1957), Mont Pelerin Society.

WRITINGS: Ceylon Currency and Banking, Longmans (Madras, India), 1941; *The Bombay Plan,* Karnatak Press, 1944; *Post-War Depression,* Kitabistan, 1944; *Sterling Assets of the Reserve Bank of India,* Oxford University Press (Bombay, India), 1946; *Problems of Indian Economic De-*

velopment, University of Madras, 1958; *Stability of the Indian Rupee,* Harold Laski Institute of Political Science, 1959; *Indian Planning and Economic Development,* Asia Publishing House (Bombay, India), 1963; *Indian Economic Policy,* Popular Prakashan, 1967; *PL 480 Aid and India's Food Problem,* East-West Press, 1974. Contributor to learned journals, popular magazines, and newspapers in India, England, Italy, Germany, and the United States, including *Fortune.*

WORK IN PROGRESS: Writing articles for newspapers and magazines "assessing the economic policies of our new government."

SIDELIGHTS: Shenoy told *CA* that he has been "a consistent opponent of governmental planning, deficit financing, and controls. I believe the free market pricing system to be the best method achieving economic development." His work has taken him to France, British Guiana, Hong Kong, Italy, Japan, Luxembourg, Mexico, Singapore, Thailand, England, Venezuela, and the United States.

* * *

SHEPHERD, Jean (Parker) 1929-

PERSONAL: Born July 26, 1929, in Chicago, Ill.; son of Jean P. (a clerk) and Anne (Heinrichs) Shepherd; married Leigh Brown (a writer), March, 1977. *Education:* Attended University of Maryland, 1948, and Indiana University, 1949-50. *Residence:* Washington, N.J. *Agent:* Leigh Brown, R.D. 1, Box 28, Washington, N.J. 07882.

CAREER: Actor in television and radio; writer. Has also been a staff member of radio stations WLW, Cincinnati, 1951-53, KYW, Philadelphia, 1954-57, and WOR, New York City, 1958—. Special instructor at New York University, 1969. As an actor has had four one-man shows at Carnegie Hall and has appeared in off-Broadway plays.

MEMBER: Authors Guild of Authors League of America, American Radio Relay League, Aircraft Owners and Pilots Association, Overseas Press Club, Dutch Treat Club. *Awards, honors:* Most original fiction award from Indiana University, 1966; best humor and satire award from *Playboy,* 1967, 1968, 1970, 1971; Mark Twain Award from International Platform Speakers Association, 1976.

WRITINGS: The America of George Ade, Putnam, 1961; *In God We Trust: All Others Pay Cash* (novel), Doubleday, 1967; *Wanda Hickey's Night of Golden Memories and Other Disasters* (stories), Doubleday, 1972; *The Ferrari in the Bedroom* (stories and essays), Dodd, 1973; *The Phantom of the Open Hearth,* Doubleday, 1977. Author of columns in *Village Voice,* 1960-67, and *Car and Driver,* 1968-77. Contributing editor of *Playboy* and *Car and Driver.*

WORK IN PROGRESS: Giant Country, a novel; a major television series for American Broadcasting Co.

AVOCATIONAL INTERESTS: Amateur radio operator, private pilot.

* * *

SHEPPARD, Roger 1939-

PERSONAL: Born January 2, 1939, in Dorsetshire, England; son of Frederick (a plumber) and Sybil (a music teacher; maiden name, Lander) Sheppard; married Judith Gerrans (a copywriter), October 1, 1966; children: Jackie, Anna, Michael. *Education:* Attended school in Swanage, England. *Politics:* None. *Religion:* None. *Home:* 117 Kent House Rd., Beckenham, Kent, England. *Office:* National Portrait Gallery, Trafalgar Sq., London W.C.1, England.

CAREER: Bookseller of second-hand and antiquarian books, 1956-68; Royal Institute of British Architects, London, England, specialist architectural bookseller, 1968-72; Architectural Press, London, sales manager, 1972-77; National Portrait Gallery, London, manager of publications, 1977—. *Member:* Private Libraries Association, Bibliographical Society, Powys Society, Society of Dorset Men.

WRITINGS: Science Fiction Traders Handbook, Trigon, 1978; *Walking the Dorset Cursus,* Abbey Press, in press.

Editor: (With Richard Threadgill and John Holmes) *Paper Houses,* Schocken, 1974; (with wife, Judith Sheppard) *International Directory of Book Collectors,* Trigon, 1976, 2nd edition, 1978; *Societies for Book Collectors,* Trigon, 1978; (with J. Sheppard) *Publishing Your First Book,* Trigon, 1978; *Publishers in the U.S.A. and Their Addresses,* Trigon, 1978; *Instant Houses,* Trigon, in press.

SIDELIGHTS: Sheppard told CA he is motivated by a desire to find out things. "I have compulsively compiled directories in fields not many people seem to be interested in. I am also interested in unusual buildings (and materials for building), futures of all kinds, including projections for the year 2000, and science fiction." *Avocational interests:* Exploring ancient pre-Roman sites in the countryside.

* * *

SHERE, Dennis 1940-

PERSONAL: Born November 29, 1940, in Cleveland, Ohio; son of William (a laborer) and Susan (Laskay) Shere; married Maureen Elizabeth Jones, September 4, 1965; children: Rebecca Lynn, David Matthew, Stephen Andrew. *Education:* Ohio University, B.S., 1963, M.S., 1964. *Religion:* Protestant. *Home:* 66 East Dixon Ave., Dayton, Ohio 45419. *Office: Journal Herald,* 37 South Ludlow St., Dayton, Ohio 45401.

CAREER/WRITINGS: Dayton Daily News, Dayton, Ohio, reporter, 1966-69; Bowling Green State University, Bowling Green, Ohio, assistant professor of journalism, 1969-70; *Detroit News,* Detroit, Mich., business and city editor, 1970-75; *Journal Herald,* Dayton, editor, 1975—. *Military service:* U.S. Army, 1964-66; became first lieutenant. *Member:* Sigma Delta Chi, Kiwanis.

* * *

SHERMAN, Dan(iel Michael) 1950-

PERSONAL: Born July 31, 1950, in Los Angeles, Calif.; son of Lawrence James and Charlotte Zelda Sherman. *Education:* Attended University of Oregon; received B.A. from University of California, Northridge. *Politics:* "American." *Religion:* Jewish. *Home:* 1300 Chautauqua Blvd., Pacific Palisades, Calif. 90027. *Agent:* Richard Curtis, 156 East 52nd St., New York, N.Y. 10022.

CAREER: Free-lance journalist and public relations copywriter, 1972-74; *Los Angeles Voice,* Los Angeles, Calif., editor, 1974-75; free-lance writer, 1975—. *Member:* American Society of Journalists and Authors.

WRITINGS: The Mole, Arbor House, 1977; *Riddle,* Arbor House, 1977; (with Robin Williamson) *The Glory Trap,* Walker & Co., 1977. Author of play, "The Cult of Rags."

WORK IN PROGRESS: A novel.

SIDELIGHTS: Sherman writes: "It is not enough for the writer to lead the reader from passage to passage. He must never cease wrestling with the language, never shy from vital problems: moral, social, especially spiritual. For the writer is an artist and it is the artist who dreams the dreams of a civilization.''

* * *

SHERMAN, Harold (Morrow) 1898-

PERSONAL: Born July 13, 1898, in Traverse City, Mich.; son of Thomas Henry and Alcinda E. (Morrow) Sherman; married Martha Frances Bain, September 26, 1920; children: Mary Alcinda (Mrs. Bernard J. Kobiella), Marcia Anne (Mrs. Wendell R. Smith). Education: Attended University of Michigan, 1918-19. Politics: Democrat. Religion: ''Nonsectarian.'' Home address: Highway 5, South Mountain View, Ark. 72560. Office: ESP Research Associates Foundation, 1630 Union National Plaza Building, Little Rock, Ark. 72201.

CAREER: Marion Chronicle, Marion, Ind., reporter, 1921-24; free-lance writer, 1924-35; CBS-Radio, writer and commentator of ''Your Key to Happiness'' in New York, N.Y., 1935-36, and Chicago, Ill., 1943; free-lance writer, 1936-64; ESP Research Associates Foundation, Little Rock, Ark., founder, president, and director, 1964—, also director of annual workshop. Investigator, experimenter, and lecturer on extra-sensory perception. Co-developer of Blanchard Springs Caverns. Member: Authors Guild of Authors League of America (life member), Dramatists Guild, Lions.

WRITINGS—Fiction: Fight 'em, Big Three, Appleton, 1926; Mayfield's Fighting Five, Appleton, 1926; Touchdown!, Grosset, 1927; Beyond the Dog's Nose, Appleton, 1927; (with Hawthorne Daniel) Cameron MacBain, Backwoodsman, Appleton, 1927; Get 'em, Mayfield, Appleton, 1927; Hit by Pitcher, Grosset, 1928; Block That Kick!, Grosset, 1928; Bases Full!: ''Ernie Challenges the World'', Grosset, 1928; Safe!, Grosset, 1928; Over the Line, Goldsmith Publishing, 1929; Don Rader, Trailblazer, Grosset, 1929; Flashing Steel, Grosset, 1929; Hit and Run!, Grosset, 1929.

Hold That Line!, Grosset, 1930; Flying Steel and Other Hockey Stories, Grosset, 1930; Ding Palmer, Air Detective, Grosset, 1930; Batter Up!: A Story of American Legion Junior Baseball, Grosset, 1930; Number Forty-Four, and Other Football Stories, Grosset, 1930, reprinted, Books for Libraries, 1972; Shoot That Ball!, and Other Basketball Stories, Grosset, 1930; The Land of Monsters, Grosset, 1931; It's a Pass!, Goldsmith Publishing, 1931; Slashing Sticks and Other Hockey Stories, Grosset, 1931; Strike Him Out!, Goldsmith Publishing, 1931; Goal to Go!, Grosset, 1931; Interference and Other Football Stories, Goldsmith Publishing, 1932, reprinted, Books for Libraries, 1971; Down the Ice, and Other Winter Sport Stories, Goldsmith Publishing, 1932; Double Play! and Other Baseball Stories, Grosset, 1932; Crashing Through!, Grosset, 1932; Under the Basket, and Other Basketball Stories, Goldsmith Publishing, 1932; The Tennis Terror, and Other Tennis Stories, Goldsmith Publishing, 1932; Let Freedom Ring!: A Novel of These Turbulent Times, N. H. White, Jr., 1932; Tahara among African Tribes, Goldsmith Publishing, 1933; Tahara: Boy King of the Desert, Goldsmith Publishing, 1933; Tahara: Boy Mystic of India, Goldsmith Publishing, 1933; Tahara in the Land of Yucatan, Goldsmith Publishing, 1933; Call of the Land: A Novel of High Adventure in 4-H Club Work, M. A. Donohue, 1948.

Nonfiction: Your Key to Happiness, H. C. Kinsey, 1935; Your Key to Married Happiness, Putnam, 1944; Your Key to Youth Problems, Putnam, 1945; Your Key to Romance, Pegasus Books, 1948; You Live after Death, Creative Age Press, 1949; You Can Stop Drinking, Creative Age Press, 1950, reprinted as Anyone Can Stop Drinking (Even You!), C. & R. Anthony, 1959; (with George Hubert Wilkins) Thoughts Through Space, Creative Age Press, 1942, 1951, reprinted, Fawcett, 1973; Know Your Own Mind: An Amazing Revelation of Your Inner Consciousness, C. & R. Anthony, 1953; Adventures in Thinking, Master Publications, 1956; (with Claude Myron Bristol) TNT, the Power within You: How to Release the Forces inside You and Get What You Want!, Prentice-Hall, 1957; How to Turn Failure into Success, Prentice-Hall, 1958; How to Use the Power of Prayer, C. & R. Anthony, 1958.

How to Make ESP Work for You, DeVorss, 1964; How to Solve Mysteries of Your Mind and Soul: A Way to Find a Philosophy of Life that Meets the Needs of Today, DeVorss, 1965; The New TNT: Miraculous Power within You, Prentice-Hall, 1954, revised edition, 1966; Wonder Healers of the Philippines, DeVorss, 1967; Your Mysterious Powers of ESP: The New Medium of Communication, World Publishing, 1969; How to Foresee and Control Your Future, Fawcett, 1970; How to Take Yourself Apart and Put Yourself Back Together Again, Fawcett, 1971; The Harold Sherman ESP Manual, Human Development Associates, 1972; (with Ambrose Worrall and Olga Worrall) Your Power to Heal: How to Work with the God Power within You to Regain Health of Body and Mind, Harper, 1972; You Can Communicate with the Unseen World, Fawcett, 1974; How to Know What to Believe, Fawcett, 1976; How to Picture What You Want, Fawcett, 1978.

Other: ''Her Supporting Cast'' (play), 1933; ''The Little Black Book'' (play), 1935; ''The Adventures of Mark Twain'' (screenplay), Warner Brothers, 1942.

WORK IN PROGRESS: ESP research and lectures.

SIDELIGHTS: Thoughts Through Space is a book Sherman wrote to describe mind-to-mind communication experiments conducted between New York City and the Wilkins expedition three thousand miles to the north, in which he claims seventy per cent accuracy as a receiver of thoughts. Since then, his entire career has been devoted to psychic research and has gone beyond simple mind-to-mind communication experiments. He has conducted research on psychic surgery in the Philippines on two occasions, and Wonder Healers of the Philippines is one of the results of his studies.

Sherman believes that everyone possesses at least a latent extra-sensory perception ability, and through his foundation and his books (which have been translated and published abroad), he attempts to open up new areas for research and bring the information to the general reader.

He has made three record albums, ''How to Develop ESP,'' 1964, ''Advanced Techniques of ESP,'' 1964, and ''How to Foretell Your Future,'' 1964, and two cassette series, ''Know Your Own Mind'' and ''The Big Fight and How You Can Win'' (formerly ''Anyone Can Stop Drinking'').

* * *

SHERR, Paul C(linton) 1920-

PERSONAL: Born March 22, 1920, in Allentown, Pa.; son of Berne (a tailor) and Eleanor Sherr; married Jane Ickrath, September 15, 1946 (divorced); married Virginia Truitt (a physician), April 28, 1957; children: Donald, Paul, Suzanne, Gregory. Education: Muhlenberg College, B.A., 1957; Lehigh University, M.A., 1960; University of Pennsylvania, Ph.D., 1965. Politics: Democrat. Religion: Unitarian-Universalist. Home: 47 Crescent Dr., Holland, Pa. 18966. Of-

fice: Department of English, Rider College, Lawrenceville, N.J. 08648.

CAREER: Rider College, Lawrenceville, N.J., professor of English, 1965—, chairman of department, 1965-77. *Member:* Modern Language Association of America, American Association of University Professors, Multi-Ethnic Literatures of the United States, Northeast Modern Language Association, Omicron Delta Kappa.

WRITINGS: The Short Story and the Oral Tradition, Boyd & Fraser, 1970; (with Bertram L. Mott, Jr.) *Writing Fundamentals for Business Students,* Rider College Press, 1977. Contributor to journals in history, black studies, psychoanalysis, education, and library science.

WORK IN PROGRESS: The Hero as Orphaned Adolescent; new edition of *Writing Fundamentals for Business Students,* entitled *Writing for Business.*

SIDELIGHTS: Sherr writes: "As a college teacher, I often found available classroom teaching materials unsatisfactory for my purposes; consequently, I frequently composed my own. I prefer to write about such matters because by so doing, I combine my interest in teaching with that of writing. As a youth, I had intensive training in music, a regimen that developed my sense of order and my sensitivity to sound."

AVOCATIONAL INTERESTS: Playing clarinet.

* * *

SHERROD, Robert (Lee) 1909-

PERSONAL: Born February 8, 1909, in Thomas County, Ga.; son of Joseph Arnold (a lumberman) and Victoria Ellen (Evers) Sherrod; married Elizabeth Hudson, October 8, 1936 (died December 21, 1958); married Margaret Carson Ruff (a public relations counselor), May 5, 1961 (divorced, 1972); married Mary Gay Labrot Leonhardt, August 26, 1972 (died July 12, 1978); children: (first marriage) John Hudson, Robert Lee, Jr. *Education:* University of Georgia, A.B., 1929. *Politics:* Democrat. *Religion:* Episcopalian. *Home:* 4000 Massachusetts Ave. N.W., Washington, D.C. 20016. *Office:* 4000 Cathedral Ave. N.W., Washington, D.C. 20016.

CAREER: Atlanta Constitution, Atlanta, Ga., campus correspondent, 1927-29, reporter, 1929-30; *Palm Beach Daily News,* Palm Beach, Fla., reporter, 1931-32; *Hampton Chronicle,* Westhampton Beach, N.Y., reporter, 1932-34; *New York Herald Tribune,* New York, N.Y., reporter and stringer, 1932-35; *Time,* New York City, Washington correspondent, 1935-42, associate editor, 1942-52, war correspondent in the South Pacific, 1942-45, senior correspondent in the Far East, 1945-48; chief Pentagon correspondent for *Time* and *Life,* 1949-52; *Saturday Evening Post,* Philadelphia, Pa., Far East correspondent, 1952-55, managing editor, 1955-62, editor-in-chief, 1962-63, editor-at-large, 1963-65; Curtis Publishing Co., Philadelphia, Pa., vice-president and editorial coordinator, 1965-66; *Life,* contract writer, 1967-69; free-lance writer, 1969—. Member of President's Committee to Employ the Handicapped, 1958-73, U.S. Marine Corps history advisory committee, 1973-76, and University of Georgia president's advisory committee, 1975—. Member of board of trustees of Correspondents Fund, 1963—.

MEMBER: National Press Club, Overseas Press Club, Sigma Delta Chi, Alpha Tau Omega, Century Association, Federal City Club, Military Order of Carabao. *Awards, honors:* Commendation from U.S. Navy, 1943, for covering the Battles of Attu and Tarawa, and Pacific theater ribbon;

award from Headliners Club, 1944, for war reporting; Benjamin Franklin Award from University of Illinois, 1955, for best article on foreign affairs; certificate from Overseas Press Club, 1956, for excellence in reporting foreign events.

WRITINGS: Tarawa: The Story of a Battle, Duell, Sloan & Pearce, 1944, 3rd edition, 1973; *On to Westward: War in the Central Pacific,* Duell, Sloan & Pearce, 1945; (author of text) *Life's Picture History of World War II,* Time, Inc., 1950; *History of Marine Corps Aviation in World War II,* Combat Forces Press, 1952; (author of text) *Kobunsha's Picture History of the Pacific War* (in Japanese; translated by Goro Nakano), Kobunsha, 1952, 4th edition, 1960; (contributor) Edgar M. Cartwright, editor, *Apollo Expeditions to the Moon,* U.S. Government Printing Office, 1975. Contributor to journalism magazines and newspapers.

WORK IN PROGRESS: A biography of Douglas MacArthur, for Harper.

SIDELIGHTS: Sherrod told *CA:* "My major journalistic interest, 1935-41, was American politics; 1941-55, military and foreign affairs, chiefly the Pacific and Asia; from 1966 to the present I have been writing on the military and space. Obviously, I love to travel, which has always been a motivation. The last time I counted, I had crossed the Pacific forty-six times, the Atlantic twenty-two times, and had been around the world six times—not a record by any means, but an indication of motivation. It is fun to find out what is on the other side of the hill—or ocean.

"It is also interesting to learn what really happened. Thus I have turned more and more to history, and I must report that we journalists frequently don't get things right. Sometimes we are conned into errors; other times we surmise wrong. But correcting journalism is what history is all about."

AVOCATIONAL INTERESTS: Collecting books.

BIOGRAPHICAL/CRITICAL SOURCES: New York Times, March 26, 1962; *Philadelphia Evening Bulletin,* March 27, 1962.

* * *

SHETTLES, Landrum Brewer 1909-

PERSONAL: Born November 21, 1909, in Pontotoc, Miss.; son of Basil Manly and Sue (Mounce) Shettles; married Priscilla Elinor Schmidt, December 18, 1948; children: Susan Flora, Frances Louise, Lana Brewer, Landrum Brewer, David Ernest, Harold Manly and Alice Annmarie (twins). *Education:* Mississippi College, B.A., 1933; University of New Mexico, M.S., 1934; Johns Hopkins University, Ph.D., 1937, M.D., 1943. *Home:* 9 Highland Ave., Randolph, Vt. 05060. *Office:* Gifford Memorial Hospital, 44 South Main St., Randolph, Vt. 05060.

CAREER: Mississippi College, Clinton, instructor in biology, 1932-33; U.S. Bureau of Fisheries, New Mexico, biologist, 1934; Johns Hopkins University, Baltimore, Md., instructor in biology, 1934-37, research fellow, 1937-38; National Committee on Maternal Health, New York City, research fellow, 1938-43; Johns Hopkins University, intern, 1943-44; Columbia-Presbyterian Medical Center, New York City, resident in obstetrics and gynecology, 1947-51, attending obstetrician and gynecologist, 1951-73; attending obstetrician-gynecologist at New York City's Doctors Hospital, Polyclinic, and Flower-Fifth Ave. Hospital, all 1974-75; Gifford Memorial Hospital, Randolph, Vt., attending obstetrician-gynecologist, 1975—. Diplomate of American Board of Obstetrics and Gynecology. Associate professor at Columbia University, 1951-73; Anglo-American lecturer at

Royal College of Obstetricians and Gynecologists, 1959. Private practice in obstetrics and gynecology, 1951-75. Research director for New York Fertility Research Foundation, 1974-75; consultant to Office of Naval Research. *Military service:* U.S. Army, Medical Corps, 1944-46; became major.

MEMBER: World Medical Association (fellow), Pan American Medical Association, American Medical Association, American College of Obstetricians and Gynecologists (fellow), American Cancer Society (fellow), American Association for the Advancement of Science (fellow), American Society of Zoologists, American Physiological Society, Society for Experimental Biology and Medicine, Harvey Society, Society of University Gynecologists, Royal Society of Health (fellow), Vermont Medical Society, New York State Medical Association, New York County Medical Association, Phi Beta Kappa, Sigma Xi, Omicron Delta Kappa, Gamma Alpha. *Awards, honors:* Markle Foundation scholarship for Columbia University, 1951-56; Ortho Medal from American Society for the Study of Fertility, Sterility, and Allied Subjects, 1960; D.Sc. from Mississippi College, 1966.

WRITINGS: Ovum Humanum: Growth, Maturation, Nourishment, Fertilization, and Early Development, Hafner, 1960; (with David M. Rorvik) *Your Baby's Sex: Now You Can Choose,* Dodd, 1970, revised edition published as *Choose Your Baby's Sex,* 1977; (with Roberts Rugh) *From Conception to Birth: The Drama of Life's Beginnings,* Harper, 1971; *Life's Beginnings,* Johns Hopkins Press, in press. Contributor to journals.

SIDELIGHTS: Shettles's extensive research in biology, physiology, and medicine led him to the discovery and identification of male- and female-producing sperm.

*   *   *

SHEVIN, David (Avram) 1951-

PERSONAL: Born June 1, 1951, in Rochester, N.Y.; son of Nathan (an urban developer) and Ella (a child welfare worker; maiden name, Drexler) Shevin. *Education:* Attended Mount Angel College and Deep Springs College, 1969-72; Lewis & Clark College, B.A., 1973; Bowling Green State University, M.F.A., 1976; University of Cincinnati, doctoral study, 1976—. *Religion:* Jewish. *Home:* 3300 Jefferson Ave., #10, Cincinnati, Ohio 45220.

CAREER: Scrantom's, Rochester, N.Y., book store manager, 1972-73; writer, 1973—.

WRITINGS—All poetry: (With Jonathan Weisberger) *Musics,* privately printed, 1972; *The World Series,* Maidstone, 1974; *Expecting Ginger Rogers,* Armchair Press, 1975, 2nd edition, 1978; *Camptown Spaces,* Anti-Ocean Press, 1977; *The Stop Book,* Konglomerati Press, 1978. Contributor of articles and poems to literary journals, including *Parnassus, Poetry Now, Marilyn,* and *Margins.*

WORK IN PROGRESS: You Break Up Inside, translations of Israeli poet Arye Sivan; *Einat,* poems.

SIDELIGHTS: Shevin writes: "Imagine punching your way out of the sweet womb of sorrow. Sparks fly, huh? And the knuckles bleed from the hard salt crystals in the tears. Soft walls don't break down easy. Whining bulldozers still richochet from their old momentum, or sit in failure alley drinking Genessee cream ale. Imagine that you are in love with the sweat and can't sleep on the velvet bed. The obvious facts are too shaped, like in *Schjeldahl:* cows know the secret of pastoral poetry. So you take off the dark shirt and wear your words instead. It doesn't matter if there is a way

out or not, 'cuz you think there is and there are colors out there. Rainbows are pasted all over the animals."

*   *   *

SHIH, Vincent Y(u) C(hung) 1903-

PERSONAL: Born February 17, 1903, in China; came to the United States in 1945, naturalized citizen, 1956; son of Hsin-tsang (a minister) and Chousan (Chou) Shih; married Shih-J Wang; children: William. *Education:* Fukien Christian University, B.A., 1925; Yenching University, M.A., 1930; University of Southern California, Ph.D., 1939. *Home:* 28002 Ridgebrook Court, Rancho Palos Verdes, Calif. 90274.

CAREER: University of Washington, Seattle, assistant professor, 1945-51, associate professor, 1951-56, professor of Chinese philosophy and literature, 1956-73, professor emeritus, 1973—; writer, 1973—. Visiting professor at Taiwan National University, San Francisco State University, and University of Southern California. Adviser to the governor of Szechuan during the Sino-Japanese War. *Member:* Association for Asian Studies.

WRITINGS: The Literary Mind and the Carving of Dragons, Columbia University Press, 1959, bilingual edition, Chung Hwa Books, 1970; *Taiping Ideology: Its Sources, Interpretations, and Influences,* University of Washington Press, 1967; *Collected Essays on Literary Criticism,* Lien-Ching Publishing House, 1976; *Collected Philosophical Essays,* Lien-Ching Publishing House, 1976.

WORK IN PROGRESS: A History of Chinese Literary Criticism; The Dream of Red Chamber and Enlightenment.

SIDELIGHTS: Shih writes: "In *The Dream of Red Chamber and Enlightenment* I propose to do something which is the most important aspect of the novel, but which has never been attempted before. The history of Chinese literary criticism has always been my aim, diverted by other studies demanded of me by circumstances."

*   *   *

SHINE, Ted 1931-

PERSONAL: Born April 26, 1931, in Baton Rouge, La.; son of Theodis Wesley and Bessie (Herson) Shine. *Education:* Howard University, B.A., 1953; Iowa State University, M.A., 1958; University of California, Santa Barbara, Ph.D., 1971. *Politics:* Democrat. *Religion:* Baptist. *Home:* 10717 Cox Lane, Dallas, Tex. 75229. *Agent:* Flora Roberts, Inc., 65 East 55th St., New York, N.Y. 10022. *Office:* P.O. Box 2082, Prairie View, Tex. 77445.

CAREER: Dillard University, New Orleans, La., instructor in drama and English, 1960-61; Howard University, Washington, D.C., assistant professor of drama, 1961-67; Prairie View A. & M. University, Prairie View, Tex., professor and head of department of drama, 1967—. Member of theater panel of Texas Commission of the Arts. *Military service:* U.S. Army, 1955-57. *Member:* American Theatre Association, Texas Educational Theatre Association.

WRITINGS: Sho Is Hot in the Cotton Patch (one-act play; first produced in Washington, D.C. at Howard University, 1950), Encore, 1966; *Shoes,* Encore, 1967; *Morning, Noon, and Night* (three-act play; first produced in Washington, D.C. at Howard University, 1964), Negro Universities Press, 1969; *Contribution* (one-act play; first produced in New York City, 1967), Chilton, 1972; *Herbert the Third* (one-act play; first produced in Wichita Falls, Tex. at Midwestern University, October, 1975), Free Press, 1974; (co-editor with James V. Hatch) *Black Theatre U.S.: An Anthology of Plays,* Free Press, 1974.

WORK IN PROGRESS: "Sid and Byron," a television series about a middle-aged black man and the retarded grandson he has chosen to raise.

SIDELIGHTS: Shine comments: "Motivation for my work stems from life itself—a sad face, a broken heart, a trembling voice, a cry in the night. The purpose of drama for me continues to be to teach and to please, and hopefully my work will emerge realistically—uplifting the dignity of mankind."

* * *

SHOENIGHT, Aloise 1914-
(Aloise Tracy)

PERSONAL: Born November 20, 1914, in Bridgeport, Ill.; daughter of William Fitch (an oil field superintendent) and Carrie E. (Milhous) Souers; married James Richard Tracy, September 18, 1946 (died August 1, 1972); married Hurley F. Shoenight (a farmer), June 25, 1976. *Education:* Eastern Illinois University, B.Ed., 1937. *Politics:* Republican. *Religion:* Southern Baptist. *Home address:* Route 3, Box 1107, West Riverwood Dr., Foley, Ala. 36535.

CAREER: Elementary school teacher in Westfield, Ill., 1937-38, and Bridgeport, Ill., 1938-46; writer, 1946—. *Member:* American Poetry League, American Poets Fellowship Society (honorary life member), Illinois State Poetry Society (charter member), Alabama State Poetry Society, Pensters (chaplain, 1974—).

WRITINGS—Books of poems; all under name Aloise Tracy: *His Handiwork,* Blue River Press, 1954; *Memory Is a Poet,* Windfall Press, 1964; *The Silken Web,* Prairie Press, 1965; *A Merry Heart,* Prairie Press, 1966; *In Two or Three Tomorrows,* Prairie Press, 1968; *All Flesh Is Grass,* Merchants Press, 1971; *Beyond the Edge,* Merchants Press, 1973.

SIDELIGHTS: Aloise Tracy writes: "I believe in good, clean writing. Humor and brevity are important fundamentals, also.

"Traveling has always been of interest to me; but the last few years, trips have necessarily been short. Interesting people, I've found, are in one's home area as well as hundreds of miles away. Listening is learning anywhere."

* * *

SHORE, Jane 1947-

PERSONAL: Born March 10, 1947, in Newark, N.J.; daughter of George and Essie Shore. *Education:* Goddard College, B.A., 1969; University of Iowa, M.F.A., 1971. *Home:* 153 C Mount Auburn St., Cambridge, Mass. 02138.

CAREER: Radcliffe Institute, Cambridge, Mass., fellow in poetry, 1971-73; Harvard University, Cambridge, Briggs-Copeland Lecturer in English, 1973—. Has given poetry readings. *Member:* Academy of American Poets (local chairperson, 1976-77). *Awards, honors:* Bess Hokin Prize from *Poetry,* 1973; Borestone Mountain poetry awards, 1973, 1975; grant from Massachusetts Endowment for the Arts and Humanities, 1976-77; Juniper Prize from University of Massachusetts Press, 1977, for *Eye Level;* Robert Frost fellowship for Breadloaf Writers Conference, 1977; grant from National Endowment for the Arts, 1978-79.

WRITINGS: Lying Down in the Olive Press (poetry chapbook), Goddard Journal Press, 1969; *Eye Level* (poems), University of Massachusetts Press, 1977.

Work represented in anthologies, including *Ten American Poets,* edited by James Atlas, Carcanet Press, 1973; *Out of This World: Poems from the Hawkeye State,* edited by Gildner, Iowa State University Press, 1975; *The Blacksmith Anthology,* 1976. Contributor of poems to literary magazines and popular periodicals, including *New Republic, Antioch Review,* and *American Review. Ploughshares,* member of editorial board, 1973-74, editor, 1977.

* * *

SHORT, Robert L(ester) 1932-

PERSONAL: Born August 3, 1932, in Big Spring, Tex.; son of Lester Marshall (a druggist) and Hazel T. (Hobbs) Short; married Ellen Kay Coale, May 27, 1966; children: Rebecca Grace, Sarah Elizabeth, Christopher. *Education:* University of Oklahoma, B.A., 1953; Southern Methodist University, B.D., 1957; North Texas State University, M.A., 1961; doctoral study at Garrett Theological Seminary. *Politics:* Independent. *Home and office:* 3030 Isabella, Evanston, Ill. 60201.

CAREER: Ordained Methodist minister. Margo Jones Theatre, Dallas, Tex., actor, 1959-60; Dallas Council of Churches, Dallas, director of radio and television, 1960-61; North Texas State University, Denton, instructor in English and philosophy, 1961-63; writer, 1963—. Lecturer throughout United States and Europe. *Member:* International Bonhoeffer Society, Karl Barth Society of North America, Authors Guild of Authors League of America. *Awards, honors:* Robert F. Ferguson Memorial Award, 1974, for *A Time to Be Born—A Time to Die.*

WRITINGS: The Gospel According to Peanuts, John Knox, 1964; *The Parables of Peanuts,* Harper, 1968; *A Time to Be Born—A Time to Die,* Harper, 1973; *Something to Believe In,* Harper, 1978. Contributor to religious periodicals and newspapers.

WORK IN PROGRESS: Research on systematic theology.

* * *

SHORTT, Terence Michael 1911-

PERSONAL: Born March 1, 1911, in Winnipeg, Manitoba, Canada; son of Henry (a trainman) and Emma (an artist; maiden name, McMeekan) Shortt; married Audrey Helen Bell, August 7, 1939. *Education:* Attended Winnipeg School of Art. *Home:* 127 Glencairn Ave., Toronto, Ontario, Canada M4R 1N1.

CAREER: Royal Ontario Museum, Toronto, Ontario, assistant, 1930-38, artist-ornithologist, 1939-48, chief of display department, 1949-76; writer and artist, 1976—. *Member:* American Ornithologists Union (life elective member), Cleveland Museum of Natural History (honorary curator, 1976), Explorers Club (fellow).

WRITINGS: Not as the Crow Flies (self-illustrated), McClelland & Stewart, 1975; *Wild Birds of the Americas* (self-illustrated), Houghton, 1977.

Illustrator: Lester L. Snyder, *The Hawks and Owls of Ontario,* University of Toronto Press, 1932; W. Perkins Bull, *From Hummingbird to Eagle,* Canadiana, 1936; W. Stewart Wallace, editor, *Encyclopedia of Canada,* University Associates of Canada, 1936; Francis H. Kortright, *Ducks, Geese, and Swans of North America,* American Wildlife Institute, 1943; Snyder, *Canadian Birds,* Canadian Nature, 1944; Richard M. Saunders, *Flashing Wings,* McClelland & Stewart, 1947; Raymond Camp, editor, *The Hunter's Encyclopedia,* Stackpole & Heck, 1948; *Nature Unspoiled,* Carling Conservation Club, 1949.

James A. Munro, *Birds of Canada's Mountain Parks,* King's Printer, 1950; Robert B. Stringfellow, editor, *The Standard Book of Hunting and Shooting,* Greystone Press, 1950; Herbert Brandt, *Arizona and Its Bird Life,* Bird Research Foundation, 1951; Snyder, *Ontario Birds,* Clarke-Irwin, 1951; Clifford Wilson, *North of Fifty-Five Degrees,* Ryerson, 1954; Fred C. Bodsworth, *Last of the Curlews,* Dodd, 1955; Lorus J. Milne and Margery Milne, *World of Night,* Harper, 1956; James L. Baillie, *Ontario Grouse,* Royal Ontario Museum, 1956; Snyder, *Arctic Birds of Canada,* University of Toronto Press, 1957; Ray W. Salt and A. L. Wilk, *Birds of Alberta,* Department of Economic Affairs, Edmonton, 1958. Richard H. Pough, *Audubon Western Bird Guide,* Doubleday, 1957.

H. C. Andrews, H. H. Wiebe, H. G. Hedges, and D. E. Farwell, *Science Activities,* Gage, 1960; Alfred M. Bailey and Alfred J. Niedrach, *Birds of Colorado,* Denver Museum of Natural History, 1965; John Livingston and Lister Sinclair, *Darwin and the Galapagos,* Canadian Broadcasting Corporation, 1966; Randolph L. Peterson, *The Mammals of Eastern Canada,* Oxford University Press, 1966; W. B. Scott and E. J. Crossman, *Freshwater Fishes of Canada,* Fisheries Research Board, 1973; John P. S. Mackenzie, *The Complete Outdoorsman's Guide to Birds of Eastern North America,* Pagurian, 1976; Mackenzie, *Birds in Peril,* Houghton, 1977.

Contributor to scientific and popular journals.

WORK IN PROGRESS: Birds of Madagascar, watercolor studies; a history of wildlife in art; work on African, Asian, and Galapagos birds.

SIDELIGHTS: Shortt writes: "I am by training, vocation and choice a painter-illustrator; writing has been largely an adjunctive activity. In my artwork I have specialized in portraits of birds, particularly their faces. Each of the more than 2500 kinds with which I have had field experience has its own 'species individuality' which transcends mere feather pattern and color. To capture on paper the avian personalities has been my effort; it must be admitted that all fall short of the artistry of the reality. I am also intrigued by the variety of styles of bird flight and have attempted to record the flying mannerisms of many species.

"I have filled many sketchbooks with quick pencil sketches from life of bird postures, gait and wing action. But birds are not long suffering models and most of these sketches of wild birds are, to all but me, well-nigh indecipherable, resembling the scribbled scrawls on memo pads beside the telephone. Part of retirement activity is to 'translate' these to comprehensible form (otherwise will have wasted an immensity of time and paper!).

"My views on 'art' are uncomplicated. Fulfillment in life is largely a by-product of sharing. Creative work, whether it be writing, painting, sculpting or music, simply expands one's capacity to share, and I would rather share pleasant things than unpleasant ones. I believe in a light-hearted approach to most everything. Frequent communion with wilderness is a stimulus to this. I have little patience with angry people who habitually look upon the darker side of things and talk about the drudgery and pain of creative work. Writing and painting are joyous occupations. If they should ever begin to cause me boredom or anguish I shall discontinue them."

Shortt has participated in or led more than thirty expeditions, including travel to Mexico, Trinidad & Tobago, Ecuador and the Galapagos Islands, the Bahamas, India, Thailand, Burma, Hong Kong, Japan, Kenya, Tanzania, the Seychelles, Madagascar, and South Africa. He has been actively involved in conservation work, with such organizations as Ducks Unlimited, World Wildlife Fund, World Wilderness Congress, and Pan-African Ornithological Congress.

As an educator, his exhibits (especially for children) include dioramas of extinct passenger pigeons, black bears, the Arctic tundra, the African plains, and Bushmaster, Trinidad rain forest.

His watercolor field studies include more than a thousand species of birds, and he has sketches of perhaps another thousand. His watercolors have been exhibited all over the world, including Johannesburg, South Africa, the United States, and the National Museum of Canada.

BIOGRAPHICAL/CRITICAL SOURCES: Reader's Digest, Canadian edition, January, 1973; *Nature Canada,* July-September, 1974; *Maclean's,* May 16, 1977; *International Wildlife,* May-June, 1977.

* * *

SHOWERS, Renald E(dward) 1935-

PERSONAL: Born July 27, 1935, in DuBois, Pa.; son of Louis H. (a meat salesman) and Christine (Laing) Showers; married Eleanor Eby, July 21, 1962; children: Renee Dawn, Marbeth Noel. *Education:* Philadelphia College of Bible, diploma, 1956; Wheaton College, Wheaton, Ill., B.A., 1958; Dallas Theological Seminary, M.Th., 1962; Grace Theological Seminary, D.Th., 1975. *Politics:* Republican. *Residence:* Wheaton, Ill. *Office:* Moody Bible Institute, 820 North LaSalle, Chicago, Ill. 60610.

CAREER: Ordained Baptist minister, 1962; Lancaster Bible College, Lancaster, Pa., instructor in Bible, theology, and English, 1962-65; pastor of Protestant churches in Egg Harbor, N.J., 1965-66, and Philadelphia, Pa., 1966-68; Philadelphia College of Bible, Philadelphia, Pa., instructor, 1968-70, assistant professor, 1970-74, associate professor of Bible doctrine and church history, 1974-77; Moody Bible Institute, Chicago, Ill., instructor in Bible and theology, 1977—. Speaker at Bible conferences. *Member:* Evangelical Theological Society.

WRITINGS: Liberty and Love in Life With Christ, Philadelphia College of Bible, 1973; *What on Earth Is God Doing?: Satan's Conflict with God,* Loizeaux Brothers, 1973. Contributor to magazines.

WORK IN PROGRESS: The Biblical Concept of Marriage and *The New Nature.*

AVOCATIONAL INTERESTS: Travel (including Israel).

* * *

SHUCHMAN, Abraham 1919-1978

July 26, 1919—May 31, 1978; Russian-born educator and author. Shuchman taught at the Columbia University Graduate School of Business and served as a consultant to several large corporations, including Western Electric. He wrote several books on business subjects and contributed articles to science journals. Shuchman died in Long Island, N.Y. Obituaries and other sources: *American Men and Women of Science: The Social and Behavioral Sciences,* 12th edition, Bowker, 1973; *Who's Who in Consulting,* 2nd edition, Gale, 1973; *New York Times,* June 1, 1978.

* * *

SHULL, Margaret Anne Wyse 1940-
(Peg Shull; Annie Windsor)

PERSONAL: Born September 21, 1940, in Hornell, N.Y.;

daughter of Harry O. (a civil engineer) and Roberta (Windsor) Wyse; divorced; children: Robert Nicholson, Teresa Elisabeth, John Elrond. *Education:* University of Iowa, B.A., 1962, M.A., 1965; attended New York Theological Seminary, 1971-72, Union Theological Seminary, New York, N.Y., 1972, Lexington Theological Seminary, 1974-75, and Nashotah House, 1976-77. *Politics:* "More-or-less Republican." *Religion:* Episcopalian. *Home:* 242 Glendover Rd., Lexington, Ky. 40503.

CAREER: Manticore Press, Iowa City, Iowa, designer and printer, 1964-66; *Middlesboro Daily News,* Middlesboro, Ky., reporter, photographer, and reviewer, 1966; Grolier, Inc., New York City, photographic researcher, 1966-67; Hawthorn Books, Inc., New York City, editorial assistant, 1967-68, assistant juvenile editor, 1968; Goodway, Inc., New York City, editorial supervisor, 1969-70; *Herald,* New York City, secretary, 1971, photographer, 1972; free-lance writer, photographer, and editor, 1972—. *Member:* Society of St. Francis, Episcopal Church Women, Kentucky Guild of Artists and Craftsmen. *Awards, honors:* Photography prize from Kentucky Press Photographers Association, 1966.

WRITINGS: (Under name Peg Shull) *Children of Appalachia* (juvenile picture book; with own photographs), Messner, 1967. Reporter, editor, and photographer for *Church Advocate,* 1973-76. Contributor to religious magazines and to *Appalachian Journal* (sometimes under pseudonym Annie Windsor).

WORK IN PROGRESS: The Forest Winter, a juvenile novel; an adult fantasy; a popular approach to the Old Testament.

SIDELIGHTS: Margaret Shull writes: "I wrote *Children of Appalachia* because I wanted people outside the hill country to see that there is beauty there as well as poverty, and I think I pretty much succeeded. I really had no other motivation to write until I found in systematic theology a sufficient body of material to delight me for several lifetimes. Since most theologians use a technical language and are bound in imposing-looking books, I hope (I expect immodestly) to translate without diluting some thoughts, some concepts that please me for people who would not attempt to study theology otherwise."

AVOCATIONAL INTERESTS: Cooking, gardening, hiking, playing the dulcimer and singing.

*   *   *

SHULL, Peg
See SHULL, Margaret Anne Wyse

*   *   *

SHUSTER, George Nauman   1894-1977

PERSONAL: Born August 27, 1894, in Lancaster, Wis.; son of Anthony and Elizabeth (Nauman) Shuster; married Doris Parks Cunningham, June 25, 1924; children: Robert George. *Education:* University of Notre Dame, A.B., 1915, A.M., 1920; University of Poitiers (France), Certificat d'Aptitude, 1919; Columbia University, graduate study, 1925-26, Ph.D., 1940. *Religion:* Roman Catholic. *Home:* 2819 York Rd., South Bend, Ind. 46614.

CAREER: University of Notre Dame, South Bend, Ind., head of English department, 1920-24; St. Joseph's College, Brooklyn, N.Y., professor of English, 1924-35; Columbia University, New York City, fellow of the Social Science Research Council, 1937-39; Hunter College (now of the City University of New York), New York City, dean and acting president, 1939-40, president, 1940-60, president emeritus, 1960-77; University of Notre Dame, assistant to the president and director of Center for the Study of Man in Contemporary Society, 1961-71, trustee, 1961-77, professor emeritus of English, 1971-77. Professor of English at Brooklyn Polytechnic Institute, 1924-25. Member of Enemy Alien Board in New York City, 1942-45; member of general advisory committee of U.S. State Department Division of Cultural Relations, 1944-45; chairman of Historical Commission to Germany, 1945; adviser to American delegation to London Conference on International Education, 1945; delegate to UNESCO Conference in Paris, 1946, 1958; chairman of U.S. National Commission for UNESCO, 1954; U.S. representative to executive board of UNESCO, 1958-64. Member of University of Chicago Commission on the Freedom of the Press, 1944-47; chairman of Committee on Discrimination in the Nation's Capitol, 1947; chairman of board of trustees of Institute of International Education, 1948-51. Land Commissioner for Bavaria, 1950-51. Also worked as chairman of Picker Foundation and as a member of board of directors of Public Broadcasting. Carnegie Endowment for International Peace, director, 1954-64, honorary director, 1964-77; president of Pestalozzi Foundation, 1955; director of Fund for Republic. *Military service:* U.S. Army; served in Intelligence Section during World War I; became sergeant.

MEMBER: Modern Language Association of America, Academy of Arts and Sciences, Council on Foreign Relations. *Awards, honors:* Carl Schurz Memorial Foundation fellow in Germany, 1930-31; Oberlaender Trust fellow in Germany, 1932; LL.D. from St. Thomas College, 1950 and Columbia University, 1954; Mus.D. from New York College of Music, 1954; Christopher Awards, 1954 and 1957; Butler medal from Columbia University, 1954; decorated Chevalier, Legion of Honor, 1955; Litt.D. from Jewish Theological Seminary, 1956, and Loyola University, 1957; L.H.D. from Dropsie College, 1957; Ph.D. honoris causa from University of Freiburg, 1957; LL.D. from Manhattan College, 1958; Litt.D. from Seton Hill College, 1958; En.d.U. ●om University of Free Berlin, 1958; L.H.D. from Hunter College (now of the City University of New York), 1960; Laetore medal from University of Notre Dame, 1960; LL.D. from Stonehill College, 1964, and St. Mary's College, 1965; Pax Christi award from St. John's University, 1965; L.H.D. from Mundelein College, 1966, and Indiana University, 1968; Reinhold Niebuhr Award from University of Notre Dame, 1975; named Senator of University of Munich, 1975; recipient of Great Gold Medal of Honor (Austrian Republic) and Knight Commander's Cross of Order of Merit (Germany).

WRITINGS: The Catholic Spirit in Modern English Literature, Macmillan, 1922, reprinted, Books for Libraries, 1967; *English Literature,* Allyn & Bacon, 1926; *The Hill of Happiness* (short stories), D. Appleton, 1926, reprinted, Books for Libraries, 1971; *The Catholic Spirit in America,* Dial, 1927; *The Catholic Church and Current Literature,* Macmillan, 1930; *The Germans,* Dial, 1932; *Strong Man Rules: An Interpretation of Germany Today,* D. Appleton, 1934; *Like a Mighty Army: Hitler Versus Established Religion,* D. Appleton, 1935; *Brother Flo: An Imaginative Biography,* Macmillan, 1938; *Look Away!* (fiction), Macmillan, 1939.

The English Ode from Milton to Keats, Columbia University Press, 1940, reprinted, Peter Smith, 1964; (with Arnold Bergstraesser) *Germany: A Short History,* Norton, 1944; *Cultural Cooperation and the Peace: The Difficulties and Objectives of International Cultural Understanding,* Bruce

Publishing, 1953; *Religion Behind the Iron Curtain,* Macmillan, 1954; *In Silence I Speak: The Story of Cardinal Mindszenty Today and of Hungary's "New Order,"* Farrar, Straus, 1956; *Education and Moral Wisdom,* Harper, 1960; *The Ground I Walked On: Reflections of a College President,* Farrar, Straus, 1961, 2nd enlarged edition, University of Notre Dame Press, 1969; *UNESCO: Assessment and Promise,* Harper, 1963; *Catholic Education in a Changing World,* Holt, 1967; *On the Side of Truth: George N. Shuster,* edited by Vincent P. Lannie, University of Notre Dame Press, 1974.

Editor: *The World's Great Catholic Literature,* Macmillan, 1942, new enlarged edition, Dimension Books, 1964; *The Problem of Population,* University of Notre Dame Press, Volume II: *Practical Catholic Applications,* 1964, Volume III: *Educational Considerations,* 1965 (Shuster was not associated with Volume I); *Freedom and Authority in the West,* University of Notre Dame Press, 1967; *Saint Thomas Aquinas,* Mackay, 1969, Heritage Press, 1971; (with Ralph E. Thorson) *Evolution in Perspective,* University of Notre Dame Press, 1970.

Commonweal, associate editor, 1925-29, managing editor, 1929-37; member of board of editors of *Encyclopaedia Britannica,* 1959-68.

BIOGRAPHICAL/CRITICAL SOURCES: New York Times Book Review, February 18, 1968; *Commonweal,* March 15, 1968. Obituaries: *New York Times,* January 27, 1977; *Current Biography,* March, 1977; *AB Bookman's Weekly,* May 9, 1977.

(Died January 25, 1977, in South Bend, Ind.)

[Sketch verified by wife, Doris Shuster]

*   *   *

SIANO, Mary M(artha) 1924-

PERSONAL: Born February 23, 1924, in Centreville, N.J.; daughter of Albert Umberto (a farmer) and Stella (Genovese) Siano. *Education:* Attended high school in Keyport, N.J. *Politics:* Democrat. *Religion:* Christian. *Home:* 37 Shore Haven Park Rd., Hazlet, N.J. 07730.

CAREER: Free-lance writer, 1970—. Has worked as farm helper, sewing operator, domestic servant, and piano teacher. *Member:* International Poetry Association (life member), Society of Children's Book Writers, American Poets Fellowship, Pierson Mettler Associates, Songwriters' Cooperative, New Jersey Poetry Society, Pennsylvania Poetry Society, Texas Poetry Society.

WRITINGS: Through the Years (poems), Dorrance, 1972; *Vibrations* (poems), Prairie Poet Books, 1974. Work represented in several anthologies, including *Yearbook of Modern Poetry,* 1971, 1973, 1976; *Outstanding Contemporary Poetry,* 1972; *Melody of the Muse,* 1973.

WORK IN PROGRESS: "Young Mary," a song, for the record album "So Many Ways to Say I Love You."

SIDELIGHTS: Siano writes: "I am now combining the talents of poetry and writing with my aptitude for music, having many songs recorded. My love and appreciation for music and poetry dates back to growing up on a farm, where I studied music, and later taught."

*   *   *

SIBLEY, Susan
See KINNICUTT, Susan Sibley

SIDER, Don 1933-

PERSONAL: Born January 11, 1933, in Chicago, Ill.; son of Seymour and Isabel (Klawans) Sider; married Margot Janoff (a realtor), March 20, 1955; children: Todd, Dean, Darby. *Education:* University of Miami, B.A., 1954. *Politics:* Independent Democrat. *Religion:* Jewish. *Home:* 6700 Pine Creek Court, McLean, Va. 22101. *Office:* Time, 888 16th St. N.W., Washington, D.C. 20006.

CAREER/WRITINGS: St. Petersburg Times, St. Petersburg, Fla., news features editor, 1956-66; *Time,* New York City, staff correspondent, 1966-69; Pioneer Press Papers, Chicago, Ill., editor, 1969-72; *Time,* staff correspondent in Washington, D.C., 1972—. Notable assignments include coverage of the Vietnam War. Contributor to periodicals, including *Parade, Chicago Tribune,* and *Chicago Sun-Times. Military service:* U.S. Army, 1954-56. *Member:* Sigma Delta Chi. *Awards, honors:* Roy Howard Award, 1972.

SIDELIGHTS: Sider told *CA* that the most engaging aspect of his work is "the fact that it never is work until you must return to face the typewriter. But by then, you're committed, so you do it. Then you go out and report again, unmindful that the real work will follow when you get back to that typewriter." *Avocational interests:* Sport parachuting.

*   *   *

SIEGEL, Ben 1925-

PERSONAL: Born July 6, 1925, in Cleveland, Ohio; son of David and Nellie (Lansky) Siegel; married Ruth Fink (a secretary), August 12, 1956; children: Sharon, Kenneth. *Education:* San Diego State Teachers College (now San Diego State University), B.A. (honors), 1948; University of California, Los Angeles, M.A., 1950; University of Southern California, Ph.D., 1956. *Home:* 239 Monterrey Dr., Claremont, Calif. 91711. *Office:* Department of English and Modern Languages, California State Polytechnic University, Pomona, Calif. 91768.

CAREER: University of Southern California, Los Angeles, lecturer in English, 1952-57; California State Polytechnic University, Pomona, assistant professor, 1957-62, associate professor, 1962-66, professor of English, 1966—, chairman of department, 1957-65. Lecturer at Earl Warren Institute of Ethics and Morals, University of Judaism, 1974. Editorial consultant for Charles Scribner's Sons, Harper & Row, Scott, Foresman, Dickenson Publishing Co., and Harcourt Brace Jovanovich, Inc. *Military service:* U.S. Army, Infantry, 1943-46; became staff sergeant; received Bronze Star, two Purple Hearts, and four battle stars. *Member:* Modern Language Association of America, American Studies Association, American Humor Studies Association, Popular Culture Association. *Awards, honors:* Danforth fellow, summer, 1959.

WRITINGS: (With Joseph Gaer) *The Puritan Heritage,* New American Library, 1964; (editor with William Davenport) *Biography Past and Present,* Scribner, 1965; (author of teacher's manual) Davenport and Leonard Brown, editors, *A Quarto of Modern Literature,* Scribner, 1966; (author of teacher's manual) Paul A. Jorgensen and Frederick B. Shroyer, editors, *A College Treasury,* Scribner, 1967; *Isaac Bashevis Singer,* University of Minnesota Press, 1969; *The Controversial Sholem Asch,* Bowling Green University Popular Press, 1976. Contributor of articles and reviews to literature, drama, and literary magazines, including *Northwest Review,* and newspapers.

WORK IN PROGRESS: Monographs on modern American humor, Saul Bellow, Philip Roth, and Isaac Bashevis Singer.

SIDELIGHTS: Siegel writes: "For some years, I have collected materials in American humor or the American comic literary tradition. My focal point has been 'angry humor in American writing.' I mean by this the various satiric-moralistic ways in which major literary figures (Bellow, Roth, Singer) and popular humorists have contributed to American thought, values, and writing. More recently, I have been intrigued by the humorous techniques, styles, and devices of the mass media. I am now tracing and analyzing not only recent comic trends in American fiction (black humorists, absurdists, surrealists), but also the different forms of social and political humor helping to shape our national culture or temper. This includes, therefore, a close study of the above-mentioned 'movie, radio, television, record, and newspaper comics.' In short, I am attempting to pinpoint the varied forms of satire, parody, burlesque, light verse, and caricature used in dealing with and commenting on the realities of contemporary politics, religion, business, sexism, education, ethnic relations, and urban problems."

* * *

SIEGEL, June 1929-

PERSONAL: Born December 11, 1929, in Brooklyn, N.Y.; daughter of Louis H. (a physician) and Lillian (a high school Latin teacher; maiden name, Hirsch) Sigler; married Eugene Siegel (a certified public accountant), June 19, 1953; children: Evan, Eric, Claudia. *Education:* Attended Sorbonne, University of Paris, 1949-50; Wellesley College, B.A., 1951; Columbia University, M.A., 1955, Ph.D., 1963. *Politics:* "Still Liberal." *Religion:* Jewish. *Home:* 6 Carol Lane, New Rochelle, N.Y. 10804.

CAREER: Metro-Goldwyn-Mayer, New York City, subtitle writer, 1952-53; Columbia University, New York City, associate in French, 1963-68; writer. *Member:* Phi Beta Kappa. *Awards, honors:* Danforth fellowship, 1960-61; American Association of University Women fellowship, 1961; Woodbridge fellowship, 1962.

WRITINGS—Musical plays: "Housewives' Cantata" (one-act; music by Mira Spektor), first produced in New York City at Theatre at Noon, November 5, 1973; (with Miriam Fond) "Men, Women, and Why It Won't Work" (two-act; music by David Warrack), first produced in New York City at Mama Gail's Dinner Theatre, October 22, 1975; (lyricist) "Three for All" (two-act; book by Marcia Kesselman; music by Irwin Webb), first produced in Philadelphia at Cafe Society, April 28, 1977.

Contributor of articles and poems to magazines, including *Diderot Studies, Romanic Review, Gravida,* and *Lazarus.*

WORK IN PROGRESS: A musical adaptation of Shakespeare's *Much Ado About Nothing;* research on Diderot and Richardson.

SIDELIGHTS: June Siegel writes: "I have had a midstream change of careers from scholarship to lyric-writing. It came about partly by chance, but it was a chance that was a long time in the making. I felt the need to abandon the established texts and create my own. The dimension of music was a revelation, the demands of collaboration a joy, and the reaction of an audience like the immediacy of a successful class—to the tenth power."

SIFFORD, (Charles) Darrell 1931-

PERSONAL: Born September 19, 1931, in Moberly, Mo.; son of Charles Dewey and Hazel Odell (Bland) Sifford; married Verna Mae Angerer, April 18, 1954 (separated); children: Jay, Grant. *Education:* University of Missouri, B.J., 1953. *Home:* 1808 Meadow Dr., Norristown, Pa. 19403. *Office:* Philadelphia Inquirer, 400 North Broad St., Philadelphia, Pa. 19101.

CAREER/WRITINGS: Columbia Missourian, Columbia, Mo., news reporter, 1952-53; *Jefferson City News-Tribune,* Jefferson City, Mo., sports editor, 1955-56, city editor, 1956-61, managing editor, 1961-62; *Louisville Courier-Journal,* Louisville, Ky., night city editor, 1962-66; *Charlotte News,* Charlotte, N.C., executive editor, 1966-76; *Philadelphia Inquirer,* Philadelphia, Pa., columnist, 1976—. Also author of thrice-weekly syndicated column for Knight News Service, 1972—. Lecturer. *Military service:* U.S. Army Corps of Engineers, 1953-55. *Member:* Associated Press Managing Editors Association. *Awards, honors:* National Epilepsy Foundation writing award, 1972; North Carolina Mental Health writing award, 1973.

* * *

SIK, Endre 1891-1978

April 2, 1891—April 10, 1978; Hungarian diplomat, lawyer, authority on African affairs, and author. During World War I, Sik was taken prisoner in Russia where, following the Bolshevik Revolution, he remained and worked for the press. He later returned to Hungary and eventually became foreign minister. In 1967, he received the Lenin Peace Prize. Sik wrote prolifically on the subject of African affairs, including the book, *History of Black Africa.* He died in Budapest, Hungary. Obituaries and other sources: *The International Who's Who,* Europa, 1977; *New York Times,* April 11, 1978.

* * *

SILBER, Kate 1902-

PERSONAL: Born December 16, 1902, in Germany, emigrated to Scotland, 1939; daughter of Wilhelm and Lisbeth (Abraham) Silber. *Education:* Augusta-Schule (Berlin, Germany), teaching diploma, 1927; University of Berlin, D.Phil., 1932; Cambridge University, certificate, 1941; University of Edinburgh, M.A., 1951. *Residence:* Edinburgh, Scotland.

CAREER: Teacher in elementary and high schools in Berlin, Germany, 1933-39; teacher of German in girls' school in Edinburgh, Scotland, 1942-46; University of Edinburgh, Edinburgh, teacher of adult education at Settlement College, 1943-54, assistant lecturer at the university, 1944-63, senior lecturer in German, 1963-73. Writer, 1932—. Teacher of German at Moray House Teacher's Training College, 1945-53. *Member:* Conference of University Teachers of German in Great Britain and Ireland, Deutsche Erziehungswissenschaftliche Gesellschaft (German Society for the Science of Education).

WRITINGS: Anna Pestalozzi-Schulthess und der Frauenkreis um Pestalozzi (title means "Anna Pestalozzi-Schulthess and the Circle of Women Around Pestalozzi"), Walter de Gruyter, 1932; *Pestalozzi: Der Mensch und sein Werk,* Quelle & Meyer, 1957, English version by author published as *Pestalozzi: The Man and His Work,* Routledge & Kegan Paul, 1960, Schocken, 1974, 4th revised British edition, 1976; (editor) *Pestalozzis Beziehungen zu England und Amerika* (title means "Pestalozzi's Relationship to England

and America''), Conzett & Huber, 1963. Contributor to *Encyclopaedia Britannica, Dictionary of Christian Education,* and *Kindler's Enzyklopaedie,* and of articles and reviews to education, history, and German studies journals in Switzerland, Germany, and England.

WORK IN PROGRESS: Co-editor with Emanuel Dejung of the critical edition of Pestalozzi's *Letters,* volumes 11, 12, and 13, and *Works,* volumes 26 and 27.

SIDELIGHTS: Kate Silber told *CA:* "Pestalozzi, the Man and His Work is the only comprehensive study of Pestalozzi's life and the interpretation of his works existing in English, based on the original sources. It shows that his ideas were far head of his time, are relevant to present-day problems, and in many respects not yet fully realized. *Avocational interests:* Music.

* * *

SILVERMAN, Sydel 1933-

PERSONAL: Born May 20, 1933, in Chicago, Ill.; daughter of Joseph (a rabbi) and Elizabeth (Bassman) Finfer; married Mel Silverman, December 27, 1953 (died, September, 1966); married Eric R. Wolf (an anthropologist), March 18, 1972; children: (first marriage) Eve Rachel, Julie Beth. *Education:* Attended University of Illinois, 1951-52; University of Chicago, M.A., 1957; Columbia University, Ph.D., 1963. *Home address:* Taxter Rd., Elmsford, N.Y. 10523. *Office:* Department of Anthropology, City University of New York, 33 West 42nd St., New York, N.Y. 10036.

CAREER: Queens College of the City University of New York, Flushing, N.Y., 1962—, began as lecturer, professor of anthropology, 1973—Executive officer of City University of New York doctoral program in anthropology, 1975—. *Member:* American Anthropological Association.

WRITINGS: Three Bells of Civilization, Columbia University Press, 1975. Contributor to anthropology and ethnology journals.

WORK IN PROGRESS: Editing *Anthropological Ancestors* (tentative title).

* * *

SIMMONS, Blake
  See WALLMANN, Jeffrey M(iner)

* * *

SIMMONS, Judy Dothard 1944-

PERSONAL: Born August 29, 1944, in Westerly, R.I.; daughter of Edward Everett (an accountant) and Amanda Dothard (a teacher; maiden name, Bledsoe) Simmons. *Education:* California State University, Sacramento, B.A. (honors), 1967; also attended Iona College, 1976. *Home:* 531 South Ninth Ave., Mount Vernon, N.Y. 10550.

CAREER: Teacher and counselor at Utah State Industrial School, Ogden; sales correspondent for Harcourt, Brace & World Publishing Co., San Francisco, Calif.; teacher and counselor at Rodman Job Corps Center, New Bedford, Mass.; American Telephone & Telegraph—Long Lines, accounting operations supervisor in broadcast billing, 1968-70, public relations staff supervisor in policy and public affairs, 1970-73, division staff supervisor in personnel and administration, 1973-74; Columbia University, New York, N.Y., guest instructor in creative writing, 1974; affirmative action consultant for Black Swan Enterprises, 1974-75; staff writer and copy editor for *Black Enterprise,* 1976—. Has

given readings and interviews on radio and television, and at cultural and educational centers.

AWARDS, HONORS: Certificate of achievement from Federation of Protestant Welfare Agencies, 1974; grant from Poets and Writers, Inc.

WRITINGS: Judith's Blues, Broadside Press, 1973.

Work represented in anthologies, including *Giant Talk,* edited by Quincy Troupe, Random House, 1975; *Drum Voices,* edited by Eugene Redmond, Doubleday, 1976; *Celebration,* edited by Arnold Adoff, Follett, 1977. Contributor of articles and reviews to magazines, including *Black Enterprise.*

* * *

SIMON, Hilda Rita 1921-

PERSONAL: Born November 22, 1921, in Santa Ana, Calif. *Education:* Educated in Germany. *Residence:* New Paltz, N.Y.

CAREER: Author and illustrator.

WRITINGS—All self-illustrated: *The Amazing Book of Birds,* Hart Publishing, 1958, revised edition published as *The Young Pathfinder's Book of Birds,* 1962; *Exploring the World of Social Insects,* Vanguard, 1962; *The Study of Birds Made Simple,* Made Simple Books, 1962; *Wonders of the Butterfly World,* Dodd, 1963; *The Young Pathfinder's Book of Snakes,* Hart Publishing, 1963; (with David Mooney) *Hart's Maps of New York City,* Hart Publishing, 1964; *Wonders of Hummingbirds,* Dodd, 1964; *Insect Masquerades,* Viking, 1968; *Feathers, Plain and Fancy,* Viking, 1969; *Milkweed Butterflies: Monarchs, Models, and Mimics,* Vanguard, 1969; *Partners, Guests, and Parasites: Coexistence in Nature,* Viking, 1970; *Living Lanterns: Luminescence in Animals,* Viking, 1971; *Our Six-Legged Friends and Allies: Ecology in Your Backyard,* Vanguard, 1971; *The Splendor of Iridescence: Structural Colors in the Animal World,* Dodd, 1971; *Dragonflies,* Viking, 1972; *Chameleons and Other Quick-Change Artists,* Dodd, 1973; *Snakes: The Facts and the Folklore,* Viking, 1973; *Frogs and Toads of the World,* Lippincott, 1975; *The Private Lives of Orchids,* Lippincott, 1975; *Strange Breeding Habits of Aquarium Fish,* Dodd, 1975; *Snails of Land and Sea,* Vanguard, 1976; *The Courtship of Birds,* Dodd, 1977; *The Date Palm: Bread of the Desert,* Dodd, 1978.

Other: (Illustrator) Ruth Brindze, *Story of the Trade Winds,* Vanguard, 1960; *Songbirds Nature Crammer,* Ken Publishing, 1964; (translator) Fabian von Schlabrendorff, *The Secret War against Hitler,* Pitman, 1965.

SIDELIGHTS: Miss Simon's interest in nature and painting began when she was a child. Over the years she has experimented with several different techniques and presently works with watercolor, pencil, and pen-and-ink.

Simon describes the habits and flying patterns of hummingbirds in *Wonders of Hummingbirds.* A reviewer for *Horn Book* noted, "Children who already consider these lovely birds as favorites will appreciate having them faithfully represented in unusually inviting illustrations. Delicate line and jewel tones successfully convey the hummingbird's graceful hovering flight and its incessant activity."

Simon's *Insect Masquerades* gives examples of the various means of camouflage used by insects and offers possible theories on how such methods of disguise might have been developed through evolution. "*Insect Masquerade* is much more than a book about insects," wrote *Books and Book-*

men. ''Immensely readable and remarkably well-illustrated, it heightens the sense of wonder and leaves questions to ponder in the mind.'' A *Book World* critic commented, ''Miss Simon has created a book about them [insects] that is not only fascinating but also exquisitely beautiful.''

The development and function of feathers was discussed in *Feathers: Plain and Fancy.* A critic for *Young Reader's Review* said: ''The superb illustrations should awaken an interest in the text, and once a child starts reading it . . . he'll be hooked. This book contains the most absorbing details about the subject, and it is not a technical or difficult-to-understand book. The style is clear, straightforward, and yet detailed.''

Color and light served as the topics for two of Miss Simon's nature books in 1971. Her *Living Lanterns: Luminescence in Animals* gives a descriptive analysis of how light is emitted from various animal species. ''Meticulous four-color drawings of animal forms balance the informative text of an unusually good book in the field of natural science,'' commented Zena Sutherland in an article for *Saturday Review.* Miss Simon's *The Splendor of Iridescence: Structural Colors in the Animal World* examines the science of optics and its relation to the colorful appearance of different animals and insects. A reviewer for the *New Yorker* observed, ''Her [Miss Simon's] mind is clear and her hand is firm, and her book is lucid in expression and beautifully (and lucidly) illustrated with brilliantly colored drawings.''

Simon told *CA:* ''My lifelong interest in animals led to a careful study of a variety of pets such as snakes and other reptiles, frogs, and small mammals. Successful attempts to restock the Monarch population in the New Paltz area by mass-raising these butterflies from eggs inspired me to write *Milkweed Butterflies. The Date Palm: Bread of the Desert* was inspired by my father's involvement in the establishment of the date industry in California before World War I. Thus all my books are based upon areas of personal observation, study, and knowledge of the subjects chosen, with animal behavior high on the list of special interests.''

BIOGRAPHICAL/CRITICAL SOURCES: Horn Book, April, 1965, February, 1974; *Natural History,* November, 1965; *Book World,* November 3, 1968; *Young Reader's Review,* October, 1969; *Books and Bookmen,* December, 1969; *New Yorker,* May 15, 1971; *Saturday Review,* August 21, 1971; *Bulletin of the Center for Children's Books,* May, 1974.

* * *

SIMON, Louis M(ortimer) 1906-

PERSONAL: Born October 25, 1906, in Salt Lake City, Utah; son of Adolph (a merchant) and Stella (a photographer; maiden name, Furchgott) Simon; married Edith Morrisey (an administrator), October 23, 1941; children: Anthony Frederick. *Education:* Attended University of Pennsylvania, 1923-24, Harvard University, 1924-25, and Yale University, 1925-27. *Residence:* New York, N.Y. *Office:* Actors' Fund of America, 1501 Broadway, New York, N.Y. 10036.

CAREER: Private secretary to Max Reinhardt in Berlin, Germany, and Hollywood, Calif., 1928; Theatre Guild, New York City, stage manager, 1929-30; Garrick Gaieties, New York City, production stage manager, 1930; Arthur Hopkins, New York City, stage manager, 1931-32; co-director of ''Run, Little Chillun'' in New York City, 1933; Robert Rockmore, New York City, supervisor of municipal theatre project, 1933-36; Federal Theatre, Newark, N.J., New Jersey state director, 1936-37, New York state produc-

tion director, 1938-39; director of New York City productions for Warner Brothers, Shubert's, and Robert Rockmore, 1939-41; worked for Veteran's Administration, Washington, D.C., 1946-47, and for Veterans' Hospital camp shows in New York City, 1948-49; Actors' Equity Association, New York City, executive secretary, 1949-52; American Theatre Wing, New York City, director of professional training program, 1952-58; organized a theatre in Long Island, N.Y., 1959; worked for Mineola Theatre in Long Island, 1959-61; Commonwealth of Pennsylvania, Harrisburg, executive secretary of Gettysburg Centennial Commission, 1961-65; Actors' Fund of America, New York City, director of public relations, 1965—. Former technical director for League of Composers; executive secretary for Associated Actors and Artists of America, 1950-53. Civilian adviser and chief liaison during theatrical production of ''This Is the Army,'' 1942; director of Veterans Administration Special Services entertainment, 1945; managing director of Veterans Hospital Camp Shows, 1948. *Military service:* U.S. Army, 1941-46; served in Pacific theater; became major. *Member:* American National Theatre and Academy (member of board of directors).

WRITINGS: Gettysburg Centennial, Commonwealth of Pennsylvania, 1964; *A History of the Actors Fund of America,* Theatre Arts, 1972. Contributor to magazines and newspapers, including *New Yorker, Newsday,* and *New Republic.*

WORK IN PROGRESS: ''I am presently cooperating with an oral history program of the Research Center for the Federal Theatre Project at George Mason University. This might be an incentive to write an autobiography covering my entire theatrical career.''

SIDELIGHTS: Simon writes: ''The motivation for *A History of the Actors Fund of America* was to make salient facts about this oldest current theatrical charity accessible to researchers, and also to provide potential financial supporters of the Fund with authentic information about its work and goals.

''Although I started out with ideas of creative accomplishment in the theatrical field, the degree of success to which I aspired did not materialize. At the same time, experience with the Federal Theatre, and later in Army special services, led me to the conviction that I possessed administrative talents that were capable of rather unique adaptation to theatre organizations (not primarily concerned with theatrical productions) because of my experience with the production side of theatre and the temperaments of people in production and the stresses to which they are subjected.''

AVOCATIONAL INTERESTS: Gardening, carpentry.

* * *

SIMONDS, John Ormsbee 1913-

PERSONAL: Born March 11, 1913, in Jamestown, N.D.; son of Guy Wallace and Marguerite (Ormsbee) Simonds; married Marjorie C. Todd, May 1, 1943; children: Taye Anne Simonds Townley, John Todd, Polly Jean, Leslie Brook. *Education:* Michigan State University, B.S., 1935; Harvard University, M.L.A., 1939. *Politics:* Liberal. *Religion:* Presbyterian. *Home:* 17 Penhurst Rd., Pittsburgh, Pa. 15202. *Office:* Environmental Planning & Design Partnership, 100 Ross St., Pittsburgh, Pa. 15219.

CAREER: Worked as partner of Simonds & Simonds (landscape architecture planners), 1939-70; Environmental Planning & Design Partnership, Pittsburgh, Pa., partner, 1970—.

Partner of Collins, Simonds & Simonds, 1952-70. Associated with Carnegie-Mellon University, 1955-67; visiting critic at Cornell University, Yale University, University of California, and Inter-American Planning & Housing Center (Bogota, Colombia). Member of board of directors of Hubbard Educational Trust. Consultant to Department of Housing & Urban Development, U.S. Department of Transportation, National Park Service, and U.S. Army Corps of Engineers.

MEMBER: American Society of Landscape Architects (fellow; president, 1963-65; president of Foundation, 1965-67), American Society of Planning Officials, Urban Land Institute, Royal Society of the Arts, Royal Town Planning Institute (honorary corresponding member). *Awards, honors:* D.Sc. from Michigan State University, 1968; medal from American Society of Landscape Architects, 1973.

WRITINGS: Landscape Architecture, McGraw, 1961; (editor) *The Freeway in the City,* U.S. Government Printing Office, 1968; *Earthscape: A Manual of Environmental Planning and Design,* McGraw, 1978. Contributor to architecture and engineering journals. Also editor of reports, including *The Profession of Landscape Architecture,* 1963, and *Virginia's Common Wealth,* 1965.

WORK IN PROGRESS: A textbook on community planning; a survey of American landscape architecture; a book of animal and nature stories for children; a book on "Florida Crackers"; autobiographical sketches.

SIDELIGHTS: Simonds comments: "Of all human endeavors, writing may be at once the most demanding and most rewarding. As a process it sharpens the powers of observation, develops the capability of organization, stimulates creativity, extends the dimensions of expression, and intensifies the experience of living."

BIOGRAPHICAL/CRITICAL SOURCES: Engineering News Record, March 9, 1972.

*   *   *

SIMONETTA, Linda   1948-

PERSONAL: Born January 26, 1948, in Ann Arbor, Mich.; daughter of Stanley Gerald (a sales manager) and Frances (Raes) Richardson; married Sam Simonetta (an elementary school principal), April 4, 1971; children: Scott. *Education:* University of Northern Iowa, B.A., 1970. *Home:* 5113 Thistle Pl., Loveland, Colo. 80537.

CAREER: Elementary school teacher in public schools in Englewood, Colo., 1970-74, and Loveland, Colo., 1974-75.

WRITINGS: (With husband, Sam Simonetta) *Trappers, Trains, and Mining Claims,* Pruett, 1976.

SIDELIGHTS: Linda Simonetta writes: "It was through our working with children in the elementary classroom that my husband and I became aware of the void in children's literature which dealt with Colorado history. There was a definite interest within the children as we read to them from adult books or told from memory of the colorful people who lived in Colorado's past. But nowhere was there printed material on the reading level of a ten-year-old that captured the excitement of early-day Colorado. This fact, coupled with our own fascination for the state's history, served as the source of our inspiration to write *Trappers, Trains, and Mining Claims.*

"History, in general, and Colorado history in particular, is fascinating to us. We have many pieces of antique furniture in our house that date back to the years that our book cov-

ers. Besides their beauty, it is good to help assure their continuance so that future generations may know the quality of earlier Americans' contribution to our country. I suppose this basically says that we appreciate the efforts of those who have come before and that, hopefully, there will be those in the future who will feel similarly toward us."

AVOCATIONAL INTERESTS: Collecting and refinishing antique furniture, hiking, skiing, gardening.

*   *   *

SIMONETTA, Sam   1936-

PERSONAL: Born January 7, 1936, in Easton, Pa.; son of Samuel and Erma (Riedlinger) Simonetta; married Linda Richardson (an elementary school teacher), April 4, 1971; children: Scott. *Education:* Miami-Dade Junior College, A.A., 1967; Florida Atlantic University, B.S., 1969; Western State College, Gunnison, Colo., M.A., 1972. *Home:* 5113 Thistle Pl., Loveland, Colo. 80537. *Office:* Centennial Elementary School, Loveland, Colo. 80537.

CAREER: Elementary school teacher in public schools of Englewood, Colo., 1969-74; Loveland Public Schools, Loveland, Colo., assistant principal, 1974-76, principal of Centennial Elementary School, 1976—.

WRITINGS: (With wife, Linda Simonetta) *Trappers, Trains, and Mining Claims,* Pruett, 1976.

AVOCATIONAL INTERESTS: Collecting and refinishing antique furniture, hiking, skiing, gardening.

*   *   *

SIMPSON, George Eaton   1904-

PERSONAL: Born October 4, 1904, in Knoxville, Iowa; son of Lawrence E. and M. Grace (Curtis) Simpson; married Eleanor Brown, September 4, 1930; children: Jon E., A. Louise, Nancy B., G. Curtis. *Education:* Coe College, B.S., 1926; University of Missouri, M.A., 1927; University of Pennsylvania, Ph.D., 1934. *Home:* 319 Reamer Pl., Oberlin, Ohio 44074.

CAREER: Wisconsin State College, Superior, instructor in sociology, 1927-28; Temple University, Philadelphia, Pa., instructor, 1928-34, assistant professor of sociology, 1934-39; Pennsylvania State University, University Park, associate professor, 1939-43, professor of sociology, 1943-47, head of department, 1942-47; Oberlin College, Oberlin, Ohio, professor of sociology and anthropology, 1947-71, professor emeritus, 1971—, chairman of sociology and anthropology, 1947-69. Assistant professor at West Virginia State University, summers, 1933, 1939; visiting lecturer in Kingston, Jamaica, 1946, 1953; visiting professor at University of Pennsylvania, summer, 1952, Columbia University, summer, 1954, and Northwestern University, summer, 1956. Chairman of national advisory screening committee for Fulbright Awards in Sociology, 1959-62; consultant to National Science Foundation and National Endowment for the Humanities.

MEMBER: American Sociological Association (fellow), American Anthropological Association (fellow), American Association of University Professors, American Folklore Society (past second vice-president), Archaeological Institute of America, African Studies Association, Royal Anthropological Institute of Great Britain and Ireland (fellow), Central States Anthropological Society, Ohio Academy of Science (fellow), Philadelphia Anthropological Society (past president), Phi Beta Kappa, Sigma Xi, Phi Kappa Phi. *Awards, honors:* Social Science Research Council fellow,

1936-37 (Haiti); grants from American Philosophical Society for Jamaica, 1953, and Nigeria, 1964, from National Institute of Mental Health and U.S. Public Health Service for Trinidad, 1960, and Nigeria, 1964, and from Joint Committee on African Studies for Nigeria, 1964; Wellcome Medal from Royal Anthropological Institute of Great Britain and Ireland, 1957; Anisfield-Wolf Award in Race Relations from *Saturday Review of Literature*, 1958, for *Racial and Cultural Minorities*; D.H.L. from Oberlin College, 1976.

WRITINGS: The Negro in the Philadelphia Press, University of Pennsylvania Press, 1936; (with J. M. Yinger) *Racial and Cultural Minorities*, Harper, 1953, 4th edition, 1972; *Jamaican Revivalist Cults*, Institute of Social and Economic Studies, University of the West Indies, 1956; *The Shango Cult in Trinidad*, Institute of Caribbean Studies, University of Puerto Rico, 1965; *Caribbean Papers*, Centro Intercultural de Documentacion, 1970; *Religious Cults of the Caribbean*, Institute of Caribbean Studies, University of Puerto Rico, 1970; *Melville J. Herskovits*, Columbia University Press, 1973; *Yoruba and Medicine in Ibadan*, Ibadan University Press, in press; *Black Religions in the New World*, Columbia University Press, in press. Contributor to *International Encyclopedia of the Social Sciences* and to scholarly journals. Associate editor of *American Sociologist*, 1965-69; advisory editor of *Phylon*, 1963—.

WORK IN PROGRESS: Fifth edition of *Racial and Cultural Minorities*, with J. M. Yinger.

SIDELIGHTS: Simpson told *CA:* "Because it seemed to me in the middle 1930's that most writers on Haiti gave undue attention to *vodun*, I was determined not to emphasize the role of the cult in my work. In doing field work, however, this syncretistic religion proved to be the most interesting aspect of peasant culture, and I have published more on *vodun* than on other phases of Haitian peasant life. Later, I investigated revivalist cults in Jamaica and Trinidad, the Shango cult in Trinidad, the Kele cult in St. Lucia, and the Ras Tafari movement in Jamaica. In *Black Religions in the New World*, materials on these and other cults of the Caribbean, together with studies by others of cults and sects in South America, the United States, Canada, and England, are related to reports of the experiences Afro-Americans have had in the historical Christian churches in the New World."

Simpson has made two record albums for Folkways Records: "Jamaican Cult Music," 1954, and "Cult Music of Trinidad," 1961.

*   *   *

SIMPSON, R(onald) A(lbert)   1929-

PERSONAL: Born February 1, 1929, in Melbourne, Australia; son of Herbert Albert (a cooper) and Louise (Rigg) Simpson; married Shirley Athale Pamela Bowles (a research officer), August 27, 1955; children: Meredith, Warwick. *Education:* Melbourne Teachers' College, certificate, 1951; Royal Melbourne Institute of Technology, diploma, 1967. *Politics:* None. *Religion:* None. *Home:* 29 Omama Rd., Melbourne, Victoria 3163, Australia. *Office:* Caulfield Institute of Technology, 900 Dandenong Rd., Melbourne, Victoria 3145, Australia.

CAREER: Worked as a primary school teacher in Melbourne, Australia, and in England, 1951-57; art teacher in secondary schools in Melbourne, 1958-61; Department of Education, Melbourne, sub-editor, 1962-67; Caulfield Institute of Technology, Melbourne, senior lecturer and head of department of fine arts, 1968—. Liaison officer, Adelaide

Festival of Arts. *Member:* Australian Society of Authors. *Awards, honors:* Australia Council Literature Board special grant to travel, 1977.

WRITINGS—All poetry: *The Walk Along the Beach*, Edwards & Shaw, 1960; *This Real Pompeii*, Jacaranda Press, 1964; *After the Assassination*, Jacaranda Press, 1968; *Diver*, University of Queensland Press, 1972; *Poems from Murrumbeena*, University of Queensland Press, 1976.

Contributor of literary criticism to periodicals, including *Age* (Melbourne), *Quandrant*, and *The Bulletin*. Poetry editor, *The Bulletin*, 1963-65, and *The Age*, 1969—.

WORK IN PROGRESS: The Forbidden City; a book of poems; a report of a visit to England and the United States.

SIDELIGHTS: Simpson told *CA:* "I feel, and hope, my poetry has moved from preoccupations with formal neatness toward a kind of poetry that is more flexible. I have worked toward experimental regions where language is meant to be stripped of its essentials: 'Student,' 'Diver,' 'Hardiman's Progress' are poems in which I have tried to be more truthful—perhaps an impossibility: artists are not merely 'strippers,' because they must know what to conceal. However, this is the Stripper Age. I want my poetry to be far more interesting in terms of form. I have always thought of myself as being a visual writer—that is, a person who finds satisfaction in the image: my recent experiments in 'concrete poetry' are by-products of this.

"During the sixties and seventies I have tried to achieve more flexible ways, forms in poetry. At the moment I am very interested in prose poems. Too many of the poems in *Walk Along the Beach* now strike me as being flat, mannered and merely dull. There were forty five poems in that collection, and these days about twenty five of them seem worthwhile to me; but I'm probably being too optimistic here.

"The book of poems I am now working on is a continuation of my last book, *Poems from Murrumbeena*. The grant from the Literature Board of the Australia Council was a considerable help to me, and I was able to write a batch of poems while overseas."

*   *   *

SINCLAIR, Grace
See WALLMANN, Jeffrey M(iner)

*   *   *

SINCLAIR, Miranda   1948-
(Miranda Seymour)

PERSONAL: Born August 8, 1948, in Nottinghamshire, England; daughter of George Fitzroy (a magistrate) and Rosemary Scott (Ellis) Seymour; married Andrew Sinclair (a writer and historian), October 24, 1972; children: Merlin George. *Education:* Educated privately. *Home:* 15 Hanover Ter., London N.W.1, England; and Kombitsi, Corfu. *Agent:* Felicity Bryans, Curtis Brown Ltd., 1 Craven Hill, London W.2, England; and John Cushman Associates, Inc., 25 West 43rd St., New York, N.Y. 10036.

CAREER: Worked in art galleries, Christie's Auction Rooms, as a plumber's assistant, and as a journalist for *Daily Express;* editor, Lorrimer Publishing; free-lance writer. Member of Samaritans Task Force.

WRITINGS—Under name Miranda Seymour: *Stones of Maggiare*, Houghton, 1974; *Bride of Sforza*, Hutchinson, 1975; *Count Manfred*, Coward, 1976; *Daughter of Darkness*, Hutchinson, 1977, Coward, 1978. Stories anthologized in *Over Twenty-One*, Harper.

WORK IN PROGRESS: The Goddess, a historical novel about Helen of Troy; stories about a Greek village.

SIDELIGHTS: Miranda Sinclair writes: "I wrote three historical novels because I enjoy researching and trying to work out why people acted as they did. For me they are also a good way of learning how to write. A novel with a message does not leave room for the inexperienced to practice style. In my short stories, I draw a lot from my travels.

"I should like to stimulate interest, to make people go back and read the classics again after reading *The Goddess*—to stop people thinking that it is dull or difficult to read 'heavy history.'

"My strongest admiration is for Kazantzakis, in whom message and history, past and present, synthesize with a force and relish for life which few modern writers can convey."

*   *   *

SINNING, Wayne E.   1931-

PERSONAL: Born March 30, 1931, in Worthing, S.D.; son of Tom (a farmer) and Edith (Jones) Sinning; married Jane Mumford, June 14, 1958; children: Thomas, Martha, Nancy, Edith. *Education:* South Dakota State University, B.Sc., 1953, M.Sc., 1956; University of Oregon, Ph.D., 1966. *Home:* 5909 Horning Rd., Kent, Ohio 44240. *Office:* Applied Physiology Research Laboratory, Kent State University, Kent, Ohio 44242.

CAREER: High school science teacher and athletic coach in Lennox, S.D., 1956-57; South Dakota State University, Brookings, 1957-61, began as instructor, became assistant professor of physical education; Montana State University, Missoula, assistant professor of physical education and director of laboratory, 1962-64; Springfield College, Springfield, Mass., 1964-76, began as associate professor, became professor of physical education, Buxton Professor, 1974-76, director of Physiological Research Laboratory; Kent State University, Kent, Ohio, professor of physical education and director of Applied Physiology Research Laboratory, 1976—. *Military service:* U.S. Naval Reserve, active duty, 1953-55.

MEMBER: American Alliance for Health, Physical Education and Recreation (member of Kinesiology Council, 1969, 1971; chairman of Physical Fitness Council, 1975-76), American College of Sports Medicine (member of regional board of trustees, 1976—).

WRITINGS: (With P. V. Karpovich) *Physiology of Muscular Activity,* Saunders, 7th edition, 1971; (editor with C. Myers and L. Golding) *The Y's Way to Physical Fitness,* Association Press, 1973; *Experiments and Demonstrations in Exercise Physiology,* Saunders, 1975; (contributor) P. K. Wilson, editor, *Adult Fitness: Cardiac Rehabilitation,* University Park Press, 1975; (contributor) M. Adrian and J. Brame, editors, *NAGWAS Research Reports,* Volume III, American Alliance for Health, Physical Education and Recreation, 1977. Contributor to professional journals. Member of board of associate editors of *Research Quarterly;* guest reviewer for *Medicine and Science in Sports.* Member of editorial board of "International Research Monograph Series in Physical Education," Prentice-Hall.

WORK IN PROGRESS: Physiology of Muscular Activity, 8th edition, with M. Foss, for Saunders; research on body composition and human performance, and physical fitness education.

SKARTVEDT, Dan (L.)   1945-

PERSONAL: Born September 17, 1945, in Morning Sun, Iowa; son of Roy S. (a farmer) and Ruth E. (a nurse; maiden name, Snapp) Skartvedt. *Education:* University of Northern Iowa, B.A., 1966; University of Oregon, M.S., 1967. *Home:* 1001 South Frederick, Apt. 1041, Arlington, Va. 22204. *Office: Journal of Commerce,* 1325 E St. N.W., Washington, D.C. 20004.

CAREER/WRITINGS: KGLO-TV, Mason City, Iowa, news anchorman, 1970-71; Prentice-Hall Publications, Washington, D.C., reporter, 1972-73; *Journal of Commerce,* Washington, D.C., reporter, 1974—. Notable assignments include coverage of energy crisis during Arab oil embargo, interviewing William Simon, "death watch" at White House during Nixon resignation, and 1976 Republican National Convention. Author, with Morton Kondracke, of profile on President Ford for Capital Hill News Service Voters Guide Series, 1976. *Military service:* U.S. Army, 1968-69. *Member:* White House Correspondents' Association.

SIDELIGHTS: Skartvedt told *CA:* "I find Washington as immensely stimulating and interesting place to work—can't think of anyplace I'd rather be as a journalist." Skartvedt speaks Swahili and French. *Avocational interests:* Rock-climbing, scuba-diving, traveling.

*   *   *

SKELLINGS, Edmund   1932-

PERSONAL: Born March 12, 1932, in Ludlow, Mass.; son of R. T. and Lolita Skellings; married Louise Noah (an associate professor), 1960. *Education:* University of Massachusetts, B.A., 1957; University of Iowa, Ph.D., 1962. *Residence:* Dania, Fla. *Office:* 600 N.E. Second Place, Dania, Fla. 33004.

CAREER: Poet. University of Iowa, Iowa City, teacher in Iowa Writer's Workshop, 1957-62; Maryland State College (now University of Maryland, Eastern Shore), Princess Anne, associate professor of English, 1962-63, chairman of department of English, 1963; University of Alaska, Fairbanks, associate professor of English and director of writer's workshop, 1963-68; Florida Atlantic University, Boca Raton, assistant professor of English, 1968-73; Florida International University, Miami, founder and executive director of International Institute for Creative Communication, 1973-76. Visiting Professor at University of Massachusetts, 1965. Director of state writer's conferences in Maryland, 1963, Alaska, 1967, and Florida, 1976. Worked for Office of Economic Opportunity's Project Upward Bound, 1967-68. Coordinator of Southern Florida's Artist-in-the-Schools programs, 1974-76. Served as consultant to Prentice-Hall Publishing, Inc., United Fund, Hercules Power Company, and Cessna Aircraft Corporation, 1963-76. *Member:* Alaska Flying Poets (founder). *Awards, honors:* Received National Humanities Foundation citation for teaching excellence, 1968; nominated for Pulitzer Prize, 1976, for *Heart Attacks.*

WRITINGS: Duels and Duets, Qara Press, 1961; *The Comma Cat* (juvenile), Cornell, 1962; *The Marriage Fire,* Qara Press, 1963; *Heart Attacks,* University of Florida Press, 1976; *Face Value,* University of Florida Press, 1977; *Showing My Age,* University of Florida Press, 1978. Contributor to numerous periodicals, including *Miami, Midwestern University Quarterly, New England Quarterly,* and *Writer.* Editor of *Collegian,* 1956, *Quarterly,* 1957, *Poetry Alaska,* 1968, Florida Arts Council Literature Panel, 1975-76; poetry editor of *Miami,* 1975-76.

SIDELIGHTS: "Poetry should have as wide a range as possible," Skellings has said. Often referred to as the "electronic poet," Skellings employs a variety of audio devices to create a new type of poetry which he calls "perfoems." "Everyone in America has been writing 8½ x 11 poems for years," Skellings told an interviewer. "The typewriter has determined the size of the poem. The 8½ x 11 poem is gone. But this is where we are and there's no turning back now. This is the poetry of the few-ture."

Skellings has recorded *The Marriage Fire* and *Duels and Duets* for RCA Victor.

AVOCATIONAL INTERESTS: Parachuting, auto racing, airplane flying.

BIOGRAPHICAL/CRITICAL SOURCES: National Center for Audio Experimentation, April, 1973; *Fort Lauderdale News and Sun-Sentinel,* February 2, 1975; *Miami Herald,* August 29, 1976.

* * *

SKIPPER, G. C. 1939-

PERSONAL: Born March 22, 1939, in Ozark, Ala.; son of G. C. (a railroad worker) and Ada (Price) Skipper; married Dorothy Wright (a secretary), March 26, 1960; children: Richard Craig, Lisa Ann. *Education:* University of Alabama, B.A., 1961. *Home:* 1924 Flintshire Dr., Schaumburg, Ill. 60194. *Agent:* Jack Dierks, Porter, Gould & Dierks, 215 West Ohio, Chicago, Ill. 60610. *Office:* Hunter Publishing Co., 53 West Jackson, Chicago, Ill. 60604.

CAREER: Huntsville Times, Huntsville, Ala., reporter and columnist, 1961-65; United Airlines, Chicago, Ill., public relations agent, 1966-70; *Travel Weekly,* Chicago, Midwest news bureau chief, 1970-72; Hitchcock Publishing Co., Wheaton, Ill., executive editor, 1973-76; currently employed as editor of *Motor Service* magazine, Hunter Publishing Co., Chicago. Has also worked as folk and rock pianist.

WRITINGS: And the Angels Rage (novel), Touchstone Publishing, 1972; *The Ghost in the Church* (juvenile), Children's Press, 1976; *A Night in the Attic* (juvenile), Children's Press, 1977; *The Ghost at Manor House* (juvenile), Children's Press, 1978.

WORK IN PROGRESS: Triad Summer, a novel; *Asylum for a Mad Woman,* a novel based on the life of Annie Palmer, the "White Witch of Jamaica"; *Christmas Haunting,* a children's book.

SIDELIGHTS: Skipper writes: "I've known since I was twelve years old that I not only wanted to write, but *had* to write. Some have labeled this obsession 'talent,' but in reality it's more like a disease. As to the reason why, I'm still trying to figure that out. Insanity helps a whole lot and if you keep your insanity you'll be okay. The worst thing in the world for a writer is to become a 'well-rounded individual.' Writers, I guess, are an egotistical lot—they'd have to be to think they've got anything to say, much less believe people want to hear it. Whew!

"I grew up in Alabama, in the deep South, and I've seen how ridiculous other areas of the country have been in imagining what 'the South' is 'really like.' Now, like country music, suddenly it's 'in' to be Southern—and the worst thing in the world is a Professional Southerner. I believe all creativity springs out of an individual or a section of the country that has known defeat. The South is the only area of the United States that has been defeated. I think that accounts, at least partially, for the Faulkners, the Weltys, the Jacksons, et cetera, et cetera. New York is getting there, too, in its own unique way—hence, the Mailers. In other words all this man-it's-a-rough-miserable-world-type-stuff is good fodder to sprout writers. Outside playing God, I think creativity—in this case in writing—is one of the most honorable, honest contributions Man can make. If it's really good, it survives everything. Any other profession, say a thousand years from now, will look just downright silly—if I can paraphrase Hemingway.

"There's only a handful of good writers around today, hidden among the mass of academic phonies. I mean good in the creative sense of Hemingway, Faulkner and Fitzgerald. Maybe these writers are hidden because the selling of fiction has been reduced to computerized marketing exercised by publishers. Yeah, I know all us word merchants can't be Hemingway and all editors can't be Max Perkins—but it sure would be refreshing to see a novel make it on merit rather than hype. There is a need now in the United States—not for entertainment (there's plenty of that)—but for literature. I'd like to contribute my limited amount to filling that gap."

* * *

SKLAR, Morty 1935-

PERSONAL: Born November 28, 1935, in New York, N.Y.; son of Jack and Selma (Ehrlich) Sklar. *Education:* Attended Queens College (now of the City University of New York), 1957-61; University of Iowa, B.A., 1973. *Politics:* "Human-need oriented." *Religion:* "Born Jewish." *Home and office address:* P.O. Box 1585, Iowa City, Iowa 52240.

CAREER: Sklar Wholesale Hardware, Flushing, N.Y., clerk and salesman, 1960-70; Veterans Administration Hospital, Iowa City, Iowa, drug counselor, 1972-73; City of Iowa City, bus driver, 1973-76; Spirit That Moves Us Press, Iowa City, owner, editor, and publisher, 1974—. Waiter, ice cream salesman, thief, junkie, and rehabilitee, 1960-70. Member of New Pioneer Food Co-Operative and Tenants United for Action. *Military service:* U.S. Army, 1954-56. *Member:* Committee of Small Press Editors and Publishers, Coordinating Council of Literary Magazines, Actualists. *Awards, honors:* Grants from Iowa Department of Public Instruction, 1975-76, Iowa Arts Council, 1976-78, National Endowment for the Arts, 1976-78, and Coordinating Council of Literary Magazines, 1976-78.

WRITINGS: Riverside (poetry), Emmess Press, 1974; *The Night We Stood Up for Our Rights* (poetry), Toothpaste Press, 1977; (editor) *The Actualist Anthology,* Spirit That Moves Us Press, 1977; (editor) *Editors' Choice: An Anthology of Literature and Graphics from the U.S. Small Press, 1965-1977,* Spirit That Moves Us Press, in press. Contributor of poems, stories, articles, and reviews to literary journals.

WORK IN PROGRESS: Getting Up, an autobiographical novel.

SIDELIGHTS: Sklar writes: "Besides the silent communication that went on in early family relationships, writing was the first really expressive thing I did. I believe that honesty is the most important thing to me in writing—along with a communication of energy and an expression of emotion. The first writer who turned me on was Jack Kerouac. I like very little of what I read, and I am a tough editor. When something gets through to me, then I remember what it's all about."

SKURDENIS, Juliann V.
   See SKURDENIS-SMIRCICH, Juliann V(eronica)

*   *   *

SKURDENIS-SMIRCICH, Juliann V(eronica)   1942-
   (Juliann V. Skurdenis)

PERSONAL: Born July 13, 1942, in Brooklyn, N.Y.; daughter of Julius J. and Anna (Zilys) Skurdenis; married Lawrence J. Smircich (a banker), August 21, 1965. *Education:* College of New Rochelle, A.B., 1964; Columbia University, M.S., 1966; Hunter College of the City University of New York, M.A., 1974. *Residence:* Pelham Manor, N.Y. *Office:* Department of Library, Bronx Community College, University Ave. & 181st St., Bronx, N.Y. 10453.

CAREER: Brooklyn Public Library, Brooklyn, N.Y., young adult librarian, 1964-66; Kingsborough Community College, Brooklyn, periodicals librarian and instructor in library science, 1966-67; Pratt Institute, Brooklyn, acquisitions librarian and instructor in library science, 1967-68; Bronx Community College, Bronx, N.Y., instructor, 1968-71, assistant professor, 1971-75, associate professor of library science, 1975—, and of acquisitions at the library, 1968-71, head of technical services, 1975—. *Member:* American Association of University Professors, National Organization for Women, Library Association of the City University of New York (member of executive council, 1968-73, 1976-77), City University of New York Women's Coalition.

WRITINGS—All under name Juliann V. Skurdenis: (With husband, Lawrence J. Smircich) *Walk Straight Through the Square,* McKay, 1976; (with L. J. Smircich) *More Walk Straight Through the Square,* McKay, 1977.

WORK IN PROGRESS: Another walking tour book.

SIDELIGHTS: Juliann Skurdenis-Smircich told *CA:* "I love to travel and I love to write and have been extremely fortunate to be able to unite my two loves in the books of walking tours of small European towns which have appeared in the past two years. I am a firm believer (maybe fanatic is the better word) in the fact that the only way people can really experience Europe is to walk—through cathedrals, marketplaces, museums, back streets. My books were written primarily for myself, because I think this is the only way to travel. They have been my personal guidebooks: having these walks published and used by other travelers only increases the pleasure. As for future travel plans, we are going to the Soviet Union and Greece, and I could list the next ten jaunts after that (which are still in the daydream stage). All or none of these trips may materialize into books or articles. I would like them to."

AVOCATIONAL INTERESTS: Traveling, daydreaming about traveling, gardening, opera, attending ballet, "sitting through infinite numbers of old American films of the thirties and forties," cats.

*   *   *

SLATEN, Yeffe Kimball   1914(?)-1978

1914(?)—April 11, 1978; American Indian artist and author. A noted expert in the field of American Indian culture, Slaten was most interested in space exploration and the southwestern area of the United States. She held numerous exhibits at various institutions, including the Rehn Gallery and National Academy in New York. Her works are displayed permanently at the Department of the Interior in Washington, D.C., the Museum of Fine Arts in Boston. She wrote *The Art of American Indian Cooking.* She died in Santa Fe, N.M. Obituaries and other sources: *New York Times,* April 12, 1978.

*   *   *

SLETHOLT, Erik   1919-

PERSONAL: Born July 23, 1919, in Norway; came to the United States in 1976; son of Ole A. (an Army major) and Elsa (an accountant; maiden name, Jacobsen) Sletholt; married Ciska H. Van Keyzerswaard (an interior decorator), October 1, 1948. *Education:* Attended University of Oslo, 1939-40, 1947-48, and University of Toronto, 1949-50. *Politics:* Conservative. *Religion:* Lutheran. *Home and office:* 625 Rim Rd., Pasadena, Calif. 91107.

CAREER: United Nations Relief & Rehabilitation Administration, Bremen, Germany, chief welfare officer and movements officer, 1946, director of displaced persons camps in the U.S. Zone, 1946-47; U.S. Army, Fulda, Germany, screening officer in displaced persons operations, 1947; Canadian Broadcasting Corp., writer and radio commentator in Toronto, Ontario, 1948-51, in Calgary, Alberta, 1948-56; Western Travel Service, Inc., Calgary, owner and operator, 1952-63; business consultant in Los Angeles, Calif., 1963-64; free-lance writer, 1964—. Norwegian honorary consul in Calgary, 1956-63. *Military service:* British Army, Intelligence Service, undercover agent, forward interrogator of prisoners of war at Akershus Prison for War Criminals, 1945; became lieutenant.

WRITINGS: Daktary (title means "Doctor"), Green, 1969; *Jesse James: Bandit og folkehelt* (title means "Jesse James: Outlaw and Folkhero"), Green, 1970; *Venner med pels og venner med fjaer,* Green, 1970, translation by Oliver Stallybrass published as *Wild and Tame: A View of Animals,* Scribner, 1975; *Kolsas Mysteriet* (title means "The Kolsasaas Mystery"), Green, 1971; *Drobak Mysteriet* (title means "The Drobak Mystery"), Green, 1971; *Hvorfor ble de doemt: Mord og motiver* (an evaluation of the American legal system; title means "Why Were They Convicted?"), Aschehoug, 1975; *Spin-off Benefits from the Space Research* (in Norwegian), Aschehoug, 1976.

Contributor of more than twelve hundred articles to Norwegian and European magazines including *Norwegian Oil Review* and *Hjemmet.* Contributor and North American editor of *Naa.* Associate editor of *International Trade Forum,* 1970-73.

WORK IN PROGRESS: Another animal book.

SIDELIGHTS: Sletholt told *CA:* "I have done extensive studies on psychic abilities in animals, particularly telepathic communication and ESP which animals possess to a far greater degree than humans.

Sletholt has lectured in North America and Europe.

*   *   *

SLONIMSKY, Yuri   1902-1978

March 12, 1920—April 23, 1978; Russian ballet critic and historian, and author. As a critic, Slonimsky was called "a spokesman for Soviet ballet in the West," and was one of the first to study nineteenth-century international ballet. He lectured on the subject of ballet in Leningrad and Moscow. Slonimsky wrote *Evenings of Young Ballet* in collaboration with New York City Ballet director George Ballachine, a friend since the 1920's. Among other works, Slonimsky wrote scholarly monographs on the nineteenth-century ballets, "La Sylphide" and "Giselle," and a study of Tchaikovsky and ballet. He died in Leningrad, U.S.S.R. Obituaries and other sources: *New York Times,* May 23, 1978.

SMALL, Bertrice 1937-

PERSONAL: Born December 9, 1937, in New York, N.Y.; daughter of David R. (a broadcaster) and Doris S. (a broadcaster) Williams; married George S. Small (a photographer and designer), October 5, 1963; children: Thomas David. Education: Attended Western College for Women, 1955-58, and Katharine Gibbs Secretarial School, 1958-59. Politics: "I vote for candidates, not parties." Religion: Anglican. Agent: James Seligmann Agency, 280 Madison Ave., New York, N.Y. 10016.

CAREER: Secretary in New York, N.Y., 1959-61; Edward Petry & Co., New York City, sales assistant, 1961-63; freelance writer, 1969—. Member: Southold Association of Merchants (member of board of directors, 1977-78).

WRITINGS: The Kadin (historical romance), Avon, 1978; Love Wild and Fair (historical romance), Avon, 1978.

WORK IN PROGRESS: Two historical books.

SIDELIGHTS: Bertrice Small comments: "I am the one reader in a hundred thousand who will go and check a historical fact and I become highly irritated if that fact is not fact; or if the author has used too much literary license. Therefore I try to write for the same people as myself, and be as accurate as possible. However I find different historians have different viewpoints that color their histories. Where history is foggy, or disputed, imagination can go wild! And in my case does!"

* * *

SMITH, Dwight C(hichester), Jr. 1930-

PERSONAL: Born June 23, 1930, in Bellingham, Wash.; son of Dwight C. (a clergyman) and Josephine (a social worker; maiden name, Wood) Smith; married Rachel Stryker (a teacher), July 11, 1953; children: Dwight C. III, Gerald S., David B. Education: Yale University, B.A. (with distinction), 1951; Syracuse University, M.P.A., 1952. Religion: Presbyterian. Home: 10 Cherry Tree Rd., Loudonville, N.Y. 12211. Office: State University of New York at Albany, 1400 Washington Ave., Albany, N.Y. 12222.

CAREER: U.S. State Department, Washington, D.C., clerk for Bureau of United Nations Affairs, summers, 1949-50; U.S. Navy Department, Washington, D.C., budget analyst for Bureau of Ships, 1952-53; Connecticut State Division of the Budget, Hartford, management analyst, 1956; Maryland State Department of Finance and Control, Baltimore, budget analyst, 1957-60; Indiana University, Bloomington, assistant director of Institute of Training for Public Service, 1960-65; New York State Identification and Intelligence System (NYSIIS), Albany, assistant deputy director for systems planning and research, 1965-67; State University of New York at Albany, director of institutional research, 1967—. Visiting associate professor at John Jay College of Criminal Justice of the City University of New York, 1967-73. Military service: U.S. Army, Counter Intelligence Corps, agent, 1953-56. Member: Association for Institutional Research, American Society of Criminology.

WRITINGS: The Mafia Mystique, Basic Books, 1975.

WORK IN PROGRESS: "Further development of a theory of illicit enterprise."

SIDELIGHTS: Smith told CA: "My interest in organized crime and Mafia began in 1965, when I was asked by NYSIIS to think about designing a computer system that would help State lawmen as they tried to control organized crime. I quickly learned that I had been asked to create computer logic from a collection of misinformation, misrepresentation, half truths, whole fictions, misplaced analogies, and myths.

"I discovered that accepted stories about a Mafia in Sicily were historic fiction; that claims that a Mafia had emigrated to the United States were false history; and that a belief in the post-Prohibition organization of crime by an American Mafia was based on an unstated assumption that no one but Italians were involved in organized criminal activities. Without a Mafia to explain it I realized that what my lawmen friends saw was just successful businessmen who were willing to deal in illegal goods and services if there were customers to buy them. Then it became clear that loan sharks were bankers, that fences were retailers, and that narcotics or cigarette smugglers were importers; and that they could be controlled only by understanding how a market system permits them to be both illegal and successful.

"This line of thought has led me to the construction of a theory of 'illicit enterprise' to explain both organized crime and white-collar crime as market-driven business activities that can be analyzed, evaluated and controlled by the same general rules that apply to legitimate businesses. This theory has a logic that Mafia theories lack; and it is more compatible and consistent with other theories of deviance, ethnic mobility, organizational behavior, etc. It also provides new ways of asking questions about philosophy, ethnics, history, rhetoric and administration. In short the concept of illicit enterprise gives us exciting and provocative ways of looking at American civilization and American public policy."

* * *

SMITH, Elske v(an)P(anhuys) 1929-

PERSONAL: Born November 9, 1929, in Monaco; came to the United States in 1943, naturalized citizen, 1952; daughter of J.A.E.A. and Vera (Craven) vanPanhuys; married Henry J. Smith; children: Ralph Andrew, Kenneth Alan. Education: Radcliffe College, B.S., 1950, M.A., 1951, Ph.D., 1955. Home: 5005 Westpath Ter., Bethesda, Md. 20016. Office: Astronomy Program, University of Maryland, College Park, Md. 20742.

CAREER: Sacramento Park Observatory, Sunspot, N.M., research associate, 1955-62; Joint Institute for Laboratory Astrophysics, Boulder, Colo., visiting fellow, 1962-63; University of Maryland, College Park, associate professor, 1963-75, professor of astronomy, 1975—, assistant provost of division of mathematical and physical sciences and engineerings, 1973—. Member: International Astronomical Union, American Astronomical Society (treasurer of solar physics division, 1970-74; councilor), American Association for the Advancement of Science, Astronomical Society of the Pacific, Phi Beta Kappa (president of Maryland chapter, 1974-75), Sigma Xi.

WRITINGS: (With husband, Henry J. Smith) Solar Flares (monograph), Macmillan, 1963; (with K. C. Jacobs) Introductory Astronomy and Astrophysics, Saunders, 1973. Contributor to Covert Discrimination and Women in the Sciences, edited by J. Ramaly. Also contributor to solar physics and astronomy journals including Astrophysical Journal.

WORK IN PROGRESS: Tentatively planning a course on women in the sciences.

SIDELIGHTS: Smith told CA: "Solar Flares is a monograph written and published just prior to the opening up of solar physics by space research. The book presents a summary of the state of knowledge in the early sixties and therefore seemed as a useful reference to those space experiments. However, it became out of date in a few years—a circumstance not unusual for scientific monographs."

* * *

SMITH, Gene 1924-

PERSONAL: Born May 19, 1924, in Somerville, Mass.; son of Eugene F. (a civil servant) and Anne (an office manager; maiden name, Belban) Smith; married Jayne Wiethoff, August 28, 1948 (died, 1963); married Lois Wollenweber (a publicist), February 27, 1965; children: Eric C., Luke H., Brooke A., Scott E. *Education:* Dartmouth College, A.B. (cum laude), 1949; Columbia University, B.S., 1950. *Religion:* Protestant. *Home:* Kingswood Drive, Orangeberg, N.Y. 10962. *Office: The Trib,* 711 Third Ave., New York, N.Y. 10017.

CAREER/WRITINGS: Wall Street Journal, New York City, reporter, 1950-52; *New York Herald Tribune,* New York City, reporter, 1952-55; *New York Times,* New York City, reporter, 1955-77; *The Trib,* New York City, senior editor, 1977—. *Military service:* U.S. Army, 1943-46; received Combat Infantry Award and three Battle Stars. *Member:* New York Financial Writers Association (director, 1970), Deadline Club, New York Press Club, New England Society in New York, Sigma Delta Chi, Ramapo Youth Hockey Association (vice-president, 1975—, head coach), Mid-Atlantic Amateur Hockey Association (vice-president, 1973-75).

WORK IN PROGRESS: Collaborating with Matthew J. Culligan on a book about libel, *The Exquisitive Art of Character Assassination.*

* * *

SMITH, Harry 1936-

PERSONAL: Born October 15, 1936, in New York, N.Y.; son of Harry Joseph (a banker) and May A. (Dinkelmeyer) Smith; married Marion Camilla Petschek (a psychologist), February 21, 1959; children: Tristram, Lisa, Rebecca. *Education:* Brown University, A.B., 1957, further study, 1957-58. *Politics:* "Harmless anarchist." *Residence:* Brooklyn, N.Y. *Office:* Generalist Association, 5 Beekman St., New York, N.Y. 10038.

CAREER: Southbridge Evening News, Southbridge, Mass., reporter, photographer, and sports editor, 1958; *Worcester Telegram,* Worcester, Mass., reporter-photographer, 1959; *Modern Server* (alcoholic beverage industry trade publication), New York City, managing editor, 1959-61; *Recess* (legal newspaper), New York City, editor-in-chief, 1962-63; *Smith,* New York City, publisher, 1964—. *Member:* International P.E.N., Committee of Small Magazine Editors and Publishers (member of board of directors, 1968-74; chairman, 1971-73), Coordinating Council of Literary Magazines, Generalist Association (president, 1972—). *Awards, honors:* Lucile Medwick Memorial Award from International P.E.N., 1976.

WRITINGS: Rainscent (lyric poetry), Stephen Dwoskin, 1962; *Trinity* (epic poem), Horizon Press, 1975; *The Early Poems,* Ghost Dance Press, 1977; *Summer Woman* (love poems), Allegra Press, 1978; (translator) Menke Katz, *Water-Rose* (poems), Allegra Press, 1978. Editor-in-chief of *Newsletter on the State of Culture,* 1968—.

SIDELIGHTS: Smith writes: "The poet is the primal revolutionary. The poet is everyman."

SMITH, Herbert F(rancis) 1922-

PERSONAL: Born December 31, 1922, in Buffalo, N.Y.; son of John Francis (a mechanic) and Clara (Otto) Smith. *Education:* Attended Canisius College, 1949, St. Philip Neri School for Delayed Vocations, Boston, 1950, and Loyola Seminary, Shrub Oak, N.Y.; Fordham University, M.A., 1961; Woodstock College, Woodstock, Md., S.T.B., 1963. *Politics:* Democrat. *Home and office:* Jesuit Community, St. Joseph College, Philadelphia, Pa. 19131.

CAREER: American Radio Institute, Buffalo, N.Y., instructor in radio-television, 1948-50; entered Society of Jesus (Jesuits), 1951, ordained Roman Catholic priest, 1962; teacher of math, English, and religion at Roman Catholic high school in Baltimore, Md., 1958-59; director of spiritual programs and retreats, 1965-75; producer-director and writer for "Who Will Believe Our Report?" on WIBF-FM Radio, 1976—. Writer, 1954—. Moderator of Xavier-Damians Christian Life Community. Regular speaker for "International Sacred Heart" radio program.

WRITINGS: Living for Resurrection, Joseph F. Wagner, 1970; *The Lord Experience,* Liturgical Press, 1973; *God Day by Day,* Our Sunday Visitor, 1973; *The Pilgrim Contemplative: Early Years,* Liturgical Press, 1977; *The Pilgrim Contemplative: Mature Years,* Liturgical Press, 1977. Author of "The Sunday Mass in Focus" in *Catholic Standard and Times* and *Magnificat,* 1967-69. Contributor to *Catholic Encyclopedia for School and Home.* Contributor to religious publications and newspapers.

WORK IN PROGRESS: Research on prayer and personal growth, and on the mystery of Christ.

SIDELIGHTS: Smith told *CA:* "I'm of the breed of wayfarers and explorers of the Absolute. My journey is interior, in the uncharted realms of the spirit. My bodily passages across America are external expressions of the inner travels—mere epiphenomena. My struggles are with more than human powers. I have gone from knowing Christ to knowing that Christ is Mystery and life is a mysterious evolution that carries us into His depths. I have captured what I could of this mystery in *The Pilgrim Contemplative.*"

* * *

SMITH, Jon R(ichard) 1946-

PERSONAL: Born May 31, 1946, in Kettering, England; son of Tom (a schoolmaster) and Margaret (a botanist; maiden name, Oates) Smith; married Lamenda Barrett, 1965 (divorced, 1971); children: James Brunel. *Education:* Attended University of Keele, 1964-65. *Politics:* "Basically Socialist." *Religion:* "Pantheist of sorts." *Home:* Waskerley, Thurlestone, Kingsbridge, Devonshire, England.

CAREER: Musician (played guitar and managed small bands), 1965-75; South Devon Jazz Workshop, Dartington, England, director, 1970-72; writer, 1972—.

WRITINGS: (With John Jenkins) *Electric Music,* Indiana University Press, 1976.

WORK IN PROGRESS: Electric Music Effects, with Jenkins; research on local history, especially Devonshire in the Dark Ages, and industrial archaeology in southwestern England, and on the history of the Italian motorcycle.

SIDELIGHTS: Smith writes: "I had no particular motivation for writing before *Electric Music.* Having found I rather enjoyed writing, I think I may well try other ventures in this field. Music has been a dominant interest for me so far, but my taste is catholic and includes such things as motorcycles, engineering generally, local history and topography, railway history and related sociology, mineralogy, etc., providing little financial return but plenty of challenges.''

* * *

SMITH, Kenneth Lee 1925-

PERSONAL: Born January 5, 1925, in Virginia; son of George Lee and Margaret (Bonnewell) Smith; married Esther Ward Shrieves (a banker), August 19, 1953; children: Matthew Kenneth, Meredith Ann, Michael Lee. *Education:* University of Richmond, B.A., 1945; Crozer Theological Seminary, B.D.,1948; Duke University, Ph.D., 1959. *Politics:* Democrat. *Religion:* American Baptist. *Home:* 50 Evandale Rd., Rochester, N.Y. 14618. *Office:* Department of Theology and Ethics, Colgate Rochester Divinity School, 1100 South Goodman St., Rochester, N.Y. 14620.

CAREER: Ordained American Baptist minister, 1948; Crozer Theological Seminary, Chester, Pa., assistant professor, 1950-53, associate professor, 1953-59, professor of Christian ethics, 1959-70; Colgate Rochester Divinity School, Rochester, N.Y., professor, 1970-75, Mrs. John Prize Crozer Professor of Applied Theology, 1975—. Past member of Pennsylvania Social Service Committee and Delaware County Housing Authority; past chairman of board of directors of Chester's Office of Economic Opportunity program. Guest on "Today Show" and "Look Up and Live." *Member:* National Association for the Advancement of Colored People, Association of Christian Ethics (vice-president, 1955-58), American Academy of Religion, People (past member of executive committee in Chester).

WRITINGS: Search for the Beloved Community: The Thinking of Martin Luther King, Jr., Judson, 1974. Contributor to Baptist journals.

AVOCATIONAL INTERESTS: Politics, prison reform, fishing, bowling, little league baseball.

* * *

SMITH, Merritt Roe 1940-

PERSONAL: Born November 14, 1940, in Waverly, N.Y.; son of Wilson N. (an optometrist) and Eleanor (a teacher; maiden name, Fitzgerald) Smith; married Bronwyn M. Mellquist (an editor), August 24, 1974. *Education:* Georgetown University, A.B., 1963; Pennsylvania State University, M.A., 1965, Ph.D., 1971. *Home:* 258 Canyon Dr., Columbus, Ohio 43214.

CAREER: Ohio State University, Columbus, assistant professor, 1970-75, associate professor of history, 1975—. Visiting professor at University of Pennsylvania, 1976. Member of board of trustees of American Precision Museum. Consultant to Franklin Institute. *Member:* American Historical Association, Organization of American Historians, American Association for the Advancement of Science, Society for the History of Technology (member of executive council), Society for Industrial Archeology. *Awards, honors:* American Philosophical Society grant, 1974; Harvard-Newcomen fellow at Harvard University, 1974-75; Frederick Jackson Turner Award from Organization of American Historians, 1977, for *Harpers Ferry Armory and the New Technology;* nominated for Pulitzer Prize, 1977, for *Harpers Ferry Armory and the New Technology;* fellow of Regional Economic History Research Center at Eleutherian Mills Library, 1978-79.

WRITINGS: (Contributor) Ian M. G. Quimby and P. A. Earl, editors, *Technological Innovation and the Decorative Arts,* University Press of Virginia, 1974; (contributor) B. Franklin Cooling, editor, *War, Business, and American Society,* Kennikat, 1977; *Harpers Ferry Armory and the New Technology,* Cornell University Press, 1977; (contributor) Carroll Pursell, editor, *Technology in America,* Voice of America, 1978.

Contributor to professional journals. Associate editor for Johns Hopkins Press. Member of editorial board of *Business History Review;* advisory editor of *Technology and Culture.*

WORK IN PROGRESS: Mechanizing America: Technology, Society, and the Republic, 1790-1876, publication expected in 1980; research for a comparative study of early industrial communities in nineteenth-century America.

SIDELIGHTS: Smith comments: "I am particularly interested in how people respond to change in early industrial societies and in developing countries generally."

* * *

SMITH, Norman Lewis 1941-

PERSONAL: Born October 9, 1941, in Elizabeth, N.J.; son of Charles Wesson (a self-employed businessman) and Genevieve (Smart) Smith; married Susan Renner (associate editor of *Popular Science*), February 5, 1972. *Education:* Attended Oxford University, 1962; Georgetown University, A.B., 1963; further study at University of Madrid, 1965. *Home and office:* 20 Fifth Ave., New York, N.Y. 10011.

CAREER: True, New York City, articles editor, 1965-70; *Signature,* New York City, senior editor, 1970-71; *Sport,* New York City, managing editor, 1971-74; Playboy Press, New York City, managing editor, 1974-75; free-lance writer, 1975—. Chairman of education for Juvenile Diabetes Foundation, 1977-78. *Member:* Authors Guild of Authors League of America.

WRITINGS: (With Tom Seaver) *How I Would Pitch to Babe Ruth,* Playboy Press, 1974; (with Jim Gott) *Amphibian: The Adventures of a Professional Diver,* Playboy Press, 1975; *The Return of Billy the Kid,* Coward, 1977. Contributor to popular magazines, including *Travel and Leisure, Sport,* and *Free Enterprise.*

WORK IN PROGRESS: Sports and Games Almanac; Dwelling With Dwarfs, a novel.

* * *

SMITH, Patrick 1936-

PERSONAL: Born October 29, 1936, in Cork, Ireland; son of Joseph (a physician) and Elizabeth (Gunne) Smith; married Berit Kaspar (a translator), November 29, 1961; children: Kathleen Barbro Helena, Nicholas Edvard Patrick. *Education:* National University of Ireland, University College, Dublin, B.Arch., 1960. *Home:* Pontonjaergatan 16, 11237 Stockholm, Sweden.

CAREER: Architect in London, England, and Stockholm, Sweden, 1960-74; writer, 1974—. *Member:* Foerfattarfoerbundet, Arkitektfoerbundet, Svenska Arkitekters Riksfoerbund, Society of Authors, Royal Institute of Architects (Ireland).

WRITINGS—Novels: *Having and Wanting,* R. Hale, 1970; *In London One Summer,* R. Hale, 1973; *En Liten Stad paa Irland* (title means "A Small Town in Ireland"), Bonniers, 1976; *Haer foer att stanna* (title means "Here to Stay"), Bonniers, 1977; *The End of Something,* R. Hale, 1978; (translator) Goeran Palm, *The Flight from Work,* Cambridge University Press, 1978. Contributor to British and Swedish architectural journals. Contributing editor of *New World Architecture,* 1965-68.

WORK IN PROGRESS: A novel in Swedish; a book on Ireland.

SIDELIGHTS: Smith writes: "I work mainly as a novelist. I changed to writing in Swedish in 1976. (I have lived here since 1960.) My ambition as a writer is (as one reviewer commented) 'to see the world exactly as it is, with crystal clarity.' Not until we force ourselves to see how the world around us functions (as opposed to how it is supposed to function) can we properly set about changing it. I do not believe very much in writing for posterity. I write my books in the hope of affecting those I live amongst—and also in the hope of entertaining them.

"I do not plan to return to architecture. As long as a handful of people are interested in reading what I write, I shall go on writing."

*   *   *

SMITH, Patrick D(avis)   1927-

PERSONAL: Born October 8, 1927, in Mendenhall, Miss.; son of John D., Sr. (a politician) and Nora (Eubanks) Smith; married Iris Doty, August 1, 1948; children: Patrick D., Jr., Jane (Mrs. Charles Schneider). *Education:* Hinds Junior College, A.A., 1944; University of Mississippi, B.A., 1947, M.A., 1959. *Politics:* "I have been both a Democrat and a Republican." *Religion:* Baptist. *Home:* 1370 Island Dr., Merritt Island, Fla. 32952.

CAREER: Owner and operator of an automobile dealership and a cattle ranch in Mendenhall, Miss., 1948-56; Sperry Rand Corp., Vickers Division, Jackson, Miss., director of public relations, 1956-58; Hinds Junior College, Raymond, Miss., director of public relations, 1959-62; University of Mississippi, Oxford, director of public information, 1962-66; Brevard Community College, Cocoa, Fla., director of college relations, 1966—. *Military service:* U.S. Merchant Marine, 1945; served in North Africa and Europe.

MEMBER: American Association of Community and Junior Colleges, American College Public Relations Association (district director, 1968), Council for the Advancement and Support of Education, Authors Guild of Authors League of America, Florida Association of Community Colleges, Cape Canaveral Public Relations Association (chairman, 1976).

WRITINGS: The River Is Home (novel), Little, Brown, 1953; *The Beginning* (novel), Exposition, 1967; *Forever Island* (novel), Norton, 1973; *Angel City* (novel), Valkyrie Press, 1978; *Allapattah* (novel), Valkyrie Press, in press. Correspondent in Korea, 1953. Contributor to newspapers.

WORK IN PROGRESS: A novel based on the life of the "Florida Cracker" cowman in the nineteenth and early twentieth centuries, completion expected, 1979.

SIDELIGHTS: Smith told *CA:* "My novels reflect the plight of the underdogs in life. *The River Is Home* portrays the life of people called 'swamp rats' who lived along the Pearl River in South Mississippi and Louisiana at the turn of the century. *The Beginning* is about the struggles of poor whites and blacks in the South during the 1960's civil rights movement. *Forever Island* tells the story of what happens to an old Seminole Indian and his family and a white settler when a section of the Florida Everglades is destroyed by development. *Angel City* is about slavery among modern-day migrant workers; and *Allapattah* (a Seminole word for crocodile) tells the plight of the younger generation of Seminoles.

"In order to write *Forever Island,* I lived among the Seminoles in the Florida Everglades. The novel has been published in seventeen foreign countries. I also lived in several migrant camps prior to writing *Angel City.*

"These underdogs in life are *real people* although they are basically unknown to the majority of the reading public. I have devoted my writing talent to researching their ways of life and putting this into print in hopes that my novels might in some way improve their status in life."

AVOCATIONAL INTERESTS: Boating, gardening, exploring wilderness areas.

*   *   *

SMITH, Philip Chadwick Foster   1939-

PERSONAL: Born February 17, 1939, in Salem, Mass.; son of Philip Horton (an architect) and Elinor Colby (Mahoney) Smith; married Jane Fillis de Ledesma (a teacher), July 4, 1964; children: Alexandra Chadwick, Hillary Webb. *Education:* Harvard University, B.A., 1961, graduate study, 1961-63. *Politics:* Republican. *Religion:* Protestant. *Residence:* Salem, Mass. *Office:* Peabody Museum, East India Sq., Salem, Mass. 01970.

CAREER: Free-lance architectural draftsman and model maker, 1959-63; Peabody Museum, Salem, Mass., museum assistant, 1963-66, curator of maritime history, 1966—, editor of museum publications, 1978—. Managing editor of *American Neptune,* 1969—. Chairman of Peabody Museum Marine Associates, 1964-74. Member of design review board of Salem Redevelopment Authority, 1969-72. Member of board of trustees of Ropes Memorial, 1968—, board of directors of Historic Salem, Inc., 1966, and board of managers of Salem Home for Aged Women, 1968-70.

MEMBER: International Congress of Maritime Museums, North American Society for Oceanic History (member of council, 1976—), Council of American Maritime Museums (member of national board of directors, 1977—), Marine Society (England; honorary governor, 1968—), Society for Nautical Research (England), Colonial Society of Massachusetts (member of council, 1976-77), Massachusetts Historical Society, Bostonian Society (curator of maritime history, 1967—), Salem Marine Society, Salem Athenaeum, Marblehead Historical Society, Club of Odd Volumes, Essex Institute.

WRITINGS: A History of the Marine Society at Salem, 1766-1966, Salem Marine Society, 1966; *Portraits of the Marine Society at Salem in New-England,* Salem Marine Society, 1972; (editor) *Michele Felice Corne, 1752-1845: Versatile Neapolitan Painter of Salem, Boston, and Newport,* Peabody Museum, 1972; (editor) *The Journals of Ashley Bowen (1728-1813) of Marblehead,* Colonial Society of Massachusetts, 1973; *The Frigate Essex Papers: Building the Salem Frigate, 1798-1799,* Peabody Museum, 1974; *East India Marine Hall, 1824-1972,* Peabody Museum, 1974; *Captain Samuel Tucker (1747-1833), Continental Navy,* Essex Institute, 1976; *Fired by Manley Zeal: A Naval Fiasco of the American Revolution,* Peabody Museum, 1977; (contributor) Bryant F. Tolles, Jr., editor, *Dr. Bentley's Salem: Diary of a Town,* Essex Institute, 1977; *The Artful Roux: Marine Painters of Marseille,* Peabody Museum, 1978.

Illustrator: Edith Mary Webb, *Presents* (juvenile), privately printed, 1974. Contributor of more than a hundred articles and reviews to museum catalogs, magazines, and newspapers, including *American Neptune* and *Historic Preserva-*

tion. Member of board of editors of Essex Institute's *Historical Collections,* 1975—, and "The Samuel McIntire Papers," 1977—.

WORK IN PROGRESS: A biography of U.S. Navy constructor Josiah Fox; several novels; a children's book.

AVOCATIONAL INTERESTS· Bookbinding, marble paper making, woodcarving, model making, cabinetmaking, oil painting (seascapes and portraits).

* * *

SMITH, Ralph Alexander 1929-

PERSONAL: Born June 12, 1929, in Ellwood City, Pa.; son of J. and B. V. (Campbell) Smith; married Christiane M. Kolbe, November, 1955. *Education:* Columbia University, A.B., 1954, M.A., 1959, Ed.D., 1962. *Home:* 1310 West John St., Champaign, Ill. 61820. *Office:* Department of Educational Policy Studies, University of Illinois, Champaign, Ill. 61801.

CAREER: Kent State University, Kent, Ohio, instructor in art history and art education, 1959-61; Wisconsin State University (now University of Wisconsin), Oshkosh, assistant professor of art history and art education, 1961-63; State University of New York College at New Paltz, assistant professor of art history and art education, 1963-64; University of Illinois, Champaign, assistant professor, 1964-67, associate professor, 1967-71, professor of aesthetic education, 1971-74, professor of cultural and educational policy, 1975—, member of executive committee of Bureau of Educational Research, 1972—. De Francesco Memorial Lecturer at Kutztown State College, 1974; guest lecturer at colleges and universities. Member of board of governors of Institute for the Study of the Arts in Education, 1974-75; member of board of trustees of National Center for the Study of Art in Education, 1974-76; project and institute director for National Endowment for the Humanities; consultant to Kettering Foundation and Canada Council. *Military service:* U.S. Army, Medical Corps, 1954-57; served in Germany.

MEMBER: International Society for Education Through Art, Philosophy of Education Society, American Society for Aesthetics, National Art Education Association, National Association for Humanities Education, American Educational Studies Association, Council for Policy Studies in Art Education, Council for Research in Music Education, World Future Society, Illinois Art Education Association. *Awards, honors:* Manuel Barkan Memorial Award from National Art Education Association, 1973, for "Art and Aesthetic Statesmanship in American Education."

WRITINGS: (Editor and contributor) *Aesthetics and Criticism in Art Education: Problems in Defining, Explaining, and Evaluating Art,* Rand McNally, 1966; (editor and contributor) *Aesthetic Concepts and Education,* University of Illinois Press, 1966; (editor and contributor) *Aesthetics and Problems of Education,* University of Illinois Press, 1971; (editor and contributor) *Aesthetic Education Today: Problems and Prospects,* Division of Art Education, Ohio State University, 1973; (editor and contributor) *Regaining Educational Leadership: Critical Essays on PBTE/CBTE, Behavioral Objectives, and Accountability,* Wiley, 1975.

Contributor: Donald Carver and Thomas Sergiovanni, editors, *Organizations and Human Behavior: Focus on Schools,* McGraw, 1969; Shiela Schwartz, editor, *Readings in the Humanities,* Macmillan, 1970; Dwight Allen and Eli Seitman, editors, *The Teachers Handbook,* Scott Publish-

ing, 1970; Richard Colwell, editor, *An Approach to Aesthetic Education,* two volumes, College of Education, University of Illinois, 1970; George Pappas, editor, *Concepts and Art Education,* Macmillan, 1970; editors, *Challenges from the Future,* Kodansha, 1971; John Katz, editor, *Approaches to the Teaching of Film,* Little, Brown, 1971; *Toward an Aesthetic Education,* Music Educators National Conference, 1971; R. W. Hostrop, editor, *Accountability for Educational Results,* Linnet Books, 1973; Margaret Gillet and J. L. Laska, editors, *Foundation Studies in Education: Justifications and New Directions,* Scarecrow, 1973; K. B. Hoyt and J. R. Hebeler, editors, *Career Education for Gifted and Talented Students,* Olympus, 1974; *Papers on Educational Reform,* Volume IV, Open Court, 1974; George Hardiman and Theodore Zernich, editors, *Curricular Considerations for Visual Arts Education,* Stipes, 1974. Also contributor to *Art and Aesthetics: An Agenda for the Future.*

Author of script, "Dial for Educational Information Service." Contributor of about seventy-five articles and reviews to learned journals. Founder and editor of *Journal of Aesthetic Education,* 1966—; past member of editorial board of *Studies in Art Education.*

WORK IN PROGRESS: Essays on the subject of art, culture, and education.

SIDELIGHTS: Smith told *CA:* "I'm interested in cultural criticism, especially the ways in which social, political, and economic forces influence attitudes towards the arts and education."

* * *

SMITH, Red
See SMITH, Walter W(ellesley)

* * *

SMITH, Russell E. 1932-

PERSONAL: Born January 21, 1932, in Windsor, Mo.; son of William R. and Gladys (Petty) Smith; married wife, Mary Ann; children: Kent, Samuel, Nathan, Rachel. *Education:* University of Missouri, B.S., 1956, M.A., 1957; University of Wisconsin, Madison, M.S.S.W., 1961. *Politics:* Democrat. *Religion:* Episcopalian. *Home:* 405 Fiesta Ave., Davis, Calif. 95616. *Office:* 6000 Jay St., Sacramento, Calif. 95819.

CAREER: Child welfare worker for Dane County, Madison, Wis., 1958-61; supervisor of social services for Rock County, Janesville, Wis., 1961-63; State of California, Sacramento, training officer, 1963-64; California State University, Sacramento, professor, 1964—. Member of Yolo County Family Service Board; chairman of Sacramento County Welfare Advisory Committee. *Military service:* U.S. Navy, 1951-55.

WRITINGS: (With Dorothy Zietz) *Welfare in America,* Wiley, 1971; (with Alan D. Wade) *American Social Policy and Services,* Mosby, 1979. Contributor to *Collier's Encyclopedia Yearbook.* Contributor to social studies, education, history, and economic journals.

AVOCATIONAL INTERESTS: European travel.

* * *

SMITH, Sharon 1947-

PERSONAL: Born July 18, 1947, in California; married Randolph Phillips Huber (a filmmaker and teacher of film),

April 21, 1973; children: Christine Teresa. *Education:* Middlebury College, B.A., 1968; University of Southern California, M.A., 1973. *Religion:* Episcopalian. *Home address:* R.F.D. 1, Box 106, Hartland, Me. 04943.

CAREER: Writer, 1975—.

WRITINGS: (Contributor) Barbara Stanford, editor, *On Being Female,* Washington Square Press, 1974; *Women Who Make Movies,* Hopkinson & Blake, 1975.

WORK IN PROGRESS: Frostpocket Farm, the autobiographical story of a young couple's first two years in Maine; research for *And Mice Don't Bark,* a murder mystery set in central Maine.

* * *

SMITH, W(illiam) David   1928-

PERSONAL: Born November 30, 1928, in Neath, Wales; son of Albert G. and Gwladys M. Smith; married Joan Mali Williams (a lecturer), December 24, 1952; children: Deborah Elizabeth Mali. *Education:* University of Wales, University College, Aberystwyth, B.A., 1949, diploma in education, 1950; Loughborough College of Education, diploma, 1951; University of East Anglia, M.Phil., 1971. *Religion:* Church of England. *Home:* 127 Greenways Eaton, Norwich NR4 6PD, England. *Office:* Keswick Hall, Norwich NR4 6TL, England.

CAREER: Assistant master of private school in Lichfield, England, 1954-58; adviser for schools in Cambridgeshire, England, 1960-65; Keswick Hall, Norwich, England, lecturer in history of education and history of physical education, director of in-service education, and head of department of physical education, 1965—. *Military service:* Royal Air Force, education officer, 1951-54; became flying officer. *Member:* International Association for the History of Physical Education and Sport (HISPA), History of Education Society.

WRITINGS: Stretching Their Bodies: The History of Physical Education, David & Charles, 1974. Contributor of articles and reviews to journals. Editor of *Bulletin of Physical Education,* 1969-70.

WORK IN PROGRESS: Education and Society in Norwich, 1800-1914.

SIDELIGHTS: Smith writes: "I am interested in applying research methods of social scientists and of historians to the evaluation of physical activities in society and to the development of physical education in schools.

"I am interested in the social history of education, especially as revealed in the microcosm of a small city: the contribution of literacy and education to the aspirations and satisfaction of man in a modern industrial society."

AVOCATIONAL INTERESTS: Walking, sailing, gardening, theater, opera.

* * *

SMITH, Walter W(ellesley)   1905-
(Red Smith)

PERSONAL: Born September 25, 1905, in Green Bay, Wis.; son of Walter Philip (in wholesale produce) and Ida (Richardson) Smith; married Catherine Cody, February 11, 1933 (died February 19, 1967); married Phyllis Warner (an artist), November 8, 1968; children: (first marriage) Catherine (Mrs. J. David Halloran), Terence Fitzgerald. *Education:* University of Notre Dame, A.B., 1927. *Politics:* "Liberal?" *Religion:* Roman Catholic. *Home:* 510 West Rd.,

New Canaan, Conn. 06840. *Office:* New York Times, 229 West 43rd St., New York, N.Y. 10036.

CAREER: Milwaukee Sentinel, Milwaukee, Wis., cub reporter, 1927-28; *St. Louis Star,* St. Louis, Mo., copyreader and sports writer, 1928-36; *Philadelphia Record,* Philadelphia, Pa., sports reporter and columnist, 1936-45; *New York Herald Tribune,* New York City, author of "Views of Sport" column, 1945-66; *New York World-Journal-Tribune,* New York City, author of "Views of Sport" column, 1966-67; author of "Views of Sport" column for Publishers Hall Syndicate (now Field Newspapers Syndicate), 1967-71; New York Times Syndicate, New York City, sports columnist, 1971—. *Member:* Society of the Silurians, Players Club. *Awards, honors:* Received journalism award from National Headliners Club, 1945; Grantland Rice Memorial Award from Sportsmanship Brotherhood of New York, 1956; LL.D. from University of Notre Dame, 1968; Pulitzer Prize for Commentary, 1976; and many annual sportscaster and sportswriter awards.

WRITINGS—All under name Red Smith: (Editor) *Selected Sports Stories* (from *Saturday Evening Post*), A. S. Barnes, 1949; *Out of the Red* (collected columns), Knopf, 1950; *Views of Sport* (collected columns), Knopf, 1954; *Red Smith's Sports Annual,* Crown, 1961; *The Best of Red Smith,* edited by Verna Reamer, F. Watts, 1963; *Red Smith on Fishing Around the World,* Doubleday, 1963; *Strawberries in the Wintertime: The Sporting World of Red Smith,* Quadrangle, 1974; *Red Smith's Favorite Sports Stories,* Norton, 1976. Contributor to popular magazines.

SIDELIGHTS: Smith told *CA:* "I never wanted to be anything but a newspaper stiff. I have been one without interruption for fifty-one years, and I am proud of it." *Avocational interests:* Fishing.

* * *

SMITS, Teo
See SMITS, Theodore R(ichard)

* * *

SMITS, Theodore R(ichard)   1905-
(Teo Smits)

PERSONAL: Born April 24, 1905, in Jackson, Mich.; son of Bastian (a clergyman) and Helen (Hull) Smits; married Anna Mary Wells, September 5, 1931 (divorced June 13, 1952); married Pamela Ada Seward (an executive secretary), September 22, 1952; children: (first marriage) Jean Marie Smits Miles, Helen Lida, Gerrit (deceased); (second marriage) Richard Winston. *Education:* Attended Michigan State University, 1922-23. *Home:* 601 East 20th St., New York, N.Y. 10010.

CAREER: Lansing State Journal, Lansing, Mich., state and telegraph editor, 1924-29; International News Service, New York City, city editor, 1929-31, manager of Los Angeles bureau, 1931-34; Associated Press, New York City, city editor in Los Angeles, Calif., 1934-37, chief of bureaus in Salt Lake City, Utah, 1937-39, and Detroit, Mich., 1939-46, general sports editor in New York City, 1946-69; AMF, Inc., White Plains, N.Y., editorial adviser for Leisure Time Products, 1969-74; *Armchair Quarterback,* New York City, editor, 1976—.

WRITINGS—Under name Teo Smits: (Editor) *The Year in Sports,* Prentice-Hall, 1958; *The Game of Soccer,* Prentice-Hall, 1968; *Soccer for the American Boy,* Prentice-Hall, 1970; *Soccer, American Style,* Doubleday, 1976.

WORK IN PROGRESS: Pitching and Catching, for Doubleday.

SIDELIGHTS: While with Associated Press, Smits was in charge of world coverage for the Olympics from 1948 to 1968.

* * *

SMYSER, Adam A(lbert) 1920-

PERSONAL: Born December 18, 1920, in York, Pa.; son of Adam M. (a businessman) and Miriam (Stein) Smyser; married Elizabeth Avery (a television hostess), December 25, 1943; children: Heidi O., Avery R. *Education:* Pennsylvania State University, B.A., 1941. *Politics:* Republican. *Home:* 2144 Mott-Smith Dr., Honolulu, Hawaii 96822. *Office: Honolulu Star-Bulletin,* P.O. Box 3080, Honolulu, Hawaii 96802.

CAREER/WRITINGS: Pittsburgh Press, Pittsburgh, Pa., rewrite man, 1941-42; *Honolulu Star-Bulletin,* Honolulu, Hawaii, member of staff, 1946-52, city editor, 1953-60, managing editor, 1960-65, editor, 1966—. Contributor of articles to *Business Week,* McGraw-Hill magazines, and other periodicals. Member of board of directors, Aloha United Fund, Friends of East-West Center, Foundation for Study in Hawaii and Abroad, National Council on Crime and Delinquency, and Oahu Cancer Society. *Military service:* U.S. Naval Reserve, 1942-46. *Member:* American Civil Liberties Union, American Society of Newspaper Editors, United Nations Association, Honolulu Chamber of Commerce (director), Honolulu Press Club, Sigma Delta Chi.

* * *

SNELL, David 1936-

PERSONAL: Born September 6, 1936, in Lansing, Mich.; son of Clair John (a minister) and Iva (a teacher; maiden name, Hawkins) Snell; married wife, Mary Lou, July 15, 1961; children: Christopher Storey. *Education:* Graduated from Michigan State University, 1960. *Home:* 5227 Greenpoint Dr., Stone Mountain, Ga. 30088. *Agent:* N. S. Bienstock, Inc., 10 Columbus Circle, New York, N.Y. 10019. *Office:* ABC News, 10 Perimeter Park, Atlanta, Ga. 30341.

CAREER/WRITINGS: WIBM Radio, Jackson, Mich., news reporter, 1961; WJRT-TV, Flint, Mich., news reporter, 1962-64; WKJG-TV, Fort Wayne, Ind., news reporter, 1965; American Broadcasting Co. (ABC) News, New York City, news reporter, 1966—. Notable assignments include coverage of the war in Vietnam, the Nixon and Muskie campaigns in 1968, riots in Attica, slayings at Jackson State, and the Apollo splashdowns.

* * *

SNODGRASS, Joan Gay 1934-

PERSONAL: Born October 4, 1934, in Pittsburgh, Pa.; daughter of William Rodney and Grace (Dietrich) Snodgrass. *Education:* Pennsylvania State University, B.S., 1955; University of Pennsylvania, Ph.D., 1966. *Home:* 110 Bleecker St., Apt. 22-E, New York, N.Y. 10012. *Office:* Department of Psychology, New York University, 6 Washington Pl., New York, N.Y. 10003.

CAREER: New York University, New York, N.Y., assistant professor, 1966-70, associate professor of psychology, 1966—, coordinator of graduate experimental psychology program, 1976—. *Member:* American Psychological Association, Psychonomic Society, Eastern Psychological Association, New York Academy of Sciences, Sigma Xi, Psi Chi.

WRITINGS: (Contributor) Bertram Scharf, editor, *Experimental Sensory Psychology,* Scott, Foresman, 1975; *The Numbers Game: Statistics for Psychology,* Oxford University Press, 1977; (with Gail Levy) *Human Experimental Psychology,* Little, Brown, 1978. Contributor to psychology journals. Consulting editor of *Journal of Experimental Psychology.*

SIDELIGHTS: Snodgrass told *CA:* "My training as an experimental psychologist began in third grade when our teacher informed us that a 'q' missing a following 'u' would fall over. I raced home to test the assertion and discovered that, like many other assertions, it was false. Since that early experience, I have broadened my research interests to include esthetices, vusual memory, mathematical models for memory processes, and more generally the role of pictorial symbols in communication."

* * *

SNOOK, I(van) A(ugustine) 1933-

PERSONAL: Born March 27, 1933, in New Zealand; son of John Thomas (a shopkeeper) and Mary Monica (Granger) Snook; married Josephine Carde (a speech therapist), January 16, 1965; children: Kathryn, John, David. *Education:* University of Canterbury, B.A., 1962, M.A., 1965; University of Illinois, Ph.D., 1968. *Home:* 56 Birdwood Ave., Christchurch, New Zealand. *Office:* Department of Education, University of Canterbury, Christchurch, New Zealand.

CAREER: Teacher at school in Christchurch, New Zealand, 1961-65; University of Canterbury, Christchurch, New Zealand, lecturer, 1968-71, senior lecturer, 1972-76, reader in education, 1977—.

WRITINGS: (With H. S. Broudy, R. D. Szoke, and M. J. Parsons) *Philosophy of Education,* University of Illinois Press, 1967; *Indoctrination and Education,* Routledge & Kegan Paul, 1972; *Concepts of Indoctrination,* Routledge & Kegan Paul, 1972; (with Colin McGeorge) *More Than Talk,* New Zealand Department of Education, 1977. Associate editor of *New Zealand Journal of Educational Studies.*

WORK IN PROGRESS: The Right to Educate and the Right to Be Educated, with Colin Lankshear.

* * *

SOBEL, B. Z. 1933-

PERSONAL: Born October 28, 1933, in New York; son of Louis (a baker) and Esther (Ingber) Sobel; married Michal Steinberg (a historian), June 2, 1953; children: Minda, Daniel, Noam. *Education:* Brooklyn College (now of the City University of New York), B.A., 1955; New School for Social Research, M.A., 1956, Ph.D., 1964. *Politics:* "Guiltfree liberal." *Religion:* Jewish. *Home:* 37 Ruth St., Haifa, Israel. *Office:* Haifa University, Haifa, Israel.

CAREER: Former executive of B'nai B'rith Anti-Defamation League; former lecturer at Miami University and Brandeis University; Haifa University, Haifa, Israel, lecturer, dean of faculty of social sciences, 1970-73, director of overseas study programs, 1977—. Member of Israel Board of Higher Education, 1971-76. *Member:* Israel Sociological Society.

WRITINGS: Hebrew Christianity: The Thirteenth Tribe, Wiley, 1974. Contributor to Jewish studies and religious studies journals.

WORK IN PROGRESS: A book on the impact of the Six-Day War on Israeli society.

SOLDO, John J(oseph) 1945-

PERSONAL: Born May 16, 1945, in Brooklyn, N.Y.; son of Victor (a carpenter) and Mildred (a seamstress; maiden name, Ferrari) Soldo; married Martha Schwink, August 22, 1968 (divorced, April, 1971). *Education:* Fordham University, B.A. (magna cum laude), 1966; Harvard University, M.A., 1968, Ph.D., 1972; other graduate study at King's College, Cambridge, 1969. *Politics:* "Middle." *Religion:* Roman Catholic. *Home:* 238 Ave. U, Brooklyn, N.Y. 11223.

CAREER: Wells College, Aurora, N.Y., assistant professor of English, 1971-72; City University of New York, New York City, assistant professor of English at Bronx Community College and Kingsborough Community College, 1972-73; Columbia University, New York City, assistant professor of English, 1973-77; free-lance writer, 1977—. *Member:* Modern Language Association of America, American Studies Association, Society for Values in Higher Education, Poets and Writers, New York Poetry Forum. *Awards, honors:* Award for poetry from Academy des Beaux Arts, 1976.

WRITINGS: Delano in America and Other Early Poems, Pearl Press, 1974.

Plays: "Delano's Destiny" (poetic drama), first produced in Santa Fe, N.M., at St. John's College, August, 1970; "Delano in America" (with music, mime, and dance), first produced in New York City at St. Paul's Chapel, April, 1974; "Waves Clapping Like Angels" (one-act), first produced in New York City at Glines Theater, October, 1978.

Work represented in *Americana Anthology.* Contributor of poems, articles, and reviews to magazines, including *NewsArt, Margins, New Earth,* and *Columbia Review.*

WORK IN PROGRESS: The High Roller, a novel; *Stocks and Blonds,* a music book, with lyrics; books of poems, including *Odes and Cycles, Sonnets for Our Risorgimento, Mirrors for the Harmony of Sex, Passage to Philia* (dramatic poem), *Now Old with My Youth,* and *Flower, Children, Oh My Antonios.*

SIDELIGHTS: Soldo comments: "I began writing poetry again while living in England during 1969-70. Being in a different culture and living in the country provided a great stimulus."

*   *   *

SOLYN, Paul 1951-

PERSONAL: Born December 23, 1951, in Youngstown, Ohio; son of S. Paul (an insurance agent) and Margaret (Barnes) Solyn. *Education:* Oberlin College, A.B., 1973; Indiana University, M.A., 1974. *Politics:* Democrat. *Home:* 413 South Henderson, #14, Bloomington, Ind. 47401. *Office:* Department of English, Indiana University, Bloomington, Ind. 47401.

CAREER: Indiana University, Bloomington, associate instructor in English, 1976—. Puppeteer and director of publicity for Puck Players Puppet Theatre, 1976—. Member of board of directors of Bloomington Area Arts Council, 1977-80; member of Bloomington Poetry Workshop. *Member:* Modern Language Association of America, Society for the Study of Midwestern Literature, Midwest Modern Language Association.

WRITINGS: Mistress Quickly's Garden (poetry), Raintree Press, 1978. Contributor of poems and translations to literary journals, including *New Letters, Northeast, Dimension,* and *International Poetry Review,* and of articles to *Regionalism and the Female Imagination* and *Indiana Writes.*

WORK IN PROGRESS: Hearsay, poems; adapting Dickens' *A Christmas Carol* for puppet theater; a libretto for an opera about Martha Mitchell; studying the work of Harriette Simpson Arnow.

SIDELIGHTS: Solyn writes: "Living in the Midwest seems to have made some difference in my writing—or, the awareness of writing in the Midwest has made some difference. Since I do not believe in biographical interpretations of literature, I am reluctant to say much about this."

*   *   *

SONNEBORN, Harry L(ee) 1919-

PERSONAL: Born June 4, 1919, in Detroit, Mich.; son of Arthur B. (a manufacturing representative) and Lois (Speer) Sonneborn; married Jacquelyn Panetti, July 21, 1943; children: Carolyn (Mrs. Wilhelm Mayr), Susan (Mrs. Joel Myerson), Prudence. *Education:* University of Michigan, B.A., 1940. *Home:* 1021 East Ogden Ave., Milwaukee, Wis. 53202. *Office: Milwaukee Sentinel,* 918 North 4th St., Milwaukee, Wis. 53201.

CAREER/WRITINGS: Grand Rapids Press, Grand Rapids, Mich., reporter and copy editor, 1940-41; *Milwaukee Journal,* Milwaukee, Wis., copy editor, special news and city editor, 1941-62; *Milwaukee Sentinel,* Milwaukee, managing editor, 1962—. *Military service:* U.S. Naval Reserve, 1942-45; became lieutenant. *Member:* Associated Press Managing Editors (director, 1964-70; treasurer, 1970), Milwaukee Press Club (president, 1960-61), Sigma Delta Chi, Theta Chi, Unitarian Club.

*   *   *

SORIN, Gerald 1940-

PERSONAL: Born October 23, 1940, in Brooklyn, N.Y.; son of John (a foreman) and Ruth (a secretary; maiden name, Gass) Sorin; married Myra Cohen (a language teacher), June 9, 1962; children: Anna Bess. *Education:* Columbia University, A.B., 1962, Ph.D., 1969; Wayne State University, M.A., 1964. *Politics:* Democratic Socialist. *Religion:* Jewish. *Home:* 28 Woodland Dr., New Paltz, N.Y. 12561. *Office:* Department of History, State University of New York College at New Paltz, New Paltz, N.Y. 12561.

CAREER: State University of New York College at New Paltz, assistant professor, 1965-70, associate professor, 1970-77, professor of history, 1977—. *Member:* Organization of American Historians, American Studies Association, Social Science History Association, Group for the Use of Psychology in History, Southern Historical Association. *Awards, honors:* Danforth associate, 1970—.

WRITINGS: New York Abolitionists: A Case Study of Political Radicalism, Greenwood Press, 1971; *Abolitionism: A New Perspective,* Praeger, 1972.

WORK IN PROGRESS: The Times and Life of Martin Van Buren.

SIDELIGHTS: Sorin comments: "History gives me a weapon with which to negotiate a tentative peace with a chaotic universe." *Avocational interests:* Jogging forty miles a week, theatre.

*   *   *

SORRENTINO, Gilbert 1929-

PERSONAL: Born April 27, 1929, in Brooklyn, N.Y.; son of August E. and Ann (Davis) Sorrentino; married Elsene Wiessner (divorced); married Vivian Victoria Ortiz; children: Jesse, Delia, Christopher. *Education:* Attended Brooklyn College (now of the City University of New York), 1950-51, 1955-57. *Residence:* New York, N.Y. *Agent:* Mel Berger, William Morris Agency, Inc., 1350 Avenue of the Americas, New York, N.Y. 10019.

CAREER: "At least twenty-five jobs of all sorts," 1947-65; *Neon* (magazine), New York City, editor and publisher, 1956-60; Grove Press, New York City, editor, 1965-70. *Military service:* U.S. Army, 1951-53; served in medical corps. *Member:* American P.E.N. *Awards, honors:* Guggenheim fellowship, 1973; National Endowment for the Arts grant, 1974; Samuel S. Fels Award in fiction, 1974, for "Catechism"; Creative Artists Public Service grant, 1975.

WRITINGS: The Darkness Surrounds Us (poetry), Jargon Society, 1960; *Black and White* (poetry), Totem/Corinth, 1964; *The Sky Changes* (novel), Hill & Wang, 1966; *The Perfect Fiction* (poetry), Norton, 1968; *Steelwork* (novel), Pantheon, 1970; *Imaginative Qualities of Actual Things* (novel), Pantheon, 1971; *Corrosive Sublimate* (poetry), Black Sparrow, 1971; *Splendide-Hotel* (short story; limited edition), New Directions, 1973; *Flawless Play Restored: The Masque of Fungo* (play), Black Sparrow, 1974; *A Dozen Oranges*, Black Sparrow, 1976; *Sulpiciae Elegidid* (translations), Perishable Press, 1977; *White Snail*, Black Sparrow, 1977; *The Orangery*, University of Texas Press, 1977.

Work has been represented in anthologies, including *The New American Poetry, 1945-1960*, edited by Donald Hall, Grove, 1960; *Poesia Americana del '900*, Guanda, 1963; *The New Writing in the U.S.A.*, Penguin, 1967. Contributor to *Nation, New York Times, Esquire, Partisan Review, TriQuarterly, Colorado Review, Book Week, Harper's, New York Times Book Review, Poetry, New Directions in Prose and Poetry, Chelsea, Shenandoah, Spectrum,* and others. *Kulchur*, guest editor, Number 4, 1961, literary editor, 1961-63.

WORK IN PROGRESS: An untitled novel.

SIDELIGHTS: "My books speak for me," Sorrentino told *CA*, but critics and reviewers have written fairly extensively about Sorrentino's work. Shaun O'Connell commented: "Sorrentino, a writer of considerable stylistic range, is able, too, to rein in this headlong, galloping prose—evocative of the breathless hysteria of kids at those matinees—and show in lyrical detail the kind of minimal satisfactions these same boys can find for themselves as they grow up in the forties."

Roy Skodnick called Sorrentino a "master of the urban blues" who "delights in the world's arbitrary creation of trash and formal beauty . . . (and) allows both into the poem."

Sorrentino's first book of poetry, *The Darkness Surrounds Us,* was found "somber, sardonic, vulnerable" by Eric Mottram. He remarked: "Sorrentino revolts against the perversion of the *polis*—New York—and moves only warily into the romantic blandishments of landscape nature. . . . Most of the poems move where there is most difficulty, where anger and vindictiveness, in sometimes hopeless uncontrol, are countered by a need for love—it's a raw, vulnerable place for a poem to emerge, and the 'I' of the poem is often lyrically on edge." Mottram also noted the influence of Pound and Olson. While the "urgencies and embattlements" of *Black and White* occasionally lead to "awkwardness and stridency" the book was found to be remarkably honest. *The Perfect Fiction* has what Mottram termed "a platonic idea . . . of reality" and in comparison to *Black and White* has "an almost Stephens-like formality of imposed calm."

Jerome Klinkowitz observed that "Sorrentino will not tell stories: 'Prose will kill you if you give it an inch, i.e., if you try and substitute it for the world,' he remarks in 'Imaginative Qualities.'" Henry Weinfield added: "Sorrentino himself has written fine poems; but because the author has succumbed to the self-hatred and impotence that are so characteristic of our time. He has dramatized this self-hatred; he has not gone beyond it, and in the end his book only mires us more deeply in the vacuous corridors of the Splendide-Hotel."

Donald Phelps recognized "the heroism of Sorrentino's attitude in *Corrosive Sublimate*" as 'the most resiliently stoic kind, counting his resources, checking his defenses. He has at last defined his geography by declaring his vulnerability: his recognition of, and testimony to, the adjoining void as the definition of his own unrealized, undeclared power."

BIOGRAPHICAL/CRITICAL SOURCES: Nation, June 21, 1971; *Modern Occasions*, winter, 1972; *Grosseteste Review*, 1973; *Village Voice*, November 22, 1973; *VORT*, fall, 1974; Jerome Klinkowitz, *Literary Disruptions*, University of Illinois Press, 1975; *Contemporary Literary Criticism*, Gale, Volume 3, 1975, Volume 7, 1977; Klinkowitz, *The Life of Fiction*, University of Illinois Press, 1977.

*   *   *

SOSSAMAN, Stephen 1944-

PERSONAL: Born June 19, 1944, in Bryn Mawr, Pa.; son of Henry Maguire and Dorothy (Mitsch) Sossaman; married Rosario Perignat (a teacher and artist), January 23, 1966; children: Christine, Emily. *Education:* Columbia University, B.A., 1970; State University of New York at Stony Brook, M.A., 1971; doctoral study at New York University, 1972—. *Residence:* Huntington, Mass. *Office:* Department of English, Westfield State College, Westfield, Mass. 01085.

CAREER: Worked as advertising copywriter for various companies, 1970-72; Kingsborough Community College, Brooklyn, N.Y., part-time teacher of English, 1971-72; higher education officer, 1972-75; Westfield State College, Westfield, Mass., assistant professor of English, 1975—. *Military service:* U.S. Army, Artillery, 1966-68; served in Vietnam. *Member:* Modern Language Association of America, Dickens Fellowship.

WRITINGS: Death in the Bronx Zoo (poetry broadside), Sceptre Press, 1974; *The My Tho Laundry and Other Poems from the Indochina War*, Tideline Press, 1977; *Anonyms* (prose poems), Little River Press, 1978. Contributor to literary journals, antiques magazines, and newspapers in the United States, Canada, Australia, and New Zealand, including *Paris Review, Southern Humanities Review, Cottonwood Review,* and *Dickens Studies Newsletter.*

WORK IN PROGRESS: A study of poet Charles Olson; a play about a repertory company; fiction set in Vietnam.

SIDELIGHTS: Sossaman writes: "While war confirmed my long-standing cynicism about the human animal, it also taught me that combat is a complex, often exhilarating yet terrible human condition which eludes the usual simplicities of most of our "war literature" and of our intellectual stances. Combat is humbling to the writer for it is so intense, pure, ghastly and illuminating as to render adequate literary transformation both essential and nearly impossible.

"Of the many writers who have doubtless influenced me, three stand out as especially effective in alerting me to my own potentials, limitations, and goals as a writer. They are William Faulkner, Lawrence Durrell, and Gabriel Garcia Marquez.

"I hope eventually to have written a few intensely crafted yet fully felt and meaningful works; I hope never to crank out works merely because I fancy myself a writer."

* * *

SOUTHALL, Aidan (William) 1920-

PERSONAL: Born September 11, 1920, in England; son of William (a priest) and Vida (Ibbotson) Southall; married Isis Ragheb, October 8, 1966 (died January 6, 1973); married Christine Obbo (a university teacher), August 1, 1975; children: Aidan Mark, Lucinda Primrose. Education: Cambridge University, B.A., 1942, M.A., 1957; University of London, Ph.D., 1952. Office: Department of Anthropology, University of Wisconsin, 1180 Observatory Dr., Madison, Wis. 53706.

CAREER: Makerere University, Kampala, Uganda, 1945-64, began as lecturer, became professor, chairman of East African Institute of Social Research, 1957-61, dean of Faculty of Social Sciences, 1962-64; Syracuse University, Syracuse, N.Y., professor of anthropology, 1964-69; University of Wisconsin, Madison, professor of anthropology, 1969—. Member: International African Institute, American Anthropological Association, Association of Social Anthropologists, African Studies Association (member of board of directors), Royal Anthropological Institute.

WRITINGS: Lineage Formation Among the Luo, International African Institute, 1952; Alur Society: A Study in Processes and Types of Domination, Heffer, 1956; (with P. C. W. Gutkind) Townsmen in the Making: Kampala and Its Suburbs, Makerere University, 1957; (editor) Urban Anthropology: Cross Cultural Studies of the Urbanization Process, Oxford University Press, 1973; Cities in Time and Space, Oxford University Press, 1978. Contributor of more than fifty articles to scholarly journals. Former editor of Uganda Journal.

WORK IN PROGRESS: Research on small urban centers in rural development in Africa.

SIDELIGHTS: Southall speaks French, Alur, and Luganda; he has conducted long-term research in Africa and Madagascar.

* * *

SPAKE, Amanda 1947-

PERSONAL: Born July 17, 1947, in Long Beach, Calif.; daughter of Gorman Owen (a salesman) and Marie (Citlau) Spake. Education: University of California, Irvine, B.A., 1970. Home: 1176 A South Van Ness, San Francisco, Calif. 94110. Agent: Elaine Markson, 44 Greenwich, New York, N.Y. 10011. Office: Mother Jones, 607 Market St., San Francisco, Calif. 94105.

CAREER/WRITINGS: College Press Service, Washington, D.C., editor, 1970-71; Chronicle of Higher Education, Washington, D.C., writer, 1971-72; free-lance writer in Washington, D.C., 1972-77; Washington Newsworks, Washington, D.C., editor, 1976-77; Mother Jones, San Francisco, Calif., managing editor, 1977—. Contributor of articles to periodicals, including Washington Post, New Times, and Progressive. Member: Washington Independent Writers.

WORK IN PROGRESS: Abnormal Occurences/Incredible Events; a book on nuclear power.

SIDELIGHTS: Spake wrote: "For me, writing is one of the most important ways to reach people politically. The mass media is one of the best educational tools this country has today. Communicating with people is everything to me and I'm never happy unless I'm writing."

CA asked Spake how the format and stance of Mother Jones has changed since its inception. She responded: "The initial format of Mother Jones was to be a progressive, mass market journal of arts and opinion, aimed at an educated readership—something slightly more literate than New Times and for an older audience than Rolling Stone.

"The magazine has changed in that it is still a progressive mass market journal—however, it has moved heavily into news and investigative articles as well as opinion and personal pieces of a political/social and cultural nature. The audience is fairly affluent, has an average age of 31, older than Rolling Stone and New Times. It has recently moved from entirely subscriber based to newsstand and subscriber circulated. Total circulation is around 180,000 on a nationwide level. And it remains independent, owned by a staff-controlled foundation."

* * *

SPANN, Gloria Carter 1926-

PERSONAL: Born October 22, 1926, in Plains, Ga.; daughter of J. Earl (a farmer and warehouse man) and Lillian (a registered nurse; maiden name, Gordy) Carter; married Walter G. Spann (a farmer), December 15, 1950; children: William. Education: Attended Georgia Southwestern College and Patterson Business School. Home address: P.O. Box 309, Plains, Ga. 31780. Agent: Bill Adler, 1230 Sixth Ave., New York, N.Y. 10020.

CAREER: Accountant, 1950-76; writer, 1976—.

WRITINGS: (With Lillian Carter) Away from Home: Letters to My Family, Simon & Schuster, 1977.

* * *

SPARKIA, Roy (Bernard) 1924-
(Mitchell Caine)

PERSONAL: Born October 31, 1924, in Owosso, Mich.; son of John Henry and Anne (Bessinger) Sparkia; married Renee Nemerov (a graphic artist and sculptress), October 19, 1947; children: Alisa Anne. Education: Attended Art Students League, New York, N.Y., 1941-42, University of Shrivenham, 1945-46, Columbia University, 1947-48, and New York University, 1950-51. Politics: "Nonpartisan." Religion: Agnostic. Home: 2858 Holiday Pines, Traverse City, Mich. 49684. Agent: Lyle Kenyon Engel, Schillings Crossing Rd., Canaan, N.Y. 12029.

CAREER: Writer. Also works as stained glass artist (one series is permanently installed in the Empire State Building), designer, art studio director, engineering draftsman, and technical writer. Editor for McGraw's Technical Writing Service, 1951-52. Military service: U.S. Army, Engineer Combat Group, 1942-45; served in Europe; became staff sergeant. Member: Authors Guild of Authors League of America. Awards, honors: American Institute of Decorators Award, 1960, for design in plastics.

WRITINGS—All novels: Boss Man, Lion Books, 1954; Build My Gallows High, Fawcett, 1956; The Vanishing Vixen, Fawcett, 1959; Doctors and Lovers, Pyramid Publications, 1960; Doctors and Sinners, Pyramid Publications, 1961; Swap, New American Library, 1967; Bitter Fruit, New American Library, 1970; The Love Eaters, McFadden-Bartell, 1971; Operating Room Four, Pyramid Publications, 1973; The Dirty Rotten Truth, New American Library,

1973; *Paradise County,* Dell, 1974; *The Golden People,* Pyramid Publications, 1976; (under pseudonym Mitchell Caine) *Creole Surgeon,* Gold Medal, 1977.

WORK IN PROGRESS: Regimental Surgeon (under pseudonym Mitchell Caine), a sequel to *Creole Surgeon,* with other volumes on medicine in history to follow.

SIDELIGHTS: Sparkia writes: "In 1951 (I think) I was afforded the rare opportunity to be one of Saul Bellow's two students at New York University. Each student met with Mr. Bellow on different days so we each had the full benefit of his undivided attention. My sessions with him were usually spent on a park bench in Washington Square Park, and were exhilarating. I also studied with Paul Gallico at Columbia.

"I think the novel today is in a terrible plight; a really good novelist has never had a worse time for getting published, and the commercial field is competitive beyond belief."

BIOGRAPHICAL/CRITICAL SOURCES: Grand Rapids Press, March 5, 1978.

*   *   *

SPECTOR, Samuel I(ra) 1924-

PERSONAL: Born July 29, 1924, in New York, N.Y.; son of Benjamin and Julia (Cohen) Spector; married Virginia Elliott (a librarian), March 9, 1947; children: Julianne Spector Tullis, Tom. *Education:* American University, LL.B., 1954; Georgia State University, M.B.A., 1967, D.B.A., 1969. *Home:* 117 Glendale Rd., Rome, Ga. 30161. *Office:* Garden Lakes Co., 2400 Garden Lakes Co., Rome, Ga. 30161.

CAREER: Employed by U.S. Government, 1946-55; Garden Lakes Co., Rome, Ga., vice-president, 1955-66; Berry College, Mount Berry, Ga., professor of business, 1968-76, chairman of department, 1974-76; Garden Lakes Co., president, 1975—. Home builder, realtor, and land developer. Mediator for Federal Mediation and Conciliation Service; local director of Goodwill Industries. *Military service:* U.S. Army, Office of Strategic Services, 1943-45; served in Burma. *Member:* National Association of Home Builders of the United States, National Association of Realtors, Georgia Home Builders Association (past member of state board of directors), Rome Home Builders Association (past president).

WRITINGS: Zoning in a Changing Urban Environment, Georgia State University, 1971. Contributor to technical journals.

SIDELIGHTS: Spector told *CA:* "My book reviewed the origin of zoning laws and its current application. Zoning was found to be used as a device for discrimination causing serious distortions in the supply and demand for certain types of land, and a major factor in urban decay. I believe that in spite of the continuing discriminatory use of zoning and its adverse impact on urban property values, most people blindly seek solutions in more restrictive regulations."

*   *   *

SPEIZMAN, Morris 1905-

PERSONAL: Born August 31, 1905, in Lodz, Poland; came to the United States in 1906, naturalized citizen, 1938; son of David (a textile executive) and Elka Speizman; married Sylvia Valenstein, March 4, 1934; children: Lawrence Jay, Robert Stephen. *Education:* Philadelphia Textile School, diploma, 1927. *Politics:* Democrat. *Religion:* Jewish. *Home:* 435 Colville Rd., Charlotte, N.C. 28207. *Office:* Speizman Industries, 508 West Fifth St., Charlotte, N.C. 28231.

CAREER: Speizman Industries (textile mill machinery business), Charlotte, N.C., chairman of board of directors, 1936—. President of Mint Museum of Art, 1973-75. Chairman of board of directors of Mercy Hospital, 1967-77. President of World Council of Synagogues, 1972-74.

WRITINGS: This Week's Miracle, Graham Publishing, 1968; *A Little Sense and a Lot of Hutzpah,* Graham Publishing, 1970; *Our Brave New World,* Graham Publishing, 1975; *The Jews of Charlotte, North Carolina,* McNally & Loftin, 1977. Contributor to textile trade journals.

SIDELIGHTS: Speizman told *CA:* "To my mind, one of the most important inventions of the twentieth century is the electronic dictating machine. It has taken the drudgery out of writing."

*   *   *

SPELMAN, Mary 1934-
(Mary Lockwood, Mary Towne)

PERSONAL: Born March 14, 1934, in Brooklyn, N.Y.; daughter of Edward Towne (an executive with American Telephone & Telegraph Co.) and Ann (a teacher; maiden name, Hamilton) Lockwood; married James B. Spelman (a merchant), January, 1959; children: two daughters, one son. *Education:* Smith College, B.A. (summa cum laude), 1955. *Residence:* West Redding, Conn. *Agent:* Henriette Neatrour, Curtis Brown Ltd., 575 Madison Ave., New York, N.Y. 10022.

CAREER: Scholastic Magazines, Inc., New York, N.Y., editor and copywriter, 1955-57; teacher of English at private school in Seattle, Wash., 1957-58; free-lance writer, 1958—. Instructor at Institute of Children's Literature, 1975—. *Member:* Authors Guild of Authors League of America, National Organization for Women, Common Cause, Phi Beta Kappa.

WRITINGS—Adult novels, under pseudonym Mary Lockwood: *Child of Light,* Morrow, 1963; *The Accessory* (Mystery Guild selection), Random House, 1968.

Children's books, under pseudonym Mary Towne: *The Glass Room,* Farrar, Straus, 1971; *First Serve* (Junior Literary Guild selection), Atheneum, 1976; *Goldenrod* (Junior Literary Guild selection), Atheneum, 1977.

SIDELIGHTS: Mary Spelman writes: "In the field of adult fiction, I have wanted to experiment with a variety of forms and subject matter—with the result that I have three unpublished masterpieces to set against my two published novels! But I go on trying. In writing for the young, I enjoy the challenge of constructing what are really miniature novels—the disciplines of economy and clarity."

BIOGRAPHICAL/CRITICAL SOURCES: Junior Literary Guild, September, 1977.

*   *   *

SPENCER, Terence (John Bew) 1915-1978

May 21, 1915—March, 1978; English educator, editor, and author. Spencer was director of the Shakespeare Institute in Birmingham, England, and an educator at University of Birmingham. He wrote scholarly books, including *Elizabethan Love Stories, Shakespeare: The Roman Plays,* and *Byron and the Greek Tradition.* He edited and contributed to literary works and contributed articles to journals in his field. Spencer died in England. Obituaries and other sources: *Who's Who in the World,* 2nd edition, Marquis, 1973; *Who's Who,* 126th edition, St. Martin's, 1974; *AB Bookman's Weekly,* May 8, 1978.

SPIEGEL, Steven L(ee) 1941-

PERSONAL: Born April 7, 1941, in Los Angeles, Calif.; son of Sol (an accountant) and Claire (Saltzman) Spiegel; married Fredelle Zaiman (an educational publicist), June 13, 1965; children: Mira, Nina, Avishalom. *Education:* University of Southern California, B.A., 1962; Harvard University, M.A., 1966, Ph.D., 1967. *Religion:* Jewish. *Home:* 1137 South Alfred St., Los Angeles, Calif. 90035. *Office:* Department of Political Science, University of California, Los Angeles, Calif. 90024.

CAREER: University of California, Los Angeles, assistant professor, 1966-73, associate professor of political science, 1973—. Fellow of Institute of War and Peace Studies, Columbia University, 1969-70; fellow of Johns Hopkins University School of Advanced International Studies, 1973-75. *Member:* International Studies Association, American Political Science Association, Society for Values in Higher Education, Phi Beta Kappa, Phi Kappa Phi, Pi Sigma Alpha. *Awards, honors:* Guggenheim fellowship, 1973-74.

WRITINGS: (With Louis Cantori) *The International Politics of Regions: A Comparative Approach,* Prentice-Hall, 1970; (editor with Kenneth Waltz) *Conflict in World Politics,* Winthrop Publishing, 1971; *Dominance and Diversity: The International Hierarchy,* Little, Brown, 1972; (editor) *At Issue: Politics in the World Arena,* St. Martin's, 1973, 2nd edition, 1977. Contributor to political science and international studies journals.

WORK IN PROGRESS: The War for Washington: The Other Arab-Israeli Conflict.

SIDELIGHTS: Spiegel writes: "My latest research interest is American policy toward the Arab-Israeli dispute, the manner in which American policy is formulated, the kinds of groups which attempt to influence foreign policy. I am concerned with this question because I believe it to be one of the most fascinating problems of American foreign policy in the present era, and because an examination of those groups which attempt to influence American policy on the subject tells us a great deal about the nature of American society and the way in which we formulate foreign policy generally. I am also concerned with broader problems of American foreign policy, the objectives of the United States in foreign affairs, and policy options with respect to a broad range of specific issues."

*   *   *

SPIELBERG, Steven 1947-

PERSONAL: Born December, 1947, in Cincinnati, Ohio. *Education:* Attended California State College (now University), Long Beach. *Residence:* Beverly Hills, Calif. *Office:* Amblin' Productions, 4000 Warner Blvd., Burbank, Calif. 91522.

CAREER: Universal City Studios, Inc., Universal City, Calif., director of television series episodes, television films, and motion pictures, 1968-75; director of motion pictures, 1975—; writer, 1977—. Director of television series episodes of "Marcus Welby, M.D.," "Owen Marshall," "The Name of the Game," "The Psychiatrist," and "Columbo," of television films including "Night Gallery," "Something Evil," and "Duel," and of motion pictures including "The Sugarland Express," "Jaws," and "Close Encounters of the Third Kind." *Awards, honors:* Won film contest for "Escape to Nowhere"; won prizes at Atlanta Film Festival and Venice Film Festival for "Amblin'"; nomination for best director from Academy of Motion Picture Arts and Sciences, 1977, for "Close Encounters of the Third Kind."

WRITINGS: Close Encounters of the Third Kind, Dell, 1977. Also author and director of the screenplay "Close Encounters of the Third Kind," and author and director of amateur films including "Escape to Nowhere," "Firelight," and "Amblin'."

SIDELIGHTS: "Making movies is an illusion," Spielberg told an interviewer, "a technical illusion that people fall for, and my job is to take that technique and hide it so well that never once are you taken out of your chair and reminded of where you are." The definition of film as illusion is an accurate summation of Spielberg's cinematic accomplishments, one exemplified in a *Time* review which noted his reliance "on both the immediacy of illusion and the safety it provides." And Pauline Kael called him "an entertainer—a magician in the age of movies" who is "probably the most gifted American director who's dedicated to sheer entertainment."

Because of his devotion to illusion and entertainment, Spielberg is often considered a throwback to an earlier era of film, an era of action and excitement. "Spielberg closely resembles those oldtime directors who disregarded the cerebrum and went right for the viscera," wrote Arthur Cooper, adding: "He is a virtuoso of action." Reviewing Spielberg's first film, "The Sugarland Express," Paul Zimmerman cited the director's "breath-taking command of action" and his "vitality and excitement." In a review which mentioned Spielberg's "rather old-fashioned, very American way of making a movie," *Time* deemed "Jaws" "wonderfully crafted, a movie whose every shock is a devastating surprise." Although curiously silent about his penchant for action, Spielberg has revealed the motivation behind his particular style. "We're [Spielberg and peers including Martin Scorsese, Brian De Palma, and George Lucas] interested in well-crafted, intelligent movies that can appeal to millions of people," he said. "We're not interested in making small critical successes that nobody goes to see."

"The Sugarland Express," made by Spielberg when he was only twenty-six, immediately established him as a whiz kid. Critics praised his film as a "satiric but strangely beautiful vision of an America on wheels" that, according to Kael, "has so much eagerness and flash and talent" that "it marks the debut of a new-style, new-generation Hollywood hand." The critical success of Spielberg's tale of a young couple's attempt to kidnap their own child ultimately garnered Spielberg enough exposure to land the directorship of "Jaws."

Cooper reviewed "Jaws" as "a grisly film, often ugly as sin, which achieves precisely what it set out to accomplish—scare the hell out of you. As such, it's destined to become a classic the way all truly terrifying movies, good or bad, become classics of a kind." The story of a small, oceanside community mysteriously plagued by a man-eating shark, "Jaws" became the all-time leading money-maker, establishing Spielberg as Hollywood's latest new wave success. Spielberg's filmmaking was lauded for its "subtly correct camera placement and meticulous editing." "He twists our guts with false alarms," reported *Time,* giving us the real thing with heart-stopping suddenness." Evidently, Spielberg invested much of his own feelings into the film. "I wanted to do 'Jaws' for hostile reasons," he said. "I read it and felt that I had been attacked. It terrified me, and I wanted to strike back."

The success of "Jaws" provided Spielberg with the opportunity to direct his own screenplay about visitors from outer space, "Close Encounters of the Third Kind." Hailed by Kael as "the most innocent of all technological-marvel movies, and one of the most satisfying," "Close Encounters of the Third Kind" revealed Spielberg's fascination with UFO's and those who claim to have seen them. "UFO's for me, represent a cultural phenomenon rather than a fantasy one," he stated. "Whether they're real or not real, they've certainly affected everyone's life." And in another interview, Spielberg said: "Every film I find out a little more about myself. I've discovered I've got this preoccupation with ordinary people pursued by large forces. A personal movie for me is one about people with obsessions."

If Spielberg is obsessed with anything cinematically, it is machines. In reviewing "The Sugarland Express," Zimmerman wrote: "In this world the cars are as eloquent as the characters." Spielberg's television film, "Duel," concerns a man being hunted by a truck in the desert. "Jaws" was praised more for the believeability of the mechanical shark than the characters, as was "Close Encounters of the Third Kind." Spielberg himself commented on this obsession in *Newsweek*. "My father brought home a transistor one day, when I was fifteen," recalled Spielberg. "He said, 'This is the new age.' I put it into my mouth and swallowed it."

Confident of his filmmaking ability, Spielberg once claimed: "I could make 'Jaws' every year if I really wanted to." Now he is interested in expanding the variety of films being released. "There are so many movies I want to make," he said. "I used to sit around wondering why nobody would make a movie about this subject or that one. Now I can make those missing movies myself."

AVOCATIONAL INTERESTS: Audio-visual gimmicks, custard pies, skeet shooting.

BIOGRAPHICAL/CRITICAL SOURCES: New Yorker, March 18, 1974, November 28, 1977; *Newsweek,* April 8, 1974, June 23, 1975, November 21, 1977; *Time,* June 23, 1975; *New York,* November 7, 1977; *New York Times,* November 13, 1977.*

* * *

SPIVAK, Talbot 1937-

PERSONAL: Born April 6, 1937, in Philadelphia, Pa.; son of Louis (a lawyer) and Elane (a painter; maiden name, Kopf) Spivak. *Education:* Trinity College, Hartford, Conn., B.A., 1959; Cornell University, M.A., 1962; University of Iowa, Ph.D., 1976. *Politics:* Democrat. *Home:* 614 West North St., Geneva, N.Y. 14456. *Office:* Department of English and Comparative Literature, Hobart & William Smith Colleges, Geneva, N.Y. 14456.

CAREER: Augustana College, Rock Island, Ill., instructor in French, 1967-74; Hobart & William Smith Colleges, Geneva, N.Y., assistant professor of English and comparative literature, 1976—. *Member:* Modern Language Association of America.

WRITINGS: The Bride Wore the Traditional Gold (novel), Knopf, 1972.

WORK IN PROGRESS: Two novels, "one historical, one personal."

SIDELIGHTS: Spivak told *CA:* "My first novel is both a love story and a farce. The two poles—serious and comic—seem to characterize most of my writing (as, indeed, they characterize much contemporary writing). Most interesting for me is to see how much I am a product of my time both in the subjects I choose to write about and in the way I write."

SRERE, Benson M. 1928-

PERSONAL: Born August 13, 1928, in Rock Island, Ill.; son of Jacob H. (a tire merchant) and Margaret (Weinstein) Srere; married Betty Cerruti, June 20, 1957; children: David, Anne, Peter. *Education:* University of Southern California, B.A., 1949. *Home:* 44 Witherbee Ave., Pelham Manor, N.Y. 10803.

CAREER/WRITINGS: United Press International, New York City, newsman in Los Angeles, Calif., 1948-56; *Good Housekeeping,* New York City, 1956-76, began as associate editor, became executive editor and vice president; King Features Syndicate, New York City, vice president and general manager, 1976—. *Member:* Overseas Press Club, Phi Beta Kappa, Phi Kappa Phi, Sigma Delta Chi, Phi Eta Sigma.

* * *

STAEBLER, Neil 1905-

PERSONAL: Born July 11, 1905, in Ann Arbor, Mich.; son of Edward W. (a merchant) and Magdalena (a community service worker; maiden name, Dold) Staebler; married Burnette Bradley (a theater director), February 8, 1935; children: Elizabeth Staebler Brewer, Michael. *Education:* University of Michigan, A.B., 1926. *Religion:* Unitarian-Universalist. *Home:* 530 N St. S.W., Washington, D.C. 20024. *Office:* 408 Wolverine Bldg., 202 Washington, Ann Arbor, Mich. 48104.

CAREER: Staebler & Son, Ann Arbor, Mich., partner, 1915-47, proprietor, 1947—. Treasurer of Staebler-Kempf Oil Co., 1926-51; president of Michigan Capital & Service, Inc., 1965-70, director, 1975—. Professor at University of Massachusetts, 1962; fellow at Kennedy Institute of Politics, 1975. Chairman of Michigan Democratic State Committee, 1950-61; member of Democratic National Committee, 1961-75; Democratic member of Congress, 1963-64; member of Federal Election Commission, 1975—. Chief of building materials for Office of Price Administration, 1942-43. *Military service:* U.S. Navy, 1943-45; became first lieutenant.

MEMBER: American Economic Association, American Political Science Association, National Association for the Advancement of Colored People, Detroit Economic Club. *Awards, honors:* LL.D. from University of Michigan, 1962.

WRITINGS: (With Douglas Ross) *How to Argue with a Conservative,* Grossman, 1967.

WORK IN PROGRESS: A book on government and politics.

* * *

STALEY, (Alvah) Eugene 1906-

PERSONAL: Born July 3, 1906, in Friend, Neb.; son of Alvah H. (a school superintendent) and Helen T. (Browne) Staley; married Phyllis E. Parker, December 19, 1936; children: Pamela Staley Herr, Thomas E. *Education:* Hastings College, A.B. (magna cum laude), 1925; University of Chicago, Ph.D., 1928, postdoctoral study, 1928-29. *Politics:* Democrat. *Religion:* Unitarian-Universalist. *Home:* 455 Seale Ave., Palo Alto, Calif. 94301.

CAREER: University of Chicago, Chicago, Ill., assistant professor of economics, 1931-37; Fletcher School of Law and Diplomacy, Medford, Mass., 1937-44, began as associate professor, became professor of international economic relations; Johns Hopkins School of Advanced International

Studies, Washington, D.C., professor of international economic relations, 1944-45; Bay Area Institute of Pacific Relations, San Francisco, Calif., director, 1945-46; World Affairs Council of Northern California, San Francisco, founding executive director, 1947-49; Stanford Research Institute, Menlo Park, Calif., senior international economist, 1950-65; Stanford University, Stanford, Calif., professor of education at International Development Education Center, 1965-68; Ford Foundation, India Office, New Delhi, program specialist on occupational education, 1968-73; writer and researcher, 1973—. Assistant professor at Institut de Hautes Etudes Internationales (Geneva, Switzerland), 1934-35; lecturer at Stanford University, 1945-46. Research associate at Hoover Institution and Library on War, Revolution and Peace, 1948-50; senior specialist at East-West Center, 1965, and senior fellow of its Technology and Development Institute, 1975. Economist for U.S. State Department Office of Relief and Rehabilitation Operations, 1943; staff member of United Nations Relief and Rehabilitation Administration, 1944; secretariat member of United Nations Conference on International Organization (Charter Conference), 1945; chief economist of Cuban mission for International Bank for Reconstruction and Development, 1950-51; member of Committee on Education and Human Resource Development of Education and World Affairs, 1964-68; participant in international conferences and symposia; consultant in numerous countries, including Pakistan, Egypt, India, Thailand, and in the South Pacific, and to U.S. government agencies.

MEMBER: Society for International Development, American Association for the Advancement of Science, Council on Foreign Relations. *Awards, honors:* Social Science Research Council fellowship for Europe, 1929-31; Ford Foundation grants, 1958-65.

WRITINGS: History of the Illinois State Federation of Labor, University of Chicago Press, 1930; *War and the Private Investor: A Study of the Interrelations of International Politics and International Private Investment,* Doubleday, 1935; *Raw Materials in Peace and War,* Council on Foreign Relations, 1937; *World Economy in Transition,* Council on Foreign Relations, 1939; *World Economic Development: Effects on Established Industrial Countries,* International Labour Office, 1944; (contributor) Hans W. Weigert and Vilhjalmur Stefansson, editors, *Compass of the World,* Macmillan, 1944; *Raw Materials Problems and Policies,* Department of Economics, League of Nations, 1946.

(Contributor) *Report on Cuba,* International Bank for Reconstruction and Development, 1951; (editor) *Creating an Industrial Civilization,* Harper, 1952; (with Neil Houston) *A Manual of Industrial Development,* Stanford Research Institute, 1954; *The Future of Underdeveloped Countries: Political Implications of Economic Development,* Harper, 1954, revised edition, 1961; *The American Citizen's Stake in the Progress of Less Developed Areas of the World,* U.S. Government Printing Office, 1954, revised edition, 1957; (with Guy Benveniste) *Possible Nonmilitary Scientific Developments and Their Potential Impact on Foreign Policy Problems of the United States,* Stanford Research Institute, 1959; (with Richard Morse) *Modern Small Industry for Developing Countries,* McGraw, 1965.

Planning Occupational Education and Training for Development, Orient Longmans, 1970, Praeger, 1971; *Work-Oriented General Education,* Popular Prakashan, 1973. Contributor of articles and reviews to economic, political science, and scientific journals.

WORK IN PROGRESS: The Expanding "We": Shared Values and Common Problems of Humankind (tentative title), a five-part textbook for high school, junior college, and adult students.

SIDELIGHTS: Staley writes: "My chief motivation in current writing comes from the strong feeling that each of us should do what little he can to nudge the human race toward knowledge and attitudes that are essential to survival, or at least to a reasonably civilized survival, in this unprecedented era of world-wide interdependence. Recognition that many problems are insoluble these days unless there is enough support for constructive action at the world community level is vital. In the 'race between education and catastrophe' (a phrase from H. G. Wells, I believe) I'm on the side of education."

Staley's books have been published in Spanish, French, Italian, and Japanese.

*   *   *

STALEY, Thomas F(abian)   1935-

PERSONAL: Born August 13, 1935, in Pittsburgh, Pa.; son of Fabian Richard and Mary (McNulty) Staley; married Carolyn O'Brien, September 3, 1960; children: Thomas Fabian, Caroline Ann, Mary Elizabeth, Timothy X. *Education:* Regis College, A.B. and B.S., both 1957; University of Tulsa, M.A., 1958; University of Pittsburgh, Ph.D., 1962. *Home:* 3018 South Trenton, Tulsa, Okla. 74120. *Office:* Department of English, University of Tulsa, Tulsa, Okla. 74104.

CAREER: Rollins College, Winter Park, Fla., assistant professor of English, 1961-62; University of Tulsa, Tulsa, Okla., assistant professor, 1962-67, associate professor, 1967-69, professor of English, 1969—, Trustees' Professor of Modern Literature, 1977—, dean of Graduate School, 1969-77, acting vice-president for academic affairs, 1977. Fulbright professor in Italy, 1966-67, spring, 1971; visiting professor at University of Pittsburgh, 1967, 1970, and State University of New York at Buffalo, summer, 1974. Chairman of International James Joyce Symposium, 1971, 1973, co-chairman, 1967, 1969, 1977; president of James Joyce Foundation, 1969-73 (member of board of directors, 1967—). Chairman of board of directors of Undercroft Montessori School, 1969-70, and Marquette School, 1969-70; member of board of directors of Cascia Hall Preparatory School; director of Graduate Institute of Modern Letters, 1970—. Member of advisory board of Tulsa Arts and Humanities Council, 1970—; member of Tulsa City-County Library Commission, 1974.

MEMBER: American Association of University Professors, Modern Language Association of America, Anglo-Irish Studies Association, American Committee for Irish Studies, James Joyce Society, South Central Modern Language Association (section chairman, 1965-66, 1968-69, 1970-71, 1975-76), Midwest Association of Graduate Schools, Tulsa Tennis Club, Friends of the Tulsa County Library (member of board of directors, 1971—). *Awards, honors:* Danforth associate, 1962-66, senior associate, 1967—; American Council of Learned Societies grant, 1969.

WRITINGS: (Editor) *James Joyce Today: Essays on the Major Works,* Indiana University Press, 1966; (contributor) Lester Zimmerman, editor, *Jonathan Swift: Tercentenary Essays* (monograph), University of Tulsa, 1967; (editor with H. J. Mooney, Jr., and contributor) *The Shapeless God: Essays on the Modern Novel,* University of Pittsburgh Press, 1968; *James Joyce's Portrait of the Artist,* Littlefield,

Adams, 1968; (editor with Zimmerman) *Literature and Theology* (monograph), University of Tulsa, 1969; (editor with James R. Baker) *Dubliners: A Critical Handbook,* Wadsworth, 1969; (editor) *Italo Svevo: Essays on His Work* (monograph), University of Tulsa, 1969; (contributor) W. T. Zyla, editor, *James Joyce: His Place in World Literature,* Texas Tech Press, 1969.

(Editor with Bernard Benstock, and contributor) *Approaches to Ulysses: Ten Essays,* University of Pittsburgh Press, 1970; (editor) *Ulysses: Fifty Years,* University of Indiana Press, 1974; (contributor) Richard Finnerman, editor, *Anglo-Irish Literature: A Review of the Research,* Modern Language Association of America, 1976; *Dorothy Richardson,* Twayne, 1976; (with Benstock) *Approaches to Joyce's Portrait: Ten Essays,* University of Pittsburgh Press, 1976. Executive director of monograph series at University of Tulsa. Contributor to *Twentieth Century Literature Encyclopedia* and *New Catholic Encyclopedia.* Contributor of about forty articles to literature journals and literary magazines, including *Italica, American Book Collector, Commonweal,* and *Nimrod.* Editor of *James Joyce Quarterly;* associate editor of *South Central Modern Language Association Bulletin,* 1973-75; guest editor of *Modern Fiction Studies,* spring, 1972; member of board of editors of *Twentieth Century Literature;* advisory editor of *Virginia Woolf Quarterly.*

WORK IN PROGRESS: James Joyce: The Trieste Years; books on Jean Rhys and Margaret Drabble; a critical study of Italo Svevo; the introduction for the Dutch translation of *Flush,* by Virginia Woolf.

SIDELIGHTS: Staley writes: ''Although my primary critical interest is in James Joyce, I have tried to spell this compelling activity with work on other writers. I am presently completing a critical study of Jean Rhys which will be published by Macmillan.''

* * *

STALLONE, Sylvester (Enzio) 1946-
(Q. Moonblood)

PERSONAL: Born July 6, 1946, in New York, N.Y.; son of Frank (a hairdresser) and Jacqueline (Labofish) Stallone; married Sasha Czack, 1974; children: Sage Moonblood. *Education:* Attended University of Miami, 1967-69. *Residence:* Coldwater Canyon, Calif. *Office:* c/o G. P. Putnam & Sons, 200 Madison Ave., New York, N.Y. 10016.

CAREER: Motion picture actor and director, screenwriter, and author. Actor in motion pictures, including ''Bananas,'' 1971, ''Lords of Flatbush,'' 1974, '' Death Race 2000,'' 1975, ''Prisoner of Second Avenue,'' 1975, ''Rocky,'' 1976, and ''F.I.S.T.,'' 1978. *Awards, honors:* Received People's Choice Award for best actor and nominations from Academy of Motion Picture Arts and Sciences for best actor and best screenplay, all 1976, all for ''Rocky.''

WRITINGS: Paradise Alley, Putnam, 1977.

Screenplays: (Author of additional dialogue) ''Lords of Flatbush,'' 1974; ''Rocky,'' United Artists, 1976; (with Joe Eszterhas) ''F.I.S.T.,'' United Artists, 1978; (and director) ''Paradise Alley'' (adapted from the novel), Universal, 1978.

Also author of scripts for the television series ''A Touch of Evil,'' under the pseudonym Q. Moonblood, including ''The Monster of Manchester,'' ''Heart to Heart,'' and ''The Ballad of Butcher Bloom.'' Other scripts include ''Cry Full, Whisper Empty—in the Same Breath,'' an alternate ''Rocky'' and a ''Rocky'' sequel, and ''Bodyguard.''

SIDELIGHTS: ''I just did your chart and you are not going to get into show business for seven and one-half years,'' Stallone's mother told him eight years ago. ''And when you do, you will make it as a writer.''

''That was absurd,'' recalled Stallone in reference to his mother's prophecy. ''I was a total failure in English. I had gotten seven Fs in English through high school.''

''I couldn't even write a bad check,'' he continued. ''I couldn't even write graffiti.'' But Stallone did turn to writing as a means of support, and his career was launched when he wrote the screenplay for the Oscar-winning film of 1976, ''Rocky.'' The tale of a nobody boxer given a chance at the heavyweight title, ''Rocky'' proved Stallone's worth as an actor as well as a screenwriter, but not without some opposition first.

''If I had been a screenwriter the size of Buck Henry then things would have been different,'' Stallone told an interviewer. ''But I had the size to be a heavyweight like Rocky. Now the point was, was I marketable?'' Evidently, the studio didn't think so and they offered Stallone huge sums of money to let someone else play the part. ''They were offering me $265,000 and five percent of the gross,'' he said. ''But I was more desperate than hungry.''

Stallone finally won out and got the part. His performance earned him an Oscar nomination and critics praised his ''pre-Brando'' and ''unaffected and unsubtle'' style. ''I am at the beginning of a new cycle of actors,'' Stallone told *Newsweek,* adding that ''we are going to see the communicative actor, the actor who will be a hero, the actor who will inspire confidence and imitativeness to his viewers. Positiveness!'' Stallone told *CA* that ''Richard Dreyfuss's win [Academy Award, 1977] is an affirmation of this.''

The parallel between Stallone's career and his writings is obvious. Like the boxer in ''Rocky,'' the labor leader in ''F.I.S.T.,'' and the hustler in ''Paradise Alley,'' Stallone started nowhere but saw his chance and made the most of it. ''I got my shot and Rocky gets his,'' remarked Stallone, ''that's the parallel.'' But he also noted: ''I'd never let myself get into the situation that Rocky does, and not have anything to fall back on. Though I came close. But if this hadn't panned out, I would have gone back to writing.''

Stallone dismisses those critics who dislike his ''make the most of yourself'' attitude as easily as he does those who excessively praise his work. ''I think I'm clever,'' he said. ''As for splitting an atom, no. Maybe a coconut.''

BIOGRAPHICAL/CRITICAL SOURCES: Time, November 15, 1976, December 13, 1976; *Newsweek,* November 29, 1976, April 11, 1977, June 27, 1977; *Mademoiselle,* January, 1977; *Writer's Digest,* July, 1977.

* * *

STANDARD, William L. 1900(?)-1978

1900(?)—May 6, 1978; lawyer and author. In his legal work, Standard specialized in the welfare of merchant seamen. He was the author of a book and numerous articles on international and admiralty law. The founder and first chairman of the Lawyers Committee on American Policy Toward Vietnam, Standard also wrote *Aggression: Our Asian Disaster.* He died in Manhattan, N.Y. Obituaries and other sources: *New York Times,* May 7, 1978.

* * *

STANDIFORD, Lester A(lan) 1945-

PERSONAL: Born October 30, 1945, in Cambridge, Ohio;

son of R. Allan and Lucille F. (Patterson) Standiford; married Margaret Ann Spence (a public school teacher), June 13, 1970. *Education:* Muskingum College, B.A., 1967; Columbia University, graduate study, 1967; University of Utah, M.A., 1970, Ph.D. (honors), 1973. *Home:* 778 Camino Real, El Paso, Tex. 79922. *Agent:* John Sterling, Paul R. Reynolds, Inc., 12 East 41st St., New York, N.Y. 10017. *Office:* Department of English, University of Texas, El Paso, Tex. 79968.

CAREER: Ameritel Enterprises, Inc., Columbus, Ohio, administrator of nursing home, 1970, restaurant manager, 1972; University of Texas, El Paso, assistant professor of English, 1973—. Visiting professor at Baylor University, summer, 1974. Has given readings in Texas, New Mexico, and Utah. *Military service:* U.S. Air Force Reserve, 1963-69. *Member:* Rocky Mountain Modern Language Association. *Awards, honors:* Short story award from Utah Fine Arts Institute, 1971, for "Closing the Sarasota Road."

WRITINGS: (Contributor) W. T. Zyla, editor, *Ethnic Literatures Since 1776: The Many Voices of America*, Texas Tech University Press, 1978; *Armadillo Country Safari* (poems), Endeavors in Humanity Press, 1977.

Work anthologized in about eight collections, including *Death Was Our Escort*, edited by Hugo Eckback, Moorpark Press, 1974; *New and Experimental Literature*, edited by James P. White, Texas Center for Writers Press, 1976; *The Southwest: A Contemporary Anthology*, edited by Karl Yopp, Yarbrough Mountain Press, 1977. Contributor of articles, stories, and poems to literary journals, including *Occident, Kansas Quarterly, Beloit Poetry Journal*, and *Quetzal*, and newspapers.

WORK IN PROGRESS: Guerin's Nine Lives: A Segmented Novel; The Summer We Lost Yellowstone.

SIDELIGHTS: Standiford told *CA:* "When I begin a novel, I always ask myself, 'What shouldn't a writer do?' and then I try to choose one of those major DON'TS to incorporate into the work at hand. Guerin is an eighty-year-old schnorrer, a man about to die, a man with a number of disgusting habits. I have tried to make him an engaging protagonist despite all that. Still, with the next book, I may try to do all the RIGHT things and see if the movies like it. So much for philosophy."

                              *   *   *

STANLEY, Timothy Wadsworth 1927-

PERSONAL: Born September 28, 1927, in New Britain, Conn.; son of Maurice and Margaret Stowell (Sammond) Stanley; married Nadia Leon, June 7, 1952; children: Timothy Wadsworth III, Alessandra Maria, Christopher Maurice, Flavia Margaret. *Education:* Yale University, A.B., 1950; Harvard University, LL.B., 1955, Ph.D., 1957. *Religion:* Congregationalist. *Residence:* Washington, D.C. *Office:* International Economic Policy Association, 1625 Eye St. N.W., Washington, D.C. 20006.

CAREER: Office of the Secretary of Defense, Washington, D.C., staff member, 1955-56; White House, Washington, D.C., member of staff, 1957-59; Department of Defense, Washington, D.C., special assistant in international security affairs to assistant secretary of defense, 1959-63, division director of policy planning staff, 1963-65, assistant to Secretary of Defense for North Atlantic Treaty Organization force planning in Paris, France, 1965-67, defense adviser and minister to North Atlantic Treaty Organization in Brussels, Belgium, 1967-69; Johns Hopkins University, School of

Advanced International Studies, Washington, D.C., visiting professor of international relations and research associate at Washington Center of Foreign Policy Research, 1969-70; International Economic Policy Association, Washington, D.C., executive vice-president, 1970-74, president, 1974—, president of International Economic Studies Institute, 1974—. Admitted to Connecticut bar, 1956, and Bar of U.S. Supreme Court. Adjunct professor at George Washington University, 1958-61; visiting research fellow at Council on Foreign Relations, 1962-63. Member of board of directors of Atlantic Council of the United States; member of State Department advisory committee on transnational enterprises; former member of European Advisory Council; consultant to Arms Control & Disarmament Agency. *Military service:* U.S. Army, 1946-48, 1951-52; became first lieutenant.

MEMBER: International Institute for Strategic Studies, Council on Foreign Relations, Metropolitan Club, Federal City Club, Yale Club. *Awards, honors:* Distinguished civilian service medal from Department of Defense, 1969, for U.S. mission to North Atlantic Treaty Organization.

WRITINGS: American Defense and National Security, Public Affairs Press, 1955; *NATO in Transition*, Praeger, 1965; (with D. M. Whitt) *Detente Diplomacy*, University Press of Cambridge, 1970; (with John Newhouse and others) *U.S. Troops in Europe*, Brookings Institution, 1971; *The U.S. Balance of Payments: From Crisis to Controversy*, International Economic Policy Association, 1972; (co-author) *Raw Materials and Foreign Policy*, International Economic Studies Institute, 1976. Also author of *NATO in the Seventies*, 1970. Contributor to professional journals.

                              *   *   *

STARKIE, Walter F(itzwilliam) 1894-1976

PERSONAL: Born August 9, 1894, in Killiney, Dublin, Ireland; son of W.J.M. (a scholar and high government official) and May C. (a scholar; maiden name, Walsh) Starkie; married Italia Augusta Porchietti, August 10, 1921; children: Alma Starkie Herrero, Landi William. *Education:* Trinity College (Dublin), B.A., 1917, M.A., 1920, Ph.D., 1924; also studied at Royal Irish Academy of Music. *Politics:* Conservative. *Religion:* Catholic. *Residence:* Madrid, Spain.

CAREER: Trinity College, Dublin, Ireland, lecturer in Romance languages, 1920; University of London, King's College, London, England, lecturer in modern Spanish drama, 1923; Trinity College and Dublin University, Dublin, professor of Spanish and lecturer in Italian literature, 1926-47; British Institute, Madrid, Spain, director, 1940-54; University of Madrid, Madrid, special lecturer in English literature, 1948-56; gave lectures throughout United States, 1956-57; University of Texas, Austin, visiting professor of Romance languages, 1958; New York University, New York, N.Y., visiting professor, 1959; University of Kansas, Lawrence, visiting professor, 1960; University of Colorado, Boulder, visiting professor, 1960; Menninger Foundation of Psychiatric Research, Topeka, Kan., Sloan Professor, 1961; University of California, Los Angeles, professor-in-residence, 1961-70. Lecturer throughout Europe; director of Irish National (Abbey) Theatre, 1927-42; visiting professor of Romance languages at University of Chicago, 1930; Lord Northcliffe Lecturer in Literature at University of London, 1936; gave lectures in Central and South America, 1950. Representative of the British Council in Spain, 1940-52. *Wartime service:* Served with Young Men's Christian Association attached to British Expeditionary Forces in Italy during World War I.

MEMBER: Royal Society of Arts (fellow), Royal Society of Literature (fellow), Royal Irish Academy, Irish Academy of Letters, Spanish Academy (corresponding member), Academy of History. *Awards, honors:* Litt. D. from Trinity College (Hartford, Conn.), 1930; Commander of the Order of the British Empire, 1948; Companion of the Order of St. Michael and St. George, 1954; Knight of the Order of Alfonso XII; Knight of the Order of the Crown of Italy; Chevalier de la Legion d'Honneur; Commander of the Order of Isabel the Catholic; lifetime honorary fellow of Trinity College, Dublin.

WRITINGS: Jacinto Benavente, Oxford University Press, 1924; *Luigi Pirandello,* Dutton, 1926, 3rd revised and enlarged edition, 1965; *Raggle-Taggle: Adventures with a Fiddle in Hungary and Roumania,* Dutton, 1933, new edition, J. Murray, 1964; *Spanish Raggle-Taggle: Adventures with a Fiddle in North Spain,* J. Murphy, 1934, Dutton, 1935, reprinted, Chivers, 1973; *Don Gypsy: Adventures With a Fiddle in Barbary, Andalusia, and La Mancha,* J. Murray, 1936, Dutton, 1937; *The Waveless Plain: An Italian Autobiography,* Dutton, 1938; *Grand Inquisitor,* Hodder & Stoughton, 1940.

(Translator and author of preface) Ramon Menendez Pidal, *The Spaniards in Their History,* Norton, 1950; *In Sara's Tents,* Dutton, 1953; (editor and translator) Miguel de Cervantes Saavedra, *Don Quixote of La Mancha: An Abridged Version,* St. Martin's Press, 1954; *The Road to Santiago: Pilgrims of St. James,* Dutton, 1957; *Spain: A Musician's Journey Through Time and Space,* three volumes, E.D.I.S.L.I. (Geneva), 1958; (translator) Lope Felix de Vega Carpio, *Peribanez and the Commendador of Ocana,* University of Colorado Libraries, 1962; *Scholars and Gypsies: An Autobiography,* University of California Press, 1963; (editor and translator) Miguel de Cervantes Saavedra, *Don Quixote of La Mancha* (complete version), New American Library, 1964; (editor and translator) *Eight Spanish Plays of the Golden Age,* Modern Library, 1964; (with A. Norman Jeffares) *Homage to Yeats, 1865-1965,* University of California, 1966.

Also author of *Il Teatro contemporaneo inglese,* 1926, *Writers, Modern Spain,* 1929, *The Dukes of Alba,* 1959, and *The House of Alba,* 1973. Also translator of *Tiger Juan* by Ramon Perez de Ayala, 1933. Contributor to *Enciclopedia Italiana, Encyclopaedia Britannica, Americana, Chambers's,* and *Grove's Dictionary of Music,* and of articles to *Saturday Review, Fortnightly,* and *Contemporary Review.*

OBITUARIES: New York Times, November 9, 1976; *Current Biography,* February, 1977.*

(Died November 2, 1976, in Madrid, Spain)

* * *

STARR, Jerold M. 1941-

PERSONAL: Born May 12, 1941, in Detroit, Mich.; son of Nathan (in advertising) and Roberta (part-owner and manager of a trailer park; maiden name, Martin) Starr; married Judith Eisele (in social work), August 22, 1964; children: Jason, Zachary. *Education:* Wayne State University, Ph.B., 1964; Brandeis University, Ph.D., 1970. *Home:* 113 Jackson Ave., Morgantown, W.Va. 26505. *Office:* Department of Sociology, West Virginia University, Morgantown, W.Va. 26506.

CAREER: University of Pennsylvania, Philadelphia, assistant professor of sociology, 1969-76; West Virginia University, Morgantown, associate professor of sociology, 1976—.

Consultant to community legal services. *Member:* American Sociological Association, Gerontological Society, American Civil Liberties Union.

WRITINGS: (With C. V. Thrall) *Technology, Power, and Social Change,* Lexington Books, 1972; *Social Structure and Social Personality,* Little, Brown, 1974; (with R. S. Laufer) *Youth and the Struggle for History,* Longman, 1978. Contributor to sociology and education journals.

WORK IN PROGRESS: Public Opinion in Mass Society.

SIDELIGHTS: Starr comments: "I am interested in the dynamic relationship between social structure and life course organization through history, with particular focus on the stage of youth and the relation of youth movements and social change."

AVOCATIONAL INTERESTS: Good wine, art, music, theater, travel (especially Asia and Europe).

* * *

STARR, John Bryan 1939-

PERSONAL: Born June 15, 1939, in Berkeley, Calif.; son of Leonidas Arthur and Bernice Luise (Bryan) Starr; married Marilyn Elaine Ballou (a teacher), February 18, 1962; children: Lynne Ballou, Katherine Anne. *Education:* Dartmouth College, B.A., 1961; University of California, Berkeley, M.A., 1966, Ph.D., 1971. *Home:* 2 Roslyn Court, Oakland, Calif. 94618. *Office:* Department of Political Science, University of California, Berkeley, Calif. 94720.

CAREER: University of California, Berkeley, assistant professor of political science, 1969—. *Military service:* U.S. Navy, 1961-65; became lieutenant. *Member:* American Political Science Association, Association for Asian Studies. *Awards, honors:* Postdoctoral fellowship from Social Science Research Council and American Council of Learned Societies, 1970-71.

WRITINGS: Ideology and Culture: An Introduction to the Dialectic of Contemporary Chinese Politics, Harper, 1973; *Continuing the Revolution: Studies in the Political Thought of Mao,* Princeton University Press, 1978. Editor of monograph series for Center for Chinese Studies at University of California, Berkeley. Contributor to Asian studies journals. Member of editorial board of *Asian Survey* and *Modern China.*

WORK IN PROGRESS: Research on local political history of Changsha (capital of Hunan Province), from 1800 to the present.

SIDELIGHTS: Starr told *CA:* "My interest in Chinese politics arose somewhat indirectly. Growing up in California I became acquainted with Japanese culture and developed an interest in pursuing the study of Japan. At the time I was a student there Dartmouth College offered no coursework on Japan or in the Japanese language. I pursued instead a research project which took me to Southeast Asia during my senior year. It was during this trip that my interest in China arose and grew. My first book attempts to provide the beginning student, in a college or university course on Chinese politics, information concerning (and a set of perspectives for viewing and understanding) the Chinese political system since 1949. My more recent book, *Continuing the Revolution,* is a thematic study of the political thought of Mao as it evolved during the course of his career as a revolutionary leader, particularly during the last two decades of his life."

START, Clarissa
  See LIPPERT, Clarissa Start

* * *

STAUDERMAN, Albert P(hilip)   1910-
  (Alan Phillips)

PERSONAL: Born October 5, 1910, in Mount Vernon, N.Y.; son of Edward (a clergyman) and Elizabeth (Wagner) Stauderman; married Martha L. Williamson (an artist), August 5, 1934; children: Albert Philip, Jr., Susan Lisbeth Stauderman Neubauer. Education: Wagner College, B.A., 1931; Hartwick Lutheran Seminary, B.D., 1935; further graduate study at Columbia University, 1935-37. Politics: Independent. Home: 999 Welsh Rd., Huntingdon Valley, Pa. 19006. Office: 2900 Queen Lane, Philadelphia, Pa. 19129.

CAREER: New York Times, New York, N.Y., reporter, sports writer, and copy editor, 1930-35; ordained Lutheran minister; pastor of Lutheran church in Teaneck, N.J., 1935-51; Lutheran, Philadelphia, Pa., associate editor, 1951-69, executive editor, 1969-70, editor, 1971—. Managing editor of Muhlenberg Press, 1951-62. Member of Teaneck Assistance Board, 1941-51; president of New Jersey Conference of the Lutheran Church of America, 1945-48, 1950-51.

MEMBER: Associated Church Press, National Lutheran Editors, Germantown Cricket Club. Awards, honors: D.D. from Wagner College, 1952; distinguished service award from Lutheran Brotherhood, 1963; Litt.D. from Susquehanna University, 1972; editorial award from Freedoms Foundation, 1973.

WRITINGS: Understanding My Congregation, Muhlenberg Press, 1948; My Congregation at Work, Muhlenberg Press, 1952; Earth Has No Sorrow, Fortress, 1955, revised edition, 1975; Our New Church, Muhlenberg Press, 1960; Facts About Lutherans, Fortress, 1972. Also author of novels under pseudonym Alan Phillips. Contributor to encyclopedias. Contributor of several hundred articles to magazines and newspapers.

WORK IN PROGRESS: A Reader's Guide to the Bible.

SIDELIGHTS: Stauderman has attended church conferences in Sweden, Finland, Kenya, India, France, and the Netherlands.

* * *

STEDMAN, James Murphy   1938-

PERSONAL: Born July 6, 1938, in Lockhart, Tex.; son of James W. (a dentist) and Mary Ann (Murphy) Stedman; married Susan Cathrine Bradley, August 11, 1961; children: James B., Mary Lynn, Matthew J., Anne K. Education: Rockhurst College, A.B., 1961; St. Louis University, M.A., 1962, Ph.D., 1966; also studied at Temple University. Politics: "Moderate." Religion: Roman Catholic. Office: Department of Psychiatry, University of Texas Health Science Center at San Antonio, 7709 Floyd Curl Dr., San Antonio, Tex. 78229.

CAREER: University of Texas Health Science Center at San Antonio, assistant professor, 1969-74, associate professor of psychiatry, 1968—. Diplomate of American Board of Professional Psychology. Chairman of workshops and institutes. Member: American Psychological Association.

WRITINGS: (Editor with William F. Patton and Kay Walton, and contributor) Clinical Studies in Behavior Therapy with Children, Adolescents, and Their Families, C. C

Thomas, 1973; (contributor) John D. Krumboltz and C. E. Thoresen, editors, Counseling Methods, Holt, 1976. Contributor to psychology and psychiatry journals.

WORK IN PROGRESS: Semi-Depressed: A Native Son Psychologist Looks at Southwest Conference Football; or, How to Cope When We Blow the Cotton Bowl.

SIDELIGHTS: Stedman writes: "My study of philosophy, even though restricted to the undergraduate level for the most part, influenced and still influences my 'worldview.' Whatever scholar there is in me has its roots there, rather than primarily in psychology.

"I am also crucially interested in revitalizing marriage as an institution, and work with my wife in the Marriage Encounter Movement. We consider this to be the most important work in which we are involved."

* * *

STEEGER, Henry   1929(?)-1978

1929(?)—July 3, 1978; American businessman, film maker, and editor. Steeger was vice-president and associate publisher of Popular Publications before entering the sporting goods business and making adventure films. He was also editor of Media Industry Newsletter and Argosy, and contributed regularly to Financial World. He died in New York, N.Y. Obituaries and other sources: New York Times, July 6, 1978.

* * *

STEFANSSON, Thorsteinn   1912-

PERSONAL: Born December 1, 1912, in Lodmundarfiord, Iceland; son of Stefan (a farmer) and Herborg (Bjoernsdottir) Thorsteinsson. Politics: "Individualism and social justice." Religion: "Faith in After-Life." Home: Langdraget 13 DK-2720, Vanlose, Denmark.

CAREER: Writer. Worked as cowman, fisherman, dockworker, hodman, debt collector, language teacher, and translator. Member: Dansk Forfatterforening. Awards, honors: Hans Christian Andersen Medal from Danish literary committee of judges, 1958, for The Golden Future.

WRITINGS—In English: Den gyldne Fremtid (novel), Nyt Nordisk Forlag, 1958, translation by the author published as The Golden Future, Oxford University Press, 1974.

Other; all novels, except as indicated: Fra oedrum hnetti (title means "From Another Planet"), [Reykjavik], 1935; Dalen (title means "The Valley"), Nyt Nordisk Forlag, 1942; Als het hart in woorden zingt (title means "When the Heart Sings"), Zuid-Hollandsche, 1950; (contributor) Datskaya Novella XIX-XX, Leningrad, 1967; Wo sich die Wege Kreuzen (title means "At Crossroads"), Herder Verlag, 1976; Dybgroenne tun (title means "Deep Green Tuns"), Birgitte Hoevrings Biblioteksforlag, 1976; Soelvglitrende hav (title means "Silvery Ocean"), Birgitte Hoevrings Biblioteksforlag, 1976; Paa lovens grund (short stories; title means "With the Sanction of the Law"), Birgitte Hoevrings Biblioteksforlag, 1977; Forlevelsesringen (title means "The Engagement Ring"), Birgitte Hoevrings Biblioteksforlag, 1977; (translator) Olafur Johann Sigurdsson, The Nest, Gyldendal, 1978. Also author of radio drama, "Lagsystir manns" (title means "Comradeship With a Man"), 1975. Contributor of short stories to literary periodicals, including Norseman, American-Scandinavian Review, Vaerldens, Beraettare, Ord och Bild, and Eimreidin.

WORK IN PROGRESS: Translating The Wedding Gown by Kristmann Gudmundsson.

SIDELIGHTS: Stefansson told *CA:* "All fiction must represent the greatest drama: Life itself." *Avocational interests:* Outdoor life, swimming, psychic research, protecting animals and environments.

* * *

STEIG, William 1907-

PERSONAL: Born November 14, 1907, in New York, N.Y.; son of Joseph (a painter) and Laura (a painter; maiden name, Ebel) Steig; married Elizabeth Mead, January 2, 1936 (divorced); married Kari Homestead, 1950 (divorced, 1963); married Stephanie Healey, December 12, 1964 (divorced, December, 1966); married Jeanne Doron, 1969; children: (first marriage) Lucy, Jeremy; (second marriage) Margit Laura. *Education:* Attended City College (now of the City University of New York), 1923-25, and National School of Design, 1925-29. *Address:* R.F.D. #1, Box KH2, Kent, Conn. 06757.

CAREER: Cartoonist for *New Yorker,* 1930—; author of children's books, and illustrator, 1968—. Former cartoonist for *Life, Judge, Vanity Fair,* and *Collier's.* Has exhibited wood sculptures. *Awards, honors:* Caldecott Medal, 1970, for *Sylvester and the Magic Pebble; Amos & Boris* was listed among the *New York Times* choice of best illustrated children's books of the year, 1971; Christopher Award (children's book category), 1972, for *Dominic;* runner-up for National Book Award (children's book category), 1972, for *Amos & Boris; Amos & Boris, Abel's Island,* and *The Amazing Bone* were listed among the children's book showcase selections in 1972, 1977, and 1977, respectively; William Allen White Children's Book Award, 1975, for *Dominic;* runner-up for the Newbery Medal, 1977, for *Abel's Island;* runner-up for Caldecott Medal, 1977, for *The Amazing Bone.*

WRITINGS—Cartoons; all self-illustrated: *Man About Town,* R. Long & R. Smith, 1932; *About People: A Book of Symbolical Drawings,* Random House, 1939; *The Lonely Ones,* Duell, Sloan, 1942, reprinted, Windmill Books, 1970; *Small Fry,* Duell, Sloan, 1944; *All Embarrassed,* Duell, Sloan, 1944; *Persistent Faces,* Duell, Sloan, 1945; *Till Death Do Us Part,* Duell, Sloan, 1947; *The Agony in the Kindergarten,* Duell, Sloan, 1950; *The Rejected Lovers,* Knopf, 1951, reprinted, Dover, 1973; *The Steig Album: Seven Complete Books,* Duell, Sloan, 1953; *Dreams of Glory, and Other Drawings,* Knopf, 1953; *Male/Female,* Farrar, Straus, 1971.

For young people; all fiction, except as noted: *C D B!* (word games), Windmill Books, 1968; *Roland, the Minstrel Pig,* Windmill Books, 1968; *Sylvester and the Magic Pebble,* Windmill Books, 1969; *The Bad Island,* Windmill Books, 1969; *An Eye for Elephants* (limericks), Windmill Books, 1970; *The Bad Speller* (anecdotes), Windmill Books, 1970; *Amos & Boris,* Farrar, Straus, 1971; *Dominic,* Farrar, Straus, 1972; *The Real Thief,* Farrar, Straus, 1973; *Farmer Palmer's Wagon Ride,* Farrar, Straus, 1974; *The Amazing Bone,* Farrar, Straus, 1976; *Abel's Island,* Farrar, Straus, 1976; *Caleb & Kate,* Farrar, Straus, 1977.

Illustrator: Wilhelm Reich, *Listen, Little Man!,* translation by Theodore P. Wolfe, Orgone Institute Press, 1948, reprinted, Octagon Books, 1971.

SIDELIGHTS: "Humor is of many kinds," William Steig once commented. "Mine takes life seriously." Steig, the penetratingly observant caricaturist of the neurotic in us all, has, through his drawings, made us laugh at our faults and shortcomings. He insists that he does not draw people, but rather, character traits which are illustrative of the psychopathology of everyday strife. He is not concerned with current events and problems, but with eternal problems. His drawings become the medium through which he criticizes people for caring too much about what they are.

In the preface to *Lonely Ones,* Wolcott Gibbs explained that Steig had sketched "impressions of people . . . set off from the rest of the world by certain private obsessions." A *Books* reviewer concurred and noted: "They are certainly 'fantastic but recognizable,' as anyone will agree who glances up from them to look round at the occupants of a subway car or of the office where he works. That is why they are so cruel and so frightening and so funny." A *New Republic* critic wrote: "Mr. Steig's vision of mankind is awesome and awful; certainly to one reviewer this latest work of a humorist is anything but funny. But it isn't singular, except in degree. You need only have ridden with your eyes open in a New York subway during rush hour to recognize many of Mr. Steig's obsessed types."

All Embarrassed is a collection of drawings depicting bewildered adults in embarrassing situations. A *Weekly Book Review* critic commented: "As in all the best comic or satiric art, these Steig pictures have a caustic, sobering, and philosophic quality: they call upon introspection and self-judgment. And while they make us laugh or shudder, or see in some hippopotamus-like face or lax torso the fearful likeness of a neighbor, they also do a pretty thorough job of slapping the stuffing out of our own unreasonable cocky little selves. The method has changed slightly, but Steig is still a master-hand at x-raying human beings." *Book Week* noted: "With admirable economy of means and the assistance of only an occasional laconic caption he manages to imbue his stylized drawings with devastating meaning." *Commonweal* found the collection "a bit savage, but piercing in its misanthropy and insight into our vagaries."

One hundred drawings of children doing a variety of things, in addition to just being kids, are collected in *Small Fry.* A *New York Times* critic observed: "What they prove to the parents and elders is that eight-year-olds do not change from one generation to another, that the world of childhood is compounded of miniature terrors and glorious day-dreams, and that Mr. Steig—not to put too fine a point upon it—is wonderful. He is wonderful because, by what must be a combination of recollection and acute observation, he is at once funny and honest and sympathetic."

In 1968 Steig began to write and illustrate children's books which have won him much critical acclaim and numerous awards. Steig commented on his new career: "I came into this second profession in the seventh decade of my life, not knowing what to expect. Cartooning, my other profession, is extremely peaceful. One submits his drawings to magazines and gets back either a check or the drawings. There are no meetings, no celebrations of anything, no medals, and almost no mail. One hardly knows for whom he is working. About three admirers write each year, and occasionally one meets one in person and is praised for something he didn't do. One has lots of time to meditate and wait for Enlightenment.

"Writing for children is a different kettle of fish. Not only does one write and illustrate, but one is asked to go places and authenticate what he has written by autographing it, one is invited to attend seminars and discuss how to do what you do, one gets lots of mail (in responding to which he is saved from idleness), and so forth. Not all of it is as much fun as the writing and the drawing. But winning is definitely fun. I never understood what was missing from my life until this began to happen. It feels darn good, like being dubbed into knighthood. I've even taken to buying medals in the antique shope in my territory to have the feeling repeated."

BIOGRAPHICAL/CRITICAL SOURCES: Books, January 17, 1943; *New Republic,* January 25, 1943; *Book Week,* June 18, 1944; *Commonweal,* June 30, 1944, November 22, 1968; *Weekly Book Review,* July 23, 1944; *New York Times,* November 19, 1944, February 20, 1971, November 14, 1972, December 6, 1976; *Publishers Weekly,* March 10, 1968; *Saturday Review,* October 19, 1968, March 22, 1969; *New York Times Book Review,* November 24, 1968, February 16, 1969, November 13, 1977; Doris De Montreville and Donna Hill, editors, *Third Book of Junior Authors,* H. W. Wilson, 1972; *Hartford Courant,* September 8, 1974; *Children's Literature Review,* Volume 2, Gale, 1976.

* * *

STEIGER, Paul E(rnest) 1942-

PERSONAL: Born August 15, 1942, in New York, N.Y.; son of Ernest (a certified public accountant) and Mary (a teacher; maiden name, Walsh) Steiger; married JoAnn McKenna (a research executive), August 29, 1964; children: Erika, Laura. *Education:* Yale University, B.A., 1964. *Office: Los Angeles Times,* Times-Mirror Sq., Los Angeles, Calif. 90053.

CAREER: Wall Street Journal, New York, N.Y., staff reporter in San Francisco, Calif., 1966-68; *Los Angeles Times,* Los Angeles, Calif., financial staff writer, 1968-71, economic correspondent, 1971-78, financial editor, 1978—. *Awards, honors:* John Hancock Award for Excellence from John Hancock Mutual Life Insurance Co., 1970, for excellence in business and financial writing; Gerald Loeb Award from Loeb Foundation of University of California, 1974, for distinguished business and financial journalism.

WRITINGS: (With John F. Lawrence) *The Seventies Crash,* World Publishing, 1970.

* * *

STEIN, Dona

PERSONAL: Born in Boston, Mass.; daughter of Frank Joseph and Regina (Bigler) Luongo; married Robert Allen Stein; children: Benjamin Allen. *Education:* Clark University, A.B., 1960, M.A., 1969. *Home:* 361 Wolcott St., Auburndale, Mass. 02166.

CAREER: Lasell Junior College, Newton, Mass., instructor, 1969-73, assistant professor of English, 1973-75; Fitchburg State College, Fitchburg, Mass., part-time instructor in English, 1976—. Has participated and directed poetry workshops; has given poetry readings in the New York-New England area. *Awards, honors:* Grants and scholarships for Bread Loaf Writers' Conference, 1973, 1977; Grolier Poetry Prize, 1976; Massachusetts Council of the Arts fellowship, 1976; fellowship for Yaddo, 1978; residence grant for Helene Wurlitzer Foundation, 1979.

WRITINGS: Children of the Mafiosi (poems), West End Press, 1977.

Work represented in *Cameos: Small Press Women Poets,* edited by Felice Newman, Crossing Press, 1978. Contributor of nearly sixty poems and reviews to literary magazines, including *Epoch, Island, Denver Quarterly,* and *Dark Horse.*

WORK IN PROGRESS: The Wing Factory, poems.

STEINBACK, William (Clarence) 1943-

PERSONAL: Born April 13, 1943, in Emporia, Kan.; son of Willard T. and Maybelle (Moore) Steinback; married Susan Bray (a professor of education), December 16, 1967. *Education:* Atlantic Christian College, B.S., 1966; Radford College, M.S., 1967; University of Virginia, Ed. D., 1971. *Politics:* Democrat. *Home:* 2218 Minnetonka Dr., Cedar Falls, Iowa 50613. *Office:* Division of Special Education, University of Northern Iowa, Cedar Falls, Iowa 50613.

CAREER: Virginia State College, Petersburg, assistant professor of special education, 1971-73; University of Florida, Gainesville, assistant professor of special education, 1973-74; University of Northern Iowa, Cedar Falls, associate professor of special education, 1974—. *Member:* American Association for the Education of the Severely and Profoundly Handicapped, Council for Exceptional Children.

WRITINGS: (With wife, Susan Bray Steinback, J. S. Payne, and R. A. Payne) *Establishing a Token Economy in the Classroom,* C. E. Merrill, 1973; (with S. B. Steinback) *Classroom Discipline: A Positive Approach,* C. C Thomas, 1975. Contributor to *Exceptional Children.*

WORK IN PROGRESS: A book on the education of the severely behaviorally disordered.

* * *

STEINBRUNER, John David 1941-

PERSONAL: Born July 12, 1941, in Denver, Colo.; son of Robert Joseph and Louise (Stegner) Steinbruner; married Maureen Strain (a planner), June 18, 1963; children: David, Gregory. *Education:* Stanford University, A.B., 1963; graduate study at University of Freiburg, 1963-64; Massachusetts Institute of Technology, Ph.D., 1968. *Politics:* Democrat. *Religion:* Roman Catholic. *Home:* 148 Cold Spring St., New Haven, Conn. *Office:* Yale University, 60 Sachem St., New Haven, Conn. 06520.

CAREER: Harvard University, Cambridge, Mass., assistant professor, 1969-73, associate professor, 1973-76; Yale University, New Haven, Conn., associate professor, 1976—.

WRITINGS: (With H. Jacoby) *Clearing the Air: Federal Policy on Automotive Emissions,* Ballinger, 1973; *The Cybernetic Theory of Decision,* Princeton University Press, 1974.

* * *

STEINHARDT, Milton 1909-

PERSONAL: Born November 13, 1909, in Miami, Okla.; son of Herman (a merchant) and Hedwig (Fleischaker) Steinhardt; married Ilse Boral, June 15, 1933; children: Robert. *Education:* Attended University of Kansas, 1926-28; Eastman School of Music, B.Mus., 1936, M.Mus., 1937; New York University, Ph.D., 1950. *Home:* 1331 Strong Ave., Lawrence, Kan. 66044.

CAREER: Central Washington College of Education (now Central Washington State College), Ellensburg, assistant professor of music, 1938-42; Michigan State University, East Lansing, instructor in music history, 1948-50; Ohio University, Athens, associate professor of music history, 1950-51; University of Kansas, Lawrence, professor of music history and literature, 1951-75, professor emeritus, 1975—. *Military service:* U.S. Army, Signal Corps, 1942-45.

MEMBER: International Musicological Society, American Musicological Society, Renaissance Society of America,

Vereniging voor Nederlandse Muziekgeschedenis, Gesellschaft zur Herausgabe von Denkmaeler der Tonkunst in Oesterreich. *Awards, honors:* Fulbright grant, 1958; Guggenheim fellowships, 1958, 1965.

WRITINGS: Jacobus Vaet and His Motets, Michigan State College Press, 1951; (editor) *Jacobus Vaet: The Complete Works,* Volumes 98, 100, 103/04, 108/09, 113/14, 116, 118, Denkmaeler der Tonkunst in Oesterreich, 1961-68; (editor) *Alard du Gaucquier: The Complete Works,* Volume 123, Denkmaeler der Tonkunst in Oesterreich, 1971; (editor) Philippe de Monte, *New Complete Edition,* Series A: *Motets,* University of Leuven Press, Volumes 1 and 2, 1975. Contributor to *Grove's Dictionary of Music and Musicians.* Contributor of articles and reviews to music journals.

WORK IN PROGRESS: Editing motets of Philippe de Monte; research on sacred music of the Renaissance.

* * *

STEINHOFF, Dan 1911-

PERSONAL: Born December 16, 1911, in Spokane, Wash.; son of Dan (an engineer) and Bartha (Van Os) Steinhoff; married Alberta Jill Cook, June 1, 1962. *Education:* University of Washington, Seattle, B.B.A., 1934; Northwestern University, graduate study, 1934-36; University of Michigan, M.A., 1941; University of Havana, D.S.Sc., 1951. *Religion:* Methodist. *Home:* 1437 Sopera Ave., Coral Gables, Fla. 33134. *Office:* Department of Business Management, University of Miami, Coral Gables, Fla. 33124.

CAREER: Bank of California, Portland, Ore., credit officer, 1934-37; Antioch College, Yellow Springs, Ohio, assistant professor of business administration, 1941-42; University of Miami, Coral Gables, Fla., 1946—, began as assistant professor, currently professor of business management, dean of Evening Division, 1950-62, dean of Division of Continuing Education, 1962-63, chairman of department of business management, 1969-73. Director of Industrial Research, Inc.; consultant to utility and plastics companies. *Military service:* U.S. Army, 1941-45; became second lieutenant.

MEMBER: Association of University Evening Colleges, Association of Urban Universities, Southeastern Adult Education Association, Beta Gamma Sigma, Phi Delta Kappa, Chi Pi, Delta Sigma Pi, Newcomen Society, Order of Artus, Exchange Club (Coral Gables).

WRITINGS: Small Business Management Fundamentals, McGraw, 1974, 2nd edition, 1978; *Small Business: Cases and Essays,* Grid Publishing, 1975; (with Bruce Yuill) *Developing Managers in Organization,* Wiley, 1975; *The World of Business,* McGraw, 1978. Also author of *Purchasing Management,* 1978, and *Accounting for Non-Accounting Majors,* 1978.

SIDELIGHTS: Steinhoff writes that his goal as a writer is to "adjust textbooks to the new generation." His seminars on every continent have taken him around the world twice.

* * *

STEINLE, Paul (Michael) 1939-

PERSONAL: Born February 26, 1939, in Chillicothe, Ohio; son of Ray Charles (a pharmacist) and Janice (Schmidt) Steinle; married Peggy Printz (a journalist), January 11, 1970. *Education:* Amherst College, B.A., 1962; Syracuse University, graduate study, 1964-65; Harvard University, M.B.A., 1976. *Office:* WIXT-TV, Shoppingtown, DeWitt, N.Y. 13214.

CAREER: WBZ-TV, Boston, Mass., reporter and producer, 1965-69; Westinghouse Broadcasting, Group W, radio correspondent and bureau chief in Saigon, Vietnam, 1969-71, and Hong Kong, 1972-74; WCVB-TV, Boston, financial editor, 1974-77; free-lance writer and broadcaster, 1977; WIXT-TV, Syracuse, N.Y., news director, 1978—. President of Actualities, Inc. *Member:* Overseas Press Club, Foreign Correspondents Club (Hong Kong), Southeast Asia Foreign Correspondents Club. *Awards, honors:* Public service award from New England United Press International, 1968, for "Boston: A Part of the Dream"; citation from Overseas Press Club, 1972, for radio reporting.

WRITINGS: (With wife, Peggy Printz) *Commune: Life in Rural China,* Dodd, 1977.

Films: "Auerbach and the Celtics," WBZ-TV, 1966; "Boston: A Part of the Dream," WBZ-TV, April, 1968; "Commune," Westinghouse Broadcasting, 1973.

Radio scripts: "Failure in United States Foreign Policy: The South Vietnamese Election," Westinghouse Broadcasting, September, 1970; "Heroin and the American G.I.'s," Westinghouse Broadcasting, 1971; "The Spirit of Survival," Westinghouse Broadcasting, March, 1973; "Cambodia: The Curtain of Silence," National Public Radio, October, 1977.

WORK IN PROGRESS: A management textbook for local TV news operations, tentatively entitled, *Television News.*

* * *

STEMPEL, Guido H(ermann) III 1928-

PERSONAL: Born August 13, 1928, in Bloomington, Ind.; son of Guido H. (a chemist) and Alice (a pianist; maiden name, Menninger) Stempel; married Anne Elliott (a social worker), August 30, 1952; children: Ralph, Carl, Jane. *Education:* Attended Carnegie Institute of Technology (now Carnegie-Mellon University), 1945-46; Indiana University, A.B., 1949, A.M., 1951; University of Wisconsin, Madison, Ph.D., 1954. *Politics:* Democrat. *Religion:* Methodist. *Home:* 7 Lamar Dr., Athens, Ohio 45701. *Office:* School of Journalism, Ohio University, Athens, Ohio 45701.

CAREER: Frankfort Times, Frankfort, Ind., sports editor, 1949-50; Pennsylvania State University, State College, instructor, 1955-57, assistant professor of journalism, 1957; Central Michigan University, Mount Pleasant, associate professor, 1957-63, professor of journalism, 1963-65; Ohio University, Athens, associate professor, 1965-68, professor of journalism, 1968—, director of School of Journalism, 1972—. *Military service:* U.S. Army, information specialist, 1954-55. *Member:* Association for Education in Journalism (chairman of research committee, 1968-71), Sigma Delta Chi.

WRITINGS: Global Mass Communication, Harcourt, 1978; (editor with Bruce Westley) *Research Methods in Mass Communications,* Prentice-Hall, 1979. Contributor to scholarly journals and journalism magazines. Editor of *Journalism Quarterly,* 1972—.

WORK IN PROGRESS: Study of trends in newspaper format.

* * *

STEPHENS, A. Ray 1932-

PERSONAL: Born August 1, 1932, in Vernon, Tex.; son of Eddie Wendell and Harriett (Killough) Stephens; married Linda Delaplain (a teacher), November 28, 1954; children: David Ray, Linda Ann. *Education:* Western Oklahoma

State College, A.A., 1952; University of Oklahoma, B.A., 1954, M.A., 1957; University of Texas, Ph.D., 1962. *Politics:* Democrat. *Religion:* Methoeist. *Home:* 619 Ridgecrest Circle, Denton, Tex. 76201. *Office:* Department of History, North Texas State University, Denton, Tex. 76203.

CAREER: Texas A & M University, College Station, professor of history, 1962-65; North Texas State University, Denton, professor of history, 1965—. Member of Denton City Council, 1975-77; chairman of Denton Young Men's Christian Association board of management, 1974-75. *Military service:* U.S. Army, 1954-56. *Member:* Organization of American Historians, Western History Association, Southwestern Social Science Association, Texas State Historical Association, Phi Alpha Theta (local president, 1956-57, 1958-59).

WRITINGS: The Taft Ranch: A Texas Principality, University of Texas Press, 1964; (author of introduction) Lester R. Dillon, Jr., *American Artillery in the Mexican War, 1846-1847,* Presidial Press, 1975. Contributor of articles and reviews to regional history and library journals.

WORK IN PROGRESS: A History of Texas; A Historical Atlas of Texas; editing *The Reminiscences of Abner Doubleday.*

* * *

STEPHENS, Charles
    See GOLDIN, Stephen

* * *

STEPHENS, Martha (Thomas) 1937-

PERSONAL: Born March 19, 1937, in Waycross, Ga.; daughter of Bernard L. (a salesman) and Evelyn (Stephens) Thomas; married V. Jerome Stephens (a professor of political science), August 13, 1962; children: Daniel, Paige, Shelley. *Education:* Georgia State College for Women, A.B., 1958; University of Georgia, M.A., 1962; Indiana University, Ph.D., 1967. *Politics:* "Reform Socialist." *Religion:* None. *Residence:* Cincinnati, Ohio. *Office:* Department of English, University of Cincinnati, Cincinnati, Ohio 45221.

CAREER: Worked as waitress, secretary, and high school teacher until 1967; University of Cincinnati, Cincinnati, Ohio, 1967—, began as assistant professor, became professor of English. Active in campus-reform organizations, civil rights groups, and medical reform actions. Consultant to Time-Life Books.

WRITINGS: The Question of Flannery O'Connor, Louisiana State University Press, 1973; *Cast a Wistful Eye* (novel), Macmillan, 1977. Contributor of articles and reviews to academic journals.

WORK IN PROGRESS: Another novel of the South; children's stories "of a humorous and odd variety."

SIDELIGHTS: Martha Stephens comments: "Most of my writing is set in the South." *Avocational interests:* Gardening, opera, children, reform politics, medicine and consumer problems, American dialects.

* * *

STEPHENS, Rosemary 1924-
    (Leslie Carswell)

PERSONAL: Born December 4, 1924, in Waycross, Ga.; daughter of Matthew Paul and Pearl (Vining) Carswell; married Harold W. Stephens (a professor of mathematics), June 4, 1946; children: Diana Patricia Brooks. *Education:* Mem-

phis State University, B.A. (summa cum laude), 1963; University of Mississippi, M.A., 1965, Ph.D., 1971. *Politics:* Independent. *Religion:* Episcopalian. *Home:* 64 North Yates Rd., Memphis, Tenn. 38117.

CAREER: St. Petersburg Times, St. Petersburg, Fla., reporter and literary editor, 1943-46; *Gainesville Sun,* Gainesville, Fla., society editor, 1948-50; *Muncie Evening Press,* Muncie, Ind., reporter, 1952-54; University of Mississippi, Oxford, instructor in English, 1963-65; free-lance writer, 1967—. Featured speaker at writers' conferences.

MEMBER: National League of American Pen Women (organizer and vice-president of local branch, 1974-76; fiction editor of *Pen Woman,* 1974-78; National Letters Chairman, 1976-78), National Federation of Press Women, Tennessee Woman's Press and Authors Club (president, 1973-75), Poetry Society of Tennessee (president, 1972-74). *Awards, honors:* Martha Foley Distinctive Short Story Award, 1972, for "Pink Roses"; national awards from National League of American Pen Women, 1972, for "The Nightingale," 1974, for "Christmas Come, Christmas Gone" and "The Animal," and 1976, for "Politician in the Family"; Tennessee Governor's Award, 1973, for contributions to poetry; dramatic poetry award from New York Poetry Forum, 1974, for "Turned On"; Golden Owl Award from Tennessee Pen Women, 1975, for a variety of national publications; Pikeville College Award, 1976, and fiction award from National Press Women, 1977, both for "The Neighborhood"; Women of Achievement Award from Tennessee Woman's Press and Author's Club, 1977.

WRITINGS: (Under pseudonym Leslie Carswell) *Silver Dollar Mystery* (juvenile), Scholastic Book Services, 1971; (under pseudonym Leslie Carswell) *Mystery of the Spider's Web* (juvenile), Scholastic Book Services, 1975; *Eve's Navel* (poetry), South & West, 1976.

Work represented in anthologies, including *Today's Stories from Seventeen,* Macmillan, 1971; *Universe Ahead,* Atheneum, 1975; *Phantoms and Fantasies,* Harper, 1977. Contributor of articles, poems, and stories to academic journals, juvenile magazines, and literary journals, including *Southern Poetry Review, Voices International, American Transcendental Quarterly,* and *Seventeen.*

WORK IN PROGRESS: Green Horse, Green Rider, a novel, for Harcourt; *Mystery of the Barking Dog,* a juvenile novel for Scholastic Book Services; *Wild Dogs and Other Poems;* short stories.

SIDELIGHTS: Rosemary Stephens writes: "My writings are varied, ranging from novels for teenagers (which are used in public schools in the United States and Canada) to academic articles for university professors, and include short stories in both popular and literary magazines, essays, reviews, and poetry. I find writing as a career enjoyable, frustrating, rewarding, and challenging."

* * *

STERLING, Donald J(ustus), Jr. 1927-

PERSONAL: Born September 27, 1927, in Portland, Ore.; son of Donald Justus (an editor) and Adelaide (Armstrong) Sterling; married Julie Ann Courteol, June 7, 1963; children: Sarah L., William J., John C. *Education:* Princeton University, B.A., 1948; graduate study at Harvard University, 1955-56. *Politics:* Democrat. *Home:* 1718 S.W. Myrtle St., Portland, Ore. 97201. *Office: Oregon Journal,* 1320 S.W. Broadway, Portland, Ore. 97201.

CAREER/WRITINGS: Denver Post, Denver, Colo., reporter, 1948-52; *Oregon Journal,* Portland, Ore., reporter, assistant city editor, and associate editor, 1952-71, editor, 1971—. President, Tri-County Community Council, 1972-73. *Member:* American Society of Newspaper Editors, Oregon Historical Society, Nieman Fellows, Sigma Delta Chi, Phi Beta Kappa, City Club of Portland (president, 1973-74), Multnomah Athletic Club (Portland, Ore.), Dial Lodge (Princeton, N.J.). *Awards, honors:* Nieman fellowship, 1955-56; English-Speaking Union traveling fellowship, 1959; Izaak Walton League Golden Beaver Award, 1969; Oregon Newspaper Publishers Association President's Award, 1975.

* * *

STETTNER, Irving 1922-

PERSONAL: Born November 7, 1922, in Brooklyn, N.Y.; son of Morris (a carpenter) and Nettie (Falk) Stettner; children: Mona. *Education:* Attended Columbia University, 1946-47. *Politics:* None. *Religion:* None. *Home:* 129 Second Ave., #14, New York, N.Y. 10003.

CAREER: Has worked variously as a farmer, free-lance writer, painter, door-to-door salesman, seaman, cafe sketch artist, and carpenter. Work exhibited at five one-man shows in New York City. *Military service:* U.S. Army, Signal Corps, 1942-45.

WRITINGS: On the Second Avenue Patrol: Selected Poems, Home Planet Publications, 1976; *Anna: A Bicentennial Poem,* Amphora Press, 1977; *Jo Ann in the White House* (one-act play; first produced in New York City at Theatre Genesis, March 30, 1978), X Press Press, 1977; *Go-Stop-Go Greyhound America* (poem), Downtown Press, 1977; (with Alexander Kohav) *Resolutions in Spring* (poems), Stroker, 1977. Contributor of poems to more than thirty-five magazines in the United States and abroad, including Greece, Italy, Poland, and France. Editor of *Stroker.*

WORK IN PROGRESS: An autobiographical novel.

SIDELIGHTS: Stettner writes: "I have been living in Paris for five years; it has been a rich experience. Hard times—but I've learned the meaning of the saying 'To be poor is to be rich.' I have no philosophy in my writing; primarily expression, and I enjoy doing it. I feel little rapport with other poets now in America—except Jack Hirschman, John Brandi, etc.—the post-Beat poets. I'm astonished at the recognition my work is receiving in Italy, where it has been translated."

BIOGRAPHICAL/CRITICAL SOURCES: Northeast Rising Sun, Number 3; *Small Press Review,* Number 51; *Hydria,* Number 19.

* * *

STEVENS, David Harrison 1884-

PERSONAL: Born December 20, 1884, in Berlin, Wis.; son of William Waters (a clergyman) and Katherine (McCoy) Stevens; married Ruth Frances Davis (a writer), March 26, 1915 (died December 8, 1974); children: John Scott, Anne Elizabeth Stevens Hobler, Barbara Scott Monroe. *Education:* Lawrence University, A.B., 1906, A.M., 1910; Harvard University, A.M., 1912; University of Chicago, Ph.D., 1914. *Politics:* Democrat. *Religion:* Presbyterian. *Home and office address:* P.O. Box 154, Ephraim, Wis. 54211.

CAREER: High school teacher of Latin and English in Merrill, Wis., 1906-07; Northwestern University, Evanston, Ill., instructor in English, 1908-11; University of Chicago, Chica-

go, Ill., instructor, 1914-18, assistant professor, 1919-23, associate professor, 1923-25, professor of English, 1925-30, dean of College of Arts, Literature, and Science, 1920-22, assistant to president, 1926-30; Rockefeller Foundation, New York, N.Y., director of humanities, 1932-60; Huntington Library, Pasadena, Calif., research associate, 1951-52; University of Helsinki, Helsinki, Finland, lecturer in English, 1964. Vice-president of General Education Board, 1930-38; member of committee of inter-American artistic and cultural relations of Office of the Coordinator of Inter-American Affairs, 1940-44; member of education mission to Japan, 1946. Member of board of trustees of Lawrence University, 1950-70. *Military service:* U.S. Army, on cipher staff in Military Intelligence, 1918-19; became captain. *Member:* Modern Language Association of America, American Library Association (honorary life member; president of Ephraim Foundation, 1952-54), Phi Beta Kappa. *Awards, honors:* LL.D. from Lawrence University, 1931; citation from Wisconsin Academy of Sciences, Arts and Letters, 1974.

WRITINGS: Party Politics and English Journalism, 1702-1742, G. Banta, 1916, reprinted, Russell & Russell, 1967; (editor and contributor with wife, Ruth Davis Stevens) *The Home Guide to Good Reading,* Frederick J. Drake & Co., 1920; *The Stevens Handbook of Punctuation,* Century Co., 1923; *College Composition,* Century Co., 1927; (editor) *Types of English Drama, 1660-1780,* Ginn, 1923; *The Teaching of College Composition,* Century Co., 1927; *Milton Papers,* University of Chicago Press, 1927, reprinted, AMS Press, 1975; *Reference Guide to Milton: From 1800 to the Present Day,* University of Chicago Press, 1930, reprinted, Russell & Russell, 1967; *The Changing Humanities: An Appraisal of Old Values and New Uses,* Harper, 1953; (editor) *Ten Talents in the American Theatre,* University of Oklahoma Press, 1957; *Reference Guide to Milton,* Duquesne University Press, 1960; (editor with wife, Ruth Frances Stevens) *American Patriotic Prose and Verse,* Books for Libraries, 1970; *A Time of Humanities, an Oral History: Recollections of David H. Stevens,* edited by Robert E. Yahnke, Wisconsin Academy of Sciences, Arts and Letters, 1976; *Where Are the Humanities?,* Wisconsin Academy of Sciences, Arts and Letters, 1976. Contributor to professional journals and popular magazines.

SIDELIGHTS: Stevens writes: "I have traveled from Germany to Japan, supporting special courses in foreign languages for war value, 1933-45, and so established American centers for unusual languages; I brought unusual scholars from Germany to save them, as part of my duties during World War II, as well as saving works of art and libraries to be returned after 1945."

AVOCATIONAL INTERESTS: Writing on local history.

* * *

STEVENS, Sharon 1949-

PERSONAL: Born June 14, 1949, in Chicago, Ill.; daughter of Clarence B. (with a railroad company) and Erma (a teacher; maiden name, Collins) Stevens. *Education:* Northern Illinois University, B.S., 1967. *Office:* NBC, 30 Rockefeller Plaza, New York, N.Y. 10020.

CAREER/WRITINGS: Independent Bulletin, Chicago, Ill., reporter and teen editor, 1964-67; Headstart, Chicago, teacher's aide, 1967-69; *Chatham Citizen,* Chicago, reporter, 1971; WBBM-Radio, Chicago, reporter, anchorperson, and writer and producer of documentaries, 1971-75; National Broadcasting Co. (NBC), New York, N.Y., anchorperson for radio network, 1975—. Notable assignments include coverage of the Karen Quinlan hearings, 1975, national Republican and Democratic conventions, 1976, and the Ronald Reagan presidential campaign. *Member:* National Association of Black Journalists, New York Press Club. *Awards, honors:* Michele Clark fellowship, Columbia University, 1972; Young Women's Christian Association Black Achievers Award, 1975; National Association of Media Women Award, 1975; Outstanding Young Women of America Award, 1977.

SIDELIGHTS: Stevens told *CA:* "The most important guideline in this business is to be fair. Unfortunately, this has not always been the case in covering stories involving minorities. I would like to see the day when these kinds of stories are considered 'news' and treated accordingly, instead of 'special stories,' reported on every now and then." *Avocational interests:* Theatre.

* * *

STEVENSON, Henry M(iller)   1914-

PERSONAL: Born February 25, 1914, in Birmingham, Ala.; son of Henry Munn (a clergyman) and Mayme Gene (a teacher; maiden name, Fuller) Stevenson; married Rosa Belle Ard (a teacher), November 11, 1939; children: Nell (Mrs. Charles Sanders), Ernest, Henry, Jr., James. *Education:* Birmingham-Southern College, B.A., 1935; University of Alabama, M.S., 1939; Cornell University, Ph.D., 1943. *Politics:* Independent. *Religion:* Methodist. *Home:* 905 Briarcliffe Rd., Tallahassee, Fla. 32303. *Office;* Tall Timbers Research Station, Route 1, Box 160, Tallahassee, Fla. 32303.

CAREER: Alabama Cooperative Wildlife Research Unit, Auburn, research associate, summer, 1943; University of Mississippi, Oxford, acting associate professor of biology, 1943-44; Memphis State College, Memphis, Tenn., instructor in biology, summer, 1944; Emory and Henry College, Emory, Va., associate professor of biology, 1944-46; Florida State University, Tallahassee, assistant professor, 1946-52, associate professor of zoology, 1952-75, professor emeritus, 1975—, curator of birds, 1965-75; Tall Timbers Research Station, Tallahassee, Fla., research fellow, 1975—. Ecological consultant with Conservation Consultants, 1973—.

MEMBER: American Ornithologists Union, Wilson Ornithological Society, Alabama Ornithological Society, Florida Ornithological Society.

WRITINGS: A Key to Florida Birds, Peninsular Publishing, 1960; *Vertebrates of Florida: Identification and Distribution,* University Presses of Florida, 1976. Contributor of more than one hundred seventy articles to nature studies journals, particularly ornithology journals.

WORK IN PROGRESS: A book on Florida birds; research on distribution, migration, and taxonomy of birds, especially through the use of quantitative field data.

SIDELIGHTS: Stevenson's interest in studying birds and collecting specimens has taken him to Mexico, Ecuador, and Panama.

AVOCATIONAL INTERESTS: Music (choir soloist), sports.

* * *

STEWART, A(gnes) C(harlotte)

PERSONAL: Born in Liverpool, England; married Robert Frederick Stewart (a mechanical engineer); children: Sheila Therese (Mrs. Andrew Philip Thomson). *Education:* Privately educated. *Politics:* "None: I despair of them all!" *Religion:* Church of England. *Home:* Knowetop, Corsock, Castle Douglas, Kirkcudbrightshire, Scotland, DG7 3EB.

CAREER: Writer. *Member:* Society of Women Writers and Journalists. *Awards, honors:* Edgar Allen Poe Award, 1972, from Mystery Writers of America for *Elizabeth's Tower;* award of merit, 1977, from Scottish Arts Council for *Beyond the Boundary.*

WRITINGS—All young adult novels: *The Boat in the Reeds* (illustrated by Christopher Brooker), Blackie & Son, 1960, Bradbury, 1970; *Falcon's Crag,* Blackie & Son, 1969; *The Quarry Line Mystery,* Faber, 1971, Nelson, 1973; *Elizabeth's Tower,* S. G. Phillips, 1972; *Dark Dove,* S. G. Phillips, 1974; *Ossian House,* Blackie & Son, 1974, S. G. Phillips, 1976; *Beyond the Boundary,* Blackie & Son, 1976; *Silas and Con,* Atheneum, 1977; *Brother Raimon Returns,* Blackie & Son, 1978.

WORK IN PROGRESS: A sequel to *Falcon's Crag;* research for a story about highland clearances.

SIDELIGHTS: Stewart told *CA:* "I grew up in a small seaside town in Cheshire, England, where the high spring tides often came over into our garden. My sole companion of my own age was my elder sister, as we were educated at first by a series of governesses. When I was in my teens we moved to a cottage in Kent and there my lifelong love of animals and gardens had a chance to develop. It was the first of a long series of country cottages peopled with a wide variety of animals, from my daughter's white mice, via guinea-pigs, hamsters, hens, ducks, geese, Siamese cats and goats to my favourites, retrievers, both labrador and flat-coated. Fortunately my husband—a mechanical engineer—and my daughter share my love of the country and animals.

"I cannot remember a time when I did not want to write but there never seemed any opportunity; then my daughter went to boarding school and for a time gardens and animals gave place to a first-floor flat in a 400-year-old Dorset manor house and my only companions from eight-thirty until six were my two labradors. It could not have been a better place to start to write and I have continued to do so ever since.

"My daughter is now married and my husband and I live in a shepherd's cottage high amongst the Galloway hills in Scotland. We renovated it ourselves and it has one of the loveliest views anyone could wish for, and a garden and animals once again fill a large part of my life. I am very interested in wildlife too and seventy acres of marsh and moor which we own has been accepted by the Scottish Wildlife Trust as a nature reserve. We have planted eight acres of conifers as a windbreak, doing much of the planting ourselves, and made a mile-and-a-half long trail. Two small lochs provide homes for wild duck and winter quarters for whooper swans and also supply us with brown trout fishing.

"An added interest these last few years has been the lending of a bungalow I own to groups of physically handicapped children for holidays. I have always wanted to be able to do something of this kind and it has proved a very rewarding experience.

"When indoors, apart from writing, I cook and knit and I always must have something at hand to read. My husband paints—he did the end papers for *The Quarry Line Mystery*—and he types all my manuscripts. I write all my stories in longhand and then read them to my tape recorder—a great help in balancing the sentences.

"My writing naturally reflects my interests and the backgrounds of my stories are ones I know well and love. I began many of my books with no idea of what the plot would be; I just started with an idea, a scene or a character that interested me and wrote on—it was often more like writing down a story I was being told than inventing one. Any guidance or morals my stories may have, develop as a natural part of them, often unseen by me until later: they are never put in deliberately.

"I did not intend to write for young people, I began writing for my daughter and it went on from there. I have written adult stories that have been well-liked and kept for consideration but finally returned. I find a great satisfaction in writing books for young people and would not now wish to change.

"A well-known English critic once wrote: 'If I know and like a man I am careful never to read his books and if I enjoy a book I take pains to avoid meeting the author.' If this questionnaire is rather incomplete it is because I too strongly believe that authors and their work are things better kept apart. My books appear under my initials only to avoid my personal identity becoming imposed upon the story. Nothing about me can possibly be as interesting as a stranger in a tower, a mystery train running against signals or an invisible boy whistling in the Highland hills."

* * *

STEWART, Kenneth N. 1901-1978

June 6, 1901—February 22, 1978; American educator, journalism critic, and journalist. Stewart was an educator at New York University, Columbia University, the University of Michigan, and other universities. In addition, he worked as a reporter, editor, and critic at over twelve newspapers, including *New York Times, Paris Herald,* and *New York Herald Tribune.* He died in Menlo Park, Calif. Obituaries and other sources: *Directory of American Scholars,* Volume II: *English, Speech, and Drama,* 6th edition, Bowker, 1974; *New York Times,* February 25, 1978.

* * *

STINGER, Charles L(ewis) 1944-

PERSONAL: Born March 19, 1944, in Waverley, N.Y.; son of Gilbert B. (a newspaper editor) and Helen (Olmstead) Stinger; married Patricia Freres, June 15, 1968; children: Owen A., Katherine L. *Education:* Hobart College (now Hobart & William Smith Colleges), B.A. (summa cum laude), 1966; Stanford University, M.A., 1967, Ph.D., 1971. *Politics:* "Much-derided liberalism." *Religion:* Roman Catholic. *Home:* 234 Parker Ave., Buffalo, N.Y. 14214. *Office:* Department of History, State University of New York at Buffalo, Amherst Campus, Buffalo, N.Y. 14261.

CAREER: State University of New York at Buffalo, Amherst campus, assistant professor, 1973-77, associate professor of history, 1977—. *Member:* American Historical Association, Renaissance Society of America, American Society for Reformation Research. *Awards, honors:* Woodrow Wilson fellow, 1966-67; Fulbright fellow in Italy, 1969-70; fellowship from Harvard University's Center for Italian Renaissance Studies in Florence, Italy, 1972-73; American Council of Learned Societies grant for Rome, summer, 1977.

WRITINGS: Humanism and the Church Fathers: Ambrogio Traversari (1386-1439) and Christian Antiquity in the Italian Renaissance, State University of New York Press, 1977.

WORK IN PROGRESS: Research for *The Renaissance in Rome, 1447-1527,* publication by Harvard University Press expected in 1980.

SIDELIGHTS: Stinger comments: "My fascination with the Italian Renaissance began with a course I took as a sophomore at Hobart. I have now been to Italy five separate times in the process of doing historical research. If anything, I am even more intrigued by the mysteriously creative and dynamic age which was the Renaissance in Italy, an age which continues to inspire us to exploit our human potentialities for artistic and intellectual achievement. Perhaps my most satisfying endeavor is teaching a course of 'Renaissance civilization.' No other teaching experience has captured so well the multi-dimensionality of the Italian Renaissance."

* * *

STINNETTE, Charles R(oy), Jr. 1914-

PERSONAL: Born June 18, 1914, in Asheville, N.C.; son of Charles Roy (a businessman) and Grace (Graham) Stinnette; married Nancy Virginia Riddle, June 14, 1937; children: Graham Long, Cynthia Lynn. *Education:* North Carolina State University, B.S., 1937; Union Theological Seminary, New York, N.Y., M.Div., 1940; Hartford Theological Seminary, S.T.M., 1942; William Alanson White Institute for Psychiatry, certificate, 1950; Columbia University, Ph.D., 1950. *Politics:* Liberal. *Home:* 1509 Indian Dr., Enid, Okla. 73701.

CAREER: Ordained Episcopal minister, 1941; curate of Episcopal church in Hartford, Conn., 1940-42, assistant pastor in New York City, 1946-48; University of Rochester, Rochester, N.Y., professor of religion and chaplain, 1948-50; rector of Episcopal church in Rochester, 1950-52; Washington Cathedral, Washington, D.C., canon and associate warden of College of Preachers, 1952-56; Union Theological Seminary, New York City, associate professor, 1956-59; professor of psychiatry and religion, 1959-62; University of Chicago, Chicago, Ill., professor of pastoral theology and psychiatry, 1962-71; Phillips University, Enid, Okla., professor of theology of the ministry, 1971—. Visiting professor at Union Theological Seminary; lecturer at schools and conferences. Clinical associate of Illinois State Psychiatric Hospital, 1965—. Member of National Committee on Health and Human Values. *Military service:* U.S. Army, chaplain, 1943-46; served in Okinawa; received Bronze Star. U.S. Army Reserve, 1946-74; became colonel.

WRITINGS: Faith and Freedom, Seabury, 1955; *Faith, Freedom, and Selfhood,* Seabury, 1959; *Grace and the Search of Our Heart,* Association Press, 1962; *Learning in the Theological Perspective,* Association Press, 1965. Contributor to religious periodicals.

WORK IN PROGRESS: Moral Discernment and Morphology in Ministry: Essays in Practical Theology; The Presence of the City: Care, Prophecy, and Ministry in American Theology.

SIDELIGHTS: Stinnette comments briefly: "As a writer my primary aim is to relate theology and philosophy to human activities in aesthetics, political life, and humane education and humane living."

* * *

STONE, Alma 1908-

PERSONAL: Born December 31, 1908, in Jasper, Tex.; daughter of Arthur Kyle and Alma (a teacher; maiden name, Adams) Stone. *Education:* Attended Southern Methodist University, 1925-26, Bradford Academy, 1926-27, and Columbia University. *Politics:* Democrat. *Home:* 523 West

112th St., New York, N.Y. 10025. *Agent:* Candida Donadio, 111 West 57th St., New York, N.Y. 10019. *Office:* Sarah Lawrence College Library, Bronxville, N.Y. 10708.

CAREER: Central News Agency of China, New York, N.Y., research assistant, 1941-43; Sarah Lawrence College, Bronxville, N.Y., music librarian, 1946-48, archivist, 1954-76. *Awards, honors:* O. Henry Award, 1959, for first chapter of *The Bible Salesman.*

WRITINGS: The Harvard Tree (novel), Houghton, 1954; *The Bible Salesman* (novel), Doubleday, 1962; *The Banishment* (short stories and novella), Doubleday, 1973.

WORK IN PROGRESS: "An in-depth comparison of the Open Road philosophy of Walt Whitman and the Campfire Girls: all the rough new prizes in poncho rolling and beaded head bands, the End of the Trail with the accouchezing and squatting and stifling. Clarified by relevant footnotes from Henry James: Prose, in order to be good poetry, must first be good prose."

SIDELIGHTS: Coleman Rosenberger reviewed *The Harvard Tree* for the *New York Herald Tribune:* "In her first novel Alma Stone tells, with artistry and poignance and humor, the story of a town in her native Texas during a summer soon after the first world war. The qualities here, the mood and the manner, are not those which we normally associate with Texas. Miss Stone is a prose stylist who sustains her tone with a sure control throughout her relatively long novel."

Stone's most recent work, *The Banishment,* was reviewed in the *New York Times Book Review:* "Three short stories and a novella make up this nosegay to the downtrodden, which includes unexpected candidates for compassion, like 'the orphan shrimp' and 'eggplants begging to be pulled,' as well as selected short subjects. The author's mixture of down-home diction and creative nonsense offers humorous surprises. It's as though you were expecting Eudora Welty and ran into Al Capp."

AVOCATIONAL INTERESTS: "Helping old people (or young people, or people), feeding pigeons and sleeping with cats."

BIOGRAPHICAL/CRITICAL SOURCES: New Yorker, September 18, 1954; *New York Times,* September 19, 1954; *New York Herald Tribune,* September 26, 1954; *New York Times Book Review,* May 13, 1962, November 18, 1973; *Time,* May 25, 1962.

*　　*　　*

STONE, Charles Sumner, Jr.　1924-
(Chuck Stone)

PERSONAL: Born July 21, 1924, in St. Louis, Mo.; son of Charles Sumner and Madalene (Chafin) Stone; married Louise Davis, October 4, 1958; children: Krishna, Allegra, Charles III. *Education:* Wesleyan University, A.B., 1948; University of Chicago, M.A., 1950. *Office: Philadelphia Daily News,* Philadelphia, Pa.

CAREER: Regional field representative for World Politics and American Foreign Policy adult education discussion programs, 1952-56; Cooperative for American Relief Everywhere (CARE), New York City, overseas representative to Egypt, Gaza, and India, 1956-57; *New York Age,* New York City, editorial consultant, 1957-58, editor, 1958-60; American Committee on Africa, New York City, associate director, 1960; *Washington Afro-American,* Washington, D.C., editor and White House correspondent, 1960-63; *Chicago Daily Defender,* Chicago, Ill., editor-in-chief, 1963-64; spe-

cial assistant to U.S. Congressman Adam Clayton Powell, 1965-67; editorial research specialist for U.S. Congressman Robert N. C. Nix, 1968; Trinity College, Hartford, Conn., John T. Dorrance Visiting Professor of Government, 1969; NBC-TV New York City, commentator on "Today" show, 1969-70; Educational Testing Service, Princeton, N.J., director of minority affairs and educational opportunities, 1970-72; Antioch-Putney Graduate School of Education, Philadelphia, Pa., lecturer in sociology, 1973; *Philadelphia Daily News* and Universal Press Syndicate, Philadelphia, columnist, 1973—. Part-time lecturer in journalism at Columbia College, 1963-64. Has served as member of National Workshop on Testing in Education and Employment steering committee, Creative and Visual Arts Panel, American Revolution Bicentennial Commission, and Wesleyan University board of trustees, and Pennsylvania State Board of Colleges and University Directors. *Military service:* U.S. Army Air Forces, 1943-45.

MEMBER: National Conference of Black Political Scientists, Black Academy of Arts and Letters (fellow and founding member). *Awards, honors:* Award for best column of the year from National Newspaper Publishers Association, 1960; named "Journalist of the Year" by Capital Press Club, Washington, D.C., 1961; Annual Distinguished Citizen's award from Frontiers International, Inc., Washington, D.C., 1963; named "Outstanding Citizen of the Year" by Congress of Racial Equality (CORE), Chicago chapter, 1964; Award of Merit for journalism from Alpha Phi Alpha, Chicago, Ill., 1965; Politician-in-Residence at Morgan State College Institute of Political Education, 1969; named "Alpha Man of the Year" by Alpha Phi Alpha, Philadelphia, Pa., 1973.

WRITINGS—Under name Chuck Stone: *Tell It Like It Is* (essays), Trident, 1968; *Black Political Power in America* (nonfiction), Bobbs-Merrill, 1968; *King Strut* (novel), Bobbs-Merrill, 1970.

Work represented in anthologies, including *The Black Power Revolt: A Collection of Essays,* edited by Floyd Barbour, Sargent, 1968. Contributing editor, *Black Scholar;* member of board of advisers, *Contact.*

SIDELIGHTS: As an editor and columnist with Black newspapers in three large American cities, Stone has been recognized as an outstanding journalist. *Best Sellers* called his first collection of essays, *Tell It Like It Is,* "a welcome addition to the thoughtful Negro approach to the racial situation in the United States." Emphasizing Stone's objectivity, the reviewer added: "Stone is neither an Uncle Tom nor a torch-throwing rioter. What he has to say is sound common sense said with trenchant humor and pungent wit."

Oscar A. Bouise noted Stone's "microscopic scrutiny" of the "political panorama" in *Black Political Power in America,* declaring: "He rakes the coals of party politics; he digs into the ashes of big city machines, revealing some interesting secrets of racial, national, religious, and underworld politics. He probes the North; he slaps the South. He lays bare personalities and secret weapons of success in what is revealed as a dirty game of survival of the fittest, the most wily, the most conscienceless—even sometimes the most inhumane." While acknowledging that Stone possesses the "gift of a good journalist: the facile statement," Bouise also observed that this style is "at times too glib for a real historical study" leading Stone into "portraying politicians as extremes." Bouise called *Black Political Power in America* a "book which had to be written" and concluded that "no writer is better equipped than Chuck Stone is for the task."

Citing Stone's "facile style, . . . love of creative language and expression, . . . keen wit, . . . dedication to the subject," Bouise said the author's technique "cannot be equalled, let alone surpassed."

Stone's experiences in Washington, first as an assistant to Representative Adam Clayton Powell, then to Representative Robert N. C. Nix, inspired his novel, *King Strut*. Oscar Bouise called it "a hard hitting book" with a "tongue-in-cheek manner." Again he praised Stone as a "stylist of the first order (journalistic, that is)" and labeled him a "heavy-handed, bludgeon-wielding, Swiftian satirist." "This could be a serious book, if it were not so funny," wrote Bouise, "[and] it would be a funny book if it were not so serious."

BIOGRAPHICAL/CRITICAL SOURCES: Best Sellers, February 1, 1968, December 1, 1968, November 15, 1970; *Washington Post,* July 11, 1969.*

*　　*　　*

STONE, Chuck
See STONE, Charles Sumner, Jr.

*　　*　　*

STONE, Joan 1930-

PERSONAL: Born October 22, 1930, in Port Angeles, Wash.; daughter of William David and Florence (Burdick) Duncan; married Donald H. Stone, July 11, 1949 (divorced); children: Bruce, Duncan, Duane, Todd, Anne Stone Weixel. *Education:* University of Washington, Seattle, B.A., 1970, M.A., 1974, Ph.C., 1976, Ph.D., 1978. *Home:* 4460 184th Ave. S.E., Issaquah, Wash. 98027. *Office:* Department of English, Colorado College, Colorado Springs, Colo. 80903.

CAREER: University of Washington, Seattle, director of creative writing workshop, 1973; University of Montana, Missoula, lecturer in English, 1974; Colorado College, Colorado Springs, lecturer in English, 1977—. Member of board of advisers, Washington State Volunteer Lawyers for the Arts. *Awards, honors:* Pacific Northwest Writers award, 1968; American Academy of Poets awards, 1969, 1970, and 1972; Borestone Mountain award, 1973, for "Birthday Poem."

WRITINGS: The Swimmer and Other Poems, Sea Penn Press, 1975; *Alba* (poetry), Sea Penn Press, 1976; *Seven Poems,* Press at Colorado College, 1978; *A Question for My Brother Who Knows the Weather* (poetry), Succor Press, in press.

Work represented in *The Academy of American Poets University and College Prizes, 1967-1973,* edited by Daniel Hoffman, 1974. Contributor of about ninety poems to magazines, including *Yale Review, Texas Quarterly, Southern Poetry Review, Georgia Review,* and *Poetry Now.*

WORK IN PROGRESS: Research on Robert Frost, with a book expected to result.

SIDELIGHTS: Joan Stone comments: "Nothing contributes to my writing so much as the fact that I like people and spend time trying to understand them and therefore myself."

AVOCATIONAL INTERESTS: Volleyball, swimming, cross-country skiing, pottery, needlepoint, travel in the Orient and Europe, gardening, remodeling houses, raising pigs, cooking.

*　　*　　*

STONE, Ronald H. 1939-

PERSONAL: Born March 26, 1939, in Humboldt, Iowa; son of Hubert Henry (a contractor) and Bernice (a teacher; maiden name, Tilton) Stone; married Joann Loftus (divorced); children: Randall Warren, Patricia Bernice. *Education:* Morningside College, B.A., 1960; Union Theological Seminary, New York, N.Y., B.D., 1963; Columbia University, Ph.D., 1968. *Politics:* Democrat. *Religion:* Presbyterian. *Home:* 1112 King Ave., Pittsburgh, Pa. 15206. *Office:* Pittsburgh Theological Seminary, 616 Highland Ave., Pittsburgh, Pa. 15206.

CAREER: United Church of Christ, New York City, assistant to secretary of international relations, 1961-63; Morningside College, Sioux City, Iowa, instructor, summers, 1964, 1965; Union Theological Seminary, New York City, instructor in social ethics, 1967-68; Columbia University, New York City, assistant professor of religion, 1968-69; Pittsburgh Theological Seminary, Pittsburgh, Pa., associate professor of ethics, 1970-72, professor of social ethics, 1972—. Visiting instructor in ethics, Vassar College, 1967; lecturer at Union Theological Seminary, 1968-69; adjunct professor and coordinator of doctoral program in religious studies at University of Pittsburgh, 1974-77. *Member:* American Society of Christian Ethics, American Academy of Religion, American Association of University Professors, Society for Values in Higher Education. *Awards, honors: Reinhold Niebuhr: Prophet to Politician* was named by *New York Times Book Review* as noteworthy title, 1972; Association of Theological Schools fellowships, 1972 and 1975.

WRITINGS: (Editor and author of introduction) *Reinhold Niebuhr, Faith and Politics: Essays on Religion, Social and Political Thought in a Technological Age,* Braziller, 1968; *Reinhold Niebuhr: Prophet to Politician,* Abingdon, 1972; *Realism and Hope* (essays), University Press of America, 1977; (editor and author of introduction) Gustavo Gutierrez and Richard M. Shaull, *Liberation and Change,* John Knox, 1977. Contributor to journals, including *Commonweal, Religion in Life, Christianity and Crisis,* and *Worldview.* Editor of *Social Action,* 1968.

BIOGRAPHICAL/CRITICAL SOURCES: New York Times Book Review, October 6, 1968, March 5, 1972; *Best Sellers,* February 15, 1972; *Commonweal,* May 5, 1972.

*　　*　　*

STOUT, George L(eslie) 1897-1978

October 5, 1897—July 1, 1978; American authority on art restoration and author. Stout was director of the Isabella Steward Gardner Museum in Boston before becoming a consultant at institutions on the West Coast. He was one of the first to use scientific techniques in restoring art works, and played a part in the development of camouflage during World War II. He also worked with a group concerned with monuments, fine arts, and archives, under the direction of Dwight D. Eisenhower. He wrote *Treasures From the Isabella Stewart Gardner Museum, The Care of Pictures,* and other books, in addition to articles for publications in his field. He died in Stanford, Calif. Obituaries and other sources: *Who's Who in American Art,* Bowker, 1973; *Who's Who in America,* 38th edition, Marquis, 1974; *Washington Post,* July 6, 1978.

*　　*　　*

STOWE, Leland 1899-

PERSONAL: Born November 10, 1899, in Southbury, Conn.; son of Frank Philip (in lumber business) and Eva Sarah (Noe) Stowe; married Ruth F. Bernot, September 27, 1924 (marriage ended); married Theodora F. Calauz, June

17, 1952; children: (first marriage) Bruce B., Alan A. *Education:* Wesleyan University, Middletown, Conn., B.A., 1921. *Politics:* Independent. *Religion:* Protestant. *Home:* 801 Greenhills Dr., Ann Arbor, Mich. 48105.

CAREER: Worcester Telegram, Worcester, Mass., reporter, 1921-22; *New York Herald,* New York City, staff reporter, 1923-24; news editor for *Pathe News,* 1924-26; *New York Herald Tribune,* New York City, staff reporter, 1924, 1926, Paris correspondent, 1926-35, political correspondent in North and South America, 1936-39; *Chicago Daily News,* Chicago, Ill., war correspondent in England, Finland, Norway, Hungary, Yugoslavia, Bulgaria, Romania, Turkey, Albania, and Greece, 1939-40, and in China, Burma, India, Thailand, Malaya, Indo-China, Iran, the Soviet Union, and Libya, 1941-43; American Broadcasting Co., New York City, radio commentator, 1944-46; lecturer and free-lance writer, 1947—; University of Michigan, Ann Arbor, professor of journalism, 1956—. Free-lance war correspondent in France, Belgium, and Germany, 1944, and Italy and Greece, 1945; radio commentator for Mutual Broadcasting System, 1945-46; director of news and information service of Radio Free Europe, 1952-54.

AWARDS, HONORS: Pulitzer prize for foreign correspondence, 1930, for covering events in Paris in 1929; Legion of Honor (France), 1931; M.A. from Wesleyan University, 1936, and Harvard University, 1945; distinguished service awards from Sigma Delta Chi, Overseas Press Club of America, and University of Missouri's School of Journalism, all 1941, for war reporting from Finland and Norway; LL.D. from Wesleyan University, 1944, and Hobart College, 1946; Military Cross (Greece), 1945; James L. McConaughty Award from Wesleyan University, 1963.

WRITINGS: Nazi Means War, Faber, 1933, Whittlesey House, 1934; *No Other Road to Freedom,* Knopf, 1941; *They Shall Not Sleep,* Knopf, 1943; *While Time Remains,* Knopf, 1946; *Target: You,* Random House, 1949; *Conquest by Terror: The Story of Satellite Europe,* Random House, 1951; *Crusoe of Lonesome Lake,* Random House, 1959. Contributor of about a hundred articles to national magazines, including *Life, Look, Nation, New Republic,* and *Harper's.* Foreign editor of *Reporter,* 1949-50; roving editor of *Reader's Digest,* 1955-76.

WORK IN PROGRESS: Research for a biography of Canadian frontiersman Tom Lamb of Manitoba.

SIDELIGHTS: Stowe writes that his chief motivation is "to inform the public in the United States and other countries of important political and social developments directly affecting their lives." His writings and lectures (totaling over three hundred in the United States) included major forewarnings of the coming of World War II (1933-39), the assured ultimate victory of Britain and her allies over Nazi Germany (1941-43), the spread of Communist regimes and controls in Europe and China as a result of World War II (1941-45), and the inevitable Soviet nuclear menace to the United States (1946-57).

He adds: "I am certain that the Soviet-American proliferation of nuclear missiles and other related weapons, still uncurbed, constitutes the greatest, almost inestimable peril not only to our people but to most of mankind. Next to this the energy crisis—certain to afflict Western nations in the 1980's—threatens to undermine, if not destroy, democratic governments, including our own and much or most of free enterprise systems as we now know them."

STRICKLAND, Charles E(verett)   1930-

PERSONAL: Born September 13, 1930, in Amarillo, Tex.; son of George Strum (a chef) and Bertha Irene (Barton) Strickland; married Eycke M. Laabs (a potter), December 8, 1956; children: Nils, Kirsten. *Education:* Southwest Missouri State College, B.S., 1952; further study at University of Copenhagen, 1953-54; University of Wisconsin, Madison, M.S., 1959, Ph.D., 1963. *Politics:* Democrat. *Religion:* Protestant. *Home:* 1787 Vickers Circle, Decatur, Ga. 30030. *Office:* Department of History, Emory University, Atlanta, Ga. 30322.

CAREER: American Forces Network, Frankfurt, Germany, reporter and newswriter, 1956-58; University of Wisconsin, Madison, assistant professor of history of education, 1962-63; Emory University, Atlanta, Ga., assistant professor, 1963-69, associate professor of history, 1969—. Research fellow at Charles Warren Center for Studies in American History, Harvard University, 1968-69; consultant to National Endowment for the Humanities. *Military service:* U.S. Army, 1955-57. *Member:* American Historical Association, Organization of American Historians, American Studies Association, History of Education Society (member of board of directors, 1969-70). *Awards, honors:* Fulbright fellow, 1953-54.

WRITINGS: (Editor with Charles Burgess) *Health, Growth, and Heredity: G. Stanley Hall on Natural Education,* Teachers College Press, 1965. Contributor to *Encyclopedia of Education.* Contributor to history and education journals.

WORK IN PROGRESS: The Family in the Art and Life of Louisa May Alcott; Success in America: The Myth and the Reality.

*   *   *

STROEYER, Poul   1923-

PERSONAL: Born July 13, 1923, in Copenhagen, Denmark; son of Peter Stroyer Pedersen and Olga Esbensen; married Solveig Lauritzen, August 20, 1947; children: Poul, Jr., Pia Marianne, Per-Erik. *Education:* Educated in Copenhagen, Denmark. *Home:* Ymervaegen 18, 182 63 Djursholm, Sweden.

CAREER: Writer; illustrator; cartoonist. Political cartoons, illustrations, and paintings have been exhibited in European countries, Canada, and Japan; paintings are represented in Swedish museums. *Member:* Association of Illustrators (Sweden), Organization of Artists (Sweden), Union of Authors (Sweden), Association of Journalists (Sweden). *Awards, honors:* German Children's Book prize, 1961, for *PP and His Big Horn;* Elsa Beskowplaketten, 1967, for children's books.

WRITINGS—All self-illustrated: *Bubus jungletur* (juvenile; title means "Bubus' Trip in the Jungle"), Wilhelm Hansen, 1948; *Stroeyers dagbook* (title means "Stroeyer's Daybook"), Almqvist & Wiksell, published annually, 1954—; *PP och hans stora horn* (juvenile; title means "PP and His Big Horn"), Almqvist & Wiksell, 1956; *Bytt aer bytt* (juvenile), Almqvist & Wiksell, 1960, translation by Maria Cimino published as *It's a Deal,* McDowell, Obolensky; *Utan ord* (title means "Without Words"), Almqvist & Wiksell, 1963; *PP fixar allt* (juvenile; title means "PP Fixes Everything"), Askild & Kaernekull, 1972; *Guld, Groenland och Transsib* (title means "Gold, Greenland and Transsib"), Almqvist & Wiksell, 1974.

Illustrator; juveniles: Sven Ingvar, *Alla tiders Joje,* Raben &

Sjoegren, 1950; Lennart Hellsing, *Summa summarum,* Raben & Sjoegren, 1950; Hellsing, *Den kraangliga kraakan,* Raben & Sjoegren, 1953, translation by Nancy and Edward Maze published as *The Cantankerous Crow,* Astor-Honor, 1962; Ingemar Hasselblad, *Agusta aaker ut,* O. Eklund, 1954; Gunnar Brolund, *Grabben paa maanen,* O. Eklund, 1954; Margit Holmberg, *Tre smaa skoeldpaddor,* O. Eklund, 1954; Hellsing, *Den flygande trumman,* Raben & Sjoegren, 1954; Hellsing, *Krakel Spektakel-boken,* Raben & Sjoegren, 1959; Hellsing, *ABC,* Raben & Sjoegren, 1961; Olle Holmberg, *Sotarpojken och prinsessan,* Bo Cavefors, 1964; *Sjoeroevarbok,* Raben & Sjoegren, 1965, translation by William J. Smith published as *The Pirate Book,* Delacorte, 1972; Hellsing, *Boken om Bagar Bengtsson,* Raben & Sjoegren, 1966; Hellsing, *Boken om Kasper,* Raben & Sjoegren, 1971; Hellsing, *Haer dansar herr gurka,* Raben & Sjoegren, 1977.

Illustrator; for adults: Gallie Akerhielm, *Konsten att tjusa mannen,* Wahlstroem & Widstrand, 1950; Edward Clausen and Knud Lundberg, *Aet, drick och var smaert,* Raben & Sjoegren, 1951; Clausen and Lundberg, *Mat som goer Er smaert,* Raben & Sjoegren, 1951; Clausen and Lundberg, *Baettre nerver—baettre humoer,* Raben & Sjoegren, 1953; Chic Sale, *The Specialist,* Forum, 1953; Torsten Ehrenmark, *Petmoijs besyaerligheter,* Lindqvists Foerlag, 1953; Cello, *Lika vaenligt somvanligt,* Gebers, 1953; Mark Spade, *Fagotter paa loepande band* (title means "How to Run a Bassoon Factory"), Forum, 1954; Ehrenmark, *Foer soemnloesa dagar,* Lindqvists Foerlag, 1954; Cello, *Saa, skoerda och saa vidare,* Gebers, 1954; Ehrenmark, *Petmoijs petitesser,* Lindqvists Foerlag, 1955; Cello, *Foerlaat en yngling,* Gebers, 1955; Herman Stolpe, *Boecker paa oede oe,* KFs Bokfoerlag, 1956; Axel Wallengren, *Falstaf Fakirs vitterlek,* Gebers, 1956; Cello, *Skum paa ytan,* Gebers, 1956; Stig Jaerrel, *Lapp pae luckan,* Wahlstroem & Widstrand, 1957; Cello, *Det gamla spelet om en far,* Gebers, 1957; Lundberg, *Fin form paa laett saett,* Raben & Sjoegren, 1958; Clausen and Lundberg, *Spis, drik og bliv sund,* Branner og Korch, 1958; Lundberg, *Bedre examen-lettere,* Branner og Korch, 1958; Cello, *Med pegasen i botten,* Gebers, 1958; Clausen, *Pengene og livet,* Branner og Korch, 1959; Cello, *Laett faerdiga stycken,* Gebers, 1959.

Bertil Gillqvist, *Saelj med Bertil Gillqvist,* Forum, 1960; Cello, *Bara foer lust,* Gebers, 1961; Cello, *Familjens flintis,* Gebers, 1962; Clausen, *Pengar aer inte allt,* Sparfraemjandets Foerlag, 1963; Cello, *En hoeg repriser till hoegre priser,* Gebers, 1963; Goeran Smith, *Service,* Prisma, 1964; Cello, *Aarsberaettelse,* Gebers, 1964; Cello, *Cellos glada ark,* Gebers, 1965; Cello, *Stora jubelboken,* Gebers, 1966; Axel Johansson, *Faafaengens kemi,* AV Carlsons, 1966; Ehrenmark, *Aarets Ehrenmark,* Aahlen & Aakerlunds Foerlag, published annually, 1966—; Cello, *Valsen gaar,* Gebers, 1967; Cello, *Cellos lilla lila,* Gebers, 1968; Cello, *Cellos godbitar,* Gebers, 1969.

Cello, *Bland tomtar och troll,* Gebers, 1970; Bertil Dahlgren, *Laerarens lilla groena,* Tempus Foerlag, 1970; Maj-Britt Baehrendtz, *Roer paa dig,* LTs Foerlag, 1970; Ehrenmark, *En smoergaasaetares bekaennelser,* Askild & Kaernekull, 1970; Cello, *Rapport fraan kaasoergaarden,* Gebers, 1971; Cello, *Till min egen lilla skatt,* Gebers, 1972; Ning-tsu Malmqvist, *Att aeta med pinnar i Sverige,* Forum, 1972.

Creator of a daily political cartoon "Stroeyers dagbok" (title means "Stroeyer's Daybook"), in *Dagens Nyheter,* Stockholm (a daily newspaper). Contributor of articles to *Dagens Nyheter.* Author of television scripts.

SIDELIGHTS: Poul Stroeyer wrote and illustrated his first children's book in one day, when he was twenty years old. It was published four years later. "Luckily," he told *CA,* "I lived in Sweden at that time and was therefore spared the awful experience of reading the reviews, with the exception of one which my parents forwarded to me from Denmark. This particular review stated—if my memory does not fail me—that 'the drawings are better than the text.' I felt that the reviewer had been very kind, since I had expected the verdict that the text was even worse than the drawings.

"In any event, I decided to abstain from writing the text of children's books and instead be content with illustrating them. It was not until 1956 that I dared to try a second time and now I wrote in Swedish, my acquired language. This book, *PP and His Big Horn,* later appeared in Germany where it was awarded the German Children's Book prize."

Stroeyer's books have been translated into Danish, German, English, and Japanese. He has traveled to approximately seventy countries.

*   *   *

STROYER, Poul
See STROEYER, Poul

*   *   *

STRUTTON, William Harold 1918-

PERSONAL: Born February 23, 1918, in Moonta, South Australia; son of Cecil George (a banker) and Mabel (Phillips) Strutton; married Louise Virginia O'Hara Hibbert, April 10, 1970; children: Mark, Julia, Amanda. *Education:* Attended Adelaide University. *Home:* Osbrooks, Capel, Surrey RH5 5JN, England. *Agent:* John Farquharson Ltd., 15 Red Lion Sq., London WC1R 4QW, England.

CAREER: Journalist, novelist, and author of scripts for film and television. Australian Consolidated Press, Adelaide, member of London bureau, 1945-58. *Military service:* Australian Army; became sergeant. *Member:* Writers Guild, Crime Writers Association, Critics Circle.

WRITINGS: A Jury of Angels, Hodder & Stoughton, 1957; (with Michael Pearson) *The Secret Invaders,* Hodder & Stoughton, 1958, British Book Center, 1959, published as *The Beachhead Spies,* Ace Books; *Island of Terrible Friends,* Hodder & Stoughton, 1961, Norton, 1962; *Doctor Who and the Zarbi,* Frederick Muller, 1965; *The Carpaccio Caper,* Coward, 1973 (published in England as *A Glut of Virgins,* William Macdonald, 1974).

Also author of screenplays, including "Assignment K," Columbia Pictures, 1968, and documentary screenplays for Rank Organisation.

WORK IN PROGRESS: No False Dawn, for Macdonald & James; *A Ghost From Iberia.*

SIDELIGHTS: Strutton told *CA* that his interests are catholic, "but with special emphasis on art, crime and travel." He has traveled widely in Western Europe and the Middle and Far East.

*   *   *

SUESSMAN, Irving 1908-

PERSONAL: Born December 25, 1908, in New York, N.Y.; son of Samuel A. (a diamond merchant) and Elka (Shurack) Suessman; married Cornelia Jessey (a writer), May 6, 1932. *Education:* University of California, Los Angeles, B.A., 1929, M.A., 1932, Ph.D., 1936; also attended

University of California, Berkeley, 1930-36, and Boalt School of Law, 1930-35. *Politics:* Democrat. *Religion:* Roman Catholic. *Home:* 269 Cypress Dr., #1, Laguna Beach, Calif. 92651. *Office: Way,* 109 Golden Gate Ave., San Francisco, Calif. 94109.

CAREER: Actor with MacLoon Productions, Los Angeles, Calif., 1929-32, and Stratford-on-Avon Shakespearean Co., 1931; English teacher at public schools in Oakland and Riverside, Calif., 1934-70, chairman of department, 1950-70. Professor of English at Dominican College, San Rafael, Calif., 1936-39. Guest lecturer at colleges and universities in California, Arizona, and Colorado. Producer at Don Quixote Marionette Theatre; director for Oakland Children's Theatre; has appeared in feature films. *Member:* International P.E.N., Authors Guild of Authors League of America, Third Order of St. Francis.

WRITINGS: (With wife, Cornelia Suessman) *The Pilgrim Reader,* Herald Press, 1966; (with C. Suessman) *How to Read a Dirty Book,* Templegate, 1967; (with C. Suessman) *This Train Is Bound for Glory,* Herald Press, 1969; (with C. Suessman) *As Others See Us,* Sheed, 1971; (with C. Suessman) *Thomas Merton: A Biography,* Macmillan, 1977.

Plays: "Lot's Wife" (two-act), first produced in Berkeley, Calif., at Little Theatre, 1935; "Francis and Lady Poverty" (one-act), first produced in California at San Juan Bautista Mission Auditorium, 1976.

Contributor of several hundred articles, poems, and reviews to magazines, including *Saturday Review, America, Catholic Digest,* and *Desert Call.* Contributing editor of *Way.*

WORK IN PROGRESS: A Marvelous Piece of Luck, a novel; *Engendered Into Morning,* a novel; *The Eve Helix and the Damascus Connection,* a book on creative interpretations of literature and Scripture.

SIDELIGHTS: Suessman comments: "The thrust of my writing: humanism, religious humanism, civil rights, art, creativity, language, literature, reading—what our humanity is about! I am also a painter and have exhibited my work in Palm Springs and San Francisco. My paintings (a series of creative biblical interpretations) have appeared in *Way* magazine over a period of years."

*   *   *

SUGGS, Willie Kathryn 1950-

PERSONAL: Born October 7, 1950, in Holly Springs, Miss.; daughter of Wilson Cedell (a repairman) and Catherine (Snow) Suggs. *Education:* Marquette University, B.A., 1972; Columbia University, M.A., 1973. *Home:* 503 West 121st St., New York, N.Y. 10027. *Agent:* Helen Merrill, 337 West 22nd St., New York, N.Y. 10011. *Office:* ABC-TV, 7 West 66th St., New York, N.Y. 10023.

CAREER/WRITINGS: WITI-TV6, Milwaukee, Wis., reporter, film editor, producer, 1968-72; American Broadcasting Co. (ABC), New York, N.Y., production associate, 1972-73, newswriter and assignment editor for ABC Evening News, 1973, writer, researcher, and field producer of series, "Americans All," 1973-75, writer, producer, and editor of network news syndication, 1976—. Notable assignments include coverage of the McGovern-Shriver campaign, 1972, and the Nixon inaugural, 1973. Contributor to *Confrontation/Change Review, Essence, Unique,* and *Black Enterprise.* Member of Frederick Douglass Creative Arts Center and New York Upbeat. *Member:* Writers Guild of America, East. *Awards, honors:* Received awards from National Association of Media Women, 1975, for "Puerto Ri-

can Traveling Theater," and 1976, for "My Name Is John Belindo," "An Interview With Diana Ross," "Dr. Jane Wright," and "New Orleans and All That Jazz."

WORK IN PROGRESS: A novel about a local television station; a collection of short stories; a history of theatre; a textbook on contemporary broadcast news.

SIDELIGHTS: Suggs told *CA:* "Television news is the most exciting journalism writing today. To coherently marry script to picture is a craft requiring an intimate knowledge of two completely different fields. This complexity makes the achievement all the more rewarding. The discipline required to write under pressure for a specified length, to embellish when the picture fails, and even more important, to know when few if any words are necessary, is the surest test of a writer's abilities. To write well, it is necessary to be well read. Journalists are notoriously bookish. The natural extension for a journalist, print or broadcast, is the truly creative writing of novels, short stories, and poetry."

AVOCATIONAL INTERESTS: Photography, horseback riding, documentaries and foreign films, reading, travel.

*   *   *

SULLIVAN, Michael B. 1938-

PERSONAL: Born June 17, 1938; married. *Education:* Earned A.B. from Fordham College, and M.S. from Columbia University. *Home:* 14, rue Michel Servet, 1206 Geneva, Switzerland.

CAREER/WRITINGS: Providence Journal, Providence, R.I., reporter, 1964; *Barron's,* New York City, associate editor, 1964-65; free-lance journalist in Cairo, Egypt, 1965-67; McGraw-Hill World News, Paris, France, staff correspondent, 1967-75; *Business International,* New York City, editorial director for Middle East region based in Geneva, Switzerland, 1975—. Notable assignments include coverage of economic, technological, financial, and industrial developments in France and economic and business conditions in the Middle East. Former contributor to *Business Week, Newsweek, New York Herald-Tribune,* and other periodicals. Writer of book-length reports on individual Middle East countries. *Awards, honors:* Fulbright fellowship in Arab Affairs at American University in Cairo, 1965-66.

*   *   *

SULLIVAN, Richard 1908-

PERSONAL: Born November 29, 1908, in Kenosha, Wis.; son of Thomas A. (a merchant) and Rose (Pitts) Sullivan; married Mabel Priddis, May 2, 1932; children: Jill Sullivan Keiffer, Molly. *Education:* University of Notre Dame, A.B., 1930; also attended Art Institute of Chicago, 1930-31. *Religion:* Roman Catholic. *Home:* 1093 Riverside Dr., South Bend, Ind. 46616. *Agent:* Russell & Volkening, Inc., 551 Fifth Ave., New York, N.Y. 10017. *Office:* Memorial Library, University of Notre Dame, G-3, Notre Dame, Ind. 46556.

CAREER: Free-lance writer, 1931-36; University of Notre Dame, Notre Dame, Ind., member of faculty, 1936-52, professor of English, 1952-76; free-lance writer, 1976—.

WRITINGS: Our Lady's Tumbler (one-act play), Dramatic Publishing, 1940; *Summer After Summer* (novel), Doubleday, 1942; *Dark Continent* (novel), Doubleday, 1943; *The World of Idella May* (novel), Doubleday, 1946; *First Citizen* (novel), Holt, 1948; *Fresh and Open Sky* (stories), Holt, 1950; *Notre Dame* (nonfiction), Holt, 1951; *311 Congress Court* (novel), Holt, 1953; *The Three Kings* (novel), Harcourt, 1956.

Also author of radio and television plays. Work represented in anthologies. Contributor of about seventy-five stories and one thousand reviews to newspapers.

WORK IN PROGRESS: A novel; stories and poems.

* * *

SULLIVAN, Sheila 1927-
(Sheila Bathurst)

PERSONAL: Born January 29, 1927, in Malaya; daughter of Henry (a civil servant) and Georgina (a psychologist; maiden name, McCormick) Bathurst; married David Sullivan (a barrister), August 16, 1952; children: Oriel, Tessa, Jocelyn. *Education:* Oxford University, M.A. (honors), 1948. *Religion:* None. *Home:* Wyldes, North End, London N.W.3, England. *Agent:* Curtis Brown Ltd., 1 Craven Hill, London, England.

CAREER: Oxford University Press, Oxford, England, member of publicity and editorial staffs, 1948-51; French Lycee de London, London, England, teacher of English, 1952-55; free-lance writer and editor, 1955—. *Member:* Friends of the Earth, Conservation Society.

WRITINGS: (Under name Sheila Bathurst) *The Blind Beggar's Daughter* (children's opera libretto), Novello, 1951; (editor) *Critics on Chaucer,* Allen & Unwin, 1971; (editor) *Critics on T. S. Eliot,* Allen & Unwin, 1972; *Summer Rising* (novel), Weidenfeld & Nicolson, 1975; (contributor and illustrations editor), Margaret Drabble, editor, *The Genius of Thomas Hardy,* Weidenfeld & Nicolson, 1976.

WORK IN PROGRESS: A sequel to *Summer Rising.*

SIDELIGHTS: Sheila Sullivan comments briefly: "I am deeply interested in problems of ecology and the environment, the care (now and in the future) of this planet, and possible alternative futures of man on earth."

* * *

SUMMERS, Robert 1922-

PERSONAL: Born June 20, 1922, in Gary, Ind.; son of Frank (a pharmacist) and Ella (Lipton) Samuelson; married Anita Arrow (an economist), March 29, 1953; children: Lawrence Henry, Richard Frederic, John Steven. *Education:* University of Chicago, B.S., 1943; further study at King's College, Cambridge, 1951-52; Stanford University, Ph.D., 1956. *Home:* 641 Revere Rd., Merion Station, Pa. 19066. *Office:* Department of Economics, University of Pennsylvania, Philadelphia, Pa. 19066.

CAREER: Stanford University, Stanford, Calif., instructor in economics, 1949-50, research associate, 1950-51; Yale University, New Haven, Conn., instructor, 1952-56, assistant professor of economics, 1956-59, staff member of Cowles Foundation for Research in Economics, 1955-59; University of Pennsylvania, Philadelphia, associate professor, 1959-67, professor of economics, 1967—. Visiting professor at Rutgers University, 1964—. Economist for RAND Corp., 1959-60, consultant, 1960—. *Military service:* U.S. Army, 1944-46.

MEMBER: International Association for Research on Income and Wealth, American Economic Association, American Statistical Association, Econometric Society, American Association of University Professors. *Awards, honors:* Social Science Research Council fellowship for Cambridge University, 1951-52; National Science Foundation grants, 1957-59, 1963-66; Ford Foundation fellowship for London School of Economics and Political Science, 1966-67; M.A. from University of Pennsylvania, 1971.

WRITINGS: (Co-author) *A System of International Comparisons of Gross Product and Purchasing Power,* Johns Hopkins Press, 1965; (with Lawrence R. Klein) *The Wharton Index of Capacity Utilization,* Economic Research Unit, University of Pennsylvania, 1966; (with T. Marschak and T. Glennan) *Strategy for Research and Development,* Springer-Verlag, 1967; (co-author) *Studies in the Microeconomics of Development,* Springer-Verlag, 1967. Contributor to economics journals.

WORK IN PROGRESS: A book on international comparisons.

* * *

SUTHERLAND, Margaret 1941-

PERSONAL: Born September 16, 1941, in Auckland, New Zealand; daughter of William Charles and Dorothy Genevieve (Bolton) Mansfield; married Alan Sutherland (a business consultant), December 12, 1959; children: Roger Anthony, Claire Frances, David Alan. *Education:* Educated in Auckland, New Zealand. *Religion:* "Subud." *Home:* 16 Manuka Rd., Titirangi, Auckland, New Zealand.

CAREER: Writer, 1968—.

WRITINGS: *The Fledgling* (novel), Heinemann, 1974; *Hello, I'm Karen* (juvenile), Methuen, 1974, Coward, 1976; *The Love Contract* (novel), Heinemann, 1976; *Getting Through* (stories), Heinemann, 1977.

SIDELIGHTS: Margaret Sutherland writes: "I like to write for pleasure and discovery. There are a lot of other things I enjoy, like music, animals, my home and family, and thinking about God. I am training to be a nurse. I started this before I got married, and did not expect to be able to finish it. Now I know that if I don't mind working at it, I can do most things I am drawn to."

* * *

SUTTON, Felix 1910(?)-

PERSONAL: Born in West Virginia. *Education:* Earned diploma from West Virginia University. *Residence:* Wilton, Conn.

CAREER: Has worked as a sports reporter and as a copy writer for an advertising agency; author of books for young people.

WRITINGS: *The Big Book of Dogs* (illustrated by Percy Leason), Grosset, 1952; *Mighty Mouse* (illustrated by Chad), Treasure Books, 1953; *Mighty Mouse: Dinky Learns to Fly* (illustrated by Chad), Treasure Books, 1953; *The Big Treasure Book of Wheels: 70 Things that Move on Wheels* (illustrated by Art Seiden), Grosset, 1953, published as *The Big Book of Wheels: 70 Things that Move on Wheels,* 1965; *The Big Treasure Book of Clowns* (illustrated by James Schucker), Grosset, 1953, published as *The Book of Clowns,* 1966; *Mighty Mouse and the Sacred Scarecrow* (illustrated by Chad), Treasure Books, 1954; *The Big Book of Cars* (illustrated by Tom Hill), Grosset, 1954; *The Magic Clown* (illustrated by Schucker), Treasure Books, 1954; *Let's Take a Trip in Our Car* (illustrated by Schucker), Treasure Books, 1954; *The Big Book of Wild Animals* (illustrated by Bob Kuhn), Grosset, 1954; *The Nine Friendly Dogs* (illustrated by June Goldsborough), Wonder Books, 1954; (with Gladys E. Cook) *The Big Book of Cats,* Grosset, 1954.

Adventures of the Range Rider (illustrated by Louis Glanzman), Wonder Books, 1955; *The Terry Bears Win the Cub*

Scout Badge (illustrated by J. Robert Moore), Treasure Books, 1955; *Mighty Mouse, Santa's Helper* (illustrated by Chad), Treasure Books, 1955; *The Picture Story of Davy Crockett* (illustrated by H. B. Vestal), Wonder Books, 1955; *Daniel Boone* (illustrated by De Witt Whistler Jayne), Grosset, 1956; *Wild Bill Hickok* (illustrated by Jon Nielsen), Wonder Books, 1956; *We Were There at the Battle of Lexington and Concord* (illustrated by Vestal), Grosset, 1958; *We Were There at Pearl Harbor* (illustrated by Frank Vaughn), Grosset, 1957; (with Leon A. Hausman) *The Illustrated Book of the Sea* (illustrated by Art Renshaw and Herman Bischoff), Grosset, 1957; *Skin Diving for Sunken Treasure*, Young America Books, 1957; *Dangerous Safari: Big Game Hunting in Africa*, Young America Books, 1958; (with Leon Jason) *The Terrytoons Playhouse* (illustrated by Chad), Grosset, 1958; *Hot Rock of Hondo: Prospecting for Uranium in the Western Badlands*, Young America Books, 1958; *The Illustrated Book about Africa* (illustrated by Vestal), Grosset, 1959.

Big Game Hunter: Carl Akeley, Messner, 1960; *The How and Why Wonder Book of Our Earth* (illustrated by John Hull), Grosset, 1960; *The Planet We Live On* (illustrated by Hull), Grosset, 1960; *We Were There at the First Airplane Flight* (illustrated by Laszlo Matulay), Grosset, 1960; *The City under the Sea*, Duell, Sloan, 1961; *The Valiant Virginian: Stonewall Jackson*, Messner, 1961; *The How and Why Wonder Book of World War II* (illustrated by Darrell Sweet), Grosset, 1962; (with Charles F. Gieg) *The Last Voyage of the Albatross*, Duell, Sloan, 1962; *The Big Book of Dogs* (illustrated by Percy Leason), Grosset, 1962; *The Illustrated Book about Europe* (illustrated by Hull), Grosset, 1962; *The How and Why Wonder Book of Winning of the West* (illustrated by Leonard Vosburgh), Grosset, 1963; *The How and Why Wonder Book of the Moon* (illustrated by Raul Mina Mora), Grosset, 1963; *The How and Why Wonder Book of the American Revolution* (illustrated by Vosburgh), Grosset, 1963; *Horses of America* (illustrated by Walter J. Wilwerding), Putnam, 1964; *The How and Why Wonder Book of the First World War* (illustrated by Robert Doremus), Grosset, 1964; *The How and Why Wonder Book of North American Indians* (illustrated by Vosburgh), Grosset, 1965; (with Earl S. Miers) *America During Four Wars* (illustrated by Vosburgh), Grosset, 1965; (with V. Phillips Weaver) *Discoverers of America: Primitive Man to Spanish Conquerors* (illustrated by Vosburgh), Grosset, 1965.

The How and Why Wonder Book of Deserts, Grosset, 1966; *West Virginia*, Coward, 1968; *Master of Ballyhoo: The Story of P. T. Barnum*, Putnam, 1968; *The How and Why Wonder Book of Our Earth* (illustrated by Hull), Grosset, 1969; *Getting to Know Virginia* (illustrated by Paul Frame), Coward, 1969; (with Alvin Maurer) *Conquest of the Moon* (illustrated by R. M. Mora), Grosset, 1969; *Sons of Liberty* (illustrated by Bill Barss), Messner, 1969; *Indian Chiefs of the West* (illustrated by Russell Hoover), Messner, 1970; *The Big Show: A History of the Circus*, Doubleday, 1971.

Adapter of books for children, including, Eric M. Knight, *Lassie Come-Home;* Johanna Spyri, *Heidi: Child of the Mountains;* Mark Twain, *Adventures of Tom Sawyer;* Herman Melville, *Moby Dick;* Albert P. Terhune, *Lad, a Dog;* Johann D. Wyss, *The Swiss Family Robinson;* Robert Louis Stevenson, *Kidnapped.*

BIOGRAPHICAL/CRITICAL SOURCES: Kirkus, July 1, 1959; *Saturday Review,* May 7, 1960.*

SUTTON, Robert M(ize)   1915-

PERSONAL: Born December 15, 1915, in Bunker Hill, Ill.; son of Robert E. Lee (a postal employee) and Mary E. (Mize) Sutton; married Elizabeth S. Blair, June 19, 1942; children: Sarah M. Sutton Mager, William R., David B., Mary E. Sutton Vitoux. *Education:* Shurtleff College, A.B., 1937; University of Illinois, A.M., 1938, Ph.D., 1948. *Politics:* Independent. *Religion:* Baptist. *Home:* 1207 South Busey Ave., Urbana, Ill. 61801. *Office:* Department of History, University of Illinois, 309 Gregory Hall, Urbana, Ill. 61801.

CAREER: High school history teacher in Bunker Hill, Ill., 1938-42; University of Illinois, Urbana, instructor, 1948-51, assistant professor, 1951-57, associate professor, 1957-63, professor of history, 1963—, chairman of department, 1972-74, associate dean of Graduate College, 1958-66, director of Illinois Historical Survey, 1964—. Member of board of trustees of Northern Baptist Theological Seminary. *Military service:* U.S. Army Air Forces, 1942-46; became staff sergeant.

MEMBER: American Historical Association, Organization of American Historians, American Association for State and Local History, Illinois Historical Society (past president; past member of board of directors), Urbana Exchange Club (president, 1973), Phi Kappa Phi. *Awards, honors:* D.H.L. from Wheaton College, Wheaton, Ill., 1971.

WRITINGS: (With Fritiof Ander and others) *Lincoln Images,* Augustana Book Concern, 1960; *A History of Illinois in Paintings,* University of Illinois Press, 1968; *The Heartland: Pages from Illinois History,* Deerpath Publishing, 1975; (with Maynard J. Brickford and Dennis F. Walle) *Manuscripts Guide to Collections at the University of Illinois at Urbana-Champaign,* University of Illinois Press, 1976.

Contributor to academic journals. Member of board of editors of *Chicago History* and *Illinois Studies in the Social Studies.*

WORK IN PROGRESS: Illinois: The Forgotten Years, 1772-1778.

SIDELIGHTS: Sutton writes: "The history of Illinois which now covers more than three centuries of discovery, exploration, settlement, and development is exciting and full of variety, and its study is rich and rewarding. Her lands have been occupied successively by Indians, Frenchmen, Englishmen, and Americans of many national backgrounds. Competing interests and sharply conflicting points of view have clashed within her borders. She has furnished important figures in almost every realm of human activity—leaders in government at the state, national, and international levels as well as pathfinders and pacesetters in the fields of religion, education, science, commerce, and industry. No wonder the closing words of the official state song read: 'Not without thy wondrous story, Illinois, can be writ the nation's glory, Illinois.' "

*   *   *

SWANSON, Gloria Borseth   1927-

PERSONAL: Born May 14, 1927, in Red Wing, Minn.; daughter of Olaf M. (in sales) and Edythe (a violinist; maiden name, Grow) Borseth; married John Leonard Swanson (a store manager), June 1, 1957; children: Thomas John, Ann Marie. *Education:* Macalester College, B.A., 1951; further study at University of Minnesota, 1954-55, 1965-66. *Politics:* Independent Republican. *Religion:* Protestant. *Home address:* Box E, Hallock, Minn. 56728.

CAREER: Teacher of English and music in elementary and high schools in Henderson, Minn., 1951-54, Kasson-Mantorville, Minn., 1954-55, Albert Lea, Minn., 1955-56, and Hallock, Minn., 1958-59; remedial reading teacher, 1968-69; currently substitute teacher. Piano teacher, 1962—. Member of board of trustees of local library; church choir director and organist. *Member:* Hallock Federated Women's Club.

WRITINGS: (Contributor) *Our Northwest Corner,* Taylor Publishing, 1976; (with Virginia Ott) *The Man with a Million Ideas: Fred Jones, Genius Inventor,* Lerner, 1977. Author of several dozen columns for local newspaper, *Kittson County Enterprise.*

WORK IN PROGRESS: For children, a biography of Dr. Anne Carlsen, administrator of Jamestown, N.D., Crippled Children's School and Hospital.

SIDELIGHTS: Gloria Swanson comments: "The black inventor, Fred McKinley Jones, spent eighteen years of his life in Hallock, Minn., a town of fifteen hundred, far from the city where he eventually became an important pioneer in transport refrigeration. Writing his biography and seeing it published proves that a writer can find material wherever he or she happens to be! When people ask me why I do not quit giving piano lessons and concentrate on writing, my reply is, 'I make more money giving piano lessons!' My writing is done in rare spare moments. It is an enjoyable hobby."

* * *

SWANSON, Gustav A. 1910-

PERSONAL: Born February 13, 1910, in Minn.; son of Gustaf A. (an electrician) and Pauline H. Swanson; married Evadene Burris (a writer); children: Hildegarde Swanson Morgan, Evedene Swanson Gale, Arthur B. *Education:* University of Minnesota, B.A., 1930, M.A., 1932, Ph.D., 1937. *Politics:* Independent. *Home:* 620 Mathews, #115, Fort Collins, Colo. 80521. *Office:* Department of Fishery & Wildlife, Colorado State University, Fort Collins, Colo. 80523.

CAREER: University of Minnesota, Minneapolis, assistant professor, 1937-44, associate professor of wildlife management, 1942-44; U.S. Department of the Interior, Fish & Wildlife Service, Washington, D.C., chief of Division of Wildlife, 1946-48; Cornell University, Ithaca, N.Y., professor of conservation, 1948-66, head of department, 1948-66, executive director of Laboratory of Ornithology, 1958-61; Colorado State University, Fort Collins, professor of wildlife administration, law, and policy, and head of department of fishery and wildlife biology, 1966-75, professor emeritus, 1975—. Member of National Academy of Sciences/National Research Council board on agriculture and renewable resources, 1974-77; consultant to New York State Joint Legislative Committee on Natural Resources and to National Wildlife Federation and Nature Conservancy (England).

MEMBER: International Association of Wildlife Agencies, American Ornithologists Union, American Association for the Advancement of Science (fellow), American Institute of Biological Sciences, National Audubon Society (member of board of directors, 1950-56), American Society of Mammalogists, National Wildlife Federation, Wildlife Society (honorary member; president, 1954-55), Wilson Ornithological Society (treasurer, 1938-42). *Awards, honors:* Fulbright fellow in Denmark, 1961-62, and at University of New England (Australia), 1968; fellow of Rochester Museum, 1956; Aldo Leopold Memorial Medal from Wildlife Society, 1973.

WRITINGS: (With Thaddeus Surber and T. S. Roberts) *Mammals of Minnesota,* Minnesota Department of Conservation, 1945; (editor) *The Use and Effects of Pesticides,* New York Joint Committee on Natural Resources, 1963; (with Theodore Shields and others) *Fish and Wildlife Resources on the Public Lands,* Colorado State University, 1969; (with D. R. Allardance, G. E. Radosevich, K. E. Koebel) *Water Law in Relation to Environmental Quality,* Colorado State University, 1974. Also contributor to *Wildlife in America,* edited by Howard Brokaw, 1978. Contributor to scientific journals. Editor of *Journal of Wildlife Management,* 1949-53.

WORK IN PROGRESS: A book on wildlife administration, law, and policy, with John Gottschalk; a book on management of non-game birds, with R. A. Ryder.

SIDELIGHTS: Swanson comments: "I have been interested in wildlife, especially birds, and natural history all my life, and count it good fortune to have been able to have a career in this general area, which has also served as my hobby."

BIOGRAPHICAL/CRITICAL SOURCES: *Journal of Wildlife Management,* Volume XXXVII, number 3, 1973.

* * *

SWARTHOUT, Doris L(ouise) 1931-

PERSONAL: Born April 26, 1931, in Utica, N.Y.; daughter of Maurice A. (a laborer) and Mildred (Mace) Bickford; married Dick L. Swarthout (a teacher and bookseller), June 18, 1950; children: Douglas, Dawn. *Education:* Attended high school in Lock Haven, Pa. *Politics:* Republican. *Religion:* Unitarian-Universalist. *Home:* Berry Hill Farm, Deansboro, N.Y. 13328.

CAREER: Berry Hill Book Shop (rare and used books), Deansboro, N.Y., co-owner, 1968—.

WRITINGS: *An Age of Flowers: Nature—Sense and Sentiment in Victorian America* (Ecological Book Club selection), Chatham Press, 1975. Contributor to magazines, including *Americana* and *Nineteenth Century.*

WORK IN PROGRESS: *A Practical Guide for the Sentimental Garden;* research for a book on the life and work of poet Clinton Scollard; *Representative American Women Illustrators, 1880-1915.*

SIDELIGHTS: Aside from her work in the book shop, Doris Swarthout collects rare nineteenth-century books and maps, as well as other "paper antiques" such as cards and posters. She has been recognized as an authority on Victorian times, but her major interest is in the Victorian woman, the subject of many of her lectures.

AVOCATIONAL INTERESTS: Organic gardening, flowers (especially Victorian roses), raising rare and exotic poultry.

BIOGRAPHICAL/CRITICAL SOURCES: *Utica Observer-Dispatch,* January 23, 1977.

* * *

SWEET, Paul R(obinson) 1907-

PERSONAL: Born March 14, 1907, in Willow Grove, Pa.; son of William Warren (a historian) and Louise M. (Neill) Sweet; married Katharyn Grummann, 1937; children: Sarah (Mrs. Gerald Rosen), William Walker. *Education:* DePauw University, A.B., 1929; attended University of Goettingen and University of Munich, 1929-30, and University of Chicago, 1930-31; University of Wisconsin, Madison, Ph.D., 1934. *Home:* 443 Clifton Blvd., East Lansing, Mich. 48823.

CAREER: Associated with Birmingham-Southern College, Birmingham, Ala., 1934-36; Bates College, Lewiston, Maine, assistant professor of history, 1936-45; University of Chicago, Chicago, Ill., assistant professor of history, 1946-47; Colby College, Waterville, Maine, associate professor of history, 1947-48; U.S. Department of State, Washington, D.C., editor-in-chief of "Documents on German Foreign Policy, 1918-1945," 1948-59, first secretary at American embassy in Bonn, Germany, 1959-63, consul-general at consulate in Stuttgart, Germany, 1963-67; Michigan State University, East Lansing, professor of history, 1968—. Member: American Historical Association. Awards, honors: Medal of Freedom award.

WRITINGS: Friedrich von Gentz: Defender of the Old Order, University of Wisconsin Press, 1941, reprinted, Greenwood Press, 1970; (with others) The Tragedy of Austria, Gollancz, 1948; Wilhelm von Humboldt: A Biography, Ohio State University Press, Volume I: 1767-1808, 1978, Volume II: 1808-1835, in press. Also co-author of Festschrift fuer Heinrich Benedikt, 1957. Contributor to history and philosophy journals.

*   *   *

SWENSON, Allan A(rmstrong)   1933-

PERSONAL: Born December 26, 1933, in Passaic, N.J.; son of Harold O. (an attorney) and Amy T. (Dugdale) Swenson; married Sheila Jane Kerr Haglund; children: Peter Jon, Drew Erik, Boyd Allan, Meade Christopher. Education: Rutgers University, B.A., 1955. Religion: Protestant. Home address: Windrows Farm, P.O. Box 94, Kennebunk, Maine 04043. Agent: Anita Diamant, Writer's Workshop, Inc., 52 East 42nd St., New York, N.Y. 10017.

CAREER: National Broadcasting Co., New York, N.Y., writer and producer of garden and farm programs for radio and television, 1955; Armstrong Associates, Inc. (nursery and house plant mail order business), Basking Ridge, N.J. and Kennebunk, Maine, owner and president, 1957—. Writer, 1955—. Host of "Gardener's Notebook" for Enterprise Broadcast Features, 1966; appears regularly on "Good Day," WCVB-TV; producer of syndicated radio programs and television specials. Lecturer and garden consultant. Military service: U.S. Army, Intelligence, 1955-57; became captain.

MEMBER: American Society of Authors and Journalists, American Federation of Radio and Television Artists, International Horticultural Fellowship of Rotarians, Garden Writers of America, Overseas Press Club, Deadline Club, Sigma Delta Chi.

WRITINGS: The Practical Book of Organic Gardening, Award Books, 1974; Inflation Fighter's Victory Gardening, Ballantine, 1975; Terrariums: Your Complete Guide, Fawcett, 1975; My Own Herb Garden (juvenile), Rodale Press, 1976; Allan A. Swenson's Big Fun to Grow Book (juvenile), McKay, 1977; Cultivating Carnivorous Plants, Doubleday, 1977; World Beneath Your Feet, McKay, 1978; World Above Your Head, McKay, 1978; Starting Over, A & W Publishing, 1978; Plan Your Own Landscape, Grosset & Dunlap, 1978; Landscape You Can Eat, McKay, 1978.

Author of "Gardener's Notebook," a column syndicated by Newspaper Enterprise Association to about three hundred fifty newspapers, 1958—. Contributor to outdoor and farm journals.

WORK IN PROGRESS: Nine books; The Gardener's Almanac.

SIDELIGHTS: Swenson told CA: "I have a philosophy, if it's good news, dig it out and write about it, whether gardening books, children's books, nature books, columns or radio-tv shows. The world needs and wants good news, so I concentrate on it."

*   *   *

SWENSSON, Paul S.   1907-

PERSONAL: Born November 11, 1907, in Woburn, Mass.; son of G. Sigfried and Minnie E. (Hamburg) Swensson; married Mildred G. C. Johnson, July 4, 1932; children: J. Kenneth, Paula Kay Cerkvenik. Education: Gustave Adolphus College, B.A., 1928. Home: 11130 Wedge Rd., Reston, Va.

CAREER/WRITINGS: Minneapolis Tribune, Minneapolis, Minn., managing editor, 1950-55; Minneapolis Star, Minneapolis, managing editor, 1956-61; Wall Street Journal Foundation, New York, N.Y., executive director of the newspaper fund, 1961-68; Temple University, Philadelphia, Pa., professor, 1968-70; American Press Institute, Reston, Va., director, 1971-75; newspaper consultant in Reston, 1975—. Contributor of articles to journalism publications and to Encyclopedia for Education, Volume 5. Awards, honors: D.H.L. from Gustave Adolphus College, 1961.

*   *   *

SYDNOR, Charles W(right), Jr.   1943-

PERSONAL: Born August 26, 1943, in Jefferson City, Tenn.; son of Charles W. (an attorney) and Frances Q. (a teacher) Sydnor; married Linda Edwards (a teacher), June 19, 1965; children: Matthew David, Daniel Charles, Emily Ruth-Marie. Education: Emory & Henry College, B.A., 1965; Vanderbilt University, M.A., 1967, Ph.D., 1971; attended Albert-Ludwigs Universitaet, 1968-69. Religion: Methodist. Home address: Box 26-J, Fox Hill Rd., Rice, Va. 23966. Office: Department of History, Longwood College, Farmville, Va. 23901.

CAREER: Ohio State University, Columbus, instructor in history, 1969-72; Longwood College, Farmville, Va., assistant professor, 1972-77, associate professor of history, 1977—. President and chairman of board of directors of Research Productions Ltd., 1975—. Visiting assistant professor at Vanderbilt University, summer, 1974. Member: Conference Group for Central European History, American Committee for the History of the Second World War, Southern Historical Association.

WRITINGS: Soldiers of Destruction: The S.S. Death's Head Division, 1933-1945, Princeton University Press, 1977; (contributor) Hans A. Schmitt, editor, American Occupation in Europe After World War II, University Press of Kansas, 1978.

Films: "Adolf Hitler: 1889-1945," Public Broadcasting System, 1978; "Occupied Germany: The American Legacy," George C. Marshall Research Foundation. Contributor to history journals.

WORK IN PROGRESS: Research for a biography of Reinhard Heydrich, Himmler's deputy as chief of the Gestapo; The Social and Political History of the S.S. Officer Corps; Ideology and Strategy in the Planning and Conduct of the German War in Russia, 1941-1945; a textbook on modern German history, for college students.

SIDELIGHTS: Sydnor told CA: "Soldiers of Destruction is a multi-dimensional analysis of one of the most powerful and destructive military forces in history. The book is based almost exclusively upon a variety of SS manuscript materials deposited in various German archives and upon the massive collection of captured German Army records now on microfilm in the National Archives in Washington, D.C. *Soldiers of Destruction* relates the political and military experience of the SS Death's Head Division (SS Totenkopfdivision) to the institutional development of the SS, the ideological objectives of Nazi Germany, and the attempted implementation of Hitler's war aims.

"'Adolf Hitler: 1889-1945,' a 90 minute video tape biographical documentary, is the first such program of its kind in the United States, created, written and produced by a historian who is a specialist in modern German history.

"'Occupied Germany' views the American role in postwar Germany and Europe within the context of American foreign policy after 1945. The occupation policies which culminated in the development of the Marshall Plan and the comprehensive economic and social programs for the reconstruction of Europe were the most positive, far-sighted, and enduring accomplishments yet achieved by American diplomacy in this century.''

* * *

SYKES, Alrene

PERSONAL: Born in Australia; daughter of Alton and Sarah (Waters) Sykes. *Education:* University of Sydney, B.A. (honors), 1951; University of Queensland, M.A., 1967. *Residence:* Bellbowrie, Queensland, Australia. *Office:* Department of English, University of Queensland, St. Lucia, Brisbane, Queensland 4067, Australia.

CAREER: Australian Broadcasting Commission, Sydney, Australia, play editor, 1952-61; University of Queensland, Brisbane, Australia, lecturer, 1961-68, senior lecturer in English, 1968—. *Member:* International Theatre Institute (Queensland representative), Australian Society of Authors.

WRITINGS: Harold Pinter, Humanities, 1970; (editor) *Five Plays for Radio,* Currency Press, 1975; (editor) *Five Plays,* University of Queensland Press, 1976; (editor) *Can't You Hear Me Talking To You?,* University of Queensland Press, 1978; *ZD and Other Plays,* University of Queensland Press, 1978. Author of more than fifty radio scripts and radio play adaptations. Contributor to literature journals.

WORK IN PROGRESS: A book on Australian drama.

SIDELIGHTS: Sykes told *CA:* "Searching for new writers and new plays is a major interest. I have been involved in many play competitions."

* * *

SYLVESTER, Richard Standish 1926-1978

November 30, 1926—July 9, 1978; American educator and editor. Sylvester taught at Yale University since 1956 where he was executive editor of the Yale editions of *The Complete Works of St. Thomas More.* A scholar of English Renaissance literature, Sylvester received an honorary doctorate in humane letters from Georgetown University in 1978, which commended him for having "humanized our culture with the breadth of his knowledge." He died in New Haven, Conn. Obituaries and other sources: *The Author's and Writer's Who's Who,* 6th edition, Burke's Peerage, 1971; *Directory of American Scholars,* Volume II: *English, Speech, and Drama,* 6th edition, Bowker, 1974; *Who's Who in America,* 39th edition, Marquis, 1976; *New York Times,* July 11, 1978. (See index for *CA* sketch)

* * *

SYMONS, (H. B.) Scott 1933-

PERSONAL: Born July 13, 1933, in Toronto, Ontario, Canada. *Education:* University of Toronto, B.A., 1955; King's College, Cambridge, M.A.; Sorbonne, University of Paris, Diplome d'Etudes Superieures. *Residence:* Newfoundland, Canada. *Office:* University of Toronto, Toronto, Ontario, Canada.

CAREER: Writer. Worked as curator of Sigmund Samuel Canadiana Collection and Canadiana Gallery of Royal Ontario Museum, Toronto; assistant professor of fine art at University of Toronto; taught contemporary art at University of Pennsylvania. Editorialist and reporter for various Canadian journals. Consultant to Smithsonian Institution. *Awards, honors:* Beta Sigma Phi award, 1968; senior arts grant from Canada Council, 1973.

WRITINGS: Combat Journal of Place d'Armes (novel), McClelland & Stewart, 1967; *Civic Square* (novel), McClelland & Stewart, 1969; *Heritage: A Romantic Look at Early Canadian Furniture,* New York Graphic Society, 1971. Contributor to periodicals including *Montreal Presse, Montreal Nouveau Journal, Toronto Telegram,* and *Quebec Chronicle Telegram.*

BIOGRAPHICAL/CRITICAL SOURCES: Canadian Forum, May, 1967.*

T

TAGIURI, Renato 1919-

PERSONAL: Born April 28, 1919, in Milan, Italy; came to the United States in 1947, naturalized citizen, 1951. *Education:* McGill University, B.Sc., 1945, M.Sc., 1946; Harvard University, Ph.D., 1951. *Home:* 432 Concord Rd., Weston, Mass. 02193. *Office:* Graduate School of Business Administration, Harvard University, Boston, Mass. 02163.

CAREER: Harvard University, Cambridge, Mass., lecturer, 1951-58, associate professor, 1958-62, professor of social sciences, 1962—. Consultant to government and private organizations. *Member:* American Psychological Association (fellow), Massachusetts Psychological Association (fellow). *Awards, honors:* Commonwealth Fund fellow, 1953-57.

WRITINGS: (Editor with Luigi Petrullo, and contributor) *Person Perception and Interpersonal Behavior,* Stanford University Press, 1958; (editor with J. L. Moreno and others) *Reader in Sociometry,* Free Press, 1960; (editor) *Research Needs in Executive Selection,* Division of Research, Graduate School of Business Administration, Harvard University, 1961; (with Atilla Baransel) *Human Aspects of Organizations* (published in Turkish), Husnutabiat Matbaasi (Istanbul), 1966; (editor with G. H. Litwin) *Organizational Climate: Exploration of a Concept,* Division of Research, Graduate School of Business Administration, Harvard University, 1968; (with P. R. Lawrence, Rosalind Barnett, and D. C. Dunphy) *Behavioral Science Concepts in Case Analysis: The Relationship of Ideas to Management Action,* Division of Research, Graduate School of Business Administration, Harvard University, 1969; (with J. D. Glover and R. M. Hower) *The Administrator: Cases on Human Aspects of Management,* 5th edition (Tagiuri was not associated with earlier editions), Irwin, 1973. Contributor to *Handbook of Social Psychology,* 1954, 1969.

Contributor to encyclopedias and professional journals.

WORK IN PROGRESS: Revising *The Administrator* with J. D. Glover.

*   *   *

TAGLIAFERRI, Aldo 1931-

PERSONAL: Born December 21, 1931, in Milan, Italy; son of Gino and Velia Tagliaferri; married Monique Harpignies, December 24, 1958; children: Elisa, Alma. *Education:* Universita Bocconi, D.Foreign Lit., 1957. *Home:* Montevideo 19, Milan 20144, Italy.

CAREER: Il Giorno, Milan, Italy, translator and writer, 1959-69; Feltrinelli Publishing House, Milan, chief literary editor, 1969—. *Awards, honors:* Commonwealth Fellowship, 1957, for Yale University, and 1958, for Berkeley College.

WRITINGS: Beckett e l'iperdeterminazione letteraria (title means "Beckett and Literary Overdetermination"), 1967, revised edition published as *Beckett et la Surdetermination litteraire,* Payot, 1977; *Fabulous Ancestors,* Africana Publishing, 1974. Also author of *L'estetica dell'oggettive* (title means "The Aesthetics of Objectivity"), 1969. Translator into Italian of R. D. Laing's *Politics of Experience.*

Work anthologized in *Sessualita e politica,* edited by A. Verdiglione, Feltrinelli (Milan), 1976, Penguin, 1978. Contributor to Italian, French, and American journals.

WORK IN PROGRESS: A collection of essays on psychoanalysis, many previously published in magazines.

SIDELIGHTS: Tagliaferri writes: "I consider my study of African sculpture to be a hobby. My travel in West Africa gave me some competence in this subject, but my main field of interest is still aesthetics and psychoanalysis."

*   *   *

TARNOPOL, Lester 1913-

PERSONAL: Born February 23, 1913, in Haverhill, Mass.; son of Morris (a tailor) and Sarah (Goldshine) Tarnopol; married second wife, Muriel Dubinsky (a professor), July 1, 1956; children: K. Lee, David H., Matthew J., Daniel I. *Education:* Massachusetts Institute of Technology, B.S., 1934, M.S., 1935; Harvard University, Sc.D., 1938. *Home:* 769 Edgewood Rd., San Mateo, Calif. 94402.

CAREER: University of Kentucky, Lexington, assistant professor, 1938-40, associate professor of physical metallurgy, 1940-41; Raytheon Production Co., Newton, Mass., chief metallurgist, 1941-43; Loyola University, Los Angeles, Calif., professor of mathematics, 1943-44; Van Tuyl Engineering Co., Los Angeles, consulting engineer, 1944-45; University of Southern California, Los Angeles, lecturer in physics, metallurgy, and mechanical engineering, 1945-46; Douglas Aircraft Co., Santa Monica, Calif., engineer, 1946-47; City College of San Francisco, San Francisco, Calif., professor of engineering and industrial psychology, 1947—. President of Tarnopol & Associates, 1950—.

MEMBER: American Society for Metals, American Society of Safety Engineers, American Institute of Mining, Metallurgical and Petroleum Engineers, Indian Institute of Metals, Sigma Xi. *Awards, honors:* Research awards from American Institute of Mining, Metallurgical and Petroleum Engineers, 1941, Lincoln Arc Welding Foundation, 1947, and American Society of Safety Engineers, 1972; plaque from American Society of Safety Engineers, 1963.

WRITINGS: Handbook for Airborne Radar Direction Finder, U.S. Navy, 1944; *Handbook for Airborne Recording Machine*, U.S. Navy, 1944; *Fundamentals of Vacuum Tube Manufacturing: Vacuum Tube Materials*, Eitel-McCullough, 1960; *Motivation in Human Relations*, American Society of Training Directors, 1963; (contributor) Keith Davis and W. Scott, editors, *Readings in Human Relations*, McGraw, 1964; *Learning Disabilities: Introduction to Educational and Medical Management*, C. C Thomas, 1969; (contributor) W. Grzynkowicz and J. E. Sturch, editors, *Readings in Diagnosis for Prescriptive Teaching*, Associated Educational Services Corp., 1969; *Learning Disorders in Children: Diagnosis, Medication, Education*, Little, Brown, 1971; *Detecting and Diagnosing Educationally/Neurologically Handicapped Children*, Network for Continuing Medical Education, 1971; *Treating Educationally/Neurologically Handicapped Children*, Network for Continuing Medical Education, 1971; (with wife, Muriel Tarnopol) *Reading Disabilities: An International Perspective*, University Park Press, 1976; (with M. Tarnopol) *Brain Function and Reading Disabilities*, University Park Press, 1977. Contributor of about forty articles to professional journals.

WORK IN PROGRESS: Assessment of Children With Learning Disabilities.

SIDELIGHTS: Tarnopol's books have been translated into Japanese, Spanish, Italian, Russian, and Portuguese.

* * *

TARSAIDZE, Alexandre 1901-1978

June 22, 1901—February 25, 1978; Georgian-born American public relations executive and author. A refugee from the Bolshevik Revolution, Tarsaidze came to the United States in 1923, and worked as a diamond buyer and president of a perfume company before founding his own public relations firm in the 1950's. In addition to writing articles for New York City's Russian-language press, he wrote two books, *Czars and Presidents: A Story of a Forgotten Friendship* and *Katia, Wife Before God,* a biography of Princess Catherine Yourievskaya. Tarsaidze died in New York, N.Y. Obituaries and other sources: *Who's Who in America*, 39th edition, Marquis, 1976; *New York Times*, February 28, 1978. (See index for *CA* sketch)

* * *

TAYLOR, Charles Lewis 1935-

PERSONAL: Born November 8, 1935, in Ware Shoals, S.C.; son of Lee and Sue (Brissey) Taylor; married Mary Millican, June 1, 1958; children: Susan, James. *Education:* Carson Newman College, B.A., 1957; Yale University, M.A., 1959, Ph.D., 1963. *Politics:* Democrat. *Religion:* Presbyterian. *Office:* Department of Political Science, Virginia Polytechnic Institute & State University, Blacksburg, Va. 24601.

CAREER: College of William & Mary, Williamsburg, Va., assistant professor of political science, 1962-66; Yale University, New Haven, Conn., research director, 1966-70; Virginia Polytechnic Institute & State University, Blacksburg, professor of political science, 1970—. *Awards, honors:* Fulbright grant; National Science Foundation fellowship.

WRITINGS: (Editor) *Aggregate Data Analysis*, Mouton, 1968; (with Michael C. Hudson) *World Handbook of Political and Social Indicators*, Yale University Press, 2nd edition, 1972. Contributor to political science journals.

WORK IN PROGRESS: Collecting cross-national aggregate data for 150 countries; research on British working-class history.

* * *

TAYLOR, (George) Frederick 1928-

PERSONAL: Born February 28, 1928, in Portland, Ore.; son of George Noble and Ida Elizabeth (Dixon) Taylor; married Georga Bray, October 6, 1951; children: Amelia Ruth, Ross Noble. *Education:* University of Oregon, B.S., 1950. *Home:* 154 Unadilla Rd., Ridgewood, N.J. 07450. *Office: Wall Street Journal*, 22 Cortland St., New York, N.Y. 10007.

CAREER/WRITINGS: Astoria Budget, Astoria, Ore., reporter, 1950-52; *Portland Oregonian*, Portland, Ore., reporter, 1952-54; *Wall Street Journal*, New York, N.Y., copyreader, 1955-57, reporter, 1957-59, Detroit bureau chief, 1959-64, Washington correspondent, 1964-68, assistant managing editor, 1968-69, managing editor, 1970—. *Military service:* U.S. Air Force, 1955-57; became first lieutenant. *Member:* American Society of Newspaper Editors.

* * *

TAYLOR, Ian 1944-

PERSONAL: Born March 11, 1944, in Sheffield, England; son of Charles W. (a librarian) and Eveline Sara (a librarian) Taylor; married Ruth Marion Jamieson (a teacher), February 5, 1977; children: Sara Jean. *Education:* University of Durham, B.A., 1965; Cambridge University, diploma in criminology, 1966. *Office:* Centre for Criminological Studies, University of Sheffield, Sheffield S11 7AD, England.

CAREER: Research assistant at University of Durham, 1966-68; University of Glasgow, Glasgow, Scotland, assistant lecturer in sociology, 1968-69; Queen's University, Kingston, Ontario, visiting lecturer in sociology, 1969-70; research fellow in sociology, University of Bradford, 1970-71; University of Sheffield, Sheffield, England, lecturer in criminology, 1971-75, senior lecturer in criminology at Centre for Criminological Studies, 1975—. Visiting professor, McMaster University, Hamilton, Ontario, 1977-78. *Member:* National Deviancy Conference.

WRITINGS: (Editor with Laurie Taylor) *Politics and Deviance*, Penguin, 1973; (with Paul Walton and Jock Young) *The New Criminology: For a Social Theory of Deviance*, Routledge & Kegan Paul, 1973; (editor with Walton and Young, and contributor) *Critical Criminology*, Routledge & Kegan Paul, 1975; (editor with Herman Bianchi and Mario Simondi) *Deviance and Control in Europe*, Wiley, 1975; *Crime at the End of the Welfare State*, Macmillan, 1978. Contributor of more than sixty articles and reviews to scholarly journals in England and the United States.

SIDELIGHTS: Taylor writes: "My work is concerned with the politics of crime and crime control, with a special interest in the differences between Europe and North America. Canadian developments are a special personal interest."

TAYLOR, James C(hapman) 1937-

PERSONAL: Born January 11, 1937, in Glendale, Calif.; son of James C. (a manager) and Alma (Bereley) Taylor; married Linda Gilman, November, 1964 (divorced, October, 1974); children: James C., Jr. *Education:* San Diego State College (now University), A.B., 1963; University of Michigan, M.A., 1965, Ph.D., 1969. *Home:* 756 Haverford Ave., Pacific Palisades, Calif. 90272.

CAREER: Mechanic, 1954-58; Pacific Telephone, Los Angeles, Calif., commercial representative, 1958-62; Farbinfabriken Bayer, Leverkusen, West Germany, industrial psychologist trainee, 1963; University of Michigan, Institute for Social Research, Ann Arbor, assistant project director, 1964-68, project director, 1969-70; University of Technology, Loughborough, Leicestershire, England, research fellow, 1970-71; University of California, Los Angeles, assistant professor of sociotechnical systems, 1972—, research fellow at Institute of Industrial Relations, Center for Quality of Working Life, 1975—. Organizational design consultant. *Military service:* U.S. Army Reserve, 1954-62; became sergeant. *Member:* American Psychological Association.

WRITINGS: Technology and Organizational Change, Institute for Social Research, University of Michigan, 1971; (with D. G. Bowers) *Survey of Organizations,* Institute for Social Research, University of Michigan, 1972; (editor with L. E. Davis) *Design of Jobs,* Penguin, 1973, 2nd edition, Goodyear Publishing, 1978.

WORK IN PROGRESS: Systems Analysis: The Design of White Collar Work; research on socio-technical analysis and design of organizations.

SIDELIGHTS: Taylor writes: "I am centrally concerned with improving the quality of working life of organizational employees."

* * *

TAYLOR, Kamala (Purnaiya) 1924- (Kamala Markandaya)

PERSONAL: Born in 1924, in India; married; children: Kim (daughter). *Education:* Attended University of Madras. *Religion:* Hindu-Brahmin. *Residence:* London, England. *Agent:* John Farquharson Ltd., 15 Red Lion Sq., London W.C.1, England.

CAREER: Worked briefly for a small weekly newspaper in India; immigrated to England in 1948; currently free-lance writer. *Member:* Society of Authors. *Awards, honors:* Nectar in a Sieve was named Notable Book of 1955 by the American Library Association; National Association of Independent Schools Award, 1967.

WRITINGS—Under pseudonym Kamala Markandaya: *Nectar in a Sieve* (Book-of-the-Month Club selection), Putnam (London), 1954, John Day, 1955; *Some Inner Fury,* Putnam, 1955, John Day, 1956; *A Silence of Desire,* Putnam, 1960, John Day, 1961; *Possession,* John Day, 1963; *A Handful of Rice,* John Day, 1966; *The Coffer Dams,* John Day, 1969; *The Nowhere Man,* John Day, 1972; *Two Virgins,* John Day, 1973; *The Golden Honeycombs,* John Day, 1977. Contributor of fiction and articles to Indian and British publications.

SIDELIGHTS: Nectar in a Sieve is actually Kamala Taylor's third novel. It was highly praised for its accurate picture of Indian village life. Donald Barr of the *New York Times* wrote: "The basis of eloquence is knowledge, and *Nectar in a Sieve* has a wonderful, quiet authority over our sympathies because [Kamala Taylor] is manifestly an au-

thority on village life in India. Because of what she knows, she has been able to write a story without reticence or excess." "It is a powerful book," commented critic J. F. Muehl of *Saturday Review,* "but the power is in the content. . . . You read it because it answers so many real questions: What is the day-to-day life of the villager like? How does a village woman really think of herself? What goes through the minds of people who are starving?"

Reviewing *Two Virgins,* a *New Yorker* critic observed: "[Kamala Taylor] writes in a forthright, almost breakneck style that could have been paced a little less relentlessly but could not be more precise or lucid. From the minutiae of the girls' lives we learn a great deal about the fabric of life in India today. They are constantly choosing between Eastern and Western ways of looking at the world—in their school, at home, in their language, and in their attitudes toward their own ripening sexuality, of which they are both keenly aware. . . . Both their stories are fascinating and demonstrate that [Taylor] writes as well about such universal feelings as lust, friendship, envy, and pride as she does about matters idiosyncratic to her country."

BIOGRAPHICAL/CRITICAL SOURCES: Times Literary Supplement, Saturday 10, 1954, June 12, 1969; *Kirkus Reviews,* February 1, 1955; *Saturday Review,* May 14, 1955, June 14, 1969; *Time,* May 16, 1955; *Christian Science Monitor,* May 26, 1955, October 10, 1973; *New Yorker,* May 23, 1955, October 22, 1973; *Commonweal,* August 19, 1955; *Best Sellers,* June 1, 1969, October 15, 1973; *Contemporary Literary Criticism,* Volume 8, Gale, 1978.

* * *

TAYLOR, Michael J. H. 1949-

PERSONAL: Born June 12, 1949, in Middlesex, England; son of John W. R. and Doris A. Taylor; married wife, Isobel, June, 1974. *Education:* Attended secondary school in Surbiton, England. *Home:* 12 Westcott Way, Cheam, Surrey, England.

CAREER: Writer.

WRITINGS: (With father, John W. R. Taylor, and Kenneth Munson) *Jane's Pocket Book of Military Transport and Training Aircraft,* Macdonald & Jane's, 1974; (with Munson and J. Taylor) *Jane's Pocket Book of Commercial Transport Aircraft,* Macdonald & Jane's, 1974; (with Munson and J. Taylor) *Jane's Pocket Book of Light Aircraft,* Macdonald & Jane's, 1974; (with J. Taylor) *Helicopters of the World,* Ian Allen, 1976; (with J. Taylor) *Missiles of the World,* revised edition, Ian Allen, 1976; *Jane's Pocket Book of Research and Experimental Aircraft,* Macdonald & Jane's, 1976; *Jane's Pocket Book of Homebuilt Aircraft,* Macdonald & Jane's, 1977; (with David Mondey and J. Taylor) *The Guinness Book of Air Facts and Feats,* Guinness, revised edition, 1977. Also author of, with Munson and J. Taylor, *Jane's Pocket Book of Major Combat Aircraft,* Macdonald & Jane's, and contributor to *All the World's Aircraft,* Macdonald & Jane's. Editor of *Aircraft Illustrated,* 1976-77.

WORK IN PROGRESS: Military Aircraft Between the Wars; Encyclopedia of Aircraft; Jane's Pocket Book of Helicopters.

* * *

TAYLOR, Ronald L(ee) 1938-

PERSONAL: Born January 25, 1938, in Oakland, Calif.; son of Francis J. and Ida (Hester) Taylor; divorced; children: Ronald, Damon. *Education:* San Jose State College (now University), B.A. (honors), 1960; University of Minnesota, M.S., 1962, Ph.D., 1964. *Home:* 700 South Lake Ave., Apt. 221, Pasadena, Calif. 91106. *Office:* Department of the Chief Medical Examiner, Coroner's Office, 1104 North Mission Rd., Los Angeles, Calif. 90033.

CAREER: University of California, Irvine, assistant research pathologist, 1964-69, instructor in developmental and cell biology, 1969; California State College, San Bernardino, assistant professor, 1969-71, associate professor of biology, 1971-73; University of Southern California, Los Angeles, associate clinical professor of pathology, 1973—. Director of Forensic Laboratories for Los Angeles Coroner's Office, 1973—. Founder, member of board of directors, and executive vice-president of American Institute of Forensic Science, 1975—. Conducted research in the Marshall Islands for Atomic Energy Commission, 1971. *Military service:* U.S. Naval Reserve, 1955-63.

MEMBER: American Association for the Advancement of Science, American Institute for Biological Sciences, Society for Invertebrate Pathology, Electron Microscopy Society of America, American Academy of Forensic Sciences, California Association of Criminologists, Southern California Society for Electron Microscopy, Sigma Xi.

WRITINGS: Butterflies in My Stomach; or, Insects in Human Nutrition, Woodbridge Press, 1975; (with B. J. Carter) *Entertaining With Insects; or, the Original Guide to Insect Cookery,* Woodbridge Press, in press. Contributor to scientific journals.

* * *

TAYLOR, Sydney (Brenner) 1904(?)-1978

1904(?)—February 12, 1978; American camp counsellor and writer. Taylor was an actress and dancer before becoming a counsellor for Cejwin Camps in 1942, a position she held into the late 1960's. Best known for her stories of the first generation of American Jews in New York's Lower East Side, the *All-of-a-Kind Family* books, she won the Charles W. Follett Award in 1951, and the Schwartz Juvenile Book Award in 1952. In addition to several other juvenile books, Taylor wrote, directed, and choreographed her own plays. The fifth in her famous series, *Ella of All-of-a-Kind Family,* was published after her death. She died in Queens, N.Y. Obituaries and other sources: *Authors of Books for Young People,* Scarecrow, 1967; *More Books by More People,* Citation Press, 1974; *New York Times,* February 14, 1978. (See index for *CA* sketch)

* * *

TEMPLE, Paul
See DURBRIDGE, Francis (Henry)

* * *

TENNENBAUM, Silvia 1928-

PERSONAL: Born March 10, 1928, in Germany; daughter of Erich Pfeiffer-Belli (a journalist) and Lotti (Stern) Steinberg; married Lloyd Tennenbaum (a rabbi and therapist); children: Jeremy, David, Raphael. *Education:* Barnard College, B.A. (cum laude), 1950. *Politics:* "Left of center, but active in Democratic Party." *Religion:* Jewish. *Home:* 763 Fireplace Rd., East Hampton, N.Y. 11937. *Agent:* Maxine Groffsky, 2 Fifth Ave., New York, N.Y. 10011.

CAREER: Writer and art tour lecturer. Committeewoman and treasurer of East Hampton Town Democratic Committee.

WRITINGS: (Contributor) Richard Yates, editor, *Stories for the Sixties,* Bantam, 1963; *Rachel, The Rabbi's Wife,* Morrow, 1978. Contributor of short stories to *Present Tense* and *American Review.* Contributor of articles and book reviews to *Midstream* and *Newsday. Member:* P.E.N.

WORK IN PROGRESS: A novel tracing a German-Jewish family before and after the rise of Hitler, in Germany and United States.

SIDELIGHTS: Tennenbaum told *CA:* "I have always been a writer. For a long time I didn't know it, I wrote for my own pleasure, for my escape, for my best friend, for my fantasy life, for my sanity perhaps—but I thought I would become a painter. I didn't give up that idea until I was married and a mother and finally recognized that I could never catch up to the painters but was already among the writers.

"I was born in Germany so English is my second language, but it is the one in which my education took place, the language of my dreams and thoughts, of my children and my husband. My life was undoubtably shaped by my emigration from Germany and the experience, however limited, of National Socialism and the persecution of the Jews.

"When I am writing, I try to read only 'good' books, so that I may not be 'affected' (like a pregnant woman) by mediocre matter. I think that *Anna Karenina* is probably the most important book for me—but I am basically less a reader than a 'looker.'"

AVOCATIONAL INTERESTS: Museums and art gallerys, movies, baseball, traveling.

BIOGRAPHICAL/CRITICAL SOURCES: Newsday, January 8, 1978; *New York Times Book Review,* January 11, 1978, January 22, 1978, February 24, 1978; *Newsweek,* February 6, 1978.

* * *

TERRY, Megan 1932-

PERSONAL: Born July 22, 1932, in Seattle, Wash. *Education:* Attended Banff School of Fine Arts, 1950-52, 1956, and University of Alberta, 1952-53; University of Washington, B.Ed., 1956. *Agent:* Elisabeth Marton, 96 Fifth Ave., New York, N.Y. 10011.

CAREER: Cornish School of Allied Arts, Seattle, Wash., drama teacher, 1954-56; Open Theatre, New York, N.Y., director of Playwright's Workshop, 1963-68; currently playwright-in-residence at Omaha Magic Theatre, Omaha, Neb. Writer-in-residence at Yale University, 1966-67; founding member of New York Theatre Strategy, 1971; founding member of Women's Theatre Council, New York, 1971; adjunct professor of theatre at University of Nebraska at Omaha. Playwright and lecturer. *Awards, honors:* Stanley Drama Award, 1965, for "Hot House"; Office of Advanced Drama Research Award, 1965, 1969; ABC-Yale University Fellowship, 1966; Rockefeller grant, 1968, 1974; WGBH award, 1968, for "Sanibel and Captiva"; Latin American Festival award, 1969, for "Keep Tightly Closed in a Cool Dry Place"; Obie Award from *Village Voice,* 1970, for "Approaching Simone"; Earplay Radio Award, 1972, for "American Wedding Ritual"; National Endowment for the Arts grant, 1972; Creative Artists Public Service (CAPS) grant, 1973; Guggenheim fellowship, 1978.

WRITINGS—Plays: Calm Down Mother (one-act; first produced in New York City at Open Theatre, 1965) Samuel French, 1966; *Ex-Miss Copper Queen on a Set of Pills* (one-act; first produced Off-Broadway at Cherry Lane Theatre, 1963), published in *Playwrights for Tomorrow: A Collection of Plays,* Volume I, edited by Arthur H. Ballet, University of Minnesota Press, 1966, published in *The People vs. Ranchman [and] Ex-Miss Copper Queen on a Set of Pills: Two Plays,* Dramatists Play Service, 1968, published separately by Samuel French, 1970; "Keep Tightly Closed in a Cool Dry Place" (one-act; first produced in New York City at Open Theatre, 1965), published in *Tulane Drama Review,* summer, 1966 (also see below); "Viet Rock" (three-act; first produced in New York City at Open Theatre, 1966, produced Off-Broadway at Martinique Theatre, November 10, 1966), published in *Tulane Drama Review,* fall, 1966 (also see below); *The People vs. Ranchman* (three-act; first produced in Minneapolis at Firehouse Theatre, 1967, produced Off-Broadway at Fortune Theatre, October 27, 1968), published in *The People vs. Ranchman [and] Ex-Miss Copper Queen on a Set of Pills: Two Plays,* Dramatists Play Service, 1968, published separately by Samuel French, 1970; "The Magic Realists" (one-act; first produced in New York City at Open Theatre, 1966, produced Off-Broadway at La Mama Experimental Theatre Club, 1966), published in *Best One-Act Plays of 1968,* edited by Stanley Richards, Chilton Press, 1969 (also see below).

"The Tommy Allen Show," first produced in Los Angeles at College of the Immaculate Heart, 1969), published in *Scripts 2,* December, 1971; *Megan Terry's Home: or Future Soap* (three-act; televised in 1968, produced in London at As Theatre, 1974), Samuel French, 1972; "Massachusetts Trust" (first produced in Waltham, Mass. at Brandeis University Theatre, 1968), published in *The Off-Off Broadway Book,* edited by Albert Poland and Bruce Mailman, Bobbs-Merrill, 1972; *Couplings and Groupings,* Pantheon, 1973; "American Wedding Ritual Monitored/Transmitted by the Planet Jupiter" (one-act; broadcast in 1972), published in *Places: A Journal of Theatre,* Volume I, 1973; *Approaching Simone* (three-act; first produced in Boston at Boston University Theatre, February 25, 1970), Feminist Press, 1973; *The Pioneer, and Pro-Game* (two one-act plays; first produced in New York City at Genesis Theatre, November, 1974), Ragnarok Press, 1975; *Hothouse* (three-act; first produced Off-Off-Broadway at Circle Theatre, February, 1974), Samuel French, 1975; (with Sam Shepard and Jean-Claude Van Itallie) *Nightwalk* (first produced in New York City at Theatre of St. Clements, September 8, 1973), Bobbs-Merrill, 1975; *Willie-Willa-Bill's Dope Garden* (one-act), Ragnarok Press, 1977.

Collections of plays: *Viet Rock; Comings and Goings; Keep Tightly Closed in a Cool Dry Place; The Gloaming, Oh My Darling: Four Plays* (contains "Viet Rock" [see above]; "Comings and Goings," first produced in New York City at Open Theatre, 1966, produced Off-Broadway at La Mama Experimental Theatre Club, 1966; "Keep Tightly Closed in a Cool Dry Place" [see above]; "The Gloaming, Oh My Darling," first produced in Minneapolis at Firehouse Theatre, 1965, produced in Los Angeles at Company Theatre, January 13, 1972), Simon & Schuster, 1967; *Three One-Act Plays* (includes "The Magic Realists" [see above]; "Sanibel and Captiva," broadcast in 1968; "One More Little Drinkie," televised in 1969), Samuel French, 1971.

Unpublished plays: "Beach Grass," first produced in Seattle at Cornish Players Theatre, 1955; "Seascape," first produced in Seattle at Cornish Players Theatre, 1955; "Go Out and Move the Car," first produced in Seattle at Cornish Players Theatre, 1955; "The Dirt Boat," televised in 1955; "New York Comedy: Two," first produced in Sarasota, N.Y., at Sarasota Gallery Theatre, 1961; "When My Girlfriend Was Still All Flowers," first produced in New York

City at Open Theatre, 1963; "Eat at Joe's," first produced in New York City at Open Theatre, 1963; "The Key Is on the Bottom," first produced in Los Angeles at Mark Taper Forum, 1968; "Jack-Jack," first produced in Minneapolis at Firehouse Theatre, 1968; "Changes," first produced Off-Broadway at La Mama Experimental Theatre Club, 1968.

"Grooving," first produced in New York City at Brooklyn Academy of Music, 1972; (with Jo Ann Schmidman) "Choose a Spot on the Floor," first produced in Omaha at Omaha Magic Theatre, 1972; "Susan Perutz at the Manhattan Theatre Club," first produced in New York City at Manhattan Theatre Club, 1973; "St. Hydro Clemency; or, A Funhouse of the Lord: An Energizing Event," first produced in New York City at St. Clement's Church, May 24, 1973; (with others) "All Them Women," first produced in New York City at Westbeth Playwright's Feminist Cooperative, January 11, 1974; "We Can Feed Everybody Here," first produced in New York City at Westbeth Playwright's Feminist Cooperative, January, 1974; "Babes in the Bighouse," first produced in Omaha at Omaha Magic Theatre, 1974; "The Narco Linguini Bust," first produced in Omaha at Omaha Magic Theatre, 1974; "100,001 Horror Stories of the Plains," first produced in Omaha at Omaha Magic Theatre, 1976; "Brazil Fado: You're Always with Me," first produced in Omaha at Omaha Magic Theatre, 1977; "Lady Rose's Brazil Hide Out," first produced in Omaha at Omaha Magic Theatre, 1977; "American King's English for Queens," first produced in Omaha at Omaha Magic Theatre, 1978.

Also author of lyrics for "Thoughts," a musical by Lamar Alford, first produced Off-Broadway at Theatre de Lys, March 19, 1973. Contributor to *New York Times* and *Valhalla: A Modern Drama Issue.*

Plays represented in numerous anthologies, including "Calm Down Mother" in *Eight Plays From Off-Off Broadway,* edited by M. T. Smith and N. Orzel, Bobbs-Merrill, 1966, and *Plays By and About Women,* edited by V. Sullivan and James Hatch, Vintage Books, 1974; "The Gloaming, Oh My Darling" in *The Norton Introduction to Literature,* edited by Carl E. Bain and others, Norton, 1973; "Sanibel and Captiva" in *Spontaneous Combustion: Eight New American Plays,* edited by Rochelle Owens, Drama Book Specialists, 1973; "Approaching Simone" in *Women in Drama: An Anthology,* edited by Harriett Kriegel, New American Library, 1975.

SIDELIGHTS: Megan Terry has distinguished herself as a playwright of the "New Theatre" in America, a phenomenon which grew out of the tumult of the 1960's. John Lahr characterized New Theatre as a "response to Broadway's inability to sustain a theatre pertinent to the times. . . . The rapid ferment of theatrical innovation parallels the national political frustration. Revolutions in the arts are easier to pull off than ones in society. The theatrical styles which struggle to emerge are not mere self-indulgence but a protest against the world and an attempt to refashion it." Both the themes and innovative staging of Terry's plays have reflected her commitment to social change and her conviction that the theatre plays a vital role in moving and influencing people. "In the streets and in the theatre—there are the last two places in America where you can still tell the truth," she declared.

Creating a theatre relevant to the needs and experiences of the audience of the sixties required a new process of playwrighting. Megan Terry emphasized the necessity of close interaction between playwright and actors in developing a script, and several of her plays evolved from an exchange of ideas among the entire troupe. Through improvisational exercises and continual revision they sought together to create a vivid experience for their audiences and to communicate through use of all the senses. "Who says only words make great drama?" Terry challenged. "The theatre should make use of the total man, the total society, the total universe, spiritual and material." Declaring "I want my audience to feel rather than think," Terry summarized the philosophy which her plays have incarnated.

Critics differed sharply over this issue in their reviews of "The People vs. Ranchman" in 1968. Haskel Frankel praised the performance, saying, "While I doubt I understood everything Megan Terry has in her mind . . . I spent an evening witnessing real theatre, and that's more than good enough. Whether full understanding eluded me, feeling never did." Others contended that Terry's goal of creating a purely emotional experience for the audience had backfired. A *Time* critic maintained that even though "Ranchman" was "devoid of intellectual content," it was "likely to leave a mature playgoer doing more thinking than feeling." Walter Kerr elaborated upon the nature of this intellectual response, observing that "the audience begins to draw some sort of line for itself" when the playwright refuses to do so. "Megan Terry draws no lines, intellectual or emotional," he noted. "Substituting placards and noise for any sort of precision, she splatters the working of the mind across the premises as indifferently as she splatters actors across five platforms." In response to the chaos, the minds of the viewers had to begin "talking back if only to avoid being drowned." Kerr concluded: "When the thunderbolt hurled at us in no more than a blob, we try to catch it, give it some kind of form, and toss it back. The playwright has challenged us. But because the challenge is so all-inclusive and therefore so imprecise, [she] has only challenged us to challenge [her]."

"Approaching Simone" revealed the more serious and reverent qualities of Megan Terry's creative genius. Clive Barnes described it as "a mind-shaking dramatic collage that tries to search out and describe the febrile genius of Simone Weil, the young philosopher and mystic who committed suicide by starvation in 1943." John Lahr added, "Miss Terry's respect for the nobility of Weil's struggle . . . gives her play an honesty, gentleness, and vulnerability lacking in the shrill vigor of most of her other work." Though it might appear that Terry had diverged radically from her themes of protest, Lahr emphasized the common theme of "martyrdom" which gave a continuity to her work.

BIOGRAPHICAL/CRITICAL SOURCES: Village Voice, October 31, 1968, March 12, 1970; *Time,* November 8, 1968; *New York Times,* November 10, 1968, March 9, 1970; *National Observer,* November 11, 1968; *Newsweek,* November 11, 1968; *London Magazine,* December, 1968.

* * *

TERZANI, Tiziano 1938-

PERSONAL: Born September 14, 1938, in Florence, Italy; son of Gerardo (an artisan) Terzani; married Angela Staude (a writer); children: Folco, Saskia. *Education:* University of Pisa, Ph.D., 1961; Columbia University, M.I.A., 1969. *Politics:* "Left wing in capitalist countries, right wing in Communist countries." *Address:* Via San Carlo 7, Firenze, Italy. *Agent:* Eric Linder, 2 Corso Matteotti, Milano, Italy. *Office: Der Spiegel,* 2 Kennedy Ter., Hong Kong.

CAREER: Lawyer in Florence, Italy, 1962-63; businessman, 1963-67; *Der Spiegel,* Hamburg, West Germany, correspondent in Singapore, 1971-75, and Hong Kong, 1975—.

WRITINGS: Pelle di Leopardo (title means "Leopard Skin"), Feltrinelli, 1973; *Giai Phong!: The Fall and Liberation of Saigon,* St. Martin's, 1976.

WORK IN PROGRESS: A novel on Indochina.

SIDELIGHTS: Terzani writes: "I am a journalist and I don't see what else I could be. If I was born rich a century ago I would have traveled the world and written letters to my friends. I am doing just that and I am getting paid for it."

* * *

TEUSCHER, Robert H(erman) 1934-

PERSONAL: Born February 13, 1934, in Rock Island, Ill.; son of Herman (a factory worker) and Marie I. (Martin) Teuscher; married Millena K. Thornberry Horton (a psychotherapist), July 4, 1976. *Education:* St. John's College, A.A., 1953; Concordia Seminary, B.A., 1955; further study at Christ Seminary, 1977—. *Religion:* Lutheran. *Home:* 7230 S. Winchester, St. Louis, Mo. 63121. *Office: St. Louis Globe-Democrat,* 12th and Delmar, St. Louis, Mo. 63101.

CAREER/WRITINGS: Rock Island Argus, Rock Island, Ill., reporter, 1960-66; *St. Louis Globe-Democrat,* St. Louis, Mo., investigative reporter, 1966—. Notable assignments include coverage of investigation of the administration of former Governor Warren E. Hearnes of Missouri, ongoing investigations of organized crime in unions and the financial world, and the investigation of multi-million dollar tax shelters. *Military service:* U.S. Army, 1956-60. *Member:* Investigative Reporters and Editors. *Awards, honors:* Ruth Porter Memorial Award, 1972; Connie Rosenbaum Award from Sigma Delta Chi, 1975.

SIDELIGHTS: Teuscher told *CA:* "One of the highlights of my career was participation in the Arizona Project under the sponsorship of the Investigative Reporters and Editors. My work is detailed in Michael Wendland's *The Arizona Project.* I am presently in the slow process of changing professions, hoping to combine education and background in theology, psychology and journalism in the treatment of alcoholism, with a target date of 1983 for the changeover."

BIOGRAPHICAL/CRITICAL SOURCES: Michael Wendland, *The Arizona Project,* Sheed, 1977.

* * *

THATCHER, David 1922-

PERSONAL: Born April 28, 1922, in Chattanooga, Tenn.; son of Alfred (a manufacturer) and Miriam (a teacher; maiden name, Hines) Thatcher; married Shirley Tannenbaum (an editor), June 21, 1947; children: Ellen Thatcher Rubino, Mavis, Todd. *Education:* Swarthmore College, B.A., 1947; University of Pennsylvania, M.A., 1949; University of California, Berkeley, Ed.D., 1965. *Office:* California State College at Sonoma, Rehnert Park, Calif. 94928.

CAREER: Elementary school teacher, 1951-56; curriculum consultant, 1956-60; principal of elementary school, 1964-69; presently employed by California State College at Sonoma, Rehnert Park. *Military service:* U.S. Army, 1943-46. *Member:* International Transactional Analysis Association, Association for Supervision and Curriculum Development, Phi Delta Kappa.

WRITINGS: Teaching, Loving, and Self-Directed Learning, Goodyear Publishing, 1973. Contributor to education journals.

WORK IN PROGRESS: A book on the functions of teaching and learning; a short book on intrinsic motivation.

SIDELIGHTS: Thatcher writes: "I am interested in conservation, solar energy, living more simply, and being as self-sufficient as possible. I now have a solar collector which heats the house and the hot water." Avocational interests: Travel.

* * *

THEKAEKARA, Matthew P(othen)   1914-1976

PERSONAL: Born March 21, 1914, in Changanachery, Kerala, India; came to United States, 1952; naturalized U.S. citizen, 1962; son of Pothen Chacko (a teacher) and Miriam (Kannampuzha) Thekaekara. Education: Madras University, B.A., 1937, M.Sc., 1939; Sacred Heart College, licentiate in philosophy, 1942; Johns Hopkins University, Ph.D., 1956. Home: 6607 Adrian St., New Carrollton, Md. 20784.

CAREER: St. Aloysius College, Mangalore, India, assistant professor of physics, 1939-41; St. Joseph's College, Madras, India, assistant professor of physics, 1941-44; ordained Roman Catholic priest in order of Society of Jesus (S.J.; Jesuits), in Kurseong, India, 1946; on lecture tour in France, 1947; Loyola College, Madras, associate professor of physics and chairman of the department, 1948-52; Johns Hopkins University, Baltimore, Md., instructor in physics, 1952-56; Georgetown University, Washington, D.C., assistant professor, 1957-60, associate professor of physics and astronomy, 1960-64, acting chairman of physics department, 1960-62; Goddard Space Flight Center of National Aeronautics and Space Administration (NASA), Greenbelt, Md., research physicist, 1964-76. Inventor of the mercury pool as a precision tool of alignment for observing orbits, 1964, and of the cone radiometer, 1965. Resident priest, Ascension Church, Halethorpe, Md., 1964-70; visiting professor, Pace College, 1965-70.

MEMBER: Optical Society of America (founder and president of National Capital Section), American Institute of Physics, American Association of Physics Teachers, International Solar Energy Society, Institute of Environmental Science, All-India Catholic University Federation for Catholic Students (founder of American branch), Phi Beta Kappa, Sigma Xi. Awards, honors: NASA Quality Performance Award, 1969, Quality Performance Award and Exceptional Performance Award, both 1970; Space Environmental Award from the Institute of Environmental Sciences, 1971.

WRITINGS: The Story of Jesus, Little Flower Press (Calcutta), 1947; Planning for India, Saran Jivan Press, 1947; Thoughts Twice Dyed, 1960, published as Meditations for All Seasons, Pageant Press, 1964; Recent Advances in Astro-Geophysics, Georgetown University Press, 1962; (editor) The Solar Constant and the Solar Spectrum Measured From a Research Aircraft, National Aeronautics and Space Administration, 1970; (editor) The Energy Crisis and Energy From the Sun, Goddard Space Flight Center, 1974.

Columnist, Calcutta Herald, 1945-48. Contributor of articles to scientific journals and periodicals, including Eucharistic Congress and Morning Star. Assistant editor, Modern Student, 1945-48.

SIDELIGHTS: Thekaekara's most important contribution to science, according to the Washington Post, "was considered to be his recalculation of the solar constant—the measurable amount of life-giving energy that travels from the earth to the sun." Thekaekara concluded that the solar constant was 1.940 calories per square centimeter per minute—a figure three percent lower than the previously accepted figure. This meant that the intensity of visible sunlight reaching the earth was in actuality eight percent less than scientists had calculated. The ramifications of Thekaera's recalculation were felt in such diverse areas as weather prediction, discovering the causes of major climatic change, and the design and functioning of spacecrafts. In his early experiments at NASA, Thekaekara attempted to recreate sunlight in a test chamber, and later headed a team of thirty scientists who outfitted a flying laboratory to test his theories. Thekaekara's other notable contributions to science include his invention of the mercury pool as a tool of the alignment of instruments for orbiting observations, and the cone radiometer.

Thekaekara once said of his dual careers as scientist and priest: "Man's searching mind is the same and God is the author of all truth. A scientist who is all science is hardly human. And a priest is not to be confined to the sacristy and sanctuary, less so today than ever before."

OBITUARIES: Washington Post, November 27, 1976.*

(Died November 25, 1976, in Prince George County, Md.)

* * *

THIBAULT, John C(rowell)   1922-

PERSONAL: Surname is pronounced Tee-bowe; born April 26, 1922, in Spalding, Mich.; son of John Craske (a railroad employee) and Lillian (a teacher; maiden name, Crowell) Tebo; married Barbara Story (a bank teller), May 10, 1960; children: Nicole. Education: Xavier University, Cincinnati, Ohio, Litt.B., 1944; Alma College, A.B., 1954; Loyola University, Chicago, Ill., M.A., 1947; University of Illinois, Ph.D., 1960. Home address: Route 1, Harrisburg, Mo. 65256. Office: Department of Classical Studies, University of Missouri, 420-B G.C.B., Columbia, Mo. 65201.

CAREER: University of California, Santa Barbara, assistant professor of classical studies, 1960-65; University of Missouri—Columbia, associate professor, 1965-71, professor of classical studies, 1971—, chairman of department, 1967—. Member: American Philological Association, Classical Association of the Midwest and South.

WRITINGS: The Mystery of Ovid's Exile, University of California Press, 1964.

WORK IN PROGRESS: The Works of Ovid: Sixteenth Century Neo-Latin Works in England; The Greek Myths.

* * *

THOM, James Alexander   1933-

PERSONAL: Born May 28, 1933, in Gosport, Ind.; son of Jay Webb (a physician) and Julia (a physician; maiden name, Swain) Thom; married Cody Sweet (an international platform lecturer), May 16, 1975. Education: Butler University, B.A., 1960. Office: 9560 West Mallory Rd., Bloomington, Ind. 47401.

CAREER: Indianapolis Star, Indianapolis, Ind., business editor, 1964-67; Saturday Evening Post, Indianapolis, senior editor, 1971; communications director for state trade association, 1971-73; free-lance writer, 1973—. Lecturer at Indiana University, 1977—. Military service: U.S. Marine Corps, 1953-56; served in Korea; became sergeant.

WRITINGS: Let the Sun Shine In (inspirational essays), C. R. Gibson, 1976; Spectator Sport, Avon, 1978; George Rogers Clark: Long Knife, Avon, 1979. Contributor to popular magazines, including Reader's Digest, National Geographic, and Country Gentleman. Editor and contributing writer, Nuggets magazine, 1967—.

WORK IN PROGRESS: No Thank You, nonfiction; the first novel of a projected trilogy.

SIDELIGHTS: Thom writes: "No book or article is begun until some concept has asserted itself *irresistibly* in my mind. If I can't weed it out mentally, then I nurture it into whatever it calls for. My feeling is that if I can't put it aside after two or three months, then it's a compelling enough concept that should be meaningful for at least a few people. The idea is always the primary motivation. Then, as I must support myself, I try to write it clearly and entertainingly enough that it will sell well. I am concerned with the cruelty, thoughtlessness, and grossness of many of America's 'amusements,' and try often to state the case for reflectiveness and simplicity, both in nonfiction and fiction."

AVOCATIONAL INTERESTS: Sculpture, outdoor activities.

*   *   *

THOMAS, Bob
See THOMAS, Robert J(oseph)

*   *   *

THOMAS, Denis 1922-

PERSONAL: Born July 23, 1922, in London, England; son of John Tracy and Violet Warren (Gunston) Thomas; married Joyce Betts; children: David Martin, Stephen Matthew, James Christian, Paul Warren. *Education:* St. Edmund Hall, Oxford, B.A. (honors), 1949. *Home:* Coach House, Oakwood Close, Chislehurst, Kent, England.

CAREER: United Nations World, London, England, executive editor, 1950-51; Penguin Books, Harmondsworth, England, publicity manager, 1951-52; *Ingot,* London, editor and writer, 1952-57; Associated Newspapers, London, critic and leader writer, 1957-61; Independent Television News, London, deputy editor, 1961-64; *Advertising Quarterly,* London, editor, 1964—. Managing editor and editorial director for Quadrangle Publications; director of Peter Bloomfield & Co. Freeman of the City of London. *Member:* Society of Authors, Institute of Journalists, Association of Art Historians.

WRITINGS: Challenge in Fleet Street: A Candid Commentary on Today's National Newspapers, Truth Publishing, 1957; (editor) *Personal Opinion: An Anthology,* Thomas Nelson, 1963; *The Story of Newspapers* (juvenile), Methuen, 1965; *Competition in Radio,* Institute of Economic Affairs, 1965, 2nd edition, 1966; *Advertising,* Institute of Economic Affairs, 1965, revised edition, Longmans, Green, 1969; *Thomas Churchyard of Woodbridge,* Quadrangle, 1966; *The Visible Persuaders,* Hutchinson, 1967; *Copyright and the Creative Artist: The Protection of Intellectual Property With Special Reference to Music,* Institute of Economic Affairs, 1967; (editor) *A Village in Kent: The Historic and Cultural Heritage of New Ash Green,* Quadrangle, 1967; (editor) *The Connoisseur's Concise Encyclopaedia of Antiques,* two volumes, Sphere, 1969.

The Mind of Economic Man: An Anthology, Quadrangle, 1970; (editor with Ian Bennett) *The Price Guide to English Watercolours, 1750-1900,* Antique Collectors' Club, 1971; *The Impressionists,* Hamlyn, 1975; *Picasso and His Art,* Galahad Books, 1975; *Abstract Painting,* Dutton, 1976; *Battle Art: The Artist at War,* Phaidon, 1977.

Also co-author of *Television: From Monopoly to Competition,* 1962. Contributor to *Connoisseur, Antique Collector,* and *Listener.* Editor of *Economic Age,* 1968-70.

THOMAS, F(ranklin) Richard 1940-

PERSONAL: Born August 1, 1940, in Evansville, Ind.; son of Franklin Albert (a refrigeration engineer) and Lydia (a nurse; maiden name, Klausmeier) Thomas; married Sharon Kay Myers (a teacher), June 2, 1962; children: Severn Rhyl (son), Caerllion (daughter). *Education:* Purdue University, A.B., 1963, M.A., 1964; further graduate study at University of Minnesota, 1965; Indiana University, Ph.D., 1970. *Home:* 704 Beech St., East Lansing, Mich. 48823. *Office:* Department of American Thought and Language, Michigan State University, East Lansing, Mich. 48824.

CAREER: Purdue University, Calumet Campus, Calumet, Ind., instructor, 1969-70, assistant professor of English, 1970-71; Michigan State University, East Lansing, assistant professor, 1971-76, associate professor of American thought and language, 1976—. Has given poetry readings in the United States and Denmark, and on radio and television programs. *Member:* American Studies Association, Poets and Writers, Committee of Small Magazine Editors and Publishers, Coordinating Council of Literary Magazines, Society for the Study of Midwestern Literature, Associated Writing Programs, Fulbright Alumni Association. *Awards, honors:* Fulbright teaching grant for Copenhagen, Denmark, 1974-75; National Endowment for the Arts grant for *Centering,* 1978.

WRITINGS: Fat Grass (poetry chapbook), Nosferatu Press, 1970; (editor with Charles B. Tinkham, and contributor) *The Day After Yesterday* (anthology of Midwestern poets), Catalyst Press, 1971; (editor with Roger Pfingston and Richard Pflum, and contributor) *Stoney Lonesome: Forty Poets,* Nosferato Press, 1971.

Work represented in anthologies, including *A Globe of Fruit,* 1963; *Stoney Lonesome,* 1969; *Other Men's Flowers: A Continuing Anthology of the Best Poems From Today's Poetry Magazines and Literary Journals.* Contributor of more than a hundred poems, articles, and a story to magazines, including *Poet Lore, Beloit Poetry Journal, Sparrow,* and *Midwest.* Editor of *Centering: A Magazine of Poetry,* 1973—; former assistant editor of *Purdue English Notes, Quartet: A Magazine of the Arts, Abstracts of Folklore Studies,* and *Trial Flight;* former associate editor of *Bard.*

WORK IN PROGRESS: A book of poems and essays; editing *Years: Anthology of a Community,* publication expected in 1981.

SIDELIGHTS: Thomas writes: "In this shrinking world I consider interpersonal communication to be vital. My belief is illustrated by my work in progress. A special anthology issue of *Centering* will reveal, through poems, Danish poets' reactions to America; and the book of poems and essays will reveal my own reactions to the space in which I live; the short personal essays illustrate the motivating influences behind my poems."

AVOCATIONAL INTERESTS: Swimming, building with wood.

*   *   *

THOMAS, Robert J(oseph) 1922-
(Bob Thomas)

PERSONAL: Born January 26, 1922, in San Diego, Calif.; son of George H. (an editor and publicist) and Marguerite (Creelman) Thomas; married Patricia Thompson, September 6, 1947; children: Nancy Katherine, Janet Elizabeth, Caroline Brooke. *Education:* Attended University of California, Los Angeles, 1939-43. *Agent:* William Morris Agency, 1350 Avenue of the Americas, New York, N.Y. 10019. *Office:* Associated Press, 1111 South Hill St., Los Angeles, Calif. 90015.

CAREER: Associated Press, Los Angeles, Calif., staff writer, 1943—. Public lecturer; guest on radio and television programs. *Member:* Beta Theta Pi.

WRITINGS—Under name Bob Thomas: *Walt Disney: The Art of Animation,* Simon & Schuster, 1958; *Walt Disney: Magician of the Movies,* Grosset & Dunlap, 1967; *King Cohn,* Putnam, 1967; (with Tom Gries) *Will Penny, Star,* Ballentine, 1968; *Donna DeVarona: Gold Medal Winner,* Doubleday, 1968; *Thalberg: Life and Legend,* Doubleday, 1969; *Selznick,* Doubleday, 1970; *The Heart of Hollywood,* Price, Stern, 1971; (with Arthur Samish) *The Secret Boss of California,* Crown, 1971; *Winchell,* Doubleday, 1971; *Weekend Thirty-Three,* Doubleday, 1972; *Directors in Action,* Bobbs-Merrill, 1973; *Marlon: Portrait of the Rebel as an Artist,* Random House, 1973; (with Noah Dietrich) *Howard: The Amazing Mr. Hughes,* Fawcett, 1972; *Bud and Lou,* Lippincott, 1977; (with Bob Hope) *The Road to Hollywood: My Thirty-Five Year Love Affair With the Movies,* Doubleday, 1977.

Also author of *Flesh Merchants* (novel), 1958, and *The Massie Case,* 1966. Columnist. Contributor to magazines. Editor of *Action,* 1968—.

*   *   *

THOMPSON, China
See LEWIS, Mary (Christianna Milne)

*   *   *

THOMPSON, Josiah   1935-

PERSONAL: Born Janury 17, 1935 in East Liverpool, Ohio; son of Josiah D. (a salesman) and Marion (Postles) Thompson; married Nancy Willis, December 28, 1958; children: Lis, Everson. *Education:* Yale University, B.A., 1957, M.A., 1962, Ph.D., 1964; attended Oxford University, 1959-60. *Office:* Department of Philosophy, Haverford College, Haverford, Pa. 19041.

CAREER: Haverford College, Haverford, Pa., assistant professor, 1965-70, associate professor, 1970-76, professor of philosophy, 1976—. *Military service:* U.S. Navy, 1957-59; became lieutenant junior grade. *Awards, honors:* Guggenheim fellow, 1969-70.

WRITINGS: The Lonely Labyrinth (criticism), Southern Illinois University Press, 1967; *Six Seconds in Dallas* (history), Random House, 1967; (editor) *Kierkegaard: A Collection of Critical Essays,* Doubleday, 1972; *Kierkegaard,* Knopf, 1973.

WORK IN PROGRESS: A biography of Friedrich Nietzsche; a novel.

*   *   *

THOMPSON, Paul   1943-

PERSONAL: Born November 23, 1943, in Hitchin, England; son of Philip John and Doris (Swann) Thompson; married Janet Catriona (employed by British Broadcasting Corp.), May 8, 1965; children: Karen Nicola. *Education:* Attended school in Hitchin, England. *Politics:* Socialist. *Home:* 24 Carlton Hill, London N.W.8, England. *Agent:* Michael Imison, Jan van Loewen Ltd., 81-83 Shaftesbury Ave., London W1V 8BX, England.

CAREER: Professional actor and theater director, 1964-74;

Morley College, London, England, director of Theatre School, 1974—. Writer-in-residence at National Theatre. *Awards, honors:* Art Council bursary, 1976.

WRITINGS—Musical plays: *The Children's Crusade* (first produced in London, England at National Youth Theatre, September, 1973), Heinemann, 1975; *The Motor Show* (first produced in Dogenham, England at Leys Hall, March 1974; produced in London at Half Moon Theatre, April, 1974), Pluto Press, 1975; *By Common Consent* (first produced at National Youth Theatre, September 9, 1974), Heinemann, 1976; *The Lorenzaccio Story* (first produced in Stratford-upon-Avon, England at The Other Place, July 4, 1977), Pluto Press, 1978.

WORK IN PROGRESS: Research for a play about Picasso.

*   *   *

THOMPSON, Robert Elliott   1921-

PERSONAL: Born June 28, 1921, in Los Angeles, Calif.; son of Robert W. and Sadie (Berry) Thompson; married Mary C. Mattern, February 27, 1954; children: Robert Elliott, Monica Louise. *Education:* Indiana University, A.B., 1949. *Religion:* Episcopalian. *Home:* 1818 Parkside Dr. E., Seattle, Wash. 98112. *Office: Seattle Post-Intelligencer,* 521 Wall St., Seattle, Wash. 98121.

CAREER: Fort Wayne Journal-Gazette, Fort Wayne, Ind., reporter, 1949-51; reporter for International News Service, 1951-58; *New York Daily News,* New York, N.Y., reporter, 1959-62; *Los Angeles Times,* Los Angeles, Calif., Washington correspondent, 1962-66; Hearst Newspapers, chief of Washington bureau, 1966-68, national editor, 1968-74; *Seattle Post-Intelligencer,* Seattle, Wash., publisher, 1974—, author of weekly column. Ernie Pyle Lecturer at Indiana University; has given lectures all over the United States. Chairman of House and Senate correspondents standing committee, 1961. *Military service:* U.S. Naval Reserve, active duty, 1942-45.

MEMBER: White House Correspondents Association (president, 1966-67), National Press Club, Federal City Club, Seattle Chamber of Commerce (member of board of trustees, 1974—), Downtown Seattle Development Association (member of board of trustees, 1974—), Broadmoor Golf Club, Rainier Club, Harbor Club, Washington Athletic Club, Rotary International.

WRITINGS: (With Hortense Myers) *Robert Kennedy: The Brother Within,* Macmillan, 1962.

*   *   *

THOMPSON, William A(ncker)   1931-

PERSONAL: Born April 26, 1931, in Syracuse, N.Y.; son of Frederick Howe and Ellen (Ancker) Thompson; married Sally Whitmer; children: Cary Howe, Paige Whitmer. *Education:* Springfield College, B.S., 1953; California State University, Long Beach, M.A., 1961; further study at University of Southern California. *Home:* 2708 Petaluma Ave., Long Beach, Calif. 90815. *Office:* 4901 East Carson St., Long Beach, Calif. 90808.

CAREER: Wendell P. Clark Memorial, Wenchindon, Mass., physical director, 1957-58; Long Beach City College, Long Beach, Calif., associate professor of physical education and director of intramural-recreational sports, 1958—. In sales and promotions, California Sports Inc., 1960-77. *Military service:* U.S. Marine Corps Reserve, 1954-56; became first lieutenant. *Member:* National Intramural-Recreational Sports Association (past president), National Education Association, American Surfing Association, California Teachers Association, California Association for Health, Physical Education and Recreation.

WRITINGS: Modern Sports Officiating, W. C. Brown, 1974; (contributor) Intramural Readings, Prentice-Hall, 1976. Contributor to professional journals and newspapers.

WORK IN PROGRESS: Studying physical fitness and intramural-recreational sports administration; a revision of Modern Sports Officiating.

* * *

THORNTON, J(onathan) Mills III 1943-

PERSONAL: Born October 27, 1943, in Montgomery, Ala.; son of Jonathan Mills, Jr. (an investment banker) and Priscilla (Marks) Thornton. Education: Princeton University, B.A., 1966; Yale University, M.Phil., 1969, Ph.D., 1974. Religion: Episcopalian. Home: 2220 Washtenaw Ave., Ann Arbor, Mich. 48104. Office: Department of History, University of Michigan, Ann Arbor, Mich. 48109.

CAREER: University of Illinois at Chicago Circle, Chicago, instructor in history, 1971-74; University of Michigan, Ann Arbor, assistant professor, 1974-77, associate professor of history, 1977—. Involved in Alabama historical preservation activities. Member: Organization of American Historians, National Trust for Historic Preservation, Southern Historical Association, Alabama Historical Association, Princeton Club (member of Detroit board of directors, 1977—), Phi Beta Kappa. Awards, honors: Danforth fellow, 1966-74; Jules F. Landry Prize from Louisiana State University Press, 1977, for Politics and Power in a Slave Society; Guggenheim fellowship, 1978-79.

WRITINGS: Politics and Power in a Slave Society: Alabama, 1800-1860, Louisiana State University Press, 1978. Contributor to Southern history journals.

WORK IN PROGRESS: Monographs on the Montgomery bus boycott, 1955-56, and fiscal policies of nineteenth-century state governments of the lower South.

SIDELIGHTS: Thornton comments: "I specialize in the history of the American South, particularly the intellectual and political life of the region. I am also interested in the history of the Roman Republic, of China under the T'ang and Sung, and Georgian and Victorian England, and all aspects of American history."

AVOCATIONAL INTERESTS: Reading and writing poetry, serious music.

* * *

THOULESS, Robert H(enry) 1894-

PERSONAL: First syllable of surname rhymes with "cow"; born July 15, 1894, in Norwich, England; son of Henry James (an executive) and Maud (Harper) Thouless; married Priscilla Gorton, March 19, 1924; children: Susan Thouless Sobey, David. Education: Corpus Christi College, Cambridge, B.A., 1915, Ph.D., 1922. Politics: Socialist. Religion: Church of England. Home: 2 Leys Rd., Cambridge CB4 2AU, England.

CAREER: University of Manchester, Manchester, England, lecturer in psychology, 1921-26; University of Glasgow, Glasgow, Scotland, lecturer in psychology, 1926-38; Cambridge University, Cambridge, England, reader in educational psychology, 1938-61; writer and researcher, 1961—. Consultant to National Foundation for Educational Re-

search. Military service: British Army, 1917-18; served in Salonica; became second lieutenant. British Home Guard, 1941-42; became captain. Member: British Psychological Society (president, 1949), Society for Psychical Research (president, 1942-45). Awards, honors: Sc.D. from Cambridge University, 1953.

WRITINGS: Introduction to the Psychology of Religion, Cambridge University Press, 1923, revised edition, 1971; Straight and Crooked Thinking, Hodder & Stoughton, 1930, revised edition, 1974, published as How to Think Straight, Simon & Schuster, 1932; General and Social Psychology, University Tutorial Press, 1937, fourth edition, 1957; Straight Thinking in War Time, Hodder & Stoughton, 1942; Authority and Freedom, Hodder & Stoughton, 1954; Map of Educational Research, National Foundation for Educational Research, 1968; From Anecdote to Experiment in Psychical Research, Routledge & Kegan Paul, 1972. Contributor to Encyclopaedia Britannica and Chamber's Encyclopaedia. Contributor to psychology and parapsychology journals. Editor of "British Psychological Monographs," 1959-61.

WORK IN PROGRESS: Research on the bearings of parapsychology on questions of religion.

SIDELIGHTS: Thouless writes: "My religious interests led to my first book, Introduction to the Psychology of Religion, and are playing a large part in my present research. My service in the First World War made me a strong pacifist. This conviction played a large part in my most successful book, How to Think Straight. I think that the motive which drove me to write the book was my reaction against the kind of emotional thinking that was behind warlike attitudes. I revised it in 1974 not because I had changed but because I realized that the sort of things people had controversies about had changed. I tried to make its controversial matter up-to-date. In a deeper sense I realize the whole attitude of the book is out of date. Few people now seem to value the dispassionate liberalism that I was trying to promulgate: the young seem rather to go for passionate opinions on the right or the left. But this book is still sold, so it may be having some influence on thought in the direction I want.

"This attitude of dispassionate appraisal was also what I was aiming at in my book on the psychology of religion. Psychology seemed to me to provide an attitude for the sort of dispassionate study of religion that was made by William James. It was not intended to make people less devout but it was meant to encourage them to be more tolerant. Since that time, people have grown more tolerant in religious matters and also less devout. I think it is unlikely that the psychological study of religion has had much to do with either change."

* * *

THWAITES, Michael 1915-

PERSONAL: Born May 30, 1915, in Brisbane, Australia; son of Robert Ernest (a schoolmaster) and Jeine (Nelson) Thwaites; married Honor Mary Good, December 23, 1939; children: Peter, Penelope, Richard, John. Education: Attended University of Melbourne, 1934-37, and Oxford University, 1937-39 and 1946. Religion: Church of England. Home: 49 Cobby St., Campbell, Australian Capital Territory 2601, Australia.

CAREER: University of Melbourne, Parkville, Australia, lecturer in English, 1947-49; Australian Public Service, member of staff, 1950-71, assistant parliamentary librarian, 1971-76; writer, 1976—. Military service: Royal Naval (Volunteer) Reserve, 1939-45; became lieutenant commander; received Atlantic Star. *Awards, honors:* Rhodes scholar at Victoria University of Wellington, 1937; Newdigate Prize from Oxford University, 1938, for poem "Milton Blind"; King's Medal for Poetry, 1940.

WRITINGS: Milton Blind (poems), Basil Blackwell, 1938; *The Jervis Bay and Other Poems,* Putnam, 1943; *Poems of War and Peace,* F. W. Cheshire, 1968. Author of "Poetry Notebook," a weekly column in *Age,* 1950-53.

* * *

TIGAR, Michael E(dward) 1941-

PERSONAL: Born January 18, 1941, in Glendale, Calif.; son of Charles H. (a machinist) and Margaret Elizabeth (a health plan executive; maiden name, Bowers) Tigar; children: Jon Steven, Katherine Ayer. *Education:* University of California, Berkeley, B.A., 1962, J.D., 1966. *Home:* Wolford Farm, Waterford, Va. 22190. *Agent:* Ann Buchwald, 2327 Hawthorne, Washington, D.C. 20016. *Office:* Suite 201, 1302 18th St. N.W., Washington, D.C. 20036.

CAREER: Pacifica Foundation Radio, Berkeley, Calif., announcer and director of children's programs, 1959-62, European correspondent, 1962-63, associate director of public affairs in Los Angeles, Calif., 1963; summer intern with American Civil Liberties Union of Northern California, 1965; Williams & Connolly (law firm), Washington, D.C., attorney, 1966-69; University of California, Los Angeles, acting professor of law, 1969-71; Kennedy & Rhine (law firm), San Francisco, Calif., counsel, 1971-74; Williams, Connolly & Califano, Washington, D.C., attorney, 1974-75, partner, 1976-77; Tigar & Buffone (law firm), Washington, D.C., partner, 1977—. Admitted to the Bar of Washington, D.C., 1967. Free-lance journalist, 1962-63. Maintained private practice of international law in France, 1972-74. Visiting fellow at Center for the Study of Democratic Institutions, 1971; adjunct professor of law at Georgetown University, 1975-76, 1977-78; lecturer in criminal procedure at State University of New York at Buffalo, 1976-77. *Member:* Order of the Coif. *Awards, honors:* Ford Foundation fellow in international law, 1965.

WRITINGS: (With Madeleine R. Levy) *Law and the Rise of Capitalism,* Monthly Review Press, 1977.

Contributor: Norman Dorsen, editor, *The Rights of Americans,* Pantheon, 1971; Robert Lefcourt, editor, *Law Against the People,* Random House, 1971; Richard A. Falk, editor, *The Vietnam War and International Law,* Volume III: *The Widening Context,* Princeton University Press, 1972; Crocker Snow, Jr., editor, *The Unfinished Revolution,* Boston Globe, 1976.

Contributor of articles to *Harvard Law Review, Yale Law Journal, Michigan Law Review,* and other journals in his field. Editor-in-chief of *California Law Review,* 1965-66.

WORK IN PROGRESS: Capitalism and Crime.

SIDELIGHTS: When asked about the contributions of the late-1960's counter culture to the current national temperament, Tigar told *CA:* "The contribution of the radical and revolutionary movements of the 1960's cannot yet be fully measured. The young people who cared and dared and struggled helped force an unpopular President to decline re-election over the issue of a widening war. They also helped awaken that sense of governmental accountability which in turn forced another President to resign in disgrace. These are accomplishments enough to recount for now."

Some of Tigar's controversial clients have included H. Rap Brown, Angela Davis, and David Truong.

TIMPE, Eugene Frank 1926-

PERSONAL: Born September 24, 1926, in Tacoma, Wash.; son of Charles William (in automobile sales) and Olga (Hordich) Timpe; married Sally Madison, February 18, 1950; children: Leslie Charles, Stephen Frederick, Kathryn Meredith. *Education:* Occidental College, B.A., 1948; University of Southern California, M.A., 1952, Ph.D., 1960. *Residence:* Carbondale, Ill. *Office:* Department of Foreign Languages and Literatures, Southern Illinois University, Carbondale, Ill. 62901.

CAREER: El Camino College, Los Angeles, Calif., instructor in English, 1953-66; Pennsylvania State University, State College, associate professor of German and comparative literature, 1966-72; Southern Illinois University, Carbondale, professor of German and comparative literature, 1972—, chairman of department, 1972—. Fulbright teacher in Vienna, Austria, 1958-59, and Rome, Italy, 1960-61; lecturer at University of Maryland, Munich, Germany, 1963-64; visiting professor at University of Neuchatel and University of Fribourg, 1970-71. Member of Fulbright-Hays national screening committee, 1973. *Military service:* U.S. Navy, aviation cadet, 1944-45.

MEMBER: International Comparative Literature Association, Internationale Vereinigung fuer Germanische Sprachund-Literaturwissenschaft, Modern Language Association of America, American Comparative Literature Association, Association of Departments of Foreign Languages (member of executive committee, 1976-79; president, 1977), Joint National Committee on Languages, Lessing Society, Dante Society.

WRITINGS: American Literature in Germany, 1861-1872, University of North Carolina Press, 1964; (editor) *Thoreau Abroad,* Archon Books, 1971. Contributor of about twenty-five articles and reviews to scholarly journals.

WORK IN PROGRESS: Austrian Literary Rococo.

SIDELIGHTS: Timpe writes: "My major scholarly interest is comparative literature. By this I mean the study of literature (German, American, English, and Italian) in related contexts (international and interdisciplinary). This has come about largely as a result of having lived in Europe for four years, personal interest, and academic training. My article, 'Memory and Some Poetic Structures,' is an attempt to develop relationships between cognitive psychology and literature. In 1978, I was in Vienna, working on *Austrian Literary Rococo.*"

* * *

TOLAN, Stephanie S. 1942-

PERSONAL: Born October 25, 1942, in Canton, Ohio; daughter of Joseph Edward and Mary (Schroy) Stein; married Robert W. Tolan (a managing director of a theater), December 19, 1964; children: R. J. *Education:* Purdue University, B.A., 1964, M.A., 1967. *Home:* 3631 Michigan Ave., Cincinnati, Ohio 45208. *Agent:* Marilyn Marlow, Curtis Brown Ltd., 575 Madison Ave., New York, N.Y. 10022.

CAREER: Purdue University, Fort Wayne, Ind., instructor in continuing education, 1966-70; State University of New York College at Buffalo, faculty member in speech and theater, 1972; Franklin & Marshall College, Lancaster, Pa., adjunct faculty member in English, 1973-75, coordinator of continuing education, 1974-75; writer, 1975—. Lecturer at Indiana University, 1966-70; actress, performing with Curtain Call Co., 1970-71. *Member:* Actors' Equity Association.

WRITINGS: The Ledge (one-act play), Samuel French, 1968; "Not I, Said the Little Red Hen" (one-act play), first produced in New York City, 1971; *Grandpa—and Me* (juvenile), Scribner, 1978. Also author of *The Eden Papers.*

Contributor of poems to more than a dozen literary magazines, including *Roanoke Review, Descant,* and *Green River Review.*

WORK IN PROGRESS: A novel for young adults.

SIDELIGHTS: Stephanie Tolan writes: "After many years of the academic world, writing poetry and some plays while 'hiding out' behind a full-time academic career, I moved to Ohio and chose not to look for a teaching or administrative position, but to take a chance on writing full-time, writing novels, writing for 'young adults.' I find this new career, which I put off for too many years, far more challenging and fulfilling than any of the others."

* * *

TOMSON, Bernard 1909-1978

1909—May 9, 1978; American lawyer, politician, educator, and author. Tomson was a trial and appellate lawyer in private practice until his election to the District Court of Nassau County. He was later appointed by Governor Nelson A. Rockefeller to the County Court. Tomson lectured at numerous colleges, was an officer of the Nassau County Mental Health Board, and helped found the North Shore University Hospital. Tomson wrote several books on topics in his field. He died in Bronx, N.Y. Obituaries and other sources: *Who's Who in America,* 38th edition, Marquis, 1974; *New York Times,* May 11, 1978.

* * *

TONKINSON, Robert 1928-

PERSONAL: Born September 12, 1938, in Perth, Australia; came to the United States in 1968; son of John Isaac (a fitter) and Ellen E. (Broughton) Tonkinson; married Myrna R. Ewart (an anthropologist), June 12, 1971. *Education:* University of Western Australia, B.A. (honors), 1957, M.A., 1966; University of British Columbia, Ph.D., 1972; Australian National University, postdoctoral study, 1973-75. *Home:* 189 West 36th, Eugene, Ore. 97405. *Office:* Department of Anthropology, University of Oregon, Eugene, Ore. 97403.

CAREER: School teacher in Harvey, Australia, 1958-60, and Fremantle, Australia, 1961-63; University of Oregon, Eugene, assistant professor, 1971-76, associate professor of anthropology, 1976—. *Member:* American Anthropological Association (fellow), National Humanities Faculty, Association for Social Anthropology in Oceania (fellow; member of board of directors, 1975-79), Sociological Association of Australia and New Zealand, Australian Social Anthropology Association, Australian Anthropological Society.

WRITINGS: Maat Village, Efate: A Relocated Community in the New Hebrides, University of Oregon Press, 1968; *The Jigalong Mob: Aboriginal Victors of the Desert Crusade,* Cummings, 1974; *The Mardudjara Aborigines: Living the Dream in Australia's Desert,* Holt, 1978.

Contributor: R. M. Berndt, editor, *Australian Aboriginal Anthropology,* University of Western Australia Press, 1970; M. D. Lieber, editor, *Exiles and Migrants in the Pacific,* University of Hawaii Press, 1973; Berndt, editor, *Social and Cultural Change,* Australian Institute of Aboriginal Studies, 1974; L. R. Hiatt, editor, *Ethnoclassification,* Australian Institute of Aboriginal Studies, 1974; M. Howard, editor,

Aboriginal Politics in Western Australia, University of Western Australia Press, 1975.

Contributor to academic journals, including *Anthropological Forum, Pacific Affairs, Origin,* and *American Anthropologist.*

WORK IN PROGRESS: Continuing sociological research in the New Hebrides and the Australian desert.

SIDELIGHTS: Tonkinson writes: "My writings center on aspects of both traditional and postcontact cultures of desert aborigines (Australia) and Melanesians (New Hebrides); I have a major interest in social organization and ritual, but also in reactions to Western society and adaptive strategies that traditional peoples adopt in coping with contact situations, in which rapid change is occurring. I am also interested in looking at the ways continuities from the past (traditional elements) continue to shape peoples' coping strategies and provide a stable base from which to operate in dealing with powerful alien pressures. I hope to continue to be of practical assistance to the peoples I've been privileged to study, and consider this a life-long commitment."

* * *

TOPLIN, Robert Brent 1940-

PERSONAL: Born September 26, 1940, in Philadelphia, Pa.; son of Maurice C. (a businessman) and Janet (a commodities manager) Toplin; married Aida Zukowski (a college instructor in Spanish), September 3, 1962; children: Cassandra, Jennifer. *Education:* Pennsylvania State University, B.S., 1962; Rutgers University, M.A., 1965, Ph.D., 1968. *Home:* 122 Chapin Pl., Granville, Ohio 43023. *Agent:* Scott Meredith Literary Agency, 845 Third Ave., New York, N.Y. 10022. *Office:* Department of History, Denison University, Granville, Ohio 43023.

CAREER: Denison University, Granville, Ohio, assistant professor of history, 1968-74; University of Houston, Clear Lake City, Tex., associate professor of history, 1974-75; Denison University, associate professor of history, 1976—. Active in civic affairs.

MEMBER: American Historical Association, Organization of American Historians, Latin American Studies Association. *Awards, honors:* Ford Foundation grants, 1967 and 1971; National Endowment for the Humanities younger humanist fellowship, 1969, grant, 1977; American Philosophical Society fellowship, 1970.

WRITINGS: The Abolition of Slavery in Brazil, Atheneum, 1972; *Slavery and Race Relations in Latin America,* Greenwood Press, 1974; *Unchallenged Violence: An American Ordeal,* Greenwood Press, 1975; (contributor) Martin Kilson, editor, *Harvard Studies on the African Diaspora,* Harvard University Press, in press. Contributor of articles and reviews to history and Latin American studies journals.

WORK IN PROGRESS: The Black Revolution, 1954-1976; Slavery in Crisis: Abolition in the United States and Brazil; project director for "Slavery in America," a public television series.

SIDELIGHTS: Toplin told *CA* that he is "presently working on a broad-scale comparison of the abolition of slavery in the United States and Brazil which investigates race relations, the economics of slavery, abolitionist activities, the defense of slavery, and the fear of slave violence during the period of political confrontations over abolition."

TOREN, Heller

PERSONAL: Children: Paula. Education: Educated in Elmslie, England. Agent: Elaine Markson Literary Agency, Inc., 44 Greenwich Ave., New York, N.Y. 10011.

CAREER: Writer.

WRITINGS: The Performer, Belmont-Tower, 1971; Not for Beginners, Pocket Books, 1972; Strange Games, Pocket Books, 1973; For Love of a Painted Lady, Pocket Books, 1975; Lola, Berkley, 1978.

WORK IN PROGRESS: Louisa-Mia, a sequel to Lola; research for a novel set in present-day New England.

SIDELIGHTS: Heller Toren writes: "I am a six-foot red-head who would like to be invisible. I speak three languages and have lived in Tangiers, Marrakesh, Rome, Nice, Marbella, Palma, Paris, and London. I like cats, movies, surprises, and marigolds, and most of all, pounding a typewriter. I don't like sleeping, airplanes, chocolate, and cigarette smoke. It's my ambition to live to a hundred-fifty so I can finish all the books I have in my head and then to die happy, of sunstroke."

* * *

TORTOLANO, William 1930-

PERSONAL: Born January 25, 1930, in Providence, R.I.; son of William A. and Maria (Campopiano) Tortolano; married Martha Kane (a concert singer), June 18, 1960; children: William, Allegra, Jonathan. Education: Boston University, B.Mus., 1953; New England Conservatory of Music, M.Mus., 1959; University of Montreal, D.Mus., 1964. Religion: Roman Catholic. Home address: P.O. Box 93, Underhill, Vt. 05489. Office: Department of Fine Arts, St. Michael's College, Winooski, Vt. 05404.

CAREER: St. Michael's College, Winooski, Vt., assistant professor, 1960-64, associate professor, 1964-68, professor of music and fine arts, 1968—. Musical director and conductor of Vermont Philharmonic, 1974-77; member of high table at Cambridge University, 1969-70, 1974. Member: National Association of Teachers of Singing, American Guild of Organists, American Federation of Musicians, American Federation of Labor, American Musicological Society.

WRITINGS: Choral Music for Men's Voices, Scarecrow, 1974; Samuel Coleridge Taylor, Scarecrow, 1977.

WORK IN PROGRESS: Shakespeare and Music, a study of "music during the time of Shakespeare, but also Shakespeare in opera (e.g., Verdi's 'Otello'), musical theater, symphony, and songs."

* * *

TOWER, Don
See BOWER, Donald E(dward)

* * *

TOWNE, Mary
See SPELMAN, Mary

* * *

TOWNSEND, Mark
See WALLMANN, Jeffrey M(iner)

* * *

TRACEY, Hugh (Travers) 1903-1977

January 29, 1903—October, 1977; British-born authority on African music. The director of the International Library of African Music since 1947, Tracey also lectured on the subject at more than fifty universities. He wrote articles, translations, and a musical play as well as several books on his specialty, including Zulu Paradox and African Dances of the Witwatersrand Gold Mines. He died in Johannesburg, South Africa. Obituaries and other sources: AB Bookman's Weekly, February 6, 1978. (See index for CA sketch)

* * *

TRACHTENBERG, Inge 1923-

PERSONAL: Born September 18, 1923, in Berlin, Germany; came to the United States in 1940, naturalized citizen, 1943; daughter of Ernest (a salesman) and Eve (Joske) Wachenheim; married Leo Eschelbacher, February, 1941 (divorced); married Michael Trachtenberg (an executive), August 5, 1949; children: (first marriage) Michael; (second marriage) David. Education: Educated in Berlin, Germany. Politics: Democrat. Religion: Jewish. Home and office: 288 Oakwood Rd., Englewood, N.J. 07631. Agent: Susan Pollock, 65 West 55th St., New York, N.Y.

CAREER: Writer, 1971—. Member of board of advisers of Englewood Jewish Community Center; active in civic and religious affairs. Member: Authors Guild, Authors League of America. Awards, honors: First prize from Great Lakes Colleges Association, 1973, for So Slow the Dawning.

WRITINGS: So Slow the Dawning (novel), Norton, 1973; An Arranged Marriage (novel), Norton, 1975; Let My Children Live (nonfiction), Summit Books, in press. Contributor of short stories to periodicals.

SIDELIGHTS: Inge Trachtenberg writes: "I waited a long time before I could clear the time for myself in which to write. Due to family circumstances I am, to this day, not entirely free. A mixed blessing, necessitating working always under pressure! On the other hand—very rewarding personal relationships."

* * *

TRACY, Aloise
See SHOENIGHT, Aloise

* * *

TRAMBLEY, Estela Portillo 1936-

PERSONAL: Born January 16, 1936, in El Paso, Tex.; daughter of Frank (a diesel mechanic) and Delfina (Fierro) Portillo; married Robert D. Trambley (in the automobile business), 1953; children: Naurene (Mrs. Karl Klements), Joyce, Tina, Robbie, Tracey (Mrs. Kenneth Nance). Education: University of Texas, El Paso, B.A., 1957, M.A., 1977. Home: 131 Clairemont, El Paso, Tex. 79912. Office: Department of Drama, Community College, 6601 Dyer, El Paso, Tex. 79904.

CAREER: High school English teacher in El Paso, Tex., 1957-64, chairman of department, 1965-69; Community College, El Paso, resident dramatist, 1970—. Hostess of "Estela Sezs," a talk show on Radio KIZZ, 1969-70, and "Cumbres," a cultural show on KROD-TV, 1971-72. Awards, honors: Quinto Sol Award for Literature from Quinto Sol Publications Bilingual League of the San Francisco Bay Area, 1973.

WRITINGS: Days of the Swallows (drama), El Espejo Quinto Sol, 1971; Impressions (Haiku poetry), El Espejo Quinto Sol, 1972; (editor) Chicanas en literatura y Ante (title means "Chicana Women in Literature and Art"), Quinto

Sol, 1974; *Rain of Scorpions* (short stories), Tonatiuh International, 1976.

Plays: "Morality Play" (three-act musical), first produced in El Paso, Tex., at Chamizal National Theatre, 1974; "Blacklight" (three-act drama), first produced in El Paso at Chamizal National Theatre, 1975; "El Hombre Cosmico" (title means "The Cosmic Man"), first produced in El Paso at Chamizal National Theatre, 1975; "Sun Images" (musical), first produced in El Paso at Chamizal National Theatre, 1976; "Isabel and the Dancing Bear" (three-act), first produced in El Paso at Chamizal National Theatre, 1977.

Work represented in anthologies, including *We Are Chicano*, Washington Square Press, 1974; *Chicano Theatre*, Notre Dame University Press, 1976.

WORK IN PROGRESS: Two novels, *Woman of the Earth* and *Perla;* producing and directing a video film, "Por la Calle" (title means "Along the Street").

SIDELIGHTS: Estela Trambley writes: "I would like to write and produce plays that are structured in traditional form. It is another direction from the 'acto' and the sociopolitical products which, innovative as they may be, still fail to meet the standards of good theatre. My own work in drama must undergo a lot of rewriting and change to meet those standards too. Having the opportunity to experiment with live productions of my own work focuses the flaws and the strong points in my work. The writing of the novel is another kind of challenge, lonely, restrospective, and inward drama of evolutionary growth and change. A novel is 'all up to me' if it has any worth or success. Drama involves the players, the audience outside of myself. It is a more precarious challenge, more joyous than the writing of a novel because one works with people—energy outside of oneself as a writer. But the 'power of myself,' the lonely and creative elation of novel-writing is winning over. The energy is from within."

* * *

TRAVERSI, Derek A(ntona) 1912-

PERSONAL: Born November 7, 1912, in England; came to the United States in 1970; son of Hugh Antona and Marjorie (Snow) Traversi; married Concepcion Vazquez de Castro, December 29, 1944; children: Elizabeth Traversi Dunn, Margaret, John, Susan, Helen. *Education:* Oxford University, M.A., 1934, B.Litt., 1937; University of London, B.A., 1938. *Religion:* Roman Catholic. *Home:* 401 Walnut Lane, Swarthmore, Pa. 19081. *Office:* Department of English Literature, Swarthmore College, Swarthmore, Pa. 19081.

CAREER: British Institute, Madrid, Spain, director in Bilbao, Spain, 1944-45, and Barcelona, Spain, 1945-48; British Council, director of cultural relations in Montevideo, Uruguay, 1948-50, Santiago, Chile, 1950-55, Teheran, Iran, 1955-59, Madrid, Spain, 1959-66, and Rome, Italy, 1966-70; Swarthmore College, Swarthmore, Pa., professor of English, 1970—.

WRITINGS: An Approach to Shakespeare, Paladin Press, 1938, 3rd edition, two volumes, Doubleday, 1969; *Shakespeare: The Last Phase*, Stanford University Press, 1954; *Shakespeare: From "Richard II" to "Henry V"*, Stanford University Press, 1957; *Shakespeare: The Roman Plays*, Stanford University Press, 1963; *T. S. Eliot: The Longer Poems*, Harcourt, 1976. Contributor to literary journals.

WORK IN PROGRESS: Studying medieval literature, especially Chaucer and Dante.

TREANOR, John Holland 1903(?)-1978

1903(?)—March 21, 1978; American educator and author. Treanor was a teacher of English and principal in the Boston public school system for thirty years before becoming a full-time lecturer and consultant. He wrote "The Treanor English Series," a group of textbooks used in elementary schools throughout the country. He also contributed over two hundred articles to journals in his field. Treanor died in Hyattsville, Md. Obituaries and other sources: *Washington Post*, March 22, 1978.

* * *

TREASURE, G(eoffrey) R(ussell) R(ichards) 1929-

PERSONAL: Born December 16, 1929, in Shrewsbury, Shropshire, England; son of Charles Edgar and Meriall (Steward) Treasure; married Melisa Humphreys, July 29, 1967; children: Catherine, Alexandra, Magdalen, Georgiana. *Education:* Oriel College, Oxford, B.A., 1954, M.A., 1961. *Religion:* Anglican. *Office:* Harrow School, Harrow in the Hill, Middlesex, England.

CAREER: Harrow School, Harrow on the Hill, England, member of history department, 1955-68, senior history master, 1968—. *Military service:* British Army, Royal Artillery, 1949-50; became second lieutenant. *Member:* Historical Association.

WRITINGS: Who's Who in History, Basil Blackwell, Volume IV (Treasure was not associated with earlier volumes): *England, 1714-1789*, 1969, Volume V: *England, 1789-1837*, 1975; *Seventeenth-Century France*, Evans Brothers, 1966, 2nd edition, J. Murray, 1979; *Cardinal Richelieu and the Development of Absolutism*, St. Martin's, 1972; *Reason and Authority*, Macmillan, 1979. Contributor to history journals.

WORK IN PROGRESS: Life of Cardinal Mazarin.

SIDELIGHTS: Treasure writes: "My writing arises from my teaching of history. From my experience of the needs of students in the sixteen to eighteen range, I have come to think that writing which bridges the gap between specialist monograph and popular textbook account is valuable. I have been strongly influenced by the idea of the wholeness of European civilisation."

AVOCATIONAL INTERESTS: European travel (including France), nineteenth century novels.

* * *

TREAT, Ida
See BERGERET, Ida Treat

* * *

TREFFLICH, Henry (Herbert Frederick) 1908-1978

January 9, 1908—July 7, 1978; German-born American animal importer, proprieter, and author. He traveled around the world twice on a tramp steamer and worked odd jobs in New York City before starting his own business in 1931. From his famed animal dealership Trefflich sold more than 1.5 million monkeys in his forty year career, some of which were used for polio research and for the laboratory experiments leading to the Rh blood factor discovery. He co-authored two books, *They Never Talk Back*, and his 1967 autobiography, *Jungle For Sale*. Trefflich died in Bound Brook, N.J. Obituaries and other sources: *Current Biography*, Wilson, 1953; *Who's Who in America*, 39th edition, Marquis, 1976; *New York Times*, July 9, 1978. (See index for *CA* sketch)

TREHEY, Harold F. 1902(?)-1978

1902(?)—May 5, 1978; New Zealand-born priest and author. During World War II, Trehey served as a military chaplain in Africa and Italy. He was a lecturer at Catholic University and pastor of the Holy Ghost Church in Maryland. Trehey wrote *Foundation of a Modern Guild System* and *War and Depressions.* He died in Washington, D.C. Obituaries and other sources: *Washington Post,* May 10, 1978.

* * *

TRELL, Bluma L(ee) 1903-

PERSONAL: Born March 10, 1903, in New York, N.Y.; daughter of Mark (a portrait painter) and Mary (Samuels) Popkin; married Max Trell, September 6, 1924; children: Max, Jr. *Education:* New York University, LL.B., 1924, B.A., 1935, Ph.D., 1942. *Home:* 110 Bleecker St., New York, N.Y. 10012. *Office:* Department of Classics, New York University, 7 Rufus Smith Hall, New York, N.Y. 10003.

CAREER: S. L. Prager, New York City, managing attorney, 1926-28; William A. Hyman, New York City, managing attorney, 1930-32; New York University, New York City, assistant professor, 1959-61, associate professor, 1961-67, professor of classics and comparative literature, 1967-72, lecturer in classics, 1973—. Assistant in classics at University of California, Los Angeles, 1940-41, and at Hunter College (now of the City University of New York), 1941-44; lecturer at colleges and universities, professional meetings, and conferences in the United States, Italy, Denmark, Turkey, England, and Tunisia.

MEMBER: International Papyrological Society, Classical Association of the Atlantic States, American Philological Society, Archaeological Institute of America, American Numismatic Society (fellow), American Oriental Society, Royal Numismatic Society of Great Britain, British Museum Society, Ancient Civilization Group of Metropolitan New York (chairman, 1974), New York Classics Club, Columbia University Classical Seminar, New York University Colloquium in Comparative Literature, New York University Law Alumni Association (honorary life member), Phi Beta Kappa, Eta Sigma Phi. *Awards, honors:* American Council of Learned Societies grants, 1963, 1967, 1968, 1972, 1974, 1976; National Science Foundation grant, 1973; New York University, teaching award, 1974, presidential citation, 1975.

WRITINGS: The Temple of Artemis at Ephesos, American Numismatic Society, 1945; (with Martin Jessop Price) *Coins and Their Cities: Architecture on the Ancient Coins of Greece, Rome, and Palestine,* Wayne State University Press, 1977. Contributor to *Dictionary of Arts.* Contributor of articles and reviews to classics, archaeology, and numismatics journals.

WORK IN PROGRESS: New Light on the Punic West.

SIDELIGHTS: Trell is a specialist in the history of architecture, particularly buildings represented on ancient coins. Extensive research on Greek imperial coins enabled her to suggest a reconstruction of the facade of the Temple of Artemis, which is the subject of her first book. In 1973, she had a successful (and publicized) move to prevent the Metropolitan Museum in New York from selling some of its ancient coin collection.

The Munich Museum is preparing an exhibition around the book by Trell and Price which will be sent to all major museums of Europe. The British Museum is preparing a similar exhibit which will be sent to the major museums of England.

BIOGRAPHICAL/CRITICAL SOURCES: New York Times, February 1, 1973; *New York Post,* March 9, 1973, December 27, 1975.

* * *

TRIMBLE, Marshall I(ra) 1939-

PERSONAL: Born January 16, 1939, in Mesa, Ariz.; son of Ira W. (a railroad worker) and Juanita Trimble; married Gena Powell (a high school mathematics teacher), August 9, 1974. *Education:* Attended Phoenix College, 1956-58; Arizona State University, B.A., 1961, M.A., 1963. *Home:* 6401 East Hummingbird Lane, Paradise Valley, Ariz. 85253. *Office:* Department of Southwest Studies, Scottsdale Community College, Scottsdale, Ariz. 85251.

CAREER: Professional folksinger, 1966-69; high school teacher of Southwest history in Scottsdale, Ariz., 1969—. Arizona history teacher and director of Southwest studies at Scottsdale College, 1970—; Arizona history teacher at Mesa College, 1970—. President of Arizona Department Council on Abandoned Military Posts; member of Cowboy Hall of Fame. *Military service:* U.S. Marine Corps, 1956. *Member:* Western Historical Society, Arizona Historical Society, Scottsdale Historical Society, Tempe Historical Society.

WRITINGS: Arizona: A Panoramic History of a Frontier State, Doubleday, 1977.

WORK IN PROGRESS: A novel about Arizona in the early 1900's; a contemporary history of the brush country cowboys.

SIDELIGHTS: Trimble writes: "My primary interest is the West. My family came to Texas in the 1840's; my great grandfather was a lawman at Pleasanton, Tex.; my grandfather was a railroader along the Mexican border in the early 1900's; my father was raised at Langtry, Tex., along the Mexican border. I also learned much from traveling throughout the West as an entertainer."

BIOGRAPHICAL/CRITICAL SOURCES: Phoenix Gazette, January 12, 1974; *Arizona Highways,* April, 1976; *Arizona Republic,* June 6, 1976, May 13, 1977, July 3, 1977, July 10, 1977; *Scottsdale Progress,* June 24, 1976, August 3, 1977; *Phoenix,* November, 1976.

* * *

TRIMMER, Joseph F(rancis) 1941-

PERSONAL: Born August 4, 1941, in Cortland, N.Y.; son of Francis W. (a clergyman) and Margaret (Sieber) Trimmer; married Carol L. Straley (a congressional aide), June 12, 1966; children: Robert Gorden. *Education:* Colgate University, B.A., 1963; Purdue University, M.A., 1966, Ph.D., 1968. *Home:* 409 Tyrone Dr., Muncie, Ind. 47304. *Office:* Department of English, Ball State University, Muncie, Ind. 47306.

CAREER: Ball State University, Muncie, Ind., assistant professor, 1968-72, associate professor of English, 1972—.

WRITINGS: A Casebook on Ralph Ellison's Invisible Man, Crowell, 1972; *Black American Literature: Notes on the Problems of Definition* (monograph), Ball State University, 1972; (with Robert R. Kettler) *American Oblique: Writing About the American Experience,* Houghton, 1976; *The National Book Award for Fiction: An Index to the First Twenty-Five Years,* G. K. Hall, 1978.

AVOCATIONAL INTERESTS: Photography.

TROWBRIDGE, Leslie Walter 1920-

PERSONAL: Born May 21, 1920, in Curtiss, Wis.; son of Donald H. (a farmer) and Anna (Koerner) Trowbridge; married Dorothee Kohring, August 31, 1946; children: David E., Thomas L., Edith L., Howard J. Education: Wisconsin State College (now University of Wisconsin), Stevens Point, B.S., 1940; University of Chicago, M.S., 1948; University of Wisconsin, Madison, M.S., 1953; University of Michigan, Ph.D., 1961. Religion: Methodist. Home: 2001 21st St., Greeley, Colo. 80631. Office: Department of Science Education, University of Northern Colorado, 357 Ross Hall, Greeley, Colo. 80639.

CAREER: Teacher at state elementary school in Milladore, Wis., 1941; elementary school science teacher in Lake Geneva, Wis., 1946; high school physics teacher in Wisconsin Rapids, Wis., 1947-54; University of Michigan, Ann Arbor, science teacher at university school, 1954-62; University of Northern Colorado, Greeley, assistant professor, 1962, associate professor, 1962-70, professor of science education and meteorology, 1970—, chairperson of department of science education, 1966—. Summer lecturer at College of Guam, 1967. Military service: U.S. Army Air Forces, meteorologist, 1942-46; served in China-Burma-India theater; became first lieutenant.

MEMBER: National Science Teachers Association (president, 1973), Council for the Advancement of Research in Science Teaching, National Association for Research in Science Teaching, Central Association of Science and Mathematics Teachers, Colorado Science Teachers Association, Phi Delta Kappa, Lambda Sigma Tau, Sigma Zeta, Kiwanis International. Awards, honors: Fellow of New York University, 1969-70.

WRITINGS: (With Sund) Teaching Science by Inquiry, C. E. Merrill, 1967, new edition, 1973; (with Sund, Tillery, and Olson) Elementary Science, Teaching Activities, 1970; (with Sund, MacCracken, and others) Science Through Discovery, L. W. Singer, 1970, new edition, 1972; (with Sund and Tillery) Elementary Science Discovery Lessons, Allyn & Bacon, 1970, new edition, 1972; Experiments in Meteorology: Investigations for the Amateur Scientist, Doubleday, 1970, new edition, 1973. Also author, with Sund, of Student-Centered Teaching in the Secondary School, 1974, and with Weinberg and Turner, Action in Physical Science, 1977. Contributor to education journals.

* * *

TRUBITT, Allen R(oy) 1931-

PERSONAL: Born August 24, 1931, in Chicago, Ill.; son of Harry (a draper) and Jennie (Swerdloff) Trubitt; married Anita Oberlander (a teacher), February 2, 1957 (divorced, December, 1973); children: David, Lisa. Education: Roosevelt University, B.Mus.Ed., 1953, M.Mus.Ed., 1954; Indiana University, D.Mus., 1964. Home: 920 Ward Ave., #13-E, Honolulu, Hawaii 96814. Office: Department of Music, University of Hawaii, 2411 Dole St., Honolulu, Hawaii 96822.

CAREER: Indiana University of Pennsylvania, Indiana, assistant professor, 1957-62, associate professor of music, 1962-64; University of Hawaii, Honolulu, professor of music, 1964—, chairman of department, 1971-75. Member of board of directors of Biographical Research Corp. Member of Seventh Army Symphony Orchestra and Honolulu Symphony Orchestra. Military service: U.S. Army, 1954-56. Member: American String Teachers Association. Awards, honors: Winner of Greenwood Press choral competition,

1966, with "The Carol of the Bird"; winner of Hawaii Bicentennial Commission choral competition, 1976, with "An American Letter."

WRITINGS: A Comprehensive Introduction to Musical Literature, Addison-Wesley, 1974; (with Robert S. Hines) Ear Training and Sight Singing, two volumes, G. Schirmer, 1978.

Author of about fifty musical compositions, including "Three Songs on the Shortness of Life," Roger Dean, 1973; "Ann Rutledge," Roger Dean, 1975; "Markings," Roger Dean, 1976; "What Any Lover Learns," G. Schirmer, 1978; "Cotton Mather," G. Schirmer, 1978.

WORK IN PROGRESS: "Mani," a tone poem for band; "Cyrano de Bergerac," a theatre piece.

SIDELIGHTS: Trubitt told CA: "My career has been rather typical of many composers in the United States today. Primarily I am a teacher, centered in the university, which has become the focal point for most contemporary music composition and performance. Many of my pieces have been composed specifically for students and faculty performers. In addition to teaching theory and composition, I am a cellist and conductor."

* * *

TRUSCOTT, Robert Blake 1944-

PERSONAL: Born September 30, 1944, in Bronx, N.Y.; son of Francis Charles and Virginia (Schrader) Truscott; married Kamala Brush (a library administrator), June 20, 1967. Education: Rutgers University, B.A. (cum laude), 1966; Johns Hopkins University, M.A., 1967. Home and office: 88 Guilden St., New Brunswick, N.J. 08901.

CAREER: Rutgers University Bookstore, New Brunswick, N.J., trade book manager, 1967-70; Powell House (conference center), Old Chatham, N.Y., maintenance overseer, 1971-72; Trenton State College, Trenton, N.J., instructor in English, 1973-74; Jersey City State College, Jersey City, N.J., instructor in English, 1973-74; Rutgers University, New Brunswick, instructor in English at Douglass College, 1975-76; Middlesex County College, Edison, N.J., instructor in English, 1976-77; Rutgers University, instructor in English, 1977—. Leader of poetry workshops; co-founder of Kilmer House Poetry Center.

MEMBER: Poets and Writers, College English Association, Associated Writing Programs, Poets and Writers of New Jersey, Phi Beta Kappa. Awards, honors: Poetry prize from Poet Lore, 1972, for "Ulysses."

WRITINGS: Sojourn Among Strangers (poems), Olivant, 1967. Author of "Journalview," a review column in Stone Country, 1973—. Contributor of about one hundred poems and reviews to literary journals, including Virginia Quarterly Review, Nimrod, Mississippi Review, and California Quarterly.

WORK IN PROGRESS—Books of poems: Harlow's Glass; Lost Men, Lost Pages; Far Rockaway's Guitars.

SIDELIGHTS: Truscott writes: "I play the piano. Gershwin, Joplin, Fats Waller, Earl Hines, Jelly Roll Morton, James P. Johnson are my heroes. Maybe I turned to poetry because my fingers couldn't do the walking over those tough keys. I listen to them, try to absorb their technique through the permeable layers of my brain, and then play bad versions of their songs. Art Tatum is impossible. Rubenstein (A.) puts Chopin back on the map.

"I am fascinated by time and man's relation to it, at once

mortal and immortal. I take pictures, movies, and keep a family album. I look into history. I look into its eyes.

"When I was fourteen I went to England, and when I returned in a year, I was a poet. I have been writing and publishing ever since. I write poetry because I want to; because it is the most difficult pursuit a man can endeavor in the realm of words, possibly in anything, and I want to be one human being who does it well. The challenge is just too good to avoid; everything else is dross. Everything else is noise. I want to make music. And I write for another reason: poetry, any sort of writing really, makes me, not me, it. When we write we become ourselves; we become human at last. I have never thought of myself as anything other than poet-musician.

"I want to write one of everything: one great novel, one great play, one great epic poem, one great horror story, one great essay, one great lyric poem, one great history, one great criticism, one. . . .

"I also want to survive. I teach creative writing because I have to be in the Big Buck world. All of it bores me—except for the occasional student with the special awareness, with the talent. Then I get unbored. Occasionally, I learn things as well. But the rewards of teaching are not what they used to be—at least if we are to believe Highet—and the market dwindles and the students get worse. I do what I can to reverse the trend. Sometimes it works, sometimes it doesn't."

AVOCATIONAL INTERESTS: Making movies, collecting silent films (especially Charlie Chaplin's), history.

*   *   *

TRYTHALL, Anthony John   1927-

PERSONAL: Born March 30, 1927, in Rugby, England; son of Eric Stewart (an engineer) and Irene (Hollingham) Trythall; married Celia Haddon (a teacher), August 2, 1952; children: Timothy, Peter, Susan. *Education:* St. Edmund Hall, Oxford, B.A. (honors), 1947, diploma in education (with distinction), 1951; University of London, diploma in education, 1962, M.A. (with distinction), 1969. *Religion:* Church of England. *Residence:* London, England. *Office:* Headquarters, United Kingdom Land Forces, Wilton, Salisbury, Wiltshire, England.

CAREER: Schoolmaster in Coventry, England, 1951-53; British Army, Royal Educational Corps, career officer, 1953—, served in Malaya, 1954-56, in War Office, 1956-62, on the Rhine, 1962-66, education adviser to Regular Commissions Board, 1969-71, lecturer in war studies and international relations, 1971-72, chief inspector of army education, 1973-74, Ministry of Defense, 1974-76, chief education officer for United Kingdom Land Forces, 1976—, present rank, brigadier. Lecturer at War College. *Military service:* British Army, 1948-49; served in Egypt and Akaba; became captain. *Awards, honors:* Trench Gascoigne Prize from Royal United Services Institution, 1969.

WRITINGS: Boney Fuller: Soldier, Strategist, Writer, 1878-1966, Rutgers University Press, 1977, published in England as *Boney Fuller: The Intellectual General, 1878-1966,* Cassell, 1977. Contributor to military journals.

WORK IN PROGRESS: A book on Hore-Belisha at the War Office, 1937-40.

SIDELIGHTS: Trythall writes: "By profession I am both an Army officer and an educationalist. My interests lie in the field of war studies and history—history with a military flavour, but not campaign history. My chief current area of interest is focused on those military arenas (Defence Minis-

tries, Academies, and Headquarters, as well as battlefields) in which there is, or was, a perceptible and documentable interaction between political, technological, economic, and social change on the one hand and military activities, doctrines, and institutions on the other. It was this interest which drove me on in my research on Fuller. How could anyone believe that horses were better vehicles of war than tanks or armoured cars? It is this which motivates me in trying to sort out the whole Hore-Belisha affair. How could so able and successful a Secretary of State for War be sacked just as the Panzers were about to roll in 1940?

"As I have a foot in both the military and civilian camps I believe that I have some important qualifications for this sort of research and writing. In order to make real sense of civil-military interaction it is necessary first to understand the small print and the nuances on both sides. This is particularly important for anyone dealing with the British military in relation to the British political establishment where deep pitfalls lie in wait for those whose knowledge of either the Royal Green Jackets or the Parliamentary Labour Party is only superficial.

"Being still a serving soldier I am also deeply interested in the theory of war, and deterrence, but my historical training leads me to suppose that such theories are by no means absolute; just as the ways in which wars are fought (and not fought) or deterrence achieved will be greatly influenced by changes in political aims, social values, economic circumstances, or in the nature and cost of weapons and equipment."

AVOCATIONAL INTERESTS: Classical music, reading biographies, visiting Cornwall, "finding good food and wine at reasonable prices."

*   *   *

TUFTS, Eleanor

PERSONAL: Born in Exeter, N.H.; daughter of James A. (in business) and Hazel (a teacher; maiden name, Weinbeck) Tufts. *Education:* Simmons College, B.S., 1949; Harvard University, M.A., 1957; New York University, Ph.D., 1971. *Politics:* Democrat. *Religion:* Unitarian-Universalist. *Office:* Department of Fine Arts, Southern Methodist University, Dallas, Tex. 75275.

CAREER: Boston University, Boston, Mass., executive secretary, 1950-56; Council on International Educational Exchange, New York City, director of program development, 1957-60; World University Service, New York City, associate director, 1960-64; University of Bridgeport, Bridgeport, Conn., assistant professor of art history, 1964-66; Southern Connecticut State College, New Haven, associate professor of art history, 1966-74; Southern Methodist University, Dallas, Tex., professor of art history, 1974—. Trustee of Dallas Museum of Fine Arts. *Member:* College Art Association, American Association of University Professors (local vice-president, 1972-74, 1975-76). *Awards, honors:* National Endowment for the Humanities grant, summer, 1974.

WRITINGS: Our Hidden Heritage: Five Centuries of Women Artists, Paddington, 1974. Contributor to art journals.

WORK IN PROGRESS: Luis Melendez: His Life and Works, publication expected in 1980; *Women Artists in the Renaissance,* publication expected in 1981.

AVOCATIONAL INTERESTS: Music, travel.

BIOGRAPHICAL/CRITICAL SOURCES: Simmons Re-

view, Volume 56, number 1, 1973; *Dallas Morning News,* November 17, 1974.

* * *

TULL, James E. 1913-

PERSONAL: Born September 1, 1913, in Monticello, Ark.; son of Jacob Franklin (a clergyman) and Fannie (Jackson) Tull; married Virginia Tompkins (a public school music supervisor), October 15, 1937; children: Anne, James F. *Education:* Ouachita College, B.A., 1935; Baylor University, M.A., 1936; Southern Baptist Theological Seminary, Th.M., 1941; Columbia University, Ph.D., 1960. *Politics:* Democrat. *Home address:* P.O. Box 484, Wake Forest, N.C. 27587. *Office:* Department of Theology, Southeastern Baptist Theological Seminary, Wake Forest, N.C. 27587.

CAREER: Ordained Baptist minister; pastor of Baptist churches in Frankfort, Ky., 1938-41, and Blacksburg, Va., 1948-50; Southeastern Baptist Theological Seminary, Wake Forest, N.C., instructor, 1955-60, professor of theology, 1960—. *Military service:* U.S. Army Air Forces, chaplain, 1941-46. U.S. Air Force Reserve, chaplain, 1946-66; became major. *Member:* Lions Club.

WRITINGS: Shapers of Baptist Thought, Judson, 1972; *Take the Stand: A Theology of Witnessing,* Convention Press, 1972. Also author of *The Atoning Gospel.* Contributor to magazines.

SIDELIGHTS: Tull writes: "I have passed the age when I had a keen desire to see my name in print. My principal interests have been preaching and teaching, and I came to authorship late in my career. I have written because I wanted to say some things, not because I particularly cared to establish even a modest reputation as an author. My principal interest is to interpret Christian doctrines to students in such a way that they will become informed and competent pastoral theologians."

AVOCATIONAL INTERESTS: Travel (Europe, India, China, Mexico, Central America, the Caribbean), hiking.

* * *

TURLINGTON, Catherine (Isabel) Hackett 1900(?)-1978

1900(?)—April 1, 1978; American journalist and author. Turlington began her career as a reporter for the *Christian Science Monitor* in 1920, and later became a columnist for the *Washington Star* in the 1940's. Her book, *Three to Make Ready,* is based on observations she made of her three daughters, as well as materials that were used in her weekly column. Turlington died in Washington, D.C. Obituaries and other sources: *Washington Post,* April 4, 1978.

* * *

TURNAGE, Anne Shaw 1927-

PERSONAL: Born August 19, 1927, in Aliceville, Ala.; daughter of James Spann and Eunice (Morris) Shaw; married Maclyn Neil Turnage (a clergyman, professor, and writer), June 18, 1954; children: Lynn Anne, James Neil, Laurin Shaw. *Education:* Attended University of Alabama, 1945-49, and Presbyterian School of Christian Education, 1949-50. *Religion:* Presbyterian. *Home:* 1204 Confederate Ave., Richmond, Va. 23227.

CAREER: Writer.

*WRITINGS—*All with husband, Mac N. Turnage: *Global Consciousness,* Friendship, 1974; *People, Families, and*

God, John Knox, 1976; *More Than You Dare to Ask: The First Year of Living With Cancer,* John Knox, 1976; *Explorations Into Faith,* United Presbyterian Church of the United States of America, 1977. Author of church curriculum materials.

* * *

TURNAGE, Mac(lyn) N(eil) 1927-

PERSONAL: Born August 31, 1927, in D'lo, Miss.; son of Fletcher Neal and Maxine (McLaurin) Turnage; married Anne Shaw (a writer), June 18, 1954; children: Lynn Anne, James Neil, Laurin Shaw. *Education:* Southwestern College at Memphis, B.A. (honors), 1948; Union Theological Seminary, Richmond, Va., B.D., 1952, Th.M., 1955. *Home:* 1204 Confederate Ave., Richmond, Va. 23227. *Office:* Office of the Dean, Union Theological Seminary, 3401 Brook Rd., Richmond, Va. 23227.

CAREER: Ordained Presbyterian minister, 1952; Synod of Mississippi, Jackson, regional director of Christian education, 1952-54; pastor of Presbyterian churches in Pontotoc, Miss., 1955-58, Victoria, Tex., 1958-67, and Tokyo, Japan, 1967-71; Union Theological Seminary, Richmond, Va., interim director of field education, 1971-72, associate professor of ministry and academic adviser, 1972—.

*WRITINGS—*All with wife, Anne Turnage: *Global Consciousness,* Friendship, 1974; *People, Families, and God,* John Knox, 1976; *More Than You Dare to Ask: The First Year of Living With Cancer,* John Knox, 1976; *Explorations Into Faith,* United Presbyterian Church of the United States of America, 1977. Author of church curriculum material.

* * *

TURNER, Gladys T(ressia) 1935-

PERSONAL: Born September 16, 1935, in Tamo, Ark.; daughter of Willis J. and Mary (Bluford) Turner; married Frederick M. Finney (an economist), July 1, 1972. *Education:* Arkansas Agricultural, Mechanical, and Normal College (now University of Arkansas), B.A., 1957; Atlanta University, M.S.W., 1959; also attended Rutgers University, Smith College, and University of Cincinnati. *Religion:* Presbyterian. *Home:* 1107 Lexington Ave., Dayton, Ohio 45407. *Office:* Day-Mont West Community Mental Health Center, 601 Infirmary Rd., Dayton, Ohio 45426.

CAREER: Veterans Administration Hospital, Dayton, Ohio, clinical social worker, 1959-63; Franklin County Welfare Department, Columbus, Ohio, casework supervisor, 1964; Barney Children's Medical Center, Dayton, Ohio, social work administrator, 1965-75; Day-Mont West Community Mental Health Center, Dayton, Ohio, social work administrator, 1975—. Adjunct assistant professor at Wright State University, 1970-76. *Member:* National Association of Social Workers (local president, 1974-76), American Civil Liberties Union.

WRITINGS: The Autobiography of Tammy: A Life Full of Love and Fun, Challenge Books, 1978. Contributing editor of *Confrontation/CHANGE Review.*

SIDELIGHTS: Turner told *CA:* "*Autobiography of Tammy: A Life Full of Love and Fun* is a story for children and cat lovers. It is fiction that accounts the births, siblings, parents and growth of a young cat during her early years and adulthood. I wrote this story while recuperating from major surgery. Tammy, the cat in question was one of a litter of kittens born to an adult male cat that had been given to me by a co-worker, and a female cat that had been given to my husband sometime later. Tammy, along with her sister, and mother were my constant companions during my recovery. In the process of their presence and closeness, I could 'feel' and 'experience' what their lives may be like, and found myself writing the book.

"As a result of writing this book, I have explored the possibility of writing additional childrens' books."

*   *   *

TURNER, John H(enry) 1938-

PERSONAL: Born June 23, 1938, in Jersey City, N.J.; son of Harry (a real estate agent) and Bertha (Hall) Turner. *Education:* Fairleigh Dickinson University, B.S., 1966; City College of the City University of New York, M.B.A., 1968; City University of New York, Ph.D., 1972. *Home:* 370 F River Rd., Nutley, N.J. 07110. *Office:* Department of Administrative Sciences, Montclair State College, Upper Montclair, N.J. 07043.

CAREER: Exxon Corp., Florham Park, N.J., supervisor, 1955-68; Polytechnic Institute of Brooklyn, Brooklyn, N.Y., assistant professor of management, 1969-71; Montclair State College, Upper Montclair, N.J., professor of administrative services, 1972—. Private consultant to government and industry. *Military service:* U.S. Army, 1957-60. *Member:* Academy of Management, American Management Association, American Institute of Decision Sciences, American Humanist Association, International Transactional Analysis Association.

WRITINGS: Studies in Managerial Process and Organizational Behavior, Scott, Foresman, 1972.

WORK IN PROGRESS: A book on interpersonal relationships.

SIDELIGHTS: Turner writes: "My basic interest is in behavioral science, especially as applied to work and business situations. My first book covered a broad spectrum of behavioral topics and their ramifications in organizational settings. I am currently writing my second book in which I focus on the different types of relationships that people have with one another. To my surprise, I have found relatively little systematic work done on this extremely important topic. In recent years, marriage and divorce have received increasing attention in the nonfiction literature along with other approaches that emphasize individual self-development. It is my intent to cover the 'middle ground' between the individual and marriage by exploring interpersonal affairs ranging from casual acquaintances to primary relationships. The purpose of this book is to assist people in improving the quality of their personal interactions with others and it is being written for a wide general audience. I intend to do follow-up work on relationships in specialized settings such as work and school."

*   *   *

TURNER, Ralph V(ernon) 1939-

PERSONAL: Born August 27, 1939, in Forrest City, Ark.; son of V. O. (a planter) and Thelma (Smith) Turner. *Education:* University of Arkansas, B.A., 1957, M.A., 1958; attended University of Poitiers, 1957-58; Johns Hopkins University, Ph.D., 1962. *Residence:* Tallahassee, Fla. *Office:* Department of History, Florida State University, Tallahassee, Fla.

CAREER: Florida State University, Tallahassee, assistant professor of history, 1962-66; Ohio University, Athens, associate professor of history, 1966-70; Florida State Universi-

ty, professor of history, 1970—. *Member:* American Historical Association, Mediaeval Academy of America, Conference on British Studies, Selden Society, Pipe Roll Society. *Awards, honors:* Fulbright scholarship for France, 1957-58.

WRITINGS: The King and His Courts, Cornell University Press, 1968. Contributor to history journals, including *Journal of British Studies, American Journal of Legal History,* and *Speculum.*

WORK IN PROGRESS: A collective biographical study of the earliest common law judges, in the late twelfth and early thirteenth centuries.

SIDELIGHTS: Turner writes: "My chief research interest is medieval English legal and constitutional history, a field where one has a distinct, limited body of sources to master. Also, there is a grand tradition of scholarship to follow, and there is the feeling that studies in that field have more relevance for us today than any other area of medieval studies. My secondary interest is Italian Renaissance, and I spend as much time in Italy as possible. Perhaps study of the Renaissance is appealing because it raises so many questions in so many spheres: questions of historical interpretations, of aesthetics, of values, etc."

*   *   *

TURNER, Robert C(lemens) 1908-

PERSONAL: Born March 2, 1908, in Hiram, Ohio; son of James Jesse and Bertha Irene (Clemens) Turner; married Lenora Adeline Habink, December 29, 1934; children: Roderick Habink, Alice Carol Turner Boggs. *Education:* Hiram College, A.B., 1930; Northwestern University, M.B.A., 1932; Ohio State University, Ph.D., 1937. *Home:* 915 South Highland, Bloomington, Ind. 47401. *Office:* School of Business, Indiana University, Bloomington, Ind. 47401.

CAREER: Hiram College, Hiram, Ohio, director of Warren branch, 1932-35; Wayne University (now Wayne State University), Detroit, Mich., instructor, 1937-40, assistant professor of economics, 1940-41; War Production Board, Washington, D.C., economist, 1941-42, deputy director, 1942-43, director of Foreign Division, 1943-45; Civilian Production Administration, Washington, D.C., director of Bureau of International Supply, 1945-46; Office of War Mobilization and Reconversion, Washington, D.C., adviser on international operations, 1946-47; economic adviser to the White House staff in Washington, D.C., 1947-48; Indiana University, Bloomington, professor of business administration, 1948-61, distinguished professor of business economics and public policy, 1961—, chairman of department, 1957-61, vice-chancellor of Bloomington campus, 1969-73. Deputy U.S. member of Combined Raw Materials Board, 1945; member of President's Council of Economic Advisers, 1952-53, and President's Commission on Budget Concepts, 1967; assistant director of U.S. Bureau of the Budget, 1961-62; consultant to the comptroller-general of the United States and the governments of India and the Philippines. Visiting professor at University of the Philippines, 1968-69.

MEMBER: American Economic Association, Midwest Economic Association, Indiana Academy of the Social Sciences (president, 1955-56), Beta Gamma Sigma.

WRITINGS: Member Bank Borrowing, Ohio State University Press, 1939; *Export Control,* School for Advanced International Studies, 1947; *An Economic Portrait of Indiana in 1970,* Indiana University, 1956; *Lectures on Economic Growth,* Tulane University, 1960; (contributor) *Federal Credit Programs,* Prentice-Hall, 1963; (with John Lewis)

Business Conditions Analysis, McGraw, 1967. Contributor to journals and magazines.

WORK IN PROGRESS: Several journal articles.

* * *

TURNER, Robert F(oster) 1944-

PERSONAL: Born February 14, 1944, in Atlanta, Ga.; son of Edwin W. (a physician) and Martha (Williams) Turner. *Education:* Indiana University, B.A., 1968; graduate study at Stanford University, 1972-73. *Politics:* "Jeffersonian Republican." *Home:* 116 Roberts Lane, Apt. 401, Alexandria, Va. 22314. *Office:* 353 Russell Senate Office Building, Washington, D.C. 20510.

CAREER: Stanford University, Hoover Institution on War, Revolution and Peace, Stanford, Calif., research associate and public affairs fellow, 1971-74; U.S. Senate, Washington, D.C., legislative assistant to Senator Robert Griffin, 1974—. *Military service:* U.S. Army, Armor Branch, 1968-71; served in Vietnam; became captain; received Expert Infantryman Badge, Joint Services Commendation medal, and Army Commendation medal with oak leaf cluster.

WRITINGS: Myths of the Vietnam War: The Pentagon Papers Reconsidered, American Friends of Vietnam, 1972; *Vietnamese Communism: Its Origins and Development,* Hoover Institution, 1975.

Also contributor to *U.S. Defense Policy for the 1980's: Issues and Alternatives,* edited by James E. Dornan, 1978. Regional editor (for Asia and the Pacific) of *Yearbook on International Communist Affairs,* 1973-74.

WORK IN PROGRESS: Emphasizing U.S. National Security.

SIDELIGHTS: Turner writes: "Extensive foreign travel beginning in 1954 and resulting exposure to a variety of political systems contributed to development of my classical liberal political and economic views, with emphasis on maximum individual political and economic freedom, limited government and individual responsibility. I have generally supported goals of U.S. efforts to assist other peoples to resist aggression from totalitarian forces (of the left or right), including U.S. objectives (as distinct from methods) in Southeast Asia.

"During the Vietnam War I was a frequent participant in teach-ins and debates across the United States. While in the Army I was assigned to U.S. Embassy in Saigon as analyst of North Vietnamese and Viet Cong affairs. Upon return to United States in December, 1971, I decided to write *Vietnamese Communism* to correct misconceptions in minds of most Americans about the nature of the subject."

AVOCATIONAL INTERESTS: Tennis, backpacking, photography.

* * *

TURVILLE-PETRE, Edward Oswald Gabriel 1908-1978

March 25, 1908—February, 1978; British educator and author. Turville-Petre lectured at University of Iceland and Oxford University for over fifteen years before becoming professor of ancient Icelandic literature and antiquities at Oxford in 1953. A contributor to *Folklore, Mediaeval Studies,* and other professional journals, he also authored several books in the field of Old Norse literature, including *Origins of Icelandic Literature* and *Myth and Religion of the North: The Religion of Ancient Scandinavia.* He died in England.

Obituaries and other sources: *Who's Who,* 130th edition, St. Martin's, 1978; *AB Bookman's Weekly,* May 8, 1978. (See index for *CA* sketch)

* * *

TUTTLE, Russell (Howard) 1939-

PERSONAL: Born August 18, 1939, in Marion, Ohio; son of Richard Nelson and Mary Jane (King) Tuttle; married Marlene Benjamin, June 1, 1968; children: Nicole Irene, Matthew Richard Russell. *Education:* Ohio State University, B.Sc., 1961, M.A., 1962; University of California, Berkeley, Ph.D., 1965. *Residence:* Chicago, Ill. *Office:* Department of Anthropology, University of Chicago, 1126 East 59th St., Chicago, Ill. 60637.

CAREER: University of Chicago, Chicago, Ill., instructor, 1964-66, assistant professor of anatomy and anthropology, 1966-69, assistant professor of anthropology and evolutionary biology, 1969-70, associate professor, 1970-76, professor, 1976—. Visiting professor at Kyoto University, 1974.

MEMBER: International Primatological Society, International Association of Human Biologists, American Anthropological Association, American Association for the Advancement of Science, American Association of Physical Anthropologists, Society for Vertebrate Paleontology, American Society of Naturalists, Phi Beta Kappa, Sigma Xi. *Awards, honors:* U.S. Public Health Service career development award, 1968-73.

WRITINGS: (Editor) *The Functional and Evolutionary Biology of Primates,* Aldine, 1972; (editor) *Primate Functional Morphology and Evolution,* Mouton, 1975; (editor) *Paleoanthropology: Morphology and Paleoecology,* Mouton, 1975; (editor) *Socioecology and Psychology of Primates,* Mouton, 1975. Contributor to science and anthropology journals.

WORK IN PROGRESS: Research on the problem of brachiation and hominid evolution, the manner in which current studies of apes have elucidated the human career and condition, and primate evolution, with special emphasis on the anthropoid primates.

SIDELIGHTS: Tuttle writes: "Though my primary research has been anatomical studies of living apes, monkeys, and man, results are brought to bear on problems of anthropoid behavior and evolution. I have conducted field studies of monkeys and other mammals at waterholes and in forests of Sri Lanka, Rhodesia, Kenya, and Tanzania. Experimental studies on primate locomotion and comparative morphology have been conducted at primate research centers and museums in Switzerland, Italy, and the United States. The history of the development of major problems in evolutionary anthropology fascinates me, and I hope to pursue several of them in the near future."

AVOCATIONAL INTERESTS: Classical music (especially opera), handball, swimming.

* * *

TYERMAN, Hugo 1880-1977

1880—September, 1977; British journalist, editor, and author. Tyerman was the picture editor of Arthur Mee's *Children's Encyclopedia,* and succeeded Mee as editor of the *Children's Newspaper.* He was author of *Essex,* the first volume of "The King's England" series. Tyerman died in England. Obituaries and other sources: *The Author's and Writer's Who's Who,* 6th edition, Burke's Peerage, 1971; *AB Bookman's Weekly,* February 6, 1978.

TYLER, David B(udlong) 1899-

PERSONAL: Born October 15, 1899, in Brooklyn, N.Y.; son of Walter Lincoln (a manufacturer) and May Louise (Cowperthwaite) Tyler; married Katharine Ide Haskell, September 2, 1930 (died November 23, 1956); married Elizabeth Rintoul Sloan, October 11, 1958; children: John C., Susan Tyler Faison, Sandra R. *Education:* Williams College, B.A., 1921; Oxford University, A.B., 1926; Columbia University, M.A., 1932, Ph.D., 1939. *Politics:* Republican. *Religion:* Episcopalian. *Home:* 207 Benedict Rd., Staten Island, N.Y. 10304.

CAREER: Western Electric Co., New York, N.Y., clerk, 1922-24; history teacher at private school in Brooklyn, N.Y., 1926-28; Hobart College, Geneva, N.Y., faculty member in history, 1929-31; Brooklyn College (now of the City University of New York), Brooklyn, N.Y., faculty member in history, 1934-36; Wagner College, Staten Island, N.Y., instructor, then assistant professor, 1939-43, associate professor, 1947-49, professor of history, 1949-70, professor emeritus, 1970—; writer, 1970—. Visiting professor at University of Delaware, 1954-56. Assistant historian for U.S. Maritime Commission, 1946-47. *Military service:* U.S. Naval Reserve, Air Combat Intelligence, active duty, 1943-45; became lieutenant commander. *Member:* American Historical Association, Long Island Historical Society, Staten Island Historical Society.

WRITINGS: Steam Conquers the Atlantic, Appleton, 1939; *The Bay and River Delaware: A Pictorial History,* Cornell Maritime, 1955; *The American Clyde,* University of Delaware Press, 1958; *The Wilkes Expedition,* American Philosophical Society, 1968. Contributor to *American Neptune.*

WORK IN PROGRESS: The Journal of an Ex-Whaler Fighting Tuberculosis in Minnesota, 1861-62.

SIDELIGHTS: As a boy, Tyler sailed on Great South Bay, and maritime (and English) history have always been among his interests.

TYLER, S(amuel) Lyman 1920-

PERSONAL: Born March 27, 1920, in Attica, Ark.; son of Rufus B. (a farmer) and Mary Ann (Hogan) Tyler; married Bessie Marie Rohde (a radiology technologist), April 9, 1943; children: Marie Ann Tyler Stuver, Michael, Susan, Steven. *Education:* University of Utah, B.S., 1949, Ph.D., 1951. *Religion:* Church of Jesus Christ of Latter-day Saints (Mormons). *Home:* 1017 Douglas, Salt Lake City, Utah 84105. *Office:* Department of History, University of Utah, Salt Lake City, Utah 84112.

CAREER: Brigham Young University, Provo, Utah, assistant professor, 1952-58, associate professor, 1958-61, professor of history, 1961-66, historian and librarian, 1952-66; University of Utah, Salt Lake City, professor of history and historian, 1966—, dean, 1967-71; director of American West Center, 1971—. *Military service:* U.S. Navy, 1943-45. *Member:* Western History Association, Utah Historical Society. *Awards, honors:* Social Science Research Council fellowship, 1951-52.

WRITINGS: The Ute People: A Bibliography, Brigham Young University Press, 1964; *Indian Affairs: A Study of Termination,* Brigham Young University Press, 1964; *Indian Affairs: A Study of Changes in Policy,* Brigham Young University Press, 1964; *Montana Gold Rush Diary of Kate Dunlap,* University of Utah Press, 1969; *A History of Indian Policy,* U.S. Government Printing Office, 1974. Contributor of articles, mainly on American Indians, to scholarly journals.

WORK IN PROGRESS: The Indian Cause Before the Law of Nations; The Indian Cause in the Laws of the Indies.

SIDELIGHTS: Tyler writes: "I have a continuing interest in relations between European-American and Native Peoples, particularly in the Americas and the Pacific."

U

UDE, Wayne 1946-

PERSONAL: Surname is pronounced *You*-dee; born March 23, 1946, in Minneapolis, Minn.; son of Vernon Richard and Jeanne (Boutelle) Ude; married Pattie Lee Cowell (a teacher), June 2, 1972. *Education:* University of Montana, B.A., 1969; University of Massachusetts, M.F.A., 1974. *Politics:* "Radical Jeffersonian democracy." *Religion:* "Sacralist." *Home:* 931 Vanderbilt Court, Fort Collins, Colo. 80521. *Office:* Department of English, Colorado State University, Fort Collins, Colo. 80521.

CAREER: Community Action Program, Fort Belknap Indian Reservation, Mont., executive director, 1970-71, member of reservation planning board, 1971; Council on Aging, Amherst, Mass., executive director, 1974-76; Colorado State University, Fort Collins, assistant professor of English, 1976—. *Member:* Poets and Writers, Associated Writing Programs, Western Literature Association, Southwest Indian Association, Rocky Mountain Modern Language Association.

WRITINGS: *Buffalo and Other Stories* (Small Press Book Club selection), Lynx House Press, 1975. Contributor of stories to literary journals, including *Transatlantic, Lynx, Scree, Sunday Clothes, Portland Review,* and *Salt Cedar.* Fiction editor and managing editor of *Colorado State Review.*

WORK IN PROGRESS: a novel, *Becoming Coyote;* two collections of short stories.

SIDELIGHTS: Ude writes: "I grew up in Harlem, Montana, just across the river from the Fort Balknap Indian Reservation, and early on became fascinated with the Reservation people. After graduating from the University of Montana, I was lucky enough to work on the Reservation for two years. Native American religion is a major interest to me, as is Native American folklore and poetry. Writers like Leslie Silko astound me with their integration of all these elements. I know of nothing like it in non-Indian fiction.

"I teach creative writing at Colorado State University, and whenever possible also teach native American literature. There's a rich native American literary tradition—not only in folktales and ritual poetry, but in the work of such contemporaries as Scott Momaday, James Welch, and—most of all—Leslie Silko.

"Anthropologists use the term 'marginal men' to describe young Indians who return from government schools no longer completely Indian, not yet white, and who live on the margins between two societies. My characters, most of them Indians (though I'm not), are marginal men and women in a broader sense: trapped in a present which promises only transition, never permanence, between a past and a future neither of which they have much hope of sharing. I sometimes think there is no core to America, only margins, and that we all live on those margins—we're all marginal men and women. It's that sense, that theme, which I hope raises my work beyond 'local color' and gives it some flavor, however faint, of universal meaning.

"My work tends to move—as does my mind—between older, longer forms which can contain coherences and unities, and newer, shorter forms which can contain fragments and confusions. I hope the movement is toward unities out of fragments, coherences out of confusions."

*   *   *

UDO, Reuben Kenrick 1935-

PERSONAL: Born August 8, 1935, in Ikot Ekpene, Nigeria; son of Kenrick Akpan and Umo (Udom) Udo-Ubeng; married Dora K. (a nurse tutor), December 8, 1962; children: Akanimo, Usenekong, Nene, Eno-Obong. *Education:* University of Ibadan, B.Sc., 1960; University of London, Ph.D., 1963. *Religion:* Methodist. *Home:* 7 Saunders Rd., Ibadan, Nigeria. *Office:* Department of Geography, University of Ibadan, Ibadan, Nigeria.

CAREER: University of Ibadan, Ibadan, Nigeria, 1963—, began as lecturer, became senior lecturer, professor of geography, 1972—. Researcher at Northwestern University, 1968. Chairman of Cross River State Agricultural Development Corp., 1969-72; member of National Census Board, 1972-75, and Land Use Panel, 1977. *Member:* International Union for the Scientific Study of Population, Nigerian Geographical Association (president, 1975-77), American Geographical Society.

WRITINGS: *Geographical Regions of Nigeria,* University of California Press, 1970; *Examination Guidelines for School Certificate Geography,* Heinemann, 1970; *Migrant Tenant Farmers of Nigeria,* African Universities Press, 1977. Contributor to *Collier's Encyclopedia.* Contributor to geography journals. Editor of *Nigerian Geographical Journal,* 1969-73.

WORK IN PROGRESS: *Internal Migrations in Nigeria; Land Tenure and Land Use in Nigeria.*

ULC, Otto 1930-

PERSONAL: Born March 16, 1930, in Plzen, Czechoslovakia; came to the United States in 1960, naturalized citizen, 1966; son of Frantisek (a mechanic) and Marie (Skrabek) Ulc; married Priscilla Lim, October 9, 1964; children: Ota (son). Education: Charles University, LL.D., 1953; Columbia University, M.A., 1961, Ph.D., 1964. Home: 124 Martha Rd., Binghamton, N.Y. 13903. Office: Department of Political Science, State University of New York at Binghamton, Binghamton, N.Y. 13901.

CAREER: Assistant judge of district court in Plzen Czechoslovakia, 1953-56, judge in Plzen and Stribro, 1956-59; U.S. Army, Frankfurt, Germany, civilian legal adviser, 1959-60; Grinnell College, Grinnell, Iowa, assistant professor of political science, 1964; State University of New York at Binghamton, assistant professor, 1964-71, associate professor, 1971-75, professor of political science, 1975—. Military service: Czech Army, 1953-55. Member: International Studies Association, American Political Science Association, Association for the Advancement of Slavic Studies, Czechoslovak Society of Arts and Sciences in America. Awards, honors: Fellowship from Regional Council for International Education for Taiwan, 1967; Fulbright-Hays fellowship, 1976.

WRITINGS: The Judge in a Communist State, Ohio University Press, 1972; Politics in Czechoslovakia, W. H. Freeman, 1974; Nas Clovek v Indii a na Ceylone (title means "Our Man in India and Ceylon"), Sixty-Eight Publishers, 1976. Contributor to political science and Slavic studies journals.

WORK IN PROGRESS: The Integration of Immigrants in the United States and Australia: A Comparative Study.

SIDELIGHTS: Ulc writes: "In the last ten years I have travelled rather extensively, having visited some eighty countries in five continents. Comparative government is my field of specialization; hence, I go and compare, looking for commonalities in human follies. In connection with this, I would exemplify along the lines of ethnic prejudice and arrogance. For example, in several Asian countries of today discriminatory legislation exists against the Chinese—these so-called Jews of Asia—and this legislation is very similar to that common in the Austro-Hungarian Empire of yesterday."

*   *   *

UNDERWOOD, Paul S(taats) 1915-

PERSONAL: Born December 6, 1915, in Rocky Ridge, Ohio; son of Michael Beal (a university professor and lawyer) and Margaret Pearl (a teacher; maiden name, Staats) Underwood; married Mary Lou Perkins (a free-lance artist), September 13, 1941; children: Michael Paul, Sidney Ann, Arthur. Education: Attended Ohio Northern University, 1933-35, and University of Cincinnati, 1935-36. Politics: "Uncommitted." Religion: "Unattached Protestant." Home: 5050 Olentangy River Rd., Columbus, Ohio 43214. Office: School of Journalism, Ohio State University, Columbus, Ohio 43210.

CAREER: Cincinnati Enquirer, Cincinnati, Ohio, reporter and acting city editor, 1937-44; Associated Press, reporter and editor in Cleveland, Ohio, 1944-45, editor on Latin American desk in New York City, 1945-48, correspondent from London, England, 1948-52, night editor at London Bureau, 1951-52, editor at foreign desk in New York City, 1952-56; New York Times, New York City, editor on foreign desk, 1956-58, correspondent from eastern Europe, including Yugoslavia, Bulgaria, Rumania, Hungary, Czechoslovakia, Austria, and Poland, 1958-64, main writer for "News of the Week in Review," 1964-65; Cincinnati Enquirer, member of editorial board and author of foreign affairs column, 1965-67; Ohio State University, Columbus, associate professor, 1967-75, professor of journalism, 1972—, director of international journalism program, 1972—, Maxwell Memorial Lecturer, 1966, member of community communications group at Mershon Center for Education in National Security, member of executive committee of Center for Slavic and East European Studies, 1973—. Member of national university liaison committee of U.S. Information Agency, 1968—; overseas director of eastern European tour (including the Soviet Union) for Kettering Foundation and Regional Council for International Education, 1971. Lecturer at Foreign Service Institute, 1971; guest lecturer at University of Texas, 1975. Producer of series for WOSU-Radio.

MEMBER: International Press Institute, Interamerican Press Association, American Association for the Advancement of Slavic Studies, National Press Club, Overseas Press Club of America (member of board of governors, 1965-66), Association for Education in Journalism. Awards, honors: Merit awards from New York Times, 1956, 1963; nominated for Pulitzer Prize for International Reporting, 1965; citation from Overseas Press Club, 1966, for international reporting; Kettering Foundation grants, 1972, 1973, 1973-74.

WRITINGS: Getting to Know Eastern Europe, Coward, 1966, revised edition, 1970; (contributor) James W. Markham, editor, International Communications As a Field of Study, University of Iowa Press, 1971. Contributor of several thousand articles to newspapers. Contributing editor of American Bibliography of Slavic and East European Studies, 1969-72.

SIDELIGHTS: Underwood mentions that some of his noteworthy stories covered Edvard Kardelj and the Kremlin's blacklist, Ivo Andric, Tito and his neutral policies, and Djilas as a Communist dissenter. He writes: "At this time, I am particularly interested in two subjects: the new machinery available to journalism, both print and broadcast, and its possible effects on the profession, as well as the question of what role the mass media play in the foreign policy process (in this country). In addition to my assignments in Europe, I have worked in the Middle East, North Africa, and Latin America."

AVOCATIONAL INTERESTS: Gardening, reading.

*   *   *

UNGER, Barbara 1932-

PERSONAL: Born October 2, 1932, in New York, N.Y.; daughter of David (a businessman) and Florence (a pianist; maiden name, Schuchalter) Frankel; children: Deborah, Suzanne. Education: City College (now of the City University of New York), B.A., 1957, M.A., 1957; further graduate study at New York University. Home: 68 East Maltbie Ave., Suffern, N.Y. 10901.

CAREER: Bucks Rock Work Camp, New Milford, Conn., creative writing counselor, 1958-65; educational reporter for Rockland County Citizen, 1961-63; English teacher in Nyack, N.Y., 1963-67; high school counselor in Ardsley, N.Y., 1967-69; Rockland Community College, Suffern, N.Y., assistant professor of English, 1969—.

WRITINGS: Basement (poems), Isthmus Press, 1975. Contributor of poems to Kansas Quarterly, Poet and Critic,

Cottonwood Review, Wisconsin Review, and other periodicals.

WORK IN PROGRESS: A second collection of poems.

SIDELIGHTS: Barbara Unger told *CA:* "My work as a poet deals with my life experiences as a mother, a wife, a child, a lover, a woman. I use feminist themes in some of my poems and frequently use dream imagery. My earliest poems were heavily influenced by Rimbaud and others. Recently I have read the works of poets such as Sylvia Plath, Ann Sexton, and Maxine Kumin with great interest, and my work is influenced by the theories of Carl Jung. I write in several different voices and styles and enjoy giving public readings."

* * *

UNTERMEYER, Bryna Ivens 1909-

PERSONAL: Born April 27, 1909, in New York, N.Y.; daughter of Benjamin F. (a lawyer) and Millie (Drescher) Isaacs; married Louis Untermeyer (a writer), July 23, 1948 (died, 1977). *Education:* Hunter College (now of the City University of New York), A.B., 1930. *Home address:* Great Hill Rd., Newtown, Conn. 06470. *Agent:* Shirley Fisher, McIntosh & Otis, Inc., 475 Fifth Ave., New York, N.Y. 10017.

CAREER: She (magazine), New York City, editor, 1941-46; *Seventeen,* New York City, fiction editor, 1946-57; freelance writer and editor, 1957—.

WRITINGS: (Editor) *The Seventeen Reader* (juvenile), Lippincott, 1951; (editor) *Nineteen From Seventeen* (juvenile), Lippincott, 1952; (editor) *Stories From Seventeen* (juvenile), Lippincott, 1955; (editor with husband, Louis Untermeyer) *Grimm's Fairy Tales* (juvenile), Limited Editions, 1962; (editor with L. Untermeyer) *The Golden Treasury of Children's Literature,* Golden Press, 1966; *A Memoir for Mrs. Sullivan,* Simon & Schuster, 1966.

WORK IN PROGRESS: Cats as Cats Can; a novel.

* * *

UPWARD, Edward (Falaise) 1903-

PERSONAL: Born September 9, 1903, in Romford, Essex, England; son of Harold Arthur (a doctor) and Isa (Jones) Upward; married Hilda Maude Percival, 1936; children: one son, one daughter. *Education:* Corpus Christi College, Cambridge, M.A., 1925. *Residence:* Isle of Wight. *Agent:* Candida Donadio, Candida Donadio and Associates, Inc., 111 West 57th St., New York, N.Y. 10019. *Address:* c/o William Heinemann Ltd., 15-16 Queen St., London W1X 8BE England.

CAREER: Writer. Worked as schoolmaster, 1928-62.

WRITINGS: Buddha (poetry), Cambridge University Press, 1924; (contributor) *The Mind in Chains: Socialism and the Cultural Revolution,* edited by Lewis C. Day, Folcroft, 1937; *Journey to the Border* (novel), Hogarth, 1938; *In the Thirties* (novel), Heinemann, 1962; *The Railway Accident and Other Stories,* Heinemann, 1969; *The Rotten Elements* (novel), Heinemann, 1969; *The Spiral Ascent: A Trilogy of Novels* (contains *In the Thirties, The Rotten Elements,* and *No Home But the Struggle*), Heinemann, 1977. Member of editorial board, *Ploughshare,* 1936-39.

SIDELIGHTS: "Among the literary legends of the 1930s," declared a *Times Literary Supplement* critic, "Edward Upward is surely the most legendary figure." Early in his career Upward's talent and promise were critically acclaimed. What the *Times Literary Supplement* called his

"vision of existence as a realistic nightmare" encouraged many to compare Upward's work with that of Duerer and Kafka. "But it was not his *work* that was influential; rather it was his vision of the ordinary world seen as hallucination that had genius," continued the *Times Literary Supplement.*

In an interview in *London Magazine,* Alan Ross asked Upward how he became one of those who "has a powerful private effect on the key writers of his generation, one seemingly out of all proportion to his own public image." Upward offered two possible explanations for his "influence on two or three abler contemporaries." One was the "accident of . . . having been to the same public school at the same time" as Christopher Isherwood, who had previously attended school with W. H. Auden. "My kind of imagination . . . fed on the Arabian Nights and on the engravings of Duerer and on late nineteenth century French literature, appealed to them," Upward added.

When Upward joined the Communist party, Francis Hope described him as fulfilling the role of "The Marxist . . . the left-hand marker for this raggedly dressed platoon" of writers "cultivating their own legend." In a group where "above all *roles* dominated . . . work and . . . lives," Hope saw Upward as a figure possibly "doomed to be simply the Friend" whose "public recognition" came largely from the "reflected light of *Lions and Shadows,*" Isherwood's memoir.

Yet, as an active Communist party member, Upward was not merely fulfilling a role. The *Times Literary Supplement* compared Upward's party commitment to a "religious conversion," quoting Upward: "I came to it not so much through consciousness of the political and economic situation as through despair."

For almost twenty-five years Upward stopped writing for publication. What he called an "artistic conscience" made him realize that "trying to produce a political statement and not an artistic statement . . . just wouldn't do." He explained to Ross: "It was not until 1954, when I had at last freed myself completely from my allegiance to the Party, that I was able to begin writing *In the Thirties.*"

Alan Sebrill, the main character of *In the Thirties* and *The Rotten Elements,* closely resembles Edward Upward, and the author has confirmed the use of much autobiographical material. Sebrill, like Upward, is a frustrated poet who joins the Communist party only to find his artistic ideals incompatible with his political belief. While writing *The Rotten Elements,* Upward resolved the conflict for himself. He told Ross of his discovery and of his decision that his contributions as a poet would have to have merit beyond being "versified political leading articles." Upward's novels cannot be reduced to personal statements of limited appeal; for, as the *Times Literary Supplement* observed, Upward contrasts the "need to belong" with the "need for freedom" and the "will to create" with the "will to conform."

When asked by Ross if he had avoided the "literary life as such" by choice or circumstance, Upward replied, "I would have loved to live the literary life, but I was never able to discover how to set about it."

AVOCATIONAL INTERESTS: Amateur botany and geology, reading, walking in the country.

BIOGRAPHICAL/CRITICAL SOURCES: London Magazine, June, 1969; *Spectator,* July 26, 1969; *Observer Review,* July 27, 1969; *Times Literary Supplement,* July 31, 1969; *New Statesman,* August 1, 1969.

URBANEK, Mae 1903-

PERSONAL: Born September 10, 1903, in Denver, Colo.; daughter of Boyd Byron (a farmer) and Sarah (Hotze) Bobb; married Jerry Urbanek (a rancher), December 10, 1928. *Education:* Northwestern University, B.S., 1927. *Politics:* Democrat. *Religion:* Methodist. *Home address:* Lusk, Wyo. 82225.

CAREER: Rancher, 1928—; writer, 1958—. Member of Wyoming Status of Women Commission, 1964-77. *Member:* Western Writers of America, Library, Archives & Historical Society (member of state board of directors, 1977—), Wyoming Press Women (state president, 1963-65), Wyoming Federation of Garden Clubs (state president, 1959-61), Delta Kappa Gamma.

WRITINGS: The Uncovered Wagon, Swallow Press, 1958; *Songs of the Sage,* Swallow Press, 1962; *The Second Man,* Swallow Press, 1962; *Wyoming Wonderland,* Swallow Press, 1964; *Wyoming Place Names,* Johnson Publishing Co. (Boulder, Colo.), 1967, revised edition, 1974; *Almost Up Devils Tower,* Johnson Publishing Co. (Boulder, Colo.), 1968; *Know Wyoming,* Johnson Publishing Co. (Boulder, Colo.), 1969; *Memoirs of Andrew McMaster,* Lusk Herald, 1969; *Chief Washakie,* Johnson Publishing Co. (Boulder, Colo.), 1974. State editor of *Wyoming Paintbrush,* 1961—.

WORK IN PROGRESS: Ghost Trails of Wyoming; Hands, a novel about dude ranching in Jackson Hole.

SIDELIGHTS: Mae Urbanek writes: "I love the state in which I live. All of my books are about Wyoming. I have packed into all of its wilderness areas, visited all of its ghost towns, and read most of its recorded history. I live on a ranch and am interested in preserving the ranch lands, wilderness areas, and forests of Wyoming for posterity."

*   *   *

USHER, Shaun 1937-
(Jeffrey Scott)

PERSONAL: Born May 18, 1937 in London, England; son of John Gray (an author) and Judith (a nurse; maiden name, Weir) Usher. *Education:* Educated in Somerset, England. *Religion:* Church of England. *Home:* 35 Seymour Avenue, Ewell, Epsom, Surry, England.

CAREER: London Daily Sketch, London, England, entertainment editor, 1964-72; *London Daily Mail,* London, entertainment editor, 1972-75, television critic, 1975—. *Military service:* British Army, Royal Army Ordanance Corps., 1955-59; became lance-corporal. *Member:* British Academy of Film and Television Arts, Crime Writers Association (England). *Awards:* Crime Writers Association prize for best short story, 1972 and 1973.

WRITINGS: (Under pseudonym Jeffrey Scott) *Trust Them and Die,* R. Hale, 1969; (editor with father, Gray Usher) *The Graveyard Companion* (collection of ghost and horror stories), Bailey Bros. & Swinfen, 1975; (editor with G. Usher) *Festival of Fiends* (collection of ghost and horror stories), Bailey Bros. & Swinfen, 1976.

Writer of radio play, "All Down to True Love," British Broadcasting Corp. (BBC), 1975. Contributor of more than three hundred short stories (generally under pseudonym Jeffrey Scott) to British and American magazines, including *Ellery Queen's Mystery Magazine.*

WORK IN PROGRESS: History of World Wars I and II and a history of aviation, both to be published under the author's real name.

SIDELIGHTS: Usher told *CA:* "My father, Gray Usher, is an established journalist and author, so I took it for granted that I would earn my bread in the same way. My first successful short story, anthologized and broadcast several times, and bought by U.S. television, was written when I was 15 years old. Even my army service was spent on a Pamphlet Writing Team!"

*   *   *

UTLEY, Freda 1898-1978

January 23, 1898—January 21, 1978; British-born American journalist, foreign correspondent, lecturer, and author. Utley was a member of the British Communist party until her husband was exiled to Siberia under Stalin's regime. She came to America in 1939 and served as a political adviser for American businessmen and educators. Utley is the author of numerous books, some that were written when she was a correspondent for the *Reader's Digest* in China and Germany. Utley died in Washington, D.C. Obituaries and other sources: *Current Biography,* Wilson, 1958; *Who's Who in America,* 36th edition, Marquis, 1974; *New York Times,* January 23, 1978; *Washington Post,* January 25, 1978; *Time,* February 6, 1978.

V

VAILLANT, George E. 1934-

PERSONAL: Born June 16, 1934, in New York; son of George Clapp (an archaeologist) and Suzannah (Beck) Vaillant; married Caroline Officer (a social worker), April 17, 1971; children: George Emory, John, Henry, Anne, Joanna. *Education:* Earned A.B. and M.D. from Harvard University. *Home:* 41 Holden St., Cambridge, Mass. 02138. *Office:* Cambridge Hospital, 1493 Cambridge St., Cambridge, Mass. 02139.

CAREER: Harvard University, Cambridge, Mass., professor, 1970—. Director of psychiatry training at Cambridge Hospital; member of Justice Resource Institute. *Member:* American Psychiatric Association, Boston Psychoanalytic Society. *Awards, honors:* Felix and Helene Deutsch Prize from Boston Psychoanalytic Society.

WRITINGS: Adaptation to Life, Little, Brown, 1977. Contributor of more than fifty articles to professional journals.

*   *   *

VALENSTEIN, Suzanne G(ebhart) 1928-

PERSONAL: Born July 17, 1928, in Baltimore, Md. *Office:* Department of Far Eastern Art, Metropolitan Museum of Art, Fifth Ave. and 82nd St., New York, N.Y. 10028.

CAREER: Metropolitan Museum of Art, New York, N.Y., associate curator of Far Eastern art.

WRITINGS: Ming Porcelains: A Retrospective, China Institute in America, 1970; *A Handbook of Chinese Ceramics,* Metropolitan Museum of Art, 1975; (with Julia Meech-Pekarik and Marilyn Jenkins) *Oriental Ceramics in the World's Great Collections,* Kodansha International, 1977. Contributor to *Metropolitan Museum of Art Bulletin.*

*   *   *

VANCE, Adrian 1936-

PERSONAL: Born June 7, 1936, in Chicago, Ill.; son of Arden Lowell (a teacher) and Dora (an artist; maiden name, Goff) Vance; married Carol Crosby, February 12, 1960 (divorced, September, 1970); married Evy Borggren, August 22, 1975; children: (second marriage) Vanessa. *Education:* Illinois State University, B.S., 1959; graduate study at California State College, Los Angeles. *Politics:* Democrat. *Religion:* None. *Home:* 7431 Del Zuro Dr., Hollywood, Calif. 90046. *Office:* Adrian Vance Productions, 6519 Fountain Ave., Hollywood, Calif. 90028.

CAREER: Secondary school teacher in Los Angeles, Calif., 1960-67; Adrian Vance Productions, Hollywood, Calif., owner, 1977—. Owner of AV Books; partner of Synopticon, Inc. *Awards, honors:* "Best of the year" award from *Learning,* 1976, for filmstrip series "You in the Universe."

WRITINGS: UFO's: The Eye and the Camera, Barlenmir House, 1977. Author of over two hundred thirty filmstrips.

Contributor to photography and skin diving magazines. West Coast editor of *Popular Photography;* contributing editor of *Photographic.*

WORK IN PROGRESS: Precision Diving, publication by AV Books expected in 1979; *Audio-Visual Production,* Amphoto, 1979.

SIDELIGHTS: Vance writes: "In all my writings I desire to make a contribution to the field, whether it is UFO studies, diving and underwater photography, or photography in general. My family heritage, some five generations, is in education and teaching, my own training is in that area, and most of my work continues to be of an educational nature. My two hundred thirty filmstrip productions are primarily educational, even those for financial and entertainment clients."

*   *   *

VAN DEN BOGARDE, Derek Jules Gaspard Ulric Niven 1921-
(Dirk Bogarde)

PERSONAL: Born March 28, 1921, in Hampstead, London, England; son of Ulric Jules (an art editor) and Margaret (an actress; maiden name, Niven) Van den Bogarde. *Education:* Attended Royal College of Art. *Residence:* France. *Agent:* Harbottle and Lewis, 34 South Molton St., London, W.1, England.

CAREER: Actor, under name Dirk Bogarde, in stage productions, 1939—, in motion pictures, 1948—, and television, 1964—. Contracted to J. Arthur Rank Organization, 1947-61. Actor in stage productions, including "When We Are Married," 1939, "Power Without Glory," 1947, "Point of Departure," 1950, "The Vortex," 1953, "Summertime," 1955, and "Jezebel," 1958. Actor in television productions, including "Little Moon of Alban," 1964, and "Blithe Spirit," 1966. Actor in motion pictures, including "Esther Waters," 1948, "Doctor in the House," 1954, "Doctor at

Sea," 1956, "Doctor at Large," 1957, "Victim," 1961, "Doctor in Distress," 1963, "The Servant," 1964, "Darling," 1965, "Accident," 1967, "The Damned," 1969, "Death in Venice," 1971, "The Night Porter," 1973, "Providence," 1976, and "A Bridge Too Far," 1977. *Military service:* British Army, 1940-46; became major. *Awards, honors:* Named top ten British star, 1953-54, 1956-64; named number one British moneymaking star, 1955, 1957-59; received Variety Club Award for best performance, 1961-64; best actor award from British Motion Picture Academy of Arts and Sciences, for "The Servant," 1963, and "Darling," 1965.

WRITINGS: (Under name Dirk Bogarde) *A Postillion Struck by Lightning: A Memoir,* Holt, 1977. Contributor to *Times Literary Supplement.*

WORK IN PROGRESS: Acting in the motion picture, "Despair."

SIDELIGHTS: In his biography, Bogarde commented on his need for privacy and confessed to having built a "wall" of protection around himself. "But it has been this wall," he wrote, "or tower really . . . which has allowed me to retain most of the values which I had been taught." Although his obsession for privacy has lessened his popularity, Bogarde wrote that notoriety was never his intention: "I never remotely sought, as so many of my contemporaries did, my Name in Lights—I didn't want the responsibilities that would bring; all I wanted to do was to achieve respect, acknowledgement, and honour in the profession for which I belonged."

AVOCATIONAL INTERESTS: Painting, watching television, riding horseback, gardening, music, world affairs.

BIOGRAPHICAL/CRITICAL SOURCES: Saturday Review, August 8, 1970; Dirk Bogarde, *A Postillion Struck by Lightning: A Memoir,* Holt, 1977.*

*   *   *

VANDERLIP, D(odava) George 1926-

PERSONAL: Born November 27, 1926, in the Netherlands; came to the United States in 1949, naturalized citizen, 1961; son of Gysbertus (a clergyman) and Sophia Maria (a nurse; maiden name, Rijkhoek) Van der Lip; married Dora Elaine Christy, June 23, 1956; children: Janice, Susan, Patricia, John. *Education:* McGill University, B.A., 1949; Fuller Theological Seminary, B.D., 1952, Th.M., 1953; Berkeley Baptist Divinity School, Th.M., 1956; University of Southern California, Ph.D., 1959. *Home:* 683 Mallard Rd., Wayne, Pa. 19087. *Office:* Department of Biblical Studies, Eastern Baptist Theological Seminary, Lancaster Ave. at City Line, Philadelphia, Pa. 19151.

CAREER: Ordained American Baptist minister, 1957; interim pastor of Baptist churches in Tustin, Calif., 1959, Claremont, Calif., 1960, Oxford, Pa., 1971, Norristown, Pa., 1972-73, Westmont, N.J., 1974-75, and Kennett Square, Pa., 1975-76; California Baptist Theological Seminary (now American Baptist Seminary of the West), Covina, Calif., lecturer in New Testament, 1956-59; Northern Baptist Theological Seminary, Oakbrook, Ill., associate professor, 1960-63, professor of New Testament interpretation, 1963-71, academic dean, 1966-71; Eastern Baptist Theological Seminary, Philadelphia, Pa., James A. Maxwell Professor of English Bible, 1971—. New Testament instructor on WTTW-Television in Chicago. Participated in New York University workshop in Israel; leader of tours through the Holy Land.

MEMBER: Society of Biblical Literature, American Academy of Religion, Chicago Society of Biblical Research. *Awards, honors:* Award from Christian Research Foundation, Inc., 1961, for "A Comparative Study of Certain Alleged Similarities Between the Literature of Qumran and the Fourth Gospel."

WRITINGS: Jesus, Teacher and Lord, Judson, 1964; *Paul and Romans,* Judson, 1968; *Christianity According to John,* Westminster, 1975; *Discovering a Christian Life Style,* Judson, 1978; (contributor) W. Ward Gasque, editor, *Scripture, Tradition, and Interpretation,* Eerdmans, in press, Contributor to *Baptist Leader.*

WORK IN PROGRESS: Life in Fullness, "a new look at the Gospel according to John"; *The Man Called Jesus; How to Interpret the Bible,* a study in biblical hermeneutics.

SIDELIGHTS: Vanderlip told *CA:* "In my book *Christianity According to John,* I maintain that while the Fourth Gospel is an interpretation of the life of Jesus, it contains important independent historical information about the life and teachings of Jesus.

"While my primary love is teaching in seminary and writing, I have a deep interest in working closely with the church. I enjoy preaching, conducting Bible conferences and serving as interim pastor."

*   *   *

Van DERSAL, William R(ichard) 1907-

PERSONAL: Born April 6, 1907, in Portland, Ore.; son of William Cornelius (a lawyer) and Ella Maude (Morrison) Van Dersal; married Helen Ann Jankovich, February 7, 1949 (deceased); children: Mary, Jeanne, Dianne, June Ellen, Margo. *Education:* Reed College, B.A., 1929; University of Pittsburgh, M.S., 1931, Ph.D., 1934. *Home and office:* 6 South Kensington St., Arlington, Va. 22204. *Agent:* Frances Collins, Marie Rodell-Frances Collins Literary Agency, 141 East 55th St., New York, N.Y. 10022.

CAREER: U.S. Department of Agriculture, Washington, D.C., worked with Soil Conservation Service as associate biologist, 1935-36, and biologist, 1936-38, chief of Wildlife Division, 1934-38, chief of Biology Division, 1938-42, chief of Personnel Division, 1942-46, regional chief of operations of Pacific Region in Portland, Ore., 1947-53, assistant management administrator of Soil Conservation Service, 1953-62, deputy administrator, 1962-72, instructor at Agriculture Department Graduate School, 1957—, dean, 1973-78; management consultant, 1972—. Visiting member of faculty at more than thirty universities, including Colorado State University, 1965-70, and North Carolina State University, 1971—; visiting lecturer at Columbia University, 1968-70.

MEMBER: Soil Conservation Society of America, American Geographical Society, Ecological Society of America, Wildlife Society, American Society of Plant Taxonomists, Washington Academy of Science. *Awards, honors:* Rockefeller Public Service Award, 1958; superior service award from U.S. Department of Agriculture, 1964.

WRITINGS: Native Woody Plants of the United States: Their Erosion-Control and Wildlife Values, U.S. Government Printing Office, 1938; *Ornamental American Shrubs,* Oxford University Press, 1942; *The American Land: Its History and Uses,* Oxford University Press, 1943; (with Edward H. Graham) *The Land Renewed: The Story of Soil Conservation* (juvenile), Oxford University Press, 1946, revised edition, Walck, 1968; (with Graham) *Wildlife for America: The Story of Wildlife Conservation* (juvenile),

Oxford University Press, 1949, revised edition, Walck, 1970; (with Graham) *Water for America: The Story of Water Conservation* (juvenile), Oxford University Press, 1956; *The Successful Supervisor in Government and Business,* Harper, 1962, 3rd edition, 1974; *Modern Supervisory Practice,* U.S. Department of Agriculture, 1964; (with Norman A. Berg) *Success in Supervision,* U.S. Department of Agriculture, 1965; *The Successful Manager in Government and Business,* Harper, 1974; *Why Does Your Garden Grow?: The Facts of Plant Life,* Quadrangle, 1977.

WORK IN PROGRESS: Ornamental American Shrubs and Small Trees; Environment for Americans.

SIDELIGHTS: Van Dersal's books have been published in Japan, Korea, Turkey, Egypt, Mexico, and Brazil.

*   *   *

VAN DORNE, R.
See WALLMANN, Jeffrey M(iner)

*   *   *

VANGELISTI, Paul 1945-

PERSONAL: Born September 17, 1945, in San Francisco, Calif.; son of Nicholas Thomas (an accountant) and Josephine (a saleswoman; maiden name, Zangani) Vangelisti; married Margaret Dryden, December 31, 1966; children: Tristan, Simone. *Education:* University of San Francisco, B.A., 1967; attended Trinity College, Dublin, 1967-68; University of Southern California, M.A., 1971, doctoral study, 1972. *Home:* 3209 Berkeley Ave., Los Angeles, Calif. 90026. *Office:* KPFK-Radio, 3729 Cahuenga Blvd. W., North Hollywood, Calif. 91604.

CAREER: San Francisco Department of Recreation and Parks, San Francisco, Calif., recreation director, 1967-68; University of Southern California, Los Angeles, assistant instructor in English, 1968-72; *Hollywood Reporter,* Hollywood, Calif., assignment editor, 1972-73; KPFK-Radio, North Hollywood, Calif., cultural affairs director, 1974—. Instructor in creative writing in Los Angeles public schools, 1974; instructor at Los Angeles Junior Arts Center, 1975, 1977—.

WRITINGS—Books of poems: *Communion,* Red Hill Press, 1970; *Air,* Red Hill Press, 1973; (editor with Charles Bukowski) *Anthology of Los Angeles Poets,* Red Hill Press, 1973; (editor) *Specimen 73* (catalog and anthology), Pasadena Museum, 1973; *Tender Continent,* Chatterton's Bookstore, 1974; *Pearl Harbor,* Isthmus, 1975; *Il tenero continente* (bilingual; title means "The Tender Continent"), Edizioni Geiger, 1975; *The Extravagant Room,* Red Hill Press, 1976; *Two by Two* (visual poems), Red Hill Press, 1977; *Remembering the Movies* (visual poems), Red Hill Press, 1977.

Translator: *Sixteen Poems of Vittorio Sereni,* Red Hill Press, 1971; Adriano Spatola, *Mayakovskiiiiiiij,* Red Hill Press, 1975; Giulia Niccolai, *Substitutions,* Red Hill Press, 1975; Corrado Costa, *Our Positions,* Red Hill Press, 1975; Rocco Scotellaro, *The Sky with Its Mouth Wide-Open,* Red Hill Press, 1976; Franco Beltrametti, *Another Earthquake,* Red Hill Press, 1977; Antonio Porta, *As If It Were a Rhythm,* Red Hill Press, 1978; (with Carol Lettieri) Mohammed Dib, *Omneros,* Red Hill Press, 1978; (editor and translator, with Milne Holton) *New Polish Poetry,* University of Pittsburgh Press, 1978. Co-editor of *Invisible City.*

WORK IN PROGRESS: Scapes, poems; editing and translating an anthology of Italian avant-garde writing, 1960-1976.

VAN HOUTEN, Lois 1918-

PERSONAL: Born October 31, 1918, in Paterson, N.J.; daughter of William Henry (a dentist) and Lillian (Rider) Daniels; married Melvin Van Houten (a teacher), May 19, 1942; children: Edward B., Jay W. *Education:* Attended Newark State College, 1961-62, and William Paterson College, 1963-65. *Politics:* Democrat. *Religion:* Protestant. *Home:* 16 Harlow Cres., Fairlawn, N.J. 07410.

CAREER: Nursery school teacher in Riveredge, N.J., 1961-62, New Milford, N.J., 1963-64, Fair Lawn, N.J., 1965-66, Paramus, N.J., 1967-68, Wayne, N.J., 1969-71, Ridgewood, N.J., 1972; writer, 1972—. Silversmith (designs, makes, and sells jewelry). Has given readings in New York and New Jersey; judge of arts and poetry contests and festivals.

MEMBER: New Jersey Designer Craftsmen, Poets and Writers of New Jersey, Poets and Writers of New York, Bergen Poets. *Awards, honors:* Awards from Fairlawn Festival of the Arts, 1972, for poetry; Teaneck Peace Center, 1973, for poetry; Kentucky Poetry Society of America, 1974; William Carlos Williams Poetry Center, 1975, 1976, and 1977.

WRITINGS: North Jersey Blues (city poems), Cycle Press, 1972; *Behind the Door* (poems), Stone Country Press, 1976; *The Woman Who Warped with Doors* (feminist and women's poems), Stone Country Press, 1977.

Work represented in several anthologies, including *An Anthology of American Poetry,* edited by John Nichols, American Poetry Press, 1976; *Moonchild,* edited by Ismail Erseuim, Suha Publications, 1976.

Contributor of more than a hundred poems to magazines, including *Poetry Florida* and *New Jersey Poetry Monthly.*

WORK IN PROGRESS: A fourth book, lyric poems.

SIDELIGHTS: Lois Van Houten writes: "I have been writing poetry steadily for over twenty-seven years. My first intimations of poetry came when very young, when I fell in love with 'images' in writing, rather than whole sentences. I grew up in the industrial seaboard cities of the East and wrote about cities for a long time. My last book is concerned only with women, their lives, anguish, and loss in a male-dominated society. I am closely connected with the women's movement and through that, the 'gay' movement and problems of gay women."

*   *   *

VAN MEERHAEGHE, Marcel Alfons Gilbert 1921-

PERSONAL: Born April 12, 1921, in Wetteren, Belgium. *Education:* University of Ghent, licence, 1944, Ph.D., 1946. *Home:* Zeedijk 126, Ostend, Belgium 8400. *Office:* University of Ghent, Ghent, Belgium 9000.

CAREER: Adviser to the Belgian minister of economic affairs, 1946-53; adviser to NATO Defense College, Paris, France, 1953-54; adviser to the Belgian minister of foreign trade, 1954-57; State University of Ghent, Ghent, Belgium, professor of economics, 1955—. Belgian Price Commission vice-president, 1961-64, president, 1964-69.

WRITINGS—in English: *Internationale economische betrekkingen en instellingen,* Stenfert Kroese, 1964, published as *International Economic Institutions,* Wiley, 1966, 2nd edition, St. Martin's, 1971; *Price Theory and Price Policy,* Longman, 1969, Humanities, 1970; *Economie: Een kritisch handboek,* Stenfert Kroese, 1970, published as *Economics: A Critical Approach,* Crane, Russak, 1971; *International Economics,* Crane, Russak, 1972; (contributor) William

Moskoff, editor, *Comparative National Economic Policies: A Reader for Introductory Economics*, Heath, 1973.

Books in Dutch: *Handboek van de economie* (title means "Handbook of Economics"), Elsevier, 1952, 5th edition, Stenfert Kroese, 1966; *Economische structuur van Belgisch-Kongo en Ruanda-Urundi* (title means "Economic Structure in the Belgian Congo and Ruanda-Urundi"), Ontwikkeling, 1958; *Recente bijdragen tot de theorie van de internationale economische betrekkingen* (title means "Recent Contributions to the Theory of International Economic Relations"), State University of Ghent, 1959; *Marktvormen, marktgedrag en marktresultaten in Belgie* (title means "Market Structure, Market Behavior and Market Results in Belgium"), Story Scientia, 1963; *De economie van Vlaanderen* (title means "The Economy of Flanders"), Stenfert Kroese, 1965; *Internationale economie* (title means "International Economics"), Stenfert Kroese, 1972; *Lexicon van de economie* (title means "Lexicon of Economics"), Stenfert Kroese, 1977; *De Afgunstmaatsch appij* (title means "The Envious Society"), Stenfert Kroese, 1978.

Editor and contributor: (With Jacobus Andriessen) *Theorie van de economische politiek: Een systematische overzicht met bijdragen van Nederlandse en Belgische auteurs* (title means "Theory of Economic Policy: A Systematic Survey with Contributions from Dutch and Belgian Authors"), Stenfert Kroese, 1961; *De voorwaarden tot economische groei in Afrika* (title means "Conditions for Economic Growth in Africa"), State University of Ghent, 1963; *Economics: Britain and the EEC*, Longman, 1969.

Contributor in Dutch: Max Lamberty and Rene F. Lissens, editors, *Vlaanderen door de eeuwen heen* (title means "Flanders Throughout the Centuries"), two volumes, 3rd edition, Elsevier, 1951-52; Theo Luyckx, editor, *Liber Memoralis 1913-1960*, State University of Ghent, 1960; Guy Schrans and J. Flamme, editors, *Economisch en financieel recht vandaag II* (title means "Economic and Financial Law Today"), State University of Ghent, 1973; Roelf L. Haan, Hershel Visser, and W. Maarse Nzn, editors, *Model en mogelijkheid* (title means "Models and Possibilities"), Jan Haan, 1974; *Liber amicorum Professor Baron Jean van Houtte*, Elsevier Sequoia, 1976.

Contributor in other languages: (In French) *Livre Blanc: L'Apport de la Belgique dans le developpement de l'Afrique Centrale* (title means "White Book: The Contribution of Belgium to the Development of Central Africa"), Academie Royale des Sciences d'Outre-Mer, 1962; Tullio Bagiotti, editor, *Essays in Honour of Marco Fanno*, Volume II: *Investigations in Economic Theory and Methodology*, Cedam, 1966; (in German) H. K. Schneider and C. Watrin, editors, *Macht und oekonomisches Gesetz* (title means "Power and Economic Law"), [Berlin], 1973.

Contributor to publications of various colloquia and conferences, including International Economic Associations conferences and a colloquium on economic planning at the University of Brussels. Columnist, *Trends*. Contributor of numerous articles to *Revue Economique*, *Rivista Internazionali di Scienze Economiche e Commerciali*, *Kylos*, *Economia Internazionale*, *Economisch-Statistische Berichten*, and other journals in his field.

*   *   *

VAN WAGENEN, Gertrude   1893-1978

May 23, 1893—February 8, 1978; American scientist, educator, and author. Van Wagenen, one of the first scientists to study glandular excretions and their effect on reproductive processes, was associate professor and lecturer at Yale University. She wrote two books and numerous scientific papers. Obituaries and other sources: *American Men and Women of Science: The Physical and Biological Sciences*, 12th edition, Bowker, 1971-73; *New York Times*, February 10, 1978.

*   *   *

VARDAMIS, Alex A.   1934-

PERSONAL: Born September 10, 1934, in Bangor, Maine; son of Alex G. (owner of a grocery and drug store) and Pauline (a businesswoman; maiden name, Georges) Vardamis; married Frances Diem (a novelist), June 29, 1957; children: Sharon Megan, Daniel Christopher. *Education:* U.S. Military Academy, B.S., 1957; Columbia University, M.A., 1967, Ph.D., 1970. *Politics:* "Skeptical." *Religion:* Protestant. *Home:* 1 Soldiers Field Park, Apt. 602, Boston, Mass. 02163. *Office:* Program for Science and International Affairs, Harvard University, 9 Divinity Ave., Cambridge, Mass. 02138.

CAREER: U.S. Army, career officer, 1957—, qualified as parachutist, commanding officer of artillery battalion in Ingolstadt, Germany, 1962-63, assistant exchange officer to German artillery in Ulm, 1963-64, instructor at U.S. Military Academy, 1967, assistant professor of English, 1970, executive officer of Office of the Deputy Chief of Staff for Military Operations in Vietnam, 1971-72, commander of artillery group in Muenster, Germany, 1972-74, chief of Special Ammunition Support Command in Rheindahlen, Germany, 1974-75, instructor at University of Vermont, 1975-77, fellow of Harvard University program for science and international affairs, 1977—, present rank, colonel.

MEMBER: Modern Language Association of America, Association of Graduates of U.S. Military Academy, Columbia Graduate Faculties Association. *Awards, honors*—Military: Bronze Star, Army Commendation Medal with oak leaf cluster.

WRITINGS: The Critical Reputation of Robinson Jeffers, Shoe String, 1972. Contributor of poems and reviews to literary magazines and *Military Review*.

WORK IN PROGRESS: A book on the role of nuclear arms control in diminishing probability of war.

SIDELIGHTS: Vardamis writes that most of his time is taken up by military activities, but that he has a keen interest in twentieth-century American poetry, and has found time for extensive research on Randall Jarrell and Robinson Jeffers.

*   *   *

VARLEY, H(erbert) Paul   1931-

PERSONAL: Born February 8, 1931, in Paterson, N.J.; son of Herbert P. (an automobile dealer) and Katharine L. (Norcross) Varley; married Betty Jane Geiskopf (a model), December 24, 1960; children: two stepdaughters. *Education:* Lehigh University, B.A., 1952; Columbia University, M.A., 1961, Ph.D., 1964. *Home:* 1500 Palisade Ave., 6E, Fort Lee, N.J. 07024. *Office:* Department of East Asian Languages and Studies, 414 Kent Hall, Columbia University, New York, N.Y. 10027.

CAREER: University of Hawaii, Honolulu, assistant professor of Japanese history, 1964-65; Columbia University, New York, N.Y., assistant professor, 1965-69, associate professor, 1970-75, professor of Japanese history, 1976—. *Military service:* U.S. Army, 1952-54.

WRITINGS: The Onin War, Columbia University Press, 1967; *A Syllabus of Japanese Civilization,* Columbia University Press, 1968; *The Samurai,* Weidenfeld & Nicolson, 1970; *Imperial Restoration in Medieval Japan,* Columbia University Press, 1971; *Japanese Culture: A Short History,* Praeger, 1973.

WORK IN PROGRESS: Translating a fourteenth-century work on imperial legitimacy in Japan, *Jinno Shotoki;* research on the culture of the Higashiyama epoch of medieval Japan.

SIDELIGHTS: Varley writes that one of his interests is sleight-of-hand, close-up magic. "I am active in magic organizations, and have studied close-up with Slydini, a noted magician based in New York."

* * *

VARMA, Monika 1916-

PERSONAL: Born August 5, 1916, in Allahbad, India; daughter of Lalit Mohan (a judge) and Manorama (Chatterji) Banerji; married Krishna Kumar Varma (a bank director), February 1, 1938; children: Jayant, Sanjaya (sons). *Education:* Privately educated in India. *Religion:* Hindu. *Home:* Sokra Nala Farm, P.O. Krishnak Nagar, Raipur M.P. India 492001.

CAREER: Agriculturist, poet, writer, and translator. *Member:* World Poetry Society Intercontinental, International Academy of Poets (founding fellow), Maharishi Institute of Creative Intelligence, Armed Forces Women's Welfare Organizations. *Awards, honors: Caravan* magazine poetry prize, 1956, 1958; National Short Story prize, 1970; World Poetry Society Intercontinental distinguished service citation, 1971, 1973; Creative Arts Fund award, 1976.

WRITINGS—Poetry; all published by Writers Workshop, Calcutta, except as indicated: *Dargonflies Draw Flame,* 1962; *Gita Govinda and Other Poems,* 1966; *Green Leaves and Gold,* 1970; *Quartered Questions and Queries,* 1971; *Past Imperative,* 1972; *Across the Vast Spaces,* United Writers, Calcutta, 1975; *Alakananda,* 1976.

Prose: *Facing Four: A Critical Opinion of Four Indian Women Writing in English,* Writers Workshop, Calcutta, 1974; *Lord Krishna,* Vikas Publishing House, 1978.

Translator: *A Bunch of Poems* (Tagore poems translated from Bengali to English), 1966; Jayadeva, *Gita Givinda* (poems translated from Sanskrit to English), 1968; Bibhuti Bhusan Banerjee, *Panther Panchali* (prose translated from Bengali to English), 1973.

Writer of monthly news column for *Trend* magazine. Contributor of articles, short stories, translations, and poetry to periodicals including *Illustrated Weekly of India, Women's Era, Miscellany, Quest, Dialogue,* and *Indian Verse.*

WORK IN PROGRESS: A translation of five Bengali stories; a collection of children's stories; *Crucible of Time,* a collection of essays; *Verities and Varieties,* a book about Hinduism in practice and concept.

SIDELIGHTS: Asked to comment on her poetry, Varma told *CA:* "On analysis I find that, though it has not been a conscious effort, the metaphysical idiom is a vital aspect of my poetry. Nature herself teaches one, on the philosophical plane, to see every object as a symbol of being related to each other: whether it is a star in the sky or an inanimate pebble on the floor of the earth. The technical term for this outlook is called hylozoism.

"The Greek tragic sense looked upon Fate as inexorable,

the Hindu sages teach us to look upon life as the interaction of formed objects. In poetry, as in philosophy, one can only say what has been experienced by that one particular person—this 'I.' Universality lies in the outlook and not in the dogma."

Varma has also reflected upon the various literary influences in her work. As an Indian woman writing in English she has been touched by works from many lands. But, finally, she feels, "it should be realized that the metaphors are totally Indian and based on Indian philosophy," traceable to the Sanskrit classics. She puts it this way: "If the Lake Poets were influenced by their environment, my environment has also, always, had a profound effect on me."

* * *

VAUGHAN, David 1924-

PERSONAL: Born May 17, 1924, in London, England; son of Albert George (a company secretary) and Rose (Stocks) Vaughan. *Education:* Attended Wadham College, Oxford, 1942-43, and School of American Ballet, 1950-55; also studied with Marie Rambert, Audrey de Vos, Merce Cunningham, Antony Tudor, and Richard Thomas. *Home:* 222 East 10th St., New York, N.Y. 10003. *Agent:* Robert Cornfield, Wallace, Aitken & Sheil, Inc., 118 East 61st St., New York, N.Y. 10022. *Office:* Cunningham Dance Foundation, 463 West St., New York, N.Y. 10014.

CAREER: Dance Associates, New York City, co-founder and performer, 1951-55; professional dancer in companies operated by James Waring, 1952-58, Louis Johnson 1953, Paul Taylor, 1954, Shirley Broughton, 1956, and Katherine Litz, 1960; Judson Poets' Theater, New York City, choreographer and performer, 1965—. Senior artist with U.S. Terpsichore Ballet Co., 1974—; has arranged exhibitions. Administrator of Merce Cunningham Studio (and occasionally of the dance company), 1959-72; member of Cunningham Dance Foundation (archivist, 1976); president of James Waring Dance Foundation. Faculty member at University of Chicago, summer, 1975. *Military service:* British Army, 1943-47; became staff sergeant.

MEMBER: Actors' Equity Association, American Federation of Television and Radio Artists. *Awards, honors:* Grant from Igram Merrill Foundation, 1974; De La Torre Bueno Prize from Wesleyan University Press and Dance Perspectives Foundation, 1976, for *Frederick Ashton and His Ballets;* Guggenheim fellowhip, 1978.

WRITINGS: The Royal Ballet at Covent Garden, Dance Books, 1975; *Lynn Seymour,* Dance Horizons, 1976; (editor with Mary Clarke) *Encyclopedia of Dance and Ballet,* Putnam, 1977; *Frederick Ashton and His Ballets,* Knopf, 1977. Contributor to dance magazines and journals, including *About the House, Financial Times, Sequence,* and *Sight and Sound.* Associate editor of *Ballet Review;* associate critic for *Dance.*

WORK IN PROGRESS: The Choreography of Merce Cunningham, for Knopf.

SIDELIGHTS: Vaughan comments: "Dance has been my vocation and avocation for as long as I can remember—whether as performer or spectator or writer. I also like to sing and for seven years have given an annual concert, with Al Carmines, of songs by such writers as Irving Berlin, Gershwin, and Kern."

* * *

VIGNA, Judith 1936-

PERSONAL: Surname is pronounced *Veen*-ya; born April

27, 1936, in Gedney, England; came to the United States in 1958, naturalized citizen, 1968; daughter of John (a physician) and Audrey Stephenson (Brackenridge) Pankhurst; married Arnaldo Vigna, December, 1960 (separated). *Education:* Attended St. Martin's School of Art, 1956, and School of Visual Arts, 1960; student at Queens College of the City University of New York, 1973—. *Residence:* Whitestone, N.Y. *Agent:* Curtis Brown Ltd., 575 Madison Ave., New York, N.Y. 10022.

CAREER: Lincolnshire Standard, Boston, England, journalist and artist, 1953-55; Dorville House, London, England, public relations assistant, 1955-57; Henry Morgan Co., Montreal, Quebec, advertising copywriter, 1957-58; Young & Rubicam, Inc., New York, N.Y., copywriter, 1958-65; free-lance writer and illustrator, 1965—. Worked with emotionally-disturbed children as art therapist. *Member:* Authors Guild of Authors League of America.

WRITINGS—Self-illustrated children's books: *Gregory's Stitches,* Albert Whitman, 1974; *The Little Boy Who Loved Dirt and Almost Became a Superslob,* Albert Whitman, 1975; *Couldn't We Have a Turtle Instead?,* Albert Whitman, 1975; *Everyone Goes as a Pumpkin,* Albert Whitman, 1977; *Anyhow, I'm Glad I Tried,* Albert Whitman, 1978.

WORK IN PROGRESS: Stories for children, with emphasis on everyday childhood problems.

SIDELIGHTS: Judith Vigna writes: "An addiction to books as a child in England—particularly those of Beatrix Potter and Kenneth Grahame—motivated me early on to write and illustrate children's books, but I did not realize that ambition until quite recently.

"My goal in putting together a picture-book is to approach common childhood problems such as a new baby or loss of a precious possession, with a humorous touch that can help a child over a painful experience. Most of the situations I present in my books are dug up from my own childhood—remembering uncomfortable feelings, minor calamities (that seemed major at the time!)—or overwhelming joy. In trying to keep in touch with a child's feelings, I find it helpful to remember that many of the emotions we experience as adults are enormously intensified in children. Always acknowledging the marvelous sense of humor children have, I try to combine these emotions with a bit of fun and whimsy.

"Courses in psychology, a special interest in art therapy, plus some volunteer work with emotionally-disturbed children, have contributed to my background."

AVOCATIONAL INTERESTS: Portrait painting, music, skiing, books, travel.

*   *   *

VINCENT, R(aymond) J(ohn) 1943-

PERSONAL: Born February 28, 1943, in London, England; son of Patrick John Russell (a bank official) and Barbara Jean (a teacher; maiden name, Tucker) Vincent; married Angela Murray (a teacher), October 26, 1966; children: Geraint. *Education:* University of Wales, B.A., 1965, diploma in education, 1966; University of Leicester, M.A., 1967; Australian National University, Ph.D., 1971. *Politics:* Social Democrat. *Religion:* "Lapsed Anglican." *Home:* 23 Lichfield St., Stone, Staffordshire, England. *Office:* Department of International Relations, University of Keele, Keele, Staffordshire 5T5 5BG, England.

CAREER: Princeton University, Princeton, N.J., visiting research fellow, 1972-73; International Institute for Strategic Studies, London, England, research associate, 1973-74; Australian National University, Canberra, research fellow, 1974-76; University of Keele, Keele, England, lecturer in international relations, 1976—. Member of council of London Institute of World Affairs. *Member:* International Institute for Strategic Studies, Royal Institute of International Affairs, British International Studies Association.

WRITINGS: Nonintervention and International Order, Princeton University Press, 1974; *Military Power and Political Influence: The Soviet Union and Western Europe,* International Institute for Strategic Studies, 1975. Contributor to *Yearbook of World Affairs* and international studies journals.

WORK IN PROGRESS: The Idea of World Security; The Diplomacy of Economic Justice; Cultural Approaches to World Politics.

*   *   *

VINCENT, Theodore G. 1936-

PERSONAL: Born February 24, 1936, in Washington, D.C.; son of Theodore J. (a teacher) and Billie (a teacher; maiden name, Botson) Vincent; married wife Toni, September 22, 1958 (divorced, June, 1968); married wife Selma, January 15, 1969; children: Theodore B., Frederick L., Marilyn Mavis. *Education:* Los Angeles Community College, A.A., 1957; University of California, Los Angeles, B.A., 1959; University of California, Berkeley, M.A., 1963. *Politics:* Socialist. *Religion:* None. *Home:* 2333 Fulton, Berkeley, Calif. 94704.

CAREER: San Jose State College, San Jose, Calif., instructor in Extension Division, 1966-67; University of California, Berkeley, lecturer in sociology, 1968-69; University of California, Los Angeles, instructor in history, 1973-74; writer, 1974—. *Member:* Industrial Workers of the World, National Association for the Advancement of Colored People, Congress of Racial Equality.

WRITINGS: Black Power and the Garvey Movement, Ramparts, 1970; *Voices of a Black Nation,* Ramparts, 1972. Author of series "Black Power Origins," on KPFA-Radio, 1968-69, and "Sporting Life: Historical Sketches of American Athletics," on KPFA-Radio, 1975-77.

WORK IN PROGRESS: The Politics of Sport, tracing social and political conflict in athletics.

*   *   *

VINSON, Jane 1927-

PERSONAL: Born February 5, 1927, in Oakland, Calif. *Education:* Stanford University, A.B., 1948, M.A., 1968; Nova University, Ed.D., 1975. *Residence:* Carmichael, Calif. *Office:* California State Department of Education, 721 Capitol Mall, Sacramento, Calif. 95814.

CAREER: Elementary school teacher in Sacramento, Calif., Tachikawa, Japan, and Cupertino, Calif., 1948-65; resource and demonstration teacher in Sacramento, 1965; district specialist in English as a second language in Sacramento, 1966-70; California State Department of Education, Sacramento, reading consultant, 1970-76, administrator in elementary education, 1976—. *Member:* International Reading Association, Teachers of English as a Second Language, California Writers Club, Delta Kappa Gamma.

WRITINGS: The Magic of English: Beginning Experiences in English as a Second Language, Harper, 1968, workbook, 1970. Editor of *Focus on Compensatory Education.*

WORK IN PROGRESS: Revising *The Magic of English* and its workbook; three additional workbooks to accompany *The Magic of English.*

AVOCATIONAL INTERESTS: Travel (including Europe, Japan, and Thailand), photography, gardening.

* * *

VINTON, Iris

PERSONAL: Born in West Point, Miss.; daughter of William and Maud (Best) Vinton. *Education:* University of Texas, Permanent State Teachers Certificate, 1923; Incarnate World College, A.B., 1928. *Residence:* New York, N.Y.

CAREER: Worked as a teacher in Texas; assistant to director of National Recreation Association Education Department, 1929-36; editor-in-chief of *You and Your Child* magazine, 1936-40; associate editor for Breskin Publishing Co., 1940-44; publications department director for Boys' Clubs of America, 1944-64; author, editor, and consultant on children's books. *Member:* Women's National Book Association (former member of the board of managers), Pen and Brush Club, Boys' Clubs Professional Association (honorary member).

WRITINGS: Just Babies (one-act play), Walter Baker, 1939; *Laffy of the Navy Salvage Divers* (illustrated by Addison Burbank), Dodd, 1944; *Flying Ebony* (illustrated by Marc Simont), Dodd, 1947; (with Constance Rittenhouse) *Abbie Higgins, Young Group Work Executive,* Dodd, 1950; *The Black Horse Company,* Dodd, 1950; *Passage to Texas* (illustrated by Kathleen Elgin), Aladdin Books, 1952; *The Story of Robert E. Lee* (illustrated by John Alan Maxwell), Grosset, 1952; *The Story of John Paul Jones* (illustrated by Edward A. Wilson), Grosset, 1953; *The Story of Stephen Decatur* (illustrated by Graham Kaye), Grosset, 1954; *Boy on the Mayflower* (illustrated by Jon Nielsen), Four Winds Press, 1957; *Longbow Island* (illustrated by Laszlo Matulay), Dodd, 1957; *We Were There with Jean Lafitte at New Orleans* (illustrated by Robert Glaubke), Grosset, 1957; *The Story of Edith Cavell* (illustrated by Gerald McCann), Grosset, 1959.

(Editor) Eleanor Porter, *Pollyanna* (illustrated by Isabelle Dawson), Grosset, 1960; *Look out for Pirates!* (illustrated by H. B. Vestal), Beginner Books, 1961; (editor) Leslie Wolff, *Science and the Forester* (illustrated by Kerry Lee), Criterion, 1961; *Now that You Are Nine* (illustrated by Leonhard Shortall), Association Press, 1963; *The Story of President Kennedy* (illustrated by Carl Cassler), Grosset, 1966; *Missy and the Mountain Lion* (illustrated by Leo Summers), L. W. Singer, 1967; *The Folkways Omnibus of Children's Games* (illustrated by Alex D'Amato), Stackpole, 1970.

SIDELIGHTS: Flying Ebony told the adventures of a young boy and his horse during the mid 1800's. A *New York Times* critic observed, "There is adequate action in the good story . . . and there is also rich historical atmosphere and fine family feeling." *Black Horse Company,* a sequel to *Flying Ebony,* related how the youth and his animal friend worked to salvage an old abandoned schooner. In reviewing *Black Horse Company,* a critic for the *Saturday Review of Literature* wrote: "The plot is skillfully developed to provide suspense and drama; the characterization of minor as well as major figures is vigorous and full-bodied. . . . Her [Vinton's] book has the ring of authenticity and a wealth of description and explanation that give it value even more than its action."

In *Longbow Island* the author told the adventures of six boys on an archaeological expedition. "Maybe it is a little melodramatic at the end, but it is all good reading because the boys are made real. . . . The nice part about it is that each [boy] in his own way contributes to the success of the venture, and they have a whale of a time. So will the reader," commented a critic for the *New York Times.*

Vinton's latest book is *The Folkways Omnibus of Children's Games.* A reviewer for the *Christian Science Monitor* noted: "[This is] a valuable source-book of games for the young; but it is far more than that. It tells where each game comes from in both time and place; and the historical notes often make a distant age and country suddenly come alive for us. . . ."

BIOGRAPHICAL/CRITICAL SOURCES: New York Times, July 6, 1947, June 23, 1957; *Saturday Review of Literature,* May 13, 1950; *Christian Science Monitor,* August 29, 1970.*

* * *

VISSCHER, Maurice B(olks) 1901-

PERSONAL: Born August 25, 1901, in Holland, Mich.; son of Joannes W. (a teacher) and Everdiena (Bolks) Visscher; married Janet Gertrude Pieters, August 12, 1925; children: Barbara Ruth Visscher Kahn, William Maurits, Janet Constance Visscher Simpson, Pieter Bernard. *Education:* Hope College, B.A., 1922; University of Minnesota, M.S., 1924, Ph.D., 1925, M.D., 1931; also attended University of London, 1925-26, and University of Chicago, 1926-27. *Politics:* Independent. *Religion:* Unitarian-Universalist. *Office:* Department of Physiology, University of Minnesota, 424 Millard Hall, Minneapolis, Minn. 55455.

CAREER: University of Tennessee, Memphis, associate professor, 1927-28, professor of physiology, 1928-29, head of department, 1927-29; University of Southern California, Los Angeles, professor of physiology and pharmacology and head of department, 1929-31; University of Illinois, Chicago, professor of physiology and head of department, 1931-36; University of Minnesota, Minneapolis, professor, 1936-68, distinguished service professor, 1960-70, Regents' Professor of Physiology, 1967-70, professor emeritus, 1970—, head of department, 1936-68. Scientific chairman of Italian nutrition mission, 1945; co-director of medical nutrition study for United Nations Relief & Rehabilitation Administration-Unitarian Service Committee, 1945-46; chairman of World Health Organization-Unitarian Service Committee medical mission to Austria, 1948, and National Research Council committee on UNESCO, 1950-52.

MEMBER: International Union of Physiological Sciences (secretary-general, 1953-59; chairman of U.S. national committee, 1960-69), Council of International Organizations of Medical Sciences (member of board of directors, 1952-55; president, 1952-65), American Medical Association, American Association for the Advancement of Science, American Association of University Professors, National Academy of Sciences, American Academy of Arts and Sciences (fellow), American Philosophical Society, American Physiological Society (president, 1948-49), National Society for Medical Research (vice-president, 1952-55; president, 1965-77), American Heart Association (member of board of directors, 1947-54), American Cancer Society (member of national board of directors, 1952-54), American Chemical Society, American Association of Science Workers (president, 1947-48), Society for Experimental Biology and Medicine (vice-president, 1965-67; president, 1967-69), Gesellschaft der

Aertz in Wien (corresponding member), Gesellschaft der Chirurgen Wiens (honorary member), Asociacion Medica Argentina (corresponding member), New York Academy of Sciences (fellow), Minnesota Pathological Society, Minnesota Academy of Medicine, Hennepin County Medical Society (honorary member), Academy of Medicine (Chicago), St. Paul Surgical Society (honorary member), Sigma Xi, Alpha Omega Alpha. *Awards, honors:* Distinguished service award from American Cancer Society, 1955; research achievement award from American Heart Association, 1962; Wiggins Award from Circulation Section of American Physiological Association, 1973, for distinguished research in cardiovascular physiology; achievement award from American Physiological Society, 1974; merit award from Group Health Plan of Minnesota, 1976.

WRITINGS: (With Paul W. Smith) *Experimental Physiology,* Lea & Febiger, 1935; (editor) *Chemistry and Medicine,* University of Minnesota Press, 1940; (editor with Francisco Grande) *Claude Bernard and Experimental Medicine,* Schenkman, 1967; (editor and contributor) *Humanistic Perspectives in Medical Ethics,* Prometheus Books, 1972; *Constraints and Imperatives in Medical Ethics,* C. C Thomas, 1975. Contributor of about two hundred articles to scientific journals. President of board of trustees of *Biological Abstracts,* 1949-53; chairman of editorial committee of *Handbook of Physiology,* 1958-66.

WORK IN PROGRESS: A manuscript on the history of legislation in the field of animal experimentation.

SIDELIGHTS: Visscher writes: "I am interested in various aspects of medical and other scientific ethical problems, and concerned with humanistic approaches to philosophy and religion. My main thesis in *Constraints and Imperatives in Medical Ethics* is that it is imperative for physicians to carry out investigation in relation to the care of patients if they are to follow the first rule of medical ethics, which is, first of all do no harm. When one is ignorant of the causes of particular disease states or of methods to treat them, one does not know whether one is doing harm by recommending any particular course of action or inaction. It is only possible to know by thorough scientific investigation of the disorder. This in essence puts the shoe on the other foot as far as ethical considerations are concerned. Most persons who have considered the problem have dealt with the constraints and have ignored the imperatives."

BIOGRAPHICAL/CRITICAL SOURCES: University of Minnesota *Medical Bulletin,* winter, 1977.

*   *   *

VO-DINH, Mai   1933-

PERSONAL: Born November 14, 1933, in Hue, Vietnam; came to United States, 1960, naturalized citizen, 1976; son of Thang (a civil servant) and Do-Thi (Hanh) Vo-Dinh; married Helen Coutant Webb (a teacher), August 17, 1964; children: Katherine, Hannah. *Education:* Attended University of Lyon, Academie de la Grande Chaumiere, and Ecole Nationale Superieure des Beaux-Arts, 1959. *Home:* Stonevale, RFD #1, Burkittsville, Md. 21718.

CAREER: Artist and author. Artist-in-Residence, Synechia Arts Center, 1974. *Member:* International Association of Artists, Artists Equity Association of New York. *Awards, honors:* Christopher Foundation Award, 1975.

WRITINGS: (Self-illustrated) *The Toad Is the Emperor's Uncle,* Doubleday, 1970; (self-illustrated) *The Jade Song,* Chelsea House, 1970; *Views of a Vietnam Artist* (lecture), Southern Illinois University Press, 1972.

Portfolios: *Unicorn Broadsheet #4,* Unicorn Press, 1969; *Let's Stand Beside Each Other,* Fellowship Publications, 1969; *Recent Works by Vo-Dinh,* Suzuki Graphics, 1972; *The Woodcuts of Vo-Dinh,* Hoa-Binh Press, 1974.

Illustrator: *Birds, Frogs, and Moonlight,* translation by Sylvia Cassedy and Kunihiro Suetake, Doubleday, 1967; Nhat Hanh, *The Cry of Vietnam,* Unicorn Press, 1968; (and translator) Doan-Quoc-Sy, *The Stranded Fish,* Sang-Tao Press, 1971; (and translator) Hanh, *The Path of Return Continues the Journey,* Hoa-Binh Press, 1972; James Kirkup, *The Magic Drum,* Knopf, 1973; Helen Coutant, *First Snow,* Knopf, 1974; Hanh and Daniel Berrigan, *The Raft Is Not the Shore,* Beacon Press, 1975; (poetry) Hanh, *ZEN Poems,* Unicorn Press, 1976; Hanh, *The Miracle of Mindfulness,* Beacon Press, 1976; Ron Roy, *One Thousand Pints of Water,* Knopf, 1978.

WORK IN PROGRESS: Writing a collection of short stories in English; translating a collection of short stories by leading contemporary Vietnamese writers.

SIDELIGHTS: Vo-Dinh told *CA:* "Naturally, the war in Vietnam affected me, an artist, profoundly as it did, in other ways, all Vietnamese. An entire generation grew up, lived, and died with it. Yet, my work cannot, except for occasional flarings of outrage and sorrow, be called violent or pessimistic. If anything, the war between Vietnamese and between Vietnamese and Americans has reinforced my faith in the miracle of life. It is a faith beyond hope or despair.

"Surprisingly enough, the paintings that I, born and bred in Vietnam, am most fond of are by two Britishers, Francis Bacon and Graham Sutherland. I also like Georgia O'Keefe, a great American lady, very much.

"My opinion of modern art? I hope it counts! Modern art is but a reflection of modern life. Do you know the story from that Buddhist text?: 'A man gallops by on his horse. Someone shouts at him: "Where are you going?" The man hollers back: "Don't know! Ask the horse!" ' "

*   *   *

VOELCKER, Hunce   1940-

PERSONAL: Born June 28, 1940, in Danville, Pa.; son of Henry H. and Mary Hildagard (McVey) Voelcker. *Education:* Villanova University, A.B., 1962; graduate study at City College of the City University of New York, 1963-64. *Politics:* "Hope for the best present." *Religion:* "Dreams of the timeless." *Home and office address:* P.O. Box 11, Duncans Mills, Calif. 95430.

CAREER: Writer. Substitute teacher for public schools in New York, N.Y., 1963-65.

WRITINGS: The Hart Crane Voyages, Brownstone Press, 1967; *Logan* (novel), Cowstone Press, 1969; *Songs for the Revolution* (poems), Cowstone Press, 1970; *Parade of Gumdrop* (prose), Hoddypoll Press, 1971; *Sillycomb* (novel), Panjandrum Press, 1974; *Within the Rose* (poem), Panjandrum Press, 1977.

WORK IN PROGRESS: A novel, "which doubles as a thorough explication of Hart Crane's *The Bridge.*"

SIDELIGHTS: Voelcker writes: "Anyone, as Jack Spicer used to say, who wants to know more than these vital statistics, should write to me personally and ask."

*   *   *

VOGEL, John H., Jr.   1950-

PERSONAL: Born April 16, 1950, in New York, N.Y.; son

of John H. (a banker) and Helen (a teacher; maiden name, Wolff) Vogel; married Judith Barnes (a librarian), September 28, 1974. *Education:* Attended University of Lancaster, 1970-71; Carleton College, B.A. (magna cum laude), 1972; University of Virginia, M.A. *Agent:* Curtis Brown Ltd., 60 East 56th St., New York, N.Y. 10022.

CAREER: High school English teacher in Winchester, Va., 1974-76; NICO Construction, New York, N.Y., construction superintendent, 1976-77; Ward & Ward, Cary, N.C., construction superintendent, 1977—. *Member:* Phi Beta Kappa.

WRITINGS: (With Martha Munzer) *New Towns: Building Cities from Scratch* (juvenile), Knopf, 1974.

*   *   *

VOGEL, Stanley M(orton)   1921-

PERSONAL: Born January 21, 1921, in Norwalk, Conn.; son of Morris (a realtor) and Betty (Jacobson) Vogel. *Education:* New York University, A.B., 1942; Yale University, M.A., 1945, Ph.D., 1949; postdoctoral study at Oxford University, 1950, and Harvard University, 1958, 1975. *Home:* 69 Hancock St., Boston, Mass. 02114. *Office:* Department of English, Suffolk University, Boston, Mass. 02114.

CAREER: Princeton University, Princeton, N.J., instructor in English, 1947-48; Suffolk University, Boston, Mass., instructor, 1948-49, assistant professor, 1949-55, associate professor, 1955-58, professor of English, 1958—, chairman of department, 1961-78. Lecturer at Emerson College, 1952-61. Proprietor of Boston Athenaeum. *Military service:* U.S. Army Air Forces, 1943-45. *Member:* International Reading Association, Modern Language Association of America, College English Association, Harvard Musical Association, Phi Beta Kappa, Phi Alpha Theta, Phi Alpha Tau.

WRITINGS: German Literary Influences on the American Transcendentalists, Yale University Press, 1955, 2nd edition, Archon Books, 1970. Also author of student outline series, with Ella M. Murphy, all published by Student Outlines Co.: *American Literature,* two volumes, 1961; *The English Novel in the Nineteenth Century,* 1967; *David Copperfield,* 1967; *Great Expectations,* 1967; *Bleak House,* 1967; *Martin Chuzzlewit,* 1967; *The Mill on the Floss,* 1967, *Adam Bede,* 1967; *Middlemarch,* 1967; *Jane Eyre and Villette,* 1967; *Wuthering Heights,* 1967.

WORK IN PROGRESS: The English Novel in the Eighteenth Century.

AVOCATIONAL INTERESTS: World travel (Iron Curtain countries, Asia, Africa, North and South America).

*   *   *

von MALTITZ, Horst   1905-

PERSONAL: Born October 25, 1905, in Germany; son of Hans and Elsa von Maltitz; married Frances Willard (a writer), July 8, 1939. *Education:* Earned law degree from a German university. *Politics:* Democrat. *Religion:* None. *Home:* 151 Goodhill Rd., Weston, Conn. 06883.

CAREER: Senior partner with Von Maltitz, Derenberg, Kunin & Janssen (attorneys), 1929-67.

WRITINGS: The Evolution of Hitler's Germany: The Ideology, the Personality, the Moment, McGraw, 1973.

WORK IN PROGRESS: Research on German history.

W

WACIUMA, Wanjohi 1938-

PERSONAL: Born September 22, 1938, in Kenya; son of Lewis Kaguru (a health worker) and Bertha (Wangui) Waciuma. *Education:* Attended Makerere University; Harvard University, B.A.; City University of New York, Ph.D. *Home:* 3203 Oakmont Blvd., Austin, Tex. 78703.

CAREER: Brooklyn College of the City University of New York, Brooklyn, N.Y., 1969-76, began as lecturer, became assistant professor; writer, 1976—. *Member:* International Studies Association, African Studies Association.

WRITINGS: Intervention in the Spanish Floridas, 1801-1913: A Study of Jeffersonian Foreign Policy, Branden Press, 1977.

WORK IN PROGRESS: United States Security Assistance to Africa, 1960-1976: A Study of Imperialism; American Doctrine versus Bolivarian Principles, 1810-1826; A Study of African Mineral Resources.

SIDELIGHTS: Waciuma writes: ''A considerable amount of the written history is a cover-up. My mission is to try and uncover a little of that history. My first attempt was *Intervention in the Spanish Floridas, 1801-1813: A Study of Jeffersonian Foreign Policy.* That work has received good reviews.''

*   *   *

WADE, Nicholas (Michael Landon) 1942-

PERSONAL: Born May 17, 1942, in England; came to the United States in 1970; son of Michael Rubens and Laurien Wade. *Education:* King's College, Cambridge, M.A., 1963. *Home:* 104 Hodge's Lane, Takoma Park, Md. 20012. *Office: Science,* 1515 Massachusetts Ave. N.W., Washington, D.C. 20005.

CAREER: Nature, London, England, deputy editor and Washington correspondent, 1967-70; *Science,* Washington, D.C., staff writer, 1971—.

WRITINGS: The Ultimate Experiment, Walker & Co., 1977. Author of ''Letter From Washington,'' a monthly column in *Trends in Biomedical Sciences.* Contributor to *Civil Liberties Review.*

*   *   *

WADLEY, Susan S(now) 1943-

PERSONAL: Born November 18, 1943, in Baltimore, Md.; daughter of Chester Page (a certified public accountant) and Ellen (a secretary; maiden name, Foster) Wadley; married Bruce W. Derr (a professor), December 28, 1971; children: Shona Snow. *Education:* Carleton College, A.B. (with distinction), 1965; attended Delhi University, 1963-64; University of Chicago, M.A., 1967, Ph.D. (with distinction), 1973. *Residence:* Syracuse, N.Y. *Office:* Department of Anthropology, Syracuse University, Syracuse, N.Y. 13210.

CAREER: Syracuse University, Syracuse, N.Y., instructor, 1970-73, assistant professor, 1973-76, associate professor of anthropology, 1976—, director of foreign and comparative studies program, 1978—. Conducted field studies in India, 1963-64, 1967-69, 1974-75. *Member:* American Anthropological Association (fellow), Association for Asian Studies. *Awards, honors:* Grants from National Science Foundation, 1967-68, American Institute of Indian Studies, 1974-75, and National Endowment for the Humanities, 1977.

WRITINGS: Shakti: Power in the Conceptual Structure of Karimpur Religion, University of Chicago Press, 1975; (contributor) Agehananda Bharati, editor, *Rituals, Cults, and Shamanism: The Realm of the Extra Human,* Mouton, 1976; (contributor) Kenneth David, editor, *The New Wind: Changing Identities in South Asia,* Mouton, 1977; (with Doranne Jacobson) *Women in India: Two Perspectives,* Manohar Book Service, 1977; (contributor) *Women and National Development,* University of Chicago Press, 1977; (co-author of introduction) Charlotte V. Wiser, *Four Families of Karimpur,* Foreign and Comparative Studies Program, Syracuse University, 1978. Contributor to sociology journals.

WORK IN PROGRESS: Studying the goddess of smallpox in North India, legitimation of folk rituals in medieval India, and folklore in north India.

SIDELIGHTS: Wadley told *CA:* ''My first trip to India was as an undergraduate and I quickly came to love it. After contemplating various options for post BA work, I chose anthropology, though I knew nothing of it as a discipline when I began graduate training. My interests were spurred by linguistics, resulting in fieldwork that focused on oral traditions and other forms of verbal phenomena. I continue to work with various kinds of texts and symbolic systems. I have spent over two years in the village known as Karimpur and my 'family and friends' there contributed as much to my understanding of the texts and words with which I deal as does any of my more formal training.''

WAGGAMAN, William Henry   1884(?)-1978

1884(?)—February 1, 1978; American chemist, metallurgist, industrial analyst, and author. Waggaman was considered to be an expert in phosphate fertilizers. While working for the Department of Agriculture, he helped to design special furnaces for the production of superphosphate from raw rock. Waggaman contributed articles to the *Saturday Evening Post, Collier's* magazine, and authored a book about phosphate research. He died in Washington, D.C. Obituaries and other sources: *Washington Post,* February 4, 1978.

*   *   *

WAGNER, Ray Jay   1931-

PERSONAL: Born June 30, 1931, in New York, N.Y.; son of Cornelius (in communications) and Theresa (a seamstress; maiden name, Hanghofer) Wagner; married Carmela Sigari (a clothing designer), September 24, 1960; children: Nicole. *Education:* Attended City College of the City University of New York, 1951-55, and New School for Social Research, 1966. *Politics:* Social Democrat. *Religion:* Roman Catholic. *Home:* 391 Port Royal, Foster City, Calif. 94404. *Office:* 1633 Bayshore, Burlingame, Calif. 94010.

CAREER: Brooklyn Eagle, Brooklyn, N.Y., Associated Press wire editor, 1962; Graybar Electric Co., New York, N.Y., editor, 1962-71; Global Press, Cleveland, Ohio, editorial writer, 1972; free-lance writer, 1972—. Guest on television and radio programs, including "To Tell the Truth". and "John McKinney Show." *Member:* Authors Guild of Authors League of America.

WRITINGS: (With John S. Potter) *Treasure Hunters,* Fawcett, 1962; *Fifty U.S. Treasure Wrecks,* Wagner Marine Expeditions, 1968. Contributor to popular magazines, including *Argosy, Stag, All Outdoors, Western Treasures* and *Skin Diver.* Editor of *Outlook* and *Counter Points.*

WORK IN PROGRESS: Short stories and magazine articles.

SIDELIGHTS: Wagner writes: "I am an adventure story writer, with a basic interest in sea stories. I am a former East Coaster, and now reside on the West Coast. I have gone on numerous treasure hunting expeditions, headed Wagner Marine Expeditions, and have been successful in raising treasure in New York Harbor."

BIOGRAPHICAL/CRITICAL SOURCES: This Week, July 31, 1966; *New York Daily News,* February 12, 1967.

*   *   *

WALKER, Greta   1927-

PERSONAL: Born December 31, 1927, in Los Angeles, Calif.; daughter of Leon H. (a retail furniture dealer) and Birdye (Ecker) Markson; children: David. *Education:* University of California, Los Angeles, B.A., 1949. *Residence:* New York, N.Y. *Agent:* Virginia Barber, 44 Greenwich Ave., New York, N.Y. 10011.

CAREER: Actress in New York, N.Y., appearing in Broadway and Off-Broadway productions, on television, and in summer stock, 1956-68; writer, 1968—. *Member:* International P.E.N., American Society of Journalists and Authors.

WRITINGS: Women Today: Ten Profiles (young adult), Hawthorn, 1975; *Modeling Careers* (young adult), F. Watts, 1976; *Walt Disney* (juvenile), Putnam, 1977; *Living on Your Own* (young adult), F. Watts, 1977; (with Luciana Avedon) *Frankly Forty,* Rawson Associates, in press. Contributor to magazines.

SIDELIGHTS: Greta Walker writes: "Much of my writing is in the self-help area. My goal, always, is to avoid the simple solutions of most self-help writing and to present life situations and problems as realistically as possible. In addition, I give workshops for women where, again, I attempt to expose the old myths we live by, and to present fresh ideas that will help women take greater control of their lives."

*   *   *

WALKER, Peter N.   1936-
(Christopher Coram, Tom Ferris, Nicholas Rhea)

PERSONAL: Born May 18, 1936, in Glaisdale, North Yorkshire, England; son of Norman Walker (an insurance agent) and Eva Mary Rhea Walker (a teacher); married Rhoda Mary Smith (a shorthand typist), January 10, 1959; children: Janet, Andrew, Patricia, Sarah. *Education:* Educated in England. *Religion:* Roman Catholic. *Home:* Coram Cottage, Ampleforth, York YO6 4DX, England. *Agent:* Laurence Pollinger, 18, Maddox Street, London W1R OEU, England. *Office:* North Yorkshire Police, Police HQ, Neuby Wiske Hall, Northallerton, Yorkshire, England.

CAREER: Writer; police officer. Lecturer at law and police training schools. *Military service:* Royal Air Force, 1954-56; became corporal. *Member:* Crime Writers' Association (England), Society of Authors, Writers Guild, Nottingham Writers' Club (vice-president), Yorkshire Dialect Society (member of council). *Awards, honors:* Second prize from Queen's Police Gold Medal Essay Competition, 1967.

WRITINGS—All published by R. Hale, except as noted: *Carnaby and the Goalbreakers,* 1967; *Carnaby and the Hijackers,* 1967; *Carnaby and the Assassins,* 1968; (under pseudonym Christopher Coram) *A Call to Danger,* 1968; *Carnaby and the Conspirators,* 1969; (under Coram pseudonym) *A Call to Die,* 1969; (under pseudonym Tom Ferris) *Espionage for a Lady,* 1969.

Carnaby and the Saboteurs, 1970; (under Coram pseudonym) *Death in Ptarmigan Forest,* 1970; *Fatal Accident,* 1970; *Panda One on Duty,* 1971; *A History of Courts of Law,* David & Charles, 1971; *Carnaby and the Eliminators,* 1971; *Special Duty,* 1971; *Carnaby and the Demonstrators,* 1972; *Panda One Investigates,* 1972; *Identification Parade,* 1972; *Illustrated History of Punishment,* David & Charles, 1973; *Major Incident,* 1974; *The Dovingsby Death,* 1975; *Murder by the Lake,* 1975; *Carnaby and the Kidnappers,* 1976; *The MacIntyre Plot,* 1976; *Missing From Home,* 1977; *Witchcraft for Panda One,* 1978; *Target Criminal,* 1978; (under pseudonym Nicholas Rhea) *Constable on the Hill,* 1978.

Writer of weekly column, "Countryman's Diary," in *Darlington Times* and *Stockton Times.* Contributor of articles on folklore and rural matters (generally under pseudonym Nicholas Rhea) to periodicals, and contributor to police publications. Editor of *Police Box.*

WORK IN PROGRESS: More crime novels; nonfiction.

*   *   *

WALKER, T. Michael   1937-
(Michael White Elk)

PERSONAL: Born November 2, 1937, in Aurora, Ill.; son of Hugh F. (a "jack of all trades") and Irene E. (a factory worker; maiden name, McCurdy) Walker; married Kay Kerpus (marriage ended); married Debra Winkleman, October, 1972 (marriage ended, May, 1976); married Patricia Mallory, August, 1977; children: Pamela, Connie, Stefani,

Sol, Arianna Miel. *Education:* San Francisco State University, B.A., 1962, M.A., 1963. *Politics:* "Ingelligent, whenever possible." *Religion:* "Deep. Mystical. Direct!" *Home:* 516a Capitola Rd. Extension, Santa Cruz, Calif. 95062.

CAREER: San Francisco Police Deparment, San Francisco, Calif., police patrolman and fingerprint technician, 1960-62; San Francisco State College, San Francisco, instructor in writing, 1963-66; Cabrillo Community College, Santa Cruz, Calif., instructor in creative writing and literature, 1969—. *Member:* International Society of General Semantics, American Federation of Teachers.

WRITINGS: Voices: From the Bottom of the World—A Policeman's Journal, Grove, 1972.

Author of "A Way From the World" (ten-act comedy; first produced in San Francisco at San Francisco State College, May, 1962), published in *Transfer,* May, 1963.

Contributor to *Ecology, San Francisco* magazine, and *San Jose Mercury,* and to *Sundaze* under pseudonym Michael White Elk.

WORK IN PROGRESS: Festival of Life, "a novel of the 1970's dealing with the radical changes of consciousness in California and their affects on a group of musicians and educators, madmen and freaks. Homebirths, hang-gliding, flea markets, moon festivals, rock-concerts, barn-burning, and drugs form just a few of the elements of this poetic attempt to catch the tenor of our time"; poems and nonfiction articles.

SIDELIGHTS: Walker told *CA:* "Although I have been writing professionally for twenty years, I am one of thousands of writers who have found it easier to make a continuous ongoing income teaching others to write, rather than risking the market extremes and uncertainties of freelancing. I don't agree with G. B. Shaw's devastating quote: 'Those who can do, those who can't teach.' I both do *and* teach, but with five children to support I have had to parcel out my time in tablespoons. I have written five novels to the one I published, half a dozen full-length plays and television scripts to the one on file at San Francisco State College as my Master's thesis, twenty stories for every one sold. But I don't have an agent, nor do I keep recycling my stories after they have been returned from five or six editors. I'm always more interested in the new story or poem in process. The past is behind me, falls away, gathers dust in the corner of my study. Alas! My faith is that eventually my time will come. Meanwhile, I continue to write every day.

"I play piano, drums, Greek bouzookie, Turkish *saz,* Persian *Santoor,* and Arabic *dumbeg* (drums). I have been a professional Middle-Eastern musician for ten years, supplementing my income that way, and studied music in Turkey during my sabbatical leave in 1974-75 when I travelled to India and back overland with my family. I have also worked with jazz, blues, and rock bands in the Bay Area for twenty years and am greatly joyful that I *don't have to* struggle to make a living at this art which I enjoy. Music has been a bridge between my teaching and writing, a wordless interval between correcting student papers and writing my own stories. It is through the magic of music that I transmute the critic into the creator. It becomes my meditation, my means of centering, tuning my inner ear to the infinite faint voice of the muse who is always whispering to those who have ears to hear.

"For me, writing and music, poetry and song are two parts of the same stuff, the same steady flow from the inside out which pours through us all. Some translate it in mathematics and science, others burst into song or dance. What difference? I follow the path of my heart wherever it leads, working hard at my art as I go. The main thing for me is to have fun and to love what I do. Even teaching becomes part of the dance and all experiences get stirred into the psychic-soup from which art grows, emerging unexpected in its own sweet time. My task is to stay open to that flow and keep my chops up to channel it is well as I can."

*   *   *

WALKER, William G(eorge)   1928-

PERSONAL: Born September 2, 1928, in Narrabri, New South Wales, Australia; son of William Neville (a school principal) and Lily (Dugdale) Walker; married Sheila Margaret Truman (a teacher and librarian), August 24, 1951; children: John William, Allan David, Philip Gregory, Margaret Anne, Katherine Louise. *Education:* Balmain Teachers College, certificate, 1947; University of Sydney, B.A. (honors), 1952, M.A. (honors), 1955; University of Illinois, Ph.D., 1958. *Home:* 132 Jeffrey St., Armidale, New South Wales, Australia 2350. *Office:* Faculty of Education, University of New England, Armidale, New South Wales, Australia 2351.

CAREER: Elementary school teacher in Sydney, Australia, 1948-51; Wagga Teachers College, Wagga, Australia, lecturer in education, 1952-56; Armidale Teachers College, Armidale, Australia, lecturer in education, 1959-61; University of New England, Armidale, Australia, senior lecturer, 1962-65, associate professor, 1966-67, professor of education, 1968—, dean of faculty of education, 1970-76, chairman of professorial board, 1978—. Visiting professor at University of California, Berkeley, 1966, University of Illinois, 1966, 1971, University of Oregon, 1966, and University of Hawaii's East-West Center, 1971, 1977. Member of council of Armidale School, Armidale College of Advanced Education, Victorian Institute of Educational Administration, and Australian College of Education.

MEMBER: Commonwealth Council for Educational Administration (president, 1974—), Sydney Teachers Club, Phi Delta Kappa. *Awards, honors:* Fulbright grant, 1956-58; Carnegie Foundation travel grant, 1958-59; American Council of Learned Societies fellowship, 1971-72; fellow of Australian College of Education, 1972; fellow of Commonweal Council for Educational Administration, 1978.

WRITINGS: (With A. R. Crane) *Peter Board,* Australian Council for Educational Research, 1957; (with Crane and G. W. Basset) *Headmasters for Better Schools,* University of Queensland Press, 1963, 3rd edition, 1974; *The Principal at Work,* University of Queensland Press, 1965, 3rd edition, 1973; (with George Baron and Dan H. Cooper) *Educational Administration: International Perspectives,* Rand McNally, 1969.

Theory and Practice in Educational Administration, University of Queensland Press, 1970; *School, College, and University,* University of Queensland Press, 1972; (with Carolyn Steel and J. E. Mumford) *Education in Five English-Speaking Countries: A Glossary of Terms,* University of Queensland Press, 1973; (with Crane and A. R. Thomas) *Explorations in Educational Administration,* University of Queensland Press, 1973. General editor of a series on educational administration and organization for University of Queensland Press. Editor of *Journal of Educational Administration,* 1963—; special editor of *International Review of Education,* 1976.

WORK IN PROGRESS: Power and Politics in American

and Australian Education; The Governance of Australian Universities; Values, Policy, and Administration in Education.

SIDELIGHTS: Walker writes: "My main interests lie in the administration of education through research, publication, editorial work, leadership of associations, and travel. My special interests are the United States and countries of the Commonwealth nations.

"I am most interested in the area of theories underlying administrative behaviour and in the management of higher education institutions. Most of the academic attention given to theory in recent years has centered upon hard theory arising from the social sciences, but it is my view that soft theory arising from philosophy, ethics and religion, for example, which is most fundamental in shaping administrative behaviour. I would like to see more attention paid to the theoretical base underlying both the practice of administration and the preparation of educational administrators. I am interested in implementing this movement through publication of books, journal articles and tapes, the development of simulations and the running of workshops."

* * *

WALL, Bennett H(arrison) 1914-

PERSONAL: Born December 7, 1914, in Raleigh, N.C.; son of Bennett L. (a pharmacist) and Evie (Harrison) Wall; married Maie Johnson, February, 1933 (divorced, February, 1968); married Neva White (an administrative assistant), September 27, 1968; children: Maie John Wall Clark, Diana Wall Freckman, Ann Bennett. *Education:* Wake Forest University, B.A., 1933; University of North Carolina, M.A., 1941, Ph.D., 1946. *Politics:* Democrat. *Home:* 6320 South Claiborne Ave., New Orleans, La. 70125. *Office:* Department of History, Tulane University, New Orleans, La. 70118.

CAREER: North Carolina State University, Raleigh, instructor in history, 1942-43; University of North Carolina, Chapel Hill, instructor in history, 1943-44; University of Kentucky, Lexington, instructor, 1944-46, assistant professor, 1946-52, associate professor of history, 1952-65; Tulane University, New Orleans, La., associate professor, 1965-69, professor of history, 1969—, head of department, 1968-73.

MEMBER: Organization of American Historians, Agricultural History Society, Business History Society, Economic History Association, Explorations in Economic History, Southern Historical Association, Western History Association, Newcomen Society, Louisiana Historical Association (president, 1975), North Carolina Historical and Literary Association.

WRITINGS: (With George S. Gibb) *Teagle of Jersey Standard,* Tulane University Press, 1974. Contributor to history journals.

WORK IN PROGRESS: A History of Exxon, 1950-1975.

SIDELIGHTS: Wall told *CA:* "I have had an interest in economic history since graduate school. The opportunity to do the Exxon study provided an opportunity to analyze the development of a major business institution and the persons who made possible its growth and adaptation to world society. I thought I'd try to unravel and make understandable some of these decisions and events."

* * *

WALLACE, Michael David 1943-

PERSONAL: Born November 14, 1943, in Montreal, Quebec, Canada; son of Philip Russell (a scientist) and Jean Elizabeth (a nutritionist; maiden name, Young) Wallace; married Eileen Anne Retka, May 10, 1968 (separated, 1976); children: Ian Alexander, Heather Anne. *Education:* McGill University, B.A., 1964, M.A., 1965; University of Michigan, Ph.D., 1970. *Politics:* New Democratic Party of Canada. *Office:* Department of Political Science, University of British Columbia, Vancouver, British Columbia, Canada.

CAREER: University of British Columbia, Vancouver, assistant professor, 1968-73, associate professor of political science, 1973—. Member of governing council of Institute of International Relations. Visiting professor at University of Michigan, 1972-73. Western regional chairman of Canadian Coalition for Nuclear Responsibility, 1976-77. *Member:* International Studies Association, Canadian Peace Research and Education Association, Canadian Political Science Association, American Political Science Association.

WRITINGS: War and Rank Among Nations, Heath, 1973. Contributor to peace studies and other academic journals.

WORK IN PROGRESS: A study of the relationship between the growth of world armaments and the likelihood of regional and global war.

SIDELIGHTS: Wallace writes: "Basically, I'm a 'peacenik' who refuses to stop merely because Vietnam is over. I strongly believe that the enormous growth in the production and trade of conventional as well as nuclear weapons and materials could easily lead to an holocaust. Thus, both my academic work and my politics are directed toward preventing this. If we should be successful, I would have time for my hobbies."

AVOCATIONAL INTERESTS: Medieval art and architecture, wilderness hiking, sex ("in no particular order").

* * *

WALLACE-CRABBE, Chris(topher Keith) 1934-

PERSONAL: Born May 6, 1934, in Richmond, Victoria, Australia; son of Kenneth Eyre (a journalist) and Phyllis Vera May (a pianist; maiden name, Cock) Wallace-Crabbe. *Education:* University of Melbourne, B.A., 1956, M.A., 1963. *Politics:* Socialist. *Home:* 28 Silver St., Eltham, Victoria 3095, Australia. *Office:* Department of English, University of Melbourne, Parkville, Victoria 3052, Australia.

CAREER: Royal Mint, Melbourne, Australia, junior technical officer, 1951-52; Gas & Fuel Corp., Melbourne, Australia, clerical officer, 1954-55; Haileybury College, Brighton, Australia, teacher, 1957-58; University of Melbourne, Parkville, Australia, senior lecturer in English, 1968-76, reader in English, 1976—. Visiting fellow at University of Exeter, 1973. *Military service:* Royal Australian Air Force, 1952-53. *Awards, honors:* Harkness fellow at Yale University, 1965-67.

WRITINGS: The Music of Division (verse), Angus & Robertson, 1959; *In Light and Darkness* (verse), Angus & Robertson, 1963; (editor) *Six Voices,* Angus & Robertson, 1963, revised edition, 1974; *The Rebel General* (verse), Angus & Robertson, 1967; *Where the Wind Came* (verse), Angus & Robertson, 1971; (editor) *The Australian Nationalists,* Oxford University Press, 1971; *Selected Poems,* Angus & Robertson, 1973; *Melbourne or the Bush: Essays on Literature and Society,* Angus & Robertson, 1974; *Act in the Noon* (verse), Cotswold Press, 1975; *Splinters* (novel), *The Foundations of Joy* (verse), Angus & Robertson, 1976.

WORK IN PROGRESS: A novel, a book of essays on currents in modern poetry, and an anthology of verse for children.

SIDELIGHTS: Wallace-Crabbe told *CA:* "My writing has for some time been influenced by modern Italian poetry, and by the visual arts, so that Florence became a natural place to stay and work in 1978. While there, I was not only able to make progress with the main projects which I had in hand, but also to translate some of the poetry of Eugenio Montale. It seems to me that submitting oneself to the pressures of a foreign culture for some time can creatively inform and reinforce that rootedness in home-soil which is for me an essential part of one's writing. What is more, a good deal of modern Italian poetry takes the live landscape as its prime source of metaphors in ways that have immense relevance for an Australian poet. I also found the tensions of Italian political life at once disturbing and stimulating. Further details about my own cultural sources will be found in *Melbourne or the Bush.*"

*   *   *

WALLMANN, Jeffrey M(iner)   1941-
   (Phyllis Baxter, Nick Carter, Leon DaSilva, Amanda Hart Douglass, Helga Goering, Carlotta Graham, Milton Granby, Donald Heflin, Peter Jensen, Matthew Miner, Richard Mountbatten, John Reskind, Jackson Robard, Grant Roberts, Bill Saxon, Scott Sheldon, Blake Simmons, Grace Sinclair, Mark Townsend, R. Van Dorne, Carole Wilson)

PERSONAL: Born December 5, 1941, in Seattle, Wash.; son of George Rudolph (an architect) and Elizabeth (a teacher; maiden name, Biggs) Wallmann; married Helga Eikefet (a translator), December 1, 1974. *Education:* Portland State University, B.S., 1962. *Home:* Impasse Scarouget 4, 06190 Roquebrune-Cap-Martin, France. *Agent:* Richard Curtis, 156 East 52nd St., New York, N.Y. 10022.

CAREER: Dale Systems, New York, N.Y., private investigator, 1962-63; Dohrmann Co., San Francisco, Calif., assistant buyer, manager, and public money bidder, 1964-66; became manufacturer's representative in electronics industry in San Francisco area, 1966-69; Salgscentralen Skribent AS and London Films International, public relations director in Denmark, 1969; full-time novelist, 1969—. *Member:* Mystery Writers of America, Science Fiction Writers of America, Western Writers of America, Crime Writers Association.

WRITINGS: The Spiral Web, Signet, 1969; *Judas Cross,* Random House, 1974; *Clean Sweep,* Barrie & Jenkins, 1976, Avon, 1977; *Purgatory 1: Deathtrack* (science fiction), Manor, 1978.

All published by Tiberon: (Under pseudonym Mark Townsend) *White Captive,* 1969; (under pseudonym Richard Mountbatten) *Spell of the Beast,* 1969; (under pseudonym R. Van Dorne) *The Desolate Cove,* 1970; (under pseudonym Carole Wilson) *Karen and Mother,* 1971; (under pseudonym Grace Sinclair) *Mother's Share,* 1971; (under pseudonym Phyllis Baxter) *Homework at Teacher's,* 1972; (under pseudonym Bill Saxon) *The Terrorists,* 1972; (under pseudonym Saxon) *Junkyard Rape,* 1973; (under pseudonym Helga Goering) *Piano Teacher,* 1973; (under pseudonym Townsend) *Teenage Teaser,* 1973; (under pseudonym Blake Simmons) *Faculty Advisor,* 1973; (under pseudonym Milton Granby) *The Lady Dentist,* 1973; (under pseudonym Donald Heflin) *Teacher's Exposure,* 1973; (under pseudonym Carlotta Graham) *Prowl Car Cirl,* Filandia, 1973; (under pseudonym Nick Carter) *Hour of the Wolf,* Award, 1973.

(Under pseudonym Carter) *Ice Trap Terror,* Award, 1974; (under pseudonym Leon DaSilva) *Green Hell* (nonfiction), Tower-Belmont, 1976; (under pseudonym DaSilva) *Angolan Breakout* (nonfiction), Tower-Belmont, 1976; (under pseudonym Scott Sheldon) *The Ikon,* Futura, 1977; (under pseudonym Amanda Hart Douglass) *Jamaica,* Leisure Books, 1978.

Under pseudonym Peter Jensen; all published by Liverpool: *A Mother's Love,* 1969; *The Virgin Couple,* 1970; *Her Honor the Judge,* 1970; *Ravished,* 1971; *Father and Son,* 1971.

Under pseudonym John Reskind; all published by Tiberon: *The Unholy Master,* 1969; *Parksburg Saga* (six volumes), 1970; *Caesar Conquers,* 1972; *Caesar's Revenge,* 1972; *Caesar Comes Home,* 1972; *The Senator's Secretary,* 1974.

Under pseudonym Jackson Robard; all published by Tiberon: *Gang Initiation,* 1971; *Present for Teacher,* 1972; *Teacher's Lounge,* 1972.

Under pseudonym Grant Roberts; all published by Liverpool: *The Reluctant Couple,* 1969; *Wayward Wives,* 1970; *Rajah,* 1971.

Work has been represented in many anthologies. Contributor of fiction, sometimes under pseudonym Matthew Miner, to various magazines, including *Argosy, Ellery Queen's Mystery Magazine, Alfred Hitchcock's Mystery Magazine, Mike Shayne's Mystery Magazine, Zane Grey Western, Venture Science Fiction, Oui,* and *TV Guide.*

WORK IN PROGRESS: Sigma One, Abbatoir, The Blockbuster, and other novels.

SIDELIGHTS: In attempting to compile a list of his books, Wallmann encounters the difficulties of a prolific writer who uses a variety of pseudonyms and writes in several genres, often for original paperback publication, and frequently for smaller houses which are less than efficient in keeping records.

Wallmann writes: "Going strictly by income derived (the only way to go!), I've sold more than fifty novels and somewhere around fifty novelettes, short stories and articles since I started full-time writing in 1969. Also to my credit are eleven book translations, and I've been translated into six languages.

"I have also been anthologized. In addition to the book publishers listed above, I have been published by the Playboy Press, and by science fiction, mystery, and western magazines, some oddball men's magazines and a few short-lived magazines like *Coven 13.* Plus, as I mentioned, anthologies including *Best Detective Stories of the Year* and Random House's Alfred Hitchcock series.

"The hardcover stuff under my own name is easy to list, and for that matter so are most of the pure contract jobs done under pseudonyms or house names like "Nick Carter." But, over the years, some of my paperpulp has been published under names and titles chosen by the companies after they've accepted my manuscripts, and even I don't know how they end up. It's hard enough to get marginal publishers to send author's copies—living in France makes it downright impossible. So it's a bit of a shock to browse through a second-hand bookshop in New York City and come up with something I had written as *Enemy Legion* by Matthew Miner appearing in print as *White Captive* by Mark Townsend. This is especially true in what is referred to as 'ephemeral' writing. And I'm not sure anyone would *want* to know about all this stuff."

WAPLES, Douglas 1893-1978

1893—May 4, 1978; American social scientist, communications specialist, and author of books in his field. Waples began graduate level research and the study of communications at the University of Chicago. He was credited for developing the University of Chicago Graduate Library School. Waples died in Washington Island, Wis. Obituaries and other sources: *New York Times,* May 6, 1978.

*　　*　　*

WARD, Anne G. 1932-

PERSONAL: Born August 9, 1932, in Leeds, England; daughter of F. (an architect) and H. (Stanyon) Milnes; married John B. Ward, June 14, 1956 (divorced, 1963). *Education:* University of Leeds, B.A. (honors), 1955; University of London, Ph.D., 1963, visual arts diploma, 1976. *Residence:* London, England.

CAREER: Academic Publishing, London, England, editor, 1963-68; Workers Education Association, London, England, lecturer, 1974—. Translator. Tutor for extramural department of University of London, 1974—. Free-lance translator of art and archaeology books from French into English.

WRITINGS: The Quest for Theseus, Pall Mall, 1970; *Venice,* Ian Allan, 1972; *Yugoslavia,* Ian Allan, 1975; *Adventures in Archaeology,* Hamlyn Group, 1977.

WORK IN PROGRESS: Research on fourth-century Greek sculpture.

*　　*　　*

WARD, J(oseph) Neville 1915-

PERSONAL: Born April 17, 1915, in Oxenhope, Yorkshire, England; son of John (a clergyman) and Mary (Jones) Ward; married Joy Evans, January 24, 1942; children: Christopher John, Mark Howard. *Education:* Exeter College, Oxford, B.A., 1937, M.A., 1965; University of Manchester, B.D., 1940, M.A., 1942. *Home:* 66 Mount Rd., Canterbury, Kent, England.

CAREER: Ordained Methodist minister, 1942; minister of Methodist churches in Bockenham, Kent, England, 1950-56, Coulsdon, Surrey, England, 1956-62, Marylebone, London, England, 1962-67, and Bath, Somerset, England, 1967-74; Canterbury Methodist Circuit, Kent, minister, 1974—. Member of board of governors at Kingswood School. Chaplain at University of London, 1962-67, and University of Bath, 1967-74.

WRITINGS: The Use of Praying, Epworth, 1967; *Five for Sorrow, Ten for Joy,* Epworth, 1971; *Friday Afternoon,* Epworth, 1976; *The Following Plough,* Epworth, 1978. Contributor of articles and reviews to magazines, including *Church Times.*

WORK IN PROGRESS: "Preparation of material dealing with the exposition of the Lord's Prayer and the factor of willingness to change in the process of conversion."

SIDELIGHTS: Ward told *CA:* "I see the church's current debate with the world as primarily intellectual and concerning the credibility of the Christian interpretation of life. I consider its major need as the discovery of a new, fresh, interesting language for the communication of its faith." *Avocational interests:* Music, novels, poetry, calligraphy, gardening, the countryside.

*　　*　　*

WARDLE, (John) Irving 1929-

PERSONAL: Born July 20, 1929, in Bolton, England; son of John (a journalist) and Nellie (a pianist; maiden name, Partington) Wardle; married third wife, Elizabeth Rosalind Grist, January, 1976; children: Benjamin, Thomas, Alexander, Judith. *Education:* Wadham College, Oxford, B.A., 1949; Royal College of Music, A.R.C.M., 1955. *Home:* 51 Richmond Rd., New Barnet, Hertfordshire, England. *Agent:* Deborah Rogers Ltd., 5-11 Mortimer St., London W1N 7RH, England. *Office: Times,* Gray's Inn Rd., London WC1X 8E2, England.

CAREER: Times Literary Supplement, London, England, sub-editor, 1956-59; *Observer,* London, England, assistant theater critic, 1959-63; *Times,* London, England, theater critic, 1963—. *Military service:* British Army, 1950-52.

WRITINGS: The Theatres of George Devine (biography), J. Cape, 1978. Also author of "The Houseboy" (play), first produced in London, England, at Open Space Theatre, 1973. Editor of *Gambit,* 1971-74.

WORK IN PROGRESS: Research for a book on British stage directors since 1956.

SIDELIGHTS: Wardle told *CA:* "Playwriting is something to which I wish to return after spending more than five years on *The Theatres of George Devine.* The book is really a repayment of a debt to George Devine, whose English Stage Company began operating at the Royal Court Theatre at around the same time that I began writing newspaper reviews. I owe him and that company an immeasurable debt for the satisfaction I have had out of my own job as a reviewer. A lot of other people, in and out of the English theatre, would say the same thing. The book also amounts to an account of the development of the company tradition in the English theatre from the turn of the 1930's as Devine—variously allied with John Gielgud, Michel Saint-Denis, and Komisarjevsky—was at the centre of this movement for a good twenty-five years before he finally took control of a company of his own at the Royal Court in 1956. In writing the book, therefore, I was hoping to combine a biography with a rather neglected but, I think, extremely important stretch of British theatre history."

AVOCATIONAL INTERESTS: Music.

*　　*　　*

WARDMAN, Alan 1926-

PERSONAL: Born April 28, 1926, in London, England; son of Oswald (a teacher) and Kate Louise Wardman; married Judith Ann Booth (a copy editor), July 28, 1962. *Education:* Earned degree from St. John's College, Cambridge (first class honors), 1951. *Politics:* "Usually conservative." *Religion:* None. *Home:* 19 Marlborough Ave., Reading, Berkshire, England. *Office:* Department of Classics, University of Reading, Reading, Berkshire, England.

CAREER: Epping Hospital, Epping, England, nursing orderly, 1944-48; University of Reading, Reading, England, lecturer, 1951-74, reader in classics, 1974—. *Member:* Hellenic Society. *Awards, honors:* Gold Cup for duplicate bridge, 1970.

WRITINGS: (Contributor) Renford Bambrough, editor, *The Philosophy of Aristotle,* Mentor Books, 1963; *Plutarch's Lives,* University of California Press, 1974; *Rome's Debt to Greece,* Elek, 1976, St. Martin's, 1977. Contributor to philology and classical studies journals.

WORK IN PROGRESS: Religions and Political Order in the Roman World.

SIDELIGHTS: Wardman comments: "My principal interest is in the history of ideas in later classical antiquity to see how knowledge of Greek thought affected the nature of Plutarch's biographies, and how the Romans sought to compare themselves with the Greeks, past and present.'' *Avocational interests:* Duplicate bridge.

*   *   *

WARNER, Sylvia Townsend   1893-1978

December 6, 1893—May 1, 1978; British novelist, poet, short-story writer, biographer, translator, and editor who claimed to have started writing accidently when she was given small sheets of paper with a ''particularly tempting surface.'' Her intended career as a musicologist was abandoned to pursue her writing, a profession which produced seven novels, twelve collections of short stories, five volumes of poetry, and four biographies, including *Jane Austen: 1775-1817.* Warner was best known for her short stories, many of which appeared in *New Yorker.* Her last collection, *Kingdoms of Elfin,* was issued in 1976. She died in Maiden Newton, Dorsetshire, England. Obituaries and other sources: *The Reader's Encyclopedia,* 2nd edition, Crowell, 1965; *The New Century Handbook of English Literature,* revised edition, Appleton, 1967; *Twentieth Century Writing: A Reader's Guide to Contemporary Literature,* Transatlantic, 1969; *Longman Companion to Twentieth Century Literature,* Longman, 1970; *The Penguin Companion to English Literature,* McGraw, 1971; *The Reader's Adviser: A Layman's Guide to Literature,* Volume I: *The Best in American and British Fiction, Poetry, Essays, Literary Biography, Bibliography, and Reference,* 12th edition, Bowker, 1974; *Contemporary Novelists,* 2nd edition, St. Martin's, 1976; *The Writer's Directory, 1976-78,* St. Martin's, 1976; *Who's Who in Twentieth Century Literature,* Holt, 1976; *Who's Who in the World,* 3rd edition, Marquis, 1976; *Who's Who,* 130th edition, St. Martin's, 1978; *Publisher's Weekly,* May 29, 1978. (See index for *CA* sketch)

*   *   *

WARREN, David   1943-
(D. Featherstone)

PERSONAL: Born October 20, 1943, in Watertown, N.Y.; son of Ernest Neal (a professor) and Dorothy (Failing) Warren. *Education:* Cornell University, B.A., 1966, M.F.A., 1969. *Home:* 514 Edgewood Pl., Ithaca, N.Y. 14850. *Agent:* Maximilian Becker, 115 East 82nd St., New York, N.Y. 10028.

CAREER: Writer, 1969—. Has worked as painter, carpenter, and teacher.

WRITINGS: The World According to Two Feathers (novel), Ithaca House, 1973; *Natural Bone* (novel), Ithaca House, 1978. Author of ''Outdoors,'' a column in *Grapevine Press.* Contributor to newspapers, under pseudonym D. Featherstone.

*   *   *

WARREN, Joyce W(illiams)   1935-

PERSONAL: Born June 16, 1935, in Springfield, Mass.; daughter of Robert F. (a fireman) and Violet (a teacher; maiden name, Hill) Williams; married Frank A. Warren III (a professor), January 29, 1955; children: Victoria, Catherine, Charlotte. *Education:* Brown University, A.B., 1957, M.A., 1960; doctoral study at Columbia University, 1972—. *Home:* 141 Elm St., Roslyn Heights, N.Y. 11577. *Agent:* Dorothy Markinko, McIntosh & Otis, Inc., 475 Fifth Ave., New York, N.Y. 10017.

CAREER: Brown University, Providence, R.I., librarian, 1957-59; Hobart College (now Hobart & William Smith College), Geneva, N.Y., librarian, 1960-61; Queens College of the City University of New York, Flushing, N.Y., lecturer in English, 1963-71; *Roslyn News,* Roslyn, N.Y., author of environmental column, ''Helpful Hints,'' 1971-76; freelance writer, 1976—. Member of board of trustees of Bryant Library (Roslyn), 1971-76. *Member:* Roslyn Environmental Association (vice-president, 1970-76), Roslyn Heights Civic Association (chairman, 1969-76), Phi Beta Kappa.

WRITINGS: A Mouse to Be Free (juvenile), Sea Cliff Press, 1973. Contributor to literary journals.

WORK IN PROGRESS: Three children's books, a sequel to *A Mouse to Be Free, Dogs Don't Make You Cry,* and *The Old Man and the Toad;* research on the ''American Narcissus.''

SIDELIGHTS: Joyce Warren writes: ''I grew up in Springfield, Mass., with an older brother and a little black dog. My father was from Yorkshire, England, and my mother from Nova Scotia, Canada, and they both loved to tell stories about their childhoods. My father also told me many tales of fantasy, and when I was very little, my older brother used to tell me adventure stories at night from his bedroom across the hall.

''I also did a lot of reading, and I remember weekly walks to the library. My mother did not drive, and although the walk was a long one, we both looked forward to it.

''Today I live with my husband and three daughters and a little black dog in an old house on Long Island. My principal interests are still reading and writing. Last year our family spent the year in Cambridge, England, which was a marvelous experience.''

AVOCATIONAL INTERESTS: Playing the guitar, songwriting.

*   *   *

WASHBURN, Mark   1948-

PERSONAL: Born December 19, 1948, in Youngstown, Ohio; son of George Arthur (an engineer) and Kathryn (Youngs) Washburn. *Education:* Princeton University, A.B., 1970; Duke University, M.A.T., 1972. *Home:* 74 Thorndike St., Cambridge, Mass. 02141. *Agent:* John Hartnett, 14 Sutton Pl. S., New York, N.Y.

CAREER: Renaissance magazine, Boston, Mass., fiction editor, 1973-76; free-lance writer, 1976—. Partner of Intramedia Associates (design and editorial firm), 1974-75. Editor of *Bay State Historical League Bulletin,* 1974-76.

WRITINGS: Armageddon Game (novel), Putnam, 1977; *Mars at Last!* (nonfiction), Putnam, 1977.

WORK IN PROGRESS: A suspense novel set in the near future; a historical novel set in the nineteenth century.

SIDELIGHTS: Washburn writes: ''By chance, it happens that I am writing on my twenty-ninth birthday. At the same age, Fitzgerald had already written *The Great Gatsby,* and Keats had been dead for three years. On the other hand, Conrad was still sailing ships and speaking Polish. It averages out, I suppose.

''Despite occasional sidetrips into fields such as teaching and cab driving, my central ambition has always been to be a writer; I am still somewhat astonished to realize that I have made it. But it's a precarious business. If things go badly, my thirtieth birthday could find me driving a cab again.

''I mention this element of risk because I've found that, in my own case, at least, it is one of the major factors determining what, if anything, I write. I don't yet have the luxury (does anyone?) of writing only what I want to write. My choices have to be made with at least one eye fixed on the marketplace. Do I dare spend a year or two laboring over some 'serious' work that's important to me? Or should I take the safer route by churning out pop entertainment? Do I swing for the fences, or do I bunt?

"At the moment, I'm trying to do both—playing red *and* black and hoping the ball doesn't stop on double zero. That may not be the best strategy, but it's the best one that *I* can come up with.

"In a sense, however, this may be a false choice. The part of me that yearns to write another *The Great Gatsby* is appalled by the part of me that would be satisfied with another *Valley of the Dolls* and a lot of quick cash. And yet I have too much pride to grind out nothing but pulp. If I have to write a cheap thriller to pay the rent, then, by God, it's going to be a *good* cheap thriller. And if I do have a *The Great Gatsby* in me, it probably won't get written if I can't make a living in the meantime.

"My point is that staying afloat in this business involves making some tough choices, but I don't think they have to be exclusive choices. I hope not, anyway."

*   *   *

WASSERMAN, John L.   1938-

PERSONAL: Born August 13, 1938, in California; son of Louis (a professor) and Caroline (a professor; maiden name, Leland) Wasserman. *Education:* Attended Whitman College, 1957-59, College of Marin, 1960-61, and San Francisco State College (now University), 1961-63. *Residence:* San Francisco, Calif. *Office: San Francisco Chronicle*, San Francisco, Calif. 94119.

CAREER/WRITINGS: San Francisco Chronicle, San Francisco, Calif., theatre, film, and entertainment critic, and author of column, 1963—. Has worked as critic and show host on radio and television, and taught courses in journalism, media, and the arts at San Francisco State University. Contributor of articles to *Variety, Life, Time, Saturday Review, TV Guide, Coast,* and *Rolling Stone. Member:* American Federation of Television and Radio Artists, Newspaper Guild, Screen Extras Guild.

SIDELIGHTS: Wasserman told *CA:* "I consider film and pop music vital to society, but not the writing about same, which is mostly bad. I don't take many things seriously. I enjoy satire, both as audience and perpetrator. My primary interest other than writing is music. I have visited twenty-two countries. I like to write about the very good and the very bad. Mediocrity is boring. Ambrose Bierce's *Devil's Dictionary* is the greatest book ever written."

*   *   *

WATERS, Chocolate   1949-

PERSONAL: Birth-given name, Marianne; born January 21, 1949, in Aberdeen, Md.; daughter of Emory Lee and Pauline Reba (a businesswoman; maiden name, Buller) Waters. *Education:* Lock Haven State College, B.A., 1971. *Politics:* Independent. *Religion:* "Wiccan." *Office address:* P.O. Box 18641, Denver, Colo. 80218.

CAREER: Grand Prix Management, Denver, Colo., housepainter, 1971-74; Women Who Paint, Denver, Colo., owner, 1974—. *Member:* Feminist Writers Guild. *Awards, honors:* Journalistic achievement award from *Mount Joy Bulletin,*

1967, for editing *Tribe News* and *Tomahawk* magazine; two certificates of achievement from Colorado Press Women, 1975, for column and interviews for *Tribe News.*

WRITINGS: To the man reporter From the Denver Post (poems), Eggplant Press, 1975; *Take Me Like a Photograph* (poems and short stories), Eggplant Press, 1977. Columnist, "Scraps From Mama's Table," for *Big Mama Rag.* Contributor to numerous periodicals, including *Christopher Street, Lesbian Tide, Plexus, Her-self, Albatross,* and *Moving Out.*

WORK IN PROGRESS: A collection of stories.

SIDELIGHTS: Waters told *CA:* "I am a radical feminist which means that I identify on all levels with women and the issues of women in a patriarchal society. I am most concerned with the development of female value systems and their potential in a world which is primarily operated on the masculine ideals of violence and aggression. It is this perspective as it is applied on a personal level which I seek to explore in all of the writing I do . . . read my poetry and you'll get the point."

*   *   *

WATERS, Marianne
See WATERS, Chocolate

*   *   *

WATKINS, Jane   1929-

PERSONAL: Born August 23, 1929, in Boston, Mass.; daughter of John H. (an economist) and Jessie (Monroe) Williams; children: Cynthia, David Cushman, Catherine Cushman, Nicholas. *Education:* Radcliffe College, B.A., 1951. *Home:* 19 Cottage St., Cambridge, Mass. 02139. *Agent:* Lynn Nesbit, International Creative Management, 40 West 57th St., New York, N.Y. 10019. *Office:* Harvard University, 17 Quincy St., Cambridge, Mass. 02138.

CAREER: Worked in New York City in advertising and copywriting for New Directions and William Morrow and Co., 1951-60; copy-editor, rewriter, and free-lance writer, 1960-74; Harvard University, Cambridge, Mass., administrative assistant, 1972—. Fellow, MacDowell Colony, 1978.

WRITINGS: Family Affairs (novel), Harper, 1977.

WORK IN PROGRESS: Another novel.

SIDELIGHTS: Watkins told *CA:* "*Family Affairs* is a novel about a 40-year-old woman, Alma Thomas, her relationship to her elderly father, her husband and her two teenage children, and her emotional coming of age. In her struggle to stand apart from her past, she goes back in her mind to understand, forgive and be free of it. It is a novel of three generations and three sets of values.

"I began work on this novel in 1974 largely because short stories I had written, systematically turned down for publication, grew longer and more complex. It seemed clear that I needed more space to say what was on my mind."

*   *   *

WATSON, Barbara Bellow

PERSONAL: Born in Philadelphia, Pa.; daughter of Jacob Iram and Pauline (Throne) Bellow; married Goodwin Watson, June 23, 1946 (divorced, 1970); children: David G., Jonathan S., Robert N. *Education:* University of Wisconsin, Madison, A.B., 1942; Columbia University, M.A., 1944, Ph.D., 1963. *Home:* 7 East 86th St., New York, N.Y. 10028. *Office:* Department of English, City College of the City University of New York, New York, N.Y. 10031.

CAREER: Southern Connecticut State College, New Haven, instructor in English, 1960-61; Adelphi University, Garden City, N.Y., instructor in English, 1961-63; City College of the City University of New York, New York, N.Y., assistant professor, 1963-69, associate professor, 1970-73, professor of English, 1974—, director of Women's Studies, 1972—. Member: Amnesty International, Modern Language Association of America, College English Association, National Council of Teachers of English, American Association of University Professors, American Association of University Women, American Civil Liberties Union, Shaw Society of America, Feminist Press (member of advisory committee), Women's Caucus for the Modern Languages, National Organization for Women, American Jewish Congress, Andiron Club.

WRITINGS: A Shavian Guide to the Intelligent Woman, Norton, 1964, 2nd edition, 1972; (contributor) Warren S. Smith, editor, Critical Edition of Bernard Shaw's Plays, Norton, 1970; (contributor) Norman Friedman, editor, E. E. Cummings: A Collection of Critical Essays, Spectrum, 1971; (author of introduction) Bernard Shaw, An Unsocial Socialist, Norton, 1972; (contributor) Robert K. Morris, editor, Old Lines, New Forces: Essays on the Contemporary British Novel, 1960-1970, Associated University Presses, 1976; (editor and contributor) Women's Studies: The Social Realities, Harper's College Press, 1976; (contributor) Rodelle Weintraub, editor, Bernard Shaw: Fabian Feminist, Pennsylvania State University Press, 1977. Contributor of poems and articles to literary and popular magazines, including New Yorker, Harper's, Prairie Schooner, and Poetry. Member of editorial board of Shaw Review.

WORK IN PROGRESS: Essays on women, literature, and power; a critical study of Elizabeth Bowen.

SIDELIGHTS: Barbara Watson comments: "Two interests converge in my first book: feminism and the work of Bernard Shaw. My next major project will be a new look at both subjects in the light of the considerable changes that have taken place in my own views and in the culture at large since the book was written."

*　　*　　*

WATSON, Billy 1938-

PERSONAL: Born September 7, 1938, in Pitts, Ga.; son of James W. (a farmer and barber) and Jewel (Hutchinson) Watson; married Helen Turk, July 9, 1964; children: Kimberly Paige, Kevin Turk. Education: University of Georgia, A.B., 1960; graduate study at Georgia State University, 1966-67. Religion: Presbyterian. Home: 1138 Ousley Place, Macon, Ga. 31204. Office: Macon Telegraph, 120 Broadway, Macon, Ga. 31208.

CAREER/WRITINGS: Cordele Dispatch, Cordele, Ga., reporter and copy editor, 1960-61; Macon Telegraph, Macon, Ga., Atlanta bureau chief, 1963-67, copy editor, 1967-69, Sunday editor, 1969-72, managing editor, 1972-75, editor, 1975-78, executive editor, 1978—, weekly columnist, 1975—. Notable assignments include coverage of Georgia General Assembly, 1963-67, and Democratic National Conventions, 1964 and 1976. Journalism instructor at Mercer University, 1970—. Member of local boards of Human Relations Council, 1971-75, American Red Cross, 1976—, Middle Georgia Historical Society, 1975—, and American Cancer Society, 1978—. Military service: U.S. Army, 1961-63; became specialist 5. Member: Associated Press Managing Editors Association, Society of Professional Journalists. Awards, honors: Received feature writing award from Geor-

gia Associated Press, 1969; United Press International editorial writing award, 1977; Georgia Press Association editorial writing award and column writing award, 1977.

SIDELIGHTS: Watson writes: "I'm interested in journalism education, which I feel is essential to long-range improvement of newspapering in this country. As editor of the Macon Telegraph and as journalism instructor at Mercer University, I continually emphasize the need for greater commitment to accurate, fair, and unbiased presentation of news. At the same time, as supervisor of the Telegraph's editorial page, I feel a responsibility to speak out forcefully and clearly in columns and editorials on current controversial issues. If reader confidence in the press is not to continue deteriorating, these separate functions must be more clearly distinguished in the readers' minds. This is one of the prime challenges facing the press now."

*　　*　　*

WATSON, George (Henry) 1936-

PERSONAL: Born July 27, 1936, in Birmingham, Ala., son of George H. (an editor) and Grace (Carr) Watson. Education: Harvard University, A.B., 1959; Columbia University, M.A., 1960. Residence: Georgetown, Washington, D.C. Office: ABC News, 1124 Connecticut Ave., Washington, D.C. 20007.

CAREER/WRITINGS: Worked as a reporter for the Detroit News, Detroit, Mich., and the Washington Post, Washington, D.C., during the early 1960's; American Broadcasting Co. (ABC) News, New York, N.Y., radio news writer in Washington, D.C., London bureau chief, 1970-75, White House correspondent, 1975-76, vice president and Washington bureau chief, 1976—. Notable assignments include coverage of Soviet Premier Kosygin's meeting with President Johnson, the Tet offensive in Vietnam in 1968, the U.S. invasion of Cambodia in 1970, the conflict in Northern Ireland, President Nixon's summit trip to Moscow in 1972, the Middle East War of 1973, the Portuguese Revolution of 1974, and the Helsinki summit meeting of 1975. Member: Overseas Press Club, National Press Club, Sigma Delta Chi. Awards, honors: Overseas Press Club award for best foreign affairs documentary, 1971, for "Terror in Northern Ireland."

*　　*　　*

WATSON, Helen Orr 1892-1978

December 1, 1892—February 1, 1978; American educator and author best known for her stories about heroic feats of animals in the United States armed forces. Among Watson's writings are Top Kick: U.S. Army Horse, Chanco: U.S. Homing Pigeon, and Shavetail Sam: U.S. Army Mule. Watson served briefly as president of National League of American Pen Women. She died in Pittsburgh, Pa. Obituaries and other sources: Foremost Women in Communications, Bowker, 1970; Authors of Books for Young People, 2nd edition, Scarecrow, 1971; Washington Post, February 4, 1978. (See index for CA sketch)

*　　*　　*

WATSON, Patty Jo (Andersen) 1932-

PERSONAL: Born April 26, 1932, in Superior, Neb.; married Richard A. Watson (a professor of philosophy), 1955; children: Anna. Education: University of Chicago, M.A., 1956, Ph.D., 1959; also attended University of Michigan, 1957-58, and University of Minnesota, 1958-59. Office:

Department of Anthropology, Washington University, St. Louis, Mo. 63130.

CAREER: University of Chicago, Chicago, Ill., archaeological field assistant on Oriental Institute's Iraq-Jarmo project, 1954-55, archaeologist and ethnographer on Iranian prehistory project, 1959-60; University of California, Los Angeles, instructor in anthropology, 1961; University of Michigan, Ann Arbor, lecturer in anthropology, summers, 1962-63; University of Chicago, Oriental Institute, research associate, 1964, 1967; Washington University, St. Louis, Mo., assistant professor, 1969-70, associate professor, 1970-73, professor of anthropology, 1973—. Instructor at University of Southern California and Los Angeles State College of Applied Arts and Sciences (now California State University, Los Angeles), 1961.

MEMBER: Middle East Studies Association of North America, American Anthropological Association (fellow), Society for American Archaeology, Archaeological Institute of America, American Schools of Oriental Research. *Awards, honors:* National Science Foundation grants, for Iran, 1959-60, and Turkey, 1968, 1970, also 1969-72; Illinois State Museum Society grant, 1963; Cave Research Foundation fellow.

WRITINGS: Prehistory of Salts Cave, Kentucky, Illinois State Museum, 1969; (with husband, Richard A. Watson) *Man and Nature: An Anthropological Essay in Human Ecology,* Harcourt, 1969; (with Steven A. Leblanc and Charles L. Redman) *Explanation in Archaeology,* Columbia University Press, 1971; (contributor) editors, *Research and Theory in Current Archaeology,* Wiley, 1973; *Archaeology in the Mammoth Cave Area,* Academic Press, 1974. Contributor of more than twenty articles to professional journals. Editor of *Archaeology;* associate editor of *American Anthropologist,* 1973—.

*   *   *

WATSON, Richard A(llan)   1931-

PERSONAL: Born February 23, 1931, in New Market, Iowa; son of Roscoe Richard (a secondary school superintendent) and Daisy Belle (Penwell) Watson; married Patty Jo Andersen (a professor of anthropology), 1955; children: Anna. *Education:* University of Iowa, B.A., 1953, M.A., 1957, Ph.D., 1961; attended University of Michigan, 1957-59; University of Minnesota, M.S., 1959. *Agent:* Roberta Pryor, International Creative Management, 40 West 57th St., New York, N.Y. 10019. *Office:* Department of Philosophy, Washington University, St. Louis, Mo. 63130.

CAREER: University of Michigan, Ann Arbor, instructor in philosophy, 1961-64; Washington University, St. Louis, Mo., assistant professor, 1964-67, associate professor, 1967-74, professor of philosophy, 1974—. Fellow of Center for Advanced Study in the Behavioral Sciences, 1967-68; president of Cave Research Foundation, 1965-67. *Member:* American Philosophical Association (trustee), National Parks and Conservation Association. *Awards, honors:* American Council of Learned Societies fellowship, 1967-68.

WRITINGS: Downfall of Cartesianism, 1673-1712, Nijhoff, 1966; (with wife, Patty Jo Watson) *Man and Nature: An Anthropological Essay in Human Ecology,* Harcourt, 1969; (with Roger W. Brucer) *The Longest Cave,* Knopf, 1976. Editor of series "Classics of Speleology," for Johnson Reprint, and "Speleologia," for Zephyrus Press.

WATSON, Russell   1939-

PERSONAL: Born December 1, 1939, in New Brunswick, N.J.; son of Russell E., Jr., and Sarah (Stevens) Watson; married Susan Waterbury, June 3, 1967; children: Sarah, Jane. *Education:* Princeton University, A.B., 1962. *Religion:* Episcopalian. *Home:* 35 Station Rd., Irvington, N.Y. 10533. *Office: Newsweek,* 444 Madison Ave., New York, N.Y. 10533.

CAREER/WRITINGS: Wall Street Journal, New York City, reporter and copy editor, 1962-66; *Newsweek,* New York City, writer, 1966-71, senior editor, 1971-75, foreign editor, 1975—. Notable assignments include coverage of the war in Vietnam and the Watergate investigation. Vestryman, Church of St. Barnabas, Irvington, N.Y. *Military service:* U.S. Army Reserve, 1963-69; became staff sergeant. *Member:* Princeton Club. *Awards, honors:* Sigma Delta Chi Award, 1975, for story on President Ford's Halloween massacre.

*   *   *

WATT, Donald Cameron   1928-

PERSONAL: Born May 17, 1928, in Rugby, England; son of Robert Cameron (a schoolmaster) and Barbara (Bidwell) Watt; married Marianne Ruth Grau, December 28, 1951 (died, 1962); married Felicia Cobb Stanley, December 29, 1962; children: (first marriage) Ewen Cameron; (second marriage) Cathryn Cameron (stepdaughter). *Education:* Oriel College, Oxford, Oxford, B.A., 1951, M.A., 1954. *Agent:* A. D. Peters & Co., 12 Buckingham St., London W.C.2, England. *Office:* London School of Economics and Political Science, University of London, Houghton St., London WC2A 2AE, England.

CAREER: Assistant editor in British Foreign Office, 1951-54; University of London, London School of Economics and Political Science, London, England, assistant lecturer, 1954-56, lecturer, 1956-62, senior lecturer, 1962-66, reader, 1966-72, professor of international history, 1972—. *Survey* editor for Royal Institute of International Affairs, 1962-71; official historian for Cabinet Office. Member of advisory committee of British National Film Archive; historical adviser to British Broadcasting Corp. television series, "The Mighty Continent." Chairman of Greenwich Forum. *Military service:* British Army, Intelligence Corps, 1946-48.

MEMBER: International Institute of Strategic Studies, Royal Historical Society (fellow), Association of Contemporary Historians (chairman), Royal Institute of International Affairs, Royal United Services Institute, Friends of the Royal Academy, Anglo-German Group of Historians, Players Theatre Club, Playboy Club. *Awards, honors:* Rockefeller fellow at Institute for Advanced International Studies (Washington, D.C.), 1960-61.

WRITINGS: (Editor with J. B. Donne) *Oxford Poetry, 1950,* Blackwell's Oxford, 1950; *Britain and the Suez Canal,* Oxford University press, 1956; (editor) *Documents on the Suez Crisis,* Oxford University Press, 1957; *Britain Looks to Germany,* Oswald Wolf, 1965; *Personalities and Policies: Studies in the Formulation of British Foreign Policy in the Twentieth Century,* University of Notre Dame Press, 1965; (editor) *Documents on International Affairs, 1961-63,* three volumes, Oxford University Press, 1965-71; (editor) *Survey of International Affairs, 1961-63,* three volumes, Oxford University Press, 1966-77; (editor with Kenneth Bourne) *Studies in International History,* Longmans, Green, 1967; (with Frank Spencer and Neville Brown) *A History of the World in the Twentieth Century,* Hodder & Stoughton,

1967, Morrow, 1968; (editor and author of introduction) *Hitler's Mein Kampf,* Hutchinson, 1969; (editor) *Contemporary History in Europe,* Allen & Unwin, 1969; (editor with James Mayall) *Current British Foreign Policy, 1970-72,* three volumes, Temple Smith, 1975; *Too Serious a Business: European Armed Forces and the Coming of the Second World War,* University of California Press, 1976.

Author of material for "War and Society," for Open University television. Contributor to academic journals in England, Italy, France, Germany, and the United States. Editor of newsletter of European Association of American Studies, 1962-66; member of editorial board of *Political Quarterly,* 1969—, and *Marine Policy,* 1978—.

WORK IN PROGRESS: How War Came, covering the years 1938-39; *Studies in American Foreign Policy; International Relations, 1945-1975;* "Studying Britain and the sea in the contemporary world."

SIDELIGHTS: Watt's main interests are American foreign policy, Germany, the Middle East, and maritime affairs; he has visited Switzerland, Austria, Canada, France, Germany, the Netherlands, Belgium, Denmark, Italy, Japan and United States. *Avocational interests:* Cats, exploring London.

*   *   *

WAYNE, Anderson
See DRESSER, Davis

*   *   *

WEBB, Margot S. 1914-

PERSONAL: Born March 18, 1914, in New York, N.Y.; married William Webb (deceased); children: Mrs. Marjorie Roachford, Mrs. Danielle Hesselman. *Education:* Hunter College (now of the City University of New York), B.A., 1940; Columbia University, M.A., 1948; further study at Columbia University and University of Ghana. *Home:* 11 Bayview Ave., West Amityville, N.Y. 11701. *Office:* Dept. of History, Molloy College, 1000 Hempstead Ave., Rockville Centre, N.Y. 11570.

CAREER: Worked as a junior high school teacher in New York City, 1944-70; instructor in history and black studies at Fordham University, New York City; presently instructor in history at Molloy College, Rockville Centre, N.Y. Has also worked as a professional dancer. *Member:* Association for the Study of Negro Life and History, National Association for the Advancement of Colored People (NAACP), American Heritage Society, African American Teachers Association, Suffolk Afro-American Cooperative Library, Caritas Guild, Phi Delta Kappa. *Awards, honors:* Council on Interracial Books for Children Award for story idea and original research, 1970, for "Letters from Uncle David"; Mary McLeod Bethune Award, 1970.

WRITINGS: Pioneers in Blues and Jazz, Garrad, 1971. Also author of *The Afro-American and U.S. Industry,* 1969. Author of "Afro-American Dimension" column in *Long Island Weekly Voice.**

*   *   *

WEBB, Willard 1903-1978

1903—May 7, 1978; American librarian, brigadier general in the U.S. Army, and author. Webb was chief of the stack and readers division for the Library of Congress. In 1940 he commanded a tank battalion that took part in the invasion of Leyte and Okinawa. Webb wrote twelve plays, a television

script, and two books. He died in Washington, D.C. Obituaries and other sources: *Washington Post,* May 11, 1978.

*   *   *

WEBER, Sherwood J. 1919(?)-1978

1919(?)—June 6, 1978; American educator, editor, and author. Weber served as the chairman of the English and humanities department at Pratt Institute for eleven years. He edited several books on reading and writing and authored several books on literature. Weber wrote articles for the *Saturday Review* and the *New York Times Book Review.* He died in New York, N.Y. Obituaries and other sources: *Publishers Weekly,* June 19, 1978.

*   *   *

WEBER, William A(lfred) 1918-

PERSONAL: Born November 16, 1918, in New York, N.Y.; son of Henry Paul (a pharmacist) and Emilie (Rilke) Weber; married Selma Ruth Herrmann, August 5, 1940; children: Linna Weber Mueller-Wille, Eunice Weber Fulker, Erica Weber Rice. *Education:* Iowa State University, B.S., 1940; Washington State University, M.S., 1942, Ph.D., 1946. *Home:* 1905 Bluff, Boulder, Colo. 80302. *Office:* Museum, University of Colorado, Boulder, Colo. 80309.

CAREER: University of Colorado, Boulder, instructor, 1946-52, assistant professor, 1952-55, associate professor, 1955-62, professor of biology, 1962—, curator of Herbarium, 1962—.

WRITINGS: Rocky Mountain Flora: Handbook of Plants of the Colorado Front Range, University of Colorado Press, 1953, 5th edition, Colorado Associated Universities Press, 1976; (with R. C. Beidleman and C. F. Yocum) *Wildlife of the Southern Rocky Mountains,* Naturegraph, 1967; (contributor) *Grand Canyon,* Geographischer Verlag Bern, 1971; (with Barry Johnston) *Natural History Inventory of Colorado,* Volume I: *Vascular Plants, Lichens and Bryophytes,* University of Colorado Museum, 1976; *Theodore D. A. Cockerell: Letters from West Cliff, Colorado, 1887-1889,* Colorado Associated Universities Press, 1976. Contributor to scientific periodicals.

WORK IN PROGRESS: Bryophytes of the Galapagos Islands, with S. R. Gradstein; *Lichens of the Galapagos Islands.*

*   *   *

WEBERMAN, Ben(jamin) 1923-

PERSONAL: Born March 27, 1923, in New York, N.Y.; son of Sol and Sadie (Wolfe) Weberman; married Sylvia Berger, November 15, 1947; children: Nancy, Lynn. *Education:* City College of the City University of New York, B.S., 1943; New York University, M.B.A., 1955. *Home:* 1 Albert Court, Kings Point, N.Y. 11024. *Office: Forbes,* 60 Fifth Ave., New York, N.Y. 10011.

CAREER/WRITINGS: New York Journal of Commerce, New York City, financial editor, 1951-55; *New York Herald Tribune,* New York City, financial editor, 1955-63; *American Banker,* New York City, financial editor, 1963-76; *Forbes,* New York City, economics editor, 1976—. *Military service:* U.S. Army, 1943-46. *Member:* New York Financial Writers Association (vice-president, 1971), Municipal Forum, Silurians, Bankers Club, Lambs Club, Sigma Delta Chi.

WEBSTER, Jan 1924-

PERSONAL: Born August 10, 1924, in Blantyre, Scotland; daughter of William (a grocer) and Maggie (a nurse; maiden name, Henderson) McCallum; married Andrew Drew Webster (a newspaper editor), August 10, 1946; children: Lyn Margaret, Stephen William. *Education:* Attended Hamilton Academy, 1938-40. *Politics:* "Uncommitted." *Religion:* Presbyterian. *Home:* 12 Upper Shirley Rd., Croydon CR0 5EA, England.

CAREER: Border Mail, Kelso, Scotland, journalist, 1941; Kemsley Newspapers, Glasgow, Scotland, journalist in Glasgow, 1942-46, and London, 1946-48; free-lance journalist, 1948-60, and fiction writer, 1948—.

WRITINGS: Colliers Row (novel), Lippincott, 1977.

WORK IN PROGRESS: Saturday City and another volume, the last two volumes of a trilogy begun with *Colliers Row.*

SIDELIGHTS: Jan Webster writes: "Chiefly, my aim is to present the Scots, not as the pawky, kilt-wearing, haggis-eating figures of popular conception, but as the thrusting, exciting, ambitious 'repressed romantics' (this last according to Welshman Richard Burton!) they really are. No tiny nation has contributed so much to the world and it is time Scotland stepped out from England's shadow to enjoy a cultural Renaissance."

BIOGRAPHICAL/CRITICAL SOURCES: Weekend Scotsman, March 19, 1977; *Croydon Advertiser,* April 29, 1977.

*   *   *

WEDBERG, Anders 1913-1978

1913—February, 1978; Swedish philosopher, professor, and author. Wedberg taught for several years at American universities where he developed the logical and mathematical methods that soon were to be characteristic of much of his work. He wrote a book on Plato's philosophy of mathematics and published another book on the history of philosophy. Wedberg died in Sweden. Obituaries and other sources: *New York Times,* February 23, 1978.

*   *   *

WEDDERBURN, K(enneth) W(illiam) 1927-

PERSONAL: Born April 13, 1927, in London, England; son of Herbert John (a scalemaker) and Mabel (Hollands) Wedderburn; married Nina Salaman, 1951 (marriage ended, 1961); married Dorothy Cole, 1962 (marriage ended, 1969); married Frances Ann Knight, August 22, 1969; children: (first marriage) Sarah Louise Wedderburn Walsh, David Roland, Lucy Rachel; (third marriage) Jonathan Michael. *Education:* Queen's College, Cambridge, B.A., 1948, LL.B., 1949, M.A., 1951. *Politics:* Socialist. *Religion:* None. *Home:* 29 Woodside Ave., London N.6, England. *Office:* London School of Economics and Political Science, University of London, London W.C.2, England.

CAREER: Called to the Bar at Middle Temple, 1953; Cambridge University, Cambridge, England, fellow of Clare College, 1952-64, tutor, 1957-60, assistant lecturer, 1953-55, lecturer in law, 1955-64; University of London, London School of Economics and Political Science, London, England, Cassel Professor of Commercial Law, 1964—. Visiting professor at University of California, Los Angeles, 1967; and Harvard University, 1969-70. Member of staff panel for Civil Service and Post Office Arbitration Tribunals; independent chairman of Trades Union Congress' Independent Review Committee. *Military service:* Royal Air Force, 1949-51; became flight lieutenant. *Member:* Industrial Law Society (vice-president), Haldane Society (vice-president). *Awards, honors:* Named Lord Wedderburn of Charlton, 1977.

WRITINGS: (Editor) Sutton and Shannon, *Contracts,* Butterworths, 5th edition, 1956, 6th edition, 1963; *The Worker and the Law,* Penguin, 1965, 2nd edition, 1971; *Cases and Materials on Labour Law,* Cambridge University Press, 1967; (with P. L. Davies) *Employment Grievances and Disputes Procedures in Britain,* University of California Press, 1969; (editor with L.C.B. Gower, O. Weaver, and A. E. Park) *Gower's Modern Company Law,* Stevens, 1969; (editor) Clerk and Lindsell, *Torts,* Stevens, 15th edition, 1969; (editor with B. Aaron) *Industrial Conflict: A Comparative Survey,* Longman, 1972. Contributor to law journals. General editor of *Modern Law Review,* 1970—.

WORK IN PROGRESS: Comparative Labour Law; Discrimination in Employment.

SIDELIGHTS: Wedderburn told *CA:* "I foresee both company law and labour law developing in ways which will provide for workers a new influence and power in the decision making process in industry."

*   *   *

WEEKS, John (Stafford) 1928-

PERSONAL: Born January 29, 1928, in Frimley, Surrey, England; son of Robert (an army officer) and Gladys (a school matron; maiden name, Hughes) Weeks; married Barbara Jane Kirk (an artist), October 2, 1954; children: Sarah, Caroline, Isabel. *Education:* Royal Military Academy, Sandhurst, B.Sc., 1948; Royal Military College of Science, P.T.S.C., 1960. *Politics:* Conservative. *Religion:* Church of England. *Home and office:* Dairy Farm, Bentham, Purton, Swindon, Wiltshire SN5 9HZ, England. *Agent:* Sheila Watson, Bolt & Watson Ltd., 8 Old Queen St., London S.W.1, England.

CAREER: British Army, career officer, 1945-78; member of parachute teams, 1962-63, instructor in infantry weapons at Royal Military College of Science, 1966-68, currently instructor in management. Retiring as colonel. *Member:* British Institute of Management.

WRITINGS: Infantry Weapons of World War II, Ballantine, 1972; (with Ian V. Hogg) *Military Small Arms of the Twentieth Century,* Arms & Armour Press, 1973, 3rd edition, 1977; *Men Against Tanks,* David & Charles, 1975; *Airborne Equipment,* David & Charles, 1976; *World Pistols,* Arms & Armour Press, 1978. Contributor to *Jane's Weapon Systems, Jane's Infantry Weapons, Brassey's Infantry Weapons, Encyclopedia of Land Warfare,* and *Encyclopedia of Tanks and Armoured Vehicles.* Contributor of articles and reviews to gun magazines and military newspapers in England and the United States, including *Gun Review, Airgun World,* and *War Monthly.*

SIDELIGHTS: Weeks writes: "I am interested in my subject; more than that, I get completely immersed in it. This is motivation enough to me. I don't need the complicated feelings and attitudes that some writers seem to require. I have no particular message to give to the world, I take it as I find it and make the best of it. I suffer from a wide variety of expensive interests. I live in the country and take part in country sports. I am utterly opposed to those activists whose only intention is to force their viewpoints on everyone else and destroy our present institutions."

AVOCATIONAL INTERESTS: Photography, restoring and driving old cars, shooting, following beagles, gardening.

*   *   *

WEER, William
  See KAUFMAN, I(sadore)

*   *   *

WEHRWEIN, Austin C(arl)   1916-

PERSONAL: Born January 12, 1916, in Austin, Tex.; son of George S. (a university professor) and Anna (a teacher; maiden name, Ruby) Wehrwein; married Judith V. Oakes, 1950; children: Sven Austin, Paul, Peter, Joanna Judith. *Education:* University of Wisconsin-Madison, B.A., 1937; Columbia University, LL.B., 1940; attended London School of Economics and Political Science, London, 1948. *Home:* 6208 Wyman Ave., Edina, Minn. 55436. *Office: Minneapolis Star,* 425 Portland Ave., Minneapolis, Minn. 55488.

CAREER/WRITINGS: United Press International, New York City, reporter for Washington Bureau, 1941-43, 1946-48; information specialist for Economic Cooperation Administration in London, Copenhagen, Oslo, and Stockholm, 1948-51; *Milwaukee Journal,* Milwaukee, Wis., financial writer, 1951-53; Time, Inc., New York City, staff correspondent in Chicago, 1953-55; *Chicago Sun-Times,* Chicago, Ill., reporter, 1955-56, financial editor, 1956-57; *New York Times,* New York City, chief of Chicago bureau, 1957-66; *Star,* Minneapolis, Minn., editorial writer, 1966—. Contributor to *Washington Post, London Economist,* and *Collier's Year Book;* correspondent for *Christian Science Monitor,* and *Progressive Chronicle of Higher Education. Military service:* U.S. Army Air Forces, 1943-45; member of staff, *Stars and Stripes,* Shanghai, China, 1945-46. *Awards, honors:* Pulitzer Prize, 1953, for international reporting; Distinguished Journalism award, University of Wisconsin, 1963; American Bar Association Gavel award, 1961 and 1971.

SIDELIGHTS: Wehrwein told *CA:* "Nobody should go to work as a reporter today without a clean determination to write at least one book by age thirty. My generation perceived that need to become independent—'Free agents'—if you will—but did not, or could not, do much about it. The alternative is to decide at the outset to rise (fall?) via management; the only national starting point for that is a hard-sell school of business administration—but that's another story, one for a directory of 'The Bosses of Contemporary Journalists.'"

*   *   *

WEIGLE, Luther Allan   1880-1976

PERSONAL: Born September 11, 1880, in Littlestown, Pa.; son of Elias Daniel (a clergyman) and Hannah (Bream) Weigle; married Clara Boxrud, June 15, 1909 (died, 1964); children: Richard, Luther Allen, Jr., Margaret (Mrs. William F. Quillian, Jr.), Ruth (Mrs. Arthur C. Guyton). *Education:* Gettysburg College, B.A., 1900, M.A., 1903; further study at Lutheran Theological Seminary, Gettysburg, 1900-02; Yale University, Ph.D., 1905. *Home:* 142 Cold Spring St., New Haven, Conn. 06511.

CAREER: Ordained minister of Lutheran Church, 1903; pastor in Bridgeport, Conn., 1903-04; Carleton College, Northfield, Minn., professor of philosophy, 1905-16, dean, 1910-15; Yale University, New Haven, Conn., Horace Bushnell Professor of Christian Nurture, 1916-24, Sterling Professor of Religious Education, 1924-29, dean of Divinity School, 1928-49, dean emeritus, 1949-76. Holman Lecturer at Lutheran Theological Seminary (Gettysburg, Pa.), 1921; Sprunt Lecturer at Union Theological Seminary, 1925, 1938; Avera Lecturer at Duke University, 1926; Duncan Lecturer at Presbyterian Theological Seminary (Louisville, Ky.), 1926; Norton Lecturer at Southern Baptist Theological Seminary (Louisville, Ky.),1928; Pond Lecturer at Bangor Theological Seminary, 1937; visiting lecturer at Hebrew Union College (Cincinnati, Ohio), 1942. Chairman of World Council of Christian Education and Sunday School Association, 1928-58; Conference of Theological Seminaries of the United States and Canada, president, 1929, chairman of executive committee, 1930-49; Federal Council of Churches, chairman of administrative committee, 1929-32, president, 1940-42; chairman of committee which edited Revised Standard Version of the Bible, 1930-70; chairman of planning committee of National Council of Churches of Christ, U.S.A., 1941-50; chairman of committee revising Apocrypha, 1953-70. Trustee of Northfield Schools, and Hazen Foundation; Yale in China, president, 1946-56, trustee.

MEMBER: American Philosophical Association, American Psychological Association, Phi Beta Kappa. *Awards, honors:* D.D. from Carleton College, 1916, Gettysburg College, 1917, Queen's University, 1941, Princeton University, 1946, and Yale University, 1950; Litt.D. from Muhlenberg College, 1925; LL.D. from Dickinson College, 1933, Gettysburg College, 1934, and Wittenburg College, 1949; S.T.D. from Ohio University, 1934, and Berkeley Divinity School, 1950; J.U.D. from Boston University, 1939; L.H.D. from Otterbein College, 1952, and Lambuth College 1960; Gutenberg award from Chicago Bible Society, 1959; Wilbur Cross medal from Yale University, 1967; recipient of distinguished service citations from Congregational Churches, A.M.E. Zion Church, National Council of Churches, and Boy Scouts of America.

WRITINGS: The Pupil and the Teacher, Lutheran Publication Society, 1911, abridged edition, 1917, new edition with additional notes, 1929; *The Pupil,* Morehouse Publishing, 1918; *The Teacher,* Morehouse Publishing, 1918; (with Henry H. Tweedy) *Training the Devotional Life,* Pilgrim Press, 1919; *Talks to Sunday School Teachers,* Doran, 1920; *The Training of Children in the Christian Family,* Pilgrim Press, 1922; *American Idealism,* Yale University Press, 1928; (contributor) Miao Chu-seng, editor, *Education for Service in the Christian Church in China,* National Committee for Christian Religious Education in China, 1935; *We Are Able,* Harper & Bros., 1937; *Jesus and the Educational Method,* Abingdon, 1939.

The English New Testament from Tyndale to the Revised Standard Version, Abingdon, 1949; *The Living Word: Some Bible Words Explained,* Thomas Nelson, 1956; *Bible Words in Living Language,* Thomas Nelson, 1957; (with Ronald Bridges) *The Bible Work-Book,* Thomas Nelson, 1960; (editor) *The New Testament Octapla,* Thomas Nelson, 1962; (editor) *The Genesis Octapla,* Thomas Nelson, 1965; *The Glory Years: From the Life of Luther Allan Weigle,* Friendship, 1976.

OBITUARIES: New York Times, September 3, 1976; *Washington Post,* September 4, 1976.*

(Died September 2, 1976, in New Haven, Conn.)

*   *   *

WEINBERGER, Leon J.   1926-

PERSONAL: Born August 23, 1926, in Poland; son of Jacob

A. (a merchant) and Rachel (Wallach) Weinberger; married Estelle Greenberg (a teacher), February 7, 1954; children: Gary, David, Lisa. *Education:* Mesifta Torah Vodaath, rabbi, 1956; Clark University, B.A., 1957; Brandeis University, M.A., 1959, Ph.D., 1963; Jewish Theological Seminary, M.L.H., 1964. *Politics:* Republican. *Residence:* Tuscaloosa, Ala. *Office:* University of Alabama, P.O. Box 6173, University, Ala. 35486.

CAREER: Associate rabbi of Jewish congregation in Worcester, Mass., 1956-59, assistant rabbi in Newton Centre, Mass., 1959-61, rabbi in Milford, Conn., 1961-63; University of Alabama, University, director of B'nai B'rith Hillel Foundation, 1963-64, professor, 1964—. Chaplain for Tuscaloosa Veterans Administration Hospital, 1964—.

MEMBER: American Association of University Professors (local president, 1971-72), American Oriental Society, American Academy of Religion, Association for Jewish Studies, Danforth Foundation Association, B'nai B'rith (member of state executive commission, 1968-71). *Awards, honors:* National Endowment for the Humanities grant, 1971-73; grant from American Academy for Jewish Research, 1975; award from American Association of University Presses, 1974, for *Jewish Prince in Moslem Spain*.

WRITINGS: (Translator and author of introduction and notes) *Jewish Prince in Moslem Spain: Selected Poems of Samuel Ibn Nagrela*, University of Alabama Press, 1973; (editor) *Anthology of Hebrew Poetry in Greece, Anatolia, and the Balkans*, Hebrew Union College Press, 1975. Also author of *Romaniote Penitentials for the Days of Awe*. General editor of "Judaic Studies," University of Alabama Press. Contributor to professional journals.

WORK IN PROGRESS: *Comparative Religion in the Secondary School; Hebrew Poetry in Kastoria*.

SIDELIGHTS: Weinberger writes: "My motivation in writing is to communicate with readers and to share with them a body of knowledge and some insights that I find stimulating. My current interests are in Hebrew language and literature (most of my books and articles are written in Hebrew) and in comparative religion. I have competence in some half-dozen Semitic languages and some half-dozen Indo-European languages."

*   *   *

WEINMAN, Paul 1940-

PERSONAL: Born April 11, 1940, in Albany, N.Y.; son of Philip Pius (a house builder) and Jessie (Thomas) Weinman; children: Erika, Heidi, Stefan. *Education:* Harpur College, B.A., 1962. *Home:* 156 Fairlawn Ave., Albany, N.Y. 12203.

CAREER: New York State Museum, Albany, museum education supervisor, 1963—. *Member:* New York State Archaeological Association (fellow). *Awards, honors:* Achievement award from New York State Archaeological Association.

WRITINGS: My Sister's Underwear, Zeitgeist, 1969. Also author of two full-length and six one-act plays. Contributor of poems to several literary magazines.

*   *   *

WEISBURD, Martin Harold 1940(?)-1978

1940(?)—January 5, 1978; American research microbiologist, and author. Weisburd worked with the New York City Department of Health and lectured in New York City colleges. He wrote a book on laboratory work in microbiology.

Weisburd died in New York, N.Y. Obituaries and other sources: *New York Times,* January 8, 1978.

*   *   *

WEISS, Nancy J(oan) 1944-

PERSONAL: Born February 14, 1944, in Newark, N.J.; daughter of William (a businessman) and Ruth Sylvia (Puder) Weiss. *Education:* Smith College, B.A. (summa cum laude), 1965; Harvard University, M.A., 1966, Ph.D., 1970. *Politics:* Democrat. *Religion:* Jewish. *Residence:* Princeton, N.J. *Office:* Department of History, Princeton University, Princeton, N.J. 08540.

CAREER: Princeton University, Princeton, N.J., assistant professor, 1969-75, associate professor of history, 1975—. Member of board of trustees of Woodrow Wilson National Fellowship Foundation; member of board of directors of Mid-Atlantic Higher Education Resource Services for Women; member of historical advisory committee of Energy Research & Development Administration; member of board of counselors of Smith College's advisory committee on Afro-American Studies, 1969—; consultant to Ford Foundation.

MEMBER: American Historical Association, Organization of American Historians (chairman of committee on the status of women, 1972-75), Association for the Study of Afro-American Life and History, Coordinating Committee on Women in the Historical Profession, Southern Historical Association, Smith College Alumnae Association (member of board of directors, 1970-73), Phi Beta Kappa. *Awards, honors:* Woodrow Wilson fellowship, 1965; postdoctoral fellowships from Charles Warren Center at Harvard University and Radcliffe Institute, both 1976-77.

WRITINGS: Charles Francis Murphy, 1858-1924: Respectability and Responsibility in Tammany Politics, Smith College, 1968; (with J. M. McPherson, J. M. Banner, Jr., and others) *Blacks in America: Bibliographical Essays*, Doubleday, 1971; (contributor) *Twentieth Century America: Recent Interpretations*, Harcourt, 1972; *The National Urban League, 1910-1940*, Oxford University Press, 1974. Contributor to political science journals.

WORK IN PROGRESS: A book on blacks and the New Deal.

*   *   *

WELLER, Sheila 1945-

PERSONAL: Born September 16, 1945, in New York, N.Y.; daughter of Daniel (a neurosurgeon) and Helen (a journalist and editor; maiden name, Hover) Weller. *Education:* University of California, Berkeley, B.A., 1967. *Politics:* Democrat. *Religion:* Jewish. *Home and office:* 39 Jane St., New York, N.Y. 10014. *Agent:* Elaine Markson Literary Agency, Inc., 44 Greenwich Ave., New York, N.Y. 10011.

CAREER: Free-lance writer, 1970—. *Awards, honors:* Woodrow Wilson fellowship, 1963.

WRITINGS: Hansel and Gretel in Beverly Hills (novel), Morrow, 1978. Contributor to magazines and newspapers, including *Ms., New Times, Rolling Stone, Cosmopolitan,* and *Intellectual Digest*.

SIDELIGHTS: Sheila Weller writes: "My novel began as a short story I did while in Joseph Heller's fiction workshop at City College of the City University of New York. It's about the odd couple friendship of a salty, down-but-not-defeated fifty-four-year-old divorcee and her forty-year-old gay hairdresser and what I hope it's 'about' are the unique survival mechanisms, the ironic language, the idiosyncratic and possibly 'superior' vision of people who have been defined as social orphans—people outside of the conventional Noah's Ark couples world. As an unmarried woman, I have an affinity for these people. There's a lot of subculture dialogue in the book—gay, Jewish, black—survival talk that's always interested me. The style is rather sitcom-ish. What can I say? I'm a Hollywood kid.''

* * *

WELLMAN, Frederick L(ovejoy) 1897-

PERSONAL: Born June 6, 1897, in Kamundongo, Angola; son of Frederick C. (a physician, missionary, writer, and artist) and Lydia (a teacher; maiden name, Isely) Wellman; married Dora U'Ren, November 26, 1932; children: F. Creighton. *Education:* Wichita State University, B.A., 1920; University of Wisconsin, Madison, M.S., 1924, Ph.D., 1928. *Politics:* Democrat. *Religion:* Methodist. *Home:* 1504 Ridge Rd., Raleigh, N.C. 27607. *Office:* Department of Plant Pathology, North Carolina State University, Raleigh, N.C. 27607.

CAREER: United Fruit Co., pathologist in Honduras and Guatemala, 1929-30; U.S. Department of Agriculture, Washington, D.C., associate pathologist, 1931-36, senior pathologist and regional consultant, 1936-57; University of Puerto Rico, Rio Piedras, research advisor in plant pathology and head of department, 1958-63; North Carolina State University, Raleigh, visiting professor of plant pathology, 1963-67, professor emeritus, 1967—. Founder and director of United States-El Salvador Agricultural Experiment Station; head of World Coffee Mission to Europe, Africa, the Orient, and the Americas. Plant explorer in Turkey, 1936. Member of board of directors of Wala County Shelter, Workshop, and Rehabilitation Center; volunteer worker with the mentally retarded and emotionally disturbed.

MEMBER: American Phytopathological Society (fellow; founder and first president), American Association for the Advancement of Science (fellow).

WRITINGS: Clubroot of Crucifers, U.S. Government Printing Office, 1930; (with H. W. Westover) *Report on Plant Exploration in Turkey,* U.S. Department of Agriculture, 1937; *Control of Southern Celery Mosaic in Florida by Removing Weeds That Serve as Sources of Mosaic Infection,* U.S. Government Printing Office, 1937; (with Dorothy J. Blaisdell) *Differences in Growth Characters and Pathogenicity of Fusarium Wilt Isolations Tested on Three Tomato Varieties,* U.S. Government Printing Office, 1940; *Plant Diseases of El Salvador,* Cafe de Salvador, 1945; *Around the World on Coffee Rust,* U.S. Department of Agriculture, Office of Foreign Agricultural Relations, 1952; *Enfermedades, insectos y malezas del cafe: Y su control mediante el uso de productos quimicos* (title means "Insects and Diseases of Coffee"), Instituto Interamericano de Ciencias Agricolas, 1956; (editor) P. J. Cramer, *Coffee Research in Indonesia,* Inter-American Institute of Agricultural Sciences, 1957; *Coffee: Botany, Cultivation, and Utilization,* Interscience Publishers, 1961; *Plant Diseases: An Introduction for the Layman,* Natural History Press, 1971; *Tropical American Plant Disease: Neotropical Phytopathology Problems,* Scarecrow, 1972; *Dictionary of Tropical American Crops and Their Diseases,* Scarecrow, 1977.

Contributor of about three hundred articles to scientific journals.

WELLS, Henry W(illis) 1895-1978

1895—March 22, 1978; American educator, museum curator, and author. Wells wrote articles examining Sanskrit drama and the classical drama of China, India, and Japan. He wrote more than twenty-five books on literature, poetry, and drama and contributed to journals in India, Taiwan, and Japan. Wells died in New York, N.Y. Obituaries and other sources: *New York Times,* March 24, 1978.

* * *

WELLS, Jessica
   See BUCKLAND, Raymond

* * *

WELSH, Ken 1941-

PERSONAL: Born August 22, 1941, in Melbourne, Australia; son of John Alexander (a pastry cook) and Marian (Blockey) Welsh; married Ann Richardson, April 13, 1963; children: Benjamin, Marcos, Carina. *Education:* Attended school in Warrnambool and Ballarat, Australia. *Residence:* Torremolinos, Spain. *Agent:* Richard Gollner, 17 Ave. Mansions, Finchley Rd., London NW3 7AX, England.

CAREER: General Television Corp. (GTV-9), Melbourne, Australia, comedy writer, 1964-65; Willard-King Organization, Melbourne, television comedy writer and assistant producer, 1965-66; free-lance writer, 1966-70; *Lookout,* Torremolinos, Spain, assistant editor, 1970-72, features editor, 1972—. *Military service:* Royal Australian Air Force, 1958-64.

WRITINGS: Them That Helps Themselves, Horwitz, 1968; *Hitch-Hiker's Guide to Europe: How to See Europe by the Skin of Your Teeth,* Pan Books, 1971, 6th edition, 1979, Stein & Day, 1972; *Costa del Sol* (with own photographs; published simultaneously in ten languages), Berlitz, 1976; *Costa Brava* (with own photographs; published in ten languages), Berlitz, 1977; *Mallorca and Menorca* (with own photographs; in ten languages), Berlitz, 1978; *Concentration Soldier,* Sphere, 1978; *One for the Spike* (adventure), Masnum, in press.

Photographer: Ken Bernstein, *Ibiza,* Berlitz, 1976; Bernstein, *Costa Dorada,* Berlitz, 1977; David Henderson, *Costa Blanca,* Berlitz, in press.

WORK IN PROGRESS: Fear for the Hero, an adventure novel; "The Devil Never Sleeps," a filmscript; "Buccaneer!," a television series outline.

SIDELIGHTS: Welsh told *CA:* "*Hitch-Hiker's Guide* arose out of hitching and other travel experience in Europe. I've visited about forty countries and covered maybe 150,000 miles. Don't hitch much now—I find cars and aeroplanes more efficient, but research on recent editions has been painstaking, using my own experiences, those of scores of travellers, plus the youth departments of a dozen national tourist offices. The *Guide* is often referred to by reviewers as "the hitch-hiker's bible." It's also published in Italian, Finnish, and Japanese. Apart from hitching, I now concentrate on fiction (using my travel experiences) and travel photography.

AVOCATIONAL INTERESTS: Cinema.

* * *

WENNER, Kate 1947-

PERSONAL: Born November 17, 1947, in San Francisco, Calif.; daughter of Edward (in business) and Sim (a writer)

Wenner. *Education:* Radcliffe College, B.A. (cum laude), 1970; attended University of Grenoble, summer, 1964, and Center for Intercultural Documentation, Cuernavaca, Mexico, 1971. *Residence:* New York, N.Y. *Agent:* Elaine Markson Literary Agency, Inc., 44 Greenwich Ave., New York, N.Y. 10011.

CAREER: Ruvuma Development Association, Songea, Tanzania, community development worker in Litowa, 1966-67; Center for War/Peace Studies, Cambridge, Mass., researcher, 1968-69; Training for Community Action Projects, Cambridge, project director, 1970; Family Day Care Program, Cambridge, assistant educational director, 1971; University of Massachusetts, Amherst, creative writing teacher for "Project Self," 1973-74, editor for crime and delinquency program, 1973-75; *Berkshire Sampler, Berkshire Eagle,* Pittsfield, Mass., staff features writer, 1977; Bronx Teachers and Writers Collaborative, New York City, elementary school creative writing teacher, 1978—; Hunter College (of the City University of New York), New York City, creative writing teacher in adult learning program, 1978—. Creative writing teacher at Berkshire County Jail and House of Corrections, 1974; editorial and research consultant to Model Education Program Evaluation, Catholic University, 1977. *Awards, honors:* Michael Rockefeller Memorial Fellowship, 1971-72, for Peru; scholarship from Business and Professional Women's Foundation, 1975.

WRITINGS: Shambu Letu, Houghton, 1970. Staff features writer for *Berkshire Eagle,* summer, 1977. Contributor to periodicals, including *New York Times* and *Village Voice.*

WORK IN PROGRESS: A novel "about a young woman obsessed with the inevitability of nuclear war."

SIDELIGHTS: "My first book, *Shamba Letu,* describes a year I spent living in a communal village in East Africa," Wenner told *CA.* "I worked as a volunteer through a student program at Harvard. My work included everything from organizing a cooperative day care center to driving pregnant women thirty miles in a Landrover to the hospital. The book tells the story of the beginning of a grass roots African socialist movement which later became the basis for Tanzania's national 'ujamaa' policy. Tanzania now has a widespread program of ujamaa villages in which community members work and hold property communally. The book also tells my own story as a young American confronting new ideas and a new and alien culture, and tells the story of my sometimes rocky growth into a new maturity through working and living in an isolated African Bush village."

Shamba Letu was published in a German edition and was a condensed book selection in the international edition of *Reader's Digest.*

In addition to living a year in Peru under the Michael Rockefeller fellowship, Wenner traveled overland from Mexico City to Urshaia, Argentina, the most southernly town in the world.

* * *

WENTWORTH, Elise H(ughes) 1931-

PERSONAL: Born March 20, 1931, in Atlanta, Ga.; daughter of Edward Thomas (a lawyer) and Julia (Flint) Hughes; married Wayne E. Wentworth (a professor of chemistry), July 3, 1954; children: Katherine, Randall, Gregg, Richard. *Education:* Attended Agnes Scott College, 1948-49; Florida Southern College, A.B., 1952; Florida State University, M.A., 1954. *Religion:* Episcopal. *Home:* 1911 Knoboak Circle, Houston, Tex. 77080.

CAREER: Teacher of exceptional children in Auburndale, Fla., Private speech therapist and counselor, 1956—. Teacher of English and speech (and counselor) in Lakeland, Fla., 1952-53. *Member:* American Association of University Women.

WRITINGS: Listen to Your Heart, Houghton, 1974.

WORK IN PROGRESS: The Reconstruction Era in Texas; a historical novel, following a Scotch-Irish-Welsh family's immigration to the United States and development in this country.

SIDELIGHTS: Elise Wentworth comments: *"Listen to Your Heart* grew out of a strong desire to help parents of handicapped children in their struggle toward acceptance of their children and their consequently altered lives, hopes, and dreams.

"Traveling and history are my primary interests. Several trips to Europe and Britain have only whetted and sharpened my desire to explain today in the light of the past."

* * *

WERNE, Benjamin 1904-1978

April 15, 1904—July 2, 1978; Russian-born American educator, attorney, rabbi, and author. While serving as a labor relations lawyer, Werne was consul to the New York State Conference of Mayors and the Nassau Physicians Guild. He devoted himself to writing and lecturing in 1965, and wrote over twelve books on labor relations and labor law. Werne died in Long Island, N.Y. Obituaries and other sources: *Who's Who in World Jewry,* Pitman, 1972; *New York Times,* July 5, 1978.

* * *

THE WESTERN SPY
See DILLON, John M(yles)

* * *

WESTIN, Av(ram) 1929-

PERSONAL: Born July 29, 1929, in New York, N.Y.; son of Elliot and Harriet (Radin) Westin; married Sandra Glick, April 24, 1954 (divorced, 1969); married Kathleen Lingo, May 17, 1970; children: Marc. *Education:* New York University, B.A., 1949; Columbia University, M.A., 1958. *Office:* ABC News, 7 West 66th St., New York, N.Y. 10023.

CAREER: Columbia Broadcasting System (CBS), New York City, copyboy, 1949-50, radio newswriter, 1950-53, news editor for "CBS Morning News," 1953-55, director of "CBS Six O'Clock Report," 1955-56, director of "CBS Morning News," 1956-57, producer for special programs unit, 1958, producer of "CBS Reports," 1959-60, European producer, 1960-63, producer of "CBS Morning News," 1963-65, executive producer for elections and special events, 1965-67; Columbia University, New York City, executive director of Public Broadcasting Laboratory, 1967-69; American Broadcasting Corporation (ABC), New York City, executive producer of "ABC News," 1969—, vice-president of "ABC News," 1976—. Notable assignments include coverage of Dwight Eisenhower in South America; Richard Nixon in China and Soviet Union. Fellow in communications policy at Duke University, 1974—. President of Awestin Productions, 1976-77.

MEMBER: National Academy of Television Arts and Sciences (trustee, 1974-78). *Awards, honors:* George Foster

Peabody awards, 1958, for series on the Mid East, 1959, for "The Population Explosion," 1973, for "ABC News Clean-up," and 1974, for Sadat biography; Emmy awards, 1959, for "The Population Explosion," 1967, for "Crisis in the Cities," and 1972, for coverage of Richard Nixon; and many other awards and honors.

WRITINGS: National Citizenship Test, Bantam, 1965; (with Stephanie Shaffer) *Heroes and Heroin,* Bantam, 1971.

SIDELIGHTS: A major influence in television, Westin drew from his experience at Columbia Broadcasting System (including three years as the first writer and producer for Europe) to attempt "a fourth news network" with the Public Broadcasting Laboratory. "It was a dark period," said Westin, "I was the wrong man for the job." Westin took charge of "ABC News" in 1969 and immediately made changes, instituting the now-standard quote and graphic projection behind the commentator, fast paced reporting which allowed for more stories, more economically oriented features, and the "whip around" where variously located reporters commented on the same subject.

As director of documentaries for ABC, Westin created "Close Up," the forerunner of the investigative news show. "One of the secrets of "Close Up," Westin said, "is that we don't do the universe. We set our own areas for investigation to a very narrow area."

Self assured, Westin enjoys the creative opportunities television provides: "There's nothing concrete in television and that's where the innovation comes from. You'll never hear around here, 'It can't be done.'"

AVOCATIONAL INTERESTS: Painting toy soldiers, collecting front pages.

BIOGRAPHICAL/CRITICAL SOURCES: Broadcasting, November 4, 1974; *New York Times,* April 13, 1975.

*   *   *

WESTOFF, Leslie Aldridge   1928-

PERSONAL: Born February 5, 1928, in New York, N.Y.; married Clay S. Felker (a magazine editor; divorced); married John W. Aldridge (a literary critic; divorced); married Charles F. Westoff (a demographer), August 5, 1969; children: Geoffrey. *Education:* Attended New York University, University of Zurich, Duke University, and Columbia University; University of Arizona, B.A., 1951. *Home address:* Drakes Corner Rd., Princeton, N.J. 08540.

CAREER: Arizona Daily Star, Tucson, Ariz., feature writer, 1950-51; *Women's Wear Daily,* New York City, editor, 1952-54; *Mademoiselle,* New York City, assistant editor, 1954-56; WDBJ-TV, Roanoke, Va., moderator of "College on Camera," 1961-62; University of Michigan, Ann Arbor, editor, 1966-67; free-lance writer, 1968—. *Member:* Authors Guild of Authors League of America.

WRITINGS: (With husband, Charles F. Westoff) *From Now to Zero: Fertility, Contraception, and Abortion in America,* Little, Brown, 1971; *The Second Time Around: Remarriage in America,* Viking, 1977. Contributor to popular magazines, including *New York, McCall's, Holiday, New York Times Magazine,* and *Esquire,* and newspapers.

WORK IN PROGRESS: A book about women to be published by Simon & Schuster in 1980.

SIDELIGHTS: Leslie Aldridge writes: "I was majoring in science in college until I published a poem in the *Duke University Archive,* the literary magazine. This drew the attention of the college newspaper editor, who gave me assign-

ments and whom I later married. At this point I became very interested in writing. I developed a passionate curiosity for facts and experience, and in doing research for my magazine articles and books have learned much more than I ever did in college. Writing has been my real education, as well as an entertainment, and without it I'd be terribly bored. It is constantly new and challenging and satisfying, though of course one suffers as one does with any work one tries to do well. However, if one can write, one does not have the choice of whether to write or not. One is driven, and must write."

*   *   *

WHEATLEY, Agnes
See CANTOR, Eli

*   *   *

WHEELER, (Robert Eric) Mortimer   1890-1976

PERSONAL: Born September 10, 1890, in Glasgow, Scotland; son of Robert Mortimer (a university lecturer and newspaper editor) and Emily (Baynes) Wheeler; married Tessa Verney (an archaeologist), 1914 (died, 1936); married Mavis de Vere Cole, 1939 (divorced, 1942); married Margaret Norfolk, October 6, 1945; children: (first marriage) Michael Mortimer. *Education:* University of London, B.A., 1910, M.A., 1912, D.Litt., 1920. *Address:* British Academy, Burlington House, London W1V 0NS, England.

CAREER: National Museum of Wales, Cardiff, keeper of archaeology department, 1920-24, museum director, 1924-26; London Museum, London, England, keeper and secretary, 1926-44; director-general of archaeology for government of India, 1944-48; adviser on archaeological matters, Dominion of Pakistan, 1948-50. University of Wales, University College of South Wales and Monmouthshire, Cardiff, lecturer in archaeology, 1920-24; University of London, London, fellow of University College, 1922-76, honorary director of Institute of Archaeology, 1934-44, professor of the archaeology of the Roman provinces, 1944-55, honorary fellow, School of Oriental and African Studies, 1970, British Academy, London, fellow, and lecturer to Royal Academy, 1965-76. Rhys Lecturer, British Academy, 1929; Norman Lockyer Lecturer, British Association, 1937; Dalrymple Lecturer, University of Glasgow, 1937; Lewis Fry Lecturer, University of Bristol, 1937; Rhind Lecturer, University of Edinburgh, 1951; Norton Lecturer, Archaeological Institute of America, 1952; Hobhouse Lecturer, University of London, 1955; Queen's Lecturer in Berlin, 1968. Commissioner, Royal Commission on Historical Monuments, 1939-58; chairman, Ancient Monuments Board for England, 1964-66. Trustee, British Museum, 1963-73. Directed excavations at Colchester, 1917, 1920, Carnarvon, 1921-23, Brecon, 1924-25, Caerleoon, 1926-27, Lydney, 1928-29, St. Albans, 1930-33, Maiden Castle in Dorset, 1934-37, Brittany, 1938, Normandy, 1939, India, 1944-48, Pakistan, 1950, 1958, and Stanwich in York, 1951-52; led government missions from India to Iran and Afghanistan, 1945-46. *Military service:* British Army, 1917-19, served in France, Italy, and Germany, mentioned in dispatches, received military cross for valor, 1918, 1939-43, served in Africa and Italy; became brigadier general.

MEMBER: Society of Antiquaries (fellow; president, 1954-59; director, 1940-44, 1949-54), British Association (president of conference of delegates, 1933; president of section H, 1954), Museum Association (president, 1937-38), Royal Society (fellow), Royal Archaeological Institute (president, 1951-53), Cambrian Archaeological Association (president,

1931), Indian Museum Association (president, 1947-48), Pakistan Museum Association (president, 1949-50), German Archaeological Institute (corresponding member), Archaeological Institute of America (honorary member), South Eastern Union of Scientific Societies (president, 1931), New York Academy of Sciences (honorary life member). *Awards, honors:* Companion, Order of the Indian Empire, 1947; University of London Petrie Medal, 1950; knighted, 1952; Sitara-i-Pakistan, 1964; companion of honor, 1967; Lucy Wharton Drexel Medal from University of Pennsylvania. Honorary degrees include D.Litt. from University of Bristol, University of Delhi, Oxford University, University of Wales and University of Ireland, and D.Sc. from University of Bradford.

WRITINGS: Prehistoric and Roman Wales, Clarendon Press, 1925; *London and the Saxons,* London Museum, 1935; *Twenty-five Years of the London Museum,* Cambridge University Press, 1937; *Maiden Castle, Dorset,* Oxford University Press for Society of Antiquaries, 1943; *Five Thousand Years of Pakistan: An Archaeological Outline,* C. Johnson, 1950; *Rome Beyond the Imperial Frontiers,* Bell, 1954; *Archaeology From the Earth,* Clarendon Press, 1954, Penguin, 1961; *Still Digging: Interleaves From an Antiquary's Notebook* (autobiography), M. Joseph, 1955; (with Katherine M. Richardson) *Hill-Forts of Northern France,* Oxford University Press for Society of Antiquaries, 1957; *Early India and Pakistan: To Ashoka,* Praeger, 1959, revised edition, 1968.

Charsada, a Metropolis of the North-West Frontier, Oxford University Press for the Government of Pakistan and British Academy, 1962; *Roman Art and Architecture,* Praeger, 1964; (editor) *Splendors of the East: Temples, Tombs, Palaces and Fortresses of Asia,* Putnam, 1965; (author of introduction and commentary) Roger Wood, *Roman Africa in Color,* McGraw, 1966; *Alms for Oblivion: An Antiquary's Scrapbook,* Weidenfeld & Nicolson, 1966; *Flames Over Persepolis: Turning-Point in History,* Morrow, 1968; (editor) Sir Winston Leonard Spencer Churchill, *History of the English Speaking Peoples,* B.P.C. Publishing, 1969; *The British Academy, 1949-1968,* Oxford University Press, 1970; *The Iron Age and Its Hill-Forts,* Southampton University Archaeological Society, 1971.

Pamphlets: *Wales and Archaeology,* H. Milford, 1930; (with Tessa Verney Wheeler) *The Roman Amphitheatre at Caerleon,* Clowes, 1931; *The Roman Amphitheatre, Caerleon, Monmouthshire,* His Majesty's Stationery Office, 1943; *Aspects of the Ascent of a Civilization,* Oxford University Press, 1955; *Impact and Imprint: Greeks and Romans Beyond the Himalayas,* King's College, 1959; *Roman Archaeology in Wales: A Tribute to V. E. Nash-Williams,* British Broadcasting Corp., 1957; (with V. E. Nash-Williams) *Caerleon Roman Amphitheatre and Prysg Field Barrack Buildings,* Her Majesty's Stationery Office, 1970; *Maiden Castle: Dorset,* Her Majesty's Stationery Office, 1972.

Also author of *London and the Vikings,* 1927, *London in Roman Times,* 1930, and *Parliament and the Premiership,* 1931. Writer of reports and monographs on digs and excavations. Contributor to journals in his field.

SIDELIGHTS: In a review of *Alms for Oblivion,* a *Times Literary Supplement* critic credited Wheeler with the recent increase of interest in archaeology: "At a time when archaeology is popular as never before, and when it is increasing our knowledge of the past at an unprecedented rate, it is not easy to recall how recent this all is and how much of it is owed to Sir Mortimer himself, to the excavational techniques which he perfected between the wars on sites such as Verulaminum and Maiden Castle and to the standards of meticulous, imaginative presentation which he set in publishing them."

In this book of essays, "Sir Mortimer does well to remind us with his customary vigour that the purpose of excavation is neither the magpie accumulation of random information about the past nor the enrichment of museums. We dig up objects to learn about the people who made them and used them. People not things. To Sir Mortimer it is above all the humanity of archaeological studies that gives them value today," wrote the *Times Literary Supplement.*

BIOGRAPHICAL/CRITICAL SOURCES: Times Literary Supplement, September 21, 1967.*

(Died July 22, 1976, in Leatherhead, England)

* * *

WHEELOCK, John Hall 1886-1978

September 9, 1886—March 22, 1978; American editor and poet. Wheelock was known both for his poetry and for his association with publisher Charles Scribner's Sons where he became chief editor. Wheelock worked with Kennan Rawlings, James Truslow Adams, and Thomas Wolfe. A major contribution of Wheelock's to publishing was the introduction of the "Poets of Today" series in which previously unpublished poets were presented together as opposed to appearing separately in single, thin, volumes. As a poet, he was considered a traditionalist. He received an increase in critical attention after his retirement from Scribner's. Wheelock died in New York, N.Y. Obituaries and other sources: *The Oxford Companion to American Literature,* 4th edition, Oxford University Press, 1965; *The Reader's Encyclopedia,* 2nd edition, Crowell, 1965; *New York Times Book Review,* November 15, 1970; *The Author's and Writer's Who's Who,* 6th edition, Burke's Peerage, 1971; *South Atlantic Quarterly,* spring, 1973; *The Reader's Adviser: A Layman's Guide to Literature,* Volume I: *The Best in American and British Fiction, Poetry, Essays, Literary Biography, Bibliography, and Reference,* 12th edition, Bowker, 1974; *International Who's Who,* 39th edition, Europa, 1975; *Paris Review,* fall, 1976; *The Writers Directory, 1976-78,* St. Martin's, 1976; *Who's Who in America,* 40th edition, Marquis, 1977; *New York Times,* March 23, 1978; *Washington Post,* March 24, 1978; *Newsweek,* April 3, 1978; *Time,* April 3, 1978. (See index for *CA* sketch)

* * *

WHITE, Alicen

PERSONAL: Born in Scotland; daughter of John Hermann (a flour mill owner) and Mary (Thompson) White. *Education:* University of British Columbia, received B.A.; Smith College, received M.A. *Home:* 63 East River Rd., Rumson, N.J. 07760. *Agent:* Frieda Fishbein, 353 West 57th St., New York, N.Y. 10019.

CAREER: Teacher of English and drama in preparatory schools; American Red Cross, program director in Italy, 1943-46; University of Kentucky, Lafayette, instructor in English, 1947-48; U.S. Army, information and education administrator in Germany and England, 1948-53; Girl Scouts of the United States, program department executive, 1953-66; "Let Us Entertain You," partner and performer, 1966—. Writer. Has worked in Off-Broadway theatres, and as a member of the Paravent Players in Providence, R.I. *Member:* Mystery Writers of America, Authors League of

America. *Awards, honors:* Scroll from Mystery Writers of America for *Nor Spell Nor Charm.*

WRITINGS: A Bouquet of Poems for Choral Speaking, Triad, 1966; *Dirge for a Lady* (mystery-suspense novel), Lancer, 1968; *Nor Spell Nor Charm* (suspense novel), Lancer, 1971; *Evil that Walks Invisible* (suspense novel), Dell, 1973; *Walter in Love,* Lothrop, 1973; *The Traitor Within* (suspense novel), Dell, 1974; *The Watching Eye* (suspense novel), Dell, 1977. Also author (with Marthe Coe and Ann Roos) of *Brownies Own Song Book,* 1968.

SIDELIGHTS: White told *CA:* "In addition to writing, I am a partner in a turn-of-the-century music hall program as singer and diseuse." Before touring with "Let Us Entertain You," an entertainment done in song, mime, and verse, White studied acting in Vancouver, British Columbia, at the Everyman Theatre School in London, England, and with Gene Frankel in New York City.

White has traveled extensively in Europe, and has visited Morocco, Algeria, Tunisia, Mexico, Bermuda, the Bahamas, and Jamaica.

* * *

WHITE, Maury 1919-

PERSONAL: Born January 28, 1919, in Algona, Iowa; son of Joseph R. (an owner of a weekly newspaper) and Lillian V. (a postmistress) White; married Virginia June Rockhold (office manager of a firm of certified public accountants), June 6, 1950. *Education:* Drake University, B.A., 1942. *Politics:* Democrat. *Religion:* Roman Catholic. *Home:* 5709 Grand Ave., Des Moines, Iowa 50312. *Office: Des Moines Register & Tribune,* P.O. Box 957, Des Moines, Iowa 50304.

CAREER: Des Moines Tribune, Des Moines, Iowa, sports writer, 1946-59; *Des Moines Register,* Des Moines, sports writer, 1960-65, author of sports column "Maury White," 1965—. *Military service:* U.S. Navy, 1942-46; became lieutenant senior grade. *Member:* Football Writers Association of America (president, 1967), Golf Writers of America, Basketball Writers of America, Track Writers Association, American Association of Baseball Writers. *Awards, honors:* First prize from Basketball Writers of America, 1962, for game story; silver anniversary award from *Sports Illustrated,* 1966; first prize from Golf Writers of America, 1971, for sport column; named national sportswriter of the year by Catholic Youth Organization, 1972; special recognition from National Collegiate Athletic Association, 1972; Jake Wade Award from College Sports Information Directors, 1977.

WRITINGS: (With six others) *The College Game,* Bobbs-Merrill, 1974.

Work anthologized in *Best Sports Stories.* Contributor to sports publications.

SIDELIGHTS: White has covered every kind of sports event, from Olympic Games, to the World Series, the Sugar Bowl, the Ali-Norton fight in 1976, and college football. He writes: "As the long-time custodian of a sports column, I lean heavily on looking at people, humor, joy, and sadness, rather than getting too deeply involved in the technical aspects. I grew up in the back shops of weekly newspapers owned by my father. He died a few weeks after I finished high school. My mother and I ran the paper for two years during the Depression, then things got better and I was able to attend Drake University on a football scholarship. I started working for the *Register* part-time, and it became permanent."

WHITE, Norval (Crawford) 1926-

PERSONAL: Born June 12, 1926, in New York, N.Y.; son of William Crawford (a surgeon) and Caroline (a social worker; maiden name, Taylor) White; married Joyce Lee (a psychologist), May 24, 1958; children: William, Thomas, Gordon, Alistair. *Education:* Massachusetts Institute of Technology, B.S., 1949; attended Ecole des Beaux-Arts, 1954; Princeton University, M.F.A., 1955. *Politics:* Democrat. *Religion:* Congregationalist. *Home:* 145 State St., Brooklyn, N.Y. 11201. *Agent:* Virginia Barber, 44 Greenwich Ave., New York, N.Y. 10011.

CAREER: Norval White, New York City, principal, 1959-62; Rowan & White, New York City, partner, 1962-66; writer, 1967—; Gruzen & Partners, New York City, partner, 1967-70; City College of the City University of New York, New York City, professor and chairman of School of Architecture, 1970—. Registered architect in Michigan, New Jersey, New York, Pennsylvania, and Virginia; certified by National Council of Architectural Registration Boards; has designed public and private buildings, including apartment houses, hospitals, and police headquarters. Member of New York City Community Planning Board, 1961-65; founding president of Architectural Renewal Committee in Harlem, 1965-68; president of New York Fine Arts Federation, 1969—; trustee, Brooklyn Museum, 1973—; commissioner, New York City Art Commission, 1975—. *Military service:* U.S. Naval Reserve, active duty, 1944-46.

MEMBER: American Institute of Architects (fellow; member of local executive committee, 1965-66), Society of Architectural Historians, New York State Association of Architects, Municipal Art Society (vice-president, 1968—). *Awards, honors:* Margaret Biddle fellowship, American School of Fine Arts, Fontainebleau, 1954; medal from New Jersey chapter of American Institute of Architects, 1955, national award of merit, 1962, Harry B. Rutkins Memorial Award from New York chapter, 1965; certificate of merit from New York State Association of Architects, 1961.

WRITINGS: American Institute of Architects Guide to New York City, Macmillan, 1967, revised edition, 1968, 3rd edition, 1978; *The Architecture Book,* Knopf, 1976.

WORK IN PROGRESS: Places, "a personal appraisal of places I have experienced and relished throughout the world, such as Versailles, Uxmal, the Piazza San Marco, the Galle Place, Brooklyn Heights."

* * *

WHITE, Rhea A(melia) 1931-

PERSONAL: Given name is pronounced *Ray*-a; born May 6, 1931, in Utica, N.Y.; daughter of John Raymond (a banker) and Rhea (Parry) White. *Education:* Attended Utica College and Syracuse University, 1949-51; Pennsylvania State University, A.B., 1953; Pratt Institute, M.L.S., 1965. *Politics:* Democrat. *Religion:* "I do not subscribe to any specific creed or sect." *Residence:* Dix Hills, N.Y. *Agent:* John Boswell, International Literary Management, Inc., 767 Fifth Ave., Suite 601, New York, N.Y. 10022. *Office:* East Meadow Public Library, Front St. & Newbridge Ave., East Meadow, N.Y. 11554.

CAREER: Duke University, Durham, N.C., research fellow, 1954-58; American Society for Psychical Research, New York, N.Y., research and editorial associate, 1959-62; Menninger Foundation, Topeka, Kan., research fellow, 1962-65; American Society for Psychical Research, director of information, 1965—. Assistant reference librarian in East

Meadow, N.Y., 1965—. Librarian for psychiatry department at Maimonides Hospital, 1965-67. Managing editor of *Advances in Parapsychological Research: A Biennial Review.*

MEMBER: American Library Association, Special Libraries Association, American Association for the Advancement of Science, American Society for Psychical Research, Parapsychological Association (charter member; member of council, 1958, 1960-63), Association for Transpersonal Psychology, Society for Psychical Research (England), Analytical Psychology Club of New York, Beta Phi Mu. *Awards, honors:* Hans Peter Luhn Award from local chapter of American Documentation Institute, 1965.

WRITINGS: (With Laura A. Dale) *Parapsychology: Sources of Information,* Scarecrow, 1973; (contributor) E. D. Mitchell and other editors, *Psychic Exploration,* Putnam, 1974; (editor) *Surveys in Parapsychology,* Scarecrow, 1976; (contributor) Stanley Krippner, editor, *Advances in Parapsychological Research,* Volume I, Plenum, 1977; (with Michael Murphy) *Spiritual Underground in Sports,* Addison-Wesley, 1978; *Bibliography and Index of Parapsychological Periodicals in English, 1937-1977,* Scarecrow, in press.

Author of a column on parapsychological publications, in *Newsletter of the American Society for Psychical Research.* Contributor to *Handbook of Parapsychology.* Contributor of articles and reviews to psychology and parapsychology journals. Editor of *Journal of the American Society for Psychical Research,* 1959-62.

WORK IN PROGRESS: *Bibliography and Index of Articles Relevant to Parapsychology, Appearing in Non-Parapsychological Periodicals,* for Scarecrow.

SIDELIGHTS: Rhea White writes: "My first choice of a vocation was professional golfing, but I wasn't that good even as an amateur, so I had to scrap that idea. The first ten years of my professional life were in parapsychology, where I became involved in the experimenter effect as a possible door to the larger question of the role of the observer not only in parapsychology but in science, and indeed in life in general. Next I obtained a master's degree in librarianship so I could be financially independent and free to think my own thoughts re parapsychology, which I never could get anyone to pay me for—to be paid you had to think 'their' thoughts. Since library school I have been involved in a combination of the two fields through compiling reference works in parapsychology. I am also interested in transpersonal psychology, analytical (Jungian) psychology, mysticism, and creativity, especially in women. I am especially intrigued by the mental phenomena associated with participation in motor activity, mainly in sports, but in things like picking apples as well."

AVOCATIONAL INTERESTS: Gardening, cooking, beachcombing, hiking, rock music, reading.

*   *   *

WHITE, Suzanne   1938-

PERSONAL: Born November 21, 1938, in Buffalo, N.Y.; daughter of George W. (a butcher) and Elva (McMullen) Hoskins; married Thomas Alexander White (a cinematographer; divorced); children: April Daisy, Autumn Lee. *Education:* Buffalo State College of Education, B.S., 1959. *Politics:* None. *Religion:* None. *Home:* 22 Rue de la Tombe Issoire, Paris 75014, France. *Office:* 21 Locust Pl., Locust Valley, N.Y. 11560.

CAREER: Has worked as teacher, press attache, fashion journalist, model, translator, and seller of fireworks and shoes; writer, 1972—.

WRITINGS: *Suzanne White's Book of Chinese Chance,* M. Evans, 1976; *Ladyfingers* (novel), Playboy Press, 1977. Contributor to magazines and newspapers, including *Cosmopolitan* and *Newsday.*

WORK IN PROGRESS: A novel; a nonfiction book for women over thirty-five.

SIDELIGHTS: Suzanne White writes: "As a woman writer I feel that my objective is to reach out to my fellow women in order to share with them experiences which have taught or assisted me throughout my life. It is through these sharings that I hope to show my readers how easy it is to be independent and comfortable in one's skin, providing one assumes the proper attitudes about life. I deplore the surfeit of psychoanalytical reasonings afoot in our country today and believe that, barring total psychosis, we can all learn to get along better if we arm ourselves with courage, education, altruism, and self-confidence."

*   *   *

WHITE ELK, Michael
See WALKER, T. Michael

*   *   *

WHITEHEAD, Edward   1908-1978

May 20, 1908—April 16, 1978; British commander in the Royal Navy, businessman, celebrity, and author. Whitehead was destined to become the name synonymous with Schweppes tonic water when his picture appeared in a Schweppes advertisement in 1953. His beard and English bearing converted the American public to "Schweppervesence" and established Whitehead as a world renowned celebrity. Popularity didn't diminish Whitehead's stature as a responsible businessman. While he was president of the company's American subsidiary, the price of the tonic water dropped seventy-five percent. Whitehead was awarded the Order of the British Empire. In 1965 he became chairman of the British Exports Marketing Advisory Committee. He authored numerous articles, as well as a book entitled *How to Live the Good Life.* Whitehead died in Petersfield, England. Obituaries and other sources: *Current Biography,* Wilson, 1967; *Celebrity Register,* 3rd edition, Simon and Schuster, 1973; *Who's Who,* 126th edition, St. Martin's, 1974; *Washington Post,* April 4, 1978.

*   *.   *

WHITEHEAD, James   1936-

PERSONAL: Born March 15, 1936, in St. Louis, Mo.; married Gen Graeber; children: seven. *Education:* Vanderbilt University, B.A., 1959, M.A., 1960; University of Iowa, M.F.A., 1965. *Office:* Department of English, University of Arkansas, Fayetteville, Ark. 72701.

CAREER: Millsaps College, Jackson, Miss., member of the faculty, 1960-63; presently associate professor of English, University of Arkansas. *Awards, honors:* Bread Loaf Writers Conference Robert Frost Fellowship, 1967; Guggenheim grant, 1972.

WRITINGS: *Domains* (poetry), Louisiana State University Press, 1966; (contributor) John William Corrington and Miller Williams, editors, *Southern Writing in the Sixties,* Louisiana State University Press, 1967; (contributor) Paul Engle, editor, *Midland 2,* Random House, 1970; *Joiner* (novel), Knopf, 1971.

SIDELIGHTS: Daniel B. Marin, a former colleague of James Whitehead at University of Iowa, recalled: "Jim was about six feet four, well over 200 pounds. He had played football at Vanderbilt and still seemed very self-conscious of his size—probably because little guys can say whatever they want and you have to leave them alone. At Iowa he lived near a golf course in a corrugated steel shack with only two or three rooms—and he had a wife and some children. He's a very likable, articulate man, quietly aggressive, a fierce Southerner."

Joiner is a novel about football and sweethearts in college. R. V. Cassill, Whitehead's former teacher, wrote in *New York Times Book Review* that "what Whitehead has achieved is to sound the full range of the Deep South's exultation and lament. . . . His tirade makes an awesome, fearful and glorious impact on the mind and ear." H. L. Van Brunt, in an article for *Saturday Review,* felt that the "plot progresses like a broken-field runner with a trick knee. The pace is sometimes creaky. . . . The book is larded with quotations from obscure military historians. The author's intent may well have been to draw the analogy between war and football; in practice, however, his digressions on this subject merely . . . hold up the action."

BIOGRAPHICAL/CRITICAL SOURCES: New York Times Book Review, November 7, 1971; *Saturday Review,* December 25, 1971.*

*   *   *

WHITEHEAD, Raymond Leslie   1933-

PERSONAL: Born November 17, 1933, in Buffalo, N.Y.; son of Sherwood Earl (a worker) and Verna (Kresge) Whitehead; married Rhea Menzel (in education and administration), June 12, 1957; children: Cynthia, Beth, Sara. *Education:* Elmhurst College, B.A., 1955; Union Theological Seminary, New York, N.Y., M.Div., 1960, Ph.D., 1973. *Religion:* Protestant. *Home:* 50 Tyrrel Ave., Toronto, Ontario, Canada M6G 2G2. *Office:* China Programme, Canadian Council of Churches, 40 St. Clair Ave. E., Toronto, Ontario, Canada M4T 1M9.

CAREER: Ordained minister of United Church of Christ, 1961; Hong Kong Council of Churches, Kowloon, industrial social worker, 1961-65; Council of Churches, Kowloon, Hong Kong, Asia research consultant, 1967-76; Canadian Council of Churches, Toronto, Ontario, 1976—. Lecturer at Chinese University of Hong Kong, 1967-76. *Member:* Association of Asian Studies, American Society of Christian Ethics, Committee of Concerned Asian Scholars, Canadian Society for Asian Studies.

WRITINGS: (With Dorothy Kehl, Frank Kehl, and wife, Rhea Whitehead) *China!: Inside the People's Republic,* Bantam, 1972; *Love and Struggle in Mao's Thought,* Orbis, 1977; (editor with wife, Rhea Whitehead) *China: Search for Community,* Friendship, 1978. Contributor to Christian periodicals and newspapers.

WORK IN PROGRESS: Theological/Ethical Implications of Chinese Revolution for Christians.

SIDELIGHTS: Whitehead tells *CA* that he traveled to Hong Kong and India, 1955-56. In 1971 and 1977, he visited the People's Republic of China; during the first trip, he had an interview with Chou En-lai; Whitehead himself speaks Chinese. He has also traveled in Japan, Southeast Asia, South Asia, and Africa.

Whitehead commented on the current scene in China: "Significant changes have taken place in China since the deaths of Mao Tse-tung and Chou En-lai in 1976. A China visit in 1977 gave opportunity for first hand observation of some of these changes.

"First, there seems to be a greater sense of national unity. This reflects the resolution of the struggle, which was taking place largely behind the scenes, between the 'Gang of Four' (a faction which included Mao's wife, Chiang Ching) and the group of the new Chairman of the party, Hua Kuo-feng.

"Second, in part resulting from this unity, there has been an increase in morale among farmers and workers, more orderliness in production, and a greater productivity in general.

"In the midst of this, Christian leaders, including Catholic bishops not mentioned in the public media for over a decade, have a degree of prominence again. Several have been mentioned as attending national meetings. It should not be concluded from this that there will be a new flowering of Christian thought in China. Any basic change in the status of Christianity is still a long way in the future. Some contact between Chinese Christians, and Christians from other countries is now a distinct possibility, however."

*   *   *

WHITEHILL, Arthur M(urray, Jr.)   1919-

PERSONAL: Born November 26, 1919, in Bronxville, N.Y.; son of Arthur Murray (a stock broker) and Rebecca Elizabeth (a singer; maiden name, Dubbs) Whitehill; married Rose Douglas Moore, 1942 (divorced, 1974); married Lynn Harumi Matsuhaga, 1975; children: A. Murray, III, Barbara Douglass. *Education:* University of Virginia, B.S., 1942, M.A., 1944, Ph.D., 1945. *Home:* 250 Kawaihae St., Apt. 10-C, Honolulu, Hawaii 96825. *Office:* College of Business Administration, University of Hawaii, Honolulu, Hawaii 96822.

CAREER: University of Virginia, Charlottesville, research assistant, 1945-47; Harvard University, Cambridge, Mass., visiting fellow, 1947-48; University of North Carolina, Chapel Hill, assistant professor of business administration, 1949-55; R. J. Reynolds Professor of Human Relations in Industry, 1955-65; University of Hawaii, Honolulu, professor of international management, 1965—, professor-in-residence for overseas program in Tokyo, 1966, and Okinawa, 1972, senior scholar at East-West Center, 1963-64, senior specialist, 1965-66. Fulbright lecturer at Keio University, 1957-58; visiting lecturer at University of Maryland's European Division in England and Germany, 1969-70; member of affiliate faculty of Japan-America Institute of Management Sciences, 1972. Has conducted research in Europe, Japan and Korea. Consultant to industrial firms and government agencies in the United States and Japan.

MEMBER: Association for Education in International Business, Academy of Management. *Awards, honors:* American Philosophical Society fellow in Japan, 1959-62.

WRITINGS: Personnel Relations: The Human Aspects of Administration, McGraw, 1955; *Cases on Human Relations in Management,* McGraw, 1958; *Cultural Values in Worker-Management Relations* (monograph), School of Business Administration, University of North Carolina, 1962; (with Richard P. Calhoon and E. William Noland) *The Other Worker: A Cross-Cultural Study of Industrial Relations in the United States and Japan,* East-West Center Press, 1968; (with Shinichi Takezawa) *Developing Managerial Talent in the Pacific-Asia Area* (monograph), Advisory Council on International Relations, University of Hawaii, 1974; (with P. E. Jacob) *The Automobile Worker: A Multi-National*

Perspective (monograph), Multinational Study of Automation and Industrial Workers, 1975. Contributor of articles and reviews to personnel, management, and social studies journals, and to *Rotarian.*

WORK IN PROGRESS: Workways: Japan and the United States, 1960-1976, with Shinichi Takezawa, publication expected in 1979; *Personnel Administration: An International Perspective*, publication expected in 1980.

SIDELIGHTS: Whitehill told *CA:* "As co-principal researcher for the U.S. team for the fifteen nation study of 'Automation and Industrial Workers,' I have since 1972 participated in a number of international meetings in Germany, Austria, Poland, and the U.S.S.R. The first volume of national reports from the project will be published in 1978."

* * *

WHITEHILL, Walter Muir 1905-1978

September 28, 1905—March 5, 1978; American museum director, librarian, and author. Whitehill served as assistant director of Peabody Museum of Salem, Mass., and as director and librarian of Boston Athenaeum. A member of Massachusetts Historical Commission, he wrote several books on Boston, including *The Boston Public Library* and *Boston: A Topographical History.* Whitehill also published books on American maritime history, and was founding editor of *American Neptune: A Quarterly Journal of Maritime History.* He died in Boston, Mass. Obituaries and other sources: *Current Biography*, Wilson, 1960, May, 1978; *Directory of American Scholars*, Volume I, *History*, 6th edition, Bowker, 1974; *Who's Who in American Art*, 12th edition, Bowker, 1976; *Time*, March 20, 1978; *Who's Who in America*, 40th edition, Marquis, 1978. (See index for *CA* sketch)

* * *

WHITINGTON, R(ichard) S. 1912-

PERSONAL: Born June 30, 1912, Adelaide, Australia; son of Guy and Violet (Haynes) Whitington; children: Richard Mark, James Jerome. *Education:* University of Adelaide, LL.B. *Religion:* Church of England. *Home and office address:* Polgeto di Umbertide 06019, Italy.

CAREER: Former solicitor in Adelaide, Australia; sports writer and editor, in cities, including Adelaide, Sydney, Australia and Johannesburg, South Africa, 1938-63; freelance writer, 1963—. *Military service:* Australian Army, Second Australian Imperial Force, 1939-46; became captain. *Member:* Society of Australian Authors.

WRITINGS: (With Keith Ross Miller) *Cricket Caravan*, Latimer House, 1950; *Perchance to Bowl*, N. Kaye, 1961; *John Reid's Kiwis: New Zealand Cricketers in South Africa, 1961-62*, Whitcombe & Tombs, 1962; *Bradman, Benaud and Goddard's Cinderellas*, H. Timmins, 1964; *The Vic Richardson Story*, Rigby, 1967; *Simpson's Safari: South African Test Series, 1966-67*, H. Timmins, 1967; *The Quiet Australian: The Lindsay Hassett Story*, Heinemann, 1969; *Fours Galore: The West Indians and Their Tour of Australia, 1968-69*, Cassell Australia, 1969; *Time of the Tiger: The Bill O'Reilly Story*, Routledge & Kegan Paul, 1970; *Sir Frank: The Frank Packer Story*, Cassell Australia, 1971; *Captains Outrageous: Cricket in the Seventies*, Routledge & Kegan Paul, 1972; *An Illustrated History of Australian Cricket*, Lansdowne, 1972; (with George Hele) *Bodyline Umpire*, Rigby, 1974; *The Courage Book of Australian Test Cricket, 1877-1974*, Wren, 1974; *Great Moments in Austral-*

ian Sport, Macmillan, 1974; *An Illustrated History of Australian Tennis*, Macmillan (Australia), 1975, St. Martin's, 1976; *The Champions*, Macmillan (Australia), 1976.

WORK IN PROGRESS: Two biographies.

* * *

WHITLEY, Oliver R. 1918-

PERSONAL: Born October 21, 1918, in Lebanon, Mo.; son of Oliver M. and Cora E. Whitley; married Daphne M. Palmer (an executive secretary), March 29, 1975. *Education:* Drake University, B.A., 1940, M.A., 1941; Yale University, B.D., 1944, Ph.D., 1952. *Politics:* Democrat. *Home:* 2464 East Fremont Ct., Littleton, Colo. 80122. *Office:* Department of Sociology of Religion, Iliff School of Theology, 2201 South University, Denver, Colo. 80210.

CAREER: Ordained minister, 1940; Phillips University, Enid, Okla., associate professor of sociology, 1953-56; Iliff School of Theology, Denver, Colo., associate professor, 1956-59, professor of sociology of religion, 1959—. *Military service:* U.S. Navy, Chaplains' Corps, 1944-47; became lieutenant. *Member:* American Sociological Association, Society for the Scientific Study of Religion, Religious Research Association. *Awards, honors:* Manuscript award from Bethany Press, 1958, for *Trumpet Call of Reformation.*

WRITINGS: Trumpet Call of Reformation, Bethany Press, 1959; *Religious Behavior: Where Sociology and Religion Meet*, Prentice-Hall, 1964; *The Church: Mirror or Window?*, Bethany Press, 1969. Contributor to sociology and religion journals.

WORK IN PROGRESS: Research on sociological models and theological reflection.

* * *

WHITWORTH, John McKelvie 1942-

PERSONAL: Born June 8, 1942, in Douglas, Isle of Man; son of Alan John (a journalist) and Helen (Farquhar) Whitworth; married Barbara Koschorreck (a teacher), 1975; children: John Henry. *Education:* University of Leicester, B.A. (honors), 1967; Oxford University, D.Phil., 1971. *Religion:* None. *Home:* 7345 Ridge Dr., Burnaby, British Columbia, Canada V5A 1B4. *Office:* Department of Sociology and Anthropology, Simon Fraser University, Burnaby, British Columbia, Canada.

CAREER: Simon Fraser University, Burnaby, British Columbia, instructor, 1967-71, assistant professor, 1971-76, associate professor of sociology, 1976—. *Member:* Conference Internationale de Sociologie de Religion, Canadian Association of African Studies.

WRITINGS: God's Blueprints: A Sociological Study of Three Utopian Sects, Routledge & Kegan Paul, 1975. Contributor to sociology journals.

WORK IN PROGRESS: Research on social theory and history of ideas, with publication expected to result.

* * *

WHORTON, James C(lifton) 1942-

PERSONAL: Born October 31, 1942, in North Carolina; son of Charles C. (a machinist) and Margaret (Brite) Whorton; married Sue Moseley (a teacher), December 21, 1963; children: Adrian. *Education:* Duke University, B.S., 1964; University of Wisconsin, Madison, Ph.D., 1969. *Politics:* "Apolitical." *Religion:* None. *Office:* Department of Biomedical History, University of Washington, Seattle, Wash. 98195.

CAREER: University of Washington, Seattle, postdoctoral fellow, 1969-70, instructor, 1970-73, assistant professor, 1973-77, associate professor of biomedical history, 1977—. *Member:* American Association for the History of Medicine.

WRITINGS: Before Silent Spring (nonfiction), Princeton University Press, 1975.

WORK IN PROGRESS: Physiologic Optimism in the Progressive Period.

* * *

WICKERS, David 1944-

PERSONAL: Born May 7, 1944, in England; son of Charles (a government official) and Molly (Hall) Wickers. *Education:* Churchill College, Cambridge, B.A. (honors), 1966; Royal College of Art, diploma in film and television, 1967. *Religion:* None. *Home:* Church Cottage, Wood Dalling, Norwich, Norfolk NR11 6SN, England.

CAREER: Travel tour operator and director of European operations for an agency in Lucerne, Switzerland, 1967-68; West Sussex College of Art, Worthing, Sussex, England, lecturer in film and photography, 1968-69; Toltenhaur Technical College, London, England, lecturer in liberal studies, 1969-73; Waltham Forest Technical College, London, lecturer in department of general education, 1973-76; free-lance writer, 1976—. Exhibited photographs at Hornsey Gallery, London, 1977. *Member:* Henry Doubleday Research Association, Ramblers Association. *Awards, honors:* M.A. from Cambridge University, 1970.

WRITINGS: Commercial Life, Harrap, 1972, new edition, 1975; *The Complete Urban Farmer: Growing Your Own Fruit and Vegetables in Town,* Viking, 1976; *Indoor Farming,* J. Friedmann, 1977; *Britain at Your Feet* (on backpacking), J. Friedmann, 1978; *Let's Grow Food,* J. Friedmann, 1978.

For children: (With John Tuey) *How to Make Things Grow,* Van Nostrand, 1972; (with Tuey) *How to Be a Scientist at Home,* Van Nostrand, 1972; (with Sharon Finmark) *How to Make Your Own Kinetics,* Van Nostrand, 1972; (with Finmark) *How to Make Magic,* Studio Vista, 1974; (with Finmark) *How to Make Jewelry from Junk,* Studio Vista, 1975; *The Play Outside Book,* Studio Vista, 1975; (with Tuey) *Making Moving Pictures,* Studio Vista, 1976; *The Camp Fire Book,* Studio Vista, 1976; (with Tuey) *Making Science Fun,* Studio Vista, 1976. Comedy script writer for British television and radio. Contributor of articles and photographs to magazines and newspapers.

SIDELIGHTS: Wickers comments: "Most of my work in the next two years will be the setting up and running of an urban homestead project. This involves the conversion of an ordinary terraced house in London in order to realise its full productive potential with regard to intensive food production (fruit, vegetables and animals, fish farming, chickens, and bees) and energy conservation and creation (insulation, solar heat, wind power, etc.). The project is being sponsored partly by the Greater London Council."

AVOCATIONAL INTERESTS: Travel, especially in North and South America, Eastern and Western Europe, North and West Africa, the Middle East; photography.

* * *

WIDDEMER, Margaret 1884-1978

September 30, 1884—July 14, 1978; American novelist, writer, and poet. Widdemer began writing poetry as a child and continued to write until 1968, when she published her last book at the age of 84. Although Widdemer's fiction placed her on the bestseller list at the age of twenty-one with the publication of *The Rose Garden Husband,* she is best remembered as a poet. *The Factories and Other Poems,* her first volume of poetry, was published in 1917, and in 1919, she won the American Poetry Society's prize for *The Old Road to Paradise.* Widdemer is the recipient of many other literary awards. She is the author of over thirty-two books, numerous short stories, serials, articles, and essays. Widdemer died in Gloversville, N.Y. Obituaries and other sources: *Who's Who in America,* 39th edition, Marquis, 1976; *New York Times,* July 15, 1978.

* * *

WIEGHART, James G. 1933-

PERSONAL: Born August 16, 1933, in Chicago, Ill.; son of Oscar F. (an engineer) and Mary (a seamstress; maiden name, Rill) Wieghart; married Sharon Hulin (an administrative assistant), August 13, 1955; children: Michelle, Elizabeth, Bridget, Rebecca. *Education:* Attended Central Michigan University, 1954; University of Wisconsin, B.A. (with honors), 1958. *Politics:* Democrat. *Religion:* Roman Catholic. *Home:* 5510 Nevada Ave. N.W., Washington, D.C. 20015. *Office: New York News,* National Press Building, Washington, D.C. 20045.

CAREER/WRITINGS: Milwaukee Journal, Milwaukee, Wis., reporter, 1958-62; *Milwaukee Sentinel,* Milwaukee, reporter, 1962-65; press secretary for Wisconsin senator William Proxmire, 1965; *Milwaukee Sentinel,* Washington bureau chief, 1966-69; *New York News,* Washington, D.C., correspondent, 1969-75, Washington bureau chief, 1975—. Author of "Capitol Stuff" syndicated column, Knight News Service. Notable assignments include coverage of Watergate, and U.S. presidential campaigns in 1968, 1972, and 1976. *Military service:* U.S. Army, 1951-54; became corporal. *Member:* National Press Club (member of board of governors, 1970), Sigma Delta Chi, Gridiron.

* * *

WIER, Allen 1946-

PERSONAL: Surname is pronounced like "wire"; born September 9, 1946, in San Antonio, Tex.; son of Ralph A. (a salesman) and George Ann (a social worker; maiden name, Marrs) Wier; married wife Dara (a poet and professor, April 2, 1969. *Education:* Baylor University, B.A., 1968; Louisiana State University, M.A., 1970; Bowling Green State University, M.F.A., 1974. *Politics:* "Usually Democrat." *Religion:* "Backslid Southern Baptist." *Home address:* Route 2, Box 374, Hollins, Va. 24019. *Agent:* Irene Tumulty, Julian Bach Literary Agency, Inc., 3 East 48th St., New York, N.Y. 10017. *Office:* Department of English, Hollins College, Hollins College, Va. 24020.

CAREER: Yard clerk for Kansas City Southern Railroad, 1966-67; All-Tex Ranch Supply, Waco, Tex., laborer, 1967-68; Longwood College, Farmville, Va., instructor in English, 1970-72; Carnegie-Mellon University, Pittsburgh, Pa., assistant professor of English, 1974-75; Hollins College, Hollins College, Va., assistant professor of English, 1975—. *Member:* Associated Writing Programs, P.E.N. *Awards, honors:* Creative writing fellowship from National Endowment for the Arts, 1974.

WRITINGS: Things About to Disappear (stories), Louisiana State University Press, 1978; *Blanco* (novel), Louisiana State University Press, 1978.

Work anthologized in *Carry Me Back*, Gallimaufry Press; *Intro 6*, Doubleday; *Itinerary I* and *Itinerary IV*, Bowling Green University Press.

Contributor of stories to literary magazines, including *Southern Review, Carolina Quarterly, Black Warrior Review, Georgia Review, Window,* and *New River Review.*

WORK IN PROGRESS: Two novels, one titled *Departing as Air;* stories.

SIDELIGHTS: Wier writes: "I am especially interested in the possibilities of language—images, textures are important in my work. Thematically much of my work deals with ways in which the imagination, magic, can transform our losses, can hold and share all the dreams and visions and events that must disappear."

* * *

WIER, Dara 1949-

PERSONAL: Surname is pronounced like "wire"; born December 30, 1949, in New Orleans, La.; daughter of Arthur Joseph (a director of vocational rehabilitation services) and Grace (a teacher; maiden name, Barrois) Dixon; married Allen Wier (a writer and teacher), April 2, 1969. *Education:* Attended Louisiana State University, 1967-70; Longwood College, B.S., 1971; Bowling Green State University, M.F.A., 1974. *Home address:* Route 2, Box 374, Hollins, Va. 24019. *Office:* Department of English, Hollins College, Hollins, Va. 24020.

CAREER: University of Pittsburgh, Pittsburgh, Pa., instructor in English, 1974-75; Hollins College, Hollins, Va., instructor, 1975-76, assistant professor of English, 1977—. Has given poetry readings. *Member:* Authors Guild of Authors League of America, Associated Writing Programs.

WRITINGS: Blood, Hook, & Eye (poems), University of Texas Press, 1977.

Work anthologized in *A Circle Is the Perfect Line*, 1974; *Intro Six*, Doubleday, 1974; *Fiction and Poetry by Texas Women*, 1975; *Mothers and Daughters*, 1978. Contributor of more than one hundred poems, stories, and reviews to literary magazines and popular journals, including *Southern Review, New Republic, North American Review, Quartet,* and *Hollins Critic.*

WORK IN PROGRESS—Selection of poems: *All You Have in Common*, for Bowling Green State University Press; *The Eight-Step Grapevine; The Book of Knowledge.*

SIDELIGHTS: Dara Wier writes: "Because I think the best poetry embodies mystery which evokes contemplation, I wish my own work to be acts of and instigators of meditation."

* * *

WIGHT, James Alfred 1916-
(James Herriot)

Personal: Born October 3, 1916; son of James Henry and Hannah Wight; married Joan Catherine Danbury, 1941; children: two. *Education:* Attended Glasgow Veterinary College. *Residence:* England.

CAREER: General practitioner in veterinary medicine in England, 1940—. *Military service:* Royal Air Force. *Member:* British Veterinary Association.

WRITINGS—All under pseudonym James Herriot: *If Only They Could Talk*, M. Joseph, 1970; *It Should Happen to a Vet*, M. Joseph, 1972; *All Creatures Great and Small*, St.

Martin's, 1972; *Let Sleeping Vets Lie*, M. Joseph, 1973; *All Things Bright and Beautiful*, St. Martin's, 1974; *Vet in Harness*, Pan Books, 1976; *Vets Might Fly*, M. Joseph, 1976; *All Things Wise and Wonderful*, St. Martin's, 1977.

SIDELIGHTS: In his extensive article on James Herriot in *Smithsonian* magazine, Timothy Green writes that "actually Herriot is not the literary vet's real name; Siegfried Farnon is a pseudonym, too. Even Darrowby, the town in the Dales where they practice, is a composite of two communities. Such secrecy is required by British veterinary etiquette, which does not permit any form of advertising—and being the author of a best seller might be construed that way." The best sellers are, of course, three books on the life of a country vet.

Reviewing Herriot's first book, *All Creatures Great and Small*, Nelson Bryant writes: "Herriot's book is more than a collection of well-told anecdotes and sharply drawn personalities. Laced through it is the author's growing awareness that he is in the right place doing the right thing.... Herriot charms because he delights in life, embraces it with sensitivity and gusto and writes with grace. Reading him, one is reminded that there are still, nearly 40 years after the time of this story, country places where the wind blows clean, places where men and women find pleasure in hard work and simple living."

In his review of *All Things Bright and Beautiful* Paul Showers states that Herriot's second book "does not confine itself to a specialist's account of his specialty . . . rather it is James Herriot's enthusiastic endorsement of a simple, unpretentious life." Showers continued and described Herriot as a "man who actually enjoys his work without worrying about the Protestant Ethic; he finds satisfaction in testing his skill against challenges of different kinds. Beyond that, he delights in the day-to-day process of living even when things aren't going too well. It's reassuring to come across an affirmation of this sort every now and then, even though it seems to be inspired more readily by the remote past than the immediate present."

Richard Lingeman agrees, but also states that "what allays one's pleasure, though, is a sense of formula creeping into the stories, of mechanical plot-shifts, as though Herriot were straining to heighten and point up a diminishing store of materials; he also skirts close to Disneyization, i.e., rule by lovable animals. On the whole, *All Things Wise and Wonderful* is as ingratiating as the previous one; niceness still triumphs, but this time around, it's a near thing."

Has success changed Herriot's life? Green writes that "Herriot displays almost boyish delight at his sudden fame and fortune. 'I'm on a gorgeous wicket,' he says cheerfully. 'No one had thought of writing funny books about cows and pigs before. And it's nice to make people laugh.'" Some disruption does occur in the simple life of this country vet. In addition to the many visitors who want to meet this famous vet, the postman at times delivers "to his surgery the hundreds of fan letters addressed variously, 'James Herriot, COUNTRY VET, Darrowby, England.'"

When questioned about his profession by Green, Herriot replied: "It can be rough and dirty, and the accident rate is high. In the old days with lots of horses, it used to be really tough, because if a horse kicks you it can mean a broken leg. My daughter Rosemary was mad keen to be a country vet, but I talked her out of it, so she's a doctor instead, which is the next best thing."

BIOGRAPHICAL/CRITICAL SOURCES: Observer, February 13, 1972, May 27, 1973, August 22, 1976; *New*

Statesman, March 10, 1972, August 20, 1976; *New York Times,* December 14, 1972, September 24, 1974; *New York Times Book Review,* February 18, 1973, November 3, 1974, September 18, 1977; *Time,* February 19, 1973; *Books and Bookmen,* October, 1973; *English Journal,* December, 1973; *Atlantic Monthly,* August, 1974, October, 1974; *Smithsonian,* November, 1974; *Book World,* December 8, 1974, September 14, 1975, December 5, 1976, September 11, 1977; *National Observer,* December 28, 1974; *House and Garden,* December, 1975.*

* * *

WILCOX, Michael (Denys) 1943-

PERSONAL: Born June 6, 1943, in Totnes, Devonshire, England; son of Denys Robert (a headmaster) and Phyllis (Warren) Wilcox. *Education:* Borough Road College, Isleworth, England, teacher's certificate, 1966; University of London, B.A. (honors), 1972. *Religion:* Agnostic. *Home:* Tower Cottage, Ninebanks, Hexham, Northumberland, England.

CAREER: Teacher of English at Priors Court School near Newbury, England, 1966-68, and technical school in Haydon Bridge, Nortumberland, England, 1968-69; West Denton High School, Newcastle upon Tyne, England, teacher of English and head of department, 1972-74; playwright, 1974—. *Member:* Theatre Writers Union, Northern Playwrights Society (founding member), Teesside Playwrights Society (chairperson, 1977-78). *Awards, honors:* British Arts Council bursary, 1976.

WRITINGS: Standard Procedure (two-act play; first produced by British Broadcasting Corp. on "Afternoon Theatre," 1978), Iron Press, 1978.

Unpublished plays: "The Boy Who Cried Stop" (one-act), first produced in Newcastle upon Tyne, England, by Stagecoach (of the Tyneside Theatre Company), November, 1974; "The Atom Bomb Project" (two-act), first produced by Stagecoach, March 10, 1975; "Roar Like Spears" (two-act), first produced in Montevallo, Ala., at Drama Institute, July 6, 1975; "Grimm Tales" (one-act), first produced by Stagecoach, December, 1975; "The Blacketts of Bright Street" (two-act), first produced in Stockton on Tees, England, at Dovecot Arts Centre, July 7, 1977; "The Phantom of the Fells" (one-act), first produced in Newcastle upon Tyne, England, by Live Theatre, October 7, 1977; "Pioneers" (two-act), first produced at Dovecot Arts Centre, November 22, 1977; "Mowgli" (two-act), first produced at Dovecot Arts Centre, March 15, 1978; "Rents" (two-act), first produced in Edinburgh, Scotland, at Traverse Theatre, January, 1979.

Other: "Dekka and Dava" (one-act play), 1974; "Great for Our Mark" (one-act play), 1975; "Aesop's Fables" (one-act play), 1975; "Crossfire and a Broken Glass" (television script), 1975; "Territories" (screenplay), 1976; "Shadows of the War" (screenplay), 1976; "Chicks in the Wood" (two-act pantomime), 1977.

WORK IN PROGRESS: Revising some earlier plays, including "Pioneers."

SIDELIGHTS: Wilcox writes: "I used to write puppet plays when I was a boy, and tour them round one or two of the local schools, and entertain the boys at my father's boarding school. Then my interest in the theatre was smothered by a whole lot of other things—the death of my father, being sent away to a traditional English boarding school, trying to satisfy the demands being made on me to be a super-athlete when I would rather have gone off fishing. I trained as a teacher and started using drama with kids to explore ideas with them, and find new ways of being articulate together.

"Becoming a playwright after a difficult spell at a Newcastle comprehensive school seemed the logical way of getting my life back together again. There was a twenty-year gap between those puppet plays and my fist professional play for Stagecoach. I felt I was starting to grow again.

"I was a founding member of the Northern Playwrights Society, which we set up to promote the work of playwrights working in the northeast of England. This has proved a great success, and a lot of us are selling a lot of interesting work at the moment. Futures look exciting.

"I've got a hell of a lot of plays in me. I like working with people on projects. I'm working with Chris Parr and Peter Lichtenfels at the Traverse Theatre in Edinburgh at the moment. I like my work to be challenged while I'm at the researching/writing stage. I also like to challenge the work of the company and director during rehearsals and know exactly what's going on.

"I want to get into television, but although producers make encouraging noises in my direction, none of them have taken me on yet. They seem nervous at the content of the plays I offer them, particularly the homosexual themes. I wish the British film industry had half the guts of the best films coming out of America.

"There are signs that things are beginning to go my way. I've just finished a year as resident playwright at one of the northeast's arts centres, and a local television company is showing a lot of interest at the moment. I'm impatient. I want to keep building, and I need the support of the best people in the business. I want to keep growing. . . ."

* * *

WILCOX, Richard L. 1918-1978

1918—May 8, 1978; American public relations executive, journalist, and author. Wilcox covered stories in the Pacific and European theatres of World War II while he was a member of the staff of *Life* magazine. He later joined the Coast Guard, where he served as a public information officer. It was during this time that Wilcox won the Philippines Liberation Medal and the Fifth Fleet Commendation Medal. He is the author of two books and numerous magazine articles. Wilcox died in New York, N.Y. Obituaries and other sources: *New York Times,* May 12, 1978.

* * *

WILCOX, Robert K(alleen) 1943-

PERSONAL: Born July 21, 1943, in Indianapolis, Ind.; son of Jacob Guire (a real estate broker) and Agnes (a real estate broker; maiden name, Kalleen) Wilcox; married Begona de Amezola; children: Robert Guire. *Education:* Attended University of Oklahoma, 1962-64, and Miami-Dade Junior College, 1964; University of Florida, B.S., 1966. *Home and office:* 3851 Stewart Ave., Coconut Grove, Fla. 33133. *Agent:* Jet Associates, 124 East 84th St., New York, N.Y. 10028.

CAREER: Gainesville Sun, Gainesville, Fla., part-time reporter, 1964-66; *Miami News,* Miami, Fla., police reporter, 1966-67, general assignments reporter, 1967-69, religion editor, 1970-73; free-lance writer, 1973—. Stringer for *New York Times,* 1973—. *Military service:* U.S. Air Force Reserve, 1967-77; became first lieutenant. *Member:* Sigma

Delta Chi. *Awards, honors:* Supple Memorial Award from Religion Newswriters Association, 1970.

WRITINGS: The Mysterious Deaths at Ann Arbor, Popular Library, 1977; *Shroud,* Macmillan, 1977.

Author of "The Seer," a film script.

Contributor to magazines and newspapers, including *New York Times, Probe the Beyond, Tropic* and *Family Weekly.*

WORK IN PROGRESS: Books on scientific evidence for life after death and the air war in Vietnam; *The Seer* (tentative title), a novel; a novel on the Basques, of the mountains in northern Spain.

SIDELIGHTS: Wilcox writes: "I have an interest in religion—not so much the theology, but the cultural trappings that go with it. I suspect this will always have an influence on my writing. Although I don't know why, I also seem to gravitate toward crime as a subject in my writings. My long-term ambition is to become prolific in fiction, and thus pursue a career in both fiction and nonfiction, writing many books in the process. I like writing books best of all because it allows me the time to understand a subject and write about it to the best of my ability. I also think books are the best way to make money in writing."

*   *   *

WILDENHAIN, Marguerite 1896-

PERSONAL: Born October 11, 1896, in Lyons, France; came to the United States in 1940, naturalized citizen, 1945; daughter of Theodore (a businessman) and Rose (Calmann) Friedlaender; married Frans R. Wildenhain (an artist), 1930 (divorced). *Education:* Attended Berlin School for Applied Arts, 1917-19, and Bauhaus, 1919-25; Halle/Saale, master degree, 1926. *Home and office address:* Pond Farm Pottery, Guerneville, Calif. 95446.

CAREER: Porcelain designer for a factory in Thuringia, Germany, 1917-19; Kunstgewerve Schule, Haale Saale, Germany, teacher of pottery making and head of ceramic department, 1925-33; co-owner of pottery workshop in Putten, Gelderland, Netherlands, 1933-40; California College of Arts and Crafts, Oakland, ceramics teacher, 1940-42; Pond Farm Pottery, Guerneville, Calif., owner, 1942—, director of Pond Farm Summer School, 1948—. Pottery has been exhibited in the United States and abroad, and is represented in museums and permanent collections. *Awards, honors:* Numerous awards for pottery since 1926, including a second prize from "Arts and Techniques," an international exhibition in Paris, 1937; D.Humanities from Luther College, 1969.

WRITINGS: Pottery: Form and Expression, Reinhold, 1959; *The Invisible Core: A Potter's Life and Thoughts,* Reinhold, 1973. Contributor to magazines.

SIDELIGHTS: Marguerite Wildenhain has written: "My teachers were the potter Max Krehan and the sculptor Gerhard Marcks. The first one taught me all about the craft and the latter made me understand the problems of form, sculpture, and art.... I learned to be a craftsman as a way of life and that it meant you had to think.... I have always been deeply grateful for this serious and basic education that conveyed to the student not only a technique and facts but also a high degree of ethical and artistic integrity.

"Trained as I was in the tradition of European pottery and in the creative and high artistic milieu of the Weimar Bauhaus, I recognized what the main difficulty in producing good pottery in our time was. We had lost a really intense and collected knowledge of a craft, of both the materials and the form and thus lost the fusion of the technique and the artistic possibilities of a craft in one piece of work. There were many craftsmen who had good techniques but whose pots were deadly boring, had no character nor beauty of their own; and on the other hand there were 'artists' who tried to express something without the least knowledge of the materials or the technique. These two poles had to be united again if the craft was ever to have cultural importance and a human, educational value.

"It is important to be as basically honest as possible in one's search for artistic expression. For what makes a pot good, whether made now or a thousand years ago, is that its form, its lines, its decoration are alive, skillfully made and expressive of the time, country and man that made it....

"Realizing that in our time most pots will have to be made by the machine on a large scale, I have formerly made many models for mass-production. Today though, I feel that it is increasingly important to stress again the value of the way of life of a craftsman and to try to educate young people to a basic understanding of what is the essence of a life dedicated to an idea that is not based on success and money, but on human independence and dignity."

*   *   *

WILKINSON, Paul 1937-

PERSONAL: Born May 9, 1937, in Harrow, Middlesex, England; son of Walter Ross and Joan Rosemary Wilkinson; married Susan Flook (a medical social worker); children: Rachel, John, Charles. *Education:* University of Wales College at Swansea, B.A., 1959, M.A., 1968. *Office:* Department of Politics, University College, University of Wales, P.O. Box 78, Cardiff CF1 1XL, Wales.

CAREER: University of Wales, University College, Cardiff, assistant lecturer, 1966-68, lecturer, 1968-75, senior lecturer in politics, 1975—. Chairman of Youth Movement Archive Advisory Committee. *Military service:* Royal Air Force, 1959-65. *Member:* International Institute for Strategic Studies, Royal United Services Institute for Defense Studies.

WRITINGS: Social Movement, Praeger, 1971; *Political Terrorism,* Halsted, 1974; *Terrorism versus Liberal Democracy: The Problems of Response,* Institute for the Study of Conflict, 1976; *Terrorism and the Liberal State,* Macmillan (England), 1977, New York University Press, 1978; (editor and contributor) *Terrorism: Theory and Practice,* Westview Press, 1978. Contributor to political science journals, including *World Today,* and newspapers. Member of editorial board of *Terrorism: An International Journal.*

WORK IN PROGRESS: Rules of War, for Dent; research on international terrorism; a monograph on Western defense, for Macmillan.

SIDELIGHTS: Wilkinson writes: "I am best known for my studies of terrorism and civil violence. Writing from the perspective of liberal democratic philosophy, I have consistently and passionately condemned terrorism as an unmitigated evil. I believe that terrorist violence is inherently morally unjustifiable becouse it involves the murder and maiming of the innocent. Whatever terrorists may say, there are always alternative forms of protest, opposition and resistance available which do not necessitate the deliberate and systematic murder of the innocent.

"The major preoccupations of my recent work have been the protection of the life and rights of the innocent, and the design of policies and measures at both national and international levels to defeat terrorism in ways fully compatible with liberal democracy and the rule of law. I am currently engaged in a major study of the efforts to revise and extend the humanitarian laws of war, and the problems of their enforcement in major armed conflicts.''

AVOCATIONAL INTERESTS: Modern Poetry, modern painting, walking.

BIOGRAPHICAL/CRITICAL SOURCES: Terrorism: An International Journal, Volume I, number 2, 1978.

* * *

WILL, George F. 1941-

PERSONAL: Born May 4, 1941, in Champaign, Ill.; son of Frederick L. (a professor) and Louise Will; married Madeleine C. Marion, September 4, 1967; children: Jonathan, Geoffrey. *Education:* Trinity College, B.A., 1962; attended Magdalen College, Oxford, 1962-64; Princeton University, Ph.D., 1967. *Home:* 4 Melrose, Chevy Chase, Md. 20015.

CAREER/WRITINGS: Michigan State University, East Lansing, professor of politics, 1967-68; University of Toronto, Toronto, Ontario, professor of politics, 1968-69; U.S. Senate, Washington, D.C., congressional aide to Senator Alcott of Colorado, 1970-72; *National Review,* New York City, Washington editor, 1972-76; *Newsweek,* New York City, contributing editor, 1975—; Washington Post Writers Group, Washington, D.C., author of syndicated column, 1974—. *Awards, honors:* Pulitzer Prize, 1977, for distinguished commentary.

* * *

WILLIAMS, Guy Neal 1953-

PERSONAL: Born October 31, 1953, in Waycross, Ga.; son of Kenneth E. (an official with the Department of Housing and Urban Development) and Elaine (Graham) Williams; married Gail Macbeth, December 29, 1973. *Education:* Attended public schools in Atlanta, Ga., and Philadelphia, Pa. *Home:* 1437 Kenwood St., Winston-Salem, N.C. 27103. *Office: Winston-Salem Journal,* 416 North Marshall, Winston-Salem, N.C. 27102.

CAREER/WRITINGS: Free-lance writer. Has worked variously as a housepainter, gravedigger, and bricklayer; currently reporter for *Winston-Salem Journal,* Winston-Salem, N.C. Notable assignments include three months living and working with migrant farmworkers in Pennsylvania in 1976, and a series of articles about drug smuggling along the Outer Banks of North Carolina. *Awards, honors:* Sidney Hillman Prize and Clarion Award from Women in Communications, both 1976, both for the article ''The Mushroom Pickers.''

WORK IN PROGRESS: Damaged Goods, a novel.

SIDELIGHTS: Williams writes: ''Motivation and circumstance are fairly closely tied, I suppose. When I lived in Philadelphia, I wrote for magazines and newspapers there. Now that I live in Winston-Salem, I write for the newspaper here. There seems to be enough interesting stuff to go around.

''As for viewpoints, I seem to be well qualified to do things other reporters don't want to. I haven't studied journalism, or anything else for that matter. I haven't approached reporting as a calling or even as a definite career. That seems to help. For some reason, though, I end up drawing the assignments no one else wants. I get the misfits, which is how I like it.''

WILLIAMS, Harold R(oger) 1935-

PERSONAL: Born August 22, 1935, in Arcade, N.Y.; son of Harry A. and Gertrude A. Williams; married L. Dorothy Preuschoff (a teacher), April 23, 1955; children: Theresa Lynn, Mark Roger. *Education:* State University of New York at Binghamton, B.A., 1961; Pennsylvania State University, M.A., 1962; University of Nebraska, Ph.D., 1966; postdoctoral study at Harvard University, 1969-70. *Home:* 415 Suzanne, Kent, Ohio 44240. *Office:* Department of Economics, College of Business Administration, Kent State University, Kent, Ohio 44242.

CAREER: University of Nebraska, Lincoln, instructor in economics, 1965-66; Kent State University, Kent, Ohio, assistant professor, 1966-68, associate professor, 1968-72, professor of economics, 1972—, chairman of department, 1974—. *Military service:* U.S. Army, Intelligence, 1954-57; served in the Far East.

MEMBER: International Economic Association, Academy of International Business, American Economic Association, Association for Evolutionary Economics, Midwest Finance Association, Midwest Economic Association (vice-president, 1969-70), Southern Economic Association, Ohio Association of Economists and Political Scientists, Omicron Delta Epsilon, Beta Gamma Sigma, Pi Gamma Mu. *Awards, honors:* National Science Foundation fellowship, 1969-70.

WRITINGS: Macroeconomics: Problems and Concepts, Norton, 1967, revised edition, 1974, 3rd edition, 1978; *Macroeconomic Analysis: Selected Readings,* Appleton, 1969; (with John Huffnagle) *Money, Banking, and Monetary Theory: Problems and Concepts,* Harper, 1969, 3rd edition, 1977; (with Henry Woudenberg) *Money and Banking Manual* (to accompany *The Economics of Money and Banking,* by Lester V. Chandler), Harper, 1969, 3rd edition, 1977. Contributor to business and economic journals.

WORK IN PROGRESS: International Economics, for Norton; research on the impact of exchange rate systems on the marginal efficiency of foreign direct investment and, more generally, on multilateral trade negotiations, the General Agreement on Tariffs and Trade (GATT), the Tokyo Round, and U.S. international trade reform; *Energy Demand and Conservation in the OECD Countries,* with Randall Mount; *U.S. Competitive Position in World Steel Trade: Problems and Prospects.*

AVOCATIONAL INTERESTS: Travel (Korea, Japan, England, Germany, Egypt), jogging, bicycling, tennis.

* * *

WILLIS, Roy (Geoffrey) 1927-

PERSONAL: Born September 15, 1927, in London, England; son of Edward Ernest (a businessman) and Doris (Connel) Willis; married Audrey Grant, June 7, 1968 (separated, 1972); children: Joseph, Maryam. *Education:* Attended school in Brentwood, England. *Politics:* Independent. *Religion:* ''Not yet.'' *Home:* 18 Viewforth Gardens, Edinburgh EH10 4ET, Scotland. *Office:* Centre of African Studies, University of Edinburgh, Edinburgh, Scotland.

CAREER: Romford Recorder, Romford, England, apprentice reporter, 1944-45; Betterwear Products Ltd., Romford, business trainee, 1946-51; reporter for *The Grocer,* 1951-53; *Northern News,* Zambia, Rhodesia, reporter, 1953-55; *Uganda Argus,* Kampala, Uganda, sub-editor, 1955-58; Reuters News Agency, London, England, sub-editor, 1958-60; Oxford University, Oxford, England, lecturer in social anthropology, 1960-65; University of London, University College, London, lecturer in social anthropology, 1965-67; University of Edinburgh, Edinburgh, Scotland, lecturer and reader in social anthropology, 1967—. Participated in anthropological research in Tanzania, 1962-64, 1966, and 1967. *Military service:* British Army, Royal Artillery, 1945-46. *Member:* Association of Social Anthropologists.

WRITINGS: Man and Beast, Hart-Davis, 1974; *There Was a Certain Man* (on the spoken art of the Fipa of southwest Tanzania), Oxford University Press, 1978.

WORK IN PROGRESS: Ideology and Dominion: The Consensual State in Ufipa, about the history and sociology of the Fipa people of Tanzania; anthropology of Britain.

SIDELIGHTS: Willis writes: "My major and developing interests include social and cultural anthropology, cosmology, parapsychology, humanistic psychology, and philosophy. Writing, for me, is both self-discovery and discovery of the world and ultimately these are the same. The enormous advantage of getting older is that the material of one's own experience becomes so much more abundant, complex, and meaningful. This means that the world is expanding in a way which I find delightful."

* * *

WILLNOW, Ronald D. 1933-

PERSONAL: Born March 12, 1933, in Adrian, Mich.; son of Wilbur A. and Irene (Sword) Willnow Daniels; married Onnalee Thompson (an instructor of nursing), August 24, 1957; children: Lindle, Randall, Evan. *Education:* Adrian College, B.A., 1954; University of Michigan, M.A., 1959. *Religion:* Unitarian. *Home:* 7432 Cornell Ave., University City, Mo. 63130. *Office: St. Louis Post-Dispatch,* 900 North Twelfth Blvd., St. Louis, Mo. 63101.

CAREER/WRITINGS: St. Louis Post-Dispatch, St. Louis, Mo., general assignment reporter, 1959-61, state capital correspondent, 1961-66, assistant city editor, 1966-70, city editor, 1970-75, news editor, 1975—. *Member:* Society of Professional Journalists (regional director), Mid-American Press Institute (member of board of directors), St. Louis Journalism Foundation (chairman), Press Club of Metropolitan St. Louis, Sigma Delta Chi.

* * *

WILLRICH, Mason 1933-

PERSONAL: Born May 30, 1933, in Los Angeles, Calif.; married Patricia Rowe; children: four. *Education:* Yale University, B.A. (magna cum laude), 1954; University of California, Berkeley, J.D., 1960. *Office:* Rockefeller Foundation, 1133 Avenue of the Americas, New York, N.Y. 10036.

CAREER: Pillsbury, Madison & Sutro, San Francisco, Calif., associate attorney, specializing in corporation law and securities regulation, 1960-62; U.S. Arms Control & Disarmament Agency, Washington, D.C., attorney adviser, 1962-64, assistant general counsel, 1964-65, also member of U.S. delegations to International Atomic Energy Agency (Vienna) and Eighteen-Nation Disarmament Committee (Geneva); University of Virginia, Charlottesville, associate professor, 1965-68, professor of law, 1968-76, John C. Stennis Professor of Law, 1976—, director of Center for the Study of Science, Technology, and Public Policy, 1968-73. Director of International Relations Division of Rockefeller Foundation, 1976—. Admitted to Bars of California, Virginia, and the U.S. Supreme Court. Guest lecturer at Academy

of Sciences (Soviet Union) Institute of the United States of America, 1971; sesquicentennial associate of Center for Advanced Studies, 1973-74; lecturer at Stanford University, 1974; visiting research fellow at Royal Institute of International Affairs, 1975; visiting professor at Massachusetts Institute of Technology, 1976, and at Woodrow Wilson School of Public and International Affairs, Princeton University, 1977. Member of technical advisory board of Virginia State Air Pollution Control Board, 1971-76; member of working groups on North Atlantic Treaty Organization security and nuclear fuels policy of Atlantic Council of the United States, 1975-77; member of board on energy studies of National Academy of Sciences-National Academy of Engineering Commission on Natural Resources, 1975-77. Has testified before the U.S. Senate and House of Representatives; consultant to U.S. Congress, RAND Corp., and U.S. Naval War College.

MEMBER: American Society of International Law (member of executive council, 1967-70; chairman of panel on international energy policy, 1974-75), American Association for the Advancement of Science, Council on Foreign Relations, Phi Beta Kappa, Coif. *Awards, honors:* Guggenheim fellowship, 1973.

WRITINGS: Non-Proliferation Treaty: Framework for Nuclear Arms Control, Michie Co., 1969; (editor with Bennett Boskey) *Nuclear Proliferation: Prospects for Control,* Dunellen, 1970; (contributor) Richard A. Falk and Cyril E. Black, editors, *The Future of the International Legal Order,* Volume III: *Conflict Management,* Princeton University Press, 1971; (editor and contributor) *Civil Nuclear Power and International Security,* Praeger, 1971; *Global Politics of Nuclear Energy,* Praeger, 1971; (editor and contributor) *International Safeguards and Nuclear Industry,* Johns Hopkins Press, 1973; (editor with John B. Rhinelander, and contributor) *SALT: The Moscow Agreements and Beyond,* Free Press, 1974; (with Theodore B. Taylor) *Nuclear Theft: Risks and Safeguards,* Ballinger, 1974; *Energy and World Politics,* Free Press, 1975; *Administration of Energy Shortages: Natural Gas and Petroleum,* Ballinger, 1976; (with Richard K. Lester) *Radioactive Waste Management and Regulation,* Free Press, 1976. Contributor of about twenty articles to professional journals.

* * *

WILMOT, Anthony 1933-
(Anthony Raoul)

PERSONAL: Born August 5, 1933, in Peterborough, England; son of Leonard (an engineer) and Lucy (Wilson) Wilmot; married second wife, Shelagh Shone (a free-lance writer), December, 1971; children: Alexis Jane. *Education:* Educated in England. *Home:* 3 Lansdowne Ct., 1 Lansdowne Rd., Wimbledon, London SW 20, England.

CAREER: Employed as a horticultural worker, student draftsman, wine packer, and newspaper circulation representative in London, England, 1950-55; worked as newspaper reporter and magazine feature writer, 1955-68; became magazine rewriter, editor of children's books, and fiction writer, 1968—. *Military service:* Royal Air Force, 1952-54. *Member:* Crime Writers Association, London Press Club. *Awards, honors:* Crime Writers Association short story award, 1972, for "Requiem for a Flea"; Edgar Wallace Award, 1974.

WRITINGS: The Last Bohemian, McDonald & Janes, 1975; (editor and contributor) *The Gourmet Crook Book,* Everest Books, 1976. Work has been represented in *John*

Creasey Bedside Books (mystery anthologies). Contributor of short stories, sometimes under pseudonym Anthony Raoul, to periodicals, including *Argosy, London Evening News,* and *She.*

WORK IN PROGRESS: Editing and compiling a companion volume to *The Gourmet Crook Book,* to be titled *The Railway Crook Book.*

* * *

WILSHIRE, Bruce W(ithington) 1932-

PERSONAL: Born February 8, 1932, in Los Angeles, Calif.; son of Gilbert B. and June W. Wilshire; married Donna Welch (an actress, playwright, and director), August 15, 1959; children: Gilbert, Rebekah. *Education:* University of Southern California, B.A. (honors), 1953; New York University, M.A., 1960, Ph.D., 1966; studied at American Theatre Wing, 1955-56, and American Shakespeare Festival Academy, 1956-57. *Office:* Department of Philosophy, Rutgers University, New Brunswick, N.J. 08903.

CAREER: Teacher of philosophy in public schools in New York, N.Y., 1959-62; New York University, New York, N.Y., instructor in philosophy, 1963-66; Purdue University, Indianapolis, Ind., associate professor of philosophy, 1966-69; Rutgers University, New Brunswick, N.J., professor of philosophy, 1969—. *Member:* Society for Phenomenology and Existential Philosophy (co-executive secretary, 1974-77). *Awards, honors:* National Endowment for the Humanities grant for younger scholars, 1968-69; travel grant from Rutgers Research Council for Poland, 1973-74, 1978.

WRITINGS: (Editor and contributor) *Romanticism and Evolution: The Nineteenth Century,* Putnam, 1968; *William James and Phenomenology: A Study of "The Principles of Psychology",* Indiana University Press, 1968; *Metaphysics: An Introduction to Philosophy,* Pegasus, 1969; (editor and author of introduction) *William James: The Essential Writings,* Harper, 1971; (editor with Ronald Bruzina) *Selected Studies in Phenomenology and Existential Philosophy,* Volume VII: *Cross Currents in Phenomenology,* Nijhoff, 1978.

WORK IN PROGRESS: Role Playing, Transformation, and Identity: A Study of Theatre and of the Theatrical Metaphor for Existence.

* * *

WILSON, Carole

See WALLMANN, Jeffrey M(iner)

* * *

WILSON, Howard Hazen 1908-1978

July 2, 1908—March 8, 1978; American historian, educator, and author. Wilson began his career with the U.S. Air Force in international relations and intelligence research. Later, he was employed by the federal government as an assistant economist for the Department of Commerce, and division assistant for American Republic Affairs at the State Department. Wilson lectured on international relations at American universities and authored nine books on history and international politics. He died in Washington, D.C. Obituaries and other sources: *Who's Who in the South and Southwest,* 15th edition, Marquis, 1976; *Washington Post,* March 11, 1978.

* * *

WILSON, Michael 1914-1978

July 1, 1914—April 9, 1978; American educator, short story author, and screenwriter. Wilson is best known for his Academy Award winning film, "A Place in the Sun." He found it almost impossible to get work as a screenwriter after he was blacklisted during the McCarthy era for alleged membership in the Communist party. Hollywood producers denied Wilson an Academy Award for "Friendly Persuasion" in 1957, because of his leftist connections. His other films include "Bridge On the River Kwai," "The Sandpiper," "Planet of the Apes," and "Che." Wilson has also written short stories. He died in Beverly Hills, Calif. Obituaries and other sources: *International Motion Picture Almanac,* Quigley, 1975; *New York Times,* April 10, 1978; *Washington Post,* April 11, 1978; *Newsweek,* April 24, 1978.

* * *

WILSON, Paul C(arroll) 1944-

PERSONAL: Born April 21, 1944, in Washington, D.C.; son of Carroll Louis and Mary (a pony breeder; maiden name, Bischoff) Wilson; married Bonny Bouck (an administrator), May 22, 1971. *Education:* Harvard University, B.A. (magna cum laude), 1966; Trinity College, Cambridge, graduate study; University of Virginia, M.A., 1973, Ph.D., 1976. *Home address:* Route 1, Box 240, Fairfield, Va. 24435. *Office:* Department of English, Virginia Military Institute, Lexington, Va. 24450.

CAREER: Virginia Military Institute, Lexington, assistant professor of English, 1976—. Restorer of antique and classic cars.

WRITINGS: Modern Rowing, Stackpole, 1969; *Chrome Dreams: Automobile Styling since 1893,* Chilton, 1976.

WORK IN PROGRESS: A novel, *Always Afternoon,* about an American's difficulties in adjusting to British ways; a book on the inventors of the sewing machine; research on Pope and Boswell.

SIDELIGHTS: Wilson writes: "I see no reason why serious scholarship need be dull reading, nor why lively writing need be superficial, yet daily I meet scholars who are contemptuous of writing they can quickly understand (perhaps a hint that they lack confidence in their intellects?), and I see readers giving credit for profundity to books that are merely turgid. Both attitudes outrage me. My writing is an experiment to see how far complex ideas can be made accessible to the common reader without oversimplification. If the experiment has not always been successful, at least I still believe that the goal is worthwhile."

AVOCATIONAL INTERESTS: Competitive rowing (rowing coach; member of U.S. world championship team, 1970, and U.S. Olympic team, 1972).

* * *

WILSON, Robley (Conant), Jr. 1930-

PERSONAL: Born June 15, 1930, in Brunswick, Maine; son of Robley Conant (a teacher) and Dorothy (Stimpson) Wilson; married Charlotte Lehon, August 20, 1955; children: Stephen, Philip. *Education:* Bowdoin College, B.A., 1957; Indiana University, graduate study, 1960; University of Iowa, M.F.A., 1968. *Home:* 6105 Westbrook Rd., Route 3, Cedar Falls, Iowa 50613. *Office:* Department of English, University of Northern Iowa, Cedar Falls, Iowa 50613.

CAREER: Valparaiso University, Valparaiso, Ind., instructor in English and Russian, 1958-63; University of Northern Iowa, Cedar Falls, assistant professor, 1968-70, associate professor, 1970-75, professor of English, 1975—. Has given readings and lectures at colleges and universities all over the

United States. *Military service:* U.S. Air Force, 1951-55; became staff sergeant.

WRITINGS: All That Lovemaking (poems), Country Print, 1961; (editor with Stephen Minot) *Three Stances of Modern Fiction: A Critical Anthology,* Winthrop Publishing, 1972; *Returning to the Body* (poetry chapbook), Juniper Press, 1977; *The Pleasures of Manhood* (stories), University of Illinois Press, 1977; *Living Alone* (fiction), Fiction International, 1978.

Poems and stories anthologized in ten collections, including *All Our Secrets Are the Same,* Norton; *Three Genres,* Prentice-Hall; *Interpreting Literature,*Holt. Contributor of poems and stories to literary journals and popular magazines, including *Antaeus, Esquire, Nation,* and *New Yorker.* Editor of *North American Review,* 1969—.

* * *

WINDSOR, Annie
See SHULL, Margaret Anne Wyse

* * *

WINGATE, John 1920-

PERSONAL: Born March 15, 1920, in Carbis Bay, Cornwall, England; son of Allan and Joyce (Heriz-Smith) Wingate; children: Susan Wingate Tuckett, Christopher. *Education:* Attended Royal Naval College, Dartmouth, England. *Politics:* "I would burn all the flags." *Home:* 2 Rue Pierre Brossolette, 92130 Issy-les-Moulineaux, France.

CAREER: Horticulturist, 1947-51; schoolmaster at Fonthill, Sussex and Aysgarth, Yorkshire, and housemaster at Milton Abbey, Dorset, 1953-65; warden at Calshot Activities Center, Calshot, Hampshire, 1965-70; free-lance writer, 1970—. *Military service:* Royal Navy, 1933-46, 1951-52; received Distinguished Service Cross; mentioned in dispatches. *Member:* Authors' Society, Naval Records Society, Army and Navy Club.

WRITINGS—Juvenile: *Submariner Sinclair,* G. Newnes, 1959; *Timmy-the-One,* G. Newnes, 1960; *Sinclair in Command: A Submariner Sinclair Story,* G. Newnes, 1961; *Nuclear Captain: The Fourth Story of Submariner Sinclair,* Macdonald & Co., 1962; *Sub-Zero: A Submariner Sinclair Story,* Macdonald & Co., 1963; *Torpedo Shila: The FAA Raid on Toronto,* Macdonald & Co., 1964; *Never So Proud, Crete, May, 1941: The Battle and Evacuation,* Meredith, 1966; *Full Fathom Five: A Submariner Sinclair Story,* Heinemann, 1967; *In the Blow,* Heinemann, 1968; *Last Ditch: The English Channel and Dieppe Raid, 1939-1943,* Heinemann, 1971.

Other: *H.M.S. Dreadnought, Battleship, 1906-1920,* Profile Publications, 1970; (editor) *Warships in Profile,* Doubleday, 1972; *Below the Horizon,* Arthur Barker, 1974, St. Martin's, 1975; *The Sea Above Them,* Arthur Barker, 1975, St. Martin's, 1976; *Oil Strike,* St. Martin's, 1976; *Avalanche,* St. Martin's, 1977; *Black Tide,* Weidenfeld & Nicolson, 1977; *Red Mutiny,* Weidenfeld & Nicolson, 1978; *Target Risk,* Weidenfeld & Nicolson, 1978.

WORK IN PROGRESS: A novel, for Weidenfeld & Nicolson.

SIDELIGHTS: Wingate told *CA:* "I wrote the juvenile "Submarine Sinclair" series (fiction-based-on-fact) for two good reasons: to eat (I was a schoolmaster), and to tell youth what submarining was all about. In my other novels, I aim to entertain, but behind the stories lies my view that the assets of this planet, particularly in and beneath the sea, will have

to be shared by the nations of the world and not grabbed by force, as is being done at the moment. Our last storehouse is the sea, whence man crawled. If we continue to violate, pollute, and plunder it, it is not difficult to forecast the end of life on our planet: a dead sea (almost there in the Mediterranean), a dead surface, ergo, no evaporation, deserts, an oxygen lack and chlorophyll imbalance. . . . There's still time, but not much.

"Through my novels I hope to make people think. The politicians fail—perhaps writers might succeed?"

* * *

WINNEGRAD, Mark Harris 1948-

PERSONAL: Born November 11, 1948, in Bronx, N.Y.; son of Joseph (an accountant) and Bella (a teacher; maiden name, Polivy) Winnegrad. *Education:* Herbert H. Lehman College of the City University of New York, B.A., 1971, M.A., 1976; Queens College of the City University of New York, M.L.S., 1973. *Home:* 1450 Parkchester Rd., Bronx, N.Y. 10462. *Office:* New York City Finance Administration, New York, N.Y.

CAREER: New York City Finance Administration, New York, N.Y., investigator, 1977—. *Member:* American Philatelic Society (Writer's Unit), Society of Philaticians, American Topical Association, Graphics Philately Association (president, 1977—), Journalists, Authors and Poets on Stamps Study Group, Junior Philatelists of America, Beta Phi Mu. *Awards, honors:* Compex Award from Ben Reeves Philatelic Literature Competition, 1974, for "French History from the French Revolution Through World War I as Depicted in French Philately"; Bronze Award from Filatelic Fiesta, 1976, for *Spirits of the Revolution.*

WRITINGS: Highlights of the History of Printing as Depicted on Postage Stamps, Boxwood Press, 1973; *Printing on Stamps,* Graphics Philately Association, 1975. Also author of *Spirits of the Revolution: American History as Depicted in the Commemorative Postage Stamps of the United States,* Junior Philatelists of America. Contributor to philatelic journals.

WORK IN PROGRESS: Revising *Printing on Stamps;* studying French history through French philately; research on philately and the vertical file.

SIDELIGHTS; Winnegrad told *CA:* "The idea of studying history through philately began to develop after I'd collected stamps for a few years, and realized that a country's postal emissions are mirrors in miniature of its history, rather than mere currency of communication through the mails. By then I had joined the major philatelic societies in the United States and had begun to write the articles about American history on stamps which would eventually be published as *Spirits of the Revolution.* Elated by the success of this handbook, and because I'd majored in history and French as an undergraduate, I turned to studying French history through French stamps.

"I've written about American and French history through philately for essentially three reasons. The first is to better enable the collector of French or American stamps to 'write up' his collection by providing him with information about the historical significance of the people, places, and events which are honored on the stamps in his collection. The second reason is to help the topical collector of 'History on Stamps' and his more specialized colleagues who collect 'French History on Stamps' or 'American History on Stamps' to get the 'story behind the stamp.' Knowing this background information, especially when the subjects of the stamps are representative of the most important highlights of each country's history, makes a stamp collection so much more enjoyable. The third reason is to provide a practical and interesting method to teach American or French culture and history, for there are many teachers who also collect stamps, and any philatelist worth his salt knows the educational value of stamps and stamp collecting.''

* * *

WINTER, Gordon 1912-

PERSONAL: Born May 17, 1912, in London, England; son of Arthur (a company director) and Ottilie Winter; married Mary Jackson, October 22, 1939 (divorced, 1943); married Elspeth Kerr Bone (a teacher), November 6, 1948; children: William, Andrew, Lucinda. Education: Attended Camberley Staff College, 1943. Politics: Conservative. Religion: Church of England. Home: Noble Tree End, Hildenborough, Kent, England. Office: Country Life, Kings Reach Tower, Stamford St., London S.E. 1, England.

CAREER: British Broadcasting Corp., London, England, staff member, 1937-57; Country Life, London, chief assistant editor, 1957-77, consultant editor, 1977—. Member of board of directors of Lighthouse Books, 1947-53. Military service: British Army, Royal Artillery, 1936-45; became lieutenant colonel. Member: Royal Ocean Racing Club, London Rowing Club, Leander Club.

WRITINGS: The Horseman's Wcek-End Book, Seeley Service, 1936; (with wife, Elspeth Winter) Ourselves in Canada, Seeley Service, 1958; A Country Camera, David & Charles, 1966; A Cockney Camera, Chatto & Windus, 1971; The Golden Years, David & Charles, 1975; The Country Life Picture Book of Britain, Country Life, 1978. Author of material for radio and television. Member of editorial staff of Field, 1932—, and Listener, 1937-39. Director of Fortnightly Review, 1938-53.

WORK IN PROGRESS: Revising The Horseman's Week-End Book; another book.

SIDELIGHTS: Winter comments: ''The principal activity of my lifetime and of my writings has been the defence of the beauty of the countryside of the United Kingdom, which I regard as the source of inspiration for our English civilisation. The weekly magazine, Country Life, reflects all my personal interests.''

* * *

WINTERFELD, Henry 1901-
(Manfred Michael)

PERSONAL: Born April 9, 1901, in Hamburg, Germany; came to the United States in 1940, naturalized citizen, 1946; son of Max (a composer of operettas) and Rosa (Wagner) Winterfeld; married Elsbeth Michael (a toy designer), April 9, 1923; children: Thomas. Education: Attended Stern's Academy of Music. Home address: Roque Bluffs, Machias, Maine 04654. Agent: Joan Daves, 515 Madison Ave., New York, N.Y. 10022.

CAREER: Playwright and screenwriter, 1923-45; author of books for children, 1937—.

WRITINGS—Books for children: (Under pseudonym Manfred Michael) Timpetill: Die Stadt ohne Eltern, Corrodi, 1937, translation by Kyrill Schabert published as Trouble at Timpetill (under name Henry Winterfeld), Harcourt, 1965; Caius ist ein Dummkopf: Eine lustige und spannende Detektivgeschichte fuer Kinder, Blanvalet, 1953, translation by Richard and Clara Winston published as Detectives in Togas, Harcourt, 1956; Kommt ein Maedchen geflogen: Eine fast unglaubliche Geschichte fuer Kinder, Blanvalet, 1956, translation by Schabert published as Star Girl (Parents' Magazine Book Club selection), Harcourt, 1957, Avon, 1976; Telegramm aus Lilliput: Eine phantastische Geschichte nur fuer Kinder, Blanvalet, 1958, translation by Schabert published as Castaways in Lilliput, Harcourt, 1960; Caius geht ein Licht auf, Blanvalet, 1969, translation by Edith McCormick published as Mystery of the Roman Ransom, Harcourt, 1971.

Books not translated into English: Pimmi Pferdeschwang: Eine koenigliche Unterhaltung fuer junge Maedchen (title means ''Pimmy Ponytail''), Blanvalet, 1967; Der Letzte der Sekundaner: Eine haarstraeubende Erzaehlung (title means ''The Last of the Sekundaner''), Blanvalet, 1971; Caius in der Klemme (title means ''Caius in Trouble''), Blanvalet, 1976.

Plays: ''Schloss im Nebel'' (title means ''Manor in the Fog''), first produced in Ostrava, Czechoslovakia, 1937.

Screenplays: ''Privatsekretaerin'' (title means ''Private Secretary''), produced by Universium Film Aktiengesellschaft (UFA), 1929; ''Maedchen zum Heitaten'' (title means ''Girls to Marry''), produced by UFA, 1931; ''Einer Frau muss man alles verzeihen'' (title means ''You Have to Forgive a Woman''), produced by UFA, 1932; ''Das Fravenparadies'' (title means ''A Paradise for Women''), [Vienna], 1936.

SIDELIGHTS: Winterfeld wrote: ''I started studying the piano at Stern's Academy of Music in Berlin, together with Claudio Arrau and Frederick Loewe. I couldn't compete with them and switched to the profession of writing.

''In 1933 I left Germany and went to Austria. There I wrote Timpetill. I wanted somehow to entertain my son Thomas, who was sick with scarlet fever. Surprisingly other people liked the story too. Since then I have written only children's books. It's painful but I do it because I love children so much. Most of my best friends are children.

''We live in Maine, on the ocean, and even have a little private beach all to ourselves. Each summer we give a Young People's Garden Party for the children of our friends the lobster men, clam diggers, and other neighbors. It's great fun!''

Winterfeld's books have been published, sometimes under the pseudonym Manfred Michael, in Switzerland, England, the Netherlands, France, Norway, Sweden, Japan, Italy, Australia, and Yugoslavia.

* * *

WINTLE, Justin (Beecham) 1949-
(Justin Beecham)

PERSONAL: Born May 24, 1949, in London, England; son of Francis Julian (a film producer) and Anne (a writer; maiden name, Ellis) Wintle; married Hiroko Uehara, March 1, 1975. Education: Magdalen College, Oxford, B.A. (honors), 1972. Politics: ''Social individualism.'' Religion: None. Residence: London, England. Agent: Curtis Brown Ltd., 1 Craven Hill, London W.2, England.

CAREER: Inter-Action Trust Ltd. (community arts association), London, England, trainee director at Almost Free Theatre, 1972-74; writer, 1974—.

WRITINGS: (With Ed Berman) The Fun Art Bus, Eyre Methuen, 1973; (under pseudonym Justin Beecham) Olga (biography), Two Continents Publishing, 1974; (with Emma Fisher) *The Pied Piper* (interviews with writers for children), Two Continents Publishing, 1975; (editor with Richard Kenin) *Dictionary of Biographical Quotation,* Knopf, 1978. Contributor to magazines and newspapers, including *New Society.*

WORK IN PROGRESS: Fiction.

SIDELIGHTS: Wintle writes: *"The Fun Art Bus* is an account of an experimental theatre project of the same name which was launched in 1972 and is still running. It consists of a converted double-decker bus with a miniature theatre on the top deck, with enough space for three or four actors to perform. The idea is that the bus takes a fairly light-hearted kind of theatre to areas of the urban community which do not possess their own theatres, among people who do not regularly go to the theatre. All this was devised by Ed Berman, the director of Inter-Action Trust, which specializes in such work. My book is simply an account of how the bus was developed, how it has been used, and contains five or six short plays by various playwrights.

"My most important books is the *Dictionary of Biographical Quotations.* It is the first of several reference books I have devised and am editing. My general feelings are: reference books are important because they serve as a reminder of the width of culture, and through that hopefully give people some immunity toward ideologies of whatever kind, to keep alive the sense of alternatives. My 'social individualism' is not an ideology, except in that it is ideologically opposed to ideologies. It involves following one's own interests, but with thought for other people, i.e. paying reasonable taxes. For the last decade people have seen rights as an end not a means, so now it's time to start thinking again about why we want all the rights we can get."

AVOCATIONAL INTERESTS: Travel (Europe, the United States, Thailand), reference books, history of ideas.

*　　*　　*

WISE, Leonard

PERSONAL: Born in Hudson, N.Y. *Home and office:* 10322½ Almayo Ave., Los Angeles, Calif. 90064.

CAREER: Writer. *Military service:* U.S. Army, paratrooper.

WRITINGS: The Big Biazarro (novel), Doubleday, 1977; *The Diggstown Ringers* (novel), Doubleday, 1978.

*　　*　　*

WISEMAN, Adele　1928-

PERSONAL: Born in 1928, in Winnipeg, Manitoba, Canada. *Address:* c/o Macmillan Company of Canada Ltd., St. Martin's House, 70 Bond St., Toronto, Canada M5B 1X3.

CAREER: Teacher of English at MacDonald College, McGill University, Montreal, Quebec. *Awards, honors:* Beta Sigma Chi award, Governor General's award, and National Conference of Christians and Jews Brotherhood award, all 1957, all for *The Sacrifice;* Guggenheim fellowship, 1957.

WRITINGS: The Sacrifice (novel), Viking, 1956; (with Joe Rosenthal) *Old Markets, New World,* Macmillan, 1964; *Crackpot,* Macmillan, 1974.

SIDELIGHTS: Reviewing *The Sacrifice,* Saul Maloff wrote: "Adele Wiseman's brilliant and moving first novel, *The Sacrifice,* differs from the older pattern of Jewish fiction in important respects. Miss Wiseman cannot avoid the themes of the difficulty of love and the constant threat of rebellion and estrangement, but her perception of the predicament includes the possibility of reconciliation." A critic from the *New York Times Book Review* stated that *"The Sacrifice* is not a book of unrelieved gloom, of dark metaphysical probings or moral assessments. It is eminently readable, rich in Jewish folklore and *genre* wit which . . . has about it the unmistakeable air of authenticity."

Several critics praised Wiseman's ability to go beyond the scope of a modern ethnic story and create a timeless parable of universal interest. *New Yorker* said *The Sacrifice* was "so concentrated and so well balanced inside the domestic circle that the time could be now or forty years ago." Even though "Avrom and his little family rarely move beyond the range" of their home, Stuart Keate said, "the people they encounter, and the problems they face, are universal: the making of new friends, creation of a home in one room, the testing of ancient faiths in unfamiliar surroundings."

BIOGRAPHICAL/CRITICAL SOURCES: Christian Science Monitor, September 13, 1956; *Saturday Review,* September 15, 1956; *Chicago Sunday Tribune,* September 16, 1956; *New York Herald Tribune Book Review,* September 16, 1956; *New York Times Book Review,* September 16, 1956; *New Yorker,* September 29, 1956; *Time,* October 22, 1956; *Times Literary Supplement,* November 9, 1956; *New Republic,* November 12, 1956.*

*　　*　　*

WISEMAN, Robert F(rederick)　1935-

PERSONAL: Born January 22, 1935, in Pine City, Minn.; son of George D. (an electrician) and Helen V. (Engler) Wiseman; married Geneva Lamyrta Ripley, August 19, 1956; children: George, Bret, Russell, Carey, Natasha, Justin, Ruth. *Education:* University of Montana, B.S., 1961; also attended Montana State University and River Falls State College. *Religion:* Methodist. *Home address:* R.R. 2, Burns Lake, British Columbia, Canada V0J 1E0.

CAREER: Sailor on the Great Lakes, 1953, 1956; miner in Kellogg, Idaho, 1956; Bureau of Land Management, natural resource specialist in Lewistown, Mont., 1961-67, Burns, Ore., 1967-71, and Anchorage, Alaska, 1971-76; cattle rancher in British Columbia, 1976—. *Military service:* U.S. Army, paratrooper, 1953-55.

WRITINGS: The Complete Horseshoeing Guide, University of Oklahoma Press, 1968; *How to Shoe Your Horse,* Farnham Horse Products, 1971.

SIDELIGHTS: Wiseman wrote that during his years as a conservationist he "wrote *The Complete Horseshoeing Guide,* chased wild horses, competed in rodeos, and enjoyed the beauty and vastness of Montana and Oregon. In 1971 we moved to Alaska where I worked first as a smokejumper and then as a natural resource specialist over much of Alaska, including the Aleutian Islands where most of Alaska's cattle ranching takes place.

"We are now building a cattle ranch in beautiful British Columbia where we have a herd of one hundred thirty cattle and horses. We are located on the edge of the wilderness and are experiencing fantastic adventures which may someday be the basis for another book."

AVOCATIONAL INTERESTS: Flying (private pilot), hang gliding.

*　　*　　*

WITHERSPOON, Mary Elizabeth　1919-

PERSONAL: Born June 14, 1919, in Marianna, Fla.; daughter of Cecil (a building contractor) and Janie (a writer; maiden name, Smith) Rhyne; married Jack Witherspoon (an engineer), July 13, 1942; children: John, David, Bill. *Education:* Attended Florida State College for Women (now Florida State University), 1936-38; University of North Carolina, A.B., 1941; University of Tennessee, M.A., 1963. *Politics:* Independent. *Religion:* Society of Friends (Quakers). *Home and office address:* Route 4, Box 821, Panama City, Fla. 32405.

CAREER: Free-lance writer, 1942—. Instructor at University of Tennessee and Knoxville College during the 1960's. Past member of board of trustees of Knox County Library. *Member:* League of Women Voters.

WRITINGS: Somebody Speak for Katy (novel), Dodd, 1950; *The Morning Cool* (novel), Macmillan, 1972. Contributor of poems and stories to magazines.

WORK IN PROGRESS: Watercolor (tentative title), a novel about Americans in Florence, Italy, during the 1966 flood.

SIDELIGHTS: Mary Witherspoon writes: "I am concerned with 'social issues,' as all three of my novels clearly show; but for me there are no uncontaminated causes, no heroes, and no clean-cut remedies. There is nature, there are work and nonsense, laughter and children, discovery and art. Music is probably the highest form of art, and writing next. I strive to be an artist."

*   *   *

WITKER, Kristi

PERSONAL: Born in New York, N.Y. *Education:* Attended Sorbonne, University of Paris, 1964-65. *Politics:* Democrat. *Religion:* Protestant. *Home:* 116 East 91st St., New York, N.Y. 10028.

CAREER: American Heritage Publishing Co., New York City, editor, 1965-70; deputy press secretary, George McGovern U.S. presidential campaign, 1972; *Time,* New York City, stringer photographer, 1972; ABC-TV News, New York City, correspondent, 1974-75; WABC-TV, New York City, reporter for "Eyewitness News," 1975-77; WPIX-TV News, New York City, co-anchorperson of Sunday news program, 1977. Member of board of directors, Irvington House for Medical Research. *Member:* Authors Guild of Authors League of America, Writer's Guild, American Federation of Television and Radio Artists, National Academy of Television Arts and Sciences, Overseas Press Club, American Cancer Society (member of board of directors), American Society for Prevention of Cruelty to Animals (member of board of directors). *Awards, honors:* Prize from *Newsweek,* 1972, for excellence in campaign photography.

WRITINGS: (With Jay Jacobs) *Bobby,* Dell, 1968; (with Jacobs) *R.F.K.: His Life and Death,* Dell, 1968; (with Jacobs) *The Horizon Book of Great Cathedrals,* Horizon Publishing, 1968; (editor) *The Temperance Song Book,* McGraw, 1970; (editor) *How to Become a Super-Salesman,* McGraw, 1970; (editor) *How to Be an Absolutely Smashing Public Speaker without Saying Anything,* McGraw, 1970; (editor) *The American Heritage History of the American People,* American Heritage Publishing, 1971; *How to Lose Everything in Politics Except Massachusetts,* Mason & Lipscomb, 1974.

Contributor: Oliver Jensen, editor, *American Album,* American Heritage Publishing, 1968; Wendy Buehr, editor, *American Manners and Morals,* American Heritage Publishing, 1969; Norman Kotker, editor, *The Horizon Book of the Arts of China,* Horizon Publishing, 1969; Norman Kotker, editor, *The Horizon History of China,* Horizon Publishing, 1969; Patricia Lawford, editor, *That Shining Hour,* Halliday Lithograph Co., 1970; William Van den Heuvel and Milton Gwirtzman, editors, *On His Own,* Doubleday, 1970; Lester David, editor, *Ethel,* Dell, 1971.

Author of monthly column, "Strictly for Kicks," in *Art Gallery,* 1968-72. Contributor of articles and photographs to magazines, newspapers, and syndicates in the United States and abroad, including *New York Times, Washington Post, Vogue, Redbook, Boston Globe, Philadelphia Bulletin, People, Cosmopolitan,* and *Time.*

WORK IN PROGRESS: An autobiography.

SIDELIGHTS: Kristi Witker has traveled in Europe, Asia, and South America, including the Soviet Union and Cuba, where she interviewed Fidel Castro in 1969. She also arranged the interview between news commentator Walter Cronkite and Robert Vesco in Costa Rica in 1974. She has appeared on such television programs as "Today," "Tomorrow," "Good Morning America," and "To Tell the Truth." She has acted in eight films, including six Japanese movies, as well as television commercials and an off-Broadway play.

BIOGRAPHICAL/CRITICAL SOURCES: Beirut Daily Star, March, 1970; *Sarasota Herald-Tribune,* November 26, 1973, May 13, 1974; *New York Post,* May 13, 1974; *Chicago Tribune,* June 2, 1974; *Stanford Advocate,* July 17, 1974; *St. Louis Globe-Democrat,* July, 1974; *Money,* September, 1976.

*   *   *

WOHL, James P(aul) 1937-
(James Coltrane)

PERSONAL: Born October 3, 1937, in New York; son of Joseph (a lawyer) and Mae (Kreshover) Wohl; children: Frederic, Kristin, Jenifer. *Education:* Attended Princeton University, 1955-56, and New York University, 1960; Stanford University, A.B., 1962, J.D., 1963. *Politics:* None. *Home address:* P.O. Box 362, Hilo, Hawaii 96720. *Agent:* Robert Mills Ltd., 156 East 52nd St., New York, N.Y. 10022. *Office:* 60 Keawe St., Hilo, Hawaii 96720.

CAREER: Carlsmith, Carlsmith, Wichman & Case, Honolulu, Hawaii, attorney, 1963-68; Fried, Frank, Harris, Shriver & Jacobsen, New York, N.Y., attorney, 1968-69; Hawaii Land Corp., Hilo, Hawaii, president, 1969—. President of Hawaii Media Advisory Council, 1963—.

WRITINGS: The Nirvana Contracts (novel), Bobbs-Merrill, 1977; (under pseudonym James Coltrane) *Talon* (novel), Bobbs-Merrill, 1978; *The Blind Trust Kills,* Bobbs-Merrill, 1978.

WORK IN PROGRESS: A screenplay, "The Circuit"; a non-fiction book, *Downside Risk;* a short story collection, *The Conspiracy;* a novel, *The Indian Giver.*

*   *   *

WOLFE, Charles Keith 1943-
(Kaw Henricks)

PERSONAL: Born August 14, 1943, in Sedalia, Mo.; son of Jesse Orville (in sales) and Dilla (a teacher; maiden name, Stacey) Wolfe; married Mary Dean King, August 21, 1966; children: Marian Stacey, Cynthia Dean. *Education:* Southwest Missouri State University, B.A., 1965; University of Kansas, M.A., 1967, Ph.D., 1971. *Home:* 1210 Bond Court,

Murfreesboro, Tenn. 37130. *Office:* P.O. Box 201, Middle Tennessee State University, Murfreesboro, Tenn. 37132.

CAREER: Park Central Hospital, Springfield, Mo., surgical technician, 1961-65; University of Kansas, Lawrence, instructor for correspondence school, 1969-71; Middle Tennessee State University, Murfreesboro, assistant professor, 1970-75, associate professor of English, 1975—. Advisor of Tennessee Arts Commission, 1975—; Advisor to National Endowment of Arts, 1977—; also consultant to British Broadcasting Corp. *Member:* National Popular Culture Association, National Academy of Recording Arts and Sciences, American Folklore Society, South Atlantic Modern Language Association, Tennessee Folklore Society, Tennessee College English Association, Tennessee Jazz and Blues Society. *Awards, honors:* Woodrow Wilson fellowship, 1965-67.

WRITINGS: (Editor) *Planets and Dimensions,* Mirage Press, 1973; *Grand Ole Opry: The Early Years, 1925-35,* Old Time Music, 1975; (contributor) Bill Malone and Judith McCulloh, editors, *Stars of Country Music,* University of Illinois Press, 1975; *Tennessee Strings,* University of Tennessee Press, 1977; (editor) Alton Delmore, *Truth Is Stranger Than Fiction: The Autobiography of Alton Delmore,* Country Music Foundation Press, 1978; (with Jlaus Kunnke) *Riley Puckett,* Archiv Fuer Populare Musik, 1978; (with William C. Levy, Douglas Green, Bob Pinson, Nick Tosches, and others) *Illustrated History of Country Music,* Doubleday, 1979; (with Thomas Burton, Ambrose Manning, David Evans, Jack Hurley) *Three Tennessee Folksingers,* University of Tennessee Press, 1979. Author of "From the Fiddling Archives," a column in *Devil's Box.* Contributor of more than eighty articles and reviews, sometimes under pseudonym Kaw Henricks, to magazines, including *Southern Exposure.* Co-editor of *Tennessee Folklore Society Bulletin.* Book editor of *Journal of Country Music.*

WORK IN PROGRESS: A book on Anglo-American gospel music, for University of Illinois Press; studying early history of the recording industry; a biography of Uncle Dave Macon.

SIDELIGHTS: Wolfe writes: "I have produced over twenty albums of folk music, and assisted in the production of three television shows in this area. I am interested in many aspects of southern life and culture, and much of my work is a direct result of extensive field research.

"I am vitally concerned with helping southerners to see the dignity and worth of their own folk and popular culture, and to try to show how these cultures reflect the humanism, the values, and the unique regional identity of the area. Unlike many people interested in documenting southern culture, I grew up in the culture, and have shared first-hand the kinds of experiences that molded it. I enjoy working in the field, doing personal interviews with people, and talking with them about their music and their lives. At times I feel quite desparate about documenting the older folk culture before it is too late; too many of the musicians I have recorded and interviewed have passed on in the last five years. The last generation of 'pre-media' people is now approaching its seventh and eighth decade, and when they are gone we will have lost a great resource. I want to do as much as I can toward establishing a sense of cultural ecology in the region, and, indeed, across the country."

* * *

WOLFF, Diane 1945-

PERSONAL: Born October 12, 1945, in New York, N.Y.;

daughter of Irving M. (an attorney) and Catherine (Halkett) Wolff; married Wallace Gorell, June 25, 1977. *Education:* Briarcliff College, A.A. (magna cum laude), 1965; Columbia University, B.A., 1968. *Politics:* "Feminist, food radical, environmental crank, and medical anarchist." *Home:* 1850 Arch St., #6, Berkeley, Calif. 94709. *Agent:* Elaine Markson Literary Agency, Inc., 44 Greenwich Ave., New York, N.Y. 10014.

CAREER: Free-lance writer. Has worked as an editor and gold dealer. *Member:* Authors Guild of Authors League of America.

WRITINGS: An Easy Guide to Everyday Chinese, Harper, 1974; *Chinese Writing: An Introduction,* Holt, 1975. Contributor to *American Poetry Review* and *Village Voice.*

WORK IN PROGRESS: Love-Slave of the Tropix Heads North, a novel.

SIDELIGHTS: Wolff told *CA:* "For years I was captive in a Chinese prison—library research—and my only crime was a fascination with the long ago and far away, the east side of the mind. I have escaped into the near and now, and the contrast thrills me right down to my very small feet. I've also traded fact for fiction. The novel-in-progress deals with a woman in bondage trying to get her locks off." *Avocational interests:* Psychosomatic exercise, mind-jogging, and gossip.

* * *

WOLFF, Janet 1943-

PERSONAL: Born March 25, 1943, in Manchester, England; daughter of Arthur (a chemist and company director) and Rosabelle (Noar) Wolff. *Education:* University of Birmingham, B.S.S. (first class honors), 1968, Ph.D., 1972; also attended London School of Contemporary Dance, 1970-72. *Politics:* "Feminist/socialist." *Religion:* "(Jewish) atheist." *Home:* 5 St. John's Ter., Leeds 3, England. *Office:* Department of Sociology, University of Leeds, Leeds, England.

CAREER: Worked as a secretary in Manchester, England, 1963-65; University of Leeds, Leeds, England, lecturer in sociology, 1973—. *Member:* British Sociological Association (member of executive committee, 1977-79), Association of Scientific, Technical, and Management Staffs.

WRITINGS: Hermeneutic Philosophy and the Sociology of Art, Routledge & Kegan Paul, 1975; (editor with Jane Routh) *The Sociology of Literature: Theoretical Approaches* (monograph), University of Keele, 1977. Contributor to sociology journals. Member of editorial board of *Sociology,* 1976—.

WORK IN PROGRESS: Research on the sociology of contemporary dance, women and social stratification, literature, culture, and ideology; research on the development of the arts in nineteenth-century Manchester.

AVOCATIONAL INTERESTS: Modern dance (watching and performing), music (especially chamber music and rock music), cinema.

* * *

WOLK, Allan 1936-

PERSONAL: Born December 27, 1936, in New York; son of Kalman and Lee (Blazer) Wolk; married Iris Fleischman, January 31, 1960; children: Michele, Glenn, Brian. *Education:* City College (now of the City University of New York), B.A., 1958, M.A., 1961; New York University, Ph.D., 1970. *Politics:* "Democrat-Humanist." *Religion:*

Jewish. *Home:* 96 Third St., New City, N.Y. 10956. *Agent:* Charles Byrne, 1133 Avenue of the Americas, New York, N.Y. 10036. *Office:* Department of Social Sciences, Bronx Community College, University Ave. and West 181st St., Bronx, N.Y. 10453.

CAREER: Junior high school social studies teacher in Bronx, N.Y., 1960-65; Bronx Community College (now of the City University of New York), Bronx, N.Y., adjunct lecturer, 1963-65, instructor, 1965-68, assistant professor, 1968-71, associate professor, 1971-75, professor of political science, 1975—, college ombudsman, 1975—. Member of executive committee of Rockland County Affirmative Action Advisory Committee, 1974-75. *Member:* Authors Guild of Authors League of America, American Civil Liberties Union, Common Cause (member of local board of directors and Rockland County coordinator, 1975).

WRITINGS: The Presidency and Black Civil Rights: Eisenhower to Nixon, Fairleigh Dickinson University Press, 1971; *Gunfighters of the West,* Dexter Press, 1976; *Indian Legends,* Dexter Press, 1977; *The Naming of America,* Thomas Nelson, 1978; *Words That Came from Names of People and Places,* Thomas Nelson, in press; *Incredible Names of People and Places,* Thomas Nelson, in press. Author of "Word Trivia," a column in *Rockland Review* and other newspapers, 1977—.

WORK IN PROGRESS: The Pros Look at Politics, descriptions of the political system in the words of politicians themselves; editing and writing material for *Living Together in America: The Basics of Psychology, Sociology, Economics, and American Government,* for young people; *Human Rights Heroines,* vignettes of American women involved in human rights causes; *The Constitution in Plain Language,* for young people; *Dr. Wolk's Fairy Tales,* stories of the animal kingdom humanized, from a human rights point of view; "Grow Old Along with Me," a three-act play, about an elderly couple who can't escape an urban ghetto; "Casanova Meets Catherine," a two-act play depicting and enlarging upon the historic meeting between Casanova and the ruler of Russia.

SIDELIGHTS: Wolk writes: "A great deal of my writing—and teaching, is propelled by a sense of frustration with the many unjust inhumanities that occur in the world's societies. I believe that the written word can play an important part in educating and thus motivating the have-nots to try to get their rightful, proportionate share of the pie.

"My academic activities, as college ombudsman, and in other capacities, have often been directed to prod the powers-that-be into recognizing the rights of others.

"It is essential that those who have the ability to influence others, whether through writing of other means, consider it their sacred duty to use this power to bring about a better world."

*　　*　　*

WOOD, Edgar A(llardyce) 1907-
(Kerry Wood)

PERSONAL: Born June 2, 1907, in New York, N.Y.; moved to Canada, 1909, naturalized citizen, 1973; son of William Campbell (an insurance agent) and Elizabeth (Callon) Wood; married Marjorie Marshall, February 10, 1936; children: Rondo (daughter), Heather Kathleen (Mrs. Patrick David F. Ion), Walden Gregory. *Education:* Attended public schools in Alberta. *Religion:* Protestant. *Residence:* Red Deer, Alberta, Canada.

CAREER: Full-time free-lance writer, 1924—. Local correspondent for five Alberta newspapers, 1926-36, columnist, 1926-73; archery tackle manufacturer, 1937-44; radio broadcaster and scriptwriter for Canadian Broadcasting Corp. (CBC) and independent stations, 1939-73; television scriptwriter for the programs "Rope Around the Sun" and "The Outrider," and writer and performer of programs "The Kerry Wood Storybook," "Outdoors with Kerry Wood," and "Playtime" for CBC, 1958-65. Secretary-treasurer of Red Deer Public Library board, 1930-45. *Member:* Alberta Natural History Society (life member; sanctuary chairman, 1936-64; former president, secretary-treasurer, and committee chairman), Alberta Federation of Naturalists (life member). *Awards, honors*—For books: *Cowboy Yarns for Young Folk* was named runner-up children's book of the year by the Canadian Library Association, 1951; Governor-General medals for juvenile literature, 1955, for *The Map-Maker,* and 1957, for *The Great Chief;* first Vicky Metcalf award from Canadian Authors Association, 1963, for "consistently good writing of material inspirational to Canadian youth." Other awards include grants from John S. Ewart Foundation, 1954 and 1957, and from Canada Council, 1960; Alberta Historical Society award of the year, 1965; LL.D. from University of Alberta, 1969; achievement award from Government of Alberta, 1975.

WRITINGS—All under name Kerry Wood; all juveniles, except as noted: (Self-illustrated with A. H. Short) *The Magpie Menace,* privately printed, 1936; *Robbing the Roost* (adapted from author's radio script), privately printed, 1938; *I'm a Gaggle Man Myself* (adapted from author's radio script), privately printed, 1940; *Three Mile Bend,* Ryerson Press, 1945; *Birds and Animals in the Rockies,* H. R. Larson, 1946; *A Nature Guide for Farmers* (adult), H. R. Larson, 1947.

Cowboy Yarns for Young Folk, Copp Clark, 1951; (self-illustrated) *The Sanctuary,* privately printed, 1952; *Wild Winter,* Houghton, 1954; *The Map-Maker,* Macmillan (Toronto), 1955; *Willowdale,* McClelland & Stewart, 1956; *The Great Chief,* Macmillan, 1957; *The Queen's Cowboy,* Macmillan, 1960; *Great Horned Mac Owl,* privately printed, 1961; *The Boy and The Buffalo,* Macmillan, 1963; *Mickey the Beaver and Others,* Macmillan, 1964; *A Lifetime of Service: George Moon,* privately printed, 1966; (self-illustrated) *A Corner of Canada,* privately printed, 1966; *A Time for Fun,* privately printed, 1967; *Samson's Long Ride,* Collins (Toronto), 1968; *The Medicine Man,* privately printed, 1968.

(Self-illustrated with wife, Marjorie Wood) *The Creek,* privately printed, 1970; *The Icelandic-Canadian Poet: Stephan G. Stephansson,* privately printed, 1974; (illustrated with photographs by the author and others) *Red Deer: A Love Story,* privately printed, 1975; (illustrated by M. Wood) *Bessie, The Coo,* privately printed, 1975.

Work represented in over seventy school texts and fifty anthologies. Writer of an estimated sixty-two hundred short stories, eight thousand magazine articles for Canadian, American, and British publications, nine thousand newspaper columns, over three hundred television scripts.

WORK IN PROGRESS: Articles and short stories, "no book at the moment."

SIDELIGHTS: Wood decided to become a writer at the age of twelve and has been a full-time professional since the age of sixteen. His career began when a school administrator urged him to drop out of high school and spend the time writing. Since that day he left school in 1926, he has worn out nineteen typewriters and gained the distinction of being one of only three Canadian authors who were able to live off their writings during the Depression. A devoted naturalist, Wood is especially proud of helping to establish twenty-six wildlife sanctuaries across North America.

"My love of nature developed in early childhood and increased steadily," Wood wrote. "Through its study grew my interest in Indians and their history; personal friends among them added to my profound respect.

"My scholarly father encouraged and guided me through a wide course of reading, making sure that I understood the books. From him and helpful librarians came my determination to write, and the advice and confidence of a high school teacher precipitated the career. The family background of nine ministers and deaconesses, plus the absorbing responsibilities in the Scouting movement, perhaps, helped a natural tendency toward service. The writings of P. A. Taverner, ornithologist, Henry David Thoreau, naturalist-philosopher, plus those of Peter McArthur and Robert Stead were certainly influential.

"I have always felt that writing for children is an important part of my work. A writer should exhibit sincerity, a feeling of accurate knowledge throughout his book. There should be a story achievement, even though it may contain some sadness. It should have believably natural characters, usually some humor, be of interest to both children and adults, having values which endure regardless of age, locality or era. A book may instruct,, but sarcasm and satire should never be used in children's literature.

"Two of the most gratifying honors that have come to me are the Vicky Metcalf Award, and the librarians' estimate in 1969 that 500,000 Canadian children annually read my books.

"Two of the most interesting audiences I have ever addressed were the New York State Librarians in conference at Lake Placid, and a group of holidayers under the auspices of the Institute of the Blind at Sylvan Lake, Alberta. The former: listeners kept rising and leaving the hall, then returning with many more delegates in tow! The latter: I had gauged my talk to be attuned to their ears and what nature they were hearing, rather than to their eyes and what they might see around their camping area. Both groups' responses were tremendously enthusiastic.

"Of very great influence and help in my lifetime have been the members of my family: my elder brother, Thaddy, until his death in 1918, my father throughout his life, and my wife, Marjorie, and our three children. Marjorie's encouragement and assistance in our forty years of happy marriage have been of considerable strength to me."

AVOCATIONAL INTERESTS: Walking, nature observations, nature-oriented handicrafts (especially archery and wood carving).

BIOGRAPHICAL/CRITICAL SOURCES: Calgary Herald, May 5, 1965; *Vancouver Sun,* February 10, 1967; *Ottawa Citizen,* September 20, 1969; *Western Producer,* August 30, 1973; *Red Deer Advocate,* June 2-June 15, 1976.

*   *   *

WOOD, Gordon R(eid)   1913-

PERSONAL: Born February 27, 1913, in Charleston, W.Va.; son of Gordon G. and Doll (Reid) Wood; married wife, Sara, 1946; children: Reid. *Education:* Davidson College, A.B., 1935; Duke University, M.A., 1937; Princeton University, A.M. and Ph.D., 1941. *Office:* Department of

English, Southern Illinois University, Edwardsville, Ill. 62025.

CAREER: Appalachian State Teachers College (now Appalachian State University), Boone, N.C., assistant professor of English, 1941-42; Davidson College, Davidson, N.C., assistant professor of English, 1946-48; University of Chattanooga, Chattanooga, Tenn., associate professor, 1948-58, professor of English, 1958-63; Southern Illinois University, Edwardsville, professor of English, 1963—, chairman of department, 1964-66. *Military service:* U.S. Army, 1941-46, instructor at U.S. Army University in France, 1945-46. U.S. Army Reserve, 1946-63; became lieutenant colonel.

MEMBER: American Association of University Professors, American Dialect Society, Association for Computer Linguistics, Modern Language Association of America, South Atlantic Modern Language Association, Midwest Modern Language Association, Phi Beta Kappa. *Awards, honors:* Grants from Carnegie Foundation, 1947, 1950, Southern Fellowship Fund, 1955, American Philosophical Society, 1960, and National Council of Teachers of English, 1971-72.

WRITINGS: (With Frederic G. Cassidy) *A List of Words from Tennessee* [and] *Report of a Recent Project of Collecting* (the former by Wood, the latter by Cassidy), University of Alabama Press, 1958; *Word Distribution in the Interior South,* University of Alabama Press, 1961; *Dialectology by Computer,* International Conference on Computer Linguistics, 1969; *Vocabulary Change: A Study of Variation in Regional Words in Eight of the Southern States,* Southern Illinois University Press, 1970; (contributor) *Dialectology: Problems and Perspectives,* University of Tennessee Press, 1971. Contributor to speech and language journals.

WORK IN PROGRESS: A computer-assisted analysis of Sidney's sonnet style.

*   *   *

WOOD, John Thomas   1939-

PERSONAL: Born June 10, 1939, in Washington, D.C.; son of Thomas E. and Lula (Brown) Wood; children: Greg, Chris. *Education:* Attended University of Virginia, 1958-59; San Diego State University, B.A., 1962; Union Graduate School, Ph.D., 1978. *Office:* Center for Studies of the Person, 1125 Torrey Pines Rd., La Jolla, Calif. 92037.

CAREER: Center for Studies of the Person, La Jolla, Calif., staff member and group leader, 1969—. Instructor at San Diego State University, 1976, 1977, and University of California, San Diego.

WRITINGS: How Do You Feel? (non-fiction), Prentice-Hall, 1974; *What Are You Afraid Of?* (non-fiction), Prentice-Hall, 1975; *Love Poems to Someone Else,* Bear Pause Press, 1976. Part-time correspondent for *Time,* 1973-77.

WORK IN PROGRESS: Growing Up Male, "in search of the essence of a man-child."

SIDELIGHTS: Woods told *CA:* "*How Do You Feel?* is a very personal book, a series of first person statements from me and my colleagues about thirty-one different feelings. *What Are You Afraid Of?* is less personal, more an exploration of what fear is and how it affects our lives and how we can use it in a more positive way. *Growing Up Male* is an autobiographical study of how one man learned his masculine behavior. It is heavy with memoirs, anecdotes, heroes, and family photos."

WOOD, Kerry
    See WOOD, Edgar A(llardyce)

*   *   *

WOOD, Peggy   1892-1978

February 9, 1892—March 18, 1978; American stage, screen, and television actress, singer and author. Wood reached stardom in 1917, with her performance in Maytime, but is most widely remembered as the Norwegian mother in the CBS-TV series "Mama" which ran from 1947 through 1957. Noel Coward's "Blithe Spirit," which opened in 1942, was a highlight in Wood's career; she performed in the play as a USO entertainer in England and France. In 1966 she was nominated for an Academy Award as best supporting actress for her portrayal of the Mother Superior in "The Sound of Music." Wood taught acting classes in New York universities and was president of the American National Theatre and Academy from 1959 to 1966. Her autobiography, *How Young You Look: Memoirs of a Middle-Sized Actress,* was published in 1941, and *Arts and Flowers,* a memoir of her career, was published in 1963. She was an author of other books, as well as articles about the entertainment industry for newspapers and magazines. Wood died in Stamford, Conn. Obituaries and other sources: *Current Biography,* Wilson, 1942, 1953, May, 1968; *The Biographical Enclopaedia and Who's Who of the American Theatre,* James Heineman, 1966; *Who's Who in the East,* 14th edition, Marquis, 1973; *International Motion Picture Almanac,* Quigley, 1975; *Who's Who in the Theatre,* 16th edition, Pitman, 1977; *New York Times,* March 19, 1978; *Time,* April 4, 1978.

*   *   *

**WOODHAM-SMITH, Cecil (Blanche Fitzgerald) 1896-1977
(Janet Gordon)**

PERSONAL: Born in 1896, in Tenby, Wales; daughter of James (a military officer) and Blanche Elizabeth (Philipps) Fitzgerald; married George Ivon Woodham-Smith (a solicitor), April 3, 1928 (died, 1968); children: Elizabeth Sarah (Mrs. B.B.W. Goodden), Charles James. *Education:* Graduated from St. Hilda's College, Oxford. *Home:* 44 Mount St., London W.1, England.

CAREER: Writer, biographer, and historian. Worked in an advertising agency until 1928. *Awards, honors:* Awarded James Tait Black Memorial Prize, 1950, for *Florence Nightingale;* named Commander of the Order of the British Empire, 1960; D.Litt from National University of Ireland, 1964, and St. Andrew's University, 1965; named honorary fellow of St. Hilda's College, Oxford, 1967; awarded A.C. Benson Medal for contributions to literature, 1969.

WRITINGS: Florence Nightingale, 1820-1910, Constable, 1950, McGraw, 1951, abridged version published as *Lonely Crusader: The Life of Florence Nightingale, 1820-1910,* Whittlesey House, 1951 (published in England as *Lady-in-Chief: The Story of Florence Nightingale,* Metheuen, 1953); *The Reason Why,* McGraw, 1953, 2nd edition, 1971, original edition published as *The Charge of the Light Brigade,* New American Library, 1953; *The Great Hunger: Ireland 1845-1849,* Harper, 1962; *Queen Victoria: Her Life and Times,* Hamish Hamilton, 1972, published as *Queen Victoria: From Her Birth to the Death of the Prince Consort,* Knopf, 1972.

Under pseudonym Janet Gordon: *April Sky,* Hutchinson, 1938; *Tennis Star,* Hutchinson, 1939; *Just Off Bond Street,* Hurst, 1940.

WORK IN PROGRESS: A second volume of her biography of Queen Victoria.

SIDELIGHTS: Woodham-Smith summarized her views on the writing of history: "The historian's task is to make the past live again, to find out the truth and make it real. He does not need the assistance of novelty to attract his readers, he needs historical imagination, the capacity so to live in the past that it becomes as actual as the present."

BIOGRAPHICAL/CRITICAL SOURCES: New York Times Book Review, July 1, 1954. Obituaries: *New York Times,* March 17, 1977; *Washington Post,* March 19, 1977; *Newsweek,* March 28, 1977; *Time,* March 28, 1977; *Current Biography,* May, 1977; *AB Bookman's Weekly,* May 9, 1977.*

(Died March 16, 1977, in London, England)

*   *   *

WOODS, William

PERSONAL: Born in New York; married Kato Havas (a violinist), May 17, 1940 (divorced, 1961); married Kit Pharaoh (a teacher), March 4, 1965; children: Susanna Woods Egan, Pamela Woods Thomas, Catherine, Alison, Jonathan, Jason, Thomasin. *Education:* University of North Carolina, B.A., 1936; University of Iowa, M.A., 1939. *Politics:* "Left." *Religion:* None. *Home:* Yat, Glascwm, Llandrindod Wells, Wales. *Agent:* Curtis Brown Ltd., 575 Madison Ave., New York, N.Y. 10022.

CAREER: Writer. Chairman of the village of Llandrindod Wells. *Military service:* U.S. Army, Infantry, 1942. *Member:* Royal Society of Literature (fellow), Savage Club.

WRITINGS: The Edge of Darkness, Lippincott, 1942; *The Street of Seven Monks,* Little, Brown, 1948; *Manuela,* Hill & Wang, 1957; *The Mask,* Hill & Wang, 1960; *A Mermaid in Nikoli,* Hill & Wang, 1967; *Poland: Eagle in the East,* Hill & Wang, 1969; *A History of the Devil,* Putnam, 1973; *A Casebook of Witchcraft,* Putnam, 1974; *England in the Age of Chaucer,* Stein & Day, 1976. Author of more than fifty television plays and six film scripts.

WORK IN PROGRESS: A biography of King Alfred.

SIDELIGHTS: Woods writes: "Nothing any author says about his own motivation is of the slightest value. And nothing he may feel about liberty, justice, truth, or the eternal verities can possibly be condensed into a paragraph. I have travelled America, Europe and parts of Africa. I speak German, Slovenian, French, some Polish. I know something of the Middle Ages and intend to know more. I love women, whisky, and literary history, not in any particular order of preference. I possess the best library of English poetry I know of in private hands. I enjoy life more than most, and if I were to drop dead tomorrow would consider I had been well served by my creator."

*   *   *

WOOLARD, Edgar   1899(?)-1978

1899(?)—June 17, 1978; American meteorologist, astronomer, educator and author. Woolard was director of the Nautical Almanac Office of the U.S. Naval Observatory and authored several books on meteorology and astronomy. He died in Kingman, Ariz. Obituaries and other sources: *Washington Post,* June 21, 1978.

*   *   *

WOOLDRIDGE, Rhoda   1906-

PERSONAL: Born May 25, 1906, in Buckner, Mo.; daughter of Walter James (a farmer) and Georgia (Tucker) Phillips; married Clinton Prather Wooldridge (a dentist), September 13, 1930 (died, 1962); children: Clinton Prather, Jr., Georgia Wooldridge Reardon. *Education:* Earned B.A. from University of Missouri; also attended Stephens College. *Politics:* Democrat. *Religion:* Methodist. *Home address:* Route 2, Independence, Mo. 64058.

CAREER: Writer, 1962—. Farmer in Independence, Mo. Historical consultant, 1968—.

WRITINGS: Hannah's Brave Year, Bobbs-Merrill, 1964; *That's the Way,* Bobbs-Merrill, 1965; *Hannah's House,* Independence Press (Independence, Mo.), 1971; *And Oh! How Proudly,* Independence Press (Independence, Mo.), 1972; *Chouteau and the Founding of St. Louis,* Independence Press (Independence, Mo.), 1975.

WORK IN PROGRESS: The Flood of Hannah's Town, based on the flood of the Missouri River in 1844.

SIDELIGHTS: "I started writing from need of a family," Wooldridge told *CA.* "My husband died suddenly and I was unprepared for being left alone. My daughter was in school at Missouri University at that time. I found it was more pleasant to spend time with her in Columbia and do research in the university archives than to rattle around alone in an oversize house."

* * *

WORTHLEY, Jean Reese 1925-

PERSONAL: Born February 23, 1925, in Pasadena, Calif.; daughter of Francis Sydney (a lawyer) and Waiva (Dean) Reese; married Elmer George Worthley (an environmentalist), June 19, 1948; children: Elmer George, Jr., William, Kimball, Waiva, Heather, Asa. *Education:* Goucher College, A.B., 1944; University of Massachusetts, M.S., 1948; University of Maryland, further graduate study, 1949-51. *Politics:* Republican. *Religion:* Episcopalian. *Home:* 11821 Bonita Ave., Owings Mills, Md. 21117. *Office:* Maryland Center for Public Broadcasting, Owings Mills, Md. 21117.

CAREER: Director and teacher at nursery school-kindergarten in Owings Mills, Md., 1955-69; Maryland Center for Public Broadcasting, Owings Mills, executive producer, 1969—, also presents the series "Hodgepodge Lodge." *Military service:* U.S. Navy, Women Accepted for Volunteer Emergency Service (WAVES), 1945-46. *Member:* National Association of Educational Broadcasters, American Nature Study Society, League of Women Voters, Maryland Congress of Parents and Teachers, Natural History Society of Maryland, Maryland Ornithological Society, Sierra Club, Wilson Society. *Awards, honors:* Ohio State Award, 1971, for television series "Hodgepodge Lodge"; national 4-H alumni award, 1973; Public Affairs Broadcasts award from Odyssey Institute, 1977, for "Day Care" series; International Meditation Society award, 1977, for "Inspiration and Information."

WRITINGS: The Complete Family Nature Guide, Doubleday, 1976.

SIDELIGHTS: Jean Worthley writes: "I feel very fortunate that the state of Maryland opted to build their public television center next to my family farm and that, because of my thirteen years of teaching other people's children and successfully coping with our own six, I managed to get my present job where I aim to acquaint a broad audience with the wonders of nature and important ecological principles. I am presently producing a new series with my husband, 'On Nature's Trail.'"

WREN, Thomas Edward 1938-

PERSONAL: Born July 16, 1938, in Kansas City, Mo.; son of Alfred A. and Mary (O'Connor) Wren; married Carol Thompson (a teacher), 1969; children: Kathleen. *Education:* St. Mary's College, Winona, Minn., B.A. (cum laude), 1959, M.Ed., 1965; De Paul University, M.A. (English), 1962; Loyola University, Chicago, Ill., M.A. (philosophy), 1965; Northwestern University, Ph.D., 1969. *Home:* 807 Hinman Ave., Evanston, Ill. 60202. *Office:* Department of Philosophy, Loyola University, 820 North Michigan, Chicago, Ill. 60611.

CAREER: St. Mary's College, Winona, Minn., instructor in philosophy, 1963; Lewis University, Lockport, Ill., instructor in philosophy, 1965; Loyola University, Chicago, Ill., instructor, 1966-67, assistant professor, 1968-73, associate professor of philosophy, 1973—. Lecturer at Northwestern University, 1967; lecturer at University of Maryland (in Rome, Italy), 1969; did research at University of Freiburg, summer, 1969, University of Tuebingen, summer, 1971, and Oxford University, 1976-77.

MEMBER: American Philosophical Association. *Awards, honors:* Fellowship from Northwestern University, 1968, and Carnegie Foundation Institute in Ethics, 1972; National Endowment for the Humanities grant, summer, 1975; Spencer Foundation grant, 1976; Loyola University grant, 1977.

WRITINGS: Agency and Urgency: The Origin of Moral Obligation, Precedent Publishing, 1974; (editor and contributor) *The Personal Universe: Essays in Honor of John Macmurray,* Humanities, 1975; (editor) *Revolution or Reform?: A Confrontation Between Karl Popper and Herbert Marcuse,* New University Press, 1976; (contributor) Florence Hestler and Lois Kutchner, editors, *Philosophical Aspects of Death and Dying,* MSS Press, 1978. Editor of series "Studies in Ethics and Society," for New University Press; consulting editor of *Listening.* Contributor to philosophy and psychology journals.

WORK IN PROGRESS: A monograph on moral psychology.

* * *

WRIGHT, Arthur Frederick 1913-1976

PERSONAL: Born December 3, 1913, in Portland, Ore.; son of Charles Frederick and Georgiana (Gwynne) Wright; married Mary Clabaugh (a professor of history), July 6, 1940 (died in June, 1970); married Marya Wankowicz Welch, March 4, 1972; children: (first marriage) Charles Duncan, Jonathan Arthur. *Education:* Stanford University, A.B., 1935; Oxford University, B.Litt., 1937; Harvard University, A.M., 1940, Ph.D., 1947. *Residence:* Guilford, Conn. *Office:* 328 Hall of Graduate Studies, Yale University, New Haven, Conn. 06520.

CAREER: Stanford University, Stanford, Calif., assistant professor, 1947-51, associate professor, 1951-58, professor of history, 1958-59, chairman of commission of East Asian research, 1956-59; Yale University, New Haven, Conn., professor, 1959-61, Charles Seymour Professor of History, 1961-76, executive secretary of Concilium of International Studies, 1961-65, chairman of council on East Asian studies, 1961-62, 1968-69. Chairman of Committee on Studies of Chinese Civilization of the American Council of Learned Societies, 1963-73. Member of board of governors of Institute of Current World Affairs, 1961-66. *Member:* American Historical Association, American Association of University Professors, Association for Asian Studies (member of board of directors, 1951-58; vice-president, 1963-64; president, 1964-65). *Awards, honors:* Rockefeller fellowship for Harvard University, 1937-39; Guggenheim fellowship for University of Kyoto, 1953-54; honorary M.A. from Yale University, 1959.

WRITINGS: (Editor) *Studies in Chinese Thought,* University of Chicago Press, 1953; *Buddhism in Chinese History,* Stanford University Press, 1959; (editor with David S. Nivison) *Confucianism in Action,* Stanford University Press, 1959; (editor) *The Confucian Persuasion,* Stanford University Press, 1960; (editor with Denis Twitchett) *Confucian Personalities,* Stanford University Press, 1962; (editor and author of introduction) *Confucianism and Chinese Civilization,* Atheneum, 1964; (editor) Etienne Balazs, *Chinese Civilization and Bureaucracy: Variations on a Theme,* Yale University Press, 1964; (editor with Twitchett) *Perspectives on the T'ang,* Yale University Press, 1973.

Far Eastern Quarterly, associate editor, 1950-51, editor, 1951-55; adviser to editorial board of *Encyclopaedia Britannica,* 1957-60.

SIDELIGHTS: Wright and his wife spent two and a half years in a prison camp after their arrest by Japanese authorities in Peking on December 7, 1941. They returned to Peking after World War II to study postwar conditions there. Wright also participated in an archaeological expedition to China in 1974.

OBITUARIES: New York Times, August 14, 1976.*

(Died August 11, 1976, in New London, Conn.)

* * *

WRIGHT, Benjamin Fletcher   1900-1976

PERSONAL: Born February 8, 1900, in Austin, Tex.; son of Benjamin Fletcher and Mary (Blandford) Wright; married Alexa Rhea, 1926; children: David, Janet (Mrs. Paul E. Jones, Jr.). *Education:* University of Texas, A.B. and A.M., 1921; Harvard University, Ph.D., 1925. *Home:* 1415 Walthen Ave., Austin, Tex. 78703.

CAREER: University of Texas, Austin, instructor, 1922-24, adjunct professor of government, 1925-26; Harvard University, Cambridge, Mass., instructor, 1926-28, assistant professor, 1928-40, associate professor, 1940-45, professor of government, 1945-49, chairman of department, 1942-46, chairman of committee on general education, 1946-49; Smith College, Northampton, Mass., president, 1949-59; Center for Advanced Studies in the Behavioral Sciences, Stanford, Calif., fellow, 1959-60; University of Texas, professor of government, 1960-75. Lowell Lecturer in Boston, 1947; member of faculty of Salzburg Seminar on American Studies, 1947, 1949; Bacon Lecturer at Boston University, 1957; Jefferson Memorial Lecturer at University of California, Berkeley, 1964; visiting professor of government at Harvard University, 1966-67. *Military service:* U.S. Army, Infantry, 1918. *Member:* American Academy of Arts and Sciences, American Political Science Association. *Awards, honors:* LL.D. from Amherst College, 1950, Mt. Holyoke College, 1958, and University of Pittsburgh, 1962; Litt.D. from American International College, 1958.

WRITINGS: The Merit System in American States, With Special Reference to Texas, University of Texas, 1923; *American Interpretations of Natural Law: A Study in the History of Political Thought,* Harvard University Press, 1931, reprinted, Russell, 1962; *The Contract Clause of the Constitution,* Harvard University Press, 1938; *The Growth of American Constitutional Law,* Houghton, 1942, reprint-

ed, University of Chicago Press, 1967; *Consensus and Continuity, 1776-1787,* Boston University Press, 1958; *Five Public Philosophies of Walter Lippmann,* University of Texas Press, 1973. Also co-author of *General Education in a Free Society.*

Editor: *A Source Book of American Political Theory,* Macmillan, 1929; John Calyer Ranney and Gwendolyn M. Carter, *The Major Foreign Powers: The Governments of Great Britain, France, the Soviet Union, and China,* Harcourt, 1949; Alexander Hamilton, *The Federalist,* Harvard University Press, 1961. Contributor to *Saturday Review* and other periodicals.

OBITUARIES: New York Times, November 30, 1976; *Current Biography,* March, 1977.*

(Died November 28, 1976, in Austin, Tex.)

* * *

WRIGHT, Cynthia Challed   1953-

PERSONAL: Born April 1, 1953, in Cedar Rapids, Iowa; daughter of Eugene Frank (a pharmacist) and Priscilla (Patterson) Challed; married Richard Wright (a naval officer), April 1, 1972; children: Jennifer Rae. *Education:* Attended University of Iowa, 1971-72. *Home:* 3 Fowler Court, New London, Conn. 06320.

CAREER: Writer, 1975—.

WRITINGS—Historical romances: *Caroline,* Ballantine, 1977; *Touch the Sun,* Ballantine, 1978.

WORK IN PROGRESS: A third historical romance, set in New London during the Revolutionary War; research for a fourth book, set in Rome around 100 A.D.

SIDELIGHTS: Cynthia Wright comments: "My career, which has just begun, is a dream come true for me. *Caroline* was my hobby. I knew the odds and had little hope of being published, yet I had to try. Now I believe in pursuing one's dreams, no matter how elusive they may seem.

"I chose historical romance. I enjoy writing love stories, and I also feel that they can have an impact on readers' lives. I avoid the violent, degrading aspects of the current genre, instead emphasizing women's strengths and capabilities. I try to leave the reader feeling positive about herself and her ability to deal with life."

AVOCATIONAL INTERESTS: Reading, exploring New England, European travel.

* * *

WRIGHT, Rosalie Muller   1942-

PERSONAL: Born June 20, 1942, in Newark, N.J.; daughter of Charles and Angela (Fortunato) Muller; married Lynn Wright, January 13, 1962 (divorced); children: James Anthony Meador II, Geoffrey Shepard. *Education:* Temple University, B.A., 1965. *Home:* 2036 Queens Lane, San Mateo, Calif. 94402. *Office: San Francisco Examiner,* 110 South 5th St., San Francisco, Calif. 94119.

CAREER/WRITINGS: Suburban Life, Orange, N.J., managing editor, 1960-62; *Philadelphia,* Philadelphia, Pa., assistant editor, 1963-64, managing editor, 1969-73; *Womensports,* San Mateo, Calif., editor, 1973-75; *City Magazine,* San Francisco, Calif., consulting editor, 1975-76; *San Francisco Examiner,* San Francisco, scene editor, 1976—. Lecturer, University of California at Berkeley. Contributor to *Compton's Encyclopedia,* 1975. *Member:* Old Town Historical Society (Philadelphia; member of board of directors, 1971-73), Sigma Delta Chi. *Awards, honors:* Penney-Missouri award from *Womensport*, 1974, for editorial excellence.

* * *

WRISTON, Henry M(erritt) 1889-1978

July 4, 1889—March 8, 1978; American university president, government servant, and author. Wriston was a professor at Wesleyan University before serving as president of Lawrence College (now University) until 1937, and Brown University until 1955. Never limiting himself to the academic world, he served on several governmental committees and is credited with instituting the 1950's reforms making the U.S. Foreign Service more efficient. Wriston was also president of the American Assembly, the Council on Foreign Relations, and both the Association of American Colleges and the Association of American Universities. The recipient of thirty-four honorary degrees, he authored numerous books, including *Diplomacy in a Democracy* and *Rugged Individualism*. Wriston died in New York, N.Y. Obituaries and other sources: *Current Biography*, Wilson, 1952, May, 1978; *Who's Who in America*, 39th edition, Marquis, 1976; *The International Who's Who*, Europa, 1977; *Washington Post*, March 9, 1978. (See index for *CA* sketch)

* * *

WUORIO, Eva-Lis 1918-

PERSONAL: Name is pronounced A-va-lees *Worr*-y-oh; born in 1918, in Finland; emigrated to Canada about 1929. *Education:* Educated in Finland and Canada.

CAREER: Employed by *Toronto Evening Telegram* and *Toronto Globe and Mail;* became assistant editor for *Maclean's Magazine;* author. *Awards, honors:* The Island of Fish in the Trees was selected by the *New York Times* as one of the Best Illustrated Children's Books of the Year in 1962.

WRITINGS: Return of the Viking (illustrated by William Winter), Clarke, Irwin, 1955; *The Canadian Twins* (illustrated by Balant S. Biro), J. Cape, 1956; *The Island of Fish in the Trees* (illustrated by Edward Ardizzone), World Publishing, 1962; *The Woman with the Portuguese Basket*, Dobson, 1963, Holt, 1964; *The Land of Right Up and Down* (illustrated by Ardizzone), World Publishing, 1964; *Tal and the Magic Barruget* (illustrated by Bettina Bauer Ehrlich), World Publishing, 1965; *Z for Zaborra*, Dobson, 1965, Holt, 1966; *Midsummer Lokki*, Holt, 1966; *October Treasure* (illustrated by Carolyn Cather), Holt, 1966; *Forbidden Adventure* (illustrated by Bernadette Watts), Whiting & Wheaton, 1967; *Kali and the Golden Mirror* (illustrated by Ardizzone), World Publishing, 1967; *Venture at Midsummer*, Holt, 1967; *Save Alice!*, Holt, 1968; *The Happiness Flower* (illustrated by Don Bolognese), World Publishing, 1969; *The Singing Canoe* (illustrated by Irving Boker), World Publishing, 1969; *Code: Polonaise*, Holt, 1971; *To Fight in Silence*, Holt, 1973.

SIDELIGHTS: Though Eva-Lis Wuorio left Finland for Canada at the age of eleven, she carried with pride her vivid images of that Scandinavian country. The author often relied on her first-hand knowledge of the Finnish culture and history in setting up the background for her stories. In *Midsummer Lokki* she wove a tale of international intrigue involving a young Canadian of Finnish heritage. "Along with good mystery and action is a complete, enticing travelog of Finland," wrote a critic for *Publishers Weekly*. However, a reviewer for the *New York Times Book Review* observed: "She [Wuorio] doesn't handle her male protagonist convinc-

ingly . . . and she applies a serious treatment to a light and foolish plot of international malefaction. What keeps one reading is a great deal of Finnish local color, culture and history. . . ."

The author spent several months on the island of Skyros (located on the Aegean Sea) and incorporated its atmosphere in her book, *Kali and the Golden Mirror*. The plot dealt with a young girl on an archaeological dig, but as in Wuorio's previous books, it was the story's descriptive location that attracted the critic's eye. "Eva-Lis Wuorio has brought the physical beauty of her milieu into sharp focus and has sustained the spirit of the islanders," noted Shulamith Oppenheim in a review for the *New York Times*.

Wuorio continued to capture the mood and characterizations of a particular environment in her latest book, *To Fight in Silence*. In this suspenseful story the author focuses on the countries of Norway and Denmark during World War II. A reviewer for the *Bulletin of the Center for Children's Books* wrote, "The pace is fast and exciting, the characters well-defined, the setting vividly evoked."

BIOGRAPHICAL/CRITICAL SOURCES: Saturday Review, November 10, 1962; *New York Times Book Review*, August 14, 1966, May 14, 1967, June 18, 1967; *Publishers Weekly*, January 30, 1967; *Bulletin of the Center for Children's Books*, November, 1973.*

* * *

WYCHERLEY, R(ichard) E(rnest) 1909-

PERSONAL: Born February 18, 1909, in Hadley, Shropshire, England; son of Richard Stanton (a furniture dealer) and Anne (Jennings) Wycherley; married Mabel Howden, April 2, 1937; children: Richard Donald. *Education:* Queen's College, Cambridge, B.A., 1930, M.A., 1936. *Home:* Orchard, Llangoed, Anglesey, Gwynedd LL58 8NR, Wales. *Office:* Department of Classics, University College of North Wales, Bangor, Gwynedd, Wales.

CAREER: University of Manchester, Manchester, England, lecturer in classics, 1932-45; University College of North Wales, Bangor, professor of Greek, 1945-74, professor emeritus, 1974—. Visiting member at Princeton University's Institute for Advanced Study, 1951-52, 1957-58, 1966-67. *Military service:* British Home Guard, 1940-45. *Member:* Classical Association, Society for the Promotion of Hellenic Studies, Anglesey Antiquarians.

WRITINGS: Companion Volume to Pausanias, Heinemann, 1935, 2nd edition, 1955; *How the Greeks Built Cities*, Macmillan (England), 1949, 2nd edition, 1962, Norton, 1976; *Athenian Agora*, Volume III: *Literary and Epigraphical Testimonia*, American School of Classical Studies, Princeton University Press, 1957, (with H. A. Thompson) Volume XIV: *The Agora of Athens*, Princeton University Press, 1972; *The Stones of Athens*, Princeton University Press, 1978. Contributor to archaeology and classical studies journals, and to newspapers.

WORK IN PROGRESS: A book about a representative series of about twelve Greek cities.

SIDELIGHTS: Wycherley comments: "In teaching I have covered a wide field in classics, both in Greek and Latin and in classical studies without the languages. In writing for publication I have made it my chief job to combine the results of archaeological work with literary studies so as to get a better understanding of the life of the ancient Greek cities, especially Athens."

AVOCATIONAL INTERESTS: Travel, gardening, wine making.

WYNAND, Derk 1944-

PERSONAL: Born June 12, 1944, in Bad Suderode, Germany; son of Jan W. (an engineer) and Odette E. (Bergamy) Wynand; married W. Eva Kortemme, May 8, 1971. *Education:* University of British Columbia, B.A., 1966, M.A., 1969. *Home:* 440 Simcoe St., #430, Victoria, British Columbia, Canada V8V 1L3. *Office:* Department of Creative Writing, University of Victoria, Victoria, British Columbia, Canada.

CAREER: University of Victoria, Victoria, British Columbia, visiting lecturer, 1969-71, lecturer in English, 1971-73, assistant professor of creative writing, 1973—. *Member:* American Literary Translators Association. *Awards, honors:* French Government Book Award, 1963, for proficiency in French; Canada Council grants, 1969, 1976.

WRITINGS: Locus, Fiddlehead Poetry Books, 1971; *Snowscapes* (poems and prose poems), Sono Nis Press, 1974; *Pointwise,* Fiddlehead Poetry Books, 1979.

Author of "Cyanide" (radio play), Canadian Broadcasting Corp., 1975. Contributor of more than a hundred poems and translations to literary journals, including *Fiddlehead, Expression,* and *Chicago Review.* Guest editor of *Malahat Review,* 1976.

WORK IN PROGRESS: Second Person, a book of poems; *One Cook, Once Dreaming,* "a book of approximate fables, prose poems, and short stories."

SIDELIGHTS: Wynand writes: "Though I write mostly poetry and prose pieces, I am intrigued by the possibilities of the 'new radio play' written in Germany and Austria. The Canadian Broadcasting Corp. has broadcast my translations of such plays by Dieter Wellershoff, Juergen Becker, Helmut Heissenbuettel, Wolf Wondratschek, Ernst Jandl, and Friederike Mayroecker. The rapidly aging 'new radio play,' influenced by Mallarme, Bense, Gage, and others, is less concerned than are most North American radio plays with verisimilitude (linear plots and 'realistic' interior monologues, etc.), but more with words and sounds as a semiotic system, with concrete music. This is not new to North American artists, of course, though it may well be to most of our producers."

*   *   *

WYSOR, Bettie 1928-

PERSONAL: Born June 28, 1928, in Lebanon, Va.; daughter of William Clearance (a contractor) and Stella (a teacher; maiden name, Snead) Wysor. *Education:* Attended Virginia Intermont College, 1946-48, and College of William and Mary, 1949. *Politics:* Democrat. *Religion:* Episcopal. *Home and office:* 151 East 83rd St., New York, N.Y. 10028. *Agent:* Roslyn Targ Literary Agency, Inc., 250 West 57th St., Suite 1932, New York, N.Y. 10019.

CAREER: Gas Appliance Manufacturer's Association, Washington, D.C., editor of *Newsletter,* 1950; Barter Theatre, Abingdon, Va., resident playwright, 1952; John Moses Associates, New York City, writer, 1953-54, assistant producer, 1953, producer, 1954; N. W. Ayer & Sons, Inc., New York City, advertising film writer, 1955-57; J. Walter Thompson, Inc., New York City, advertising film writer, 1958; Benton & Bowles, Inc., New York City, advertising film writer, 1959-61; D'Arcy, Inc., New York City, advertising film writer, 1962-64; free-lance magazine feature writer, 1965—. Consultant to Dramatists Guild.

MEMBER: Dramatists Guild, Authors League of America, American Archaeological Association, Audubon Society, Southampton Democratic Club. *Awards, honors:* Merit award from Advertising Writers Association of New York, 1963; first and second place in product category from American Television Festival, 1964.

WRITINGS: The Lesbian Myth: Conversations and Insights, Random House, 1974; *To Remember Tina,* Stein & Day, 1975.

Author of "Chessmen of Time" (dramatic poem), first performed in Abingdon, Va. at Barter Theatre, 1951; "Poet in Seven" (three-act play), first produced at Barter Theatre, 1952.

Writer of commercial-industrial films.

Author of column "Arts & Antiques—The Collectors" in *Arts and Antiques,* 1970-72. Contributor to popular magazines, including *Harper's Bazaar, Vogue, New Woman,* and *Ladies' Home Journal.* Contributing editor of *Town and Country;* editor of Dramatists Guild national newsletter.

WORK IN PROGRESS: The Scorpio Plan, a novel.

SIDELIGHTS: Wysor commented: "*The Lesbian Myth: Conversations & Insights* was a nonfiction exploration of social, theological, psychological, medical, and literary concepts of the subject, as well as conversations with women about their life-styles.

"*To Remember Tina* was based on a partially true story of an event which occurred during World War II, and was told to me by an American painter who lived on the Dalmation coast just prior to the outbreak of the war, and knew the leading character. Twenty years after he told me what he knew of the story, I was traveling in Yugoslavia and went to the island of Korcula, where Christina had lived during the war. I was able to locate some of the partisans who had been on the island and had participated in the event the book concerns—they told me the rest of the story the painter Edward Melcarth did not know. He died in Venice three months before the book was published—the book is dedicated to him."

One of Wysor's interests is Greco-Roman archaeology, and she has traveled extensively to sites in Greece, Turkey, and Italy.

AVOCATIONAL INTERESTS: Sailing and gardening.

Y

YAMADA, Mitsuye (May) 1923-

PERSONAL: Born July 5, 1923, in Fukuoka, Japan; came to the United States in 1926, naturalized citizen, 1955; daughter of Jack Kaichiro (an interpreter) and Hide (a seamstress; maiden name, Shiraki) Yasutake; married Yoshikazu Yamada (a research chemist); children: Jeni, Stephen, Douglas, Hedi. *Education:* New York University, B.A., 1947; University of Chicago, M.A., 1953; further graduate study at University of California, Irvine. *Home:* 6151 Sierra Bravo Rd., Irvine, Calif. 92715. *Office:* Department of English, Cypress College, 9200 Valley View Ave., Cypress, Calif. 90630.

CAREER: Fullerton College, Fullerton, Calif., instructor, 1966-69; Cypress College, Cypress, Calif., instructor, 1969-76, associate professor of English, 1976—, coordinator of women's program, 1975—. Lecturer at workshops and women's conferences. Has given poetry readings in California.

MEMBER: International Women's Writing Guild, Amnesty International, National Women's Political Caucus, Council for Interracial Books, American Civil Liberties Union, Center for the Study of Democratic Institutions, Academy of American Poets, Poets and Writers, Pacific Asian American Center (member of board of directors; chairperson).

WRITINGS: Camp Notes and Other Poems, Shameless Hussy Press, 1976.

Work anthologized in *Poetry from Violence,* Lighthouse, 1976; *The Japanese-American Anthology,* 1976. Contributor to literary magazines, including *Velvet Wings, Willmore City,* and *Plexus.*

WORK IN PROGRESS: A novel; a theater project focusing on the Asian American women's experience.

SIDELIGHTS: Mitsuye Yamada's parents were U.S. residents at the time of her birth, merely making a brief visit to Japan in 1923. She spent most of her childhood in Seattle, and some time during World War II in Minidoka Relocation Center in Idaho.

She writes: "Poetry to me means making connections. Poetry simply tells what is happening. I can express in poetry what is happening to me better than any other genre, because what is happening now is invariably closely linked with what has happened in the past. Poetry is then a continuous process of making connections as I live my life. It holds my life together. It keeps me connected to the people and events around me.

"I find myself, as I get older, assuming a more political stance in my writings. I have moved from writing intensely personal poetry to writing essays on social and political issues. The reason for this progression in my writings (some of my poet friends tell me that it is regression) is that my identity as an Asian American and my identity as a woman is just beginning to merge within me as a singular identity and I am feeling a missionary zeal to let others know about it."

* * *

YAMAMOTO, J(erry) Isamu 1947-

PERSONAL: Born December 9, 1947, in Denver, Colo.; son of Shuichi (a gardener) and Agnes Yamamoto. *Education:* San Jose State University, A.B., 1971. *Politics:* Independent. *Religion:* Christian. *Residence:* San Jose, Calif. *Office:* Spiritual Counterfeits Project, 1925 Vine, Berkeley, Calif. 94709.

CAREER: Spiritual Counterfeits Project, Berkeley, Calif., staff writer, 1975—. *Member:* U.S. Chess Federation.

WRITINGS: The Moon Doctrine (booklet), Inter-Varsity Press, 1976; *The Puppet Master* (nonfiction), Inter-Varsity Press, 1977; *Hare Krishna* (booklet), Inter-Varsity Press, 1978.

WORK IN PROGRESS: Babylon Resurrected, nonfiction, publication expected in 1980.

SIDELIGHTS: Yamamoto writes: "I feel called by God to share the good news of Jesus Christ. That is why I am in a Christian ministry—the Berkeley Christian Coalition. I am interested in religious cults and the occult, and I have traveled through forty American states and Canada, speaking on that subject." *Avocational interests:* Chess, tennis, theater, literature.

* * *

YANEV, Peter (Ivanov) 1946-

PERSONAL: Born June 27, 1946, in Sofia, Bulgaria; came to the United States in 1961, naturalized citizen, 1974; son of Ivan P. (a diplomat) and Ivanka (an accountant; maiden name, Ivanova) Yanev; married Kay Marie Philbrick (a zoologist), July 9, 1971. *Education:* University of California, Berkeley, B.S., 1968; Massachusetts Institute of Technology, M.S., 1970. *Home:* 35 Glorietta Court, Orinda, Calif. 94563. *Office:* URS/J.A. Blume & Associates, 130 Jessie St., San Francisco, Calif. 94105.

CAREER: Bechtel Power Corp., San Francisco, Calif., civil and structural engineer, 1970-74; URS J.A. Blume & Associates, San Francisco, Calif., project manager, 1974—. Lecturer to technical and nontechnical audiences, including university students; guest on television and radio programs; consulting civil engineer. *Member:* Earthquake Engineering Research Institute, American Society of Civil Engineers, Seismological Society of America, American Nuclear Society, Structural Engineers Association of California.

WRITINGS: Peace of Mind in Earthquake Country, Chronicle Books, 1974. Author of "Living in Earthquake Country," a multi-media show at Oakland Museum. Contributor to technical and popular magazines.

SIDELIGHTS: Yanev writes: "My professional involvement includes large structures, from hospitals to refineries to nuclear power plants—primarily seismic and other safety-related designs. Since most people in the West and its earthquake areas live in small buildings that require minimal engineering attention, or have received none, I am continuing to attempt to educate these people about the realities of earthquakes. I am trying to dispel the various myths about quakes, and instead to describe the engineering solutions and scientific facts. I am working on the earthquake design (protection) of nuclear power plants and related experimental and waste (nuclear) storage facilities. Other research includes projects sponsored by the National Science Foundation and the U.S. Geological Survey. A particular interest involves the effects of earthquakes and other cataclysmic geologic events on history and archaeology from biblical times to the present."

AVOCATIONAL INTERESTS: Travel (Europe, Asia, Central America), skiing, photography, remodeling his home, history, archaeology, collecting stamps, geology.

*   *   *

YESELSON, Abraham   1921-1978

1921—May 3, 1978; American educator, labor consultant, authority on international affairs, lecturer, and author. Yeselson lectured for American universities, the U.S. Department of Labor, and appeared on several television programs. In 1975-76, Yeselson testified at the U.S. Senate's Foreign Relations Committee hearing as the Rutgers University delegate for the U.S. Mission to the United Nations. He wrote many articles and books on foreign policy and labor history. Yeselson died in New Brunswick, N.J. Obituaries and other sources: *New York Times,* May 5, 1978.

*   *   *

YOAKUM, Robert   1922-

PERSONAL: Born March 8, 1922, in Phoenix, Ariz.; son of Guy D. (a minister) and Eunice (Abbot) Yoakum; married Alice Blum (a lawyer), May 30, 1953; children: Elizabeth, Ellen, Robert. *Education:* Attended Northwestern University, 1940-42, and University of Chicago, 1945-47. *Religion:* "Agnostic." *Home:* Millerton Rd., Lakeville, Conn. 06039. *Agent:* Sterling Lord Agency, Inc., 660 Madison Ave., New York, N.Y. 10021. *Office:* Yoakum Features, Reservoir Rd., Lakeville, Conn. 06039.

CAREER/WRITINGS: Free-lance journalist in Europe, 1947-48; Reuters News Service, Paris, France, correspondent, 1948-49; *New York Herald Tribune,* New York, N.Y.,

Paris city editor, 1949-52; World Veterans Federation, Paris, deputy secretary general, 1952-56; free-lance journalist in Greenwich and Lakeville, Conn., 1956-72; columnist, 1972—. Notable assignments include series on the Marshall Plan, and coverage of French labor unions, North African independence movements, and congressional ethics. Author of syndicated humor column, "Another Look"; contributor to *Columbia Journalism Review.* Member of executive board of Center for Information on America in Washington, Conn., 1972—; president of Sharon Creative Arts Foundation, 1976—. *Military service:* U.S. Air Force, 1942-45; became staff sergeant; received Bronze Star and six battle stars.

SIDELIGHTS: Yoakum writes: "While city editor of the European edition of the *Herald Tribune* (now *International Herald Tribune*), I earned money on the side ($10) co-authoring an occasionally humorous column entitled 'Mostly About People.' The other by-line was Art Buchwald. I left the column and the paper for a long stint of world-saving and serious writing—afflictions inherited from my Congregational minister writer father, who did both better. During a year-long stay in London, I decided to return to humor writing, partly out of envy of Buchwald's success, partly because I enjoyed it more (and stopped feeling guilty about enjoying it more), partly because there was less competition, and partly because the world was pretty well saved. The first humor columns were printed in the *London Sunday Times,* in which they still occasionally appear."

*   *   *

YORKE, Ritchie   1944-

PERSONAL: Born January 12, 1944, in Brisbane, Australia; son of Alf George (a store executive) and Joyce (a nurse; maiden name, Hislop) Annable; married Annette Carter, April 9, 1966 (marriage ended, 1977); children: Samantha, Christie. *Education:* Educated in Australia. *Politics:* "Apolitical." *Religion:* "Nature as the Supreme God." *Home and office:* 15 Austin Crescent, Toronto, Ontario, Canada M5R 142.

CAREER: Sports reporter, newswriter, radio broadcaster, and rock music promoter in Brisbane, Australia, 1960-66; managed rock musician Normie Rowe and promoted Spencer Davis Group for Island Records, in England, 1966-67; worked in Toronto, Ontario, as writer of promotional copy for CTV and as broadcaster for CHUM-FM, 1967-70; free-lance writer, 1970—. Notable assignments include coverage of the Beatles breakup, and John and Yoko Lennon's "War Is Over" campaign. Talent consultant for several record companies. Canadian Composers, Authors, and Publishers Association. *Awards, honors:* Received Canadian Music Journalist of the Year award, 1971; syndicated documentary award from *Billboard,* 1977, for "The Evolution of Rock: The Music that Made the World Turn 'Round."

WRITINGS: Lowdown on the English Pop Scene, Horwitz, 1967; *Axes, Chops, and Licks,* Hurtig, 1971; (contributor) *The Rolling Stone Rock 'n' Roll Reader,* Bantam, 1974; *Into the Music: The Van Morrison Biography,* Charisma/Futura, 1975; *The Led Zeppelin Biography,* Two Continents, 1976; *The History of Rock 'n' Roll,* Two Continents, 1976; (contributor) *Montreux Jazz,* Editions de la Tour Laussanne (Switzerland), 1976. Also author of radio script "The Evolution of Rock: The Music That Made the World Turn 'Round."

Popular music critic and columnist for *Toronto Telegram* and *Toronto Globe and Mail,* 1967-70. Contributor to *Roll-*

ing Stone, Detroit Free Press, Los Angeles Times, Melody Maker, Circus, and other publications. Associate editor of Jazz and Pop, music editor of Modern Hi Fi, and Canadian editor of Billboard, all 1967-73.

WORK IN PROGRESS: "The creation of a serious novel set in these tormented times."

SIDELIGHTS: Yorke came to Canada in 1967 after declining an offer to manage British rock group "Traffic." An ambitious rock critic and promoter, Yorke was appalled at the pop music situation in Canada. "The way that the press responded to Canadian artists simply amazed me," he said. "Canadian artists were always cut up so badly, and the headline artists, usually American, always praised out of all proportion, even when they were inferior." Yorke began "exposing the nonsense and supporting the Canadian scene." He organized the Maple Music Junkit which brought European pop figures to Canada to hear Canadian pop music, arranged the Procol Harum-Edmonton Symphony concert which resulted in a gold album, and quit newspaper work to join John Lennon's "War Is Over" campaign. Yorke's actions were cited by Canadian radio-Television Commission chairman, Pierre Juneau: "Much credit for the success of Canadian pop music must go to the specialists—pop music reporters and columnists such as Ritchie Yorke." Yorke's Axes, Chops, and Licks was instrumental in drawing attention to Canadian pop groups as a separate entity from their American counterparts. Yorke said: "Kids seem to believe in Canada now—but the cultural overspill almost drown us. The American dream used to be the Canadian dream, too."

Yorke was among the first pop music journalists to support the British rock group Led Zeppelin. A follower since the band's early days, Yorke emceed many of their concerts and eventually documented their rise in The Led Zeppelin Biography. Yorke claims his journalistic approach was the reason he could establish a comradery with Led Zeppelin. "I used to be a critic," he said, "but later, I just interviewed. This is the era of the non-critic. There's no room for critics on pop music because people don't need them. People make their own judgments."

Yorke's position in the pop music world has afforded him an insider's view of the action. His insight has provided an objective, if cynical, perspective: "The promise of the sixties was so deep, so committed. If only all the kids in the world could get together—we were such idealists. And now it's all come down to millionaires making a quarter of a million more dollars in a couple of hours."

BIOGRAPHICAL/CRITICAL SOURCES: Miss Chatelaine, summer, 1972; Canadian Composer, October, 1976.

*   *   *

YOSELOFF, Thomas 1913-
(Thomas Young)

PERSONAL: Born September 8, 1913, in Sioux, Iowa; son of Morris and Sarah (Robinowitz) Yoseloff; married Sara Rothfuss, April 30, 1938 (marriage ended); married Lauretta Sellitti, April 23, 1964; children: (first marriage) Julien David, Mark Lawrence; (second marriage) Tamar Rachel. Education: University of Iowa, A.B., 1934. Home address: Montrose Rd., Colts Neck, N.J. 07722. Office: A. S. Barnes & Co., Inc., Forsgate Dr., Cranbury, N.J. 08512.

CAREER: A. S. Barnes & Co., Inc., Cranbury, N.J., president, 1958-70, chairman of board of directors, 1970—. President and chairman of board of directors of Rosemont Pub-

lishing & Printing Corp., 1969—; chairman of board of directors of Associated University presses, 1969—. Member: Phi Beta Kappa, Sigma Delta Chi, Delta Sigma Rho. Awards, honors: Award of merit from Bucknell University, 1975.

WRITINGS: (Under pseudonym Thomas Young) Profit in Postage Stamps: A Study of Mint United States Issues as an Investment, Harbinger House, 1940, 2nd edition, B. Ackerman, 1945; (under pseudonym Thomas Young) Dogs for Democracy: The Story of America's Canine Heroes in the Global War, B. Ackerman, 1944; (with Lillian Stuckey) The Merry Adventures of Till Eulenspiegel, B. Ackerman, 1944; (editor) Seven Poets in Search of an Answer: A Poetic Symposium, B. Ackerman, 1944; A Fellow of Infinite Jest, Prentice-Hall, 1945, reprinted, Greenwood Press, 1970; The Further Adventures of Till Eulenspiegel, T. Yoseloff, 1957; (editor) Voyage to America, A. S. Barnes, 1961; (editor) Comic Almanac, A. S. Barnes, 1963; The Time of My Life, A. S. Barnes, 1978.

*   *   *

YOUD, Samuel 1922-
(John Christopher, Hilary Ford, William Godfrey, Peter Graaf, Peter Nichols, Anthony Rye)

PERSONAL: Born in 1922, in Knowsley, Lancashire, England; children: one son, four daughters. Education: Attended Peter Symond's School, Winchester. Home: Guernsey, Channel Islands.

CAREER: Novelist and author of books for young people. Free-lance writer, 1946-48; worked in information bureau of diamond cutting organization, 1948-58; full time professional writer, 1958—. Military service: British Army. Awards, honors: Rockefeller Foundation Grant, 1946-48; Christopher Award, 1970, for The Guardians; Guardian Award for Children's Fiction, 1971, for The Guardians.

WRITINGS: Babel Itself, Cassell, 1951; The Brave Conquerors, Cassell, 1952; Crown and Anchor, Cassell, 1953; Palace of Strangers, Cassell, 1954; The Opportunist, Harper, 1955 (published in England as Holly Ash, Cassell, 1955); The Choice, Simon & Schuster, 1961; Messages of Love, Simon & Schuster, 1961; The Summers at Accorn, Longmans, Green, 1963; The Burning Bird, Longmans, Green, 1964.

Under pseudonym John Christopher: The Twenty-Second Century, Grayson, 1954; The Year of the Comet, M. Joseph, 1955; No Blade of Grass, Avon, 1956 (published in England as The Death of Grass, M. Joseph, 1956); The Caves of Night, Simon & Schuster, 1959; The White Voyage, Simon & Schuster, 1960 (published in England as The Long Voyage, Eyre & Spottiswoode, 1960); The Long Winter, Simon & Schuster, 1962 (published in England as The World of Winter, Eyre & Spottiswoode, 1962); Sweeney's Island, Simon & Schuster, 1964 (published in England as Cloud on Silver, Hodder, Stoughton, 1964); The Possessors, Simon & Schuster, 1965; The Ragged Edge, Simon & Schuster, 1966 (published in England as A Wrinkle in the Skin, Hodder & Stoughton, 1965); The Little People, Simon & Schuster, 1967; Wild Jack, Macmillan, 1974.

Under pseudonym John Christopher; for young people: The Tripod Trilogy, Macmillan, Book I: The White Mountains, 1967, Book II: The City of Gold and Lead, 1967, Book III: The Pool of Fire, 1968; Pendulum, Simon & Schuster, 1968; The Lotus Caves, Macmillan, 1969; The Guardians, Macmillan, 1970; The Prince in Waiting, Macmillan, 1970; Beyond the Burning Lands, Macmillan, 1971; The Sword of the

Spirits, Macmillan, 1972; *Dom and Va,* Macmillan, 1973.

Under pseudonym Hilary Ford: *Felix Walking,* Simon & Schuster, 1958; *Felix Running,* Eyre & Spottiswoode, 1959; *Bella on the Roof,* Longmans, Green, 1965.

Under pseudonym William Godfrey: *Malleson at Melbourne,* Museum Press, 1956; *The Friendly Game,* M. Joseph, 1957.

Under pseudonym Peter Graaf: *Give the Devil His Due,* Mill, 1957 (published in England as *Dust and the Curious Boy,* M. Joseph, 1957); *Daughter Fair,* M. Joseph, 1958; *The Sapphire Conference,* M. Joseph, 1959; *The Gull's Kiss,* P. Davies, 1962.

Under pseudonym Peter Nichols: *Patchwork of Death,* Holt, 1965.

Under pseudonym Anthony Rye: *The Inn of the Birds* (poems), J. Cape, 1947; *Giant's Arrow,* Gollancz, 1956, reprinted under the author's real name, Simon & Schuster, 1960; *Poems from Selborne,* Sidgwick, 1962; *Gilbert White and His Selborne,* Kimber, 1970.

SIDELIGHTS: Samuel Youd began his career writing traditional novels under his own name. While well received critically, they had very little success commercially. From the mid-1950's on, in an attempt to find a successful format, Youd experimented with almost every kind of novelistic genre, using a different pseudonym for each. Detective stories were written under the pseudonyms Peter Graaf and Peter Nichols, cricketing books under William Godfrey, and gay and funny farces concerning the tribulations of a novelist's rise to fame under the pseudonym Hilary Ford.

Youd's greatest success, however, has been achieved under the pseudonym John Christopher. In these books for adults, usually described as science fiction, the author is most concerned with the way in which human behavior patterns are altered under stress. *No Blade of Grass* tells the story of the near future, in which a plague, starting in China, destroys all of the grasslands of Asia and Europe. The book describes the attempt of one group of English people who try to get from London to an isolated farm in western England.

The Long Winter describes the second Ice Age and the subsequent migration of people to the south. The *Chicago Tribune* commented: "Christopher's invention is appallingly plausible, and so is the wealth of detail with which he builds up his picture. The life of English refugees in Lagos, for example, is based beyond doubt on the whole history of refugees in our time, combined with the special aspects of Negro life in the Union of South Africa. It is out of such materials that this chillingly impressive book has been compounded."

According to John Rowe Townsend in *A Sense of Story:* "The adult novels contain a good deal of sex and violence: not automatically 'unsuitable' for children, who are well enough aware that sex and violence exist, but here handled in a way that requires an adult understanding and frame of reference. Sex is not simply a matter of the sexual act; it is a force working on people in obscure and powerful ways. Violence in these novels is no mere 'bang-you're-dead' matter; it can be disturbingly brutal and casual, or the outcome of complicated social and psychological processes."

The John Christopher books for children assume that the reader has less knowledge and experience of the world, but not less intelligence. They are very serious and show the author at his best. *The White Mountains* is the first book in the "Tripod" trilogy, and was described by the *London Times* as: "A remarkable story, somewhat abruptly concluded. It belongs to the school of science-fiction which puts

philosophy before technology and is not afraid of telling an exciting story." The *Christian Science Monitor* commented: "It doesn't matter whether or not one has read the earlier books of the trilogy, each stands by itself and each tells a good straight yarn."

BIOGRAPHICAL/CRITICAL SOURCES: Chicago Tribune, July 1, 1962; *Times* (London), May 25, 1967; *Christian Science Monitor,* November 7, 1968; John Rowe Townsend, *A Sense of Story,* Longman, 1971.*

*   *   *

YOUMANS, Marlene   1953-

PERSONAL: Born November 22, 1953, in Aiken, S.C.; daughter of Hubert L. (a professor of chemistry) and Mary (a librarian; maiden name, Morris) Youmans. *Education:* Hollins College, B.A., 1974; Brown University, M.A., 1976; doctoral study at University of North Carolina, 1976—. *Religion:* Christian. *Address:* c/o P.O. Box 375A, Cullowhee, N.C. 28723 (permanent); and 501 North Greensboro St., Carrboro, N.C. 27510. *Office:* Office 310, Greenlaw Hall, University of North Carolina, Chapel Hill, N.C. 27514.

CAREER: University of North Carolina at Chapel Hill, teaching assistant in English, 1977—. Teacher at Sanford, N.C. Senior Citizens Humanities Center, 1977. *Awards, honors:* Gertrude Claytor Prize from Academy of American Poets, 1974.

WRITINGS: (Contributor) David Clouthier, editor, *Copper Beech Translations,* Copper Beech Press, 1975; (with Paul Acker and Paul Corrigan) *A Terse Set* (poems), Windfall Press, 1976.

Work represented in *Intro Eight,* Doubleday. Contributor of poems to literary magazines, including *South Carolina Review, Black Warrior Review, Southern Poetry Review,* and *Hanging Loose.*

WORK IN PROGRESS: Melancholy: or, the Yellow Boat, poems.

SIDELIGHTS: Youmans told *CA:* "I ask from my poems that their ideas, things, and emotions be sensuous, graspable, that they be as carefully fitted and jointured as a carpenter's desk, that they hunt out what is intense and common, 'avoicing' as far as possible realms of escape and unattainable perfections."

*   *   *

YOUNG, Norman J(ames)   1930-

PERSONAL: Born July 31, 1930, in Australia; son of Andrew (a builder) and Doris (Christie) Young; married Barbara Mae Silver (a secretary), August 28, 1954; children: Graeme, Paul. *Education:* University of Melbourne, B.A. (honors), 1953; Drew Theological Seminary, B.D. (summa cum laude), 1956; Drew University, Ph.D., 1959. *Home and office:* 4 Queen's College, Parkville, Victoria 3052, Australia.

CAREER: Ordained Methodist minister; pastor of churches in Melbourne, Victoria, Australia, 1954, and in Summit, N.J., 1955-59; Drew University, Madison, N.J., lecturer in philosophy, 1958-59; King's College, Brisbane, Australia, lecturer in theology and deputy master, 1960-63; University of Melbourne, Queen's College, Melbourne, Australia, professor of theology, 1964—. President of Victorian Methodist Conference, 1975-77. *Awards, honors:* Tipple fellowship for Drew University.

WRITINGS: History and Existential Theology, Westminster, 1969; *Creator, Creation, and Faith,* Westminster, 1976.

WORK IN PROGRESS: Research on the variation in views concerning the relationship between the first-century Jesus and the twentieth-century social ethics.

SIDELIGHTS: Young writes: "My main motivation in writing is to make available to those not necessarily trained in theology the relevance of recent scholarly research and writing in the area of theology and Biblical study. I have been preoccupied for many years with the ecumenical movement, actively involved in Australia and at the world level."

* * *

YOUNG, Thomas
 See YOSELOFF, Thomas

Z

ZALESKI, Eugene 1918-

PERSONAL: Born August 27, 1918, in Lwow, Poland; son of Eugeniusz (a lawyer) and Jadwiga (Umanska) Zaleski; married Isabelle Cotton (a civil servant), June 15, 1950; children: Stephane. *Education:* University of Jean Casimir (Poland), M.Law, 1940; University of Paris, J.D., 1949; Ecole Pratique des Hautes Etudes (Sorbonne), diploma, 1961. *Religion:* Roman Catholic. *Residence:* Paris, France. *Office:* Centre National de la Recherche Scientifique, E.R. 129, 27 rue Paul-Bert, 94200 Ivry, France.

CAREER: Centre National de la Recherche Scientifique (University Secretariat), Paris, France, researchist, 1951-62, research director, 1962-67, director of economic research, 1968—. Professor at Institut d'Etudes Politiques, Paris, 1969—; professor at University of Paris, 1975—. *Military service:* Polish Army, 1942-48. *Awards, honors:* Silver Medal from Centre National de la Recherche Scientifique, 1963.

WRITINGS: Les Courants commerciaux de l'Europe danubienne au cours de la premiere moitie du vingtieme siecle (title means "The Commercial Currents of Eastern Europe during the First Half of the Twentieth Century"), Librairie generale de droit et de jurisprudence, 1952; *Mouvements ouvriers et socialistes: Chronologie et bibliographie* (title means "Worker and Socialist Movements: Chronology and Bibliography"), two volumes, Editions Ouvrieres, 1956-57.

Planification de la croissance et fluctuations economiques en U.R.S.S., Societe d'edition d'enseignement superieur, Volume I: *1918-1932,* 1962, translation by Marie-Christine MacAndrew and G. Warren Nutter published as *Planning for Economic Growth in the Soviet Union, 1918-1932,* University of North Carolina Press, 1971, Volume II: *1933-52,* 1978, translation by MacAndrew and John H. Moore published as *Stalinist Planning for Economic Growth, 1933-52,* University of North Carolina Press, 1978; *Planning Reforms in the Soviet Union, 1962-66,* translated by MacAndrew and Nutter, University of North Carolina Press, 1967; (with J. P. Kozlowski, H. Wienert, R. W. Davies, M. J. Berry, and R. Amann) *Science Policy in the U.S.S.R.,* Organisation for Economic Cooperation and Development (Paris), 1969.

Editor of *Revue d'Etudes Comparatives Est-Ouest,* 1970—.

ZALLER, Robert 1940-

PERSONAL: Born March 19, 1940, in New York, N.Y.; son of Abraham Morris (an attorney) and Sylvia (Borenstein) Zaller; married Lili Bita (a writer and actress), January 19, 1968; children: Philip Rethis, Kimon Rethis (stepchildren). *Education:* Queens College (now of the City University of New York), B.A., 1960; graduate study at Brown University, 1960-61; Washington University, St. Louis, Mo., M.A., 1963, Ph.D., 1968. *Home:* 5901 Southwest 51st St., Miami, Fla. 33155. *Office:* Department of History, University of Miami, Coral Gables, Fla. 33124.

CAREER: Queens College of the City University of New York, Flushing, N.Y., lecturer in history, 1967-68; University of California, Santa Barbara, visiting assistant professor of history, 1968-69; Nassau Community College, Garden City, N.Y., visiting assistant professor of sociology, 1970-72; University of Miami, Coral Gables, Fla., assistant professor, 1972-75, associate professor of history, 1975—. *Member:* American Historical Association, Conference on British Studies, Phi Beta Kappa, Phi Alpha Theta. *Awards, honors:* Prize from Phi Alpha Theta, 1972, for *The Parliament of 1621.*

WRITINGS: The Year One (poems), Blue Oak Press, 1969; *The Parliament of 1621* (nonfiction), University of California Press, 1971; *Lives of the Poet* (poems), Barlenmir House, 1974; (editor) *A Casebook on Anais Nin* (criticism), New American Library, 1974; *Wind Songs* (poetry chapbook), Ragnarok Press, 1976.

Translator of books by wife, Lili Bita: *Lightning in the Flesh,* Athens Publishing, 1968; *Erotes,* Guevara Press, 1969; *Furies,* Hors Commerce Press, 1969; *Blood Sketches,* Guevara Press, 1973; *Sacrifice, Exile, Night,* Ragnarok Press, 1976; *I Crave the Bitter Sea,* Ragnarok Press, 1978.

Plays: "Ampersand" (one-act), first produced in Miami, Fla. at University of Miami, May 19, 1973; "The Elevator" (one-act), first produced in Miami at Upstage Theatre, February 13, 1976; "Pelf" (one-act), 1976; "The Mayor of Nagasaki" (one-act), first produced at Upstage Theatre, November 19, 1976, produced on WCKT-TV, October 1, 1977; "Sauna" (one-act), 1976; "The Shrink" (one-act), first produced at Upstage Theatre, March 11, 1977; "Lockup" (one-act), 1977; "Crawlspace" (one-act), 1978.

Work anthologized in *For Neruda/for Chile,* edited by Walter Lowenfels, Beacon Press, 1975. Contributor of articles, translations, a play, and reviews to literary journals, including *Massachusetts Review, Studies in Romanticism,* and *Southern Literary Journal.*

WORK IN PROGRESS: The Cliffs of Solitude, a study of Robinson Jeffers; editing *Biographical Dictionary of British Radicals in the Seventeenth Century* with Richard L. Greaves, for Harvester Press.

SIDELIGHTS: Zaller writes: "The Greek landscape is indispensable to me. So is my wife, Lili Bita, whose interest and example led me into poetry and the theatre. I am fascinated by speech, as act or expression, in dramatic dialogue or poetic voice. Language is the collective victory of the human race, and each use of it, even shabby or false, is still an astonishment in the world. Every stage infers the whole universe; all theatre and verse start from this fact, and ultimately come home to it. What goes on in between is a matter of taste, talent and invention.

"As for myself, I think a single line can be drawn through my work in various genres, should any care to do so. I suppose my plays can be called political in the sense that they deal with power relationships, but I intend no overt reference to parties or events, nor have I any cause to plead. My subjects arise from the happenstance of a name or image, random event or dream. Once the kernel is established, the rest follows as inexorably as chess. In writing a play I often surprise myself, but in the end I am never surpirsed at all. No poem, on the other hand, no matter how deliberately willed, has ever been anything *but* a surprise."

*   *   *

ZALZANICK, Sheldon   1928-

PERSONAL: Born August 6, 1928, in Bronx, N.Y.; son of Samuel (a shopkeeper) and Esther (a shopkeeper; maiden name, Schneiderman) Zalzanick; married Vera Altobelli (a teacher of English), April 4, 1953; children: Andrea. *Education:* New York University, B.A., 1948; Columbia University, M.A., 1950. *Home:* 458 West 246 St., Bronx, N.Y. 10471. *Office:* 60 Fifth Ave., New York, N.Y. 10011.

CAREER/WRITINGS: High school English teacher in New York City, 1950-52; *Newsweek,* New York City, associate editor, 1952-56; Manning Public Relations, New York City, vice-president, 1956-59; *Forbes,* New York City, senior editor, 1959-63; *New York Herald Tribune,* New York City, founding editor of "New York," Sunday supplement, 1963-64, Sunday editor, 1964-66; General Learning Corp., staff writer, 1966-67; *Fortune* magazine, New York City, associate editor, 1967-69; *New York,* New York City, vice-president and editorial director, 1969-76; *Forbes,* managing editor, 1976—.

*   *   *

ZAMPAGLIONE, Gerardo   1917-

PERSONAL: Born November 18, 1917, in Rome, Italy; son of Arturo and Alessandra (Quagliotti) Zampaglione; married Anna Spataro, February, 1951; children: Arturo, Giuseppe. *Education:* University of Rome, degree in law, 1939, degree in political science, 1945. *Religion:* Roman Catholic. *Home address:* Ministry of Foreign Affairs, Rome, Italy. *Office:* Italian Embassy, P.O. Box 1008, Islamabad, Pakistan.

CAREER: Worked as journalist, 1945-48; official of Italian senate, 1948; Italian Ministry of Foreign Affairs, Rome, member of staff, 1949-51, Italian consul in Toronto, Canada, 1951-53, Italian consul in Stuttgart, West Germany, 1953-58; Council of Ministers of the European Communities, Brus-

sels, Belgium, director general, 1961-73; Italian ambassador to Kuwait, 1974-77, and Pakistan, 1977—. *Military service:* Italian Army, 1940-45; became captain.

WRITINGS: Italy, Benn, 1956; *Diritto consolare* (title means "Consular Law"), two volumes, Stamperia Nazionale, 1956, 2nd edition, 1970; *Breve storia dell' integrazione europa* (title means "Short History of European Unity"), Edizioni Cinque Luna, 1957, 2nd edition, 1958; *L'Idea della pace nel mondo antico,* Edizioni ERI-RAI, 1967, translation by Richard Dunn published as *The Idea of Peace in Antiquity,* University of Notre Dame Press, 1973; *Storia del Kuwait* (title means "History of Kuwait"), Edizioni ERI-RAI, 1978. Contributor of articles on peace and pacifism, the political and economic unity of Europe, and consular law and practice to magazines.

WORK IN PROGRESS: Foreign Politics of a United Europe.

SIDELIGHTS: Zampaglione writes: "I am confident that European unity will perhaps be the greatest achievement of our era. Its political, economic, and social implications will in fact be so far reaching that all countries of the world will be affected by it.

"Having served for over eleven years in the capacity of director general for general affairs of the Council of Ministers of the European Communities, I have collected firsthand experience and evidence that European unity is not only desirable but also possible. As a matter of fact it is the most practicable and feasible way to defend democracy, of giving the world stability, security, and of raising the standard of living of all human beings. European unity will also be a guarantee for peace. The moment when Europe will be one, having abolished borders which generally lack moral and economic justification because they are simply the result of past antagonism and wars, it will be possible to solve, in spirit of brotherly cooperation, the problems of poverty, distress, and underdevelopment which are the origin of wars.

"This explains why, side by side with the problems of European unity, I have during my lifetime also been interested in pacifism in general and ways and means to enforce lasting peace among nations of the world. I have consequently tried to investigate if peace was just an ideal and a hope of our times and if it was not deeply rooted in the past of humanity and in the speculations of ancient philosophers, reformers, theologians, etc. It has been as a consequence of this research that I have written my essay on the 'History of Peace in Antiquity.' I have now in mind to pursue this research with reference to medieval and modern times and to the Eastern societies and to their trends of thought and historic traditions.

"My book *Diritto consolare* (Consular Law) is today considered the standard book for the Italian Consular Service and is adopted as such by the Italian Diplomatic and Consular Representatives."

*   *   *

ZEI, Alki

PERSONAL: Born in Greece; married a stage director and writer. *Education:* Studied at the Moscow Institute of Cinema.

CAREER: Author. *Awards, honors:* Mildred L. Batchelder Awards, 1970, for *Wildcat under Glass,* and 1974, for *Petros' War.*

WRITINGS—For children: *Wildcat Under Glass* (translation by Edward Fenton of *To Kaplani Tis Vitrinas*), Holt,

1968; *Petros' War* (translation by Fenton of *O Megalos Peripatos Tou Petrou*), Dutton, 1972.

SIDELIGHTS: Alki Zei grew up in Greece, but has lived in France, Italy, and parts of the Soviet Union, including Uzbekistan. Her book *Wildcat Under Glass* was originally published in Greek and later translated into English and Russian. The story told how the Fascist take-over of Greece during the 1930's affected the lives of Greek citizens, both young and old. "The writing is rich in characterization, convincing in its incidents, and totally rewarding for the reader in its vivid theme of the meaning of freedom and democracy," commented a reviewer for *Horn Book*. A critic for the *National Observer* noted, "Told in the first person, *Wildcat* speaks with remarkable fidelity to the accent and tone of a young teen-ager experiencing challenge, uncertainty, and fear for the first time." Similarly, a reviewer for *Books Abroad* wrote: "The author is not without skill in reproducing accurately, idyllically, the state of childhood as it experiences the consequence of the political change on a little island of the Aegean. The whole novel breathes the gentle sensitivity of a firsthand experience, its emotional and psychological impact, which is amply enriched and heightened throughout by an imaginative touch."

BIOGRAPHICAL/CRITICAL SOURCES: Horn Book, June, 1968; *National Observer,* October 21, 1968; *Book Abroad,* Spring, 1969.*

* * *

ZEITLIN, Solomon 1888(?)-1976

PERSONAL: Born in Russia. *Education:* Dropsie College (now University), Ph.D., 1917. *Religion:* Jewish. *Residence:* Philadelphia, Pa.

CAREER: Dropsie University, Philadelphia, Pa., professor of history and rabbinics until 1976.

WRITINGS: Josephus on Jesus, Dropsie College, 1931; *The History of the Second Jewish Commonwealth,* Dropsie College, 1933; *Maimonides: A Biography,* Bloch Publishing, 1935, 2nd edition, 1955; *The Book of Jubilees: Its Character and Its Significance,* Dropsie College, 1939; *Who Crucified Jesus?,* Harper, 1942, 4th edition, 1964; *Religious and Secular Leadership,* Dropsie College, 1943.

(Author of introduction and commentary) *The First Book of Maccabees,* Harper, 1950; (author of introduction) *The Zadokite Fragments,* Dropsie College, 1952; (editor) *The Second Book of Maccabees,* Harper, 1954; *The Dead Sea Scrolls and Modern Scholarship,* Dropsie College, 1956; *The Rise and Fall of the Judaean State: A Political, Social, and Religious History of the Second Commonwealth,* Jewish Publication Society, Volume 1, 1962, Volume 2, 1967, Volume 3, 1977; *Studies in the Early History of Judaism,* four volumes, Ktav, beginning 1973.

Contributor of several hundred articles to scholarly journals. Editor of *Jewish Quarterly Review.*

SIDELIGHTS: Moses Aberbach called Zeitlin "the stormy petrel of Jewish scholarship" and "an uncompromising fighter where scholarly truth is concerned." A noted scholar in the fields of history and rabbinics, Zeitlin was especially recognized for his dissenting views on the subject of the Dead Sea scrolls. Battling against the prevailing view of the scholarly establishment, he forcefully maintained his conviction that they were written by scribes during the Middle Ages and therefore worthless for the historical study of the period. He sharply criticized faulty scholarship and stressed the extreme importance of primary sources. "A scholar must utilize the sources," he said. "He must be a master of the sources, and not depend on somebody else or on translations. But now our scholars neglect the fundamentals." Aberbach characterized him briefly as "the *enfant terrible* of Jewish scholarship who is not afraid to defy the whole and cry out, 'The emperor is naked.'"

BIOGRAPHICAL/CRITICAL SOURCES: Jewish Quarterly Review, winter, 1968-69; *New York Times,* February 13, 1972. Obituaries: *New York Times,* December 30, 1976.*

(Died December 28, 1976, in Philadelphia, Pa.)

* * *

ZELIGS, Meyer A(aron) 1909-1978

March 20, 1909—March 20, 1978; American psychoanalyst and author. His controversial defense of Alger Hiss, *Friendship and Fratricide,* concluded that Whittaker Chambers was a psychopathic personality. Most interested in "the role of psychoanalytic investigation in the research of contemporary as well as historical figures," Zeligs contributed to journals in his field and was working on *Nixon, Hiss, and Chambers,* a sequel to *Friendship and Fratricide,* before his death in San Francisco, Calif. Obituaries and other sources: *Who's Who in America,* 39th edition, Marquis, 1976; *New York Times,* March 22, 1978. (See index for *CA* sketch)

* * *

ZELLAN, Audrey Penn 1950-

PERSONAL: Born May 4, 1950, in Tacoma Park, Md.; daughter of Harry Joseph (a lawyer and business manager) and Rose (Miller) Penn; married Lester Zellan (a lighting technician), December 19, 1970; children: Garth Lee. *Education:* Attended National Ballet School, 1965-68, University of Maryland, 1967-68, and New York City dance and acting schools, 1968-70. *Politics:* Democrat. *Religion:* Jewish. *Home and office:* 14323 Georgia Ave., #203, Silver Spring, Md. 20906. *Agent:* Richard Sheldon, 75 West 68th St., New York, N.Y. 10023.

CAREER: Professional actress in Washington, D.C., and New York, N.Y., on national tours, and in summer stock productions, 1965-70; professional ballet dancer, 1967-75; writer, 1975—. Dance coach for Olympic gymnasts and ice skaters, 1973-75. *Member:* Council on Physical Fitness, Arthritis Association.

WRITINGS—Juveniles: *Happy Apple Told Me,* Independence Press (Independence, Mo.), 1975.

WORK IN PROGRESS—Juveniles: *Blue Out of Season; Albert and the Pentapus; No Bones About Driftiss; How to Visit Grandma Becky; Garth and the Giant Bubble; The Mystery of Mason's Gold,* the story of Brookeville, Md., the U.S. capital for one day; *847 Avenue C,* a mystery.

SIDELIGHTS: Audrey Zellan writes: "In August of 1975, I collapsed while dancing, ending a twenty-year battle with juvenile rheumatoid arthritis. I remained in bed, unable to walk or work for the next eighteen months. During the time that followed, as I became stronger, I worked with friends and a cassette to finish the book I had already begun, and go on to complete four more books. I now wear hand braces, and can walk, so I am back at the typewriter. It is very important for me to write, because it's the only outlet I have left. My aim is to have enough money to support a diagnostic program at Children's Hospital."

BIOGRAPHICAL/CRITICAL SOURCES: Publishers Weekly, February 24, 1975; *Washington Star,* October 3, 1975.

ZERMAN, Melvyn Bernard 1930-

PERSONAL: Born July 10, 1930, in New York, N.Y.; son of Abraham (in real estate) and Ida (Belsky) Zirman; married Miriam Baron, September 14, 1952; children: Andrew, Jared, Lenore. *Education:* University of Michigan, B.A., 1952; Columbia University, M.A., 1953. *Politics:* Democrat. *Religion:* Jewish. *Home:* 110-37 68th St., Forest Hills, N.Y. 11375. *Agent:* Phyllis Seidel, 164 East 90th St., New York, N.Y. 10028. *Office:* Harper & Row Publishers, Inc., 10 East 53rd St., New York, N.Y. 10022.

CAREER: Harper & Row Publishers, Inc., New York, N.Y., assistant to sales manager, 1959-64, sales department office manager, 1964-67, assistant director of sales, 1968-70, trade sales manager, 1970-77, administrative sales manager, 1977—.

WRITINGS: Call the Final Witness (nonfiction), Harper, 1977.

WORK IN PROGRESS: A book for young people on the jury system, for Crowell.

SIDELIGHTS: Zerman writes: "In the almost-forgotten past I had thoughts of becoming a professional writer. Those thoughts were put aside for too many years until, in a very real sense, a subject discovered me. My experiences as a juror on a murder trial awakened a dormant ambition and eventually resulted in my first book."

*　　*　　*

ZIMNIK, Reiner 1930-

PERSONAL: Born December 13, 1930, in Beuthen, Upper Silesia (now East Germany); son of a city clerk. *Education:* Attended the Academy of Art, Munich, Germany. *Home:* Munich, Germany.

CAREER: Worked in a carpentry shop in Bavaria; author and illustrator of books for children. *Awards, honors: Jonah, the Fisherman* and *Little Owl* were listed among the New York Times Choice of Best Illustrated Children's Books in 1956 and 1962, respectively.

WRITINGS: Xaver, der Ringelstecher, und das Gelbe Ross, G. Parcus Verlag (Munich), 1954; *Jonas, der Angler* (self-illustrated), G. Parcus Verlag, 1954, translation by Richard Winston and Clara Winston published as *Jonah, the Fisherman,* Pantheon, 1956; *Der Baer und die Leute* (self-illustrated), G. Parcus Verlag, 1954, translation by Nina Ignatowicz published as *The Bear and the People,* Harper, 1971; *Der Kran,* C. Dressler (Berlin), 1956, translation by N. Ignatowicz and F. N. Monjo published as *The Crane,* Harper, 1970; *Der Stolze Schimmel,* C. Dressler, 1956, translation published as *The Proud Circus Horse,* Pantheon, 1957; *Die Trommler Fuer eine Bessere Zeit,* C. Dressler, 1958, translation by E. M. Hatt published as *Drummer of Dreams,* Faber, 1960; *Der Regen-Otto,* G. Lentz (Munich), 1958.

Der Kleine Bruelltiger (self-illustrated), C. Dressler, 1960, translation published as *The Little Roaring Tiger,* Pantheon, 1961; (with Hanne Axmann) *Die Geschichte vom Kaeuzchen,* translation published as *Little Owl,* Atheneum, 1962; *Der Baer auf dem Motorrad* (self-illustrated), translation by Cornelia Schaeffer published as *The Bear on the Motorcycle,* Antheneum, 1963, revised edition published as *The Bear on the Motorbike,* Methuen, 1974; *Lektro und die Feurwehr,* Diogenes Verlag (Zurich), 1964; *Die Ballade von Augustus und den Lokomotiven,* Diogenes Verlag, 1967; *Geschichten vom Lektro,* Buechergilde Gutenberg (Frankfort), 1968; *Der Kleine Millionaer,* Diogenes Verlag, 1969;

Professor Daniel J. Koopermans' Entdeckung und Erforschung des Schneemenschen, Diogenes Verlag, 1971; *Bills Ballonfahrt* (self-illustrated), Diogenes Verlag, 1972, translation by Richard Whittingham published as *Billy's Balloon Ride,* Hubbard Press, 1974.

Illustrator: Beatrice De Regniers, *The Snow Party,* Pantheon, 1959.

SIDELIGHTS: Reviewing Zimnick's *The Proud Circus Horse,* New York Herald Tribune Book Review stated: "Young children can enjoy it as they do Andersen's tales. The black and white illustrations have not the marvelous rhythmic sweep of those in *Jonah, the Fisherman,* but there is the same power and wit in the line. The proud horse himself has tremendous individuality and charm." *New York Times* had similar praise for the book and for its "sensitive, highly original writer. There is even more feeling and verbal beauty in this book than in [Zimmick's] successful first, *Jonah and the Fisherman.*"

Other books by Zimnick have received equal critical acclaim for their originality and feeling. Of *The Little Roaring Tiger,* for example, *New York Times Book Review* observed: "Again Reiner Zimnick . . . writes with unusual sensitivity. His impressive prose evokes an emotional response in the reader who becomes really involved in the tiger's plight. This is superior reading, plus delightful illustrations." Similarly, in its review of *The Crane, Times Literary Supplement* stated: "Illustrations are still of the utmost importance for children under nine. The visual orgy of modern picture-books isn't far behind them, and children want pictures they can read, pictures that really elaborate on the text. This is exactly what Reiner Zimnick provides. . . . This is a very moral story . . . [that] could have been all rather tedious and pious, but the wittiness of the drawings also pervades the text. On the whole, the moral is handled lightly, and the story itself is absorbing."

BIOGRAPHICAL/CRITICAL SOURCES: Kirkus Reviews, April 1, 1956; *New York Times,* July 22, 1956; *Saturday Review,* September 22, 1956; *New York Herald Tribune Book Review,* November 17, 1957; *Times Literary Supplement,* October 16, 1969; R. Stumm, *Graphis,* 1973-74; *Children's Literature Review,* Volume 3, Gale, 1978.*

*　　*　　*

ZODROW, John 1944-

PERSONAL: Born October 20, 1944, in Colby, Kan.; son of John Paul (a rancher) and Leona (a chef; maiden name, Heim) Zodrow. *Education:* Loyola University, Los Angeles, Calif., B.A., 1969, M.A., 1971. *Home:* 12961 Mulholland Dr., Beverly Hills, Calif. 90210. *Agent:* Gary Cosay, 9744 Wilshire Blvd., #310, Beverly Hills, Calif. 90212.

CAREER: Seminarian, studying for the Roman Catholic priesthood, 1958-67; radio producer, filmmaker, and writer, 1967—. *Member:* Writers Guild of America (West). *Awards, honors:* Award from National Catholic Theatre Conference, 1967; Ethel Percy Andrus Award, 1969, for "Raisin Wine"; Ohio State Award, 1977, for television drama "All Out."

WRITINGS: Bright Green Hell (novel), Dell, 1978; *The Coming* (novel), Dell, 1979.

Scripts: "The Ultimate Thrill" (filmscript), Centaur Films, 1975; "Kate Bliss and the Tickertape Kid" (television film), ABC, 1978; "The Hunter" (filmscript), Paramount, 1979. Writer for television series "Insight," 1971—.

WORK IN PROGRESS: Death Wind, "the story of a tornado, taking human characteristics."

SIDELIGHTS: Zodrow comments: "I am interested in telling stories in which the characters are tried by extreme circumstances. My first novel concerns a young girl of thirteen, thrust into the Amazon jungle. In six months, she becomes a woman. In that book, as in all my others, I write heavily-plotted, strongly action-oriented stories. But—and this is important—always there are several levels running, simplistic, yet converging finally for a complex, psychological insight. My one and only dictum as a writer? Never bore."

AVOCATIONAL INTERESTS: Tennis, hiking, coon hunting.

*   *   *

ZUKOFSKY, Louis 1904-1978

January 23, 1904—May 12, 1978; American poet and novelist. Zukofsky received little public attention for his poetry during his lifetime but other poets considered him one of America's finest. T. S. Eliot once nominated him for a Guggenheim fellowship and poets such as Marianne Moore praised his work. Some of Zukofsky's best known poems are "A-24" and "A." Primarily an objectivist, Zukofsky also wrote critical essays and a novel, *Little,* which *New York Times* critic John Leonard deemed a "brilliant parody." Zukofsky was a close friend of other important poets of his time, including William Carlos Williams and Ezra Pound. He died in Port Jefferson, N.Y. Obituaries and other sources: *The Penguin Companion to American Literature,* McGraw, 1971; *Webster's New World Companion to English and American Literature,* World Publishing, 1973; *The Reader's Adviser: A Layman's Guide to Literature,* Volume I: *The Best in American and British Fiction, Poetry, Essays, Literary Biography, Bibliography, and Reference,* 12th edition, Bowker, 1974; *World Authors, 1950-1970,* Wilson, 1975; *The Writers Directory, 1976-78,* St. Martin's, 1976; *Who's Who in Twentieth Century Literature,* Holt, 1976; *New York Times,* May 14, 1978. (See index for *CA* sketch)

*   *   *

ZUWIYYA, Jalal (Zakariya) 1932-

PERSONAL: Born October 12, 1932, in Sidon, Lebanon; came to the United States in 1962, naturalized citizen, 1967; son of Zakariya (a businessman) and Kawther (Kaddourah) Zuwiyya; married Nancy Emily Bennett (an English teacher), January 28, 1964; children: Zachary David, Joseph Samir, Rami Jalal. *Education:* American University of Beirut, B.B.A., 1954; State University of New York College at Geneseo, M.L.S., 1963; State University of New York at Binghamton, M.A., 1971. *Home:* 4632 Salem Dr., Binghamton, N.Y. 13903. *Office:* University Library, State University of New York at Binghamton, Binghamton, N.Y. 13901.

CAREER: Coca-Cola Bottling Co., Kuwait City, Kuwait, chief accountant, 1954-55; American Embassy, Beirut, Lebanon, reference librarian, 1956-62; Queensborough Public Library, New York, N.Y., junior librarian, 1963-64; State University of New York at Binghamton, assistant librarian, 1964-68, associate librarian, 1968-71, librarian, 1971—. Translator from English to Arabic and Arabic to English. *Member:* Middle East Association of North America, American Library Association, Middle East Librarians Association, Association of College and Research Librarians, Middle East Institute, State University of New York Faculty Association of Middle East Studies, Islamic Organization of the Southern Tier.

WRITINGS: The Parliamentary Election of Lebanon of 1968, E. J. Brill, 1972; *The Near East: South West Asia, North Africa,* Scarecrow, 1975.

WORK IN PROGRESS: Research on Lebanon's civil war, 1976-77.

SIDELIGHTS: Zuwiyya writes: "Throughout my professional career, I have seen many proposals and attended discussions on the faculty status of the academic librarian. I believe strongly that the librarians should continue to strive for parity with the teaching faculty in all respects. This should include salary, workload, time, sabbatical, governance, and other academic benefits and obligations. However, in order to reach this goal, and rightfully so, university administrators and teaching faculty expect the librarians, individually and collectively, to work toward earning this parity. The path to follow would be for the librarians to advance their graduate education and specialization, and to contribute increasingly to the different fields of education. Furthermore, many of today's American Library Association-accredited schools should also revamp their curricula and raise their admission requirements in order to better prepare their graduates to become faculty members in every sense of the word.

"My primary interest is public service and the providing of information and research assistance. My field of specialization is the Middle East and North Africa. Arabic and French are dominant languages in that area. Proficiency in the two languages is essential for the successful performance of my duties. I have also travelled extensively to that part of the world and have first-hand knowledge of the people and culture of the Easterners."

AVOCATIONAL INTERESTS: Reading, sports, travel.

*   *   *

ZWIBAK, Jacques 1902-
(Andrei Sedych)

PERSONAL: Born August 14, 1902, in Pheodosia, Russia; came to the United States in 1942, naturalized citizen, 1947; son of Moses (a journalist) and Sophie (Rubin) Zwibak; married Eugenia Lipovsky (an actress, using stage name Jenny Grey), May 14, 1932. *Education:* School of Political Sciences, Paris, France, diploma, 1926. *Home:* 114 West 70th St., New York, N.Y. 10023. *Office: Novoye Russkoye Slovo,* 243 West 56th St., New York, N.Y. 10019.

CAREER: Dernieres Nouvelles, Paris, France, parliamentary correspondent, 1924-40; *Novoye Russkoye Slovo,* New York City, city editor, 1942-65, managing editor, 1965-73, editor-in-chief, 1973—. President of Russian Literary Foundation for Russian Writers Abroad, 1973—; vice-president of American Organization for Rehabilitation Through Training Federation (member of board of directors, and member of executive committee). *Member:* International P.E.N. (Writers in Exile), Academy of Political Science. *Awards, honors:* Named man of the year by American Organization for Rehabilitation Through Training Federation (ORT), 1968.

WRITINGS—Under pseudonym Andrei Sedych: Zemlia obetovannaia, Novoye Russkoye Slovo, 1966, translation by Elizabeth Reynolds Hapgood published as *This Land of Israel,* Macmillan, 1967.

In Russian: *Staryi Parizh* (title means "The Old Paris"), Povolotzki, 1926; *Montmartre,* Povolotzki, 1927; *Tam: Gdie byla Rossia* (title means "Where Russia Used to Be"), Povolotzki, 1930; *Tam: Gdie zhill koroli* (title means "There Where the Kings Resided"), Povolotzki, 1930; *Liudi za bortom* (title means "Men Overboard"), O. Zeluk, 1933; *Doroga cherez okean* (title means "The Road Across the

Ocean''), Novoye Zhurnal, 1942; *Zvezdochety s Bosfora* (title means ''Stargazers From the Bosphorus''), Novoye Russkoye Slovo, 1948; *Sumasshedshii sharmanshchik* (title means ''The Crazy Organ Grinder''), Novoye Russkoye Slovo, 1951; *Tol'ko o liudiakh* (title means ''Only About People''), Novoye Russkoye Slovo, 1955; *Dalekie Blizkie* (title means ''The Near Ones—Far Away''), Novoye Russkoye Slovo, 1962; *Zamelo tebia snegom, Rossia* (title means ''Snow Has Covered You, Russia''), Novoye Russkoye Slovo, 1964; *Ierusalem: Imia radostnoe* (title means ''Jerusalem: Joyous Name''), Novoye Russkoye Slovo, 1969; *Krymskie Rasskazy* (title means ''Tales From the Crimea''), Novoye Russkoye Slovo, 1978. Contributor of articles and stories to Russian magazines and newspapers.

WORK IN PROGRESS: A second book of literary reminiscences.

CONTEMPORARY AUTHORS

CUMULATIVE INDEX VOLUMES 1-80

This index includes references to all entries in the series listed below.
References in the index are identified as follows:

Volume number only—*Contemporary Authors* Original Volumes
R after number—*Contemporary Authors* Revised Volumes
CAP before number—*Contemporary Authors—Permanent Series*
CLC before number—*Contemporary Literary Criticism,* Volumes 1-9
SATA before number—*Something About the Author,* Volumes 1-13

A

A. A.
  See Willis, (George) Anthony Armstrong
Aaker, David A(llen) 1938- 49-52
Aalto, (Hugo) Alvar (Henrik)
  1898-1976 Obituary 65-68
Aardema, Verna (Norbera) 1911- 7-8R
  See also SATA 4
Aaron, Benjamin 1915- 23-24R
Aaron, Chester 1923- 21-22R
  See also SATA 9
Aaron, Daniel 1912- 13-14R
Aaron, James Ethridge 1927- 23-24R
Aaronovitch, Sam 1919- 13-14R
Aarons, Edward S(idney)
  1916-1975 Obituary 57-60
Aaronson, Bernard S(eymour) 1924- 29-32R
Aarsleff, Hans 1925- 21-22R
Aaseng, Rolf E(dward) 1923- 49-52
Abajian, James De Tar 1914- 65-68
Abarbanel, Karin 1950- 65-68
Abbaanano, Nicola 1901- 33-36R
Abbas, Khwaja Ahmad 1914- 57-60
Abbazia, Patrick 1937- 57-60
Abbe, Elfriede (Martha) 1919- 15-16R
Abbe, George (Bancroft) 1911- 25-28R
Abbey, Edward 1927- 45-48
Abbey, Merrill R. 1905- 1R
Abbot, Charles G(reeley) 1872-1973 77-80
  Obituary 45-48
Abbott, Alice
  See Borland, Kathryn Kilby
  and Speicher, Helen Ross S(mith)
Abbott, Anthony S. 1935- 17-18R
Abbott, Carl (John) 1944- 65-68
Abbott, Claude Colleer 1889- 7-8R
Abbott, Freeland K(night) 1919-1971 CAP-2
  Earlier sketch in CA 25-28
Abbott, H(orace) Porter 1940- 45-48
Abbott, James H(amilton) 1924- 77-80
Abbott, Jerry (Lynn) 1938- 45-48
Abbott, John J(amison) 1930- 17-18R
Abbott, John Janisen 17-18R
Abbott, Manager Henry
  See Stratemeyer, Edward L.
Abbott, Martin 1922-1977 33-36R
Abbott, May L(aura) 1916- 9-10R
Abbott, R(obert) Tucker 1919- 9-10R
Abbott, Raymond H(erbert) 1942- 57-60
Abbott, Richard H(enry) 1936- 33-36R
Abbott, Rowland A(ubrey) S(amuel) 1909- 53-56
Abbott, Sidney 1937- 41-44R
Abbott, Walter M(atthew) 1923- 11-12R
Abbotts, John 1947- 73-76
Abboushi, W(asif) F(ahmi) 1931- 29-32R
Abcarian, Richard 1929- 33-36R
Abdallah, Omar
  See Humbaraci, D(emir) Arslan
Abdel-Malek, Anouar 1924- 29-32R
Abdelsamad, Moustafa H(assan) 1941- 53-56
Abdul, Raoul 1929- 29-32R
  See also SATA 12
Abe, Kobo 1924- 65-68
  See also CLC 8
Abel, Alan (Irwin) 1928- 19-20R
Abel, Bob 1931- 65-68
Abel, Elie 1920- 61-64
Abel, Ernest L(awrence) 1943- 41-44R
Abel, Jeanne 1937- 19-20R
Abel, Lionel 1910- 61-64
Abel, Raymond 1911- SATA-12
Abel, Reuben 1911- 37-40R
Abel, Theodora M(ead) 1899- 57-60
Abel, Theodore 1896- 23-24R
Abell, George O(gden) 1927- 9-10R
Abell, Kathleen 1938- 49-52
  See also SATA 9
Abella, Irving Martin 1940- 49-52
Abels, Jules 1913- 61-64
Abel-Smith, Brian 1926- 21-22R
Abelson, Raziel A. 1921- 11-12R
Abelson, Robert P(aul) 1928- 41-44R
Abend, Norman A(nchel) 1931- 33-36R
Aber, William M(cKee) 1929- 57-60
Aberbach, Joel D(avid) 1940- 45-48
Aberg, Sherrill E. 1924- 21-22R
Aberle, David F(riend) 1918- 21-22R
Aberle, John Wayne 1919- 1R
Aberle, Kathleen Gough 1925- 13-14R
Abernathy, David M(yles) 1933- 53-56
Abernathy, (M.) Elton 1913- 17-18R
Abernathy, M(abra) Glenn 1921- 13-14R
Abernethy, Francis Edward 1925- 21-22R
Abernethy, George Lawrence 1910- 2R
Abernethy, Peter L(ink) 1935- 69-72
Abernethy, Robert G(ordon) 1927- 21-22R
  See also SATA 5
Abernethy, Thomas Perkins 1890- CAP-1
  Earlier sketch in CA 19-20
Abisch, Roslyn Kroop 1927- 21-22R
  See also SATA 9
Abisch, Roz
  See Abisch, Roslyn Kroop
Ableman, Paul 1927- 61-64
Abler, Ronald 1939- 53-56
Abodaher, David J. (Naiph) 1919- 17-18R
Abrahall, Clare Hoskyns
  See Hoskyns-Abrahall, Clare (Constance
    Drury)
Abraham, Claude K(urt) 1931- 23-24R
Abraham, Henry Julian 1921- 5-6R
Abraham, Willard 1916- 13-14R
Abraham, William E. 1934- 13-14R
Abraham, William I(srael) 1919- 25-28R
Abrahams, Howard Phineas 1904- 57-60
Abrahams, Peter (Henry) 1919- 57-60
  See also CLC 4
Abrahams, R(aphael) G(arvin) 1934- 25-28R
Abrahams, Robert David 1905- CAP-2
  Earlier sketch in CA 33-36
Abrahams, Roger D. 1933- 11-12R
  See also SATA 4
Abrahams, William Miller 1919- 61-64
Abrahamsen, David 1903- 65-68
Abram, H(arry) S(hore) 1931-1977 29-32R
Abramowitz, Jack 1918- 7-8R
Abrams, Charles 1901-1970 CAP-2
  Earlier sketch in CA 23-24
Abrams, George J(oseph) 1918- 61-64
Abrams, Joy 1941- 77-80
Abrams, M(eyer) H(oward) 1912- 57-60
Abrams, Peter D(avid) 1936- 33-36R
Abrams, Richard M. 1932- 13-14R
Abrams, Sam(uel) 1935- 21-22R
Abramson, Doris E. 1925- 25-28R
Abramson, Harold J(ulian) 1934- 45-48
Abramson, Joan 1932- 25-28R
Abramson, Martin 1921- 49-52
Abramson, Michael 1944- 69-72
Abramson, Paul R(obert) 1937- 61-64
Abrash, Merritt 1930- 23-24R
Abrecht, Mary Ellen (Benson) 1945- 69-72
Abreu, Maria Isabel 1919- 45-48
Abse, Dannie 1923- 53-56
  See also CLC 7
Abse, David Wilfred 1915- 49-52
Abshire, David M. 1926- 23-24R
Abt, Clark C(laus) 1929- 69-72
Abt, Lawrence Edwin 1915- 33-36R
Abu Jaber, Kamel S. 1932- 21-22R
Abu-Lughod, Ibrahim Ali 1929- 5-6R
Abu-Lughod, Janet L(ouise) 1928- 65-68
Abun-Nasr, Jamil Miri 1932- 69-72
Academic Investor
  See Reddaway, W(illiam) Brian
Accola, Louis W(ayne) 1937- 29-32R
Ace, Goodman 1899- 61-64
Achard, George
  See Torress, Tereska (Szwarc)
Achard, Marcel
  See Ferreol, Marcel Auguste
Achebe, Chinua 1930- 4R
  See also CLC 1, 3, 5, 7
Acheson, Dean (Gooderham) 1893-1971 CAP-2
  Obituary 33-36R
  Earlier sketch in CA 25-28
Acheson, Patricia Castles 1924- 3R
Achtemeier, Elizabeth (Rice) 1926- 17-18R
Achtemeier, Paul J(ohn) 1927- 17-18R
Achyut
  See Birla, Lakshminiwas
Acker, Duane Calvin 1931- 33-36R
Acker, Helen 73-76
Acker, William R. B.
  1910(?)-1974 Obituary 49-52
Ackerman, Bruce A. 1943- 53-56
Ackerman, Carl W(illiam) 1890-1970 73-76
  Obituary 29-32R
Ackerman, Diane 1948- 57-60
Ackerman, Edward A.
  1911-1973 Obituary 41-44R
Ackerman, Eugene (Francis) 1888-1974 SATA-10
Ackerman, Gerald M(artin) 1928- 45-48
Ackerman, J. Mark 1939- 53-56
Ackerman, James S(loss) 1919- 9-10R
Ackerman, Nathan W(ard) 1908-1971 CAP-2
  Earlier sketch in CA 29-32
Ackerman, Robert E(dwin) 1928- 45-48
Ackerson, Duane (Wright, Jr.) 1942- 33-36R
Ackland, Rodney 1908- 57-60
Ackley, Charles Walton 1913- 41-44R
Ackley, Hugh Gardner 1915- 61-64
Ackley, Randall William 1931- 53-56
Ackoff, Russell L(incoln) 1919- 41-44R
Ackroyd, Peter R(unham) 1917- 25-28R
Ackworth, Robert Charles 1923- 5-6R
Acland, James H. 1917- 41-44R
Acquaye, Alfred Allotey 1939- 25-28R
Acre, Stephen
  See Gruber, Frank
Acred, Arthur 1926- 25-28R
Acton, Harold Mario Mitchell 1904- 4R
Acton, Jay 1949- 45-48
Acton, Thomas (Alan) 1948- 57-60
Aczel, Tamas 1921- 49-52
Adachi, Barbara (Curtis) 1924- 49-52
Adair, Ian 1942- 69-72
Adair, James R. 1923- 19-20R
Adair, John G(lenn) 1933- 49-52
Adair, Margaret Weeks ?-1971 CAP-1
  Earlier sketch in CA 13-14
  See also SATA 10
Adam, Ben
  See Drachman, Julian M(oses)
Adam, Cornel
  See Lengyel, Cornel Adam
Adam, Helen 1909- 19-20R
Adam, Michael 1919- 53-56
Adam, Ruth (Augusta) 1907- 23-24R
Adam, Thomas R(itchie) 1900- CAP-1
  Earlier sketch in CA 19-20
Adamczewski, Zygmunt 1921- 15-16R
Adamec, Ludwig W(arren) 1924- 23-24R
Adamov, Arthur 1908-1970 CAP-2
  Obituary 25-28R
  Earlier sketch in CA 17-18
  See also CLC 4
Adams, A. Don
  See Cleveland, Philip Jerome
Adams, A. John 1931- 33-36R
Adams, Adrienne 1906- 49-52
  See also SATA 8
Adams, Alice 1926- CLC-6
Adams, Anne H(utchinson) 1935- 41-44R
Adams, Annette
  See Rowland, D(onald) S(ydney)
Adams, Ansel (Easton) 1902- 21-22R
Adams, Arthur E(ugene) 1917- 7-8R
Adams, Arthur Merrihew 1908- 53-56
Adams, Betsy
  See Pitcher, Gladys
Adams, Charles J(oseph) 1924- 17-18R
Adams, Christopher
  See Hopkins, Kenneth
Adams, Cindy 23-24R
Adams, Clifton 1919- 13-14R
Adams, Clinton 1918- 33-36R
Adams, Don(ald Kendrick) 1925- 33-36R
Adams, E(lie) M(aynard) 1919- 3R
Adams, Elsie B(onita) 1932- 69-72
Adams, F(rank) Ramsay 1883-1963 7-8R
Adams, Florence 1932- 49-52
Adams, Francis A(lexandre)
  1874-1975 Obituary 61-64
Adams, Frank C(lyde) 1916- 69-72
Adams, George Worthington 1905- 41-44R
Adams, Georgia Sachs 1913- 37-40R
Adams, Graham, Jr. 1928- 17-18R
Adams, Harlen M(artin) 1904- CAP-1
  Earlier sketch in CA 13-14
Adams, Harriet S(tratemeyer) 19-20R
  See also SATA 1
Adams, Harrison
  See Stratemeyer, Edward L.
Adams, Hazard 1926- 9-10R
  See also SATA 6
Adams, Henry H(itch) 1917- 21-22R
Adams, Henry Mason 1907- CAP-1
  Earlier sketch in CA 17-18
Adams, Henry T.
  See Ransom, Jay Ellis
Adams, Herbert Mayow 1893- CAP-2
  Earlier sketch in CA 25-28
Adams, J(ames) Donald 1891- 2R
Adams, James E(dward) 1941- 73-76
Adams, James F(rederick) 1927- 19-20R
Adams, James Luther 1901- 41-44R
Adams, James R(owe) 1934- 41-44R
Adams, Joey 1911- 49-52
Adams, John Clarke 1910- 3R
Adams, John F(estus) 1930- 33-36R
Adams, John Paul
  See Kinnaird, Clark
Adams, John R. 1900- 25-28R
Adams, Julian 1919- 25-28R
Adams, Kramer A. 1920- 11-12R
Adams, L(ouis) Jerold 1939- 49-52
Adams, Laura 1943- 53-56
Adams, Laurie 1941- 53-56
Adams, Leon D(avid) 1905- 45-48
Adams, Leonie (Fuller) 1899- CAP-1
  Earlier sketch in CA 9-10
Adams, Lowell
  See Joseph, James Herz
Adams, Marion 1932- 41-44R
Adams, Michael (Evelyn) 1920- 33-36R
Adams, Nathan Miller 1934- 45-48
Adams, Paul L(ieber) 1924- 61-64
Adams, Percy G(uy) 1914- 4R
Adams, Ramon Frederick
  1889-1976 Obituary 65-68
Adams, Richard 1920- 49-52
  See also CLC 4, 5
  See also SATA 7
Adams, Richard N(ewbold) 1924- 29-32R
Adams, Richard P(errill) 1917-1977 CAP-2
  Obituary 69-72
  Earlier sketch in CA 33-36
Adams, Robert (Franklin) 1932- 69-72
Adams, Robert Martin 1915- 5-6R
Adams, Robert McCormick 1926- 61-64
Adams, Robert P. 1910- 13-14R
Adams, Russell B(aird), Jr. 1937- 69-72
Adams, Russell L. 1930- 53-56
Adams, Sally Pepper 41-44R
Adams, Sam 1934- 57-60
Adams, Sexton 1936- 25-28R
Adams, T(homas) W(illiam) 1933- 25-28R
Adams, Terrence Dean 1935- 33-36R
Adams, Theodore Floyd 1898- CAP-1
  Earlier sketch in CA 11-12
Adams, Thomas F. 1927- 15-16R
Adams, Walter 1922- 2R
Adamson, David Grant 1927- 15-16R
Adamson, Donald 1939- 53-56
Adamson, Ed(ward Joseph)
  1915(?)-1972 Obituary 37-40R
Adamson, Frank
  See Adams, Robert (Franklin)
Adamson, Gareth 1925- 13-14R
Adamson, Graham
  See Groom, Arthur William
Adamson, Hans Christian 1890-1968 5-6R
Adamson, Joe
  See Adamson, Joseph III
Adamson, Joseph III 1945- 45-48
Adamson, Joy (-Friederike Victoria) 1910- 69-72
  See also SATA 11
Adamson, Wendy Writson 1942- 53-56
Adamson, William Robert 1927- 23-24R
Adas, Michael 1943- 53-56

Hogg, Garry 1902- 23-24R
See also SATA 2
Hogg, Helen (Battles) Sawyer 1905- 69-72
Hogg, Ian V(ernon) 1926- 29-32R
Hogg, Quintin McGarel 1907- CAP-1
Earlier sketch in CA 11-12
Hogg, Robert (Lawrence) 1942- 53-56
Hogg, W(illiam) Richey 1921- 2R
Hoggart, Richard 1918- 9-10R
Hogins, James Burl 1936- 53-56
Hogner, Dorothy Childs 33-36R
See also SATA 4
Hogner, Nils 1893-1970 77-80
Hogrefe, Pearl CAP-1
Earlier sketch in CA 15-16
Hogrogian, Nonny 1932- 45-48
See also SATA 7
Hogue, Arthur R(eed) 1906- 37-40R
Hogue, C(harles) B(illy) 1928- 69-72
Hogue, Richard 1946- 49-52
Hohenberg, Dorothy Lannuier
1905(?)-1977 Obituary 73-76
Hohenberg, John 1906- 13-14R
Hohenberg, Paul M(arcel) 1933- 25-28R
Hohendahl, Peter Uwe 1936- 45-48
Hohenstein, Henry J(ohn) 1931- 53-56
Hohimer, Frank 1928- 57-60
Hohlfelder, Robert Lane 1938- 45-48
Hohn, Hazel (Stamper) 7-8R
Hohnen, David 1925- 21-22R
Hohoff, Tay
See Torrey, Therese von Hohoff
Hoig, Stan(ley Warlick) 1924- 1R
Hoijer, Harry 1904-1976 73-76
Obituary 65-68
Hoisington, Harland
1896(?)-1973 Obituary 45-48
Hoke, Helen L. 1903- 73-76
Hoke, John (Lindsay) 1925- 41-44R
See also SATA 7
Holaday, Allan Gibson 1916- 37-40R
Holbeche, Philippa Jack 1919- CAP-1
Earlier sketch in CA 9-10
Holberg, Ruth L(angland) 1889- 5-6R
See also SATA 1
Holbik, Karel 1920- 37-40R
Holbo, Paul Sothe 1929- 25-28R
Holborn, Hajo 1902-1969 .... CAP-2
Earlier sketch in CA 25-28
Holborn, Louise W. 1898-19(?) CAP-2
Earlier sketch in CA 25-28
Holbrook, Bill 1921- 61-64
Holbrook, David (Kenneth) 1923- 7-8R
Holbrook, Peter
See Glick, Carl (Cannon)
Holbrook, Sabra
See Erickson, Sabra Rollins
Holbrook, Stewart Hall 1893-1964 .... CAP-1
Earlier sketch in CA 9-10
See also SATA 2
Holck, Manfred, Jr. 1930- 19-20R
Holcomb, George L. 1911- 45-48
Holcomb, Jerry (Leona) 1927- 25-28R
Holcombe, Arthur N(orman) 1884-1977 .. CAP-2
Obituary 73-76
Earlier sketch in CA 29-32
Holden, David (Shipley) 1924-1977 ..... 41-44R
Holden, Donald 1931- 45-48
Holden, Inez 1906-1974 Obituary 53-56
Holden, Jonathan 1941- 45-48
Holden, Matthew, Jr. 1931- 57-60
Holden, Molly 1927- 25-28R
Holden, Paul E. 1894(?)-1976 Obituary ... 65-68
Holden, Raymond (Peckham) 1894-1972 .. 7-8R
Obituary 37-40R
Holden, Vincent F. 1911-1972 Obituary . 37-40R
Holden, W(illis) Sprague 1909-1973 .... 1R
Obituary 45-48
Holder, Glenn 1906- 41-44R
Holder, William G. 1937- 25-28R
Holdheim, William Wolfgang 1926- 1R
Holding, Charles H. 1897- CAP-1
Earlier sketch in CA 11-12
Holding, James (Clark Carlisle, Jr.) 1907- 25-28R
See also SATA 3
Holdren, Bob R. 1922- 37-40R
Holdren, John P(aul) 1944- 33-36R
Holdsworth, Irene CAP-1
Earlier sketch in CA 9-10
Holdsworth, Mary (Zvegintzov) 1908- CAP-1
Earlier sketch in CA 15-16
Holenstein, Elmar 1937- 65-68
Holiday, F(rederick) W(illiam) 1921- 25-28R
Holisher, Desider 1901-1972 .... CAP-2
Obituary 37-40R
Earlier sketch in CA 19-20
See also SATA 6
Holl, Adelaide Hinkle 1910- 4R
See also SATA 8
Holl, Jack M. 1937- 57-60
Holladay, Sylvia A(gnes) 1936- 57-60
Holladay, William L(ee) 1926- 53-56
Holland, Alma Boice 29-32R
Holland, Barbara A(dams) 1925- 57-60
Holland, Cecelia (Anastasia) 1943- 17-18R
Holland, Cecil Fletcher
1907-1978 Obituary 77-80
Holland, Deborah K(atherine) 1947- 57-60
Holland, DeWitte T(almage) 1923- 45-48
Holland, Francis Ross, Jr. 1927- 33-36R
Holland, Glen A. 1920- 37-40R
Holland, Hilda 1901(?)-1975 Obituary 57-60
Holland, Isabelle 1920- 21-22R
See also SATA 8
Holland, James Gordon 1927- 1R
Holland, James R. 1944- 37-40R
Holland, Janice 1913-1962 73-76
Holland, John L(ewis) 1919- 25-28R
Holland, Joyce (Flint) 1921- 5-6R
Holland, Katrin
See Albrand, Martha
Holland, Kel
See Whittington, Harry
Holland, Kenneth J(ohn) 1918- 33-36R
Holland, Laurence B(edwell) 1920- 19-20R
Holland, Lynwood M. 1905- 41-44R
Holland, Marion 1908- 61-64
See also SATA 6
Holland, Norman N(orwood) 1927- 17-18R
Holland, Robert 1940- 33-36R
Holland, Thomas E(dward) 1934- 53-56
Holland, Tim 1931- 57-60
Holland, Vyvyan (Beresford)
1886-1967 Obituary 25-28R
Hollander, A(rie) Nicolaas Jan den
See den Hollander, A(rie) Nicolaas Jan
Hollander, Herbert S.
1904(?)-1976 Obituary 69-72
Hollander, John 1929- 4R
See also CLC 2, 5, 8
See also SATA 13
Hollander, Lee M. 1880- 1R
Hollander, Paul 1932- 37-40R
Hollander, Robert 1933- 13-14R
Hollander, Sophie Smith 1911- 15-16R
Hollander, Stanley C(harles) 1919- 37-40R
Hollander, Zander 1923- 65-68
Hollaway, Otto 1903- 69-72
Hollenweger, Walter J(acob) 1927- 53-56
Holler, Ronald F. 1938- 53-56
Holles, Everett R. 1904(?)-1978 Obituary .. 77-80
Holles, Robert Owen 1926- 7-8R
Holley, Bobbie Lee 1927- 33-36R
Holley, Edward Gailon 1927- 7-8R
Holley, I(rving) B(rinton), Jr. 1919- 37-40R
Holli, Melvin G(eorge) 1933- 25-28R
Hollick, Ann L(orraine) 1941- 57-60
Holliday, Barbara Gregg 1917- 73-76
Holliday, James
See Gray, Simon
Holliday, Joe
See Holliday, Joseph
Holliday, Joseph 1910- CAP-2
Earlier sketch in CA 29-32
See also SATA 11
Hollingshead, August deBelmont 1907- .. 13-14R
Hollingshead, (Ronald) Kyle 1941- 23-24R
Hollingsworth, Harold M(arvin) 1932- 53-56
Hollingsworth, J(oseph) Rogers 1932- .. 13-14R
Hollingsworth, Lyman B(urgess) 1919- 45-48
Hollingsworth, Mary H(ead) 1910- 69-72
Hollingsworth, Paul M. 1932- 29-32R
Hollis, (Maurice) Christopher 1902-1977 ... 73-76
Obituary 69-72
Hollis, Daniel W(alker) 1922- 5-6R
Hollis, Harry Newcombe, Jr. 1938- 57-60
Hollis, Helen Rice 1908- 61-64
Hollis, James R(ussell) 1940- 41-44R
Hollis, Jim
See Summers, Hollis (Spurgeon, Jr.)
Hollis, Joseph W(illiam) 1922- 25-28R
Hollis, Lucile U(ssery) 1921- 25-28R
Hollister, Bernard C(laiborne) 1938- 49-52
Hollister, C. Warren 1930- 4R
Hollister, Charles A(mmon) 1918- 17-18R
Hollister, George E(rwin) 1905- CAP-2
Earlier sketch in CA 17-18
Hollister, Leo E. 1920- 23-24R
Hollmann, Clide John 1896-1966 .... 7-8R
Hollo, Anselm 1934- 21-22R
Hollom, Philip Arthur Dominic 1912- 15-16R
Hollon, W. Eugene 1913- 1R
Holloway, Brenda W(ilmar) 1908- CAP-1
Earlier sketch in CA 9-10
Holloway, (Rufus) Emory 1885-1977 49-52
Obituary 73-76
Holloway, (Percival) Geoffrey 1918- 49-52
Holloway, George (Edward Talbot) 1921- . 25-28R
Holloway, Harry (Albert) 1925- 11-12R
Holloway, James Y(oung) 1927- 53-56
Holloway, John 1920- 7-8R
Holloway, Mark 1917- 21-22R
Holloway, Maurice 1920- 11-12R
Holloway, Robert J. 1921- 15-16R
Holloway, Teresa (Bragunier) 1906- 19-20R
Holloway, W(illiam) V(ernon) 1903- 1R
Hollowood, Albert Bernard 1910- 9-10R
Holly, J(ohn) Fred 1915- 5-6R
Holly, J. Hunter
See Holly, Joan C(arol)
Holly, Joan C(arol) 1932- 4R
Hollyday, Frederic B(lackmar) M(umford)
1928- 45-48
Holm, (Else) Anne (Lise) 1922- 19-20R
See also SATA 1
Holm, Don(ald Raymond) 1918- 33-36R
Holm, Marilyn D. (Franzen) 1944- 19-20R
Holm, Sven (Aage) 1902- CAP-1
Earlier sketch in CA 11-12
Holman, C(larence) Hugh 1914- 5-6R
Holman, Dennis (Idris) 1915- 9-10R
Holman, Felice 1919- 7-8R
See also SATA 7
Holman, Harriet R. 1912- 37-40R
Holman, L(loyd) Bruce 1939- 61-64
Holman, William R(oger) 1926- 49-52
Holmans, Alan Edward 1934- 3R
Holme, K. E.
See Hill, (John Edward) Christopher
Holme, Thea 1903- 41-44R
Holmelund, Paul 1890- 7-8R
Holmer, Paul L(eroy) 1916- 37-40R
Holmes, Arthur F. 1924- 33-36R
Holmes, C. Raymond 1929- 57-60
Holmes, Charles M(ason) 1923- 29-32R
Holmes, Charles S(hiveley) 1916-1976 .. 41-44R
Obituary 61-64
Holmes, Colin 1938- 25-28R
Holmes, David Charles 1919- 9-10R
Holmes, David M(orton) 1929- 33-36R
Holmes, Douglas 1933- 41-44R
Holmes, Edward M(orris) 1910- 37-40R
Holmes, Efner Tudor 1949- 65-68
Holmes, Geoffrey (Shorter) 1928- 25-28R
Holmes, H. H.
See White, William A(nthony) P(arker)
Holmes, Jack D(avid) L(azarus) 1930- ... 41-44R
Holmes, Jay
See Holmes, Joseph Everett
Holmes, John
See Souster, (Holmes) Raymond
Holmes, John Clellon 1926- 9-10R
Holmes, Joseph Everett 1922- 3R
Holmes, Kenneth L(loyd) 1915- 37-40R
Holmes, Lowell D(on) 1925- 33-36R
Holmes, Marjorie 1910- 3R
Holmes, Martin (Rivington) 1905- 49-52
Holmes, (John) Michael (Aleister) 1931- . 25-28R
Holmes, Michael Stephan 1942- 77-80
Holmes, Nancy 1921- 69-72
Holmes, Parker Manfred 1895- CAP-1
Earlier sketch in CA 13-14
Holmes, Paul Allen 1901- CAP-2
Earlier sketch in CA 19-20
Holmes, Paul Carter 1926- 23-24R
Holmes, Rick
See Hardwick, Richard Holmes, Jr.
Holmes, Robert A(lexander) 1943- 57-60
Holmes, Robert L(awrence) 1935- 41-44R
Holmes, Tommy 1903-1975 Obituary 57-60
Holmes, Urban T(igner) 1900-1972 ...... CAP-2
Earlier sketch in CA 21-22
Holmes, W(ilfred) J(ay) 1900- 29-32R
Holmes, William Kersley 1882- CAP-1
Earlier sketch in CA 9-10
Holmquist, Anders 1933- 29-32R
Holmquist, Eve 1921- 53-56
See also SATA 11
Holmstrand, Marie Juline (Gunderson)
1908- 5-6R
Holmstrom, (John) Edwin 1898- CAP-1
Earlier sketch in CA 11-12
Holmstrom, Lynda Lytle 1939- 33-36R
Holmvik, Oyvind 1914- 19-20R
Holquist, (James) Michael 1935- 45-48
Holroyd, Michael (de Courcy Fraser) 1935- . 53-56
Holsaert, Eunice ?-1974 Obituary 53-56
Holsinger, Jane Lumley 17-18R
Holsopple, Barbara 1943- 73-76
Holst, Johan J(oergen) 1937- 25-28R
Holst, Lawrence E(berhardt) 1929- 61-64
Holsti, Kalevi J(acque) 1935- 23-24R
Holsti, Ole R(udolf) 1933- 25-28R
Holt, Edgar Crawshaw 1900-1975 .... 3R
Obituary 61-64
Holt, Gavin
See Rodda, Charles
Holt, Helen
See Paine, Lauran (Bosworth)
Holt, (Laurence) James 1939- 25-28R
Holt, John (Robert) 1926- 25-28R
Holt, John (Caldwell) 1923- 69-72
Holt, John Agee 1920- 1R
Holt, L. Emmett, Jr. 1895-1974 Obituary .. 53-56
Holt, Lee E(lbert) 1912- 13-14R
Holt, Margaret 1937- 17-18R
See also SATA 4
Holt, Michael (Paul) 1929- 53-56
See also SATA 13
Holt, Robert R(utherford) 1917- 41-44R
Holt, Robert T. 1928- 37-40R
Holt, Rochelle L(ynn) 1946- 57-60
Holt, Stephen
See Thompson, Harlan H.
Holt, Tex
See Joscelyn, Archie L.
Holt, Thelma Jewett 1913- 29-32R
Holt, Victoria
See Hibbert, Eleanor Burford
Holt, William 1897-1977 .... CAP-1
Obituary 69-72
Earlier sketch in CA 17-18
Holtan, Orley I. 1933- 33-36R
Holter, Don W. 1905- 37-40R
Holthusen, Hans Egon 1913- 45-48
Holtje, Herbert F(ranklin) 1931- 61-64
Holton, Felicia Antonelli 1921- 69-72
Holton, Gerald (James) 1922- 15-16R
Holton, Leonard
See Wibberley, Leonard (Patrick O'Connor)
Holton, (William) Milne 1931- 41-44R
Holtrop, William Frans 1908- 57-60
Holtz, Avraham 1934- 29-32R
Holtzman, Abraham 1921- 3R
Holtzman, Jerome 1926- 53-56
Holtzman, Paul D(ouglas) 1918- 33-36R
Holtzman, Wayne H(arold) 1923- 37-40R
Holub, Miroslav 1923- 21-22R
See also CLC 4
Holway, John 1929- 57-60
Holyer, Erna Maria 1925- 29-32R
Holyer, Ernie
See Holyer, Erna Maria
Holz, Loretta (Marie) 1943- 65-68
Holz, Robert K(enneth) 1930- 53-56
Holzapfel, Rudolf Patrick 1938- CAP-1
Earlier sketch in CA 11-12
Holzberger, William George 1932- 53-56
Holzer, Hans 1920- 13-14R
Holzman, Franklyn Dunn 1918- 61-64
Holzman, Philip Seidman 1922- 37-40R
Holzman, Robert Stuart 1907- 1R
Homan, Robert Anthony 1929- 7-8R
Homans, Peter 1930- 23-24R
Homburger, Erik
See Erikson, Erik H(omburger)
Homer, Frederic D(onald) 1939- 65-68
Homer, Williams Innes 1929- 15-16R
Homoras
See Nuttall, Jeff
Homrighausen, Elmer George 1900- 45-48
Homsher, Lola Mae 1913- 2R
Homze, Alma C. 1932- 29-32R
Homze, Edward L. 1930- 33-36R
Honan, Park 1928- 77-80
Honce, Charles E. 1895-1975 Obituary 61-64
Honderich, Ted 1933- 33-36R
Hone, Joseph 1937- 65-68
Hone, Ralph E(merson) 1913- 23-24R
Honey, P(atrick) J(ames) 1922- 13-14R
Honey, William (Houghton) 1910- 33-36R
Honeycombe, Gordon 1936- 77-80
Honeycutt, Benjamin L(awrence) 1938- 57-60
Honeycutt, Roy L(ee), Jr. 1926- 41-44R
Honeyman, Brenda
See Clarke, Brenda Margaret Lilian
Hong, Edna H. 1913- 21-22R
Hong, Howard V(incent) 1912- 21-22R
Honig, Donald 1931- 19-20R
Honig, Edwin 1919- 7-8R
Honig, Louis 1911-1977 77-80
Obituary 73-76
Honigfeld, Gilbert
See Howard, Gilbert
Honigmann, E(rnest) A(nselm) J(oachim)
1927- 21-22R
Honigmann, John J(oseph) 1914- 1R
Honnalgere, Gopal 1944- 73-76
Honness, Elizabeth H. 1904- 25-28R
See also SATA 2
Honnold, John Otis, Jr. 1915- 15-16R
Honore, Antony Maurice 1921- 3R
Honourable Member for X
See de Chair, Somerset (Struben)
Hoobler, Dorothy 69-72
Hoobler, Thomas 69-72
Hood, David Crockett 1937- 37-40R
Hood, Donald W(ilbur) 1918- 37-40R
Hood, Dora (Ridout) 1885- CAP-2
Earlier sketch in CA 17-18
Hood, F(rancis) C(ampbell) 1895-1971 ... CAP-1
Earlier sketch in CA 13-14
Hood, Graham 1936- 77-80
Hood, Hugh (John Blagdon) 1928- 49-52
Hood, Joseph F. 1925- 33-36R
See also SATA 4
Hood, Margaret Page 1892- 3R
Hood, Robert E. 1926- 23-24R
Hood, (Martin) Sinclair (Frankland) 1917- 21-22R
Hoofnagle, Keith Lundy 1941- 15-16R
Hoogasian-Villa, Susie 1921- 17-18R
Hoogenboom, Ari (Arthur) 1927- 45-48
Hoogenboom, Olive 1927- 23-24R
Hoogestraat, Wayne E. 7-8R
Hook, Andrew 1932- 53-56
Hook, Diana ffarington 1918- 61-64
Hook, Donald D(wight) 1928- 53-56
Hook, Frank S(cott) 1922- 23-24R
Hook, J(ulius) N(icholas) 1913- 5-6R
Hook, Sidney 1902- 11-12R
Hooke, Nina Warner 1907- 73-76
Hooker, Clifford Alan 1942- 49-52
Hooker, Craig Michael 1951- 57-60
Hooker, James Ralph 1929- 21-22R
Hooker, (Peter) Jeremy 1941- 77-80
Hooker, Ruth 1920- 69-72
Hookham, Hilda Henriette (Kuttner) 1915- . 9-10R
Hooks, G(aylor) Eugene 1927- 4R
Hooks, Gene
See Hooks, G(aylor) Eugene
Hoole, Daryl Van Dam 1934- 23-24R
Hooper, Douglas 1927- 25-28R
Hooper, John W(illiam) 1926- 29-32R
Hooper, Walter (McGehee) 1931- 17-18R
Hooper, William Loyd 1931- 5-6R
Hoopes, Clement R. 1906- 73-76
Hoopes, Donelson F(arquhar) 1932- 33-36R
Hoopes, James 1944- 65-68
Hoopes, Ned E(dward) 1932- 17-18R
Hoopes, Robert Griffith 1920- 2R
Hoopes, Roy 1922- 21-22R
See also SATA 11
Hoops, Richard A(llen) 1933- 41-44R
Hoos, Ida Russakoff 1912- 19-20R
Hooson, David J. M. 1926- 19-20R
Hooten, William J(arvis) 1900- 61-64
Hooton, Charles
See Rowe, Vivian C(laud)
Hoover, Calvin Bryce 1897-1974 .... CAP-1
Obituary 49-52
Earlier sketch in CA 13-14
Hoover, Dorothy Estheryne 1918- 49-52
Hoover, Dwight W(esley) 1926- 33-36R
Hoover, Edgar M. 1907- 13-14R
Hoover, F(rancis) Louis 1913- 41-44R
Hoover, Hardy 1902- 29-32R
Hoover, Helen (Drusilla Blackburn) 1910- 21-22R
See also SATA 12
Hoover, J(ohn) Edgar 1895-1972 .... 3R
Obituary 33-36R
Hoover, John P. 1910- 53-56
Hoover, Kenneth H(arding) 1920- 57-60
Hoover, Marjorie L(awson) 1910- 41-44R
Hopcraft, Arthur 1932- 25-28R
Hope, A(lec) D(erwent) 1907- 21-22R
See also CLC 3
Hope, A(shley) Guy 1914- 25-28R
Hope, Andrew
See Hern, (George) Anthony
Hope, C(harles) E(velyn) G(raham)
1900-1971 .... CAP-1
Earlier sketch in CA 15-16
Hope, Felix
See Williamson, Claude C(harles) H.